GENERAL INFORMATION AND MAINTENANCE

block. The letter in the code identifies the engine by displacement (cu.in.), carburetor type and compression ratio.

The undersize/oversize bearing letter codes, located on the boss directly above the oil filter, are as follows:

Letter B indicates 0.010 in. oversized cylinder bore.
Letter M indicates 0.010 in. undersized main bearings.
Letter P indicates 0.010 in. undersized connecting rod bearings.
Letter C indicates 0.010 in. oversized camshaft block bores.

Transmission

Manual Transmissions

AISIN AX4/5/15

The AX4 is a 4-speed synchromesh manual transmission. The AX5 and AX15 are 5-speed synchromesh manual transmissions. The shift mechanism in all is integral and mounted in the shift tower portion of the housing. The transmission identification code for the Aisin AX4/5/15 transmissions is located on the bottom of the transmission case near the filler plug. The first three numbers identify the date of manufacture (e.g. 902 = 1989, February). The next series of numbers is the serial number.

BA 10/5

The BA10/5 is a 5-speed, synchromesh manual transmission. The shifter is mounted in the transmissions intermediate case. The BA 10/5 identification code is located on a tag, riveted to the left side of the transmission. The plate provides build date, part number, and serial number identification.

Automatic Transmissions

AW-4

The AW-4 is a 4-speed, electronically controlled automatic transmission. The identification plate is attached to the right side of the transmission case.

Transfer Case

The identification plate for all New Process transfer cases is attached to the rear of the case. The I.D. plate provides model number, assembly number, serial number and low range ratio. The transfer case serial number is also the build date (e.g. 8-10-89 = August 10, 1989).

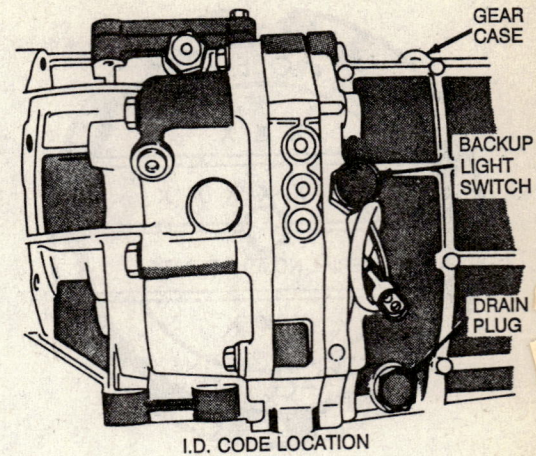

AX15 Identification code location

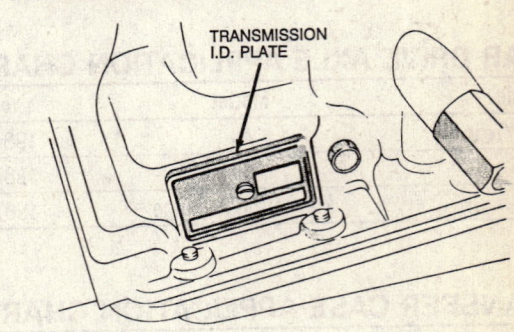

AW-4 Identification code location

MANUAL TRANSMISSION APPLICATION CHART

Transmission Types	Years
Warner T4 4-speed	1984 w/4-150
Warner T5 5-speed	1984 all
AISIN AX4 4-speed	1984–87 w/4-150
AISIN AX5 5-speed	1984–91 all
BA 10/5 5-speed	1987–89 all
AISIN AX15	1989–91 w/6-243

NOTE: The T4 and T5 were used in 1984 only, as substitutes for the AX4 and AX5 during a production shortage.

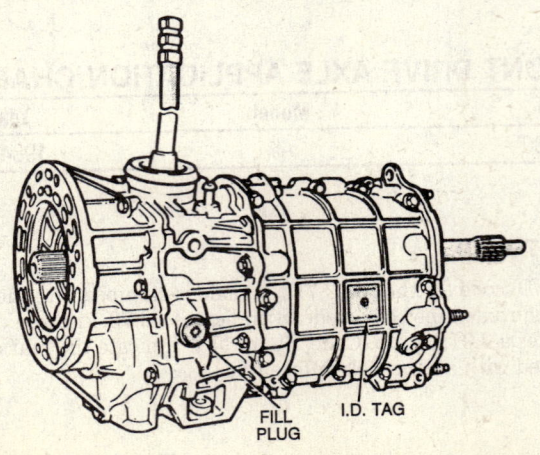

BA10/5 Identification code location

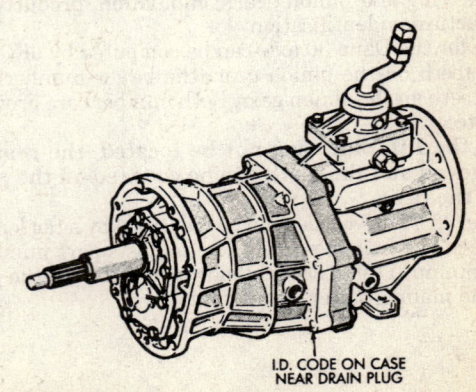

AX4/5 Identification code location

1-11

1 GENERAL INFORMATION AND MAINTENANCE

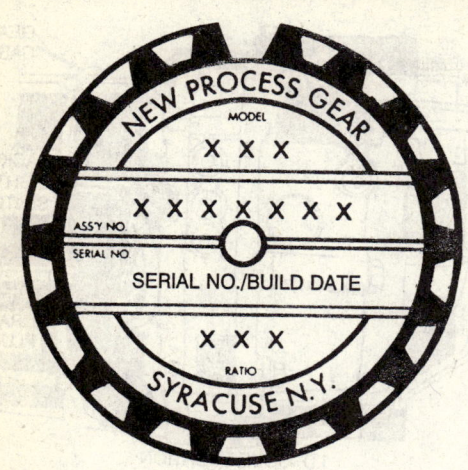

New process identification plate

REAR DRIVE AXLE APPLICATION CHART

Axle	Model	Years
AMC 7 9/16 in.	All	1984–86
Dana 35	All	1987–91
Dana 44	Metric Ton Package	1987–91

TRANSFER CASE APPLICATION CHART

Transfer Case Types	Years
New Process 207	1984–87 all
New Process 228	1985–87 w/auto trans.
New Process 229	1984 w/auto. trans.
New Process 231	1988–91 all
New Process 242	1987–91 w/auto. trans.

Drive Axles

Dana 30/35/44

Dana model 30 drive axles can be identified by an I.D. plate attached to the right side of the cover housing. Information on the tag includes- ring and pinion gear combination, production date and manufacturers identification.

Gear ratio for the Dana 30 axle can be computed by dividing the number of teeth on the pinion gear (the larger number) by the number of teeth on the pinion gear. Both numbers are provided on the I.D. plate.

NOTE: If the I.D. plate can not be located, the rear cover can be removed and the teeth can be counted on the gears to determine the ratio.

Dana model 35/44 drive axles can be identified by a tag located on the left side of the housing cover. The tag lists part number and gear ratio. Stamped into the right side axle shaft are the production date and manufacturers identification.

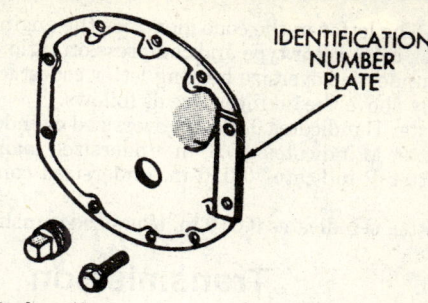

Dana 30 I.D. plate location

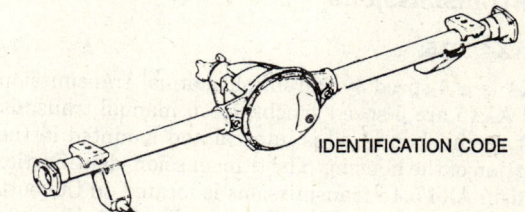

AMC 7 9/16 in. I.D. plate location

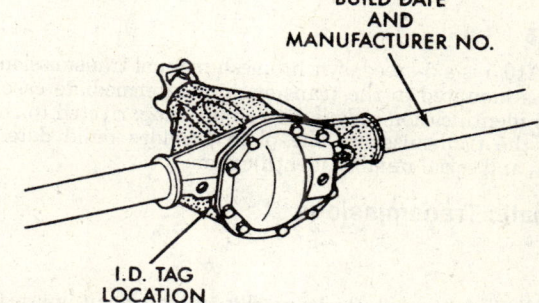

Dana 35/44 I.D. plate location

AUTOMATIC TRANSMISSION APPLICATION CHART

Transmission	Years
Chrysler 903 3-speed	1984–86
AISIN/Warner AW4 4-speed	1986–91

FRONT DRIVE AXLE APPLICATION CHART

Axle	Model	Years
Dana 30	All	1984–91

AMC 7 9/16 in.

The I.D. code for the AMC 7 9/16 in. axle is stamped into the right hand side axle tube boss. Code 'S' indicates a 3.73:1 ratio. Code 'T' indicates a 3.31:1 ratio. Code 'SS' or 'TT' indicate the rear axle is equipped with a Trac-Lok differential.

GENERAL INFORMATION AND MAINTENANCE 1

ROUTINE MAINTENANCE

Air Cleaner

SERVICING

Engines with the dry paper type filter should have the filter replaced every 30,000 miles. Under dusty conditions, the element should be checked weekly, or more often if conditions warrant, and should be replaced at the first signs of clogging.

On engines using a dry paper filter with the polyurethane wrap, the wrap should be carefully removed every 6,000 miles. Shake the dirt from the wrap, DO NOT WASH IT, squeeze the oil out by pressing it flat between two rags, then liberally soak it with SAE 10W-30 engine oil. Squeeze it flat to remove excess oil. At the same time, direct compressed air at the inside of the paper element to remove dirt. Replace the paper element every 30,000 miles, or sooner if necessary.

REMOVAL AND INSTALLATION

1. Remove air cleaner cover and filter element.
2. Clean filter element by gently blowing trapped debris from the filter with compressed air. Direct the air in the opposite direction of normal flow. Keep the air nozzle at lease two inches away from the filter to avoid damage to the filter.
3. If the filter element has become saturated with oil, replace it and inspect the crankcase ventilating system for proper operation.
4. Clean the air cleaner cover and body.
5. Install the air cleaner element and cover.

Fuel Filter

SERVICING

The inline fuel filter should be cleaned or replaced every 30,000 miles. If the vehicle is driven in abnormally dirty conditions or if contaminated gasoline was put in the gas tank, the filter could become clogged before 30,000 miles. The fuel sediment bowl type filter need not be serviced unless there is evidence of foreign matter (e.g., water, dirt) visible in the bowl. If there is, remove and empty the bowl, wipe it dry with a clean cloth and replace it.

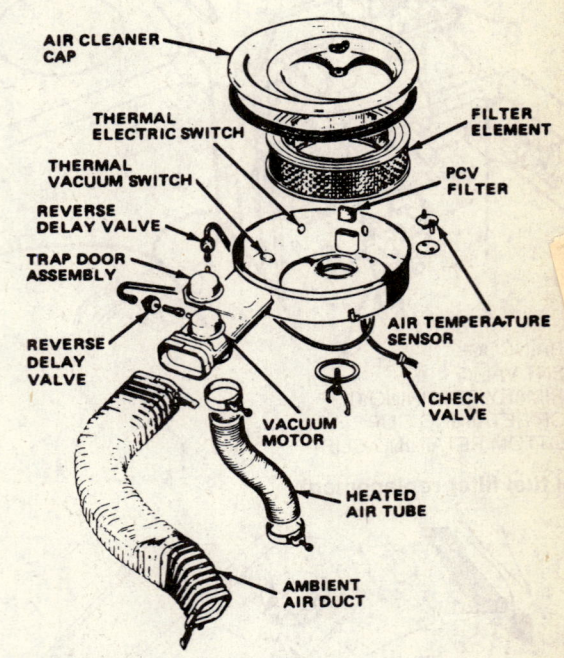

Carbureted engine air cleaner

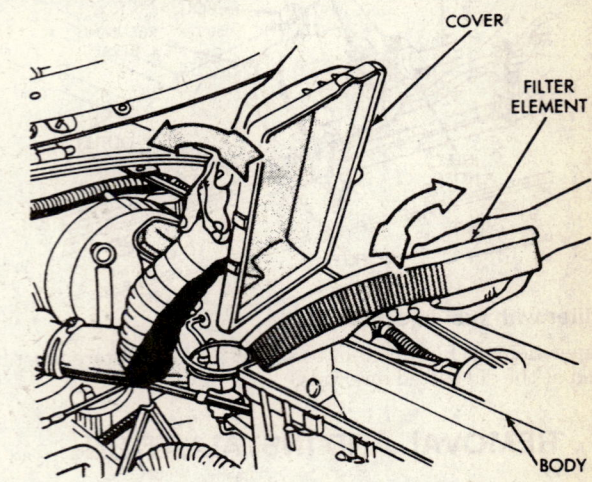

Air filter replacement on fuel injection engines

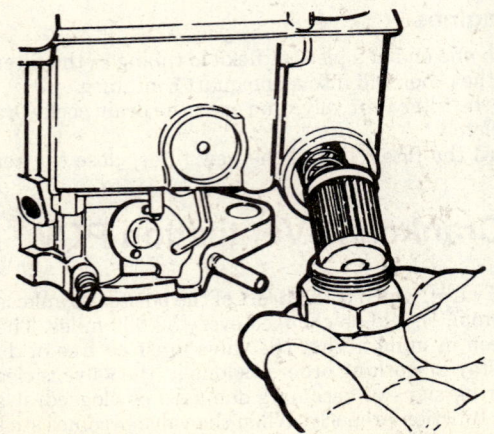

Fuel filter for 6-2.8L

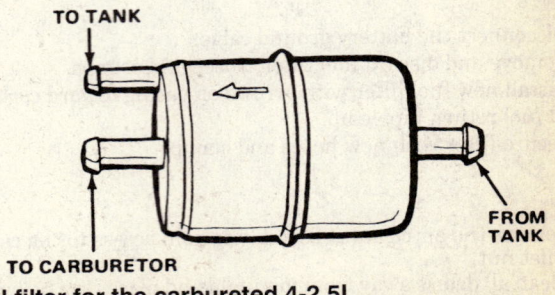

Fuel filter for the carbureted 4-2.5L

1-13

1 GENERAL INFORMATION AND MAINTENANCE

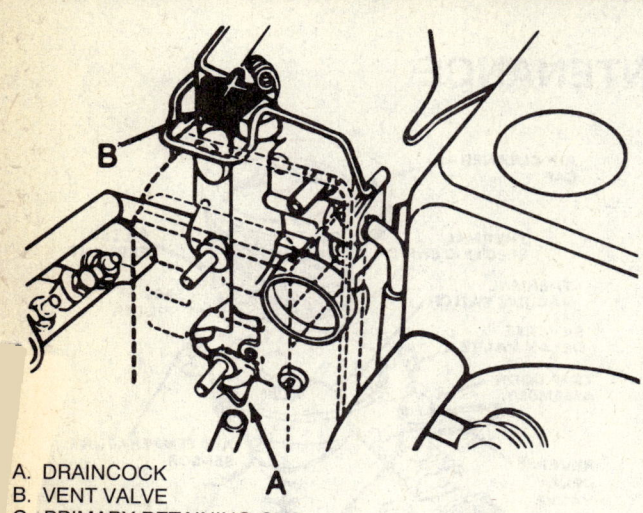

A. DRAINCOCK
B. VENT VALVE
C. PRIMARY RETAINING CLIP
D. TOP RETAINING CLIP
E. BOTTOM RETAINING CLIP

Diesel fuel filter replacement

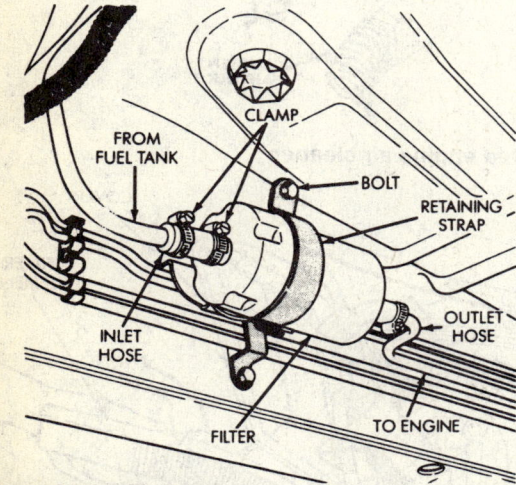

Fuel filter with fuel injection

The paper element filter cannot be serviced. These filters must be replaced at the suggested intervals.

REMOVAL AND INSTALLATION

Carbureted Engines

4-2.5L

1. Disconnect the battery ground cable.
2. Remove and discard fuel filter, hoses and clamps.
3. Install new fuel filter with arrows on casing toward carburetor and fuel return nipple up.
4. Secure filter with new hoses and clamps.

6-2.8L

1. Remove the air cleaner assembly to gain access to the carburetor inlet nut.
2. Clean all debris away from manifold and place rags below the fuel line and inlet nut to absorb any fuel spillage.
3. Hold the large inlet nut with a wrench and loosen the fuel line fitting with a *flare nut* wrench. (This wrench is made to prevent stripping of the fuel line fitting).
4. Pull the fuel pipe from the carburetor and catch any fuel with a clean rag. Next, unscrew the large nut. There is a spring behind the nut, so be careful. Remove the spring and the old filter.
5. Install the new filter and, if you are at all in doubt about its condition, a new gasket behind the inlet nut. Tighten the inlet nut carefully, because the carburetor is made of very soft metal and the threads could EASILY strip with disastrous results! Hold the inlet nut securely while tightening the fuel line fitting.

Gasoline Fuel Injection

The filter on both the 4-2.5L TBI and 6-4.0L is located under the truck, mounted on the frame rail on the driver's side.

4-2.5L TBI

1. Disconnect the battery ground cable.
2. Remove the fuel tank filler cap.
3. Raise and support the rear end on jackstands.
4. Remove the hoses and clamps from the filter.
5. Remove the filter strap bolt and remove the filter.

NOTE: The filter is marked for installation. IN goes towards the fuel tank; OUT towards the engine.

6. Place the new filter on the frame rail and tighten the strap bolt to 106 in. lbs.
7. Install and securely clamp the hoses.

6-4.0L

1. Disconnect the battery ground cable.
2. Remove the fuel tank filler cap.
3. Remove the cap from the pressure test port on the fuel rail in the engine compartment.

—— **CAUTION** ——
DON'T ALLOW FUEL TO SPRAY OR SPILL ON THE ENGINE OR EXHAUST MANIFOLD! PLACE HEAVY SHOP TOWELS UNDER THE PRESSURE PORT TO ABSORB ANY ESCAPED FUEL!

4. Using a small pin punch, push the test port valve inward to relieve fuel system pressure.
5. Install the test port cap.
6. Raise and support the rear end on jackstands.
7. Remove the hoses and clamps from the filter.
8. Remove the filter strap bolt and remove the filter.

NOTE: The filter is marked for installation. IN goes towards the fuel tank; OUT towards the engine.

9. Place the new filter on the frame rail and tighten the strap bolt to 106 in. lbs.
10. Install and securely clamp the hoses.

Diesel Engines

1. Attach one end of a piece of flexible tubing to the filter drain cock. Run the other end into a one quart container.
2. Open the filter vent valve and open the drain cock. Drain the filter completely.
3. Discard the filter. Install the new filter, close the vent and drain cock.

Crankcase Ventilation PCV

The PCV valve, which is the heart of the positive crankcase ventilation system, should be changed every 30,000 miles. The main thing to keep in mind is that the valve must be free of dirt and residue to stay in working order. As long as the valve is clean and is not showing signs of becoming damaged or clogged, it should perform its function properly. When the valve becomes sticky and will not operate freely, it should be replaced.

The PCV valve is used to control the rate at which crankcase vapors are returned to the intake manifold. The action of the valve

GENERAL INFORMATION AND MAINTENANCE 1

plunger is controlled by intake manifold vacuum and the spring. During deceleration and idle, when manifold vacuum is high, it overcomes the tension of the valve spring and the plunger bottoms in the manifold end of the valve housing. Because of the valve construction, it reduces, but does not stop, the passage of vapors to the intake manifold. When the engine is lightly accelerated or operated at constant speed, spring tension matches intake manifold vacuum pull and the plunger takes a mid-position in the valve body, allowing more vapors to flow into the manifold.

SERVICING

An inoperative PCV system will cause rough idling, sludge and oil dilution. In the event erratic idle, never attempt to compensate by disconnecting the PCV system. Disconnecting the PCV system will adversely affect engine ventilation. It could also shorten engine life through the buildup of sludge.

To inspect the PCV valve, proceed as follows:

1. With the engine idling, remove the PCV valve from the rocker cover. If the valve is not plugged, a hissing sound will be heard. A strong vacuum should be felt when you place your finger over the valve.
2. Reinstall the PCV valve and allow about a minute for pressure to drop.
3. Remove the crankcase intake air cleaner. Cover the opening in the rocker cover with a piece of stiff paper. The paper should be sucked against the opening with noticeable force.
4. With the engine stopped, remove the PCV valve and shake it. A rattle or clicking should be heard to indicate that the valve is free.
5. If the system meets the tests in Steps 1, 2, 3, and 4 (above), no further service is required, unless replacement is specified in the Maintenance Intervals Chart. If the system does not meet the tests, the valve should be replaced with a new one.

NOTE: Do not attempt to clean a PCV valve.

6. With a new PCV valve installed, if the paper is not sucked against the crankcase air intake opening (see Step 2), it will be necessary to clean the PCV valve hose and the passage in the lower part of the carburetor.
7. Clean the line with Combustion Chamber Conditioner or similar solvent. Do not leave the hoses in solvent for more than $4\frac{1}{2}$ hour. Allow the line to air dry.

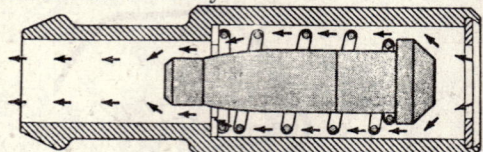

Vapor flow through PCV valve

8. Remove the carburetor and HAND turn a $4\frac{1}{4}$ in. drill through the passages to dislodge solid particles and blow clean.

NOTE: It is not necessary to disassembly the carburetor for this operation. If necessary, use a smaller drill, so that no metal is removed.

9. After checking and/or servicing the Crankcase Ventilation System, any components that do not allow passage or air to the intake manifold should be replaced.

The PCV valve is located in the valve cover on all PCV equipped engines.

Crankcase Ventilation (CCV) System

The Crankcase Ventilation (CCV) System performs the same function as the conventional PCV system but without the use of a vacuum controlled valve. When in operation fresh air enters the

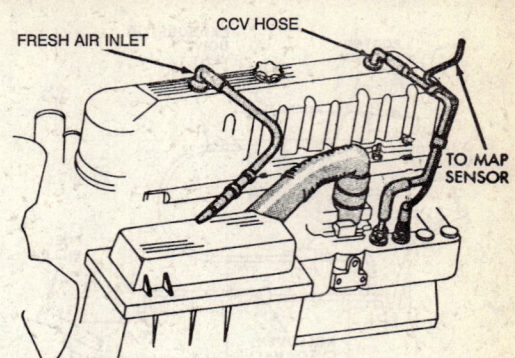

6-4.0L crankcase ventilation system

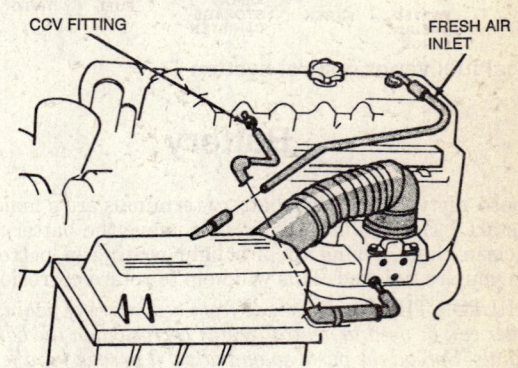

4-2.5L crankcase ventilation system

engine through an inlet and is mixed with crankcase vapors. Manifold vacuum draws the vapor/air mixture through a fixed size orifice and into the intake manifold. The vapors are then burned off during combustion.

There is no servicing to the CCV system unless one of the components gets clogged or fails.

Evaporative Canister

All models have fuel evaporative emission control systems which include an evaporative storage canister. The purpose of this charcoal canister is to store gasoline vapors until they can be drawn into the engine and burned along with the air/fuel mixture. The air filter in the bottom of the canister, if so equipped, should be replaced every 30,000 miles.

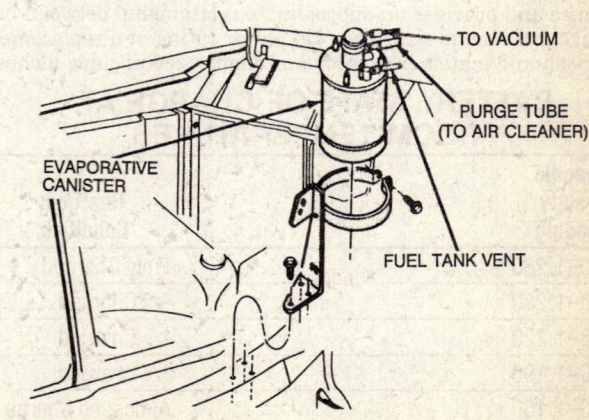

Fuel vapor storage canister

1-15

1 GENERAL INFORMATION AND MAINTENANCE

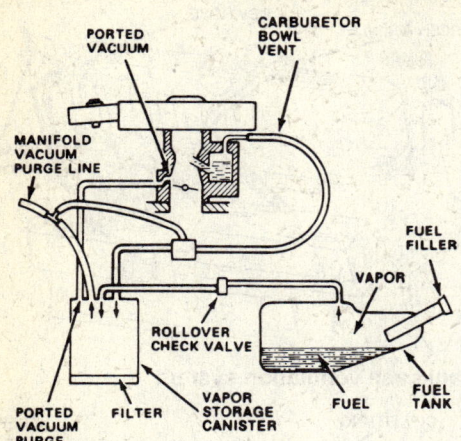

Typical fuel vapor control system

Battery

Loose, dirty, or corroded battery terminals are a major cause of "no-start." Every 3 months or so, remove the battery terminals and clean them, giving them a light coating of petroleum jelly when you are finished. This will help to retard corrosion.

CHILTON TIP: *A paste made from a mixture of baking soda and water can be used to neutralize any corrosion on the battery or terminals. Spread the paste on and allow it to soak for a few minutes. Rinse the paste with water and dry.*

Check the battery cables for signs of wear or chafing and replace any cable or terminal that looks marginal. Battery terminals can be easily cleaned. Inexpensive terminal cleaning tools are an excellent investment that will pay for themselves many times over. They can usually be purchased from any well-equipped auto store or parts department. Side terminal batteries require a different tool to clean the threads in the battery case.

Unless you have a maintenance-free battery, check the electrolyte level (see Battery under Fluid Level Checks in this Section) and check the specific gravity of each cell. Be sure that the vent holes in each cell cap are not blocked by grease or dirt. The vent holes allow hydrogen gas, formed by the chemical reaction in the battery, to escape safely.

REPLACEMENT BATTERIES

The cold power rating of a battery measures battery starting performance and provides an approximate relationship between battery size and engine size. The cold power rating of a replacement battery should match or exceed your engine size in cubic inches.

BATTERY STATE OF CHARGE AT ROOM TEMPERATURE

Specific Gravity Reading	Charged Condition
1.260–1.280	Fully Charged
1.230–1.250	¾ Charged
1.200–1.220	½ Charged
1.170–1.190	¼ Charged
1.140–1.160	Almost no Charge
1.110–1.130	No Charge

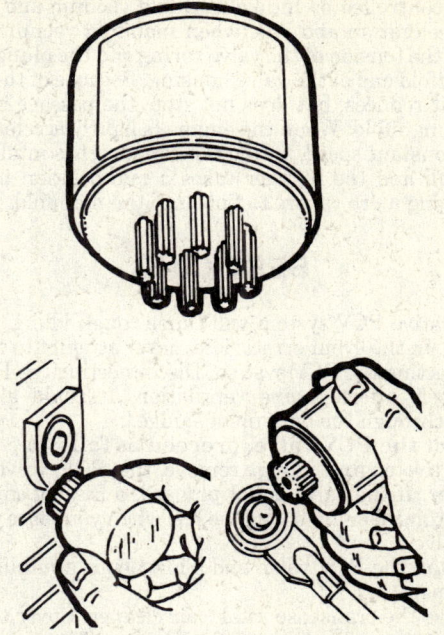

Special tools are available for cleaning the terminals and cable clamps on side terminal batteries

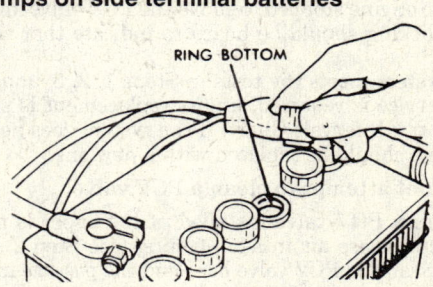

Fill each battery cell to the bottom of the split ring with distilled water

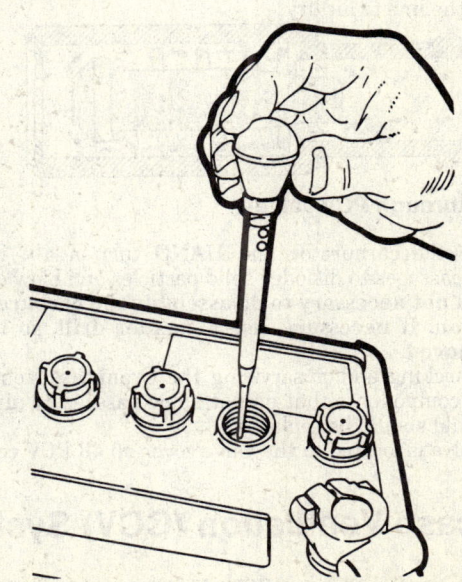

The specific gravity of the battery can be checked with a simple float-type hydrometer

GENERAL INFORMATION AND MAINTENANCE 1

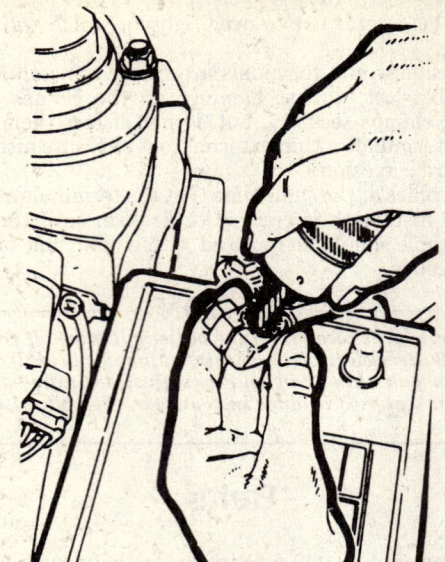

Cleaning the inside of the cable end

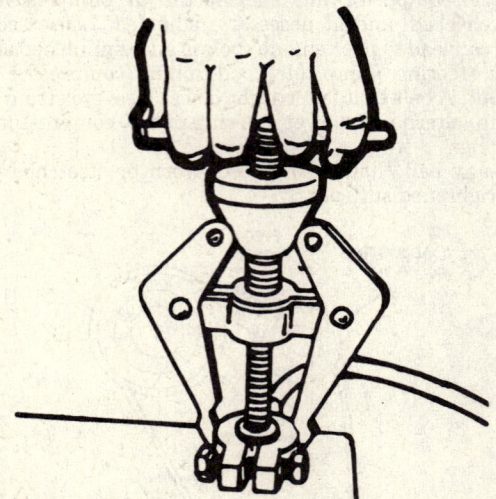

Use a small puller to remove the battery cables

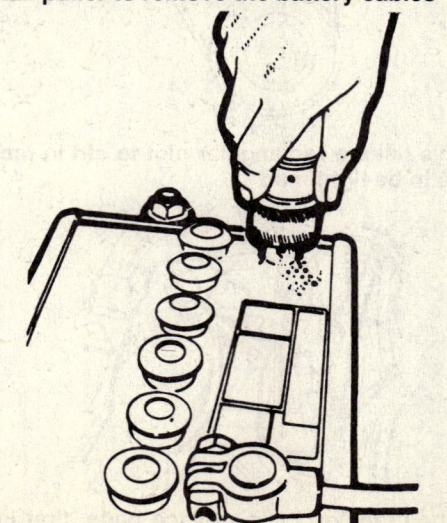

Cleaning the battery terminal

FLUID LEVEL
EXCEPT MAINTENANCE FREE BATTERIES

Check the battery electrolyte level at least once a month, or more often in hot weather or during periods of extended truck operation. The level can be checked through the case on translucent polypropylene batteries; the cell caps must be removed on other models. The electrolyte level in each cell should be kept filled to the split ring inside, or the line marked on the outside of the case.

If the level is low, add only distilled water, or colorless, odorless drinking water, through the opening until the level is correct. Each cell is completely separate from the others, so each must be checked and filled individually.

If water is added in freezing weather, the truck should be driven several miles to allow the water to mix with the electrolyte. Otherwise, the battery could freeze.

SPECIFIC GRAVITY
EXCEPT MAINTENANCE FREE BATTERIES

At least once a year, check the specific gravity of the battery. It should be between 1.20 in.Hg and 1.26 in.Hg at room temperature.

The specific gravity can be checked with the use of an hydrometer, an inexpensive instrument available from many sources, including auto parts stores. The hydrometer has a squeeze bulb at one end and a nozzle at the other. Battery electrolyte is sucked into the hydrometer until the float is lifted from its seat. The specific gravity is then read by noting the position of the float. Generally, if after charging, the specific gravity between any two cells varies more than 50 points (0.50), the battery is bad and should be replaced.

It is not possible to check the specific gravity in this manner on sealed (maintenance free) batteries. Instead, the indicator built into the top of the case must be relied upon to display any signs of battery deterioration. If the indicator is dark, the battery can be assumed to be OK. If the indicator is light, the specific gravity is low, and the battery should be charged or replaced.

CABLES AND CLAMPS

Once a year, the battery terminals and the cable clamps should be cleaned. Loosen the clamps and remove the cables, negative cable first. On batteries with posts on top, the use of a puller specially made for the purpose is recommended. These are inexpensive, and available in auto parts stores. Side terminal battery cables are secured with a bolt.

Clean the cable lamps and the battery terminal with a wire brush, until all corrosion, grease, etc., is removed and the metal is shiny. It is especially important to clean the inside of the clamp thoroughly, since a small deposit of foreign material or oxidation there will prevent a sound electrical connection and inhibit either starting or charging. Special tools are available for cleaning these parts, one type for conventional batteries and another type for side terminal batteries.

Before installing the cables, loosen the battery holddown clamp or strap, remove the battery and check the battery tray. Clear it of any debris, and check it for soundness. Rust should be wire brushed away, and the metal given a coat of anti-rust paint.

CHILTON TIP: *Many companies are now offering special rubberized coatings for battery trays. These coatings come in an aerosol can and can be applied to prevent the effects of battery acid corrosion.*

Replace the battery and tighten the holddown clamp or strap se-

1 GENERAL INFORMATION AND MAINTENANCE

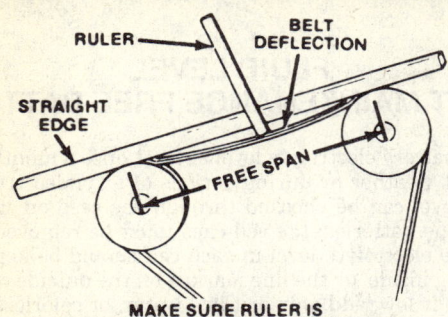

Measuring belt deflection

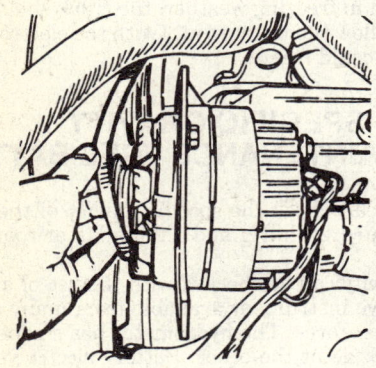

Slip the new belt over the pulley

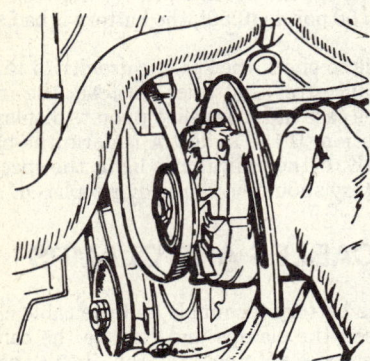

Push the component toward the engine and slip off the belt

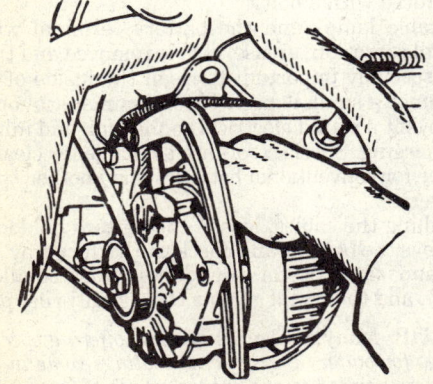

Pull outward on the component and tighten the mounting bolts

curely, but be careful not to over tighten, which will crack the battery case.

After the clamps and terminals are clean, reinstall the cables, negative cable last; do not hammer on the clamps to install. Tighten the clamps securely, but do not distort them. Give the clamps and terminals a thin external coat of grease after installation, to retard corrosion.

Check the cables at the same time that the terminals are cleaned. If the cable insulation is cracked or broken, or if the ends are frayed, the cable should be replaced with a new cable of the same length and gauge.

― CAUTION ―
Keep flame or sparks away from the battery; it gives off explosive hydrogen gas. Battery electrolyte contains sulphuric acid. If you should splash any on your skin or in your eyes, flush the affected area with plenty of clear water. If it lands in your eyes, get medical help immediately.

Belts

Once a year or at 30,000 mile intervals, the tension (and condition) of the alternator, power steering (if so equipped), air conditioning (if so equipped), and Thermactor air pump drive belts should be checked, and, if necessary, adjusted. Loose accessory drive belts can lead to poor engine cooling and diminished alternator, power steering pump, air conditioning compressor or air pump output. A belt that is too tight places a severe strain on the water pump, alternator, power steering pump, compressor or air pump bearings.

Replace any belt that is so glazed, worn or stretched that it cannot be tightened sufficiently.

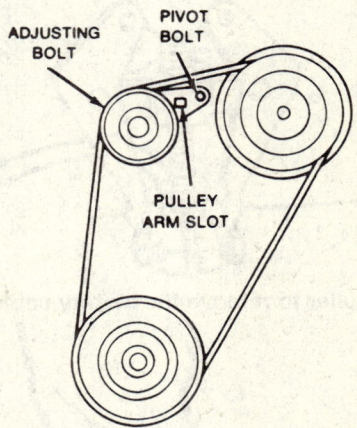

Some pulleys have a rectangular slot to aid in moving the accessories to be tightened

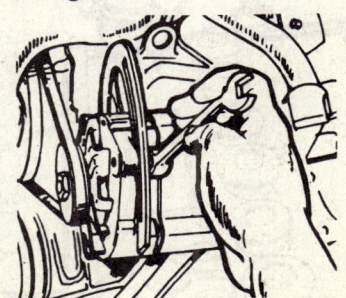

To adjust belt tension or to replace belts, first loosen the component's mounting and adjusting bolts slightly

1-18

GENERAL INFORMATION AND MAINTENANCE 1

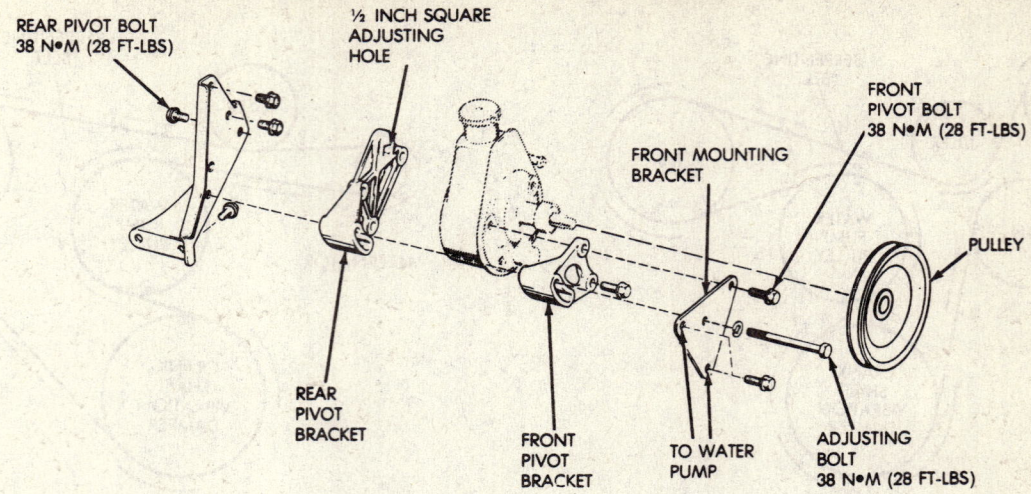

Power steering pump adjustment points on a 4-2.5L with a V-belt

NOTE: The material used in late model drive belts is such that the belts do not show wear. Replace belts at least every three years.

On vehicles with matched belts, replace both belts. New 4 1/2 in., 3/8 in. and 15/32 in. wide belts are to be adjusted to a tension of 140-160 lbs.; 4 1/4 in. wide belts are adjusted to 80 lbs., measured on a belt tension gauge. Any belt that has been operating for a minimum of 10 minutes is considered a used belt. In the first 10 minutes, the belt should stretch to its maximum extent. After 10 minutes, stop the engine and recheck the belt tension. Belt tension for a used belt should be maintained at 90-115 lbs. (except 4 1/4 in. wide belts) or 60 lbs. (4 1/4 in. wide belts).

Proper belt tension for a new serpentine belt accessory belt drive is 180-200 lbs. For a used serpentine belt the proper tension is 140-160 lbs.

ADJUSTMENTS FOR ALL V-BELTS

— CAUTION —

On models equipped with an electric cooling fan, disconnect the negative battery cable or fan motor wiring harness connector before replacing or adjusting drive belts. The fan may come on, under certain circumstances, even though the ignition is off.

Alternator (Fan Drive) Belt

1. Position the ruler perpendicular to the drive belt at its longest straight run. Test the tightness of the belt by pressing it firmly with your thumb. The deflection should not exceed 4 1/4 in.
2. If the deflection exceeds 4 1/4 in., loosen the alternator mounting and adjusting arm bolts.
3. Place a 1 in. open-end or adjustable wrench on the adjusting ridge cast on the body, and pull on the wrench until the proper tension is achieved.
4. Holding the alternator in place to maintain tension, tighten the adjusting arm bolt. Recheck the belt tension. When the belt is properly tensioned, tighten the alternator mounting bolt.

Power Steering Drive Belt

1. Hold a ruler perpendicularly to the drive belt at its longest run, test the tightness of the belt by pressing it firmly with your thumb. The deflection should not exceed 4 1/4 in.
2. To adjust the belt tension, loosen the adjusting and mounting bolts on the front face of the steering pump cover plate (hub side).
3. Using a pry bar or broom handle on the pump hub, move the power steering pump toward or away from the engine until the proper tension is reached. Do not pry against the reservoir as it is relatively soft and easily deformed.
4. Holding the pump in place, tighten the adjusting arm bolt and then recheck the belt tension. When the belt is properly tensioned tighten the mounting bolts.

Air Conditioning Compressor Drive Belt

1. Position a ruler perpendicular to the drive belt at its longest run. Test the tightness of the belt by pressing it firmly with your thumb. The deflection should not exceed 4 1/4 in.
2. If the engine is equipped with an idler pulley, loosen the idler pulley adjusting bolt, insert a pry bar between the pulley and the engine (or in the idler pulley adjusting slot), and adjust the tension accordingly. If the engine is not equipped with an idler pulley, the alternator must be moved to accomplish this adjustment, as outlined under Alternator (Fan Drive) Belt.
3. When the proper tension is reached, tighten the idler pulley adjusting bolt (if so equipped) or the alternator adjusting and mounting bolts.

Air Pump Drive Belt

1. Position a ruler perpendicular to the drive belt at its longest run. Test the tightness of the belt by pressing it firmly with your thumb. The deflection should be about 4 1/4 in.
2. To adjust the belt tension, loosen the adjusting arm bolt

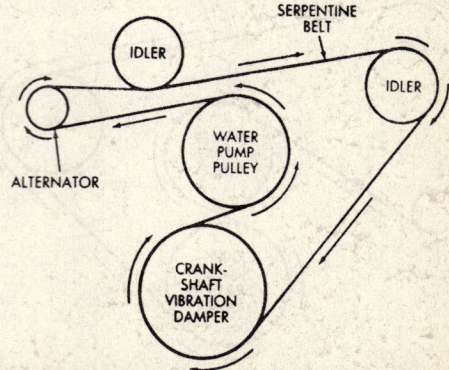

Serpentine belt installation on a 4-2.5L with an alternator only

1-19

1 GENERAL INFORMATION AND MAINTENANCE

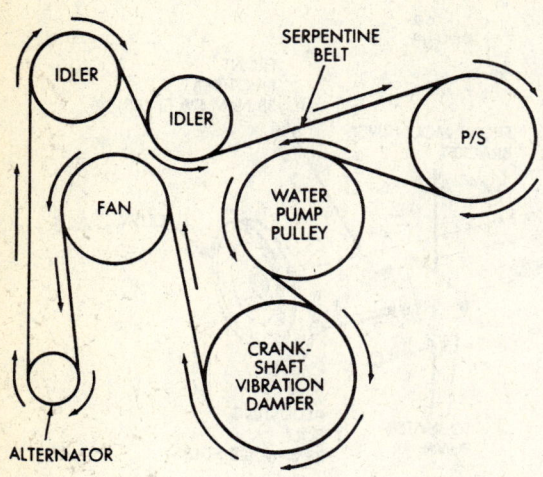

Serpentine belt installation on a 6-4.0L with an alternator and power steering

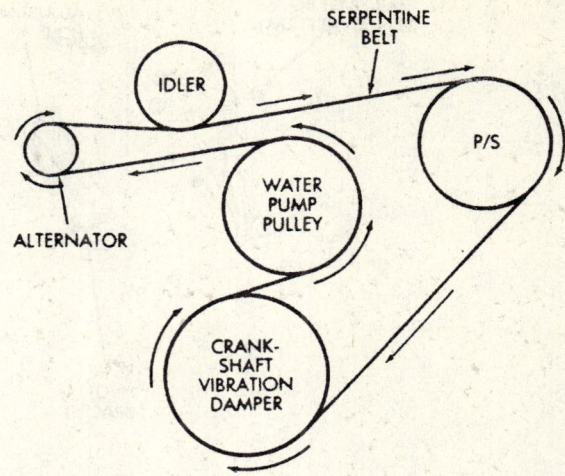

Serpentine belt installation on a 4-2.5L with an alternator and power steering

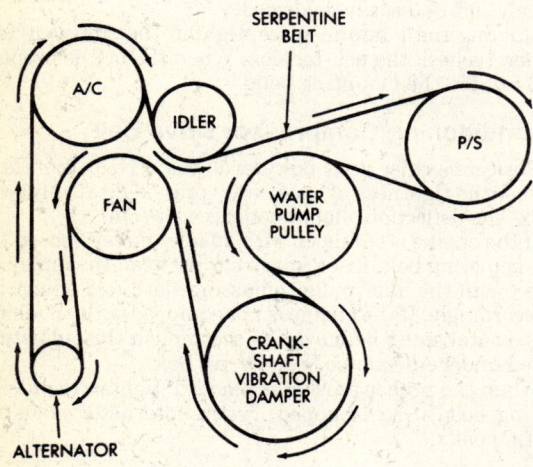

Serpentine belt installation on a 6-4.0L with an alternator, air conditioning and power steering

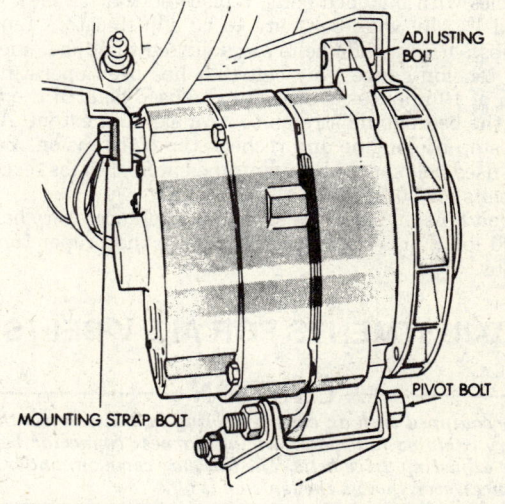

Alternator adjustment points on a 4-2.5L with a V-belt

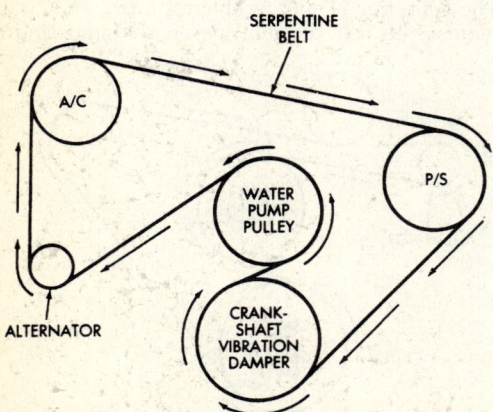

Serpentine belt installation on a 4-2.5L with an alternator, air conditioning and power steering

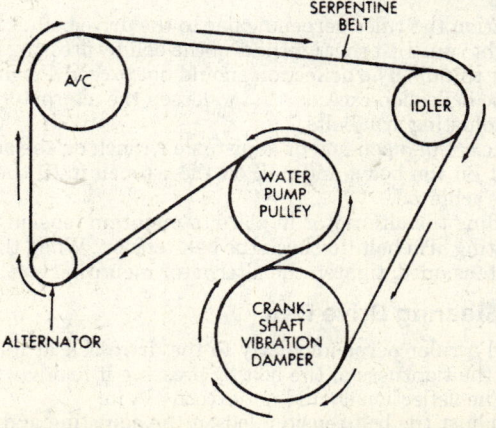

Serpentine belt installation on a 4-2.5L with an alternator and air conditioning

1-20

GENERAL INFORMATION AND MAINTENANCE 1

HOW TO SPOT WORN V-BELTS

V–Belts are vital to efficient engine operation—they drive the fan, water pump and other accessories. They require little maintenance (occasional tightening) but they will not last forever. Slipping or failure of the V–belt will lead to overheating. If your V–belt looks like any of these, it should be replaced.

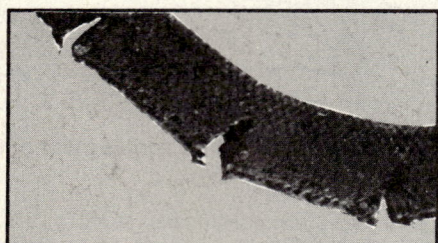

Cracking or Weathering

This belt has deep cracks, which cause it to flex. Too much flexing leads to heat build–up and premature failure. These cracks can be caused by using the belt on a pulley that is too small. Notched belts are available for small diameter pulleys.

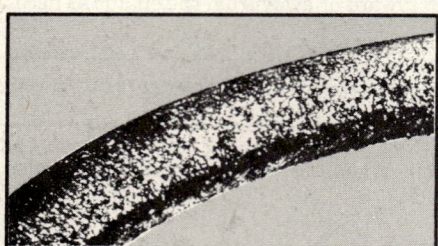

Softening (Grease and Oil)

Oil and grease on a belt can cause the belt's rubber compounds to soften and separate from the reinforcing cords that hold the belt together. The belt will first slip, then finally fail altogether.

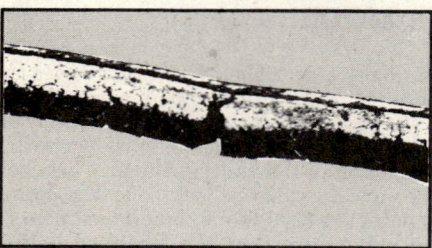

Glazing

Glazing is caused by a belt that is slipping. A slipping belt can cause a run-down battery, erratic power steering, overheating or poor accessory performance. The more the belt slips, the more glazing will be built up on the surface of the belt. The more the belt is glazed, the more it will slip. If the glazing is light, tighten the belt.

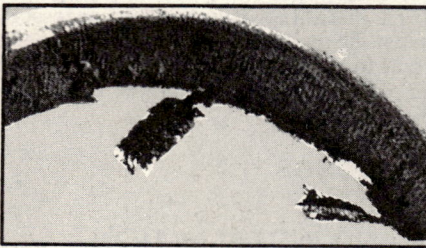

Worn Cover

The cover of this belt is worn off and is peeling away. The reinforcing cords will begin to wear and the belt will shortly break. When the belt cover wears in spots or has a rough jagged appearance, check the pulley grooves for roughness.

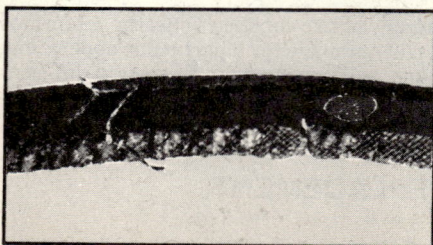

Separation

This belt is on the verge of breaking and leaving you stranded. The layers of the belt are separating and the reinforcing cords are exposed. It's just a matter of time before it breaks completely.

1 GENERAL INFORMATION AND MAINTENANCE

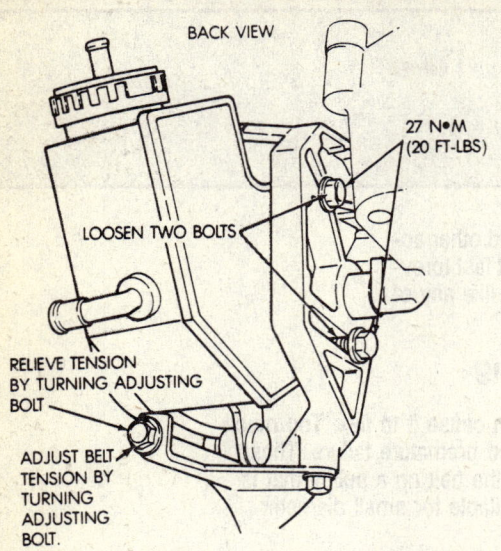

Power steering adjustment points on all engines with a serpentine belt — rear view

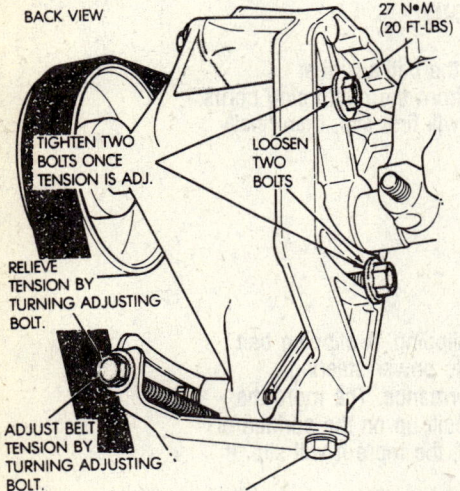

Serpentine belt adjustment points on 4-2.5L engines without power steering — rear view

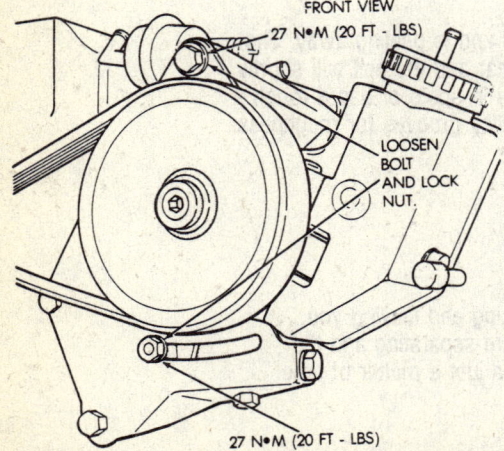

Power steering adjustment points on all engines with a serpentine belt — front view

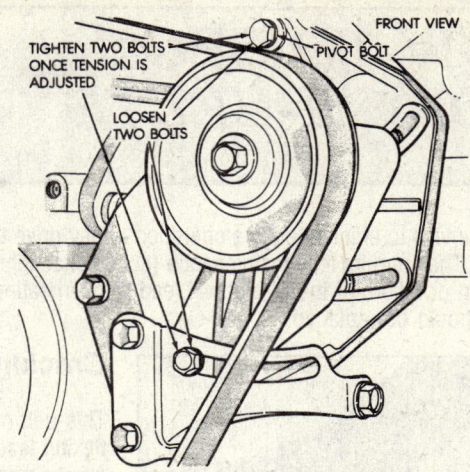

Serpentine belt adjustment points on 4-2.5L engines without power steering — front view

slightly. If necessary, also loosen the mounting belt slightly.

3. Using a pry bar or broom handle, pry against the pump rear cover to move the pump toward or away from the engine as necessary.

— CAUTION —
Do not pry against the pump housing itself, as damage to the housing may result.

4. Holding the pump in place, tighten the adjusting arm bolt and recheck the tension. When the belt is properly tensioned, tighten the mounting bolt.

SERPENTINE (SINGLE) DRIVE BELT MODELS

Some models feature a single, wide, ribbed V-belt that drives the water pump, alternator, air pump and (on some models) the air conditioner compressor and power steering pump. To install a new belt, loosen the bracket lock bolt, retract the belt tensioner with a pry bar and slide the old belt off of the pulleys. Slip on a new belt and release the tensioner and tighten the lock bolt. The spring powered tensioner eliminates the need for periodic adjustments.

WARNING: Check to make sure that the V-ribbed belt is located properly in all drive pulleys before applying tensioner pressure. When installing a serpentine accessory drive belt, the belt must be routed correctly. If not, the engine may overheat due to the water pump rotating in the wrong direction. Refer to the appropriate drive belt schematic for the correct belt routing.

Hoses

REMOVAL AND INSTALLATION

Radiator hoses are generally of two constructions, the preformed (molded) type, which is custom made for a particular application, and the spring-loaded type, which is made to fit several different applications. Heater hoses are all of the same general construction.

REPLACEMENT

Inspect the condition of the radiator and heater hoses periodically. Early spring and at the beginning of the fall or winter, when

GENERAL INFORMATION AND MAINTENANCE 1

9. The compressor is now isolated from the system. The service valves may be removed from the compressor.

RECYCLING

R12 refrigerant is a chloroflorocarbon (CFC) that can contribute to the depletion of the ozone layer in the upper atmosphere. Ozone filters out harmful radiation from the sun. To assist in protecting the ozone layer, Jeep/Eagle recommends that an R12 refrigerant recycling device be used in any service which requires discharging the air conditioning system.

DISCHARGING THE SYSTEM

1. Remove the caps from the high and low pressure charging valves in the high and low pressure lines.
2. Turn both manifold gauge set hand valves to the fully closed (clockwise) position.
3. Connect the manifold gauge set.
4. If the gauge set hoses do not have the gauge port actuating pins, install fitting adapters on the manifold gauge set hoses. If the truck does not have a service access gauge port valve, connect the gauge set low pressure hose to the evaporator service access gauge port valve.
5. Place the end of the center hose away from you and the truck.
6. Open the low pressure gauge valve slightly and allow the system pressure to bleed off.
7. When the system is just about empty, open the high pressure valve very slowly to avoid losing an excessive amount of refrigerant oil. Allow any remaining refrigerant to escape.

EVACUATING THE SYSTEM

NOTE: This procedure requires the use of a vacuum pump.

1. Connect the manifold gauge set.
2. Discharge the system.
3. Make sure that the low pressure gauge set hose is connected to the low pressure service gauge port on the top center of the accumulator/drier assembly and the high pressure hose connected to the high pressure service gauge port on the compressor discharge line.
4. Connect the center service hose to the inlet fitting of the vacuum pump.
5. Turn both gauge set valves to the wide open position.
6. Start the pump and note the low side gauge reading.
7. Operate the pump until the low pressure gauge reads 25-30 in.Hg. Continue running the vacuum pump for 10 minutes more. If you've replaced some component in the system, run the pump for an additional 20-30 minutes.
8. Leak test the system. Close both gauge set valves. Turn off the pump. The needle should remain stationary at the point at which the pump was turned off. If the needle drops to zero rapidly, there is a leak in the system which must be repaired.

LEAK TESTING

Some leak tests can be performed with a soapy water solution. There must be at least a 4½ lb. charge in the system for a leak to be detected. The most extensive leak tests are performed with either a Halide flame type leak tester or the more preferable electronic leak tester.

In either case, the equipment is expensive, and the use of a Halide detector can be **extremely** hazardous!

CHARGING THE SYSTEM

CAUTION
NEVER OPEN THE HIGH PRESSURE SIDE WITH A CAN OF REFRIGERANT CONNECTED TO THE SYSTEM! OPENING THE HIGH PRESSURE SIDE WILL OVER PRESSURIZE THE CAN, CAUSING IT TO EXPLODE!

Systems With Sight Glass

In this procedure the refrigerant enters the suction side of the system as a vapor while the compressor is running. Before proceeding, the system should be in a partial vacuum after adequate evacuation. Both hand valves on the gauge manifold should be closed.

1. Attach both test hoses to their respective service valve ports. Mid-position manually operated service valves, if present.
2. Install the dispensing valve (closed position) on the refrigerant container. (Single and multiple refrigerant manifolds are available to accommodate one to four 15 oz. cans.)
3. Attach the center charging hose to the refrigerant container valve.
4. Open dispensing valve on the refrigerant container.
5. Loosen the center charging hose coupler where it connects to the gauge manifold to allow the escaping refrigerant to purge the hose of contaminants.
6. Tighten the center charging hose connector.
7. Purge the low pressure test hose at the gauge manifold.
8. Start the truck engine, roll down the truck windows and adjust the air conditioner to maximum cooling. The truck engine should be at normal operating temperature before proceeding. The heated environment helps the liquid vaporize more efficiently.
9. Crack open the low side hand valve on the manifold. Manipulate the valve so that the refrigerant that enters the system does not cause the low side pressure to exceed 40 psi. Too sudden a surge may permit the entrance of unwanted liquid to the compressor. Since liquids cannot be compressed, the compressor will suffer damage if compelled to attempt it. If the suction side of the system remains in a vacuum, the system is blocked. Locate and correct the condition before proceeding any further.

NOTE: Placing the refrigerant can in a container of warm water (no hotter than +125°F [+51.6°C]) will speed the charging process. Slight agitation of the can is helpful too, but be careful not to turn the can upside down.

Systems Without Sight Glass

1. Connect the gauge set.
2. Close (clockwise) both gauge set valves.
3. Connect the center hose to the refrigerant can opener valve.
4. Make sure the dispensing valve is closed, that is, the needle is raised, and connect the valve to the can. Open the valve, puncturing the can with the needle.
5. Loosen the center hose fitting at the pressure gauge, allowing refrigerant to purge the hose of contaminates. When the air is bled, tighten the fitting.

CAUTION
IF THE LOW PRESSURE GAUGE SET HOSE IS NOT CONNECTED TO THE ACCUMULATOR/DRIER, KEEP THE CAN IN AN UPRIGHT POSITION!

6. Disconnect the wire harness snap-lock connector from the clutch cycling pressure switch and install a jumper wire across the two terminals of the connector.
7. Open the low side gauge set valve and the can valve.
8. Allow refrigerant to be drawn into the system.
9. When no more refrigerant is drawn into the system, start the engine and run it at about 1,500 rpm. Turn on the system and

1-27

1 GENERAL INFORMATION AND MAINTENANCE

Troubleshooting Basic Air Conditioning Problems

Problem	Cause	Solution
There's little or no air coming from the vents (and you're sure it's on)	• The A/C fuse is blown • Broken or loose wires or connections • The on/off switch is defective	• Check and/or replace fuse • Check and/or repair connections • Replace switch
The air coming from the vents is not cool enough	• Windows and air vent wings open • The compressor belt is slipping • Heater is on • Condenser is clogged with debris • Refrigerant has escaped through a leak in the system • Receiver/drier is plugged	• Close windows and vent wings • Tighten or replace compressor belt • Shut heater off • Clean the condenser • Check system • Service system
The air has an odor	• Vacuum system is disrupted • Odor producing substances on the evaporator case • Condensation has collected in the bottom of the evaporator housing	• Have the system checked/repaired • Clean the evaporator case • Clean the evaporator housing drains
System is noisy or vibrating	• Compressor belt or mountings loose • Air in the system	• Tighten or replace belt; tighten mounting bolts • Have the system serviced

Sight glass condition
    Constant bubbles, foam or oil streaks
    Clear sight glass, but no cold air
    Clear sight glass, but air is cold
    Clouded with milky fluid
	• Undercharged system
	• No refrigerant at all
	• System is OK
	• Receiver drier is leaking dessicant
		• Charge the system
		• Check and charge the system
		• Have system checked

Large difference in temperature of lines	• System undercharged	• Charge and leak test the system
Compressor noise	• Broken valves • Overcharged • Incorrect oil level • Piston slap • Broken rings • Drive belt pulley bolts are loose	• Replace the valve plate • Discharge, evacuate and install the correct charge • Isolate the compressor and check the oil level. Correct as necessary. • Replace the compressor • Replace the compressor • Tighten with the correct torque specification
Excessive vibration	• Incorrect belt tension • Clutch loose • Overcharged • Pulley is misaligned	• Adjust the belt tension • Tighten the clutch • Discharge, evacuate and install the correct charge • Align the pulley
Condensation dripping in the passenger compartment	• Drain hose plugged or improperly positioned • Insulation removed or improperly installed	• Clean the drain hose and check for proper installation • Replace the insulation on the expansion valve and hoses

GENERAL INFORMATION AND MAINTENANCE 1

Troubleshooting Basic Air Conditioning Problems (cont.)

Problem	Cause	Solution
Frozen evaporator coil	• Faulty thermostat • Thermostat capillary tube improperly installed • Thermostat not adjusted properly	• Replace the thermostat • Install the capillary tube correctly • Adjust the thermostat
Low side low—high side low	• System refrigerant is low • Expansion valve is restricted	• Evacuate, leak test and charge the system • Replace the expansion valve
Low side high—high side low	• Internal leak in the compressor—worn	• Remove the compressor cylinder head and inspect the compressor. Replace the valve plate assembly if necessary. If the compressor pistons, rings or
Low side high—high side low (cont.)		cylinders are excessively worn or scored replace the compressor
	• Cylinder head gasket is leaking • Expansion valve is defective • Drive belt slipping	• Install a replacement cylinder head gasket • Replace the expansion valve • Adjust the belt tension
Low side high—high side high	• Condenser fins obstructed • Air in the system • Expansion valve is defective • Loose or worn fan belts	• Clean the condenser fins • Evacuate, leak test and charge the system • Replace the expansion valve • Adjust or replace the belts as necessary
Low side low—high side high	• Expansion valve is defective • Restriction in the refrigerant hose	• Replace the expansion valve • Check the hose for kinks—replace if necessary
Low side low—high side high	• Restriction in the receiver/drier • Restriction in the condenser	• Replace the receiver/drier • Replace the condenser
Low side and high normal (inadequate cooling)	• Air in the system • Moisture in the system	• Evacuate, leak test and charge the system • Evacuate, leak test and charge the system

operate it at the full high position. The compressor will operate and pull refrigerant gas into the system.

NOTE: To help speed the process, the can may be placed, upright, in a pan of warm water, not exceeding 125°F (52°C).

10. If more than one can of refrigerant is needed, close the dispensing valve and gauge set low side valve when the can is empty and connect a new can. Repeat the charging process until no more refrigerant is drawn into the system. The frost line on the outside of the can will indicate what portion of the can has been used.

── **CAUTION** ──
NEVER ALLOW THE HIGH PRESSURE SIDE READING TO EXCEED 240 psi.

11. When the charging process has been completed, close the gauge set valve and dispensing valve. Remove the jumper wire and reconnect the cycling clutch wire. Run the system for at least five minutes to allow it to normalize. Low pressure side reading should be 4-25 psi; high pressure reading should be 120-210 psi at an ambient temperature of 70-90°F (21-32°C).

12. Loosen both service hoses at the gauges to allow any refrigerant to escape. Remove the gauge set and install the dust caps on the service valves.

NOTE: Multi-can dispensers are available which allow a simultaneous hook-up of up to four 1 lb. cans of R-12.

WARNING: Before operating the system, make sure the service valves are in the BACK-SEATED position. Damage to the compressor will occur if the system is operated with either valve in the FRONT-SEATED position.

1 GENERAL INFORMATION AND MAINTENANCE

CAUTION

Never exceed the recommended maximum charge for the system! The maximum charge for an evacuated (fully empty) system is 38 oz.

CHECKING COMPRESSOR OIL

Use this procedure to check compressor (system) oil level for routine maintenance or when checking oil level after replacing a system component other than the compressor. See Compressor Removal and Installation for alternate procedure.
1. Start and operate the engine at idle for 10 minutes with the air conditioning ON.
2. Stop the engine and disconnect the magnetic clutch feed wire.
3. Front-seat the discharge and suction service valves.
4. Determine the mounting angle (usually 0°) by positioning an angle gauge across the front mounting ears.
5. Remove the oil filler plug. Position internal parts by rotating the front plate counterweight to 30° angle.
6. Insert the dipstick tool (J29642-B) to its STOP position.
7. Remove the dipstick and count the increments of oil. Fill or drain to 3-5 increments.
8. Reinstall the oil filler plug and torque to 7 ft.lbs.

Windshield Wipers

Intense heat from the sun, snow, and ice, road oils and the chemicals used in windshield washer solvent combine to deteriorate the rubber wiper refills. The refills should be replaced about twice a year or whenever the blades begin to streak or chatter.

WIPER REFILL REPLACEMENT

Normally, if the wipers are not cleaning the windshield properly, only the refill has to be replaced. The blade and arm usually require replacement only in the event of damage. It is not necessary (except on new Tridon® refills) to remove the arm or the blade to replace the refill (rubber part), though you may have to position the arm higher on the glass. You can do this turning the ignition switch on and operating the wipers. When they are positioned where they are accessible, turn the ignition switch off.

There are several types of refills and your vehicle could have any kind, since aftermarket blades and arms may not use exactly the same type refill as the original equipment.

Most Anco® styles use a release button that is pushed down to allow the refill to slide out of the yoke jaws. The new refill slides in and locks in place.

Some Trico® refills are removed by locating where the metal backing strip or the refill is wider. Insert a small screwdriver blade between the frame and metal backing strip. Press down to release the refill from the retaining tab.

Other Trico® blades are unlocked at one end by squeezing 2 metal tabs, and the refill is slid out of the frame jaws. When the new refill is installed, the tabs will click into place, locking the refill.

The polycarbonate type is held in place by a locking lever that is pushed downward out of the groove in the arm to free the refill. When the new refill is installed, it will lock in place automatically.

The Tridon® refill has a plastic backing strip with a notch about 1 in. (25mm) from the end. Hold the blade (frame) on a hard surface so that the frame is tightly bowed. Grip the tip of the backing strip and pull up while twisting counterclockwise. The backing strip will snap out of the retaining tab. Do this for the remaining tabs until the refill is free of the arm. The length of these refills is molded into the end and they should be replaced with identical types.

No matter which type of refill you use, be sure that all of the frame claws engage the refill.

WARNING: Do not attempt to operate windshield wipers with out refills installed. Unrepairable scratching of the windshield will occur.

Tires and Wheels

The tires should be rotated as specified in the Maintenance Intervals Chart. Refer to the accompanying illustrations for the recommended rotation patterns.

The tires on your truck should have built-in tread wear indicators, which appear as $4^{1}/_{2}$ in. (12.7mm) bands when the tread depth gets as low as $1/_{16}$ in. (1.6mm). When the indicators appear in 2 or more adjacent grooves, it's time for new tires.

For optimum tire life, you should keep the tires properly inflated, rotate them often and have the wheel alignment checked periodically.

Pressures should be checked before driving, since pressure can increase as much as 6 psi due to heat. It is a good idea to have an accurate gauge and to check pressures weekly. Not all gauges on service station air pumps are to be trusted. In general, truck type tires require higher pressures and flotation type tires, lower pressures.

TIRE ROTATION

It is recommended that you have the tires rotated and the balance checked every 7,500 miles. There is no way to give a tire rotation diagram for every combination of tires and vehicles, but the

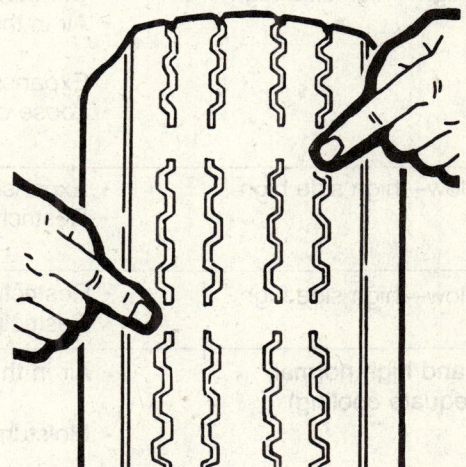

Tread wear indicators are built into all new tires. When they appear, it's time to replace the tires

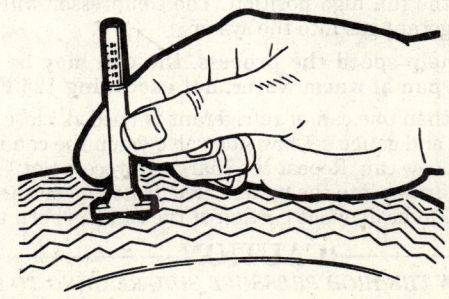

Tread depth can also be checked with an inexpensive gauge made for the purpose

GENERAL INFORMATION AND MAINTENANCE

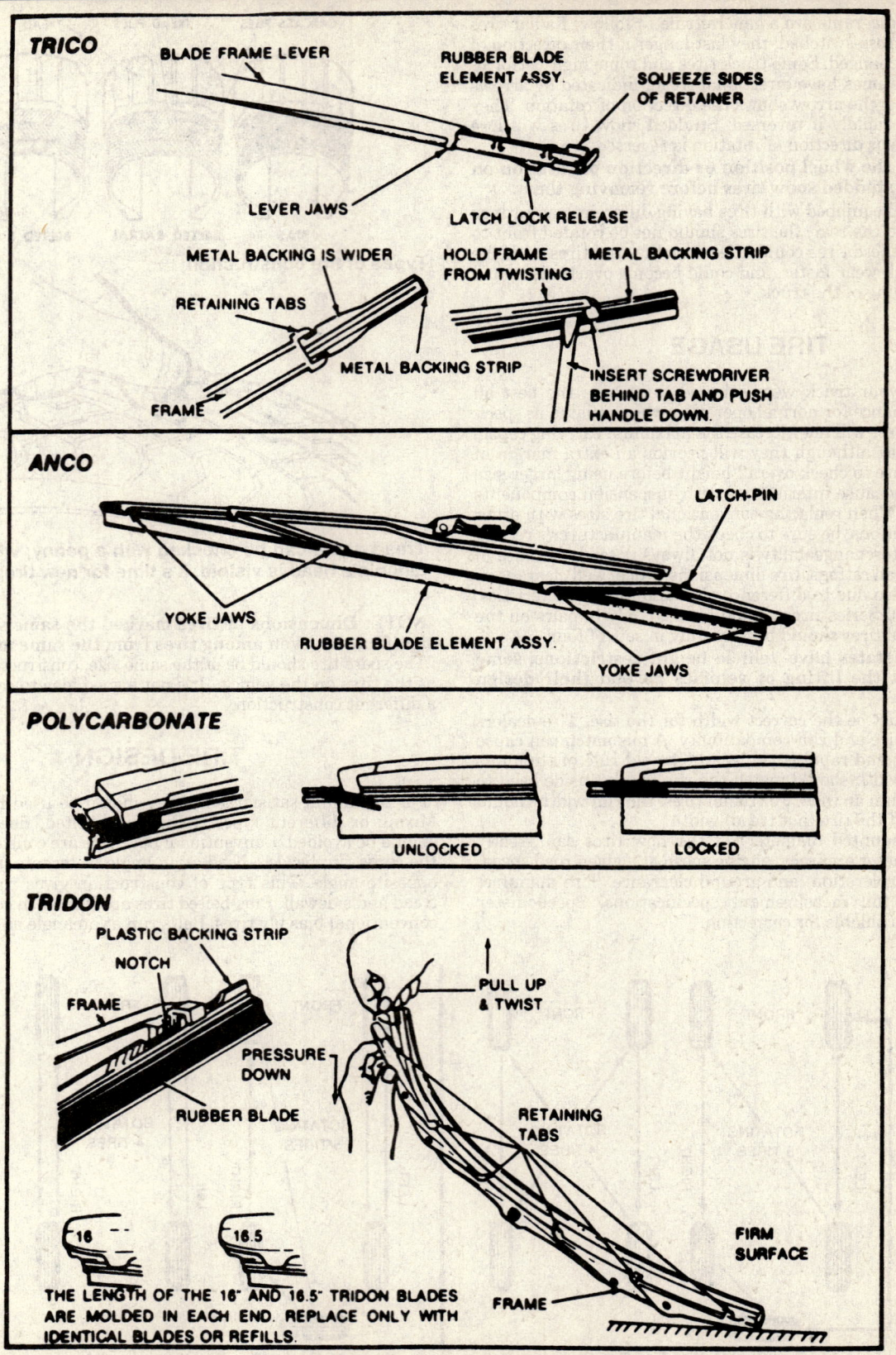

Popular styles of wiper refills

1 GENERAL INFORMATION AND MAINTENANCE

accompanying diagrams are a general rule to follow. Radial tires should not be cross-switched; they last longer if their direction of rotation is not changed. Some truck tires and some high-performance tires sometimes have directional tread, indicated by arrows on the sidewalls; the arrow shows the direction of rotation. They will wear very rapidly if reversed. Studded snow tires will lose their studs if their direction of rotation is reversed.

NOTE: Mark the wheel position or direction of rotation on radial tires or studded snow tires before removing them.

If your truck is equipped with tires having different load ratings on the front and the rear, the tires should not be rotated front to rear. Rotating these tires could affect tire life (the tires with the lower rating will wear faster, and could become overloaded), and upset the handling of the truck.

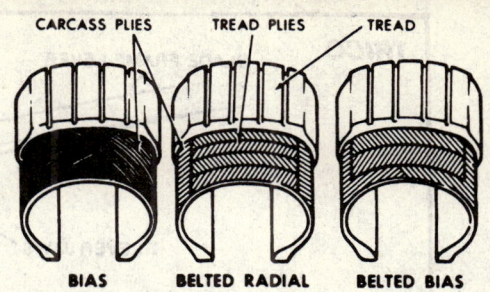

Types of tire construction

TIRE USAGE

The tires on your truck were selected to provide the best all around performance for normal operation when inflated as specified. Oversize tires will not increase the maximum carrying capacity of the vehicle, although they will provide an extra margin of tread life. Be sure to check overall height before using larger size tires which may cause interference with suspension components or wheel wells. When replacing conventional tire sizes with other tire size designations, be sure to check the manufacturer's recommendations. Interchangeability is not always possible because of differences in load ratings, tire dimensions, wheel well clearances, and rim size. Also due to differences in handling characteristics, 70 Series and 60 Series tires should be used only in pairs on the same axle; radial tires should be used only in sets of four.

NOTE: Many states have vehicle height restrictions; some states prohibit the lifting of vehicles beyond their design limits.

The wheels must be the correct width for the tire. Tire dealers have charts of tire and rim compatibility. A mismatch can cause sloppy handling and rapid tread wear. The old rule of thumb is that the tread width should match the rim width (inside bead to inside bead) within an inch. For radial tires, the rim width should be 80% or less of the tire (not tread) width.

The height (mounted diameter) of the new tires can greatly change speedometer accuracy, engine speed at a given road speed, fuel mileage, acceleration, and ground clearance. Tire manufacturers furnish full measurement specifications. Speedometer drive gears are available for correction.

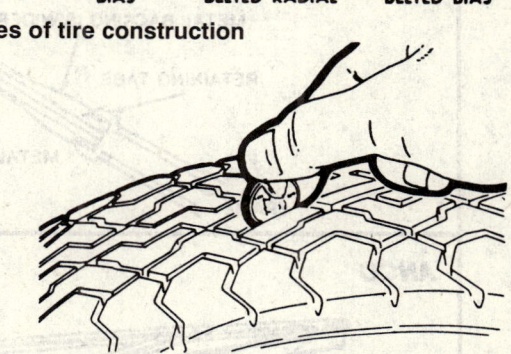

Tread depth can be checked with a penny; when the top of Lincoln's head is visible, it's time for new tires

NOTE: Dimensions of tires marked the same size may vary significantly, even among tires from the same manufacturer.

The spare tire should be of the same size, construction and design as the tires on the vehicle. It's not a good idea to carry a spare of a different construction.

TIRE DESIGN

For maximum satisfaction, tires should be used in sets of five. Mixing or different types (radial, bias-belted, fiberglass belted) should be avoided. Conventional bias tires are constructed so that the cords run bead-to-bead at an angle. Alternate plies run at an opposite angle. This type of construction gives rigidity to both tread and sidewall. Bias-belted tires are similar in construction to conventional bias ply tires. Belts run at an angle and also at a 90°

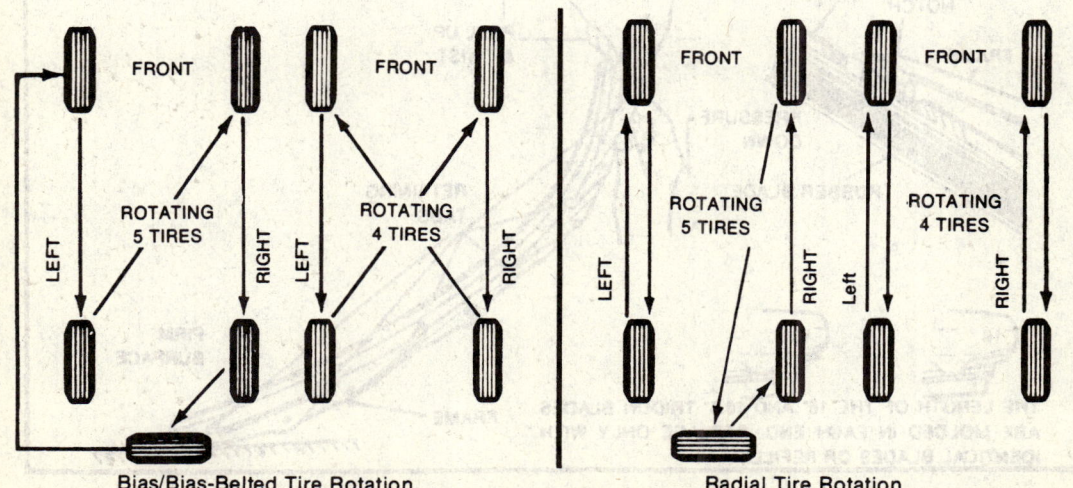

Tire rotation

GENERAL INFORMATION AND MAINTENANCE

Tire Size Comparison Chart

"Letter" sizes			Inch Sizes	Metric-inch Sizes		
"60 Series"	"70 Series"	"78 Series"	1965–77	"60 Series"	"70 Series"	"80 Series"
		Y78-12	5.50-12, 5.60-12 6.00-12	165/60-12	165/70-12	155-12
		W78-13	5.20-13	165/60-13	145/70-13	135-13
		Y78-13	5.60-13	175/60-13	155/70-13	145-13
			6.15-13	185/60-13	165/70-13	155-13, P155/80-13
A60-13	A70-13	A78-13	6.40-13	195/60-13	175/70-13	165-13
B60-13	B70-13	B78-13	6.70-13	205/60-13	185/70-13	175-13
			6.90-13			
C60-13	C70-13	C78-13	7.00-13	215/60-13	195/70-13	185-13
D60-13	D70-13	D78-13	7.25-13			
E60-13	E70-13	E78-13	7.75-13			195-13
			5.20-14	165/60-14	145/70-14	135-14
			5.60-14	175/60-14	155/70-14	145-14
			5.90-14			
A60-14	A70-14	A78-14	6.15-14	185/60-14	165/70-14	155-14
	B70-14	B78-14	6.45-14	195/60-14	175/70-14	165-14
	C70-14	C78-14	6.95-14	205/60-14	185/70-14	175-14
D60-14	D70-14	D78-14				
E60-14	E70-14	E78-14	7.35-14	215/60-14	195/70-14	185-14
F60-14	F70-14	F78-14, F83-14	7.75-14	225/60-14	200/70-14	195-14
G60-14	G70-14	G77-14, G78-14	8.25-14	235/60-14	205/70-14	205-14
H60-14	H70-14	H78-14	8.55-14	245/60-14	215/70-14	215-14
J60-14	J70-14	J78-14	8.85-14	255/60-14	225/70-14	225-14
L60-14	L70-14		9.15-14	265/60-14	235/70-14	
	A70-15	A78-15	5.60-15	185/60-15	165/70-15	155-15
B60-15	B70-15	B78-15	6.35-15	195/60-15	175/70-15	165-15
C60-15	C70-15	C78-15	6.85-15	205/60-15	185/70-15	175-15
	D70-15	D78-15				
E60-15	E70-15	E78-15	7.35-15	215/60-15	195/70-15	185-15
F60-15	F70-15	F78-15	7.75-15	225/60-15	205/70-15	195-15
G60-15	G70-15	G78-15	8.15-15/8.25-15	235/60-15	215/70-15	205-15
H60-15	H70-15	H78-15	8.45-15/8.55-15	245/60-15	225/70-15	215-15
J60-15	J70-15	J78-15	8.85-15/8.90-15	255/60-15	235/70-15	225-15
	K70-15		9.00-15	265/60-15	245/70-15	230-15
L60-15	L70-15	L78-15, L84-15	9.15-15			235-15
	M70-15	M78-15				255-15
		N78-15				

Note: Every size tire is not listed and many size comparisons are approximate, based on load ratings. Wider tires than those supplied new with the vehicle, should always be checked for clearance.

1-33

1 GENERAL INFORMATION AND MAINTENANCE

Troubleshooting Basic Wheel Problems

Problem	Cause	Solution
The car's front end vibrates at high speed	• The wheels are out of balance • Wheels are out of alignment	• Have wheels balanced • Have wheel alignment checked/adjusted
Car pulls to either side	• Wheels are out of alignment • Unequal tire pressure • Different size tires or wheels	• Have wheel alignment checked/adjusted • Check/adjust tire pressure • Change tires or wheels to same size
The car's wheel(s) wobbles	• Loose wheel lug nuts • Wheels out of balance • Damaged wheel • Wheels are out of alignment • Worn or damaged ball joint • Excessive play in the steering linkage (usually due to worn parts) • Defective shock absorber	• Tighten wheel lug nuts • Have tires balanced • Raise car and spin the wheel. If the wheel is bent, it should be replaced • Have wheel alignment checked/adjusted • Check ball joints • Check steering linkage • Check shock absorbers
Tires wear unevenly or prematurely	• Incorrect wheel size • Wheels are out of balance • Wheels are out of alignment	• Check if wheel and tire size are compatible • Have wheels balanced • Have wheel alignment checked/adjusted

Troubleshooting Basic Tire Problems

Problem	Cause	Solution
The car's front end vibrates at high speeds and the steering wheel shakes	• Wheels out of balance • Front end needs aligning	• Have wheels balanced • Have front end alignment checked
The car pulls to one side while cruising	• Unequal tire pressure (car will usually pull to the low side) • Mismatched tires • Front end needs aligning	• Check/adjust tire pressure • Be sure tires are of the same type and size • Have front end alignment checked
Abnormal, excessive or uneven tire wear See "How to Read Tire Wear"	• Infrequent tire rotation • Improper tire pressure • Sudden stops/starts or high speed on curves	• Rotate tires more frequently to equalize wear • Check/adjust pressure • Correct driving habits
Tire squeals	• Improper tire pressure • Front end needs aligning	• Check/adjust tire pressure • Have front end alignment checked

GENERAL INFORMATION AND MAINTENANCE

Condition	Rapid Wear at Shoulders	Rapid Wear at Center	Cracked Treads	Wear on One Side	Feathered Edge	Bald Spots	Scalloped Wear
Effect							
Cause	Under-inflation or lack of rotation	Over-inflation or lack of rotation	Under-inflation or excessive speed*	Excessive camber	Incorrect toe	Unbalanced wheel or tire defect*	Lack of rotation of tires or worn or out-of-alignment suspension.
Correction	Adjust pressure to specifications when tires are cool rotate tires			Adjust camber to specifications	Adjust toe-in to specifications	Dynamic or static balance wheels	Rotate tires and inspect suspension see Group 2

*HAVE TIRE INSPECTED FOR FURTHER USE.

Vehicle	GVW Rating		Tire Size	Tire Pressure (psi) Normal Load[1]				Tire Pressure (psi) Maximum Load[2]				Wheel Sizes (Inches)
				Sustained Driving 65 mph (105 km/h)		Under 65 mph (105 km/h)		Sustained Driving 65 mph (105 km/h)		Under 65 mph (105 km/h)		
	lbs	kg		Front	Rear	Front	Rear	Front	Rear	Front	Rear	
	4850	2200	P195/75R15	33	33	33	33	35	35	33	33	Aluminum Wheel is 15 × 7
			P205/75R15	30	30	30	30	33	33	30	30	
			P215/75R15	30	30	30	30	33	33	30	30	15 × 6
			P225/75R15	30	30	30	30	33	33	30	30	15 × 7
			P215/65R15	30	30	30	30	33	33	30	30	
			Compact Spare			60	60			60	60	
	4640	2105	P195/75R15	33	33	33	33	35	35	33	33	Aluminum Wheel is 15 × 7
			P205/75R15	30	30	30	30	33	33	30	30	
			P215/75R15	30	30	30	30	33	33	30	30	15 × 6
			P225/75R15	30	30	30	30	33	33	30	30	15 × 7
			P225/70R15	30	35	30	35	33	35	30	35	
			Compact Spare			60	60			60	60	

angle to the bead, as in the radial tire. Tread life is improved considerably over the conventional bias tire. The radial tire differs in construction. Instead of the carcass plies running at an angle of 90° to each other, they run at an angle of 90° to the bead. This gives the tread a great deal of rigidity, the sidewall a great deal of flexibility, and accounts for the characteristic bulge associated with radial tires.

When radial tires are used, tire sizes and wheel diameters should be selected to maintain ground clearance and tire load capacity equivalent to the minimum specified tire. Radial tires should always be used in sets of five, but in an emergency, radial tires can be used with caution on the rear axle only. If this is done, both tires on the rear should be of radial design.

WARNING: Radial tires should never be used on only the front axle!

FLUIDS AND LUBRICANTS

Oil and Fuel Recommendations

All gasoline engines are designed to run on unleaded gasoline.

The Diesel engine in your Jeep is designed to run on No.2 Diesel fuel with a cetane rating of 40. For operation when the outdoor air temperature is consistently below freezing, the use of No.1 Diesel fuel or the addition of a cold weather additive, is recommended.

Fuel makers produce two grades of diesel fuel, No. 1 and No. 2, for use in automotive diesel engines. Generally speaking, No. 2 fuel is recommended over No. 1 for driving in temperatures above 20°F (−7°C). In fact, in many areas, No. 2 diesel is the only fuel available. By comparison, No. 2 diesel fuel is less volatile than No. 1 fuel, and gives better fuel economy. No. 2 fuel is also a better injection pump lubricant.

Two important characteristics of diesel fuel are its cetane number and its viscosity.

The cetane number of a diesel fuel refers to the ease with which a diesel fuel ignites. High cetane numbers mean that the fuel will ignite with relative ease or that it ignites well at low temperatures. Naturally, the lower the cetane number, the higher the temperature must be to ignite the fuel. Most commercial fuels have cetane numbers that range from 35 to 65. No. 1 diesel fuel generally has a higher cetane rating than No. 2 fuel.

Viscosity is the ability of a liquid, in this case diesel fuel, to flow. Using straight No. 2 diesel fuel below 20°F (−7°C) can cause problems, because this fuel tends to become cloudy, meaning wax crystals begin forming in the fuel. 20°F (−7°C) is often call the cloud point for No. 2 fuel. In extremely cold weather, No. 2 fuel can stop flowing altogether. In either case, fuel flow is restricted, which can result in no start condition or poor engine performance. Fuel manufacturers often winterize No. 2 diesel fuel by using various fuel additives and blends (no. 1 diesel fuel, kerosene, etc.) to lower its winter time viscosity. Generally speaking, though, No. 1 diesel fuel is more satisfactory in extremely cold weather.

1 GENERAL INFORMATION AND MAINTENANCE

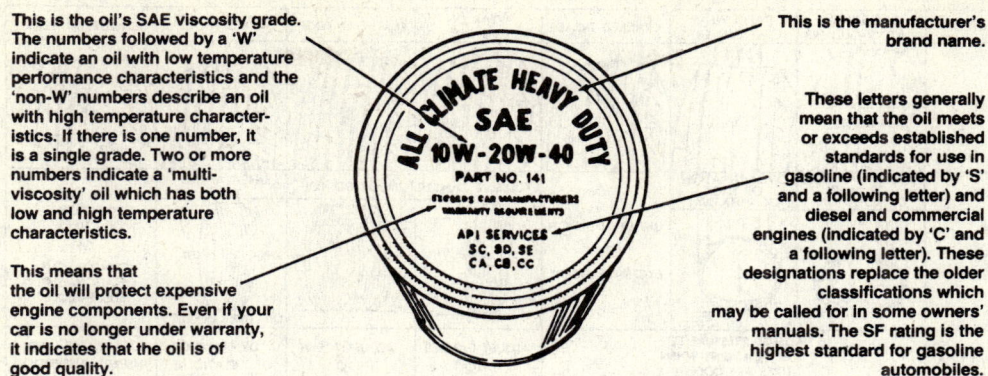

This is the oil's SAE viscosity grade. The numbers followed by a 'W' indicate an oil with low temperature performance characteristics and the 'non-W' numbers describe an oil with high temperature characteristics. If there is one number, it is a single grade. Two or more numbers indicate a 'multi-viscosity' oil which has both low and high temperature characteristics.

This means that the oil will protect expensive engine components. Even if your car is no longer under warranty, it indicates that the oil is of good quality.

This is the manufacturer's brand name.

These letters generally mean that the oil meets or exceeds established standards for use in gasoline (indicated by 'S' and a following letter) and diesel and commercial engines (indicated by 'C' and a following letter). These designations replace the older classifications which may be called for in some owners' manuals. The SF rating is the highest standard for gasoline automobiles.

The top of the oil can will tell you all you need to know about the oil

NOTE: No. 1 and No. 2 diesel fuels will mix and burn with no ill effects, although the engine manufacturer will undoubtedly recommend one or the other. Consult the owner's manual for information.

Depending on local climate, most fuel manufacturers make winterized No. 2 fuel available seasonally.

Many automobile manufacturers publish pamphlets giving the locations of diesel fuel stations nationwide. Contact the local dealer for information.

Do not substitute home heating oil for automotive diesel fuel. While in some cases, home heating oil refinement levels equal those of diesel fuel, many times they are far below diesel engine requirements. The result of using dirty home heating oil will be a clogged fuel system, in which case the entire system may have to be dismantled and cleaned.

One more word on diesel fuels. Don't thin diesel fuel with gasoline in cold weather. The lighter gasoline, which is more explosive, will cause rough running at the very least, and may cause extensive damage to the fuel system if enough is used.

Many factors help to determine the proper oil for your Jeep. The big question is what viscosity to use and when. The whole question of viscosity revolves around the lowest anticipated ambient temperature to be encountered before your next oil change. The recommended viscosity ratings for temperatures ranging from below 0° to above 32° are listed in the accompanying illustration.

Oil viscosities should be chosen from those oils recommended for the lowest anticipated temperatures during the oil change interval. Due to the need for an oil that embodies both good lubrication at high temperatures and easy cranking in cold weather, multi-grade oils have been developed. Basically, a multigrade oil is thinner at low temperatures and thicker at high temperatures. For example, a 10W-40 oil (the W stands for winter) exhibits the characteristics of a 10 weight (SAE 10) oil when the truck is first started and the oil is cold. Its lighter weight allows it to travel to the lubricating surfaces quicker and offer less resistance to starter motor cranking than, say, a straight 30 weight (SAE 30) oil. But after the engine reaches operating temperature, the 10W-40 oil begins acting like straight 40 weight (SAE 40) oil, its heavier weight providing greater lubrication with less chance of foaming than a straight 30 weight oil.

The SAE grade number indicates the viscosity of the engine oil, or its ability to lubricate under a given temperature. The lower the SAE grade number, the lighter the oil; the lower the viscosity, the easier it is to crank the engine in cold weather.

The API (American Petroleum Institute) designation indicates the classification of engine oil for use under given operating conditions. For gasoline engines, only oils designated for Service SF/SG, or just SG, should be used. For Diesel engines, use only those oils designated Service SG/CD. These oils provide maximum engine protection. Both the SAE grade number and the API designation can be found on the top of a can of oil.

NOTE: Non-detergent or straight mineral oils should not be used.

Engine Oil

OIL LEVEL CHECK

First, it is necessary to make sure that your vehicle is on a level surface to ensure an accurate reading. Then, raise the hood, position the hold-up rod, if so equipped, and measure the oil with the dipstick which is on the right side of 4-cylinder engines and on the left of 6-cylinder engines. Add oil through valve cover filler hole. If the oil is below the half mark, add a quart of oil, then recheck the level. If the level is still not reading full, add only $4^{1}/_{2}$ quart at a time, until the dipstick reads full. Do not overfill the engine. When you check the oil in any engine, make sure that you allow sufficient time for all the oil to drain back into the crankcase after stopping the engine or else you will only measure a fraction of the actual amount. A minute or so should be enough time.

OIL AND FILTER CHANGE

— CAUTION —
The EPA warns that prolonged contact with used engine oil may cause a number of skin disorders, including cancer! You should make every effort to minimize your exposure to used engine oil. Protective gloves should be worn when changing the oil. Wash your hands and any other exposed skin areas as soon as possible after exposure to used engine oil. Soap and water, or waterless hand cleaner should be used.

The engine oil is to be changed every 7,500 miles. The oil should be changed more frequently, however, under conditions such as:
- Driving in dusty conditions
- Continuous trailer pulling or RV use
- Extensive or prolonged idling
- Extensive short trip operation in freezing temperatures (when the engine is not thoroughly warmed up)
- Frequent long runs at high speeds and high ambient temperatures
- Stop-and-go service, such as delivery trucks,

If any of these conditions exist, the recommended oil and filter change interval should be reduced to every 3,000 miles. Operation of the engine in severe conditions, such as a dust storm, volcanic ash or deep water, may require an immediate oil and filter change.

Before draining the oil, make sure that the engine is at operating

GENERAL INFORMATION AND MAINTENANCE 1

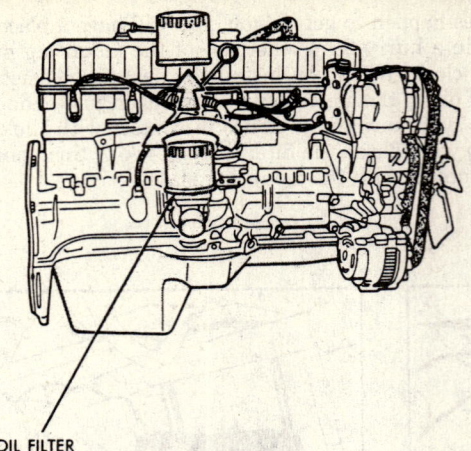

6-4.0L oil filter location

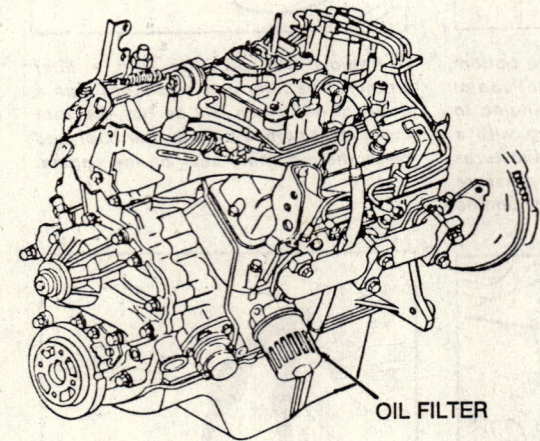

6-2.8L oil filter location

Lowest Air Temperature Anticipated	Multiviscosity Engine Oil
Above 40°F	SAE 10W-30, 40, 50 or 20W-40, 50
Above 32°F	SAE 10W-30 or 10W-40
Above 0°F	SAE 10W-30 or 10W-40
Below 0°F	SAE 5W-20 or 5W-30
	Single-Viscosity Engine Oil
Above 40°F	SAE 30 or 40
Above 32°F	SAE 20W-20
Above 0°F	SAE 20
Below 0°F	SAE 10W

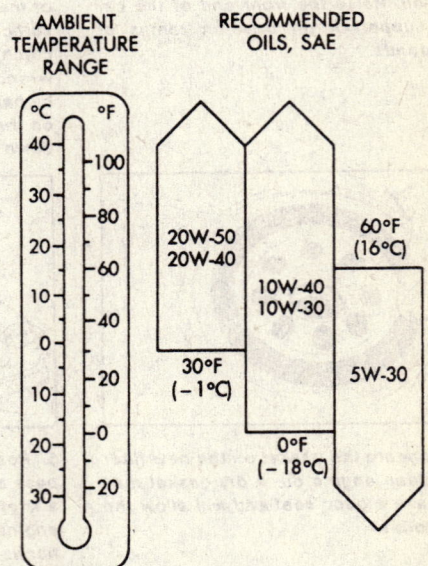

Recommended viscosity grades

temperature. Hot oil will hold more impurities in suspension and will flow better, allowing it to remove more oil and dirt.

Drain the oil into a suitable receptacle. After the drain plug is loosened, unscrew the plug with your fingers, using a rag to shield your fingers from the heat. Push in on the plug as you unscrew it so you can feel when all of the screw threads are out of the hole. You can then remove the plug quickly with the minimum amount of oil running down your arm. You will also have the plug in your hand and not in the bottom of a pan of hot oil. Be careful of the oil. If it is at operating temperatures, it is hot enough to burn you or at least make you uncomfortable.

On the 4-2.5L engines, the filter is located on the right hand side of the engine.

On the 4-126 Turbo Diesel, the filter is remotely mounted, inline with the oil cooler.

On the 6-2.8L, the filter is on the left side at the front.

On the 6-4.0L, the filter is located on the lower, center right side of the engine.

To remove a spin-on filter, you will need an oil filter wrench since the heat from the engine may have made it too tight to remove by hand. A filter wrench can be obtained at an auto parts store and is well worth the investment, since it will save you a lot of grief. Loosen the filter with the filter wrench.

CHILTON TIP: *When using a band type oil filter wrench to remove an oil filter, place the wrench as high up on the filter as possible (closest to the filter mounting pad). This will reduce the*

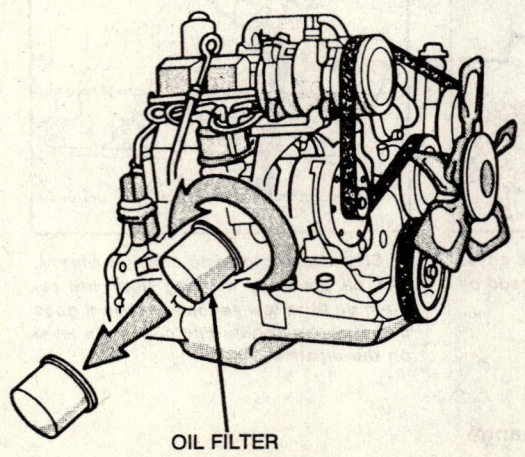

4-2.5L oil filter location

1-37

1 GENERAL INFORMATION AND MAINTENANCE

chance of crushing the oil filter and making it very difficult to remove

With a rag wrapped around the filter, unscrew the filter from the oil pump housing. Be careful of hot oil that might run down the side of the filter.

Make sure that you have a pan under the filter before you start to remove it from the engine to avoid a mess and, if some of the hot oil does happen to get on you, you will have a place to dump the filter in a hurry. Wipe the base of the mounting pad with a clean, dry cloth. When you install the new filter, smear a small amount of oil on the gasket with your finger, just enough to coat the entire surface where it comes in contact with the mounting pad. When you tighten the filter, turn it $4^{1}/_{4}$-$^{3}/_{4}$ turn more after it comes in contact with the mounting plate.

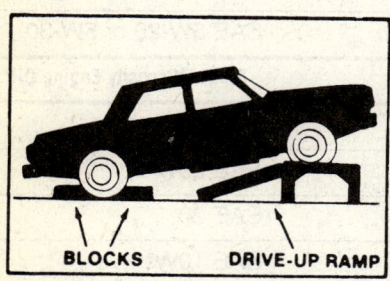
1. Warm the car up before changing your oil. Raise the front end of the car and support it on drive-on ramps or jackstands.

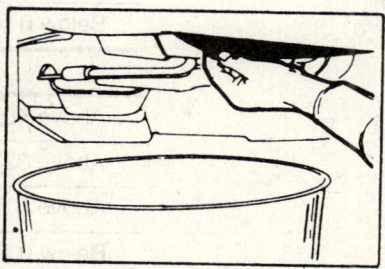
2. Locate the drain plug on the bottom of the oil pan and slide a low flat pan of sufficient capacity under the engine to catch the oil. Loosen the plug with a wrench and turn it out the last few turns by hand. Keep a steady inward pressure on the plug to avoid hot oil from running down your arm.

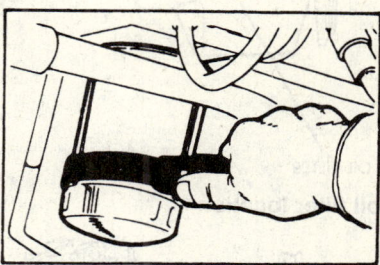
3. Remove the oil filter with a filter wrench. The filter can hold more than a quart of oil, which will be hot. Be sure the gasket comes off with the filter and clean the mounting base on the engine.

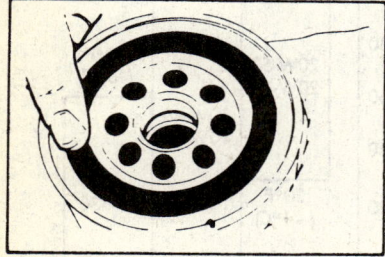
4. Lubricate the gasket on the new filter with clean engine oil. A dry gasket may not make a good seal and will allow the filter to leak.

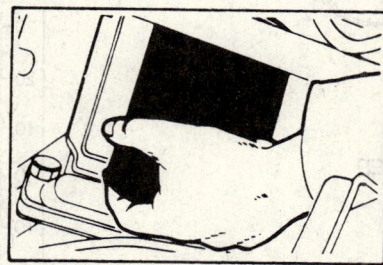
5. Position a new filter on the mounting base and spin it on by hand. Do not use a wrench. When the gasket contacts the engine, tighten it another ½–1 turn by hand.

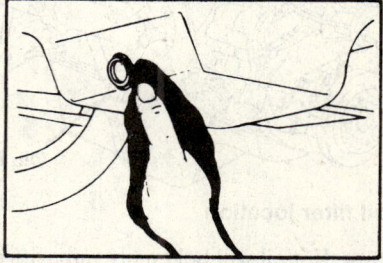
6. Using a rag, clean the drain plug and the area around the drain hole in the oil pan.

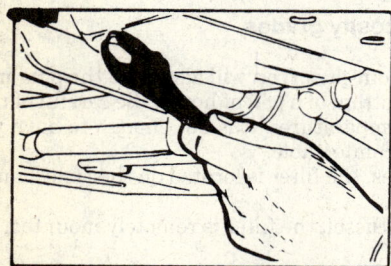
7. Install the drain plug and tighten it finger-tight. If you feel resistance, stop and be sure you are not cross-threading the plug. Finally, tighten the plug with a wrench.

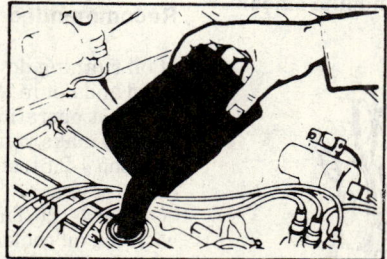
8. Locate the oil cap on the valve cover. An oil spout is the easiest way to add oil, but a funnel will do just as well.

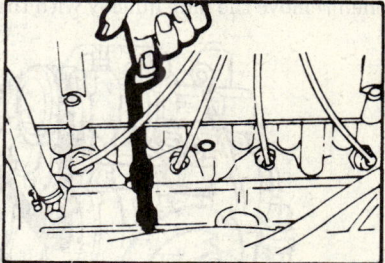
9. Start the engine and check for leaks. The oil pressure warning light will remain on for a few seconds; when it goes out, stop the engine and check the level on the dipstick.

9 easy steps to a safe oil change

GENERAL INFORMATION AND MAINTENANCE 1

Manual Transmissions

FLUID RECOMMENDATIONS

Recommended lubricant for AX 4/5/15 and BA 10/5 manual transmissions is SAE 75W-90, API Grade GL-5 gear lubricant. Warner T4 & T5 manual transmissions use DEXRON®II automatic transmission fluid.

FLUID LEVEL CHECK

The level of lubricant in the transmission should be maintained at the filler hole on all manual transmissions. This hole is locate on the right side of the transmission.

FLUID CHANGE

The lubricant in the manual transmission should be changed every 30,000 miles. To accomplish this, remove the drain plug which is located at the bottom of the transmission or on the side near the bottom. Allow all the lubricant to run out before replacing the plug. Refill using the recommended lubricant.

Transfer Case

FLUID RECOMMENDATION

All transfer cases use Dexron®II automatic transmission fluid.

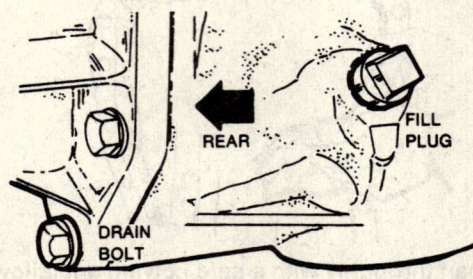

Manual transmission fill and drain plugs, using a tailshaft bolt as the drain plug

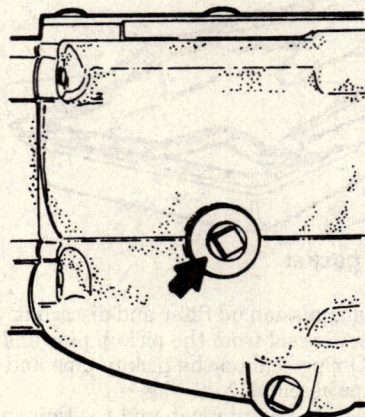

Manual transmission fill and drain plugs with the drain plug at the bottom center

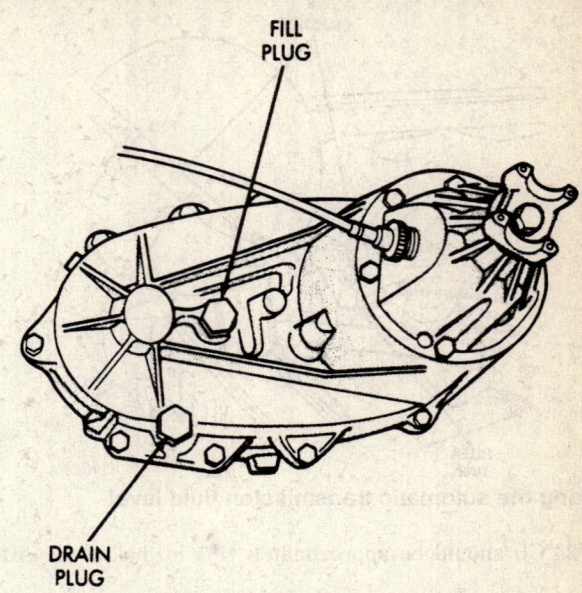

Transfer case drain and fill plugs

FLUID LEVEL CHECK

Fluid should be maintained at the level of the filler plug hole. When you check the lubricant, make sure that the vehicle is level so that you get a true reading. When the filler plug is removed, the lubricant should run out of the hole. If there is lubricant present at the hole, you know that the case is filled to the proper level. Replace the plug quickly for a minimum loss of lubricant. If lubricant does not run out of the hole when the plug is removed, lubricant should be added. Replace the plug as soon as the lubricant reaches the level of the hole.

FLUID CHANGE

All transfer cases are to be serviced at the same time and in the same manner as the manual transmissions. The transfer case has its own drain plug which should be opened; do not rely on the transmission drain plug to completely drain the transfer case (if interconnected). Once the transfer case has been drained, replace the drain plug, remove the fill plug and fill to the specified level with lubricant.

Automatic Transmission

FLUID RECOMMENDATIONS

Use only DEXRON® II automatic transmission fluid.

FLUID LEVEL CHECK

The fluid level in automatic transmissions is checked with a dipstick located in the filler pipe at the right rear of the engine. The fluid level should be maintained between the ADD and FULL marks on the end of the dipstick with the automatic transmission fluid at normal operating temperatures. To raise the level from the ADD mark to the FULL mark, requires the addition of one pint of fluid. The fluid level with the fluid at room temperature

1 GENERAL INFORMATION AND MAINTENANCE

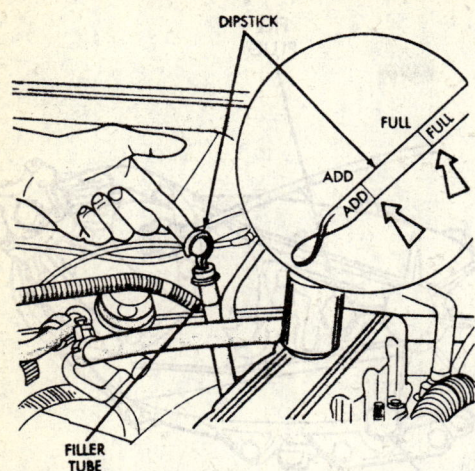

Checking the automatic transmission fluid level

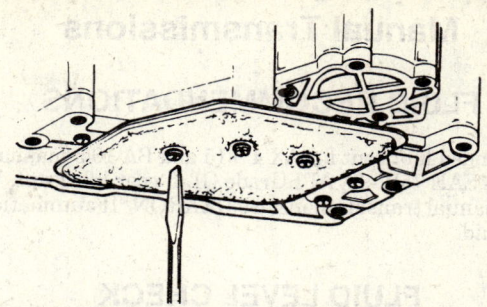

Removing the automatic transmission filter

(75°F [24°C]) should be approximately 4¼ in. below the ADD mark.

NOTE: In checking the automatic transmission fluid, insert the dipstick in the filler tube with the markings toward the center of the truck. Also, remember that the FULL mark on the dipstick is the indication of the level of the automatic transmission fluid when it is at operating temperature. This temperature is only obtained after at least 15 miles of expressway driving or the equivalent of city driving.

To check the automatic transmission fluid level, follow the procedure given below. This procedure is applicable either when the fluid is at room temperature or at operating temperature.

1. With the transmission in Park, the engine running at idle speed, the foot brake applied and the vehicle resting on level ground, move the transmission gear selector through each of the gear positions, including Reverse, allowing time for the transmission to engage. Return the shift selector to the Park position and apply the parking brake. Do not turn the engine off, but leave it running at idle speed.
2. Clean all dirt from around the transmission dipstick cap and the end of the filler tube.
3. Pull the dipstick out of the tube, wipe it off with a clean cloth, and push it back into the tube all the way, making sure that it seats completely.
4. Pull the dipstick out of the tube again and read the level of the fluid on the stick. The level should be between the ADD and FULL marks. Do not overfill the transmission because this will cause foaming, loss of fluid through the vent and malfunctioning of the transmission.

NOTE: Transmission fluid should be clear and free of foreign material. If the fluid is dark brown or black in color and smells burnt, the fluid has been overheated and should be replaced.

FLUID AND FILTER CHANGE

The transmission fluid in an automatic transmission should be changed every 30,000 miles of normal driving or every 15,000 miles of driving under abnormal or severe conditions. All models use Dexron®II fluid. The fluid should be drained immediately after the vehicle has been driven for at least 20 minutes at expressway speeds or the equivalent of city driving, before it has had the chance to cool. Follow the procedure given below:

1. Drain the automatic transmission fluid from the transmission into an appropriate container, by removing the transmission bottom pan screws, pan and gasket.

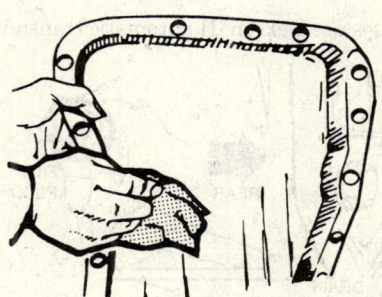

Clean the pan throughly with a safe solvent and allow to air dry

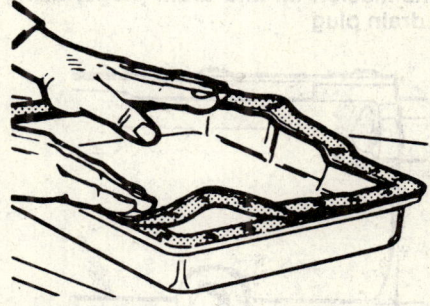

Install a new pan gasket

2. Remove the transmission oil filter and discard it.
3. Remove the O-ring seal from the pickup pipe and discard it.
4. Install a new O-ring seal on the pickup pipe and install the new oil filter and pipe assembly.
5. Thoroughly clean the bottom pan and position a new gasket on the pan mating surface. Install the bottom pan and secure it with the attaching screws, torqued to 10-13 ft. lbs.
6. Pour about 4 quarts of automatic transmission fluid in the

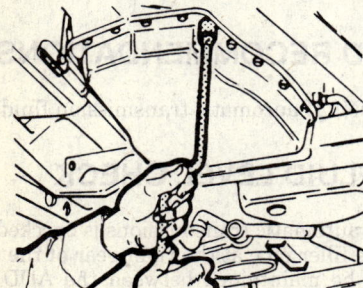

Many late model vehicles have no drain plug. Loosen the pan bolts and allow one corner of the pan to hang, so that the fluid drains out.

GENERAL INFORMATION AND MAINTENANCE 1

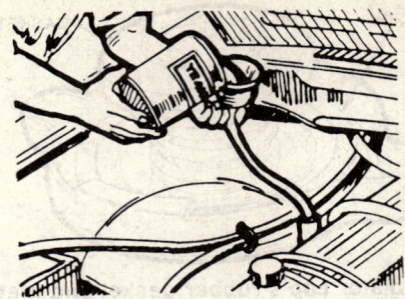

Fill the transmission with the required amount of fluid. DO NOT OVERFILL. Start the engine and run the selector through all the shift points. Check the fluid and add as necessary

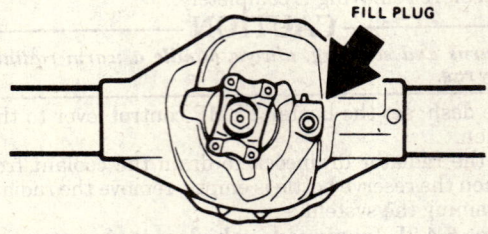

AMC axle fill plug location

filler pipe. Make sure that the funnel, container, hose or any other item used to assist in filling the transmission is clean.

7. Start the engine. DO NOT race it. Allow the engine to idle for a few minutes.

8. Place the selector lever in Park and apply the parking brake. With the transmission fluid at operating temperatures, check the fluid level; add fluid to bring the level to the FULL mark.

Front and Rear Axle

FLUID RECOMMENDATIONS

The standard front and rear axle differentials use SAE 75W/90, API grade GL 5 hypoid gear lubricant. SAE 80W-140 API grade GL 5 hypoid gear lubricant is recommended when trailer towing. With Trac-Lok® (limit slip) differentials, add a container of Trac-Lok® Lubricant additive.

FLUID LEVEL CHECK

Check the level of the oil in the differential housing every 7,500 miles under normal driving conditions and every 3,000 miles if the vehicle is used in severe driving conditions. The level should be up to the filler hole. When you remove the filler plug, the oil should start to run out. If it does not, add fluid to obtain an acceptable level.

FLUID CHANGE

The lubricant should be changed every 30,000 miles. Under severe conditions the lubricant should be changed every 15,000 miles. If running in deep water, change the lubricant daily.

Follow the procedure given below for changing the lubricant in the front and rear axle differentials:

1. Remove the axle differential housing cover and allow the lubricant to drain out into a proper container.
2. Install the differential housing cover and a new gasket.

NOTE: Some rear axle covers are not equipped with a gasket. If a gasket is not used, seal cover using RTV sealant.

3. Tighten the cover attaching bolts to 15-25 ft. lbs.
4. Remove the fill plug and add new lubricant to the fill hole level.
5. Replace the fill plug.

NOTE: Trac-Lok® (limited-slip) differentials may be cleaned only by disassembling the unit and wiping with clean, lint-free rags.

Coolant

---- CAUTION ----
When draining the coolant, keep in mind that cats and dogs are attracted by the ethylene glycol antifreeze, and are quite likely to drink any that is left in an uncovered container or in puddles on the ground. This will prove fatal in sufficient quantity. Always drain the coolant into a sealable container. Coolant should be reused unless it is contaminated or several years old.

COOLANT CHECK AND CHANGE

On systems without a coolant recovery tank, the engine coolant level should be maintained 1-2 in. below the bottom of the radiator filler neck when the engine is at air temperature and 1 in. below the bottom of the filler neck when the engine is hot.

On systems with a coolant recovery tank, maintain the coolant level at the level marks on the recovery bottle.

For best protection against freezing and overheating, maintain an approximate 50% water and 50% ethylene glycol antifreeze mixture in the cooling system. Do not mix different brands of antifreeze to avoid possible chemical damage to the cooling system.

Avoid using water that is known to have a high alkaline content or is very hard, except in emergency situations. Drain and flush the cooling system as soon as possible after using such water.

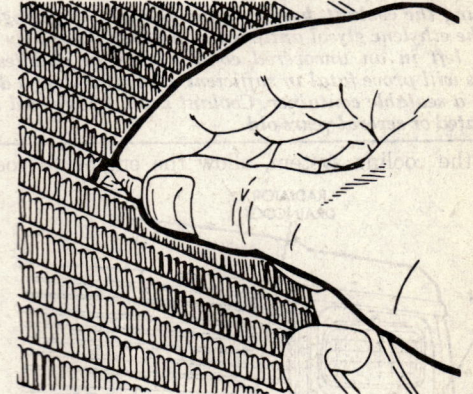

Keep the radiator fins clear for maximum cooling

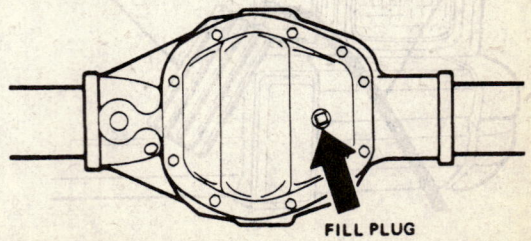

Dana axle fill plug location

1-41

1 GENERAL INFORMATION AND MAINTENANCE

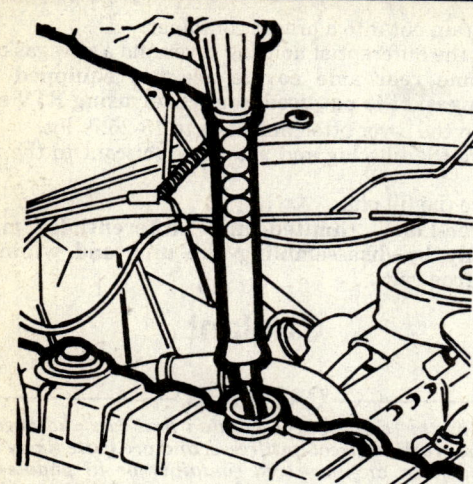

Coolant protection can be checked with a simple float-type tester

CAUTION

Cover the radiator cap with a thick cloth before removing it from a radiator in a vehicle that is hot. Turn the cap counterclockwise slowly until pressure can be heard escaping. Allow all pressure to escape from the radiator before completely removing the radiator cap. It is best to allow the engine to cool if possible, before removing the radiator cap.

NOTE: Never add cold water to an overheated engine while the engine is not running.

After filling the radiator, run the engine until it reaches normal operating temperature, to make sure that the thermostat has opened and all the air is bled from the system.

DRAINING, FLUSHING AND REFILLING

CAUTION

When draining the coolant, keep in mind that cats and dogs are attracted by the ethylene glycol antifreeze, and are quite likely to drink any that is left in an uncovered container or in puddles on the ground. This will prove fatal in sufficient quantity. Always drain the coolant into a sealable container. Coolant should be reused unless it is contaminated or several years old.

To drain the cooling system, allow the engine to cool down

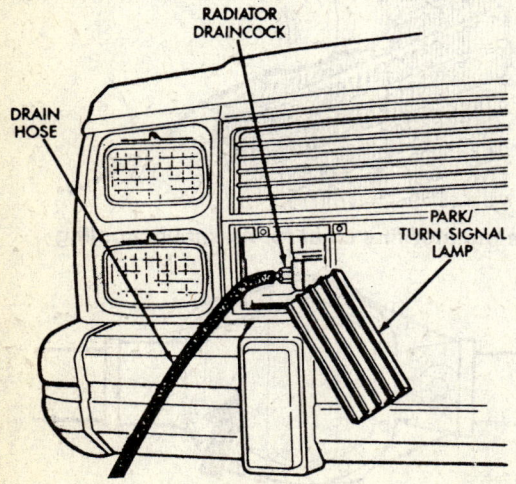

Draincock access — Remove parking lamp

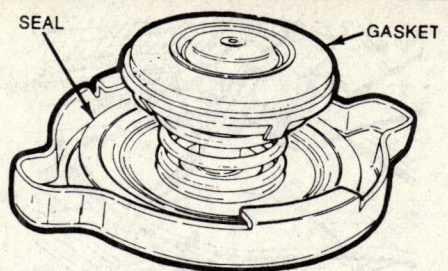

Check the radiator cap's rubber gasket and metal seal for deterioration at least once a year

BEFORE ATTEMPTING TO REMOVE THE RADIATOR CAP. Then turn the cap until it hisses. Wait until all pressure is off the cap before removing it completely.

CAUTION

To avoid burns and scalding, always handle a warm radiator cap with a heavy rag.

1. At the dash, set the heater TEMP control lever to the fully HOT position.
2. Open the radiator draincock to drain the coolant from the system. When the reserve bottle is empty, remove the radiator cap to finish draining the system.

NOTE: On 6-4.0L equipped vehicles it is necessary to remove the left turn signal lamp and/or the grill to gain access to the draincock. Attach a piece of 4 1/4 in. ID hose to the draincock to facilitate draining of the coolant.

3. Drain the coolant from the engine by removing the drain plug located on the left side of the block.
4. Flush the system with water until the fluid runs clear.
5. Close the draincock, replace the plug(s), and refill the radiator to the top with a 50/50 mix of ethylene glycol antifreeze. Fill coolant reserve bottle to FULL mark. Reinstall the radiator cap and coolant reserve bottle top.

NOTE: If not equipped with a coolant reserve tank, fill the system to 3/4-1 1/4 in. from the bottom of the filler neck.

6. Operate the engine at 2,000 rpm for a few minutes and check the system for signs of leaks.
7. Turn off engine and allow it to cool. Check coolant in reserve bottle and add if necessary to bring level up to the FULL mark.

RADIATOR CAP INSPECTION

Allow the engine to cool sufficiently before attempting to remove the radiator cap. Use a rag to cover the cap, then remove by pressing down and turning counterclockwise to the first stop. If any

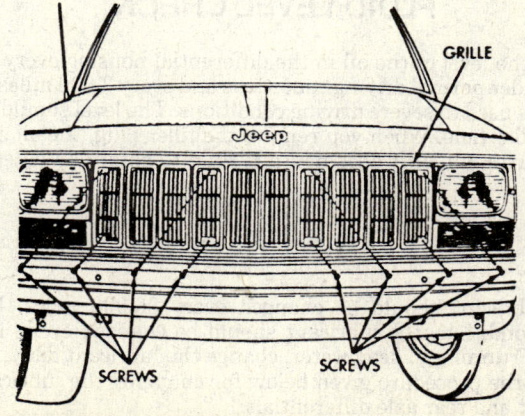

Draincock access — Remove grille

1-42

GENERAL INFORMATION AND MAINTENANCE 1

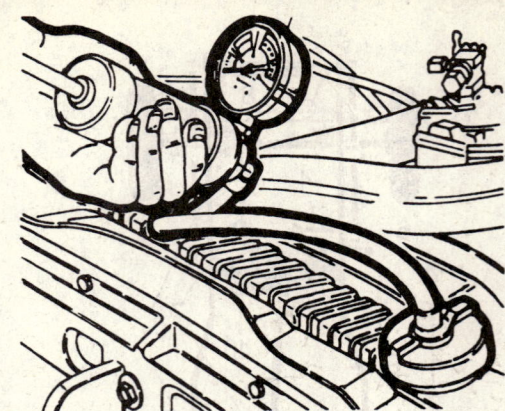

The system should be pressure tested once a year

hissing is noted (indicating the release of pressure), wait until the hissing stops completely, then press down again and turn counter-clockwise until the cap can be removed.

CAUTION

DO NOT attempt to remove the radiator cap while the engine is hot. Severe personal injury from steam burns can result.

Check the condition of the radiator cap gasket and seal inside of the cap. The radiator cap is designed to seal the cooling system under normal operating conditions which allows the build up of a certain amount of pressure (this pressure rating is stamped or printed on the cap). The pressure in the system raises the boiling point of the coolant to help prevent overheating. If the radiator cap does not seal, the boiling point of the coolant is lowered and overheating will occur. If the cap must be replaced, purchase the new cap according to the pressure rating which is specified for your vehicle.

Prior to installing the radiator cap, inspect and clean the filler neck. If you are reusing the old cap, clean it thoroughly with clear water. After turning the cap on, make sure the arrows align with the overflow hose.

Brake and/or Clutch Master Cylinder

FLUID RECOMMENDATIONS

The only brake fluid recommended for Jeep vehicles with standard or anti-lock brakes is a fluid meeting DOT 3 specifications.

FLUID LEVEL CHECK

Standard Power Brake System

The master cylinder reservoir is located under the hood, on the left side of the firewall. Before removing the master cylinder reservoir cap, make sure the vehicle is resting on level ground and clean all dirt away from the top of the master cylinder. Pry off the retaining clip or unscrew the holddown bolt and remove the cap. The fluid level should be within $4^{1}/_{4}$ in. of the top of the reservoir on both single and dual master cylinders. **Use new brake fluid only when adding fluid to the reservoir.**

If the level of the fluid is less than half the volume of the reservoir, it is advised that you check the brake system for leaks. Leaks in a hydraulic brake system most commonly occur at the wheel cylinders. Leaks may also occur in brake lines running down the frame.

There is a rubber diaphragm in the top of the master cylinder cap. As the fluid level lowers in the reservoir due to normal brake shoe wear or leakage, the diaphragm takes up the space. This acts

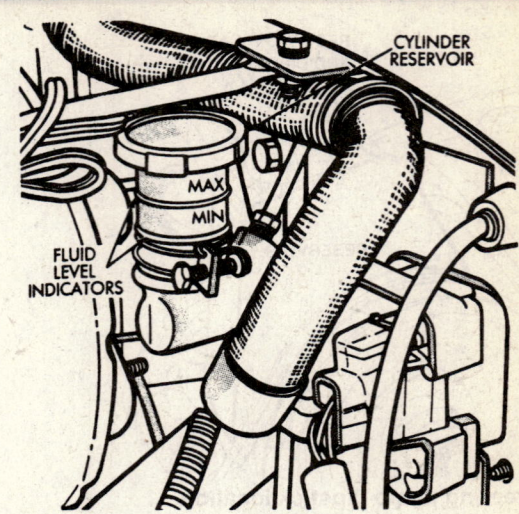

Clutch master cylinder fluid level

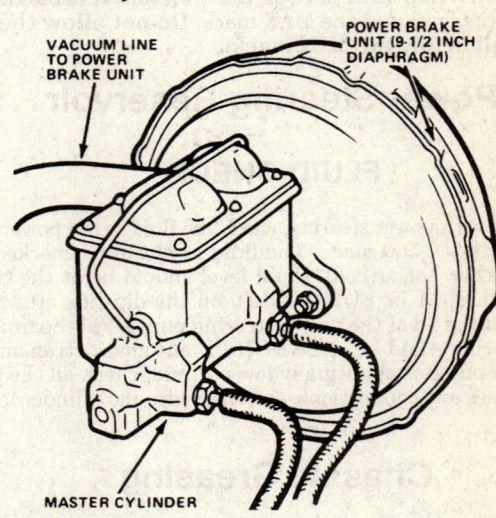

Typical master cylinder

to prevent the loss of brake fluid out of the vented cap and to prevent contamination of the brake fluid by dirt. After filling the master cylinder to the proper level with brake fluid, but before replacing the cap, fold the rubber diaphragm up into the cap, then replace the cap on the reservoir and tighten the retaining bolt or snap the retaining clip into place.

WARNING: Do not allow brake fluid to come in contact with painted components on the vehicle. If left on any painted surface it will dissolve the paint.

Anti-Lock Brake System

The anti-lock brake system reservoir is located next to the windshield washer fluid reservoir.

The brake fluid level should be at the MAX indicator mark on the reservoir. If not, add brake fluid as necessary to obtain the proper level. Do not overfill.

WARNING: Over-filling could cause fluid overflow and possible reservoir damage when the pump begins cycling.

Hydraulic Clutch Fluid

The only fluid recommended for use in Jeep hydraulic clutch systems is DOT 3 approved brake fluid.

The fluid level for the hydraulic clutch system must remain be-

1-43

1 GENERAL INFORMATION AND MAINTENANCE

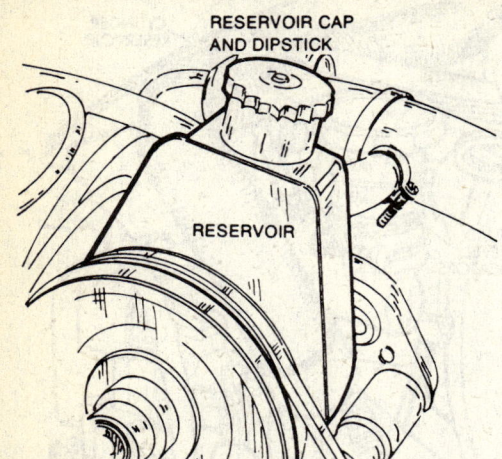

Power steering pump dipstick location

tween the MIN and MAX lines on the reservoir. If necessary, add fluid until the level is at the MAX mark. **Do not allow the fluid level to fall below the MIN mark.**

Power Steering Reservoir

FLUID CHECK

On models with power steering, check the fluid in the power steering pump every 7,500 miles. The fluid level can be checked with the fluid either hot or cold. Fluid level should be at the correct point (FULL HOT or FULL COLD) on the dipstick attached to the inside of the lid of the power steering pump. Fill the unit with power steering fluid or DEXRON®II automatic transmission fluid. If the pump is abnormally low on fluid, check all the power steering hoses and connections, and the hydraulic cylinder for possible leaks.

Chassis Greasing

The lubrication chart indicates where the grease fittings are located. The vehicle should be greased according to the intervals in the Preventive Maintenance Schedule at the end of this Section.

Water resistant EP chassis lubricant (grease) should be used for all chassis grease points.

Every year or 7,500 miles the front suspension ball points, both upper and lower on each side of the truck, must be greased. Most trucks covered in this guide should be equipped with grease nipples on the ball joints, although some may have plugs which must be removed and nipples fitted. Some late model trucks have lifetime lubricated chassis components which can not be serviced.

WARNING: Do not pump so much grease into the ball joint that excess grease squeezes out of the rubber boot. This destroys the watertight seal.

Jack up the front end of the truck and safely support it with jackstands. Block the rear wheels and firmly apply the parking brake. If the truck has been parked in temperatures below 20°F for any length of time, park it in a heated garage for an hour or so until the ball joints loosen up enough to accept the grease.

Depending on which front wheel you work on first, turn the wheel and tire outward, either full-lock right or full-lock left. You now have the ends of the upper and lower suspension control arms in front of you; the grease nipples are visible pointing up (top ball joint) and down (lower ball joint) through the end of each control arm. If the nipples are not accessible enough, remove the wheel and tire. Wipe all debris from the nipples or from around the plugs

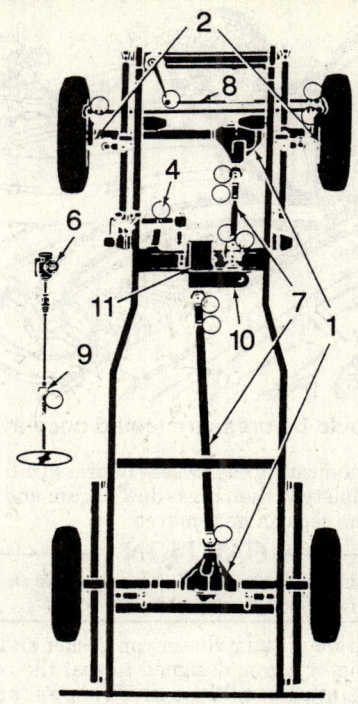

1. Differentials
2. Front wheel bearings
3. Not used
4. Clutch lever and linkage
6. Manual steering gear
7. Driveshafts
8. Steering linkage
9. Steering shaft U-joint
10. Transfer case
11. Transmission

Wagoneer, Cherokee and Comanche chassis maintenance points

(if installed). If plugs are on the truck, remove them and install grease nipples in the holes (nipples are available in various thread sizes at most auto parts stores). Using a hand operated, low pressure grease gun loaded with a quality chassis grease, grease the ball joint only until the rubber joint boot begins to swell out.

Steering Linkage

The steering linkage should be greased at the same interval as the ball joints. Grease nipples are installed on the steering tie rod ends on most models. Wipe all dirt from around the fittings at each tie rod end. Using a hand operated, low pressure grease gun loaded with a suitable chassis grease, grease the linkage until the old grease begins to squeeze out around the tie rod ends. Wipe off the nipples and any excess grease. Also grease the nipples on the steering idler arms.

Parking Brake Linkage

Use chassis grease on the parking brake cable where it contacts the cable guides, levers and linkage.

Automatic Transmission Linkage

Apply a small amount of clean engine oil to the kickdown and shift linkage points at 7,500 mile intervals.

Outside Vehicle Maintenance

Lock Cylinders

Apply graphite lubricant sparingly through the key slot. Insert the key and operate the lock several times to be sure that the lubricant is worked into the lock cylinder.

1-44

GENERAL INFORMATION AND MAINTENANCE 1

Door Hinges and Hinge Checks

Spray a white lubricant on the hinge pivot points to eliminate any binding conditions. Open and close the door several times to be sure that the lubricant is evenly and thoroughly distributed.

Tailgate

Spray a white lubricant on all of the pivot and friction surfaces to eliminate any squeaks or binds. Work the tailgate to distribute the lubricant

Body Drain Holes

Be sure that the drain holes in the doors and rocker panels are cleared of obstruction. A small screwdriver can be used to clear them of any debris.

Front Wheel Bearings

PACKING AND ADJUSTMENT

NOTE: Sodium-based grease is not compatible with lithium-based grease. Read the package labels and be careful not to mix the two types. If there is any doubt as to the type of grease used, completely clean the old grease from the bearing and hub before replacing.

Before handling the bearings, there are a few things that you should remember to do and not to do.

Remember to DO the following:
- Remove all outside dirt from the housing before exposing the bearing.
- Treat a used bearing as gently as you would a new one.
- Work with clean tools in clean surroundings.
- Use clean, dry canvas gloves, or at least clean, dry hands.
- Clean solvents and flushing fluids are a must.
- Use clean paper when laying out the bearings to dry.
- Protect disassembled bearings from rust and dirt. Cover them up.
- Use clean rags to wipe bearings.
- Keep the bearings in oil-proof paper when they are to be stored or are not in use.
- Clean the inside of the housing before replacing the bearing.

Do NOT do the following:
- Don't work in dirty surroundings.
- Don't use dirty, chipped or damaged tools.
- Try not to work on wooden work benches or use wooden mallets.
- Don't handle bearings with dirty or moist hands.
- Do not use gasoline for cleaning; use a safe solvent.

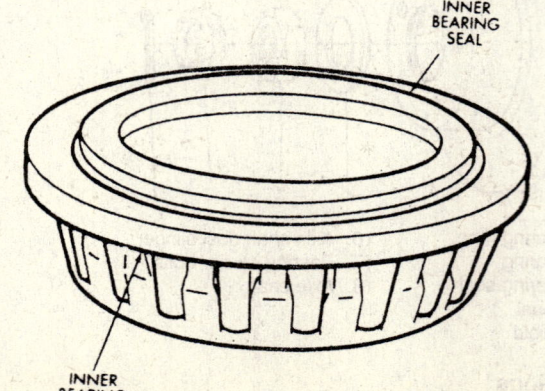

Inner bearing and seal

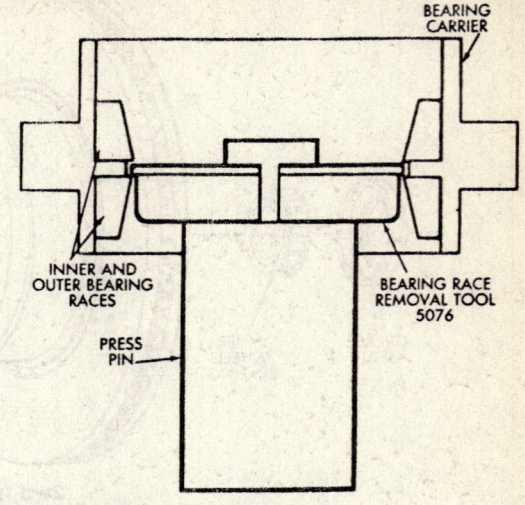

Bearing race removal tools

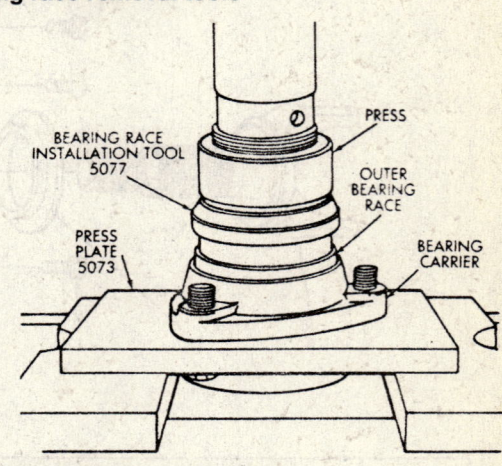

Outer bearing race installation

- Do not spin-dry bearings with compressed air. They will be damaged.
- Do not spin dirty bearings.
- Avoid using cotton waste or dirty cloths to wipe bearings.
- Try not to scratch or nick bearing surfaces.
- Do not allow the bearing to come in contact with dirt or rust at any time.

2-Wheel Drive

1. Raise and support the front end on jackstands.
2. Remove the wheels.
3. Remove the caliper without disconnecting the brake line. Suspend it out of the way using a piece of wire to prevent damage.
4. Remove the grease cap, cotter pin, nut cap, nut, and washer from the spindle. Discard the cotter pin.
5. Slowly remove the hub and rotor, catch the outer bearing as it falls.
6. Carefully drive out the inner bearing and seal from the hub, using a wood block.
7. Inspect the bearing races for excessive wear, pitting or grooves. If they are cracked or grooved, or if pitting and excess wear is present, drive them out with a drift or punch.
8. Check the bearing for excess wear, pitting or cracks, or excess looseness.

NOTE: If it is necessary to replace either the bearing or the race, replace both. Never replace just a bearing or a race.

1-45

1 GENERAL INFORMATION AND MAINTENANCE

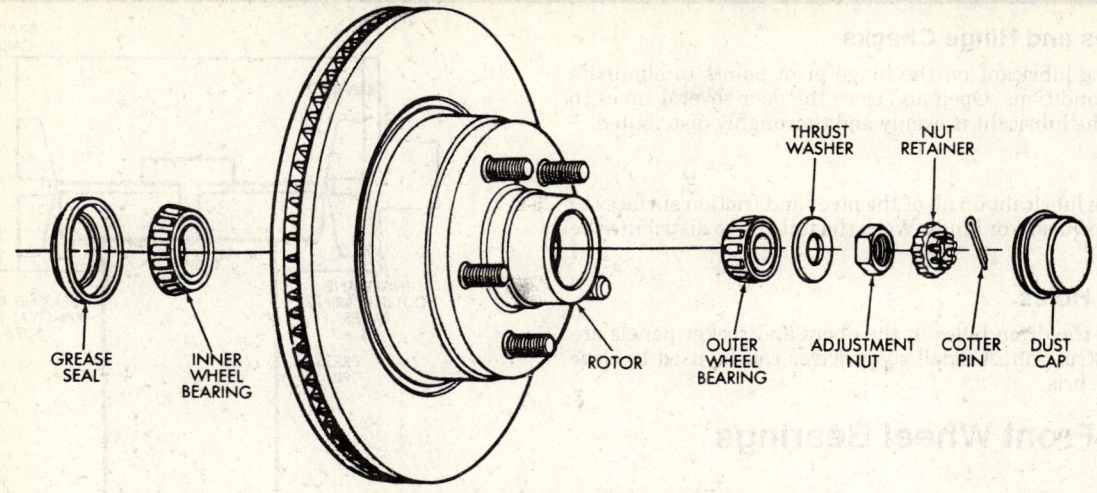

2wd front wheel bearings

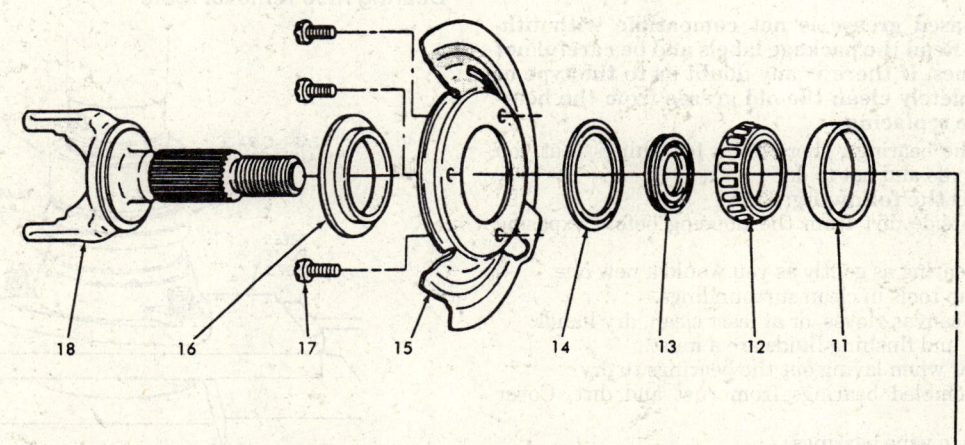

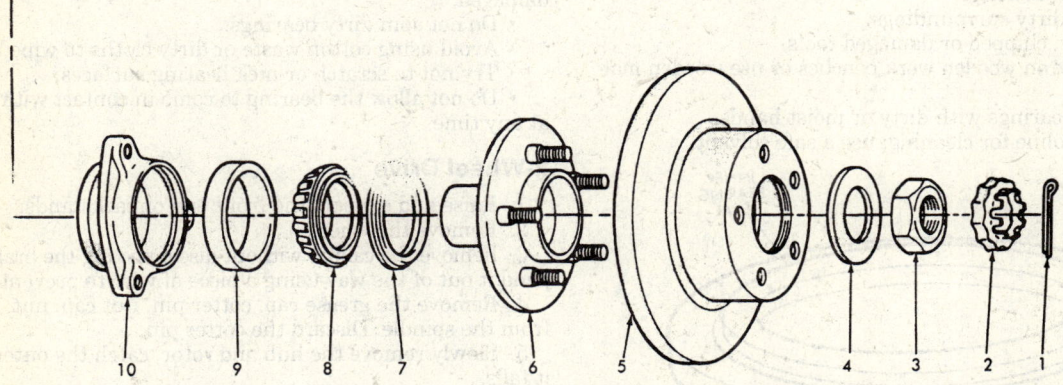

1. Cotter pin
2. Nut retainer
3. Nut
4. Washer
5. Brake rotor
6. Hub
7. Outer bearing seal
8. Outer bearing
9. Outer bearing race
10. Bearing carrier
11. Inner bearing race
12. Inner bearing
13. Inner bearing seal
14. Carrier seal
15. Rotor shield
16. Axle shaft dust slinger
17. Bearing carrier bolts
18. Axle shaft

4wd front wheel bearings

GENERAL INFORMATION AND MAINTENANCE 1

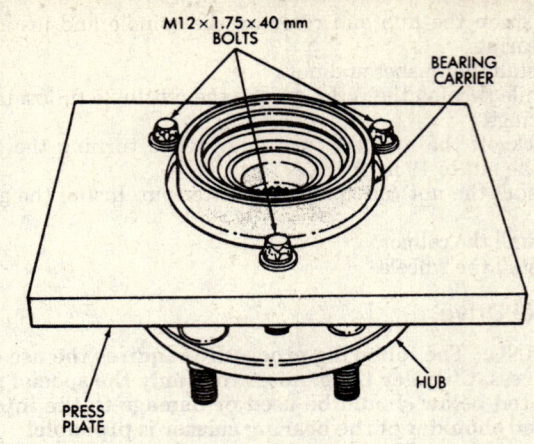

Hub and bearing carrier in a press plate

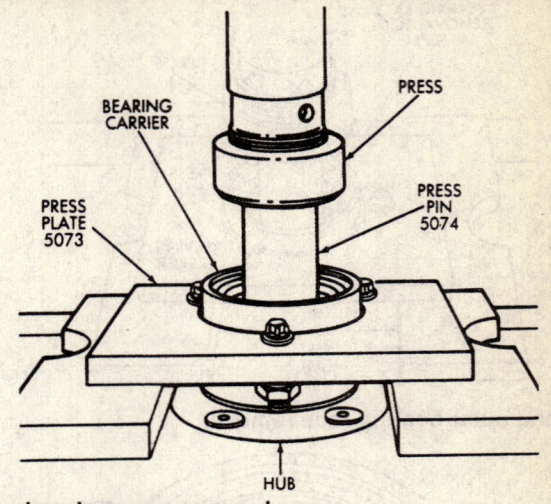

Inner bearing cage removal

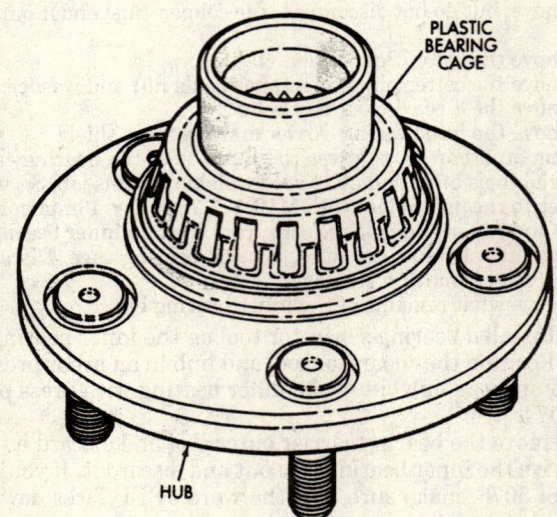

Inner bearing cage removal

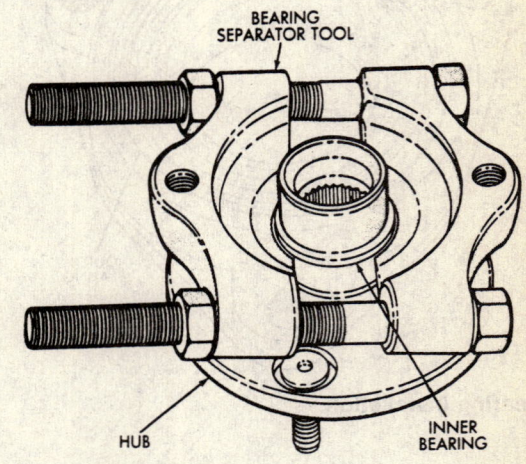

Bearing separator tool

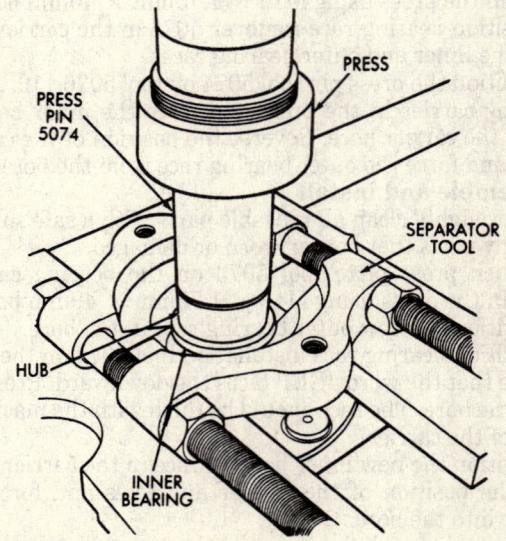

Hub and inner bearing separation

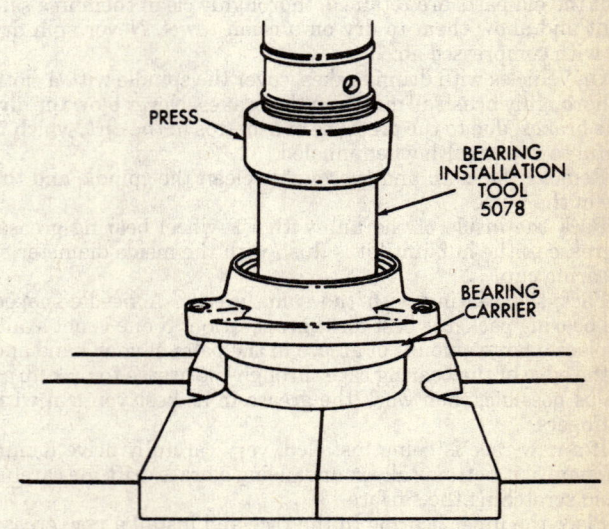

Inner bearing removal

1-47

1 GENERAL INFORMATION AND MAINTENANCE

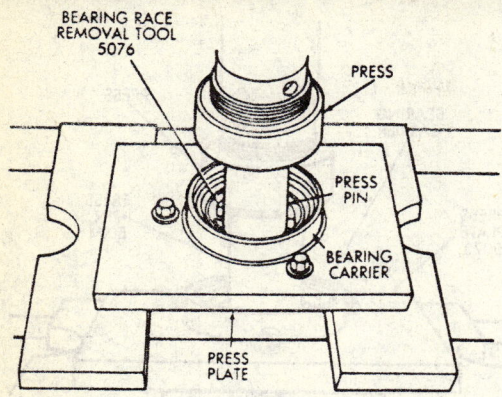

Inner and outer bearing race removal

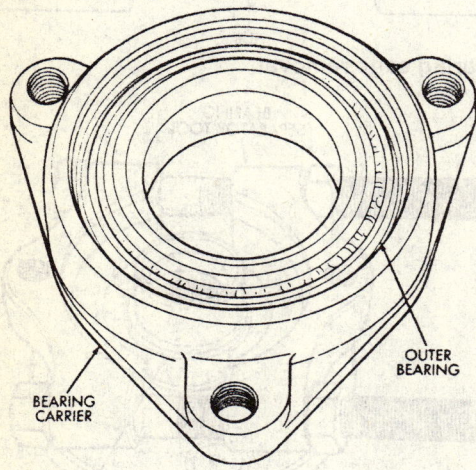

Outer bearing installation

These parts wear in a mating pattern. If just one is replaced, premature failure of the new part will result.

9. If the old parts are retained, thoroughly clean them in a safe solvent and allow them to dry on a clean towel. Never spin dry them with compressed air.
10. On vehicles with drum brakes, cover the spindle with a cloth and thoroughly brush all dirt from the brakes. Never blow the dirt off the brakes, due to the presence of asbestos in the dirt, which is harmful to your health when inhaled.
11. Remove the cloth and thoroughly clean the spindle and the inside of the hub.
12. Pack the inside of the hub with EP wheel bearing grease. Add grease to the hub until it is flush with the inside diameter of the bearing cup.
13. Pack the bearing with the same grease. A needle-shaped wheel bearing packer is best for this operation. If one is not available, place a large amount of grease in the palm of your hand and slide the edge of the bearing cage through the grease to pick up as much as possible, then work the grease in as best you can with your fingers.
14. If a new race is being installed, very carefully drive it into position until it bottoms all around, using a brass drift. Be careful to avoid scratching the surface.
15. Place the inner bearing in the race and install a new grease seal.
16. Clean and repack the hub and bearings, install the inner bearing and a new seal.
17. Clean the rotor contact surface if necessary.

18. Position the hub and rotor on the spindle and install the outer bearing.
19. Install the washer and nut.
20. While turning the rotor, torque the nut to 25 ft. lbs. to seat the bearings.
21. Back off the nut $4\frac{1}{2}$ turn, and, while turning the rotor, torque the nut to 19 in. lbs.
22. Install the nut cap and a new cotter pin. Install the grease cap.
23. Install the caliper.
24. Install the wheels.

4-Wheel Drive

WARNING: The following procedure requires the use of an arbor press. Chrysler Corp. notes that only the special press tools listed below should be used or damage to the internal machined shoulder of the bearing carrier is probable!

1. Raise and support the front end on jackstands.
2. Remove the wheels.
3. Remove, but do not disconnect, the caliper. Suspend it out of the way.
4. Remove the rotor. See Section 9.
5. Remove the cotter pin, nut retainer, axle nut and washer.
6. Remove the 3 bearing carrier bolts.
7. Remove the hub/bearing carrier and the rotor shield.
8. Using an arbor press, press the hub out of the bearing carrier. Special tools 5073 and 5074 are available for this job. Secure the carrier to the press plate with M12 × 1.75mm × 40mm bolts.
9. Cut and remove the plastic cage from the hub inner bearing. Using diagonal pliers or tin snips, cut the bearing cage. Discard the rollers after removing the cage.
10. Remove what remains of the inner bearing by:
    a. Install a bearing separator tool on the inner bearing.
    b. Position the separator tool and hub in an arbor press.
    c. Force the hub out of the inner bearing with press pin tool 5074.
11. Remove the bearing carrier outer seal and discard it.
12. Drive the inner bearing seal out and discard it. If you're using tool 5078, make sure that the word JEEP faces downward.
13. Attach press plate tool 5073 to the rear of the carrier. Secure it in the press using M12 × 1.75mm × 40mm bolts.
14. Position bearing race remover 5076 in the carrier bore between the inner and outer bearing races.
15. Position the press pin tool 5074 on tool 5076. 16. Place the bearing carrier in the press and force the inner bearing race from the carrier bore. Reverse the position of the carrier and tools and force the outer bearing race from the bore.

To assemble and install

17. Thoroughly clean all reusable parts with a safe solvent. Discard any parts that appear worn or damaged.
18. Attach press plate tool 5073 on the bearing carrier. Secure it in the press using M12 × 1.75mm × 40mm bolts.
19. Position the new outer bearing race in the bore.
20. Position bearing race installation tool 5077 on the race. Make sure that the word JEEP faces the downward. Press the race into the bore. The race should be flush with the machined shoulder of the carrier.
21. Position the new inner bearing race in the carrier bore. Reverse the position of the carrier and tools and force the inner race into the bore.
22. Thoroughly pack the new outer bearing with wheel bearing grease. Make sure that the bearing is fully packed.
23. Coat the race with wheel bearing grease and place the bearing in the bore.

GENERAL INFORMATION AND MAINTENANCE 1

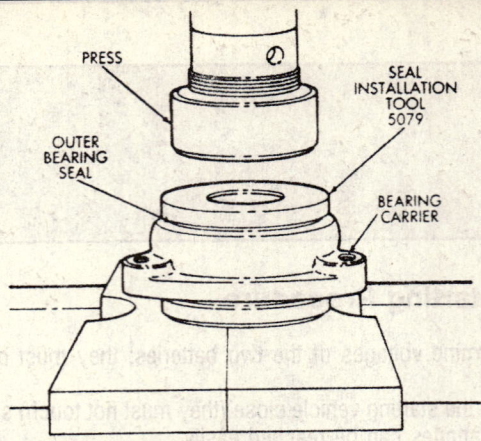

Outer bearing seal installation

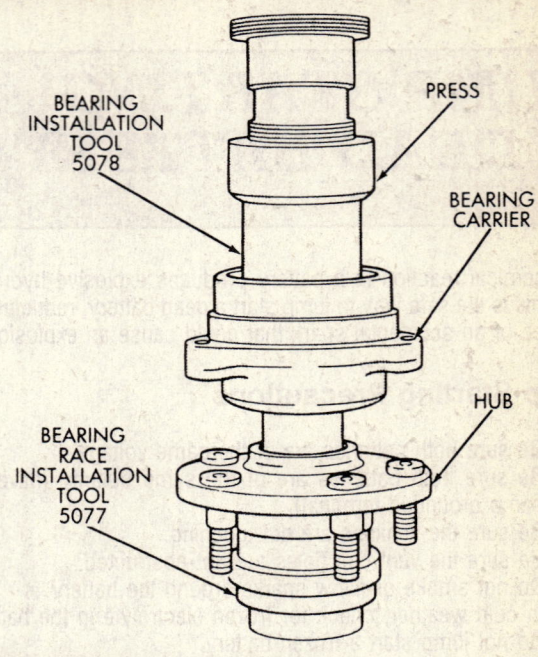

Joining the hub and bearing carrier

24. Place the new outer seal on the bearing and position bearing installation tool 5079 on the seal. Place the carrier in the press and force the seal into the bore. Apply wheel bearing grease to the seal lip.

25. Insert the hub through the seal and outer bearing and into the bearing carrier bore.

26. Install bearing installation tool 5078 into the rear of the bearing carrier bore and place the race installation tool 5077 on the front of the hub. Make sure that the word JEEP on 5077 is facing the hub.

27. Place the assembly in the press and force the hub shaft into the carrier bore.

28. Pack the new inner bearing with wheel bearing grease. Make sure that the bearing is thoroughly packed.

29. Coat the inner seal lip with wheel bearing grease and place it on the inner bearing.

30. Coat the inner bearing race with wheel bearing grease.

31. Place the carrier in a press along with tool 5077. The word JEEP on 5077 must face the hub. Position the bearing and seal in the carrier. Place seal installation tool 5080 on the seal.

32. Force the bearing and seal into the bore and onto the hub shaft.

WARNING: Use extreme care when forcing the assembly into position! The carrier must rotate freely after installation of the bearing! Do not attempt to eliminate bearing lash with the press. Final bearing preload is attained by tightening the drive axle nut.

33. Install the new outer seal on the carrier.

34. Thoroughly clean the axle shaft and apply a thin coating of lithium-based grease to the splines and seal contact surfaces.

35. Install the slinger, rotor shield and hub/bearing assembly on the axle shaft.

36. Coat the carrier bolt threads with Loctite®, install them and torque them to 75 ft. lbs.

37. Install the rotor and caliper. See Section 9.

38. Install the washer and axle shaft nut. Torque the nut to 175 ft. lbs.

39. Install the nut retainer and cotter pin. NEVER back off the nut to install the cotter pin! ALWAYS advance it!

40. Install the wheel.

JUMP STARTING A DUAL-BATTERY DIESEL

Trucks equipped with the diesel engine utilize two 12 volt batteries, one on either side of the engine compartment. The batteries are connected in a parallel circuit (positive terminal to positive terminal, negative terminal to negative terminal). Hooking the batteries up in parallel circuit increases battery cranking power without increasing total battery voltage output. Output remains at 12 volts.

─── **CAUTION** ───
NEVER hook the batteries up in a series circut or the entire electrical system will go up in smoke, especially the starter

On the other hand, hooking two 12 volt batteries up in a series circuit (positive terminal to negative terminal, positive terminal to negative terminal) increases total battery output to 24 volts (12 volts plus 12 volts).

In the event that a diesel pickup needs to be jump started, use the following procedure.

1. Turn all lights off.
2. Turn on the heater blower motor to remove transient voltage.
3. Connect one jumper cable to the passenger side battery positive (+) terminal and the other cable clamp to the positive (+) terminal to the booster (good) battery.
4. Connect one end of the other jumper cable to the negative (−) terminal of the booster (good) battery and the other cable clamp to an engine bolt head, alternator bracket or other solid, metallic point on the diesel engine. DO NOT connect this clamp to the negative (−) terminal of the bad battery.

1 GENERAL INFORMATION AND MAINTENANCE

JUMP STARTING A DEAD BATTERY

The chemical reaction in a battery produces explosive hydrogen gas. This is the safe way to jump start a dead battery, reducing the chances of an accidental spark that could cause an explosion.

Jump Starting Precautions

1. Be sure both batteries are of the same voltage.
2. Be sure both batteries are of the same polarity (have the same grounded terminal).
3. Be sure the vehicles are not touching.
4. Be sure the vent cap holes are not obstructed.
5. Do not smoke or allow sparks around the battery.
6. In cold weather, check for frozen electrolyte in the battery. Do not jump start a frozen battery.
7. Do not allow electrolyte on your skin or clothing.
8. Be sure the electrolyte is not frozen.

CAUTION: Make certin that the ignition key, in the vehicle with the dead battery, is in the OFF position. Connecting cables to vehicles with on-board computers will result in computer destruction if the key is not in the OFF position.

Jump Starting Procedure

1. Determine voltages of the two batteries; they must be the same.
2. Bring the starting vehicle close (they must not touch) so that the batteries can be reached easily.
3. Turn off all accessories and both engines. Put both vehicles in Neutral or Park and set the handbrake.
4. Cover the cell caps with a rag—do not cover terminals.
5. If the terminals on the run-down battery are heavily corroded, clean them.
6. Identify the positive and negative posts on both batteries and connect the cables in the order shown.
7. Start the engine of the starting vehicle and run it at fast idle. Try to start the car with the dead battery. Crank it for no more than 10 seconds at a time and let it cool for 20 seconds in between tries.
8. If it doesn't start in 3 tries, there is something else wrong.
9. Disconnect the cables in the reverse order.
10. Replace the cell covers and dispose of the rags.

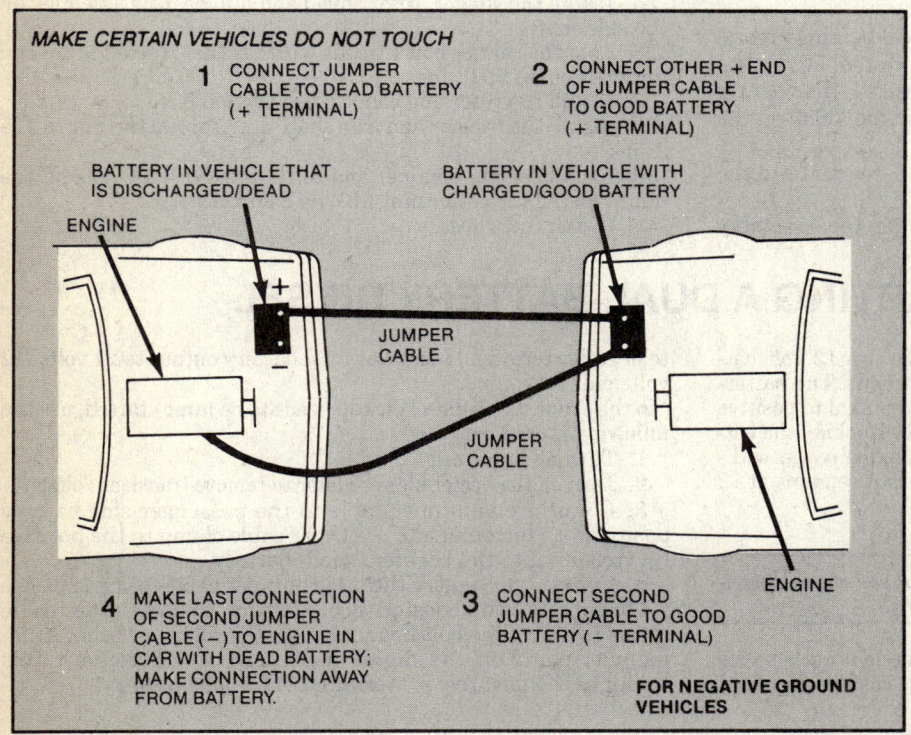

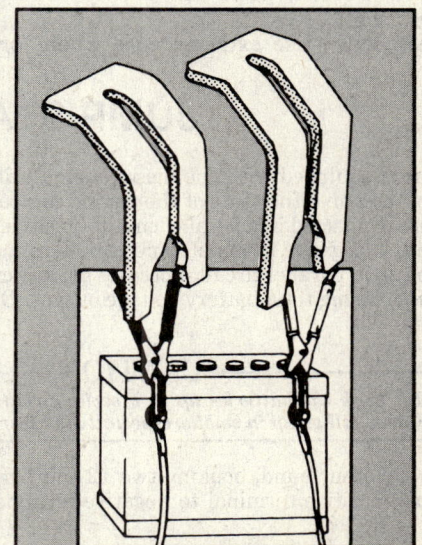

Side terminal batteries occasionally pose a problem when connecting jumper cables. There frequently isn't enough room to clamp the cables without touching sheet metal. Side terminal adaptors are available to alleviate this problem and should be removed after use

GENERAL INFORMATION AND MAINTENANCE 1

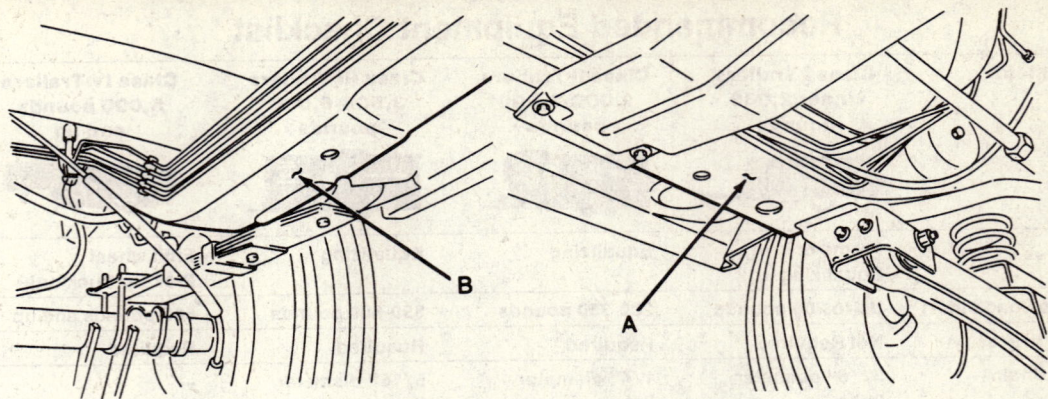

Jacking points

— CAUTION —
Be very careful to keep the jumper cables away from moving parts (cooling fan, belts, etc.) on both engines.

5. Start the engine of the donor truck and run at moderate speed.
6. Start the engine of the diesel.
7. When the diesel starts, remove the cable from the engine block before disconnecting the positive terminal.

JACKING AND HOISTING

Scissors jacks or hydraulic jacks are recommended for all Jeep vehicles. To change a tire, place the jack beneath the spring plate, below the axle, near the wheel to be changed.

Make sure that you are on level ground, that the transmission is in Reverse or with automatic transmissions, Park; the parking brake is set, and the tire diagonally opposite to the one to be changed is blocked so that it will not roll. Loosen the lug nuts before you jack the wheel to be changed completely free of the ground.

If you use a hoist, make sure that the pads of the hoist are located in such a way as to lift on the Jeep frame and not on a shock absorber mount, floor boards, oil pan, or any other part that cannot support the full weight of the vehicle.

PUSHING AND TOWING

To push-start your vehicle (manual transmissions only), follow the procedures below. Check to make sure that the bumpers of both vehicles are aligned so neither will be damaged. Be sure that all electrical system components are turned off (headlights, heater, blower, etc.). Turn on the ignition switch. Place the shift lever in first or second and push in the clutch pedal. At about 15 mph, signal the driver of the pushing vehicle to fall back, depress the accelerator pedal, and release the clutch pedal slowly. The engine should start.

When you are doing the pushing or pulling, make sure that the two bumpers match so you won't damage the vehicle you are to push. Another good idea is to put an old tire in between the two vehicles. If the bumpers don't match, perhaps you should tow the other vehicle. If the other vehicle is just stuck, use first gear to slowly push it out. Tell the driver of the other vehicle to go slowly, too. Try to keep your Jeep right up against the other vehicle while you are pushing. If the two vehicles do separate, stop and start over again instead of trying to catch up and ramming the other vehicle. Also try, as much as possible, to avoid riding or slipping the clutch. Low range makes this easy. When the other vehicle gains enough traction, it should pull away from your vehicle.

If you have to tow the other vehicle, make sure that the tow chain or rope is sufficiently long and strong, and that it is attached securely to both vehicles at a strong place. Attach the chain at a point on the frame or as close to it as possible. Once again, go slowly and tell the other driver to do the same. Warn the other driver not to allow too much slack in the line when he gains traction and can move under his own power. Otherwise he may run over the tow line and damage both vehicles. If your Jeep has to be towed by a tow truck, it can be towed forward for any distance just as long as it is done fairly slowly. If your Jeep has to be towed backward, remove the front axle drive flanges to prevent the front differential from rotating. If the drive flanges are removed, improvise a cover to keep out dust and dirt.

TRAILER TOWING

Jeep vehicles have long been popular as trailer towing vehicles. Their strong construction, 4-wheel drive and wide range of engine/transmission combinations make them ideal for towing campers, boat trailers and utility trailers.

Factory trailer towing packages are available on most Jeep vehicles. However, if you are installing a trailer hitch and wiring on your Jeep, there are a few things that you ought to know.

Trailer Weight

Trailer weight is the first, and most important, factor in determining whether or not your vehicle is suitable for towing the trailer you have in mind. The horsepower-to-weight ratio should be calculated. The basic standard is a ratio of 35:1. That is, 35 pounds of GVW for every horsepower.

1-51

1 GENERAL INFORMATION AND MAINTENANCE

Recommended Equipment Checklist

Equipment	Class I Trailers Under 2,000 pounds	Class II Trailers 2,000-3,500 pounds	Class III Trailers 3,500-6,000 pounds	Class IV Trailers 6,000 pounds and up
Hitch	Frame or Equalizing	Equalizing	Equalizing	Fifth wheel Pick-up truck only
Tongue Load Limit**	Up to 200 pounds	200-350 pounds	350-600 pounds	600 pounds and up
Trailer Brakes	Not Required	Required	Required	Required
Safety Chain	3/16" diameter links	1/4" diameter links	5/16" diameter links	—
Fender Mounted Mirrors	Useful, but not necessary	Recommended	Recommended	Recommended
Turn Signal Flasher	Standard	Constant Rate or heavy duty	Constant Rate or heavy duty	Constant Rate or heavy duty
Coolant Recovery System	Recommended	Required	Required	Required
Transmission Oil Cooler	Recommended	Recommended	Recommended	Recommended
Engine Oil Cooler	Recommended	Recommended	Recommended	Recommended
Air Adjustable Shock Absorbers	Recommended	Recommended	Recommended	Recommended
Flex or Clutch Fan	Recommended	Recommended	Recommended	Recommended
Tires	***	***	***	***

NOTE: The information in this chart is a guide. Check the manufacturer's recommendations for your car if in doubt.

*Local laws may require specific equipment such as trailer brakes or fender mounted mirrors. Check your local laws. Hitch weight is usually 10-15% of trailer gross weight and should be measured with trailer loaded.

**Most manufacturer's do not recommend towing trailers of over 1,000 pounds with compacts. Some intermediates cannot tow Class III trailers.

***Check manufacturer's recommendations for your specific car/trailer combination.

—Does not apply

To calculate this ratio, multiply you engine's rated horsepower by 35, then subtract the weight of the vehicle, including passengers and luggage. The resulting figure is the ideal maximum trailer weight that you can tow. One point to consider: a numerically higher axle ratio can offset what appears to be a low trailer weight. If the weight of the trailer that you have in mind is somewhat higher than the weight you just calculated, you might consider changing your rear axle ratio to compensate.

Hitch Weight

There are three kinds of hitches: bumper mounted, frame mounted, and load equalizing.

Bumper mounted hitches are those which attach solely to the vehicle's bumper. Many states prohibit towing with this type of hitch, when it attaches to the vehicle's stock bumper, since it subjects the bumper to stresses for which it was not designed. Aftermarket rear step bumpers, designed for trailer towing, are acceptable for use with bumper mounted hitches.

Frame mounted hitches can be of the type which bolts to two or more points on the frame, plus the bumper, or just to several points on the frame. Frame mounted hitches can also be of the tongue type, for Class I towing, or, of the receiver type, for classes II and III.

Load equalizing hitches are usually used for large trailers. Most equalizing hitches are welded in place and use equalizing bars and chains to level the vehicle after the trailer is hooked up.

The bolt-on hitches are the most common, since they are relatively easy to install.

Check the gross weight rating of your trailer. Tongue weight is usually figured as 10% of gross trailer weight. Therefore, a trailer with a maximum gross weight of 2,000 lb. will have a maximum tongue weight of 200 lb. Class I trailers fall into this category. Class II trailers are those with a gross weight rating of 2,000-3,500 lb., while Class III trailers fall into the 3,500-6,000 lb. category. Class IV trailers are those over 6,000 lb. and are for use with fifth wheel trucks, only.

When you've determined the hitch that you'll need, follow the manufacturer's installation instructions, exactly, especially when it comes to fastener torques. The hitch will subjected to a lot of stress and good hitches come with hardened bolts. Never substitute an inferior bolt for a hardened bolt.

Wiring

Wiring the car for towing is fairly easy. There are a number of good wiring kits available and these should be used, rather than trying to design your own. All trailers will need brake lights and turn signals as well as tail lights and side marker lights. Most states require extra marker lights for overwide trailers. Also, most

GENERAL INFORMATION AND MAINTENANCE 1

states have recently required back-up lights for trailers, and most trailer manufacturers have been building trailers with back-up lights for several years.

Additionally, some Class I, most Class II and just about all Class III trailers will have electric brakes.

Add to this number an accessories wire, to operate trailer internal equipment or to charge the trailer's battery, and you can have as many as seven wires in the harness.

Determine the equipment on your trailer and buy the wiring kit necessary. The kit will contain all the wires needed, plus a plug adapter set which included the female plug, mounted on the bumper or hitch, and the male plug, wired into, or plugged into the trailer harness.

When installing the kit, follow the manufacturer's instructions. The color coding of the wires is standard throughout the industry. One point to note: some domestic vehicles, and most imported vehicles, have separate turn signals. On most domestic vehicles, the brake lights and rear turn signals operate with the same bulb. For those vehicles with separate turn signals, you can purchase an isolation unit so that the brake lights won't blink whenever the turn signals are operated, or, you can go to your local electronics supply house and buy four diodes to wire in series with the brake and turn signal bulbs. Diodes will isolate the brake and turn signals. The choice is yours. The isolation units are simple and quick to install, but far more expensive than the diodes. The diodes, however, require more work to install properly, since they require the cutting of each bulb's wire and soldering in place of the diode.

One, final point, the best kits are those with a spring loaded cover on the vehicle mounted socket. This cover prevent dirt and moisture from corroding the terminals. Never let the vehicle socket hang loosely; always mount it securely to the bumper or hitch.

Cooling

ENGINE

One of the most common, if not THE most common, problems associated with trailer towing is engine overheating.

With factory installed trailer towing packages, a heavy duty cooling system is usually included. Heavy duty cooling systems are available as optional equipment on most Jeep vehicles, with or without a trailer package. If you have one of these extra-capacity systems, you shouldn't have any overheating problems.

If you have a standard cooling system, without an expansion tank, you'll definitely need to get an aftermarket expansion tank kit, preferably one with at least a 2 quart capacity. These kits are easily installed on the radiator's overflow hose, and come with a pressure cap designed for expansion tanks.

Another helpful accessory is a Flex Fan. These fan are large diameter units are designed to provide more airflow at low speeds, with blades that have deeply cupped surfaces. The blades then flex, or flatten out, at high speed, when less cooling air is needed. These fans are far lighter in weight than stock fans, requiring less horsepower to drive them. Also, they are far quieter than stock fans.

If you do decide to replace your stock fan with a flex fan, note that if your Jeep has a fan clutch, a spacer between the flex fan and water pump hub will be needed.

Aftermarket engine oil coolers are helpful for prolonging engine oil life and reducing overall engine temperatures. Both of these factors increase engine life.

While not absolutely necessary in towing Class I and some Class II trailers, they are recommended for heavier Class II and all Class III towing.

Engine oil cooler systems consist of an adapter, screwed on in place of the oil filter, a remote filter mounting and a multi-tube, finned heat exchanger, which is mounted in front of the radiator or air conditioning condenser.

TRANSMISSION

An automatic transmission is usually recommended for trailer towing. Modern automatics have proven reliable and, of course, easy to operate, in trailer towing.

The increased load of a trailer, however, causes an increase in the temperature of the automatic transmission fluid. Heat is the worst enemy of an automatic transmission. As the temperature of the fluid increases, the life of the fluid decreases.

It is essential, therefore, that you install an automatic transmission cooler.

The cooler, which consists of a multi-tube, finned heat exchanger, is usually installed in front of the radiator or air conditioning compressor, and hooked inline with the transmission cooler tank inlet line. Follow the cooler manufacturer's installation instructions.

Select a cooler of at least adequate capacity, based upon the combined gross weights of the Jeep and trailer.

Cooler manufacturers recommend that you use an aftermarket cooler in addition to, and not instead of, the present cooling tank in your Jeep radiator. If you do want to use it in place of the radiator cooling tank, get a cooler at least two sizes larger than normally necessary.

One note: the transmission cooler can, sometimes, cause slow or harsh shifting in the transmission during cold weather, until the fluid has a chance to come up to normal operating temperature. Some coolers can be purchased with or retrofitted with a temperature bypass valve which will allow fluid flow through the cooler only when the fluid has reached operating temperature, or above.

1 GENERAL INFORMATION AND MAINTENANCE

CAPACITIES CHART

Engine	Crank-case Inc. Filter (qt.)	Transmission (pt.)			Transfer Case		Drive Axle (pt.)		Fuel Tank (gal.)	Cooling System (qt.)	
		4-sp	5-sp	Auto.	Man.	Auto.	Front	Rear		w/AC	wo/AC
4-126	5.5	—	7.0	—	4.5	7.0	2.5	2.5	①	9.0	9.0
4-150	4.0	②	③	15.8	4.5	6.0	④	2.5	①⑦	10.0	10.0
6-173	5.0	②	③	15.8	4.5	6.0	④	2.5	①	12.0	12.0
6-243	6.0	②	③	17.0	⑤	⑤	2.5	⑥	⑦	12.0	12.0

① Standard: 13.5
   Optional: 20.2
② AX4 w/4WD: 7.4
   w/2WD: 7.8
   T4: 3.9
③ T5: 4.5
   AX5 w/4WD: 7.0
   w/2WD: 7.4
   BA 10/5 w/4WD: 4.9
   w/2WD: 5.2
   AX15 w/2WD: 6.7
   w/4WD: 6.75

④ Without Selec Trac: 3.0
   With Selec Trac: 4.5
   Add 5 oz. for Selec Trac disconnect housing
⑤ NP-208: 6.0
   NP-231: 2.2
   NP-242: 3.0
⑥ Standard Axle: 2.5
   Heavy Duty: 3.0
⑦ Comanche short bed: 18.5
   Comanche long bed: 23.5
   Wagoneer/Cherokee: 20.2

PREVENTIVE MAINTENANCE CHART

Interval	Item	Service
Every 7,500 miles	Engine oil and filter	Change
	Oil filler cap	Clean
	Steering gear	Check level
	Power steering reservoir	Check level
	Differentials	Check level
	Manual transmission	Check level
	Transfer case	Check level
	Automatic transmission	Check level
	Steering Linkage	EP chassis lube
	Universal joints	EP chassis lube
	Exhaust system	Check
Every 30,000 miles	Automatic transmission	Change fluid/filter
	Manual transmission	Change fluid
	Transfer case	Change fluid
	Spark plugs	Replace
	Air filter	Replace
	Drive belts	Inspect/adjust
	Fuel filter	Replace
	Coolant ①	Replace
	PCV valve	Replace
	Brakes	Check
	Wheel bearings	Clean/repack
Every 60,000 miles	Drive belts	Replace
	Ignition wires	Replace
	Distributor cap/rotor	Replace
	Battery	Replace

① or 36 months (24 months thereafter)

Engine Performance and Tune-Up

QUICK REFERENCE INDEX

Electronic ignition	2-5
1984-85 AMC SSI System	2-5
Delco HEI System	2-7
1986-90 AMC SSI System	2-10
Chrysler SBEC System	2-16
Firing Orders	2-4
Idle speed and mixture adjustment	2-20
Ignition Timing	2-18
Tune-up Charts	2-3
Valve lash adjustment	2-20

GENERAL INDEX

Carburetor Adjustments	2-20	Ignition timing	2-18	Procedures	2-2
Electronic Ignition		Spark plugs	2-2	Spark plugs	2-2
1984-85 AMC SSI System	2-5	Spark plug wires	2-4	Spark plug wires	2-4
Delco HEI System	2-7	Specifications Charts	2-3	Specifications	2-3
1986-90 AMC SSI System	2-10	Timing	2-18	Valve lash adjustment	2-20
Chrysler SBEC System	2-16	Tune-up		Wiring	
Firing orders	2-4	Idle speed and mixture	2-20	Spark plug	2-4
Idle speed and mixture adjustment	2-20	Ignition timing	2-18		

2 ENGINE PERFORMANCE AND TUNE-UP

TUNE-UP PROCEDURES

In order to extract the full measure of performance and economy from your engine it is essential that it be properly tuned at regular intervals. A regular tune-up will keep your Jeep's engine running smoothly and will prevent the annoying minor breakdowns and poor performance associated with an untuned engine.

A complete tune-up should be performed every year. If the Jeep is operated under severe conditions, such as trailer towing, prolonged idling, continual stop and start driving, or if starting or running problems are noticed, a tune-up should be performed more often. It is assumed that the routine maintenance described in Section 1 has been kept up, as this will have a decided effect on the results of a tune-up. All applicable steps should be followed in order — the result will be a complete tune-up.

If the specifications on the tune-up sticker in the engine compartment disagree with the Tune-Up Specifications chart in this Section, the figures on the sticker must be used. The sticker often reflects changes made during the production run.

Spark Plugs

A typical spark plug consists of a metal shell surrounding a ceramic insulator. A metal electrode extends downward through the center of the insulator and protrudes a small distance. Located at the end of the plug and attached to the side of the outer metal shell is the side electrode. The side electrode bends in at a 90° angle so that its tip is even with, and parallel to, the tip of the center electrode. The distance between these two electrodes (measured in thousandths of an inch) is called the spark plug gap. The spark plug in no way produces a spark, but merely provides a gap across which the current can arc. The coil produces anywhere from 20,000 to 40,000 volts which travels to the distributor where it is distributed through the spark plug wires to the spark plugs. The current passes along the center electrode and jumps the gap to the side electrode. This arc ignites the air/fuel mixture in the combustion chamber.

Spark plugs ignite the air and fuel mixture in the cylinder as the piston reaches the top of the compression stroke. The controlled explosion that results forces the piston down, turning the crankshaft and the rest of the drive train.

The average life of a spark plug is dependent on a number of factors: the mechanical condition of the engine; the type of engine; the type of fuel; driving conditions; and the driver.

When you remove the spark plugs, check their condition. They are a good indicator of engine condition (however, this is not always true with today's high energy ignitions). It is a good idea to remove the spark plugs at regular intervals, such as every 2,000 or 3,000 miles, just so you can keep an eye on the mechanical state of your engine.

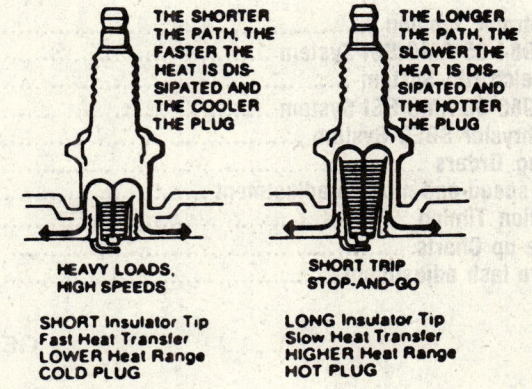

Spark plug heat range

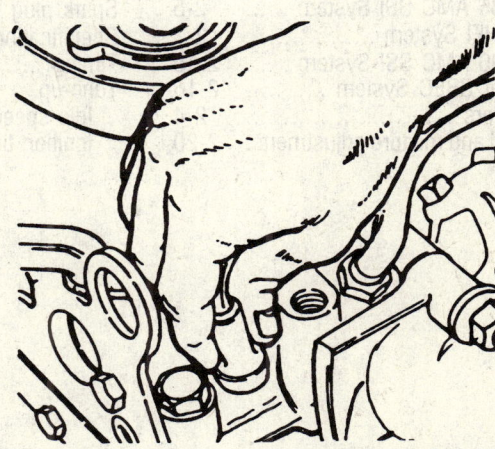

Twist and pull on the rubber boot to remove the spark plug wire; never pull on the wire itself

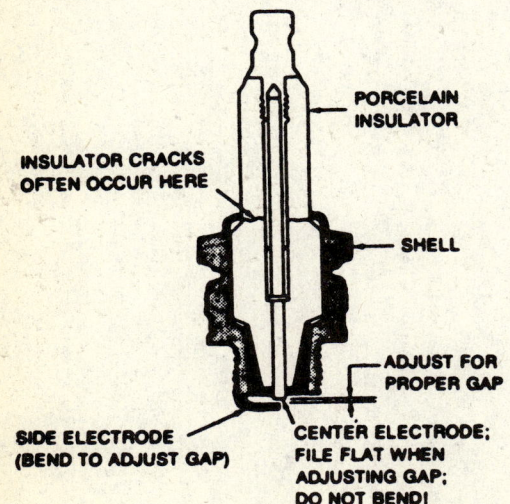

Cross section of a spark plug

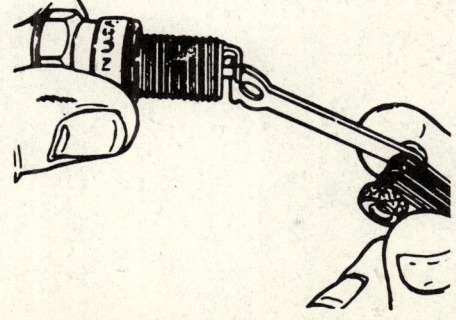

Adjust the electrode gap by bending the side electrode

2-2

ENGINE PERFORMANCE AND TUNE-UP 2

TUNE-UP SPECIFICATIONS GASOLINE ENGINES

Years	Engines	Spark Plugs Type	Gap (in.)	Ignition Timing (deg.) Man. Trans.	Ignition Timing (deg.) Auto. Trans.	Valve Clearance In.	Valve Clearance Exh.	Idle Speed Man. Trans.	Idle Speed Auto. Trans.
1984–85	4-150	RFN-12LY	0.035	12B	12B	Hyd.	Hyd.	750	750
	6-173	R43CTS	0.041	10B	10B	Hyd.	Hyd.	750	750
1986	4-150	RC-12LYC	0.035	①	①	Hyd.	Hyd.	①	①
	6-173	R43CTS	0.041	12B	10B	Hyd.	Hyd.	700	700
1987–90	4-150	RC-12LYC	0.035	①	①	Hyd.	Hyd.	①	①
	6-243	RC-9YC	0.035	①	①	Hyd.	Hyd.	①	①
1991	4-150	RC-12LYC	0.035	①	①	Hyd.	Hyd.	①	①
	6-243	RC-12LYC	0.035	①	①	Hyd.	Hyd.	①	①

① Not adjustable

TUNE-UP SPECIFICATIONS DIESEL ENGINES

Engine	Injection Timing (deg.)	(mm)	Nozzle Opening Pressure (psi)	Idle Speed (rpm) wo/sol.	Idle Speed (rpm) w/sol.	Valve Clearance Cold (in.) Int.	Valve Clearance Cold (in.) Exh.
4-126	8B	0.82 ± 0.02	1,885	800	1,100	0.008	0.010

A small deposit of light tan or gray material on a spark plug that has been used for any period of time is to be considered normal.

The gap between the center electrode and the side or ground electrode can be expected to increase not more than 0.001 in. (0.025mm) every 1,000 miles (1,609 km) under normal conditions.

When a spark plug is functioning normally or, more accurately, when a plug is installed in the engine that is functioning properly, the plugs can be taken out, cleaned, regapped, and reinstalled in the engine without doing the engine any harm.

When, and if, a plug fouls and beings to misfire, you will have to investigate, correct the cause of the fouling, and either clean or replace the plug.

There are several reasons why a spark plug will foul. You can learn which is at fault by just looking at the plug. A few of the most common reasons for plug fouling are listed below with an explanation of what the plug will look like. Solutions to the problems are also offered.

SPARK PLUG HEAT RANGE

Spark plug heat range is the ability of the plug to dissipate heat. The longer the insulator (or the farther it extends into the engine), the hotter the plug will operate; the shorter the insulator the cooler it will operate. A plug that absorbs little heat and remains too cool will quickly accumulate deposits of oil and carbon since it is not hot enough to burn them off. This leads to plug fouling and consequently to misfiring. A plug that absorbs too much heat will have no deposits, but, due to the excessive heat, the electrodes will burn away quickly and in some instances, preignition may result.

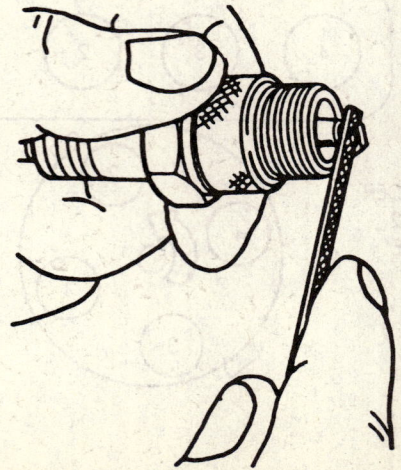

Plugs that are in good condition can be filed and re-used

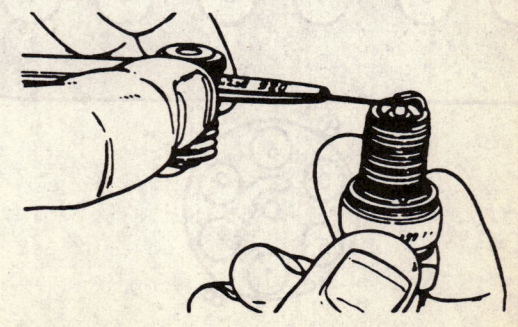

Always use a wire gauge to check the electrode gap

2 ENGINE PERFORMANCE AND TUNE-UP

Preignition takes place when plug tips get so hot that they glow sufficiently to ignite the fuel/air mixture before the actual spark occurs. This early ignition will usually cause a pinging during low speeds and heavy loads.

The general rule of thumb for choosing the correct heat range when picking a spark plug is: if most of your driving is long distance, high speed travel, use a colder plug; if most of your driving is stop and go, use a hotter plug. Original equipment plugs are compromise plugs, but most people never have occasion to change their plugs from the factory recommended heat range.

REMOVAL

1. Number and remove the spark plug wires one at a time. Remove the wire from the end of the spark plug by grasping the wire by the rubber boot. If the boot sticks to the plug, remove it by twisting and pulling at the same time. Do not pull the wire itself.
2. Use a $^{13}/_{16}$ in. spark plug socket to loosen all of the plugs about two turns.
3. If compressed air is available, blow off the area around the spark plug holes. Otherwise, use a rag or a brush to clean the area. Be careful not to allow any foreign material to drop into the spark plug holes.
4. Remove the plugs by unscrewing them the rest of the way from the engine.

INSPECTION

Check the plugs for deposits and wear (see special section on how to check your spark plugs). If they are going to be reinstalled, clean the plugs thoroughly. Remember that any kind of deposit will decrease the efficiency of the plug. Plugs can be cleaned on a spark plug cleaning machine (available through local tool dealers), or you can do an acceptable job of cleaning with a stiff brush.

Check spark plug gap before installation. The ground electrode must be aligned with the center electrode and the specified size wire gauge should pass through the gap with a slight drag. If the electrodes are worn, it is possible to file them level.

INSTALLATION

1. Insert the plugs in the spark plug hole and tighten them hand tight. Take care not to cross-thread them.

CHILTON TIP: *In hard to reach areas, a small length of tubing pushed on to the tip of the spark plug, can aid in getting the plug started in the hole.*

2. Tighten the plugs to the torque figure specified in the Tune-Up chart in this Section.
3. Install the spark plug wires on their plugs. Make sure that each wire is firmly connected to each plug.

CHECKING AND REPLACING SPARK PLUG CABLES

Visually inspect the spark plug cables for burns, cuts, or breaks in the insulation. Check the spark plug boots and the nipples on the distributor cap and coil. Replace any damaged wiring. If no physical damage is obvious, the wires can be checked with an ohmmeter for excessive resistance. (See the HEI plug Wire Resistance Chart).

When installing a new set of spark plug cables, replace the cables one at a time so there will be no mixup. Start by replacing the longest cable first. Install the boot firmly over the spark plug. Route the wire exactly the same as the original. Insert the nipple firmly into the tower on the distributor cap.

Before starting the Jeep, recheck that the wires are correctly installed by tracing each wire back to the distributor cap and checking the firing order.

FIRING ORDERS

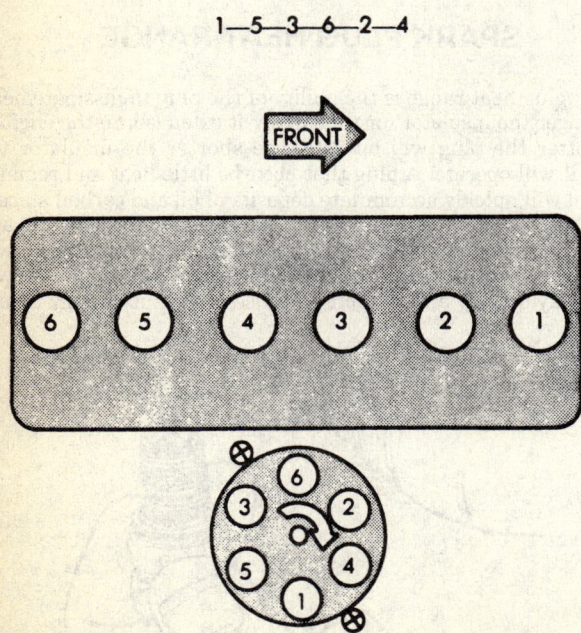

6-4.0L engine firing order

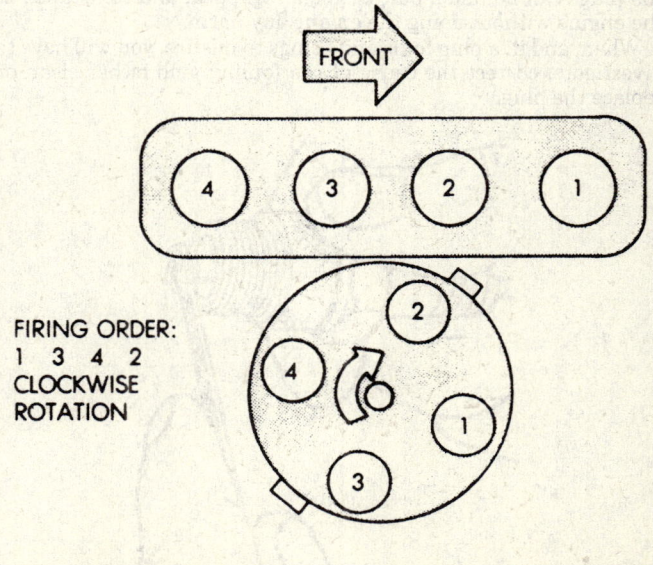

4-2.5L engine firing order 1989-91

ENGINE PERFORMANCE AND TUNE-UP 2

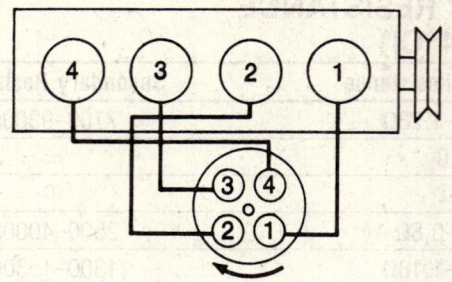

Distributor wiring and firing order: 4-2.5L 1984-88

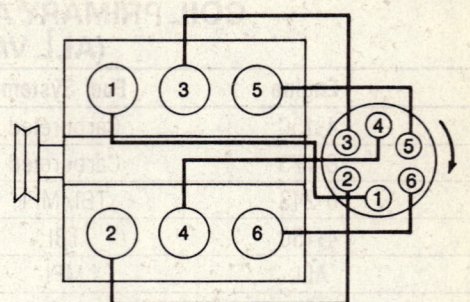

Distributor wiring and firing order: 6-2.8L

ELECTRONIC IGNITION SYSTEMS

All ignition systems are made up of two systems — Primary Circuit and Secondary Circuit. In performing service testing on these systems it helps to follow a specific sequence and avoid oversight of a minor problem.

The first step in diagnosis of an ignition problem is to perform a complete visual inspection for obvious defects. Loose or cut wires and physically damaged components should be identified and repaired before any further testing is done.

The second step is to identify which circuit — primary or secondary — is malfunctioning.

The primary circuit consists of:
- the ignition switch
- the battery to ignition coil wiring
- the ignition coil primary wiring
- all wires connected to the electronic ignition control unit and the distributor pickup coil assembly
- the electronic ignition control unit
- the distributor

The secondary circuit consists of:
- the ignition coil secondary wiring
- all high voltage wires attached to the distributor cap, coil and spark plugs
- the distributor cap
- the distributor rotor
- the spark plugs

Once the malfunctioning system is determined, further testing and ultimately repair can be accomplished.

The starting point for ignition testing is the secondary circuit. Testing of this circuit will determine if spark is reaching the cylinders. If the cylinders do not get a spark to ignite the air/fuel mixture (in addition to compression of the mixture and the air/fuel mixture itself), the engine will not run.

Perform the following tests as a first step in diagnosis of an ignition problem.

Secondary Circuit Test

NOTE: Intermittent failure may be caused by loose or corroded terminals, defective or missing components, inadequate ground connections or defective wiring.

1. Disconnect the coil wire from the center of the distributor cap.

NOTE: Twist the rubber boot slightly in either direction, then grasp the boot and pull straight up. Do not pull on the wire, and do not use pliers.

2. Hold the wire $1/4–1/2$ in. (6–12mm) from a ground with a pair of insulated pliers and a heavy glove. As the engine is cranked, watch for a spark.

3. If a spark appears, reconnect the coil wire. Remove the wire from one spark plug, and test for a spark as above.

—— CAUTION ——
Do not remove the spark plug wires from cylinder 3 on the 4-2.5L. Use of an HEI spark tester is recommended for the 6-2.8L engine.

4. If a spark occurs in both coil and all spark plug wires, the problem is in the fuel system or ignition timing. If no spark occurs, check for a defective rotor, cap, or spark plug wires.

5. If no spark occurs from the coil wire in Step 2, perform the coil secondary winding test.

Coil Primary Winding Test

1. Check the coil for cracks, carbon tracks, etc., and replace as necessary.
2. Remove the connectors (wires) from the (+) and (−) terminals of the coil.
3. Connect an ohmmeter (set to the low scale) to the coil (+) and (−) terminals. If the reading is not within specifications (see coil primary and secondary resistance chart), replace the coil.

Coil Secondary Winding Test

1. Assure that the ignition switch is OFF and remove the coil wire from the coil.
2. Set the ohmmeter for the X1000 scale. Connect it to the brass contact on the coil and to either the (+) or (−) terminal on the coil.
3. If the resistance is not within specifications, replace the coil.

American Motors Solid State Ignition (SSI) System

The SSI system is standard equipment on all 1984–85 American Motors built engines.

The system consists of a sensor and toothed trigger wheel inside the distributor, and a permanently sealed electronic control unit which determines dwell, in addition to the coil, ignition wires, and spark plugs.

The trigger wheel rotates on the distributor shaft. As one of its teeth nears the sensor magnet, the magnetic field shifts toward the tooth. When the tooth and sensor are aligned, the magnetic field is shifted to its maximum, signaling the electronic control unit to switch off the coil primary current. This starts an electronic timer inside the control unit, which allows the primary current to remain off only long enough for the spark plug to fire. The timer adjusts the amount of time primary current is off according to conditions, thus automatically adjusting dwell. There is also a special circuit within the control unit to detect and ignore spuri-

2 ENGINE PERFORMANCE AND TUNE-UP

COIL PRIMARY AND SECONDARY RESISTANCE
(ALL VALUES AT 75°F [24°C])

Year	Engine	Fuel System	Primary Resistance	Secondary Resistance
1984–88	4-150	Carbureted	1.13–1.23Ω	7700–9300Ω
	6-173	Carbureted	0	∞
1987–90	6-243	TBI/MFI	①	①
1989–90	4-150	TBI	0.4–0.8Ω	2500–4000Ω
1991 ②	ALL	MFI	0.97–1.18Ω	11300–15300Ω
1991 ③	ALL	MFI	0.95–1.20Ω	11300–15300Ω

① Must use Diagnostic Readout Box (DRB II) Diagnostic Computer
② Manufactured by Diamond
③ Manufactured by Toyodenso

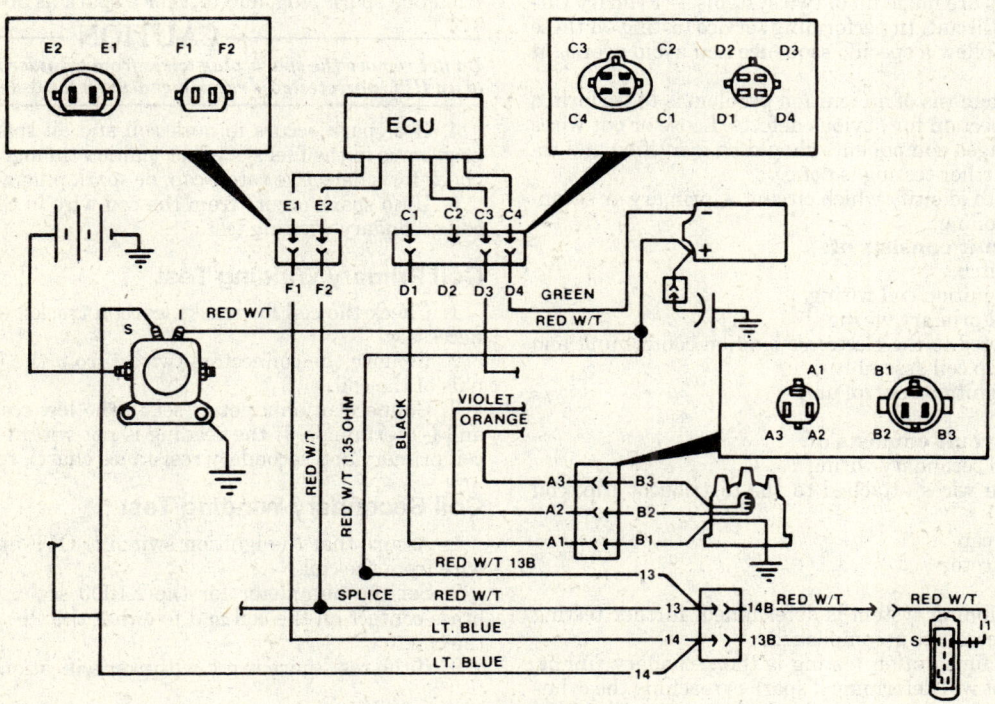

4-2.5L SSI wiring diagram

ous signals. Spark timing is adjusted by both mechanical (centrifugal) and vacuum advance.

A wire of 1.35Ω resistance is spliced into the ignition feed to reduce voltage to the coil during running conditions. The resistance wire is bypassed when the engine is being started so that full battery voltage may be supplied to the coil. Bypass is accomplished by the I-terminal on the solenoid.

DIAGNOSIS

Checking Vacuum Advance

1. Bring the engine to operating temperature.
2. Disconnect the three-wire connector to the vacuum input switches, and disconnect and plug the vacuum hose from the distributor vacuum advance.
3. Connect a vacuum pump (available through local tool distributors) to the vacuum advance unit.
4. Connect a timing light to the No. 1 spark plug wire, and a tachometer to the negative terminal on the coil.
5. Start engine and increase engine speed.
6. While observing the timing degree scale with a timing light, apply vacuum to the distributor vacuum advance unit. If timing advances, the unit is functioning properly. If timing does not advance, replace the vacuum advance unit.
7. Stop engine, remove all test equipment, replace the three-wire connector and vacuum advance hose

Checking Centrifugal (Mechanical) Advance

1. Bring the engine to operating temperature.
2. Disconnect the three-wire connector to the vacuum input switches, and disconnect and plug the vacuum hose from the distributor vacuum advance.
3. Connect a timing light to the NO. 1 spark plug wire.

ENGINE PERFORMANCE AND TUNE-UP 2

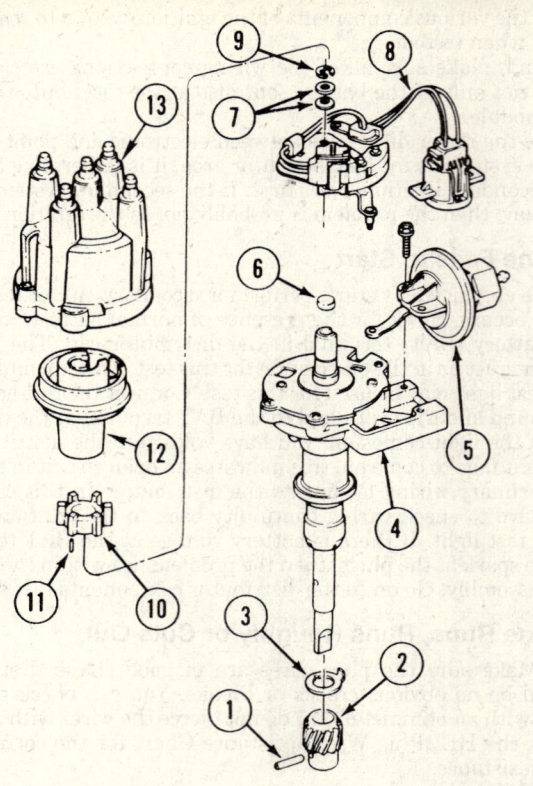

1. Pin
2. Gear
3. Washer
4. Distributor body
5. Vacuum advance mechanism
6. Wick
7. Washers
8. Pickup coil
9. Retainer
10. Trigger wheel
11. Pin
12. Rotor
13. Cap

4-2.5L SSI distributor

4. With the engine idling, slowly increase the speed and observe the timing mark. Timing should advance smoothly as engine speed increases. If timing advances unevenly, check and repair the centrifugal advance unit.
5. Stop engine, remove all test equipment, replace the three-wire connector and vacuum advance hose

Current Flow Test

1. Remove the connector from the coil. The terminals inside the connector are held in by plastic barbs. In order to remove the terminal from the connector you must carefully depress the barb and pull the terminal out. Remove both the (+) and (–) terminals from the connector.
2. Connect an ammeter between the positive terminal on the coil and the disconnected positive wire terminal. Connect a jumper wire from the coil negative terminal to a known good ground.
3. Turn the ignition switch ON.
4. The flow should be about 7 amps. If the flow is greater than 7.6 amps, replace the ignition coil.
5. Leave the ammeter connected to the coil. Remove the jumper wire and connect the coil green wire to the negative terminal. The current flow should be about 4 amps. If the current flow is less than 3.5 amps, check for poor connections in the 4-wire (control unit) and 3-wire (distributor) connectors. Also check for poor ground at the ground screw inside the distributor. If current flow is greater than 5 amps, the control unit is defective.

6. Start the engine.
7. Check for current flow between 2.0 and 2.4 amps. If current flow is not within specifications, the control unit is defective.

COMPONENT REPLACEMENT

Rotor

1. Loosen attaching screws and remove distributor cap.
2. Remove rotor by pulling straight up.
3. Apply a thin coating of dielectric compound to the tip of the rotor blade and reinstall rotor and cap.

Vacuum Advance

1. Remove the distributor cap and rotor.
2. Disconnect the vacuum hose from the vacuum advance unit.
3. Remove the two vacuum advance retaining screws.
4. Tilt the vacuum advance unit to disengage the link from the pickup coil pin. It may be necessary to loosen the base plate screws for necessary clearance.
5. Insert an allen wrench into the vacuum hose tube of the old unit and count the number of clockwise turns necessary to bottom the adjusting screw.
6. Turn the adjusting screw of the new unit clockwise to bottom, then counter clockwise the same number of turns in the above step.
7. When installing the new unit, insure that the link is engaged on the pin of the pickup coil.
8. Install and tighten all screws. Replace the rotor and cap.
9. Check ignition timing and adjust if required, then connect the vacuum advance hose to the unit.

Delco High Energy Ignition (HEI) System — 6–2.8L

The General Motors HEI system is a pulse triggered, transistor controlled, inductive discharge ignition system. The entire HEI system is contained within the distributor cap.

The distributor, in addition to housing the mechanical and vacuum advance mechanisms, contains the ignition coil (except on some inline six engines), the electronic control module, and the magnetic triggering device. The magnetic pick-up assembly contains a permanent magnet, a pole piece with internal teeth, and a pick-up coil (not to be confused with the ignition coil).

In the HEI system, as in other electronic ignition systems, the breaker points have been replaced with an electronic switch — a transistor, which is located within the control module. This switching transistor performs the same function the points did in a conventional ignition system; it simply turns coil primary current on and off at the correct time. Essentially then, electronic and conventional ignition systems operate on the same principle.

The module which houses the switching transistor is controlled (turned on and off) by a magnetically generated impulse induced in the pick-up coil. When the teeth of the rotating timer align with the teeth of the pole piece, the induced voltage in the pick-up coil signals the electronic module to open the coil primary circuit. The primary current then decreases, and a high voltage is induced in the ignition coil secondary windings, which is then directed through the rotor and spark plug wires to fire the spark plugs.

In essence, the pick-up coil module system simply replaces the conventional breaker points and condenser. The condenser found within the distributor is for radio suppression purposes only and has nothing to do with the ignition process. The module automatically controls the dwell period, increasing it with increasing engine speed. Since dwell is automatically controlled, it cannot be adjusted. The module itself is non-adjustable and non-repairable and must be replaced if found defective.

2 ENGINE PERFORMANCE AND TUNE-UP

HEI SYSTEM PRECAUTIONS

Before going on to troubleshooting, take note of the following precautions.

Timing Light Use

Inductive pick-up timing lights are the best type to use with HEI. Timing lights which connect between the spark plug and the spark plug wire occasionally (not always) give false readings.

Spark Plug Wires

The plug wires used with HEI systems are of a different construction than conventional wires. When replacing them, make sure you get the correct wires, since conventional wires won't carry the voltage. Also handle them carefully to avoid cracking or splitting them and **never** pierce them while testing.

Tachometer Use

Not all tachometers will operate or read correctly when used on an HEI system. While some tachometers may give a reading, this does not necessarily mean the reading is correct. In addition, some tachometers hook up differently from others. Check with the tachometer manufacturer to determine if your unit will work. Dwell is controlled by the electronic module and cannot be adjusted.

HEI System Testers

Instruments designed specifically for testing HEI systems are available from several tool manufacturers. The Distributor Module Tester performs a variety of tests, but may be cost prohibitive. On the other hand, the HEI Spark Tester is inexpensive, and insures that you will not short out the ignition module while performing secondary circuit tests.

TROUBLESHOOTING THE HEI SYSTEM

The symptoms of a defective component within the HEI system are exactly the same as those you would encounter in a conventional system. Some of these symptoms are:
- Hard or no starting
- Rough idle
- Poor fuel economy
- Engine misses under load or while accelerating

If you suspect a problem in the ignition system, there are certain preliminary checks which you should carry out before you begin to check the electronic portions of the system.

First, it is extremely important to make sure that the Jeep's battery is in good condition. A defective or poorly charged battery will cause the various components of the ignition system to read incorrectly when tested.

Second, make sure all of the wiring connections are clean and tight, not only at the battery, but also at the distributor cap, coil and module.

Since the major difference between electronic and point type ignition systems is in the distributor area, it is imperative to check the secondary ignition wires first. If the secondary system checks out okay, then the problem is probably not in the ignition system.

Engine Fails to Start

If the engine won't start, perform a secondary circuit test. If no spark occurs, check for the presence of normal battery voltage at the battery (BAT) terminal in the distributor cap. The ignition switch must be in the on position for this test. Either a multitester or a test light may be used for this test. Connect the test light wire to ground and the probe end to the BAT terminal at the distributor. If the light comes on, you have voltage to the distributor. If the light fails to come on, this indicates an open circuit in the ignition primary wiring leading to the distributor. In this case, you will have to check wiring continuity back to the ignition switch using test light. If there is battery voltage at the BAT terminal, but no spark at the plugs, then the problem lies within the distributor assembly. Go on to the distributor components test section.

Engine Runs, Runs Roughly or Cuts Out

1. Make sure the plug wires are in good shape first. There should be no obvious cracks or breaks. You can check the plug wires with an ohmmeter, but do not pierce the wires with a probe. Check the HEI Plug Wire Resistance Chart for the correct plug wire resistance.

2. If the plug wires are okay, remove the cap assembly, and check for moisture, cracks, chips, or carbon tracks, or any other high voltage leaks or failures. Replace the cap if you find any defects. Make sure the timer wheel rotates when the engine is cranked. If all components are functional, go on to the distributor components test section.

Distributor Components Testing

ELECTRONIC MODULE

An approved electronic module tester must be used to test the module. Purchase of such a unit may be cost prohibitive.

An easier less expensive way to determine module failure is to carry a new spare module. This spare module can be used for testing purposes only until a replacement module is needed.

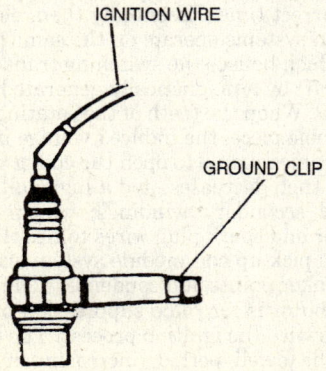

HEI spark tester

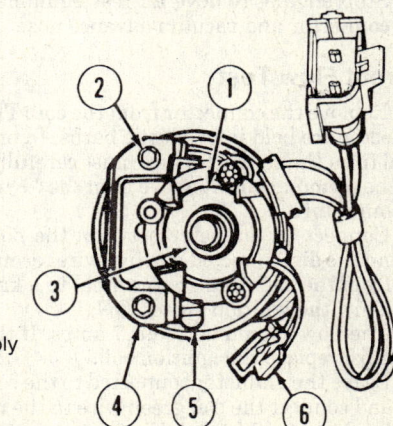

1. Pickup coil assembly
2. Screw
3. Snap ring
4. Electronic module
5. 'P' terminal
6. Pickup coil connector

6-2.8L HEI distributor

ENGINE PERFORMANCE AND TUNE-UP 2

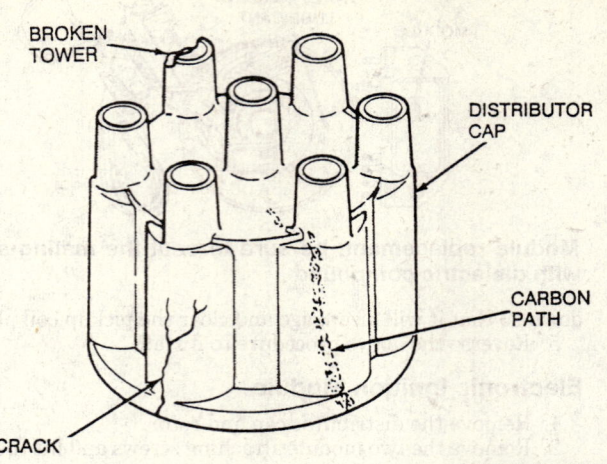

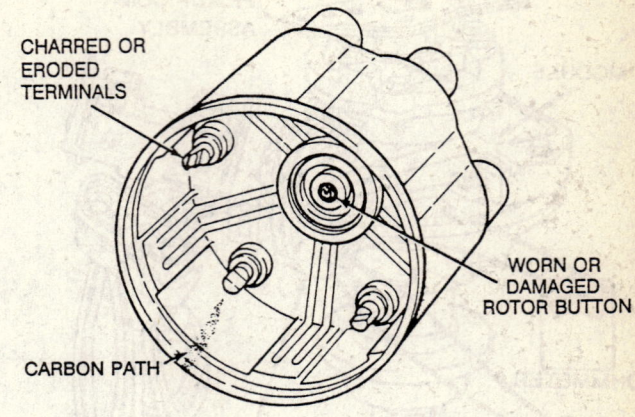

Distributor cap inspection

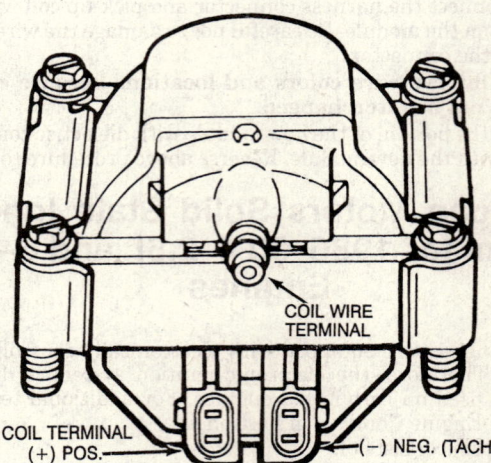

6-2.8L ignition coil

HEI PLUG WIRE RESISTANCE

Wire Length (inches)	Minimum Ohms	Maximum Ohms
Up to 15	3,000	10,000
15–25	4,000	15,000
25–35	6,000	20,000
Over 35	8,000	25,000

PICKUP COIL

1. Identify the two pickup coil wires (usually one green and one white wire) and unplug the connector from the ignition module.
2. Connect an ohmmeter (use mid scale) to one of the pickup coil connector terminals and the distributor housing.
3. Connect a vacuum pump to the vacuum advance unit (if equipped) and operate while observing the ohmmeter.
4. The ohmmeter should indicate infinite resistance at all times. if not, replace the pickup coil.
5. Next, connect the ohmmeter to both pickup coil connector terminals.
6. Operate the vacuum pump and observe the ohmmeter throughout the vacuum range.

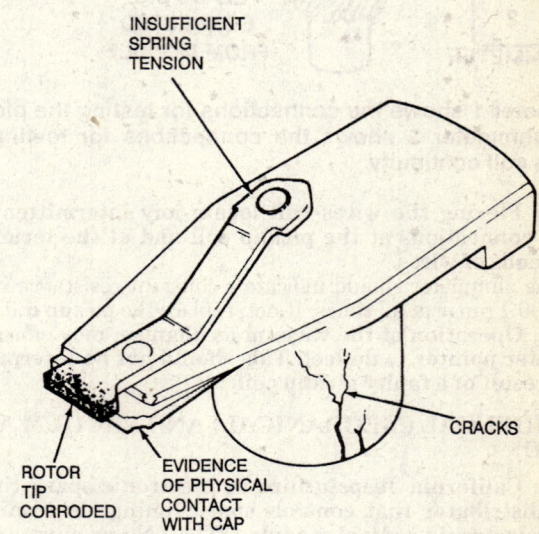

Distributor rotor inspection

a. EST signal
b. EST ref pulse
c. EST bypass
d. EST distributor ground
e. (+) battery
f. (−) coil

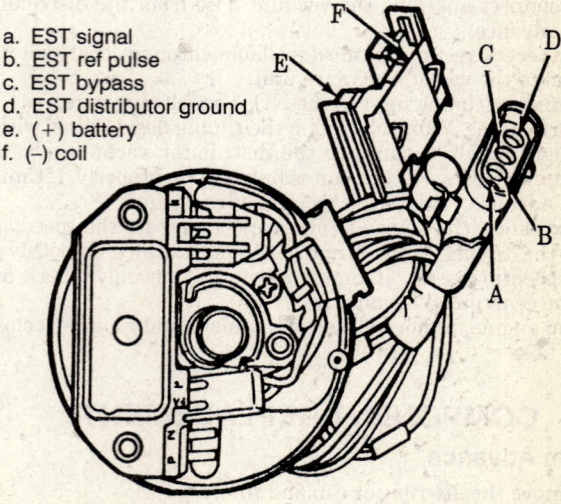

6-2.8L HEI electronic spark timing (California only) distributor

2-9

2 ENGINE PERFORMANCE AND TUNE-UP

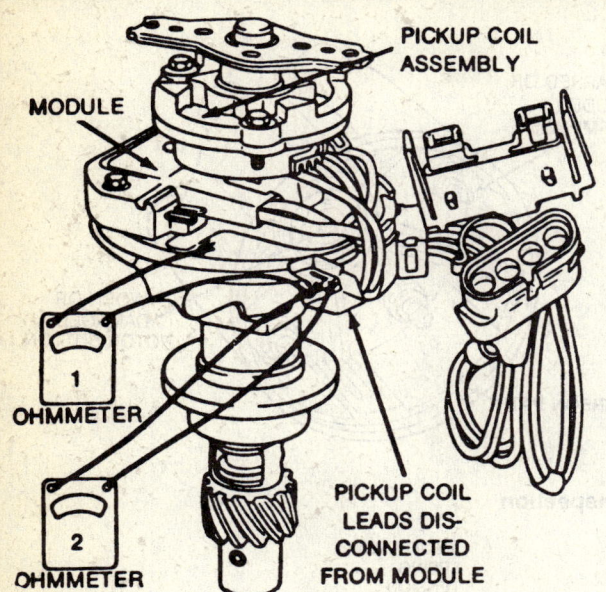

Ohmmeter 1 shows the connections for testing the pick-up coil. Ohmmeter 2 shows the connections for testing the pickup coil continuity

NOTE: Flexing the wires will locate any intermittent defective connections at the pickup coil and at the terminals on the ends of wires.

7. The ohmmeter should indicate a constant resistance in the 500–1500Ω range at all times. If not, replace the pickup coil.

NOTE: Operation of the vacuum mechanism may cause the ohmmeter pointer to deflect. This should not be interpreted as the result of a faulty pickup coil.

CENTRIFUGAL (MECHANICAL) AND VACUUM ADVANCE

NOTE: California Jeeps utilize an electronic spark timing (EST) distributor that controls spark timing electronically by the electronic control module (ECM). No vacuum or mechanical advance are used.

1. Bring the engine to operating temperature.
2. Disconnect and plug the vacuum hose from the distributor vacuum advance.
3. Connect a vacuum pump (available through local tool distributors) to the vacuum advance unit.
4. Connect a timing light to the NO. 1 spark plug wire.
5. Start engine. While observing the timing degree scale with a timing light, apply vacuum to the distributor vacuum advance unit. If timing advances, the unit is functioning properly. If timing does not advance, replace the vacuum advance unit.
6. Next, allow the engine to idle, slowly increase the speed and observe the timing mark. Timing should advance smoothly as engine speed increases. If timing advances unevenly, check and repair the centrifugal advance unit.
7. Stop engine, remove all test equipment and replace vacuum advance hose

COMPONENT REPLACEMENT

Vacuum Advance

1. Remove the distributor cap and rotor.
2. Disconnect the vacuum hose from the vacuum advance unit.
3. Remove the two vacuum advance retaining screws.
4. Turn pickup coil assembly clockwise and push mechanism

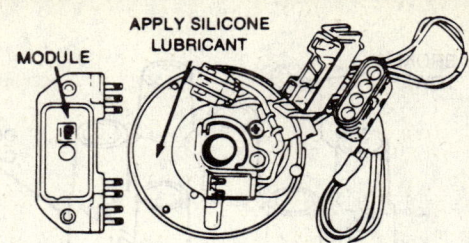

Module replacement; be sure to coat the mating surfaces with dielectric compound

down so that it will disengage and clear the pickup coil plate.
5. Reverse the above procedure to install.

Electronic Ignition Module

1. Remove the distributor cap and rotor.
2. Remove the two module attaching screws and lift the module up.
3. Disconnect the harness connector and pick-up coil wire connectors from the module. Be careful not to damage the wires when removing the connector.

NOTE: Observe wire colors and locations because connectors must not be interchanged.

4. Coat the bottom of the new module with dielectric compound supplied with the new module. Reverse above procedure to install.

American Motors Solid State Ignition System for 1986–90 4–2.5L and 6–4.0L Engines

These engines are equipped with electronically controlled fuel injection. Therefore, the electronic ignition system is different from that used on carbureted engines. For additional tests, see Electronic Engine Controls in Section 4.

The system consists of:
- a solid state ignition control module (ICM)
- an electronic control module (ECU)
- a forty tooth rotor in the distributor

The ignition control module (mounted on the right side of the shock tower area) consists of a solid state ignition circuit and an integrated ignition coil each of which can be removed and serviced separately. Spark timing control is determined by the ICM and is not adjustable.

The amount of spark advance provided is based on five input

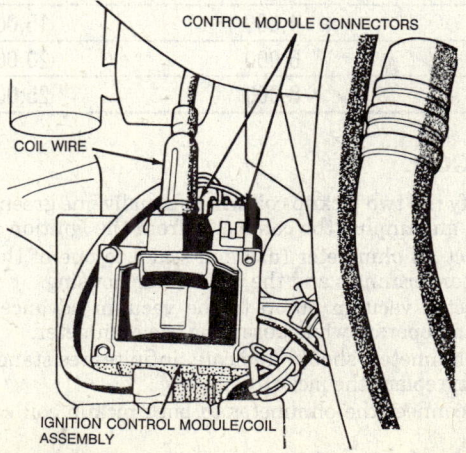

Ignition control module

ENGINE PERFORMANCE AND TUNE-UP 2

factors. The factors are coolant temperature, manifold absolute pressure, engine speed, manifold air temperature and throttle position (see TPS in Section 5).

Electrical feed to the ICM is through terminal A of connector 1 (see illustration). Electrical feed occurs only when the ignition switch is in the START and RUN positions. Terminal B of connector 1 is grounded at the engine oil dipstick bracket, along with the ECU ground wire and the O_2 sensor ground.

DIAGNOSIS

4–2.5L TBI 1986–90

DIAGNOSTIC CONNECTOR

Primary system diagnosis is made through the diagnostic connector, using an appropriate diagnostic computer. The diagnostic connector allows a primary circuit test (D1–2 B+ engine ON), and

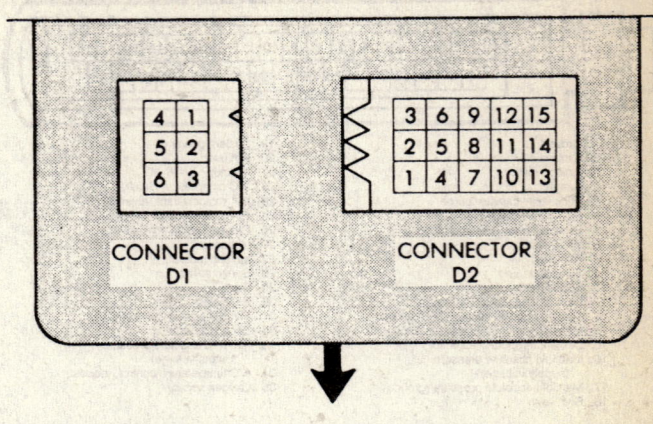

1989-90 6-4.0L MFI diagnostic connector

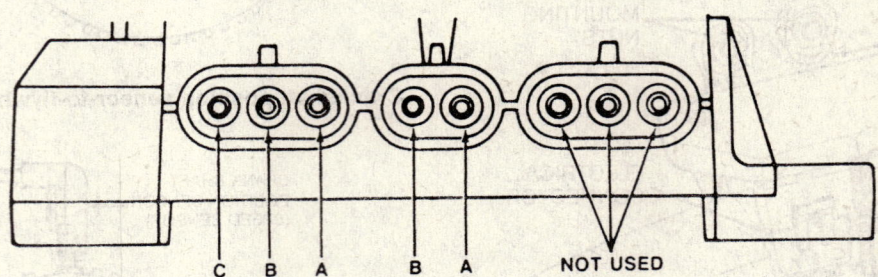

CONNECTOR 1:
A - Ignition (+)
B - Ground (−)
C - Tach Signal Diagnostic Connector
D1 - Pin 1

CONNECTOR 2:
A - Not Used
B - ECU Square Wave Output Ignition Coil Interface

Ignition control module connector

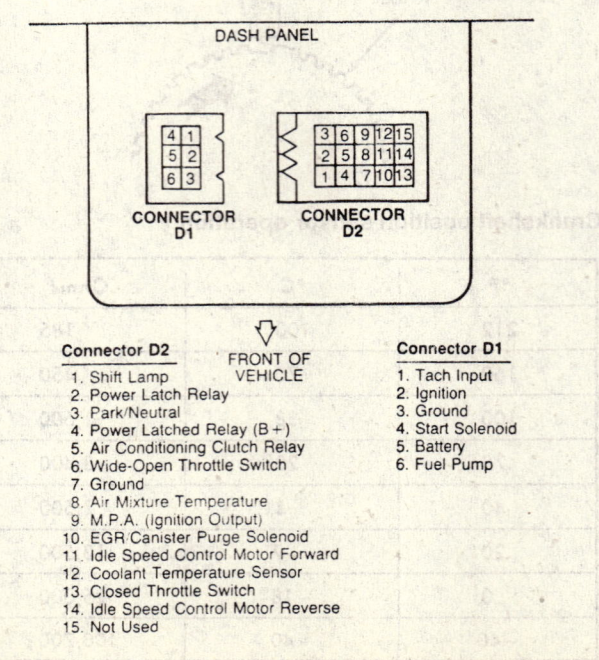

1986-88 4-2.5L TBI diagnostic connector

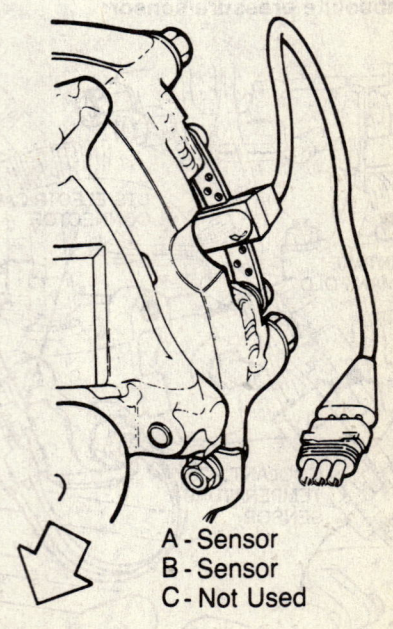

Crankshaft position sensor

2-11

2 ENGINE PERFORMANCE AND TUNE-UP

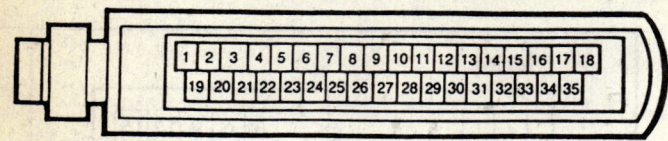

1. Ground
2. Ground
3. Ignition switch
4. Battery
5. EGR valve/canister purge
6. Fuel pump relay
7. System power relay (latch relay)
8. WOT switch
9. Not used
10. System ground
11. Speed sensor
12. Park/neutral switch (A/T only)
13. Throttle position sensor (TPS) ground
14. Manifold air/fuel temperature sensor
15. Coolant temperature sensor
16. Manifold absolute pressure (supply voltage)
17. Manifold absolute pressure (ground)
18. Shift lamp
19. System power (B+)
20. Not used
21. Injector
22. A/C compressor clutch
23. ISA motor retract (reverse)
24. ISA motor extend (forward)
25. Closed throttle (idle) switch
26. Not used
27. Ignition (output)
28. Speed sensor
29. Start
30. A/C select
31. Throttle position sensor (TPS)
32. Sensor ground
33. Manifold absolute pressure (output voltage)
34. A/C temperature control (request)
35. Oxygen sensor

1986-88 4-2.5L TBI ECU connector

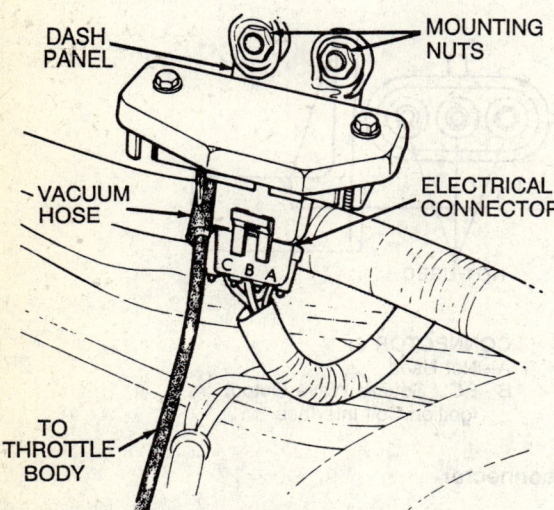

Manifold absolute pressure sensor

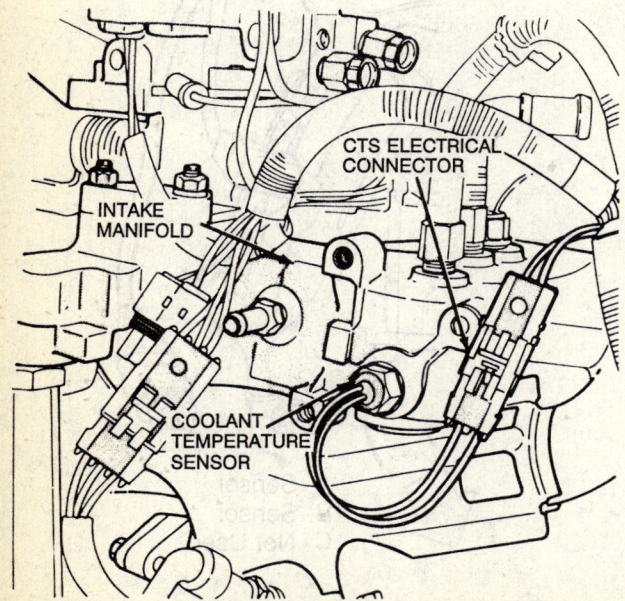

4-2.5L TBI coolant temperature sensor

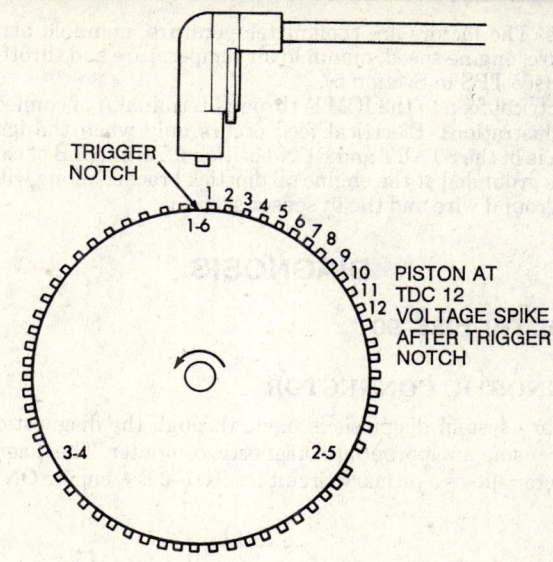

Crankshaft position sensor-to-flywheel TDC position

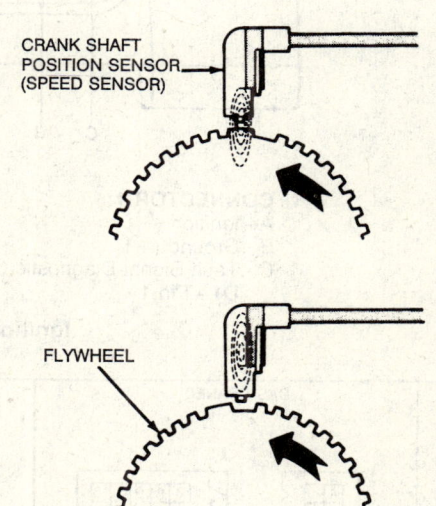

Crankshaft position sensor operation

°F	°C	Ohms
212	100	185
160	70	450
100	38	1,600
70	20	3,400
40	4	7,500
20	-7	13,500
0	-18	25,000
-40	-40	100,700

MAT/CTS temperature to resistance values

ENGINE PERFORMANCE AND TUNE-UP 2

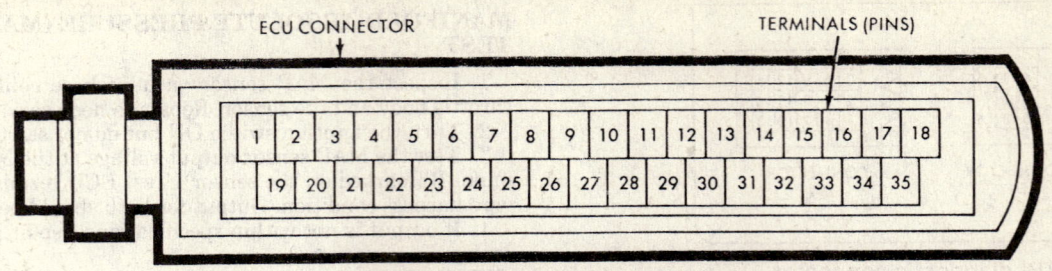

1989-90 4-2.5L TBI ECU connector

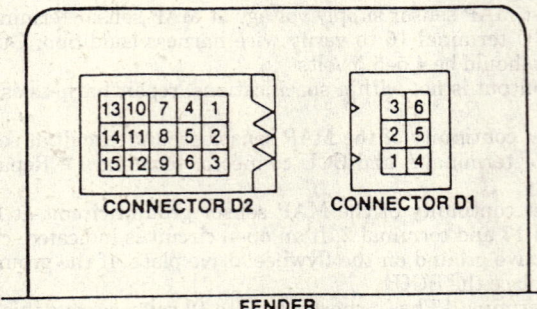

Connector D1
1. Tach (rpm) Voltage (Input)
2. Ignition
3. Ground
4. Starter Motor Relay
5. Battery
6. Fuel Pump

Connector D2
1. ECU Data Output
2. System Power Relay
3. Park/Neutral Switch
4. System Power (B+)
5. A/C Clutch
6. WOT Switch
7. Ground
8. Air/Fuel Temperature Sensor
9. Ignition Power Module
10. EGR Valve/Canister Purge Solenoid
11. ISA Motor Forward
12. Coolant Temperature Sensor
13. Closed Throttle Switch
14. ISA Motor Reverse
15. Automatic Transmission Diagnosis

1984-85 4-2.5L TBI diagnostic connector

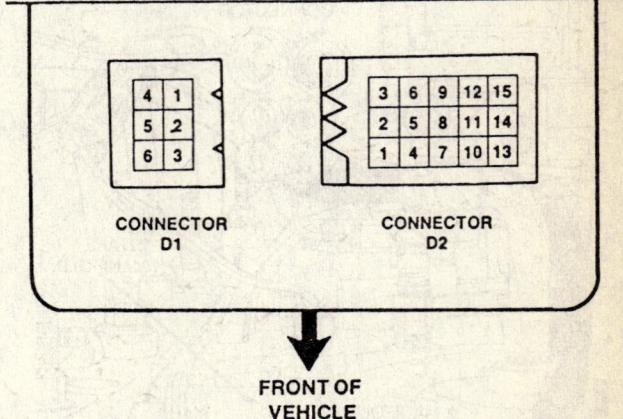

Connector D2
1. Shift Lamp
2. Power Latch Relay
3. Park/Neutral
4. Power Latch Relay (B+)
5. Air Conditioning Clutch Relay
6. WOT Switch
7. Ground
8. Air/Fuel Temperature
9. M.P.A. (Ignition Output)
10. EGR/Canister Purge Solenoid
11. ISA Motor Forward
12. Coolant Temperature Sensor
13. Closed Throttle Switch
14. ISA Motor Reverse
15. Not Used.

Connector D1
1. Tach Input
2. Ignition
3. Ground
4. Start Solenoid
5. Battery
6. Fuel Pump

1986-88 4-2.5L TBI diagnostic connector

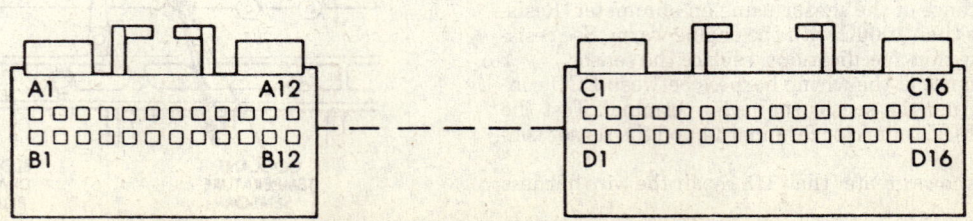

1989-90 6-4.0L MFI ECU connector

2-13

2 ENGINE PERFORMANCE AND TUNE-UP

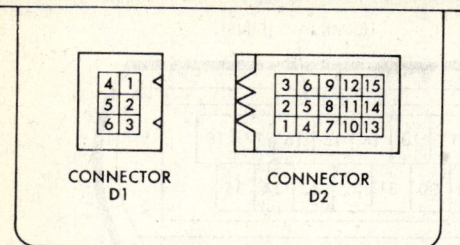

1989-90 4-2.5L TBI diagnostic connector

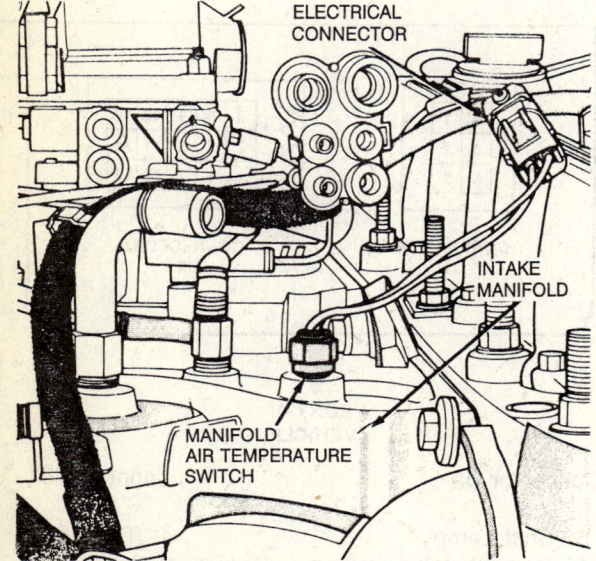

4-2.5L TBI Manifold air/fuel temperature switch

an engine speed (RPM) test (D1–1). D1–3 is used for vehicle ground. See illustration for connector locations.

COOLANT TEMPERATURE SENSOR (CTS) TEST

1. Disconnect the wire harness connector from the coolant temperature sensor located on the intake manifold.
2. Test the resistance of the sensor using an ohmmeter. Resistance should be less than 1000Ω with the engine warm. See resistance chart. If not within specifications, replace the sensor.
3. Test the resistance of the wiring harness between ECU connector terminal 15 and the sensor connector terminal. Test the resistance between ECU connector terminal 32 and the sensor connector terminal.
4. If the reading shows infinite, find and repair the open circuit (break) in the wire harness.
5. Reconnect the wire harness connector.

MANIFOLD AIR/FUEL TEMPERATURE (MAT) SENSOR TEST

1. Disconnect the wire harness connector.
2. Test the resistance of the sensor using an ohmmeter. Resistance should be less than 1000Ω with the engine warm. See resistance chart. If not within specifications, replace the sensor.
3. Test the resistance of the wiring harness between ECU connector terminal 32 and the sensor connector terminal. Test the resistance between ECU connector terminal 14 and the sensor connector terminal.
4. If the reading shows greater than 1Ω, repair the wire harness as necessary.
5. Reconnect the wire harness connector.

MANIFOLD ABSOLUTE PRESSURE (MAP) SENSOR TEST

1. Inspect the MAP sensor vacuum hose connections at the throttle body and the sensor. Repair as necessary.
2. Turn the ignition switch ON but do not start the engine.
3. Test the MAP sensor output voltage at the MAP sensor terminal B (marked on the sensor). Test ECU terminal 33 to verify wire harness condition. Output for both should be 4–5 volts.
4. If output is not within specifications, repair harness as necessary.

NOTE: The voltage should drop to 1.5–2.1 volts with a hot, idling engine.

5. Test MAP sensor supply voltage at MAP sensor terminal C. Test ECU terminal 16 to verify wire harness condition. Output for both should be 4.5–5.5 volts.
6. If output is not within specifications, repair harness as necessary.
7. Test continuity of the MAP sensor ground circuit at sensor connector terminal A and ECU connector terminal 17. Repair as necessary.
8. Test continuity of the MAP sensor ground circuit at ECU terminal 17 and terminal 2. If an open circuit is indicated, check for defective ground on the flywheel/drive plate. If the ground is good, replace the ECU.
9. If terminal 17 has a short circuit to 12 volts, correct this condition before replacing the ECU.

CRANKSHAFT POSITION SENSOR (CPS) TEST

1. Disconnect the speed sensor connector from the wire harness.
2. Test the resistance across terminals A and B (marked on connector). Resistance should be between 125–275Ω with a hot engine.
3. Replace the sensor if readings are not within specifications.

6–4.0L MFI 1987–90

COOLANT TEMPERATURE SENSOR (CTS) TEST

1. Disconnect the wire harness connector from the coolant temperature sensor located on the intake manifold.
2. Test the resistance of the sensor using an ohmmeter. Resistance should be less than 1000Ω with the engine warm. See resistance chart. If not within specifications, replace the sensor.
3. Test the resistance of the wiring harness between ECU con-

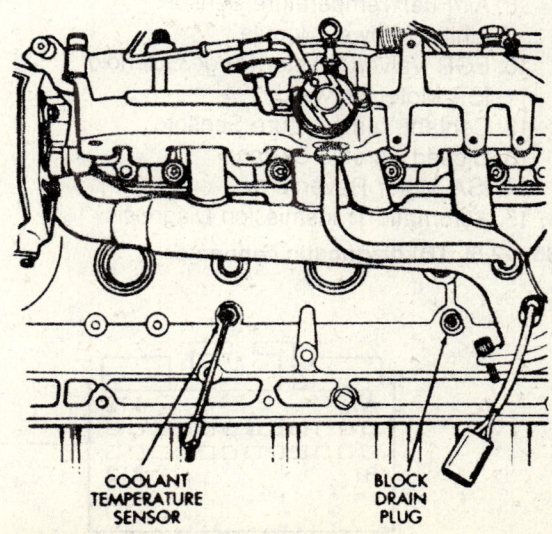

6-4.0L MFI coolant temperature sensor

ENGINE PERFORMANCE AND TUNE-UP 2

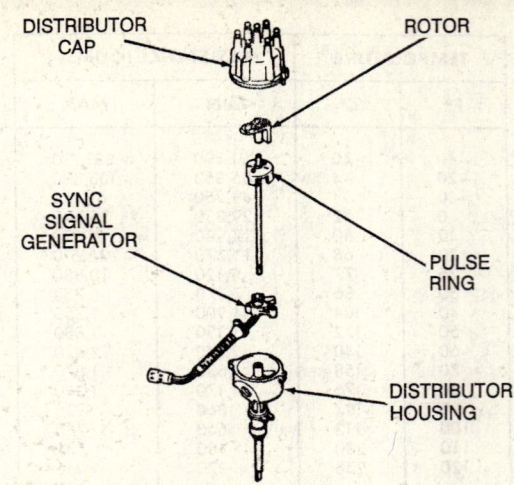

Sync signal generator and pulse ring

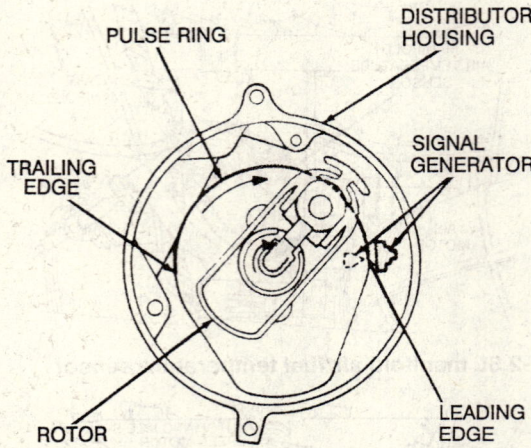

Sync signal generator operation

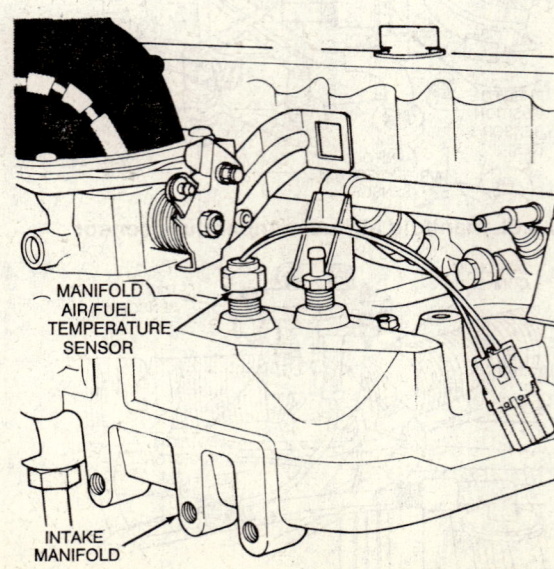

6-4.0L MFI manifold air/fuel temperature sensor

nector terminal D-3 and the sensor connector terminal. Test the resistance between ECU connector terminal C-10 and the sensor connector terminal.
  4. If the reading shows infinite, find and repair the open circuit (break) in the wire harness.
  5. Reconnect the wire harness connector.

MANIFOLD AIR/FUEL TEMPERATURE (MAT) SENSOR TEST

  1. Disconnect the wire harness connector.
  2. Test the resistance of the sensor using an ohmmeter. Resistance should be less than 1000Ω with the engine warm. See resistance chart. If not within specifications, replace the sensor.
  3. Test the resistance of the wiring harness between ECU connector terminal D-3 and the sensor connector terminal. Test the resistance between ECU connector terminal C-8 and the sensor connector terminal.
  4. If the reading shows greater than 1Ω, repair the wire harness as necessary.
  5. Reconnect the wire harness connector.

MANIFOLD ABSOLUTE PRESSURE (MAP) SENSOR TEST

  1. Inspect the MAP sensor vacuum hose connections at the throttle body and the sensor. Repair as necessary.
  2. Turn the ignition switch ON but do not start the engine.
  3. Test the MAP sensor output voltage at the MAP sensor terminal B (marked on the sensor). Test ECU terminal C-6 to verify wire harness condition. Output for both should be 4-5 volts.
  4. If output is not within specifications, repair harness as necessary.

NOTE: The voltage should drop to 0.5-1.5 volts with a hot, idling engine.

  5. Test MAP sensor supply voltage at MAP sensor terminal C. Test ECU terminal C-14 to verify wire harness condition. Output for both should be 4.5-5.5 volts.
  6. If output is not within specifications, repair harness as necessary.
  7. Test continuity of the MAP sensor ground circuit at sensor connector terminal A and ECU connector terminal D-3. Repair as necessary.
  8. Test continuity of the MAP sensor ground circuit at ECU terminal D-3 and terminal B-11. If an open circuit is indicated, check for defective ground on the flywheel/drive plate. If the ground is good, replace the ECU.
  9. If terminal D-3 has a short circuit to 12 volts, correct this condition before replacing the ECU.

CRANKSHAFT POSITION SENSOR (CPS) TEST

  1. Disconnect the CPS connector from the wire harness.
  2. Test the resistance across terminals A and B (marked on connector). Resistance should be between 125-275Ω with a hot engine.
  3. Replace the sensor if readings are not within specifications.

SYNC PULSE (STATOR) TEST

NOTE: For this test an analog voltmeter is needed.

  1. Insert the voltmeter (+) positive lead into the BLUE wire and the (-) lead into the GRAY (with tracer) wire at the distributor connector. Insert the leads into the backside of the distributor connector to make contact with the terminals.

NOTE: Do not remove the distributor connector from the distributor.

  2. Set the voltmeter on a 15 volt A/C scale and turn the ignition key ON.
  3. The voltmeter should show about 5.0 volts. If there is no voltage, perform the following sequence of tests in order:

2-15

2 ENGINE PERFORMANCE AND TUNE-UP

a. Check voltmeter leads for good contact.
b. If there is still no voltage, remove ECU and check for voltage at C-16 and ground with the harness connected.
c. If there is still no voltage, perform vehicle test using an appropriate diagnostic computer.

4. If voltage is present, check continuity between the BLUE wire at the distributor connector and ECU terminal C-16. If there is no continuity, repair the harness as necessary.
5. Check for continuity between the GRAY (with tracer) wire at the distributor connector and ECU terminal C-5. If there is no continuity, repair the harness as necessary.
6. Check for continuity between the BLACK wire at the distributor connector and ground. If there is no continuity, repair the harness as necessary.
7. Observe the voltmeter while cranking the engine. The needle should fluctuate back and forth to verify proper stator operation. If there is no fluctuation, replace the stator.

Single Board Engine Controller (SBEC) Ignition System

The multi-point, fuel injected engines for 1991 are operated by a Single Board Engine Controller.
The ignition system consists of:
- an ignition coil
- an ignition distributor containing a rotor and fuel sync sensor
- an engine controller
- a crankshaft position sensor

The amount of spark advance provided by the engine controller is based on five input factors. The factors are coolant temperature, manifold absolute pressure, engine speed, manifold air temperature and throttle position (see TPS in Section 5).
Base ignition timing is not adjustable. The controller opens and closes the ignition coil ground circuit to adjust ignition timing for changing engine operating conditions.

DIAGNOSIS

4-2.5L and 6-4.0L MFI

COOLANT TEMPERATURE SENSOR (CTS) TEST

1. Disconnect the wire harness connector from the coolant temperature sensor located on the intake manifold.
2. Test the resistance of the sensor using an ohmmeter. Resistance should be less than 1000Ω with the engine warm. See resistance chart. If not within specifications, replace the sensor.
3. Test the resistance of the wiring harness between ECU connector terminal 2 and the sensor connector terminal. Test the resistance between ECU connector terminal 4 and the sensor connector terminal.
4. If the reading shows infinite, find and repair the open circuit (break) in the wire harness.
5. Reconnect the wire harness connector.

MANIFOLD AIR/FUEL TEMPERATURE (MAT) SENSOR TEST

1. Disconnect the wire harness connector.
2. Test the resistance of the sensor using an ohmmeter. Resistance should be less than 1000Ω with the engine warm. See resistance chart. If not within specifications, replace the sensor.
3. Test the resistance of the wiring harness between ECU connector terminal 21 and the sensor connector terminal. Test the resistance between ECU connector terminal 4 and the sensor connector terminal.

TEMPERATURE		RESISTANCE (OHMS)	
F°	C°	MIN	MAX
-40	-40	291,490	381,710
-20	-4	85,850	108,390
-10	14	49,250	61,430
0	32	29,330	35,990
10	50	17,990	21,810
20	68	11,370	13,610
25	77	9,120	10,880
30	86	7,370	8,750
40	104	4,900	5,750
50	122	3,330	3,880
60	140	2,310	2,670
70	158	1,630	1,870
80	176	1,170	1,340
90	194	860	970
100	212	640	720
110	230	480	540
120	248	370	410

1991 MAT/CTS temperature to resistance chart

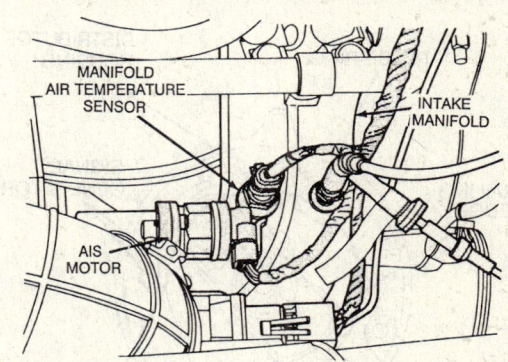

1991 4-2.5L manifold air/fuel temperature sensor

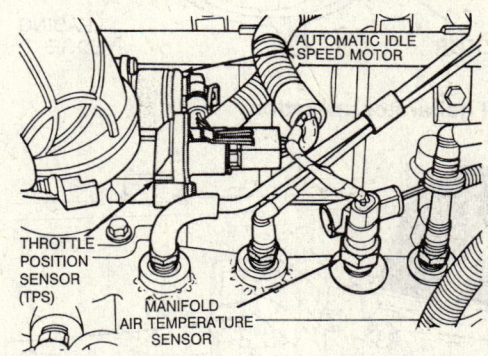

1991 6-4.0L manifold air/fuel temperature sensor

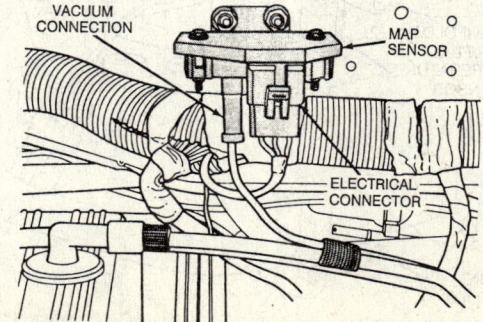

1991 manifold absolute pressure sensor

ENGINE PERFORMANCE AND TUNE-UP 2

CAV	WIRE COLOR	DESCRIPTION
1	DG/RD*	MAP SENSOR
2	TN/BK*	COOLANT SENSOR
3	RD	DIRECT BATTERY VOLTAGE
4	BK/LB*	SENSOR GROUND (ENGINE CONTROLLER)
5	BK/WT*	GROUND SENSOR FOR FUEL SENDER
6	VT/WT*	5-VOLT OUTPUT (TO MAP & TPS)
7	OR	8-VOLT OUTPUT (TO DISTRIBUTOR PICKUP)
8	BR	START SIGNAL
9	DB	IGNITION CIRCUIT SENSE
10	DB/OR*	P/S PRESSURE SENSOR
11	BK/TN*	POWER GROUND
12	BK/TN*	POWER GROUND
13	LB/BR*	INJECTOR NO. 4
14	YL/WT*	INJECTOR NO. 3
15	TN	INJECTOR NO. 2
16	WT/DB*	INJECTOR NO. 1
17		
18		
19	GY	IGNITION COIL
20	DG	ALTERNATOR FIELD CONTROL
21	BK/RD*	MANIFOLD AIR TEMPERATURE (MAT) SENSOR
22	OR/DB*	THROTTLE POSITION SENSOR
23		
24	GY/BK*	CRANKSHAFT POSITION SENSOR (CPS)
25	PK	DIAGNOSTIC CONNECTOR
26		
27	LB	A/C REQUEST
28	LG	A/C SELECT
29	WT/PK*	BRAKE SWITCH
30	BK/TN*	PARK/NEUTRAL SWITCH (AUTO TRANS. ONLY)
31		
32	BK/PK*	CHECK ENGINE LAMP
33	TN/RD*	SPEED CONTROL VACUUM SOLENOID
34	DB/OR*	A/C CLUTCH RELAY
35		
36	DG/YL*	ALTERNATOR LAMP

CAV	WIRE COLOR	DESCRIPTION
37	RD/DB*	BALLAST BYPASS RESISTOR
38		
39	GY/RD*	AIS MOTOR (TERMINAL D)
40	BR/WT*	AIS MOTOR (TERMINAL B)
41	BK/DG*	OXYGEN SENSOR
42		
43	GY/LB*	TACH SIGNAL OUTPUT (VEHICLE W/TACHOMETER)
44	TN/YL*	SYNC SENSOR
45	LG	DIAGNOSTIC CONNECTOR
46		
47	WT/OR*	VEHICLE DISTANCE (SPEED) SENSOR
48	BR/RD*	SPEED CONTROL COAST/SET
49	YL/RD*	SPEED CONTROL ON/OFF
50	WT/LG*	SPEED CONTROL RESUME/ACCEL
51	DB/YL*	FUEL PUMP RELAY/ASD RELAY
52		
53	LG/RD*	SPEED CONTROL VENT SOLENOID
54	OR/BK*	SHIFT INDICATOR LIGHT (MANUAL TRANS. ONLY)
55		
56	GY/PK*	EMISSION MAINTENANCE REMINDER
57	DG/OR*	ALTERNATOR OUTPUT
58		
59	VT/BK*	AIS MOTOR (TERMINAL A)
60	YL/BK*	AIS MOTOR (TERMINAL C)

WIRE COLOR CODES		
BK BLACK	LB LIGHT BLUE	VT VIOLET
BR BROWN	LG LIGHT GREEN	WT WHITE
DB DARK BLUE	OR ORANGE	YL YELLOW
DG DARK GREEN	PK PINK	* WITH TRACER
GY GRAY	RD RED	
	TN TAN	

1991 ECU connector

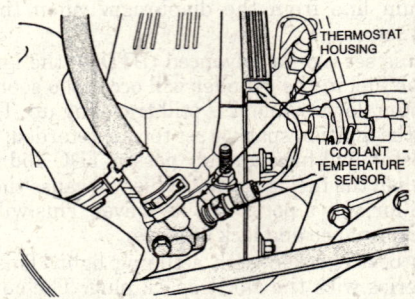

1991 coolant temperature sensor

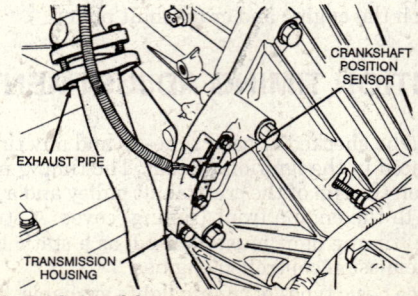

1991 crankshaft position sensor

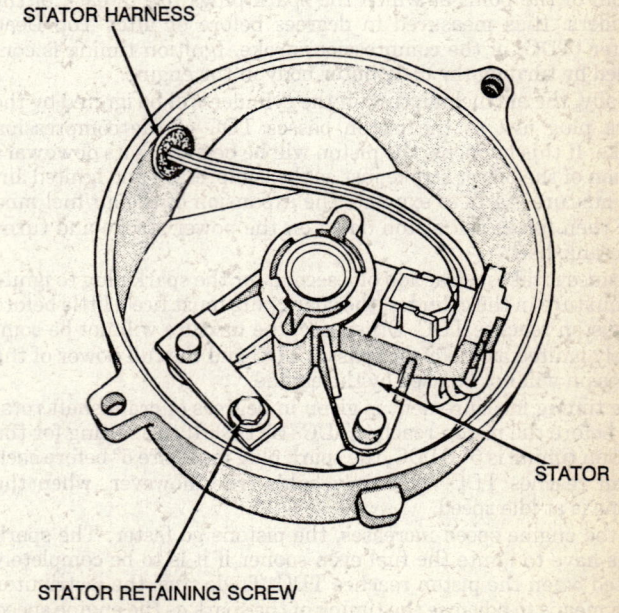

1991 sync signal generator

2-17

2 ENGINE PERFORMANCE AND TUNE-UP

4. If the reading shows greater than 1Ω, repair the wire harness as necessary.
5. Reconnect the wire harness connector.

MANIFOLD ABSOLUTE PRESSURE (MAP) SENSOR TEST

1. Inspect the MAP sensor vacuum hose connections at the throttle body and the sensor. Repair as necessary.
2. Turn the ignition switch ON but do not start the engine.
3. Test the MAP sensor output voltage at the MAP sensor terminal B (marked on the sensor). Test ECU terminal 5 to verify wire harness condition. Output for both should be 4–5 volts.
4. If output is not within specifications, repair harness as necessary.

NOTE: The voltage should drop to 1.5–2.1 volts with a hot, idling engine.

5. Test MAP sensor supply voltage at MAP sensor terminal C. Test ECU terminal 6 to verify wire harness condition. Output for both should be 4.5–5.5 volts.
6. If output is not within specifications, repair harness as necessary.
7. Test continuity of the MAP sensor ground circuit at sensor connector terminal A and ECU connector terminal 4. Repair as necessary.
8. Test continuity of the MAP sensor ground circuit at ECU terminal 4 and terminal 11. If an open circuit is indicated, check for defective ground on the flywheel/drive plate. If the ground is good, replace the ECU.
9. If terminal 4 has a short circuit to 12 volts, correct this condition before replacing the ECU.

CRANKSHAFT POSITION SENSOR (CPS) TEST

1. Disconnect the CPS connector from the wire harness.
2. Test the resistance across terminals A and B (marked on connector). Resistance should be between 125–275Ω with a hot engine.
3. Replace the sensor if readings are not within specifications.

SYNC PULSE (STATOR) TEST

NOTE: For this test an analog voltmeter is needed.

1. Insert the voltmeter (+) positive lead into the TAN (with yellow tracer) wire and the (–) lead into the BLACK (with blue tracer) wire at the distributor connector. Insert the leads into the backside of the distributor connector to make contact with the terminals. Set the voltmeter on a 15 volt A/C scale.

NOTE: Do not remove the distributor connector from the distributor.

2. Remove the distributor cap and rotate the engine until the pulse ring enters the sync signal generator. Turn the ignition key ON.
3. The voltmeter should show about 5.0 volts. If there is no voltage, check voltmeter leads for good contact.
4. If there is still no voltage, check for voltage at the supply (orange) wire.
5. If there is no voltage present at the supply (orange) wire, remove ECU and check for voltage at terminal 7 and ground with the harness connected.
6. If there is still no voltage, perform vehicle test using an appropriate diagnostic computer.
7. If voltage is present at the supply wire (orange), replace the sync sensor.
8. If voltage is present at terminal 7 but not at the supply wire (orange), check continuity between the supply wire at the distributor connector and ECU terminal 7. If there is no continuity, repair the harness as necessary.
9. Check for continuity between the ground circuit wire at the distributor connector and ground. If there is no continuity, repair the harness as necessary.
10. Observe the voltmeter while cranking the engine. The needle should fluctuate back and forth between 0 and 5 volts to verify proper stator operation. If there is no fluctuation, replace the stator.

IGNITION TIMING

Ignition timing is the measurement, in degrees of crankshaft rotation, of the point at which the spark plugs fire in each of the cylinders. It is measured in degrees before or after Top Dead Center (TDC) of the compression stroke. Ignition timing is controlled by turning the distributor body in the engine.

Ideally, the air/fuel mixture in the cylinder will be ignited by the spark plug just as the piston passes TDC of the compression stroke. If this happens, the piston will be beginning its downward motion of the power stroke just as the compressed and ignited air/fuel mixture starts to expand. The expansion of the air/fuel mixture then forces the piston down on the power stroke and turns the crankshaft.

Because it takes a fraction of a second for the spark plug to ignite the mixture in the cylinder, the spark plug must fire a little before the piston reaches TDC. Otherwise, the mixture will not be completely ignited as the piston passes TDC and the full power of the explosion will not be used by the engine.

The timing measurement is given in degrees of crankshaft rotation before the piston reaches TDC (BTDC). If the setting for the ignition timing is 5° BTDC, the spark plug must fire 5° before each piston reaches TDC. This only holds true, however, when the engine is at idle speed.

As the engine speed increases, the pistons go faster. The spark plugs have to ignite the fuel even sooner if it is to be completely ignited when the piston reaches TDC. To do this, the distributor has a means to advance the timing of the spark as the engine speed increases. This is accomplished by input from the electronic ignition control module and other computer sources. If the distributor is equipped with a vacuum advance unit, it is necessary to disconnect the vacuum line from the diaphragm when the ignition timing is being set.

If the ignition is set too far advanced (BTDC), the ignition and expansion of the fuel in the cylinder will occur too soon and tend to force the piston down while it is still traveling up. This causes engine ping. If the ignition spark is set too far retarded, after TDC (ATDC), the piston will have already passed TDC and started on its way down when the fuel is ignited. This will cause the piston to be forced down for only a portion of its travel. This will result in poor engine performance and lack of power.

The timing is best checked with a timing light. This device is connected in series with the No. 1 spark plug. The current that fires the spark plug also causes the timing light to flash.

When the engine is running, the timing light is aimed at the timing marks on the engine and crankshaft pulley.

IGNITION TIMING ADJUSTMENT

Timing should be checked at each tune-up and any time components are replaced in the ignition system. The timing marks consist of a notch on the rim of the crankshaft pulley and a graduated scale attached to the engine front (timing) cover. A stroboscopic flash (dynamic) timing light must be used, as a static light is too inaccurate for emission controlled engines.

There are three basic types of timing lights available. The first is a simple neon bulb with two wire connections. One wire connects

ENGINE PERFORMANCE AND TUNE-UP 2

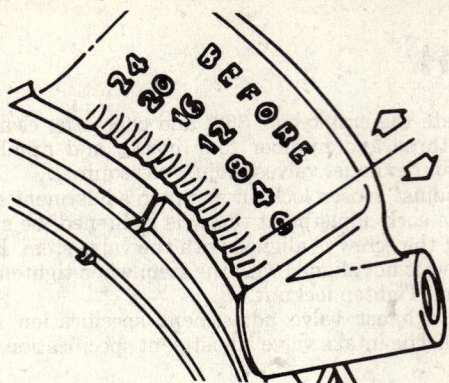

4-2.5L timing marks

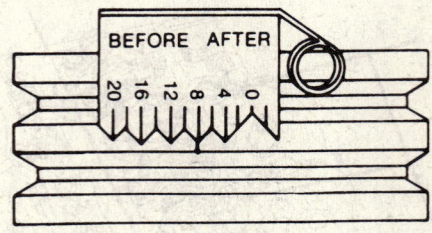

6-2.8L timing marks

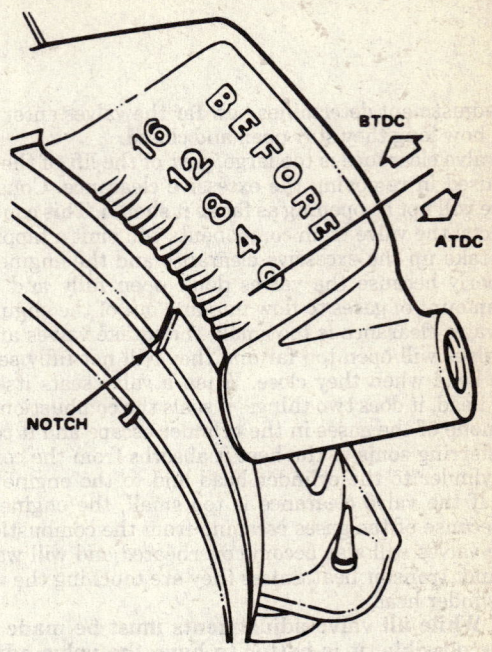

6-4.0L timing marks

to the spark plug terminal and the other plugs into the end of the spark plug wire for the No. 1 cylinder, thus connecting the light in series with the spark plug. This type of light is pretty dim and must be held very close to the timing marks to be seen. Sometimes a dark corner has to be sought out to see the flash at all. This type of light is very inexpensive. The second type operates from the car battery — two alligator clips connect to the battery terminals, while an adapter enables a third clip to be connected to the No. 1 spark plug and wire. This type provides a nice bright flash that you can see even in bright sunlight. It is the type most often seen in professional shops. The third type replaces the battery power source with 110 volt current.

4–2.5L Carbureted

---- CAUTION ----
Use extreme caution when the engine is running. Do not stand in a direct line with the fan. Do not put your hands near the pulleys, belts or fan. Do not wear loose clothing.

1. Warm up the engine to normal operating temperature. Stop the engine and connect the timing light to the No. 1 spark plug wire and a tachometer to the negative (distributor) side of the coil.
2. Clean off the timing marks and mark the pulley notch and timing scale with white chalk.
3. Disconnect the three-wire connector to the vacuum input switches and disconnect and plug the vacuum hose from the vacuum advance unit.
4. Start the engine and adjust the idle to 1600 rpm.
5. Aim the timing light at the pointer marks. Be careful not to touch the fan, because it may appear to be standing still. If the pulley notch isn't aligned with the proper timing mark (refer to the Tune-Up Specifications chart), the timing will have to be adjusted.

NOTE: TDC or Top Dead Center corresponds to 0, or Before Top Dead Center, may be shown as A for Advanced on a timing scale. R on a timing scale means Retarded, corresponding to ATDC, or After Top Dead Center.

6. Loosen the distributor clamp locknut. Local tool distributors have special wrenches that make this task a lot easier. Turn the distributor slowly to adjust the timing, holding it by the base and not the cap. Turn counterclockwise to advance timing (toward BTDC), and clockwise to retard (toward TDC or ATDC).
7. Tighten the locknut. Check the timing again, in case the distributor moved slightly as you tightened it.
8. Replace the distributor vacuum line and three wire connector. Correct the idle speed to that specified in the Tune-Up Specifications chart.
9. Stop the engine and disconnect the timing light and tachometer.

6–2.8L

1. Warm up the engine to normal operating temperature. Stop the engine and connect the timing light to the No. 1 spark plug wire and a tachometer to the **Tach** terminal on the distributor cap.

NOTE: Most tachometers require a special clip to attach the meter to the distributor. This clip may or may not be included with the tachometer.

2. Clean off the timing marks and mark the pulley notch and timing scale with white chalk.
3. Disconnect and plug the vacuum hose from the vacuum advance unit (if equipped).
4. Start the engine aim the timing light at the pointer marks. Be careful not to touch the fan, because it may appear to be standing still. If the pulley notch isn't aligned with the proper timing mark (refer to the Tune-Up Specifications chart), the timing will have to be adjusted.
5. Loosen the distributor clamp locknut. Turn the distributor slowly to adjust the timing, holding it by the base and not the cap. Turn counterclockwise to advance timing (toward BTDC), and clockwise to retard (toward TDC or ATDC).
7. Tighten the locknut. Check the timing again, in case the distributor moved slightly as you tightened it.
8. Replace the distributor vacuum line and correct the idle speed to that specified in the Tune-Up Specifications chart.
9. Stop the engine and disconnect the timing light.

2 ENGINE PERFORMANCE AND TUNE-UP

VALVE LASH

Valve adjustment determines how far the valves enter the cylinder and how long they stay open and closed.

If the valve clearance is too large, part of the lift of the camshaft will be used in removing the excessive clearance. Consequently, the valve will not be opening as far as it should. This condition has two effects: the valve train components will emit a tapping sound as they take up the excessive clearance and the engine will perform poorly because the valves don't open fully and allow the proper amount of gases to flow into and out of the engine.

If the valve clearance is too small, the intake valves and the exhaust valves will open too far and they will not fully seat on the cylinder head when they close. When a valve seats itself on the cylinder head, it does two things: it seals the combustion chamber so that none of the gases in the cylinder escape and it cools itself by transferring some of the heat it absorbs from the combustion in the cylinder to the cylinder head and to the engine's cooling system. If the valve clearance is too small, the engine will run poorly because of the gases escaping from the combustion chamber. The valves will also become overheated and will warp, since they cannot transfer heat unless they are touching the valve seat in the cylinder head.

NOTE: While all valve adjustments must be made as accurately as possible, it is better to have the valve adjustment slightly loose than slightly tight, as a burned valve may result from overly tight adjustments.

The 4–2.1L Diesel engines have adjustable valves. All other engines have hydraulic valve lifters which maintain a zero clearance.

ADJUSTMENT

4–2.1L Diesel Engine

1. Be sure that the engine is cold before adjusting the valves. Remove the valve cover.
2. Set the no.1 cylinder to TDC on the compression stroke and check the valve clearance of number one and number two intake and number one and number three exhaust valves. Adjust as required.

NOTE: The no.1 cylinder is located at the flywheel end of the engine.

3. Rotate the crankshaft 360° and check the clearance of the number three and number four intake and number two and number four exhaust valves. Adjust as required.
4. To adjust, loosen locknut and turn adjustment screw as necessary. As each adjustment screw is tightened, be sure that the bottom of the screw is aligned with the valve stem. If the adjustment screw is not aligned with the stem when tightened, the stem could bend. Tighten locknut.
5. The exhaust valve adjustment specification is 0.010 in. (0.25mm). The intake valve adjustment specification is 0.008 in.

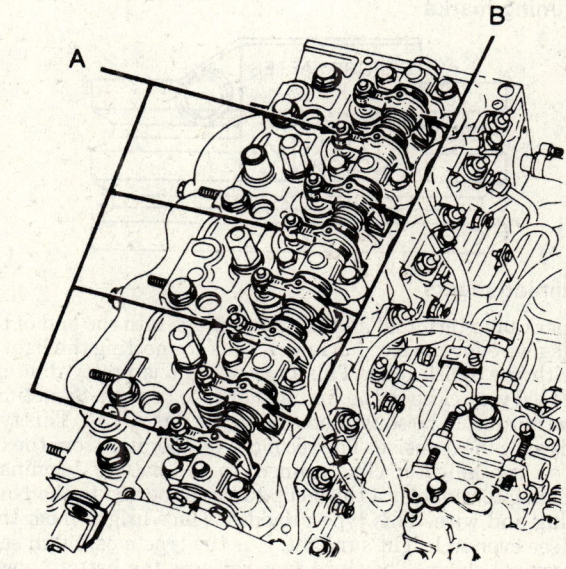

A. Intake valve rocker arms
B. Exhaust valve rocker arms

4-2.1L valve arrangement

FUEL SYSTEM

This section contains only tune-up adjustment procedures for fuel systems. Descriptions, adjustments, and overhaul procedures for fuel system components can be found in Section 5.

IDLE SPEED AND MIXTURE ADJUSTMENTS

1984

4-150

1. Fully warm up the engine.
2. Check the choke fast idle adjustment: Disconnect and plug the EGR valve vacuum hose. Position the fast idle adjustment screw on the second step of the fast idle cam with the transmission in neutral. Adjust the fast idle speed to 2,000 rpm for manual transmission and 2,300 rpm for automatic transmission. Allow the throttle to return to normal curb idle and reconnect the EGR vacuum hose.
3. To adjust the Sol-Vac Vacuum Actuator: Remove the

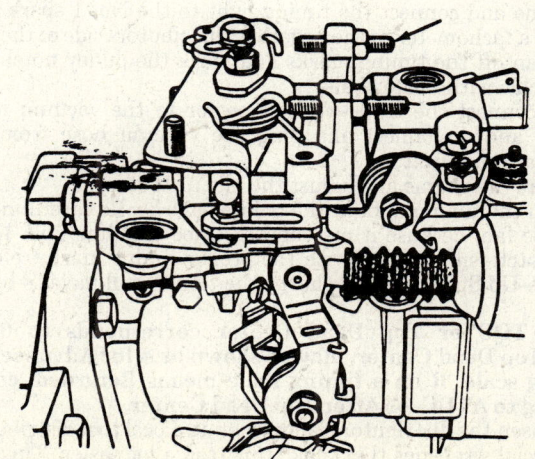

The arrow indicates the diesel idle speed adjusting screw

ENGINE PERFORMANCE AND TUNE-UP 2

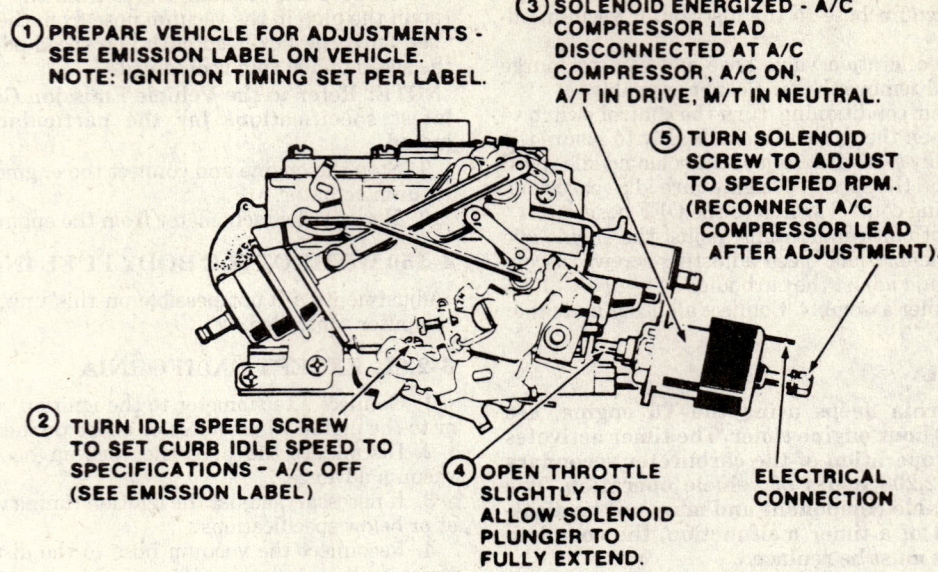

Idle speed adjustment — without A/C — E2SE

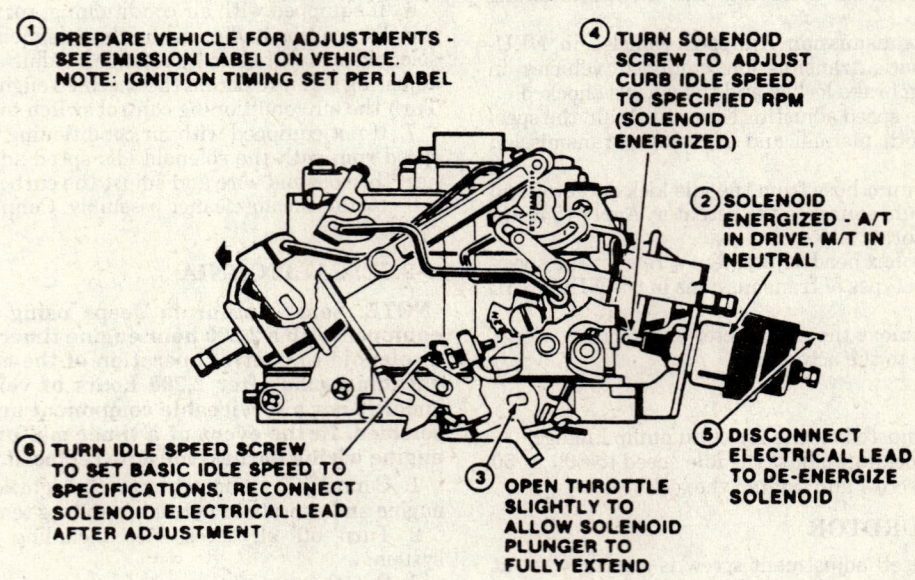

Idle speed adjustment — with A/C — E2SE

vacuum hose from the vacuum actuator and plug the hose. Connect an external vacuum source to the actuator and apply 10–15 in.Hg of vacuum to the actuator. Shift the transmission to Neutral. Adjust the idle speed to the following rpm using the vacuum actuator adjustment screw on the throttle lever: 850 rpm for automatic transmission 950 rpm for manual transmission. The adjustment is made with all accessories turned off.

NOTE: The curb idle should always be adjusted after vacuum actuator adjustment.

4. To adjust the curb idle: Remove the vacuum hose from the Sol-Vac vacuum actuator and plug the hose. Shift the transmission into Neutral. Adjust the curb idle using the 1/4 in. (6mm) hex-head adjustment screw on the end of the Sol-Vac unit. Set the speed to 750 rpm for manual transmission, 700 rpm for automatic

transmission. Reconnect the vacuum hose to the vacuum actuator.

NOTE: Engine speed will vary 10–30 rpm during this mode due to the closed loop fuel control.

5. To adjust the TRC (Anti-Diesel): The TRC screw is preset at the factory and should not require adjustment. However, to check adjustment, the screw should be 3/4 turn from closed throttle position.

6–2.8L, EXCEPT CALIFORNIA

1. Connect a tachometer to the ignition coil negative terminal or to the pigtail wire connector above the heater blower motor.
2. Disconnect the plug the vacuum hose at the distributor vacuum advance.
3. If necessary, adjust the ignition timing with the engine speed

2-21

2 ENGINE PERFORMANCE AND TUNE-UP

at or below specifications.

4. Reconnect the vacuum hose to the distributor vacuum advance unit.

5. Disconnect the deceleration valve hose and canister purge hose. Plug the hose and remove the air cleaner assembly.

6. If equipped with air conditioning, turn the control switch to the ON position and open the throttle momentarily to insure the solenoid armature is fully extended. Adjust the solenoid idle speed adjusting screw to obtain the specified engine curb idle speed rpm. Turn the air conditioning control switch to the OFF position.

7. If not equipped with air conditioning, adjust the engine idle speed rpm with the solenoid idle speed adjusting screw. Disconnect the solenoid wire and adjust the curb idle.

8. Install the air cleaner assembly. Connect all hoses and other connections.

6–2.8L, CALIFORNIA

NOTE: Some California Jeeps using the V6 engine, are equipped with a 2,200 hour engine timer. The timer activates a solenoid to control operation of the carburetor secondary vacuum brake after 2,200 hours of vehicle operation. The timer is not a serviceable component and must not be disassembled. In the event of a timer malfunction, the complete engine wiring harness must be replaced.

1. Connect a tachometer to the ignition system. Start the engine and operate to normal operating temperature.

2. Turn off all accessories including the air conditioning system.

3. Put the manual transmission equipped vehicles in NEUTRAL and the automatic transmission equipped vehicles in DRIVE with the parking brake locked and the wheels chocked.

4. Adjust the curb idle speed adjusting screw to obtain the specified rpm of 700 for both manual and automatic transmission equipped vehicles.

5. Disconnect the vacuum hose from the idle kick actuator and connect an outside vacuum source to the actuator. Apply 15 in.Hg of vacuum to the actuator.

6. Adjust the actuator hex head adjustment screw for the specified 1,200 rpm with both types of transmissions in the NEUTRAL position.

7. Stop the engine, remove the tachometer and vacuum pump. Install the vacuum hose to the actuator.

1985–87 DIESEL

1. The idle speed is adjusted on the injection pump linkage.

2. Loosen the screw locknut, adjust the idle speed to 800 ± 50 rpm with the adjusting screw and tighten the locknut.

4–150 W/YFA CARBURETOR

1. The TRC (anti-Diesel) adjustment screw is statically set at $3/4$ turn from the throttle valve closed position during factory assembly and does not normally require readjustment. Should this adjustment be required, turn the adjustment screw counterclockwise to the throttle plate closed position and then turn the screw clockwise $3/4$ turn.

2. Connect a tachometer to the ignition coil TACH wire connector.

3. Place the transmission in NEUTRAL and lock the parking brake.

4. Start the engine and allow it to reach normal operating temperature.

5. Connect an external vacuum source to the Sol-Vac vacuum actuator and apply 10–15 in.Hg of vacuum. Plug the engine vacuum hose.

6. Adjust the vacuum actuator until an engine speed of approximately 1,000 rpm is achieved.

NOTE: Refer to the Vehicle Emission Control Information Label for the latest specifications for the particular engine being adjusted.

7. Remove the vacuum source from the vacuum actuator and retain the plug in the vacuum hose from the engine.

8. Turn the hex-head curb idle speed adjustment screw until the speed of 500 rpm is obtained.

NOTE: Refer to the Vehicle Emission Control Label for the latest specifications for the particular engine being adjusted.

9. Stop the engine and connect the engine vacuum hose to the vacuum actuator.

10. Remove the tachometer from the engine.

4–150 W/THROTTLE BODY FUEL INJECTION

Adjustments are not possible on this unit, as all functions are computer controlled.

6–2.8L, EXCEPT CALIFORNIA

1. Connect a tachometer to the ignition coil negative terminal or to the pigtail wire connector above the heater blower motor.

2. Disconnect the plug the vacuum hose at the distributor vacuum advance.

3. If necessary, adjust the ignition timing with the engine speed at or below specifications.

4. Reconnect the vacuum hose to the distributor vacuum advance unit.

5. Disconnect the deceleration valve hose and canister purge hose. Plug the hose and remove the air cleaner assembly.

6. If equipped with air conditioning, turn the control switch to the ON position and open the throttle momentarily to insure the solenoid armature is fully extended. Adjust the solenoid idle speed adjusting screw to obtain the specified engine curb idle speed rpm. Turn the air conditioning control switch to the OFF position.

7. If not equipped with air conditioning, adjust the engine idle speed rpm with the solenoid idle speed adjusting screw. Disconnect the solenoid wire and adjust the curb idle.

8. Install the air cleaner assembly. Connect all hoses and other connections.

6–2.8L, CALIFORNIA

NOTE: Some California Jeeps using the V6 engine, are equipped with a 2,200 hour engine timer. The timer activates a solenoid to control operation of the carburetor secondary vacuum brake after 2,200 hours of vehicle operation. The timer is not a serviceable component and must not be disassembled. In the event of a timer malfunction, the complete engine wiring harness must be replaced.

1. Connect a tachometer to the ignition system. Start the engine and operate to normal operating temperature.

2. Turn off all accessories including the air conditioning system.

3. Put the manual transmission equipped vehicles in NEUTRAL and the automatic transmission equipped vehicles in DRIVE with the parking brake locked and the wheels chocked.

4. Adjust the curb idle speed adjusting screw to obtain the specified rpm of 700 for both manual and automatic transmission equipped vehicles.

5. Disconnect the vacuum hose from the idle kick actuator and connect an outside vacuum source to the actuator. Apply 15 in.Hg of vacuum to the actuator.

6. Adjust the actuator hex head adjustment screw for the specified 1,200 rpm with both types of transmissions in the NEUTRAL position.

7. Stop the engine, remove the tachometer and vacuum pump. Install the vacuum hose to the actuator.

1988–91

The 4–150 TBI, the 4–150 MFI and 6–4.0L MFI are all fuel injected. Routine adjustments are computer controlled. No routine idle speed adjustments are possible.

Engine and Engine Overhaul

QUICK REFERENCE INDEX

Alternator and Regulator Specifications Chart	3-14	Exhaust System	3-92
Camshaft Specifications Chart	3-26	General Engine Specifications Chart	3-28
Crankshaft and Connecting Rod Specifications Chart	3-29	Piston Specifications Chart	3-29
Engine Electrical Systems	3-2	Piston Ring Specifications Chart	3-29
Engine Mechanical Systems	3-25	Starter Specifications Chart	3-21
Engine Torque Specifications Chart	3-28	Valve Specifications Chart	3-28

GENERAL INDEX

Air conditioning
  Compressor 3-49
  Condenser 3-54
Alternator
  Alternator precautions 3-5
  Operation 3-5
  Overhaul 3-6
  Removal and installation 3-6
  Specifications 3-14
  Testing 3-10
  Troubleshooting 3-6
Battery 3-13
Camshaft
  Bearings 3-80
  Inspection 3-80
  Removal and Installation 3-78
  Specifications 3-26
Catalytic converter 3-93
Charging system 3-5
Coil (ignition) 3-3
Compression testing 3-25
Compressor 3-49
Condenser 3-54
Connecting rods and bearings
  Service 3-81
  Specifications 3-29
Crankshaft
  Service 3-89
  Specifications 3-29
Cylinder head
  Cleaning and inspection 3-60
  Removal and installation 3-56
  Resurfacing 3-60
Cylinder liners 3-85
Distributor 3-3
Engine
  Block heater 3-80
  Camshaft 3-78
  Camshaft bearings 3-80
  Compression testing 3-25
  Connecting rods and bearings 3-81
  Crankshaft 3-89
  Crankshaft damper 3-67
  Cylinder head 3-56
  Cylinder liners 3-85
  Cylinders 3-81
  Description 3-24
  Exhaust manifold 3-48
  Fan 3-52
  Flywheel 3-92
  Freeze plugs 3-80

Front (timing) cover 3-71
Front seal 3-71
Intake manifold 3-44
Lifters 3-66
Main bearings 3-89
Oil pan 3-67
Oil pump 3-69
Overhaul techniques 3-24
Piston pin 3-81
Pistons 3-81
Rear main seal 3-86
Removal and installation 3-26
Ring gear 3-92
Rings 3-82
Rocker arms 3-42
Side cover 3-41
Specifications 3-28
Thermostat 3-44
Timing belt 3-74
Timing chain 3-75
Timing covers 3-71
Timing gears 3-75
Troubleshooting 3-30
Turbocharger 3-49
Valve (rocker) cover 3-41
Valve guides 3-64
Valves 3-61
Valve seats 3-61
Valve springs 3-63
Valve stem seal 3-65
Water pump 3-54
Exhaust manifold 3-48
Exhaust pipe 3-92
Exhaust system 3-92
Fan 3-52
Flywheel and ring gear 3-92
Freeze plugs 3-80
Ignition Coil 3-3
Ignition Module 3-3
Intake manifold 3-44
Liners 3-85
Main bearings 3-89
Manifolds
  Intake 3-44
  Exhaust 3-48
Module (ignition) 3-3
Muffler 3-93
Oil pan 3-67
Oil pump 3-69
Piston pin 3-81

Pistons 3-81
Radiator 3-50
Rear main oil seal 3-86
Regulator 3-13
Ring gear 3-92
Rings 3-82
Rocker arms 3-42
Specifications Charts
  Alternator and regulator 3-14
  Camshaft 3-26
  Crankshaft and connecting rod 3-29
  Fastener markings and torque
    standards 3-27
  General engine 3-28
  Piston and ring 3-29
  Starter 3-21
  Torque 3-28
  Valves 3-28
Starter
  Installation 3-20
  Overhaul
    Bosch 3-18
    Delco 3-16
    Mitsubishi 3-19
    Motorcraft 3-15
  Removal 3-15
  Relay 3-23
  Solenoid 3-20
  Specifications 3-21
  Troubleshooting 3-13, 22
  Stripped threads 3-25
Tailpipe 3-93
Thermostat 3-44
Timing belt 3-74
Timing chain 3-75
Timing gears 3-75
Torque specifications 3-28
Troubleshooting
  Battery and starting systems 3-22
  Charging system 3-13
  Cooling system 3-33
  Engine mechanical 3-30
Turbocharger 3-49
Valve guides 3-64
Valve lifters 3-66
Valve seats 3-61
Valve service 3-61
Valve specifications 3-28
Valve springs 3-63
Valve stem seals 3-65

3-1

3 ENGINE AND ENGINE OVERHAUL

ENGINE ELECTRICAL

Understanding the Engine Electrical System

The engine electrical system can be broken down into three separate and distinct systems:
1. The starting system.
2. The charging system.
3. The ignition system.

BATTERY AND STARTING SYSTEM

Basic Operating Principles

The battery is the first link in the chain of mechanisms which work together to provide cranking of the automobile engine. In most modern cars, the battery is a lead/acid electrochemical device consisting of six 2v subsections connected in series so the unit is capable of producing approximately 12v of electrical pressure. Each subsection, or cell, consists of a series of positive and negative plates held a short distance apart in a solution of sulfuric acid and water. The two types of plates are of dissimilar metals. This causes a chemical reaction to be set up, and it is this reaction which produces current flow from the battery when its positive and negative terminals are connected to an electrical appliance such as a lamp or motor. The continued transfer of electrons would eventually convert the sulfuric acid in the electrolyte to water, and make the two plates identical in chemical composition. As electrical energy is removed from the battery, its voltage output tends to drop. Thus, measuring battery voltage and battery electrolyte composition are two ways of checking the ability of the unit to supply power. During the starting of the engine, electrical energy is removed from the battery. However, if the charging circuit is in good condition and the operating conditions are normal, the power removed from the battery will be replaced by the generator (or alternator) which will force electrons back through the battery, reversing the normal flow, and restoring the battery to its original chemical state.

The battery and starting motor are linked by very heavy electrical cables designed to minimize resistance to the flow of current. Generally, the major power supply cable that leaves the battery goes directly to the starter, while other electrical system needs are supplied by a smaller cable. During starter operation, power flows from the battery to the starter and is grounded through the car's frame and the battery's negative ground strap.

The starting motor is a specially designed, direct current electric motor capable of producing a very great amount of power for its size. One thing that allows the motor to produce a great deal of power is its tremendous rotating speed. It drives the engine through a tiny pinion gear (attached to the starter's armature), which drives the very large flywheel ring gear at a greatly reduced speed. Another factor allowing it to produce so much power is that only intermittent operation is required of it. This, little allowance for air circulation is required, and the windings can be built into a very small space.

The starter solenoid is a magnetic device which employs the small current supplied by the starting switch circuit of the ignition switch. This magnetic action moves a plunger which mechanically engages the starter and electrically closes the heavy switch which connects it to the battery. The starting switch circuit consists of the starting switch contained within the ignition switch, a transmission neutral safety switch or clutch pedal switch, and the wiring necessary to connect these in series with the starter solenoid or relay.

A pinion, which is a small gear, is mounted to a one-way drive clutch. This clutch is splined to the starter armature shaft. When the ignition switch is moved to the **start** position, the solenoid plunger slides the pinion toward the flywheel ring gear via a collar and spring. If the teeth on the pinion and flywheel match properly, the pinion will engage the flywheel immediately. If the gear teeth butt one another, the spring will be compressed and will force the gears to mesh as soon as the starter turns far enough to allow them to do so. As the solenoid plunger reaches the end of its travel, it closes the contacts that connect the battery and starter and then the engine is cranked.

As soon as the engine starts, the flywheel ring gear begins turning fast enough to drive the pinion at an extremely high rate of speed. At this point, the one-way clutch begins allowing the pinion to spin faster than the starter shaft so that the starter will not operate at excessive speed. When the ignition switch is released from the starter position, the solenoid is de-energized, and a spring contained within the solenoid assembly pulls the gear out of mesh and interrupts the current flow to the starter.

Some starter employ a separate relay, mounted away from the starter, to switch the motor and solenoid current on and off. The relay thus replaces the solenoid electrical switch, buy does not eliminate the need for a solenoid mounted on the starter used to mechanically engage the starter drive gears. The relay is used to reduce the amount of current the starting switch must carry.

THE CHARGING SYSTEM

Basic Operating Principles

The automobile charging system provides electrical power for operation of the vehicle's ignition and starting systems and all the electrical accessories. The battery services as an electrical surge or storage tank, storing (in chemical form) the energy originally produced by the engine driven generator. The system also provides a means of regulating generator output to protect the battery from being overcharged and to avoid excessive voltage to the accessories.

The storage battery is a chemical device incorporating parallel lead plates in a tank containing a sulfuric acid/water solution. Adjacent plates are slightly dissimilar, and the chemical reaction of the two dissimilar plates produces electrical energy when the battery is connected to a load such as the starter motor. The chemical reaction is reversible, so that when the generator is producing a voltage (electrical pressure) greater than that produced by the battery, electricity is forced into the battery, and the battery is returned to its fully charged state.

The vehicle's generator is driven mechanically, through V-belts, by the engine crankshaft. It consists of two coils of fine wire, one stationary (the stator), and one movable (the rotor). The rotor may also be known as the armature, and consists of fine wire wrapped around an iron core which is mounted on a shaft. The electricity which flows through the two coils of wire (provided initially by the battery in some cases) creates an intense magnetic field around both rotor and stator, and the interaction between the two fields creates voltage, allowing the generator to power the accessories and charge the battery.

There are two types of generators: the earlier is the direct current (DC) type. The current produced by the DC generator is generated in the armature and carried off the spinning armature by stationary brushes contacting the commutator. The commutator is a series of smooth metal contact plates on the end of the armature. The commutator is a series of smooth metal contact plates on the end of the armature. The commutator plates, which are separated from one another by a very short gap, are connected to the armature circuits so that current will flow in one directions

ENGINE AND ENGINE OVERHAUL 3

only in the wires carrying the generator output. The generator stator consists of two stationary coils of wire which draw some of the output current of the generator to form a powerful magnetic field and create the interaction of fields which generates the voltage. The generator field is wired in series with the regulator.

Newer automobiles use alternating current generators or alternators, because they are more efficient, can be rotated at higher speeds, and have fewer brush problems. In an alternator, the field rotates while all the current produced passes only through the stator winding. The brushes bear against continuous slip rings rather than a commutator. This causes the current produced to periodically reverse the direction of its flow. Diodes (electrical one-way switches) block the flow of current from traveling in the wrong direction. A series of diodes is wired together to permit the alternating flow of the stator to be converted to a pulsating, but unidirectional flow at the alternator output. The alternator's field is wired in series with the voltage regulator.

The regulator consists of several circuits. Each circuit has a core, or magnetic coil of wire, which operates a switch. Each switch is connected to ground through one or more resistors. The coil of wire responds directly to system voltage. When the voltage reaches the required level, the magnetic field created by the winding of wire closes the switch and inserts a resistance into the generator field circuit, thus reducing the output. The contacts of the switch cycle open and close many times each second to precisely control voltage.

While alternators are self-limiting as far as maximum current is concerned, DC generators employ a current regulating circuit which responds directly to the total amount of current flowing through the generator circuit rather than to the output voltage. The current regulator is similar to the voltage regulator except that all system current must flow through the energizing coil on its way to the various accessories.

Ignition Coil

REMOVAL AND INSTALLATION

1. Disconnect the battery ground.
2. Disconnect the 3 wires from the coil.
3. Disconnect the condenser connector from the coil, if equipped.
4. Unbolt and remove the coil.
5. Installation is the reverse of removal.

Ignition Control Module

REMOVAL AND INSTALLATION

4-2.5L

The module is located on the right shock tower sheet metal. To replace it, simply unplug the wiring and remove the mounting screws.

6-2.8L

1. Remove the distributor cap and rotor.
2. Remove the 2 control module screws and lift up on the module.
3. Disconnect the pick-up coil wire connector from the module. Note the color coding of the wires. Disconnect the wiring harness connector.

NOTE: If you're going to reuse the module, don't wipe the grease from the module base. If a new module is being installed, a package of silicone dielectric compound should come with the new module. Spread the compound on the metal face of the module and on the distributor base where

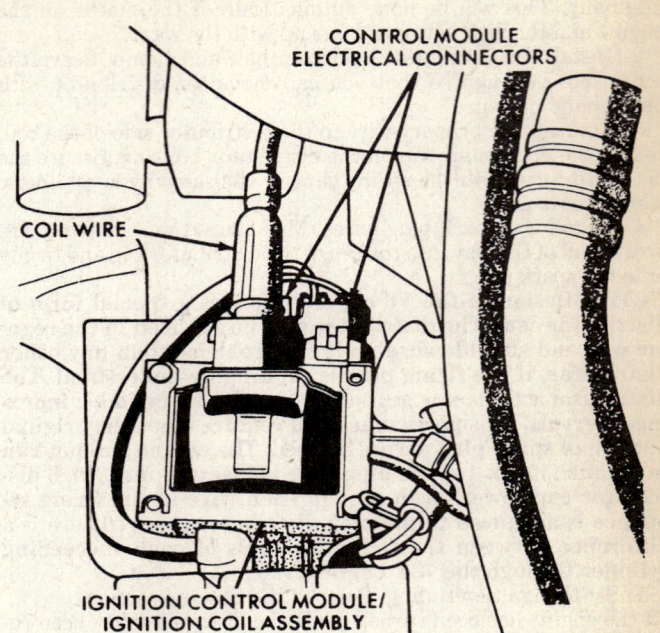

6-4.0L ignition control module

the module seats. The compound is necessary for module cooling.

4. Installation is the reverse of removal.

6-4.0L

The ignition control module is mounted on the ignition coil. To replace it, simply disconnect the wiring connectors and remove the fasteners.

Distributor

REMOVAL

All ENGINES

1. Remove the high-tension wires from the distributor cap terminal towers, noting their positions to assure correct reassembly. For diagrams of firing orders and distributor wiring, refer to the tune-up and troubleshooting section.
2. Remove the primary lead from the terminal post at the side of the distributor.
3. Disconnect the vacuum line if equipped.
4. Remove the distributor cap retaining hooks or screws and remove the distributor cap.
5. Note the position of the rotor in relation to the base. Scribe a mark on the base of the distributor and on the engine to facilitate reinstallation. Align the marks with the direction the metal tip of the rotor is pointing.
6. Remove the bolt that holds the distributor to the engine.
7. Lift the distributor assembly from the engine.

INSTALLATION

6-2.8L

1. Insert the distributor shaft and assembly into the engine. Line up the mark on the distributor and the one on the engine with the metal tip of the rotor. Make sure that the vacuum advance diaphragm is pointed in the same direction as it was pointed

3 ENGINE AND ENGINE OVERHAUL

originally. This will be done automatically if the marks on the engine and the distributor are line up with the rotor.

2. Install the distributor holddown bolt and clamp. Leave the screw loose enough so that you can move the distributor with heavy hand pressure.

3. Connect the primary wire to the distributor side of the coil. Install the distributor cap on the distributor housing. Secure the distributor cap with the spring clips or the screw type retainers, whichever is used.

4. Install the spark plug wires. Make sure that the wires are pressed all of the way into the top of the distributor cap and firmly onto the spark plugs.

NOTE: Design of the V6 engine requires a special form of distributor cam. The distributor may be serviced in the regular way and should cause no more problems than any other distributor, if the firing plan is thoroughly understood. The distributor cam is not ground to standard 6-cylinder indexing intervals. This particular form requires that the original pattern of spark plug wiring be used. The engine will not run in balance if No. 1 spark plug wire is inserted into No. 6 distributor cap tower, even though each wire in the firing sequence is advanced to the next distributor tower. There is a difference between the firing intervals of each succeeding cylinder through the 720° engine cycle.

5. Set the ignition timing. Refer to the tune-up section.

If the engine has been turned while the distributor has been removed, or if the marks were not drawn, it will be necessary to initially time the engine. Follow the procedure below.

INSTALLATION, ENGINE ROTATED

6-2.8L

1. If the engine has been rotated while the distributor was out, you'll have to first put the engine at Top Dead Center firing position on No. 1 cylinder. You can either remove the valve cover or No. 1 spark plug to determine engine position. Rotate the engine with a socket wrench on the nut at the center of the front pulley in the normal direction of rotation. Either feel for air being expelled forcefully through the spark plug hole or watch for the engine to rotate up to the Top Center mark without the valves moving (both valves will be closed). If the valves are moving as you approach TDC or there is no air being expelled through the plug hole, turn the engine another full turn until you get the appropriate indication as the engine approaches TDC position.

2. Start the distributor into the engine with the matchmarks between the distributor body and the engine lined up. Turn the rotor slightly until the matchmarks on the bottom of the distributor body and the bottom of the distributor shaft near the gear are aligned. Then, insert the distributor all the way into the engine. If you have trouble getting the distributor and camshaft gears to mesh, turn the rotor back and forth very slightly until the distributor can be inserted easily. If the rotor is not now lined up with the position of No. 1 plug terminal, you'll have to pull the distributor back out slightly, shift the position of the rotor appropriately, and then reinstall it.

3. Align the matchmarks between the distributor and engine. Install the distributor mounting bolt and tighten it finger tight. Reconnect the vacuum advance line and distributor wiring connector, and reinstall the cap. Reconnect the negative battery cable. Adjust the ignition timing as described in Section 2. Then, tighten the distributor mounting bolt securely.

INSTALLATION

4-2.5L and 6-4.0L

1. Clean the mounting area of the cylinder block and install a new distributor mounting gasket.

NOTE: On some models there is a fork on the distributor housing. The slot in the fork aligns with the distributor holddown bolt hole in the engine block. The distributor is correctly installed when the rotor is correctly positioned and the slot is aligned with the holddown bolt hole. On these computer controlled distributors, initial ignition timing is not adjustable.

2. Align the rotor tip with the scribe mark on the distributor housing during removal, then turn the rotor approximately 1/8 turn counterclockwise past the scribe mark.

3. Slide the distributor shaft down into the engine. It may be necessary to move the rotor and shaft slightly to engage the distributor shaft with the oil pump slot. Align the scribe mark on the distributor housing with the mark on the cylinder block.

NOTE: Ensure that the distributor is fully seated against the cylinder block. It may be necessary to slightly rotate (bump) the engine while applying light downward force to fully engage the distributor shaft with the oil pump drive gear shaft.

4. Install the distributor shaft holddown and bolt. Torque the bolt to 17 ft.lbs.

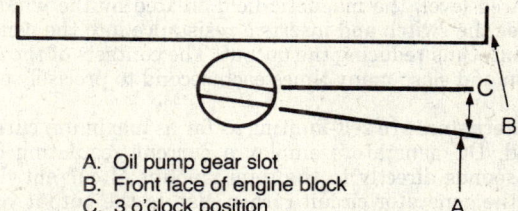

A. Oil pump gear slot
B. Front face of engine block
C. 3 o'clock position

Positioning the oil pump shaft for distributor installation on the 4-2.5L

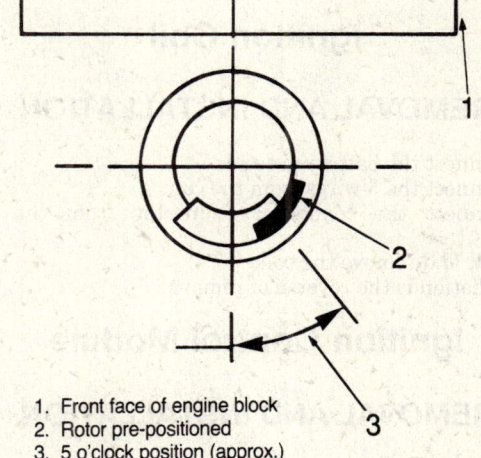

1. Front face of engine block
2. Rotor pre-positioned
3. 5 o'clock position (approx.)

Positioning the distributor rotor and shaft for installation on the 4-2.5L

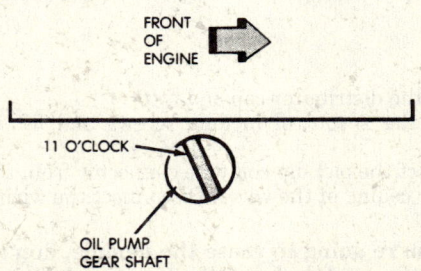

Positioning the oil pump shaft for distributor installation on the 6-4.0L

ENGINE AND ENGINE OVERHAUL 3

5. Install distributor cap and ignition wires. Insure that the wires are routed correctly before attempting to start engine.

INSTALLATION, ENGINE ROTATED

1. Rotate the engine until the No.1 piston is at TDC compression.
2. Using a flat bladed screwdriver, in the distributor hole, rotate the oil pump gear so that the slot in the oil pump shaft is in the correct position (see illustration).
3. With the distributor cap removed, install the distributor so

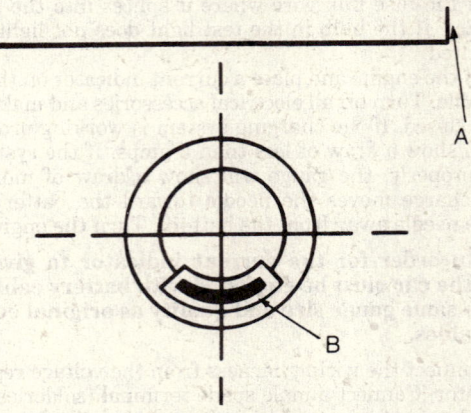

A. Front face of engine block
B. Rotor position when properly installed

Rotor position with the distributor properly installed on the 4-2.5L

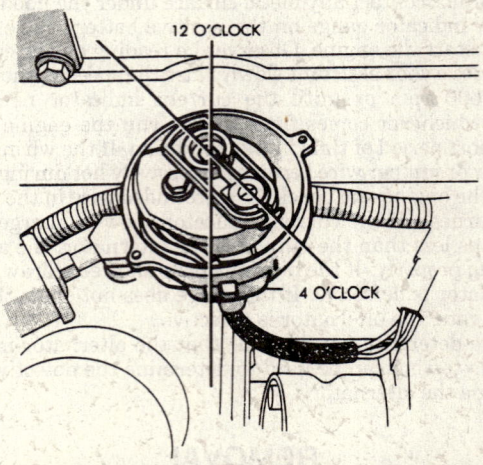

Rotor position with the distributor properly installed on the 6-4.0L

that the rotor is positioned correctly (see illustration). Insure that the distributor is fully seated against the cylinder block. If not, remove the distributor and perform the entire procedure again.
4. Tighten the holddown bolt.
5. Install distributor cap and ignition wires. Insure that the wires are routed correctly before attempting to start engine.

Alternator

The alternator charging system is a negative (−) ground system which consists of an alternator, a regulator, a charge indicator, a

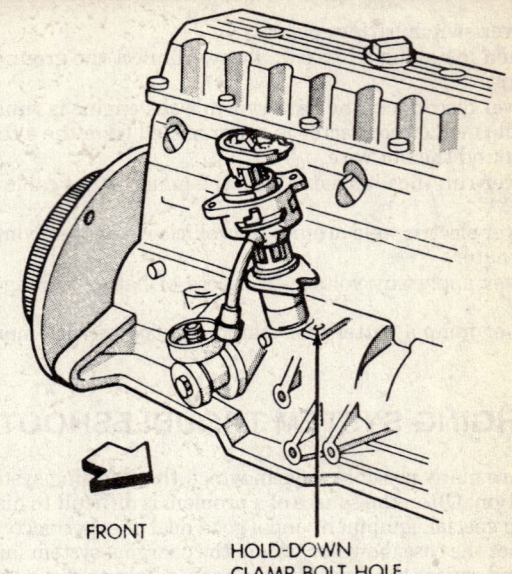

Correct positioning for distributor with non-adjustable timing

storage battery, wiring connecting the components, and fuse link wire.

The alternator is belt-driven from the engine. Energy is supplied from the alternator/regulator system to the rotating field through two brushes to two slip-rings. The slip-rings are mounted on the rotor shaft and are connected to the field coil. This energy supplied to the rotating field from the battery is called excitation current and is used to initially energize the field to begin the generation of electricity. Once the alternator starts to generate electricity, the excitation current comes from its own output rather than the battery.

The alternator produces power in the form of alternating current. The alternating current is rectified by 6 diodes into direct current. The direct current is used to charge the battery and power the rest of the electrical system.

When the ignition key is turned on, current flows from the battery, through the charging system indicator light on the instrument panel, to the voltage regulator, and to the alternator. Since the alternator is not producing any current, the alternator warning light comes on. When the engine is started, the alternator begins to produce current and turns the alternator light off. As the alternator turns and produces current, the current is divided in two ways: part to the battery to charge the battery and power the electrical components of the vehicle, and part is returned to the alternator to enable it to increase its output. In this situation, the alternator is receiving current from the battery and from itself. A voltage regulator is wired into the current supply to the alternator to prevent it from receiving too much current, causing it to in turn, produce too much current. Conversely, if the voltage regulator does not allow the alternator to receive enough current, the battery will not be fully charged and will eventually go dead.

The battery is connected to the alternator at all times, whether the ignition key is turned on or not. If the battery were shorted to ground, the alternator would also be shorted. This would damage the alternator. To prevent this, a fuse link is installed in the wiring between the battery and the alternator. If the battery is shorted, the fuse link is melted, protecting the alternator.

ALTERNATOR PRECAUTIONS

Some precautions should be taken when working on this, or any other, AC charging system.

3 ENGINE AND ENGINE OVERHAUL

1. Never switch battery polarity.
2. When installing a battery, always connect the grounded terminal first.
3. Never disconnect the battery while the engine is running.
4. If the molded connector is disconnected from the alternator, never ground the hot wire.
5. Never run the alternator with the main output cable disconnected.
6. Never electric weld around the vehicle without disconnecting the alternator.
7. Never apply any voltage in excess of battery voltage while testing.
8. Never jump a battery for starting purposes with more than 12v.

CHARGING SYSTEM TROUBLESHOOTING

There are many possible ways in which the charging system can malfunction. Often the source of a problem is difficult to diagnose, requiring special equipment and a good deal of experience. This is usually not the case, however, where the charging system fails completely and causes the dash board warning light to come on or the battery to become dead. To troubleshoot a complete system failure only two pieces of equipment are needed: a test light, to determine that current is reaching a certain point; and a current indicator (ammeter), to determine the direction of the current flow and its measurement in amps.

DIAGNOSIS

The first test which should be performed is a visual inspection of all charging system components.
1. Inspect the condition of the battery cable terminals, battery posts, connections at the engine block, starter motor solenoid and relay. All connections should be clean and tight. All wire casings should be intact. If corrosion is evident, it can be easily cleaned by using a paste made from a mixture of baking soda and water.
2. Inspect all fuses in the fuse block for tightness in their receptacles. Replace any loose or blown fuses
3. Check the electrolyte level in the battery. This can be done using a hydrometer. Add water to the battery and recharge if necessary.
4. Inspect alternator mounting bolts for tightness. Bolts should be torqued to 23–30 ft.lbs.
5. Inspect the alternator drive belt condition and tension. Adjust and/or replace as necessary. Drive belt should be torqued to 140–160 ft.lbs. if used and 180–200 ft.lbs. if new.
6. Inspect the connection at the alternator BAT terminal (usually located on the back side of the alternator). This is the alternator output to the battery. Assure that it is clean and tight.

After the visual inspection is complete, perform the following alternator and battery tests until the problem is found.
1. Turn off all electrical components on the car. Make sure the doors of the car are closed. If the car is equipped with a clock, disconnect the clock by removing the lead wire from the rear of the clock. Disconnect the positive battery cable from the battery and connect the ground wire on a test light to the disconnected positive battery cable. Touch the probe end of the test light to the positive battery post. The test light should not light. If the test light does light, there is a short or open circuit on the car.
2. Disconnect the voltage regulator wiring harness connector at the voltage regulator. Turn on the ignition key. Connect the wire on a test light to a good ground (engine bolt). Touch the probe end of a test light to the ignition wire connector into the voltage regulator wiring connector. This wire corresponds to the **I** terminal on the regulator. If the test light goes on, the charging system warning light circuit is complete. If the test light does not come on and the warning light on the instrument panel is on, either the resistor wire, which is parallel with the warning light, or the wiring to the voltage regulator, is defective. If the test light does not come on and the warning light is not on, either the bulb is defective or the power supply wire from the battery through the ignition switch to the bulb has an open circuit. Connect the wiring harness to the regulator.
3. Examine the fuse link wire in the wiring harness from the starter relay to the alternator. If the insulation on the wire is cracked or split, the fuse link may be melted. Connect a test light to the fuse link by attaching the ground wire on the test light to an engine bolt and touching the probe end of the light to the bottom of the fuse link wire where it splices into the alternator output wire. If the bulb in the test light does not light, the fuse link is melted.
4. Start the engine and place a current indicator on the positive battery cable. Turn off all electrical accessories and make sure the doors are closed. If the charging system is working properly, the gauge will show a draw of less than 5 amps. If the system is not working properly, the gauge will show a draw of more than 5 amps. A charge moves the needle toward the battery, a draw moves the needle away from the battery. Turn the engine off.

NOTE: In order for the current indicator to give a valid reading, the car must be equipped with battery cables which are of the same gauge size and quality as original equipment battery cables.

5. Disconnect the wiring harness from the voltage regulator at the regulator. Connect a male spade terminal (solderless connector) to each end of a jumper wire. Insert one end of the wire into the wiring harness connector which corresponds to the **A** terminal on the regulator. Insert the other end of the wire into the wiring harness connector which corresponds to the **F** terminal on the regulator. Position the connector with the jumper wire installed so that it cannot contact any metal surface under the hood. Position a current indicator gauge on the positive battery cable. Have an assistant start the engine. Observe the reading on the current indicator. Have your assistant slowly raise the speed of the engine to about 2,000 rpm or until the current indicator needle stops moving, whichever comes first. Do not run the engine for more than a short period of time in this condition. If the wiring harness connector or jumper wire becomes excessively hot during this test, turn off the engine and check for a grounded wire in the regulator wiring harness. If the current indicator shows a charge of about three amps less than the output of the alternator, the alternator is working properly. If the previous tests showed a draw, the voltage regulator is defective. If the gauge does not show the proper charging rate, the alternator is defective.

Once the determination is made that the alternator is at fault, off vehicle testing can be used to determine the defective component inside the alternator.

REMOVAL

1. Disconnect the battery ground.
2. Remove and tag all alternator wiring.
3. Remove the adjusting bolt, loosen the mounting bolts and remove the belt.
4. Support the alternator with your hand and remove the mounting bolts. Lift the alternator out.

ALTERNATOR OVERHAUL

Disassembly

NOTE: As the rotor and housing ends are separated, the brushes can spring out and cone in contact with lubricant. Immediately clean the brushes if they are to be reused.

ENGINE AND ENGINE OVERHAUL 3

1. Scribe a line across the front housing, stator frame and rear housing to serve as a reference point for alternator clocking during reassembly.
2. Remove the four through bolts and separate the housings by gently prying them apart. Cover the rear housing bearings and the rotor shaft with tape to protect them from dirt. If brushes are to be reused, clean them with a soft dry cloth.
3. Place alternator in a vice and remove pulley nut, lock washer, pulley, fan and outer collar. Separate the front housing from the rotor shaft.
4. Remove the three stator winding terminal attaching nuts and washers and remove stator winding terminals from the bridge rectifier terminal studs. Separate the stator from the rear housing.
5. Remove the diode trio strap terminal attaching screw from the brush holder and remove the diode trio.
6. Remove the capacitor holddown screw and disconnect the capacitor wire terminal from the bridge rectifier. Remove the capacitor.
7. Remove the bridge rectifier attaching screws and the battery wire terminal (output) stud. Remove the bridge rectifier. For assembly reference, note the insulator located between the heat sink and the rear housing.
8. Remove the remaining two brush holder screws. Note the location of all the insulator washer sleeves to facilitate correct assembly. Remove the brush holder and brushes, carefully noting their position.
9. Remove the voltage regulator. Remove the front bearing retainer plate screws, retainer plate and inner collar.
10. Press out the front bearing and slinger from the front housing with an appropriate tool. If the bearing is in good condition, it may be reused.
11. Press out the rear bearing from the rear housing using an

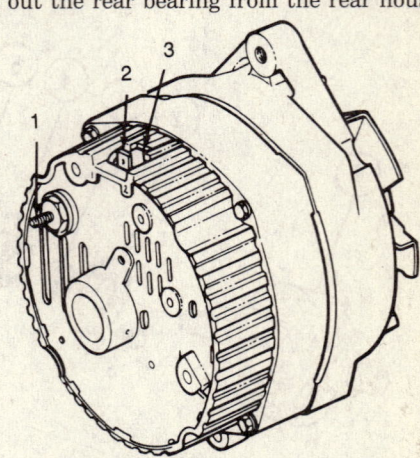

- Alternator "BAT" terminal to ground (1).
- Alternator No. 1 terminal to ground (2).
- Alternator No. 2 terminal to ground (3).

Delco alternator

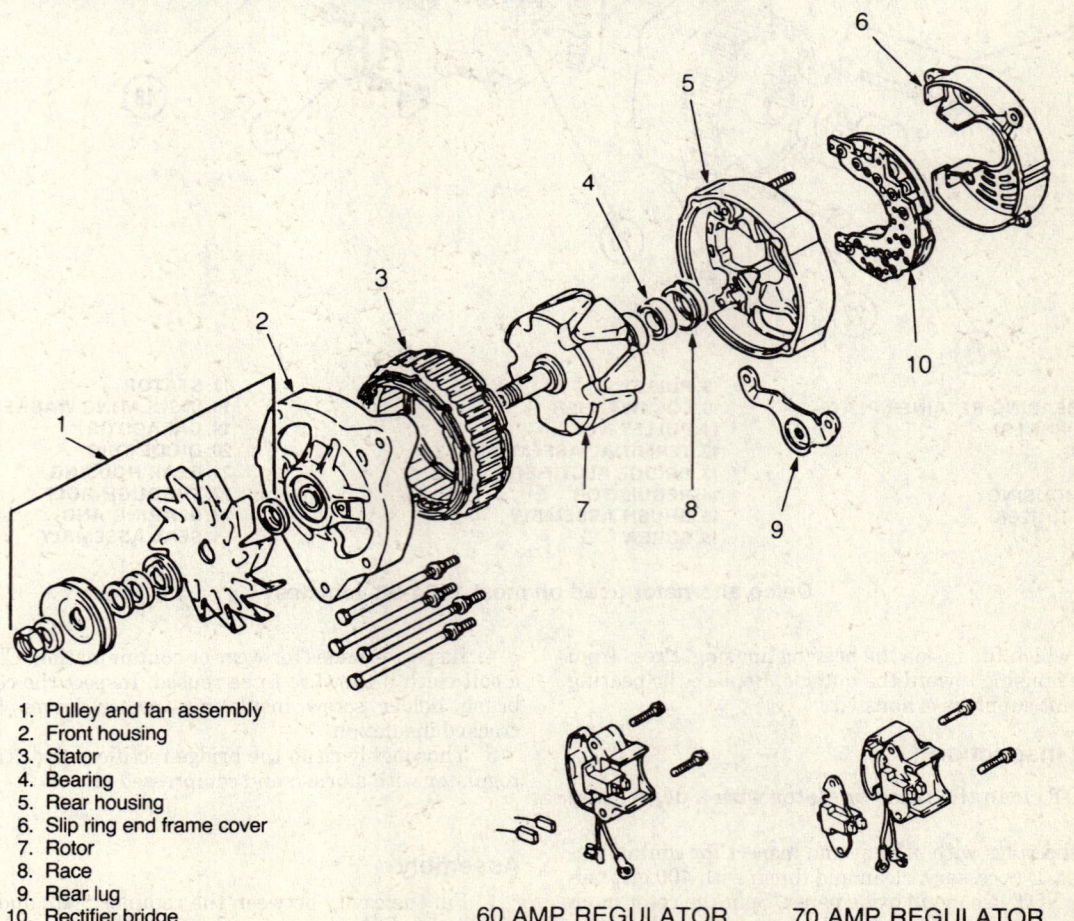

1. Pulley and fan assembly
2. Front housing
3. Stator
4. Bearing
5. Rear housing
6. Slip ring end frame cover
7. Rotor
8. Race
9. Rear lug
10. Rectifier bridge

60 AMP REGULATOR   70 AMP REGULATOR

Paris-Rhone alternator used on the 4-2.1L diesel

3-7

3 ENGINE AND ENGINE OVERHAUL

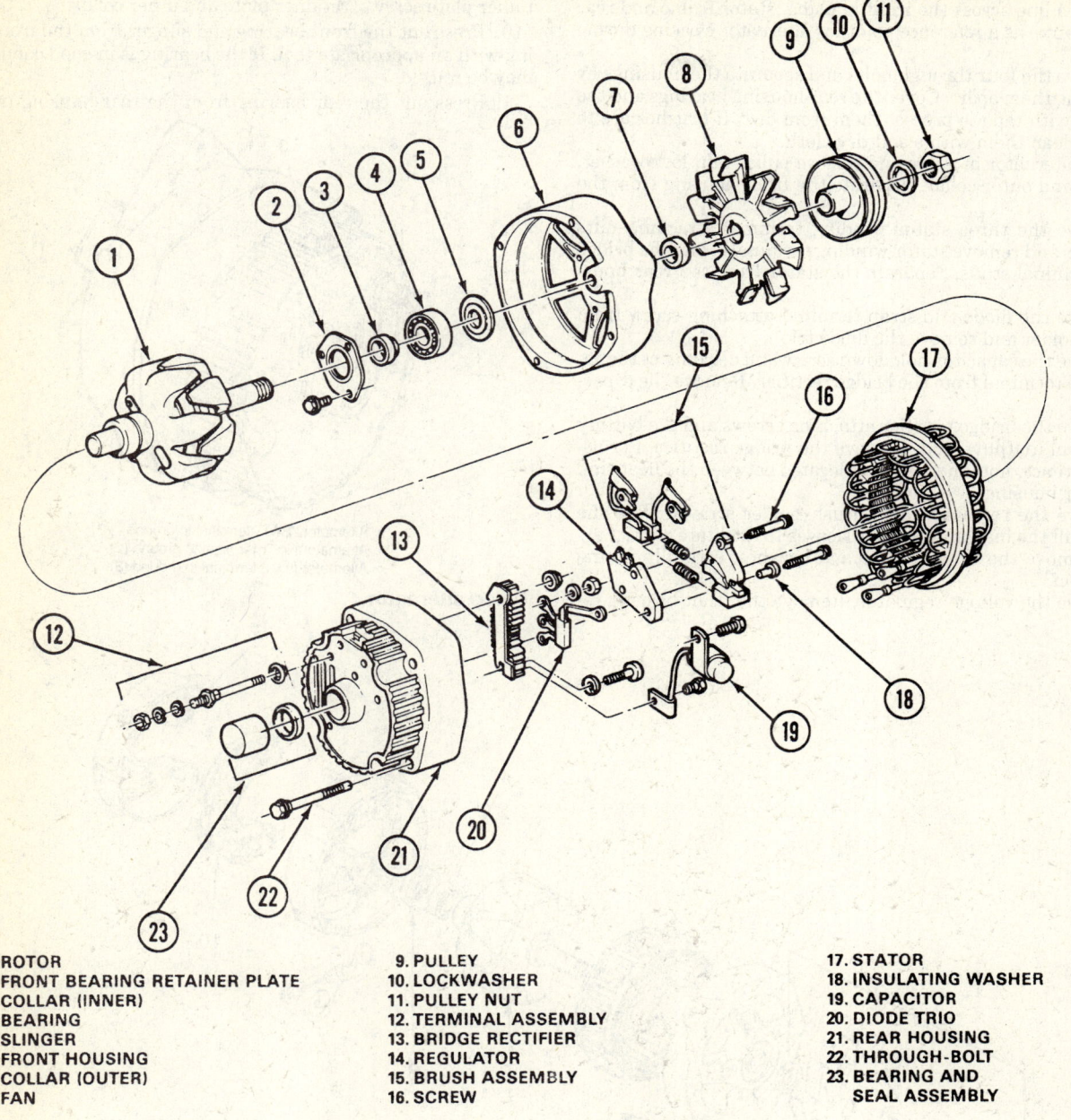

1. ROTOR
2. FRONT BEARING RETAINER PLATE
3. COLLAR (INNER)
4. BEARING
5. SLINGER
6. FRONT HOUSING
7. COLLAR (OUTER)
8. FAN
9. PULLEY
10. LOCKWASHER
11. PULLEY NUT
12. TERMINAL ASSEMBLY
13. BRIDGE RECTIFIER
14. REGULATOR
15. BRUSH ASSEMBLY
16. SCREW
17. STATOR
18. INSULATING WASHER
19. CAPACITOR
20. DIODE TRIO
21. REAR HOUSING
22. THROUGH-BOLT
23. BEARING AND SEAL ASSEMBLY

Delco alternator used on most 1984-90 vehicles

appropriate tool which fits inside the bearing housing. Press from the inside of the housing toward the outside. Replace the bearing only if its lubricant supply is exhausted.

Cleaning and Inspection

NOTE: DO NOT clean the rotor or stator with a degreasing solvent.

1. Clean the slip rings with solvent and inspect for contamination or roughness. If necessary, clean and finish with 400 grit polishing cloth. DO NOT use metal oxide paper. Spin the rotor in an appropriate support while holding the abrasive against the rings.
2. Clean the stator with alcohol.
3. Inspect the brush springs for damage or corrosion. Replace springs if there is any doubt about their condition.

4. Inspect brushes for wear or contamination. Clean them with a soft cloth if they are to be reused. Inspect the condition of the brush holder screw insulating washer/sleeves for broken or cracked insulation.
5. Thoroughly clean the bridge rectifier, diode trio and voltage regulator with a brush and compressed air.

Assembly

1. Fill the cavity between the retainer plate and front bearing ¼ full with Delco lubricant No.1948791 or equivalent.
2. Assemble the slinger and bearing into the front of the housing. Press the bearing into the housing with an appropriate tool.
3. Install the inner collar, retainer plate and screws. Install a

ENGINE AND ENGINE OVERHAUL 3

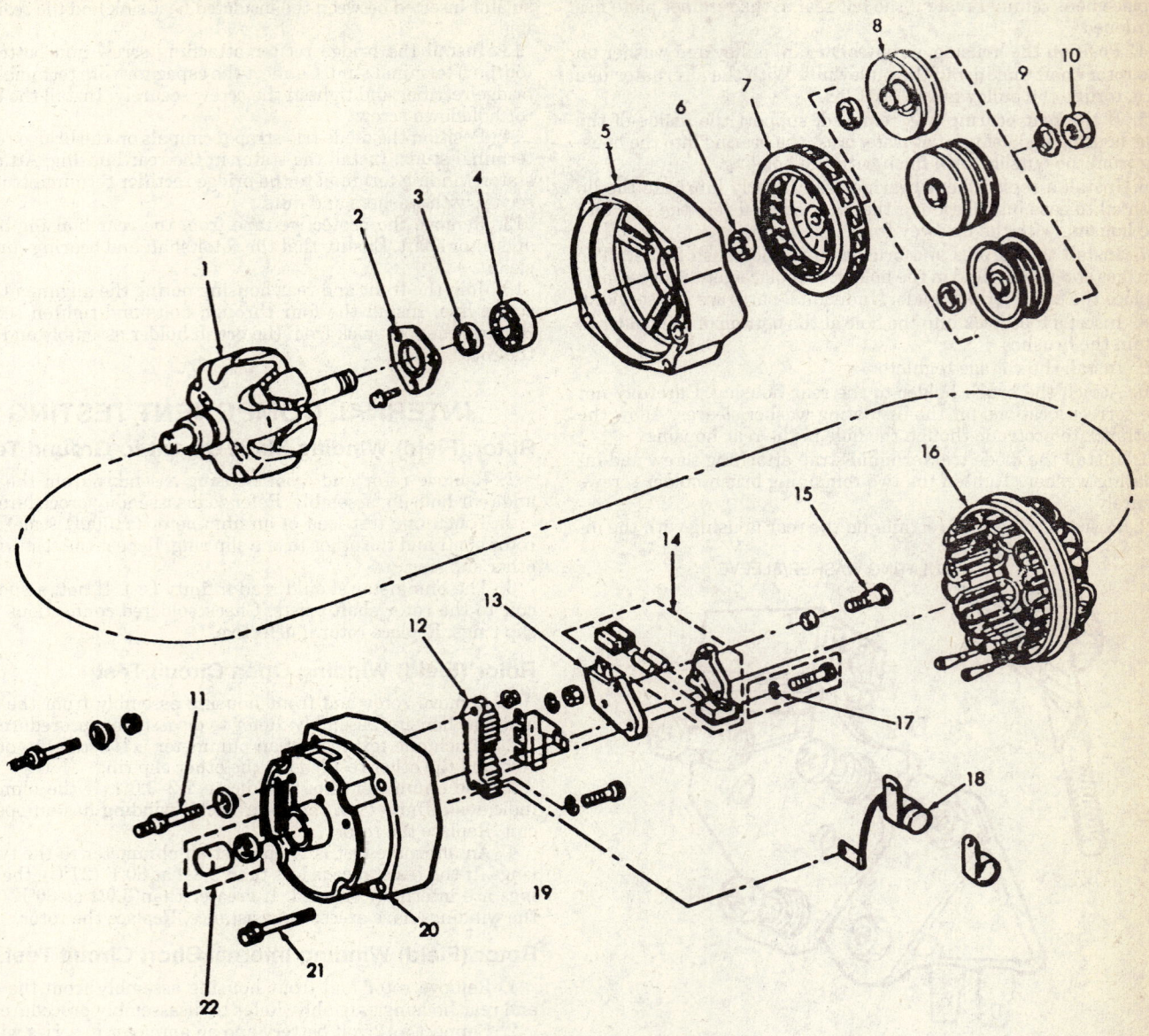

1. ROTOR
2. FRONT BEARING RETAINER PLATE
3. COLLAR (INNER)
4. BEARING
5. FT. HOUSING
6. COLLAR (INNER)
7. FAN
8. PULLEY
9. LOCKWASHER
10. PULLEY NUT
11. TERMINAL ASSEMBLY
12. BRIDGE RECTIFIER
13. REGULATOR
14. BRUSH ASSEMBLY
15. SCREW
16. STATOR
17. INSULATING WASHER
18. CAPACITOR
19. DIODE TRIO
20. REAR HOUSING
21. THROUGH-BOLT
22. BEARING AND SEAL ASSEMBLY

Nippondenso alternator used on all 1991 vehicles

3 ENGINE AND ENGINE OVERHAUL

replacement retainer plate if the felt seal in the retainer plate has hardened.

4. Position the housing, outer collar, fan, pulley and washer on the rotor shaft and install the pulley nut. With the alternator in a vice, torque the pulley nut to 50 ft.lbs.

5. If the rear bearing was removed, support the inside of the rear housing and using a flat plate, press the bearing into the housing from the outside until flush with the housing.

6. Install a replacement bearing seal. Lightly lubricate the lip with oil to ease installation of the rotor shaft. Press the seal into the housing with the lip away from the bearing.

7. Install the springs and brushes into the brush holder. The brushes should not bind in the holder. If replacement is necessary, replace the entire brush holder. Individual parts are not serviced.

8. Insert a toothpick into the hole at the bottom of the holder to retain the brushes.

9. Install the voltage regulator.

10. Attach the brush holder to the rear housing. Carefully not the correct locations for the insulating washer/sleeves. Allow the toothpick to protrude though the hole in the rear housing.

11. Install the diode trio terminal strap attaching screw and insulating washer. Tighten the two remaining brush holder screws securely.

12. Position the bridge rectifier on the rear housing with the insulator inserted between the insulated heat sink and the rear housing.

13. Install the bridge reciter attaching screw and batter wire (output) terminal stud. Connect the capacitor wire terminal to the bridge rectifier and tighten the screw securely. Install the capacitor holddown screw.

14. Position the diode trio strap terminals on the bridge rectifier terminal studs. Install the stator in the rear housing. Attach the stator winding terminal to the bridge rectifier terminal studs and secure with washers and nuts.

15. Remove the protective tape from the rear housing bearing and rotor shaft. Ensure that the rotor shaft and bearing surface is clean.

16. Join the front and rear housing noting the alignment of the scribe line. Install the four through bolts and tighten securely. Remove the toothpick from the brush holder assembly and rotate the rotor.

INTERNAL COMPONENT TESTING

Rotor (Field) Winding Short Circuit-to-Ground Test

1. Remove rotor and front housing assembly from the stator and rear housing assembly. Refer to disassembly procedure.

2. Touch one test lead of an ohmmeter (x1000Ω scale) to the rotor shaft and the other to one slip ring. Repeat the test with the other slip ring.

3. The ohmmeter should read infinity (∞). If not, a short circuit to the rotor shaft exists. Check soldered connections at the slip rings. Replace rotor if defective.

Rotor (Field) Winding Open Circuit Test

1. Remove rotor and front housing assembly from the stator and rear housing assembly. Refer to disassembly procedure.

2. Touch one test lead of an ohmmeter (x1Ω scale) to one slip ring and the other test lead to the other slip ring.

3. The ohmmeter should indicate 2.2–3.0Ω. If the ohmmeter indicates infinity (∞), the rotor (field) winding has an open circuit. Replace the rotor.

4. An alternate test is to connect an ohmmeter to the two slip rings. If the resistance is less than 2.8Ω at 80°F (27°C), the windings are internally shorted. If greater than 3.0Ω at 80°F (27°C), the windings have excessive resistance. Replace the rotor.

Rotor (Field) Winding Internal Short Circuit Test

1. Remove rotor and front housing assembly from the stator and rear housing assembly. Refer to disassembly procedure.

2. Connect a 12 volt battery and an ammeter in series with the slip rings.

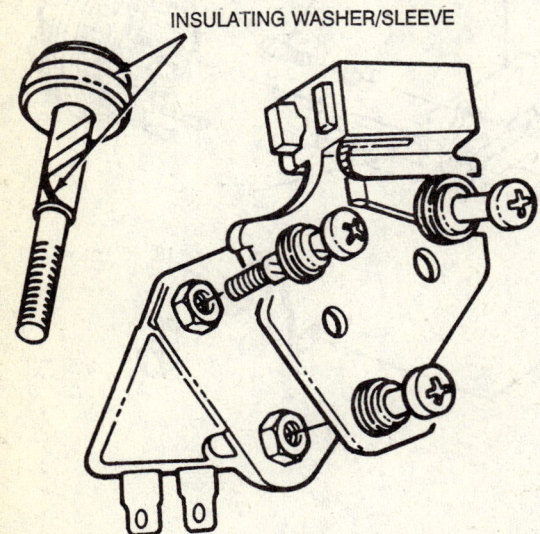

Brush holder screw insulating washer/sleeve

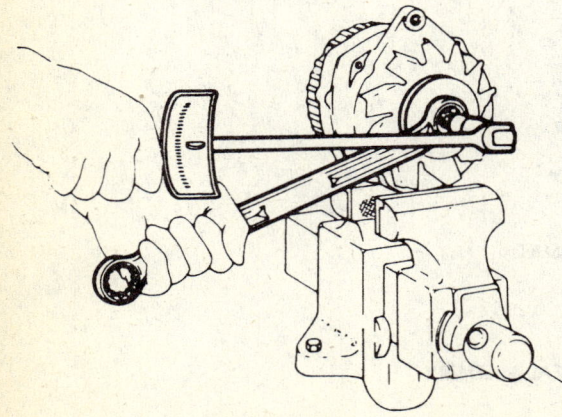

Torque the pulley nut to 50 ft. lbs.

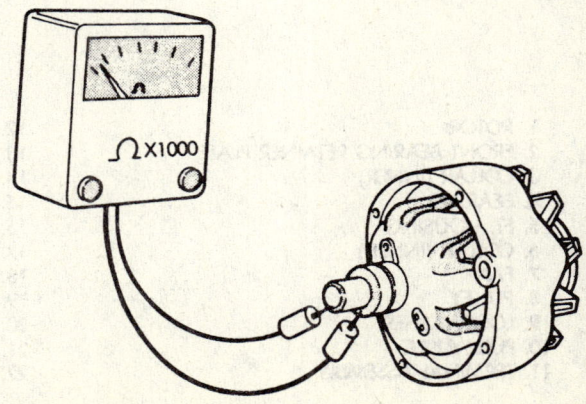

Rotor winding-short-circuit-to ground test

ENGINE AND ENGINE OVERHAUL 3

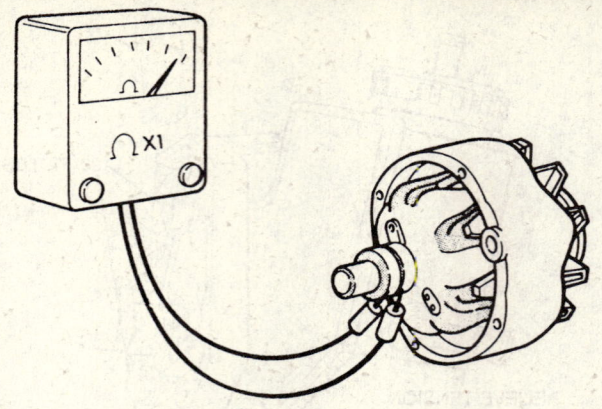

Rotor winding open circuit test

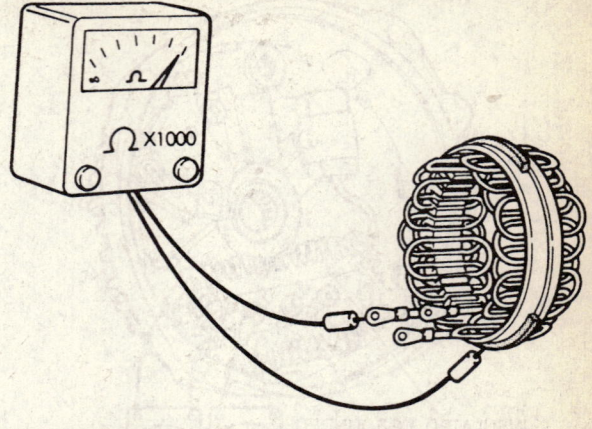

Stator windings-short-circuit to ground test

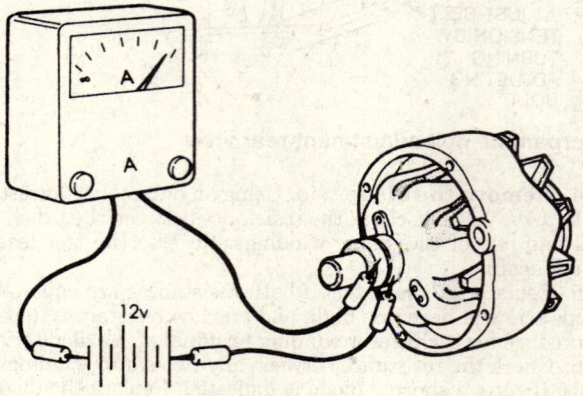

Rotor winding internal short circuit test

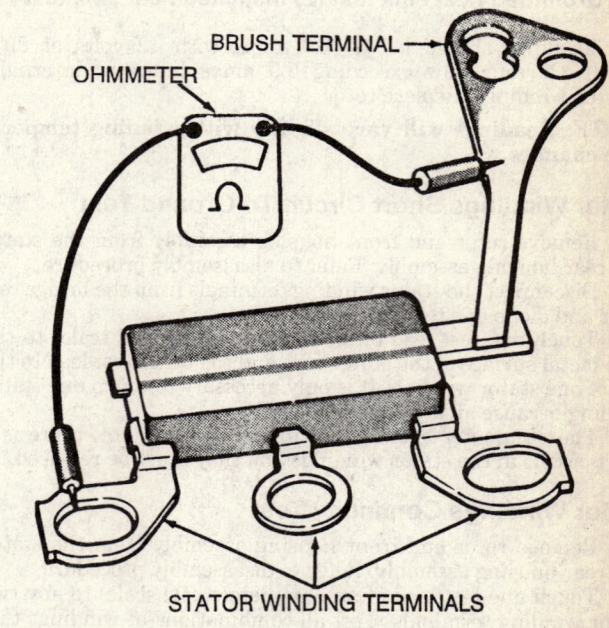

Diode trio test

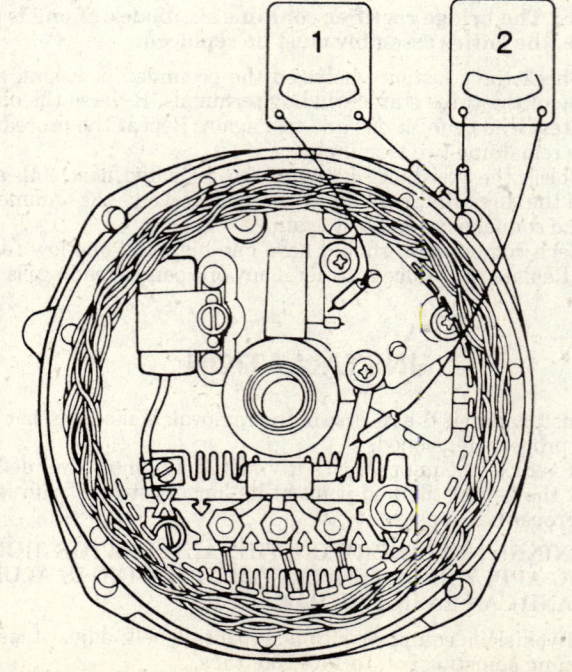

(1) Brush holder clip test (2) Diode trio insulation test

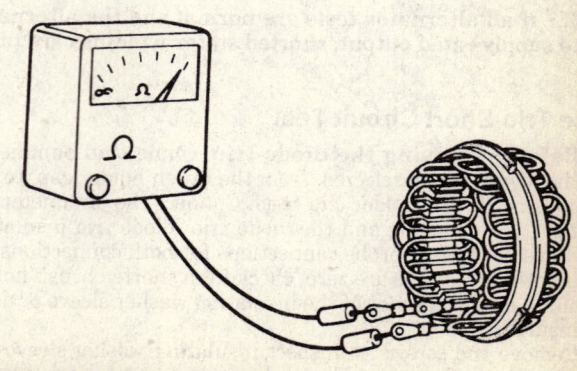

Stator windings-continuity test

3-11

3 ENGINE AND ENGINE OVERHAUL

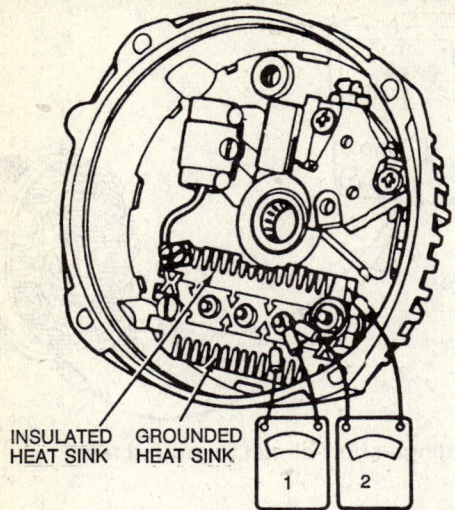

(1) Grounded heat sink test (2) Insulated heat sink test

3. Readings should be 4.0–5.0 amps with 12 volts at 80°F (27°C). Current flow exceeding 5.0 amps indicates internally shorted windings. Replace rotor.

NOTE: Readings will vary slightly with winding temperature changes.

Stator Windings Short Circuit To Ground Test

1. Remove rotor and front housing assembly from the stator and rear housing assembly. Refer to disassembly procedure.
2. Disconnect the stator winding terminals from the bridge rectifier and diode trio terminal studs.
3. Touch one test lead of an ohmmeter (x1000Ω scale) to the bare metal surface of the stator core and the other test lead to the end of one stator winding. It is only necessary to touch one stator winding because all are soldered together.
4. The ohmmeter should read infinity (∞). If not, there is a short circuit in the stator windings and they must be replaced.

Stator Windings Continuity Test

1. Remove rotor and front housing assembly from the stator and rear housing assembly. Refer to disassembly procedure.
2. Touch one test lead of an ohmmeter (x1Ω scale) to any two stator winding terminals. Test all combinations of windings this way. Equal indications should be obtained for each pair.
3. An infinity (∞) reading indicates open windings. An indication of more than 1Ω indicates a poorly soldered joint. Inspect the neutral junction splice solder connection. Resolder the connection even if it appears to be electrically and mechanically good.

NOTE: If all alternator tests are normal and the alternator fails to supply rated output, shorted stator windings are probable.

Diode Trio Short Circuit Test

1. **Before removing the diode trio**, connect an ohmmeter, with the lowest range selected, from the brush holder clip, to the rear housing (brush holder clip test). Connect the ohmmeter between the rear housing and the diode trio (diode trio insulation test). Reverse the test probe connections for both connections.
2. If both indications are zero, check for a shorted brush holder clip caused by the absence of the insulating washer/sleeve or damaged insulation.
3. Remove the screws to inspect insulating washer/sleeves. If intact, and both ohmmeter observations are identical, replace the voltage regulator.

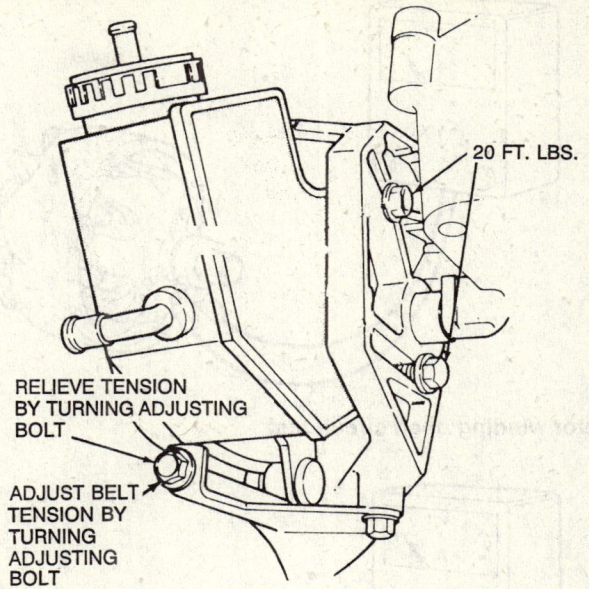

Serpentine belt adjustment-rear view

4. **Remove the diode trio.** Using an ohmmeter (lowest scale) with a 1 1/8 volt cell, check the resistance between the brush terminal and one of the stator windings. Reverse the test leads and check again.
5. Replace the diode trio if both resistances are equal. A good diode trio will have one high, and one low resistance. Repeat the procedure for each stator winding terminal of the diode trio.
6. Check the resistance between any two stator winding terminals. If zero, a shorted diode is indicated. Replace the diode trio. Repeat the test for all combinations of stator winding terminals.

Bridge Rectifier Test

NOTE: The bridge rectifier contains six diodes. If one is defective, the entire assembly must be replaced.

1. Check the resistance between the grounded heat sink and any one of the three stator winding terminals. Reverse the ohmmeter test lead connections and test again. Repeat the procedure for the remaining two terminals.
2. Check the resistance between the insulated heat sink and each of the three stator winding terminals. Reverse the ohmmeter test lead connections and test again.
3. Each combination should have one high and one low resistance. Replace the bridge rectifier if any one pair of readings is the same.

INSTALLATION

1. Installation is the reverse of the removal. Make sure that the belt is properly tensioned.
2. If vehicle is equipped with a V-belt: a 13mm (1/8 in.) deflection of the belt at the mid-point of its longest straight run indicates proper belt tension.

WARNING: NEVER PRY ON THE ALTERNATOR HOUSING TO APPLY BELT TENSION! THE HOUSING IS ALUMINUM AND CAN EASILY BE DAMAGED!

3. If vehicle is equipped with a serpentine belt: adjust tension by turning adjusting bolt to 140–160 ft.lbs.
4. Tighten all bolts, replace all wiring. Replace battery ground cable.

ENGINE AND ENGINE OVERHAUL 3

Regulator

Regulators used with alternators are transistorized (in most cases they are internally mounted in the alternator) and cannot be serviced. If one of these units proves defective, it must be replaced.

Battery

1984–91 Jeep vehicles come with a 390 cold cranking amp battery standard. This battery is of the 12 volt negative ground type. Optional on some models is a 475 cold cranking amp battery.

REMOVAL AND INSTALLATION

1. Remove the holddown screws from the battery box. Loosen the nuts that secure the cable ends to the battery terminals. Lift the battery cables from the terminals with a twisting motion. If the terminals are difficult to remove, use a battery terminal puller. Do not try to force the terminals off as this could break the plastic battery case.

NOTE: Always remove the negative (ground) battery terminal first and replace it last.

2. Using a battery lift strap, remove the battery from the vehicle.
3. Before installing the new battery, make sure that the battery terminals are clean and free from corrosion. Use a battery terminal cleaner (or sandpaper) to clean the terminals and battery posts until bright. A paste made from baking soda and water will neutralize any acid deposits. Place the battery in the vehicle, install the terminals (make sure they are installed on the correct post), and tighten the nuts on the terminals. Coat the terminals and tops of the posts with grease to prevent corrosion. Install and tighten the nuts of the battery box.

Starter

STARTING SYSTEM TROUBLESHOOTING

Starter Won't Crank The Engine
1. Dead battery.
2. Open starter circuit, such as:

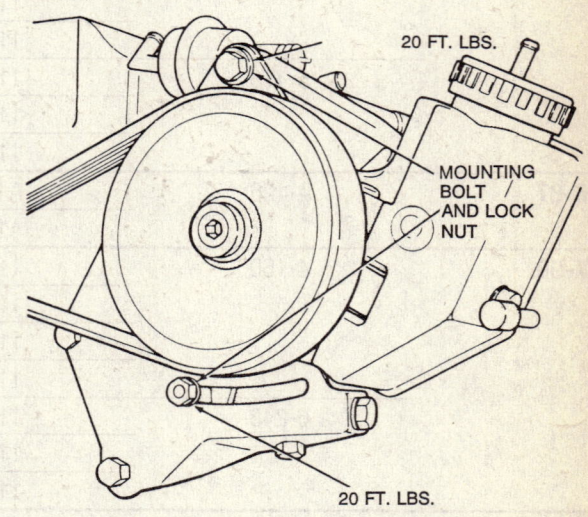

Serpentine belt adjustment-front view

Troubleshooting Basic Charging System Problems

Problem	Cause	Solution
Noisy alternator	• Loose mountings • Loose drive pulley • Worn bearings • Brush noise • Internal circuits shorted (High pitched whine)	• Tighten mounting bolts • Tighten pulley • Replace alternator • Replace alternator • Replace alternator
Squeal when starting engine or accelerating	• Glazed or loose belt	• Replace or adjust belt
Indicator light remains on or ammeter indicates discharge (engine running)	• Broken fan belt • Broken or disconnected wires • Internal alternator problems • Defective voltage regulator	• Install belt • Repair or connect wiring • Replace alternator • Replace voltage regulator
Car light bulbs continually burn out—battery needs water continually	• Alternator/regulator overcharging	• Replace voltage regulator/alternator
Car lights flare on acceleration	• Battery low • Internal alternator/regulator problems	• Charge or replace battery • Replace alternator/regulator
Low voltage output (alternator light flickers continually or ammeter needle wanders)	• Loose or worn belt • Dirty or corroded connections • Internal alternator/regulator problems	• Replace or adjust belt • Clean or replace connections • Replace alternator or regulator

3 ENGINE AND ENGINE OVERHAUL

ALTERNATOR OUTPUT SPECIFICATIONS

Year	Engine	Alternator Part. No.	Output (amps)	Regulator Volts @ 75°F
1984–87	4-150	1105044	56	13.9–14.9
		1105047	56	13.9–14.9
		1105045	66	13.9–14.9
		1105048	66	13.9–14.9
		1105049	78	13.9–14.9
		1105046	78	13.9–14.9
	6-173	1105058	56	13.9–14.9
		1105059	66	13.9–14.9
		1105060	78	13.9–14.9
1986–87	4-126	A13N117 [1]	60	N/A
		A13N108 [1]	70	N/A
1987–90	4-150	1101175	61	13.9–14.9
		1101171	61	13.9–14.9
		1101176	74	13.9–14.9
		1101172	74	13.9–14.9
	6-243	1101168	61	13.9–14.9
		1101170	85	13.9–14.9
		1101167	100	13.9–14.9
1991	All	56005684 [2]	75	13.9–15.0
		56005685 [2]	90	13.9–15.0

[1] Manufactured by Paris-Rhone
[2] Manufactured by Nippondenso
• All other alternators manufactured by Delco-Remy
N/A—Not Available

  a. Broken or loose battery cables.
  b. Inoperative starter motor solenoid.
  c. Broken or loose wire from ignition switch to solenoid.
  d. Poor solenoid or starter ground.
  e. Bad ignition switch.
3. Defective starter internal circuit, such as:
  a. Dirty or burnt commutator.
  b. Stuck, worn or broken brushes.
  c. Open or shorted armature.
  d. Open or grounded fields.
4. Starter motor mechanical faults, such as:
  a. Jammed armature end bearings.
  b. Bad bearings, allowing armature to rub fields.
  c. Bent shaft.
  d. Broken starter housing.
  e. Bad starter drive mechanism.
  f. Bad starter drive or flywheel-driven gear.
5. Engine hard or impossible to crank, such as:
  a. Hydrostatic lock, water in combustion chamber.
  b. Crankshaft seizing in bearings.
  c. Piston or ring seizing.
  d. Bent or broken connecting rod.
  e. Seizing of connecting rod bearings.
  f. Flywheel jammed or broken.

Starter Spins Freely, Won't Engage

1. Sticking or broken drive mechanism.
2. Damaged ring gear.

DIAGNOSIS

Cold Cranking Test

NOTE: The battery must be fully charged and in good condition before starting this test.

1. Connect a volt meter across the positive and negative terminals of the battery. Connect an induction meter to the positive battery cable.
2. Fully engage parking brake, place manual transmission in NEUTRAL, automatic transmission in PARK.
3. Disconnect the ignition coil wire from the distributor cap and connect a suitable jumper wire between the coil cable and a good body ground.
4. Have an assistant crank the engine by turning the ignition switch (key) to the START position. Observe the voltmeter and induction meter.
5. Replace or rebuild the starter motor if not within specifications. A cold motor will increase starter motor current.

Starter/Ground Cable Test

When performing these tests, it is important that the voltmeter be connected to the terminals, not the cables themselves.

ENGINE AND ENGINE OVERHAUL 3

Before testing, assure that the ignition control module (if equipped) is disconnected, the parking brake is set, the transmission is in PARK (automatic) or NEUTRAL (manual), and the battery is fully charged and in good condition.

1. Check voltage between the positive battery post and the center of the B+ terminal on the starter solenoid stud.
2. Check voltage between the negative battery post and the engine block.
3. Disconnect the ignition coil wire from the distributor cap and connect a suitable jumper wire between the coil cable and a good body ground.
4. Have an assistant crank the engine and measure voltage again. Voltage drop should not exceed 0.5 volts.
5. If voltage drop is greater than 0.5 volts, clean metal surfaces. Apply a thick layer of silicone grease. Install a new cadmium plated bolt and star washer on the battery terminal and a new brass nut on the starter solenoid. Retest and replace cable if not within specifications.

REMOVAL

All Except 4-2.1L Diesel

1. Disconnect the battery ground.
2. Raise and support the vehicle on jackstands.
3. On 1989–91 models equipped with a 4-2.5L engine, it is necessary to remove the exhaust clamp and bracket, and the transmission brace rod before removing the starter. See illustration.
4. Remove all wires from the starter and tag them for installation.

NOTE: It may be easier to remove the solenoid wires after lowering the starter. Support the starter before removing the wires. DO NOT LET THE STARTER HANG BY THE WIRES.

5. Remove all but one attaching bolt, support the starter (it's heavier than it looks) and remove the last bolt.
6. Lower the starter from the engine.

4-2.1L Diesel

1. Disconnect the battery ground.
2. Remove all wires from the starter and tag them for installation.
3. Raise and support the vehicle on jackstands.
4. Remove the starter upper bracket.
5. Take up the weight of the engine with a floor jack and remove the left side engine mount.
6. Remove the starter lower support bracket.
7. Support the starter (it's heavier than it looks) and remove the attaching bolts. Remove the starter.

STARTER OVERHAUL

Motorcraft

DISASSEMBLY

1. Remove the cover screw, the cover through-bolts, the starter drive end housing and the starter drive plunger lever return spring.
2. Remove the starter gear plunger lever pivot pin, the lever and the armature. Remove the stop ring retainer and the stop ring from the armature shaft (discard the ring), then the starter drive gear assembly.
3. Remove the brush end plate, the insulator assembly and the brushes from the plastic holder, then lift out the brush holder. For reassembly, note the position of the brush holder with respect to the end terminal.
4. Remove the two ground brush-to-frame screws.

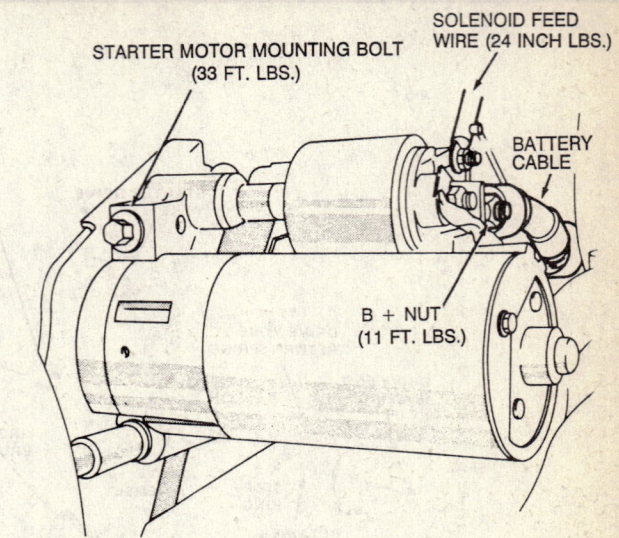

1989-91 4-2.5L starter removal/installation

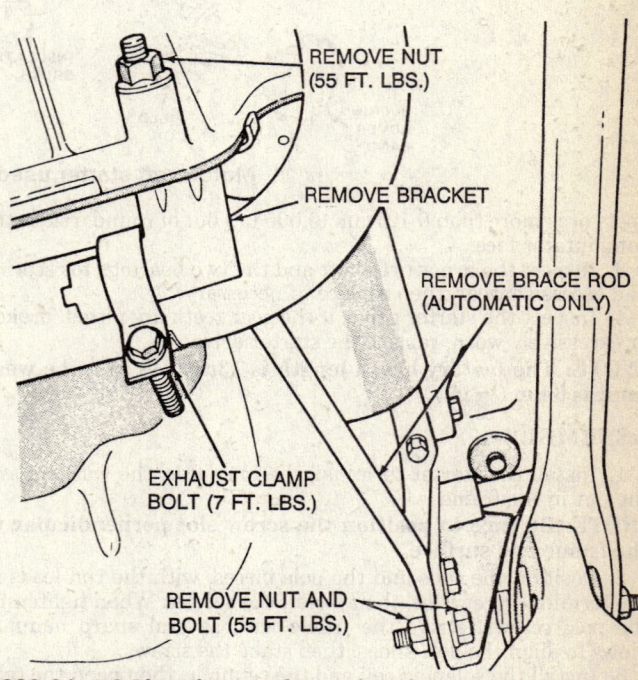

1989-91 4-2.5L exhaust clamp, bracket and transmission brace rod removal/installation

5. Bend up the sleeve's edges which are inserted in the frame's rectangular hole, then remove the sleeve and the retainer. Detach the field coil ground wire from the copper tab.
6. Remove the three coil retaining screws. Cut the field coil connection at the switch post lead, then remove the pole shoes and the coils from the frame.
7. Cut the positive brush leads from the field coils (as close to the field connection point as possible).

CLEANING AND INSPECTION

1. Check the armature and the armature windings for broken or burned insulation, open circuits or grounds.
2. Check the commutator for runout; if it is rough, has flat

3-15

3 ENGINE AND ENGINE OVERHAUL

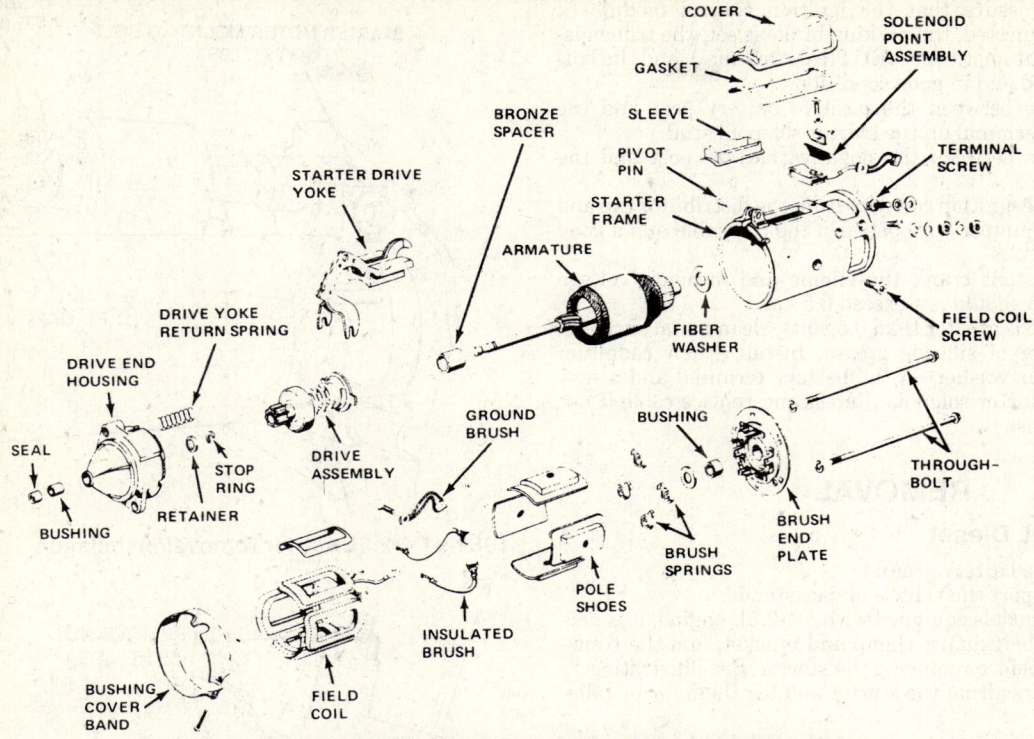

Motorcraft starter used on carbureted 4-2.5L engines

spots or is more than 0.127mm (0.005 in.) out of round, reface the commutator face.

3. Inspect the armature shaft and the two bearings for scoring and excessive wear, then replace (if necessary).

4. Inspect the starter drive; if the gear teeth are pitted, broken or excessively worn, replace the starter drive.

NOTE: The factory brush length is 13mm (1/8 in.); the wear limit is 6mm (1/4 in.).

ASSEMBLY

1. Install the starter terminal, the insulator, the washers and the nut in the frame.

NOTE: Be sure to position the screw slot perpendicular to the frame end surface.

2. Position the coils and the pole pieces, with the coil leads in the terminal screw slot, then install the screws. When tightening the pole screws, strike the frame with several sharp hammer blows to align the pole shoes, then stake the screws.

3. Install the solenoid coil and the retainer, then bend the tabs to hold the coils to the frame.

4. Using resin-core solder and a 300 watt iron, solder the field coils and the solenoid wire to the starter terminal. Check for continuity and ground connections of the assembled coils.

5. Position the solenoid coil ground terminal over the nearest ground screw hole and the ground brushes-to-starter frame, then install the screws.

6. Apply a thin coating of Lubriplate® on the armature shaft splines. Install the starter motor drive gear assembly-to-armature shaft, followed by a new stop ring and retainer. Install the armature in the starter frame.

7. Position the starter drive gear plunger lever to the frame and the starter drive assembly, then install the pivot pin. Place some grease into the end housing bore; fill it about 1/4 full, then position the drive end housing to the frame.

8. Install the brush holder and the brush springs; the positive brush leads should be positioned in their respective brush holder slots, to prevent grounding problems.

9. Install the brush end plate; be certain that the end plate insulator is in the proper position on the end plate. Install the two starter frame through-bolts and torque them to 55–75 inch lbs.

10. Install the starter drive plunger lever cover and tighten the retaining screw.

Delco-Remy

DISASSEMBLY

1. Detach the field coil connectors from the motor solenoid terminal.

NOTE: If equipped, remove solenoid mounting screws.

2. Remove the through-bolts, the commutator end frame, the field frame and the armature assembly from drive housing.

3. Remove the overrunning clutch from the armature shaft as follows:

    a. Slide the two piece thrust collar off the end of the armature shaft.

    b. Slide a standard 1/8in. pipe coupling or other spacer onto the shaft, so that the coupling end butts against the retainer edge.

    c. Using a hammer, tap the coupling end, driving the retainer towards the armature end of the snapring.

    d. Using snapring pliers, remove the snapring from its groove in the shaft, then slide the retainer and the clutch from the shaft.

4. Disassemble the field frame brush assembly by releasing the V-spring and removing the support pin. The brush holders, the brushes and the springs can now be pulled out as a unit and the leads disconnected.

NOTE: On the integral frame units, remove the brush holder from the brush support and the brush screw.

ENGINE AND ENGINE OVERHAUL 3

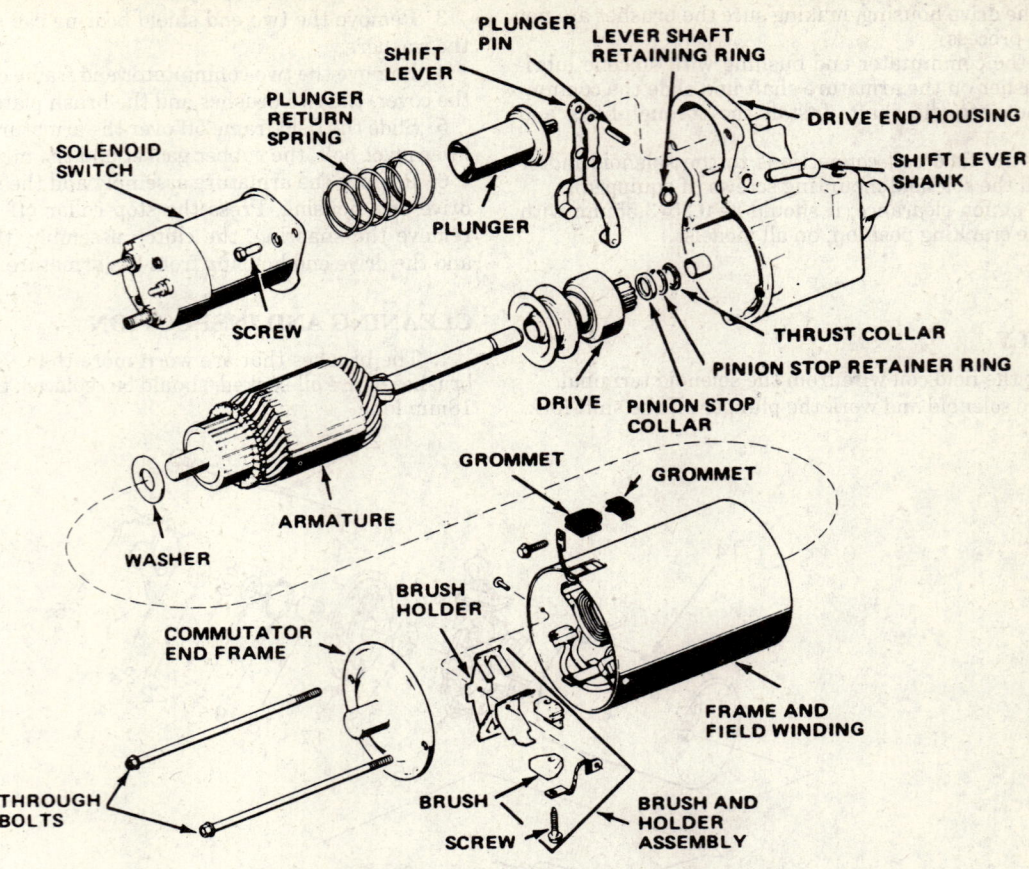

Delco-Remy starter used on the 6-2.8L

5. If equipped, separate the solenoid from the lever housing.

CLEANING AND INSPECTION

1. Clean the parts with a rag; do not immerse the parts in a solvent.

---- **CAUTION** ----

Immersion in a solvent will dissolve the grease that is packed in the clutch mechanism; it will damage the armature and the field coil insulation.

---

2. Test the overrunning clutch action; the pinion should turn freely in the overrunning direction but must not slip in the cranking direction. Check that the pinion teeth have not been chipped, cracked or excessively worn; replace the unit (if necessary).

3. Inspect the armature commutator; if the commutator is rough or out of round, it should be machined and undercut.

NOTE: Undercut the insulation between the commutator bars by 0.8mm (1/32 in.). The undercut must be the full width of the insulation and flat at the bottom; a triangular groove will not be satisfactory. Most late model starter motor use a molded armature commutator design; no attempt to undercut the insulation should be made or serious damage may result to the commutator.

ASSEMBLY

1. Install the brushes into the holders, then install solenoid (if equipped).

2. Assemble the insulated and the grounded holder together. Using the V-spring, position and assemble the unit on the support pin. Push the holders and the spring to bottom of the support, then rotate the spring to engage the slot in the support. Attach the ground wire to the grounded brush and the field lead wire to the insulated brush, then repeat this procedure for other brush sets.

3. Assemble the overrunning clutch to the armature shaft as follows:

   a. Lubricate the drive end of the shaft with silicone lubricant.

   b. Slide the clutch assembly onto the shaft with the pinion outward.

   c. Slide the retainer onto the shaft with the cupped surface facing away from the pinion.

   d. Stand the armature up on a wood surface with the commutator downward. Position the snapring on the upper end of the shaft and drive it onto the shaft with a small block of wood and a hammer, then slide the snapring into groove.

   e. Install the thrust collar onto the shaft with the shoulder next to snapring.

   f. With the retainer on one side of the snapring and the thrust collar on the other side, squeeze two sets together (with pliers) until the ring seats in the retainer. On models without a thrust collar use a washer; remember to remove the washer before continuing.

4. Lubricate the drive end bushing with silicone lubricant, then slide the armature and the clutch assembly into place, while engaging the shift lever with the clutch.

NOTE: On the non-integral starters, the shift lever may be installed in the drive gear housing first.

5. Position the field frame over the armature and apply sealer (silicone) between the frame and the solenoid case. Position the

3-17

3 ENGINE AND ENGINE OVERHAUL

frame against the drive housing, making sure the brushes are not damaged in the process.

6. Lubricate the commutator end bushing with silicone lubricant, place a washer on the armature shaft and slide the commutator end frame onto the shaft. Install the through-bolts and tighten.

7. Reconnect the field coil connections to the solenoid motor terminal. Install the solenoid mounting screws (if equipped).

8. Check the pinion clearance; it should be 0.25–3.55mm with the pinion in the cranking position, on all models.

Bosch

DISASSEMBLY

1. Disconnect the field coil wire from the solenoid terminal.
2. Remove the solenoid and work the plunger off the shift fork.
3. Remove the two end shield bearing cap screws, the cap and the washers.
4. Remove the two commutator end frame cover through-bolts, the cover, the two brushes and the brush plate.
5. Slide the field frame off over the armature. Remove the shift lever pivot bolt, the rubber gasket and the metal plate.
6. Remove the armature assembly and the shift lever from the drive end housing. Press the stop collar off the snapring, then remove the snapring, the clutch assembly, the clutch assembly and the drive end housing from the armature.

CLEANING AND INSPECTION

1. The brushes that are worn more than $1/8$ the length of new brushes or are oil-soaked, should be replaced; the new brushes are 18mm long.

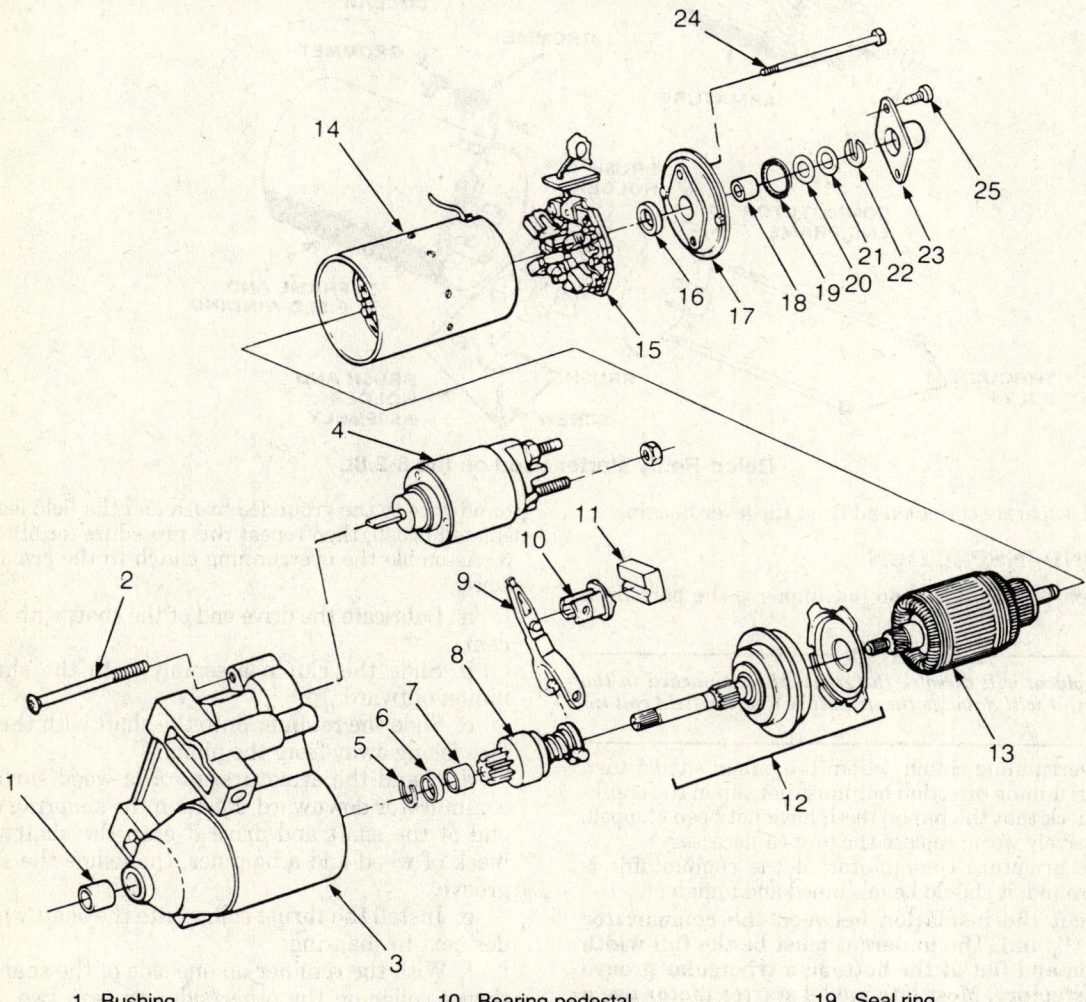

1. Bushing
2. Screw
3. Shield
4. Solenoid switch
5. Retainer
6. Stop ring
7. Bushing
8. Overrunning clutch drive
9. Fork
10. Bearing pedestal
11. Sealing rubber
12. Planetary gear system
13. Armature
14. Stator frame
15. Brush holder
16. Gasket
17. Commutator end shield
18. Bushing
19. Seal ring
20. Shim
21. Shim
22. Retaining washer
23. Closure cap
24. Hexagon screw
25. Screw

Bosch starter used on the 1986-91 4-2.5L MFI

ENGINE AND ENGINE OVERHAUL 3

2. Do not immerse the starter clutch unit in cleaning solvent; solvent will wash the lubricant from the clutch.
3. Place the drive unit on the armature shaft, then, while holding the armature, rotate the pinion.
NOTE: The drive pinion should rotate smoothly in one direction only. The pinion may not rotate easily but as long as it rotates smoothly it is in good condition. If the clutch unit does not function properly or if the pinion is worn, chipped or burred, replace the unit.

ASSEMBLY

1. Lubricate the armature shaft and the splines with SAE 10W or 30W oil.
2. Fit the drive end housing onto the armature, then install the clutch, the stop collar and the snapring onto the armature.
3. Install the shift fork pivot bolt, the rubber gasket and the metal plate. Slide the field frame into position and install the brush holder and the brushes.
4. Position the commutator end frame cover and the through-bolts.
5. Install the shim and the armature shaft lock. Check the end-play (0.050–0.300mm), then install the bearing cover.
6. Assemble the plunger to the shift fork, then install the solenoid with its mounting bolts. Connect the field wire to the solenoid.

Mitsubishi

DISASSEMBLY

1. Remove the solenoid terminal nut and disconnect the brush holder connecting wire. Remove the solenoid screws and remove the solenoid and solenoid plunger.
2. Loosen but do not remove the two screws that attach the communicator shield to the brush holder plate.
3. Remove the two through-bolts and slide the armature frame away from the overrunning clutch housing. Remove the retainer and washer, then remove the overrunning clutch housing from the armature frame.
NOTE: Take care not to lose the armature shaft ball when removing the stator frame.
4. Remove the clutch fork from the overrunning clutch and then the overrunning clutch from the armature. Remove the two screws attaching the end cover but do not remove the brush holder plate. Remove the brush feed wire by sliding the wire and connector out of the cover.
5. Install a 22mm socket on the armature shaft. Slide the socket against the communicator, then slide the brush holder onto the socket. Leave the socket in position for inspection.
6. Remove the seal from the planetary gear assembly, remove the planetary gears, and remove the gear carrier and pinion shaft from the planetary annulus gear.
7. Place a 17mm socket on the work bench and use it to support the planetary gear/overrunning clutch assembly. Use a 14mm socket to unseat the stop ring on the pinion shaft.
8. Remove the snap ring, stop ring, and overrunning clutch.

CLEANING AND INSPECTION

1. Clean the armature, armature frame, overrunning clutch, solenoid, and brush holder assembly with a clean rag and dry compressed air only. All other starter components may be cleaned with solvent.
2. Inspect stator frame and magnets for damage. The magnets can not be removed. If the frame or magnets are damaged, the entire assembly must be replaced.

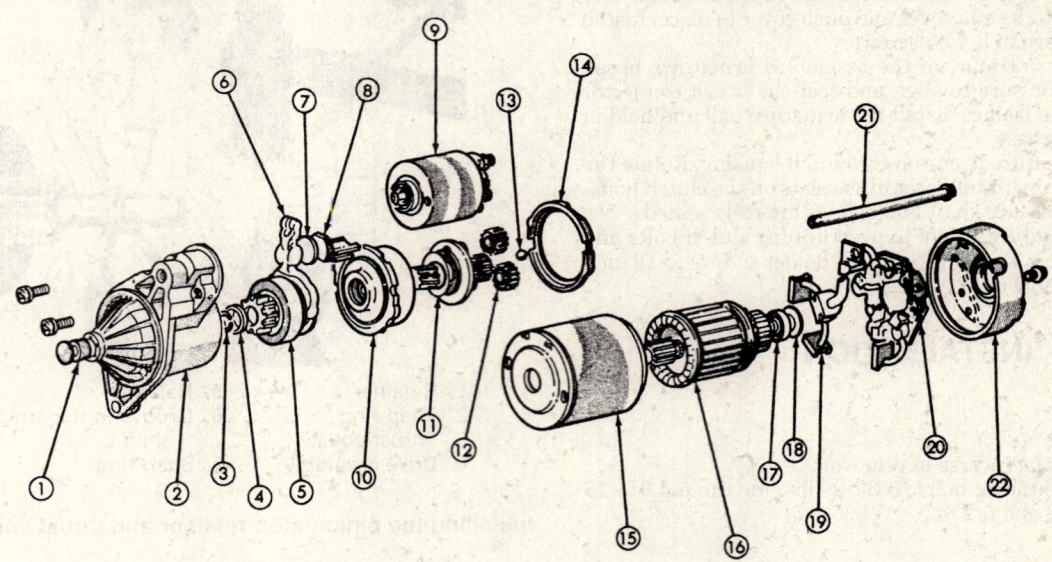

1. BUSHING
2. OVERRUNNING CLUTCH HOUSING
3. SNAP RING
4. STOP RING
5. OVERRUNNING CLUTCH
6. CLUTCH YOKE
7. YOKE WASHER
8. RETAINER
9. SOLENOID
10. PLANETARY ANNULUS GEAR
11. PLANETARY CARRIER AND PINION SHAFT
12. PLANETARY GEARS
13. ARMATURE SHAFT BALL
14. SEAL RING
15. ARMATURE FRAME AND MAGNET ASSEMBLY
16. ARMATURE
17. BEARING
18. WASHER
19. CARBON BRUSHES
20. BRUSH HOLDER
21. ARMATURE FRAME BOLTS (2)
22. END COVER

Mitsubishi starter used on the 1986-91 6-4.0L MFI

3 ENGINE AND ENGINE OVERHAUL

3. Inspect the condition of the bushing in the armature end of the drive shaft.
4. Replace the planetary gear assembly and pinion shaft if worn.
5. Inspect the armature shaft bushing and bearing. If either has worn, replace them. If contact has been made with the frame, replace the entire starter.
6. Inspect the brushes and brush holder. Replace the brushes if worn below 0.9mm (0.035 in.). Do not remove the socket unless the holder must be replaced.

ASSEMBLY

1. Install the planetary gear on the gear carrier and pinion shaft. Lubricate the drive shaft and the bushing in the overrunning clutch with SAE 20W oil, and the splines with Lubriplate. Install the overrunning clutch on the pinion shaft.
2. Install the stop ring and snap ring on the pinion shaft. Inspect the pinion shaft bushing for scratches. Polish scratches with 400–600 grit crocus cloth.
3. Slide the clutch fork on the overrunning clutch. Install the planetary/overrunning clutch assembly in the clutch housing assuring that the lugs on the planetary annulus are aligned properly.
4. Lubricate the planetary gears with chassis grease and install on the carrier shafts. Install the seal ring on the overrunning clutch housing. Position the largest lug on the seal ring at the top.
5. If replacement brushes were installed, reinsert the socket to keep the brushes in position. Position the socket against the communicator then slide the assembly on and remove the socket. Verify the brushes and retainers are fully seated.
6. Install the bearing and washer on the armature shaft. Position the end cover on the brush holder. Align the brush connector wire and grommet in the end cover and push cover in place. Install but do not tighten brush holder screws.
7. Install armature frame on the assembled armature, brush holder and shield. Be sure to align and seat the brush connector wire grommet in the frame. Install the armature ball and hold in place with chassis grease.
8. Install the armature frame on the clutch housing. Rotate the frame until the alignment tabs seat in the slots on the clutch housing. Be sure the armature shaft and splines are fully seated.
9. Install the armature frame to overrunning clutch bolts and tighten to 28 inch lbs. Tighten the brush holder screws to 18 inch lbs. Install the solenoid on the housing.

INSTALLATION

All except 4-2.1L

1. Installation is the reverse of removal.
2. Torque the mounting bolts to 33 ft. lbs. for the 6-4.0L. 18 ft.lbs. for the 4-2.5L and 6-2.8L.

4-2.1L

1. Install the starter and HAND TIGHTEN ONLY, the attaching bolts. Insure locating dowel is properly seated in hole.
2. Install the upper and lower support bracket, hand tighten only.
3. Torque the starter attaching bolts to 37 ft. lbs., then, tighten the upper bracket bolts to 37 ft. lbs. and then the lower bracket bolts, also to 37 ft. lbs.
4. Install the engine mount. Torque the engine mount-to-block bolt to 40 ft. lbs.; the engine mount-to-frame bolt to 48 ft. lbs.; the engine mount-to-bell housing bolt to 35 ft. lbs.
5. Connect all wires and lower the vehicle.

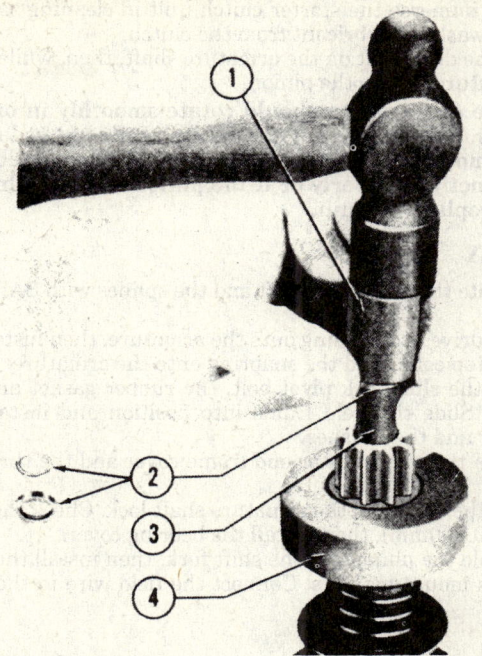

1. ½ in. pipe coupling
2. Snap-ring and retainer
3. Armature shaft
4. Drive assembly

Removing the starter drive

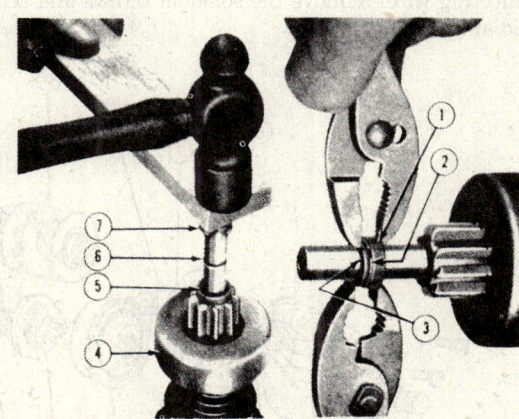

1. Retainer
2. Snap-ring
3. Thrust collar
4. Drive assembly
5. Retainer
6. Groove in the armature shaft
7. Snap-ring

Installing the pinion stop retainer and thrust collar

Starter Solenoid

TESTING

1. Before testing, assure the parking brake is set, the transmission is in PARK (automatic) or NEUTRAL (manual), and the battery is fully charged and in good condition.
2. Connect a voltmeter from the (S) terminal on the solenoid to ground. Turn the ignition switch to the START position and test for battery voltage. If battery voltage is not found, inspect the ig-

ENGINE AND ENGINE OVERHAUL 3

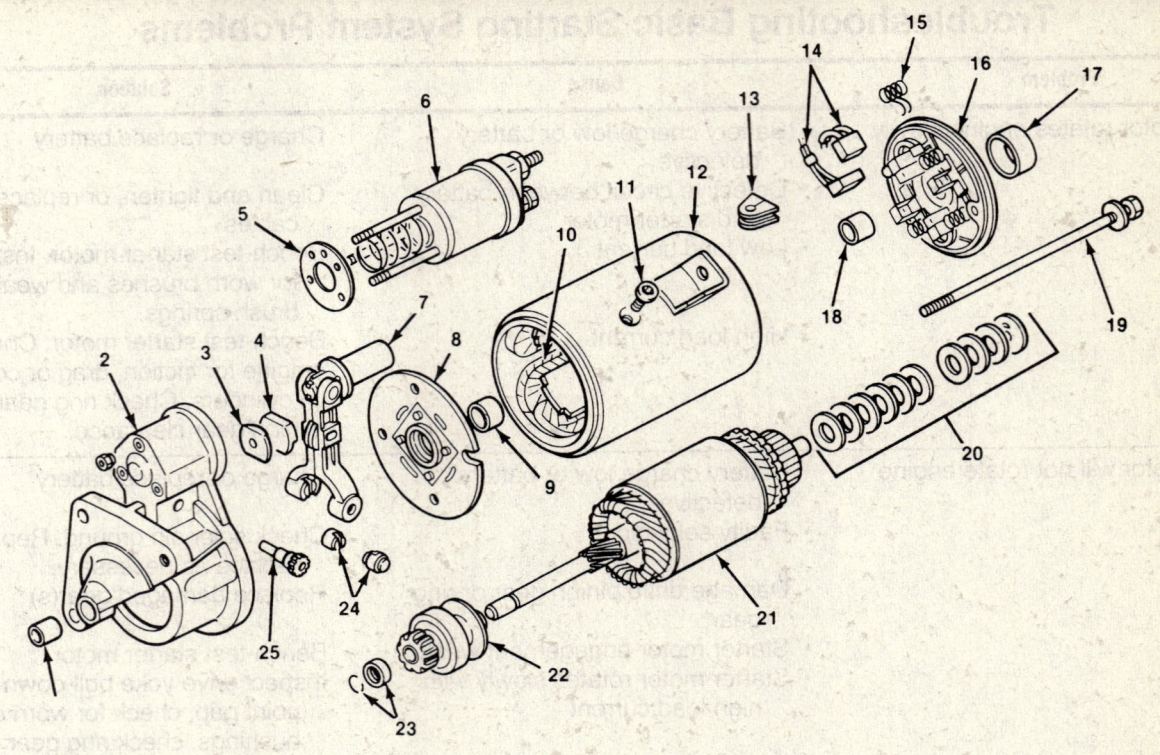

1. End housing bushing
2. Drive-end housing
3. Spacer
4. Pad
5. Solenoid plate
6. Solenoid
7. Pinion shift yoke
8. Support plate
9. Support plate bushing
10. Field winding and pole shoe sets (4)
11. Pole shoe screw (4)
12. Armature housing
13. Grommet
14. Brush set (4)
15. Brush spring (4)
16. Brush holder
17. Cap
18. Brush holder bushing
19. Through bolts (4)
20. Armature brake assembly
21. Armature
22. Starter drive pinion
23. Drive pinion stop
24. Shift yoke pivot pins
25. Shift yoke axle

Paris-Rhone starter used on the 4-2.1L

STARTER SPECIFICATIONS

Year	No. Cylinder Displacement cu. in. (liter)	MFR	Battery Volts	Cold Cranking Test Cold Cranking Volts	Cold Cranking Amps
1984–85	4-150 (2.5)	Motorcraft	12.5	9.6	120
	6-173 (2.8)	Delco	12.5	9.6	130
1986–87	4-126 (2.1)	Paris-Rhone	12.5	9.6	160
	4-150 (2.5)	Bosh	12.5	9.6	120
	6-173 (2.8)	Delco	12.5	9.6	130
	6-243 (4.0)	Mitsubishi	12.5	9.6	130
1988–91	4-150 (2.5)	Bosh	12.5	9.6	120
	6-243 (4.0)	Mitsubishi	12.5	9.6	130

3 ENGINE AND ENGINE OVERHAUL

Troubleshooting Basic Starting System Problems

Problem	Cause	Solution
Starter motor rotates engine slowly	• Battery charge low or battery defective	• Charge or replace battery
	• Defective circuit between battery and starter motor	• Clean and tighten, or replace cables
	• Low load current	• Bench-test starter motor. Inspect for worn brushes and weak brush springs.
	• High load current	• Bench-test starter motor. Check engine for friction, drag or coolant in cylinders. Check ring gear-to-pinion gear clearance.
Starter motor will not rotate engine	• Battery charge low or battery defective	• Charge or replace battery
	• Faulty solenoid	• Check solenoid ground. Repair or replace as necessary.
	• Damage drive pinion gear or ring gear	• Replace damaged gear(s)
	• Starter motor engagement weak	• Bench-test starter motor
	• Starter motor rotates slowly with high load current	• Inspect drive yoke pull-down and point gap, check for worn end bushings, check ring gear clearance
	• Engine seized	• Repair engine
Starter motor drive will not engage (solenoid known to be good)	• Defective contact point assembly	• Repair or replace contact point assembly
	• Inadequate contact point assembly ground	• Repair connection at ground screw
	• Defective hold-in coil	• Replace field winding assembly
Starter motor drive will not disengage	• Starter motor loose on flywheel housing	• Tighten mounting bolts
	• Worn drive end busing	• Replace bushing
	• Damaged ring gear teeth	• Replace ring gear or driveplate
	• Drive yoke return spring broken or missing	• Replace spring
Starter motor drive disengages prematurely	• Weak drive assembly thrust spring	• Replace drive mechanism
	• Hold-in coil defective	• Replace field winding assembly
Low load current	• Worn brushes	• Replace brushes
	• Weak brush springs	• Replace springs

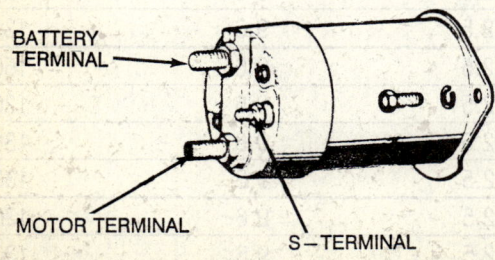

Starter mounted solenoid

nition switch circuit. If battery voltage is found, proceed to next step.

3. Connect an ohmmeter between the battery negative post and the starter solenoid mounting plate (manual) or the ground terminal (automatic). Turn the ignition switch to the START position. The ohmmeter should read zero (0). If not, repair the faulty ground.

4. If both tests are performed and the solenoid still does not energize, replace the solenoid.

ENGINE AND ENGINE OVERHAUL 3

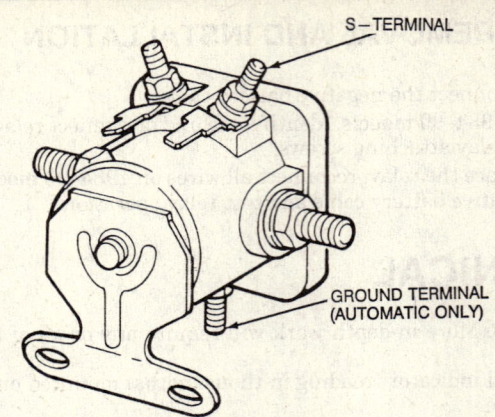

Remote mounted solenoid

REMOVAL AND INSTALLATION

Starter Mounted

NOTE: On most engines it is necessary to remove the starter. See previous section for starter removal/installation procedures

1. Disconnect negative battery cable.
2. Label and remove all wires from the solenoid. Remove the 'M' terminal bolt (Delco-Remy).
3. Remove the solenoid mounting screws. Hold the solenoid tight, there is a spring inside.
4. Remove the solenoid (by twisting on Delco-Remy units) with the armature and return spring.
5. Installation is the reverse of removal. Assure mounting surface is clean to provide a good ground.

Remotely Mounted

1. Disconnect negative battery cable.
2. Label and remove all wires from the solenoid. Remove the solenoid mounting screws.
3. Installation is the reverse of removal. Assure mounting surface is clean to provide a good ground.

Starter Relay

TESTING

1984–90

1. Insure that the transmission is in PARK (automatic) or NEUTRAL (manual) and that the parking brake is applied.
2. Turn the ignition switch to the START position and listen for the starter relay to click. If a click is heard, the relay functioning correctly. If not, go to next step.
3. Connect a jumper wire from pin G on the relay to ground. Turn the ignition switch to START and listen for click. If click is heard, repair the short to ground. If not, go to next step.
4. With starter solenoid terminal (S) disconnected (prevent terminal from touching metal parts), test for battery voltage. If battery voltage is found, replace the relay. If battery voltage is not found, repair the short to the relay terminal (SOL).

1991

1. Remove the relay from the power distribution center, located near the coolant overflow tank in the engine compartment.

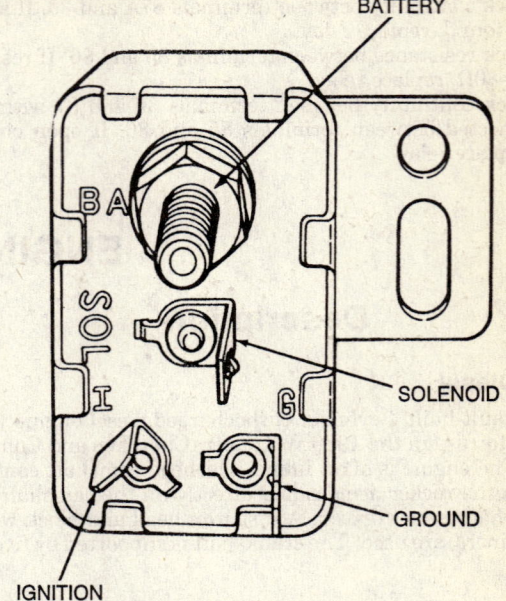

Starter relay (1984-90)

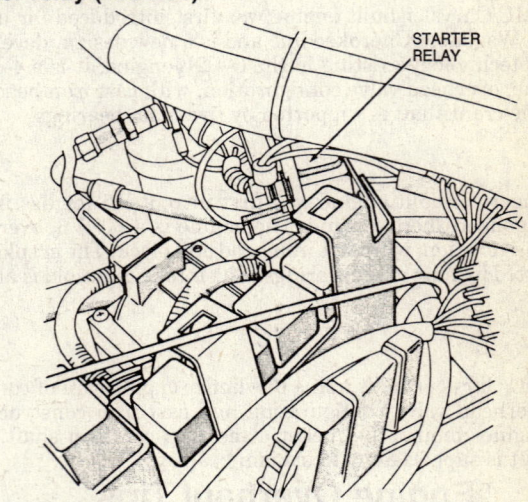

1984-90 starter relay location

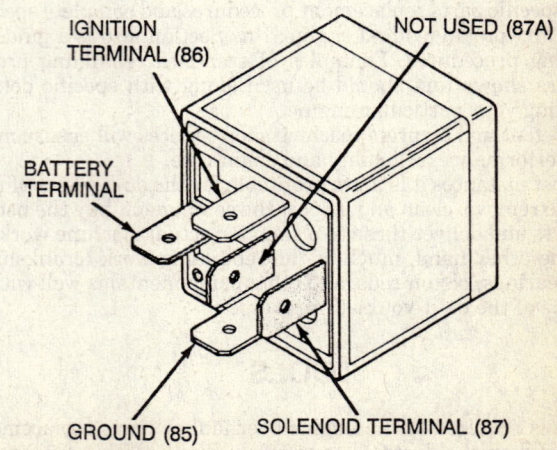

Starter relay (1991)

3-23

3 ENGINE AND ENGINE OVERHAUL

2. Check continuity between terminals 87A and 30. If an open circuit is found, replace relay.
2. Check resistance between terminals 85 and 86. If resistance is not 70–80Ω, replace relay.
2. Check continuity between terminals 30 and 87 with a battery connected between terminals 85 and 86. If open circuit is found, replace relay.

REMOVAL AND INSTALLATION

1. Disconnect the negative battery cable.
2. On 1984–90 models, identify, tag and disconnect relay wires. Remove relay attaching screws.
3. Replace the relay, reconnect all wires on 1984–90 models, replace negative battery cable and test relay operation.

ENGINE MECHANICAL

Description

4-2.1L Diesel

The Renault-built 4-cylinder turbocharged diesel engine was introduced for use in the 1986 Wagoneer, Cherokee and Comanche models. The engine is of an inline, overhead camshaft configuration, with the rocker arms riding directly on the camshaft lobes. The camshaft is belt driven. A cast iron head and block with removable liners, are used. The crankshaft is supported by five main bearings.

4-2.5L

This AMC/Chrysler-built engine was first introduced for use in the 1984 Wagoneer/Cherokee line and is a new design, developed from the technology existing in the 6-4.2L engine. It is a 4-cylinder, inline, overhead valve configuration, with cast iron head and block. The crankshaft is supported by five main bearings.

6-2.8L

This Chevrolet-built engine was first introduced for use in the 1984 Wagoneer/Cherokee line. The engine is a 60° V6, overhead valve configuration, with cast iron head and block. The crankshaft is supported by four main bearings. The intake manifold is aluminum.

6-4.0L

The AMC/Chrysler-built inline 6-cylinder engines are of conventional overhead valve configuration and cast iron construction. These engines mount the rocker arms on a common shaft. The crankshaft is supported by four main bearings.

Engine Overhaul Tips

Most engine overhaul procedures are fairly standard. In addition to specific parts replacement procedures and complete specifications for your individual engine, this Section also is a guide to rebuilding procedures. Examples of standard rebuilding procedures are shown and should be used along with specific details concerning your particular engine.

Competent and accurate machine shop services will ensure maximum performance, reliability and engine life.

In most instances it is more profitable for the do-it-yourself mechanic to remove, clean and inspect the component, buy the necessary parts and deliver these to a shop for actual machine work.

On the other hand, much of the rebuilding work (crankshaft, block, bearings, piston rods, and other components) is well within the scope of the do-it-yourself mechanic.

TOOLS

The tools required for an engine overhaul or parts replacement will depend on the depth of your involvement. With a few exceptions, they will be the tools found in a mechanic's tool kit (see Section 1). More in-depth work will require any or all of the following:
- A dial indicator (reading in thousandths) mounted on a universal base
- Micrometers and telescope gauges
- Jaw and screw-type pullers
- Scraper
- Valve spring compressor
- Ring groove cleaner
- Piston ring expander and compressor
- Ridge reamer
- Cylinder hone or glaze breaker
- Plastigage®
- Engine stand

The use of most of these tools is illustrated in this Section. Many can be rented for a one-time use from a local parts jobber or tool supply house specializing in automotive work.

Occasionally, the use of special tools is called for. See the information on Special Tools and Safety Notice in the front of this book before substituting another tool.

INSPECTION TECHNIQUES

Procedures and specifications are given in this Section for inspecting, cleaning and assessing the wear limits of most major components. Other procedures such as Magnaflux® and Zyglo® can be used to locate material flaws and stress cracks. Magnaflux® is a magnetic process applicable only to ferrous materials. The Zyglo® process coats the material with a fluorescent dye penetrant and can be used on any material to check for suspected surface cracks. The dye is sprayed onto the suspected area, wiped off and the area sprayed with a developer. Cracks will show up brightly.

OVERHAUL TIPS

Aluminum has become extremely popular for use in engines, due to its low weight. Observe the following precautions when handling aluminum parts:
- Never hot tank aluminum parts (the caustic hot tank solution will eat the aluminum.
- Remove all aluminum parts (identification tag, etc.) from engine parts prior to the tanking.
- Always coat threads lightly with engine oil or anti-seize compounds before installation, to prevent seizure.
- Never over-torque bolts or spark plugs especially in aluminum threads.

Stripped threads in any component can be repaired using any of several commercial repair kits (Heli-Coil®, Microdot®, Keenserts®, etc.).

When assembling the engine, any parts that will be frictional contact must be prelubed to provide lubrication at initial start-up. Any product specifically formulated for this purpose can be used, but engine oil is not recommended as a prelube.

When semi-permanent (locked, but removable) installation of bolts or nuts is desired, threads should be cleaned and coated with

ENGINE AND ENGINE OVERHAUL 3

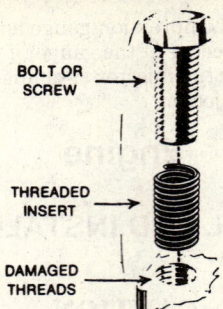

Damaged bolt holes cane be repaired with thread repair inserts

Loctite® or other similar, commercial non-hardening sealant (not recommended for use on aluminum parts).

REPAIRING DAMAGED THREADS

Several methods of repairing damaged threads are available. Heli-Coil® (shown here), Keenserts® and Microdot® are among the most widely used. All involve basically the same principle—drilling out stripped threads, tapping the hole and installing a prewound insert—making welding, plugging and oversize fasteners unnecessary.

Two types of thread repair inserts are usually supplied: a standard type for most Inch Coarse, Inch Fine, Metric Course and Metric Fine thread sizes and a spark lug type to fit most spark plug port sizes. Consult the individual manufacturer's catalog to determine exact applications. Typical thread repair kits will contain a selection of prewound threaded inserts, a tap (corresponding to the outside diameter threads of the insert) and an installation tool. Spark plug inserts usually differ because they require a tap equipped with pilot threads and a combined reamer/tap section. Most manufacturers also supply blister-packed thread repair inserts separately in addition to a master kit containing a variety of taps and inserts plus installation tools.

Before effecting a repair to a threaded hole, remove any snapped, broken or damaged bolts or studs. Penetrating oil can be used to free frozen threads; the offending item can be removed with locking pliers or with a screw or stud extractor. After the hole is clear, the thread can be repaired, as follows:

Checking Engine Compression

A noticeable lack of engine power, excessive oil consumption and/or poor fuel mileage measured over an extended period are all indicators of internal engine war. Worn piston rings, scored or worn cylinder bores, blown head gaskets, sticking or burnt valves and worn valve seats are all possible culprits here. A check of each cylinder's compression will help you locate the problems.

As mentioned in the Tools and Equipment section of Section 1, a screw-in type compression gauge is more accurate that the type you simply hold against the spark plug hole, although it takes slightly longer to use. It's worth it to obtain a more accurate reading. Follow the procedures below for gasoline and diesel engines trucks.

GASOLINE ENGINES

1. Warm up the engine to normal operating temperature.
2. Remove all spark plugs.
3. Disconnect the high tension lead from the ignition coil.
4. On fully open the throttle either by operating the carburetor throttle linkage by hand or by having an assistant floor the accelerator pedal.

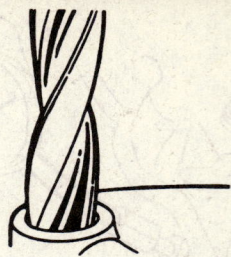

Drill out the damaged threads with specified drill. Drill completely through the hole or to the bottom of a blind hole

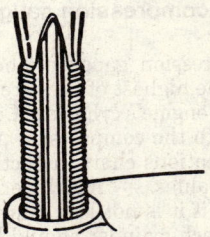

With the tap supplied, tap the hole to receive the thread insert. Keep the tap well oiled and back it out frequently to avoid clogging the threads

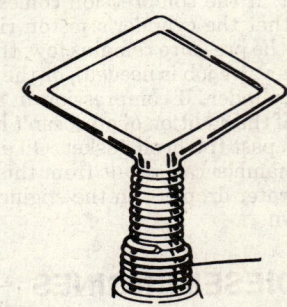

Screw the threaded insert onto the installation tool until the tang engages the slot. Screw the insert into the tapped hole until it is 1/4-1/2 turn below the surface. After installation break off the tang with a hammer and punch

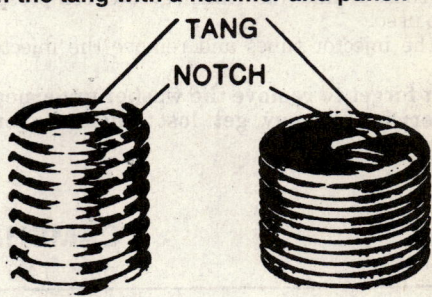

Standard thread repair insert (left) and spark plug thread insert (right)

5. Screw the compression gauge into the no.1 spark plug hole until the fitting is snug.

NOTE: Be careful not to crossthread the plug hole. On aluminum cylinder heads use extra care, as the threads in these heads are easily ruined.

6. Ask an assistant to depress the accelerator pedal fully on both carbureted and fuel injected trucks. Then, while you read the compression gauge, ask the assistant to crank the engine two or three times in short bursts using the ignition switch.

3-25

3 ENGINE AND ENGINE OVERHAUL

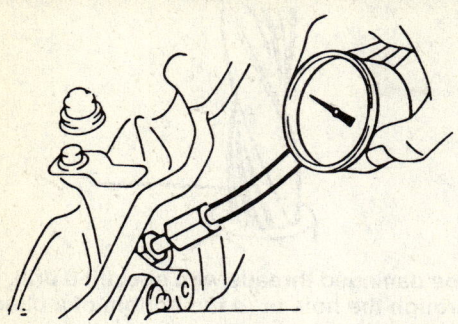

The screw-in type compression gauge is more accurate

7. Read the compression gauge at the end of each series of cranks, and record the highest of these readings. Repeat this procedure for each of the engine's cylinders. Compare the highest reading of each cylinder to the compression pressure specification in the Tune-Up Specifications chart in Section 2. The specs in this chart are maximum values. A cylinder's compression pressure is usually acceptable if it is not less than 80% of maximum. The difference between each cylinder should be no more than 12–14 pounds.

8. If a cylinder is unusually low, pour a tablespoon of clean engine oil into the cylinder through the spark plug hole and repeat the compression test. If the compression comes up after adding the oil, it indicates that the cylinder's piston rings or bore may damaged or worn. If the pressure remains low, the valves may not be seating properly (a valve job is needed), or the head gasket may be blown near that cylinder. If compression in any two adjacent cylinders is low, and if the addition of oil doesn't help the compression, there is leakage past the head gasket. Oil and coolant water in the combustion chamber can result from this problem. There may be evidence of water droplets on the engine dipstick when a head gasket has blown.

DIESEL ENGINES

Checking cylinder compression on diesel engines is basically the same procedure as on gasoline engines except for the following:

1. A special compression gauge adaptor suitable for diesel engines (because these engines have much greater compression pressures) must be used.
2. Remove the injector tubes and remove the injectors from each cylinder.

NOTE: Don't forget to remove the washer underneath each injector; otherwise, it may get lost when the engine is cranked.

3. When fitting the compression gauge adaptor to the cylinder head, make sure the bleeder of the gauge (if equipped) is closed.
4. When reinstalling the injector assemblies, install new washers underneath each injector.

Engine

REMOVAL AND INSTALLATION

4-2.1L Diesel

— **CAUTION** —
The following procedure requires the discharge of the air conditioning refrigerant. See Section 1. If you are not thoroughly familiar with the handling of refrigerant, leave this to someone who is. Severe personal injury will result from accidental contact with refrigerant.

1. Disconnect the battery cables and remove the battery. Remove the hood.
2. If equipped, remove the skid plate.
3. Drain the radiator. Remove the air cleaner assembly.

— **CAUTION** —
When draining the coolant, keep in mind that cats and dogs are attracted by the ethylene glycol antifreeze, and are quite likely to drink any that is left in an uncovered container or in puddles on the ground. This will prove fatal in sufficient quantity. Always drain the coolant into a sealable container. Coolant should be reused unless it is contaminated or several years old.

4. If equipped, discharge the air conditioning compressor. Be sure to observe all safety precautions.
5. Disconnect the radiator hoses and remove the E-clip from the bottom of the radiator.
6. Raise and support the vehicle safely. If the vehicle is equipped with automatic transmission disconnect the oil cooler lines at the radiator.
7. Remove the splash shield from the oil pan. Lower the vehicle.
8. Loosen the radiator shroud and remove the radiator fan as-

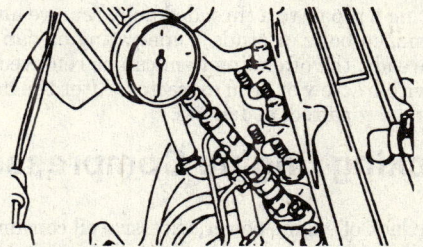

Diesel engines require a special compression adapter

CAMSHAFT SPECIFICATIONS
(All specifications in inches)

Engine	Journal Diameter					Bearing Clearance	Lobe Lift		End Play
	1	2	3	4	5		Int.	Exh.	
4-126	NA	NA	NA	NA	NA	NA	NA	NA	0.001–0.005
4-150	2.0300–2.0290	2.0200–2.0190	2.0100–2.0090	2.0000–1.9990	—	0.0010–0.0030	0.2650	0.2650	0.
6-173	1.8690–1.8670	1.8690–1.8670	1.8690–1.8670	—	—	0.0010–0.0039	0.2311	0.2625	0
6-243	2.0300–2.0290	2.0200–2.0190	2.0100–2.009	2.0000–1.9990	—	0.0010–0.0030	0.2530	0.2530	0

ENGINE AND ENGINE OVERHAUL 3

Standard Torque Specifications and Fastener Markings

In the absence of specific torques, the following chart can be used as a guide to the maximum safe torque of a particular size/grade of fastener.
- There is no torque difference for fine or coarse threads.
- Torque values are based on clean, dry threads. Reduce the value by 10% if threads are oiled prior to assembly.
- The torque required for aluminum components or fasteners is considerably less.

U.S. Bolts

SAE Grade Number	1 or 2			5			6 or 7		
Number of lines always 2 less than the grade number.									
Bolt Size (Inches)—(Thread)	Maximum Torque			Maximum Torque			Maximum Torque		
	Ft./Lbs.	Kgm	Nm	Ft./Lbs.	Kgm	Nm	Ft./Lbs.	Kgm	Nm
¼ — 20	5	0.7	6.8	8	1.1	10.8	10	1.4	13.5
— 28	6	0.8	8.1	10	1.4	13.6			
5/16 — 18	11	1.5	14.9	17	2.3	23.0	19	2.6	25.8
— 24	13	1.8	17.6	19	2.6	25.7			
3/8 — 16	18	2.5	24.4	31	4.3	42.0	34	4.7	46.0
— 24	20	2.75	27.1	35	4.8	47.5			
7/16 — 14	28	3.8	37.0	49	6.8	66.4	55	7.6	74.5
— 20	30	4.2	40.7	55	7.6	74.5			
½ — 13	39	5.4	52.8	75	10.4	101.7	85	11.75	115.2
— 20	41	5.7	55.6	85	11.7	115.2			
9/16 — 12	51	7.0	69.2	110	15.2	149.1	120	16.6	162.7
— 18	55	7.6	74.5	120	16.6	162.7			
5/8 — 11	83	11.5	112.5	150	20.7	203.3	167	23.0	226.5
— 18	95	13.1	128.8	170	23.5	230.5			
¾ — 10	105	14.5	142.3	270	37.3	366.0	280	38.7	379.6
— 16	115	15.9	155.9	295	40.8	400.0			
7/8 — 9	160	22.1	216.9	395	54.6	535.5	440	60.9	596.5
— 14	175	24.2	237.2	435	60.1	589.7			
1 — 8	236	32.5	318.6	590	81.6	799.9	660	91.3	894.8
— 14	250	34.6	338.9	660	91.3	849.8			

Metric Bolts

Relative Strength Marking	4.6, 4.8			8.8		
Bolt Markings						
Bolt Size Thread Size x Pitch (mm)	Maximum Torque			Maximum Torque		
	Ft./Lbs.	Kgm	Nm	Ft./Lbs.	Kgm	Nm
6 x 1.0	2–3	.2–.4	3–4	3–6	.4–.8	5–8
8 x 1.25	6–8	.8–1	8–12	9–14	1.2–1.9	13–19
10 x 1.25	12–17	1.5–2.3	16–23	20–29	2.7–4.0	27–39
12 x 1.25	21–32	2.9–4.4	29–43	35–53	4.8–7.3	47–72
14 x 1.5	35–52	4.8–7.1	48–70	57–85	7.8–11.7	77–110
16 x 1.5	51–77	7.0–10.6	67–100	90–120	12.4–16.5	130–160
18 x 1.5	74–110	10.2–15.1	100–150	130–170	17.9–23.4	180–230
20 x 1.5	110–140	15.1–19.3	150–190	190–240	26.2–46.9	160–320
22 x 1.5	150–190	22.0–26.2	200–260	250–320	34.5–44.1	340–430
24 x 1.5	190–240	26.2–46.9	260–320	310–410	42.7–56.5	420–550

3 ENGINE AND ENGINE OVERHAUL

GENERAL ENGINE SPECIFICATIONS

Engine	Years	Fuel System Type	SAE net Horsepower @ rpm	SAE net Torque ft. lb. @ rpm	Bore × Stroke (in.)	Comp. Ratio	Oil Press. (psi.) @ 2000 rpm
4-126	1986–87	Diesel	85 @ 3750	132 @ 2750	3.503 × 3.358	21.5:1	43
4-150	1984–85	1-bbl	83 @ 4200	116 @ 2600	3.876 × 3.188	9.2:1	40
	1986–91	TBI	117 @ 5000	135 @ 3000	3.876 × 3.188	9.2:1	40
6-173	1984–85	2-bbl	115 @ 4800	150 @ 3500	3.500 × 2.990	8.5:1	45
6-243	1987–91	MFI	150 @ 4300	210 @ 2100	3.874 × 3.441	8.8:1	40

VALVE SPECIFICATIONS

Engines	Seat Angle (deg)	Face Angle (deg)	Spring Test Pressure (lbs. @ in.)	Spring Installed Height (in.)	Stem-to-Guide Clearance (in.) Intake	Stem-to-Guide Clearance (in.) Exhaust	Stem Diameter (in.) Intake	Stem Diameter (in.) Exhaust
4-126	45	45	135 @ 1.173	1.547	0.0010–0.0030	0.0010–0.0030	0.3140	0.3140
4-150	44.5	①	②	③	0.0010–0.0030	0.0010–0.0030	0.3110–0.3120	0.3110–0.3120
6-173	46	45	195 @ 1.180	1.570	0.0010–0.0027	0.0010–0.0027	0.3410–0.3416	0.3410–0.3416
6-243	44.5	45	210 @ 1.200	1.625	0.0010–0.0030	0.0010–0.0030	0.3120	0.3120

① 1984–85: 44
   1986–89: 45
② 1984–85: 212 @ 1.203
   1986–91: 200 @ 1.216
③ 1984–85: 1.625
   1986–91: 1.640

TORQUE SPECIFICATIONS
(All specifications in ft. lbs.)

Engines	Cyl. Head	Conn. Rod	Main Bearing	Crankshaft Damper	Flywheel	Manifold Intake	Manifold Exhaust
4-126	70–77 ⑥	48	69	96	44	15–20	15–20
4-150	80–90 ⑤	30–35	75–85	75–85	50 ①	20–25	20–25 ④
6-173	65–75	34–40	63–74	66–84	45–55	20–25	22–28
6-243	②	30–35	80	80	100–110	20–25	③

① Plus a 60 degree turn
② See the illustration accompanying the text.
   Bolt #11: 100 ft. lbs.
   All other bolts: 110 ft. lbs.
③ Middle nuts: 30 ft. lbs.
   Outside nuts: 23 ft. lbs.
④ 1988–91: 30 ft. lbs.
⑤ See the illustration accompanying the text.
   Fuel Injected Engines
   Bolt #8: 100 ft. lbs.
   All other bolts: 110 ft. lbs.
⑥ First tightening 22 ft. lbs.
   Second 37 ft. lbs.
   Third 70–77 ft. lbs.
   Fourth 70–77 ft. lbs.

ENGINE AND ENGINE OVERHAUL 3

CRANKSHAFT AND CONNECTING ROD SPECIFICATIONS
(All specifications in inches)

Engines	Crankshaft Main Bearing Journal Dia.	Main Bearing Oil Clearance	Shaft End Play	Thrust on No.	Connecting Rod Journal Dia.	Connecting Rod Oil Clearance	Side Clearance
4-126	2.4750	0.0098	0.0055–0.0090	3	2.2163	0.0098	0.012–0.019
4-150	2.4996–2.5001	0.0010–0.0025	0.0015–0.0065	2	2.2080–2.2085	②	0.010–0.019
6-173	①	0.0016–0.0030	0.0020–0.0060	3	1.9980–1.9990	0.0010–0.0030	0.006–0.017
6-243	2.4996–2.5001	0.0010–0.0025	0.0015–0.0065	3	2.2080–2.2085	0.0010–0.0030	0.010–0.019

① Nos. 1, 2, 4: 2.4930–2.24940
  No. 3: 2.4920–2.4930
② 1984–85: 0.0010–0.0030
  1986–91: 0.0010–0.0025

PISTON AND RING SPECIFICATIONS
(All specifications in inches)

Engines	Ring Gap #1 Compr.	Ring Gap #2 Compr.	Ring Gap Oil Control	Ring Side Clearance #1 Compr.	Ring Side Clearance #2 Compr.	Ring Side Clearance Oil Control	Piston-to-Bore* Clearance
4-150	0.0100–0.0200	0.0100–0.0200	①	②	②	③	④
6-173	0.0098–0.0196	0.0098–0.0196	0.0200–0.0550	0.0010–0.0027	0.0015–0.0037	0.0078 max.	0.0006–0.0016
6-243	0.0100–0.0200	0.0100–0.0200	0.0100–0.0250	0.0017–0.0032	0.0017–0.0032	0.0010–0.0095	0.0009–0.0017

*Measured at the skirt
NOTE: For the 4-126 Turbo Diesel, pistons, rings and cylinder liners are installed as a matched set. Specifications for individual parts are not applicable.
① 1984–85: 0.0100–0.0250
  1986–91: 0.0150–0.0550
② 1984–85: 0.0017–0.0032
  1986–91: 0.0010–0.0032
③ 1984–85: 0.0010–0.0080
  1986–88: 0.0078 max.
  1989–91: 0.001–0.0085
④ 1984–88: 0.0006–0.0016
  1989–91: 0.0013–0.0021

sembly. Remove the shroud and the splash shield.
9. Remove the radiator and the condenser assembly from the vehicle. Remove the inner cooler.
10. Remove the exhaust shield from the manifold. Disconnect the hoses at the remote oil filter. Remove the oil filter.
11. Tag and disconnect all vacuum hoses and electrical connections. Disconnect and plug the fuel inlet and outlet lines at the fuel pump.
12. If equipped with automatic transmission, remove the left motor mount through bolt retaining nut.
13. Remove the motor mount retaining bolts. Disconnect the accelerator cable. Raise and support the vehicle safely.
14. Disconnect and drain the power steering hoses at the power steering pump.
15. Disconnect the exhaust pipe at the exhaust manifold. Remove the motor mount retaining nuts.
16. Support the engine. Remove the left motor mount bolts. On automatic transmission equipped vehicles, remove the left motor mount.
17. Remove the starter.
18. If the vehicle is equipped with automatic transmission, mark and remove the converter-to-drive plate bolts through the starter opening. Install the left motor mount and retaining bolts finger tight. Install the motor mount cushion through bolt. Remove the engine support.
19. Remove the accessible transmission-to-engine retaining bolts.
20. Lower the vehicle. Remove the remaining engine-to-transmission retaining bolts.
21. Remove the power steering pump from the engine. Remove the oil separator and disconnect the hoses. Disconnect the heater hoses.
22. Remove the reference pressure regulator from the dash panel. Install the engine lifting device and position a jack under the transmission.
23. Remove the engine from the vehicle.
To install:
24. Lower the engine into the vehicle.
NOTE: It may be necessary to remove the engine mount cushions to ease alignment of the engine.
25. On trucks with a manual transmission, slide the transmission input shaft into the clutch splines, align the flywheel housing bolt holes and install the lower bolts finger tight.
26. On trucks with an automatic transmission, align the torque

3 ENGINE AND ENGINE OVERHAUL

Troubleshooting Engine Mechanical Problems

Problem	Cause	Solution
External oil leaks	• Fuel pump gasket broken or improperly seated	• Replace gasket
	• Cylinder head cover RTV sealant broken or improperly seated	• Replace sealant; inspect cylinder head cover sealant flange and cylinder head sealant surface for distortion and cracks
	• Oil filler cap leaking or missing	• Replace cap
External oil leaks	• Oil filter gasket broken or improperly seated	• Replace oil filter
	• Oil pan side gasket broken, improperly seated or opening in RTV sealant	• Replace gasket or repair opening in sealant; inspect oil pan gasket flange for distortion
	• Oil pan front oil seal broken or improperly seated	• Replace seal; inspect timing case cover and oil pan seal flange for distortion
	• Oil pan rear oil seal broken or improperly seated	• Replace seal; inspect oil pan rear oil seal flange; inspect rear main bearing cap for cracks, plugged oil return channels, or distortion in seal groove
	• Timing case cover oil seal broken or improperly seated	• Replace seal
	• Excess oil pressure because of restricted PCV valve	• Replace PCV valve
	• Oil pan drain plug loose or has stripped threads	• Repair as necessary and tighten
	• Rear oil gallery plug loose	• Use appropriate sealant on gallery plug and tighten
	• Rear camshaft plug loose or improperly seated	• Seat camshaft plug or replace and seal, as necessary
	• Distributor base gasket damaged	• Replace gasket
Excessive oil consumption	• Oil level too high	• Drain oil to specified level
	• Oil with wrong viscosity being used	• Replace with specified oil
	• PCV valve stuck closed	• Replace PCV valve
	• Valve stem oil deflectors (or seals) are damaged, missing, or incorrect type	• Replace valve stem oil deflectors
	• Valve stems or valve guides worn	• Measure stem-to-guide clearance and repair as necessary
	• Poorly fitted or missing valve cover baffles	• Replace valve cover
	• Piston rings broken or missing	• Replace broken or missing rings
	• Scuffed piston	• Replace piston
	• Incorrect piston ring gap	• Measure ring gap, repair as necessary
	• Piston rings sticking or excessively loose in grooves	• Measure ring side clearance, repair as necessary
	• Compression rings installed upside down	• Repair as necessary
	• Cylinder walls worn, scored, or glazed	• Repair as necessary

ENGINE AND ENGINE OVERHAUL 3

Troubleshooting Engine Mechanical Problems (cont.)

Problem	Cause	Solution
	• Piston ring gaps not properly staggered	• Repair as necessary
	• Excessive main or connecting rod bearing clearance	• Measure bearing clearance, repair as necessary
No oil pressure	• Low oil level	• Add oil to correct level
	• Oil pressure gauge, warning lamp or sending unit inaccurate	• Replace oil pressure gauge or warning lamp
	• Oil pump malfunction	• Replace oil pump
	• Oil pressure relief valve sticking	• Remove and inspect oil pressure relief valve assembly
	• Oil passages on pressure side of pump obstructed	• Inspect oil passages for obstruction
	• Oil pickup screen or tube obstructed	• Inspect oil pickup for obstruction
	• Loose oil inlet tube	• Tighten or seal inlet tube
Low oil pressure	• Low oil level	• Add oil to correct level
	• Inaccurate gauge, warning lamp or sending unit	• Replace oil pressure gauge or warning lamp
	• Oil excessively thin because of dilution, poor quality, or improper grade	• Drain and refill crankcase with recommended oil
	• Excessive oil temperature	• Correct cause of overheating engine
	• Oil pressure relief spring weak or sticking	• Remove and inspect oil pressure relief valve assembly
	• Oil inlet tube and screen assembly has restriction or air leak	• Remove and inspect oil inlet tube and screen assembly. (Fill inlet tube with lacquer thinner to locate leaks.)
	• Excessive oil pump clearance	• Measure clearances
	• Excessive main, rod, or camshaft bearing clearance	• Measure bearing clearances, repair as necessary
High oil pressure	• Improper oil viscosity	• Drain and refill crankcase with correct viscosity oil
	• Oil pressure gauge or sending unit inaccurate	• Replace oil pressure gauge
	• Oil pressure relief valve sticking closed	• Remove and inspect oil pressure relief valve assembly
Main bearing noise	• Insufficient oil supply	• Inspect for low oil level and low oil pressure
	• Main bearing clearance excessive	• Measure main bearing clearance, repair as necessary
	• Bearing insert missing	• Replace missing insert
	• Crankshaft end play excessive	• Measure end play, repair as necessary
	• Improperly tightened main bearing cap bolts	• Tighten bolts with specified torque
	• Loose flywheel or drive plate	• Tighten flywheel or drive plate attaching bolts
	• Loose or damaged vibration damper	• Repair as necessary

3-31

3 ENGINE AND ENGINE OVERHAUL

Troubleshooting Engine Mechanical Problems (cont.)

Problem	Cause	Solution
Connecting rod bearing noise	• Insufficient oil supply	• Inspect for low oil level and low oil pressure
	• Carbon build-up on piston	• Remove carbon from piston crown
	• Bearing clearance excessive or bearing missing	• Measure clearance, repair as necessary
	• Crankshaft connecting rod journal out-of-round	• Measure journal dimensions, repair or replace as necessary
	• Misaligned connecting rod or cap	• Repair as necessary
	• Connecting rod bolts tightened improperly	• Tighten bolts with specified torque
Piston noise	• Piston-to-cylinder wall clearance excessive (scuffed piston)	• Measure clearance and examine piston
	• Cylinder walls excessively tapered or out-of-round	• Measure cylinder wall dimensions, rebore cylinder
	• Piston ring broken	• Replace all rings on piston
	• Loose or seized piston pin	• Measure piston-to-pin clearance, repair as necessary
	• Connecting rods misaligned	• Measure rod alignment, straighten or replace
	• Piston ring side clearance excessively loose or tight	• Measure ring side clearance, repair as necessary
	• Carbon build-up on piston is excessive	• Remove carbon from piston
Valve actuating component noise	• Insufficient oil supply	• Check for: (a) Low oil level (b) Low oil pressure (c) Plugged push rods (d) Wrong hydraulic tappets (e) Restricted oil gallery (f) Excessive tappet to bore clearance
	• Push rods worn or bent	• Replace worn or bent push rods
	• Rocker arms or pivots worn	• Replace worn rocker arms or pivots
	• Foreign objects or chips in hydraulic tappets	• Clean tappets
	• Excessive tappet leak-down	• Replace valve tappet
	• Tappet face worn	• Replace tappet; inspect corresponding cam lobe for wear
	• Broken or cocked valve springs	• Properly seat cocked springs; replace broken springs
	• Stem-to-guide clearance excessive	• Measure stem-to-guide clearance, repair as required
	• Valve bent	• Replace valve
	• Loose rocker arms	• Tighten bolts with specified torque
	• Valve seat runout excessive	• Regrind valve seat/valves
	• Missing valve lock	• Install valve lock
	• Push rod rubbing or contacting cylinder head	• Remove cylinder head and remove obstruction in head
	• Excessive engine oil (four-cylinder engine)	• Correct oil level

ENGINE AND ENGINE OVERHAUL 3

Troubleshooting the Cooling System

Problem	Cause	Solution
High temperature gauge indication—overheating	• Coolant level low • Fan belt loose • Radiator hose(s) collapsed • Radiator airflow blocked • Faulty radiator cap • Ignition timing incorrect • Idle speed low • Air trapped in cooling system • Heavy traffic driving • Incorrect cooling system component(s) installed • Faulty thermostat • Water pump shaft broken or impeller loose • Radiator tubes clogged • Cooling system clogged • Casting flash in cooling passages • Brakes dragging • Excessive engine friction • Antifreeze concentration over 68% • Missing air seals • Faulty gauge or sending unit • Loss of coolant flow caused by leakage or foaming • Viscous fan drive failed	• Replenish coolant • Adjust fan belt tension • Replace hose(s) • Remove restriction (bug screen, fog lamps, etc.) • Replace radiator cap • Adjust ignition timing • Adjust idle speed • Purge air • Operate at fast idle in neutral intermittently to cool engine • Install proper component(s) • Replace thermostat • Replace water pump • Flush radiator • Flush system • Repair or replace as necessary. Flash may be visible by removing cooling system components or removing core plugs. • Repair brakes • Repair engine • Lower antifreeze concentration percentage • Replace air seals • Repair or replace faulty component • Repair or replace leaking component, replace coolant • Replace unit
Low temperature indication—undercooling	• Thermostat stuck open • Faulty gauge or sending unit	• Replace thermostat • Repair or replace faulty component
Coolant loss—boilover	• Overfilled cooling system • Quick shutdown after hard (hot) run • Air in system resulting in occasional "burping" of coolant • Insufficient antifreeze allowing coolant boiling point to be too low • Antifreeze deteriorated because of age or contamination • Leaks due to loose hose clamps, loose nuts, bolts, drain plugs, faulty hoses, or defective radiator	• Reduce coolant level to proper specification • Allow engine to run at fast idle prior to shutdown • Purge system • Add antifreeze to raise boiling point • Replace coolant • Pressure test system to locate source of leak(s) then repair as necessary

3 ENGINE AND ENGINE OVERHAUL

Troubleshooting the Cooling System (cont.)

Problem	Cause	Solution
Coolant loss—boilover	• Faulty head gasket • Cracked head, manifold, or block • Faulty radiator cap	• Replace head gasket • Replace as necessary • Replace cap
Coolant entry into crankcase or cylinder(s)	• Faulty head gasket • Crack in head, manifold or block	• Replace head gasket • Replace as necessary
Coolant recovery system inoperative	• Coolant level low • Leak in system • Pressure cap not tight or seal missing, or leaking • Pressure cap defective • Overflow tube clogged or leaking • Recovery bottle vent restricted	• Replenish coolant to FULL mark • Pressure test to isolate leak and repair as necessary • Repair as necessary • Replace cap • Repair as necessary • Remove restriction
Noise	• Fan contacting shroud • Loose water pump impeller • Glazed fan belt • Loose fan belt • Rough surface on drive pulley • Water pump bearing worn • Belt alignment	• Reposition shroud and inspect engine mounts • Replace pump • Apply silicone or replace belt • Adjust fan belt tension • Replace pulley • Remove belt to isolate. Replace pump. • Check pulley alignment. Repair as necessary.
No coolant flow through heater core	• Restricted return inlet in water pump • Heater hose collapsed or restricted • Restricted heater core • Restricted outlet in thermostat housing • Intake manifold bypass hole in cylinder head restricted • Faulty heater control valve • Intake manifold coolant passage restricted	• Remove restriction • Remove restriction or replace hose • Remove restriction or replace core • Remove flash or restriction • Remove restriction • Replace valve • Remove restriction or replace intake manifold

NOTE: *Immediately after shutdown, the engine enters a condition known as heat soak. This is caused by the cooling system being inoperative while engine temperature is still high. If coolant temperature rises above boiling point, expansion and pressure may push some coolant out of the radiator overflow tube. If this does not occur frequently it is considered normal.*

converter housing and engine and install the lower bolts finger tight.
27. Install all remaining bolts. Torque all bolts to 30 ft. lbs.
28. Install any engine mount cushions previously removed.
29. Remove the engine lifting device.
30. If the vehicle is equipped with automatic transmission, install the converter-to-drive plate bolts through the starter opening. Torque the bolts to 40 ft. lbs.
41. Install the starter.
42. Tighten all engine mount bolts to 30 ft. lbs.
43. Install the power steering pump. Tighten the rear bracket-to-block bolt to 20 ft. lbs.; all other bolts to 28 ft. lbs.
44. Connect the exhaust pipe at the exhaust manifold.
45. Install the oil filter and lines.
46. Install the oil separator and connect the hoses.
47. Connect the heater hoses.
48. Connect all vacuum hoses and electrical connections.
49. Connect the fuel inlet and outlet lines at the fuel pump.
50. Install the reference pressure regulator from the dash panel.
51. Connect the accelerator cable.
52. Install the exhaust shield at the manifold.
53. Install the radiator and the condenser assembly from the vehicle.
54. Install the inner cooler.
55. Install the radiator fan assembly.
56. Install the shroud and the splash shield.

ENGINE AND ENGINE OVERHAUL 3

Troubleshooting the Serpentine Drive Belt

Problem	Cause	Solution
Tension sheeting fabric failure (woven fabric on outside circumference of belt has cracked or separated from body of belt)	• Grooved or backside idler pulley diameters are less than minimum recommended • Tension sheeting contacting (rubbing) stationary object • Excessive heat causing woven fabric to age • Tension sheeting splice has fractured	• Replace pulley(s) not conforming to specification • Correct rubbing condition • Replace belt • Replace belt
Noise (objectional squeal, squeak, or rumble is heard or felt while drive belt is in operation)	• Belt slippage • Bearing noise • Belt misalignment • Belt-to-pulley mismatch • Driven component inducing vibration • System resonant frequency inducing vibration	• Adjust belt • Locate and repair • Align belt/pulley(s) • Install correct belt • Locate defective driven component and repair • Vary belt tension within specifications. Replace belt.
Rib chunking (one or more ribs has separated from belt body)	• Foreign objects imbedded in pulley grooves • Installation damage • Drive loads in excess of design specifications • Insufficient internal belt adhesion	• Remove foreign objects from pulley grooves • Replace belt • Adjust belt tension • Replace belt
Rib or belt wear (belt ribs contact bottom of pulley grooves)	• Pulley(s) misaligned • Mismatch of belt and pulley groove widths • Abrasive environment • Rusted pulley(s) • Sharp or jagged pulley groove tips • Rubber deteriorated	• Align pulley(s) • Replace belt • Replace belt • Clean rust from pulley(s) • Replace pulley • Replace belt
Longitudinal belt cracking (cracks between two ribs)	• Belt has mistracked from pulley groove • Pulley groove tip has worn away rubber-to-tensile member	• Replace belt • Replace belt
Belt slips	• Belt slipping because of insufficient tension • Belt or pulley subjected to substance (belt dressing, oil, ethylene glycol) that has reduced friction • Driven component bearing failure • Belt glazed and hardened from heat and excessive slippage	• Adjust tension • Replace belt and clean pulleys • Replace faulty component bearing • Replace belt
"Groove jumping" (belt does not maintain correct position on pulley, or turns over and/or runs off pulleys)	• Insufficient belt tension • Pulley(s) not within design tolerance • Foreign object(s) in grooves	• Adjust belt tension • Replace pulley(s) • Remove foreign objects from grooves

3 ENGINE AND ENGINE OVERHAUL

Troubleshooting the Serpentine Drive Belt (cont.)

Problem	Cause	Solution
"Groove jumping" (belt does not maintain correct position on pulley, or turns over and/or runs off pulleys)	• Excessive belt speed • Pulley misalignment • Belt-to-pulley profile mismatched • Belt cordline is distorted	• Avoid excessive engine acceleration • Align pulley(s) • Install correct belt • Replace belt
Belt broken (Note: identify and correct problem before replacement belt is installed)	• Excessive tension • Tensile members damaged during belt installation • Belt turnover • Severe pulley misalignment • Bracket, pulley, or bearing failure	• Replace belt and adjust tension to specification • Replace belt • Replace belt • Align pulley(s) • Replace defective component and belt
Cord edge failure (tensile member exposed at edges of belt or separated from belt body)	• Excessive tension • Drive pulley misalignment • Belt contacting stationary object • Pulley irregularities • Improper pulley construction • Insufficient adhesion between tensile member and rubber matrix	• Adjust belt tension • Align pulley • Correct as necessary • Replace pulley • Replace pulley • Replace belt and adjust tension to specifications
Sporadic rib cracking (multiple cracks in belt ribs at random intervals)	• Ribbed pulley(s) diameter less than minimum specification • Backside bend flat pulley(s) diameter less than minimum • Excessive heat condition causing rubber to harden • Excessive belt thickness • Belt overcured • Excessive tension	• Replace pulley(s) • Replace pulley(s) • Correct heat condition as necessary • Replace belt • Replace belt • Adjust belt tension

57. Install the splash shield on the oil pan.
58. If the vehicle is equipped with automatic transmission connect the oil cooler lines at the radiator.
59. Connect the radiator hoses and install the E-clip at the bottom of the radiator.
60. Install the air conditioning compressor.
61. Evacuate, charge and leak test the air conditioning system. Be sure to observe all safety precautions. See Section 1.
62. Fill the cooling system.
63. Install the air cleaner assembly.
64. If equipped, install the skid plate.
65. Install the battery.
66. Install the hood.

4-2.5L

— **CAUTION** —
This procedure requires that on vehicles with air conditioning, the refrigerant system be discharged. See Section 1. This is a dangerous procedure. Anyone who is not thoroughly familiar with the handling of refrigerant systems should not attempt this procedure. Serious personal injury could result from the mishandling of refrigerant.

1. Disconnect the battery.
2. Matchmark the hood and hinges, and remove the hood.
3. Remove the air cleaner.
4. Drain the coolant and engine oil.

— **CAUTION** —
When draining the coolant, keep in mind that cats and dogs are attracted by the ethylene glycol antifreeze, and are quite likely to drink any that is left in an uncovered container or in puddles on the ground. This will prove fatal in sufficient quantity. Always drain the coolant into a sealable container. Coolant should be reused unless it is contaminated or several years old.

5. Remove the radiator hoses.
6. Remove the fan shroud and transmission cooler lines.
7. Discharge the refrigerant.
8. Remove the condenser and radiator.
9. Remove the fan and install a $5/16$ in. × $1/8$ in. capscrew through the pulley and into the water pump flange to maintain pulley alignment.
10. Disconnect the heater hoses.
11. Disconnect and tag all wires, hoses, and cables connected to the engine.
12. Remove the service ports from the air conditioning compressor and cap the openings.
13. Drain the power steering reservoir.
14. Remove the power steering hoses at the gear.

ENGINE AND ENGINE OVERHAUL 3

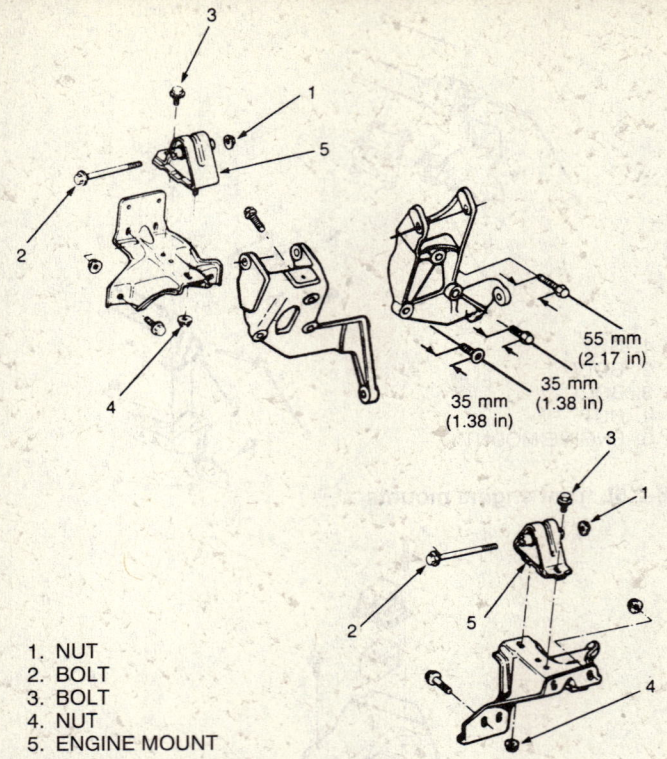

1. NUT
2. BOLT
3. BOLT
4. NUT
5. ENGINE MOUNT

Front engine mounts for the diesel

15. Remove the check valve from the power brake vacuum hose.
16. Raise and support the front end on jackstands.
17. Remove the starter.
18. Disconnect the exhaust pipe at the manifold.
19. Remove the bell housing access plate.
20. On trucks equipped with automatic transmission, match-

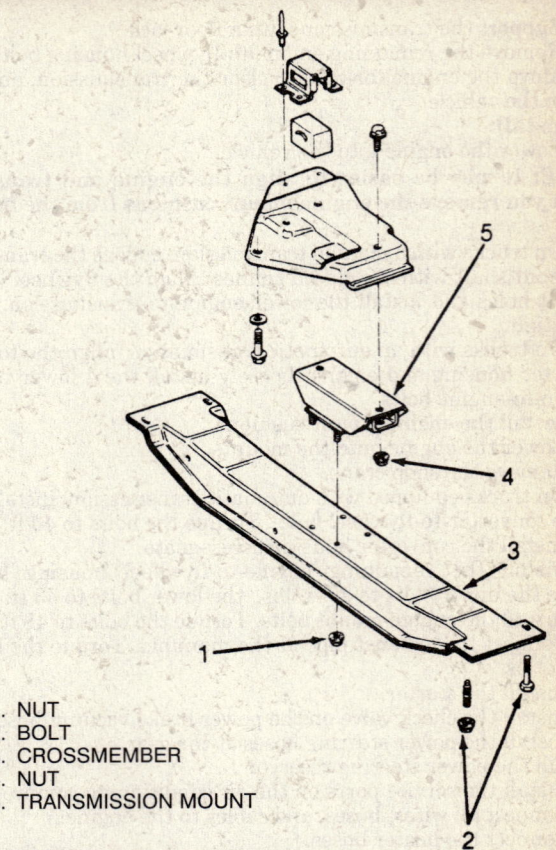

1. NUT
2. BOLT
3. CROSSMEMBER
4. NUT
5. TRANSMISSION MOUNT

Rear engine mount for the 4-2.5L

mark the torque converter and flywheel. Remove the attaching bolts.
21. Remove the upper flywheel housing-to-engine bolts; loosen the lower ones.
22. Take up the weight of the engine with a shop crane.
23. Remove the engine mount bolts.
24. Raise the engine off the mounts.

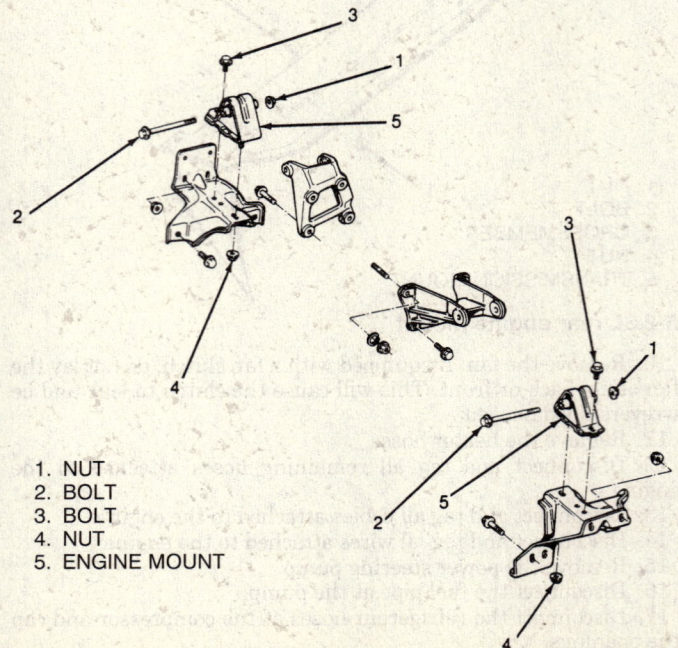

1. NUT
2. BOLT
3. BOLT
4. NUT
5. ENGINE MOUNT

Front engine mount for the 4-2.5L

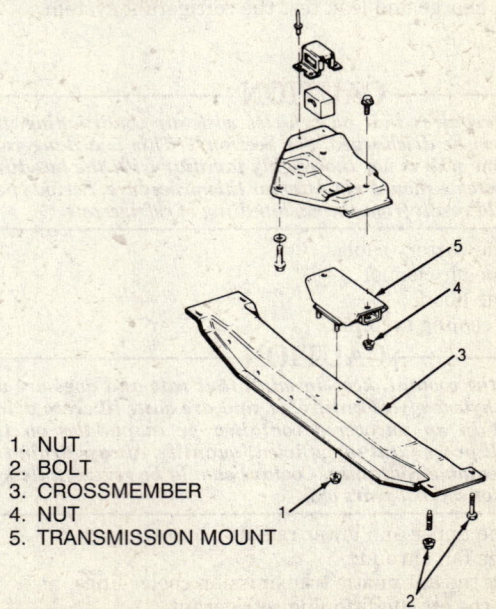

1. NUT
2. BOLT
3. CROSSMEMBER
4. NUT
5. TRANSMISSION MOUNT

Rear engine mount for the diesel

3-37

3 ENGINE AND ENGINE OVERHAUL

25. Support the transmission with a floor jack.
26. Remove the remaining engine-to-flywheel housing bolts.
27. Move the engine forward to clear the transmission, and lift it from the vehicle.

To install:

28. Lower the engine into the vehicle.

NOTE: It may be easier to align the engine and transmission if you remove the engine mount cushions from the brackets.

29. On trucks with a manual transmission, engage the transmission input shaft with the clutch splines. Align the flywheel housing bolt holes and install the lower engine-to-transmission bolts finger tight.
30. On trucks with an automatic transmission, align the torque converter housing and engine. Loosely install the 4 lower transmission-to-engine bolts.
31. Install the engine mount cushions.
32. Lower the engine onto the mounts.
33. Remove the shop crane.
34. On trucks equipped with automatic transmission, install the torque converter-to-flywheel bolts. Torque the bolts to 40 ft. lbs.
35. Install the converter housing access plate.
36. Install the remaining engine-to-flywheel housing bolts. Torque the upper bolts to 27 ft. lbs.; the lower bolts to 43 ft. lbs.
37. Install the engine mount bolts. Torque the bolts to 48 ft. lbs.
38. Connect the exhaust pipe at the manifold. Torque the bolts to 23 ft. lbs.
39. Install the starter.
40. Install the check valve on the power brake vacuum hose.
41. Install the power steering hoses at the gear.
42. Fill the power steering reservoir.
43. Install the service ports on the air conditioning compressor.
44. Connect all wires, hoses, and cables to the engine.
45. Connect the heater hoses.
47. Install the fan and pulley.
48. Install the condenser and radiator.
49. Install the fan shroud and transmission cooler lines.
50. Install the radiator hoses.
51. Fill the cooling system.
52. Fill the crankcase.
53. Install the air cleaner.
54. Install the hood.
55. Connect the battery.
56. Evacuate, charge and leak test the refrigerant system.

6-2.8L

— **CAUTION** —
This procedure requires that on vehicles with air conditioning, the refrigerant system be discharged. See Section 1. This is a dangerous procedure. Anyone who is not thoroughly familiar with the handling of refrigerant systems should not attempt this procedure. Serious personal injury could result from the mishandling of refrigerant.

1. Remove the battery cables.
2. Remove the air cleaner.
3. Remove the hood.
4. Drain the cooling system.

— **CAUTION** —
When draining the coolant, keep in mind that cats and dogs are attracted by the ethylene glycol antifreeze, and are quite likely to drink any that is left in an uncovered container or in puddles on the ground. This will prove fatal in sufficient quantity. Always drain the coolant into a sealable container. Coolant should be reused unless it is contaminated or several years old.

5. Remove the upper and lower radiator hoses.
6. Remove the fan shroud.
7. Disconnect the automatic transmission cooler lines.
8. Discharge the air conditioning refrigerant.
9. Remove the radiator/condenser assembly.

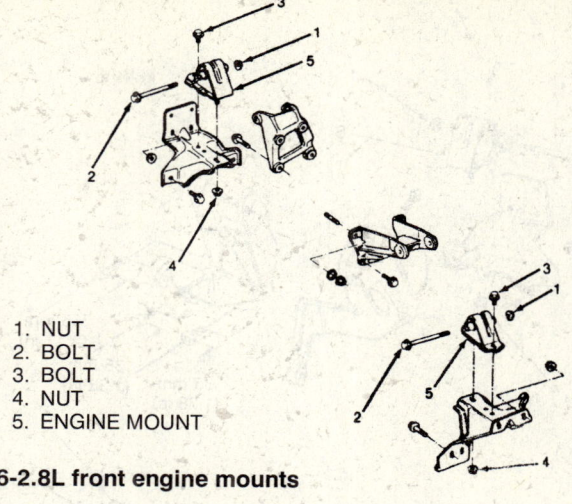

1. NUT
2. BOLT
3. BOLT
4. NUT
5. ENGINE MOUNT

6-2.8L front engine mounts

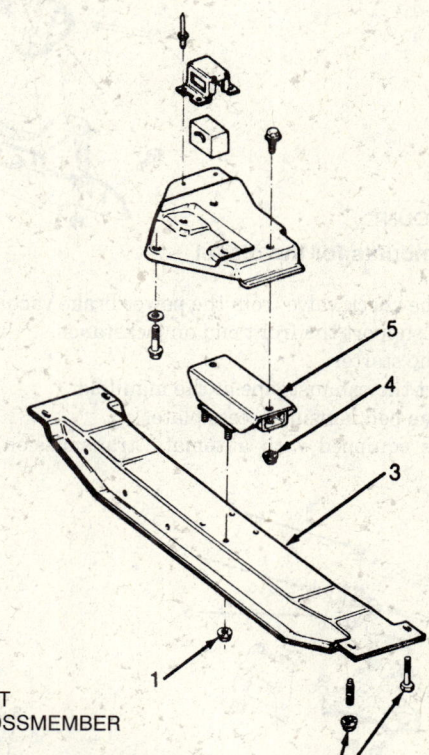

1. NUT
2. BOLT
3. CROSSMEMBER
4. NUT
5. TRANSMISSION MOUNT

6-2.8L rear engine mount

10. Remove the fan. If equipped with a fan clutch, do not lay the fan on its back or front. This will cause the clutch to leak and be irreversibly damaged.
11. Remove the heater hoses.
12. Disconnect and tag all remaining hoses attached to the engine.
13. Disconnect and tag all cables attached to the engine.
14. Disconnect and tag all wires attached to the engine.
15. Remove the power steering pump.
16. Disconnect the fuel pipe at the pump.
17. Disconnect the refrigerant hoses at the compressor and cap the openings.
18. Raise and support the truck on jackstands.
19. Disconnect the exhaust pipe at the converter flange.

ENGINE AND ENGINE OVERHAUL

20. Remove the flywheel housing access plate.
21. On vehicles equipped with automatic transmission, matchmark the converter-to-flywheel and remove the bolts.
22. Remove the flywheel housing-to-engine bolts.
23. Lower the vehicle.
24. Place a floor jack under the transmission.
25. Attach a shop crane to the engine lifting eyes.
26. Remove the engine mount bolts.
27. Lift the engine from the truck.

To install:
28. Lift the engine from the truck.

NOTE: **It will be easier to align the engine if you remove the engine support cushions.**

29. Install the flywheel housing-to-engine bolts. Finger tight.
30. Install the support cushions and lower the engine onto the mounts.
31. Install the engine mount bolts. Torque the through-bolts to 92 ft. lbs.
32. Remove the shop crane.
34. Remove the floor jack under the transmission.
35. On vehicles equipped with automatic transmission, install the converter-to-flywheel bolts. Torque the bolts to 25 ft. lbs.
36. Install the flywheel housing access plate.
37. Torque the engine-to-transmission bolts to 40 ft. lbs.
38. Connect the exhaust pipe at the converter flange.
39. Connect the refrigerant hoses at the compressor.
40. Connect the fuel pipe at the pump.
41. Install the power steering pump.
42. Connect all wires attached to the engine.
43. Connect all cables attached to the engine.
44. Connect all remaining hoses attached to the engine.
45. Install the heater hoses.
46. Install the fan.
47. Install the radiator/condenser assembly.
48. Connect the automatic transmission cooler lines.
49. Install the fan shroud.
50. Install the upper and lower radiator hoses.
51. Fill the cooling system.
52. Install the hood.
53. Install the air cleaner.
54. Install the battery cables.
55. Evacuate, charge and leak test the refrigerant system.

6-4.0L

— **CAUTION** —
This procedure requires that on vehicles with air conditioning, the refrigerant system be discharged. See Section 1. This is a dangerous procedure. Anyone who is not thoroughly familiar with the handling of refrigerant systems should not attempt this procedure. Serious personal injury could result from the mishandling of refrigerant.

1. Matchmark the hood and hinges and remove the hood.
2. Drain the engine oil.

— **CAUTION** —
The EPA warns that prolonged contact with used engine oil may cause a number of skin disorders, including cancer! You should make every effort to minimize your exposure to used engine oil. Protective gloves should be worn when changing the oil. Wash your hands and any other exposed skin areas as soon as possible after exposure to used engine oil. Soap and water, or waterless hand cleaner should be used.

3. Drain the cooling system.

— **CAUTION** —
When draining the coolant, keep in mind that cats and dogs are attracted by the ethylene glycol antifreeze, and are quite likely to drink any that is left in an uncovered container or in puddles on the ground. This will prove fatal in sufficient quantity. Always drain the coolant into a sealable container. Coolant should be reused unless it is contaminated or several years old.

4. Remove the battery.
5. Remove the air cleaner.
6. Remove the upper and lower radiator hoses.
7. Disconnect and cap the automatic transmission cooler lines.
8. Remove the fan shroud.
9. Remove the radiator.
10. Remove the electric cooling fan.

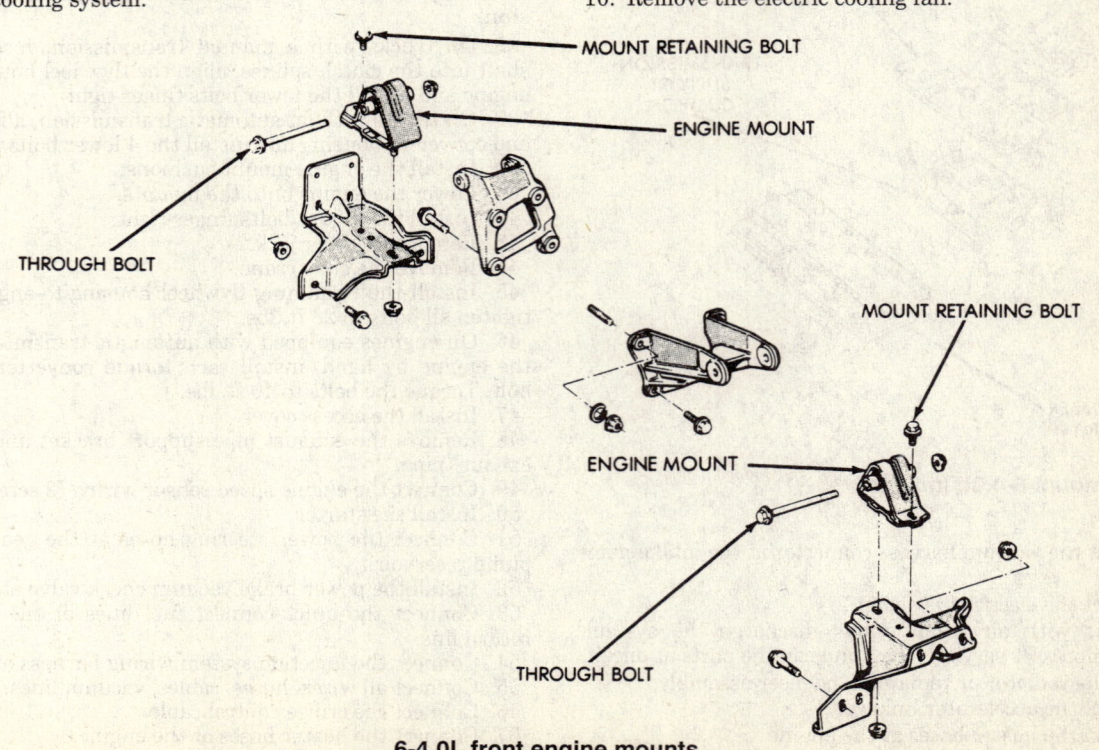

6-4.0L front engine mounts

3 ENGINE AND ENGINE OVERHAUL

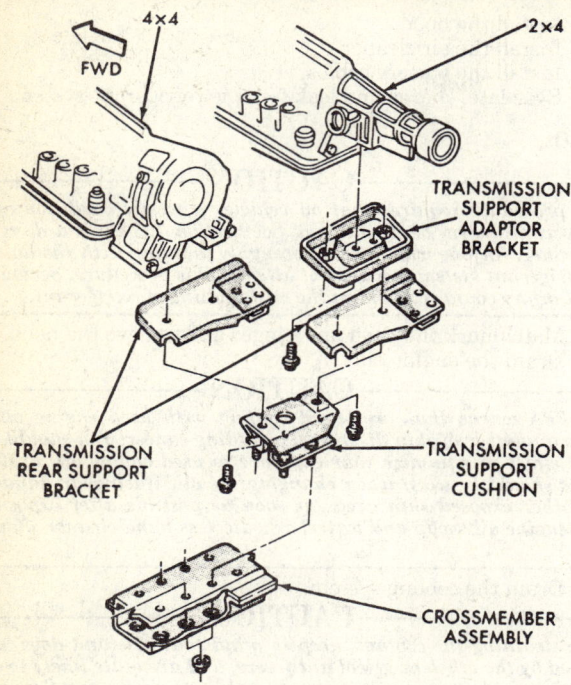

Rear engine mounts 6-4.0L (automatic)

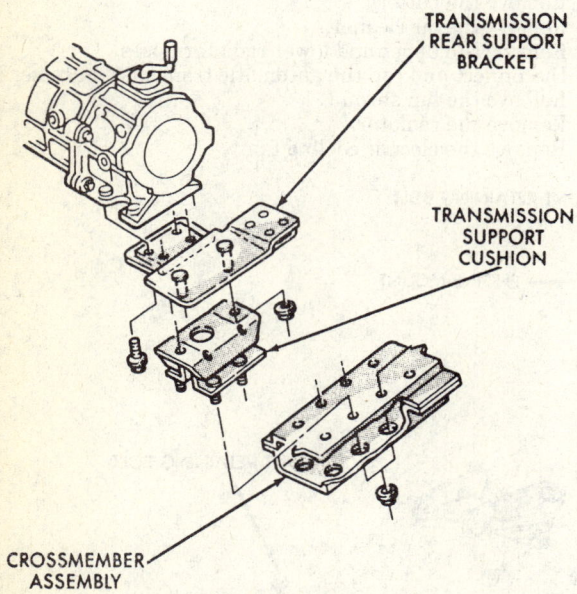

Rear engine mount 6-4.0L (manual)

11. Disconnect the vacuum harness connector at the intake manifold.
12. Disconnect the electric fan switch.
13. On trucks with air conditioning, discharge the system, remove the compressor service valves and cap the ports at once!
14. Remove the radiator or radiator/condenser assembly.
15. Disconnect the accelerator linkage.
16. Disconnect the heater hoses at the engine.
17. Disconnect the cruise control cable.

18. Disconnect and tag all wires, hoses, cables, vacuum lines, etc., connected to the engine or in the way of engine removal.
19. Disconnect the injection system wiring harness at the firewall.
20. Relieve fuel system pressure. See Section 5.
21. Disconnect the quick-connect fuel lines at the fuel rail and return line by squeezing the 2 tabs against the tube. Pull the fuel tube and retainer from the quick-connect fitting.
22. Remove the power brake vacuum check valve from the booster.
23. Disconnect the power steering hoses from the gear, drain the pump reservoir, and cap all openings.
24. Raise and support the front end on jackstands.
25. Remove the starter.
26. Disconnect the exhaust pipe at the support bracket and the manifold.
27. Disconnect the engine speed sensor wiring (2 screws).
28. Remove the exhaust pipe support bracket.
29. On engines, equipped with automatic transmission, remove the inspection cover. Matchmark the torque converter and flex plate. Turning the engine by hand, remove each torque converter-to-flex plate bolt.
30. Remove the upper flywheel housing-to-engine bolts and loosen the bottom bolts.
31. Remove the engine front support-to-frame nuts.
32. Lower the truck.
33. Take up the weight of the engine with a shop crane.
34. Support the transmission with a floor jack.
35. Remove the lower engine-to-bellhousing bolts.
36. Raise the engine, while guiding it forward and out of the vehicle.

To install:
37. Lower the engine into the vehicle. It may make it easier to align the engine and transmission if you remove the engine mount cushions.

WARNING: Be very careful to avoid damaging the trigger wheel on the flywheel on trucks with an automatic transmission!

38. On trucks with a manual transmission, insert the input shaft into the clutch splines, align the flywheel housing with the engine and install the lower bolts finger tight.
39. On trucks with an automatic transmission, align the engine and converter housing and install the 4 lower bolts finger tight.
40. Install the engine mount cushions.
41. Lower the engine onto the mounts.
42. Install the mount bolts finger tight.
43. Remove the floor jack.
44. Remove the shop crane.
45. Install the remaining flywheel housing-to-engine bolts and tighten all bolts to 28 ft. lbs..
46. On engines equipped with automatic transmission, turning the engine by hand, install each torque converter-to-flex plate bolt. Torque the bolts to 40 ft. lbs.
47. Install the access cover.
48. Remove the exhaust pipe support bracket and connect the exhaust pipe.
49. Connect the engine speed sensor wiring (2 screws).
50. Install the starter.
51. Connect the power steering hoses at the gear and fill the pump reservoir.
52. Install the power brake vacuum check valve at the booster.
53. Connect the quick-connect fuel lines at the fuel rail and return line.
54. Connect the injection system wiring harness at the firewall.
55. Connect all wires, hoses, cables, vacuum lines, etc.
56. Connect the cruise control cable.
57. Connect the heater hoses at the engine.
58. Connect the accelerator linkage.

ENGINE AND ENGINE OVERHAUL 3

59. Install the radiator or radiator/condenser assembly.
60. On trucks with air conditioning, install the compressor service valves.
61. Install the electric cooling fan.
62. Connect the electric fan switch.
63. Connect the vacuum harness connector at the intake manifold.
64. Install the fan shroud.
65. Connect the automatic transmission cooler lines.
66. Install the upper and lower radiator hoses.
67. Install the air cleaner.
68. Install the battery.
69. Fill the cooling system.
70. Fill the crankcase.
71. Install the hood.
72. Evacuate, charge and leak test the refrigerant system.

Rocker Arm (Valve) Cover

REMOVAL AND INSTALLATION

4-2.1L Diesel

1. Disconnect the negative battery cable
2. Disconnect vacuum and oil breather hoses that route over the rocker arm cover.
3. Remove the rocker arm cover retaining bolts. Remove the cover.
4. Remove the cover gasket, clean the mating surfaces and install the new gasket.
5. Install the retaining bolts and tighten them to 35 inch lbs. Reconnect vacuum and oil breather hoses that were disconnected during removal.

4-2.5L

1. Remove the air cleaner and the PCV valve molded hose.
2. Disconnect the fuel line at the fuel pump and swivel to allow removal of the rocker arm cover (carbureted 4-2.5L).
3. Remove the PCV valve from the cover. Disconnect or remove any vacuum or air hoses to provide access to the rocker arm cover.
   NOTE: To avoid damaging the rocker arm cover, DO NOT pry the cover upward until the RTV seal has been broken.
4. Remove the rocker arm cover retaining bolts. Break the RTV seal with a putty knife or razor blade. Pry on the rocker arm cover only were indicated (see illustration).
5. Thoroughly clean old sealer from head and cover. Examine rocker arm cover for cracks or bent rails.
6. Apply an 3mm (1/8in.) bead of RTV sealant along the entire length of the rocker arm cover rail. Allow the sealant to set-up for a few seconds.
7. While the sealant is still fluid, install the rocker arm cover on the cylinder head. Take care not to get any sealant on the rocker arms or valve train components.
8. Install rocker arm cover retaining bolts and tighten to 55 inch lbs.
9. Reposition and connect all previously disconnected vacuum and air hoses. Install the PCV valve and hose. Install the air cleaner.

6-2.8L

LEFT SIDE

1. Disconnect the battery cables.
2. Disconnect the hoses, wire connectors and pipe bracket. Remove the spark plug wires and clips from the retaining stud.
3. Remove the rocker arm cover retaining bolts. Break the RTV seal with a putty knife or razor blade. Pry on the rocker arm cover gently to remove.
4. Thoroughly clean old sealer from head and cover. Examine rocker arm cover for cracks or bent rails.
5. Apply an 3mm (1/8 in.) bead of RTV sealant along the entire length of the rocker arm cover rail. Allow the sealant to set-up for a few seconds.
6. While the sealant is still fluid, install the rocker arm cover on the cylinder head. Take care not to get any sealant on the rocker arms or valve train components.
7. Install rocker arm cover retaining bolts and tighten to 8 ft.lbs.
8. Connect all previously disconnected wires, hoses and brackets. Reconnect the battery cables.

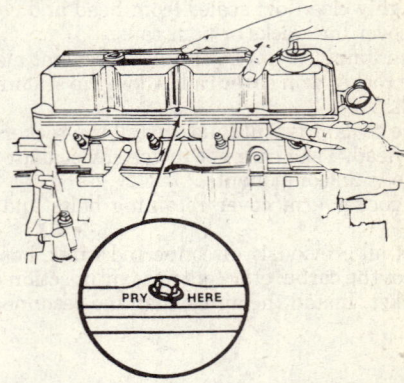

Use a putty knife or razor blade to break the RTV seal. Pry up on valve cover only where indicated

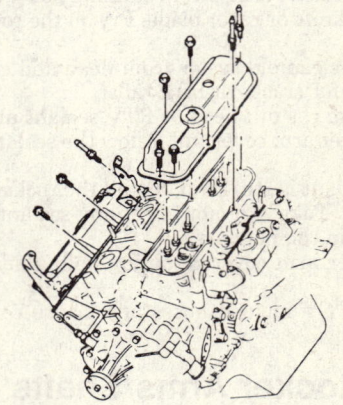

6-2.8L valve cover

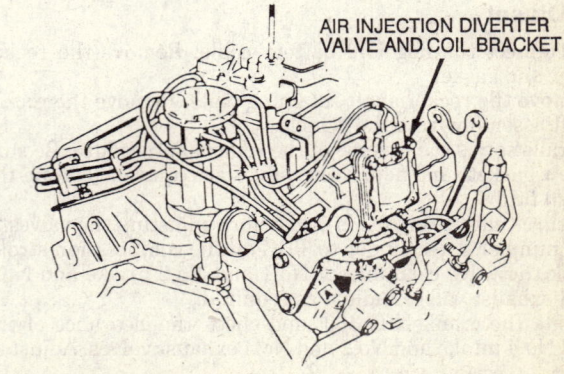

Air diverter valve and coil bracket location on the 6-2.8L

3 ENGINE AND ENGINE OVERHAUL

RIGHT SIDE

1. Disconnect the battery cables.
2. Remove the air cleaner, air injection diverter and coil bracket.
3. Disconnect the air hose from the air injection manifold, wire connectors and vacuum hoses.
4. Remove the spark plug wires and clip from the retaining stud.
5. Disconnect the carburetor controls and remove from the bracket.
6. Remove the rocker arm cover retaining bolts. Break the RTV seal with a putty knife or razor blade. Pry on the rocker arm cover gently to remove.
7. Thoroughly clean old sealer from head and cover. Examine rocker arm cover for cracks or bent rails.
8. Apply an 3mm (1/8 in.) bead of RTV sealant along the entire length of the rocker arm cover rail. Allow the sealant to set-up for a few seconds.
9. While the sealant is still fluid, install the rocker arm cover on the cylinder head. Take care not to get any sealant on the rocker arms or valve train components.
10. Install rocker arm cover retaining bolts and tighten to 8 ft.lbs.
11. Connect all previously disconnected wires, hoses and brackets. Reconnect the carburetor controls, air injection diverter valve and coil bracket. Install the air cleaner and reconnect the battery cables.

6-4.0L

1. Remove the PCV molded hoses and cruise control servo (if equipped).
2. Remove the rocker arm cover retaining bolts. Break the RTV seal with a putty knife or razor blade. Pry on the rocker arm cover gently to remove.
3. Thoroughly clean old sealer from head and cover. Examine rocker arm cover for cracks or bent rails.
4. Apply an 3mm (1/8 in.) bead of RTV sealant along the entire length of the rocker arm cover rail. Allow the sealant to set-up for a few seconds.
5. While the sealant is still fluid, install the rocker arm cover on the cylinder head. Take care not to get any sealant on the rocker arms or valve train components.
6. Install rocker arm cover retaining bolts and tighten to 55 inch lbs.
7. Install the PCV molded hoses and cruise control servo (if equipped).

Rocker Arms/Shafts

REMOVAL AND INSTALLATION

4-2.1L Diesel

1. Disconnect the negative battery cable. Remove the rocker arm cover and gasket.
2. Remove the rocker shaft retaining bolts. Remove the rocker arm shaft assembly from the vehicle.
3. Installation is the reverse of the removal procedure. Be sure to use new gaskets and adjust the valves as required. Torque the bolts to 20 ft. lbs.
4. Be sure that the engine is cold before adjusting the valves.
5. Set number one cylinder to TDC on the compression stroke and check the valve clearance of No.1 and No.2 intake and No.1 and No.3 exhaust valves. Adjust as required.
6. Rotate the crankshaft 360° and check the clearance of the No.3 and No.4 intake and No.2 and No.4 exhaust valves. Adjust as required.

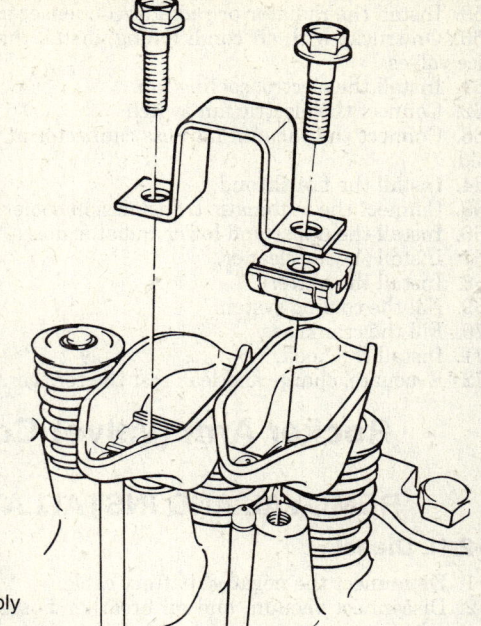

1. Capscrews
2. Bridge
3. Pivot assembly
4. Rocker arms

Rocker arm removal for the 4-2.5L and 6-4.0L

NOTE: The No.1 cylinder is located at the flywheel end of the engine.

7. To adjust, loosen the locknut and turn the adjustment screw as necessary. As each adjustment screw is tightened, be sure that the bottom of the screw is aligned with the valve stem. If the adjustment screw is not aligned with the stem when tightened, the stem could bend. Tighten the locknut.
8. The exhaust valve adjustment specification is 0.25mm (0.010 in.). The intake valve adjustment specification is 0.20mm (0.008 in.).

4-2.5L and 6-4.0L

1. Remove the rocker arm cover. Refer to Rocker Arm (Valve) Cover Removal for the procedure.

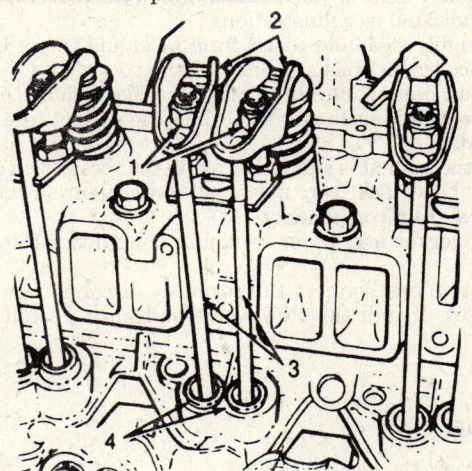

1. Rocker arm nuts
2. Rocker arms
3. Pushrods
4. Pushrod guides

6-2.8L valve train

ENGINE AND ENGINE OVERHAUL 3

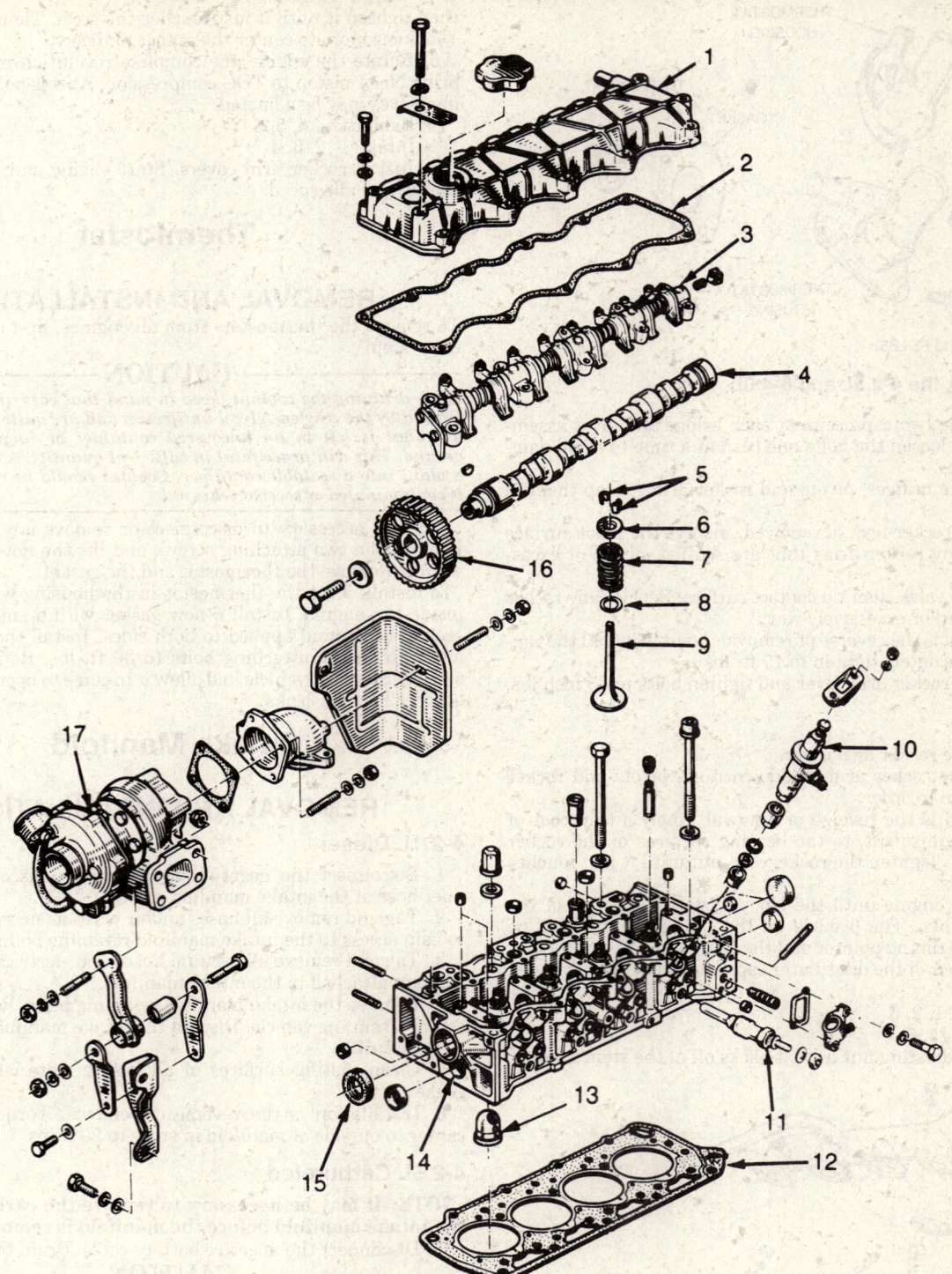

1. Cylinder head cover
2. Cylinder head cover gasket
3. Rocker arm and shaft assembly
4. Camshaft
5. Valve spring locks
6. Valve spring retainer
7. Valve spring
8. Valve spring washer
9. Valve
10. Injector
11. Glow plug
12. Cylinder head gasket
13. Pre-combustion chamber
14. Cylinder head
15. Camshaft oil seal
16. Camshaft sprocket
17. Turbocharger

Exploded view of the 4-2.1L diesel cylinder head

3-43

3 ENGINE AND ENGINE OVERHAUL

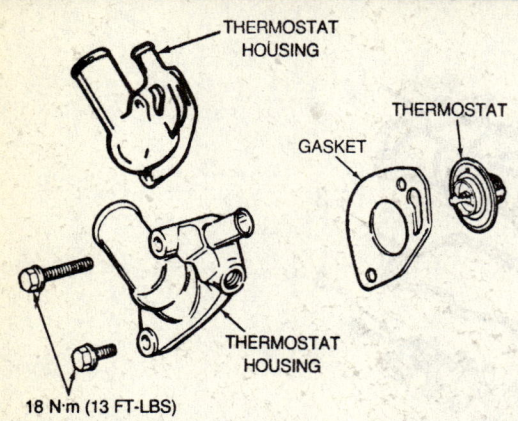

Thermostat for the 4-2.5L and 6-4.0L

2. Remove the two capscrews at each bridge and pivot assembly. Alternately loosen the bolts one turn at a time to avoid damaging the bridges.
3. Remove the bridges, pivots and rocker arms. Keep them in order.
4. While the rocker arm is removed, inspect the pivot surface area. Replace any rocker arms that are scuffed, pitted or excessively worn.
5. Inspect the valve stem tip contact surface. Replace any rocker arm that is pitted or excessively worn.
6. Installation is the reverse of removal. Loosely install the capscrews then alternately tighten to 19 ft. lbs.
7. Install the rocker arm cover and tighten bolts to 55 inch lbs.

6-2.8L

1. Remove the rocker arm cover.
2. Remove the rocker arm holddown nuts, pivots and rocker arms. Keep them in order.
3. Installation is the reverse of removal. Apply a thin coat of Molykote®, or equivalent, to the bearing surfaces of the rocker arms and pivots. Tighten the rocker arm nut until it just touches the valve stem.
4. Rotate the engine until the No. 1 piston is at TDC of the compression stroke. The 0 mark on the timing scale should be aligned with the timing pointer and the rotor should be at the No. 1 spark plug tower of the distributor cap. The following valves can be adjusted:
   - Exhaust — 1, 2, 3
   - Intake — 1, 5, 6
5. Turn the adjusting nut until it backs off of the stem slightly,

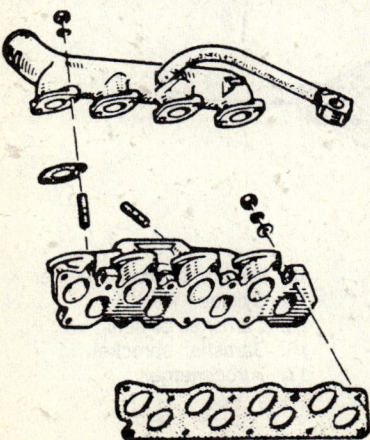

4-2.1L diesel intake and exhaust manifolds

then tighten it until it just touches the stem. Then, turn the nut $1\frac{1}{8}$ turns more to center the tappet plunger.
6. Rotate the engine one complete revolution more. This will bring No. 4 piston to TDC compression. At this point, the following valves may be adjusted:
   - Exhaust — 4, 5, 6
   - Intake — 2, 3, 4
7. Install rocker arm covers. Start engine and check ignition timing and idle speed.

Thermostat

REMOVAL AND INSTALLATION

To remove the thermostats from all engines, first drain the cooling system.

---- CAUTION ----

When draining the coolant, keep in mind that cats and dogs are attracted by the ethylene glycol antifreeze, and are quite likely to drink any that is left in an uncovered container or in puddles on the ground. This will prove fatal in sufficient quantity. Always drain the coolant into a sealable container. Coolant should be reused unless it is contaminated or several years old.

It is not necessary to disconnect or remove any of the hoses. Remove the two attaching screws and lift the housing from the engine. Remove the thermostat and the gasket.

To install, place the thermostat in the housing with the spring inside the engine. Install a new gasket with a small amount of sealing compound applied to both sides. Install the water outlet and tighten the attaching bolts to 30 ft. lbs. Refill the cooling system. Start the vehicle and allow it to come to operating temperature. Check for leaks.

Intake Manifold

REMOVAL AND INSTALLATION

4-2.1L Diesel

1. Disconnect the negative battery cable. Disconnect the air inlet hose at the intake manifold.
2. Tag and remove all hoses and/or wires as necessary in order to gain access to the intake manifold retaining bolts.
3. Tag and remove all vacuum hoses and electrical connections that are attached to the intake manifold.
4. Remove the intake manifold retaining bolts. Remove the assembly from the vehicle. Discard the intake manifold gaskets.

To Install:

5. Clean mating surfaces of all gasket material. Install new gasket.
6. Installation is the reverse of removal. Torque bolts from center to outside of manifold in steps to 20 ft.lbs.

4-2.5L Carbureted

NOTE: *It may be necessary to remove the carburetor from the intake manifold before the manifold is removed.*

1. Disconnect the negative battery cable. Drain the radiator.

---- CAUTION ----

When draining the coolant, keep in mind that cats and dogs are attracted by the ethylene glycol antifreeze, and are quite likely to drink any that is left in an uncovered container or in puddles on the ground. This will prove fatal in sufficient quantity. Always drain the coolant into a sealable container. Coolant should be reused unless it is contaminated or several years old.

---

2. Remove the air cleaner. Disconnect the fuel pipe. Remove the carburetor.
3. Disconnect the coolant hoses from the intake manifold.
4. Disconnect the throttle cable from the bellcrank.

ENGINE AND ENGINE OVERHAUL 3

5. Disconnect the PCV valve vacuum hose from the intake manifold.
6. If equipped, remove the vacuum advance CTO valve vacuum hoses.
7. Disconnect the system coolant temperature sender wire connector (located on the intake manifold). Disconnect the air temperature sensor wire, if equipped.
8. Disconnect the vacuum hose from the EGR valve.
9. On vehicles equipped with power steering remove the power steering pump and its mounting bracket. Do not detach the power steering pump hoses.
10. Disconnect the intake manifold electric heater wire connector, as required.
11. Disconnect the throttle valve linkage, if equipped with automatic transmission.
12. Disconnect the EGR valve tube from the intake manifold.
13. Remove the intake manifold attaching screws, nuts and clamps. Remove the intake manifold. Discard the gasket.
14. Clean the mating surfaces of the manifold and cylinder head.

NOTE: If the manifold is being replaced, ensure all fittings, etc., are transferred to the replacement manifold.

To install:
15. Clean the mating surfaces of the manifold and cylinder head.
16. Install the intake manifold, with a new gasket. Install intake manifold attaching screws, nuts and clamps. Using the sequence shown in the illustration, torque the bolts in steps to 23 ft.lbs.
17. Connect the EGR valve tube.
18. Connect the throttle valve linkage, if equipped with automatic transmission.
19. Connect the intake manifold electric heater wire connector, as required.
20. On vehicles equipped with power steering install the power steering pump and its mounting bracket.
21. Connect the vacuum hose to the EGR valve.
22. Connect the system coolant temperature sender wire connector (located on the intake manifold).
23. Connect the air temperature sensor wire, if equipped.
24. If equipped, install the vacuum advance CTO valve vacuum hoses.
25. Connect the PCV valve vacuum hose at the intake manifold.
26. Connect the throttle cable at the bellcrank.
27. Connect the coolant hoses at the intake manifold.
28. Install the carburetor and working in a crisscross pattern, torque the nuts to 14 ft. lbs.

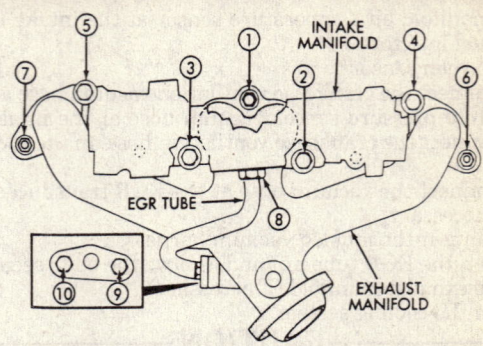

Carbureted 4-2.5L intake and exhaust manifold torquing sequence

29. Connect the fuel pipe.
30. Install the air cleaner.
31. Connect the negative battery cable.
32. Fill the cooling system.

4-2.5L MFI
1. Disconnect negative battery cable.
2. Remove the air cleaner inlet hose.
3. Loosen the accessory drive belt tension and remove the drive belt.
4. Remove the power steering pump and brackets. Support them from the radiator support with wire.
5. Remove the fuel tank filler cap to relieve the fuel tank pressure. Reinstall filler cap.
6. Disconnect the fuel supply tube from the fuel rail by squeezing the tabs of the quick connector and pulling. When disconnected, the retainer will stay on the fuel tube and the O-rings and spacer will remain in the connector. Use an 'L' shaped paper clip to remove the O-rings and spacer.

NOTE: When ever a fuel system disconnect fitting is disconnected the O-rings, spacer and retainer must be replaced.

7. Follow the instructions on the O-ring replacement kit package to install the new O-rings and spacer.
8. Disconnect the accelerator cable from the throttle body and holddown bracket. Disconnect the cruise control connector (if equipped) by loosening it with your hands. DO NOT attempt to pry off.
9. Disconnect all necessary electrical connectors:
 • the throttle position sensor
 • the idle speed sensor
 • the coolant temperature sensor at the thermostat

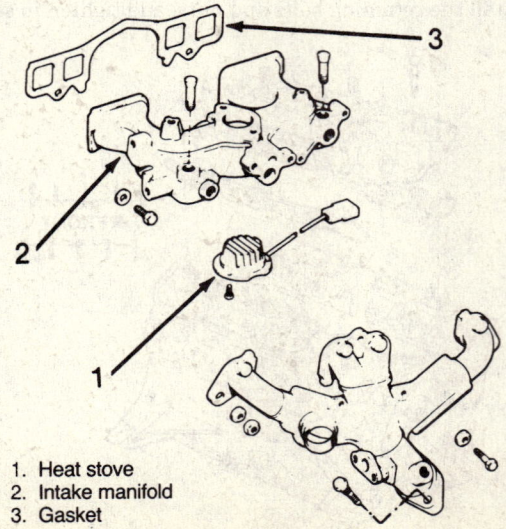

1. Heat stove
2. Intake manifold
3. Gasket

Carbureted 4-2.5L manifolds

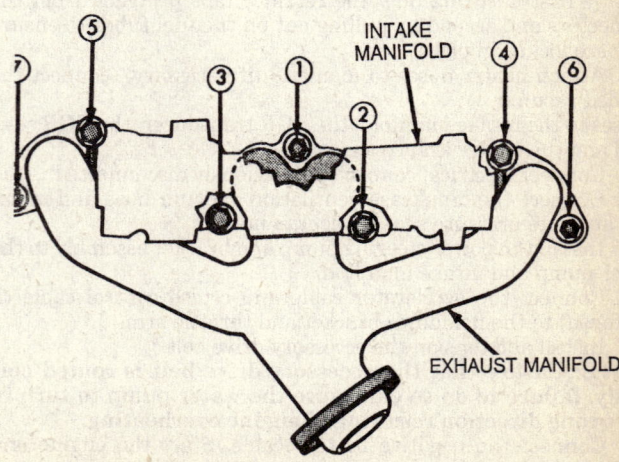

4-2.5L MFI intake and exhaust manifold torquing sequence

3-45

3 ENGINE AND ENGINE OVERHAUL

- the manifold air temperature sensor at the intake manifold
- the fuel injectors
- the oxygen sensor

10. Disconnect the crankcase ventilation vacuum hose and manifold absolute pressure sensor vacuum hose at the intake manifold. Disconnect the crankcase ventilation hose on the rocker arm cover.
11. Disconnect the vacuum hose at the EGR transducer and solenoid (if necessary).
12. Disconnect the molded vacuum harness.
13. Loosen the EGR tube nut and remove the bolts securing the tube to the exhaust manifold (if necessary).
14. Drain the cooling system.

---- **CAUTION** ----

When draining the coolant, keep in mind that cats and dogs are attracted by the ethylene glycol antifreeze, and are quite likely to drink any that is left in an uncovered container or in puddles on the ground. This will prove fatal in sufficient quantity. Always drain the coolant into a sealable container. Coolant should be reused unless it is contaminated or several years old.

15. Disconnect the vacuum brake booster hose at the intake manifold.
16. Remove bolts number 2 through 5 securing the intake manifold. Loosen bolt 1 and nuts 6 and 7.
17. Remove the intake manifold.

To install:
18. Clean the intake manifold and cylinder head mating surfaces. DO NOT allow foreign material to enter the intake manifold or cylinder head ports. Install the new intake manifold gasket over the locating dowels.
19. Position the intake manifold in place and finger tighten bolts.
20. Use a new EGR tube gasket and attach the EGR tube to the exhaust manifold. Finger tighten bolts 9 and 10. Leave the EGR tube nut at the intake manifold finger tight.
21. Tighten the fasteners in sequence and to the specified torque.

1989-90
- Fasteners 1, 6, 7, 8: 30 ft.lbs.
- Fasteners 2, 3, 4, 5: 23 ft.lbs.
- Fasteners 9 & 10: 14 ft.lbs.

1991
- Fastener 1: 30 ft.lbs.
- Fasteners 2, 3, 4, 5: 23 ft.lbs.
- Fasteners 6 & 7: 30 ft.lbs.

22. Connect the fuel return and supply tube to the connector next to the fuel rail. Don't forget to install the new O-rings. Push them into the fitting until a click is heard. Verify correct installation by first ensuring only the retainer tabs protrude from the connectors and second by pulling out on the fuel tubes to ensure they are locked in place.
23. Attach heater hoses to manifold (if necessary), connect the molded vacuum
hoses to the intake manifold, the EGR transducer, the EGR solenoid and the rocker arm cover.
24. Connect electrical connectors previously disconnected.
25. Connect the crankcase ventilation vacuum hose and manifold absolute pressure sensor vacuum hose.
26. Install the power steering pump and bracket assembly to the water pump and intake manifold.
27. Connect the accelerator cable and cruise control cable (if equipped) to the holddown bracket and throttle arm.
28. Install and tension the accessory drive belt.

NOTE: Ensure that the accessory drive belt is routed correctly. failure to do so can cause the water pump to turn in the wrong direction resulting in engine overheating.

29. Connect the negative battery cable. Start the engine and check for leaks.

6-2.8L

NOTE: It may be necessary to remove the carburetor from the intake manifold before the manifold is removed.

1. Disconnect the negative battery cable. Remove the air cleaner and rocker arm covers. Drain the coolant.

---- **CAUTION** ----

When draining the coolant, keep in mind that cats and dogs are attracted by the ethylene glycol antifreeze, and are quite likely to drink any that is left in an uncovered container or in puddles on the ground. This will prove fatal in sufficient quantity. Always drain the coolant into a sealable container. Coolant should be reused unless it is contaminated or several years old.

2. If equipped with air conditioning disconnect the compressor and move it to one side. Disconnect the spark plugs wires at the spark plugs. Disconnect the wires at the ignition coil.
3. If equipped, remove the air pump and bracket.
4. Remove the distributor cap. Mark the position of the ignition rotor in relation to the distributor body, and remove the distributor. Do not crank the engine with the distributor removed.
5. Remove the EGR valve. Remove the air hose. Disconnect the charcoal canister hoses. Remove the pipe bracket from the left cylinder head, if equipped.
6. Remove the diverter valve. Remove the power brake vacuum hose. Remove the heater and radiator hoses from the intake manifold.
7. Disconnect and label the vacuum hoses. If equipped, remove the EFE pipe from the rear of the manifold. Disconnect the coolant temperature switches.
8. Remove the carburetor linkage. Disconnect and plug the fuel line.
9. Remove the manifold retaining bolts and nuts.
10. Remove the intake manifold. Remove and discard the gaskets, and scrape off the old silicone seal from the front and rear ridges.

To Install:
11. The gaskets are marked for right and left side installation; do not interchange them. Clean the sealing surface of the engine block, and apply a 5mm wide bead of silicone sealer to each ridge.
12. Install the new gaskets onto the heads. The gaskets will have to be cut slightly to fit past the center pushrods. Do not cut any more material than necessary. Hold the gaskets in place by extending the ridge bead of sealer 6mm ($1/4$ in.) onto the gasket ends.
13. Install the intake manifold. The area between the ridges and the manifold should be completely sealed.
14. Install the retaining bolts and nuts, and tighten in sequence

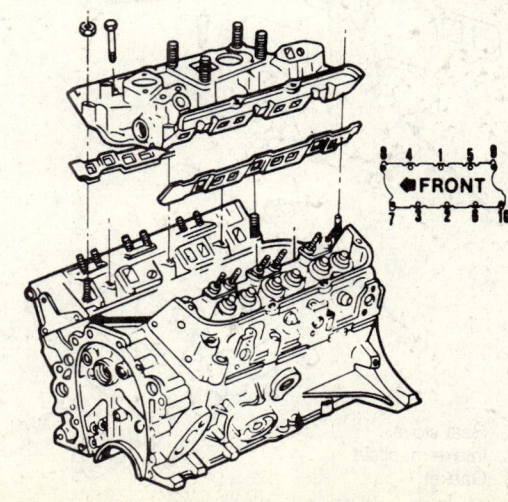

6-2.8L intake and exhaust manifold

ENGINE AND ENGINE OVERHAUL 3

to 23 ft. lbs. Do not overtighten the manifold. It is made of aluminum, and can be warped or cracked with excessive force.
15. Connect the fuel line.
16. Install the carburetor linkage.
17. Connect the vacuum hoses.
18. Install the EFE pipe at the rear of the manifold.
19. Connect the coolant temperature switches.
20. Install the diverter valve.
21. Install the power brake vacuum hose.
22. Install the heater and radiator hoses.
23. Install the EGR valve.
24. Install the air hose.
25. Connect the charcoal canister hoses.
26. Install the pipe bracket at the left cylinder head, if equipped.
27. Install the distributor.
28. Install the distributor cap.
29. Install the air pump and bracket.
30. Connect the air conditioning compressor.
31. Install the rocker arm covers.
32. Connect the spark plugs wires at the spark plugs.
33. Connect the wires at the ignition coil.
34. Connect the negative battery cable.
35. Install the air cleaner.
36. Fill the cooling system.

6-4.0L MFI

NOTE: The intake and exhaust manifold are mounted externally on the left side of the engine and are attached to the cylinder head. They are removed as a unit.
1. Disconnect the negative battery cable.
2. Remove the air cleaner.
3. Drain the cooling system.

⚠ CAUTION

When draining the coolant, keep in mind that cats and dogs are attracted by the ethylene glycol antifreeze, and are quite likely to drink any that is left in an uncovered container or in puddles on the ground. This will prove fatal in sufficient quantity. Always drain the coolant into a sealable container. Coolant should be reused unless it is contaminated or several years old.

4. Disconnect the EGR tube nuts at the intake manifold and exhaust manifold (if equipped).
5. Disconnect the accelerator cable, cruise control cable and transmission line pressure cable.
6. Disconnect the vacuum multiconnector at the intake manifold.
7. Disconnect all wiring connectors at the manifold.
8. Remove the fuel tank filler cap to relieve the fuel tank pressure. Reinstall filler cap.
9. Disconnect the fuel supply tube from the fuel rail by squeezing the tabs of the quick connector and pulling. When disconnected, the retainer will stay on the fuel tube and the O-rings and spacer will remain in the connector. Use an 'L' shaped paper clip to remove the O-rings and spacer.
NOTE: When ever a fuel system disconnect fitting is disconnected the O-rings, spacer and retainer must be replaced.
10. Follow the instructions on the O-ring replacement kit package to install the new O-rings and spacer.
11. Loosen the serpentine belt tensioner.
12. Remove the power steering pump and bracket and set it aside. Don't disconnect the hoses.
13. Remove the fuel rail and injectors.
14. Remove the intake manifold heat shield.
15. Raise and support the front end safely.
16. Disconnect the exhaust pipe at the exhaust manifold. Discard the seal.
17. Disconnect the oxygen sensor wiring at the sensor.
18. Lower the vehicle.
19. Remove the manifold attaching bolts, nuts and clamps.

20. Separate the intake manifold and exhaust manifold from the engine as an assembly, and discard the gasket.
21. If either manifold is to be replaced, they should be separated.
To install:
22. Clean the mating surface of the manifolds and the cylinder head. DO NOT allow foreign material to enter the intake or cylinder ports.
23. Install a new gasket over the alignment dowels on the head.
24. Loosely install the EGR tube to the intake and exhaust manifolds. DO NOT tighten the fasteners.
25. Position the manifold assemblies and loosely install the bolts. See the illustration and tighten the bolts as follows:

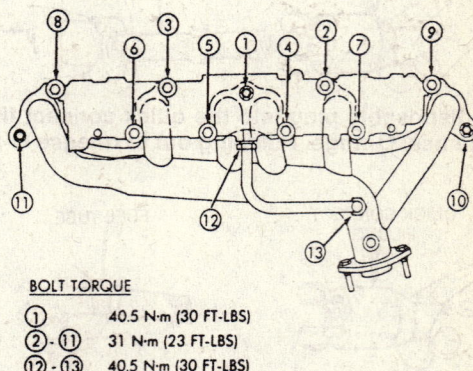

6-4.0L MFI intake and exhaust manifold torquing sequence

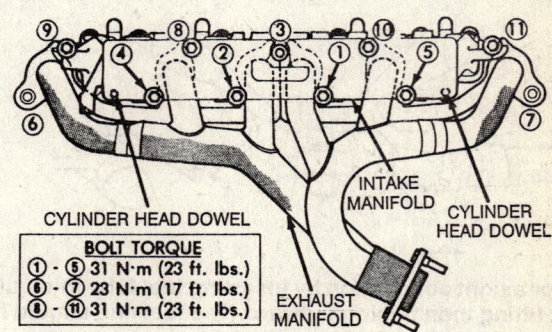

1991 6-4.0L MFI intake and exhaust manifold torquing sequence

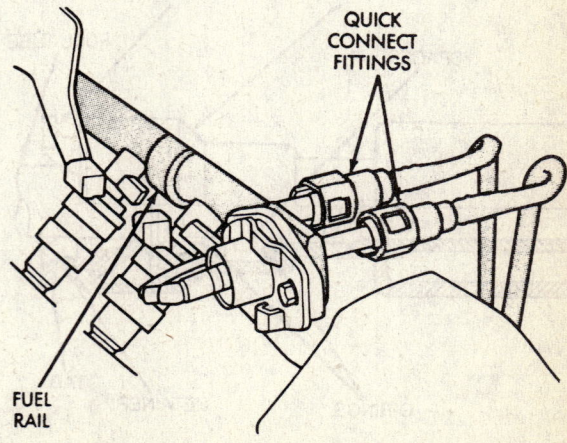

Quick connect fittings on fuel injected engines

3-47

3 ENGINE AND ENGINE OVERHAUL

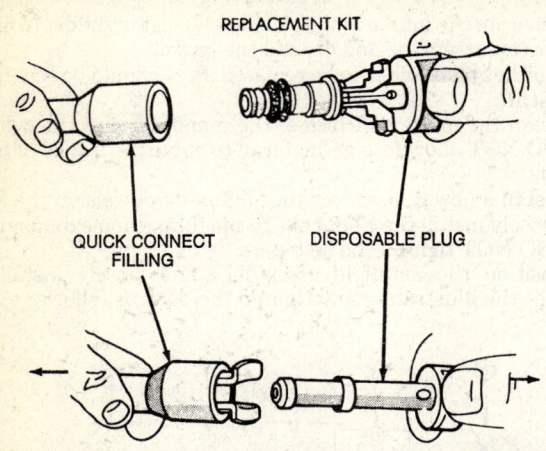

Insert the disposable plug into the quick connect fitting to position the new O-rings. Pull plug out to release O-rings

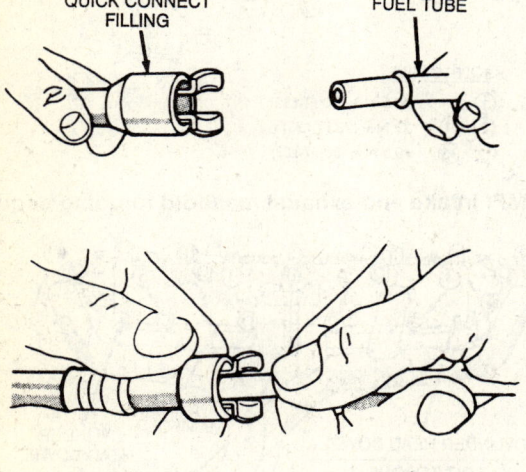

Check for a tight connection by inserting fuel tube into quick connect fitting then pulling outward. The fuel line should not come out unless the tabs are pressed

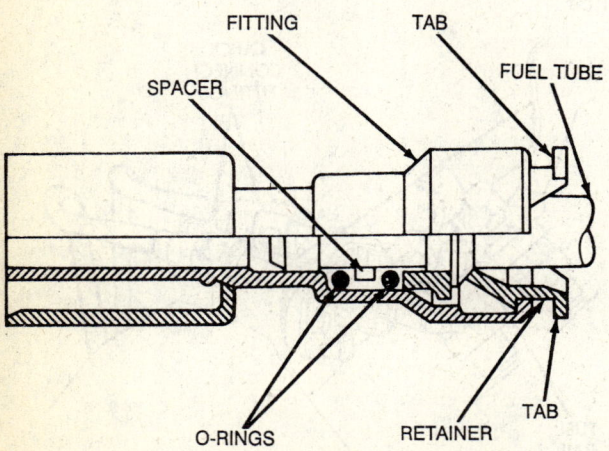

Exploded view of the quick connect fitting

1989–90
- Fastener 1: 30 ft. lbs.
- Fasteners 2 through 11: 23 ft. lbs.
- Fasteners 12 & 13: 30 ft. lbs.

1991
- Fasteners 1 through 5: 23 ft. lbs.
- Fasteners 6 & 7: 17 ft. lbs.
- Fasteners 8 through 11: 23 ft. lbs.

26. Connect the oxygen sensor wiring at the sensor.
27. Connect the exhaust pipe at the exhaust manifold.
28. Install the intake manifold heat shield.
29. Install the fuel rail and injectors.
30. Install the power steering pump and bracket and set it aside.
31. Adjust the serpentine belt tensioner.
32. Connect the fuel supply and return lines at the fuel rail. Use new O-rings at the quick-connect fittings.
33. Connect all wiring connectors at the manifold.
34. Connect the vacuum multiconnector at the intake manifold.
35. Connect the accelerator cable, cruise control cable and transmission line pressure cable.
36. Connect the EGR tube nuts at the intake manifold and exhaust manifold.
37. Fill the cooling system.
38. Install the air cleaner.
39. Connect the negative battery cable.

Exhaust Manifold

REMOVAL AND INSTALLATION

4-2.1L Diesel

1. Disconnect the negative battery cable. Remove the intake manifold.
2. Disconnect the exhaust pipe from the adapter.
3. Remove the oil supply pipe and the oil return hose from the turbocharger assembly (see illustration).
4. Disconnect the turbocharger air inlet and outlet hoses (see illustration).
5. Remove the turbocharger retaining bolts. Remove the turbocharger from the vehicle.
6. Remove the exhaust manifold retaining bolts. Remove the exhaust manifold and gasket. Discard the gasket.

To install:

7. Position the exhaust manifold and gasket on the head.
8. Install the exhaust manifold retaining bolts and torque them to 31 ft. lbs.
9. Install the turbocharger.
10. Connect the turbocharger air inlet and outlet hoses.
11. Install the oil supply pipe and the oil return hose at the turbocharger assembly.
12. Connect the exhaust pipe at the adapter.
13. Install the intake manifold.
14. Connect the negative battery cable.

4-2.5L

1. Disconnect negative battery cable.
2. Loosen the EGR tube nut at the intake manifold and tube bolts at the exhaust manifold.
3. Remove the intake manifold.
4. Raise and support the vehicle safely.
5. Disconnect the exhaust pipe at the manifold.
6. Disconnect the oxygen sensor wire.
7. Remove the intake exhaust manifold assembly.
8. If a new manifold is being installed, transfer the oxygen sensor. Torque the sensor to 35 ft. lbs.
9. Installation is the reverse of removal. See Intake Manifold Removal and Installation for torque sequence and specifications.

ENGINE AND ENGINE OVERHAUL 3

6-2.8L

LEFT SIDE

1. Disconnect the negative battery cable. Remove the air cleaner.
2. Remove the air injection hose and manifold (if equipped).
3. Remove the power steering bracket.
4. Raise and support the vehicle safely. Unbolt and remove the exhaust pipe at the manifold.
5. Unbolt and remove the manifold.
6. Clean the mating surfaces of the cylinder head and manifold. Install the manifold onto the head, and install the retaining bolts finger tight.
7. Tighten the manifold bolts in a circular pattern, working from the center to the ends, to 25 ft. lbs. in two stages.
8. Connect the exhaust pipe to the manifold.
9. The remainder of installation is the reverse of removal.

RIGHT SIDE

1. Disconnect the negative battery cable. Raise and support the vehicle safely.
2. Disconnect the exhaust pipe from the exhaust manifold.
3. Lower the vehicle. Remove the spark plug wires from the plugs. Number them first if they are not already labeled. Remove the cruise control servo from the right inner fender panel, if equipped.
4. Remove the air supply pipes from the manifold. Remove the

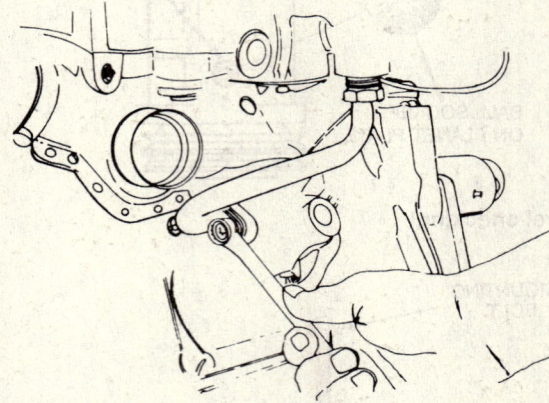

4-2.5L EGR tube installation

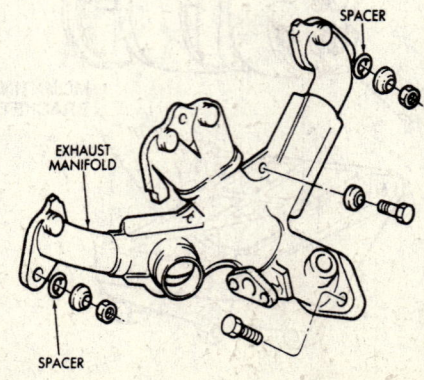

4-2.5L exhaust manifold spacers

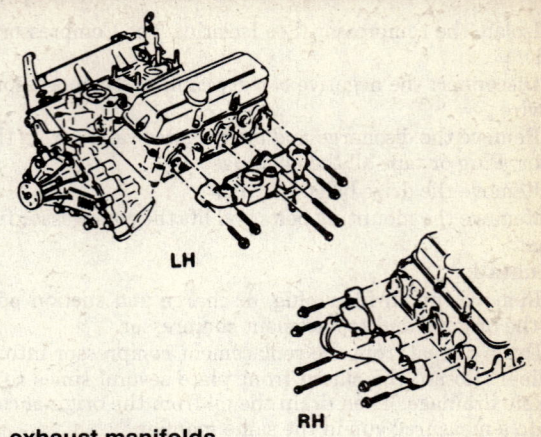

6-2.8L exhaust manifolds

Pulsair bracket bolt from the rocker cover, on models so equipped, then remove the pipe assembly.

5. Remove the manifold retaining bolts and remove the manifold.
6. Clean the mating surfaces of the cylinder head and manifold. Position the manifold against the head and install the retaining bolts finger tight.
7. Tighten the bolts in a circular pattern, working from the center to the ends, to 25 ft. lbs. in two stages.
8. Install the air supply system. Install the spark plug wires. If equipped install the cruise control servo.
9. Raise and support the vehicle safely. Connect the exhaust pipe to the manifold.

6-4.0L

The intake and exhaust manifolds of the 6-4.0L must be removed together. See Intake Manifold Removal and Installation in this section.

Turbocharger

REMOVAL AND INSTALLATION

4-2.1L Diesel

1. Disconnect the negative battery cable.
2. Remove all the necessary components in order to gain access to the turbocharger retaining bolts.
3. Disconnect the exhaust pipe flange. Remove the oil supply pipe. Remove the oil return hose.
4. Remove the turbocharger retaining bolts. Remove the turbocharger from the vehicle.

To install:

5. Position the turbocharger on the manifold.
6. Install the turbocharger retaining bolts. Torque the bolts to 31 ft. lbs.
7. Install the oil return hose.
8. Install the oil supply pipe.
9. Connect the exhaust pipe flange.
10. Install any removed components.
11. Connect the negative battery cable.

Air Conditioning Compressor

REMOVAL AND INSTALLATION

NOTE: If a replacement compressor is being installed, check the oil level in the compressor before putting the system into service.

3 ENGINE AND ENGINE OVERHAUL

1. Isolate the compressor (See Isolating The Compressor in Section 1).
2. Disconnect the negative battery cable and compressor clutch lead wire.
3. Remove the discharge and inlet service valves from the compressor. Plug or tape all the openings.
4. Remove the drive belts.
5. Remove the mounting bolts and lift the compressor from the bracket.

To install:

6. Remove the oil filler plug, discharge and suction port caps from the original and replacement compressor.
7. Drain the oil from the replacement compressor into a clean container. Rotate the clutch front plate several times to ensure complete drainage. Then drain the oil from the original compressor into a measured cup in the same manner.
8. Fill the replacement compressor with the same amount of oil drained from the original compressor plus 1 additional fluid ounce. Use Suniso 5GS compressor oil or equivalent.
9. Install the compressor on the mounting bracket and tighten the bolts to 20 ft.lbs. torque.
10. Install the drive belts. Tighten V-type belts to 120–160 ft.lbs. if new, 90–115 ft.lbs. if used. Tighten serpentine belts to 180–200 ft.lbs. if new, 140–160 ft.lbs. if used.
11. Remove the tape or plugs from all suction and discharge openings and install the service valves on the compressor.
12. Connect the battery negative cable.
13. Evacuate, charge and test the system for leaks. See Section 1.

Radiator

NOTE: On some systems the air conditioning condenser must be removed with the radiator. This involves purging the refrigerant. See Discharging The System in Section 1 for the correct procedure. Be sure to use the proper precautions as Freon® can be dangerous if not handled correctly.

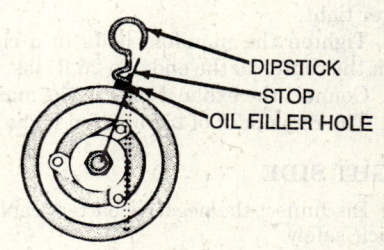

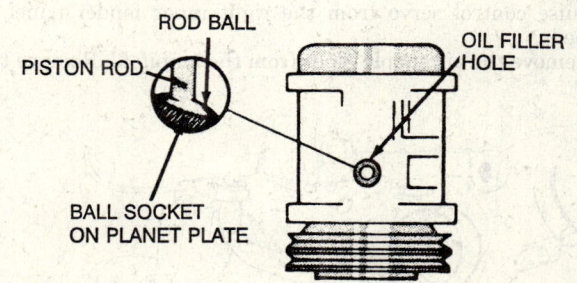

Oil level checking

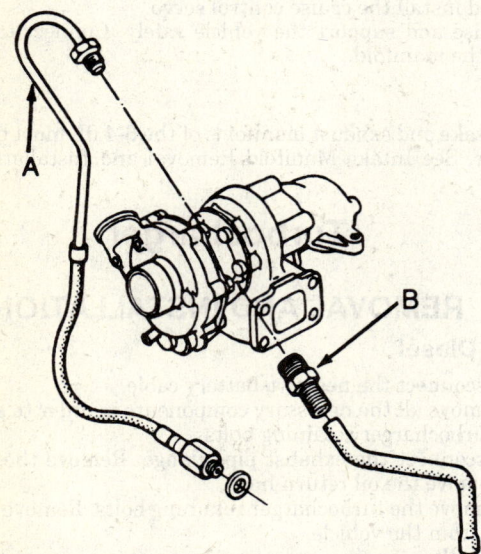

4-2.1L turbocharger oil supply (A) and return (B) lines

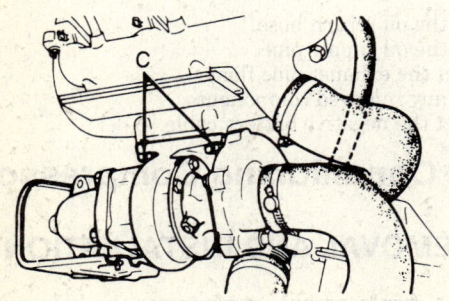

4-2.1L turbocharger mounting bolts (C)

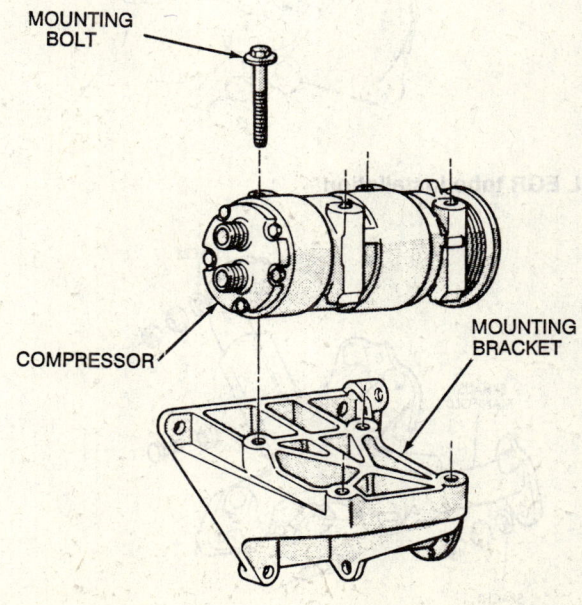

Remove/install air conditioning compressor

3-50

ENGINE AND ENGINE OVERHAUL 3

REMOVAL AND INSTALLATION

1. Disconnect the negative battery cable.

CAUTION
Do not remove the radiator cap or loosen the radiator draincock with the system hot and pressurized. Serious burns from the hot coolant can occur.

2. Remove radiator grille mounting screws and grille.
3. Drain the radiator by opening the drain cock and removing the radiator pressure cap. On some vehicles the drain cock is located on the right side of the radiator behind the park/turn signal lamp. Attach a 610mm (24 in.) long 6mm ($1/4$ in.) ID hose to the draincock to aid in removal of coolant.

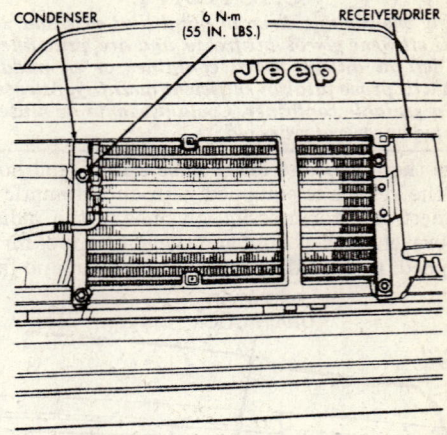
Condenser mounting screw locations on the 4-2.5L

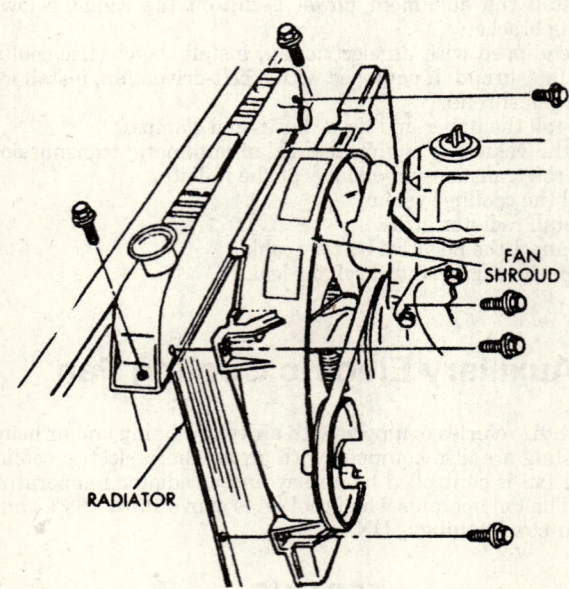
Fan shroud removal on the 4-2.5L

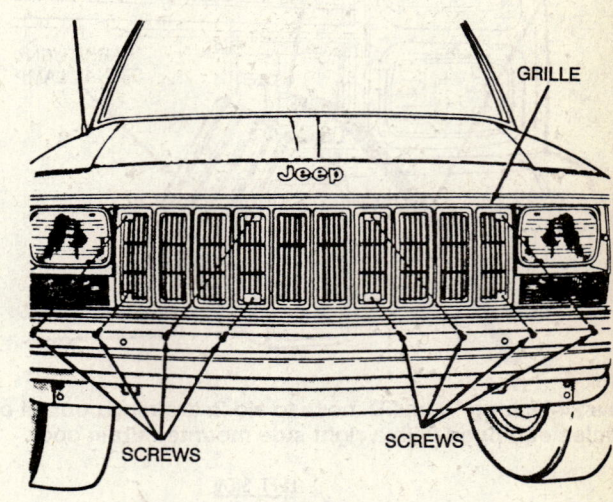
Radiator grille attaching screw locations

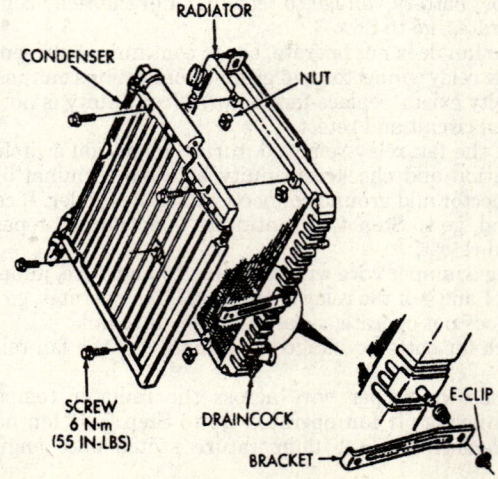
Radiator installation on the 4-2.5L

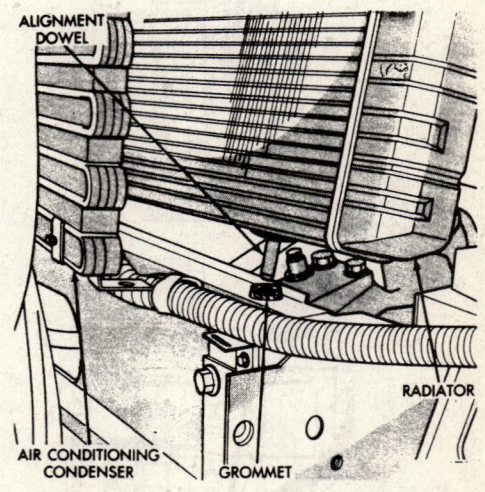
6-4.0L Radiator installation

3-51

3 ENGINE AND ENGINE OVERHAUL

CAUTION
When draining the coolant, keep in mind that cats and dogs are attracted by the ethylene glycol antifreeze, and are quite likely to drink any that is left in an uncovered container or in puddles on the ground. This will prove fatal in sufficient quantity. Always drain the coolant into a sealable container. Coolant should be reused unless it is contaminated or several years old.

4. Remove the upper and lower hose clamps and hoses at the radiator. If the vehicle is equipped with an automatic transmission, disconnect the transmission oil lines at the radiator. Plug the lines to prevent loss of fluid and the entrance of dirt.
5. If equipped, remove the electric cooling fan and fan shroud.

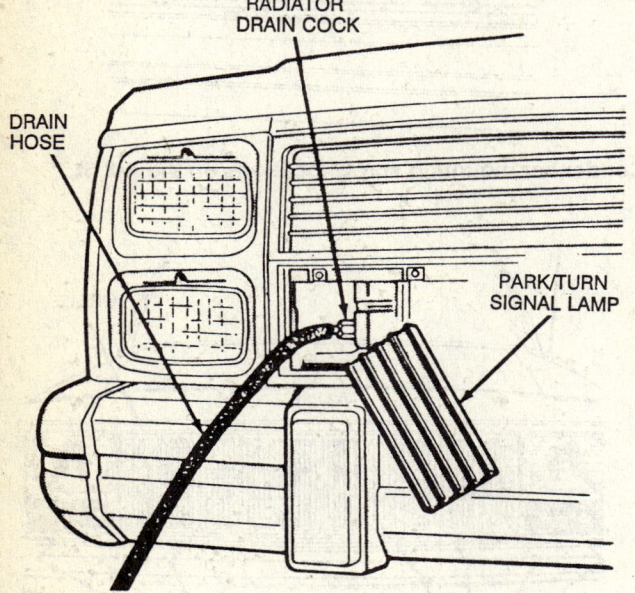

Use a 24 in. long ¼ in. I.D. hose to aid in draining coolant on vehicles equipped with a right side mounted drain cock

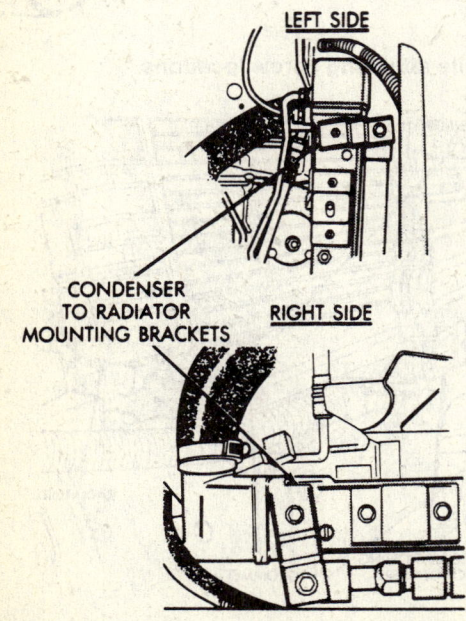

Condenser mounting brackets for the 6-4.0L

Remove mechanical fan shroud attaching screws and push shroud back against the front of the engine.
6. Remove the alignment dowel E-clip from the radiator lower mounting bracket.
7. Disconnect coolant reserve bottle hose from radiator.
8. Remove all attaching brackets and screws that secure the radiator to the radiator support.
9. Remove the air conditioning condenser to radiator mounting screws using an open end wrench.
10. Remove the radiator by lifting straight up. Take care not to damage the radiator fins.

To install:
11. Install the radiator. Take care not to damage the radiator fins. Torque the mounting screws to 36 inch lbs.
12. Install the air conditioning condenser-to-radiator mounting screws.
13. Install all attaching brackets and screws that secure the radiator to the radiator support.
14. Connect the coolant reserve bottle hose at radiator.
15. Install the alignment dowel E-clip on the radiator lower mounting bracket.
16. If equipped with an electric fan, install the electric cooling fan and fan shroud. If equipped with a belt-driven fan, install mechanical fan shroud.
17. Install the upper and lower hoses and clamps.
18. If the vehicle is equipped with an automatic transmission, connect the transmission oil lines at the radiator.
19. Fill the cooling system.
20. Install radiator grille.
21. Connect the negative battery cable.
22. Run the engine and check for leaks.

Auxiliary Electric Cooling Fan

All 6-4.0L vehicles equipped with air conditioning and/or heavy duty cooling are also equipped with an auxiliary electric cooling fan. The fan is controlled by a relay and a radiator temperature switch. The fan operates when coolant is above 190°F (88°C) and/or the air conditioning is ON.

TESTING

1. Remove fan relay. Using a jumper wire with an inline 25 amp fuse, supply battery voltage to terminal 4 of the relay connector. If fan operates, go to Step 3.
2. If the fan does not operate, check continuity between terminal 4 of the relay connector and ground connections on the fender. If continuity exists, replace fan motor. If continuity is not found, repair open circuit and retest.
3. With the fan relay removed, turn the ignition switch to the RUN position and check continuity between terminal 5 of the relay connector and ground connections on the fender. If continuity is found, go to Step 4. If continuity is not found, repair open circuit and retest.
4. Using a jumper wire with an inline 25 amp fuse, jump across terminals 1 and 4 of the relay connector. If fan operates, go to Step 5. If fan does not operate, repair fan relay fuse link.
5. Check for battery voltage at terminal 2 of the fan relay connector.
6. Connect a jumper wire across the radiator temperature switch connector. If fan operates, go to Step 7. If fan does not operate, replace radiator temperature switch once engine has cooled.
7. Check for battery voltage at terminal 2 of the fan relay connector. If battery voltage is not found, replace fan diode assembly.

ENGINE AND ENGINE OVERHAUL 3

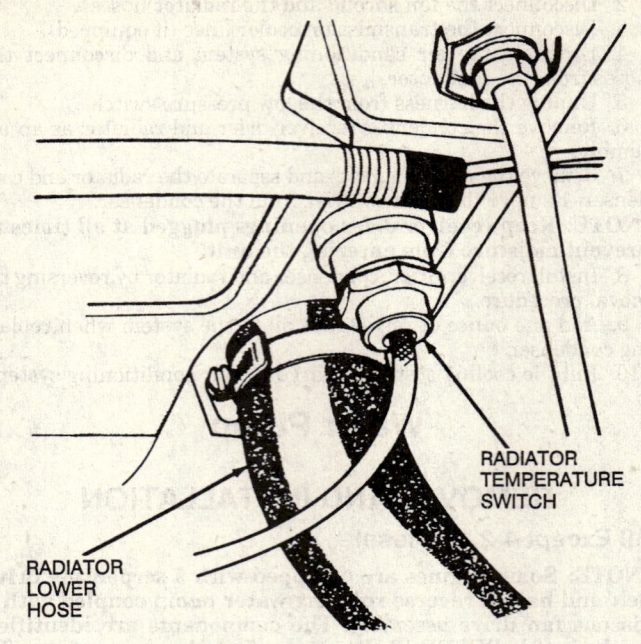

Electric cooling fan temperature switch location

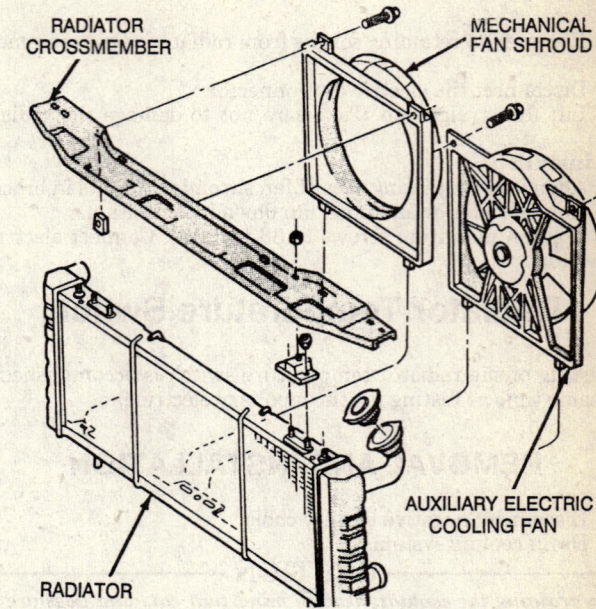

Auxiliary electric cooling fan remove/install

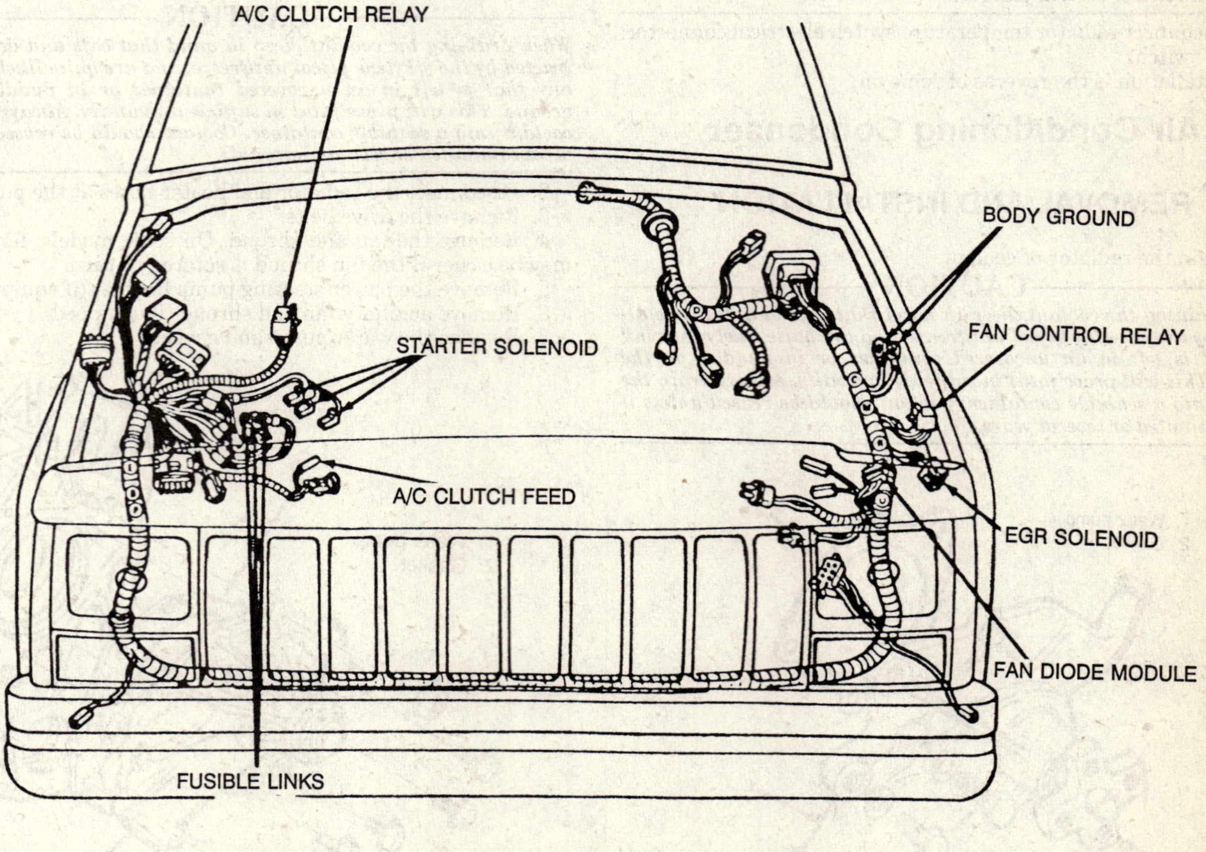

Auxiliary electric fan connector locations

3-53

3 ENGINE AND ENGINE OVERHAUL

REMOVAL AND INSTALLATION

1. Remove fan retaining screws from radiator upper crossmember.
2. Disconnect the electric fan connector.
3. Lift fan straight up. Take care not to damage the radiator fins.

To install:

4. Align lower retaining tabs of fan shroud with slots in bracket at bottom of radiator and push fan down into position.
5. Tighten mounting screws to 36 inch lbs. Connect electrical connector.

Radiator Temperature Switch

Testing of the radiator temperature switch is accomplished at the same time as testing for the auxiliary electric fan.

REMOVAL AND INSTALLATION

1. Disconnect negative battery cable.
2. Drain cooling system.

CAUTION

When draining the coolant, keep in mind that cats and dogs are attracted by the ethylene glycol antifreeze, and are quite likely to drink any that is left in an uncovered container or in puddles on the ground. This will prove fatal in sufficient quantity. Always drain the coolant into a sealable container. Coolant should be reused unless it is contaminated or several years old.

---

3. Disconnect radiator temperature switch electrical connector. Remove switch.
4. Installation is the reverse of removal.

Air Conditioning Condenser

REMOVAL AND INSTALLATION

1. Drain the radiator of coolant.

CAUTION

When draining the coolant, keep in mind that cats and dogs are attracted by the ethylene glycol antifreeze, and are quite likely to drink any that is left in an uncovered container or in puddles on the ground. This will prove fatal in sufficient quantity. Always drain the coolant into a sealable container. Coolant should be reused unless it is contaminated or several years old.

---

2. Disconnect the fan shroud and the radiator hoses.
3. Disconnect the transmission cooler lines (if equipped).
4. Evacuate the air conditioning system and disconnect the hoses from the condenser.
5. Unplug the harness from the low pressure switch.
6. Remove the condenser/receiver drier and radiator as an assembly.
7. Remove the retaining bolts and separate the radiator and condenser. Remove the receiver/drier from the condenser.

NOTE: Keep receiver/drier openings plugged at all times to prevent moisture from entering the unit.

8. Install receiver/drier, condenser and radiator by reversing removal procedure.
9. Add one ounce of refrigerant oil to the system when replacing condenser.
10. Fill the cooling system. Charge the air conditioning system.

Water Pump

REMOVAL AND INSTALLATION

All Except 4-2.1L Diesel

NOTE: Some engines are equipped with a serpentine drive belt and have a reverse rotating water pump coupled with a viscous fan drive assembly. The components are identified by the words REVERSE (R) stamped on the cover of the viscous drive and on the inner side of the fan. The word REV is also cast into the body of the water pump.

1. Drain the cooling system.

CAUTION

When draining the coolant, keep in mind that cats and dogs are attracted by the ethylene glycol antifreeze, and are quite likely to drink any that is left in an uncovered container or in puddles on the ground. This will prove fatal in sufficient quantity. Always drain the coolant into a sealable container. Coolant should be reused unless it is contaminated or several years old.

---

2. Disconnect the radiator and heater hoses at the pump.
3. Remove the drive belts.
4. Remove the fan and shroud. On some models, fan removal may be easier if the fan is rotated 1/8 turn.
5. Remove the power steering pump bracket (if equipped).
6. Remove auxiliary fan and shroud (if equipped).
7. Remove the water pump and gasket.

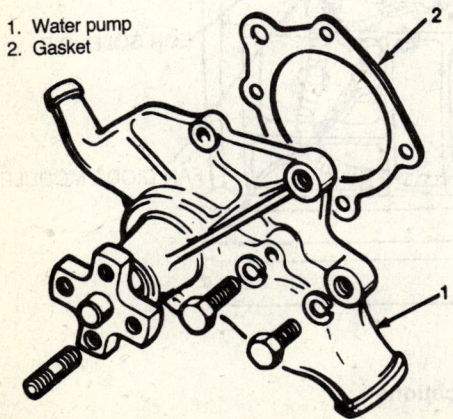

1. Water pump
2. Gasket

6-2.8L water pump

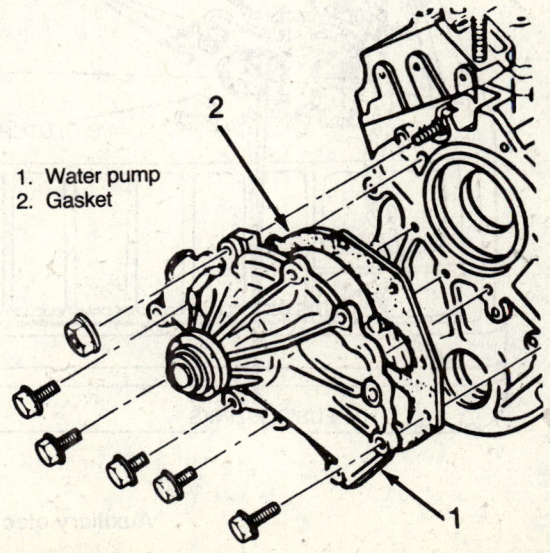

1. Water pump
2. Gasket

4-2.5L water pump

ENGINE AND ENGINE OVERHAUL 3

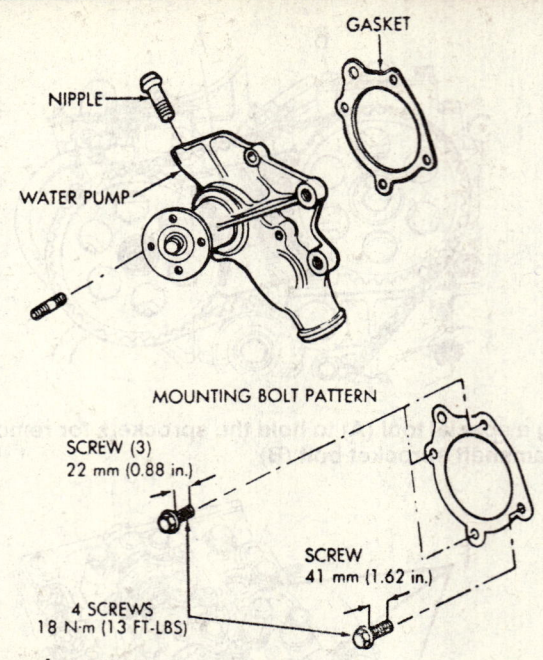

6-4.0L water pump

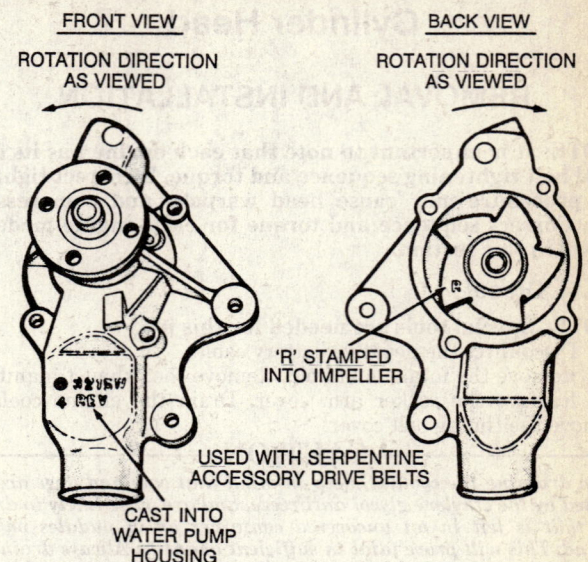

Reverse rotation water pump used with serpentine accessory drive belt

8. Clean the mating surfaces thoroughly.
9. Using a new gasket, install the pump and torque the bolts to 13 ft. lbs. Rotate the shaft to ensure it turns freely.
10. Connect radiator and heater hoses. Install fan and shroud; tighten nuts to 18 ft.lbs.

NOTE: When installing the serpentine drive belt, the belt must be routed correctly. If not, the engine may overheat due to the water pump rotating in the wrong direction.

11. Install accessory drive belts. Tension serpentine belt to 180–200 lbs. if new, 140–160 lbs. if used. Tension V-belt to 120–160 lbs. if new, 90–115 lbs. if used.
12. Fill cooling system. On 4-2.5L engines remove the coolant temperature sensor in the intake manifold to permit air to escape from the block. Reinstall the sensor when the cooling system is filled.
13. Operate the engine with the heater control valve in the HEAT position until the thermostat opens to purge air from the system. Check coolant level and fill as required.

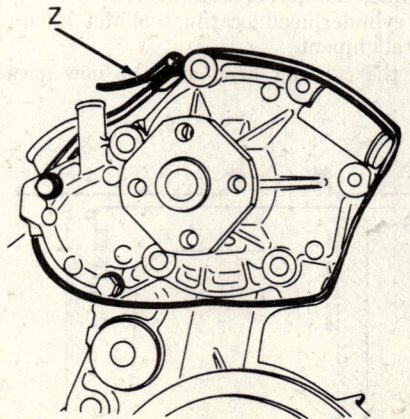

Using a strap and clip to retain the 4-2.1L timing belt tensioner

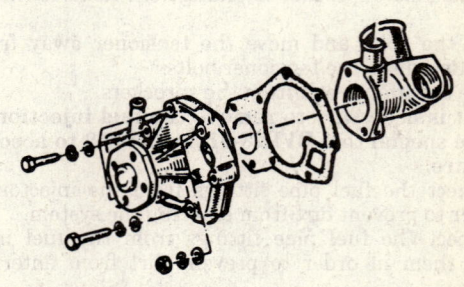

4-2.1L water pump mounting

4-2.1L Diesel

1. Disconnect the negative battery cable. Drain the engine coolant.

── CAUTION ──
When draining the coolant, keep in mind that cats and dogs are attracted by the ethylene glycol antifreeze, and are quite likely to drink any that is left in an uncovered container or in puddles on the ground. This will prove fatal in sufficient quantity. Always drain the coolant into a sealable container. Coolant should be reused unless it is contaminated or several years old.

2. Remove the coolant hose from the water pump.
3. Remove the drive belts.
4. Remove the fan and hub assembly.
5. It is not necessary to remove the timing belt tensioner. Use a long strap and clip in order to retain the timing belt tensioner plunger in place.
6. Remove the water pump retaining bolts. Remove the water pump assembly from the vehicle.
7. Clean the mating surfaces of all gasket material.
8. Do not use sealer on the new gasket. Position the gasket and pump on the engine and install the bolts. Torque the bolts to 15 ft. lbs.
9. Re-tension the timing belt.
10. Install the fan and hub, drive belts and coolant hoses.
11. Fill the cooling system.
12. Connect the battery.

3-55

3 ENGINE AND ENGINE OVERHAUL

Cylinder Head

REMOVAL AND INSTALLATION

NOTE: It is important to note that each engine has its own head bolt tightening sequence and torque. Incorrect tightening procedure may cause head warpage and compression loss. Correct sequence and torque for each engine model is shown in this section.

4-2.1L Diesel

NOTE: Special tools are needed for this job.
1. Disconnect the negative battery cable.
2. Remove the intake manifold. Remove the exhaust manifold.
3. Remove the rocker arm cover. Drain the engine coolant. Remove the timing belt cover.

CAUTION

When draining the coolant, keep in mind that cats and dogs are attracted by the ethylene glycol antifreeze, and are quite likely to drink any that is left in an uncovered container or in puddles on the ground. This will prove fatal in sufficient quantity. Always drain the coolant into a sealable container. Coolant should be reused unless it is contaminated or several years old.

4. Install sprocket holding tool MOT-854 or equivalent and remove the camshaft sprocket retaining bolt. Remove the special tool.
5. Loosen the bolts and move the tensioner away from the timing belt. Retighten the tensioner bolts.
6. Remove the timing belt from the sprockets.

NOTE: If it is necessary to remove the fuel injection pump sprocket use special tool BVI-28-01 or BVI-859 to accomplish this procedure.

7. Disconnect the fuel pipe fittings from the injectors. Plug them in order to prevent dirt from entering the system.
8. Disconnect the fuel pipe fittings from the fuel injection pump. Plug them in order to prevent dirt from entering the system.
9. Remove the fuel pipes from their mountings on the engine. Remove all hoses and connectors from the fuel injection pump.
10. Remove the injection pump retaining bolts. Remove the fuel injection pump and its mounting brackets, as an assembly, from the vehicle.
11. Remove the retaining bolts and nuts from the cylinder head. Loosen pivot bolt but do not remove it. Remove the remaining cylinder head bolts.
12. Place a block of wood against the cylinder head and tap it with a hammer in order to loosen the cylinder head gasket. The pivot movement will be minimal due to the small clearance between the studs and the cylinder head. Remove the pivot bolt from the cylinder head.
13. Remove the retaining bolts and the rocker arm shaft assembly from the cylinder head.

NOTE: Do not lift the cylinder head from the cylinder block until the gasket is completely loosened from the cylinder liners. Otherwise, the liner seals could be broken.

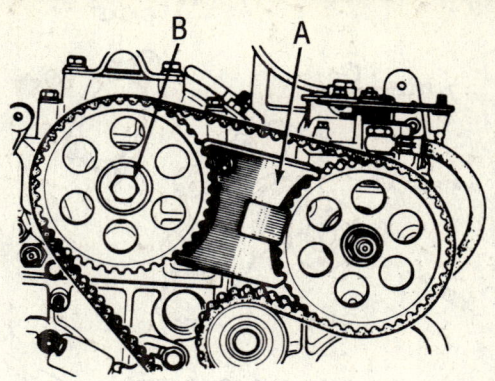

Using a special tool (A) to hold the sprockets for removal of the camshaft sprocket bolt (B)

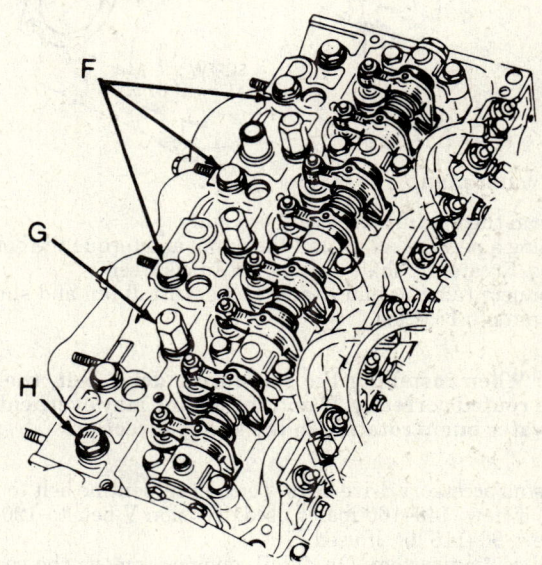

4-2.1L head bolts (F), nuts (G), and pivot bolt (H)

14. Remove the cylinder head and the gasket from the engine block. While the head is off, install liner clamp tool Mot.521-01 to hold the liners in place in the block.

To install:

15. Remove liner clamp tool Mot.521-01.
16. Position cylinder head locating tool Mot.720 on the block to insure proper alignment.
17. Position the cylinder head and the new gasket from the

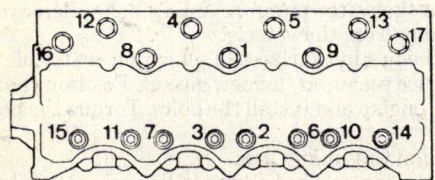

4-2.1L diesel head bolt torque sequence

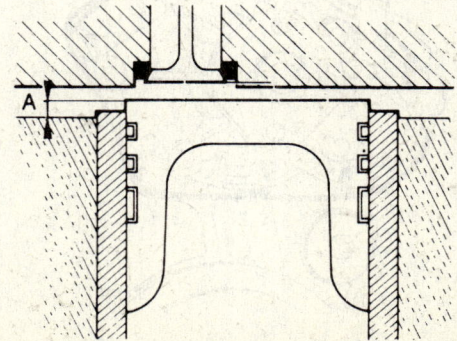

Piston protrusion measured at (A) on the 4-2.1L

3-56

ENGINE AND ENGINE OVERHAUL 3

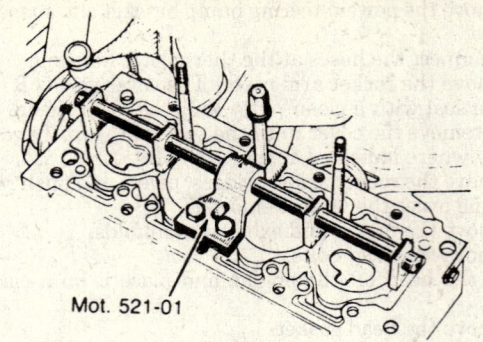

Cylinder liner clamp tool in place on the 4-2.1L block

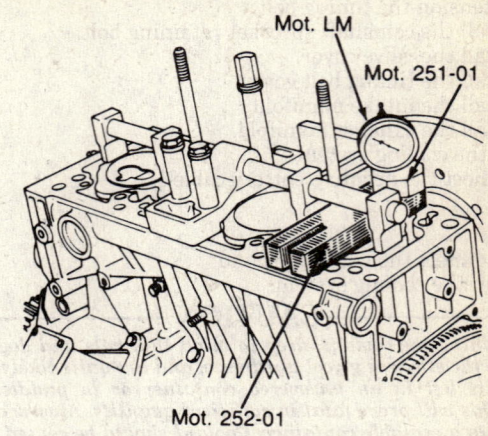

Piston protrusion measurement tools in place on the 4-2.1L

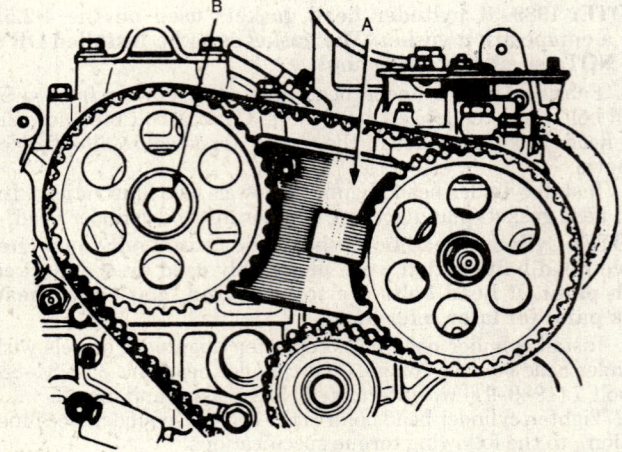

Using a special tool (A) to hold the sprockets for removal of the camshaft sprocket bolt (B)

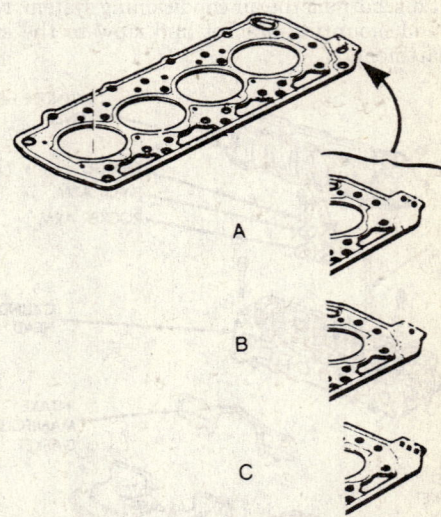

Identifying the proper head gasket thickness for the 4-2.1L: A = 1.6mm; B = 1.7mm; C = 1.8mm

engine block. Be sure that the new cylinder head gasket is positioned properly on the cylinder head and that it is the correct thickness for piston protrusion. Whenever major components, such as pistons, liners, crankshaft, etc., have been replaced, the piston protrusion must be measured to determine proper replacement head gasket thickness. Measure the protrusion as follows:

a. Rotate the crankshaft one complete revolution clockwise and bring #1 piston to a point just below and before TDC.
b. Place thrust plate tool Mot.252-01 on top of the piston.
c. Assemble dial indicator LM in block gauge Mot.251-01 and place this assembly on one side of the thrust plate.
d. Zero the indicator with the stem on the cylinder block face.
e. Place the stem on the top of the piston and rotate the crankshaft clockwise to TDC of the piston. Record the piston travel.
f. Repeat the procedure with the dial indicator on the opposite side of the block. Record the piston travel.
g. Add the two figures together and divide by two. Repeat the protrusion measurement for the three remaining pistons. The piston with the greatest protrusion should be the basis for determining gasket thickness. For example, if the amount of greatest piston protrusion is:
 • Less than 0.96mm, use a gasket 1.6mm thick
 • Between 0.96mm and 1.04mm, use a 1.7mm thick gasket
 • More than 1.04mm, use a 1.8mm thick gasket

18. Install the head bolts. Torque the cylinder head retaining bolts to 22 ft. lbs., then to 37 ft. lbs., then to 70–77 ft. lbs. Once all the bolts are tightened, recheck the torque.

NOTE: The cylinder head bolts must be retightened after the cylinder head is installed in the vehicle. Operate the engine for a minimum of twenty minutes. Allow the engine to cool for a minimum of two and one half hours. Loosen each cylinder head bolt in sequence about 1/8 turn. Then retighten in the proper sequence and torque to 70–77 ft. lbs. For the final tightening, tighten the bolts again, in sequence, without loosening them to 70–77 ft. lbs.

19. Remove tool Mot.720.
20. Install the rocker arm shaft assembly.
21. Install the fuel injection pump and its mounting brackets, as an assembly. See Section 5.
22. Install the fuel pipes on their mountings on the engine. Install all hoses and connectors on the fuel injection pump.
23. Connect the fuel pipe fittings to the fuel injection pump.
24. Connect the fuel pipe fittings from the injectors.
25. Install the timing belt.

3 ENGINE AND ENGINE OVERHAUL

26. Re-tension the timing belt.
27. Install the camshaft sprocket retaining bolt.
28. Install the valve cover.
29. Install the timing belt cover.
30. Install the intake manifold.
31. Install the exhaust manifold.
32. Fill the cooling system.
33. Connect the negative battery cable.

4-2.5L

1. Disconnect the battery ground.
2. Drain the cooling system.

CAUTION

When draining the coolant, keep in mind that cats and dogs are attracted by the ethylene glycol antifreeze, and are quite likely to drink any that is left in an uncovered container or in puddles on the ground. This will prove fatal in sufficient quantity. Always drain the coolant into a sealable container. Coolant should be reused unless it is contaminated or several years old.

---

3. Loosen the accessory drive belt and remove.
4. Without discharging the air conditioning system, remove the compressor and mounting bracket and stow to the side of the engine compartment.

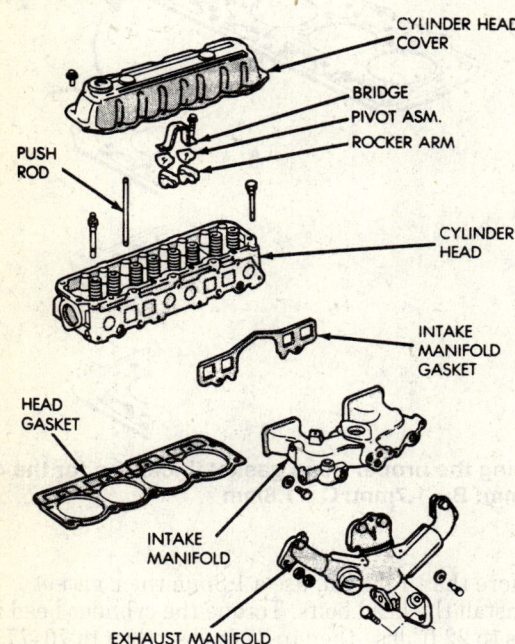

4-2.5L cylinder head components

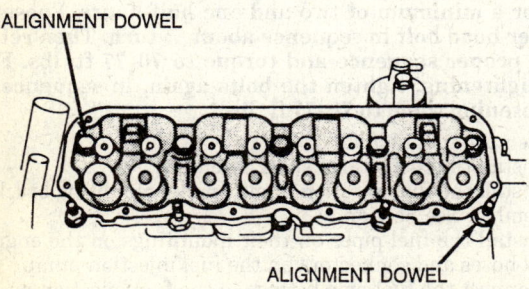

Alignment dowel placement on the 4-2.5L

5. Remove the power steering pump bracket and suspend out of the way.
6. Disconnect the hoses at the thermostat housing.
7. Remove the rocker arm cover. The cover seal is RTV sealer. Break the seal with a clean putty knife or razor blade. Don't attempt to remove the cover until the seal is broken. To remove the cover, pry where indicated at the bolt holes.
8. Remove the rocker arms, bridges, pivots and push rods. Keep them in the order they were removed!
9. Remove the intake and exhaust manifolds.
10. Remove the head bolts.
11. Lift the head off the engine and place it on a clean workbench.
12. Remove the head gasket.

To install:

13. Install the head gasket. Apply sealer to both sides of the new gasket; never to the head or block surfaces!

NOTE: 1989–91 cylinder head gaskets used on the 4-2.5L are a composition gasket. The gasket is to be installed DRY. DO NOT use sealing compound

14. Fabricate two cylinder head alignment dowels from used head bolts. Use the longest head bolts. Cut the bolt off below the hex head. Next cut a slot in the top of the dowel to allow easier removal.
15. Install cylinder head alignment dowels (see illustration). Install head gasket (manufacturer number up) and cylinder head.

NOTE: Cylinder head bolts should be reused only once. Replace head bolts which were previously used or are marked with paint. If head bolts are to be reused, mark each head with paint for later reference.

16. Install cylinder head bolts replacing alignment dowels with cylinder head bolts as you go. Coat cylinder head bolt 8 (1984–88) or bolt 7 (1989–91) with Permatex No.2 sealant and install.
17. Tighten cylinder head bolts in the correct sequence (see illustration), to the following torque specifications:

- **1984–88**
  a. Using three steps, torque all bolts in sequence (except bolt 8) to 85 ft.lbs.
  b. Torque bolt 8 to 75 ft.lbs.
- **1989–91**
  a. Tighten bolts 1 through 10 in sequence to 22 ft.lbs.
  b. Tighten bolts 1 through 10 in sequence to 45 ft.lbs.
  c. Tighten bolts 1 through 6 and 8 through 10 in sequence to 110 ft.lbs.
  d. Tighten bolt 7 to 100 ft.lbs.

NOTE: Some head bolts used on the spark plug side of the 1984 4-2.5L were improperly hardened and may break under the head during service or at head installation while torquing the bolts. Engines with the defective bolts are serial numbers 310U06 through 310U14. Whenever a broken bolt is found, replace all bolts on the spark plug side of the head with bolt #400 6593.

18. Install the rocker arm cover. The cover gasket is RTV sealer. Thoroughly clean the mating surfaces of the head and rocker cover. Run a $1/8$ inch bead of RTV sealer along the length of the sealing surface of the head. Position the cover on the head within 10 minutes of applying the sealer. Torque the cover bolts, in a crisscross pattern, to 55 inch lbs.
19. Install the intake and exhaust manifolds.
20. Connect the hoses at the thermostat housing.
21. Install power steering pump bracket and pump.
22. Install air conditioning compressor mounting bracket. Torque to 30 ft.lbs. Install compressor and torque to 20 ft.lbs.
23. Install the accessory drive belt.

NOTE: The accessory drive belt must be routed correctly. Incorrect routing can cause the water pump to turn in the opposite direction causing the engine to overheat.

ENGINE AND ENGINE OVERHAUL 3

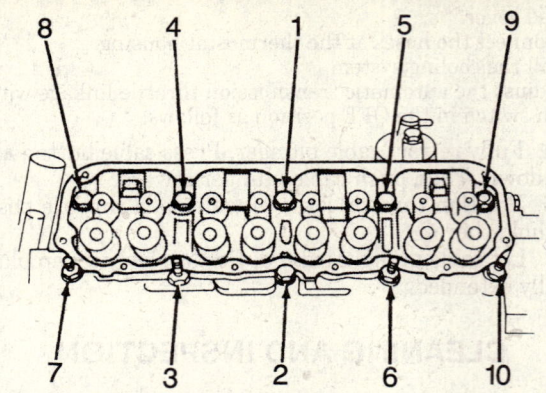

4-2.5L head bolt torque sequence

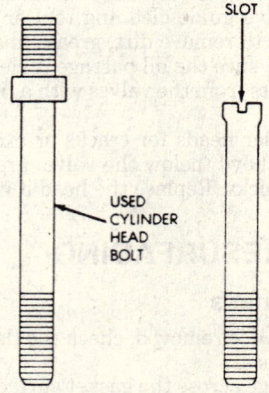

Fabricated cylinder head alignment dowels for the 4-2.5L

6. Remove the dipstick tube.
7. Loosen the rocker arm bolts and remove the pushrods. Keep the pushrods in the same order as removed.
8. Remove the cylinder head bolts in stages and in the reverse order of the tightening sequence.
9. Remove the cylinder head. Do not pry on the head to loosen it.

To install:
10. Thoroughly clean the head and block mating surfaces. All bolt holes must be free of foreign material.
11. Place a new head gasket on the block with the words **This Side Up**, up.
12. Position the cylinder head on the block.
13. Coat the cylinder head bolts with RTV silicone sealant and install them. Torque the bolts, in sequence, in three equal stages. The final stage should be 70 ft. lbs.
14. Install the pushrods, keeping them in the same order as removed.
15. Install the rocker arms.
16. Install the dipstick tube.
17. Install the power steering pump and bracket.
18. Install the exhaust manifold.
19. Install the intake manifold.
20. Connect the exhaust pipe from the exhaust manifold.
21. Fill the cooling system.
22. Connect the negative battery cable.
23. Adjust the valves.

RIGHT SIDE

1. Disconnect the negative battery cable. Raise and support the vehicle safely. Drain the coolant from the block.

CAUTION
When draining the coolant, keep in mind that cats and dogs are attracted by the ethylene glycol antifreeze, and are quite likely to drink any that is left in an uncovered container or in puddles on the ground. This will prove fatal in sufficient quantity. Always drain the coolant into a sealable container. Coolant should be reused unless it is contaminated or several years old.

2. Disconnect the exhaust pipe and lower the vehicle.
3. If equipped, remove the cruise control servo bracket.
4. Remove the alternator and air pump bracket assembly.
5. Remove the intake manifold.
6. Loosen the rocker arm nuts and remove the pushrods. Keep the pushrods in the order in which they were removed.
7. Remove the cylinder head bolts in stages and in the reverse order of the tightening sequence.
8. Remove the cylinder head. Do not pry on the cylinder head to loosen it.

To install:
9. Thoroughly clean the head and block mating surfaces. All bolt holes must be free of foreign material.
10. Place a new head gasket on the block with the words **This Side Up** facing up.
11. Position the cylinder head on the block.
12. Coat the cylinder head bolts with RTV silicone sealant and install them. Torque the bolts, in sequence, in three equal stages. The final stage should be 70 ft. lbs.
13. Install the pushrods, keeping them in the same order as removed.
14. Install the rocker arms.
15. Install the exhaust manifold.
16. Install the intake manifold.
17. Connect the exhaust pipe from the exhaust manifold.
18. Fill the cooling system.
19. Connect the negative battery cable.
20. Adjust the valve lash.

24. Fill the cooling system.
25. Connect the battery ground.

6-2.8L

LEFT SIDE

1. Disconnect the negative battery cable. Raise and support the vehicle safely. Disconnect the exhaust pipe from the exhaust manifold.
2. Drain the coolant from the block and lower the vehicle.

CAUTION
When draining the coolant, keep in mind that cats and dogs are attracted by the ethylene glycol antifreeze, and are quite likely to drink any that is left in an uncovered container or in puddles on the ground. This will prove fatal in sufficient quantity. Always drain the coolant into a sealable container. Coolant should be reused unless it is contaminated or several years old.

3. Remove the intake manifold.
4. Remove the exhaust manifold.
5. If equipped, remove the power steering pump and bracket.

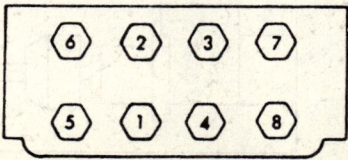

6-2.8L head bolt torque sequence

3-59

3 ENGINE AND ENGINE OVERHAUL

6-4.0L

1. Drain the cooling system and disconnect the hoses at the thermostat housing.

CAUTION
When draining the coolant, keep in mind that cats and dogs are attracted by the ethylene glycol antifreeze, and are quite likely to drink any that is left in an uncovered container or in puddles on the ground. This will prove fatal in sufficient quantity. Always drain the coolant into a sealable container. Coolant should be reused unless it is contaminated or several years old.

2. Remove the fuel line and vacuum advance hose.
3. Remove the rocker arm cover (valve cover), the gasket, the rocker arm assembly (rocker arm, pivot, bridge and capscrew), and the pushrods.

NOTE: The rocker arm assembly must be replaced in their original positions.

4. Remove the accessory drive belt by loosening the tensioner at the alternator.
5. Remove the alternator and mounting bracket. Set it aside in the engine compartment.
6. Remove the power steering pump and mounting bracket. DO NOT disconnect the hoses. Set the pump aside in the engine compartment.
7. Remove the air conditioning compressor. DO NOT disconnect the hoses. Set the compressor aside in the engine compartment.
8. Remove the intake and exhaust manifold from the cylinder head.
9. Disconnect the spark plug wires and the spark plugs to avoid damaging them.
10. Disconnect the temperature sending unit wire, ignition coil and bracket assembly from the engine.
11. Remove the ignition coil.
12. Remove the cylinder head bolts. On 1990–1991 vehicles bolt No.14 cannot be removed until the head is moved forward. Pull bolt No.14 out as far as it will go and suspend the bolt in this position by wrapping the stem of the bolt with tape. Remove the cylinder head and gasket from the block.

To install:

13. Coat a new head gasket with sealer and place it on the block. Most replacement gaskets will have the word TOP stamped on them.

NOTE: DO NOT apply sealing compound on the cylinder head and block gasket surfaces. DO NOT allow sealing compound to enter the cylinder bore.

14. Install the cylinder head and bolts. The threads of bolt No.11 must be coated with Loctite®592 sealant before installation. Tighten the bolts in sequence (see illustration) to the following torque specifications:
    a. Tighten bolts 1 through 10 in sequence to 22 ft.lbs.
    b. Tighten bolts 1 through 10 in sequence to 45 ft.lbs.
    c. Tighten bolts 1 through 6 and 8 through 10 in sequence to 110 ft.lbs.
    d. Tighten bolt 11 to 100 ft.lbs.

NOTE: Cylinder head bolts should be reused only once. Replace head bolts which were previously used or are marked with paint. If head bolts are to be reused, mark each head with paint for later reference.

15. Install the ignition coil.
16. Install spark plugs and connect the spark plug wires.
17. Install the air conditioning compressor and bracket.
18. Install the intake and exhaust manifold assembly.
19. Install the alternator and mounting bracket.
20. Install the power steering pump and bracket.
21. Adjust the serpentine belt tension.
22. Connect the temperature sending unit wire, ignition coil and bracket.
23. Install the pushrods, rocker arm assembly, gasket, and cylinder head cover.
24. Connect the hoses at the thermostat housing.
25. Fill the cooling system.
26. Adjust the automatic transmission throttle linkage with the ignition switch in the OFF position as follows:
    a. Fully retract cable plunger. Press cable button all the way down. Then push cable plunger inward.
    b. Position throttle lever in wide-open-throttle position and hold there.
    c. Let cable plunger extend. Release lever when plunger is fully extended.

CLEANING AND INSPECTION

1. With the valves installed to protect the valve seats, remove deposits from the combustion chambers and valve heads with a scraper and a wire brush. Be careful not to damage the cylinder head gasket surface. After the valves are removed, clean the valve guide bores with a valve guide cleaning tool or a bristle brush. Using cleaning solvent to remove dirt, grease and other deposits, clean all bolts holes; be sure the oil passage is clean (V6 engines).
2. Remove all deposits from the valves with a fine wire brush or buffing wheel.
3. Inspect the cylinder heads for cracks or excessively burned areas in the ports and bowl (below the valve) area. Check gasket surface for burrs and nicks. Replace the head if it is cracked.

RESURFACING

Cylinder Head Flatness

When the cylinder head is removed, check the flatness of the cylinder head gasket surfaces.

1. Place a straightedge across the gasket surface of the cylinder head. Using feeler gauges, determine the clearance at the center of the straightedge.
2. If warpage exceeds 0.076mm (0.003 in.) in a 152mm (6 in.) span, or 0.15mm (0.006 in.; 0.20mm (0.008 in.) for the diesel, over the total length, the cylinder head must be resurfaced.
3. If necessary to refinish the cylinder head gasket surface, do not plane or grind off more than 0.25mm (0.010 in.); 0.05mm (0.002 in.) for the diesel, from the original gasket surface.

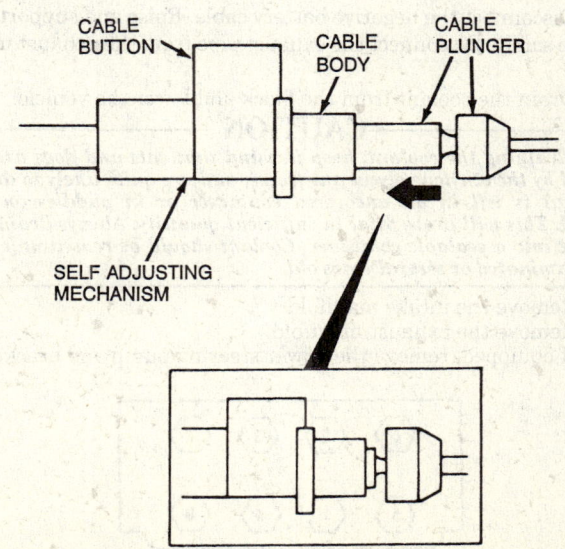

Retracting throttle cable plunger

ENGINE AND ENGINE OVERHAUL 3

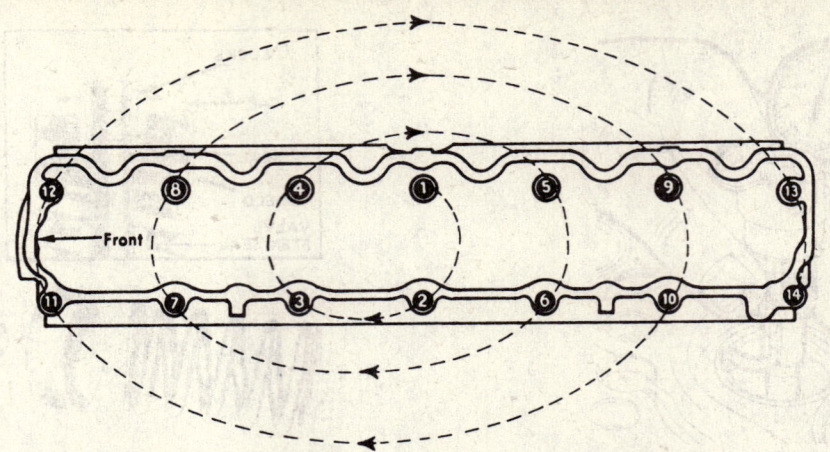

6-4.0L cylinder head bolt torque sequence

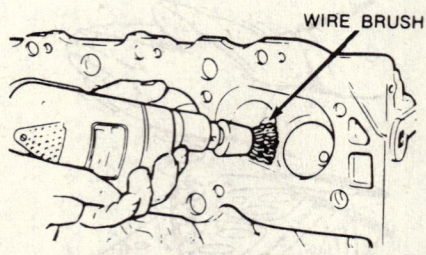

Remove all traces of carbon from the combustion chambers with a drill-mounted wire brush

NOTE: When milling the cylinder heads of V6 engines, the intake manifold mounting position is altered, and must be corrected by milling the manifold flange a proportionate amount. Consult an experienced machinist about this.

Valves

NOTE: Fabricate a valve arrangement board to use when you remove the valves, which will indicate the port in which each valve was originally installed (and which cylinder head on V6 models). Also note that the valve keys, rotators, caps, etc. should be arranged in a manner which will allow you to install them on the valve on which they were originally used.

REMOVAL

1. Remove the cylinder head.
2. Remove the rocker arm assemblies.
3. Using a spring compressor, compress the valve springs and remove the keepers (locks). Relax the compressor and remove the rotators, the springs and the lower washers (on some engines). Keep all parts in order.
4. Slide the valve seals from the stems. Replace the valve seals when service is performed or when seals have deteriorated.
5. Remove any burrs from the top of the valve stem with a jewelers file and slide the valves from the head, keeping them in order for installation.

INSPECTION

1. Clean all carbon deposits from the combustion chambers, valve ports, valve stems, valve guides and head.

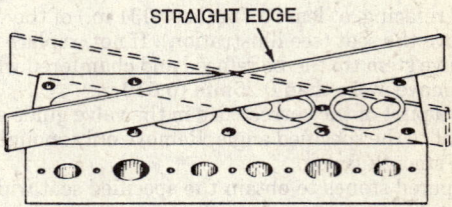

Checking cylinder head for warpage with a straight edge

2. Inspect the combustion chambers and valve ports for cracks. Inspect for cracks on the exhaust seat and the gasket surface at each coolant passage.
3. Inspect valves for burned, cracked or warped heads. Inspect for scuffed or bent valve stems.

REFACING

All engines have integral seats (they cannot be removed). Check the condition of the seats for excessive wear, pitting or cracks. Remove all traces of deposits from the seats. The seats may be refaced with a special grinding tool, to the dimensions shown in the Valve Specifications Charts.

1. Use a valve refacing machine to reface valves to the specified

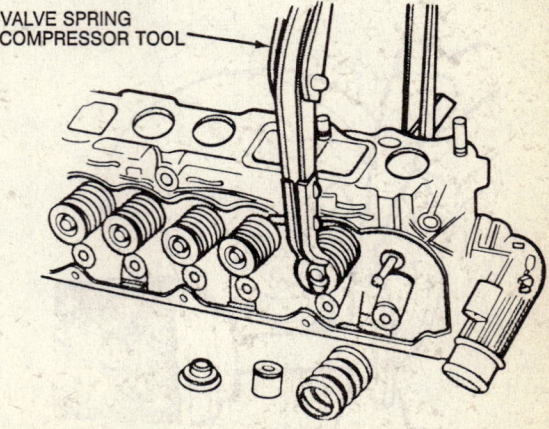

Remove valve spring and retainer with valve spring compressor

3-61

3 ENGINE AND ENGINE OVERHAUL

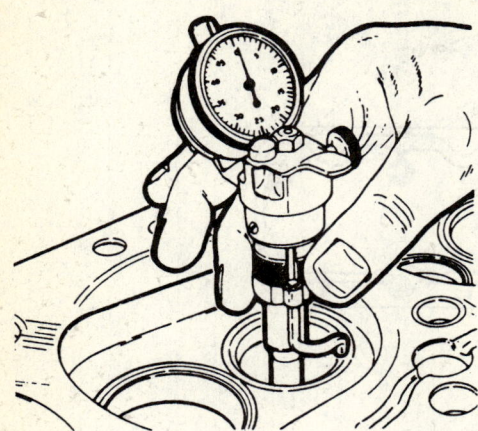

Checking valve seat runout with a dial gauge

angle. After refacing, at least 0.78mm (0.031 in.) of the valve head must be above the seat (see illustration). If not, replace the valve.

2. The valve stem tip can be refaced and chamfered when worn. DO NOT remove more than 0.25mm (0.010 in.).

3. Install a pilot of the correct size in the valve guide and reface the valve seat to the specified angle. Remove only enough material to provide a smooth finish.

4. Use tapered stones to obtain the specified seat widths when required.

5. Control valve seat runout to a maximum of 0.0635mm (0.0025 in.).

LAPPING

This procedure should be performed after the valves and seats have been refaced, to insure that each valve mates to each seat precisely.

1. Invert the cylinder head, lightly lubricate the valve stems, and install the valves in the head as numbered.

2. Coat valve seats with fine grinding compound, and attach the lapping tool suction cup to a valve head.

NOTE: Moisten the suction cup.

3. Rotate the tool between your palms, changing position and lifting the tool often to prevent grooving.

4. Lap the valve until a smooth, polished seat is evident.

5. Remove the valve and tool, and rinse away all traces of grinding compound.

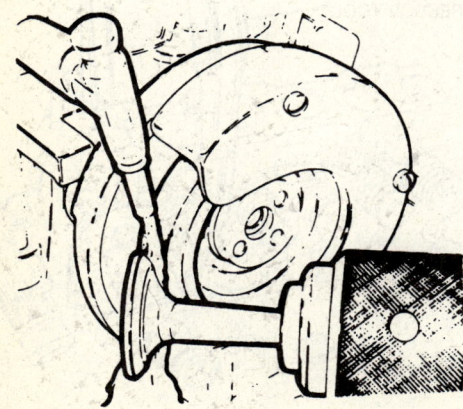

Refacing a valve on a valve grinding machine

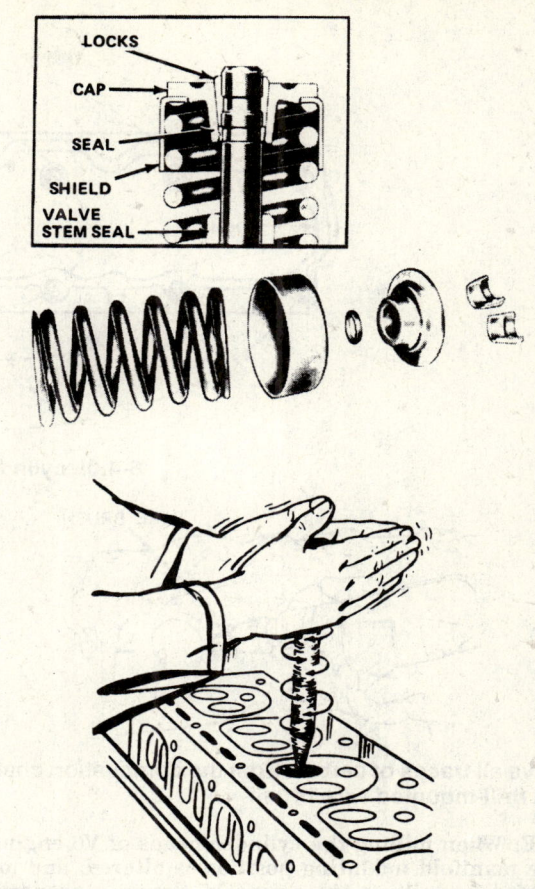

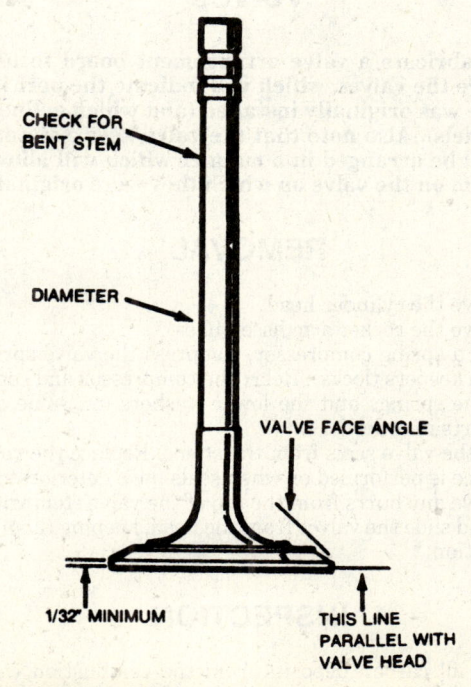

Lapping the valves by hand. The finish should be smooth; shiny and uniform

Critical valve dimensions

3-62

ENGINE AND ENGINE OVERHAUL 3

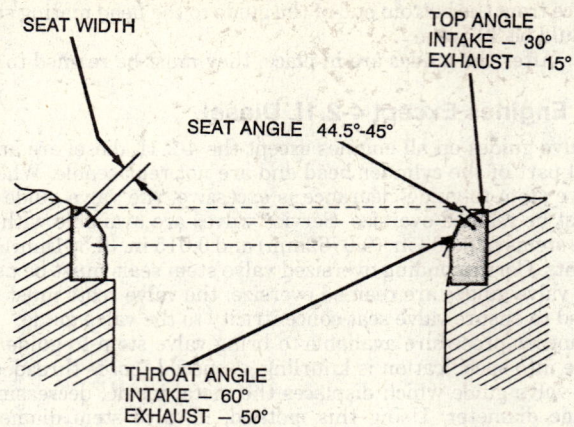

4-2.5L head bolt torque sequence

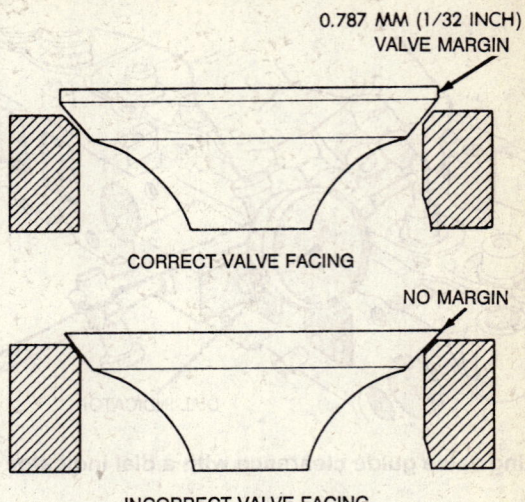

The valve facing margin must be correct for proper sealing

INSTALLATION

1. Thoroughly clean the valve stems and guides. Lightly lubricate the stem with oil and install the valve in its respective valve guide.
2. Install replacement valve stem oil seals (marked INT for intake and EXH for exhaust) over the stems and onto valve guide boss.

NOTE: If valves with oversized stems are used, oversize oil seals are required.

3. Position the valve spring and retainer on the cylinder head and compress the valve spring (with an appropriate valve spring compressor). Install valve locks and release the tool.
4. Lightly tap valve spring with a rubber hammer to ensure the spring is seated properly.
5. Install cylinder head on cylinder block.

Valve Springs

REMOVAL WITH THE CYLINDER HEAD INSTALLED

NOTE: Compressed air is required to perform this procedure. Only one valve may be serviced at a time.

1. Remove spark plug wires and spark plugs from cylinder head.
2. Remove rocker arm cover. Remove rocker arms, pivots, bridges and capscrews.
2. Bring piston to top dead center (TDC) on the compression stroke.
3. Insert an Air Hold Fitting (allows cylinder to be pressurized to keep valve closed) into the spark plug hole and pressurize the cylinder with compressed air.
4. Remove the valve spring using an appropriate valve spring compressor.

TESTING

1. Use a valve spring tester (J–22738–02) and a torque wrench to test valve spring tension. See Valve Specifications Chart. Replace any springs that are not within ± 1 lb. of all other springs.
2. Install valve spring retainer and locks on valve stem. Use a telescopic gauge to measure the installed height of the spring (from the bottom of the spring cup in the head to the bottom of the retainer). If not within specifications use valve spring shims to bring spring into specification.

NOTE: If a valve spring requires more than 2.28mm (0.090 in.) in spacers, replace the spring. Use only one shim of cor-

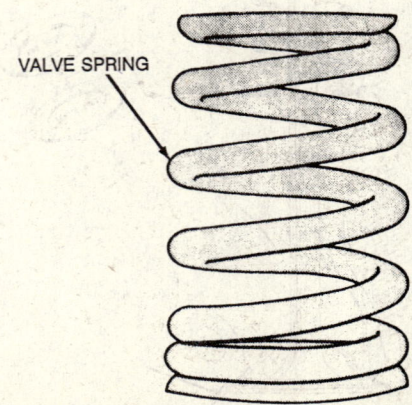

Install the valve spring with the closely wound coils toward the head

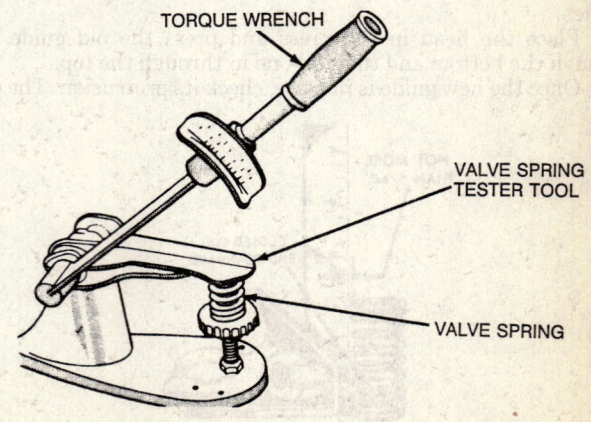

Testing valve spring tension

3-63

3 ENGINE AND ENGINE OVERHAUL

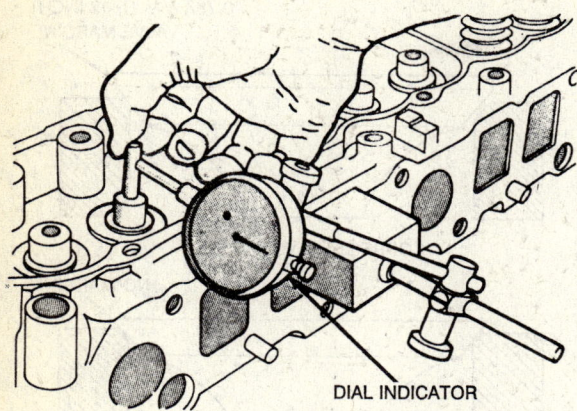

Checking valve guide clearance with a dial indicator

rect thickness per spring.

3. Place the spring on a flat surface next to a square. Measure the height of the spring, and rotate it against the edge of the square to measure distortion. If spring height varies (by comparison) by more than 1.5mm or if distortion exceeds 1.5mm, replace the spring.

INSTALLATION

1. The spring is installed with the closely wound coils toward the valve head. Always use new valve seals.
2. Use a spring compressor to install the keepers and slowly release the compressor after the keepers are in place.
3. Release the spring compressor. Tap the end of the stem with a wood mallet to insure that the keepers are securely in place.
4. Install all other parts in reverse order of removal.
5. After all springs have been installed, test for coil bind. Crank over engine while holding a paper clip between the coils of the spring. You should be able to remove the paper clip easily at maximum valve lift.

Valve Guides

REMOVAL AND INSTALLATION

4-2.1L Diesel

NOTE: A press is used for removal and installation of guides.

1. Place the head in the press and press the old guide out through the bottom and the new one in through the top.
2. Once the new guide is in place, check its protrusion. The distance from the bottom end of the guide to the head mating surface should be 32.5mm.
3. After the guides are in place, they must be reamed to 8mm.

All Engines Except 4-2.1L Diesel

Valve guides on all engines except the 4-2.1L diesel are an integral part of the cylinder head and are not replaceable. When the valve stem-to-guide clearance is excessive, the valve guide bores must be reamed oversize. Service valves are available with oversize stems in 0.003 in. (0.0762mm) and 0.015 in. (0.381mm) increments. Corresponding oversized valve stem seals must be used. If the valve guides are reamed oversize, the valve seats must be refaced to ensure valve seat concentricity to the valve guide.

Another procedure available to bring valve stem-to-guide clearance into specification is knurling. A special tool is threaded into the valve guide which displaces the metal inside, decreasing the inside diameter. Using this method, if valve stem diameter is within specification and valves are not damaged, valves may be reused.

VALVE STEM-TO-GUIDE CLEARANCE

Two procedures are provided for checking valve stem-to-guide clearance. The preferred method is very accurate and requires the use of micrometers and a telescoping gauge. The alternate method is somewhat less complicated and only requires the use of a dial indicator.

1. Remove and disassemble the cylinder head
2. Using a valve guide cleaner chucked into a drill, clean all of the valve guides.
3. Check valve stem-to-guide clearance using one of the two procedures.
4. If valve guide must be reamed, reface valve and valve seat.
5. Check valve spring tension and installed height.
6. Reassemble head using new oil seals.

Preferred Method

1. Insert a telescoping gauge into the valve stem guide bore approximately 10mm ($^3/_8$ in.) from the valve spring side of the head. Ensure that contacts are perpendicular to the cylinder head. Remove the gauge and measure it with a micrometer.
2. Repeat the measurement with contacts parallel to the cylin-

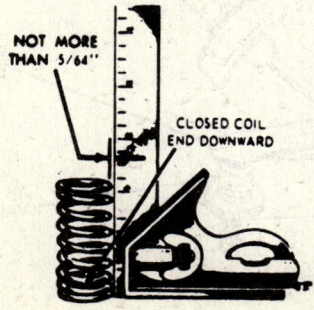

Check the valve spring free length and squareness

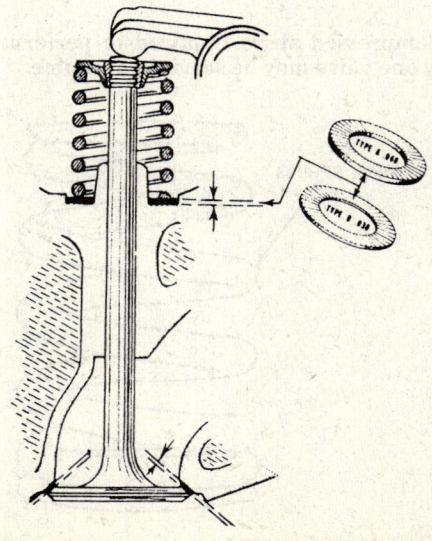

Using shims to correct valve spring installed height

ENGINE AND ENGINE OVERHAUL 3

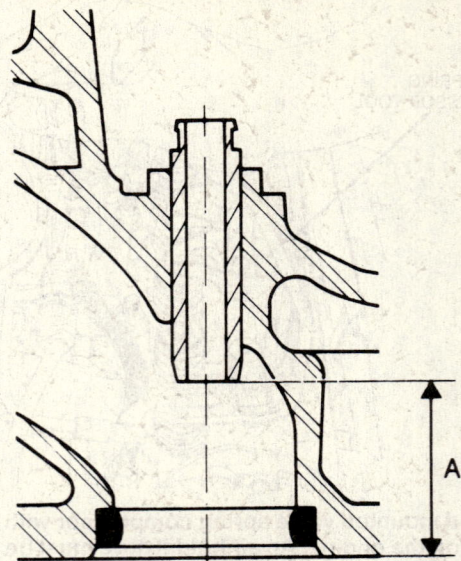

Checking valve guide protrusion on the 4-2.1L diesel

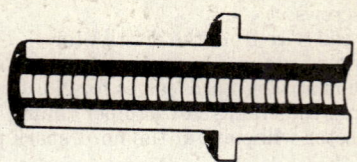

Cross section of a knurled valve guide

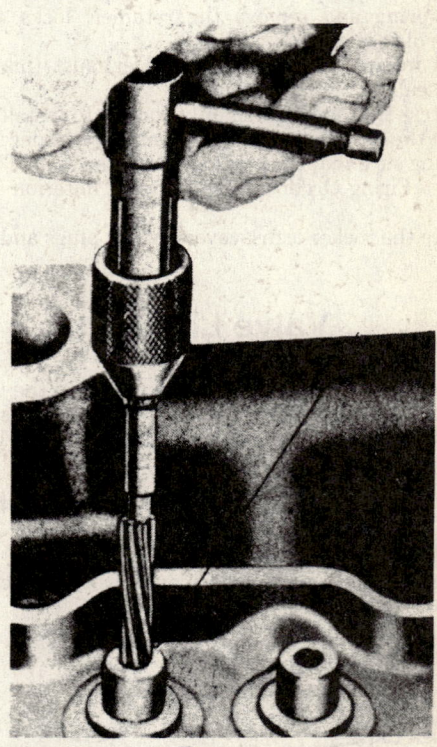

Reaming a valve guide with a hand reamer

der head.
  3. Compare parallel and perpendicular measurements to determine out of roundness. If measurements differ more than 0.0635mm (0.0025 in.), ream the guide bore to accommodate an oversize valve stem.
  4. Compare the measured valve guide bore with specifications (valve stem diameter + stem-to-guide clearance). If the measurement differs from the specification by more than 0.076mm (0.003 in.), ream the guide bore to accommodate an oversized valve stem.

Alternate Method

  1. Install each valve into its respective guide bore of the cylinder head.
  2. Mount a dial indicator so that the stem is at 90° to the valve stem, as close to the valve guide as possible.

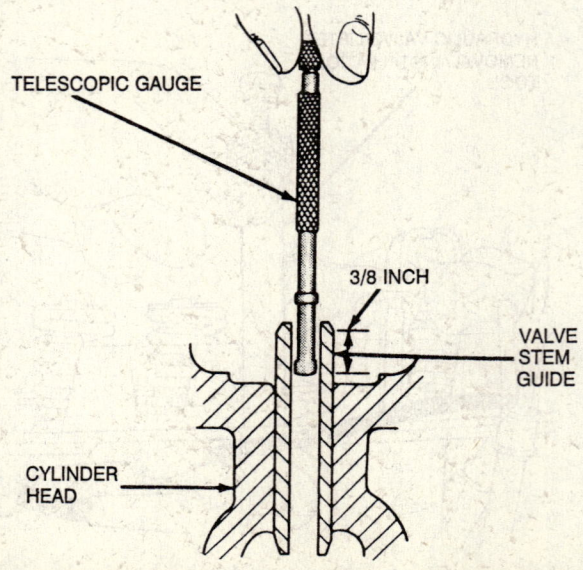

Checking valve guide clearance with a telescopic gauge and micrometer (preferred method)

  3. Move the valve off its seat, and measure the valve guide-to-stem clearance by rocking the stem back and forth to actuate the dial indicator. The correct clearance is 0.025–0.076mm (0.001–0.003 in.).
  4. The valve guide, if worn, must be repaired before the valve seats can be resurfaced. Valves with oversize stems are available to fit valve guides that are reamed oversize for repair.

Valve Stem Oil Seal

Gasoline Engines

If valve stem oil seals are found to be the cause of excessive oil consumption, they may be replaced without removing the cylinder block.

REMOVAL WITH THE CYLINDER HEAD INSTALLED

NOTE: Compressed air is required to perform this procedure. Only one valve may be serviced at a time.

  1. Remove spark plug wires and spark plugs from cylinder head.
  2. Remove rocker arm cover. Remove rocker arms, pivots,

3-65

3 ENGINE AND ENGINE OVERHAUL

bridges and capscrews.

3. Detach the coil wire from the distributor.
4. Turn the engine so that No. 1 cylinder is at Top Dead Center on the compression stroke. Both Valves for No. 1 cylinder should be fully closed and the crankshaft damper timing mark at TDC. The distributor rotor will point at the no. 1 spark plug wire location in the cap.
5. Apply 90–100 psi air pressure to No. 1 cylinder, using a spark plug air hold adaptor.
6. Use a valve spring compressor to compress each no. 1 cylinder valve spring and remove the retainer, locks and spring. Remove the old seals.
7. Install intake (marked INT) and exhaust (marked EXH) valve stem seals.
8. Compress the valve spring only enough to install the lock.
9. Repeat the operation on each successive cylinder in the firing order, making sure that the crankshaft is exactly on TDC for each cylinder. See Firing Order and Distributor Rotation in this Section.
10. Replace the rocker arms, covers, spark plugs and coil wire.

Valve Lifters

In some engines it is possible to gain access to the valve lifters without removing the intake manifold. This requires the use of Hydraulic Valve Lifter Removal/Installation Tool C-4129-A.

REMOVAL AND INSTALLATION

1. Remove the rocker arm cover.
2. Remove the rocker arm bridge and pivot assembly by alternately loosening the capscrews 1 turn at a time. Remove the push rods. Keep all components in order.
3. On the 6-2.8L, remove the intake manifold. Remove lifters using lifter removal tool.
4. On all other engines, remove the lifters through the push rod opening in the cylinder head using a lifter removal tool.

To Install:

5. Dip each lifter in MOPAR engine oil supplement and install into lifter bore using lifter tool.
6. Install all components (in their original positions) in reverse order of removal. Alternately tighten capscrews and torque 19 ft.lbs.
7. Pour remaining engine oil supplement in engine. The engine oil supplement must remain in the engine for at least 1000 miles but need not be drained until the next scheduled oil change.

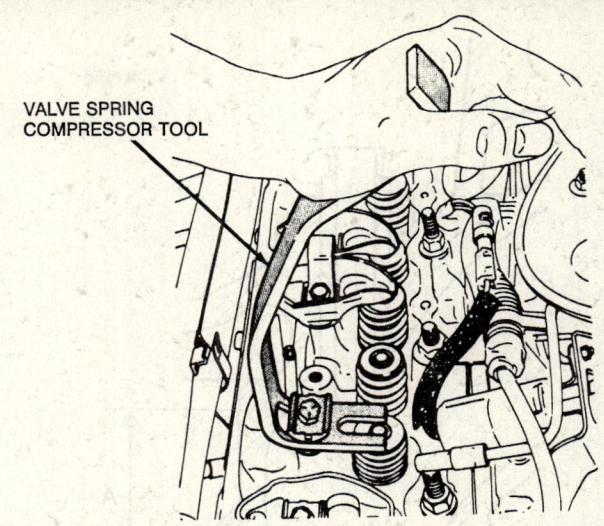

Using a stud mounted valve spring compressor with the cylinder head on the engine. An air hold fixture must be used to prevent the valve from dropping into the cylinder

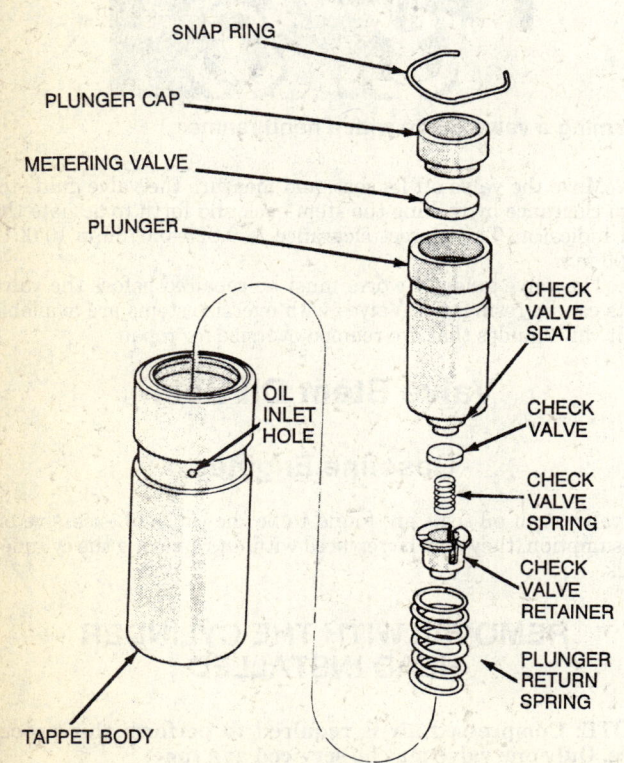

Exploded view of a hydraulic lifter

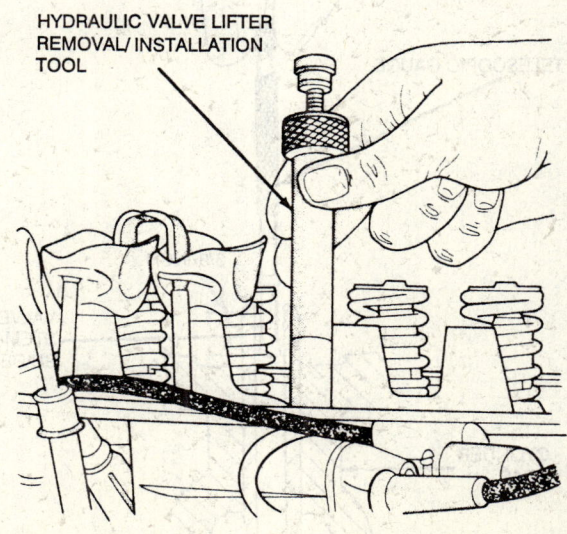

Using a lifter removal tool to ease hydraulic lifter removal/installation

ENGINE AND ENGINE OVERHAUL 3

CLEANING AND INSPECTION

1. Release snap ring and remove the plunger cap, metering valve, plunger, check valve assembly and plunger return spring from the lifter body.
2. DO NOT intermix components from other lifters. Keep all components in order.
3. Clean lifter assembly in solvent to remove varnish, gum and sludge deposits.
4. Inspect for indications of scuffing on the side and base of each lifter.
5. Inspect each lifter for concave wear with a straight edge placed across the bottom of the lifter. If the base is concave, the corresponding lobe on the camshaft is also worn. Replace the camshaft and defective tappets.
6. Install all internal components in reverse order of removal. Compress plunger using an old pushrod and install snap ring.
7. Test lifter for specified leak-down rate tolerance.

LEAK-DOWN TEST

A hydraulic lifter leak-down tool is needed to perform this test. The tool incorporates a weighted arm, degree scale and an external timer to measure lifter leak-down rate. These tools may be cost prohibitive for the average vehicle owner.

A less costly alternative is to purchase a lifter rebuild kit. This kit contains all the internal components necessary to assure proper lifter leak-down. Install this kit only if the lifter passes all external inspections. Install a new lifter if the old one is not rebuildable.

1. Place a 7.92–7.95mm (0.312–0.313 in.) diameter ball bearing on the plunger cap of the lifter.
2. Lift the ram and position lifter in the tester. Lower ram and adjust until it contacts the ball bearing. DO NOT tighten the hex nut.
3. Fill the tester cup with oil until lifter is submerged. Swing weighted arm onto the push rod and pump lifter to remove all air. After all air bubbles cease, swing weighted arm away and allow the plunger to return to normal position.
4. Adjust the nose of the ram to align the pointer with the SET mark on the scale. Tighten the hex nut.
5. Slowly swing the weighted arm onto the pushrod. Rotate the cup by turning the handle at the base of the tester clockwise 1 turn every 2 seconds.
6. Observe leak-down rate from the instant the pointer aligns with the start mark on the scale until pointer aligns with the 0.125 mark.
7. Lifter leak-down specification is 60 to 110 seconds. Discard lifters if not within specification.

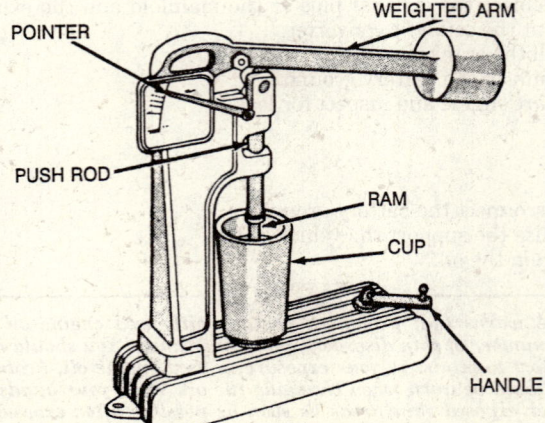

Hydraulic lifter leak-down tester

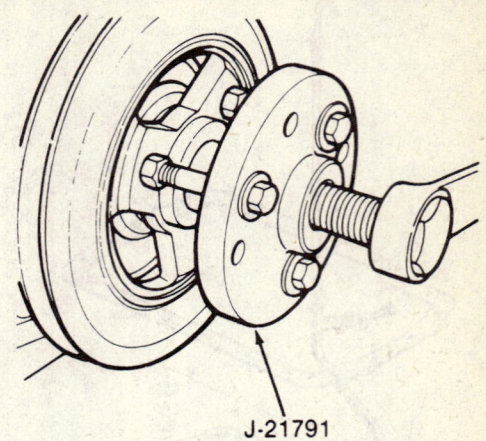

Using a puller to remove the crankshaft damper

Crankshaft Pulley (Vibration Damper)

REMOVAL AND INSTALLATION

1. Remove the fan shroud, as required.
2. On those engines with a separate pulley, remove the retaining bolts and separate the pulley from the vibration damper.
3. Remove the vibration damper/pulley retaining bolt from the crankshaft end.
4. Using a puller, remove the damper/pulley from the crankshaft.
5. Inspect the damper shaft and remove any burrs. Inspect for oil leakage from the timing chain seal. If leakage is present it may be caused by an undersized damper shaft. Install a damper shaft collar to restore correct outside diameter.
6. Place a small amount of grease on the damper shaft to ease installation. Align the key slot of the damper with the key in the crankshaft and push damper on. The damper bolt is torqued to 80 ft.lbs.
7. Install pulley and torque bolts to 20 ft.lbs.
8. Install drive belt and adjust to the specified tension.

Oil Pan

REMOVAL AND INSTALLATION

4-2.1L Diesel

1. Disconnect the negative battery cable. Raise and support the vehicle safely. Remove the converter housing shield, as required.
2. Drain the engine oil. This engine has two oil drain plugs, both must be opened.

— **CAUTION** —

The EPA warns that prolonged contact with used engine oil may cause a number of skin disorders, including cancer! You should make every effort to minimize your exposure to used engine oil. Protective gloves should be worn when changing the oil. Wash your hands and any other exposed skin areas as soon as possible after exposure to used engine oil. Soap and water, or waterless hand cleaner should be used.

3 ENGINE AND ENGINE OVERHAUL

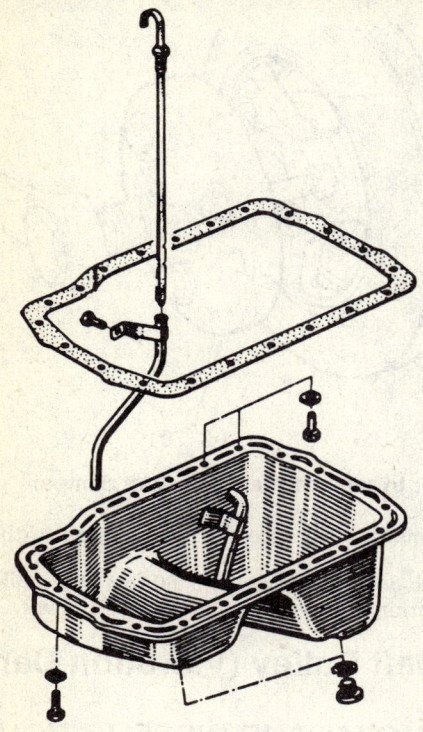

4-2.1L oil pan

3. Remove all the necessary components in order to gain access to the oil pan retaining bolts.
4. Remove the oil pan retaining bolts. Remove the oil pan from the engine.

To install:

5. Clean all gasket surfaces thoroughly. Be careful to avoid bending the oil pan mating flanges.
6. If the oil pan was assembled with RTV gasket material, run a 6mm bead of new sealer around the oil pan flanges, outboard of the mounting holes. The sealer sets in 15 minutes, so work quickly! If a gasket was used, coat the oil pan flanges with gasket sealer and place the gasket on the pan. Coat the engine block mounting surfaces with sealer.
7. Position the pan on the block and install the bolts. Torque the bolts to 79 inch lbs.
8. Install the drain plugs, fill the crankcase, run the engine and check for leaks.

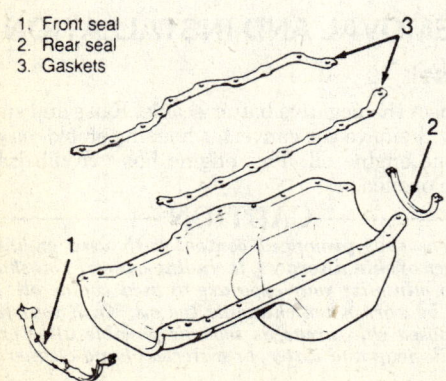

1. Front seal
2. Rear seal
3. Gaskets

4-2.5L oil pan gasket and seal positioning

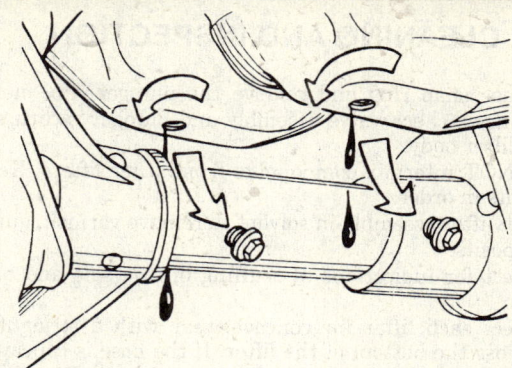

4-2.1L oil pan drain plugs

4-2.5L

1. Disconnect the battery ground.
2. Raise and support the vehicle safely.
3. Drain the oil.

— **CAUTION** —
The EPA warns that prolonged contact with used engine oil may cause a number of skin disorders, including cancer! You should make every effort to minimize exposure to used engine oil. Protective gloves should be worn when changing the oil. Wash your hands and any other exposed skin areas as soon as possible after exposure to used engine oil. Soap and water, or waterless hand cleaner should be used.

4. Disconnect the exhaust pipe at the manifold and the exhaust hanger at the catalytic converter. Lower the exhaust.
5. Remove the starter.
6. Remove the bellhousing access plate.
7. If necessary, remove the engine mount and raise the engine to gain clearance.
8. Unbolt and remove the oil pan.

To install:

9. Clean the gasket surfaces thoroughly. Remove all sludge and dirt from the oil pan sump.
10. Install a replacement seal at the bottom of the timing case cover and at the rear bearing cap.
11. Using new gaskets coated with sealer, install the oil pan and torque the $1/4$–20 bolts to 80 inch lbs.; the $5/16$–18 bolts to 11 ft. lbs.
12. Lower the engine until it is properly located on the engine mounts. Torque engine mount bolts to 48 ft.lbs.
13. Torque oil pan drain plug to 25 ft.lbs.
14. Install the bellhousing access plate.
15. Install the starter.
16. Connect the exhaust pipe at the manifold and the exhaust hanger at the catalytic converter.
17. Fill the crankcase.
18. Connect the battery ground.
19. Start engine and inspect for leaks.

6-2.8L

1. Disconnect the battery ground.
2. Raise the support the vehicle safely.
3. Drain the oil.

— **CAUTION** —
The EPA warns that prolonged contact with used engine oil may cause a number of skin disorders, including cancer! You should make every effort to minimize your exposure to used engine oil. Protective gloves should be worn when changing the oil. Wash your hands and any other exposed skin areas as soon as possible after exposure to used engine oil. Soap and water, or waterless hand cleaner should be used.

4. Remove the bellhousing access cover.

ENGINE AND ENGINE OVERHAUL 3

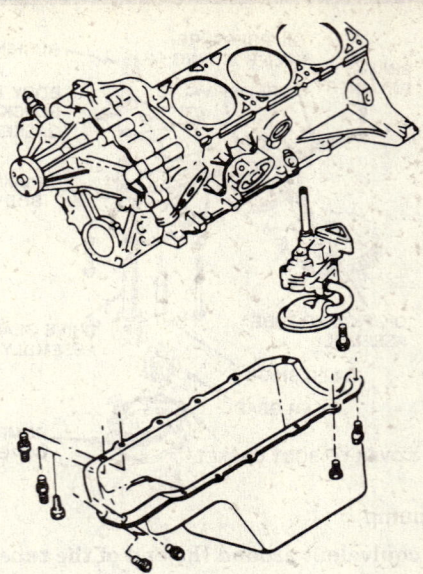

6-2.8L oil pan

5. Disconnect the exhaust pipes at the manifold.
6. Remove the starter.
7. Disconnect the exhaust pipe at the converter flange and lower the exhaust so that the 'Y' portion rests on the axle upper control arms.
8. Unbolt and remove the pan.

To install:

9. Remove all RTV gasket material. Remove all sludge and dirt from the oil pan sump.
10. Install a new rear pan seal.
11. Apply a 3mm ($1/8$ in.) bead of RTV gasket material all the way around the pan sealing surface.
12. Install the pan and torque the bolts to 12 ft. lbs.
13. Connect the exhaust pipe at the converter flange.
14. Install the starter.
15. Connect the exhaust pipes at the manifold.
16. Install the bellhousing access cover.
17. Fill the crankcase.
18. Connect the battery ground.

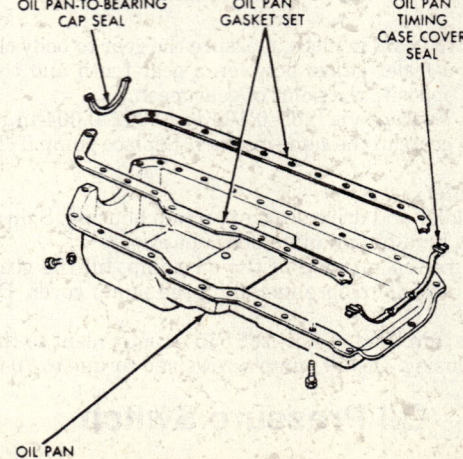

6-4.0L oil pan, seals and gaskets

6-4.0L

1. Disconnect the battery ground.
2. Raise and support the vehicle safely.
3. Drain the oil.

— **CAUTION** —

The EPA warns that prolonged contact with used engine oil may cause a number of skin disorders, including cancer! You should make every effort to minimize your exposure to used engine oil. Protective gloves should be worn when changing the oil. Wash your hands and any other exposed skin areas as soon as possible after exposure to used engine oil. Soap and water, or waterless hand cleaner should be used.

4. Disconnect the exhaust pipe at the manifold and the exhaust hanger at the catalytic converter. Lower the exhaust.
5. Remove the starter.
6. Remove the bellhousing access plate.
7. If necessary, remove the engine mount and raise the engine to gain clearance.
8. Unbolt and remove the oil pan.

To install:

9. Clean the gasket surfaces thoroughly. Remove all sludge and dirt from the oil pan sump.
10. When installing the front oil pan seal to the timing chain cover, apply a generous amount of Permatex® No. 2 to the end tabs. Also, cement the oil pan side gaskets to the mating surface on the bottom of the engine block. Coat the inside curved surface of the new oil pan rear seal with soap and apply a generous amount of Permatex® No. 2 to the gasket contacting surface of the seal end tabs.
11. Install the seal in the recess of the rear main bearing cap, making certain that it is fully seated.
12. Apply engine oil to the oil pan contacting surface of the front and rear oil pan seals.
13. Install the oil pan. Torque the $1/4$–20 bolts to 80 inch lbs.; the $5/16$–18 bolts to 11 ft.lbs.; the oil pan drain plug to 30 ft.lbs.
14. Lower the engine and install the engine mount.
15. Install the bellhousing access plate.
16. Install the starter.
17. Connect the exhaust pipe at the manifold and the exhaust hanger at the catalytic converter.
18. Fill the crankcase.
19. Connect the battery ground.

Oil Pump

REMOVAL AND INSTALLATION

4-2.1L Diesel

NOTE: Special tools are needed for this job.

1. Disconnect the negative battery cable.
2. Remove the vacuum pump along with the oil pump drive gear.
3. Remove the timing belt cover. Loosen the intermediate shaft drive sprocket using tool MOT-855 or equivalent.
4. Remove the intermediate shaft bolt, sprocket, cover, clamp plate and intermediate shaft.
5. Raise and support the vehicle safely. Drain the engine oil. Remove the oil pan.

— **CAUTION** —

The EPA warns that prolonged contact with used engine oil may cause a number of skin disorders, including cancer! You should make every effort to minimize your exposure to used engine oil. Protective gloves should be worn when changing the oil. Wash your hands and any other exposed skin areas as soon as possible after exposure to used engine oil. Soap and water, or waterless hand cleaner should be used.

3 ENGINE AND ENGINE OVERHAUL

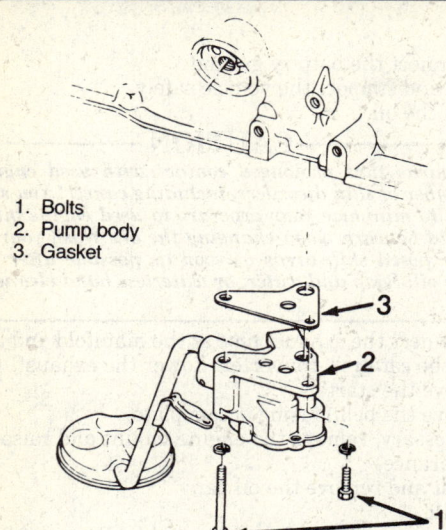

1. Bolts
2. Pump body
3. Gasket

4-2.5L oil pump

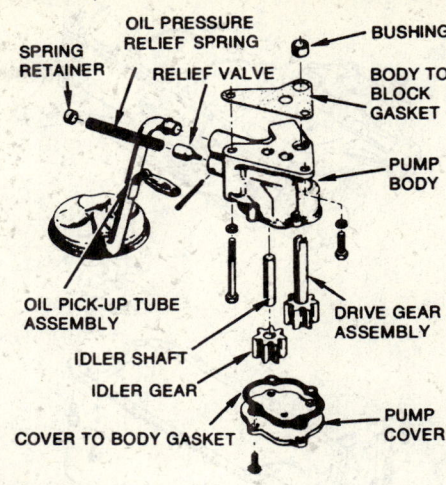

6-4.0L oil pump

6. Remove the piston skirt cooling oil jet assembly to oil pump pipe.
7. Remove the oil pump retaining bolts. Remove the oil pump.
8. Be sure that the oil pump locating dowels are in place on the pump.
9. Inspect the gears for abnormal wear, chips, looseness on the shafts, galling, and scoring.
10. Inspect the cover and cavity for breaks, cracks, distortion, and abnormal wear.
11. Install the gears into the pump cavity, and with the use of a straight edge and feeler gauge, check the gear to housing clearance.
12. Repair or replace defective components as required.
13. Install the oil pump and retaining bolts. Use a new gasket. Torque the bolts to 33 ft. lbs.
14. Install the piston skirt cooling oil jet assembly on oil pump pipe.
15. Install the oil pan.
16. Install the intermediate shaft and sprocket.
17. Install the timing belt cover.
18. Install the vacuum pump and oil pump drive gear.
19. Connect the negative battery cable.
20. Fill the crankcase.

All Except 4-2.1L Diesel

1. Remove the oil pan.

NOTE: Do not disturb the position of the oil pick-up tube and screen assembly in the pump body. If the tube is moved within the pump body, a new assembly must be installed to assure an airtight seal. Apply a thin film of Permatex® No.2 sealant or equivalent around the end of the tube prior to assembly.

2. Unbolt and remove the pump assembly from the block. Discard any gaskets.
3. Install the pump on the block, using a new gasket (if one was removed).
    a. On 4-2.5L and 6-4.0L, torque the short bolt to 10 ft.lbs. and the long bolt to 17 ft.lbs.
    b. On 6-2.8L, torque bolt to 25–30 ft.lbs.
4. Install the pan.

GEAR END CLEARANCE

1. Remove the cover retaining screws and cover from the pump body.
2. Place a straight edge across the ends of the gears and the pump body.
3. Measure the clearance between the gears and the straight edge. A 0.05–0.15mm (0.002–0.006 in.) feeler gauge should fit snugly but freely.

NOTE: It is recommended that all oil pumps, even new replacement pumps, be checked for proper clearance.

4. If gear clearance is excessive, replace the pump assembly.

GEAR TO BODY CLEARANCE

1. With both gears in place, measure the gear to body clearance by inserting a feeler gauge between a gear tooth and the pump wall directly opposite the point of gear mesh.
2. Correct clearance is 0.05–0.10mm (0.002–0.004 in.). Rotate and check all gears in the same manner. Replace pump if clearance is excessive.

To Assemble:

3. Install idler and drive gear into pump housing. Spin gears to assure that a binding condition does not exist.
4. To assure self priming of the oil pump, fill the gear cavity with petroleum jelly before installing the pump cover. DO NOT use grease.
5. Apply a thin bead of Loctite® 515 or equivalent to the top of the pump housing. Install pump screws and torque to 70 inch lbs.

Oil Pressure Switch

Location of the oil pressure switch is as follows:
• 4-2.1L; mounted on the remote oil filter housing.

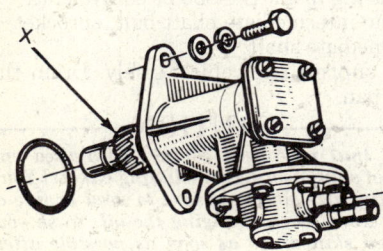

4-2.1L oil pump/vacuum pump conbination. (X) is the drive gear

ENGINE AND ENGINE OVERHAUL 3

- 4-2.5L; forward of the distributor on the right side of the engine.
- 6-2.8L; mounted on the rear rail of the lifter valley at the back of the intake manifold.
- 6-4.0L; to the rear of the distributor on the right side of the block.

TESTING

Test the oil pressure switch by turning the ignition to the RUN position. On vehicles equipped with an oil pressure gauge, disconnect the switch wiring connector at the switch. The gauge should go to 'H'. If not, touch oil pressure switch terminal 'S' to ground. The needle should go to 'L'. If not, repair the open circuit to the gauge. If OK, replace the switch.

Vehicles with an oil pressure indicator light are also tested with the ignition in the RUN position. Disconnect the switch wiring connector at the switch. Touch oil pressure switch terminal 'S' to ground. The lamp should light. If not, repair the open circuit to the light. If OK, replace the switch.

REMOVAL AND INSTALLATION

1. Disconnect the negative battery cable.
2. Remove the oil pressure switch wiring harness connector.
3. Remove the oil pressure switch.

NOTE: On some models a special socket is required to remove the switch.

4. Installation is the reverse of removal. Coat threads of switch with teflon tape. Tighten switch to 10 ft.lbs.

Timing Cover and Seal

REMOVAL AND INSTALLATION

4-2.1L Diesel

1. Disconnect the negative battery cable.
2. Remove all necessary components in order to gain access to the timing belt cover bolts.
3. Remove the timing belt cover retaining bolts. Remove the timing belt cover from the engine.
4. Installation is the reverse of removal.

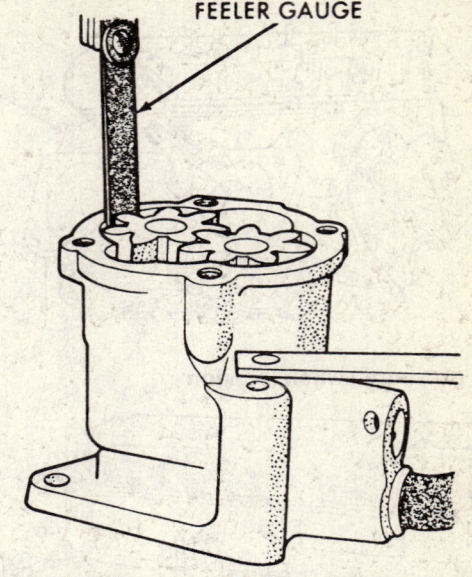

Check gear to body clearance opposite the point where the gears mesh

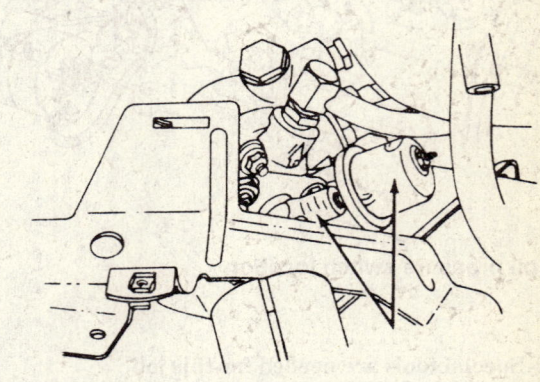

4-2.1L oil pressure switch location

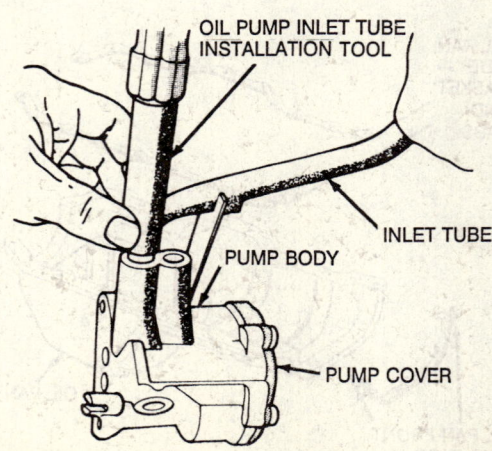

Oil tube inlet and strainer assembly. Use tool J-21882

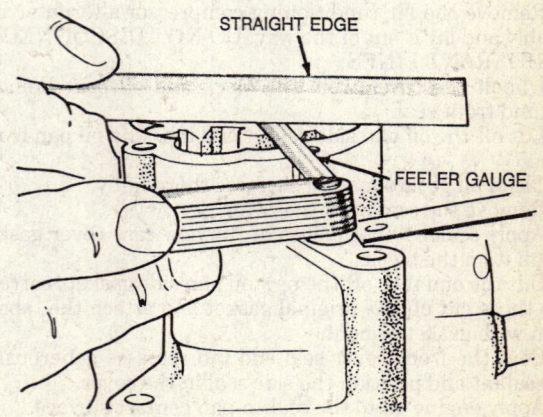

Checking gear end clearance with a feeler gauge

3-71

3 ENGINE AND ENGINE OVERHAUL

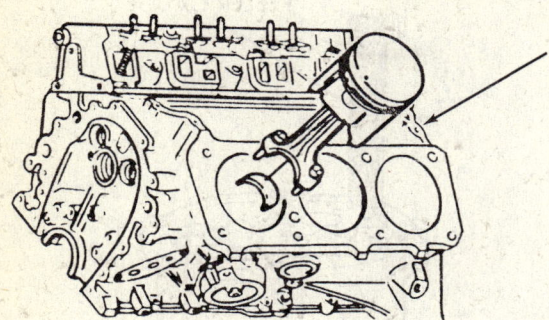

6-2.8L oil pressure switch location

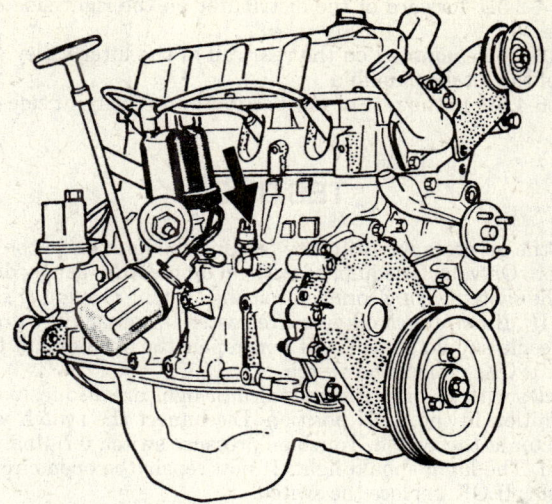

4-2.5L oil pressure switch location

17. Install the cover bolts. Tighten the cover-to-block bolts to 5 ft. lbs.; the cover-to-pan bolts to 11 ft. lbs.
18. Remove the alignment tool and position the new front seal on the tool with the seal lip facing outward. Apply a light film of sealer to the outside diameter of the seal. Lightly coat the crankshaft with clean engine oil.
19. Position the tool and seal over the end of the crankshaft and insert the Draw Screw J–9163–2 into the installation tool.
20. Tighten the nut until the tool just contacts the cover.

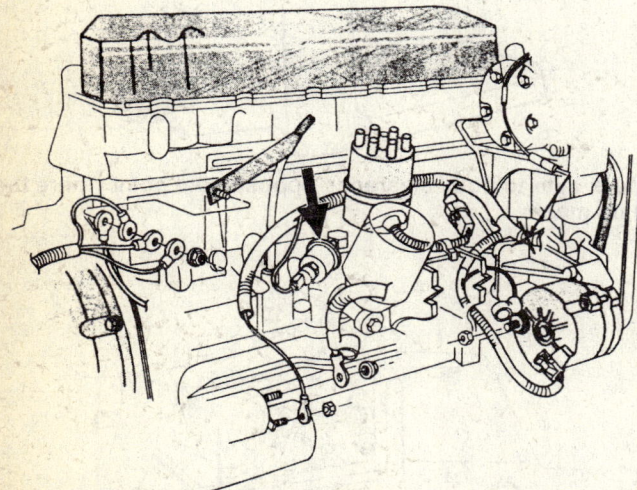

6-4.0L oil pressure switch location

4-2.5L

NOTE: Special tools are needed for this job.
1. Disconnect the battery ground.
2. Remove the drive belts and fan shroud.
3. Unscrew the vibration damper bolts and washer.
4. Using a puller, remove the vibration damper.
5. Remove the fan assembly. If the fan is equipped with a fan clutch DO NOT LAY IT DOWN! If you lay it down, the fluid will leak out of the clutch and irreversibly damage the fan.
6. Remove the air conditioning compressor/alternator bracket assembly and lay it out of the way. DO NOT DISCONNECT THE REFRIGERANT LINES!
7. Unbolt the cover from the block and oil pan. Remove the cover and front seal.
8. Cut off the oil pan side gasket end tabs and oil pan front seal tabs.
9. Clean all gasket mating surfaces thoroughly.
10. Remove the seal from the cover.
11. Apply sealer to both sides of the new case cover gasket and position it on the block.
12. Cut the end tabs off the new oil pan side gaskets corresponding to those cut off the original gasket and attach the tabs to the oil pan with gasket cement.
13. Coat the front cover seal end tab recesses generously with RTV sealant and position the side seal in the cover.
14. Apply engine oil to the seal-to-pan contact surface.
15. Position the cover on the block.
16. Insert alignment tool J–22248 into the crankshaft opening in the cover.

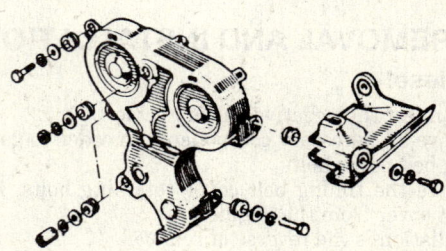

4-2.1L diesel timing belt cover

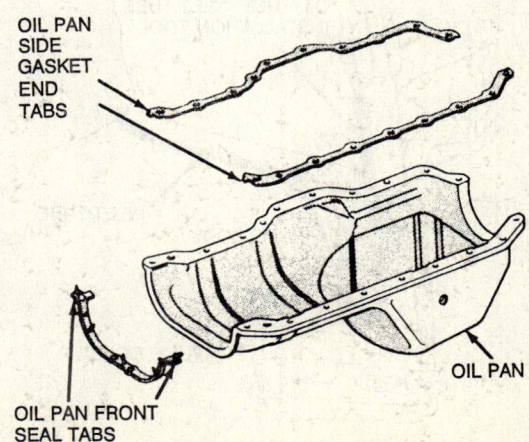

Oil pan side/front gasket seal tabs

ENGINE AND ENGINE OVERHAUL 3

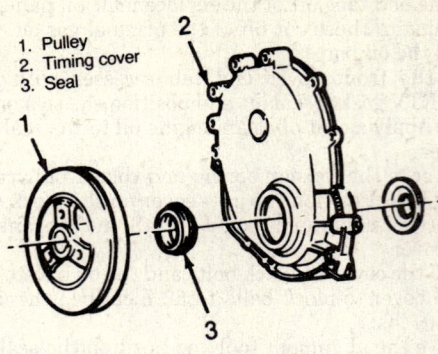

4-2.5L timing cover assembly

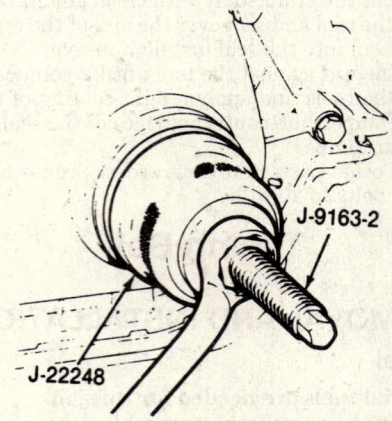

Oil seal installation tool for the 4-2.5L/6-4.0L

21. Remove the tools and apply a light film of engine oil on the vibration damper hub contact surface of the seal.
22. With the key inserted in the keyway in the crankshaft, install the vibration damper, washer and bolt. Lubricate the bolt and tighten it to 108 ft. lbs.
23. If equipped with a serpentine belt, tighten the pulley-to-damper bolts to 20 ft.lbs. Install all other parts in reverse order of removal.

6-2.8L

1. Disconnect the battery ground.
2. Remove the drive belts.
3. Remove the fan shroud.
4. Remove the fan and pulley. If the fan is equipped with a fan

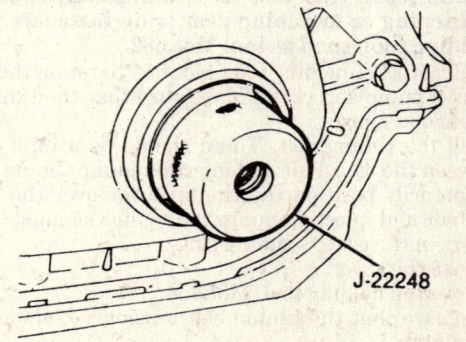

Timing cover centering tool for the 4-2.5L/6-4.0L

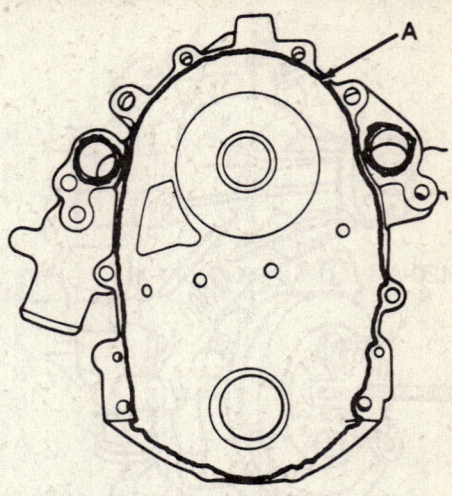

RTV sealer application on the 6-2.8L timing cover

clutch, DO NOT LAY IT ON ITS SIDE! If you do, the fluid will leak out and the fan clutch will have to be replaced.
5. Drain the cooling system.

— **CAUTION** —
When draining the coolant, keep in mind that cats and dogs are attracted by the ethylene glycol antifreeze, and are quite likely to drink any that is left in an uncovered container or in puddles on the ground. This will prove fatal in sufficient quantity. Always drain the coolant into a sealable container. Coolant should be reused unless it is contaminated or several years old.

6. Remove the air conditioning compressor and mounting bracket and position them out of the way. DO NOT DISCONNECT THE REFRIGERANT LINES!
7. Remove the water pump.
8. Remove the vibration damper retaining bolt and, using a puller, remove the damper.

NOTE: *On some vehicles the outer ring (weight) of the harmonic balancer is bonded to the hub with rubber. The balancer must be removed with a puller which acts on the inner hub only. Pulling on the outer portion of the balancer will break the rubber bond or destroy the tuning of the torsional damper.*

9. Disconnect the lower radiator hose.
10. Unbolt and remove the cover. Pry out the seal.
11. Thoroughly remove all traces of gasket material from the mating surfaces.
12. Position a new seal in the cover with the open end of the seal facing outward.
13. Apply a 2.5mm (³⁄₃₈ in.) bead of RTV silicone gasket material to the mating surfaces of the cover and block. Place the cover on the block and install the bolts. Torque the M8 x 1.25 bolts to 18 ft. lbs.; the M10 x 1.5 bolts to 30 ft. lbs. Tighten the bolts within five minutes, as the sealer will begin to set.
14. Install all other parts in reverse order of removal.

NOTE: *Breakage may occur if the balancer is hammered back onto the crankshaft. A press or special installation tool is necessary.*

6-4.0L

1. Remove the drive belts, engine fan and hub assembly, the accessory pulley and vibration damper.
2. Remove the air conditioning compressor and alternator bracket assembly and set it aside. Don't disconnect the refrigerant lines.
3. Remove the oil pan to timing chain cover screws and the screws that attach the cover to the block.

3-73

3 ENGINE AND ENGINE OVERHAUL

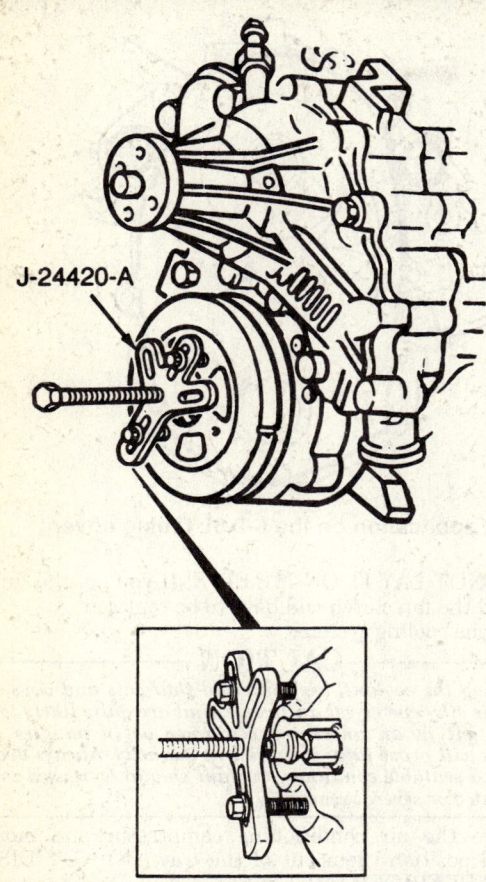

Using a puller to remove the vibration damper on the 6-2.8L

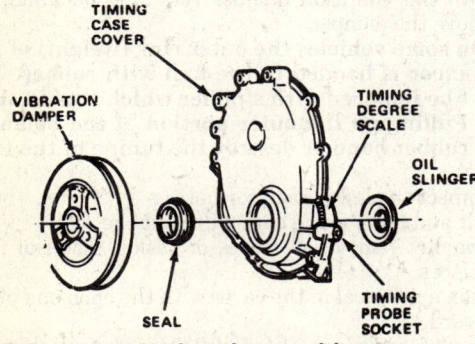

6-4.0L timing cover and seal assembly

4. Raise the timing chain cover just high enough to detach the retaining nibs of the oil pan neoprene seal from the bottom side of the cover. This must be done to prevent pulling the seal end tabs away from the tongues of the oil pan gaskets, which would cause a leak.
5. Remove the timing chain cover and gasket from the engine. Make sure the timing chain tensioner spring and thrust pin do not fall out of the preload bolt.
6. Use a razor blade to cut off the oil pan seal end tabs flush with the front face of the cylinder block and remove the seal. Clean the timing chain cover, oil pan, and cylinder block surfaces.
7. Remove the crankshaft oil seal from the timing chain cover. Thoroughly clean the mating surfaces.

To install:

8. Apply RTV gasket material to both sides of the new gasket and position the gasket on the block.
9. Cut the end tabs off of the replacement oil pan side gaskets, corresponding to those cut off of the original gasket. Cement the end tabs to the oil pan.
10. Coat the front cover end tab recesses with a generous amount of RTV gasket sealant and position the seal on the timing case cover. Apply a coat of clean engine oil to the seal-to-pan contact surfaces.
11. Make sure the tension spring and thrust pin are in place in the preload bolt. Position the case cover on the block.
12. Place cover alignment tool (J-22248) in the crankshaft opening of the cover.
13. Install the cover-to-block bolts and the oil pan-to-cover bolts. Torque the cover-to-block bolts to 62 inch lbs.; the cover-to-pan bolts to 11 ft. lbs.
14. Remove the alignment tool and position the seal on the tool with the lip facing outward.
15. Apply a light coat of sealer on the outside diameter of the seal.
16. Lightly coat the crankshaft with clean engine oil.
17. Position the tool and seal over the end of the crankshaft and insert a screw tool into the seal installation tool.
18. Tighten the nut against the tool until it contacts the cover.
19. Remove the tools and apply a light coating of engine oil on the vibration damper hub contact surface of the seal.
20. Install the damper.
21. Install all other parts in reverse order of removal. tighten the damper pulley bolts to 20 ft.lbs.

Timing Belt

REMOVAL AND INSTALLATION

4-2.1L Diesel

NOTE: Special tools are needed for this job.

1. Disconnect the negative battery cable.
2. Remove the timing belt cover.
3. Install sprocket holding tool MOT-854 or equivalent and remove the camshaft sprocket retaining bolt. Remove the special tool.
4. Loosen the bolts and move the chain tensioner away from the timing belt. Tighten the tensioner bolts.
5. Remove the timing belt from the sprockets. Inspect the belt, using the accompanying diagnosis chart.
6. If it is necessary to remove the fuel injection pump sprocket, use tools BVI-28-01 and BVI-859, or equivalent.

NOTE: The following installation steps must be followed, exactly!

7. Remove the access plug in the block, on the left side, and install the holding tool, Mot.861 in the hole. Rotate the crankshaft slowly, clockwise, until the tool drops into the TDC locating slot in the crankshaft counterweight.

NOTE: Don't use this tool as a crankshaft holding tool. When tightening or loosening gear train fasteners, use a flywheel holding tool, such as tool Mot.582.

8. Install sprocket holding tool, Mot.854 to retain the camshaft and injection pump sprockets. Make sure that the timing marks are positioned as shown.
9. Install the timing belt. There should be a total of 19 belt teeth between the camshaft and injection pump timing marks.
10. Temporarily position the timing cover over the sprockets. The camshaft and injection pump timing marks must index with the pointers in the cover's timing slots.
11. Remove the cover.
12. Remove the holding tool, Mot.854.
13. Make sure that the timing belt tensioner bolts are $1/2$ turn loose, maximum.
14. The tensioner should, automatically, bear against the belt, giving the proper belt tension. Tighten the tensioner bolts.

ENGINE AND ENGINE OVERHAUL 3

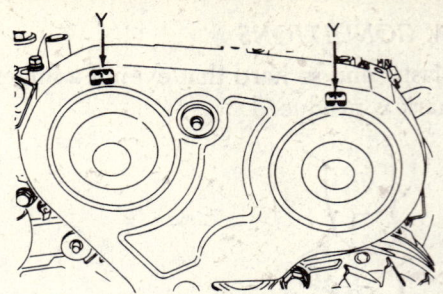

Indexing the timing cover slots and sprocket timing marks on the 4-2.1L diesel

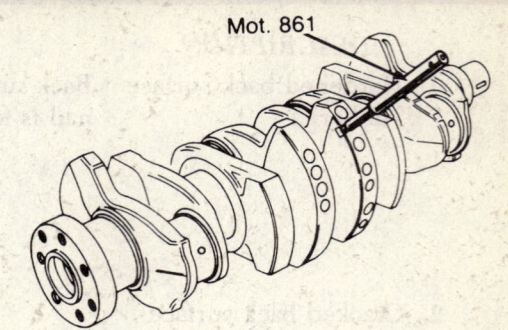

TDC locating tool in the crankshaft TDC locating slot

15. Remove the TDC locating tool and install the plug.
16. Rotate the crankshaft, slowly, CLOCKWISE, two complete revolutions.
NOTE: NEVER rotate the crankshaft counterclockwise while adjusting belt tension.
17. Loosen the tensioner bolts $1/8$ turn, maximum, then tighten them again.
18. Check the belt deflection at a point midway between the camshaft and injection pump sprockets. The belt should deflect 3–5mm.
19. Install the timing belt cover.

Timing Chain and Gears

The timing chain tensioner reduces noise and prolongs engine life. It provides a way of taking up timing chain slack which ensures correct valve timing.

REMOVAL AND INSTALLATION

4-2.5L

1. Disconnect the negative battery cable
2. Remove the fan and shroud, the accessory drive belts, vibration damper and pulley.
3. Remove the timing case cover.
4. Rotate the crankshaft so that the timing marks on the cam and crank sprockets align next to each other, as illustrated.
5. Remove the oil slinger from the crankshaft.
6. Remove the cam sprocket retaining bolt and remove the sprocket and chain. The crank sprocket may also be removed at this time. If the tensioner is to be removed, the oil pan must be removed first.
7. Prior to installation, turn the tensioner lever to the unlock (down) position.

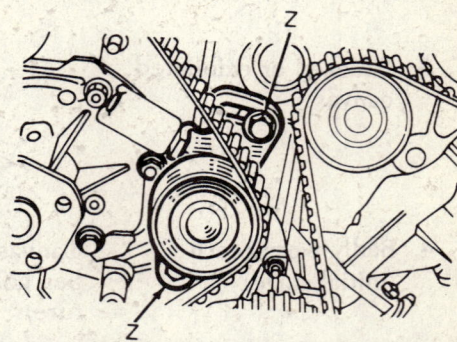

Timing belt tensioner adjusting bolts (Z) on the 4-2.1L diesel

8. Pull the tensioner block toward the tensioner to compress the spring. Hold the block and turn the tensioner lever to the lock (up) position.
9. Install the camshaft/crankshaft sprocket and timing chain together, as a unit. Ensure timing marks are aligned properly. The camshaft sprocket bolt should be torqued to 50 ft. lbs. (1984–88); 80 ft.lbs. (1989–91).
10. Install all other components in the reverse order of removal.

6-2.8L

1. Disconnect the negative battery cable.
2. Remove the timing cover.
3. Turn the crankshaft to bring the #1 piston to TDC of its

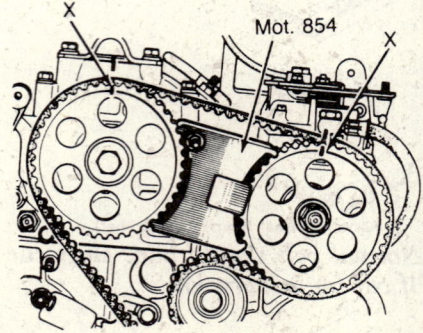

Camshaft and injection pump timing marks aligned on the 4-2.1L diesel

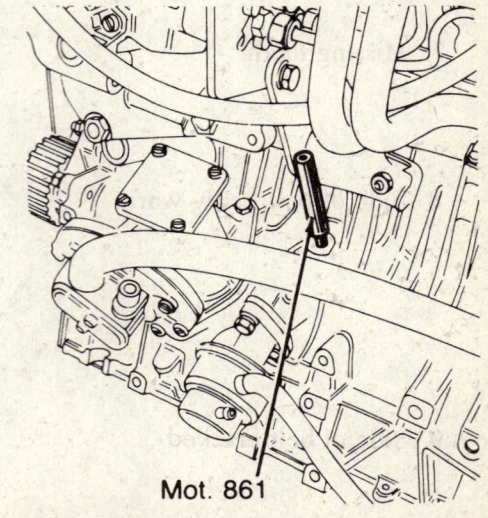

4-2.1L diesel TDC locating tool installed in the block

3-75

3 ENGINE AND ENGINE OVERHAUL

DESCRIPTION	FLAW CONDITIONS
1. Hardened back surface rubber	Back surface glossy. Non-elastic and so hard that even if a finger nail is forced into it, no mark is produced. 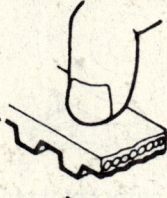
2. Cracked back surface rubber	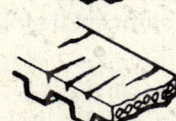
3. Cracked or exfoliated canvas	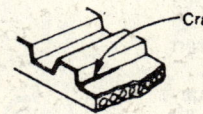 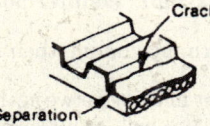 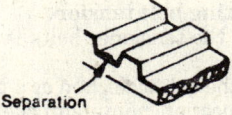
4. Badly worn teeth (initial stage)	Canvas on load side tooth flank worn (Fluffy canvas fibers, rubber gone and color changed to white, and unclear canvas texture) 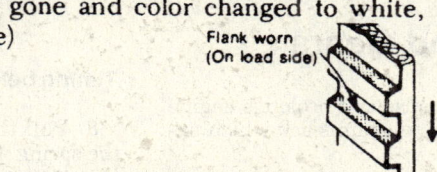
5. Badly worn teeth (last stage)	Canvas on load side tooth flank worn down and rubber exposed (tooth width reduced) 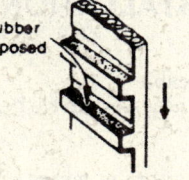
6. Cracked tooth bottom	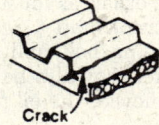
7. Missing tooth	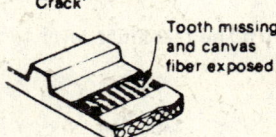
8. Side of belt badly worn	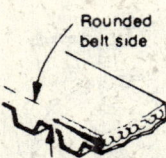 NOTE: *Normal belt should have clear-cut sides as if cut by a sharp knife.*
9. Side of belt cracked	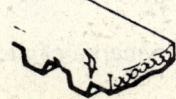

ENGINE AND ENGINE OVERHAUL 3

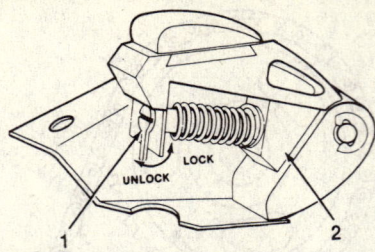

4-2.5L timing chain tensioner. (1) is the tensioner lever, (2) is the block

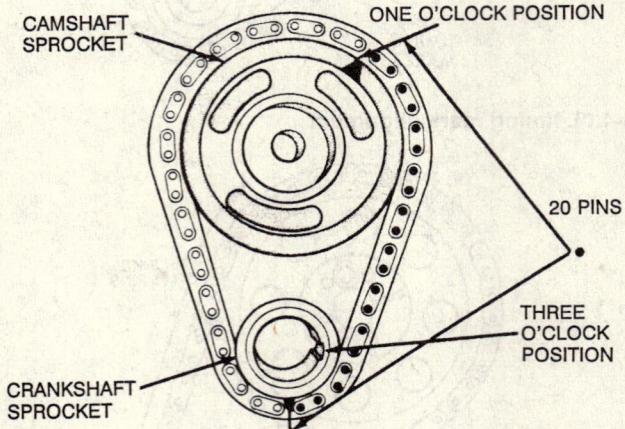

Verifying correct crankshaft/camshaft sprocket installation

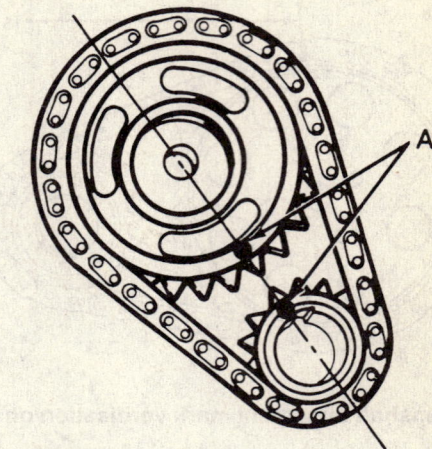

4-2.5L valve timing mark alignment

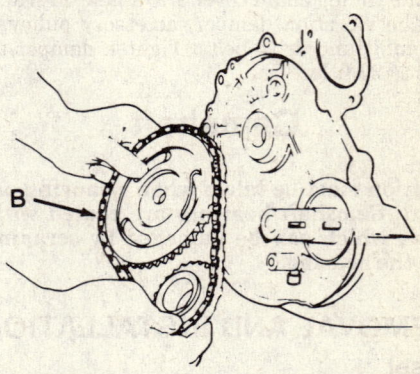

Install the timing chain and sprockets as an assembly on the 4-2.5L

compression stroke. The timing marks on the crankshaft and camshaft sprockets should be aligned as shown with the #4 cylinder in firing position.

4. Remove the camshaft sprocket and chain. If the sprocket is stuck, you can remove it by tapping it lightly with a plastic or wood mallet.
5. Lubricate the chain and sprockets with Molykote®, or equivalent. Install the cam sprocket and chain, with the timing marks aligned and the dowel in the camshaft aligned with the hole in the sprocket.
6. Install the sprocket on the camshaft and torque the cam sprocket bolts to 20 ft. lbs.
7. Install the timing cover. Reconnect the negative battery cable.

6-4.0L

On the 6-4.0L a worn or stretched timing chain will adversely affect valve timing (no chain tensioner is used). If the timing chain deflects more than 13mm ($1/8$ in.) replace it. The correct timing chain has 48 pins.

1. Remove the drive belts, engine fan and hub assembly, accessory pulley, vibration damper and timing chain cover.
2. Remove the tension spring and thrust pin from the preload bolt, if equipped.
3. Remove the oil seal from the timing chain cover.
4. Remove the camshaft sprocket retaining bolt and washer.
5. Rotate the crankshaft until the timing mark on the crankshaft sprocket is closest to and in a center line with the timing pointer of the camshaft sprocket (see illustration).
6. Remove the crankshaft sprocket, camshaft sprocket, and timing chain as an assembly. Disassemble the chain and sprockets.

To Install:

7. Assemble the timing chain, crankshaft sprocket and camshaft sprocket with the timing marks aligned.
8. Install the assembly to the crankshaft and the camshaft. Install the camshaft sprocket retaining bolt and washer and tighten to 80 ft. lbs.
9. Check the alignment of the chain and sprockets by counting the number of links or pins with the sprockets positioned as illustrated. There must be 15 pins between the marks on the sprockets.
10. Lubricate the tension spring, thrust pin and pin bore with

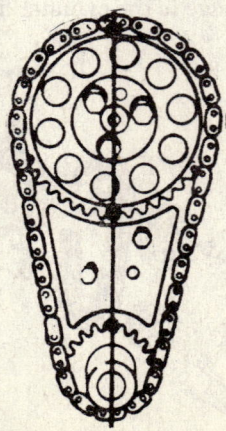

6-4.0L valve timing mark alignment

3-77

3 ENGINE AND ENGINE OVERHAUL

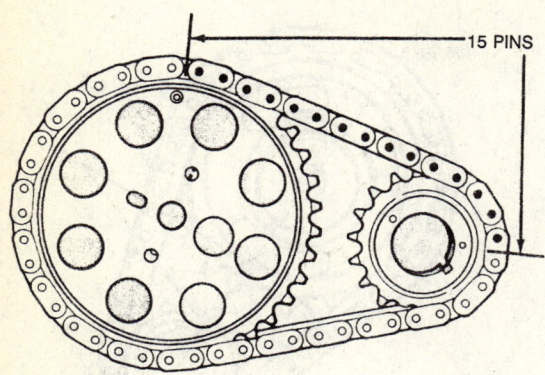

1990-91 camshaft alignment mark verification on the 6-4.0L

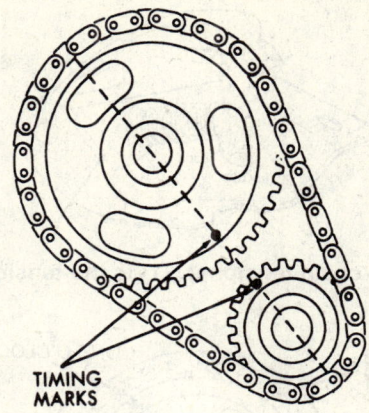

6-4.0L timing mark alignment

MOPAR engine oil supplement, or equivalent, and install.
11. Install the timing chain cover and a new oil seal.
12. Install the vibration damper, accessory pulley, engine fan and hub assembly and drive belts. Tighten damper to 80 ft.lbs.; damper bolts to 20 ft.lbs.

Camshaft

NOTE: Caution must be taken when removing or installing any camshaft. Camshaft bearings are coated with soft babbitt material, which can be damaged by scraping the cam lobes across the bearing.

REMOVAL AND INSTALLATION

4-2.1L Diesel

1. Disconnect the negative battery cable.
2. Drain the cooling system.

CAUTION

When draining the coolant, keep in mind that cats and dogs are attracted by the ethylene glycol antifreeze, and are quite likely to drink any that is left in an uncovered container or in puddles on the ground. This will prove fatal in sufficient quantity. Always drain the coolant into a sealable container. Coolant should be reused unless it is contaminated or several years old.

---

3. Remove the valve cover and timing chain cover.
4. Remove the cylinder head.

NOTE: A special cylinder head removal procedure must be followed to avoid damage to the cylinder liners. See Cylinder

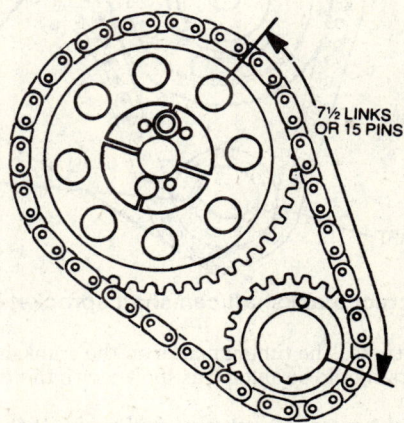

On the 6-4.0L, verify there are 15 pins between the marks when the camshaft sprocket alignment mark is at the 3 o'clock location

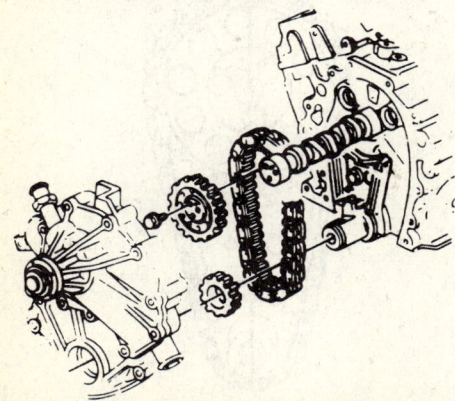

Camshaft removal/installation on the 6-2.8L

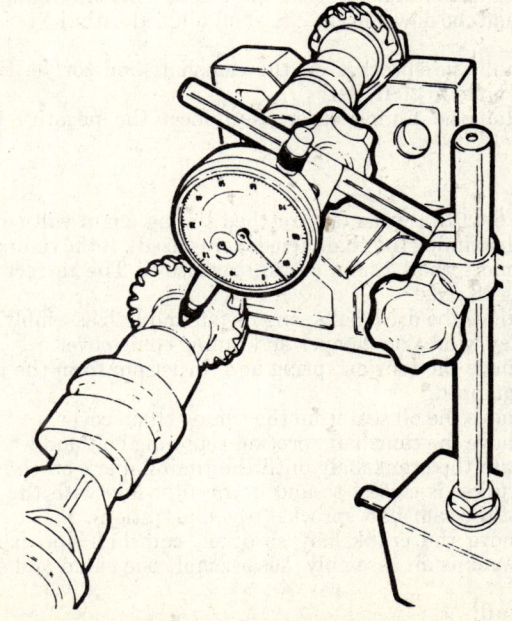

Checking the camshaft for straightness

ENGINE AND ENGINE OVERHAUL 3

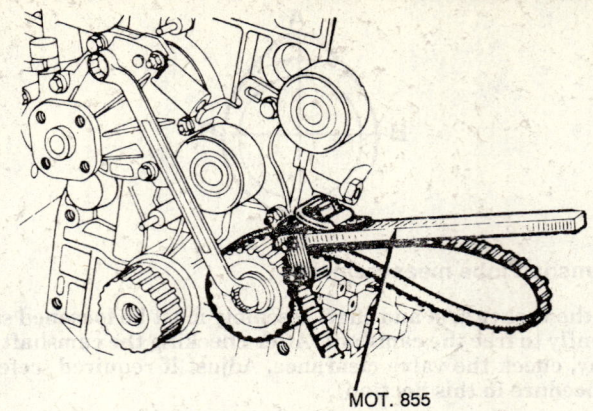

Use tool Mot. 855 to hold the camshaft sprocket while tightening the sprocket retaining bolt

Head Removal/Installation in this Section.

5. Remove the camshaft gear using tool B.Vi 28-01.
6. Remove the oil seal from the cylinder head by prying it out using a suitable tool.
7. Remove the camshaft from the cylinder head.
8. Coat the camshaft with an engine oil supplement.
9. Carefully install the camshaft in the cylinder head.
10. Install the oil seal in the cylinder.
11. Install the camshaft gear. Hold the sprocket with tool Mot.855 while tightening to 37 ft. lbs.
12. Install the cylinder head.
13. Install the valve cover and timing chain cover.
14. Fill the cooling system.
15. Connect the negative battery cable.

All Except 4-2.1L

— CAUTION —
To remove the camshaft from this engine, the air conditioning system must be discharged. See Section 1. Mishandling of refrigerant gas can cause severe personal injury. DO NOT attempt to discharge the refrigerant system if you are not completely familiar with the handling of refrigerant gas.

1. Disconnect the battery ground.
2. Drain the cooling system.

— CAUTION —
When draining the coolant, keep in mind that cats and dogs are attracted by the ethylene glycol antifreeze, and are quite likely to drink any that is left in an uncovered container or in puddles on the ground. This will prove fatal in sufficient quantity. Always drain the coolant into a sealable container. Coolant should be reused unless it is contaminated or several years old.

3. On 4-2.5L and 6-2.8L engines, discharge the air conditioning system, remove the radiator and air conditioning condenser. On 6-4.0L remove the radiator, then remove the air conditioning condenser and receiver/dryer assembly as a charged unit.
4. On pre-1990 4-2.5L engines and all 6-2.8L engines remove the fuel pump.
5. Matchmark the distributor and engine for installation. Note the rotor position by marking it on the distributor body. Unbolt and remove the distributor and wires.
5. Remove the rocker arm cover.
6. Remove the rocker arm assemblies.
7. Remove the pushrods.

NOTE: Keep everything in order for installation. If a replacement camshaft is to be installed, replace hydraulic lift-

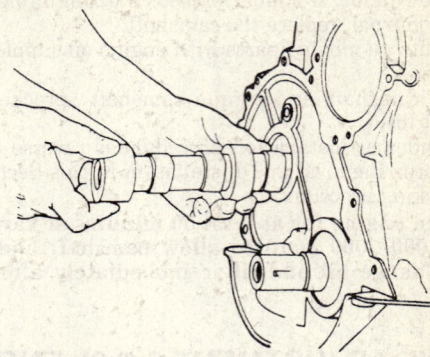

Remove/install the camshaft carefully! Camshaft bearings are coated with soft babbet material, which can be damaged by scraping the cam lobes across the bearing

ers to ensure durability of camshaft lobes and lifter bottoms.

8. Using a tool J-21884, or equivalent, remove the hydraulic lifters.
9. Remove the vibration damper and timing chain cover.

NOTE: If the camshaft sprocket appears to have been rubbing against the cover, check the oil pressure relief holes in the rear cam journal for debris.

10. Remove the timing chain and sprockets.
11. Slide the camshaft from the engine. If necessary, remove front bumper and/or grille to allow removal of camshaft through front of vehicle.
12. Inspect the cam lobes, bearing journals, bearings and distributor drive gear for wear. Replace if necessary.
13. Check camshaft for straightness. Place the camshaft in two V-blocks. Install a dial indicator so that the actuating point of the indicator rests on a camshaft bearing journal. Spin the camshaft

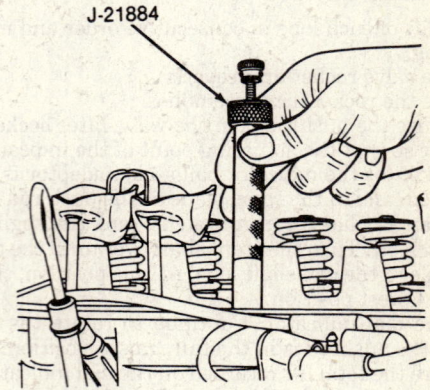

Remove the lifters from the engine using a hydraulic lifter removal/installation tool (J-21884)

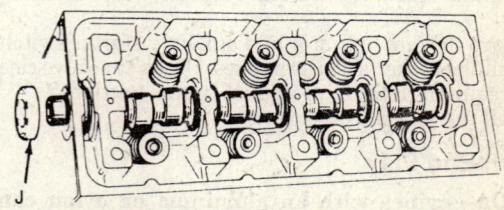

When installing a camshaft, always use a new front seal (J)

3-79

3 ENGINE AND ENGINE OVERHAUL

and note the runout. If runout exceeds 0.023mm (0.0009 in.) on any bearing journal, replace the camshaft.

14. Lubricate all moving parts with engine oil supplement prior to installation.
15. Install camshaft and torque camshaft sprocket retaining bolts to 80 ft.lbs.
16. Remainder of installation procedure is reverse of removal. See Distributor Removal and Installation in this Section for distributor clocking procedure.

NOTE: Run engine for at least 30 minutes at varying rpm's (between 1000–2000 rpm) to allow camshaft and lifters to break-in. Change oil and filter immediately after break-in period.

VALVE ADJUSTMENT 6-2.8L ENGINE

1. Tighten the rocker arm adjusting nuts until rocker arms just touch the valve stems.
2. Rotate the engine until number one piston is at TDC of the compression stroke. The '0' on the timing scale should be aligned with the timing pointer and the rotor should be at the number one spark plug tower of the distributor cap.
3. Adjust Exhaust valves 1-2-3; Intake valves 1-5-6.

NOTE: Valve arrangement on the 6-2.8L engine is as follows: RIGHT E-I-I-E-I-E, LEFT E-I-I-E-I-E.

4. Turn the adjusting nut until the rocker arm lifts off the valve stem slightly, then tighten until the rocker arm just touches the valve stem. Turn the nut $1^{1}/_{8}$ turns more to center the tappet plunger.
5. Rotate the engine one complete revolution. The number four piston should be at TDC on the compression stroke.
6. Adjust Exhaust valves 4-5-6; Intake valves 2-3-4.

CHECKING CAMSHAFT

Camshaft Lobe Lift

Check the lift of each lobe in consecutive order and make a note of the reading.

1. Remove valve rocker arm cover(s).
2. Remove the rocker arm assemblies.
3. Make sure the pushrod is in the valve lifter socket. Install a dial indicator so that the actuating point of the indicator is in the pushrod socket (or the indicator ball socket adaptor is on the end of the pushrod) and in the same plane as the push rod movement.
4. Install an auxiliary starter switch Crank the engine with the ignition switch off. Turn the crankshaft over until the tappet is on the base circle of the camshaft lobe. At this position, the pushrod will be in its lowest position.
5. Zero the dial indicator. Continue to rotate the crankshaft slowly until the pushrod is in the fully raised position.
6. Compare the total lift recorded on the dial indicator with the specification shown on the Camshaft Specification chart.
7. Check the accuracy of the original indicator reading by continuing to rotate the crankshaft and noting the highest lift recorded on the dial indicator. If the lift on any lobe is below specified wear limits listed, the camshaft and the valve lifters must be replaced.
8. Remove the dial indicator and auxiliary starter switch.
9. Install the rocker arm assemblies. Check the valve clearance. Adjust if required (refer to procedure in this Section).
10. Install the rocker arm cover(s).

Camshaft End Play

NOTE: On engines with an aluminum or nylon camshaft sprocket, prying against the sprocket, with the valve train load on the camshaft, can break or damage the sprocket. Therefore, the rocker arm adjusting nuts must be backed off,

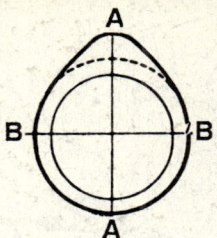

Camshaft lobe measurement

or the rocker arm and shaft assembly must be loosened sufficiently to free the camshaft. After checking the camshaft end play, check the valve clearance. Adjust if required (refer to procedure in this Section).

1. Push the camshaft toward the rear of the engine. Install a dial indicator so that the indicator point is on the camshaft sprocket attaching screw.
2. Zero the dial indicator. Position a prybar between the camshaft gear and the block. Pull the camshaft forward and release it. Compare the dial indicator reading with the specifications.
3. If the end play is excessive, check the spacer for correct installation before it is removed. If the spacer is correctly installed, replace the thrust plate.
4. Remove the dial indicator.

CAMSHAFT BEARING REPLACEMENT

1. Remove the engine following the procedures in this Section and install it on an engine stand.
2. Remove the camshaft, flywheel and crankshaft, following the appropriate procedures. Push the pistons to the top of the cylinder.
3. Remove the camshaft rear bearing bore plug. Remove the camshaft bearings with a bearing removal tool.
4. Select the proper size expanding collet and back-up nut and assemble on the mandrel. With the expanding collet collapsed, install the collet assembly in the camshaft bearing and tighten the back-up nut on the expanding mandrel until the collet fits the camshaft bearing.
5. Assemble the puller screw and extension (if necessary) and install on the expanding mandrel. Wrap a cloth around the threads of the puller screw to protect the front bearing or journal. Tighten the pulling nut against the thrust bearing and pulling plate to remove the camshaft bearing. Be sure to hold a wrench on the end of the puller screw to prevent it from turning.
6. To remove the front bearing, install the puller from the rear of the cylinder block.
7. Position the new bearings at the bearing bores, and press them in place. Be sure to center the pulling plate and puller screw to avoid damage to the bearing. Failure to use the correct expanding collet can cause severe bearing damage. Align the oil holes in the bearings with the oil holes in the cylinder block before pressing bearings into place.
8. Install the camshaft rear bearing bore plug.
9. Install the camshaft, crankshaft, flywheel and related parts, following the appropriate procedures.
10. Install the engine in the truck, following procedures described earlier in this Section.

Freeze Plugs and Block Heater

Freeze plugs are located on the side of the engine block and the front or side of the cylinder heads. Their function is to allow coolant expansion in the event of a cold weather freeze up of the cool-

ENGINE AND ENGINE OVERHAUL 3

ant. Unless you are rebuilding your engine or a freeze plug starts to leak, they require no maintenance.

Installation and removal of freeze plugs is fairly simple. Set aside all components which impede removal of the plug. Use a hammer and punch to remove the freeze plug from the block. Coat the new plug with sealer and install, using a brass drift (a large socket works well too), until the plug is flush with the block.

Block heaters are used to warm the engine coolant prior to initial start up of the engine. They are also used to prevent coolant freeze up in severe climates. The block heater replaces one of the freeze plugs and is plugged into 110v house current via an extension cord routed from the engine compartment.

Pistons and Connecting Rods Gasoline Engines

NOTE: Use care at all times when handling and servicing rods and pistons. To prevent possible damage to these units, DO NOT allow rods or pistons to strike hard objects or one another.

REMOVAL

NOTE: To ease the removal and installation of internal engine components, it is recommended that the engine be removed for servicing.

1. Remove the head(s).
2. Remove the oil pan.
3. Rotate the engine to bring each piston, in turn, to the bottom of its stroke. With the piston bottomed, use an expanding type hone to remove the ridge at the top of the cylinder. DO NOT CUT TOO DEEPLY!
4. Matchmark the rods and caps. If the pistons are to be removed from the connecting rod, mark the cylinder number on the piston with a silver pencil or quick drying paint for proper cylinder identification and cap-to-rod location. Remove the connecting rod capnuts and lift off the rod caps, keeping them in order. Install a guide hose over the rod bolt threads to prevent damage to the bearing journal and rod bolt threads.
5. Using a hammer handle, push the piston and rod assemblies up out of the block.
6. If replacement pistons are to be used, remove the piston pin

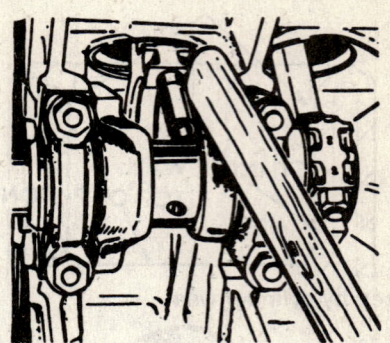
Push the piston and rod assembly out with a hammer handle

lockring (if used). Install the guide bushing of the piston pin removal/installation tool.

7. Place the piston and connecting rod assembly on a support, and place the assembly in an arbor press. Press the pin out of the connecting rod, using the appropriate piston pin tool.

CLEANING AND INSPECTION

Clean varnish from piston skirts and pins with a cleaning solvent. DO NOT WIRE BRUSH ANY PART OF THE PISTON. Remove old piston rings and clean the ring grooves with a groove cleaner. Make sure oil ring holes and slots are clean.

Inspect the piston for cracked ring lands, skirts or pin bosses, wavy or worn ring lands, scuffed or damaged skirts, eroded areas at the top of the piston. Replace pistons that are damaged or show signs of excessive wear. Inspect the grooves for nicks or burrs that might cause the rings to hang up.

Inspect connecting rod bearings for scoring and bent alignment tabs. Also check for grooving, fatigue or any sign of abnormal wear. Inspect connecting rod journals for signs of scoring, nicks, burrs or abnormal wear. Any of these conditions signal problems which should be investigated.

Using a straightedge, check the connecting rods for straightness. It is advisable to have connecting rods Magnafluxed® for cracks. The Magnaflux® process is performed by first cleaning the connecting rod. Next, the rod is sprayed with a special fluorescent dye and placed under a black-light for inspection. Cracks will show up as bright lines in the metal. This procedure is also performed on crankshafts, cylinder blocks and heads.

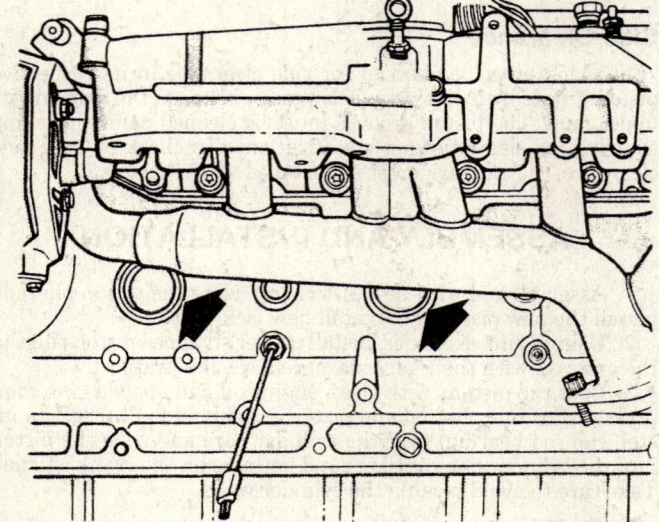
Freeze plug location

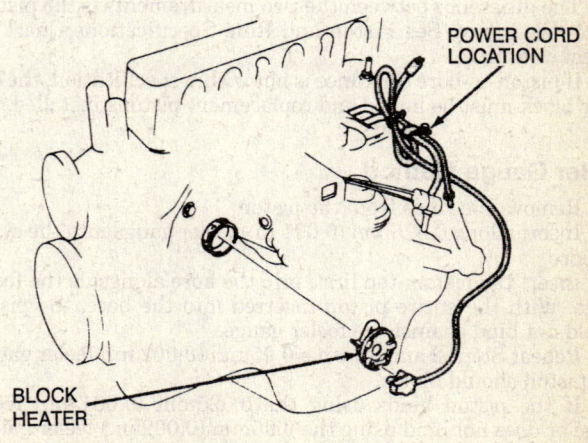
Block heater assembly

3 ENGINE AND ENGINE OVERHAUL

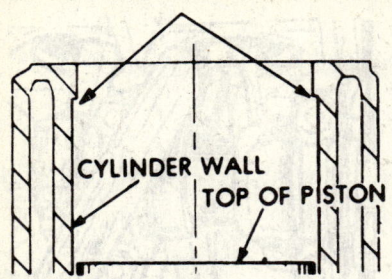

Ridge caused by cylinder wear

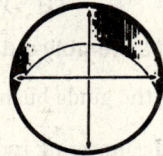

Take cylinder bore measurements at 1/2 in. below the top of the cylinder; 1/2 in. above the top of the piston at BDC. Take measurements parallel and perpendicular to the crankshaft centerline

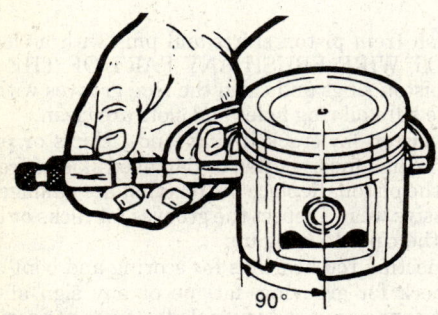

Measure the piston at 90° to the piston pin axis

PISTON FITTING

Micrometer Method

1. Measure the inside diameter of the cylinder bore at a point 50mm (2 in.) below the deck surface using a dial bore gauge.
2. Measure the outside diameter of the piston at the piston centerline and perpendicular to the piston pin bore.
3. The difference between the two measurements is the piston-to-bore clearance. See Piston and Ring Specifications Chart for correct clearance.
4. If piston-to-bore clearance is not within specification, the cylinder block must be honed and replacement pistons installed.

Feeler Gauge Method

1. Remove the rings from the piston.
2. Insert a long 0.025mm (0.001 in.) feeler gauge into the cylinder bore.
3. Insert the piston, top first, into the bore alongside the feeler gauge. With the entire piston inserted into the bore, the piston should not bind against the feeler gauge.
4. Repeat Steps 2 and 3 with a 0.05mm (0.002 in.) feeler gauge. The piston should bind.
5. If the piston binds using the 0.025mm (0.001 in.) feeler gauge or does not bind using the 0.05mm (0.002 in.) feeler gauge, the piston is not the correct size for the bore. Replace the piston and/or hone the bore to gain proper piston-to-bore clearance.

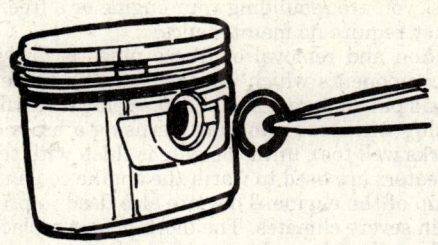

Use needle-nosed pliers to remove the piston pin clips

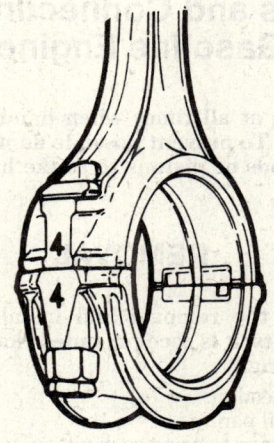

Number each rod and cap accordingly

PISTON RING REPLACEMENT

For service ring specifications and detailed installation procedures, refer to the ring manufacturers instructions. When installing new rings, gap and side clearance should be checked as follows:

Piston Ring Gap

Each ring and rail gap must be measured with the ring or rail positioned squarely and at the bottom of the ring-travel area of the bore.

Side Clearance

Each ring must be checked for side clearance in its respective piston groove by inserting a feeler gauge between the ring and its upper land. The piston grooves must be cleaned before checking the ring for side clearance specifications. To check oil ring side clearance, the oil rings must be installed on the piston.

ASSEMBLY AND INSTALLATION

1. Assemble rod with new piston and using the piston pin tool, install the new piston pin. Install new lockrings.
2. Using a ring expander, install properly gapped piston rings in the grooves, with their gaps staggered (see illustration).
3. Coat the pistons with clean engine oil and apply a ring compressor. Position the rod and piston assembly (don't forget to install the rod bearing) over the cylinder bore and slide the piston into the cylinder bore until the rod bottoms on the crank journal. Take care to avoid nicking the cylinder walls.

NOTE: The pistons will have a mark on the crown, such as a groove or notch or stamped symbol. This mark indicates the side of the piston which should face front.

ENGINE AND ENGINE OVERHAUL 3

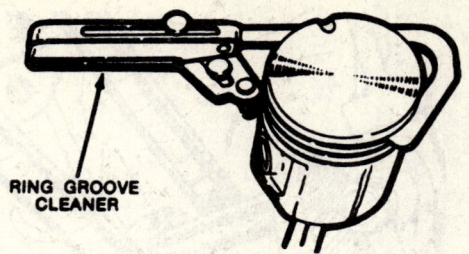

Using a ring groove cleaner

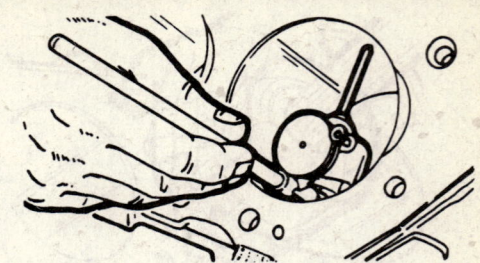

Measuring the cylinder bore with a dial gauge

4. Install the bearing caps with the stamped numbers matched. Check the rod bearing clearances with Plastigage®, using the manufacturers instructions on the package.

5. Torque the cap bolts (nuts) to specification. See the accompanying illustrations for proper piston and rod installation.

Pistons and Connecting Rods, Diesel Engines

REMOVAL AND INSTALLATION

Mark the connecting rods and rod bearing caps on the intermediate shaft side of the cylinder block with the number of the corresponding cylinder. Number one cylinder is located at the flywheel/drive plate end of the engine block. When removing, remove each connecting rod, cylinder liner and piston as a complete assembly. Each piston and cylinder liner are matched as a set, so, be sure that they are marked properly for installation. Install the assembly according to the marks made during the removal stage of the overhaul.

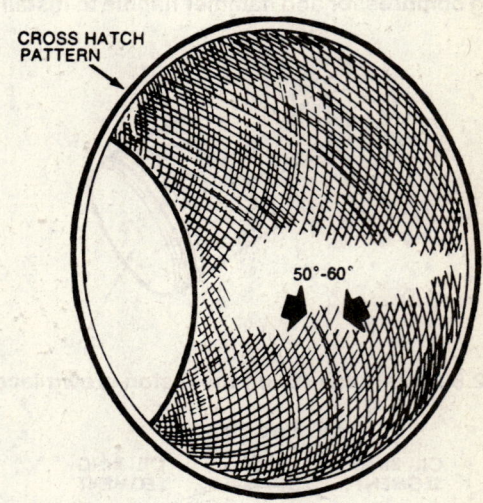

Finished cylinder after honing

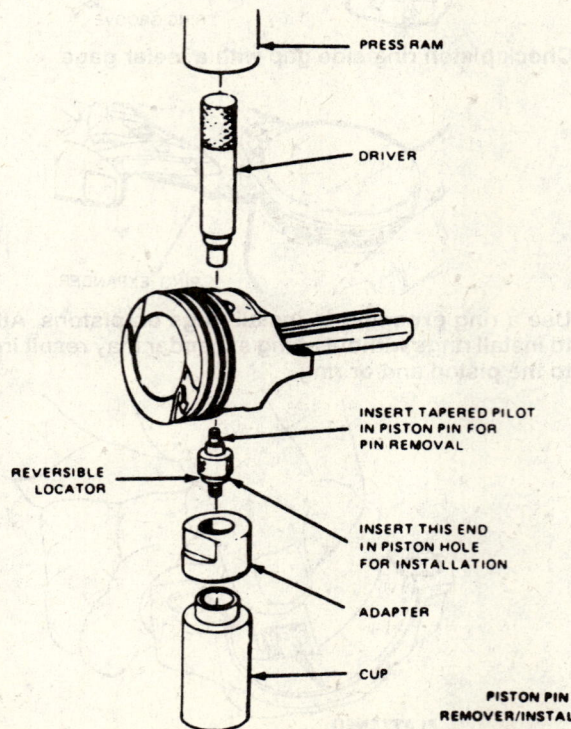

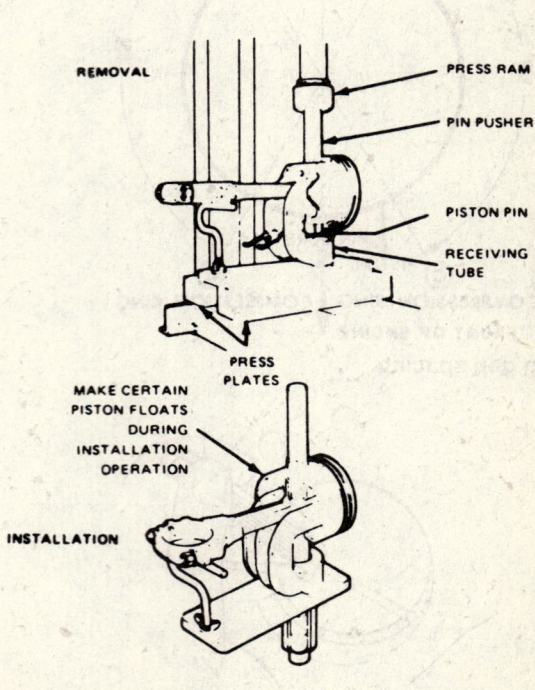

Piston pins must be pressed in with an arbor press

3-83

3 ENGINE AND ENGINE OVERHAUL

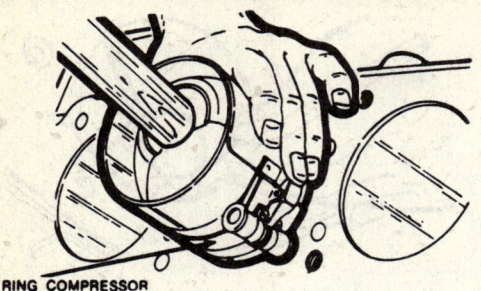
Use a ring compressor and hammer handle to install pistons

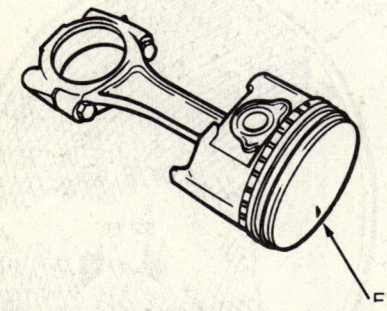
On the 6-2.8L, the notch (E) on the piston crown faces front

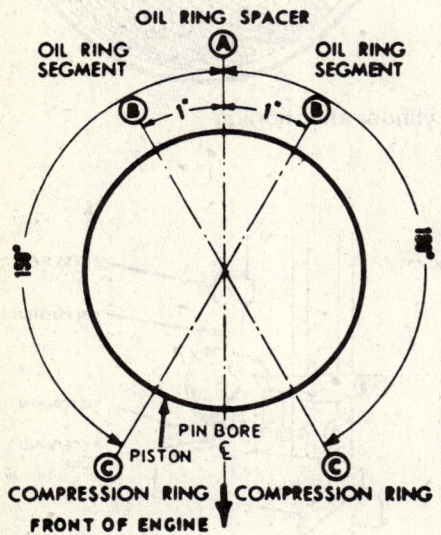
Proper ring gap spacing

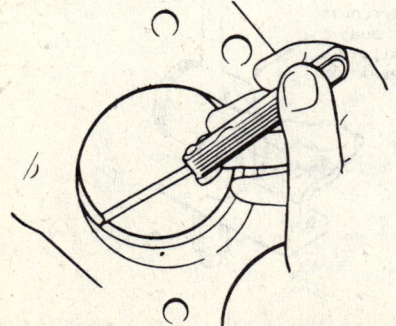
Check piston ring end gap with ring squared approximately 1 in. down in the bore

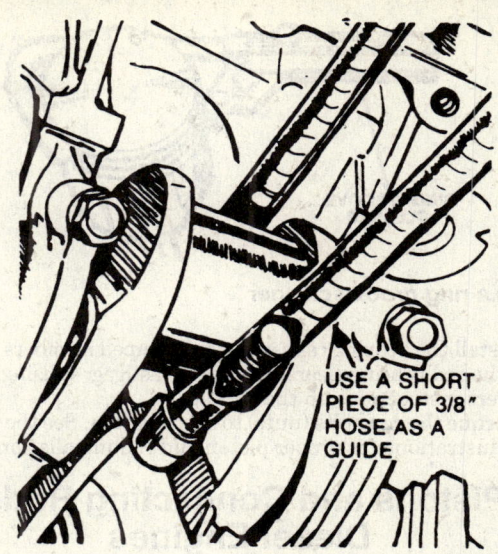
Use lengths of rubber hose to protect the crankshaft journals and cylinder walls during piston removal/installation

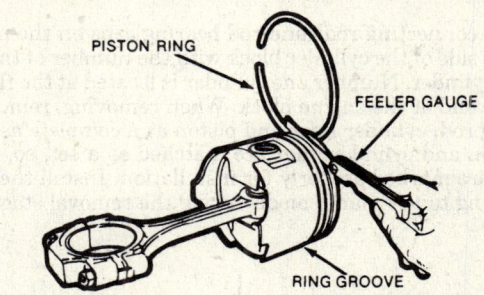
Check piston ring side gap with a feeler gage

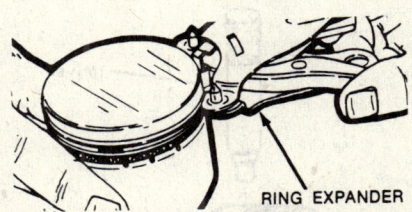
Use a ring expander to install rings on pistons. Attempting to install rings without a ring expander may result in damage to the piston and/or ring

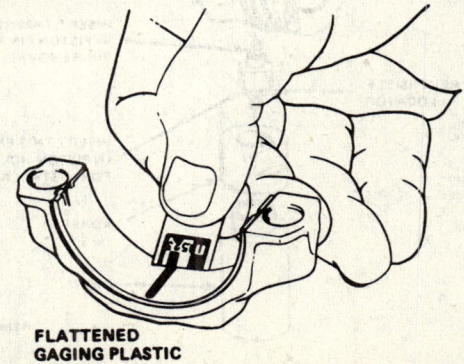
Using a Plastigage® to measure connecting rod bearing clearance

ENGINE AND ENGINE OVERHAUL 3

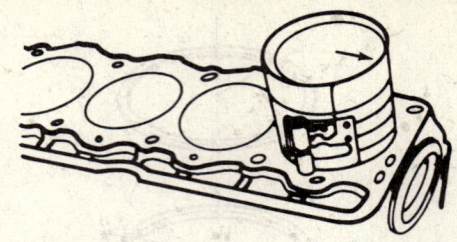

On the 4-2.5L/6-4.0L the arrow on the piston crown faces front

Cylinder Liners

REMOVAL AND INSTALLATION

4-2.1L Diesel

NOTE: Special tools are needed for this job.

1. Remove the engine from the vehicle.
2. Remove the cylinder head.
3. Remove the oil pan.
4. Number the connecting rod caps and remove them, keeping them in order.

NOTE: Number 1 cylinder is at the flywheel end.

5. Remove the cylinder liner along with the piston and connecting rod assembly.
6. Separate the piston assembly from the cylinder liner. Remove the O-ring seal and the plastic ring from the cylinder liner.
7. If the liner is going to be replaced, be sure to also replace the piston assembly, as they are a matched set.
8. Upon installation, install the piston assembly into the cylinder liner with tool MOT-851 or equivalent.

NOTE: The cylinder liners require a rubber O-ring seal and a plastic ring to provide a seal between the liner and the cylinder block, as each liner is supported by the cylinder block. The correct liner protrusion, X in the accompanying illustration, which is above the cylinder block, is achieved by close matching tolerances when the cylinder liner and block are manufactured. If replacement liners are required, the liner protrusions above the cylinder block must be measured and all the cylinder liners rearranged according to the results of the measurements.

CYLINDER LINER PROTRUSION MEASUREMENT

NOTE: Special tools are needed for this job.

1. Insert each reusable cylinder liner in its original position in the cylinder block. If applicable, insert the replacement liner in the cylinder block.
2. Install tool MOT-LM and MOT-251-01 or equivalent, on the engine block and tighten the screw clamp. Position tool MOT-252-01 or equivalent, across each cylinder liner, in turn, and secure it with tool MOT-853 or equivalent. Tighten the tool retaining bolts gradually and torque them to 37 ft. lbs. This will assure that each cylinder liner will be firmly in contact with the cylinder block.
3. Measure the protrusion, **X**, of each cylinder liner above the cylinder block using the dial indicator and block gauge. The correct specification is 0.050–0.120mm.
4. If an out-of-specification cylinder liner protrusion is measured, install a replacement liner. Measure the protrusion to determine if the cylinder block or the cylinder liner is defective.
5. With all cylinder liner protrusions within specification arrange them so that the difference in protrusion between any two adjacent liners does not exceed 0.040mm.
6. The protrusions are stepped down from the number one cylinder to the number four cylinder or from the number four cylinder to the number one cylinder.
7. When the correct cylinder liner protrusion arrangement has been determined, match each piston and connecting rod assembly

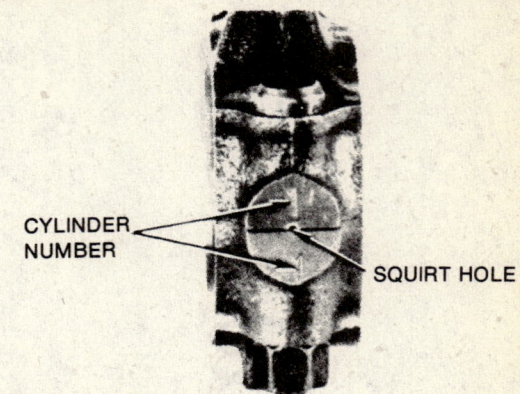

6-4.0L connecting rod and cap

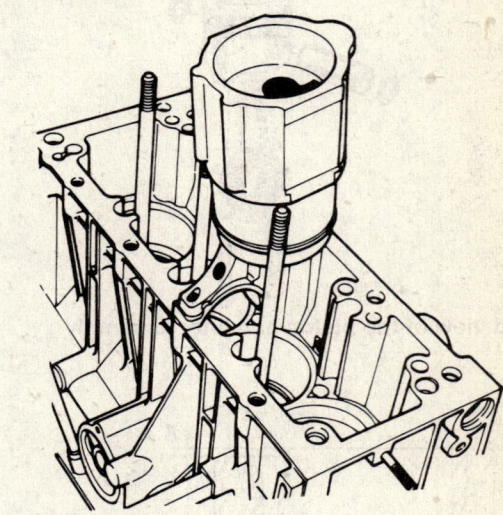

Removing the liner, piston and rod assembly

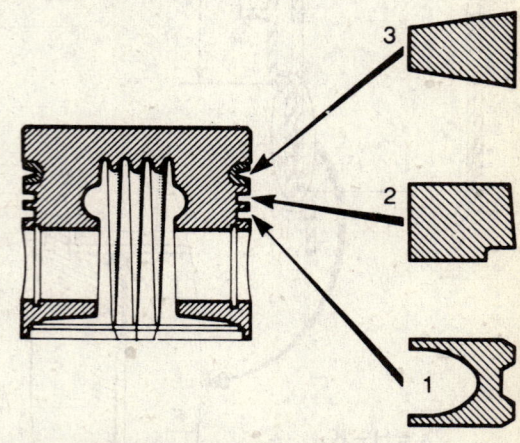

Ring installation on the 4-2.1L diesel

3-85

3 ENGINE AND ENGINE OVERHAUL

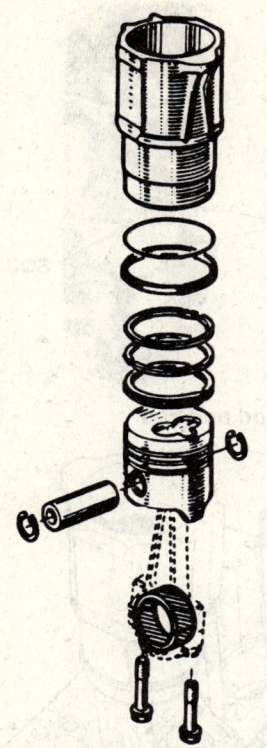

Exploded view of the piston and liner assembly

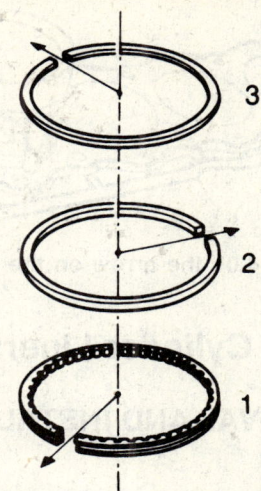

Ring gap positioning on the 4-2.1L diesel

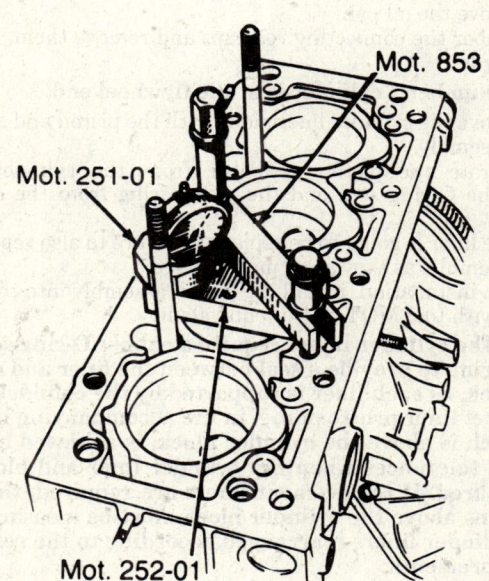

Special tools in place to measure liner protrusion

with its original liner and remark each according to the new position in the cylinder block.

Crankshaft Main Oil Seal

REPLACEMENT

4-2.1L Diesel

NOTE: Replacement front and rear main side seals are available in 2 different thicknesses: 5.4mm and 5.1mm. There are identical main seals in both the front (No.5) and rear (No.1) main bearing positions. They are replaced in an identical manner. Both ends are sealed with identical, but not interchangeable, one piece round seals.

If the end seals are being replaced, remove the engine and place it on an engine stand. If the side seals are being replaced, remove the oil pan. It advisable to replace the end seals if the side seals are leaking.

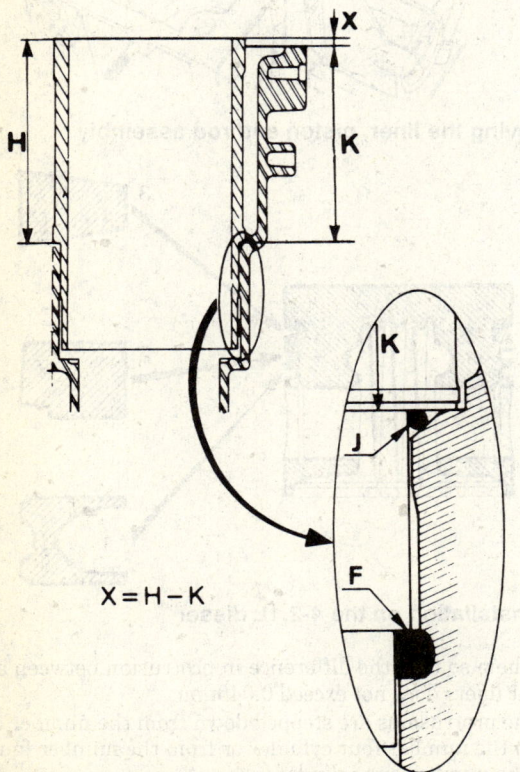

Diesel cylinder liner installation. (X) liner protrusion; (J) rubber O-ring; (F) plastic O-ring

$X = H - K$

ENGINE AND ENGINE OVERHAUL

FRONT END MAIN SEAL

1. Remove the engine.
2. Remove the timing chain and sprockets.
3. Using a sharp awl, punch a hole in the seal and pry it out of its bore.
4. Thoroughly clean the bore.
5. Coat the outer edge of the new seal with sealer and the inner sealing surface with clean engine oil.
6. Using a seal driver, such as Mot.789, drive the new seal into place.
7. Install the timing chain and sprockets, and all other related parts.
8. Install the engine.

REAR END MAIN SEAL

1. Remove the engine.
2. Remove the flywheel.
3. Using a sharp awl, punch a hole in the seal and pry it out of its bore.
4. Thoroughly clean the bore.
5. Coat the outer edge of the new seal with sealer and the inner sealing surface with clean engine oil.
6. Using a seal driver, such as Mot.788, drive the new seal into place.
7. Install the flywheel.
8. Install the engine.

FRONT END AND/OR REAR END MAIN SIDE SEALS

NOTE: Depending on working clearance, it may be necessary to remove the engine.

1. Remove the oil pan.
2. Remove the main bearing cap.
3. Remove the side seals.
4. Thoroughly clean the seal surfaces in the block and cap.
5. Replace the cap.
6. Measure the width of the seal bore.
7. If the seal bore is 5mm or less, use a 5.1mm thick seal; if it is more than 5mm, use a 5.4mm thick seal.
8. Remove the bearing cap.
9. Insert the proper side seals in the cap grooves with the grooves in the seals facing outward. Each seal should stick out from the cap about 0.2mm.
10. Lightly coat the seals with clean engine oil.
11. Cover the length of each seal with a strip of aluminum foil and install the cap and seals in the block. Don't install the cap bolts. Remove the foil.
12. Measure the side seal protrusion above the cap. Protrusion should be greater than 0.7mm.
13. Torque the bearing cap bolts to 72 ft. lbs.
14. Cut the side seals to within 0.5–0.7mm protrusion.
15. Install the oil pan.

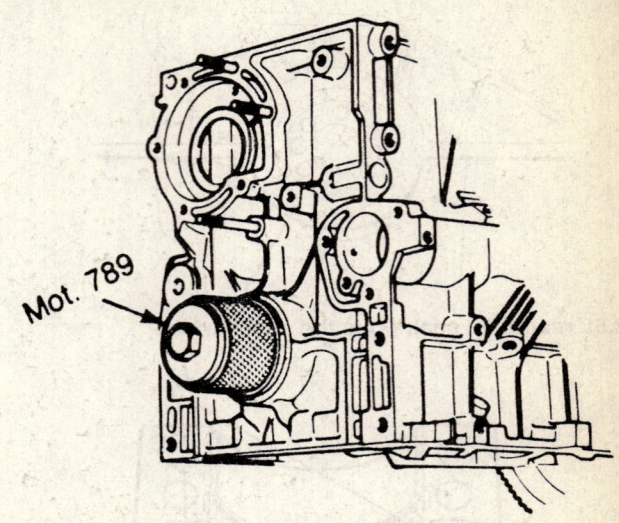
Front end main seal installation on the 4-2.1L diesel

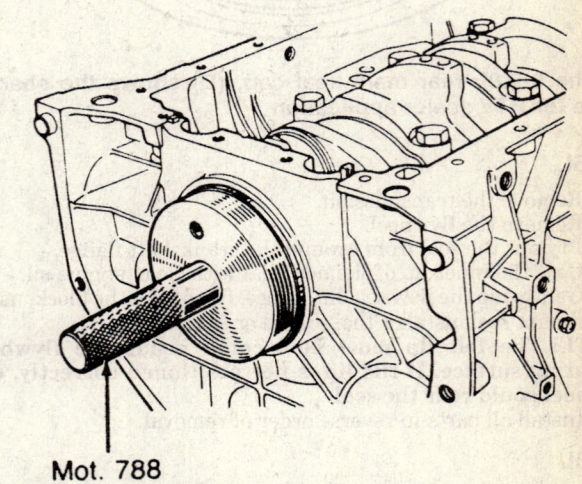
Rear end main seal on the 4-2.1L diesel

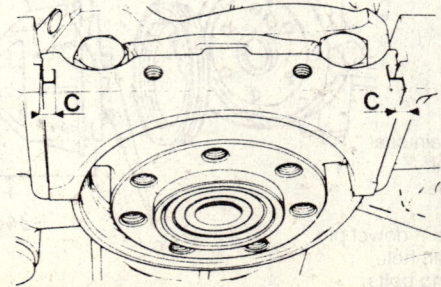
Measuring the side bore (C) on the 4-2.1L diesel

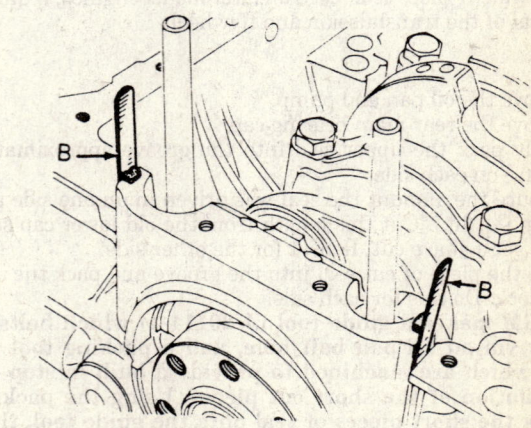
Cap and seals installed on the 4-2.1L diesel. (B) indicates foil strips covering the side seals

3 ENGINE AND ENGINE OVERHAUL

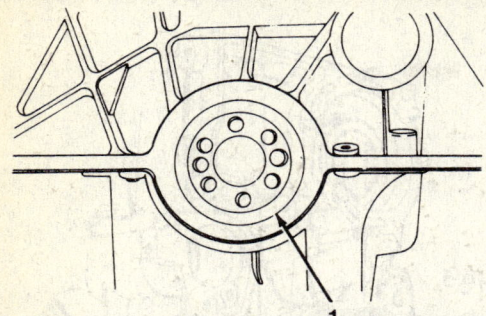

4-2.5L rear main seal. (1) is the seal surface

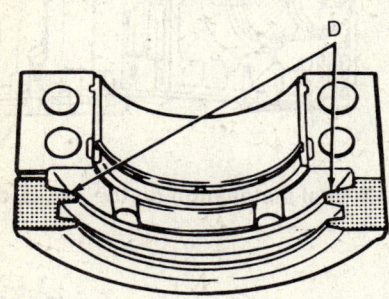

On the 6-2.8L rear main seal cap, (D) shows the shaded areas for RTV sealer application

4-2.5L

1. Remove the transmission.
2. Remove the flywheel.
3. Pry out the seal from around the crankshaft flange.
4. Coat the inner lip of the new seal with clean engine oil.
5. Gently tap the new seal into place, flush with the block, using a rear main seal installer tool (6271) or equivalent.

NOTE: The felt lip must be located inside the flywheel mounting surface. If the lip is not positioned correctly, the flywheel could rear the seal.

6. Install all parts in reverse order of removal.

6-2.8L

The General Motors-built 6-2.8L uses will have one of two different rear main seal assemblies: either a 1-piece or 2-piece seal. The 2-piece type requires removal of the rear main bearing cap for servicing. The wide, 1-piece seal, used on later model engines, requires the removal of the transmission and flywheel.

2-PIECE

1. Remove the oil pan and pump.
2. Remove the rear main bearing cap.
3. Gently pack the upper seal into the groove approximately 6mm (¼ in.) on each side.
4. Measure the amount the seal was driven in on one side and add 1.5mm (1/16 in.). Cut this length from the old lower cap seal. Be sure to get a sharp cut. Repeat for the other side.
5. Place the piece of cut seal into the groove and pack the seal into the block. Do this for each side.

NOTE: GM makes a guide tool (J-29114-1) which bolts to the block via an oil pan bolt hole, and a packing tool (J-29114-2) which are machined to provide a built-in stop for the installation of the short cut pieces. Using the packing tool, work the short pieces of seal onto the guide tool, then pack them into the block with the packing tool.

6. Install a new lower seal in the rear main cap.
7. Install a piece of Plastigage® or the equivalent on the bearing

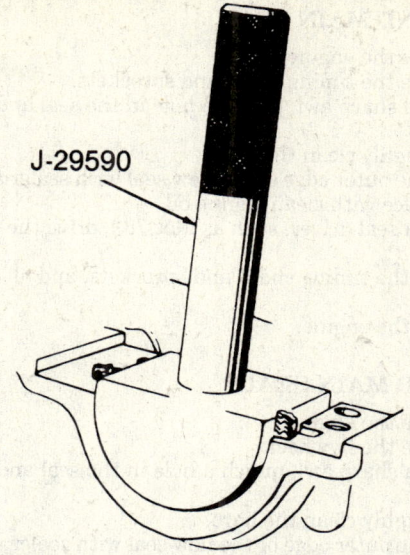

Installing the lower rear main seal in the cap

journal. Install the rear cap and tighten to 70 ft.lbs. Remove the cap and check the gauge for bearing clearance. If out of specification, the ends of the seal may be frayed or not flush, preventing the cap from proper sealing. Correct as required.

8. Clean the journal, and apply a thin film of RTV silicone sealer to the mating surfaces of the cap and block. Do not allow any sealer to get onto the journal or bearing. Install the bearing cap and tighten to 70 ft. lbs. Install the pan and pump.

1-PIECE

1. Remove transmission and flywheel.
2. Using an appropriate tool, pry the seal from around the crankshaft flange. Insert the pry tool under the seal dust lip and pry up and out.

NOTE: DO NOT allow the pry tool to contact the crankshaft journal surface.

3. Clean and lubricate the inner and outer surfaces of the replacement seal thoroughly with engine oil.
4. Install the seal on the installation tool (J-34686). Ensure the seal dust lip faces the collar of the installation tool. Seat the seal firmly against the collar of the tool.

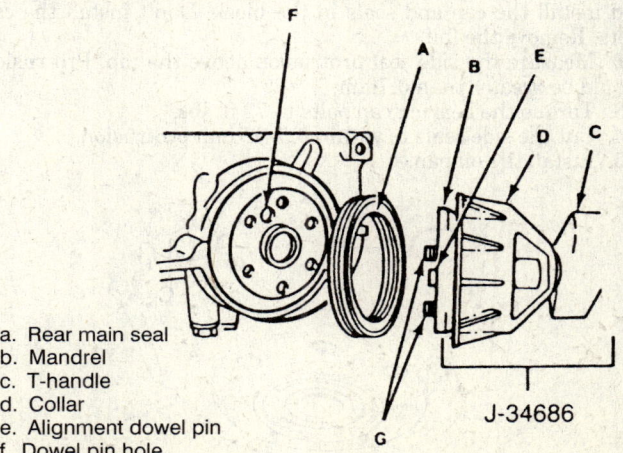

a. Rear main seal
b. Mandrel
c. T-handle
d. Collar
e. Alignment dowel pin
f. Dowel pin hole
g. Attaching bolts

Rear main seal installation tool J-34686

ENGINE AND ENGINE OVERHAUL 3

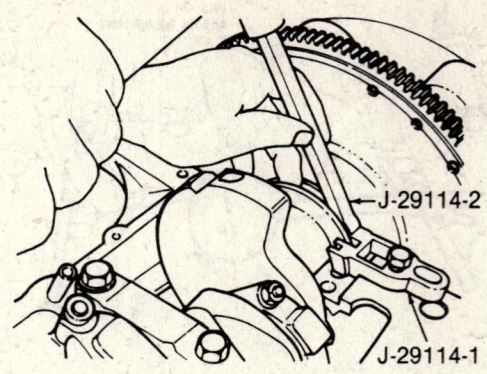

Exhaust pipe-to-converter connection

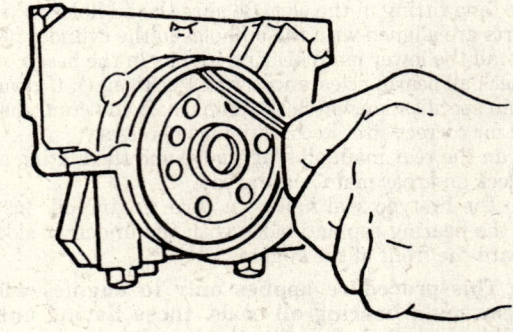

Removing the one piece rear main seal on the 6-2.8L

5. Align the dowel pin of the tool with the dowel pin hole and tighten tool to crankshaft flange with attaching bolts. tighten bolts to 24–36 ft. lbs.
6. Install the seal by tightening the T-handle of the tool until the seal is firmly seated against the block and bearing cap.
7. Fully retract the T-handle of the tool. Remove the attaching bolts and tool. Verify the seal is properly seated.
8. Install the flywheel and transmission.

6-4.0L

1. Remove the transmission.
2. Remove the flywheel or flexplate.
3. Pry the seal out from around the crankshaft flange.
4. Remove the rear main bearing cap and wipe clean the cap and crankshaft seal surfaces.
5. Apply a thin coat of engine oil to the seal surfaces of the cap and crankshaft.
6. Coat the lip of each seal half with clean engine oil.
7. Position the upper seal half in the block. The lip of the seal faces the front of the engine.
8. Coat both side of the lower seal's end tabs with RTV silicone gasket material. Don't get any on the seal lip.
9. Coat the outer, curved surface of the lower seal with soap.
10. Seat the lower seal firmly in the bearing cap recess.
11. Coat both chamfered edges of the bearing cap with RTV silicone gasket material.

WARNING: Be careful to avoid getting and RTV material on the bearing cap-to-block mating surfaces! Doing so would change the bearing clearance!

12. Install the bearing cap.
13. Torque all the main bearing caps to 80 ft. lbs.

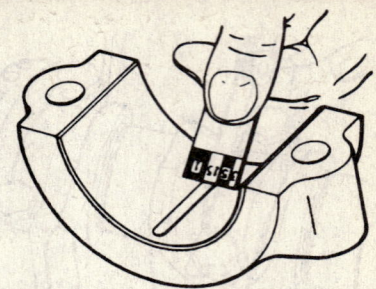

Checking rear main bearing oil clearance with Plastigage®

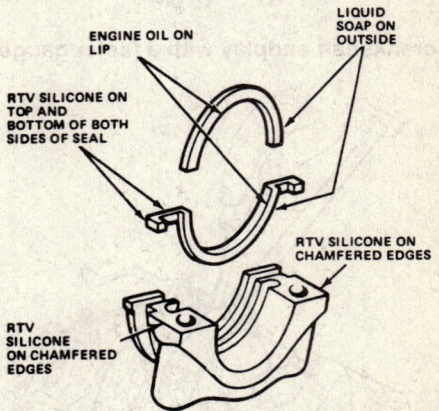

Rear main seal installation on the 6-4.0L

Crankshaft and Main Bearings

REMOVAL AND INSTALLATION

Engine Removed

1. With the engine removed from the vehicle and placed on an engine stand, disconnect the spark plug wires from the spark plugs and remove the wires and bracket assembly from the attaching stud on the rocker arm cover(s) if so equipped. Disconnect the coil to distributor high tension lead at the coil. Remove the distributor cap and spark plug wires as an assembly. Remove the spark plugs to allow easy rotation of the crankshaft.
2. Remove the fuel pump and oil filter. Slide the water pump by-pass hose clamp (if so equipped) toward the water pump. Remove the alternator and mounting brackets.
3. Remove the crankshaft pulley from the crankshaft vibration damper. Remove the capscrew and washer from the end of the crankshaft. Install a universal puller on the crankshaft vibration damper and remove the damper.
4. Remove the timing chain/belt cover and crankshaft sprockets/gears and chain/belt.
5. Invert the engine on the work stand. Remove the clutch pressure plate and disc (manual shift transmission). Remove the flywheel and engine rear cover plate (automatic transmission). Remove the oil pan and gasket. Remove the oil pump.
6. Make sure all bearing caps (main and connecting rod) are marked so that they can be installed in their original locations. Turn the crankshaft until the connecting rod from which the cap is being removed is down, and remove the bearing cap. Push the connecting rod and piston assembly up into the cylinder. Repeat this procedure until all the connecting rod bearing caps are removed.
7. Remove the main bearings caps.
8. Carefully lift the crankshaft out of the block so that the

3 ENGINE AND ENGINE OVERHAUL

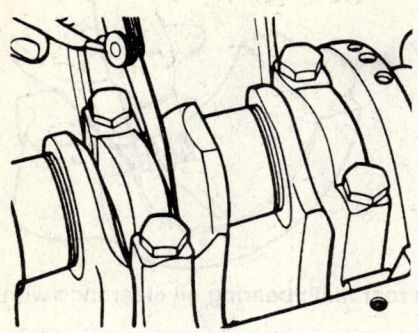

Checking crankshaft endplay with a feeler gauge

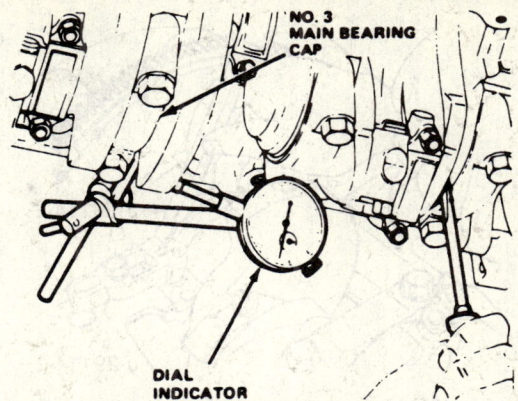

Checking crankshaft endplay with a dial indicator

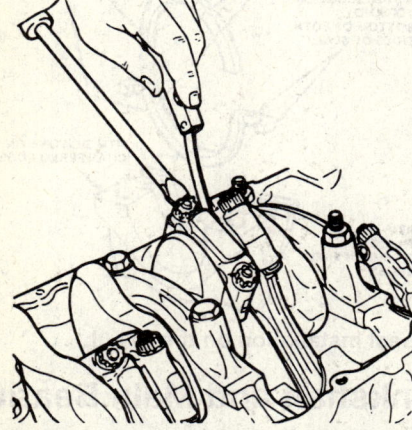

Checking rod side clearance with a flat feeler gauge. Use a small prybar to separate rods. Use this procedure again when tightening rod bolts. This will ensure the rod caps are aligned

thrust bearing surfaces are not damaged. Handle the crankshaft with care to avoid possible damage to the finished surfaces.

NOTE: If the engine is equipped with a one piece rear main seal, remove the seal prior to removing the crankshaft.

9. Remove the rear main seal from the block and rear main bearing cap.
10. Remove the main bearing inserts from the block and bearing caps.
11. Remove the connecting rod bearing inserts from the connecting rods and caps.
12. If the crankshaft main bearing journals have been refinished to a definite undersize, install the correct undersize bearings. Be sure the bearing inserts and bearing bores are clean. Foreign material under the inserts will distort the bearing and cause a failure.
13. Place the upper main bearing inserts in position in the bores with the tang fitting in the slot. Be sure the oil holes in the bearing inserts are aligned with the oil holes in the cylinder block.
14. Install the lower main bearing inserts in the bearing caps.
15. Check all bearing clearances with Plastigage®. If clearance is not within specification, check the crankshaft and crankshaft bearing bore for correct size. Recondition as necessary.
15. Clean the rear main oil seal groove and the mating surfaces of the block and rear main bearing cap.
16. Dip the lip-type seal halves in clean engine oil. Install the seals in the bearing cap and block with the undercut side of the seal toward the front of the engine.

NOTE: This procedure applies only to engines with two piece rear main bearing oil seals. those having one piece seals will be installed after the crankshaft is in place.

17. Carefully lower the crankshaft into place. Be careful not to damage the bearing surfaces.
18. Install all the bearing caps except the thrust bearing cap. Be sure the main bearing caps are installed in their original locations. Tighten the bearing cap bolts to specifications.
19. Install the thrust bearing cap with the bolts finger tight.
20. Pry the crankshaft forward against the thrust surface of the upper half of the bearing.
21. Hold the crankshaft forward and pry the thrust bearing cap to the rear. This will align the thrust surfaces of both halves of the bearing.
22. Retain the forward pressure on the crankshaft. Tighten the cap bolts to specifications.
23. Check the crankshaft end play.
24. On engines with one piece rear main bearing oil seal, coat a new crankshaft rear oil seal with oil and install using a seal driver. Inspect the seal to be sure it was not damaged during installation.
25. Install new bearing inserts in the connecting rods and caps. Check the clearance of each bearing. If clearance is not within specification, check the size of the crankshaft journal and connecting rod bore. Recondition as necessary.
26. After the connecting rod bearings have been fitted, apply a

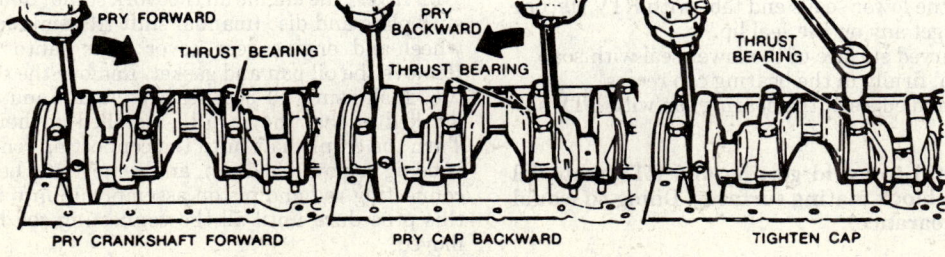

Crankshaft thrust bearing alignment

ENGINE AND ENGINE OVERHAUL 3

light coat of engine oil to the journals and bearings.
27. Turn the crankshaft throw to the bottom of its stroke. Push the piston all the way down until the rod bearing seats on the crankshaft journal.
28. Install the connecting rod cap using a feeler gauge to keep cap and rod aligned. Tighten the nuts to specification.
29. After the piston and connecting rod assemblies have been installed, check the side clearance with a feeler gauge between the connecting rods on each connecting rod crankshaft journal. Refer to Crankshaft and Connecting Rod specifications chart in this Section.
30. Install all other components in reverse order of removal.

CLEANING AND INSPECTION

Crankshaft

NOTE: handle the crankshaft carefully to avoid damage to the finish surfaces.

1. Clean the crankshaft with solvent, and blow out all oil passages with compressed air.
2. Use crocus cloth to remove any sharp edges, burrs or other imperfections which might damage the oil seal during installation or cause premature seal wear.

NOTE: Do not use crocus cloth to polish the seal surfaces. A finely polished surface may produce poor sealing or cause premature seal wear.

3. Inspect the main and connecting rod journals for cracks, scratches, grooves or scores.
4. Measure the diameter of each journal at least four places to determine out-of-round, taper or undersize condition.
5. On an engine with a manual transmission, check the fit of the clutch pilot bearing in the bore of the crankshaft. A needle roller bearing and adapter assembly is used as a clutch pilot bearing. It is inserted directly into the engine crank shaft. The bearing and adapter assembly cannot be serviced separately. A new bearing must be installed whenever a bearing is removed.

Main Bearings

1. Clean the bearing inserts and caps thoroughly in solvent, and dry them with compressed air.

NOTE: Do not scrape varnish or gum deposits from the bearing shells.

2. Inspect each bearing carefully. Bearings that have a scored, chipped, or worn surface should be replaced.
3. The copper-lead bearing base may be visible through the bearing overlay in small localized areas. This may not mean that the bearing is excessively worn. It is not necessary to replace the bearing if the bearing clearance is within recommended specifications.
4. Check the clearance of bearings that appear to be satisfactory with Plastigage® or its equivalent. If clearance is excessive, regrind the crankshaft and install undersized bearings.
5. If the journal will not clean up to maximum undersize bearing available, replace the crankshaft.
6. Always reproduce the same journal shoulder radius that existed originally. Too small a radius will result in fatigue failure of the crankshaft. Too large a radius will result in bearing failure due to radius ride of the bearing.
7. After regrinding the journals, chamfer the oil holes, then polish the journals with a #320 grit polishing cloth and engine oil. Crocus cloth may also be used as a polishing agent.

CHECKING MAIN BEARING OIL CLEARANCE

1. Check the clearance of each main bearing by using the following procedure:

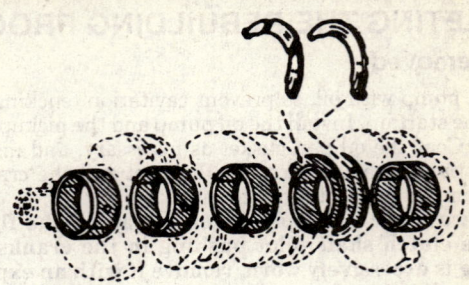

Main bearing positioning on the 4-2.1L diesel. The thrust washers are shown

   a. Place a piece of Plastigage® or its equivalent, on bearing surface across full width of bearing cap and about 6mm ($^1/_4$ in.) off center.
   b. Install cap and tighten bolts to specifications. Do not turn crankshaft while Plastigage® is in place.
   c. Remove the cap. Using Plastigage® scale, check width of Plastigage® at widest point to get the minimum clearance. Check at narrowest point to get maximum clearance. Difference between readings is taper of journal.
   d. If clearance exceeds specified limits, try a 0.0254mm (0.001 in.) or 0.051mm (0.002 in.) undersize bearing in combination with the standard bearing. Bearing clearance must be within specified limits. If standard and 0.051mm (0.002 in.) undersize bearing does not bring clearance within desired limits, refinish crankshaft journal, then install undersize bearings.

NOTE: Refer to Rear Main Oil Seal removal and installation, for special instructions in applying RTV sealer to rear main bearing cup.

3. Install all the bearing caps except the thrust bearing cap. Be sure the main bearing caps are installed in their original locations. Tighten the bearing cap bolts to specifications.
4. Install the thrust bearing cap with the bolts finger tight.
5. Pry the crankshaft forward against the thrust surface of the upper half of the bearing.
6. Hold the crankshaft forward and pry the thrust bearing cap to the rear. This will align the thrust surfaces of both halves of the bearing.
7. Retain the forward pressure on the crankshaft. Tighten the cap bolts to specifications.

CHECKING CRANKSHAFT ENDPLAY

1. Check the crankshaft end play after installing all main bearing caps and aligning thrust bearing inserts.
2. Force the crankshaft forward and then toward the rear of the engine.
3. Install a dial indicator so that the contact point rests against the crankshaft flange and the indicator axis is parallel to the crankshaft axis.
4. Zero the dial indicator. Push the crankshaft forward and note the reading on the dial.
5. If the end play exceeds the wear limit listed in the Crankshaft and Connecting Rod Specifications chart, replace the thrust bearing. If the end play is less than the minimum limit, inspect the thrust bearing faces for scratches, burrs, nicks, or dirt. If the thrust faces are not damaged or dirty, then they probably were not aligned properly. Lubricate and install the new thrust bearing and align the faces following procedures 21 through 24.

3 ENGINE AND ENGINE OVERHAUL

COMPLETING THE REBUILDING PROCESS
Engine Removed

Fill the oil pump with oil, to prevent cavitation (sucking air) on initial engine start up. Install the oil pump and the pickup tube on the engine. Coat the oil pan gasket as necessary, and install the gasket and the oil pan. Mount the flywheel and the crankshaft vibration damper and pulley on the crankshaft.

NOTE: Always use new bolts when installing the flywheel. Inspect the clutch shaft pilot bushing in the crankshaft. If the bushing is excessively worn, remove it with an expanding puller and a slide hammer, and tap a new bushing into place.

Position the engine, cylinder head side up. Lubricate the lifters, and install them into their bores. Install the cylinder head, and torque it as specified. Insert the pushrods (where applicable), and install the rocker shaft(s) (if so equipped) or position the rocker.

Install the intake and exhaust manifolds, the carburetor(s), the distributor and spark plugs. Mount all accessories and install the engine in the car. Fill the radiator with coolant, and the crankcase with high quality engine oil.

BREAK-IN PROCEDURE

Start the engine, and allow it to run at low speed for a few minutes, while checking for leaks. Stop the engine, check the oil level, and fill as necessary. Restart the engine, and fill the cooling system to capacity. Check and adjust the ignition timing. Run the engine at low to medium speed (800–2,500 rpm) for approximately $1/8$ hour, and retorque the cylinder head bolts. Road test the car, and check again for leaks.

NOTE: Some gasket manufacturers recommend not retorquing the cylinder head(s) due to the composition of the head gasket. Follow the directions in the gasket set.

Flywheel/Flexplate and Ring Gear

NOTE: Flexplate is the term for a flywheel mated with an automatic transmission.

REMOVAL AND INSTALLATION
All Engines

NOTE: The ring gear is replaceable only on engines mated with a manual transmission. Engines with automatic transmissions have ring gears which are welded to the flexplate.

1. Remove the transmission and transfer case.
2. Remove the clutch, or torque converter, from the flywheel. The flywheel bolts should be loosened a little at a time in a cross pattern to avoid warping the flywheel. On trucks with manual transmission, replace the pilot bearing in the end of the crankshaft if removing the flywheel.
3. The flywheel should be checked for cracks and glazing. It can be resurfaced by a machine shop.
4. If the ring gear is to be replaced, drill a hole in the gear between two teeth, being careful not to contact the flywheel surface. Using a cold chisel at this point, crack the ring gear and remove it.
5. Polish the inner surface of the new ring gear and heat it in an oven to about 600°F (315°C). Chill the flywheel in the freezer for a few minutes. Quickly place the ring gear on the flywheel and tap it into place, making sure that it is fully seated.

NOTE: Never heat the ring gear past 800°F (426°C), or the tempering will be destroyed.

6. Installation is the reverse of removal. Torque the bolts a little at a time in a cross pattern, to the torque figure shown in the Torque Specifications Chart.

EXHAUST SYSTEM

Safety Precautions

For a number of reasons, exhaust system work can be the most dangerous type of work to perform on your car. Always observe the following precautions:

CAUTION

Be very careful when working on or near the catalytic converter. External temperatures can reach 1,500°F (816°C) and more, causing severe burns. Removal or installation should be performed only on a cold exhaust system.

• Support the car extra securely. Not only will you often be working directly under it, but you'll frequently be using a lot of force, say, heavy hammer blows, to dislodge rusted parts. This can cause a car that's improperly supported to shift and possibly fall.
• Wear goggles. Exhaust system parts are always rusty. Metal chips can be dislodged, even when you're only turning rusted bolts. Attempting to pry pipes apart with a chisel makes the chips fly even more frequently.
• If you're using a cutting torch, keep it a great distance from either the fuel tank or lines. Stop what you're doing and feel the temperature of the fuel bearing pipes on the tank frequently. Even slight heat can expand and/or vaporize fuel, resulting in accumulated vapor, or even a liquid leak, near your torch.
• Watch where your hammer blows fall and make sure you hit squarely. You could easily tap a brake or fuel line when you hit an exhaust system part with a glancing blow. Inspect all lines and hoses in the area where you've been working.

Special Tools

A number of special exhaust system tools can be purchased from local auto supply stores. A common one is a tail pipe expander, designed to enable you to join pipes of identical diameter.

It may also be quite helpful to use solvents designed to loosen rusted bolts or flanges. Soaking rusted parts the night before you do the job can speed the work of freeing rusted parts considerably. Remember that these solvents are often flammable. Apply only to parts after they are cool!

COMPONENT REPLACEMENT

Exhaust Downpipe

1. Raise and truck on jackstands.
2. Saturate all bolts and nuts with penetrating lubricant.
3. Disconnect the downpipe from the manifold and discard the seal.
4. Support the transmission with a floor jack and remove the rear crossmember.
5. Remove the pipe-to-flywheel housing bracket.
6. Support the catalytic converter and disconnect the downpipe. Discard the gasket.
7. Installation is the reverse of removal. Use new gaskets and seals. Tighten all fasteners to 23 ft. lbs.

ENGINE AND ENGINE OVERHAUL 3

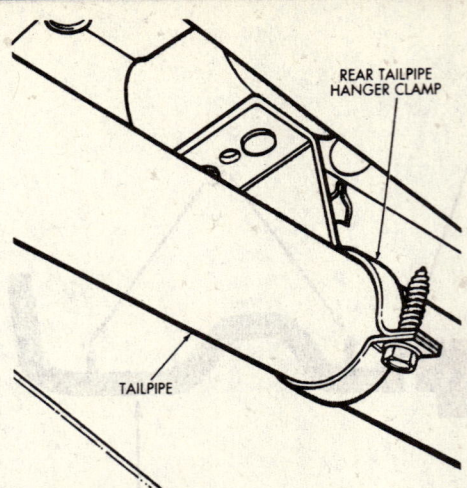

Rear tail pipe hanger

Catalytic Converter

1. Raise and truck on jackstands.
2. Saturate all bolts and nuts with penetrating lubricant.
3. Remove the converter-to-muffler clamp.
4. Heat the converter-to-muffler connection with a torch until it becomes cherry red.
5. Remove all muffler hangers and twist the muffler back-and-forth to free it from the converter.
6. Disconnect the downpipe from the converter. Discard the gasket.
7. Installation is the reverse of removal. Use new gaskets. Torque the downpipe connection to 23 ft. lbs.; the muffler clamp to 45 ft. lbs.

Muffler and Tailpipe

1. Raise and truck on jackstands.
2. Saturate all bolts and nuts with penetrating lubricant.
3. Remove the converter-to-muffler clamp.
4. Heat the converter-to-muffler connection with a torch until it becomes cherry red.
5. Remove all muffler hangers and twist the muffler back-and-forth to free it from the converter.

NOTE: Original equipment mufflers are welded to the tailpipe. Replacement mufflers and tailpipes clamp together.

6. Installation is the reverse of removal. Torque the muffler-to-converter clamp bolt to 45 ft. lbs.

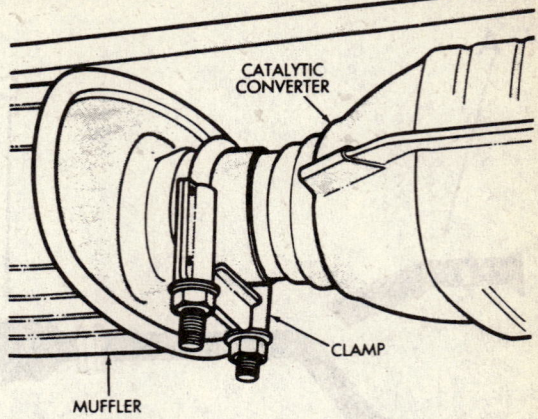

Converter-to-muffler connection

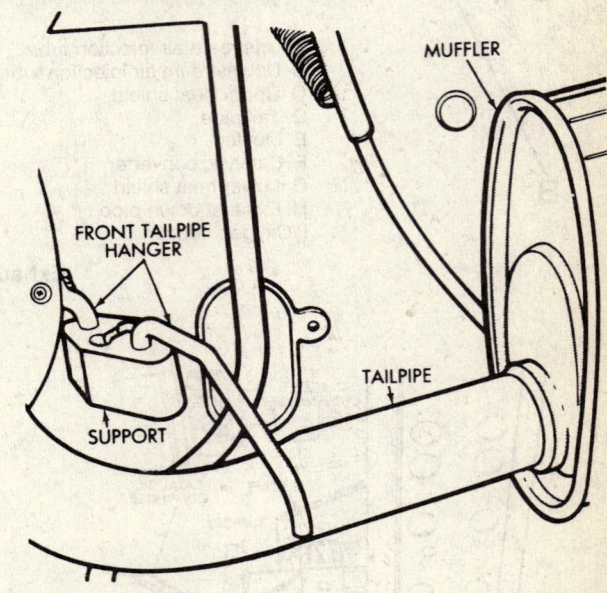

Front tail pipe hanger

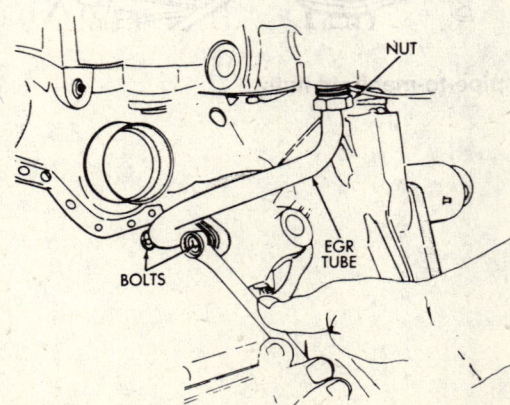

4-2.5L EGR tube

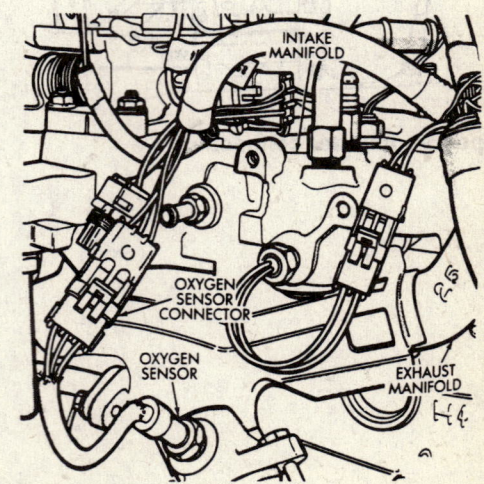

Oxygen sensor and connector

3-93

3 ENGINE AND ENGINE OVERHAUL

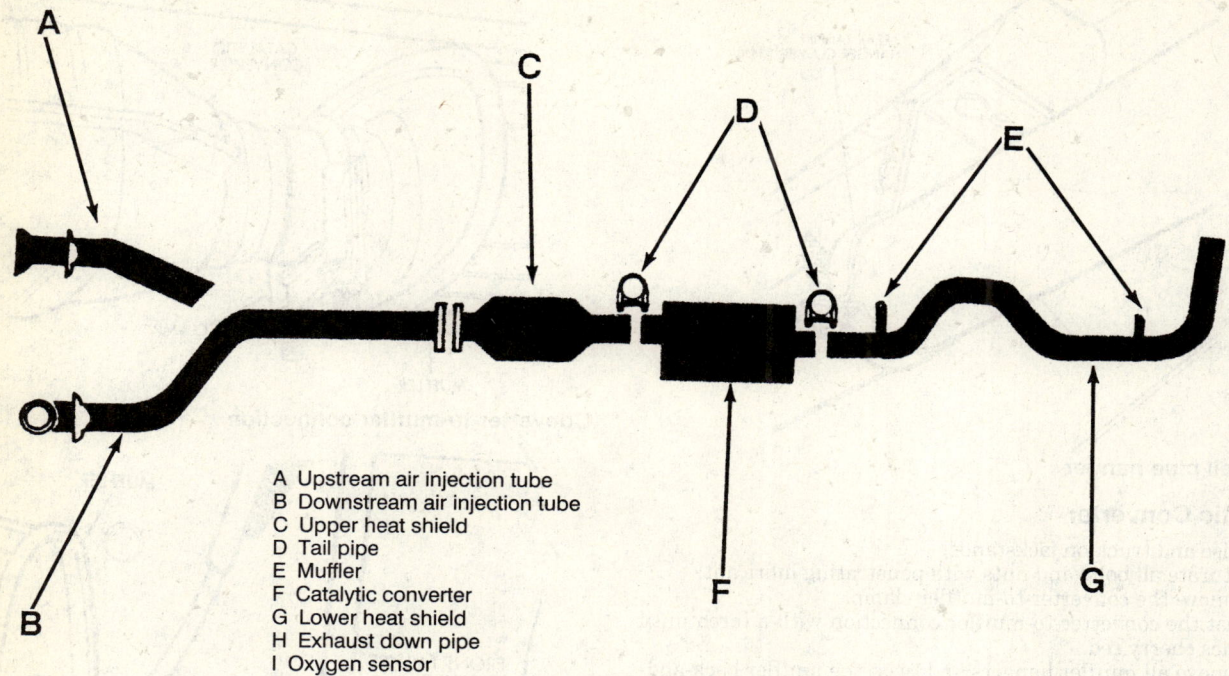

A Upstream air injection tube
B Downstream air injection tube
C Upper heat shield
D Tail pipe
E Muffler
F Catalytic converter
G Lower heat shield
H Exhaust down pipe
I Oxygen sensor

Exhaust system

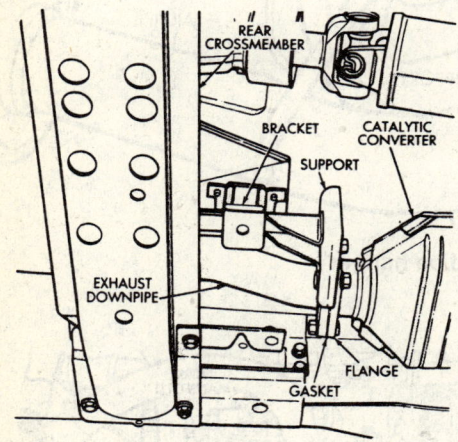

Exhaust pipe-to-converter connection

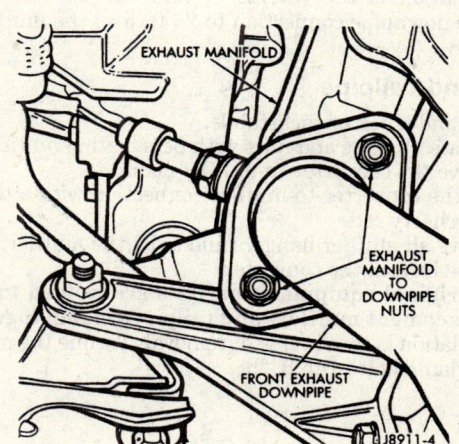

Exhaust pipe-to-manifold nuts

3-94

4 Emission Controls

QUICK REFERENCE INDEX

Electronic Engine Controls	4-12
Engine Emission Control Systems	4-2
Vacuum diagrams	4-147

GENERAL INDEX

Air pump	4-10	Chrysler MPI System	4-139	Pressure Relief/Rollover Valve	4-4
Catalytic Converter	4-9	Engine Emission controls		Evaporative canister	4-4
Crankcase ventilation valve	4-2	Air Injection Reactor	4-10	Exhaust Gas Recirculation (EGR)	
EGR valve	4-7	Catalytic converter	4-9	system	4-7
Electronic Engine Controls		Evaporative canister	4-4	Maintenance reminder light	4-2
AMC/Jeep CEC System	4-12	Exhaust Gas Recirculation		Oxygen (O_2) sensor	4-6
Jeep Self-Diagnostic System	4-47	(EGR) system	4-7	PCV valve	4-2
AMC/Jeep TBI System	4-73	Oxygen (O_2) sensor	4-6	Thermostatic air cleaner	4-5
AMC/Jeep MPI System	4-127	PCV valve	4-2	Vacuum diagrams	4-147

4 EMISSION CONTROLS

EMISSION CONTROLS

Emission control devices are designed to eliminate the chemical compounds that escape from the engine crankcase and exhaust pipe, and from evaporation of fuel in the fuel tank and carburetor. With the growing use of on-board computers, it has become possible for auto manufacturers to meet strict Federal emissions standards by using electronic engine controls to monitor operating conditions and adjust engine calibrations for the best possible performance and economy with minimum emissions.

Engine calibration has a big effect on emissions out the tailpipe. The calibration consists of spark timing, fuel mixture, choke setting, idle speed and spark plug gap. Calibrations are not a service problem as long as the engine is adjusted to the factory specifications, which are found on a sticker in the engine compartment. Engines must be adjusted to these factory specifications or emissions will be high. Additionally, emission control systems have become such an integral part of the overall engine design that peak engine performance is dependent on peak emissions system performance. This is especially true for computer controlled systems.

Any attempt to disconnect or bypass and OEM emission equipment is a violation of federal law.

The latest emission control systems use electronic instead of vacuum devices and are much more sensitive to malfunctions in any component. Following is a description of each group of controls and how they work to reduce emissions.

WARNING: Due to the complex nature of modern electronic engine control systems, comprehensive diagnosis and testing should be performed by qualified technicians. Most emissions equipment is covered under a 5 year/50,000 mile federally mandated warranty.

Emissions Maintenance Reminder Light

Most Jeep vehicles are equipped with an Emissions Maintenance Reminder (EMR) light. The EMR light comes on after the vehicle has reached 82,500 miles (132, 767 km) and informs the owner when oxygen sensor and other related emissions service is required. The light is located in the instrument cluster.

The oxygen sensor and EMR are interdependent. When the reminder light illuminates, the oxygen sensor and EMR should be replaced simultaneously. This is important in ensuring proper engine performance. Maintenance reminders for 1991 vehicles are reset using a Diagnostic Readout Box (DRB). See the DRB instruction manual for further instructions.

NOTE: Resetting or replacing the EMR without performing the required maintenance is a violation of federal law. Only after performing the required maintenance, should the EMR be reset.

The maintenance reminder for pre-1991 vehicles cannot be reset after reaching the specified mileage, the unit must be replaced. The unit is mounted on the dash panel to the right of the steering column. To replace the reminder:

• Remove the attaching screws and disconnect the reminder electrical connector.
• Install the connector to the new EMR and replace the attaching screws.
• On vehicles equipped with cruise control, the cruise control module may need to be moved to gain access to the EMR.

Crankcase Ventilation PCV/CCV

Crankcase emission control equipment is separated into two different systems: Positive Crankcase Ventilation (PVC) and Crankcase Ventilation System (CCV). The systems perform the same function, differing only in the way the exhaust gases are metered. The PVC system uses a valve, containing spring loaded plunger, which meters the amount of crankcase vapors routed to the combustion chamber based on manifold vacuum. The CCV system contains a metered orifice of a calibrated size which meters the amount of crankcase vapors drawn from the engine based on manifold vacuum.

When the engine is running, a small portion of the gases which are formed in the combustion chamber during combustion leak by the piston rings and enter the crankcase. Since these gases are under pressure, they tend to escape from the crankcase and enter

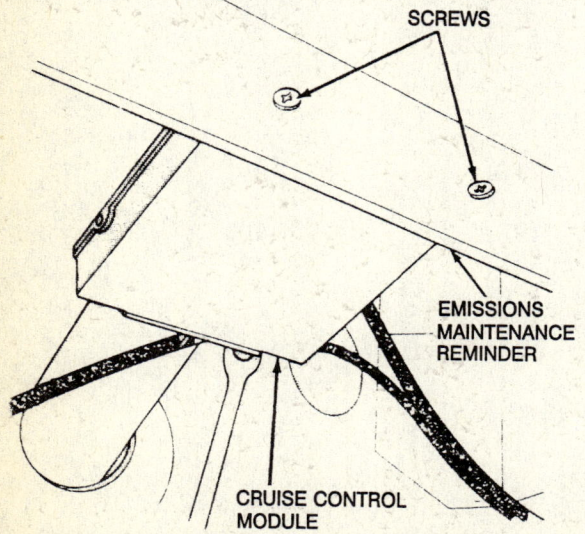

Remove the cruise control module to gain access to the emissions maintenance reminder

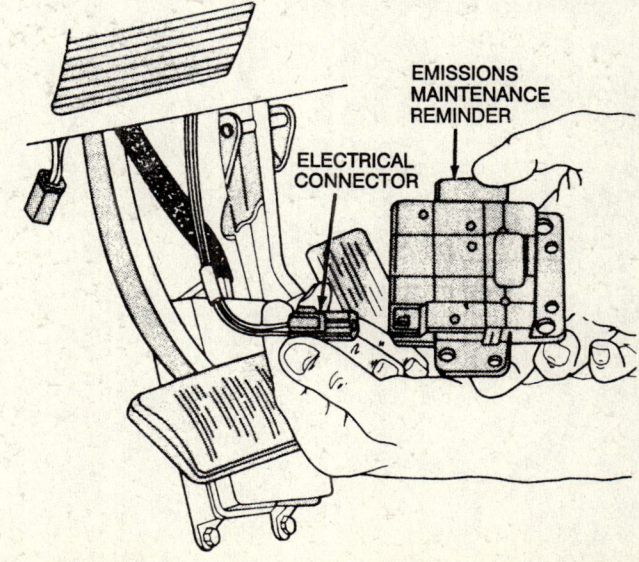

Emissions maintenance reminder removal and installation

EMISSION CONTROLS 4

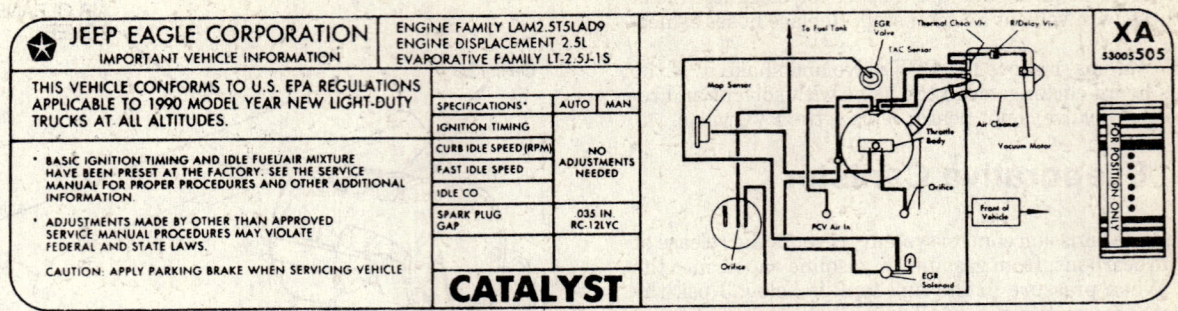

Federal vehicle emission control information label

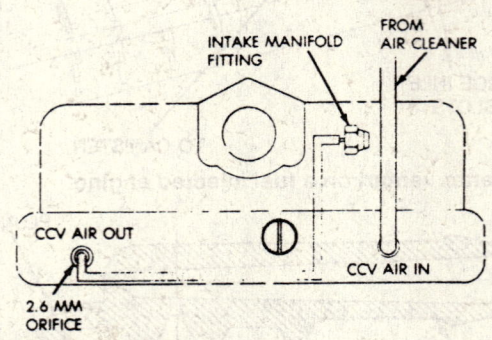

6-4.0L CCV system diagram

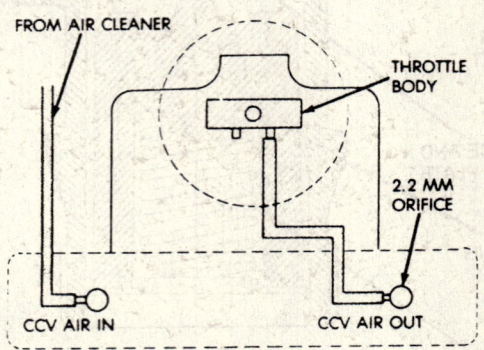

4-2.5L CCV system diagram

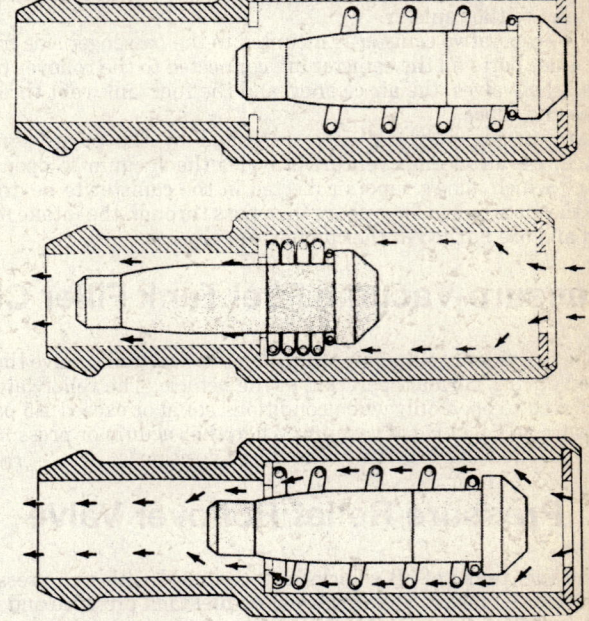

1. a. ♦ Engine off — no vapor flow
   b. High manifold vacuum — minimal vapor flow
   c. Moderate manifold vacuum — maximum vapor flow

PVC valve operation

into the atmosphere. If these gases were allowed to remain the crankcase for any length of time, they would contaminate the engine oil and cause sludge to build up. If the gases are allowed to escape into the atmosphere, they would pollute the air, as they contain unburned hydrocarbons. The crankcase emission control equipment recycles these gases back into the engine combustion chamber where they are burned.

While the engine is running, clean filtered air is drawn into the crankcase either directly through the oil filler cap, or through a filter mounted in the air cleaner assembly and connected to the oil filler cap. As the air passes through the crankcase it picks up combustion gases, carries them out of the crankcase, through the PCV valve, and into the intake manifold. After entering the intake manifold gases are drawn into the combustion chamber and burned.

The most critical component in the system is the metering device — the PCV valve in the PVC system, and the metered orifice in the CCV system — which control the amount of gases recycled into the combustion chamber. If the metering device should become clogged, gases will be prevented from escaping the crankcase by the normal route. Since the gases are under pressure, they will find a point of least resistance, usually a weak oil seal or gasket, and create an oil leak. In addition to creating oil leaks,

clogged ventilation systems also allow gases to remain in the crankcase for an extended period of time. This promotes the formation of sludge in the engine and ultimately leads to decreased engine life.

TROUBLESHOOTING

With the engine running, pull the hose (and PCV valve if equipped) from the rocker arm cover. Block off the end of the hose with your finger. The engine speed should drop at least 50 rpm when blocked. If the engine speed does not drop at least 50 rpm, a component in the system is defective. Inspect for vacuum leaks or a defective PCV valve.

CLEANING AND INSPECTION

The PVC/CCV systems require periodic inspection to ensure proper operation.
• Check all vacuum lines for signs of cracking, cuts or leaks. Replace as necessary.

4 EMISSION CONTROLS

• Remove hoses from engine and inspect for clogging. Clean any clogged hose with solvent and reinstall. Replace hoses as necessary.
• On PVC systems, remove the PCV valve and shake it. If the check valve is heard clicking, clean the valve with solvent and reinstall. If the check valve is not heard, replace the PVC valve.

Evaporative Canister

The evaporative emission control system prevents the release of unburned hydrocarbons, from gasoline or gasoline vapor, into the atmosphere. When pressure in the fuel tank is below 3 psi, the pressure relief/rollover valves open allowing fuel vapors to flow to the evaporative canister where they are absorbed by a charcoal mixture. This prevents excessive pressure build-up in the fuel system. Most canisters are equipped with a calibrated orifice at the inlet to the canister.

The evaporative canister is mounted to the passenger side frame rail. Inlet ports on the canister are connected to the rollover/pressure relief valves, the air cleaner, and the fuel tank vent through hoses and tubes.

Canister purge operation is activated by the purge shutoff switch. An air cleaner venturi provides the vacuum to open the switch which allows vapors collected in the canister to be drawn into the air stream. The vapors then pass through the intake manifold and are burned in the combustion process.

Pressure-Vacuum Fuel Tank Filler Cap

The fuel filler cap is equipped with a two-way relief valve that is closed during normal operation of the vehicle. The relief valve is calibrated to open only when conditions equal or exceed 1.5 psi of pressure or 1.8 in.Hg of vacuum. When the vacuum or pressure is relieved, the valve returns to the closed position.

Pressure Relief/Rollover Valve

The fuel tanks of all vehicles are equipped with two pressure relief/rollover valves. The valves relieve fuel tank pressure and prevent fuel flow through the fuel tank vent hoses in the event of vehicle rollover.

The valves consist of a plunger, spring, orifice and guide plate. The valve is normally open allowing fuel vapor to vent to the canister. If the bottom of the plunger is contacted by sloshing fuel,

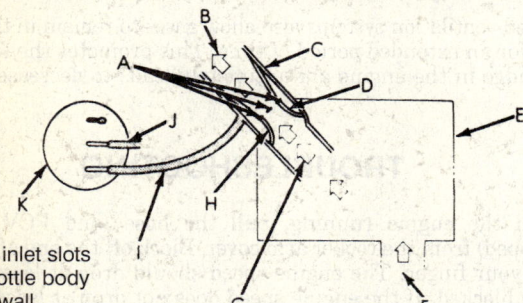

a. Purge inlet slots
b. To throttle body
c. Outer wall
d. Inner wall
e. Remote air cleaner
f. Inlet air
g. Intake air accelerated by venturi
h. Venturi
i. Canister purge line
j. To fuel tank
k. Vapor canister

Air cleaner venturi and canister purge operation

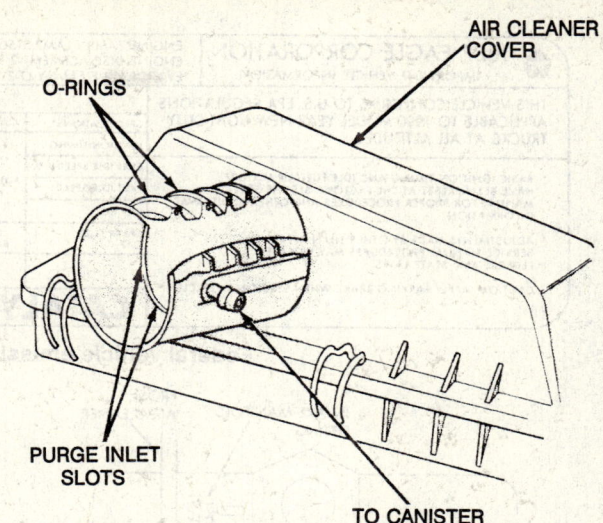

Air cleaner venturi on a fuel injected engine

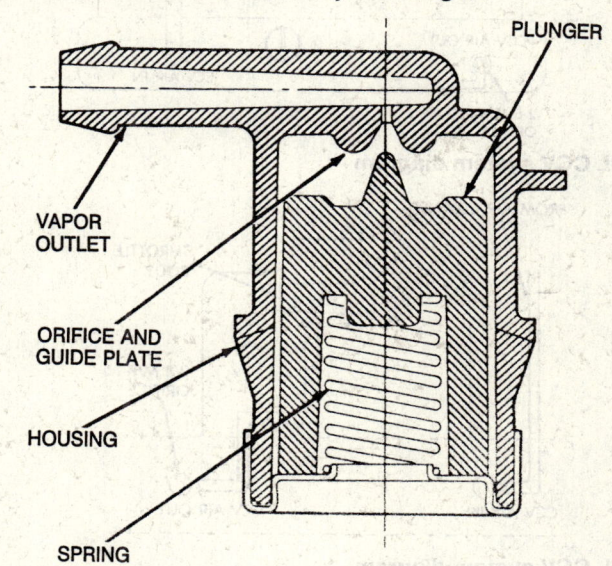

Pressure relief/rollover valve operation

the plunger seats in the guide plate preventing fuel from reaching the canister.

If the vehicle should roll over, the valve is inverted and the plunger is forced against the guide plate, preventing fuel from flowing through the vent tube.

REMOVAL AND INSTALLATION

1. Disconnect the battery negative cable.
2. Remove the fuel filler cap. On fuel injected engines, remove the cap from the pressure test port on the fuel rail (located in the engine compartment). Using an appropriate tool, push the test port valve in to relieve fuel pressure. Replace test port cap.

NOTE: DO NOT allow fuel to spill on the intake or exhaust manifolds. Use shop rags to absorb any spilled fuel.

3. Drain the fuel tank dry using a siphon pump.
4. Raise and support the vehicle safely.
5. Remove the fuel tank. See appropriate procedure in Section 5.
6. The rollover valve is seated in a grommet. Pry one side of the

EMISSION CONTROLS 4

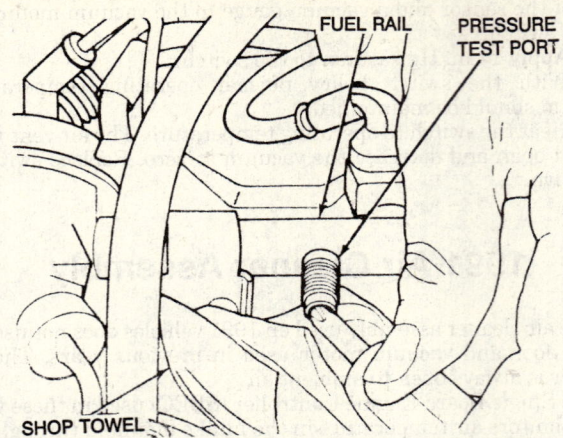

Releasing fuel pressure on a fuel injected engine

low, the air bleed valve is closed and sufficient vacuum is applied to the vacuum motor to hold the air valve in the closed (heat on) position.

As the temperature of the air entering the air cleaner approaches approximately 115°F (46°C), the air bleed valve opens to decrease the amount of vacuum applied to the vacuum motor. The diaphragm spring in the vacuum motor then moves the air valve into the open (heat off) position, allowing only underhood air to enter the air cleaner.

The air valve in the air cleaner will also open, regardless of air temperature, during heavy acceleration to obtain maximum air flow through the air cleaner.

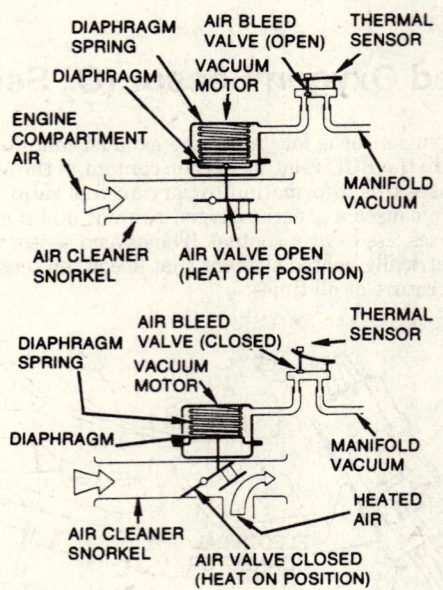

Thermostatically controlled air cleaner (TAC) operation (upper open, lower closed)

valve up and twist to remove the grommet from the tank.
7. Installation is the reverse of removal.
8. Start vehicle and check for leaks.

Thermostatically Controlled Air Cleaner System (TAC)

The TAC system is used on all engines up to 1991. It consists of a heat shroud which is integral with the right side exhaust manifold, a hot air hose and a special air cleaner assembly equipped with an air temperature sensor, a vacuum motor and air valve assembly.

The air temperature sensor incorporates an air bleed valve which regulates the amount of vacuum applied to the vacuum motor, controlling the air valve position to supply either heated air from the exhaust manifold or cool air from the engine compartment.

During the warm-up period when underhood temperatures are

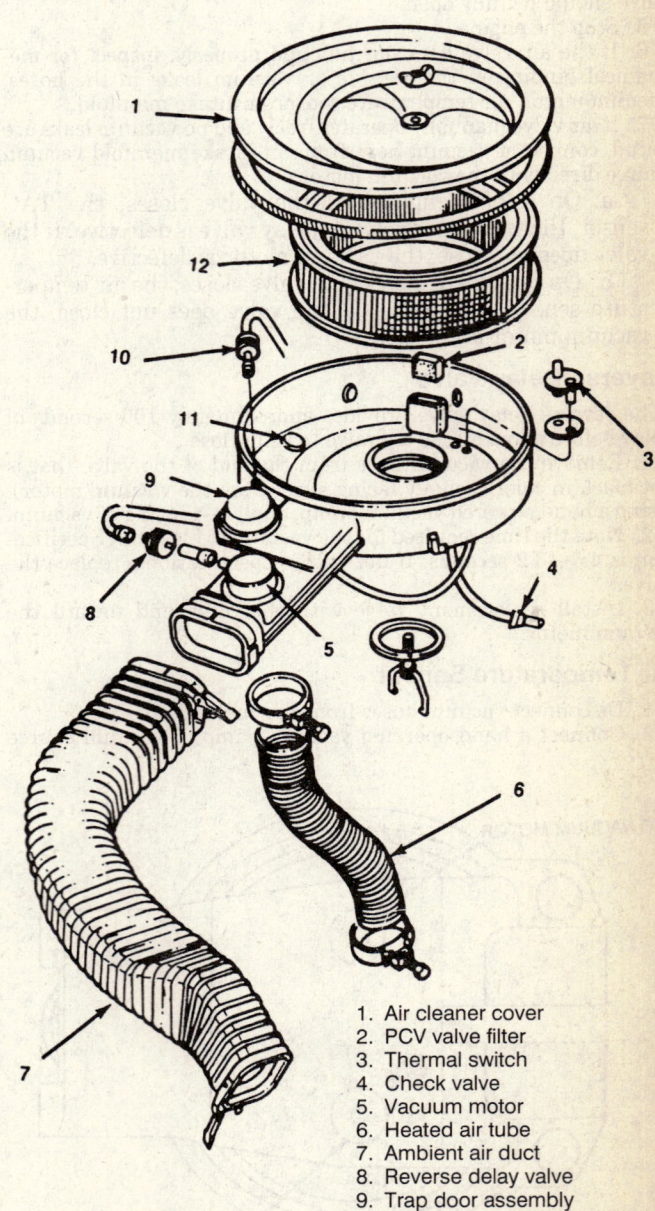

1. Air cleaner cover
2. PCV valve filter
3. Thermal switch
4. Check valve
5. Vacuum motor
6. Heated air tube
7. Ambient air duct
8. Reverse delay valve
9. Trap door assembly
10. Reverse delay valve
11. Thermal vacuum switch
12. Filter element

Thermostatically controlled air cleaner — exploded view

4-5

4 EMISSION CONTROLS

FUNCTIONAL TESTS

Vacuum Motor

1. With the engine OFF, observe the position of the air valve. It can be observed by looking down the air snorkle with a mirror. The valve should be fully open (allowing in only cool air from the snorkle).
2. Start the engine and observe the position of the air valve. It should be fully closed (allowing in only hot air from the exhaust manifold) below operating temperature.
3. Depress the throttle rapidly and release. The air valve should briefly remain stationary and then move toward the closed and then back toward the open position.
4. Warm the engine to normal operating temperature. The air valve should be fully open.
5. Stop the engine.
6. If the air valve does not function properly, inspect for mechanical binding in the snorkle or vacuum leaks in the hoses, vacuum motor, air temperature sensor or intake manifold.
7. If air valve manually operates freely and no vacuum leaks are found, connect a vacuum hose from an intake manifold vacuum source directly to the vacuum motor.
    a. On 4-2.5L engines: If the valve closes, the TAC sensor, thermal check valve or delay valve is defective. If the valve does not close, the vacuum motor is defective.
    b. On 6-4.0L engines: If the valve closes, the air temperature sensor is defective. If the valve does not close, the vacuum motor is defective.

Reverse Delay Valve

The reverse delay valve provides approximately 100 seconds of delay before allowing the air valve to fully close.

1. Remove the vacuum hose from the end of the valve that is not black in color (usually facing away from the vacuum motor). Using a hand powered vacuum pump, apply 2–4 in. Hg of vacuum.
2. Note the time required for the vacuum to bleed off. Specification is 4.5–13.2 seconds. If not within specifications, replace the valve.
3. Install replacement valve with the black end toward the vacuum motor.

Air Temperature Sensor

1. Disconnect vacuum hoses from thermal switch.
2. Connect a hand operated vacuum pump to vacuum source side of the sensor and a vacuum gauge to the vacuum motor side of the switch.
3. Apply 14 in. Hg vacuum to the switch.
4. With the switch below normal operating temperature, vacuum should be maintained.
5. Heat the switch to operating temperature. The air vent valve should open and decrease the vacuum to zero. Replace switch if defective.

1991 Air Cleaner Assembly

The air cleaner assembly used on 1991 vehicles does not use the blend door and vacuum motor used in previous years. The air cleaner is always open to ambient air.

The Single Board Engine Controller (SBEC) used in these vehicles monitors air temperature in the intake manifold through the Manifold Air Temperature (MAT) sensor. The controller adjusts injector pulse and ignition timing to compensate for air temperature.

Heated Oxygen Sensor (O_2 Sensor)

The oxygen sensor is located in the exhaust manifold and provides input to the ECU relating oxygen content of the exhaust gas. The ECU uses this information to vary air/fuel ratio. A lean air/fuel mixture causes a greater oxygen content and a rich air/fuel mixture causes less oxygen content. The oxygen sensor is equipped with an electrically heated element that keeps the sensor at operating temperature at all times.

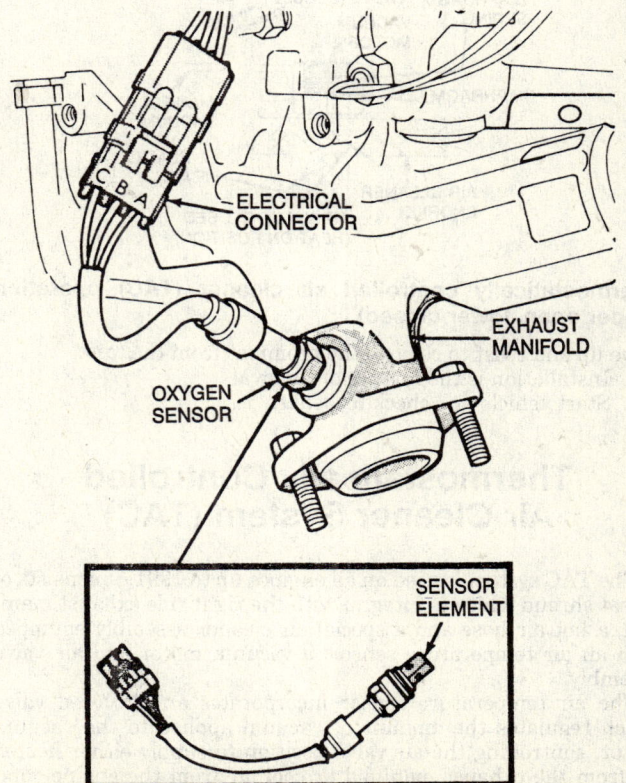

Heated oxygen sensor removal and installation

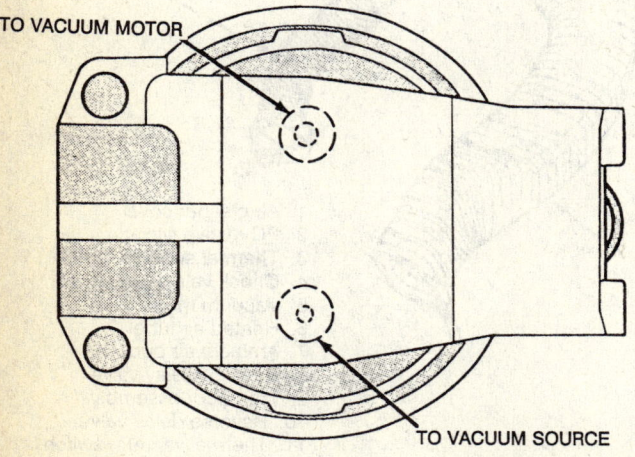

Thermal switch

EMISSION CONTROLS 4

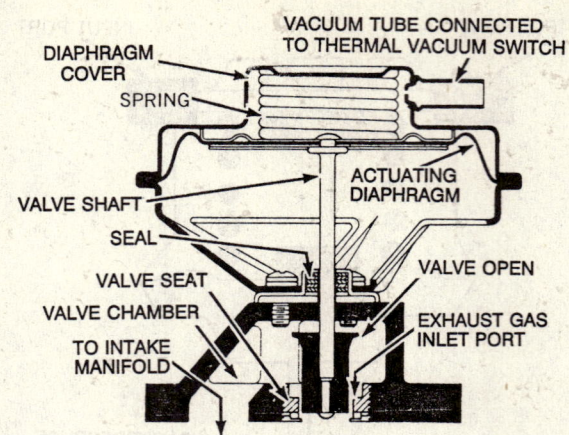

Exhaust gas recirculating valve

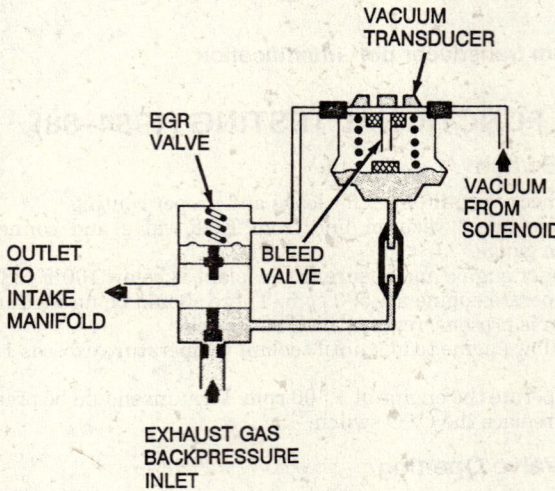

EGR system with a vacuum transducer

REMOVAL AND INSTALLATION

1. Raise the vehicle and support it safely. Allow the exhaust system to cool sufficiently to permit servicing.
2. Disconnect the wire connector from the oxygen sensor.
3. Remove the oxygen sensor from the exhaust manifold.
4. If not already done, coat the threads of the replacement sensor with anti-seize compound. Be careful not to contaminate the oxygen sensor probe with the anti-seize.
5. Install the oxygen sensor into the exhaust manifold and tighten to 22–35 ft. lbs. Reconnect the wire connector.

Exhaust Gas Recirculation (EGR) System

NOx (oxides of nitrogen) is a tailpipe emission caused by the oxidation of nitrogen in the combustion chamber. When the peak combustion temperatures go over 2500°F (1371°C) NOx is formed in excessive amounts. To keep the combustion temperatures down, exhaust gas is recirculated.

Recirculation of the exhaust gases is accomplished by having a movable valve between the exhaust and intake manifolds. Upon a predetermined demand, engine vacuum is routed to the valve, open-

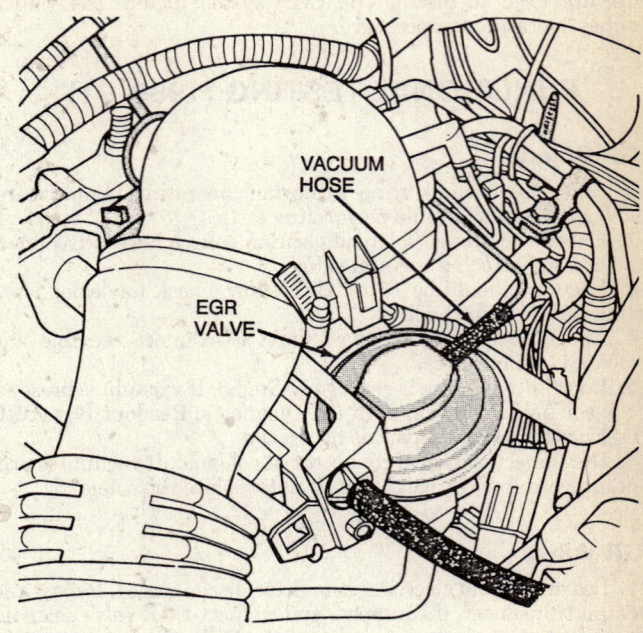

4-2.5L EGR valve location

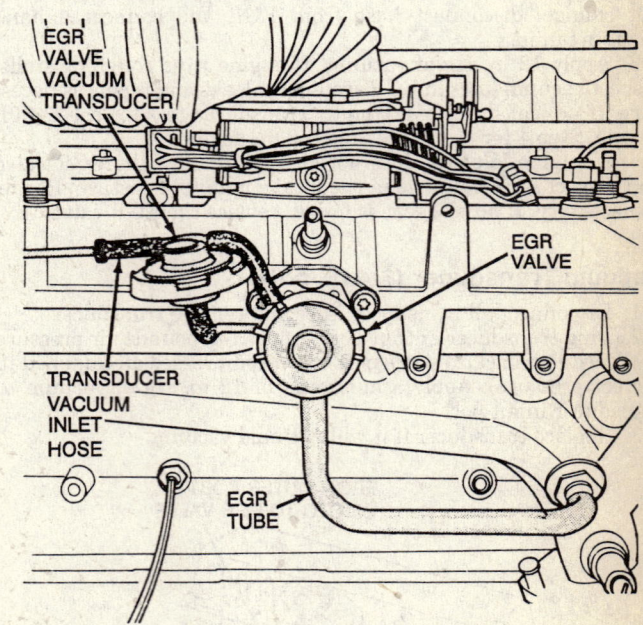

6-4.0L EGR valve and vacuum transducer

ing the connecting port and allowing exhaust gases to enter the intake tract.

The EGR valves used on Jeep vehicles fall into two categories:
• An EGR valve with no backpressure sensor which is controlled by ported vacuum only. 4-2.5L and 6-2.8L engines are equipped with this type of EGR valve.
• An EGR valve with an external backpressure sensor which is controlled by ported vacuum and backpressure. 6-4.0L engines are equipped with this type of EGR valve.

Thermal vacuum switches, which control the amount of vacuum available to the EGR valve based on air or water tempera-

4 EMISSION CONTROLS

ture, are used to disable the EGR system before the vehicle reaches operating temperature.

FUNCTIONAL TESTING (1989–91)

EGR Solenoid

1. Start engine and bring to normal operating temperature. Allow engine to idle while performing tests.
2. Check vacuum at solenoid vacuum source hose. Disconnect the hose and attach a vacuum gauge.
3. Vacuum should be 15 in. Hg. If low, check for leaks, loose fittings or kinks in the line.
4. Check vacuum at solenoid port. Disconnect the line and attach a vacuum gauge.
5. If vacuum reading is zero, go to Step 6. If vacuum is present, check solenoid operation with the Diagnostic Readout Box (DRB II) service tester and repair as necessary.
6. Disconnect electrical connector at solenoid. If vacuum is present, proceed to EGR valve test. If not, replace the solenoid.

EGR Valve

1. Leave solenoid electrical connector disconnected. Bypass the vacuum transducer, if equipped, and connect EGR valve solenoid output hose directly to the nipple on the EGR valve.
2. The engine should run roughly or stall. If this occurs, the valve is good. Proceed to the Transducer test. If engine rpm does not change, disconnect hose from EGR and connect a hand vacuum pump.
3. Apply 12 in. Hg of vacuum. If engine runs rough or stalls, inspect vacuum lines in EGR system for leaks and repair as necessary. If no leaks are found, go to Transducer test for the 6-4.0L engine; Step 4 for the 4-2.5L and 6-2.8L engines.
4. If engine idle still does not change, remove the EGR valve and inspect for a blockage in the intake manifold passage. Repair as necessary. If no blockage is found, replace the EGR valve.

Vacuum Transducer (6-4.0L only)

1. Disconnect all transducer lines and remove transducer.
2. Plug transducer output port. Apply 1–2 pounds air pressure to transducer backpressure port (used compressed air adjusted to correct pressure). Apply a minimum of 12 in. Hg of vacuum to transducer input port.
3. Replace transducer if it will not hold vacuum.

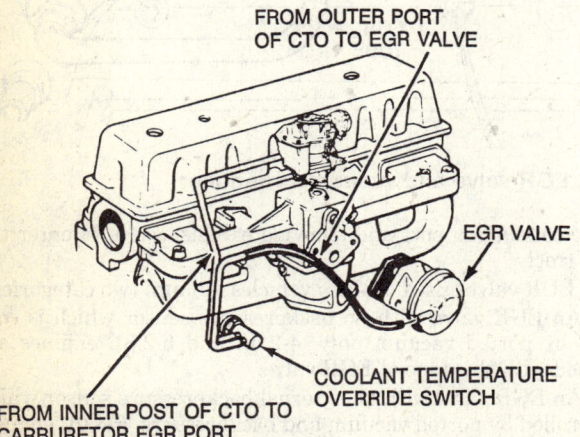

EGR system using a coolant temperature override switch

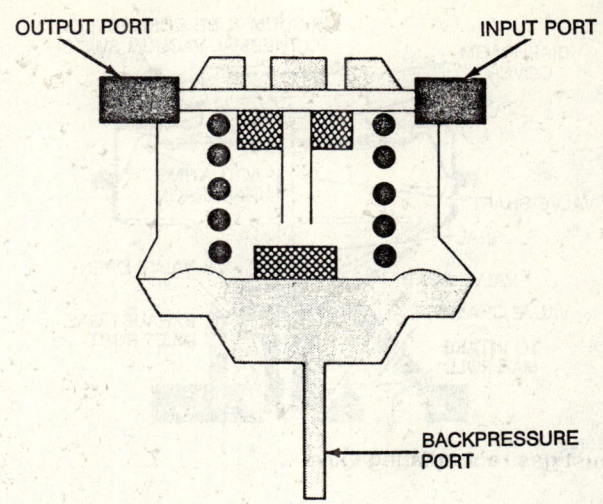

Vacuum transducer port identification

FUNCTIONAL TESTING (1984–88)

CTO Switch

1. Check vacuum lines for leaks and proper routing.
2. Disconnect vacuum line from EGR valve and connect a vacuum gauge.
3. Start engine and ensure that coolant is below 100°F (38°C).
4. Operate engine a 1,500 rpm. There should be no vacuum. If vacuum is present, replace the CTO switch.
5. Allow engine to idle until coolant temperature exceeds 115°F (46°C).
6. Operate the engine at 1,500 rpm. Vacuum should be present. If not, replace the CTO switch.

EGR Valve Opening

1. With the engine at normal operating temperature and idling, rapidly open and close the throttle to allow engine to reach 1500 rpm.
2. There should be a distinct movement in the EGR control valve diaphragm. If there is no movement check for:
   a. Faulty vacuum hose to EGR valve.
   b. Defective EGR diaphragm. Use a hand vacuum pump and test see if the EGR will hold vacuum.
   c. Defective backpressure sensor.
   d. Vacuum hose leaks.

EGR Valve Closing

1. With the engine at normal operating temperature and idling, use a protective glove and manually depress the EGR valve diaphragm. This should cause an immediate drop in engine rpm and indicate the EGR is operating correctly.
2. If there is no drop in rpm and the engine is idling properly, check for a restricted passage between the EGR valve and the intake manifold. Clean as necessary.
3. If the engine idles improperly and the rpm is not greatly affected, check for a carboned EGR valve. Clean or replace as necessary.

Thermal Vacuum Switch

1. With the engine cold and ambient air temperature in the air cleaner below 40°F (4°C), disconnect the vacuum hoses from the TVS (located on the air cleaner).

EMISSION CONTROLS 4

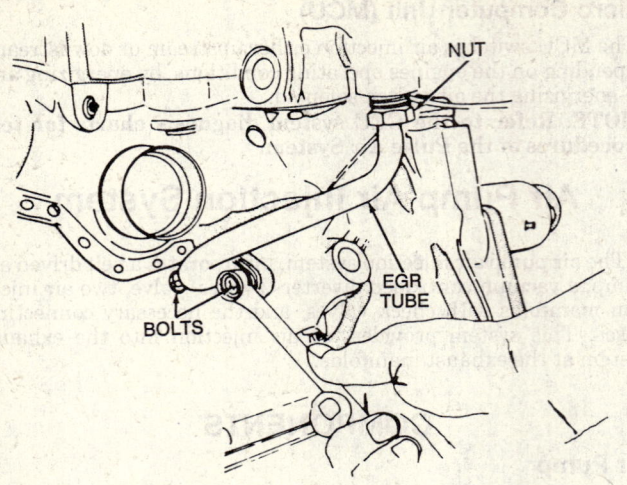

4-2.5L EGR tube

2. Connect a hand vacuum pump to the inner port and apply vacuum.
3. Vacuum should be maintained at air cleaner intake temperatures below 40°F (4°C). If vacuum is not held, check to see that temperature is below 40°F (4°C). If so, replace the TVS.
4. Start the engine and warm to normal operating temperature. With an air cleaner intake temperature above 55°F (13°C), the switch should not hold vacuum. If vacuum is held, check to see that temperatures are above 55°F (13°C). If so, replace the TVS.

NOTE: Temperatures are nominal values and the actual switching temperature may vary.

EGR Tube

REMOVAL AND INSTALLATION

1. Remove EGR tube to exhaust manifold bolts.
2. Unscrew EGR tube line nut at intake manifold. Remove EGR tube.

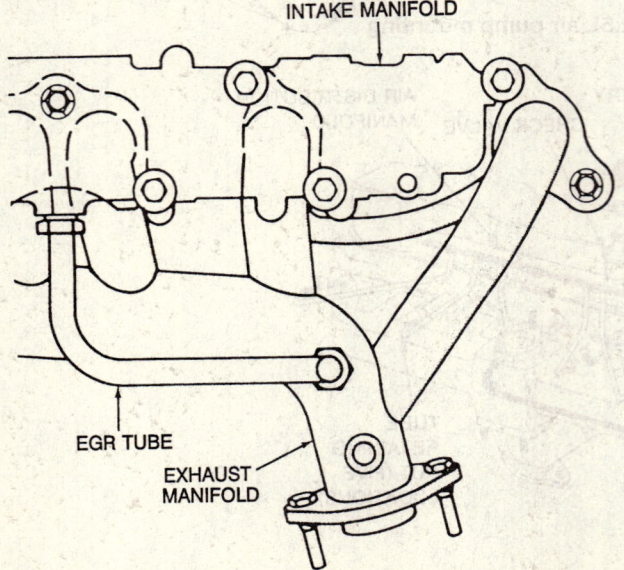

6-4.0L EGR tube

3. Install EGR tube with a new gasket. Tighten line nut to 30 ft. lbs. and exhaust manifold bolts to 14 ft. lbs.

Catalytic Converter

All gasoline engines are equipped with a catalytic converter. Most models use a single pellet-filled unit, while other models use a single monolithic type unit.

The pellet type contains beads of alumina coated with platinum and palladium, contained in a stainless steel canister. A plug is provided in the unit for replacement of the beads if they become fouled. The monolithic unit uses an extruded core resembling a honeycomb. The core layers are coated with platinum and palladium. This unit is not serviceable.

Excessive heat can cause premature failure of the catalytic converter. Although heat would be contained in the converter, the cause of overheating would come from a component other than the converter. A defective fuel system, ignition system, air injection system or other component which allows unburned fuel to

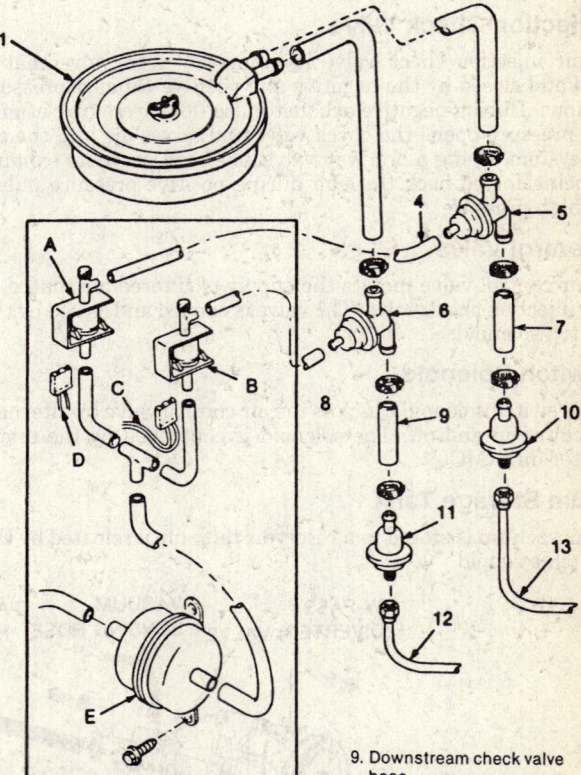

1. Air cleaner
2. Air cleaner-to-downstream air control valve vacuum hose
3. Air cleaner-to-upstream air control valve vacuum hose
4. Upstream vacuum hose
5. Upstream air control valve
6. Downstream air control valve
7. Upstream check valve hose
8. Downstream vacuum hose
9. Downstream check valve hose
10. Upstream check valve
11. Downstream check valve
12. Downstream tube-to-converter
13. Upstream Tube-to-exhaust pipe
A. Air switch solenoid (upstream)
B. Air switch solenoid (downstream)
C. Control wires from MCU (downstream)
D. Control wires from MCU (upstream)
E. Vacuum storage reservoir

Pulse air system

4-9

4 EMISSION CONTROLS

enter the converter will usually be the cause. If the converter becomes heat damaged, locate the malfunctioning component before replacing the converter.

Pulse Air System

The Pulse Air Injection System is used on the 4-2.5L engine. The system utilizes the alternating positive and negative exhaust pressure pulsations instead of an air pump to inject air into the exhaust system and produce exhaust gas oxidation. The air enters through the filtered side of the air cleaner to the air control valve. When opened by the air switch, the air control valve allows air to continue to and through the air injection check valve. The air enters the exhaust system, either upstream or down stream from the check valve, and is injected wither into the front exhaust pipe (upstream) or into the catalytic converter (downstream), depending upon the engine operating conditions. The CEC system micro computer unit (MCU) controls the switching.

COMPONENTS

Air Injection Check Valve

The air injection check valve is a one-way reed valve that is opened and closed by the negative and positive exhaust pressure pulsations. During negative exhaust pulse (low pressure), atmospheric pressure opens the check valve and forces air into the exhaust system. Being a one-way valve, the reed prevents exhaust from being forced back through during positive pressure pulsations (high pressure).

Air Control Valve

The air control valve meters the supply of filtered air routed to the air injection check valve. The valve is opened and closed by the air switch solenoid.

Air Switch Solenoid

The air switch solenoid controls the air control valve by alternating vacuum on and off. The solenoid is controlled by the micro computer unit (MCU).

Vacuum Storage Tank

Engine vacuum is stored in a reservoir tank until released by the air switch solenoid.

Micro Computer Unit (MCU)

The MCU switches air injection either upstream or downstream, depending on the engines operating conditions, by energizing and de-energizing the air switch solenoid.

NOTE: Refer to the CEC system diagnosis charts for test procedures of the Pulse Air System.

Air Pump Air Injection System

The air pump air injection system, incorporates a belt driven air pump, a vacuum controlled diverter (bypass) valve, two air injection manifolds with check valves, and the necessary connecting hoses. This system provides for air injection into the exhaust system at the exhaust manifolds.

COMPONENTS

Air Pump

The air injection pump is a positive displacement vane type which is permanently lubricated and requires little periodic maintenance. The only serviceable parts on the air pump are the filter, exhaust tube, and relief valve. The relief valve relieves the air flow

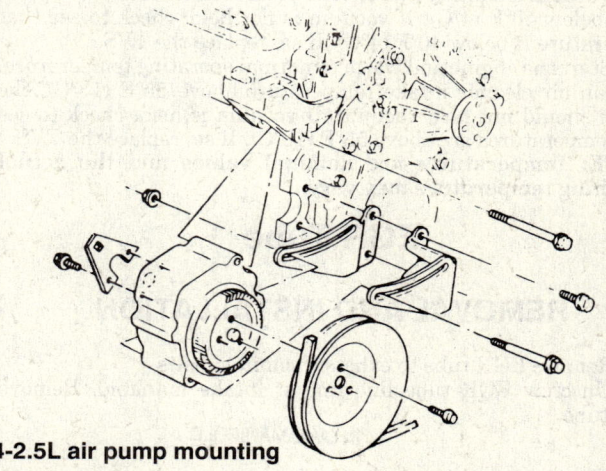

4-2.5L air pump mounting

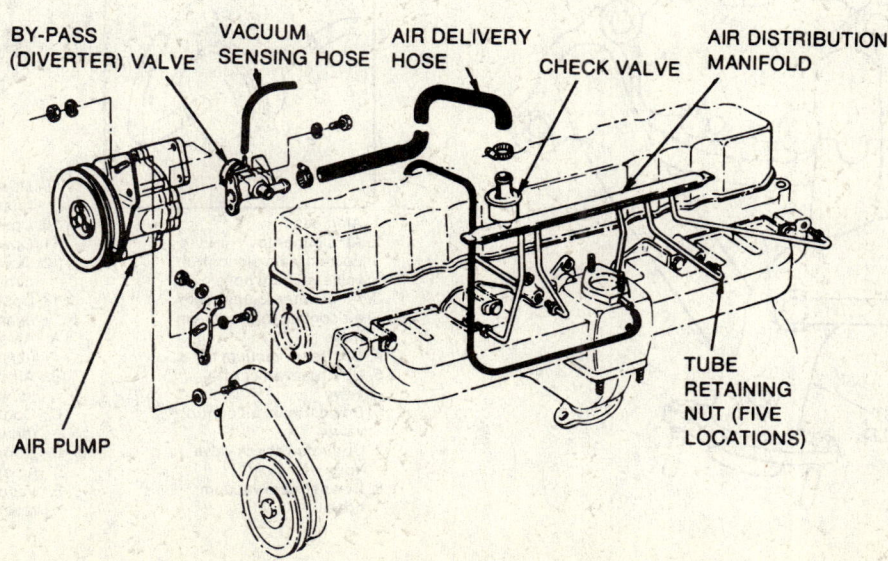

Air pump system on the 6-4.0L

EMISSION CONTROLS 4

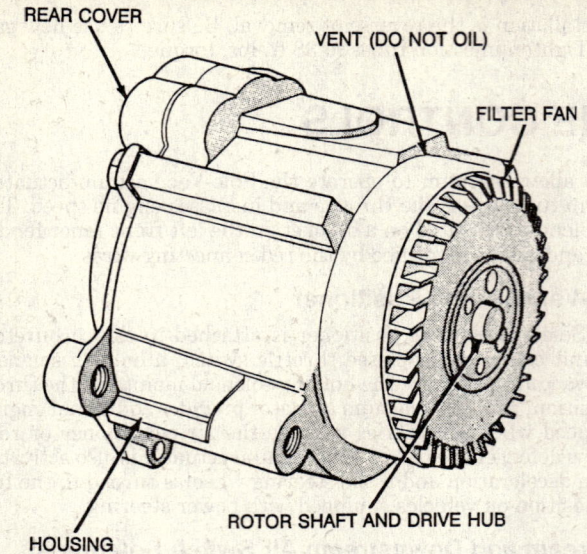

Air pump

Air Injection Tubes

The air injection tubes distribute air via the diverter valve to each of the exhaust ports. The ends of the tubes project into the ports near the exhaust valve seat.

A check valve, incorporating a stainless steel spring plunger and an asbestos seat, is integral with each air injection tube. The check valve functions to prevent the reverse flow of exhaust gas into the air pump during a malfunction of the pump or diverter valve.

FUNCTIONAL TESTING

Diverter (Bypass) Valve

ALL EXCEPT 6-2.8L

1. Start the engine and operate at idle speed.
2. Check the diverter valve vent. Little or no air should flow from the vent.
3. Accelerate engine to 2000–3000 rpm and rapidly close throttle. A strong flow of air should pass from the diverter valve vent for 3 seconds. If air does not flow or engine backfires, check for a vacuum hose leak at the diverter.

NOTE: The diverter valve vents air pump output at a manifold vacuum of 20 in. Hg or an air pump pressure of 5 psi.

4. Slowly accelerate the engine between 2500–3500 rpm. Air should begin to flow from the diverter valve vent. If vacuum is present and the valve does not function as described above, replace the valve.

6-2.8L

1. Bring engine to normal operating temperature. Remove the air cleaner cover.
2. Disconnect the lower vacuum hose from the diverter valve. Air pump output should be directed to the air cleaner.
3. Connect the vacuum hose to the diverter valve. Air pump output should be directed to the exhaust manifolds.
4. If air is not directed as described above, check to see that the vacuum source is drawing vacuum. If so, replace the diverter.

NOTE: California emissions diverter valves also function as vacuum switches. They are controlled directly by the electric control module (ECM) so that air is diverted to the air cleaner during closed throttle deceleration, high electrical load on the engine control system, the first five seconds of start up and when the engine is off.

Check Valves

1. Disconnect air hoses at the air tubes.
2. With the engine operating above idle, listen and feel for exhaust gas leakage from the check valves and tubes.

NOTE: A slight leak from the check valves is normal.

3. Replace components which are rusted through or leak excessively.

when the pump pressure reaches a preset level. This occurs at high engine rpm. This serves to prevent damage to the pump and to limit maximum exhaust manifold temperatures.

Check the air pump drive belt for proper tension and adjust as necessary. Do not pry on the die cast pump housing. Check to see if the pump is discharging air. Remove the air outlet hose at the pump. With the engine running, air should be felt at the pump outlet opening.

NOTE: DO NOT disassemble the air pump for any reason. Internal components are not serviceable. If the air pump is malfunctioning, replace the pump as a unit.

Pump Air Filter

Some air pumps are equipped with a replaceable element type air filter. The filter should be replaced every 12,000 miles under normal conditions and sooner under off-road use. Other models draw their air supply through the carburetor air filter.

Diverter (Bypass) Valve

The diverter valve has two outlets; one for each air injection tube. The valve momentarily diverts air pump output from the tubes and vents it to atmosphere during rapid deceleration. In addition, the valve functions as a pressure release for excessive air pump output.

REMOVAL AND INSTALLATION

Air Pump

1. Disconnect the output hose from the pump.
2. Loosen the mount bracket-to-pump bolts.
3. Remove the drive belt, pivot bolt and brace bolts. Remove the pump.
4. Installation is the reverse of removal. Tighten mounting bolts to 20 ft. lbs. torque.

Air Injection Tubes

1. Disconnect the air hoses at the check valve.
2. Remove the air tube fittings from the exhaust manifolds.

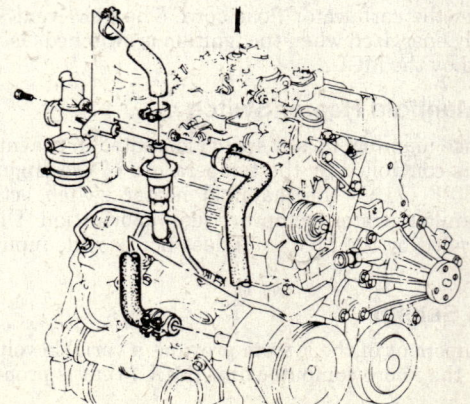

6-2.8L air diverter valve and injection tube

4-11

4 EMISSION CONTROLS

Some resistance may be encountered due to a build up of carbon on the threads. Remove the air injection tubes.

3. Installation is the reverse of removal. Be sure to use new gaskets. Tighten injection tubes to 38 ft. lbs. torque.

ELECTRONIC ENGINE CONTROLS

AMC/JEEP Computerized Emission Control (CEC) System
General Information

The Computerized Emission Control System (CEC) is used on pre-1989 gasoline engines. There are two primary modes of operation for the CEC feedback system, open loop and closed loop. The system will be in the open loop mode of operation (or a variation of it) whenever the engine operating conditions do not meet the programmed criteria for closed loop operation. During open loop operation, the air/fuel mixture is maintained at a programmed ratio that is dependent on the type of engine operation involved. The oxygen sensor data is not accepted by the system during this mode of operation.

When all input data meets the programmed criteria for closed loop operation, the exhaust gas oxygen content signal from the oxygen sensor is accepted by the computer. This results in an air/fuel mixture that will be optimum for the engine operating condition and also will correct any pre-existing mixture condition which is too lean or too rich.

NOTE: A high oxygen content in the exhaust gas indicates a lean air/fuel mixture. A low oxygen content indicates a rich air/fuel mixture. The optimum air/fuel mixture ratio is 14.7:1.

Micro Computer Unit (MCU)

The micro computer unit, or MCU, is the heart of the CEC system. The MCU receives signals from various engine sensors to constantly monitor the engine operating conditions, then it uses this information to make adjustments in order to achieve the optimum performance and economy with a minimum of engine emissions. The MCU monitors the oxygen sensor voltage and, based upon the mode of operation, generates an output control signal for the carburetor stepper motor or mixture control solenoid. If the system is in the closed loop mode of operation, the air/fuel mixture will vary according to the oxygen content in the exhaust gas and engine operating conditions. If the system is in the open loop mode of operation, the air/fuel mixture will be based on a predetermined ratio that is dependent on engine rpm. In addition, the MCU generates output signals to control ignition timing and engine idle speed, PCV flow and Pulse Air System operation.

Mixture Control Solenoid

On engines with the Carter YFA or Rochester E2SE carburetors, a mixture control (MC) solenoid is used to regulate the air/fuel mixture. During open loop operation, the MC solenoid supplies a preprogrammed amount of air to the carburetor idle circuit and main metering circuit where it mixes with the fuel. During closed loop operation, the MCU operates the MC solenoid to provide additional or less air to the fuel mixture, depending on the engine operating conditions as monitored by the various engine sensors.

Idle Relay and Solenoid

The idle relay is energized by the MCU to control the vacuum actuator portion of the Sole-Vac throttle positioner by providing a ground for the idle relay. The relay energizes the idle solenoid, which allows vacuum to operate the Sole-Vac vacuum actuator. This, in turn, opens the throttle and increases engine speed. The idle solenoid is located on a bracket on the left front inner fender panel and can be identified by the red connecting wires.

Sole-Vac Throttle Positioner

The Sole-Vac throttle positioner is attached to the carburetor. The unit consists of a closed throttle switch, a holding solenoid and a vacuum actuator. The holding solenoid maintains the throttle position, while the vacuum actuator provides additional engine idle speed when accessories such as the air conditioner or rear window defogger are in use. The vacuum actuator is also activated during deceleration and if the steering wheel is turned to the full stop position on vehicles equipped with power steering.

Upstream and Downstream Air Switch Solenoids

The upstream and downstream solenoids of the pulse air system distribute air to the exhaust pipe and catalytic converter. Both solenoids are energized by the MCU to route air into the exhaust pipe at a point after the oxygen sensor. When energized, the downstream solenoid routes air into the second bed of the dual-bed catalytic converter. This additional air reacts with the exhaust gases to reduce engine emissions.

The solenoids are located on a bracket attached to the left inner front fender panel. The idle solenoid is also located on this same bracket.

PCV Shutoff Solenoid

The positive crankcase ventilation shutoff solenoid is installed in the PCV valve hose and is energized by the MCU to turn off the crankcase ventilation system when the engine is at idle speed. An anti-diesel relay system on 4 cylinder engines, consisting of an anti-diesel relay and a delay relay, prevents engine run-on when the ignition is switched off by momentarily energizing the PCV valve solenoid when the ignition is switched off to prevent air entering below the throttle plate.

Bowl Vent Solenoid

The bowl vent solenoid is located in the hose between the carburetor bowl vent and the canister. The bowl vent solenoid is closed and allows no fuel vapor to flow when the engine is operating. When the engine is not operating, the solenoid is open and allows vapor to flow to the charcoal canister to control hydrocarbon emissions from the carburetor float bowl. The bowl vent solenoid is electrically energized when the ignition is switched ON and is not controlled by the MCU.

Intake Manifold Heater Switch

The intake manifold heater switch is located in the intake manifold and is controlled by the temperature of the engine coolant. Below 160°F (71°C) the manifold heater switch activates the intake manifold heater to improve fuel vaporization. The switch is not controlled by the MCU and does not provide input information to it.

Oxygen Sensor

This component of the system provides a variable voltage (millivolts) for the micro computer unit (MCU) that is proportional to

EMISSION CONTROLS 4

the oxygen content in the exhaust gas. In addition to the oxygen sensor, the following data senders are used to supply the MCU with engine operation data.

Knock Sensor

The knock sensor is a tuned piezoelectric crystal transducer that is located in the cylinder head. The knock sensor provides the MCU with an electrical signal that is created by vibrations that correspond to its center frequency (5550 Hz). Vibrations from engine knock (detonation) cause the crystal inside the sensor to vibrate and produce an electrical signal that is used by the MCU to selectively retard the ignition timing of any single cylinder or combination of cylinders to eliminate the knock condition.

Vacuum Switches

Two vacuum-operated electrical switches (ported and manifold) are used to detect and send throttle position data to the MCU for idle (closed), partial and wide open throttle (WOT). These switches are located together in a bracket attached to the dash panel in the engine compartment. The 4 in. Hg vacuum switch can be identified by its natural (beige) color, while the 10 in. Hg vacuum switch is green in color. The 4 in. Hg switch is controlled by ported vacuum and its electrical contact is normally in the open position when the vacuum level is less than 4 in. Hg. When the vacuum exceeds 4 in. Hg, the switch closes. The 4 in. Hg vacuum switch tells the MCU when either a closed or deep throttle condition exists.

The 10 in. Hg vacuum switch is controlled by manifold vacuum. Its electrical contact is normally closed when the vacuum level is less than 10 in. Hg; if the vacuum level exceeds 10 in. Hg, the switch opens. This switch tells the MCU that either a partial or medium throttle condition exists.

Engine RPM Voltage

This voltage is supplied from a terminal on the distributor. Until a voltage equivalent to a predetermined rpm is received by the MCU, the system remains in the open loop mode of operation. The result is a fixed rich air/fuel mixture for starting purposes.

Coolant Temperature Switch

The temperature switch supplies engine coolant temperature data to the MCU. Until the engine is sufficiently warmed (above 135°F/57°C), the system remains in the open loop mode of operation (i.e., a fixed air/fuel mixture based upon engine rpm).

Thermal Electric Switch

The thermal electric switch is located inside the air cleaner to sense the incoming air temperature and indicate a cold weather start-up condition to the MCU when the air temperature is below 50°F (10°C). Above 65°F (18°C), the switch opens to indicate a normal engine start-up condition to the MCU.

Wide Open Throttle (WOT) Switch

The wide open throttle switch is attached to the base of the carburetor by a mounting bracket. It is a mechanically operated electrical switch that is controlled by the position of the throttle. When the throttle is placed in the wide open position, a cam on the throttle shaft actuates the switch about 15°F (−9°C) before wide open position to indicate a full-throttle demand to the MCU.

Altitude Jumper Wire

The altitude jumper wire connector is located next to the MCU. The jumper wire provides the MCU with an indication of whether the vehicle is being operated above or below a 4000 ft. elevation (high altitude operation). The connector normally has no jumper wire installed. If a vehicle is to be operated in a designated high altitude area, a jumper wire must be installed.

CEC SYSTEM OPERATION

4-CYLINDER ENGINE

The open loop mode of operation occurs when:
1. Starting engine, engine is cold or air cleaner air is cold.
2. Engine is at idle speed, accelerating to partial throttle or decelerating from partial throttle to idle speed.
3. Carburetor is either at or near wide open throttle (WOT).

When any of these conditions occur, the mixture control (MC) solenoid provides a predetermined air/fuel mixture ratio for each condition. Because the air/fuel ratios are predetermined and no feedback relative to the results is accepted, this type of operation is referred to as open loop operation. All open loop operations are characterized by predetermined air/fuel mixture ratios. Each operation (except closed loop) has a specific air/fuel ratio and because more than one of the engine operational selection conditions can be present at one time, the MCU is programmed with a priority ranking for the operations. It complies with the conditions that pertain to the operation having the highest priority. The priorities are as described below.

Cold Weather Engine Start-Up and Operation

If the air cleaner air temperature is below the calibrated value (55°F or 13°C) of the thermal electric switch (TES), the air/fuel mixture is at a "rich" ratio. Lean air/fuel mixtures are not permitted for a preset period following a cold weather start-up.

At or Near Wide Open Throttle (WOT) Operation (Cold Engine)

This open loop operation occurs whenever the coolant temperature is below the calibrated switching value (95°F or 35°C) of the open loop coolant temperature switch and the WOT vacuum switch (cold) has been closed because of the decrease in manifold vacuum (less than 5 in. Hg or 17 kPa). When this open loop condition occurs the MC solenoid provides a rich air/fuel mixture for cold engine operation at wide open throttle.

NOTE: Temperature and switching vacuum levels are nominal values. The actual switching temperature or vacuum level will vary slightly from switch to switch.

At or Near Wide Open Throttle (WOT) Operation (Warm Engine)

This open loop operation occurs whenever the coolant temperature is above the calibrated switching temperature (135°F or 57°C) of the enrichment coolant temperature switch and the WOT vacuum switch (warm) has been opened because of the decrease in manifold vacuum (less than 3 in. Hg or 10 kPa). When this open loop condition occurs the MC solenoid provides a rich air/fuel mixture for warm engine operation at wide open throttle.

Adaptive Mode of Operation

This open loop operation occurs when the engine is either at idle speed, accelerating from idle speed or decelerating to idle speed. If the engine rpm (tach) voltage is less than the calibrated value and manifold vacuum is above the calibrated switching level for the adaptive vacuum switch (i.e., switch closed), an engine idle condition is assumed to exist. If the engine rpm (tach) voltage is greater than the calibrated value and manifold vacuum is above the calibrated switching level of the adaptive vacuum switch (i.e., switch closed), an engine deceleration-to-idle speed condition is assumed to exist. During the adaptive mode of operation the MC solenoid provides a predetermined air/fuel mixture.

Closed Loop Operation

Closed loop operation occurs whenever none of the open loop engine operating conditions exist. The MCU causes the MC solenoid to vary the air/fuel mixture in reaction to the voltage input from the oxygen sensor located in the exhaust manifold. The

4 EMISSION CONTROLS

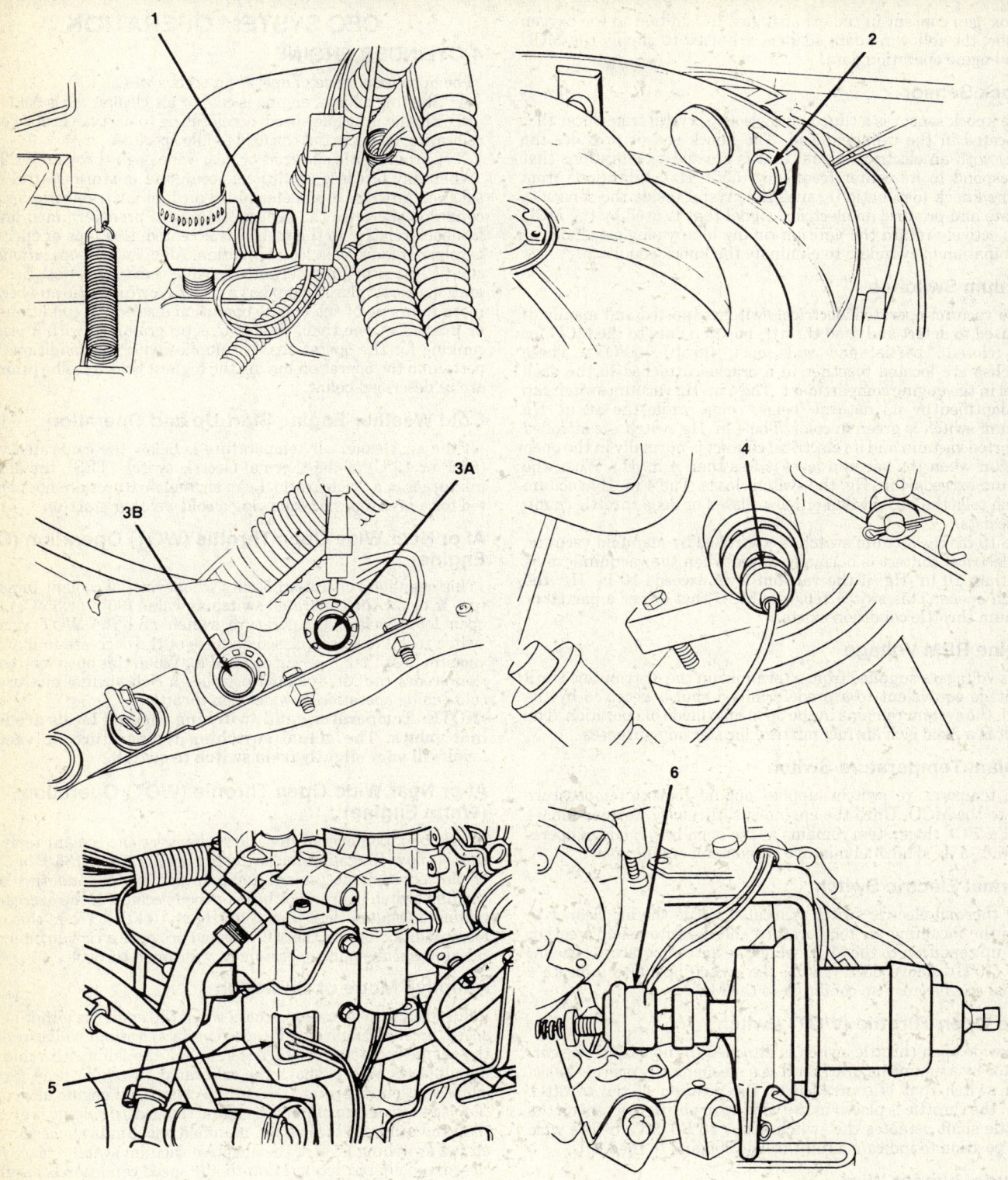

1. Coolant temperature switch
2. Thermal electric switch
3a. 4-inch hg vacuum switch (ported vacuum)
3b. 10-inch hg vacuum switch (manifold vacuum)
4. Oxygan sensor
5. Wide open throttle switch
6. Closed throttle switch

CEC system components

EMISSION CONTROLS 4

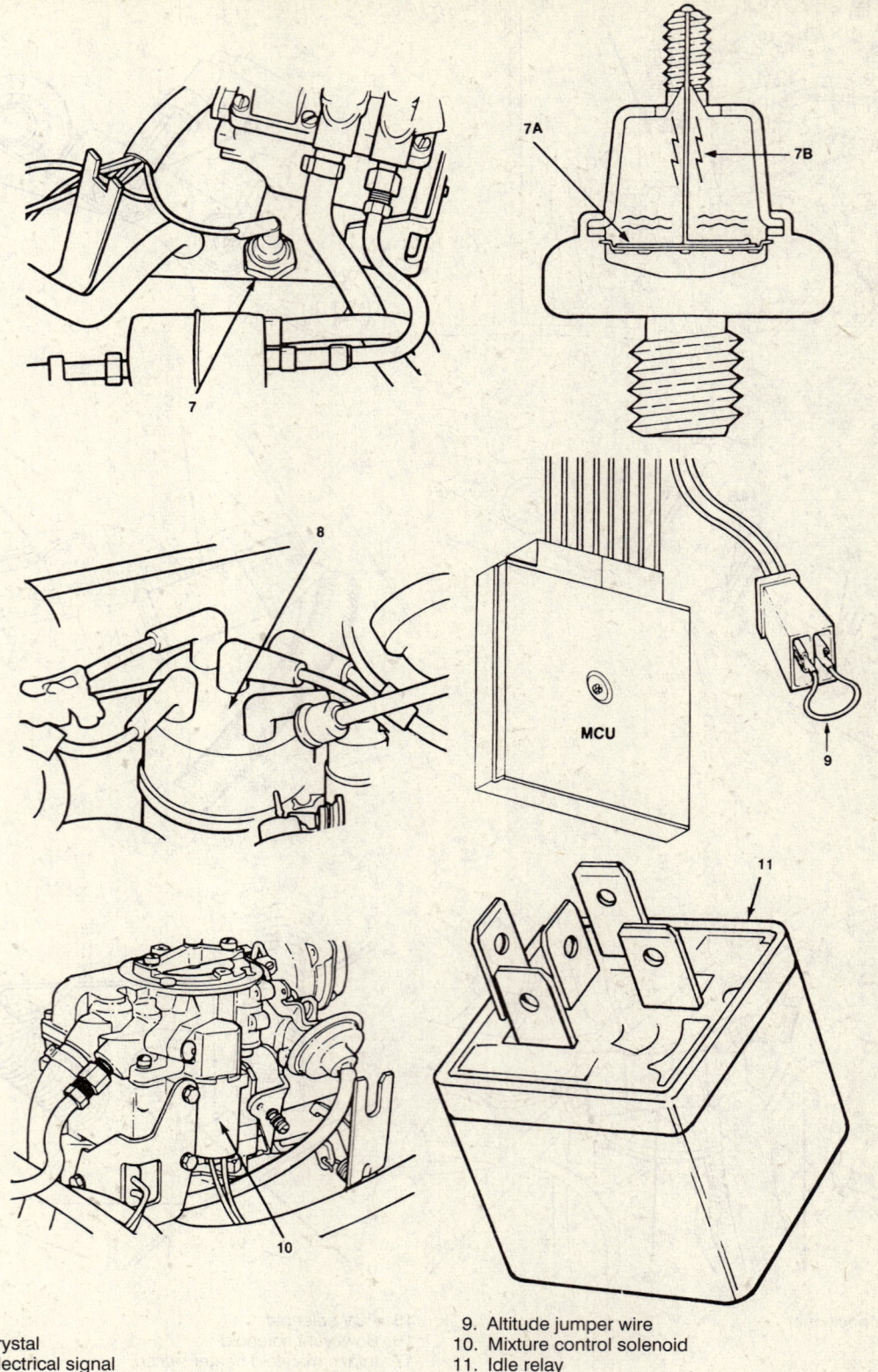

7. Knock sensor
7a. Knock sensor crystal
7b. Knock sensor electrical signal
8. Distributor
9. Altitude jumper wire
10. Mixture control solenoid
11. Idle relay

CEC system components

4 EMISSION CONTROLS

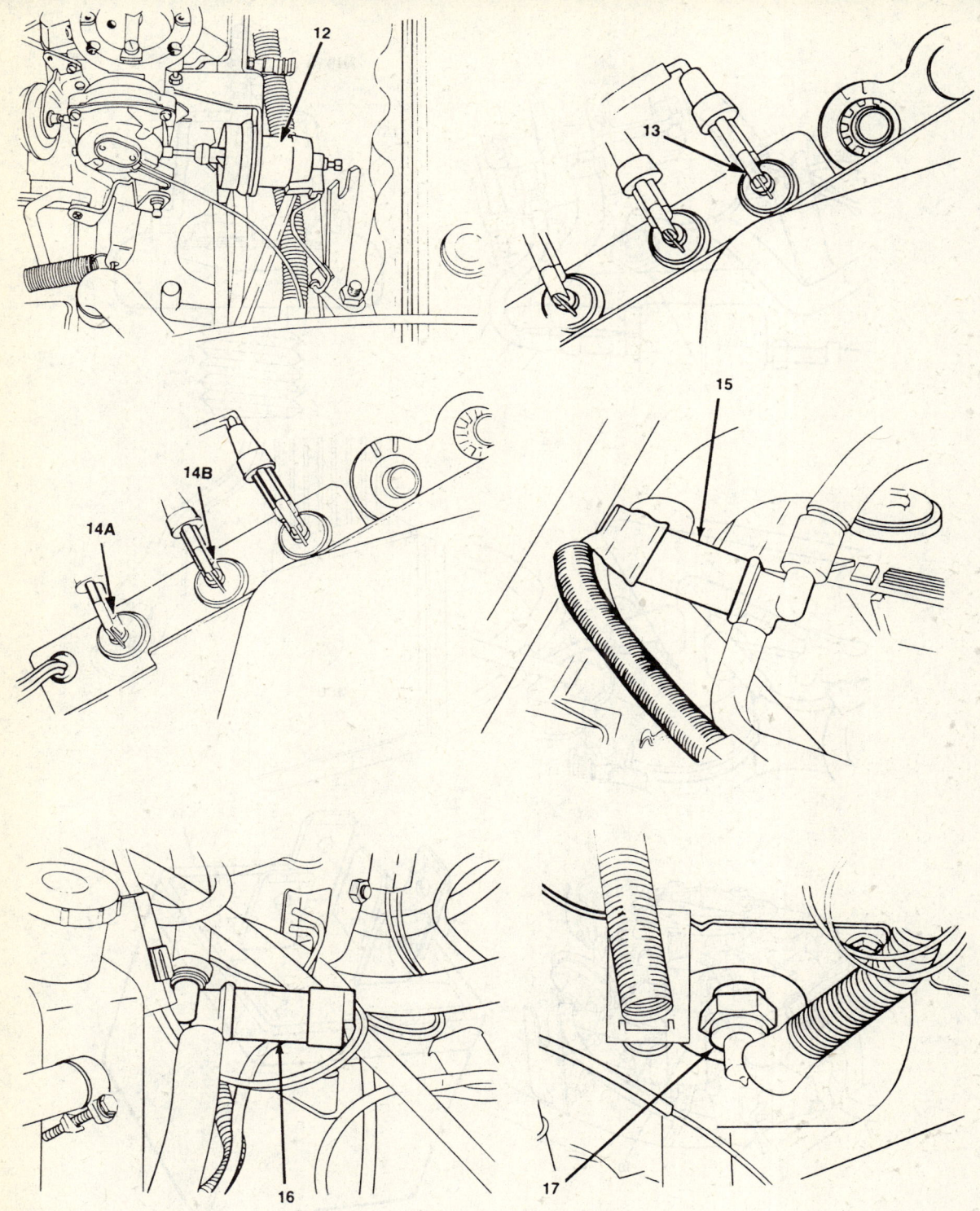

12. Sole-vac throttle positioner
13. Idle solenoid
14a. Upstream solenoid
14b. Downstream solenoid
15. PCV solenoid
16. Bowl vent solenoid
17. Intake manifold heater switch

CEC system components

EMISSION CONTROLS 4

Because the oxygen sensor only reacts to oxygen, manifold air leak or malfunction between the carburetor and sensor may cause the sensor to provide an erroneous voltage output. The engine operation characteristics never quite permit the MCU to compute a single air/fuel mixture ratio that constantly provides the optimum air/fuel mixture. Therefore, closed loop operation is characterized by constant variation of the air/fuel mixture because the MCU is forced constantly to make small corrections in an attempt to create an optimum air/fuel mixture ratio.

DIAGNOSTIC TESTS

The CEC system should be considered as a possible source of trouble only after normal tests, that would apply to a vehicle without the system, have been performed.

The CEC Fuel Feedback System incorporates a diagnostic connector to provide a means for systematic evaluation of each component that could cause an operational failure. Electronic Fuel Feedback testers, ET-501-82 and ET-501-84 or equivalent, are available to aid in the system diagnosis. When a tester is not available, other test equipment can be substituted.

The equipment required to perform the checks and tests includes a tachometer, a hand vacuum pump and a digital volt-ohmmeter (DVOM) with a minimum ohms per volt of 10 MΩ.

— CAUTION —
The use of a voltmeter with less than 10 MΩ per volt input impedance can destroy the oxygen sensor. Since it is necessary to look inside the carburetor with the engine running, observe the following precautions.

1. Shape a sheet of clear acrylic plastic at least 0.250 in. (6mm) thick and 15 in. (381mm) × 15 in. 381mm).
2. Secure the acrylic sheet with an air cleaner wing nut after the top of the air cleaner has been removed.
3. Wear eye protection whenever performing checks and tests.
4. When engine is operating, keep hands and arms clear of fan, drive pulleys and belts. Do not wear loose clothing. Do not stand in line with fan blades.
5. Do not stand in front of running car.

Basic Diagnosis

CEC SYSTEM OPERATION
6-CYLINDER ENGINE

The open loop mode of operation occurs when:
1. Starting the engine, engine is cold or air cleaner air is cold.
2. Engine is at idle speed.
3. Carburetor is either at or near wide open throttle (WOT).

When any of these conditions occur, the metering pins are driven to a predetermined (programmed) position for each condition. Because the positions are predetermined and no feedback relative to the results is accepted, this type of operation is referred to as open loop operation. The five open loop operations are characterized by the metering pins being driven to a position where they are stopped and remain stationary.

Each operation (except closed loop) has a specific metering pin position and because more than one of the operation selection conditions can be present at one time, the MCU is programmed with a priority ranking for the operations. It complies with conditions that pertain to the operation having the highest priority. The priorities are as described below.

Cold Weather Engine Start-Up and Operation

If the air cleaner air temperature is below the calibrated value of the thermal electric switch (TES), the stepper motor is positioned a predetermined number of steps rich of the initialization position and air injection is diverted upstream. Lean air/fuel mixtures are

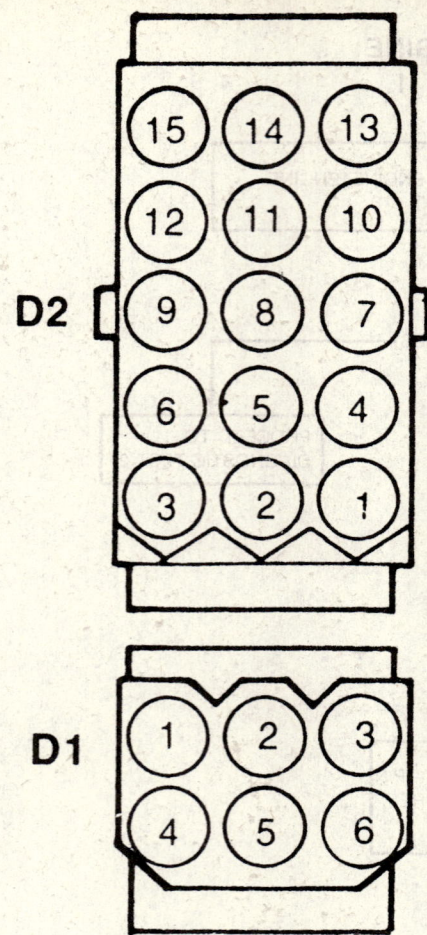

D2
1. PCV shut-off solenoid
2. Shift light
3. Altitude jumper wire
4. I₁ power
5. Downstream solenoid
6. WOT switch
7. Ground
8. Upstream solenoid
9. 10 in hg vacuum switch
10. Thermal electric switch
11. Sole-vac
12. Coolant temperature switch
13. Idle relay
14. MC solenoid
15. 4 inch Hg vacuum switch

D1
1. Tach
2. Electric choke
3. Body ground
4. Start
5. Idle solenoid
6. Not used

4-CYL CEC MCU diagnostic connector

oxygen sensor voltage varies in reaction to changes in oxygen content present in the exhaust gas. Because the content of oxygen in the exhaust gas indicates the completeness of the combustion process, it is a reliable indicator of the air/fuel mixture that is entering the combustion chamber.

4-17

4 EMISSION CONTROLS

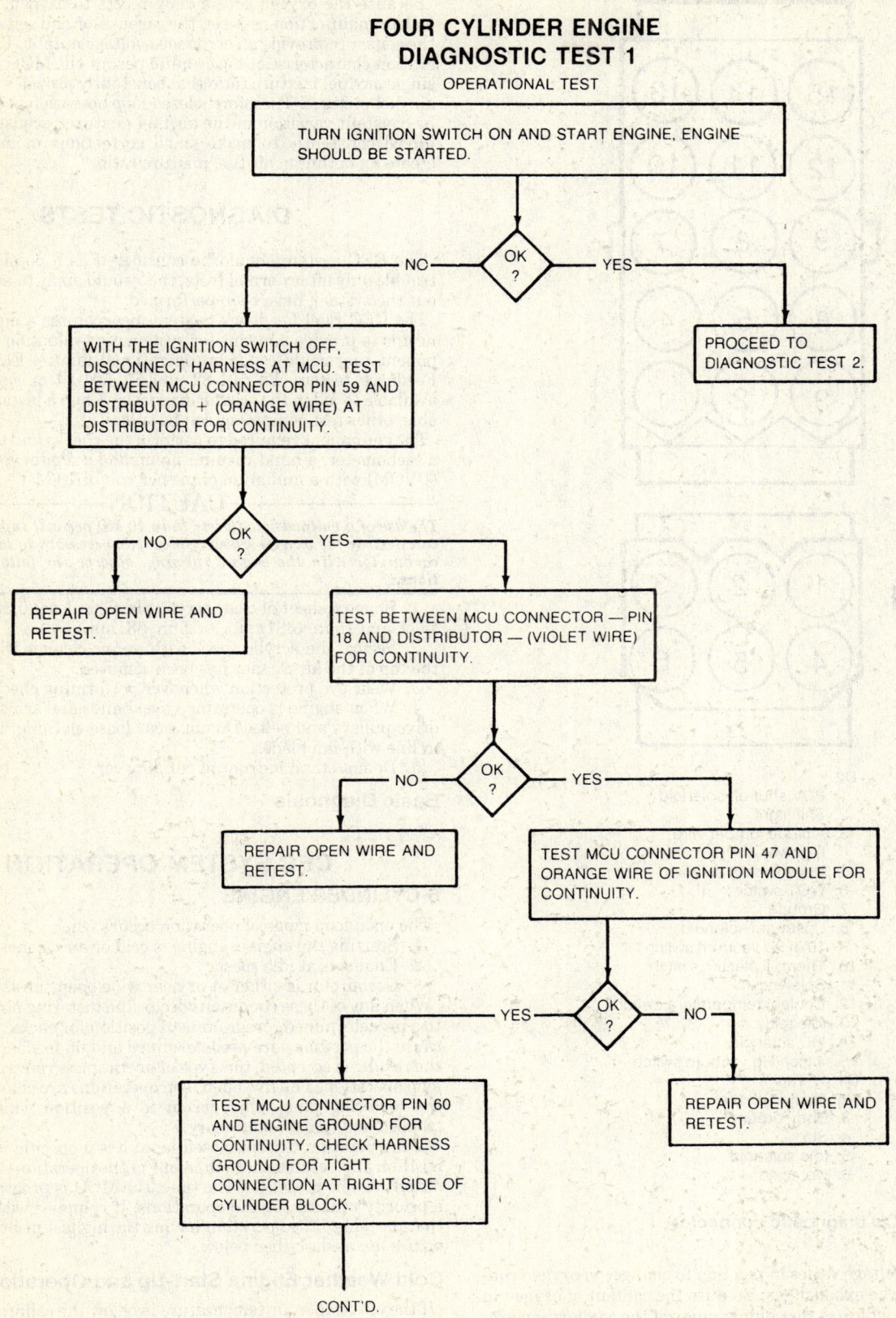

4-CYL CEC fuel feedback diagnostic charts

EMISSION CONTROLS 4

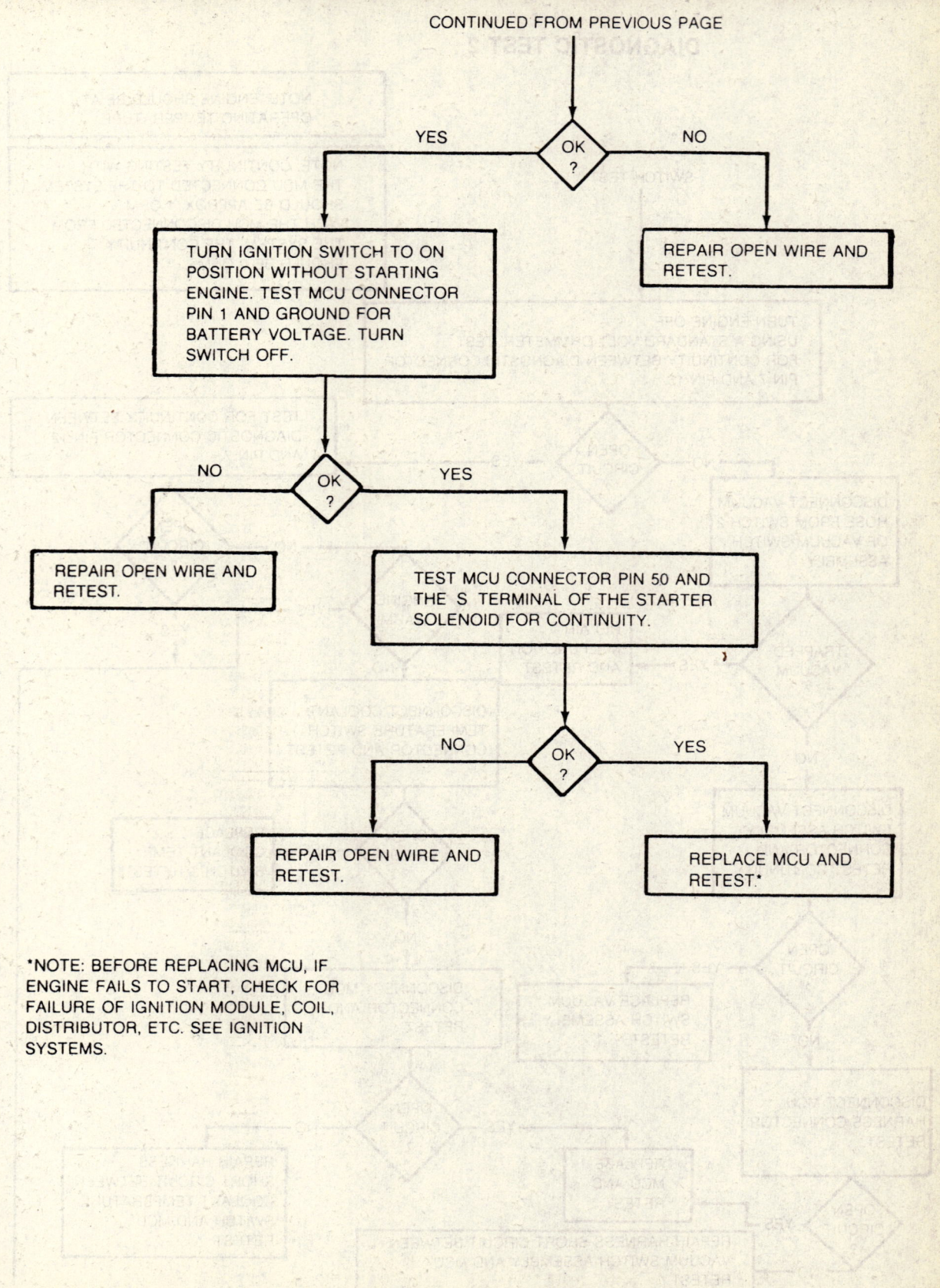

4-19

4 EMISSION CONTROLS

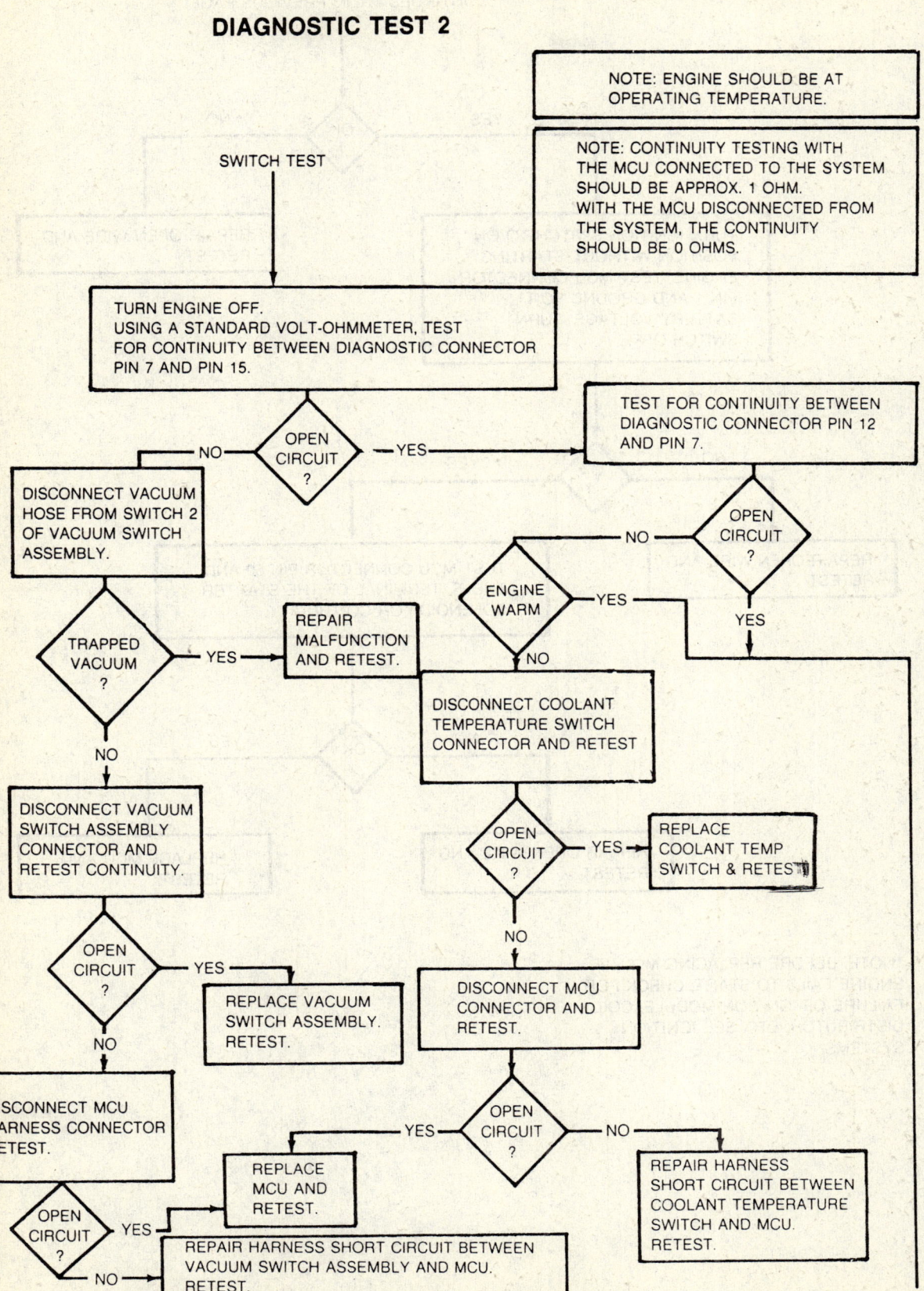

EMISSION CONTROLS 4

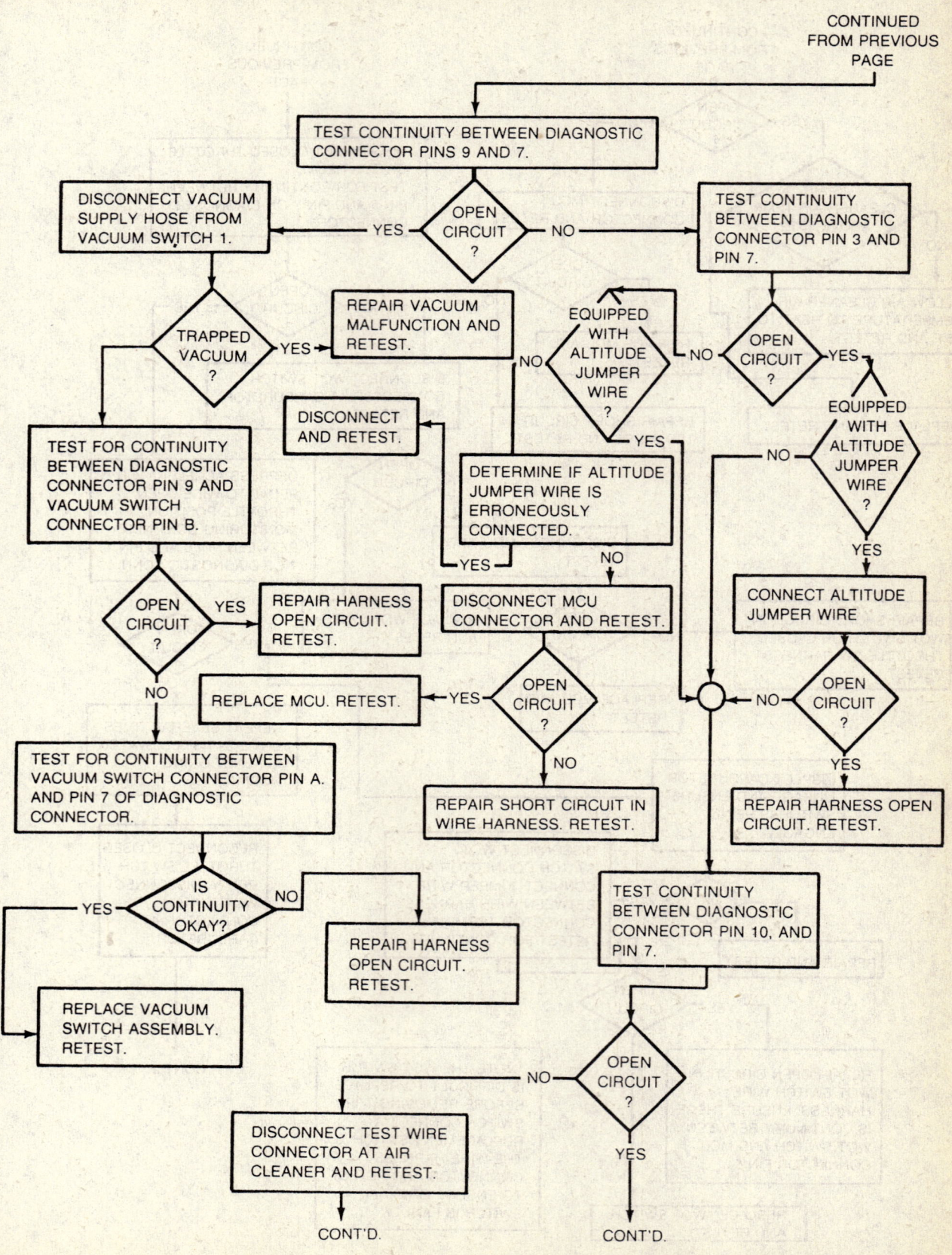

4-21

4 EMISSION CONTROLS

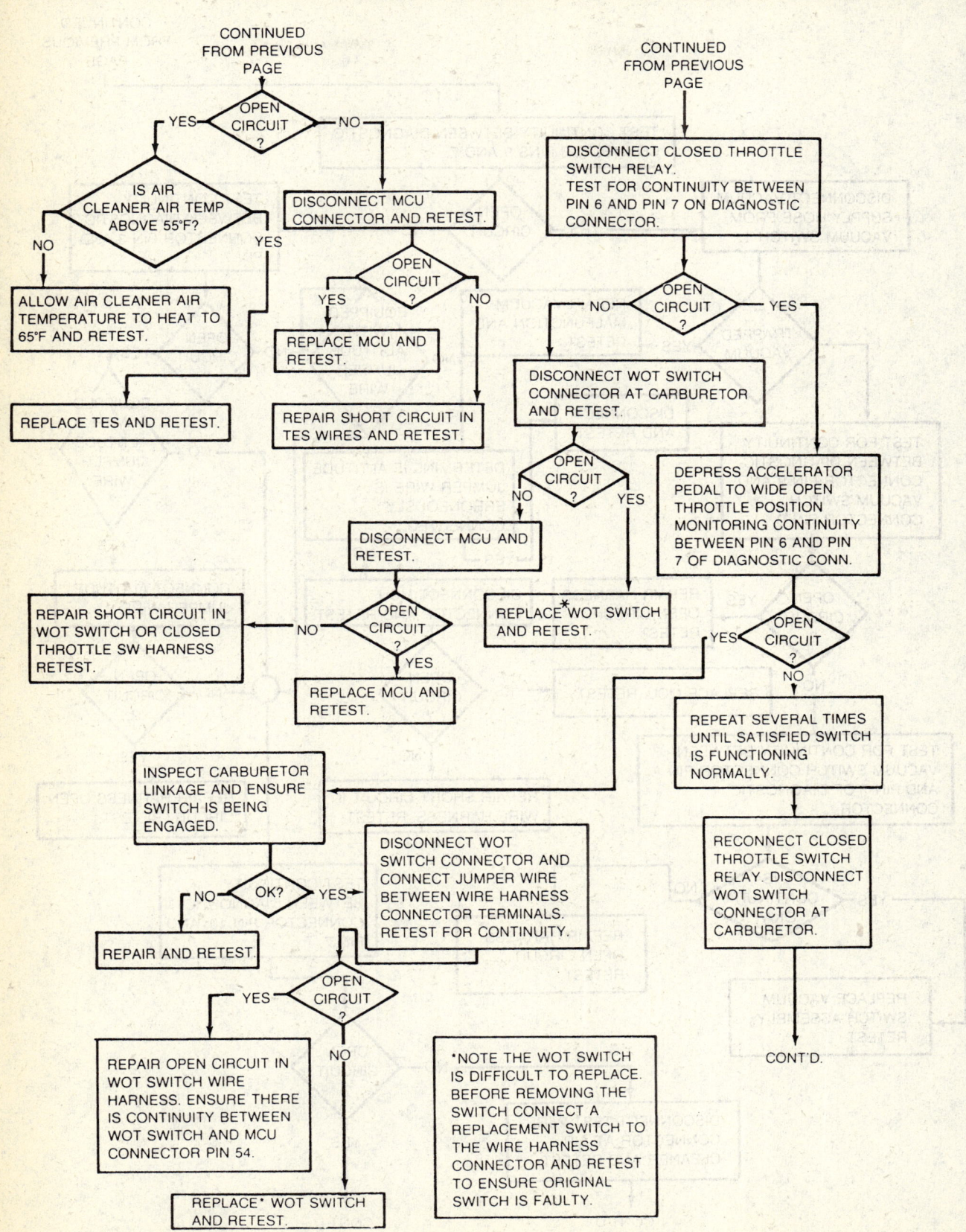

4-22

EMISSION CONTROLS 4

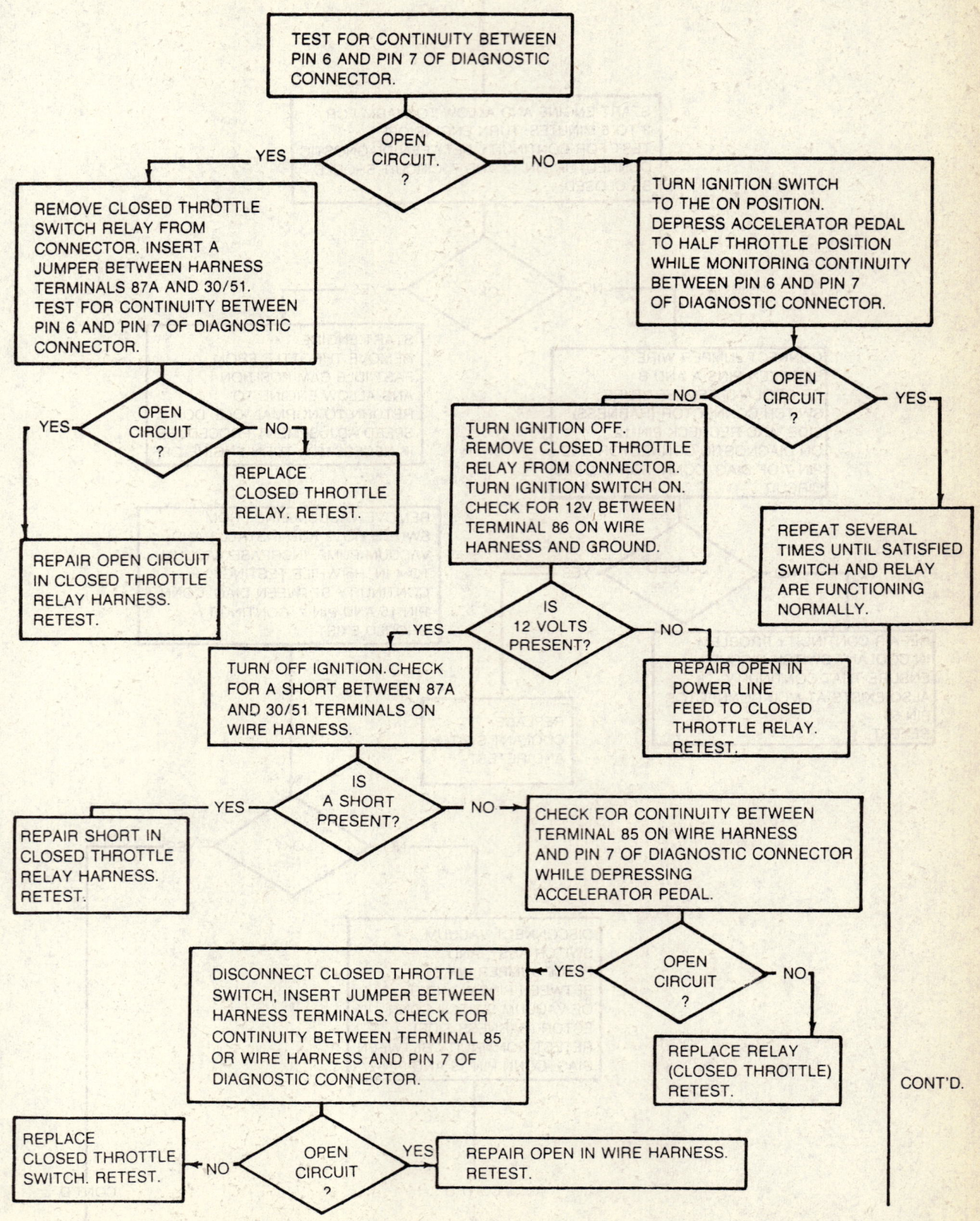

4-23

4 EMISSION CONTROLS

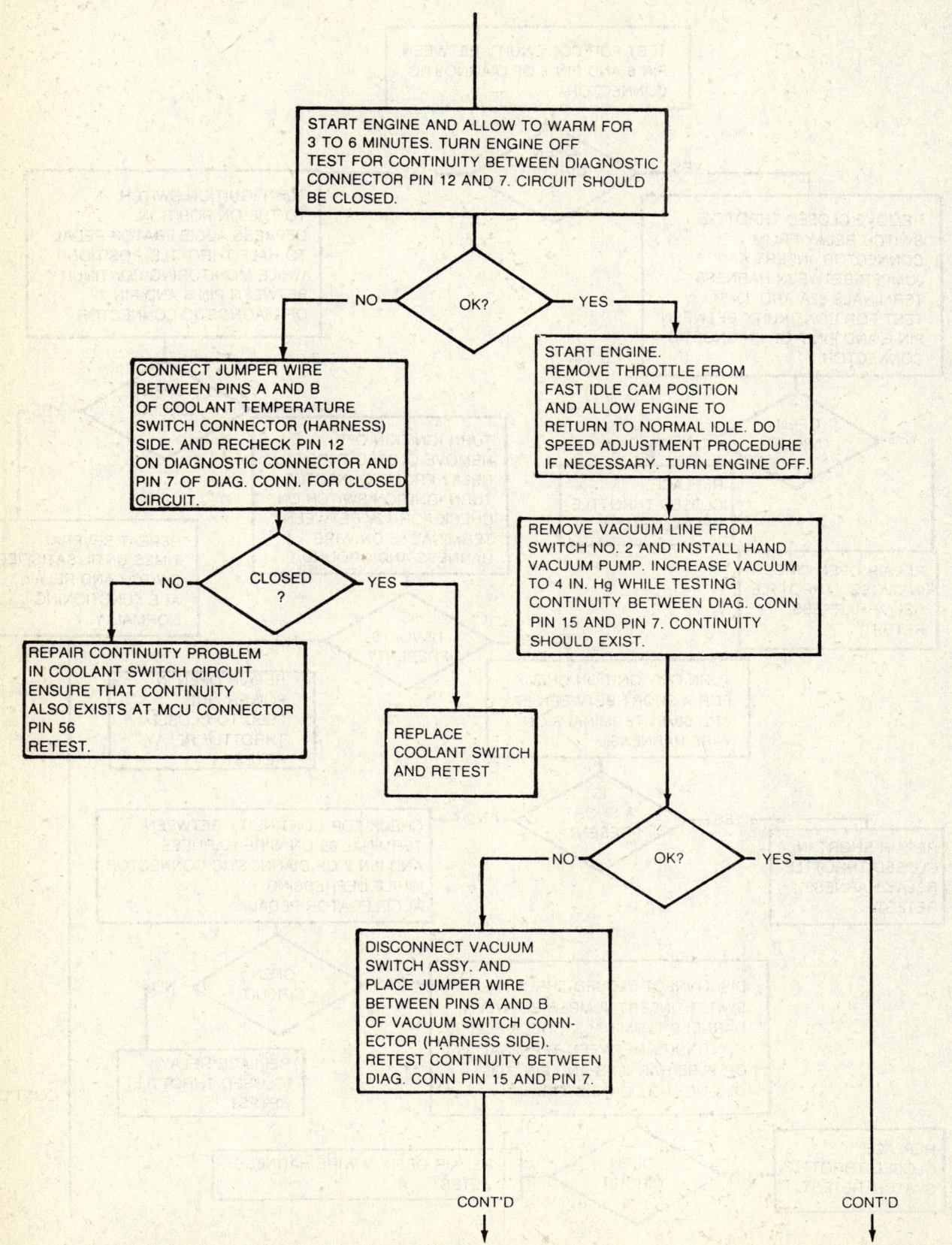

4-24

EMISSION CONTROLS 4

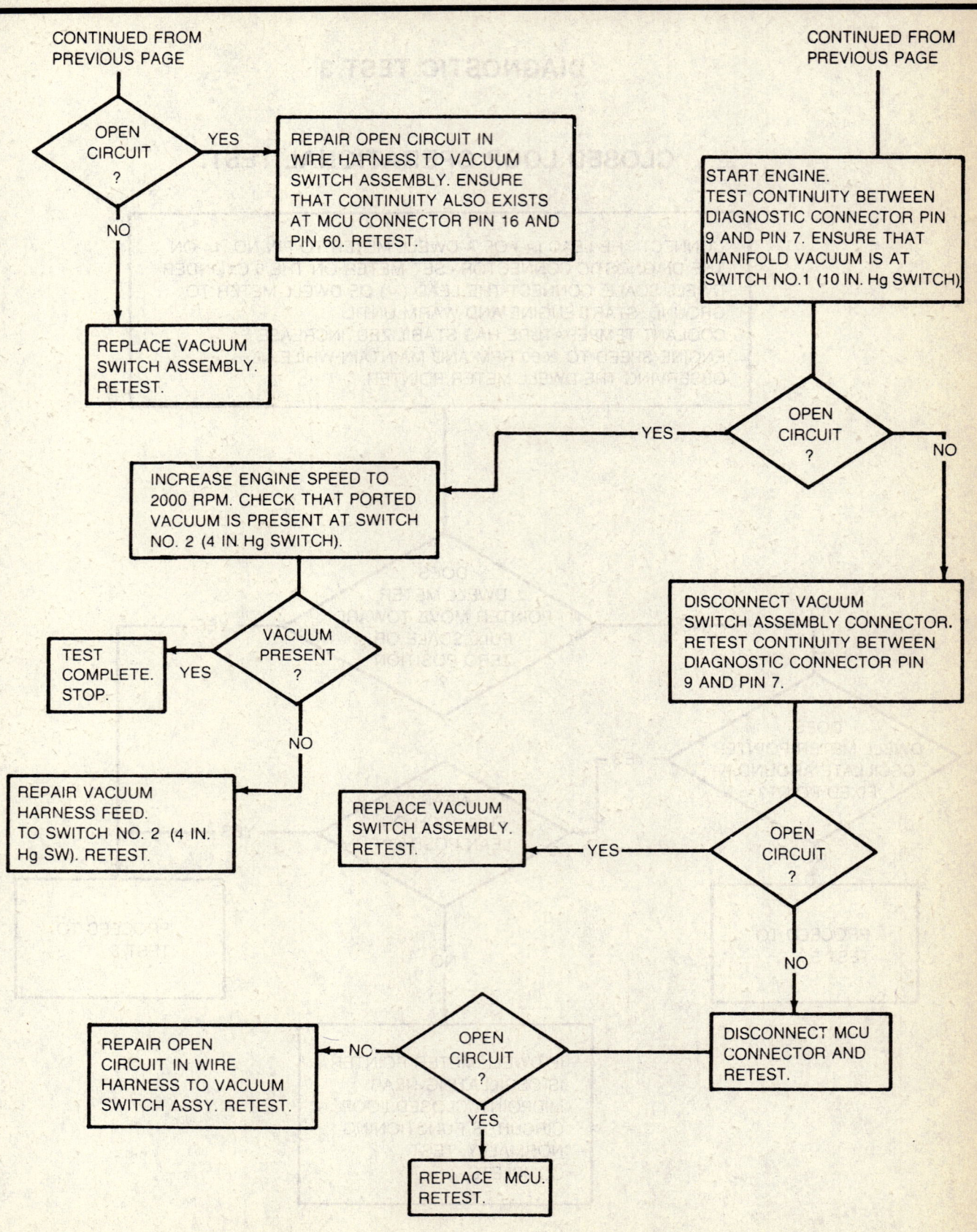

4-25

4 EMISSION CONTROLS

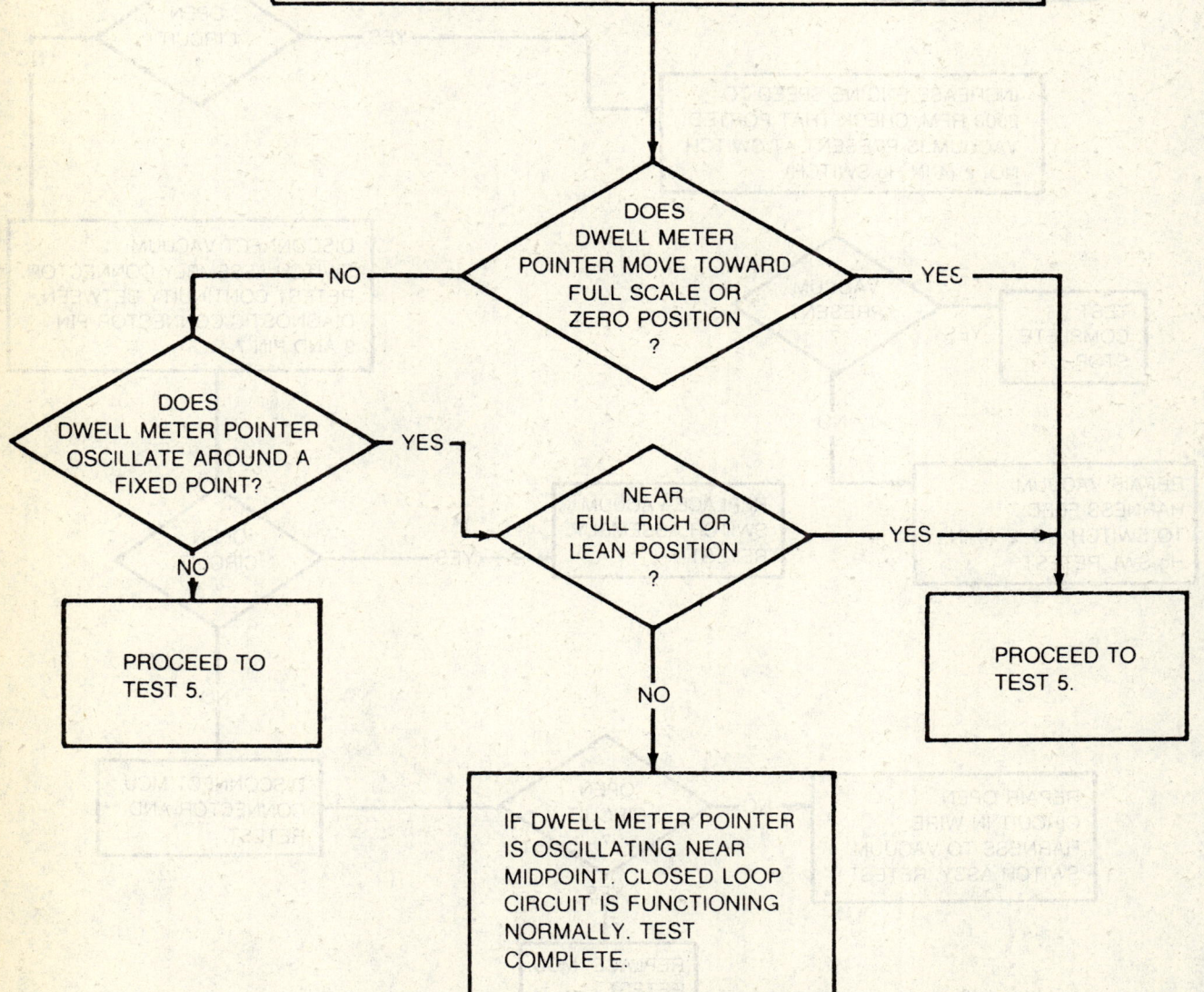

DIAGNOSTIC TEST 3

CLOSED LOOP OPERATIONAL TEST.

CONNECT THE LEAD (+) OF A DWELL METER TO PIN NO. 14 ON THE DIAGNOSTIC CONNECTOR - SET METER ON THE 6-CYLINDER DWELL SCALE. CONNECT THE LEAD (−) OF DWELL METER TO GROUND. START ENGINE AND WARM UNTIL COOLANT TEMPERATURE HAS STABILIZED. INCREASE ENGINE SPEED TO 2000 RPM AND MAINTAIN WHILE OBSERVING THE DWELL METER POINTER.

DOES DWELL METER POINTER MOVE TOWARD FULL SCALE OR ZERO POSITION?

- NO → DOES DWELL METER POINTER OSCILLATE AROUND A FIXED POINT?
  - NO → PROCEED TO TEST 5.
  - YES → NEAR FULL RICH OR LEAN POSITION?
    - YES → PROCEED TO TEST 5.
    - NO → IF DWELL METER POINTER IS OSCILLATING NEAR MIDPOINT. CLOSED LOOP CIRCUIT IS FUNCTIONING NORMALLY. TEST COMPLETE.
- YES → PROCEED TO TEST 5.

EMISSION CONTROLS 4

DIAGNOSTIC TEST 4.

KNOCK SENSOR TEST

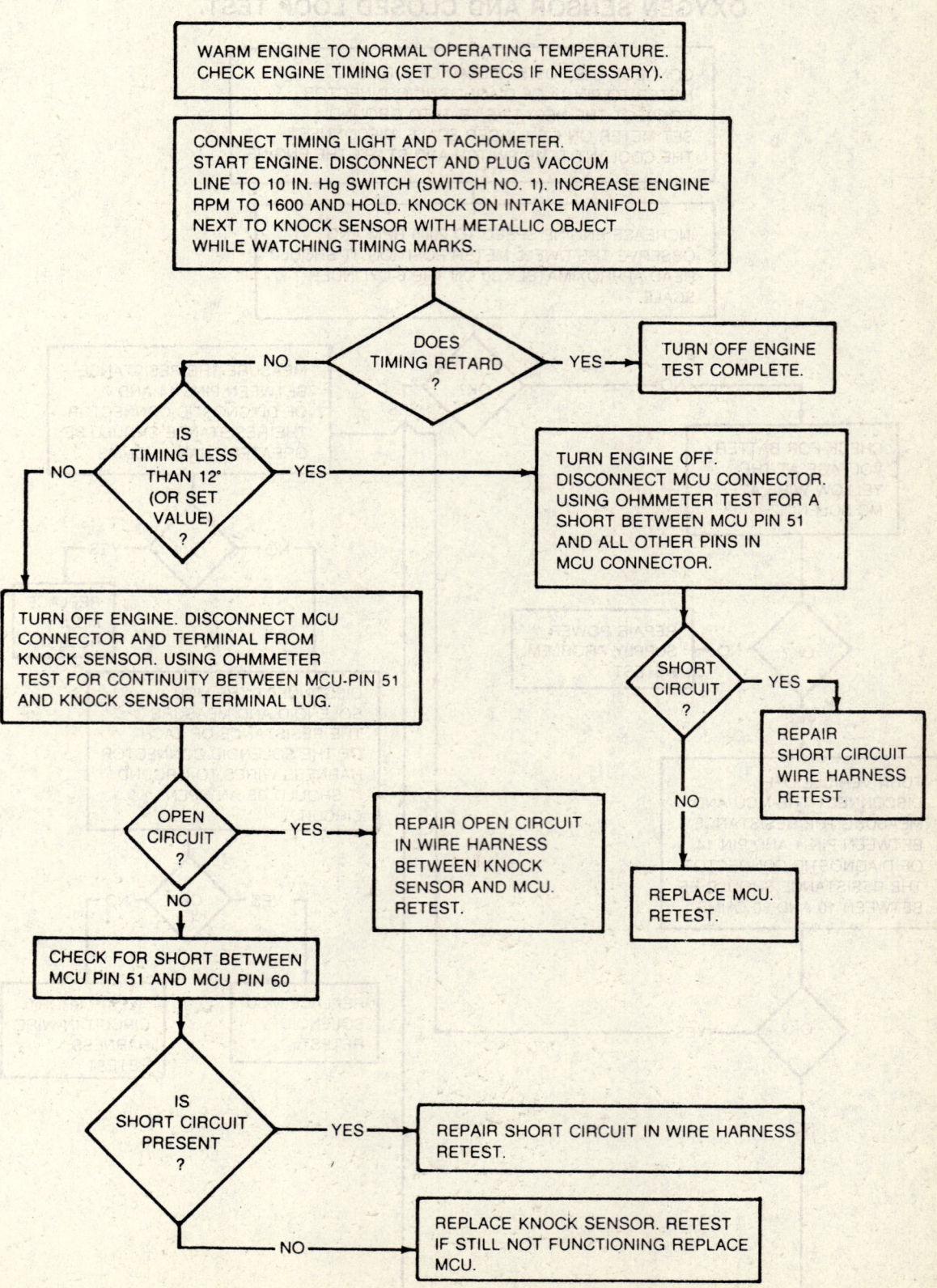

4-27

4 EMISSION CONTROLS

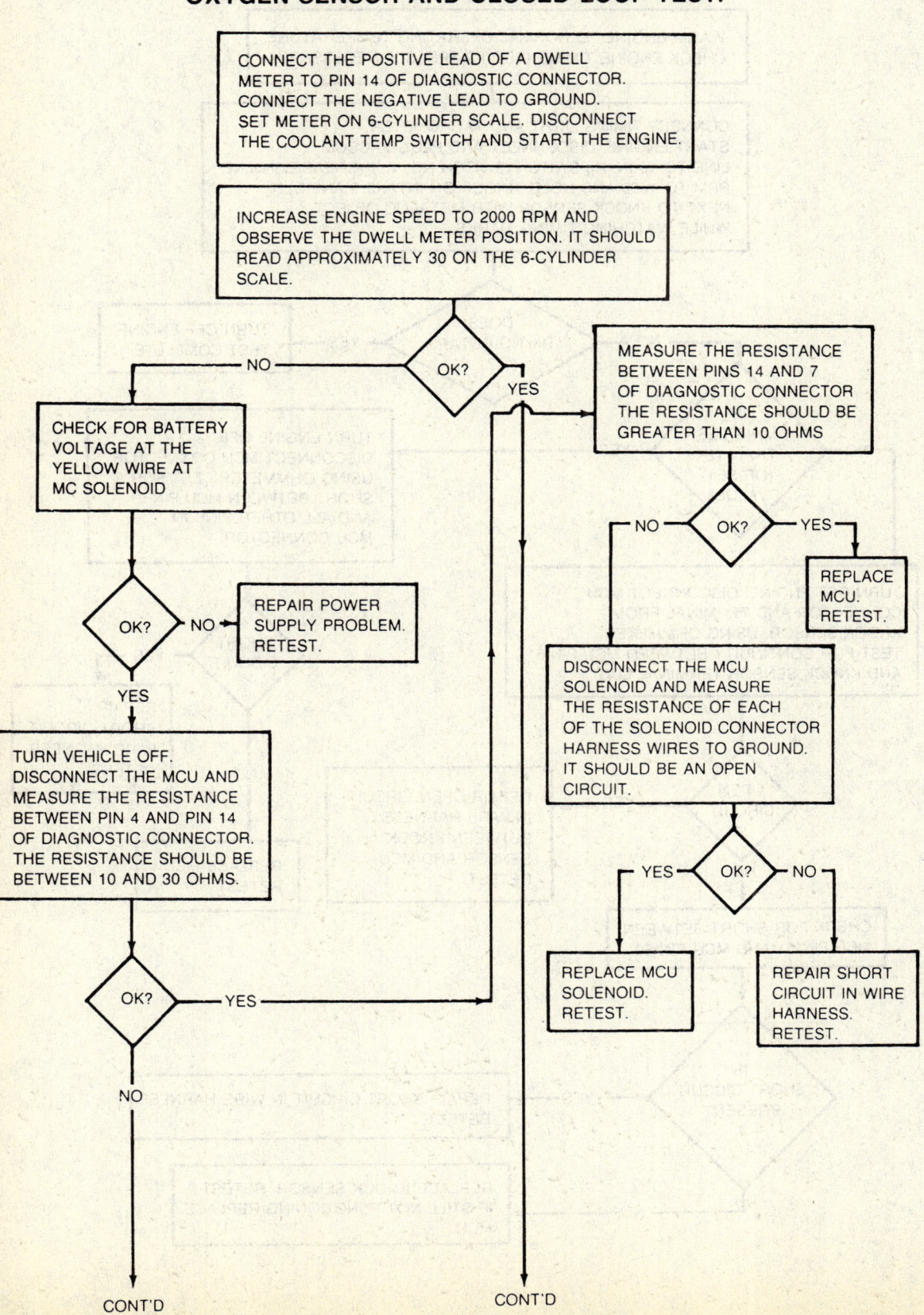

EMISSION CONTROLS 4

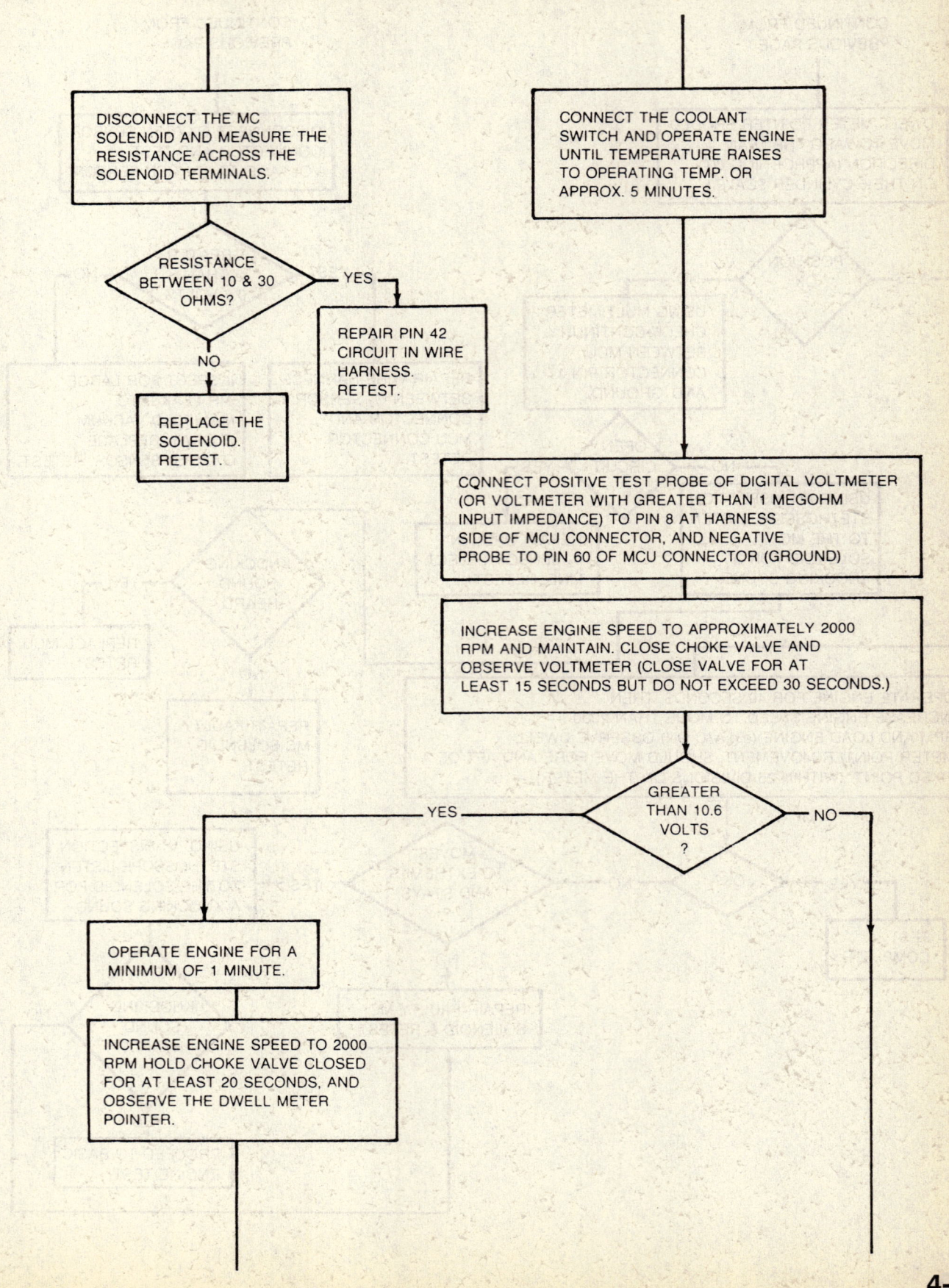

4-29

4 EMISSION CONTROLS

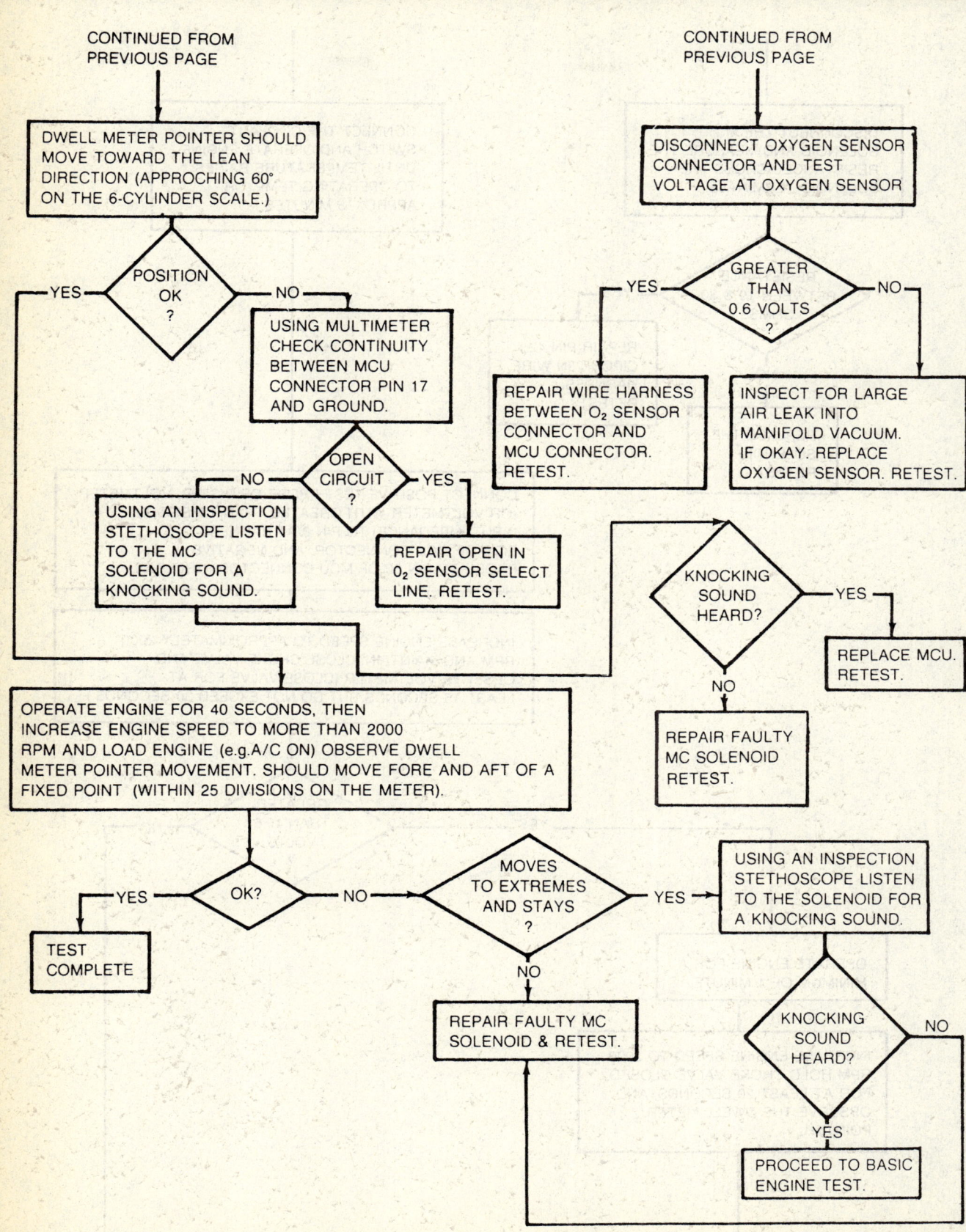

EMISSION CONTROLS 4

BASIC ENGINE TEST

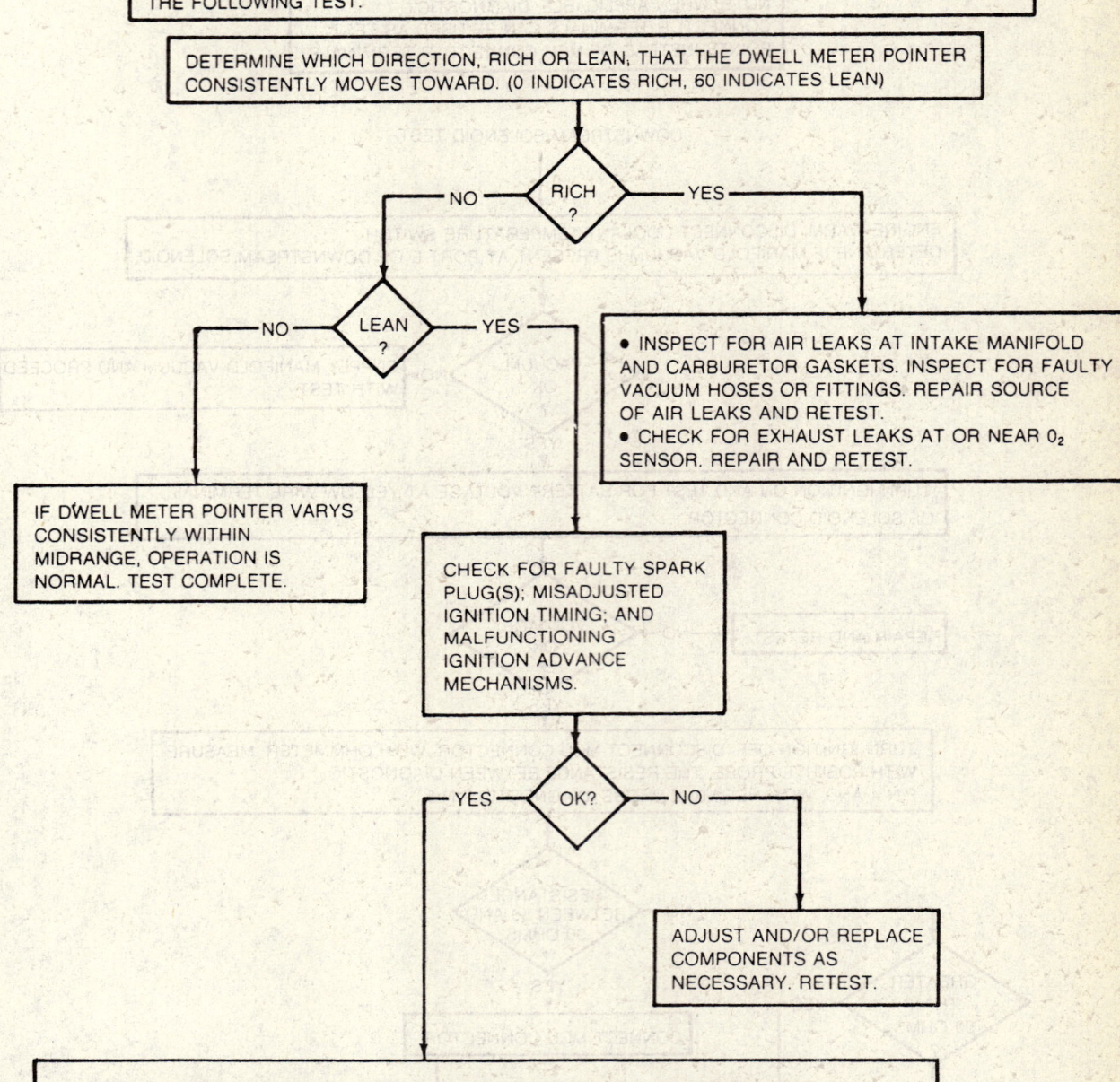

4-31

4 EMISSION CONTROLS

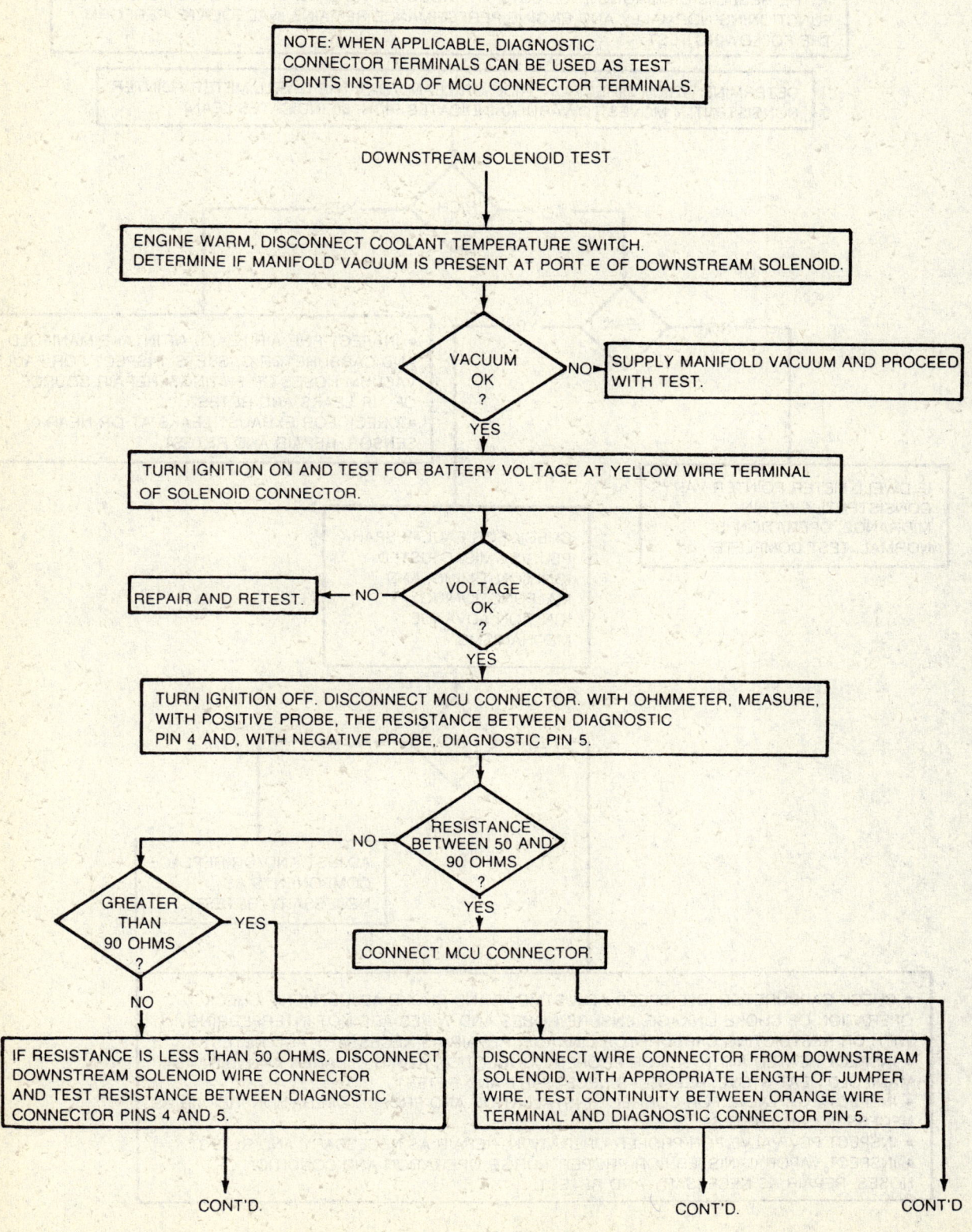

4-32

EMISSION CONTROLS 4

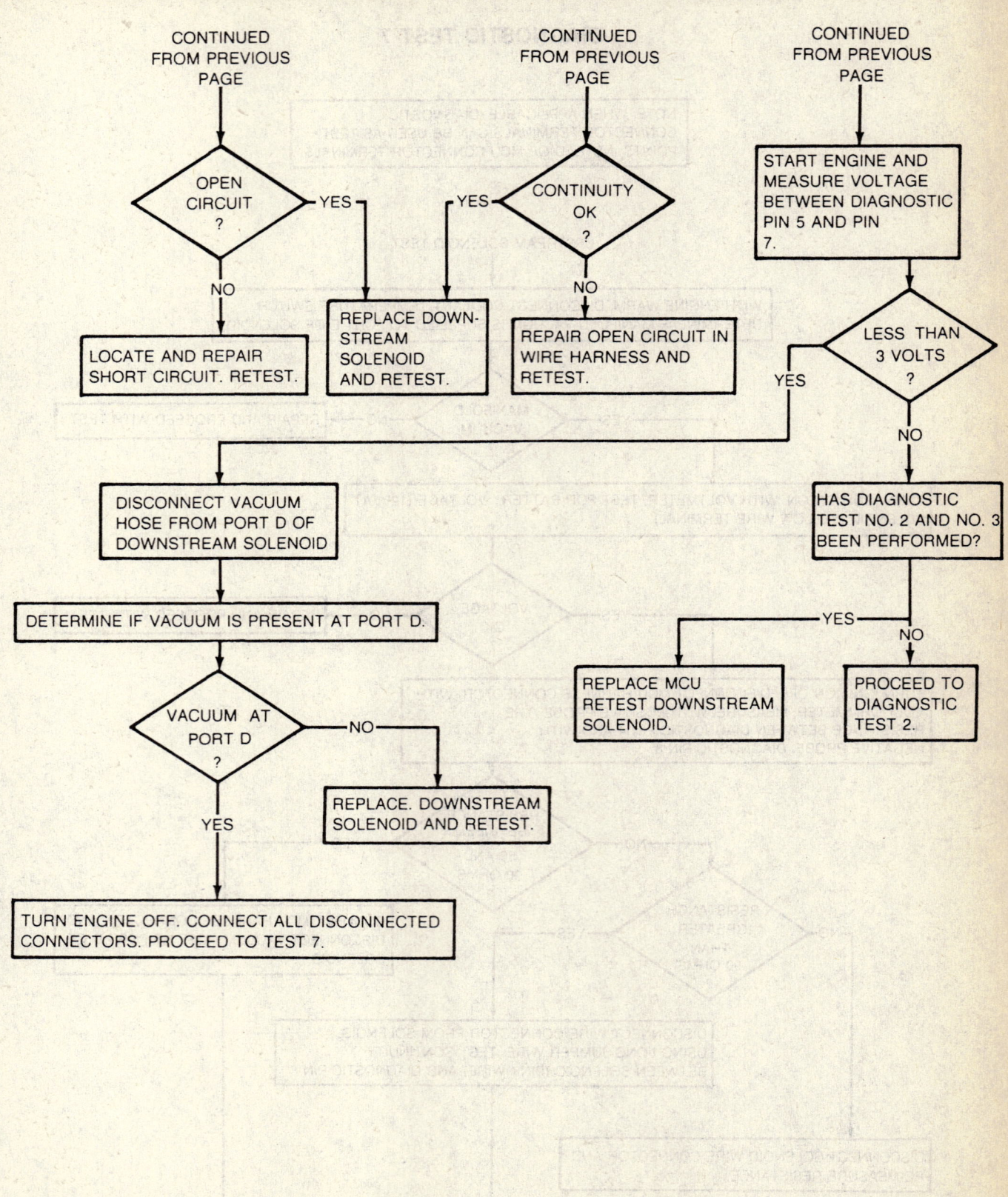

4-33

4 EMISSION CONTROLS

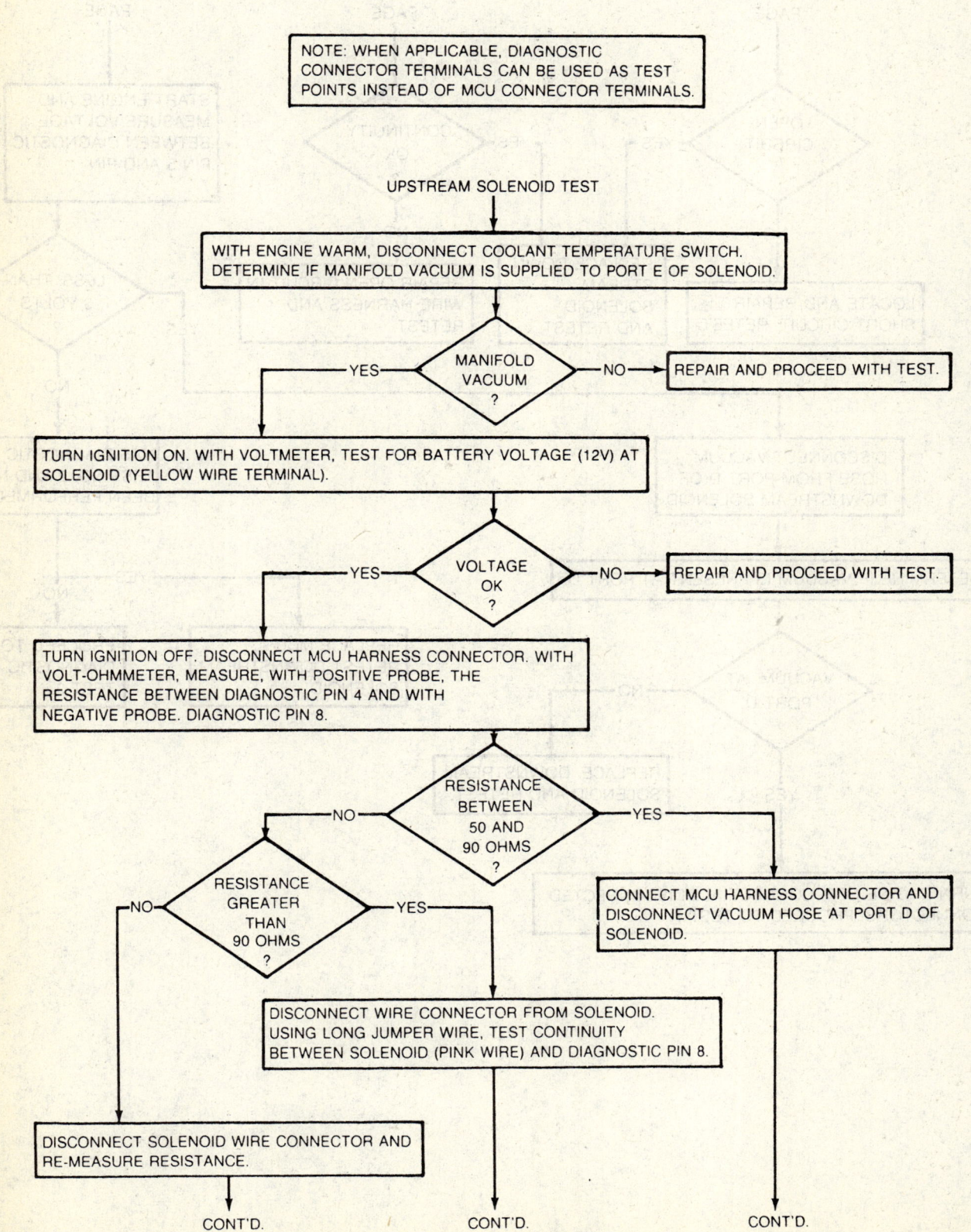

4-34

EMISSION CONTROLS 4

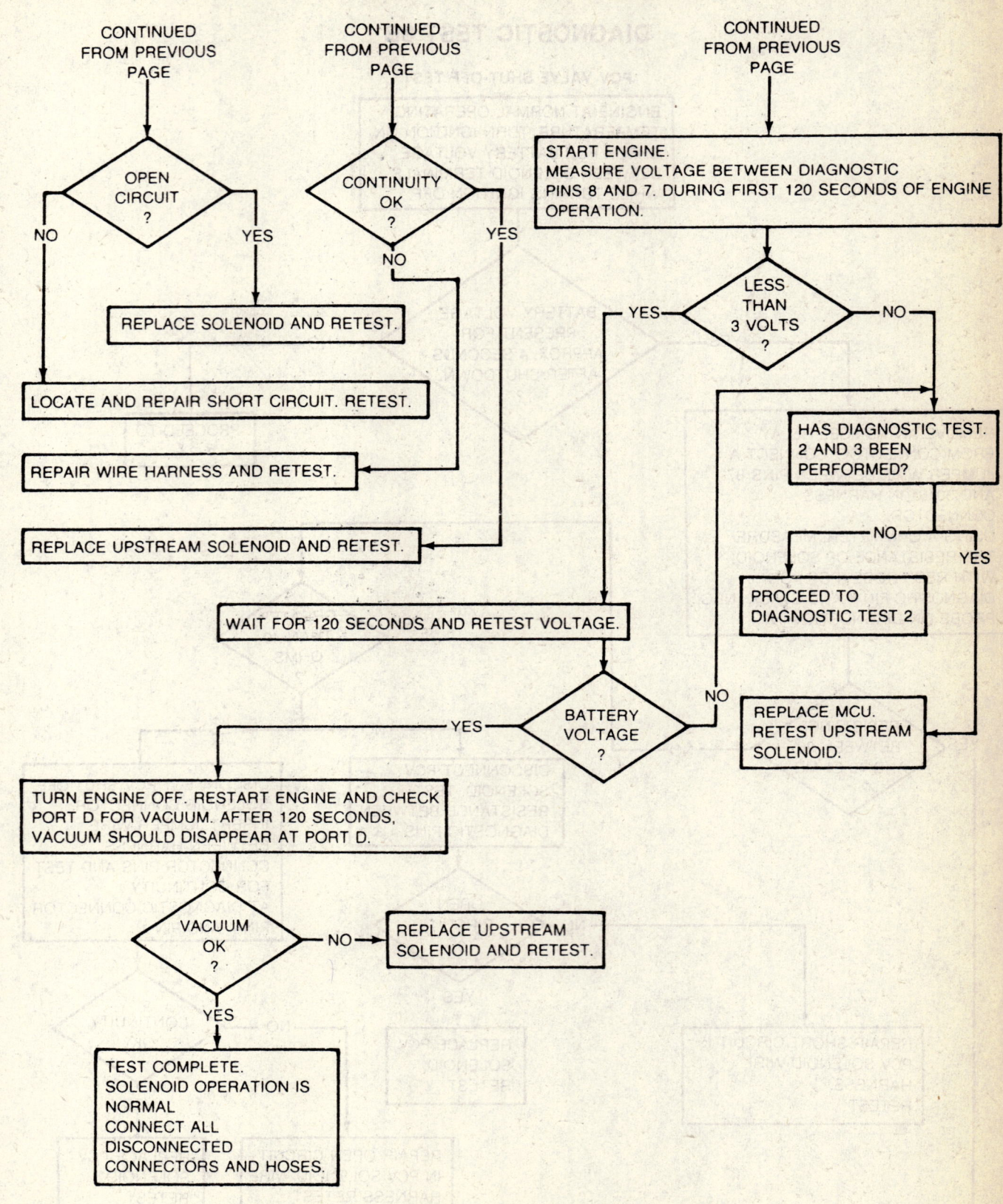

4-35

4 EMISSION CONTROLS

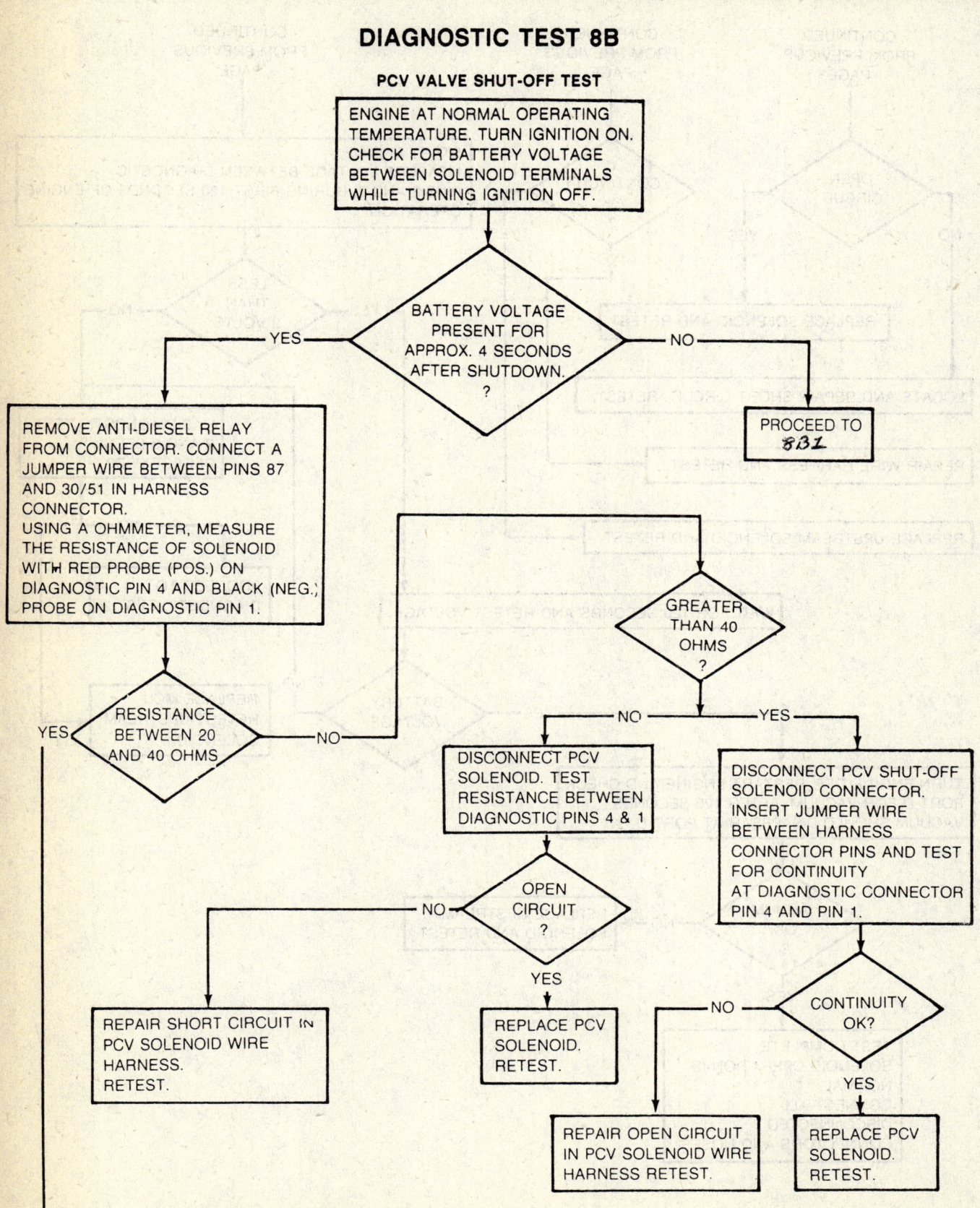

EMISSION CONTROLS 4

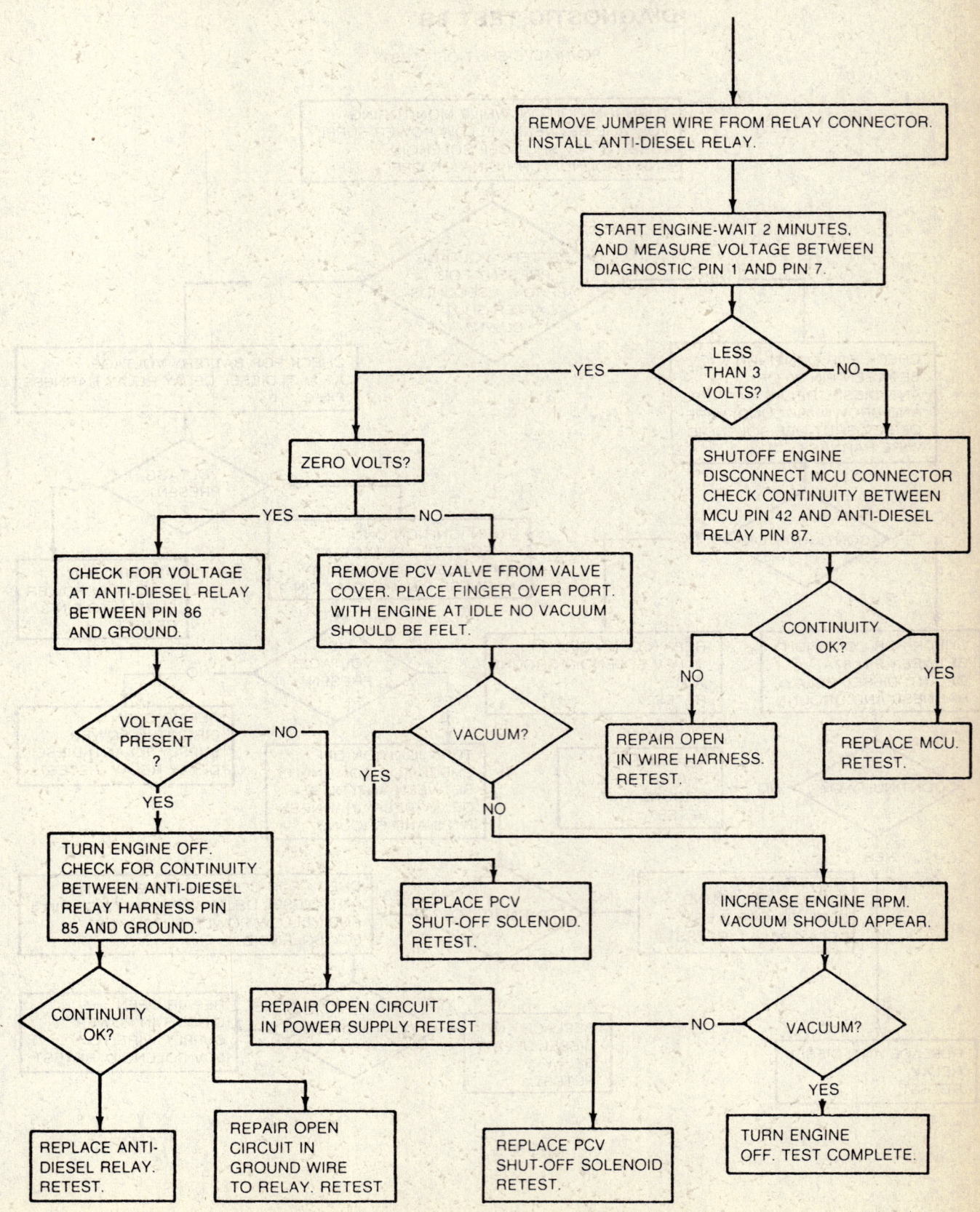

4-37

4 EMISSION CONTROLS

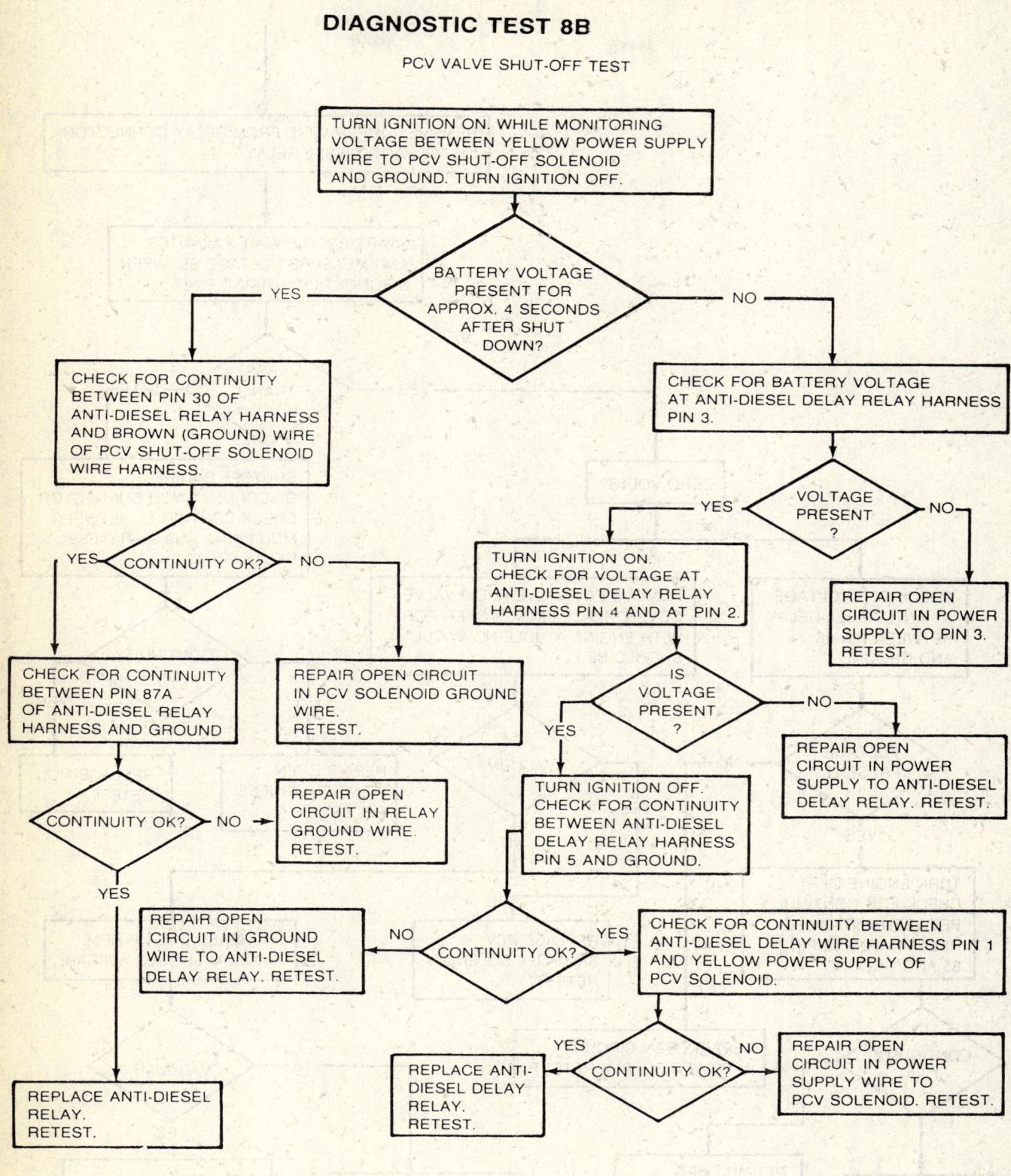

EMISSION CONTROLS 4

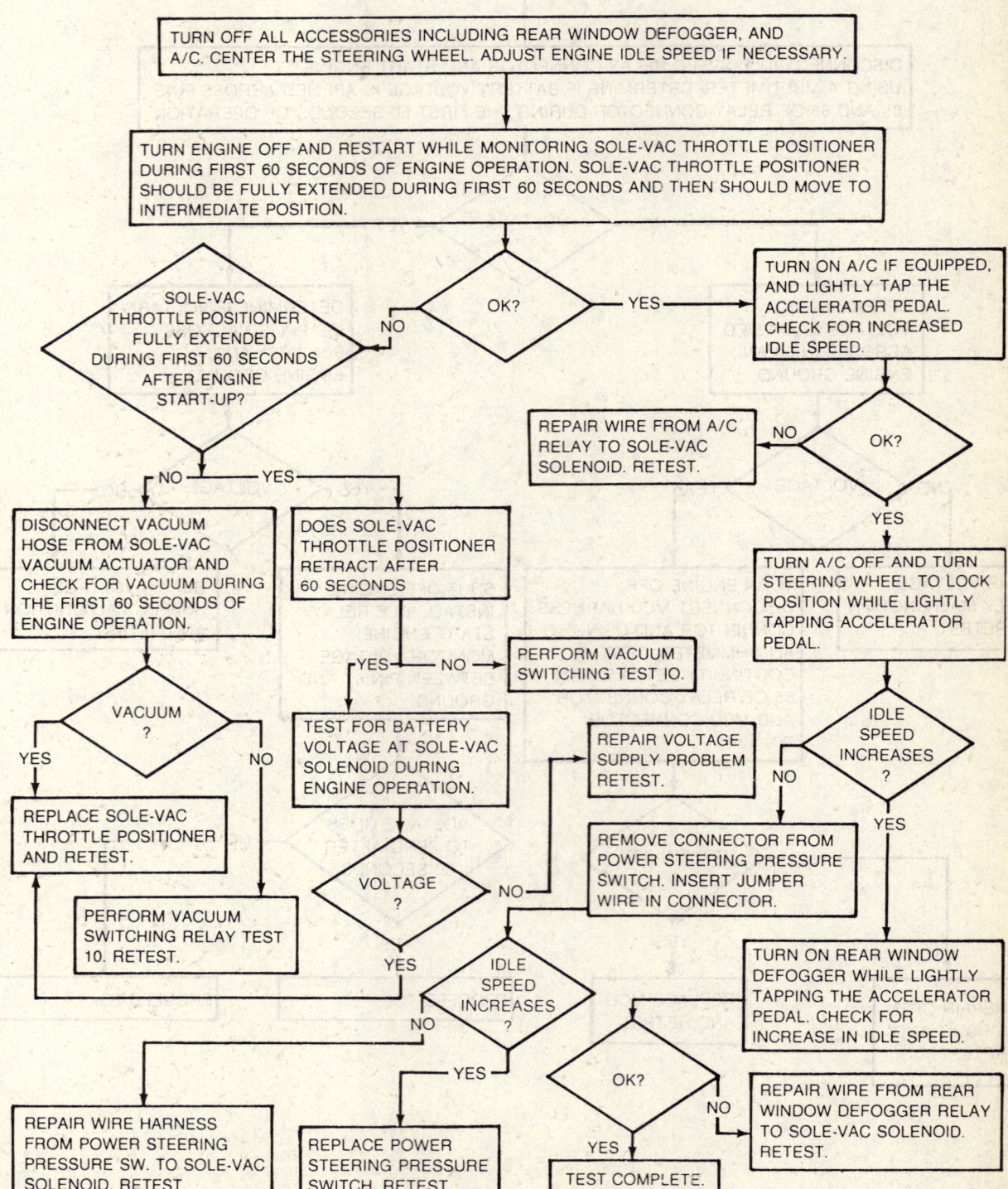

DIAGNOSTIC TEST 9
IDLE SPEED CONTROL SYSTEM TEST

4-39

4 EMISSION CONTROLS

DIAGNOSTIC TEST 10

SOLE-VAC VACUUM SWITCHING RELAY TEST

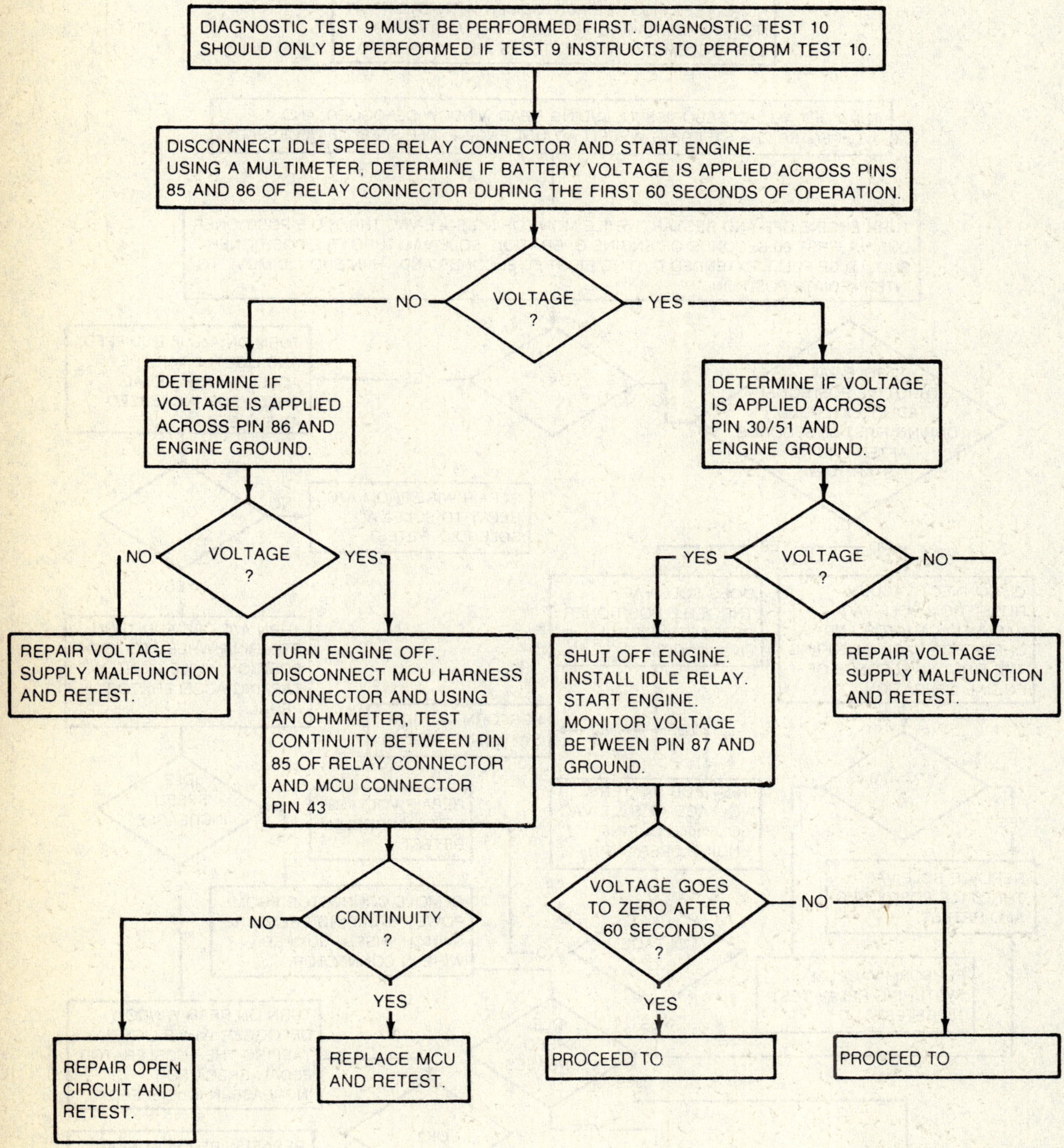

DIAGNOSTIC TEST 9 MUST BE PERFORMED FIRST. DIAGNOSTIC TEST 10 SHOULD ONLY BE PERFORMED IF TEST 9 INSTRUCTS TO PERFORM TEST 10.

↓

DISCONNECT IDLE SPEED RELAY CONNECTOR AND START ENGINE. USING A MULTIMETER, DETERMINE IF BATTERY VOLTAGE IS APPLIED ACROSS PINS 85 AND 86 OF RELAY CONNECTOR DURING THE FIRST 60 SECONDS OF OPERATION.

↓

VOLTAGE?

- NO → DETERMINE IF VOLTAGE IS APPLIED ACROSS PIN 86 AND ENGINE GROUND.
  - **VOLTAGE?**
    - NO → REPAIR VOLTAGE SUPPLY MALFUNCTION AND RETEST.
    - YES → TURN ENGINE OFF. DISCONNECT MCU HARNESS CONNECTOR AND USING AN OHMMETER, TEST CONTINUITY BETWEEN PIN 85 OF RELAY CONNECTOR AND MCU CONNECTOR PIN 43
      - **CONTINUITY?**
        - NO → REPAIR OPEN CIRCUIT AND RETEST.
        - YES → REPLACE MCU AND RETEST.

- YES → DETERMINE IF VOLTAGE IS APPLIED ACROSS PIN 30/51 AND ENGINE GROUND.
  - **VOLTAGE?**
    - YES → SHUT OFF ENGINE. INSTALL IDLE RELAY. START ENGINE. MONITOR VOLTAGE BETWEEN PIN 87 AND GROUND.
      - **VOLTAGE GOES TO ZERO AFTER 60 SECONDS?**
        - YES → PROCEED TO
        - NO → PROCEED TO
    - NO → REPAIR VOLTAGE SUPPLY MALFUNCTION AND RETEST.

4-40

EMISSION CONTROLS 4

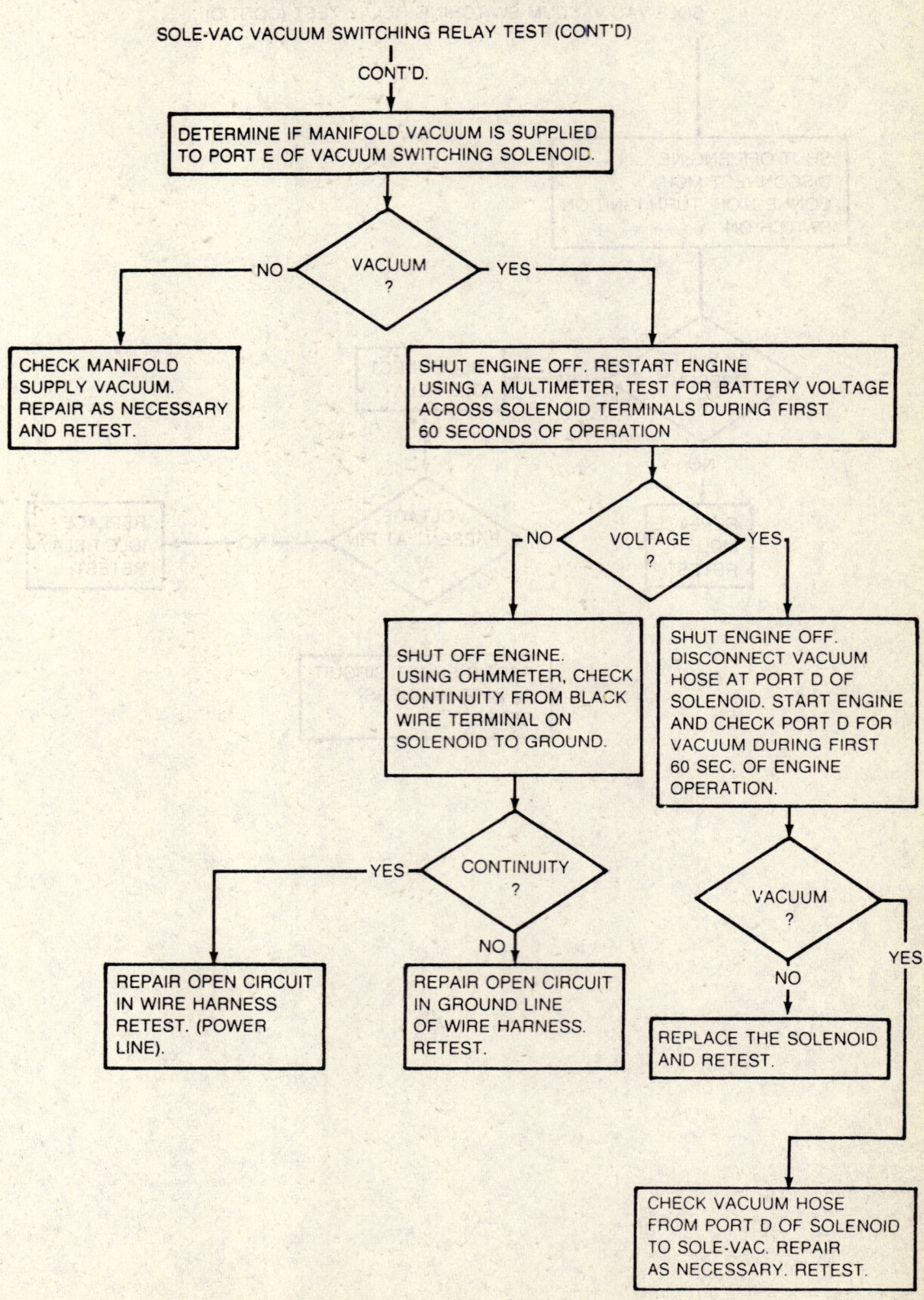

DIAGNOSTIC TEST 10 (CONT'D)

SOLE-VAC VACUUM SWITCHING RELAY TEST (CONT'D)

4-41

4 EMISSION CONTROLS

DIAGNOSTIC TEST 10 (CONT'D)
SOLE-VAC VACUUM SWITCHING RELAY TEST (CONT'D)

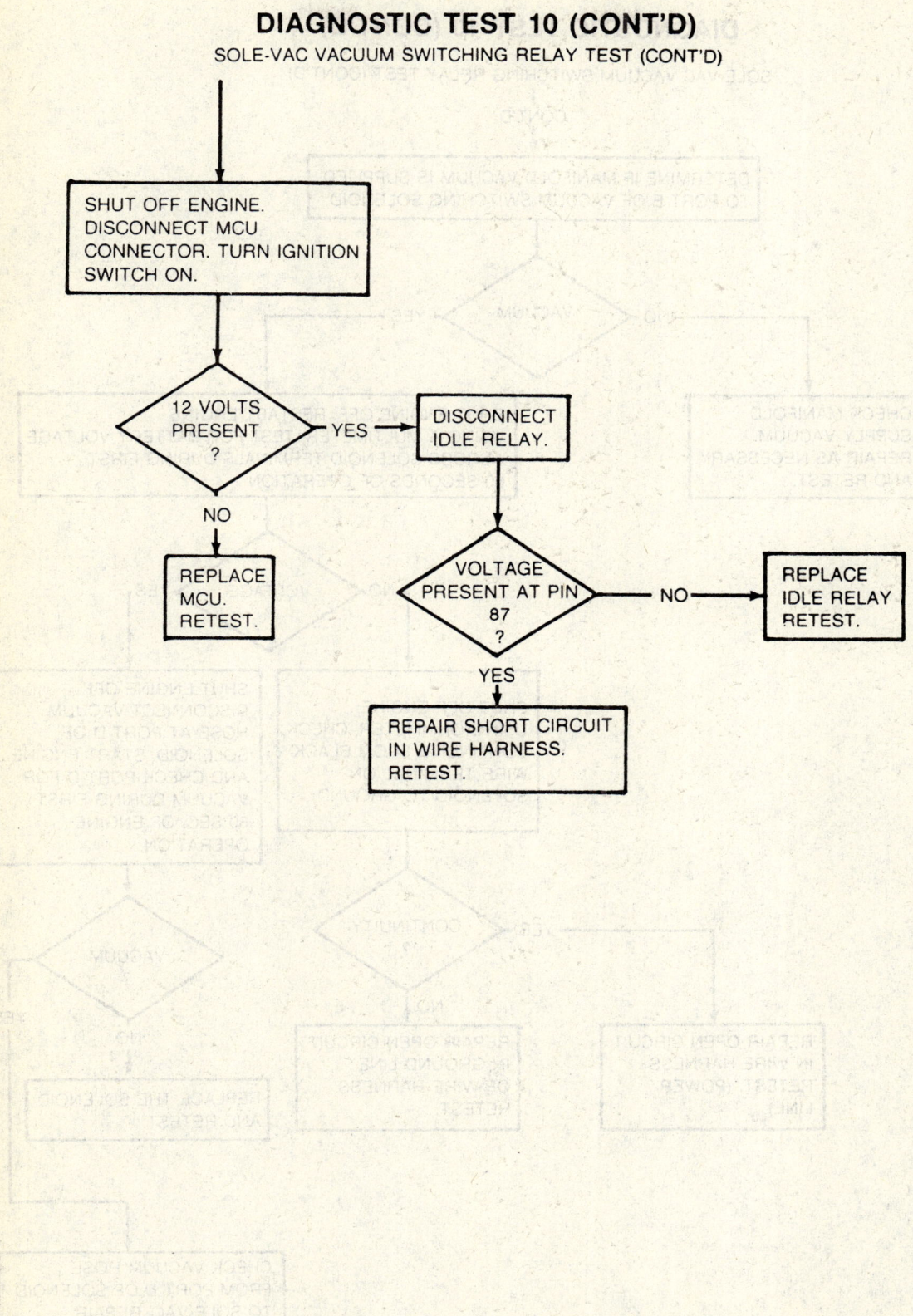

4-42

EMISSION CONTROLS 4

CEC SYSTEM

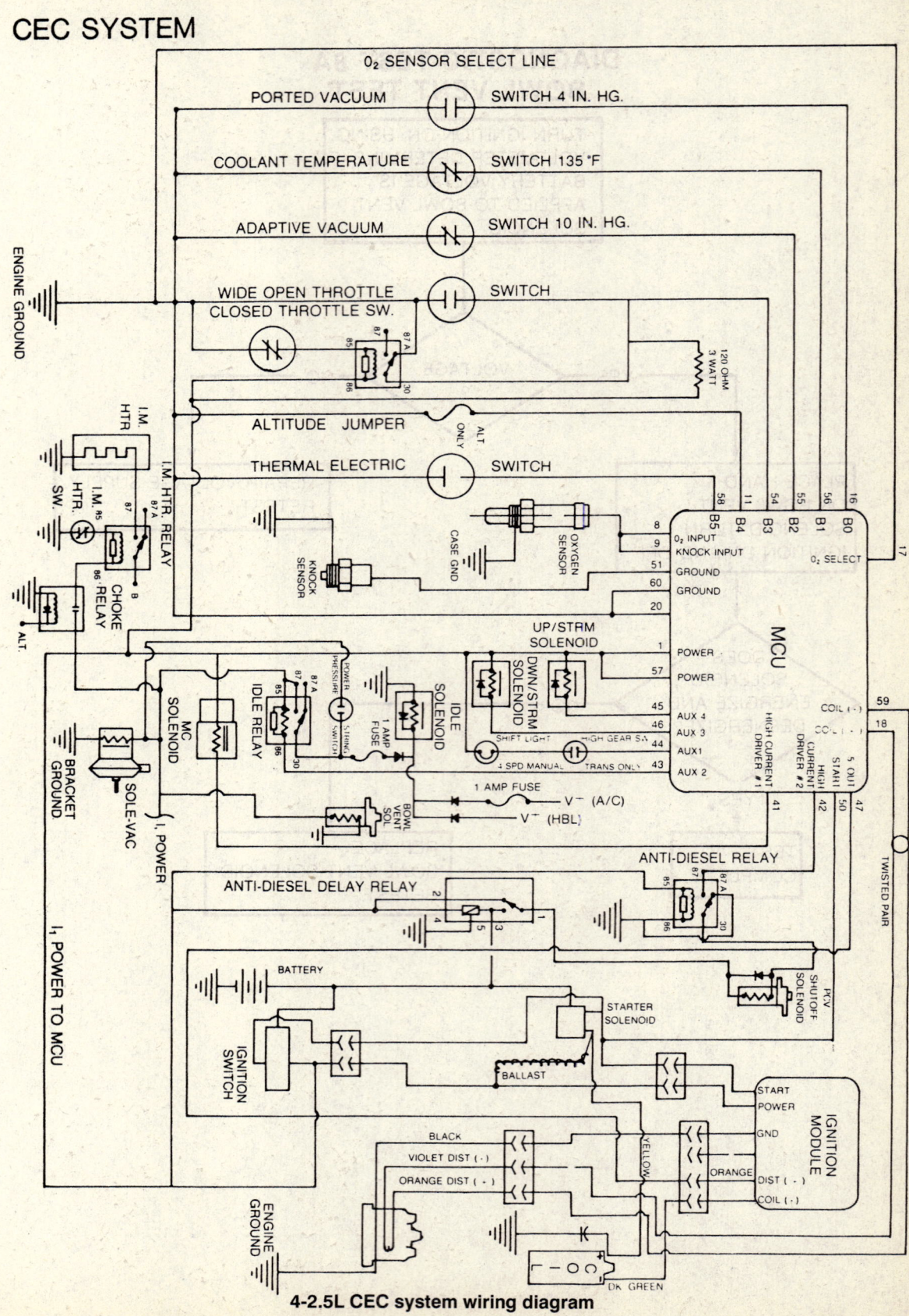

4-2.5L CEC system wiring diagram

4-43

4 EMISSION CONTROLS

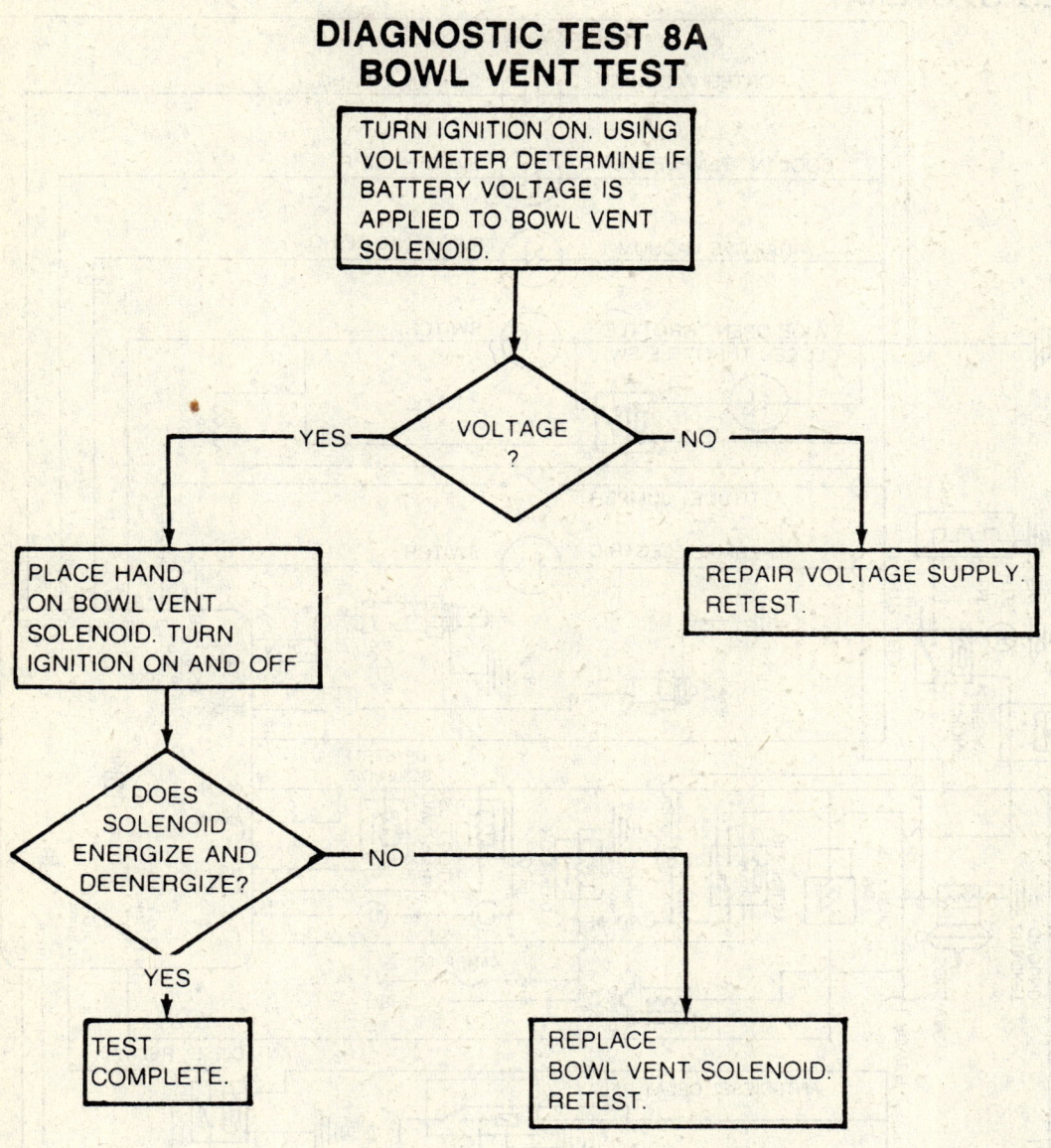

4-44

EMISSION CONTROLS 4

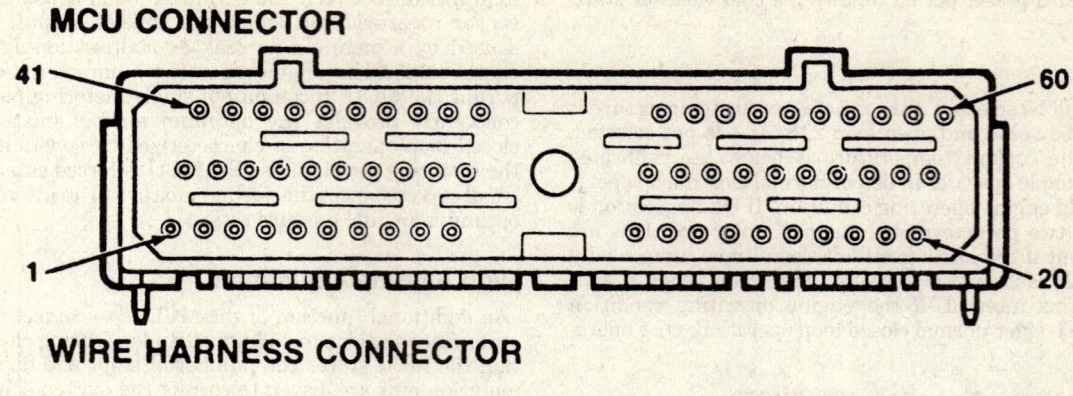

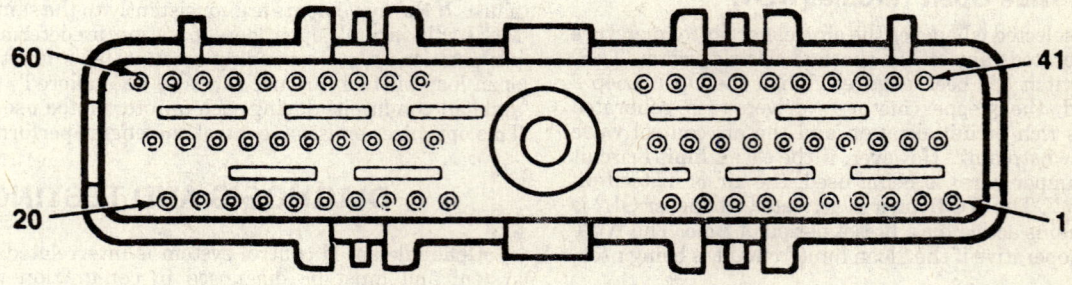

MCU wiring harness connector

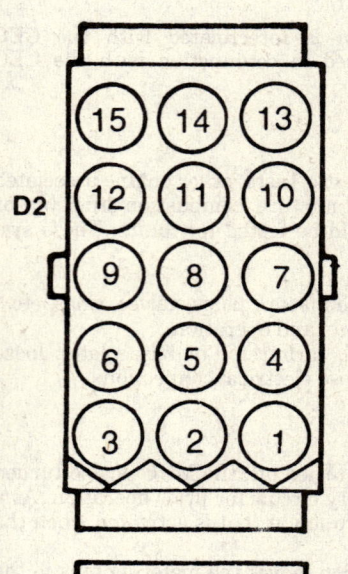

PIN FUNCTION

1 CHECK ENGINE LIGHT
2 NOT USED
3 NOT USED
4 SWITCHED B+
5 NOT USED
6 TEST CODE
7 GROUND
8 NOT USED
9 NOT USED
10 DIVERTER SOLENOID
11 EGR SOLENOID
12 NOT USED
13 INTAKE MANIFOLD HEATER RELAY
14 MC SOLENOID
15 NOT USED

1 NOT USED
2 CHOKE
3 GROUND
4 NOT USED
5 INTAKE MANIFOLD HEATER VOLTAGE
6 NOT USED

6-CYL fuel feedback diagnostic connector

4-45

4 EMISSION CONTROLS

not permitted for a preset period following a cold weather start-up.

Open Loop 1

Open Loop 1 will be selected if the air cleaner air temperature is above a calibrated value and open loop 2, 3, or 4 is not selected, and if the engine coolant temperature is below the calibrated value. The OL1 mode operates in lieu of normal closed loop operation during a cold engine operating condition. If OL1 operation is selected, one of two predetermined stepper motor positions are chosen, dependent if the altitude circuit (lean limit) jumper wire is installed. With each engine start-up, a start-up timer is activated. During this interval, if the engine operating condition would otherwise trigger normal closed loop operation, OL1 operation is selected.

Open Loop 2, Wide Open Throttle (WOT)

Open Loop 2 is selected whenever the air cleaner air temperature is above the calibrated value of the thermal electric switch (TES) and the WOT switch has been engaged. When the Open Loop 2 mode is selected, the stepper motor is driven to a calibrated number of steps rich of initialization and the air control valve switches air "downstream". However, if the "lean limit" circuit (with altitude jumper wire) is being used, the air is instead directed "upstream". The WOT timer is activated whenever OL2 is selected and remains active for a preset period of time. The WOT timer remains inoperative if the "lean limit" circuit is being used.

Open Loop 3

Open Loop 3 is selected when the ignition advance vacuum level falls below a predetermined level. When the OL3 mode is selected, the engine rpm is also determined. If the rpm (tach) voltage is greater than the calibrated value, an engine deceleration condition is assumed to exist. If the rpm (tach) voltage is less than the calibrated value, an engine idle speed condition is assumed to exist.

Open Loop 4

Open Loop 4 is selected whenever manifold vacuum falls below a predetermined level. During OL4 operation, the stepper motor is positioned at the initialization position. Air injection is switched "upstream" during OL4 operation. However, air is switch "downstream" if the extended OL4 timer is activated and if the "lean limit" circuit is not being used (without altitude jumper wire). Air is also switch "downstream" if the WOT timer is activated.

Closed Loop

Closed loop operation is selected after either OL1, OL2, OL3 or OL4 modes have been selected and the start-up timer has timed out. Air injection is routed "downstream" during closed loop operation. The predetermined "lean" air/fuel mixture ceiling is selected for a preset length of time at the onset of closed loop operation.

Closed Loop Operation

The CEC system controls the air/fuel ratio with movable air metering pins, visible from the top of the carburetor air horn, that are driven by the stepper motor. The stepper motor moves the metering pins in increments or small steps via electrical impulses generated by the MCU. The MCU causes the stepper motor to drive the metering pins to a "richer" or "leaner" position in reaction to the voltage input from the oxygen content present in the exhaust gas. Because the content of oxygen in the exhaust gas indicates the completeness of the combustion process, it is a reliable indicator of the air/fuel mixture that is entering the combustion chamber.

Because the oxygen sensor only reacts to oxygen, any air leak or malfunction between the carburetor and sensor may cause the sensor to provide an erroneous voltage output. This could be caused by a manifold air leak or malfunctioning secondary air check value. The engine operation characteristics never quite permit the MCU to compute a single metering pin position that constantly provides the optimum air/fuel mixture. Therefore, closed loop operation is characterized by constant movement of the metering pins because the MCU is forced constantly to make small corrections in the air/fuel mixture in an attempt to create an optimum air/fuel mixture ratio.

High Altitude Adjustment

An additional function of the MCU is to correct for a change in ambient conditions (e.g., high altitude). During closed loop operation the MCU stores the number of steps and direction that the metering pins are driven to correct the oxygen content of the exhaust. If the movements are consistently to the same position, the MCU will vary all open loop operation predetermined metering pin positions a corresponding amount. This function allows the open loop air/fuel mixture ratios to be "tailored" to the existing ambient conditions during each uninterrupted use of the system. This optimizes emission control and engine performance.

DIAGNOSIS AND TESTING

- The idle speed control system is interrelated with the CEC system and must be diagnosed in conjunction with the CEC System.
- The electronic ignition retard function of the ignition control module is interrelated with CEC System and must be diagnosed in conjunction with CEC System. Refer to Diagnostic Test 4 if a malfunction occurs.
- The air injection system is interrelated with the CEC System and must be diagnosed in conjunction with the CEC System.

Preliminary Tests

Before performing the Diagnostic Tests, other engine associated systems that can affect air/fuel mixture, combustion efficiency or exhaust gas composition should be tested for faults. These systems include:
1. Basic carburetor adjustments.
2. Mechanical engine operation (spark plugs, valves, rings, etc.).
3. Ignition system components and operation.
4. Gaskets (intake manifold, carburetor or base plate); loose vacuum hoses or fittings, or loose electrical connections.

Initialization

When the ignition system is turned off, the MCU is also turned off. It has no long term memory circuit for prior operation. As a result, it has an initialization function that is activated when the ignition switch is turned ON.

The MCU initialization function moves the metering pins to the predetermined starting position by first driving them all the way to the rich end stop and then driving them in the lean direction by a predetermined number of steps. No matter where they were before initialization, they will be at the correct position at the end of every initialization period. Because each open loop operation metering pin position is dependent on the initialization function, this function is the first test in the diagnostic procedure.

NOTE: The CEC System should be considered as a possible source of trouble for engine performance, fuel economy and exhaust emission complaints only after normal tests that would apply to an automobile without the system have been performed.

EMISSION CONTROLS 4

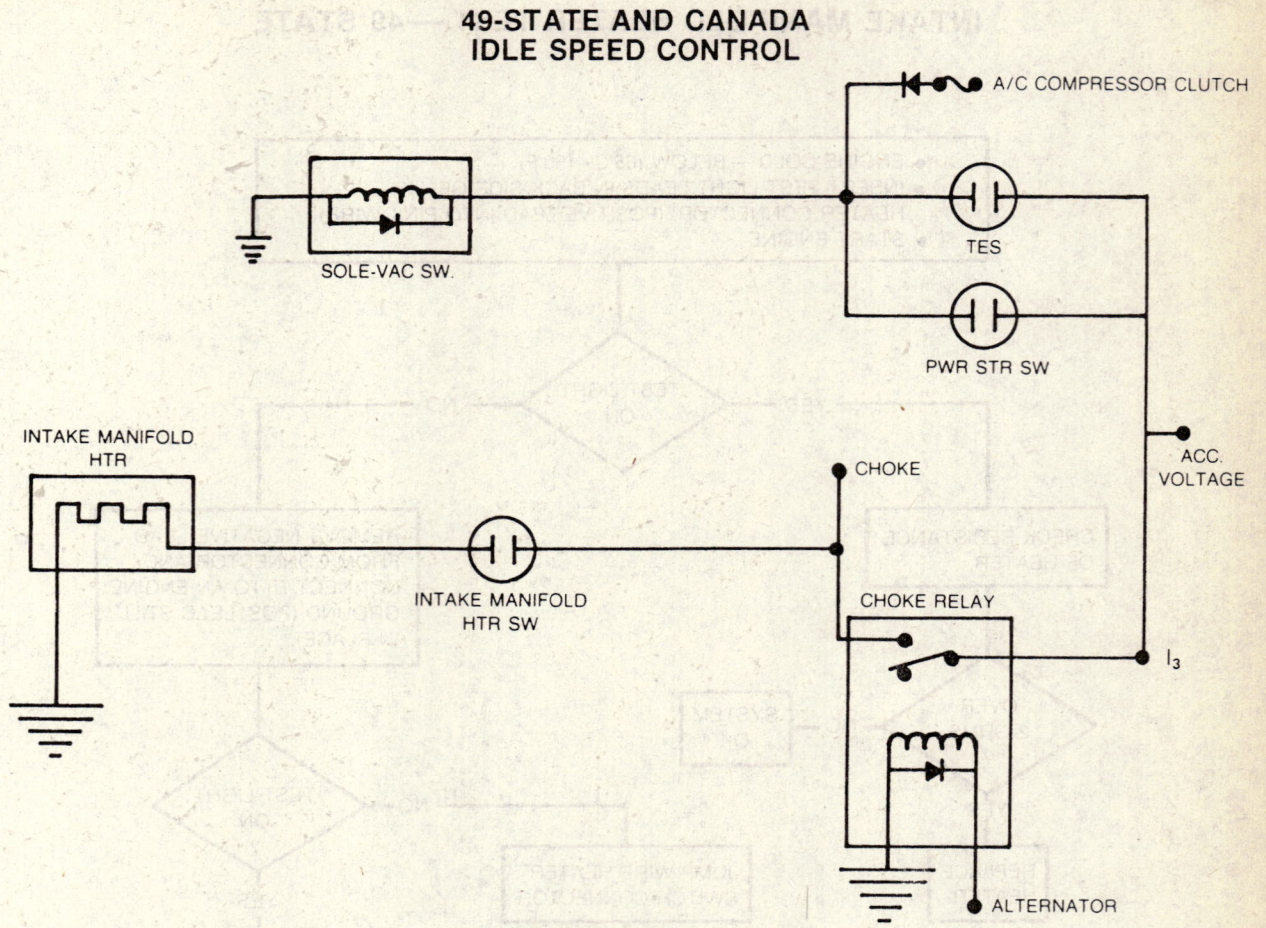

49-STATE AND CANADA IDLE SPEED CONTROL

Jeep Self-Diagnostic System

Late model Jeep vehicles equipped with a six cylinder engine and California emissions package have a self-diagnostic system with a CHECK ENGINE light mounted in the instrument panel. The self-diagnostic system is designed to detect problems most likely to occur within the various system components.

When a jumper wire is connected between the trouble code test terminals 6 and 7 of the 15-terminal diagnostic connector (D2), the CHECK ENGINE light will flash a trouble code or codes that indicate a problem area. For a bulb and system check, the CHECK ENGINE light will illuminate when the ignition switch is ON and the engine not started. If the test terminals are then grounded, the light will flash a code 12 that indicates the self-diagnostic system is operational. A code 12 consists of one flash, followed by a short pause, then two more flashes in quick succession. After a longer pause, the code will repeat two more times.

When the engine is started, the CHECK ENGINE light will remain ON momentarily and then be turned off. If the CHECK ENGINE light remains on, the self-diagnostic system has detected a problem. If the trouble code test terminals are then grounded, the trouble code will be flashed three times; if more than one trouble code is stored, each will be flashed three more times in numerical order, from the lowest to the highest numbered code. This trouble code series will repeat as long as the test terminals are grounded.

A trouble code indicates a problem in a particular circuit or component. Trouble code 14, for example, indicates a problem in the coolant sensor circuit. It should be noted that the self-diagnostic system doesn't pinpoint where the problem is in the coolant sensor circuit, which includes the coolant sensor, connector, wire harness and the electronic control unit itself. The following diagnostic charts contain procedures for isolating the problem to a particular point in the circuit to avoid the unnecessary replacement of working components. A diagnosis chart is provided for each trouble code.

Because the self-diagnostic system does not detect all possible problems, the absence of a trouble code does not necessarily mean the system is functioning normally. The System Performance Test should be performed when the self-diagnostic system does not indicate a problem, but the system operation is suspect.

All system connectors in the engine compartment are sealed against debris and moisture. Because the system operates on low voltage and low current, corrosion on the connectors can cause problems. Before repairing or replacing any component, disconnect the appropriate connector(s) and check for proper installation, bent, broken or dirty terminals or mating tabs. Clean, straighten or replace the connectors as required, then reconnect everything and recheck the system operation to see if the problem has been corrected. The system should be considered as a possible cause of trouble only after normal engine diagnosis for ignition timing, carburetor and idle speed adjustments has been performed. The electronic control module (ECM) is located in the pas-

4 EMISSION CONTROLS

INTAKE MANIFOLD HEATER TEST — 49 STATE

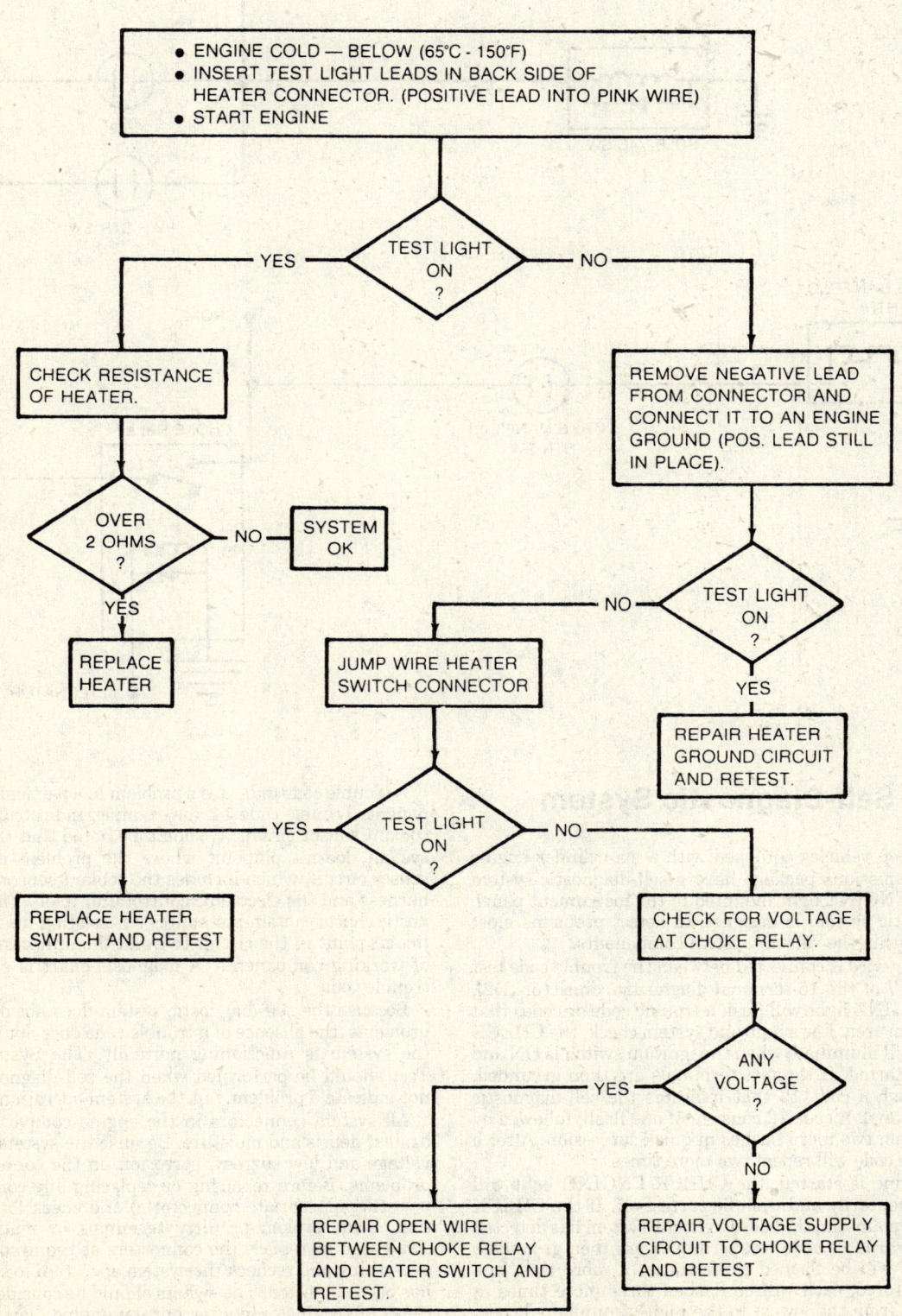

4-48

EMISSION CONTROLS 4

INTAKE MANIFOLD HEATER TEST — CALIFORNIA

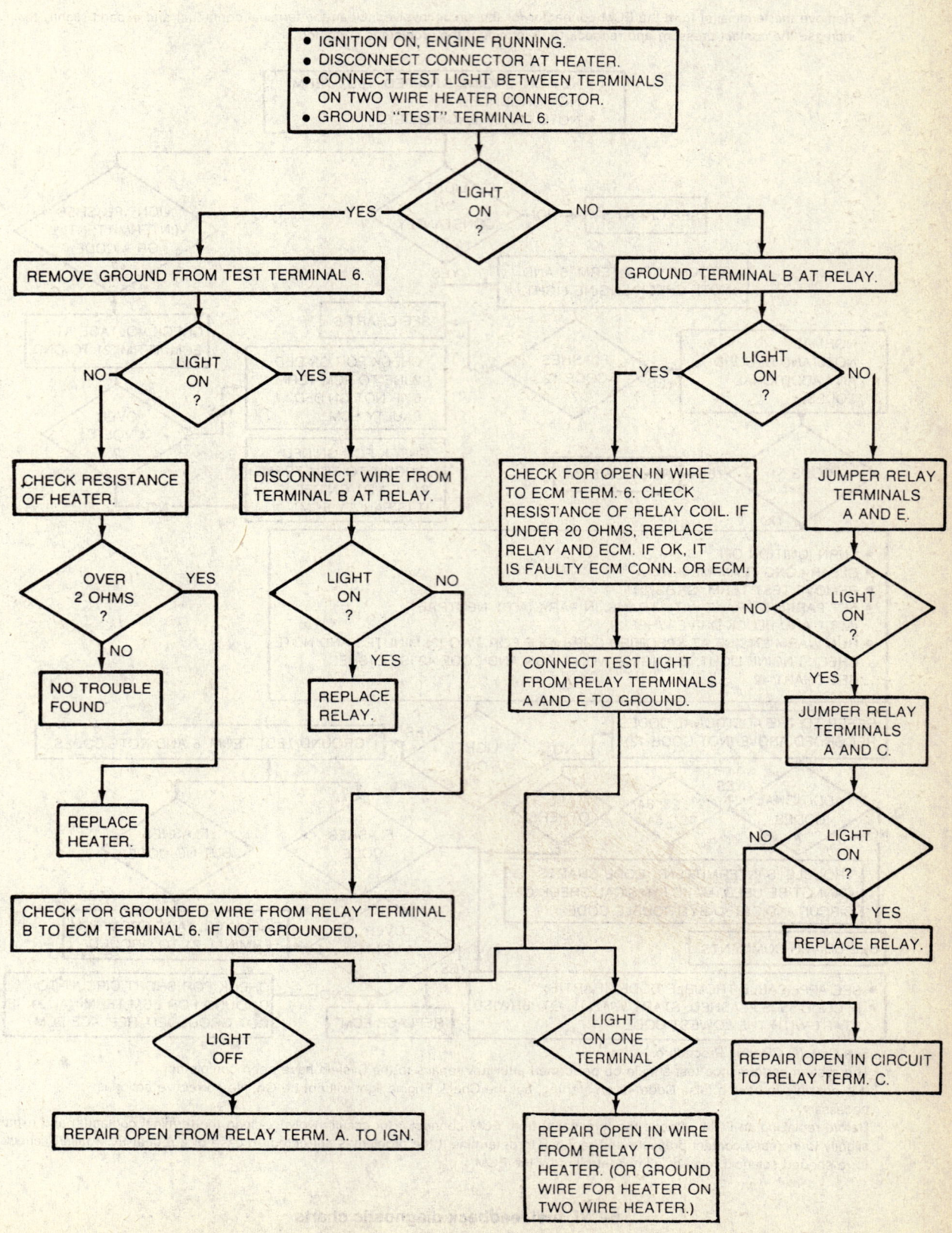

4-49

4 EMISSION CONTROLS

DIAGNOSTIC CIRCUIT TEST

- Remove the terminal(s) from the ECM connector for the circuit involved, clean the terminal contact(s) and expand slightly to increase the contact pressure and recheck to determine if the problem is corrected.

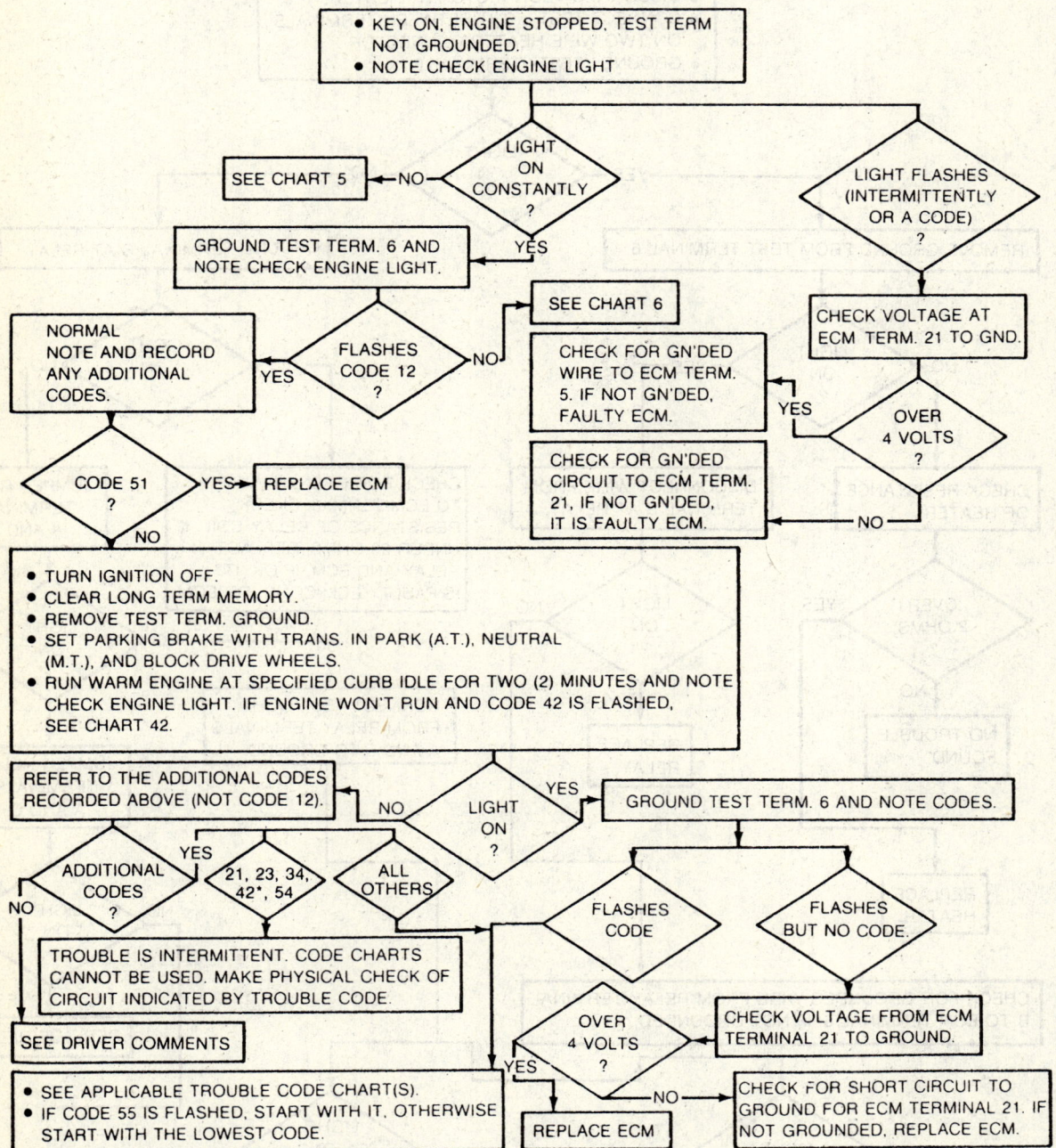

See Code(s) Clearing Procedure.
The system performance test should be performed after any repairs to the System have been completed.
* It is possible to have a false Code 42 on starting, but the Check Engine light will not be On. No corrective action is necessary.
Before replacing an ECM, remove the terminal(s) from ECM connector for circuit involved, clean the terminal contact(s) and expand slightly to increase contact pressure and recheck to determine if the problem is corrected. In case of a repeat ECM failure, check for a shorted solenoid relay or relay controlled by the ECM.

6-CYL fuel feedback diagnostic charts

EMISSION CONTROLS 4

DRIVER COMMENTS

ENGINE PERFORMANCE PROBLEM (ODOR, SURGE, FUEL ECONOMY ...)
EMISSION PROBLEM

IF THE CHECK ENGINE LIGHT IS NOT ON, NORMAL CHECKS THAT WOULD BE PERFORMED ON THE VEHICLE WITHOUT THE SYSTEM SHOULD BE DONE FIRST.

IF THE ALTERNATOR OR COOLANT LIGHT IS ON WITH THE CHECK ENGINE LIGHT, THEY SHOULD BE DIAGNOSED FIRST.

INSPECT FOR POOR CONNECTIONS AT COOLANT SENSOR, MC SOLENOID, ETC., AND POOR OR LOOSE VACUUM HOSES AND CONNECTIONS. REPAIR AS NECESSARY.

- Intermittent Check Engine light but no trouble code stored.
  - Check for intermittent connection in circuit from:
    - Ignition coil to ground and arcing at spark plug wires or plugs.
    - ECM Voltage Supply Terminals.
    - ECM Ground Terminals.
  - Loss of long-term memory.
    Grounding dwell lead for 10 seconds with test lead ungrounded should give Code 23, which should be retained after the engine is stopped and the ignition turned to RUN position.
    If it is not, ECM is defective.
  - EST wires should be kept away from the spark plug wires, distributor housing, coil and alternator. Wires from ECM Term. 13 to dist. and the shield around EST wires should have a good ground.
  - Open diode across A/C compressor clutch.

- Stalling, Rough Idle, Dieseling or Improper Idle Speed.

- Detonation (spark knock)
  Check: MAP or Vacuum Sensor output.
          EGR operation.
          TPS enrichment operation.
          HEI operation.

- Poor Performance and/or Fuel Economy.
  See EST diagnosis.

- Poor Full Throttle Performance
  See Chart 4 if equipped with TPS.

- Intermittent No-start
  - Incorrect pickup coil or ignition coil.
  - Intermittent ground connections on ECM.

- ALL OTHER COMPLAINTS
  Make system performance test on warm engine.
  (upper radiator hose hot).

The System Performance Test should be performed after any repairs to the system has been made.

4-51

4 EMISSION CONTROLS

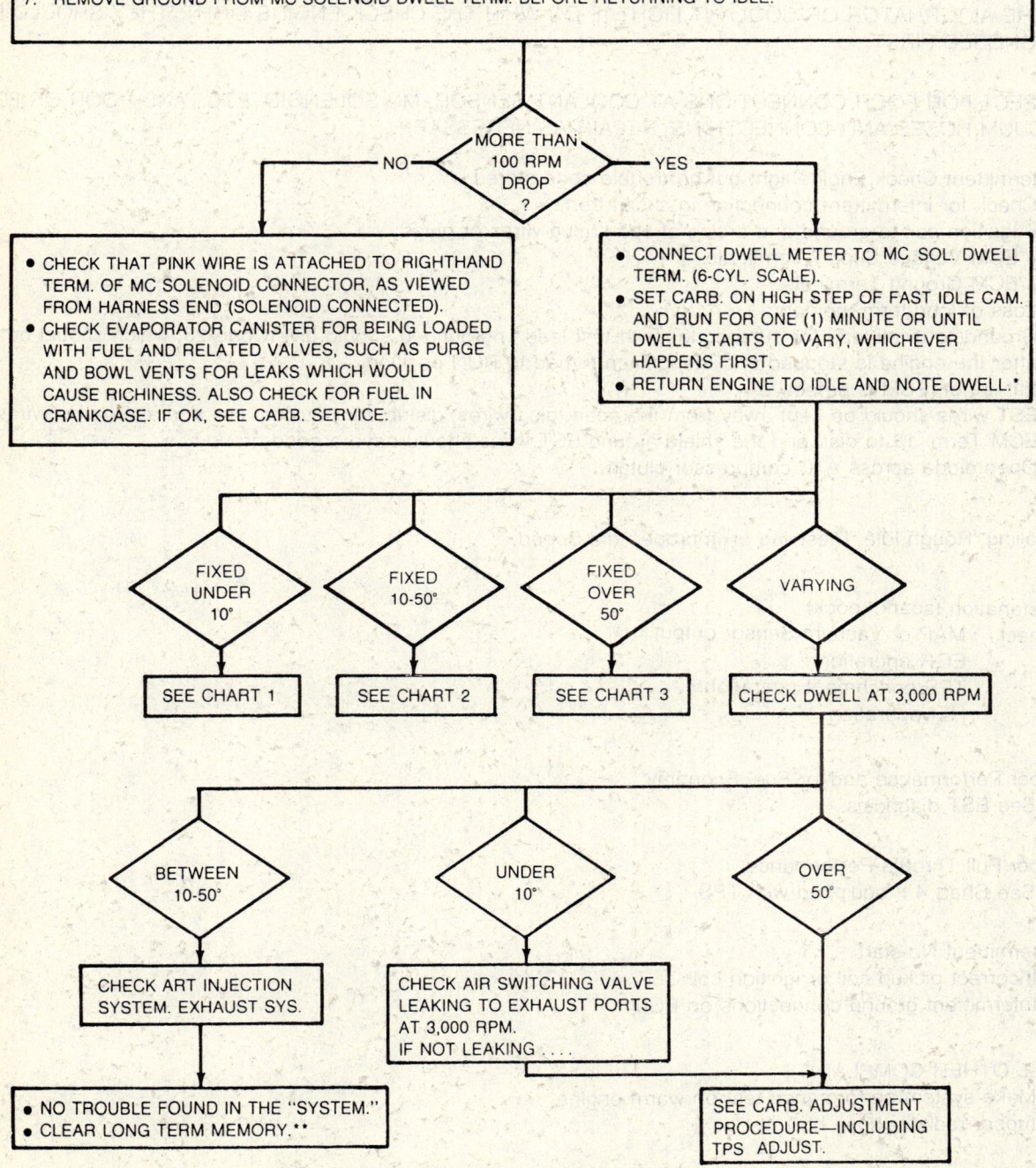

SYSTEM PERFORMANCE TEST

1. START ENGINE.
2. GROUND TEST TERMINAL 6. (MUST NOT BE GROUNDED BEFORE ENGINE IS STARTED.)
3. DISCONNECT PURGE HOSE FROM CANISTER AND PLUG IT. REMOVE, DISCONNECT BOWL VENT AT CARBURETOR.
4. CONNECT TACHOMETER.
5. DISCONNECT MIXTURE CONTROL (MC) SOLENOID AND GROUND MC SOLENOID DWELL TERM.
6. RUN ENGINE AT 3,000 RPM AND, WHILE KEEPING THROTTLE CONSTANT, CONNECT MC SOLENOID AND NOTE RPM.
7. REMOVE GROUND FROM MC SOLENOID DWELL TERM. BEFORE RETURNING TO IDLE.

MORE THAN 100 RPM DROP?

NO:
- CHECK THAT PINK WIRE IS ATTACHED TO RIGHTHAND TERM. OF MC SOLENOID CONNECTOR, AS VIEWED FROM HARNESS END (SOLENOID CONNECTED).
- CHECK EVAPORATOR CANISTER FOR BEING LOADED WITH FUEL AND RELATED VALVES, SUCH AS PURGE AND BOWL VENTS FOR LEAKS WHICH WOULD CAUSE RICHNESS. ALSO CHECK FOR FUEL IN CRANKCASE. IF OK, SEE CARB. SERVICE.

YES:
- CONNECT DWELL METER TO MC SOL. DWELL TERM. (6-CYL. SCALE).
- SET CARB. ON HIGH STEP OF FAST IDLE CAM. AND RUN FOR ONE (1) MINUTE OR UNTIL DWELL STARTS TO VARY, WHICHEVER HAPPENS FIRST.
- RETURN ENGINE TO IDLE AND NOTE DWELL.*

- FIXED UNDER 10° → SEE CHART 1
- FIXED 10-50° → SEE CHART 2
- FIXED OVER 50° → SEE CHART 3
- VARYING → CHECK DWELL AT 3,000 RPM
  - BETWEEN 10-50° → CHECK ART INJECTION SYSTEM. EXHAUST SYS.
    - NO TROUBLE FOUND IN THE "SYSTEM."
    - CLEAR LONG TERM MEMORY.**
  - UNDER 10° → CHECK AIR SWITCHING VALVE LEAKING TO EXHAUST PORTS AT 3,000 RPM. IF NOT LEAKING ....
  - OVER 50° → SEE CARB. ADJUSTMENT PROCEDURE—INCLUDING TPS ADJUST.

*Oxygen sensors may cool off at idle the and the dwell change from varying to fixed. If this happens, running the engine at fast idle will warm it up again.
**See Code(s) Clearing Procedure.

EMISSION CONTROLS 4

CHART NO. 1
DWELL FIXED UNDER 10°
(LEAN EXHAUST INDICATION)

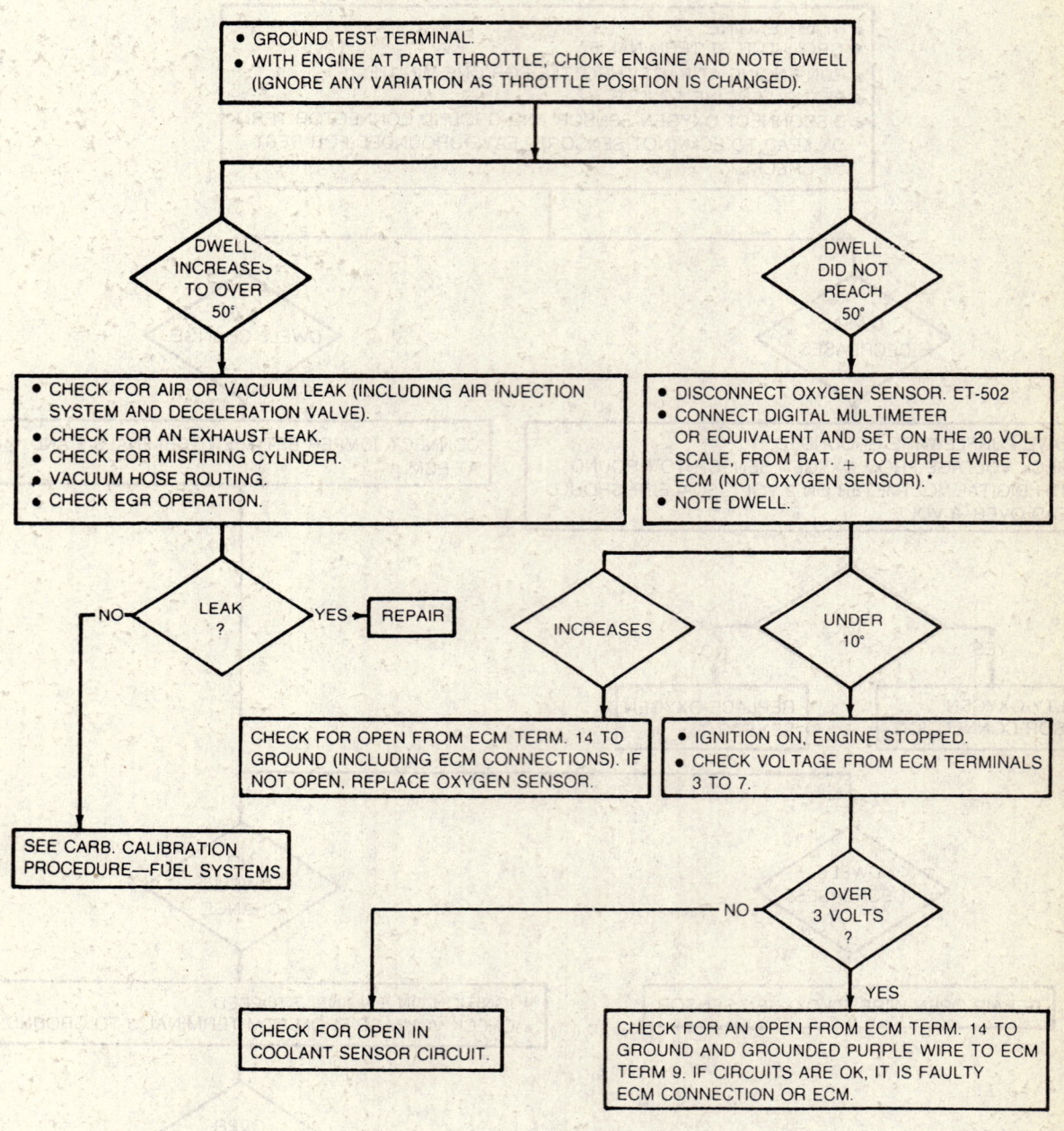

*Do Not use an ordinary voltmeter or jumper in place of digital voltmeter, because they have too little input impealance. A voltage source of 1.0V to 1.7V (such as a flashlight battery) can be connected with the Positive terminal to the purple wire and the negative terminal to ground as a jumper. If the polarity is reversed, it won't work.

4-53

4 EMISSION CONTROLS

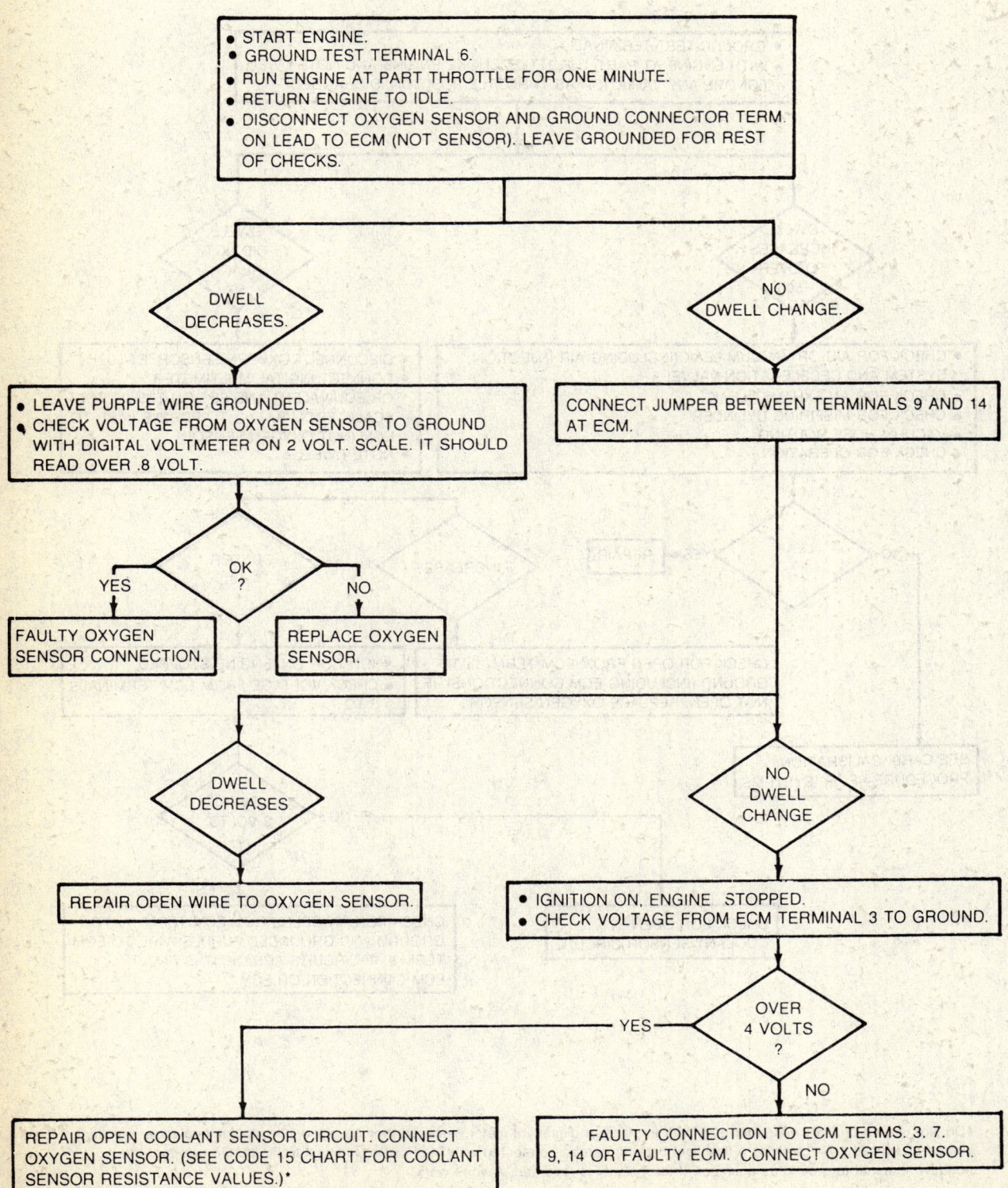

**CHART NO. 2
DWELL FIXED BETWEEN 10°-50°
OPEN COOLANT OR OXYGEN SENSOR CIRCUIT**

Check for sticking TPS plunger and adjustment and low coolant.

- START ENGINE.
- GROUND TEST TERMINAL 6.
- RUN ENGINE AT PART THROTTLE FOR ONE MINUTE.
- RETURN ENGINE TO IDLE.
- DISCONNECT OXYGEN SENSOR AND GROUND CONNECTOR TERM. ON LEAD TO ECM (NOT SENSOR). LEAVE GROUNDED FOR REST OF CHECKS.

DWELL DECREASES.
- LEAVE PURPLE WIRE GROUNDED.
- CHECK VOLTAGE FROM OXYGEN SENSOR TO GROUND WITH DIGITAL VOLTMETER ON 2 VOLT. SCALE. IT SHOULD READ OVER .8 VOLT.

OK?
- YES: FAULTY OXYGEN SENSOR CONNECTION.
- NO: REPLACE OXYGEN SENSOR.

DWELL DECREASES → REPAIR OPEN WIRE TO OXYGEN SENSOR.

NO DWELL CHANGE. → CONNECT JUMPER BETWEEN TERMINALS 9 AND 14 AT ECM.

NO DWELL CHANGE
- IGNITION ON, ENGINE STOPPED.
- CHECK VOLTAGE FROM ECM TERMINAL 3 TO GROUND.

OVER 4 VOLTS?
- YES: REPAIR OPEN COOLANT SENSOR CIRCUIT. CONNECT OXYGEN SENSOR. (SEE CODE 15 CHART FOR COOLANT SENSOR RESISTANCE VALUES.)*
- NO: FAULTY CONNECTION TO ECM TERMS. 3, 7, 9, 14 OR FAULTY ECM. CONNECT OXYGEN SENSOR.

4-54

EMISSION CONTROLS 4

CHART NO. 3
DWELL FIXED OVER 50°
RICH EXHAUST INDICATION

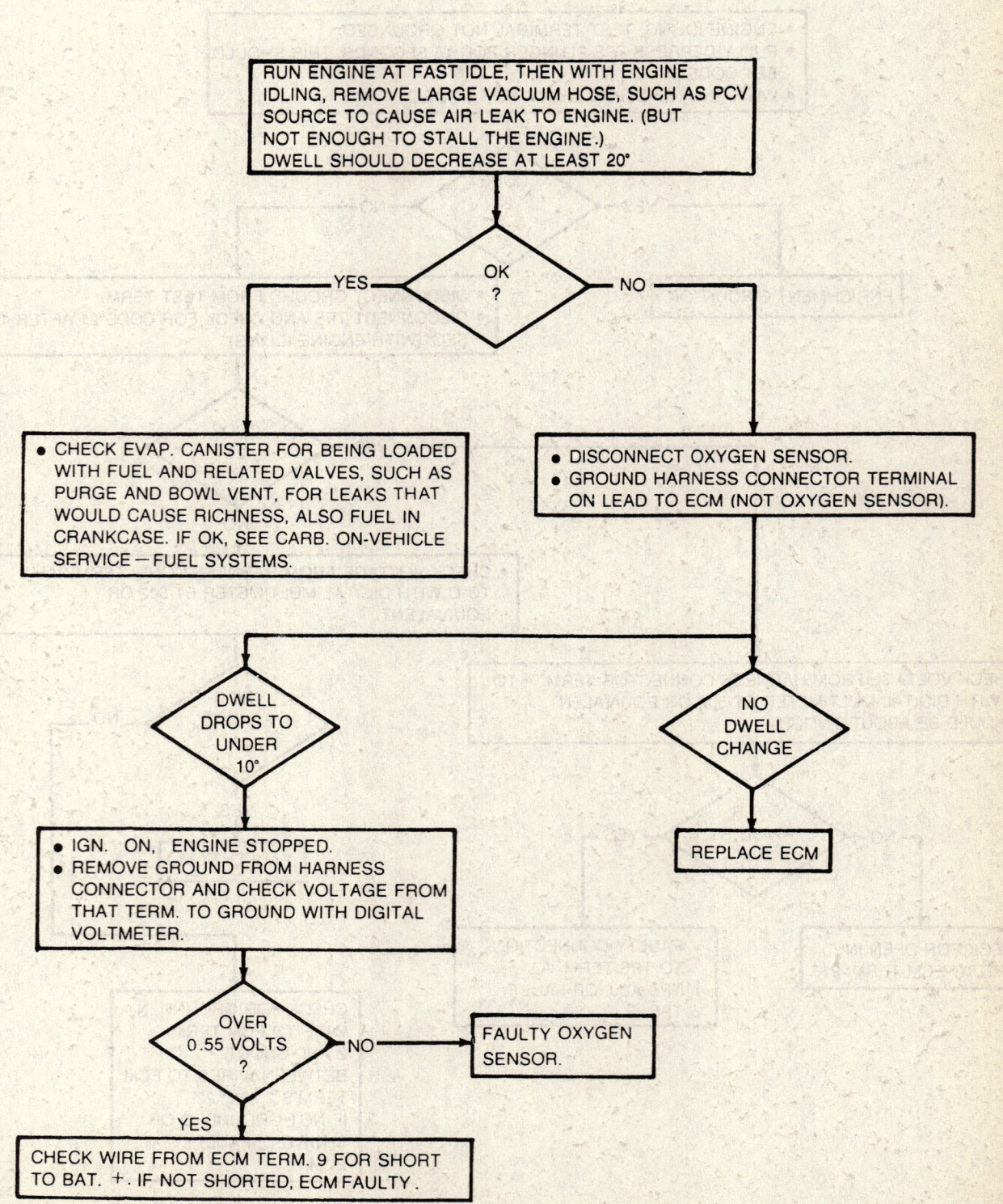

4 EMISSION CONTROLS

CHART NO. 4
TPS ENRICHMENT CHECK

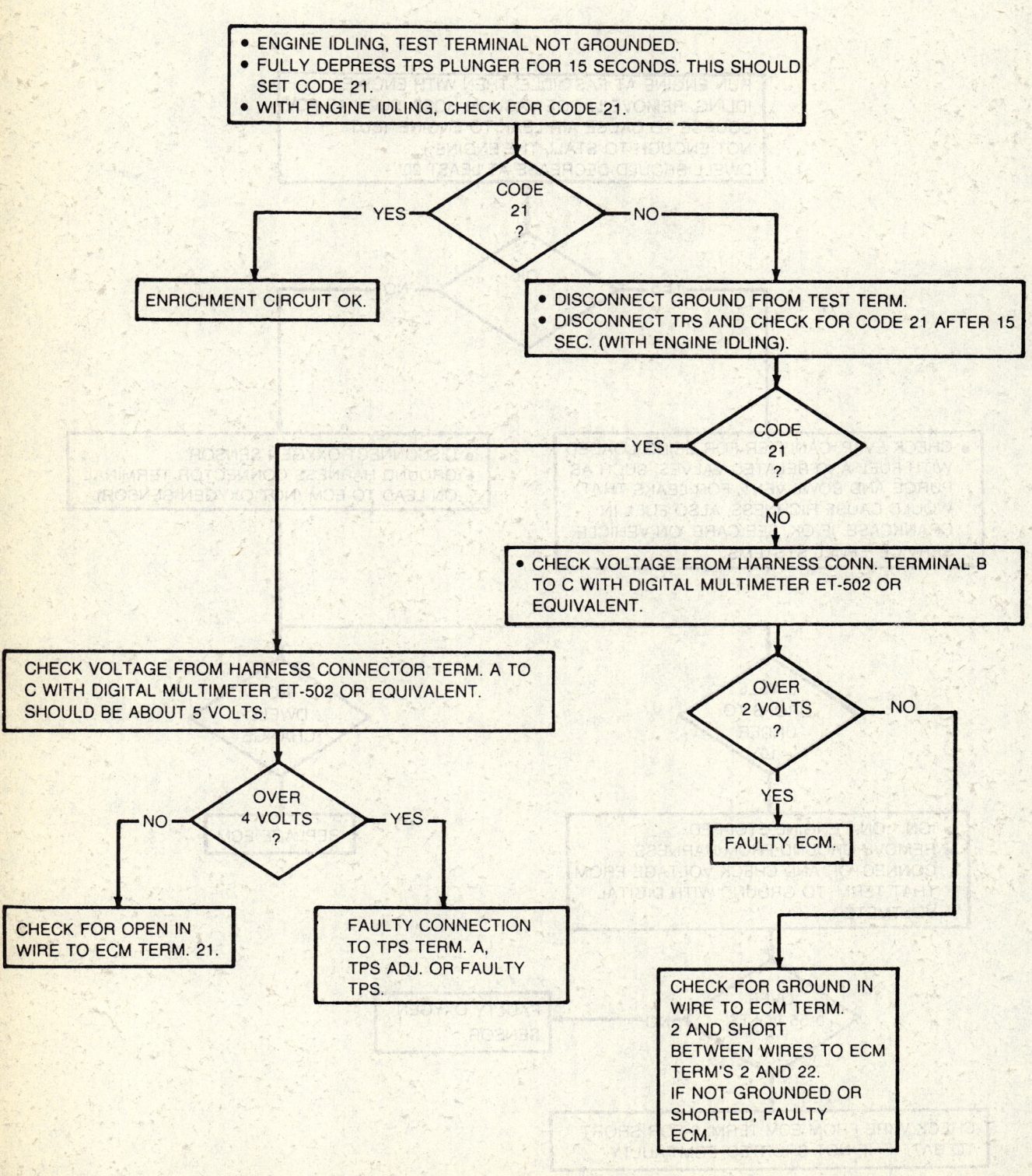

4-56

EMISSION CONTROLS 4

CHART NO. 5
CHECK ENGINE LIGHT INOPERATIVE

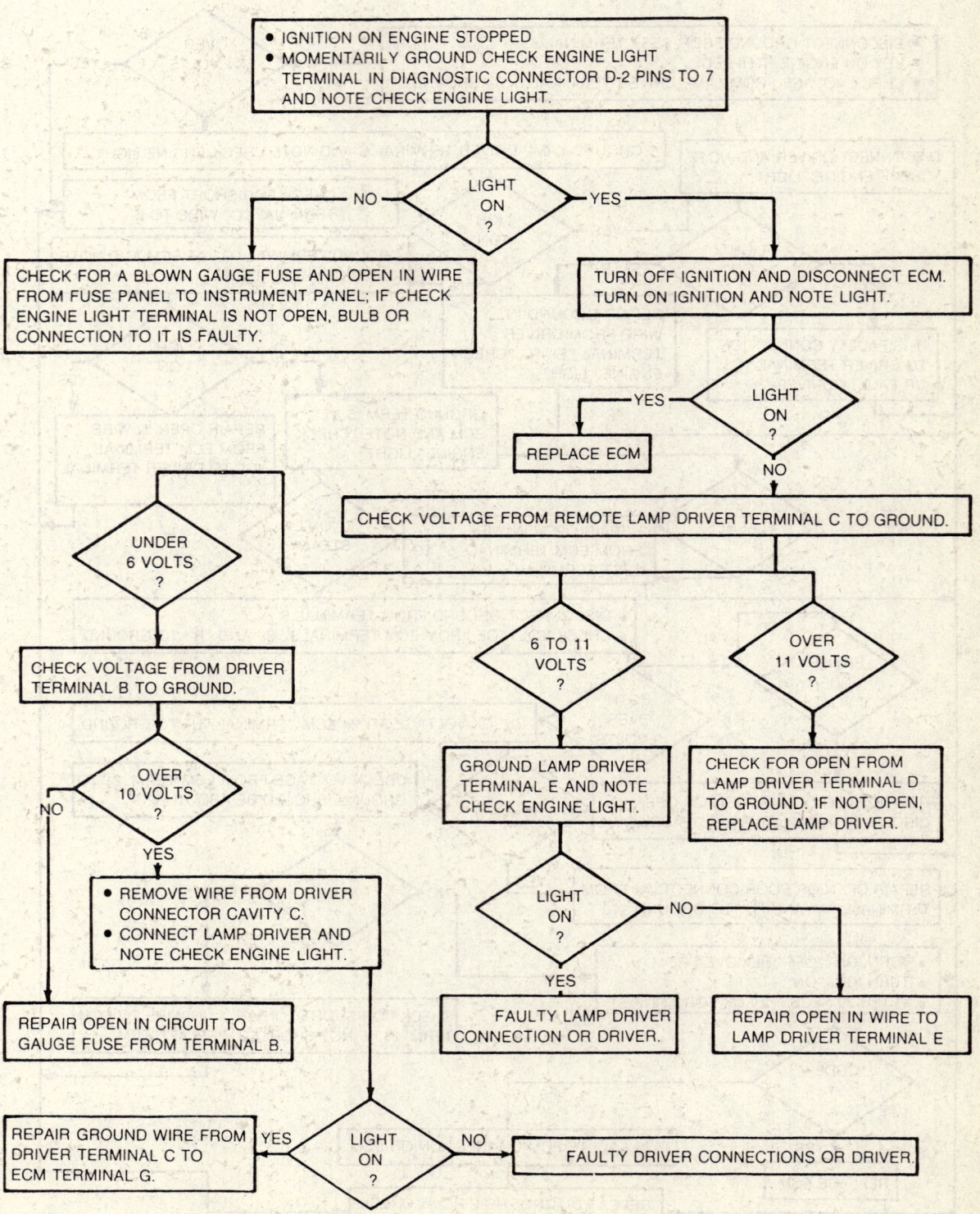

4 EMISSION CONTROLS

CHART NO. 6
CODE 12 DOES NOT FLASH
(REMOTE LAMP DRIVER IN HARNESS)
Check fuses that supply power to ECM

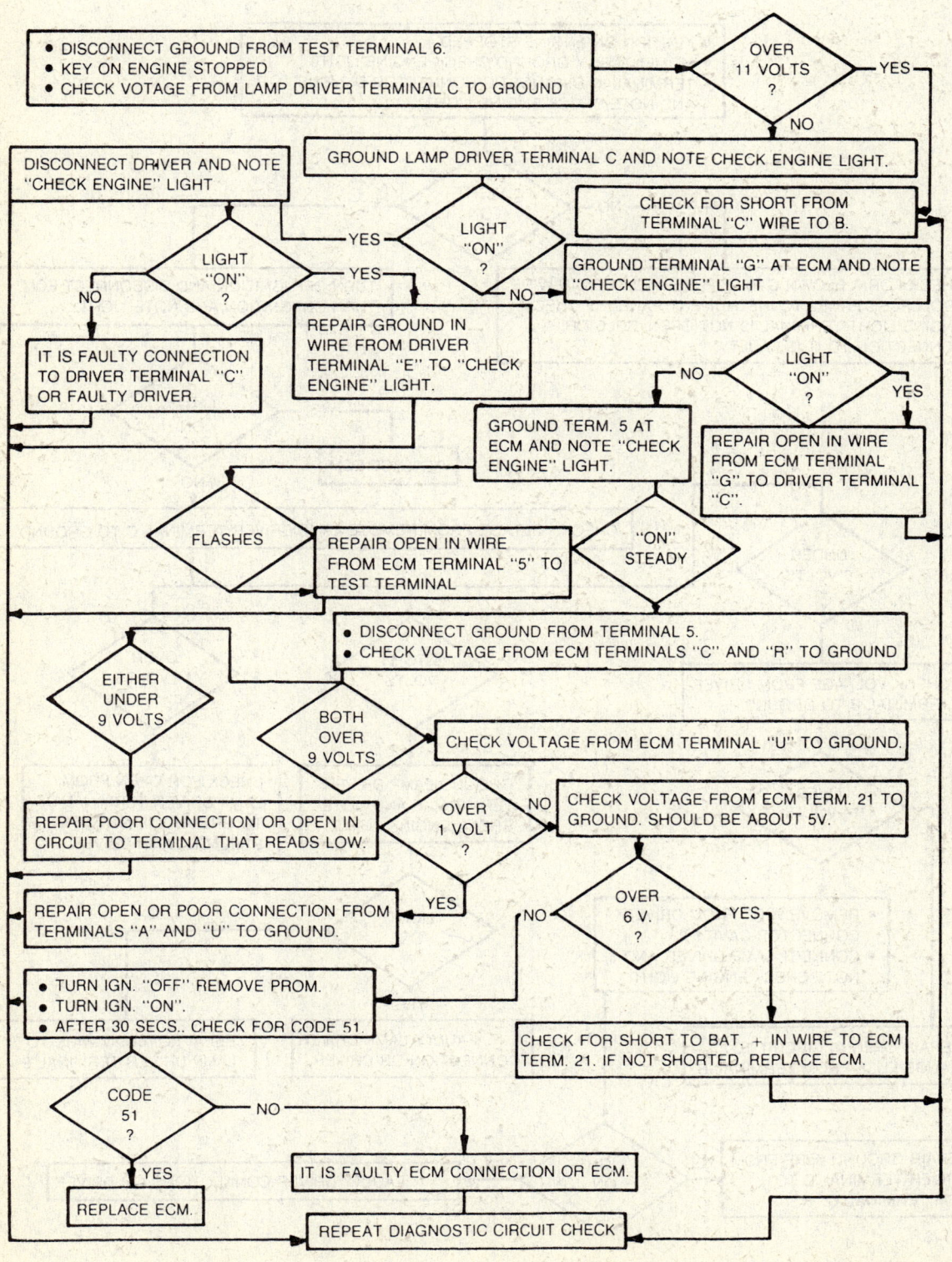

4-58

EMISSION CONTROLS 4

CHART NO. 7
VACUUM SENSOR TEST

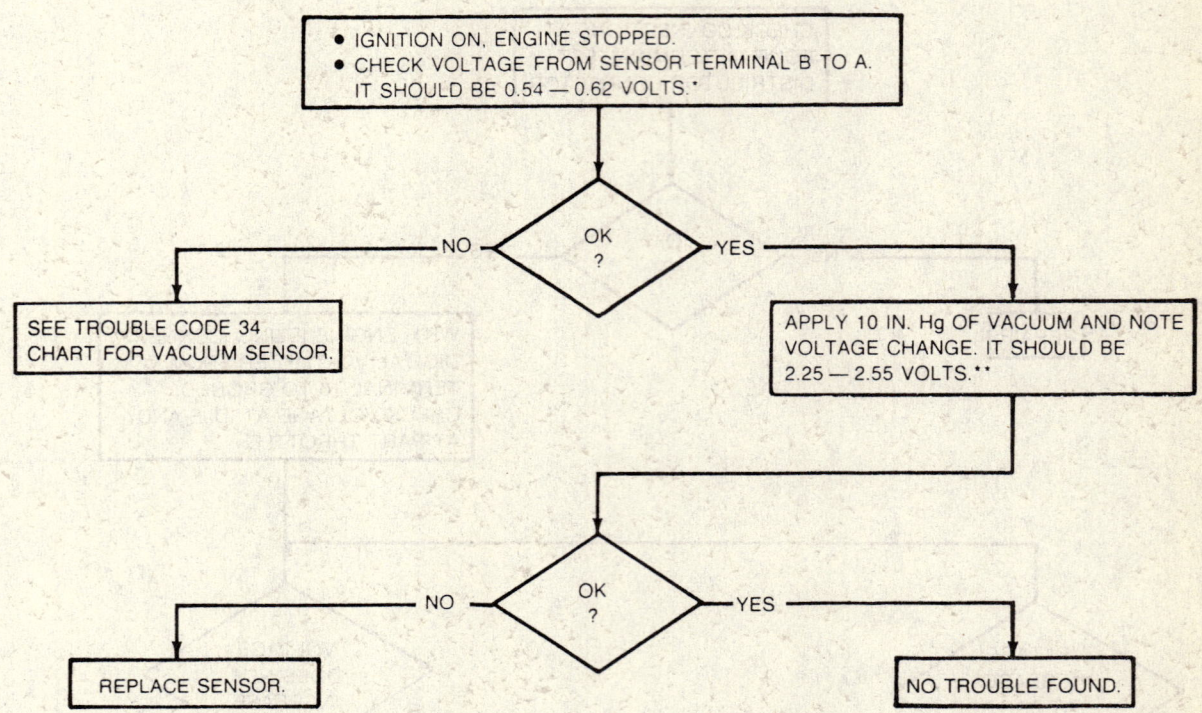

senger compartment at the right side of the steering column below the instrument panel.

TROUBLE CODE MEMORY

When a problem develops in the feedback system, the CHECK ENGINE light will illuminate and a trouble code will be stored in the on-board computer memory. If the fault is intermittent, the CHECK ENGINE light will be turned off 10 seconds after the problem disappears. The trouble code will be retained in the memory until the battery voltage to the control unit is removed. Disconnecting the battery for 10 seconds will erase all stored trouble codes.

The CHECK ENGINE light will be illuminated only if a problem exists that pertains to the conditions listed below. It takes up to 5 seconds minimum for the light to come on when a problem occurs. Code 12 is not stored in memory and any codes stored will be cleared if the problem does not reoccur within 50 engine starts. The trouble codes indicate problems as follows:

CODE 12: No distributor reference pulses to the ECM. This code is not stored in memory and will only flash while the trouble exists. This code is normal when the ignition is switched ON with the engine not running.
CODE 13: Oxygen sensor circuit. The engine must operate for up to 5 minutes at part throttle, under road load, before this code will be set.
CODE 14: Shorted coolant sensor circuit. The engine must operate for up to 5 minutes before this code will be set.
CODE 15: Open coolant sensor circuit. The engine must operate for up to 5 minutes before this code will be set.
CODE 21: Throttle position sensor circuit. The engine must operate for at least 25 seconds at curb idle speed before this code will be set.
CODE 23: Mixture control solenoid circuit is shorted or open.
CODE 34: Vacuum sensor circuit. The engine must operate for up to 5 minutes at curb idle speed before this code will be set.
CODE 41: No distributor reference pulses to the ECM at the specified engine manifold vacuum. This code will be stored in memory.
CODE 42: Electronic spark timing (EST) bypass circuit or EST circuit has short circuit to ground or an open circuit.
CODE 44: Lean exhaust indication. The engine must operate for up to 5 minutes, be in closed loop operation and at part throttle before this code will be set.
CODE 44 & 45: If these two codes appear at the same time, it indicates a problem in the oxygen sensor circuit.
CODE 45: Rich exhaust indication. The engine must operate for up to 5 minutes, be in closed loop and at part throttle before this code will be set.
CODE 51: Faulty calibration unit (PROM) or installation. It requires up to 30 seconds for this code to be set.
CODE 54: Mixture control (MC) solenoid circuit is shorted or the ECM is faulty.
CODE 55: Voltage reference has short circuit to ground (terminal 21), faulty oxygen sensor or faulty ECM.

4 EMISSION CONTROLS

TROUBLE CODE 12
NO REFERENCE PULSES TO THE ECM

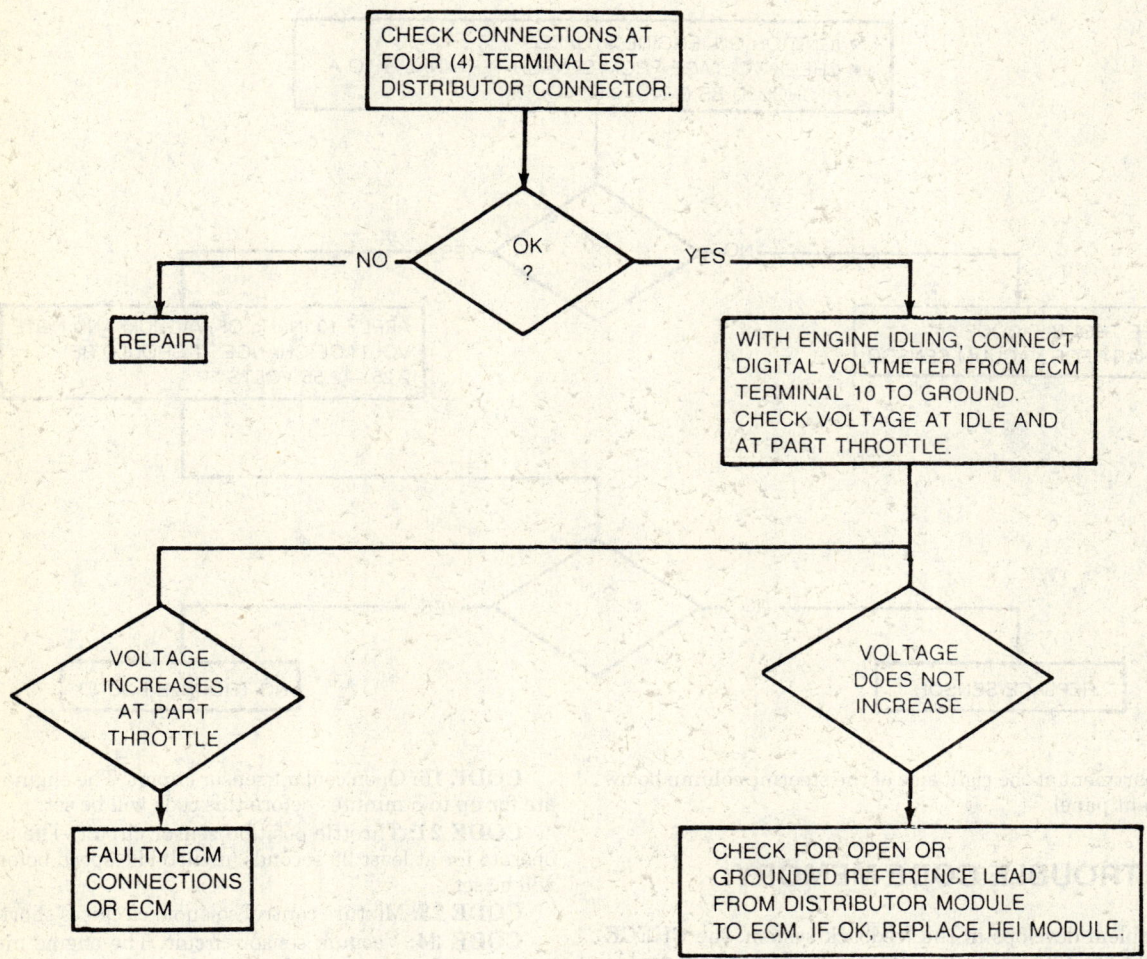

4-60

EMISSION CONTROLS 4

TROUBLE CODE 13
OPEN OXYGEN SENSOR CIRCUIT

Checking for sticking or misadjusted throttle position sensor.
If codes 13 and 21 are displayed, go to code 21 first.

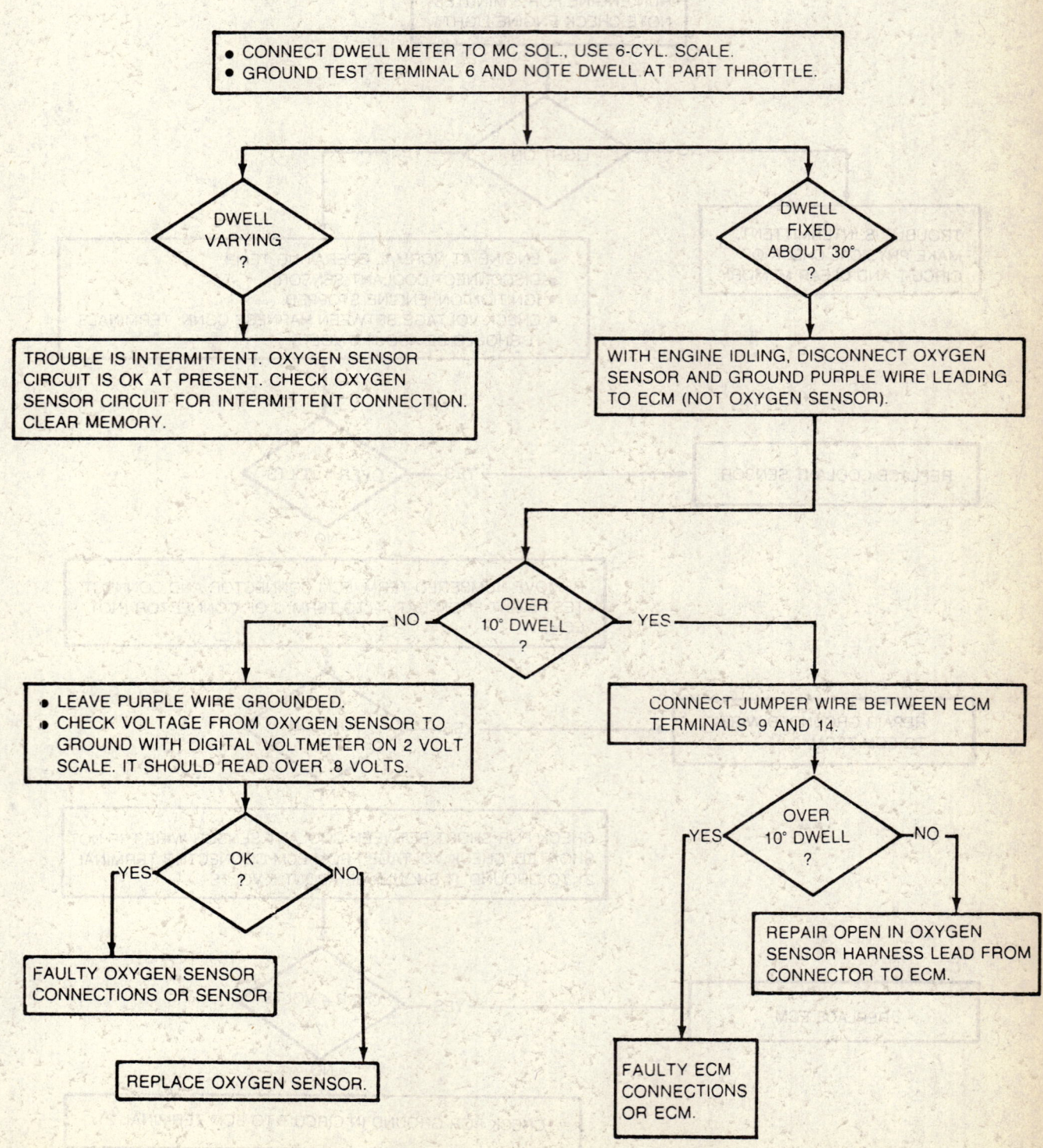

4-61

4 EMISSION CONTROLS

TROUBLE CODE 14
SHORTED COOLANT SENSOR CIRCUIT

If the engine coolant light is on, check for overheating condition first.

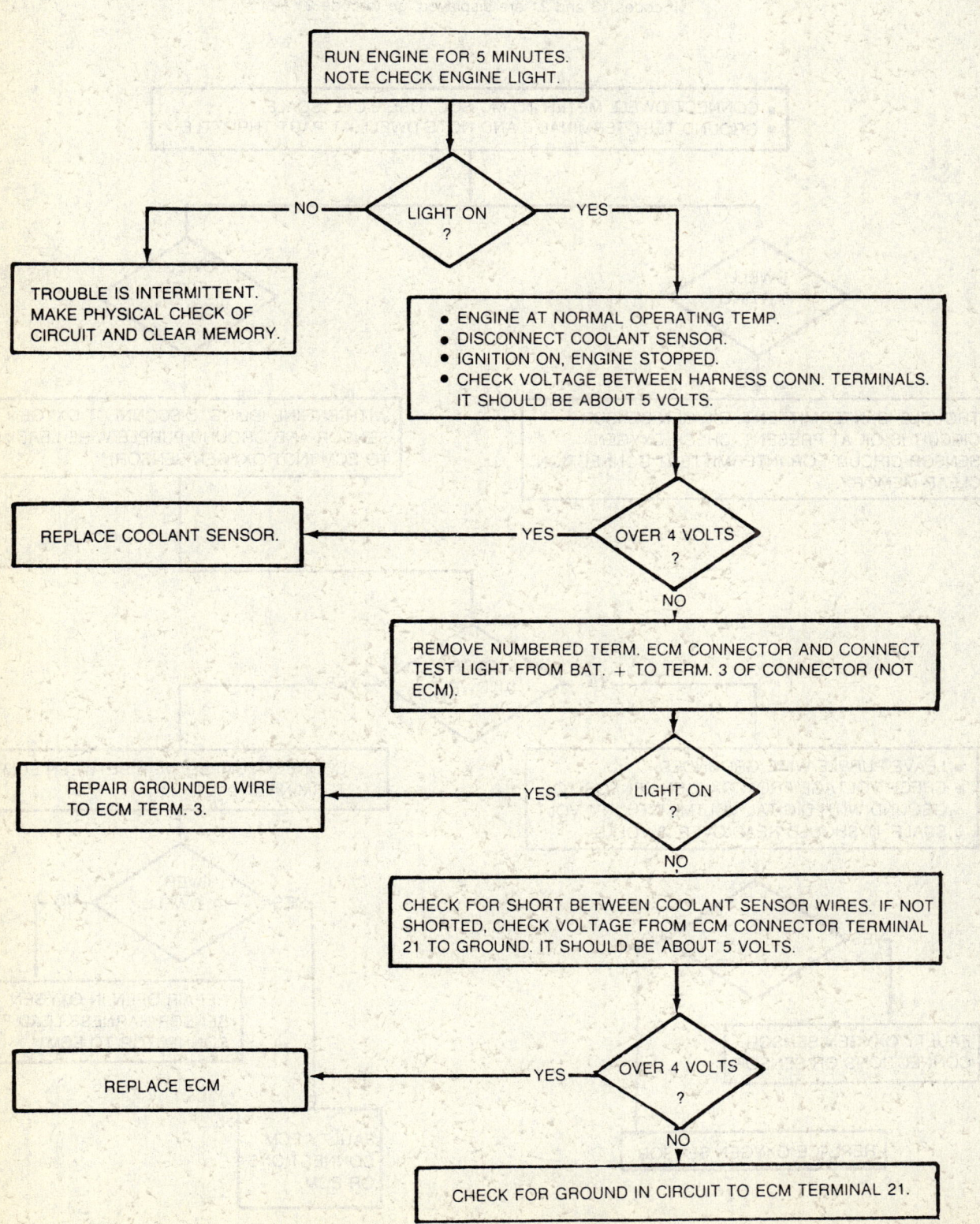

EMISSION CONTROLS 4

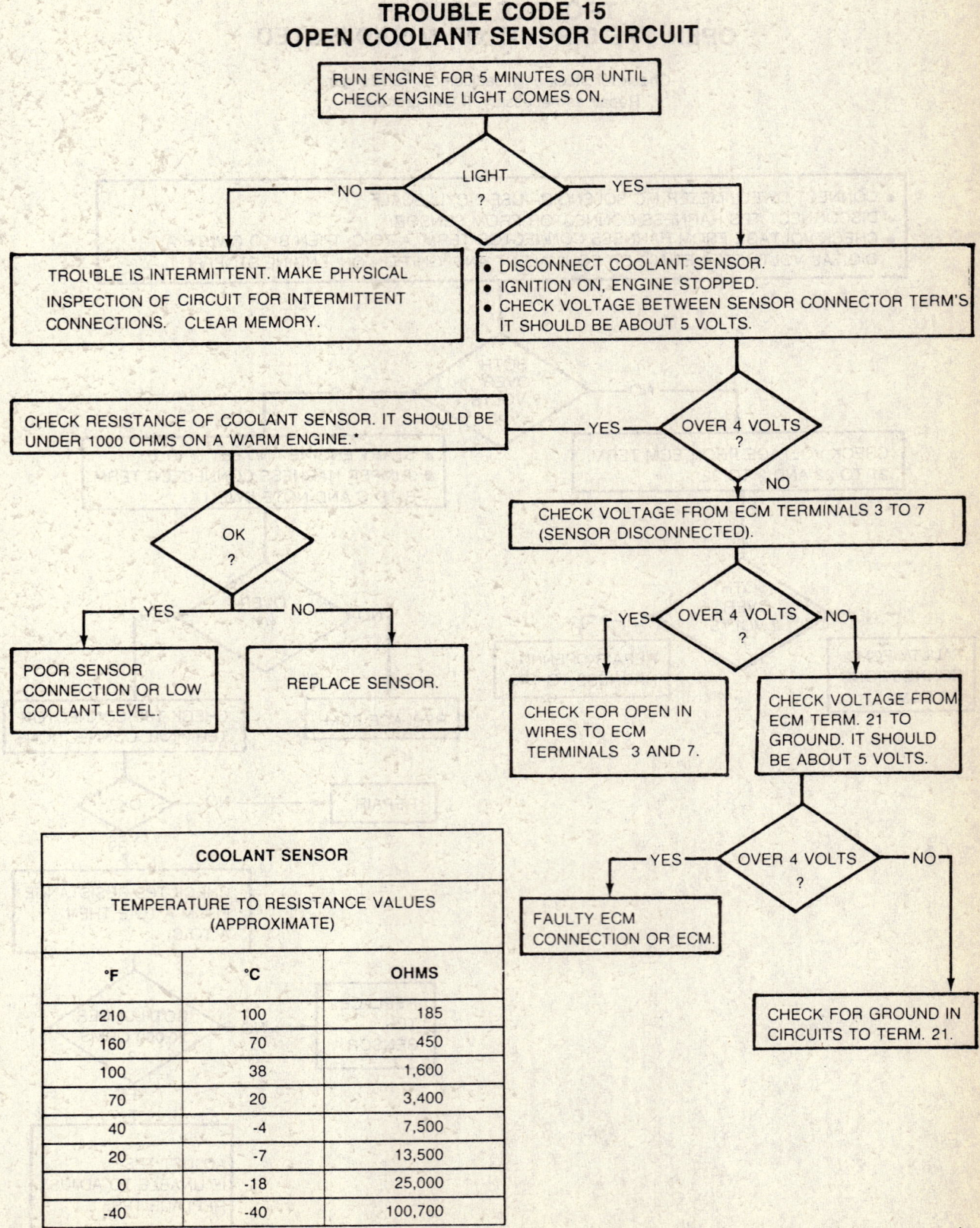

**TROUBLE CODE 15
OPEN COOLANT SENSOR CIRCUIT**

COOLANT SENSOR		
TEMPERATURE TO RESISTANCE VALUES (APPROXIMATE)		
°F	°C	OHMS
210	100	185
160	70	450
100	38	1,600
70	20	3,400
40	-4	7,500
20	-7	13,500
0	-18	25,000
-40	-40	100,700

4-63

4 EMISSION CONTROLS

TROUBLE CODE 21
OPEN TPS CIRCUIT OR MISADJUSTED

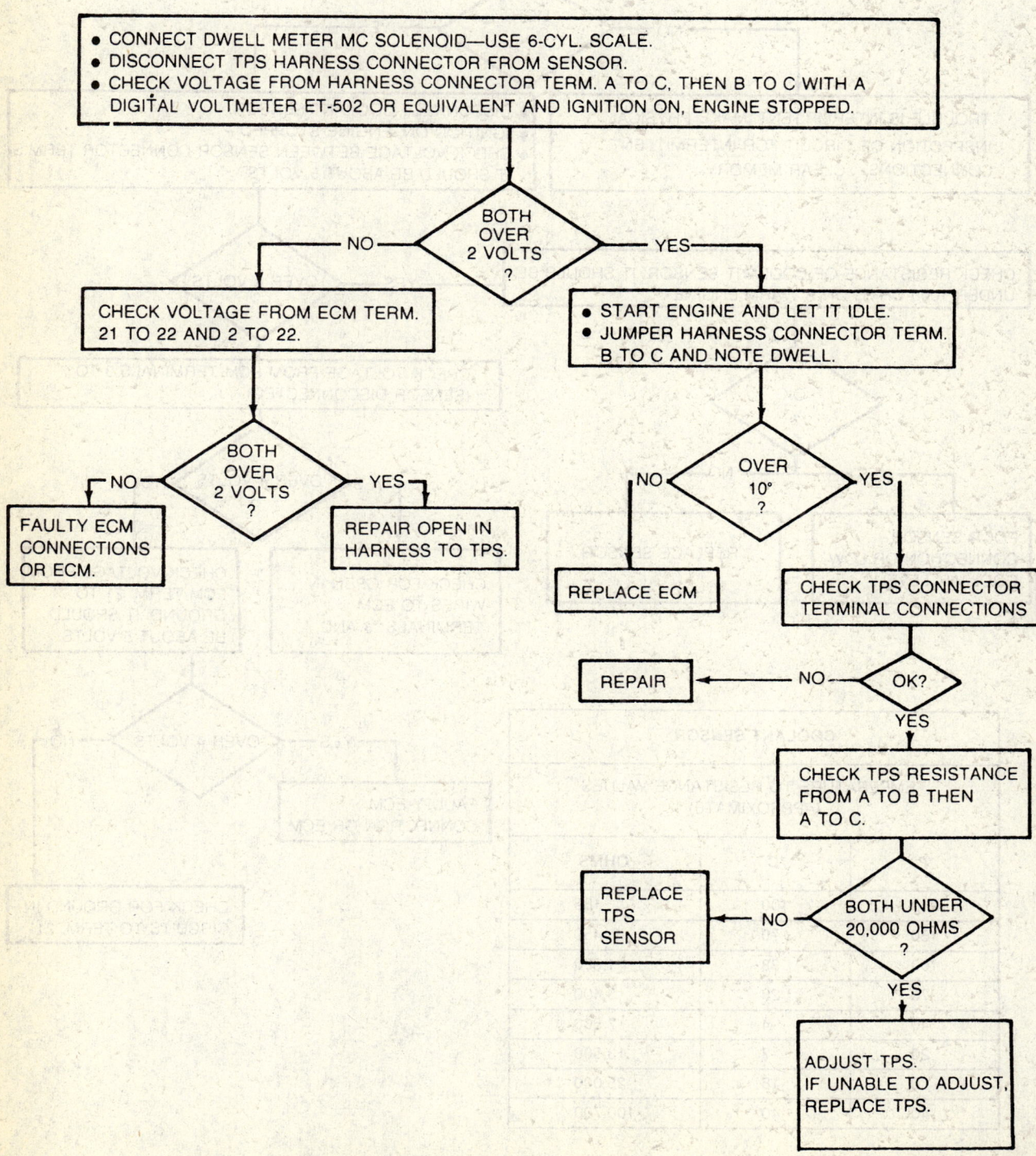

EMISSION CONTROLS 4

TROUBLE CODE 23
OPEN OR GROUNDED MC SOLENOID CIRCUIT

Check connections at MC solenoid. If O.K.: Clear memory* and recheck for code(s). If no code 23, circuit is OK.

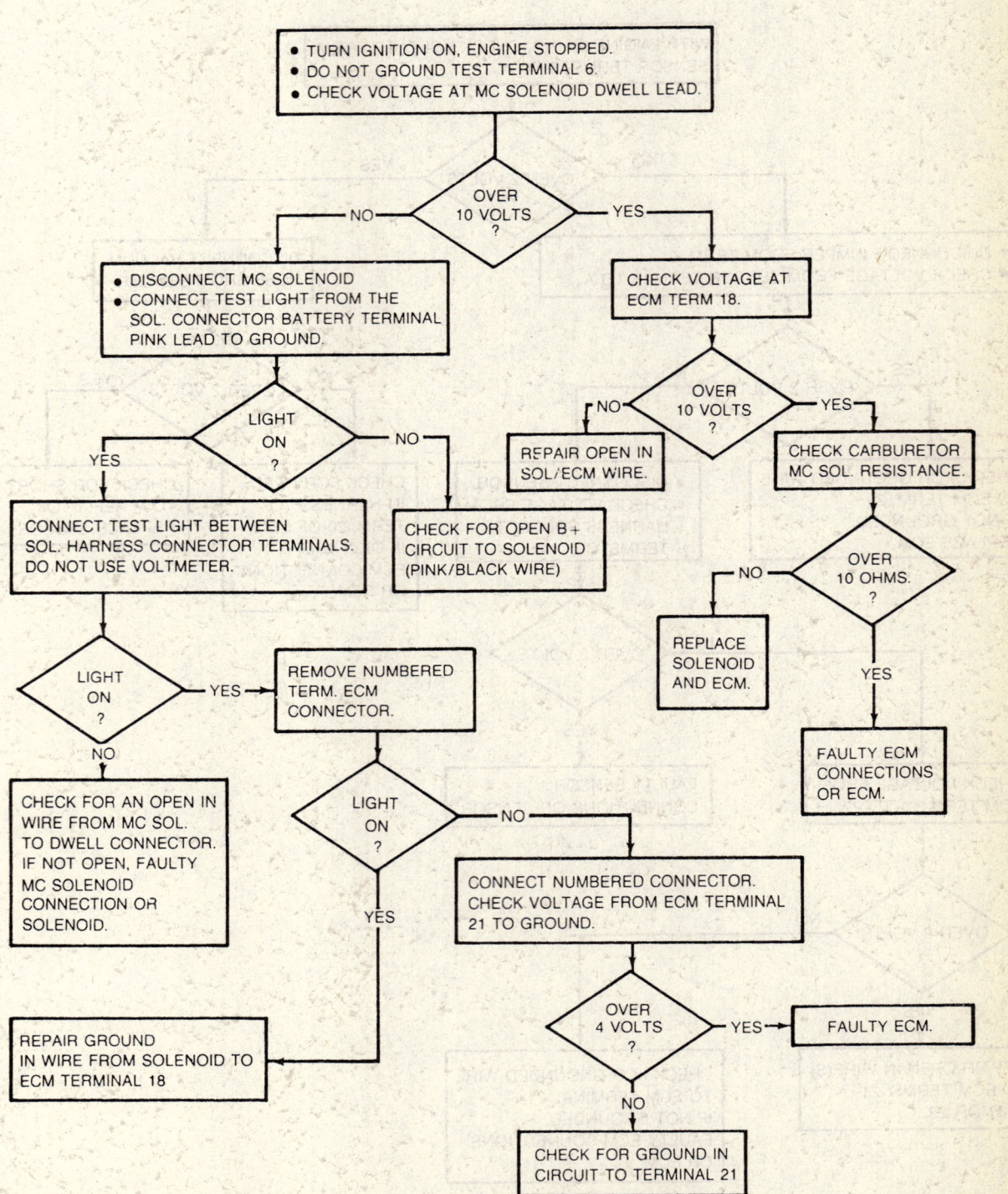

*See Code(s) Clearing Procedure

4-65

4 EMISSION CONTROLS

TROUBLE CODE 34
VACUUM SENSOR VOLTAGE TOO HIGH OR LOW

Check for over 34 kPa (10 inches Hg) of vacuum at sensor with engine idling. If not OK, repair.

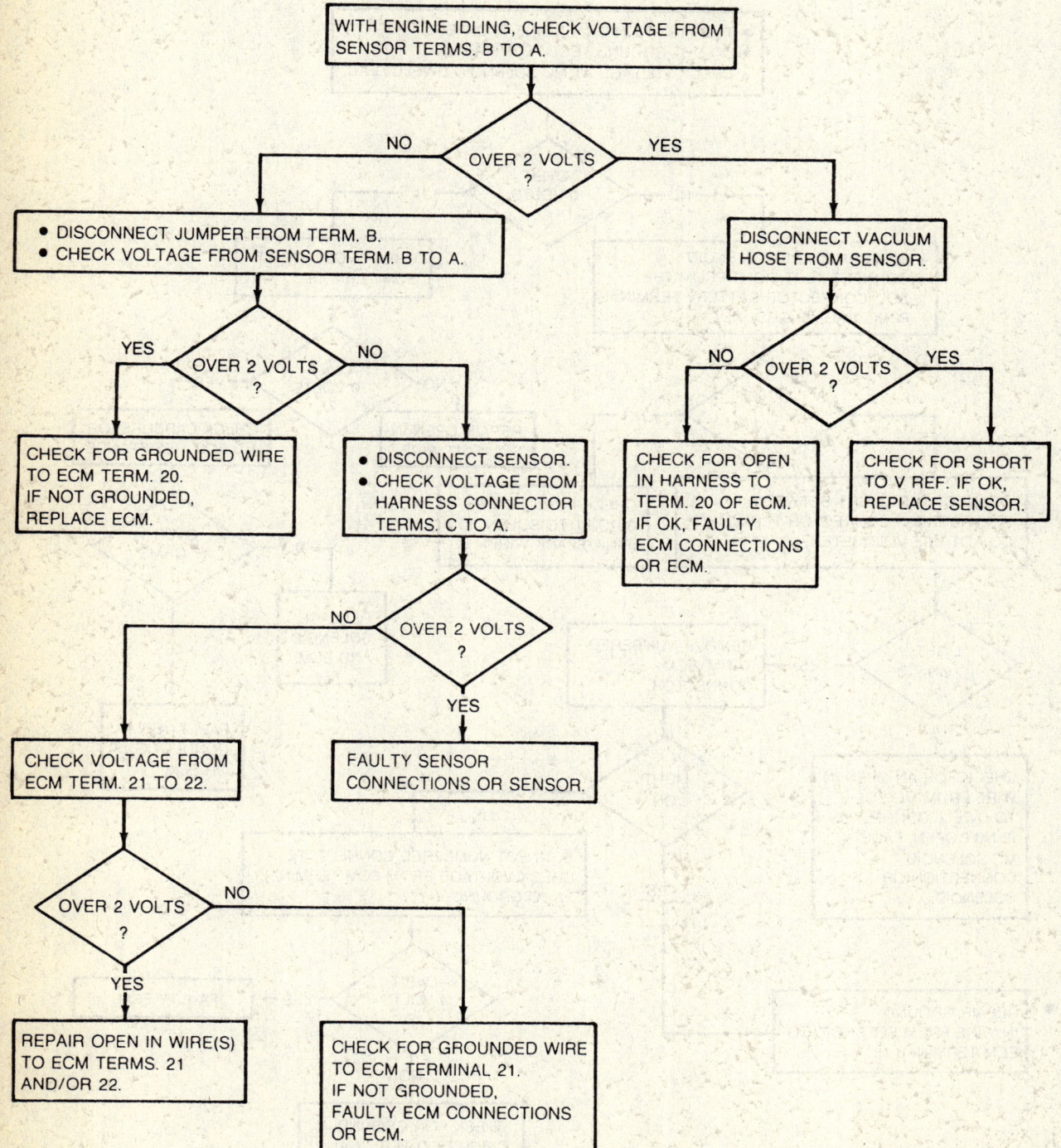

*This requires use of three jumpers between the sensor and the connector.

EMISSION CONTROLS 4

**TROUBLE CODE 41
NO DISTRIBUTOR REFERENCE SIGNAL**

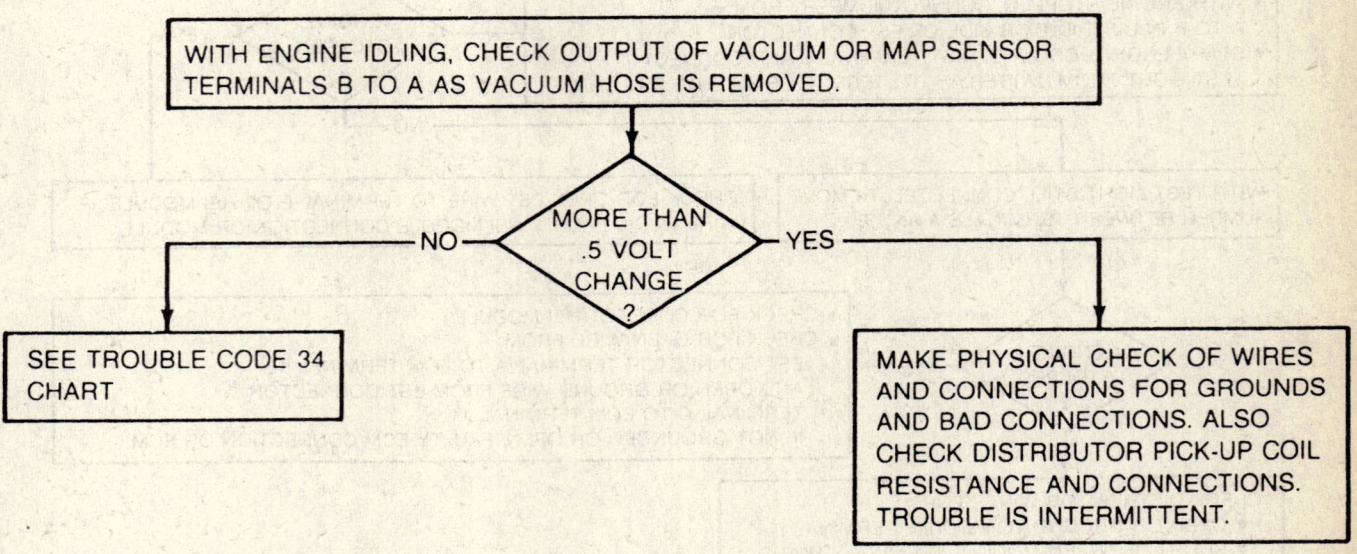

4-67

4 EMISSION CONTROLS

TROUBLE CODE 42
BYPASS OR EST PROBLEM

If vehicle will not start and run, check for grounded EST wire to ECM terminal 12.

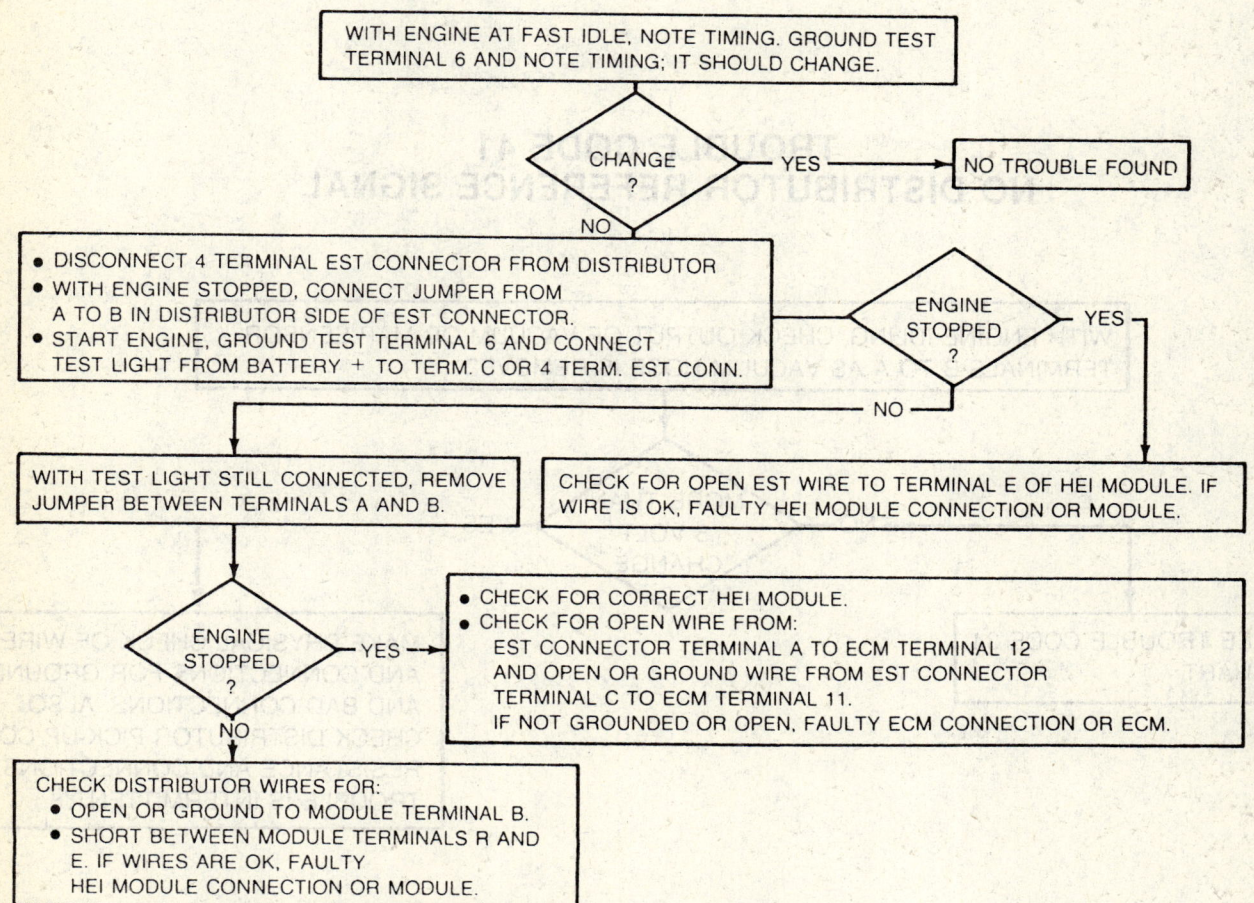

4-68

EMISSION CONTROLS 4

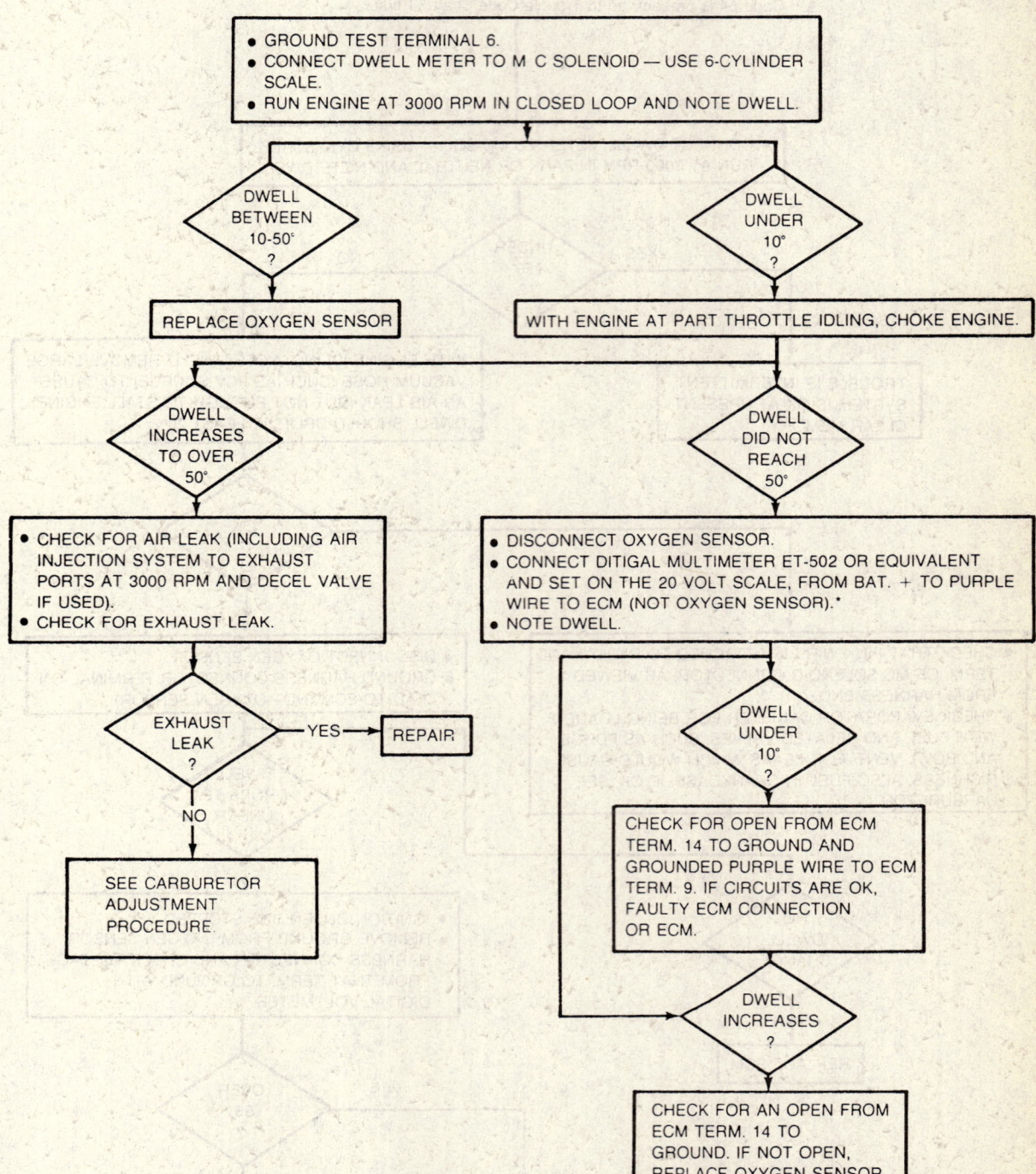

*Do not use ordinary voltmeter or jumper in place of the digital voltmeter because they have so little input impedance. A voltage source of 1.0V to 1.7V (such as a flashlight battery) can be connected with the positive terminal to the purple wire and the negative terminal to ground as a jumper. If the polarity is reversed, it won't work.

4 EMISSION CONTROLS

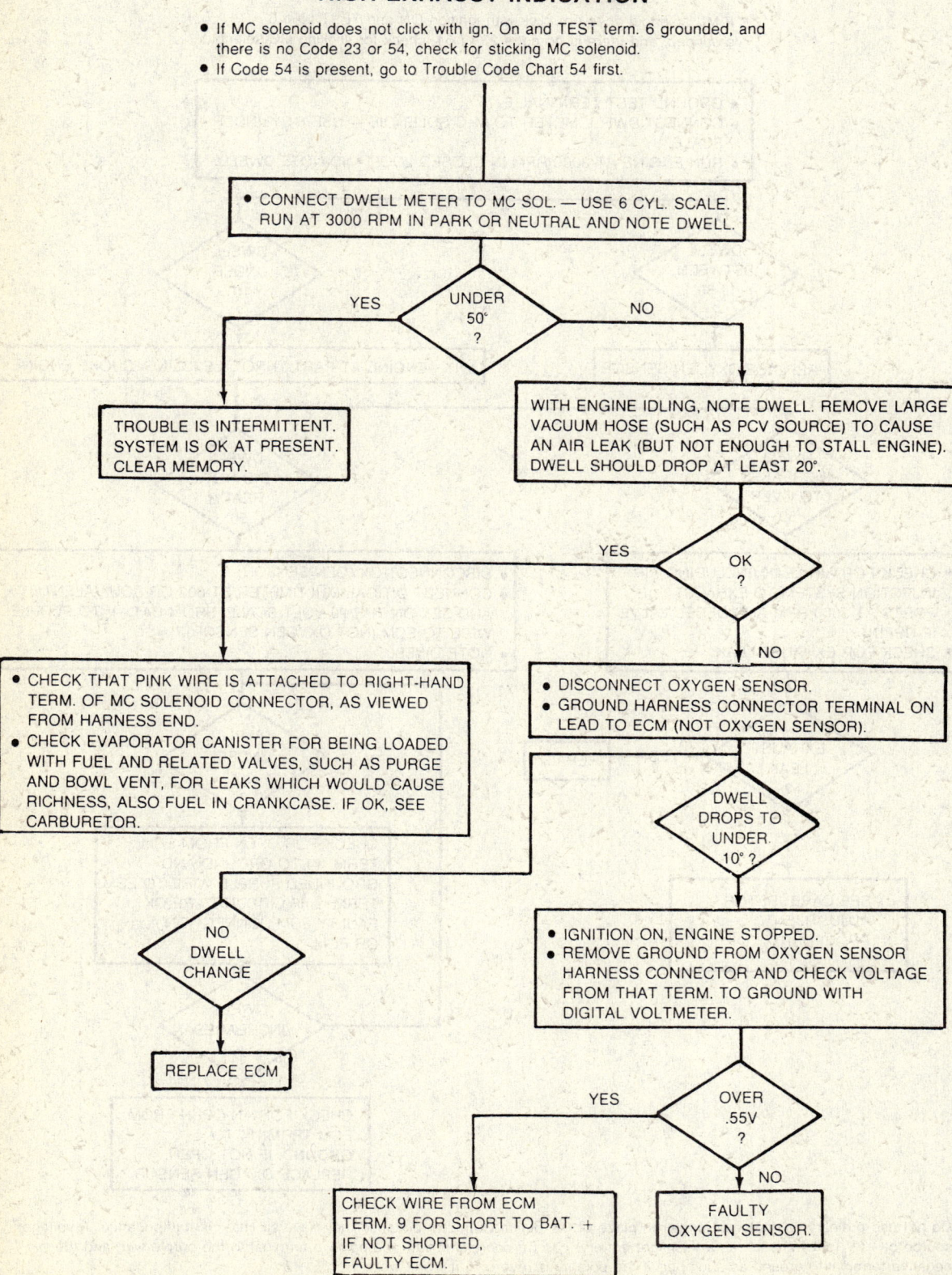

4-70

EMISSION CONTROLS 4

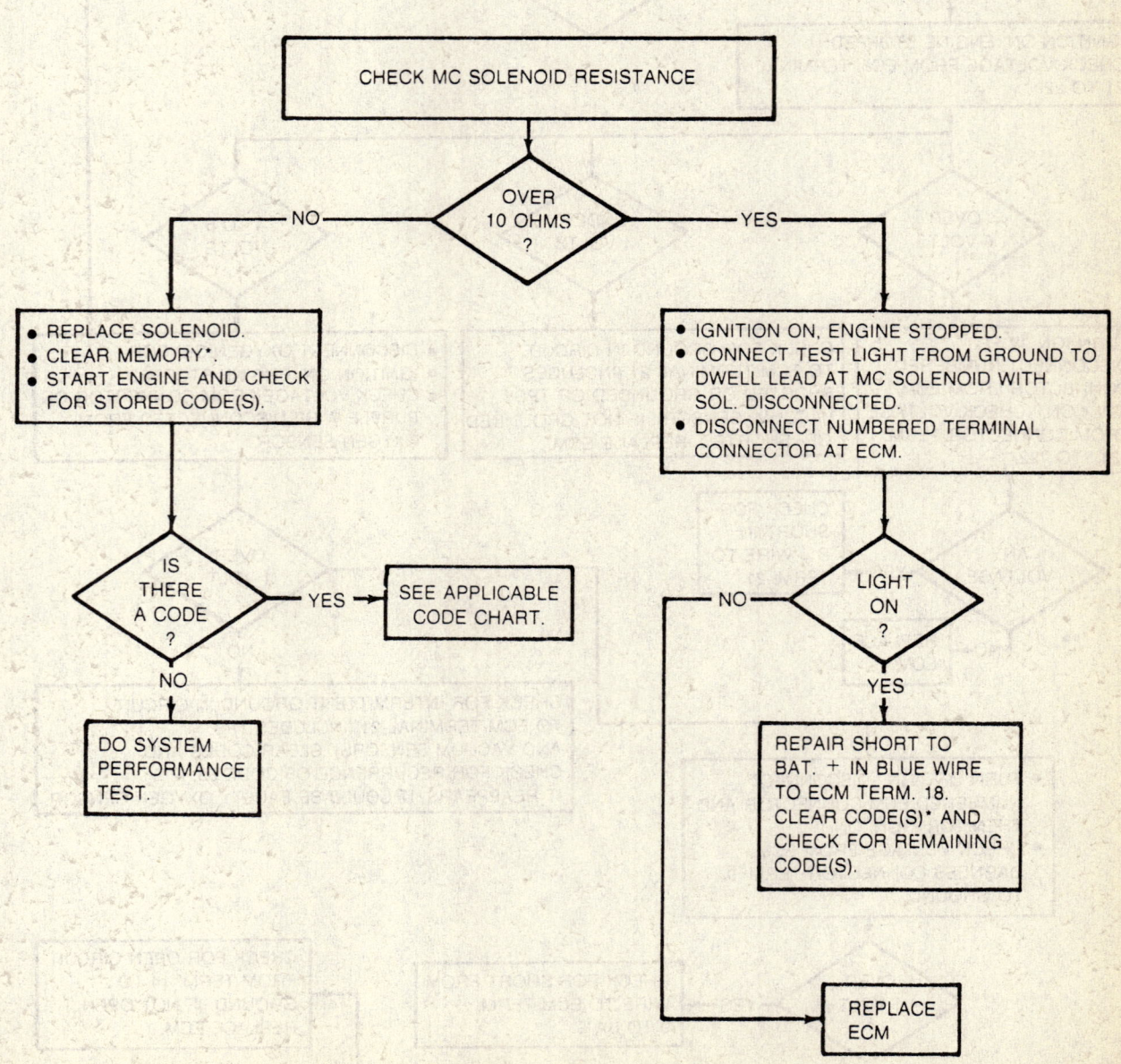

**TROUBLE CODE 51
PROM PROBLEM**

**TROUBLE CODE 54
CONSTANT HIGH VOLTAGE FROM
MC SOLENOID-TO-ECM**

4-71

4 EMISSION CONTROLS

TROUBLE CODE 55
FAULTY OXYGEN SENSOR OR ECM

Check for corrosion at ECM edgeboard connectors and terms. If present, check for coolant sensor, windshield or heater core leaks. Repair leak, clean connector terms. and replace ECM. Also, check for 4 term. EST harness being too close to electrical signals, such as spark plug wires, distributor housing, generator, etc.

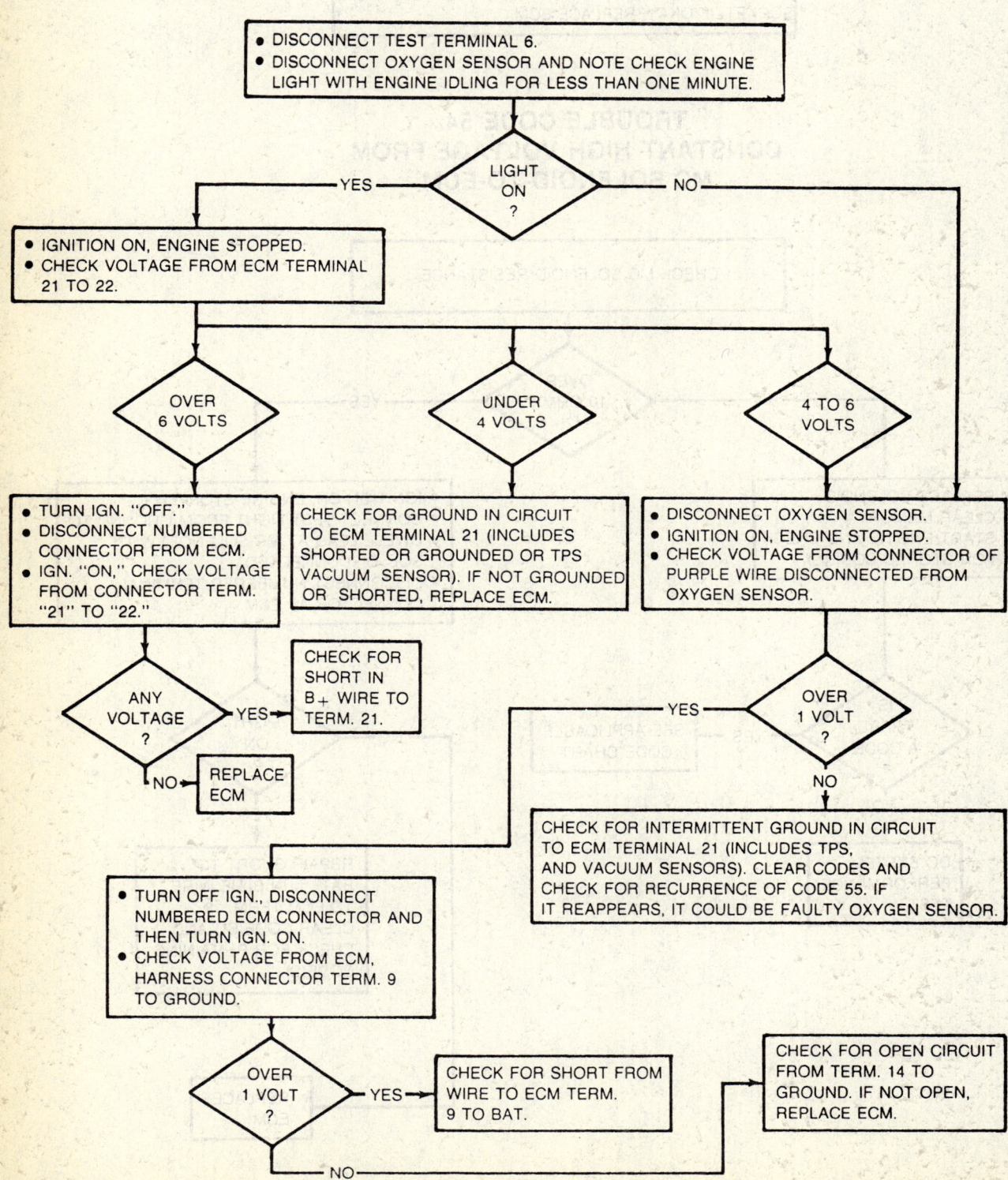

EMISSION CONTROLS 4

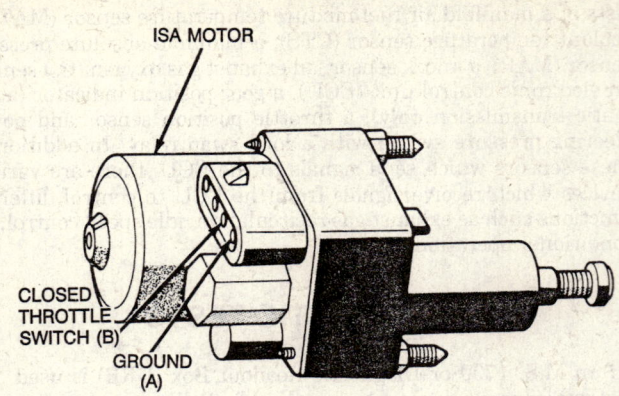

Closed throttle switch/ISA motor

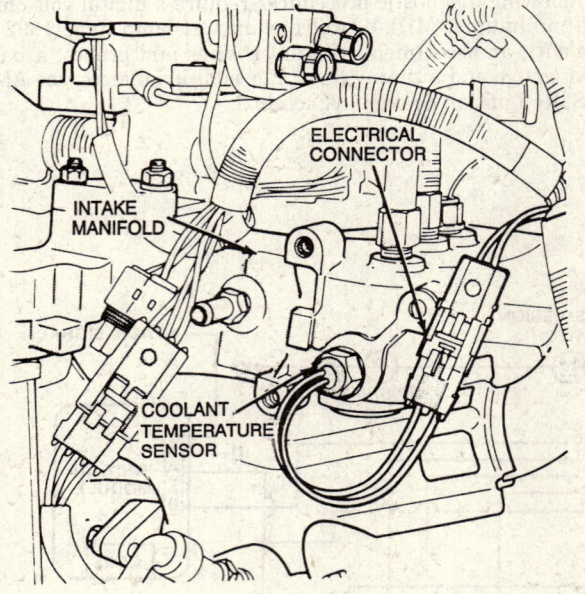

Coolant temperature sensor

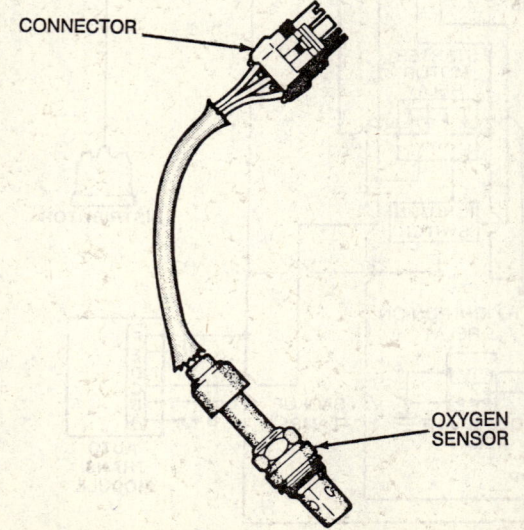

Oxygen sensor connector terminals

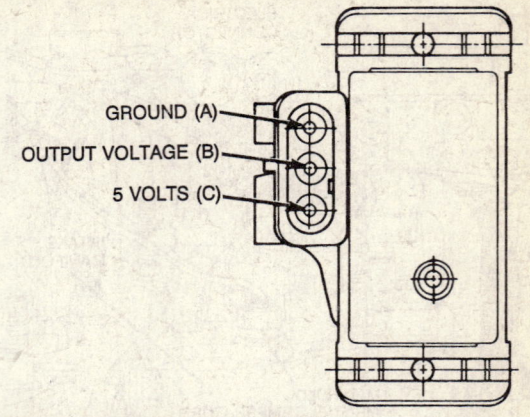

MAP sensor connector terminals

AMC/JEEP Throttle Body Fuel Injection (TBI) System

COMPONENTS AND OPERATION

The Renix throttle body fuel injection is a "pulse time" system that uses a single solenoid-type injector to meter fuel into the throttle body above the throttle blade. Fuel is metered to the engine by an electronic control unit (ECU), which controls the amount of fuel delivery according to input from various engine sensors that monitor exhaust gas oxygen content, coolant temperature, manifold absolute pressure, crankshaft position and throttle position. These sensors provide an electronic signal by varying resistance within the sensor itself. By reading the difference in resistance, the ECU can determine engine operating conditions and calculate the correct air/fuel mixture, and ignition timing under varying engine loads and temperatures. In addition, the ECU controls idle speed, emission control and fuel pump operation, the upshift indicator lamp and the A/C compressor clutch.

Renix TBI fuel injection has two main subsystems; a fuel subsystem and a control subsystem. The fuel subsystem consists of an electric fuel pump (mounted in the fuel tank), a fuel filter, a pressure regulator and the fuel injector. The control subsystem con-

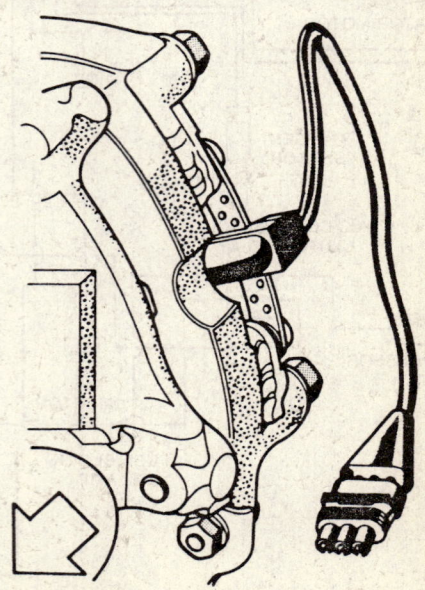

Crankshaft position (speed) sensor

4-73

4 EMISSION CONTROLS

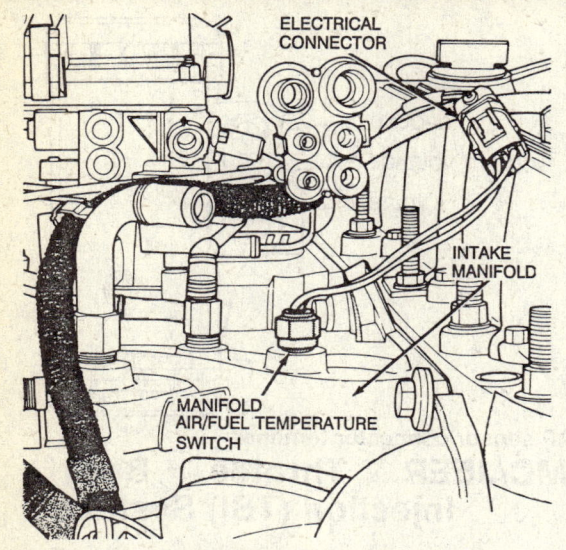

Manifold air/fuel temperature sensor

sists of a manifold air/fuel mixture temperature sensor (MAT), a coolant temperature sensor (CTS), a manifold absolute pressure sensor (MAP), a knock sensor, an exhaust gas oxygen (O_2) sensor, an electronic control unit (ECU), a gear position indicator (automatic transmission only), a throttle position sensor and power steering pressure switch with a load swap relay. In addition to these sensors which send signals to the ECU, there are various devices which receive signals from the ECU to control different functions such as exhaust gas recirculation, idle speed control, air conditioner operation, etc.

DIAGNOSTIC TESTS

If an M.S. 1700 or Diagnostic Readout Box (DRB) is used, the test procedures below are not applicable. Follow the directions included with the tester.

The following diagnostic procedures require a digital volt-ohmmeter (minimum 1 MΩ), a twelve point test lamp (type 1892 or equivalent), an assortment of jumper wires and probes, a hand vacuum gauge and a timing light. For additional tests, see AMC Solid State Ignition System in Section 2.

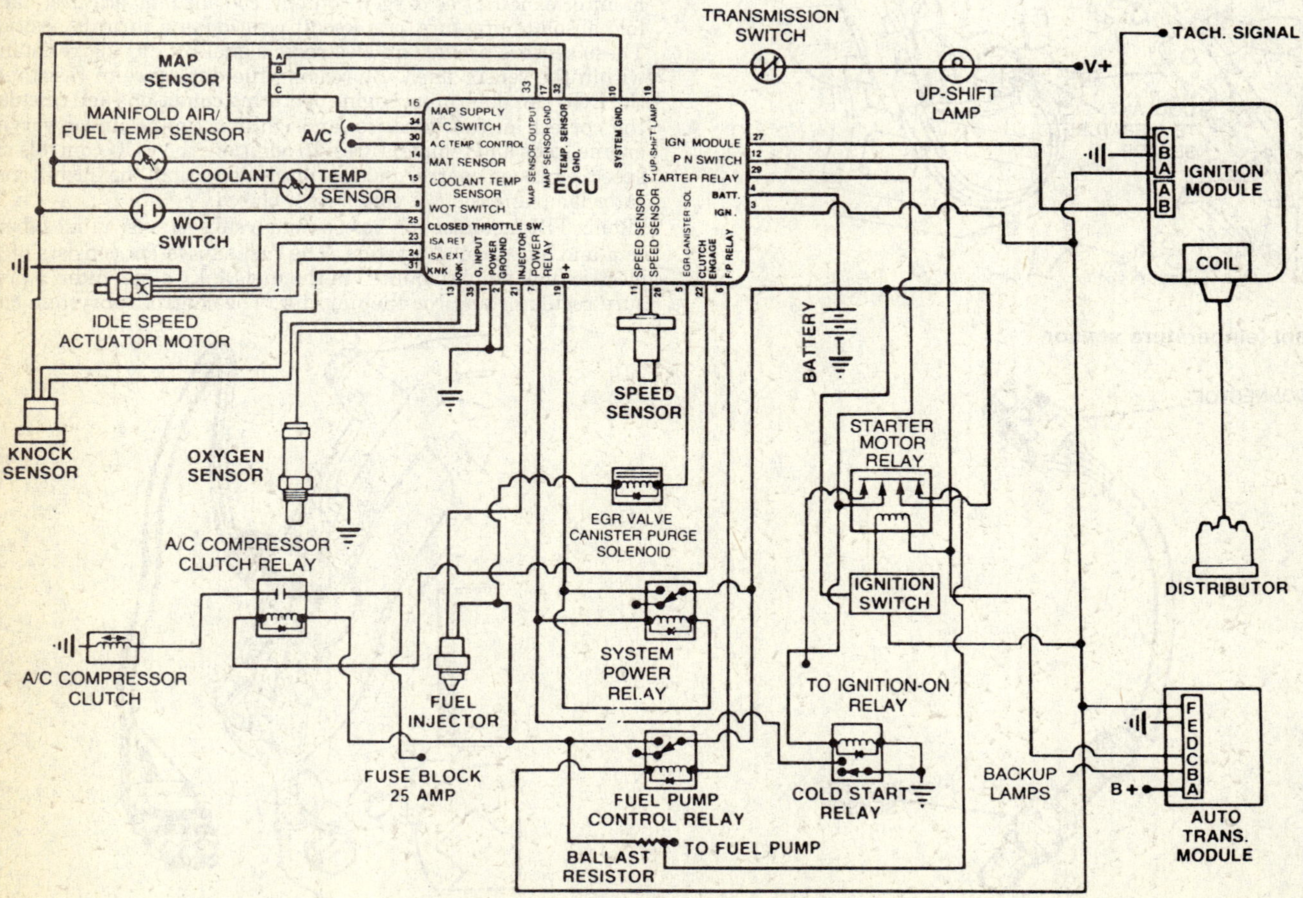

1984-85 TBI wiring diagram

EMISSION CONTROLS 4

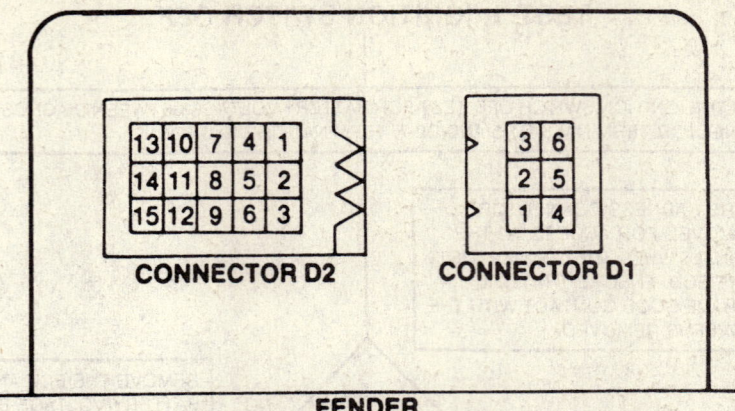

Connector D1
1. Tach (rpm) Voltage (Input)
2. Ignition
3. Ground
4. Starter Motor Relay
5. Battery
6. Fuel Pump

Connector D2
1. ECU Data Output
2. System Power Relay
3. Park/Neutral Switch
4. System Power (B+)
5. A/C Clutch
6. WOT Switch
7. Ground
8. Air/Fuel Temperature Sensor
9. Ignition Power Module
10. EGR Valve/Canister Purge Solenoid
11. ISA Motor Forward
12. Coolant Temperature Sensor
13. Closed Throttle Switch
14. ISA Motor Reverse
15. Automatic Transmission Diagnosis

1984-85 4-2.5L TBI diagnostic connector

4 EMISSION CONTROLS

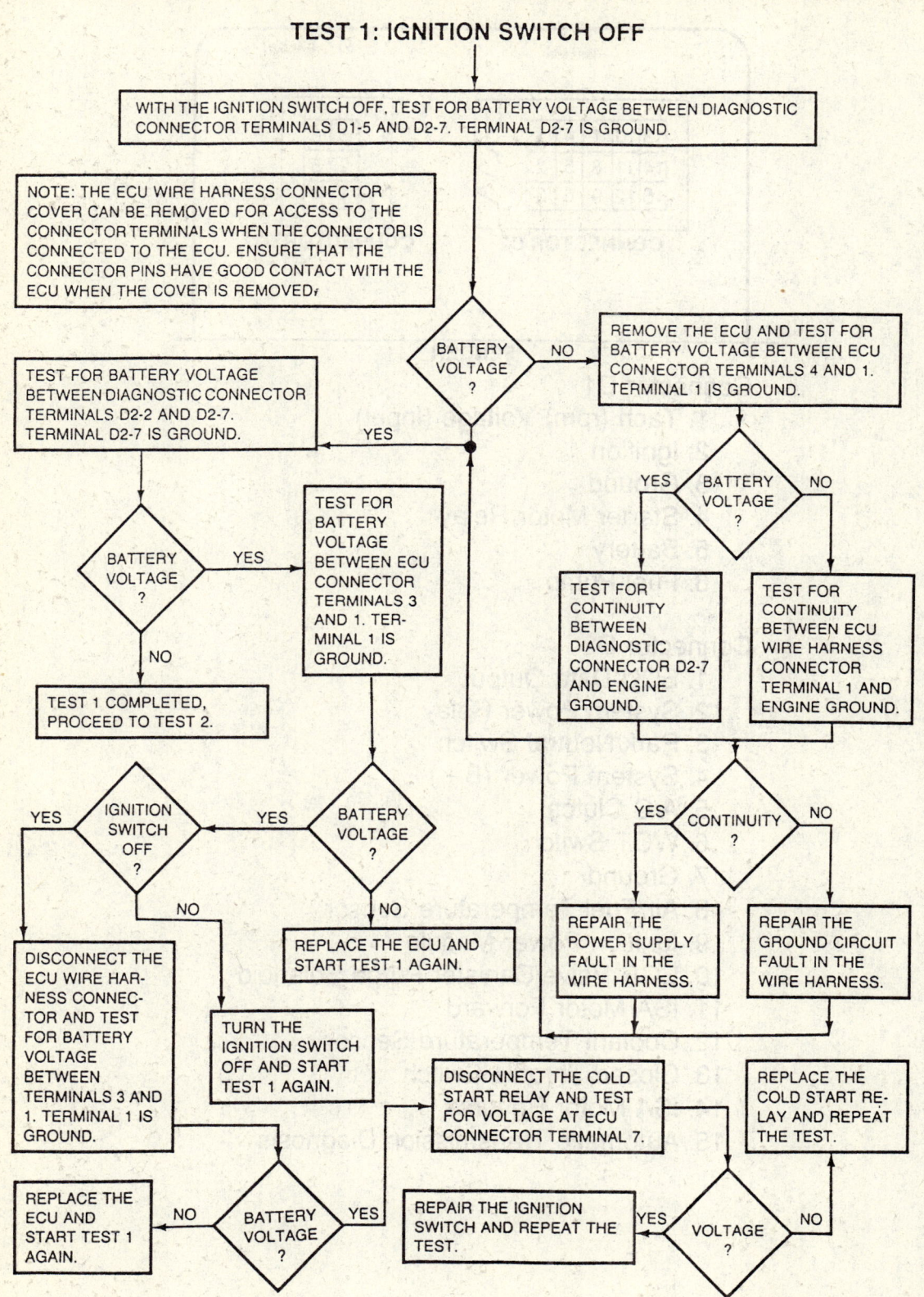

1984-85 TBI diagnostic charts

EMISSION CONTROLS 4

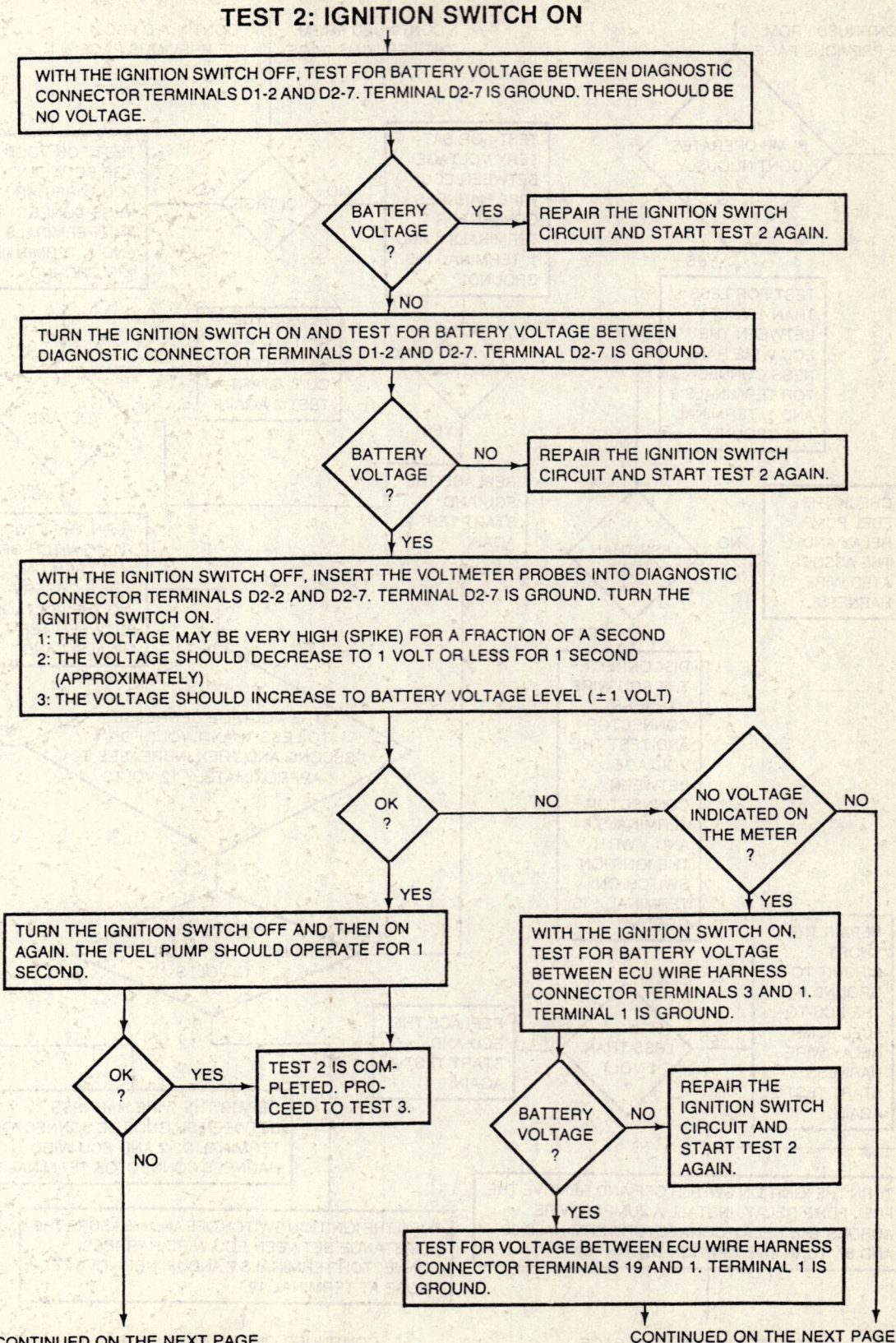

4-77

4 EMISSION CONTROLS

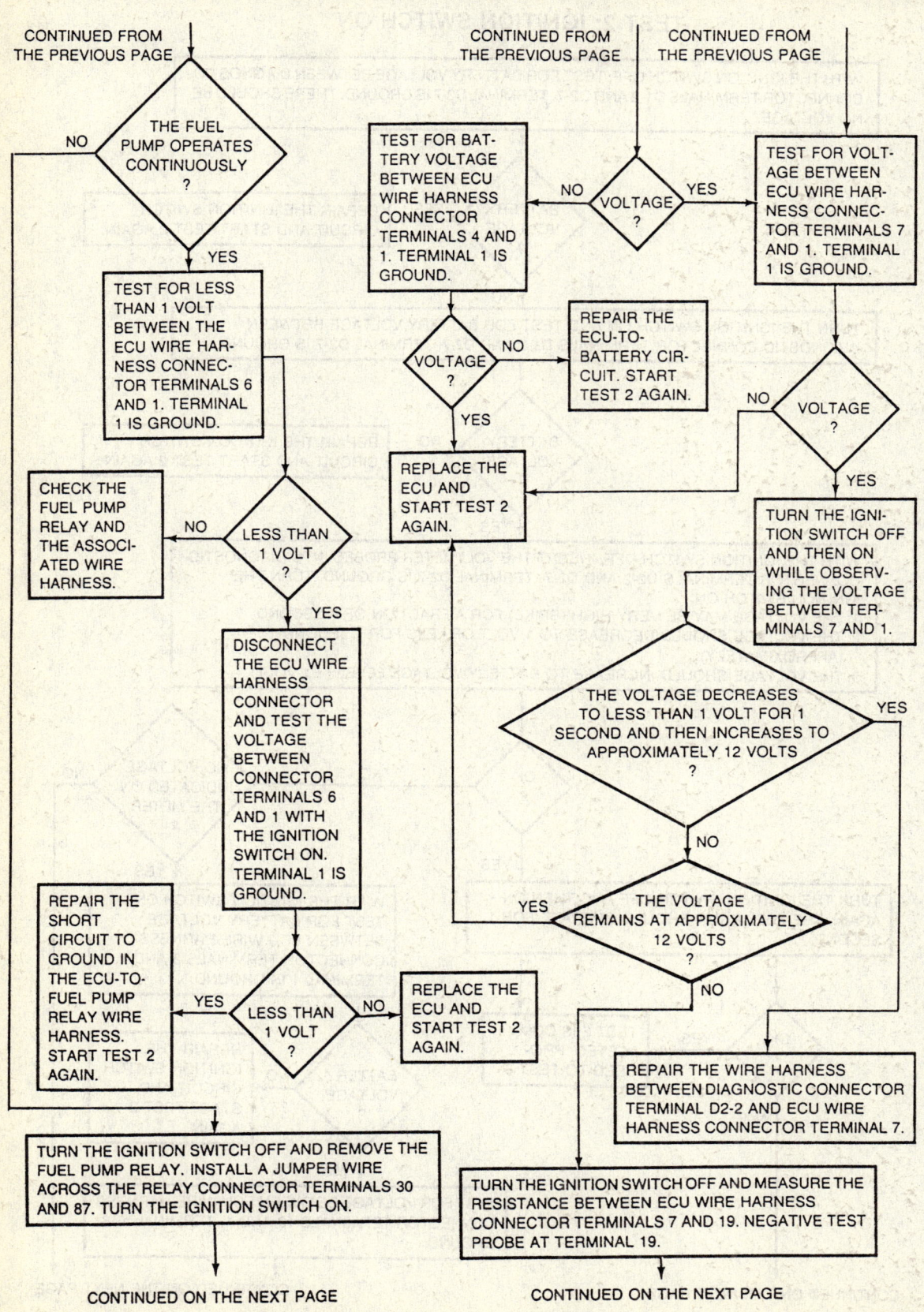

EMISSION CONTROLS 4

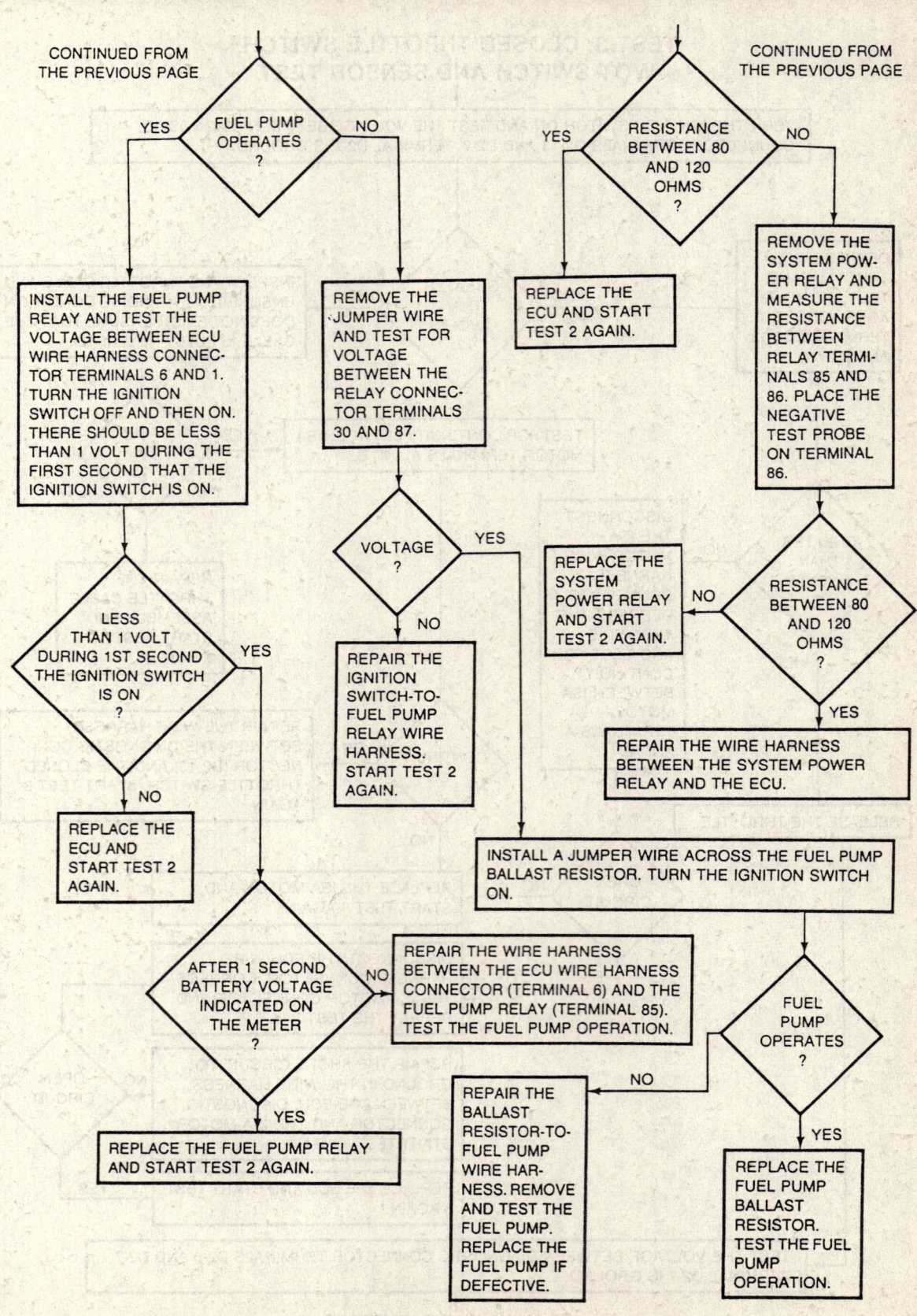

4-79

4 EMISSION CONTROLS

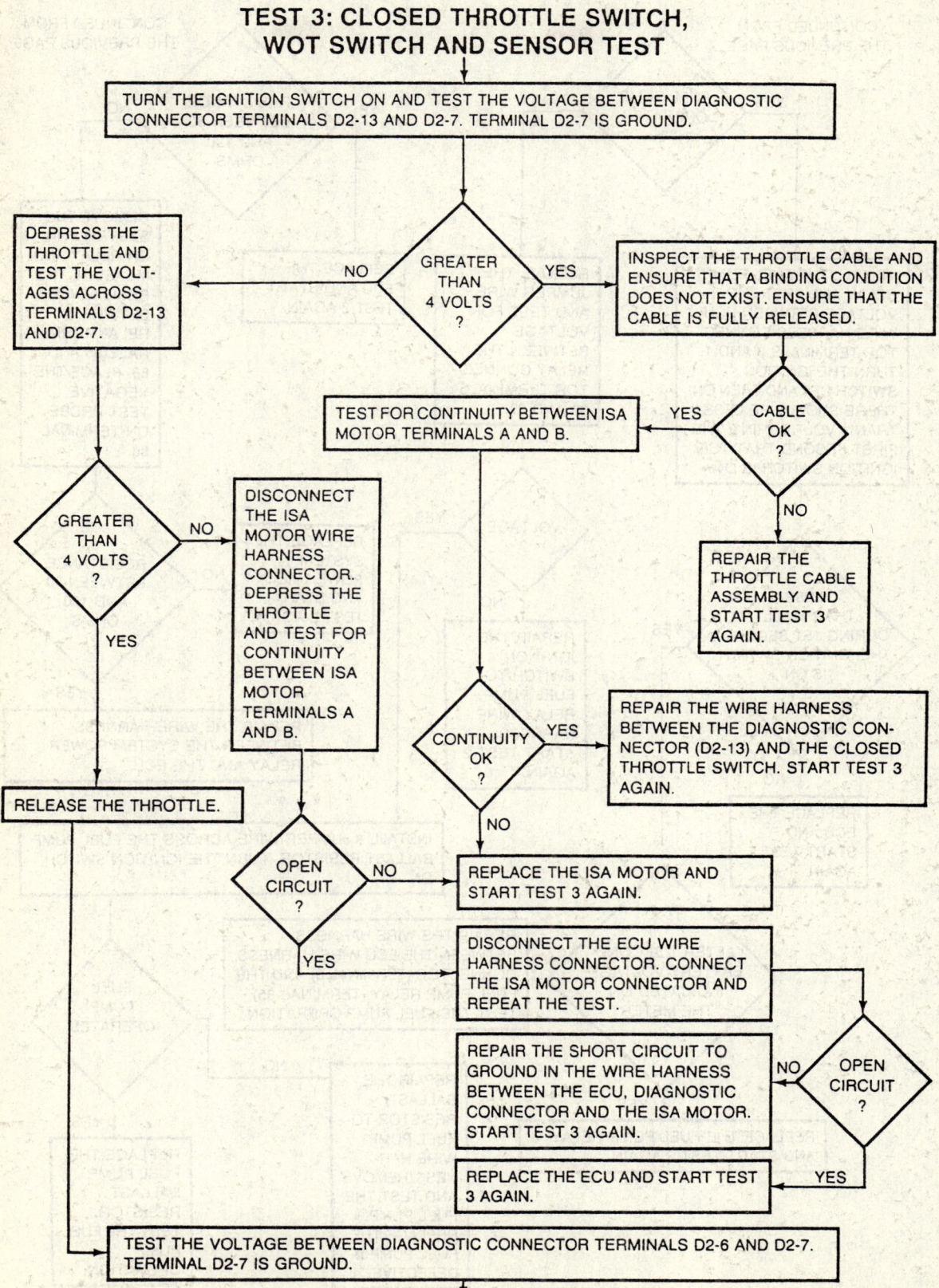

4-80

EMISSION CONTROLS 4

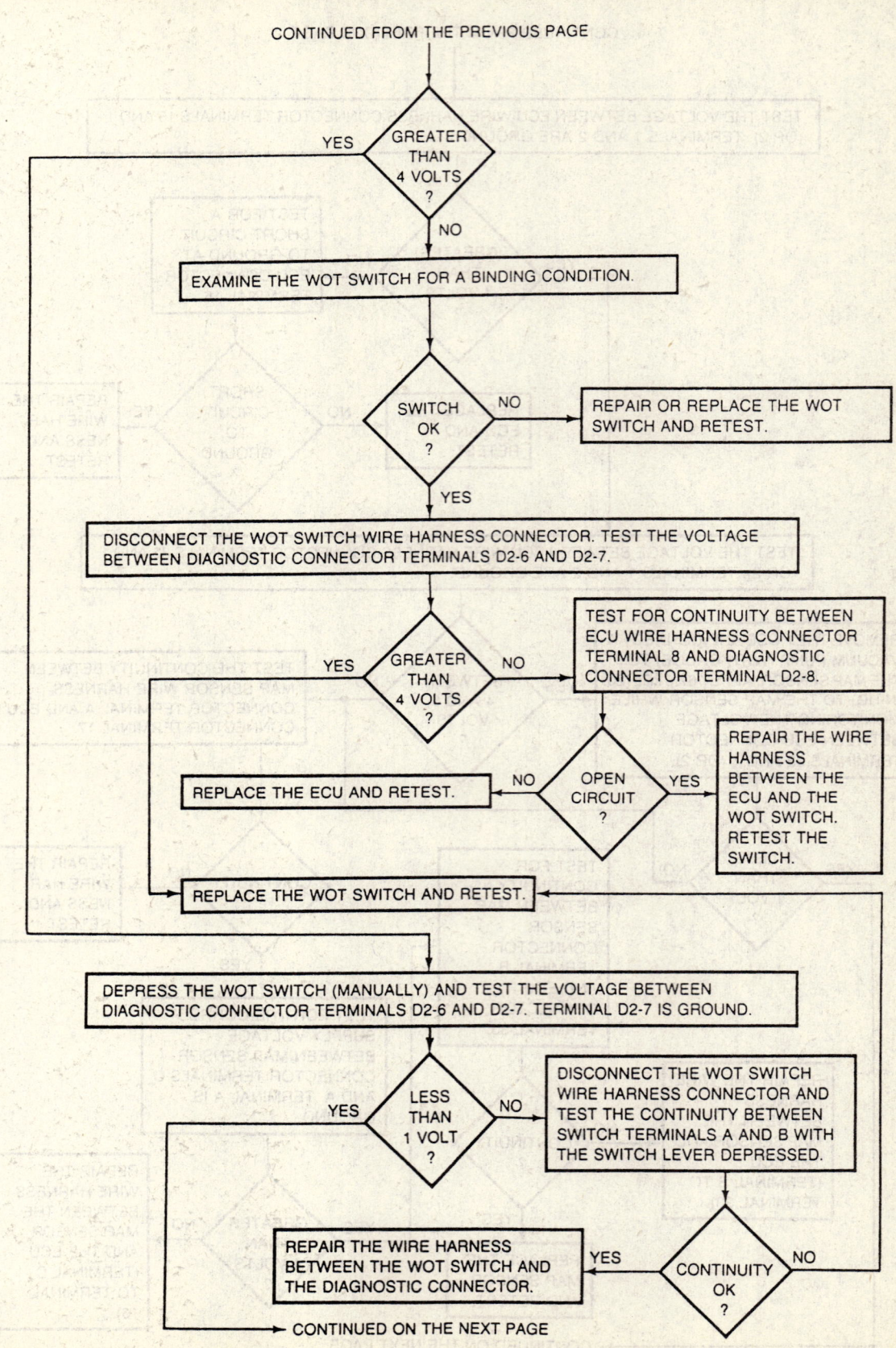

4-81

4 EMISSION CONTROLS

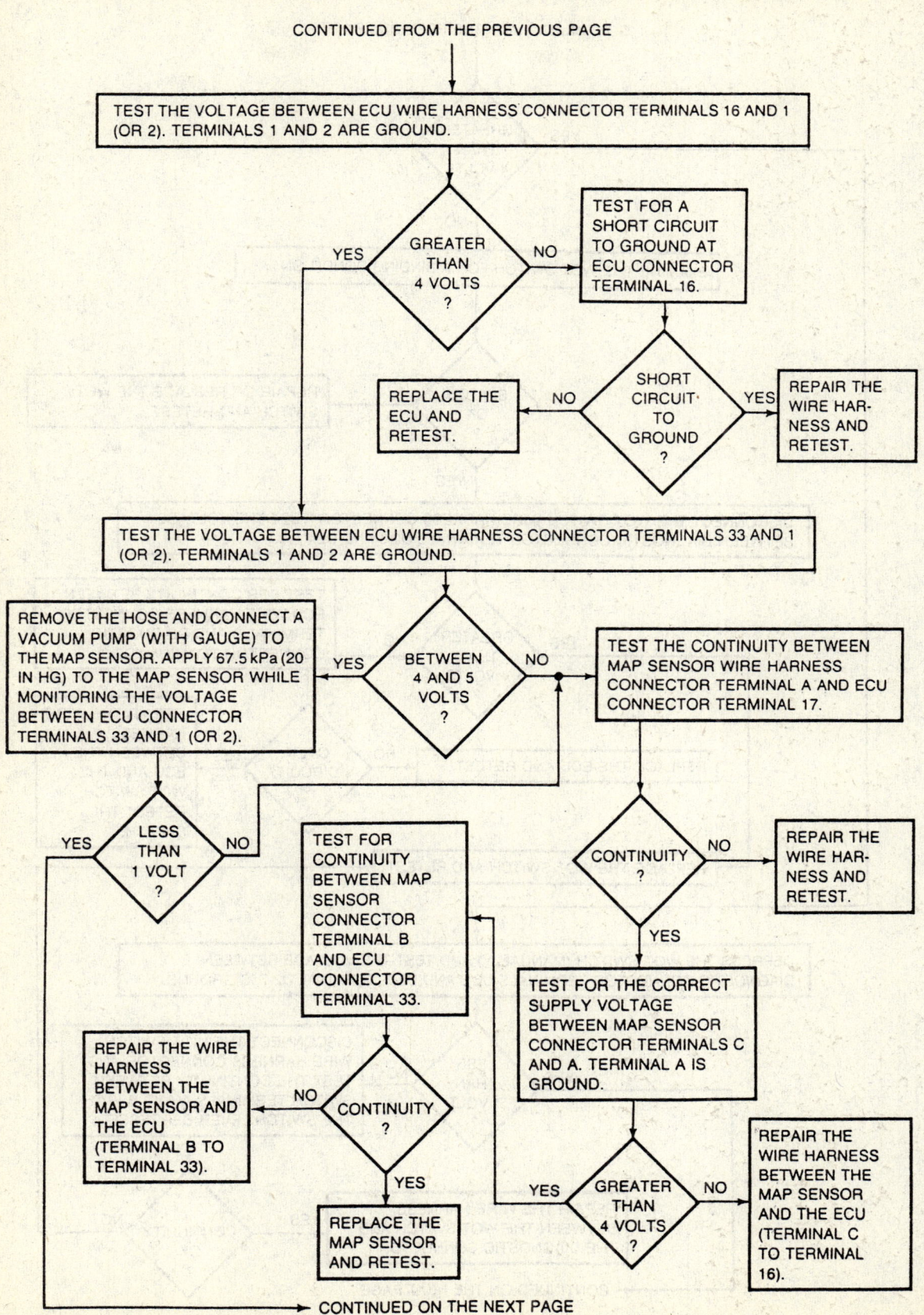

4-82

EMISSION CONTROLS 4

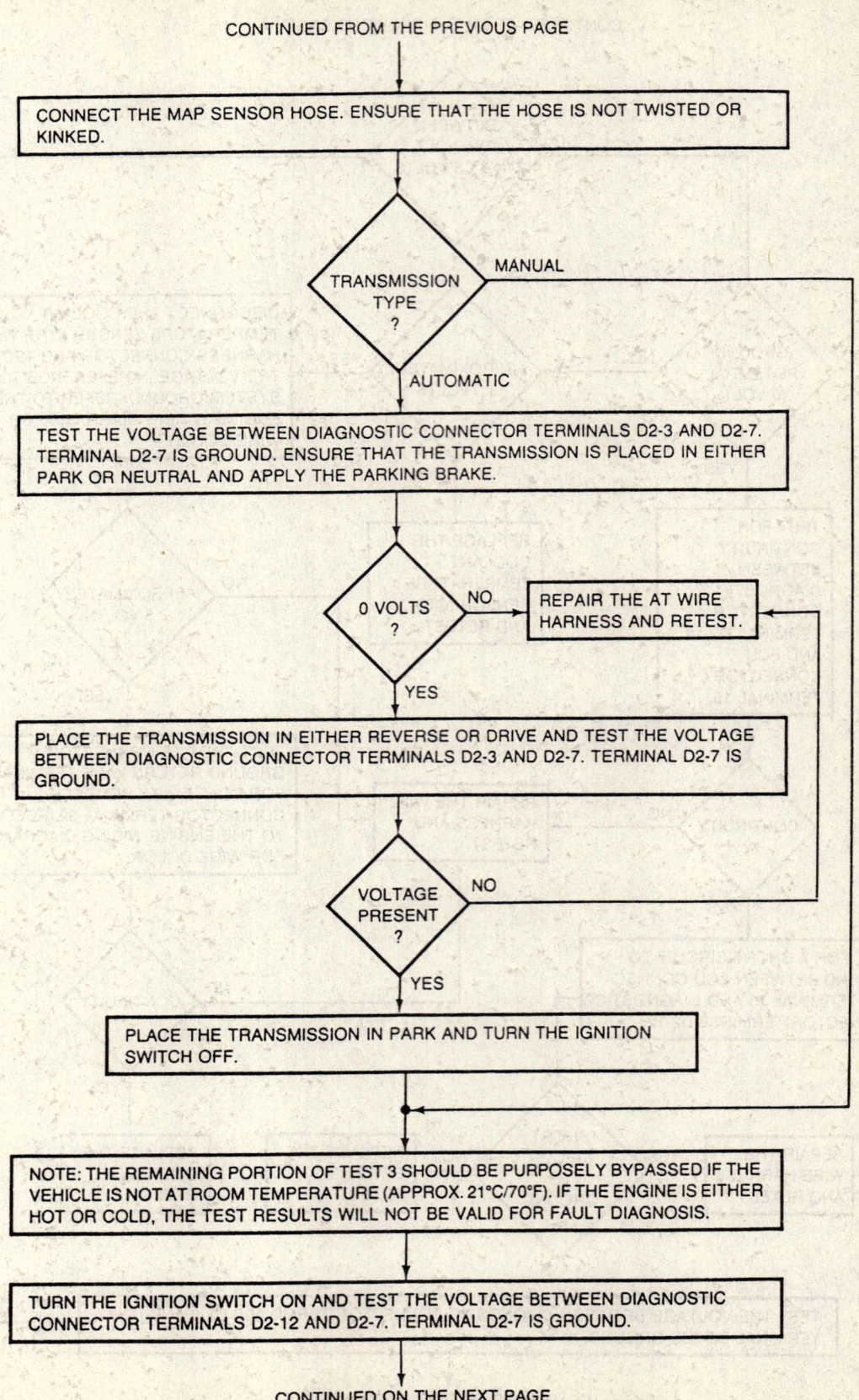

4-83

4 EMISSION CONTROLS

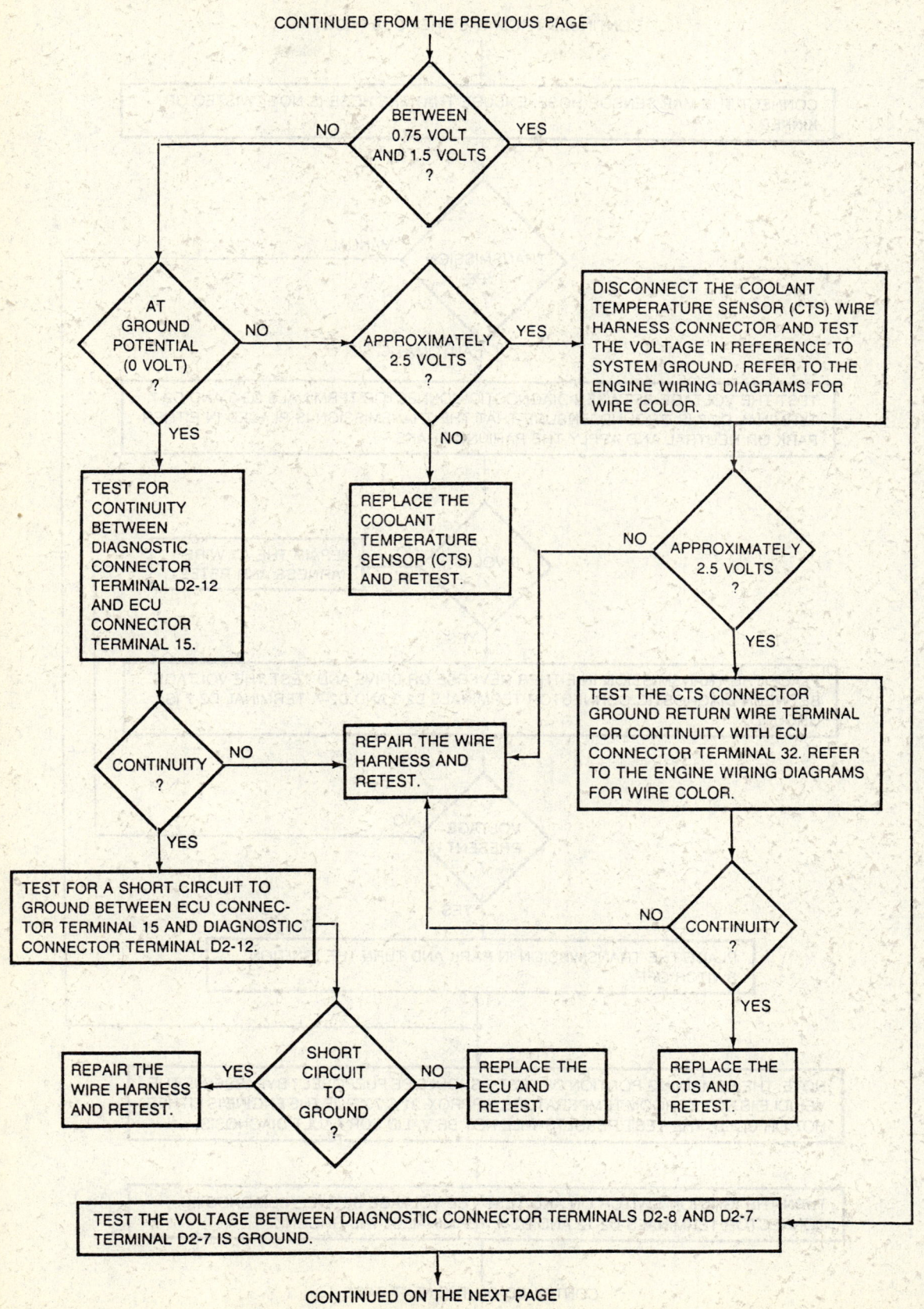

4-84

EMISSION CONTROLS 4

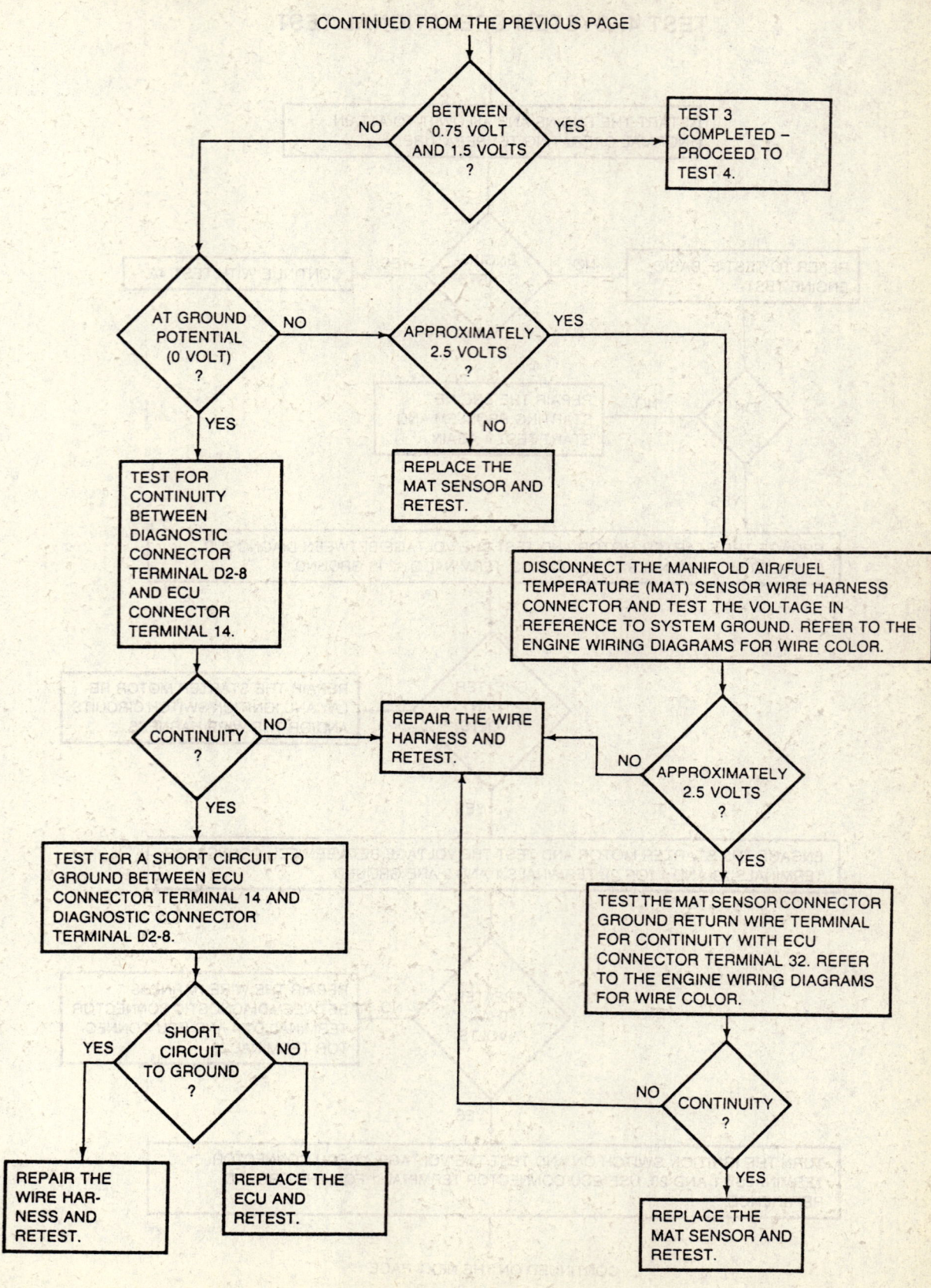

4 EMISSION CONTROLS

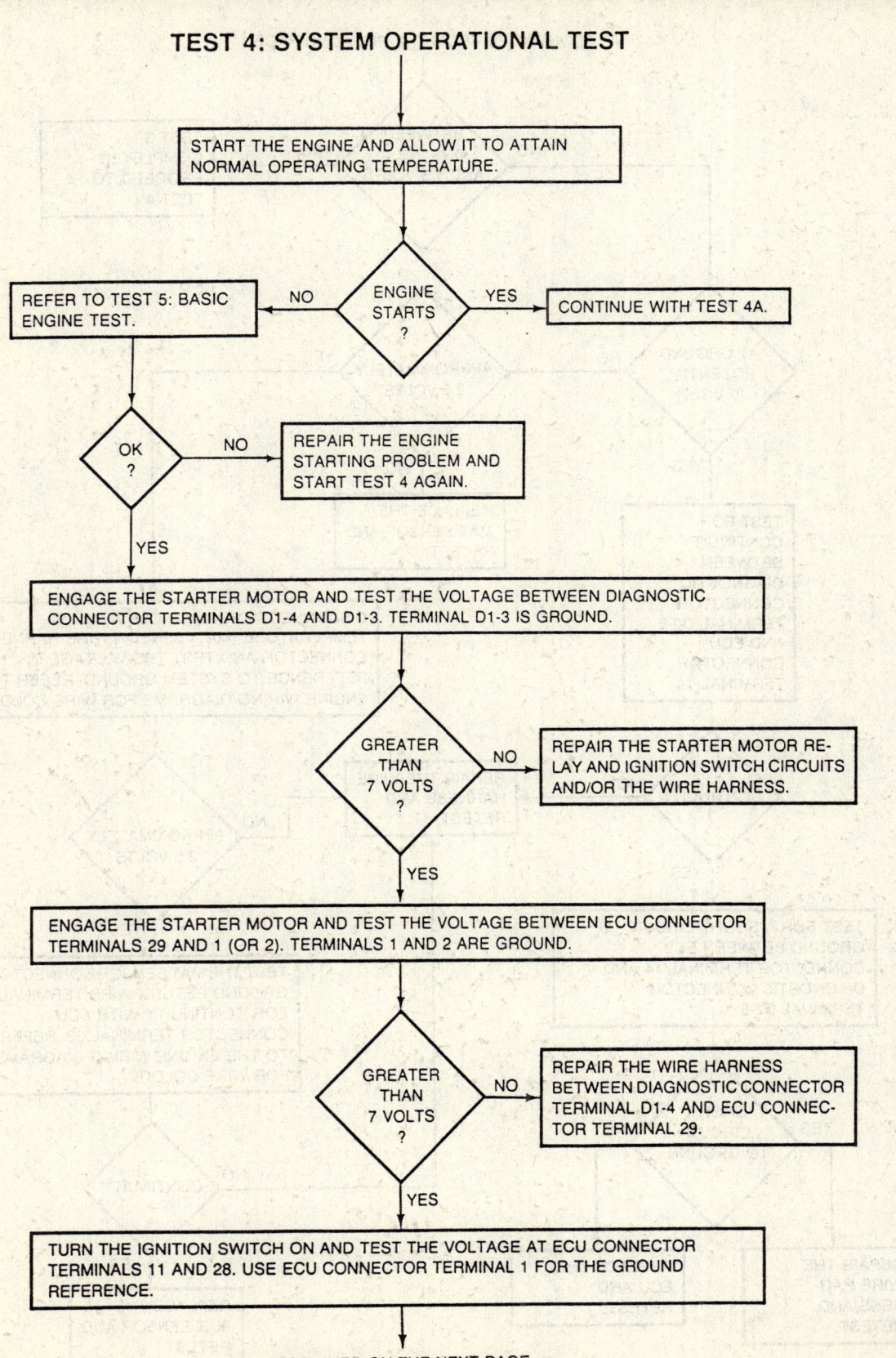

TEST 4: SYSTEM OPERATIONAL TEST

START THE ENGINE AND ALLOW IT TO ATTAIN NORMAL OPERATING TEMPERATURE.

ENGINE STARTS?
- NO → REFER TO TEST 5: BASIC ENGINE TEST.
- YES → CONTINUE WITH TEST 4A.

OK?
- NO → REPAIR THE ENGINE STARTING PROBLEM AND START TEST 4 AGAIN.
- YES ↓

ENGAGE THE STARTER MOTOR AND TEST THE VOLTAGE BETWEEN DIAGNOSTIC CONNECTOR TERMINALS D1-4 AND D1-3. TERMINAL D1-3 IS GROUND.

GREATER THAN 7 VOLTS?
- NO → REPAIR THE STARTER MOTOR RELAY AND IGNITION SWITCH CIRCUITS AND/OR THE WIRE HARNESS.
- YES ↓

ENGAGE THE STARTER MOTOR AND TEST THE VOLTAGE BETWEEN ECU CONNECTOR TERMINALS 29 AND 1 (OR 2). TERMINALS 1 AND 2 ARE GROUND.

GREATER THAN 7 VOLTS?
- NO → REPAIR THE WIRE HARNESS BETWEEN DIAGNOSTIC CONNECTOR TERMINAL D1-4 AND ECU CONNECTOR TERMINAL 29.
- YES ↓

TURN THE IGNITION SWITCH ON AND TEST THE VOLTAGE AT ECU CONNECTOR TERMINALS 11 AND 28. USE ECU CONNECTOR TERMINAL 1 FOR THE GROUND REFERENCE.

CONTINUED ON THE NEXT PAGE

EMISSION CONTROLS 4

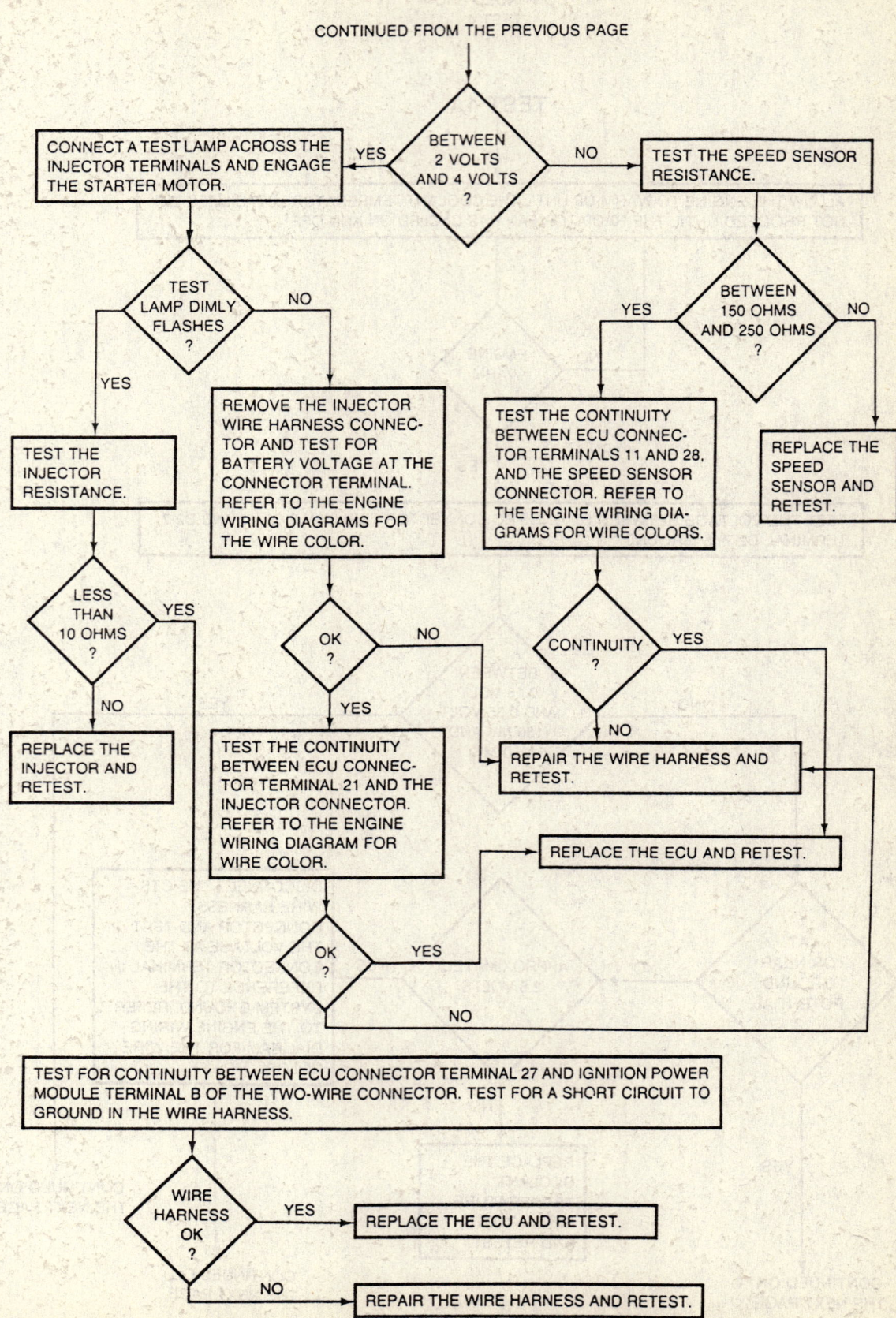

4-87

4 EMISSION CONTROLS

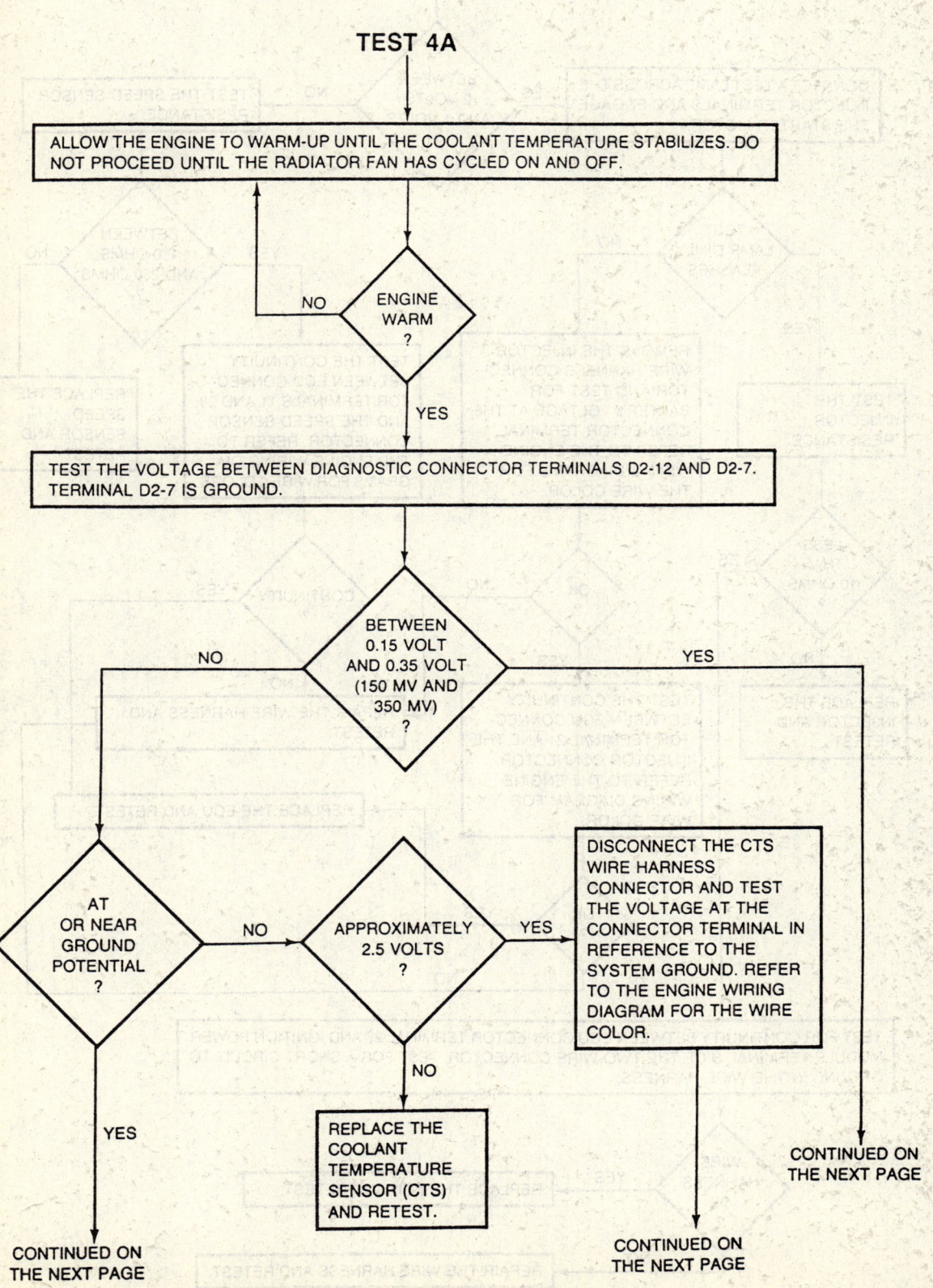

EMISSION CONTROLS 4

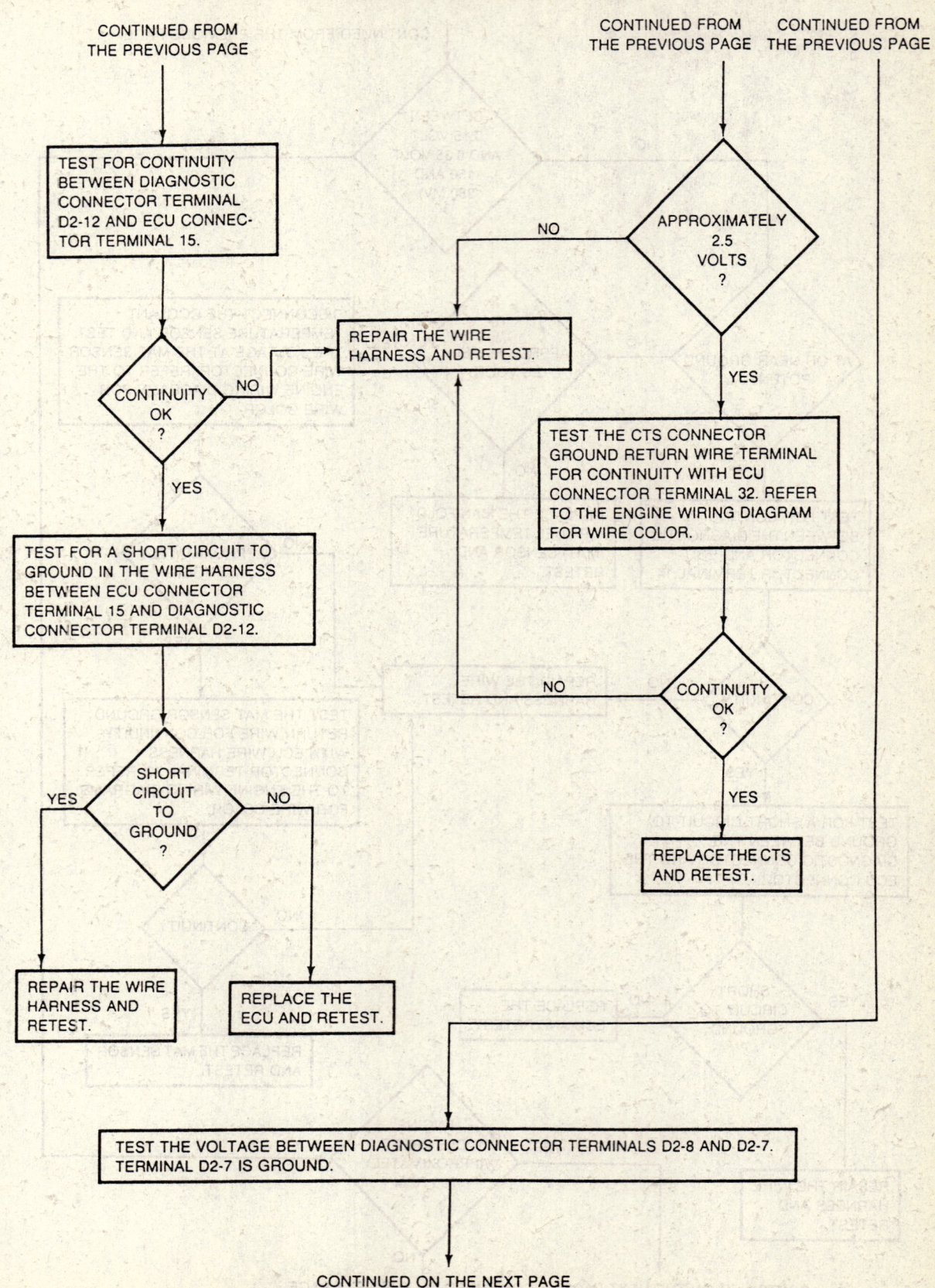

4 EMISSION CONTROLS

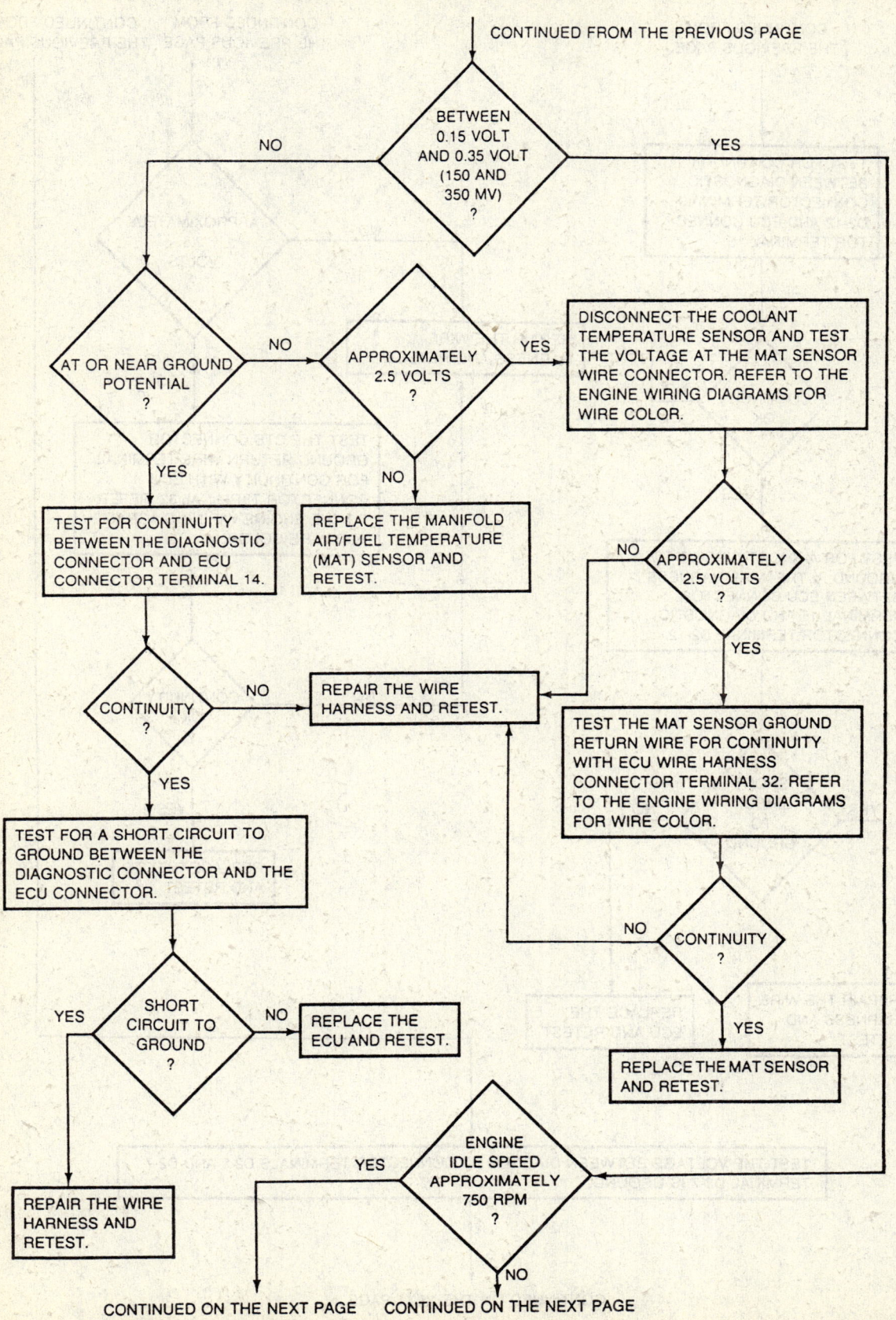

4-90

EMISSION CONTROLS 4

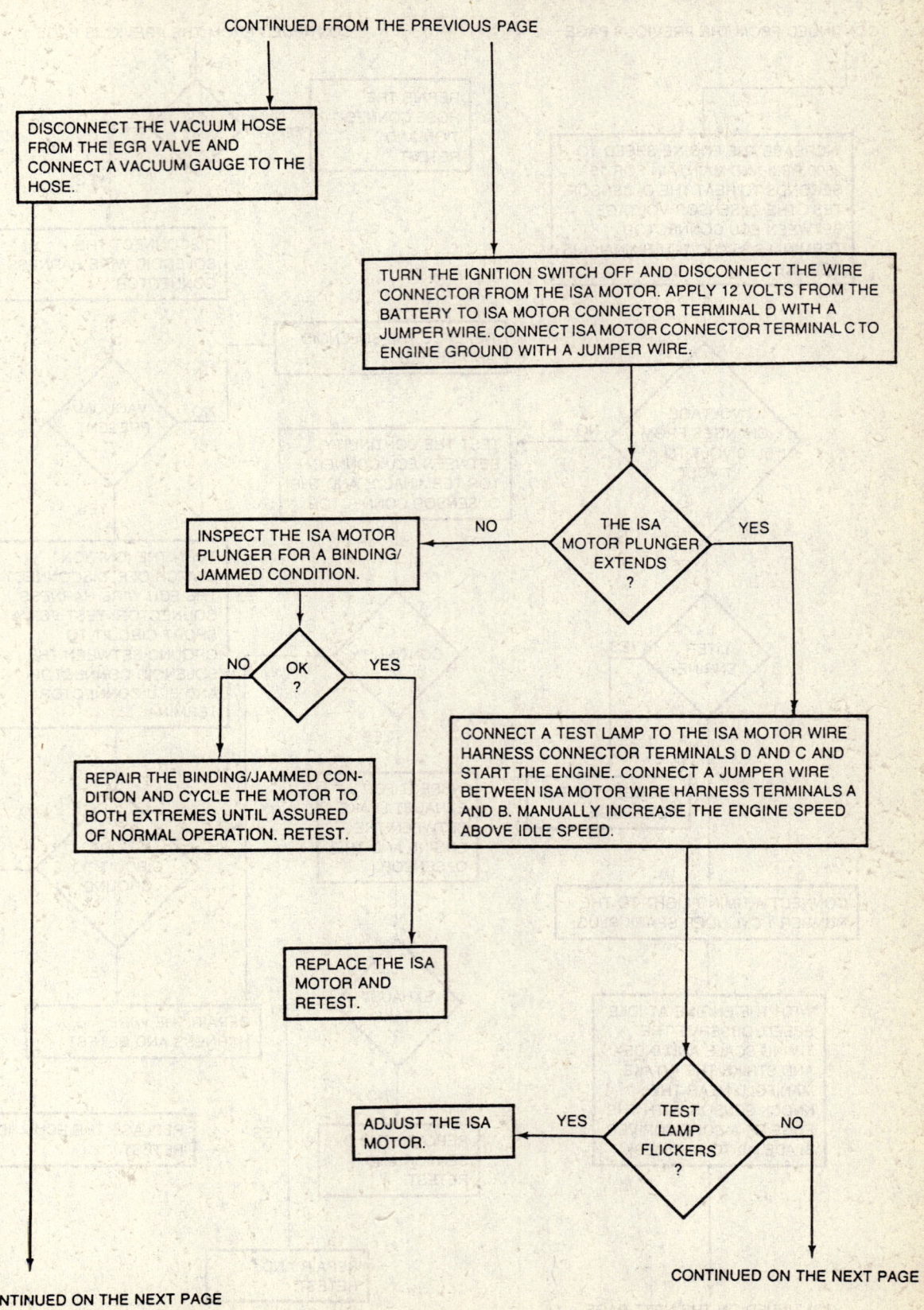

4-91

4 EMISSION CONTROLS

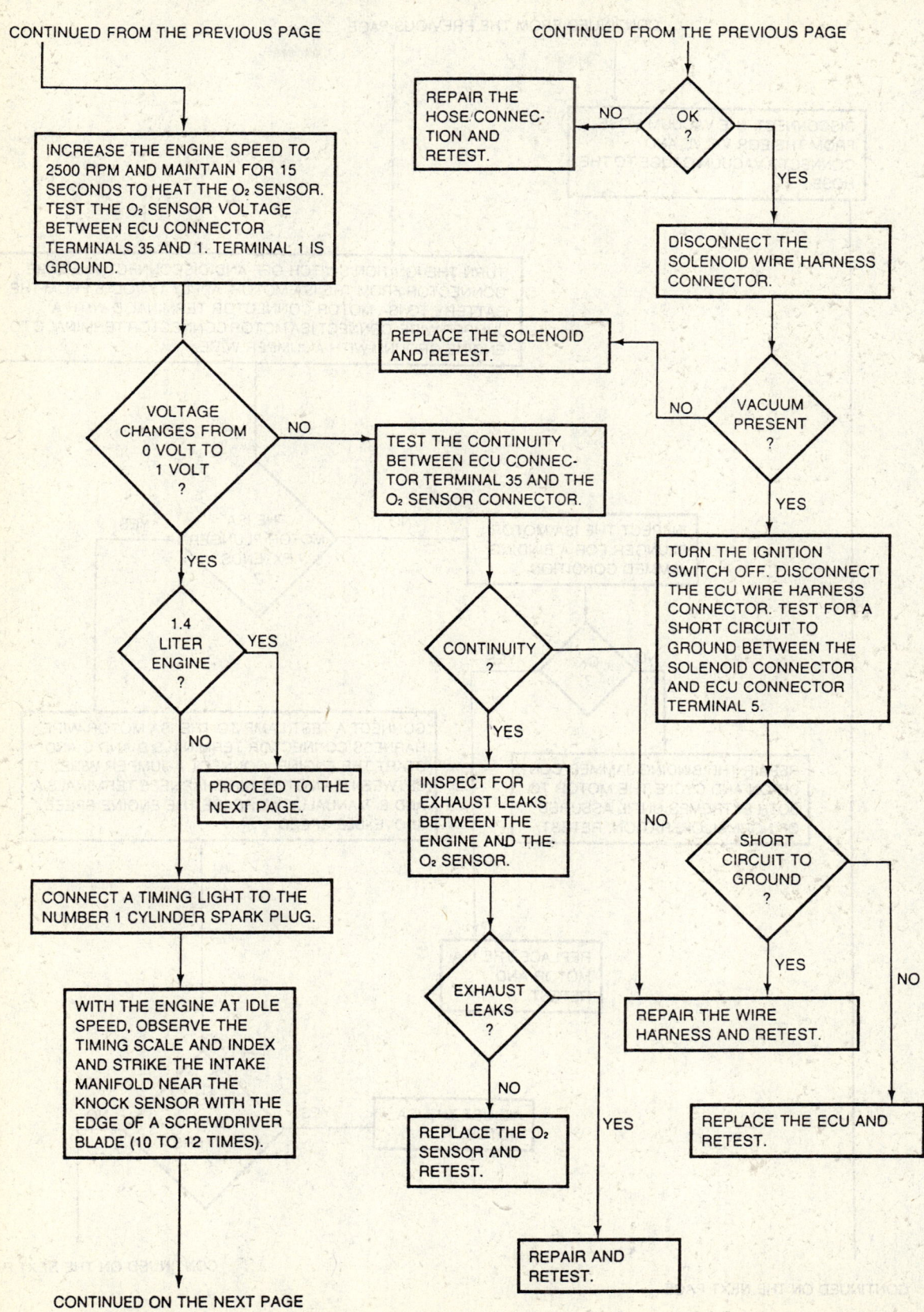

EMISSION CONTROLS 4

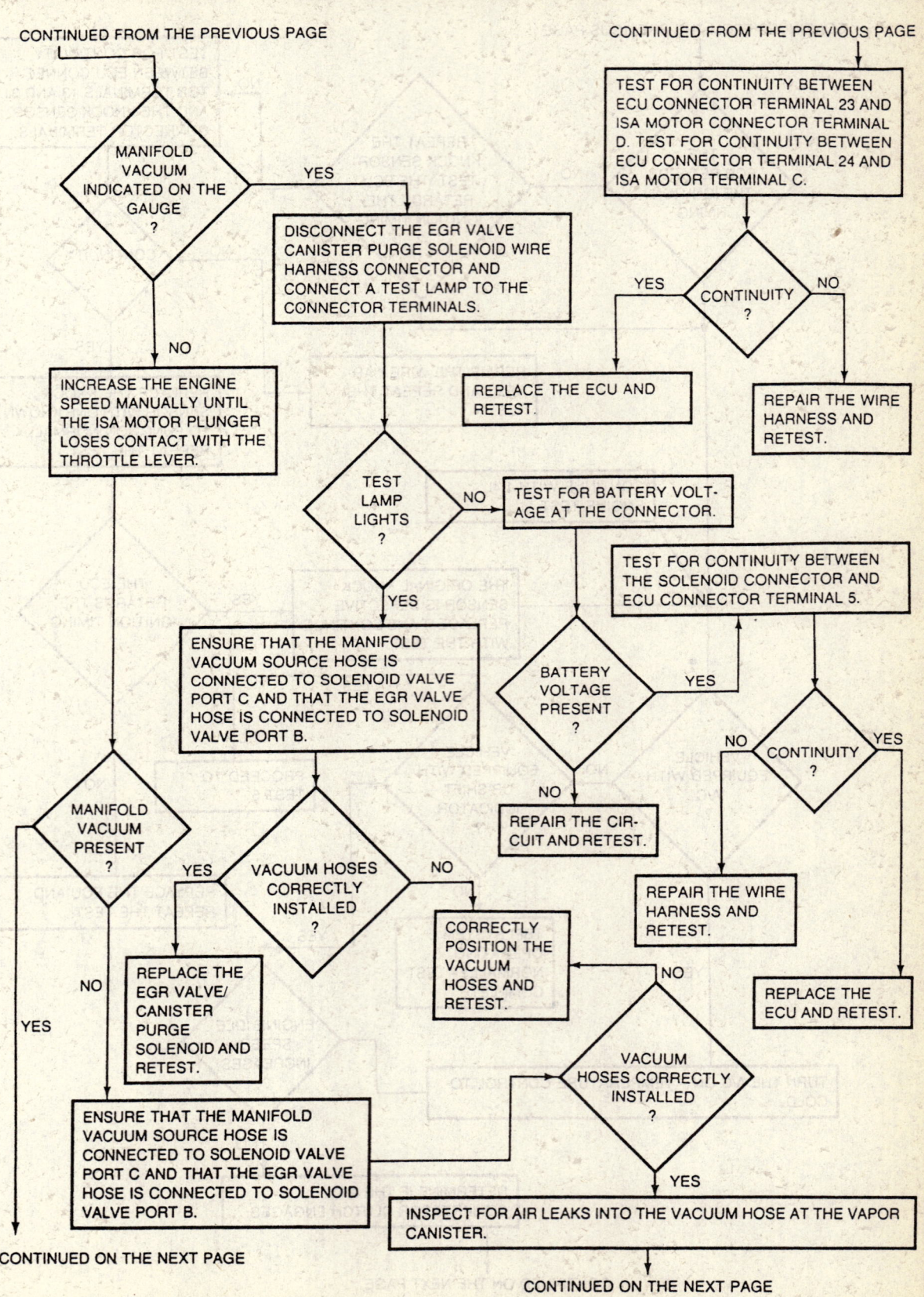

4-93

4 EMISSION CONTROLS

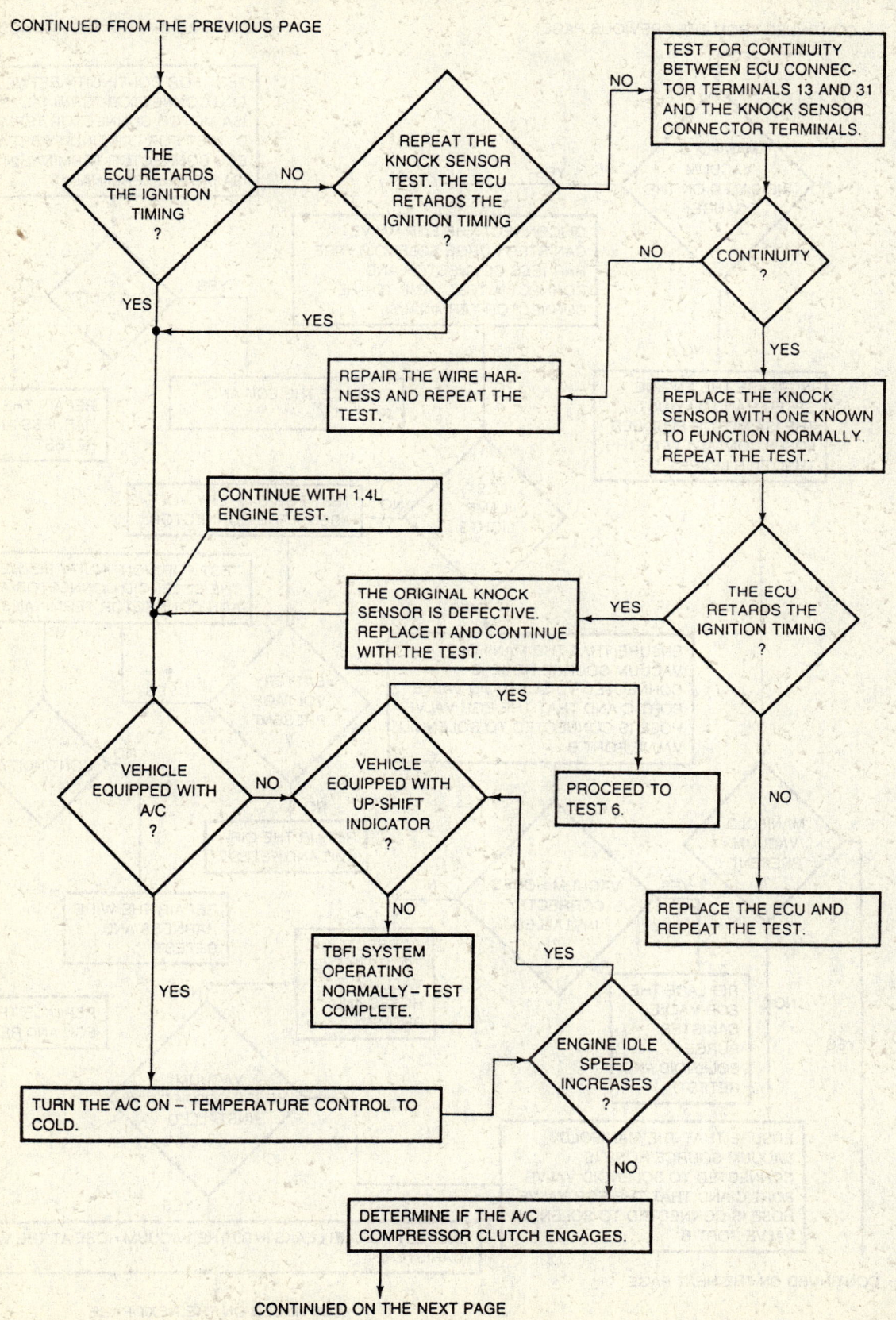

EMISSION CONTROLS 4

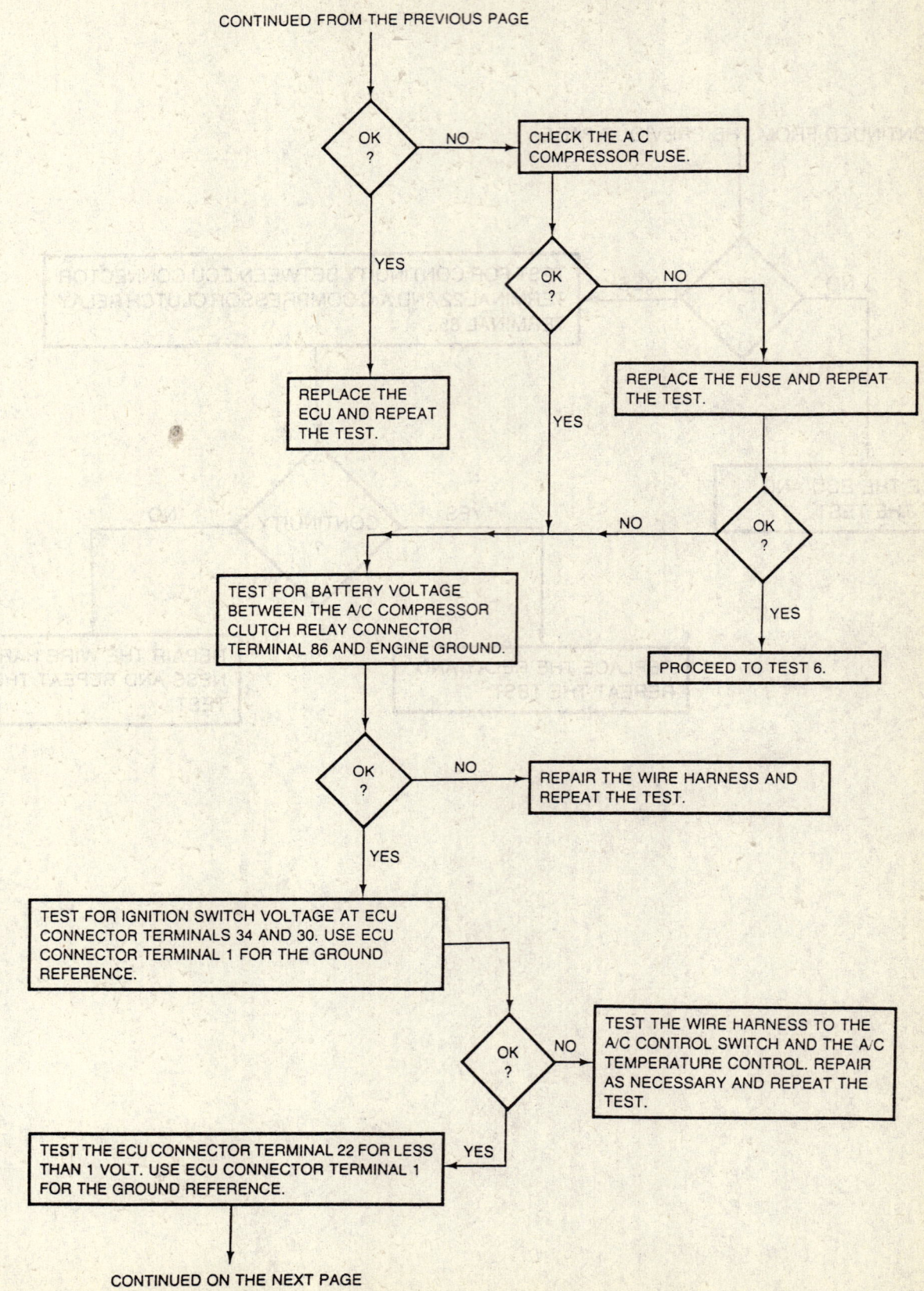

4-95

4 EMISSION CONTROLS

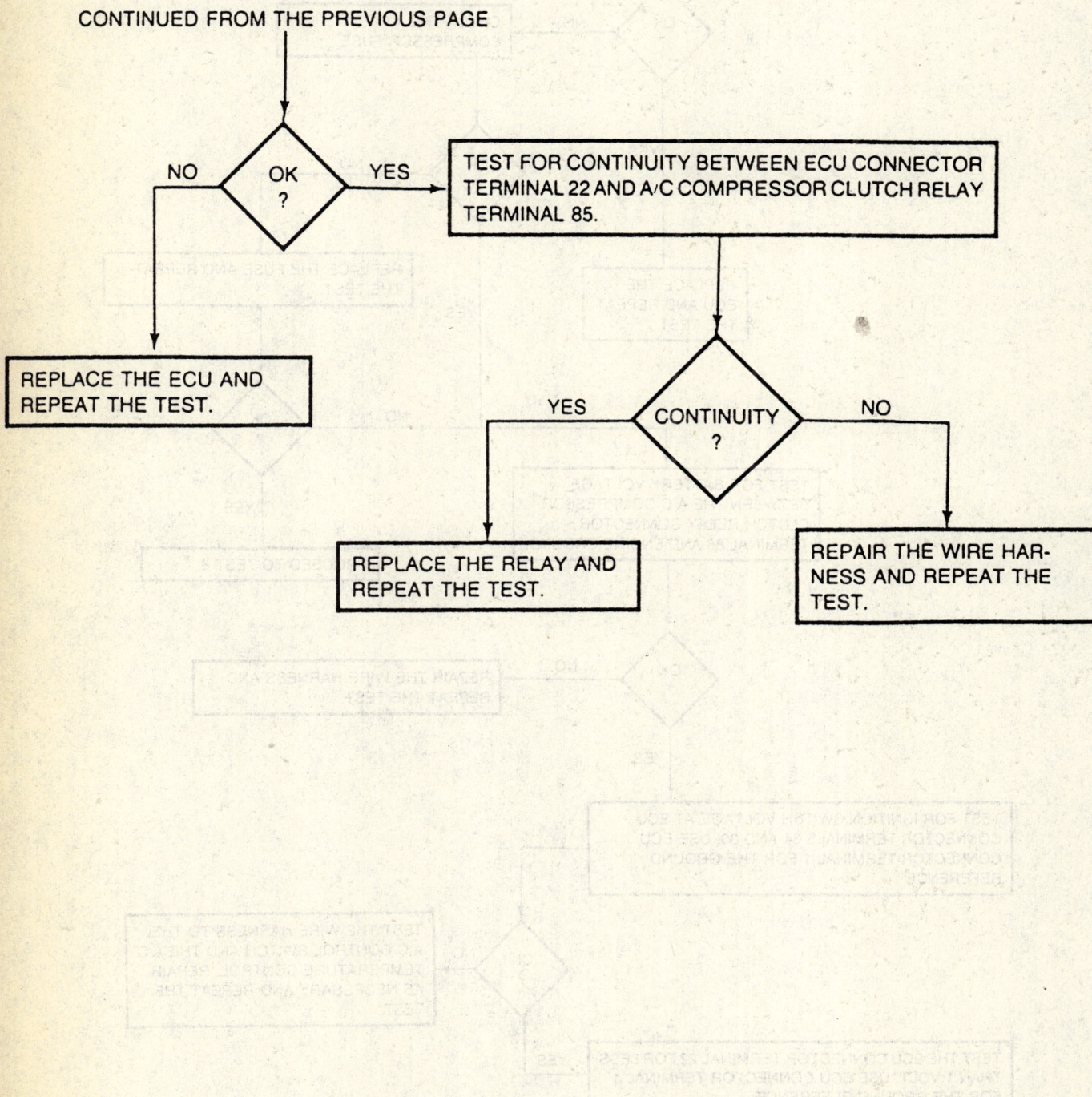

4-96

EMISSION CONTROLS 4

TEST 5: BASIC ENGINE TEST

INSPECT THE ENGINE FOR AIR LEAKS INTO THE VACUUM HOSES AND FITTINGS.

CHECK THE IGNITION POWER MODULE OPERATION AND THE IGNITION HIGH VOLTAGE.

IF FUEL IS LEAKING FROM AROUND THE BASE OF THE INJECTOR, REPLACE THE O-RING.

CHECK THE FUEL PUMP PRESSURE.

RETURN TO TEST 4.

4-97

4 EMISSION CONTROLS

TEST 6: MT UP-SHIFT TEST

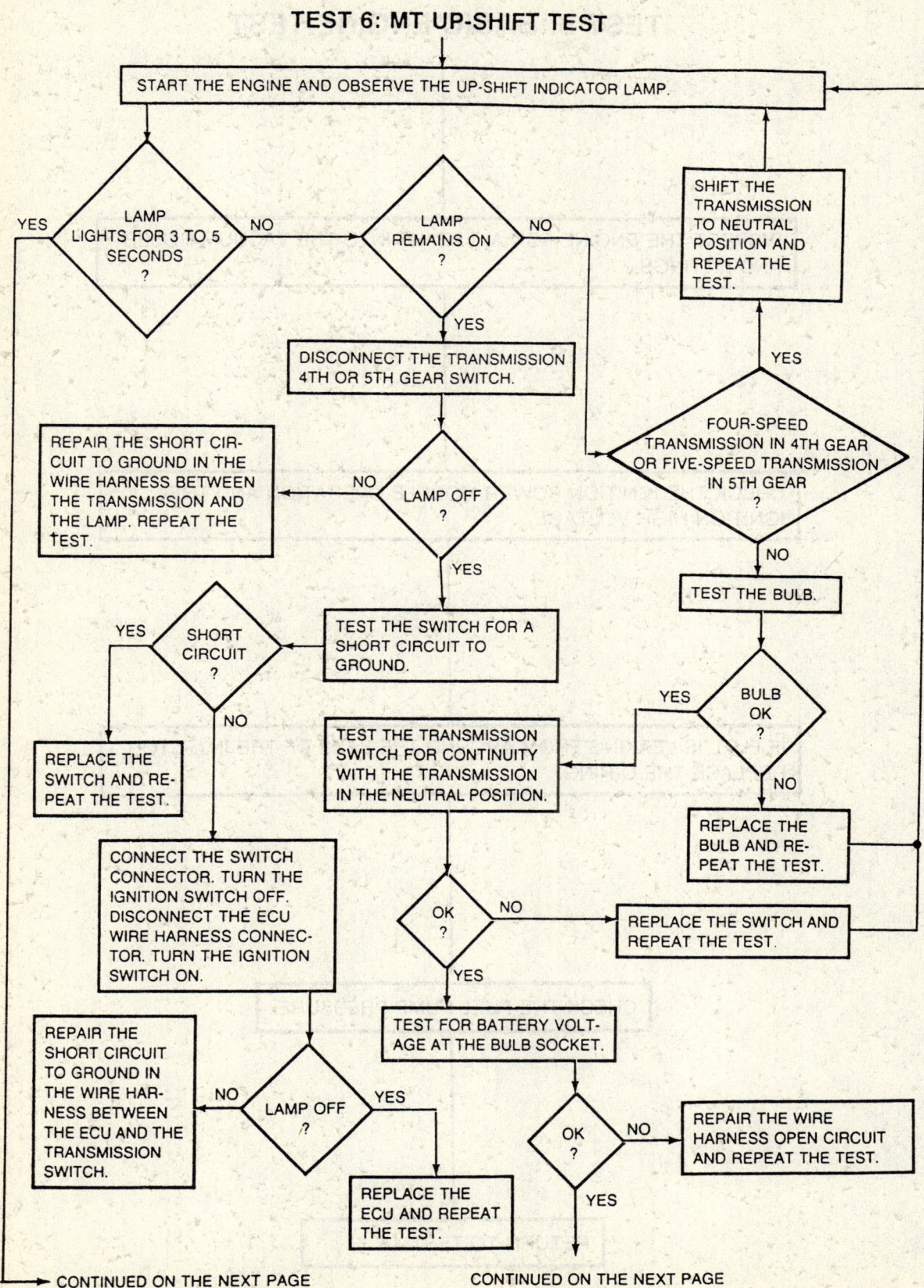

EMISSION CONTROLS 4

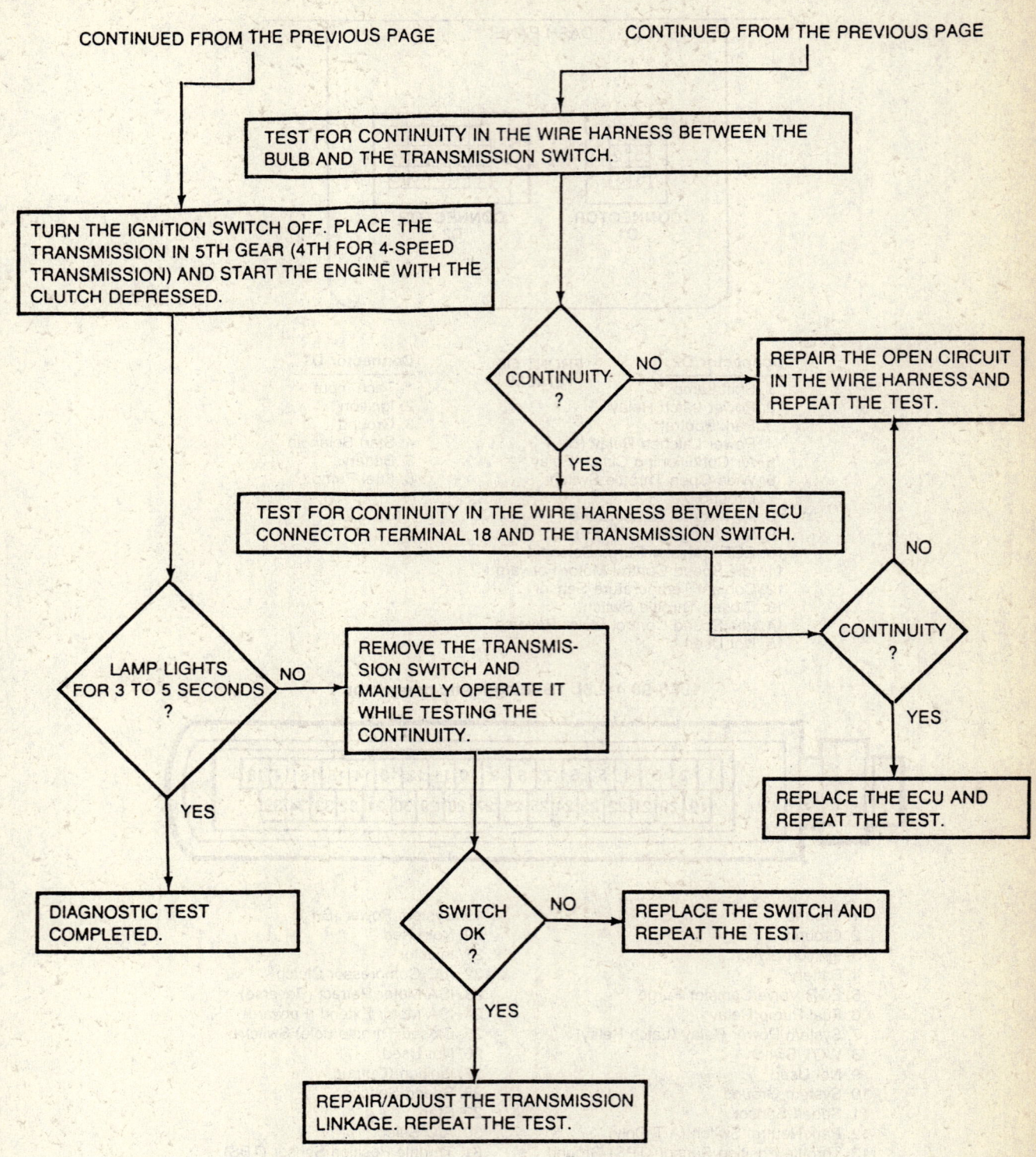

4-99

4 EMISSION CONTROLS

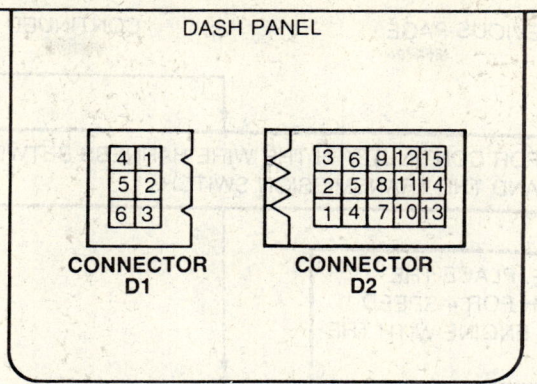

Connector D2
1. Shift Lamp
2. Power Latch Relay
3. Park/Neutral
4. Power Latched Relay (B+)
5. Air Conditioning Clutch Relay
6. Wide-Open Throttle Switch
7. Ground
8. Air Mixture Temperature
9. M.P.A. (Ignition Output)
10. EGR/Canister Purge Solenoid
11. Idle Speed Control Motor Forward
12. Coolant Temperature Sensor
13. Closed Throttle Switch
14. Idle Speed Control Motor Reverse
15. Not Used

Connector D1
1. Tach Input
2. Ignition
3. Ground
4. Start Solenoid
5. Battery
6. Fuel Pump

1986-90 4-2.5L TBI diagnostic connector

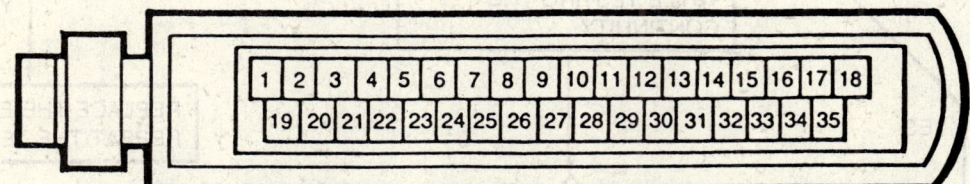

1. Ground
2. Ground
3. Ignition Switch
4. Battery
5. EGR Valve/Canister Purge
6. Fuel Pump Relay
7. System Power Relay (Latch Relay)
8. WOT Switch
9. Not Used
10. System Ground
11. Speed Sensor
12. Park/Neutral Switch (A/T Only)
13. Throttle Position Sensor (TPS) Ground
14. Manifold Air/Fuel Temperature Sensor
15. Coolant Temperature Sensor
16. Manifold Absolute Pressure (Supply Voltage)
17. Manifold Absolute Pressure (Ground)
18. Shift Lamp
19. System Power (B+)
20. Not Used
21. Injector
22. A/C Compressor Clutch
23. ISA Motor Retract (Reverse)
24. ISA Motor Extend (Forward)
25. Closed Throttle (Idle) Switch
26. Not Used
27. Ignition (Output)
28. Speed Sensor
29. Start
30. A/C Select
31. Throttle Position Sensor (TPS)
32. Sensor Ground
33. Manifold Absolute Pressure (Output Voltage)
34. A/C Temperature Control (Request)
35. Oxygen Sensor

1986-90 4-2.5L TBI ECU connector

EMISSION CONTROLS 4

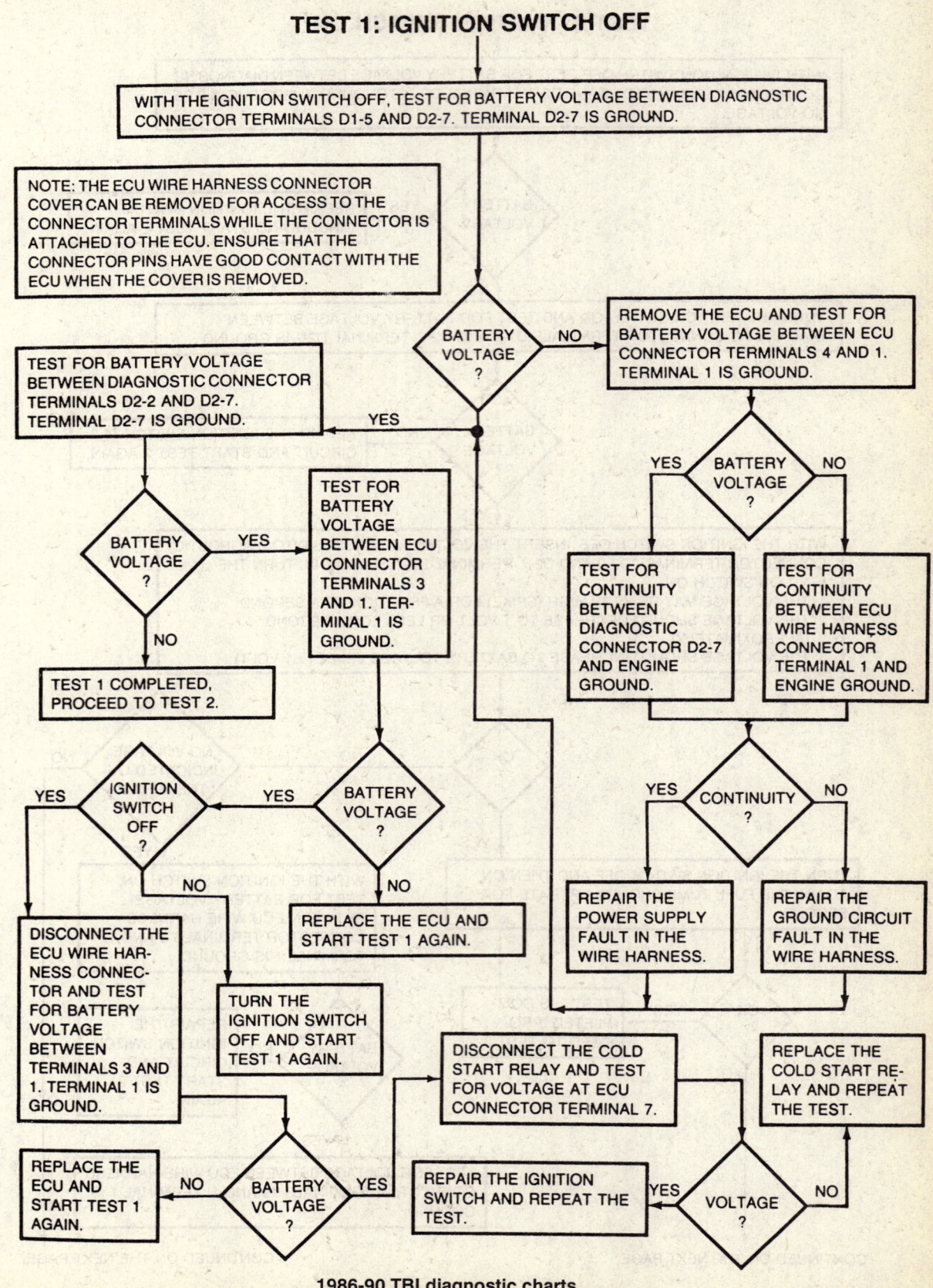

1986-90 TBI diagnostic charts

4 EMISSION CONTROLS

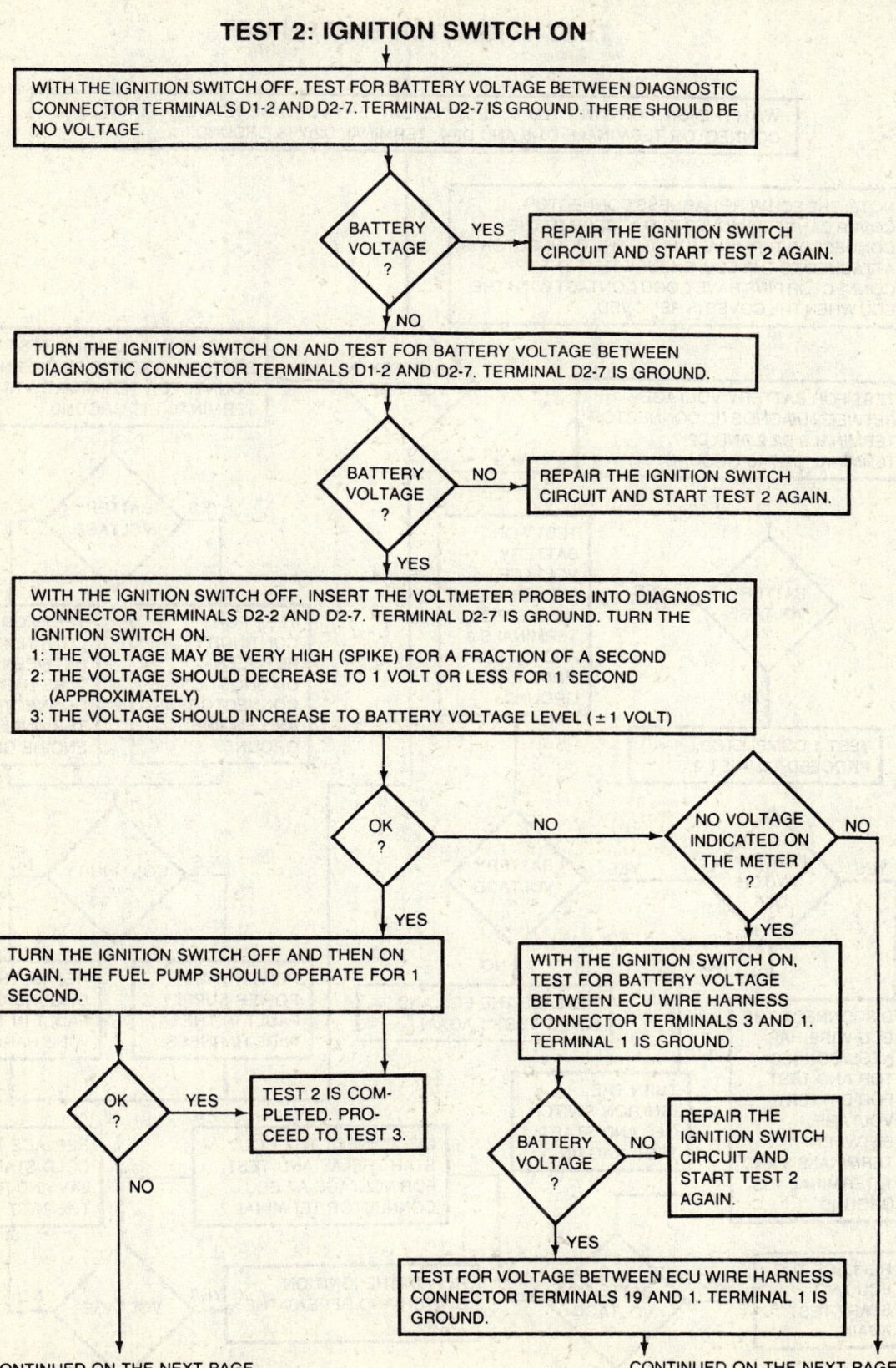

EMISSION CONTROLS 4

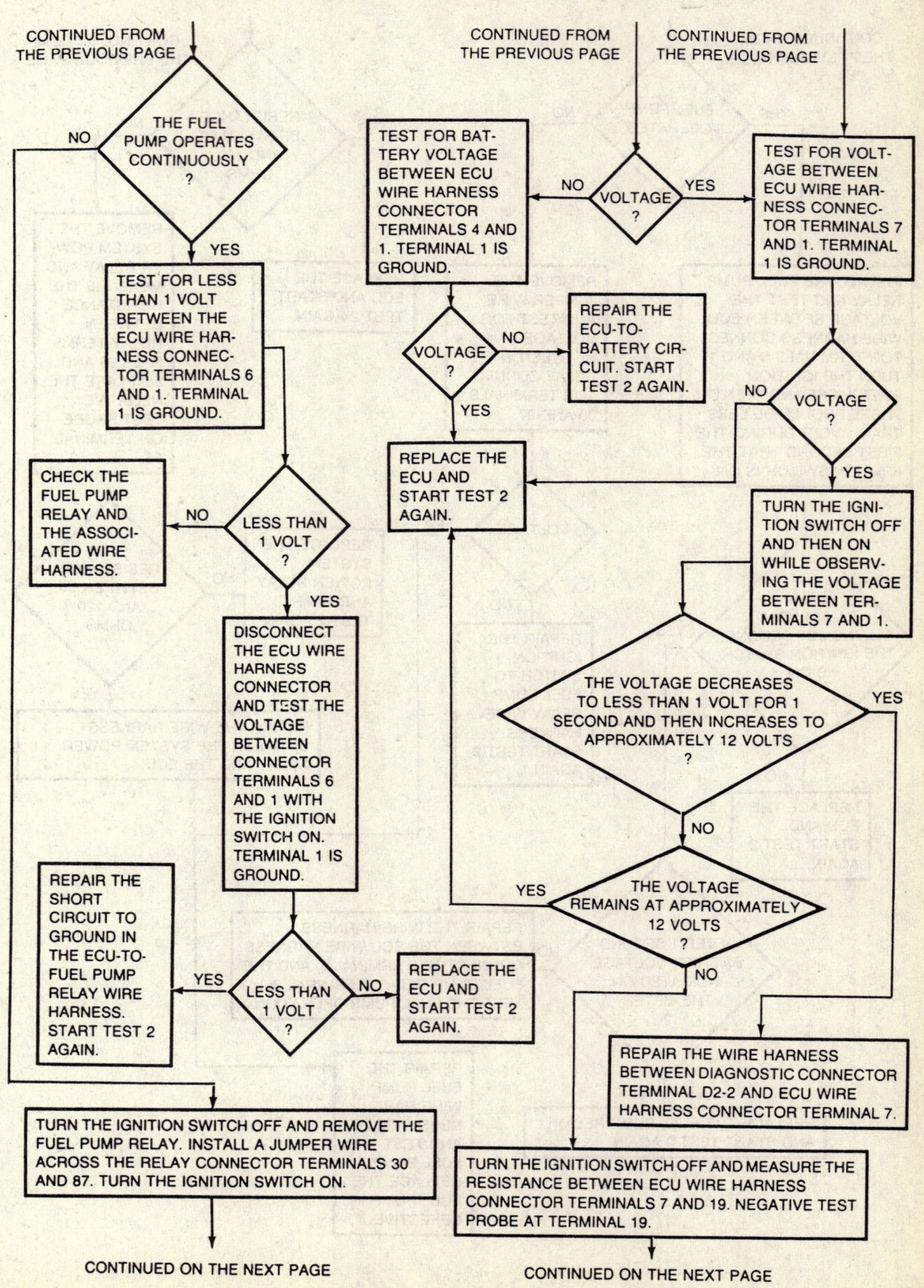

4-103

4 EMISSION CONTROLS

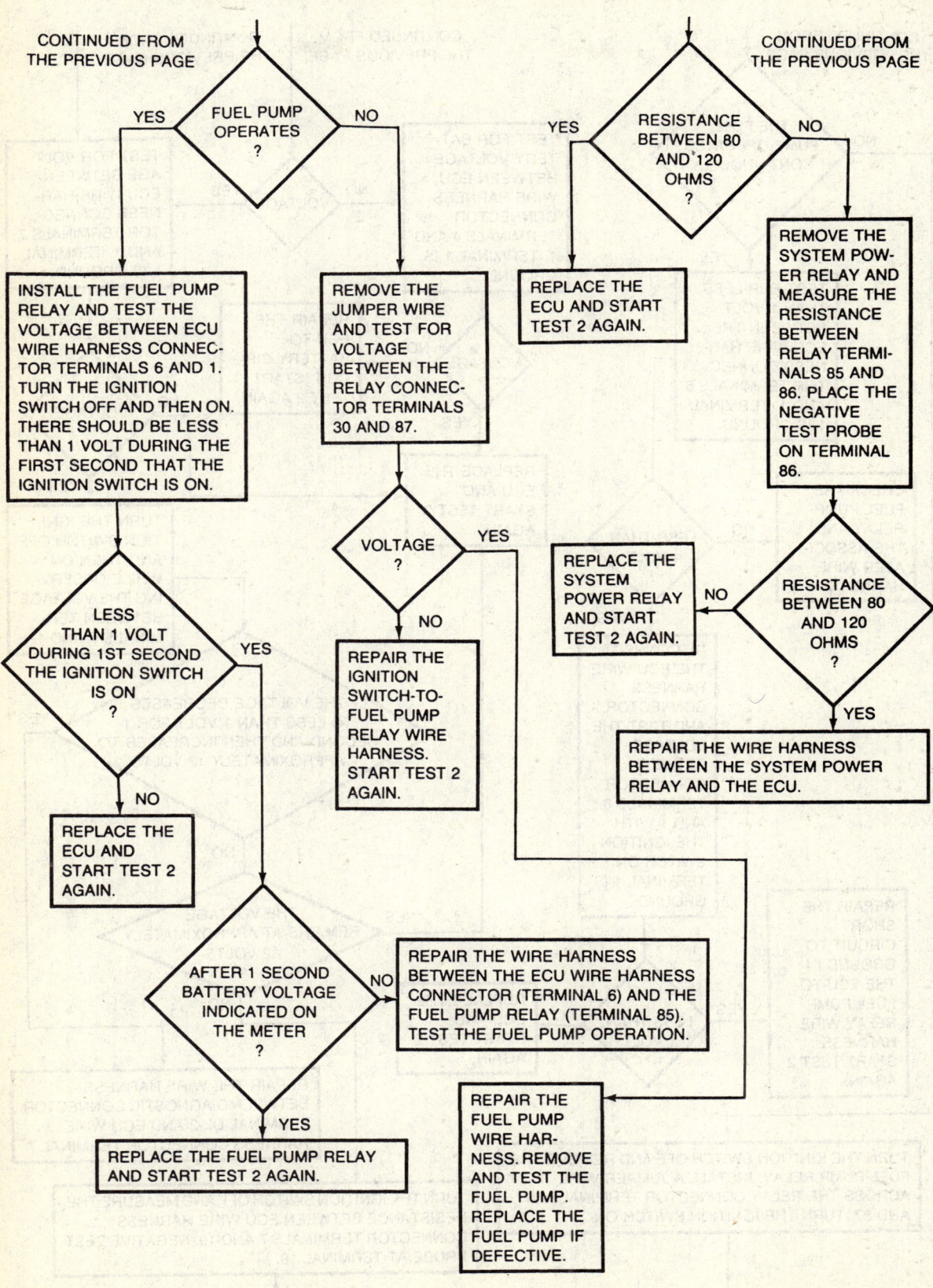

EMISSION CONTROLS 4

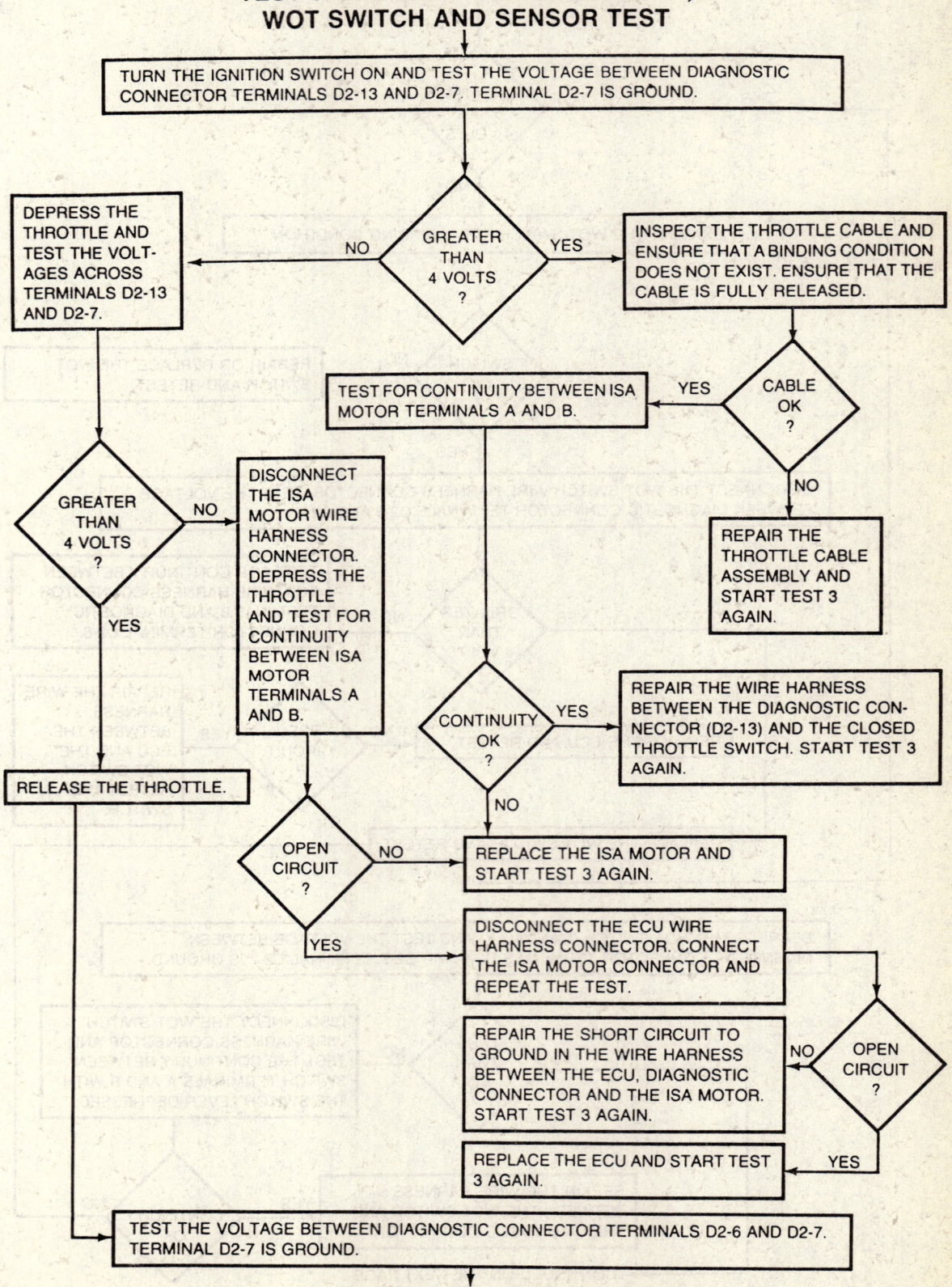

4-105

4 EMISSION CONTROLS

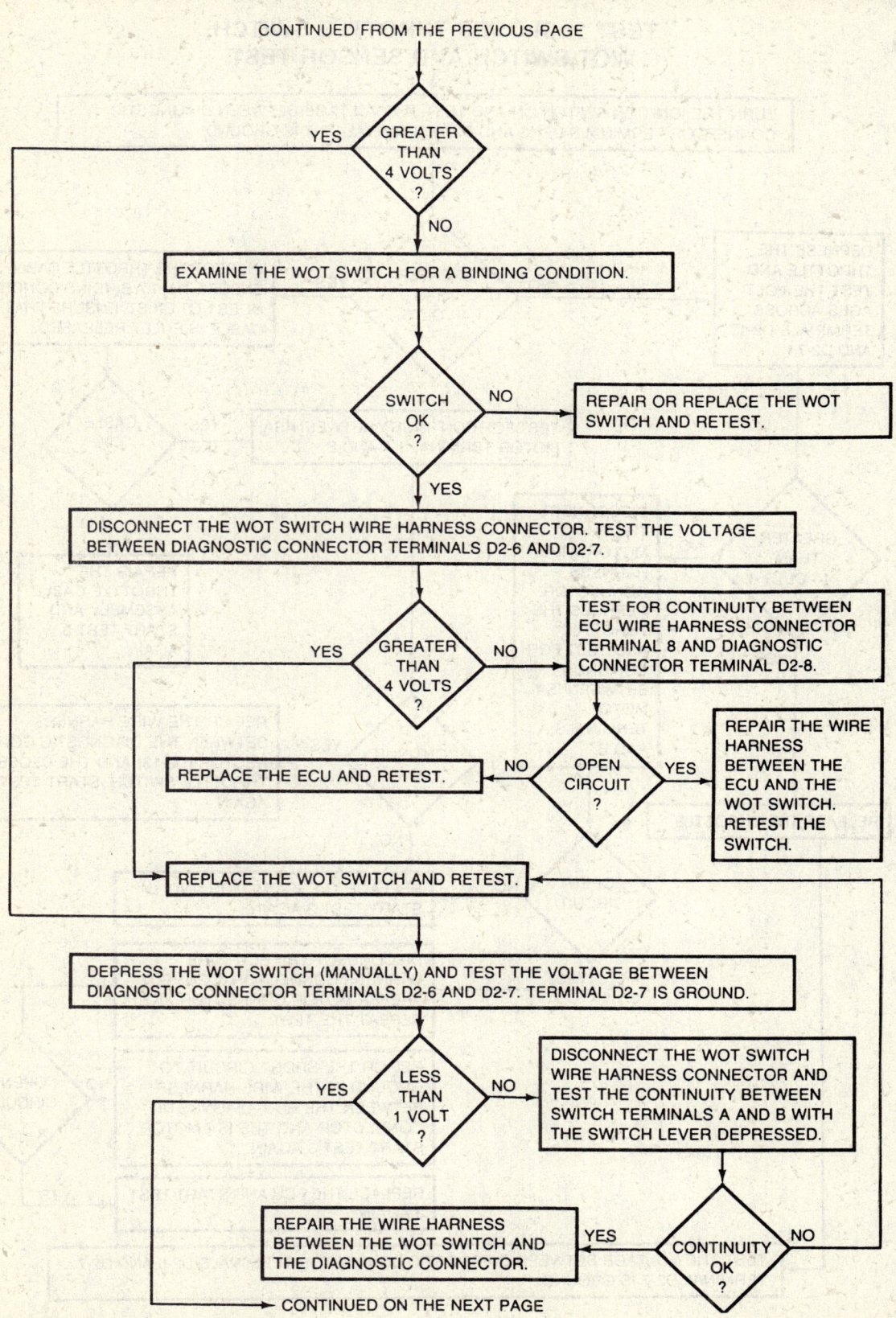

4-106

EMISSION CONTROLS 4

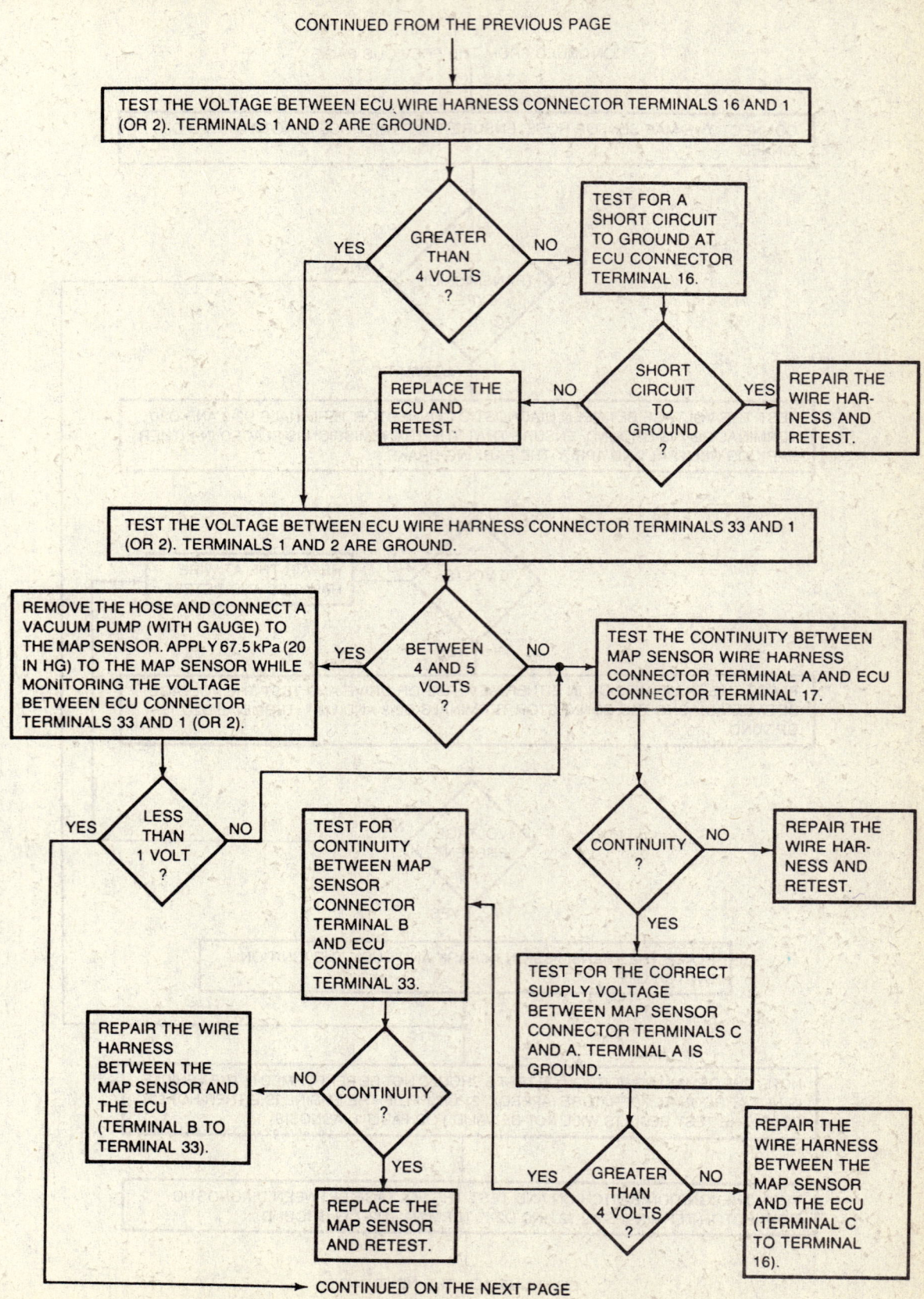

4 EMISSION CONTROLS

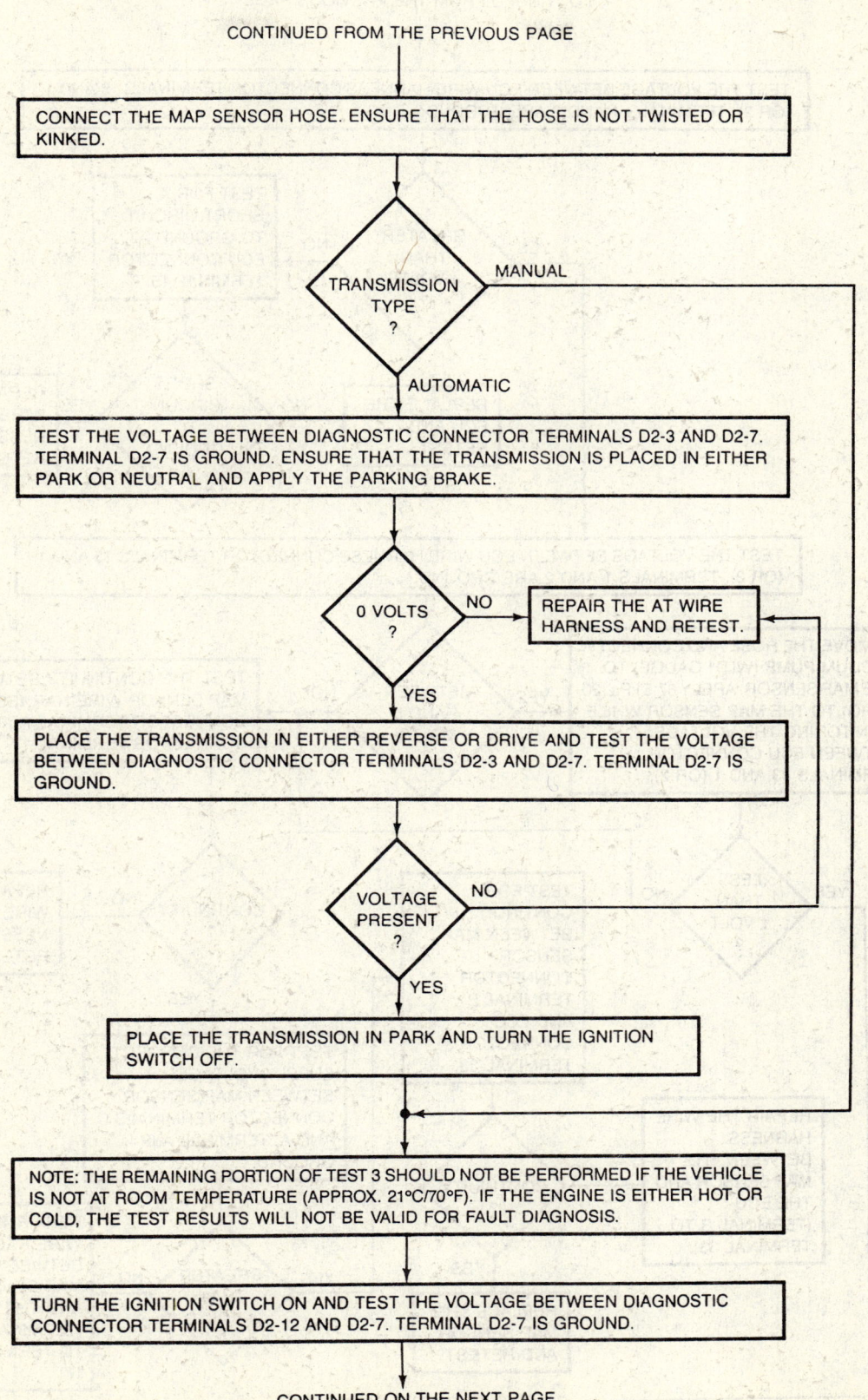

EMISSION CONTROLS 4

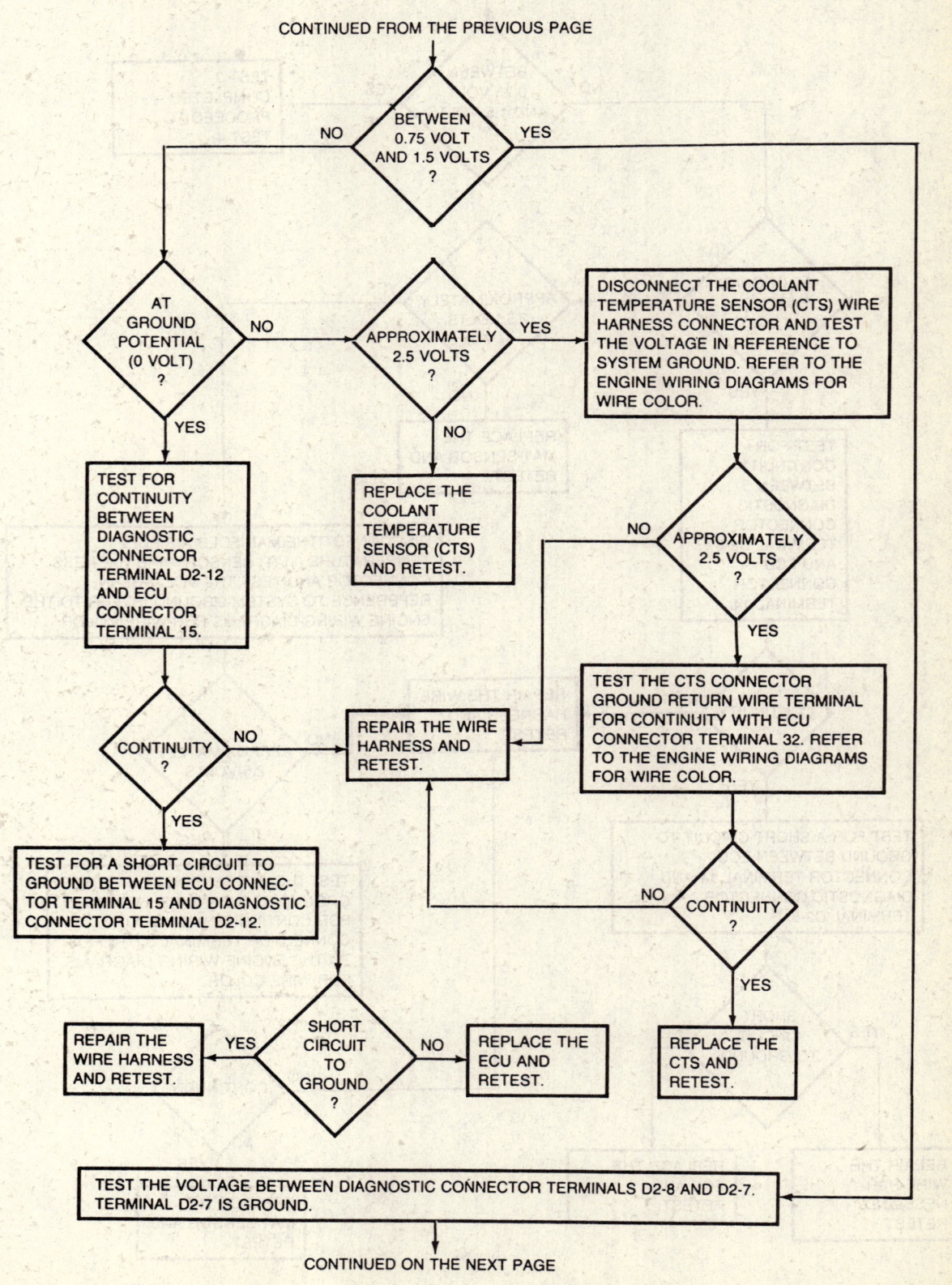

4-109

4 EMISSION CONTROLS

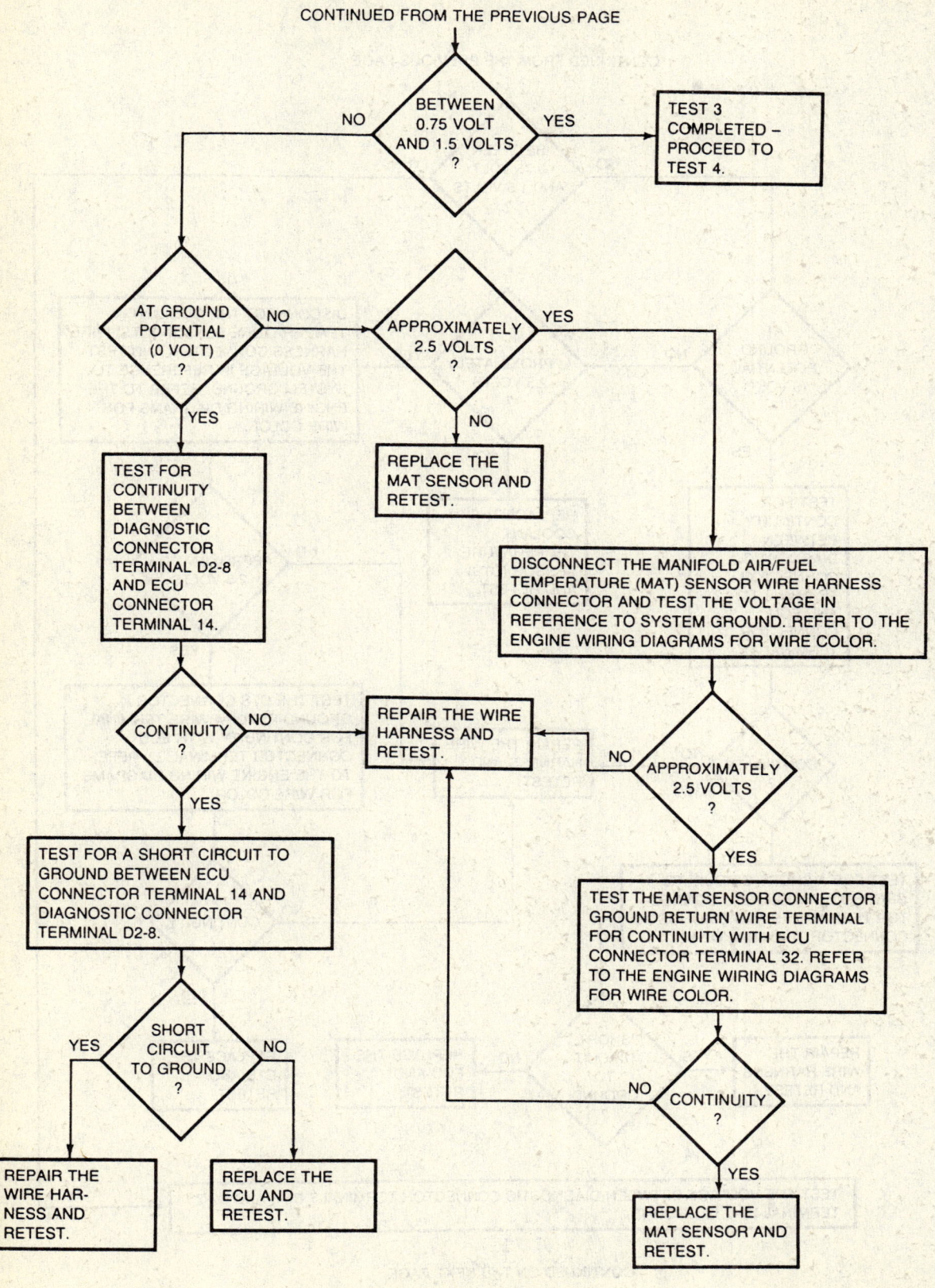

4-110

EMISSION CONTROLS 4

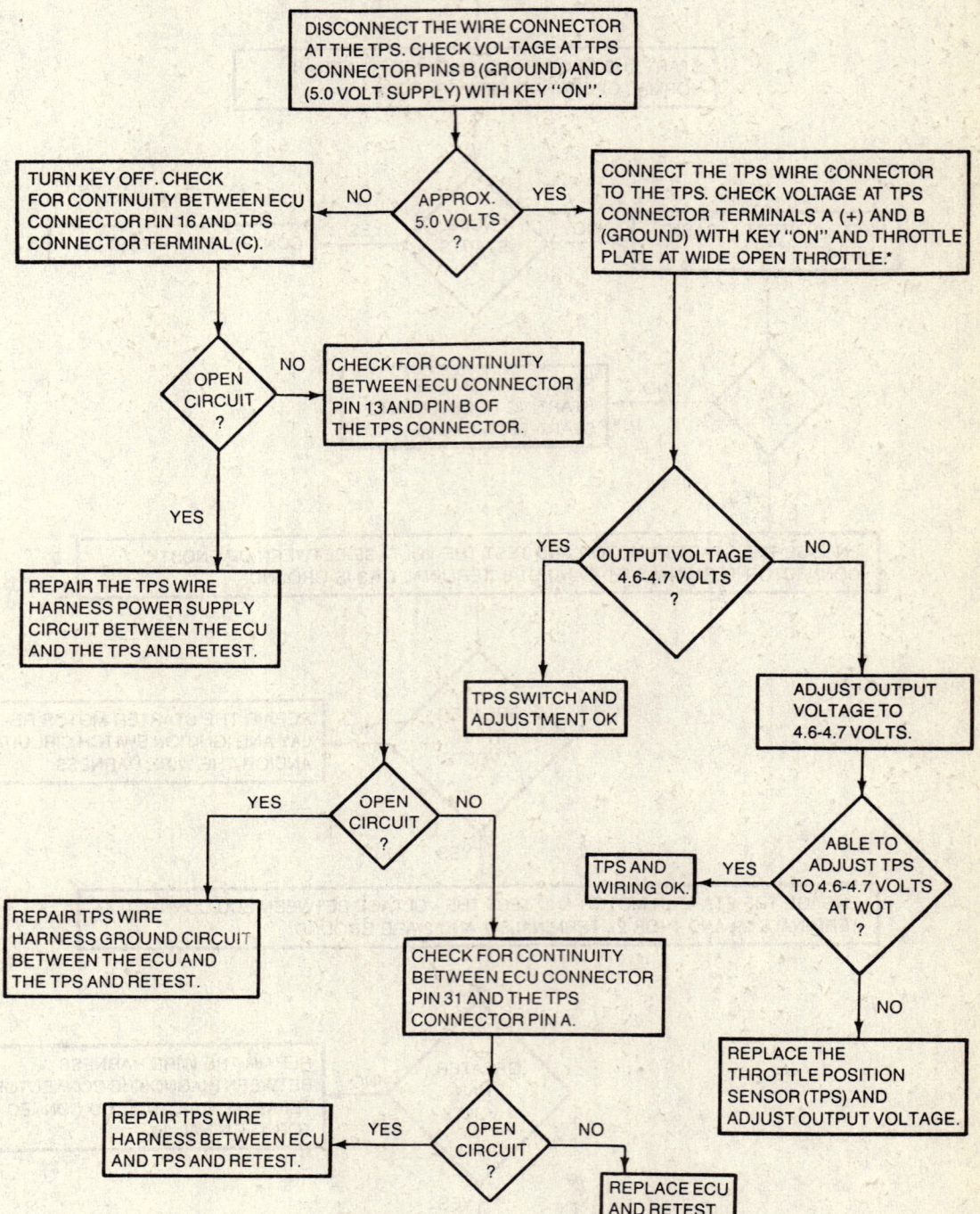

TEST 3A: THROTTLE POSITION SENSOR (TPS) TEST — 2.46L ONLY

* DO NOT UNFASTEN THE SENSOR WIRE HARNESS CONNECTOR. INSERT THE VOLTMETER TEST LEADS THROUGH THE BACK OF THE WIRE HARNESS CONNECTOR TO MAKE CONTACT WITH THE SENSOR TERMINALS. ON SOME MODELS, IT MAY ALSO BE NECESSARY TO REMOVE THE THROTTLE BODY FROM THE INTAKE MANIFOLD, TO GAIN ACCESS TO THE SENSOR WIRE HARNESS CONNECTOR.

4-111

4 EMISSION CONTROLS

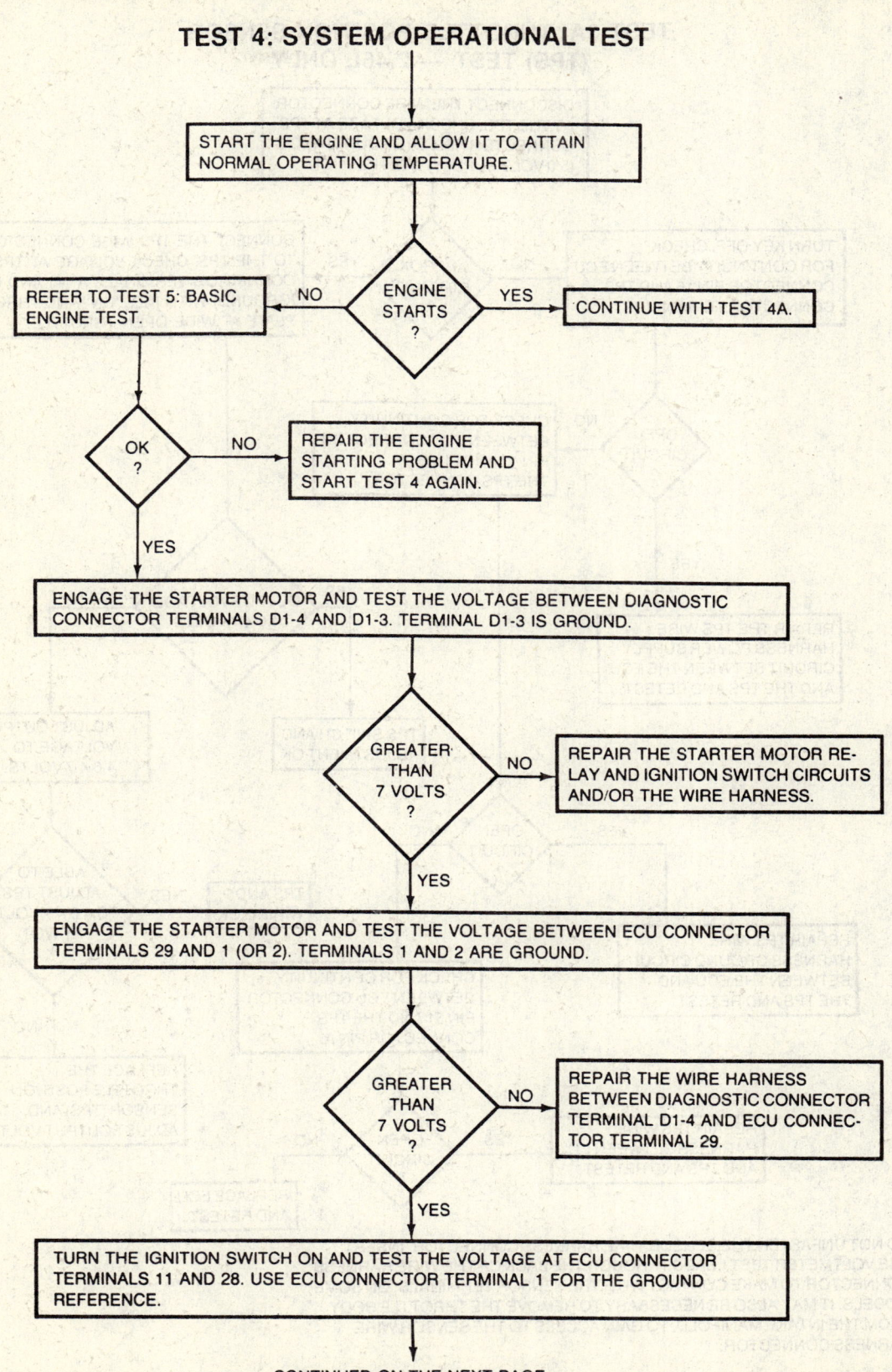

4-112

EMISSION CONTROLS 4

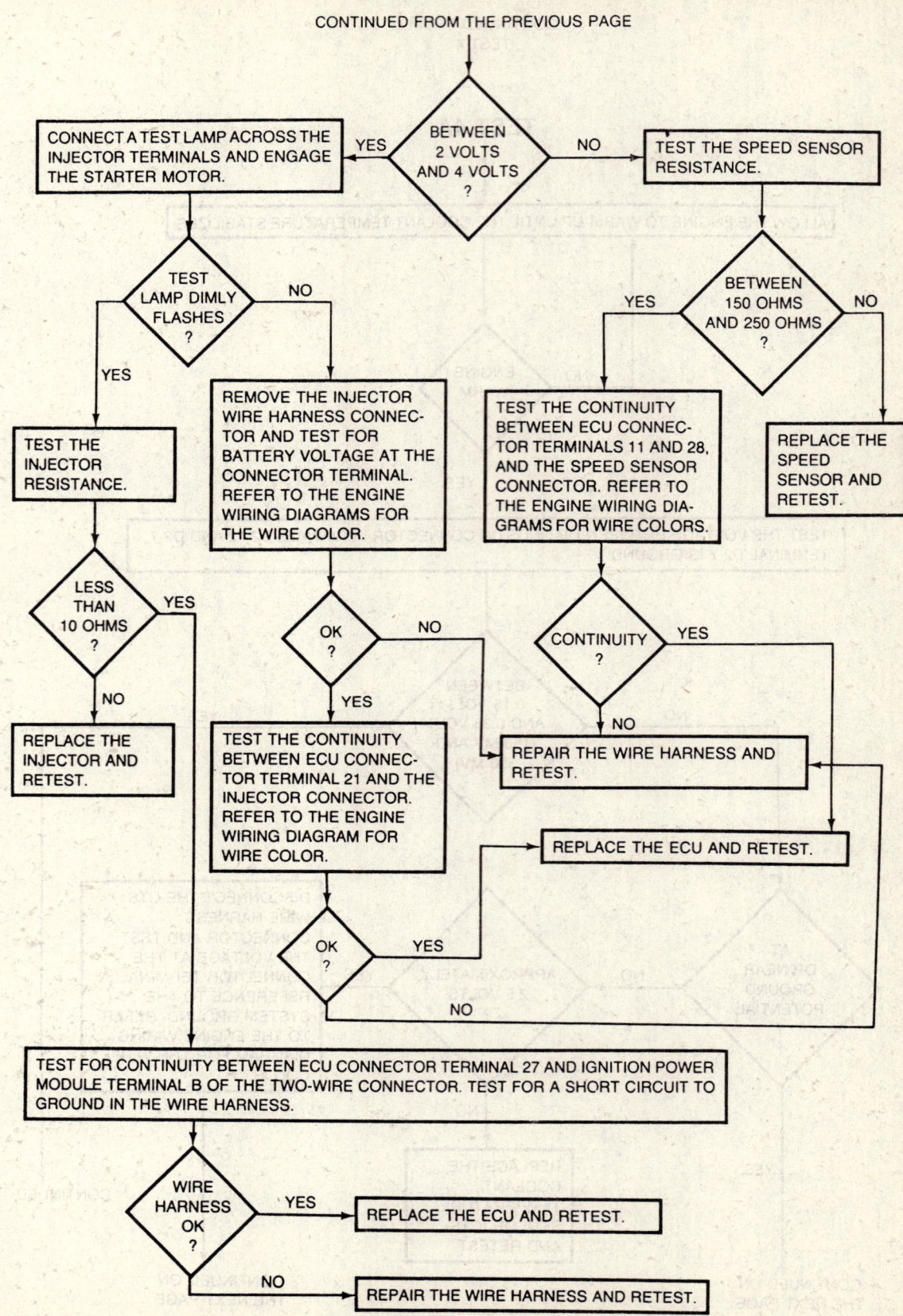

4-113

4 EMISSION CONTROLS

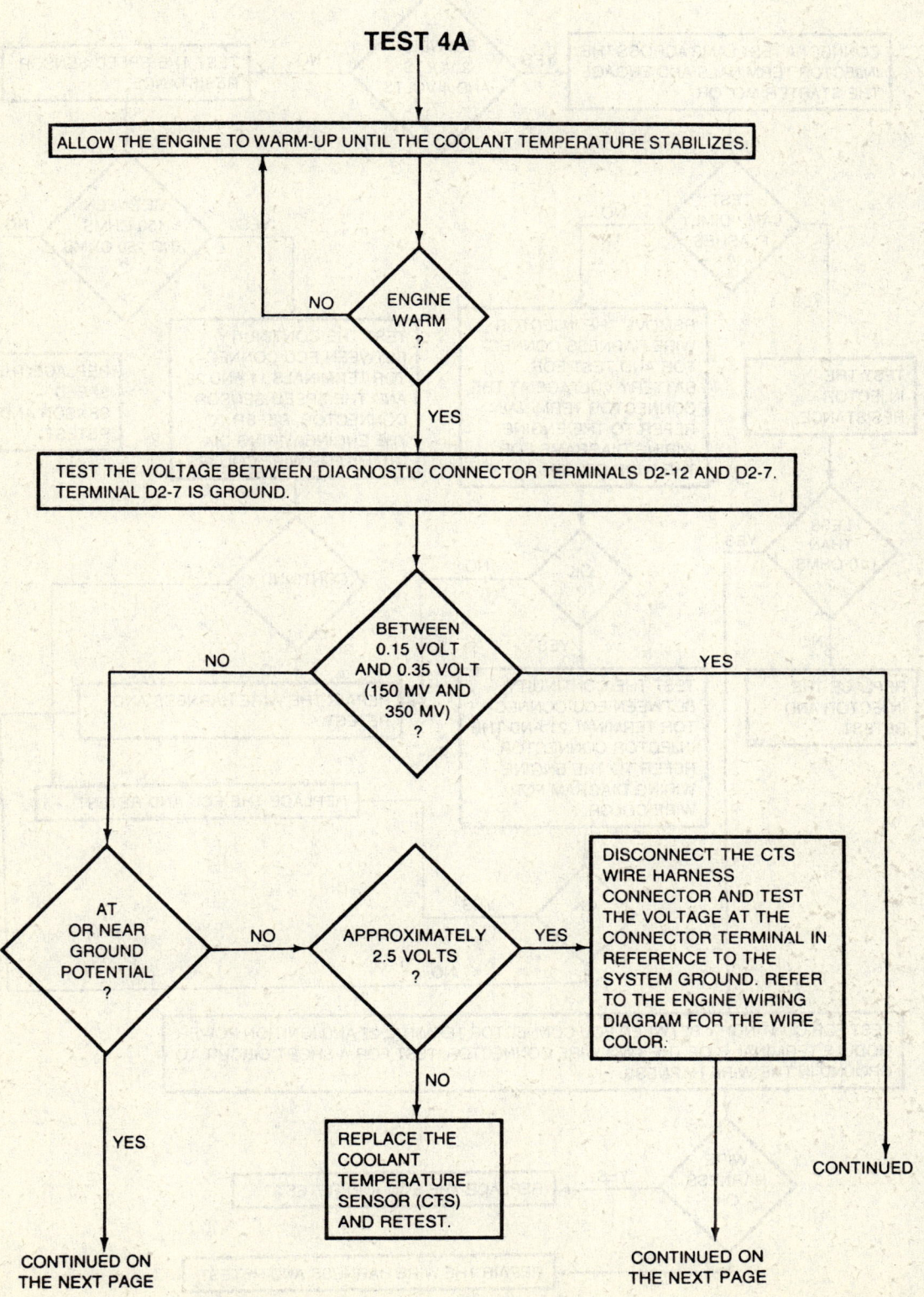

4-114

EMISSION CONTROLS 4

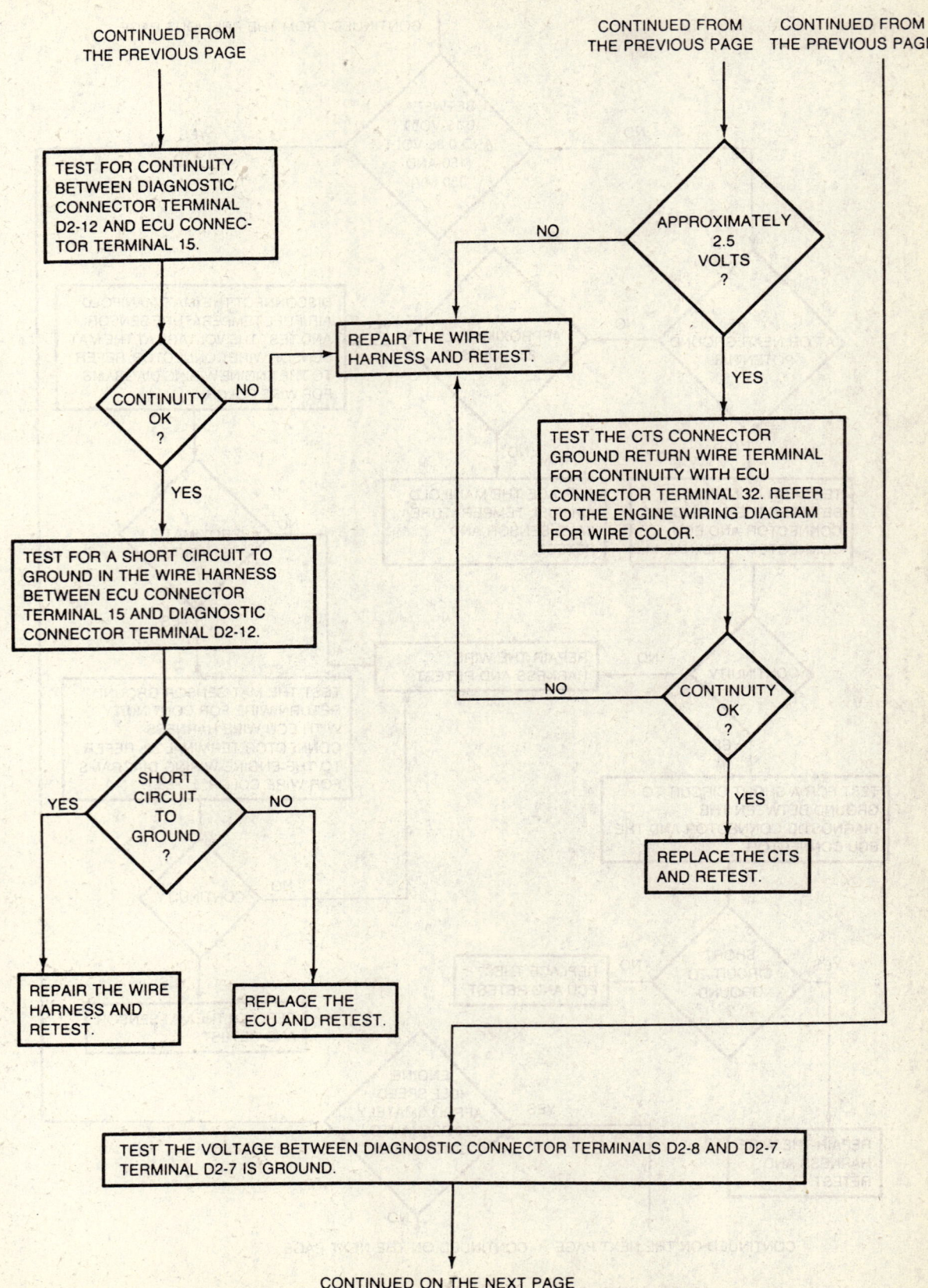

4-115

4 EMISSION CONTROLS

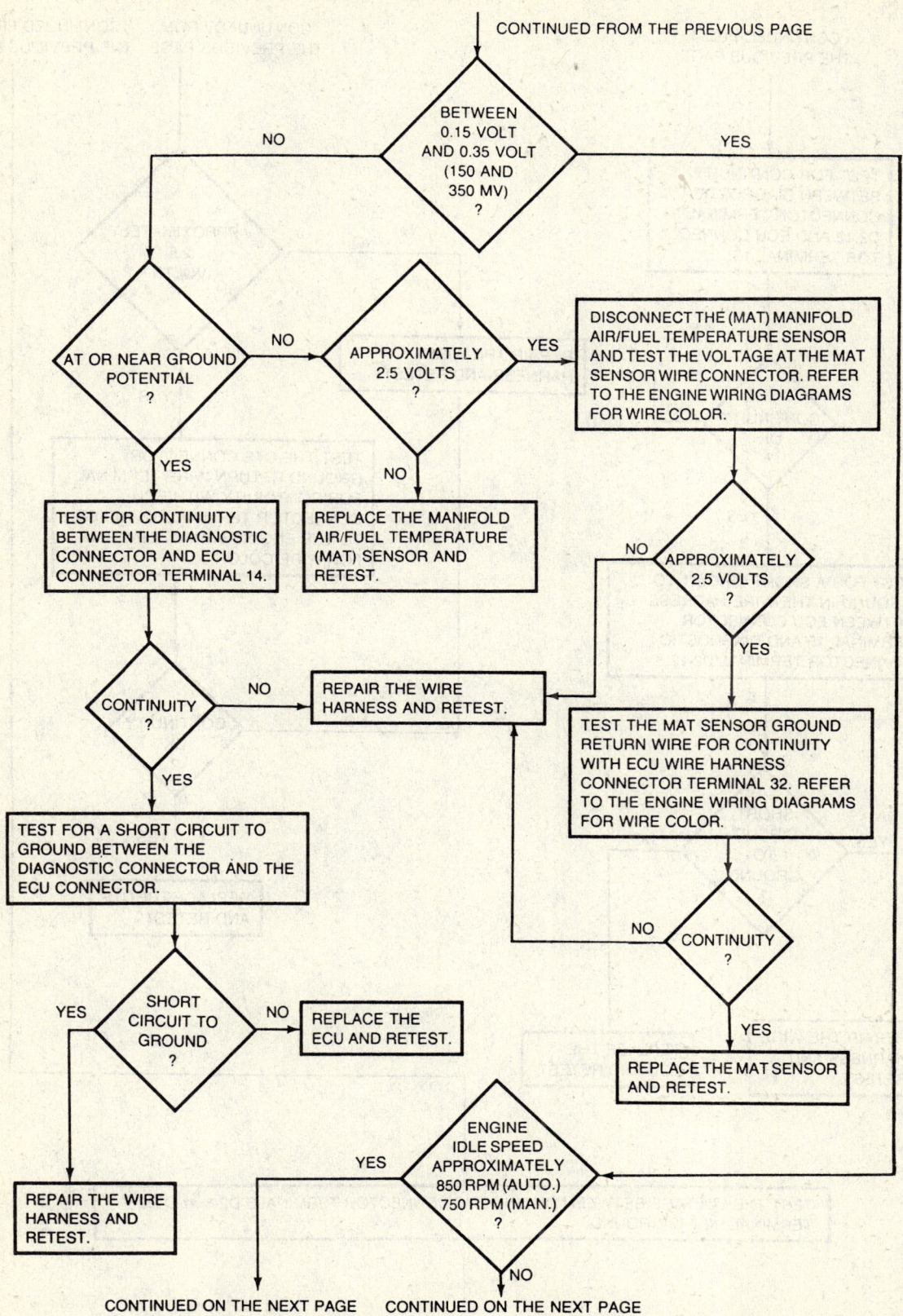

4-116

EMISSION CONTROLS 4

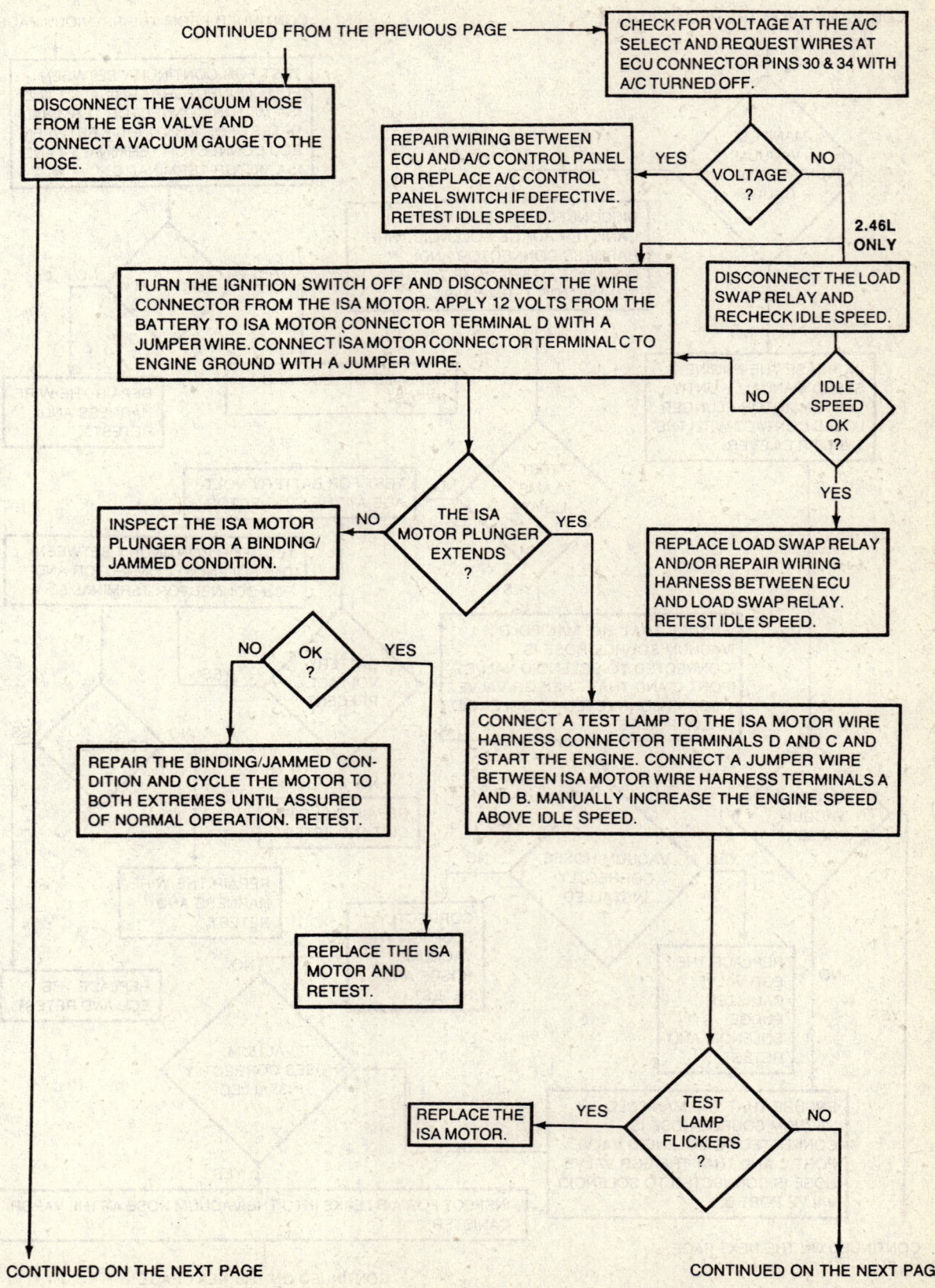

4-117

4 EMISSION CONTROLS

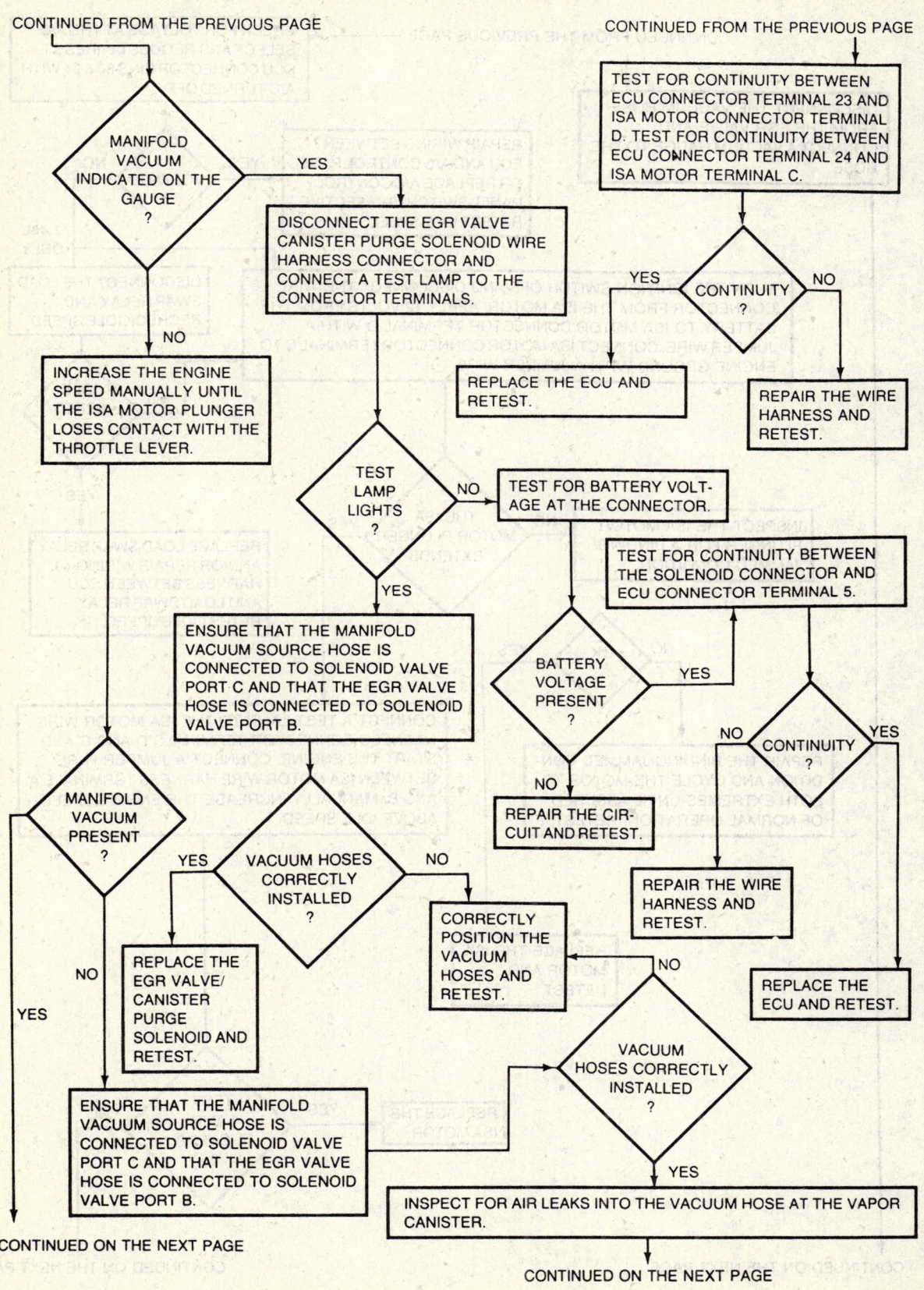

4-118

EMISSION CONTROLS 4

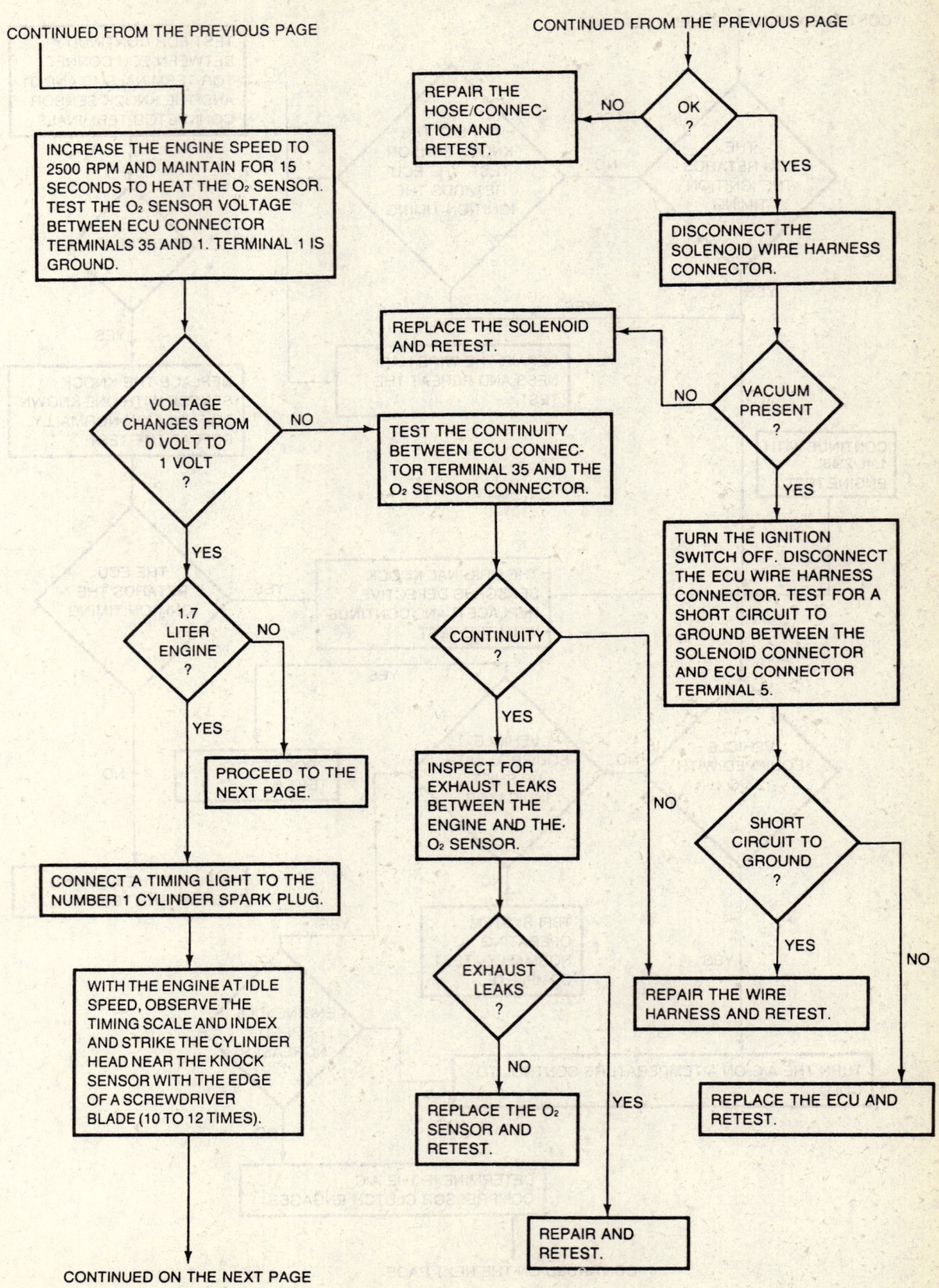

4 EMISSION CONTROLS

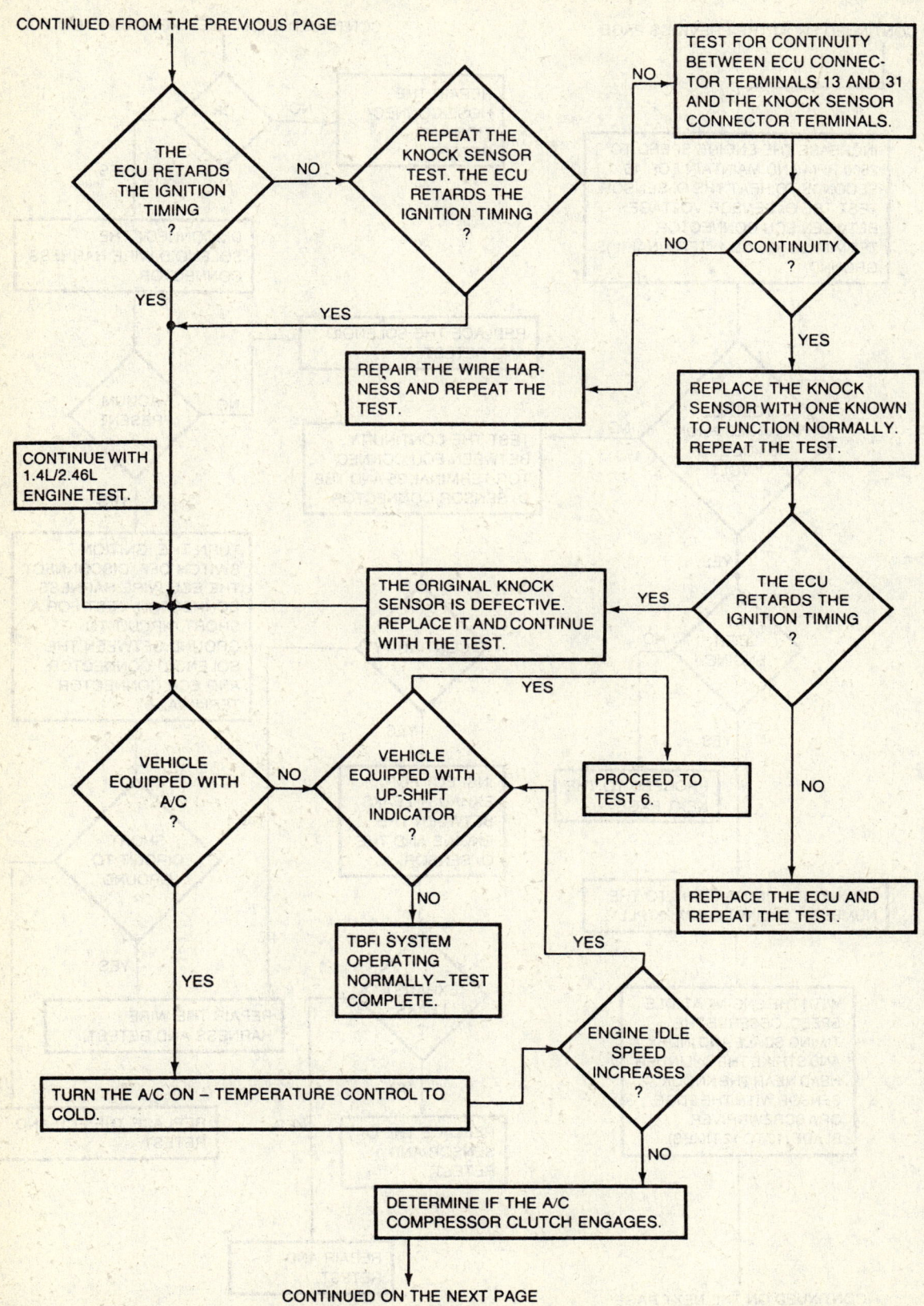

4-120

EMISSION CONTROLS 4

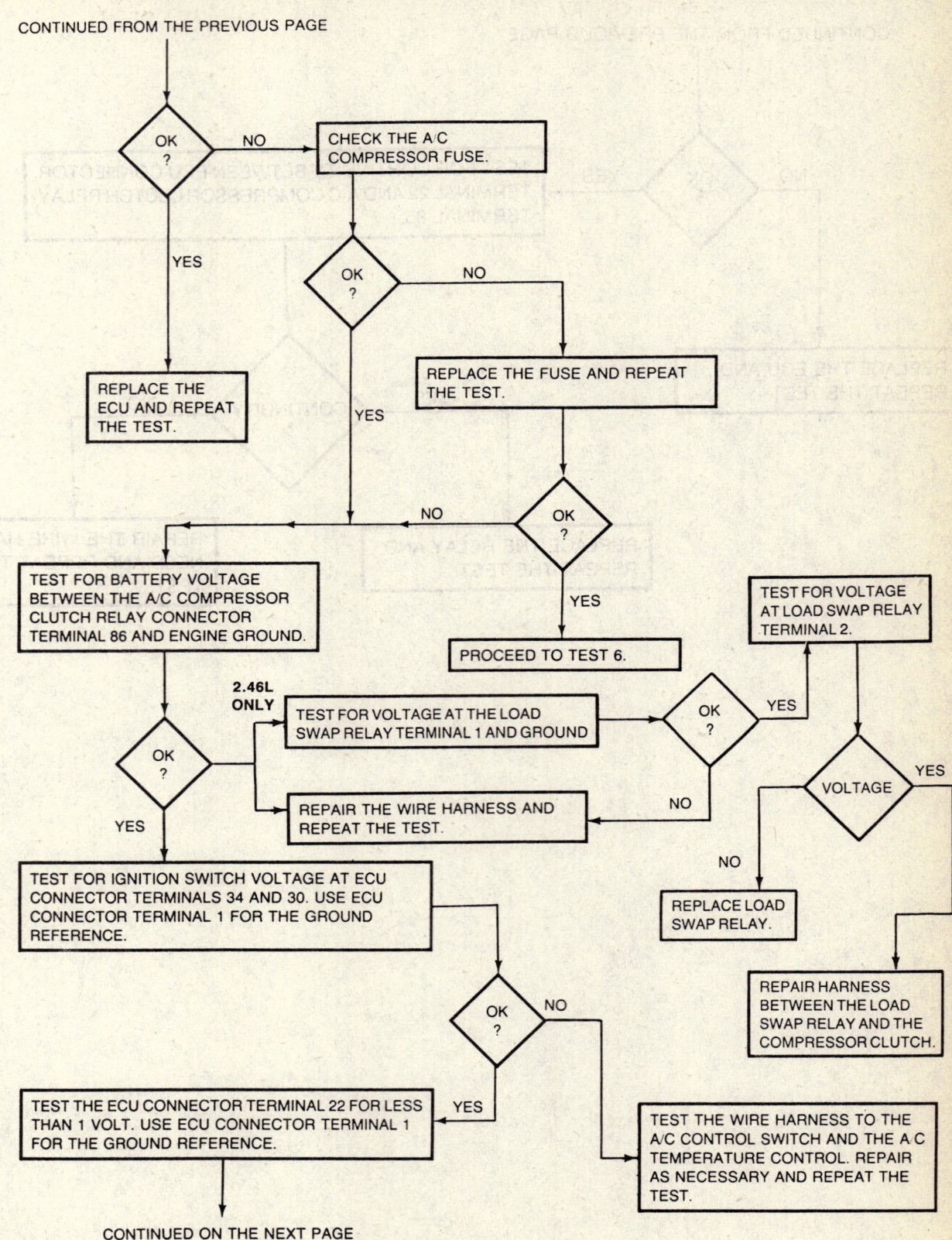

4 EMISSION CONTROLS

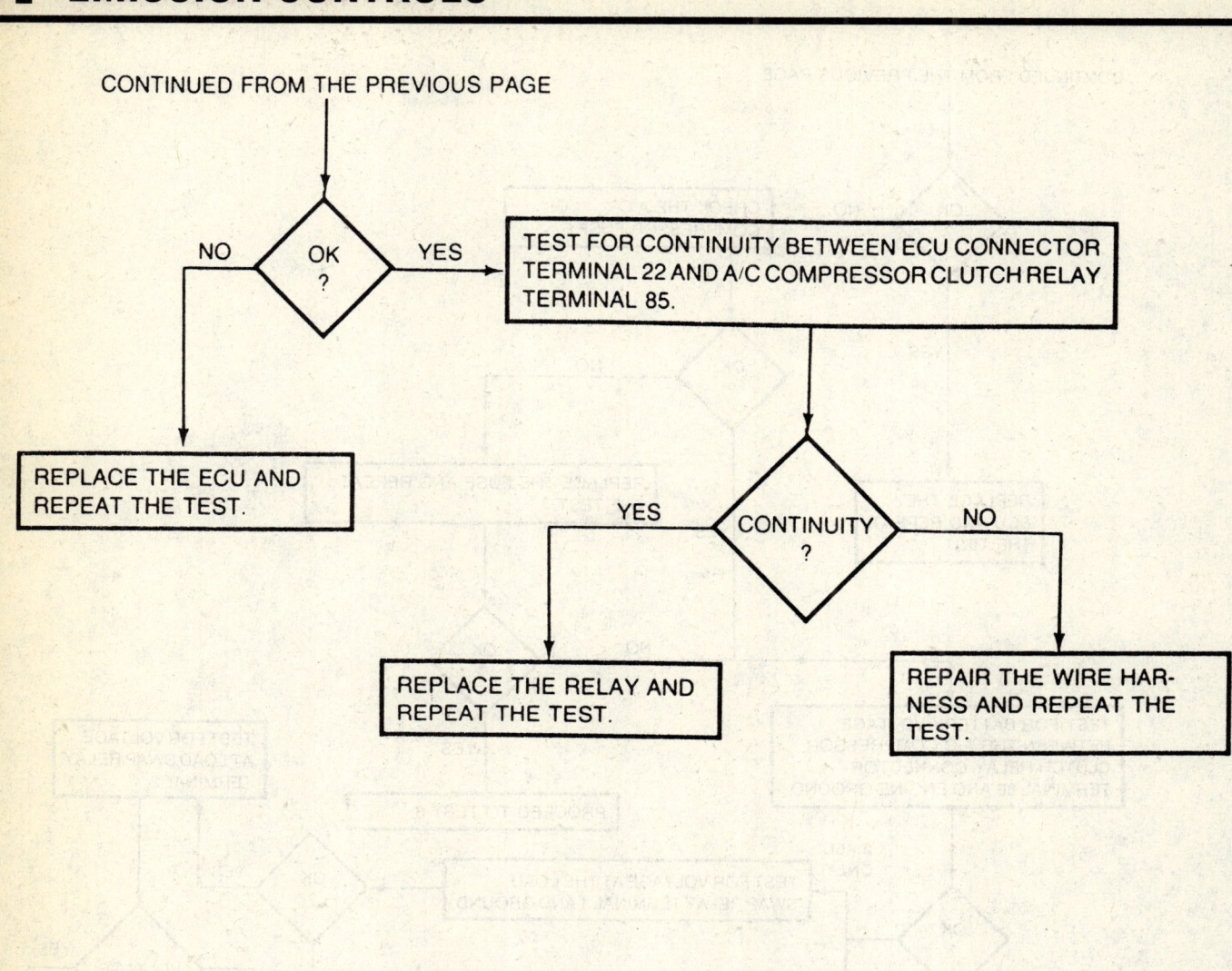

4-122

EMISSION CONTROLS 4

TEST 5: BASIC ENGINE TEST

INSPECT THE ENGINE FOR AIR LEAKS INTO THE VACUUM HOSES AND FITTINGS.

↓

CHECK THE IGNITION POWER MODULE OPERATION AND THE IGNITION HIGH VOLTAGE.

↓

IF FUEL IS LEAKING FROM AROUND THE BASE OF THE INJECTOR, REPLACE THE O-RING.

↓

CHECK THE FUEL PUMP PRESSURE.

↓

RETURN TO TEST 4.

4-123

4 EMISSION CONTROLS

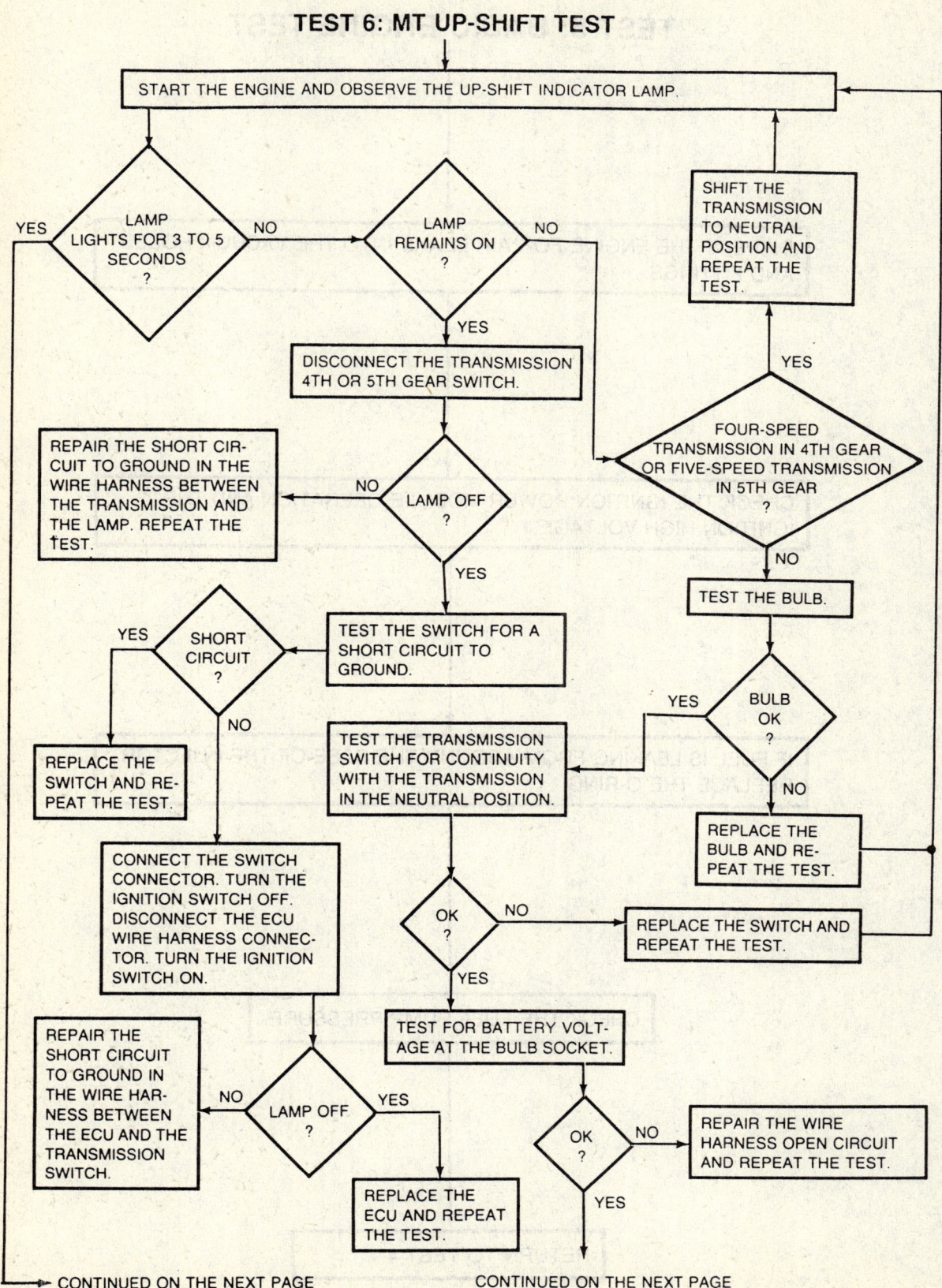

EMISSION CONTROLS 4

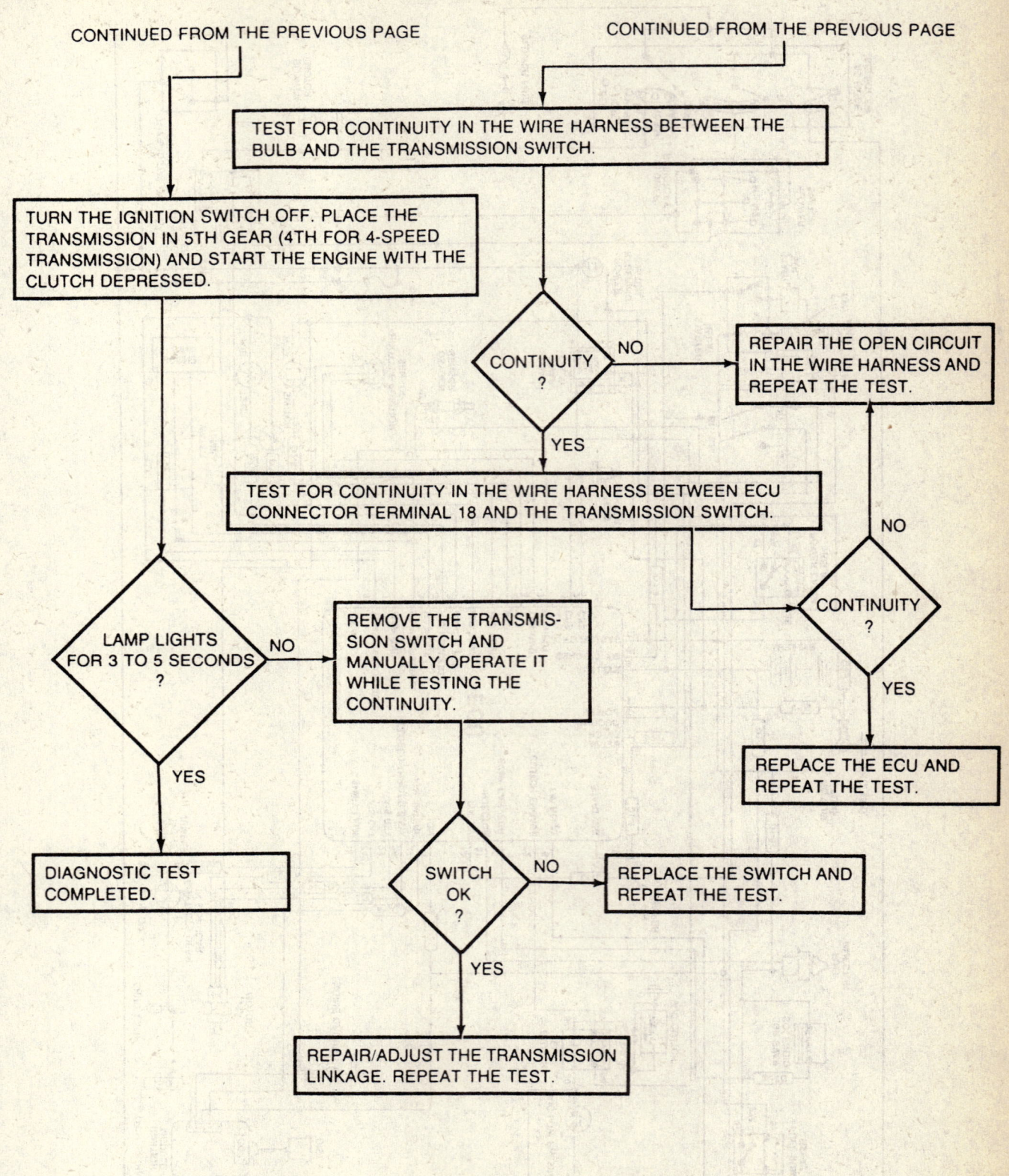

4-125

4 EMISSION CONTROLS

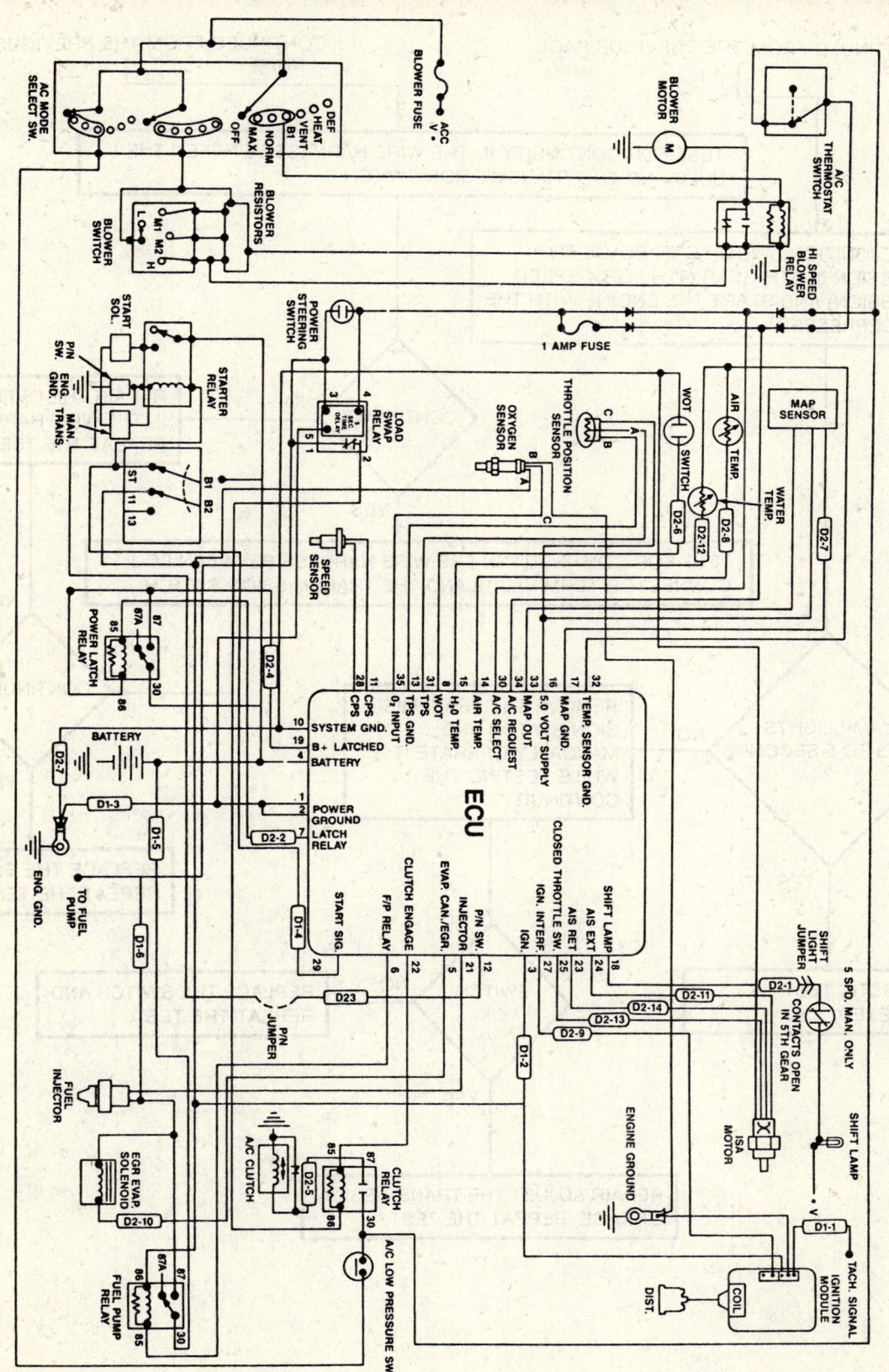

1986-90 TBI wiring diagram

EMISSION CONTROLS 4

8. Key OFF mode

Modes of operation exist as two different types. Crank, Warmup, Deceleration and WOT modes are Open Loop modes, while the Idle and Cruise modes at operating temperature are Closed Loop modes. In the Open Loop modes, the ECU receives input signals and responds only according to the preset ECU programming. In the Closed Loop modes, the ECU also receives a signal from the exhaust gas oxygen sensor which indicates whether or not the calculated injector pulse width results in the ideal air/fuel mixture of 14.7:1. By monitoring the exhaust oxygen content with the O_2 sensor, the ECU can fine tune the injector pulse width and achieve the optimum fuel mixture for all operating conditions.

System Operation

Key ON Mode

When the ignition switch is turned to the ON position (engine OFF), the ECU responds to inputs from the MAP sensor, air temperature sensor, coolant temperature sensor, throttle position switch and the battery voltage signal. The ignition switch supplies voltage to the B+ (fuel system power) relay and the ECU provides a ground path for the B+ relay to be energized. The ECU receives and stores a barometric pressure value from the MAP sensor in preparation for engine starting.

Voltage is supplied to the fuel pump relay from the B+ relay and the ECU provides a ground path for 1–3 seconds. During this period, the fuel pump relay is energized and the fuel pump pressurizes the fuel supply system. Voltage is supplied to the injectors via the fuel pump relay, but the ECU does not provide a ground path for the injector circuits. The idle regulating valve opens fully.

Crank Mode

During engine cranking, the ECU responds to inputs from the MAP sensor, engine speed sensor, air temperature sensor, throttle position switch, starter relay (automatic transmission only) and the battery voltage signal. The ballast resistor is bypassed during engine cranking. The ECU provides a ground path for the fuel pump relay and the fuel pump is energized.

The ECU restricts EGR and canister purge operation by energizing the EGR/canister purge solenoid. Voltage is supplied to the injectors and the ECU controls the injector pulse width (ON time)

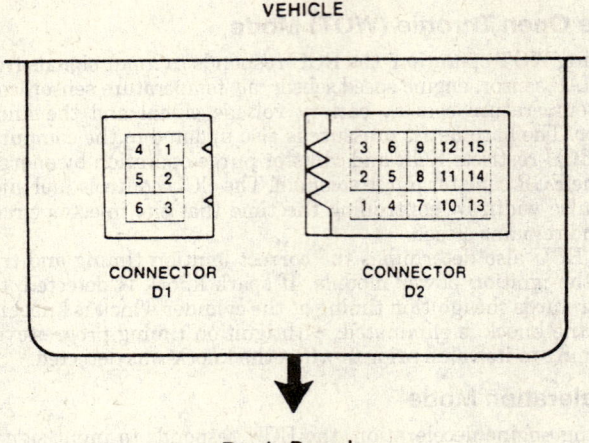

Dash Panel

Connector D1
1. Tach Signal
2. Not Used
3. ECU Ground
4. Not Used
5. Battery (+)
6. Fuel Pump (+)

Connector D2
1. ECU Output (TX)
2. RX Data (ECU)
3. Latch Relay
4. Ignition
5. Latch B+
6. A/C Clutch
7. Ignition Ground
8. Sensor Ground
9. Oxygen Sensor Heater
10. Not Used
11. Shift Lamp
12. Not Used
13. Not Used
14. Not Used
15. Automatic Transmission Diagnosis

1989-90 diagnostic connector

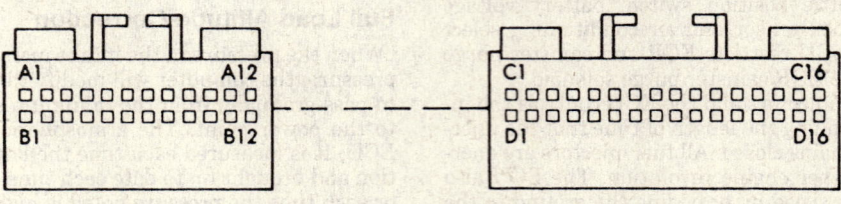

A
1. Injector #3
2. Injector #6
3. Injector #2
4. Injector #4
5. Fuel pump relay
6. Not used
7. Oxygen sensor relay
8. Shift lamp
9. Latch relay
10. EGR/Evap. Solenoid
11. Not used
12. A/C relay

B
1. Injector #1
2. Injector #5
3. AIS a
4. AIS a¹
5. AIS c
6. AIS c¹
7. Battery (+)
8. Ignition
9. Not used
10. Latched battery (+)
11. Ground
12. Ground

C
1. Speed sensor
2. A/C request
3. Start
4. P/N switch
5. Sync.
6. MAP sensor
7. TPS sensor
8. Air temperature sensor
9. Not used
10. Coolant temperature sensor
11. Injection supply
12. TX (serial data)
13. Not used
14. Map sensor supply (+)
15. TPS supply (+)
16. Sync. (+)

D
1. Speed sensor (–)
2. A/C select
3. Sensor ground
4. Not used
5. Not used
6. Not used
7. Not used
8. Knock sensor ground
9. Oxygen sensor output
10. Injection supply
11. RX (serial data)
12. Not used
13. Spark/dwell
14. Not used
15. Not used
16. Knock sensor

1989-90 ECU connector

4-129

4 EMISSION CONTROLS

by controlling the length of time that the injector circuit ground path remains completed. Based on signals received from the engine speed sensor, the ECU determines the correct ignition timing and triggers the ignition coil.

All fuel injectors are energized simultaneously, once per engine revolution, except during cold start conditions when the injectors are energized twice per engine revolution. This extra fuel delivery continues for a few seconds after the engine starts. To eliminate the possibility of the engine flooding, the ECU limits the number of times that the injectors can be energized twice per engine revolution. This limit is calculated solely on the basis of engine coolant temperature. If the coolant temperature is extremely low, the ECU increases the number of times that the double injection sequence is possible during engine start.

When the ignition switch is turned to the START position, a crank signal is sent to the ECU. If the vehicle is equipped with an automatic transmission, the starter relay prevents the signal from reaching the ECU if the transmission is not in Park or Neutral.

Warmup Mode

During engine warmup, the ECU responds to input signals from the MAP sensor, engine speed sensor, air temperature sensor, coolant temperature sensor, throttle position switch, gear indicator (automatic transmission only), air conditioning select signal (if equipped) and the knock sensor. The ECU restricts EGR and canister purge operation by energizing the EGR/canister purge solenoid.

Voltage is supplied to the injectors and the ECU controls the injector pulse width by controlling the length of time that the injector circuit ground path remains closed. All fuel injectors are energized simultaneously once per engine revolution. The ECU also establishes the correct idle speed by providing the ground to the idle regulating valve. If necessary, the idle speed is also adjusted to compensate for increased engine load during the A/C compressor operation, if equipped.

In addition to the above, the ECU determines the correct ignition timing and triggers the ignition power module. The shift indicator light is actuated if the engine speed and load conditions warrant a change to a higher gear.

Idle Mode

During engine idle, the ECU responds to input signals from the MAP sensor, engine speed sensor, air temperature sensor, coolant temperature sensor, throttle position switch, battery voltage signal, oxygen sensor, knock sensor and air conditioning select signal (if equipped). The ECU restricts EGR and canister purge operation by energizing the EGR/canister purge solenoid.

Voltage is supplied to the injectors and the ECU controls the injector pulse width by controlling the length of time that the injector circuit ground path remains closed. All fuel injectors are energized simultaneously once per engine revolution. The ECU also establishes the correct idle speed by providing the ground to the idle regulating valve. If necessary, the idle speed is also adjusted to compensate for increased engine load during the A/C compressor operation, if equipped.

In addition to the above, the ECU determines the correct ignition timing and triggers the ignition power module. By monitoring the oxygen sensor signal, the ECU can fine tune the fuel delivery by adjusting the injector pulse width (ON time), until the ideal 14.7:1 air/fuel mixture is achieved.

Cruise Mode

When the vehicle is moving at road speed, the ECU responds to input signals from the MAP sensor, engine speed sensor, air temperature sensor, coolant temperature sensor, throttle position switch, battery voltage signal, oxygen sensor, knock sensor and air conditioner select signal (if equipped). The ECU opens the ground path for the EGR/canister purge solenoid, allowing the EGR transducer and the evaporative vapor canister to receive manifold vacuum. Fuel delivery and timing control are as described under the Idle Mode.

Wide Open Throttle (WOT) Mode

During WOT operation, the ECU responds to input signals from the MAP sensor, engine speed sensor, air temperature sensor, coolant temperature sensor, battery voltage signal and the knock sensor. The barometric pressure is also updated in the computer. The ECU restricts EGR and canister purge operation by energizing the EGR/canister purge solenoid. The ECU controls fuel injector pulse width by controlling the time that the injector circuit ground remains closed.

The ECU also determines the correct ignition timing and triggers the ignition power module. If spark knock is detected, the ECU retards the ignition timing at the cylinder which is knocking until the knock is eliminated, with ignition timing progressively returning to its value prior to when the knock was detected.

Deceleration Mode

During engine deceleration, the ECU responds to input signals from the MAP sensor, engine speed sensor, air temperature sensor, coolant temperature sensor, throttle position switch and air conditioner select signal (if equipped). The ECU restricts EGR and canister purge operation by energizing the EGR/canister purge solenoid. The ECU controls fuel injector pulse width by controlling the time that the injector circuit ground remains closed, and determines correct ignition timing and triggers the ignition power module.

If the ECU receives a closed throttle signal and engine speed is over 1500 rpm, the ECU determines that the engine is in a hard deceleration condition and responds by completely shutting off fuel injection. Injection is resumed when the engine speed decreases to 1500 rpm.

Key OFF Mode

When the ignition switch is moved to the OFF position, the ECU breaks the injector ground circuit and all fuel injection stops. The ignition power module is deactivated and the ECU opens the ground circuit for the B+ relay, cutting off the voltage supply to the fuel injection circuitry.

SPECIAL OPERATING CONDITIONS

Full Load Altitude Correction

When the pressure in the intake manifold is around atmospheric pressure, the computer will modify the mixture fed to the engine to pass gradually from the minimum specific consumption point to the power point. The atmospheric pressure is stored in the ECU. It is measured each time the key is turned to the ON position and brought up to date each time the throttle is fully opened or each time the pressure noted is higher than atmospheric pressure. At higher altitude, the air is less dense and therefore has less oxygen per unit volume. To maintain a constant manifold pressure, the fuel mixture must be leaner at low load and when idling. The atmospheric pressure reading provides a basis for altitude correction.

Operation In Defect Mode

The injection system can remain operative when some of its sensors are defective. The ECU diagnoses its sensors by comparing their values to preset limits. If the value sensed does not lie between these limits, the sensor is treated as defective and the system operates in a defect mode.

If the coolant sensor is inoperative, air temperature is used in determining injection pulse width and ignition timing values. The air temperature value is then increased as a function of engine rpm to simulate coolant sensor output. If the oxygen sensor fails, open loop operation is forced.

EMISSION CONTROLS 4

Oxygen (O₂) Sensor

The oxygen sensor is located in the exhaust manifold. The voltage output from this sensor, which varies with the oxygen content in the exhaust gas, is supplied to the ECU. The O_2 sensor is equipped with a heating element that keeps the sensor at the proper operating temperature during all engine operating modes. Maintaining correct sensor temperature at all times allows the system to enter closed loop operation sooner and to remain in closed loop during periods of extended idle. Electrical feed to the O_2 sensor is through the ignition switch.

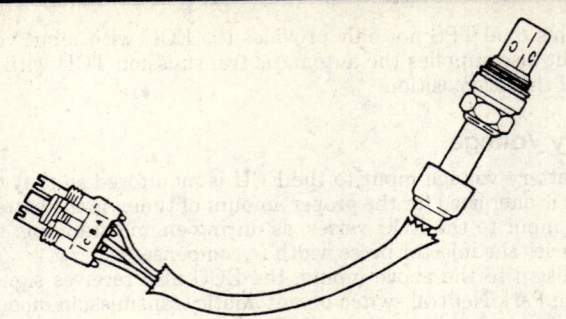

Oxygen sensor

System Components

ECU INPUTS

Coolant Temperature Sensor (CTS)

The coolant temperature sensor is located on the left side of the cylinder block, just below the exhaust manifold. The CTS provides an engine coolant temperature input to the ECU, which will then enrich the air/fuel mixture delivered by the injectors when the engine coolant is cold. Based on the CTS signal, the ECU will also control engine warmup idle speed, increase ignition advance and inhibit EGR operation when the coolant is cold.

Manifold Air Temperature (MAT) Sensor

The manifold air temperature sensor is located in the intake manifold. The MAT sensor reacts to the temperature of the air in the intake manifold and provides an input to the ECU to allow it to compensate for air density changes during high temperature operation.

Manifold Absolute Pressure (MAP) Sensor

The manifold absolute pressure sensor is mounted on the dash panel behind the engine. The MAP sensor reacts to absolute pressure in the intake manifold and provides an input voltage to the ECU. Manifold pressure is used to supply mixture density information and ambient barometric pressure information to the ECU. A hose from the intake manifold provides the input pressure.

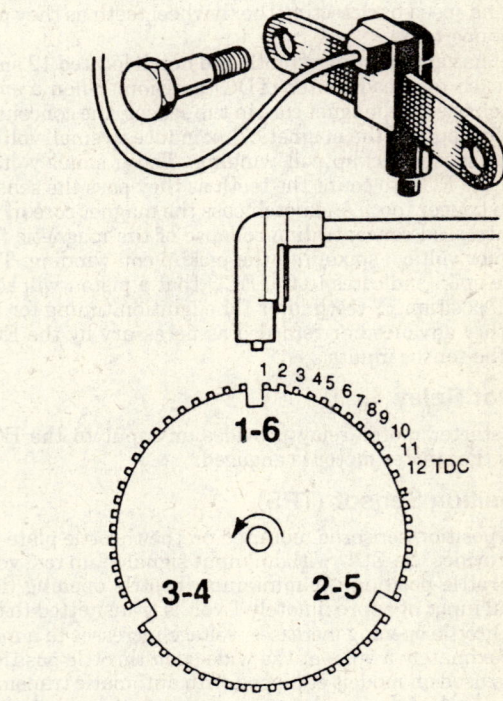

Speed sensor and flywheel teeth

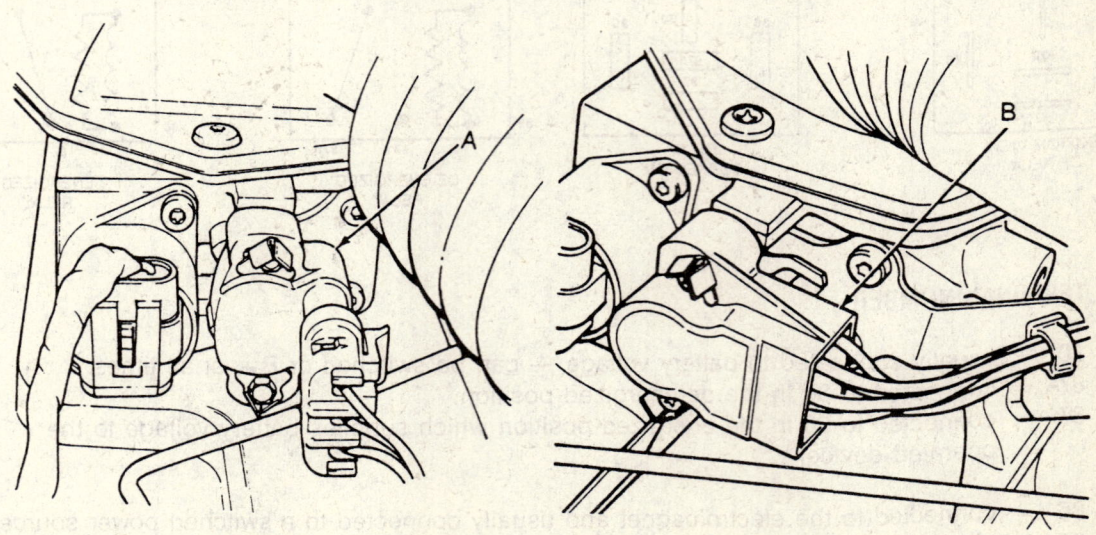

Throttle position switch (A) used on manual transmissions and (B) used on automatic transmissions

4-131

4 EMISSION CONTROLS

Knock Sensor

The knock sensor is located on the lower left side of the cylinder block, just above the oil pan. The knock sensor provides and input to the ECU that indicates detonation (knock) during engine operation. When detonation occurs, the ECU retards the ignition timing advance to eliminate the detonation at the applicable cylinder(s).

Speed Sensor

The speed sensor is secured by special shouldered bolts to the flywheel/drive plate housing. It is preset in its mounting at the factory and is non-adjustable in the field. The speed sensor senses TDC and engine speed by detecting the flywheel teeth as they pass during engine operation.

The flywheel has a large trigger tooth and notch located 12 small teeth before each top dead center (TDC) position. When a small tooth and notch pass the magnet core in the sensor, the concentration and then collapse of the magnetic flux induces a small voltage spike into the sensor pickup coil winding. These small voltage spikes enable the ECU to count the teeth as they pass the sensor.

When a large trigger tooth and notch pass the magnet core in the sensor, the increased concentration/collapse of the magnetic flux induces a higher voltage spike into the pickup coil winding. This higher voltage spike indicates to the ECU that a piston will soon be at the TDC position 12 teeth later. The ignition timing for the cylinder is either advanced or retarded as necessary by the ECU according to the sensor inputs.

Starter Motor Relay

The engine starter motor relay provides an input to the ECU that indicates the starter motor is engaged.

Throttle Position Sensor (TPS)

The throttle position sensor is mounted on the throttle plate assembly and provides the ECU with an input signal of up to 5 volts to indicate throttle position. At minimum throttle opening (idle speed), a signal input of approximately 1 volt is transmitted to the ECU. As the throttle opening increases, voltage increases to a maximum of approximately 5 volts at the wide open throttle position.

A dual TPS is used on models equipped with automatic transmission. This dual TPS not only provides the ECU with input voltages, but also supplies the automatic transmission TCU with an input of throttle position.

Battery Voltage

The battery voltage input to the ECU is monitored so that the injector is energized for the proper amount of time. As the battery voltage input to the ECU varies, as during engine cranking, the ECU varies the injector pulse width to compensate.

In addition to the above inputs, the ECU also receives signals from the Park/Neutral switch on automatic transmission models; an A/C input signal to tell the ECU when the compressor is engaged so it can raise the idle speed to compensate for the load; and

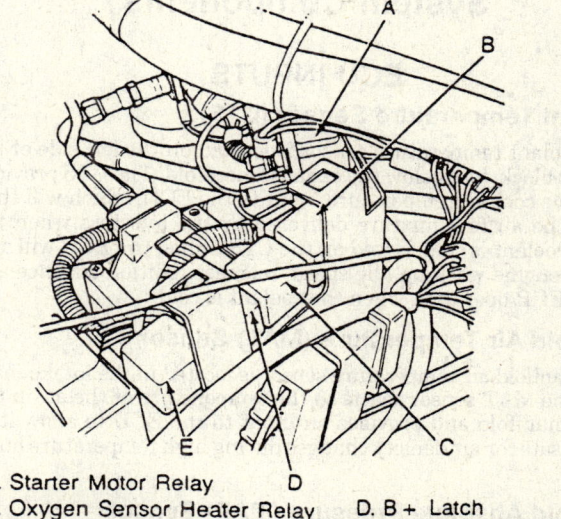

A. Starter Motor Relay
B. Oxygen Sensor Heater Relay
C. Fuel Pump Relay
D. B + Latch
E. A/C Clutch Relay

Relay locations on the 6-4.0L MPI engine

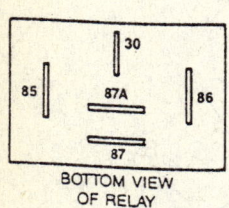 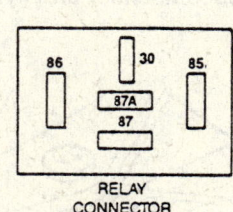 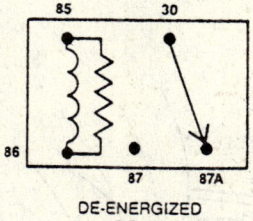 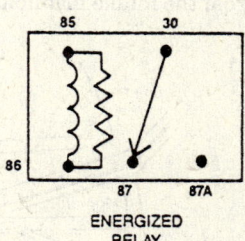

TERMINAL NUMBER

30 = usually connected to battery voltage — can be switched or B+ at all times.
87A = connected to 30 in the de-energized position.
87 = connected to 30 in the energized position which supplies battery voltage to the operated device.

86 = connected to the electromagnet and usually connected to a switched power source.
85 = also is connected to the electromagnet and is usually grounded by a switch or ECU.

Relay terminal identification

EMISSION CONTROLS 4

a sync pulse (stator) signal generated within the distributor to properly synchronize injector opening with intake valve closing.

ECU OUTPUTS

Oxygen Sensor Heater Relay

The oxygen sensor heater relay is normally closed, supplying voltage to the O_2 sensor heater under warmup and idle conditions. The O_2 heater relay is controlled by the ECU. When the speed sensor and MAP sensor reach a predetermined input, it tells the ECU that the O_2 sensor will stay heated by the exhaust gas under those conditions, and the ECU can open the O_2 sensor heater relay and cut off the voltage supply to the heater.

A/C Clutch Relay

The ECU controls the compressor clutch through the A/C clutch relay. This allows the ECU to receive a request for air conditioning from the A/C temperature control thermostat.

Temperature-to-Resistance Values (Approximate)

°F	°C	Ohms
212	100	185
160	70	450
100	38	1,600
70	20	3,400
40	4	7,500
20	-7	13,500
0	-18	25,000
-40	-40	100,700

MAT/CTS sensor resistance test chart

Ignition Control Module

Based on inputs, the ECU triggers the ignition coil to fire via the ignition control module. In this manner, the ECU can control spark timing according to engine operating conditions as reported by the various engine sensors.

Fuel Injectors

The fuel injectors are located in the intake manifold. The injectors are electronically and exclusively controlled by the ECU. The injection time duration, or pulse width, is based on engine operating conditions as reported by the various engine sensors. The ECU controls the injectors by supplying the ground; the longer the ground is supplied, the more fuel delivered to the engine.

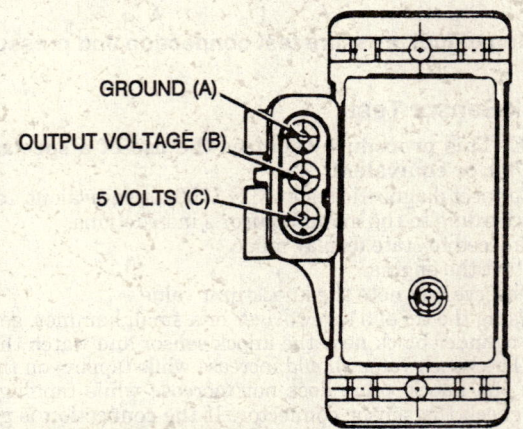

MAP sensor connector terminals

Fuel Pump Relay

The fuel pump relay is located on the right inner fender panel. Battery voltage is supplied to the relay from the ignition switch and is energized when a ground is provided by the ECU. When energized, voltage is supplied to the fuel pump.

EGR Valve Solenoid

The vacuum for the EGR valve operation is controlled by this solenoid. When energized by the ECU, the EGR valve solenoid prevents vacuum from reaching the EGR valve diaphragm. The solenoid is energized during engine warmup, closed throttle (idle), wide open throttle and rapid acceleration/deceleration conditions. If the solenoid wire connector is disconnected, the EGR valve will be operative at all times and cause driveability problems.

Upshift Indicator Lamp

The indicator lamp is normally illuminated when the ignition switch is turned to the ON position and goes out when the engine is started. The indicator will be illuminated during engine operation according to engine speed and load conditions. A switch located on the transmission prevents the lamp from being illuminated when the transmission is shifted into its highest gear. The ECU will turn off the upshift indicator if the gear change is not performed within 3–5 seconds.

Latch Relay

The latch relay is located on the right inner fender panel. This relay is initially energized during engine startup and remains energized until 3–5 seconds after the engine is stopped. This enables the ECU to extend the idle speed stepper motor for the next startup, then cease operation.

Idle Speed Stepper Motor

The idle speed stepper motor is located on the throttle plate assembly. The ECU controls the idle speed by providing the appropriate voltage outputs to move the stepper motor pin inward or outward to maintain a predetermined idle speed. There is no idle speed adjustment.

Component Testing and Diagnosis

Coolant Temperature Sensor (CTS) Test

Disconnect the wire harness connector from the CTS and measure the resistance of the sensor with a high input impedance (digital) volt-ohmmeter. The resistance should be less than 1000Ω with the engine warm. Refer to the resistance chart and replace the sensor if it is not within the range of resistance specified in the chart. Measure the resistance of the wire harness between ECU wire harness connector terminal D-3 and the sensor connector terminal, and terminal C-10 to the sensor connector terminal and repair the wire harness if an open circuit is indicated.

Manifold Air Temperature (MAT) Sensor Test

Disconnect the wire harness connector from the MAT and measure the resistance of the sensor with a high input impedance (digital) volt-ohmmeter. The resistance should be less than 1000Ω with the engine warm. Refer to the resistance chart and replace

4 EMISSION CONTROLS

the sensor if it is not within the range of resistance specified in the chart. Measure the resistance of the wire harness between ECU wire harness connector terminal D-3 and the sensor connector terminal, and terminal C-8 to the sensor connector terminal and repair the wire harness if the resistance is greater than 1Ω.

Manifold Absolute Pressure (MAP) Sensor Test

1. Inspect the MAP sensor vacuum hose connection at the throttle body and sensor and repair as necessary.
2. Test the MAP sensor output voltage at the MAP sensor connector terminal B (as marked on the sensor body) with the ignition switch ON and the engine OFF. The output voltage should be 4–5 volts.

NOTE: The voltage should drop to 0.5–1.5 volts with a hot, neutral idle speed condition.

3. Test ECU terminal C-6 for the same voltage as in Step 2 to verify the wire harness condition and repair as necessary.
4. Test the MAP sensor supply voltage at the sensor connector terminal C with the ignition ON. The voltage should be 4.5–5.5 volts. The same voltage should be present at terminal C-14 of the ECU wire harness connector. Repair or replace the wire harness as necessary. If the ECU is suspect, use Diagnostic Tester M.S.1700, or equivalent, to test ECU function.
5. Test the MAP sensor ground circuit at the sensor connector terminal A and ECU connector terminal D-3. Repair the wire harness as necessary.
6. Test the MAP sensor ground circuit at the ECU connector between terminal D-3 and terminal B-11 with an ohmmeter. If the ohmmeter indicates an open circuit, check for a defective sensor ground connection located on the right side of the cylinder block. If the ground connection is good, replace the ECU.

NOTE: If terminal D-3 has a short circuit to 12 volts, correct this condition before replacing the ECU.

Oxygen Sensor Heating Element Test

Disconnect the O₂ sensor connector and connect ohmmeter test leads to terminals **A** and **B** of the sensor connector. The resistance should be 5–7Ω. Replace the O₂ sensor if the ohmmeter displays an infinity (∞) reading. Oxygen sensor operational testing requires the use of a special tester M.S.1700, or equivalent.

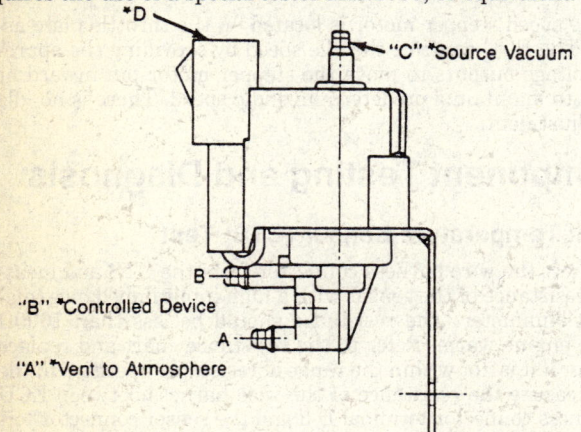

Vacuum port identification for EGR solenoid test

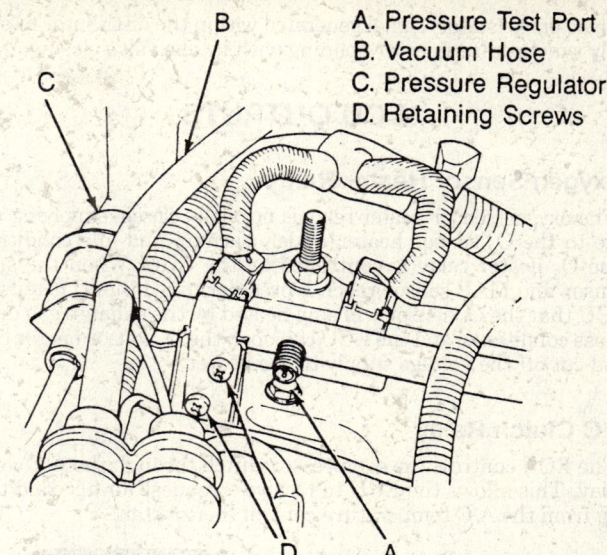

A. Pressure Test Port
B. Vacuum Hose
C. Pressure Regulator
D. Retaining Screws

Location of fuel pressure test connection and pressure regulator

Knock Sensor Test

NOTE: This procedure requires the use of a special tester M.S.1700, or equivalent.

1. Connect diagnostic tester M.S.1700, or equivalent, to the vehicle according to the manufacturer's instructions.
2. Proceed to state display mode.
3. Start the engine.
4. Observe and note the knock unit value.
5. Using the tip of a screwdriver or a small hammer, gently tap on the cylinder block near the knock sensor and watch the knock value. The knock value should increase while tapping on the block.
6. If the knock value does not increase while tapping on the block, check the sensor connector. If the connection is good, replace the knock sensor.

Speed Sensor Test

Disconnect the speed sensor connector from the ignition control module and connect an ohmmeter between terminals **A** and **B** as marked on the connector. The ohmmeter should read 125–275Ω on a hot engine. Replace the sensor if the readings are not as stated.

Relay Testing

A relay in the de-energized position should have continuity between terminals 87A and 30. Resistance values between terminals 85 and 86 is 70–80Ω for resistor relays and 81–91Ω for diode relays. Not all relays have battery voltage connected to terminal 30. Some may have battery voltage connected to terminals 87 or 87A.

Starter Motor Relay Test

1. Disconnect the wire connectors from the **I** and **G** terminals.
2. Measure the resistance between the terminals with an ohmmeter. It should be approximately 22Ω.
3. Measure the resistance between either terminal and the battery negative post. Reading should be infinite (∞). If defective, replace the relay.
4. Remove the SOL terminal wire connector and connect a voltmeter between the terminal and the battery negative post. With the ignition switch in the START position, the voltmeter should indicate battery voltage (12 volts).
5. If battery voltage is not present, check the related wiring, bulkhead connector and ignition switch adjustment.

EMISSION CONTROLS 4

INJECTOR DIAGNOSIS— Vehicle runs rough and/or has a miss

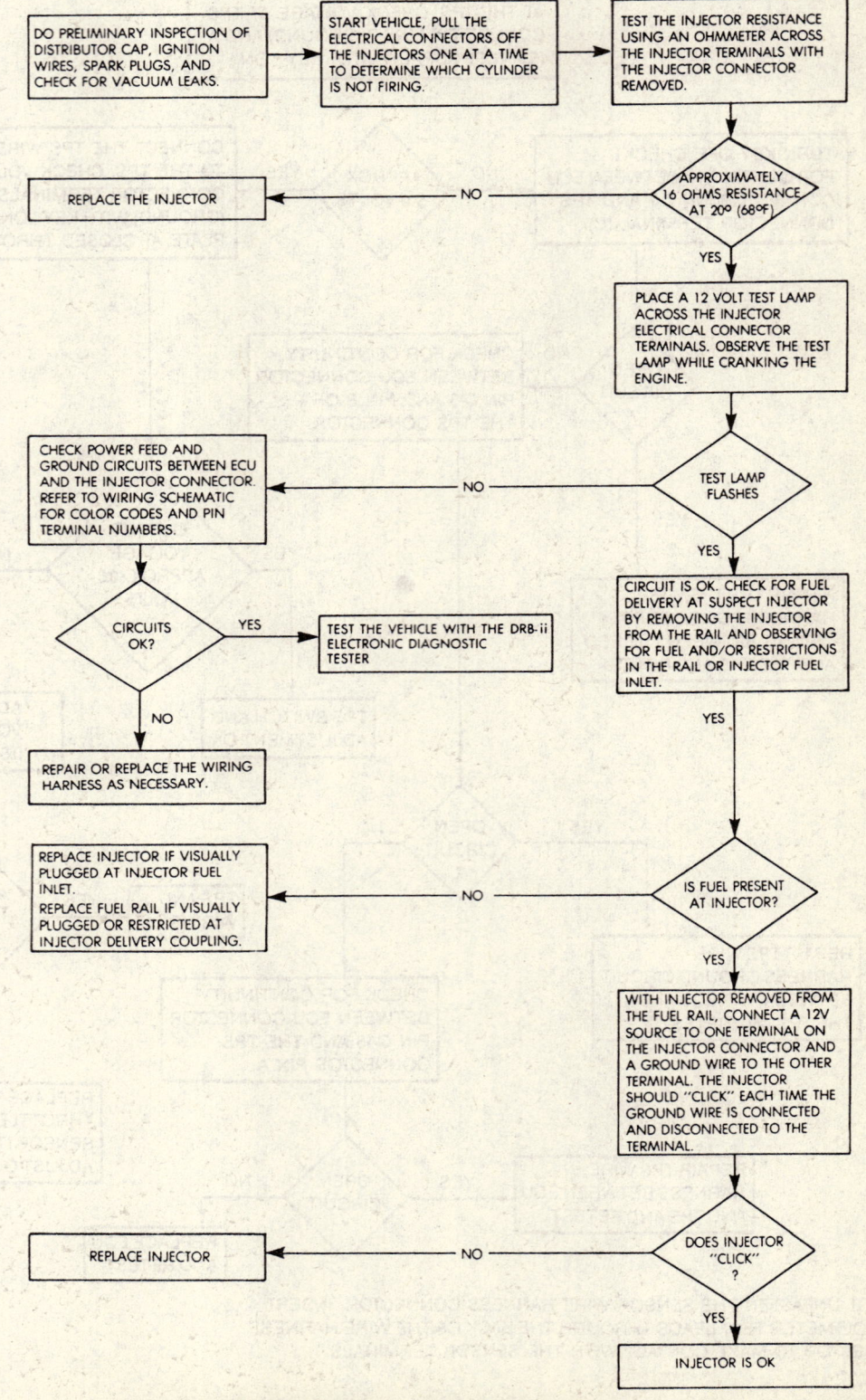

6-CYL fuel feedback diagnostic connector

4-135

4 EMISSION CONTROLS

THROTTLE POSITION SENSOR (TPS) TEST

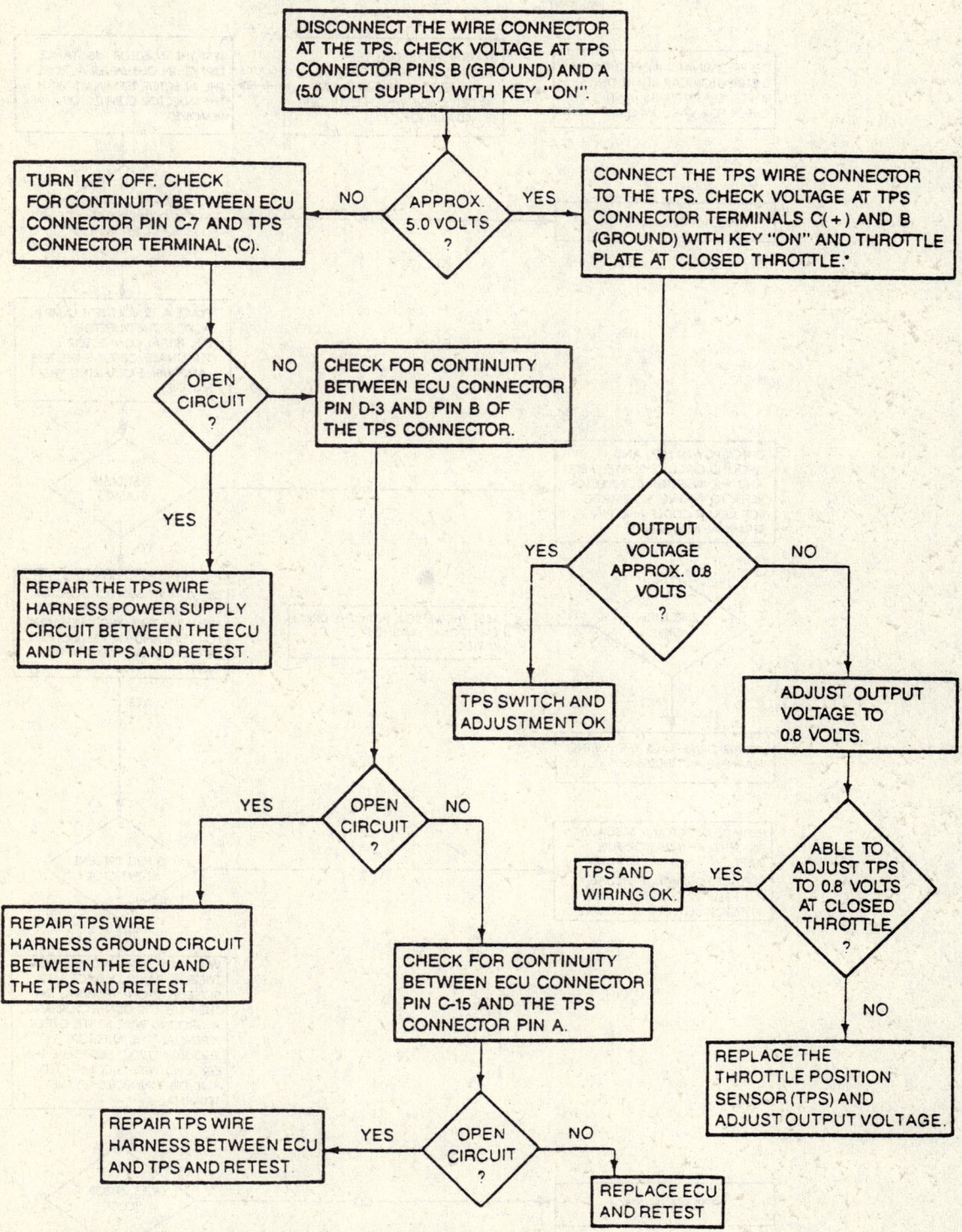

DO NOT UNFASTEN THE SENSOR WIRE HARNESS CONNECTOR. INSERT THE VOLTMETER TEST LEADS THROUGH THE BACK OF THE WIRE HARNESS CONNECTOR TO MAKE CONTACT WITH THE SENSOR TERMINALS.

4-136

EMISSION CONTROLS 4

FAULT CODE	DRBII DISPLAY	DESCRIPTION OF FAULT CONDITION
11	Ign. Reference Signal	No distributor reference signal detected during engine cranking.
13+**	Slow Change in Idle Map Signal	No variation in MAP sensor signal is detected.
	or	
	No Change in MAP from Start to Run	No difference is recognized between the engine MAP reading and the barometric pressure reading at engine start-up.
14+**	MAP Voltage Too Low	MAP sensor input below minimum acceptable voltage.
	or	
	MAP Voltage Too High	MAP sensor input above maximum acceptable voltage.
15**	No Vehicle Speed Signal	No distance sensor signal detected during road load conditions.
17	Engine Is Cold Too Long	Engine coolant temperature remains below normal operating temperatures during vehicle travel (thermostat).
21**	O₂ Signal Stays at Center	Neither rich nor lean condition is detected from the oxygen sensor input.
	or	
	O₂ Signal Shorted to Voltage	Oxygen sensor input voltage maintained above normal operating range.
22+**	Coolant Sensor Voltage Too Low	Coolant temperature sensor input below the minimum acceptable voltage.
	or	
	Coolant Sensor Voltage Too High	Coolant temperature sensor input above the maximum acceptable voltage.
23+**	Charge Temperature Sensor Voltage High	MAT sensor input above the maximum acceptable voltage.
	or	
	Charge Temperature Sensor Voltage Low	MAT sensor input below minimum acceptable voltage.
24+**	TPS Voltage High	Throttle position sensor (TPS) input below the minimum acceptable voltage.
	or	
	TPS Voltage Low	Throttle position sensor (TPS) input above the maximum acceptable voltage.

\+ Check Engine Lamp On
** Check Engine Lamp On (California Only)

4 EMISSION CONTROLS

FAULT CODE	DRBII DISPLAY	DESCRIPTION OF FAULT CONDITION
25 **	Automatic Idle Speed Motor Circuits	A shorted or open circuit detected in one or more of the automatic idle speed (AIS) motor circuits.
27 + **	Injector (number) Control Circuit	Injector output driver does not respond properly to the control signal.
33	A/C Clutch Relay Circuit	An open or shorted condition detected in the A/C clutch relay circuit.
34 only)	Speed Control Solenoid Circuits	An open or shorted condition detected in the speed control vacuum or vent solenoid circuits.
35	Radiator Fan Relay	An open or shorted condition detected in the radiator fan relay control circuit.
41 + **	Alternator Field Not Switching Properly	Alternator field not switching properly.
42	ASD Relay Circuit or No ASD Relay Voltage Sense at Controller	An open or shorted condition detected in the ASD relay control circuit. No ASD voltage sensed at controller.
44	Battery Temp. Sensor Voltage Out of Limit	Battery temperature sensor voltage out of limit.
46 + **	Charging System Voltage Too High	Charging system voltage too high.
47 + **	Charging System Voltage Too Low	Charging system voltage too low.
51 **	O₂ Signal Stays Below Center (Lean)	O₂ sensor signal stays lean.
52 **	O₂ Signal Stays Above Center (Rich)	O₂ sensor signal stays rich.
53	Internal Controller Failure or Controller Failure SPI Communications	Internal engine controller fault condition detected. No internal communication between co-processors.
54	No Sync Pickup Signal	No sync pickup signal.
62	Controller Failure EMR Miles Not Stored	Engine controller failure—EMR miles not stored.

+ Check Engine Lamp On
** Check Engine Lamp On (California Only)

EMISSION CONTROLS 4

FAULT CODE	DRBII DISPLAY	DESCRIPTION OF FAULT CONDITION
63	Controller Failure EEprom Write Denied	Engine controller failure—EEprom write denied.
76	Fuel Pump Resistor Bypass Relay Circuit	An open or shorted condition detected in the ballast resistor bypass circuit.
55	NA	Completion of fault code display on the CHECK ENGINE lamp.

+ Check Engine Lamp On
** Check Engine Lamp On (California Only)

6. If battery voltage is present but the relay isn't working, make sure the transmission is in Park or Neutral and connect terminal **I** wire harness connector, then jumper terminal **G** to ground. If the relay doesn't click, replace the relay. If the starter relay does click, repair the ground circuit.

Sync Pulse (Stator) Test

1. Insert the positive (+) lead of a voltmeter into the blue wire at the distributor connector and the negative (−) lead into the gray/white wire at the distributor connector.

NOTE: Do not disconnect the distributor connector from the distributor. Insert the voltmeter leads into the back side of the connector to make contact with the terminals.

2. Set the voltmeter on the 15 volt AC scale and turn the ignition switch ON. The voltmeter should read approximately 5 volts. If there is no voltage, check the voltmeter leads for a good connection.
3. If there is still no voltage, remove the ECU and check for voltage at pin C-16 and ground with the harness connected. If there is still no voltage present, perform a vehicle test using tester M.S.1700, or equivalent.
4. If voltage is present, check for continuity between the blue wire at the distributor connector and pin C-16 at the ECU. If there is no continuity, repair the wire harness as necessary.
5. Check for continuity between the gray/white wire at the distributor connector and pin C-5 at the ECU. If there is no continuity, repair the wire harness as necessary.
6. Check for continuity between the black wire at the distributor connector and ground. If there is no continuity, repair the wire harness as necessary.
7. Crank the engine while observing the voltmeter; the needle should fluctuate back and forth while the engine is cranking. This verifies that the stator in the distributor is operating properly. If there is no sync pulse, stator replacement is necessary.

EGR Solenoid Test

1. Verify that source vacuum is present at port **C**.
2. Remove vacuum connector at ports **A** and **B** and connect a hand vacuum pump with a gauge at port **B**.
3. Start the engine and read the vacuum level on the gauge. There should be no vacuum at port **B**.
4. Disconnect the electrical connector from the solenoid and again note the reading on the vacuum gauge. There should now be vacuum at port **B**.

5. Reconnect the electrical connector to the solenoid and remove the vacuum gauge. Reconnect all vacuum lines.

Fuel Injector Test

Disconnect the wire connector from the fuel injector and connect an ohmmeter to the injector terminals. The resistance reading should be approximately 16Ω at 68°F (20°C).

Fuel Pressure Test

1. Remove the cap from the pressure test connection on the fuel rail.
2. Connect a fuel pressure gauge (J–34730–1 or equivalent) to the pressure fitting.
3. Start the engine and read the fuel pressure. Normal pressure should be 31 psi with the vacuum hose connected to the pressure regulator and 39 psi with the vacuum hose disconnected from the pressure regulator.
4. If the fuel pressure is not to specifications, check the fuel supply and return lines for kinks or restricting bends. Before replacing the pressure regulator, check the fuel pump flow rate by connecting one end of an old A/C gauge hose to the fuel test port on the fuel rail and inserting the other end into a container of at least 1 liter capacity. A good fuel pump will deliver at least 1 liter of fuel per minute with the return line pinched off. Run the pump by installing a jumper wire into diagnostic connector terminals D1-5 and D1-6.

NOTE: Be sure to pinch off the return line or most of the fuel will be returned to the fuel tank. The fuel pressure regulator is not adjustable and must be replaced if found to be defective.

Chrysler Multi-Point Fuel Injection (MPI) System

All 1991 Jeep vehicles employ a sequential Multi-Point Fuel Injection (MPI) System. The system, similar in construction to the AMC/Jeep multi-point fuel injection system, is controlled by a Single Board Engine Controller II (SBECII). The engine controller is a pre-programmed, dual microprocessor digital computer. It regulates ignition timing, air-fuel ratio, emission control devices, charging system, speed control and idle speed.

Fuel is injected into the intake port directly above the intake valve in precise metered amounts through electrically operated in-

4 EMISSION CONTROLS

jectors. The injectors are fired in a specific sequence by the engine controller. The engine controller maintains an air/fuel ratio of 14.7/1 by constantly adjusting injector pulse width. Injector pulse width is the length of time the injector is open.

The engine controller adjusts ignition timing by controlling the ignition coil. Base ignition timing is not adjustable.

FAULT CODES

The engine controller can detect certain faults in the fuel injection system. A fault indicates that the engine controller has recognized an abnormal signal in the system. Fault codes indicate the result of a failure but never identify the failed component directly.

Fault codes can be obtained by cycling the ignition switch ON-OFF-ON-OFF-ON within 5 seconds. Fault codes will be flashed by the check engine light. Each of the flash(es) represents a digit in the fault code. See the fault code chart for description.

NOTE: A Diagnostic Readout Box (DRB) may be necessary for diagnosis of certain engine malfunctions.

SYSTEM SELF DIAGNOSTICS

The first test performed by the engine controller is for sensor output. If there is a problem with a circuit, the controller tests for an open circuit, short to ground and short to 12 volts. The second test determines if the oxygen sensor is functioning properly.

Systems not monitored by the system self diagnostics include the following:
- Fuel Pressure — The system cannot detect a clogged fuel pump filter, inline filter or a pinched fuel line. However, these could result in a rich or lean condition causing an oxygen sensor fault to be stored.
- Secondary Ignition Circuit — The system cannot detect faulty ignition coil, fouled or worn spark plugs, ignition cross firing, or open spark plug cables.
- Engine Timing — The system cannot detect an incorrectly indexed timing chain, camshaft/crankshaft sprocket, or distributor. However these may cause a rich or lean condition causing a oxygen sensor fault to be stored.
- Cylinder Compression — The system cannot detect uneven, low, or high cylinder compression.
- Exhaust System — The system cannot detect a plugged, restricted or leaking exhaust system.
- Fuel Injector Malfunctions — The system cannot detect of a fuel injector is clogged, the pintle is sticking or the wrong injector is installed. However these may cause a rich or lean condition causing a oxygen sensor fault to be stored.
- Excessive Oil Consumption — Although the system monitors the exhaust stream, it cannot detect excessive oil consumption.
- Throttle Body Air Flow — The system cannot detect a clogged or restricted air cleaner inlet or filter element.
- Evaporative System — The system cannot detect a clogged or restricted evaporative purge canister.
- Vacuum Assist — Leaks or restriction in the vacuum circuits of engine control devices are not monitored by the system. However, these could result in a MAP sensor fault being stored.
- Engine Controller System Ground — The system cannot determine a poor system ground. However, a fault code may be generated as a result of this condition.
- Engine Controller Connector Engagement — The system cannot determine spread or damaged connector pins. However, a fault code may be generated as a result of this condition.

COMPONENT TESTING

Coolant Temperature Sensor (CTS) Test

Disconnect the wire harness connector from the CTS and measure the resistance of the sensor with a high input impedance (digital) volt-ohmmeter. The resistance should be less than 1000Ω with the engine warm. Refer to the resistance chart and replace the sensor if it is not within the range of resistance specified in the chart. Measure the resistance of the wire harness between engine controller wire harness connector terminal 2 and the sensor connector terminal, and terminal 4 to the sensor connector terminal and repair the wire harness if an open circuit is indicated.

Manifold Air Temperature (MAT) Sensor Test

Disconnect the wire harness connector from the MAT and measure the resistance of the sensor with a high input impedance (digital) volt-ohmmeter. The resistance should be less than 1000Ω with the engine warm. Refer to the resistance chart and replace the sensor if it is not within the range of resistance specified in the chart. Measure the resistance of the wire harness between engine controller wire harness connector terminal 2 and the sensor connector terminal, and terminal 4 to the sensor connector terminal and repair the wire harness if the resistance is greater than 1Ω.

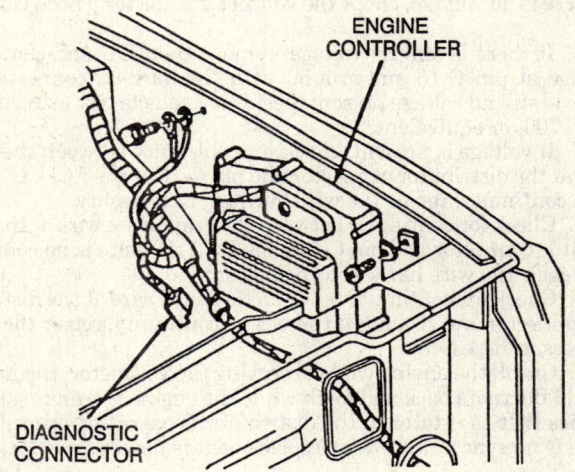

Engine controller location

Manifold Absolute Pressure (MAP) Sensor Test

1. Inspect the MAP sensor vacuum hose connection at the throttle body and sensor and repair as necessary.
2. Test the MAP sensor output voltage at the MAP sensor connector terminal B (as marked on the sensor body) with the ignition switch ON and the engine OFF. The output voltage should be 4–5 volts.

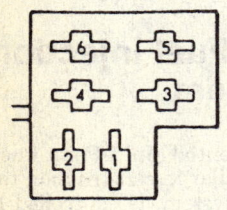

D-1	GROUND
D-2	N/C
D-3	SCI TRANS
D-4	SCI RECEIVE
D-5	IGNITION
D-6	ASD RELAY

Single board engine controller diagnostic connector diagram

EMISSION CONTROLS 4

CAV	WIRE COLOR	DESCRIPTION
1	DG/RD*	MAP SENSOR
2	TN/BK*	COOLANT SENSOR
3	RD	DIRECT BATTERY VOLTAGE
4	BK/LB*	SENSOR GROUND (ENGINE CONTROLLER)
5	BK/WT*	GROUND SENSOR FOR FUEL SENDER
6	VT/WT*	5-VOLT OUTPUT (TO MAP & TPS)
7	OR	8-VOLT OUTPUT (TO DISTRIBUTOR PICKUP)
8	BR	START SIGNAL
9	DB	IGNITION CIRCUIT SENSE
10	DB/OR*	P/S PRESSURE SENSOR
11	BK/TN*	POWER GROUND
12	BK/TN*	POWER GROUND
13	LB/BR*	INJECTOR NO. 4
14	YL/WT*	INJECTOR NO. 3
15	TN	INJECTOR NO. 2
16	WT/DB*	INJECTOR NO. 1
17		
18		
19	GY	IGNITION COIL
20	DG	ALTERNATOR FIELD CONTROL
21	BK/RD*	MANIFOLD AIR TEMPERATURE (MAT) SENSOR
22	OR/DB*	THROTTLE POSITION SENSOR
23		
24	GY/BK*	CRANKSHAFT POSITION SENSOR (CPS)
25	PK	DIAGNOSTIC CONNECTOR
26		
27	LB	A/C REQUEST
28	LG	A/C SELECT
29	WT/PK*	BRAKE SWITCH
30	BK/TN*	PARK/NEUTRAL SWITCH (AUTO TRANS. ONLY)
31		
32	BK/PK*	CHECK ENGINE LAMP
33	TN/RD*	SPEED CONTROL VACUUM SOLENOID
34	DB/OR*	A/C CLUTCH RELAY
35		
36	DG/YL*	ALTERNATOR LAMP

CAV	WIRE COLOR	DESCRIPTION
37	RD/DB*	BALLAST BYPASS RESISTOR
38		
39	GY/RD*	AIS MOTOR (TERMINAL D)
40	BR/WT*	AIS MOTOR (TERMINAL B)
41	BK/DG*	OXYGEN SENSOR
42		
43	GY/LB*	TACH SIGNAL OUTPUT (VEHICLE W/TACHOMETER)
44	TN/YL*	SYNC SENSOR
45	LG	DIAGNOSTIC CONNECTOR
46		
47	WT/OR*	VEHICLE DISTANCE (SPEED) SENSOR
48	BR/RD*	SPEED CONTROL COAST/SET
49	YL/RD*	SPEED CONTROL ON/OFF
50	WT/LG*	SPEED CONTROL RESUME/ACCEL
51	DB/YL*	FUEL PUMP RELAY/ASD RELAY
52		
53	LG/RD*	SPEED CONTROL VENT SOLENOID
54	OR/BK*	SHIFT INDICATOR LIGHT (MANUAL TRANS. ONLY)
55		
56	GY/PK*	EMISSION MAINTENANCE REMINDER
57	DG/OR*	ALTERNATOR OUTPUT
58		
59	VT/BK*	AIS MOTOR (TERMINAL A)
60	YL/BK*	AIS MOTOR (TERMINAL C)

WIRE COLOR CODES			
BK	BLACK	LB	LIGHT BLUE
BR	BROWN	LG	LIGHT GREEN
DB	DARK BLUE	OR	ORANGE
DG	DARK GREEN	PK	PINK
GY	GRAY	RD	RED
		TN	TAN
VT	VIOLET		
WT	WHITE		
YL	YELLOW		
*	WITH TRACER		

CONNECTOR TERMINAL SIDE SHOWN

2.5L engine controller connector pin identification

4 EMISSION CONTROLS

CAV	WIRE COLOR	DESCRIPTION
1	DG/RD*	MAP SENSOR
2	TN/BK*	COOLANT SENSOR
3	RD	DIRECT BATTERY VOLTAGE
4	BK/LB*	SENSOR GROUND (ENGINE CONTROLLER)
5	BK	GROUND SENSOR FOR FUEL SENDER
6	VT	5-VOLT OUTPUT (TO MAP & TPS)
7	OR	8-VOLT OUTPUT (TO DISTRIBUTOR PICKUP)
8	BR	START SIGNAL
9	DB	IGNITION CIRCUIT SENSE
10		
11	BK/TN*	POWER GROUND
12	BK/TN*	POWER GROUND
13	LB/BR*	INJECTOR NO. 4
14	YL/WT*	INJECTOR NO. 3
15	TN	INJECTOR NO. 2
16	WT/DB*	INJECTOR NO. 1
17		
18		
19	GY	IGNITION COIL
20	DG	ALTERNATOR FIELD CONTROL
21	BK/RD*	MANIFOLD AIR TEMPERATURE (MAT) SENSOR
22	OR/DB*	THROTTLE POSITION SENSOR
23		
24	GY/BK*	CRANKSHAFT POSITION SENSOR (CPS)
25	PK	DIAGNOSTIC CONNECTOR
26	VT/BR*	SECURITY ALARM MODULE
27	LB	A/C REQUEST
28	LG	A/C SELECT
29	WT/PK*	BRAKE SWITCH
30	BR/YL*	PARK/NEUTRAL SWITCH (AUTO TRANS. ONLY)
31	DB/PK*	RADIATOR FAN RELAY
32	BK/PK*	CHECK ENGINE LAMP
33	TN/RD*	SPEED CONTROL VACUUM SOLENOID
34	DB/OR*	A/C CLUTCH RELAY
35		
36	DG/YL*	ALTERNATOR LAMP
37	RD/DB*	BALLAST BYPASS RESISTOR
38	PK/BK*	INJECTOR NO. 5
39	GY/RD*	AIS MOTOR (TERMINAL D)
40	BR/WT*	AIS MOTOR (TERMINAL B)
41	BK/DG*	OXYGEN SENSOR
42		
43	GY/LB*	TACH SIGNAL OUTPUT (VEHICLE W/TACHOMETER)
44	TN/YL*	SYNC SENSOR
45	LG	DIAGNOSTIC CONNECTOR
46	WT	SECURITY ALARM MODULE
47	WT/OR*	VEHICLE DISTANCE (SPEED) SENSOR
48	BR/RD*	SPEED CONTROL COAST/SET
49	YL/RD*	SPEED CONTROL ON/OFF
50	WT/LG*	SPEED CONTROL RESUME/ACCEL
51	DB/YL*	FUEL PUMP RELAY/ASD RELAY
52		
53	LG/RD*	SPEED CONTROL VENT SOLENOID
54	OR/BK*	SHIFT INDICATOR LIGHT (MANUAL TRANS. ONLY)
55		
56	GY/PK*	EMISSION MAINTENANCE REMINDER
57	DG/OR*	ALTERNATOR OUTPUT
58	LG/BK*	INJECTOR NO. 6
59	VT/BK*	AIS MOTOR (TERMINAL A)
60	YL	AIS MOTOR (TERMINAL C)

WIRE COLOR CODES			
BK	BLACK	LB	LIGHT BLUE
BR	BROWN	LG	LIGHT GREEN
DB	DARK BLUE	OR	ORANGE
DG	DARK GREEN	PK	PINK
GY	GRAY	RD	RED
		TN	TAN
VT	VIOLET		
WT	WHITE		
YL	YELLOW		
* WITH TRACER			

CONNECTOR TERMINAL SIDE SHOWN

4.0L engine controller connector pin identification

EMISSION CONTROLS 4

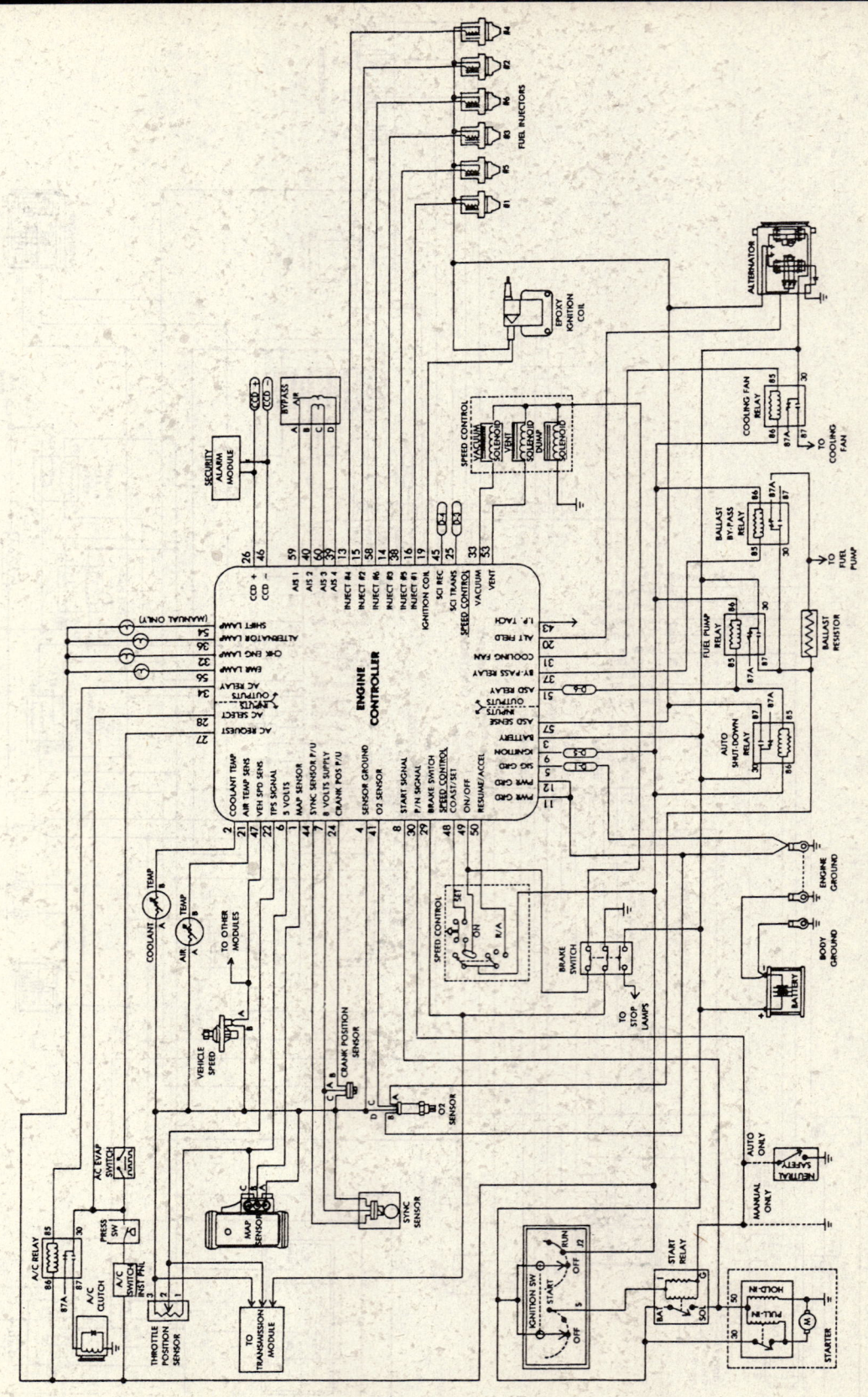

4.0L Single board engine controller wiring diagram

4-143

4 EMISSION CONTROLS

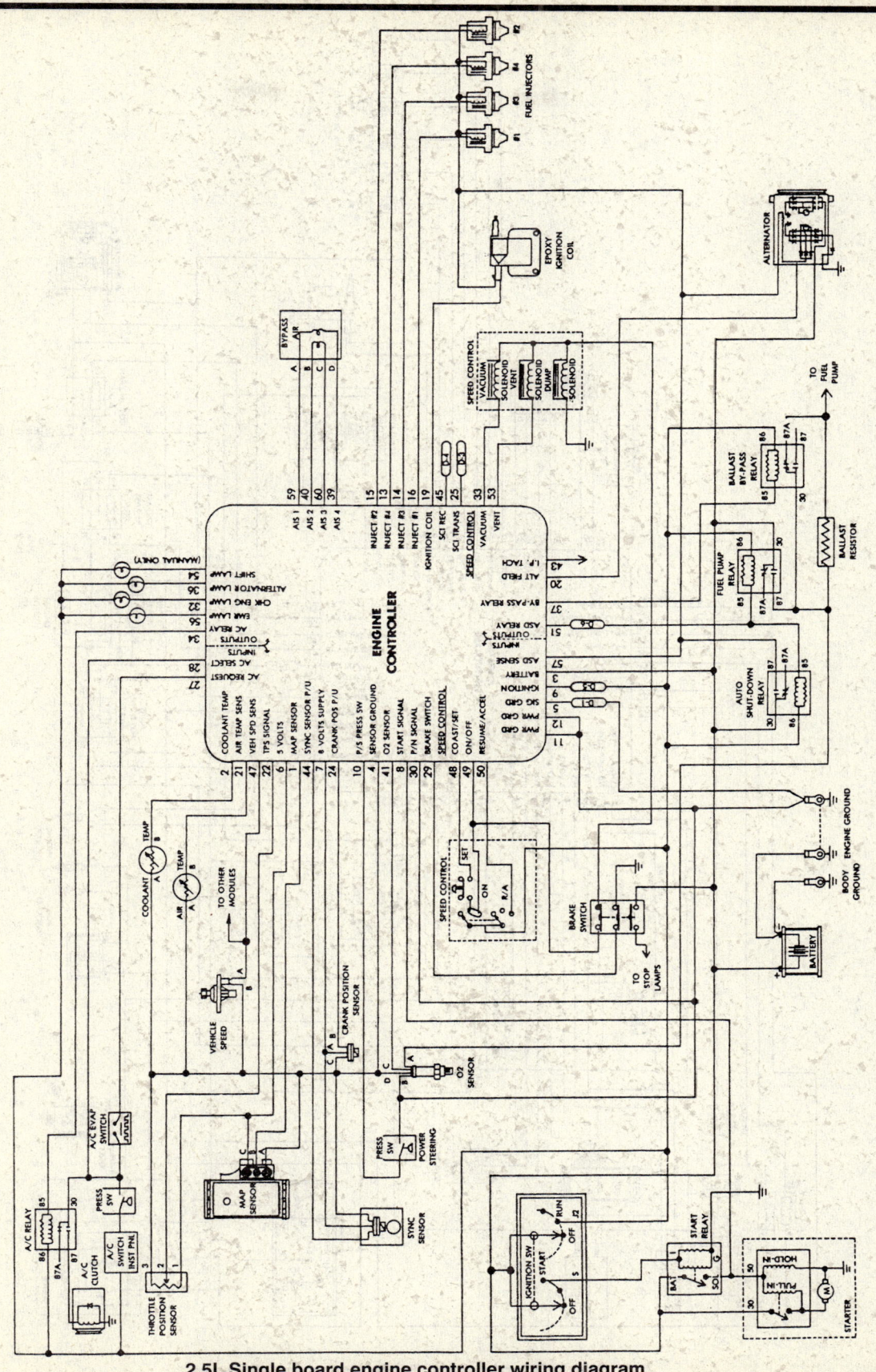

2.5L Single board engine controller wiring diagram

EMISSION CONTROLS 4

NOTE: The voltage should drop to 0.5–1.5 volts with a hot, neutral idle speed condition.

3. Test engine controller terminal 5 for the same voltage as in Step 2 to verify the wire harness condition and repair as necessary.
4. Test the MAP sensor supply voltage at the sensor connector terminal C with the ignition ON. The voltage should be 4.5–5.5 volts. The same voltage should be present at terminal 6 of the engine controller wire harness connector. Repair or replace the wire harness as necessary. If the engine controller is suspect, use Diagnostic Tester M.S.1700, or equivalent, to test engine controller function.
5. Test the MAP sensor ground circuit at the sensor connector terminal A and engine controller connector terminal 4. Repair the wire harness as necessary.
6. Test the MAP sensor ground circuit at the engine controller connector between terminal 4 and terminal 11 with an ohmmeter. If the ohmmeter indicates an open circuit, check for a defective

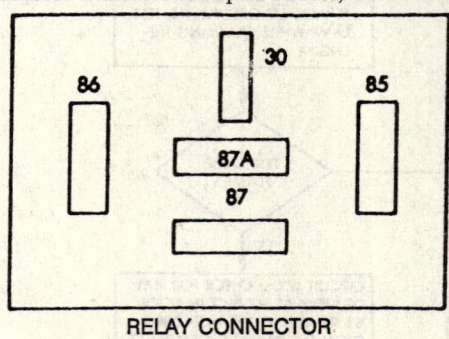
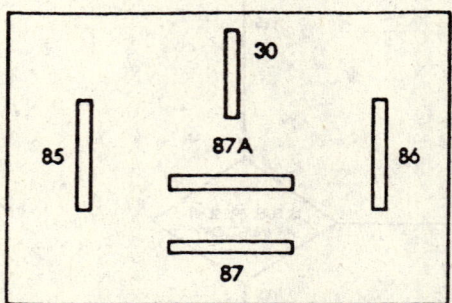

Relay diagram

sensor ground connection located on the right side of the cylinder block. If the ground connection is good, replace the engine controller.

NOTE: If terminal 4 has a short circuit to 12 volts, correct this condition before replacing the engine controller.

Oxygen Sensor Heating Element Test

Disconnect the O₂ sensor connector and connect ohmmeter test leads to terminals **A** and **B** of the sensor connector. The resistance should be 5–7Ω. Replace the O₂ sensor if the ohmmeter displays an infinity (∞) reading. Oxygen sensor operational testing requires the use of a special tester M.S.1700, or equivalent.

Crankshaft Position (Speed) Sensor Test

Disconnect the speed sensor connector from the ignition control module and connect an ohmmeter between terminals **A** and **B** as marked on the connector. The ohmmeter should read 125–275Ω

on a hot engine. Replace the sensor if the readings are not as stated.

Relay Testing

A relay in the de-energized position should have continuity between terminals 87A and 30. Resistance values between terminals 85 and 86 is 70–80Ω for resistor relays and 81–91Ω for diode relays. Not all relays have battery voltage connected to terminal 30. Some may have battery voltage connected to terminals 87 or 87A.

Starter Motor Relay Test

1. Disconnect the wire connectors from the **I** and **G** terminals.
2. Measure the resistance between the terminals with an ohmmeter. It should be approximately 22Ω.
3. Measure the resistance between either terminal and the battery negative post. Reading should be infinite (∞). If defective, replace the relay.
4. Remove the SOL terminal wire connector and connect a voltmeter between the terminal and the battery negative post. With the ignition switch in the START position, the voltmeter should indicate battery voltage (12 volts).
5. If battery voltage is not present, check the related wiring, bulkhead connector and ignition switch adjustment.
6. If battery voltage is present but the relay isn't working, make sure the transmission is in Park or Neutral and connect terminal **I** wire harness connector, then jumper terminal **G** to ground. If the relay doesn't click, replace the relay. If the starter relay does click, repair the ground circuit.

Sync Pulse (Stator) Test

1. Insert the positive (+) lead of a voltmeter into the blue wire at the distributor connector and the negative (−) lead into the gray/white wire at the distributor connector.

NOTE: Do not disconnect the distributor connector from the distributor. Insert the voltmeter leads into the back side of the connector to make contact with the terminals.

2. Set the voltmeter on the 15 volt AC scale and turn the ignition switch ON. The voltmeter should read approximately 5 volts. If there is no voltage, check the voltmeter leads for a good connection.
3. If there is still no voltage, remove the engine controller and check for voltage at pin C-16 and ground with the harness connected. If there is still no voltage present, perform a vehicle test using tester M.S.1700, or equivalent.
4. If voltage is present, check for continuity between the blue wire at the distributor connector and pin C-16 at the engine controller. If there is no continuity, repair the wire harness as necessary.
5. Check for continuity between the gray/white wire at the distributor connector and pin C-5 at the engine controller. If there is no continuity, repair the wire harness as necessary.
6. Check for continuity between the black wire at the distributor connector and ground. If there is no continuity, repair the wire harness as necessary.
7. Crank the engine while observing the voltmeter; the needle should fluctuate back and forth while the engine is cranking. This verifies that the stator in the distributor is operating properly. If there is no sync pulse, stator replacement is necessary.

EGR Solenoid Test

1. Verify that source vacuum is present at port **C**.
2. Remove vacuum connector at ports **A** and **B** and connect a hand vacuum pump with a gauge at port **B**.
3. Start the engine and read the vacuum level on the gauge. There should be no vacuum at port **B**.
4. Disconnect the electrical connector from the solenoid and

4 EMISSION CONTROLS

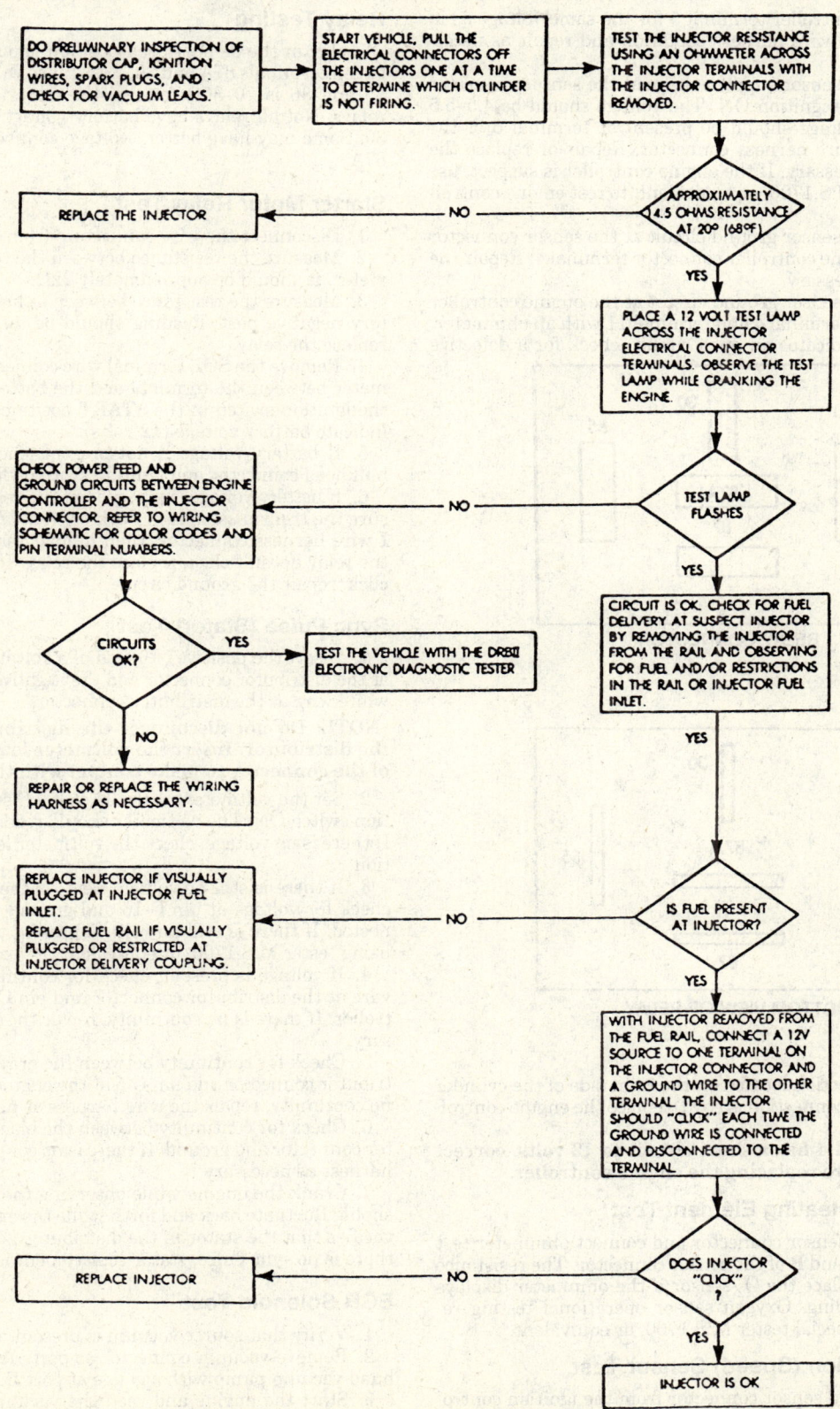

4-146

EMISSION CONTROLS 4

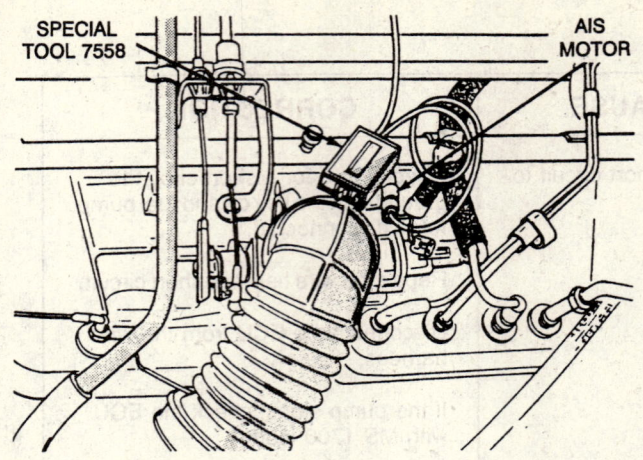

Auto idle speed motor exerciser

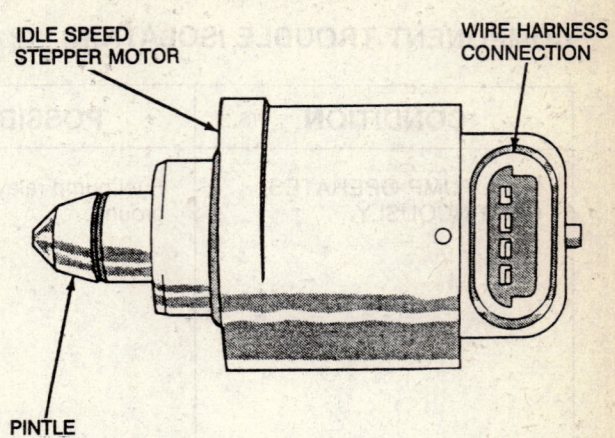

Idle speed stepper motor pintle

again note the reading on the vacuum gauge. There should now be vacuum at port **B**.

5. Reconnect the electrical connector to the solenoid and remove the vacuum gauge. Reconnect all vacuum lines.

Fuel Injector Test

Disconnect the wire connector from the fuel injector and connect an ohmmeter to the injector terminals. The resistance reading should be approximately 12.8–15.2Ω at 68°F (20°C).

Fuel Pressure Test

1. Remove the cap from the pressure test connection on the fuel rail.
2. Connect a fuel pressure gauge (J–34730–1 or equivalent) to the pressure fitting.
3. Start the engine and read the fuel pressure. Normal pressure should be 31 psi with the vacuum hose connected to the pressure regulator and 39 psi with the vacuum hose disconnected from the pressure regulator.
4. If the fuel pressure is not to specifications, check the fuel supply and return lines for kinks or restricting bends. Before replacing the pressure regulator, check the fuel pump flow rate by connecting one end of an old A/C gauge hose to the fuel test port on the fuel rail and inserting the other end into a container of at least 1 liter capacity. A good fuel pump will deliver at least 1 liter of fuel per minute with the return line pinched off.

NOTE: Be sure to pinch off the return line or most of the fuel will be returned to the fuel tank. The fuel pressure regulator is not adjustable and must be replaced if found to be defective.

Automatic Idle Speed (AIS) Motor Test

The automatic idle speed motor can be tested using exerciser tool 7558.

1. With the ignition OFF, disconnect the AIS motor wire connector at the throttle body. Plug the exerciser tool harness into the AIS motor. Connect the exerciser motor power leads to the battery. The red light on the exerciser should flash.
2. Start engine. When the switch is in the HIGH or LOW position, the light on the exerciser will flash indicating that voltage pulses are being sent to the stepper motor.
3. Move the switch to the HIGH position; the engine speed should increase. Move the switch to the LOW position; the engine speed should decrease.

    a. If engine speed changes while using the exerciser, the AIS motor is functioning properly. Disconnect the tool and reconnect the AIS harness.

    b. If the engine speed does not change, turn the ignition OFF and proceed to Step 4.

4. Remove the AIS motor from the throttle body.

NOTE: When checking AIS motor operation with the motor removed, DO NOT allow the pintle to extend more than 1/4 in. (6mm). If the pintle is extended more than 1/4 in. (6mm), it may separate from the motor. The AIS motor must be replaced if the pintle separates from the motor.

5. With the ignition switch OFF, cycle the exerciser tool switch between the HIGH and LOW positions. Observe the pintle for movement.

    a. If the pintle does not move, replace the AIS motor. Start engine and test replacement motor as described in Step 3.

    b. If the pintle operates properly, check the AIS motor bore in the throttle body for blockage and clean as necessary. Reinstall the AIS motor and retest.

4 EMISSION CONTROLS

COMPONENT TROUBLE ISOLATION

CONDITION	POSSIBLE CAUSE	CORRECTION
FUEL PUMP OPERATES CONTINUOUSLY.	Fuel pump relay has short circuit to ground.	Check Pin 6 for a short circuit to ground with the key off and fuel pump relay disconnected. Repair the wire harness short circuit. Disconnect the ECU from the wire harness. If the pump stops, check the ECU with MS 1700 tester. Disconnect the fuel pump relay and check for a short circuit. Replace the relay. Test the ECU with MS 1700 tester.
FUEL PUMP WILL NOT OPERATE FOR ONE SECOND WITH THE IGNITION SWITCH ON.	Open circuit.	Connect a jumper wire across the fuel pump relay. If the pump operates, check for battery voltage at the relay. Check the continuity between the relay and Pin 6 at the ECU. Repair the wire harness as necessary. Replace the fuel pump relay. Test the ECU with MS 1700 tester. Test for continuity between the fuel pump and the relay contacts. Check the pump ground circuit. Repair the harness as necessary.
	Fuel pump ballast resistor defective.	Replace the fuel pump ballast resistor.

4-148

EMISSION CONTROLS 4

COMPONENT TROUBLE ISOLATION (Cont'd)

CONDITION	POSSIBLE CAUSE	CORRECTION
FUEL PUMP WILL NOT OPERATE WHEN THE STARTER MOTOR IS ENGAGED.	Fuel pump defective.	Replace the fuel pump.
	Open circuit.	Connect positive battery voltage to the pump contact on the starter motor relay.
		If the pump operates, repair or replace the starter motor relay.
		If the pump does not operate, repair the wire harness between the starter motor relay and the pump side of the ballast resistor.
		Check to determine if the pump operates one second with the ignition switch on.
ISA (IDLE SPEED ACTUATOR) MOTOR DOES NOT EXTEND ON ENGINE SHUTDOWN. (SYMPTOM: SLOW, UNSATISFACTORY IDLE AFTER COLD START.)	ECU, wire harness, or motor.	Connect a test bulb between D2 Pin 14 and D2 Pin 11 with the engine operating. Shut the engine off.
		If the bulb does not light momentarily on shutdown: test the ECU with MS 1700 tester.
		If the bulb lights at shutdown: test the wire harness and connector at the ISA motor. Repair as necessary.
		Test to determine if the motor is jammed in the full retract position. Extend manually. Apply battery voltage to Pins C and D on the ISA motor.
		NOTE: The motor must be disconnected from the wire harness for all tests.
		Replace the ISA motor.

4-149

4 EMISSION CONTROLS

COMPONENT TROUBLE ISOLATION (Cont'd)

CONDITION	POSSIBLE CAUSE	CORRECTION
IDLE SPEED ERRATIC, LOW, OR HIGH CONSISTENTLY.	ISA motor inoperative.	Battery voltage supplied to motor, positive battery post connected to Pin D, and Pin C connected to ground should advance the motor plunger. Extending the motor plunger also verifies that the motor is not jammed in the extract position. All motor tests should be with the motor disconnected from the wire harness.
		Replace the ISA motor.
		Check the closed throttle switch and associated wiring.
		Refer to the test procedure.
	NO ECU output.	Connect a test lamp from Pin 23 to Pin 24 on the ECU. Remove the ISA motor from the bracket and close the CTS switch manually. With the engine warmed-up and at idle speed, manually open the throttle to a speed well above normal idle speed. The lamp should flash. Close the throttle so the speed drops well below normal idle speed. The lamp should flash.
		NOTE: Improper handling of the ISA motor outputs can result in system damage. Never connect to ground or the battery.
		If the lamp flashes on both over and under idle speed: Check the wiring harness between the ECU and the ISA motor for an open or short circuit. Recheck the ISA motor function.
		If the lamp fails to flash on either over or under speed: Check the ECU with MS 1700 tester.
ECU DOES NOT TURN OFF AFTER ENGINE SHUTDOWN. (SYMPTOM: BATTERY LOSES CHARGE WITH KEY OFF.)	Throttle position incorrect.	Check to ensure that the throttle is resting on the switch at normal idle. Connect a voltmeter from D2 Pin 13 to D1 Pin 3. Should indicate ground potential at a normal idle speed.
		Check for air leaks into vacuum. Check the closed throttle switch using the test procedure.
	MAP sensor voltage supply (ECU Pin 16). Voltage should go from 5V to zero within 30 seconds after key is turned off.	Check coolant temperature sensor. Refer to the test procedure.
		Check the starter motor relay for a short circuit. With the key off, check the relay for battery voltage.

EMISSION CONTROLS 4

COMPONENT TROUBLE ISOLATION (Cont'd)

CONDITION	POSSIBLE CAUSE	CORRECTION
EGR VALVE/CANISTER PURGE SOLENOID CONTROL IS ERRATIC. (SYMPTOMS: UNSATISFACTORY IDLE, BAD DRIVEABILITY, INACTIVE OXYGEN SENSOR.)	Defective solenoid.	Replace relay. Test the ECU with MS 1700 tester. Check ignition switch and harness for short circuit to battery voltage. Repair or replace as necessary. Check the solenoid valve. Connect the valve (out of harness) to 12V and determine if it opens and closes. Check for 12V to the solenoid valve coil. Replace the valve. Repair the wiring harness. Test the ECU with MS 1700 tester.
FUEL PRESSURE IS LOW AT TEST POINT ON THROTTLE BODY (BELOW 17.3 PSI AT IDLE). (SYMPTOMS: UNSATISFACTORY DRIVEABILITY, INACTIVE OXYGEN SENSOR, HARD COLD STARTS.)	Fuel pump malfunction.	Check the pump for proper voltage (nominally 7.5V). Check the fuel filter. Replace the filter. Replace the fuel pump ballast resistor. Repair the wiring harness. Check the fuel pressure regulator for proper function. With the engine idling, gently pinch off the rubber fuel return hose to the fuel tank. The pressure should rise greatly when the hose is restricted. Check the fuel pressure out of the pump. With a gauge directly on fuel inlet pipe (pipe dead headed at gauge), several cycles of key on should produce a pressure well over 20 psi. **WARNING:** This should only be done for a short time because the fuel system is not designed for high pressures. Install a fuel pressure regulator kit. Replace the throttle body. Replace the fuel pump.
FUEL PRESSURE HIGH AT TEST POINT ON THROTTLE BODY (OVER 17.3 PSI AT IDLE). (SYMPTOMS: UNSATISFACTORY DRIVEABILITY, HARD STARTS, BLACK SMOKE, INACTIVE OXYGEN SENSOR.)	Fuel restriction.	Check the fuel pressure with an oversize temporary fuel return pipe. Pipe should replace the existing return pipe. It should be securely fastened at the throttle body and discharge fuel into an approved closed container. If the pressure drops, replace the fuel return pipe. Inspect the fuel tank fittings and replace if restricted. If the pressure does not drop, install a fuel pressure regulator kit.

4 EMISSION CONTROLS

COMPONENT TROUBLE ISOLATION (Cont'd)

CONDITION	POSSIBLE CAUSE	CORRECTION
ENGINE WILL NOT START.	Defective WOT switch.	Refer to the WOT switch test procedure.
	Low battery voltage.	Replace or charge the battery.
	Fuel supply too low.	Replenish as necessary.
	Low fuel pressure.	Refer to the fuel pressure test. Correct as necessary. Replace the fuel filter.
	Fuel pump inoperative.	Repair or replace as necessary.
	Defective secondary ignition circuit.	Position a spark plug (with ignition wire) on the cylinder block. Engage the starter motor and observe the spark. Repair or replace the ignition power module or wiring.
	Primary ignition input to the ECU defective.	Connect a voltmeter between D1 Pin 1 and ground. With key on (engine stopped) voltage should be close to battery voltage. Check the harness and connectors between the ECU and the ignition power module. Service the ignition power module as necessary.
	No battery voltage applied to the injector (12V from one pin to chassis ground).	Check the B+ relay. Check the wire harness and connectors. Repair or replace as necessary.
	Injector resistance too high (ohmmeter should indicate less than 10 ohms).	Replace the injector.
	ECU is not switching the injector.	Remove the injector wire harness connector. Connect a test lamp across the connector. Engage the starter motor. The lamp should pulse dimly. Check the ECU with MS 1700 tester.
	Leaking injector.	Check to determine if the injector is discharging fuel when the engine is rotated by the starter motor. Install an O-ring kit if it is leaking fuel. Replace the injector if it either discharges no fuel with engine turning or drips fuel with the engine stopped.

EMISSION CONTROLS 4

COMPONENT TROUBLE ISOLATION (Cont'd)

CONDITION	POSSIBLE CAUSE	CORRECTION
ENGINE STARTS BUT WILL NOT IDLE.	No start signal voltage.	Check the start signal. Voltmeter from D1 Pin 4 to ground should indicate battery voltage when the starter motor is engaged.
		Service the starter motor relay or wire harness.
	ISA motor plunger is not extended.	Refer to the ISA motor test procedure.
	Coolant temperature sensor inoperative.	Refer to the coolant temperature sensor test procedure.
		Check to ensure that the spark plugs are not fouled or wet.
		Replace as necessary.
	Fuel pump inoperative.	Check the fuel pump.
	Ignition system malfunction.	Check the ignition system. Repair as necessary.
		Check the start signal after engaging the starter motor. Voltmeter from D1 Pin 4 to D1 Pin 3 should indicate zero volts.
		Repair wire harness as necessary.
		Check the MAP sensor. Repair as necessary.
		Test the ECU with MS 1700 tester.
DRIVEABILITY OR FUEL ECONOMY COMPLAINT.	High fuel pressure.	Check the fuel pressure.
		Test the ECU with MS 1700 tester.
		Replace the ECU if necessary.
		Check to determine if the oxygen sensor is functioning.
		Replace if necessary.
	Injector defective.	Replace the injector.
	WOT switch malfunction.	Check the WOT switch.
		Adjust, repair or replace the switch to ensure that the WOT voltage (D2 Pin 6) is low during an actual wide open throttle condition.

4-153

4 EMISSION CONTROLS

COMPONENT TROUBLE ISOLATION (Cont'd)

CONDITION	POSSIBLE CAUSE	CORRECTION
	Air filter restricted.	Check the air filter. Replace as necessary.
	EGR valve malfunction.	Check the EGR valve and hoses. Repair or replace.
	Canister purge malfunction.	Check the canister purge function. Repair as necessary.

VACUUM DIAGRAMS

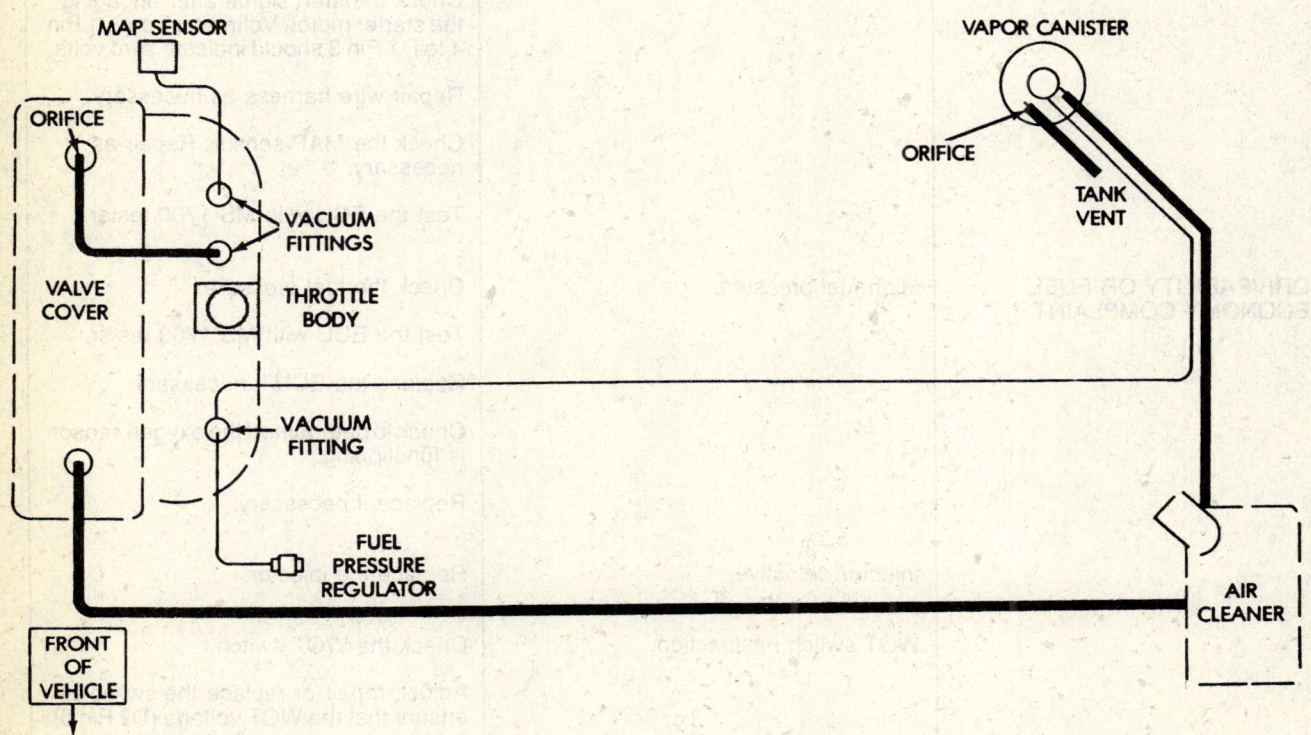

1991 4.0L vacuum diagram

4-154

EMISSION CONTROLS 4

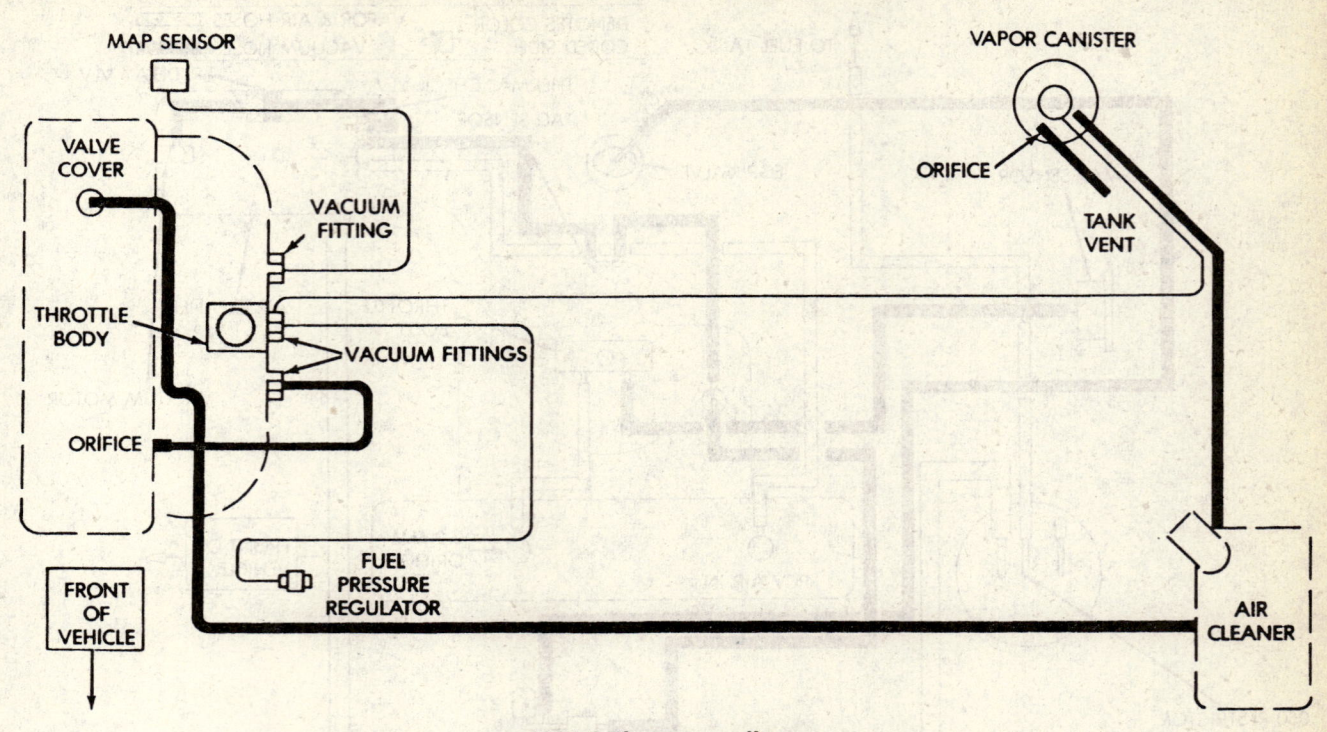

1991 2.5L vacuum diagram

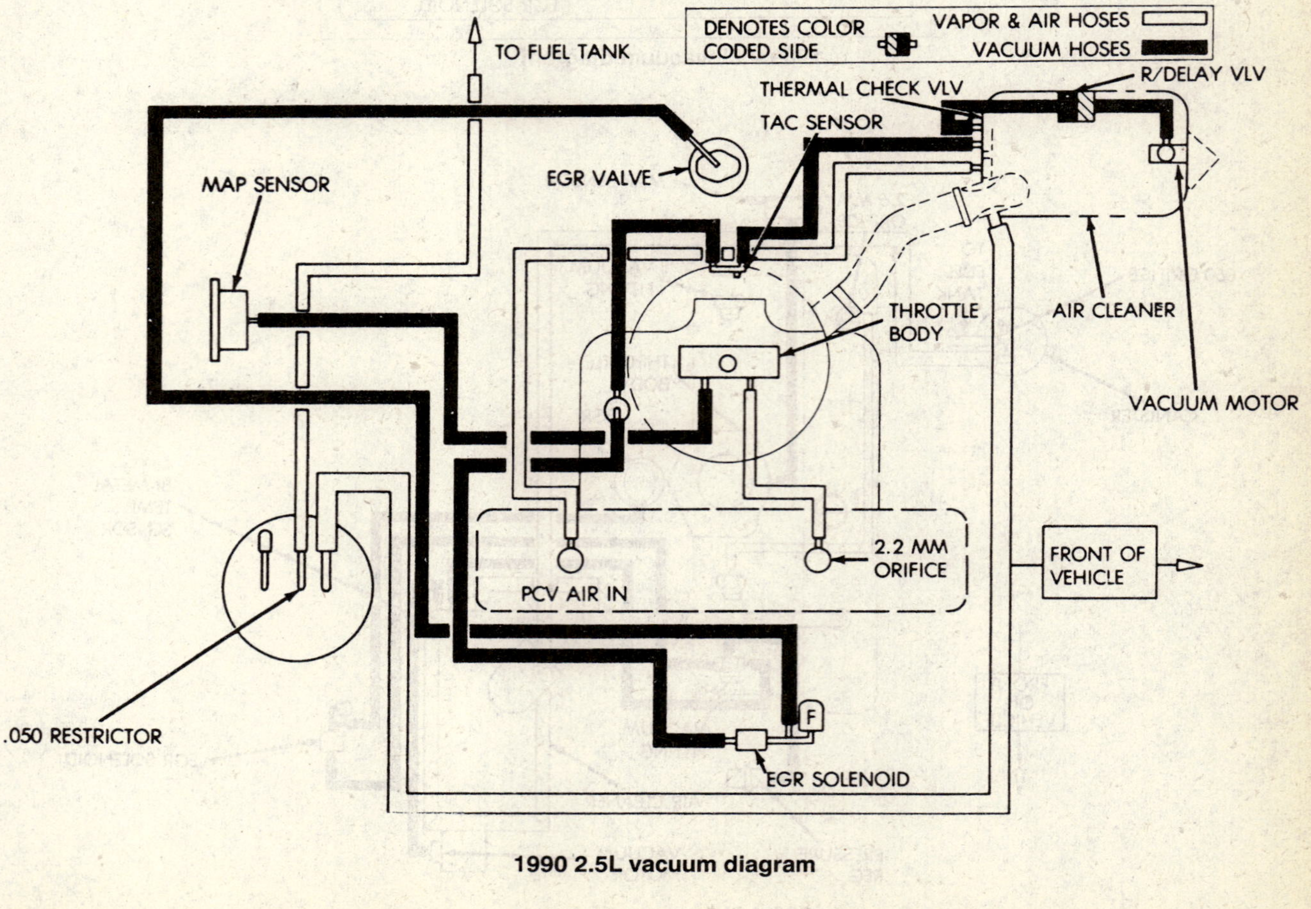

1990 2.5L vacuum diagram

4-155

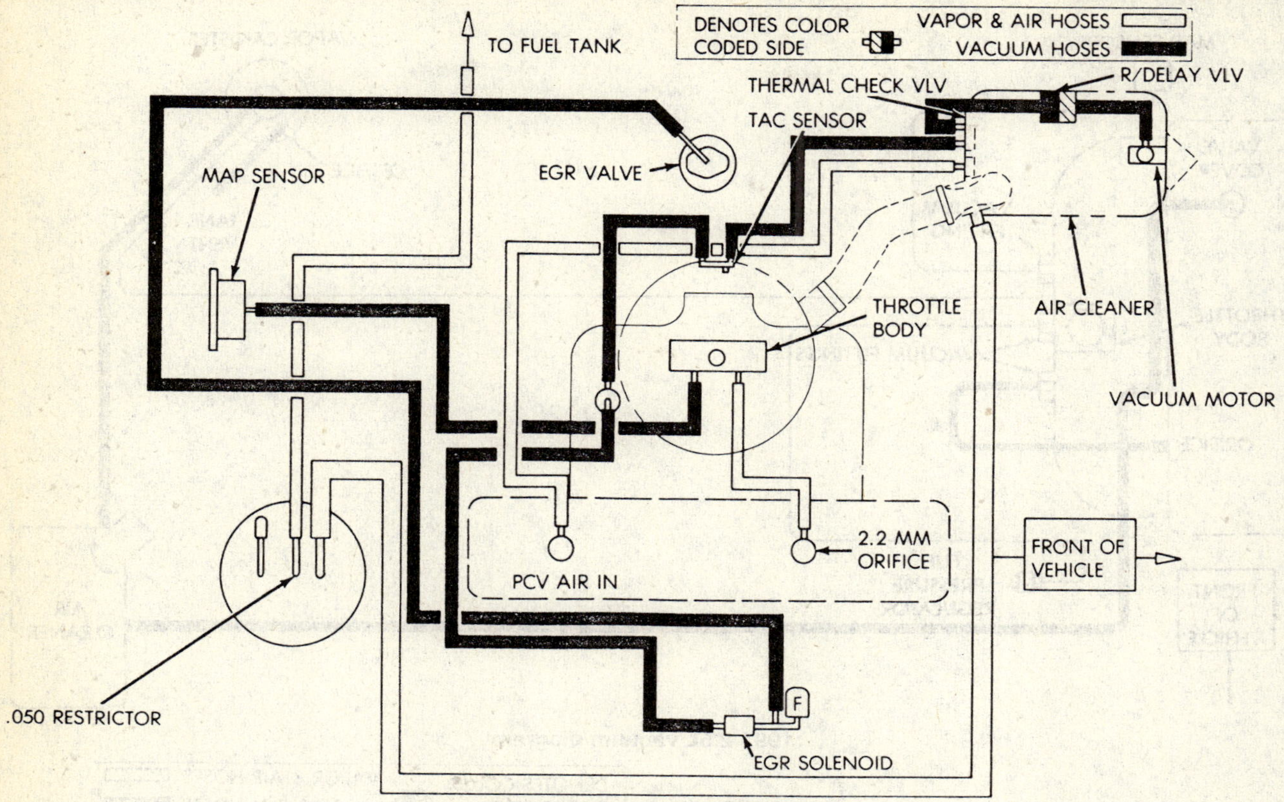

4 EMISSION CONTROLS

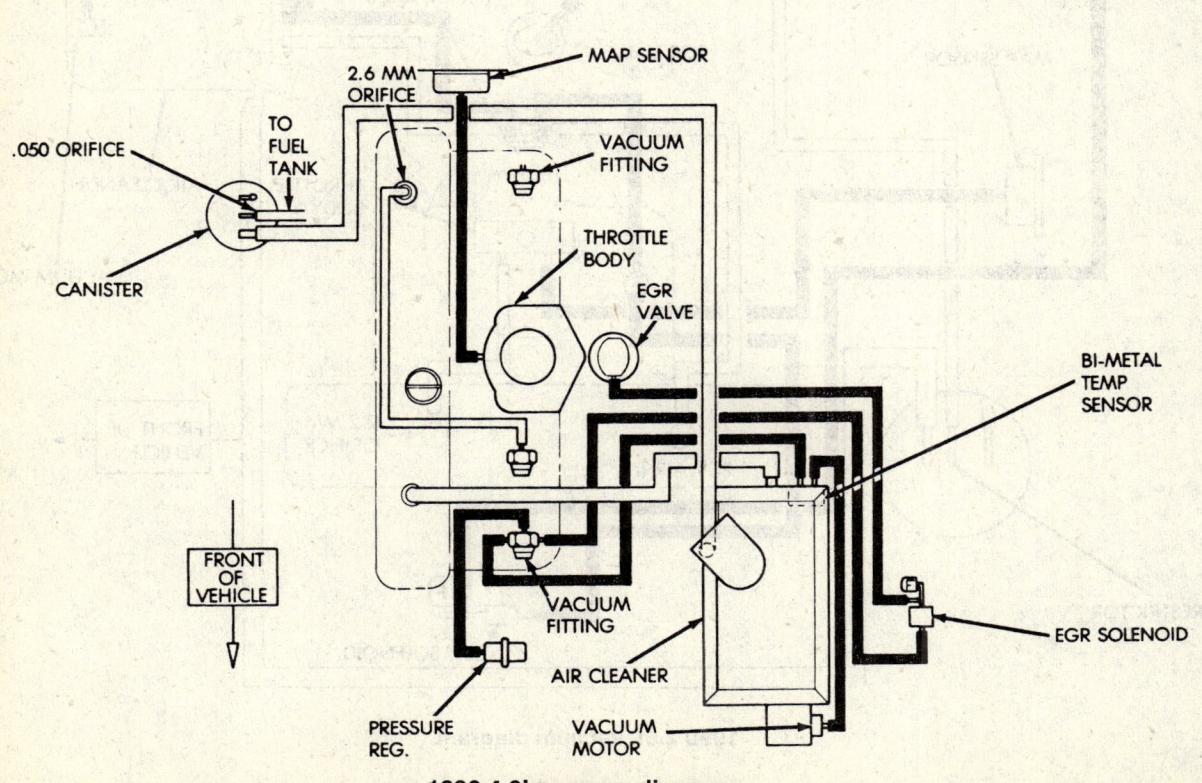

1989 2.5L vacuum diagram

1990 4.0L vacuum diagram

EMISSION CONTROLS 4

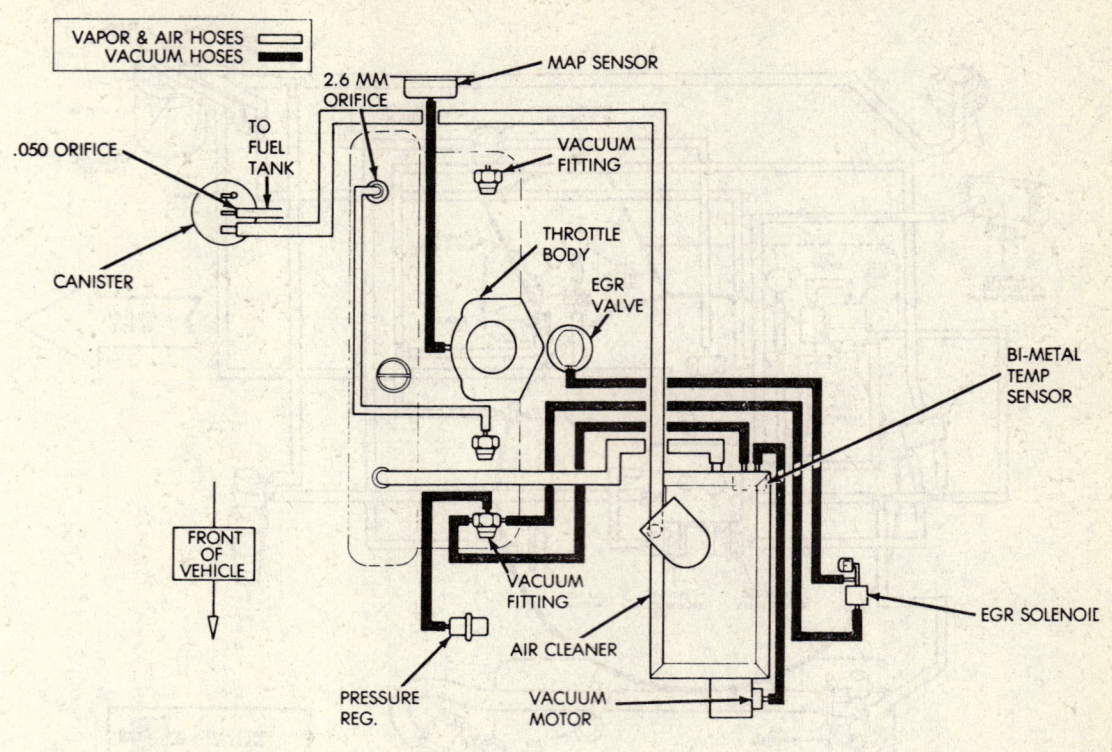

1989 4.0L vacuum diagram

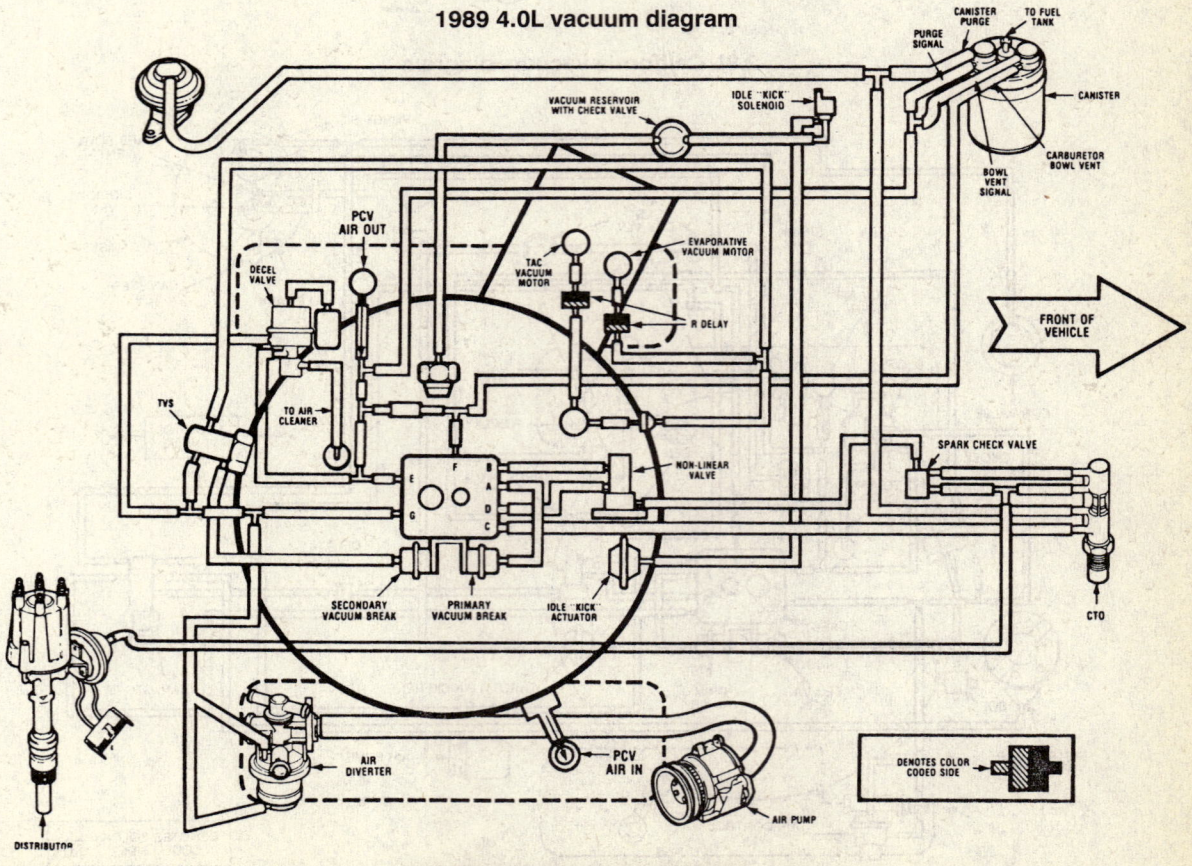

2.8L 49 state vacuum diagram

4-157

4 EMISSION CONTROLS

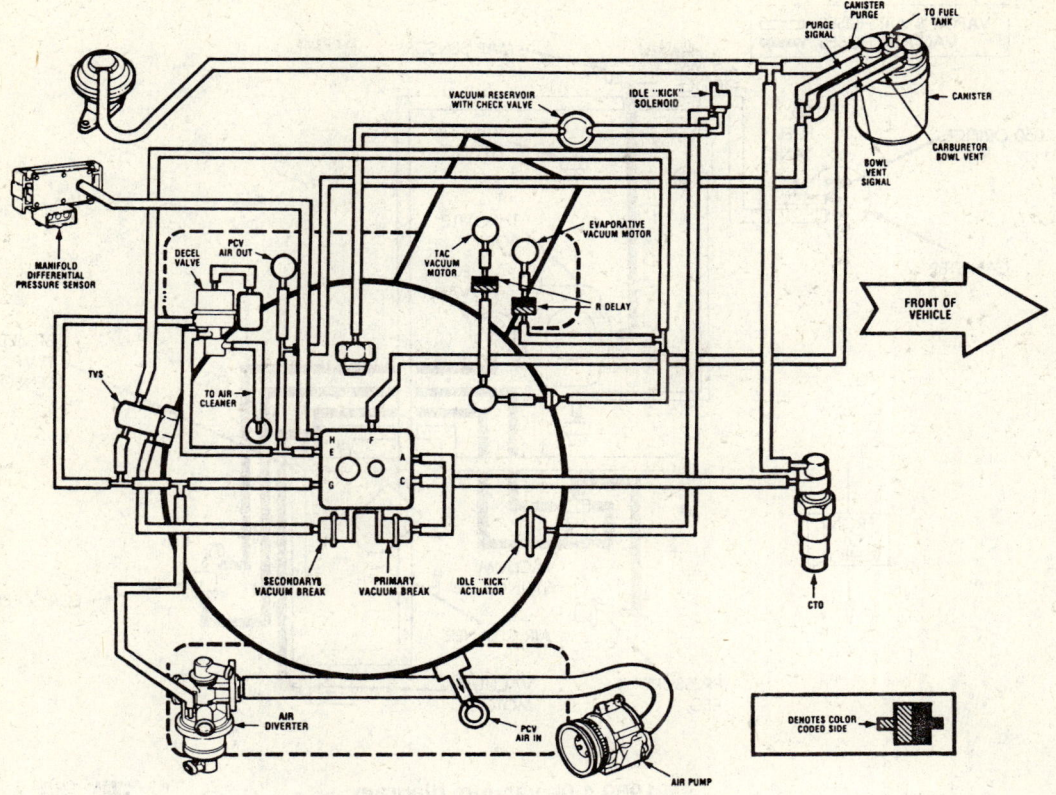

2.8L California vacuum diagram

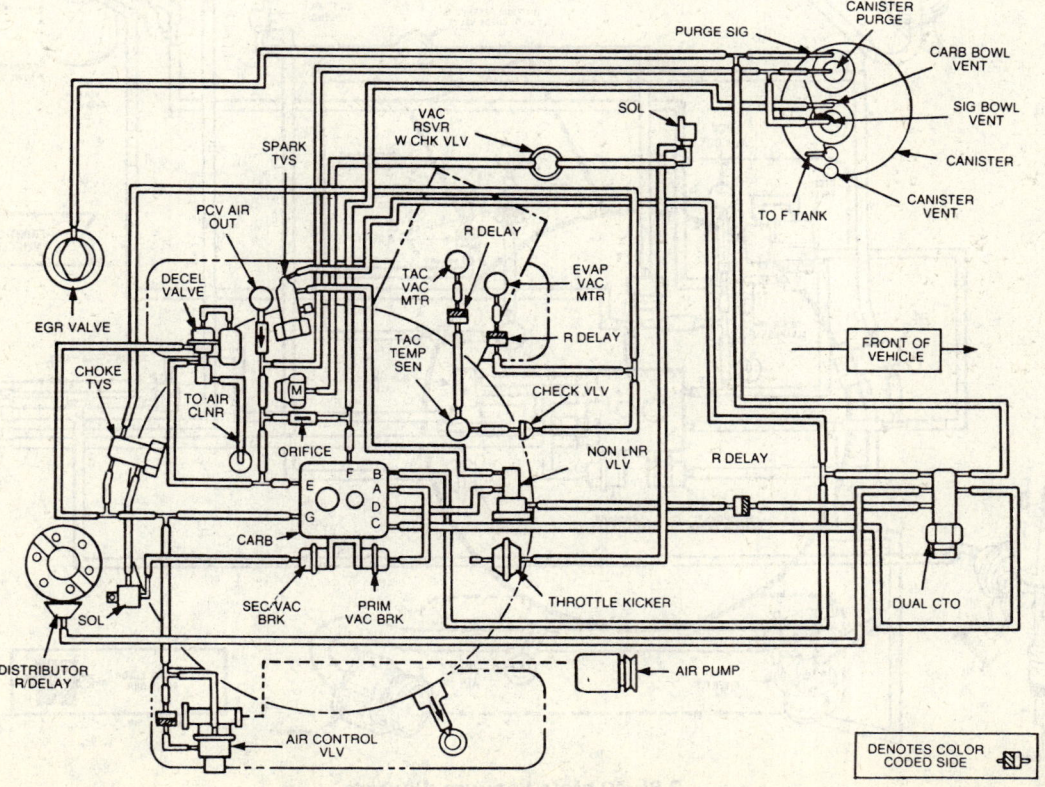

2.8L California vacuum diagram

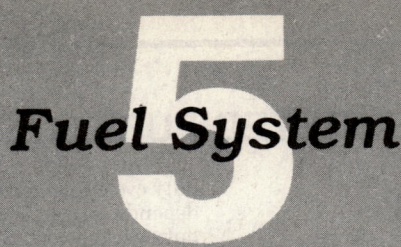

Fuel System

QUICK REFERENCE INDEX

Carbureted Fuel System	5-2
Diesel Fuel System	5-27
Fuel Injection Systems	5-20

GENERAL INDEX

Carburetor — Carter YFA
- Adjustments 5-2
- Overhaul 5-6
- Removal and Installation 5-6
- Specifications 5-4

Carburetor — Rochester 2SE/E2SE
- Adjustments 5-10
- Overhaul 5-15
- Removal and Installation 5-15
- Specifications 5-11

Diesel Fuel System
- Cold start capsule 5-30
- Cold start system 5-30
- Glow plugs 5-30
- Injection pump 5-27
- Injection timing 5-29

Injectors 5-29

Multi-Point Fuel Injection
- Coolant temperature sensor 5-24
- Crankshaft speed sensor 5-25
- Fuel pump 5-23
- Idle speed stepper motor 5-27
- Injectors 5-26
- Knock sensor 5-25
- MAP sensor 5-24
- MAT sensor 5-24
- Oxygen sensor 5-25
- Relieving fuel system pressure . 5-23
- Throttle body 5-23
- Throttle position sensor 5-25

Throttle Body Fuel injection
- Fuel body 5-20

- Fuel pressure regulator 5-21
- Fuel pump 5-20
- Idle speed actuator motor 5-23
- Injectors 5-21
- Quick-connect fuel line 5-23
- Throttle body 5-20
- Throttle position sensor 5-21
- Wide open throttle switch 5-23

Fuel pump
- Electric 5-20, 23
- Mechanical 5-2

Fuel system
- Carbureted 5-2
- Fuel injection 5-20

Fuel tank 5-31

5-1

5 FUEL SYSTEM

CARBURETED FUEL SYSTEM

Mechanical Fuel Pump

Carbureted 4-2.5L and 6-2.8L engines use a single action stamped fuel pump that is mechanically driven by an eccentric on the camshaft.

REMOVAL AND INSTALLATION

1. Disconnect the inlet and outlet fuel lines and, on the 6-2.8L engine, the fuel return line.
2. Remove the fuel pump body attaching nuts and lock washers.
3. Pull the pump and gasket or O-ring free of the engine.
NOTE: On the 6-2.8L engine, the actuating rod may fall from the engine.
4. Make sure that the mating surfaces of the fuel pump and the engine are clean.
5. Cement a new gasket to the mounting flange of the fuel pump.
6. Position the fuel pump on the engine block so that the lever of the fuel pump rests on the fuel pump cam of the camshaft.
7. Secure the fuel pump to the block with the capscrews and lock washers. tighten the capscrews to 16 ft. lbs.
8. Connect the fuel lines to the fuel pump.

FUEL PUMP TESTING

Volume Check

Disconnect the fuel line from the carburetor. Place the open end of the line into a graduated one quart container. Start the engine and operate it at a normal idle speed. The pump should deliver at least one pint in 30 seconds. Replace the pump if defective.

Pressure Check

Disconnect the fuel line at the carburetor. Install a T-fitting on the open end of the fuel line and refit the line to the carburetor. Plug a pressure gauge into the remaining opening of the T-fitting. The hose leading to the pressure gauge should not be any longer than 6 in. (152mm). On pumps with a fuel return line, the line must be plugged. Start the engine. Fuel pressures are as follows:
  4-2.5L: 4.00–5.00 psi idle
  6-2.8L: 6.00–7.50 psi idle

Carter Model YFA Feedback Carburetor, 4-2.5L Engine

DESCRIPTION

The Carter/Weber YFA carburetor consists of three main assemblies. The air horn contains the choke, vacuum break, choke plate, duty cycle solenoid, float and assembly. The main body contains the pump diaphragm assembly, metering jet, low-speed jet, accelerator pump check ball and weight, pump bleed valve and wide open throttle switch. The throttle body contains the throttle plate, throttle shaft and lever, idle mixture screw with O-ring and a tamper-proof plug.

The duty cycle solenoid is an integral part of the YFA carburetor. The control unit operates the duty cycle solenoid to provide the proper air/fuel ratio by controlling the air flow. In open loop operation, the air supplied by the duty cycle solenoid is preprogrammed. In closed loop operation, the control unit signals the duty cycle solenoid to provide additional air to the air/fuel mixture depending upon the sensor inputs to the control unit. Air from the duty cycle solenoid is then distributed to the carburetor idle circuit and main metering circuit where it mixes with the fuel.

ADJUSTMENTS

Fast Idle Speed Adjustment

1. Disconnect and plug the EGR valve vacuum hose at the valve.
2. Connect a tachometer to the ignition coil negative (TACH) terminal.
3. Place the automatic transmission in Park, or the manual transmission in Neutral, then start the engine and allow it to reach normal operating temperature.
4. Position the fast idle speed adjustment screw on the second step of the fast idle cam.
5. Turn the fast idle adjustment screw to obtain a fast idle speed of 2300 rpm (automatic transmission) or 2000 rpm (manual transmission). If the fast idle speed listed on the underhood emission sticker differs from the above, use the specification on the underhood sticker.
6. Allow the throttle to return to curb idle speed, then reconnect the EGR valve vacuum hose. Turn the ignition OFF and disconnect the tachometer.

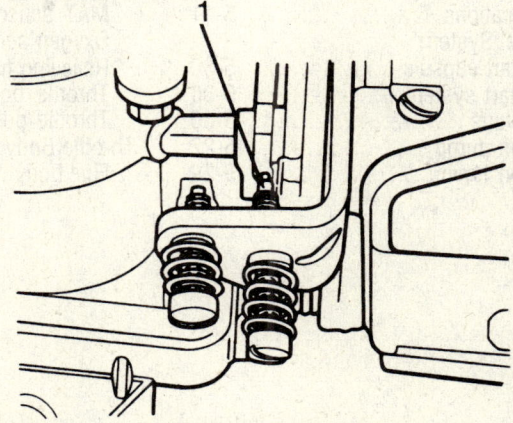

Carter YFA fast idle adjustment screw (1)

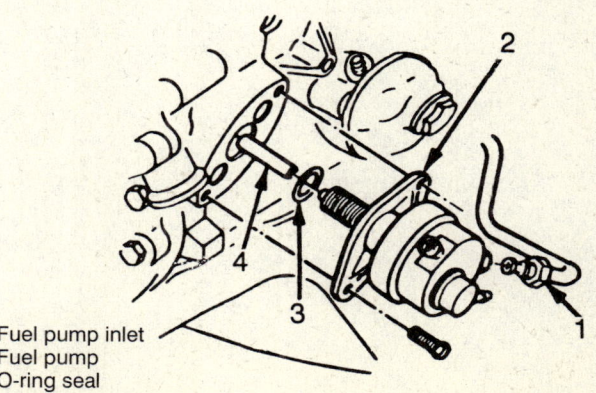

1. Fuel pump inlet
2. Fuel pump
3. O-ring seal

6-2.8L fuel pump

FUEL SYSTEM 5

Troubleshooting Basic Fuel System Problems

Problem	Cause	Solution
Engine cranks, but won't start (or is hard to start) when cold	• Empty fuel tank • Incorrect starting procedure • Defective fuel pump • No fuel in carburetor • Clogged fuel filter • Engine flooded • Defective choke	• Check for fuel in tank • Follow correct procedure • Check pump output • Check for fuel in the carburetor • Replace fuel filter • Wait 15 minutes; try again • Check choke plate
Engine cranks, but is hard to start (or does not start) when hot— (presence of fuel is assumed)	• Defective choke	• Check choke plate
Rough idle or engine runs rough	• Dirt or moisture in fuel • Clogged air filter • Faulty fuel pump	• Replace fuel filter • Replace air filter • Check fuel pump output
Engine stalls or hesitates on acceleration	• Dirt or moisture in the fuel • Dirty carburetor • Defective fuel pump • Incorrect float level, defective accelerator pump	• Replace fuel filter • Clean the carburetor • Check fuel pump output • Check carburetor
Poor gas mileage	• Clogged air filter • Dirty carburetor • Defective choke, faulty carburetor adjustment	• Replace air filter • Clean carburetor • Check carburetor
Engine is flooded (won't start accompanied by smell of raw fuel)	• Improperly adjusted choke or carburetor	• Wait 15 minutes and try again, without pumping gas pedal • If it won't start, check carburetor

Sole-Vac Vacuum Actuator Adjustment

1. Connect a tachometer to the ignition coil TACH terminal.
2. Start the engine and allow it to reach normal operating temperature.
3. This adjustment is made with the automatic transmission in DRIVE or manual transmission in NEUTRAL and all accessories turned OFF.
4. Disconnect the vacuum hose from the Sole-Vac vacuum actuator and plug. Connect an external vacuum source and apply 10-15 in. Hg (34-51 kPa) of vacuum to the actuator.

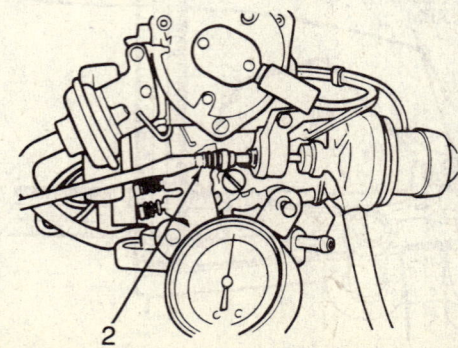

Sole-Vac adjustment screw (2)

5. Adjust the idle speed to 850 rpm (auto. trans.), 950 rpm (manual trans.) using the vacuum actuator adjustment screw on the throttle lever. Use the specifications on the underhood sticker if they differ from the above specifications.
6. Turn the ignition OFF and disconnect the tachometer and vacuum pump. The Sole-Vac curb idle speed should be adjusted following this procedure.

Sole-Vac Curb Idle Speed Adjustment

1. Connect a tachometer to the ignition coil TACH terminal.
2. Place the automatic transmission in DRIVE, or the manual transmission in NEUTRAL.
3. Start the engine and allow it to reach normal operating temperature.
4. Disconnect and plug the vacuum hose from the actuator.
5. Adjust the hex head curb idle speed adjustment screw to 700 rpm (auto. trans.) or 750 rpm (manual trans.). Use the specifications on the underhood sticker if they differ from the above specifications.
6. Turn the ignition switch OFF, then disconnect the tachometer and reconnect the vacuum actuator hose.

Float Adjustment

Remove and invert the air horn assembly and check the clearance from the top of the float to the surface of the air horn with a T-scale. The air horn should be held at eye level when gauging and the float arm should be resting on the needle pin. Do not exert

5 FUEL SYSTEM

CARTER YFA

Year	List Number	Application	Float Level mm (in) Set To	Float Level mm (in) OK Range	Initial Choke Valve Clearance mm (in) Set To	Initial Choke Valve Clearance mm (in) OK Range	Fast Idle Cam Setting Index mm (in) Set To	Fast Idle Cam Setting Index mm (in) OK Range	Automatic Choke Cover Setting Set To	Choke Unloader mm (in)	Fast Idle Speed Set To	Fast Idle Speed OK Range
1984	7701/ 7452	4-2.5L Auto 49-S	15.2 (0.600)	14.2–16.0 (0.570–0.630)	6.0 (0.240)	6.4–6.7 (0.255–0.265)	4.4 (0.175)	4.0–4.8 (0.160–0.190)	TR	7.6 (0.280)	2300*	±100
	7700/ 7453	4-2.5L Man 49-S	15.2 (0.600)	14.2–16.0 (0.570–0.630)	6.0 (0.240)	6.4–6.7 (0.255–0.265)	4.4 (0.175)	4.0–4.8 (0.160–0.190)	TR	7.6 (0.280)	2000*	±100
	7703/ 7454	4-2.5L Auto High Alt	15.2 (0.600)	14.2–16.0 (0.570–0.630)	6.0 (0.240)	6.4–6.7 (0.255–0.265)	4.4 (0.175)	4.0–4.8 (0.160–0.190)	TR	7.6 (0.280)	2300*	±100
	7702/ 7455	4-2.5L Man High Alt	15.2 (0.600)	14.2–16.0 (0.570–0.630)	6.0 (0.240)	6.4–6.7 (0.255–0.265)	4.4 (0.175)	4.0–4.8 (0.160–0.190)	TR	7.6 (0.280)	2000*	±100
1985	7705	4-2.5L Auto 49-S	15.2 (0.600)	14.2–16.0 (0.570–0.630)	7.1 (0.280)	6.7–7.5 (0.265–0.295)	4.4 (0.175)	4.0–4.8 (0.160–0.190)	TR	7.6 (0.280)	2300*	±100
	7704	4-2.5L Man 49-S	15.2 (0.600)	14.2–16.0 (0.570–0.630)	7.1 (0.280)	6.7–7.5 (0.265–0.295)	4.4 (0.175)	4.0–4.8 (0.160–0.190)	TR	7.6 (0.280)	2000*	±100
	7707	4-2.5L Auto High Alt	15.2 (0.600)	14.2–16.0 (0.570–0.630)	7.1 (0.280)	6.7–7.5 (0.265–0.295)	4.4 (0.175)	4.0–4.8 (0.160–0.190)	TR	7.6 (0.280)	2300*	±100
	7706	4-2.5L Man High Alt	15.2 (0.600)	14.2–16.0 (0.570–0.630)	7.1 (0.280)	6.7–7.5 (0.265–0.295)	4.4 (0.175)	4.0–4.8 (0.160–0.190)	TR	7.6 (0.280)	2000*	±100

*EGR Valve Disconnected and the engine fully warm.
TR—Tamper Resistant
(1) Measured at upper edge of choke valve and airhorn wall

pressure on the needle valve when measuring or adjusting the float. Bend the float arm as necessary to adjust the float level.

CAUTION
Do not bend the tab at the end of the float arm as it prevents the float from striking the bottom of the fuel bowl when empty and keeps the needle in place.

Float Drop Adjustment

Hold the air horn upright and let the float hang freely. Measure the maximum clearance from the toe end of the float to the casting surface. Hold the air horn at eye level when measuring. To adjust, bend the tab at the end of the float arm.

Metering Rod Adjustment

1. Remove the air horn. Back out the idle speed adjusting screw until the throttle plate is seated fully in its bore.
2. Press down on the upper end of the diaphragm shaft until the diaphragm bottoms in the vacuum chamber.
3. The metering rod should contact the bottom of the metering rod well. The lifter link at the outer end nearest the springs and at the supporting link should be bottomed.
4. Turn the rod adjusting screw until the metering rod just bottoms in the body casting. For final adjustment, turn the screw one additional turn clockwise.
5. Install the carburetor air horn and replacement gasket on

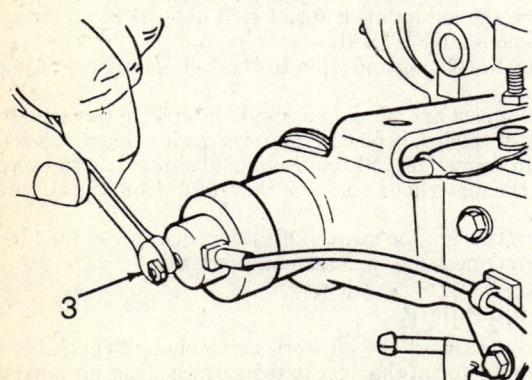

Sole-Vac curb idle speed adjustment screw (3)

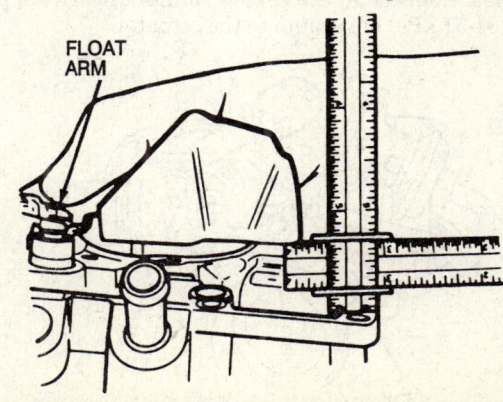

Carter YFA carburetor float level measurement

FUEL SYSTEM 5

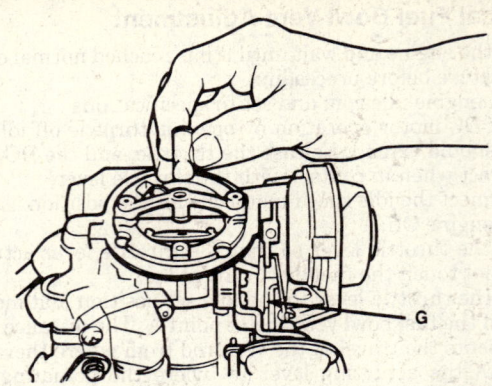

Bend the choke plate connecting rod (G) to obtain the specified clearance when adjusting the fast idle cam

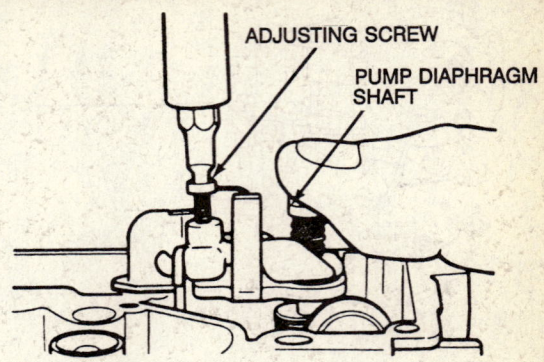

Carter YFA metering rod adjustment

the carburetor, then set the curb idle speed to specifications.

Fast Idle Cam Index Adjustment

Put the fast idle screw on the second highest step of the fast idle cam, against the shoulder of the high step. Measure the clearance between the lower edge of the choke valve and the air horn wall. It is not necessary to remove the air cleaner bracket when measuring clearance between the choke valve and air horn wall; position the gauge next to the bracket. Adjust by bending the choke plate connecting rod to obtain the specified clearance between the lower edge of the choke plate and the air horn wall.

Choke Unloader Adjustment

1. Hold the throttle lever fully open and apply pressure on the choke valve toward the closed position.
2. Measure the clearance between the lower edge of the choke valve and the air horn wall. See specifications chart.

NOTE: DO NOT bend the unloader tang DOWN.

3. Adjust by bending the unloader tang which contacts the fast idle cam. Bend toward the cam to increase clearance, away to decrease.
4. Ensure the unloader tang is at least 0.070 in. (1.8mm) from the main body flange when the throttle is open.
5. Check for full throttle opening when throttle is operated from inside vehicle.

Automatic Choke Adjustment

Loosen the choke cover retaining screws, then turn the choke cover so that the index mark on the cover lines up with the specified mark on the choke housing.

Choke Plate Pull-down Adjustment

PISTON TYPE CHOKE

NOTE: This adjustment requires that the thermostatic spring housing and gasket (choke cap) are removed. Refer to the "Choke Cap" removal procedure below.

1. Remove the air cleaner assembly, then the choke cap.
2. Bend a 0.026 in. (0.66mm) diameter wire gauge at a 90° angle approximately 1/8 in. (3mm) from one end. Insert the bent end of the gauge between the choke piston slot and the right hand slot in the choke housing. Rotate the choke piston lever counterclockwise until the gauge is shut in the piston slot.
3. Apply light pressure on the choke piston lever to hold the gauge in place, then measure the clearance between the lower edge of the choke plate and the carburetor bore using a drill with the diameter equal to the specified pull-down clearance.
4. Bend the choke piston lever to obtain the proper clearance.
5. Install the choke cap.

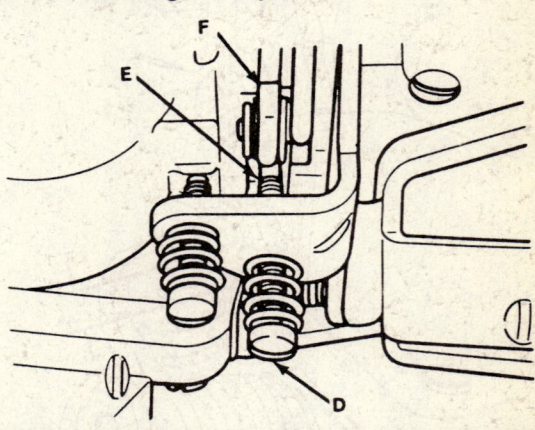

Fast idle cam index adjustment. (D) is the adjusting screw; (E) is the second step of the cam (F)

DIAPHRAGM TYPE CHOKE

1. Activate the pull-down motor by applying an external vacuum source.
2. Close the choke plate as far as possible without forcing it.
3. Using a drill of the specified size, measure the clearance between the lower edge of the choke plate and the air horn wall.
4. If adjustment is necessary, bend the choke diaphragm link as required.

Choke Cap Removal

NOTE: The automatic choke has two rivets and a screw, retaining the choke cap in place. There is a locking and indexing plate to prevent misadjustment.

1. Remove the air cleaner assembly from the carburetor.
2. Check choke cap retaining ring rivets to determine if mandrel is well below the rivet head. If mandrel appears to be at or within the rivet head thickness, drive it down or out with a 1/16 in. (1.5mm) diameter punch.
3. Use a 1/8 in. (3mm) diameter drill for drilling the rivet heads. Drill into the rivet head until the rivet head comes loose from the rivet body.
4. After the rivet head is removed, drive the remaining portion of the rivet out of the hole with a 1/8 in. (3mm) diameter punch.

NOTE: This procedure must be followed to retain the hole size.

5. Repeat Steps 1–4 for the remaining rivet.
6. Remove screw in the conventional manner.

Choke Cap Installation

1. Install choke cap gasket.
2. Install the locking and indexing plate.
3. Install the notched gasket.

5 FUEL SYSTEM

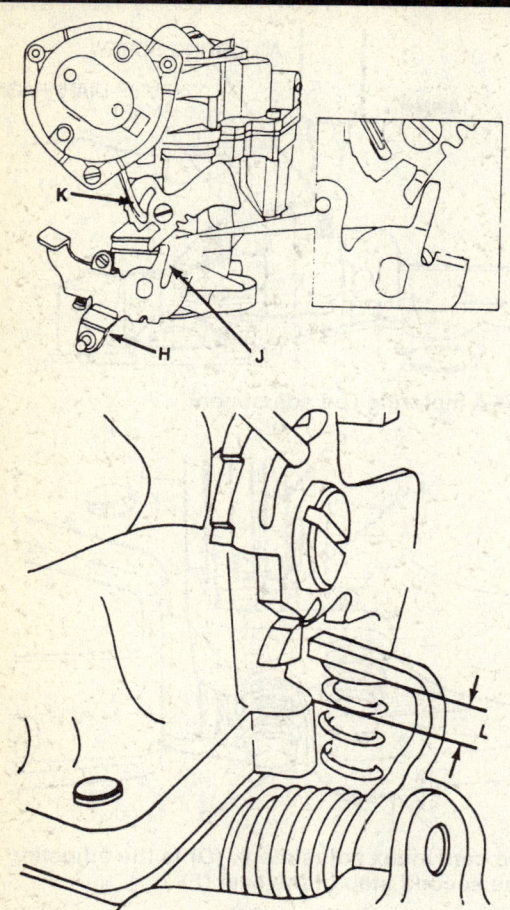

Choke unloader adjustment. (H) is the throttle lever; (J) is the unloader tang; (K) is the cam; (L) is the gap

4. Install choke cap, making certain that bi-metal loop is positioned around choke lever tang.
5. While holding cap in place, actuate choke plate to make certain bi-metal loop is properly engaged with lever tang. Set retaining clamp over choke cap and orient clamp to match holes in casting (holes are not equally spaced). Make sure retaining clamp is not upside down.
6. Place rivet in rivet gun and trigger lightly to retain rivet — 1/8 in. diameter 1/2 in. long 1/4 in. diameter head (3mm × 12.7mm × 6mm).
7. Press rivet fully into casting after passing through retaining clamp and pop rivet (mandrel breaks off).
8. Repeat this step for the remaining rivet.
9. Install screw in conventional manner. Tighten to 17–20 inch lbs.

Choke Plate Clearance (Dechoke) Adjustment

1. Remove the air cleaner assembly.
2. Hold the throttle plate fully open and close the choke plate as far as possible without forcing it. Use a drill of the proper diameter to check the clearance between the choke plate and air horn.
3. If the clearance is not within specification, adjust by bending the arm on the choke lever of the throttle lever. Bending the arm downward will decrease the clearance, and bending it upward will increase the clearance. Always recheck the clearance after making any adjustment.

Mechanical Fuel Bowl Vent Adjustment

1. Start the engine and wait until it has reached normal operating temperature before proceeding.
2. Check engine idle rpm and set to specifications.
3. Check DC motor operation by opening throttle off idle. The DC motor should extend. Release the throttle, and the DC motor should retract when in contact with the throttle lever.
4. Disconnect the idle speed motor in the idle position.
5. Turn engine Off.
6. Open the throttle lever so that the throttle lever actuating lever does not touch the fuel bowl vent rod.
7. Close the throttle lever to the idle set position and measure the travel of the fuel bowl vent rod at point A. The distance measured represents the travel of the vent rod from where there is no contact with the actuating lever to where the actuating lever moves the vent rod to the idle set position. The travel of the vent rod at point A should be 0.100–0.150 in. (2.5–3.8mm).
8. If adjustment is required, bend the throttle actuating lever at notch shown.
9. Reconnect the idle speed control motor.

Secondary Throttle Stop Screw Adjustment

Back off the screw until it does not touch the lever. Turn the screw in until it touches the lever, then turn it an additional 1/4 turn.

CARBURETOR REMOVAL AND INSTALLATION

1. Remove the air cleaner.
2. Tag and disconnect all hoses leading to the carburetor.
3. Disconnect the control shaft from the throttle lever.
4. Disconnect the inline fuel filter, pullback spring and all electrical connectors.
5. Remove the carburetor mounting nuts and lift off the carburetor.
6. Remove the carburetor mounting gasket from the spacer.
7. Clean all gasket mating surfaces on the spacer and carburetor.
8. Install a new gasket on the spacer, then install the carburetor and secure it with the mounting nuts.
9. Reconnect all vacuum hoses, fuel lines and electrical connectors. Connect the control shaft and pullback spring.
10. Install the air cleaner and adjust the curb and fast idle speed as previously described.

CARBURETOR OVERHAUL

CARTER YFA

The following procedure applies to complete overhaul with the carburetor removed from the engine. A complete disassembly is not necessary when performing adjustments. In most cases, service adjustments of individual systems may be completed without removing the carburetor from the engine. A complete carburetor overhaul includes disassembly, thorough cleaning, inspection and replacement of gaskets and worn or damaged parts. When using an overhaul kit, use all applicable parts in the kit.

NOTE: Flooding, stumble on acceleration and other performance problems are in many instances caused by the presence of dirt, water or other foreign material in the carburetor. To help in diagnosing the problem, carefully remove the carburetor from the engine without removing the fuel from the float bowl. Examine the bowl contents for contamination as the carburetor is disassembled.

FUEL SYSTEM 5

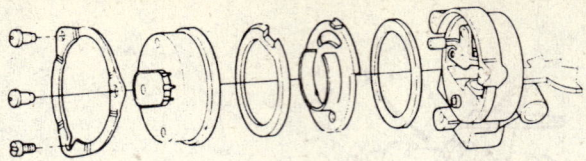

Choke cover assembly

1. Drill out the choke retainer rivet heads using a No. 30 (1/8 in. or 3mm) drill bit. After the rivet heads are removed, drive out the remaining portion of the rivets with a 1/8 in. (3mm) punch. This procedure must be followed exactly to retain the hole sizes.
2. Remove the screw holding the retainer.
3. Remove the retainer, thermostatic spring housing assembly, spring housing gasket and the locking/indexing plate.
4. Remove the vacuum break.
5. Disengage and remove the vacuum break connector link from the choke shaft lever.
6. Remove the sole-vac and the mounting bracket.
7. Remove the duty cycle solenoid from the air horn.
8. Remove the air horn attaching screws.
9. Remove the fast idle cam link.
10. Remove the air horn and gasket from the carburetor main body.
11. To remove the float from the air horn, hold the air horn bottom side up and remove the float pin and float.
12. Invert the air horn and catch the needle pin, spring and needle.
13. Remove the needle seat and gasket.
14. To remove the pump check ball and weight, turn the main body casting upside down and catch the accelerator pump check ball and weight.
15. Loosen the throttle shaft arm screw and remove the arm and pump connector link.
16. Remove the retaining screws and separate the throttle body from the main body.
17. Remove the wide open throttle switch and mounting bracket.
18. Remove the accelerator pump housing screws from the main body.
19. Lift out the pump assembly, pump lifter link and metering rod as a unit.
20. Disassemble the pump as follows:

    a. Disengage the metering rod arm spring from the metering rod.
    b. Remove the metering rod from the metering rod assembly.
    c. Compress the upper pump spring and remove the spring retainer cup.
    d. Remove the upper spring, metering rod arm assembly and pump lifter link from the pump diaphragm shaft.
    e. Compress the pump diaphragm spring and remove the pump diaphragm spring retainer, spring and pump diaphragm assembly from the pump diaphragm housing.

21. Remove the low speed jet and the main metering jet.
22. Using a sharp punch, remove the accelerator pump bleed valve plug from outside the main body casting. Loosen the bleed valve screw and remove the valve.
23. Drill out and remove the tamper proof plug. After removing the plug, count the number of turns required to seat the idle mixture screw lightly. Remove the idle mixture screw and O-ring.
24. Thoroughly clean and inspect all components and replace any that are damaged, worn or malfunctioning. Check the idle mixture screw needle for scoring or damage and replace it if any grooves are noted.
25. Install the throttle body to the main body with the retaining screws, then install the idle mixture screw.
26. Install the low speed jet and main metering jet.
27. Install the pump bleed valve and spring.
28. Install the accelerator pump assembly.

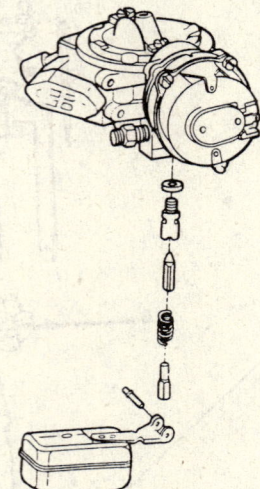

Needle and seat assembly with float

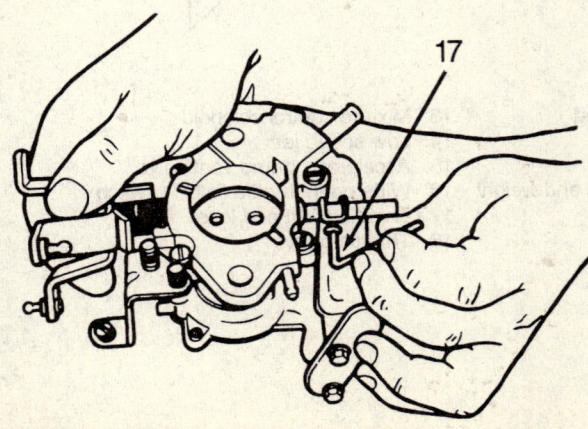

Removing the pump connector link

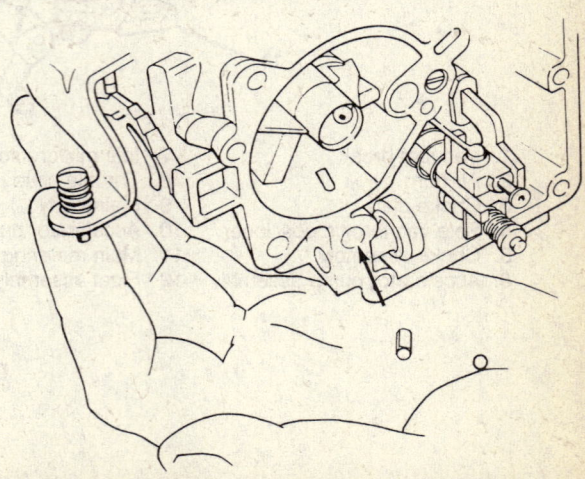

Removing the accelerator pump check ball and weight

5-7

5 FUEL SYSTEM

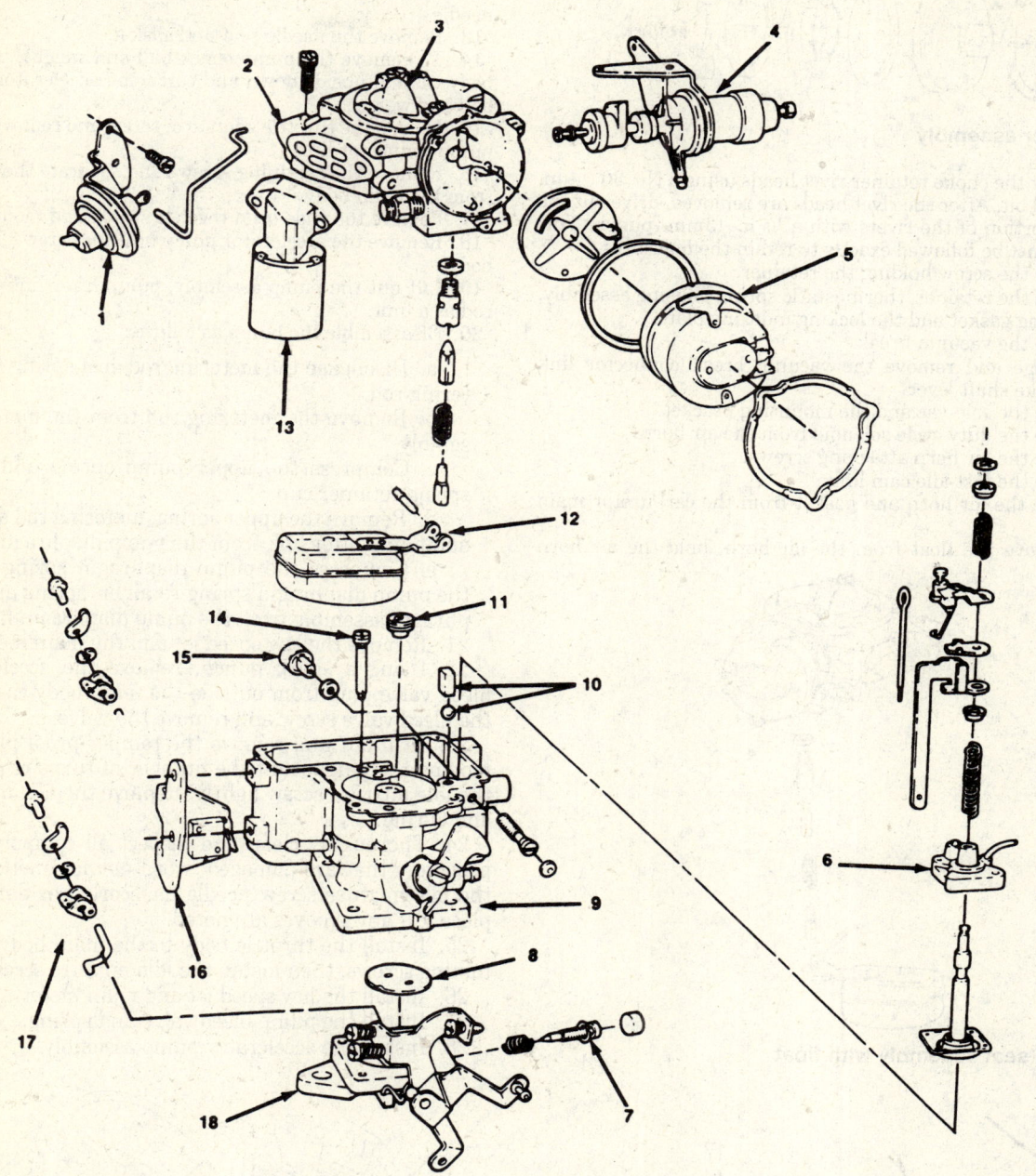

1. Vacuum break
2. Air horn
3. Choke plate
4. Sole-vac throttle positioner
5. Choke assembly
6. Accelerator pump assembly
7. Idle mixture screw with O-ring
8. Throttle plate
9. Main body
10. Accelerator pump check ball and weight
11. Main metering jet
12. Float assembly
13. Mixture control solenoid
14. Low speed jet
15. Accelerator pump vent valve
16. Wide open throttle (WOT) switch
17. Throttle shaft and lever
18. Throttle body

Carter YFA

5-8

FUEL SYSTEM 5

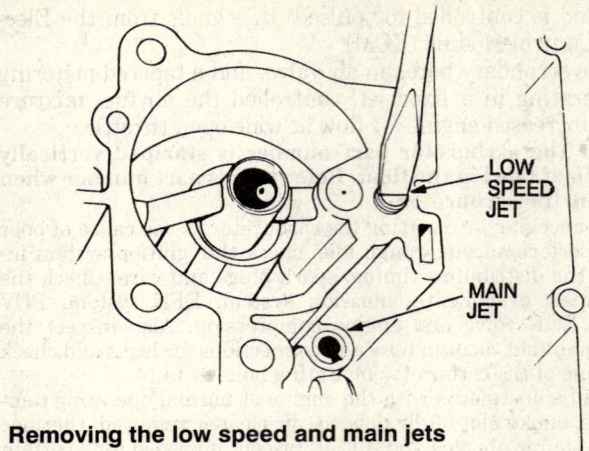

Removing the low speed and main jets

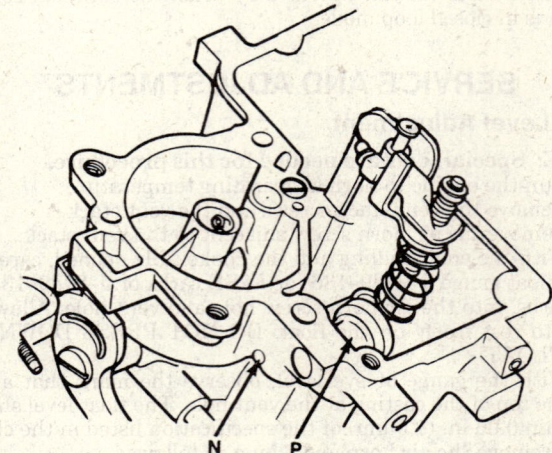

Removing the accelerator pump bleed valve plug (N) and the bleed valve (P)

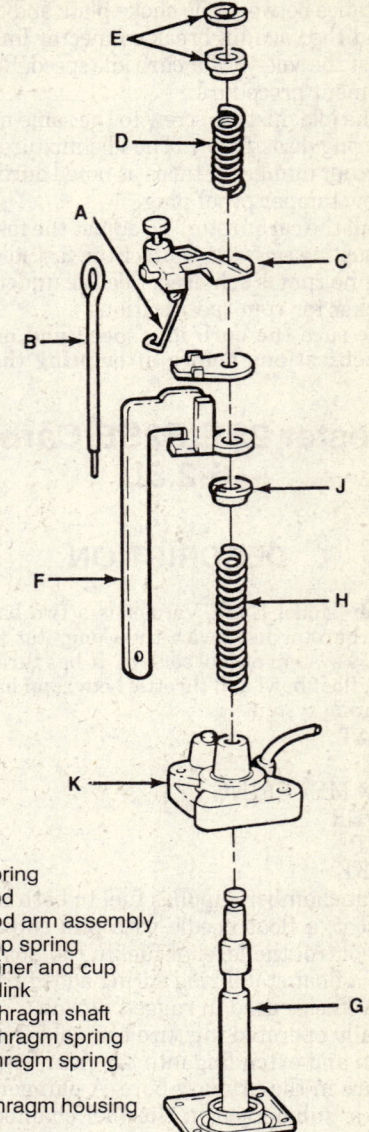

A. Rod arm spring
B. Metering rod
C. Metering rod arm assembly
D. Upper pump spring
E. Spring retainer and cup
F. Pump lifter link
G. Pump diaphragm shaft
H. Pump diaphragm spring
J. Pump diaphragm spring retainer
K. Pump diaphragm housing assembly

Carter YFA accelerator pump assembly

29. Install the pump passage tube.
30. Install the throttle shaft arm and pump connector link and retaining screw.
31. Install the wide open throttle switch actuator.
32. Install the throttle shaft retaining bolt.
33. Install the wide open throttle switch and bracket.
34. To adjust the metering rod:
   a. Make sure the idle speed adjusting screw allows the throttle plate to close tightly in the throttle bore.
   b. Press down on top of the pump diaphragm shaft until the assembly bottoms.
   c. While holding the pump diaphragm down, adjust the metering rod by turning the metering rod adjusting screw counterclockwise until the metering rod just bottoms in the main metering jet.
   d. Turn the metering rod adjusting screw clockwise one turn for final adjustment.
35. Install the needle pin, spring, needle, seat, gasket and strainer.
36. Install the float and pin.
37. Invert the air horn assembly and check the clearance from the top of the float to the bottom of the air horn with the gauge. The float arm should be resting on the needle pin. Bend the float arm as necessary to adjust the float level.
38. Install the accelerator pump check ball and weight, then install the air horn and gasket to the main body.
39. Install the fast idle cam link.
40. Install the sole-vac and mounting bracket, then install the duty cycle solenoid and gasket.
41. Install the locking and indexing plate, spring housing gasket, thermostatic spring housing assembly, choke cover retainer and attaching screws.
42. Position the fast idle cam screw on the second step of the fast idle cam and against the shoulder of the high step. Adjust by bending the fast idle cam link to obtain the specified clearance between the lower edge of the choke plate and the carburetor air horn.
43. Position the fast idle screw on the top step of the fast idle cam.
44. Seat the vacuum break using a hand vacuum pump.
45. Apply a light closing pressure to the choke plate to position the plate as far closed as possible without forcing it. Meas-

5-9

5 FUEL SYSTEM

ure the distance between the choke plate and the air horn. To adjust, bend the vacuum break connector link.

46. Adjust the sole-vac for curb idle speed. Refer to the Sole-Vac Adjustment procedure.

47. Set the idle mixture screw to the same number of turns as noted during disassembly. The idle mixture screw must be set to the **exact** number of turns as noted during disassembly. Install a new tamper proof plug.

48. Install the carburetor. To adjust the fast idle, turn the fast idle adjusting screw to contact the fast idle cam until the desired engine rpm is achieved. See the underhood emission control sticker for rpm specifications.

NOTE: Make sure the curb idle speed and mixture are adjusted to specifications before attempting the fast idle adjustment.

Rochester 2SE/E2SE Carburetor 6-2.8L

DESCRIPTION

The Rochester Model E2SE Varajet is a two barrel, two stage down-draft carburetor used with the Computer Command Control (CCC or C^3) system of fuel control. It has three major assemblies; air horn, float bowl and throttle body; and has the following six basic operating systems:

  a. FLOAT
  b. IDLE
  c. MAIN METERING
  d. POWER
  e. PUMP
  f. CHOKE

A single float chamber supplies fuel to both bores. a float, a float needle seat, a float needle with pull clip and float bowl inserts, help control the level of fuel in the float chamber. On some models, a float stabilizing spring adds further control of fuel level for vehicles used in rugged terrain.

An electrically operated mixture control solenoid, mounted in the air horn and extending into the float bowl, controls the air/fuel mixture in the primary bore. A plunger, at the end of the solenoid, is submerged in the fuel chamber of the float bowl, and is controlled (or pulsed) by signals from the Electronic Control Module (ECM).

In the secondary bore, an air valve, and a tapered metering rod operating in a fixed jet, controlled the air/fuel mixture during increased engine air flow at wide open throttle.

NOTE: The carburetor part number is stamped vertically on the float bowl in the float. Refer to this part number when servicing the carburetor.

Before checking or resetting the carburetor as the cause of poor engine performance or rough idle; check the ignition system including the distributor, timing, spark plugs and wire. Check the air cleaner, evaporative emission system, EFE system, PCV system, EGR valve and engine compression. Also inspect the intake manifold vacuum hose and connections for leaks and check the torque of the carburetor mounting bolts or nuts.

Make all adjustments with the engine at normal operating temperature, choke plate fully opened, air cleaner removed, thermac vacuum source plugged and A/C off (except if needed for a certain adjustment). Set the idle speeds only when the emission control system is in closed loop mode.

SERVICE AND ADJUSTMENTS

Float Level Adjustment

NOTE: Special tools are needed for this procedure.

1. Run the engine to normal operating temperature.
2. Remove the vent stack screws and the vent stack.
3. Remove the air horn screw adjacent to the vent stack.
4. With the engine idling and the choke fully opened, carefully insert float gauge J–9789–136 for E2SE carbs or J–9789–138 for 2SE carbs, into the air horn screw hole and vent hole. Allow the gauge to rest freely on the float. DO NOT PRESS DOWN ON THE FLOAT!
5. With the gauge at eye level, observe the mark that aligns with the top of the casting at the vent hole. The float level should be within 0.06 in. (1.5mm) of the specification listed in the chart. If not, remove the air horn and adjust as follows:

  a. Hold the retainer pin firmly in place and push the float down, lightly, against the inlet needle.

  b. Using an adjustable T-scale, at a point 3/16 in. (4.8mm) from the end of the float, at the toe, measure the distance from the float bowl top surface (gasket removed) to the top of the float at the toe. If the distance isn't as specified in the Chart, remove the float and bend the float arm as necessary.

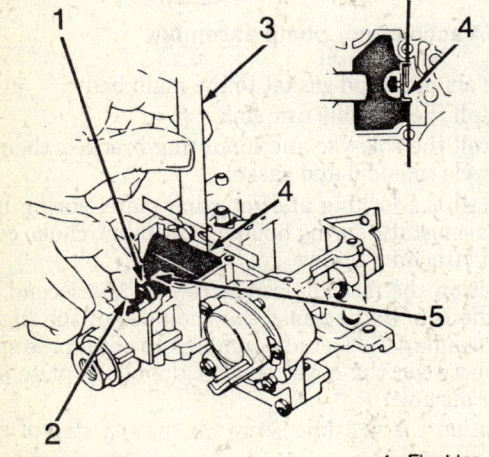

1. Retainer pin
2. Needle
3. T-scale
4. Float toe
5. Float arm

Float adjustment on the E2SE/2SE carburetor

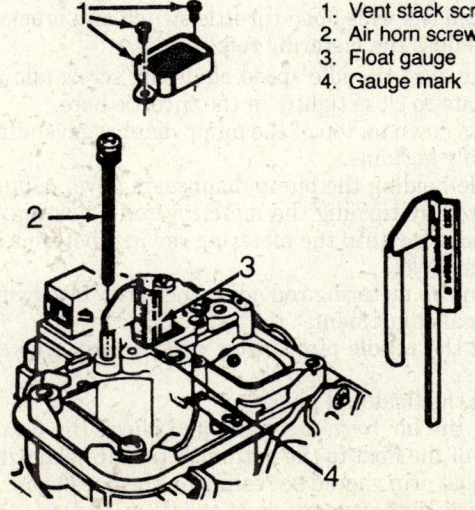

1. Vent stack screws
2. Air horn screw
3. Float gauge
4. Gauge mark

Measuring float clearance on the E2SE/2SE carburetor

FUEL SYSTEM 5

ROCHESTER 2SE/E2SE

Engine	Year	Carburetor Number	Float Level mm (in)	Air Valve Spring (Turns)	Choke Coil Lever mm (in)	Fast Idle Cam (Choke Rod) 2nd Step	Vacuum Break Primary	Air Valve Rod	Vacuum Break Secondary	Unloader
6-2.8L	1984	17084581	4.2 (5/32)	1	2.2 (0.085)	22°	26°	1°	32°	40°
		17084580	4.2 (5/32)	1	2.2 (0.085)	22°	26°	1°	32°	40°
		17084582	4.2 (5/32)	1	2.2 (0.085)	22°	26°	1°	32°	40°
		17084583	4.2 (5/32)	1	2.2 (0.085)	22°	26°	1°	32°	40°
		17084384	3.3 (1/8)	1	2.2 (0.085)	22°	25°	1°	30°	40°
	1985–86	17085380	4.2 (5/32)	1	2.2 (0.085)	22°	26°	1°	32°	40°
		17085381	4.2 (5/32)	1	2.2 (0.085)	22°	26°	1°	32°	40°
		17085382	4.2 (5/32)	1	2.2 (0.085)	22°	26°	1°	32°	40°
		17085383	4.2 (5/32)	1	2.2 (0.085)	22°	26°	1°	32°	40°
		17085384	3.3 (1/8)	1	2.2 (0.085)	22°	25°	1°	30°	40°

Throttle Position Sensor (TPS) Adjustment

A tamper-resistant plug covers the TPS adjustment screw. This plug should not be removed unless diagnosis indicates the TPS sensor is not adjusted properly or it is necessary to replace the air horn assembly, float bowl, TPS sensor or TPS adjustment screw. This is a critical adjustment that must be performed accurately and carefully to ensure proper engine performance and emission control. If TPS adjustment is indicated, proceed as follows:

1. Use a $5/64$ in. (2mm) drill bit to drill a hole in the steel cup plug covering the TPS adjustment screw. Use care in drilling to prevent damage to the adjustment screw head.
2. Use a small slide hammer to remove the steel plug from the air horn.
3. Disconnect the TPS connector and use jumper wires to connect all three terminals.
4. Connect a digital voltmeter between the TPS connector center terminal **B** and the bottom terminal **C** (ground).
5. With the ignition ON (engine OFF), turn the TPS adjustment screw to obtain 0.26 volts (260 mv) at the curb idle throttle position with the A/C off.
6. After all adjustments are complete, a new tamper-proof plug (supplied in service kits) or silicone RTV rubber sealant must be inserted into the TPS adjustment screw hole to seal the adjustment. If a plug is used, it should be installed with the cup facing outward and flush with the top of the casting.

Fast Idle Speed Adjustment

1. Place the fast idle screw on the high step of the fast idle cam.
2. Disconnect and plug the EGR valve hose and the canister purge line at the canister.
3. Set the parking brake firmly and start the engine. Place the transmission in Neutral (manual) or Park (automatic).
4. Turn the fast idle screw in or out to obtain the specified fast

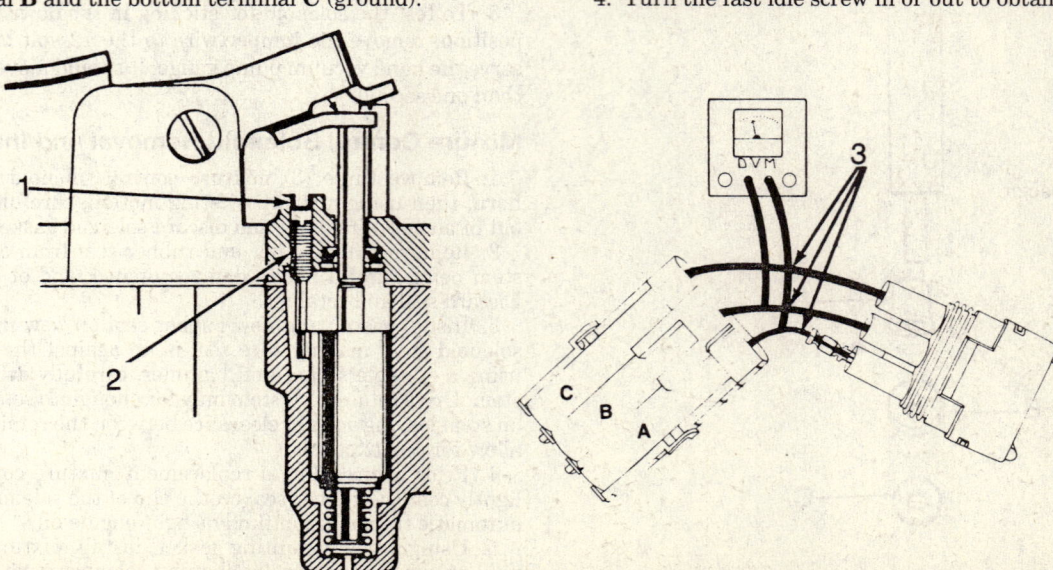

Throttle position sensor adjustment. (1) is the adjustment screw cup plug; (2) is the adjustment screw; (3) shows how to connect the jumper wires

5-11

5 FUEL SYSTEM

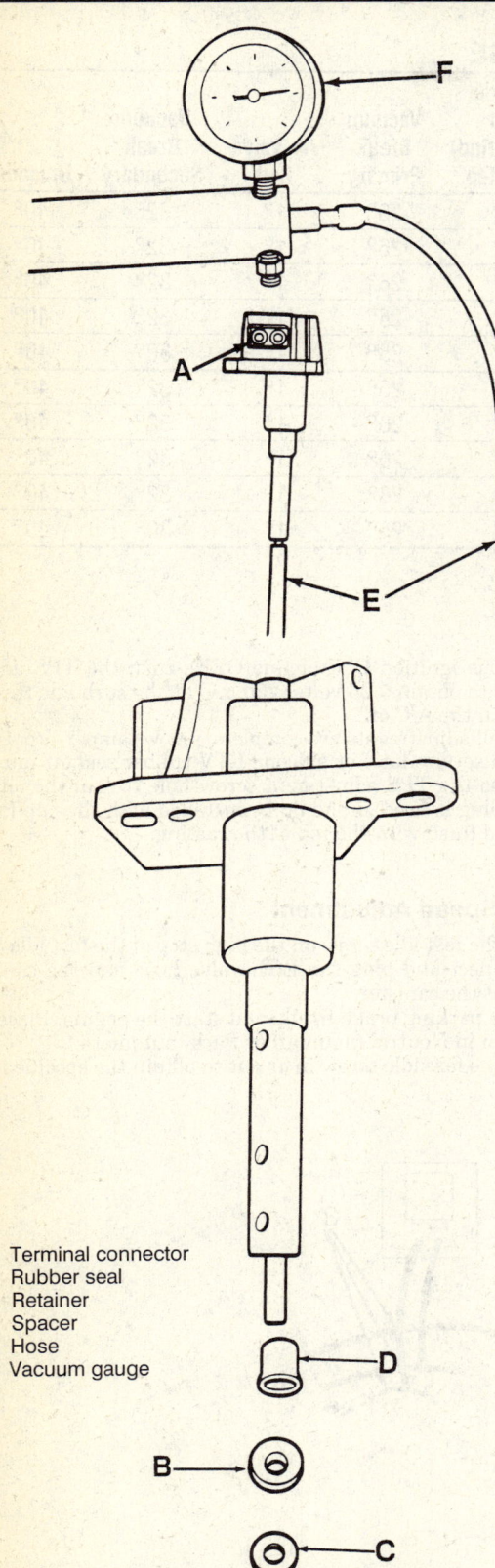

A. Terminal connector
B. Rubber seal
C. Retainer
D. Spacer
E. Hose
F. Vacuum gauge

Testing the E2SE mixture control solenoid

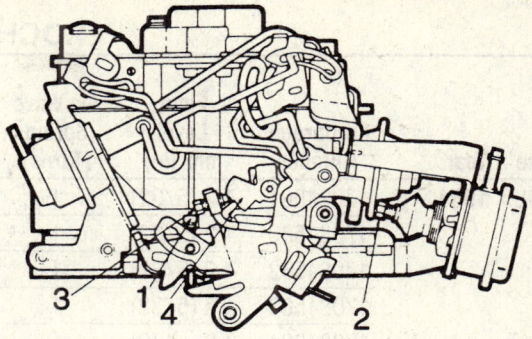

1. Idle speed screw
2. Vacuum diaphagm
3. Fast idle screw
4. Fast idle cam

2SE adjustment points

idle speed. Refer to the underhood emission sticker for fast idle speed specifications.

5. Once all adjustments are complete, reconnect the EGR valve hose and the canister purge line at the canister.

Testing Mixture Control (MC) Solenoid

E2SE CARBURETOR

If the mixture control solenoid is suspected of either sticking, binding or leaking, test it using the following procedure:

1. Connect one end of a jumper wire to either terminal of the solenoid wire connector and the other end to the positive (+) terminal of a 12 volt battery.
2. Connect one end of another jumper wire to the other terminal of the solenoid wire connector and the other end to the negative (−) terminal of the battery.
3. With the rubber seal, retainer and spacer removed from the end of the solenoid stem, attach a hose from a hand vacuum pump.
4. With the solenoid fully energized (lean position), apply at least 25 in. Hg of vacuum and time the leak-down rate from 20 to 15 in. Hg. The leak-down rate should not exceed 5 in. Hg in 5 seconds. If the leak-down rate exceeds that amount, replace the solenoid.
5. To test the solenoid for sticking in the down (de-energized) position, remove the jumper wire to the 12 volt battery and observe the hand vacuum pump gauge. It should move to zero in less than one second.

Mixture Control Solenoid Removal and Installation

1. Remove three (3) mixture control solenoid screws in the horn, then using a slight twisting motion, carefully lift solenoid out of air horn. Remove and discard solenoid gasket.
2. Remove seal retainer and rubber seal from end of solenoid stem being careful not to damage or nick end of solenoid stem. Discard seal and retainer.
3. Install spacer and new rubber seal on new mixture control solenoid stem making sure seal is up against the spacer. Then, using a suitable socket and hammer, carefully drive retainer on stem. Drive retainer on stem only far enough to retain rubber seal on stem leaving a slight clearance between the retainer and seal to allow for seal expansion.
4. Prior to installing a replacement mixture control solenoid, lightly coat the rubber seal on the end of the solenoid stem with a automatic transmission fluid or light engine oil.
5. Using a new mounting gasket, install mixture control solenoid on air horn, carefully aligning solenoid stem with recess in bottom of bowl.
6. Use a slight twisting motion of the solenoid during installa-

FUEL SYSTEM 5

tion to ensure rubber seal on stem is guided into recess in the bottom of the bowl to prevent distortion or damage to the rubber seal. Install three (3) solenoid attaching screws and tighten securely.

7. Install mixture control solenoid connector, and check for proper latching. The latch may require filing. Check colors of wires in connector for proper position. Pink wire must be on right hand terminal of connector, as viewed from harness end. If incorrect, use Tool J–28742, BT 8234–A or equivalent to remove wires from connector and replace. The System Performance Check should be performed after any repairs to the CCC system have been made.

Electric Choke Test

1. Check voltage at the choke heater connection with the engine running. If voltage is between 12 and 15 volts, replace the electric choke unit.
2. If the voltage is low or zero, check all wires and connections.
3. If Steps 1 and 2 pass the test properly, check and see if the connection on the oil pressure switch is faulty, the temperature pressure warning light will be off with the key in the ON position and the engine not running. Repair wires as required.
4. If the choke is still inoperative, replace the oil pressure switch.

Choke Coil Replacement

1. Remove air cleaner and disconnect the choke electrical connector.
2. Align a 5/32 in. (4mm) drill on the retainer rivet head and drill only enough to remove rivet head. After removing rivet heads and retainers, use a drift and small hammer to drive the remainder of the rivet from the choke housing. Use care in drilling to prevent damage to the choke cover or housing. Remove the three rivets and choke cover assembly from choke housing.
3. Remove choke coil from housing.
4. Install the choke cover and coil assembly in choke housing as follows:
   a. Install the choke cover and coil assembly in the choke housing, aligning notch in cover with raised casting projection on housing cover flange. Make sure coil pickup tank engages the inside choke coil lever.
   b. A choke cover retainer kit is required to attach the choke cover to the choke housing. Install a suitable blind rivet installing tool.
5. Connect choke electrical connector.
6. Start engine, check operation of choke and then install air cleaner.

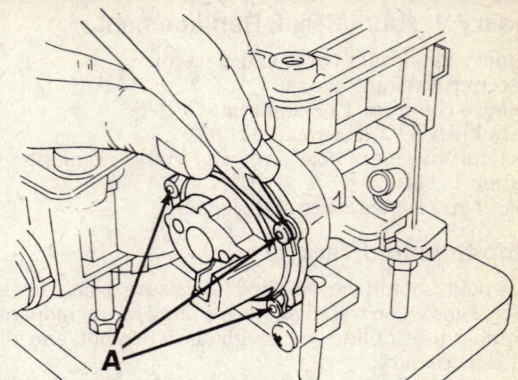

Choke coil cap rivets (A)

Choke Coil Lever Adjustment

1. Remove the three retaining screws and remove the choke cover and coil. On models with a riveted choke cover, drill out the three rivets and remove the cover and choke coil.

NOTE: A choke stat cover retainer kit is required for reassembly.

2. Place the fast idle screw on the high step of the dam.
3. Close the choke by pushing in on the intermediate choke lever. On front wheel drive models, the intermediate choke lever is behind the choke vacuum diaphragm.
4. Insert a drill or gauge of the specified size into the hole in the choke housing. The choke lever in the housing should be up against the side of the gauge.
5. If the lever does not just touch the gauge, bend the intermediate choke rod to adjust.

Electric Choke Setting

This procedure is only for those carburetors with choke covers retained by screws. Riveted choke covers are preset and non-adjustable.

1. Loosen the three retaining screws.
2. Place the fast idle screw on the high step of the cam.
3. Rotate the choke cover to align the cover mark with the specified housing mark.

NOTE: The specification "index" which appears in the specification table refers to the mark between "1 notch lean" and "1 notch rich".

Secondary Lockout Adjustment

1. Pull the choke wide open by pushing out on the intermediate choke lever.
2. Open the throttle until the end of the secondary actuating lever is opposite the toe of the lockout lever.
3. Gauge clearance between the lockout lever and secondary lever should be as specified.
4. To adjust, bend the lockout lever where it contacts the fast idle cam.

Secondary Vacuum Break TVS Test

The secondary vacuum break TVS (thermal vacuum switch), located in the air cleaner, improves cold starting and cold driveability by sensing carburetor air inlet temperature to control the carburetor secondary vacuum break.

1. With engine at normal operating temperature, the Thermal Vacuum Switch (TVS) must be open (air cleaner cover on).
2. Apply either engine or auxiliary vacuum to the TVS inlet port and check for vacuum at the outlet port (outlet port connects to secondary vacuum break).
3. If there is no vacuum, check air cleaner assembly for leaks, thermostatic air cleaner vacuum hoses and/or replace the TVS.

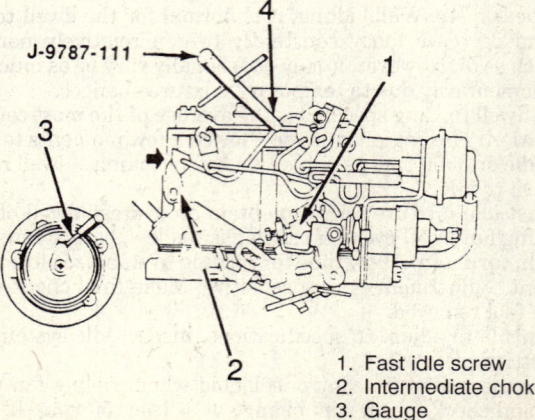

1. Fast idle screw
2. Intermediate choke lever
3. Gauge
4. Bending point on the rod

Choke coil lever adjustment

5 FUEL SYSTEM

Secondary Vacuum Break Replacement

1. Remove air cleaner cover and element.
2. Disconnect vacuum hoses.
3. Remove clip from TVS and remove TVS.
4. Install new TVS and replace clip.
5. Reconnect vacuum hoses (refer to Vehicle Emission Control Information Label).
6. Install air cleaner cover and element.

Idle Stop Solenoid Test

The solenoid should be checked to assure that the solenoid plunger extends when the solenoid is energized. an inoperative solenoid could cause stalling or a rough idle when hot, and should be replaced as necessary.

1. Turn on ignition, but do not start engine. Position transmission lever in Drive (A/T) or Neutral (M/T). On vehicles equipped with air conditioning, A/C switch must be on.
2. Open and close throttle to allow solenoid. Solenoid plunger should retract from throttle lever. Disconnect the wire at the solenoid, the solenoid plunger should retract from the throttle lever.
3. Connect solenoid wire. Plunger should move out and contact the throttle lever. Solenoid may not be strong enough to open the throttle, but the plunger should move.
4. If the plunger does not move in and out as the wire is disconnected and connected, check the voltage feed wire:
    a. If voltage is 12–15 volts, replace the solenoid.
    b. If voltage is low or zero, locate the cause of the open circuit in the solenoid feed wire and repair.

Idle Stop Solenoid Replacement

1. Remove carburetor air cleaner.
2. Disconnect electrical connector at solenoid.
3. Remove large retaining nut, tabbed lock washer, and remove solenoid.
4. To install, install the solenoid and retaining nut, bending the lock tabs against nut flats.
5. Connect electrical connector.
6. Install air cleaner and adjust idle speed as necessary.

Carburetor Pre-set Procedure

1. Remove the carburetor from the engine following normal service procedures to gain access to the plug covering the idle mixture needle.
2. To remove the plug, make two parallel cuts in the throttle body, one on each side of the plug, with a hacksaw. There is a locator point marking the casting at the plug. The cuts should extend down to the steel plug, but should not extend more than $1/8$ in. (3mm) beyond the locator point.
3. Place a flat punch at a point near the ends of the saw cuts in the throttle body. Hold the punch at a 45° angle and drive it into the throttle body until the casting breaks away and exposes the steel plug. Hold a center punch in the vertical position and drive

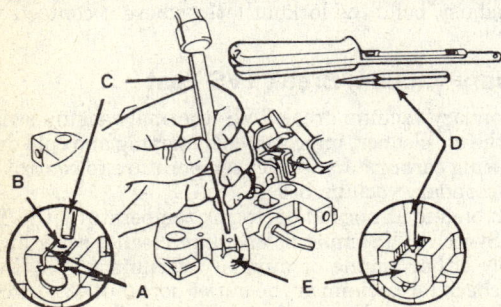

Removing the idle mixture screw cover on the 2SE/E2SE carburetor

it into the plug, then hold the punch at a 45° angle and drive the plug out of the housing. The hardened steel plug will shatter rather than remain intact. It is not necessary to remove the plug completely; instead, remove the loose pieces, then turn the idle mixture needle in until lightly seated and back out 4 turns.
4. If the plug in air horn covering the idle air has been removed, replace air horn. If plug is still in place, do not remove plug.
5. Remove vent stack screen assembly to gain access to lean mixture screw. (Be sure to reinstall vent stack screen assembly after adjustment).
6. Using tool J–28696–10 BT 7928 or equivalent, turn lean mixture screw in until lightly bottomed and back out $2^{1}/_{2}$ turns.
7. Reinstall the carburetor on the engine and perform the following:
    a. Do not install air cleaner and gasket.
    b. Disconnect the bowl vent line at carburetor.
    c. Disconnect the EGR valve hose and canister purge hose at the carburetor and cap the carburetor ports.
    d. Refer to Vehicle Emission control Information Label and observe hose from sensor and secondary vacuum break TVS. Disconnect hose at temperature sensor on air cleaner and plug open hose.
    e. Connect the positive lead of a dwell meter to the mixture control solenoid test lead (green connector). Connect the other meter lead to ground. Set dwell meter to 6 cylinder position. Connect a tachometer to distributor lead (brown connector). Tachometer should be connected to the distributor side of the tach filter if vehicle is equipped with a tachometer.
    f. Block the drive wheels.
    g. Place the transmission in Park (automatic transmission) or Neutral (manual transmission) and set the parking brake.
8. Proceed to Mixture Adjustment Procedure.

MIXTURE ADJUSTMENT PROCEDURE

1. Perform carburetor pre-set procedure.
2. Run engine on high step of fast idle cam until engine cooling fan starts to cycle (at least three minutes and until in closed loop).
3. Run the engine at 3000 rpm and adjust the lean mixture screw slowly in small increments allowing time for the dwell to stabilize after turning the screw to obtain an average dwell of 35°.
4. If dwell is too low, back screw out; if too high, turn it in. If unable to adjust to specifications, inspect main metering circuit for leaks, restrictions, etc.
5. The dwell reading of the M/C solenoid is used to determine calibration and is sensitive to changes in fuel mixture caused by heat, air leaks, etc. While idling, it is normal for the dwell to increase and decrease fairly constantly over a relatively narrow range, such as 5°. However, it may occasionally vary be as much as 10–15° momentarily due to temporary mixture changes.
6. The dwell reading specified is the average of the most consistent variation. The engine must be allowed a few moments to stabilize at idle or 3000 rpm as applicable before taking a dwell reading. Return to idle.
7. Adjust idle mixture screw to obtain an average dwell of 25° with cooling fan in off cycle. If reading is too low, back screw out. If too high, turn it in. Allow time for reading to stabilize after each adjustment. Adjustment is very sensitive. Make final check with adjusting tool removed.
8. If unable to adjust to specifications, inspect idle system for leaks, restrictions, etc.
9. Disconnect mixture control solenoid when cooling fan is in off cycle and check for an rpm change of at least 50 rpm. If rpm does not change enough, inspect idle air bleed circuit for restrictions, leaks, etc.
10. Run engine at 3000 rpm for a few moments and note dwell

FUEL SYSTEM 5

reading. Dwell should be varying with an average reading of 35°. If not at 35° average dwell: Reset lean mixture screw per Step 3. Then reset idle mixture screw to obtain 25° dwell per Step 5.

11. If at 35° average dwell: Reconnect systems disconnected earlier (purge and vent hoses, EGR valve, etc.), reinstall vent screen and set idle speed to specifications. It is not necessary to repeat the System Performance Check after proper adjustment of the carburetor.

CARBURETOR REMOVAL AND INSTALLATION

Always replace all internal gaskets that are removed. Base gasket should be inspected and replaced only if damaged. Flooding, stumble on acceleration and other performance complaints are in many instances, caused by presence of dirt, water, or other foreign matter in carburetor. To aid in diagnosis, carburetor should be carefully removed from engine without draining fuel from bowl. Contents of fuel bowl may then be examined for contamination as carburetor is disassembled. Check fuel filter.
1. Remove air cleaner and gasket.
2. Disconnect fuel pipe and vacuum lines.
3. Disconnect electrical connectors.
4. Disconnect accelerator linkage.
5. If equipped with automatic transmission, disconnect downshift cable.
6. If equipped with cruise control, disconnect linkage.
7. Remove carburetor attaching bolts.
8. Remove carburetor and EFE heater/insulator (if used).
9. Fill carburetor bowl before installing carburetor. A small supply of no-lead fuel will enable the carburetor to be filled and the operation of the float and inlet needle and seat to be checked. Operate throttle lever several times and check discharge from pump jets before installing carburetor.
10. Inspect EFE heater/insulator for damage. Be certain throttle body and EFE heater/insulator surfaces are clean.
11. Install EFE heater; insulator.
12. Install carburetor and tighten nuts alternately to the correct torque.
13. Connect downshift cable as required.
14. Connect cruise control cable as required.
15. Connect accelerator linkage.
16. Connect electrical connections.
17. Connect fuel pipe sand vacuum hoses.
18. Check base (slow) and fast idle.
19. Install air cleaner.

CARBURETOR OVERHAUL

Air Horn

1. Invert the carburetor, then remove the plug covering the idle mixture needle as previously described.
2. Install the carburetor in a suitable holding stand.
3. Remove the primary and secondary vacuum break assemblies. Be sure to take note of the linkage positions for installation.
4. Remove the three screws from the mixture control solenoid. Remove the mixture control solenoid with gasket and discard the gasket.
5. Remove the two screws from the vent stack and remove the vent stack. Remove the intermediate choke shaft link retainer at the choke lever and discard it.
6. Remove the choke link and bushing from choke lever and save the bushing.
7. Remove the retainer and bushing from the fast idle cam link and discard the retainer.

NOTE: Do not remove fast idle cam screw and cam from the float bowl. If removed, the cam might not operate prop-

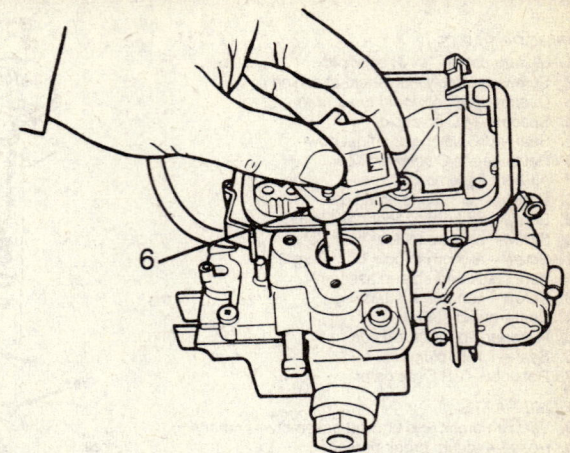

Mixture control solenoid (6) removal/installation

erly when reassembled. If needed, a replacement float bowl will include a secondary locknut lever, fast idle cam, and cam screw.

8. Remove the retainer from the pump link. Do not remove the screw attaching the pump lever to the air horn assembly. When reassembled, the screw might not hold properly.
9. Remove the seven screw assemblies of various length that retain the air horn to the carburetor and remove the air horn assembly. Tilt the air horn to disconnect fast idle cam link from the slot in fast idle cam and the pump link from the hole in the pump lever.
10. Remove the cam link from the choke lever. Be sure to line up the "squirt" on link with slot in lever.
11. Invert the air horn and remove the TPS actuator plunger. The TPS adjusting screw and plug should not be removed.
12. Remove the stakings that holds the TPS plunger seal retainer and pump stem seal retainer.
13. Remove the retainers and seals and discard them.
14. Further disassembly of the air horn is not required for cleaning purposes. The choke valve and choke valve screws, the air valve and air valve shaft should not be removed.

NOTE: Do not turn the secondary metering rod adjusting screw. The rod could come out of jet and possibly cause damage.

Float Bowl

1. Remove the accelerator pump, air horn gasket and pump return spring.
2. Remove the Throttle Position Sensor (TPS) assembly and spring. Inspect the TPS connector wires for broken insulation, which could cause grounding of the TPS.
3. Remove the upper insert and the hinge pin. Remove the float and lever assembly with the float stabilizing spring if used. Remove the float needle and pull clip.
4. Remove the lower insert, if used.
5. Remove the float needle seat and seat gasket.
6. Remove the jet and lean mixture needle assembly.

NOTE: Do not remove or change the preset adjustment of calibration needle in the metering jet unless the Computer Command Control system performance check requires it.

7. Remove the pump discharge spring guide, using a suitable slide hammer puller only.

NOTE: Do not pry the guide. Damage could occur to the sealing surfaces, and could require replacement of the float bowl.

8. Remove the spring and check ball, by inverting the bowl and catching them as they fall out.
9. Remove the fuel inlet nut and the fuel filter spring.

5 FUEL SYSTEM

AIR HORN PARTS
1. Mixture control (M/C) solenoid
2. Screw assembly—solenoid attaching
3. Gasket—M/C solenoid to air horn
4. Spacer—M/C solenoid
5. Seal—M/C solenoid to float bowl
6. Retainer—M/C solenoid seal
7. Air horn assembly
8. Gasket—air horn to float bowl
9. Screw—air horn to float bowl (short)
10. Screw—air horn to float bowl (long)
11. Screw—air horn to float bowl (large)
12. Vent stack and screen assembly
13. Screw—vent stack attaching
14. Seal—pump stem
15. Retainer—pump stem seal
16. Seal—T.P.S. plunger
17. Retainer—T.P.S. actuator

CHOKE PARTS
19. Vacuum break and bracket assembly—primary
20. Hose—vacuum break primary
21. Tee—vacuum break
22. Solenoid—idle speed
23. Retainer—idle speed solenoid
24. Nut—idle speed solenoid attaching
25. Screw—vacuum break bracket attaching
26. Link—air valve
27. Bushing—air valve link
28. Retainer—air valve link
29. Link—fast idle cam
29A. Link—fast idle cam
29B. Link—fast idle cam
29C. Bushing—link
30. Hose—vacuum break
31. Intermediate choke shaft/lever/link assembly
32. Bushing—intermediate choke link
33. Retainer—intermediate choke link
34. Vacuum break and link assembly—secondary
35. Screw—vacuum break attaching
36. Electric choke—cover and coil assembly
37. Screw—choke lever attaching
38. Choke coil lever assembly
39. Choke housing
40. Screw—choke housing attaching
41. Choke cover retainer kit
67. Screw—vacuum break bracket attaching

FLOAT BOWL PARTS
42. Nut—fuel inlet
43. Gasket—fuel inlet nut
44. Filter—fuel inlet
45. Spring—fuel filter
46. Float and lever assembly
47. Hinge pin—float
48. Upper insert—float bowl
48A. Lower insert—float bowl
49. Needle and seat assembly
50. Spring—pump return
51. Pump plunger assembly
52. Primary metering jet assembly
53. Retainer—pump discharge ball
54. Spring—pump discharge
55. Ball—pump discharge
56. Spring—T.P.S. adjusting
57. Sensor—throttle position (TPS)
58. Float bowl assembly
59. Gasket—float bowl

THROTTLE BODY PARTS
60. Retainer—pump link
61. Link—pump
62. Throttle body assembly
63. Clip—cam screw
64. Screw—fast idle cam
65. Idle needle and spring assembly
66. Screw—throttle body to float bowl
68. Screw—idle stop
69. Spring—idle stop screw
70. Gasket—insulator flange

Rochester E2SE

10. Remove the fuel filter assembly and discard it. Remove the filter gasket and discard it.

Choke Assembly and Throttle Body

1. Remove the choke cover as follows:
   a. Use a 5/32 in. (4mm) drill bit to remove the heads (only) from the rivets.
   b. Remove the choke cover retainers. Remove the remaining pieces of rivets, using drift and small hammer.
   c. Remove the electric choke cover and stat assembly.
2. Remove the stat lever screw, Stat lever, intermediate choke shaft, lever and link assembly.
3. Remove the two screws and the choke housing.
4. Remove the four screws, and the throttle body assembly from the inverted float bowl.
5. Remove the gasket, pump link and line up the "squirt" on link with the slot in the lever.
6. Count and make a record of the number of turns needed to lightly bottom the idle mixture needle (69), then back out and remove needle and spring assembly using Idle mixture socket tool J-29030-B or BT-7610-B or equivalent.
7. Do not disassemble throttle body further.

INSPECTION AND CLEANING

1. Place the metal parts in immersion carburetor cleaner.
NOTE: Do not immerse idle stop solenoid, mixture control solenoid, throttle lever actuator, TPS, electric choke, rubber and plastic parts, diaphragms, and pump in the cleaner, as they may be damaged. Plastic bushing in throttle lever will withstand normal cleaning.

2. Blow dry the parts with shop air. Be sure all fuel and air passages are free of burrs and dirt. Do not pass drill bits or wires through jets and passages.

FUEL SYSTEM 5

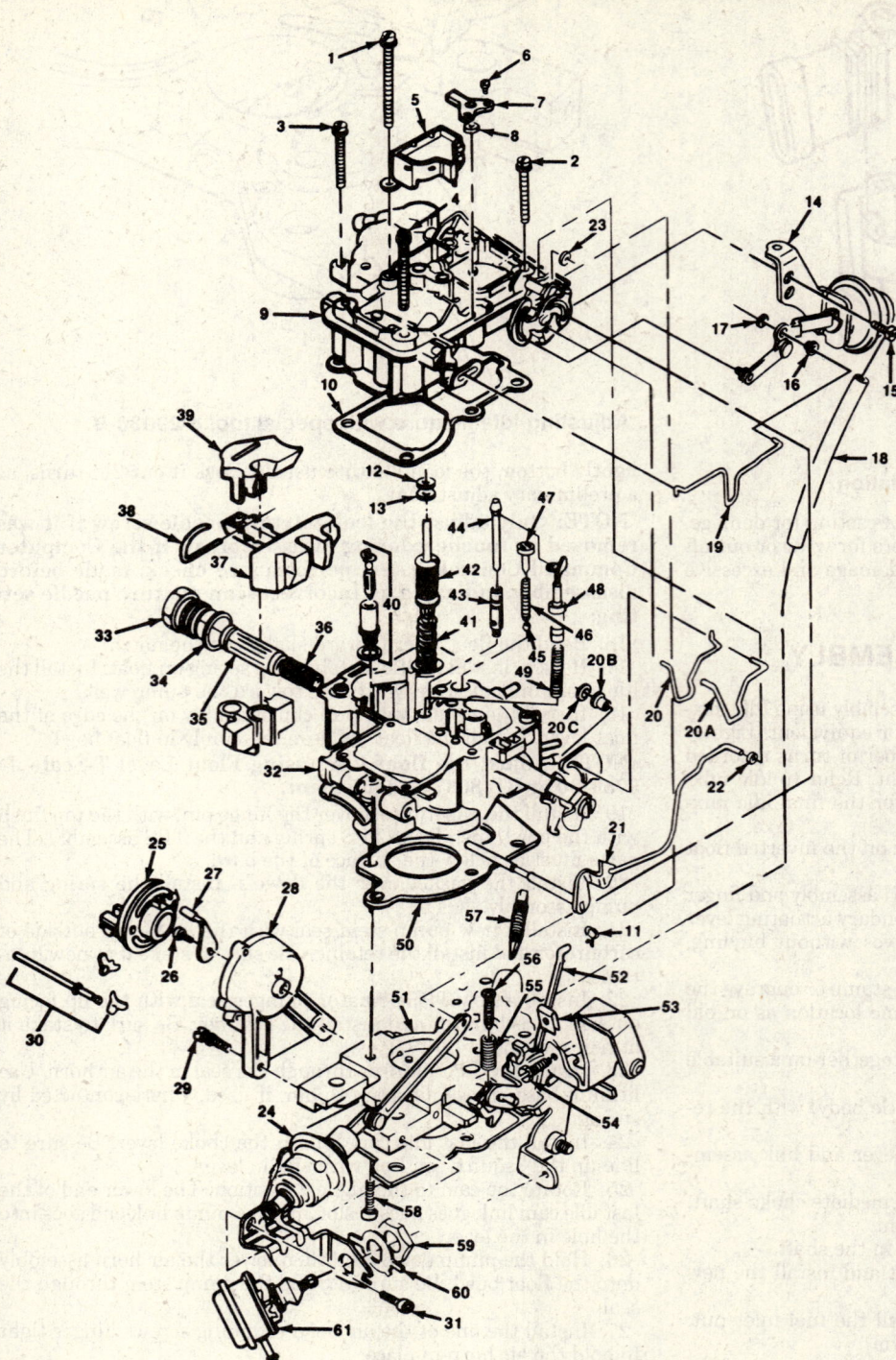

AIR HORN COMPONENTS
1. Screw—air horn (long) (2)
2. Screw—air horn (large)
3. Screw—air horn (short) (3)
4. Screw—air horn (medium)
5. Vent stack assembly
6. Screw—hot idle compensator (2)
7. Hot idle compensator
8. Gasket—hot idle compensator
9. Air horn assembly
10. Gasket—air horn
11. Retainer—pump
12. Seal—pump stem
13. Retainer—stem seal

CHOKE COMPONENTS
14. Vacuum break and bracket assembly
15. Screw—vacuum break attaching
16. Bushing—air valve—rod
17. Retainer—air valve rod
18. Hose—vacuum break—primary
19. Rod—air valve
20. Rod—fast idle cam
21. Intermediate choke shaft/lever/rod assembly
22. Bushing—intermediate choke shaft rod
23. Retainer—intermediate choke shaft rod
24. Vacuum break and bracket assembly
25. Choke cover and coil assembly
26. Screw—choke lever
27. Choke lever and contact assembly
28. Choke housing
29. Screw—choke housing (2)
30. Stat cover retainer kit
31. Screw—vacuum break attaching (2)

FLOAT BOWL COMPONENTS
32. Float bowl assembly
33. Nut—fuel inlet
34. Gasket—fuel inlet nut
35. Filter—fuel inlet
36. Spring—fuel filter
37. Float assembly
38. Hinge pin—float
39. Insert—float bowl
40. Needle and seat assembly
41. Spring—pump return
42. Pump—assembly
43. Jet—main metering
44. Rod—main metering assembly
45. Ball—pump discharge
46. Spring—pump discharge
47. Retainer—pump discharge spring
48. Power piston assembly
49. Spring—power piston

THROTTLE BODY COMPONENTS
50. Gasket—throttle body
51. Throttle body assembly
52. Pump rod
53. Clip—cam screw
54. Screw—cam
55. Spring—throttle stop screw
56. Screw—throttle stop
57. Idle needle and spring
58. Screw—throttle body attaching (4)
59. Nut—idle speed kick actuator
60. Retainer—idle speed kick actuator
61. Idle speed kick actuator

Rochester 2SE

5 FUEL SYSTEM

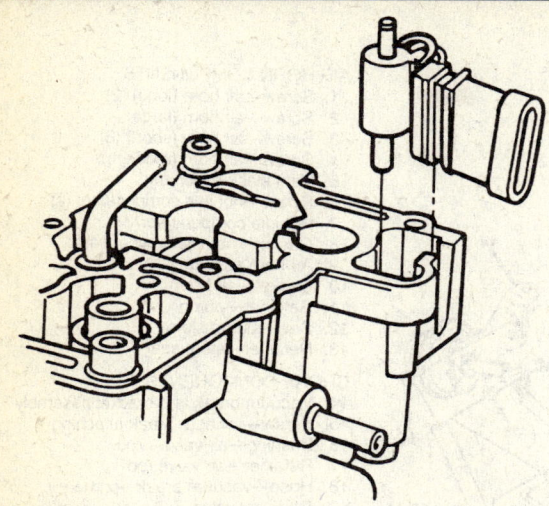

Throttle position sensor removal/installation

3. Be sure to check the mating surfaces of casting for damage. Replace if necessary. Check for holes in levers for wear or out-of-round conditions. Check the bushings for damage and excessive wear. Replace if necessary.

CARBURETOR REASSEMBLY

1. Install the mixture needle and spring assembly using Idle mixture socket tool J–29030–B or BT–7610–B or equivalent. Lightly bottom the needle and back it out the number of turns recorded during removal, as a preliminary adjustment. Refer to idle mixture adjustment procedure in this section for the final idle mixture adjustment.
2. Install the pump link and a new gasket on the inverted float bowl.
3. Install the throttle body to the float bowl assembly and finger tighten the four retaining screws. If the secondary actuating lever engages the lockout lever, and linkage moves without binding, tighten retaining screws.
4. If the float bowl assembly was replaced, stamp or engrave the model number on the new float bowl in same location as on old bowl.
5. Place the throttle body and float bowl together on a suitable carburetor holding stand.
6. Install the choke housing on the throttle body, with the retaining screws.
7. Install the intermediate choke shaft, lever and link assembly.
8. Install the choke stat lever on the intermediate choke shaft. The intermediate choke lever must be upright.
9. Install the choke lever attaching screw in the shaft.
10. Install the gasket on the fuel inlet nut and install the new filter assembly in the nut.
11. Install the filter spring and then install the fuel inlet nut. Tighten the fuel inlet nut to 18 ft. lbs. (24 Nm).

CAUTION
Tightening beyond this limit may damage gasket and could cause a fuel leak, which might result in personal injury.

12. Install the pump discharge ball and spring.
13. Install a new spring guide and tap it until the top is flush with the bowl casting.
14. Install the needle seat with gasket. If used, lower the insert.
15. Install the jet and lean mixture needle assembly. Using lean mixture adjusting tool J–28696–10 or BT–7928 or equivalent,

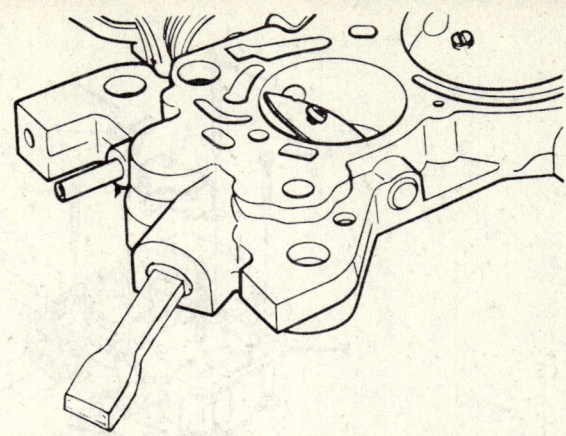

Adjusting idle mixture with special tool J-29030-B

lightly bottom the lean mixture needle. Back it out $2\frac{1}{2}$ turns, as a preliminary adjustment.

NOTE: Only adjust the lean mixture needle screw if it was removed or touched during disassembly or if the Computer Command Control system performance check, made before disassembly, indicated an incorrect lean mixture needle setting:

16. Bend the float lever upward slightly at the notch.
17. If used, install the float stabilizing spring on float. Install the hinge pin in float lever, with ends toward the pump well.
18. Install the needle with pull clip assembly on the edge of the float lever. Install the float and lever assembly in float bowl.

NOTE: Adjust the float level using Float Level T-Scale J–9789–90 or BT–8037 or equivalent.

19. Install the upper insert over the hinge pin, with the top flush with the bowl. Install the TPS spring and the TPS assembly. The parts must be below the surface of the bowl.
20. Install the gasket over the dowels. Install the spring and pump assembly.
21. Install a new pump stem seal with the lip facing outside of carburetor and install the retainer. Be sure to stake it at new locations.
22. Install a new TPS actuator plunger seal with the lip facing outside of carburetor and install the retainer. Be sure to stake it at new locations.
23. Install the TPS plunger through the seal in the air horn. Use lithium base grease, liberally to pin, if used, where contacted by spring.
24. Install the fast idle cam link in the choke lever. Be sure to line-up the "squirt" on link with slot in lever.
25. Rotate the cam to the highest position. The lower end of the fast idle cam link goes in cam slot, and the pump link end goes into the hole in the lever.
26. Hold the pump down, and then lower the air horn assembly onto the float bowl. Be sure to guide the pump stem through the seal.
27. Install the one of the air horn retaining screws, finger tight to hold the air horn in place.
28. Install the cam link in the slot of the cam. Install a new bushing and retainer to the link, with the large end of bushing facing the retainer. Check for freedom of movement.
29. Install the rest of the air horn retaining screws.
30. Install the spacer and a new seal, lightly coat the seal with automatic transmission fluid. Assemble the seal on the solenoid stem, touching the spacer.
31. Install a new retainer and a new gasket on the air horn. Install the mixture control solenoid lining up the stem with the recess in the bowl.
32. Install the solenoid retaining screws. Install the vent stack,

FUEL SYSTEM 5

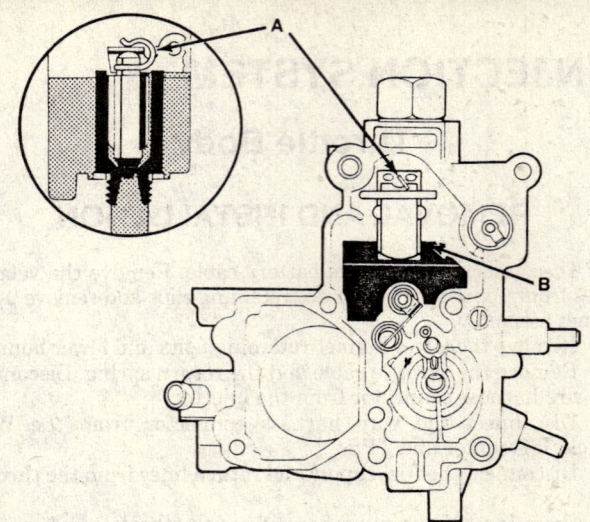

Installation of the float retaining pin (A) and float (B) on the 2SE/E2SE carburetor

with two retaining screws, (unless lean mixture needle requires on-vehicle adjustment).

33. Install a new retainer on the pump link. Adjust the air valve spring, if adjustable.
34. Install the bushing on the choke link. With the intermediate choke lever upright, install the link in the choke lever hole. Install the new link retainer.
35. The following procedures is for reassembly of any small components that have been removed from the carburetor, if part replacement is necessary or for any other reason.
    a. Install the idle stop solenoid, retainer and nut to the secondary side vacuum break bracket. Bend the retainer tab to secure nut.
    b. Install the bushing to the link and the link to the vacuum break plunger. Install the retainer to the link.
    c. Rotate the assembly, insert the end of the link in the upper slot of the choke lever. Install the bracket screws.
    d. Install the idle speed device, retainer and nut to the primary side vacuum break bracket. Bend the retainer tab to secure the nut.
    e. Install the bushing to the vacuum break link. Install the link to vacuum break plunger. Install the retainer to the link and the bushing to the air valve link. Install the link to the plunger and the retainer to the link.
36. Rotate the vacuum break assembly (primary side) and insert the end of the air valve link into the air valve lever and the vacuum break link into the lower slot of the choke lever.
37. Install the bracket screws, vacuum hose between the throttle body tube and the vacuum break assembly.
38. Install the choke thermostat lever. Install the choke cover and thermostat assembly in the choke housing.
39. If the thermostat has a "trap" (box-shaped pick-up tang), the trap surrounds the lever.
40. Line up the notch in the cover with projection on the housing flange. Install the retainers and rivets with rivet tool. If necessary, use an adapter. Adjust the choke as previously described.

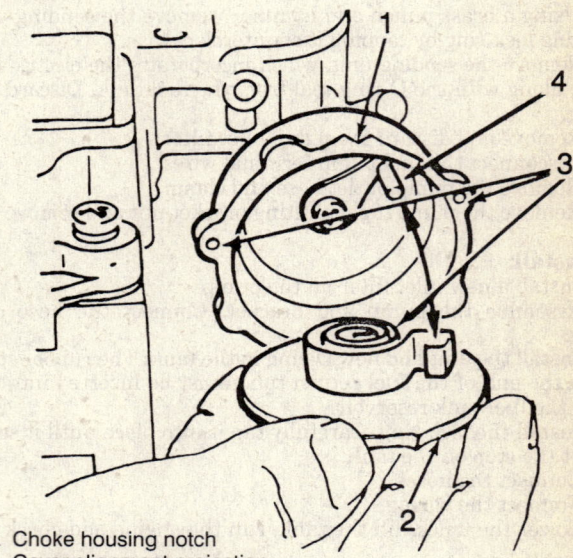

1. Choke housing notch
2. Cover alignment projection
3. Cover assembly
4. Choke coil lever

Installing the choke coil and cover.

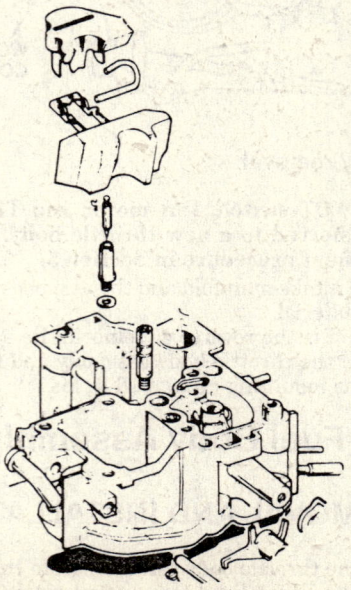

Float valve assembly removal/installation

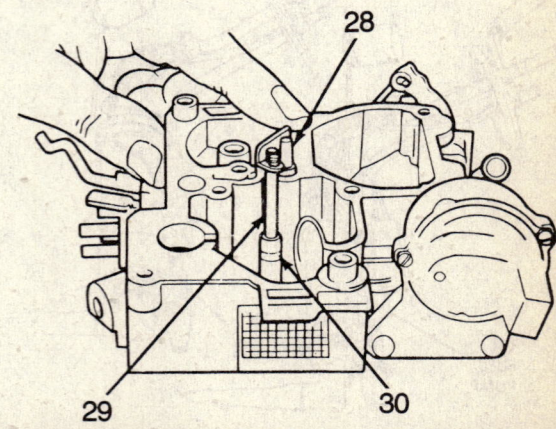

Installation of the power piston (28), metering rod (29) and metering jet (30)

5-19

5 FUEL SYSTEM

THROTTLE BODY FUEL INJECTION SYSTEM

Complete diagnostic testing and adjustment procedures for the throttle body injection system components are provided in Section 4.

Electric Fuel Pump

REMOVAL AND INSTALLATION

1. Disconnect the negative battery cable.
2. Remove the fuel tank filler cap.
3. Using a siphon hose, drain the fuel tank below 1/4 full.
4. Raise and support the rear end on jackstands.
5. Remove the fuel inlet and outlet hoses from the sending unit. Be ready to catch any spilled fuel.
6. Remove the sending unit wires.
7. Using a brass punch and hammer, remove the sending unit retaining lock ring by tapping it counterclockwise.
8. Remove the sending unit, which incorporates the electric fuel pump, along with the O-ring seal from the fuel tank. Discard the O-ring.
9. Remove and discard the pump inlet filter.
10. Disconnect the fuel pump terminal wires.
11. Remove the pump outlet hose and clamp.
12. Remove the pump top mounting bracket nut and remove the pump.

To install:

13. Install a new inlet filter on the pump.
14. Assemble the pump and bracket. Connect the hose and wiring.
15. Install the unit and new O-ring in the tank. The rubber stopper on the end of the fuel return tube must be inserted into the cup in the fuel tank reservoir.
16. Install the lock ring. Carefully tap it into place until it seats against the stop on the tank.
17. Connect the hoses.
18. Connect the wiring.
19. Lower the truck, fill the tank, run the engine and check for leaks.

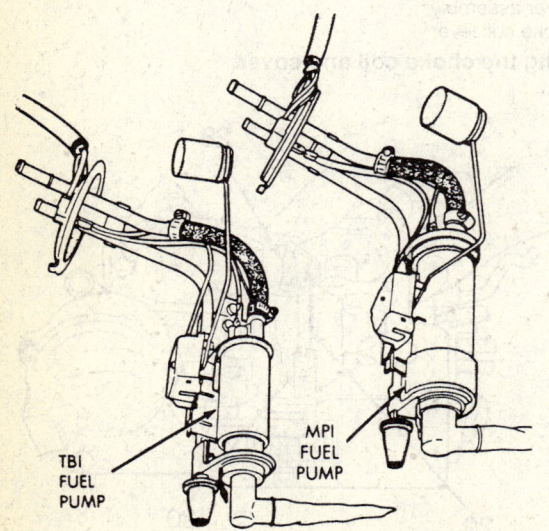

Electric fuel pumps

Throttle Body

REMOVAL AND INSTALLATION

1. Disconnect the negative battery cable. Remove the vacuum hoses from upper bonnet, release retaining clips and remove upper bonnet assembly.
2. Remove the lower bonnet retaining bolts and lower bonnet.
3. Remove the throttle cable and the return spring. Disconnect the wire harness connector from the injector.
4. Disconnect the wire harness connector from the WOT switch, ISA motor and TPS.
5. Disconnect the fuel supply and return lines from the throttle body.
6. Disconnect the vacuum hoses from the throttle body assembly. Disconnect the potentiometer wire connector.
7. Loosen throttle body retaining bolts and remove throttle body assembly from the intake manifold.

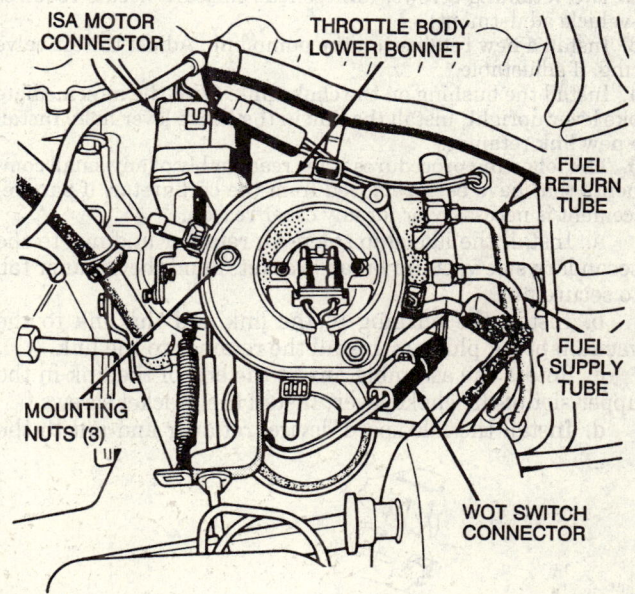

Throttle body removal

NOTE: The WOT switch, ISA motor and TPS must be adjusted if transferred to a new throttle body. See the appropriate adjustment procedure in Section 5.

8. Clean the intake manifold and throttle body mating surfaces of old gasket material.
9. Installation is the reverse of removal. Be sure to use a new gasket between the throttle body assembly and the intake manifold. Torque the mounting nuts to 16 ft. lbs.

Fuel Body Assembly

REMOVAL AND INSTALLATION

1. Remove the throttle body assembly from the vehicle.
2. Remove the Torx® head screws that retain the fuel body to the throttle body. Remove and discard the gasket.

FUEL SYSTEM 5

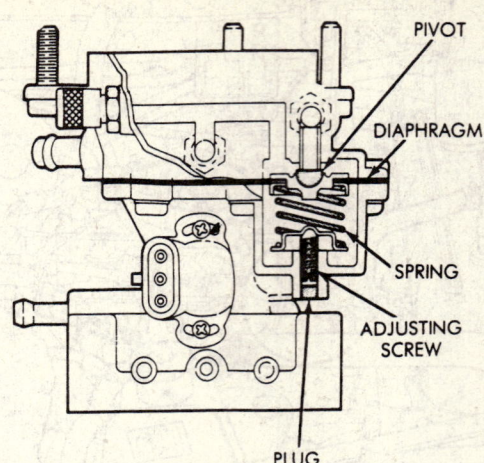

TBI fuel pressure regulator

3. Installation is the reverse of removal. Be sure to use a new gasket.

Fuel Pressure Regulator

REMOVAL AND INSTALLATION

1. Remove the throttle body assembly from the vehicle.

WARNING: To prevent spring pressure release, hold the regulator housing against the throttle body while removing the mounting screws.

2. Remove the three retaining screws that hold the pressure regulator to the fuel body.
3. Disassemble the pressure regulator assembly. Note the location of the components for reassembly. Discard the gasket.
4. Installation is the reverse of the removal procedure. Be sure to use a new gasket.

WARNING: The pressure regulator diaphragm MUST be installed with the vent hole aligned with the vent holes in the throttle body and regulator housing!

Fuel Injector

REMOVAL AND INSTALLATION

1. Disconnect the negative battery cable. Remove the air cleaner and hose assembly.
2. Remove the throttle body upper and lower bonnets.
3. Remove the fuel injector wire by compressing the tabs and pulling it upwards.
4. Remove the fuel injector retainer clip screws. Remove the fuel injector retainer clip.

NOTE: The injector has a small locating tab that fits into a slot in the bottom of the injector bore of the throttle body. DO NOT twist the injector during removal!

5. Using a small pair of pliers, gently grasp the center collar of the injector, between the electrical terminals, and carefully remove the injector using a lifting/rocking motion.
6. Discard the centering ring and the upper and lower O-rings. Never reuse these rings!
7. Installation is the reverse of the removal procedure. Lubricate both O-rings with light oil before installation. Align the tab on the injector with the slot in the throttle body.

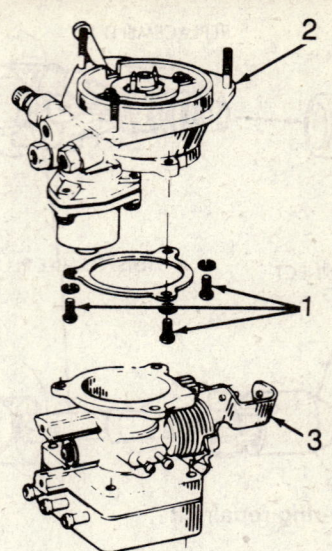

1. Fuel body retaining screws
2. Fuel body
3. Throttly body

Fuel body assembly removal/installation

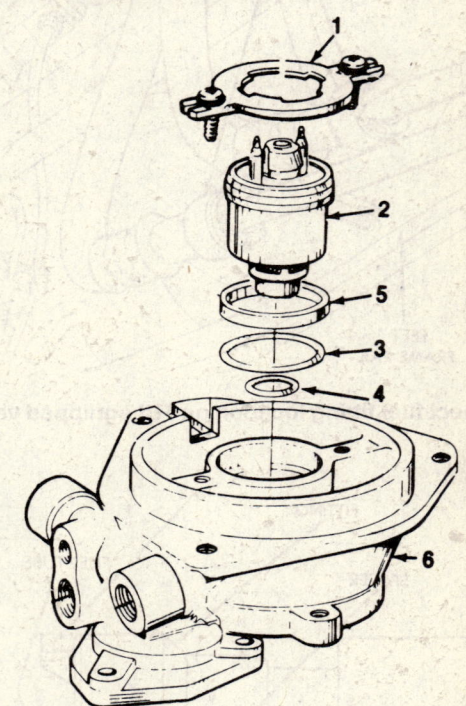

1. Retainer clip
2. Injector
3. Upper O-ring
4. Lower O-ring
5. Backup ring
6. Fuel body

Fuel injector removal/installation

Throttle Position Sensor

REMOVAL AND INSTALLATION

1. Remove the upper and lower bonnet assemblies.
2. Remove the throttle body assembly from the vehicle.

5-21

5 FUEL SYSTEM

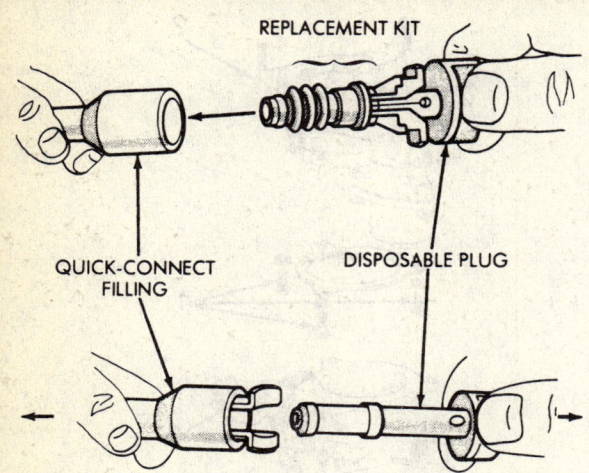

Quick-connect O-ring repair kit

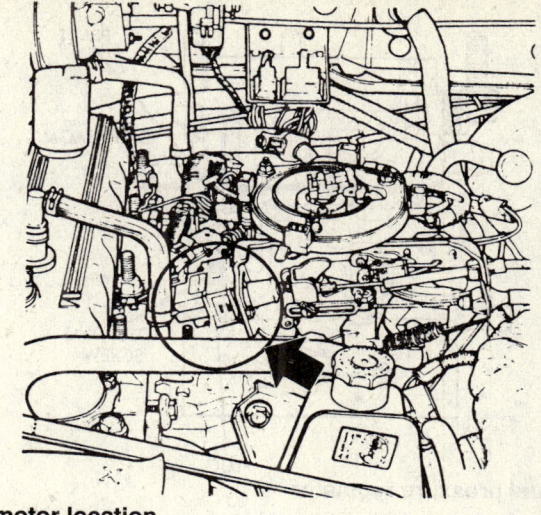

ISC motor location

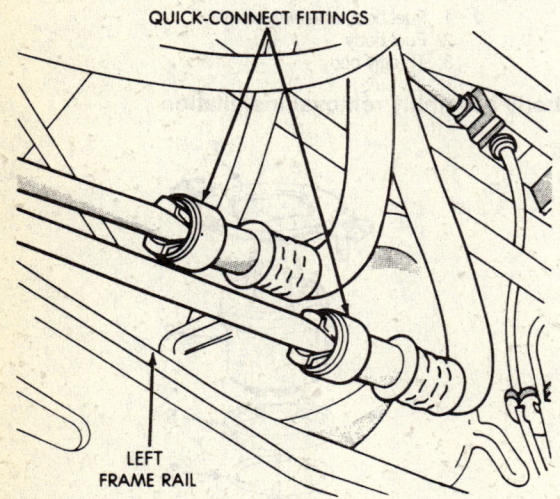

Quick-connect fuel fitting location on TBI equipped vehicles

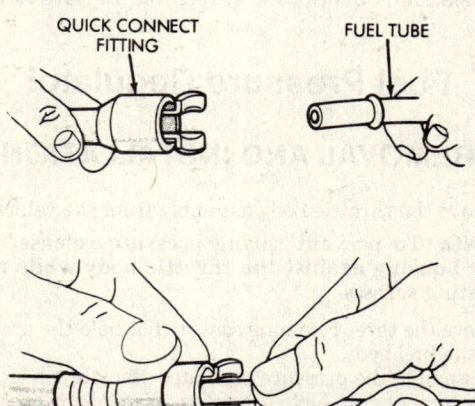

Assembling the fuel tube and quick-connect fitting. Push fuel tube into quick connect fitting and then pull apart to ensure positive engagement

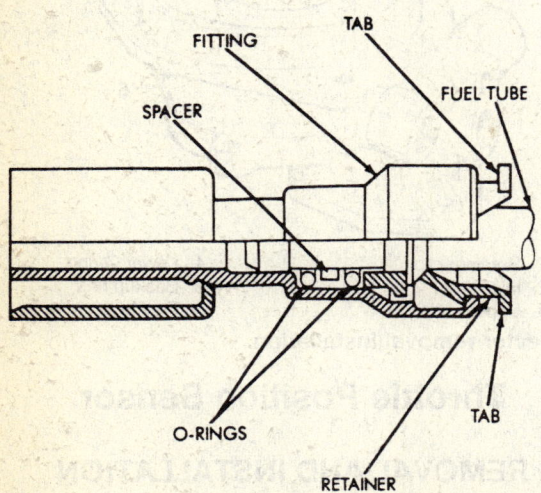

Quick-connect fuel fitting

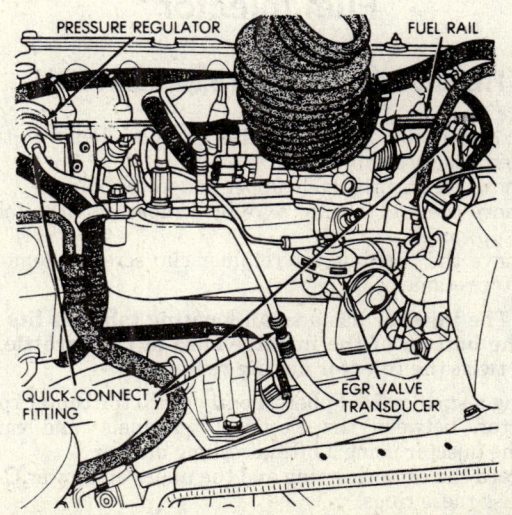

Quick-connect fuel fitting location on MPI equipped vehicles

5-22

FUEL SYSTEM 5

3. Remove the two Torx® head retaining screws holding the TPS assembly to the throttle body.
4. Remove the throttle position sensor from the throttle shaft lever.
5. Installation is the reverse of removal. Adjust the sensor as described in Section 5.

WARNING: Make sure that the sensor arm is installed UNDERNEATH the arm of the throttle valve shaft!

Idle Speed Actuator Motor

REMOVAL AND INSTALLATION

NOTE: The closed throttle switch is integral with the motor.

1. Disconnect the throttle return spring. Disconnect the wire harness connector from the motor.
2. Remove the motor to bracket retaining nuts. **Be sure to use a back-up wrench** as not to remove the motor studs which hold the motor together.
3. Remove the motor from the bracket.
4. Installation is the reverse of removal. Adjust the motor as described in Section 5.

Wide Open Throttle (WOT) Switch

REMOVAL AND INSTALLATION

1. Remove the air cleaner assembly.
2. Disconnect the throttle return spring.
3. Disconnect the throttle cable.
4. Disconnect the wire harness connector to the WOT switch.
5. Remove the two WOT switch-to-bracket mounting screws.
6. Remove the WOT switch.
7. Installation is the reverse of removal. Adjust WOT switch as described in Section 5.

Quick-Connect Fuel Line

O-RING REPLACEMENT

1. Release the fuel system pressure, then separate the quick-connect fuel line tubes at the inner fender panel by squeezing the two retaining tabs against the fuel line, then pulling the tube and retainer from the fitting.
2. Remove the two O-rings and the spacer from the fitting. This can be accomplished by using a paper clip or piece of heavy wire bent into an L-shape.
3. Remove the retainer from the fuel tube and discard the O-rings, spacer and retainer.
4. Install the new retainer assembly by pushing it into the quick-connect fitting until it clicks.
5. Grasp the disposable plastic plug and remove it from the replacement fitting. By removing only the plastic plug, the O-rings, spacer and retainer will remain in the fitting.
6. Push the fuel line into the fitting until a click is heard and the connection is complete. Give the fuel line connection a firm tug to verify that it is seated and locked properly.

MULTI-POINT FUEL INJECTION SYSTEM

Complete diagnostic testing and adjustment procedures for the multi-point fuel injection system components are provided in Section 4.

Relieving Fuel System Pressure

CAUTION

Before opening any part of the fuel system, the pressure in the system must be relieved!

1. Disconnect the negative battery cable.
2. Remove the fuel filler cap.
3. Remove the cap from the pressure test port on the fuel rail in the engine compartment.

CAUTION

DO NOT ALLOW FUEL TO SPRAY OR SPILL ON THE ENGINE EXHAUST MANIFOLD! PLACE HEAVY SHOP TOWELS UNDER THE PRESSURE PORT TO ABSORB ANY ESCAPED FUEL!

4. Using a small punch, push the test port valve in to relieve fuel system pressure.
5. Install the test port cap

Throttle Body

REMOVAL AND INSTALLATION

1. Disconnect the battery ground cable.
2. Disconnect the air inlet tube from the throttle body.
3. Tag and disconnect the wiring and hoses from the throttle body.
4. Disconnect the throttle linkage.
5. Disconnect the automatic transmission line pressure cable.
6. Remove the mounting bolts and remove the throttle body. Discard the gasket.
7. Installation is the reverse of removal. Tighten the mounting bolts to 23 ft. lbs. (pre-1991) and 9 ft. lbs. (1991)
8. If equipped with an automatic transmission, the line pressure cable MUST be adjusted! See Section 7.

Fuel Pump

REMOVAL AND INSTALLATION

1. Disconnect the negative battery cable.
2. Remove the fuel tank filler cap.
3. Relieve the fuel system pressure as described above.
4. Drain the fuel from the fuel tank.
5. Raise and support the rear end on jackstands.
6. Remove the fuel inlet and outlet hoses from the sending unit. Be ready to catch any spilled fuel.
7. Remove the sending unit wires.
8. Using a brass punch and hammer, remove the sending unit retaining lock ring by tapping it counterclockwise.
9. Remove the sending unit, which incorporates the electric fuel pump, along with the O-ring seal from the fuel tank. Discard the O-ring.
10. Remove and discard the pump inlet filter.
11. Disconnect the fuel pump terminal wires.
12. Remove the pump outlet hose and clamp.
13. Remove the pump top mounting bracket nut and remove the pump.

To install:

14. Install a new inlet filter on the pump.

5-23

5 FUEL SYSTEM

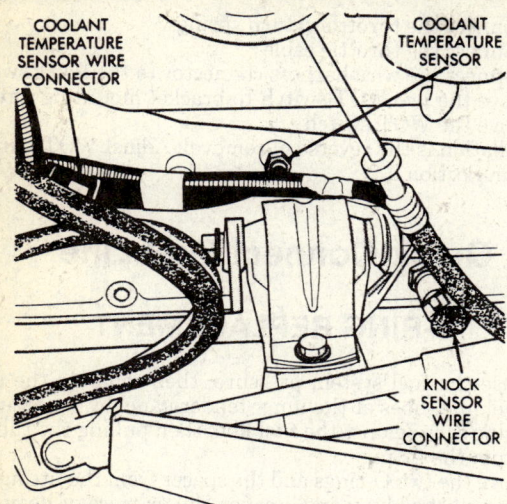

Coolant temperature sensor removal/installation

15. Assemble the pump and bracket. Connect the hose and wiring.
16. Install the unit and new O-ring in the tank. The rubber stopper on the end of the fuel return tube must be inserted into the cup in the fuel tank reservoir.
17. Install the lock ring. Carefully tap it into place until it seats against the stop on the tank.
18. Connect the hoses.
19. Connect the wiring.
20. Lower the truck, fill the tank, run the engine and check for leaks.

Coolant Temperature Sensor (CTS)

REMOVAL AND INSTALLATION

The coolant temperature sensor is located on the side of the engine block for most models. In 1991 the location was moved to the thermostat housing on top of the engine.

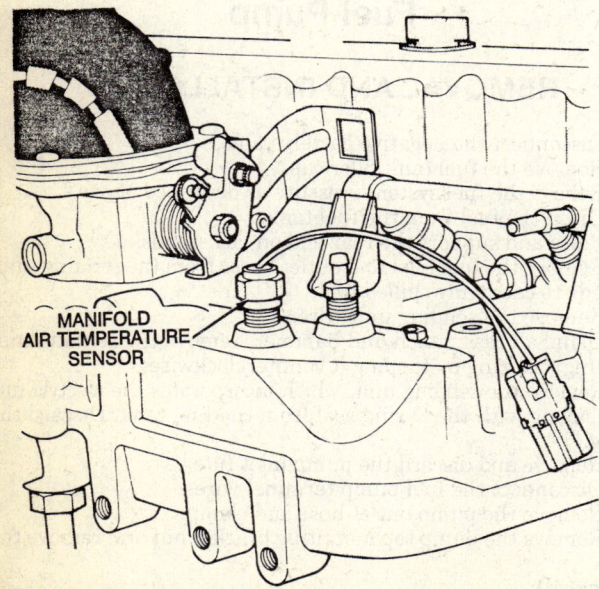

MAT sensor location

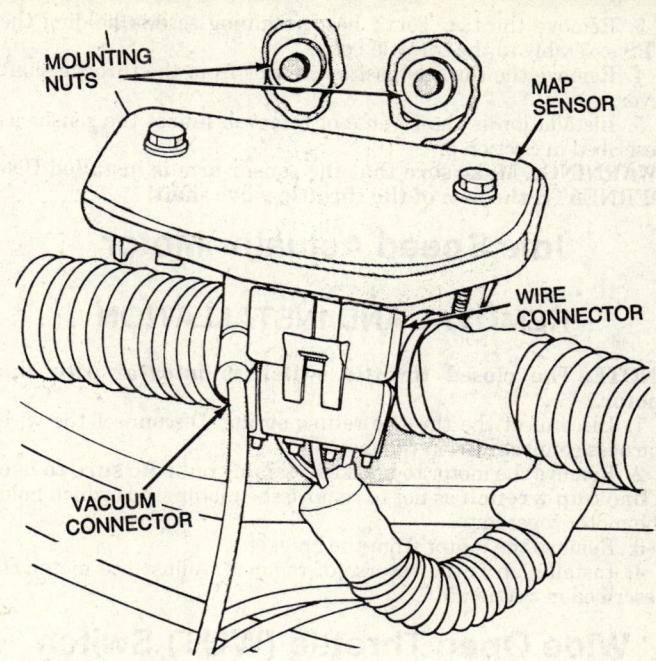

MAP sensor location

1. Drain the cooling system.

— CAUTION —
When draining the coolant, keep in mind that cats and dogs are attracted by the ethylene glycol antifreeze, and are quite likely to drink any that is left in an uncovered container or in puddles on the ground. This will prove fatal in sufficient quantity. Always drain the coolant into a sealable container. Coolant should be reused unless it is contaminated or several years old.

2. Remove the air cleaner assembly.
3. Disconnect the CTS wire connector.
4. Unscrew the CTS from the engine block.
5. Installation is the reverse of removal. Tighten the sensor to 21 ft. lbs. Refill the cooling system, start the engine and check for leaks.

Manifold Air Temperature (MAT) Sensor

REMOVAL AND INSTALLATION

The MAT sensor is removed by simply disconnecting the harness connector and removing the sensor from the intake manifold. Tighten the replacement sensor securely and install the connector.

Manifold Absolute Pressure (MAP) Sensor

REMOVAL AND INSTALLATION

1. Disconnect the MAP sensor wire harness connector.
2. Remove the MAP sensor vacuum supply hose.
3. Remove the MAP sensor retaining nuts and lift the sensor from the dash panel at the rear of the engine cylinder head cover.
4. Installation is the reverse of removal.

FUEL SYSTEM 5

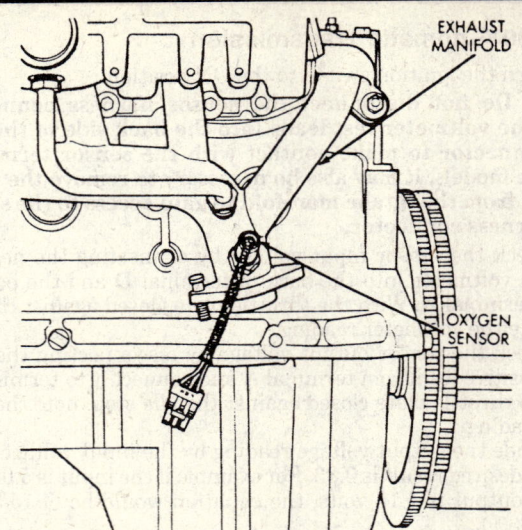

Oxygen sensor location

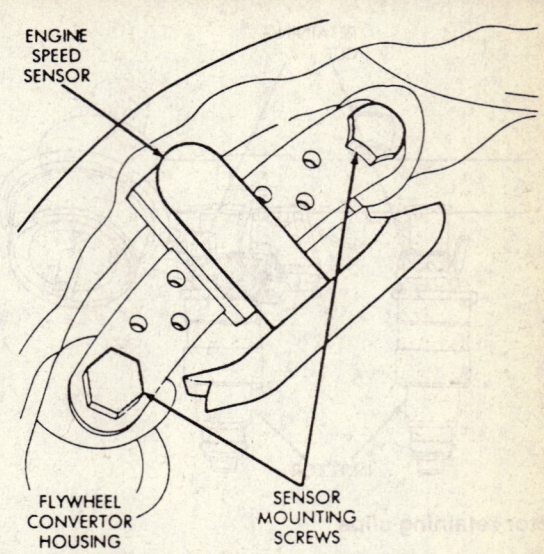

Crankshaft position (speed) sensor location

Oxygen Sensor

REMOVAL AND INSTALLATION

1. Raise the vehicle and support it safely. Allow the exhaust system to cool sufficiently to permit servicing.
2. Disconnect the wire connector from the oxygen sensor.
3. Remove the oxygen sensor from the exhaust manifold.
4. Coat the threads of the replacement sensor with anti-seize compound. Take care not to contaminate the oxygen sensor probe with anti-seize.
5. Install the oxygen sensor into the exhaust manifold and tighten to 35 ft. lbs. (48 Nm). Reconnect the wire connector.

Knock Sensor

REMOVAL AND INSTALLATION

The knock sensor can be removed from below by raising and supporting the vehicle, disconnecting the wire harness connector and then removing the knock sensor from the engine block. Install in reverse order.

Crankshaft Position (Speed) Sensor

REMOVAL AND INSTALLATION

The speed sensor can be removed by disconnecting the wire connector and removing the two shoulder bolts attaching the sensor to the transmission housing. Install in reverse order. There is no speed sensor adjustment.

Throttle Position Sensor (TPS)

REMOVAL AND INSTALLATION

1. Disconnect the TPS harness connector.
2. Bend back the lock tabs and remove the TPS retaining screws.
3. Remove the TPS from the throttle plate assembly.

4. Position the new TPS onto the throttle plate assembly, then install and snug the mounting bolts. Do not tighten the mounting bolts fully.
5. Connect the harness connector and adjust the TPS as outlined below.

TPS ADJUSTMENT

NOTE: The throttle position switch used on the 1991 Multi Point Injection system is non-adjustable.

1989–90 Manual Transmission

1. Turn the ignition switch to the ON position.

NOTE: Do not disconnect the sensor harness connector. Insert the voltmeter test leads into the back side of the harness connector to make contact with the sensor terminals.

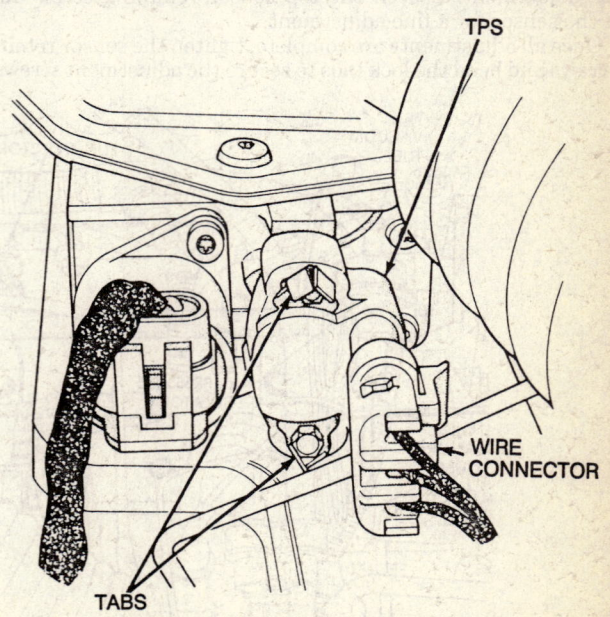

Throttle position sensor mounted to the throttle body

5-25

5 FUEL SYSTEM

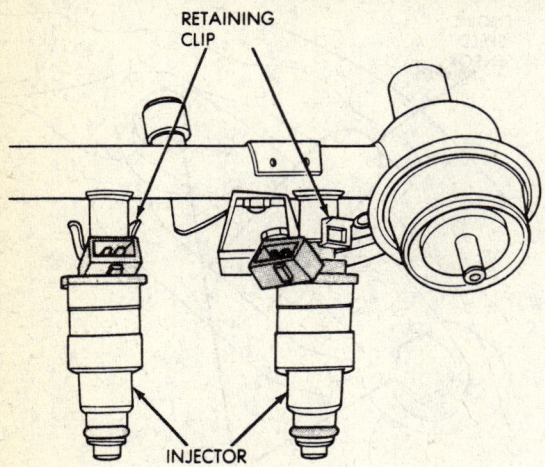

Injector retaining clips

On some models, it may also be necessary to remove the throttle body from the intake manifold to gain access to the sensor wire harness connector.

2. Check the sensor input voltage by connecting the negative lead of a voltmeter into the back of terminal **B** and the positive lead to terminal **A**. With the throttle plate closed against the idle stop, note the voltmeter reading.
3. Check the sensor output voltage by disconnecting the voltmeter positive lead from terminal **A** and connecting it to terminal **C**. With the throttle plate closed against the idle stop, note the voltmeter reading.
4. Divide the output voltage reading by the input voltage reading. The desired result is 0.17. For example if the input is 5.0 volts, and the output is 0.85 volts, the equation would be (0.85/5.0 = 0.17 or 17%).
5. If the output voltage requires adjustment, loosen the bottom mounting screw and pivot the sensor in the adjustment slot for a coarse adjustment. Loosen the top sensor retaining screw and pivot the sensor for a fine adjustment.
6. Once all adjustments are complete, tighten the sensor retaining screws and bend the lock tabs to secure the adjustment screws.

1989–90 Automatic Transmission

1. Turn the ignition switch to the ON position.

NOTE: Do not disconnect the sensor harness connector. Insert the voltmeter test leads into the back side of the harness connector to make contact with the sensor terminals. On some models, it may also be necessary to remove the throttle body from the intake manifold to gain access to the sensor wire harness connector.

2. Check the sensor input voltage by connecting the negative lead of a voltmeter into the back of terminal **D** and the positive lead to terminal **A**. With the throttle plate closed against the idle stop, note the voltmeter reading.
3. Check the sensor output voltage by disconnecting the voltmeter positive lead from terminal **A** and connect it to terminal **B**. With the throttle plate closed against the idle stop, note the voltmeter reading.
4. Divide the output voltage reading by the input voltage reading. The desired result is 0.83. For example if the input is 5.0 volts, and the output is 4.15 volts, the equation would be (4.15/5.0 = 0.83 or 83%).
5. If the output voltage requires adjustment, loosen the bottom mounting screw and pivot the sensor in the adjustment slot for a coarse adjustment. Loosen the top sensor retaining screw and pivot the sensor for a fine adjustment.
6. Once all adjustments are complete, tighten the sensor retaining screws to 50 inch lbs. and bend the lock tabs to secure the adjustment screws.

Fuel Injectors

REMOVAL AND INSTALLATION

--- **CAUTION** ---
Fuel system pressure must be relieved before disconnecting any fuel lines. Release fuel system pressure at the test connection using a suitable pressure gauge with a pressure bleed valve. Take precautions to avoid the risk of fire whenever working on or around any open fuel system.

1. Relieve fuel system pressure.
2. Disconnect the fuel lines at the ends of the fuel rail assembly.
3. Mark and disconnect the injector wire harness connectors.
4. Remove the fuel rail retaining bolts.

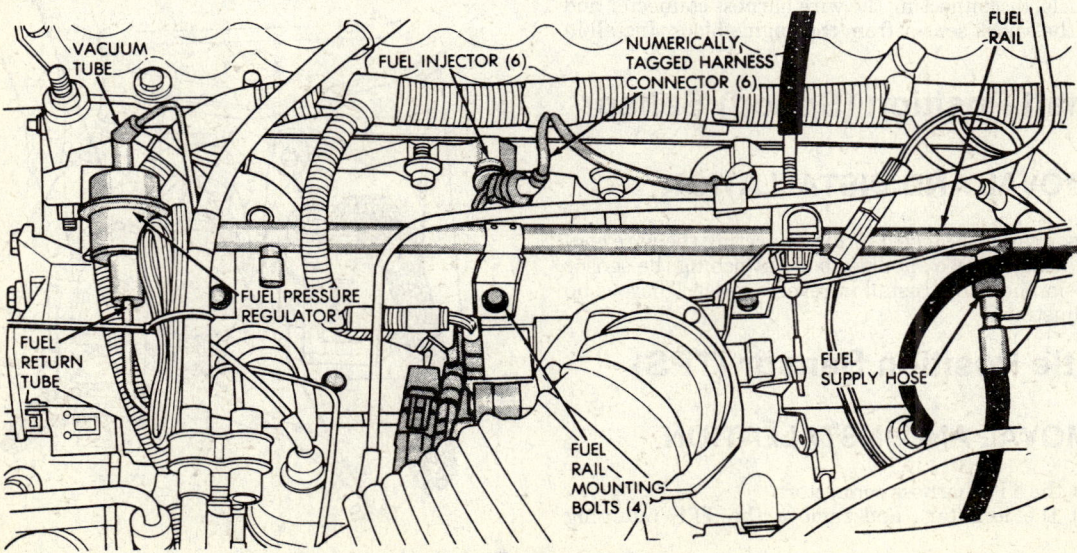

MFI fuel rail assembly

FUEL SYSTEM 5

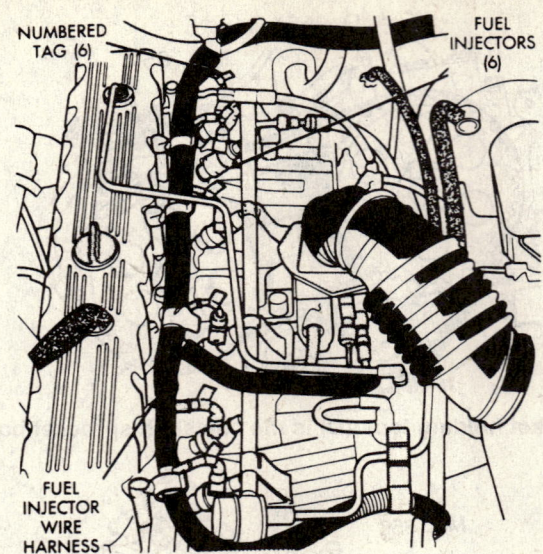

MFI injector harness

5. Disconnect the vacuum line from the fuel pressure regulator.
6. Remove the fuel rail assembly from the engine.

NOTE: **On models with automatic transmission, it may be necessary to remove the automatic transmission throttle pressure cable and bracket to remove the fuel rail assembly.**

7. Remove the clips that retain the injectors to the fuel rail and remove the injectors. An O-ring kit (part No. PN 8983 503 637) is available which consists of 6 brown seals and 7 black seals. The brown seals fit on the injector tip area and seal the injector to the intake manifold. The black seals fit on the rail end of the injector to seal the injector when it is installed into the fuel rail. The last black seal is for the fuel pressure regulator to seal the pressure regulator to the fuel rail. These seals cannot be interchanged.

8. Installation is the reverse of removal. Tighten the fuel rail mounting bolts to 20 ft. lbs. (27 Nm).

Idle Speed Stepper Motor

REMOVAL AND INSTALLATION

The idle speed stepper motor, located to the rear of the throttle position switch on the throttle body, is removed by simply disconnecting the harness connector and removing the retaining screws. Installation is the reverse of removal.

Quick-Connect Fuel Line

The procedure for installing new O-rings in the quick-connect fuel line fittings is the same for all fuel injection systems. See the appropriate procedure in the Throttle Body Injection section of this Section.

DIESEL FUEL SYSTEM

The Renault-built diesel engine uses a Bosch VE4/9F injection pump, supplying Bosch KBE 48 57 injectors. A Stanadyne fuel filter cleans the system. Boost is developed by a Garret T-2 turbocharger.

Injection Pump

REMOVAL AND INSTALLATION

NOTE: **Special tools are needed for this job.**

1. Disconnect the negative battery cable.
2. Using heavy clamps, clamp off the coolant inlet and outlet hoses at the cold start capsule. Then, disconnect them.
3. Disconnect the throttle cable and fuel shut-off solenoid wire.
4. If so equipped, disconnect the automatic transmission throttle cable, and cruise control cable.
5. Disconnect and plug the fuel delivery and return hoses.
6. Remove the alternator drive belt.
7. Remove the power steering drive belt.
8. Remove the timing belt cover.
9. Rotate the crankshaft clockwise, as viewed from the front, until #1 piston is at TDC compression. Make sure that the camshaft sprocket timing mark is aligned with the center boss on the cylinder head cover. Make sure, also, that the injection pump sprocket timing mark is aligned with the center of the boss on the injection pump.
10. Rotate the crankshaft counterclockwise, moving the sprocket timing marks by 3 timing belt teeth.
11. Install sprocket holding tool MOT-854. It may be necessary to turn the sprocket back and forth slightly to install the tool.
12. Loosen the sprocket retaining nut on the end of the injection pump shaft, and turn it out just to the end of the threads.
13. Assemble the sprocket removal tool jaws, B.Vi.48 and the short screw B.Vi.859, on the sprocket removal tool, B.Vi.28-01. 14. Attach the tool to the injection pump sprocket.
15. Disconnect all the fuel pipe fittings from the injectors. Plug the injectors to prevent dirt from entering the fuel system.
16. Disconnect the fuel pipe fittings from the fuel injection pump. Plug the fittings to prevent dirt from entering the system.
17. Remove the fuel line fittings from the vehicle. Remove all hoses and connectors from the injection pump assembly.
18. Remove the injection pump rear bracket retaining nuts.

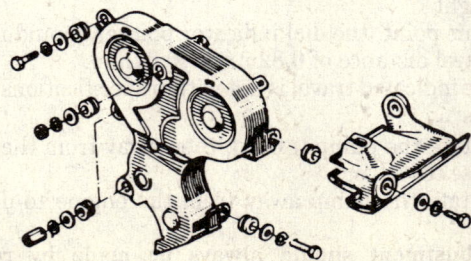

Diesel timing belt cover

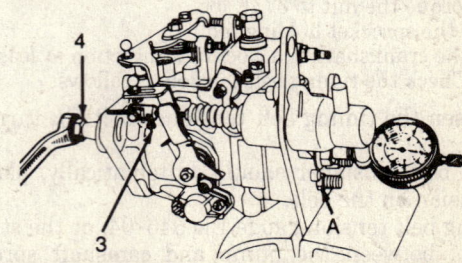

Injection pump adjustment points. (3) is the control cable screw; (4) is the injection pump shaft lock-nut; (A) is the fuel outlet fitting

5 FUEL SYSTEM

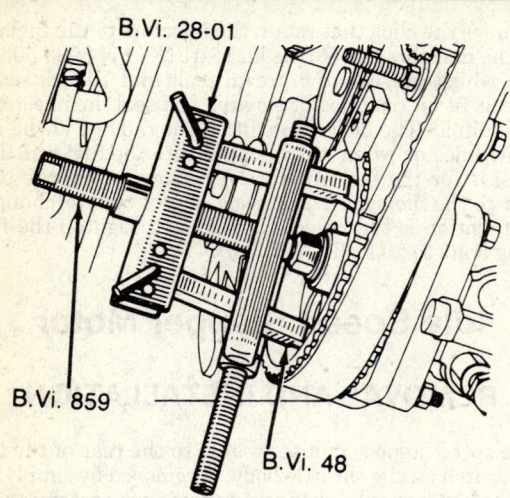

Injection pump sprocket removal tools

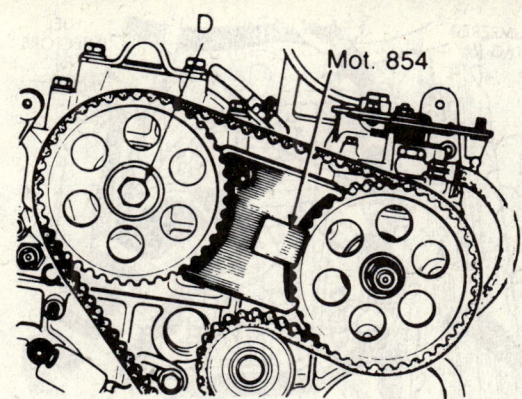

Sprocket holding tool. (D) is the camshaft sprocket bolt

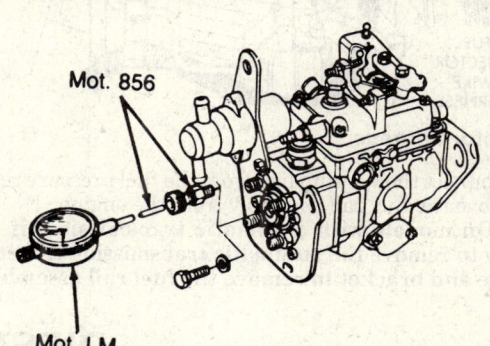

Installing the dial indicator and support tool

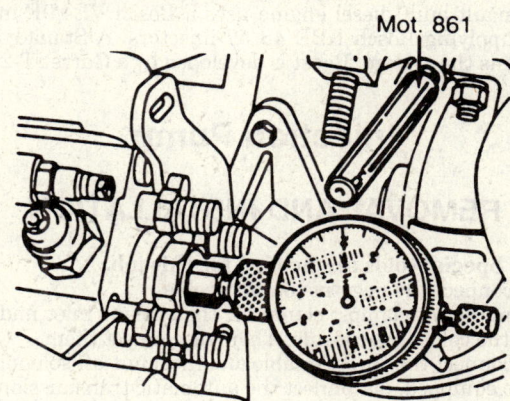

Injection timing procedure using a dial indicator

19. Remove the plastic shield from under the injection pump.
20. Remove the three retaining nuts located at the front of the injection pump. The lower nut is hard to get at. It may be necessary to remove the alternator to get a wrench on it.
21. Using the sprocket removal tool, separate the injection pump from the sprocket.
22. Remove the removal tool and the sprocket nut. The sprocket holding tool and the timing belt will hold the sprocket in plate, facilitating injection pump installation.
23. Remove the injection pump from the mounting brackets.
24. Remove the key from the shaft.
25. Remove the screw plug and copper washer located between the four high pressure fuel outlets, at the rear of the pump. Install dial indicator support tool Mot.856 in its place.
26. Install the stem of dial indicator Mot.LM in the support tool.
27. Position a locknut and nut on the end of the injection pump driveshaft.
28. Tighten the locknut against the nut.
29. Loosen the control cable set screw on the clevis, move the levers back slightly and turn the clevis pin 1/4 turn to disengage the cold start system.
30. Using the locknut, turn the pump driveshaft in the normal direction of rotation, to position the piston at bottom dead center. The dial indicator pointer will stop moving when the piston is at BDC. Zero the pointer.
31. The pump driveshaft keyway should be located just before the centerline of the number 1 fuel outlet fitting.
32. Remove the nut and locknut.
33. Insert the key in its keyway.
34. Mount the injection pump in the sprocket, aligning the key.
35. Loosely install the washers and retaining nuts on the mounting bracket studs.
36. Install the sprocket washer and retaining nut on the pump driveshaft. Torque the nut to 37 ft. lbs.
37. Remove the sprocket holding tool.
38. Rotate the crankshaft in a clockwise direction at least 2 full revolutions. Check the timing belt tension as follows:

   a. Loosen the timing belt tensioner bolts 1/2 turn each, maximum.
   b. The belt tensioner should, automatically, place the proper tension on the belt.
   c. Using belt tension gauge Ele.346–04, at the straight, upper run, between the pump and camshaft sprockets, check belt deflection. Deflection should be 3–5mm when the gauge shoulder is flush with the plunger body.

39. Remove the threaded plug from the block, just behind the pump, and insert TDC Rod Mot.861.
40. Slowly rotate the crankshaft clockwise until tool Mot.861 can be inserted into the TDC slot in the crankshaft counterweight.
41. At this point, the dial indicator pointer should indicate a piston travel distance of 0.82mm ± 0.02mm.
42. If the indicated travel is not within specifications, adjust it as follows:

   a. Rotate the pump toward, then away from the engine to increase travel, or:,
   b. Rotate the pump away from the engine to decrease lift.

NOTE: Adjustment should always be made by rotation away from the engine. That's why rotation toward the engine is necessary in Step 42a.

FUEL SYSTEM 5

43. Tighten the injection pump mounting nuts.
44. Remove the TDC Rod from the counterweight slot.
45. Observe the dial indicator and rotate the crankshaft clockwise 2 full revolutions until the rod can, once again, be installed into the counterweight hole. The dial indicator should return to 0, then move to 0.82mm ± 0.02mm. If so, injection pump static timing is correct.
46. Remove the TDC Rod and install the plug.
47. Remove the dial indicator and install the washer and screw plug in the pump.
48. Connect the high pressure lines at the injectors.
49. Compress the timing control lever and install the clevis pin in the first position on the cable clamp.
50. With the lever against the clevis, tighten the setscrew.
51. Install and tighten the pump rear support bracket nuts.
52. Install all other parts in reverse order of removal.

NOTE: Don't confuse the fuel delivery and return hose banjo bolts. The delivery banjo bolt has two 4mm diameter holes; the return banjo bolt has a calibrated orifice. Never use the banjo bolts from one pump on another!

Injectors

REMOVAL AND INSTALLATION

NOTE: A 13mm deep-well socket is necessary for this procedure.

1. Disconnect the negative battery cable.
2. Remove the fuel return hoses and fittings from the injectors.
3. Remove the high pressure lines from the injectors.
4. Remove both injector clamp nuts and washers from each injector.
5. Remove the injector clamp.
6. Pull the injector from the head.
7. Remove the copper seal and the heat shield.
8. Clean the injector bore with a brass brush.
9. Install a new heat shield and a new copper seal. Never reuse the old ones!
10. Install the injector, high pressure fuel lines (finger tight at this time), clamps, washers and nuts.
11. Tighten the high pressure fuel lines.
12. Use new washers and install the fuel return lines. Tighten the fittings to 88 inch lbs.

DIESEL INJECTION PUMP STATIC TIMING ADJUSTMENT

NOTE: Special tools are needed for this job.

1. Remove the injection pump as described above.
2. Remove the key from the shaft.
3. Remove the screw plug and copper washer located between the four high pressure fuel outlets, at the rear of the pump. Install dial indicator support tool Mot.856 in its place.
4. Install the stem of dial indicator Mot.LM in the support tool.
5. Position a locknut and nut on the end of the injection pump driveshaft.
6. Tighten the locknut against the nut.
7. Loosen the control cable set screw on the clevis, move the levers back slightly and turn the clevis pin 1/4 turn to disengage the cold start system.
8. Using the locknut, turn the pump driveshaft in the normal direction of rotation, to position the piston at bottom dead center. The dial indicator pointer will stop moving when the piston is at BDC. Zero the pointer.
9. The pump driveshaft keyway should be located just before the centerline of the number 1 fuel outlet fitting.
10. Remove the nut and locknut.
11. Insert the key in its keyway.
12. Mount the injection pump in the sprocket, aligning the key.
13. Loosely install the washers and retaining nuts on the mounting bracket studs.
14. Install the sprocket washer and retaining nut on the pump driveshaft. Torque the nut to 37 ft. lbs.
15. Remove the sprocket holding tool.
16. Rotate the crankshaft in a clockwise direction at least 2 full revolutions. Check the timing belt tension as follows:
    a. Loosen the timing belt tensioner bolts 1/2 turn each, maximum.
    b. The belt tensioner should, automatically, place the proper tension on the belt.
    c. Using belt tension gauge Ele.346–04, at the straight, upper run, between the pump and camshaft sprockets, check belt deflection. Deflection should be 3–5mm when the gauge shoulder is flush with the plunger body.
17. Remove the threaded plug from the block, just behind the pump, and insert TDC Rod Mot.861. 18. Slowly rotate the crankshaft clockwise until tool Mot.861 can be inserted into the TDC slot in the crankshaft counterweight.
19. At this point, the dial indicator pointer should indicate a piston travel distance of 0.82mm ± 0.02mm.
20. If the indicated travel is not within specifications, adjust it as follows:
    a. Rotate the pump toward, then away from the engine to increase travel, or
    b. Rotate the pump away from the engine to decrease lift.

NOTE: Adjustment should always be made by rotation away from the engine. That's why rotation toward the engine is necessary in Step 20a.

21. Tighten the injection pump mounting nuts.
22. Remove the TDC Rod from the counterweight slot.
23. Observe the dial indicator and rotate the crankshaft clockwise 2 full revolutions until the rod can, once again, be installed into the counterweight hole. The dial indicator should return to 0, then move to 0.82mm ± 0.02mm. If so, injection pump static timing is correct.
24. Remove the TDC Rod and install the plug.
25. Remove the dial indicator and install the washer and screw plug in the pump.
26. Connect the high pressure lines at the injectors.
27. Compress the timing control lever and install the clevis pin

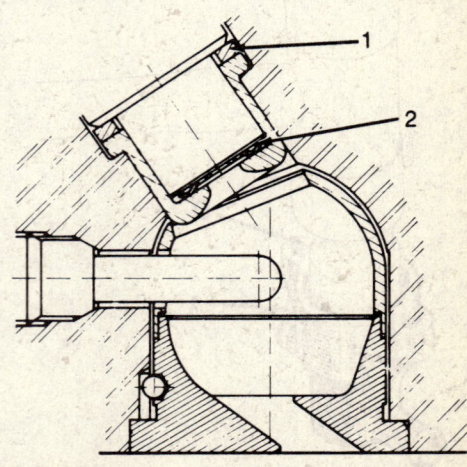

Diesel injector installed. (1) is the copper seal; (2) is the heat sheild

5-29

5 FUEL SYSTEM

in the first position on the cable clamp.
28. With the lever against the clevis, tighten the setscrew.
29. Install and tighten the pump rear support bracket nuts.
30. Install all other parts in reverse order of removal.
NOTE: Don't confuse the fuel delivery and return hose banjo bolts. The delivery banjo bolt has two 4mm diameter holes; the return banjo bolt has a calibrated orifice. Never use the banjo bolts from one pump on another!

Cold Start Capsule

REMOVAL AND INSTALLATION

NOTE: Two 6mm x 70mm threaded rods and nuts are necessary for this procedure.
1. Using heavy clamps, clamp off the coolant lines at the cold start capsule.

CAUTION
Follow this procedure exactly when removing the cold start capsule. There is a great deal of spring tension behind the housings.

2. Remove one of the capsule retaining bolts and replace it with a 6mm diameter × 70mm long threaded rod.
3. Thread a nut down the rod and tighten it.

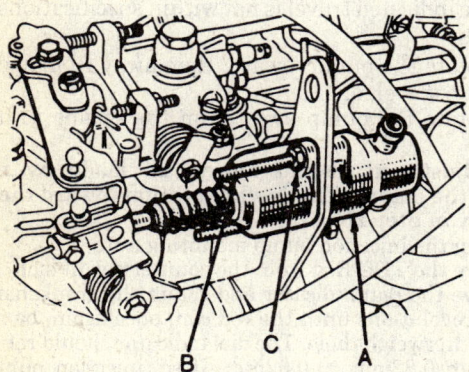
Cold start capsule A; threaded rod B; nut C

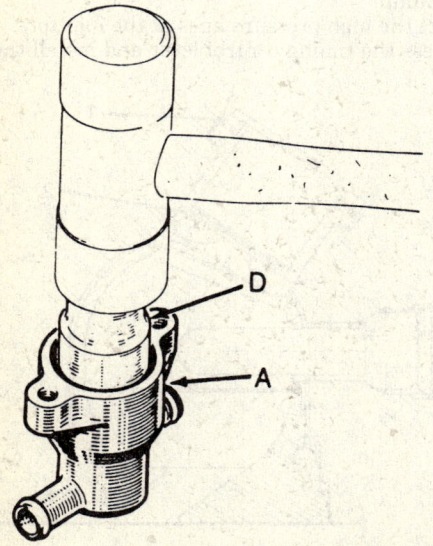
Loosening the slotted retaining nut

4. Remove the other bolt and replace it with a similar rod and nut.
5. Back off the two nuts, alternately and evenly, to release spring tension. Separate the capsule housing from the bracket and cable housing.
6. Remove the threaded rods.
7. Insert a 26mm OD section of tubing into the end of the capsule housing and hit the end sharply with a mallet to loosen the slotted retaining nut. Remove the nut, capsule and O-ring.
8. Assembly is the reverse of disassembly. Use the threaded rods to position the capsule housing, tightening them, alternately and evenly, then, replacing them, one at a time, with the bolts. Tighten the bolts securely.

Glow Plugs

REMOVAL AND INSTALLATION

1. Disconnect the battery ground.
2. Disconnect the wire from the glow plug.
3. Unscrew the glow plug from the head.
4. Installation is the reverse of removal. Use a small amount of anti-seize compound on the glow plug threads. Torque the glow plug to 20 ft. lbs.

Cold Start System

ADJUSTMENT

NOTE: The engine must be cold, shut off for at least 2½ hrs., before starting this procedure. Special tools and shims are necessary for this procedure.

1. Make sure that the timing control lever is contacting the stop. If not, loosen the setscrew and turn the clevis ¼ turn.
2. Remove the TDC slot access hole plug from the block, just behind the pump.
3. Rotate the crankshaft clockwise 2 full revolutions and insert the TDC Rod Mot.861, into the crankshaft counterweight TDC slot.
4. Move the timing control lever to the detent position.
5. Make sure that the clearance between the stop and the timing control lever is now 0.5mm. If not, turn the throttle stop adjustment screw, at the control lever, until it is.
6. Insert a 6.5mm shim between the timing control lever and the stop.
7. Insert a 3.0mm shim between the throttle lever and the idle stop screw.
8. Loosen the pivot ball nut and slide the pivot ball until it contacts the throttle lever. Tighten the nut.
9. Remove the shims.
10. The temperature of the capsule is now important. If the engine has been shut down for at least 2½ hrs., the capsule temperature should be the same as the ambient air temperature. Select a shim as follows:
  - below 66°F (19°C): 6.5mm
  - 66°F–71°F (19–22°C): 5.9mm
  - 72°F–76°F (22–24°C): 5.5mm
  - 77°F–85°F (25–29°C): 4.75mm
  - 86°F–94°F (30–34°C): 4.0mm
  - 95°F–104°F (35–40°C): 3.25mm
11. When the shim thickness has been determined, place the shim between the timing control lever and the stop.
12. Align the clevis and the throttle cable stop so that both screw heads are in the same plane.
13. Tighten the throttle cable and position the clevis and the throttle stop so that they contact the timing control lever.

FUEL SYSTEM 5

14. Tighten the throttle cable stop screw.
15. Remove the shim and make sure that the distance between the stop and the timing control lever is the same as the thickness of the shim. Correct it if necessary.
16. Start the engine and run it to normal operating temperature.
17. Make sure that the throttle lever and timing control lever are against their stops and move freely.
18. If necessary, adjust the idle with the idle adjustment screw to obtain an idle of 800 rpm.
19. Insert a 6.5mm shim between the timing control lever and its stop and measure the clearance between the throttle control lever and its stop. The clearance should be 3.0mm. If not, repeat the above adjustments.

FUEL TANK

REMOVAL AND INSTALLATION

— CAUTION —
If the vehicle is equipped with the Multi Point Fuel Injection, perform the fuel system pressure release sequence described earlier in this Section.

1. Remove the fuel filler cap.
2. Drain the fuel tank.
3. Raise and support the vehicle safely.
4. On 1986–91 Comanche, remove the rear drive shaft.
5. Disconnect all hoses and wires connected to the tank.

— CAUTION —
Wrap heavy shop towels around disconnected fuel lines to absorb spilled fuel. Be prepared to catch any fuel that is not absorbed!

6. Remove the skid plate, if equipped.
7. Remove the fuel tank shield.
8. Support the tank with a floor jack and remove the strap nuts.
9. Partially lower the tank and disconnect the tank vapor vent hoses.
10. Remove the tank.
11. Inspect for rotted or leaking fuel lines
12. Installation is the reverse of removal.
13. If 2 straps are used to secure the fuel tank, tighten them to 100 inch lbs. torque. If 3 straps are used, tighten the center strap to 43 inch lbs.; the outer straps to 65 inch lbs. torque.

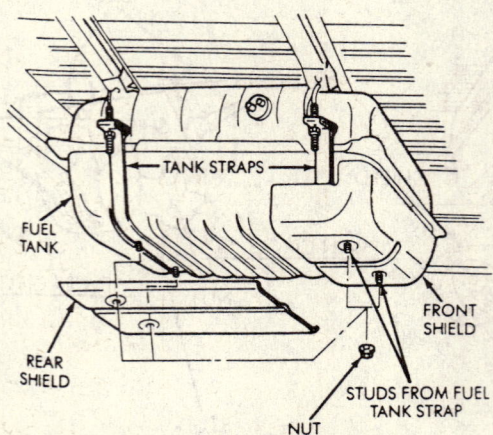
Fuel tank and shield, short bed Comanche

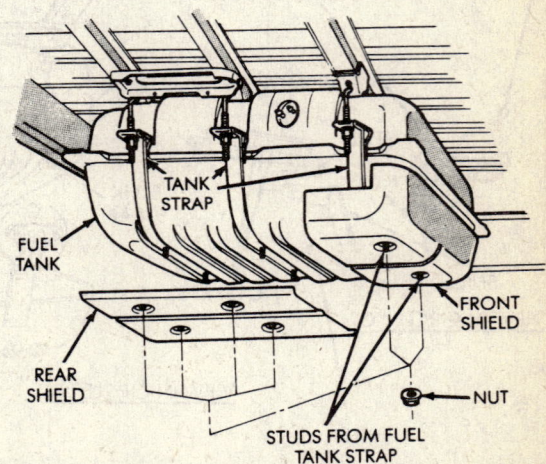
Fuel tank and shield, 2wd and 4wd long bed Comanche without skid plate

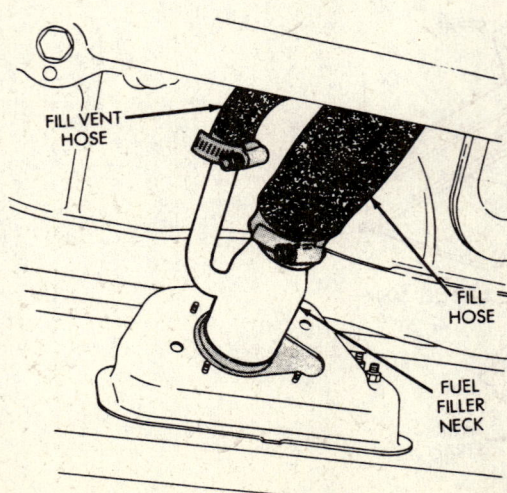
Filler neck hose removal/installation

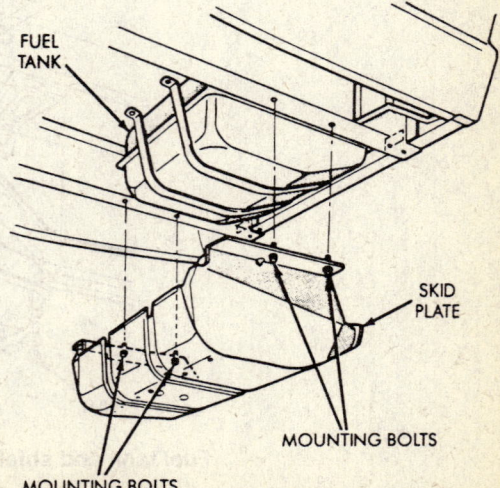
Wagoneer/Cherokee skid plate removal/installation

5-31

5 FUEL SYSTEM

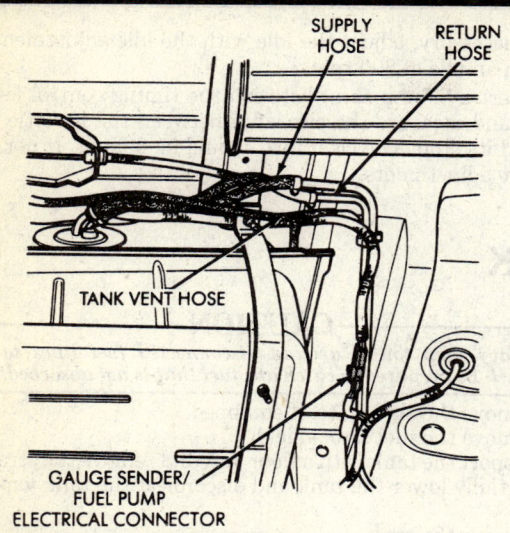

Fuel tank hose removal/installation

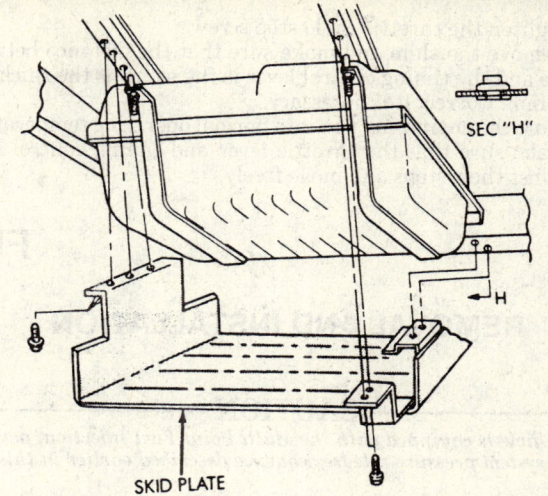

Comanche skid plate removal/installation

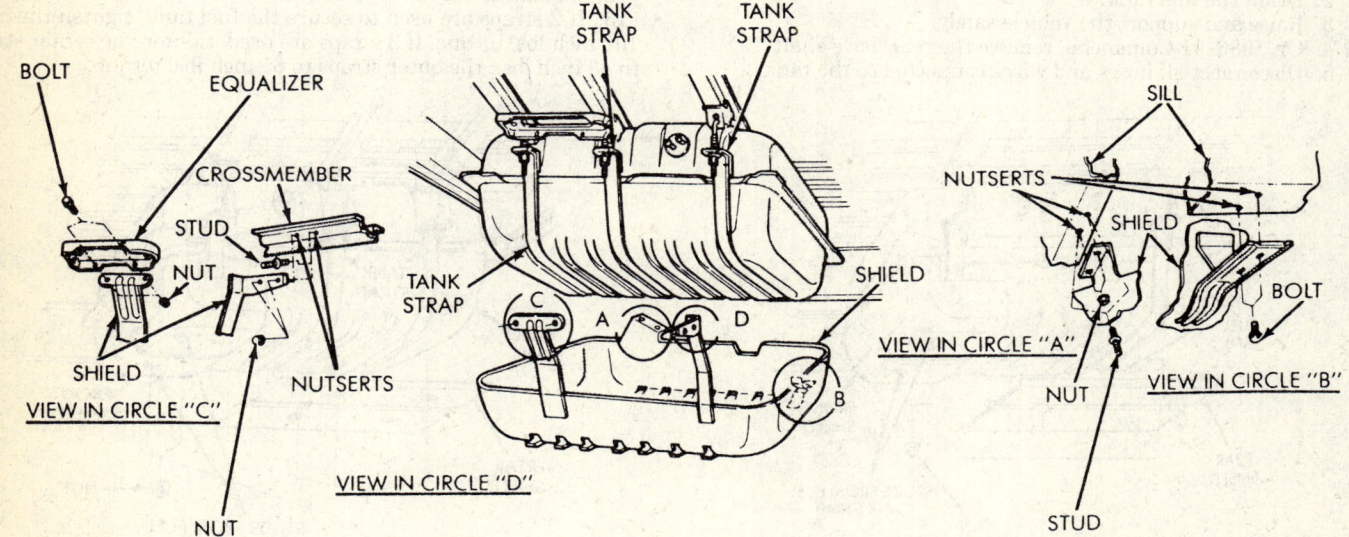

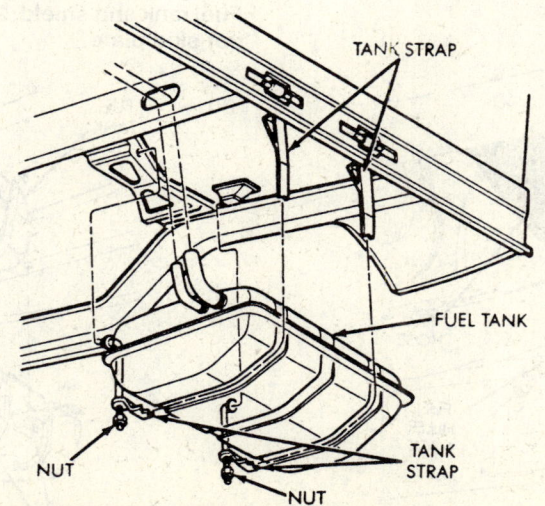

Fuel tank and shield, Wagoneer/Cherokee

Chassis Electrical 6

QUICK REFERENCE INDEX

Circuit Protection	6-39
Cruise Control	6-15
Heating and Air Conditioning	6-8
Instruments and Switches	6-28
Lighting	6-31
Radio	6-13
Theft Security System	6-21
Troubleshooting Charts	6-44
Understanding Electrical Systems	6-2
Windshield Wipers	6-14
Wiring Diagrams	6-49

GENERAL INDEX

Air conditioning
- Blower 6-8, 9
- Control panel 6-10
- Evaporator 6-9, 11
- Expansion valve 6-13
- Receiver/drier 6-13
- Water control valve 6-13

Blower motor 6-8, 9

Chassis electrical system
- Fuses 6-39
- Fusible links 6-39, 43
- Heater and air conditioning 6-8
- Instrument cluster 6-28
- Lighting 6-31
- Windshield wipers 6-14

Control panel 6-10

Cruise control
- Control module 6-16
- Control servo 6-16
- Control switch 6-16
- Diagnosis and wiring 6-17
- Operation 6-15
- Servo cable 6-20
- Speed sensor 6-16

Evaporator 6-9, 11
Fuses 6-39

Fusible links 6-39, 43
Headlights 6-32
Headlight switch 6-31

Heater
- Blower 6-8
- Control panel 6-10
- Core 6-10

Instrument cluster 6-28

Instrument Panel
- Cluster 6-28
- Gauges 6-29
- Overhead console 6-31
- Panel 6-28
- Printed circuit board 6-29
- Radio 6-13
- Speedometer 6-29

Lighting
- Fog lights 6-33
- Headlights 6-32
- Illuminated entry system 6-31
- License plate light 6-35
- Light bulb application chart 6-38
- Signal and marker lights 6-35

Marker lights 6-35
Radio 6-13
Speedometer cable 6-29

Switches
- Headlight 6-31
- Windshield wiper 6-14, 31

Theft Security System
- Control module 6-23
- Diagnosis 6-22, 24
- Door switch 6-23
- General information 6-21
- Hood switch 6-23

Trailer wiring 6-38

Troubleshooting
- Cruise control 6-17
- Gauges 6-47
- Heater 6-45
- Lights 6-46
- Theft Security System 6-22, 24
- Turn signals and flashers 6-44
- Windshield wipers 6-48

Windshield wipers
- Arm and blade 6-14
- Liftgate wiper 6-15
- Linkage 6-15
- Motor 6-14
- Switch 6-14, 31
- Troubleshooting 6-48

Wiring diagrams 6-49

6-1

6 CHASSIS ELECTRICAL

UNDERSTANDING AND TROUBLESHOOTING ELECTRICAL SYSTEMS

With the rate at which both import and domestic manufacturers are incorporating electronic control systems into their production lines, it won't be long before every new vehicle is equipped with one or more on-board computer, like the unit installed on the truck. These electronic components (with no moving parts) should theoretically last the life of the vehicle, provided nothing external happens to damage the circuits or memory chips.

While it is true that electronic components should never wear out, in the real world malfunctions do occur. It is also true that any computer-based system is extremely sensitive to electrical voltages and cannot tolerate careless or haphazard testing or service procedures. An inexperienced individual can literally do major damage looking for a minor problem by using the wrong kind of test equipment or connecting test leads or connectors with the ignition switch ON. When selecting test equipment, make sure the manufacturers instructions state that the tester is compatible with whatever type of electronic control system is being serviced. Read all instructions carefully and double check all test points before installing probes or making any test connections.

The following section outlines basic diagnosis techniques for dealing with computerized automotive control systems. Along with a general explanation of the various types of test equipment available to aid in servicing modern electronic automotive systems, basic repair techniques for wiring harnesses and connectors is given. Read the basic information before attempting any repairs or testing on any computerized system, to provide the background of information necessary to avoid the most common and obvious mistakes that can cost both time and money. Although the replacement and testing procedures are simple in themselves, the systems are not, and unless one has a thorough understanding of all components and their function within a particular computerized control system, the logical test sequence these systems demand cannot be followed. Minor malfunctions can make a big difference, so it is important to know how each component affects the operation of the overall electronic system to find the ultimate cause of a problem without replacing good components unnecessarily. It is not enough to use the correct test equipment; the test equipment must be used correctly.

Safety Precautions

— CAUTION —
Whenever working on or around any computer based microprocessor control system, always observe these general precautions to prevent the possibility of personal injury or damage to electronic components.

- Never install or remove battery cables with the key ON or the engine running. Jumper cables should be connected with the key OFF to avoid power surges that can damage electronic control units. Engines equipped with computer controlled systems should avoid both giving and getting jump starts due to the possibility of serious damage to components from arcing in the engine compartment when connections are made with the ignition ON.
- Always remove the battery cables before charging the battery. Never use a high output charger on an installed battery or attempt to use any type of "hot shot" (24 volt) starting aid.
- Exercise care when inserting test probes into connectors to insure good connections without damaging the connector or spreading the pins. Always probe connectors from the rear (wire) side, NOT the pin side, to avoid accidental shorting of terminals during test procedures.
- Never remove or attach wiring harness connectors with the ignition switch ON, especially to an electronic control unit.
- Do not drop any components during service procedures and never apply 12 volts directly to any component (like a solenoid or relay) unless instructed specifically to do so. Some component electrical windings are designed to safely handle only 4 or 5 volts and can be destroyed in seconds if 12 volts are applied directly to the connector.
- Remove the electronic control unit if the vehicle is to be placed in an environment where temperatures exceed approximately 176°F (80°C), such as a paint spray booth or when arc or gas welding near the control unit location in the car.

ORGANIZED TROUBLESHOOTING

When diagnosing a specific problem, organized troubleshooting is a must. The complexity of a modern automobile demands that you approach any problem in a logical, organized manner. There are certain troubleshooting techniques that are standard:

1. Establish when the problem occurs. Does the problem appear only under certain conditions? Were there any noises, odors, or other unusual symptoms?
2. Isolate the problem area. To do this, make some simple tests and observations; then eliminate the systems that are working properly. Check for obvious problems such as broken wires, dirty connections or split or disconnected vacuum hoses. Always check the obvious before assuming something complicated is the cause.
3. Test for problems systematically to determine the cause once the problem area is isolated. Are all the components functioning properly? Is there power going to electrical switches and motors? Is there vacuum at vacuum switches and/or actuators? Is there a mechanical problem such as bent linkage or loose mounting screws? Doing careful, systematic checks will often turn up most causes on the first inspection without wasting time checking components that have little or no relationship to the problem.
4. Test all repairs after the work is done to make sure that the problem is fixed. Some causes can be traced to more than one component, so a careful verification of repair work is important to pick up additional malfunctions that may cause a problem to reappear or a different problem to arise. A blown fuse, for example, is a simple problem that may require more than another fuse to repair. If you don't look for a problem that caused a fuse to blow, for example, a shorted wire may go undetected.

Experience has shown that most problems tend to be the result of a fairly simple and obvious cause, such as loose or corroded connectors or air leaks in the intake system; making careful inspection of components during testing essential to quick and accurate troubleshooting. Special, hand held computerized testers designed specifically for diagnosing the system are available from a variety of aftermarket sources, as well as from the vehicle manufacturer, but care should be taken that any test equipment being used is designed to diagnose that particular computer controlled system accurately without damaging the control unit (ECU) or components being tested.

NOTE: Pinpointing the exact cause of trouble in an electrical system can sometimes only be accomplished by the use of special test equipment. The following describes commonly used test equipment and explains how to put it to best use in diagnosis. In addition to the information covered below, the manufacturer's instructions booklet provided with the tester should be read and clearly understood before attempting any test procedures.

CHASSIS ELECTRICAL 6

TEST EQUIPMENT

Jumper Wires

Jumper wires are simple, yet extremely valuable, pieces of test equipment. Jumper wires are merely wires that are used to bypass sections of a circuit. The simplest type of jumper wire is merely a length of multistrand wire with an alligator clip at each end. Jumper wires are usually fabricated from lengths of standard automotive wire and whatever type of connector (alligator clip, spade connector or pin connector) that is required for the particular vehicle being tested. The well equipped tool box will have several different styles of jumper wires in several different lengths. Some jumper wires are made with three or more terminals coming from a common splice for special purpose testing. In cramped, hard-to-reach areas it is advisable to have insulated boots over the jumper wire terminals in order to prevent accidental grounding, sparks, and possible fire, especially when testing fuel system components.

Jumper wires are used primarily to locate open electrical circuits, on either the ground (−) side of the circuit or on the hot (+) side. If an electrical component fails to operate, connect the jumper wire between the component and a good ground. If the component operates only with the jumper installed, the ground circuit is open. If the ground circuit is good, but the component does not operate, the circuit between the power feed and component is open. You can sometimes connect the jumper wire directly from the battery to the hot terminal of the component, but first make sure the component uses 12 volts in operation. Some electrical components, such as fuel injectors, are designed to operate on about 4 volts and running 12 volts directly to the injector terminals can burn out the wiring. By inserting an inline fuse holder between a set of test leads, a fused jumper wire can be used for bypassing open circuits. Use a 5 amp fuse to provide protection against voltage spikes. When in doubt, use a voltmeter to check the voltage input to the component and measure how much voltage is being applied normally. By moving the jumper wire successively back from the lamp toward the power source, you can isolate the area of the circuit where the open is located. When the component stops functioning, or the power is cut off, the open is in the segment of wire between the jumper and the point previously tested.

CAUTION

Never use jumpers made from wire that is of lighter gauge than used in the circuit under test. If the jumper wire is of too small gauge, it may overheat and possibly melt. Never use jumpers to bypass high resistance loads (such as motors) in a circuit. Bypassing resistances, in effect, creates a short circuit which may, in turn, cause damage and fire. Never use a jumper for anything other than temporary bypassing of components in a circuit.

---

12 Volt Test Light

The 12 volt test light is used to check circuits and components while electrical current is flowing through them. It is used for voltage and ground tests. Twelve volt test lights come in different styles but all have three main parts; a ground clip, a probe, and a light. The most commonly used 12 volt test lights have pick-type probes. To use a 12 volt test light, connect the ground clip to a good ground and probe wherever necessary with the pick. The pick should be sharp so that it can penetrate wire insulation to make contact with the wire, without making a large hole in the insulation. The wrap-around light is handy in hard to reach areas or where it is difficult to support a wire to push a probe pick into it. To use the wrap around light, hook the wire to probed with the hook and pull the trigger. A small pick will be forced through the wire insulation into the wire core.

CAUTION

Do not use a test light to probe electronic ignition spark plug or coil wires. Never use a pick-type test light to probe wiring on computer controlled systems unless specifically instructed to do so. Any wire insulation that is pierced by the test light probe should be taped and sealed with silicone after testing.

Like the jumper wire, the 12 volt test light is used to isolate opens in circuits. But, whereas the jumper wire is used to bypass the open to operate the load, the 12 volt test light is used to locate the presence of voltage in a circuit. If the test light glows, you know that there is power up to that point; if the 12 volt test light does not glow when its probe is inserted into the wire or connector, you know that there is an open circuit (no power). Move the test light in successive steps back toward the power source until the light in the handle does glow. When it does glow, the open is between the probe and point previously probed.

NOTE: The test light does not detect that 12 volts (or any particular amount of voltage) is present; it only detects that some voltage is present. It is advisable before using the test light to touch its terminals across the battery posts to make sure the light is operating properly.

Self-Powered Test Light

The self-powered test light usually contains a 1.5 volt penlight battery. One type of self-powered test light is similar in design to the 12 volt test light. This type has both the battery and the light in the handle and pick-type probe tip. The second type has the light toward the open tip, so that the light illuminates the contact point. The self-powered test light is dual purpose piece of test equipment. It can be used to test for either open or short circuits when power is isolated from the circuit (continuity test). A powered test light should not be used on any computer controlled system or component unless specifically instructed to do so. Many engine sensors can be destroyed by even this small amount of voltage applied directly to the terminals.

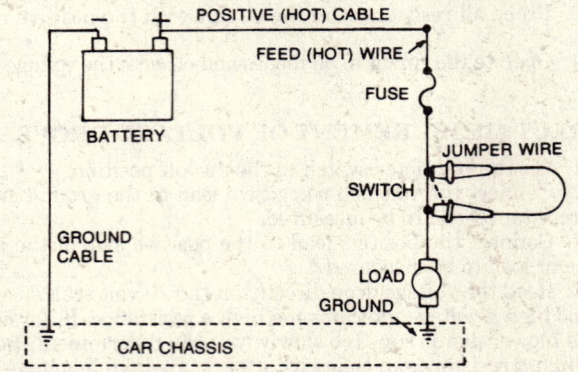

Bypassing a switch with a jumper wire

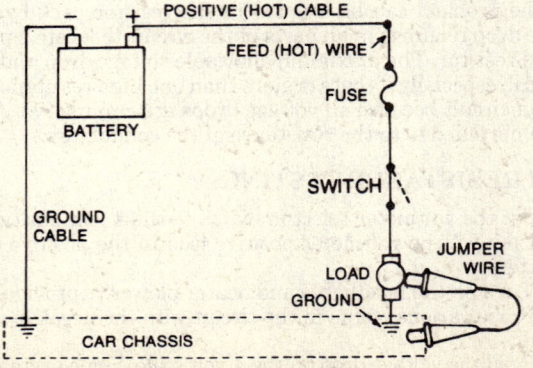

Checking for a bad ground with a jumper wire

6 CHASSIS ELECTRICAL

Open Circuit Testing

To use the self-powered test light to check for open circuits, first isolate the circuit from the vehicle's 12 volt power source by disconnecting the battery or wiring harness connector. Connect the test light ground clip to a good ground and probe sections of the circuit sequentially with the test light. (start from either end of the circuit). If the light is out, the open is between the probe and the circuit ground. If the light is on, the open is between the probe and end of the circuit toward the power source.

Short Circuit Testing

By isolating the circuit both from power and from ground, and using a self-powered test light, you can check for shorts to ground in the circuit. Isolate the circuit from power and ground. Connect the test light ground clip to a good ground and probe any easy-to-reach test point in the circuit. If the light comes on, there is a short somewhere in the circuit. To isolate the short, probe a test point at either end of the isolated circuit (the light should be on). Leave the test light probe connected and open connectors, switches, remove parts, etc., sequentially, until the light goes out. When the light goes out, the short is between the last circuit component opened and the previous circuit opened.

NOTE: The 1.5 volt battery in the test light does not provide much current. A weak battery may not provide enough power to illuminate the test light even when a complete circuit is made (especially if there are high resistances in the circuit). Always make sure that the test battery is strong. To check the battery, briefly touch the ground clip to the probe; if the light glows brightly the battery is strong enough for testing. Never use a self-powered test light to perform checks for opens or shorts when power is applied to the electrical system under test. The 12 volt vehicle power will quickly burn out the 1.5 volt light bulb in the test light.

Voltmeter

A voltmeter is used to measure voltage at any point in a circuit, or to measure the voltage drop across any part of a circuit. It can also be used to check continuity in a wire or circuit by indicating current flow from one end to the other. Voltmeters usually have various scales on the meter dial and a selector switch to allow the selection of different voltages. The voltmeter has a positive and a negative lead. To avoid damage to the meter, always connect the negative lead to the negative (–) side of circuit (to ground or nearest the ground side of the circuit) and connect the positive lead to the positive (+) side of the circuit (to the power source or the nearest power source). Note that the negative voltmeter lead will always be black and that the positive voltmeter will always be some color other than black (usually red). Depending on how the voltmeter is connected into the circuit, it has several uses.

A voltmeter can be connected either in parallel or in series with a circuit and it has a very high resistance to current flow. When connected in parallel, only a small amount of current will flow through the voltmeter current path; the rest will flow through the normal circuit current path and the circuit will work normally. When the voltmeter is connected in series with a circuit, only a small amount of current can flow through the circuit. The circuit will not work properly, but the voltmeter reading will show if the circuit is complete or not.

Available Voltage Measurement

Set the voltmeter selector switch to the 20V position and connect the meter negative lead to the negative post of the battery. Connect the positive meter lead to the positive post of the battery and turn the ignition switch ON to provide a load. Read the voltage on the meter or digital display. A well charged battery should register over 12 volts. If the meter reads below 11.5 volts, the battery power may be insufficient to operate the electrical system properly. This test determines voltage available from the battery and should be the first step in any electrical trouble diagnosis procedure. Many electrical problems, especially on computer controlled systems, can be caused by a low state of charge in the battery. Excessive corrosion at the battery cable terminals can cause a poor contact that will prevent proper charging and full battery current flow.

Normal battery voltage is 12 volts when fully charged. When the battery is supplying current to one or more circuits it is said to be "under load". When everything is off the electrical system is under a "no-load" condition. A fully charged battery may show about 12.5 volts at no load; will drop to 12 volts under medium load; and will drop even lower under heavy load. If the battery is partially discharged the voltage decrease under heavy load may be excessive, even though the battery shows 12 volts or more at no load. When allowed to discharge further, the battery's available voltage under load will decrease more severely. For this reason, it is important that the battery be fully charged during all testing procedures to avoid errors in diagnosis and incorrect test results.

Voltage Drop

When current flows through a resistance, the voltage beyond the resistance is reduced (the larger the current, the greater the reduction in voltage). When no current is flowing, there is no voltage drop because there is no current flow. All points in the circuit which are connected to the power source are at the same voltage as the power source. The total voltage drop always equals the total source voltage. In a long circuit with many connectors, a series of small, unwanted voltage drops due to corrosion at the connectors can add up to a total loss of voltage which impairs the operation of the normal loads in the circuit.

INDIRECT COMPUTATION OF VOLTAGE DROPS

1. Set the voltmeter selector switch to the 20 volt position.
2. Connect the meter negative lead to a good ground.
3. Probe all resistances in the circuit with the positive meter lead.
4. Operate the circuit in all modes and observe the voltage readings.

DIRECT MEASUREMENT OF VOLTAGE DROPS

1. Set the voltmeter switch to the 20 volt position.
2. Connect the voltmeter negative lead to the ground side of the resistance load to be measured.
3. Connect the positive lead to the positive side of the resistance or load to be measured.
4. Read the voltage drop directly on the 20 volt scale.

Too high a voltage indicates too high a resistance. If, for example, a blower motor runs too slowly, you can determine if there is too high a resistance in the resistor pack. By taking voltage drop readings in all parts of the circuit, you can isolate the problem. Too low a voltage drop indicates too low a resistance. If, for example, a blower motor runs too fast in the MED and/or LOW position, the problem can be isolated in the resistor pack by taking voltage drop readings in all parts of the circuit to locate a possibly shorted resistor. The maximum allowable voltage drop under load is critical, especially if there is more than one high resistance problem in a circuit because all voltage drops are cumulative. A small drop is normal due to the resistance of the conductors.

HIGH RESISTANCE TESTING

1. Set the voltmeter selector switch to the 4 volt position.
2. Connect the voltmeter positive lead to the positive post of the battery.
3. Turn on the headlights and heater blower to provide a load.
4. Probe various points in the circuit with the negative voltmeter lead.
5. Read the voltage drop on the 4 volt scale. Some average maximum allowable voltage drops are:

CHASSIS ELECTRICAL 6

FUSE PANEL — 7 volts
IGNITION SWITCH — 5 volts
HEADLIGHT SWITCH — 7 volts
IGNITION COIL (+) — 5 volts
ANY OTHER LOAD — 1.3 volts

NOTE: Voltage drops are all measured while a load is operating; without current flow, there will be no voltage drop.

Ohmmeter

The ohmmeter is designed to read resistance, in ohms (Ω), in a circuit or component. Although there are several different styles of ohmmeters, all will usually have a selector switch which permits the measurement of different ranges of resistance (usually the selector switch allows the multiplication of the meter reading by 10, 100, 1000, and 10,000). A calibration knob allows the meter to be set at zero for accurate measurement. Since all ohmmeters are powered by an internal battery (usually 9 volts), the ohmmeter can be used as a self-powered test light. When the ohmmeter is connected, current from the ohmmeter flows through the circuit or component being tested. Since the ohmmeter's internal resistance and voltage are known values, the amount of current flow through the meter depends on the resistance of the circuit or component being tested.

The ohmmeter can be used to perform continuity test for opens or shorts (either by observation of the meter needle or as a self-powered test light), and to read actual resistance in a circuit. It should be noted that the ohmmeter is used to check the resistance of a component or wire while there is no voltage applied to the circuit. Current flow from an outside voltage source (such as the vehicle battery) can damage the ohmmeter, so the circuit or component should be isolated from the vehicle electrical system before any testing is done. Since the ohmmeter uses its own voltage source, either lead can be connected to any test point.

NOTE: When checking diodes or other solid state components, the ohmmeter leads can only be connected one way in order to measure current flow in a single direction. Make sure the positive (+) and negative (-) terminal connections are as described in the test procedures to verify the one-way diode operation.

In using the meter for making continuity checks, do not be concerned with the actual resistance readings. Zero resistance, or any resistance readings, indicate continuity in the circuit. Infinite resistance indicates an open in the circuit. A high resistance reading where there should be none indicates a problem in the circuit. Checks for short circuits are made in the same manner as checks for open circuits except that the circuit must be isolated from both power and normal ground. Infinite resistance indicates no continuity to ground, while zero resistance indicates a dead short to ground.

RESISTANCE MEASUREMENT

The batteries in an ohmmeter will weaken with age and temperature, so the ohmmeter must be calibrated or "zeroed" before taking measurements. To zero the meter, place the selector switch in its lowest range and touch the two ohmmeter leads together. Turn the calibration knob until the meter needle is exactly on zero.

NOTE: All analog (needle) type ohmmeters must be zeroed before use, but some digital ohmmeter models are automatically calibrated when the switch is turned on. Self-calibrating digital ohmmeters do not have an adjusting knob, but its a good idea to check for a zero readout before use by touching the leads together. All computer controlled systems require the use of a digital ohmmeter with at least 10 megohms ($M\Omega$) impedance for testing. Before any test procedures are attempted, make sure the ohmmeter used is compatible with the electrical system or damage to the on-board computer could result.

To measure resistance, first isolate the circuit from the vehicle power source by disconnecting the battery cables or the harness connector. Make sure the key is OFF when disconnecting any components or the battery. Where necessary, also isolate at least one side of the circuit to be checked to avoid reading parallel resistances. Parallel circuit resistances will always give a lower reading than the actual resistance of either of the branches. When measuring the resistance of parallel circuits, the total resistance will always be lower than the smallest resistance in the circuit. Connect the meter leads to both sides of the circuit (wire or component) and read the actual measured ohms on the meter scale. Make sure the selector switch is set to the proper ohm scale for the circuit being tested to avoid misreading the ohmmeter test value.

--- **CAUTION** ---
Never use an ohmmeter with power applied to the circuit. Like the self-powered test light, the ohmmeter is designed to operate on its own power supply. The normal 12 volt automotive electrical system current could damage the meter.

Ammeters

An ammeter measures the amount of current flowing through a circuit in units called amperes or amps. Amperes are units of electron flow which indicate how fast the electrons are flowing through the circuit. Since Ohms Law dictates that current flow in a circuit is equal to the circuit voltage divided by the total circuit resistance, increasing voltage also increases the current level (amps). Likewise, any decrease in resistance will increase the amount of amps in a circuit. At normal operating voltage, most circuits have a characteristic amount of amperes, called "current draw" which can be measured using an ammeter. By referring to a specified current draw rating, measuring the amperes, and comparing the two values, one can determine what is happening within the circuit to aid in diagnosis. An open circuit, for example, will not allow any current to flow so the ammeter reading will be zero. More current flows through a heavily loaded circuit or when the charging system is operating.

An ammeter is always connected in series with the circuit being tested. All of the current that normally flows through the circuit must also flow through the ammeter; if there is any other path for the current to follow, the ammeter reading will not be accurate. The ammeter itself has very little resistance to current flow and therefore will not affect the circuit, but it will measure current draw only when the circuit is closed and electricity is flowing. Excessive current draw can blow fuses and drain the battery, while a reduced current draw can cause motors to run slowly, lights to dim and other components to not operate properly. The ammeter can help diagnose these conditions by locating the cause of the high or low reading.

Multimeters

Different combinations of test meters can be built into a single unit designed for specific tests. Some of the more common combination test devices are known as Volt/Amp testers, Tach/Dwell meters, or Digital multimeters. The Volt/Amp tester is used for charging system, starting system or battery tests and consists of a voltmeter, an ammeter and a variable resistance carbon pile. The voltmeter will usually have at least two ranges for use with 6, 12 and 24 volt systems. The ammeter also has more than one range for testing various levels of battery loads and starter current draw and the carbon pile can be adjusted to offer different amounts of resistance. The Volt/Amp tester has heavy leads to carry large amounts of current and many later models have an inductive ammeter pickup that clamps around the wire to simplify test connections. On some models, the ammeter also has a zero-center scale to allow testing of charging and starting systems without switching leads or polarity. A digital multimeter is a voltmeter, ammeter and ohmmeter combined in an instrument which gives a digital readout. These are often used when testing solid state circuits be-

6-5

6 CHASSIS ELECTRICAL

cause of their high input impedance (usually 10 megohms or more).

The tach/dwell meter combines a tachometer and a dwell (cam angle) meter and is a specialized kind of voltmeter. The tachometer scale is marked to show engine speed in rpm and the dwell scale is marked to show degrees of distributor shaft rotation. In most electronic ignition systems, dwell is determined by the control unit, but the dwell meter can also be used to check the duty cycle (operation) of some electronic engine control systems. Some tach/dwell meters are powered by an internal battery, while others take their power from the car battery in use. The battery powered testers usually require calibration much like an ohmmeter before testing.

Special Test Equipment

A variety of diagnostic tools are available to help troubleshoot and repair computerized engine control systems. The most sophisticated of these devices are the console type engine analyzers that usually occupy a garage service bay, but there are several types of aftermarket electronic testers available that will allow quick circuit tests of the engine control system by plugging directly into a special connector located in the engine compartment or under the dashboard. Several tool and equipment manufacturers offer simple, hand held testers that measure various circuit voltage levels on command to check all system components for proper operation. Although these testers usually cost about $300–$500, consider that the average computer control unit (or ECM) can cost just as much and the money saved by not replacing perfectly good sensors or components in an attempt to correct a problem could justify the purchase price of a special diagnostic tester the first time it's used.

These computerized testers can allow quick and easy test measurements while the engine is operating or while the car is being driven. In addition, the on-board computer memory can be read to access any stored trouble codes; in effect allowing the computer to tell you where it hurts and aid trouble diagnosis by pinpointing exactly which circuit or component is malfunctioning. In the same manner, repairs can be tested to make sure the problem has been corrected. The biggest advantage these special testers have is their relatively easy hookups that minimize or eliminate the chances of making the wrong connections and getting false voltage readings or damaging the computer accidentally.

NOTE: It should be remembered that these testers check voltage levels in circuits; they don't detect mechanical problems or failed components if the circuit voltage falls within the preprogrammed limits stored in the tester PROM unit. Also, most of the hand held testers are designed to work only on one or two systems made by a specific manufacturer.

A variety of aftermarket testers are available to help diagnose different computerized control systems. Owatonna Tool Company (OTC), for example, markets a device called the OTC Monitor which plugs directly into the assembly line diagnostic link (ALDL). The OTC tester makes diagnosis a simple matter of pressing the correct buttons and, by changing the internal PROM or inserting a different diagnosis cartridge, it will work on any model from full size to subcompact, over a wide range of years. An adapter is supplied with the tester to allow connection to all types of ALDL links, regardless of the number of pin terminals used. By inserting an updated PROM into the OTC tester, it can be easily updated to diagnose any new modifications of computerized control systems.

Wiring Harnesses

The average automobile contains about 1/2 mile of wiring, with hundreds of individual connections. To protect the many wires from damage and to keep them from becoming a confusing tangle, they are organized into bundles, enclosed in plastic or taped together and called wire harnesses. Different wiring harnesses serve different parts of the vehicle. Individual wires are color coded to help trace them through a harness where sections are hidden from view.

A loose or corroded connection or a replacement wire that is too small for the circuit will add extra resistance and an additional voltage drop to the circuit. A ten percent voltage drop can result in slow or erratic motor operation, for example, even though the circuit is complete. Automotive wiring or circuit conductors can be in any one of three forms:
1. Single strand wire
2. Multistrand wire
3. Printed circuitry

Single strand wire has a solid metal core and is usually used inside such components as alternators, motors, relays and other devices. Multistrand wire has a core made of many small strands of wire twisted together into a single conductor. Most of the wiring in an automotive electrical system is made up of multistrand wire, either as a single conductor or grouped together in a harness. All wiring is color coded on the insulator, either as a solid color or as a colored wire with an identification stripe. A printed circuit is a thin film of copper or other conductor that is printed on an insulator backing. Occasionally, a printed circuit is sandwiched between two sheets of plastic for more protection and flexibility. A complete printed circuit, consisting of conductors, insulating material and connectors for lamps or other components is called a printed circuit board. Printed circuitry is used in place of individual wires or harnesses in places where space is limited, such as behind instrument panels.

Wire Gauge

Since computer controlled automotive electrical systems are very sensitive to changes in resistance, the selection of properly sized wires is critical when systems are repaired. The wire gauge number is an expression of the cross section area of the conductor. The most common system for expressing wire size is the American Wire Gauge (AWG) system.

Wire cross section area is measured in circular mils. A mil is $1/1000$ in.. or 0.001 in. or 0.0254mm; a circular mil is the area of a circle one mil in diameter. For example, a conductor 1/4 in. (6mm) in diameter is 0.250 in. or 250 mils. The circular mil cross section area of the wire is 250 squared (250^2) or 62,500 circular mils. Imported car models usually use metric wire gauge designations, which is simply the cross section area of the conductor in square millimeters (mm^2).

Gauge numbers are assigned to conductors of various cross section areas. As gauge number increases, area decreases and the conductor becomes smaller. A 5 gauge conductor is smaller than a 1 gauge conductor and a 10 gauge is smaller than a 5 gauge. As the cross section area of a conductor decreases, resistance increases and so does the gauge number. A conductor with a higher gauge number will carry less current than a conductor with a lower gauge number.

NOTE: Gauge wire size refers to the size of the conductor, not the size of the complete wire. It is possible to have two wires of the same gauge with different diameters because one may have thicker insulation than the other.

12 volt automotive electrical systems generally use 10, 12, 14, 16 and 18 gauge wire. Main power distribution circuits and larger accessories usually use 10 and 12 gauge wire. Battery cables are usually 4 or 6 gauge, although 1 and 2 gauge are occasionally used. Wire length must also be considered when making repairs to a circuit. As conductor length increases, so does resistance. An 18 gauge wire, for example, can carry a 10 amp load for 10 feet without excessive voltage drop; however if a 15 foot wire is required for the same 10 amp load, it must be a 16 gauge wire.

An electrical schematic shows the electrical current paths when a circuit is operating properly. It is essential to understand how a circuit works before trying to figure out why it doesn't. Schemat-

CHASSIS ELECTRICAL 6

ics break the entire electrical system down into individual circuits and show only one particular circuit. In a schematic, no attempt is made to represent wiring and components as they physically appear on the vehicle; switches and other components are shown as simply as possible. Face views of harness connectors show the cavity or terminal locations in all multi-pin connectors to help locate test points.

If you need to backprobe a connector while it is on the component, the order of the terminals must be mentally reversed. The wire color code can help in this situation, as well as a keyway, lock tab or other reference mark.

NOTE: Wiring diagrams are not included in this book. As trucks have become more complex and available with longer option lists, wiring diagrams have grown in size and complexity. It has become almost impossible to provide a readable reproduction of a wiring diagram in a book this size. Information on ordering wiring diagrams from the vehicle manufacturer can be found in the owner's manual.

WIRING REPAIR

Soldering is a quick, efficient method of joining metals permanently. Everyone who has the occasion to make wiring repairs should know how to solder. Electrical connections that are soldered are far less likely to come apart and will conduct electricity much better than connections that are only "pig-tailed" together. The most popular (and preferred) method of soldering is with an electrical soldering gun. Soldering irons are available in many sizes and wattage ratings. Irons with higher wattage ratings deliver higher temperatures and recover lost heat faster. A small soldering iron rated for no more than 50 watts is recommended, especially on electrical systems where excess heat can damage the components being soldered.

There are three ingredients necessary for successful soldering; proper flux, good solder and sufficient heat. A soldering flux is necessary to clean the metal of tarnish, prepare it for soldering and to enable the solder to spread into tiny crevices. When soldering, always use a resin flux or resin core solder which is non-corrosive and will not attract moisture once the job is finished. Other types of flux (acid core) will leave a residue that will attract moisture and cause the wires to corrode. Tin is a unique metal with a low melting point. In a molten state, it dissolves and alloys easily with many metals. Solder is made by mixing tin with lead. The most common proportions are 40/60, 50/50 and 60/40, with the percentage of tin listed first. Low priced solders usually contain less tin, making them very difficult for a beginner to use because more heat is required to melt the solder. A common solder is 40/60 which is well suited for all-around general use, but 60/40 melts easier, has more tin for a better joint and is preferred for electrical work.

Soldering Techniques

Successful soldering requires that the metals to be joined be heated to a temperature that will melt the solder—usually 360–460°F (182–238°C). Contrary to popular belief, the purpose of the soldering iron is not to melt the solder itself, but to heat the parts being soldered to a temperature high enough to melt the solder when it is touched to the work. Melting flux-cored solder on the soldering iron will usually destroy the effectiveness of the flux.

NOTE: Soldering tips are made of copper for good heat conductivity, but must be "tinned" regularly for quick transference of heat to the project and to prevent the solder from sticking to the iron. To "tin" the iron, simply heat it and touch the flux-cored solder to the tip; the solder will flow over the hot tip. Wipe the excess off with a clean rag, but be careful as the iron will be hot.

After some use, the tip may become pitted. If so, simply dress the tip smooth with a smooth file and "tin" the tip again. An old saying holds that "metals well cleaned are half soldered." Flux-cored solder will remove oxides but rust, bits of insulation and oil or grease must be removed with a wire brush or emery cloth. For maximum strength in soldered parts, the joint must start off clean and tight. Weak joints will result in gaps too wide for the solder to bridge.

If a separate soldering flux is used, it should be brushed or swabbed on only those areas that are to be soldered. Most solders contain a core of flux and separate fluxing is unnecessary. Hold the work to be soldered firmly. It is best to solder on a wooden board, because a metal vise will only rob the piece to be soldered of heat and make it difficult to melt the solder. Hold the soldering tip with the broadest face against the work to be soldered. Apply solder under the tip close to the work, using enough solder to give a heavy film between the iron and the piece being soldered, while moving slowly and making sure the solder melts properly. Keep the work level or the solder will run to the lowest part and favor the thicker parts, because these require more heat to melt the solder. If the soldering tip overheats (the solder coating on the face of the tip burns up), it should be retinned. Once the soldering is completed, let the soldered joint stand until cool. Tape and seal all soldered wire splices after the repair has cooled.

Wire Harness and Connectors

The on-board computer (ECM) wire harness electrically connects the control unit to the various solenoids, switches and sensors used by the control system. Most connectors in the engine compartment or otherwise exposed to the elements are protected against moisture and dirt which could create oxidation and deposits on the terminals. This protection is important because of the very low voltage and current levels used by the computer and sensors. All connectors have a lock which secures the male and female terminals together, with a secondary lock holding the seal and terminal into the connector. Both terminal locks must be released when disconnecting ECM connectors.

These special connectors are weather-proof and all repairs require the use of a special terminal and the tool required to service it. This tool is used to remove the pin and sleeve terminals. If removal is attempted with an ordinary pick, there is a good chance that the terminal will be bent or deformed. Unlike standard blade type terminals, these terminals cannot be straightened once they are bent. Make certain that the connectors are properly seated and all of the sealing rings in place when connecting leads. On some models, a hinge-type flap provides a backup or secondary locking feature for the terminals. Most secondary locks are used to improve the connector reliability by retaining the terminals if the small terminal lock tangs are not positioned properly.

Molded-on connectors require complete replacement of the connection. This means splicing a new connector assembly into the harness. All splices in on-board computer systems should be soldered to insure proper contact. Use care when probing the connections or replacing terminals in them as it is possible to short between opposite terminals. If this happens to the wrong terminal pair, it is possible to damage certain components. Always use jumper wires between connectors for circuit checking and never probe through weatherproof seals.

Open circuits are often difficult to locate by sight because corrosion or terminal misalignment are hidden by the connectors. Merely wiggling a connector on a sensor or in the wiring harness may correct the open circuit condition. This should always be considered when an open circuit or a failed sensor is indicated. Intermittent problems may also be caused by oxidized or loose connections. When using a circuit tester for diagnosis, always probe connections from the wire side. Be careful not to damage sealed connectors with test probes.

All wiring harnesses should be replaced with identical parts, using the same gauge wire and connectors. When signal wires are spliced into a harness, use wire with high temperature insulation only. With the low voltage and current levels found in the system,

6 CHASSIS ELECTRICAL

it is important that the best possible connection at all wire splices be made by soldering the splices together. It is seldom necessary to replace a complete harness. If replacement is necessary, pay close attention to insure proper harness routing. Secure the harness with suitable plastic wire clamps to prevent vibrations from causing the harness to wear in spots or contact any hot components.

NOTE: Weatherproof connectors cannot be replaced with standard connectors. Instructions are provided with replacement connector and terminal packages. Some wire harnesses have mounting indicators (usually pieces of colored tape) to mark where the harness is to be secured.

In making wiring repairs, it's important that you always replace damaged wires with wires that are the same gauge as the wire being replaced. The heavier the wire, the smaller the gauge number. Wires are color-coded to aid in identification and whenever possible the same color coded wire should be used for replacement. A wire stripping and crimping tool is necessary to install solderless terminal connectors. Test all crimps by pulling on the wires; it should not be possible to pull the wires out of a good crimp.

Wires which are open, exposed or otherwise damaged are repaired by simple splicing. Where possible, if the wiring harness is accessible and the damaged place in the wire can be located, it is best to open the harness and check for all possible damage. In an inaccessible harness, the wire must be bypassed with a new insert, usually taped to the outside of the old harness.

When replacing fusible links, be sure to use fusible link wire, NOT ordinary automotive wire. Make sure the fusible segment is of the same gauge and construction as the one being replaced and double the stripped end when crimping the terminal connector for a good contact. The melted (open) fusible link segment of the wiring harness should be cut off as close to the harness as possible, then a new segment spliced in as described. In the case of a damaged fusible link that feeds two harness wires, the harness connections should be replaced with two fusible link wires so that each circuit will have its own separate protection.

NOTE: Most of the problems caused in the wiring harness are due to bad ground connections. Always check all vehicle ground connections for corrosion or looseness before performing any power feed checks to eliminate the chance of a bad ground affecting the circuit.

Repairing Hard Shell Connectors

Unlike molded connectors, the terminal contacts in hard shell connectors can be replaced. Weatherproof hard-shell connectors with the leads molded into the shell have non-replaceable terminal ends. Replacement usually involves the use of a special terminal removal tool that depress the locking tangs (barbs) on the connector terminal and allow the connector to be removed from the rear of the shell. The connector shell should be replaced if it shows any evidence of burning, melting, cracks, or breaks. Replace individual terminals that are burnt, corroded, distorted or loose.

NOTE: The insulation crimp must be tight to prevent the insulation from sliding back on the wire when the wire is pulled. The insulation must be visibly compressed under the crimp tabs, and the ends of the crimp should be turned in for a firm grip on the insulation.

The wire crimp must be made with all wire strands inside the crimp. The terminal must be fully compressed on the wire strands with the ends of the crimp tabs turned in to make a firm grip on the wire. Check all connections with an ohmmeter to insure a good contact. There should be no measurable resistance between the wire and the terminal when connected.

Mechanical Test Equipment

Vacuum Gauge

Most gauges are graduated in inches of mercury (in.Hg), although a device called a manometer reads vacuum in inches of water (in. H_2O). The normal vacuum reading usually varies between 18 and 22 in.Hg at sea level. To test engine vacuum, the vacuum gauge must be connected to a source of manifold vacuum. Many engines have a plug in the intake manifold which can be removed and replaced with an adapter fitting. Connect the vacuum gauge to the fitting with a suitable rubber hose or, if no manifold plug is available, connect the vacuum gauge to any device using manifold vacuum, such as EGR valves, etc. The vacuum gauge can be used to determine if enough vacuum is reaching a component to allow its actuation.

Hand Vacuum Pump

Small, hand-held vacuum pumps come in a variety of designs. Most have a built-in vacuum gauge and allow the component to be tested without removing it from the vehicle. Operate the pump lever or plunger to apply the correct amount of vacuum required for the test specified in the diagnosis routines. The level of vacuum in inches of Mercury (in.Hg) is indicated on the pump gauge. For some testing, an additional vacuum gauge may be necessary.

Intake manifold vacuum is used to operate various systems and devices on late model vehicles. To correctly diagnose and solve problems in vacuum control systems, a vacuum source is necessary for testing. In some cases, vacuum can be taken from the intake manifold when the engine is running, but vacuum is normally provided by a hand vacuum pump. These hand vacuum pumps have a built-in vacuum gauge that allow testing while the device is still attached to the component. For some tests, an additional vacuum gauge may be necessary.

HEATING AND AIR CONDITIONING

Blower Motor

REMOVAL AND INSTALLATION

Except the 6-4.0L

1. Disconnect the electrical connection.
2. Remove the blower motor attaching screws.
3. Remove the blower motor.
4. Remove the blower motor fan from the motor shaft for access to the motor attaching nuts.
5. Installation is the reverse of removal. Check motor for proper operation.

6-4.0L

1. Remove the coolant overflow bottle retaining strap. Remove the coolant overflow bottle and bracket.
2. On trucks with anti-lock brakes, remove the anti-lock brake pump and bracket as an assembly, and position out of the way.
3. Remove the brake hose retaining bracket screw.
4. Disconnect the blower motor wiring connector.
5. Remove the blower motor mounting screws. Remove the blower motor.
6. Remove the blower motor fan from the motor shaft for access to the motor attaching nuts.
7. Installation is the reverse of removal. Check motor for proper operation.

CHASSIS ELECTRICAL 6

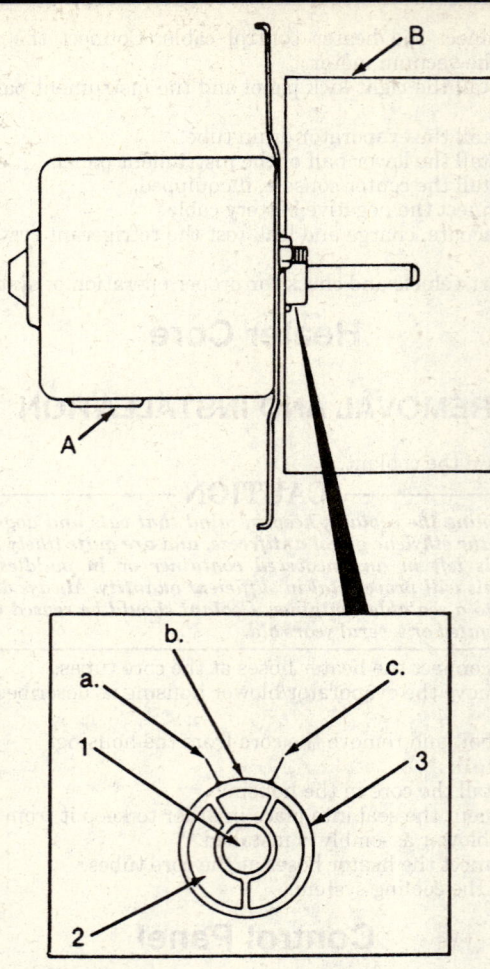

1. Motor shaft
2. Fan hub
3. Retainer clip

NOTE: Ears of retainer clip must be over flat surface on motor shaft (a, b, c).

Blower motor removal/installation

Evaporator/Blower Housing

REMOVAL AND INSTALLATION

1. Disconnect the negative battery cable.
2. Discharge the air conditioning system. See Section 1.

CAUTION
Unless you are thoroughly familiar with the handling of refrigerant gas, do not attempt to discharge the system. Mishandling of refrigerant gas can cause severe personal injury. Have the system discharged by a trained professional.

3. Disconnect the blower motor wires and vent tube.
4. If equipped, remove the center console as follows:
  a. On manual transmission models, remove the shift knob, boot and bezel.
  b. On automatic transmission models, remove the shift handle cap, plunger, spring, T-lock, shift handle and bezel.
  c. If equipped with power windows, pry switch out of console and disconnect.
  d. Remove console cover screws, cover and cover base.
5. Remove the lower half of the instrument panel.
6. Disconnect the wiring at the A/C relay, blower motor resistors and A/C thermostat. Disconnect the vacuum hoses at the vacuum motor.
7. Cut the plastic retaining strap that retains the evaporator housing to the heater core housing.
8. Disconnect and remove the heater control cable.
9. Remove the clips at the rear blower housing flange and remove the retaining screws.
10. Remove the housing attaching nuts from the studs on the engine compartment side of the firewalll.
11. Remove the evaporator drain tube.
12. Remove the right kick panel and the instrument panel support bolt.
13. Gently pull out on the right side of the dash and rotate

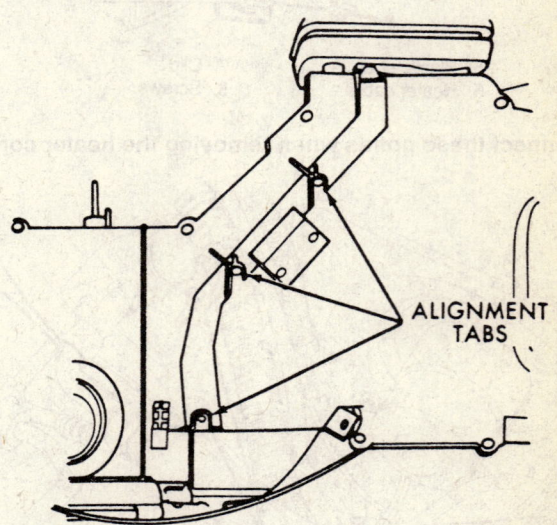

Evaporator housing removal/installation

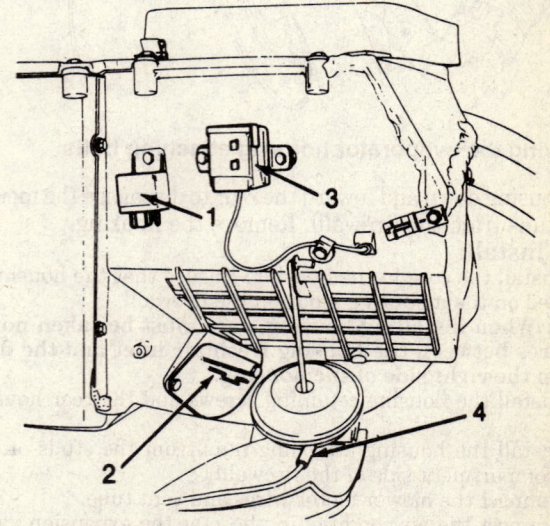

1. A.C. relay
2. A.C. resistor
3. A.C. thermostat
4. Vacuum motor

Evaporator housing component location

6-9

6 CHASSIS ELECTRICAL

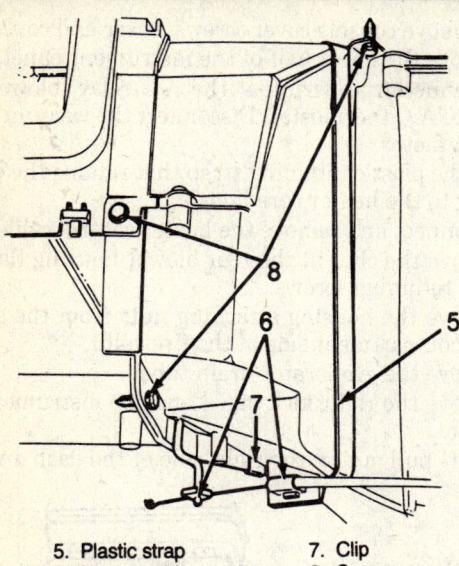

5. Plastic strap
6. Heater cable
7. Clip
8. Screws

Disconnect these points when removing the heater core

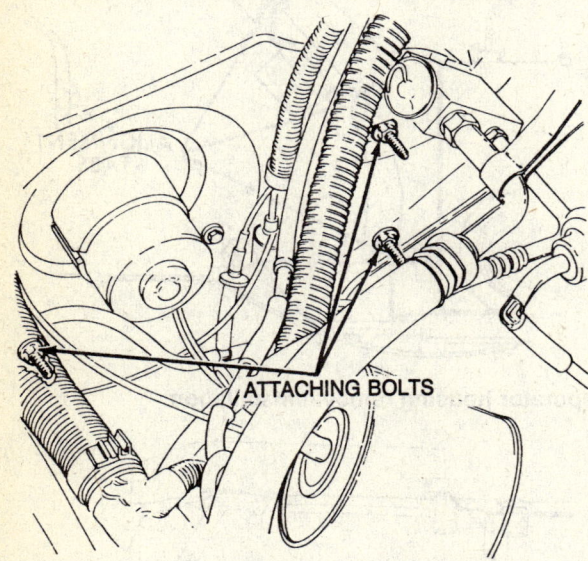

Removing the evaporator housing attaching bolts

the housing down and toward the rear to disengage the mounting studs from the firewalll. Remove the housing.

To install:

14. Install the core in the housing. Ensure that the housing is positioned on the mounting studs on the firewalll.

NOTE: When installing housing, care must be taken not to trap wires between the housing fresh air inlet and the dash panel on the right side of the housing.

15. Install the housing retaining screws and the rear housing clips.
16. Install the housing attaching nuts from the studs on the engine compartment side of the firewalll.
17. Connect the blower motor wires and vent tube.
18. Connect the air conditioning hose at the expansion valve. Always use a back-up wrench!
19. Connect the wiring at the A/C relay, blower motor resistors and A/C thermostat.
20. Connect the heater control cable. Connect the vacuum hoses at the vacuum motor.
21. Install the right kick panel and the instrument panel support bolt.
22. Install the evaporator drain tube.
23. Install the lower half of the instrument panel.
24. Install the center console, if equipped.
31. Connect the negative battery cable.
32. Evacuate, charge and leak test the refrigerant system. See Section 1.
33. Start vehicle and check for proper operation of system.

Heater Core

REMOVAL AND INSTALLATION

1. Drain the coolant.

CAUTION
When draining the coolant, keep in mind that cats and dogs are attracted by the ethylene glycol antifreeze, and are quite likely to drink any that is left in an uncovered container or in puddles on the ground. This will prove fatal in sufficient quantity. Always drain the coolant into a sealable container. Coolant should be reused unless it is contaminated or several years old.

---

2. Disconnect the heater hoses at the core tubes.
3. Remove the evaporator/blower housing as described in this section.
4. Unbolt and remove the core from the housing.

To install:

5. Install the core in the housing.
6. Cement the seal into place in order to keep it from moving when the blower assembly is installed.
7. Connect the heater hoses at the core tubes.
8. Fill the cooling system.

Control Panel

REMOVAL AND INSTALLATION

1. Disconnect the battery ground.
2. Remove the lower part of the instrument panel.
3. Remove the instrument panel bezel.

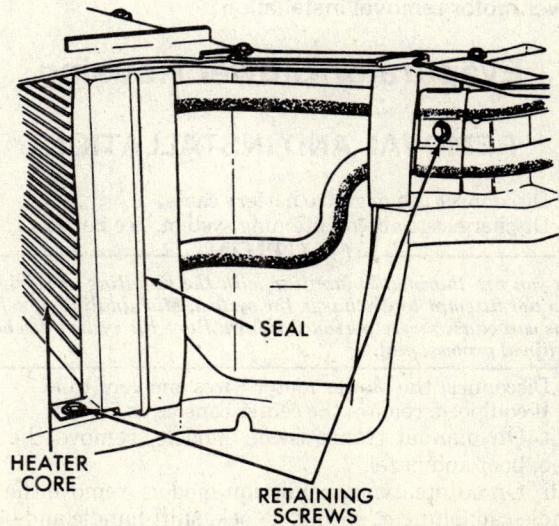

Heater core removal/installation

CHASSIS ELECTRICAL 6

4. Remove the clock.
5. Remove the radio.
6. Remove the control panel screws, pull the panel outward and disconnect and tag the hoses, wires and cable.
7. Installation is the reverse of removal. Test operation before installing instrument panel bezel.

Evaporator Core

REMOVAL AND INSTALLATION

1. Drain the coolant.

— CAUTION —
When draining the coolant, keep in mind that cats and dogs are attracted by the ethylene glycol antifreeze, and are quite likely to drink any that is left in an uncovered container or in puddles on the ground. This will prove fatal in sufficient quantity. Always drain the coolant into a sealable container. Coolant should be reused unless it is contaminated or several years old.

2. Disconnect the heater hoses at the core tubes.
3. Discharge the refrigerant.

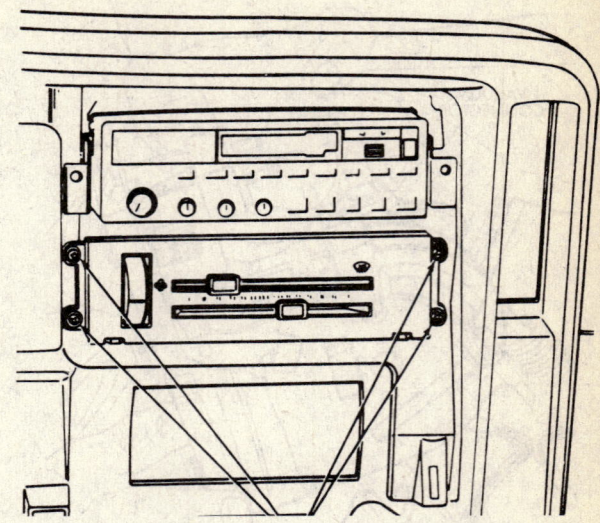
Control panel mounting screw removal

— CAUTION —
Unless you are thoroughly familiar with the handling of refrigerant gas, do not attempt to discharge the system. Mishandling of refrigerant gas can cause severe personal injury. Take the system to someone trained in refrigeration.

4. Disconnect the air conditioning hose from the expansion valve and cap all openings.
5. Disconnect the blower motor wires and vent tube.
6. Remove the center console, if equipped.
7. Remove the lower half of the instrument panel.
8. Disconnect the wiring at the A/C relay, blower motor resistors and A/C thermostat. Disconnect the vacuum hoses at the vacuum motor.
9. Cut the plastic retaining strap that retains the evaporator housing to the heater core housing.
10. Disconnect and remove the heater control cable.
11. Remove the 3 clips at the rear blower housing flange and remove the retaining screws.
12. Remove the housing attaching nuts from the studs on the engine compartment side of the firewalll.

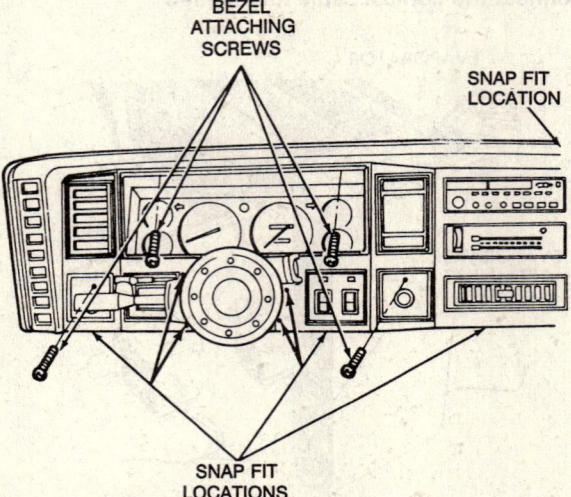
Instrument bezel removal/installation

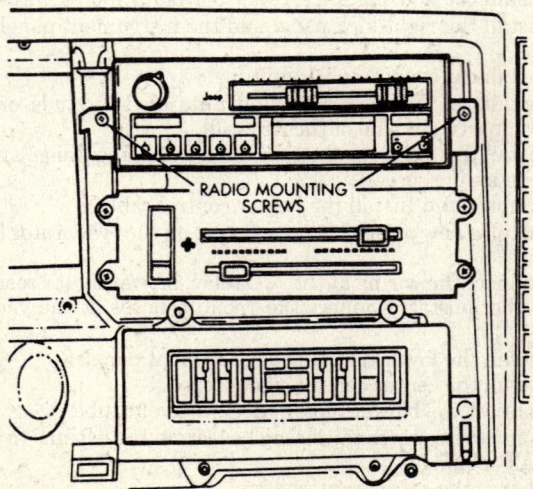
Radio attaching screw removal

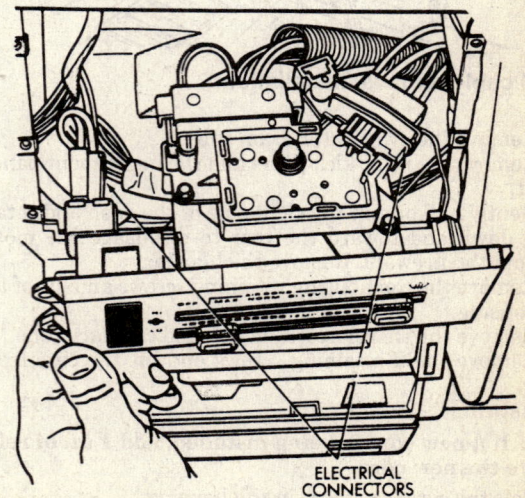
Control panel electrical connectors

6-11

6 CHASSIS ELECTRICAL

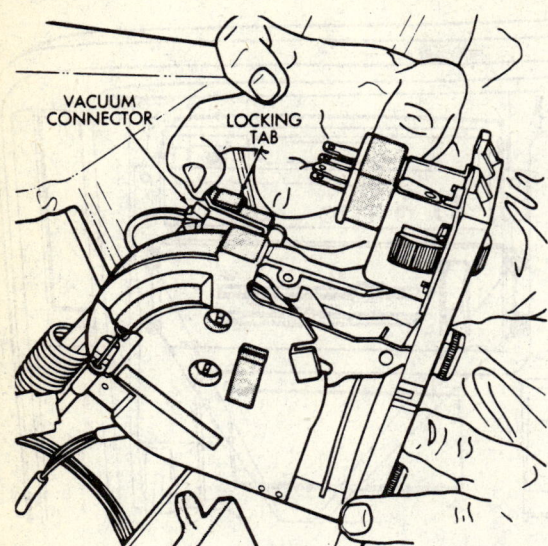

Control panel vacuum harness connector

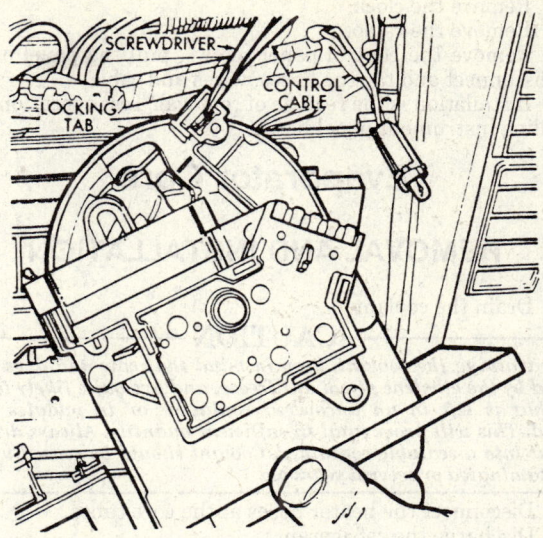

Disconnect the control cable locking tab

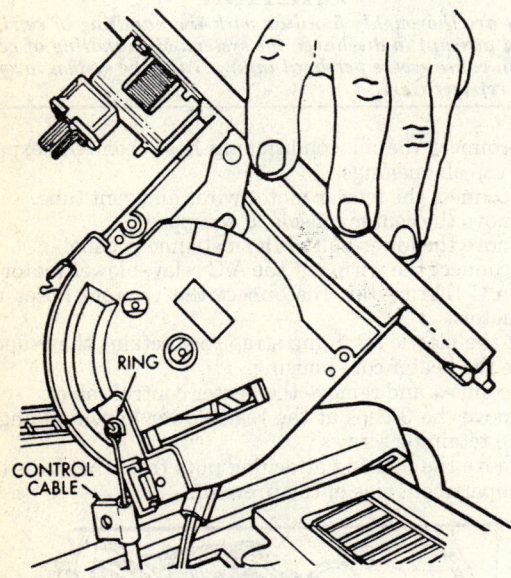

Control cable removal/installation

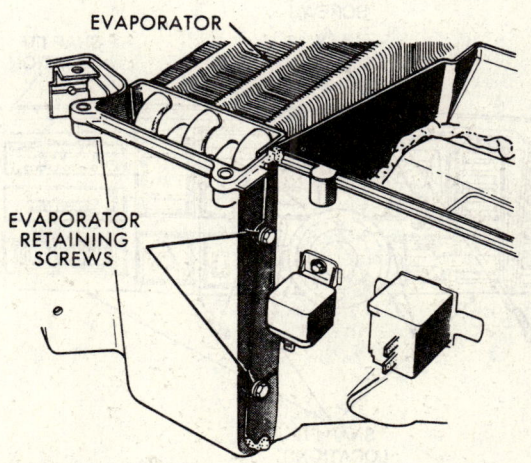

Evaporator removal/installation

13. Remove the evaporator drain tube.
14. Remove the right kick panel and the instrument panel support bolt.
15. Gently pull out on the right side of the dash and rotate the housing down and toward the rear to disengage the mounting studs from the firewalll. Remove the housing.
16. Remove the top housing retaining screws and lift of the top of the housing.
17. Remove the thermostatic switch and capillary tube.
18. Remove the 2 retaining screws and lift the core from the housing.

To install:

NOTE: If a new core is being installed, add 1 oz. of refrigerant oil to the new core.

19. Bolt the core into place in the housing.
20. Install the thermostatic switch and capillary tube.
21. Install the top of the housing.
22. Install the housing. Be careful to avoid trapping wires.
23. Install the right kick panel and the instrument panel support bolt.
24. Install the evaporator drain tube.
25. Install the housing attaching nuts on the studs on the engine compartment side of the firewalll.
26. Install the 3 clips at the rear blower housing flange and install the retaining screws.
27. Connect and Install the heater control cable.
28. Install a new plastic retaining strap on the evaporator housing.
29. Connect the wiring at the A/C relay, blower motor resistors and A/C thermostat. Connect the vacuum hoses at the vacuum motor.
30. Install the lower half of the instrument panel.
31. Install the center console, if equipped.
32. Connect the blower motor wires and vent tube.
33. Connect the air conditioning hose from the expansion valve and cap all openings.
34. Charge the refrigerant system.
35. Connect the heater hoses at the core tubes.
36. Fill the cooling system.

CHASSIS ELECTRICAL 6

Expansion Valve

REMOVAL AND INSTALLATION

1. Discharge the A/C system.

—— CAUTION ——
Unless you are thoroughly familiar with the handling of refrigerant gas, do not attempt to discharge the system. Mishandling of refrigerant gas can cause severe personal injury. Take the system to someone trained in refrigeration.

2. Remove the coolant overflow bottle and bracket, if necessary.
3. Disconnect the A/C hoses from the expansion valve.
4. Disconnect the expansion valve from the evaporator core inlet and outlet tubes. Remove the expansion valve.
5. Installation is the reverse of removal.
6. Charge the A/C system and test for leaks.

Condenser Receiver/Drier

REMOVAL AND INSTALLATION

All except 6-4.0L

1. Drain the coolant system.
2. Disconnect the fan shroud and radiator hoses.
3. On vehicles with automatic transmission, disconnect the transmission cooler lines.
4. Evacuate the A/C system and disconnect the hoses from the condenser.
5. Unplug the harness from the low pressure switch.
6. Remove the radiator and condenser as an assembly.
7. Remove the retaining bolts and separate the condenser from the radiator. Remove the receiver/drier from the condenser.

NOTE: Keep receiver/drier openings plugged at all times to prevent moisture from entering the receiver/drier.

8. Installation is the reverse of removal. Add 1 ounce of refrigerant oil to the system when replacing the condenser.

6-4.0L

1. Disconnect the fan shroud and electric fan from the radiator.
2. Remove the upper cross member and bracket.
3. Evacuate the A/C system, disconnect the A/C hoses from the condenser and plug the openings.
4. Unplug the harness from the low pressure switch.
5. Remove all attaching bolts connecting the condenser to the radiator. Remove condenser and receiver drier as an assembly.
6. Remove the receiver/drier from the condenser.

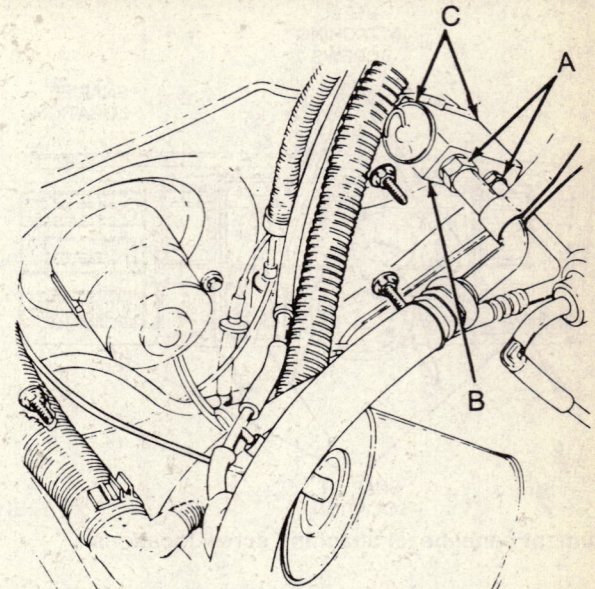

Expansion valve removal/installation. (A) air conditioning hoses; (B) expansion valve; (C) outlet tubes

NOTE: Keep receiver/drier openings plugged at all times to prevent moisture from entering the receiver/drier.

7. Installation is the reverse of removal. Add 1 ounce of refrigerant oil to the system when replacing the condenser.

Heater Control Valve

The heater control valve is spliced into the heater core hoses. It can be tested by attaching a hand vacuum pump to the valve to draw and release vacuum. If during this procedure the heating system functions properly, the valve is not defective. Check for vacuum leaks in the control panel or restrictions in the coolant system.

1. Allow the vehicle to cool before performing this procedure.
2. Label and disconnect all heater hoses attached to the valve.
3. Disconnect the vacuum hose which controls the valve.
4. Remove the valve.
5. Installation is the reverse of removal.

RADIO

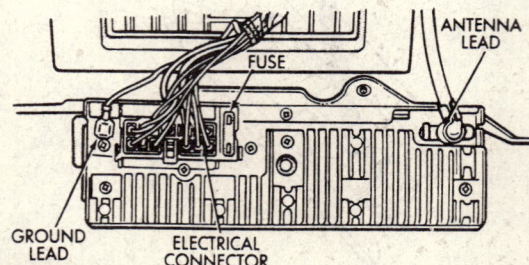

Radio wiring harness

REMOVAL AND INSTALLATION

1. Disconnect the battery ground.
2. Remove the instrument panel bezel.
3. Remove the radio attaching screws.
4. Disconnect the radio from the instrument panel wiring harness.
5. Installation is the reverse of removal.

6 CHASSIS ELECTRICAL

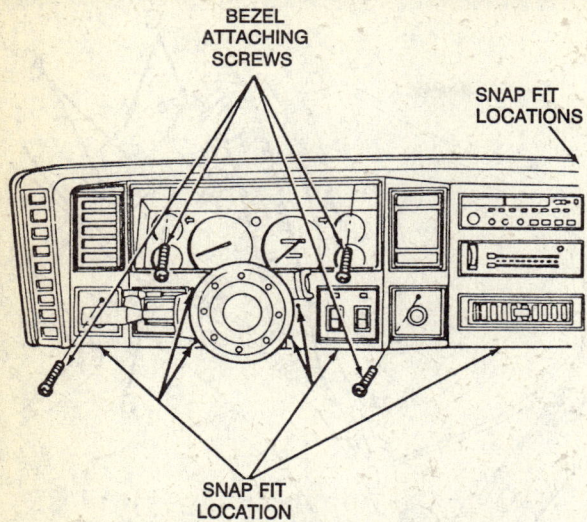
Instrument panel bezel attaching screw locations

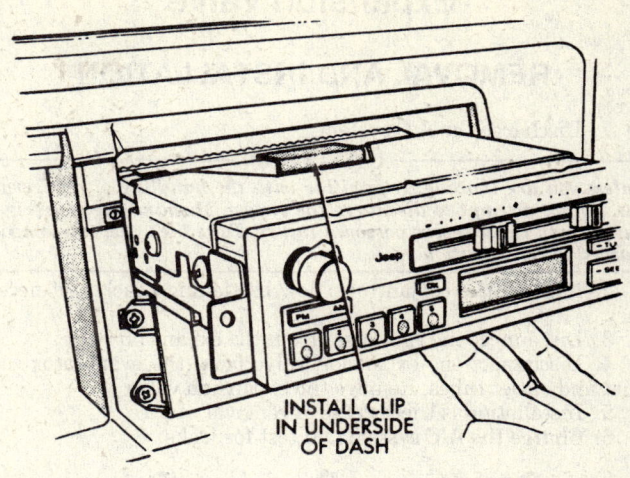
Install the clip on the under-side of the dash

WINDSHIELD WIPERS

Wiper Blade

REPLACEMENT

1. Insert a screwdriver into the spring release opening of the blade saddle and depress the spring clip. Pull the blade from the arm.
2. Push the blade saddle onto the mounting clip so that the spring clip engages the pin.

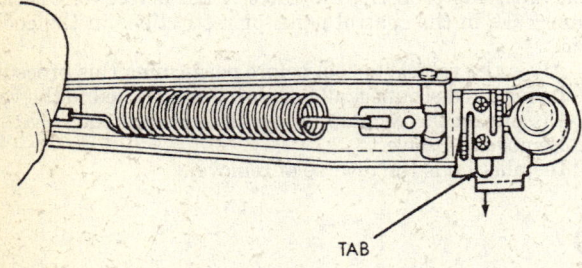
Wiper arm replacement

Wiper Arm

REPLACEMENT

1. Raise the blade end of the arm away from the windshield and move the spring tab away from the pivot shaft.
2. Disengage the auxiliary arm retainer clip from the pivot pin and pull the wiper arm from the pivot shaft.
3. Pivot the auxiliary over the pivot pin and engage the retainer clip. Push the wiper arm over the pivot shaft. Be sure that the shaft is in park and the wiper arm is positioned in the down mode.

Windshield Wiper Motor

REMOVAL AND INSTALLATION

1. Remove the wiper arm and blade assemblies.
2. Remove the cowl trim panel.
3. Disconnect the washer hose.

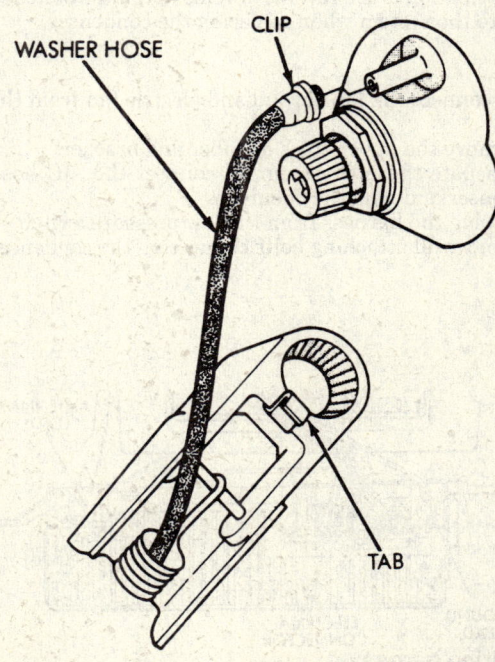
Liftgate wiper washer hose

CHASSIS ELECTRICAL 6

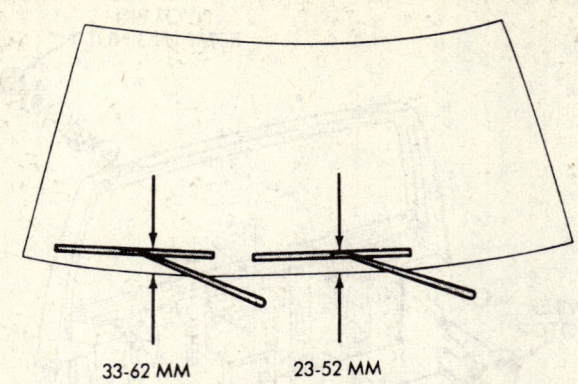

After installing wiper arms, check installed height

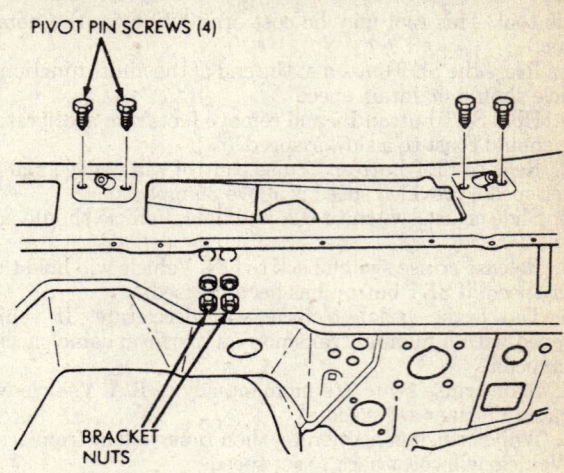

Pivot arm assembly removal/installation

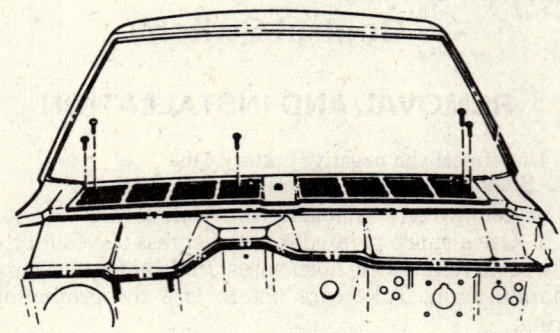

Cowl panel attaching screw location

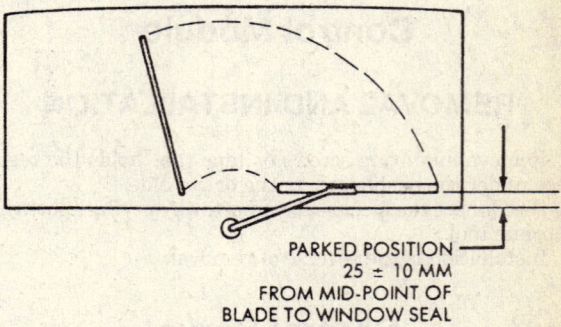

After installing the liftgate wiper, check installed height

4. Remove the cowl mounting bracket attaching nuts and pivot pin attaching screws.
5. Disconnect the wiring harness and remove the motor. DO NOT puncture the washer motor rubber boot.
6. Installation is the reverse of removal. Torque the mounting nuts to 35–50 inch lbs.

Linkage

REMOVAL AND INSTALLATION

1. Remove the wiper arms and pivot shaft nuts, washers, escutcheons and gaskets.
2. Disconnect the drive arm from the motor crank.
3. Remove individual links where necessary, to ease removal of the pivot shaft bodies.
4. Install in the reverse order of removal.

Liftgate Wiper Motor

REMOVAL AND INSTALLATION

1. Remove the wiper arm assembly.
2. Disconnect the washer hose.
3. Remove the pivot pin retaining nut.
4. Remove the liftgate interior trim panel.
5. Disconnect the wiper motor at the wiring harness.
6. Unbolt and remove the motor.
7. Installation is the reverse of removal. Torque the pivot pin attaching nut to 32 inch lbs. and the motor mounting bracket to 40 inch lbs.

CRUISE CONTROL

General Information

The Cruise Command system is electrically actuated and vacuum operated. The turn signal lever on the steering column incorporates a slide switch which has three positions OFF, ON or RESUME. A SET button is located in the end of the lever. This device is designed to operate at speeds above approximately 35 mph.

The speed control module automatically controls throttle position to maintain a speed set by the operator. The vehicle will keep the set speed unless the driver presses the brake, clutch or accelerator pedal.

Operational Check

Perform the following tests with the cruise control switch ON and vehicle speed faster than 35 mph. More comprehensive testing can be accomplished with an AM P-C-1R cruise control diag-

6 CHASSIS ELECTRICAL

nostic tool. This tool may be cost prohibitive for the home mechanic.
1. Press the SET button at the end of the multi-function lever. Vehicle should maintain speed.
2. Hold SET button IN and remove foot from accelerator. Vehicle should coast to a slower speed.
3. Release SET button. Cruise control will engage and hold a slower speed, provided speed is above 35 mph.
4. Slide cruise switch to R/A and hold. Vehicle should accelerate.
5. Release cruise switch back to ON. Vehicle will hold the new faster speed, if SET button has been pressed.
6. Tap brake pedal. Vehicle will decelerate. If vehicle is equipped with a manual transmission, perform same check with clutch pedal.
7. Slide cruise switch to momentarily to R/A. Vehicle will accelerate to former set speed.
8. While cruising, accelerate, then remove foot from accelerator. Vehicle will coast back to set speed.
9. While cruise is engaged, tap SET button. Vehicle will increase 1 mph for each time SET button is tapped.

Control Module

REMOVAL AND INSTALLATION

1. Remove mounting screws or tape that holds the regulator in place under the dashboard on the driver side.
2. Disconnect the electrical connector by prying apart with an appropriate tool.
3. Installation is the reverse of removal.

Control Servo

REMOVAL AND INSTALLATION

1. Remove the locknut holding the servo to the mounting bracket.
2. Remove the vacuum hoses from the servo and disconnect the wiring harness.
3. Remove the two nuts and cable housing from the servo.
4. Release the cable clip from the servo cable.
5. Installation is the reverse of removal. Tighten locknut to 60 inch lbs.

Speed Sensor

REMOVAL AND INSTALLATION

The speed sensor is located behind the instrument cluster.
1. Raise and support the vehicle safely.
2. Disconnect the negative battery cable.
3. Remove the spring nut holding the speedometer cable in position on the drivers side upper control arm bolt.
4. Remove the instrument panel bezel and instrument cluster. Disconnect the speedometer cable. See procedure in this Section.
5. Remove the two attaching nuts from the speed sensor. Disconnect the sensor wiring harness.
6. Installation is the reverse of removal.

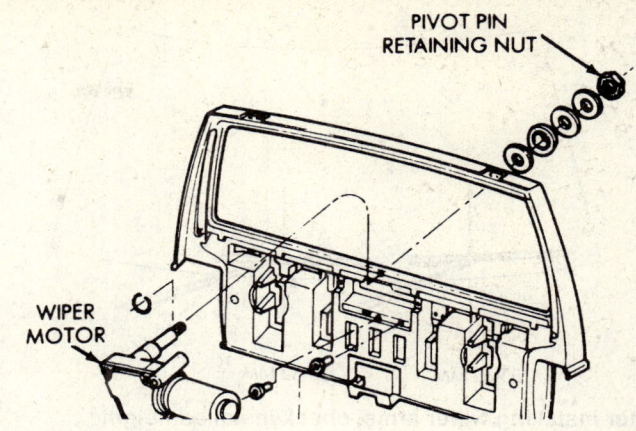

Liftgate wiper assembly

Control Switch

REMOVAL AND INSTALLATION

1. Disconnect the negative battery cable.
2a. Standard Steering Wheel:
  a. Remove screws holding the front cover.
  b. Use a sharp pointed tool to depress the connector retainer and remove the horn wires. Pull gently to remove the grounding pin. Take care not to lose the grounding pin spring.
2b. Optional Steering Wheel:
  a. Remove the horn button with a push and turn motion. Remove the rest of the horn button components.
  b. Turn ignition key to the lock position and remove the steering wheel nut and washer.
3. Scribe an alignment mark on the steering wheel inline with the mark already existing on the end of the steering column.
4. Remove the vibration damper from the steering column hub, if equipped.
5. Remove the steering wheel using a steering wheel puller.

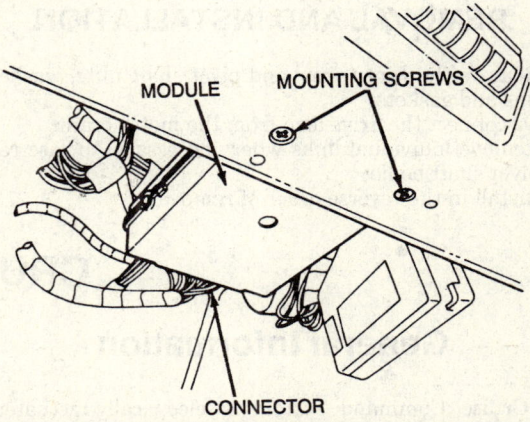

Cruise control module location, under dashboard on drivers side

CHASSIS ELECTRICAL 6

Cruise Control Diagnosis

CONDITION	POSSIBLE CAUSE	CORRECTION
A. System Does Not Engage in ON Position	(1) Restricted vacuum hose or no vacuum (2) Control switch defective (3) Control module defective (4) Speed sensor defective (5) Brake lamps defective (6) Brake lamp switch defective (7) Brake lamp switch wire disconnected (8) Open circuit between brake lamp switch and brake lamps (9) Mechanical vent valve position improperly adjusted	(1) Locate restriction or air leak and repair (2) Replace switch (3) Replace control module (4) Replace sensor (5) Replace brake lamp bulbs (6) Replace switch (7) Connect wire to switch (8) Adjust open circuit (9) Adjust vent valve position
B. Resume Feature Inoperative	(1) Defective servo ground connection (2) Control switch defective	(1) Check servo ground wire connection and repair as necessary (2) Replace switch
C. Accelerate Function Inoperative	(1) Accelerate circuit in control module inoperative (2) Cruise switch defective	(1) Replace control module (2) Replace switch
D. System Re-engages When Brake Pedal Or Clutch Is Released	(1) Control module defective (2) Mechanical vent valve not opening (3) Kink in mechanical vent valve hose (4) Brake lamp switch defective	(1) Replace control module (2) Adjust position or replace valve (3) Reroute hose to remove kink (4) Adjust or replace switch
E. Throttle Does Not Return To Idle Position	(1) Improper linkage adjustment (2) No slack in lost motion link	(1) Adjust properly (2) Adjust servo cable
F. Road Speed Changes More Than 2 MPH (3.2km/h) When Setting Speed	(1) Centering adjustment set wrong	(1) Adjust centering screw
G. Engine Accelerates When Started	(1) No slack in bead chain (2) Vacuum hose connections reversed at servo (3) Servo defective	(1) Adjust chain (2) Check connection and correct (3) Replace servo
H. System Disengages On Level Road Without Applying Brake Or Clutch	(1) Loose wire connection (2) Loose vacuum hose connection (3) Servo linkage broken (4) Defective brake lamp switch	(1) Repair connection (2) Check vacuum hose connection and repair as necessary (3) Repair linkage (4) Replace switch
I. Erratic Operation	(1) Reverse polarity (2) Servo defective (3) Control module defective	(1) Check position of speed sensor wires at connector (2) Replace servo (3) Replace control module
J. Vehicle Continues to Accelerate When Set Button is Released	(1) Servo defective (2) Control module defective	(1) Replace servo (2) Replace control module
K. System Engages But Slowly Loses Set Speed	(1) Air leak at vacuum hose connection or in hoses (2) Air leak at vent release valve at brake pedal	(1) Check hoses and connections and repair as necessary (2) Replace vacuum vent valve

6 CHASSIS ELECTRICAL

Cruise Control Wiring Diagram

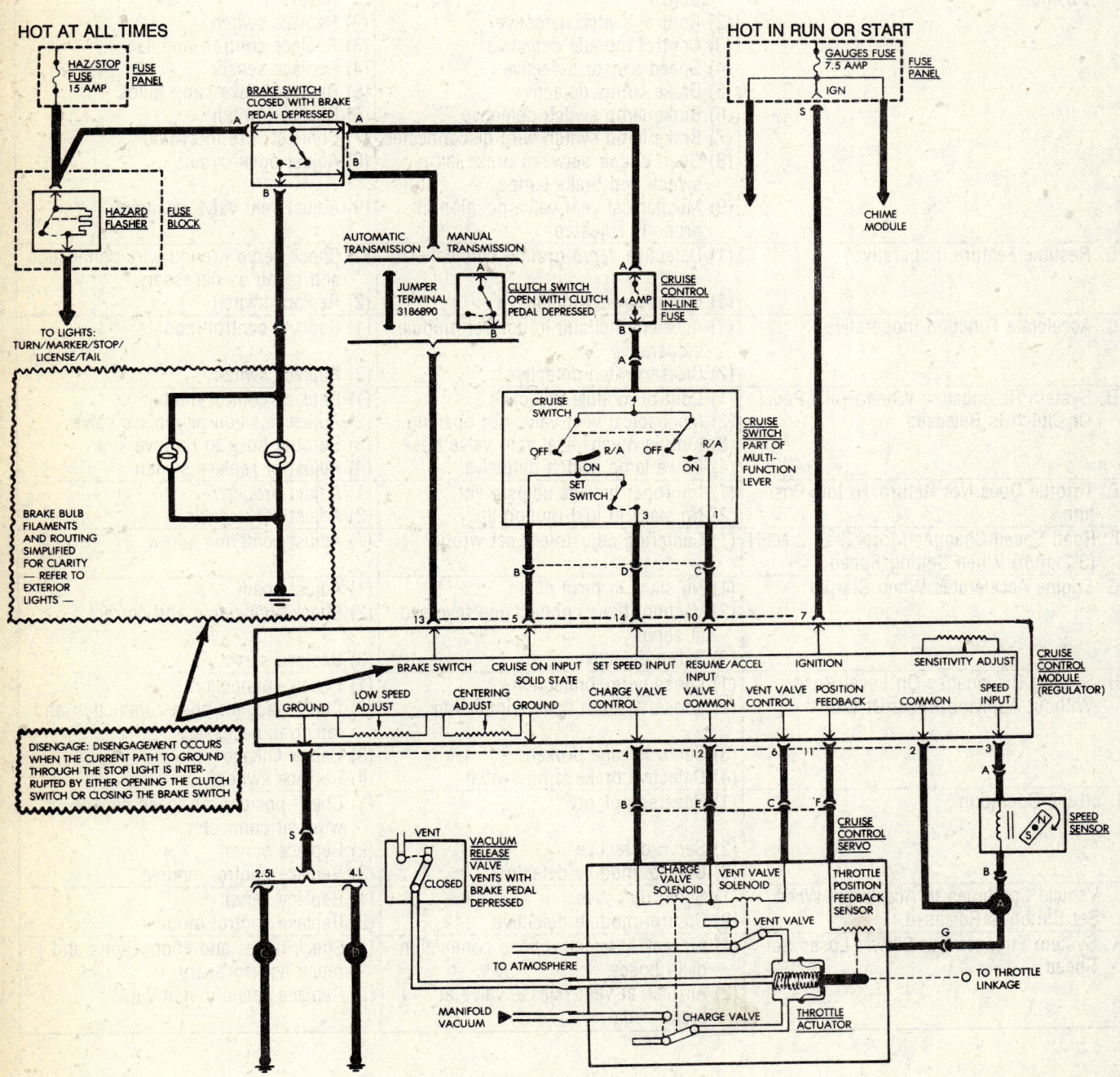

6-18

CHASSIS ELECTRICAL 6

Cruise Control Switch Testing

SET/COAST (S/C) SW	POSITION SLIDER	1-2	1-3	1-4	2-3	2-4	3-4
Normal	Off	O	O	O	O	O	O
Normal	On	O	O	O	O	C	O
Normal	R/A	C	O	C	O	C	O
Depressed	Off	O	O	O	C	O	O
Depressed	On	O	O	O	C	C	C
Depressed	R/A	C	C	C	C	C	C

C — CLOSED — ZERO OHMS (0Ω)
O — OPEN — INFINITE (∞)

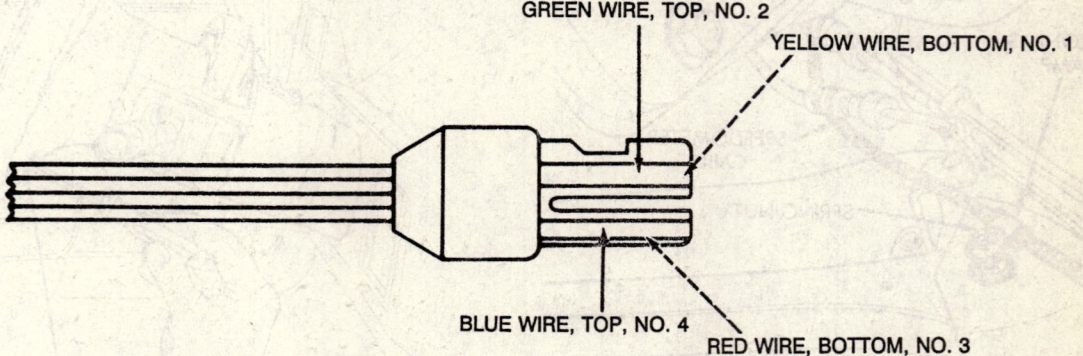

NOTE: In order to remove the steering shaft snap ring, the lock plate must be compressed. Use a lock spring compressor tool (C4156). Take care as the lock plate is under heavy tension.

6. Compress the lock plate and remove the steering shaft snap ring. Discard the snapring.
7. Remove the lock plate, canceling cam, and upper bearing preload spring. If equipped with the optional steering wheel, remove the horn button components from the canceling cam.
8. Remove the screw and hazard warning switch knob. Remove the actuator arm attaching screw.
9. Remove the turn signal switch attaching screws. Disconnect the cruise control switch wiring harness and remove from steering column.
10. Turn the ignition key to the ON position. Remove the key warning buzzer switch and retaining clip with a paper clip inserted below the retainer.

NOTE: The buzzer switch and clip must be removed as a unit. If not, the clip may drop down into the steering column.

11. Remove the ignition lock cylinder retaining screw and pull the lock out of the column.
12. Remove the screws that attach the housing and shroud assembly to the column jacket and remove the housing and shroud assembly. DO NOT let the dimmer switch rod, lock pin or lock rack fall out.
13. Remove the turn signal/wiper lever by pulling it straight out of the column. Remove the column shift cover screw if equipped with column shift.

To Install:
14. Remove the pivot screw from the housing and remove the wiper switch. Install a new switch and switch cover.
15. Push on dimmer switch rod to make sure it is connected then carefully position housing and shroud assembly to column.

NOTE: Ensure the nylon spring retainer on the lock pin is positioned forward of the retaining slot of the lock rack.

16. Position the first tooth of the gear (farthest from the block tooth) with the most forward tooth of the lock rack.
17. Install the screws that attach the housing and shroud assembly and carefully mate the housing and shroud.
18. Insert the key and lock cylinder and test that the lock pin extends fully when the key is moved to the lock position.

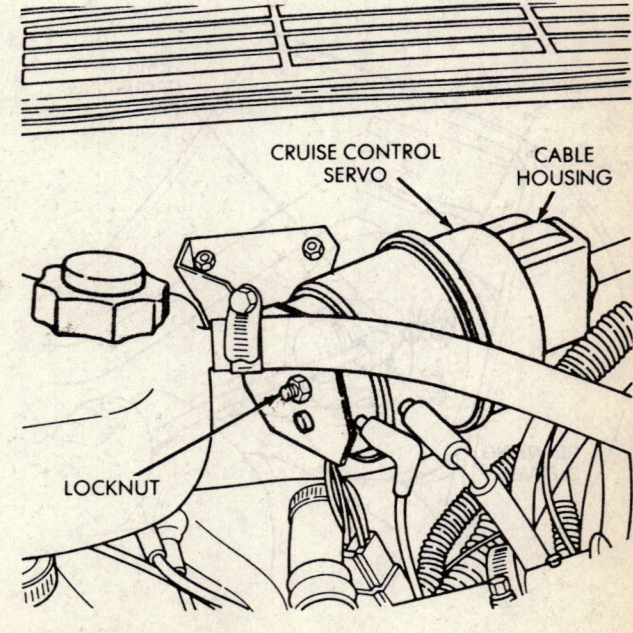

Cruise control servo

6 CHASSIS ELECTRICAL

19. Install the remaining parts in reverse order of removal.
NOTE: When installing the wiper switch, make sure the wires are laying flat on the bottom of the column.
20. On vehicles equipped with column shift, install the gear indicator cable clip with the shift indicator on NEUTRAL. Move the selector through the range and make ensure it lines up with each letter.
21. Install the steering wheel. Tighten the steering wheel nut to 25 ft. lbs. torque.

Servo Cable

REMOVAL AND INSTALLATION

1. Using finger pressure only, remove cruise control cable con-

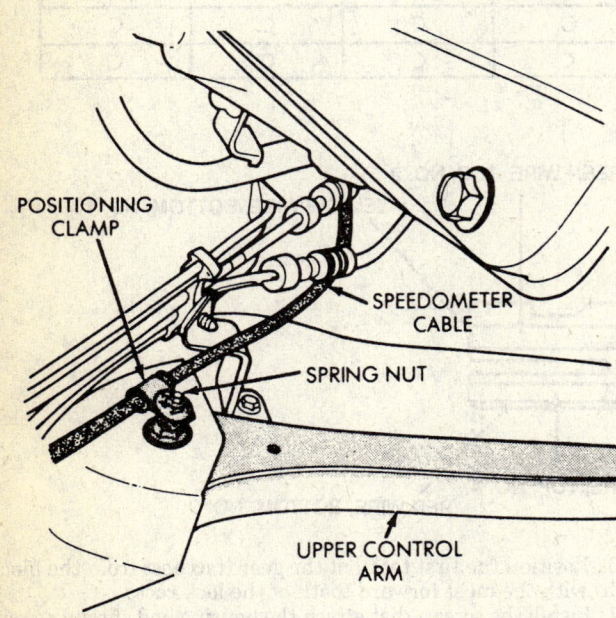

Remove speedometer cable positioning clamp

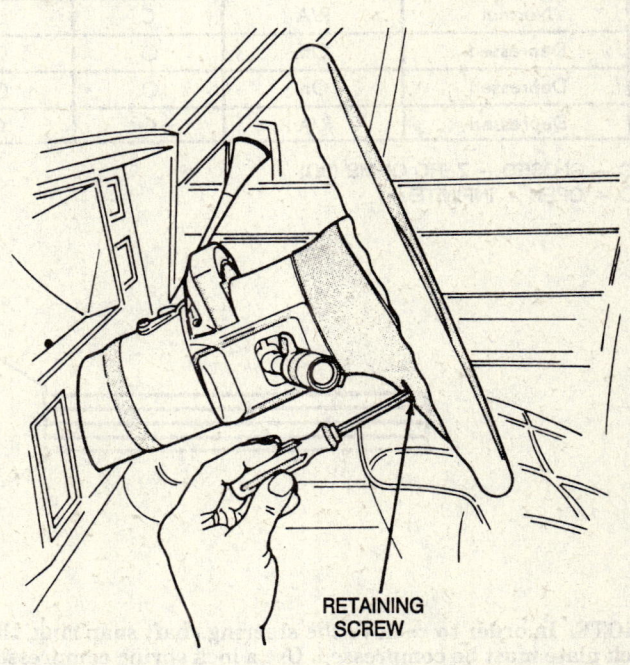

Standard steering wheel cover removal/installation

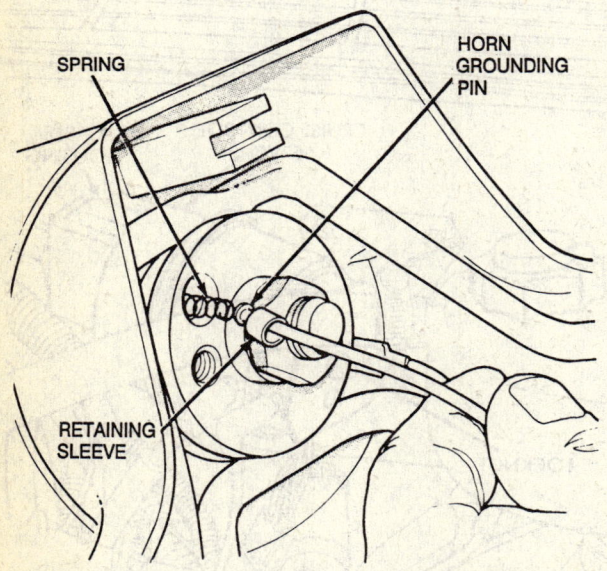

Horn ground pin removal/installation

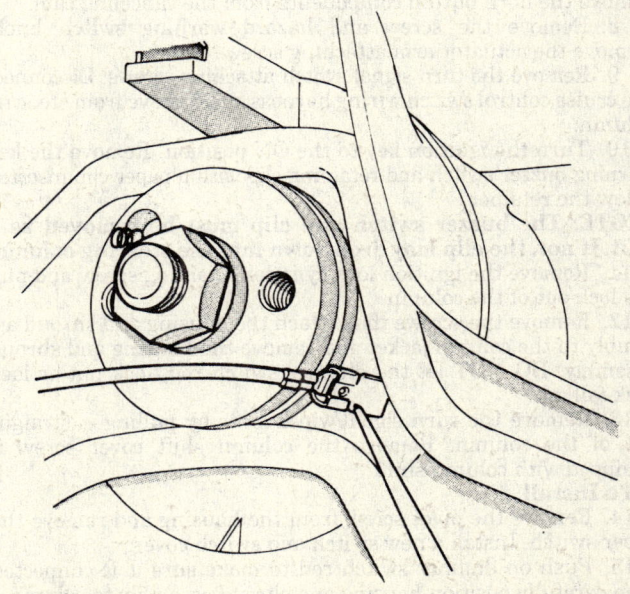

Horn wire removal

6-20

CHASSIS ELECTRICAL 6

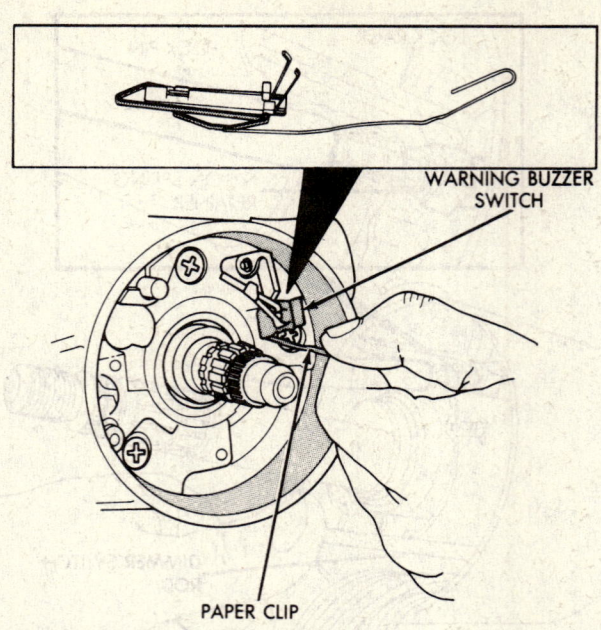

Buzzer switch removal/installation

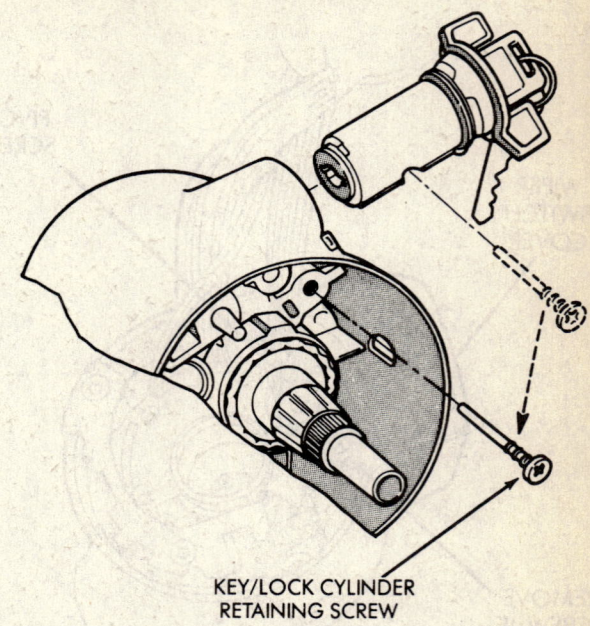

Lock cylinder removal/installation

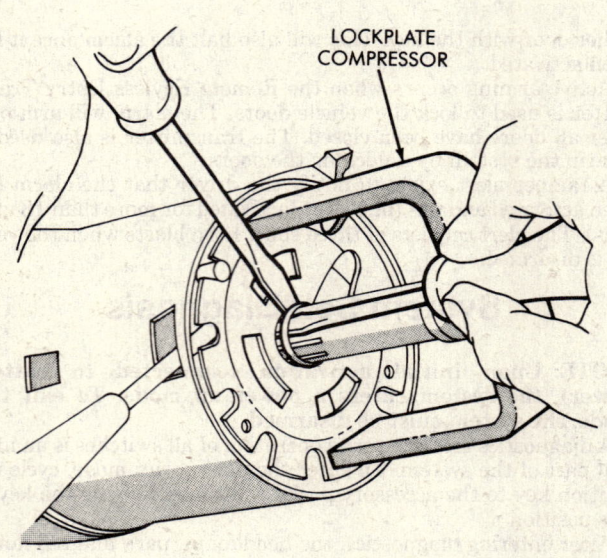

Lockplate removal/installation

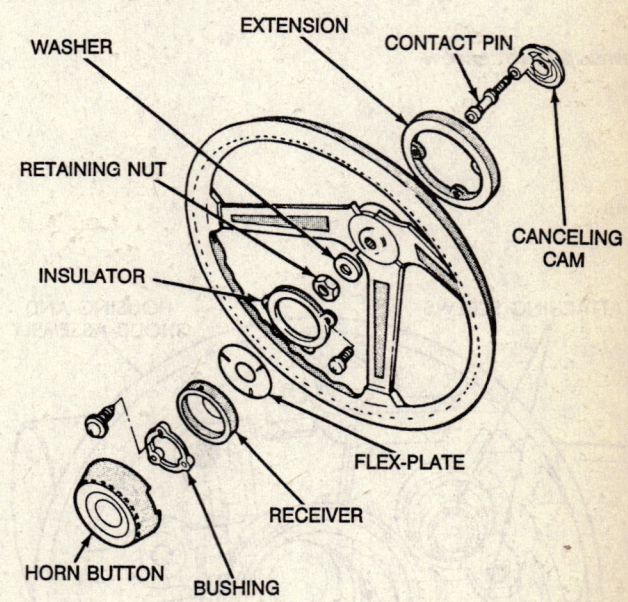

Optional steering wheel assembly

nector at bell crank. DO NOT try to pull connector off perpendicular to the bell crank.
  2. Remove MAP sensor mounting nuts and slide sensor forward off studs.

3. Remove attaching nuts and cable housing from the servo.
4. Release thee cable clip from the servo cable and remove the servo cable.
5. Installation is the reverse of removal.

VEHICLE THEFT SECURITY SYSTEM

General Information

The passive system is designed to protect against vehicle theft. If activated, the alarm sounds the horn, flashes the head lamps, park and tail lamps, and kills the engine.

Passive arming occurs upon normal vehicle exit. After exiting the vehicle, locking the doors with the power lock, and closing the door, the security lamp in the dash will flash for 15 seconds to indicate the alarm is arming. The alarm will not arm if the doors are manually locked.
Passive disarming occurs upon normal vehicle entry; unlocking

6 CHASSIS ELECTRICAL

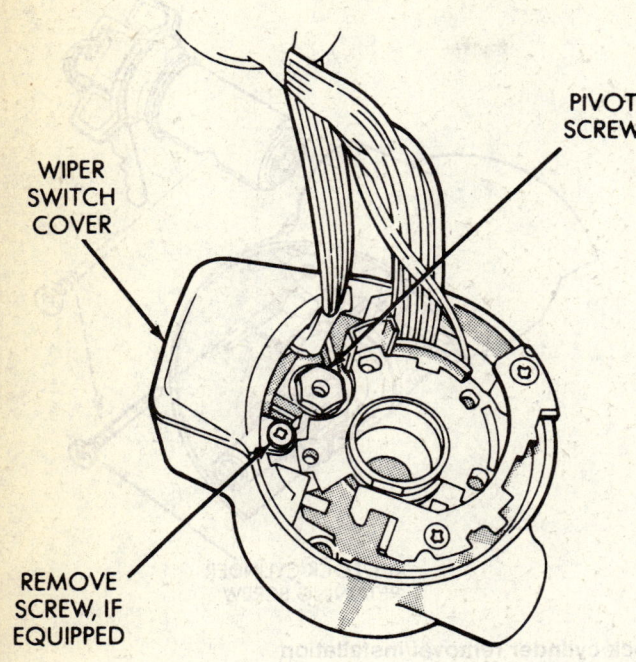

Remove pivot screw

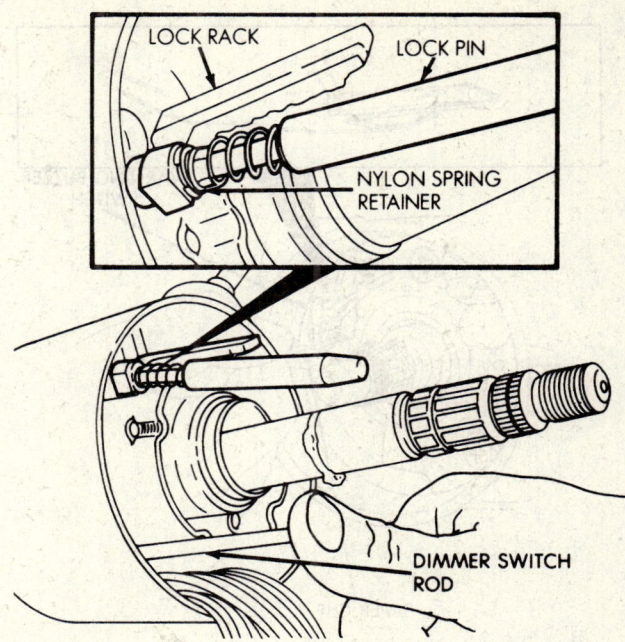

Check dimmer switch rod and lock pin

either door with the key. This will also halt the alarm once it has been activated.

Active arming occurs when the Remote Keyless Entry Transmitter is used to lock the vehicle doors. The alarm will arm only after all doors have been closed. The transmitter is also used to disarm the system by unlocking the doors.

A tamper alert exists to notify the driver that the alarm has been activated and has timed-out (activated for more than 18 minutes). The alert consists of three short horn blasts when the vehicle is disarmed.

System Self Diagnosis

NOTE: Upon initial activation (connected to battery power), the system enters a power up mode. To exit this mode, the system must be disarmed.

A diagnostics mode to verify operation of all switches is an integral part of the system. To enter the diagnostics mode, cycle the ignition key to the accessory position 3 times, leaving the key in this position.

After entering diagnostics, the headlamps, park and tail lamps will begin flashing to verify their operation. In addition, the horn will sound twice. Returning the ignition to the OFF position will stop the lamps from flashing while keeping the system in diagnostics.

While in diagnostics, a horn blast should occur at each of the tests to indicate proper operation.

NOTE: Vehicles equipped with Vehicle Anti-Theft Systems are also equipped with Illuminated Entry. Before beginning diagnostics, disable the Illuminated Entry system by unplugging the relay (TAN) located behind the instrument panel on a bracket of 3 relays.

PRELIMINARY TESTS

1. Beginning with all doors closed, open then close each door. The horn will sound when the door opens, and then again when

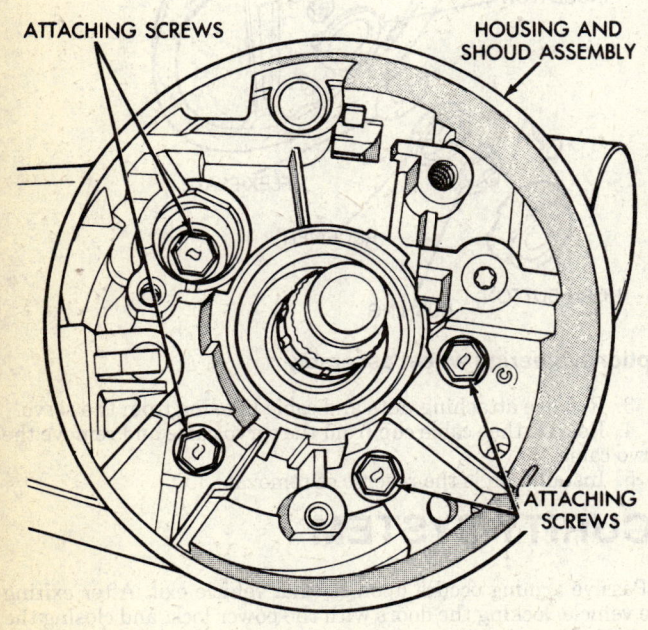

Steering column housing removal/installation

CHASSIS ELECTRICAL 6

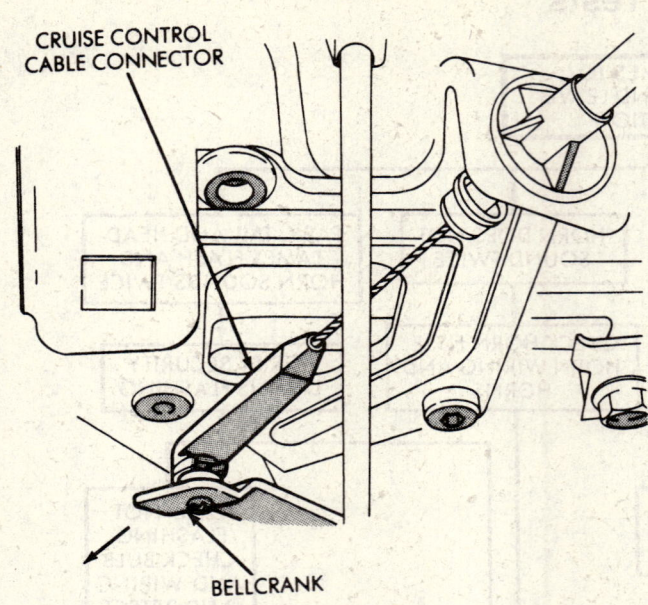

Remove bell crank connector

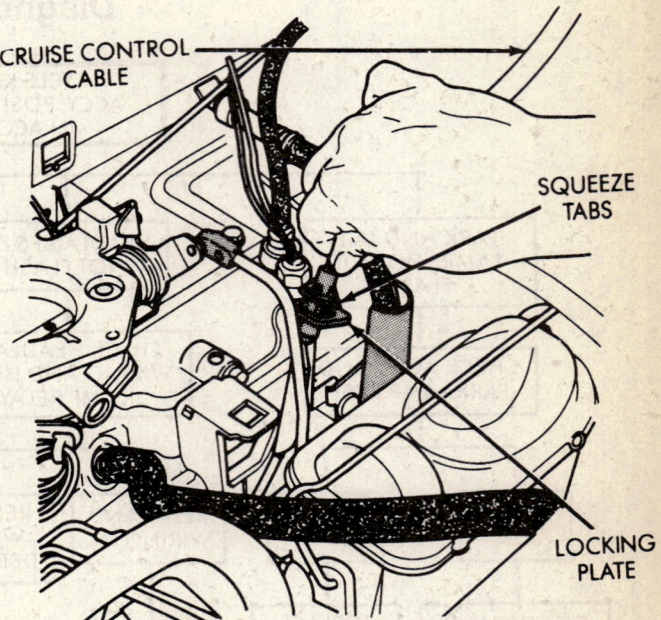

Cruise control cable to locking plate removal/installation

the door closes. There must be a 1 second delay between opening and closing the door.

2. Open, then close the hood. The horn will sound when the hood is opened and closed.

3. Activate the power door locks in both the LOCK and UNLOCK positions. The horn should sound after each activation.

4. Rotate the key in each of the door lock cylinders to the unlock position. The horn will sound as the lock closes and then again when it opens. There must be a 1 second delay between locking and unlocking the door.

5. Cycle the key to the RUN position. A single horn blast will indicate proper operation of the ignition input. This will also take the module out of diagnostic mode.

The lack of a horn blast indicates a switch failure. Check for continuity at the switch. If this is good, check for an open or shorted wire between the switch and alarm module. If the engine controller has been replaced, ensure that the replacement is equipped with a Vehicle Theft Security System circuitry.

Security System Module

REMOVAL AND INSTALLATION

1. Remove two nuts holding the module and bracket located on the drivers side of the heater housing.
2. Pull the module down and disconnect the electrical connector.
3. Installation is the reverse of removal.

Hood Switch

REMOVAL AND INSTALLATION

1. Disconnect the negative battery cable.
2. Remove the battery from the vehicle.
3. Remove the two attaching screws and remove the switch from the right inner fender.

NOTE: When replacing hood switch, always replace bracket and screws with new parts.

4. Installation is the reverse of removal.

Door Switch

REMOVAL AND INSTALLATION

1. Remove the interior door latch release assembly and control panel retaining screws.
2. Disconnect the control linkage and the wiring harness.
3. Remove the latch release and control panel assembly.
4. Remove the armrest lower retaining screws. Swing the armrest down to a vertical position and release upper clip. Pull armrest straight out to remove.
5. Remove the trim panel with a wide flat blade tool starting at the bottom of the panel. Remove the plastic water shield.
6. Pry the door switch off the back of the lock cylinder.
7. Remove the harness clip from the door sheet metal. Disconnect the harness connector and remove the switch.
8. To install the door switch, push the switch onto the lock cylinder, connect the harness and fasten clip to door.
9. The remainder of the installation procedure is the reverse of removal.

6-23

6 CHASSIS ELECTRICAL

Diagnostic Tests

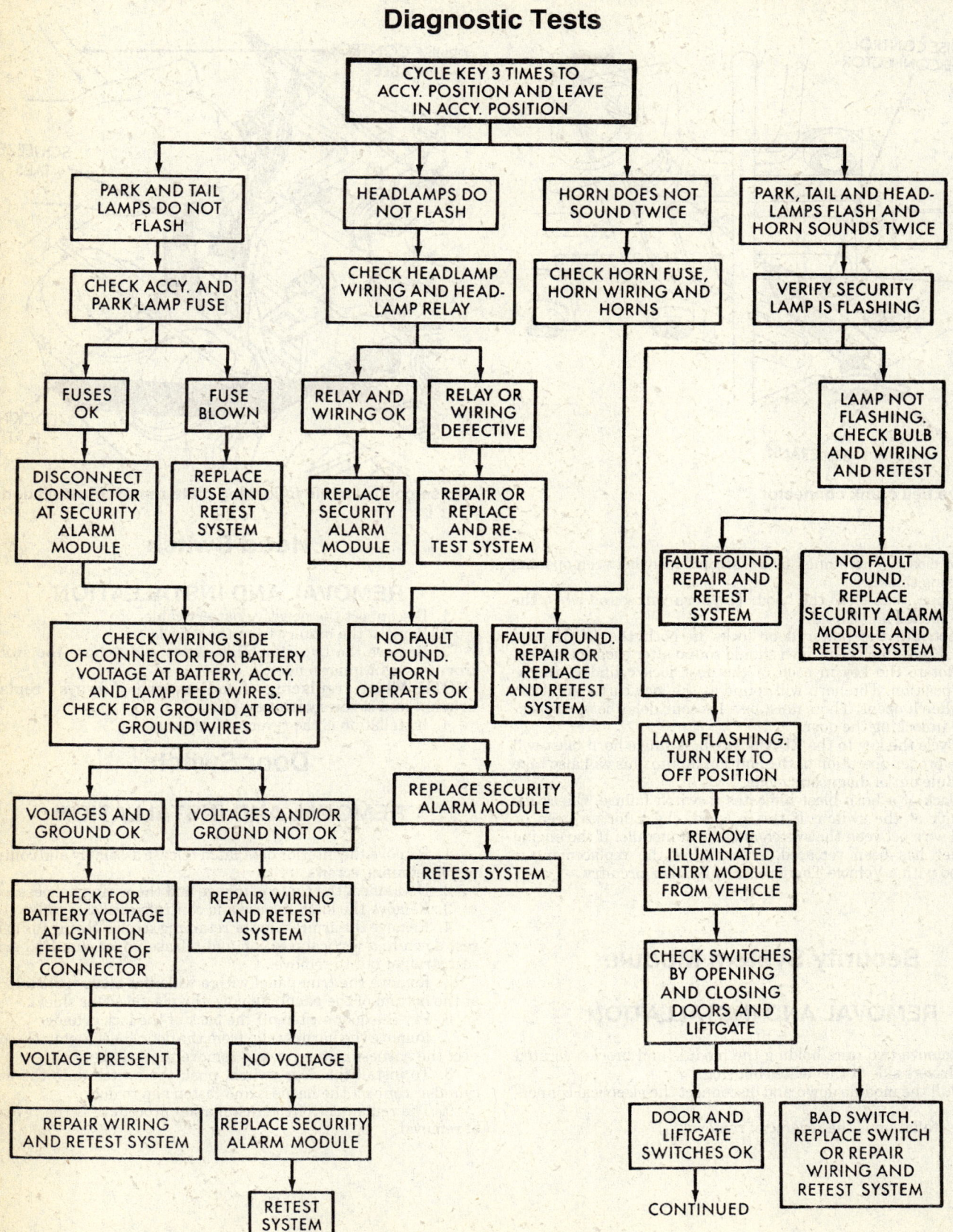

CHASSIS ELECTRICAL 6

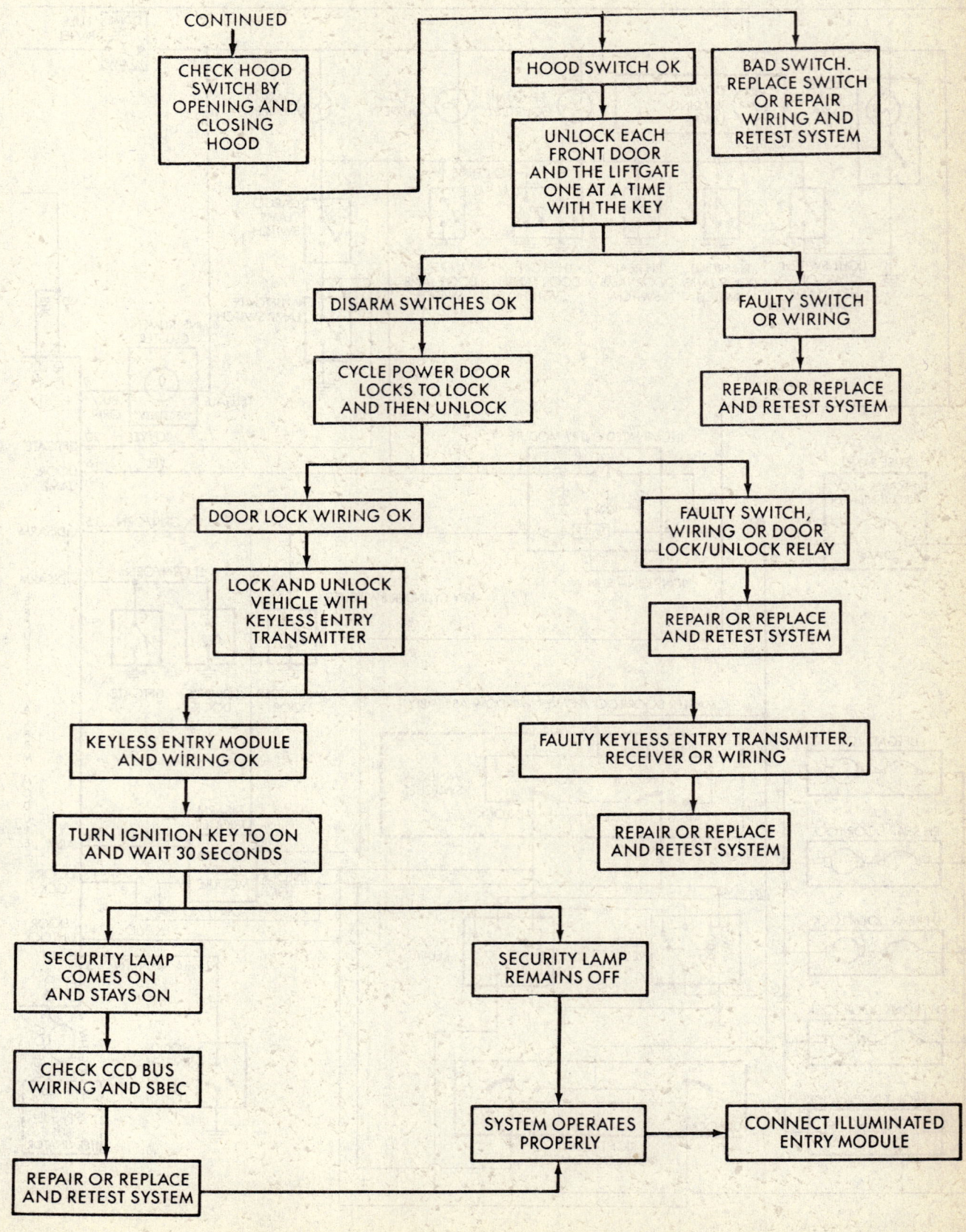

6-25

6 CHASSIS ELECTRICAL

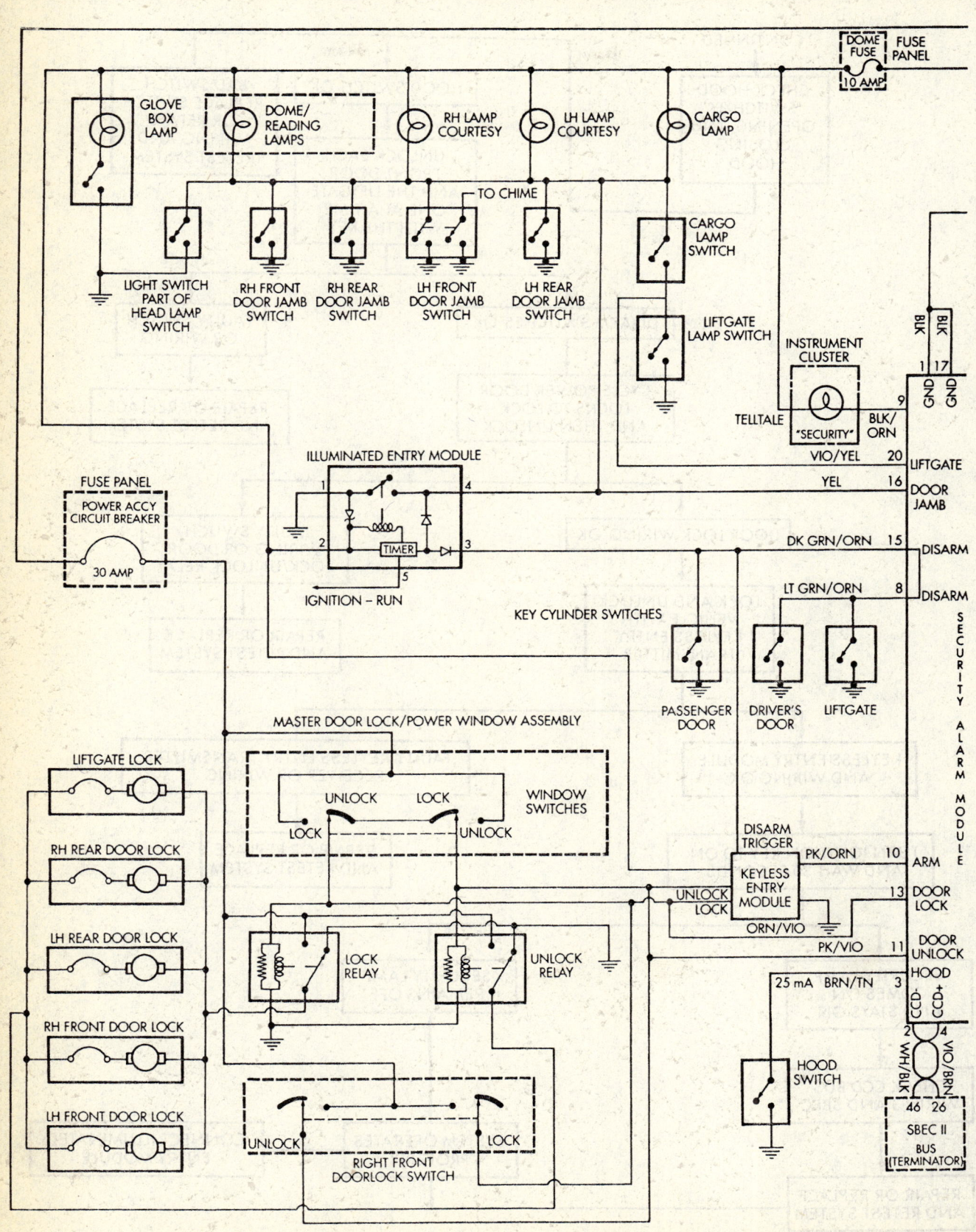

CHASSIS ELECTRICAL 6

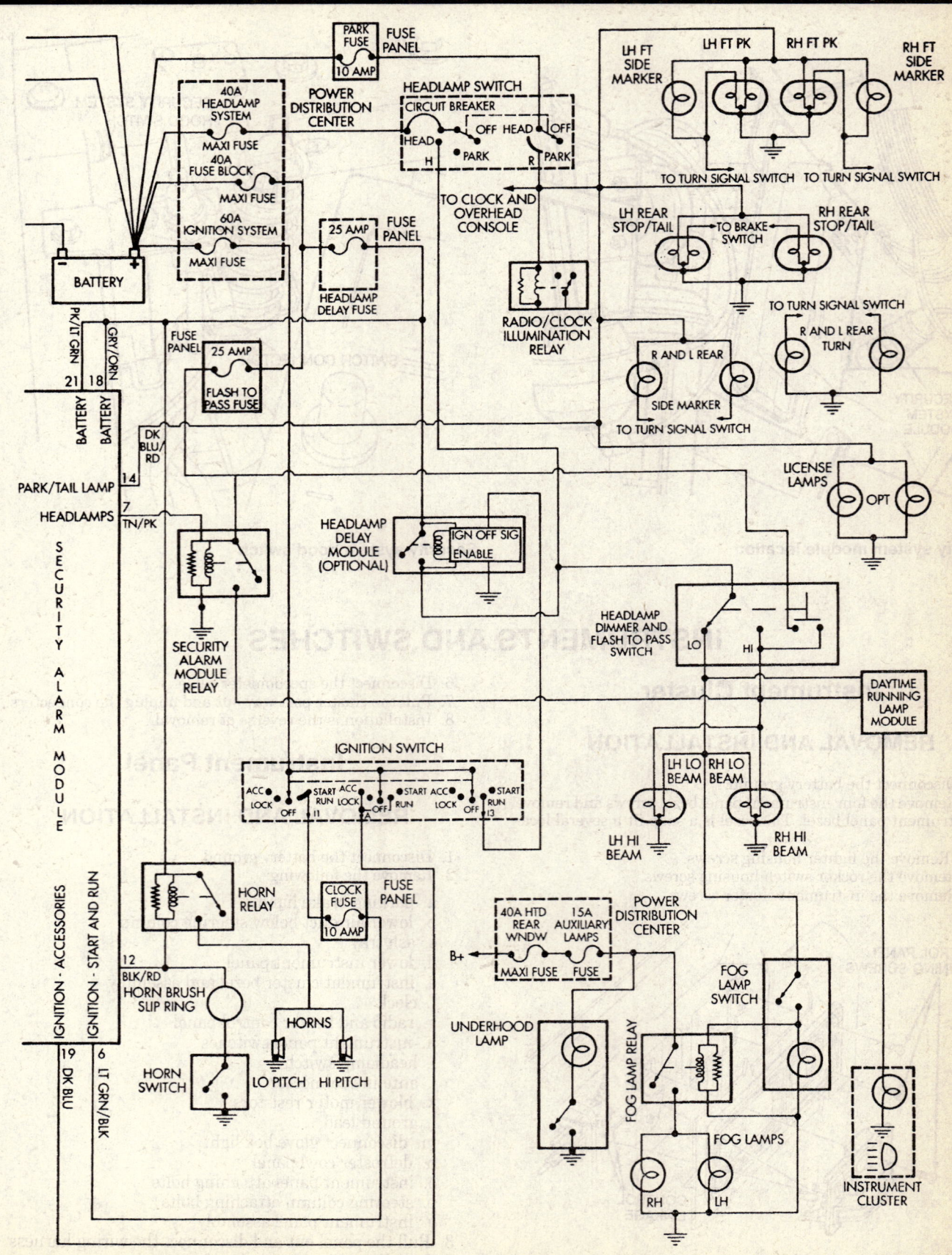

6-27

6 CHASSIS ELECTRICAL

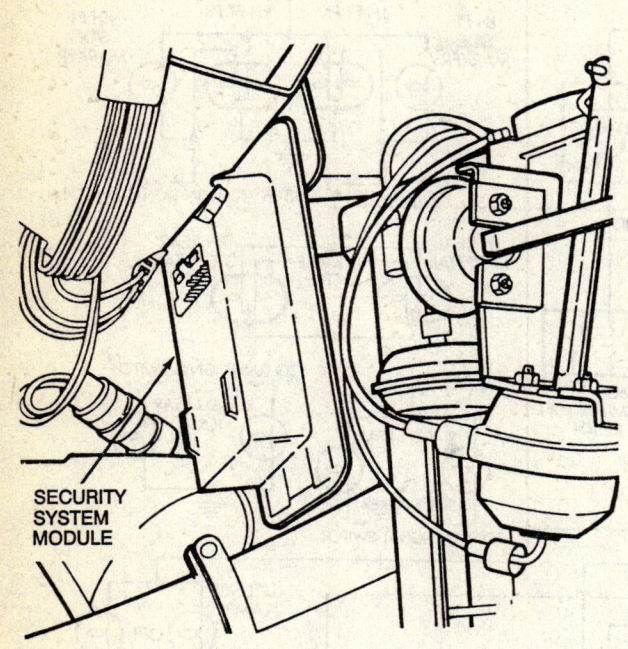

Security system module location

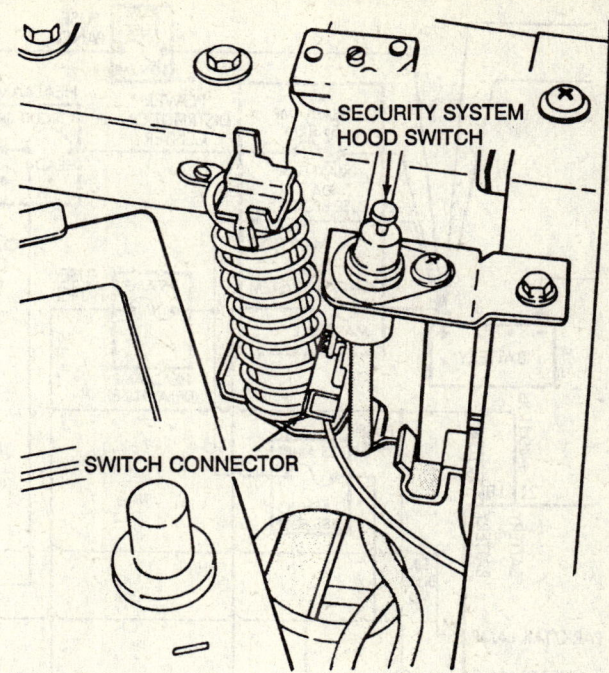

Security system hood switch

INSTRUMENTS AND SWITCHES

Instrument Cluster

REMOVAL AND INSTALLATION

1. Disconnect the battery ground.
2. Remove the four instrument panel bezel screws and remove the instrument panel bezel. The bezel is a snap fit a several locations.
3. Remove the lighter housing screws.
4. Remove the rocker switch housing screws.
5. Remove the instrument cluster screws.
6. Disconnect the speedometer cable.
7. Pull the cluster part way out and unplug the connectors.
8. Installation is the reverse of removal.

Instrument Panel

REMOVAL AND INSTALLATION

1. Disconnect the battery ground.
2. Remove the following:
   a. parking brake handle
   b. lower air duct below steering column
   c. ash tray
   d. lower instrument panel
   e. instrument cluster bezel and assembly
   f. clock
   g. radio and heater control panel
   h. instrument panel switches
   i. headlamp switch
   j. antenna connector
   k. blower motor resistors
   l. ground lead
   m. disconnect glove box light
   n. defroster cowl panel
   o. instrument panel attaching bolts
   p. steering column attaching bolts
   q. instrument panel assembly
3. Pull the panel out and disconnect the wiring harness.
4. Installation is the reverse of removal.

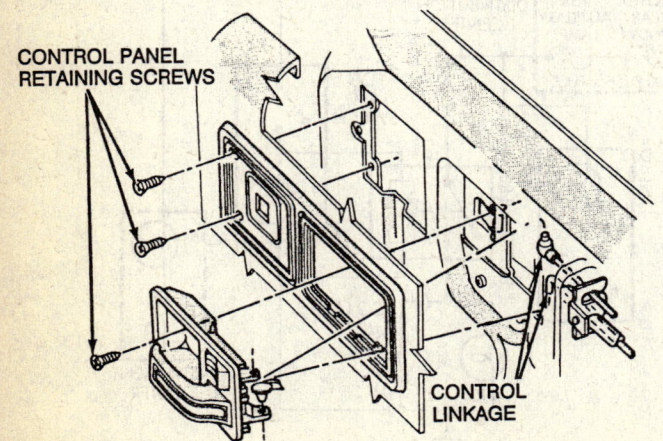

Control panel disassembly

CHASSIS ELECTRICAL 6

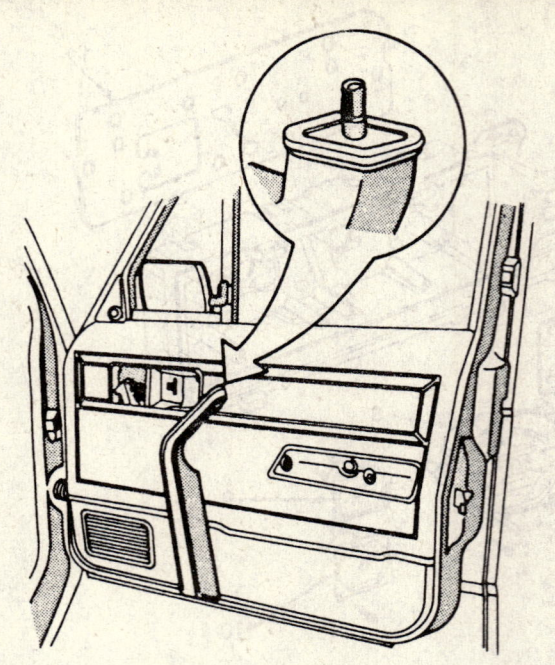

After removing the armrest attaching screws, rotate the armrest to a vertical position and pull straight out

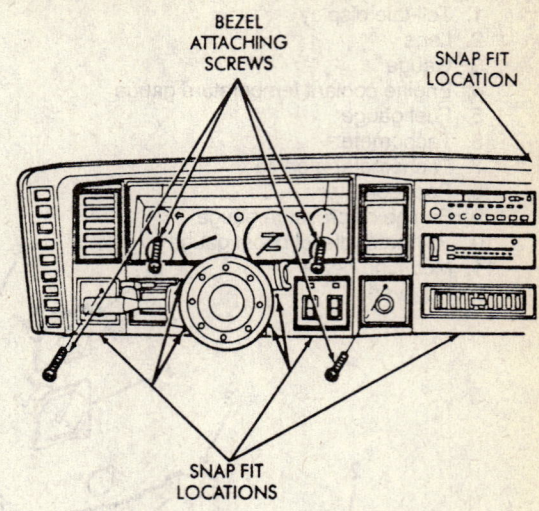

Instrument bezel removal/installation

Speedometer/Tachometer Instrument Cluster Gauges

REMOVAL AND INSTALLATION

1. Remove the instrument cluster.
2. Remove the cluster lens and gauge bezel. If equipped with a trip odometer remove the knob by gently pulling.
3. Remove attaching screws from the front and/or rear of the mounting bezel.
4. Remove the speedometer/tachometer assembly.
5. Installation is the reverse of removal.

Speedometer Cable

REPLACEMENT

1. Reach up behind the speedometer. Depress the spring tab (located on the instrument cluster) IN and pull the cable straight back. Pull the core from the sheath.
2. If the cable is broken, raise and support the vehicle and remove the cable from the transmission. Pull the broken end from the sheath.
3. When installing the cable, coat it with speedometer cable lubricant before installation.

Printed Circuit Replacement

REPLACEMENT

1. Remove the instrument cluster as described in this Section.
2. Remove all gauge attaching screws that contact the printed circuit board.
3. Remove the screw holding the cluster connector retaining strap to the bezel. Remove the strap and pivot the bezel down.
4. Remove the lamp sockets from the circuit board.
5. Remove the printed circuit including the connector.

NOTE: A separate printed circuit for the warning lights is removed by removing the warning light sockets.

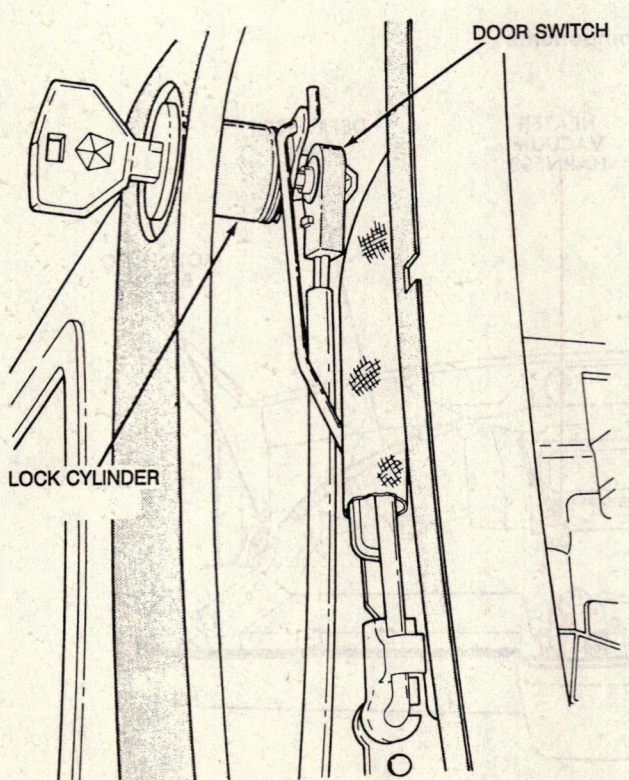

Door switch and lock cylinder assembly

6-29

6 CHASSIS ELECTRICAL

1. Tell-tale display
2. Lens
3. Gauge
4. Engine coolant temperature gauge
5. Fuel gauge
6. Tachometer
7. Tachometer module
8. Speedometer
9. Engine oil pressure gauge
10. Voltmeter/diesel boost gauge
11. Mounting bezel
12. PC overlay

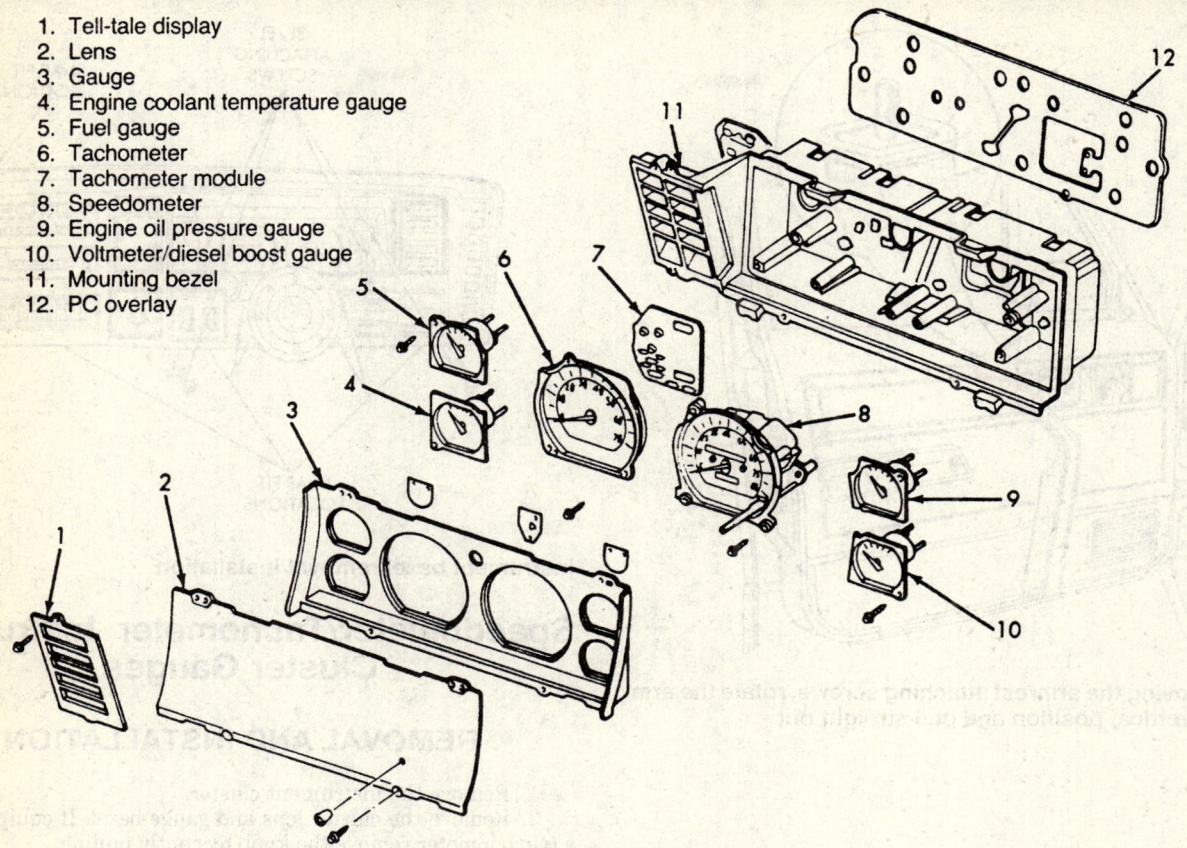

Instrument cluster components

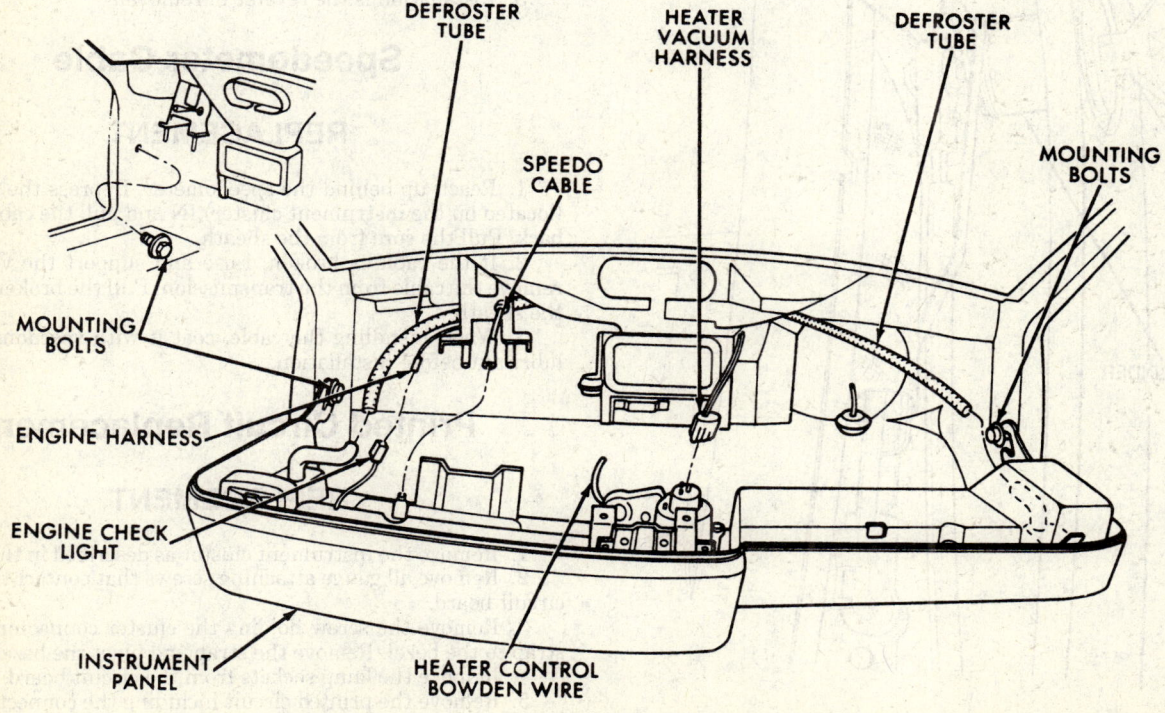

Instrument panel removal/installation

CHASSIS ELECTRICAL 6

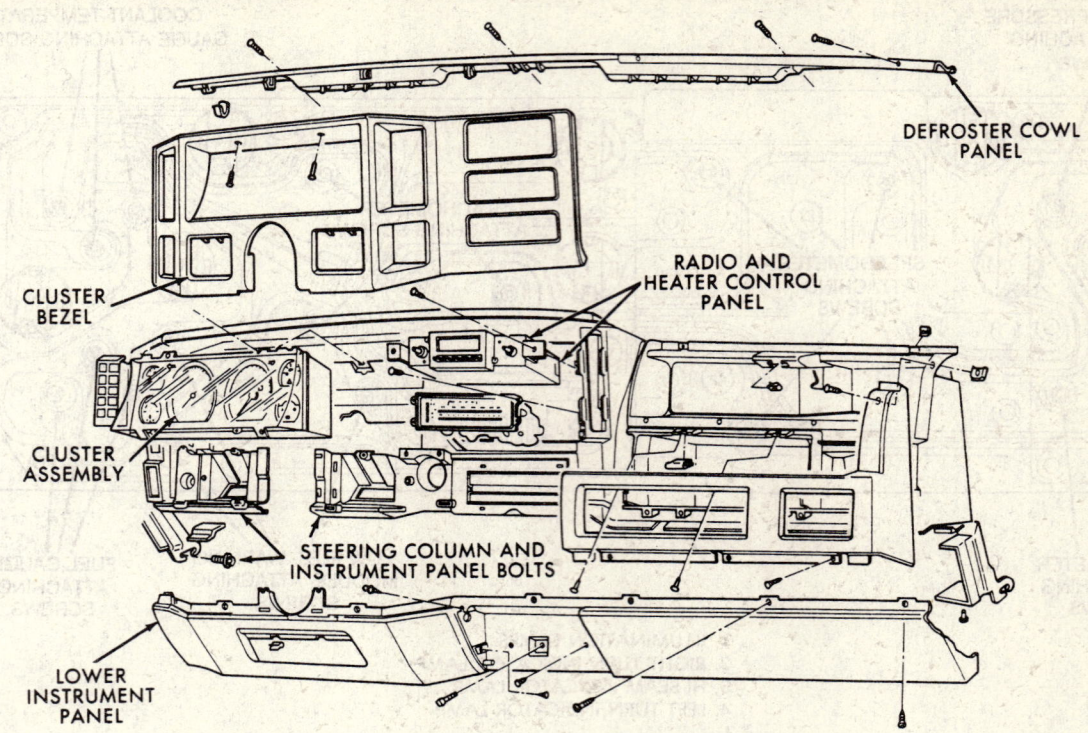

Instrument panel components

Overhead Console

REMOVAL AND INSTALLATION

1. Remove attaching screw located forward of compass.
2. Flex housing outward while pressing upward to disengage from rear bracket.
3. Slide console rearward until the console detaches from the front mounting bracket.
4. While pressing upwards on the rear of the console, slide it forward holding the front away from the headliner, until the rear detaches from the headliner and becomes free.
5. Disconnect wire harness from console and remove.
6. Installation is the reverse of removal. Be sure to flex console outward near the rear allowing engagement with the rear mounting bracket.

Windshield Wiper Switch

REMOVAL AND INSTALLATION

The wiper switch is part of the multi-function switch. See Section 8 for replacement.

Rear Window Wiper Switch

REMOVAL AND INSTALLATION

1. Remove the instrument cluster bezel.
2. Remove the switch housing panel.
3. Unplug the switch connector.
4. Installation is the reverse of removal.

Headlight Switch

REMOVAL AND INSTALLATION

1. Disconnect the battery ground cable.
2. Pull the switch to the full ON position.
3. Reach up under the panel and depress the switch shaft retainer button while pulling the switch control shaft straight out.
4. Remove the switch ferrule nut from the switch.
5. Disconnect the switch from the harness.
6. Installation is the reverse of removal.

LIGHTING

Illuminated Entry System

The Illuminated Entry System is designed to provide the driver with lighting during entry into and exit from the vehicle. The system is activated by a relay (TAN), located on a bracket (3 relays) behind the instrument panel, which receives input from the door jamb switch, keyless entry system and the ignition key. The system provides interior illumination for approximately 30 seconds.

6-31

6 CHASSIS ELECTRICAL

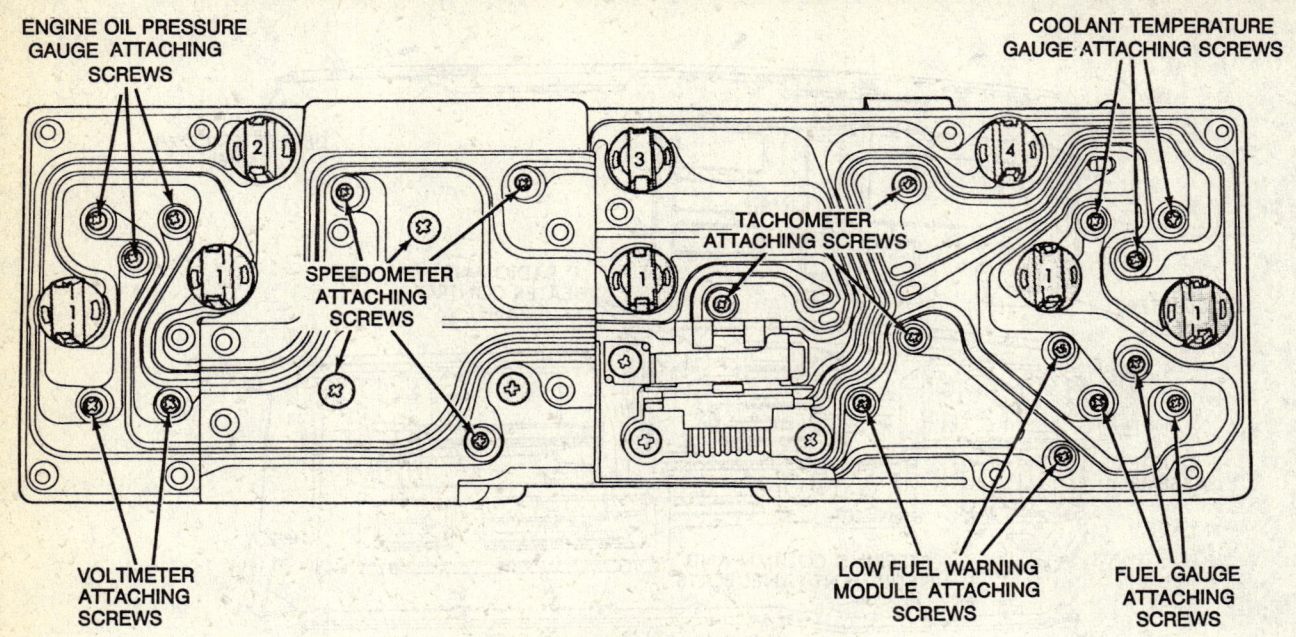

1. ILLUMINATION LAMPS
2. RIGHT TURN INDICATOR LAMP
3. HI-BEAM INDICATOR LAMP
4. LEFT TURN INDICATOR LAMP

Printed circuit panel

DIAGNOSTIC PROCEDURES

1. Ensure the ignition key is in the OFF position.
2. Open and immediately close the drivers door. Interior courtesy lamps should come on.
3. Open drivers door, enter vehicle, close door and turn ignition key to the RUN position. The courtesy lights should turn off.
4. Turn the ignition OFF and exit the vehicle. The courtesy lamps should stay ON after the door is closed.
5. From outside the vehicle, open and close the passenger door. The courtesy lamps should light.

RELAY TESTING

1. Touch Pin 4 to ground. Lamp should light for 30 seconds. If not, replace relay.
2. Touch Pin 4 to ground. Lamp should light, then touch Pin 5 to B+ and light should go out. If not, replace relay.
3. Touch Pin 3 to ground. Lamp should light, then touch Pin 5 to B+ and light should go out. If not, replace relay.

Headlights

REMOVAL AND INSTALLATION

1. Remove the headlamp bezel and retaining ring attaching screws. Remove the bezel and retaining ring.
2. Pull the headlight out, disconnect the wire harness and remove the headlight from the vehicle.
3. Install the headlight in the reverse order of removal.

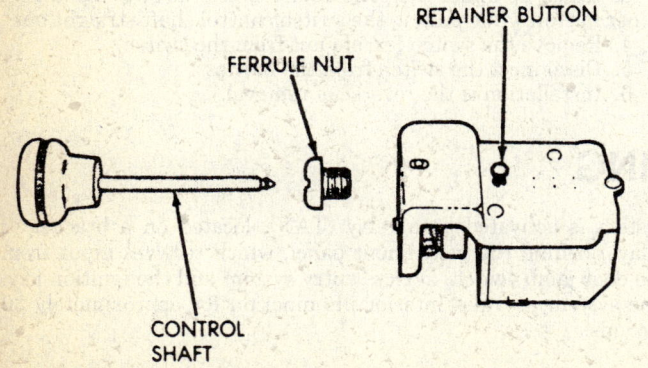

Headlight switch assembly

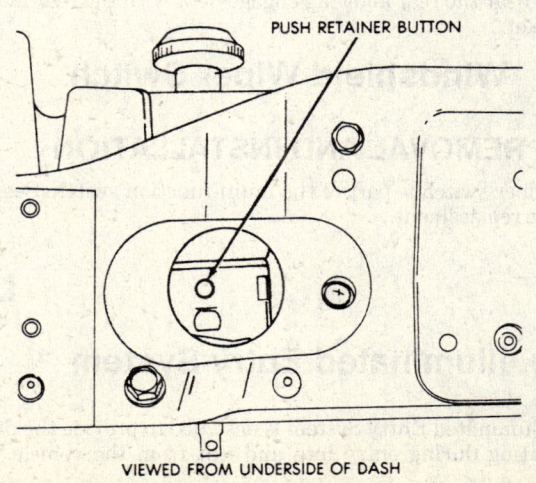

Headlight switch shaft removal

CHASSIS ELECTRICAL 6

HEADLIGHT AIMING

The headlights must be properly aimed to provide the best, safest road illumination. The lights should be checked for proper aim, and adjusted if necessary, after installing a new sealed beam unit or if the front end sheet metal has been replaced. Certain state and local authorities have requirements for headlight aiming and you should check these before adjusting.

The truck's fuel tank should be about half full when adjusting the headlights. Tires should be properly inflated, and if a heavy load is carried in the pick-up bed, it should remain there.

Horizontal and vertical aiming of each sealed beam unit is provided by two adjusting screws, which move the mounting ring in the body against the tension of the coil spring. There is no adjustment for focus; this is done during headlight manufacturing.

Fog/Driving Lights

Fog lamps are installed on the front bumper. The switch is located to the left of the steering column on the dash panel. The fog lamps are turned off by the circuit relay when the high beam driving lamps are turned on. The circuit relay is located on the right front wheelhouse panel near the blower motor.

REMOVAL AND INSTALLATION

Fog Lamp Element

1. Remove the lamp stone shields, the four bezel attaching screws, and the bezel.
2. Remove the reflector assembly from the lamp body.
3. Remove the bulb holder from the assembly. Remove the element from the bulb.

NOTE: DO NOT handle elements with your bare hands, always handle with a clean cloth. Oil from your hands will cause the element to fail.

4. Installation is the reverse of removal.

Fog Lamp Switch

The fog lamp switch is removed and installed by simply prying the switch from the instrument panel and unplugging the electrical connector.

FOGLAMP BEAM ADJUSTMENT

1. Position the vehicle on a level surface, facing a wall approximately 25 feet away. Remove the lamp stone shields and loosen the adjustment nuts.
2. Turn the fog lamps ON and adjust as follows:

    a. Distance between the light beam centers should be equal to the distance between the lamp assemblies on the bumper.

    b. Height of the light beams on the wall should be 4 inches less than the center of the lamp assemblies when mounted on the bumper.

3. Install all previously removed items after turning OFF the fog lamps.

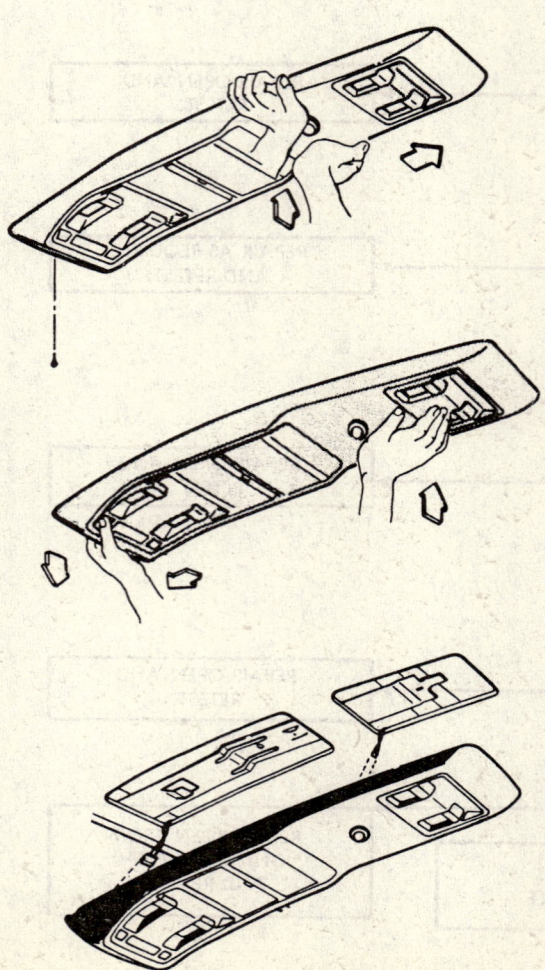

Overhead console removal/installation

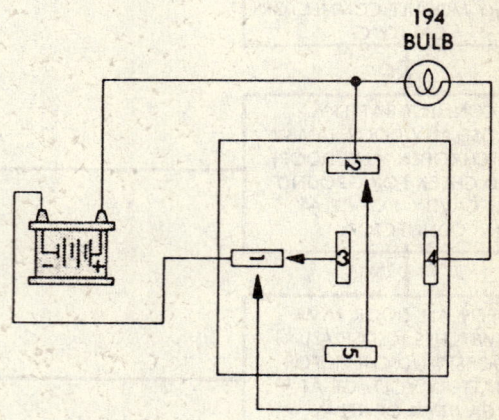

→ TEST POINTS (TOUCH MOMENTARILY)

PIN 1 GROUND
PIN 2 B+
PIN 3 KEYLESS ENTRY INPUT
PIN 4 DOOR JAMB
PIN 5 KEY IN RUN INPUT

Illuminated entry relay

6-33

6 CHASSIS ELECTRICAL

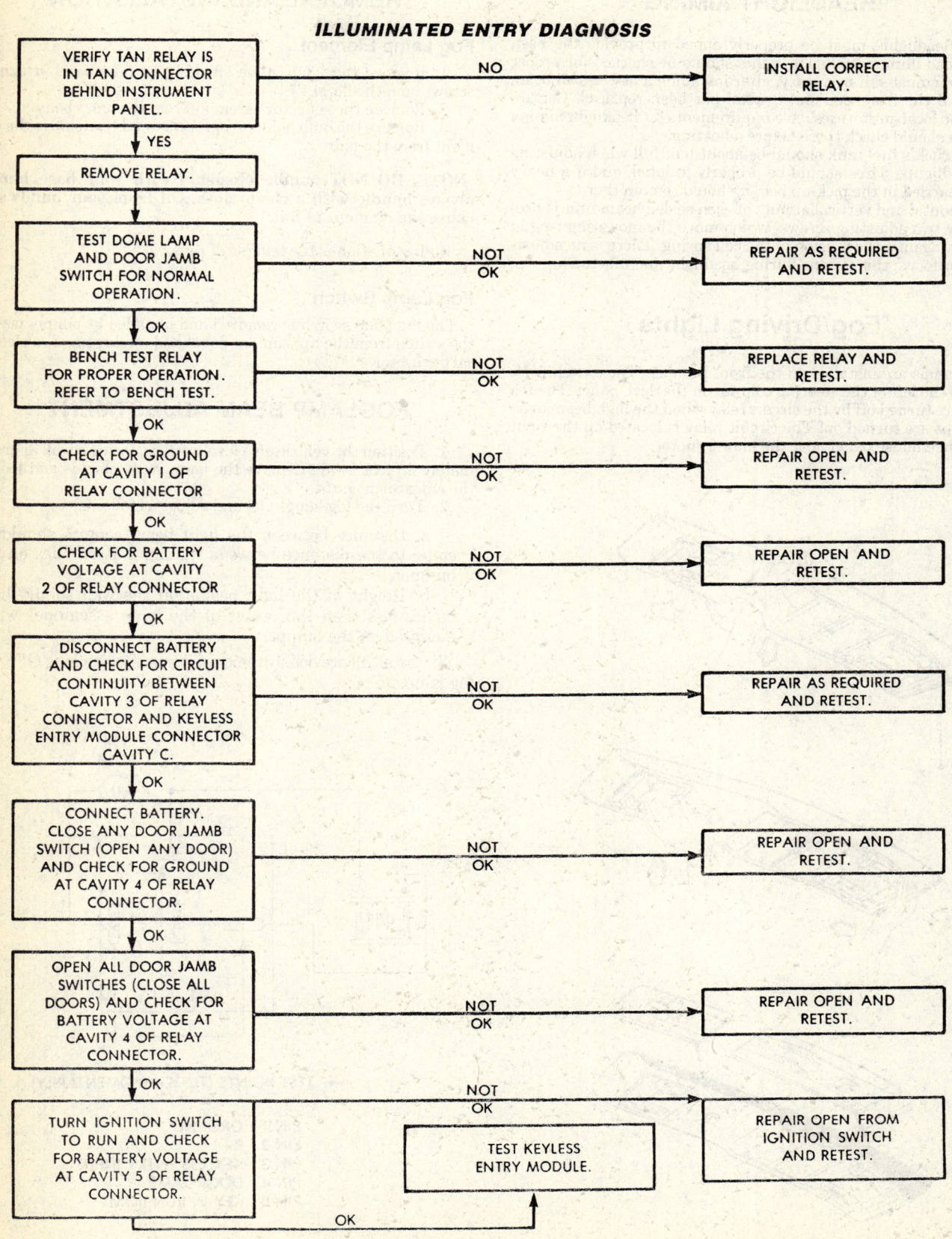

CHASSIS ELECTRICAL 6

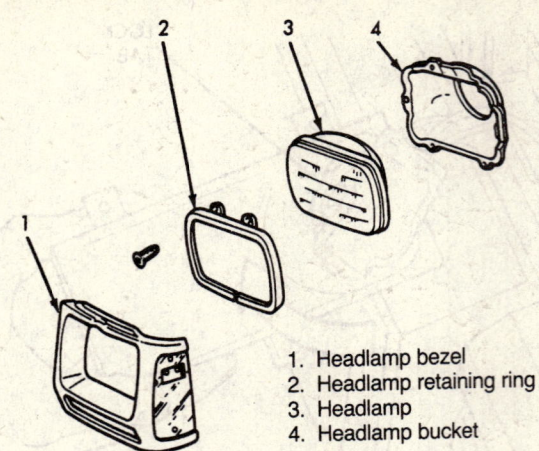

1. Headlamp bezel
2. Headlamp retaining ring
3. Headlamp
4. Headlamp bucket

Single headlamp assembly

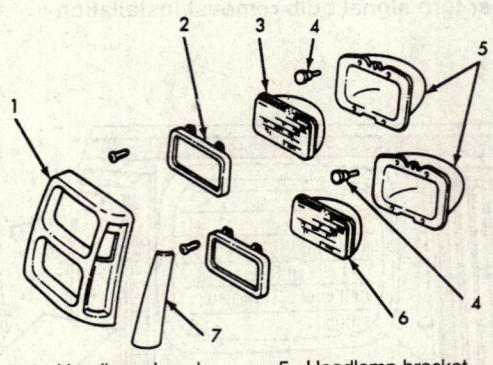

1. Headlamp bezel
2. Retaining ring
3. Headlamp (low beam)
4. Headlamp adjustors
5. Headlamp bracket
6. Headlamp (high beam)
7. Side marker

Dual headlamp assembly

Signal and Marker Lights

REMOVAL AND INSTALLATION

Front Parking/Turn Signal Lights

1. Remove the screws from the lens and separate the lens from the headlight bezel.
2. Remove the headlight bezel.
3. Remove the screws from the turn signal housing and pull it out.
4. Turn the bulb socket counterclockwise $1/3$ turn and remove it.
5. Installation is the reverse of removal.

Side Marker Lights

1. Remove the screws from the marker lens and separate the lens from the headlight bezel.
2. Pull the bulb from its socket in the back of the lens.

3. Installation is the reverse of removal.

Back-Up/Rear Turn Signal/Tail Lights

1. Remove attaching screws and pull out the tail light assembly.
2. The bulbs can be removed by turning them $1/3$ turn counterclockwise.

Dome Light

CHEROKEE/WAGONEER

Remove the dome lamp lens by squeezing it on both sides. Pull the lens down to gain access to the bulb. If removing the entire assembly, remove the housing retaining clips with a thin blade tool, lower the housing and disconnect the wiring harness.

COMANCHE

Remove the dome lamp assembly by prying outward to detach the retaining clips from the side trim panel. Pull the assembly outward and disconnect the wiring harness.

License Plate Light

WAGONEER/CHEROKEE WITHOUT SWING-OUT SPARE

Remove the two lens screws and remove the bulb hosing from liftgate. Remove bulb from housing.

WAGONEER/CHEROKEE WITH SWING-OUT SPARE

Remove screw holding lens assembly. Pry housing cover from vehicle. Remove bulb.

COMANCHE

Remove clip, located at the rear of the bumper, that retains the lamp and socket in the bumper. Slide bulb and socket out of bumper and replace bulb.

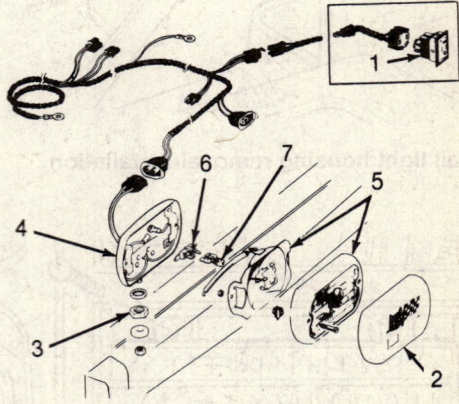

1. Instrument panel switch
2. Stone shield
3. Adjustment nut
4. Lamp body
5. Lens and reflector assembly
6. Bulb holder
7. Lamp element

Fog lamp assemblies

6-35

6 CHASSIS ELECTRICAL

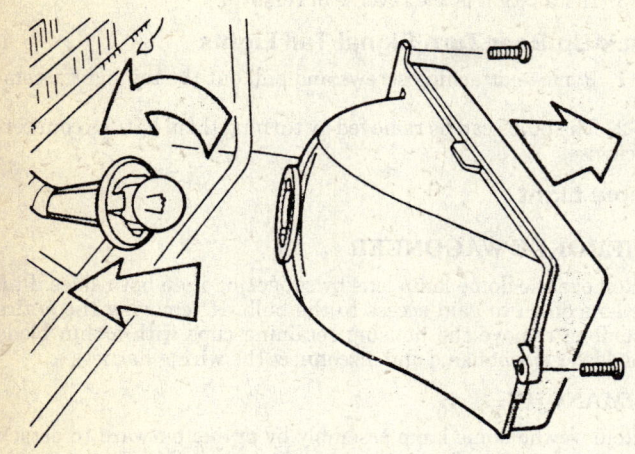

Cherokee/Comanche turn signal assembly removal/installation

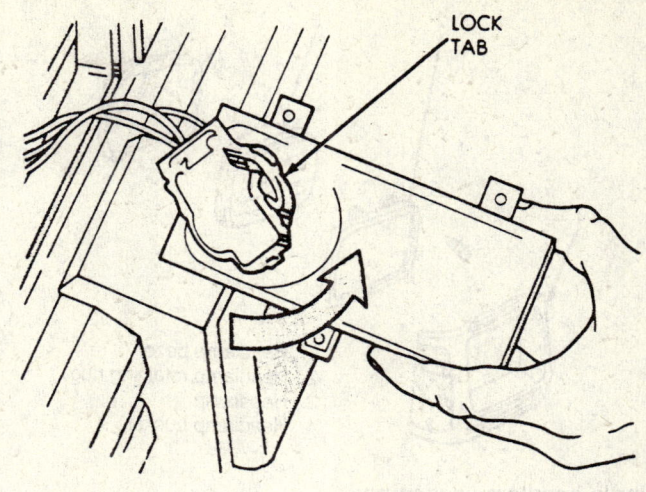

Wagoneer turn signal bulb removal/installation

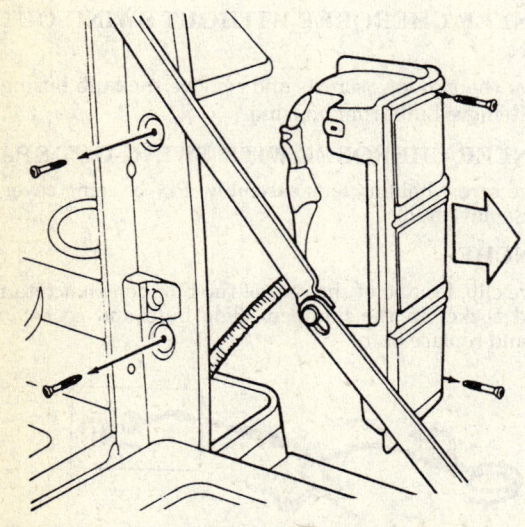

Comanche tail light housing removal/installation

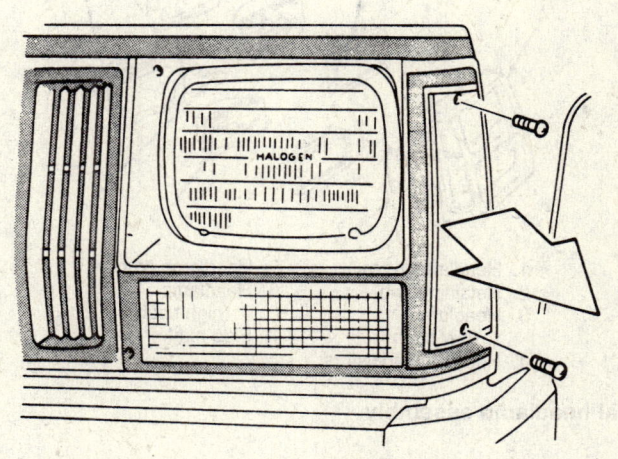

Wagoneer/Cherokee side marker lamp removal/installation

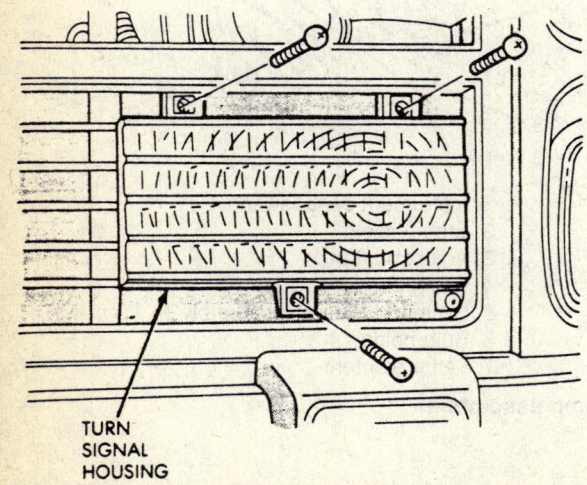

Wagoneer turn signal lens removal/installation

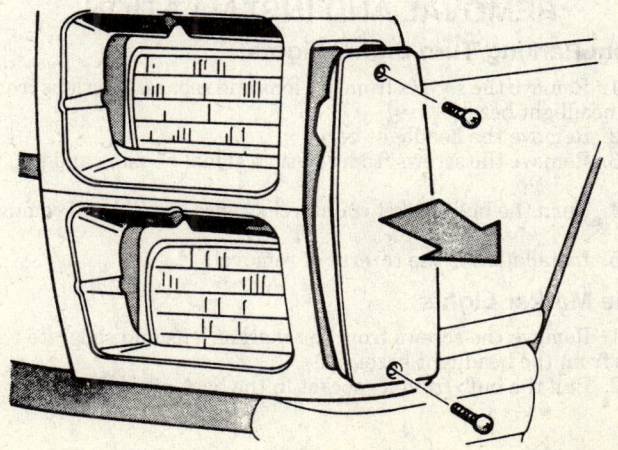

Comanche side marker lamp removal/installation

CHASSIS ELECTRICAL 6

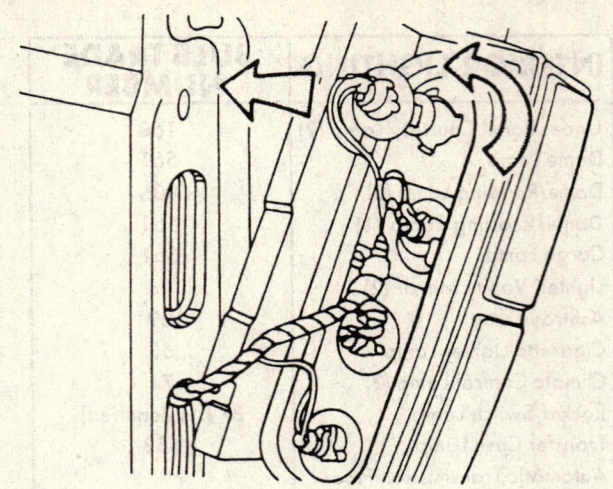
Wagoneer/Cherokee tail light bulb removal/installation

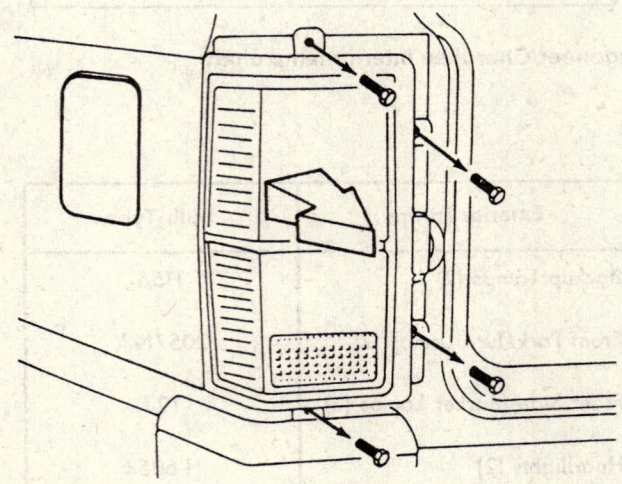
Wagoneer/Cherokee tail light housing removal/installation

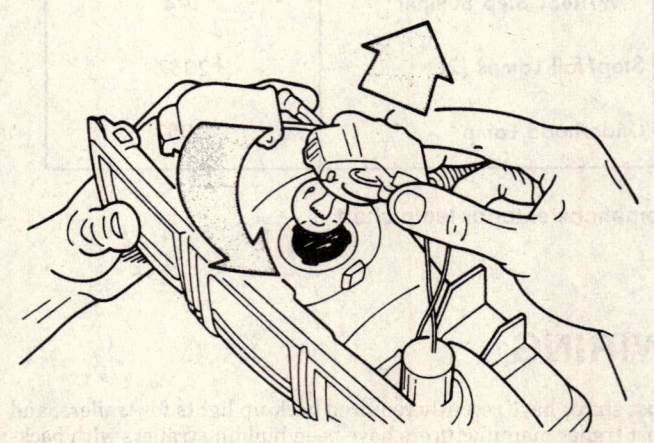
Comanche tail light housing removal/installation

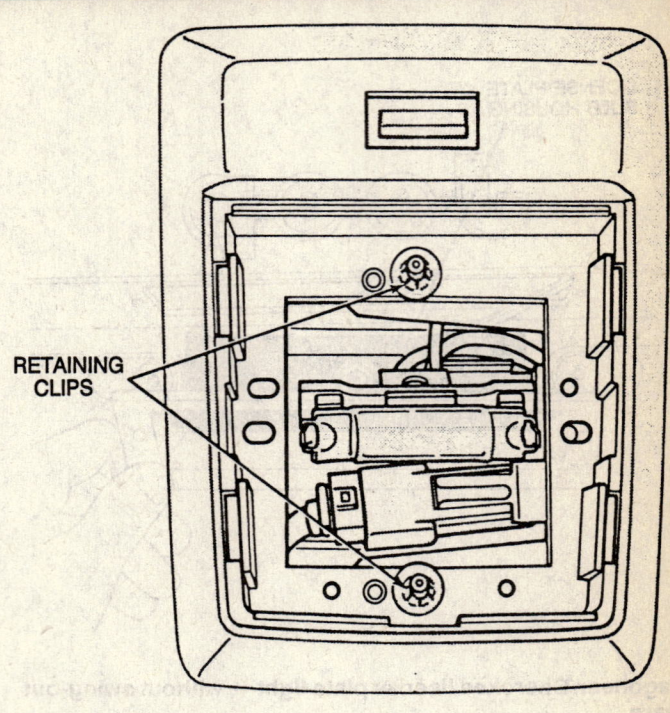
Wagoneer/Cherokee dome light

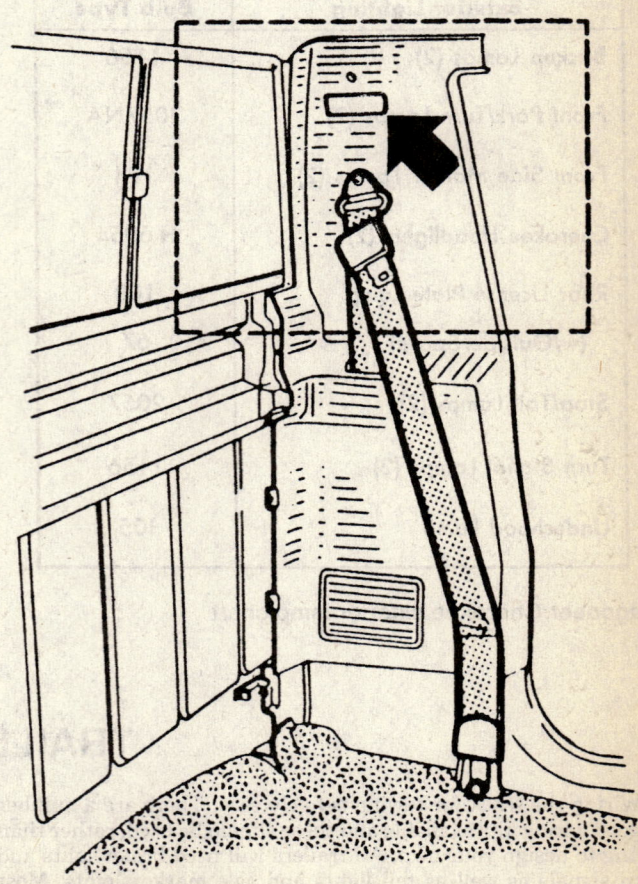
The arrow points to the Comanche dome light

6-37

6 CHASSIS ELECTRICAL

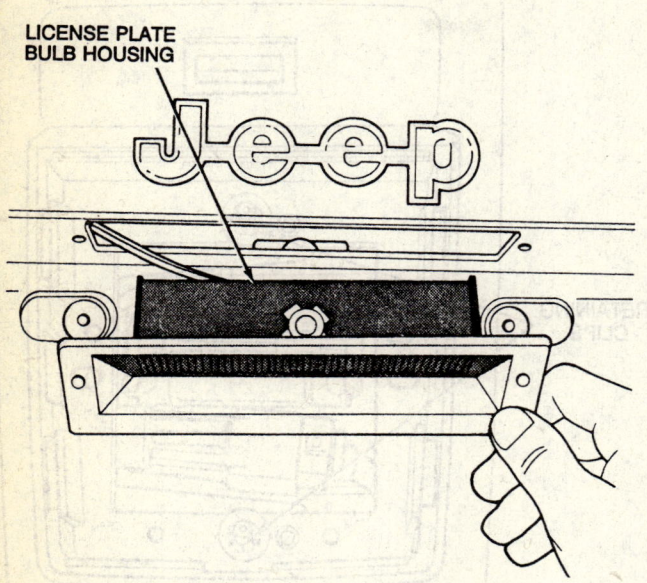

Wagoneer/Cherokee license plate light — without swing-out spare

INTERIOR LIGHTING	BULB TRADE NUMBER
Under Panel Courtesy Lamp (2)	168
Dome Lamp	561
Dome/Reading Lamp (2)	906
Dome/Reading Lamp (1)	561
Cargo Lamp	561
Lighted Vanity Mirror (2)	74
Ashtray Lamp	1891
Cigarette Lighter Lamp	53
Climate Control Lamp (2)	74
Rocker Switch Lamp	37 (As Required)
Transfer Case Lamp	658
Automatic Transmission Floor Shift Lamp	658
Glove Box Lamp	194
Overhead Console	912

Wagoneer/Cherokee interior lamp chart

Exterior Lighting	Bulb Type
Backup Lamps (2)	1156
Front Park/Turn Lamps (2)	2057NA
Front Side Marker Lamps (2)	194
Cherokee Headlights (2)	H 6054
Rear License Plate Lamp	168
(w/Outside Spare)	67
Stop/Tail Lamps (2)	2057
Turn Signal Lamps (2)	1156
Underhood Lamp	105

Wagoneer/Cherokee exterior lamp chart

Exterior Lamps	Bulb Type
Backup Lamps (2)	1156
Front Park/Turn Lamps (2)	2057NA
Front Side Marker Lamps (2)	194
Headlights (2)	H 6054
Rear License Plate Lamp	67
W/Rear Step Bumper	194
Stop/Tail Lamps (2)	2057
Underhood Lamp	105

Comanche exterior lamp chart

TRAILER WIRING

Wiring the truck for towing is fairly easy. There are a number of good wiring kits available and these should be used, rather than trying to design your own. All trailers will need brake lights and turn signals as well as tail lights and side marker lights. Most states require extra marker lights for overly wide trailers. Also, most states have recently required back-up lights for trailers, and most trailer manufacturers have been building trailers with back-up lights for several years.

Additionally, some Class I, most Class II and just about all Class III trailers will have electric brakes.

CHASSIS ELECTRICAL 6

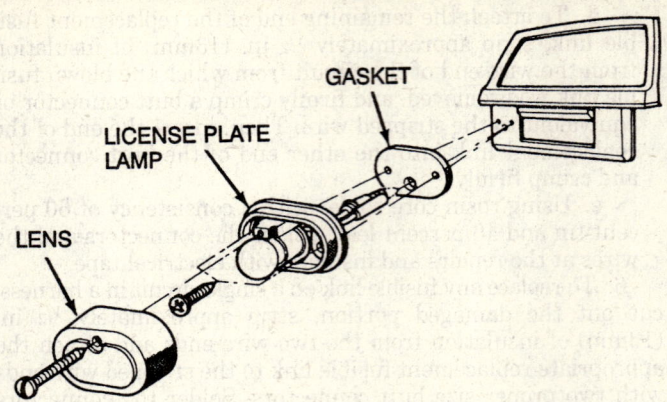

Wagoneer/Cherokee license plate light — with swing-out spare

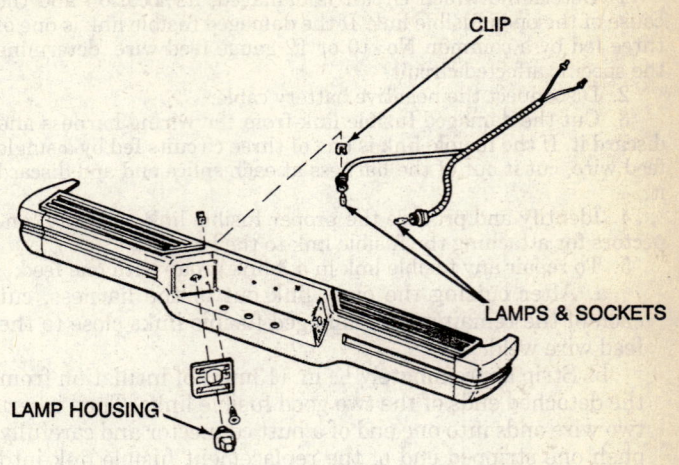

Comanche license plate light

INTERIOR LIGHTING	NUMBER OF BULBS/ BULB TRADE NUMBER
Under Panel Courtesy Light	2/168
Dome/Reading Light	2/C11-7W
Lighted Vanity Mirror	2/74
Ash Tray Light	1/1891
Cigar Lighter Light	1/53
Climate Control Panel Light	2/74
Rocker Switched Lights	1/37
Transfer Case Light	1/658
Select Drive Bezel Light	1/74
Automatic Transmission Floor Shift Light	1/658
Glove Box Light	1/194

Comanche interior lamp chart

Add to this number an accessories wire, to operate trailer internal equipment or to charge the trailer's battery, and you can have as many as seven wires in the harness.

Determine the equipment on your trailer and buy the wiring kit necessary. The kit will contain all the wires needed, plus a plug adapter set which included the female plug, mounted on the bumper or hitch, and the male plug, wired into, or plugged into the trailer harness.

When installing the kit, follow the manufacturer's instructions. The color coding of the wires is standard throughout the industry.

One point to note, some domestic vehicles, and most imported vehicles, have separate turn signals. On most domestic vehicles, the brake lights and rear turn signals operate with the same bulb. For those vehicles with separate turn signals, you can purchase an isolation unit so that the brake lights won't blink whenever the turn signals are operated, or, you can go to your local electronics supply house and buy four diodes to wire in series with the brake and turn signal bulbs. Diodes will isolate the brake and turn signals. The choice is yours. The isolation units are simple and quick to install, but far more expensive than the diodes. The diodes, however, require more work to install properly, since they require the cutting of each bulb's wire and soldering in place of the diode.

One final point, the best kits are those with a spring loaded cover on the vehicle mounted socket. This cover prevents dirt and moisture from corroding the terminals. Never let the vehicle socket hang loosely. Always mount it securely to the bumper or hitch.

CIRCUIT PROTECTION

Fuse Panel/Flashers

The fuse panel contains fuses (circuit breakers) which protect the various electrical systems. Also included are the turn signal and hazard flashers, and the chime module. The panel is located under the dash on the left hand side near the kick panel.

The Power Distribution Center contains relays and fuses which further protect the electrical systems. It is located under the hood on the right side of the engine compartment.

Fuses and relays are replaced by simply unplugging the defective unit and inserting a new one. Ensure the ignition is OFF when replacing any fuse or relay.

NOTE: Never replace any fuse or relay with one of a different rating (amperage). Damage to the vehicle or personal injury could result.

Fusible Link

The fusible link is a short length of special, Hypalon (high temperature) insulated wire, integral with the engine compartment wiring harness and should not be confused with standard wire. It is several wire gauges smaller than the circuit which it protects. Under no circumstances should a fusible link replacement repair be made using a length of standard wire cut from bulk stock or from another wiring harness.

To repair any blown fusible link use the following procedure:

6-39

6 CHASSIS ELECTRICAL

1. Determine which circuit is damaged, its location and the cause of the open fusible link. If the damaged fusible link is one of three fed by a common No. 10 or 12 gauge feed wire, determine the specific affected circuit.
2. Disconnect the negative battery cable.
3. Cut the damaged fusible link from the wiring harness and discard it. If the fusible link is one of three circuits fed by a single feed wire, cut it out of the harness at each splice end and discard it.
4. Identify and procure the proper fusible link and butt connectors for attaching the fusible link to the harness.
5. To repair any fusible link in a 3-link group with one feed:

    a. After cutting the open link out of the harness, cut each of the remaining undamaged fusible links close to the feed wire weld.

    b. Strip approximately 1/2 in. (13mm) of insulation from the detached ends of the two good fusible links. Then insert two wire ends into one end of a butt connector and carefully push one stripped end of the replacement fusible link into the same end of the butt connector and crimp all three firmly together.

NOTE: Care must be taken when fitting the three fusible links into the butt connector as the internal diameter is a snug fit for three wires. Make sure to use a proper crimping tool. Pliers, side cutters, etc. will not apply the proper crimp to retain the wires and withstand a pull test.

    c. After crimping the butt connector to the three fusible links, cut the weld portion from the feed wire and strip approximately 1/2 in. (13mm) of insulation from the cut end. Insert the stripped end into the open end of the butt connector and crimp very firmly.

    d. To attach the remaining end of the replacement fusible link, strip approximately 1/2 in. (13mm) of insulation from the wire end of the circuit from which the blown fusible link was removed, and firmly crimp a butt connector or equivalent to the stripped wire. Then, insert the end of the replacement link into the other end of the butt connector and crimp firmly.

    e. Using rosin core solder with a consistency of 60 percent tin and 40 percent lead, solder the connectors and the wires at the repairs and insulate with electrical tape.

6. To replace any fusible link on a single circuit in a harness, cut out the damaged portion, strip approximately 1/2 in. (13mm) of insulation from the two wire ends and attach the appropriate replacement fusible link to the stripped wire ends with two proper size butt connectors. Solder the connectors and wires and insulate with tape.
7. To repair any fusible link which has an eyelet terminal on one end such as the charging circuit, cut off the open fusible link behind the weld, strip approximately 1/2 in. (13mm) of insulation from the cut end and attach the appropriate new eyelet fusible link to the cut stripped wire with an appropriate size butt connector. Solder the connectors and wires at the repair and insulate with tape.
8. Connect the negative battery cable to the battery and test the system for proper operation.

NOTE: Do not mistake a resistor wire for a fusible link. The resistor wire is generally longer and has print stating, "Resistor: don't cut or splice."ca

CHASSIS ELECTRICAL 6

CAVITY	AMP/COLOR	ITEMS FUSED
18	25 AMP NAT	REAR DEFOGGER
19	5 AMP TN	INSTRUMENT PANEL LAMPS
20	5.5 AMP C/BRKR	WINDSHIELD WIPER/WINDSHIELD WASHER

AMPS	FUSE	COLOR CODE
2	PK	PINK
5	TN	TAN
7.5	VT	VIOLET
10	RD	RED
15	LT BL	LIGHT BLUE
20	YL	YELLOW
25	NAT	NATURAL

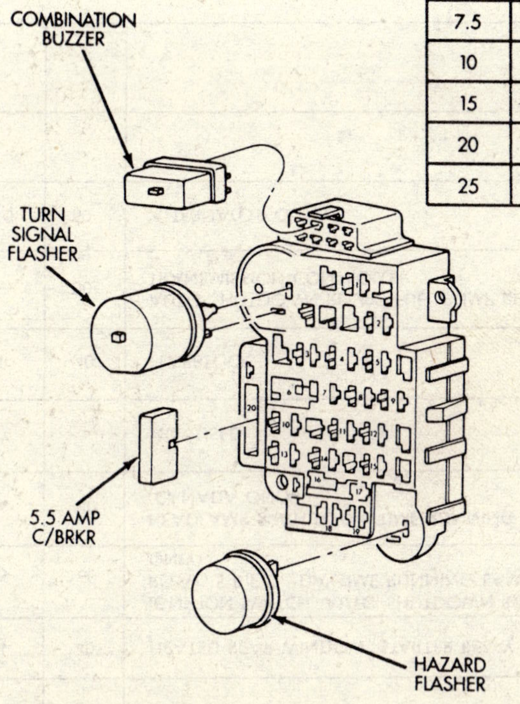

CAVITY	AMP/COLOR	ITEMS FUSED
1	25 AMP NAT	REAR WIPER, REAR WASHER
2	15 AMP LT BL	RADIO, RADIO CLOCK ILLUMINATION, CIGAR LIGHTER, DOME LAMP, LOW WASHER FLUID LAMP
3	10 AMP RD	CLOCK, EMISSION MAINTENANCE TIMER
4	15 AMP LT BL	HEADLAMP DIMMER SWITCH
5	25 AMP NAT	BLOWER MOTOR
6	30 AMP C/BRKR	POWER DOOR LOCKS, POWER SEATS, TRAILER HARNESS
7	2 AMP PK	ANTILOCK PUMP MOTOR
8	20 AMP YL	TURN SIGNAL FLASHER, HEATED REAR WINDOW
9	10 AMP RD	COURTESY; CARGO; DOME/MAP; GLOVE BOX LAMPS, RADIO, CLOCK, KEYLESS ENTRY MODULE, POWER MIRRORS
10	2 AMP PK	ANTILOCK MODULE, ANTILOCK PUMP MOTOR, BRAKE FLUID LEVEL SWITCH
11	25 AMP NAT	HEADLAMP DELAY MODULE
12	15 AMP LT BL	HAZARD FLASHER, STOP LAMP SWITCH
13	7.5 AMP VT	AUTOMATIC TRANSMISSION CONTROLS, BACK-UP LAMPS
14	10 AMP RD	RADIO, POWER ANTENNA
15	10 AMP RD	HEADLAMP SWITCH, I.P. LAMPS, CLOCK, RADIO/CLOCK ILLUMINATION, REAR LAMPS, FRONT LAMPS
16	30 AMP C/BRKR	POWER WINDOWS
17	7.5 AMP VT	INSTRUMENT CLUSTER, HEADLAMP DELAY MODULE, CHIME MODULE, CRUISE CONTROL

Fuse panel

6-41

6 CHASSIS ELECTRICAL

FUSE	AMP	FUNCTION
1	2	ABS MODULE
2	20	AUXILIARY COOLING FAN
3	15	HAZARD FLASHER/LAMPS
4	15	FOG LAMPS, UNDERHOOD LAMP, AUTOMATIC TRANSMISSION DIAGNOSTIC CONNECTOR
5	10	AUTOMATIC TRANSMISSION MODULE, POWER/COMFORT SWITCH
6	15	BALLAST, SPEED CONTROL, A/C RELAY, FAN RELAY (4.0L), DIAGNOSTIC CONNECTOR (4.0L), BACK-UP LAMPS (AUTO ONLY), SHIFT SELECTOR (AUTO ONLY)
F1	30	ABS MODULATOR RELAY
F2	60	ALTERNATOR OUTPUT
F3	30	ABS PUMP
F4	40	HEATED REAR WINDOW, STARTER RELAY
F5	60	IGNITION SWITCH, AUTO SHUTDOWN RELAY, FUEL PUMP RELAY, S.B.E.C., DAYTIME RUNNING LAMP MODULE (CANADA ONLY)
F6	40	HEADLAMP SWITCH, DAYTIME RUNNING LAMP MODULE (CANADA ONLY)
F7		NOT USED
F8	40	FUSEBLOCK
F9	30	AUTO SHUTDOWN RELAY, FUEL PUMP RELAY, S.B.E.C., TRANSMISSION CONTROLLER
F10	60	ALTERNATOR OUTPUT

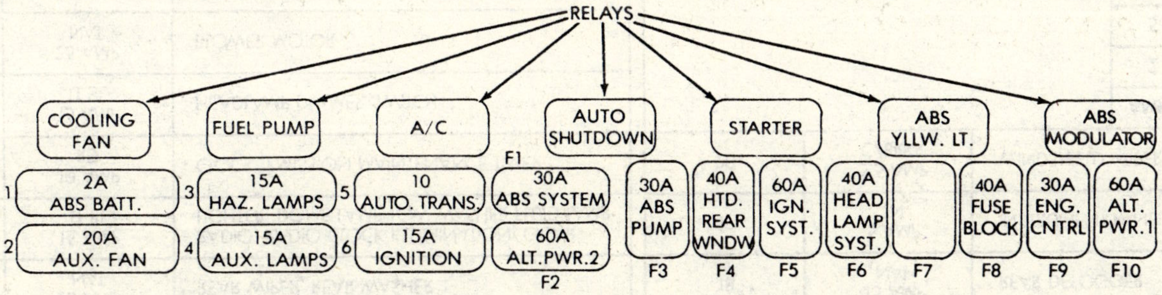

1991 Power distribution center

CHASSIS ELECTRICAL 6

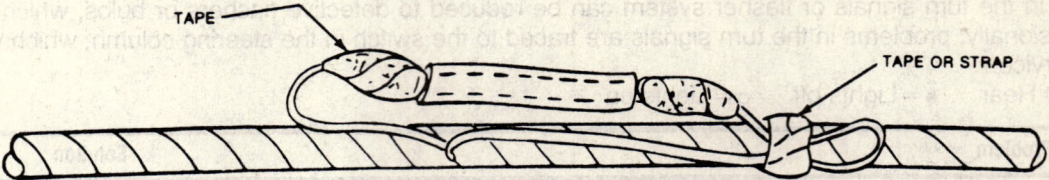

TYPICAL REPAIR USING THE SPECIAL #17 GA. (9.00" LONG-YELLOW) FUSE LINK REQUIRED FOR THE AIR/COND. CIRCUITS (2) #687E and #261A LOCATED IN THE ENGINE COMPARTMENT

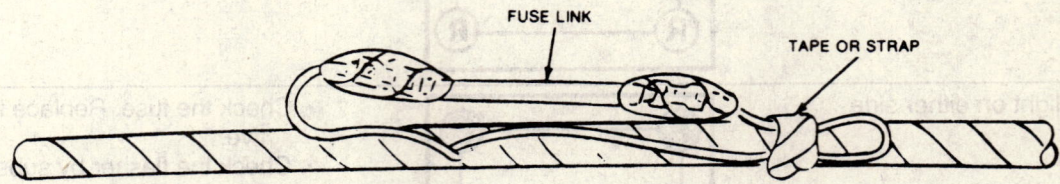

TYPICAL REPAIR FOR ANY IN-LINE FUSE LINK USING THE SPECIFIED GAUGE FUSE LINK FOR THE SPECIFIC CIRCUIT

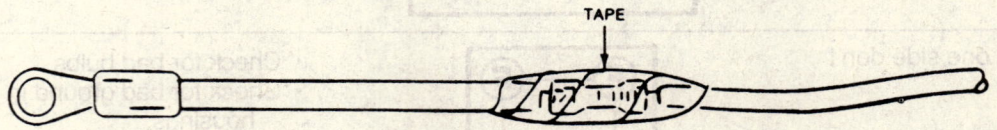

TYPICAL REPAIR USING THE EYELET TERMINAL FUSE LINK OF THE SPECIFIED GAUGE FOR ATTACHMENT TO A CIRCUIT WIRE END

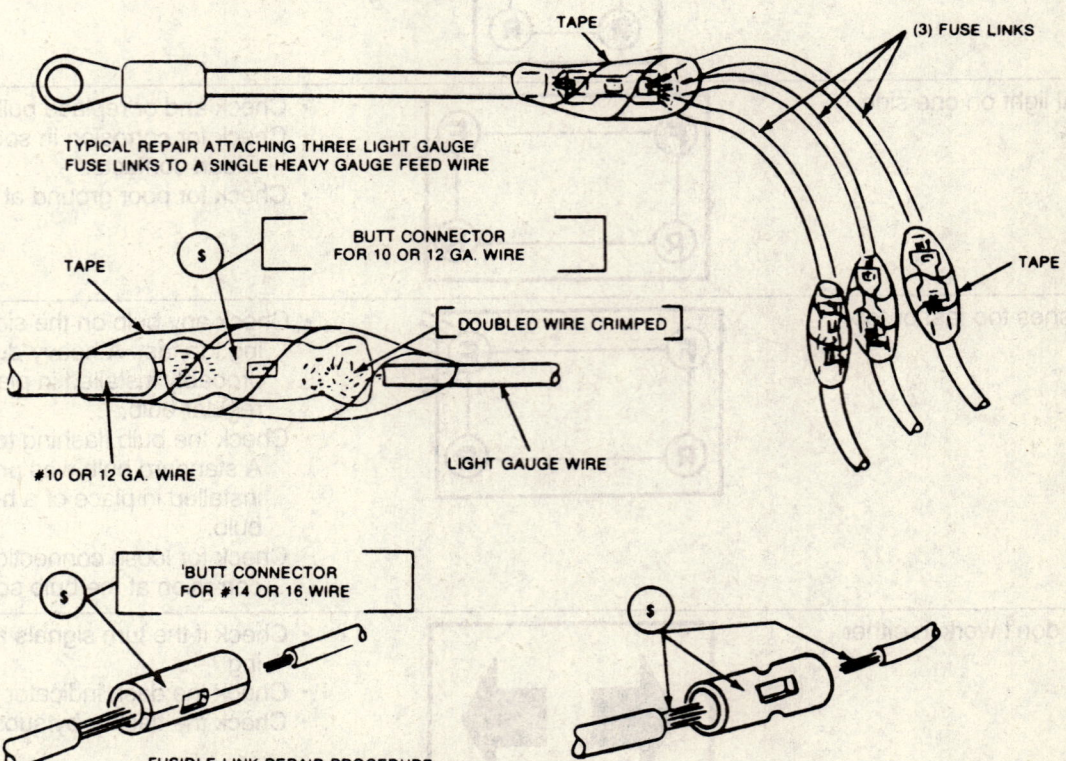

Fusible link repair

6-43

6 CHASSIS ELECTRICAL

Troubleshooting Basic Turn Signal and Flasher Problems

Most problems in the turn signals or flasher system can be reduced to defective flashers or bulbs, which are easily replaced. Occasionally, problems in the turn signals are traced to the switch in the steering column, which will require professional service.

F = Front   R = Rear   ● = Lights off   o = Lights on

Problem		Solution
Turn signals light, but do not flash	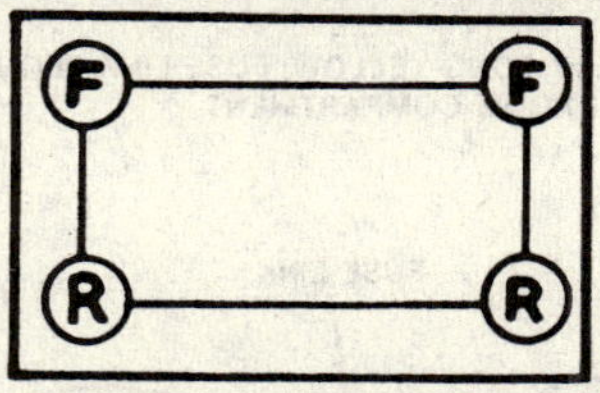	• Replace the flasher
No turn signals light on either side	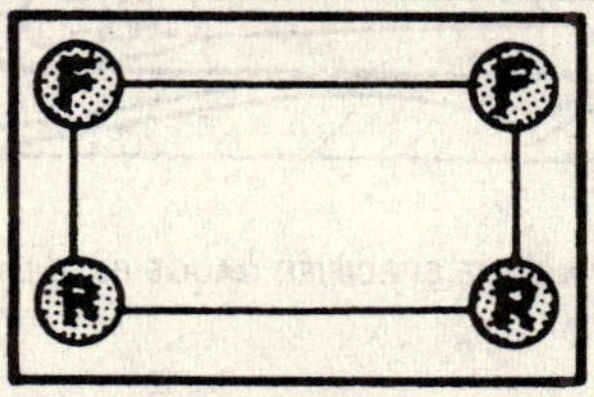	• Check the fuse. Replace if defective. • Check the flasher by substitution • Check for open circuit, short circuit or poor ground
Both turn signals on one side don't work	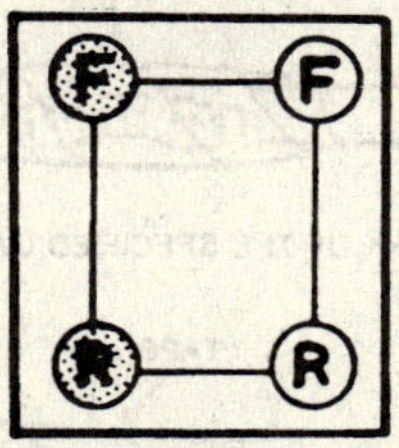	• Check for bad bulbs • Check for bad ground in both housings
One turn signal light on one side doesn't work	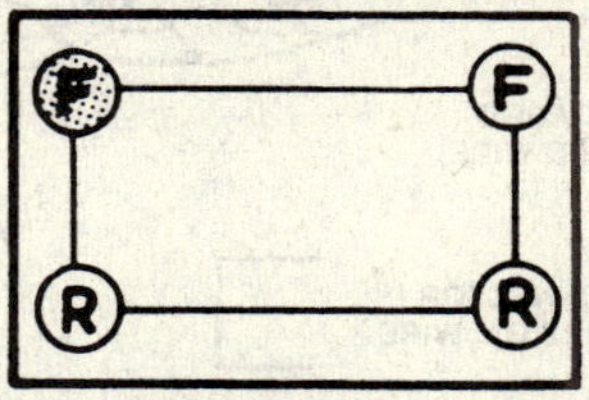	• Check and/or replace bulb • Check for corrosion in socket. Clean contacts. • Check for poor ground at socket
Turn signal flashes too fast or too slow	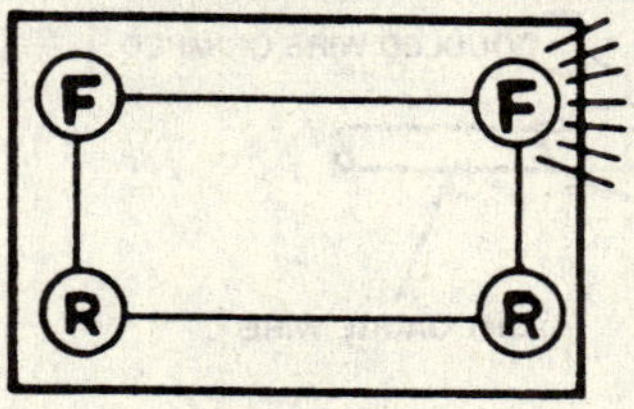	• Check any bulb on the side flashing too fast. A heavy-duty bulb is probably installed in place of a regular bulb. • Check the bulb flashing too slow. A standard bulb was probably installed in place of a heavy-duty bulb. • Check for loose connections or corrosion at the bulb socket
Indicator lights don't work in either direction	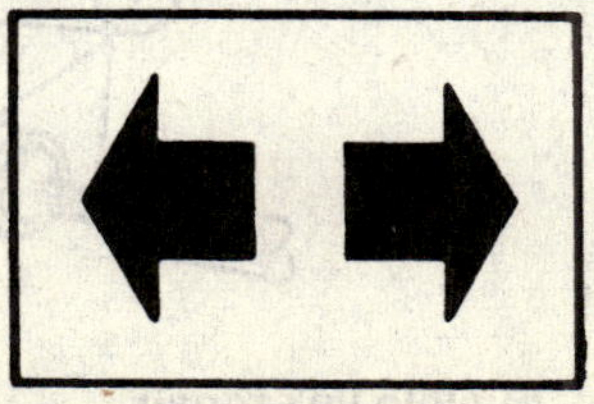	• Check if the turn signals are working • Check the dash indicator lights • Check the flasher by substitution

CHASSIS ELECTRICAL 6

Troubleshooting Basic Turn Signal and Flasher Problems

Most problems in the turn signals or flasher system can be reduced to defective flashers or bulbs, which are easily replaced. Occasionally, problems in the turn signals are traced to the switch in the steering column, which will require professional service.

F = Front   R = Rear   ● = Lights off   ○ = Lights on

Problem		Solution
One indicator light doesn't light	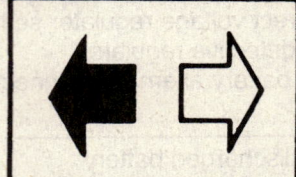	• On systems with 1 dash indicator: See if the lights work on the same side. Often the filaments have been reversed in systems combining stoplights with taillights and turn signals. Check the flasher by substitution • On systems with 2 indicators: Check the bulbs on the same side Check the indicator light bulb Check the flasher by substitution

Troubleshooting the Heater

Problem	Cause	Solution
Blower motor will not turn at any speed	• Blown fuse • Loose connection • Defective ground • Faulty switch • Faulty motor • Faulty resistor	• Replace fuse • Inspect and tighten • Clean and tighten • Replace switch • Replace motor • Replace resistor
Blower motor turns at one speed only	• Faulty switch • Faulty resistor	• Replace switch • Replace resistor
Blower motor turns but does not circulate air	• Intake blocked • Fan not secured to the motor shaft	• Clean intake • Tighten security
Heater will not heat	• Coolant does not reach proper temperature • Heater core blocked internally • Heater core air-bound • Blend-air door not in proper position	• Check and replace thermostat if necessary • Flush or replace core if necessary • Purge air from core • Adjust cable
Heater will not defrost	• Control cable adjustment incorrect • Defroster hose damaged	• Adjust control cable • Replace defroster hose

6 CHASSIS ELECTRICAL

Troubleshooting Basic Lighting Problems

Problem	Cause	Solution
Lights		
One or more lights don't work, but others do	• Defective bulb(s) • Blown fuse(s) • Dirty fuse clips or light sockets • Poor ground circuit	• Replace bulb(s) • Replace fuse(s) • Clean connections • Run ground wire from light socket housing to car frame
Lights burn out quickly	• Incorrect voltage regulator setting or defective regulator • Poor battery/alternator connections	• Replace voltage regulator • Check battery/alternator connections
Lights go dim	• Low/discharged battery • Alternator not charging • Corroded sockets or connections • Low voltage output	• Check battery • Check drive belt tension; repair or replace alternator • Clean bulb and socket contacts and connections • Replace voltage regulator
Lights flicker	• Loose connection • Poor ground • Circuit breaker operating (short circuit)	• Tighten all connections • Run ground wire from light housing to car frame • Check connections and look for bare wires
Lights "flare"—Some flare is normal on acceleration—if excessive, see "Lights Burn Out Quickly"	• High voltage setting	• Replace voltage regulator
Lights glare—approaching drivers are blinded	• Lights adjusted too high • Rear springs or shocks sagging • Rear tires soft	• Have headlights aimed • Check rear springs/shocks • Check/correct rear tire pressure
Turn Signals		
Turn signals don't work in either direction	• Blown fuse • Defective flasher • Loose connection	• Replace fuse • Replace flasher • Check/tighten all connections
Right (or left) turn signal only won't work	• Bulb burned out • Right (or left) indicator bulb burned out • Short circuit	• Replace bulb • Check/replace indicator bulb • Check/repair wiring
Flasher rate too slow or too fast	• Incorrect wattage bulb • Incorrect flasher	• Flasher bulb • Replace flasher (use a variable load flasher if you pull a trailer)
Indicator lights do not flash (burn steadily)	• Burned out bulb • Defective flasher	• Replace bulb • Replace flasher
Indicator lights do not light at all	• Burned out indicator bulb • Defective flasher	• Replace indicator bulb • Replace flasher

CHASSIS ELECTRICAL 6

Troubleshooting Basic Dash Gauge Problems

Problem	Cause	Solution
Coolant Temperature Gauge		
Gauge reads erratically or not at all	• Loose or dirty connections • Defective sending unit	• Clean/tighten connections • Bi-metal gauge: remove the wire from the sending unit. Ground the wire for an instant. If the gauge registers, replace the sending unit.
	• Defective gauge	• Magnetic gauge: disconnect the wire at the sending unit. With ignition ON gauge should register COLD. Ground the wire; gauge should register HOT.
Ammeter Gauge—Turn Headlights ON (do not start engine). Note reaction		
Ammeter shows charge	• Connections reversed on gauge	• Reinstall connections
Ammeter shows discharge	• Ammeter is OK	• Nothing
Ammeter does not move	• Loose connections or faulty wiring • Defective gauge	• Check/correct wiring • Replace gauge
Oil Pressure Gauge		
Gauge does not register or is inaccurate	• On mechanical gauge, Bourdon tube may be bent or kinked	• Check tube for kinks or bends preventing oil from reaching the gauge
	• Low oil pressure	• Remove sending unit. Idle the engine briefly. If no oil flows from sending unit hole, problem is in engine.
	• Defective gauge	• Remove the wire from the sending unit and ground it for an instant with the ignition ON. A good gauge will go to the top of the scale.
	• Defective wiring	• Check the wiring to the gauge. If it's OK and the gauge doesn't register when grounded, replace the gauge.
	• Defective sending unit	• If the wiring is OK and the gauge functions when grounded, replace the sending unit
All Gauges		
All gauges do not operate	• Blown fuse • Defective instrument regulator	• Replace fuse • Replace instrument voltage regulator
All gauges read low or erratically	• Defective or dirty instrument voltage regulator	• Clean contacts or replace
All gauges pegged	• Loss of ground between instrument voltage regulator and car • Defective instrument regulator	• Check ground • Replace regulator

6-47

6 CHASSIS ELECTRICAL

Troubleshooting Basic Dash Gauge Problems

Problem	Cause	Solution
Warning Lights		
Light(s) do not come on when ignition is ON, but engine is not started	• Defective bulb • Defective wire • Defective sending unit	• Replace bulb • Check wire from light to sending unit • Disconnect the wire from the sending unit and ground it. Replace the sending unit if the light comes on with the ignition ON.
Light comes on with engine running	• Problem in individual system • Defective sending unit	• Check system • Check sending unit (see above)

Troubleshooting Basic Windshield Wiper Problems

Problem	Cause	Solution
Electric Wipers		
Wipers do not operate— Wiper motor heats up or hums	• Internal motor defect • Bent or damaged linkage • Arms improperly installed on linking pivots	• Replace motor • Repair or replace linkage • Position linkage in park and reinstall wiper arms
Electric Wipers		
Wipers do not operate— No current to motor	• Fuse or circuit breaker blown • Loose, open or broken wiring • Defective switch • Defective or corroded terminals • No ground circuit for motor or switch	• Replace fuse or circuit breaker • Repair wiring and connections • Replace switch • Replace or clean terminals • Repair ground circuits
Wipers do not operate— Motor runs	• Linkage disconnected or broken	• Connect wiper linkage or replace broken linkage
Vacuum Wipers		
Wipers do not operate	• Control switch or cable inoperative • Loss of engine vacuum to wiper motor (broken hoses, low engine vacuum, defective vacuum/fuel pump) • Linkage broken or disconnected • Defective wiper motor	• Repair or replace switch or cable • Check vacuum lines, engine vacuum and fuel pump • Repair linkage • Replace wiper motor
Wipers stop on engine acceleration	• Leaking vacuum hoses • Dry windshield • Oversize wiper blades • Defective vacuum/fuel pump	• Repair or replace hoses • Wet windshield with washers • Replace with proper size wiper blades • Replace pump

CHASSIS ELECTRICAL 6

1989 WIRING DIAGRAMS

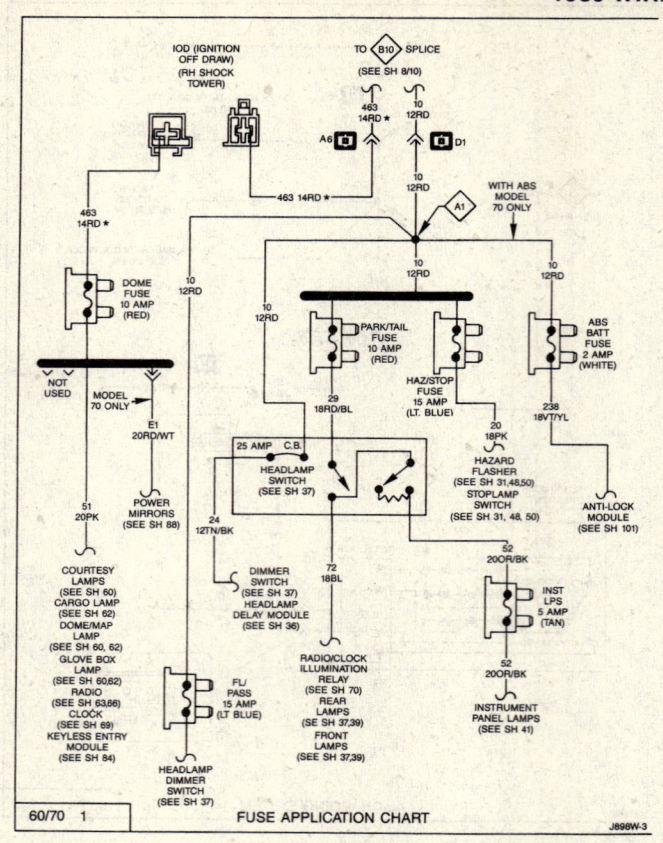
FUSE APPLICATION CHART

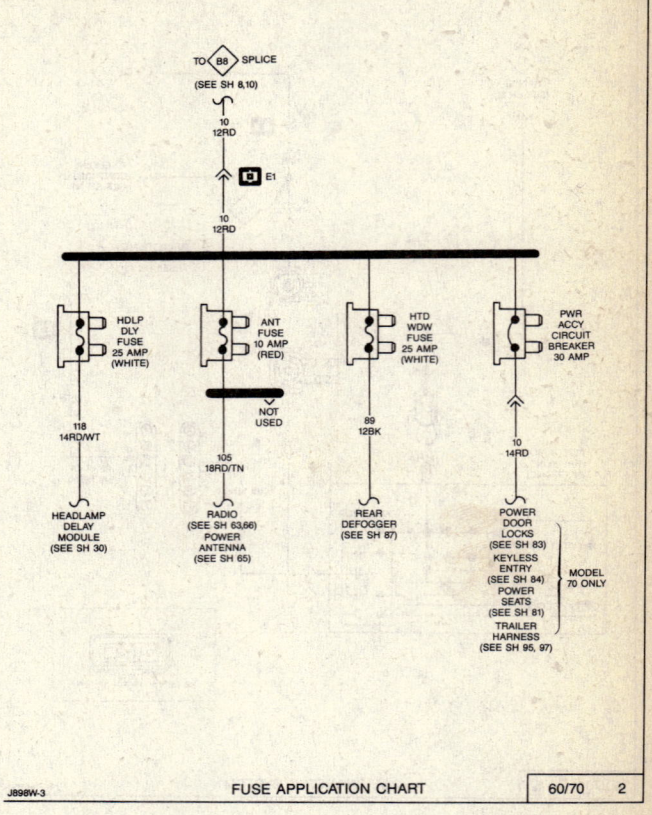
FUSE APPLICATION CHART

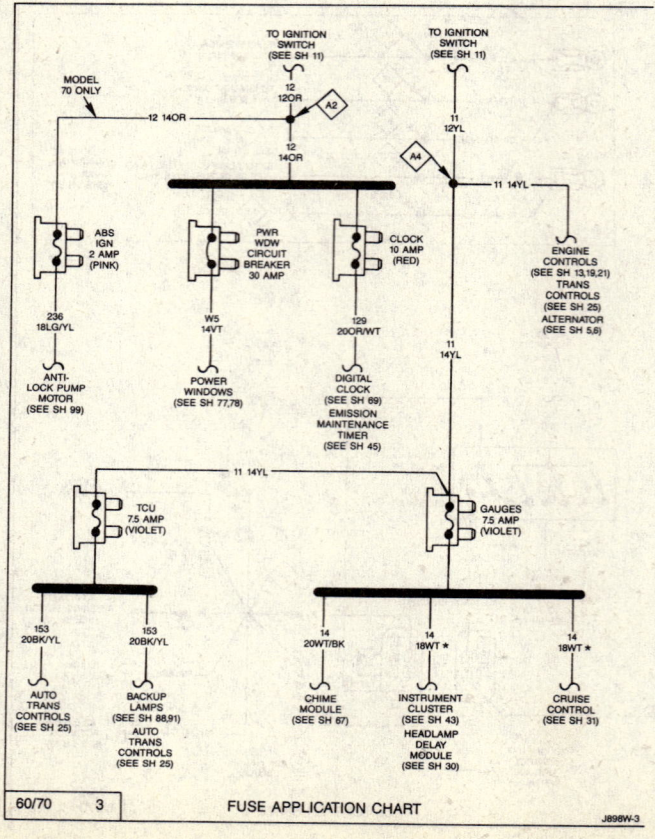
FUSE APPLICATION CHART

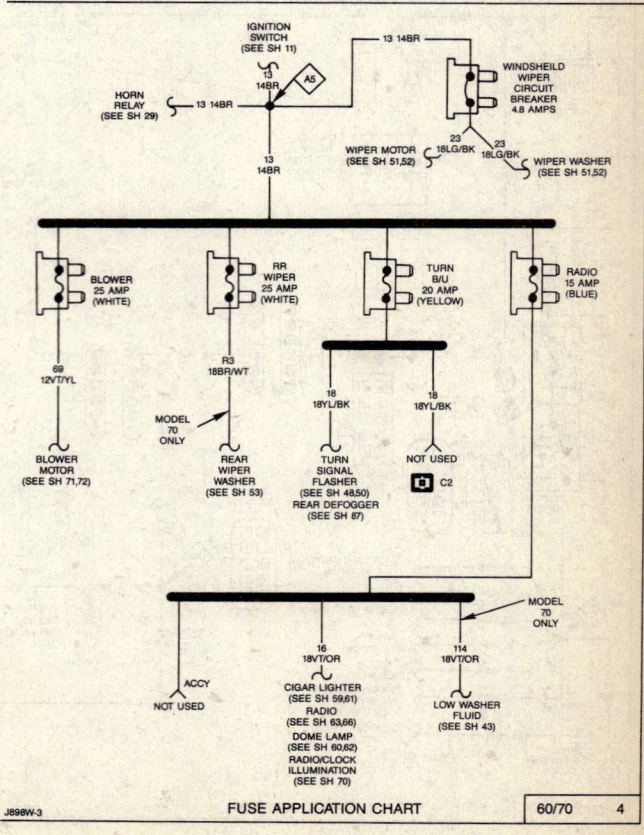
FUSE APPLICATION CHART

6-49

6 CHASSIS ELECTRICAL

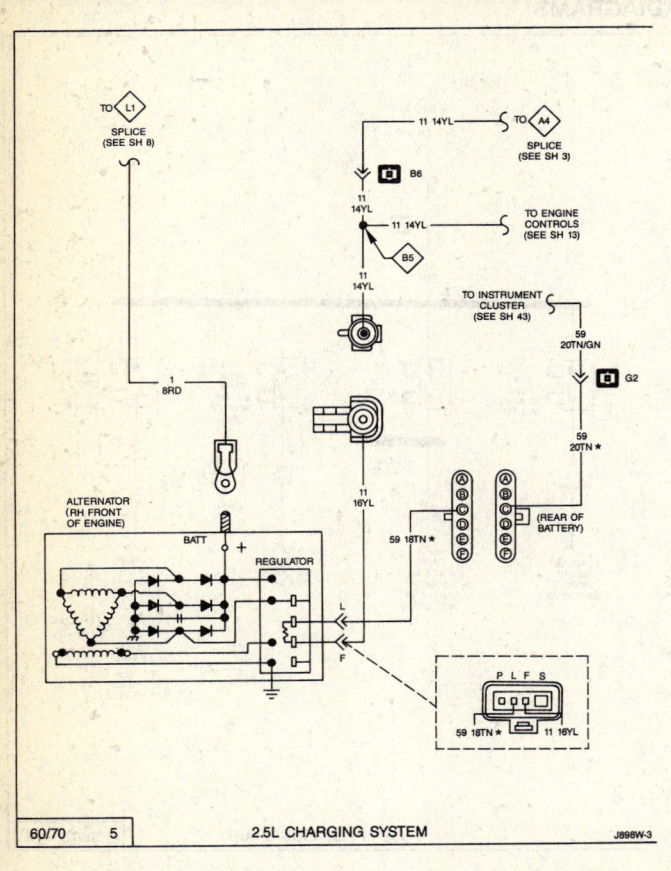

2.5L CHARGING SYSTEM

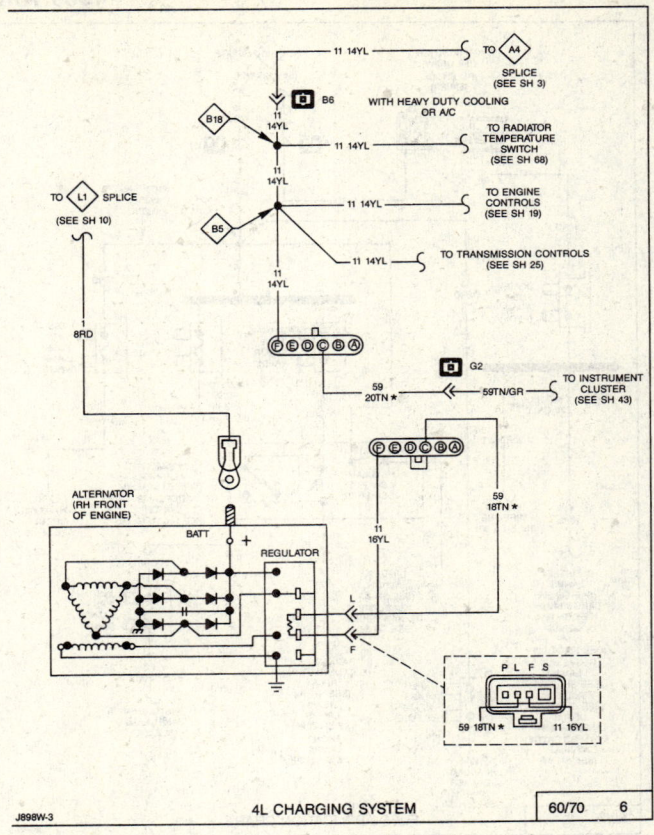

4L CHARGING SYSTEM

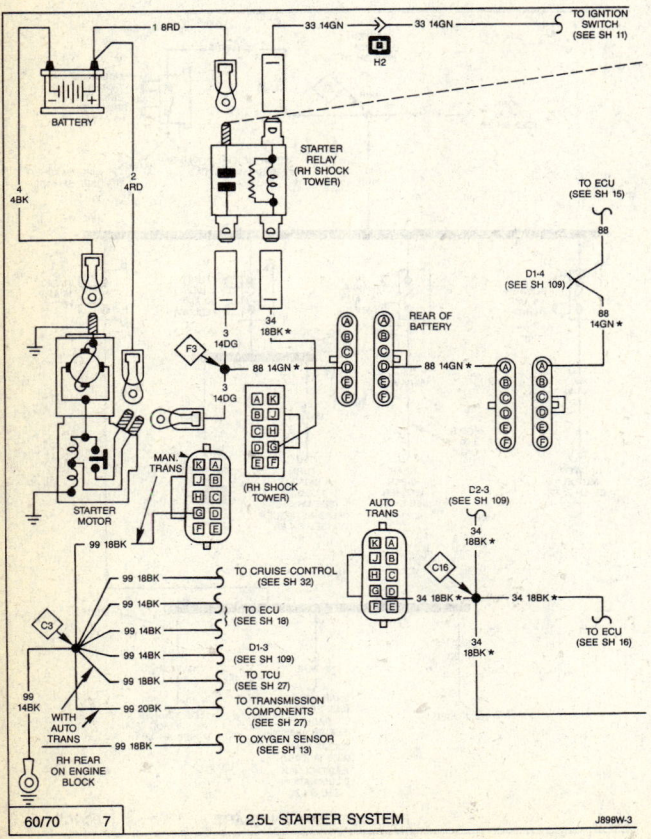

2.5L STARTER SYSTEM

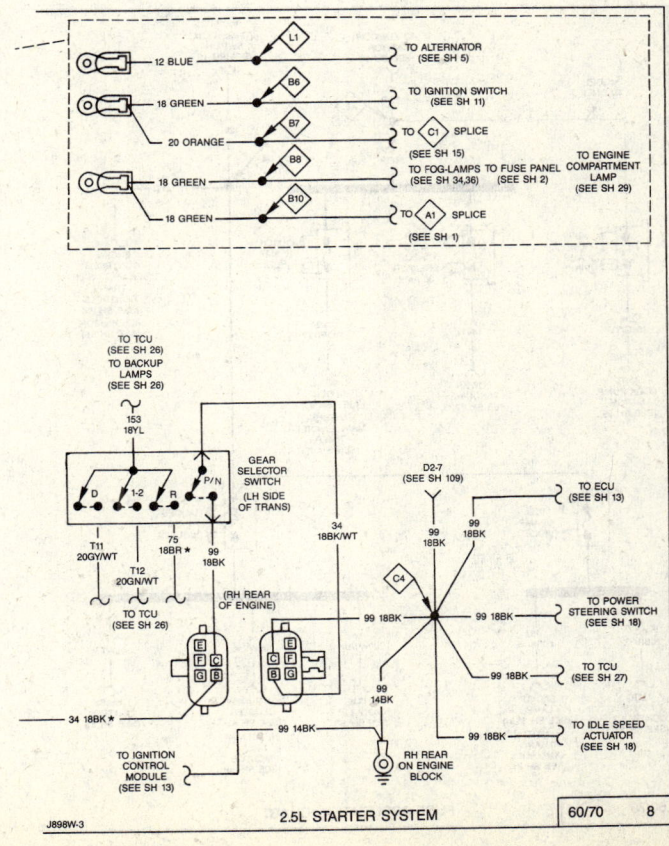

2.5L STARTER SYSTEM

CHASSIS ELECTRICAL 6

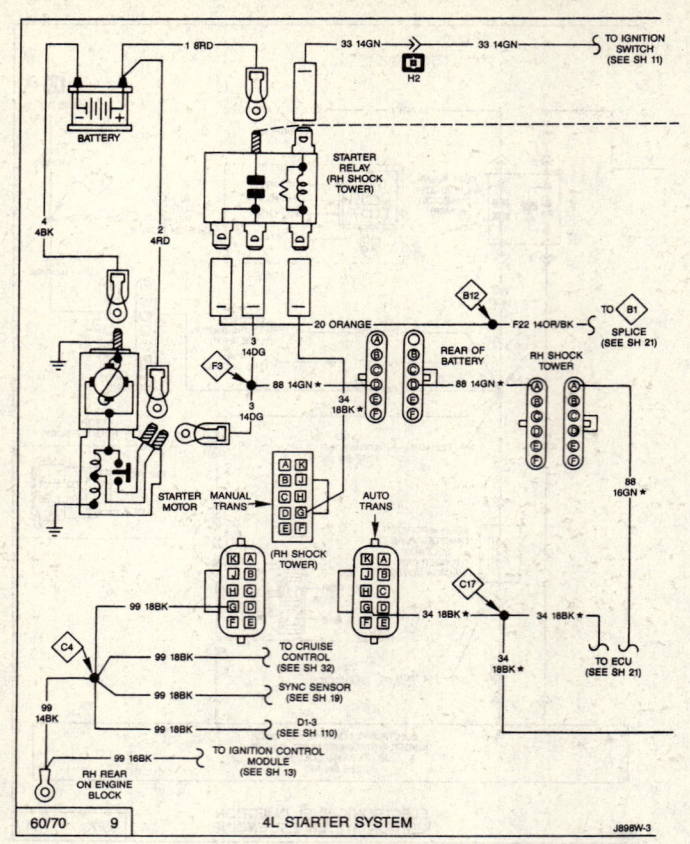

4L STARTER SYSTEM

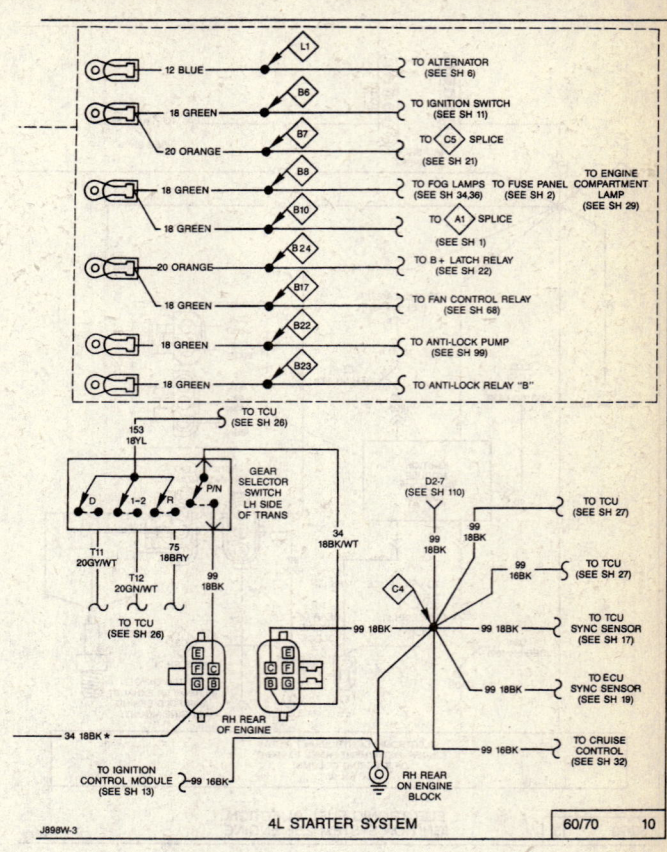

4L STARTER SYSTEM

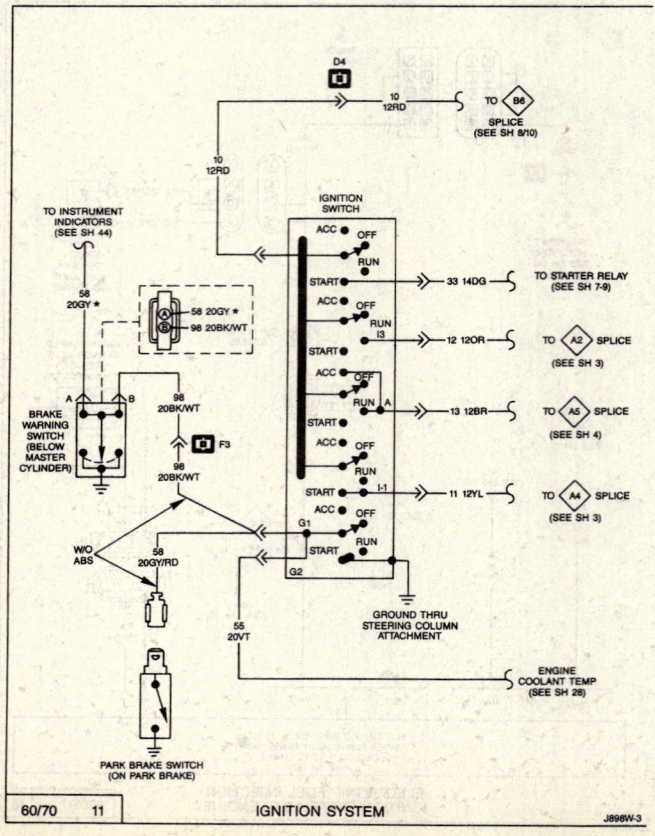

IGNITION SYSTEM

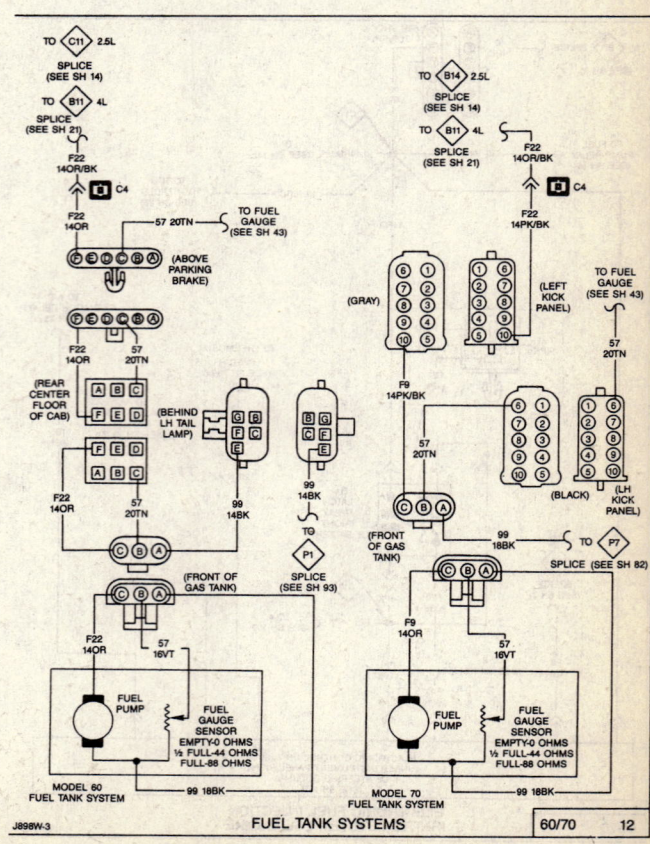

FUEL TANK SYSTEMS

6-51

6 CHASSIS ELECTRICAL

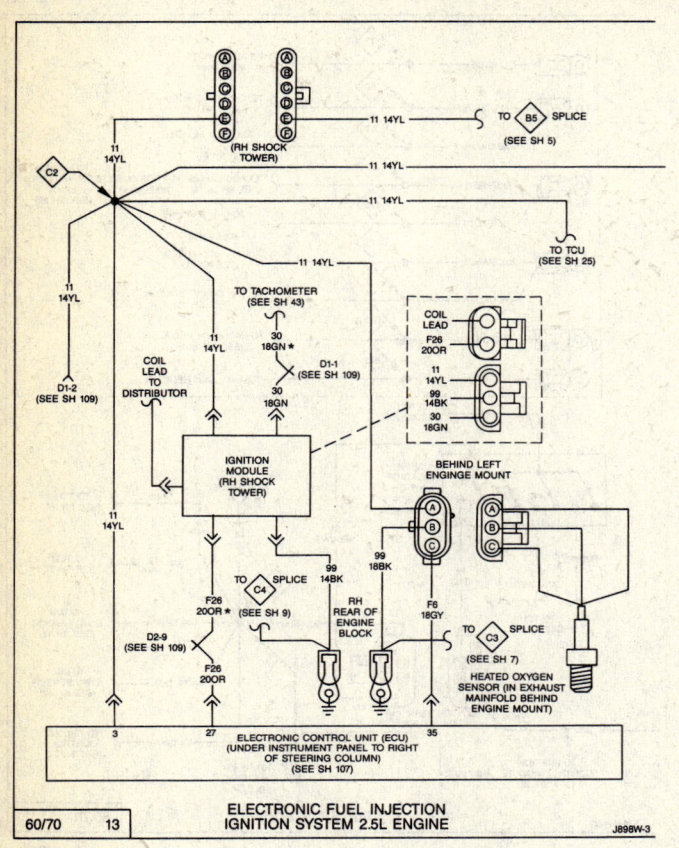
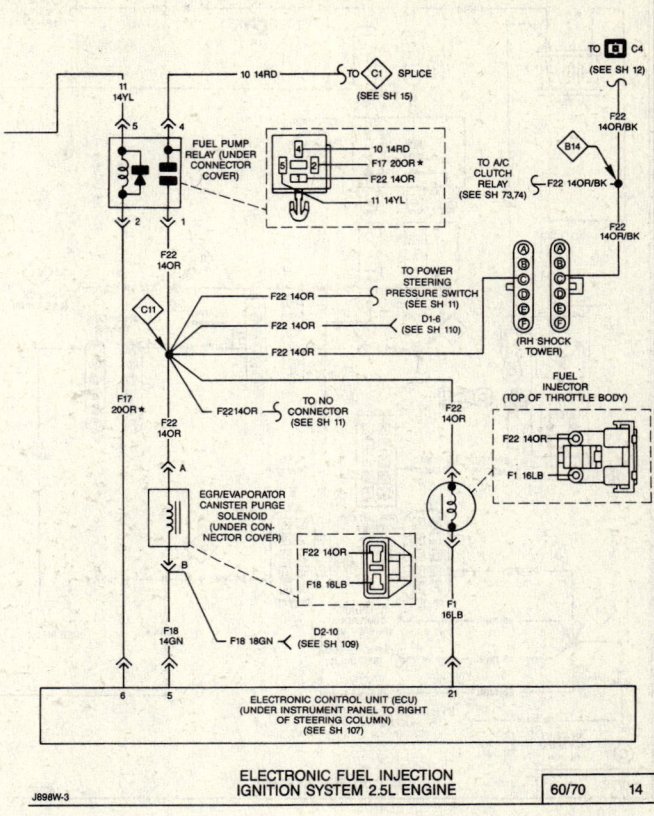
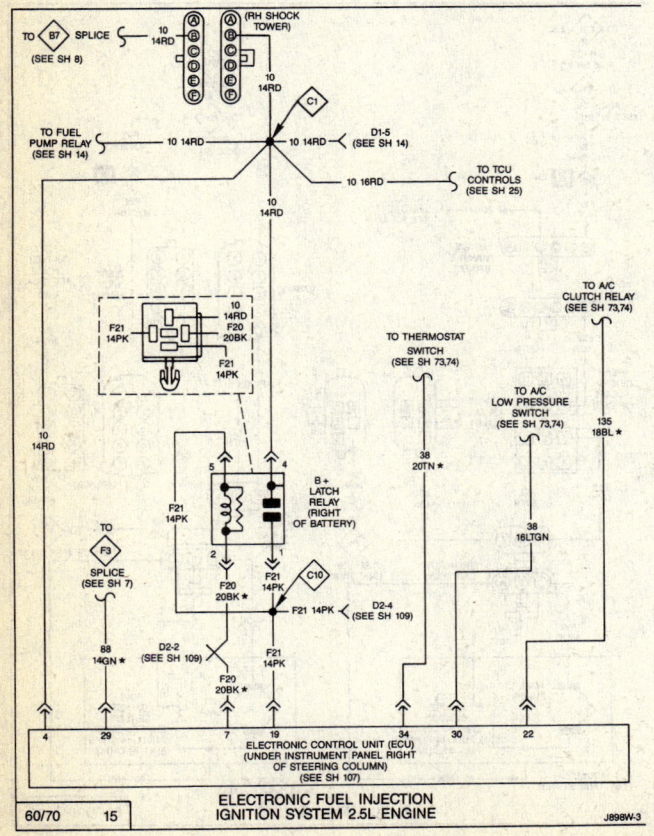
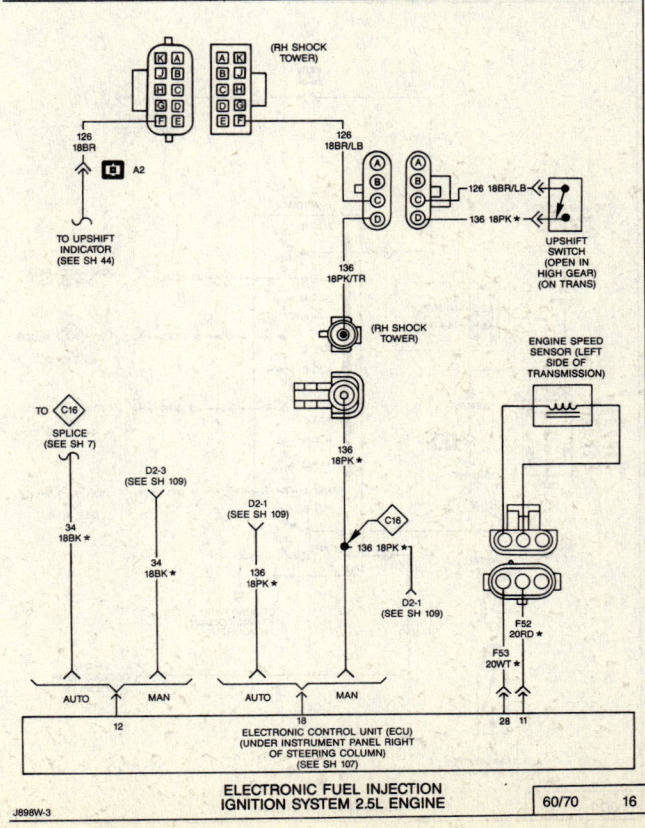

CHASSIS ELECTRICAL 6

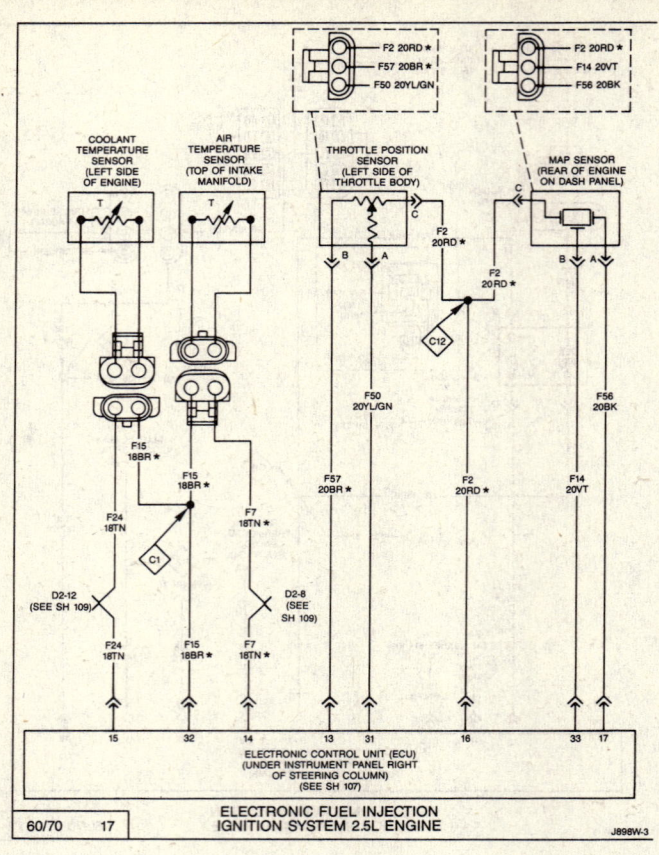
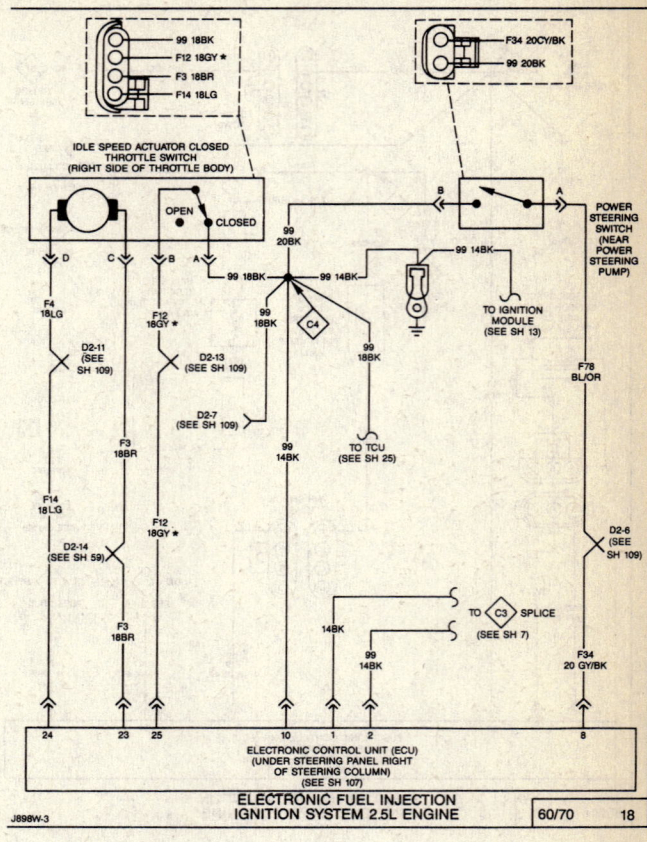
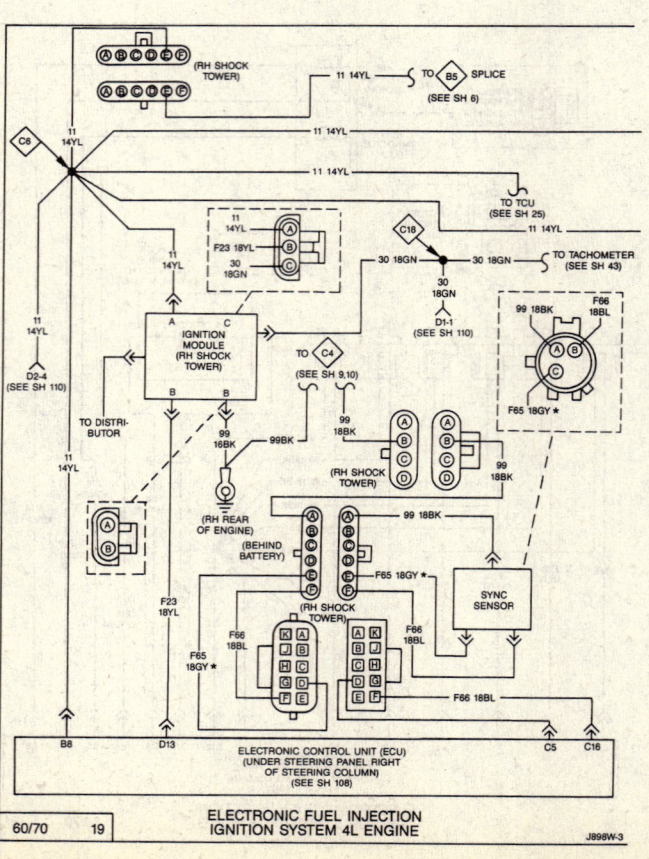
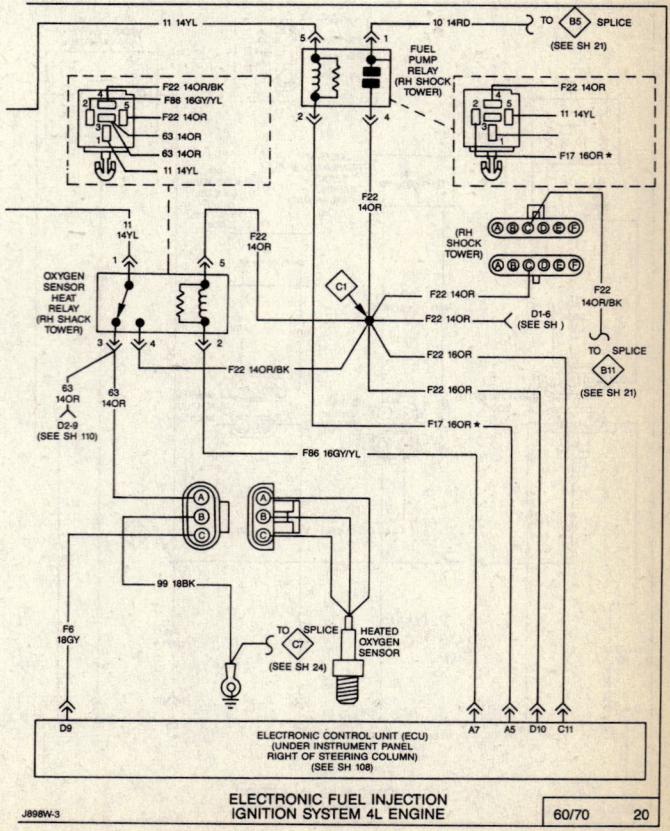

6-53

6 CHASSIS ELECTRICAL

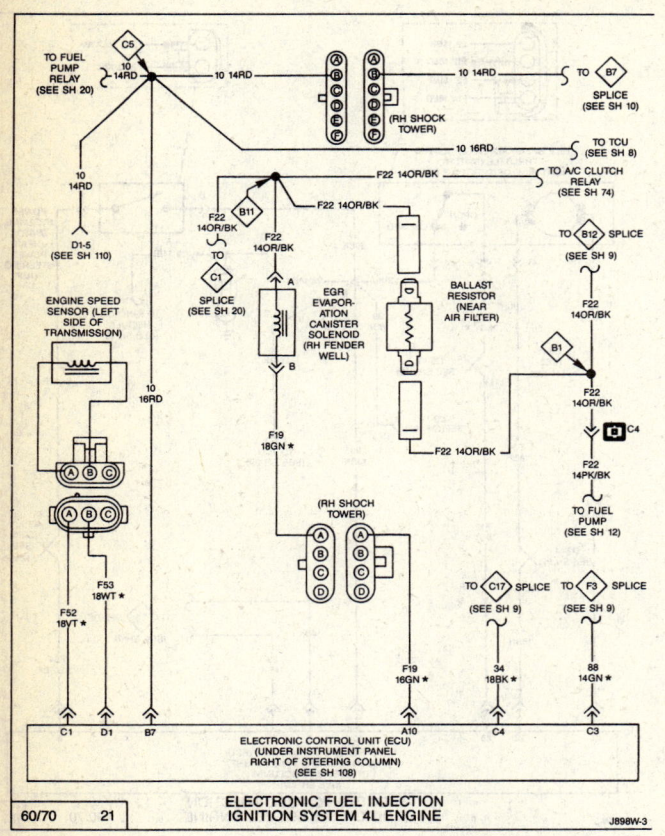
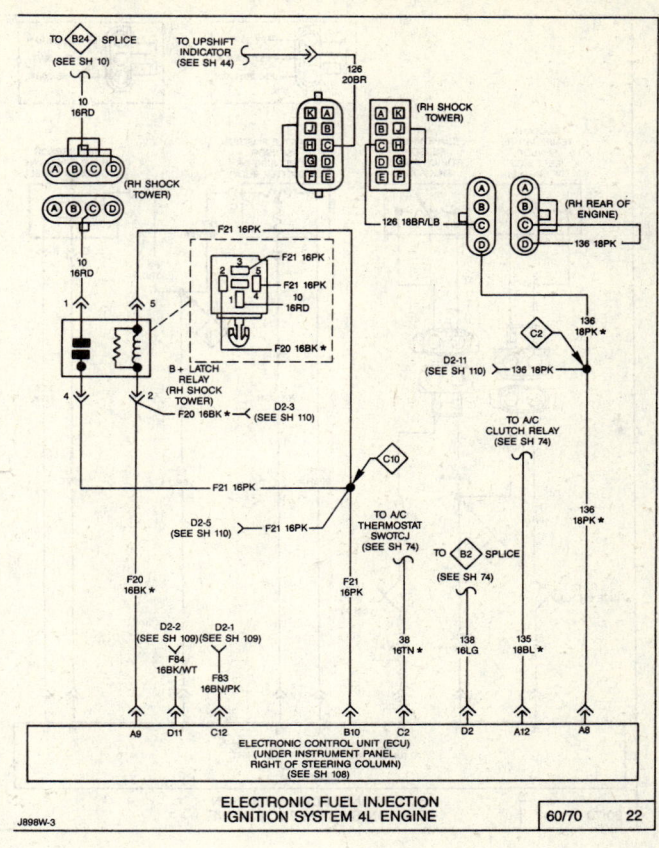
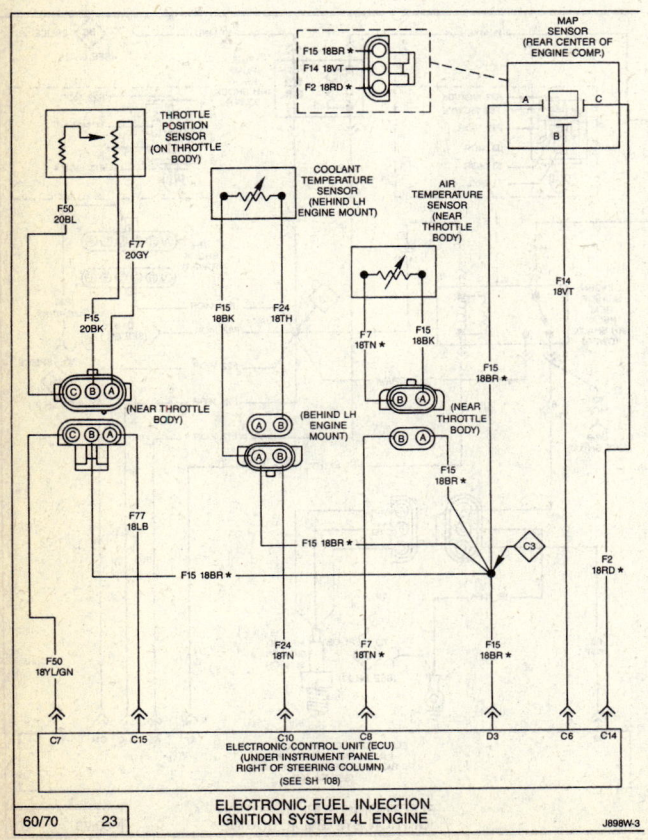
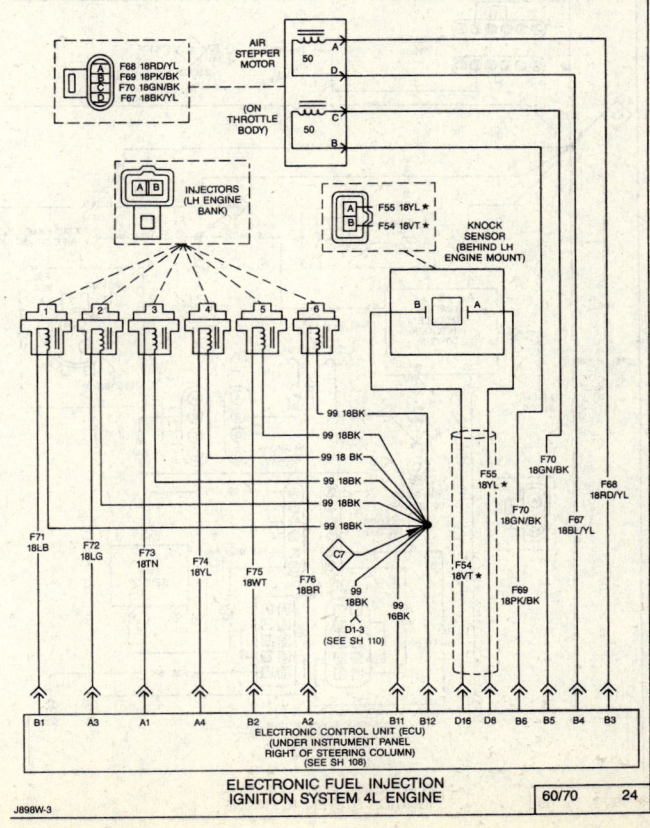

CHASSIS ELECTRICAL 6

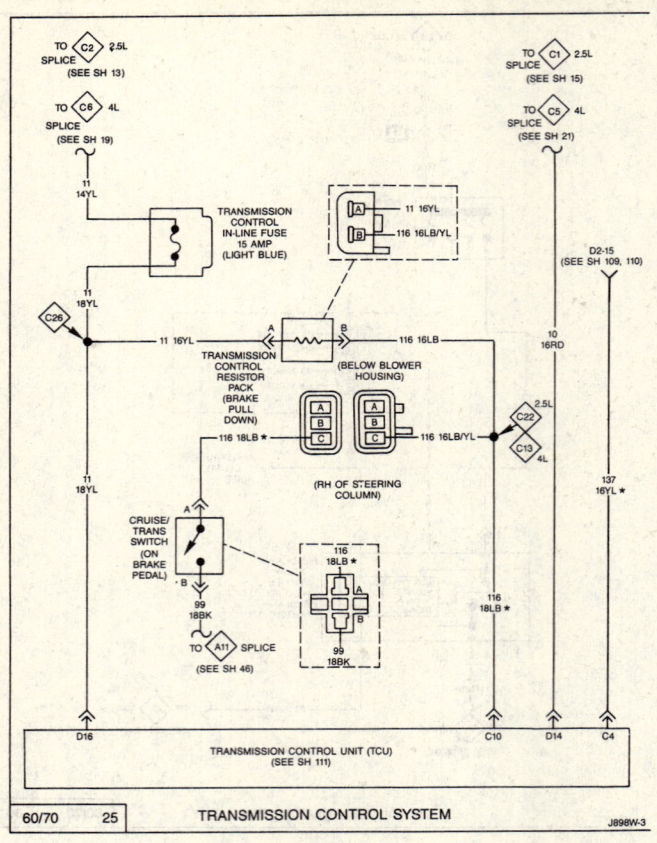

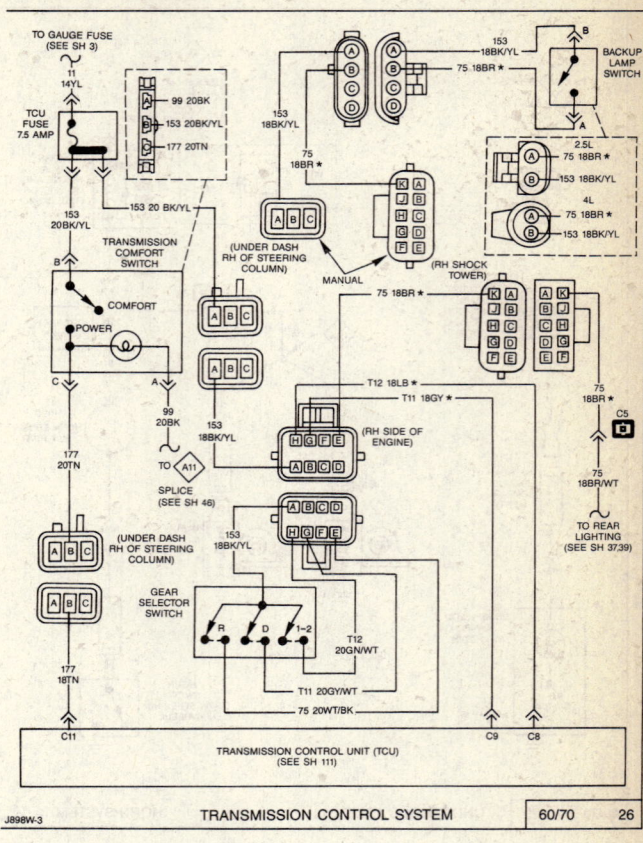

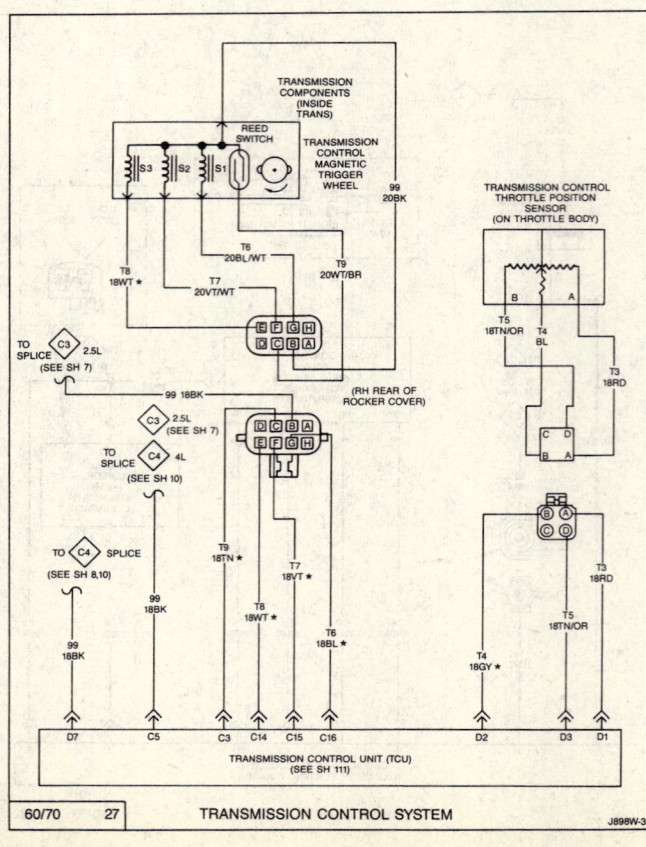

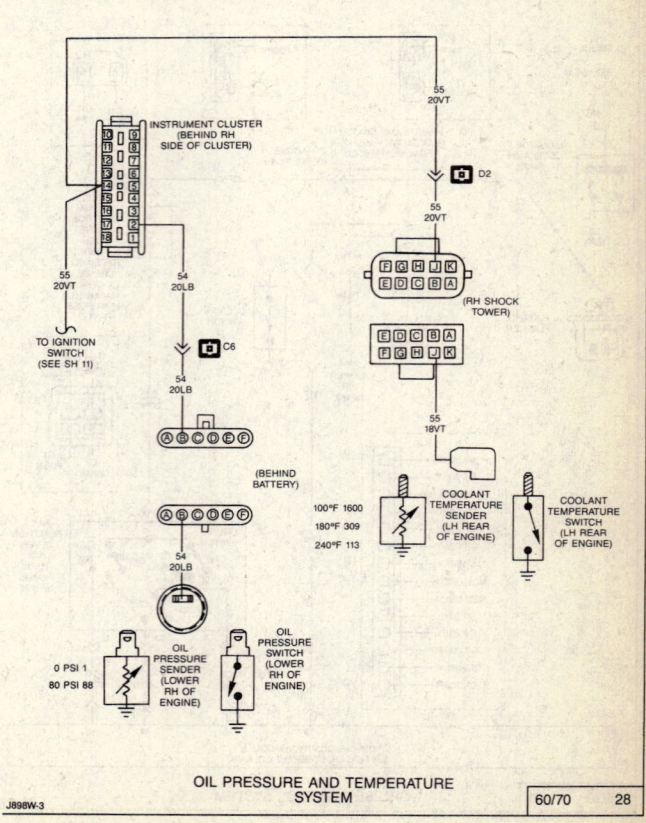

6-55

6 CHASSIS ELECTRICAL

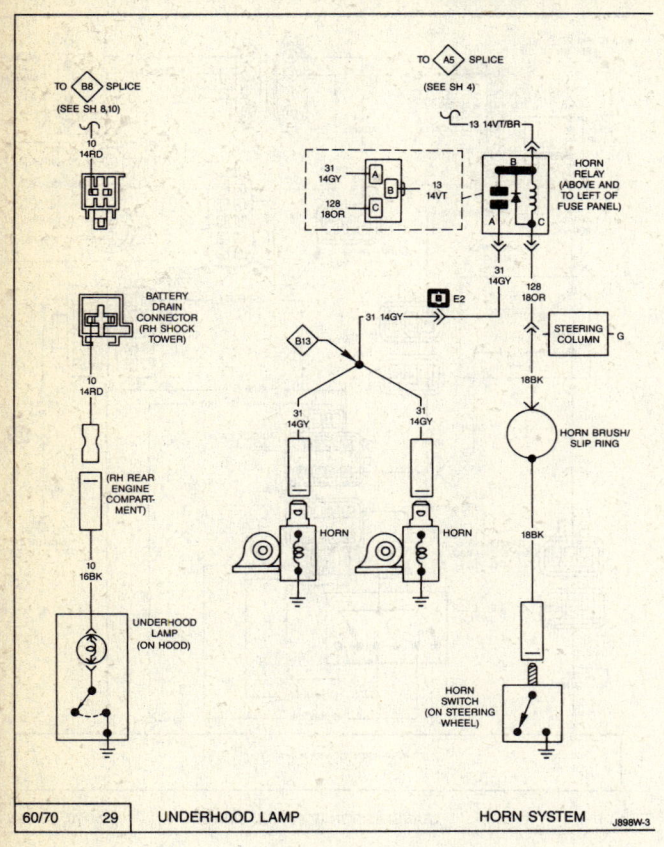

UNDERHOOD LAMP — HORN SYSTEM

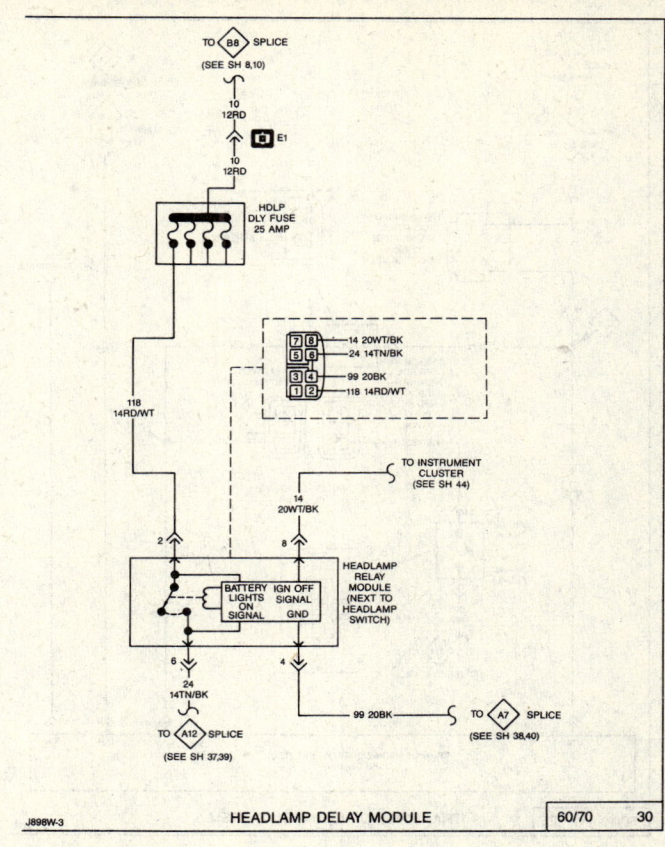

HEADLAMP DELAY MODULE

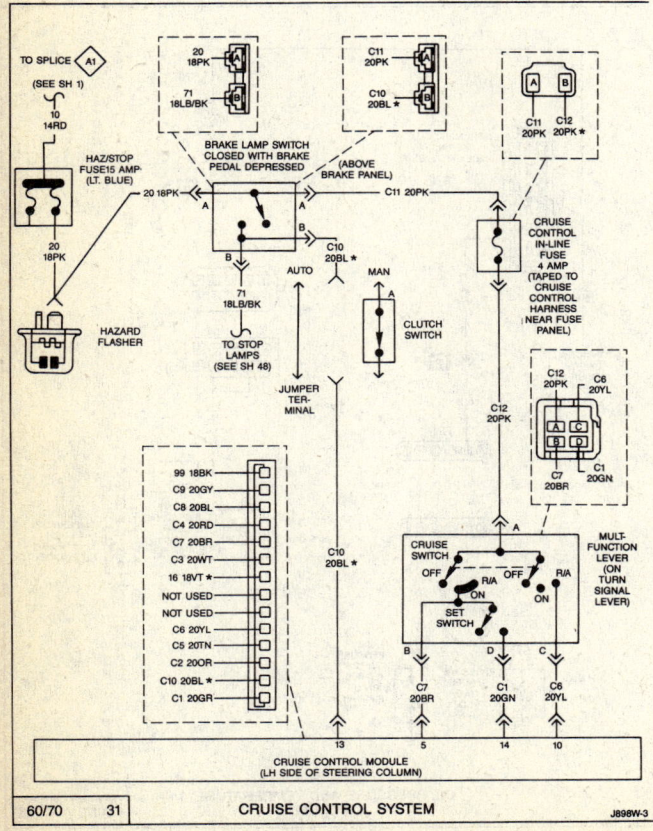

CRUISE CONTROL SYSTEM

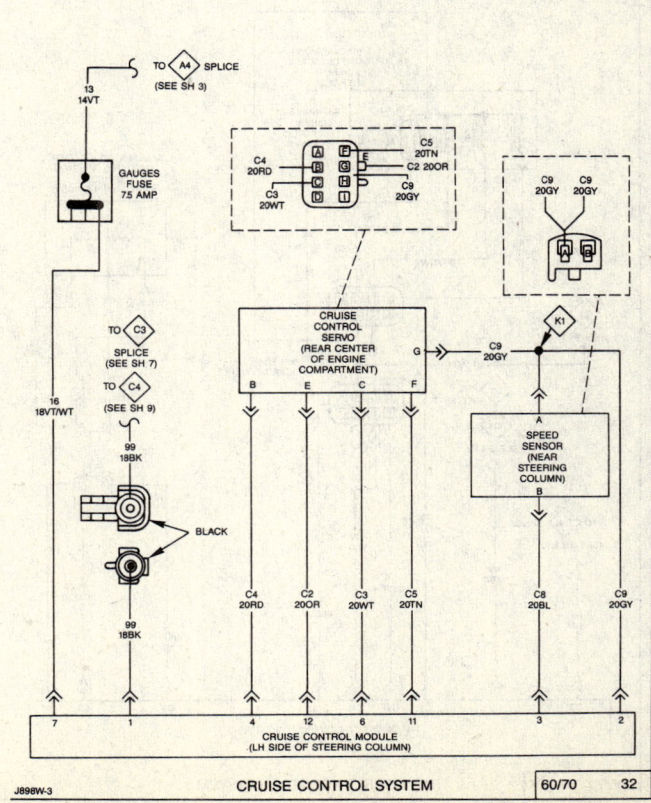

CRUISE CONTROL SYSTEM

CHASSIS ELECTRICAL 6

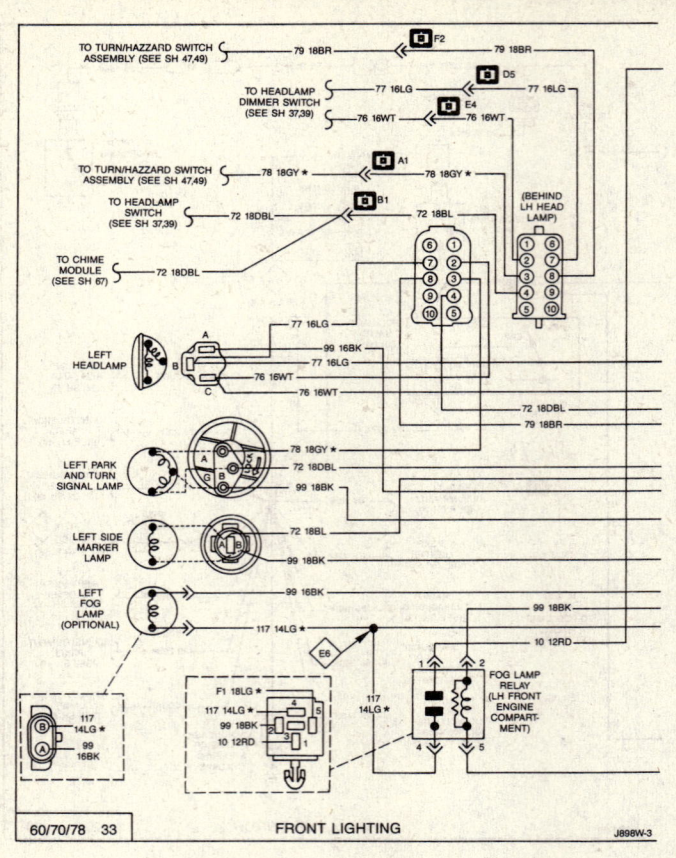

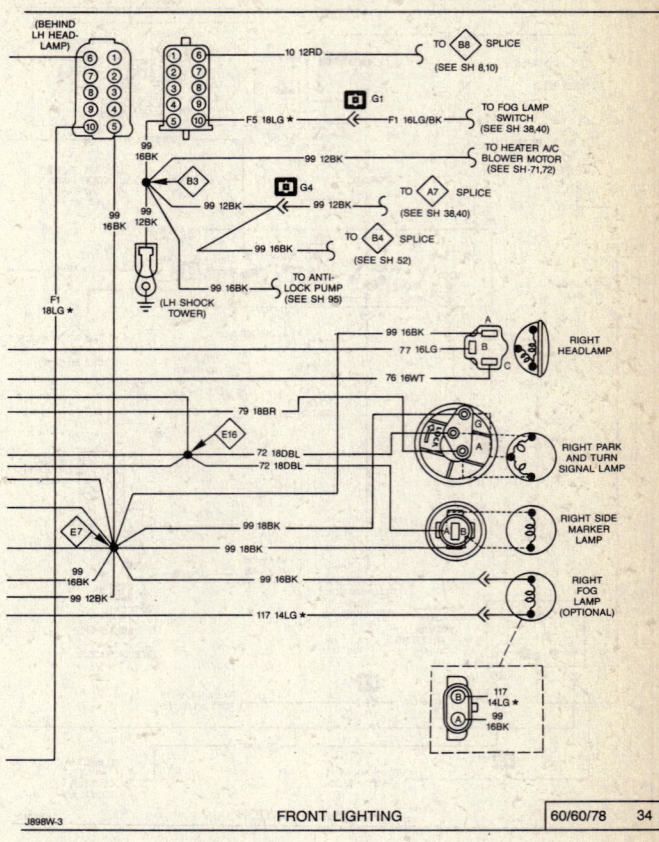

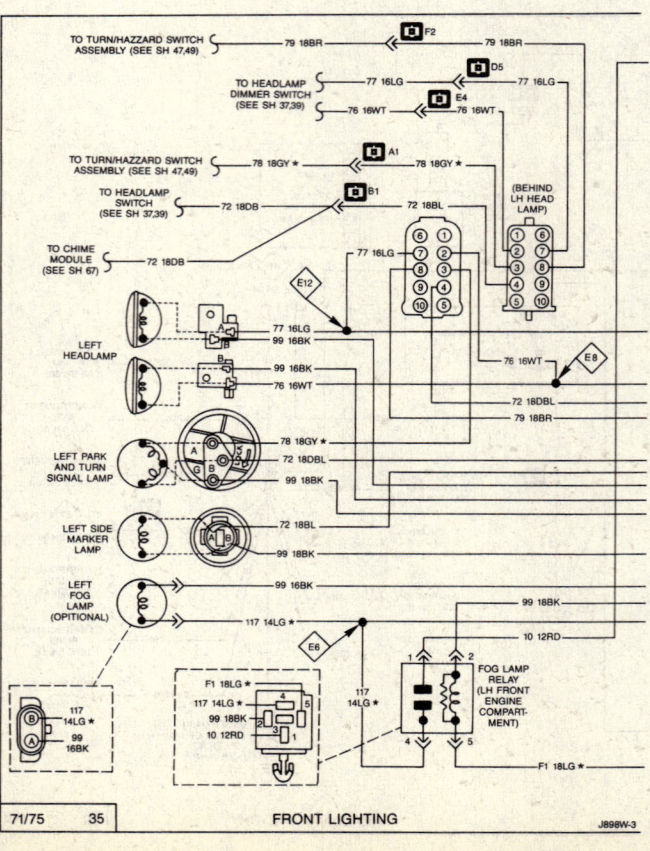

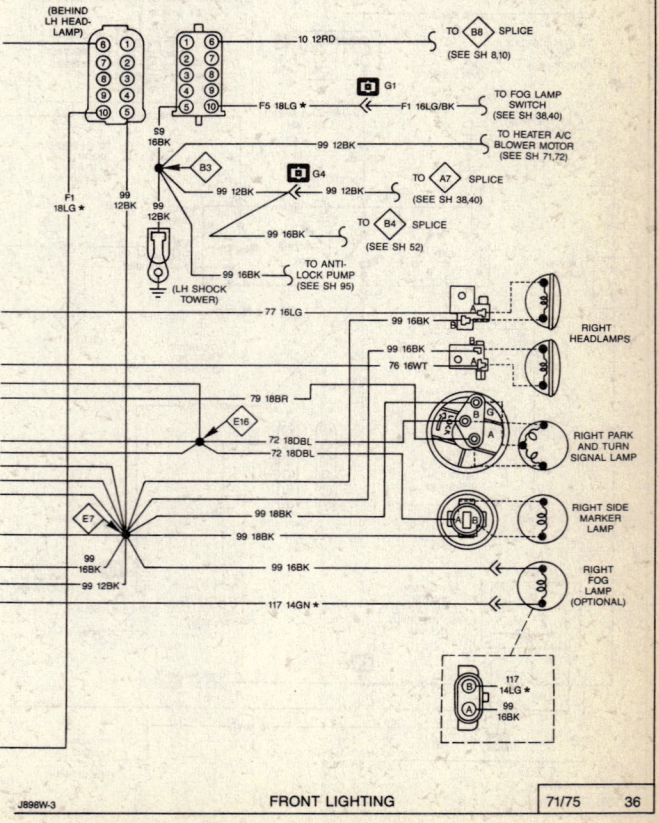

6-57

6 CHASSIS ELECTRICAL

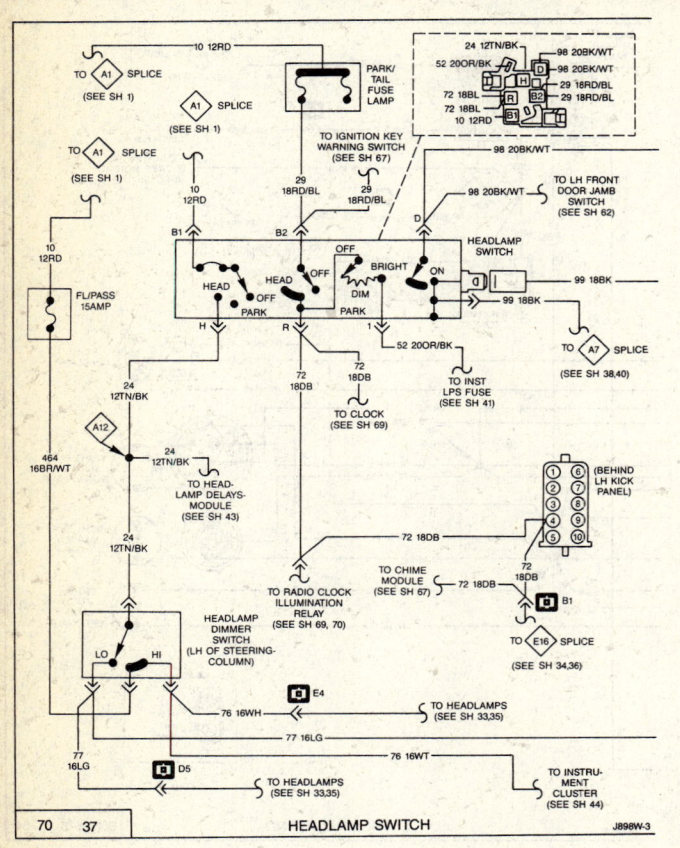
HEADLAMP SWITCH

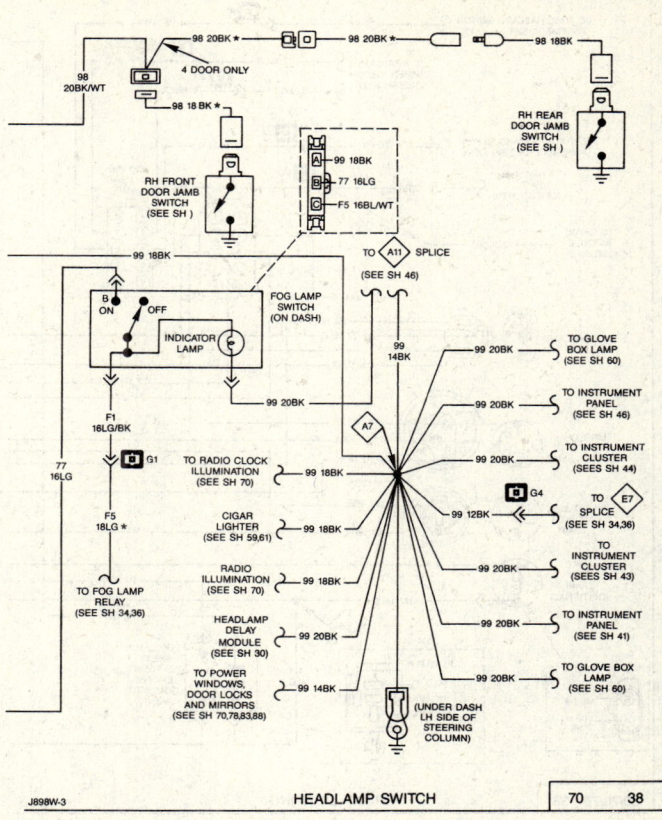
HEADLAMP SWITCH

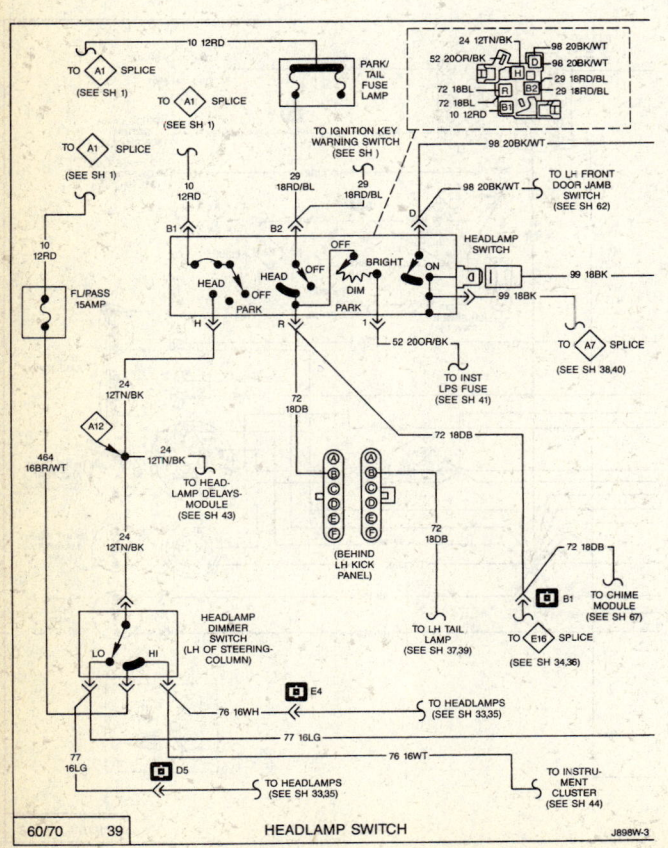
HEADLAMP SWITCH

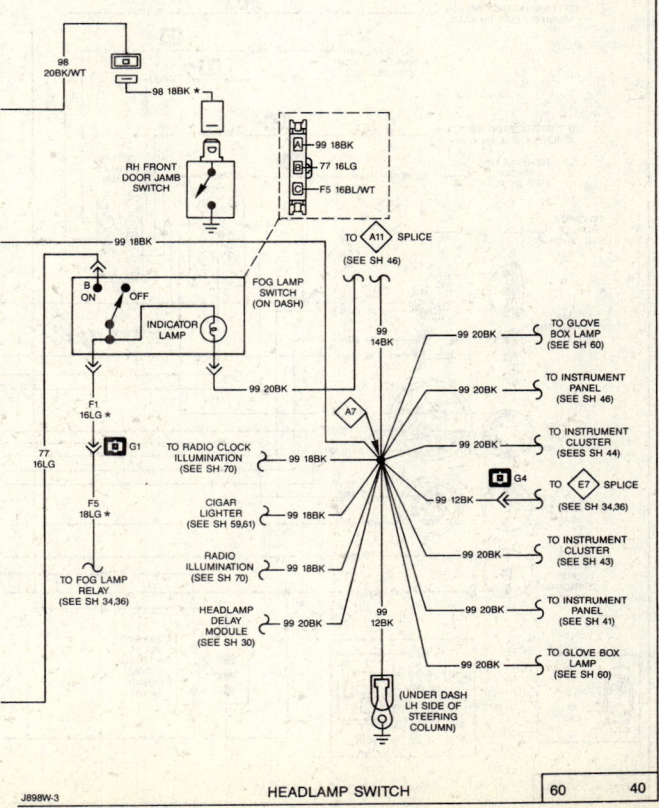
HEADLAMP SWITCH

CHASSIS ELECTRICAL 6

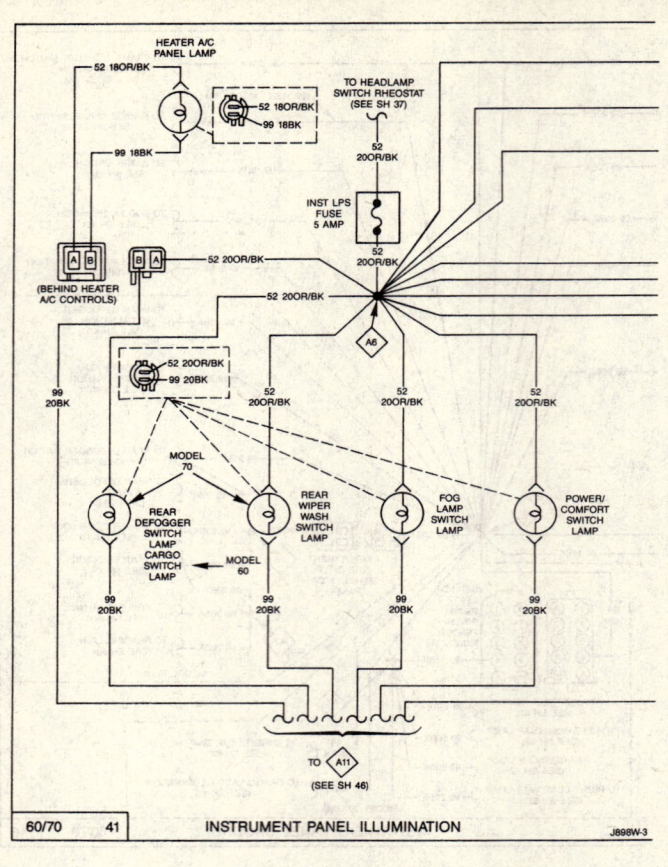

INSTRUMENT PANEL ILLUMINATION

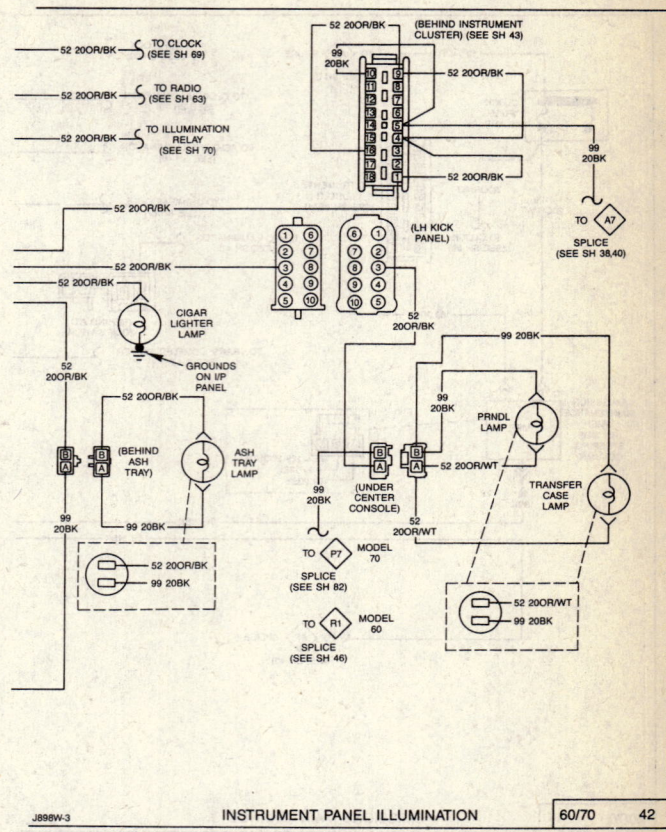

INSTRUMENT PANEL ILLUMINATION

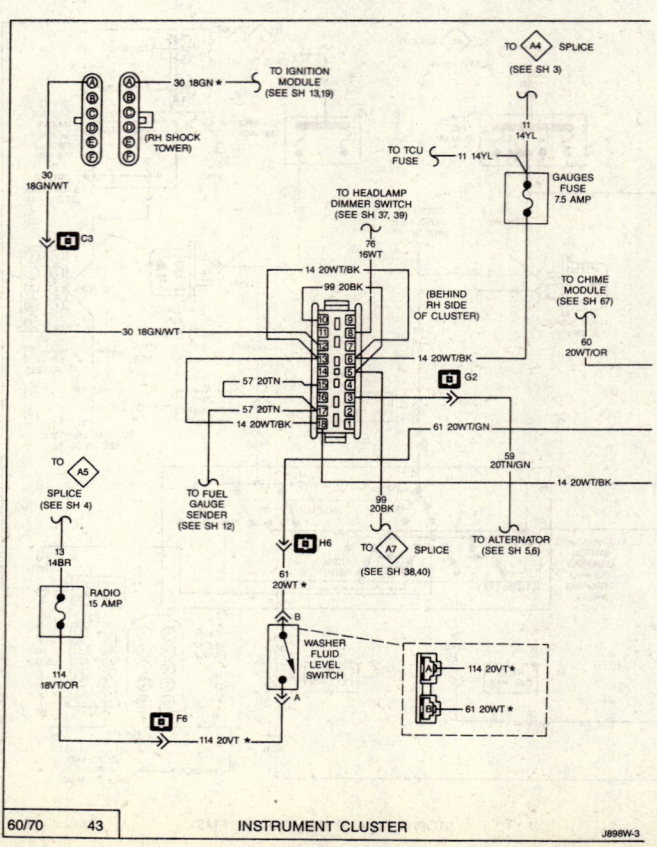

INSTRUMENT CLUSTER

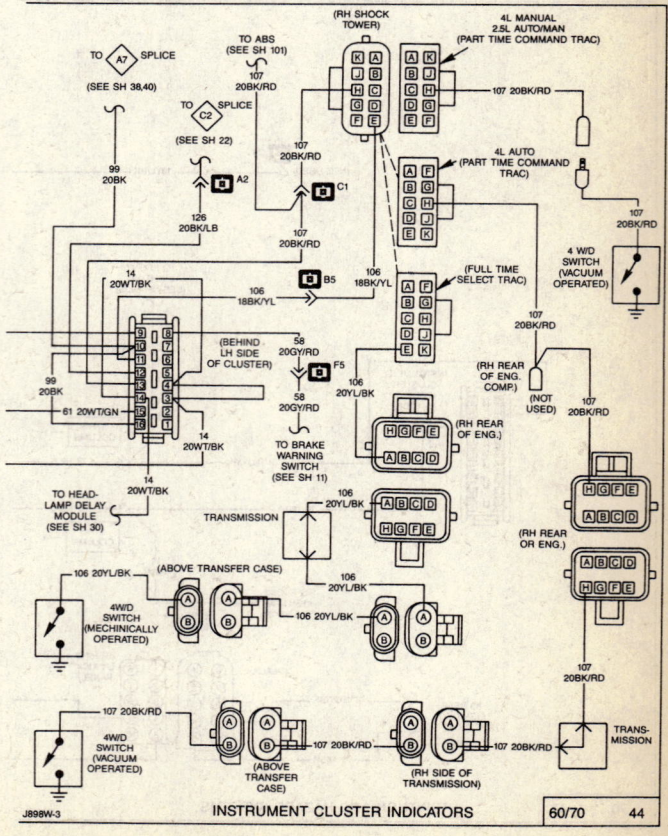

INSTRUMENT CLUSTER INDICATORS

6 CHASSIS ELECTRICAL

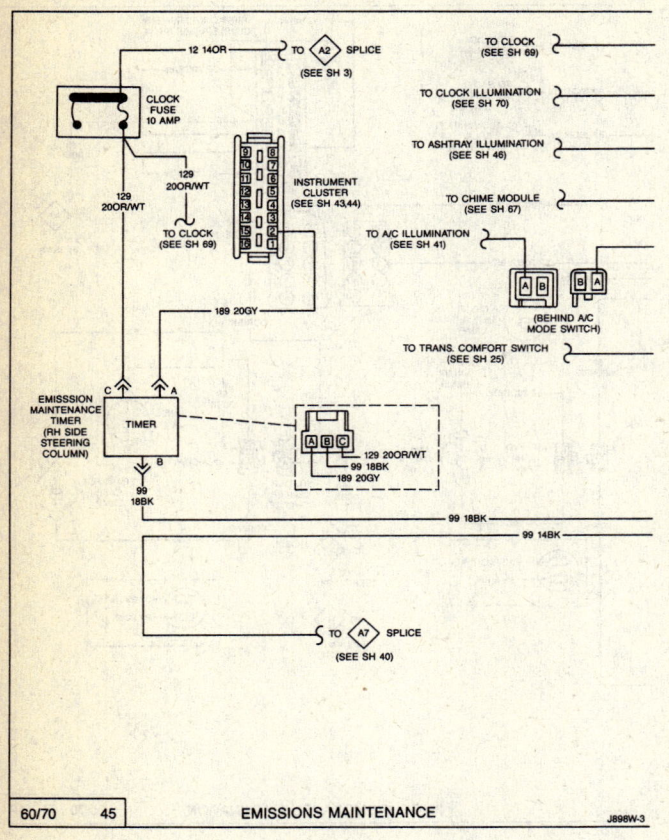

EMISSIONS MAINTENANCE

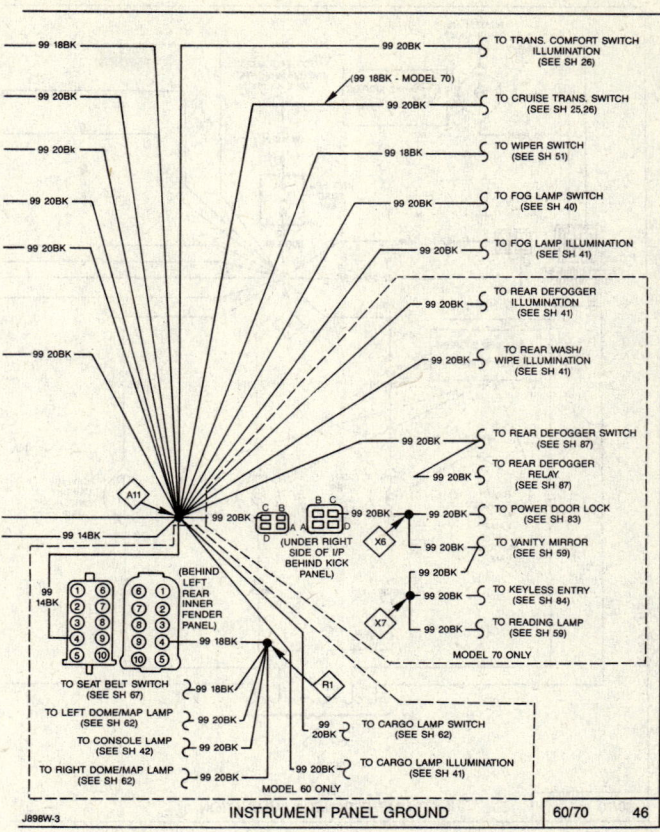

INSTRUMENT PANEL GROUND

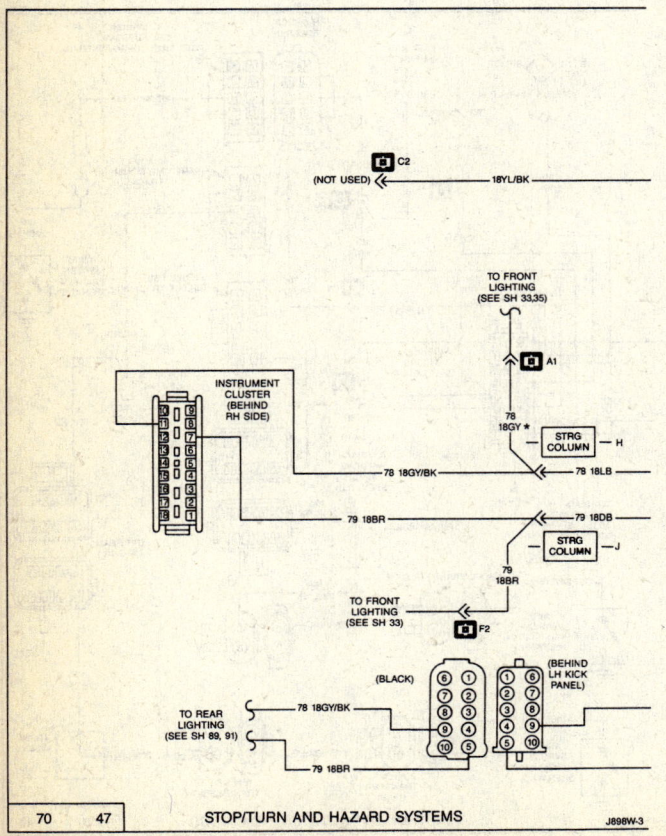

STOP/TURN AND HAZARD SYSTEMS

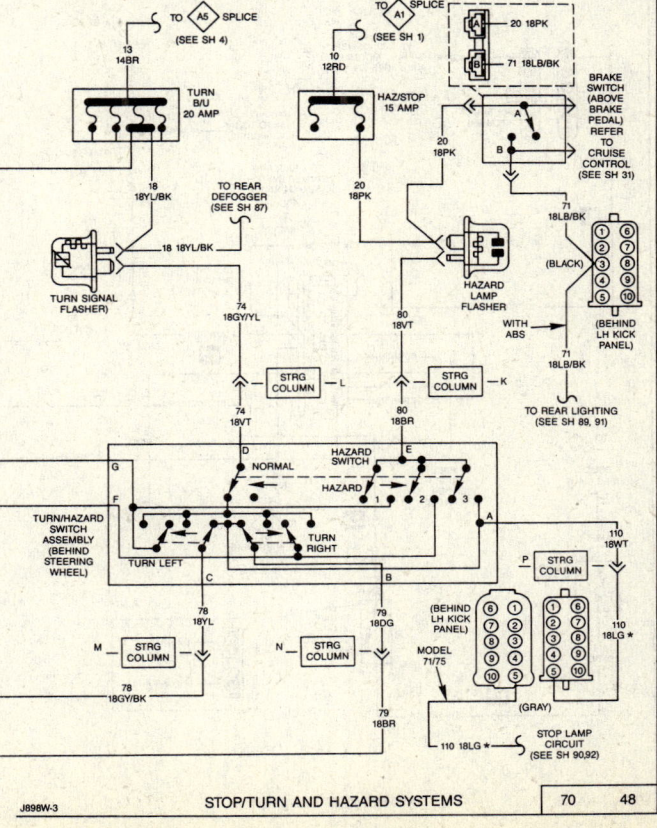

STOP/TURN AND HAZARD SYSTEMS

CHASSIS ELECTRICAL 6

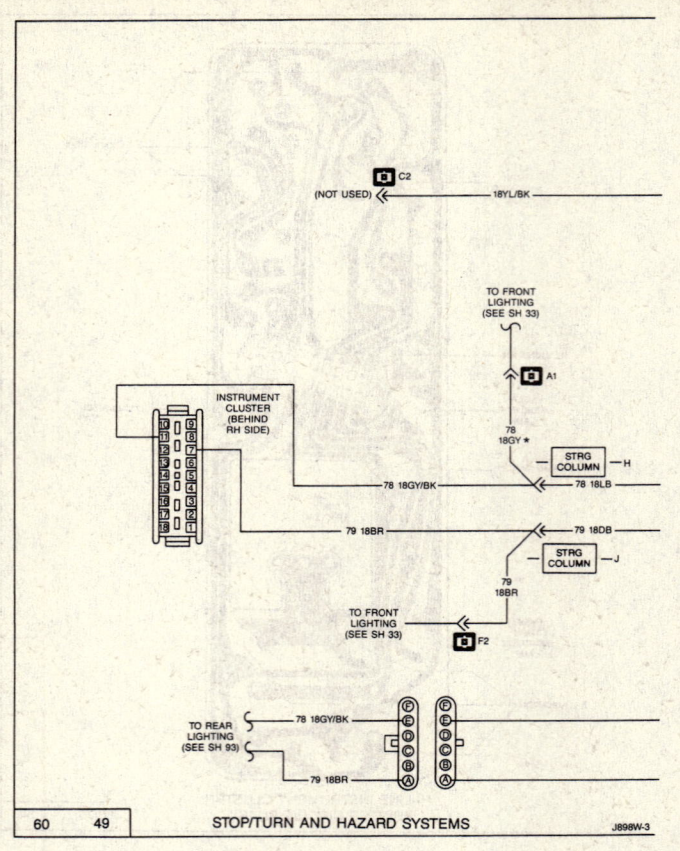

STOP/TURN AND HAZARD SYSTEMS

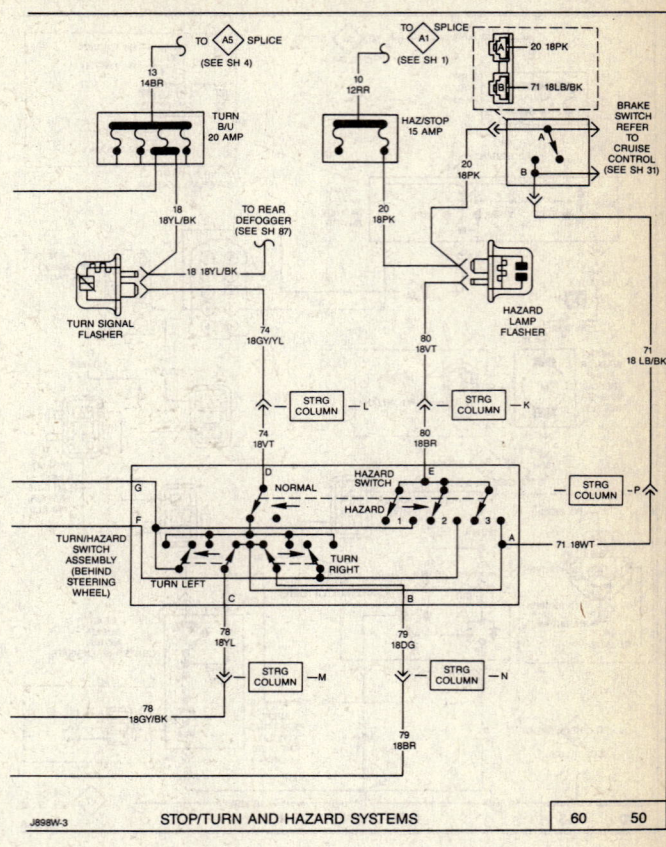

STOP/TURN AND HAZARD SYSTEMS

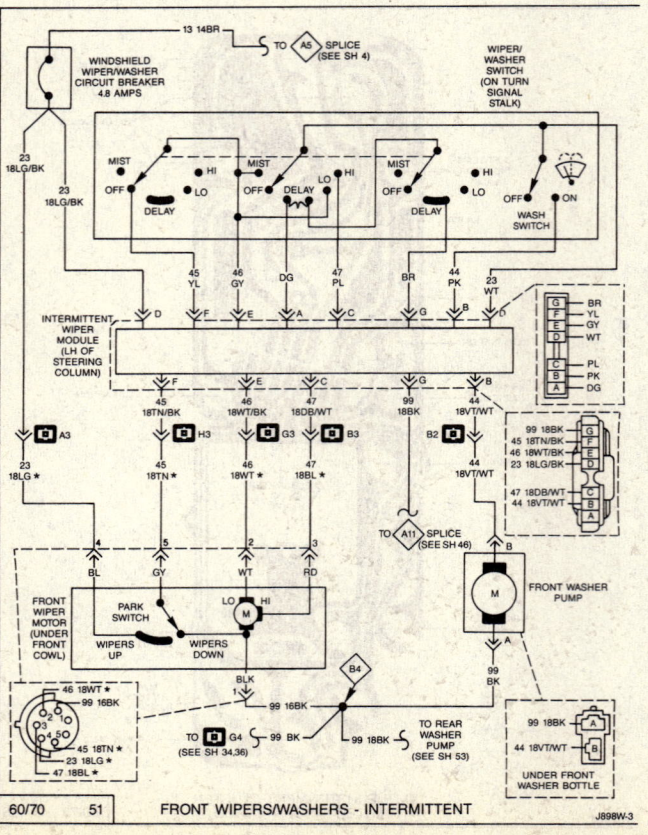

FRONT WIPERS/WASHERS - INTERMITTENT

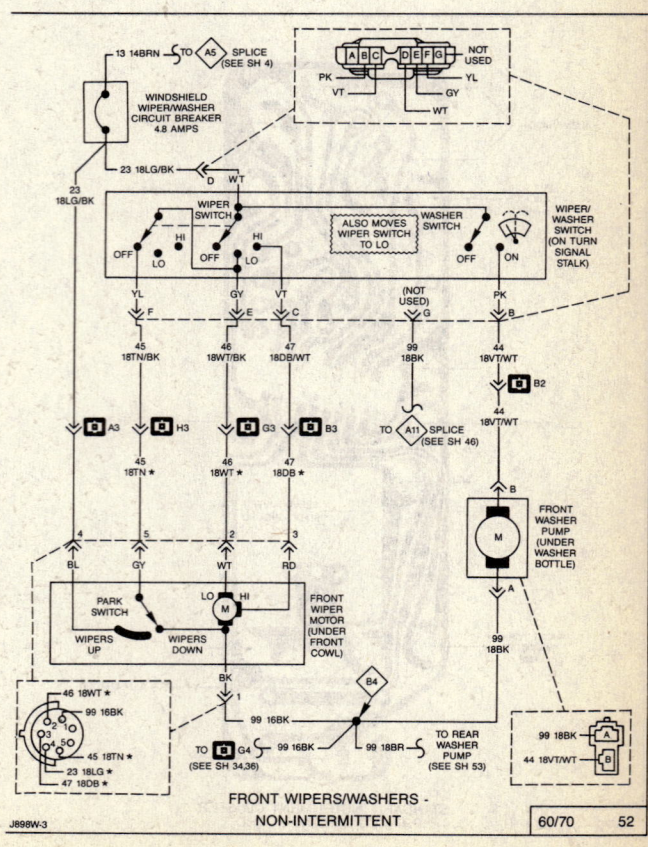

FRONT WIPERS/WASHERS - NON-INTERMITTENT

6-61

6 CHASSIS ELECTRICAL

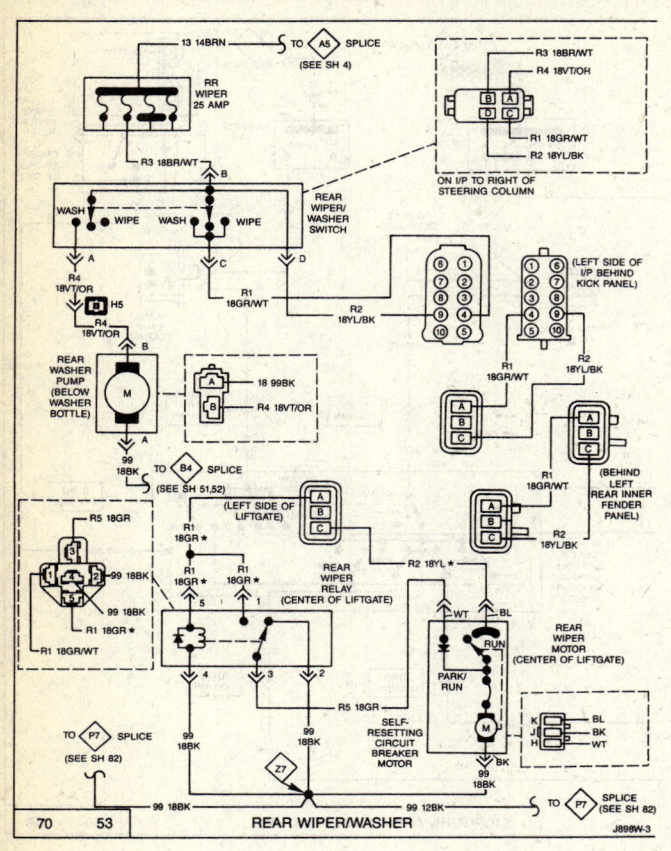

REAR WIPER/WASHER

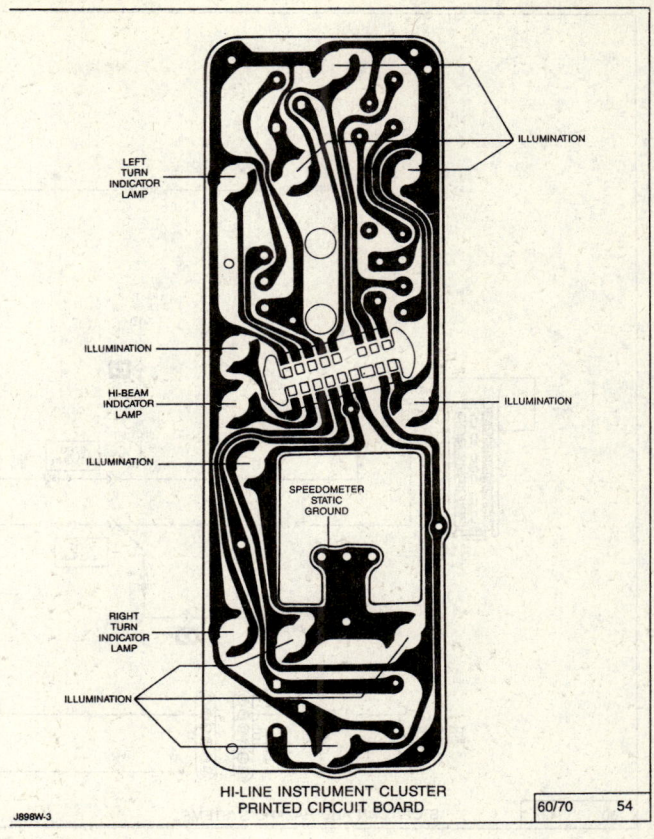

HI-LINE INSTRUMENT CLUSTER PRINTED CIRCUIT BOARD

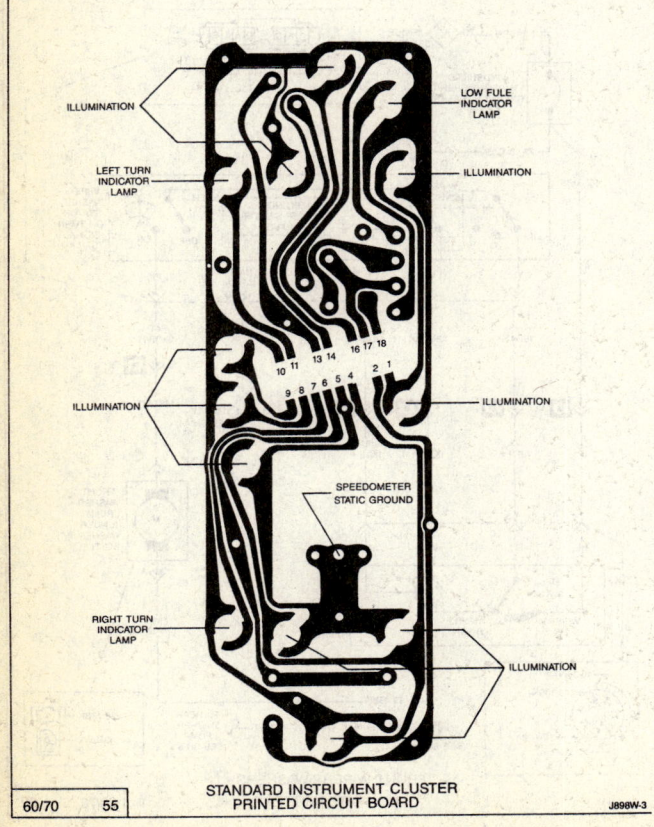

STANDARD INSTRUMENT CLUSTER PRINTED CIRCUIT BOARD

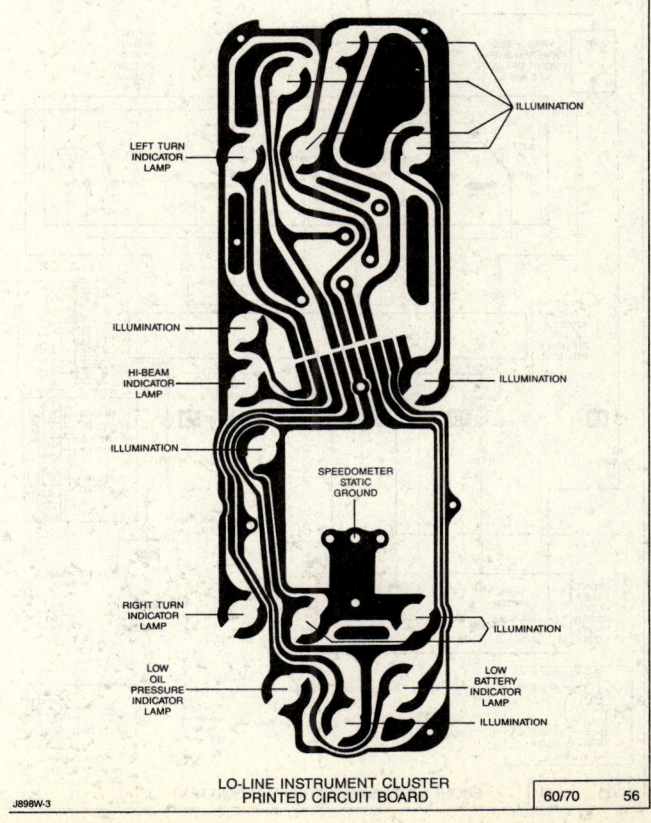

LO-LINE INSTRUMENT CLUSTER PRINTED CIRCUIT BOARD

CHASSIS ELECTRICAL 6

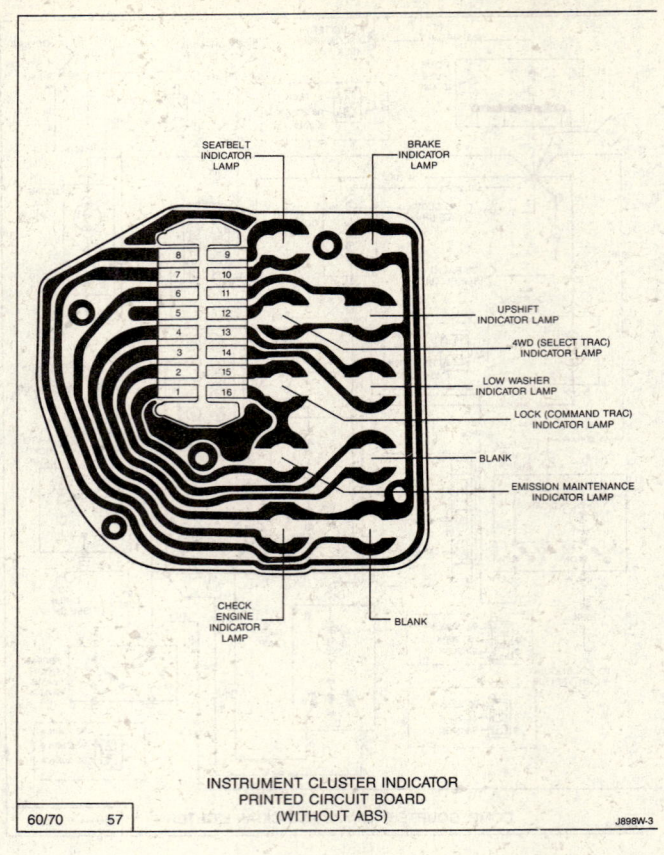

INSTRUMENT CLUSTER INDICATOR PRINTED CIRCUIT BOARD (WITHOUT ABS)

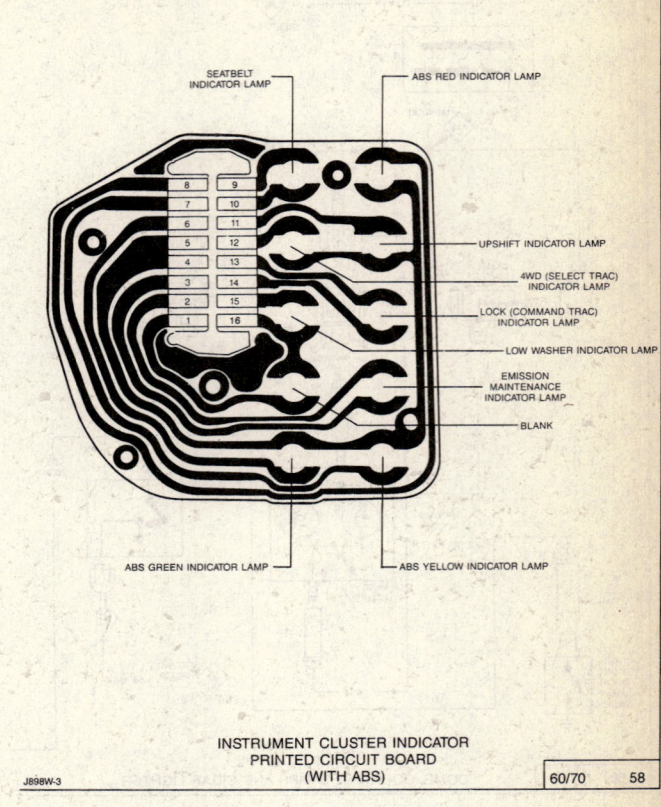

INSTRUMENT CLUSTER INDICATOR PRINTED CIRCUIT BOARD (WITH ABS)

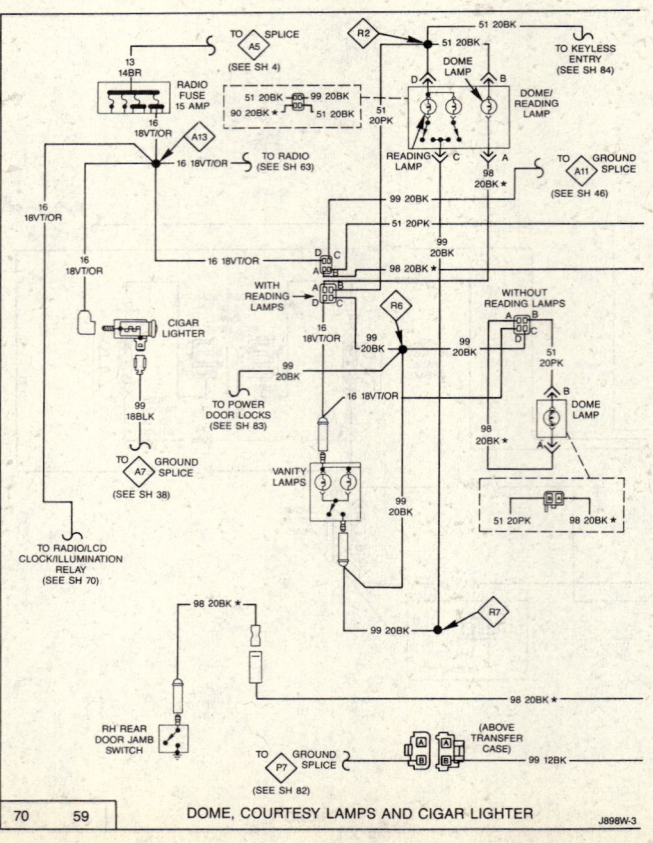

DOME, COURTESY LAMPS AND CIGAR LIGHTER

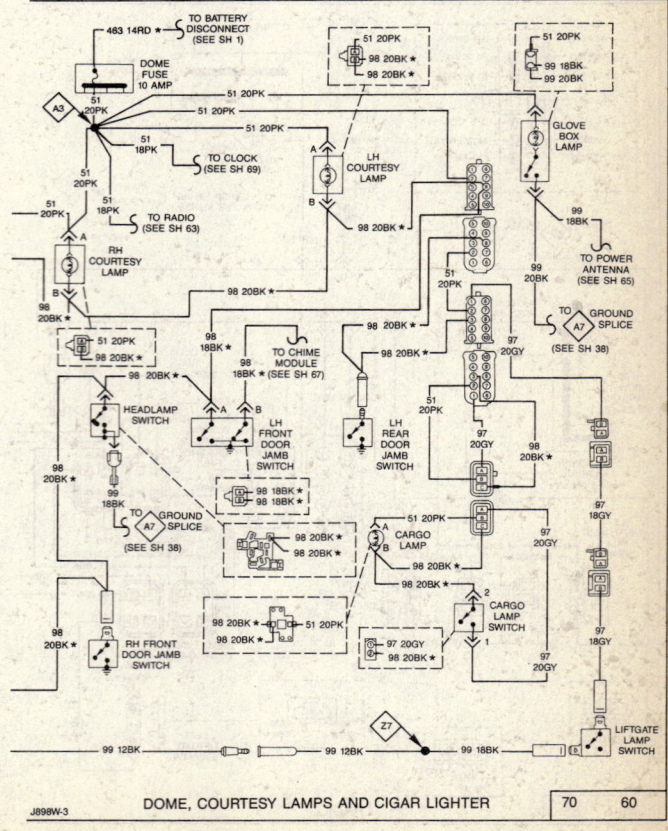

DOME, COURTESY LAMPS AND CIGAR LIGHTER

6-63

6 CHASSIS ELECTRICAL

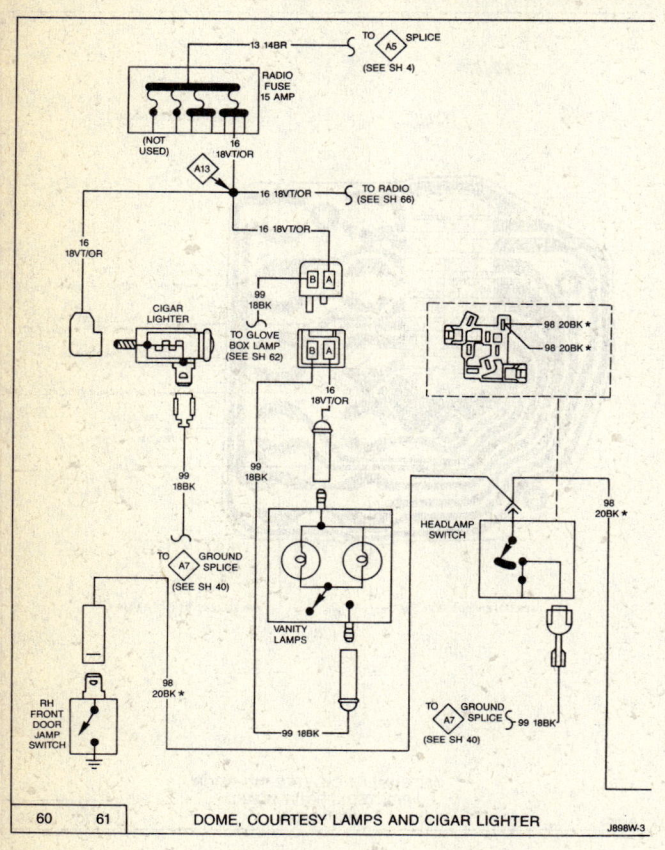

DOME, COURTESY LAMPS AND CIGAR LIGHTER

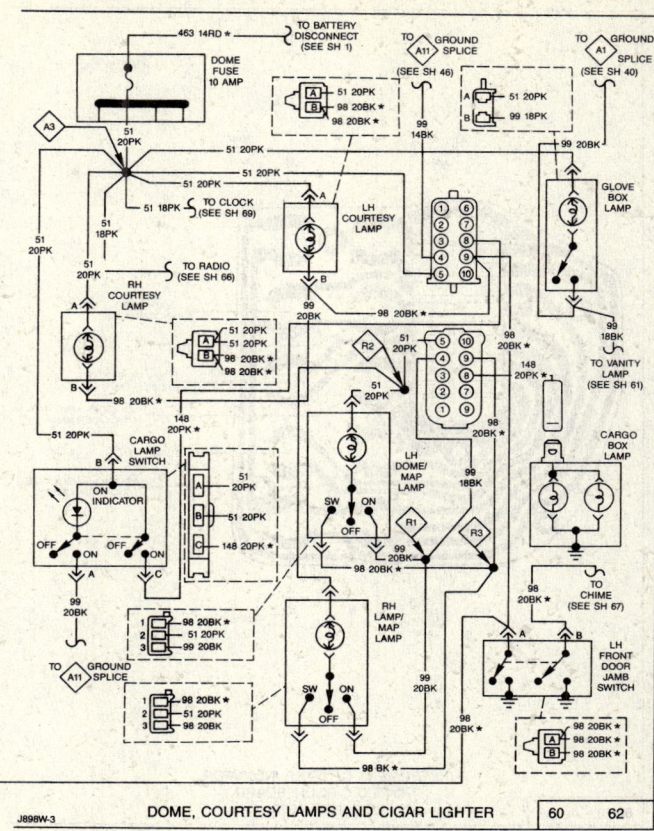

DOME, COURTESY LAMPS AND CIGAR LIGHTER

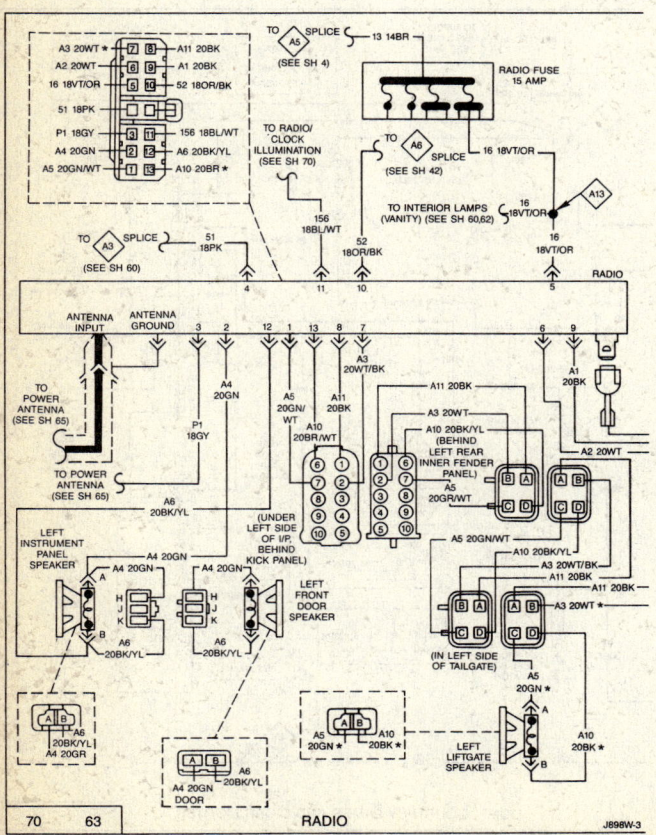

RADIO

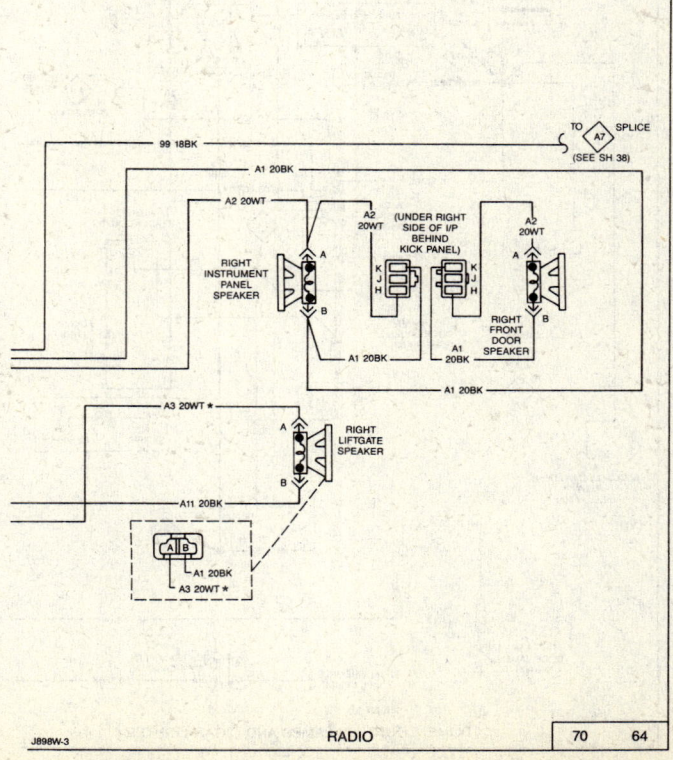

RADIO

CHASSIS ELECTRICAL 6

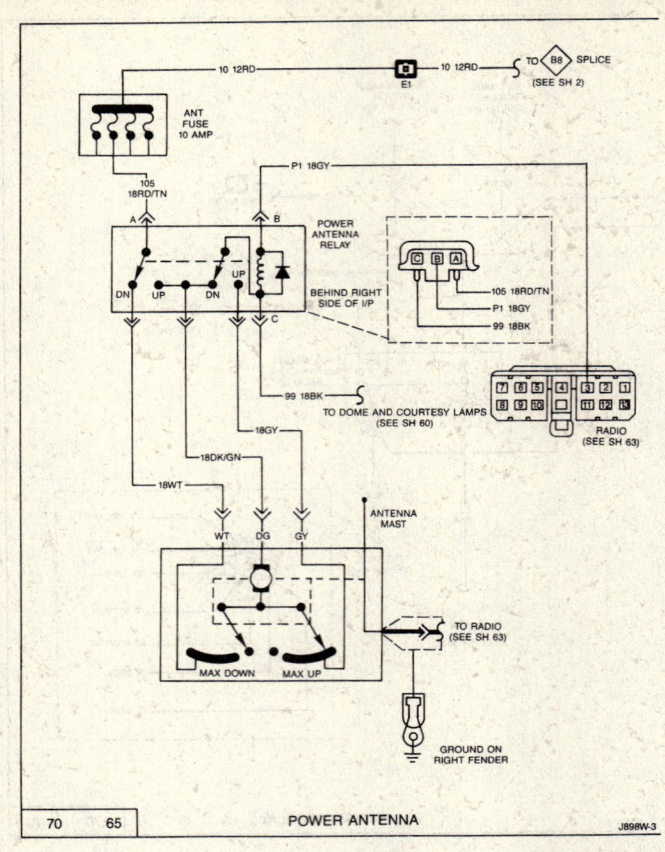
POWER ANTENNA

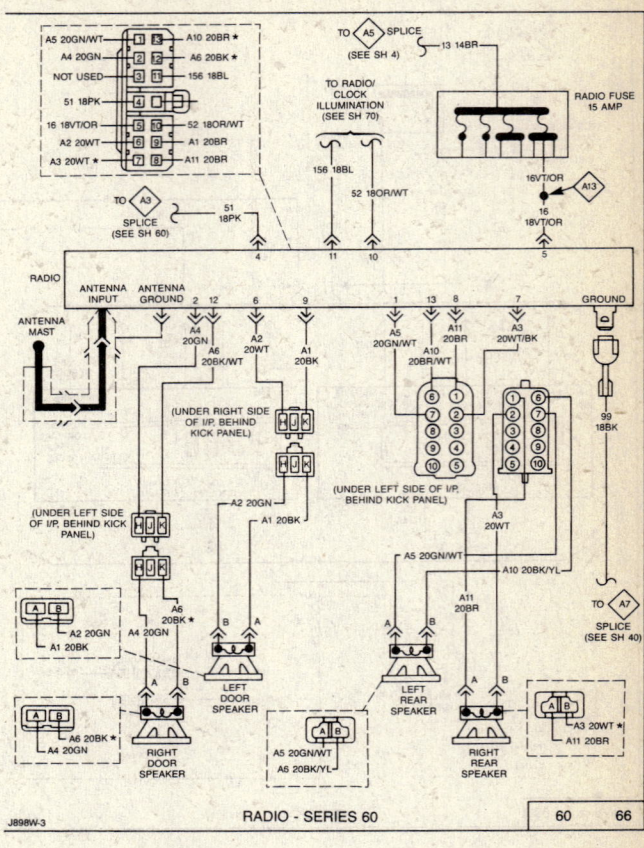
RADIO - SERIES 60

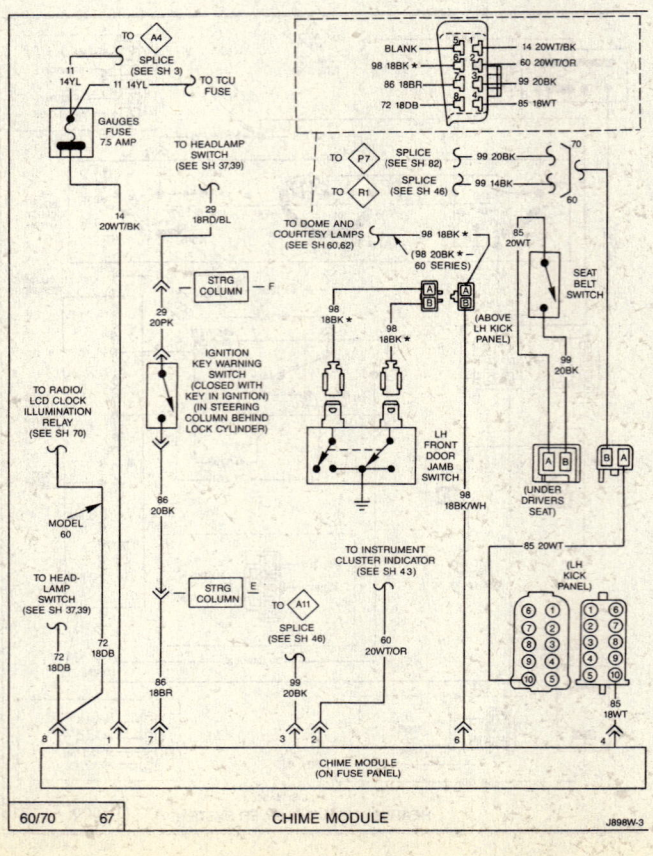
CHIME MODULE

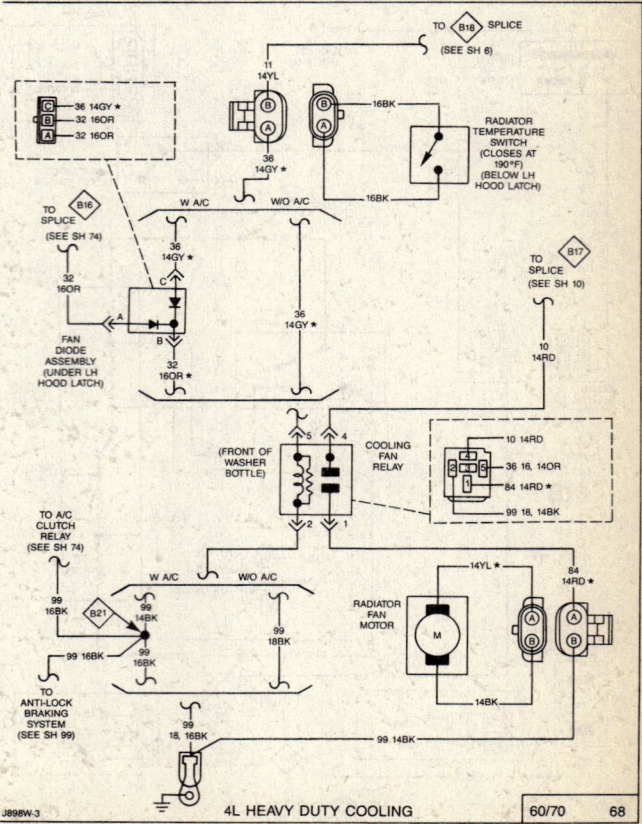
4L HEAVY DUTY COOLING

6-65

6 CHASSIS ELECTRICAL

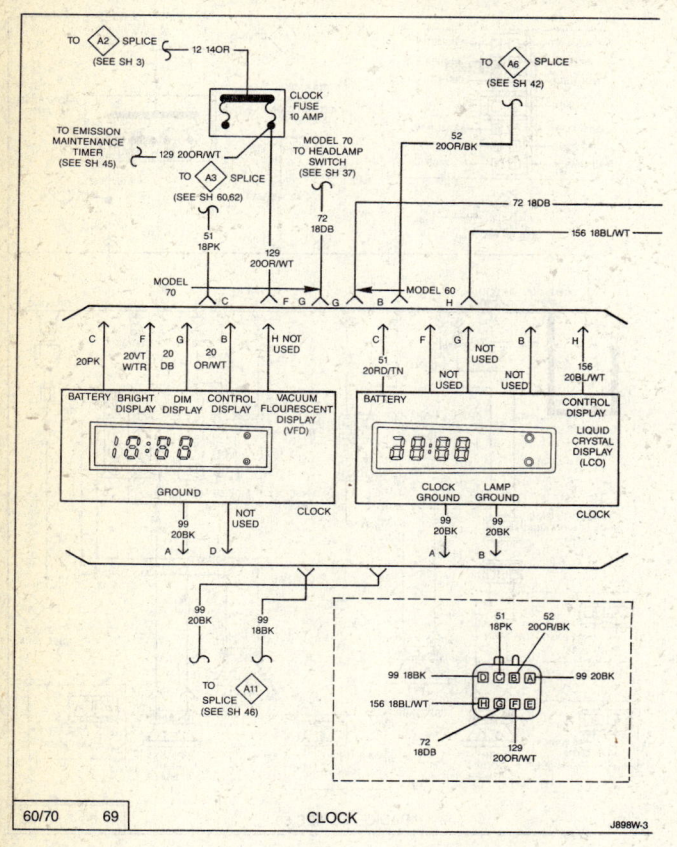

CLOCK

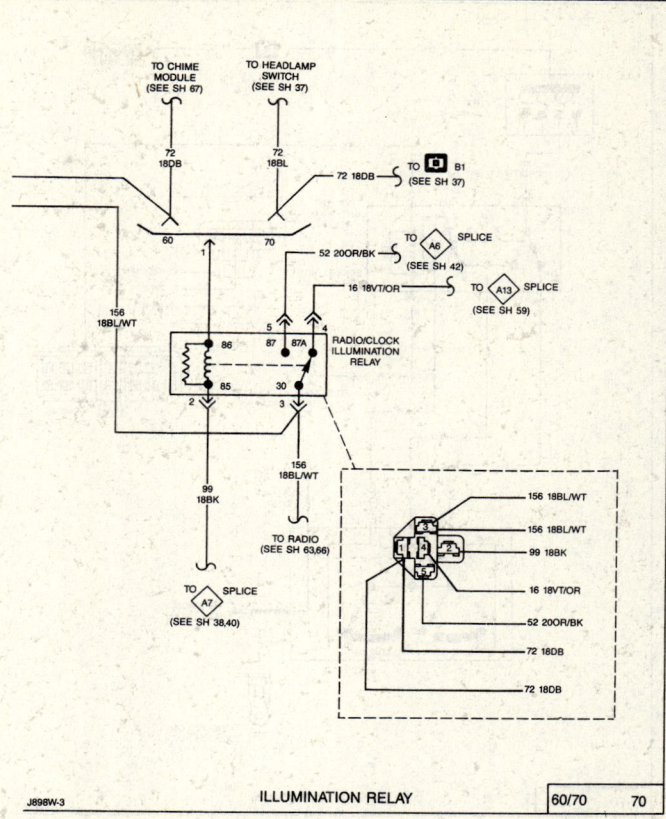

ILLUMINATION RELAY

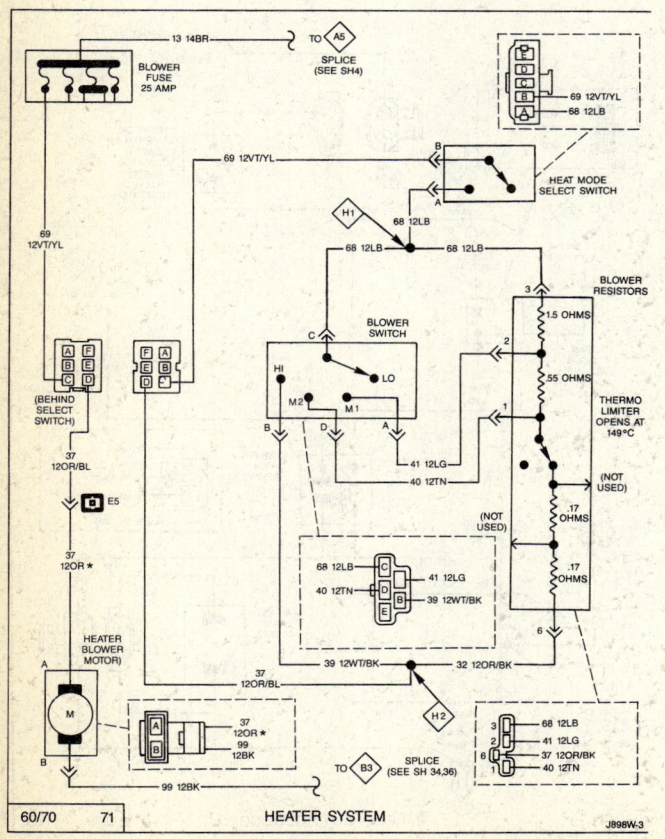

HEATER SYSTEM

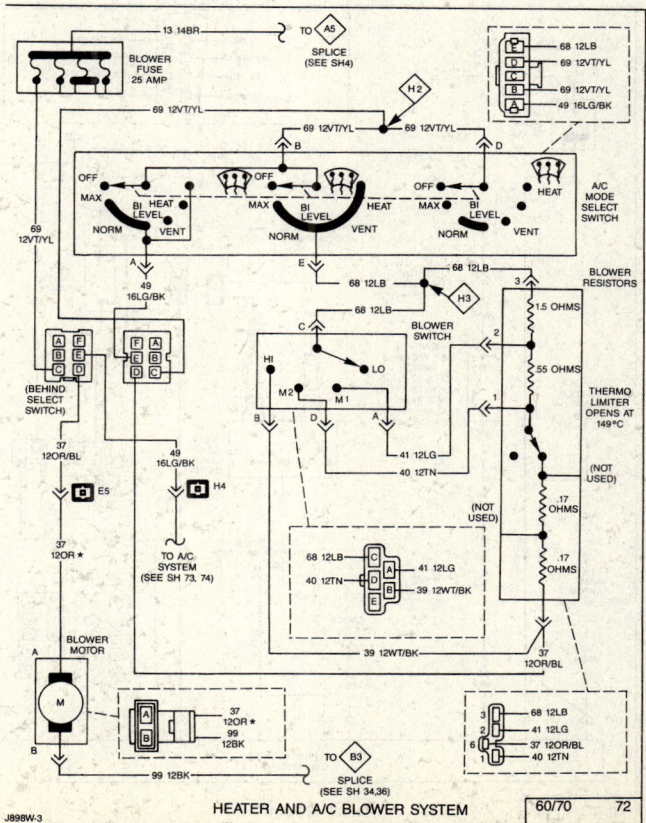

HEATER AND A/C BLOWER SYSTEM

CHASSIS ELECTRICAL 6

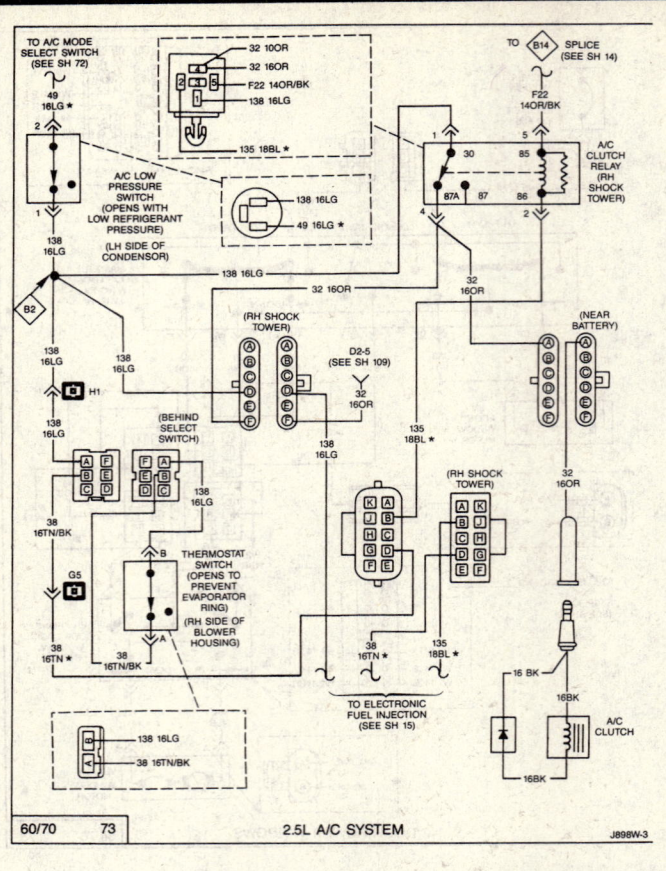

2.5L A/C SYSTEM

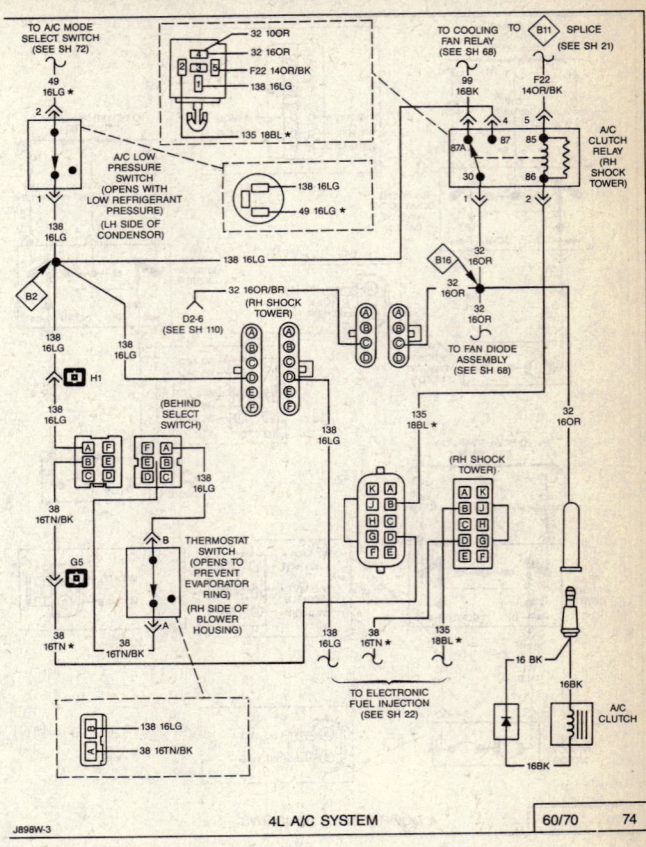

4L A/C SYSTEM

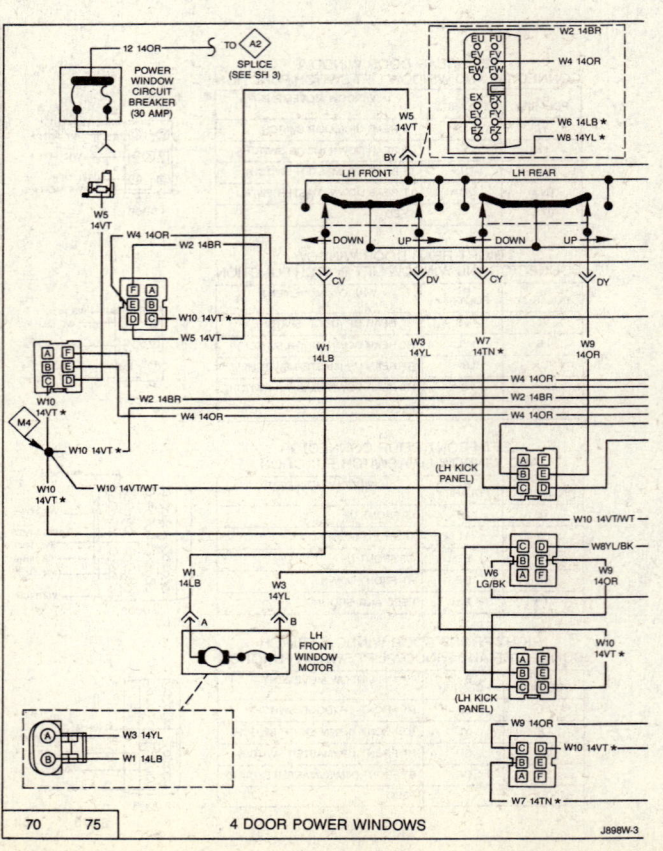

4 DOOR POWER WINDOWS

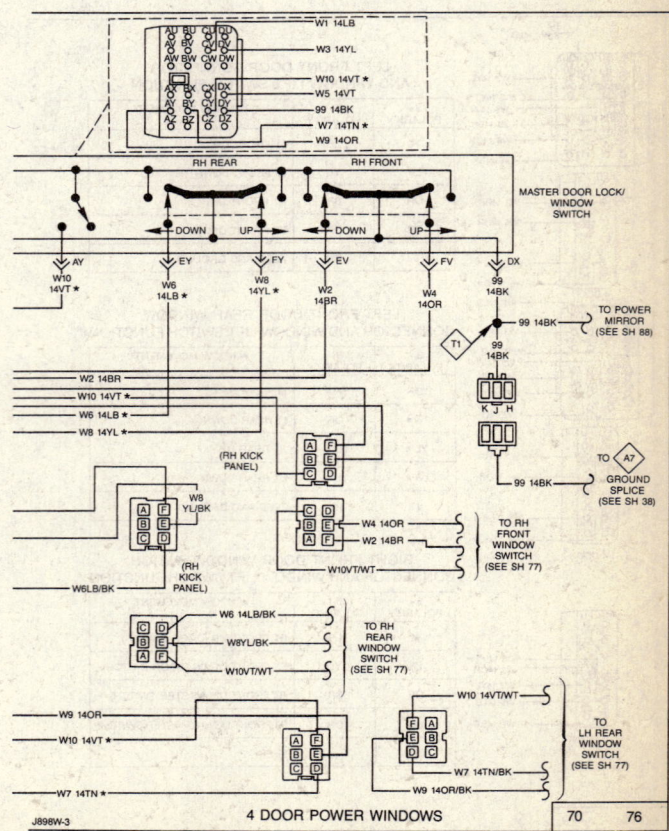

4 DOOR POWER WINDOWS

6-67

6 CHASSIS ELECTRICAL

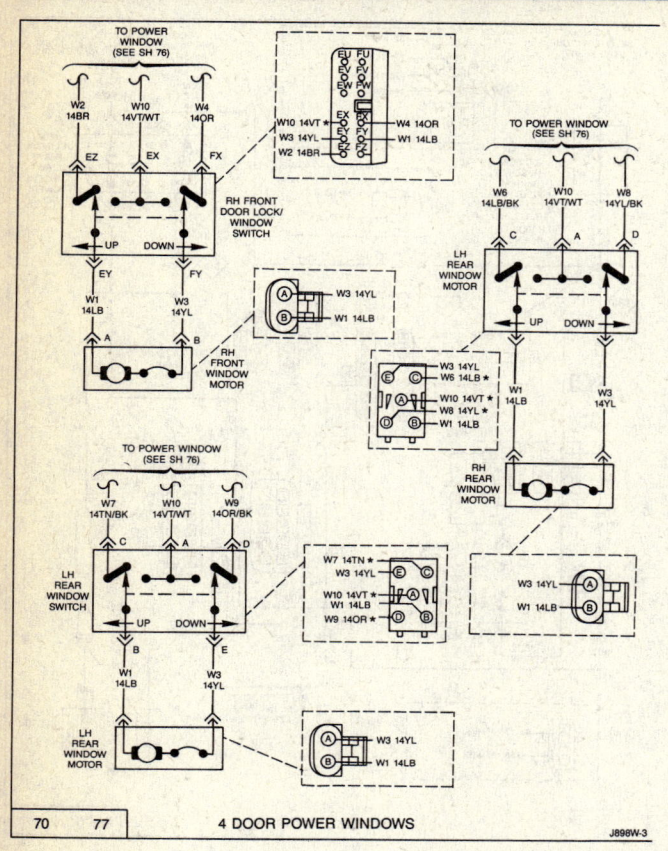

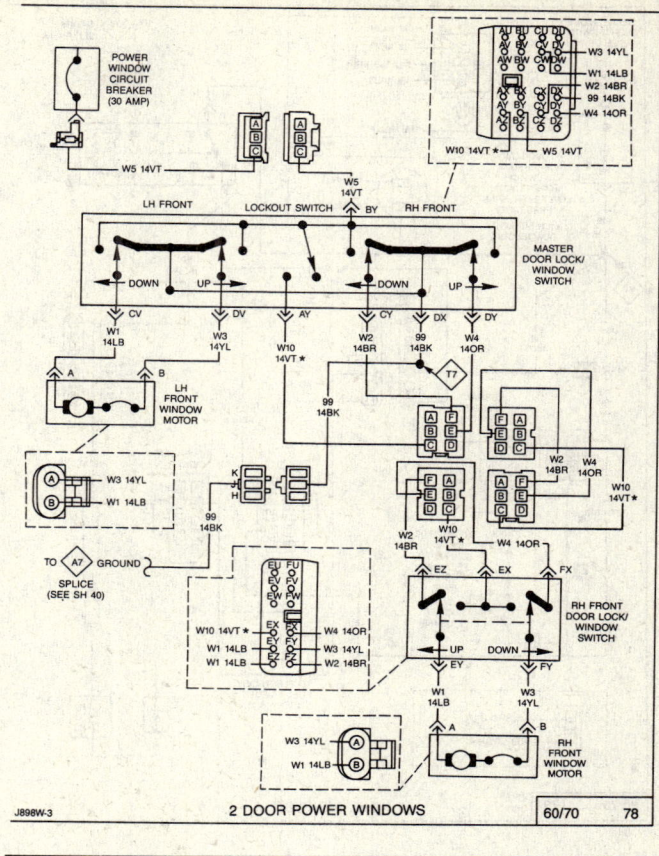

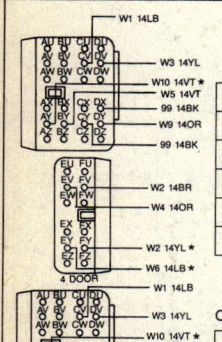

LEFT FRONT DOOR CONNECTOR AND WINDOW LIFT SWITCH FUNCTION

B+ POLARITY	B− POLARITY	WINDOW MOVEMENT
YL	LB	LT FRONT UP
LB	YL	LT FRONT DOWN
OR	BR	RT FRONT UP
BR	OR	RT FRONT DOWN
VT	BK	FEED AND GROUND

LEFT FRONT DOOR REAR WINDOW CONNECTOR AND WINDOW LIFT SWITCH FUNCTION

B+ POLARITY	B− POLARITY	WINDOW MOVEMENT
OR	TN	LT REAR UP
TN ★	OR	LT REAR DOWN
YL ★	LB ★	RT REAR UP
LB ★	YL ★	RT REAR DOWN
VT	BK	FEED AND GROUND

RIGHT FRONT DOOR WINDOW SWITCH CONNECTOR AND WINDOW LIFT SWITCH FUNCTION

B+ POLARITY	B− POLARITY	WINDOW MOVEMENT
YL	LB	RT FRONT UP (DOOR SWITCH)
LB	YL	RT FRONT DOWN (DOOR SWITCH)
OR	BR	RT FRONT UP (MASTER SWITCH)
BR	OR	RT FRONT DOWN (MASTER SWITCH)
VT ★		FEED

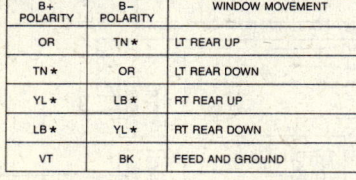

LEFT REAR DOOR WINDOW CONNECTOR AND WINDOW LIFT SWITCH FUNCTION

B+ POLARITY	B− POLARITY	WINDOW MOVEMENT
YL	LB	LT REAR UP (DOOR SWITCH)
LB	YL	LT REAR DOWN (DOOR SWITCH)
OR ★	TN ★	LT REAR UP (MASTER SWITCH)
TN ★	OR ★	LT REAR DOWN (MASTER SWITCH)
VT ★		FEED

RIGHT REAR DOOR WINDOW CONNECTOR AND WINDOW LIFT SWITCH FUNCTION

B+ POLARITY	B− POLARITY	WINDOW MOVEMENT
YL	LB	RT REAR UP (DOOR SWITCH)
LB	YL	RT REAR DOWN (DOOR SWITCH)
YL ★	LB ★	RT REAR UP (MASTER SWITCH)
LB ★	YL ★	RT REAR DOWN (MASTER SWITCH)
VT ★		FEED

LEFT FRONT DOOR CONNECTOR AND WINDOW LIFT SWITCH FUNCTION

B+ POLARITY	B− POLARITY	WINDOW MOVEMENT
YL	LB	LT FRONT UP
LB	YL	LT FRONT DOWN
OR	BR	RT FRONT UP
BR	OR	RT FRONT DOWN
VT ★	BK	FEED AND GROUND

RIGHT FRONT DOOR WINDOW SWITCH CONNECTOR AND WINDOW LIFT SWITCH FUNCTION

B+ POLARITY	B− POLARITY	WINDOW MOVEMENT
YL	LB	RT FRONT UP (DOOR SWITCH)
LB	YL	RT FRONT DOWN (DOOR SWITCH)
OR	BR	RT FRONT UP (MASTER SWITCH)
BR	OR	RT FRONT DOWN (MASTER SWITCH)
VT ★		FEED

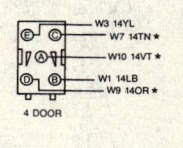
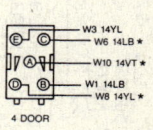
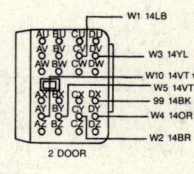
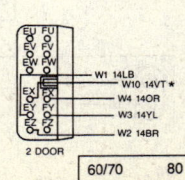

6-68

CHASSIS ELECTRICAL 6

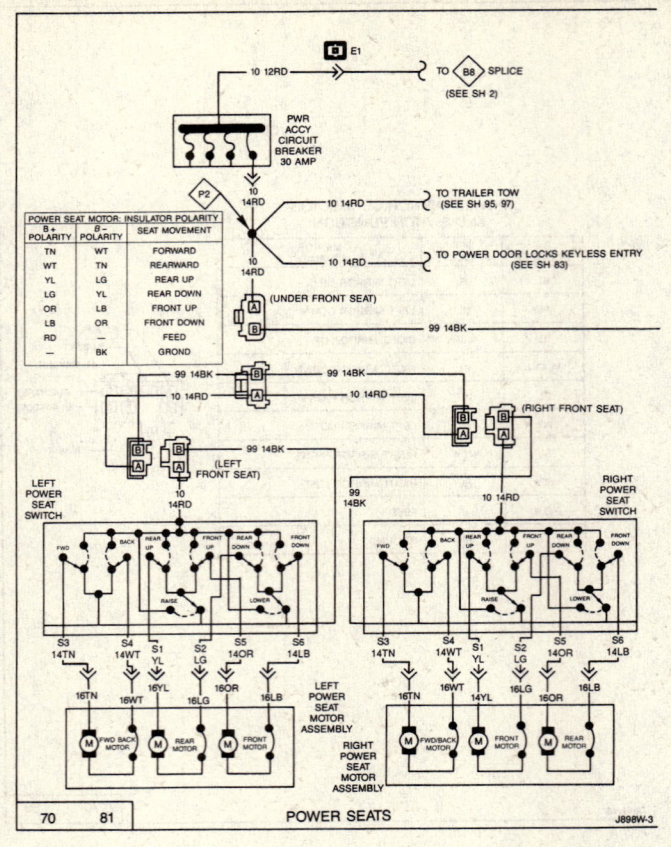

POWER SEATS

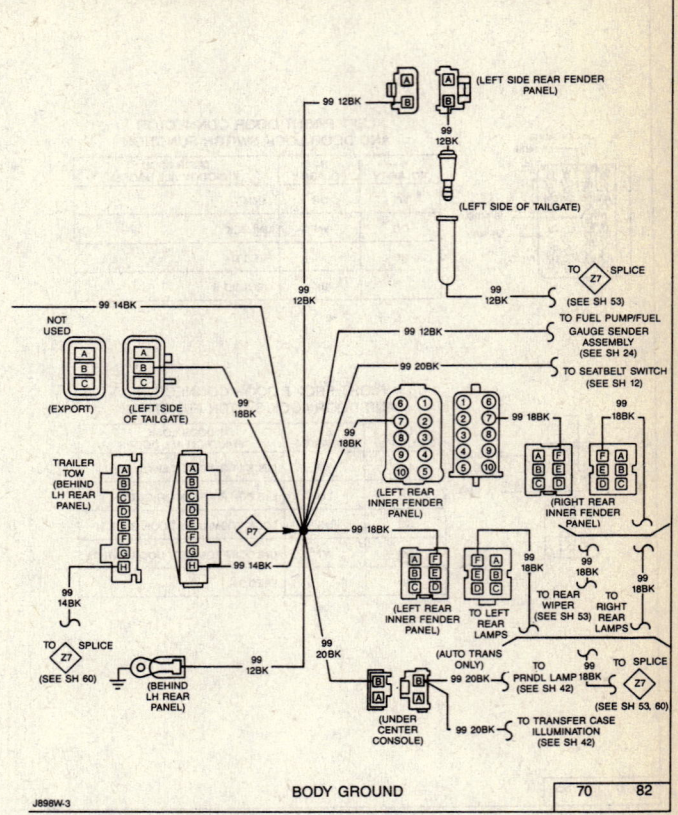

BODY GROUND

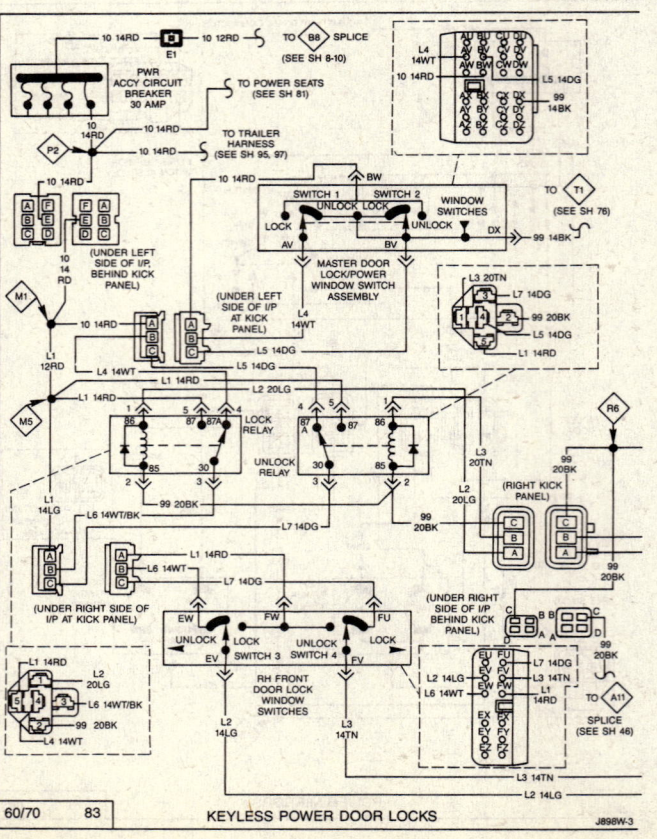

KEYLESS POWER DOOR LOCKS

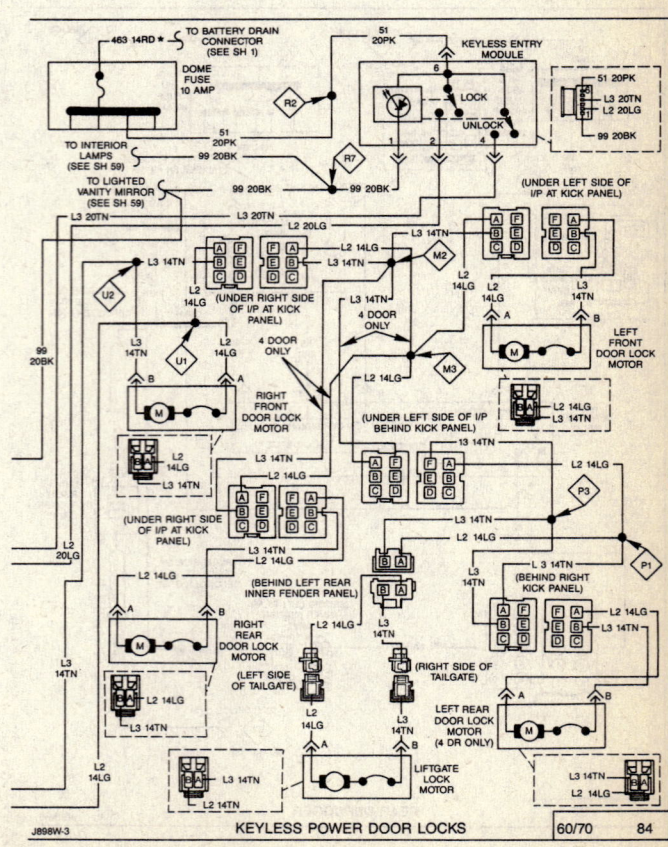

KEYLESS POWER DOOR LOCKS

6-69

6 CHASSIS ELECTRICAL

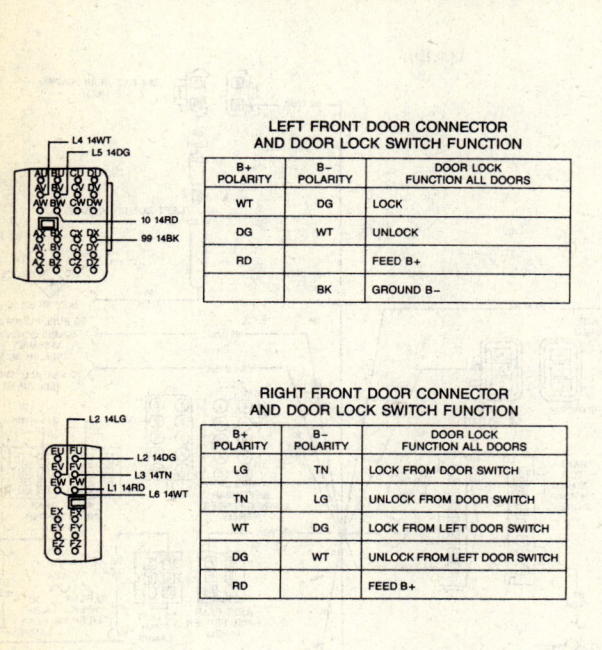

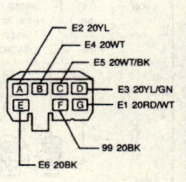

LEFT FRONT DOOR CONNECTOR AND DOOR LOCK SWITCH FUNCTION

B+ POLARITY	B− POLARITY	DOOR LOCK FUNCTION ALL DOORS
WT	DG	LOCK
DG	WT	UNLOCK
RD		FEED B+
	BK	GROUND B−

RIGHT FRONT DOOR CONNECTOR AND DOOR LOCK SWITCH FUNCTION

B+ POLARITY	B− POLARITY	DOOR LOCK FUNCTION ALL DOORS
LG	TN	LOCK FROM DOOR SWITCH
TN	LG	UNLOCK FROM DOOR SWITCH
WT	DG	LOCK FROM LEFT DOOR SWITCH
DG	WT	UNLOCK FROM LEFT DOOR SWITCH
RD		FEED B+

POWER MIRROR CONNECTOR AND SWITCH FUNCTION

B+ POLARITY	B− POLARITY	MIRROR MOVEMENT
BL	YL	LEFT MIRROR UP
YL	BL	LEFT MIRROR DOWN
BL	YL/GN	RIGHT MIRROR UP
YL/GN	BL	RIGHT MIRROR DOWN
BL	WT	LEFT MIRROR RIGHT
WT	BL	LEFT MIRROR LEFT
BL	WT *	RIGHT MIRROR RIGHT
WT *	BL	RIGHT MIRROR LEFT
RD *		FEED
	BK	GROUND

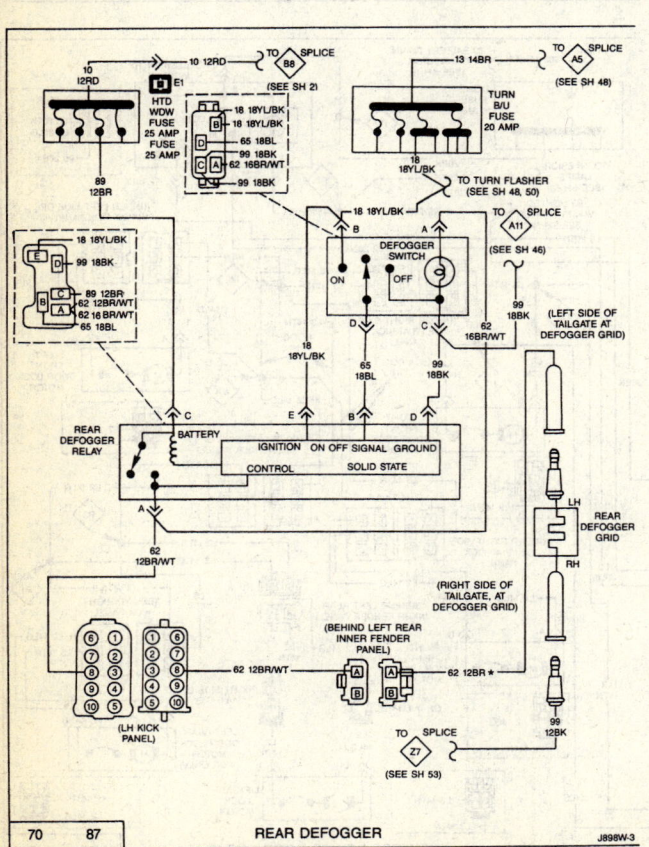

REAR DEFOGGER

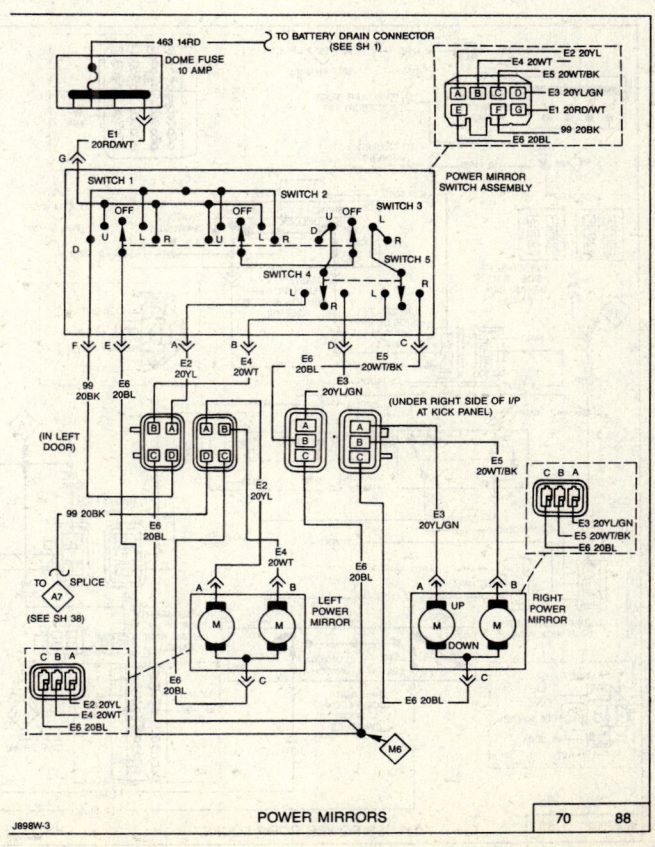

POWER MIRRORS

6-70

CHASSIS ELECTRICAL 6

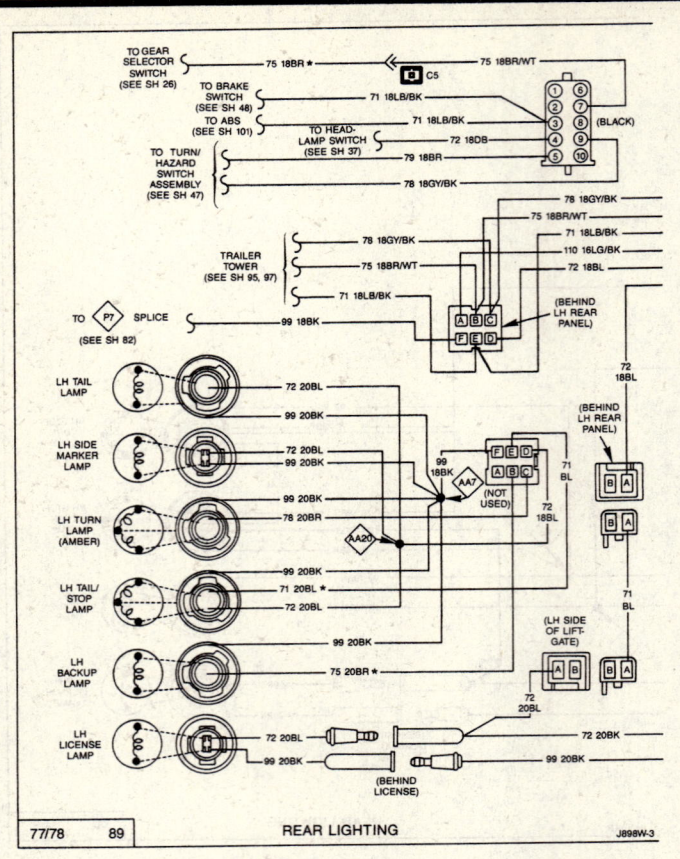
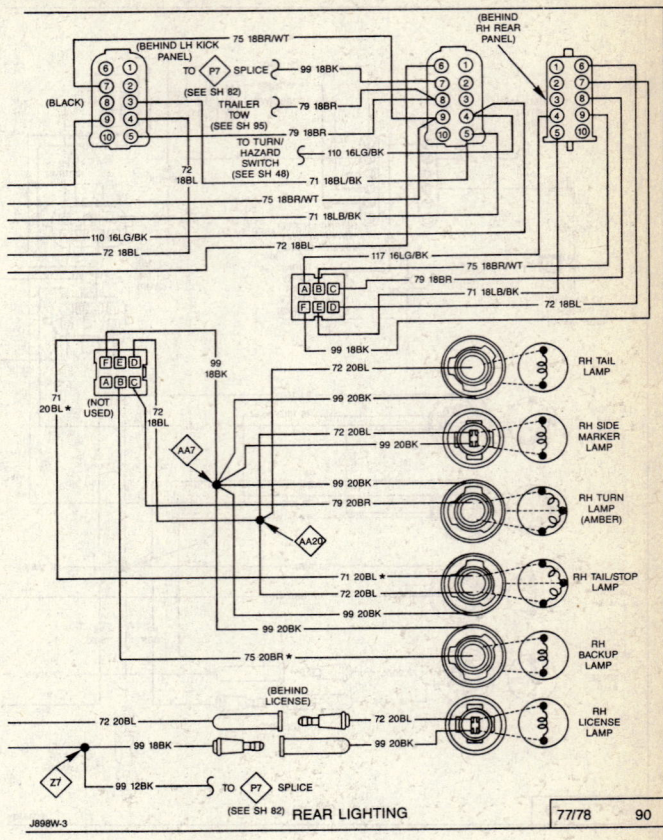
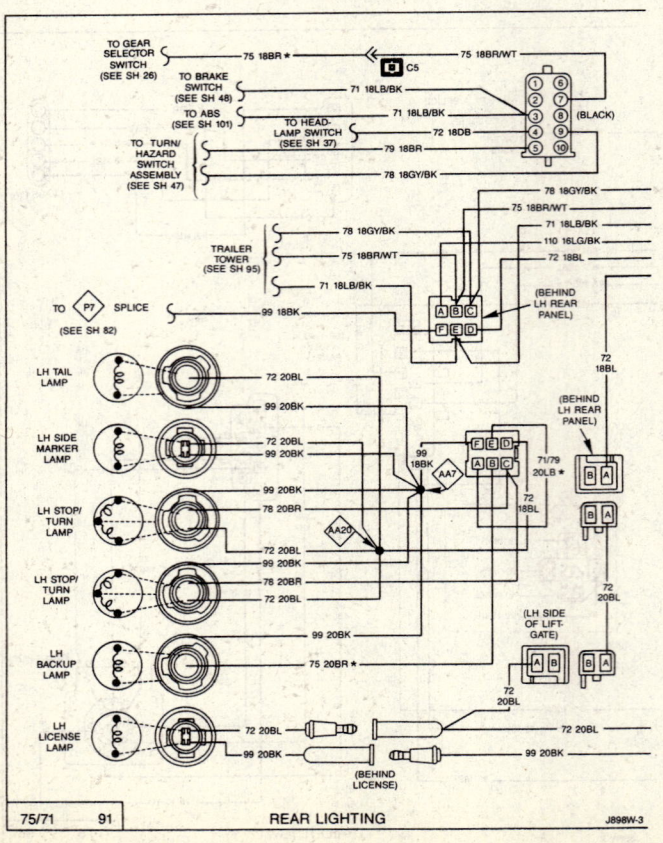
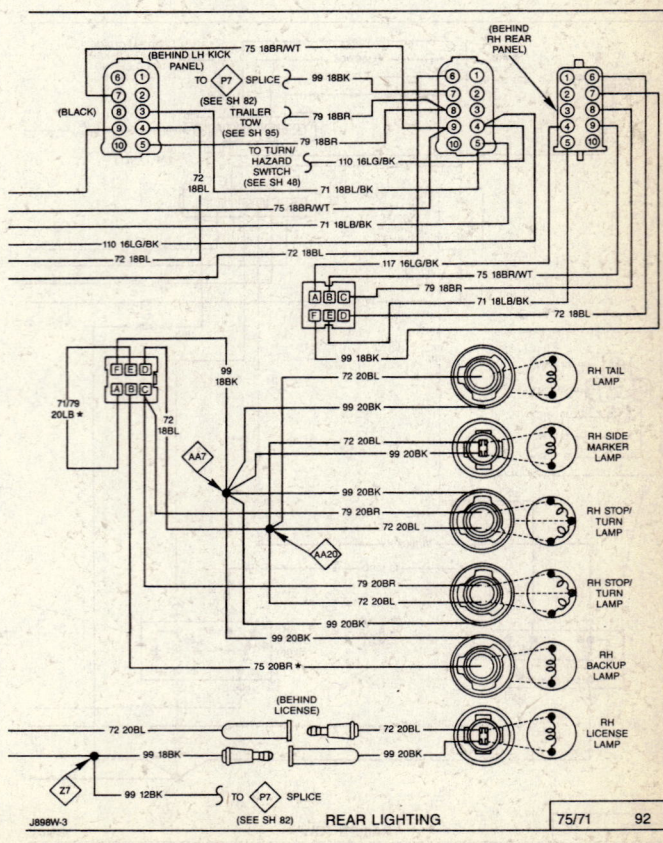

6-71

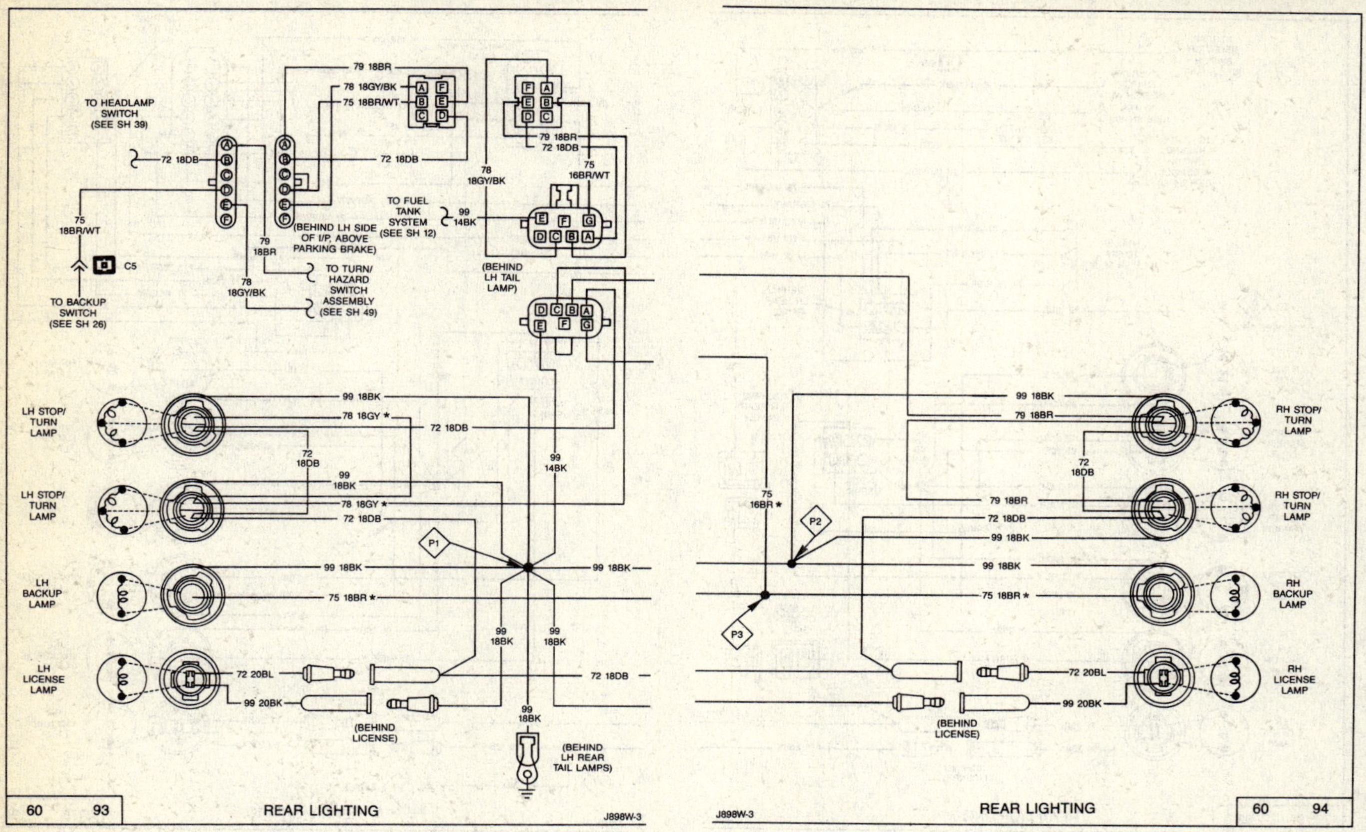
TO HEADLAMP SWITCH (SEE SH 39)
(BEHIND LH SIDE OF I/P, ABOVE PARKING BRAKE)
TO FUEL TANK SYSTEM (SEE SH 12)
(BEHIND LH TAIL LAMP)
TO TURN/ HAZARD SWITCH ASSEMBLY (SEE SH 49)
TO BACKUP SWITCH (SEE SH 26)
C5
LH STOP/ TURN LAMP
LH STOP/ TURN LAMP
LH BACKUP LAMP
LH LICENSE LAMP
P1
(BEHIND LICENSE)
(BEHIND LH REAR TAIL LAMPS)
60
93
REAR LIGHTING
J898W-3
RH STOP/ TURN LAMP
RH STOP/ TURN LAMP
RH BACKUP LAMP
RH LICENSE LAMP
P2
P3
(BEHIND LICENSE)
J898W-3
REAR LIGHTING
60
94

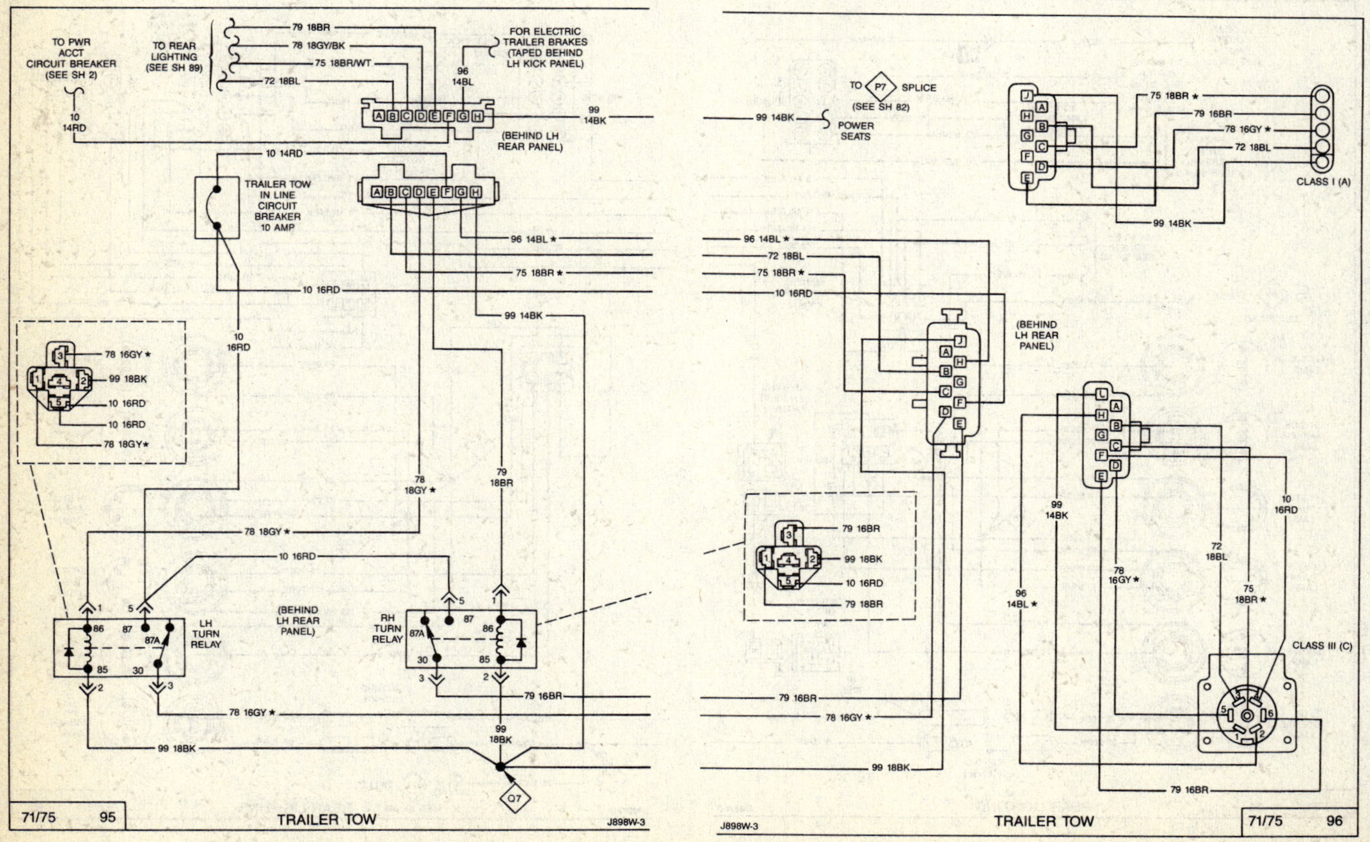
TO PWR ACCT CIRCUIT BREAKER (SEE SH 2)
TO REAR LIGHTING (SEE SH 89)
FOR ELECTRIC TRAILER BRAKES (TAPED BEHIND LH KICK PANEL)
(BEHIND LH REAR PANEL)
TRAILER TOW IN LINE CIRCUIT BREAKER 10 AMP
LH TURN RELAY
(BEHIND LH REAR PANEL)
RH TURN RELAY
Q7
71/75
95
TRAILER TOW
J898W-3
TO P7 SPLICE (SEE SH 82)
POWER SEATS
CLASS I (A)
(BEHIND LH REAR PANEL)
CLASS III (C)
J898W-3
TRAILER TOW
71/75
96

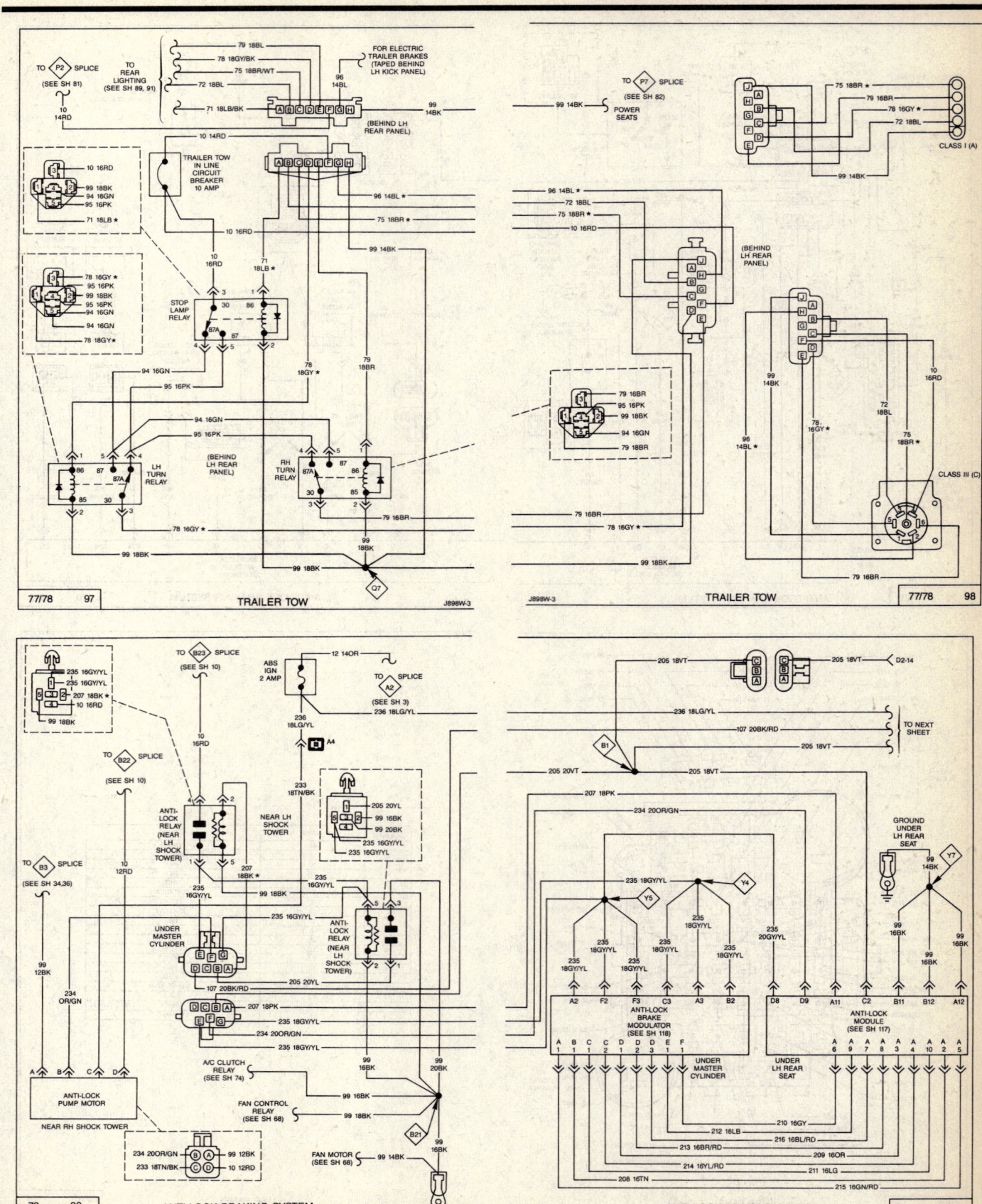

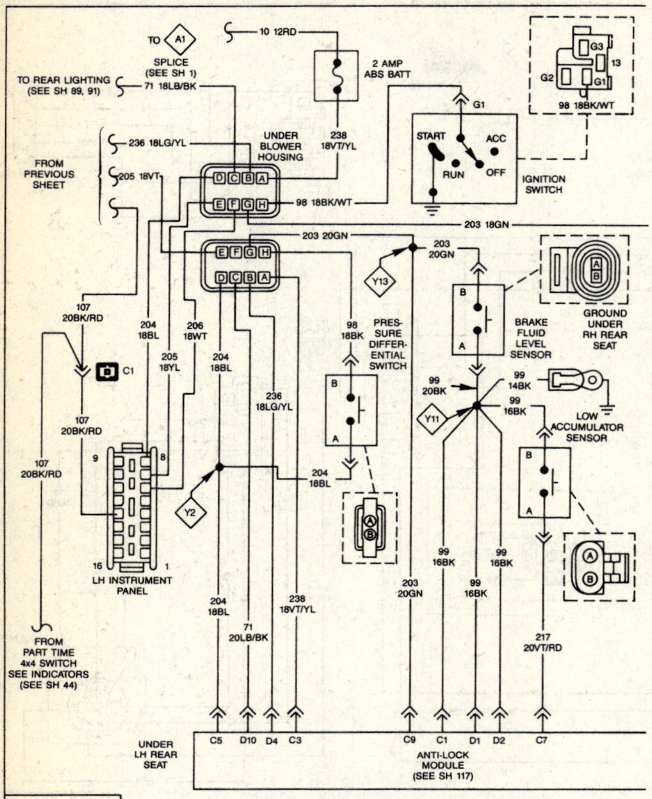

70 101 ANTI-LOCK BRAKING SYSTEM J898W-3

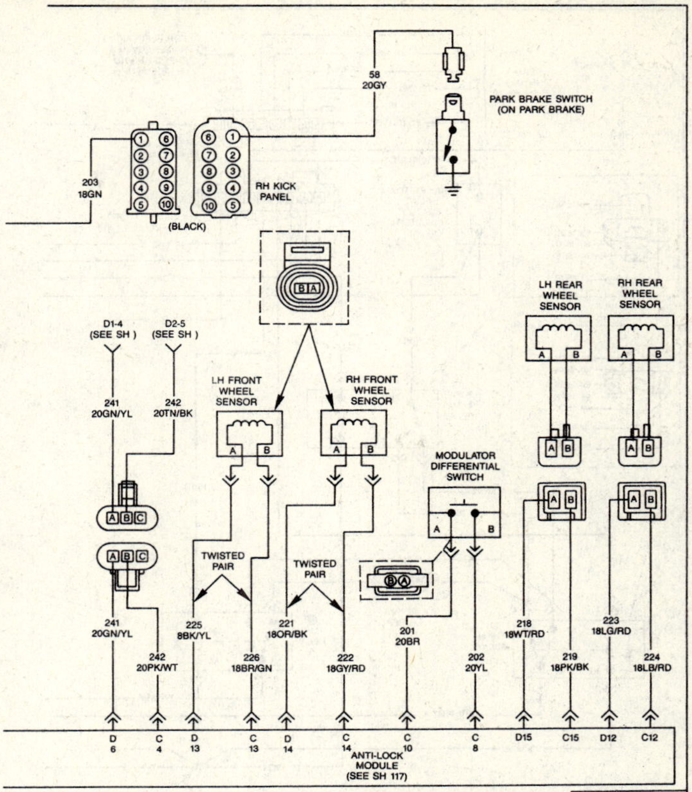

J898W-3 ANTI-LOCK BRAKING SYSTEM 70 102

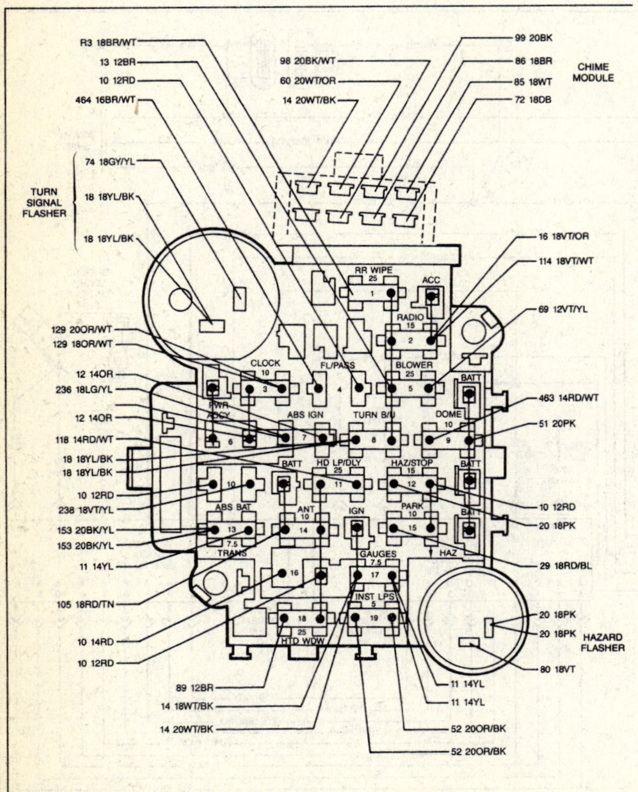

60/70 103 FUSE PANEL J898W-3

FUSE NUMBER	AMPS	COLOR
1	25	WHITE
2	15	LIGHT BLUE
3	10	RED
4	10	RED
5	25	WHITE
6	30 CIRCUIT BREAKER	SILVER CAN
7	2	WHITE
8	20	YELLOW
9	10	RED
10	2	WHITE
11	25	WHITE
12	15	LIGHT BLUE
13	7.5	VIOLET
14	10	RED
15	10	RED
16	30 CIRCUIT BREAKER	SILVER CAN
17	7.5	VIOLET
18	25	WHITE
19	5	TAN

J898W-3 FUSE PANEL 60/70 104

CHASSIS ELECTRICAL 6

Bulkhead Connector (105)

	ENGINE COMPARTMENT CIRCUITS	CAV
78 18GY *	LEFT TURN SIGNAL LAMPS	A1
126 20BR	ECU UPSHIFT INDICATOR-GROUND	A2
23 18LG *	WINDSHIELD WIPER-PARK FEED	A3
—	—	A4
—	—	A5
463 14RD *	BATTERY DRAIN DISCONNECT	A6
—	—	A7
72 18BL	PARKING LAMPS FEED	B1
44 18VT *	WINDSHIELD WASHER PUMP FEED	B2
47 18BL *	WINDSHIELD WIPER - HI SPEED	B3
—	—	B4
106 18YL/BK	4 WHEEL DRIVE SWITCH	B5
11 14YL	IGNITION CIRCUITS	B6
107 20BK/RD	4 WHEEL DRIVE SWITCH	C1
—	—	C2
30 18GN *	IGNITION MODULE - TACHOMETER	C3
F22 14OR/BK	FUEL PUMP FEED	C4
75 18BR *	BACKUP LAMPS	C5
54 20LB	OIL PRESSURE	C6
10 12RD	BATTERY	D1
55 20VT	COOLANT TEMPERATURE	D2
10 12RD	BATTERY	D4
77 16LG	LO BEAM HEADLAMPS	D5
10 12RD	BATTERY	E1
31 14GY	HORNS	E2
76 16WT	HI BEAM HEADLAMPS	E4
37 12OR *	BLOWER MOTOR FEED	E5
—	—	F1
79 18BR	RIGHT TURN SIGNAL LAMPS	F2
98 20BK *	BRAKE WARNING SWITCH W/O ABS	F3
—	—	F4
58 20GY *	BRAKE WARNING SWITCH W/O ABS	F5
114 20VT *	WINDSHIELD WASHER FLUID LEVEL	F6
F5 18LG *	FOG LAMP RELAY	G1
59 20TN	ALTERNATOR-BATTERY INDICATOR	G2
46 18WT *	WINDSHIELD WIPER-LO SPEED	G3
99 12BK	GROUND	G4
99 12BK	GROUND	G4
38	A/C REQUEST	G5
—	—	G6
138 16LG	A/C SELECT	H1
33 14GN	STARTER RELAY	H2
45 18TN *	WINDSHIELD WIPER-PARK FEED	H3
49 16LG *	A/C LOW PRESSURE SWITCH	H4
R4 18VT/OR	REAR WIPER PUMP MOTOR	H5
61 20WT *	WASHER FLUID LEVEL SWITCH	H6

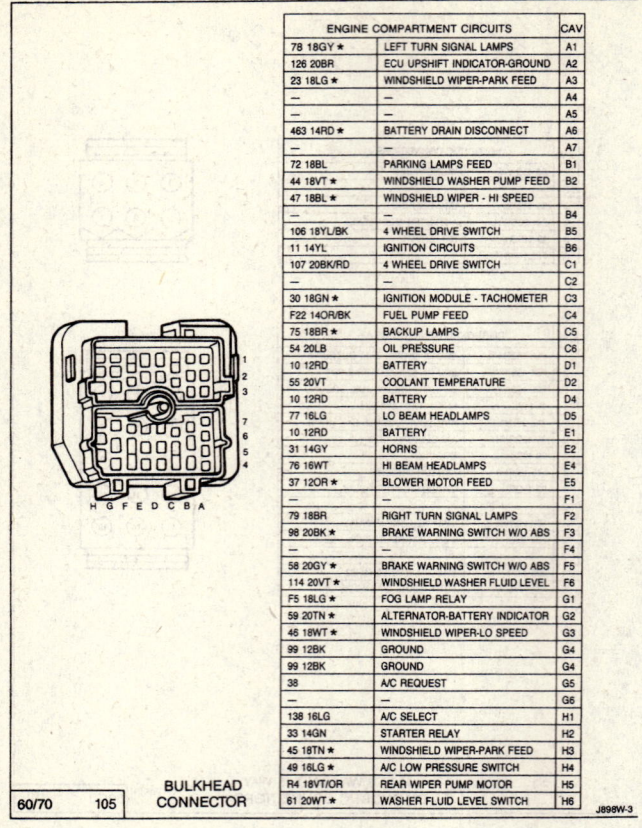

BULKHEAD CONNECTOR — 60/70 — 105

Bulkhead Connector (106)

CAV		INSTRUMENT PANEL CIRCUITS
A1	78 18GY/BK	LEFT TURN SIGNAL LAMPS
A2	126 20BK/LB	UPSHIFT INDICATOR LAMP
A3	23 18LG/BK	WINDSHIELD WIPER - PARK FEED
A4	236 18LG/YL	ANTI-LOCK PUMP FEED
A5	—	—
A6	463 14RD/WT	BATTERY DRAIN DISCONNECT
A7	—	—
B1	72 18DB	PARKING LAMPS FEED
B1	72 18DB	CHIME/BUZZER-PARKING LAMPS ON
B2	44 18VT/WT	WINDSHIELD WASHER PUMP FEED
B3	47 18DB/WT	WINDSHIELD WIPER-HI SPEED
B4	—	—
B5	106 18BK/YL	FULL TIME INDICATOR LAMP
B6	11 14YL	IGNITION SWITCH-I-1
C1	107 20BK/RD	PART TIME INDICATOR LAMP
C2	18 18YL/BK	BACKUP LAMPS FEED
C3	30 18GN/WT	TACHOMETER
C4	F9 14PK/BK	FUEL PUMP FEED
C5	75 18BR/WT	REVERSE INDICATOR
C6	54 20LB	OIL PRESSURE INDICATOR
D1	10 12RD	BATTERY
D2	55 20VT	COOLANT TEMPERATURE
D4	10 12RD	BATTERY
D5	77 16LG	DIMMER SWITCH-LO BEAM
E1	10	ACCESSORY POWER
E2	31 14GY	HORN RELAY
E4	76 16WT	DIMMER SWITCH-HI BEAM
E5	37 12OR/BL	BLOWER MOTOR FEED
F1	—	—
F2	79 18BR	RIGHT TURN SIGNAL LAMPS
F3	98 20BK *	BRAKE INDICATOR W/O ABS
F4	13 14BR	ACCESSORY IGNITION (EXPORT)
F5	58 20GY/RD	BRAKE INDICATOR
F6	114 18VT/WT	WASHER FLUID LEVEL SWITCH FEED
G1	F1 16LG/BK	FOG LAMP SWITCH
G2	59 20TN/GN	BATTERY INDICATOR LAMP
G3	46 18WT/BK	WINDSHIELD WIPER-LO FEED
G4	99 12BK	INSTRUMENT PANEL GROUND
G4	99 12BK	INSTRUMENT PANEL GROUND
G5	38 16TN/BK	A/C REQUEST
G6	12 14OR	I-3 IGNITION (EXPORT)
H1	138 16LG	A/C THERMOSTAT SWITCH
H2	33 14DG	IGNITION SWITCH-START
H3	45 18TN/BK	WINDSHIELD WIPER-PARK FEED
H4	49 16LG/BK	A/C MODE SELECTOR SWITCH
H5	R4 18VT/OR	REAR WIPER SWITCH-WASH
H6	61 20WT/GN	LOW WASHER INDICATOR

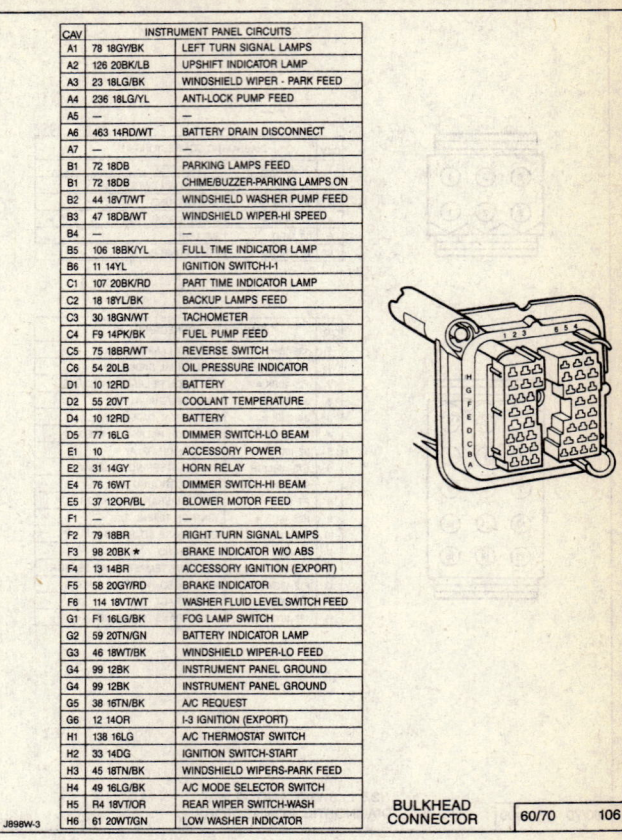

BULKHEAD CONNECTOR — 60/70 — 106

(2.5 L) 35 WAY Engine Controller Connector (107)

CAV		ECU SYSTEMS CIRCUITS
1	99 14BK	POWER GROUND
2	99 14BK	POWER GROUND
3	11 14YL	IGNITION
4	10 14RD	BATTERY
5	F18 14GN	EGR CONTROL
6	F17 20OR *	FUEL PUMP RELAY
7	F20 20BK *	LATCH RELAY
8	F78 18BL/OR	POWER STEERING INPUT
9	—	—
10	99 14BK	SYSTEM GROUND
11	F52 20RD *	ENGINE SPEED INPUT
12	34 18BK *	START SIGNAL (−)
13	F57 20BR *	TPS GROUND
14	F7 18TN *	AIR TEMP INPUT
15	F24 18TN	COOLANT TEMP INPUT
16	F2 20RD *	5 VOLT SUPPLY (TPS/MAP)
17	F56 20BK *	MAP GROUND
18	136 18PK *	UPSHIFT INDICATOR
19	F21 14PK	B + LATCH
20	—	—
21	F1 16LB	INJECTOR CONTROL
22	135 18BL *	A/C CLUTCH CONTROL
23	F3 18BR	ISCA (RETRACT)
24	F4 18LG	ISCA (EXTEND)
25	F12 18GY *	CLOSED THROTTLE INPUT
26	—	—
27	F26 20OR *	TIMING OUTPUT
28	F53 20WT *	ENGINE SPEED INPUT
29	88 14GN *	START SIGNAL (+)
30	138 16LG	A/C SELECT
31	F50 20YL/GN *	TPS INPUT
32	F15 18BR *	TEMPERATURE SENSORS GROUND
33	F14 20VT	MAP INPUT
34	38 20TN *	A/C REQUEST
35	F6 18GY	OXYGEN SENSOR INPUT

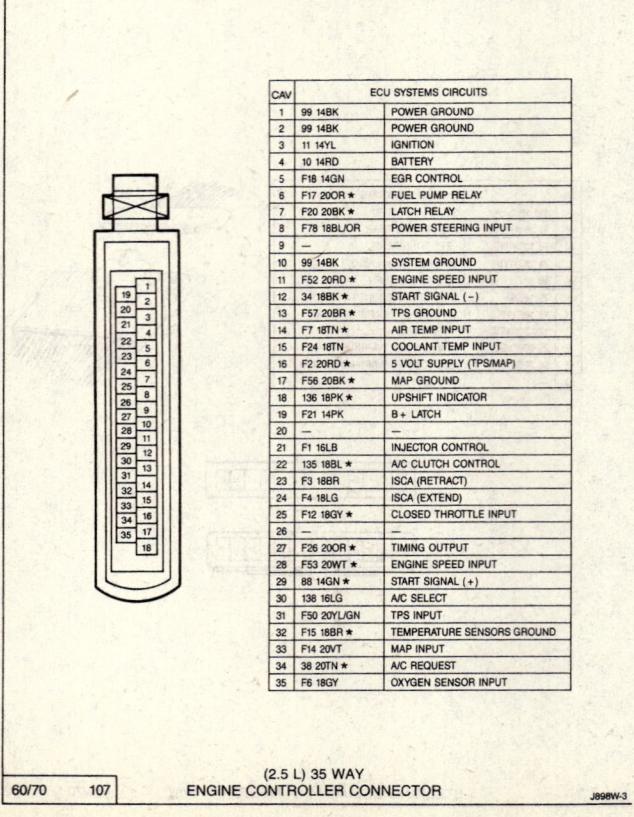

(2.5 L) 35 WAY ENGINE CONTROLLER CONNECTOR — 60/70 — 107

(4 L) 24 WAY 32 WAY Engine Controller Connector (108)

CAV		ECU SYSTEMS CIRCUITS
A1	F73 18TN	INJECTOR 3
A2	F76 18BR	INJECTOR 6
A3	F72 18LG	INJECTOR 2
A4	F74 18YL	INJECTOR 4
A5	F17 16OR *	FUEL PUMP RELAY GROUND
A6	—	—
A7	F86 16GY/YL	OXYGEN RELAY GROUND
A8	—	—
A9	F20 16BK *	B+ LATCH RELAY GROUND
A10	F19 16GN *	EGR CONTROL
A11	—	—
A12	135 18BL *	A/C CLUTCH CONTROL
B1	F71 18LB	INJECTOR 1
B2	F75 18WT	INJECTOR 5
B3	F68 18RD/YL	AIS MOTOR (A)
B4	F67 18BL/YL	AIS MOTOR (D)
B5	F70 18GN/BK	AIS MOTOR (C)
B6	F69 18BK/BK	AIS MOTOR (B)
B7	10 14RD	BATTERY
B8	11 16YL	IGNITION
B9	—	—
B10	F21 16PK	B+ LATCHED
B11	99 16BK	GROUND
B12	99 16BK	GROUND

CAV		ECU SYSTEMS CIRCUITS
C1	F52 18VT *	ENGINE SPEED INPUT
C2	38 16TN *	A/C REQUEST
C3	88 16GN *	START SIGNAL (+)
C4	34 18BK/WT	START SIGNAL (−)
C5	F65 18GY *	SYNC SIGNAL
C6	F14 18VT	MAP INPUT
C7	F50 18YL/GN *	TPS INPUT
C8	F7 18TN *	AIR TEMP INPUT
C9	—	—
C10	F24 18TN	COOLANT TEMP INPUT
C11	F22 16OR	INJECTOR FEED
C12	F83 16BR/PK	TX SERIAL DATA OUTPUT
C13	—	—
C14	F2 18RD *	MAP 5 VOLT SUPPLY
C15	F77 18LB	TPS 5 VOLT SUPPLY
C16	F66 18BL	SYNC 7.1 VOLT SUPPLE
D1	F53 18WT *	ENGINE SPEED INPUT
D2	138 16LG	A/C SELECT
D3	F15 18BR *	SENSOR GROUND
D4	—	—
D5	—	—
D6	—	—
D7	—	—
D8	F55 18YL *	KNOCK SENSOR GROUND
D9	F6 18GY	OXYGEN SENSOR INPUT
D10	F22 16OR	INJECTOR FEED
D11	F84 16BK/WT	RX SERIAL DATA INPUT
D12	—	—
D13	F23 18YL	TIMING OUTPUT
D14	—	—
D15	—	—
D16	F54 18VT *	KNOCK SENSOR INPUT

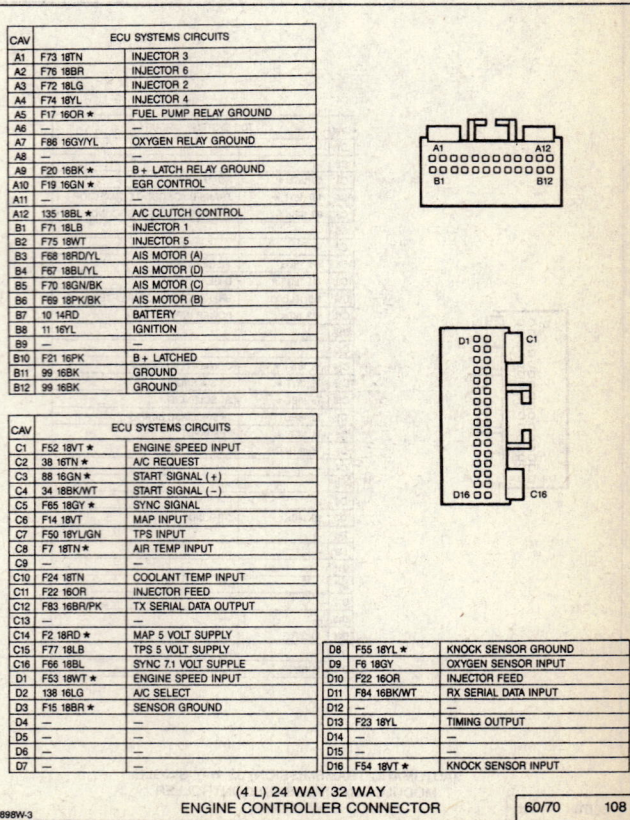

(4 L) 24 WAY 32 WAY ENGINE CONTROLLER CONNECTOR — 60/70 — 108

6-75

6 CHASSIS ELECTRICAL

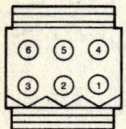

CAV	DIAGNOSTIC CONNECTORS #1	
1	30 18GN *	TACHOMETER
2	11 14YL	I-1 IGNITION SWITCH
3	99 14BK	ECU GROUND
4	88 14GN *	START SIGNAL (-)
5	10 14RD	BATTERY
6	F22 14OR	FUEL PUMP RELAY

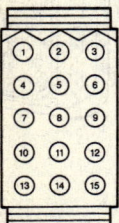

CAV	DIAGNOSTIC CONNECTORS - #2	
1	136 18PK *	UPSHIFT LAMP-MANUAL
	136 18PK *	ECU SERIAL DATA-AUTO
2	F20 20BK *	B + LATCH RELAY-COIL GROUND
3	34 18BK *	PARK/NEUTRAL-AUTO
	34 18BK *	ECU SERIAL DATA-MANUAL
4	F21 14PK	B + LATCH RELAY-COIL FEED
5	32 16OR	A/C CLUTCH RELAY
6	F78 18BL/DR	POWER STEERING PRES SW
7	99 18BK	SYSTEM GROUND
8	F7 18TN *	AIR TEMPERATURE SENSOR
9	F26 18OR *	IGNITION TIMING
10	F18 14GN	EGR PURGE SOLENOID
11	F4 18LG	ISA-EXTEND
12	F24 18TN	COOLANT TEMPERATURE SENSOR
13	F12 18GY *	ISA-CLOSED THROTTLE SWITCH
14	F3 18BR	ISA-RETRACT
15	137 16YL *	AUTO TRANS DIAGNOSIS

(2.5 L) 6 WAY AND 15 WAY DIAGNOSTIC CONNECTORS

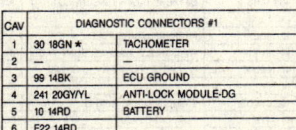

CAV	DIAGNOSTIC CONNECTORS #1	
1	30 18GN *	TACHOMETER
2	—	—
3	99 14BK	ECU GROUND
4	241 20GY/YL	ANTI-LOCK MODULE-DG
5	10 14RD	BATTERY
6	F22 14RD	

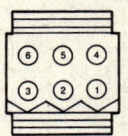

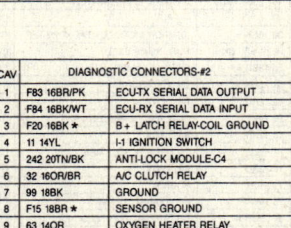

CAV	DIAGNOSTIC CONNECTORS-#2	
1	F83 16BR/PK	ECU-TX SERIAL DATA OUTPUT
2	F84 16BK/WT	ECU-RX SERIAL DATA INPUT
3	F20 16BK *	B + LATCH RELAY-COIL GROUND
4	11 14YL	I-1 IGNITION SWITCH
5	242 20TN/BK	ANTI-LOCK MODULE-C4
6	32 16OR/BR	A/C CLUTCH RELAY
7	99 18BK	GROUND
8	F15 18BR *	SENSOR GROUND
9	63 14OR	OXYGEN HEATER RELAY
10	—	—
11	136 18PK *	UPSHIFT LAMP-MANUAL
12	F21 16PK	B + LATCH RELAY (COIL FEED)
13	—	—
14	205 18VT	BRAKE ALERT-A.L.M. C2
15	137 16YL *	AUTO TRANS DIAGNOSIS-C4

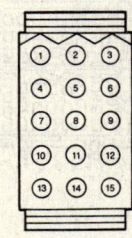

(4 L) 6 WAY AND 15 WAY DIAGNOSTIC CONNECTORS

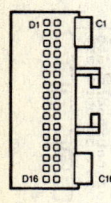

CAV	TCU SYSTEMS CIRCUITS	
C1	—	—
C2	—	—
C3	T9 18TN *	ROAD SPEED
C4	137 16YL *	TRANS DIAGNOSTIC CONNECTOR
C5	99 16BK	SHIFT POINT LOGIC GROUND
C6	—	—
C7	—	—
C8	T12 18LG	1-2 GEAR INPUT
C9	T11 18GY *	D GEAR INPUT
C10	116 16LB/YL	BRAKE/TORQUE CONVERTER
C11	177 18TN	POWER INPUT SIGNAL
C12	—	—
C13	—	—
C14	T8 18WT *	CONVERTER LOCKUP
C15	T7 18VT *	S2 SOLENOID
C16	T6 18BL *	S1 SOLENOID
D1	T3 18RD	TPS VOLTAGE SUPPLY
D2	T4 18GY *	TPS INPUT
D3	T5 18TN/OR	TPS GROUND
D4	—	—
D5	—	—
D6	—	—
D7	99 18BK	GROUND
D8	—	—
D9	—	—
D10	—	—
D11	—	—
D12	—	—
D13	—	—
D14	10 16RD	BATTERY
D15	—	—
D16	11 18YL	IGNITION

(AUTOMATIC TRAMSMISSION) 32 WAY SINGLE MODULE TRANSMISSION CONTROLLER CONNECTOR

CAV	TURN SIGNAL CIRCUITS	
P	110 18LG/BK	STOP LAMP FEED
N	79 18BR	RIGHT TURN-REAR
M	78 18GY/BK	LEFT TURN-REAR
L	74 18GY/YL	TURN SIGNAL FLASHER
K	80 18VT	HAZARD FLASHER
J	79 18BR	RIGHT TURN-FRONT/INDICATOR
H	78 18GY/BK	LEFT TURN-FRONT/INDICATOR
G	128 20GY/RD	HORN SWITCH
F	29 20RD/BL	IGNITION KEY WARNING SWITCH
E	86 20BK	IGNITION KEY WARNING SWITCH
D	—	—

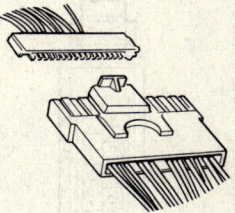

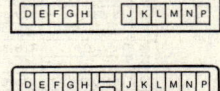
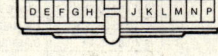

STEERING COLUMN CONNECTOR 11 WAY

CHASSIS ELECTRICAL 6

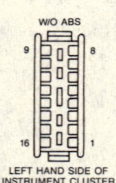

LEFT HAND SIDE OF INSTRUMENT CLUSTER (w/o ABS)

CAV	INSTRUMENT CLUSTER - INDICATOR CIRCUITS	
1	—	—
2	189 20GY	EMISSION MAINTENANCE LAMP
3	14 20WT/BK	I-1 IGNITION FEED
3	14 20WT/BK	I-1 IGNITION FEED
4	14 20WT/BK	I-1 IGNITION FEED
4	14 20WT/BK	I-1 IGNITION FEED
5	—	—
6	—	—
7	—	—
8	58 20GY/RD	BRAKE LAMP
9	60 20WT/OR	SEAT BELT LAMP
10	99 20BK	GROUND
10	99 20BK	GROUND
11	106 18BK/YL	FULL TIME LAMP
12	126 20BK/LB	UPSHIFT LAMP
13	107 20BK/RD	PART TIME LAMP
14	14 20WT/BK	I-1 IGNITION FEED
14	14 20WT/BK	I-1 IGNITION FEED
15	61 20WT/GN	LOW WASHER LAMP
16	99 20BK	GROUND

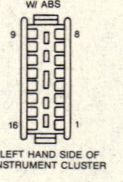

LEFT HAND SIDE OF INSTRUMENT CLUSTER (w/ ABS)

CAV	INSTRUMENT CLUSTER - INDICATOR CIRCUITS	
1	—	—
2	189 20GY	EMISSION MAINTENANCE LAMP
3	14 20WT/BK	I-1 IGNITION FEED
3	14 20WT/BK	I-1 IGNITION FEED
4	14 20WT/BK	I-1 IGNITION FEED
4	14 20WT/BK	I-1 IGNITION FEED
5	—	—
6	206 18WT	ABS-GREEN LAMP
7	205 18YL	ABS-YELLOW LAMP
8	204 18BL	ABS-RED LAMP
9	60 20WT/OR	SEAT BELT LAMP
10	99 20BK	GROUND
10	99 20BK	GROUND
11	106 18BK/YL	FULL TIME LAMP
12	126 20BK/LB	UPSHIFT LAMP
13	107 20BK/RD	PART TIME LAMP
14	14 20WT/BK	I-1 IGNITION FEED
14	14 20WT/BK	I-1 IGNITION FEED
15	61 20WT/GN	LOW WASHER LAMP
16	99 20BK	GROUND

INDICATOR CONNECTOR 16 WAY

CAV	INSTRUMENT CLUSTER-IDICATORS/GAUGES	
1	52 20OR/BK	ILLUMINATION LAMP
1	52 20OR/BK	ILLUMINATION LAMP
2	54 20LB	OIL PRESSURE
3	59 20TN/GN	BATTERY LAMP
4	52 20OR/BK	ILLUMINATION LAMP
4	52 20OR/BK	ILLUMINATION LAMP
5	99 20BK/WT	GROUND
5	99 20BK/WT	GROUND
6	14 20WT/BK	I-1 IGNITION FEED
6	14 20WT/BK	I-1 IGNITION FEED
7	79 18BR	RIGHT TURN LAMP
8	76 16WT	HI BEAM LAMP
9	52 20OR/BK	ILLUMINATION LAMP
9	52 20OR/BK	ILLUMINATION LAMP
10	99 20BK	GROUND
11	78 18GY/BK	LEFT TURN LAMP
12	30 18GN/WT	TACHOMETER
13	14 20WT/BK	I-1 IGNITION FEED
13	14 20WT/BK	I-1 IGNITION FEED
14	55 20VT	COOLANT TEMPERATURE
14	55 20VT	BULB CHECK-COOLANT
15	57 20TN	FUEL GAUGE W/O TACH
16	52 20OR/BK	ILLUMINATION LAMP
17	57 20TN	FUEL GAUGE W/O TACH
17	57 20TN	FUEL GAUGE
18	14 20WT/BK	I-1 IGNITION FEED
18	14 20WT/BK	I-1 IGNITION FEED

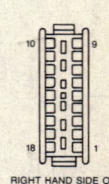

RIGHT HAND SIDE OF INSTRUMENT PANEL

INSTRUMENT CLUSTER CONNECTOR 18 WAY

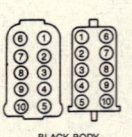

BLACK BODY CONNECTOR (LEFT HAND KICK PANEL)

CAV	BODY CONNECTOR-#1 CIRCUITS	
1	58 20GY/RD	PARK BRAKE SWITCH
2	51 20PK	CARGO LAMP FEED
3	71 18LB/BK	STOP LAMPS
4	72 18DB	ILLUMINATION RELAY
4	72 18DB	PARKING LAMPS
5	79 18BR	RIGHT TURN-REAR
6	57 20TN	FUEL GAUGE
7	75 18BR/WT	BACKUP LAMPS
8	98 20BK/WT	LEFT FRONT DOOR JAMB SWITCH
8	98 20BK/WT	COURTESY LAMPS
9	78 18GY/BK	LEFT TURN-REAR
10	85 18WT	SEAT BELT SWITCH

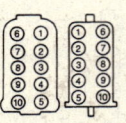

GRAY BODY CONNECTOR (LEFT HAND KICK PANEL)

CAV	BODY CONNECTOR-#2 CIRCUITS	
1	A11 20BK	SPEAKER RETURN-RIGHT REAR
2	A3 20WT/BK	SPEAKER FEED-RIGHT REAR
3	52 20OR/BK	CONSOLE ILLUMINATION
4	R1 18YL/BK	REAR WIPER MOTOR-RUN
5	110 18LG/BK	STOP LAMPS
6	A10 20BR/WT	SPEAKER RETURN-LEFT REAR
7	A5 20GR *	SPEAKER FEED-LEFT REAR
8	62 12BR/WT	REAR DEFOGGER FEED
9	R2 18YL/BR	REAR WIPER-PARK FEED
10	F9 14PK/BK	FUEL PUMP

MAIN BODY CONNECTORS

CAV	BODY CONNECTOR-#3 CIRCUITS	
1	A11 20BR	SPEAKER RETURN-RIGHT REAR
2	A3 20WT/BK	SPEAKER FEED-RIGHT REAR
3	52 20OR/BK	CONSOLE ILLUMINATION
4	99 14BK	CAB GROUND
5	51 20PK	DOME LAMPS FEED
6	A10 20BR/WT	SPEAKER RETURN-LEFT REAR
7	A5 20GN/WT	SPEAKER FEED-LEFT REAR
8	148 20PK *	CARGO BOX LAMP
9	98 20BK/WT	SWITCHED GROUND
9	98 20BK/WT	COURTESY LAMPS GROUND
10	85 20WT	SEATBELT SWITCH

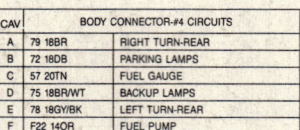

(BEHIND RH REAR PANEL)

CAV	BODY CONNECTOR-#4 CIRCUITS	
A	79 18BR	RIGHT TURN-REAR
B	72 18DB	PARKING LAMPS
C	57 20TN	FUEL GAUGE
D	75 18BR/WT	BACKUP LAMPS
E	78 18GY/BK	LEFT TURN-REAR
F	F22 14OR	FUEL PUMP

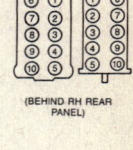

(BEHIND LEFT REAR INNER FENDER PANEL)

CAV	BODY CONNECTOR-#5 CIRCUITS	
1	97 20GY	SWITCHED GROUND
2	51 20PK	FUSED B + TO COURTESY LAMPS
3	98 20BK/WT	SWITCHED GROUND
4	110 16LB/BK	TAIL LAMPS
5	71 18LB/BK	STOP LAMPS
6	72 18BL	TAIL LAMPS
7	99 18BK	GROUND
8	79 18BR	RIGHT TURN LAMPS
9	75	
10		

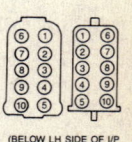

(BELOW LH SIDE OF I/P ABOVE PARKING BRAKE)

MAIN BODY CONNECTORS

6-77

CAV	BODY CONNECTOR-#3 CIRCUITS	
A2	208 16TN	BRAKE MODULATOR B1
A3	209 16OR	BRAKE MODULATOR D1
A4	214 16YL/RD	BRAKE MODULATOR C2
A5	215 16GN/RD	BRAKE MODULATOR A1
A6	210 16GY	BRAKE MODULATOR F1
A7	216 16BL/RD	BRAKE MODULATOR D3
A8	213 16BR/RD	BRAKE MODULATOR D2
A9	212 16LB	BRAKE MODULATOR E1
A10	211 16LG	BRAKE MODULATOR C1
A11	207 18PK	ANTI-LOCK RELAY B
A12	99 16BK	GROUND
B11	99 16BK	GROUND
B12	99 16BK	GROUND
C1	99 16BK	GROUND
C2	205 18VT	BRAKE ALERT
C3	238 18VT/YL	BATTERY
C4	242 20PK/WT	D2-5
C5	204 18BL	LOW BRAKE PRES. WARNING
C7	217 20VT/RD	LOW ACCUMULATOR SENSOR
C8	202 20YL	BRAKE PUMP BOOST PRES.
C9	203 20GN	BRAKE FLUID LEVEL
C10	201 20BR	BRAKE PUMP BOOST PRES.
C12	224 18LB/RD	RH REAR WHEEL SENSOR
C13	226 18BR/GN	LH FRONT WHEEL SENSOR
C14	222 18GY/RD	RH FRONT WHEEL SENSOR
C15	219 18PK/BK	LH REAR WHEEL SENSOR
D1	99 16BK	GROUND
D2	99 16BK	GROUND
D4	236 18LG/YL	IGNITION FEED
D6	241 20GN/YL	D1-4
D8	235 18GY/YL	BRAKE MODULATOR A2, F2, F3
D9	234 20OR/GN	ANTI-LOCK PUMP MOTOR
D10	71 20LB/BK	PARKING BRAKE
D12	223 18LG/RD	RH REAR WHEEL SENSOR
D13	225 18BK/YL	LH FRONT WHEEL SENSOR
D14	221 18OR/BK	RH FRONT WHEEL SENSOR
D15	218 18WT/RD	LH REAR WHEEL SENSOR

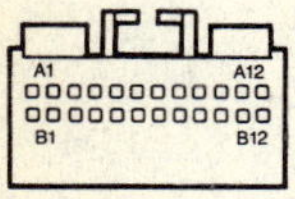

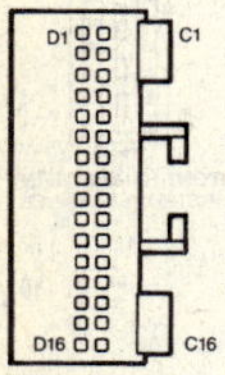

70 117 ANTI-LOCK MODULE CONNECTORS 24 WAY AND 32 WAY J898W-3

CAV	BRAKE MODULE	
A1	215 16GN/RD	A.L.M. A5
A2	235 18GY	SPLICE Y5
A3	235 18GY/YL	SPLICE Y4
B1	208 16TN	A.L.M. A2
B2	235 18GY/YL	SPLICE Y4
C1	211 16LG	A.L.M. A10
C2	214 16YL/RD	A.L.M. A4
C3	235 18GY/YL	SPLICE Y4
D1	209 16OR	A.L.M. A3
D2	213 16BR/RD	A.L.M. A8
D3	216 18BL/RD	A.L.M. A7
E1	212 16LB	A.L.M. A9
F1	210 16GY	A.L.M. A6
F2	235 18GY	SPLICE Y5
F3	235 18GY	SPLICE Y5

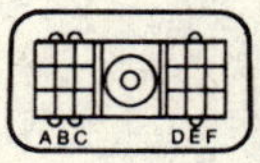

J898W-3 BRAKE MODULE 18 WAY 70 118

1990 WIRING DIAGRAMS

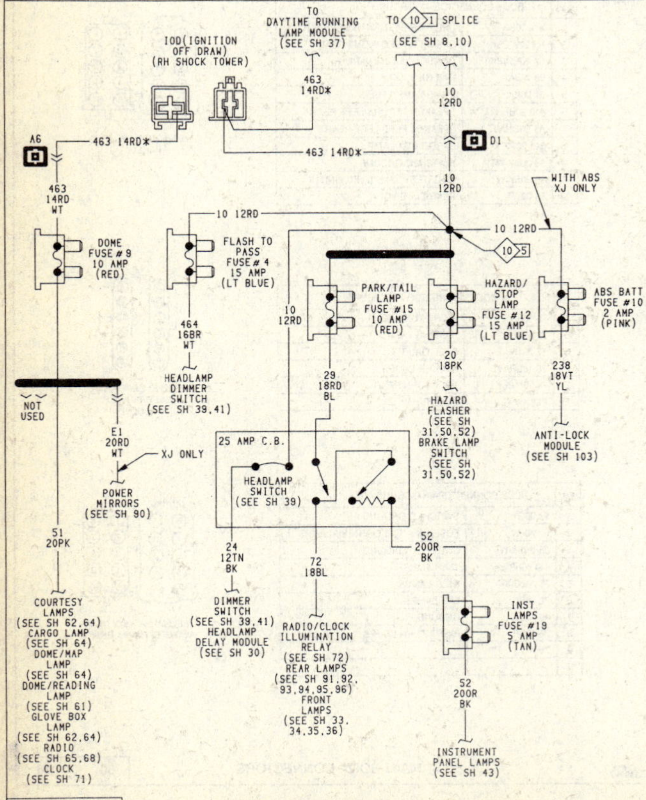

MJ-XJ 1 FUSE APPLICATION CHART J908W-3

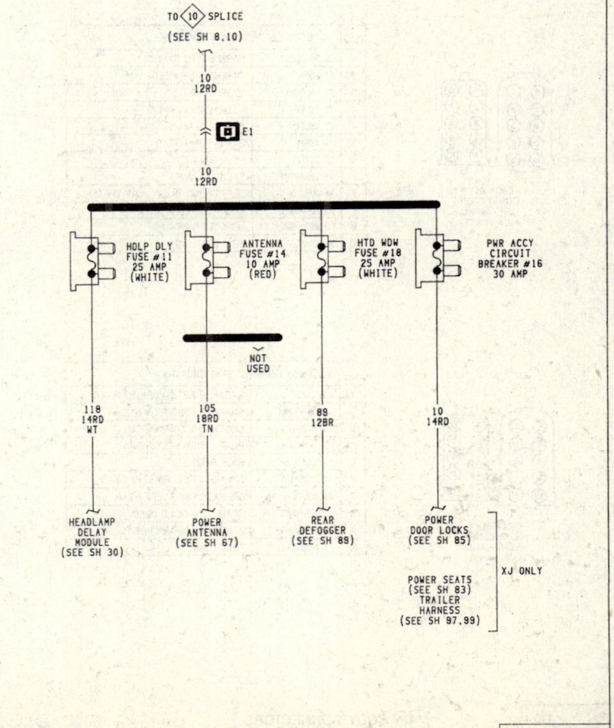

J908W-3 FUSE APPLICATION CHART MJ-XJ 2

CHASSIS ELECTRICAL 6

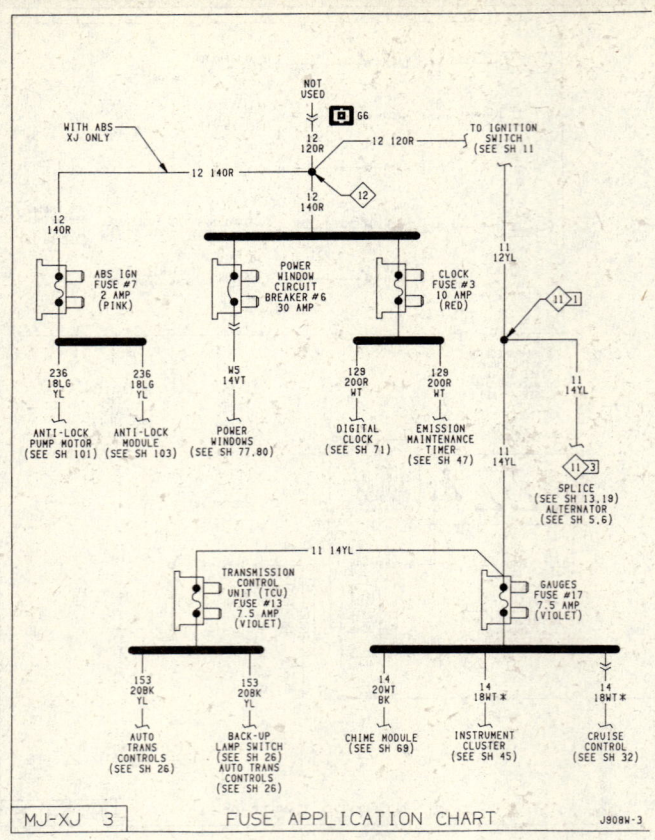

FUSE APPLICATION CHART — MJ-XJ 3

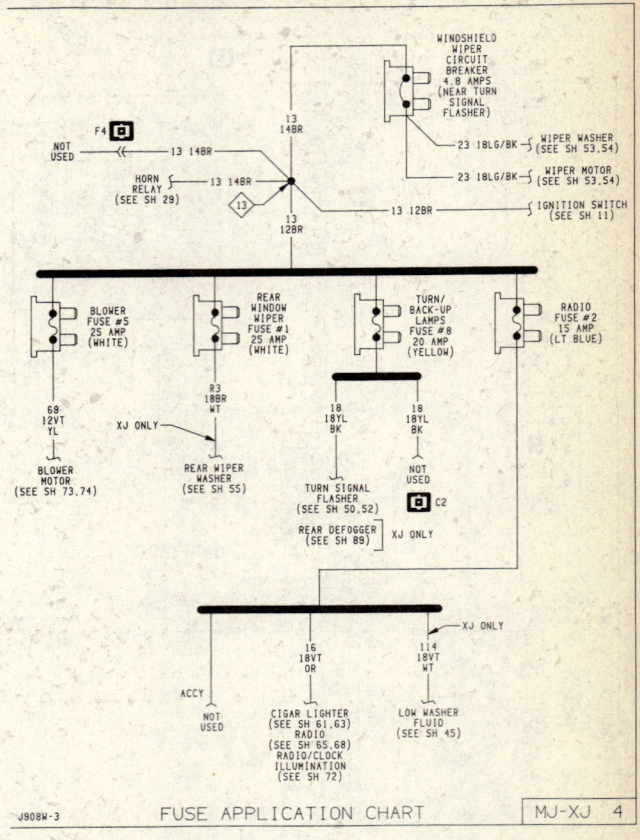

FUSE APPLICATION CHART — MJ-XJ 4

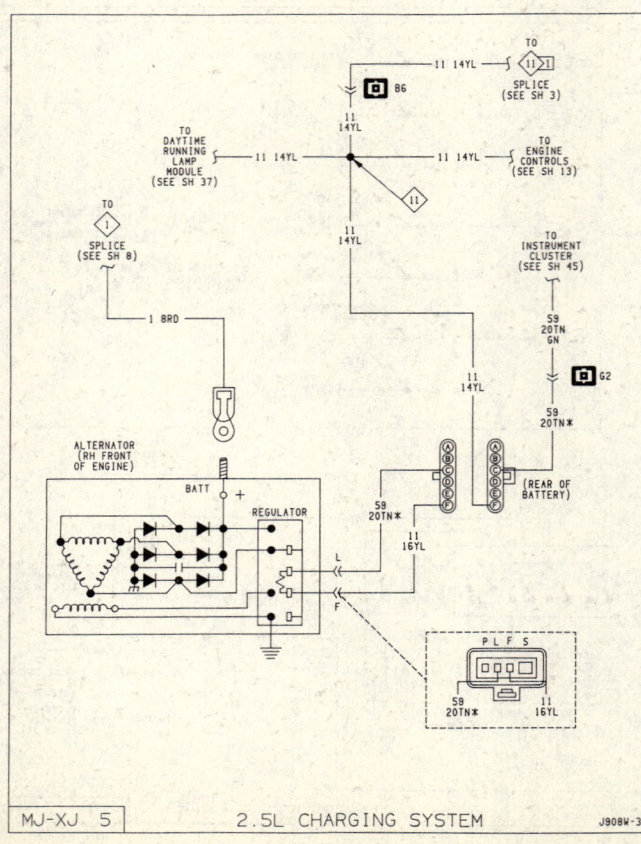

2.5L CHARGING SYSTEM — MJ-XJ 5

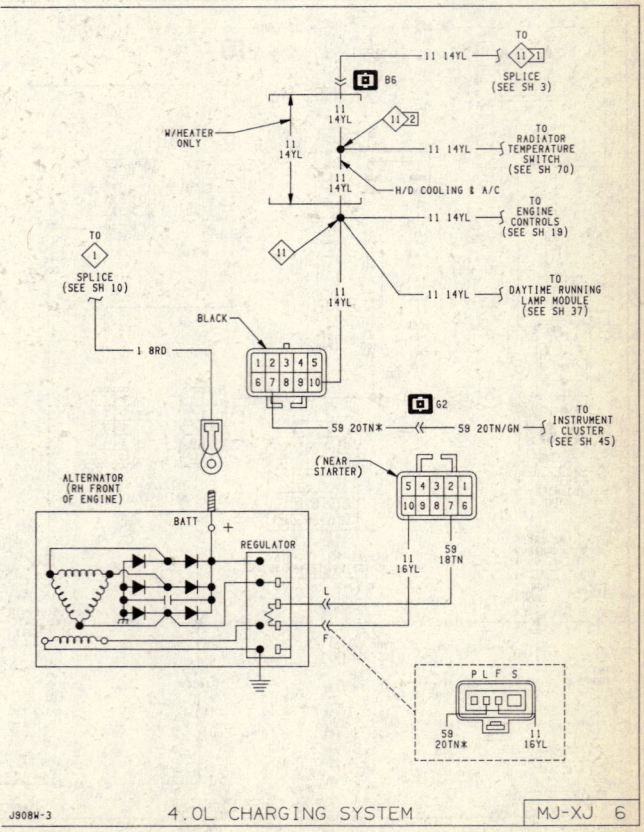

4.0L CHARGING SYSTEM — MJ-XJ 6

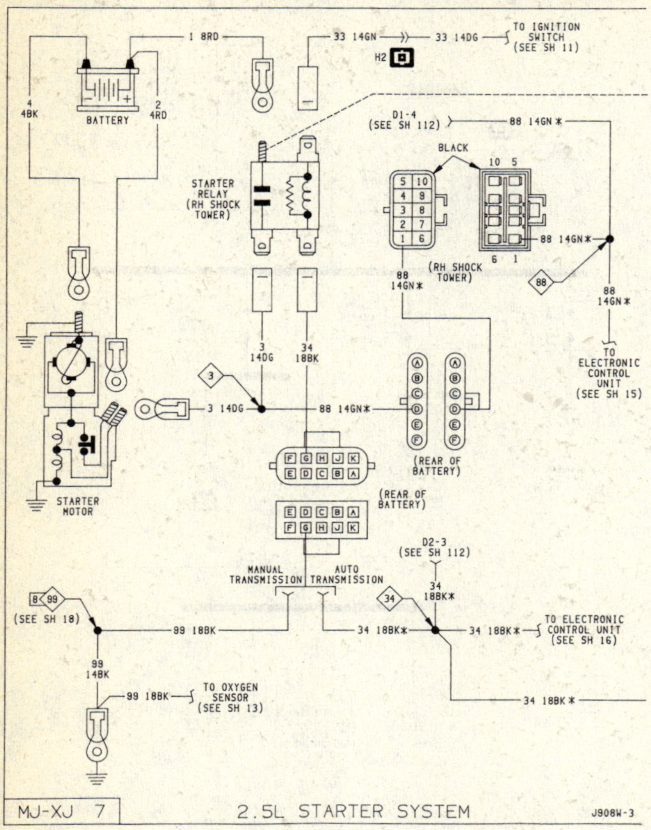

6 CHASSIS ELECTRICAL

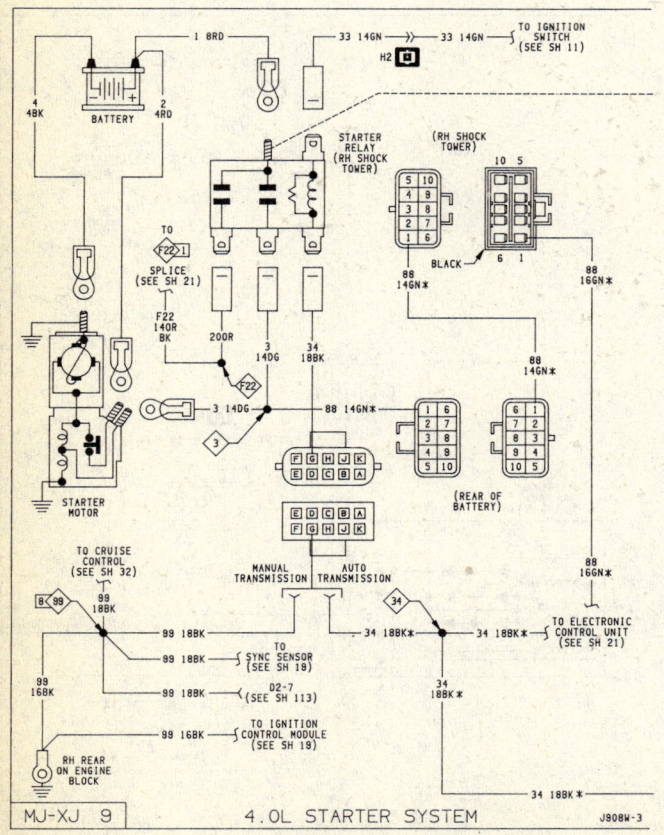
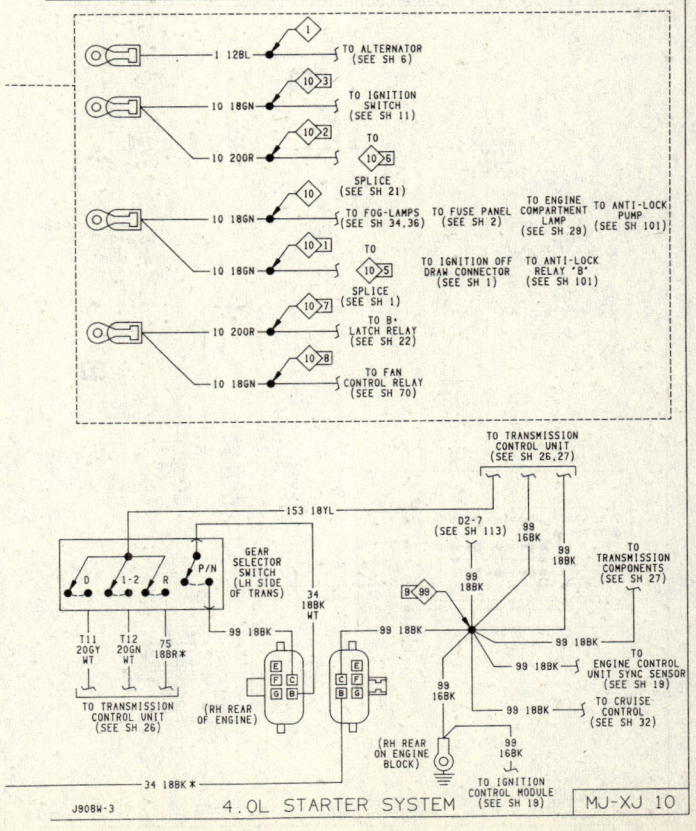

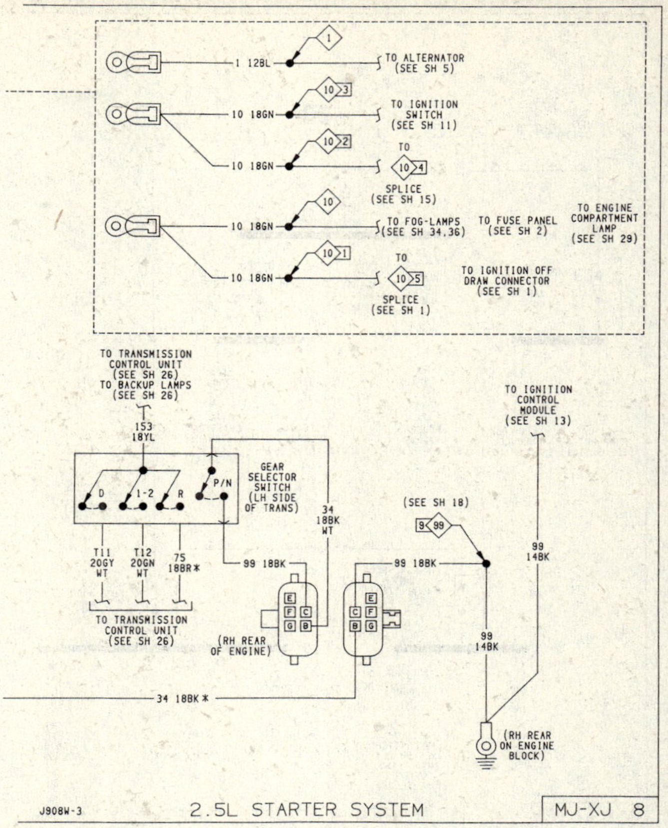

6-80

CHASSIS ELECTRICAL 6

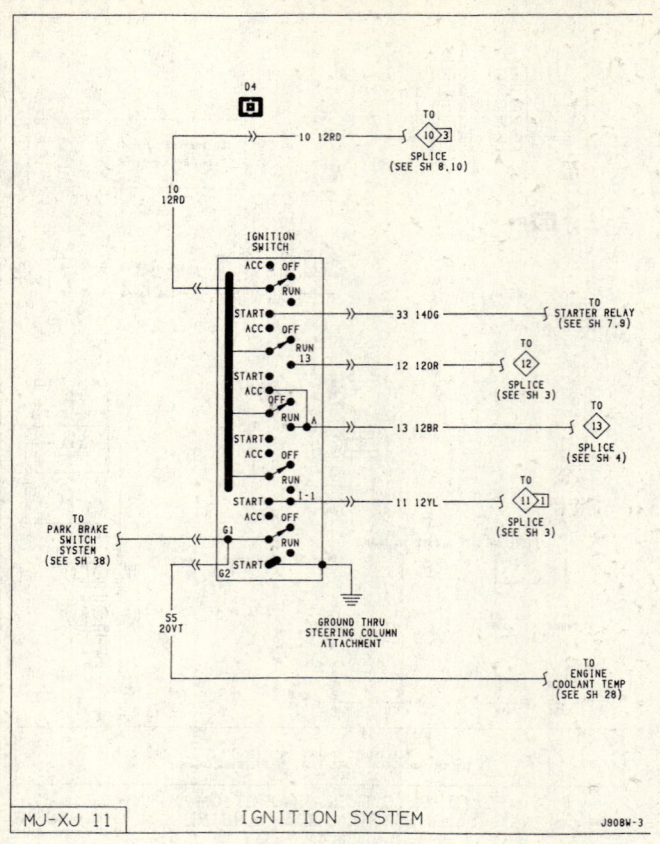

IGNITION SYSTEM — MJ-XJ 11

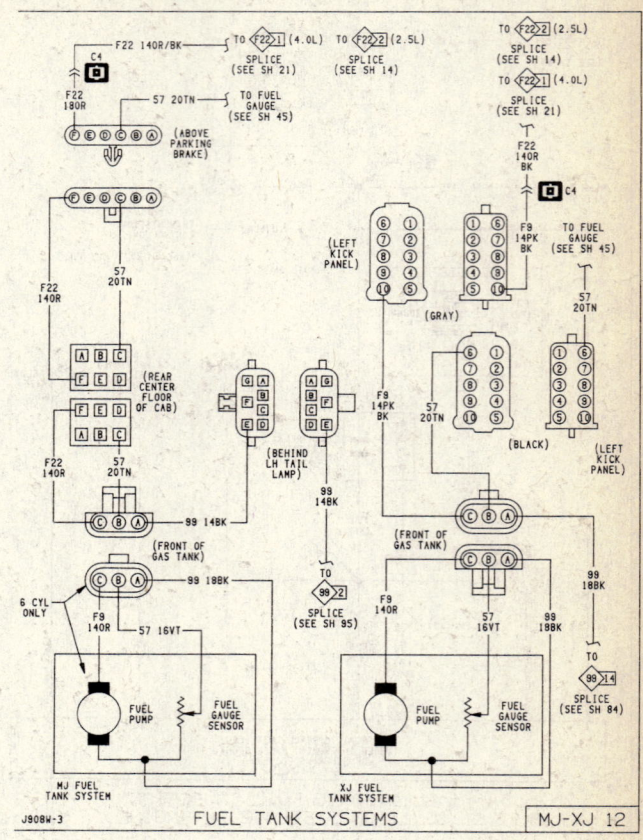

FUEL TANK SYSTEMS — MJ-XJ 12

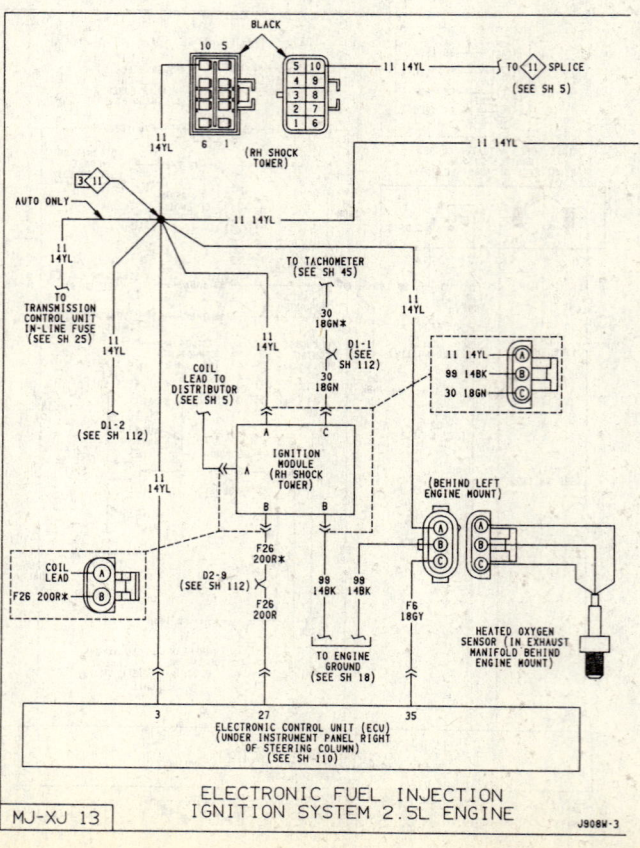

ELECTRONIC FUEL INJECTION IGNITION SYSTEM 2.5L ENGINE — MJ-XJ 13

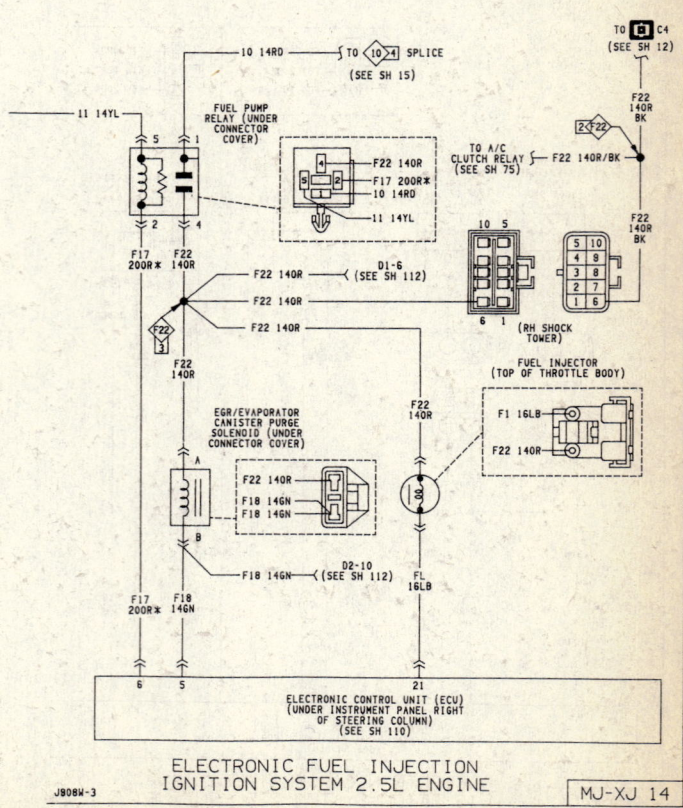

ELECTRONIC FUEL INJECTION IGNITION SYSTEM 2.5L ENGINE — MJ-XJ 14

6-81

6 CHASSIS ELECTRICAL

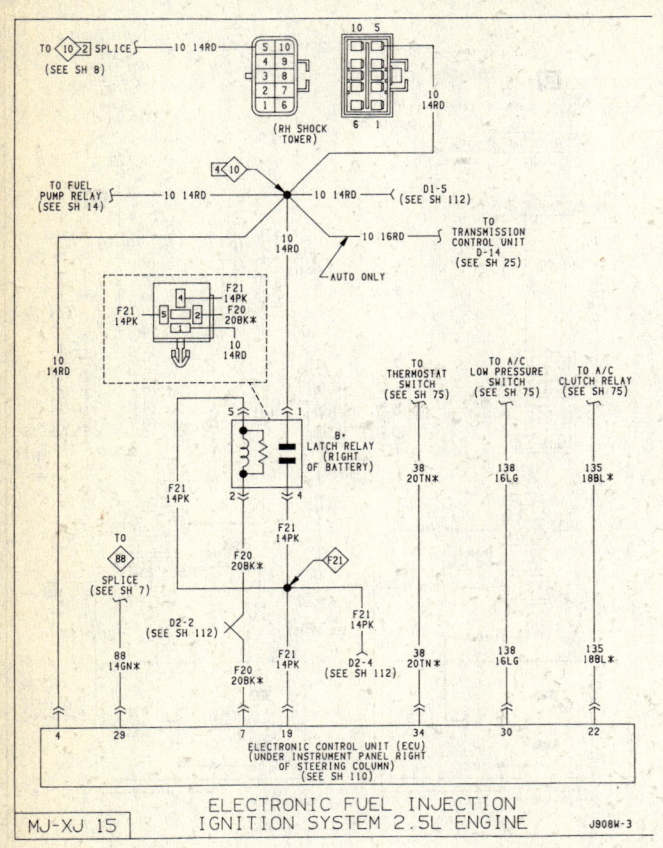

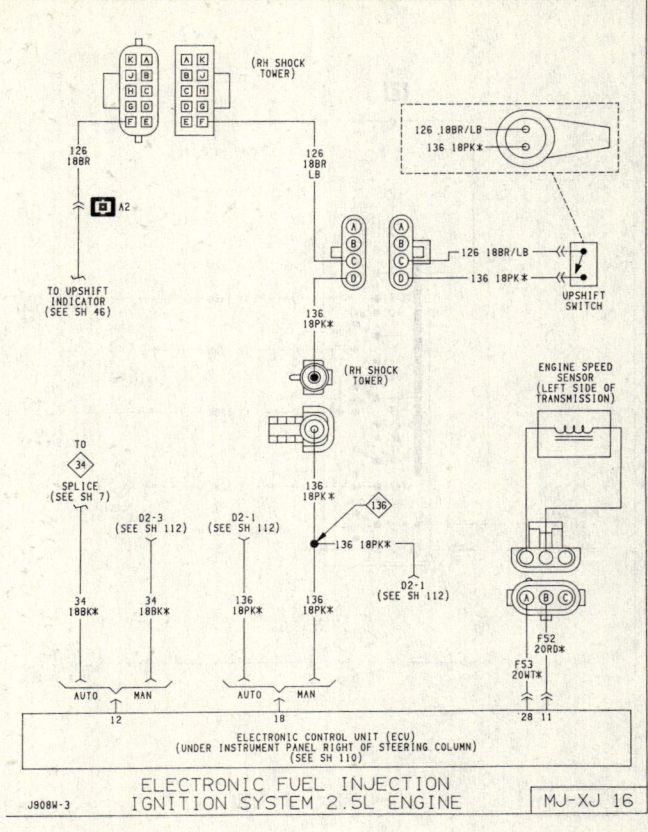

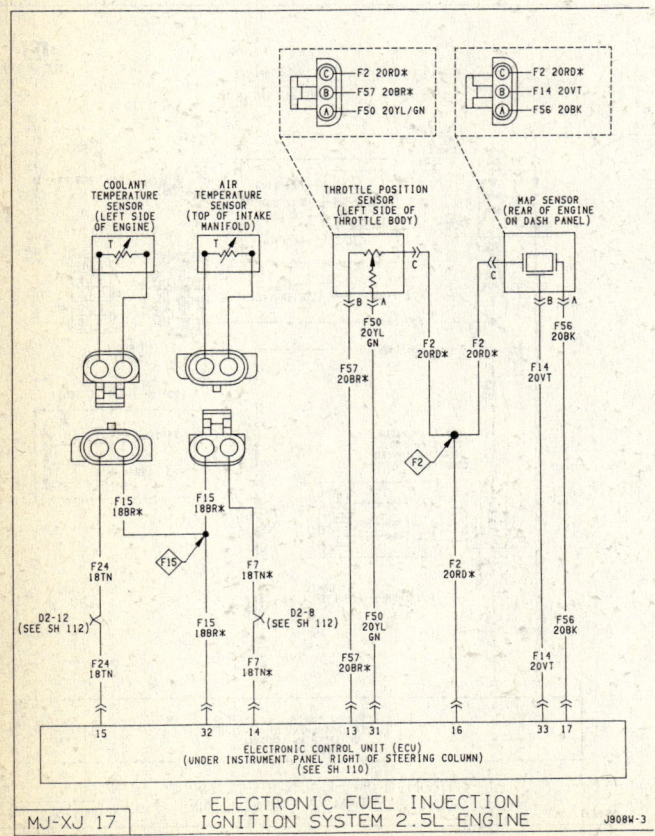

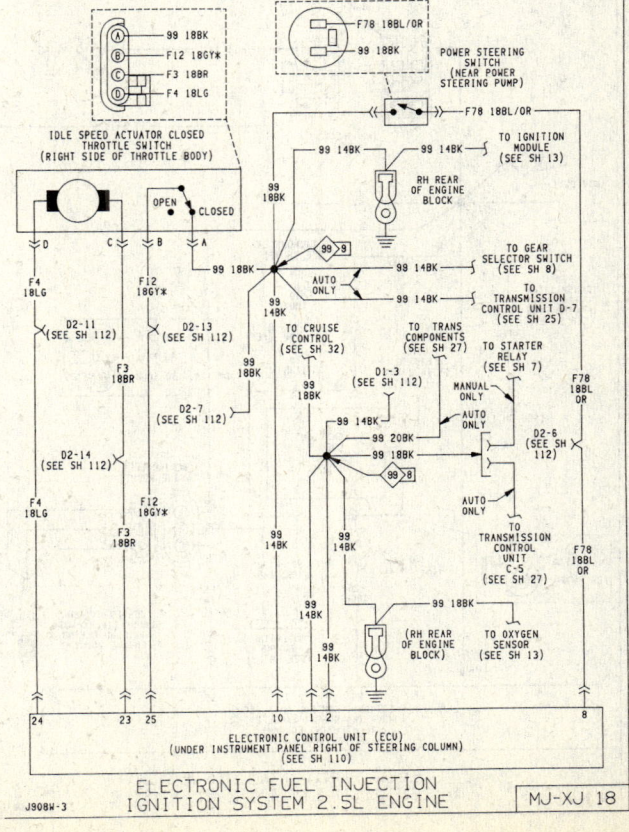

CHASSIS ELECTRICAL 6

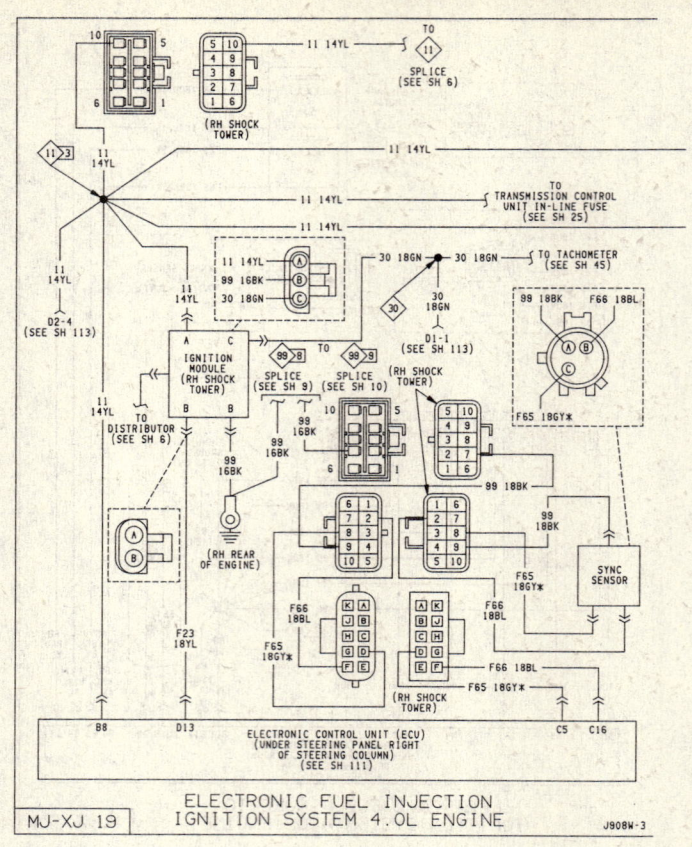

ELECTRONIC FUEL INJECTION
IGNITION SYSTEM 4.0L ENGINE
MJ-XJ 19

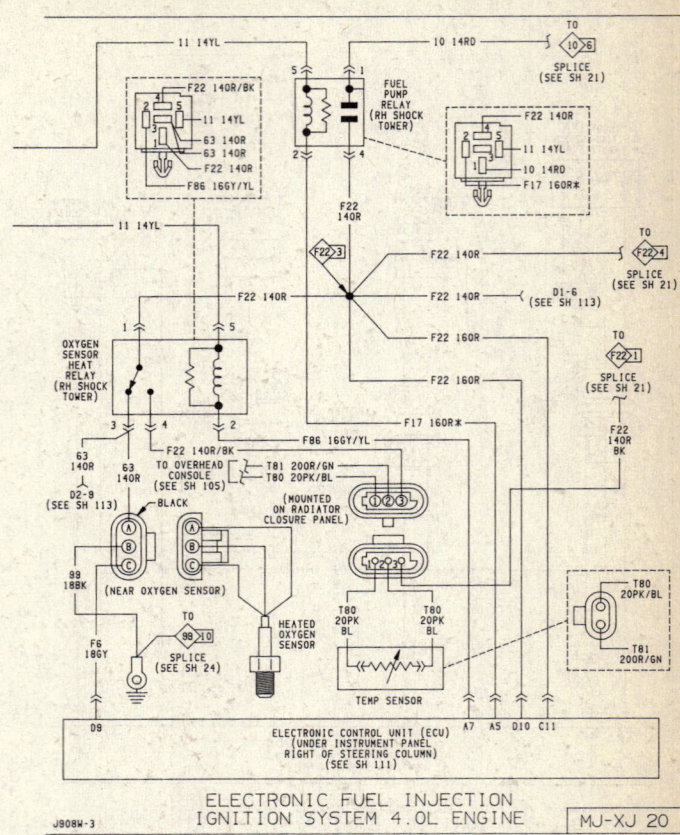

ELECTRONIC FUEL INJECTION
IGNITION SYSTEM 4.0L ENGINE
MJ-XJ 20

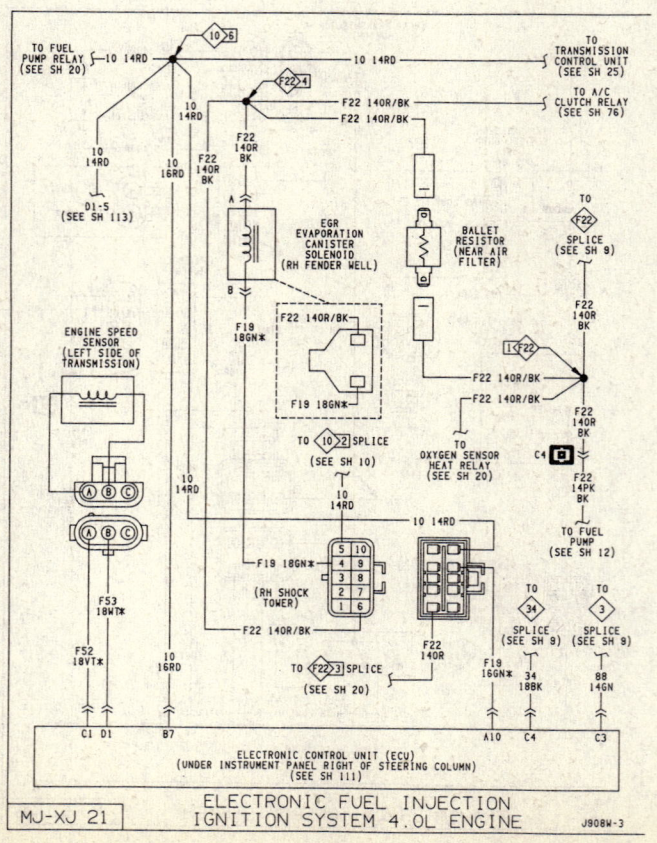

ELECTRONIC FUEL INJECTION
IGNITION SYSTEM 4.0L ENGINE
MJ-XJ 21

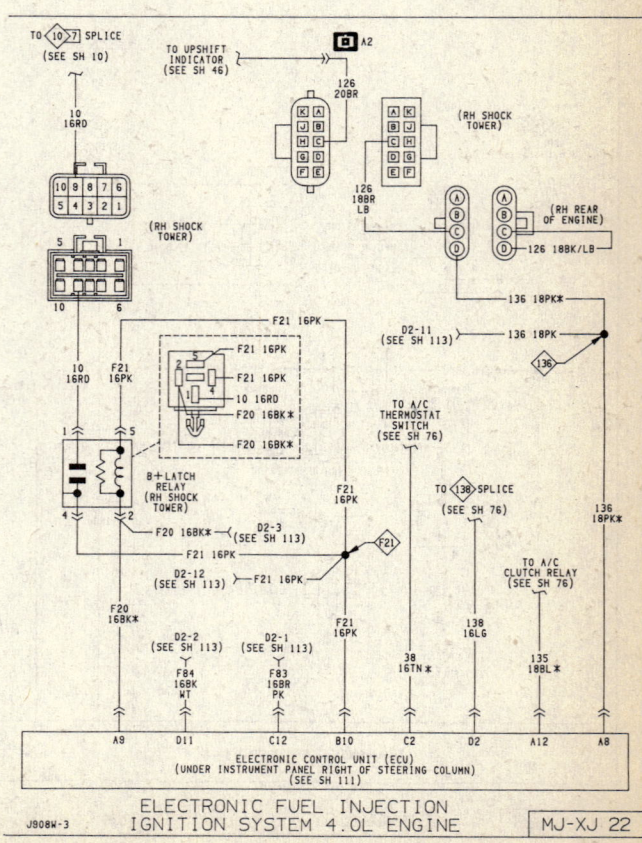

ELECTRONIC FUEL INJECTION
IGNITION SYSTEM 4.0L ENGINE
MJ-XJ 22

6-83

6 CHASSIS ELECTRICAL

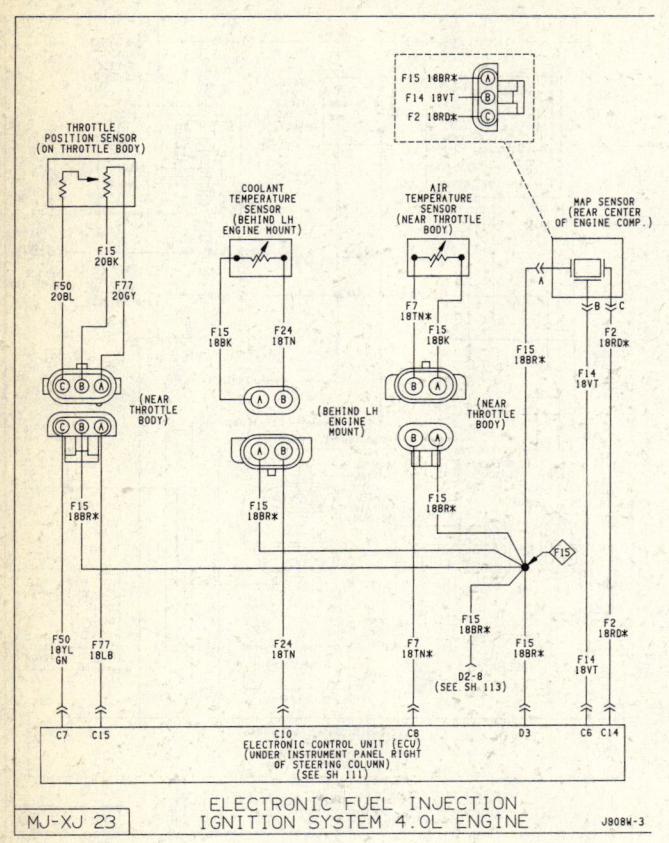

ELECTRONIC FUEL INJECTION IGNITION SYSTEM 4.0L ENGINE — MJ-XJ 23

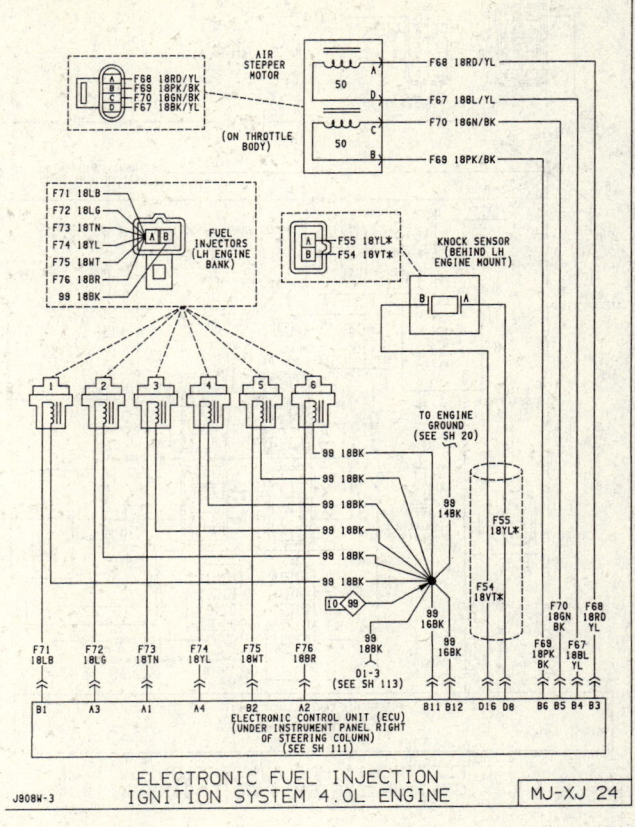

ELECTRONIC FUEL INJECTION IGNITION SYSTEM 4.0L ENGINE — MJ-XJ 24

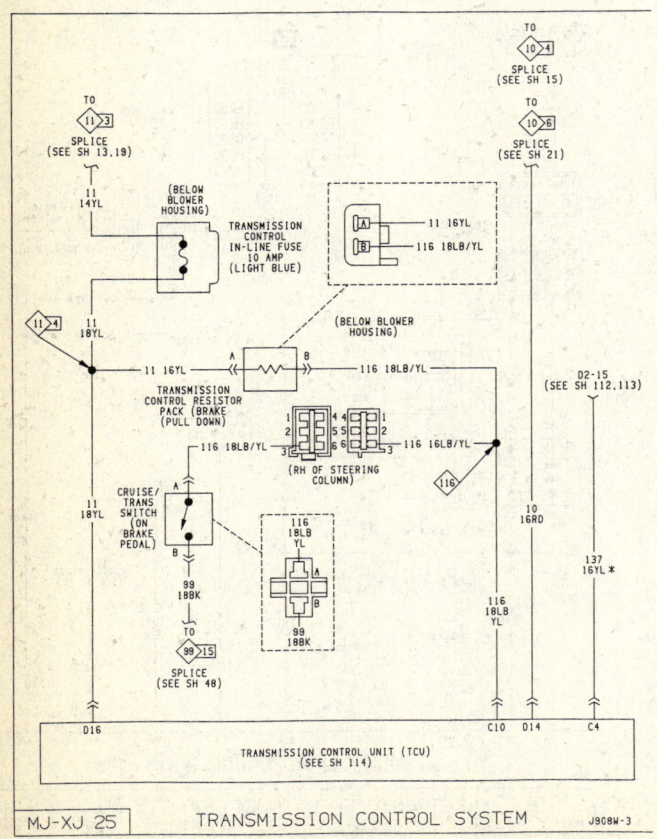

TRANSMISSION CONTROL SYSTEM — MJ-XJ 25

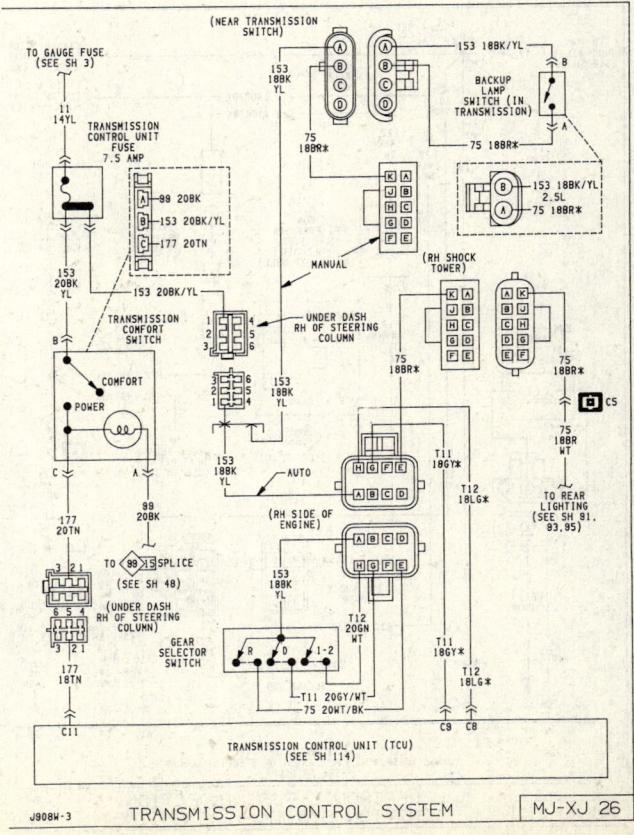

TRANSMISSION CONTROL SYSTEM — MJ-XJ 26

CHASSIS ELECTRICAL 6

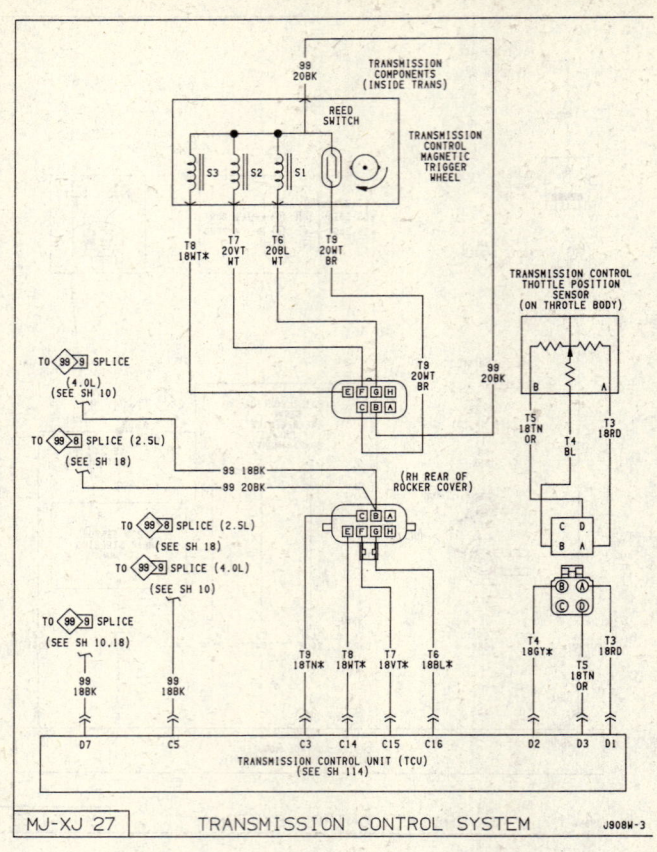

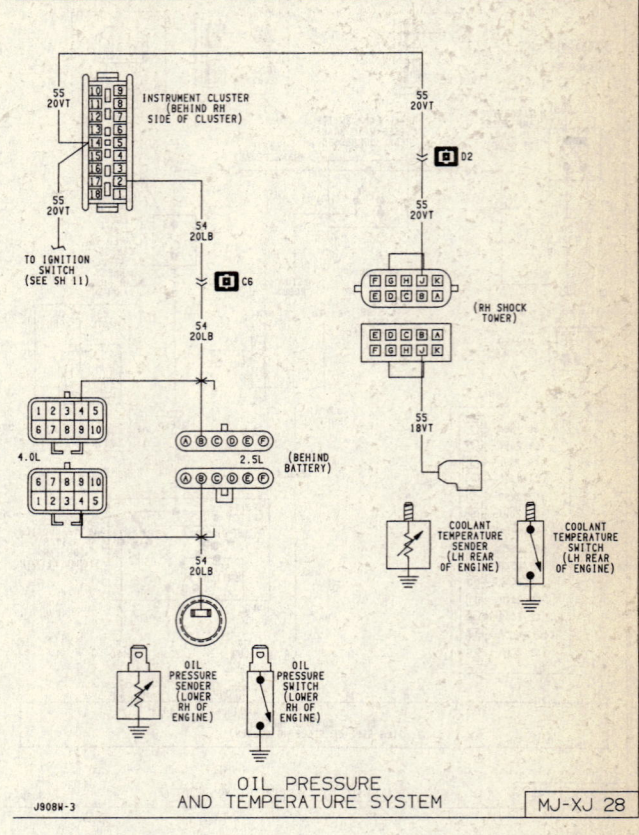

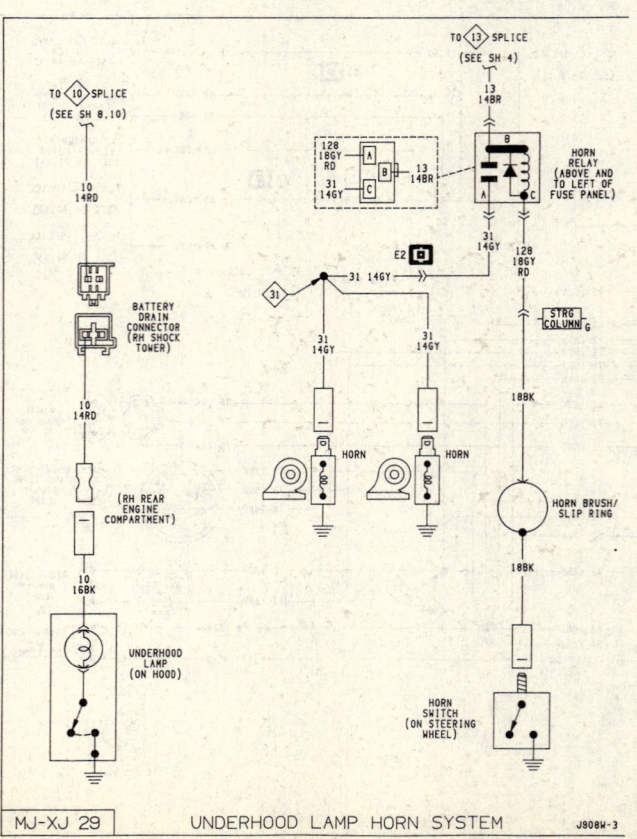

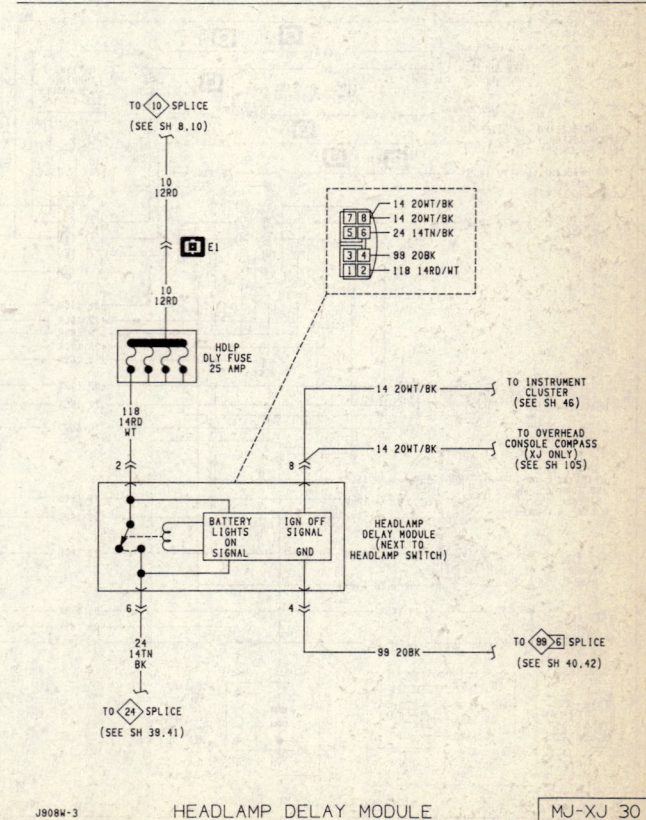

6-85

6 CHASSIS ELECTRICAL

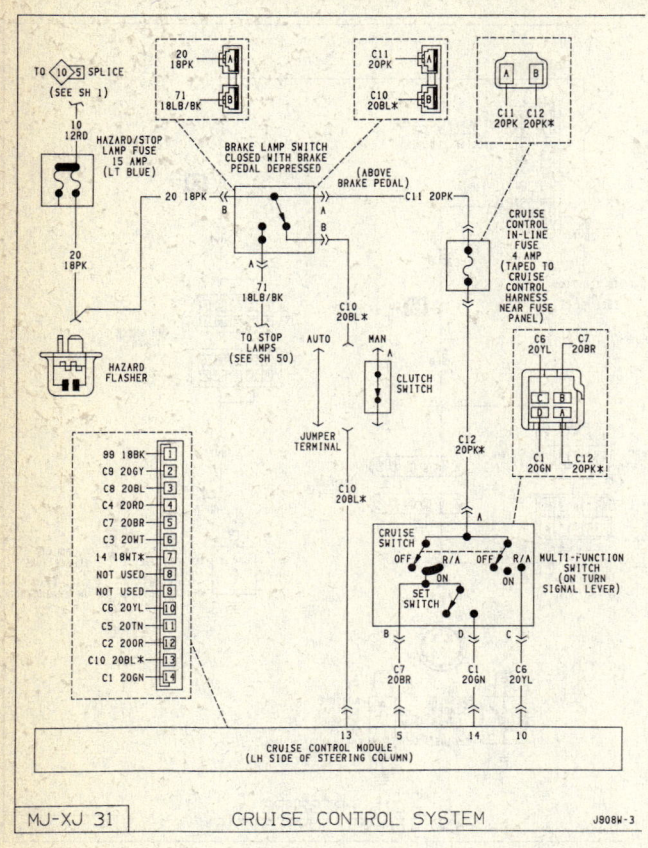

CRUISE CONTROL SYSTEM — MJ-XJ 31

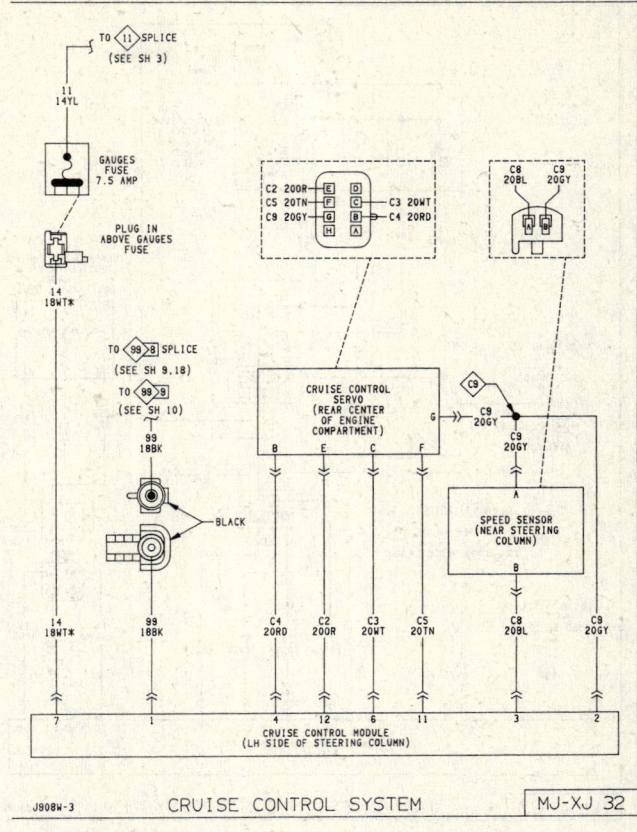

CRUISE CONTROL SYSTEM — MJ-XJ 32

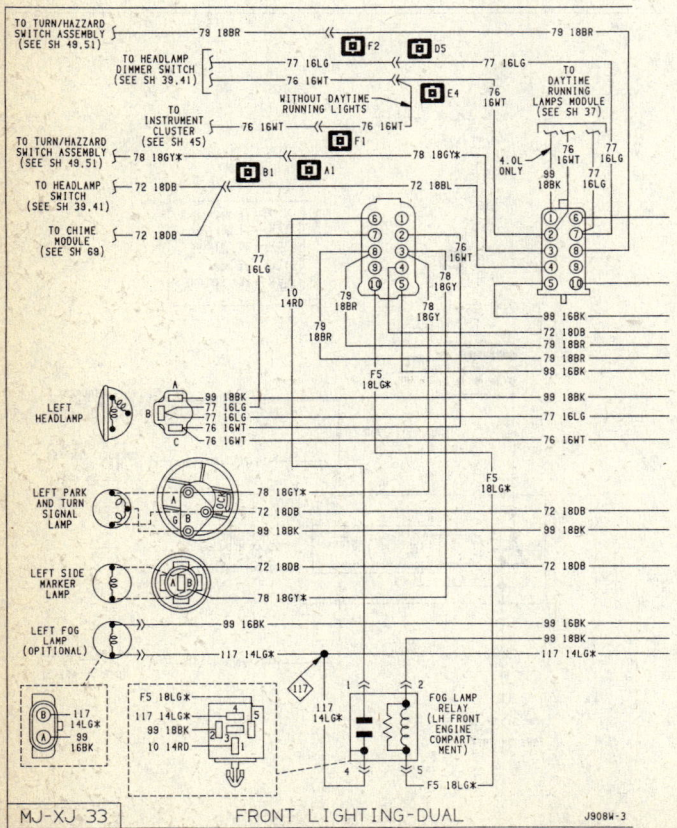

FRONT LIGHTING-DUAL — MJ-XJ 33

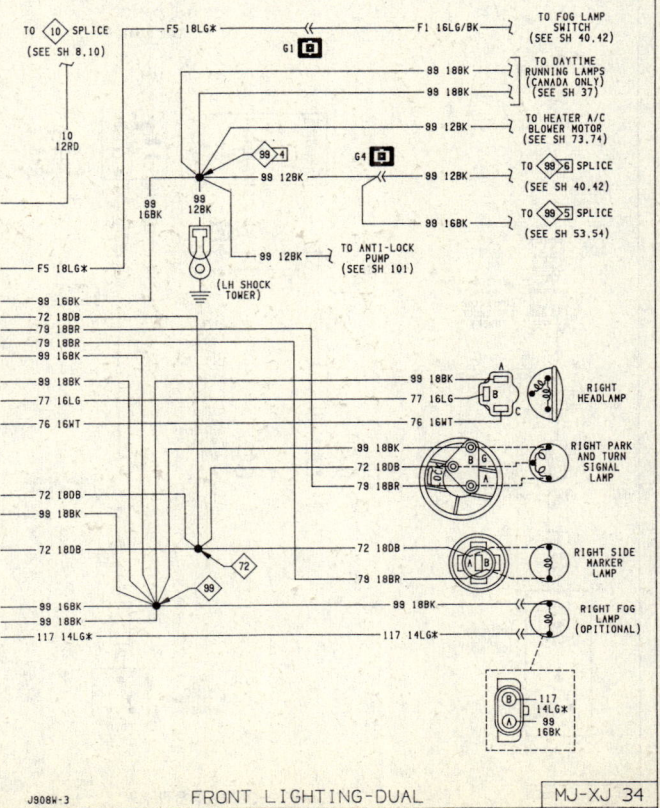

FRONT LIGHTING-DUAL — MJ-XJ 34

CHASSIS ELECTRICAL 6

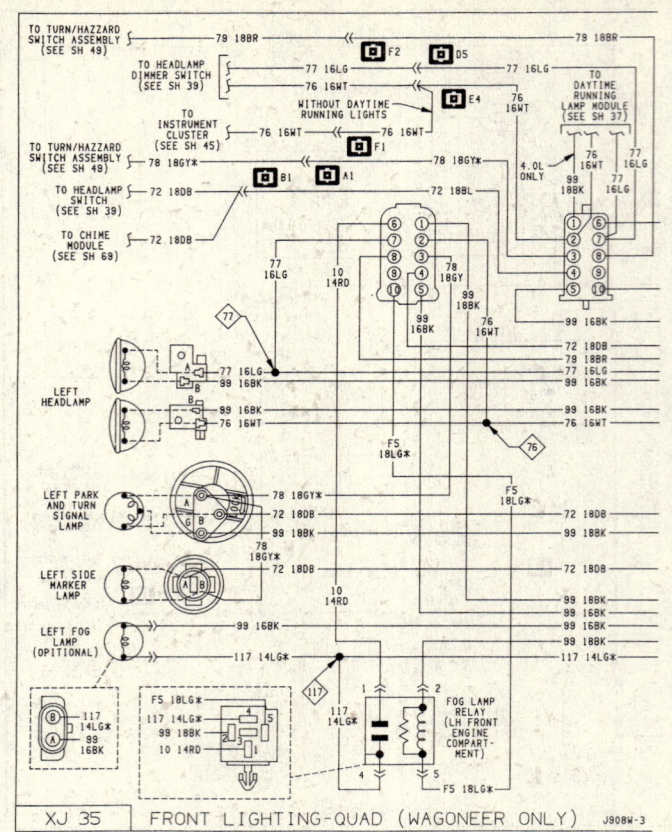

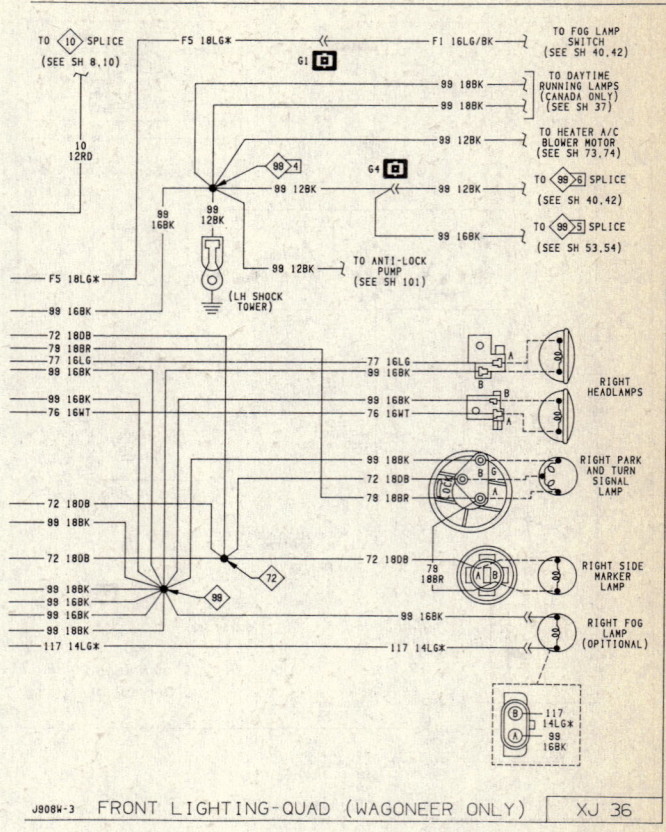

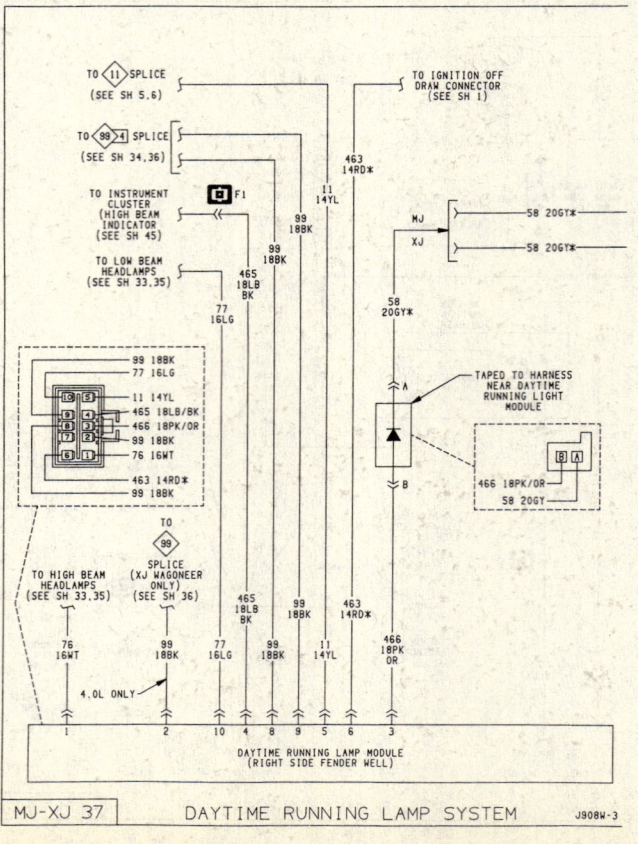

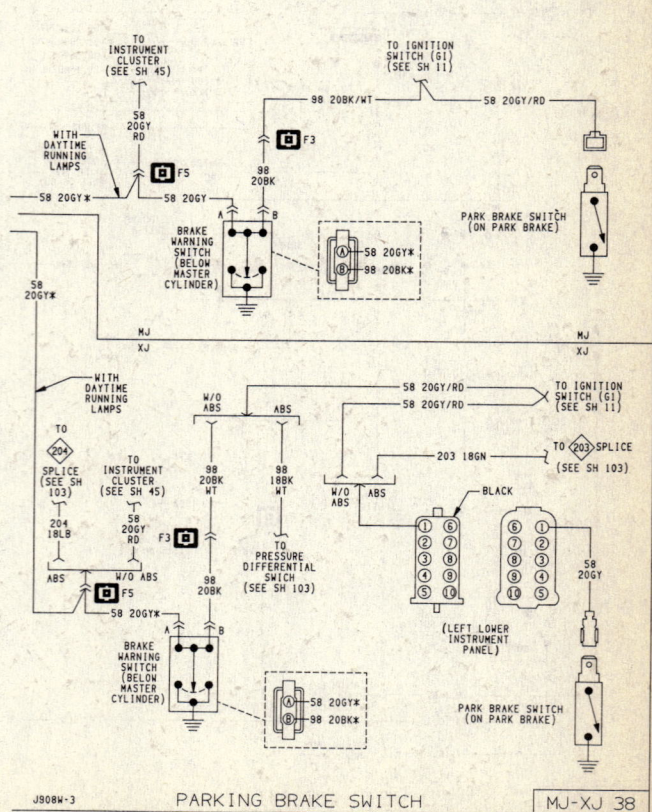

6-87

6 CHASSIS ELECTRICAL

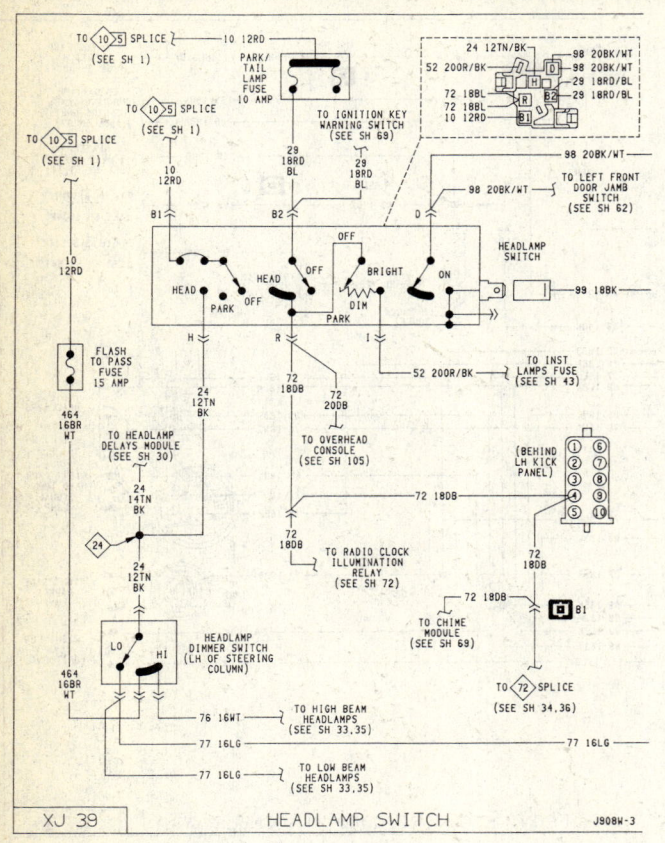
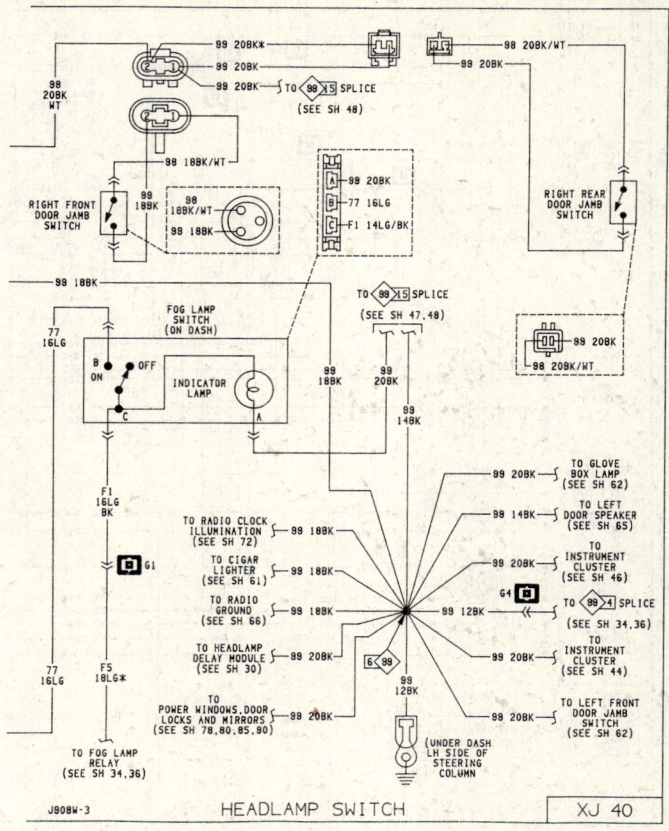
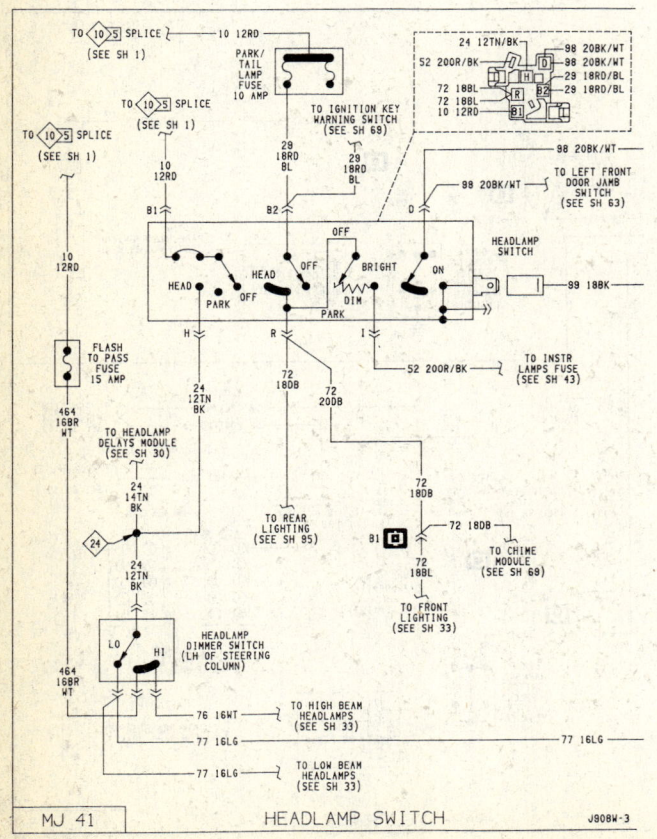
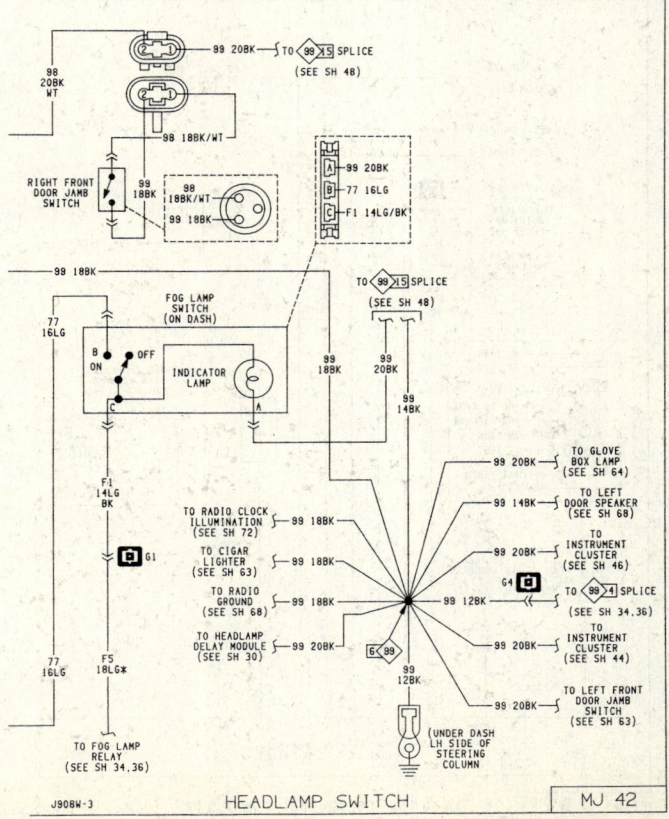

CHASSIS ELECTRICAL 6

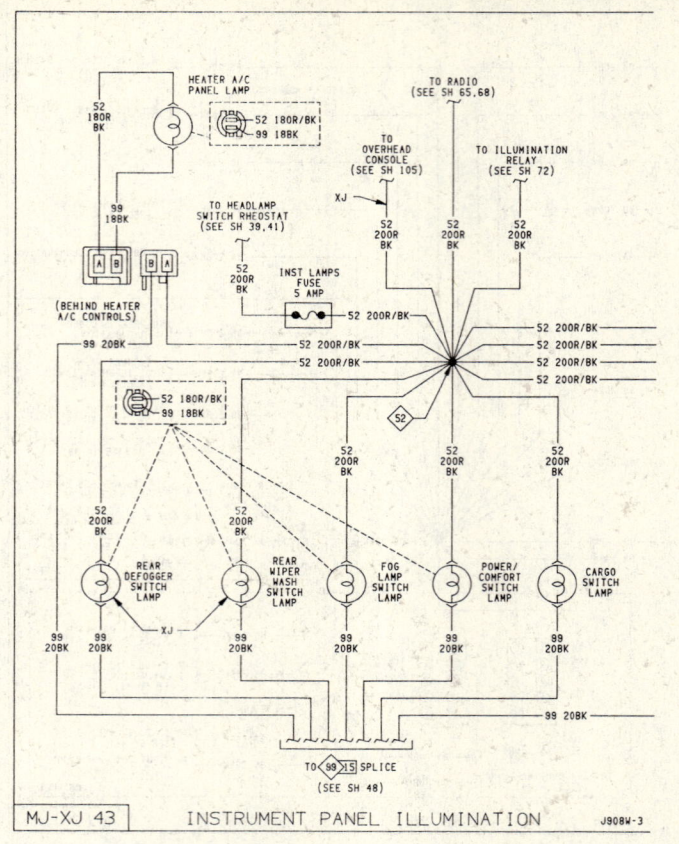

MJ-XJ 43 — INSTRUMENT PANEL ILLUMINATION

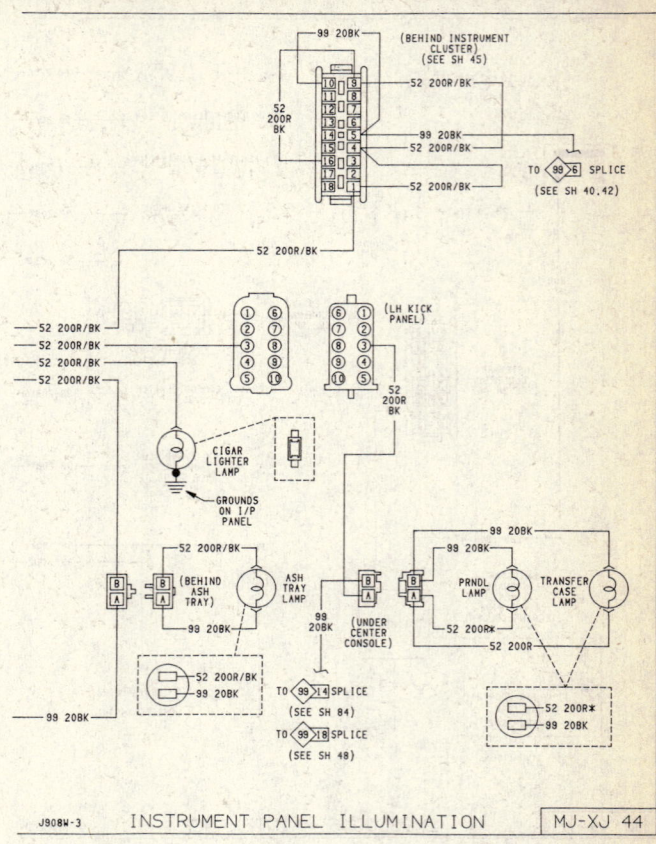

INSTRUMENT PANEL ILLUMINATION — MJ-XJ 44

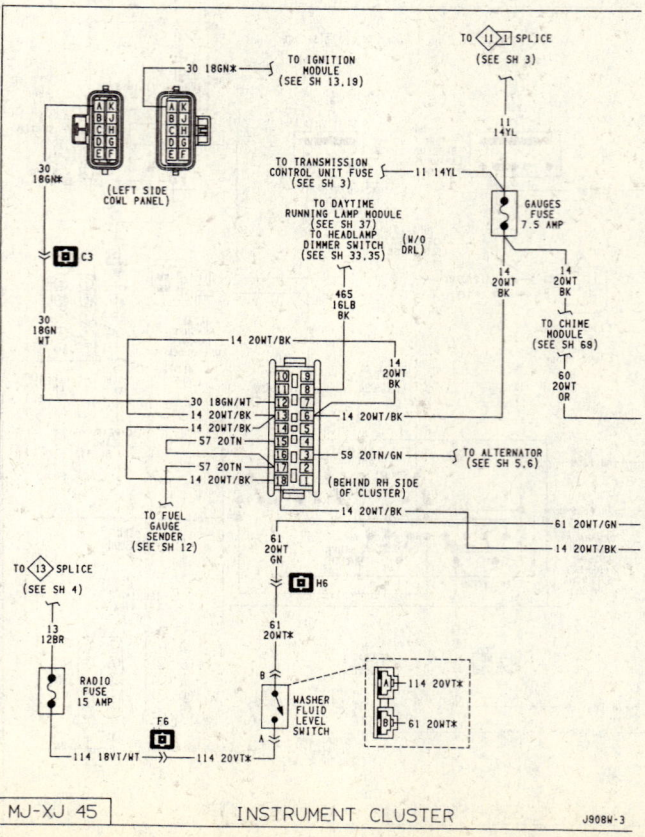

MJ-XJ 45 — INSTRUMENT CLUSTER

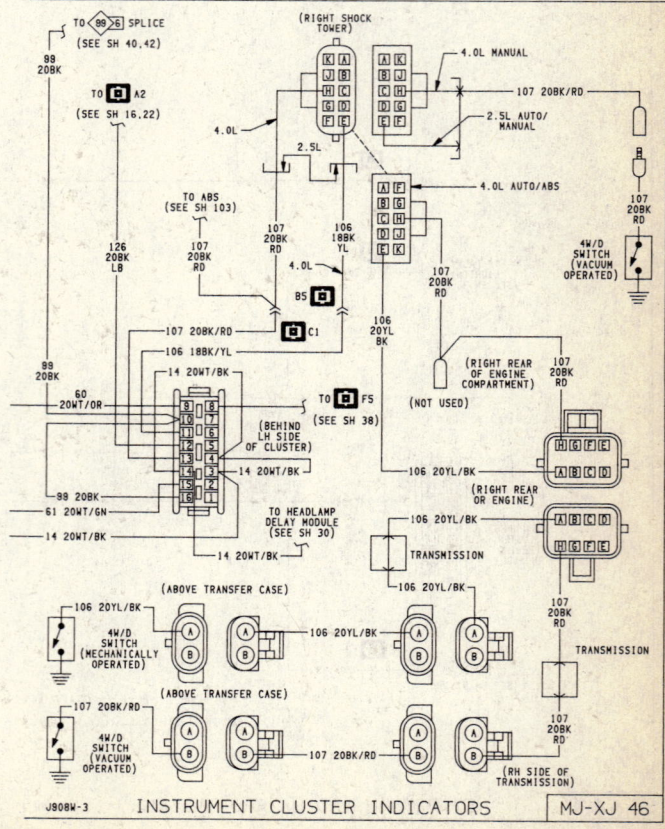

INSTRUMENT CLUSTER INDICATORS — MJ-XJ 46

6-89

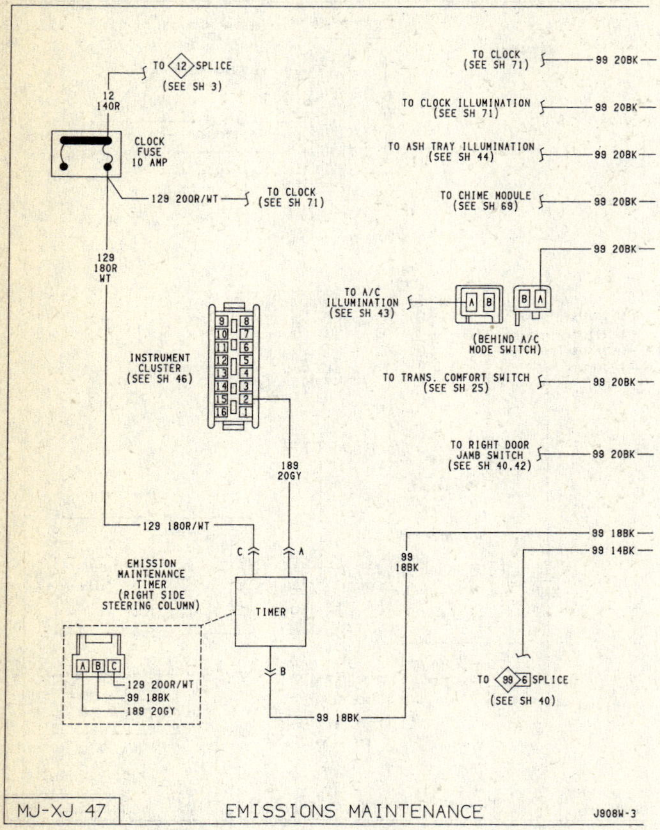
TO 12 SPLICE (SEE SH 3)
CLOCK FUSE 10 AMP
129 20OR/WT
TO CLOCK (SEE SH 71)
TO CLOCK ILLUMINATION (SEE SH 71)
TO ASH TRAY ILLUMINATION (SEE SH 44)
TO CHIME MODULE (SEE SH 68)
TO A/C ILLUMINATION (SEE SH 43)
(BEHIND A/C MODE SWITCH)
INSTRUMENT CLUSTER (SEE SH 46)
TO TRANS. COMFORT SWITCH (SEE SH 25)
TO RIGHT DOOR JAMB SWITCH (SEE SH 40,42)
99 20BK
99 18BK
99 14BK
129 18OR/WT
189 20GY
EMISSION MAINTENANCE TIMER (RIGHT SIDE STEERING COLUMN)
TIMER
TO 99 6 SPLICE (SEE SH 40)
MJ-XJ 47
EMISSIONS MAINTENANCE
J908W-3

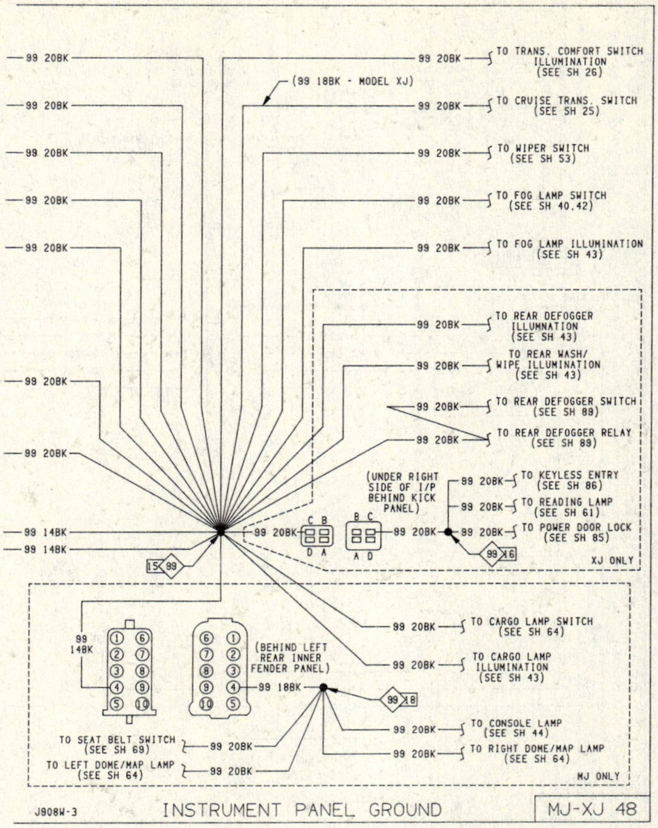
(99 18BK - MODEL XJ)
TO TRANS. COMFORT SWITCH ILLUMINATION (SEE SH 26)
TO CRUISE TRANS. SWITCH (SEE SH 25)
TO WIPER SWITCH (SEE SH 53)
TO FOG LAMP SWITCH (SEE SH 40,42)
TO FOG LAMP ILLUMINATION (SEE SH 43)
TO REAR DEFOGGER ILLUMNATION (SEE SH 43)
TO REAR WASH/WIPE ILLUMINATION (SEE SH 43)
TO REAR DEFOGGER SWITCH (SEE SH 89)
TO REAR DEFOGGER RELAY (SEE SH 89)
(UNDER RIGHT SIDE OF I/P BEHIND KICK PANEL)
TO KEYLESS ENTRY (SEE SH 86)
TO READING LAMP (SEE SH 61)
TO POWER DOOR LOCK (SEE SH 85)
XJ ONLY
(BEHIND LEFT REAR INNER FENDER PANEL)
TO CARGO LAMP SWITCH (SEE SH 64)
TO CARGO LAMP ILLUMINATION (SEE SH 43)
TO CONSOLE LAMP (SEE SH 44)
TO RIGHT DOME/MAP LAMP (SEE SH 64)
TO SEAT BELT SWITCH (SEE SH 69)
TO LEFT DOME/MAP LAMP (SEE SH 64)
MJ ONLY
J908W-3
INSTRUMENT PANEL GROUND
MJ-XJ 48

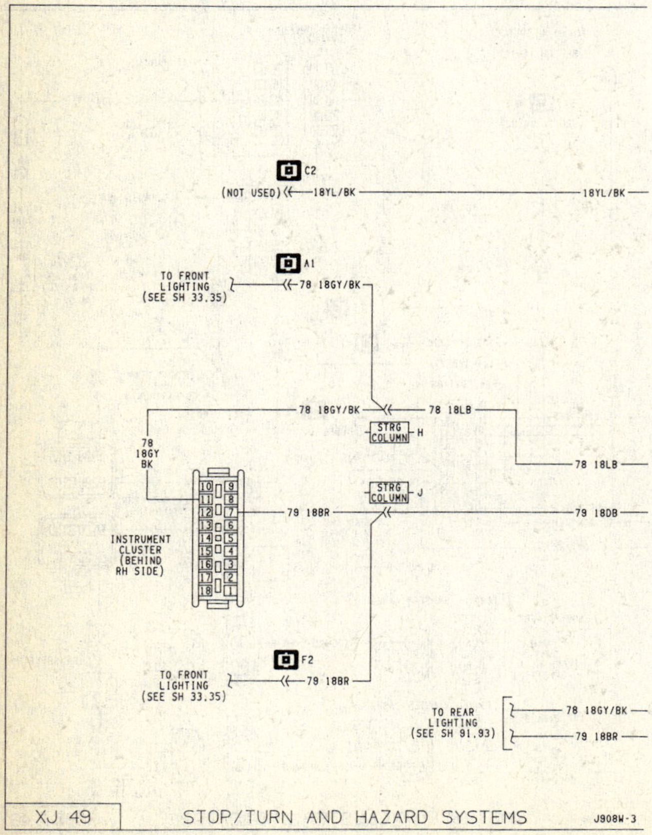
C2
(NOT USED)
18YL/BK
A1
TO FRONT LIGHTING (SEE SH 33,35)
78 18GY/BK
78 18LB
STRG COLUMN
79 18BR
79 18DB
INSTRUMENT CLUSTER (BEHIND RH SIDE)
F2
TO REAR LIGHTING (SEE SH 91,93)
XJ 49
STOP/TURN AND HAZARD SYSTEMS
J908W-3

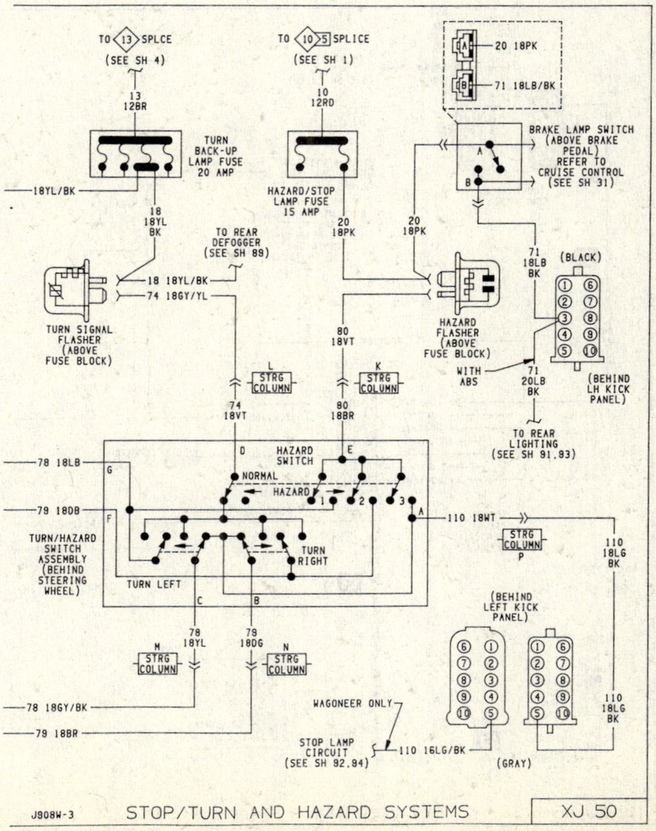
TO 13 SPLCE (SEE SH 4)
TO 10 5 SPLICE (SEE SH 1)
TURN BACK-UP LAMP FUSE 20 AMP
HAZARD/STOP LAMP FUSE 15 AMP
20 18PK
71 18LB/BK
BRAKE LAMP SWITCH (ABOVE BRAKE PEDAL) REFER TO CRUISE CONTROL (SEE SH 31)
TO REAR DEFOGGER (SEE SH 89)
TURN SIGNAL FLASHER (ABOVE FUSE BLOCK)
HAZARD FLASHER (ABOVE FUSE BLOCK)
WITH ABS
(BLACK)
(BEHIND LH KICK PANEL)
TO REAR LIGHTING (SEE SH 91,93)
STRG COLUMN
HAZARD SWITCH
NORMAL
HAZARD
TURN/HAZARD SWITCH ASSEMBLY (BEHIND STEERING WHEEL)
TURN LEFT
TURN RIGHT
110 18WT
(BEHIND LEFT KICK PANEL)
WAGONEER ONLY
STOP LAMP CIRCUIT (SEE SH 92,94)
110 16LG/BK
(GRAY)
J908W-3
STOP/TURN AND HAZARD SYSTEMS
XJ 50

CHASSIS ELECTRICAL 6

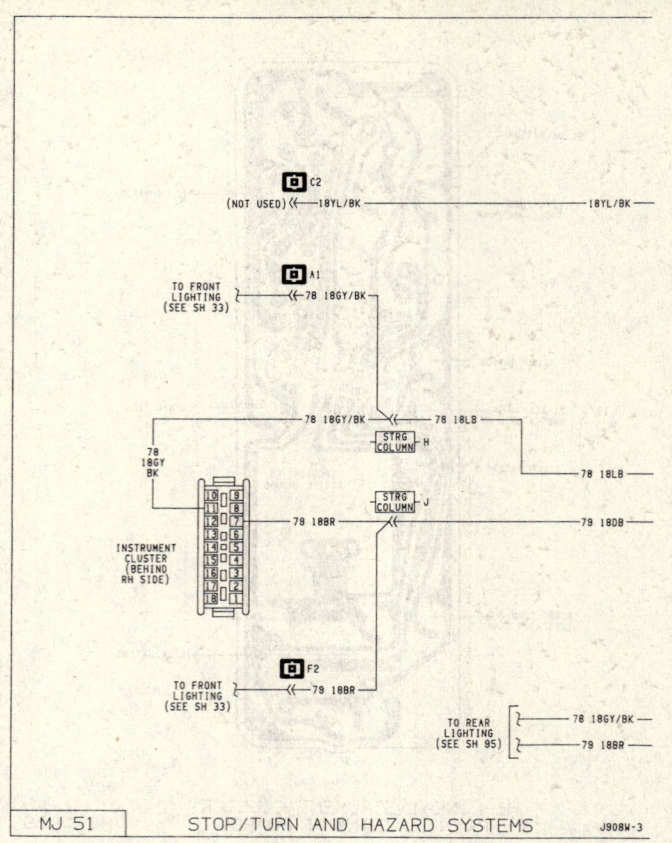

MJ 51 — STOP/TURN AND HAZARD SYSTEMS

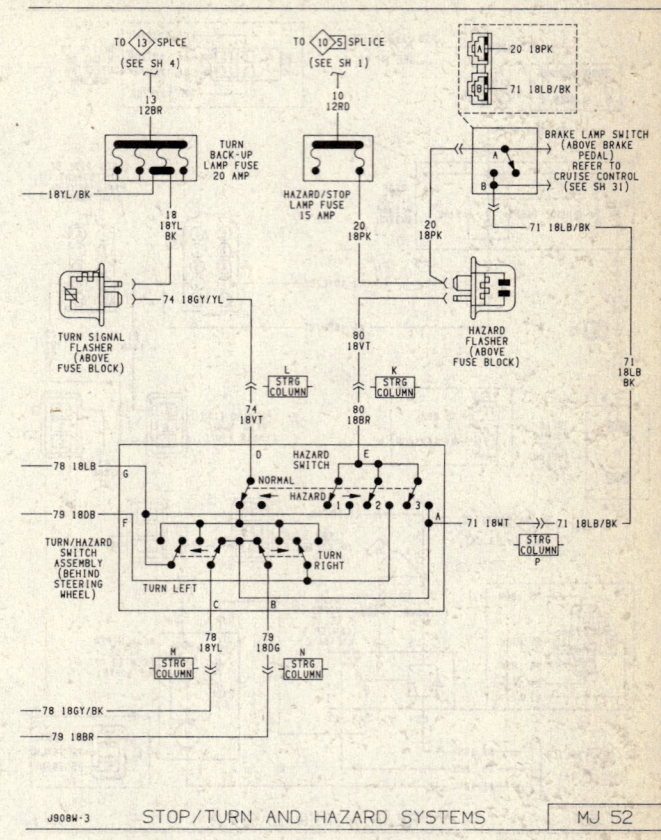

MJ 52 — STOP/TURN AND HAZARD SYSTEMS

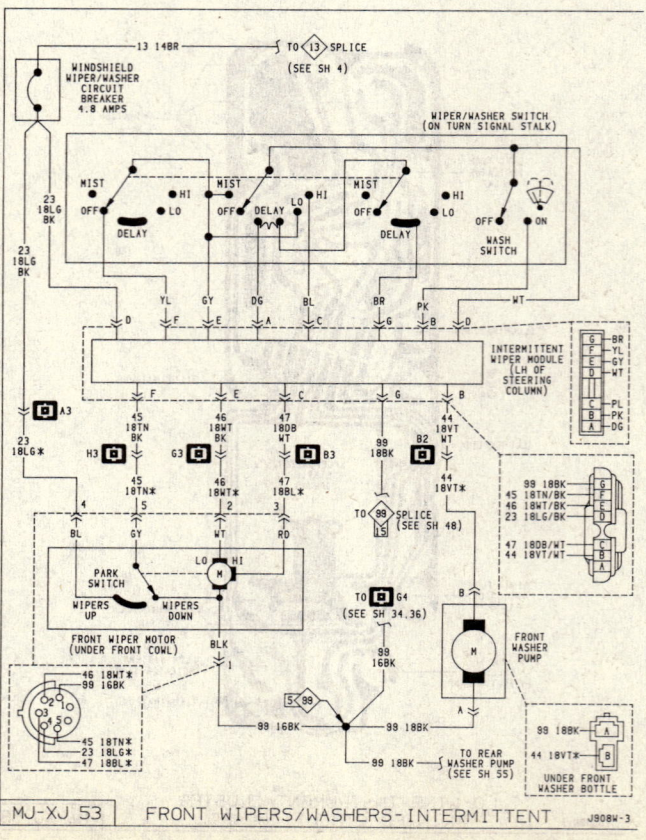

MJ-XJ 53 — FRONT WIPERS/WASHERS - INTERMITTENT

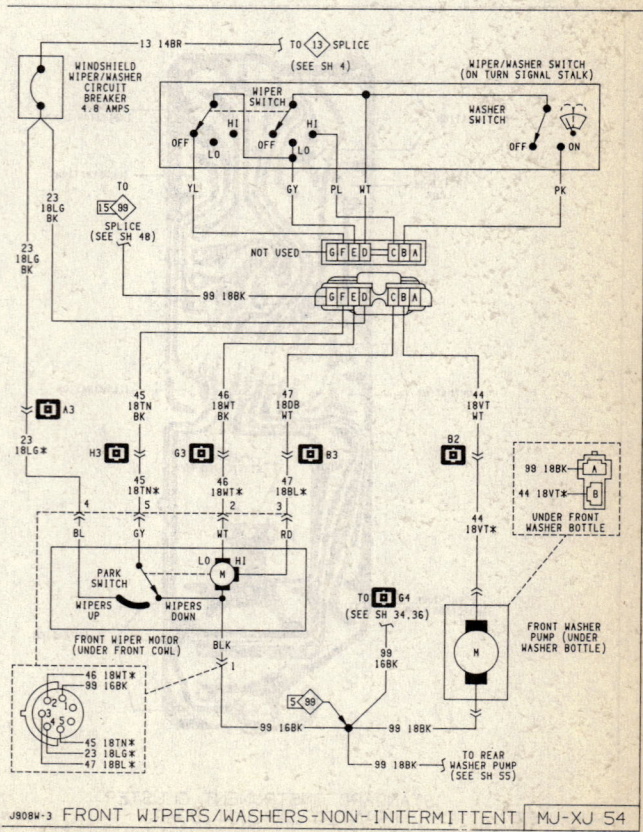

MJ-XJ 54 — FRONT WIPERS/WASHERS - NON-INTERMITTENT

6-91

6 CHASSIS ELECTRICAL

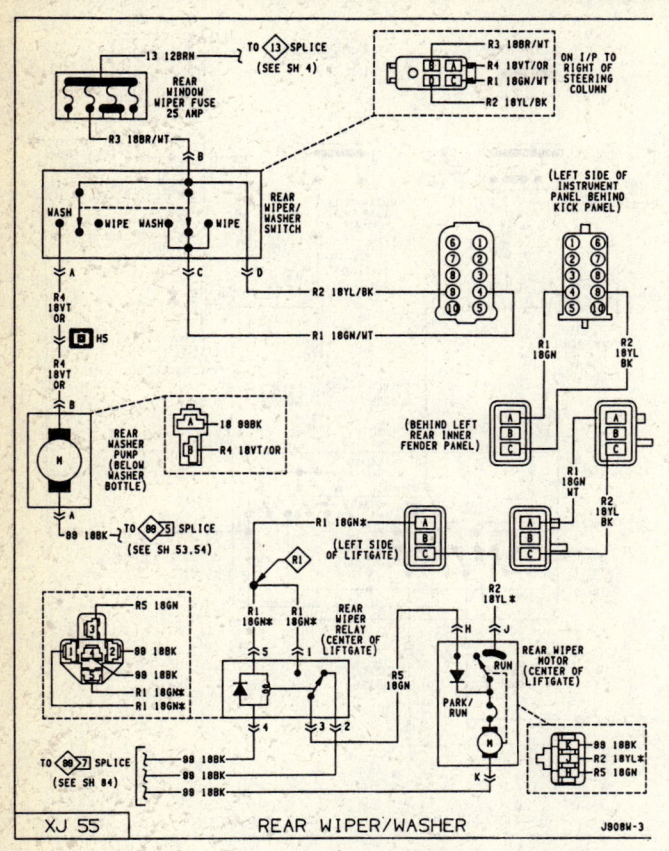

XJ 55 — REAR WIPER/WASHER

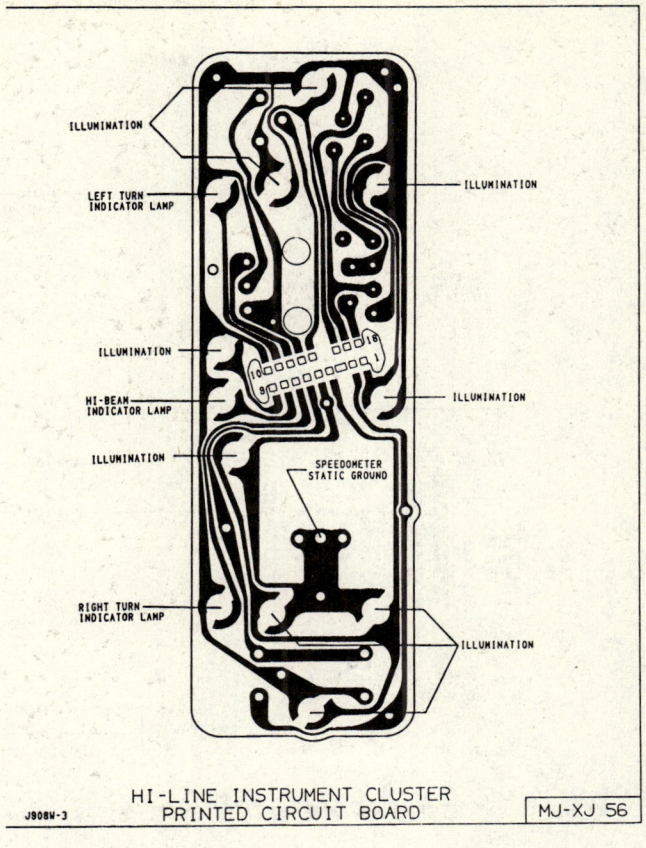

MJ-XJ 56 — HI-LINE INSTRUMENT CLUSTER PRINTED CIRCUIT BOARD

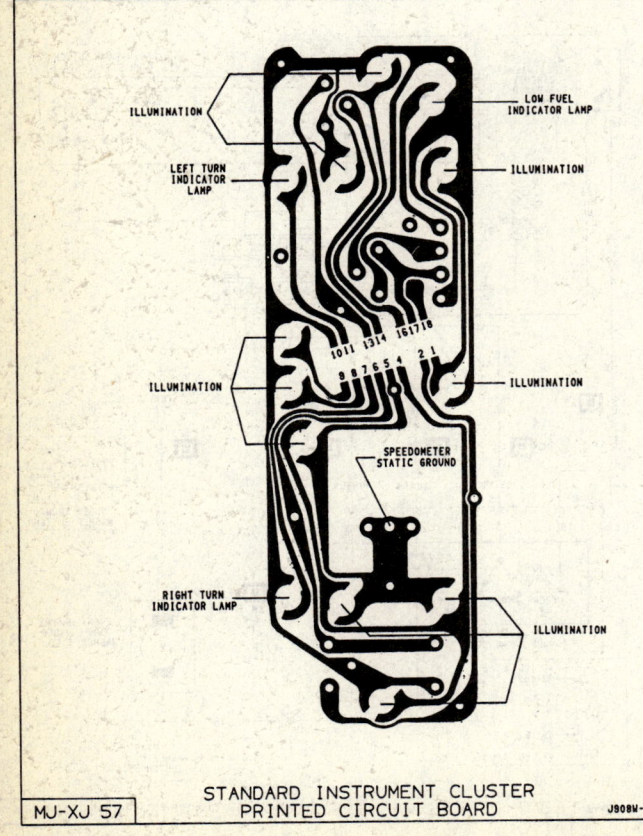

MJ-XJ 57 — STANDARD INSTRUMENT CLUSTER PRINTED CIRCUIT BOARD

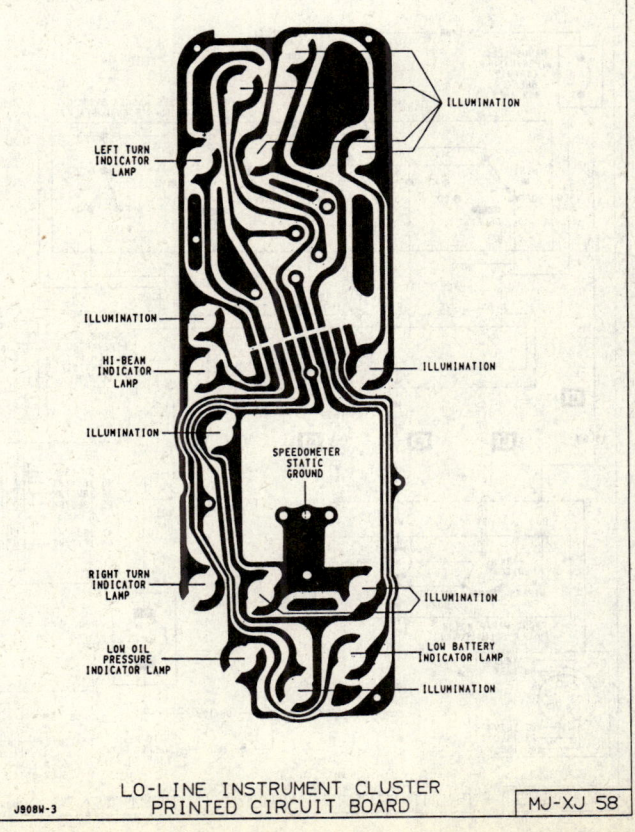

MJ-XJ 58 — LO-LINE INSTRUMENT CLUSTER PRINTED CIRCUIT BOARD

CHASSIS ELECTRICAL 6

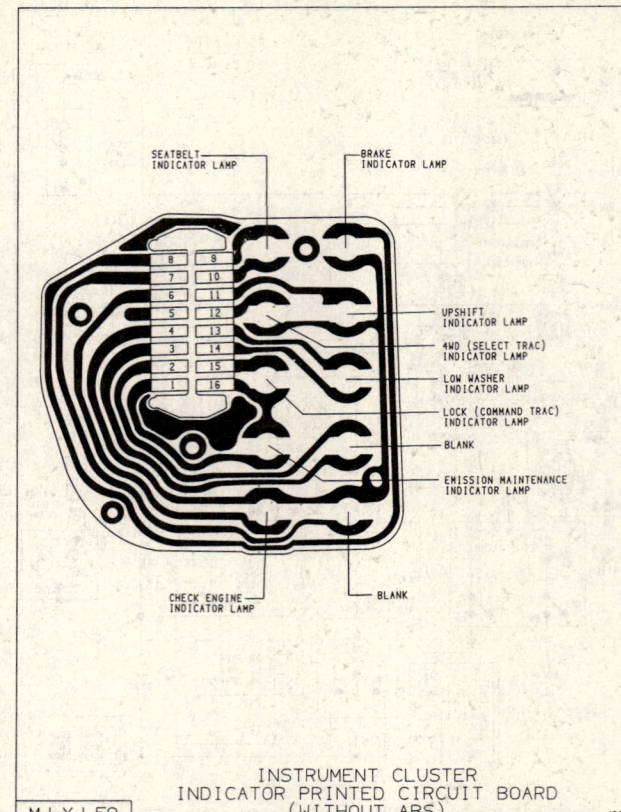

INSTRUMENT CLUSTER
INDICATOR PRINTED CIRCUIT BOARD
(WITHOUT ABS)

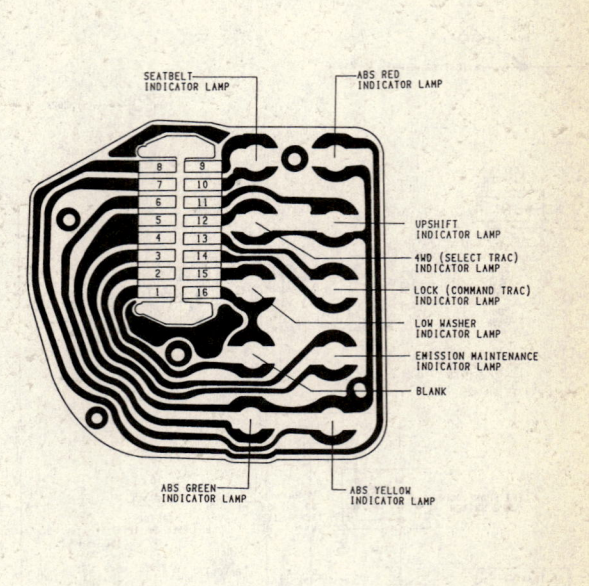

INSTRUMENT CLUSTER
INDICATOR PRINTED CIRCUIT BOARD
(WITH ABS)

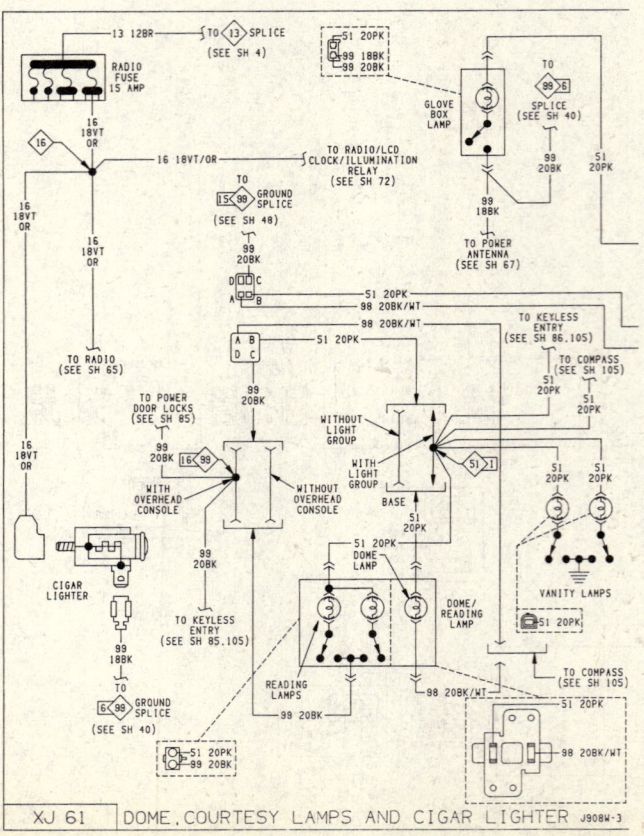

DOME, COURTESY LAMPS AND CIGAR LIGHTER

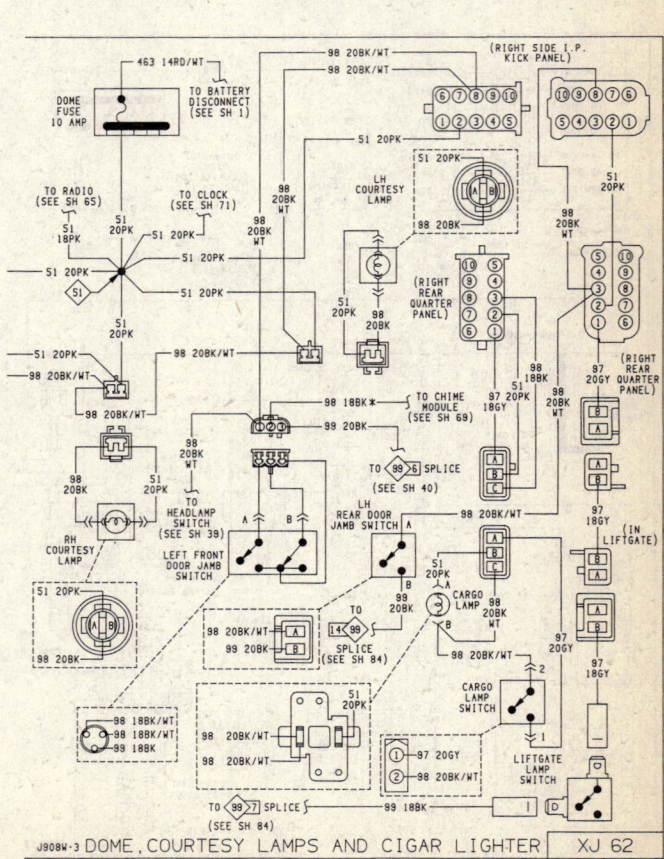

DOME, COURTESY LAMPS AND CIGAR LIGHTER

6-93

6 CHASSIS ELECTRICAL

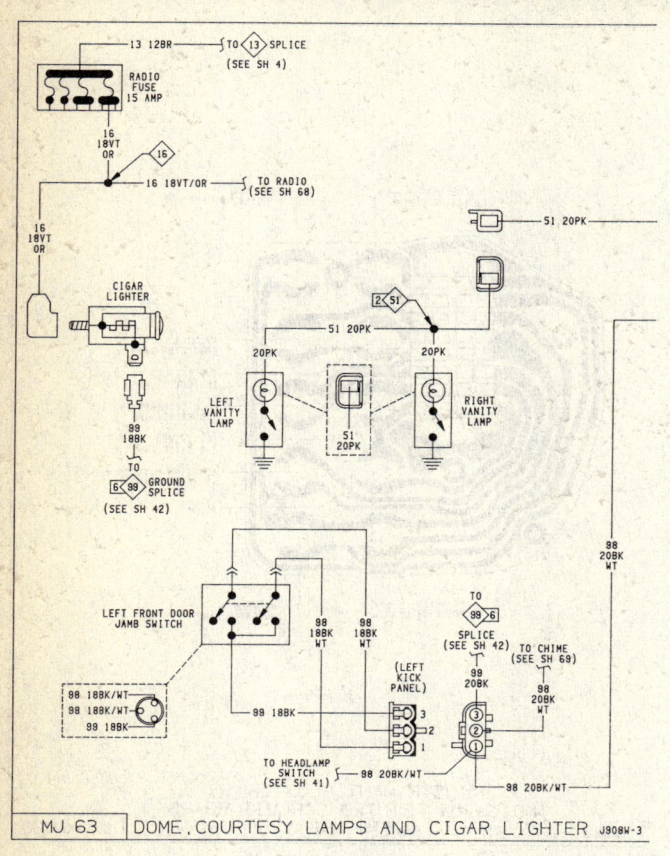

MJ 63 — DOME, COURTESY LAMPS AND CIGAR LIGHTER — J908W-3

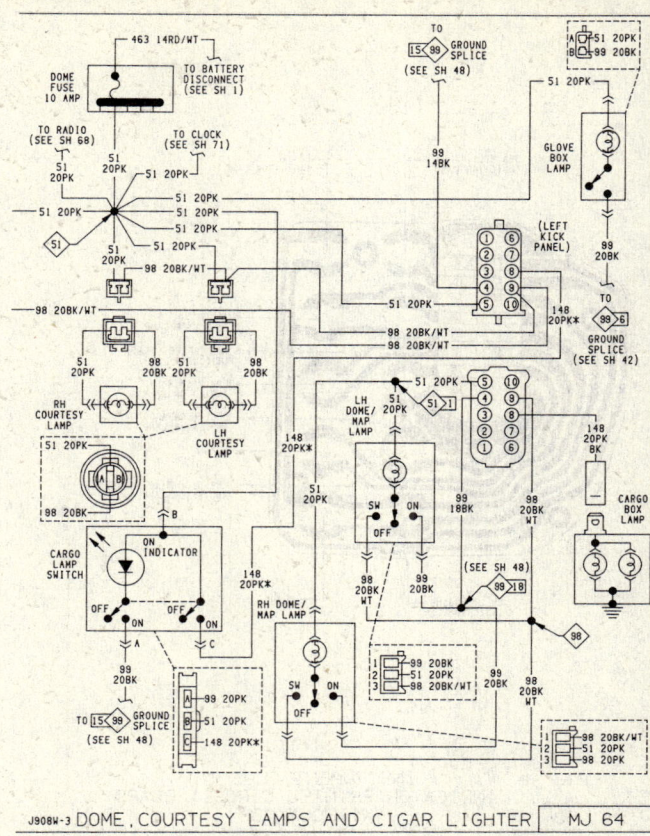

J908W-3 — DOME, COURTESY LAMPS AND CIGAR LIGHTER — MJ 64

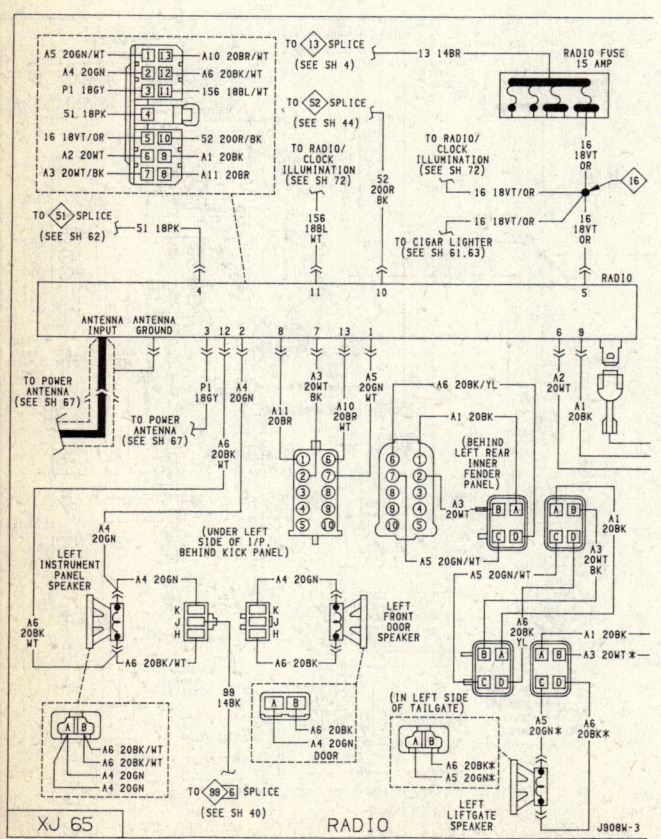

XJ 65 — RADIO — J908W-3

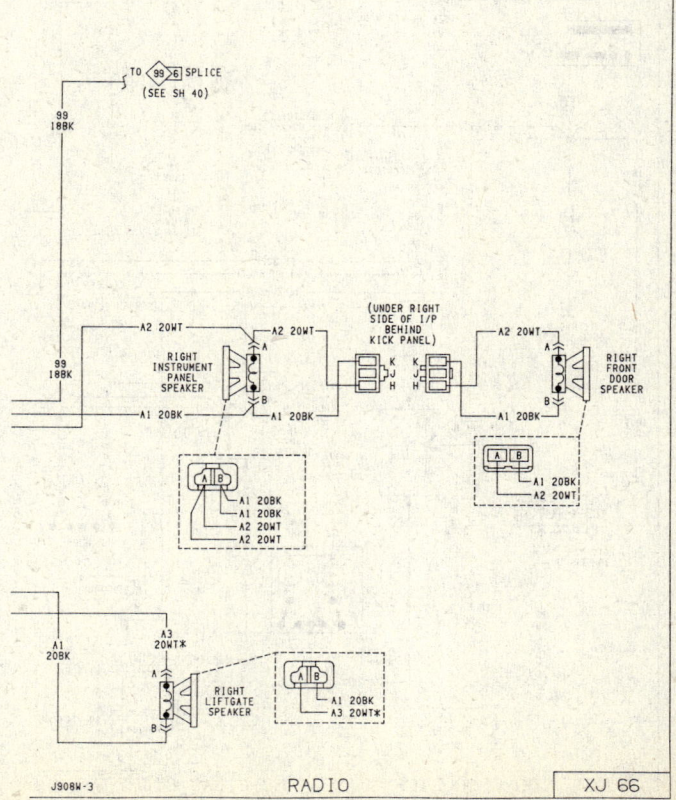

J908W-3 — RADIO — XJ 66

CHASSIS ELECTRICAL 6

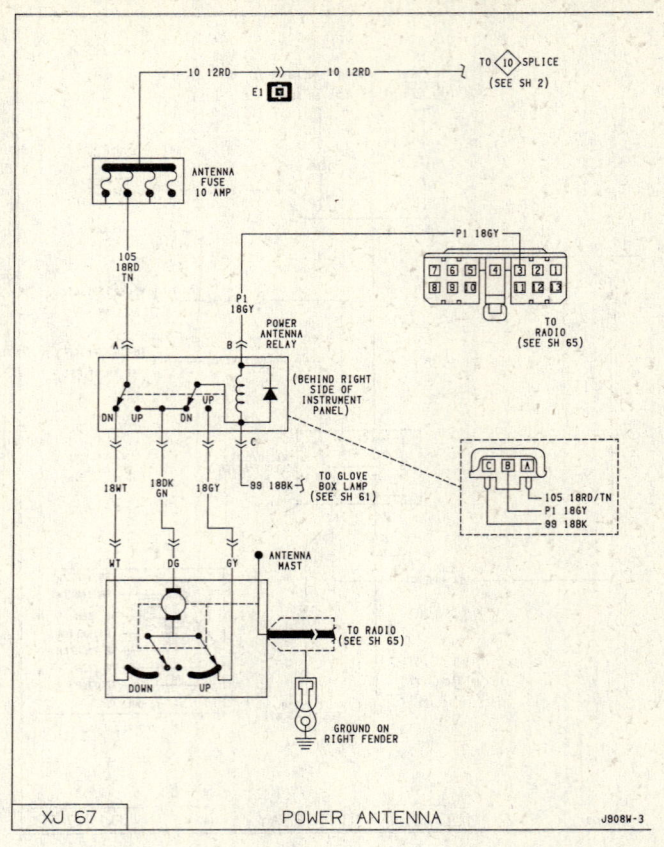

POWER ANTENNA

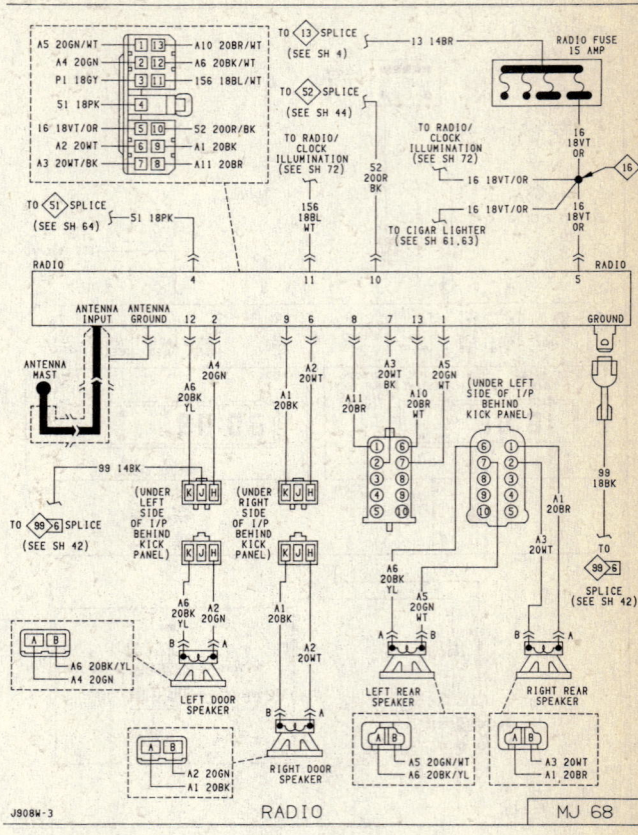

RADIO

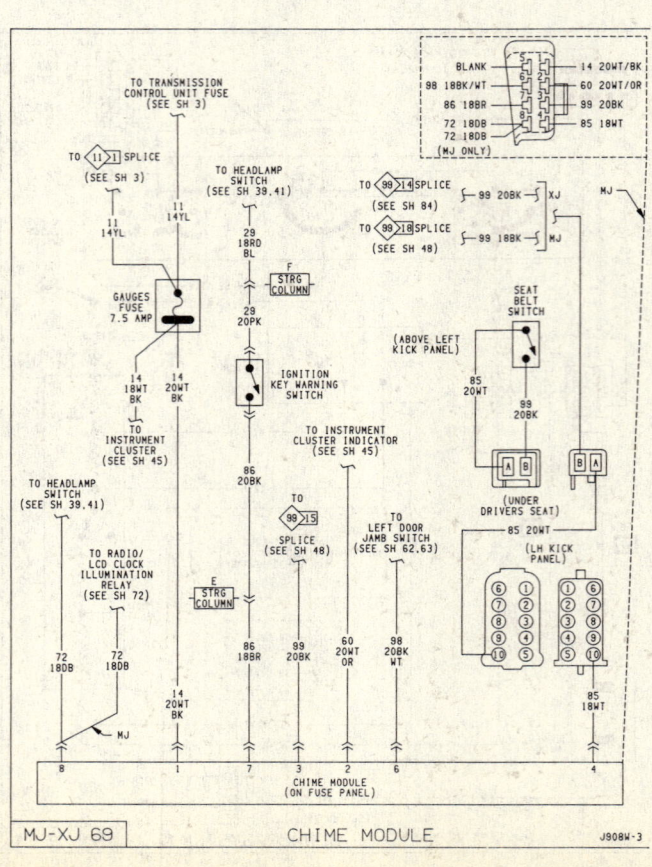

CHIME MODULE

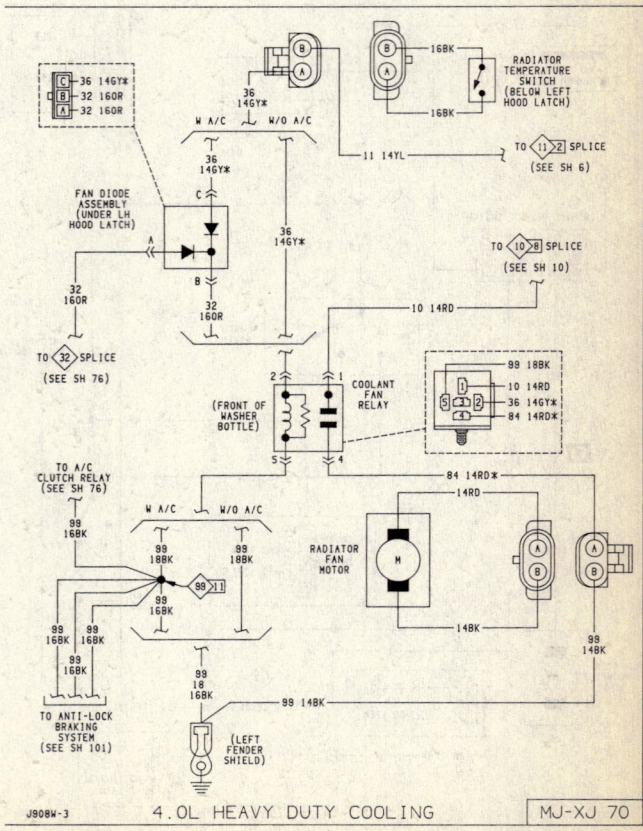

4.0L HEAVY DUTY COOLING

6-95

6 CHASSIS ELECTRICAL

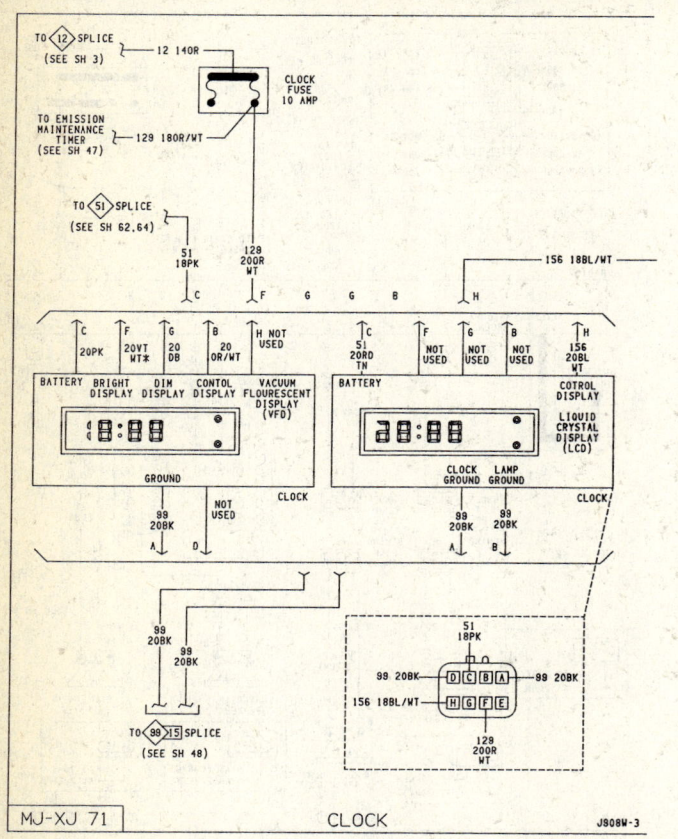

MJ-XJ 71 — CLOCK

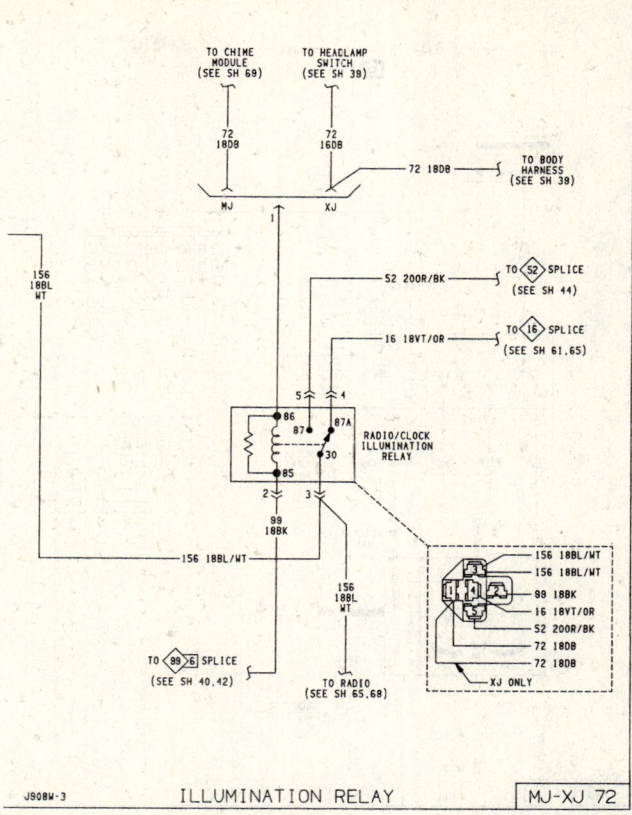

ILLUMINATION RELAY — MJ-XJ 72

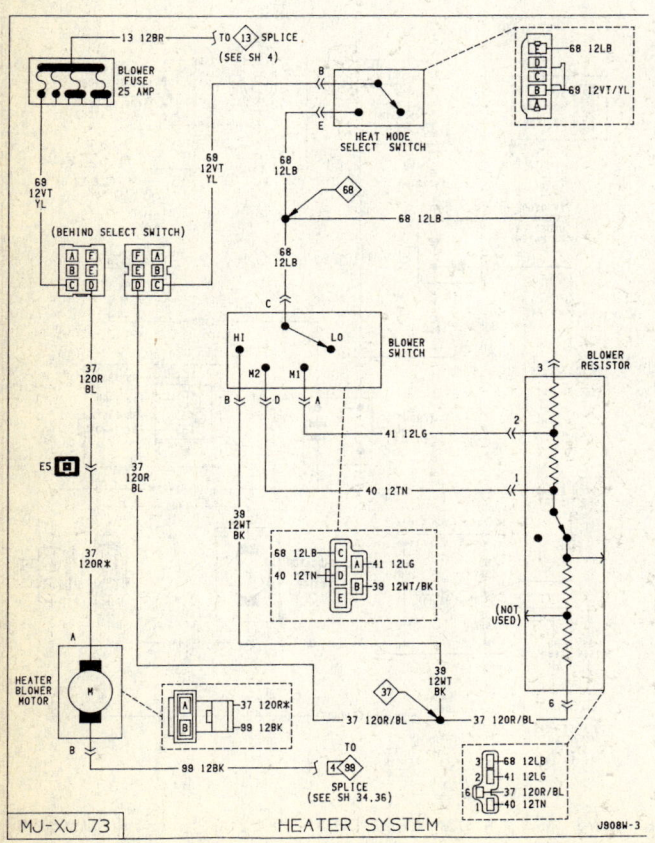

MJ-XJ 73 — HEATER SYSTEM

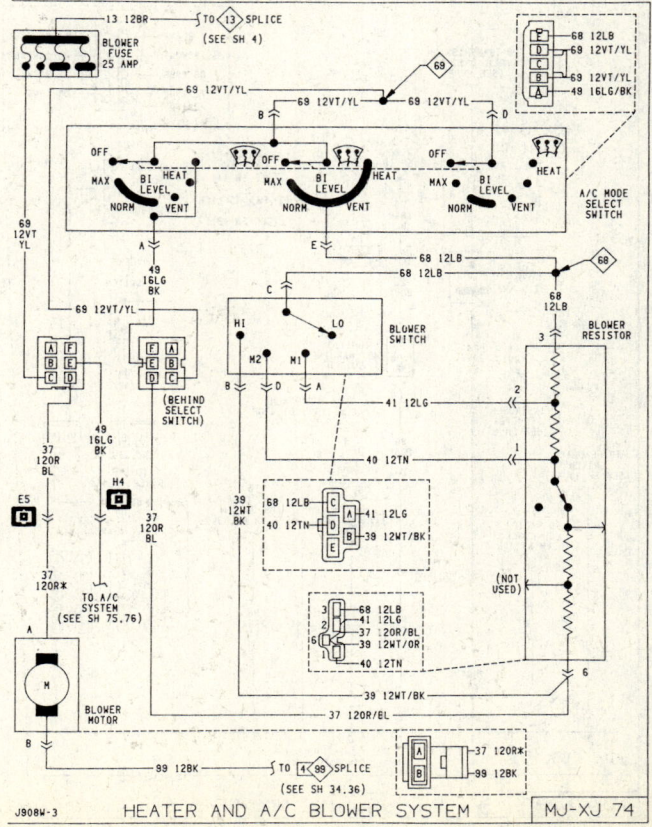

HEATER AND A/C BLOWER SYSTEM — MJ-XJ 74

CHASSIS ELECTRICAL 6

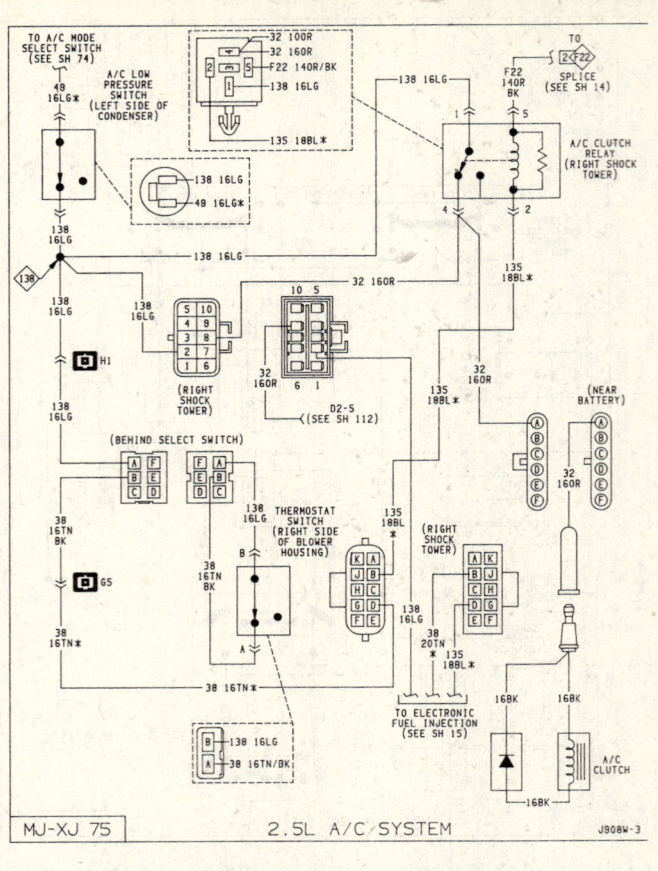

2.5L A/C SYSTEM

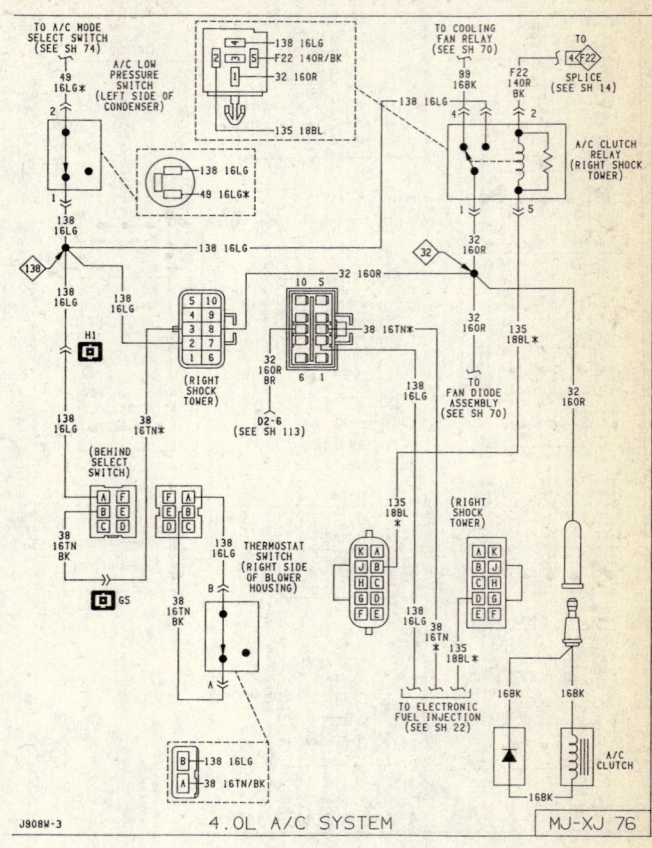

4.0L A/C SYSTEM

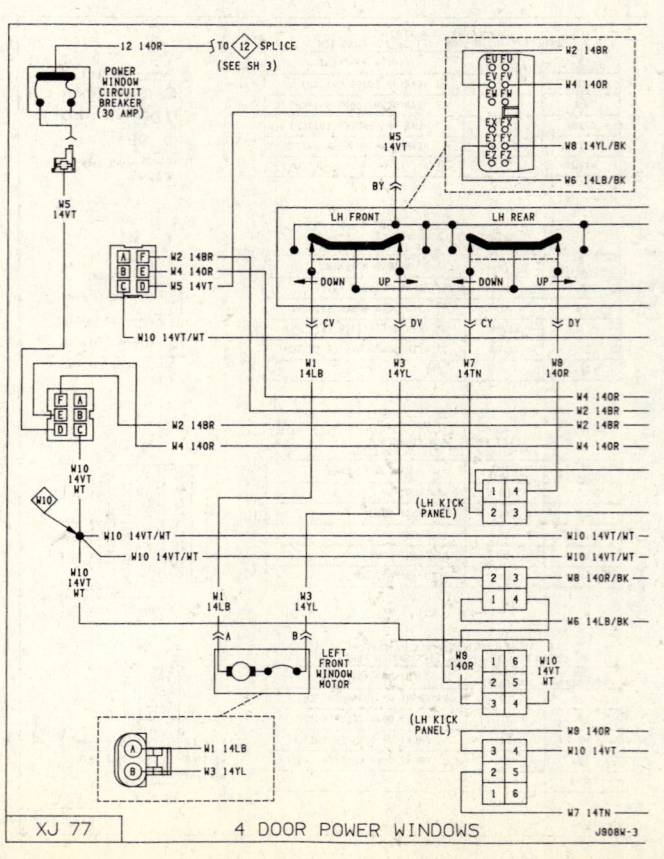

4 DOOR POWER WINDOWS

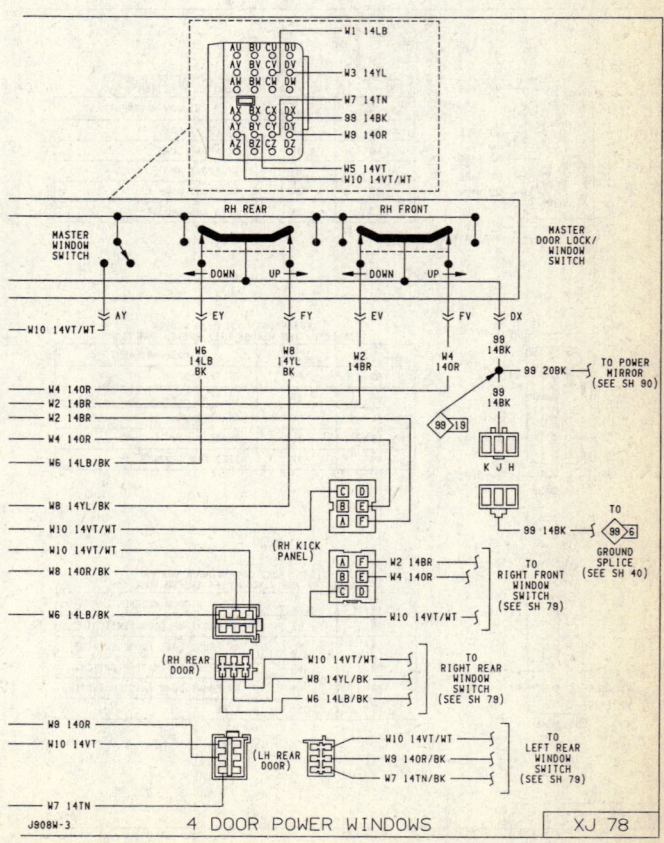

4 DOOR POWER WINDOWS

6-97

6 CHASSIS ELECTRICAL

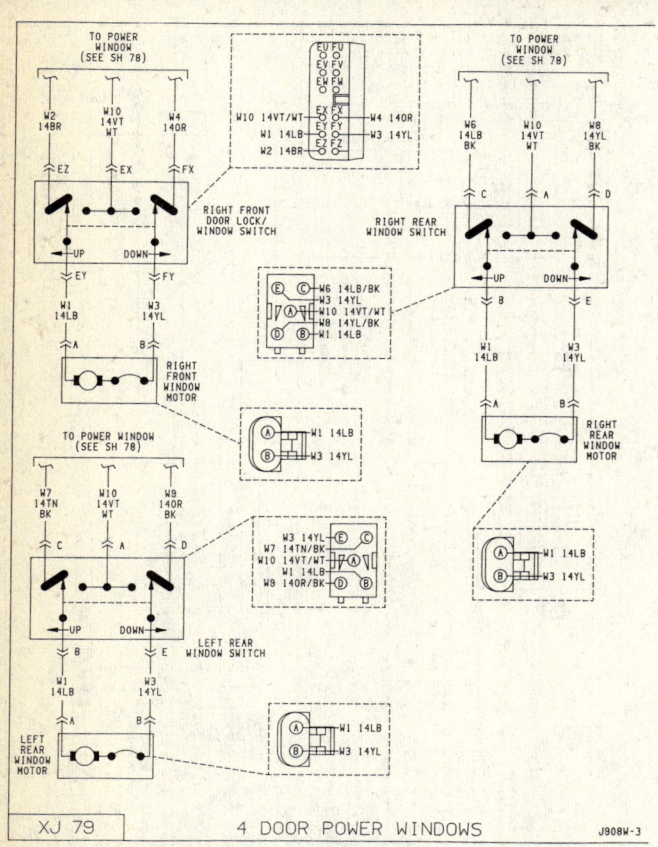

4 DOOR POWER WINDOWS — MJ-XJ 79

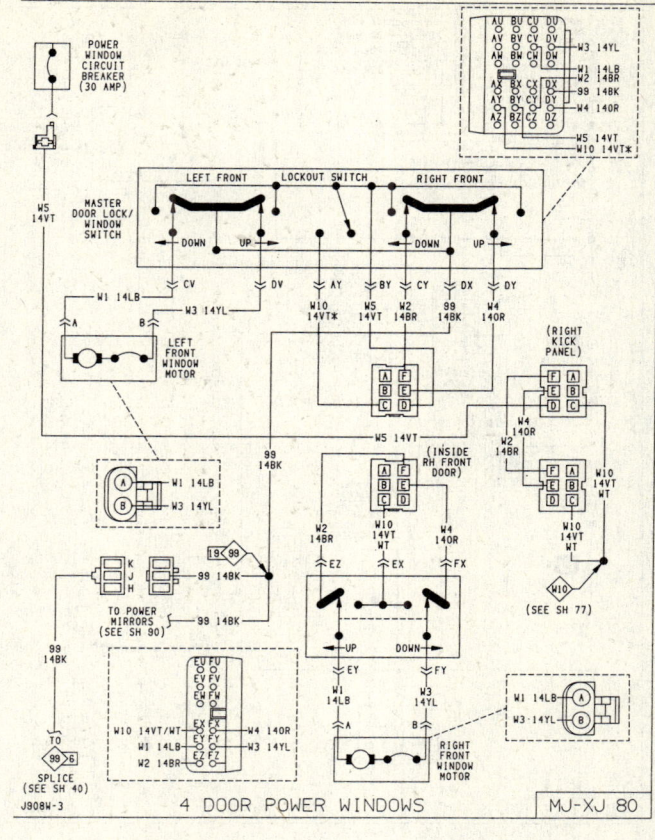

4 DOOR POWER WINDOWS — MJ-XJ 80

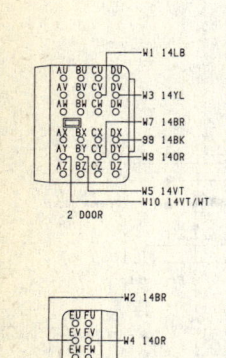

LEFT FRONT DOOR CONNECTOR AND WINDOW LIFT SWITCH FUNCTION

B+ POLARITY	B- POLARITY	WINDOW MOVEMENT
YL	LB	LT FRONT UP
LB	YL	LT FRONT DOWN
OR	BR	RT FRONT UP
BR	OR	RT FRONT DOWN
VT/WT	BK	FEED AND GROUND

2 DOOR

LEFT FRONT DOOR REAR WINDOW CONNECTOR AND WINDOW LIFT SWITCH FUNCTION

B+ POLARITY	B- POLARITY	WINDOW MOVEMENT
OR	BR	LT REAR UP
BR	OR	LT REAR DOWN
YL*	LB*	RT REAR UP
LB*	YL*	RT REAR DOWN
VT	BK	FEED AND GROUND

4 DOOR

RIGHT FRONT DOOR WINDOW SWITCH CONNECTOR AND WINDOW LIFT SWITCH FUNCTION

B+ POLARITY	B- POLARITY	WINDOW MOVEMENT
YL	LB	RT FRONT UP (DOOR SWITCH)
LB	YL	RT FRONT DOWN (DOOR SWITCH)
OR	BR	RT FRONT UP (MASTER SWITCH)
BR	OR	RT FRONT DOWN (MASTER SWITCH)
VT*	—	FEED

4 DOOR

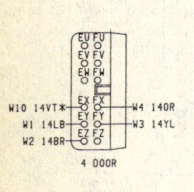

MJ-XJ 81

LEFT REAR DOOR WINDOW CONNECTOR AND WINDOW LIFT SWITCH FUNCTION

B+ POLARITY	B- POLARITY	WINDOW MOVEMENT
YL	LB	LT REAR UP (DOOR SWITCH)
LB	YL	LT REAR DOWN (DOOR SWITCH)
OR/BK	TN/BK	LT REAR UP (MASTER SWITCH)
TN/BK	OR/BK	LT REAR DOWN (MASTER SWITCH)
VT/WT	—	FEED

RIGHT REAR DOOR WINDOW CONNECTOR AND WINDOW LIFT SWITCH FUNCTION

B+ POLARITY	B- POLARITY	WINDOW MOVEMENT
YL	LB	RT REAR UP (DOOR SWITCH)
LB	YL	RT REAR DOWN (DOOR SWITCH)
YL/BK	LB/BK	RT REAR UP (MASTER SWITCH)
LB/BK	YL/BK	RT REAR DOWN (MASTER SWITCH)
VT/WT	—	FEED

LEFT FRONT DOOR CONNECTOR AND WINDOW LIFT SWITCH FUNCTION

B+ POLARITY	B- POLARITY	WINDOW MOVEMENT
YL	LB	LT FRONT UP
LB	YL	LT FRONT DOWN
OR	BR	RT FRONT UP
BR	OR	RT FRONT DOWN
VT/WT	BK	FEED AND GROUND

RIGHT FRONT DOOR WINDOW SWITCH CONNECTOR AND WINDOW LIFT SWITCH FUNCTION

B+ POLARITY	B- POLARITY	WINDOW MOVEMENT
YL	LB	RT FRONT UP (DOOR SWITCH)
LB	YL	RT FRONT DOWN (DOOR SWITCH)
OR	BR	RT FRONT UP (MASTER SWITCH)
BR	OR	RT FRONT DOWN (MASTER SWITCH)
VT*	—	FEED

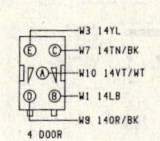
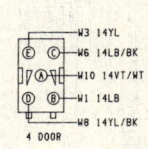
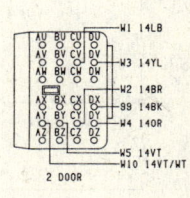
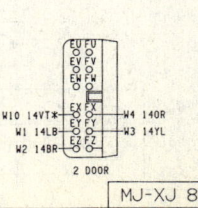

MJ-XJ 82

CHASSIS ELECTRICAL 6

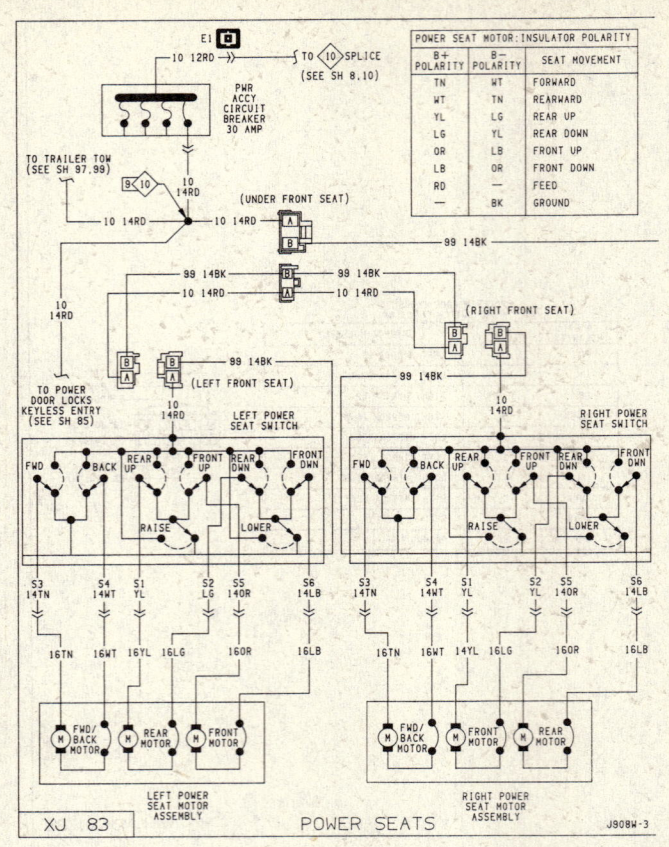

POWER SEATS — XJ 83

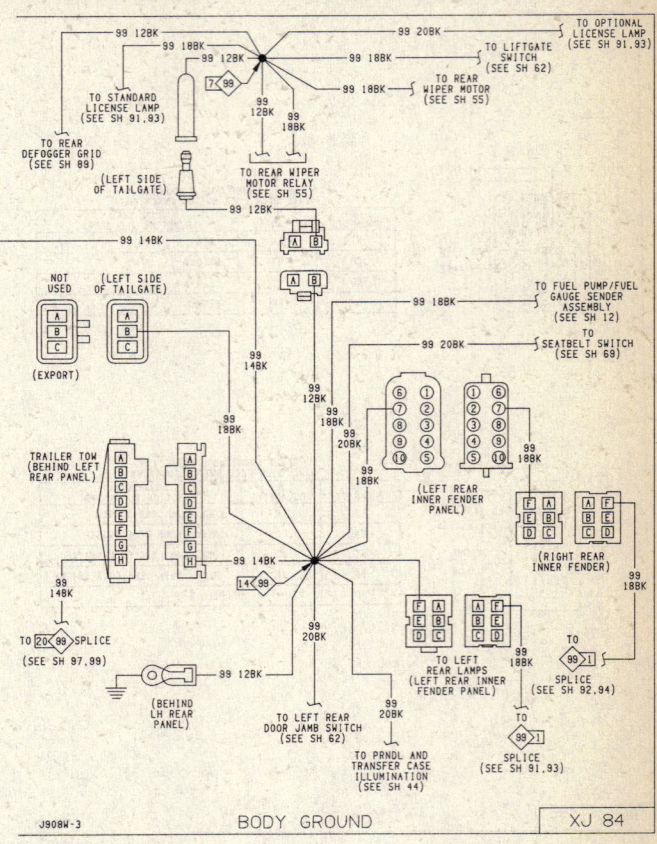

BODY GROUND — XJ 84

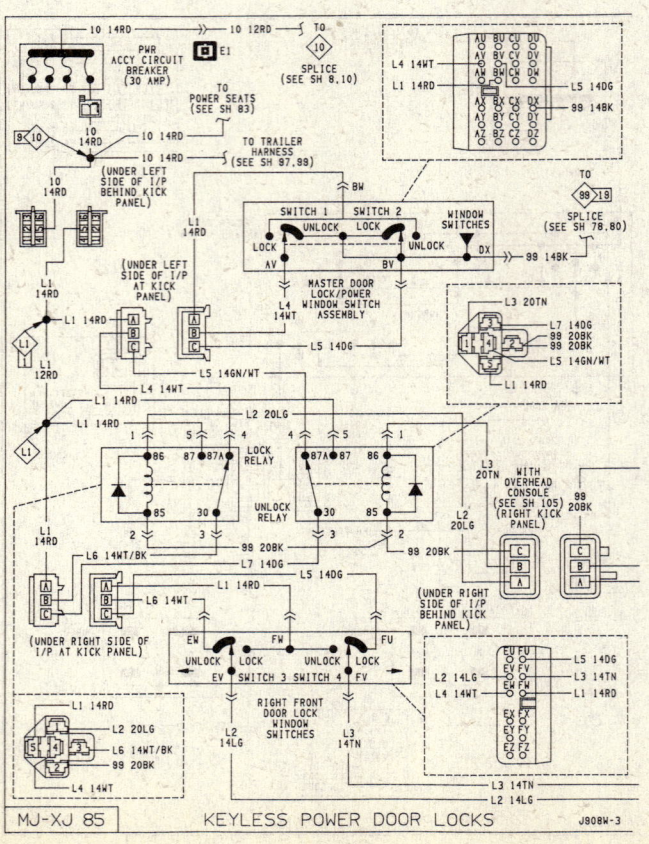

KEYLESS POWER DOOR LOCKS — MJ-XJ 85

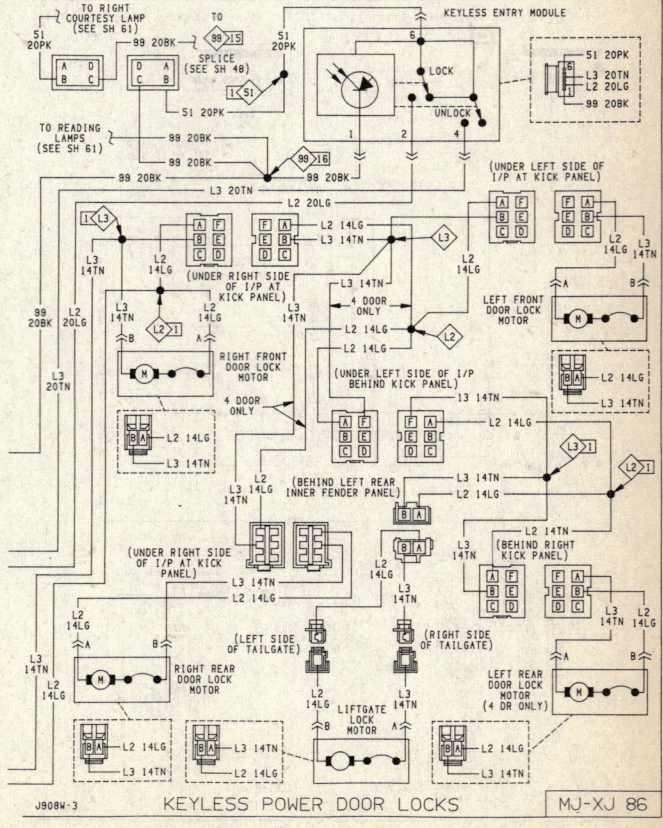

KEYLESS POWER DOOR LOCKS — MJ-XJ 86

6 CHASSIS ELECTRICAL

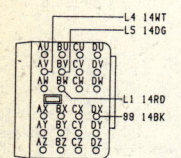

LEFT FRONT DOOR CONNECTOR AND DOOR LOCK SWITCH FUNCTION

B+ POLARITY	B− POLARITY	DOOR LOCK FUNCTION ALL DOORS
WT	DG	LOCK
DG	WT	UNLOCK
RD	—	FEED B+
—	BK	GROUND

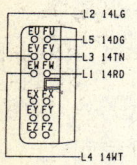

RIGHT FRONT DOOR CONNECTOR AND DOOR LOCK SWITCH FUNCTION

B+ POLARITY	B− POLARITY	DOOR LOCK FUNCTION ALL DOORS
LG	TN	LOCK FROM DOOR SWITCH
TN	LG	UNLOCK FROM DOOR SWITCH
WT	DG	LOCK FROM LEFT DOOR SWITCH
DG	WT	UNLOCK FROM LEFT DOOR SWITCH
RD	—	FEED B+

MJ-XJ 87

POWER MIRROR CONNECTOR AND SWITCH FUNCTION

B+ POLARITY	B− POLARITY	MIRROR MOVEMENT
BL	YL	LEFT MIRROR UP
YL	BL	LEFT MIRROR DOWN
BL	YL/GN	RIGHT MIRROR UP
YL/GN	BL	RIGHT MIRROR DOWN
BL	WT	LEFT MIRROR RIGHT
WT	BL	LEFT MIRROR LEFT
BL	WT*	RIGHT MIRROR RIGHT
WT*	BL	RIGHT MIRROR LEFT
RD*	—	FEED
—	BK	GROUND

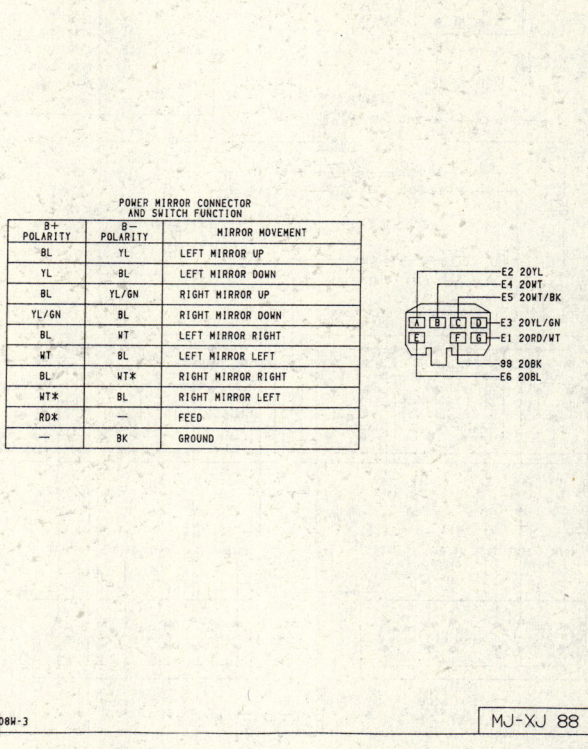

MJ-XJ 88

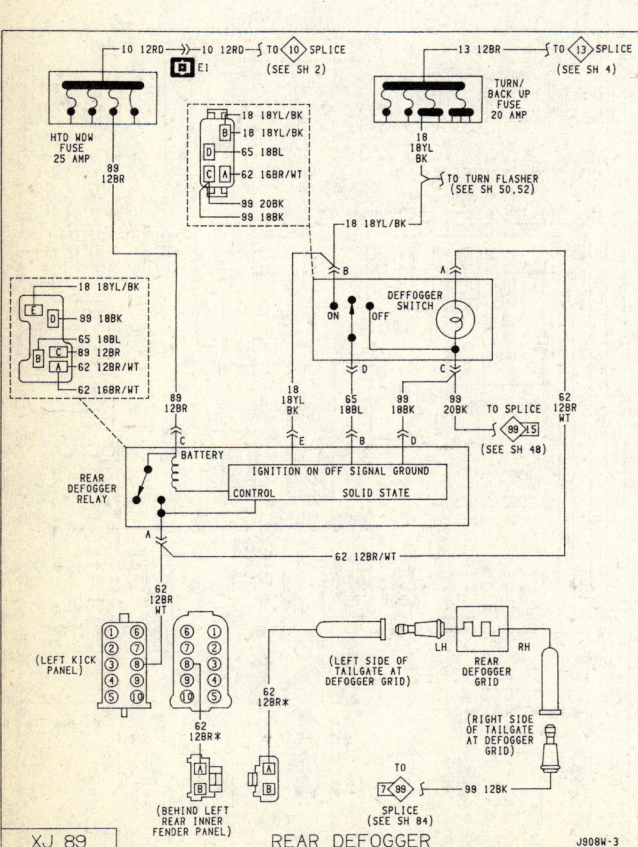

REAR DEFOGGER — XJ 89

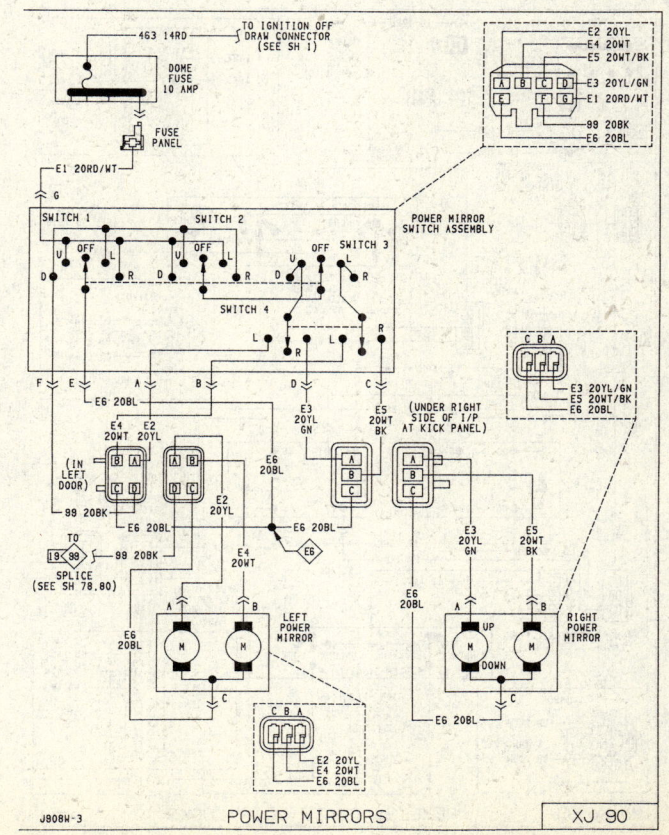

POWER MIRRORS — XJ 90

CHASSIS ELECTRICAL 6

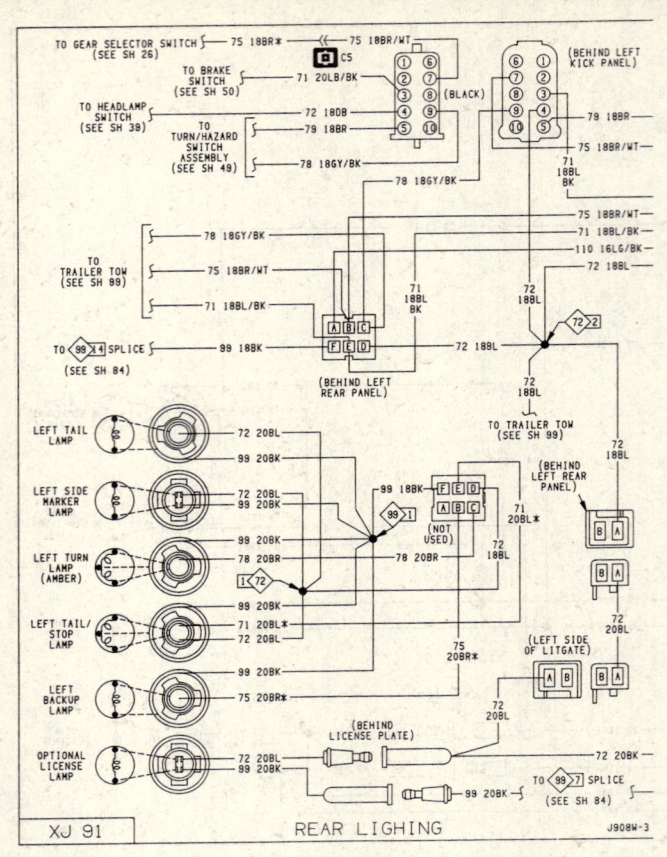

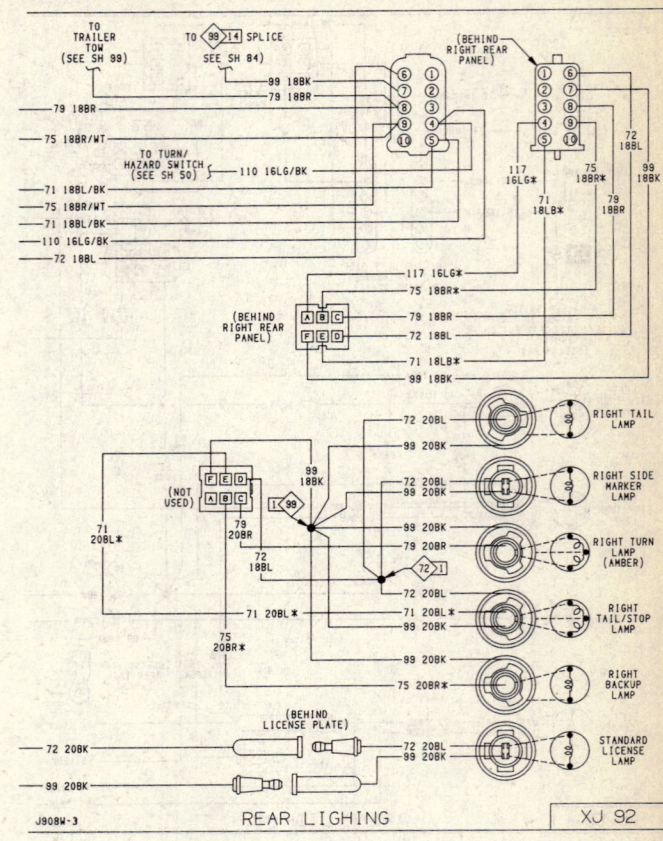

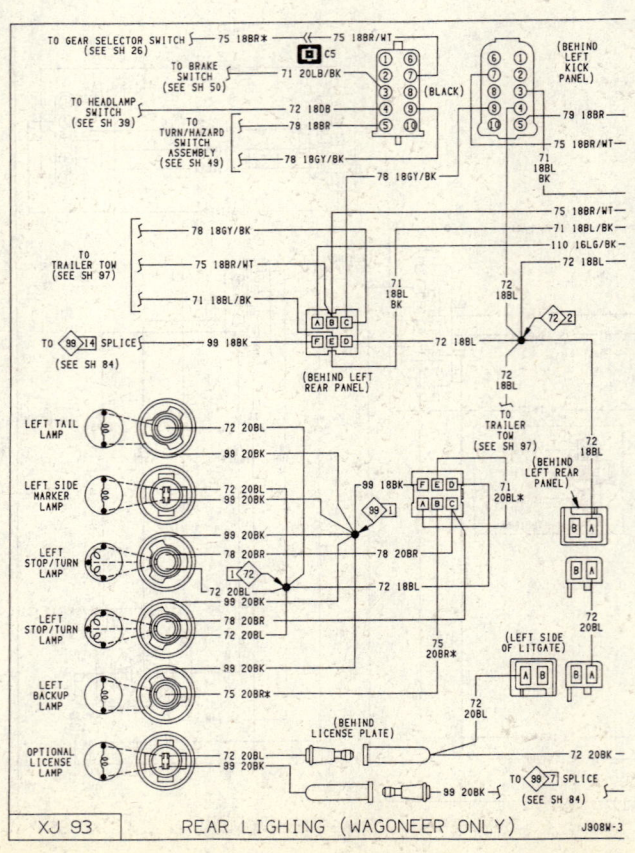

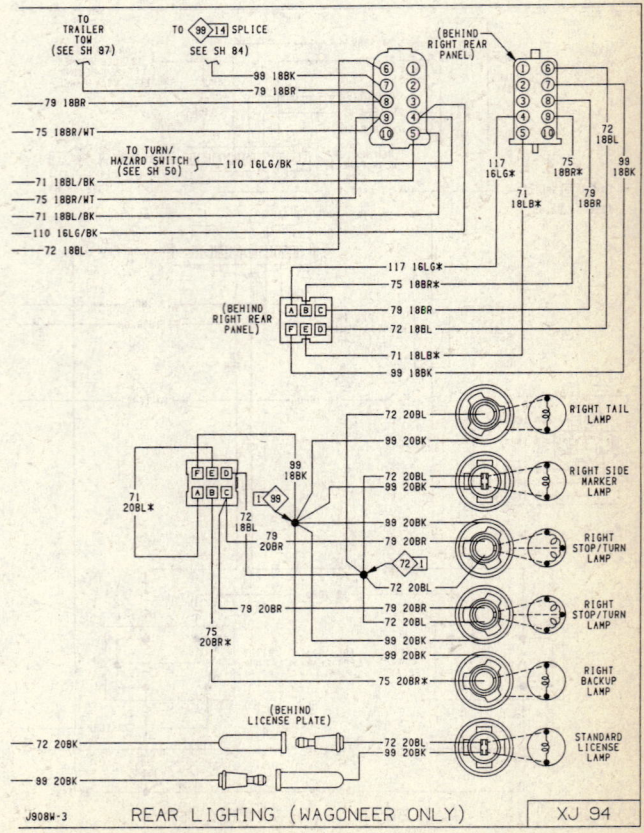

6-101

6 CHASSIS ELECTRICAL

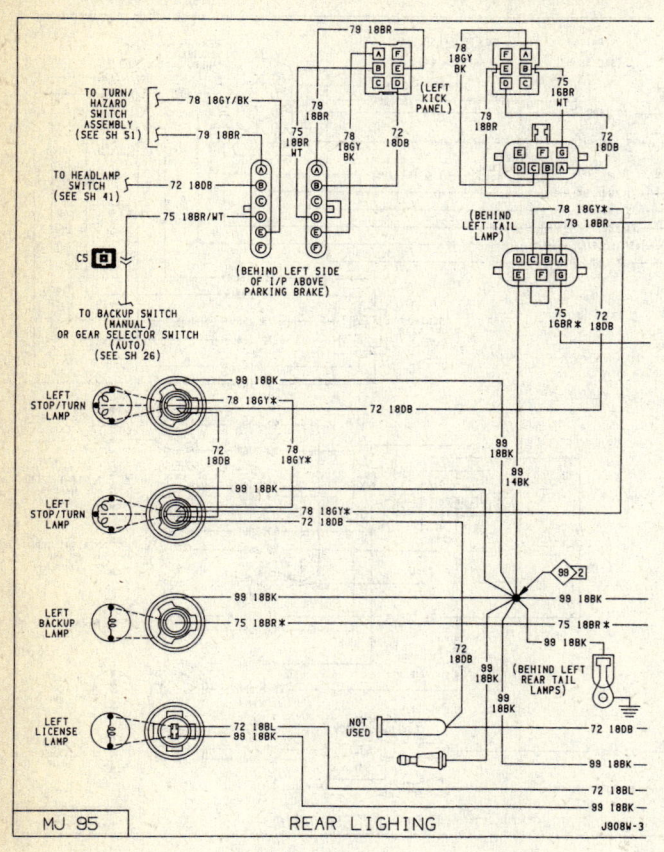

MJ 95 — REAR LIGHTING — J908W-3

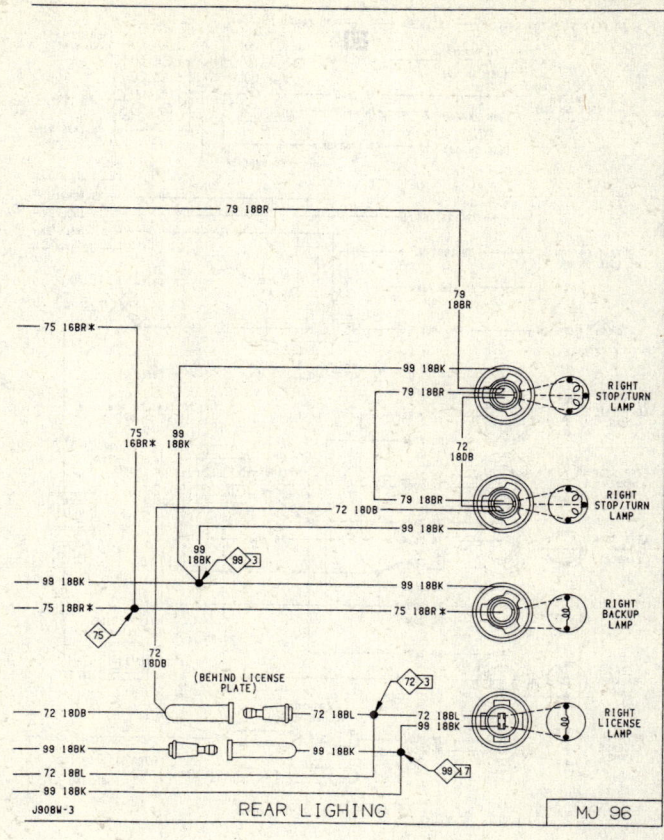

J908W-3 — REAR LIGHTING — MJ 96

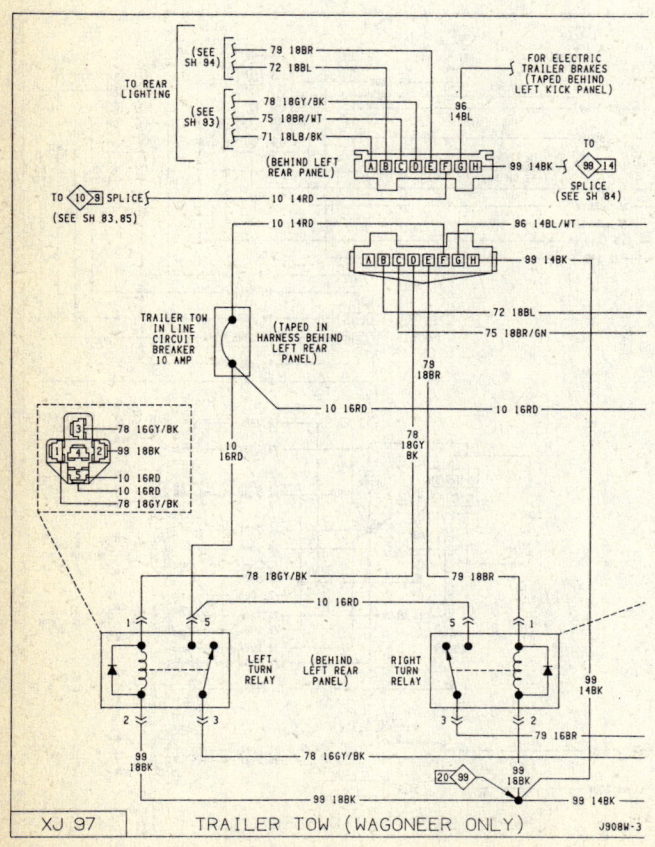

XJ 97 — TRAILER TOW (WAGONEER ONLY) — J908W-3

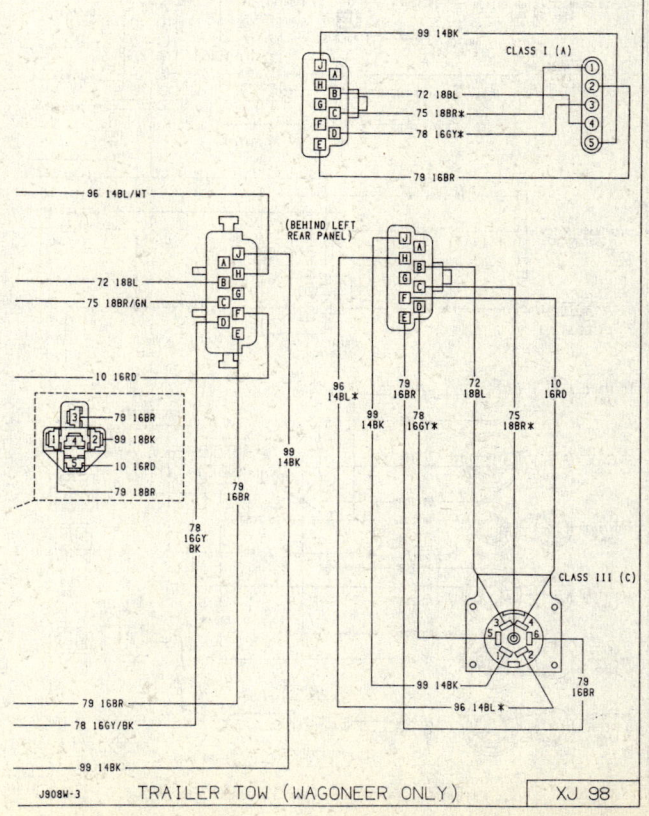

J908W-3 — TRAILER TOW (WAGONEER ONLY) — XJ 98

CHASSIS ELECTRICAL 6

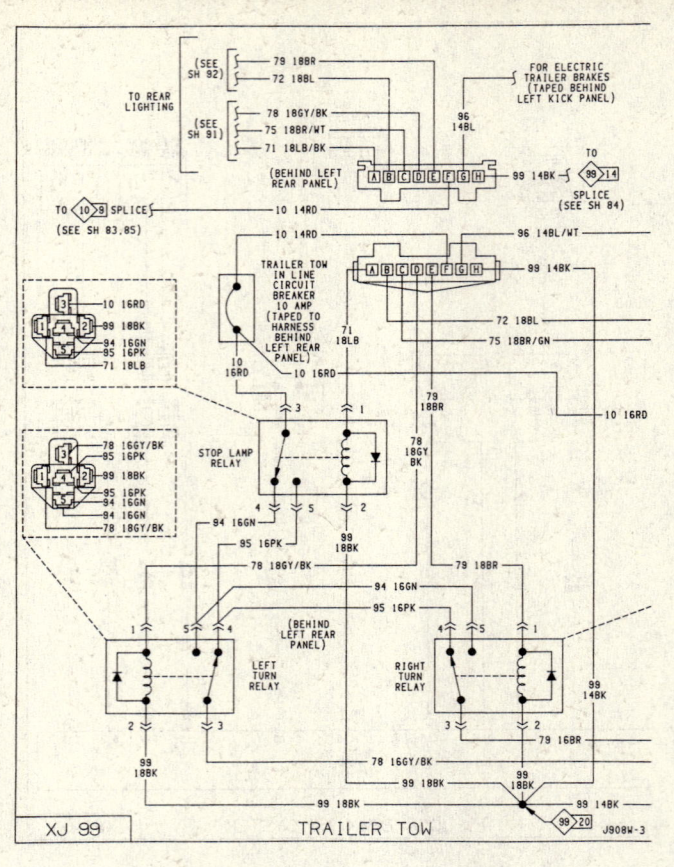

TRAILER TOW — XJ 99

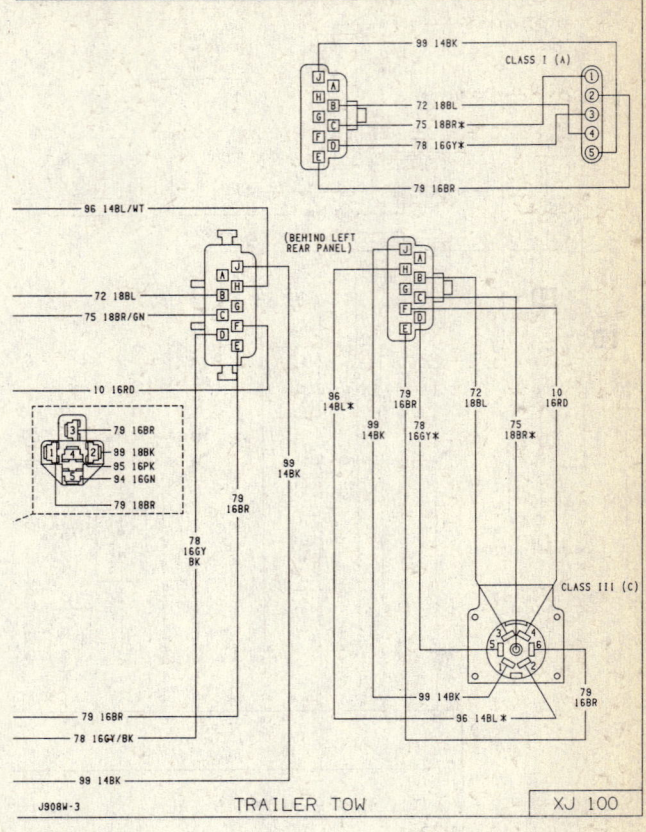

TRAILER TOW — XJ 100

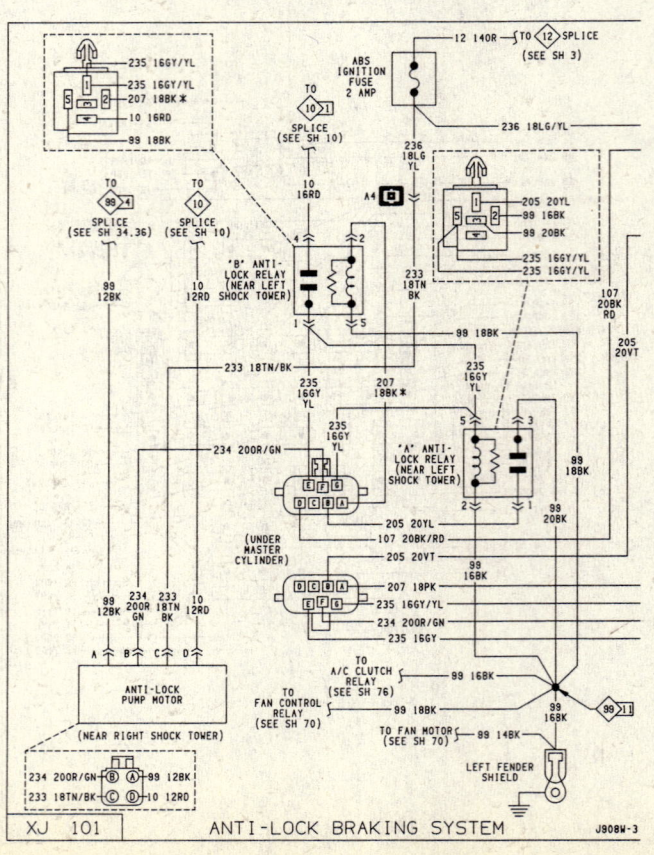

ANTI-LOCK BRAKING SYSTEM — XJ 101

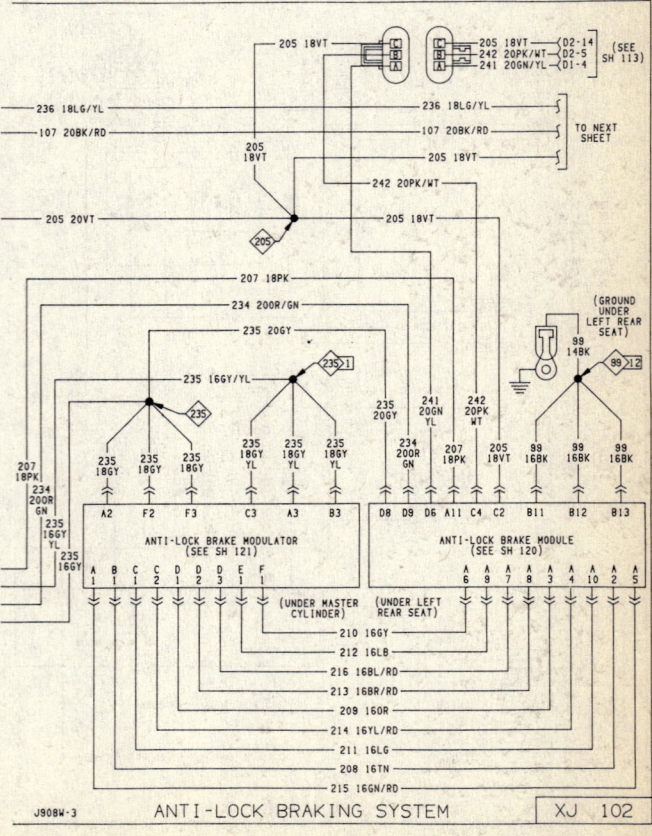

ANTI-LOCK BRAKING SYSTEM — XJ 102

6 CHASSIS ELECTRICAL

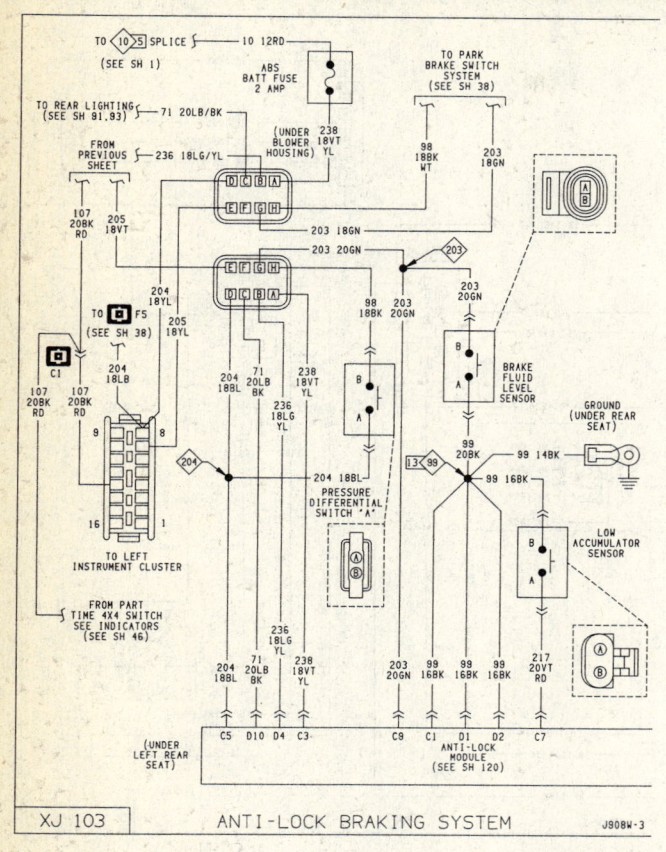

ANTI-LOCK BRAKING SYSTEM — XJ 103

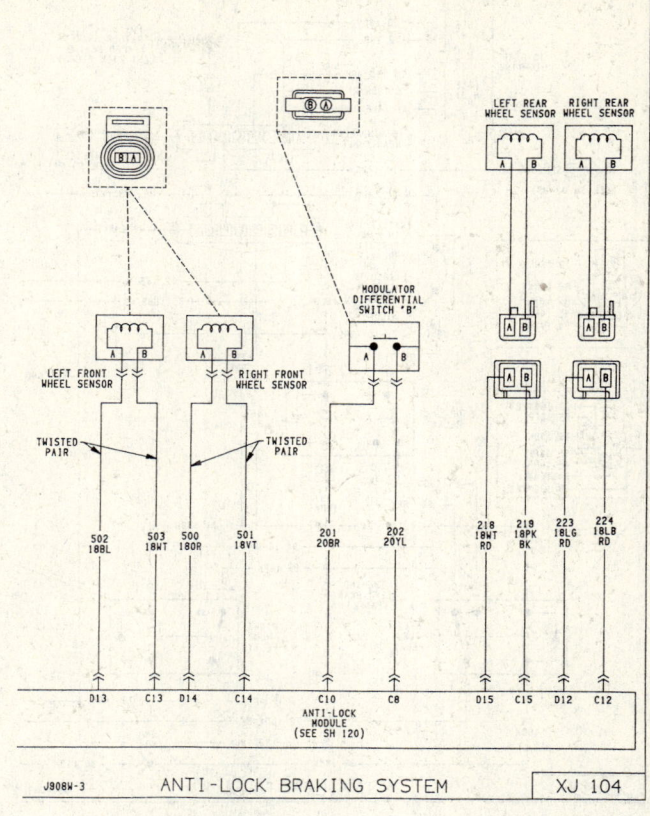

ANTI-LOCK BRAKING SYSTEM — XJ 104

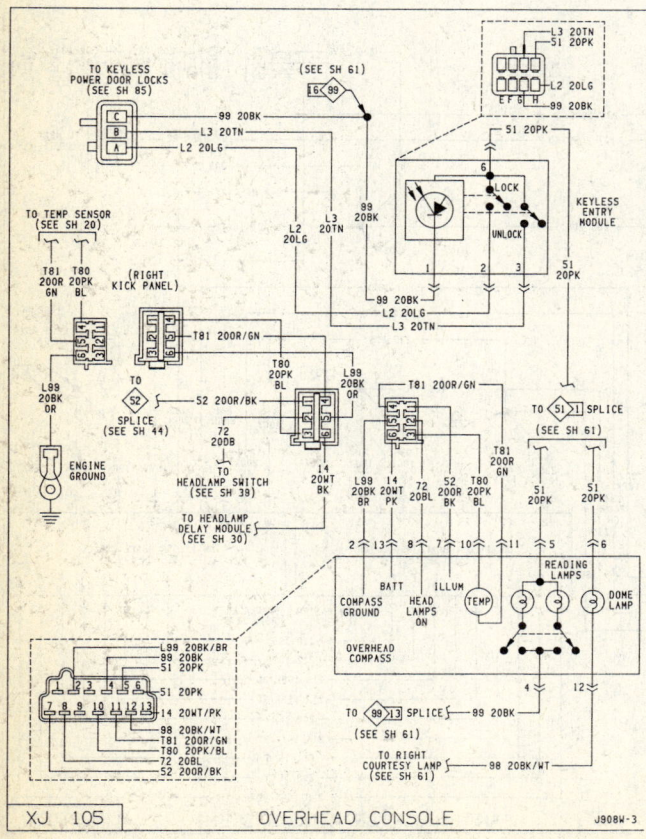

OVERHEAD CONSOLE — XJ 105

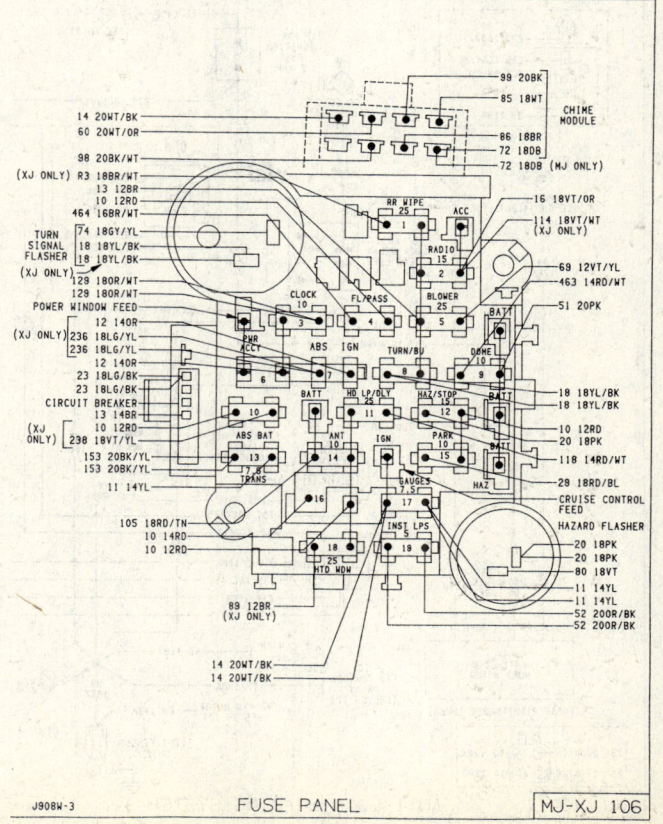

FUSE PANEL — MJ-XJ 106

CHASSIS ELECTRICAL 6

Fuse Panel (MJ-XJ 107)

FUSE NUMBER	AMPS	COLOR
1	25	WHITE
2	15	LIGHT BLUE
3	10	RED
4	15	LIGHT BLUE
5	25	WHITE
6	30 CIRCUIT BREAKER	SILVER CAN
7	2	PINK
8	20	YELLOW
9	10	RED
10	2	PINK
11	25	WHITE
12	15	LIGHT BLUE
13	7.5	VIOLET
14	10	RED
15	10	RED
16	30 CIRCUIT BREAKER	SILVER CAN
17	7.5	VIOLET
18	25	WHITE
19	5	TAN

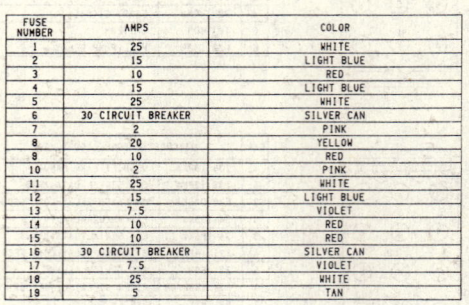

Bulkhead Connector (MJ-XJ 108)

ENGINE COMPARTMENT CIRCUITS		CAV
72 18GY*	LEFT TURN SIGNAL LAMPS	A1
126 20BR	ECU UPSHIFT INDICATOR-GROUND	A2
23 18LG*	WINDSHIELD WIPER-PARK FEED	A3
233 18TN/BK	ANTI-LOCK PUMP MOTOR	A4
—	—	A5
463 14RD*	BATTERY DRAIN DISCONNECT	A6
—	—	A7
72 18BL	PARKING LAMPS-FEED	B1
44 18VT*	WINDSHIELD WASHER PUMP FEED	B2
47 18BL*	WINDSHIELD WIPER-HI SPEED	B3
—	—	B4
106 18YL/BK	4 WHEEL DRIVE SWITCH	B5
11 14YL	IGNITION CIRCUITS	B6
107 20BK/RD	4 WHEEL DRIVE SWITCH	C1
107 20BK/RD	INSTRUMENT PANEL INDICATOR	C1
18 18YL/BK	NOT USED	C2
30 18GN*	IGNITION MODULE-TACHOMETER	C3
F22 14OR/BK	FUEL PUMP FEED	C4
75 18BR*	BACKUP LAMPS	C5
54 20LB	OIL PRESSURE	C6
10 12RD	BATTERY	D1
55 20VT	COOLANT TEMPERATURE	D2
10 12RD	BATTERY	D4
77 16LG	LO-BEAM HEADLAMPS	D5
10 12RD	BATTERY	E1
31 14GY	HORNS	E2
76 16WT	HI-BEAM HEADLAMPS	E4
37 12OR*	BLOWER MOTOR FEED	E5
76 18WT	HI-BEAM INDICATOR W/O DRL	F1
465 18LB/BK	HI-BEAM INDICATOR W/DRL	F1
79 18BR	RIGHT TURN SIGNAL LAMPS	F2
98 20BK*	BRAKE WARNING SWITCH W/O ABS	F3
13 14BR	NOT USED	F4
58 20GY*	BRAKE WARNING SWITCH W/O ABS	F5
58 18LB	BRAKE WARNING SWITCH W/DRL	F5
114 20VT*	WINDSHIELD WASHER FLUID LEVEL	F6
F5 18LG*	FOG LAMP RELAY	G1
59 20TN*	ALTERNATOR-BATTERY INDICATOR	G2
46 18WT*	WINDSHIELD WIPER-LO SPEED	G3
99 12BK	GROUND	G4
99 12BK	GROUND	G4
38 16TN*	A/C REQUEST	G5
12 14OR	NOT USED	G6
138 16LG	A/C SELECT	H1
33 14GN	STARTER RELAY	H2
45 18TN*	WINDSHIELD WIPER-PARK FEED	H3
49 16LG*	A/C LOW PRESSURE SWITCH	H4
R4 18 VT/OR	REAR WIPER PUMP MOTOR	H5
61 20WT*	WASHER FLUID LEVEL SWITCH	H6

Bulkhead Connector (MJ-XJ 109)

CAV	INSTRUMENT PANEL CIRCUITS	
A1	78 18GY/BK	LEFT TURN SIGNAL LAMPS
A2	126 20BK/LB	UPSHIFT INDICATOR LAMP
A3	23 18LG/BK	WINDSHIELD WIPER-PARK FEED
A4	236 18LG/YL	ANTI-LOCK PUMP FEED (MODEL XJ)
A5	—	—
A6	463 14RD/WT	BATTERY DRAIN DISCONNECT
A7	—	—
B1	72 18DB	PARKING LAMPS FEED
B1	72 18DB	CHIME/BUZZER-PARKING LAMPS ON
B2	44 18VT/WT	WINDSHIELD WASHER PUMP FEED
B3	47 18DB/WT	WINDSHIELD WIPER HI-SPEED
B4	—	—
B5	106 18BK/YL	FULL TIME INDICATOR LAMP
B6	11 14YL	IGNITION SWITCH I-1
C1	107 20BK/RD	PART TIME INDICATOR LAMP
C2	18 18YL/BK	BACKUP LAMPS FEED
C3	30 18GN/WT	TACHOMETER
C4	F9 14PK/BK	FUEL PUMP FEED (MODEL XJ)
C4	F22 14OR	FUEL INJECTOR (MODEL XJ)
C5	75 18BR/WT	REVERSE SWITCH
C6	54 20LB	OIL PRESSURE INDICATOR
D1	10 12RD	BATTERY
D2	55 20VT	COOLANT TEMPERATURE
D4	10 12RD	BATTERY
D5	77 16LG	DIMMER SWITCH-LO BEAM
E1	10 12RD	ACCESSORY POWER
E2	31 14GY	HORN RELAY
E4	76 16WT	DIMMER SWITCH-HI BEAM
E5	37 12OR/BL	BLOWER MOTOR FEED
F1	465 16LB/BK	HIGH BEAM INDICATOR W/DRL
F2	79 18BR	RIGHT TURN SIGNAL LAMPS
F3	98 20BK*	BRAKE INDICATOR W/O ABS (MODEL MJ)
F4	13 14BR	ACCESSORY IGNITION (EXPORT)
F5	58 20GY/RD	BRAKE INDICATOR (MODEL MJ)
F5	204 18BL	BRAKE WARNING W/ABS
F6	114 18VT/WT	WASHER FLUID LEVEL SWITCH FEED
G1	F1 16LG/BK	FOG LAMP SWITCH
G2	59 20TN/GN	BATTERY INDICATOR LAMP
G3	46 18WT/BK	WINDSHIELD WIPER-LO FEED
G4	99 12BK	INSTRUMENT PANEL GROUND
G4	—	—
G5	38 16TN/BK	A/C REQUEST
G6	12 14OR	I-3 IGNITION (EXPORT)
H1	138 16LG	A/C THERMOSTAT SWITCH
H2	33 14DG	IGNITION SWITCH-START
H3	45 18TN/BK	WINDSHIELD WIPERS-PARK FEED
H4	49 16LG/BK	A/C MODE SELECTOR SWITCH
H5	R4 18VT/OR	REAR WIPER SWITCH-WASH (MODEL XJ)
H6	61 20WT/GN	LOW WASHER INDICATOR (MODEL XJ)

(2.5L) 35 Way Engine Controller Connector (MJ-XJ 110)

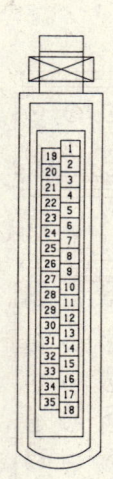

CAV		ECU SYSTEMS CIRCUITS
1	99 14BK	POWER GROUND
2	99 14BK	POWER GROUND
3	11 14YL	IGNITION
4	10 14RD	BATTERY
5	F18 14GN	EGR CONTROL
6	F17 20OR*	FUEL PUMP RELAY
7	F20 20BK*	LATCH RELAY
8	F78 18BL/OR	POWER STEERING INPUT
9	—	—
10	99 14BK	SYSTEM GROUND
11	F52 20RD*	ENGINE SPEED INPUT
12	34 18BK*	START SIGNAL (−)
13	F57 20BR*	TPS GROUND
14	F7 18TN*	AIR TEMPERATURE INPUT
15	F24 18TN	COOLANT TEMPERATURE INPUT
16	F2 20RD*	5 VOLT SUPPLY (TPS/MAP)
17	F56 20BK*	MAP GROUND
18	136 18PK*	UPSHIFT INDICATOR
19	F21 14PK	B+ LATCH
20	—	—
21	F1 16LB	INJECTOR CONTROL
22	135 16BL*	A/C CLUTCH CONTROL
23	F3 18BR	ISCA (RETRACT)
24	F4 18LG	ISCA (EXTEND)
25	F12 18GY*	CLOSED THROTTLE INPUT
26	—	—
27	F26 20OR*	TIMING OUTPUT
28	F53 20WT*	ENGINE SPEED INPUT
29	88 14GN*	START SIGNAL (+)
30	138 16LG	A/C SELECT
31	F50 20YL/GN	TPS INPUT
32	F15 18BR*	TEMPERATURE SENSORS GROUND
33	F14 20VT	MAP INPUT
34	38 20TN*	A/C REQUEST
35	F6 18GY	OXYGEN SENSOR INPUT

6-105

6 CHASSIS ELECTRICAL

CAV	ECU SYSTEMS CIRCUITS	
A1	F37 18TN	INJECTOR 3
A2	F76 18BR	INJECTOR 6
A3	F72 18LG	INJECTOR 2
A4	F74 18YL	INJECTOR 4
A5	F17 16OR*	FUEL PUMP RELAY GROUND
A6	—	—
A7	F86 16GY/YL	OXYGEN RELAY GROUND
A8	136 18PK*	UPSHIFT LAMP-MANUAL
A9	F20 16BK*	B+ LATCH RELAY GROUND
A10	F19 16GN*	EGR CONTROL
A11	—	—
A12	135 18BL*	A/C CLUTCH CONTROL
B1	F71 18LB	INJECTOR 1
B2	F75 18WT	INJECTOR 5
B3	F68 18RD/YL	AIS MOTOR (A)
B4	F67 18BL/YL	AIS MOTOR (D)
B5	F70 18GN/BK	AIS MOTOR (C)
B6	F69 18PK/BK	AIS MOTOR (B)
B7	10 16RD	BATTERY
B8	11 14YL	IGNITION
B9	—	—
B10	F21 16PK	B+ LATCHED
B11	99 16PK	GROUND
B12	99 16PK	GROUND

CAV	ECU SYSTEMS CIRCUITS	
C1	F52 18VT*	ENGINE SPEED INPUT
C2	38 16TN*	A/C REQUEST
C3	88 14GN*	START SIGNAL (+)
C4	34 18BK	START SIGNAL (−)
C5	F65 18GY*	SYNC SIGNAL
C6	F14 18VT	MAP INPUT
C7	F50 18YL/GN	TPS INPUT
C8	F7 18TN*	AIR TEMP INPUT
C9	—	—
C10	F24 18TN	COOLANT TEMP INPUT
C11	F22 16OR	INJECTOR FEED
C12	F83 16BR/PK	TX SERIAL DATA OUTPUT
C13	—	—
C14	F2 18RD*	MAP 5 VOLT SUPPLY
C15	F77 18LB	TPS 5 VOLT SUPPLY
C16	F66 18BL	SYNC 7.1 VOLT SUPPLY
D1	F53 18WT	ENGINE SPEED INPUT
D2	138 16LG	A/C SELECT
D3	F15 18BR*	SENSOR GROUND
D4	—	—
D5	—	—
D6	—	—
D7	—	—
D8	F55 18YL*	KNOCK SENSOR GROUND
D9	F6 18GY	OXYGEN SENSOR INPUT
D10	F22 16OR	INJECTOR FEED
D11	F84 16BK/WT	RX SERIAL DATA INPUT
D12	—	—
D13	F23 18YL	TIMING OUTPUT
D14	—	—
D15	—	—
D16	F54 18VT*	KNOCK SENSOR INPUT

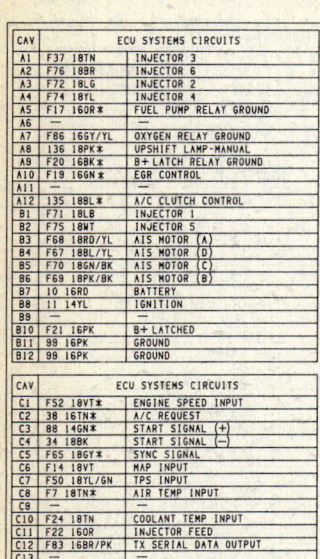
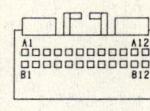
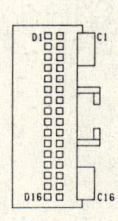

MJ-XJ 111 — (4.0L) 24 WAY/32 WAY ENGINE CONTROLLER CONNECTOR

CAV	DIAGNOSTIC CONNECTOR - #1	
1	30 18GN*	TACHOMETER
2	11 14YL	I-1 IGNITION SWITCH
3	99 14BK	ECU GROUND
4	88 14GN*	START SIGNAL (−)
5	10 14RD	BATTERY
6	F22 14OR	FUEL PUMP RELAY

CAV	DIAGNOSTIC CONNECTOR - #2	
1	136 18PK*	UPSHIFT LAMP-MANUAL
1	136 18PK*	ECU SERIAL DATA-AUTO
2	F20 20BK*	B+ LATCH RELAY-COIL GROUND
3	34 18BK*	PARK/NEUTRAL-AUTO
3	34 18BK*	ECU SERIAL DATA-MANUAL
4	F21 14PK	B+ LATCH-RELAY-COIL FEED
5	32 16OR	A/C CLUTCH RELAY
6	F78 18BL/OR	POWER STEERING PRES SWITCH
7	99 18BK	SYSTEM GROUND
8	F7 18TN*	AIR TEMPERATURE SENSOR
9	F26 18OR*	IGNITION TIMING
10	F18 14GN	EGR PURGE SOLENOID
11	F4 18LG	ISA-EXTENDED
12	F24 18TN	COOLANT TEMPERATURE SENSOR
13	F12 18GY*	ISA-CLOSED THROTTLE SWITCH
14	F3 18BR	ISA-RETRACT
15	137 16YL*	AUTO TRANS DIAGNOSIS

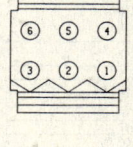
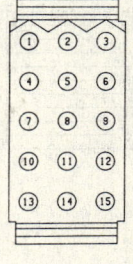

MJ-XJ 112 — (2.5L) 6 WAY AND 15 WAY DIAGNOSTIC CONNECTORS

CAV	DIAGNOSTIC CONNECTOR - #1	
1	30 18GN*	TACHOMETER
2	—	—
3	99 14BK	ECU GROUND
4	241 20GY/YL	ANTI-LOCK MODULE-DG
5	10 14RD	BATTERY
6	F22 14RD	FUEL PUMP RELAY

CAV	DIAGNOSTIC CONNECTOR - #2	
1	F83 16BR/PK	ECU-TX SERIAL DATA OUTPUT
2	F84 16BK/WT	ECU-RX SERIAL DATA INPUT
3	F20 16BK*	B+ LATCH RELAY-COIL GROUND
4	11 14YL	I-1 IGNITION SWITCH
5	242 20TN/BK	ANTI-LOCK MODULE-C4
6	32 16OR/BR	A/C CLUTCH RELAY
7	99 18BK	GROUND
8	F15 18BR*	SENSOR GROUND
9	63 14OR	OXYGEN HEATER RELAY
10	—	—
11	136 18PK*	UPSHIFT LAMP-MANUAL
12	F21 16PK	B+ LATCH RELAY (COIL FEED)
13	—	—
14	205 18VT	BRAKE ALERT-A.L.M. C2
15	136 16YL*	AUTO TRANS DIAGNOSIS-C4

MJ-XJ 113 — (4.0L) 6 WAY AND 15 WAY DIAGNOSTIC CONNECTORS

CAV	TCU SYSTEMS CIRCUITS	
C1	—	—
C2	—	—
C3	T9 18TN*	ROAD SPEED
C4	137 16YL*	TRANS DIAGNOSTIC CONNECTOR
C5	99 18BK	SHIFT POINT LOGIC GROUND
C6	—	—
C7	—	—
C8	T12 18LG	1-2 GEAR INPUT
C9	T11 18GY*	D GEAR INPUT
C10	116 18LB*	BRAKE/TORQUE CONVERTER
C11	177 18TN	POWER INPUT SIGNAL
C12	—	—
C13	—	—
C14	T8 18WT*	CONVERTER LOCKUP
C15	T7 18VT*	S2 SOLENOID
C16	T6 18BL*	S1 SOLENOID
D1	T3 18RD	TPS VOLTAGE SUPPLY
D2	T4 18GY*	TPS INPUT
D3	T5 18TN/OR	TPS GROUND
D4	—	—
D5	—	—
D6	—	—
D7	99 18BK	GROUND
D8	—	—
D9	—	—
D10	—	—
D11	—	—
D12	—	—
D13	—	—
D14	10 16RD	BATTERY
D15	—	—
D16	11 18YL	IGNITION

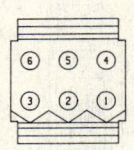
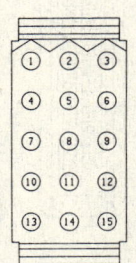

MJ-XJ 114 — (AUTOMATIC TRANSMISSION) 32 WAY SINGLE MODULE TRANSMISSION CONTROLLER CONNECTOR

CHASSIS ELECTRICAL 6

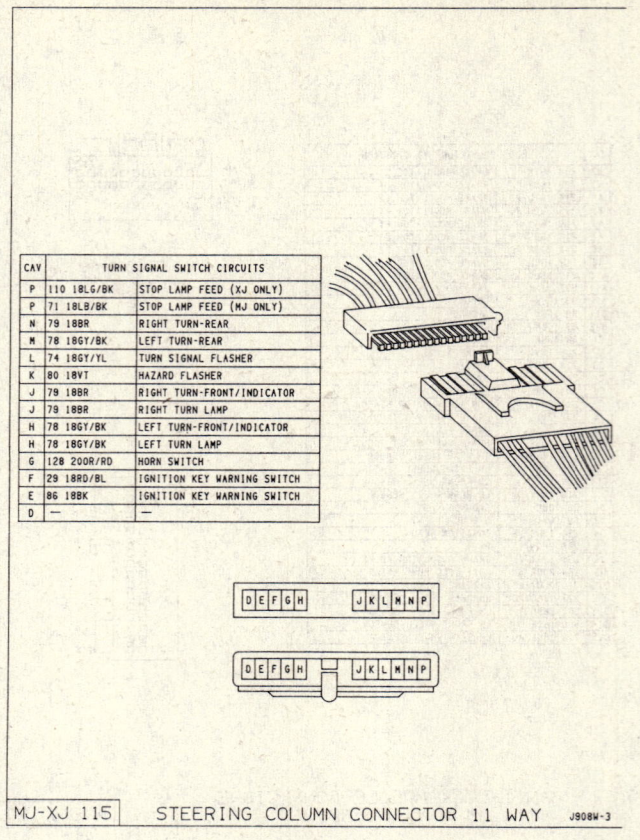

CAV		TURN SIGNAL SWITCH CIRCUITS
P	110 18LG/BK	STOP LAMP FEED (XJ ONLY)
P	71 18LB/BK	STOP LAMP FEED (MJ ONLY)
N	79 18BR	RIGHT TURN-REAR
M	78 18GY/BK	LEFT TURN-REAR
L	74 18GY/YL	TURN SIGNAL FLASHER
K	80 18VT	HAZARD FLASHER
J	79 18BR	RIGHT TURN-FRONT/INDICATOR
J	79 18BR	RIGHT TURN LAMP
H	78 18GY/BK	LEFT TURN-FRONT/INDICATOR
H	78 18GY/BK	LEFT TURN LAMP
G	128 20OR/RD	HORN SWITCH
F	29 18RD/BL	IGNITION KEY WARNING SWITCH
E	86 18BK	IGNITION KEY WARNING SWITCH
D	—	—

MJ-XJ 115 STEERING COLUMN CONNECTOR 11 WAY

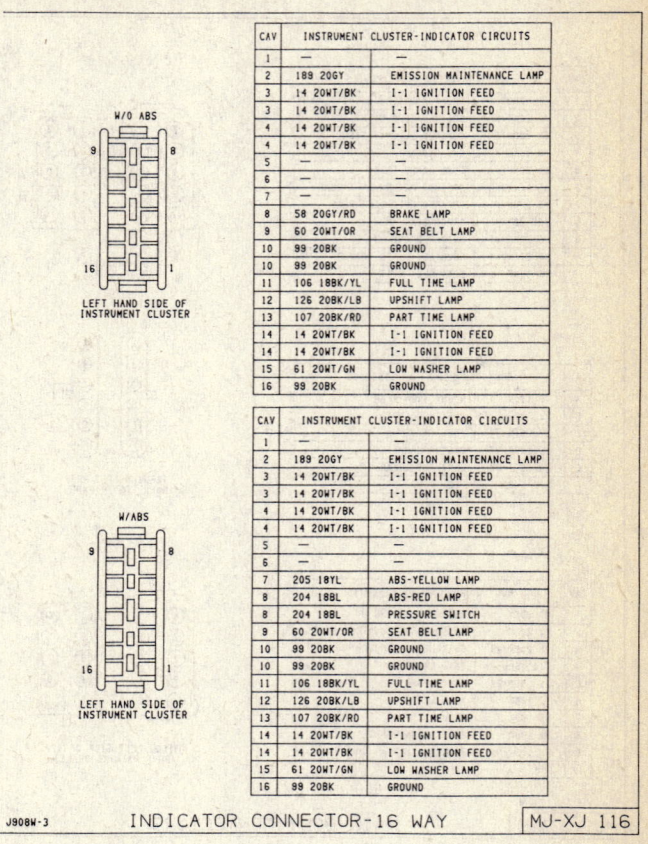

W/O ABS — LEFT HAND SIDE OF INSTRUMENT CLUSTER

CAV		INSTRUMENT CLUSTER-INDICATOR CIRCUITS
1	—	—
2	189 20GY	EMISSION MAINTENANCE LAMP
3	14 20WT/BK	I-1 IGNITION FEED
3	14 20WT/BK	I-1 IGNITION FEED
4	14 20WT/BK	I-1 IGNITION FEED
4	14 20WT/BK	I-1 IGNITION FEED
5	—	—
6	—	—
7	—	—
8	58 20GY/RD	BRAKE LAMP
9	60 20WT/OR	SEAT BELT LAMP
10	99 20BK	GROUND
10	99 20BK	GROUND
11	106 18BK/YL	FULL TIME LAMP
12	126 20BK/LB	UPSHIFT LAMP
13	107 20BK/RD	PART TIME LAMP
14	14 20WT/BK	I-1 IGNITION FEED
14	14 20WT/BK	I-1 IGNITION FEED
15	61 20WT/GN	LOW WASHER LAMP
16	99 20BK	GROUND

W/ABS — LEFT HAND SIDE OF INSTRUMENT CLUSTER

CAV		INSTRUMENT CLUSTER-INDICATOR CIRCUITS
1	—	—
2	189 20GY	EMISSION MAINTENANCE LAMP
3	14 20WT/BK	I-1 IGNITION FEED
3	14 20WT/BK	I-1 IGNITION FEED
4	14 20WT/BK	I-1 IGNITION FEED
4	14 20WT/BK	I-1 IGNITION FEED
5	—	—
6	—	—
7	205 18YL	ABS-YELLOW LAMP
8	204 18BL	ABS-RED LAMP
8	204 18BL	PRESSURE SWITCH
9	60 20WT/OR	SEAT BELT LAMP
10	99 20BK	GROUND
10	99 20BK	GROUND
11	106 18BK/YL	FULL TIME LAMP
12	126 20BK/LB	UPSHIFT LAMP
13	107 20BK/RD	PART TIME LAMP
14	14 20WT/BK	I-1 IGNITION FEED
14	14 20WT/BK	I-1 IGNITION FEED
15	61 20WT/GN	LOW WASHER LAMP
16	99 20BK	GROUND

INDICATOR CONNECTOR-16 WAY MJ-XJ 116

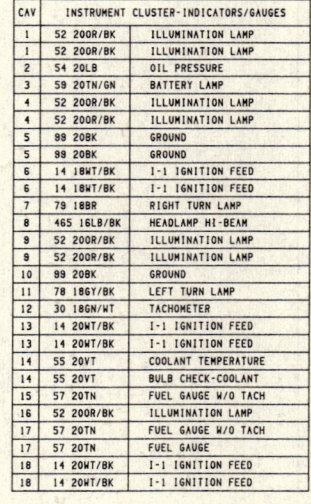

RIGHT HAND SIDE OF INSTRUMENT CLUSTER

CAV		INSTRUMENT CLUSTER-INDICATORS/GAUGES
1	52 20OR/BK	ILLUMINATION LAMP
1	52 20OR/BK	ILLUMINATION LAMP
2	54 20LB	OIL PRESSURE
3	59 20TN/GN	BATTERY LAMP
4	52 20OR/BK	ILLUMINATION LAMP
4	52 20OR/BK	ILLUMINATION LAMP
5	99 20BK	GROUND
5	99 20BK	GROUND
6	14 18WT/BK	I-1 IGNITION FEED
6	14 18WT/BK	I-1 IGNITION FEED
7	79 18BR	RIGHT TURN LAMP
8	465 16LB/BK	HEADLAMP HI-BEAM
9	52 20OR/BK	ILLUMINATION LAMP
9	52 20OR/BK	ILLUMINATION LAMP
10	99 20BK	GROUND
11	78 18GY/BK	LEFT TURN LAMP
12	30 18GN/WT	TACHOMETER
13	14 20WT/BK	I-1 IGNITION FEED
13	14 20WT/BK	I-1 IGNITION FEED
14	55 20VT	COOLANT TEMPERATURE
14	55 20VT	BULB CHECK-COOLANT
15	57 20TN	FUEL GAUGE W/O TACH
16	52 20OR/BK	ILLUMINATION LAMP
17	57 20TN	FUEL GAUGE W/O TACH
17	57 20TN	FUEL GAUGE
18	14 20WT/BK	I-1 IGNITION FEED
18	14 20WT/BK	I-1 IGNITION FEED

MJ-XJ 117 INSTRUMENT CLUSTER CONNECTOR-18 WAY

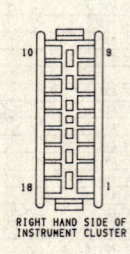

BLACK BODY CONNECTOR (LEFT HAND KICK PANEL)

CAV		BODY CONNECTOR-#1 CIRCUITS
1	58 20GY/RD	PARK BRAKE SWITCH
1	203 18GN	PARK BRAKE SWITCH (ABS)
2	51 20PK	CARGO LAMP FEED
3	71 18LB/BK	STOP LAMPS
4	72 18DB	ILLUMINATION RELAY
4	72 18DB	PARKING LAMPS
5	79 18BR	RIGHT TURN-REAR
6	57 20TN	FUEL GAUGE
7	75 18BR/WT	BACKUP LAMPS
8	98 20BK/WT	LEFT FRONT DOOR JAMB SWITCH
8	98 20BK/WT	COURTESY LAMPS
9	78 18GY/BK	LEFT TURN-REAR
10	85 18WT	SEAT BELT SWITCH

GRAY BODY CONNECTOR (LEFT HAND KICK PANEL)

CAV		BODY CONNECTOR-#2 CIRCUITS
1	A11 20BR	SPEAKER RETURN-RIGHT REAR
2	A3 20WT/BK	SPEAKER FEED-RIGHT REAR
3	52 20OR/BK	CONSOLE ILLUMINATION
4	R1 18GN/WT	REAR WIPER MOTOR-RUN
5	110 18LG/BK	STOP LAMPS
6	A10 20BR/WT	SPEAKER RETURN-LEFT REAR
7	A5 20GN/WT	SPEAKER FEED-LEFT REAR
8	62 12BR/WT	REAR DEFOGGER FEED
9	R2 18YL/BK	REAR WIPER-PARK FEED
10	F9 14PK/BK	FUEL PUMP

MAIN BODY CONNECTORS MJ-XJ 118

6-107

6 CHASSIS ELECTRICAL

CAV	BODY CONNECTOR- #3 CIRCUITS	
1	A11 20BR	SPEAKER RETURN-RIGHT REAR
2	A3 20WT/BK	SPEAKER FEED-RIGHT REAR
3	52 20OR/BK	CONSOLE ILLUMINATION
4	99 14BK	CAB GROUND
5	51 20PK	DOME LAMPS FEED
6	A10 20BR/WT	SPEAKER RETURN-LEFT REAR
7	A5 20GN/WT	SPEAKER FEED-LEFT REAR
8	148 20PK*	CARGO BOX LAMP
9	98 20BK/WT	SWITCHED GROUND
9	98 20BK/WT	COURTESY LAMPS GROUND
10	85 18WT	SEAT BELT SWITCH

CAV	BODY CONNECTOR- #4 CIRCUITS	
A	79 18BR	RIGHT TURN-REAR
B	72 18DB	PARKING LAMPS
C	57 20TN	FUEL GAUGE
D	75 18BR/WT	BACKUP LAMPS
E	78 18GY/BK	LEFT TURN-REAR
F	F22 14OR	FUEL PUMP

CAV	BODY CONNECTOR- #5 CIRCUITS	
1	97 20GY	SWITCHED GROUND
2	51 20PK	FUSED B+ TO COURTESY LAMPS
3	98 20BK/WT	SWITCHED GROUND
4	110 16LB/BK	TAIL LAMPS
5	71 18LB/BK	STOP LAMPS
6	72 18BL	TAIL LAMPS
7	99 18BK	GROUND
8	79 18BR	RIGHT TURN LAMPS
9	75 18BR/WT	BACKUP LAMPS
10	—	—

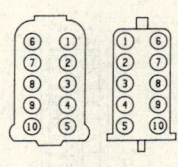
(BEHIND RIGHT REAR PANEL)

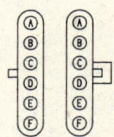
(BEHIND LEFT REAR INNER FENDER PANEL)

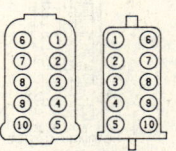
(BELOW LEFT SIDE OF I/P ABOVE PARKING BRAKE)

MJ-XJ 119 MAIN BODY CONNECTORS J908W-3

CAV	BODY CONNECTOR- #3 CIRCUITS	
A2	208 16TN	BRAKE MODULATOR B1
A3	209 16OR	BRAKE MODULATOR D1
A4	214 16YL/RD	BRAKE MODULATOR C2
A5	215 16GN/RD	BRAKE MODULATOR A1
A6	210 16GY	BRAKE MODULATOR F1
A7	216 16BL/RD	BRAKE MODULATOR D3
A8	213 16BR/RD	BRAKE MODULATOR D2
A9	212 16BL	BRAKE MODULATOR E1
A10	211 16LG	BRAKE MODULATOR C1
A11	207 18PK	ANTI-LOCK RELAY B
A12	99 16BK	GROUND
B11	99 16BK	GROUND
B12	99 16BK	GROUND
C1	99 16BK	GROUND
C2	205 18VT	BRAKE ALERT
C3	238 18VT/YL	BATTERY
C4	242 20PK/WT	D2-5
C5	204 18BL	LOW BRAKE PRESSURE WARNING
C7	217 20VT/YL	LOW ACCUMULATOR SENSOR
C8	202 20YL	BRAKE PUMP BOOST PRESSURE
C9	203 20GN	BRAKE FLUID LEVEL
C10	201 20BR	BRAKE PUMP BOOST PRESSURE
C12	224 18LB/RD	RH REAR WHEEL SENSOR
C13	503 18WT	LH FRONT WHEEL SENSOR
C14	501 18VT	RH FRONT WHEEL SENSOR
C15	219 18PK/BK	LH REAR WHEEL SENSOR
D1	99 16BK	GROUND
D2	99 16BK	GROUND
D4	236 18LG/YL	IGNITION FEED
D6	241 20GN/YL	D1-4
D8	235 18GY/YL	BRAKE MODULATOR A2,F2,F3
D9	234 20OR/GN	ANTI-LOCK PUMP MOTOR
D10	71 20LB/BK	PARKING BRAKE
D12	223 18LG/RD	RH REAR WHEEL SENSOR
D13	502 18BL	LH FRONT WHEEL SENSOR
D14	500 18OR	RH FRONT WHEEL SENSOR
D15	218 18WT/RD	LH REAR WHEEL SENSOR

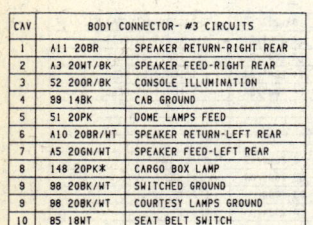

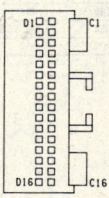

MJ-XJ 120 ANTI-LOCK MODULE CONNECTORS 24 WAY AND 32 WAY J908W-3

CAV	BRAKE MODULE	
A1	215 16GN/RD	A.L.M. A5
A2	235 18GY	SPLICE 235
A3	235 18GY/YL	SPLICE 235-1
B1	208 16TN	A.L.M. A2
B2	—	—
B3	235 18GY/YL	SPLICE 235-1
C1	211 16LG	A.L.M. A10
C2	214 16YL/RD	A.L.M. A4
C3	235 18GY/YL	SPLICE 235-1
D1	209 16OR	A.L.M. A3
D2	213 16BR/RD	A.L.M. A8
D3	216 18BL/RD	A.L.M. A7
E1	212 16LB	A.L.M. A9
F1	210 16GY	A.L.M. A6
F2	235 18GY	SPLICE 235-1
F3	235 18GY	SPLICE 235-1

MJ-XJ 121 BRAKE MODULE 18 WAY J908W-3

CHASSIS ELECTRICAL 6

1991 WIRING DIAGRAMS

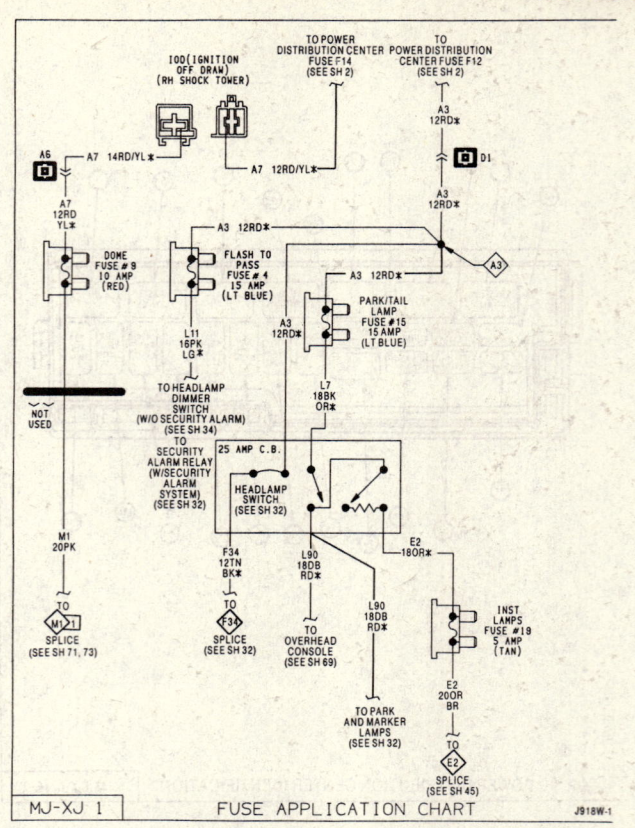
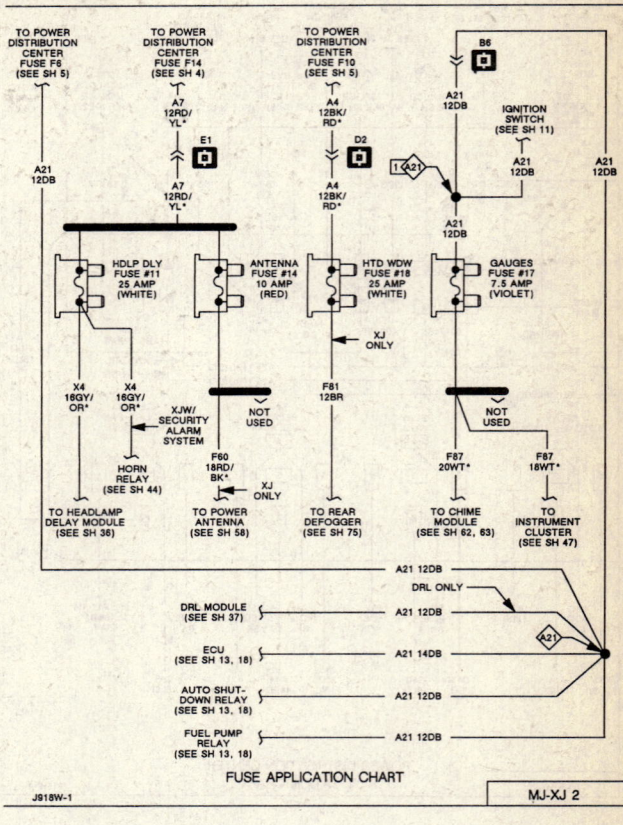
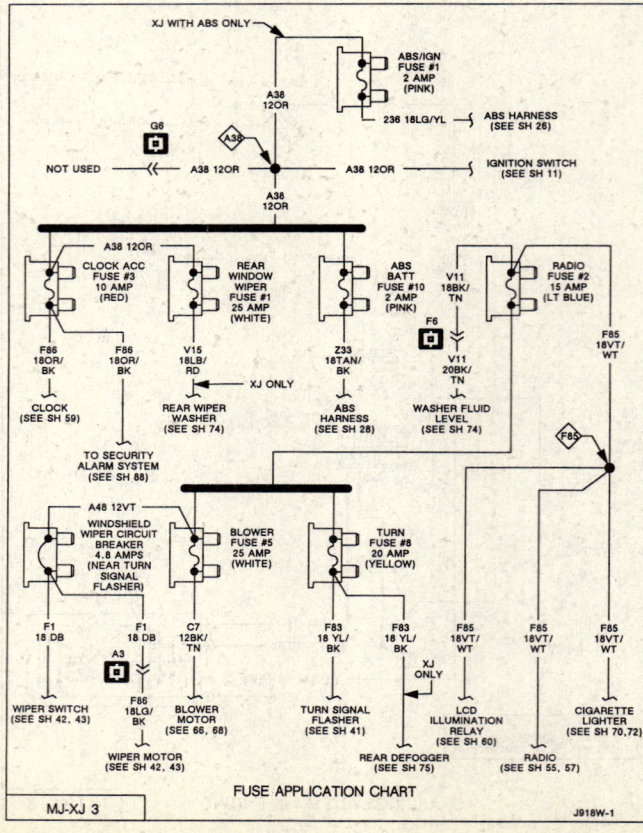
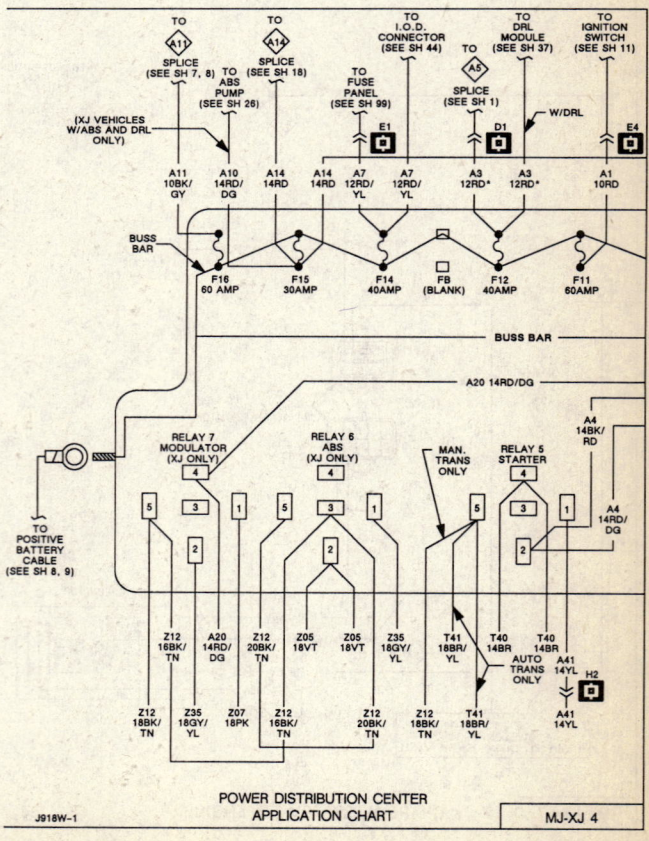

6-109

6 CHASSIS ELECTRICAL

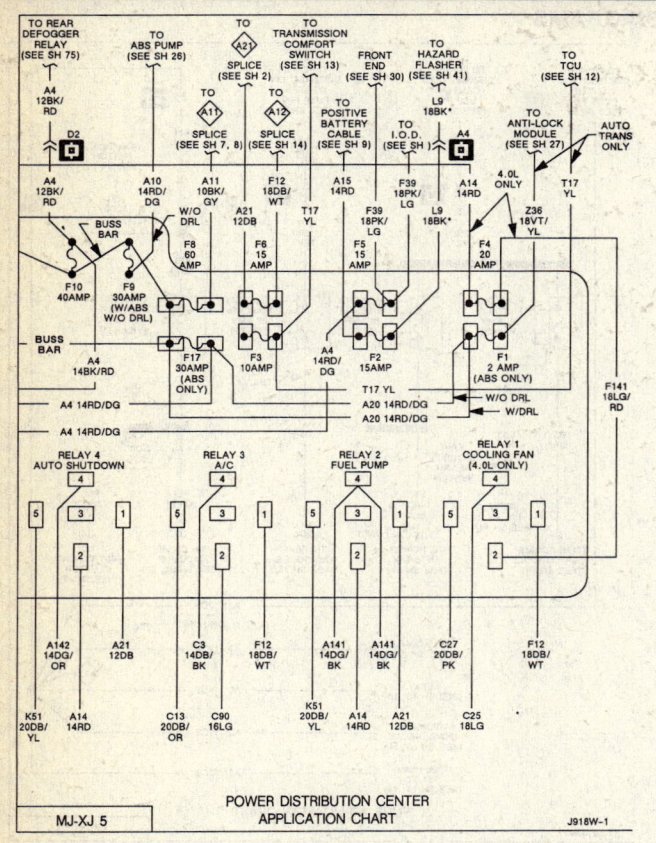

POWER DISTRIBUTION CENTER APPLICATION CHART — MJ-XJ 5

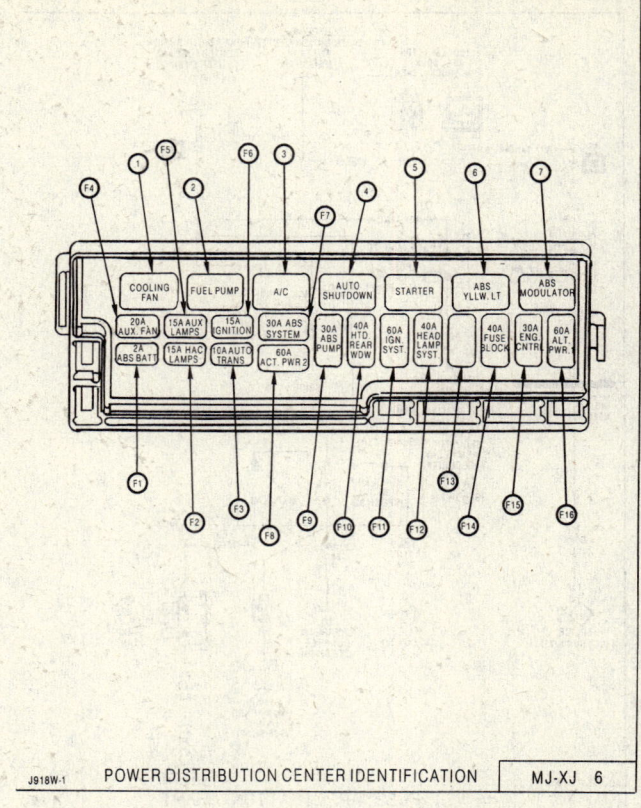

POWER DISTRIBUTION CENTER IDENTIFICATION — MJ-XJ 6

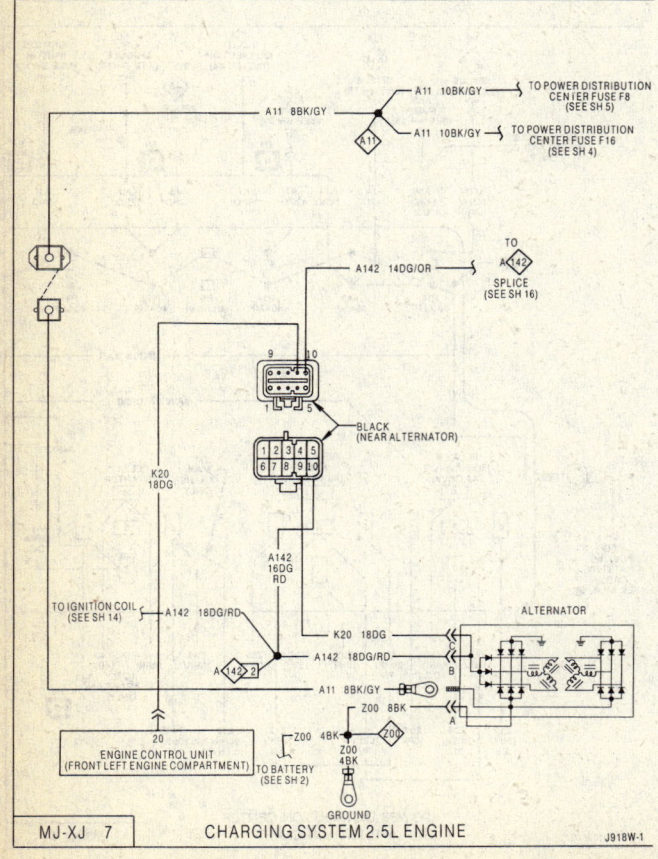

CHARGING SYSTEM 2.5L ENGINE — MJ-XJ 7

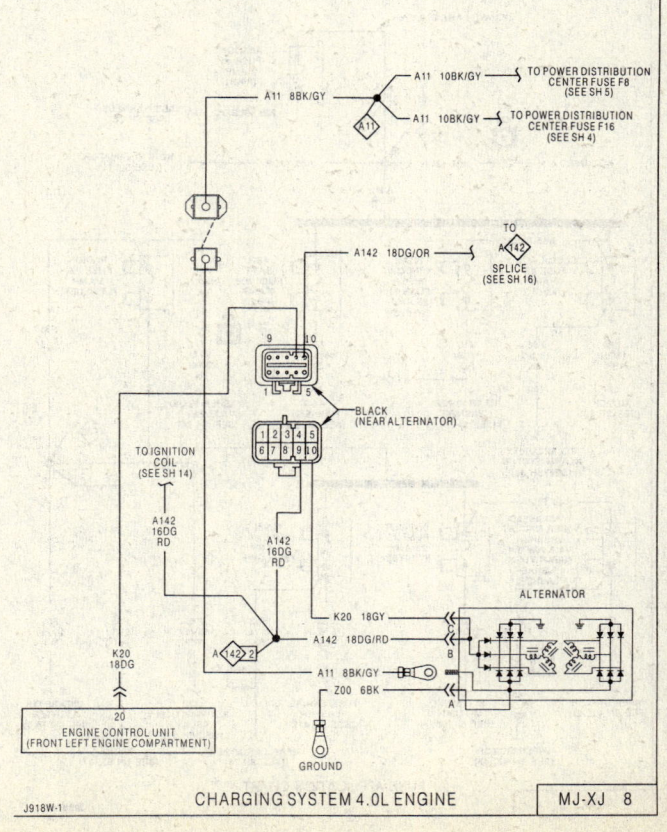

CHARGING SYSTEM 4.0L ENGINE — MJ-XJ 8

CHASSIS ELECTRICAL 6

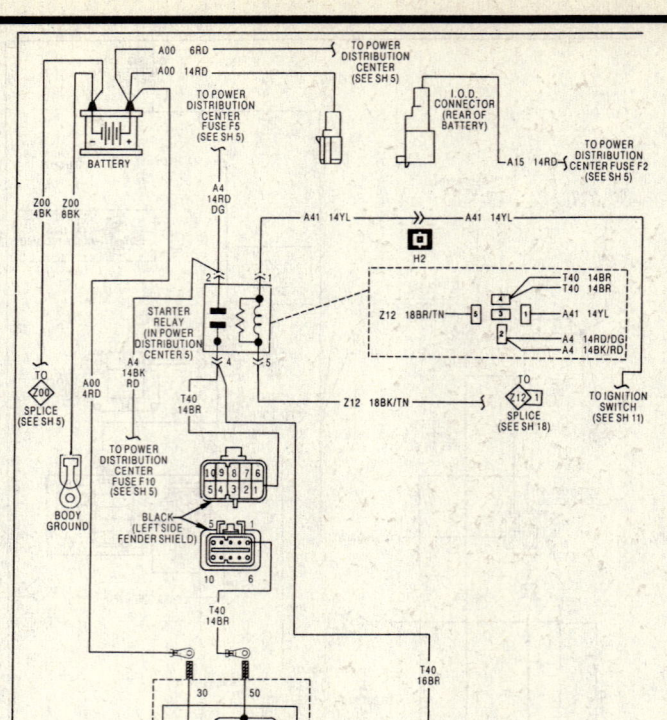

2.5L STARTER SYSTEM

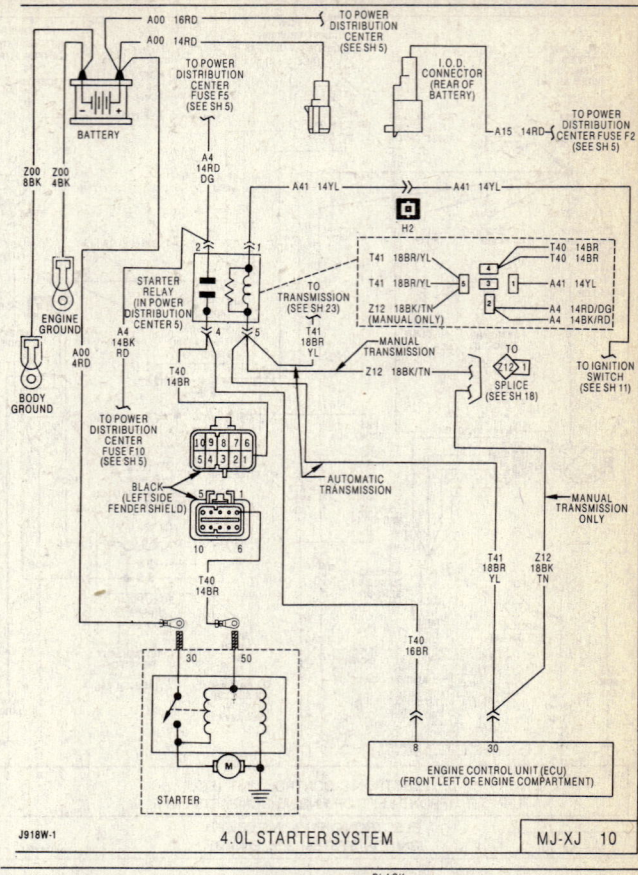

4.0L STARTER SYSTEM

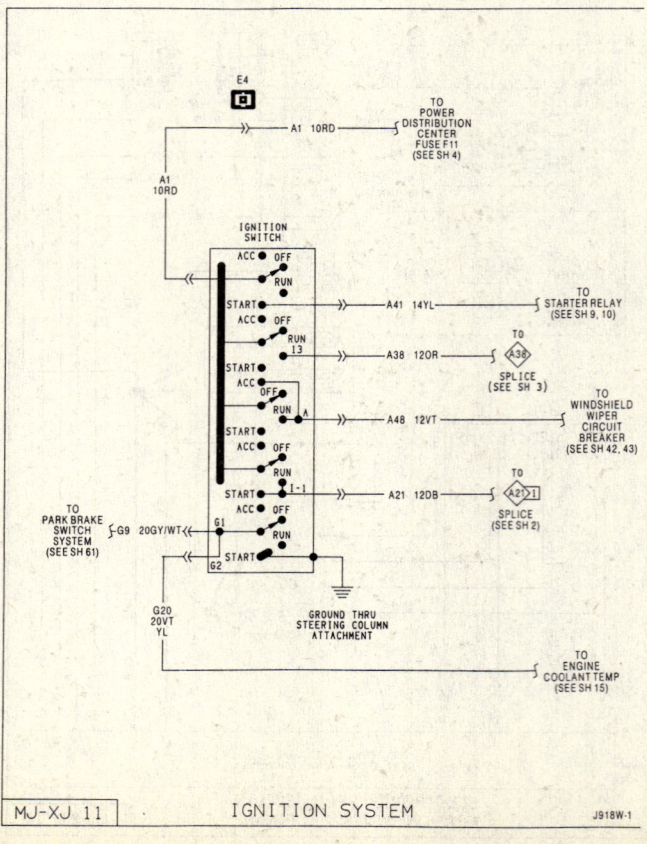

IGNITION SYSTEM

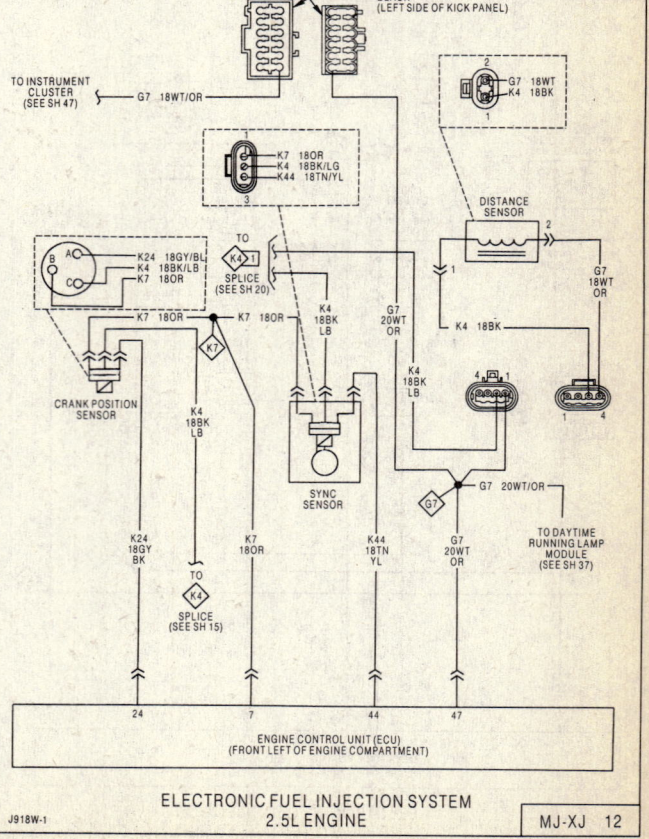

ELECTRONIC FUEL INJECTION SYSTEM
2.5L ENGINE

6 CHASSIS ELECTRICAL

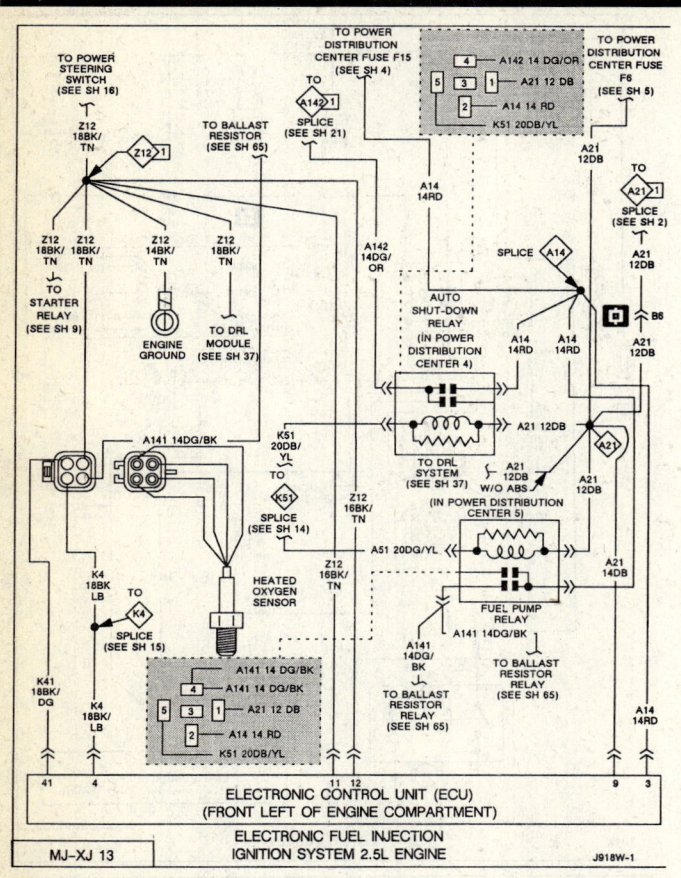
ELECTRONIC FUEL INJECTION IGNITION SYSTEM 2.5L ENGINE

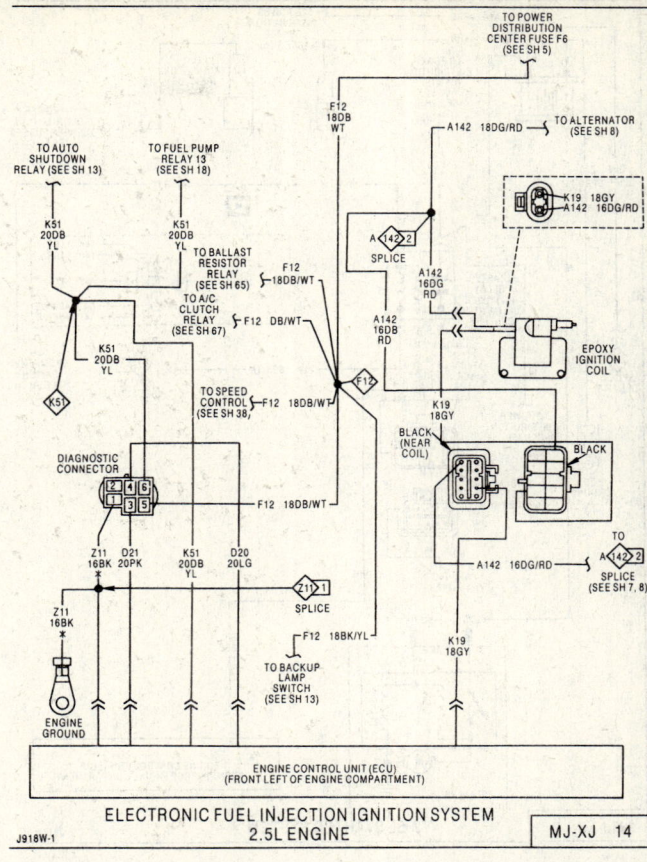
ELECTRONIC FUEL INJECTION IGNITION SYSTEM 2.5L ENGINE

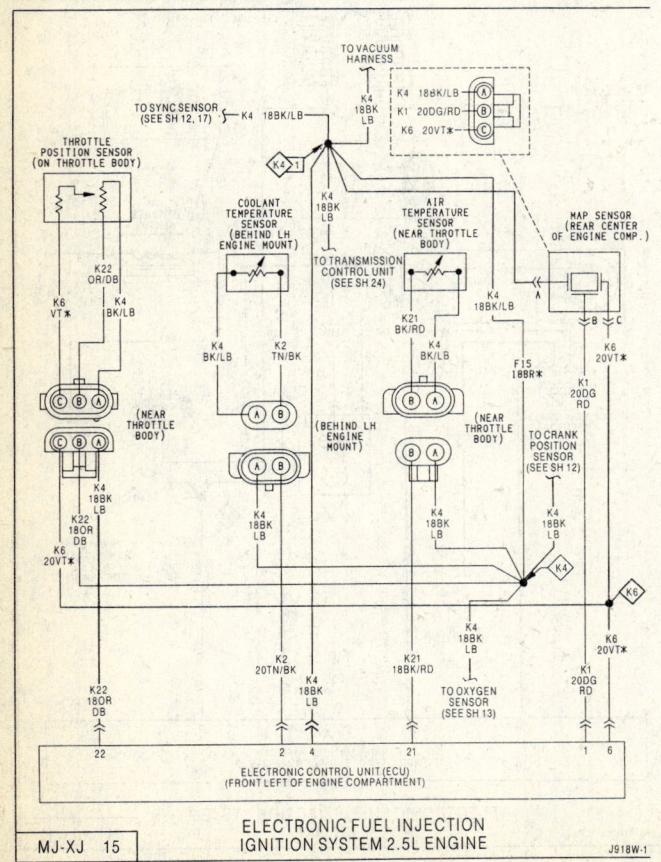
ELECTRONIC FUEL INJECTION IGNITION SYSTEM 2.5L ENGINE

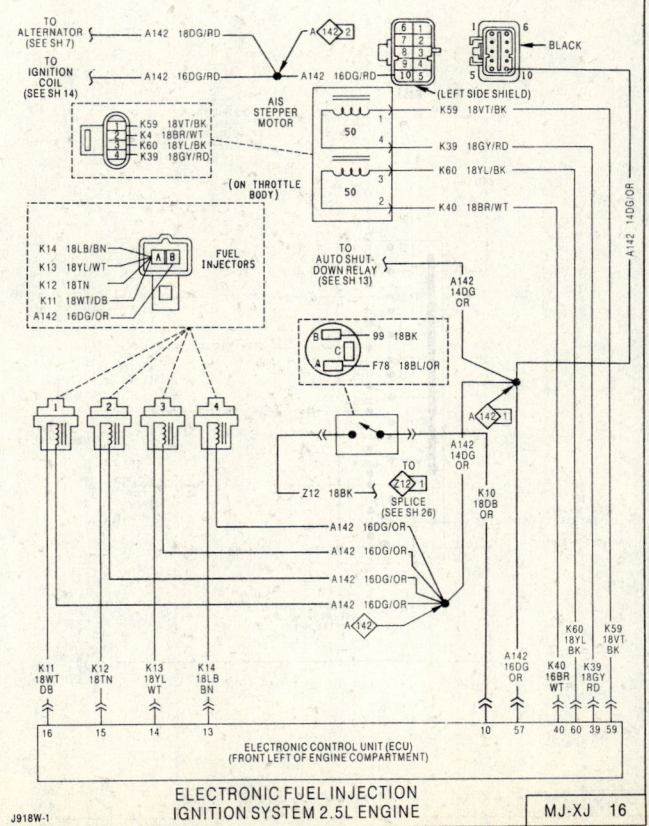
ELECTRONIC FUEL INJECTION IGNITION SYSTEM 2.5L ENGINE

CHASSIS ELECTRICAL 6

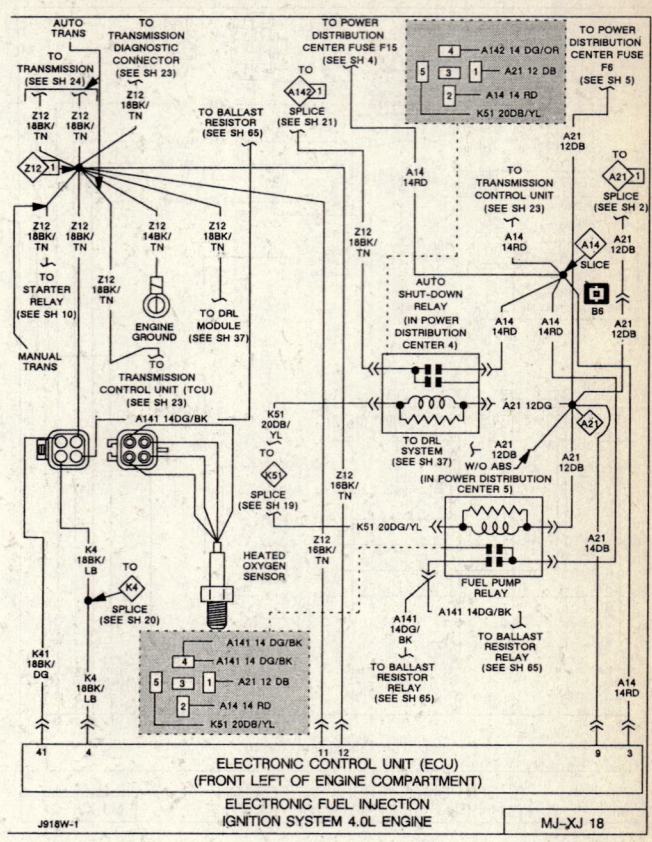
ELECTRONIC FUEL INJECTION
IGNITION SYSTEM 4.0L ENGINE
MJ-XJ 18

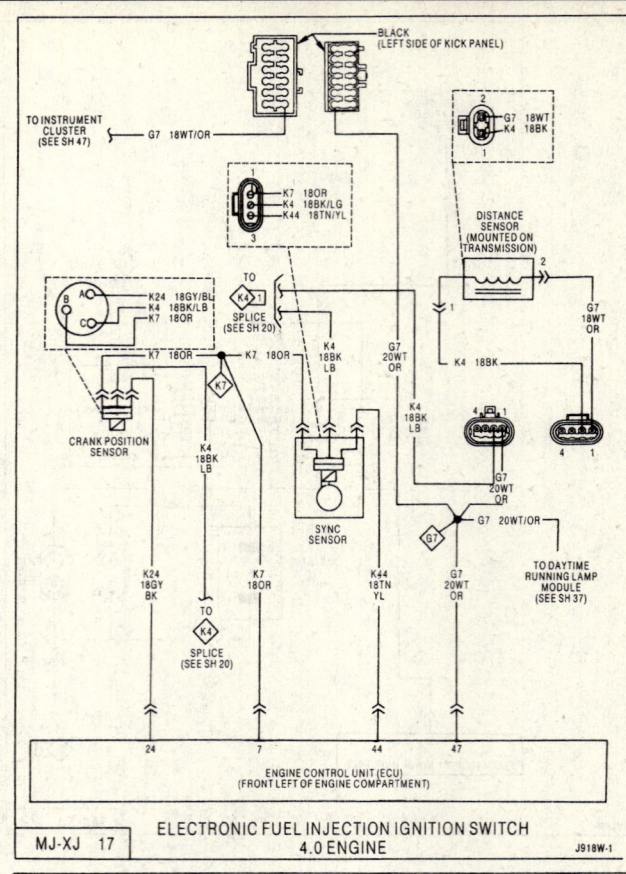
ELECTRONIC FUEL INJECTION IGNITION SWITCH
4.0 ENGINE
MJ-XJ 17

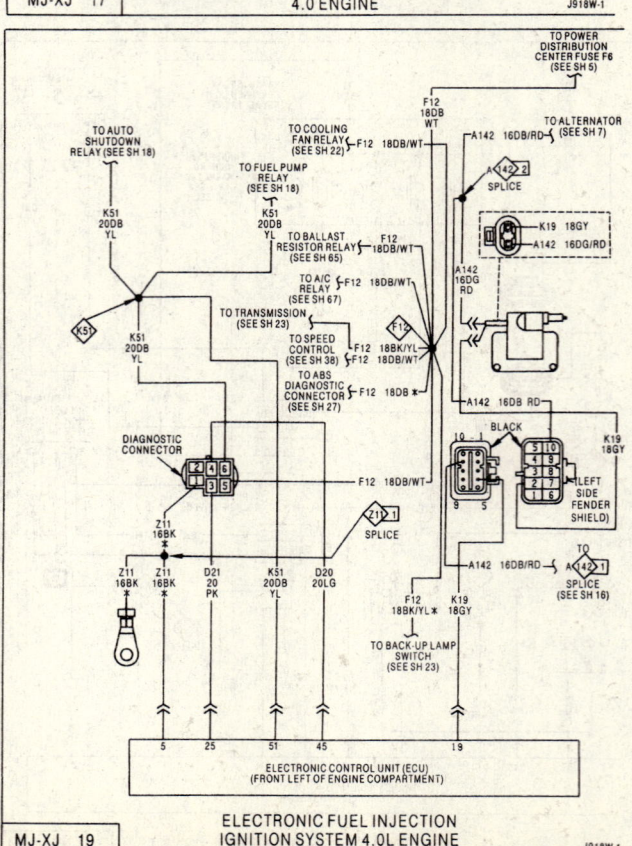
ELECTRONIC FUEL INJECTION
IGNITION SYSTEM 4.0L ENGINE
MJ-XJ 19

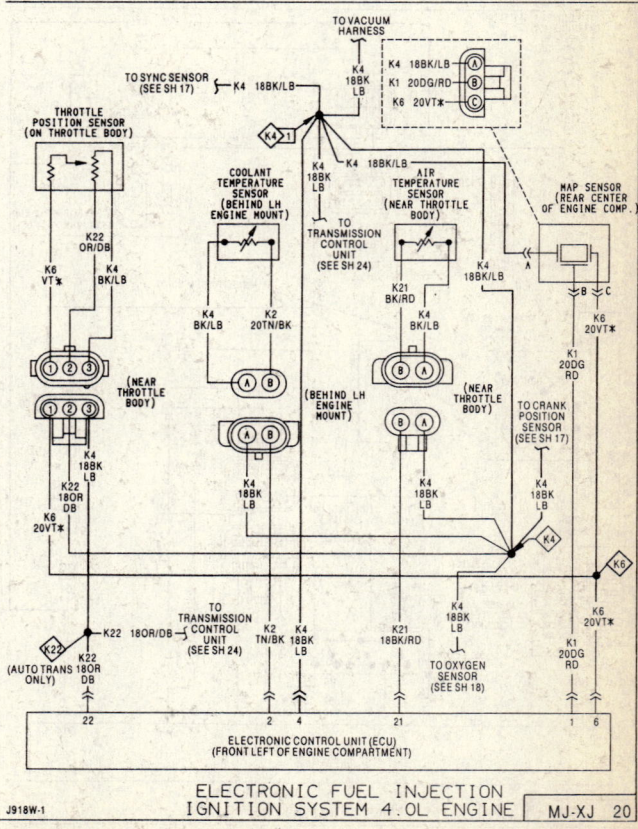
ELECTRONIC FUEL INJECTION
IGNITION SYSTEM 4.0L ENGINE
MJ-XJ 20

6 CHASSIS ELECTRICAL

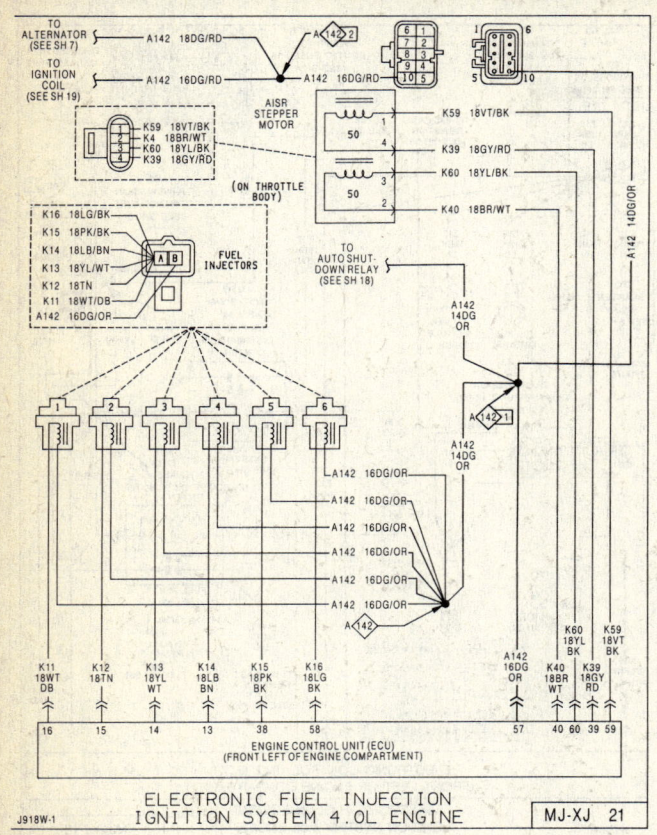
ELECTRONIC FUEL INJECTION IGNITION SYSTEM 4.0L ENGINE — MJ-XJ 21

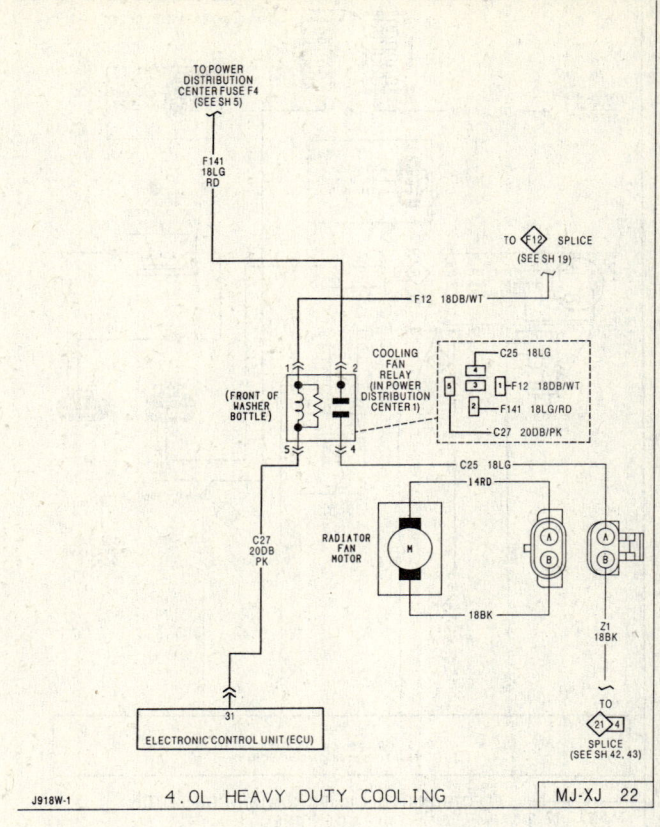
4.0L HEAVY DUTY COOLING — MJ-XJ 22

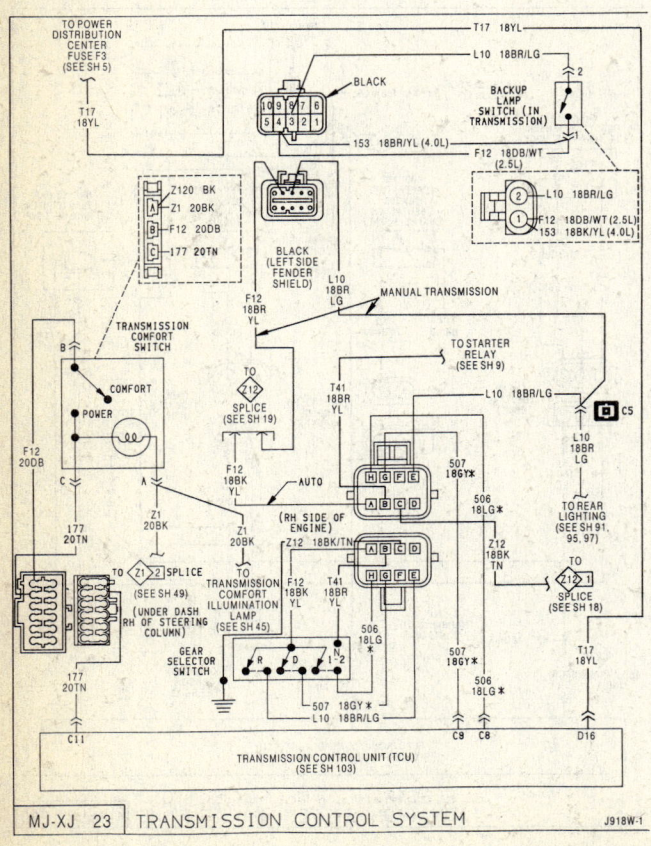
TRANSMISSION CONTROL SYSTEM — MJ-XJ 23

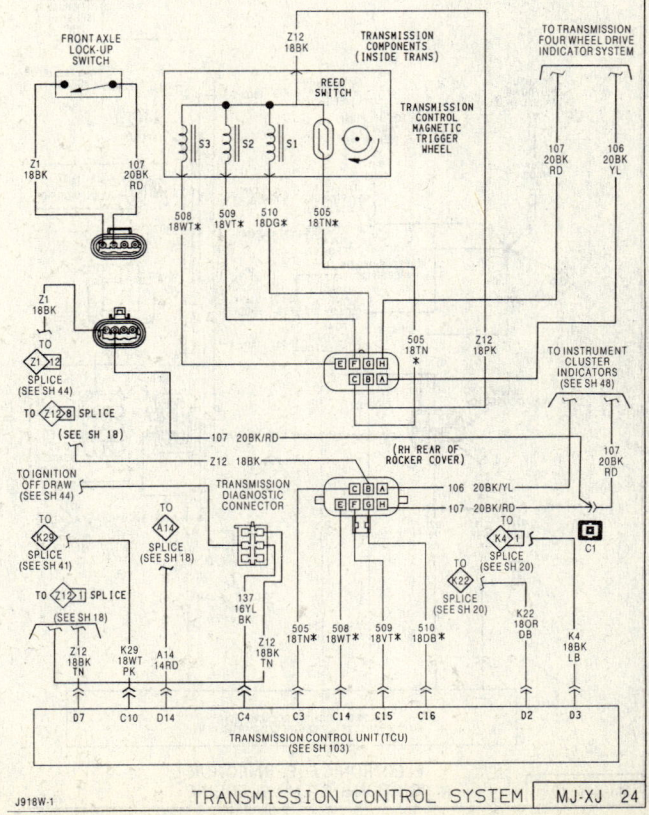
TRANSMISSION CONTROL SYSTEM — MJ-XJ 24

CHASSIS ELECTRICAL 6

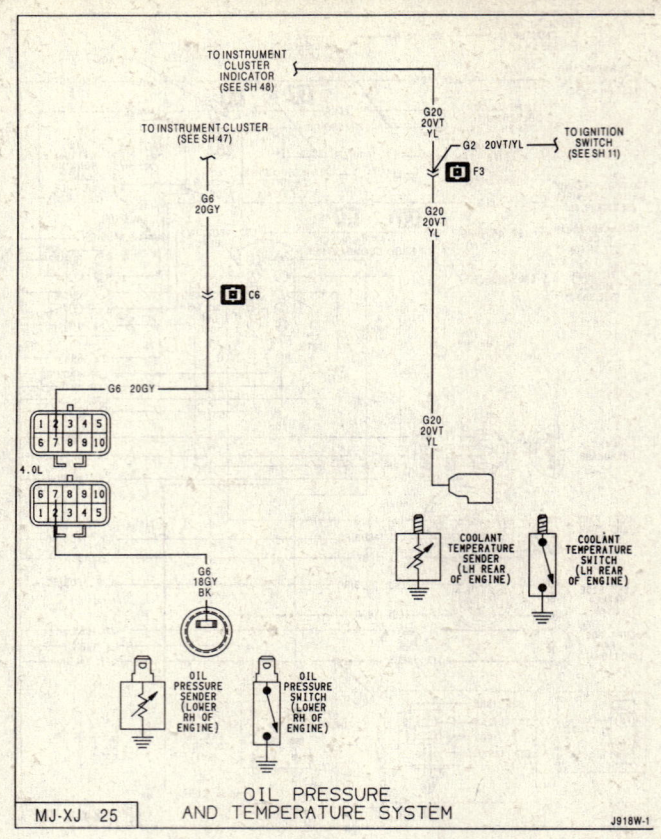
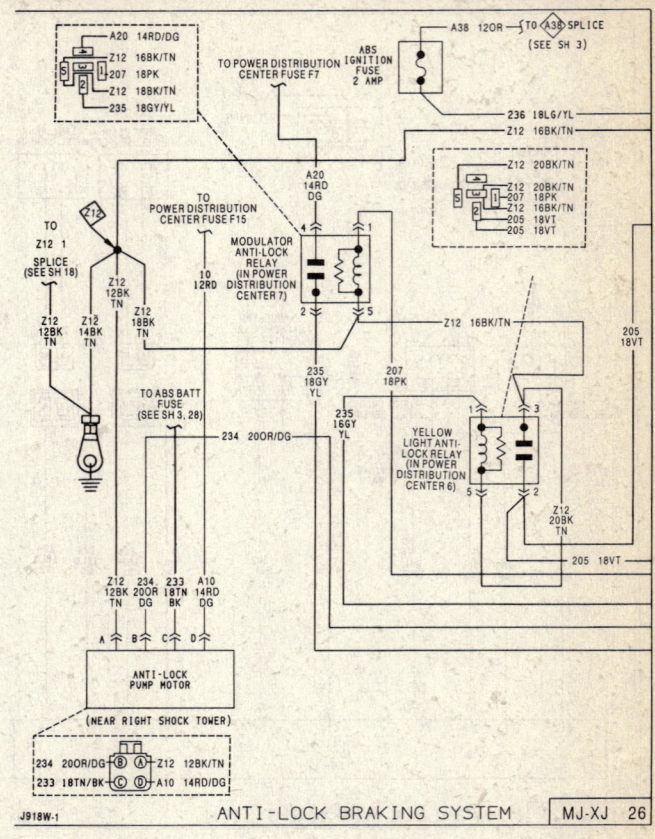
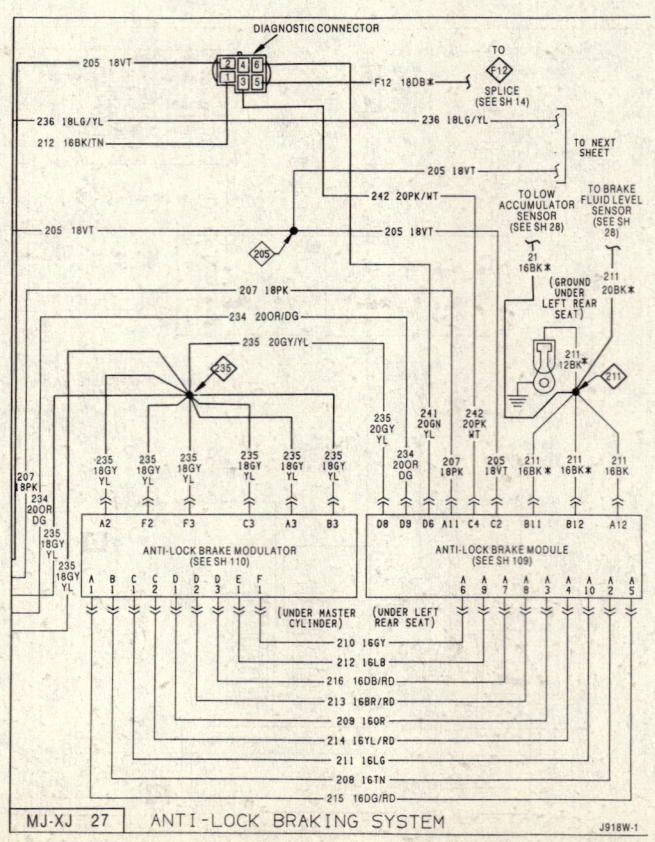
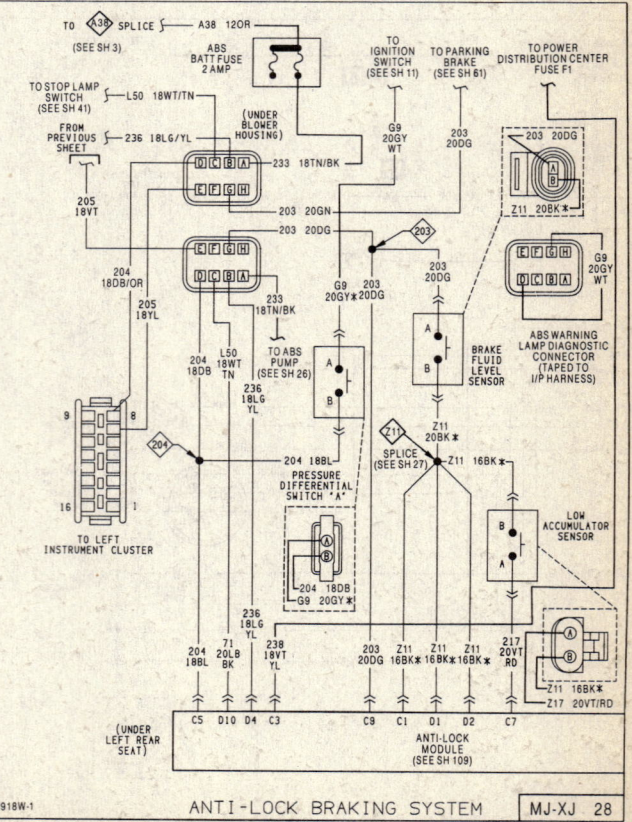

6-115

6 CHASSIS ELECTRICAL

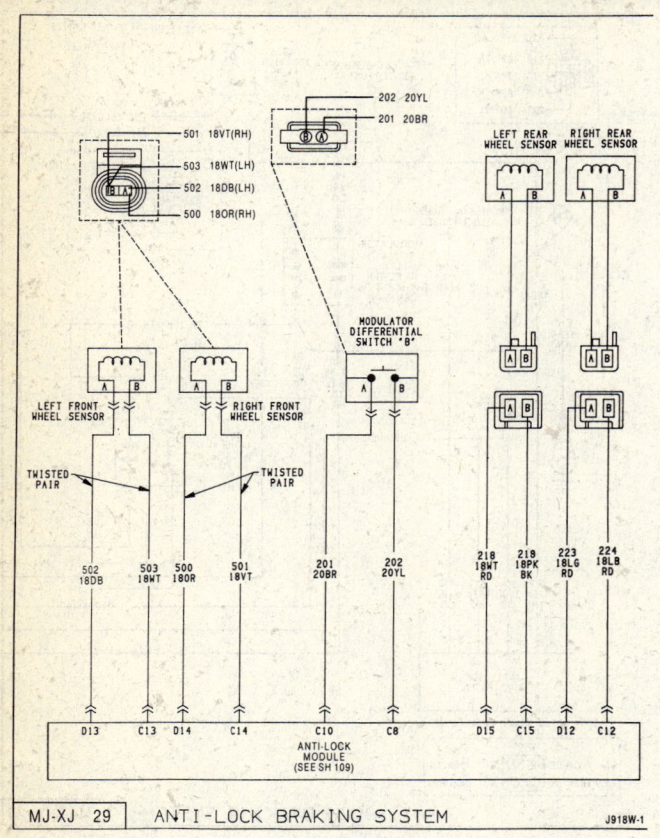

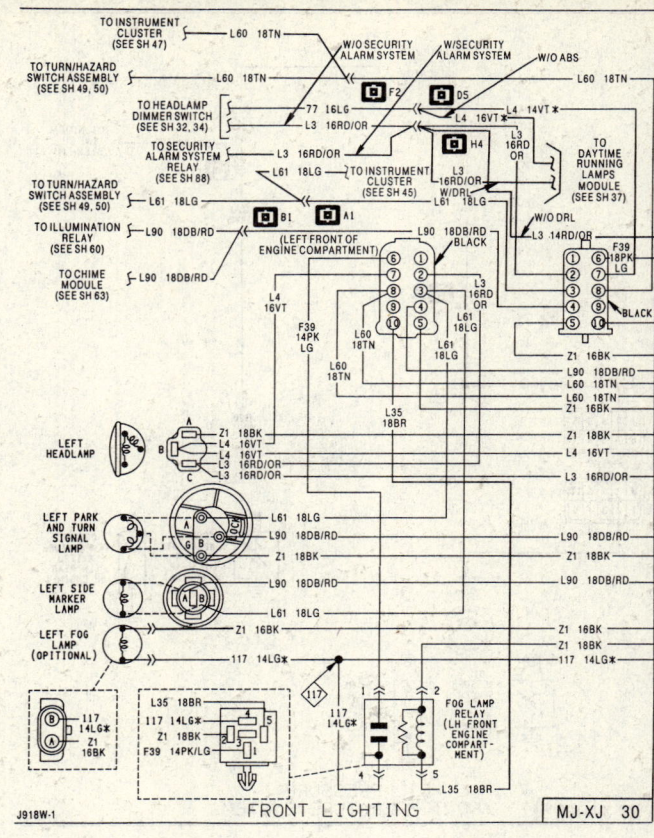

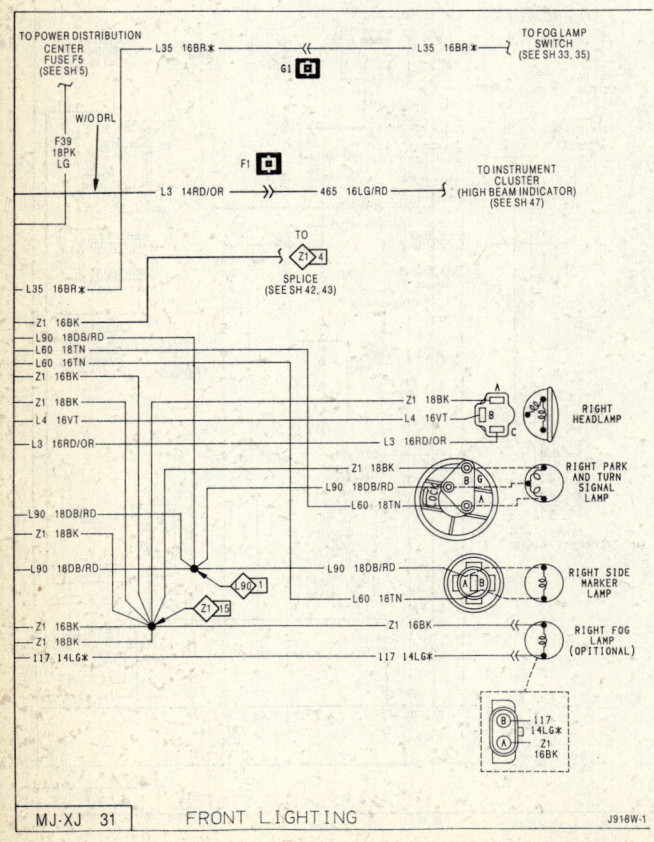

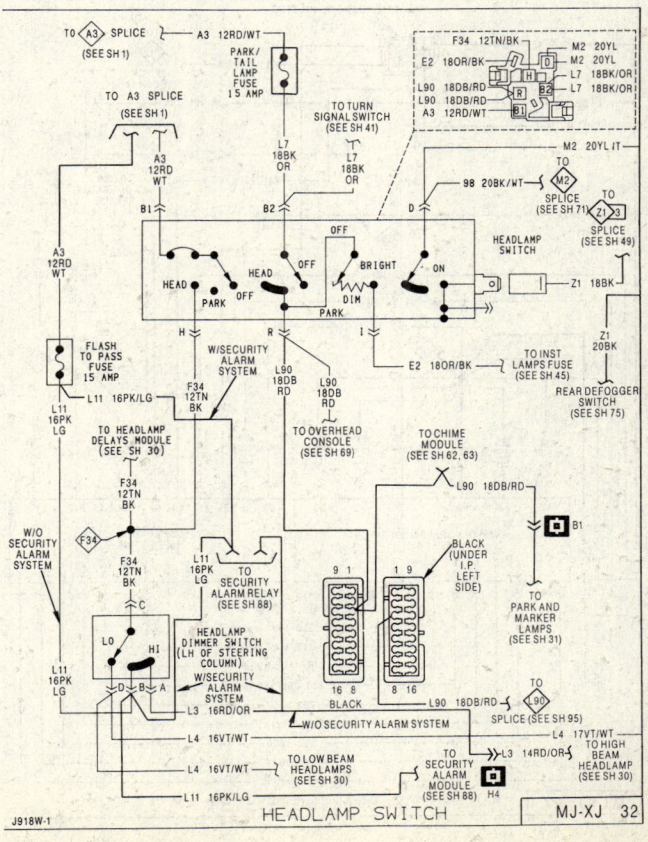

CHASSIS ELECTRICAL 6

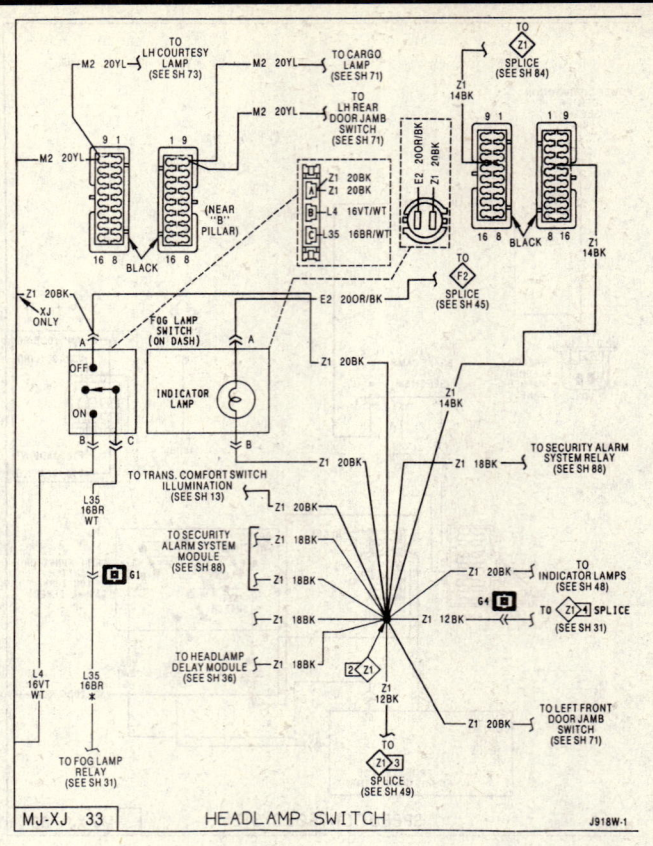
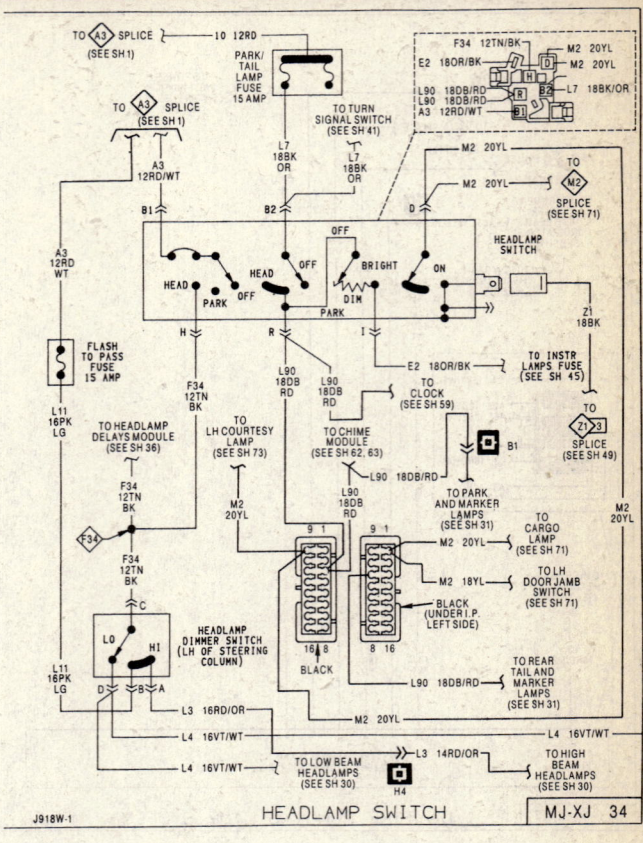
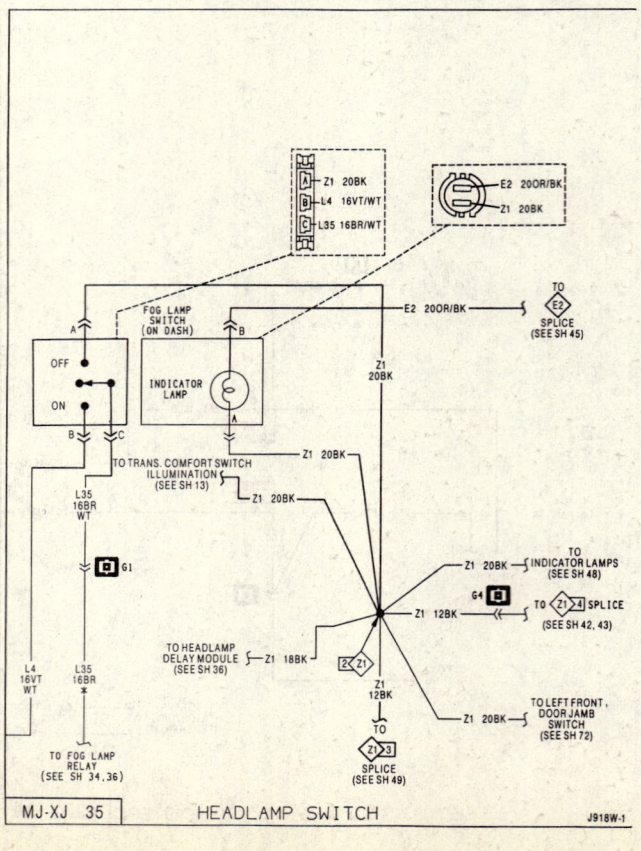
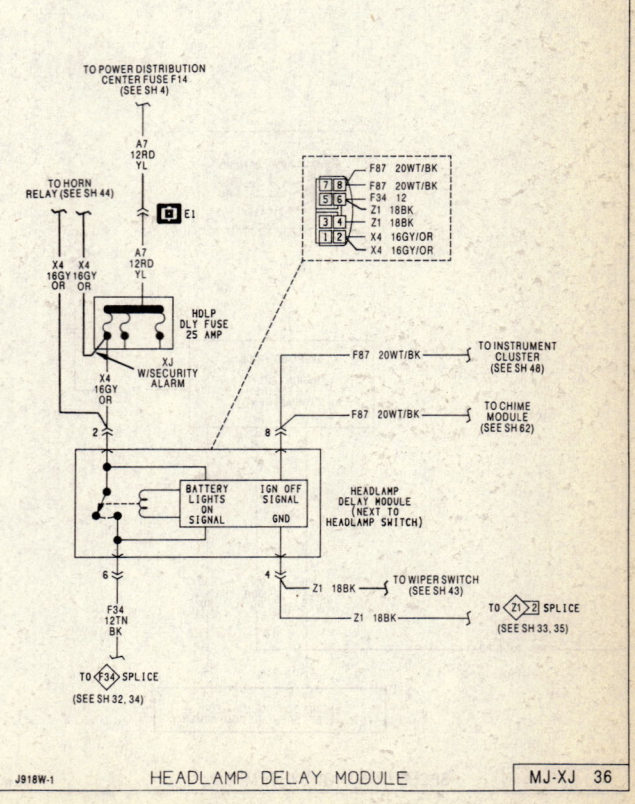

6-117

6 CHASSIS ELECTRICAL

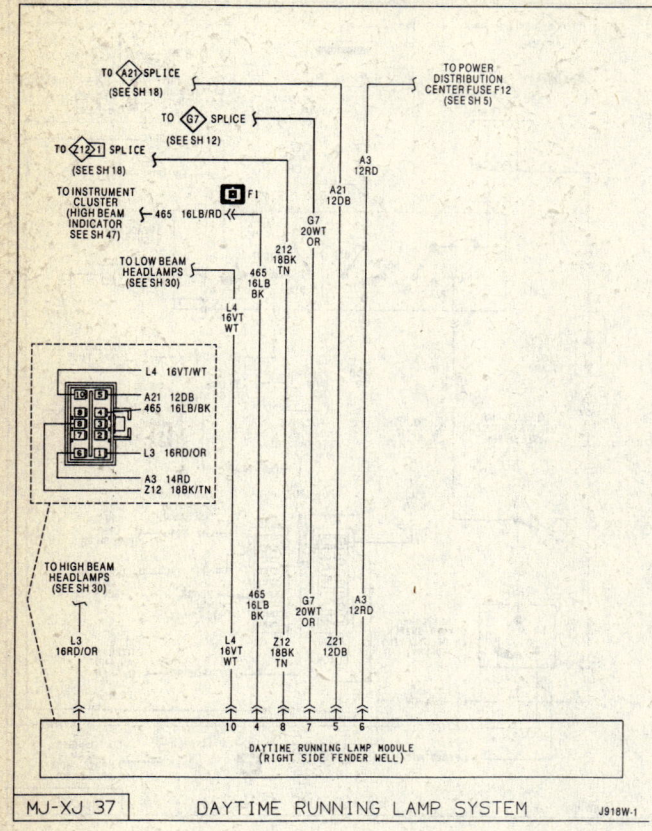

DAYTIME RUNNING LAMP SYSTEM — MJ-XJ 37

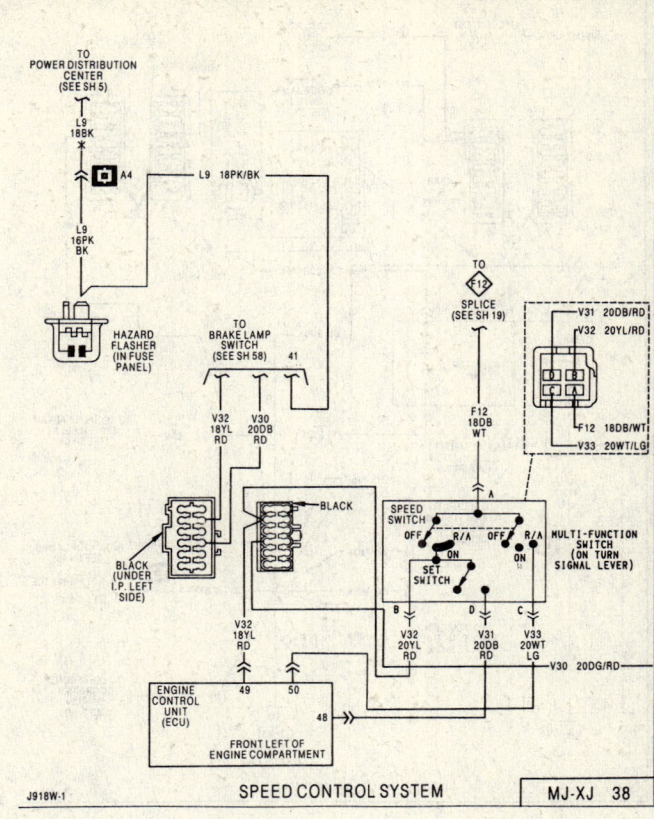

SPEED CONTROL SYSTEM — MJ-XJ 38

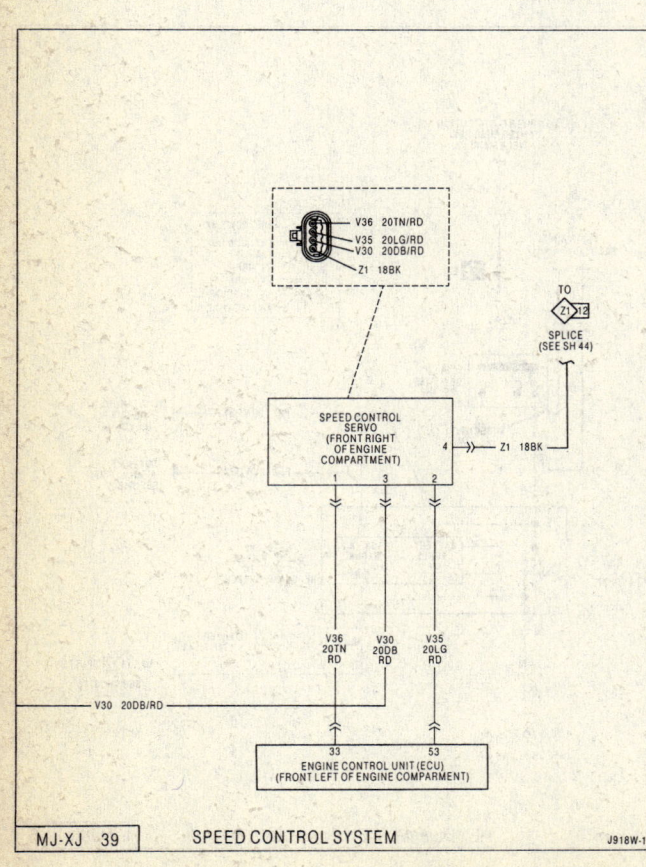

SPEED CONTROL SYSTEM — MJ-XJ 39

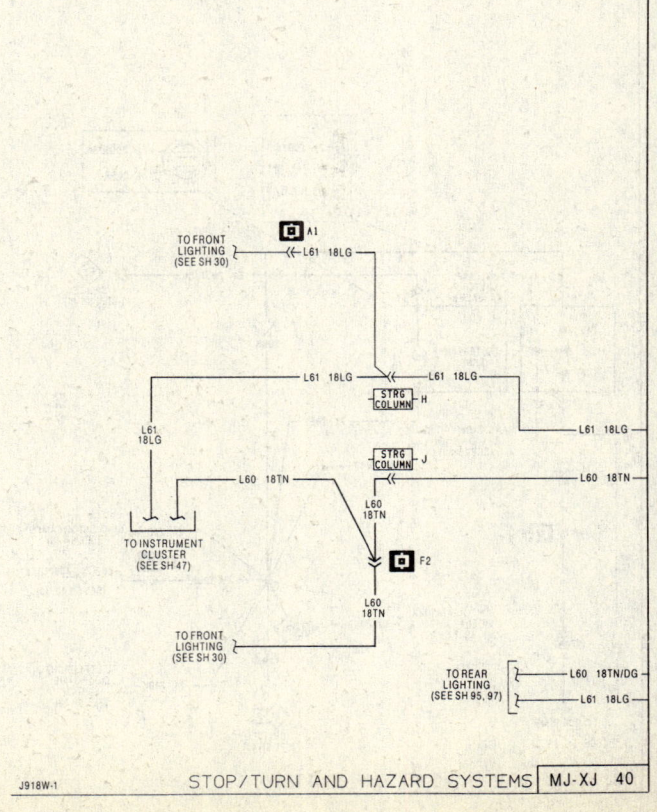

STOP/TURN AND HAZARD SYSTEMS — MJ-XJ 40

CHASSIS ELECTRICAL 6

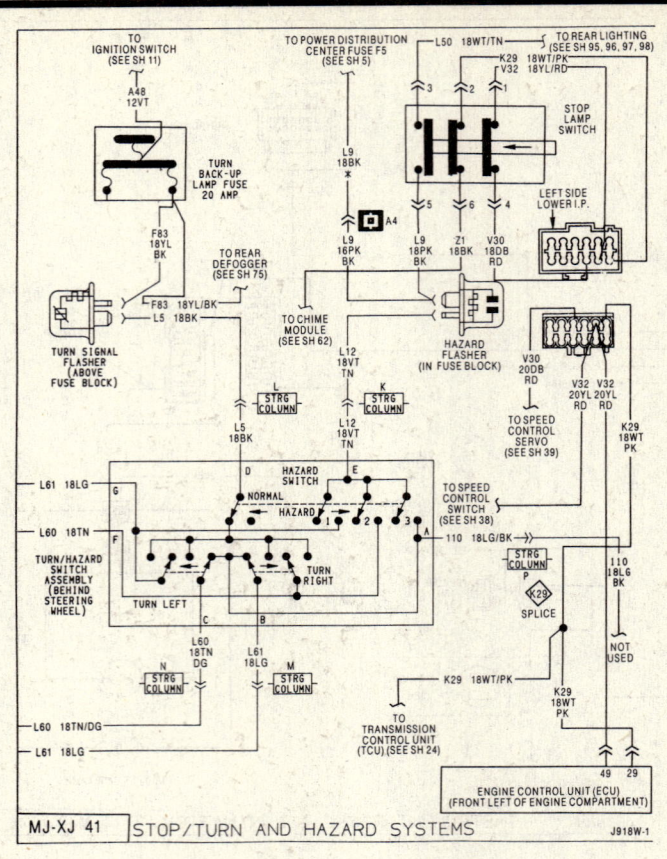

MJ-XJ 41 STOP/TURN AND HAZARD SYSTEMS

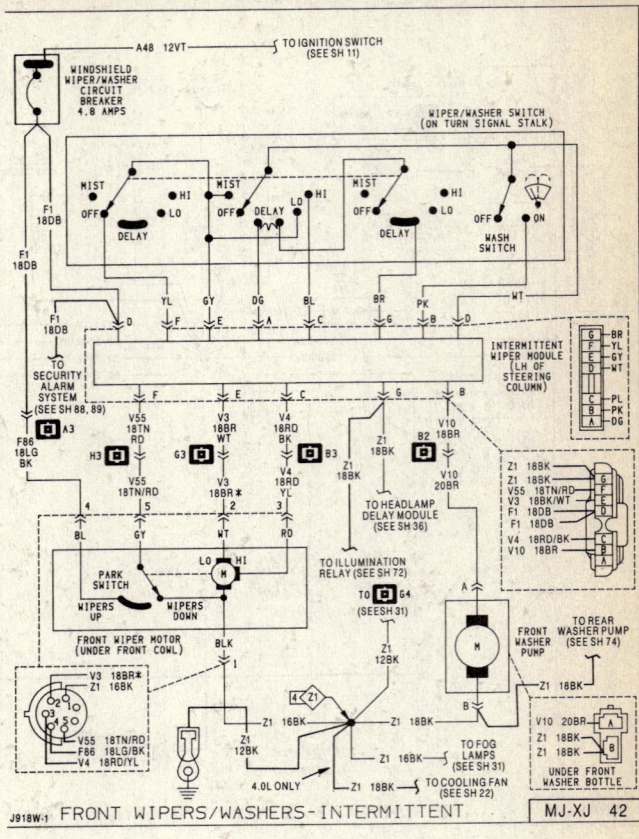

MJ-XJ 42 FRONT WIPERS/WASHERS—INTERMITTENT

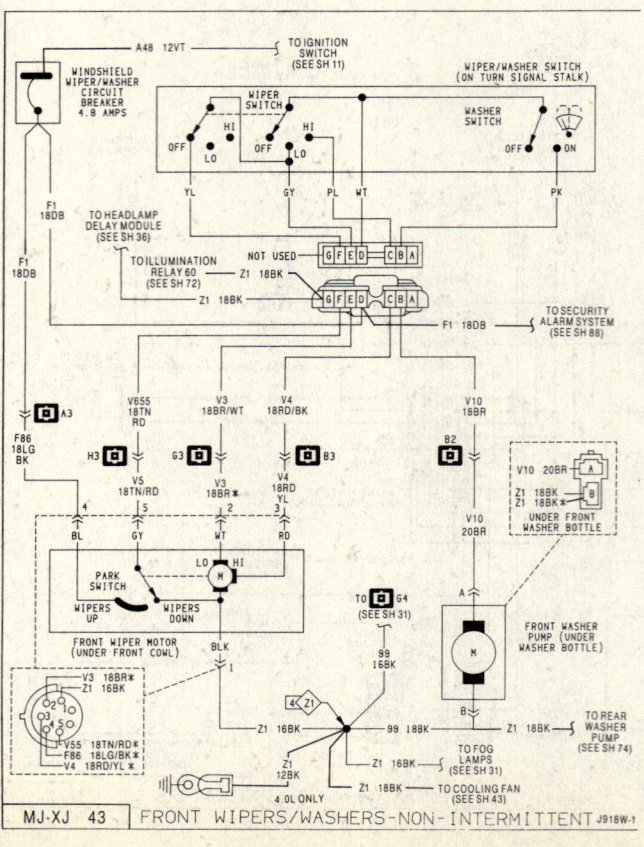

MJ-XJ 43 FRONT WIPERS/WASHERS—NON-INTERMITTENT

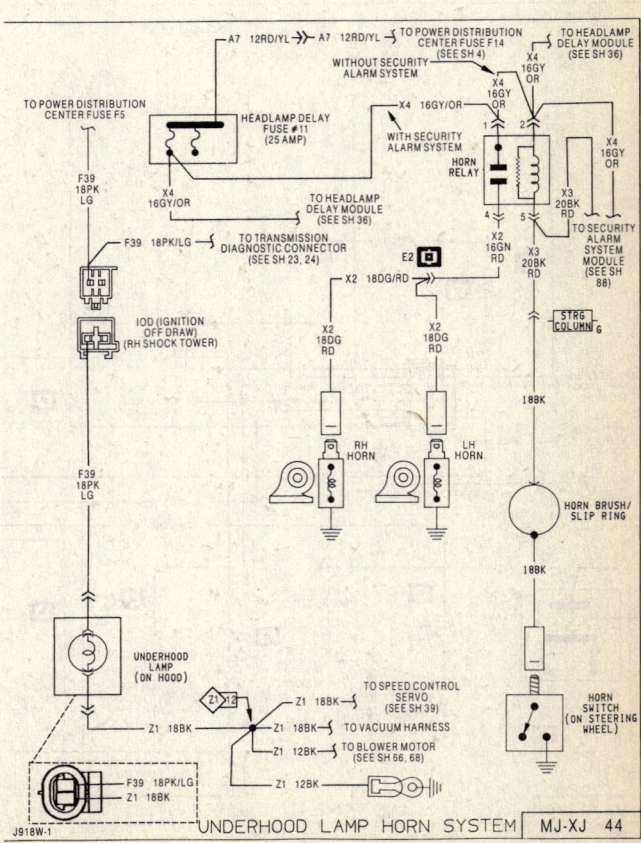

MJ-XJ 44 UNDERHOOD LAMP HORN SYSTEM

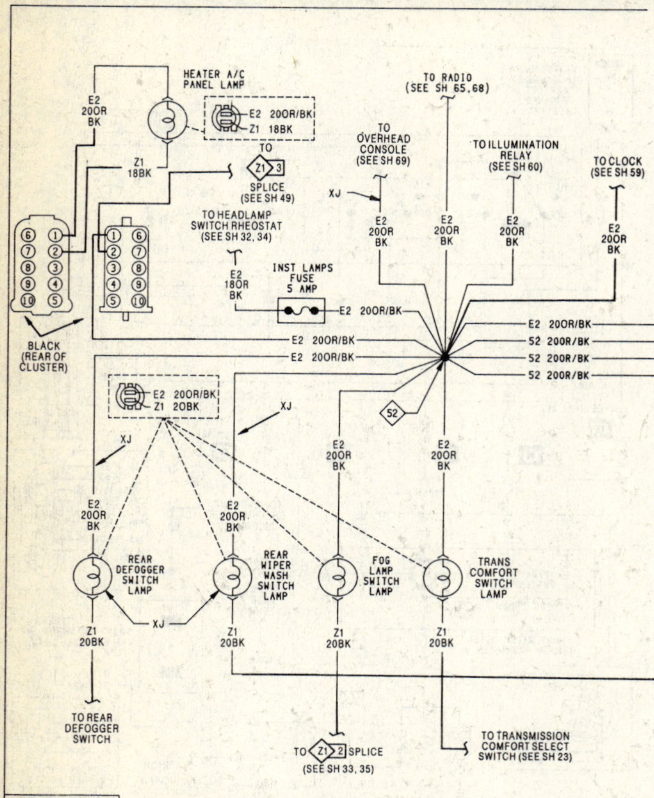

6 CHASSIS ELECTRICAL

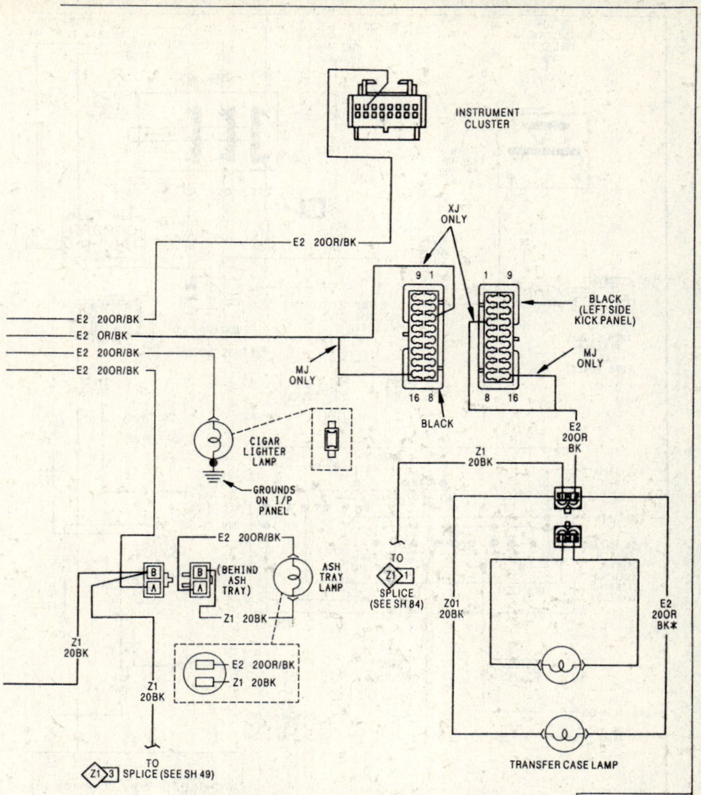

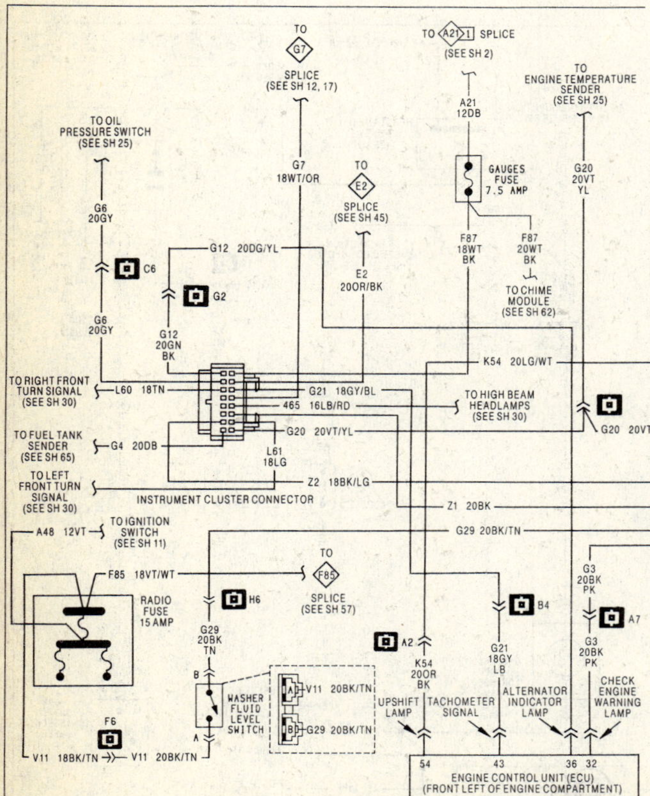

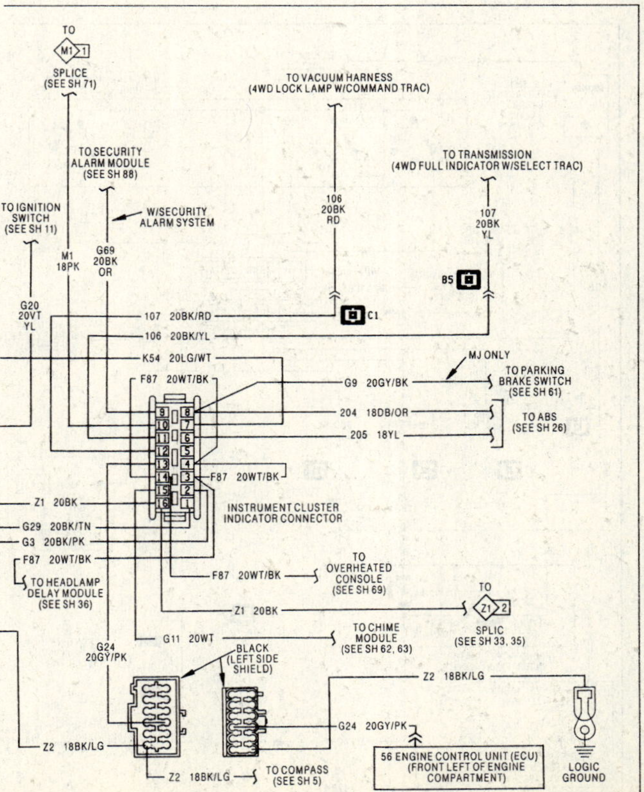

6-120

CHASSIS ELECTRICAL 6

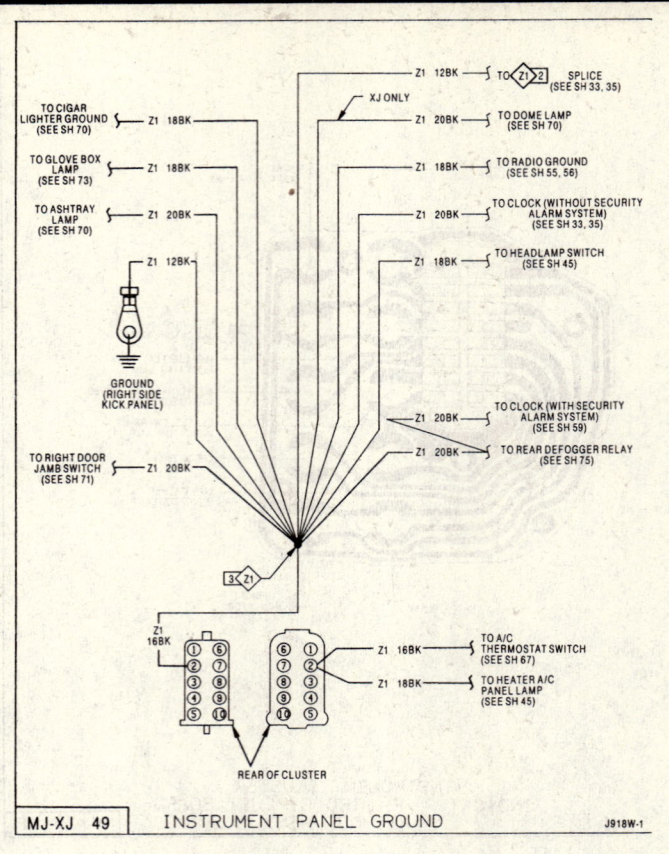

MJ-XJ 49 — INSTRUMENT PANEL GROUND

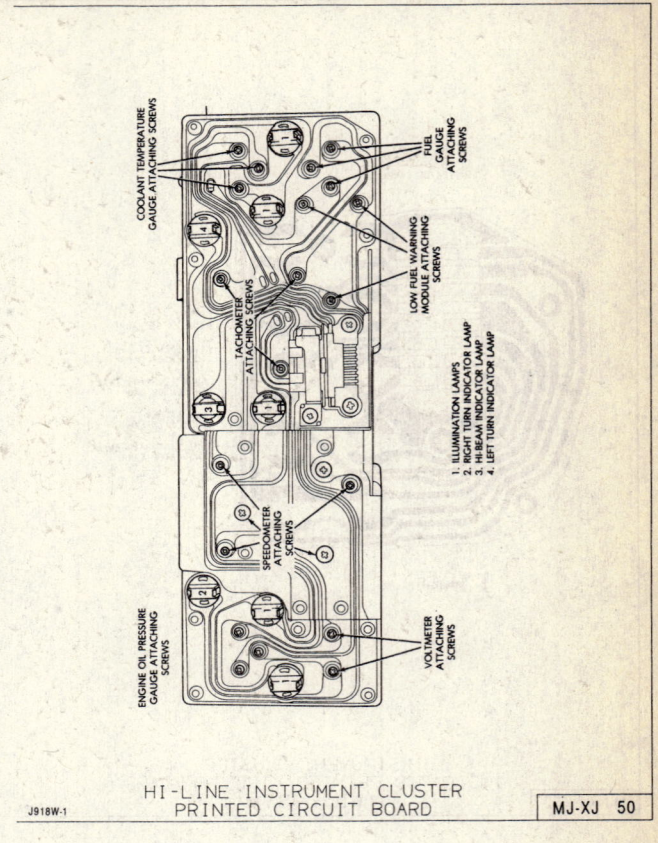

MJ-XJ 50 — HI-LINE INSTRUMENT CLUSTER PRINTED CIRCUIT BOARD

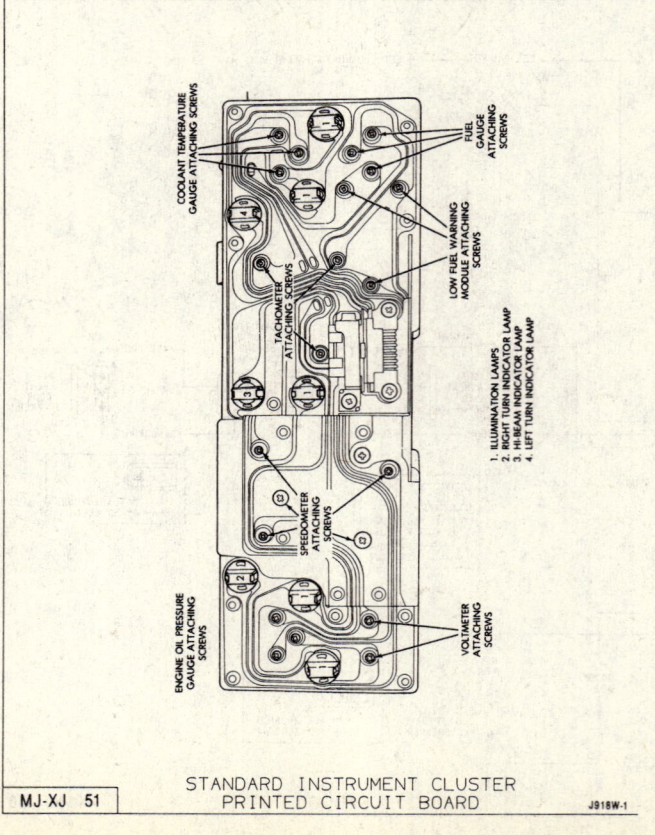

MJ-XJ 51 — STANDARD INSTRUMENT CLUSTER PRINTED CIRCUIT BOARD

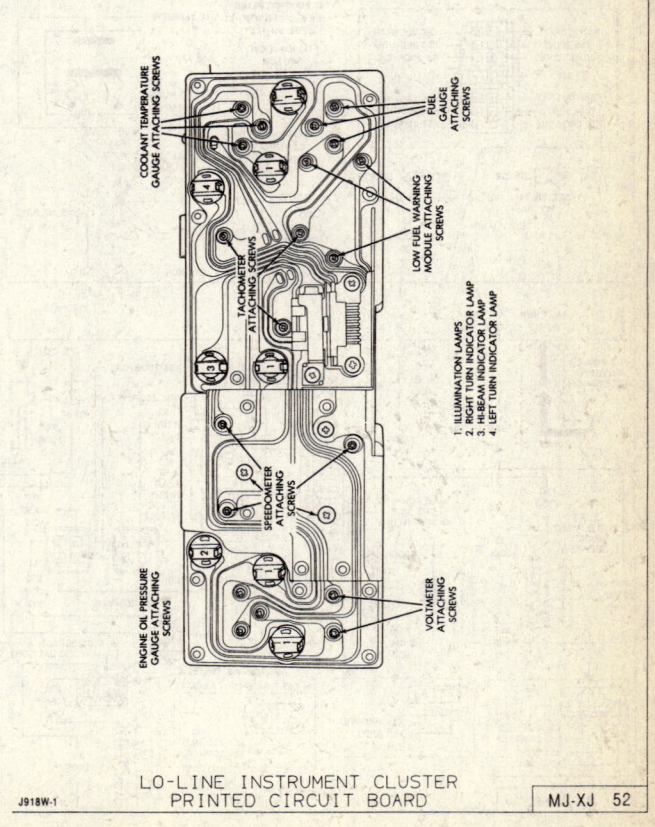

MJ-XJ 52 — LO-LINE INSTRUMENT CLUSTER PRINTED CIRCUIT BOARD

6-121

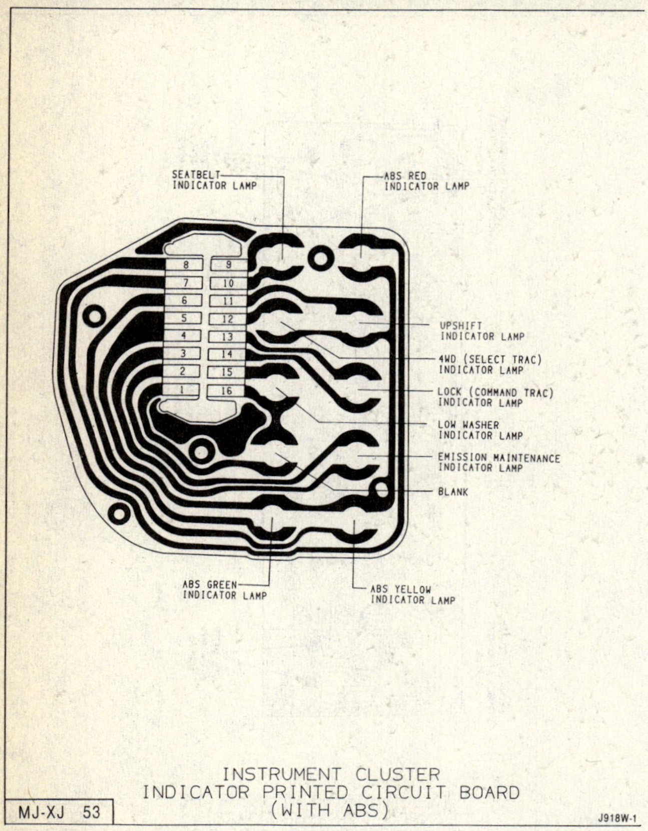

6 CHASSIS ELECTRICAL

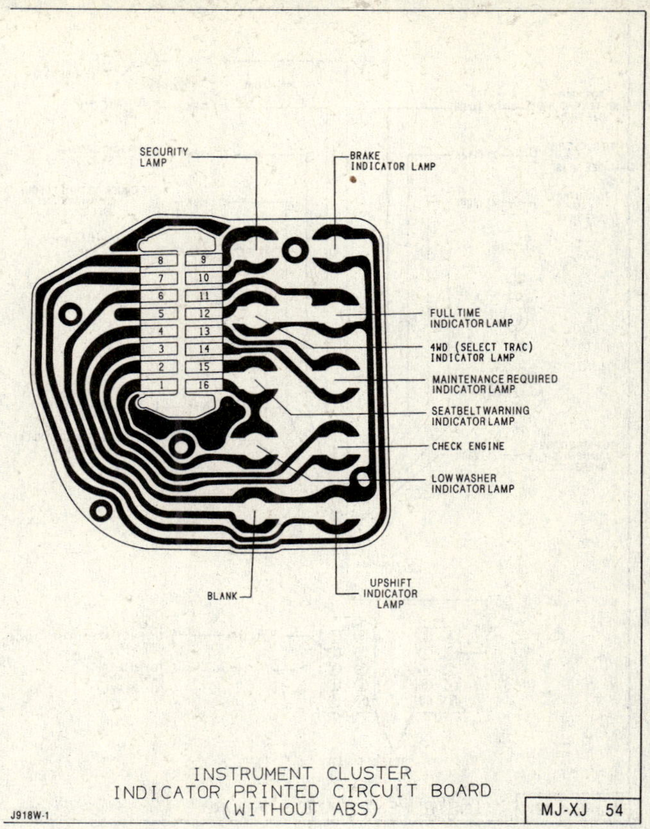

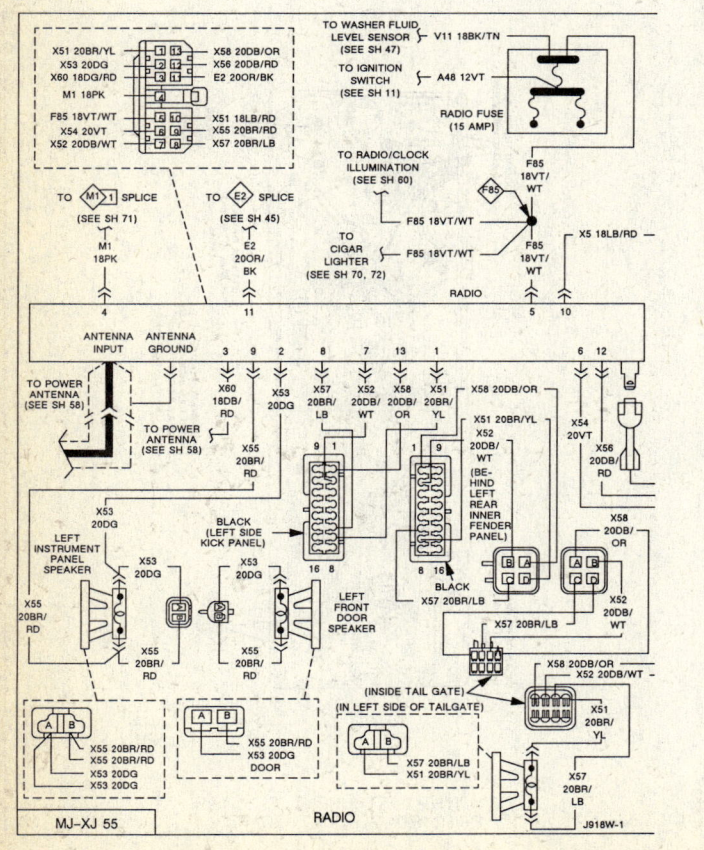

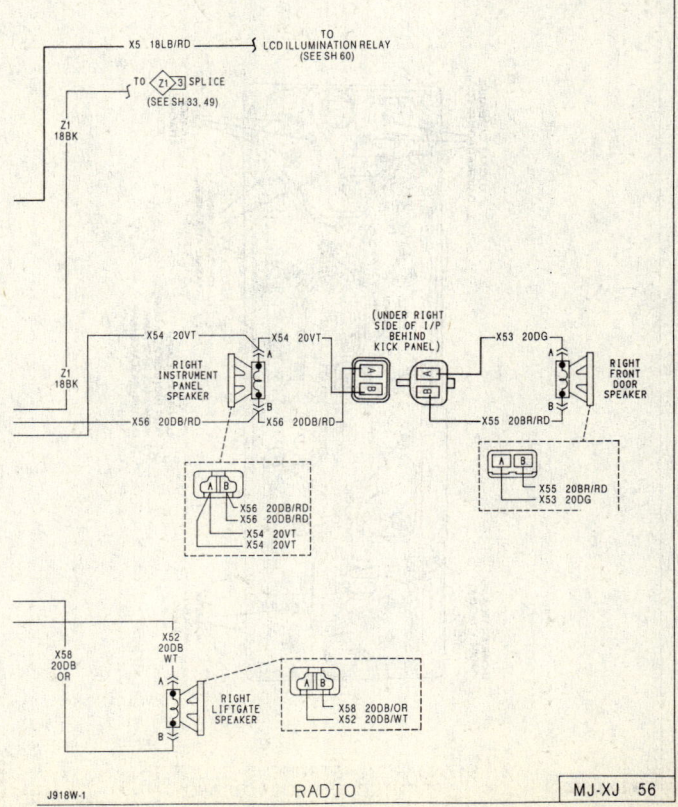

6-122

CHASSIS ELECTRICAL 6

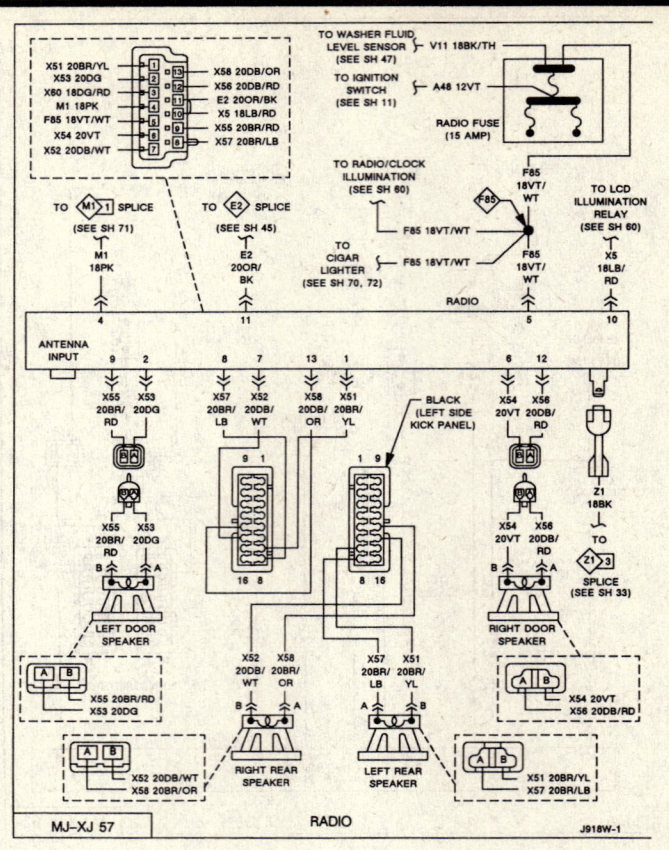

MJ-XJ 57 — RADIO

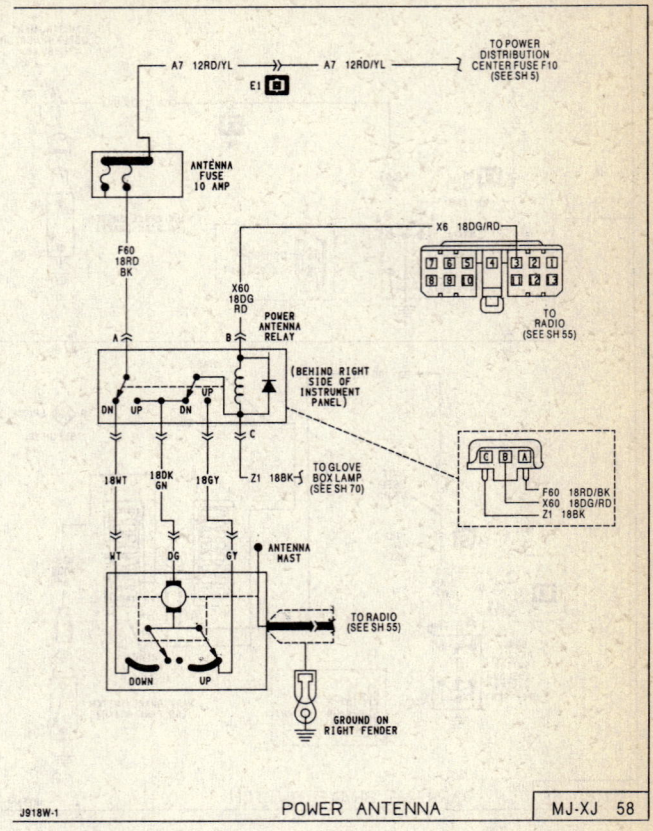

MJ-XJ 58 — POWER ANTENNA

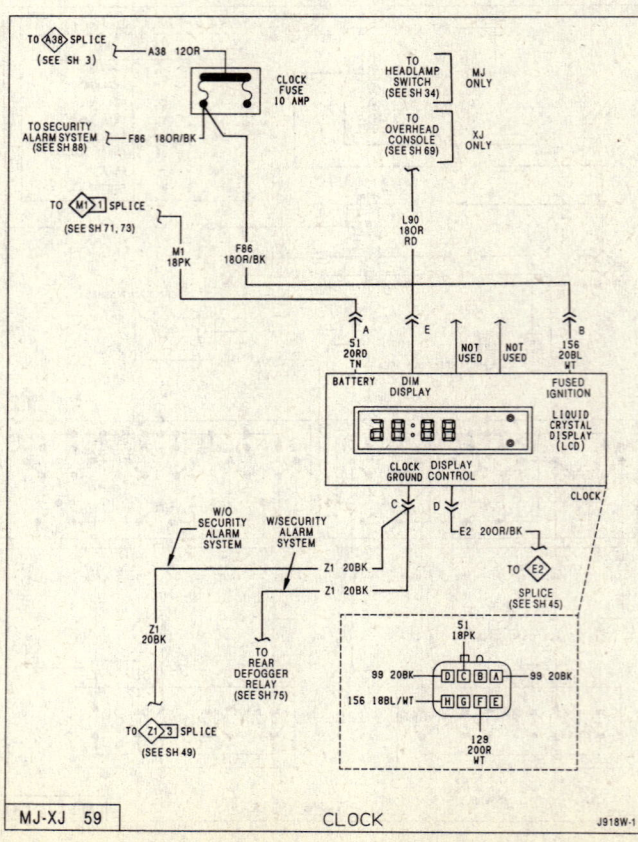

MJ-XJ 59 — CLOCK

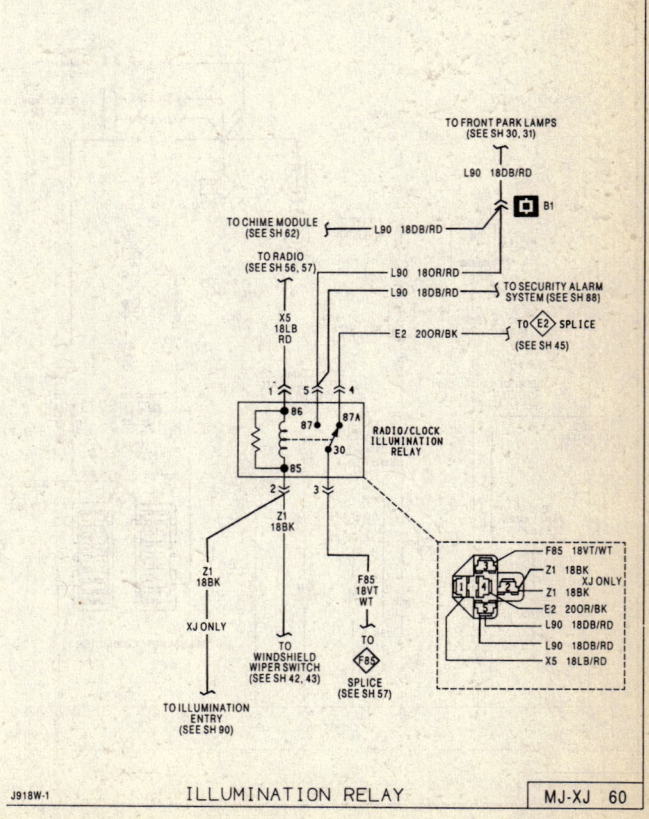

MJ-XJ 60 — ILLUMINATION RELAY

6 CHASSIS ELECTRICAL

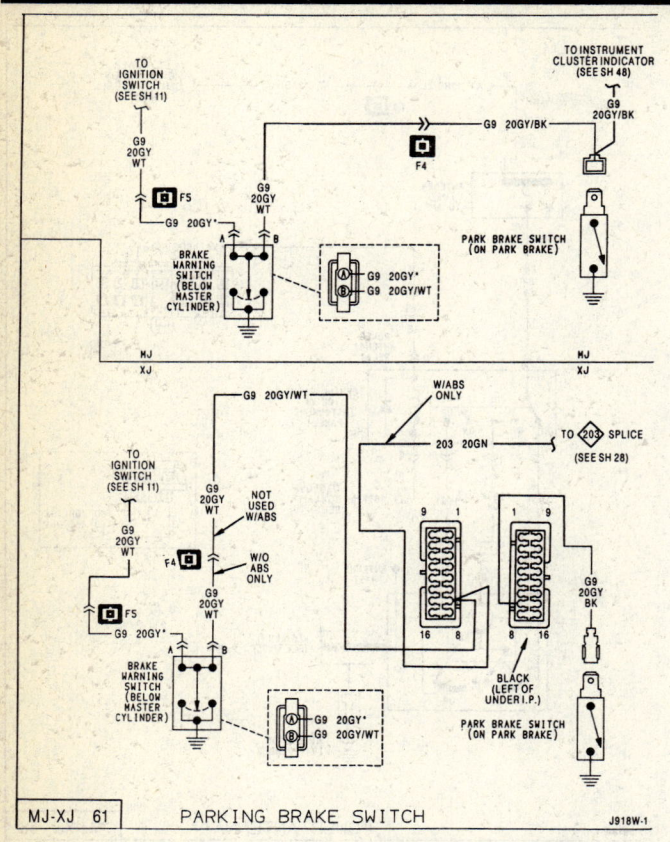

PARKING BRAKE SWITCH

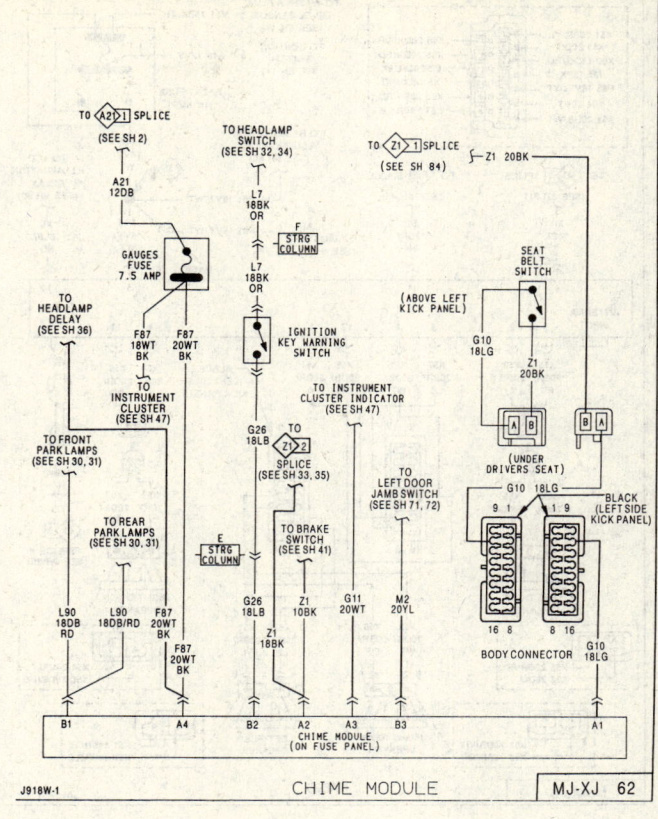

CHIME MODULE

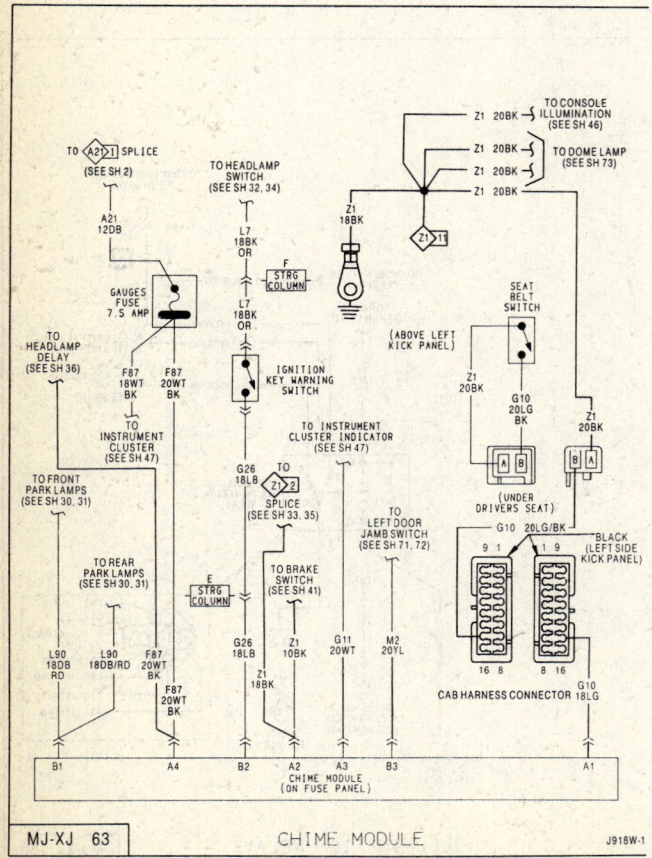

CHIME MODULE

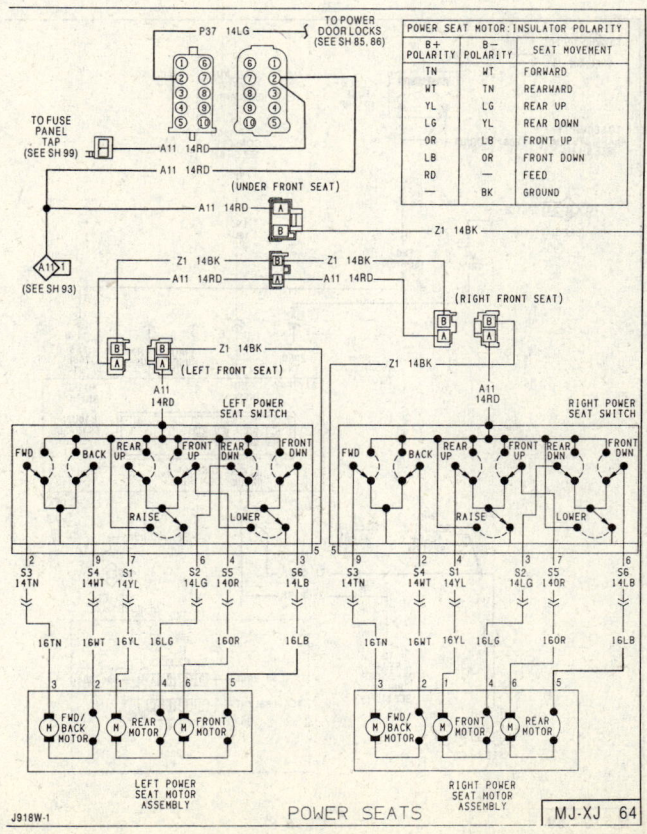

POWER SEATS

CHASSIS ELECTRICAL 6

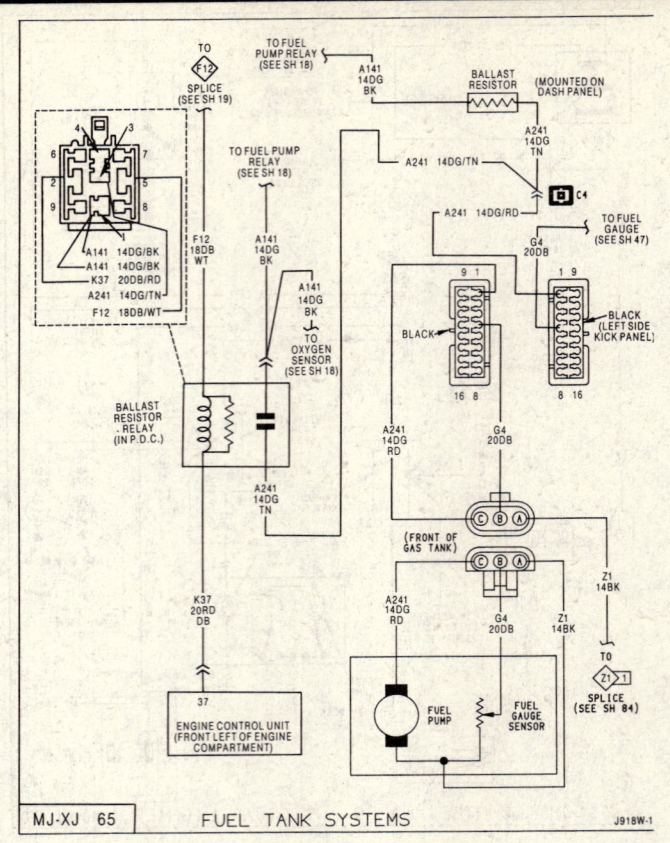

FUEL TANK SYSTEMS

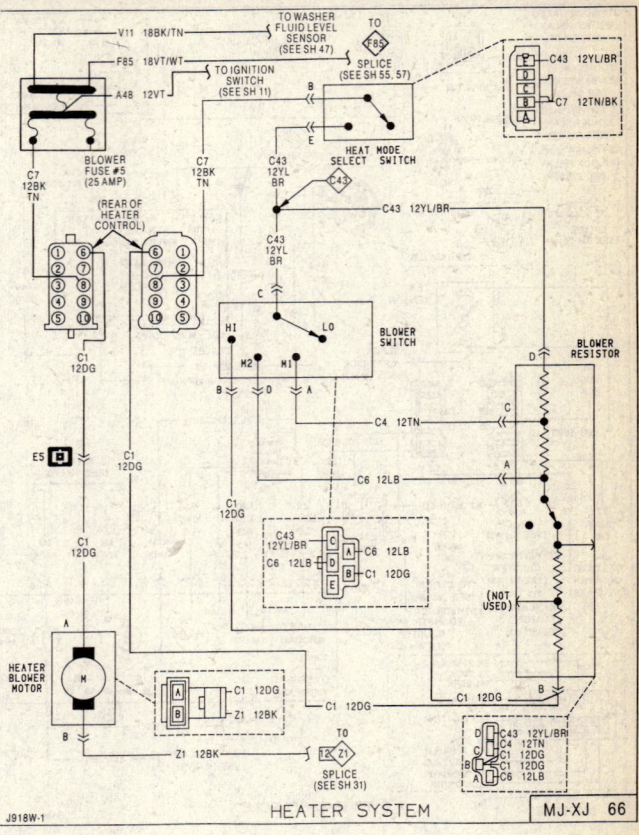

HEATER SYSTEM

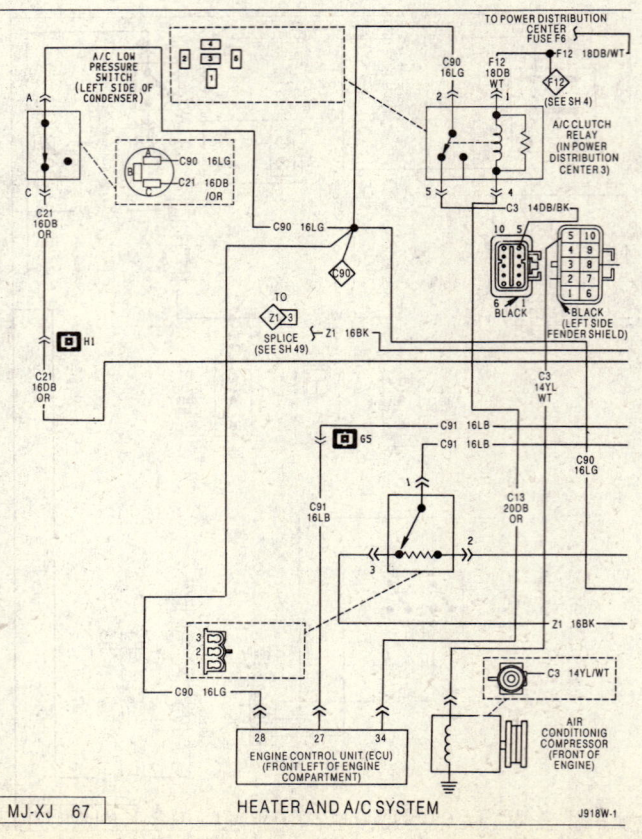

HEATER AND A/C SYSTEM

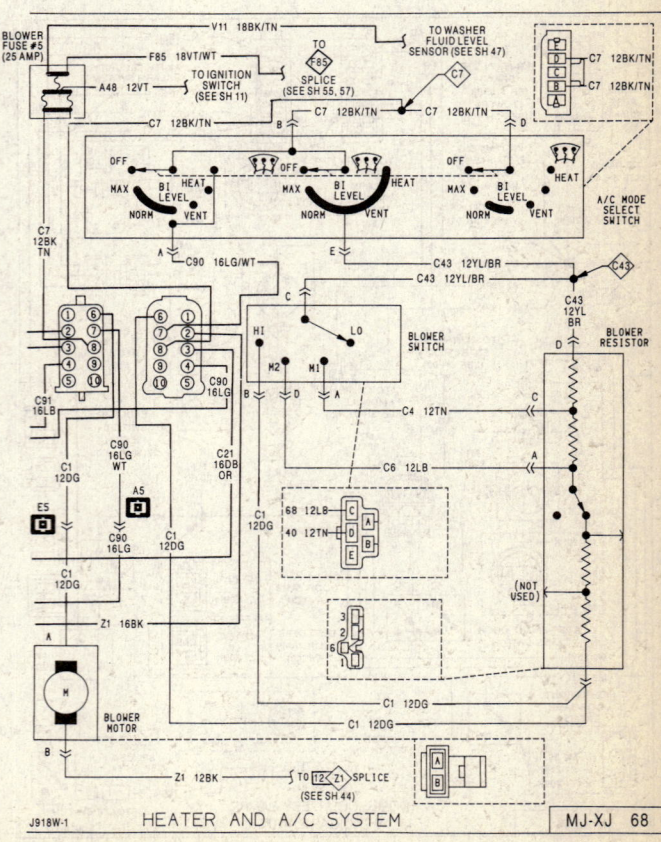

HEATER AND A/C SYSTEM

6-125

6 CHASSIS ELECTRICAL

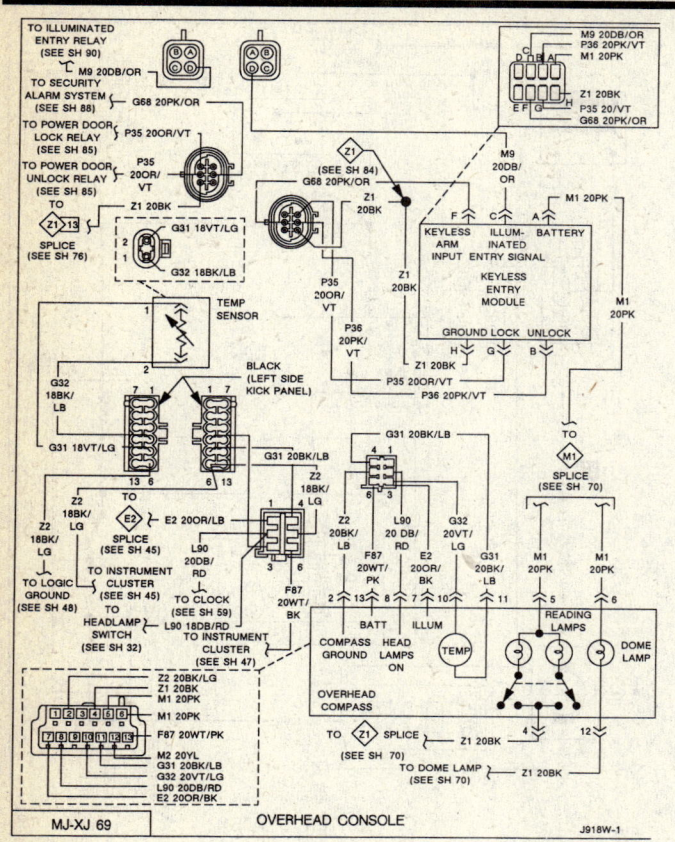

OVERHEAD CONSOLE — MJ-XJ 69

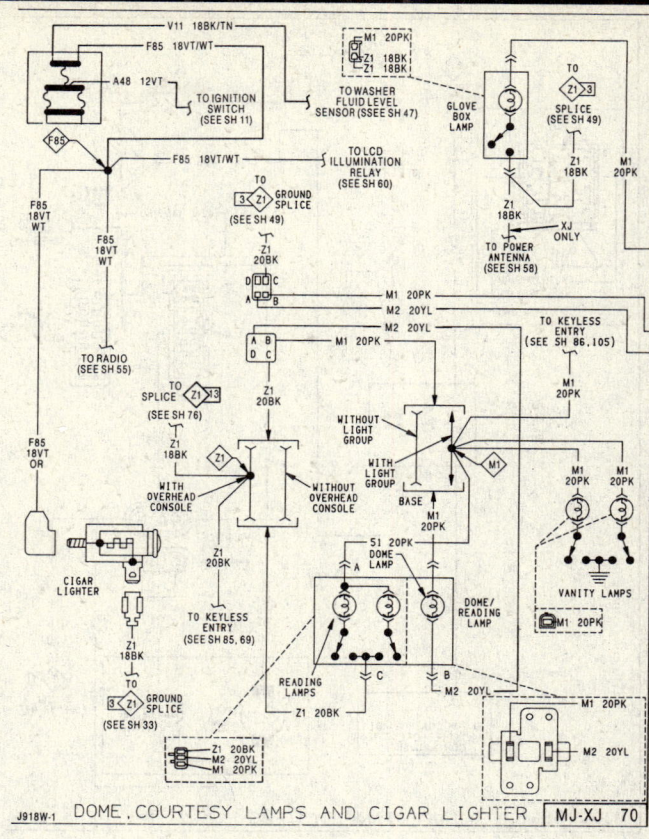

DOME, COURTESY LAMPS AND CIGAR LIGHTER — MJ-XJ 70

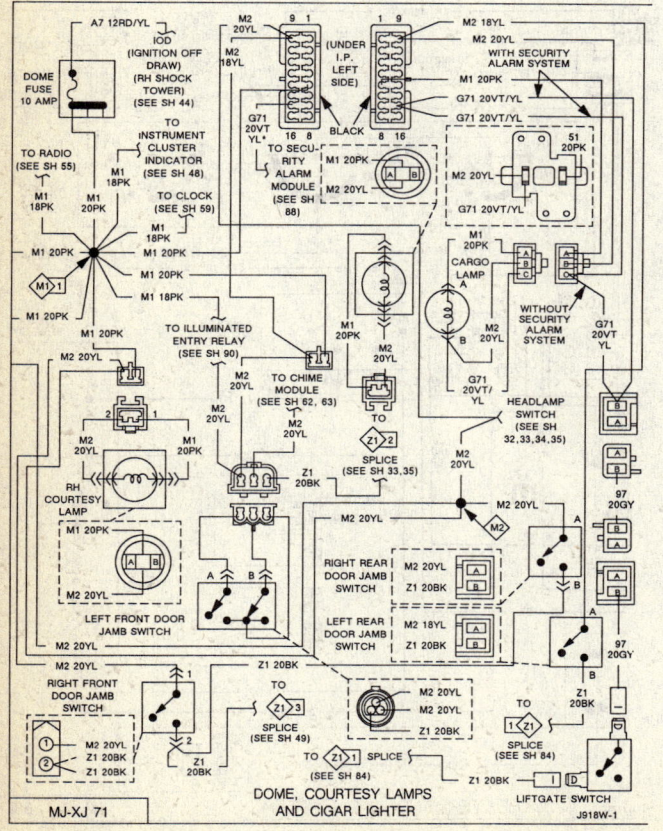

DOME, COURTESY LAMPS AND CIGAR LIGHTER — MJ-XJ 71

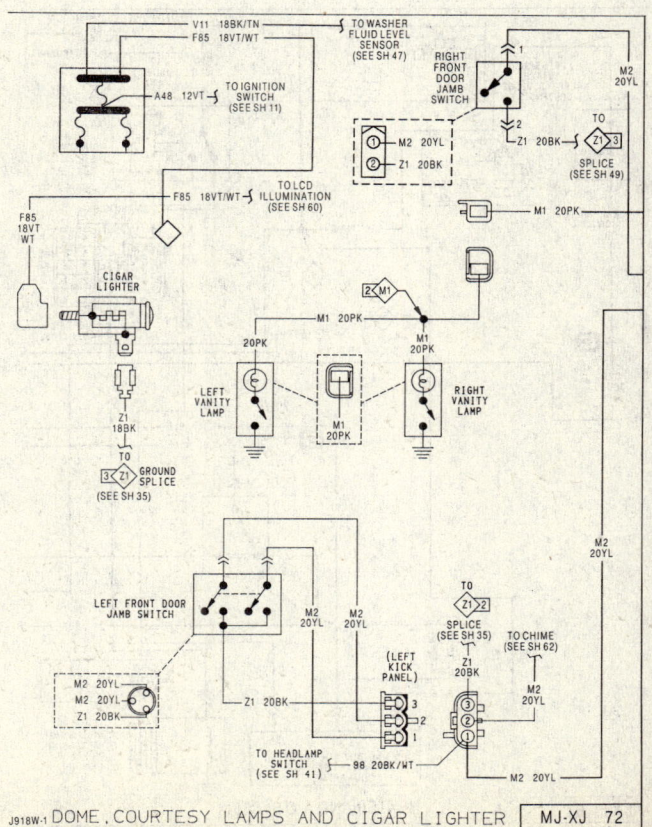

DOME, COURTESY LAMPS AND CIGAR LIGHTER — MJ-XJ 72

CHASSIS ELECTRICAL 6

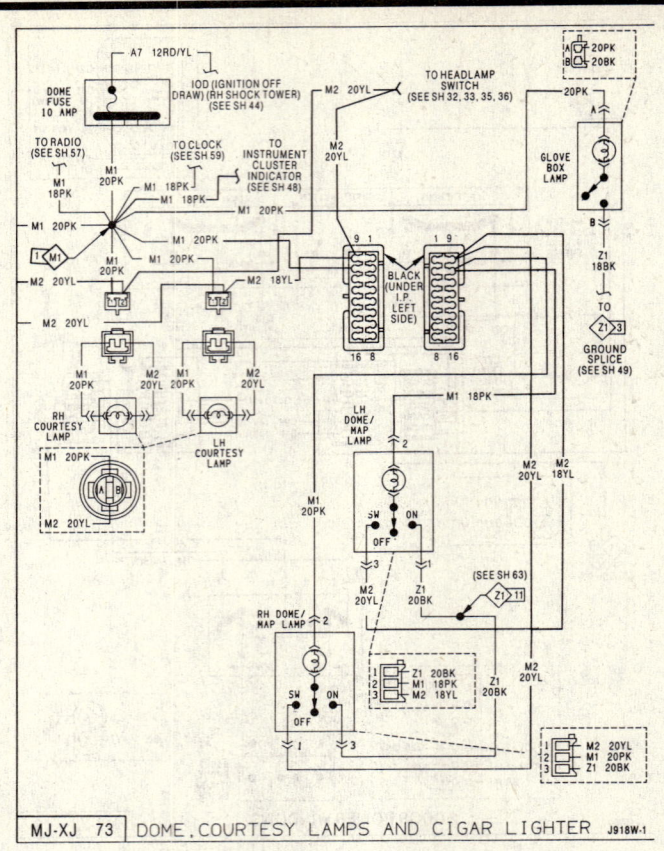

MJ-XJ 73 — DOME, COURTESY LAMPS AND CIGAR LIGHTER

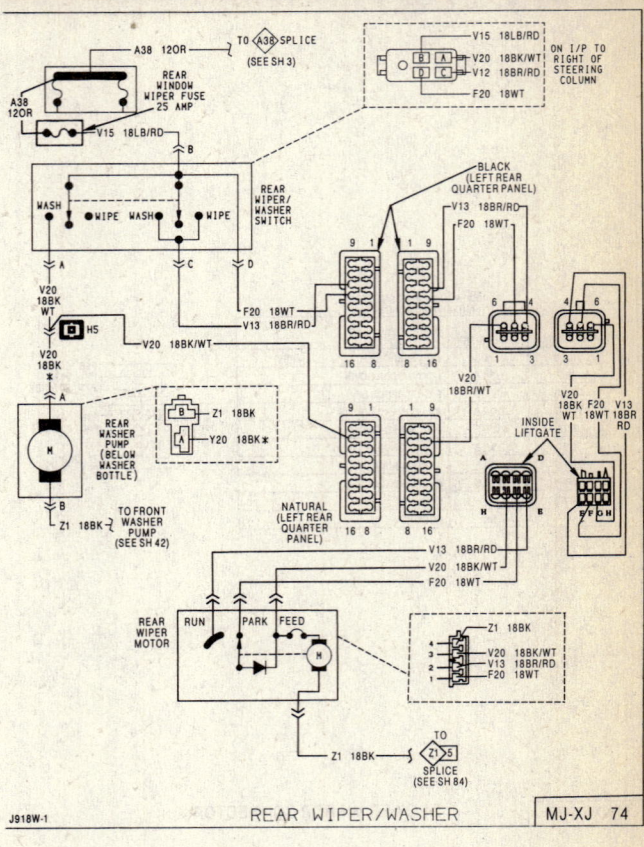

MJ-XJ 74 — REAR WIPER/WASHER

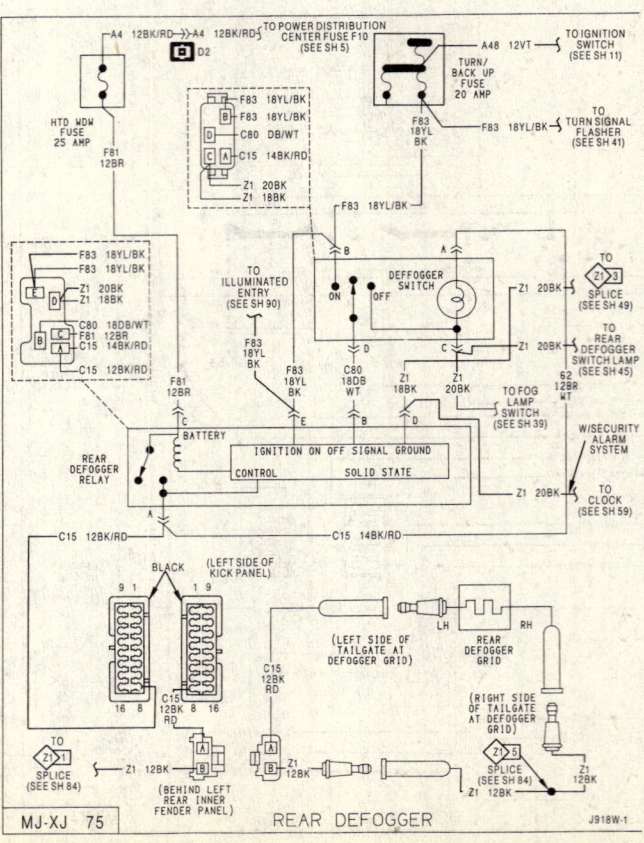

MJ-XJ 75 — REAR DEFOGGER

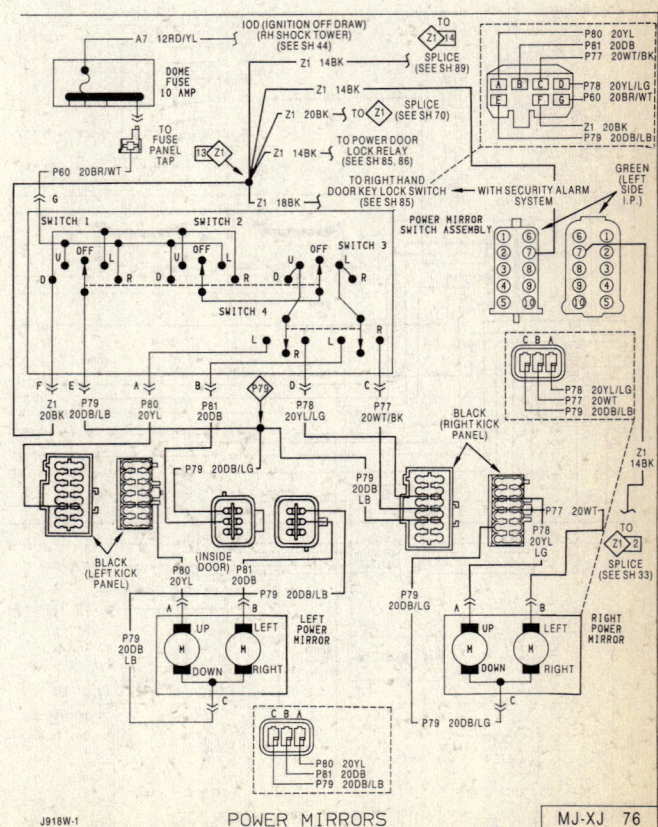

MJ-XJ 76 — POWER MIRRORS

6-127

6 CHASSIS ELECTRICAL

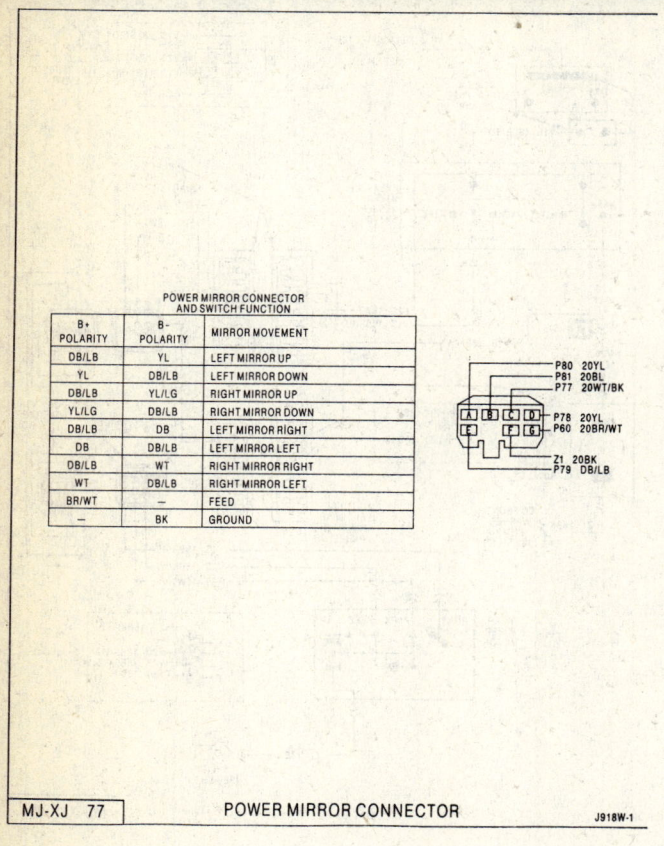

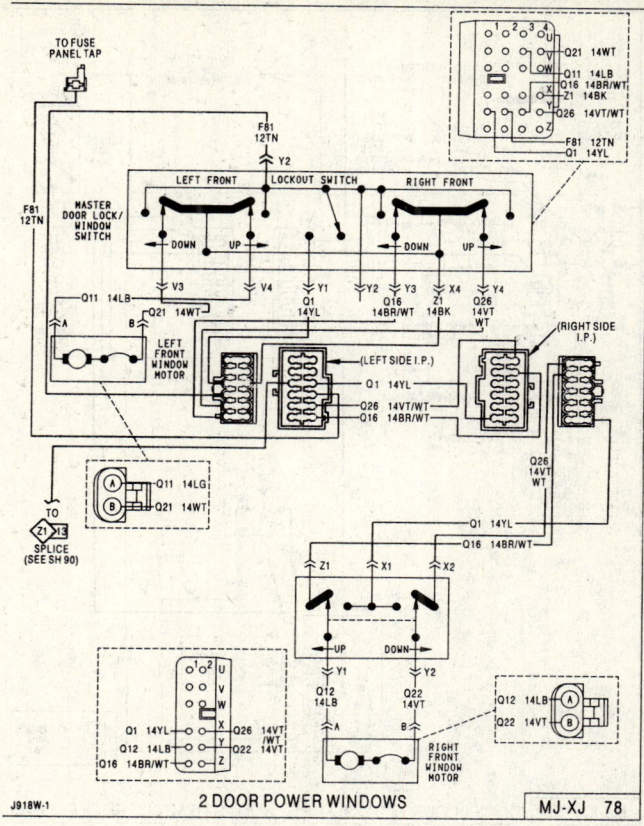

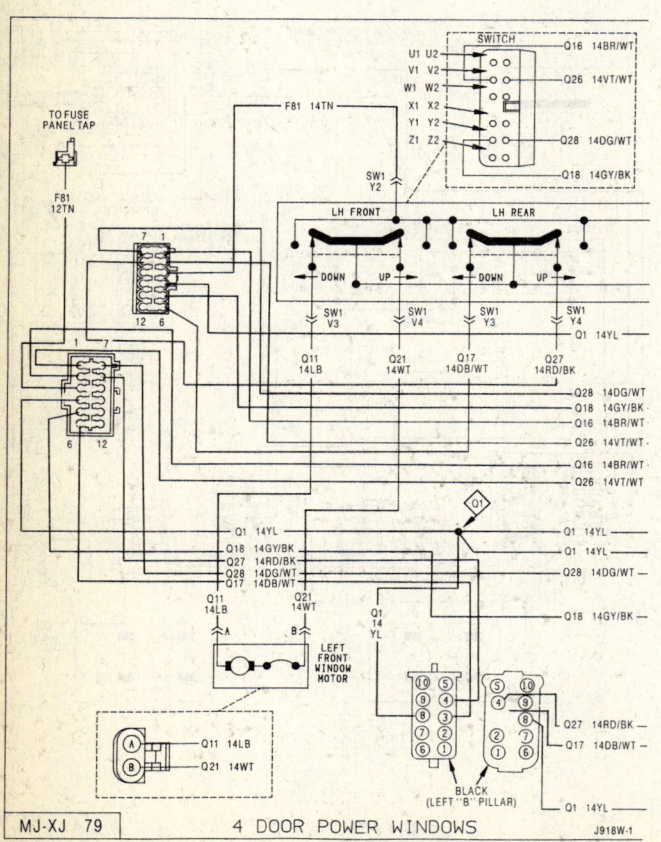

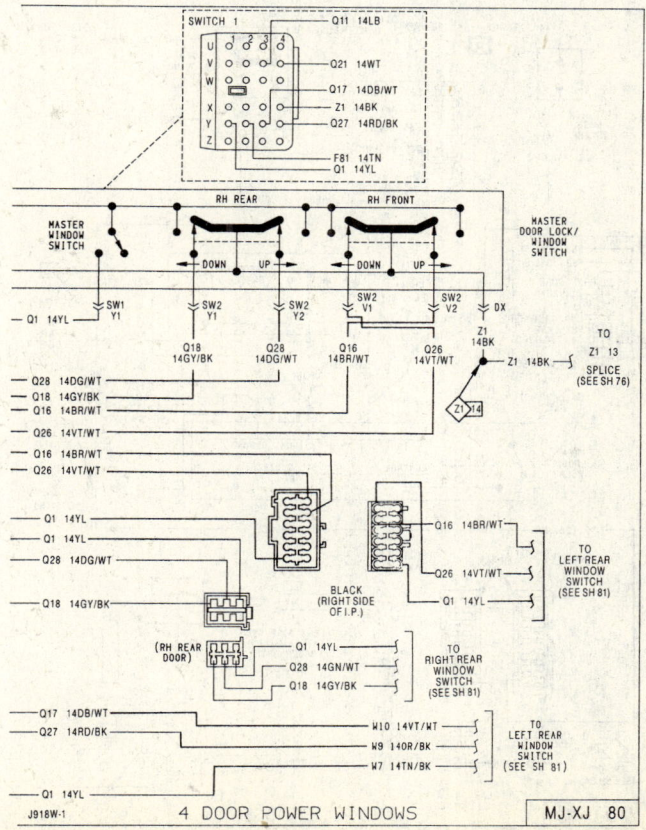

CHASSIS ELECTRICAL 6

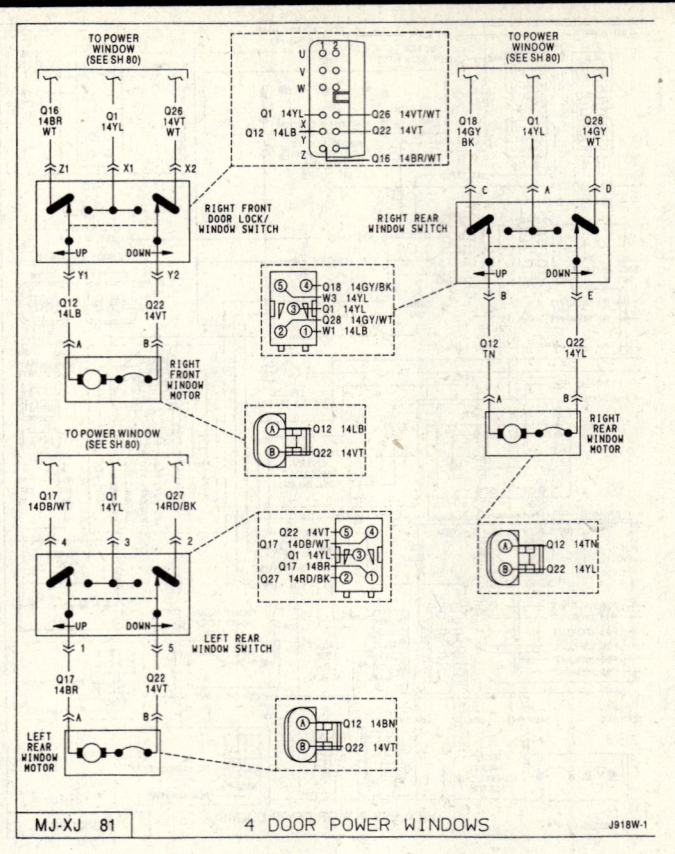

4 DOOR POWER WINDOWS — MJ-XJ 81

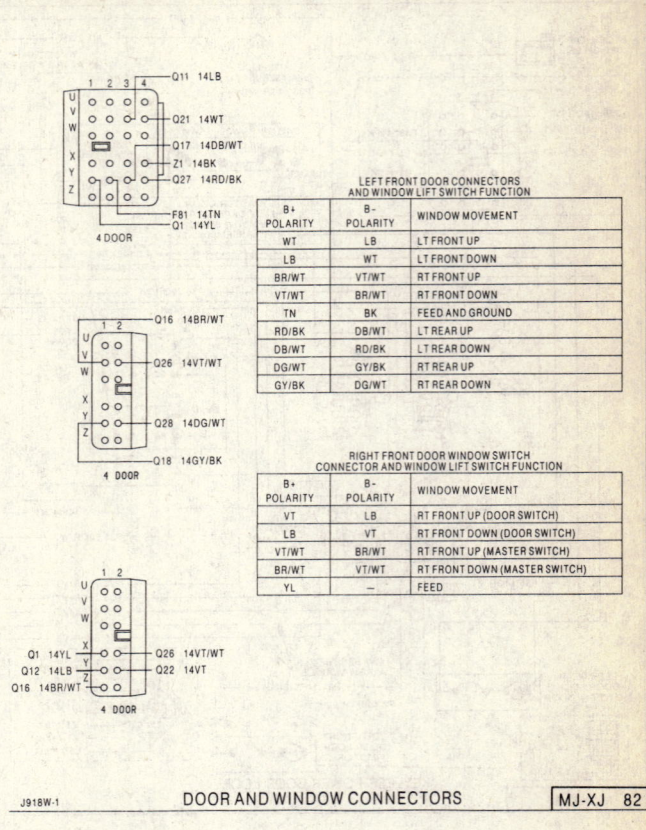

DOOR AND WINDOW CONNECTORS — MJ-XJ 82

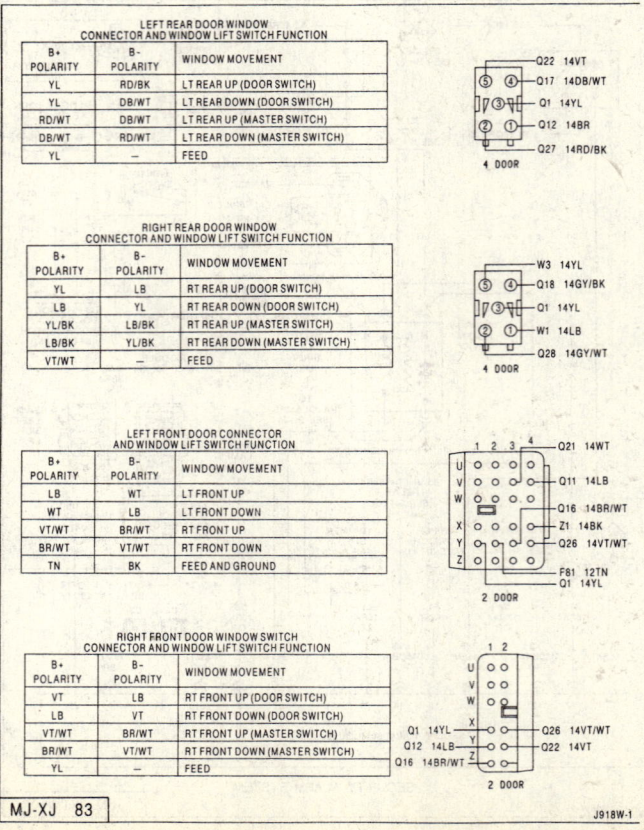

MJ-XJ 83

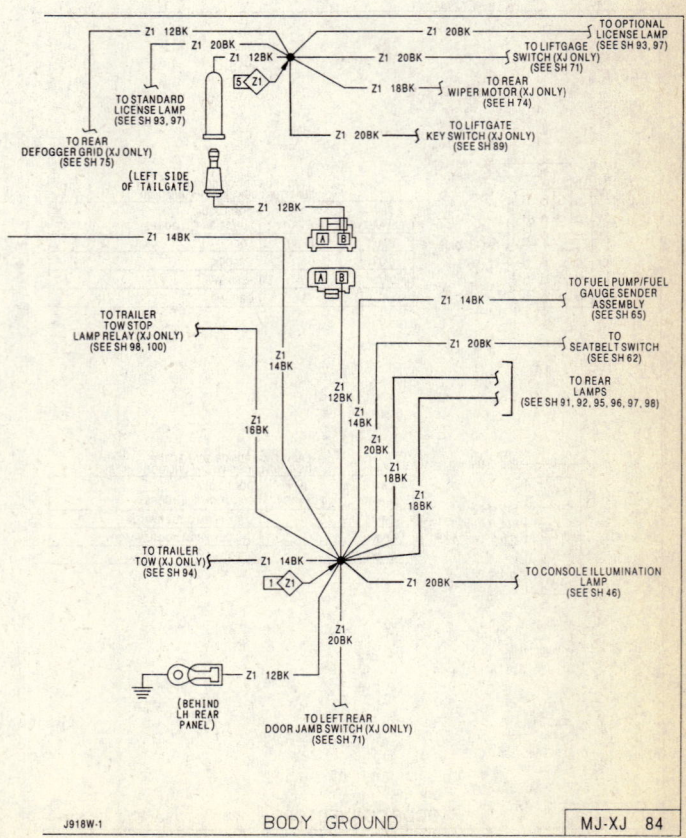

BODY GROUND — MJ-XJ 84

6 CHASSIS ELECTRICAL

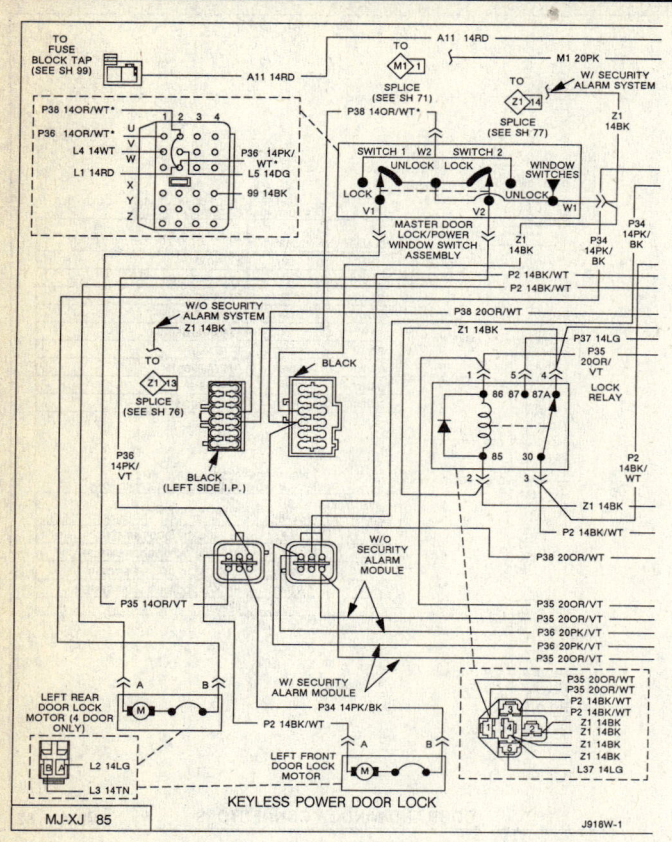
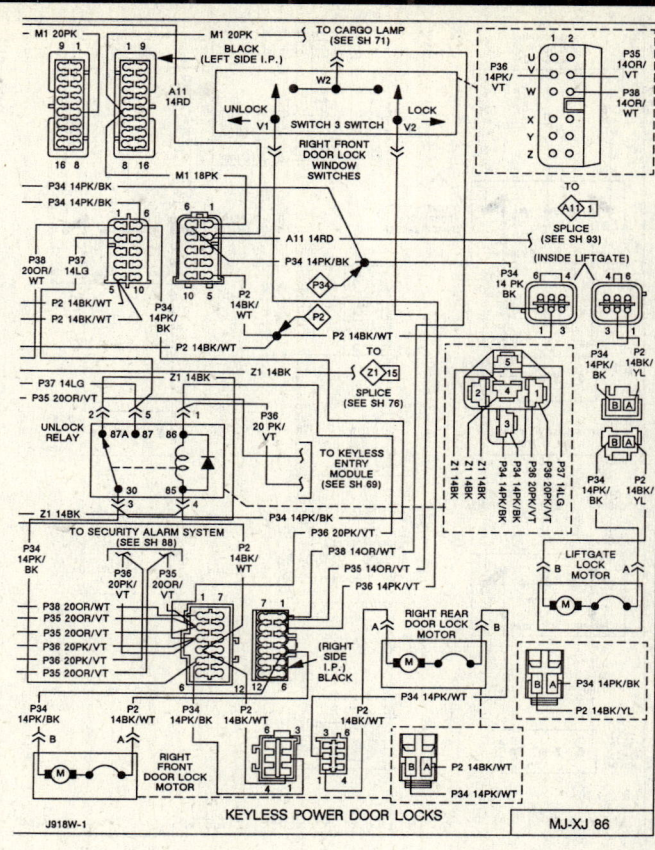
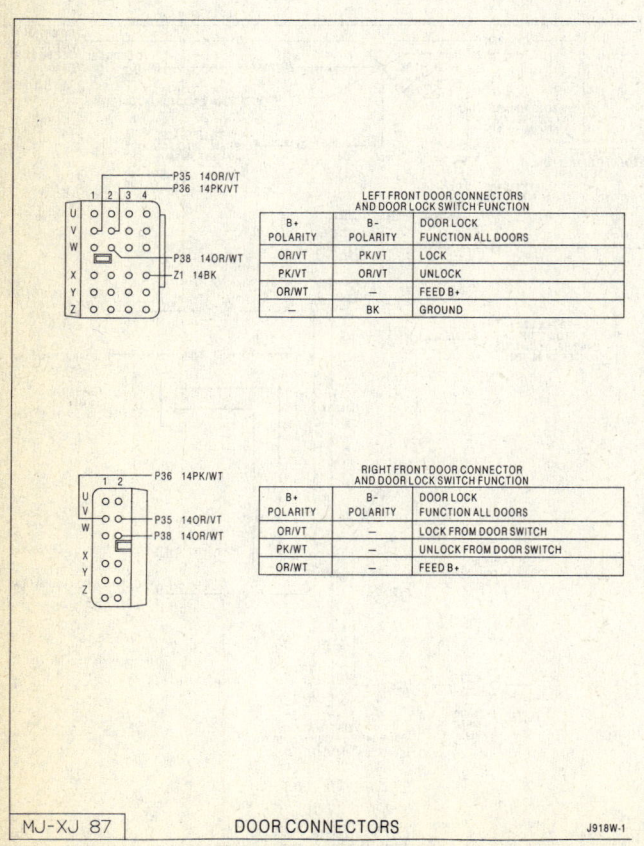
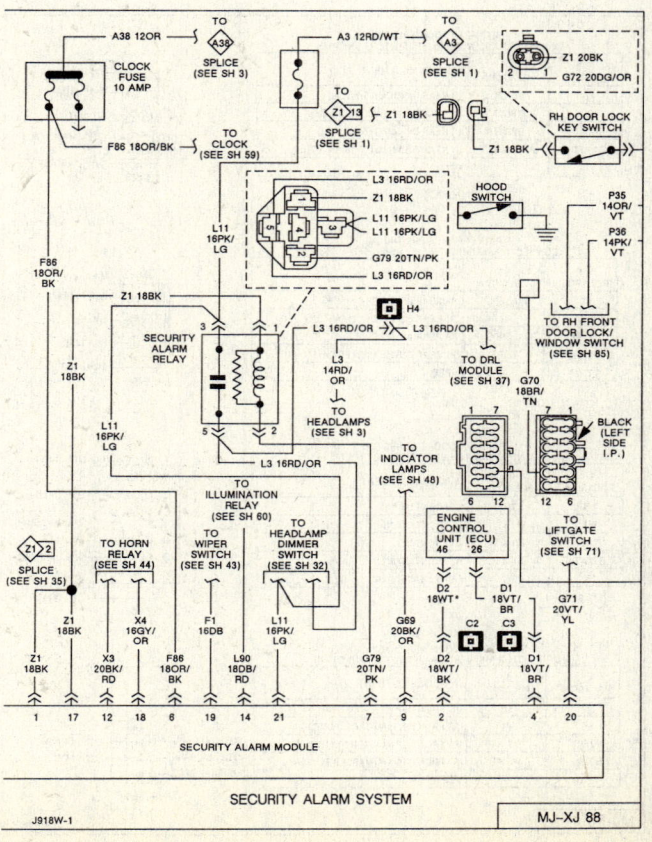

CHASSIS ELECTRICAL 6

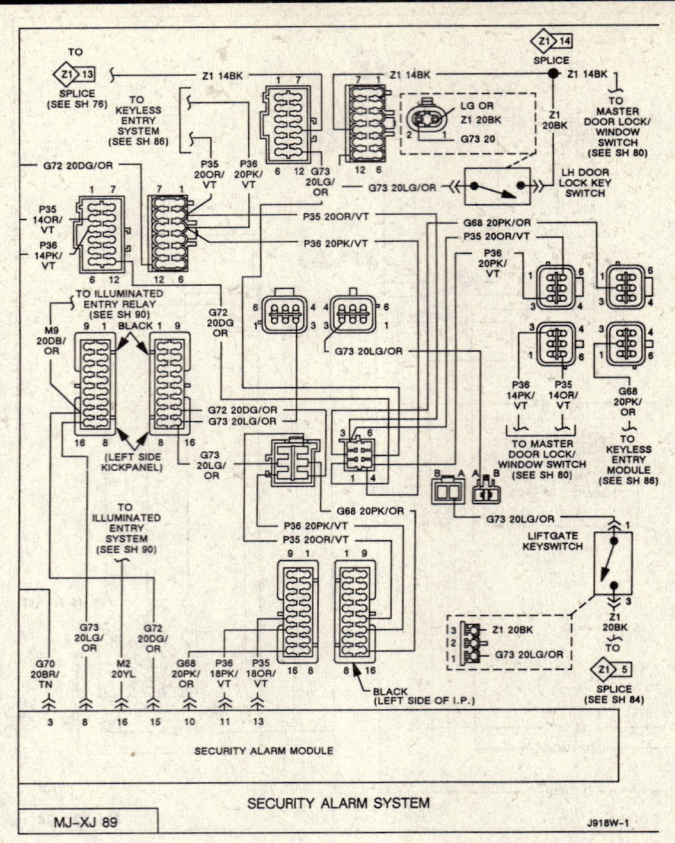

SECURITY ALARM SYSTEM

MJ-XJ 89

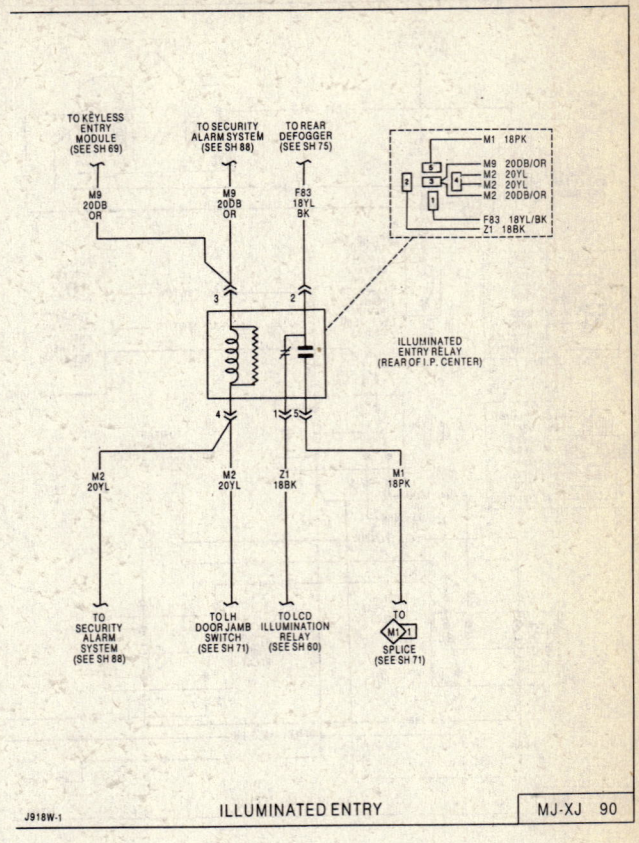

ILLUMINATED ENTRY

MJ-XJ 90

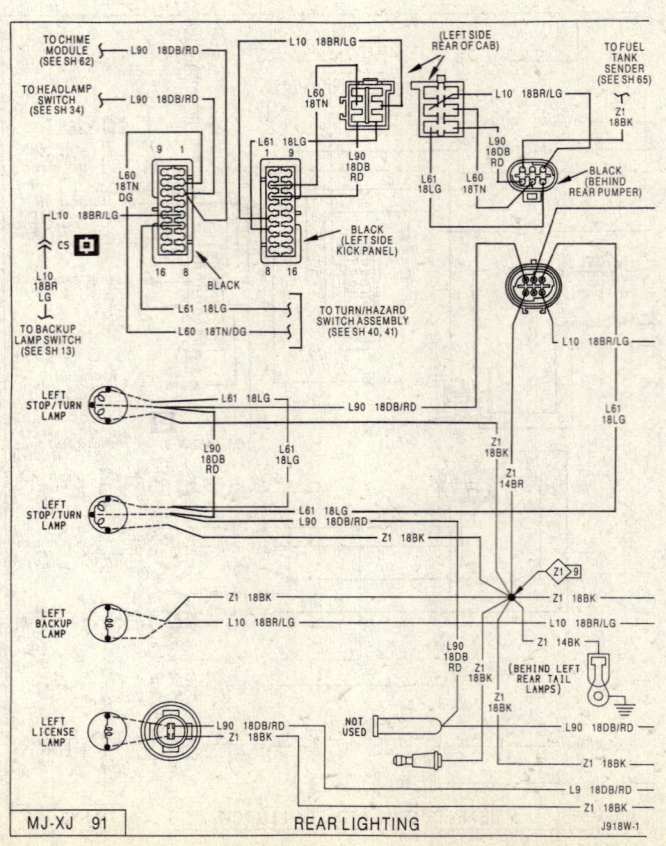

REAR LIGHTING

MJ-XJ 91

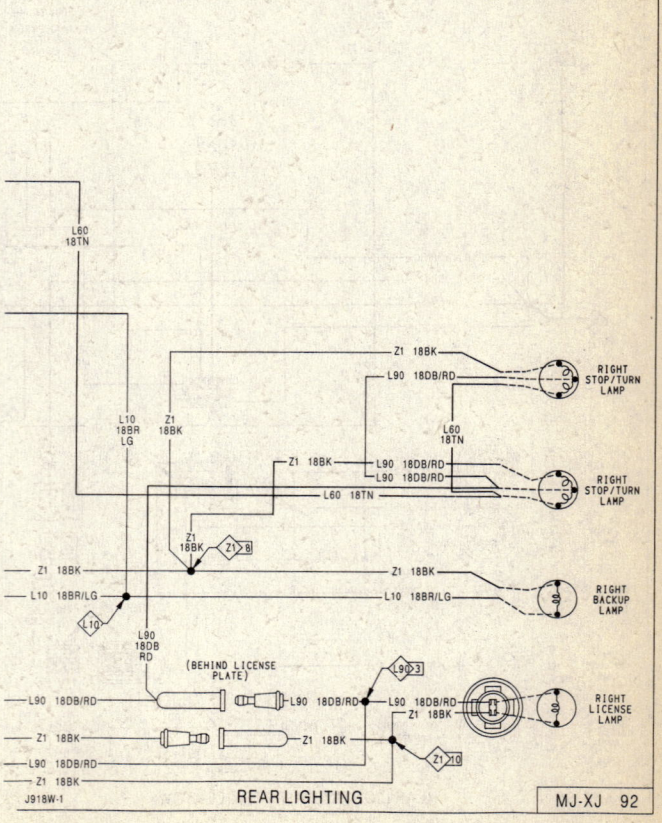

REAR LIGHTING

MJ-XJ 92

6-131

6 CHASSIS ELECTRICAL

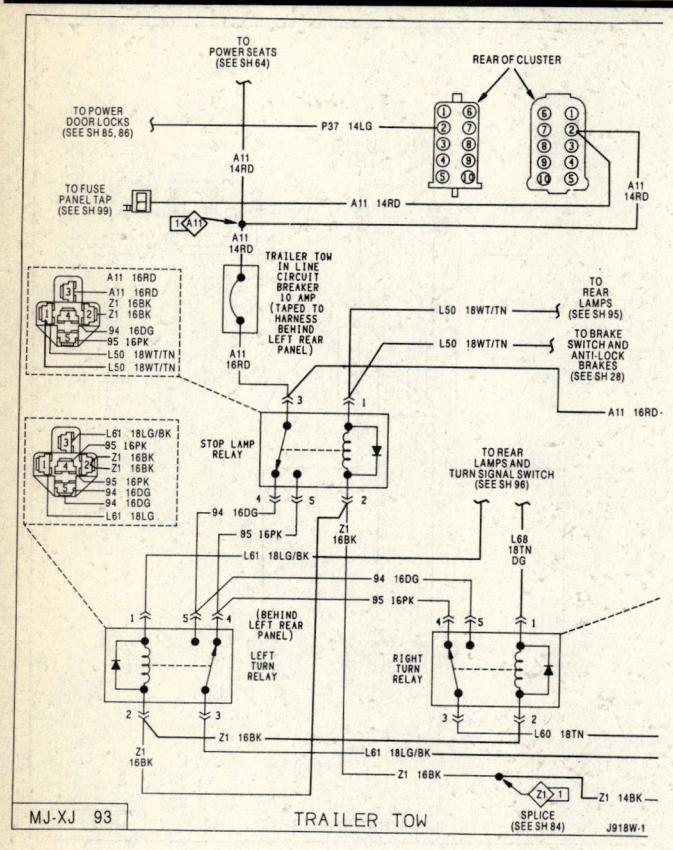

TRAILER TOW — MJ-XJ 93

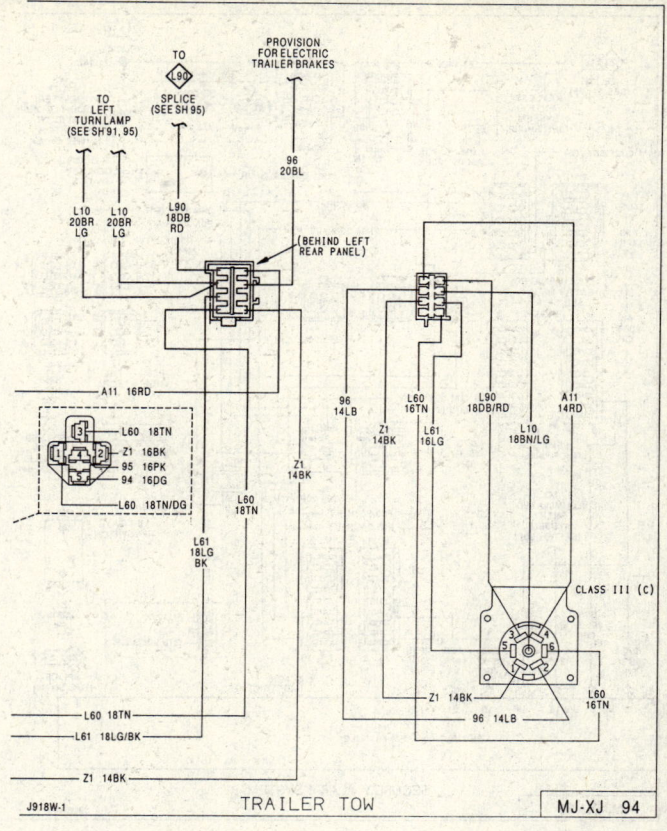

TRAILER TOW — MJ-XJ 94

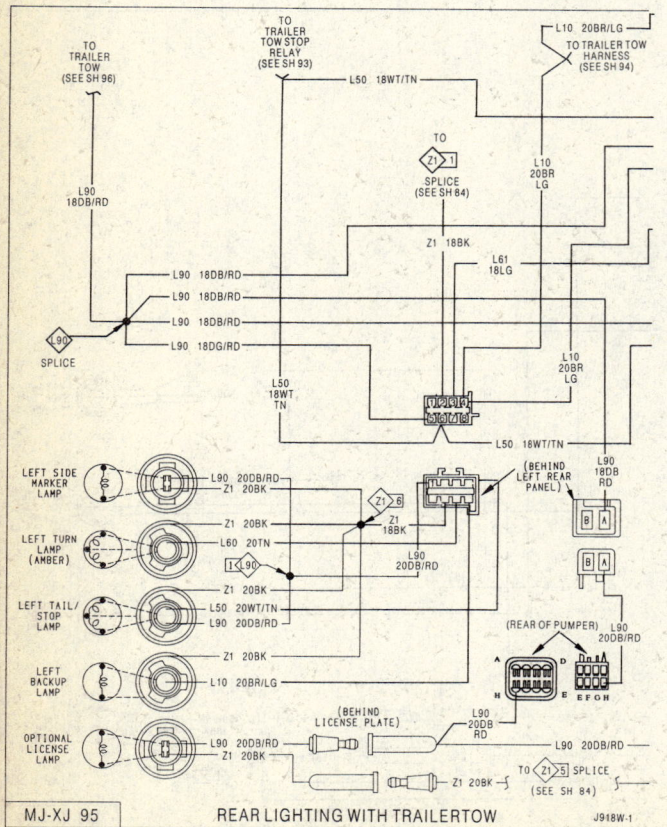

REAR LIGHTING WITH TRAILERTOW — MJ-XJ 95

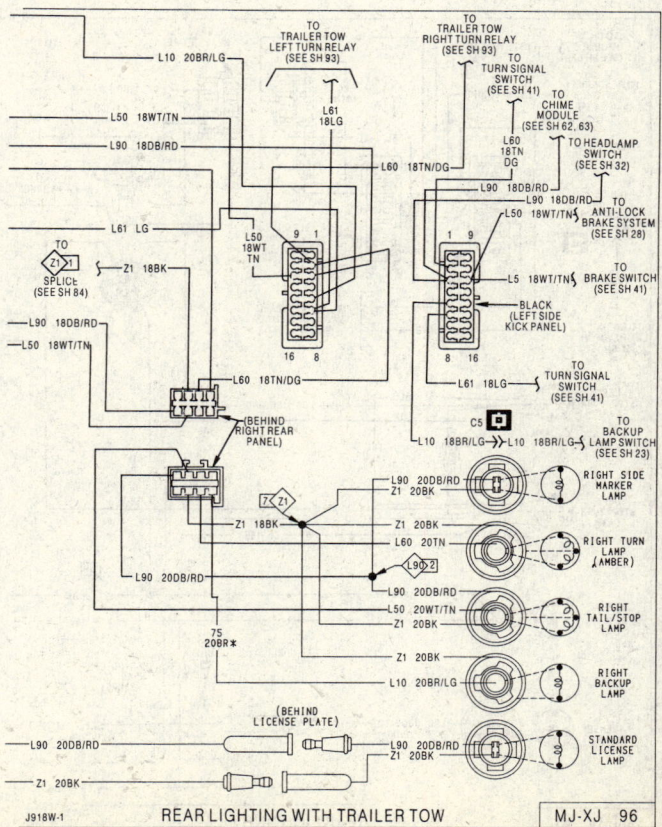

REAR LIGHTING WITH TRAILER TOW — MJ-XJ 96

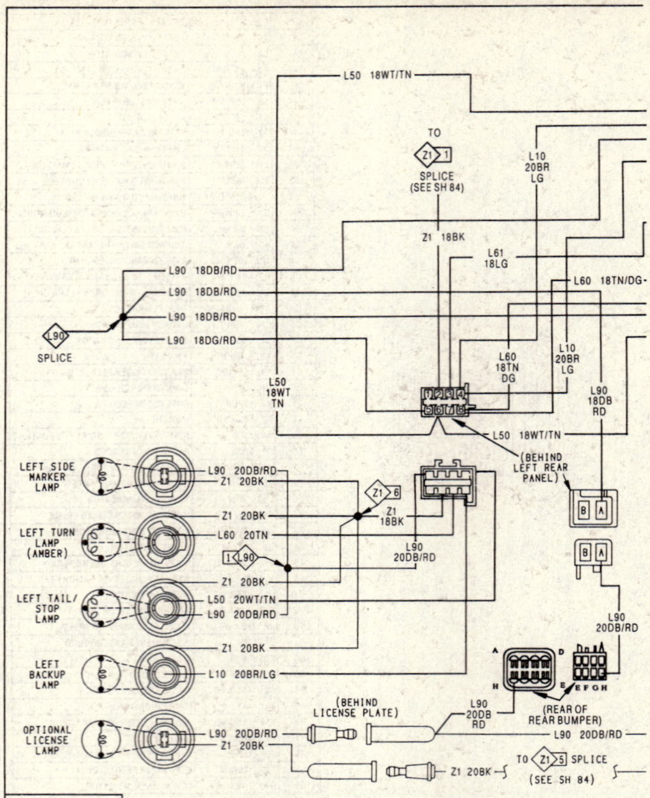

CHASSIS ELECTRICAL 6

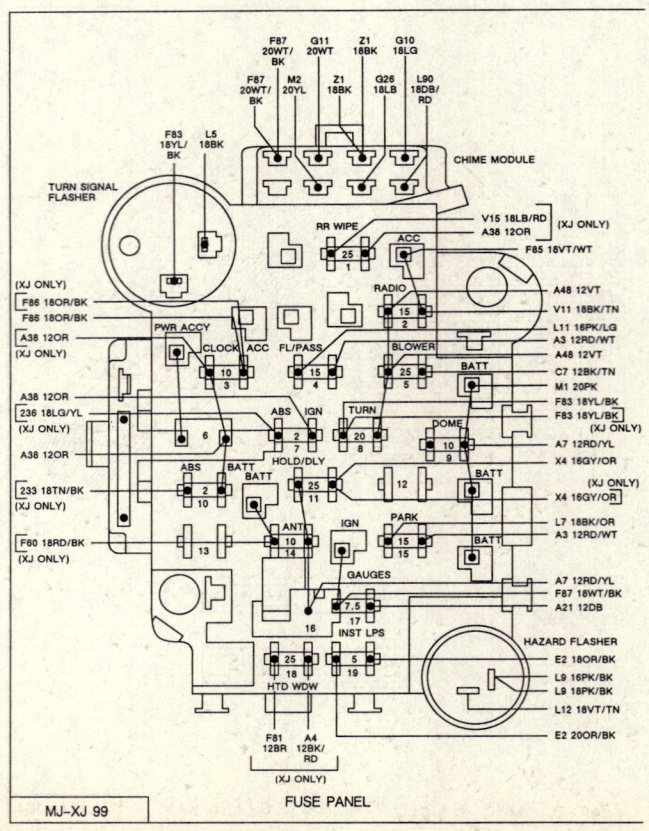

FUSE NUMBER	AMPS	COLOR
1	25	WHITE
2	15	LIGHT BLUE
3	10	RED
4	15	LIGHT BLUE
5	25	WHITE
6		
7	2	PINK
8	20	YELLOW
9	10	RED
10	2	PINK
11	25	WHITE
12		
13		
14	10	RED
15	15	LIGHT BLUE
16		
17	7.5	VIOLET
18	25	WHITE
19	5	TAN

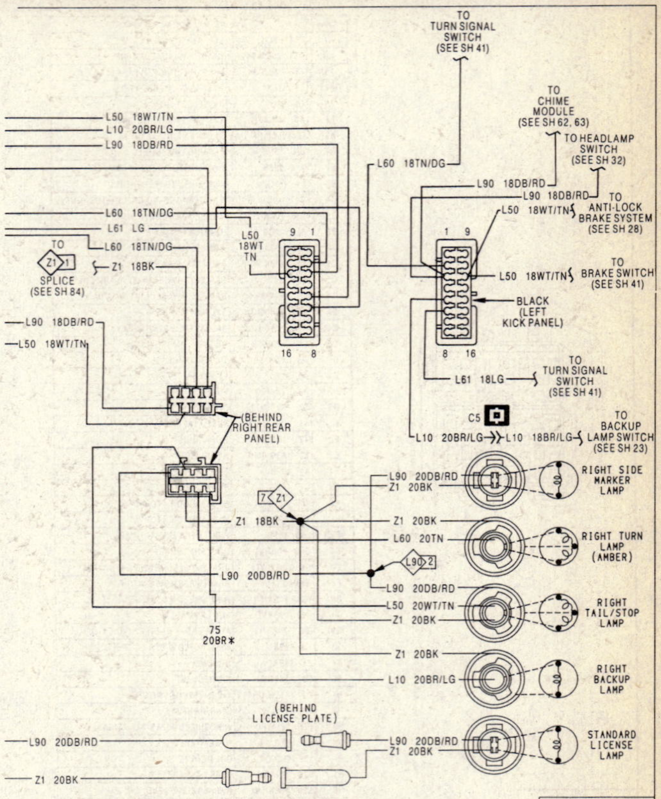

6-133

6 CHASSIS ELECTRICAL

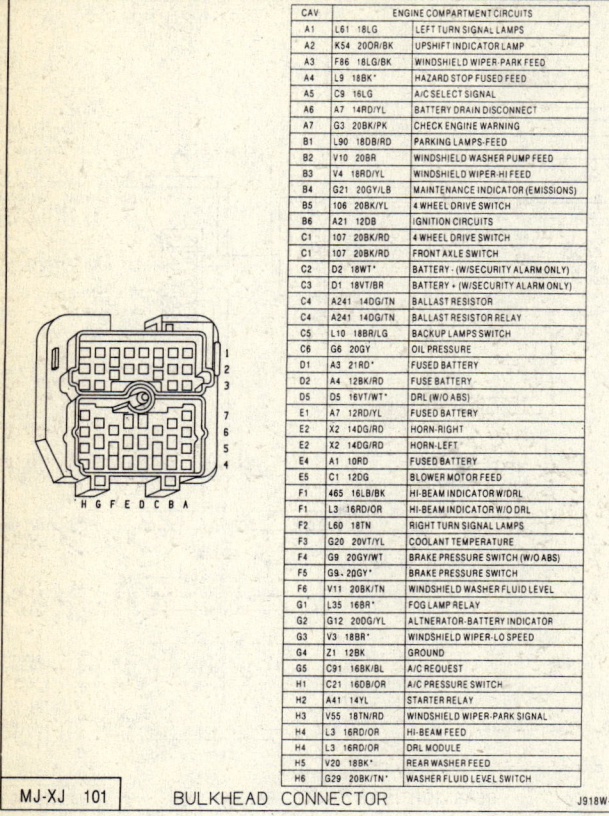

CAV	ENGINE COMPARTMENT CIRCUITS	
A1	L61 18LG	LEFT TURN SIGNAL LAMPS
A2	K54 20OR/BK	UPSHIFT INDICATOR LAMP
A3	F86 18LG/BK	WINDSHIELD WIPER-PARK FEED
A4	L9 18BK*	HAZARD STOP FUSED FEED
A5	C9 16LG	A/C SELECT SIGNAL
A6	A7 14RD/YL	BATTERY DRAIN DISCONNECT
A7	G3 20BK/PK	CHECK ENGINE WARNING
B1	L90 18DB/RD	PARKING LAMPS-FEED
B2	V10 20BR	WINDSHIELD WASHER PUMP FEED
B3	V4 18RD/YL	WINDSHIELD WIPER-HI FEED
B4	G21 20GY/LB	MAINTENANCE INDICATOR (EMISSIONS)
B5	106 20BK/YL	4 WHEEL DRIVE SWITCH
B6	A21 12DB	IGNITION CIRCUITS
C1	107 20BK/RD	4 WHEEL DRIVE SWITCH
C1	107 20BK/RD	FRONT AXLE SWITCH
C2	D2 18WT*	BATTERY - (W/SECURITY ALARM ONLY)
C3	D1 18VT/BR	BATTERY + (W/SECURITY ALARM ONLY)
C4	A241 14DG/TN	BALLAST RESISTOR
C4	A241 14DG/TN	BALLAST RESISTOR RELAY
C5	L10 18BR/LG	BACKUP LAMPS SWITCH
C6	G6 20GY	OIL PRESSURE
D1	A3 21RD*	FUSED BATTERY
D2	A4 12BK/RD	FUSE BATTERY
D5	C16 16VT/WT*	DRL (W/O ABS)
E1	A7 12RD/YL	FUSED BATTERY
E2	X2 14DG/RD	HORN-RIGHT
E2	X2 14DG/RD	HORN-LEFT
E4	A1 10RD	FUSED BATTERY
E5	C1 12DG	BLOWER MOTOR FEED
F1	465 16LB/BK	HI-BEAM INDICATOR W/DRL
F1	L3 16RD/OR	HI-BEAM INDICATOR W/O DRL
F2	L60 18TN	RIGHT TURN SIGNAL LAMPS
F3	G20 20VT/YL	COOLANT TEMPERATURE
F4	G9 20GY/WT	BRAKE PRESSURE SWITCH (W/O ABS)
F5	G9 20GY*	BRAKE PRESSURE SWITCH
F6	V11 20BK/TN	WINDSHIELD WASHER FLUID LEVEL
G1	L35 16BR*	FOG LAMP RELAY
G2	G12 200G/YL	ALTNERATOR-BATTERY INDICATOR
G3	V3 18BR*	WINDSHIELD WIPER-LO SPEED
G4	Z1 12BK	GROUND
G5	C91 16BK/BL	A/C REQUEST
H1	C21 16DB/OR	A/C PRESSURE SWITCH
H2	A41 14YL	STARTER RELAY
H3	V55 18TN/RD	WINDSHIELD WIPER-PARK SIGNAL
H4	L3 16RD/OR	HI-BEAM FEED
H4	L3 16RD/OR	DRL MODULE
H5	V20 18BK*	REAR WASHER FEED
H6	G29 20BK/TN*	WASHER FLUID LEVEL SWITCH

MJ-XJ 101   BULKHEAD CONNECTOR   J918W-1

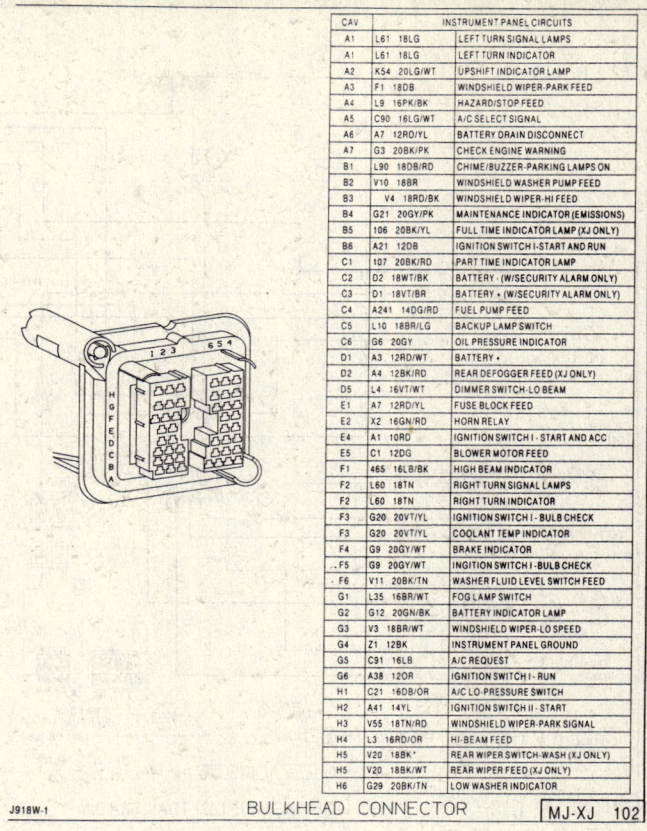

CAV	INSTRUMENT PANEL CIRCUITS	
A1	L61 18LG	LEFT TURN SIGNAL LAMPS
A1	L61 18LG	LEFT TURN INDICATOR
A2	K54 20LG/WT	UPSHIFT INDICATOR LAMP
A3	F1 18DB	WINDSHIELD WIPER-PARK FEED
A4	L9 16PK/BK	HAZARD/STOP FEED
A5	C90 16LG/WT	A/C SELECT SIGNAL
A6	A7 12RD/YL	BATTERY DRAIN DISCONNECT
A7	G3 20BK/PK	CHECK ENGINE WARNING
B1	L90 18DB/RD	CHIME/BUZZER-PARKING LAMPS ON
B2	V10 18BR	WINDSHIELD WASHER PUMP FEED
B3	V4 18RD/BK	WINDSHIELD WIPER-HI FEED
B4	G21 20GY/PK	MAINTENANCE INDICATOR (EMISSIONS)
B5	106 20BK/YL	FULL TIME INDICATOR LAMP (XJ ONLY)
B6	A21 12DB	IGNITION SWITCH I-START AND RUN
C1	107 20BK/RD	PART TIME INDICATOR LAMP
C2	D2 18WT/BK	BATTERY - (W/SECURITY ALARM ONLY)
C3	D1 18VT/BR	BATTERY + (W/SECURITY ALARM ONLY)
C4	A241 14DG/TN	FUEL PUMP FEED
C5	L10 18BR/LG	BACKUP LAMP SWITCH
C6	G6 20GY	OIL PRESSURE INDICATOR
D1	A7 12RD/WT	BATTERY +
D2	A4 12BK/RD	REAR DEFOGGER FEED (XJ ONLY)
D5	L4 16VT/WT	DIMMER SWITCH-LO BEAM
E1	A7 12RD/YL	FUSE BLOCK FEED
E2	X2 16GN/RD	HORN RELAY
E4	A1 10RD	IGNITION SWITCH I-START AND ACC
E5	C1 12DG	BLOWER MOTOR FEED
F1	465 16LB/BK	HIGH BEAM INDICATOR
F2	L60 18TN	RIGHT TURN SIGNAL LAMPS
F2	L60 18TN	RIGHT TURN INDICATOR
F3	G20 20VT/YL	IGNITION SWITCH I - BULB CHECK
F3	G20 20VT/YL	COOLANT TEMP INDICATOR
F4	G9 20GY/WT	BRAKE INDICATOR
F5	G9 20GY/WT	IGNITION SWITCH I - BULB CHECK
F6	V11 20BK/TN	WASHER FLUID LEVEL SWITCH FEED
G1	L35 16BR/WT	FOG LAMP SWITCH
G2	G12 20GN/BK	BATTERY INDICATOR LAMP
G3	V3 18BR/WT	WINDSHIELD WIPER-LO SPEED
G4	Z1 12BK	INSTRUMENT PANEL GROUND
G5	C91 16LB	A/C REQUEST
G6	A38 12OR	IGNITION SWITCH I - RUN
H1	A41 14YL	IGNITION SWITCH II - START
H2	C21 16DB/OR	A/C LO-PRESSURE SWITCH
H3	V55 18TN/RD	WINDSHIELD WIPER-PARK SIGNAL
H4	L3 16RD/OR	HI-BEAM FEED
H4	L61 18LG	LEFT TURN INDICATOR
H5	V20 18BK*	REAR WIPER SWITCH-WASH (XJ ONLY)
H5	V20 18BK/WT	REAR WIPER FEED (XJ ONLY)
H6	G29 20BK/TN*	LOW WASHER INDICATOR

BULKHEAD CONNECTOR   MJ-XJ 102

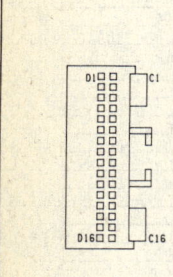

CAV	TCU SYSTEM CIRCUITS	
C1	—	—
C2	—	—
C3	505 18TN*	ROAD SPEED
C4	137 16YL/BK	TRANS DIAGNOSTIC CONNECTOR
C5	—	—
C6	—	—
C7	—	—
C8	506 18LG*	1-2 GEAR INPUT
C9	507 18GY*	D GEAR INPUT
C10	K29 18WT/PK	BRAKE/TORQUE CONVERTER
C11	177 20TN	POWER INPUT SIGNAL
C12	—	—
C13	—	—
C14	508 18WT*	CONVERTER LOCKUP
C15	509 18VT*	S2 SOLENOID
C16	510 18DB*	S1 SOLENOID
D1	—	—
D2	K22 18OR/DB	TPS INPUT
D3	K4K 18BK/LB	SENSOR GROUND
D4	—	—
D5	—	—
D6	—	—
D7	Z12 18BK/TN	GROUND
D8	—	—
D9	—	—
D10	—	—
D11	—	—
D12	—	—
D13	—	—
D14	A14 14RD	BATTERY
D15	—	—
D16	T17 18YL	IGNITION

MJ-XJ 103   (AUTOMATIC TRANSMISSION) 32 WAY SINGLE MODULE TRANSMISSION CONTROLLER CONNECTOR   J918W-1

CAV	TURN SIGNAL SWITCH CIRCUITS	
P	110 18LG/BK	NOT USED (XJ ONLY)
P	L50 18WT/TN	STOP LAMP FEED (MJ ONLY)
N	L60 18TN/DG	RIGHT TURN-REAR
M	L61 18LG	LEFT TURN-REAR
L	L5 18K	TURN SIGNAL FLASHER
K	L12 18VT/TN	HAZARD FLASHER
J	L60 18TN	RIGHT TURN-FRONT/INDICATOR
H	L61 18LG	LEFT TURN-FRONT/INDICATOR
G	X3 20BK/RD	HORN SWITCH
F	L7 18BK/OR	IGNITION KEY WARNING SWITCH
E	G26 18LB	IGNITION KEY WARNING SWITCH
D	—	—

J918W-1   STEERING COLUMN CONNECTOR 11 WAY   MJ-XJ 104

CHASSIS ELECTRICAL 6

INDICATOR CONNECTOR - 16 WAY (W/O ABS)

CAV		INSTRUMENT CLUSTER-INDICATOR CIRCUITS
1	G29 20BK/TN	LOW WASHER FLUID LAMP
2	G3 20BK/PK	CHECK ENGINE WARNING LAMP
3	F87 20WT/BK	I-1 IGNITION FEED
3	F87 20WT/BK	I-1 IGNITION FEED
4	F87 20WT/BK	I-1 IGNITION FEED
4	F87 20WT/BK	I-1 IGNITION FEED
5	—	—
6	—	—
7	K54 20LG/WT	UPSHIFT LAMP
8	G9 20BK/OR	BRAKE LAMP
9	G69 20BK/OR	SECURITY ALARM WARNING LAMP
10	M1 18PK	COURTESY LAMPS
11	106 20BK/YL	4WD FULL LAMP
12	107 20BK/RD	4WD LOCK LAMP
13	G24 20GY/PK	EMISSION MAINTENANCE LAMP
14	F87 20WT/BR	I-1 IGNITION FEED
14	F87 20WT/BK	I-1 IGNITION FEED
15	G11 20WT	SEAT BELT LAMP
16	Z1 20BK	GROUND
16	Z1 20BK	GROUND

INDICATOR CONNECTOR - 16 WAY (W/ABS)

CAV		INSTRUMENT CLUSTER-INDICATOR CIRCUITS
1	G29 20BK/TN	LOW WASHER FLUID LAMP
2	G3 20BK/PK	CHECK ENGINE WARNING LAMP
3	F87 20WT/BK	I-1 IGNITION FEED
3	F87 20WT/BK	I-1 IGNITION FEED
4	F87 20WT/BK	I-1 IGNITION FEED
4	F87 20WT/BK	I-1 IGNITION FEED
5	—	—
6	205 18YL	ABS YELLOW LAMP
7	K54 20LG/WT	UPSHIFT LAMP
8	204 18DB/OR	BRAKE LAMP
9	G69 20BK/OR	SECURITY ALARM WARNING LAMP
10	M1 18PK	COURTESY LAMPS
11	106 20BK/YL	4WD FULL LAMP
12	107 20BK/RD	4WD LOCK LAMP
13	G24 20GY/PK	EMISSION MAINTENANCE LAMP
14	F87 20WT/BK	I-1 IGNITION FEED
14	F87 20WT/BK	I-1 IGNITION FEED
15	G11 20WT	SEAT BELT LAMP
16	Z1 20BK	GROUND
16	Z1 20BK	GROUND

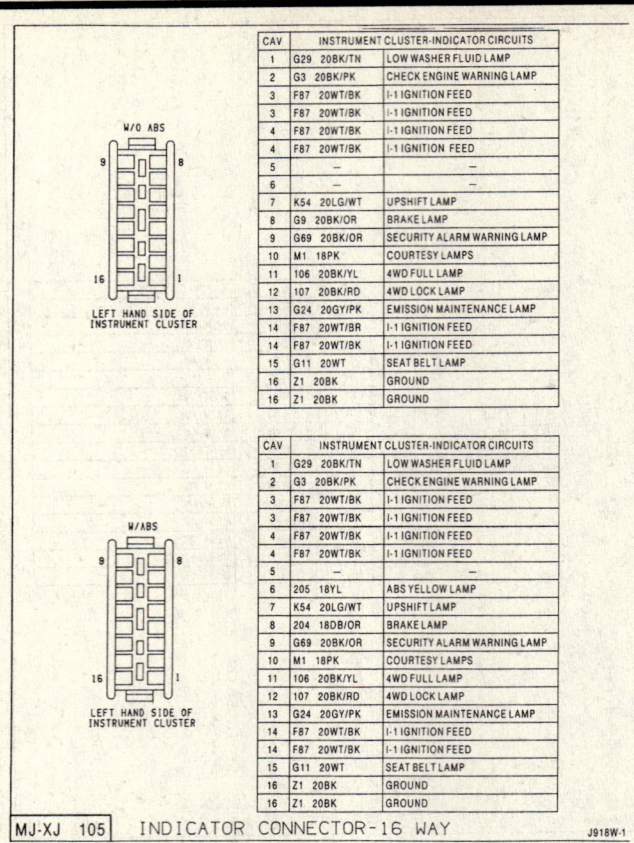

INSTRUMENT CLUSTER CONNECTOR - 16 WAY

CAV		INSTRUMENT CLUSTER-INDICATORS/GAUGES
A1	G20 20VT/YL	COOLANT TEMPERATURE
A2	L61 18LG	LEFT TURN LAMP
A3	Z1 20BK	GROUND
A4	465 16LB/RD	HEADLAMP HI-BEAM
A5	G7 18WT/OR	DISTANCE SENSOR INPUT
A6	G21 18GY/BK	TACHOMETER
A7	E2 20OR/BK	ILLUMINATION
A8	F87 18WT/BK	FUSED IGNITION
B1	G4 20DB	FUEL GAUGE
B2	Z2 18BK/LG	LOGIC GROUND
B3	—	—
B4	—	—
B5	—	—
B6	L60 18TN	RIGHT TURN LAMP
B7	G6 20GY	OIL PRESSURE
B8	—	BATTERY LAMP

MAIN BODY CONNECTORS

CAV		BODY CONNECTOR - #1 CIRCUITS
1	X58 20DB/OR	SPEAKER RETURN-RIGHT REAR
2	X52 20DB/WT	SPEAKER FEED-RIGHT REAR
3	E2 20OR/BK	ILLUMINATION
4	Z1 14BK	GROUND
5	M1 20PK	COURTESY LAMPS
6	X57 20BR/LB	SPEAKER RETURN-LEFT REAR
7	X51 20BR/YL	SPEAKER FEED-LEFT REAR
8	M2 20YL	SWITCHED GROUND
9	M2 20YL	SWITCHED GROUND
10	G10 18LG	SEAT BELT SWITCH
11	V13 18BR/RD	REAR WIPER RUN
12	F20 18WT	REAR WIPER PARK
13	P35 18OR/VT	SECURITY ALARM LOCK RELAY
14	P36 18PK/WT	SECURITY ALARM UNLOCK RELAY
15	G71 20VT/YL	SECURITY ALARM LIFTGAGE INPUT
16	G68 20PK/OR	KEYLESS ARM INPUT

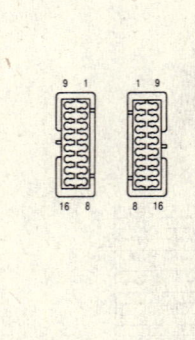

CAV		BODY CONNECTOR - #2 CIRCUITS
1	A241 14GR/RD	FUEL PUMP
2	L60 18TN/DG	RIGHT REAR TURN SIGNAL
3	L90 18DG/RD	PARKING LAMPS
3	L90 18DG/RD	PARKING LAMPS
4	G4 20DB	FUEL GAUGE
5	L10 18BR/LG	BACKUP LAMP SIGNAL
6	L61 18LG	LEFT REAR TURN SINAL
7	G9 20GY/WT	BRAKE PRESSURE WARNING SWITCH
7	203 20GN	BRAKE PRESSURE WARNING SWITCH
8	C15 12BK/RD	REAR DEFOGGER
9	110 16LG/BK	TURN/STOP FEED
10	V20 18BK/WT	REAR WASHER FEED
11	L50 18WT/TN	STOP LAMPS
11	L50 18WT/TN	STOP LAMPS
15	M9 20OR/BK	ILLUMINATED ENTRY SIGNAL
15	G72 20DG/OR	RIGHT FRONT DOOR SECURITY
16	G73 20LG/OR	LEFT FRONT DOOR SECURITY

MAIN BODY CONNECTORS

CAV		HEATING, VENTILATION, A/C CONNECTOR #3 CIRCUITS
1	E2 20OR/BK	ILLUMINATION
2	Z1 16BK	GROUND
3	C21 16DB/OR	A/C SELECT SIGNAL
4	C91 16LB	A/C SIGNAL TO EVAPORATOR
5	—	—
6	C1 12DG	BLOWER MOTOR FEED
7	C90 16LG/WT	A/C SELECT SIGNAL
8	C7 12BK/TN	HI BLOWER ENABLE
9	—	—
10	—	—

CAV		CAB HARNESS CONNECTOR - #4 CIRCUITS
1	A241 14DG/RD	FUEL PUMP
2	L60 18TN/DG	RIGHT REAR TURN SIGNAL
3	L90 18DB/RD	PARKING LAMPS
3	L90 18DB/RD	PARKING LAMPS
4	G4 20DB	FUEL GAUGE
5	L10 18BR/LG	BACKUP LAMP SIGNAL
6	L61 18LG	LEFT REAR TURN SINAL
7	X57 20BR/YL	SPEAKER FEED-LEFT REAR
8	X57 20BR/LB	SPEAKER RETURN-LEFT REAR
9	M2 18YL	SWITCHED GROUND
9	M2 18YL	SWITCHED GROUND
10	M1 20PK	COURTESY LAMPS
13	X58 20DB/OR	SPEAKER RETURN-RIGHT REAR
14	X52 20DB/WT	SPEAKER FEED-RIGHT REAR
15	G10 18LG	SEAT BELT SWITCH
16	E2 20OR/BK	ILLUMINATION

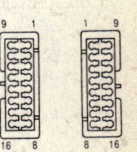

6 CHASSIS ELECTRICAL

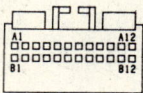

CAV			BODY CONNECTOR - CIRCUITS
A2	208	16TN	BRAKE MODULATOR B1
A3	209	16OR	BRAKE MODULATOR D1
A4	214	16YL/RD	BRAKE MODULATOR C2
A5	215	16DG/RD	BRAKE MODULATOR A1
A6	210	16GY	BRAKE MODULATOR F1
A7	216	16DB/RD	BRAKE MODULATOR D3
A8	213	16BR/RD	BRAKE MODULATOR D2
A9	212	16LB	BRAKE MODULATOR E1
A10	211	16LG	BRAKE MODULATOR C1
A11	207	18PK	ANTI-LOCK MODULATOR RELAY
A12	211	16BK*	GROUND
B11	211	16BK*	GROUND
B12	211	16BK*	GROUND
C1	211	16BK*	GROUND
C2	205	18VT	BRAKE ALERT
C3	238	18VT/YL	BATTERY
C4	242	20PK/WT	DIAGNOSTIC CONNECTOR 3
C5	204	18LB	LOW BRAKE PRESSURE WARNING
C7	217	20VT/RD	LOW ACCUMULATOR SENSOR
C8	202	20YL	BRAKE PUMP BOOST PRESSURE
C9	203	20DG	BRAKE FLUID LEVEL/PARKING BRAKE SWITCH
C10	201	12BR	BRAKE PUMP BOOST PRESSURE
C12	224	18LB/RD	RH REAR WHEEL SENSOR
C13	503	18WT	LH FRONT WHEEL SENSOR
C14	501	18VT	RH FRONT WHEEL SENSOR
C15	219	18PK/BK	LH REAR WHEEL SENSOR
D1	211	16BK*	GROUND
D2	211	16BK*	GROUND
D4	236	18LG/YL	IGNITION FEED
D6	241	20GN/YL	DIAGNOSTIC CONNECTOR 6
D8	235	20GY/YL	BRAKE MODULATOR SPLICE 235
D9	234	20OR/GN	ANTI-LOCK PUMP MOTOR B
D10	L50	18WT/TN	STOP LAMP SWITCH
D12	223	18LG/RD	RH REAR WHEEL SENSOR
D13	502	18DB	LH FRONT WHEEL SENSOR
D14	500	18OR	RH FRONT WHEEL SENSOR
D15	218	18WT/RD	LH REAR WHEEL SENSOR

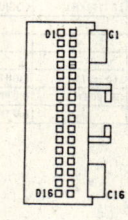

MJ-XJ 109 — ANTI-LOCK MODULE CONNECTORS 24 WAY AND 32 WAY

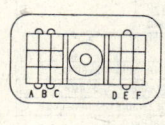

CAV			BRAKE MODULE
A1	215	16DG/RD	A.L.M. A5
A2	235	18GY/YL	SPLICE 235
A3	235	18GY/YL	SPLICE 235
B1	208	16TN	A.L.M. A2
B2	—	—	—
B3	235	18GY/YL	SPLICE 235
C1	211	16LG	A.L.M. A10
C2	214	16YL/RD	A.L.M. A4
C3	235	18GY/YL	SPLICE 235
D1	209	16OR	A.L.M. A3
D2	213	16BR/RD	A.L.M. A8
D3	216	16DB/RD	A.L.M. A7
E1	212	16LB	A.L.M. A9
F1	210	16GY	A.L.M. A6
F2	235	18GY/YL	SPLICE 235
F3	235	18GY/YL	SPLICE 235

BRAKE MODULE 18 WAY — MJ-XJ 110

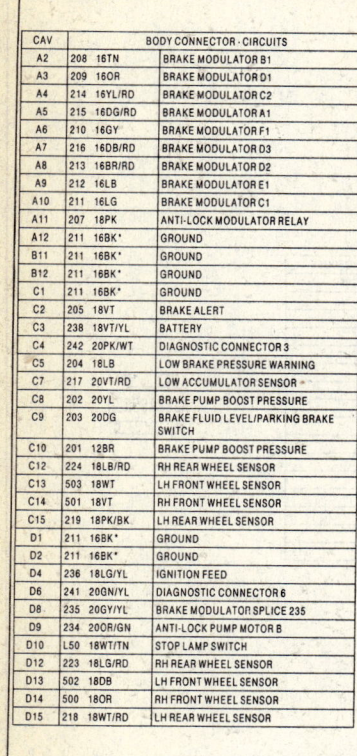

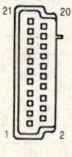

CAV			SECURITY ALARM MODULE CIRCUITS
1	Z1	18BK	GROUND
2	D2	18WT/BK	SERIAL BUSS B-
3	G70	20BR/TN	HOOD OPEN SIGNAL
4	D1	18VT/BR	SERIAL BUSS B+
6	F86	18OR/BK	FUSED IGNITION
7	G79	20TN/PK	HEADLAMP OUTPUT
8	G73	20LG/OR	LEFT FORNT DOOR KEYLOCK SIGNAL
9	G69	20BK/OR	SECURITY ALARM WARNING LAMP
10	G68	20PK/OR	KEYLESS ARM INPUT
11	P36	18PK/VT	KEYLESS UNLOCK RELAY SIGNAL
12	X3	20BK/RD	HORN OUTPUT
13	P35	18OR/VT	KEYLESS LOCK RELAY SIGNAL
14	L90	18DB/RD	PARKING LAMP OUTPUT
15	G72	20DG/OR	RIGHT FRONT DOOR KEYLESS SIGNAL
16	M2	20YL	SWITCHED GROUND
17	Z1	18BK	GROUND
18	X4	16GY/OR	HORN OUTPUT
19	F1	18DB	WIPER OUTPUT
20	G71	20VT/YL	LIFTGATE OPEN SIGNAL
21	L11	16PK/LG	FUSED BATTERY

MJ-XJ 111 — SECURITY ALARM MODULE CONNECTOR

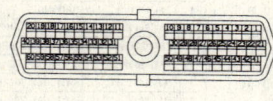

CAV			ECU SYSTEMS CIRCUITS	SHEET
1	K1	20DG/RD	MAP SENSOR	15, 20
2	K2	20TN/BK	COOLANT TEMP INPUT	15, 20
3	A14	14RD	BATTERY	13, 18
4	K4	18BK/LB	SENSOR GROUND	13, 15, 18, 20
5	Z11	16BK*	SIGNAL GROUND	14, 19
6	K6	20VT*	SENSOR 5 VOLT SUPPLY	20
7	K7	18OR	8 VOLT SUPPLY	12, 17
8	T40	16BR	START SIGNAL	9, 10
9	A21	14DB	IGNITION	13, 18
10	K10	18DB/OR	POWER STEERING SWITCH (2.5 ONLY)	16
11	Z12	16BK/TN	POWER GROUND	13, 18
12	Z12	16BK/TN	POWER GROUND	13, 18
13	K14	18LB/BR	INJECTOR 4	16, 21
14	K13	18YL/WT	INJECTOR 3	16, 21
15	K12	18TN	INJECTOR 2	16, 21
16	K11	18WT/DB	INJECTOR 1	16, 21
17				
18				
19	K19	18GY	IGNITION COIL	14, 19
20	K20	18DG	ALTNERATOR OUTPUT	7, 8
21	K21	18BK/RD	AIR TEMP SENSOR INPUT	15, 20
22	K22	20PK	THROTTLE POSITION SENSOR INPUT	15, 20
23				
24	K24	18GY/RD	CRANK POSITION SENSOR INPUT	12, 17
25	D21	20PK	DIAGNOSTIC SIGNAL	14, 19
26	D1	18VT/BR	SECURITY ALARM BATTERY OUTPUT	88
27	C91	16LB	A/C REQUEST	67
28	C90	16LG	A/C SELECT	67
29	K29	18WT	BRAKE SWITCH INPUT	41
30	T41	18BR/YL	PARK NEUTRAL SIGNAL (4.0L ONLY)	10
30	Z12	18BK/TN	PARK NEUTRAL SIGNAL (2.5 ONLY)	10

ENGINE CONTROL UNIT 60 WAY CONNECTOR — MJ-XJ 112

CHASSIS ELECTRICAL 6

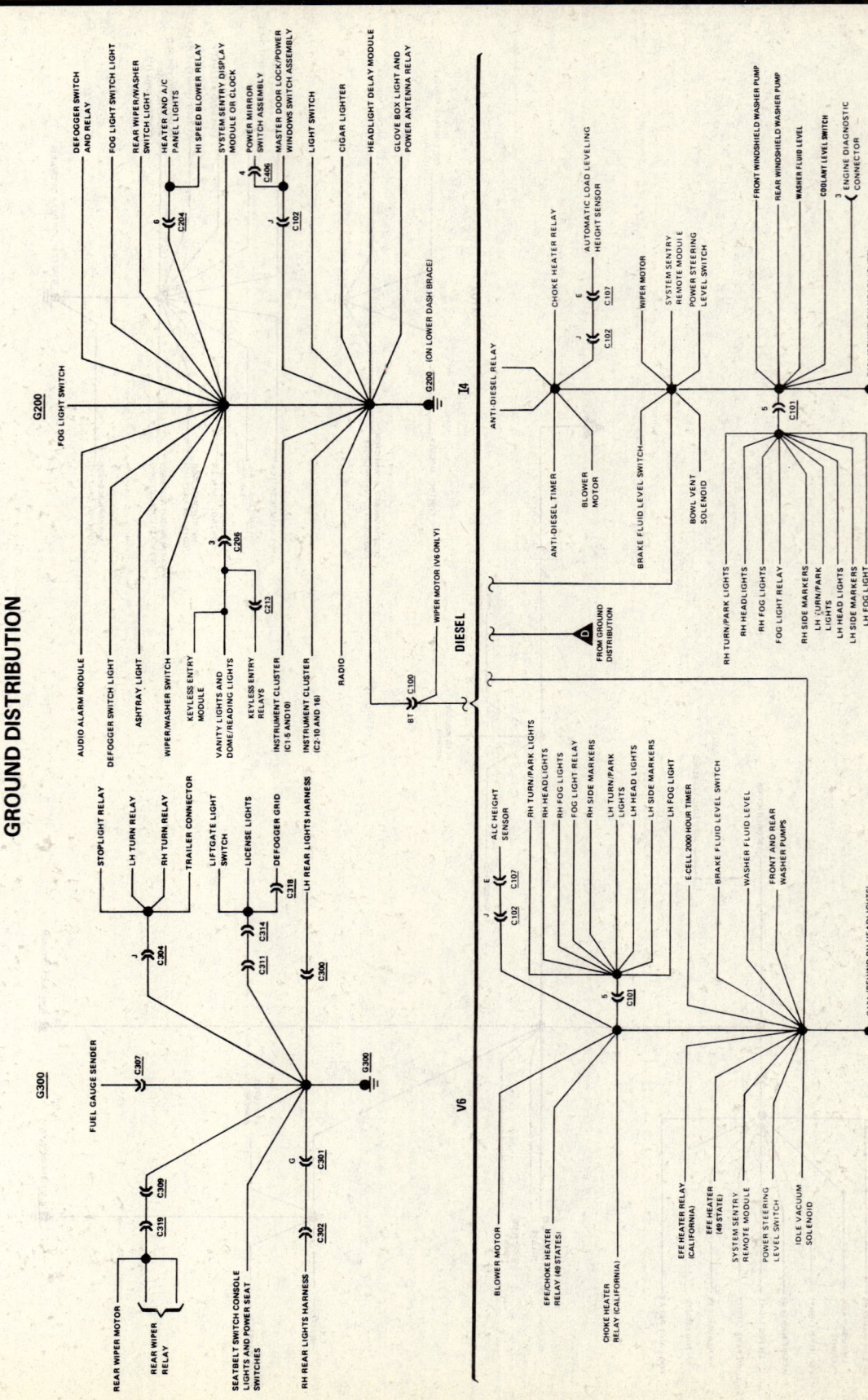

1984-85 Wagoneer and Cherokee

6-137

6 CHASSIS ELECTRICAL

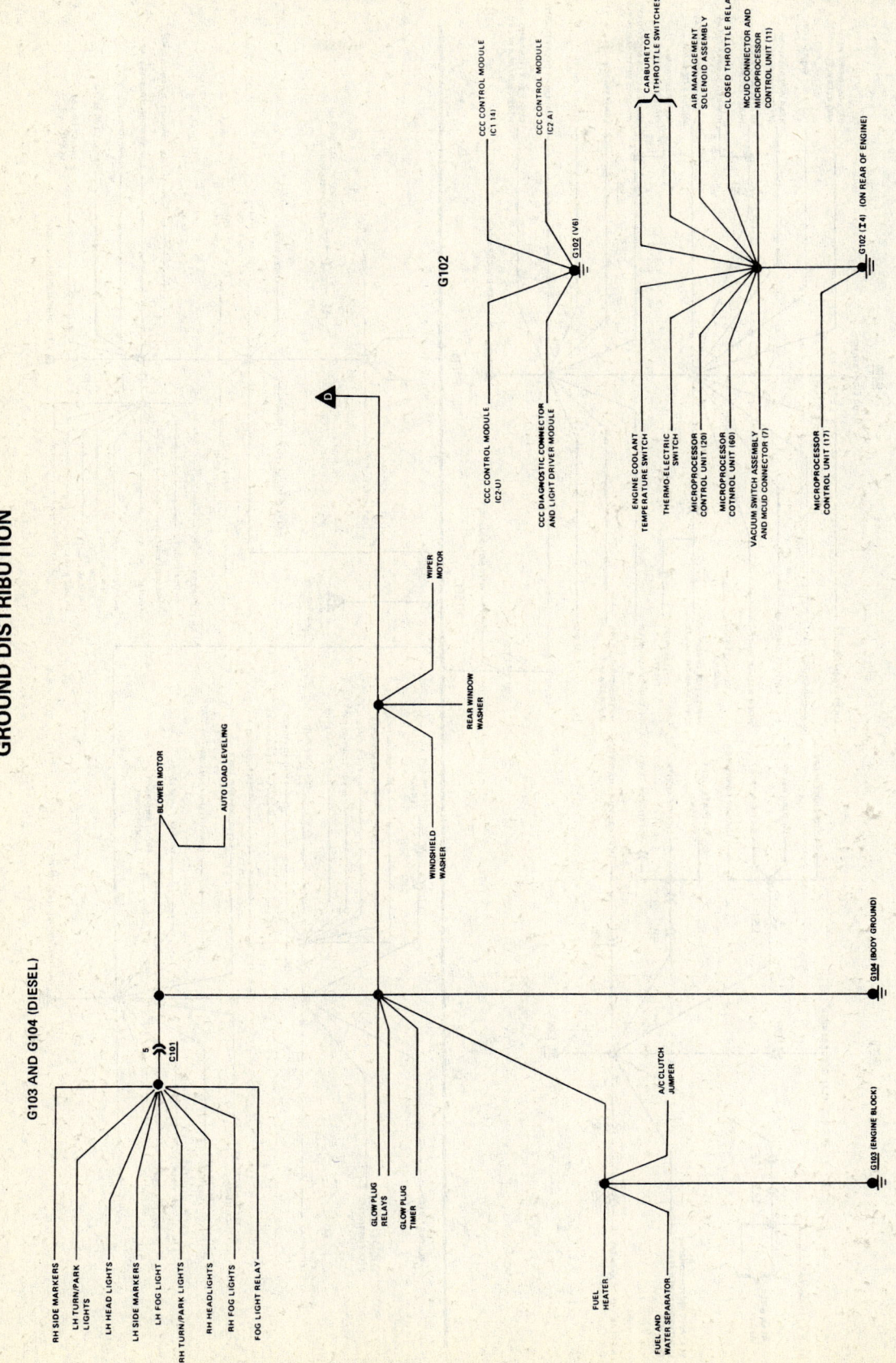

1984-85 Wagoneer and Cherokee

6-138

CHASSIS ELECTRICAL 6

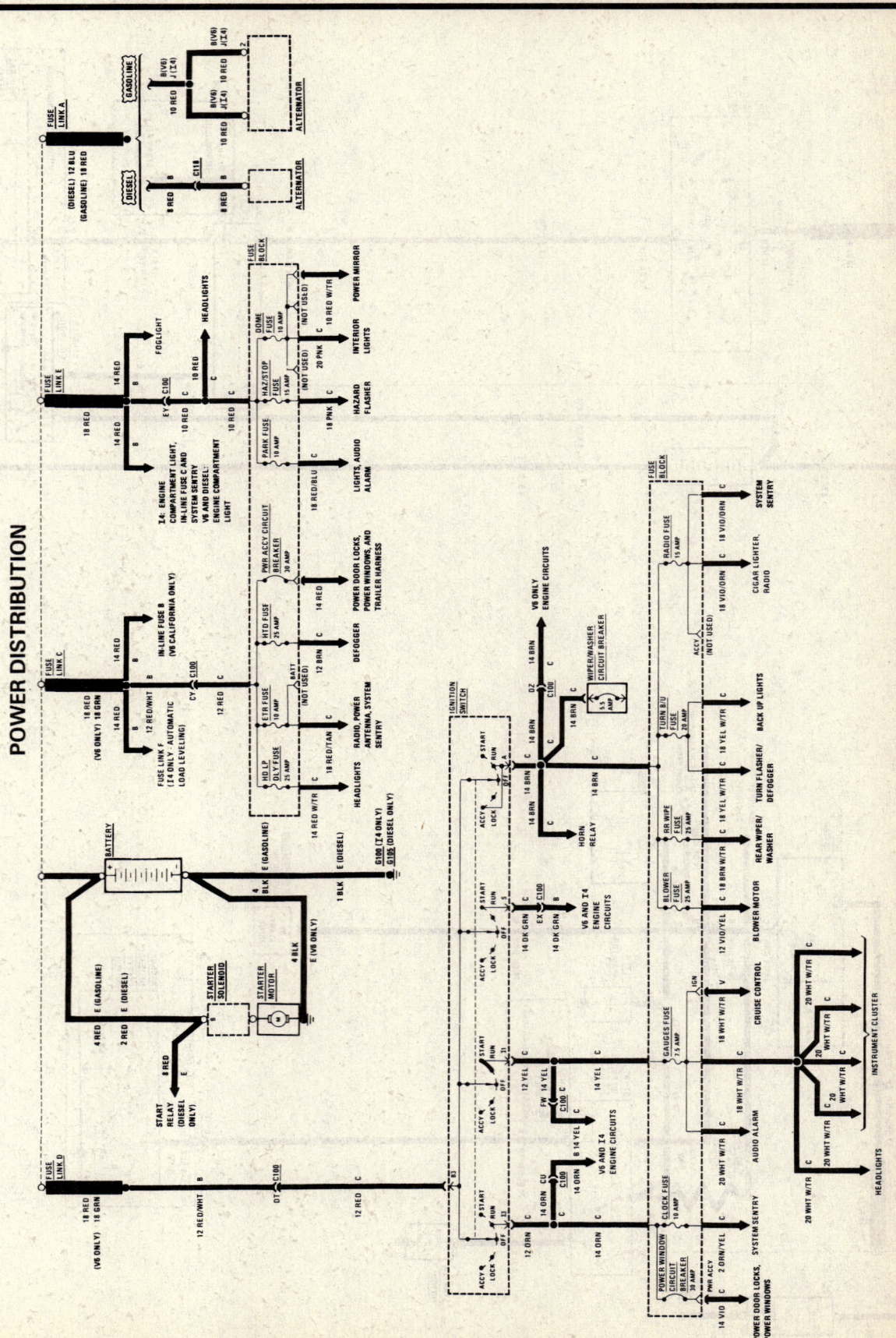

1984-85 Wagoneer and Cherokee

6-139

6 CHASSIS ELECTRICAL

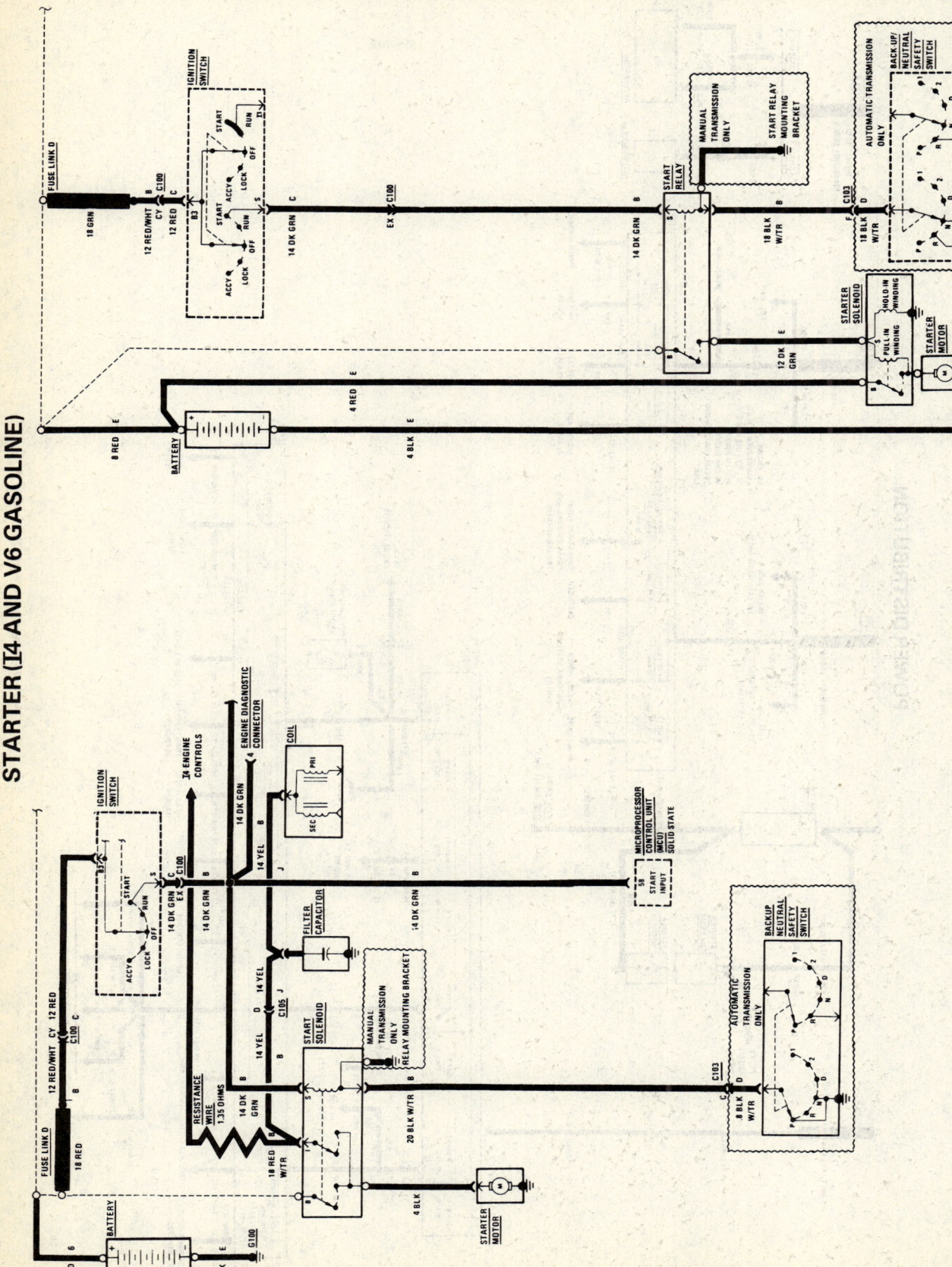

STARTER (I4 AND V6 GASOLINE)

1984-85 Wagoneer and Cherokee

6-140

CHASSIS ELECTRICAL 6

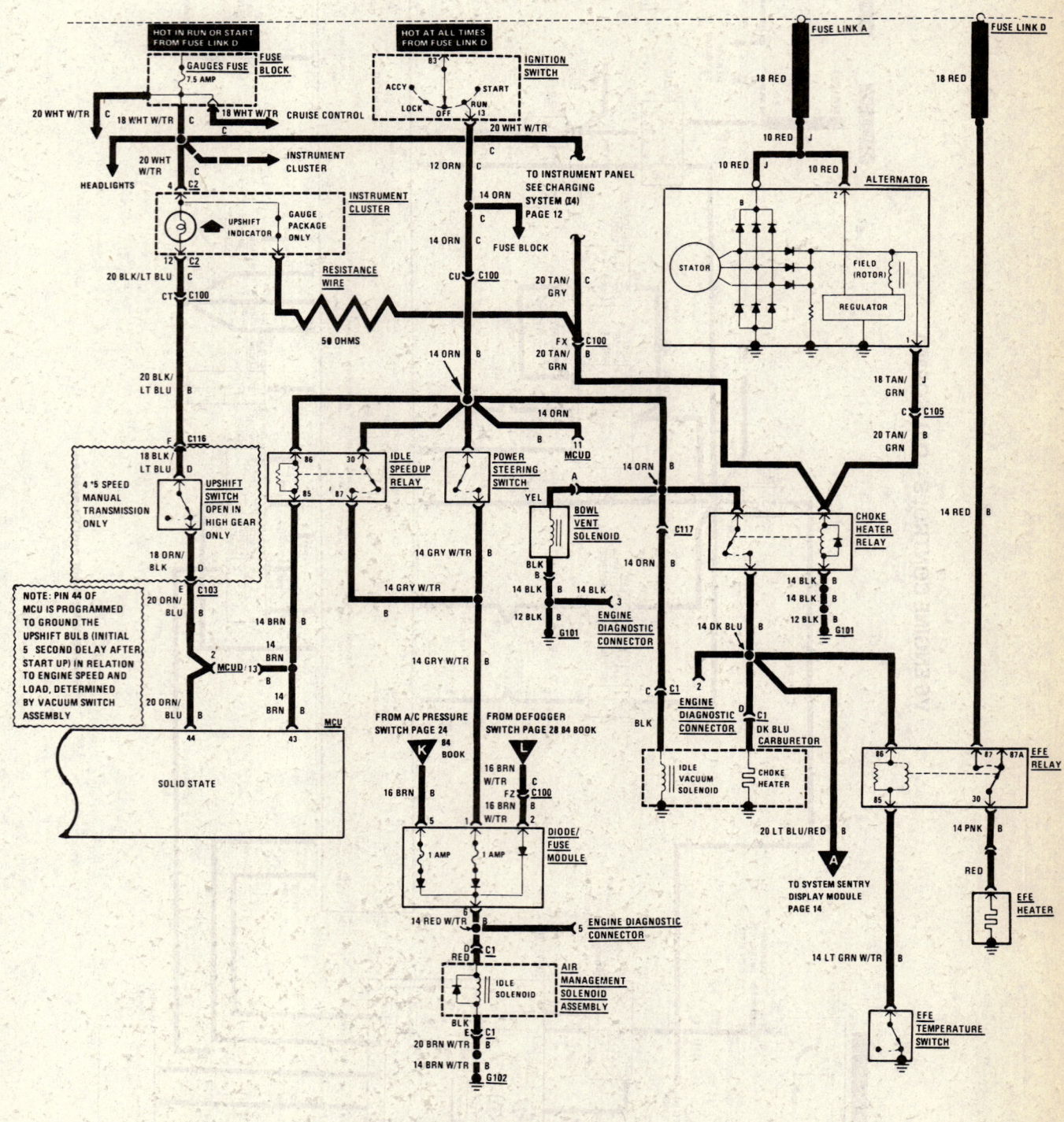

1984-85 Wagoneer and Cherokee

6-141

6 CHASSIS ELECTRICAL

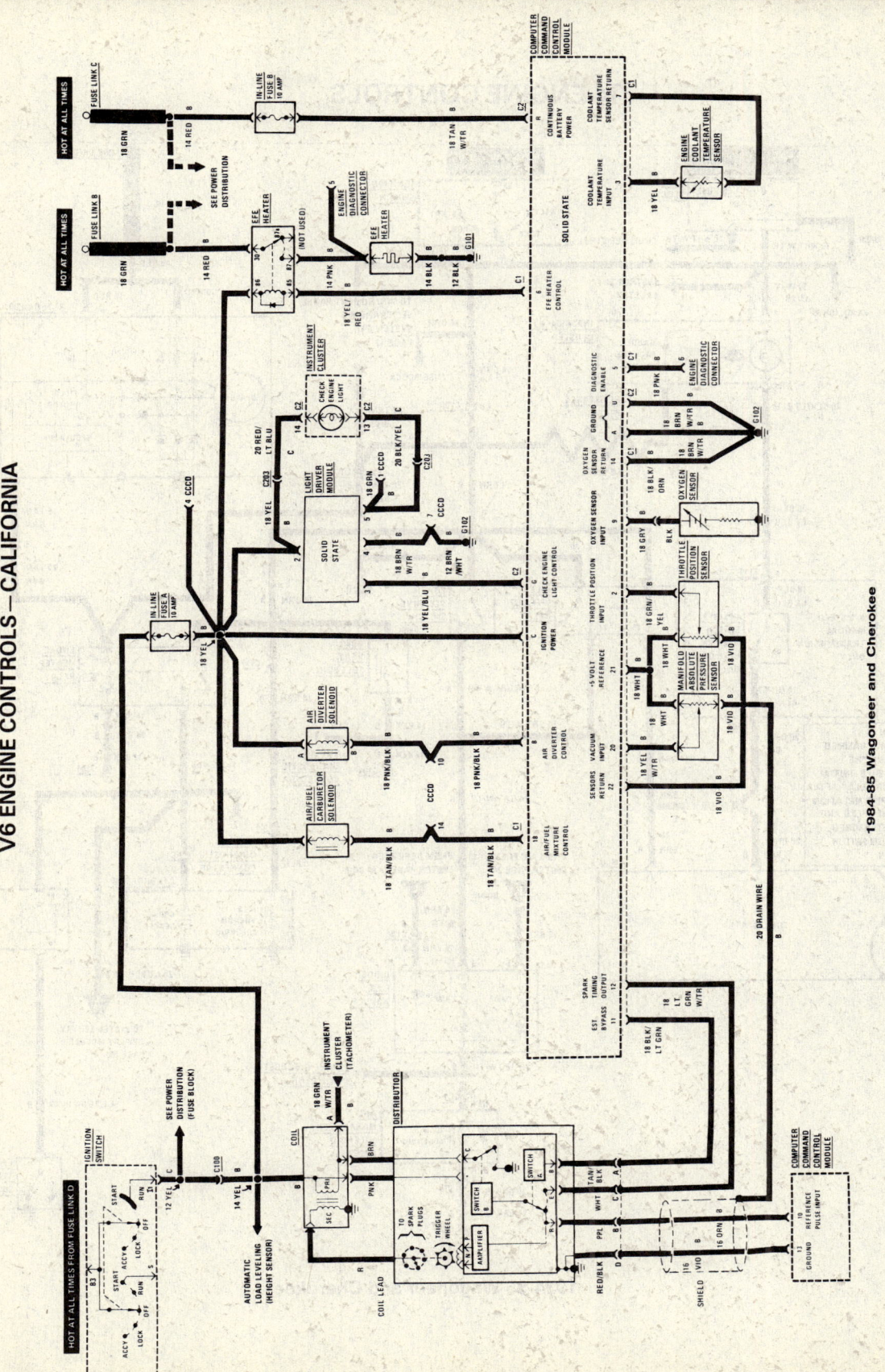

6-142

CHASSIS ELECTRICAL 6

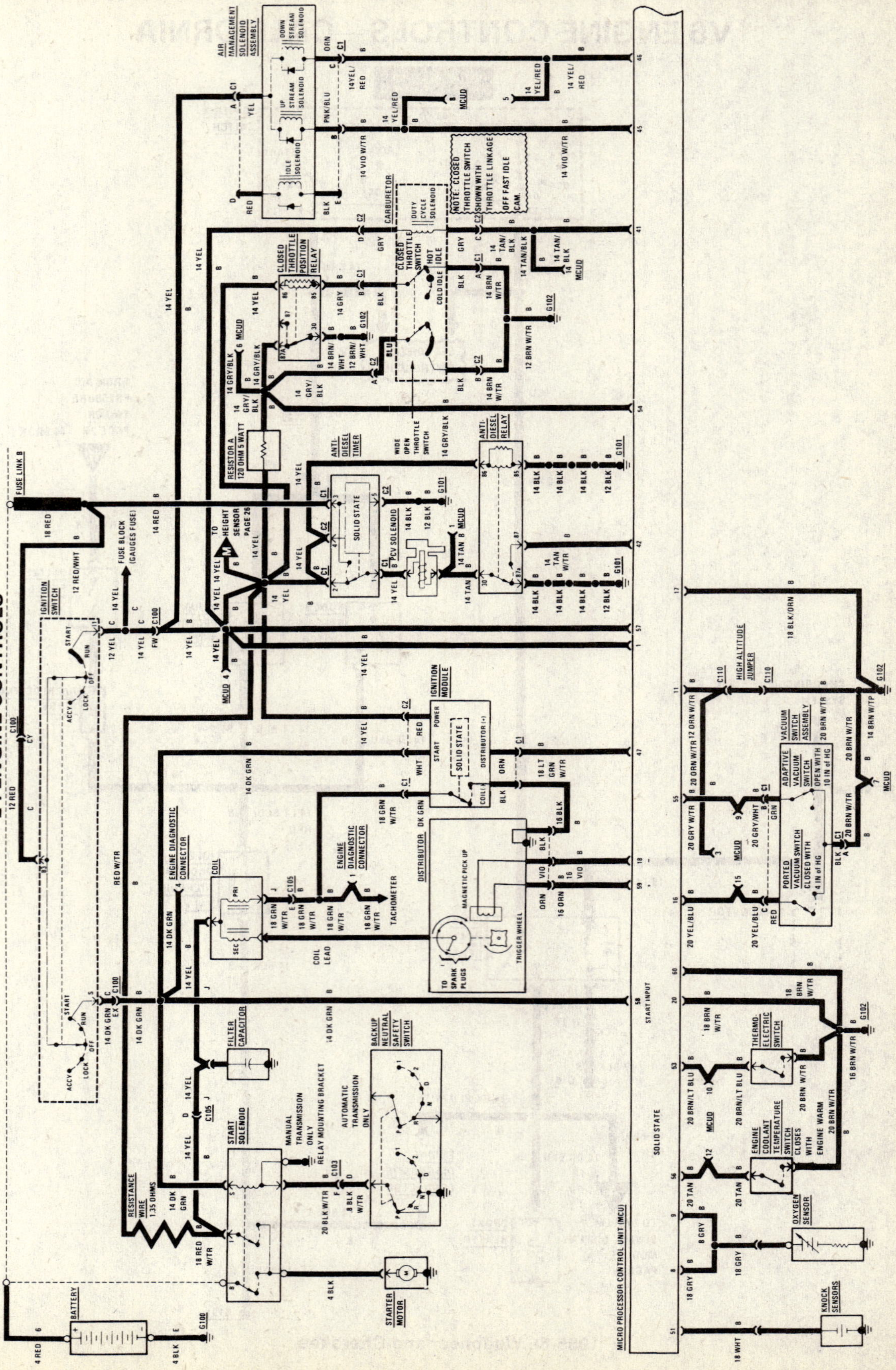

1984-85 Wagoneer and Cherokee

6-143

6 CHASSIS ELECTRICAL

V6 ENGINE CONTROLS — CALIFORNIA

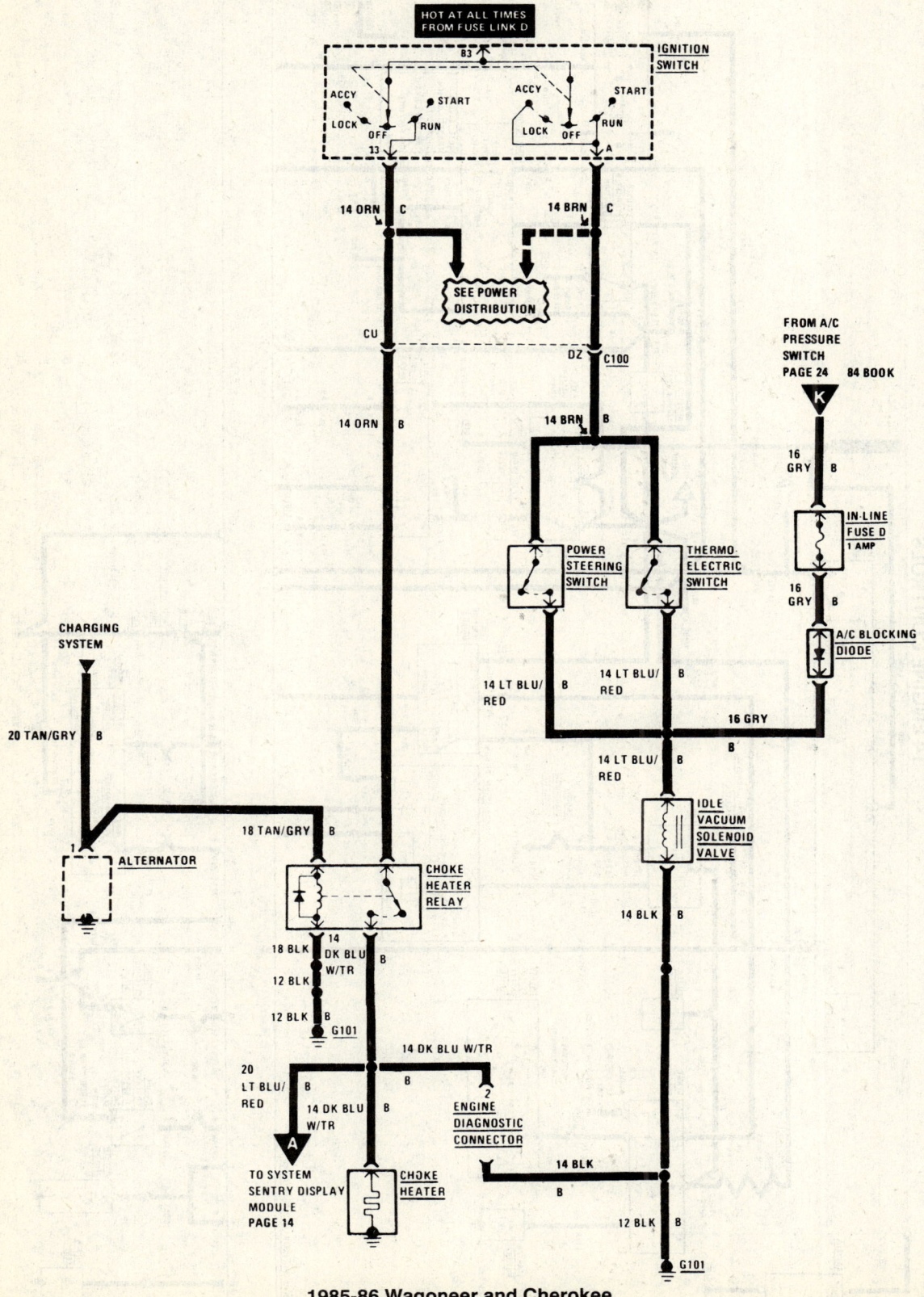

1985-86 Wagoneer and Cherokee

CHASSIS ELECTRICAL 6

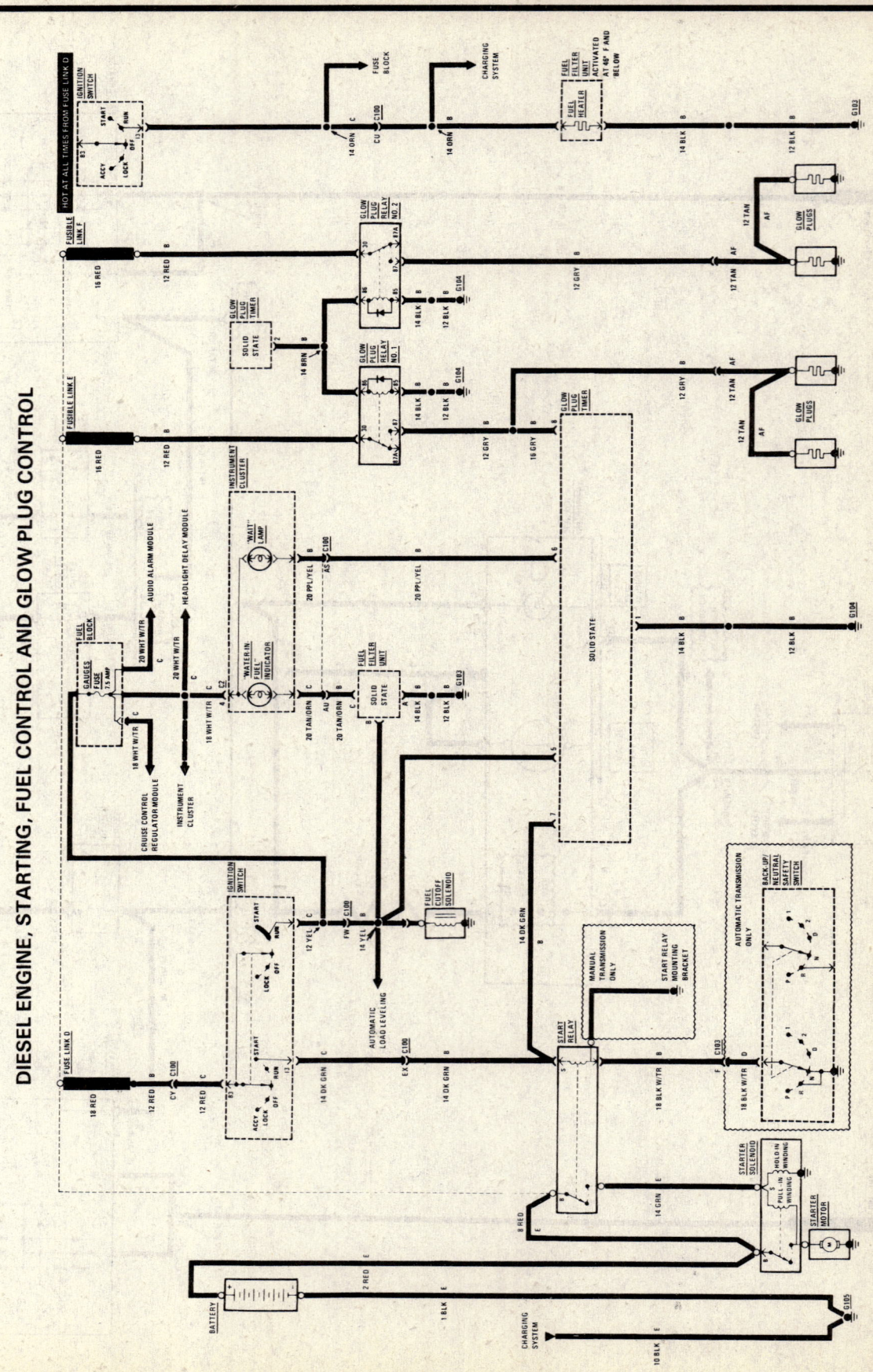

6-145

6 CHASSIS ELECTRICAL

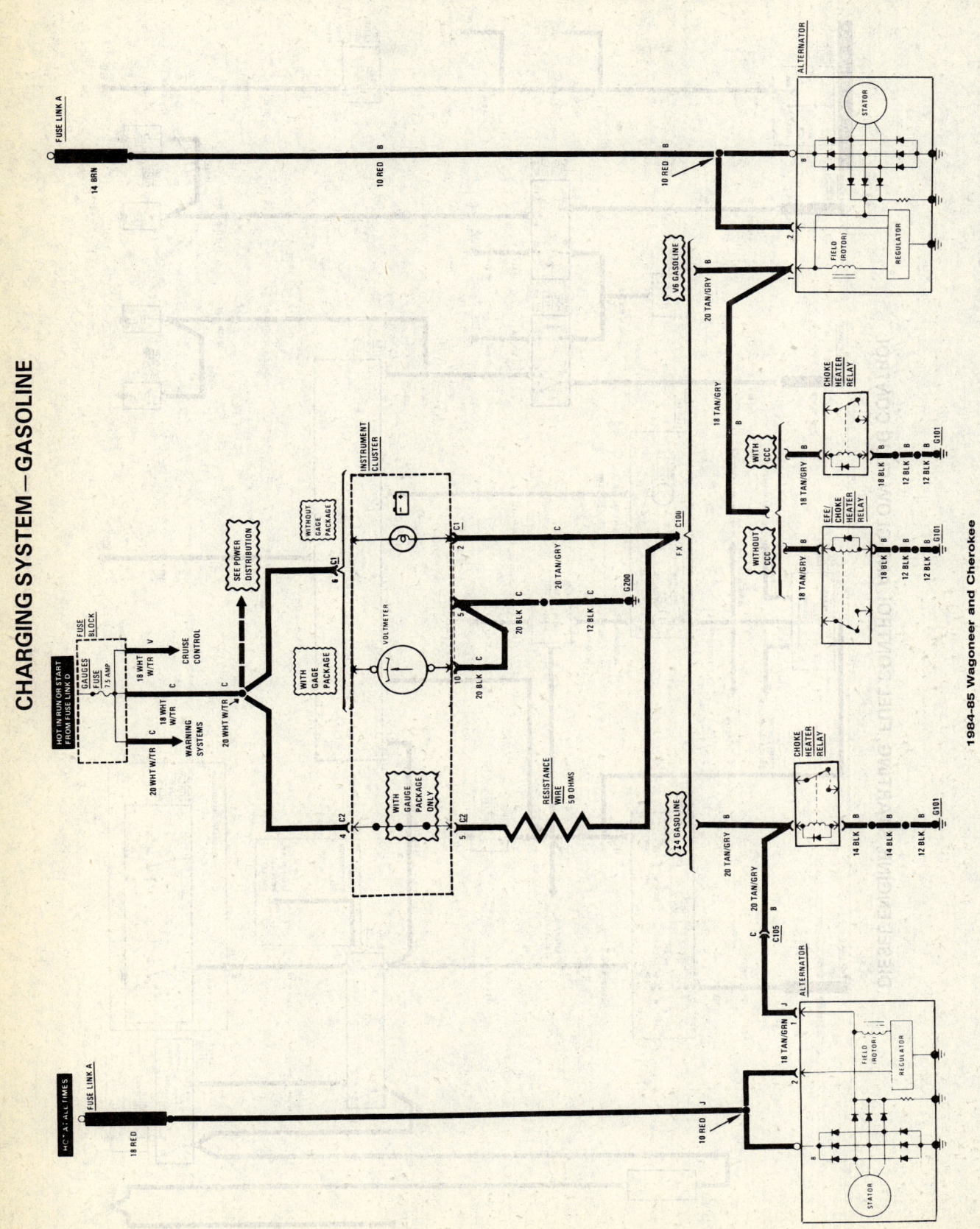

6-146

CHASSIS ELECTRICAL 6

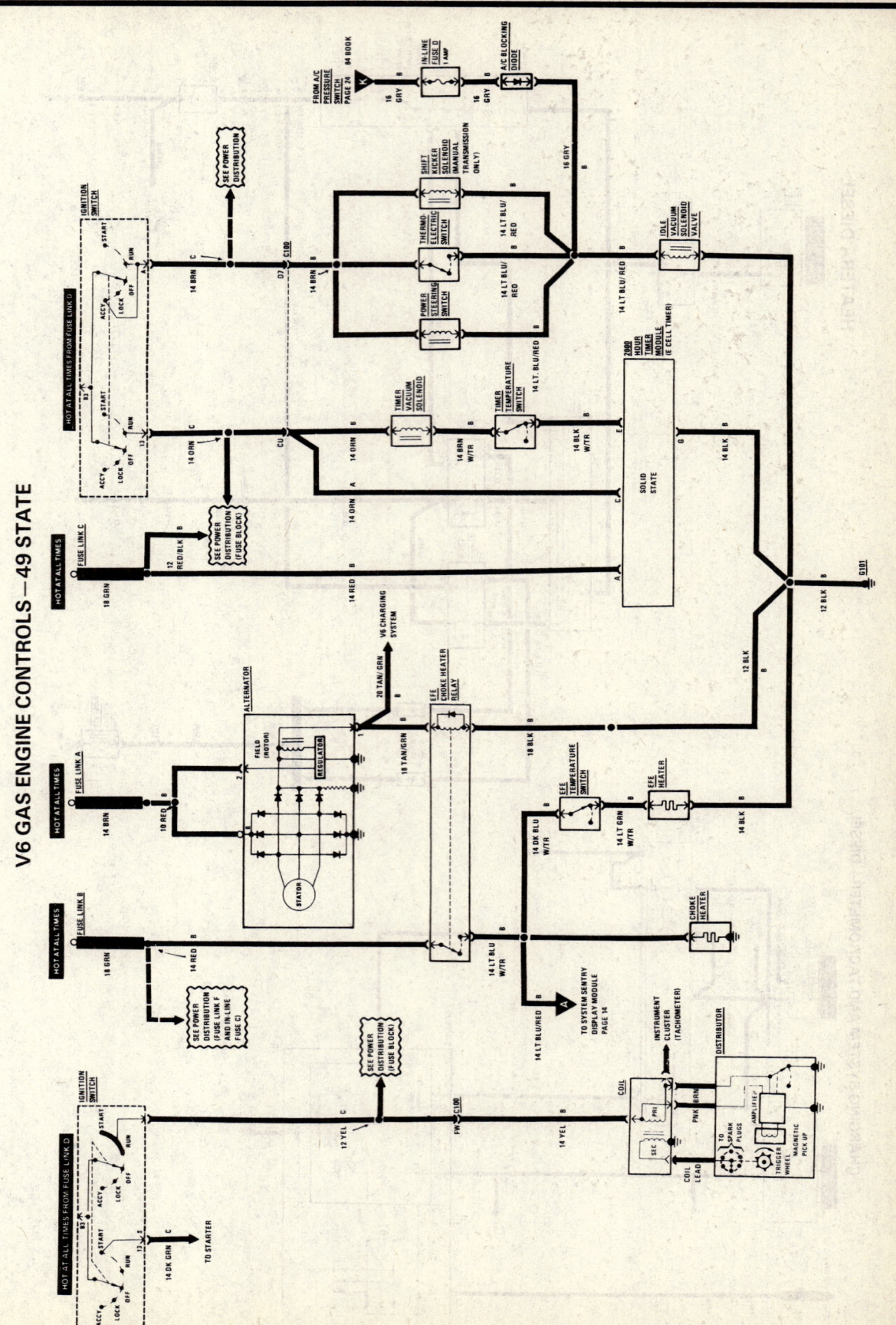

6-147

6 CHASSIS ELECTRICAL

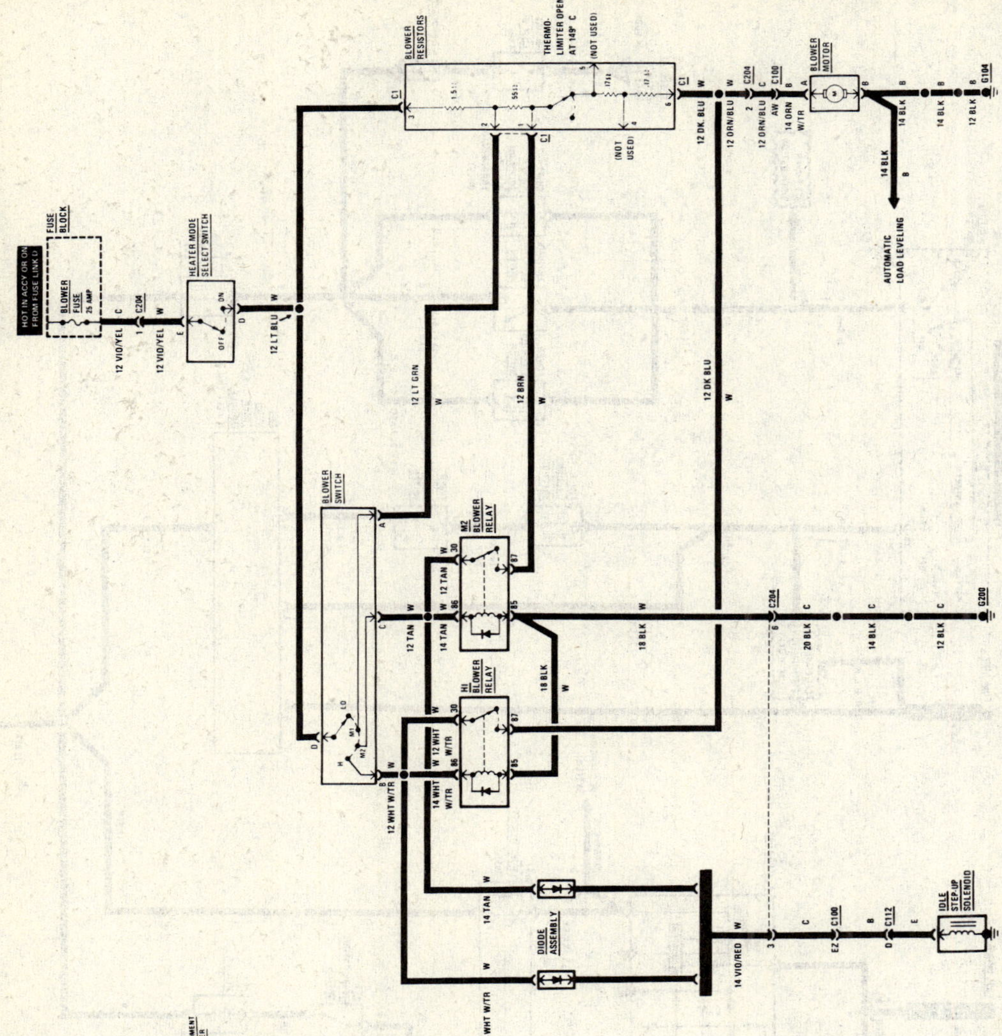

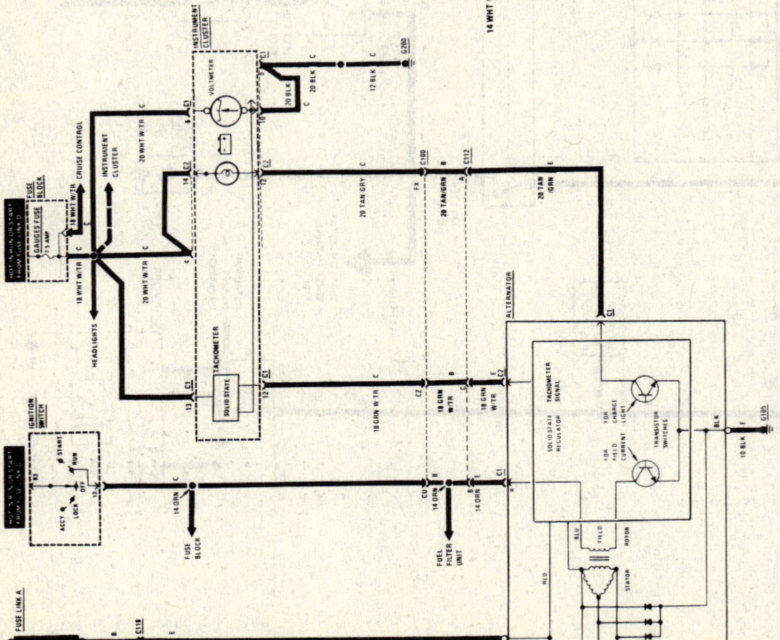

1984-85 Wagoneer and Cherokee

6-148

CHASSIS ELECTRICAL 6

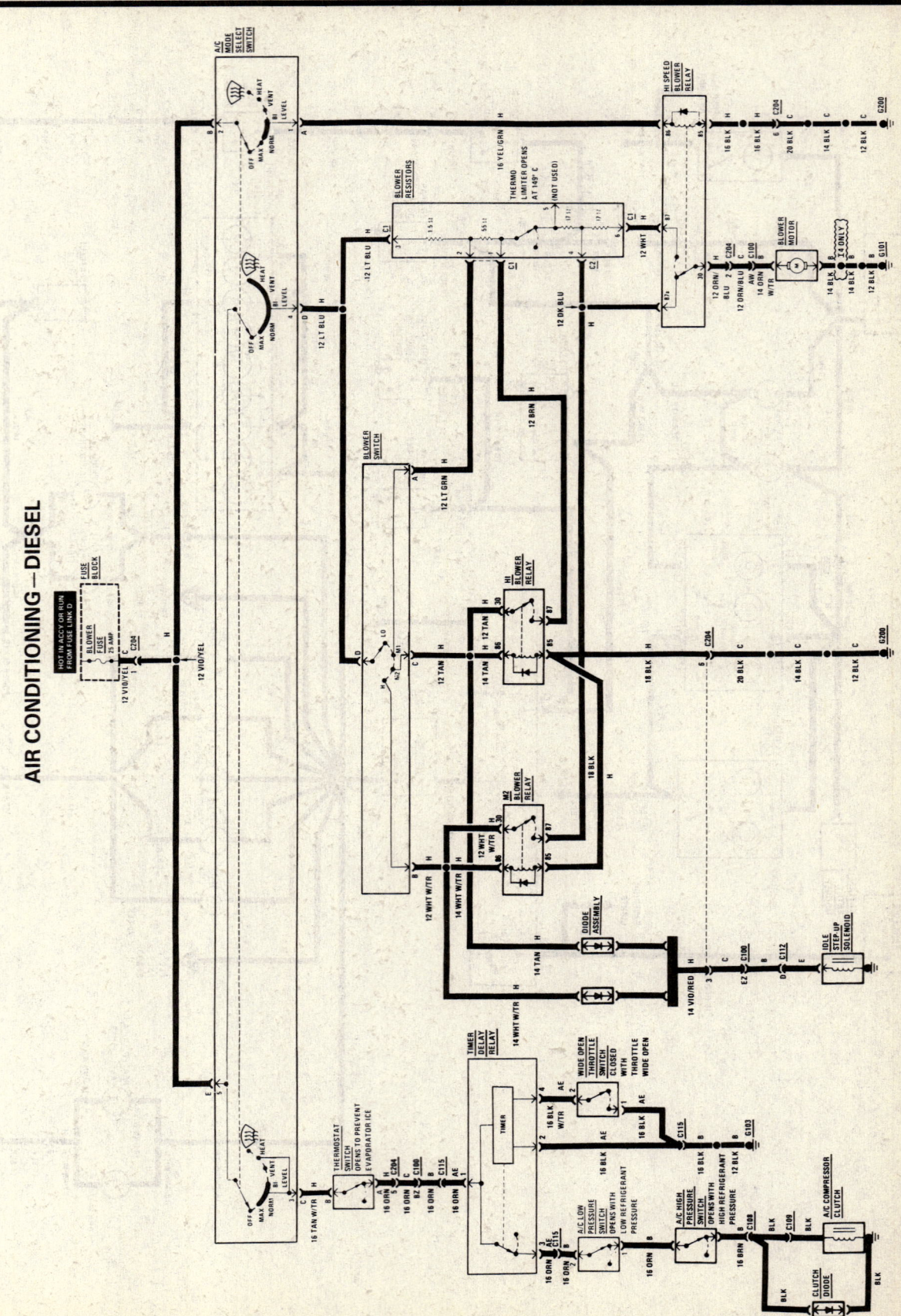

6 CHASSIS ELECTRICAL

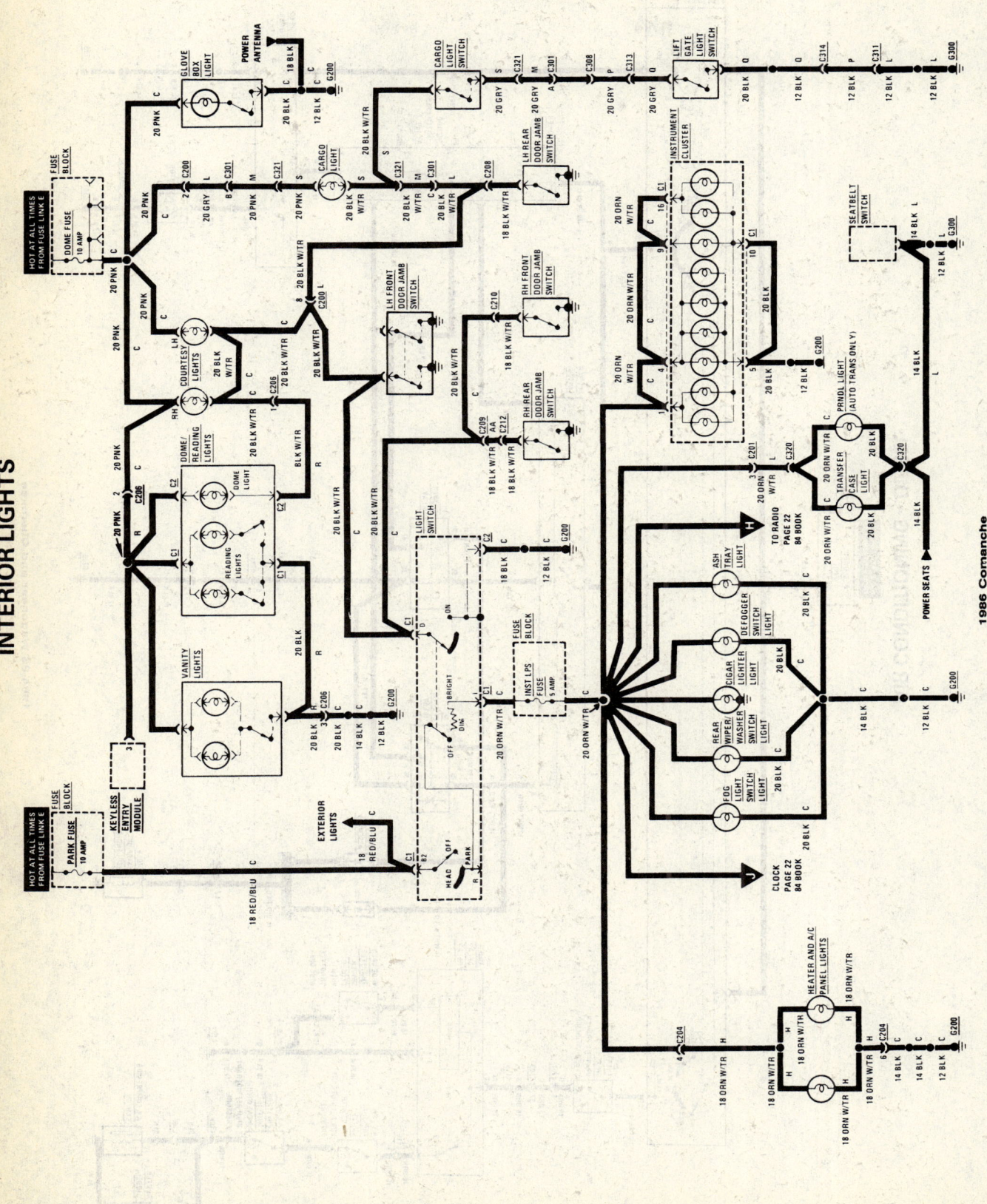

INTERIOR LIGHTS — 1986 Comanche

CHASSIS ELECTRICAL 6

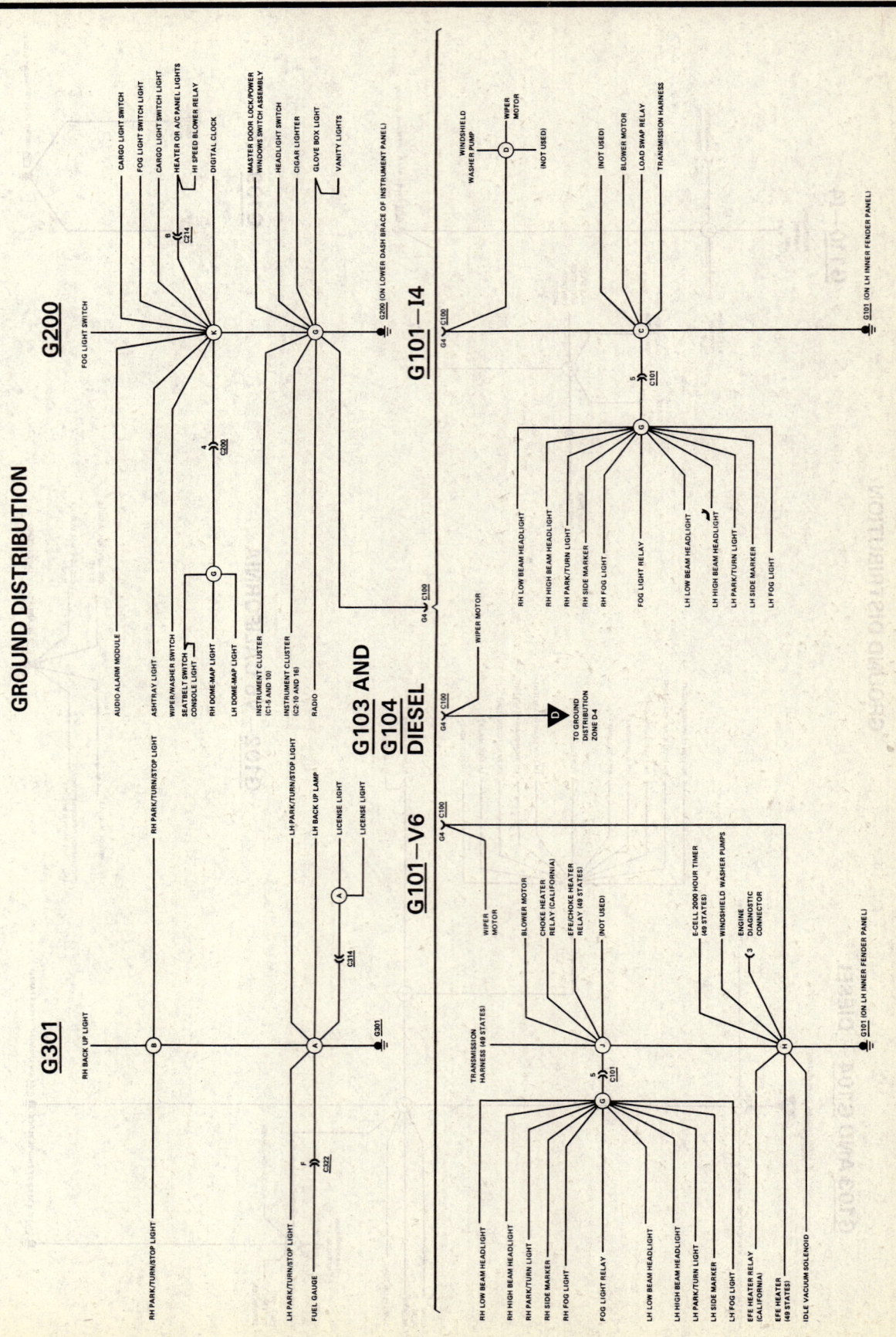

1986 Comanche

6-151

6 CHASSIS ELECTRICAL

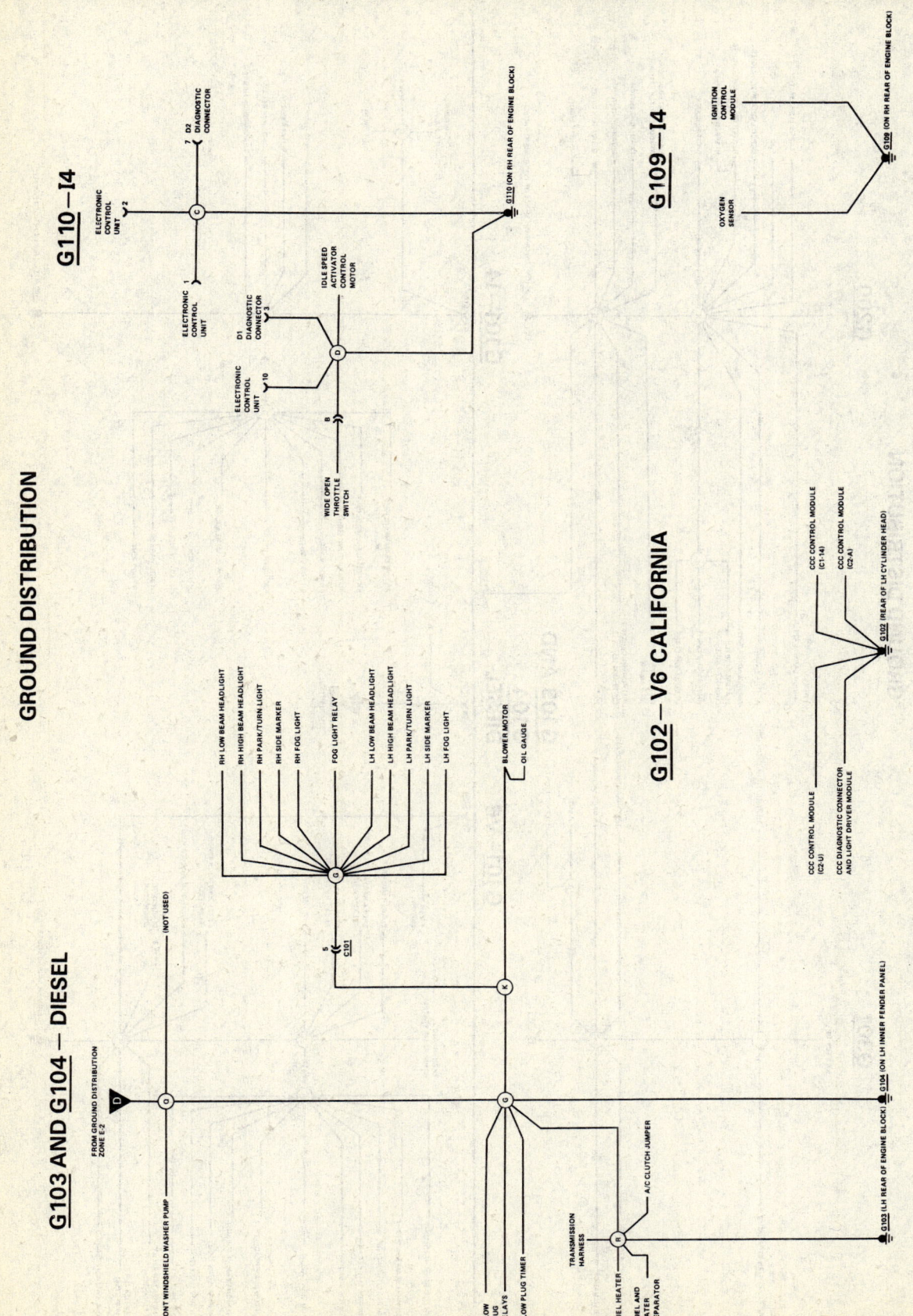

1986 Comanche

CHASSIS ELECTRICAL 6

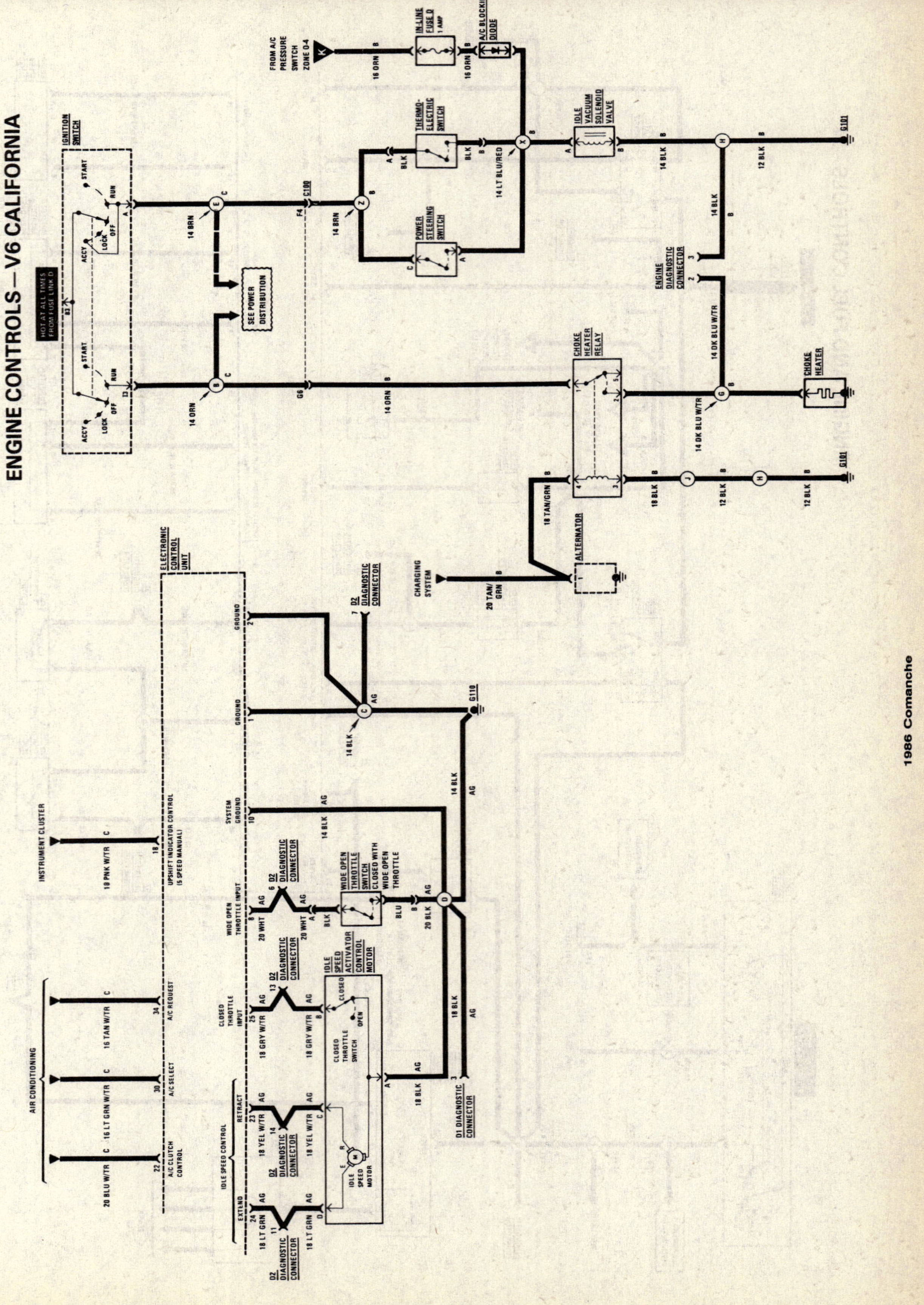

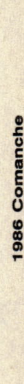

6-153

6 CHASSIS ELECTRICAL

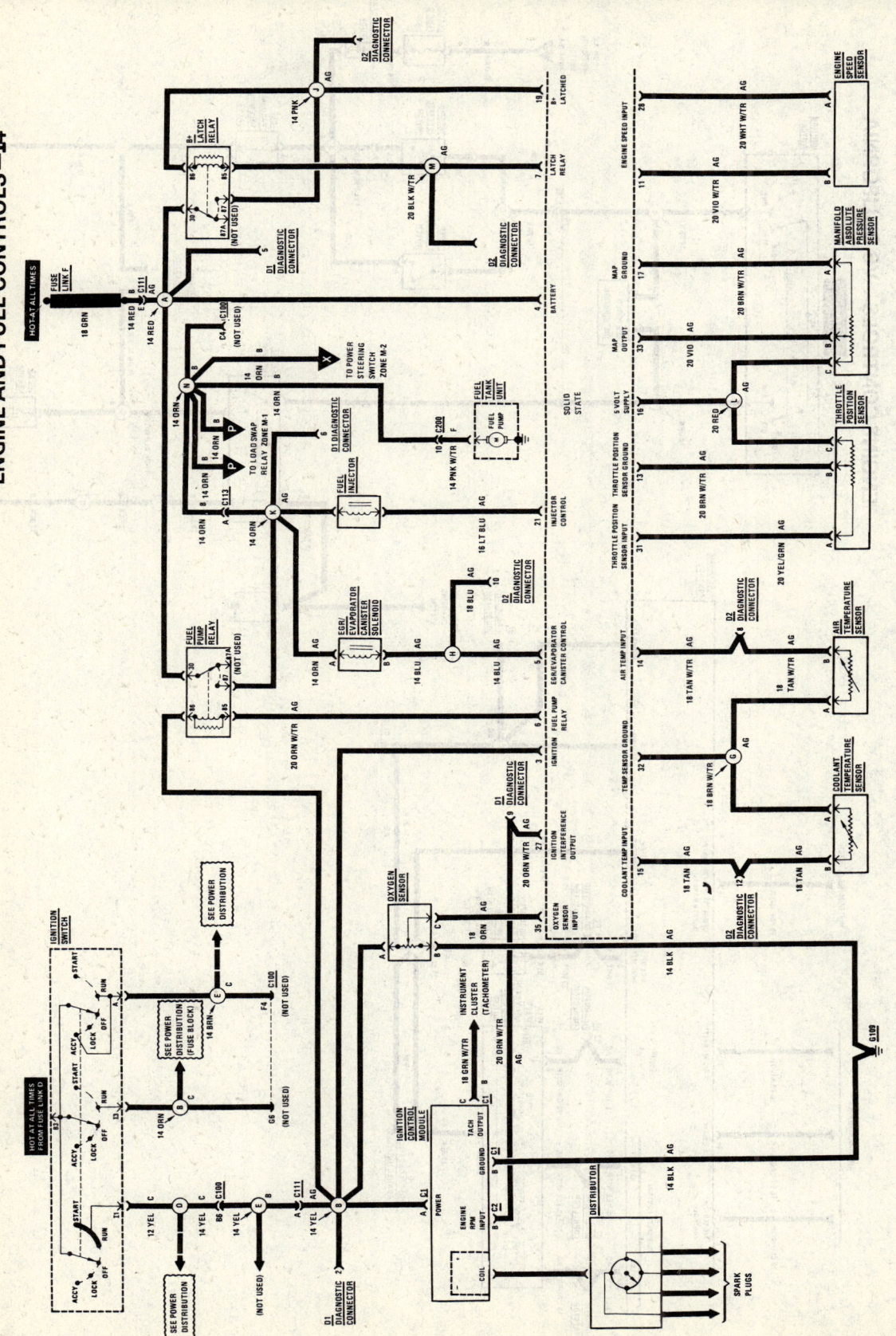

CHASSIS ELECTRICAL 6

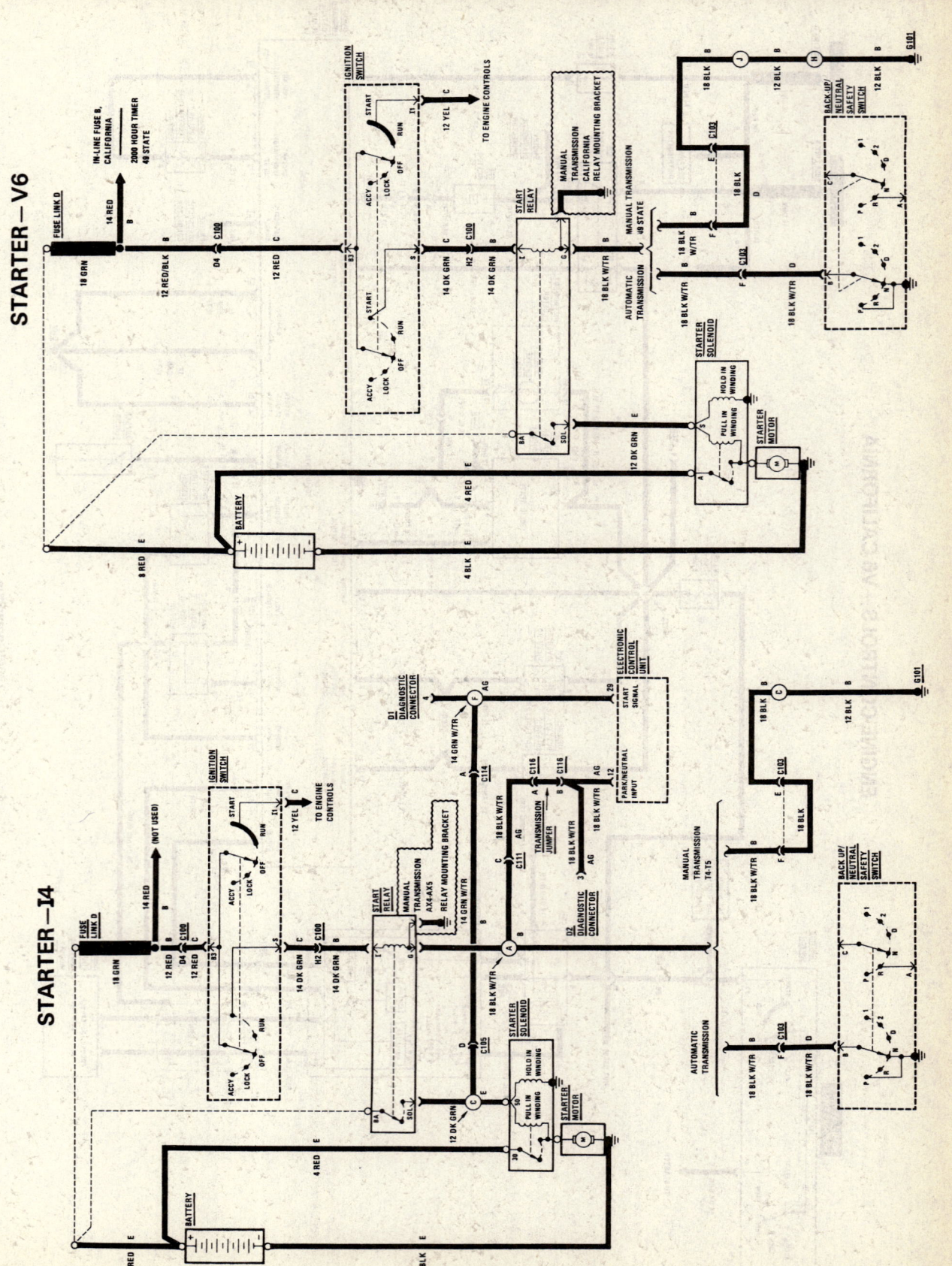

1986 Comanche

6-155

6 CHASSIS ELECTRICAL

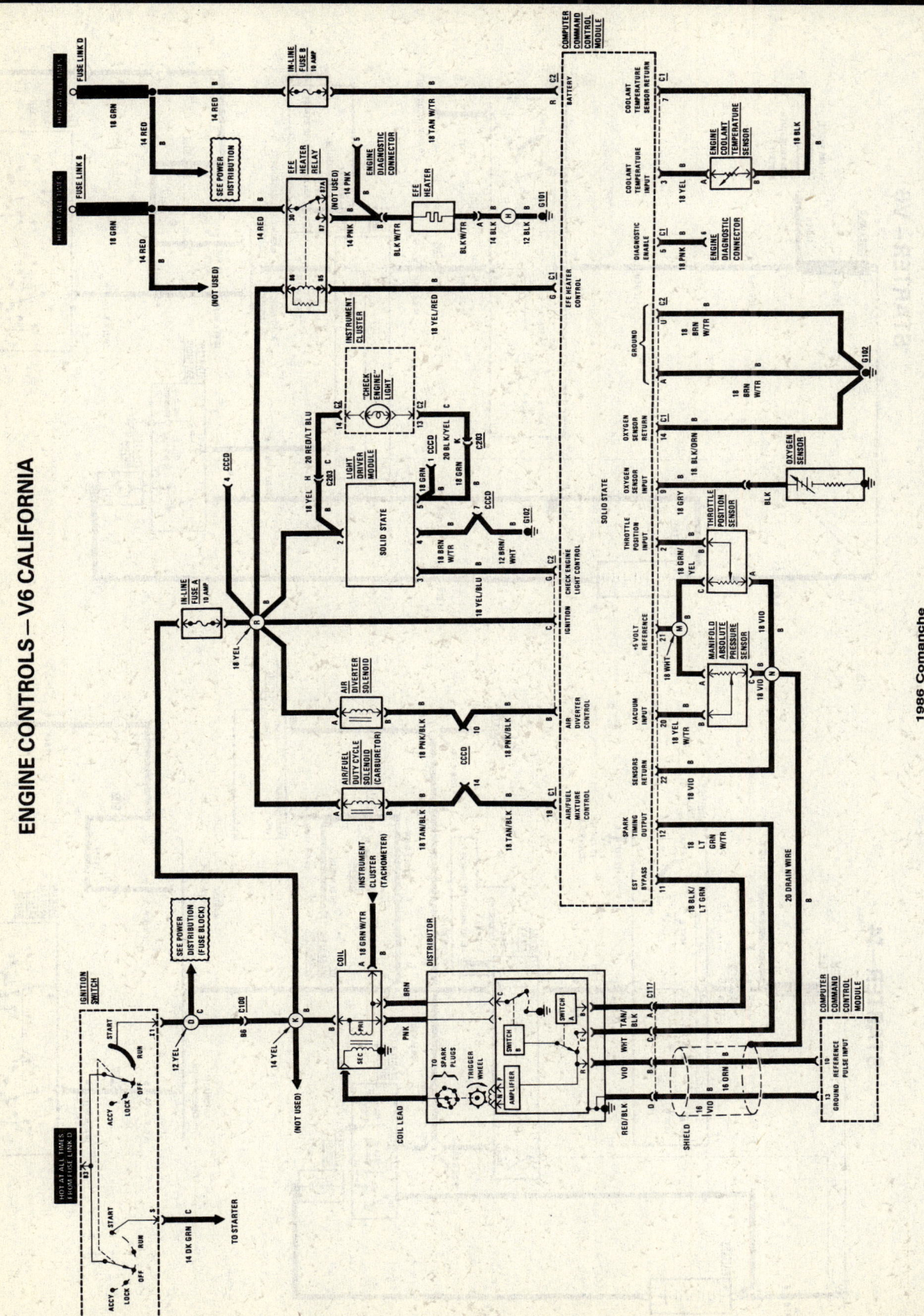

CHASSIS ELECTRICAL 6

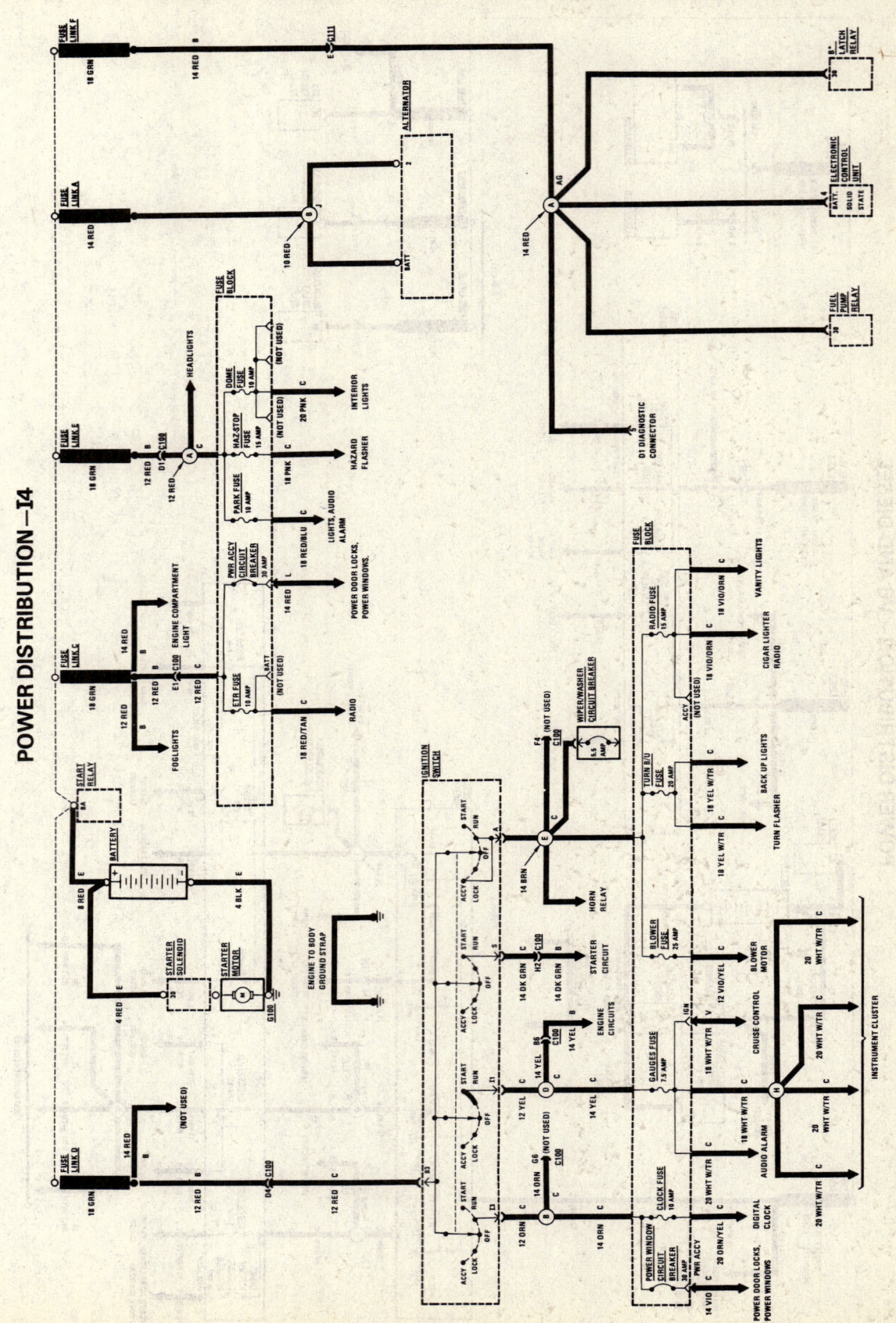

1986 Comanche

6-157

6 CHASSIS ELECTRICAL

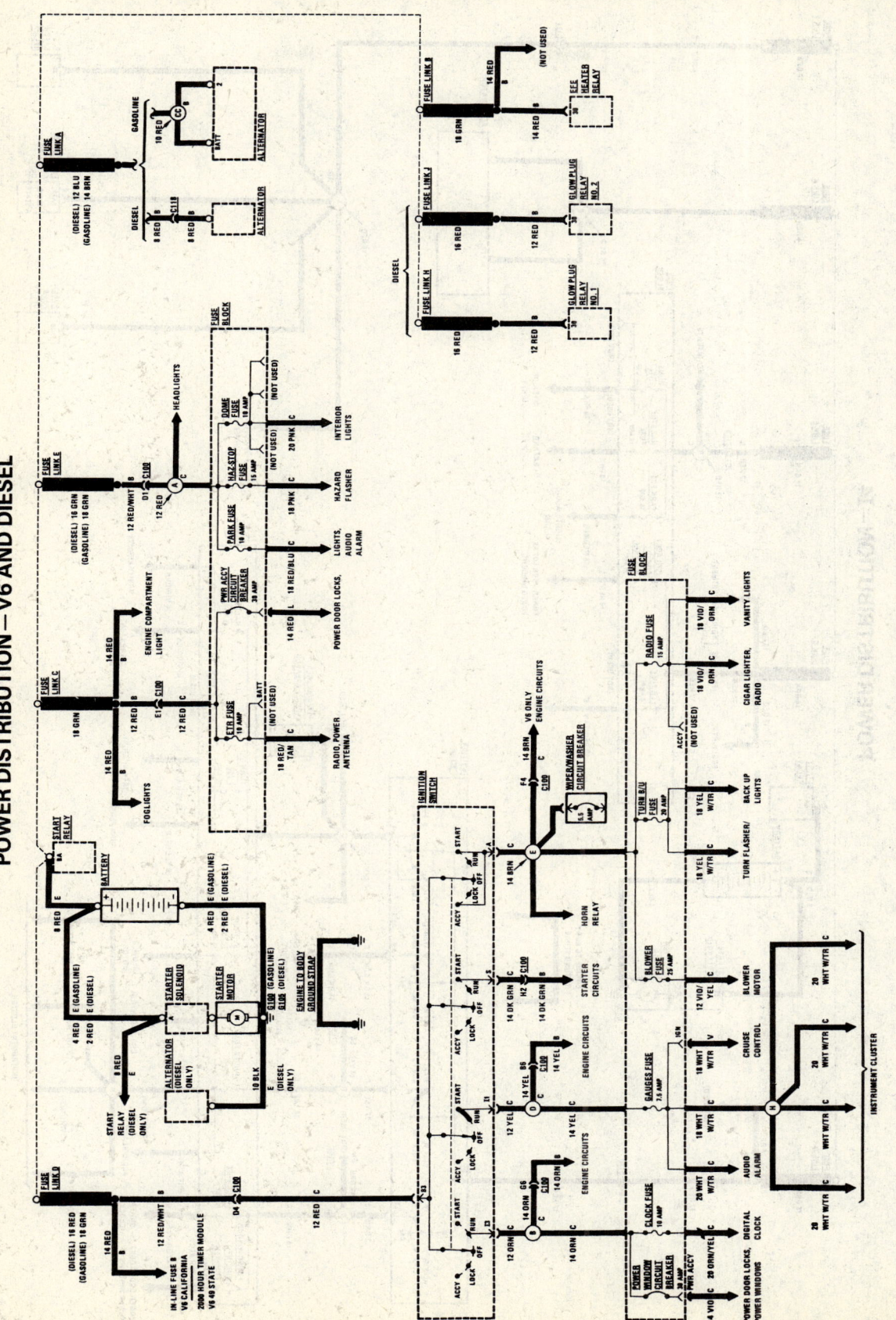

1986 Comanche

CHASSIS ELECTRICAL 6

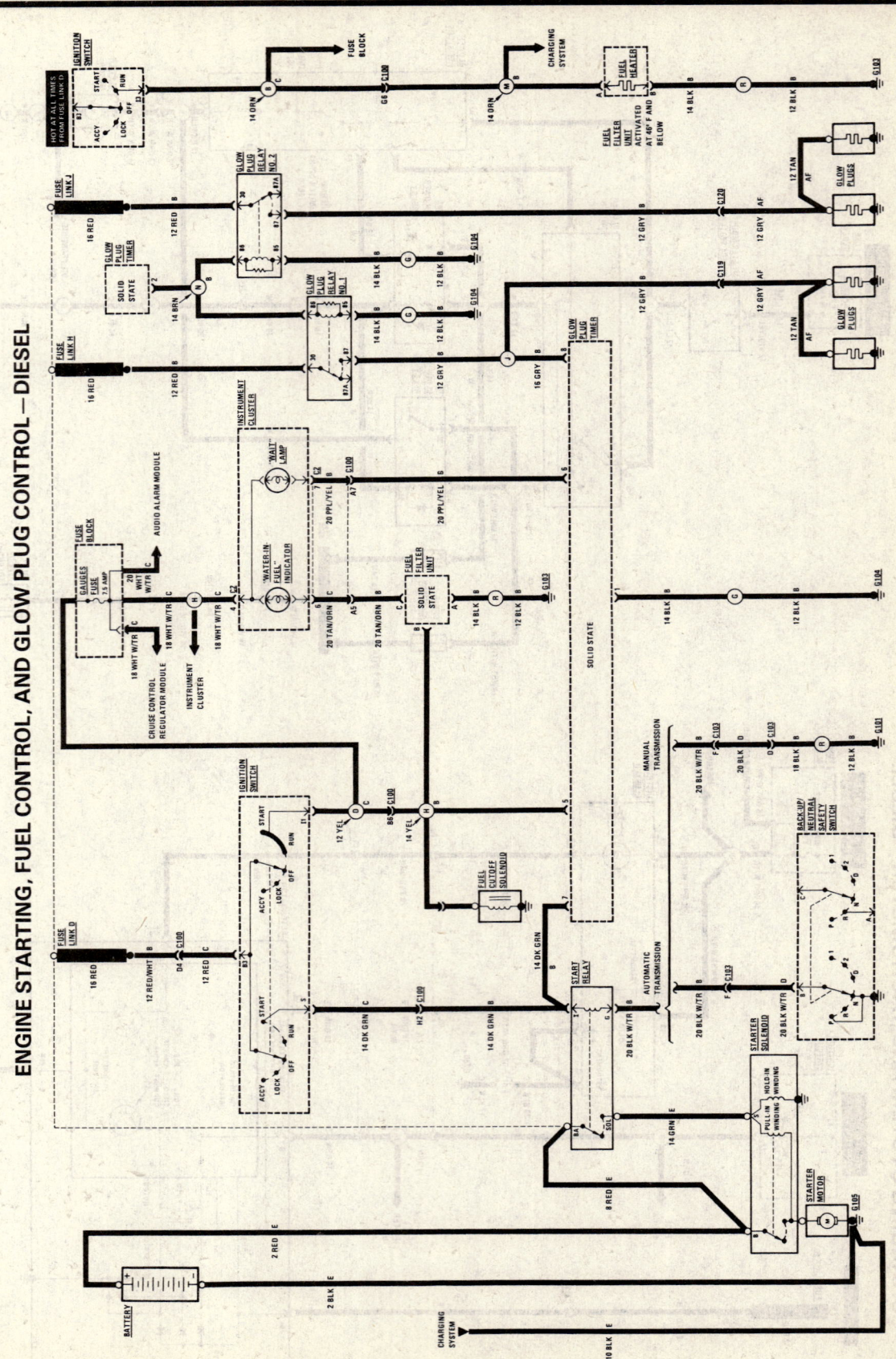

6-159

6 CHASSIS ELECTRICAL

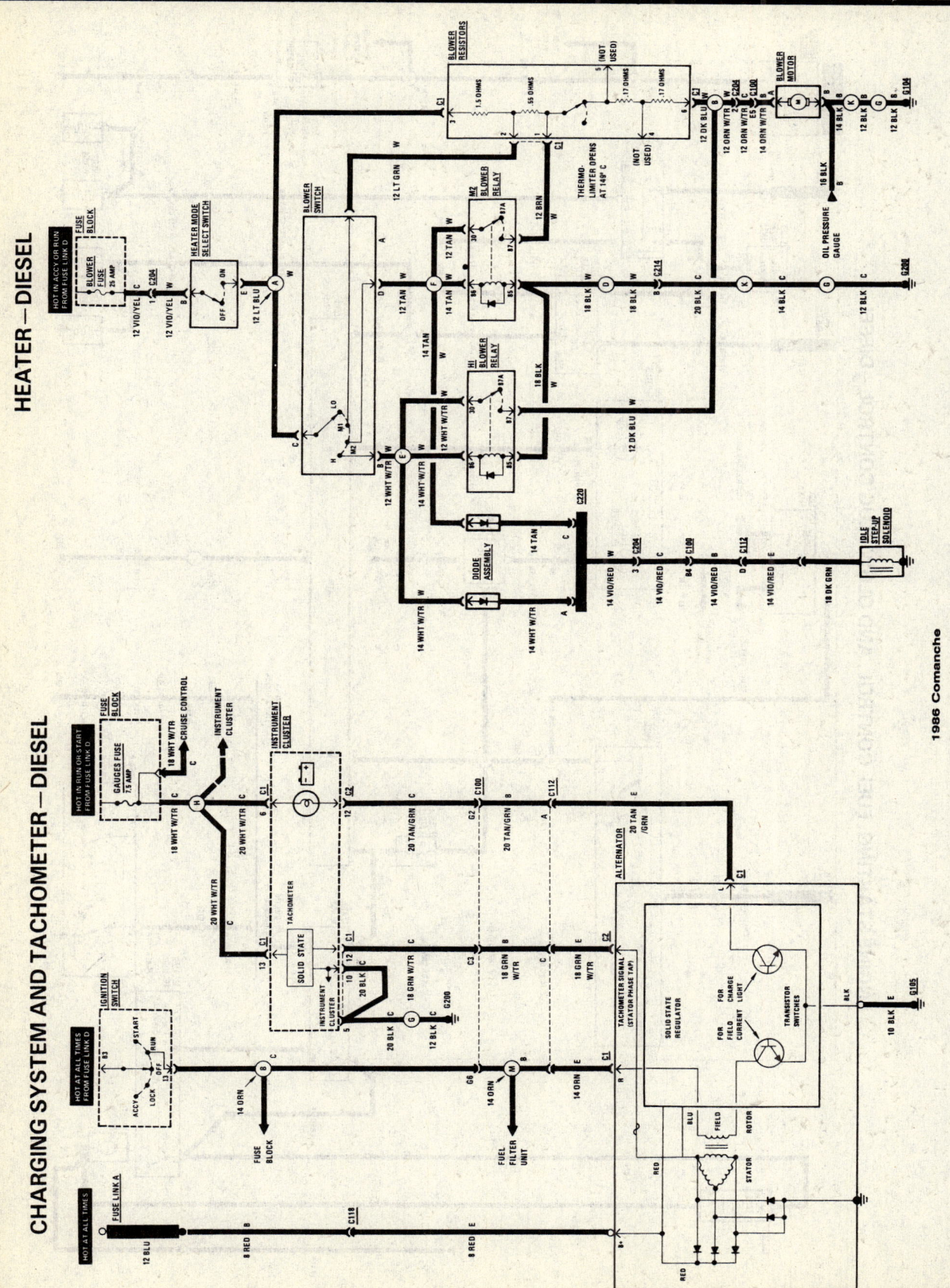

6-160

CHASSIS ELECTRICAL 6

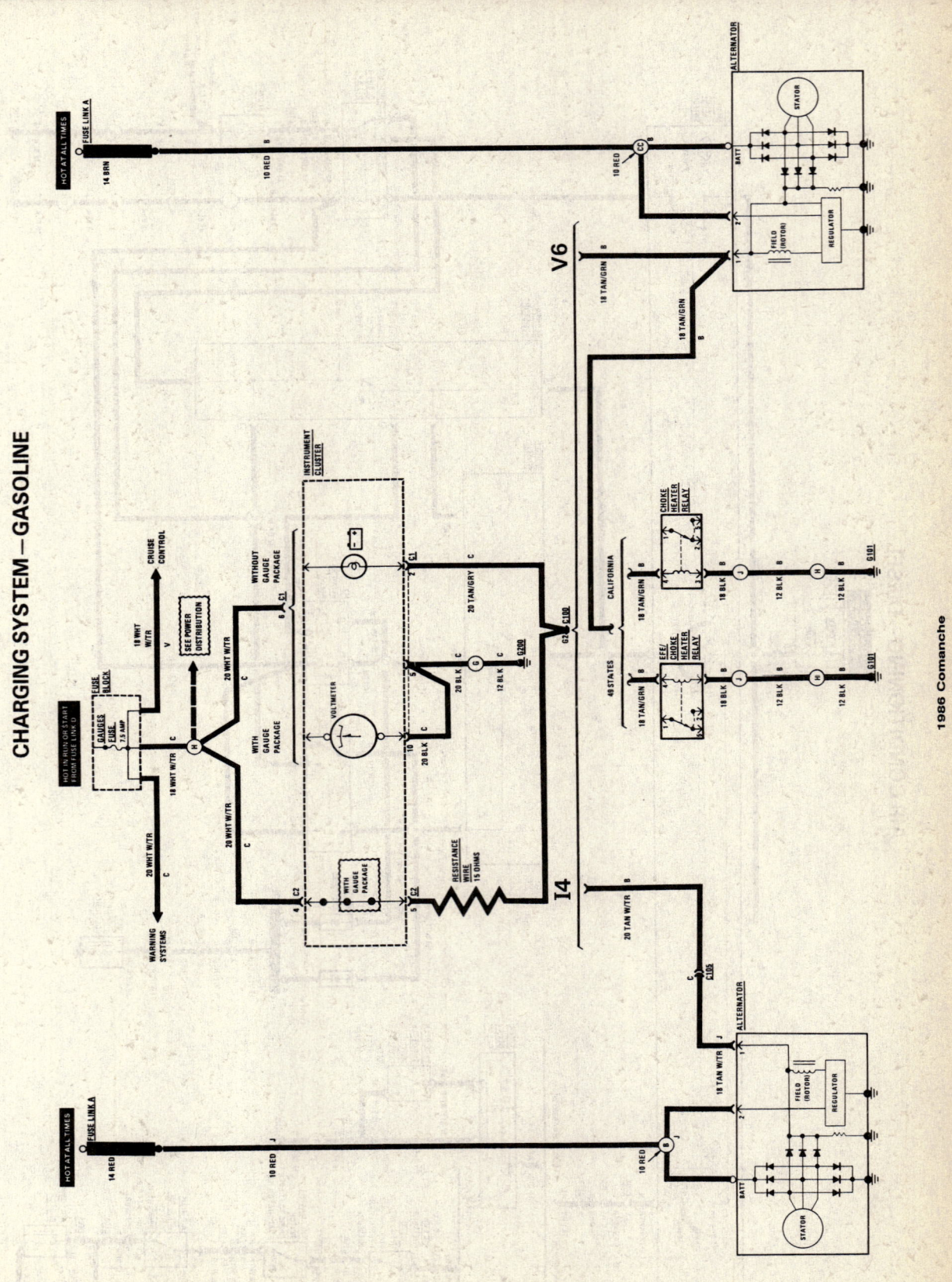

6-161

6 CHASSIS ELECTRICAL

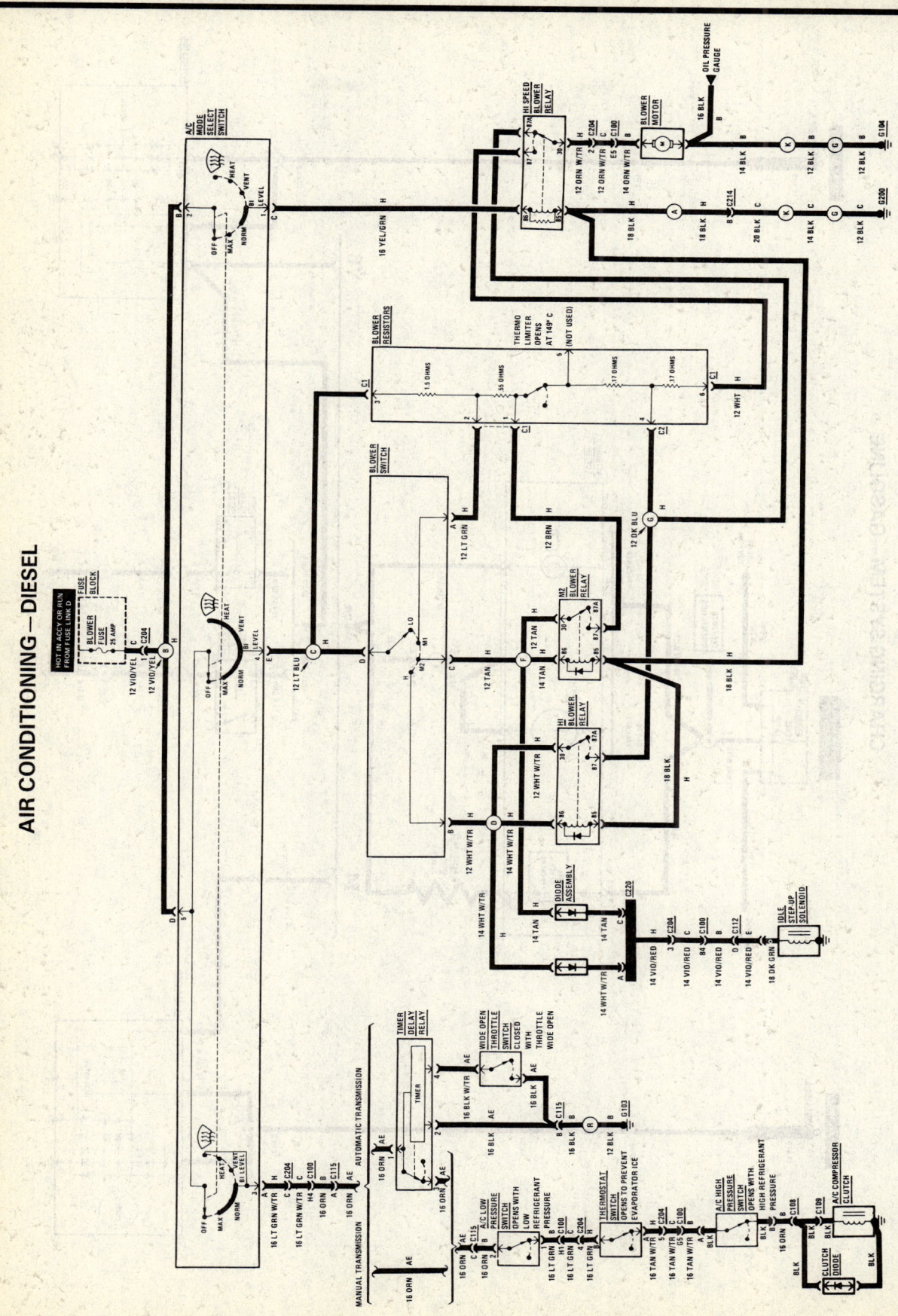

6-162

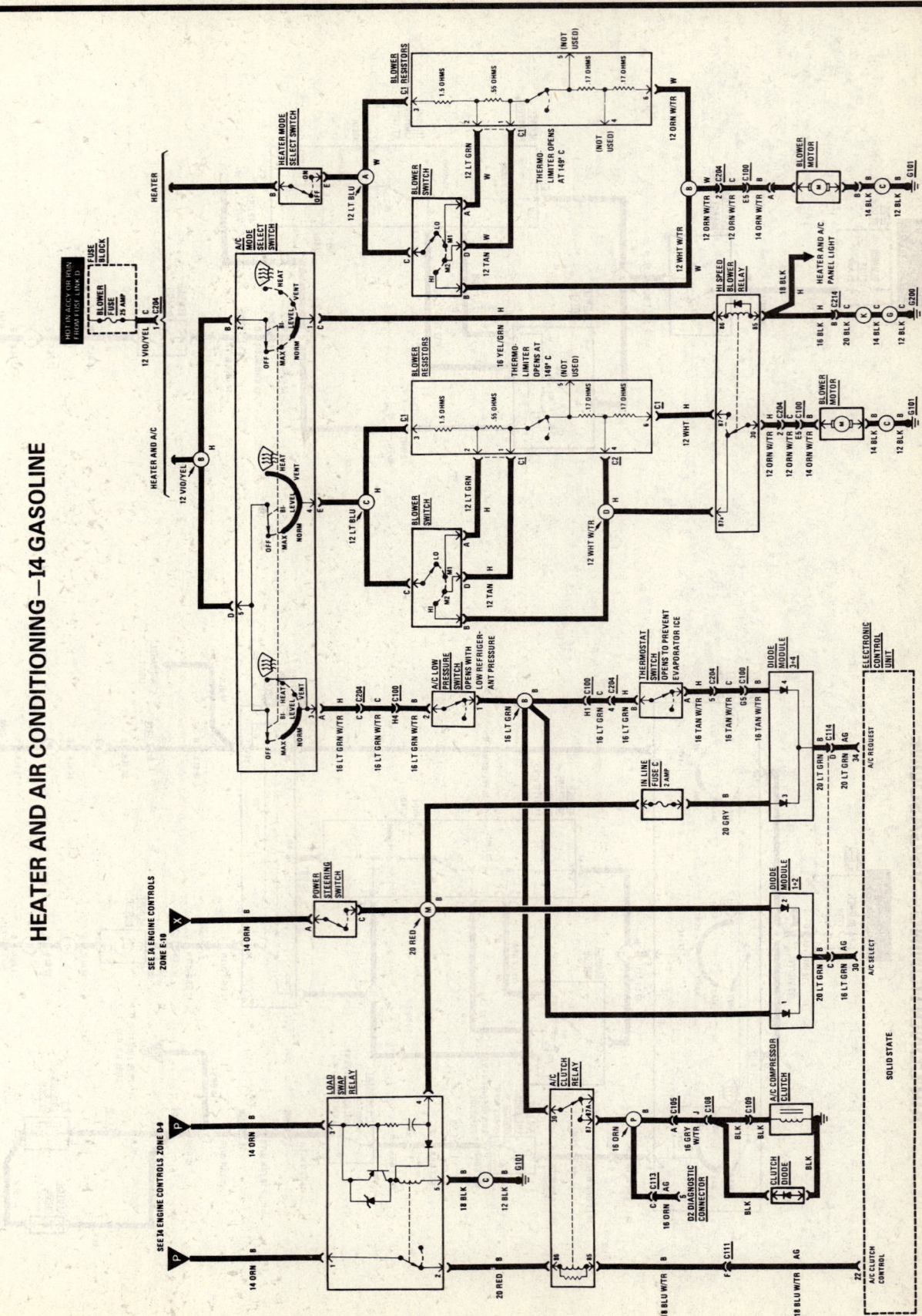

HEATER—V6 GASOLINE

AIR CONDITIONING—V6 GASOLINE

1986 Comanche

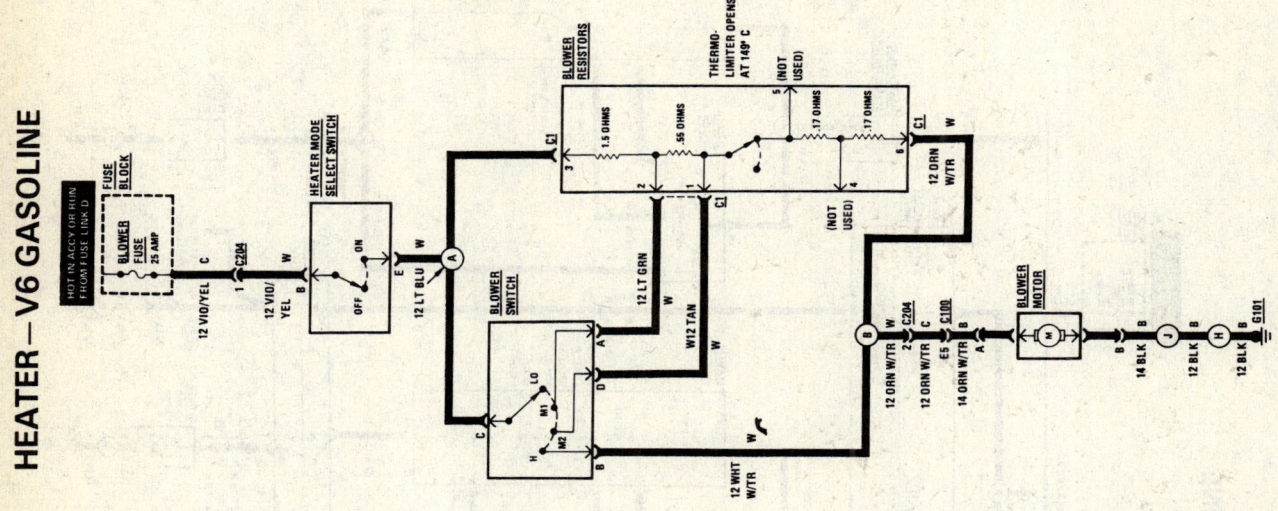

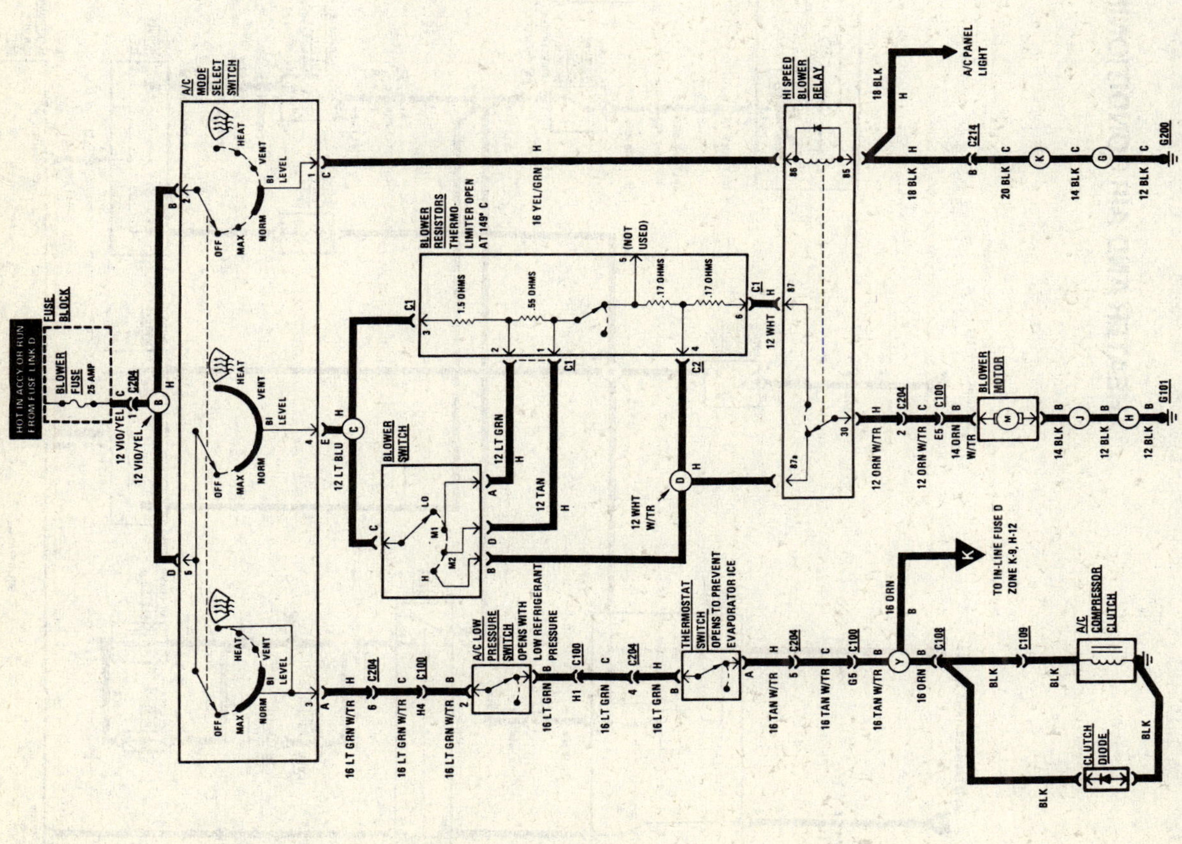

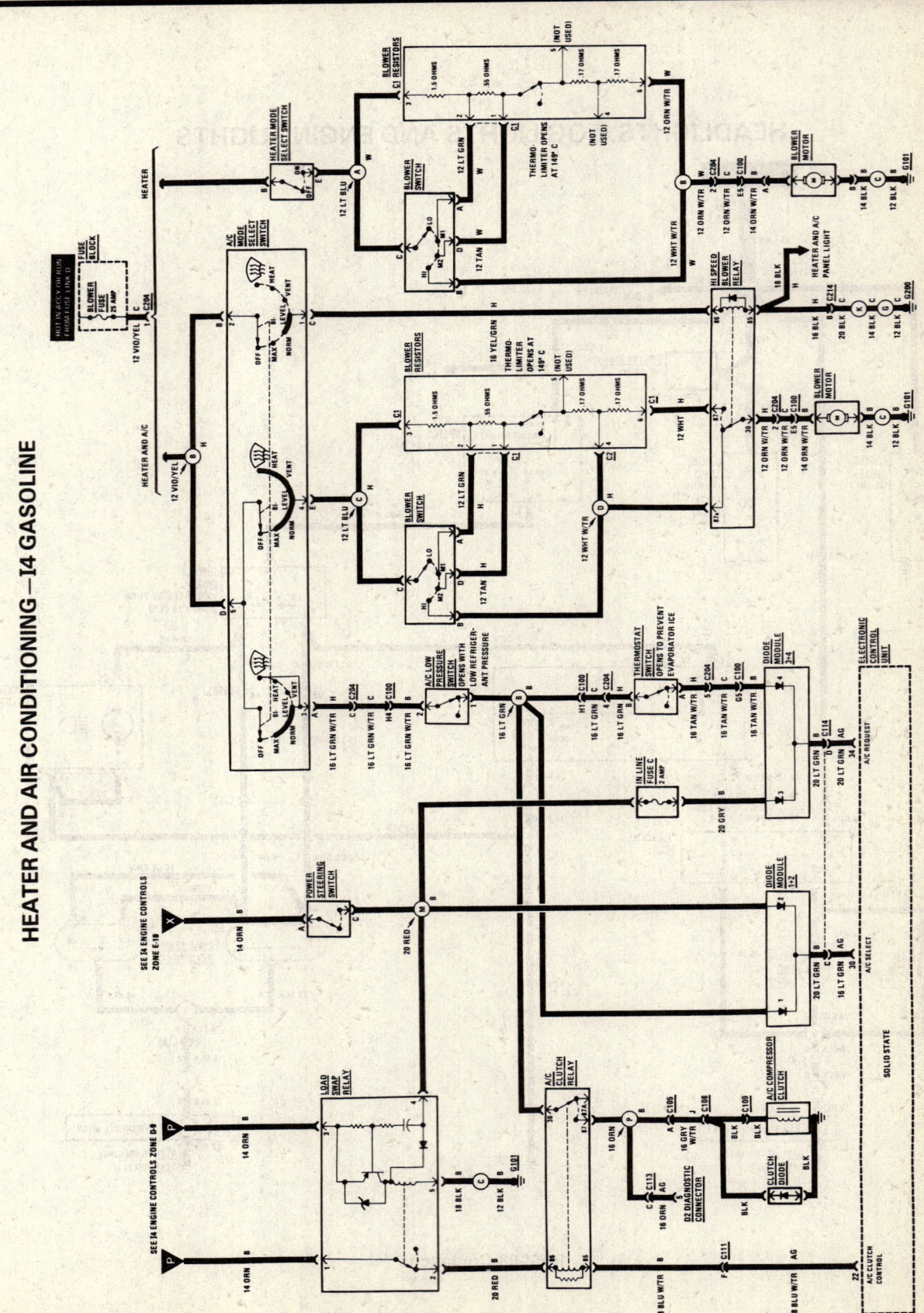

6 CHASSIS ELECTRICAL

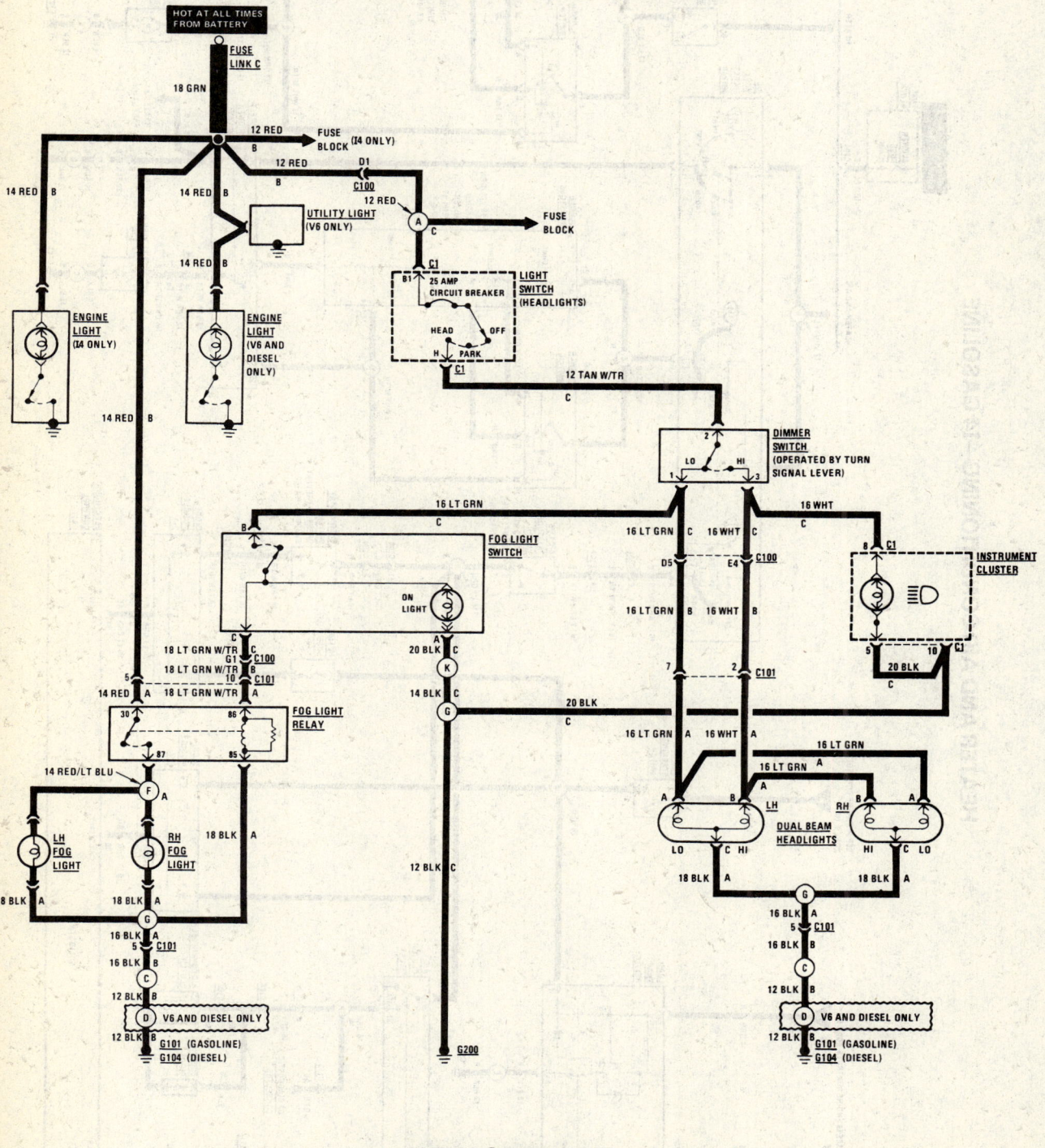

1987-88 Comanche

CHASSIS ELECTRICAL 6

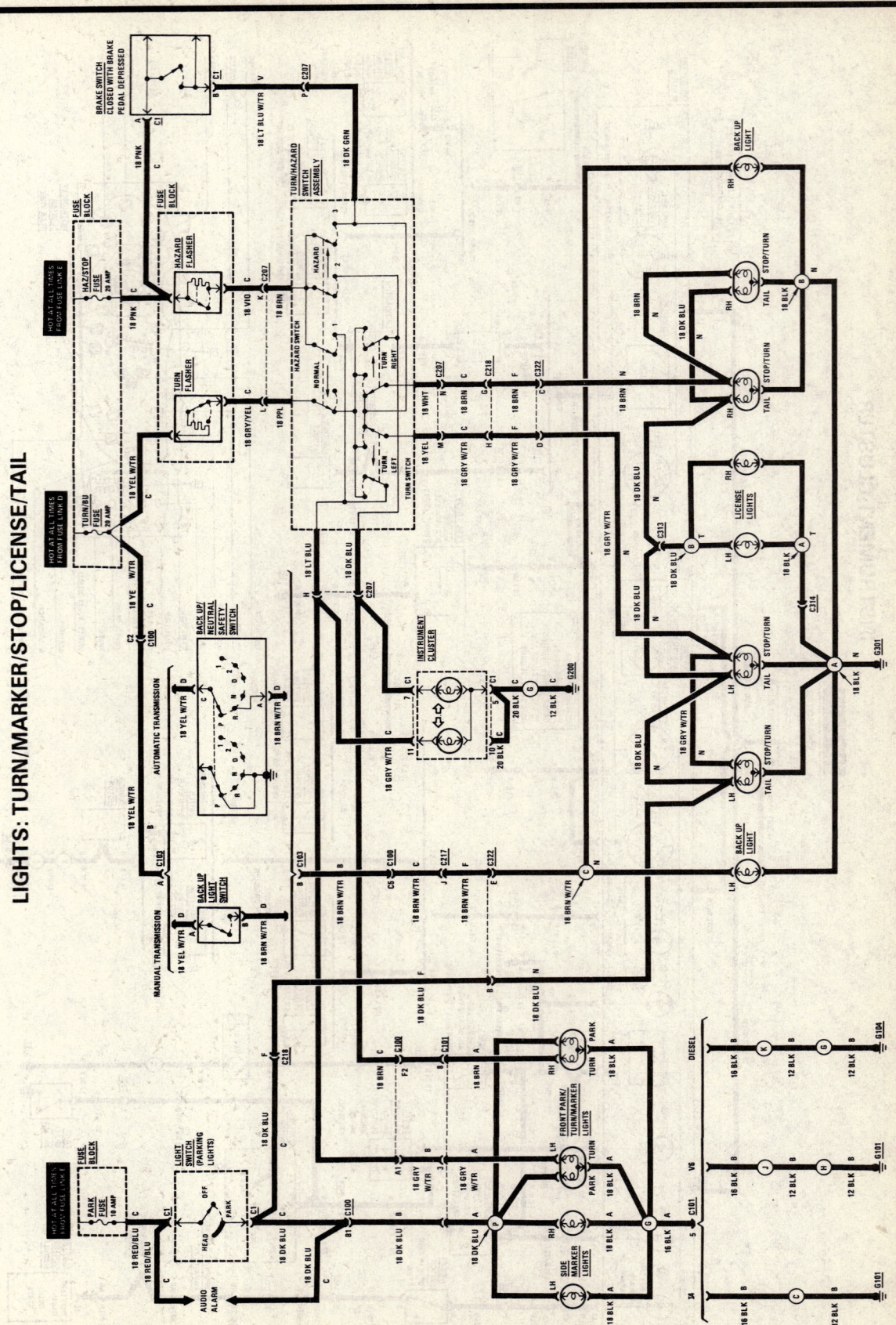

1986 Comanche

6-167

6 CHASSIS ELECTRICAL

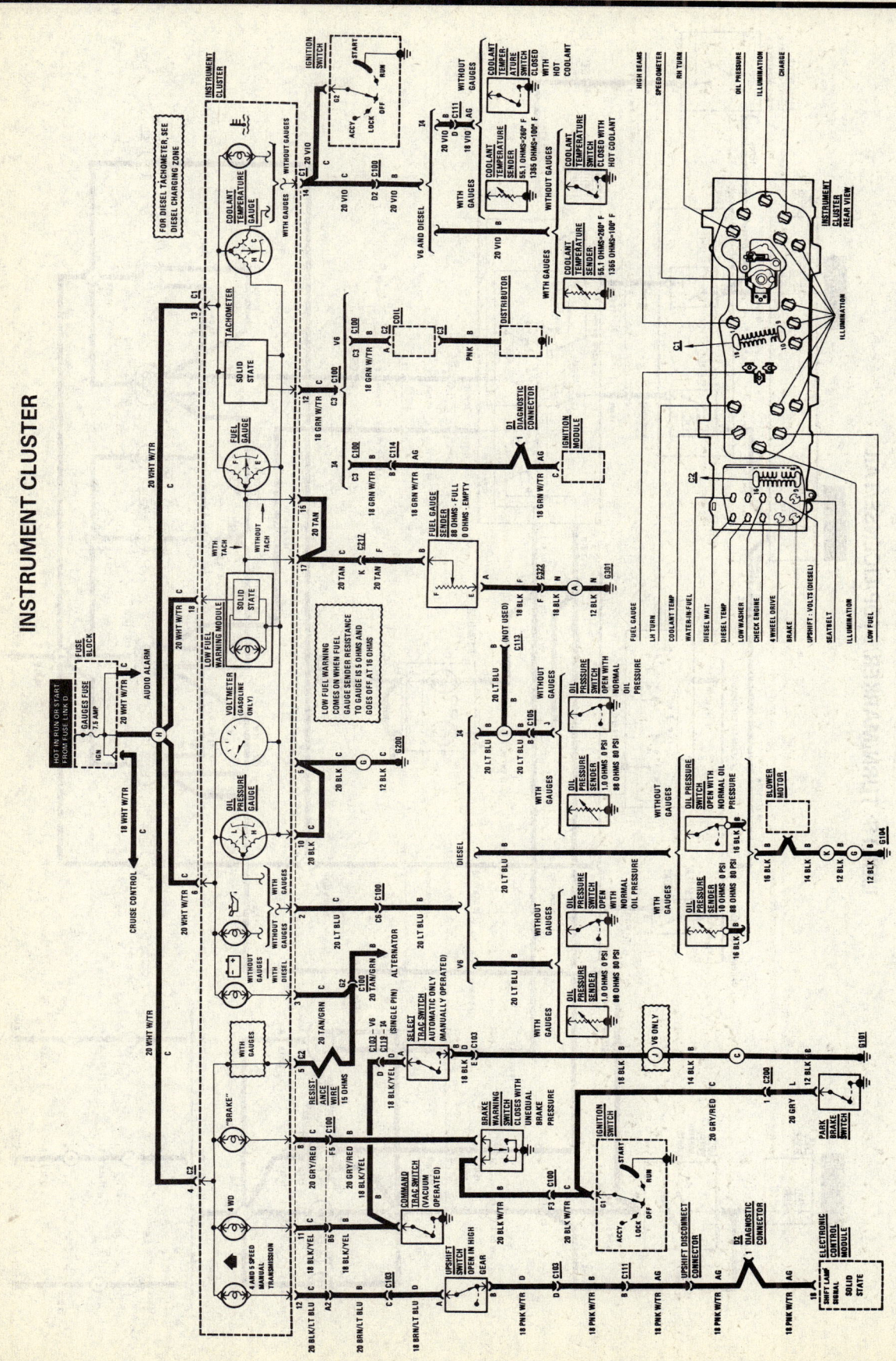

1986 Comanche

6-168

CHASSIS ELECTRICAL 6

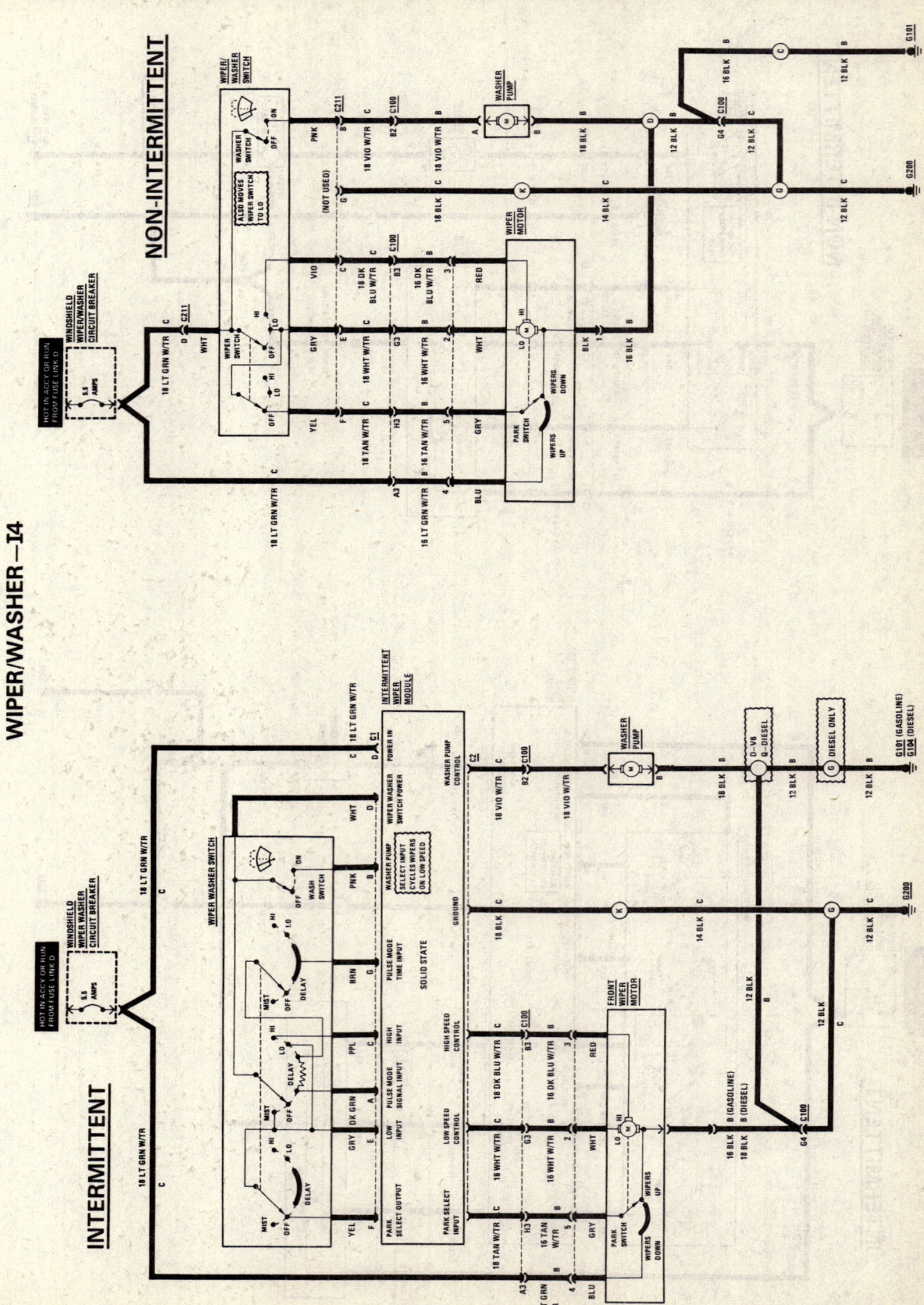

WIPER/WASHER—I4

1986 Comanche

6-169

6 CHASSIS ELECTRICAL

6-170

CHASSIS ELECTRICAL 6

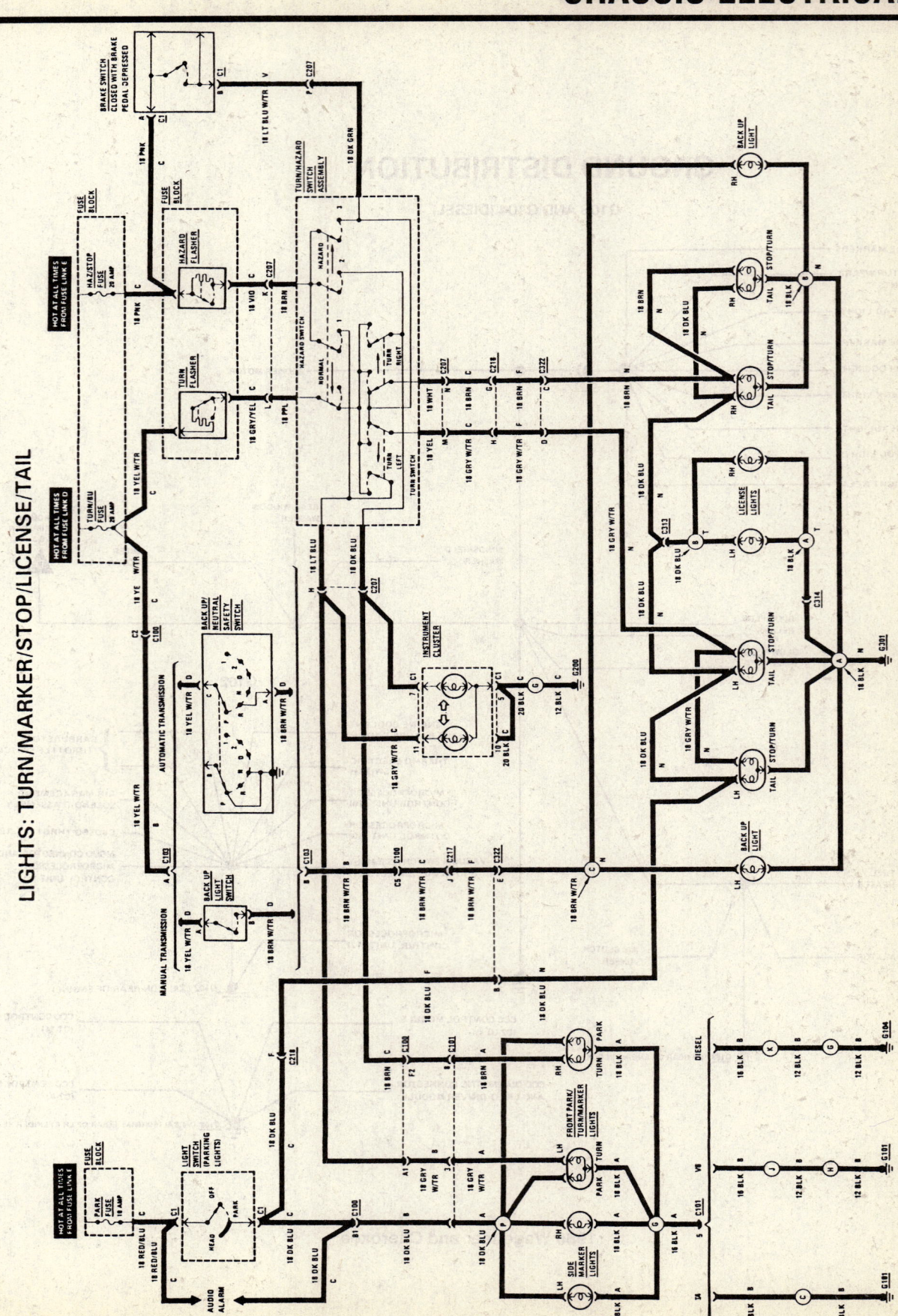

6-171

6 CHASSIS ELECTRICAL

GROUND DISTRIBUTION
G103 AND G104 (DIESEL)

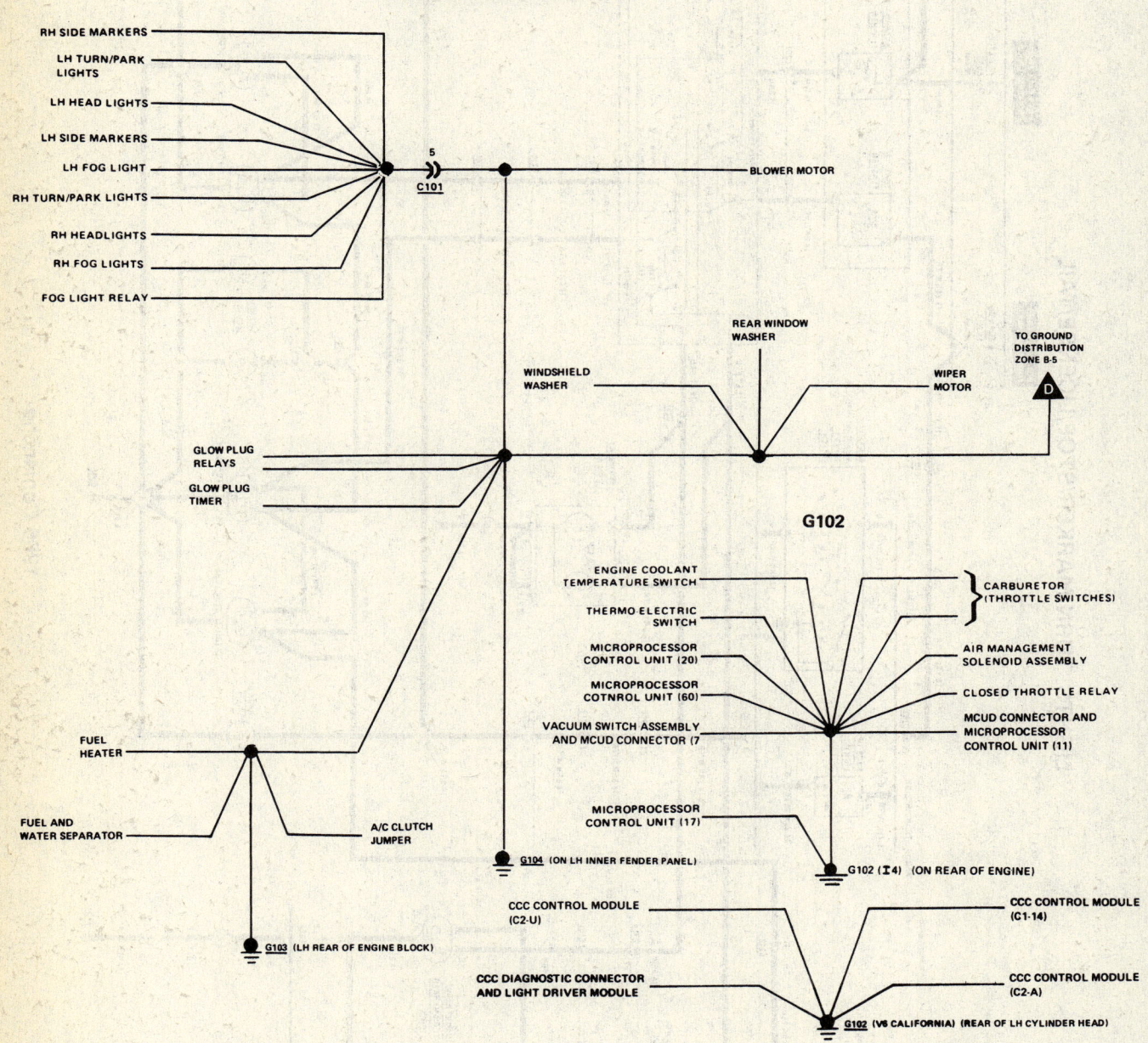

1986 Wagoneer and Cherokee

CHASSIS ELECTRICAL 6

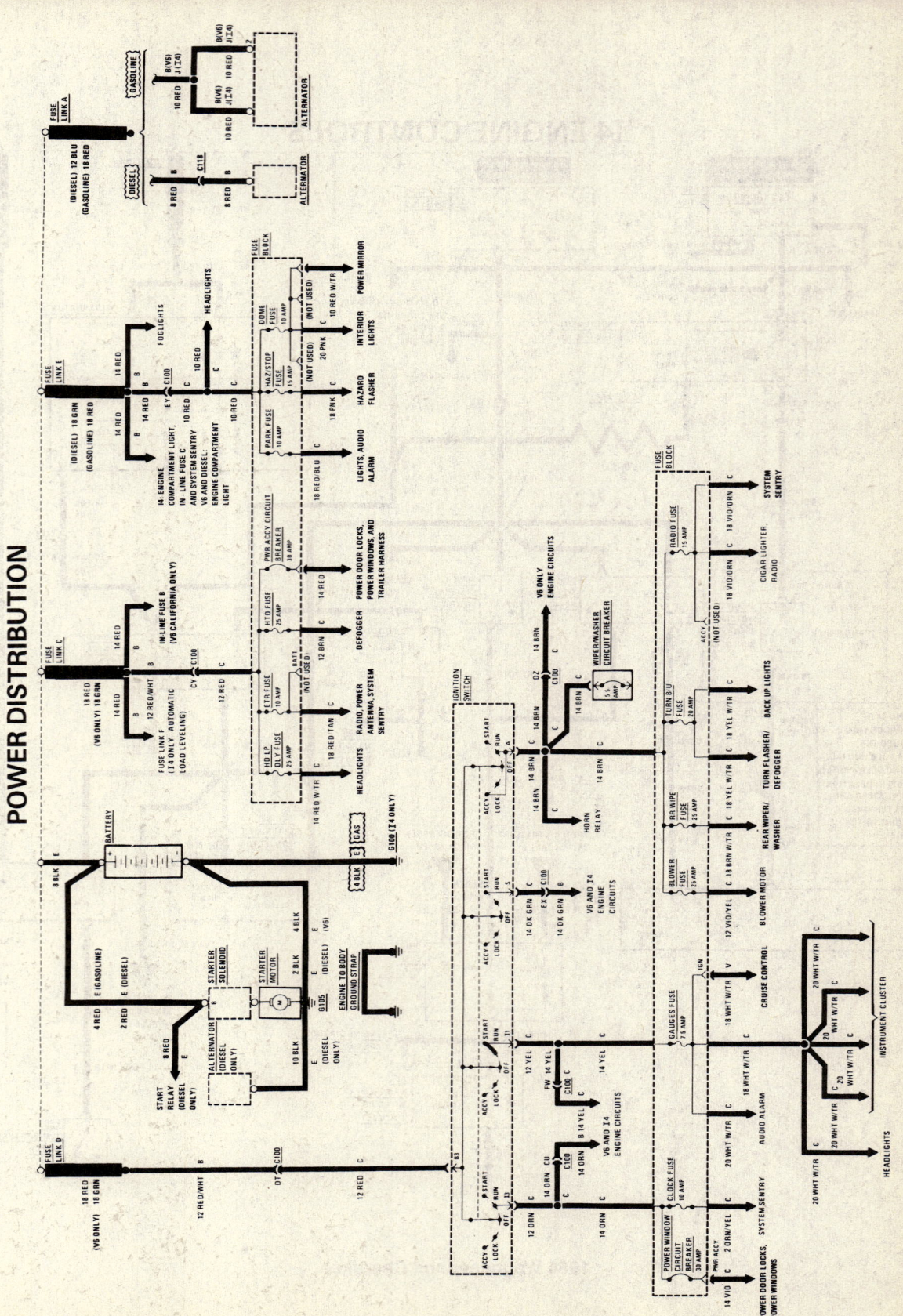

1986 Wagoneer and Cherokee

6 CHASSIS ELECTRICAL

I4 ENGINE CONTROLS

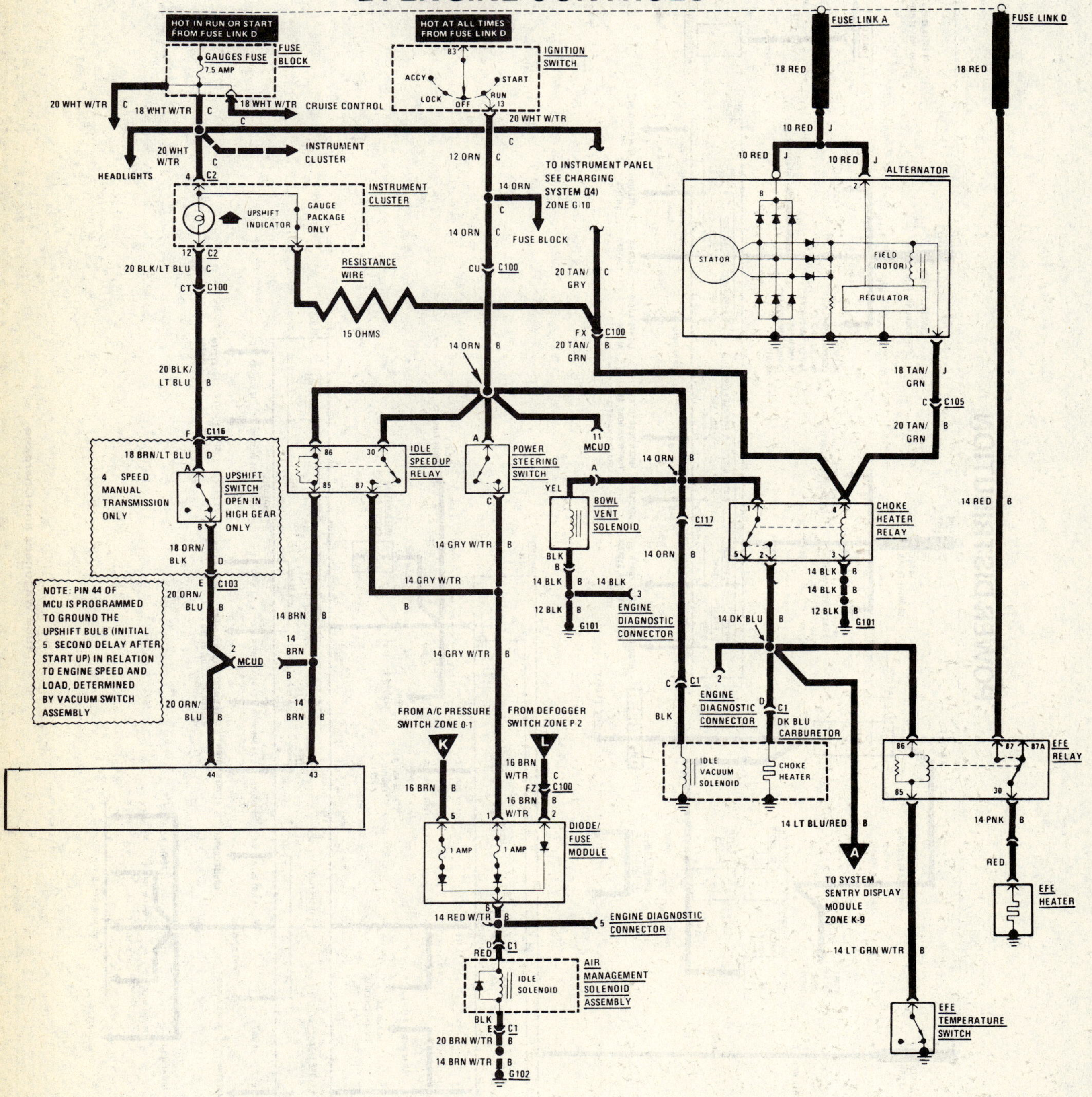

1986 Wagoneer and Cherokee

CHASSIS ELECTRICAL 6

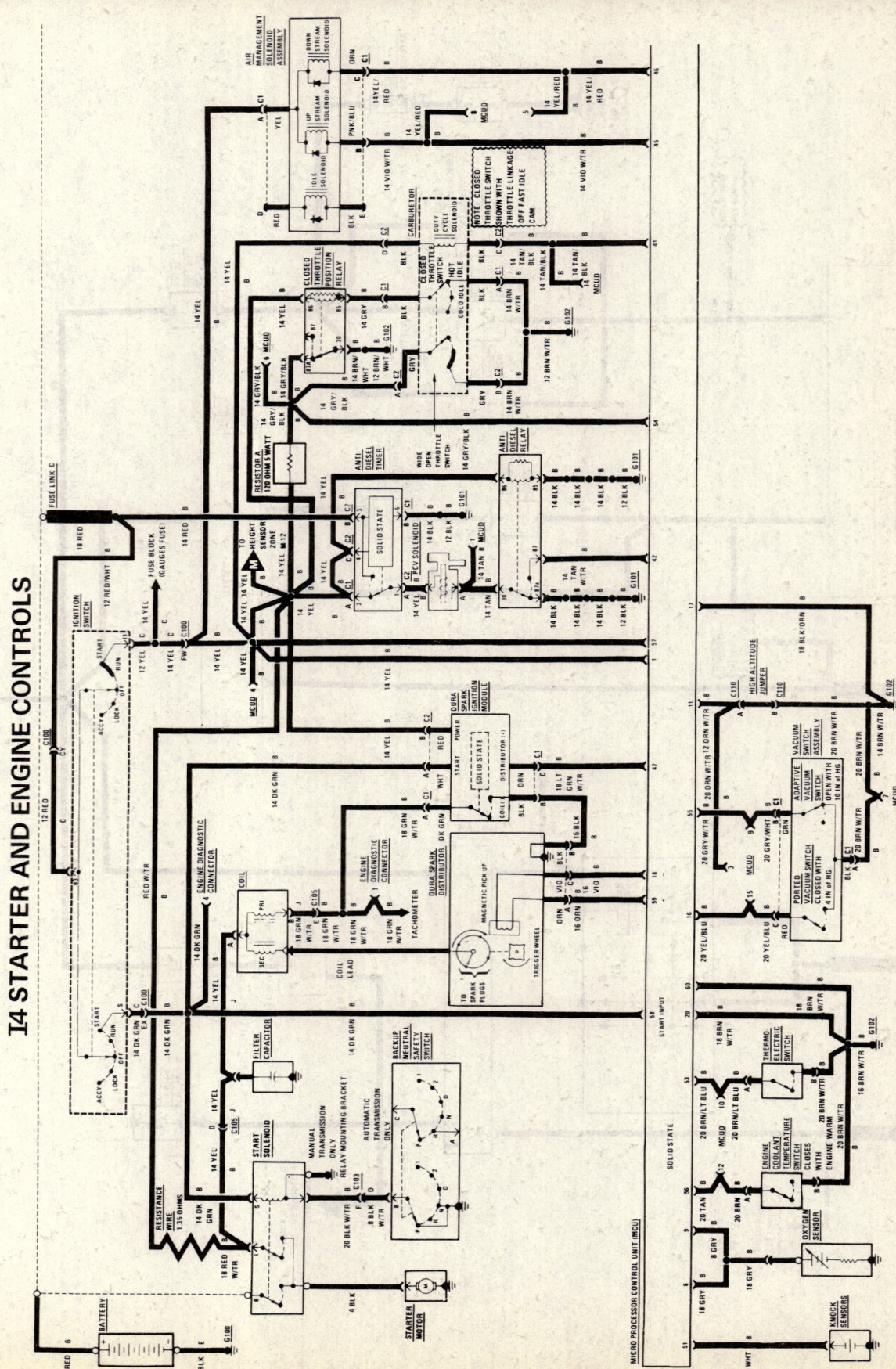

1986 Wagoneer and Cherokee — I4 Starter and Engine Controls

6-175

6 CHASSIS ELECTRICAL

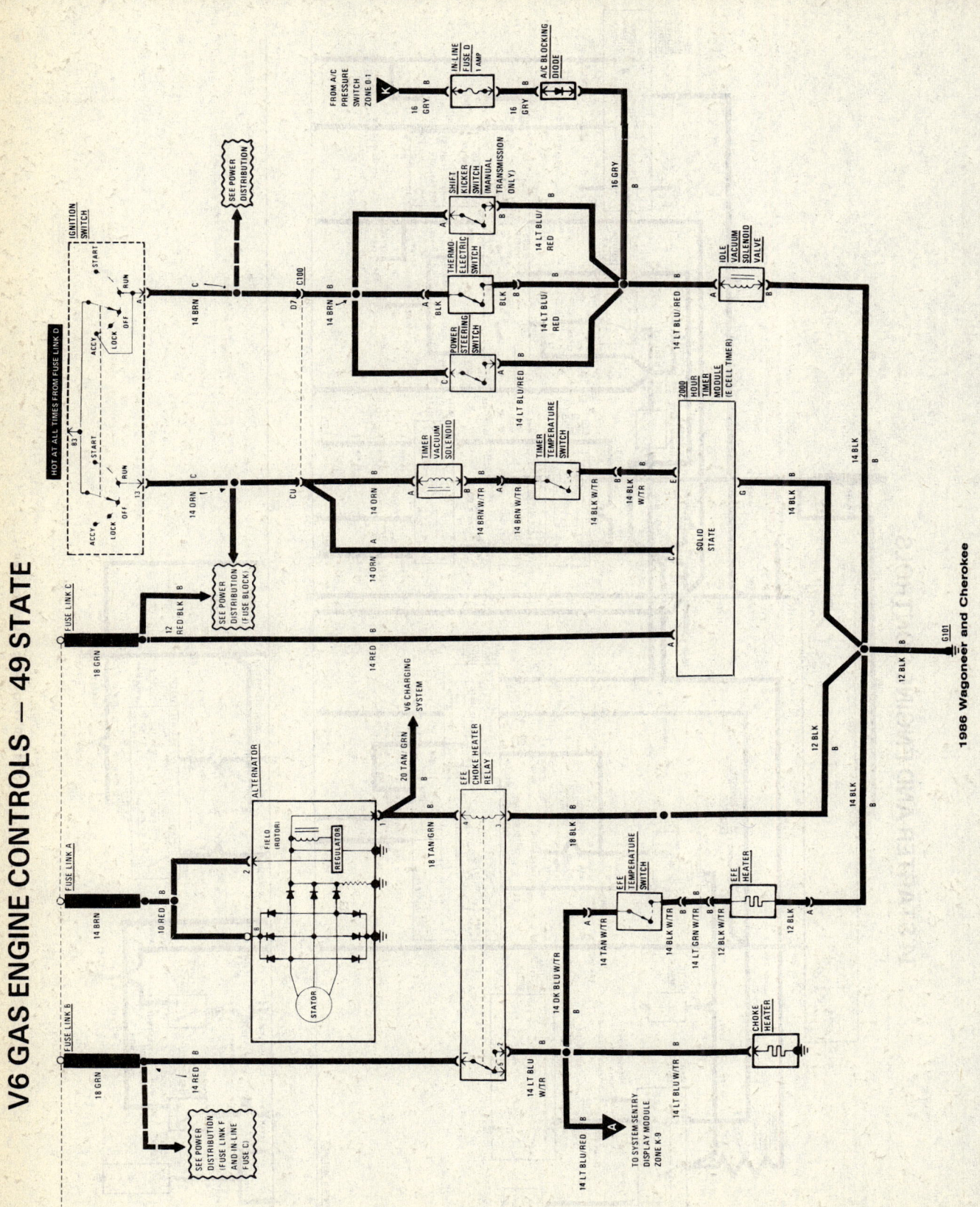

6-176

CHASSIS ELECTRICAL 6

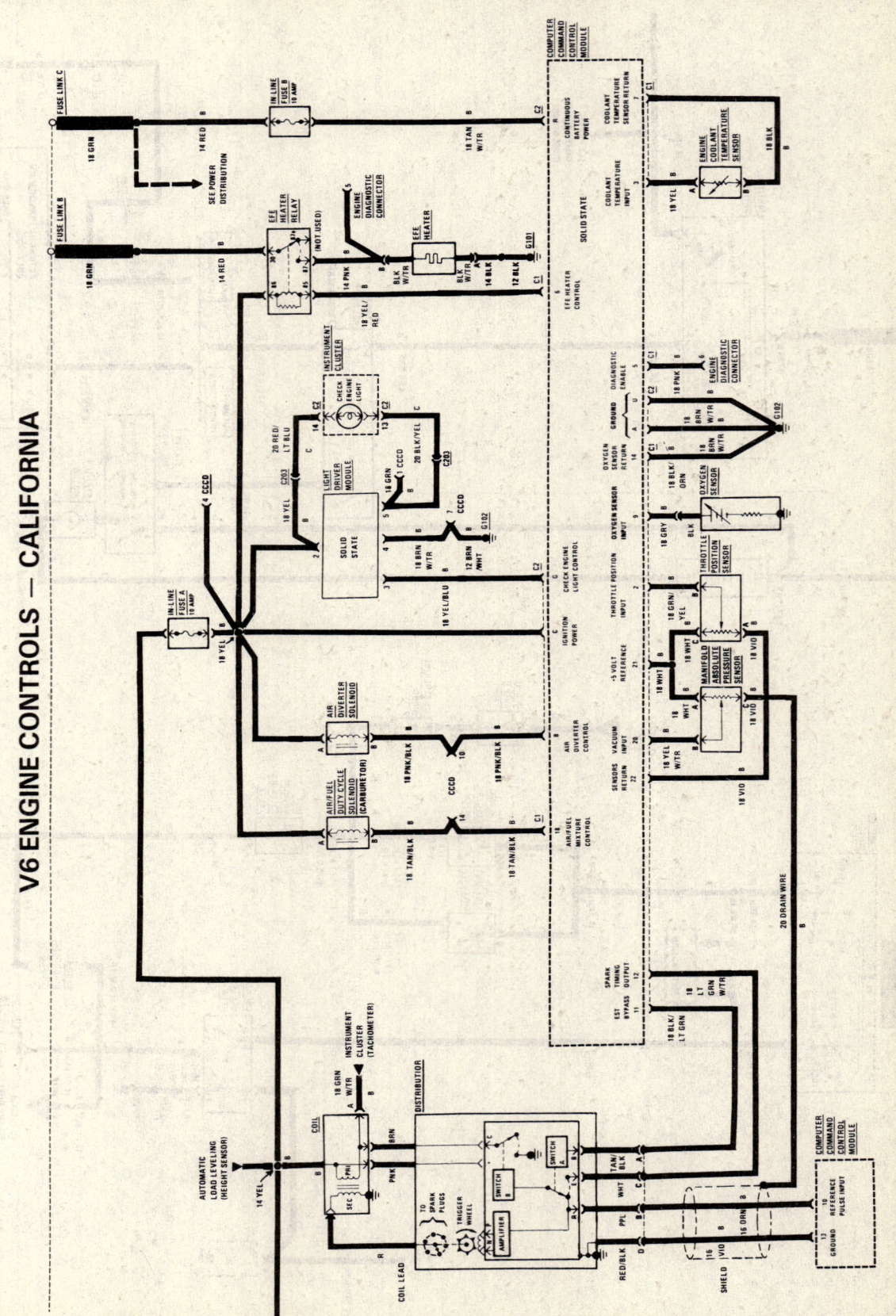

1986 Wagoneer and Cherokee

6-177

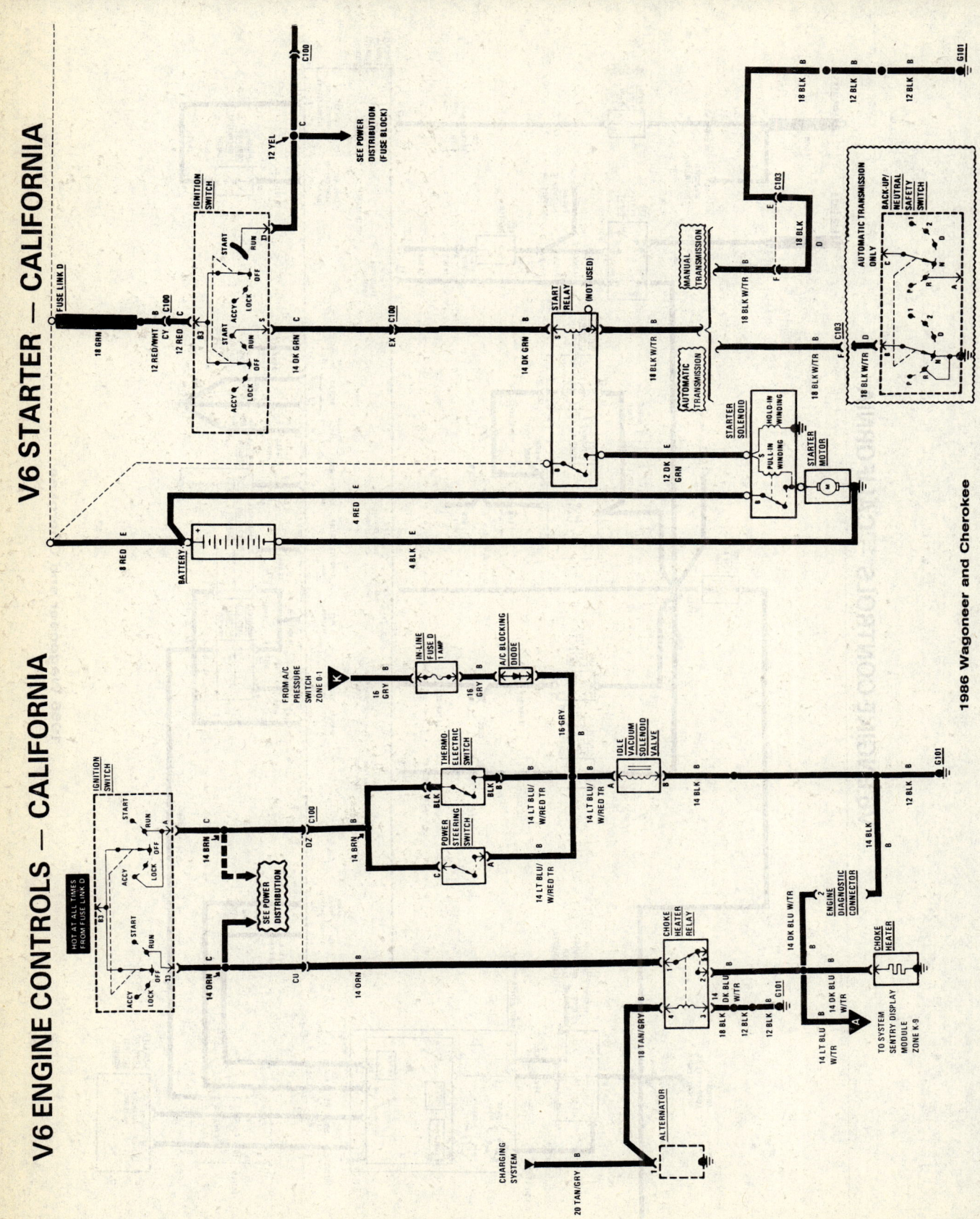

CHASSIS ELECTRICAL 6

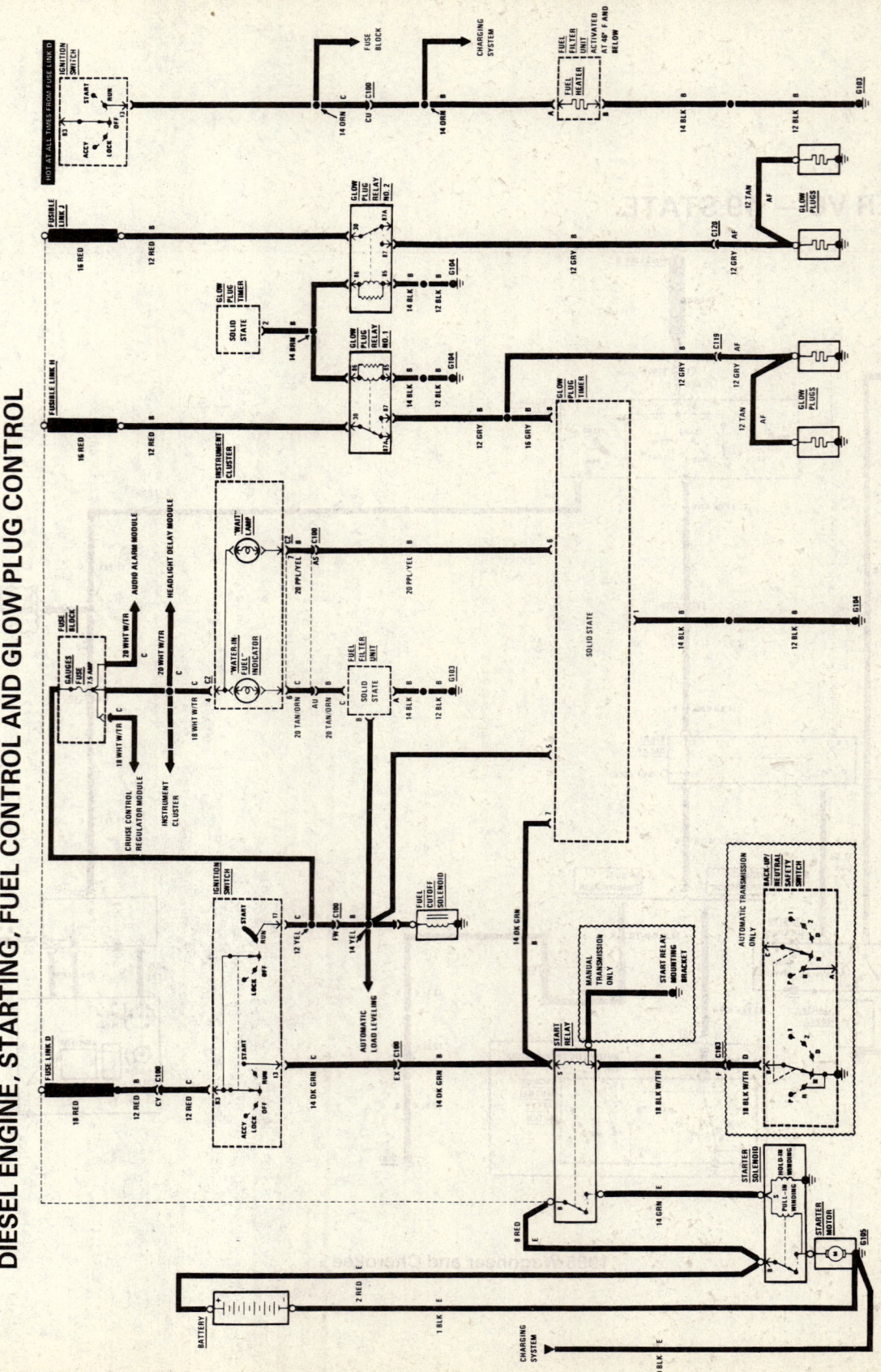

6-179

6 CHASSIS ELECTRICAL

STARTER V6 — 49 STATE

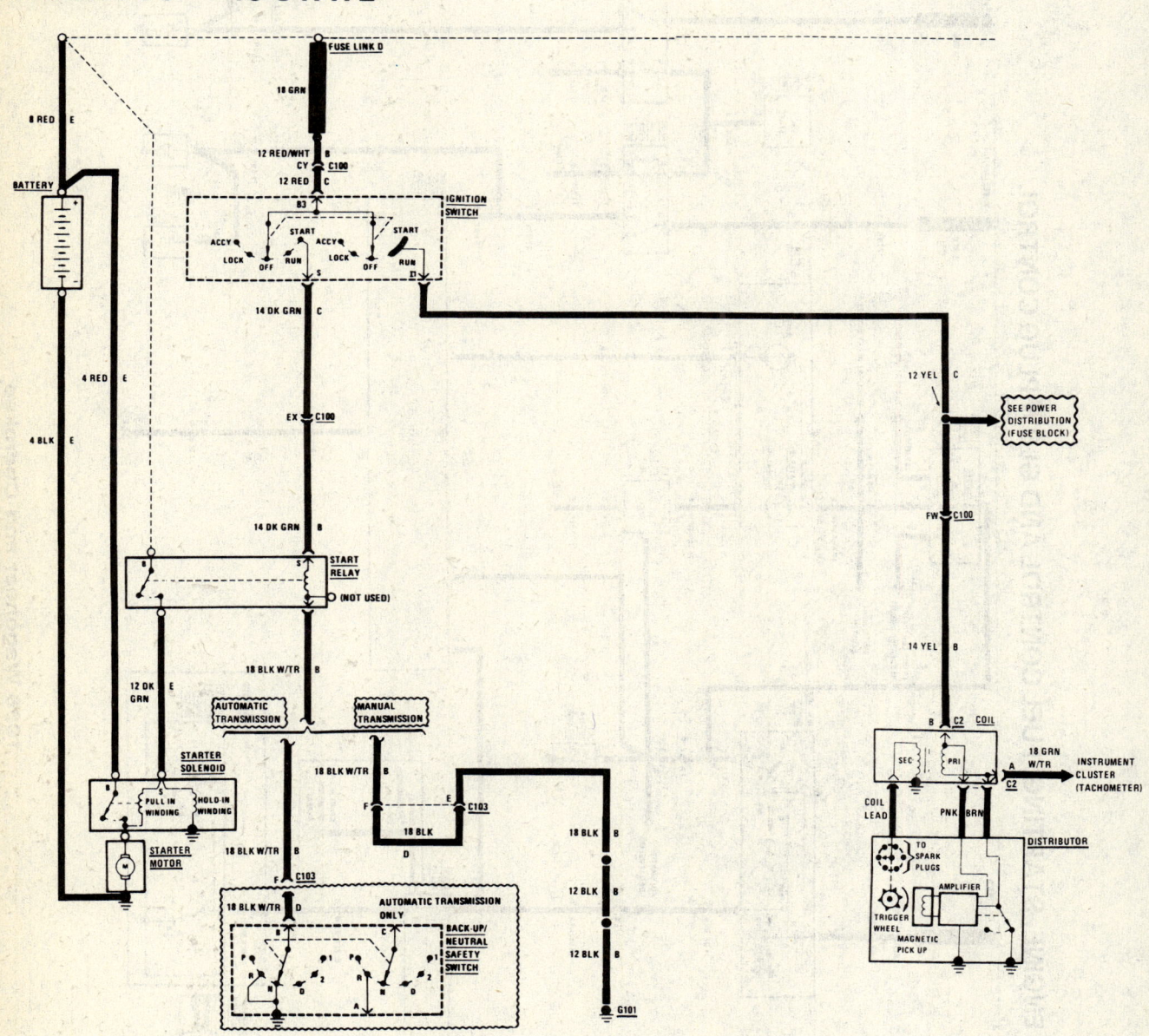

1986 Wagoneer and Cherokee

CHASSIS ELECTRICAL 6

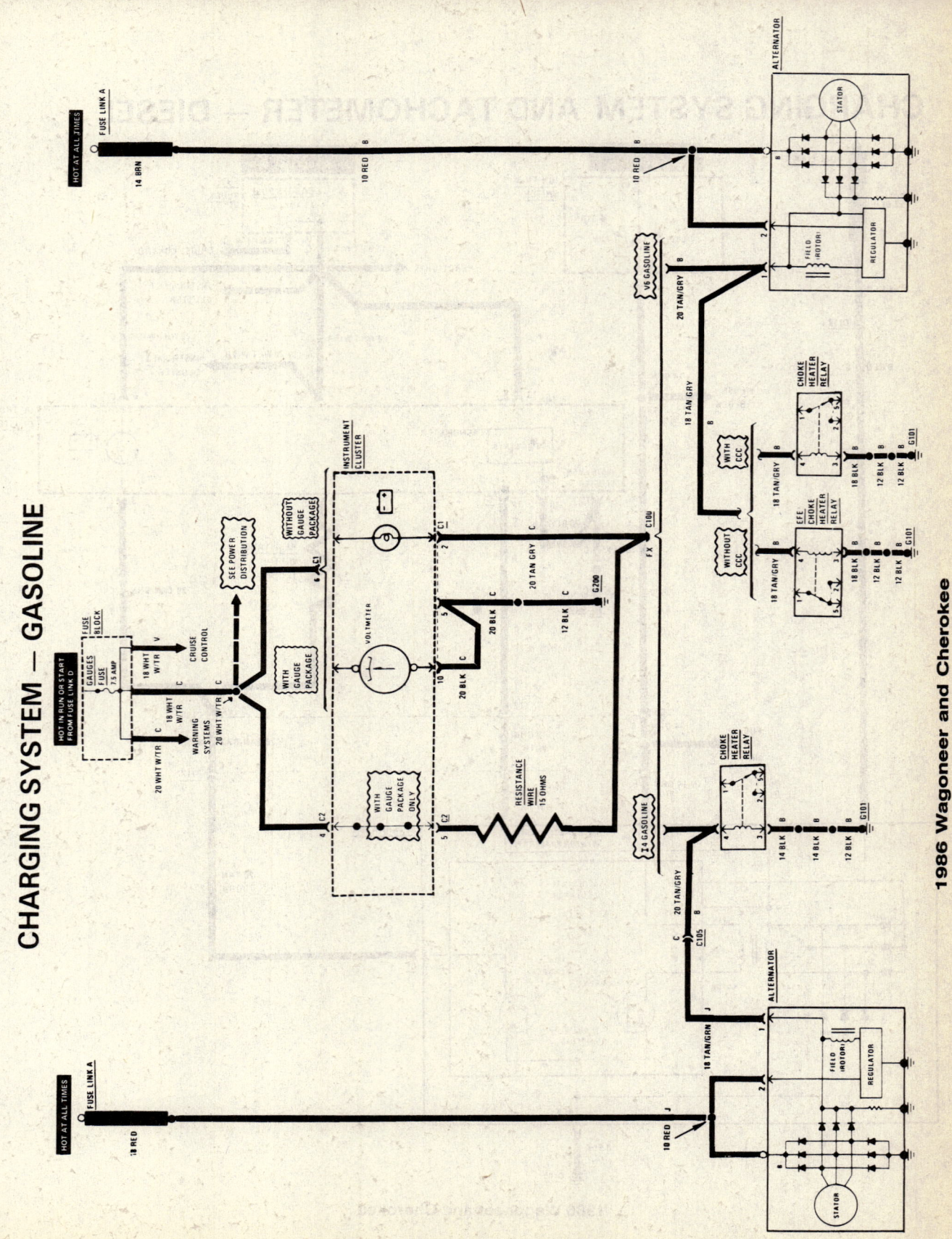

1986 Wagoneer and Cherokee

6 CHASSIS ELECTRICAL

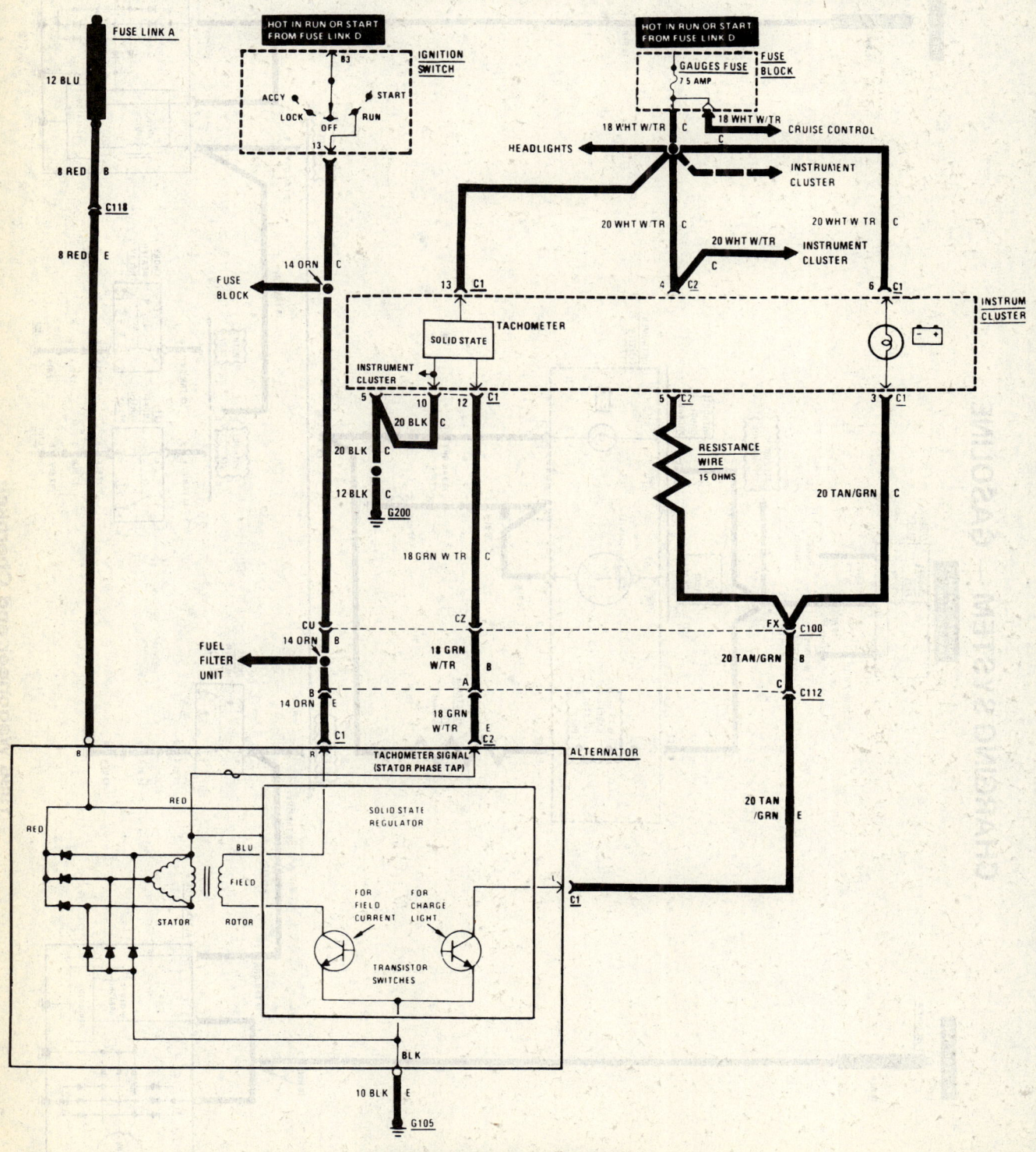

1986 Wagoneer and Cherokee

CHASSIS ELECTRICAL 6

HEATER AND AIR CONDITIONING — GASOLINE

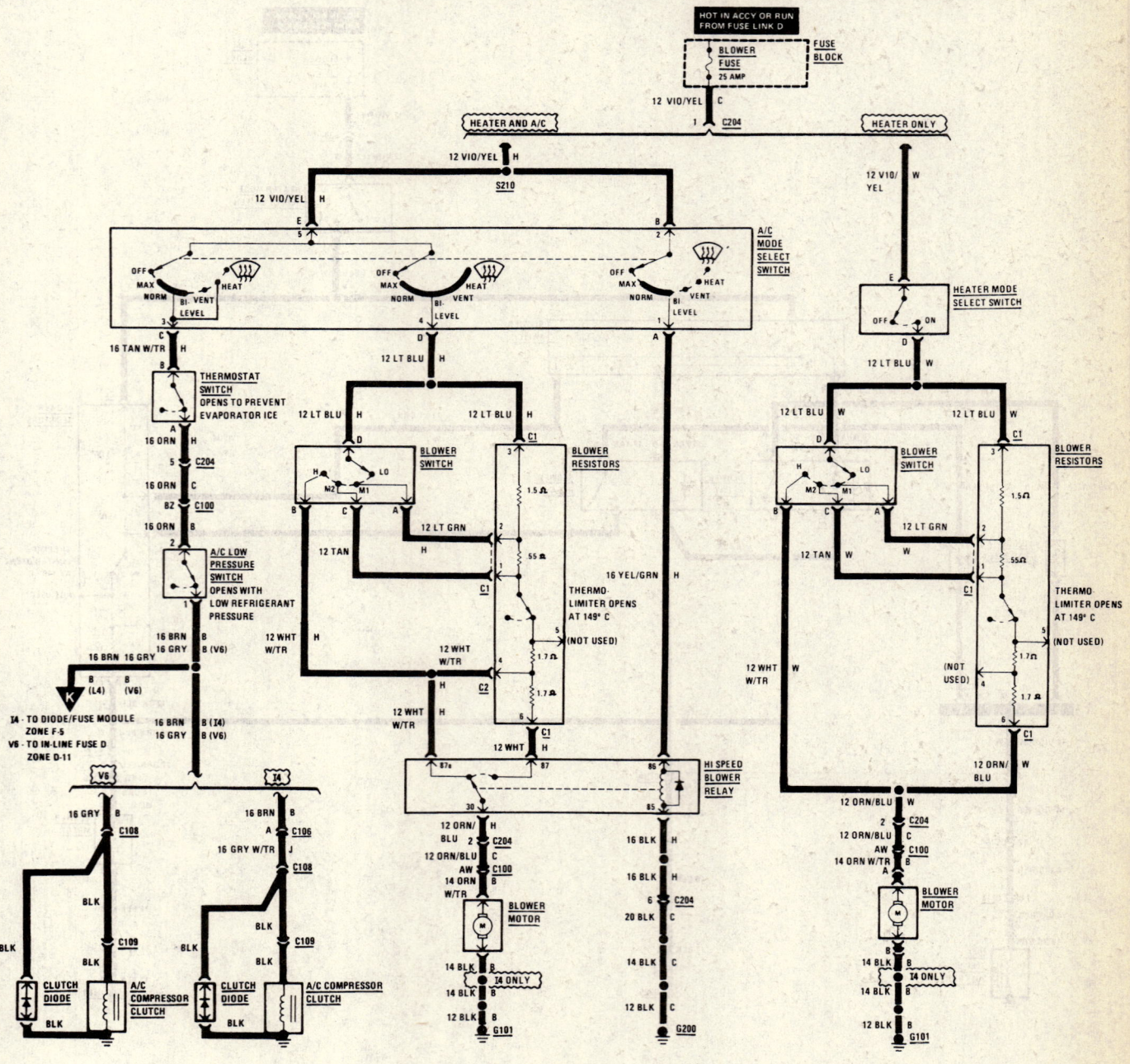

1986 Wagoneer and Cherokee

6-183

6 CHASSIS ELECTRICAL

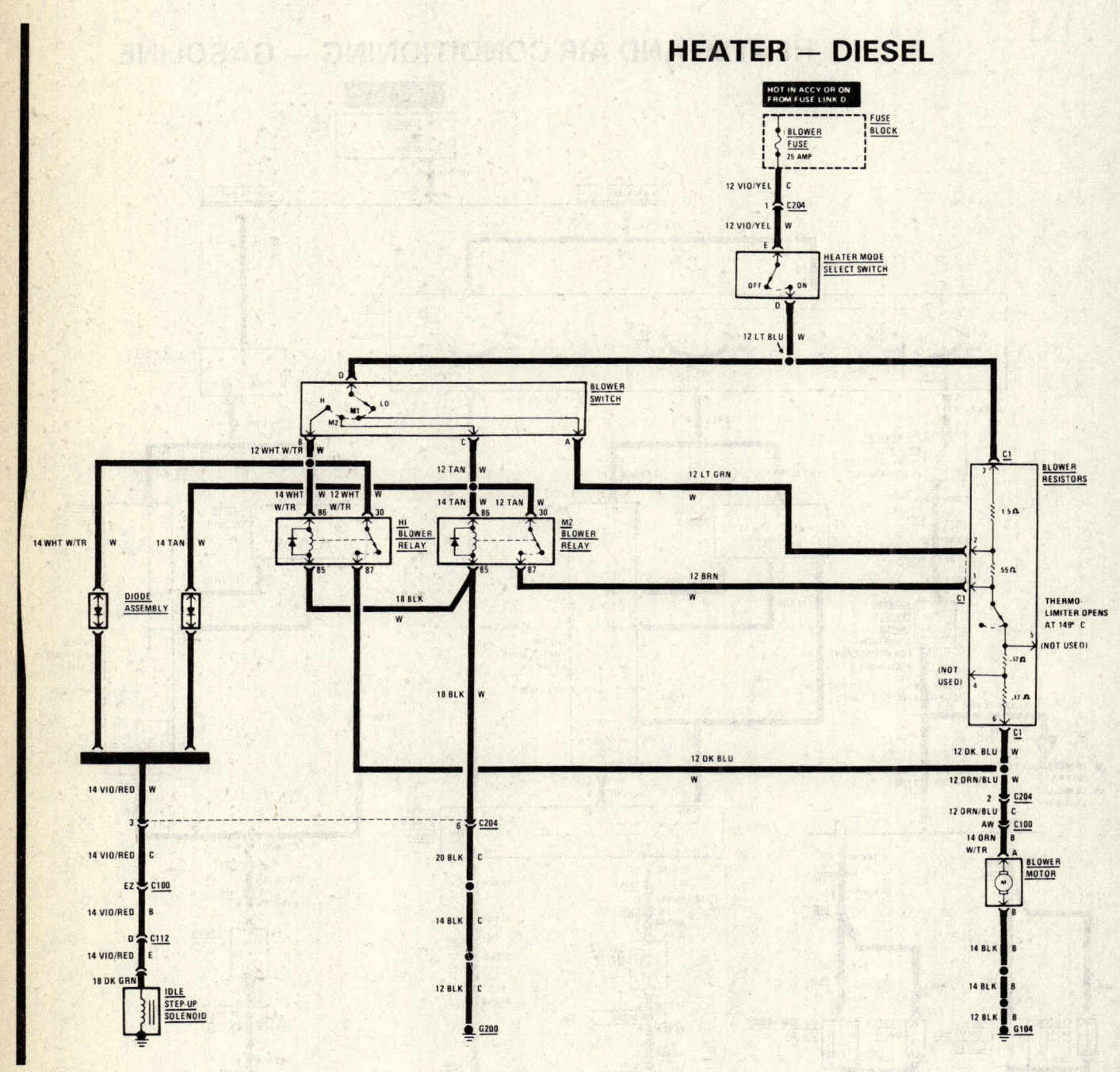

1986 Wagoneer and Cherokee

CHASSIS ELECTRICAL 6

AIR CONDITIONING – DIESEL

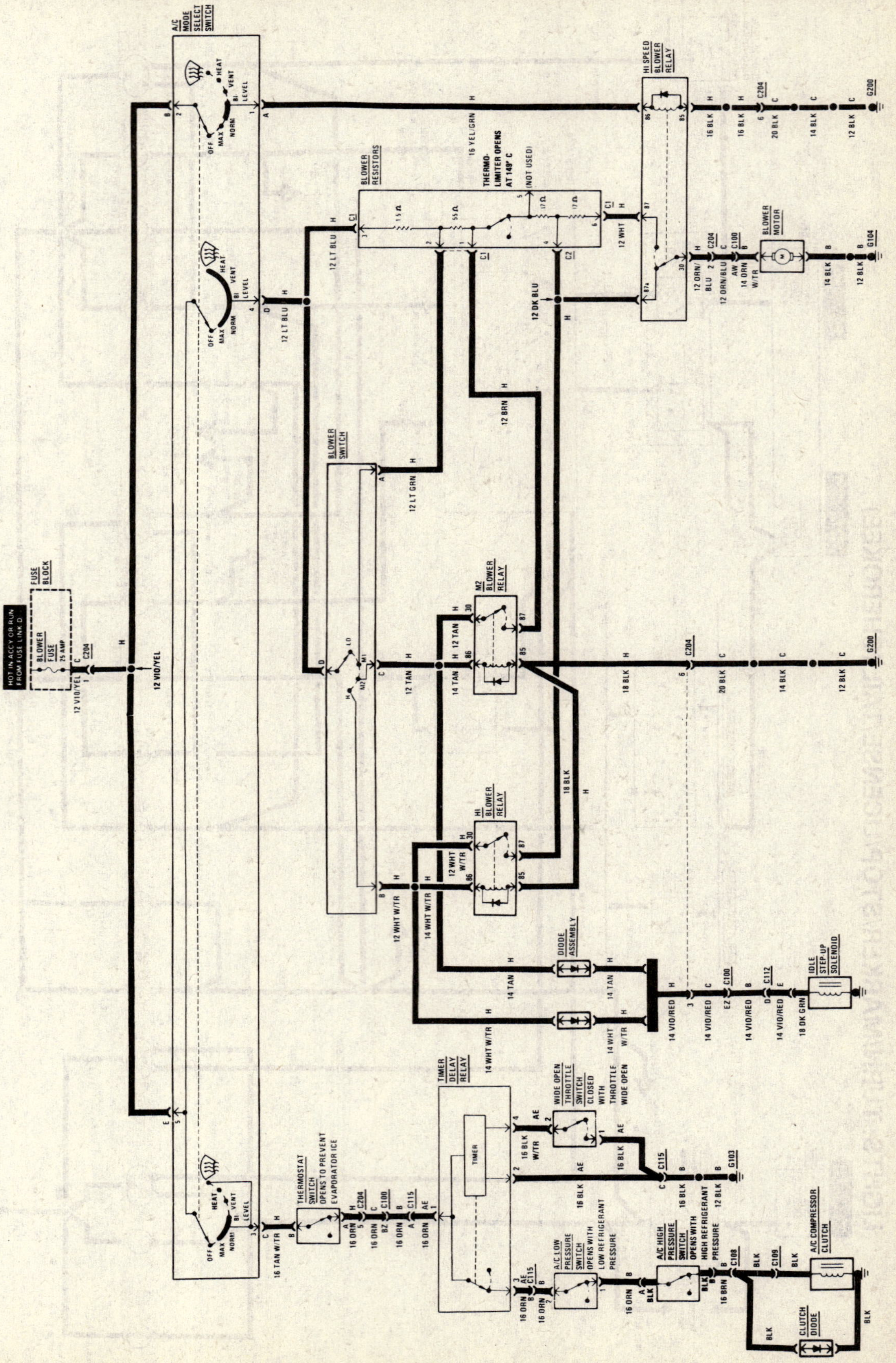

1986 Wagoneer and Cherokee

6-185

6 CHASSIS ELECTRICAL

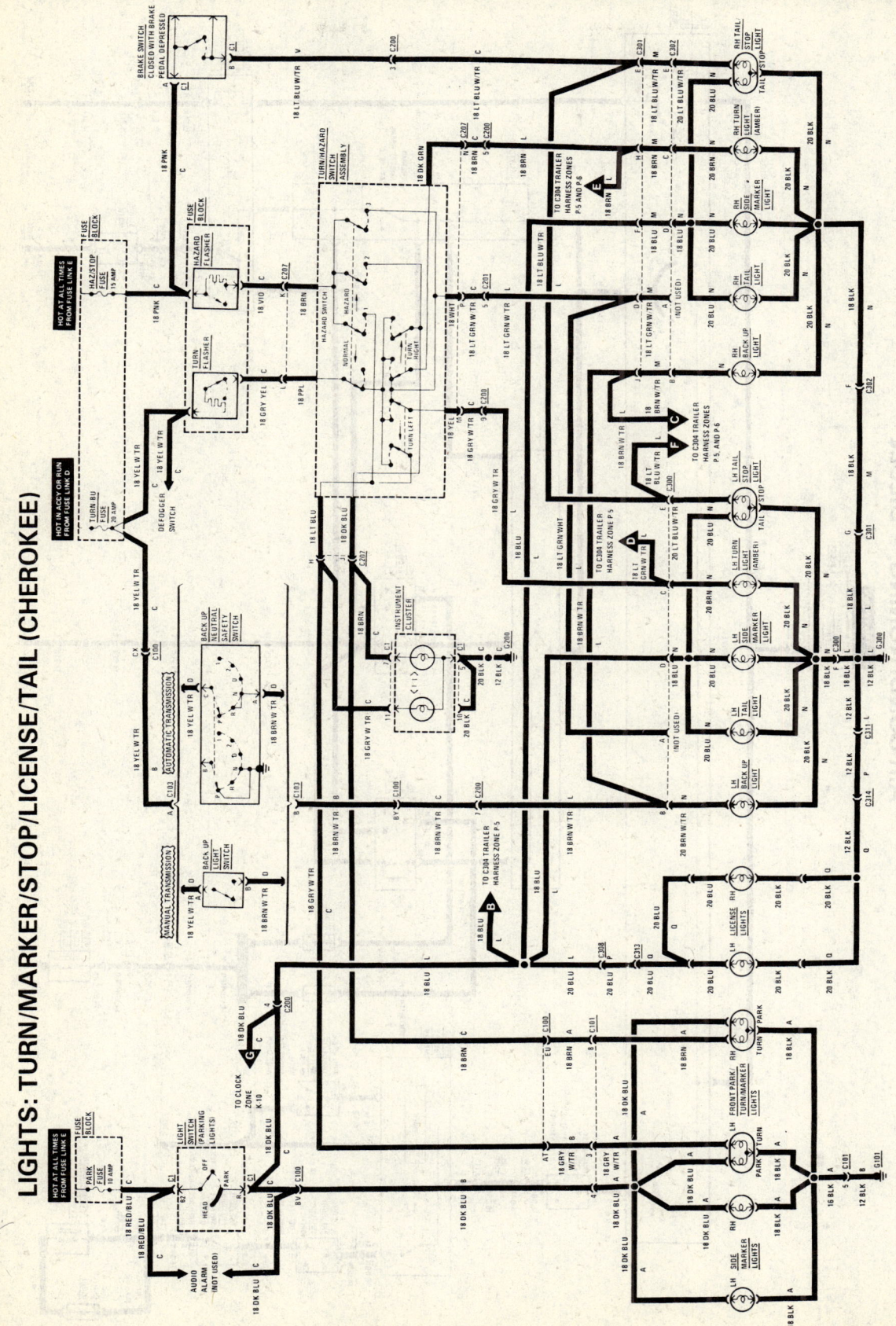

6-186

CHASSIS ELECTRICAL 6

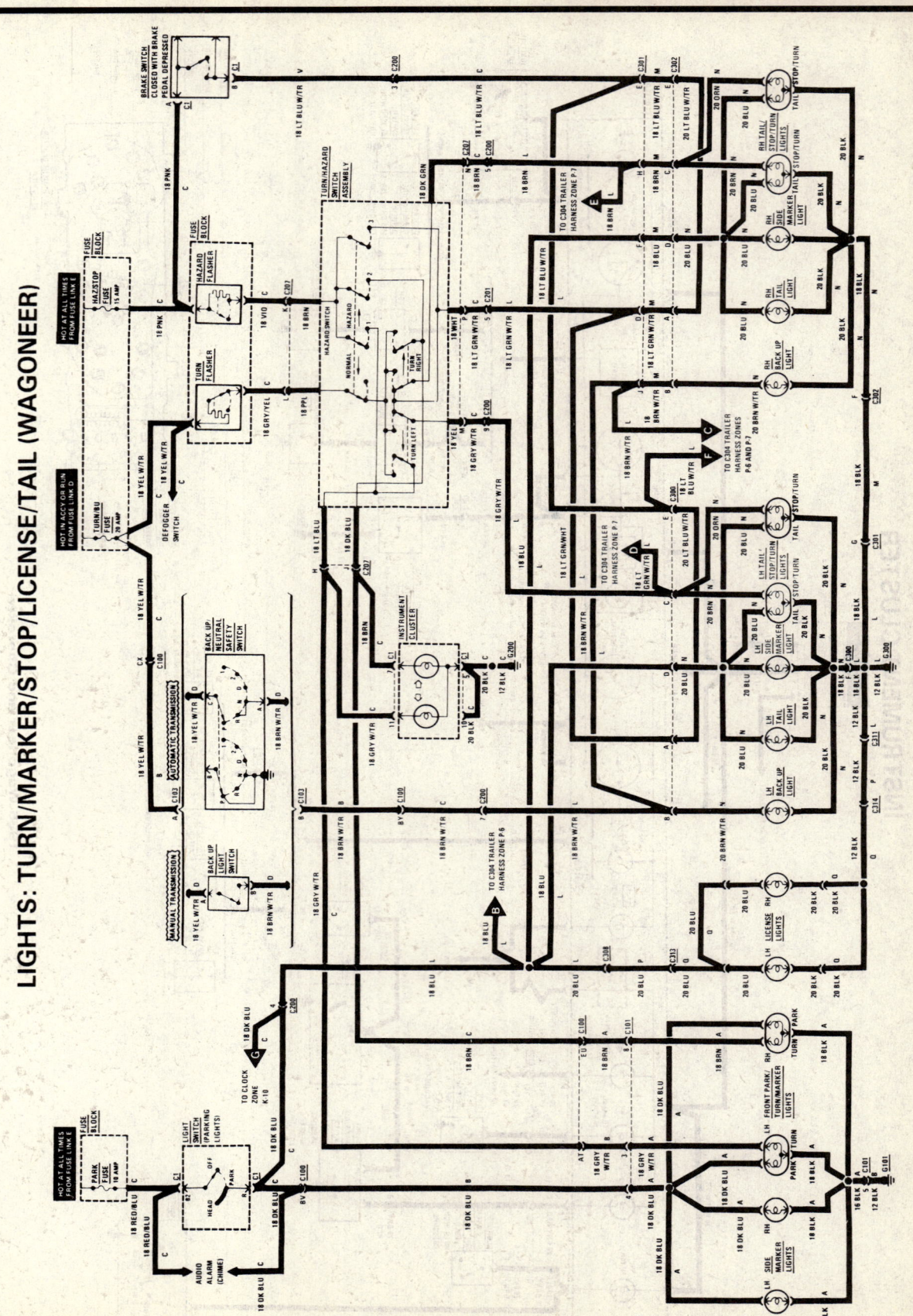

1986 Wagoneer and Cherokee

6-187

6 CHASSIS ELECTRICAL

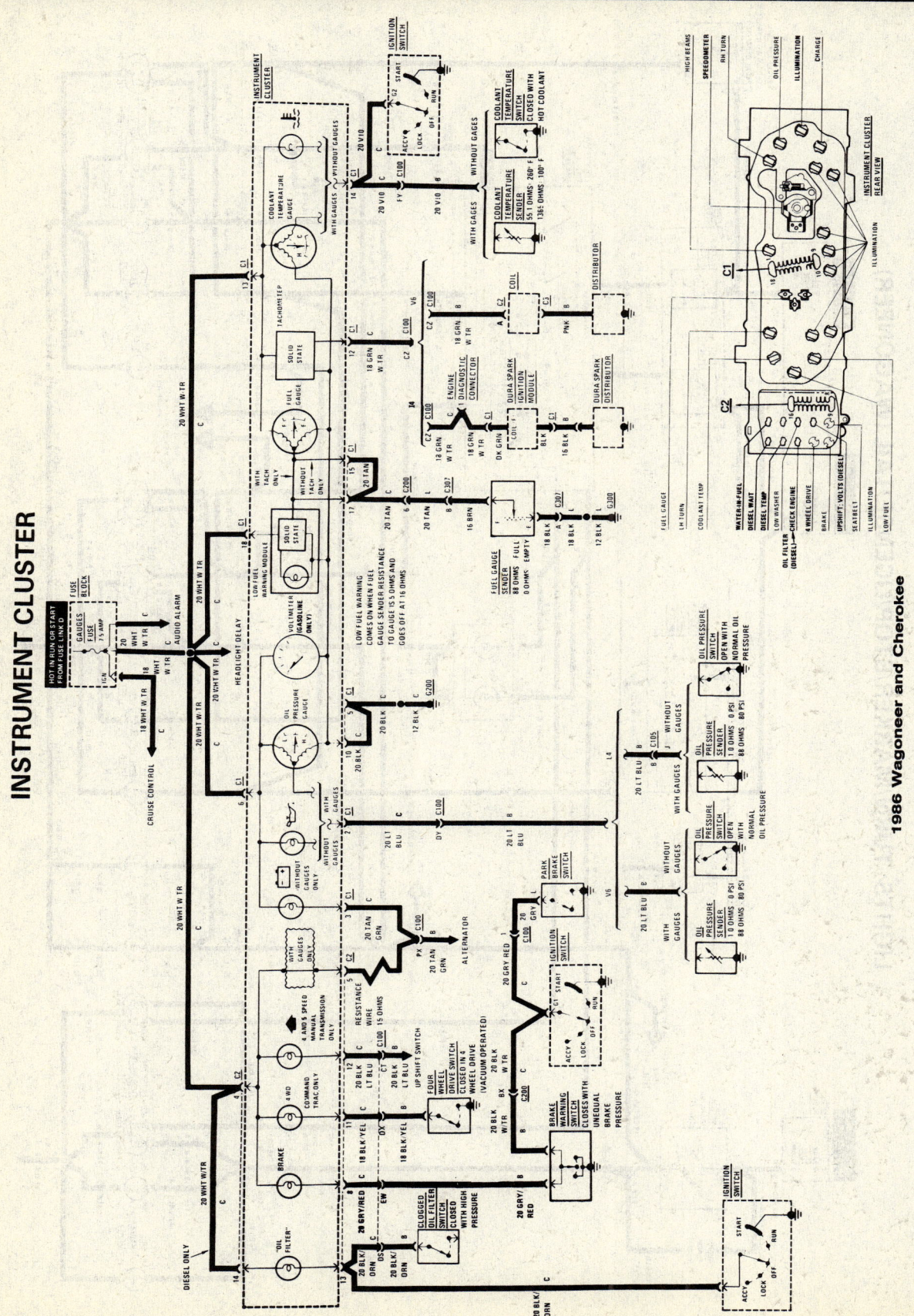

1986 Wagoneer and Cherokee

CHASSIS ELECTRICAL 6

HEADLIGHTS, FOGLIGHTS, AND ENGINE LIGHT

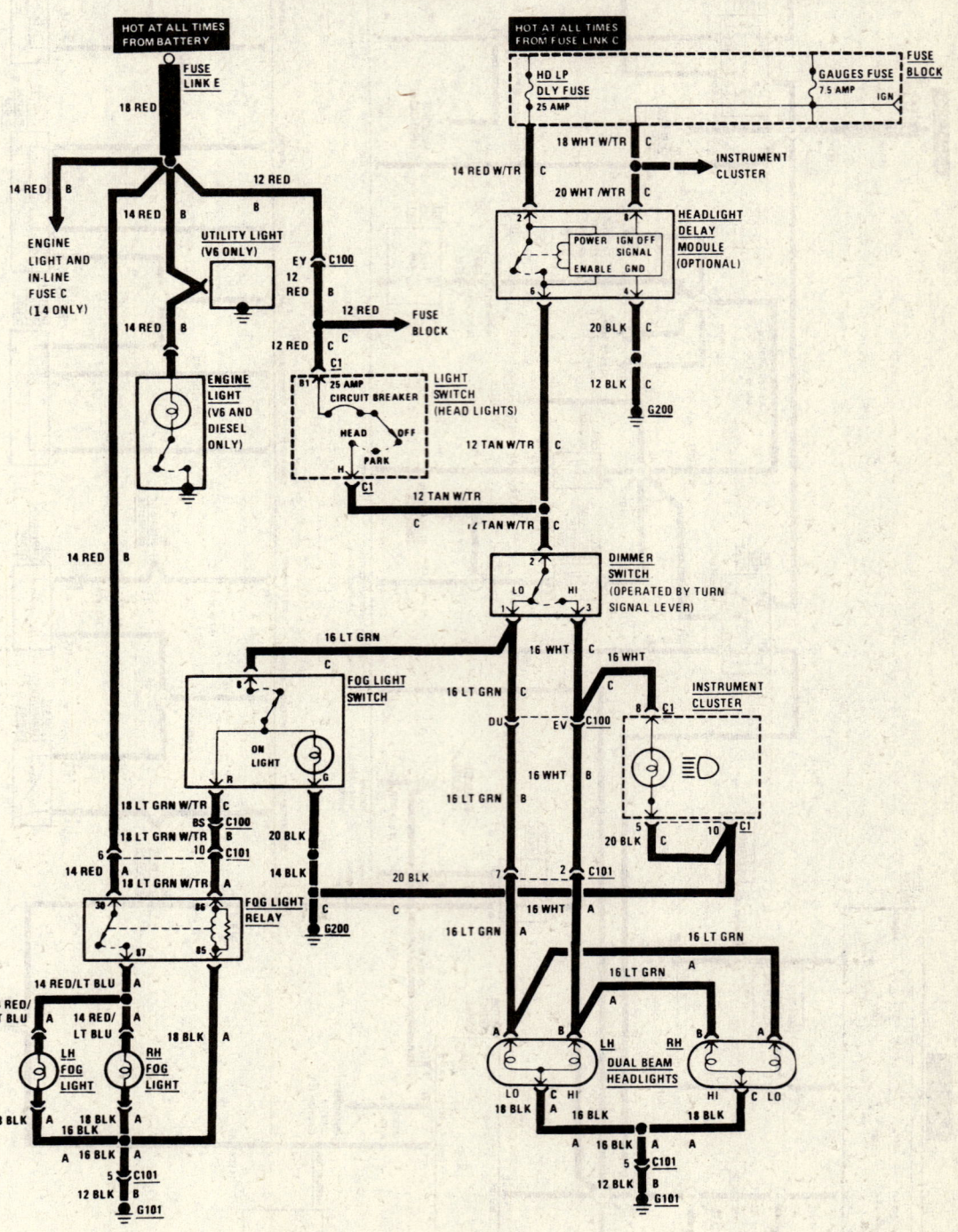

1986 Wagoneer and Cherokee

6-189

6 CHASSIS ELECTRICAL

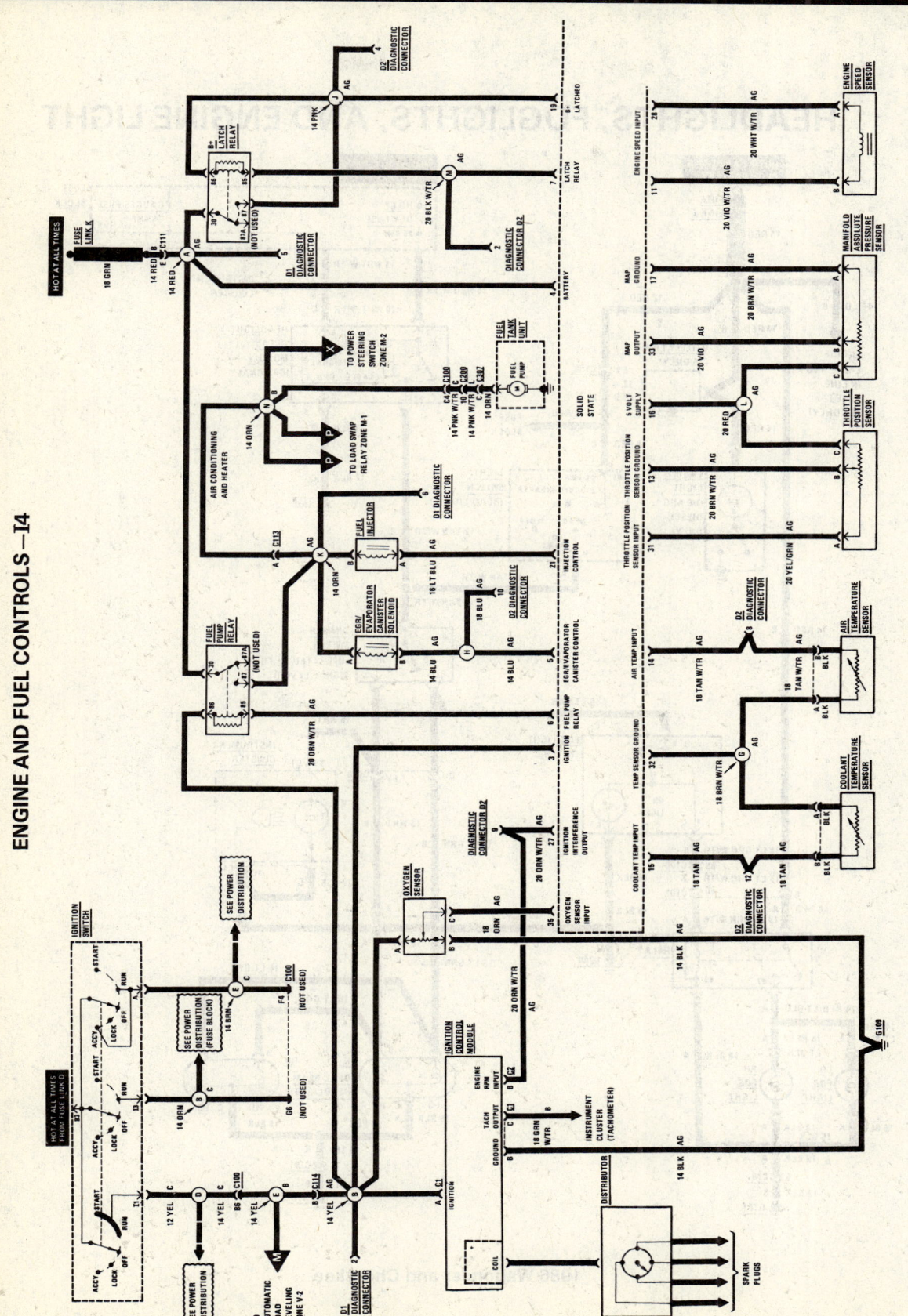

CHASSIS ELECTRICAL 6

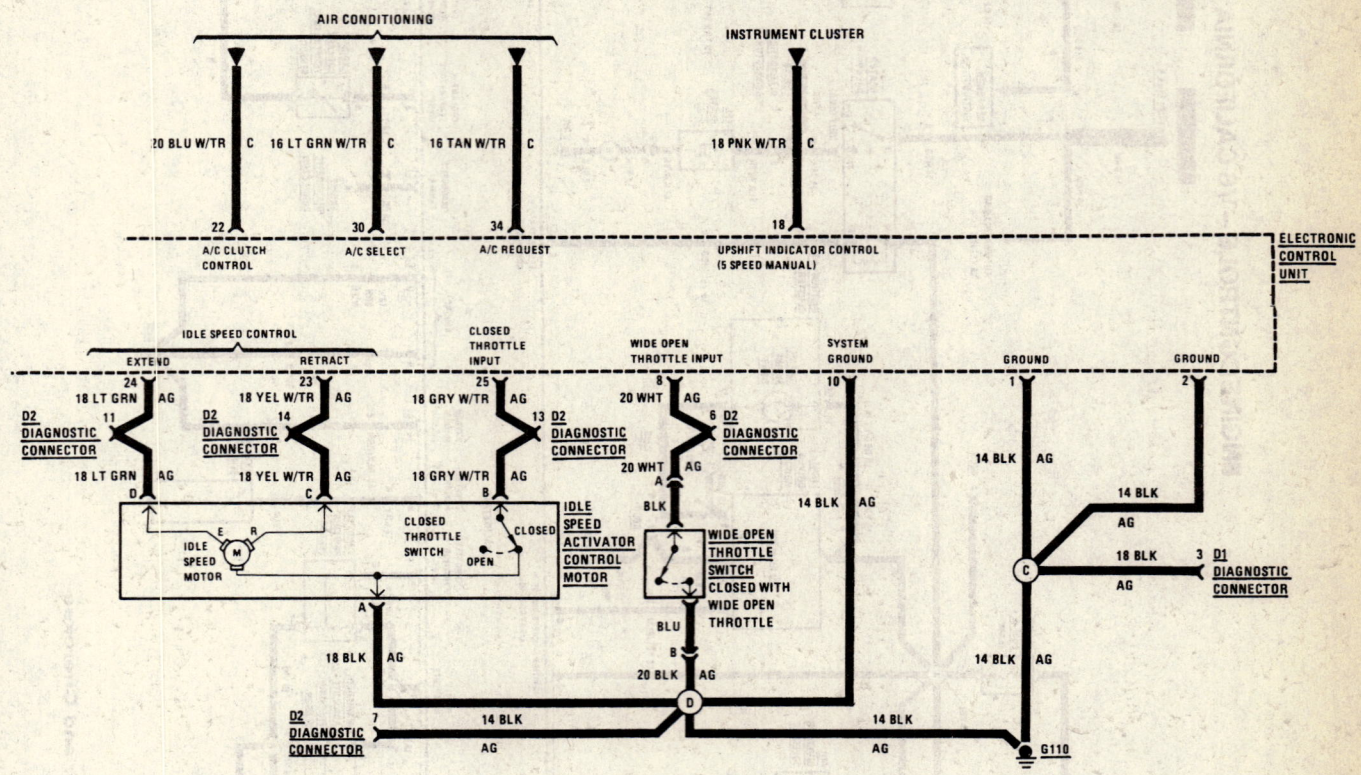

1986-88 Wagoneer and Cherokee

6-191

6 CHASSIS ELECTRICAL

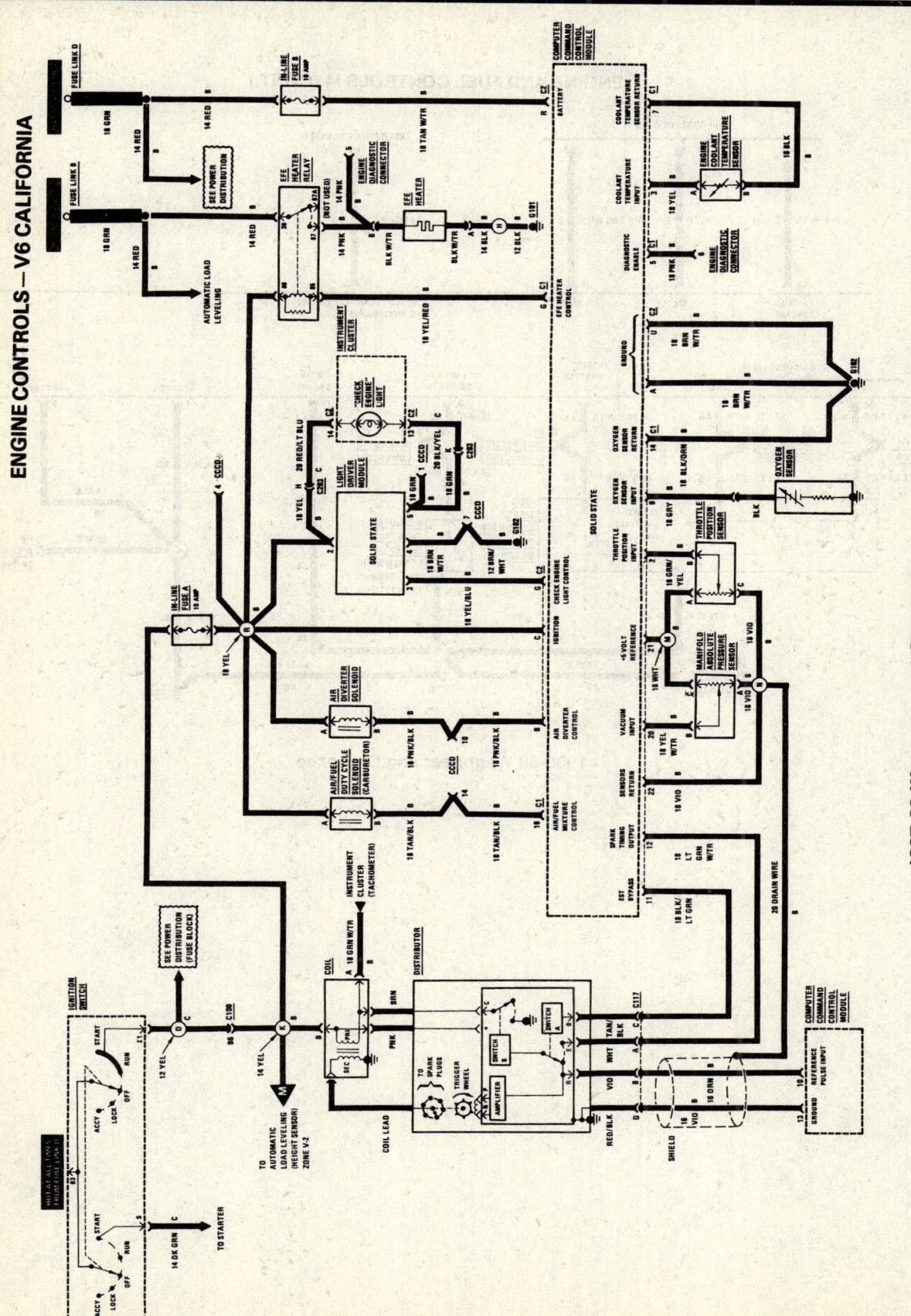

1987-88 Wagoneer and Cherokee

CHASSIS ELECTRICAL 6

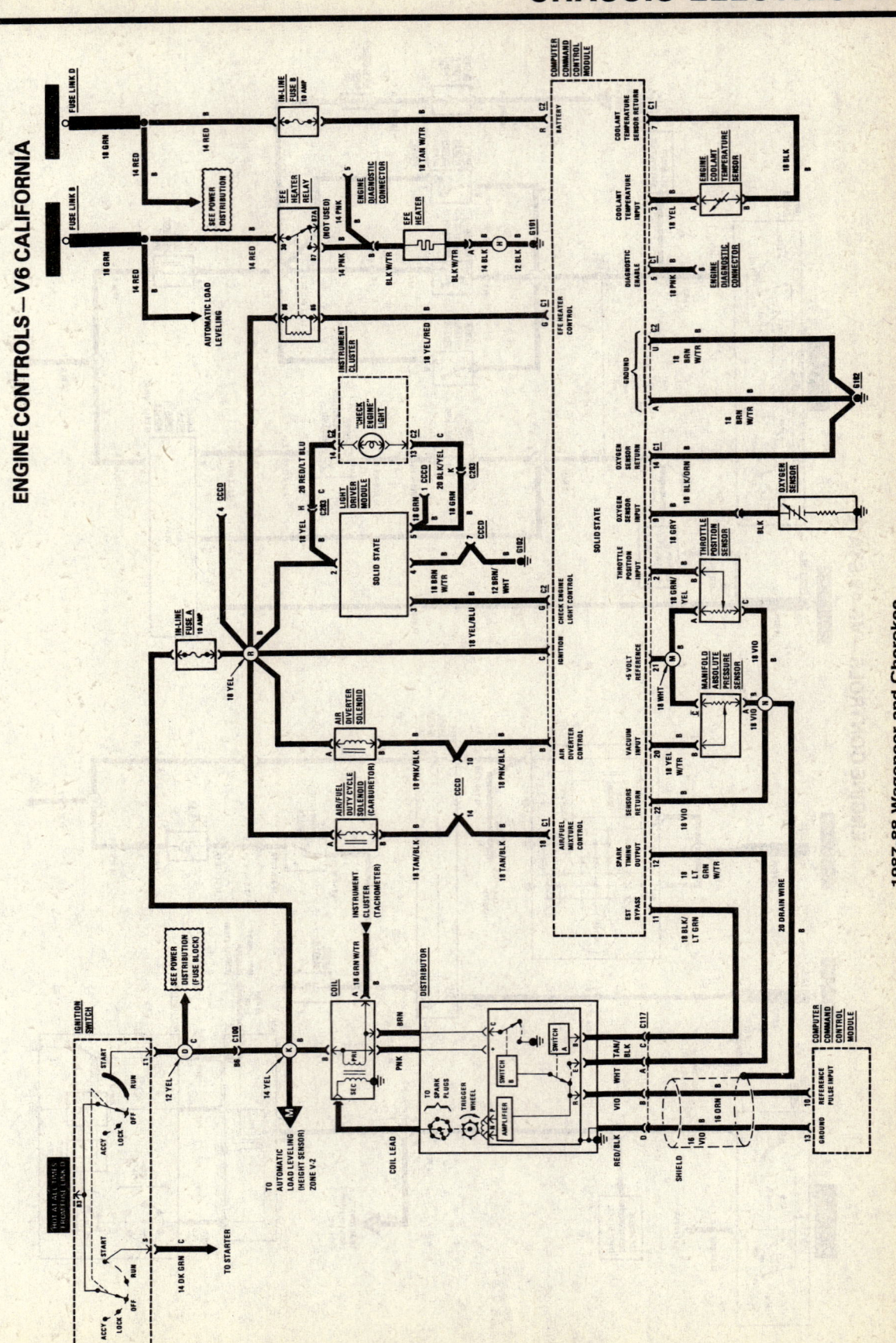

1987-88 Wagoneer and Cherokee

6-193

6 CHASSIS ELECTRICAL

ENGINE CONTROLS—V6 49 STATE

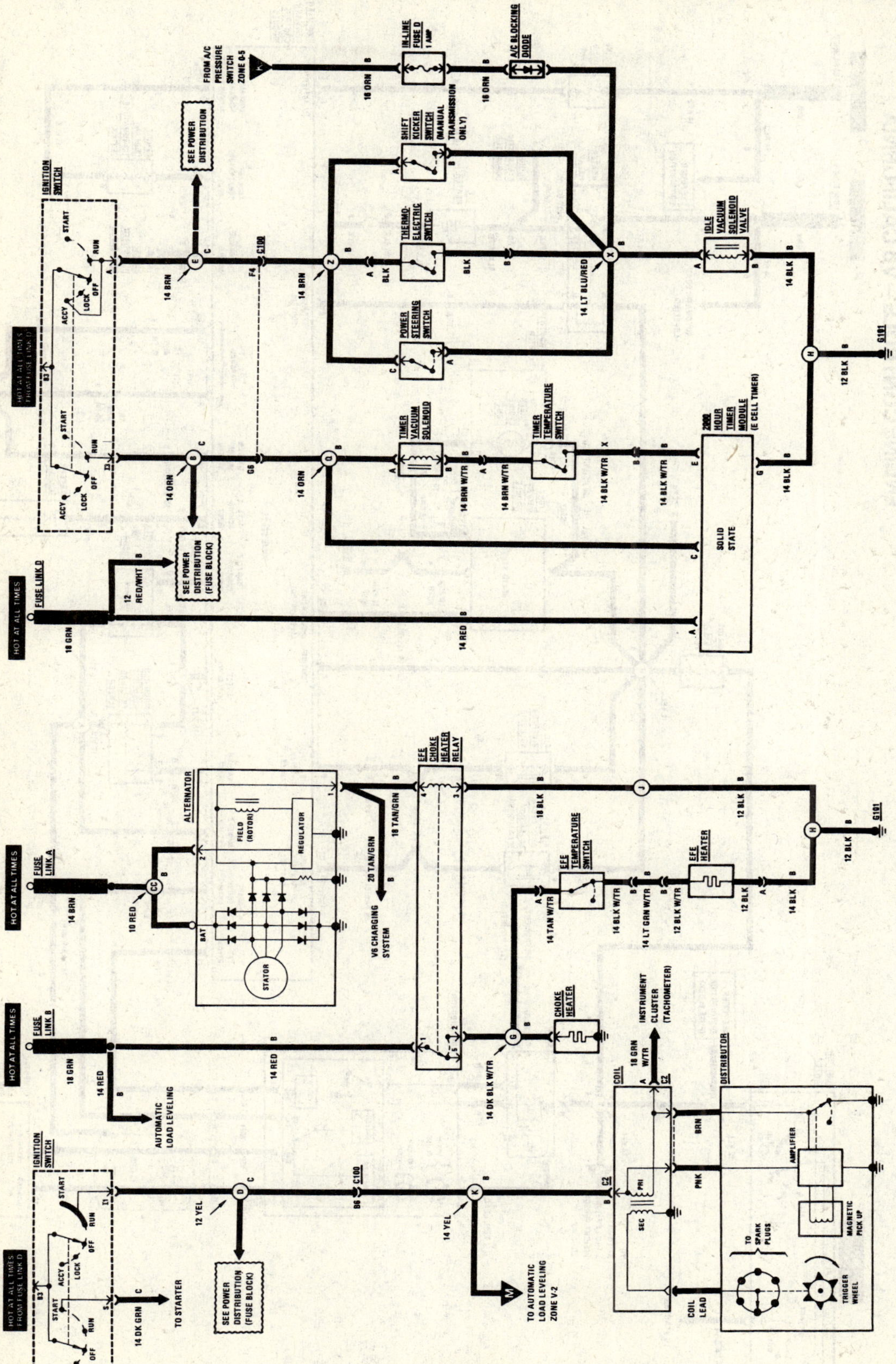

1987-88 Wagoneer and Cherokee

6-194

CHASSIS ELECTRICAL 6

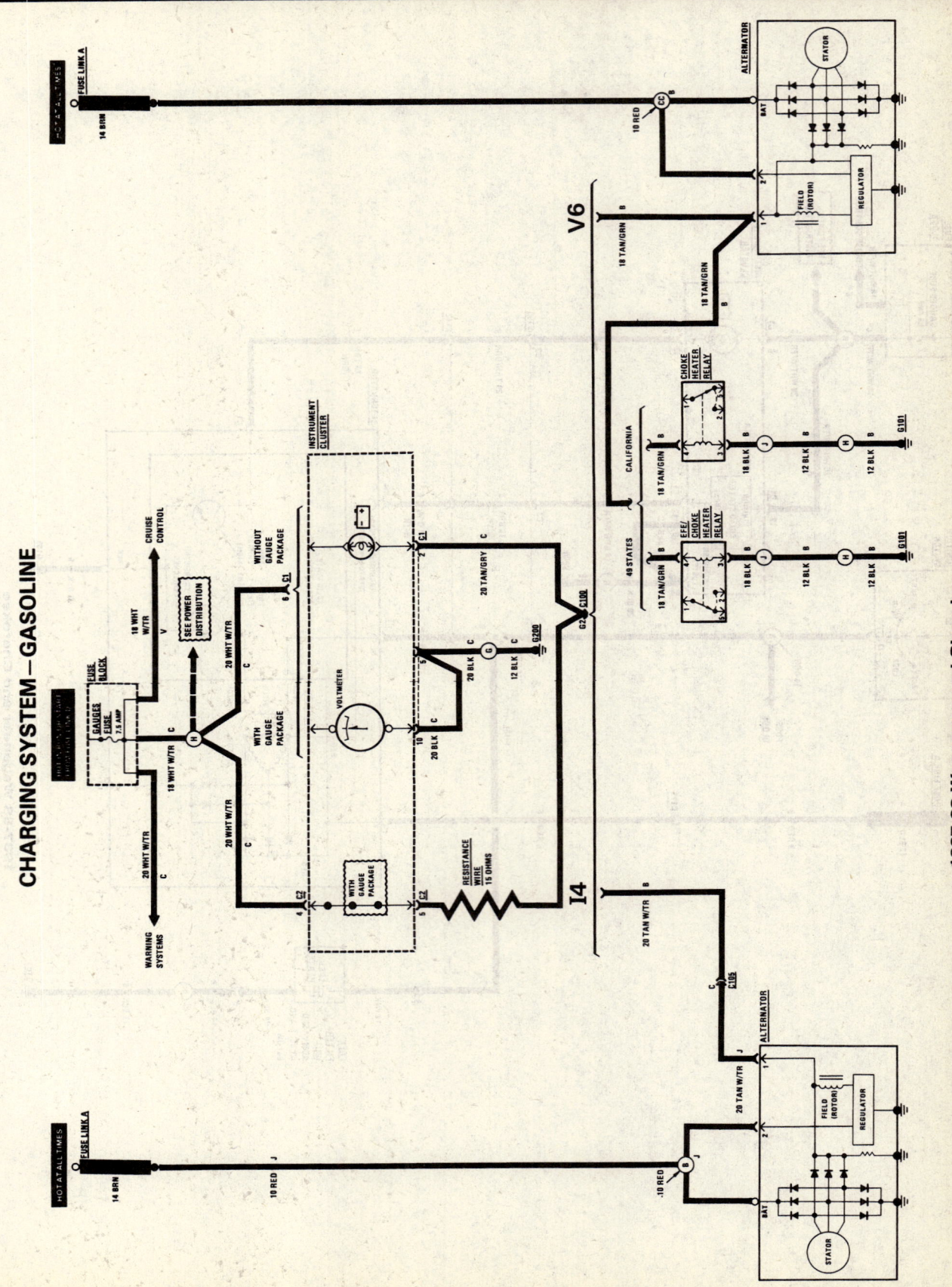

1987-88 Wagoneer and Cherokee

6-195

6 CHASSIS ELECTRICAL

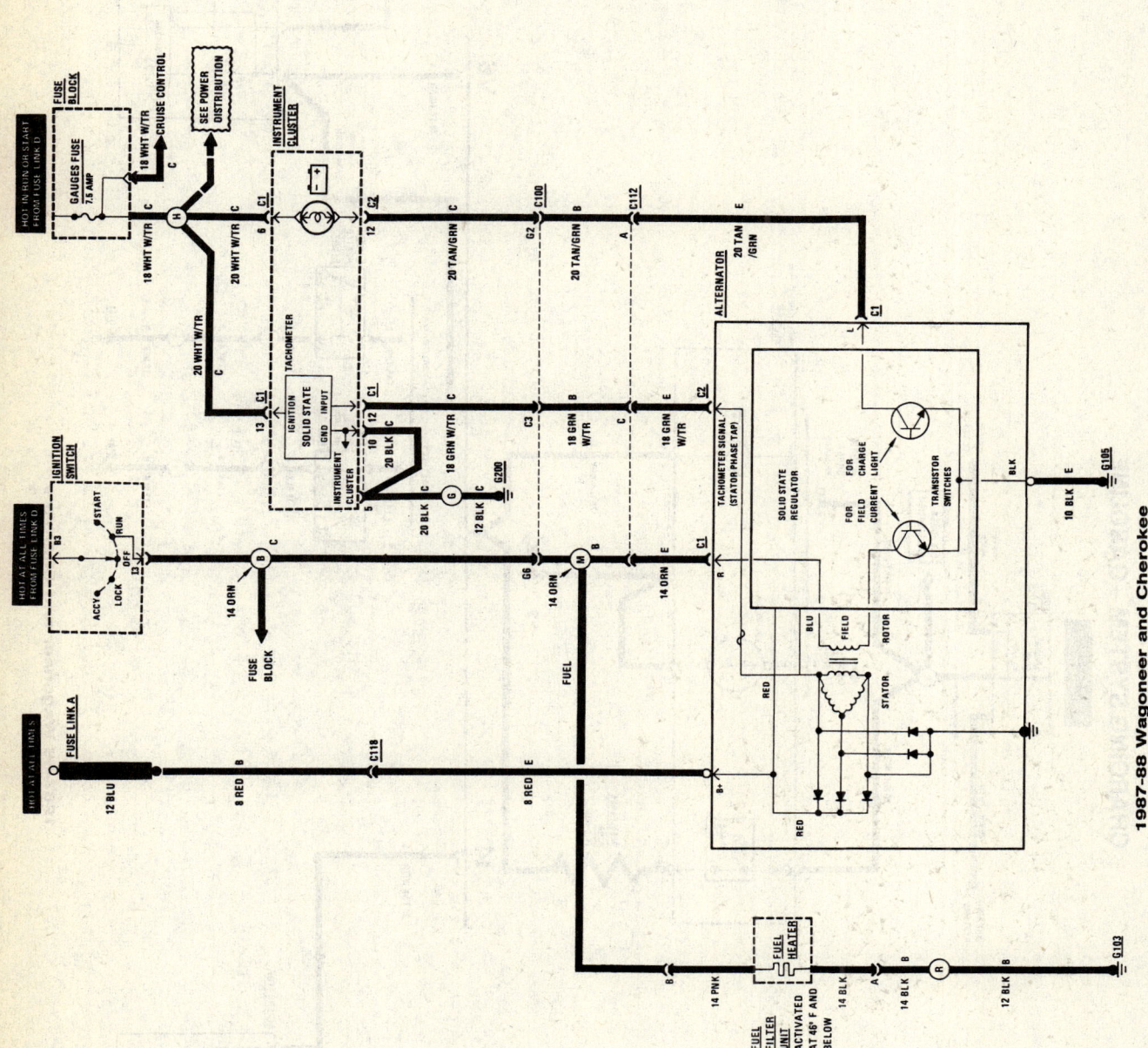

CHASSIS ELECTRICAL 6

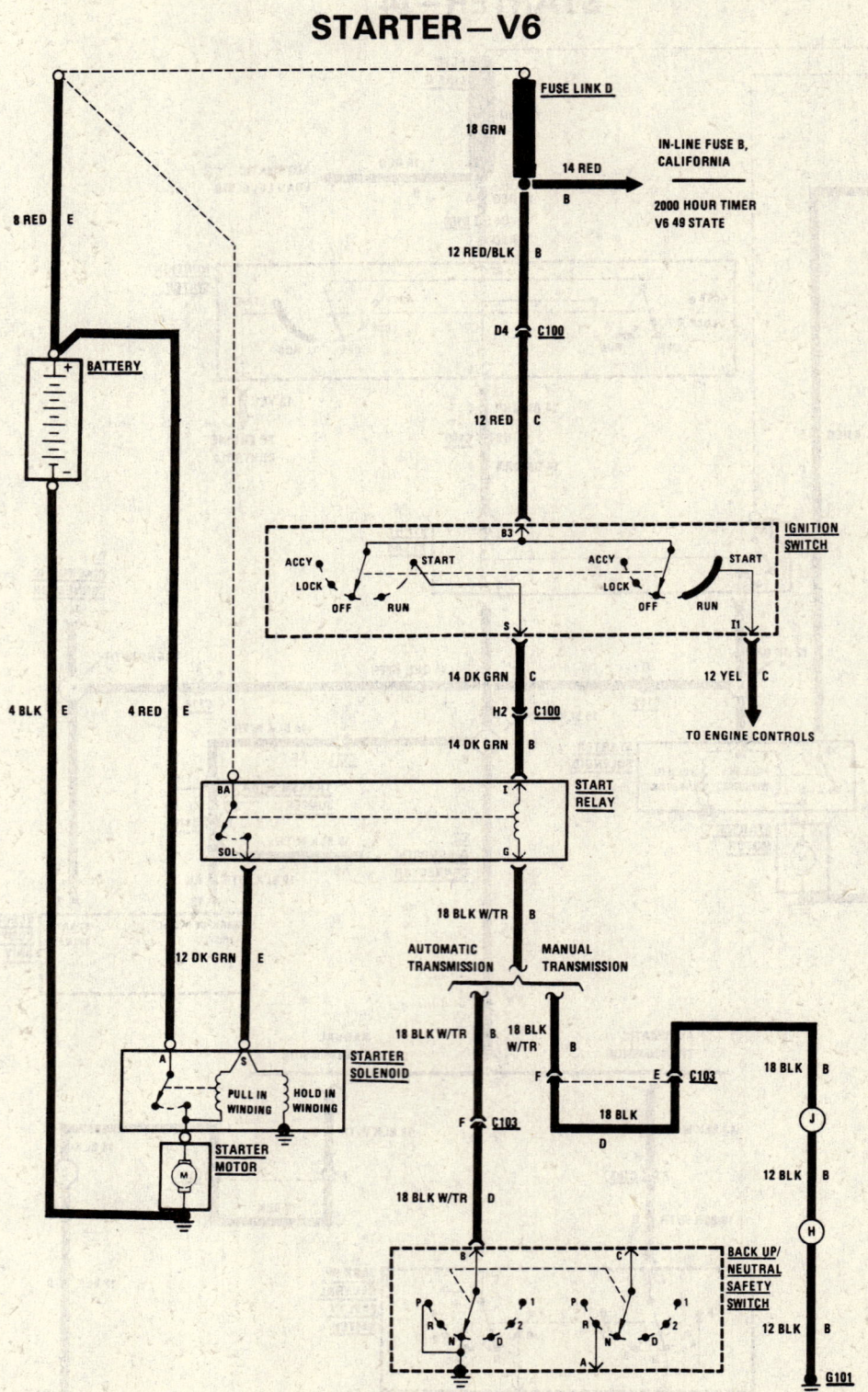

1986-88 Wagoneer and Cherokee

6-197

6 CHASSIS ELECTRICAL

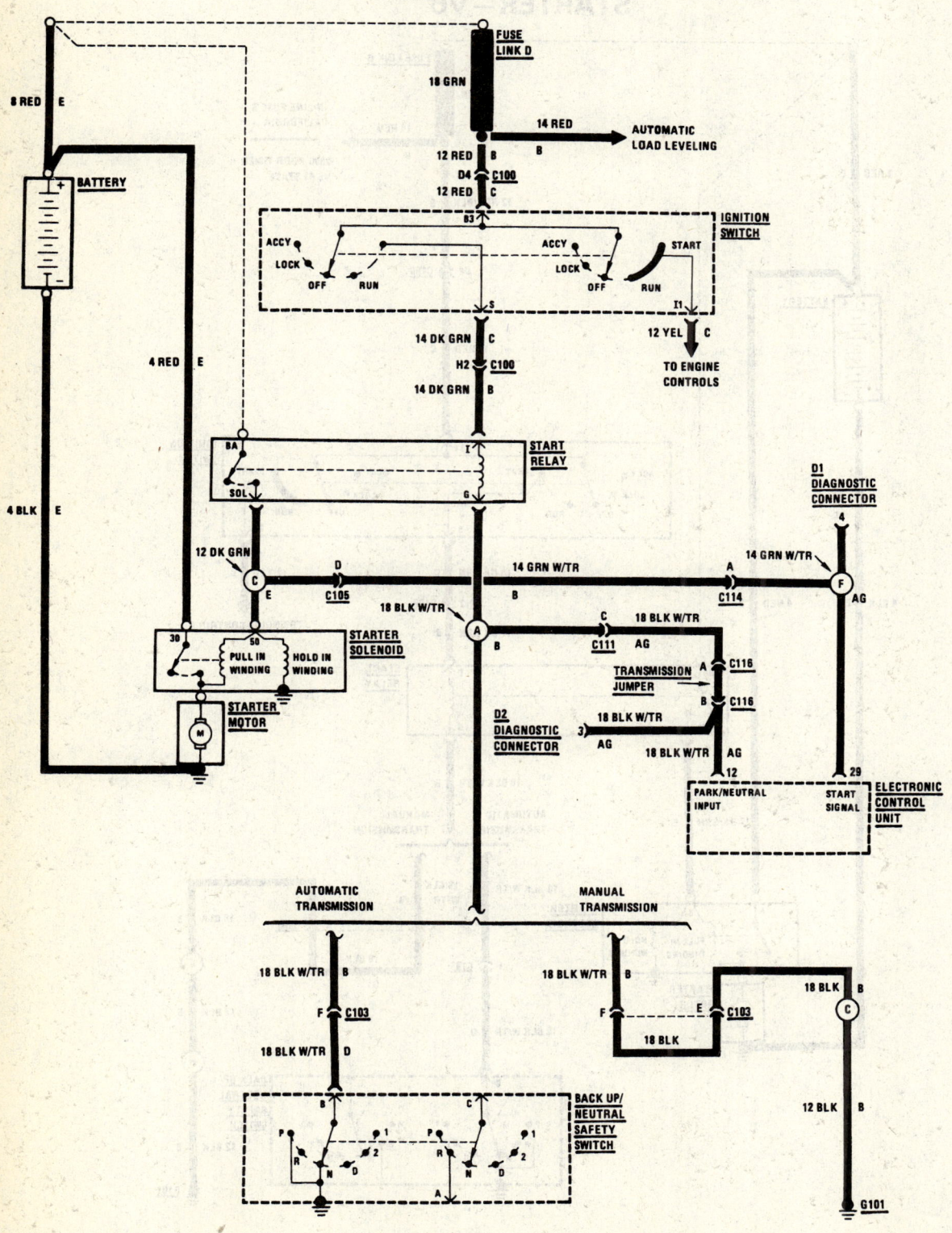

1986-88 Wagoneer and Cherokee

CHASSIS ELECTRICAL 6

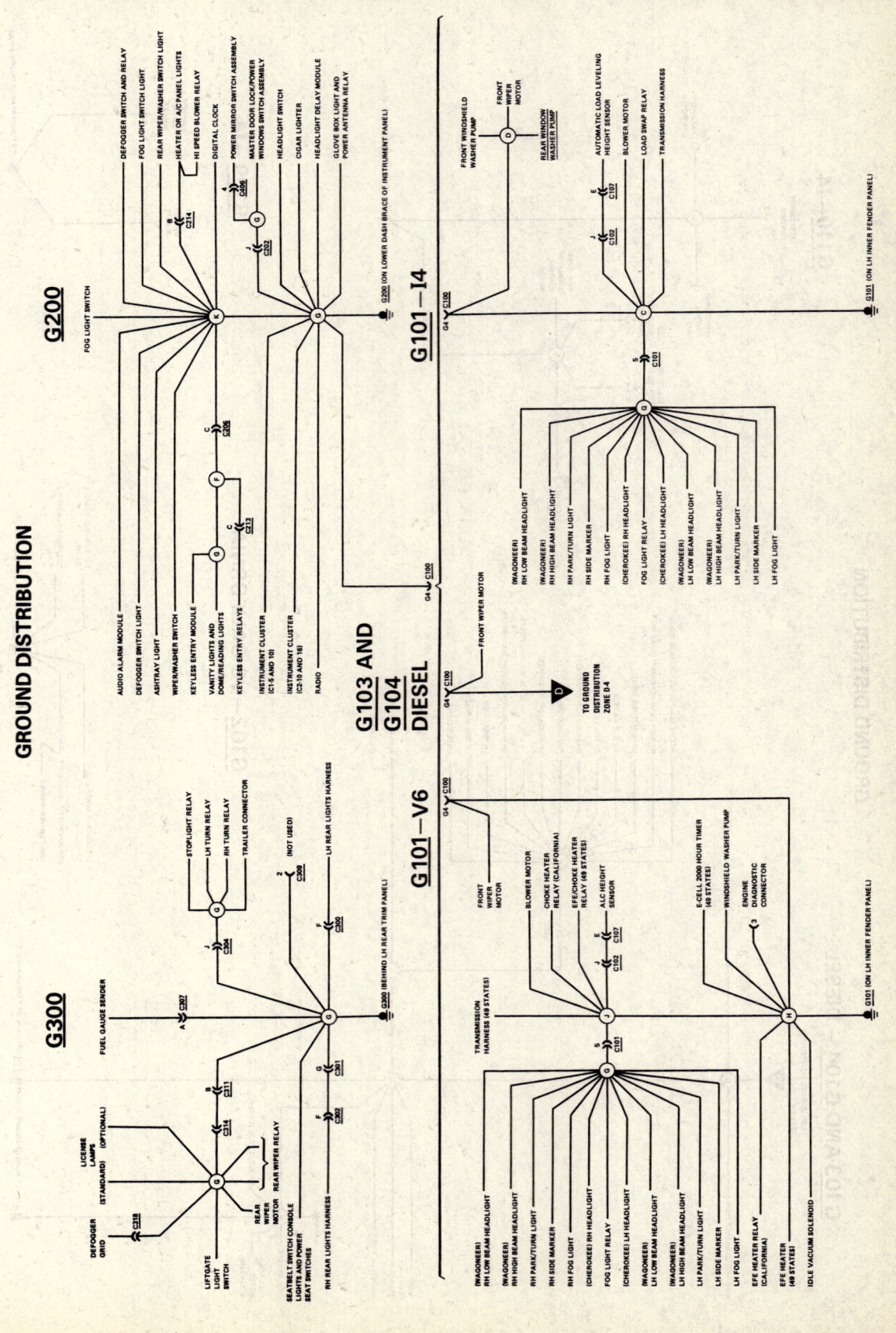

1987-88 Wagoneer and Cherokee

6-199

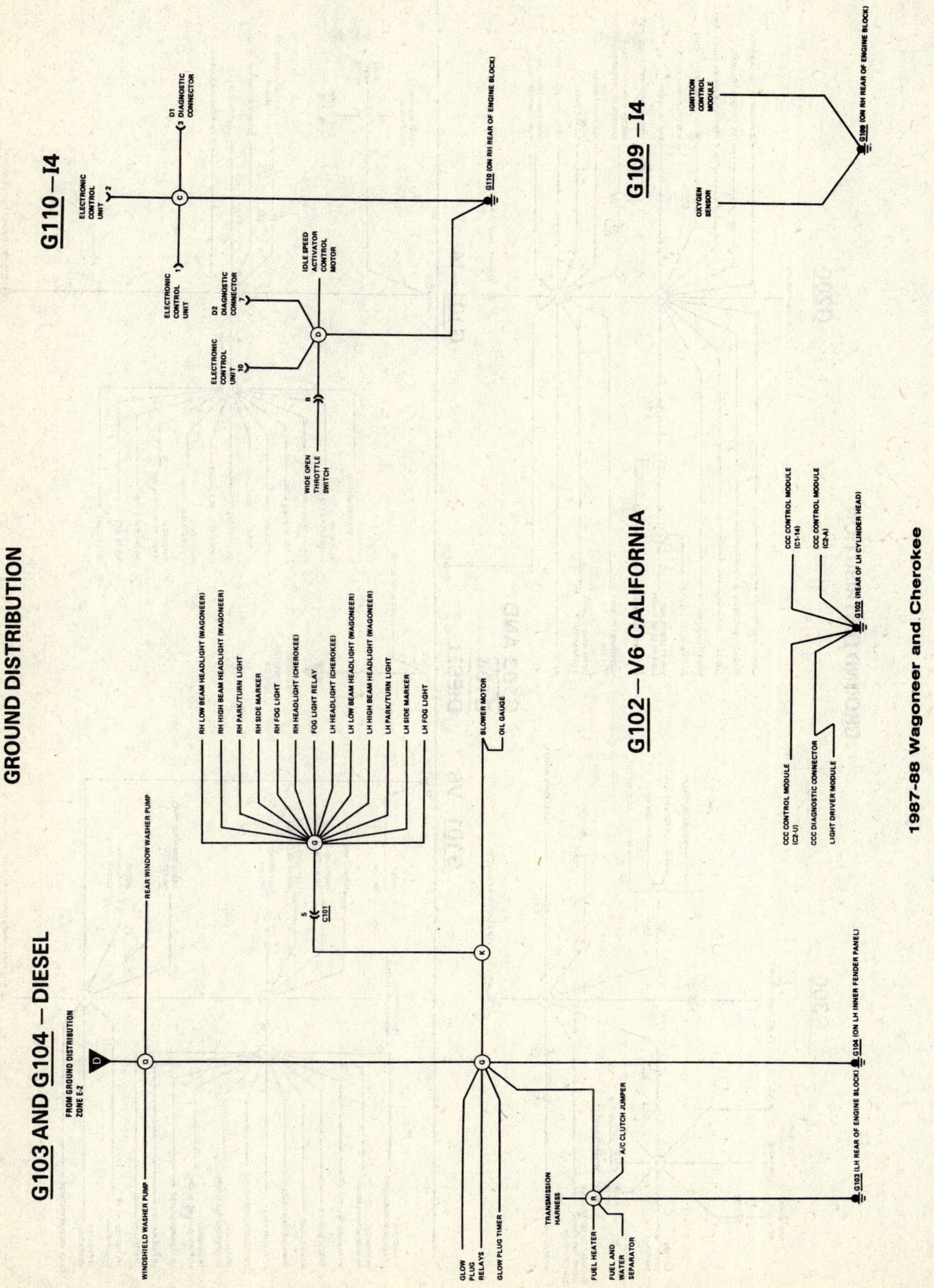

6 CHASSIS ELECTRICAL

GROUND DISTRIBUTION

G110 – I4

G109 – I4

G103 AND G104 – DIESEL

G102 – V6 CALIFORNIA

1987-88 Wagoneer and Cherokee

6-200

CHASSIS ELECTRICAL 6

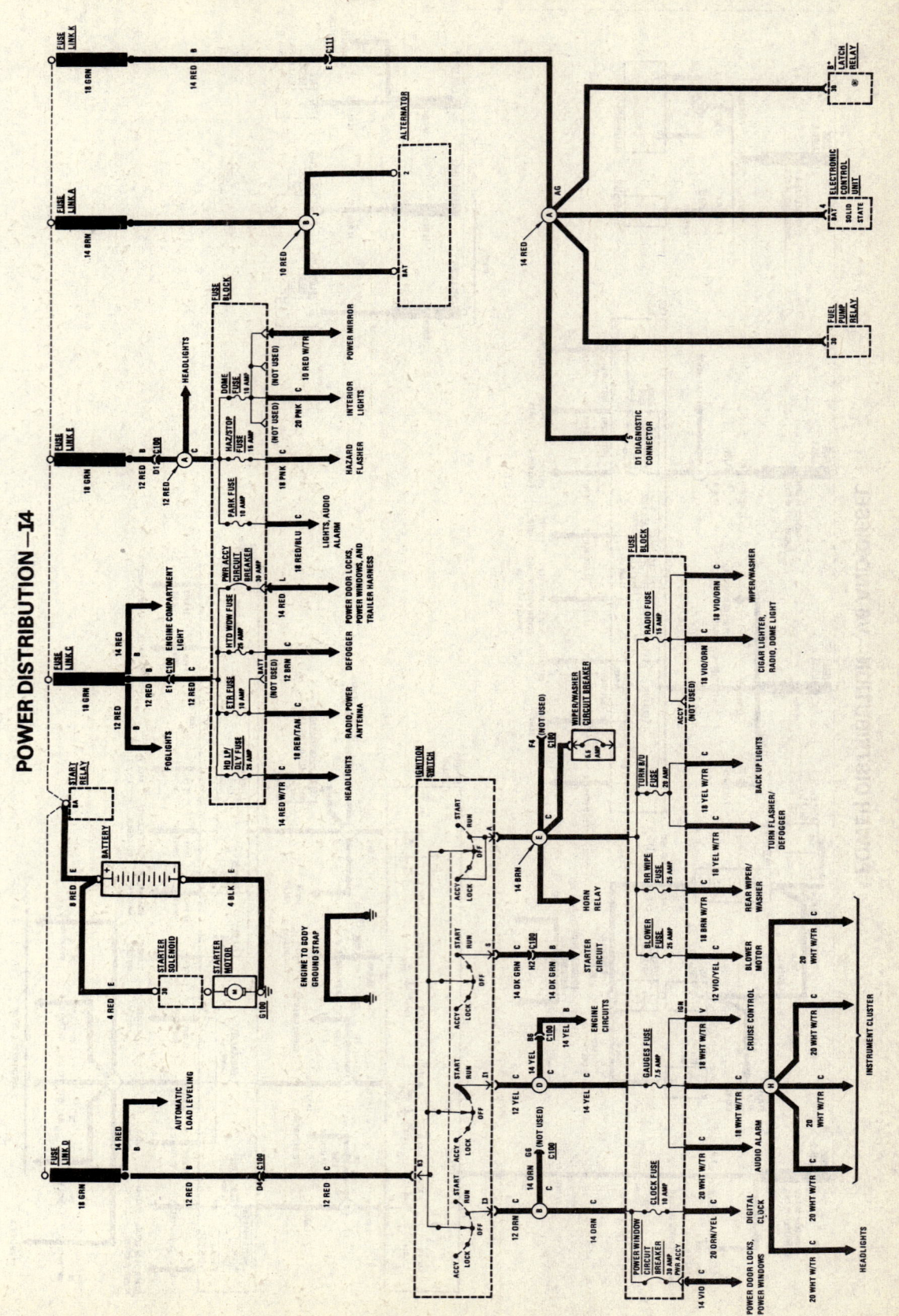

1987-88 Wagoneer and Cherokee

6 CHASSIS ELECTRICAL

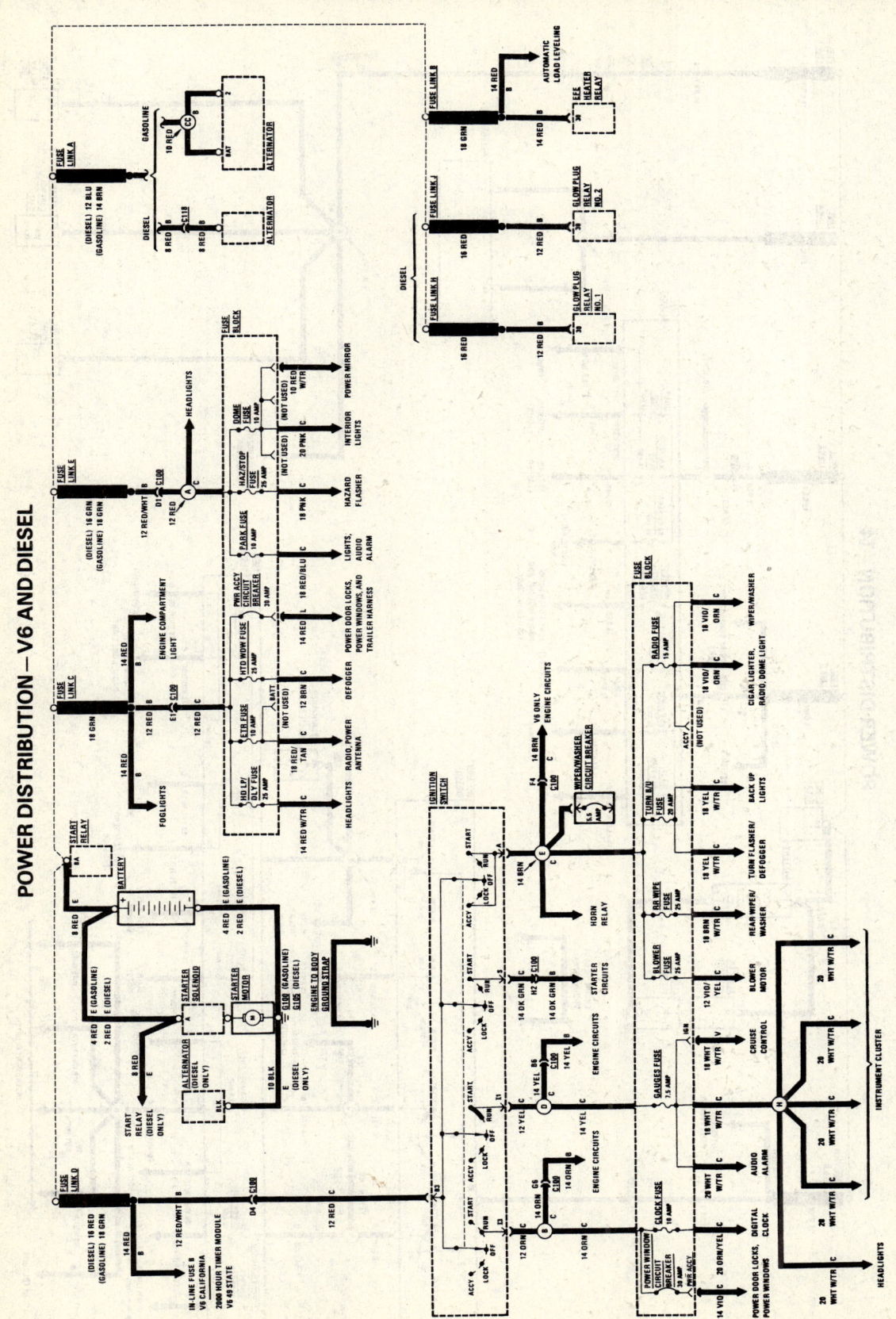

1987-88 Wagoneer and Cherokee

CHASSIS ELECTRICAL 6

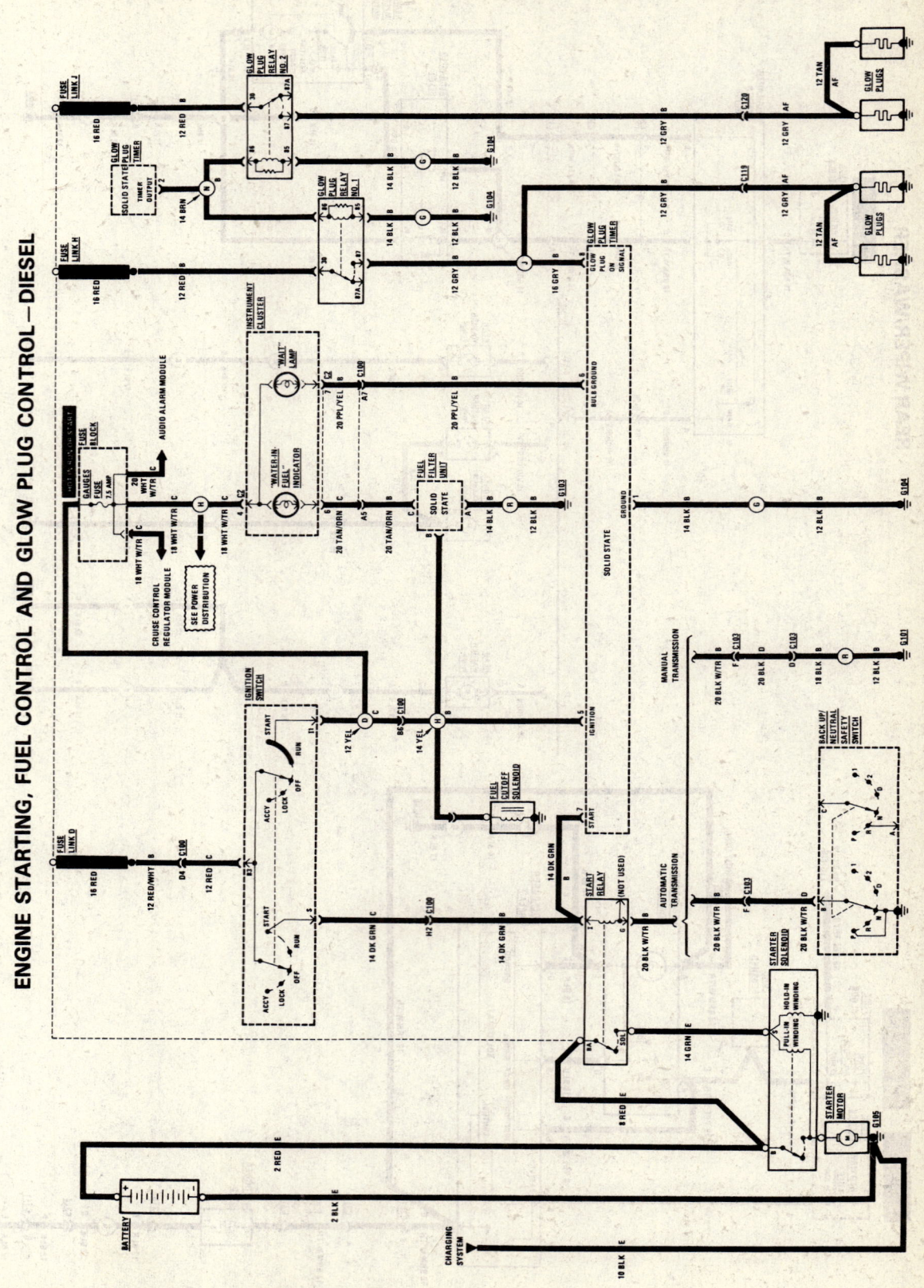

6-203

6 CHASSIS ELECTRICAL

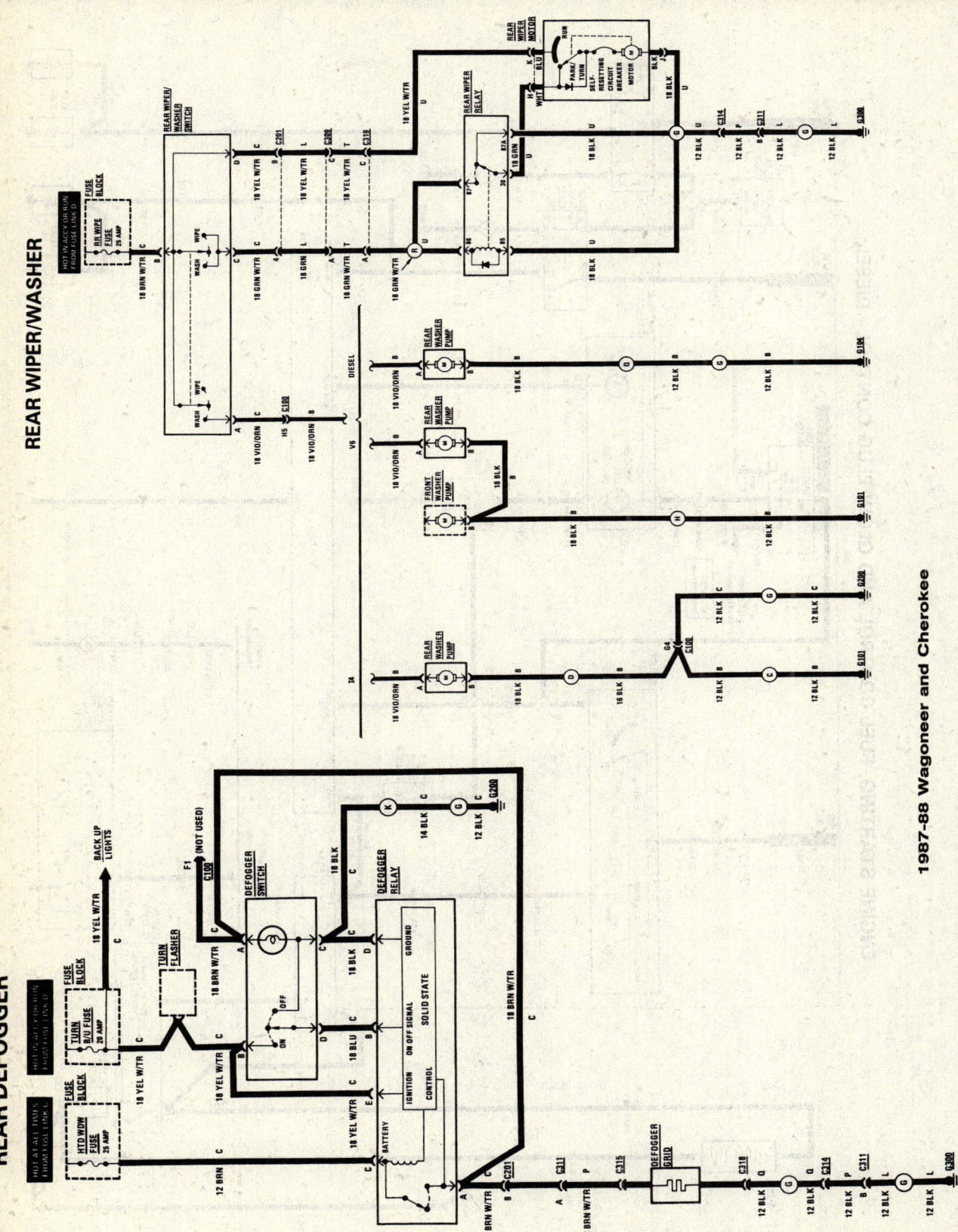

6-204

CHASSIS ELECTRICAL 6

WIPER/WASHER — V6 AND DIESEL

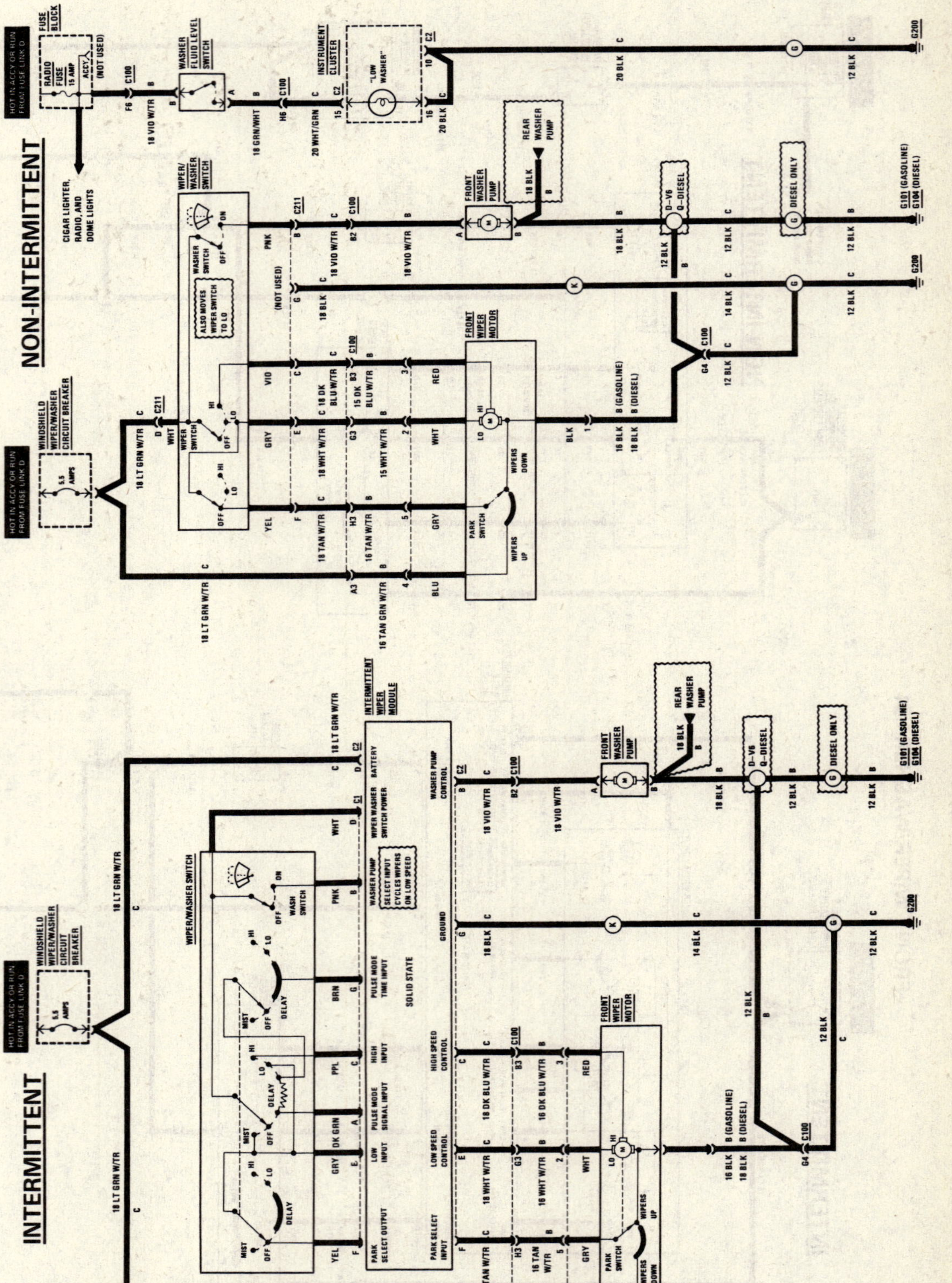

NON-INTERMITTENT

INTERMITTENT

1987-88 Wagoneer and Cherokee

6-205

6 CHASSIS ELECTRICAL

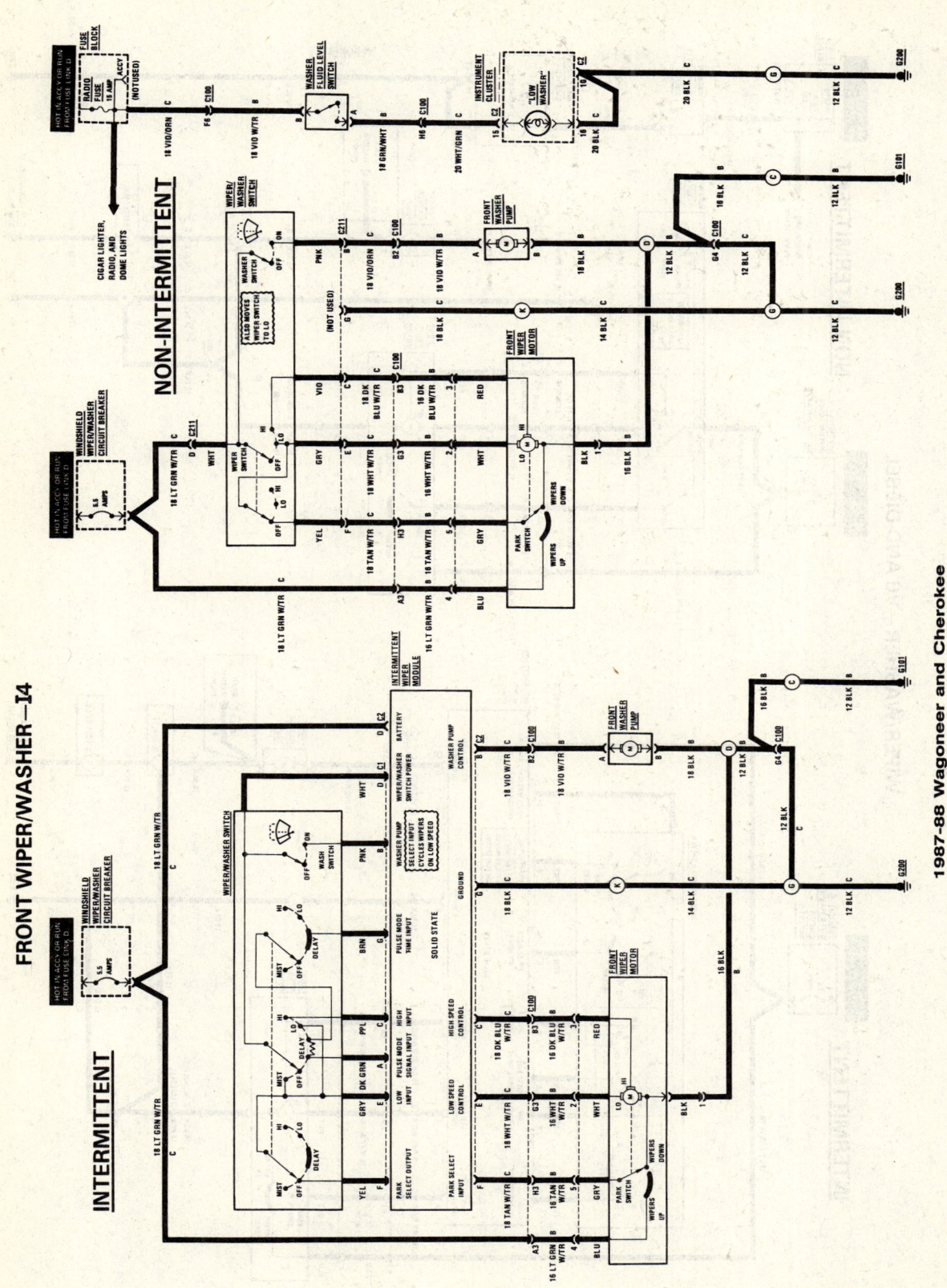

1987-88 Wagoneer and Cherokee

6-206

CHASSIS ELECTRICAL 6

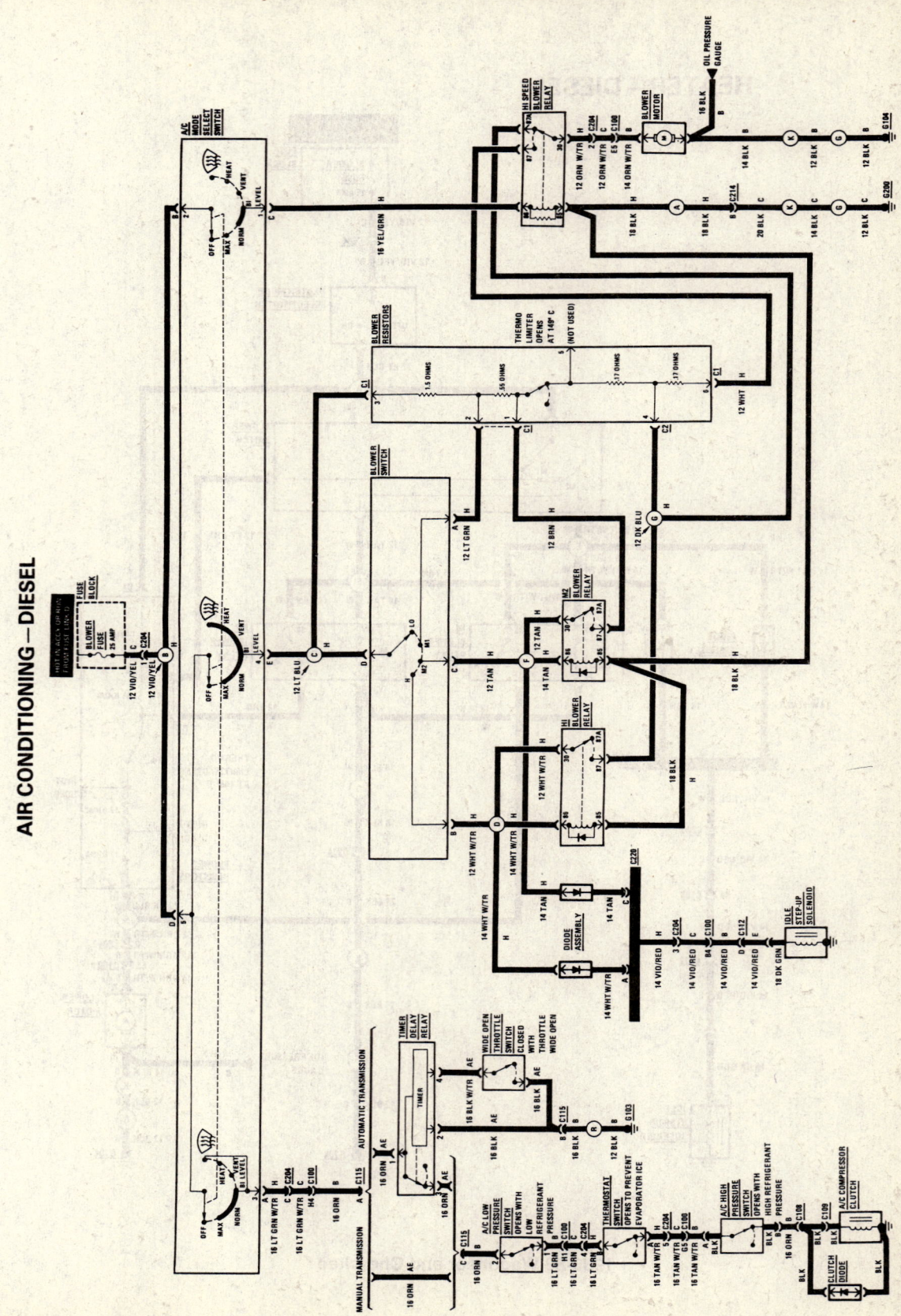

6 CHASSIS ELECTRICAL

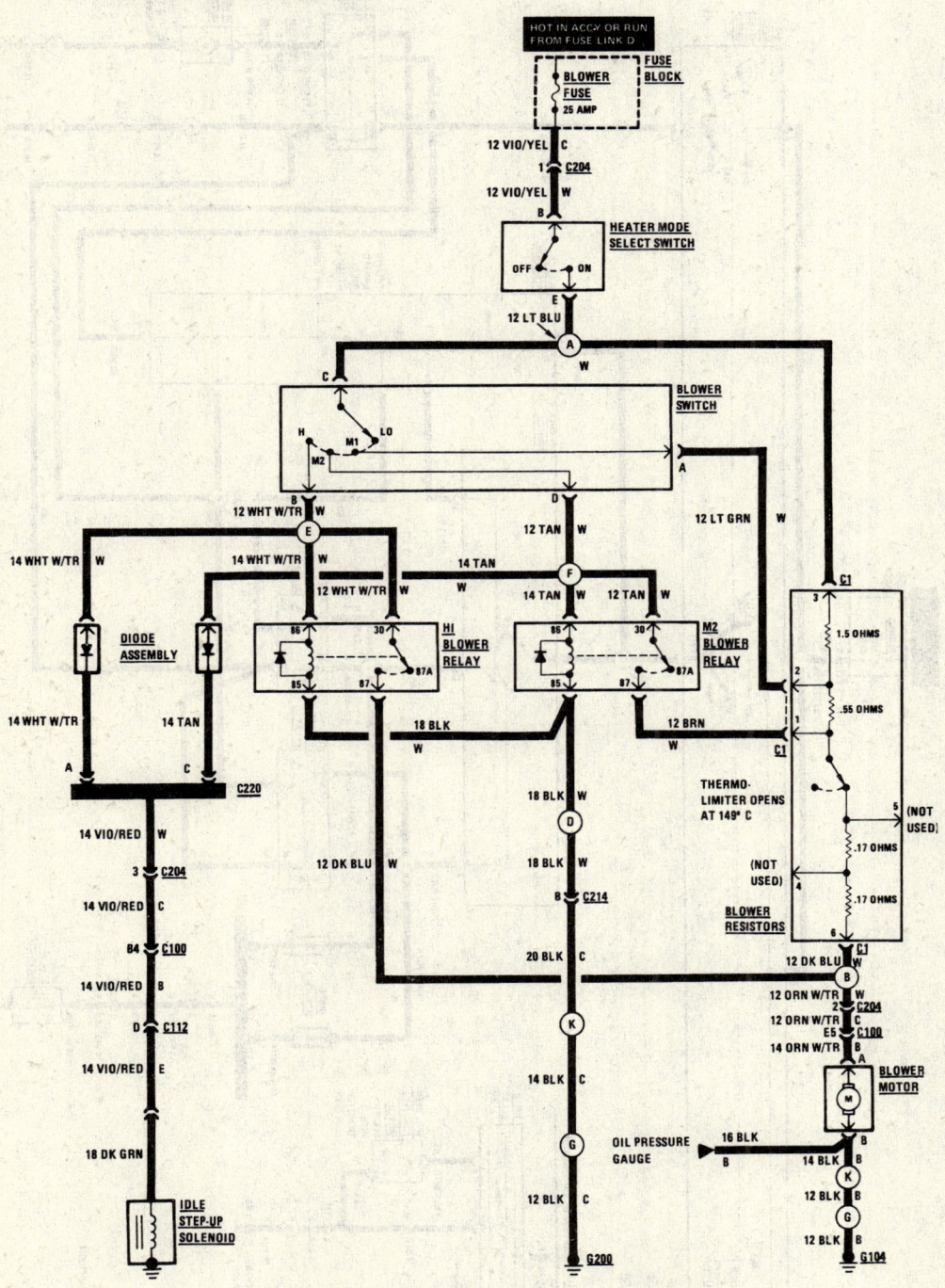

1986-88 Wagoneer and Cherokee

CHASSIS ELECTRICAL 6

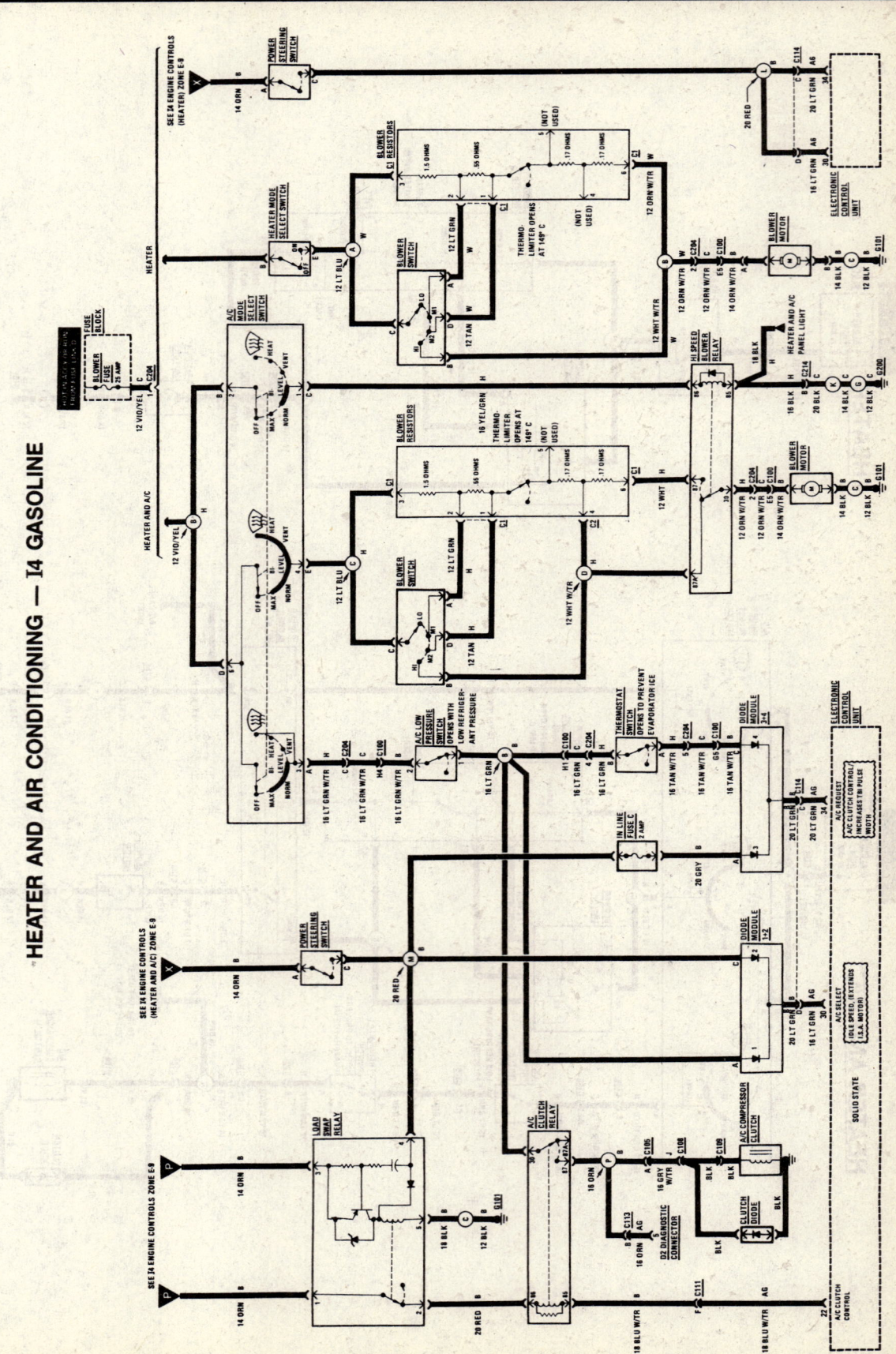

6-209

6 CHASSIS ELECTRICAL

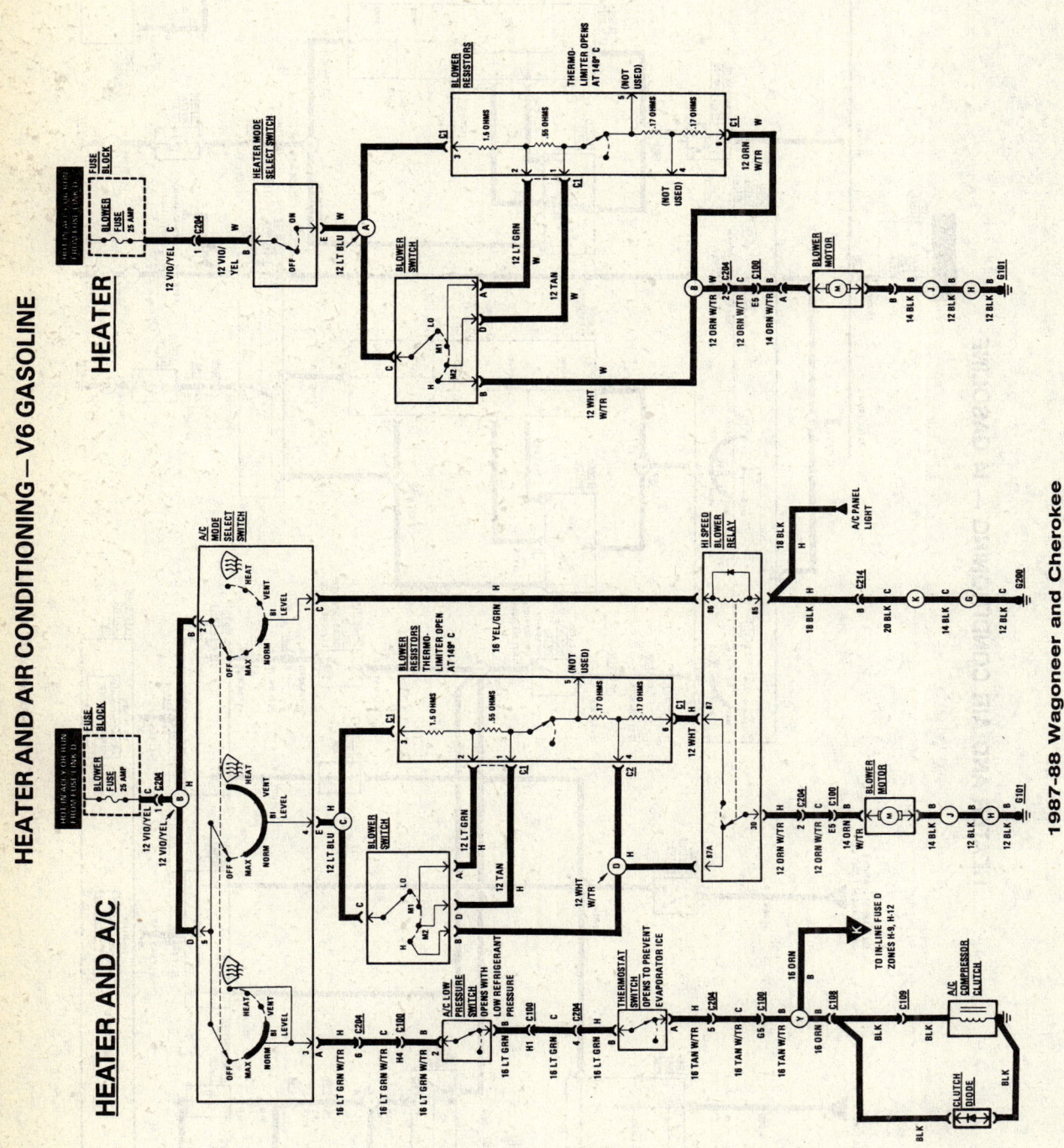

6-210

CHASSIS ELECTRICAL 6

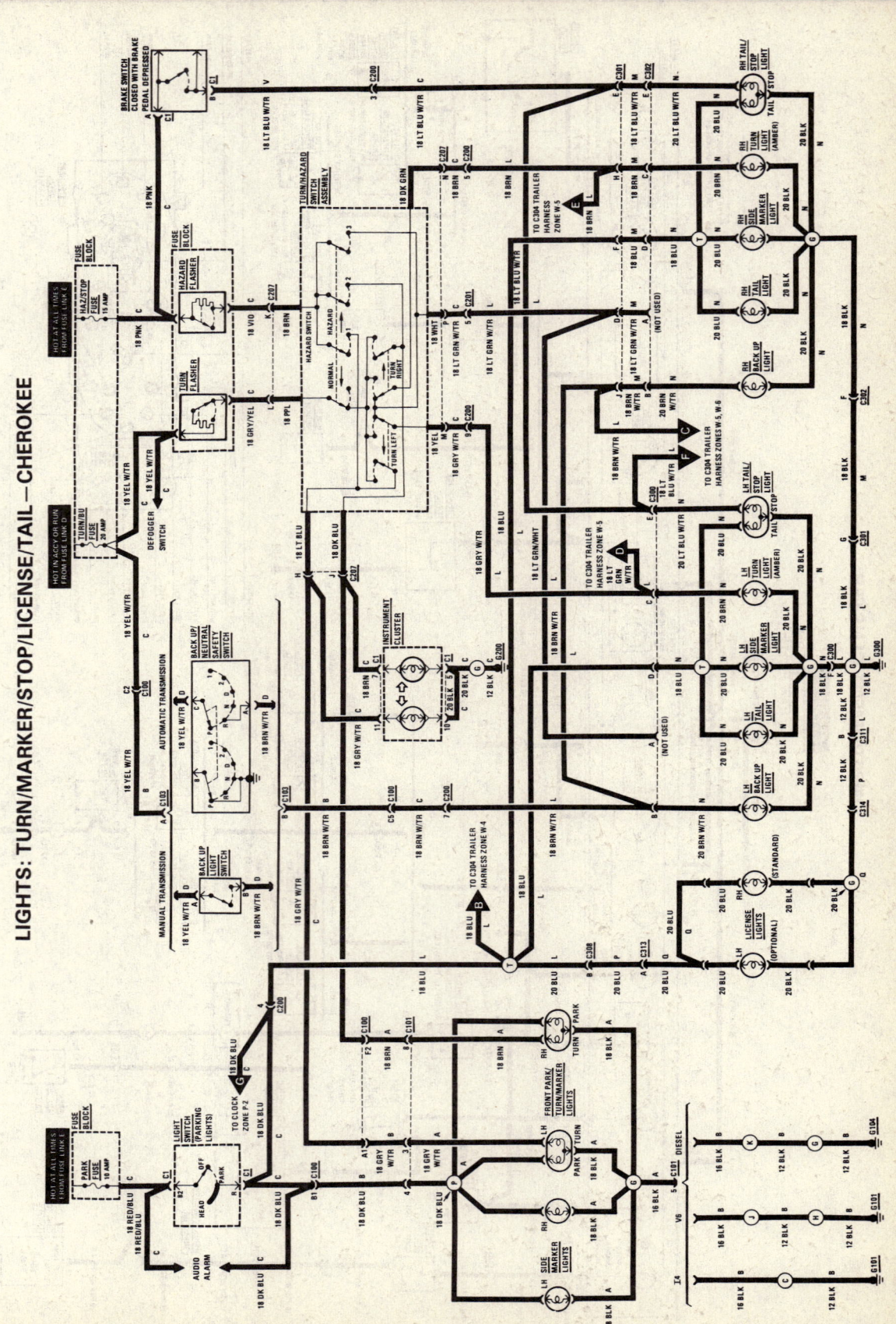

1987-88 Wagoneer and Cherokee

LIGHTS: TURN/MARKER/STOP/LICENSE/TAIL—CHEROKEE

6-211

6 CHASSIS ELECTRICAL

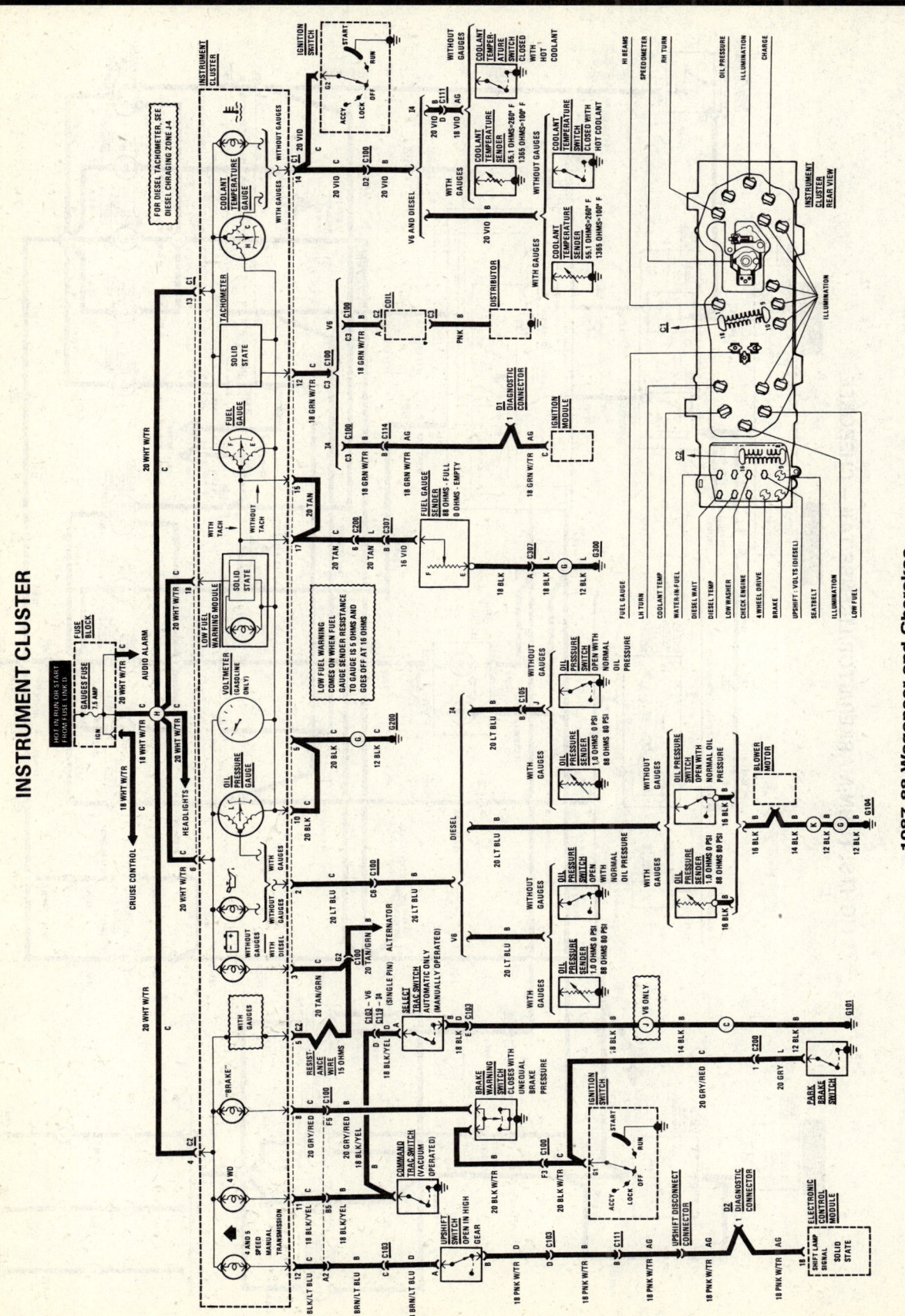

1987-88 Wagoneer and Cherokee

CHASSIS ELECTRICAL 6

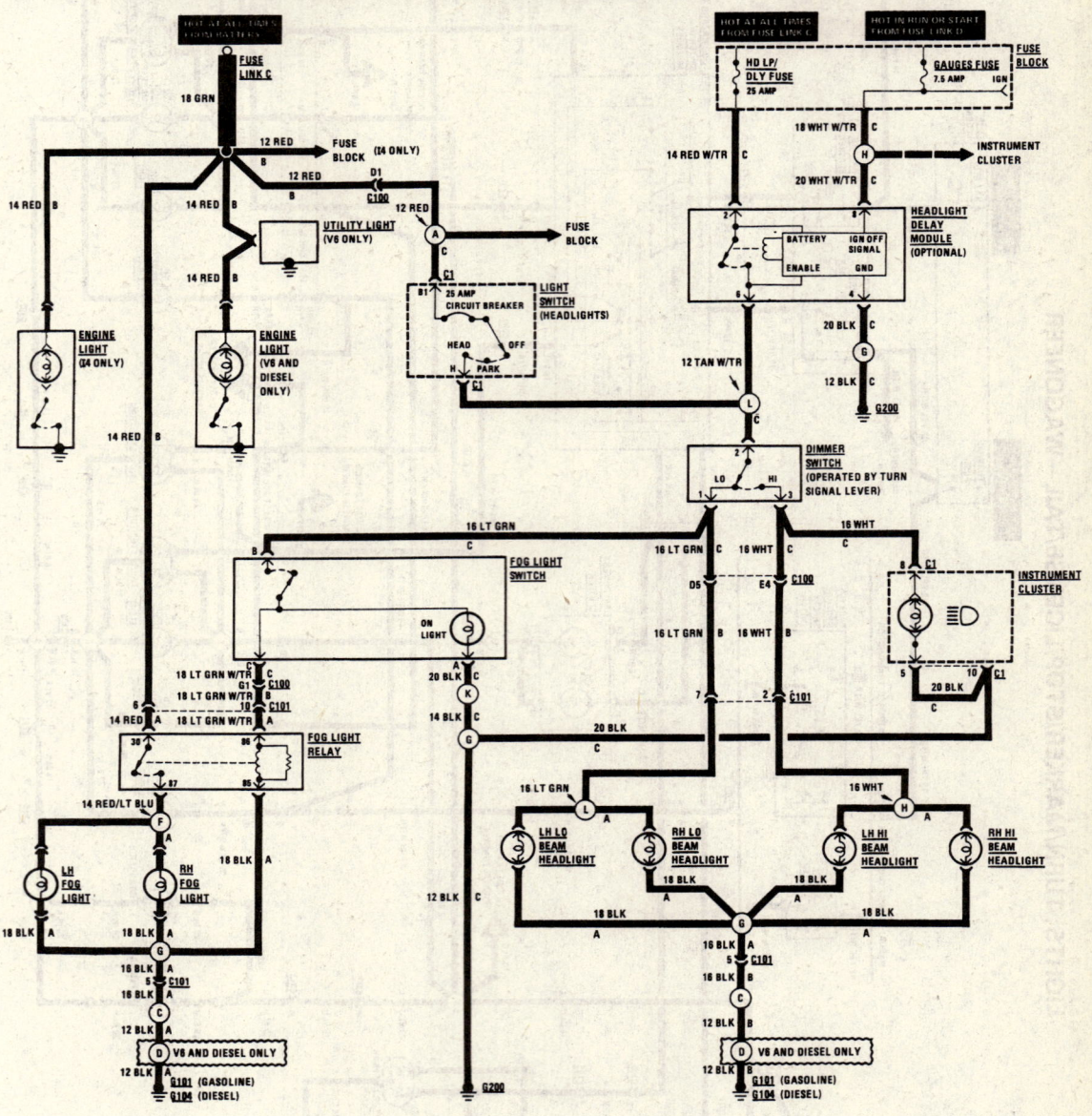

1986-88 Wagoneer and Cherokee

6-213

6 CHASSIS ELECTRICAL

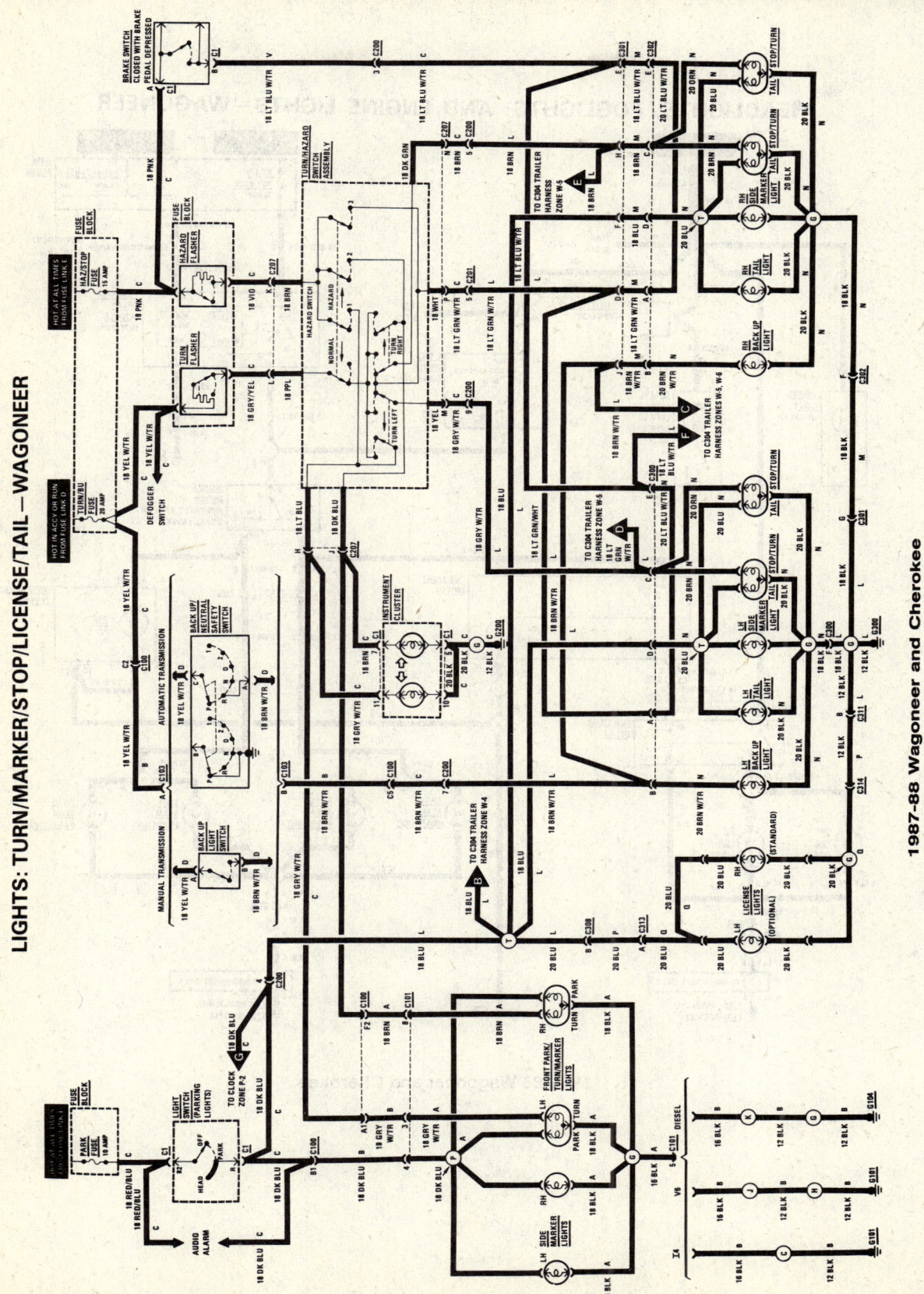

6-214

CHASSIS ELECTRICAL 6

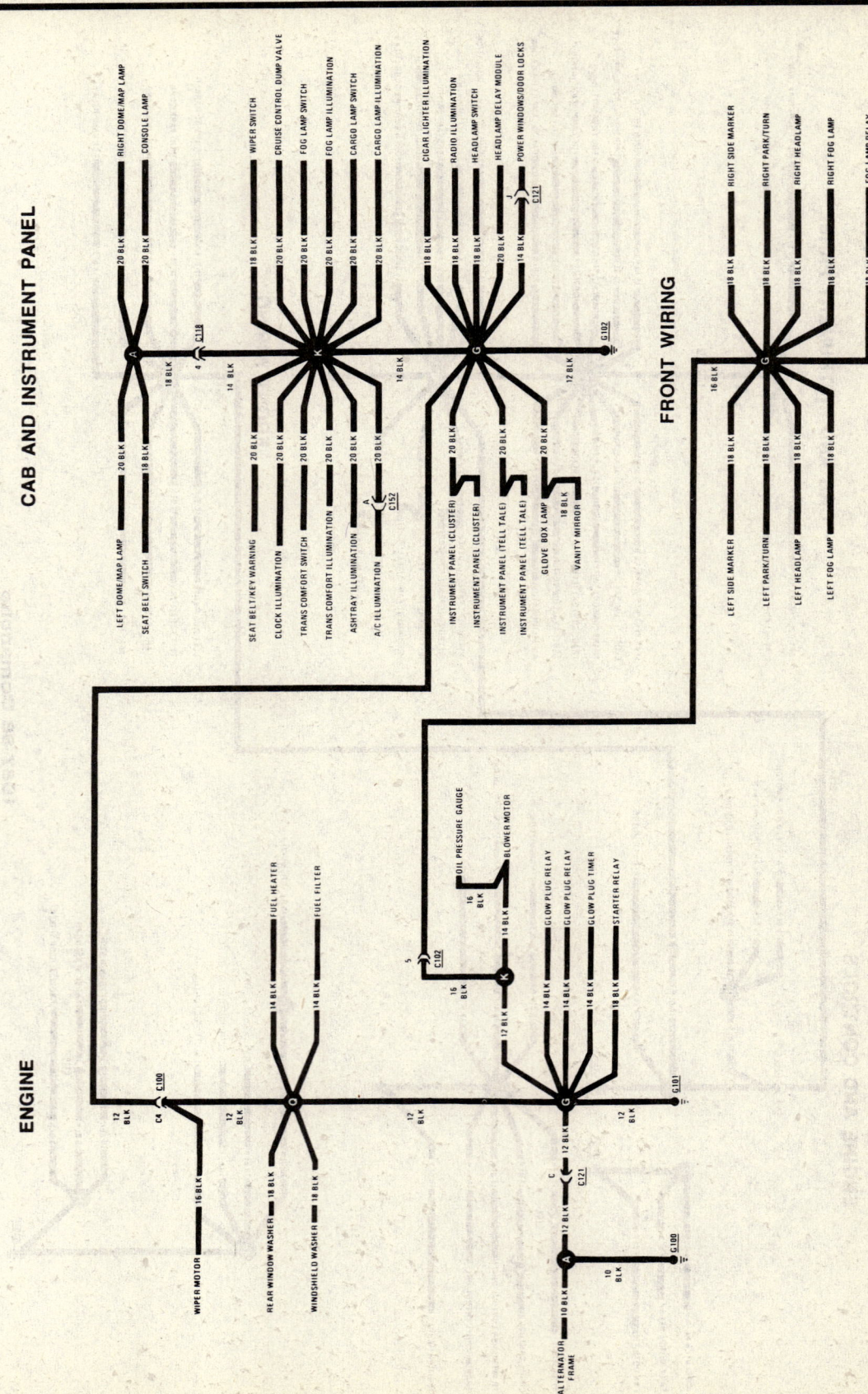

1987-88 Comanche

6-215

6 CHASSIS ELECTRICAL

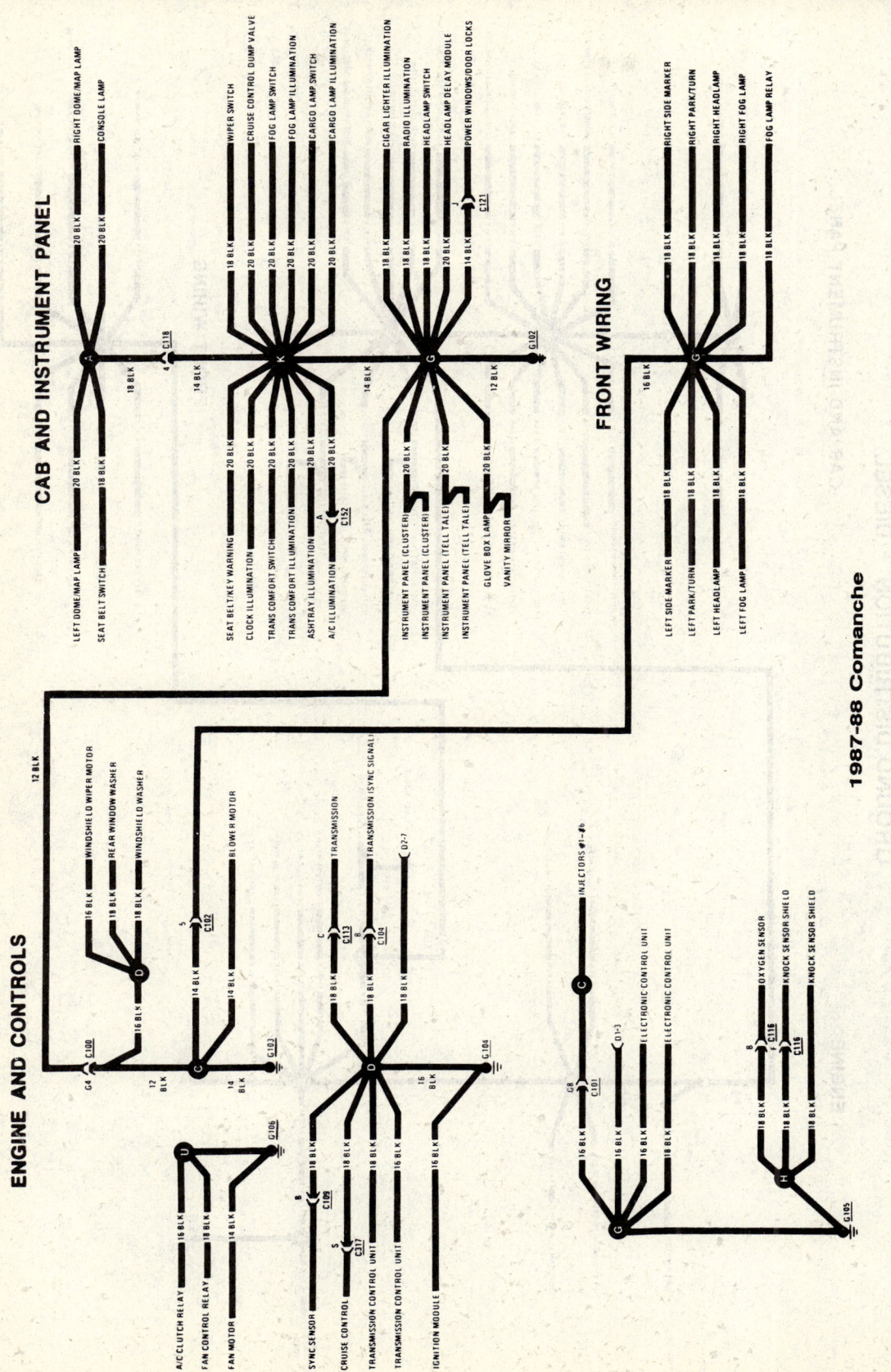

CHASSIS ELECTRICAL 6

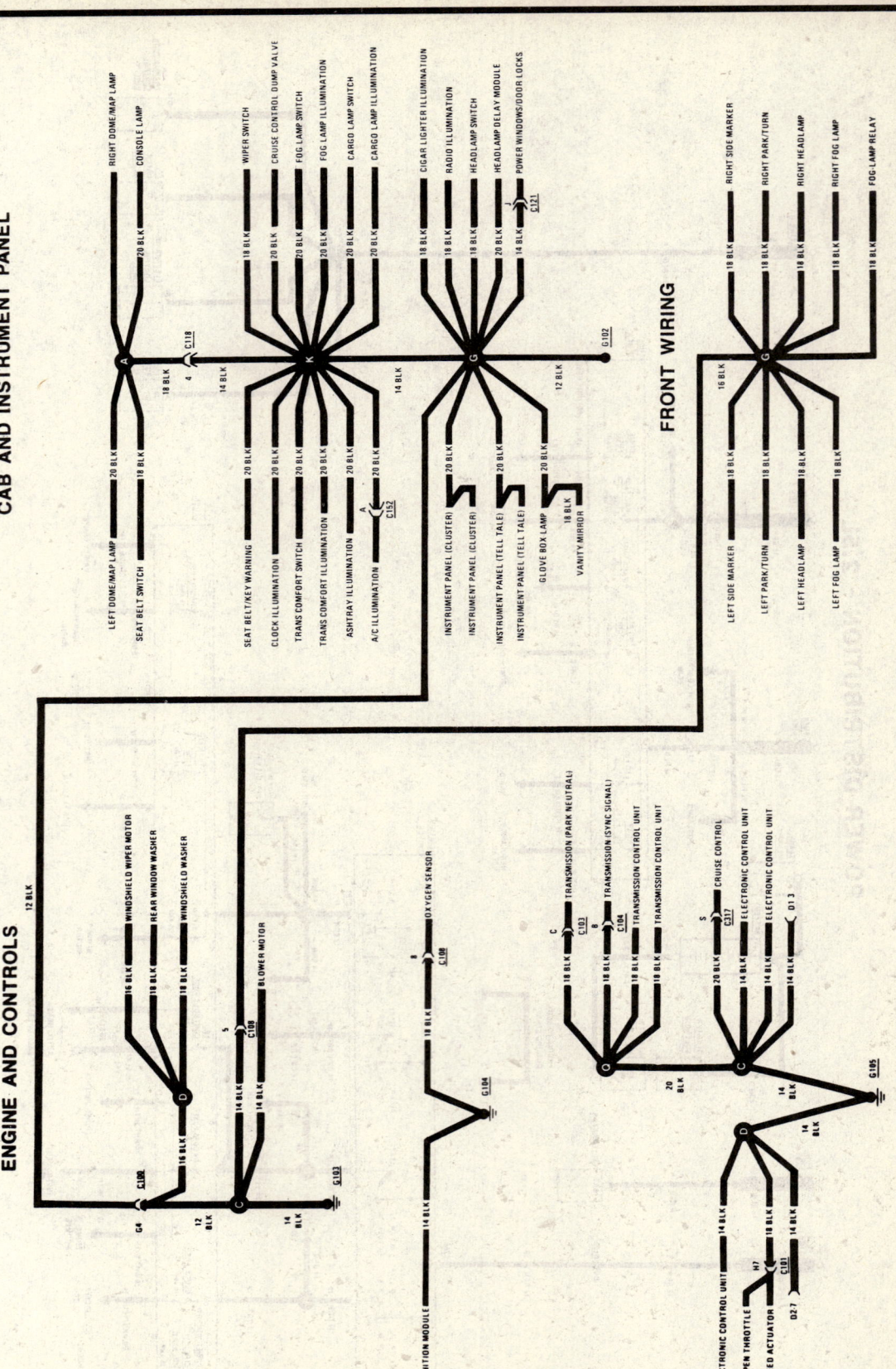

GROUND DISTRIBUTION – 2.5L ENGINE

1987-88 Comanche

6-217

6 CHASSIS ELECTRICAL

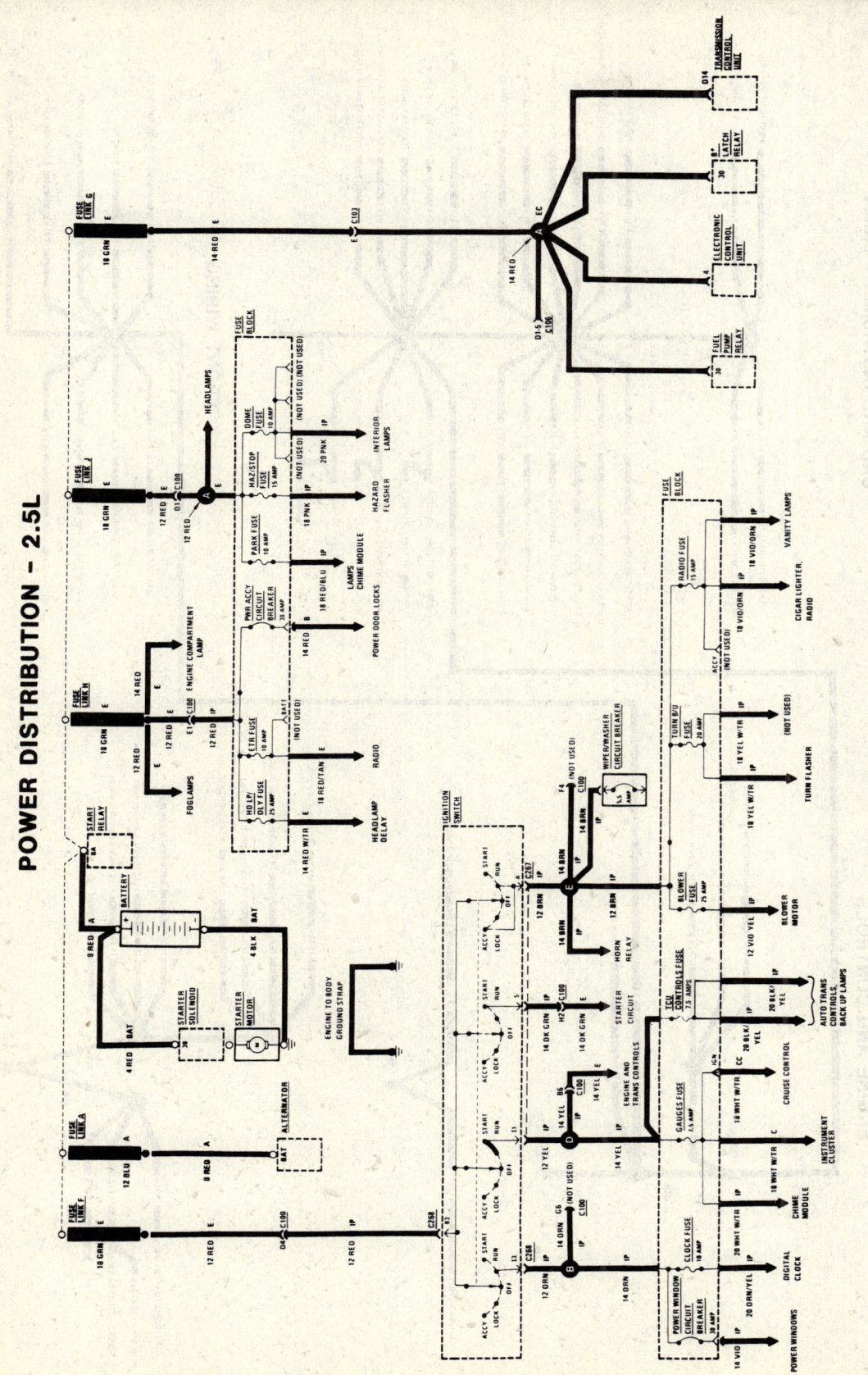

6-218

CHASSIS ELECTRICAL 6

POWER DISTRIBUTION – DIESEL

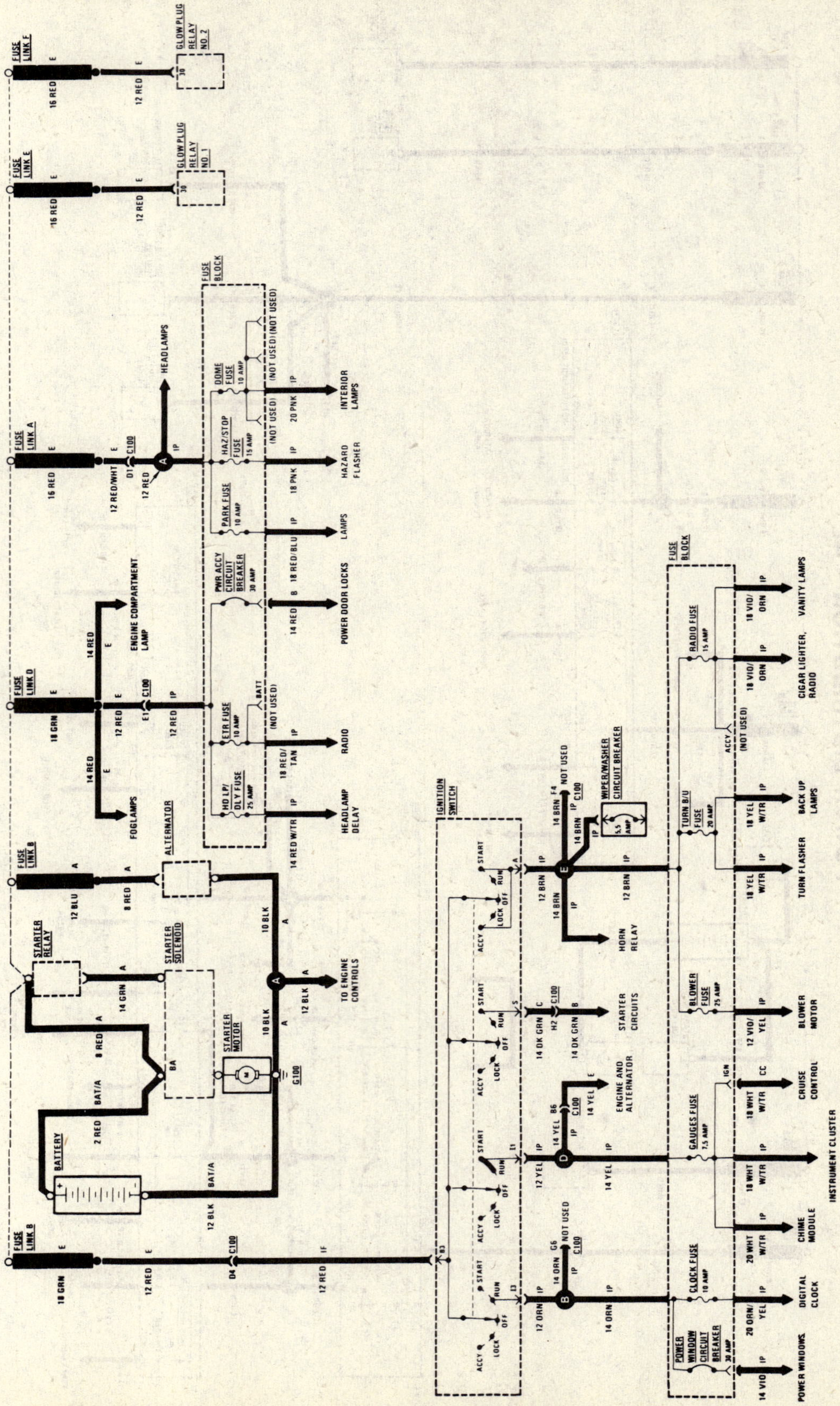

1987-88 Comanche

6-219

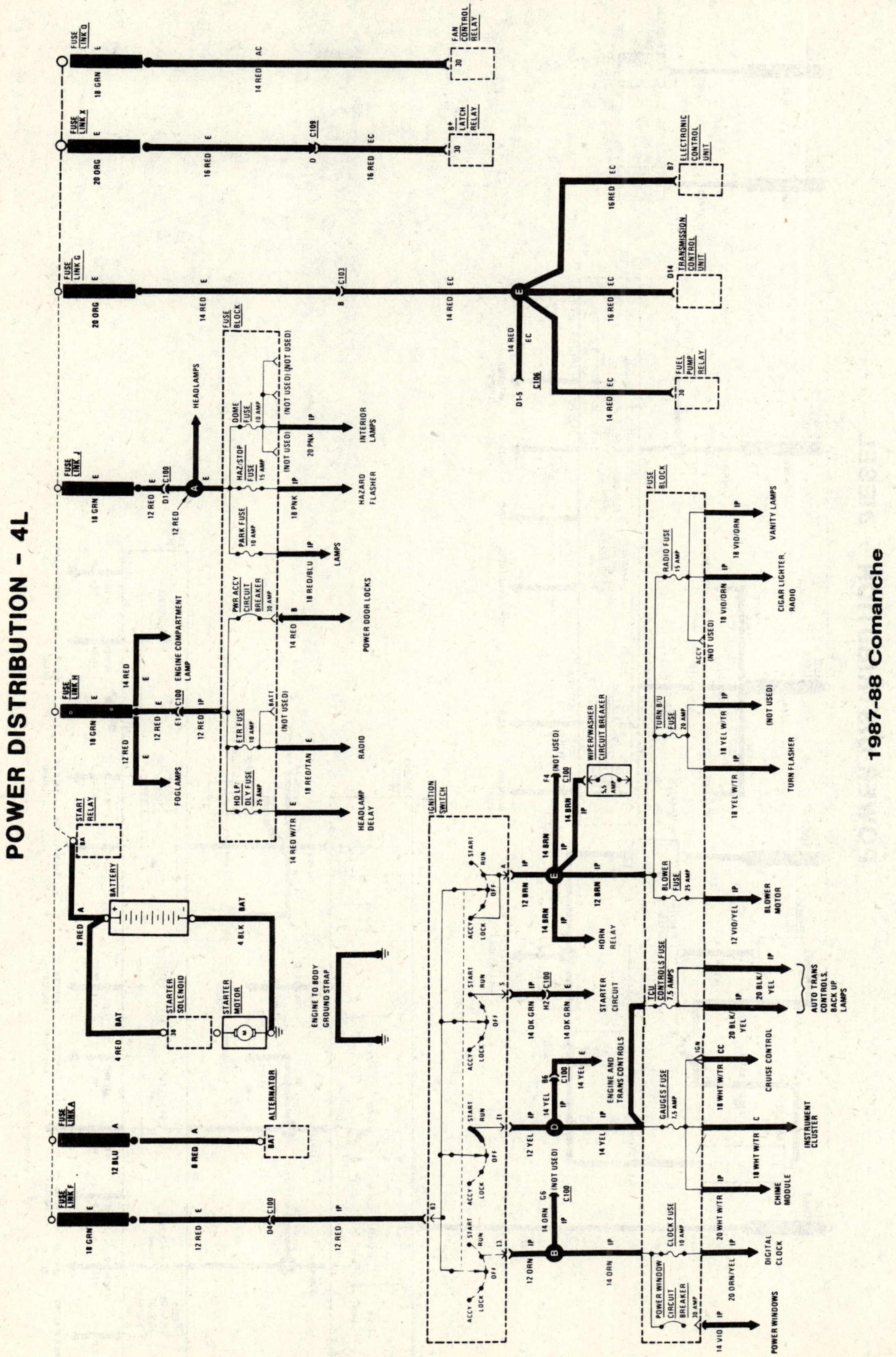

POWER DISTRIBUTION - 4L
1987-88 Comanche
FUSE LINK Q
FUSE LINK X
FUSE LINK G
FUSE LINK J
FUSE LINK H
FUSE LINK A
FUSE LINK F
FAN CONTROL RELAY
B+ LATCH RELAY
ELECTRONIC CONTROL UNIT
TRANSMISSION CONTROL UNIT
FUEL PUMP RELAY
START RELAY
BATTERY
STARTER SOLENOID
STARTER MOTOR
ALTERNATOR
ENGINE TO BODY GROUND STRAP
FUSE BLOCK
HEADLAMPS
DOME FUSE 10 AMP
HAZ/STOP FUSE 15 AMP
PARK FUSE 10 AMP
PWR ACCY CIRCUIT BREAKER 30 AMP
ETR FUSE 10 AMP
HD LP/ DLY FUSE 25 AMP
INTERIOR LAMPS
HAZARD FLASHER
LAMPS
POWER DOOR LOCKS
RADIO
HEADLAMP DELAY
FOGLAMPS
ENGINE COMPARTMENT LAMP
IGNITION SWITCH
WIPER/WASHER CIRCUIT BREAKER
HORN RELAY
STARTER CIRCUIT
ENGINE AND TRANS CONTROLS
RADIO FUSE 15 AMP
TURN B/U FUSE 20 AMP
BLOWER FUSE 25 AMP
TCU CONTROLS FUSE 7.5 AMPS
GAUGES FUSE 7.5 AMP
CLOCK FUSE 10 AMP
POWER WINDOW CIRCUIT BREAKER 30 AMP
VANITY LAMPS
CIGAR LIGHTER, RADIO
TURN FLASHER
BLOWER MOTOR
AUTO TRANS CONTROLS, BACK UP LAMPS
CRUISE CONTROL
INSTRUMENT CLUSTER
CHIME MODULE
DIGITAL CLOCK
POWER WINDOWS
(NOT USED)

CHASSIS ELECTRICAL 6

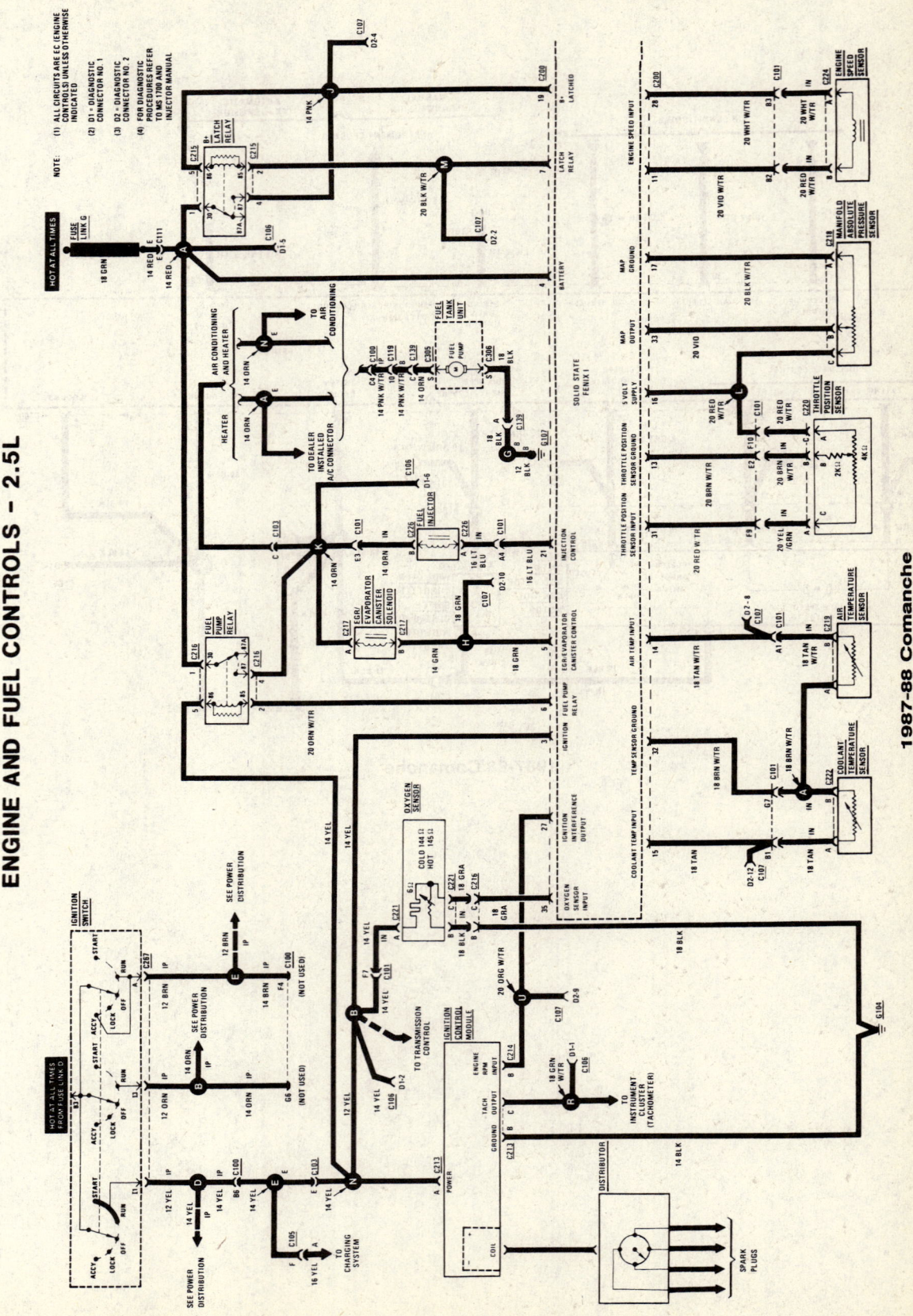

Engine and Fuel Controls – 2.5L — 1987-88 Comanche

6-221

6 CHASSIS ELECTRICAL

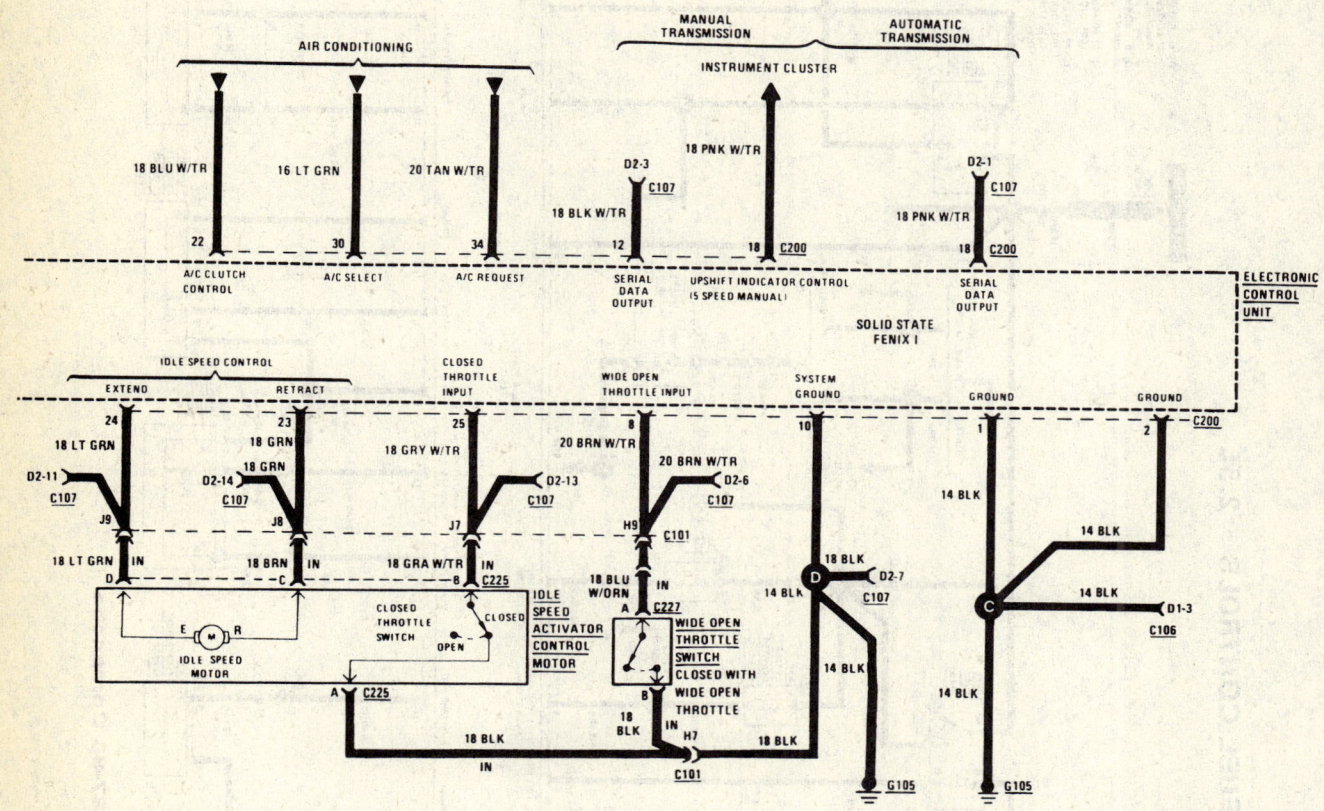

1987-88 Comanche

6-222

CHASSIS ELECTRICAL 6

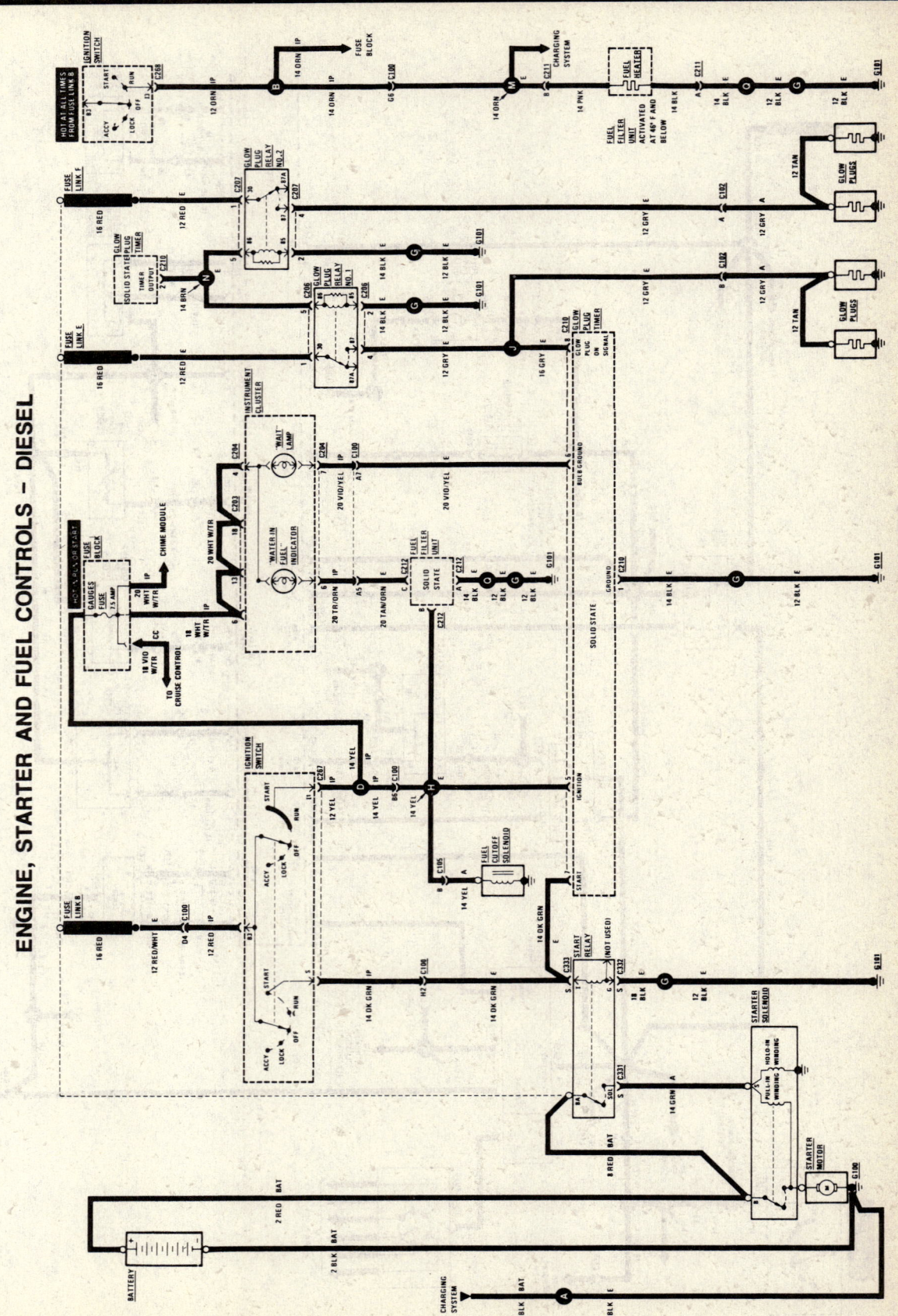

6-223

6 CHASSIS ELECTRICAL

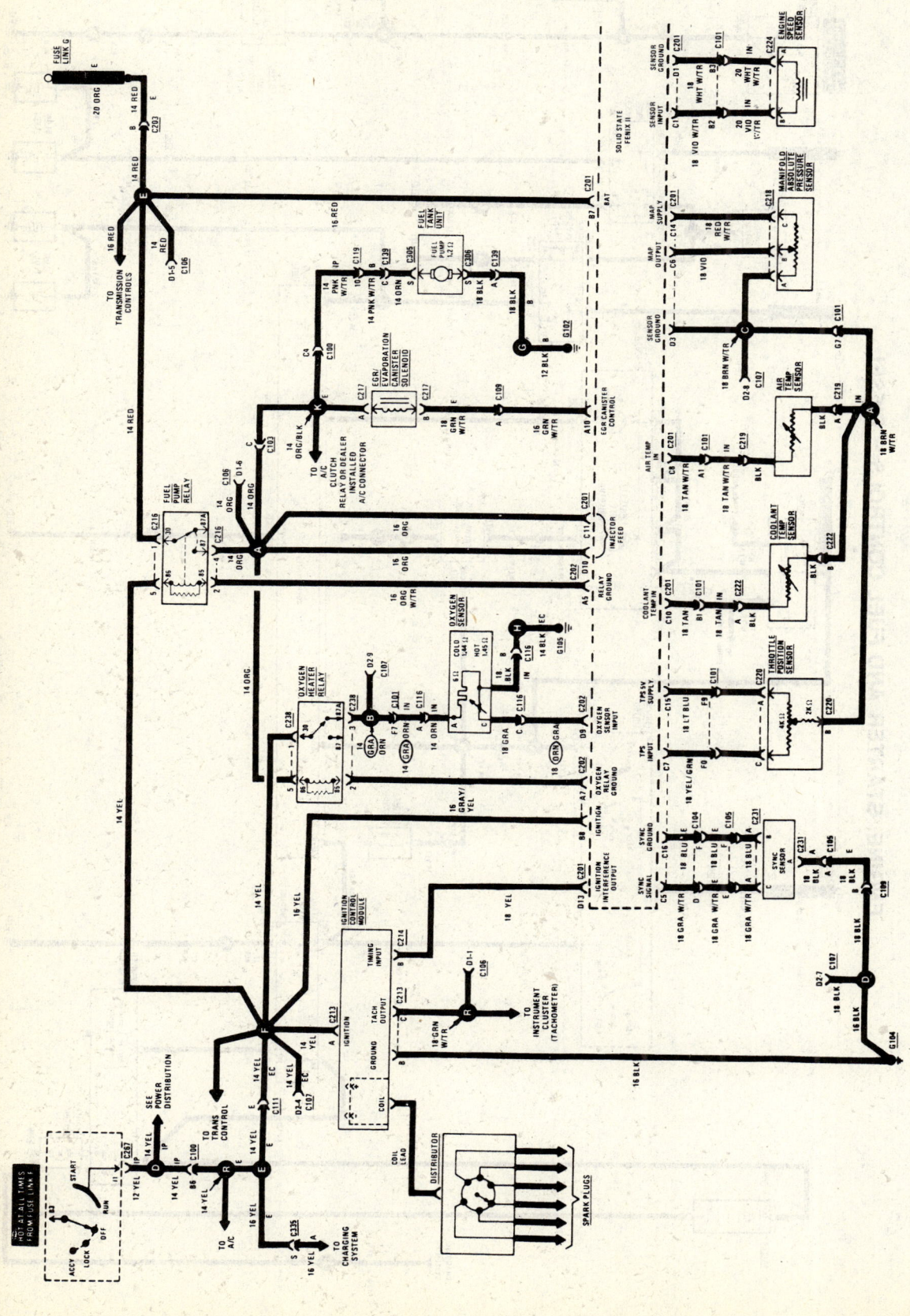

ENGINE AND FUEL CONTROLS - 4L

1987-88 Comanche

6-224

CHASSIS ELECTRICAL 6

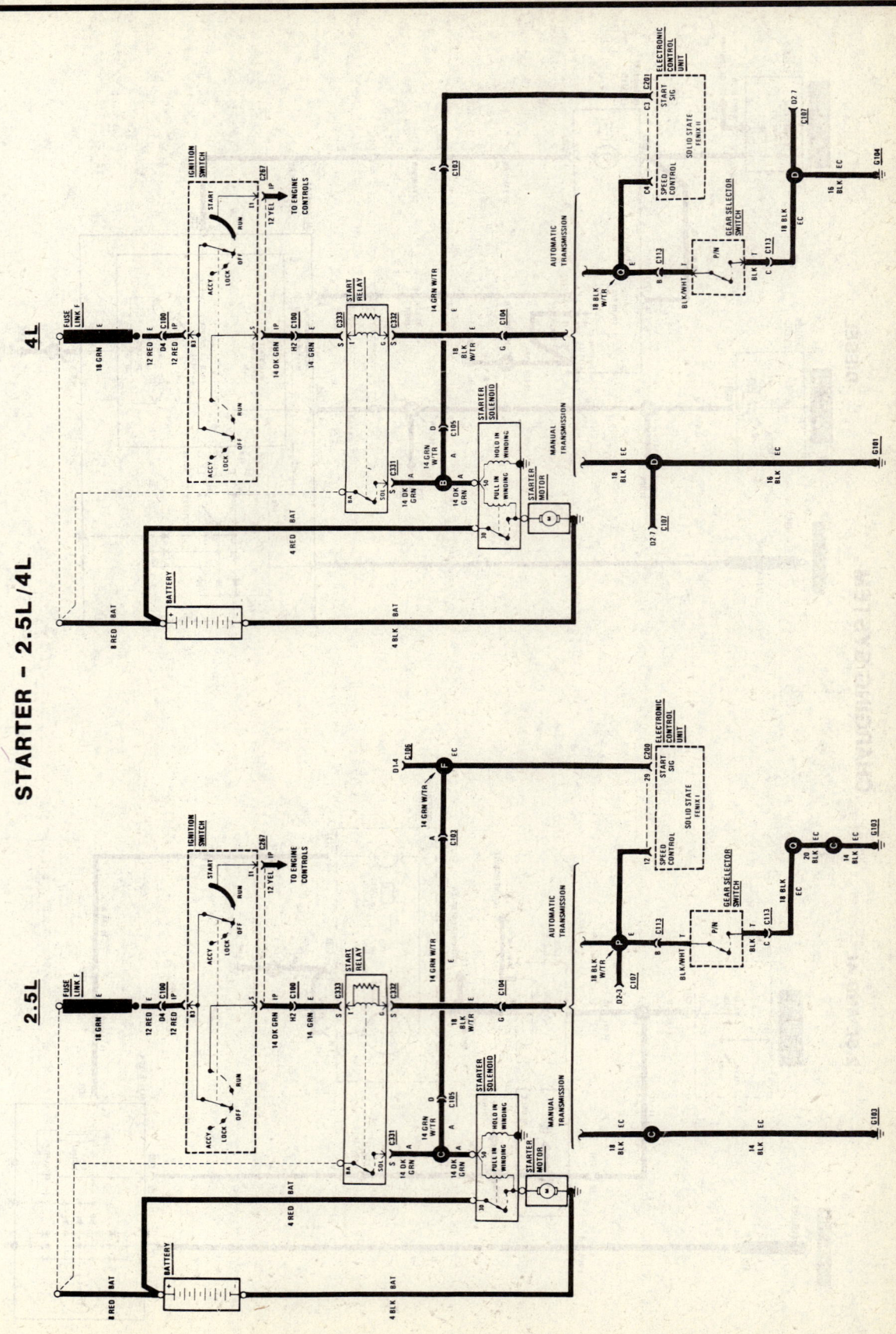

STARTER - 2.5L/4L

1987-88 Comanche

6 CHASSIS ELECTRICAL

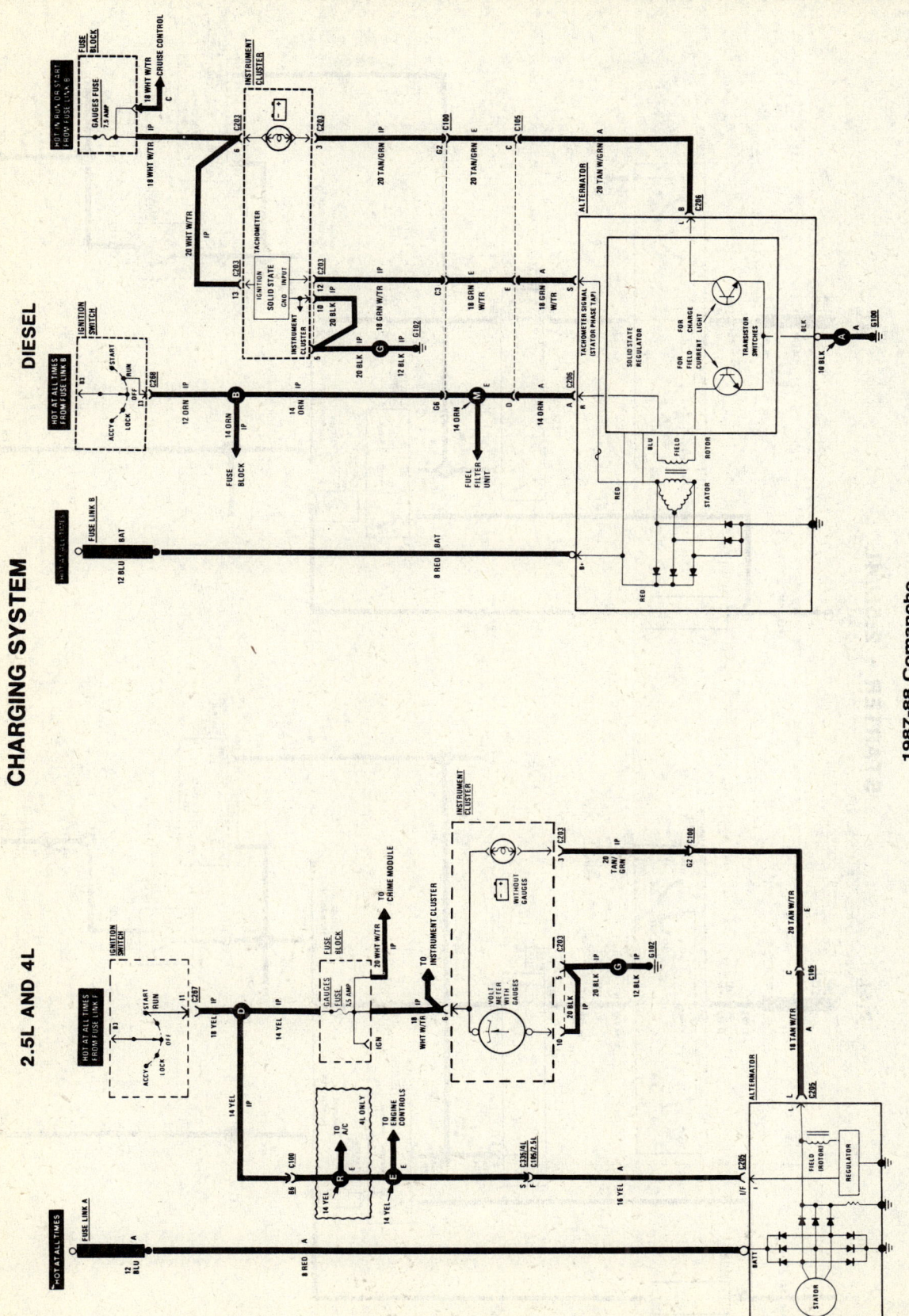

CHARGING SYSTEM — 1987-88 Comanche

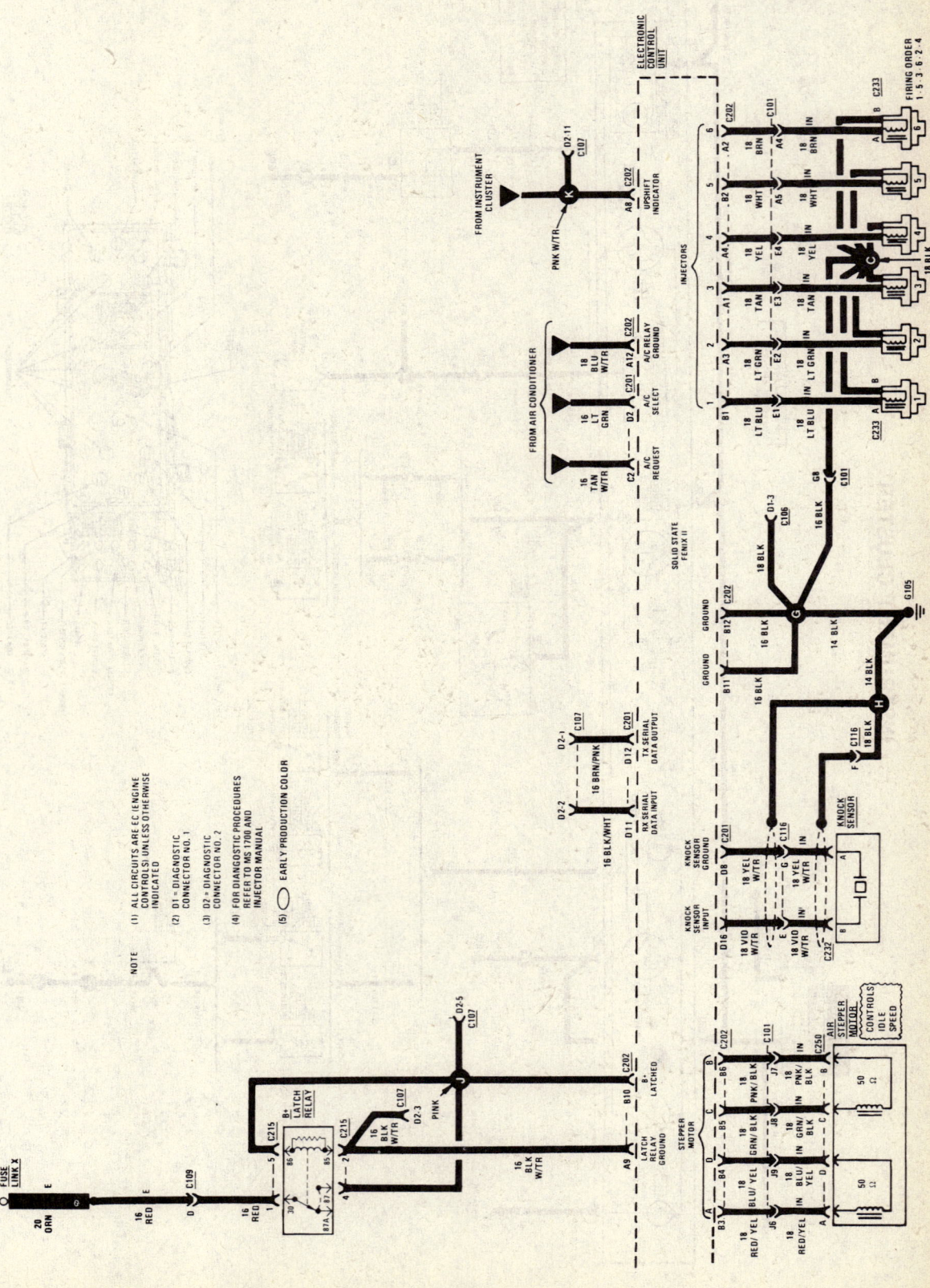

6 CHASSIS ELECTRICAL

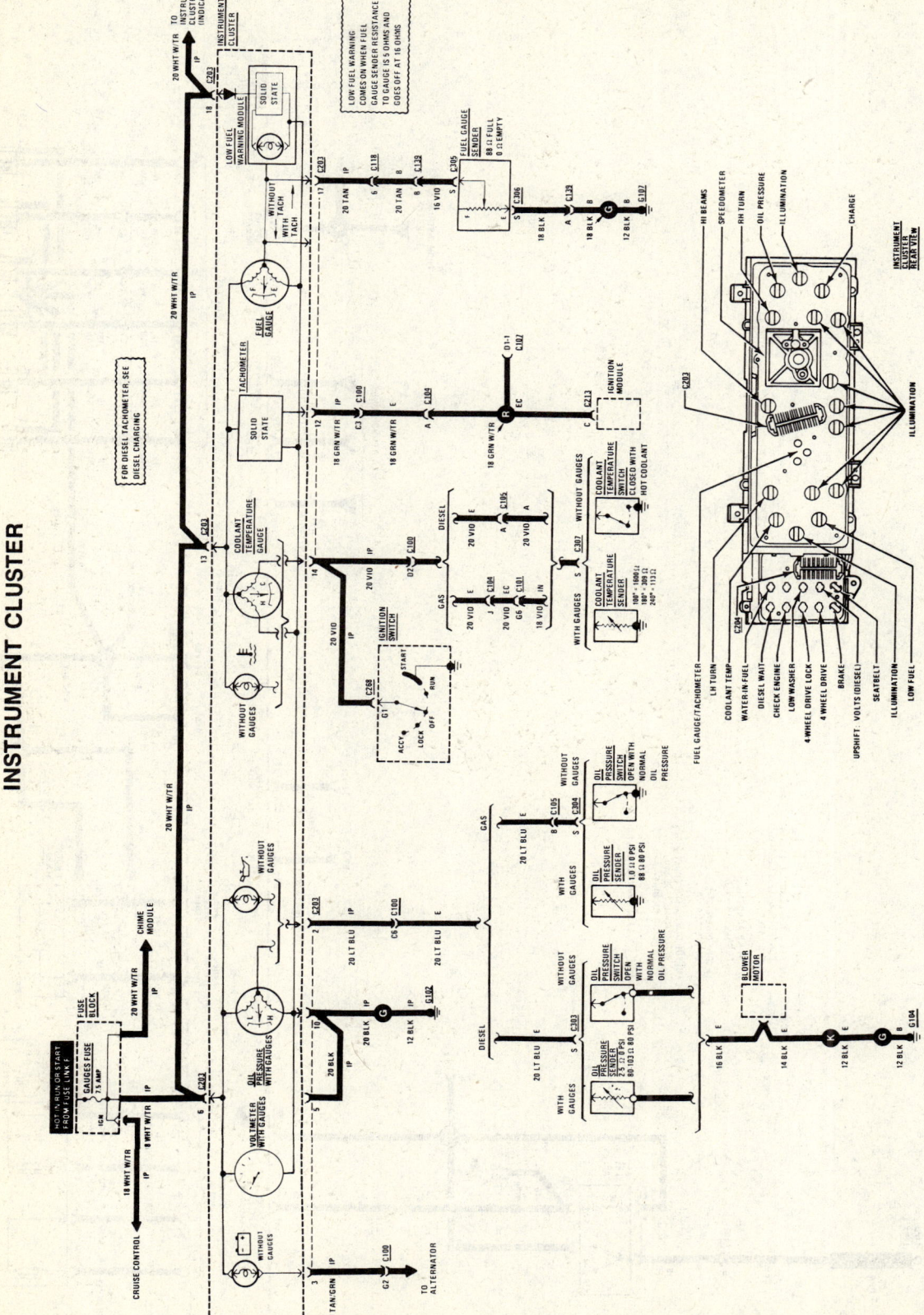

1987-88 Comanche

6-228

CHASSIS ELECTRICAL 6

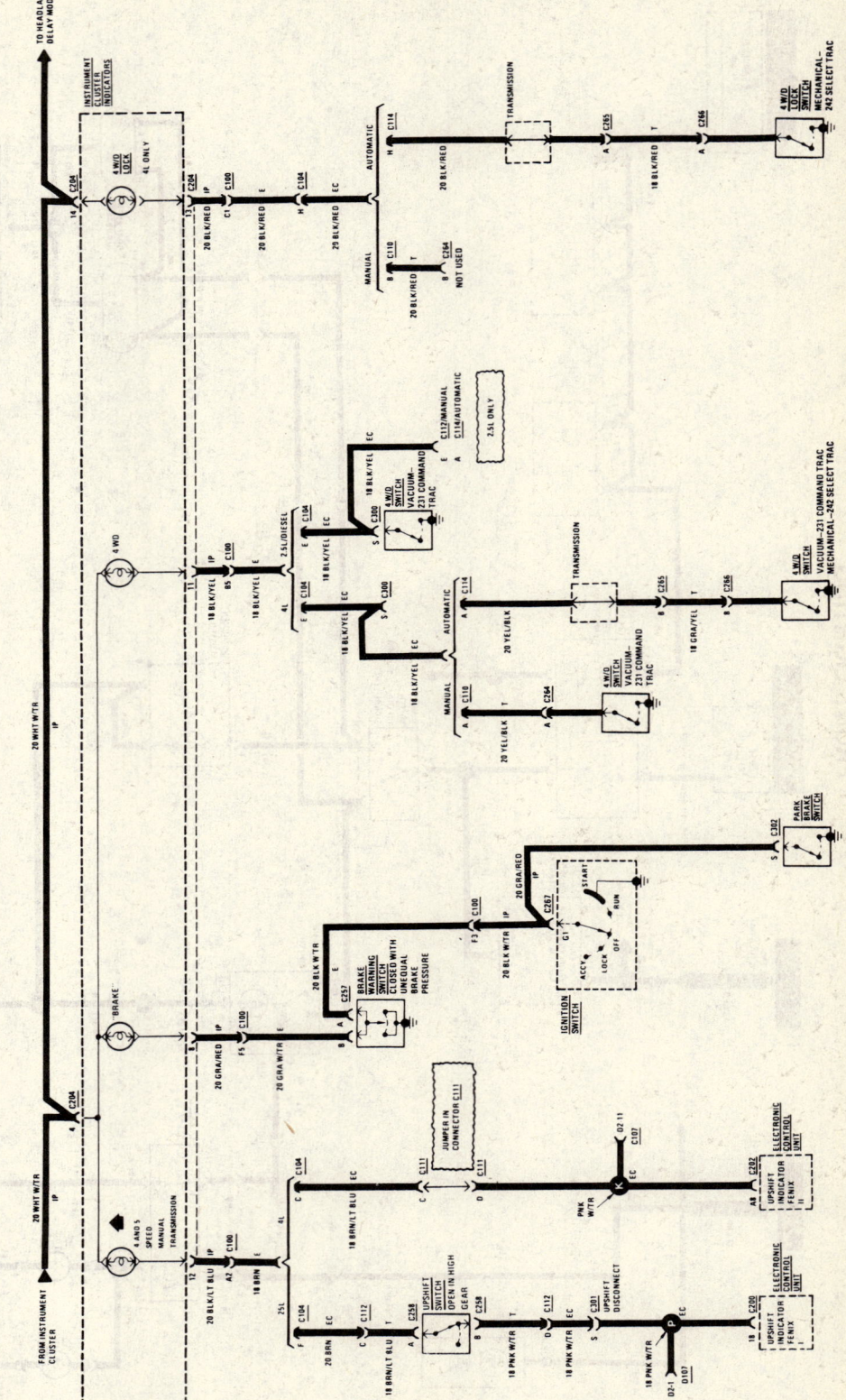

1987-88 Comanche

6 CHASSIS ELECTRICAL

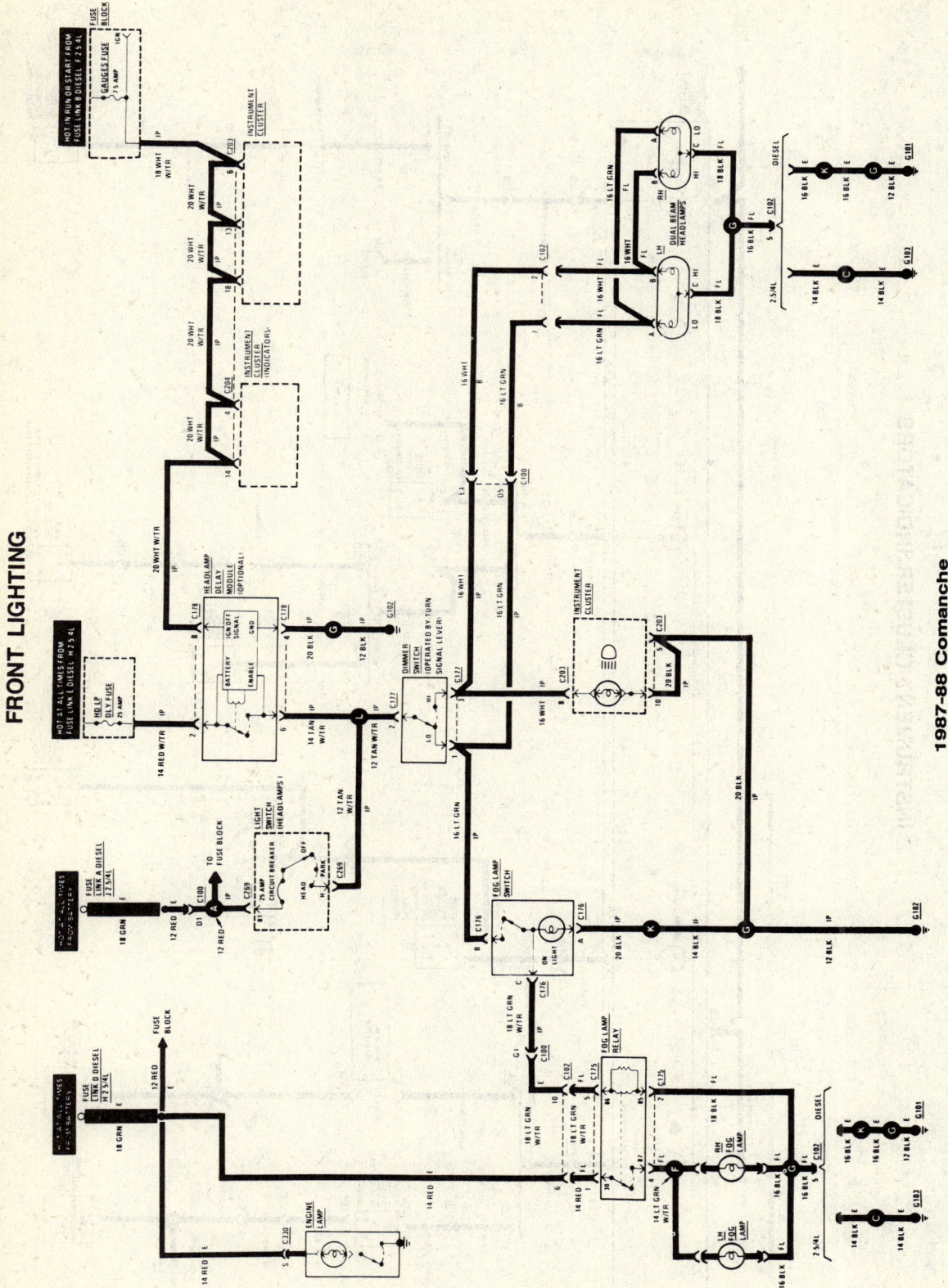

6-230

CHASSIS ELECTRICAL 6

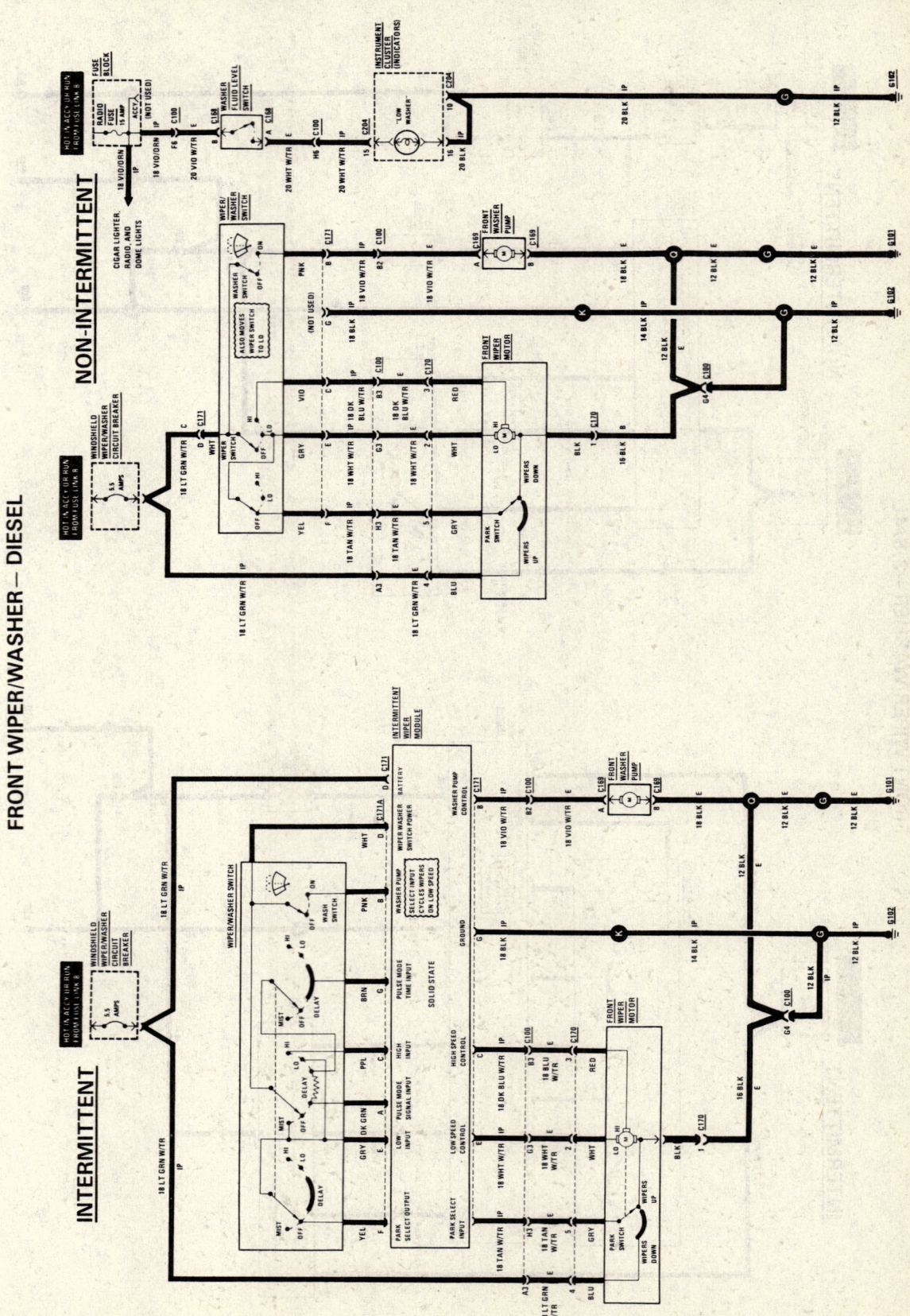

1987-88 Comanche

6 CHASSIS ELECTRICAL

FRONT WIPER/WASHER – 2.5/4L

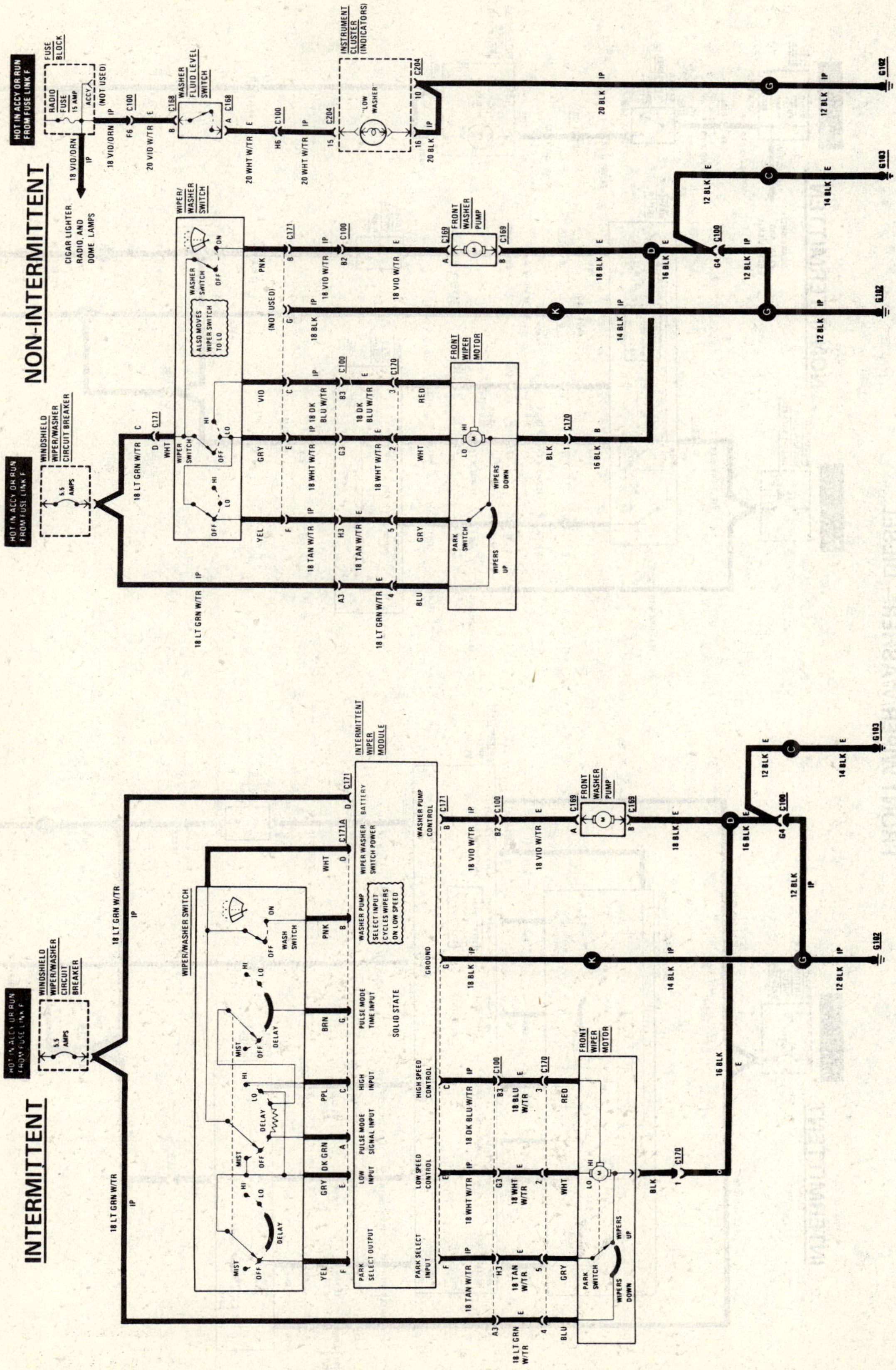

NON-INTERMITTENT

INTERMITTENT

1987-88 Comanche

6-232

CHASSIS ELECTRICAL 6

POWER REMOTE MIRRORS

REAR WIPER/WASHER

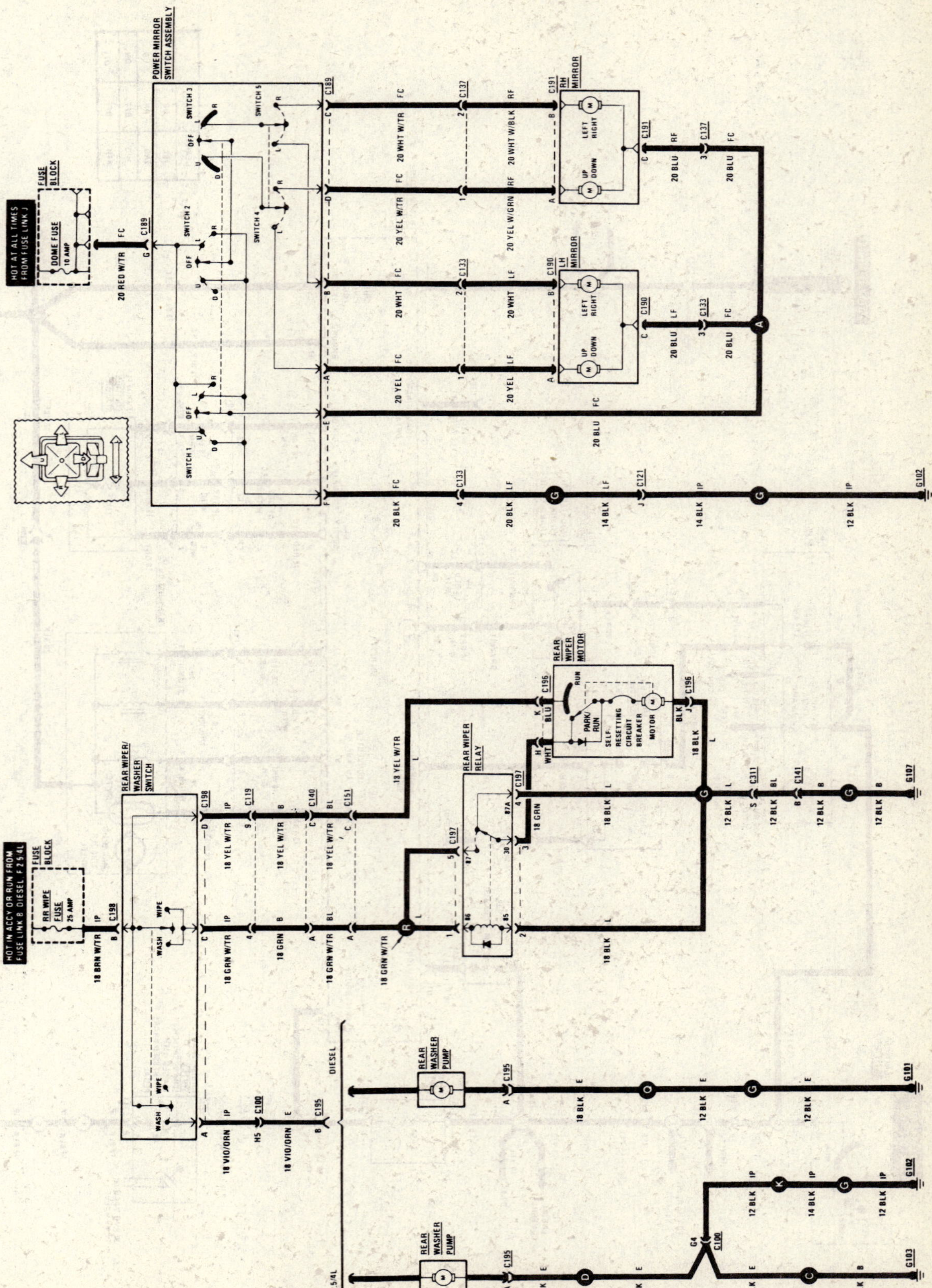

1987-88 Comanche

6-233

6 CHASSIS ELECTRICAL

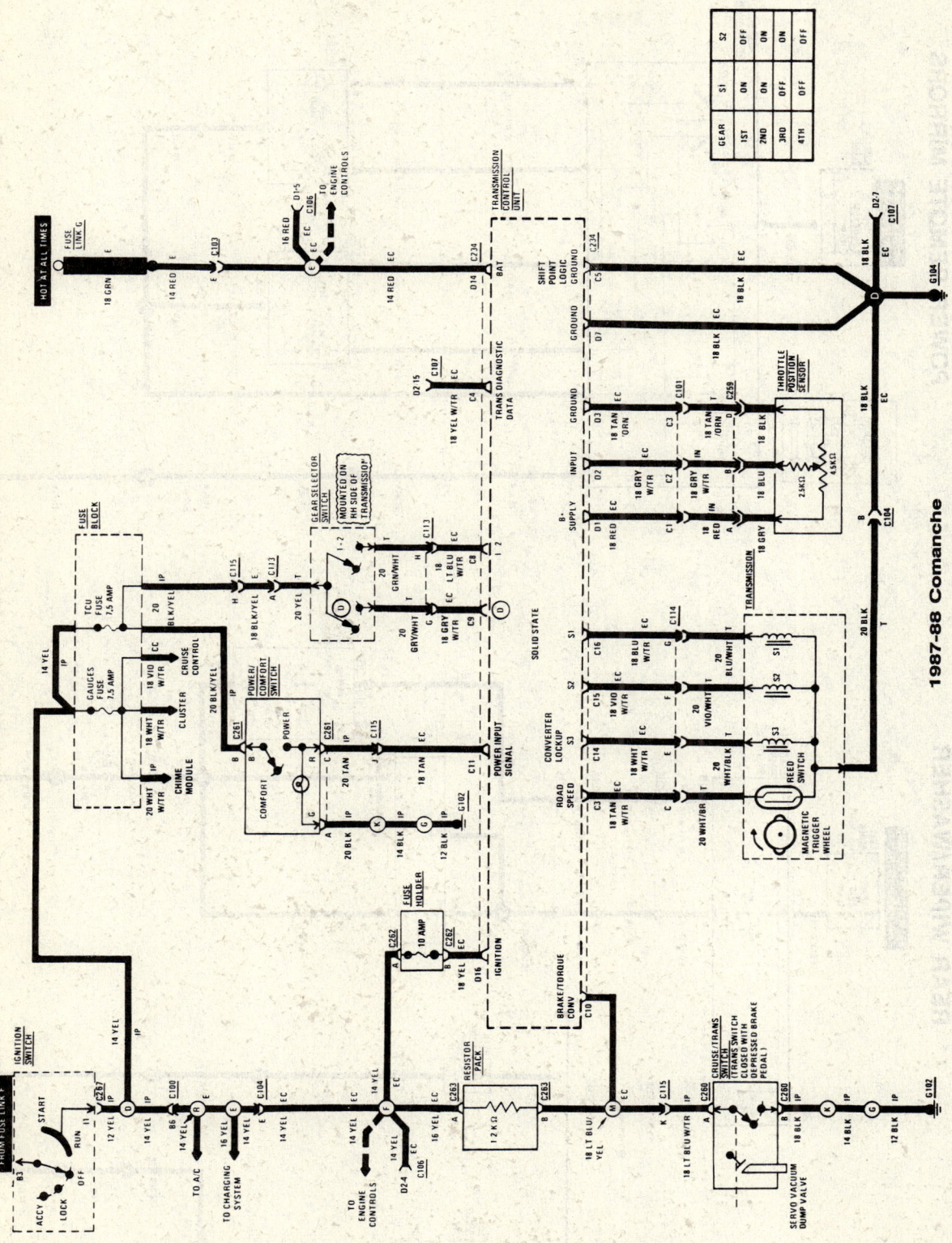

CHASSIS ELECTRICAL 6

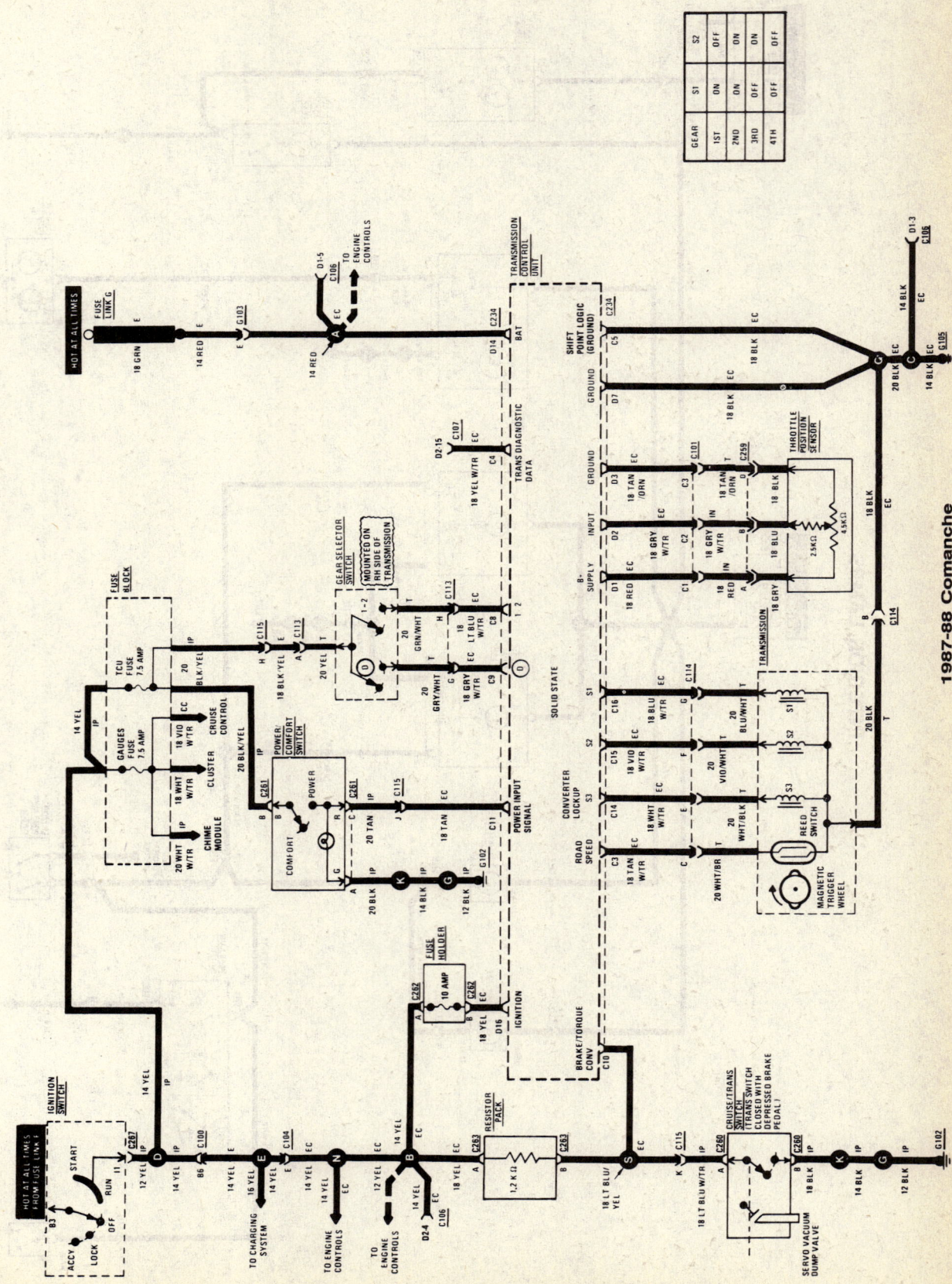

6 CHASSIS ELECTRICAL

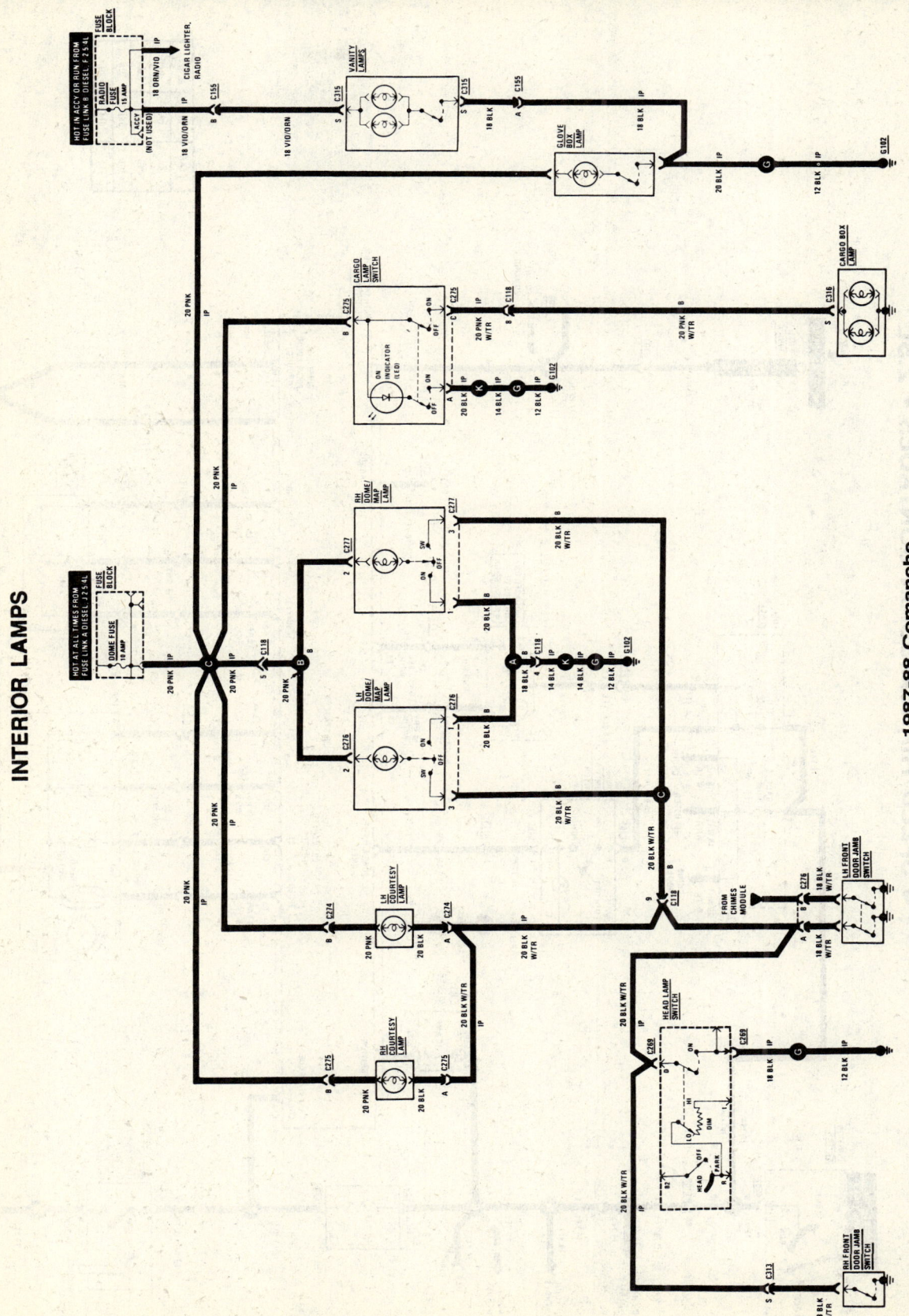

6-236

CHASSIS ELECTRICAL 6

HEATER — DIESEL

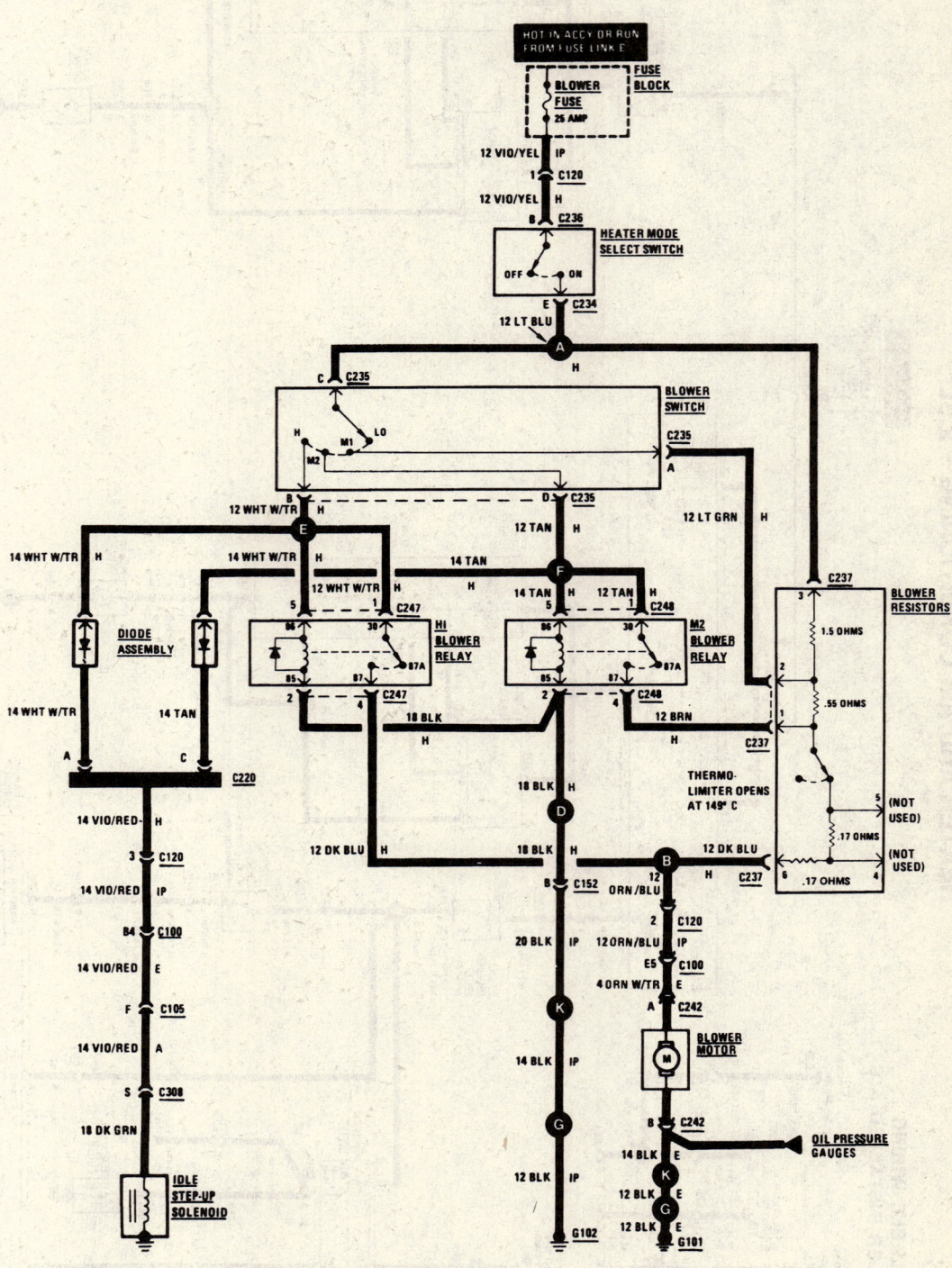

1987-88 Comanche

6-237

6 CHASSIS ELECTRICAL

HEATER AND AIR CONDITIONING – 2.5L

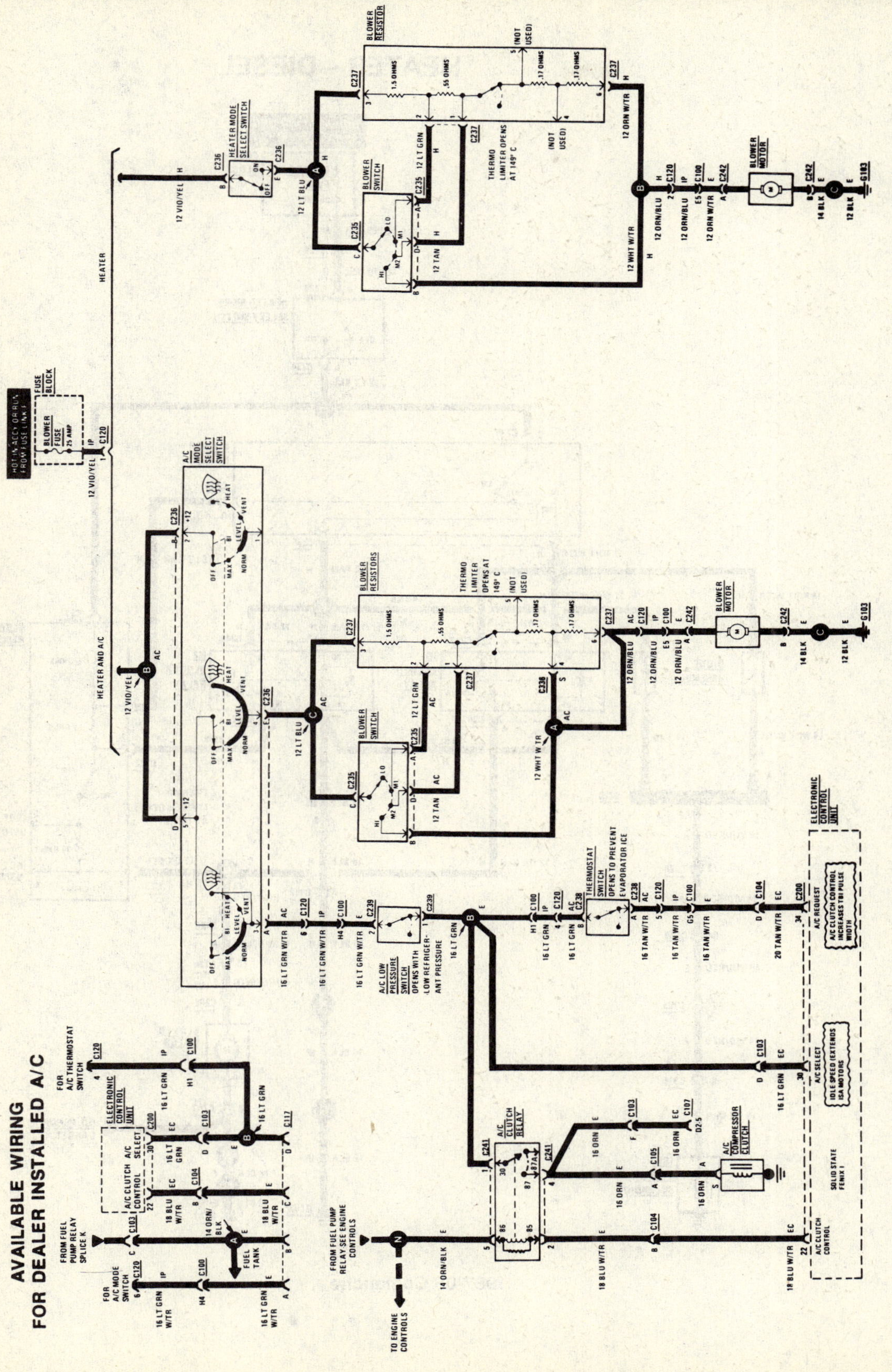

1987-88 Comanche

6-238

7

Drive Train

QUICK REFERENCE INDEX

Automatic Transmission	**7-89**
Clutch	**7-82**
Driveline	**7-153**
Front Drive Axle	**7-172**
Manual Transmission	**7-2**
Rear Axle	**7-160**
Transfer Case	**7-104**

GENERAL INDEX

Automatic transmission
  Adjustments 7-94
  Back-up light switch 7-101
  Extension housing seal 7-102
  Fluid and filter change 7-94
  Identification 7-94
  Neutral safety switch 7-101
  Oil cooler 7-94
  Operation 7-89
  Removal and installation 7-103
  Throttle cable adjustment 7-95
Axle
  Front 7-172
  Rear 7-160
Back-up Light Switch
  Automatic transmission 7-101
  Manual transmission 7-6
Clutch
  Hydraulic system bleeding 7-88
  Master cylinder 7-86
  Pedal 7-83
  Removal and installation 7-83
  Slave cylinder 7-86
  Throwout (concentric) bearing . 7-87
  Troubleshooting 7-83
Differential
  Front 7-172
  Rear 7-160
Drive axle (front)
  Axle shaft 7-172
  Axle tube bearing 7-173
  CV-joint 7-174
  Differential 7-177, 181

Hubs 7-175
  Identification 7-172
  Intermediate shaft 7-173
  Overhaul 7-177
  Pinion seal and yoke 7-173
  Removal and installation 7-175
  Shift motor 7-176
  U-joint 7-174
Drive axle (rear)
  Axle shaft and bearing 7-161
  Identification 7-161
  Overhaul 7-164
  Pinion seal 7-163
  Removal and installation 7-163
Driveshaft
  Front 7-153
  Rear 7-155
Gearshift linkage
  Automatic transmission 7-94
  Manual transmission 7-5
Manual transmission
  Back-up light switch 7-6
  Extension housing seal 7-6
  Identification 7-2
  Linkage 7-5
  Overhaul
    AX4 4-speed 7-28
    AX5 5-speed 7-39
    AX15 5-speed 7-54
    BA10/5 5-speed 7-71
    T4 4-speed 7-7
    T5 5-speed 7-17

Removal and installation
    T4 & T5 7-7
    AX4/5/15 7-27
    BA10/5 7-70
  Troubleshooting 7-3
Master cylinder 7-86
Neutral safety switch 7-101
Slave cylinder 7-86
Transfer Case
  Adjustments 7-104, 109
  Identification 7-104
  Overhaul
    NP-207 7-111
    NP-208 7-116
    NP-229 7-126
    NP-231 7-136
    NP-242 7-144
  Removal and installation
    NP-207 7-110
    NP-208 7-116
    NP-229 7-126
    NP-231 7-136
    NP-242 7-144
  Shift motor 7-110
  Troubleshooting 7-105
Troubleshooting Charts
  Automatic transmission 7-90
  Clutch 7-83
  Driveshaft 7-154
  Manual transmission 7-3
  Transfer case 7-105
U-joints 7-157

7 DRIVE TRAIN

UNDERSTANDING THE MANUAL TRANSMISSION

Because of the way an internal combustion engine breathes, it can produce torque, or twisting force, only within a narrow speed range. Most modern, overhead valve engines must turn at about 2,500 rpm to produce their peak torque. By 4,500 rpm they are producing so little torque that continued increases in engine speed produce no power increases.

The manual transmission and clutch are employed to vary the relationship between engine speed and the speed of the wheels so that adequate engine power can be produced under all circumstances. The clutch allows engine torque to be applied to the transmission input shaft gradually, due to mechanical slippage. The car can, consequently, be started smoothly from a full stop.

The transmission changes the ratio between the rotating speeds of the engine and the wheels by the use of gears. On trucks, 4-speed or 5-speed transmissions are most common. The lower gears allow full engine power to be applied to the rear wheels during acceleration at low speeds.

The transmission contains a mainshaft which passes all the way through the transmission, from the clutch to the driveshaft. This shaft is separated at one point, so that front and rear portions can turn at different speeds.

Power is transmitted by a countershaft in the lower gears and reverse. The gears of the countershaft mesh with gears on the mainshaft, allowing power to be carried from one to the other. All the countershaft gears are integral with that shaft, while several of the mainshaft gears can either rotate independently of the shaft or be locked to it. Shifting from one gear to the next causes one of the gears to be freed from rotating with the shaft and locks another to it. Gears are locked and unlocked by internal dog clutches which slide between the center of the gear and the shaft. The forward gears usually employ synchronizers; friction members which smoothly bring gear and shaft to the same speed before the toothed dog clutches are engaged.

The clutch is operating properly if:
1. It will stall the engine when released with the vehicle held stationary.
2. The shift lever can be moved freely between 1st and reverse gears when the vehicle is stationary and the clutch disengaged.

MANUAL TRANSMISSION

Identification

Warner T4/5

The T4 4-speed and the T5 5-speed manual transmissions were used on 1984 Jeep vehicles as a replacement for the AX4/5 transmissions during a production shortage. The T4 was used on vehicles equipped with 4-2.5L engines; the T5 on vehicles equipped with 6-2.8L engines.

Both transmissions have an identification tag attached at the rear of the transmission case that provides the Jeep and vendor part numbers. This information is essential when ordering replacement parts. If the tag is removed during service operations, ensure that it is securely attached to the transmission case at the original location after completion of the service operation.

Vehicles manufactured for sale in the states of Georgia and Tennessee have certain components identified by a non repeating number. For both transmissions, the number is stamped on a boss located on the left side of the transmission case.

The number used for Canadian manufactured vehicles is the body sequence number preceded by a 'C' and followed by '83' or '84' to identify the year of manufacture. The sequence number begins and ends with an asterisk (*).

Aisin AX4/5/15

The AX4 4-speed, AX5 5-speed, and the AX15 high capacity 5-speed manual transmissions have synchromesh engagement in all forward gears, controlled by a floor shift mechanism integrated into the transmission top cover. The AX4/5 are used on Jeep vehicles equipped with 4-2.5L engines; the AX15 on vehicles equipped with 6-4.0L engines.

The identification code for all transmissions is located on the bottom surface of the transmission case near the fill plug. The first number is year of manufacture. The second and third numbers indicate month of manufacture. The next series of numbers is the transmission serial number.

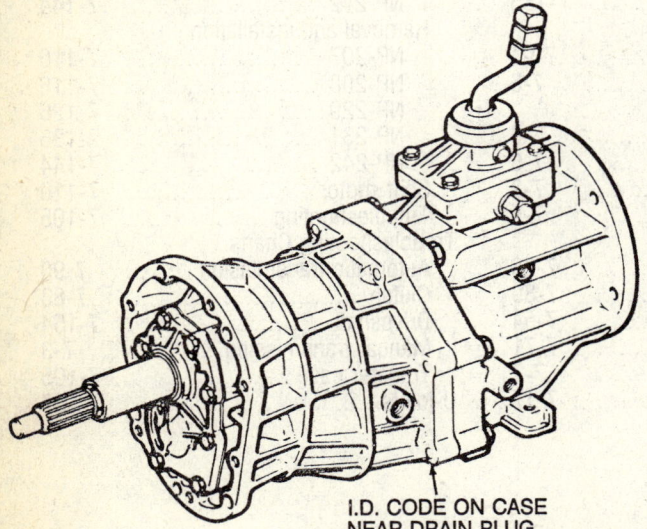

Identification code location on the AX 4/5/15

MANUAL TRANSMISSION APPLICATION CHART

Transmission Types	Years
Warner T4 4-speed	1984 w/4-150
Warner T5 5-speed	1984 all
AISIN AX4 4-speed	1984–87 w/4-150
AISIN AX5 5-speed	1984–91 all
BA 10/5 5-speed	1987–89 all
AISIN AX15	1989–91 w/6-243

NOTE: The T4 and T5 were used in 1984 only, as substitutes for the AX4 and AX5 during a production shortage.

DRIVE TRAIN 7

Troubleshooting the Manual Transmission and Transfer Case

Problem	Cause	Solution
Transmission shifts hard	• Clutch adjustment incorrect • Clutch linkage or cable binding • Shift rail binding • Internal bind in transmission caused by shift forks, selector plates, or synchronizer assemblies • Clutch housing misalignment • Incorrect lubricant • Block rings and/or cone seats worn	• Adjust clutch • Lubricate or repair as necessary • Check for mispositioned selector arm roll pin, loose cover bolts, worn shift rail bores, worn shift rail, distorted oil seal, or extension housing not aligned with case. Repair as necessary. • Remove, dissemble and inspect transmission. Replace worn or damaged components as necessary. • Check runout at rear face of clutch housing • Drain and refill transmission • Blocking ring to gear clutch tooth face clearance must be 0.030 inch or greater. If clearance is correct it may still be necessary to inspect blocking rings and cone seats for excessive wear. Repair as necessary.
Gear clash when shifting from one gear to another	• Clutch adjustment incorrect • Clutch linkage or cable binding • Clutch housing misalignment • Lubricant level low or incorrect lubricant • Gearshift components, or synchronizer assemblies worn or damaged	• Adjust clutch • Lubricate or repair as necessary • Check runout at rear of clutch housing • Drain and refill transmission and check for lubricant leaks if level was low. Repair as necessary. • Remove, disassemble and inspect transmission. Replace worn or damaged components as necessary.
Transmission noisy	• Lubricant level low or incorrect lubricant • Clutch housing-to-engine, or transmission-to-clutch housing bolts loose • Dirt, chips, foreign material in transmission • Gearshift mechanism, transmission gears, or bearing components worn or damaged • Clutch housing misalignment	• Drain and refill transmission. If lubricant level was low, check for leaks and repair as necessary. • Check and correct bolt torque as necessary • Drain, flush, and refill transmission • Remove, disassemble and inspect transmission. Replace worn or damaged components as necessary. • Check runout at rear face of clutch housing

7-3

7 DRIVE TRAIN

Troubleshooting the Manual Transmission and Transfer Case (cont.)

Problem	Cause	Solution
Jumps out of gear	• Clutch housing misalignment	• Check runout at rear face of clutch housing
	• Gearshift lever loose	• Check lever for worn fork. Tighten loose attaching bolts.
	• Offset lever nylon insert worn or lever attaching nut loose	• Remove gearshift lever and check for loose offset lever nut or worn insert. Repair or replace as necessary.
	• Gearshift mechanism, shift forks, selector plates, interlock plate, selector arm, shift rail, detent plugs, springs or shift cover worn or damaged	• Remove, disassemble and inspect transmission cover assembly. Replace worn or damaged components as necessary.
	• Clutch shaft or roller bearings worn or damaged	• Replace clutch shaft or roller bearings as necessary
Jumps out of gear (cont.)	• Gear teeth worn or tapered, synchronizer assemblies worn or damaged, excessive end play caused by worn thrust washers or output shaft gears	• Remove, disassemble, and inspect transmission. Replace worn or damaged components as necessary.
	• Pilot bushing worn	• Replace pilot bushing
Will not shift into one gear	• Gearshift selector plates, interlock plate, or selector arm, worn, damaged, or incorrectly assembled	• Remove, disassemble, and inspect transmission cover assembly. Repair or replace components as necessary.
	• Shift rail detent plunger worn, spring broken, or plug loose	• Tighten plug or replace worn or damaged components as necessary
	• Gearshift lever worn or damaged	• Replace gearshift lever
	• Synchronizer sleeves or hubs, damaged or worn	• Remove, disassemble and inspect transmission. Replace worn or damaged components.
Locked in one gear—cannot be shifted out	• Shift rail(s) worn or broken, shifter fork bent, setscrew loose, center detent plug missing or worn	• Inspect and replace worn or damaged parts
	• Broken gear teeth on countershaft gear, clutch shaft, or reverse idler gear	• Inspect and replace damaged part
	Gearshift lever broken or worn, shift mechanism in cover incorrectly assembled or broken, worn damaged gear train components	• Disassemble transmission. Replace damaged parts or assemble correctly.

DRIVE TRAIN 7

The fill plug is located on the passenger side of the adaptor housing. The drain plug is located on the bottom of the case.

BA 10/5

The BA10/5 5-speed has synchromesh engagement in all forward gears, controlled by a floor shift mechanism integrated into the transmission intermediate case.

The identification tag for the BA10/5 is riveted to the left side of the transmission case. The plate provides the transmission date of build, part number and serial number.

Gear Shift Lever

REMOVAL AND INSTALLATION

Warner T4/5

1. Remove the screws attaching the shift lever boot to the floor pan and slide the boot up.
2. Remove the bolts attaching the shift lever housing to the transmission and remove the lever and housing.
3. Installation is the reverse of removal. Make sure lever is engaged with the shift rail before tightening housing bolts to 18 ft. lbs.

Aisin AX4/5/15

1. Shift the transmission into first or third gear.
2. Raise and support the vehicle safely.
3. Support the transmission with a floor jack and remove the rear crossmember.

CHILTON TIP: *Tool manufacturers now have available a transmission cradle to fit most floor jacks. This cradle allows the transmission to be tilted horizontally and vertically, thus, easing installation.*

4. Lower the transmission assembly no more than 3 inches for access to the shift lever.

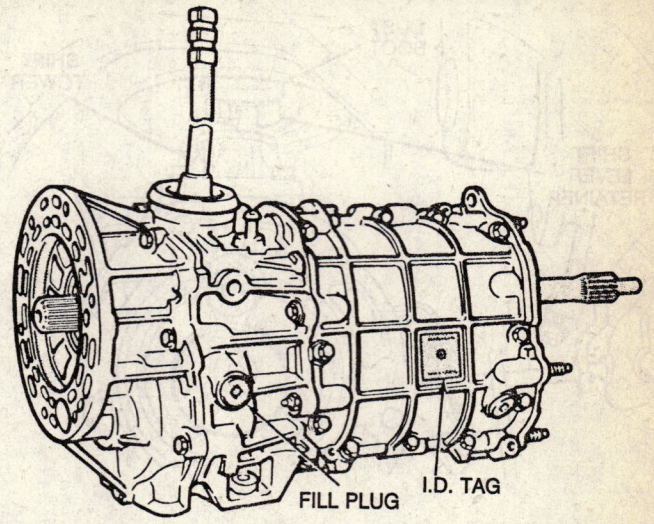
Identification code location on the BA 10/5

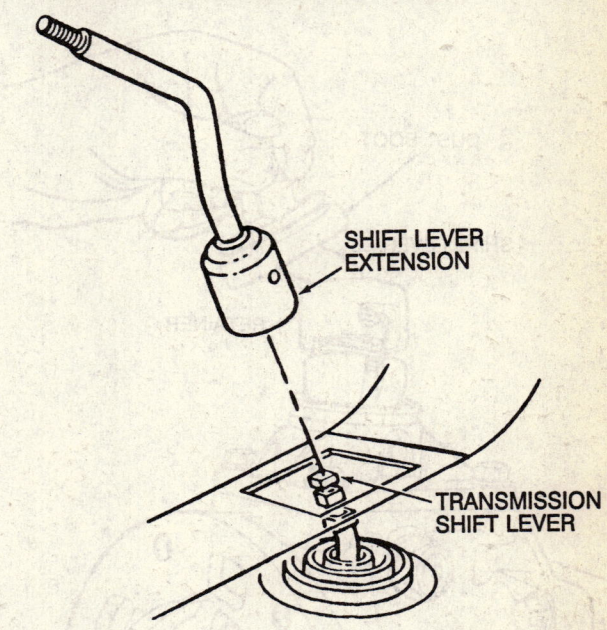
Shift lever extension removal/installation

5. Reach up and around the transmission case to unseat the shifter lever dust boot from the transmission shift tower. Move the boot upward on the shift lever for access to the retainer that secures the lever in the tower.
6. Disengage the shift lever from the transmission by pressing the shift lever retainer downward and counterclockwise. Then lift the lever and retainer out of the shift tower. You can leave the shift lever in the floor pan boot for reassembly.
7. Installation is the reverse of removal. Tighten crossmember-to-frame bolts to 30 ft. lbs.; transmission-to-crossmember bolts to 33 ft. lbs.

BA10/5

1. Remove the gearshift lever boot and remove the upper part of the console.
2. Remove the lower part of the console. Remove the inner gearshift lever boot.

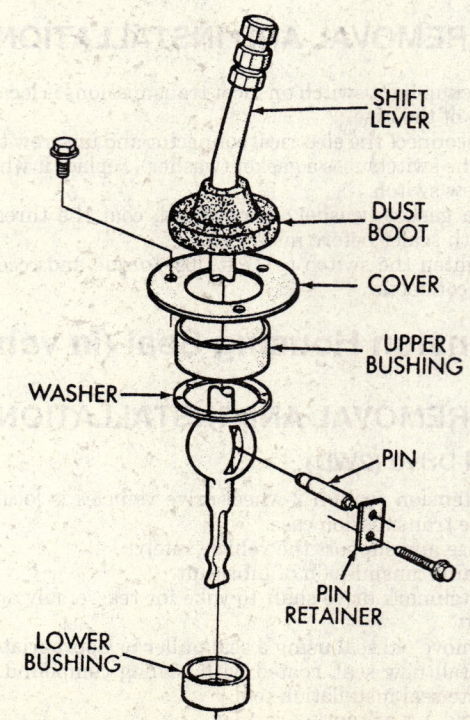
Shift lever removal/installation on the BA 10/5

7-5

7 DRIVE TRAIN

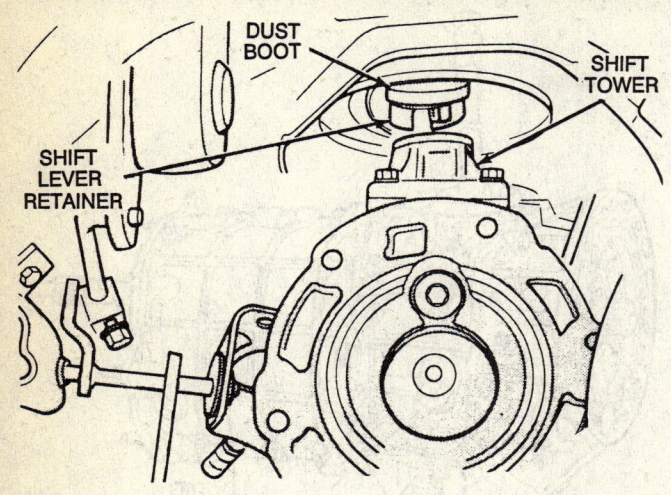

Lower the AX 4/5/15 transmission no more than 3 inches to gain access to the shift lever base

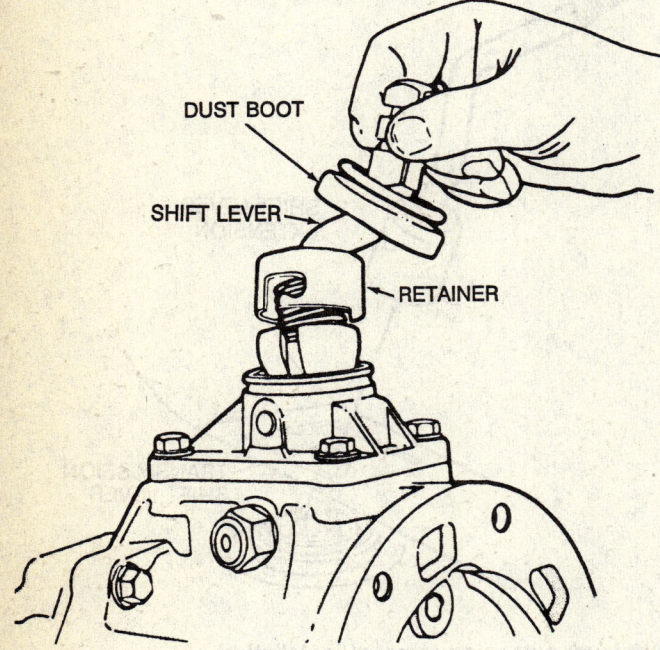

Shift lever removal/installation on the AX 4/5/15

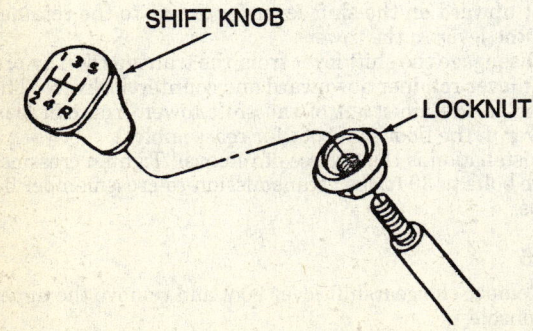

Shift knob removal

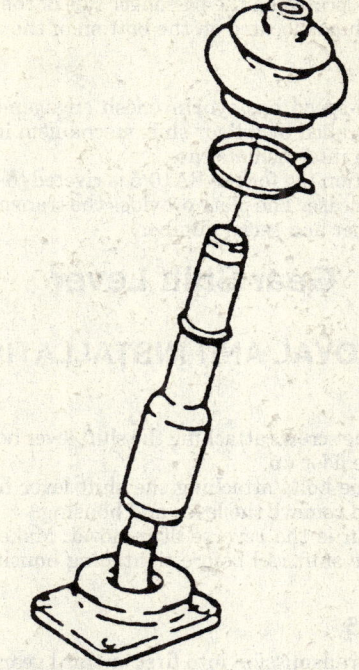

Warner T4/5 shift lever

3. Remove the gearshift lever.
NOTE: On some BA10/5 transmissions, the shift lever may be held in place with a snapring and spring washer.
4. Installation is the reverse of removal.

Backup Light Switch

REMOVAL AND INSTALLATION

The backup light switch on most transmissions is located on the right side of the case.
1. Disconnect the electrical connector and unscrew the switch.
2. If the switch uses a gasket (washer), replace it when installing the new switch.
3. If a gasket (washer) is not used, coat the threads of the switch with sealer before installation.
4. Tighten the switch to 27 ft. lbs. torque and reconnect the electrical connector.

Extension Housing Seal (in vehicle)

REMOVAL AND INSTALLATION

2-Wheel Drive (2WD)

The extension seal on 2-wheel drive vehicles is located at the rear of the transmission case.
1. Raise and support the vehicle safely.
2. Drain transmission of lubricant.
3. Matchmark drive shaft to yoke for reassembly and remove drive shaft.
4. Remove old seal using a seal puller or appropriate pry tool.
5. Install new seal, coated with sealing compound, using an appropriate seal installation tool.
NOTE: Tool J-35582 or equivalent is recommended for AX4/5/15 transmissions. Tool J-21426 or equivalent is recommended for Warner T4/5 transmissions.

DRIVE TRAIN 7

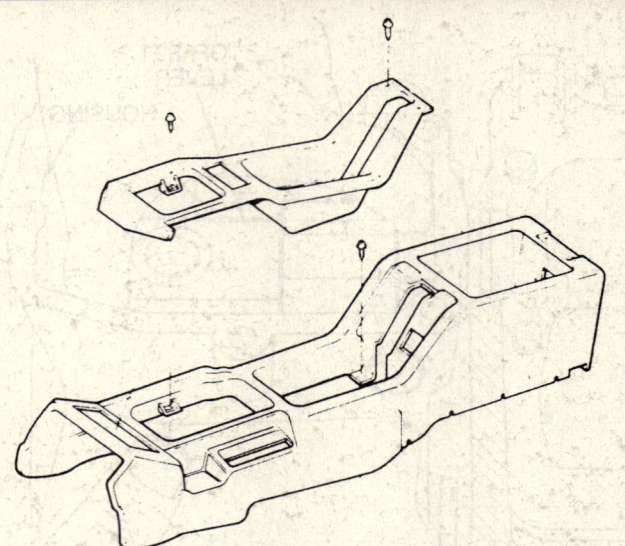

Upper and lower console removal/installation

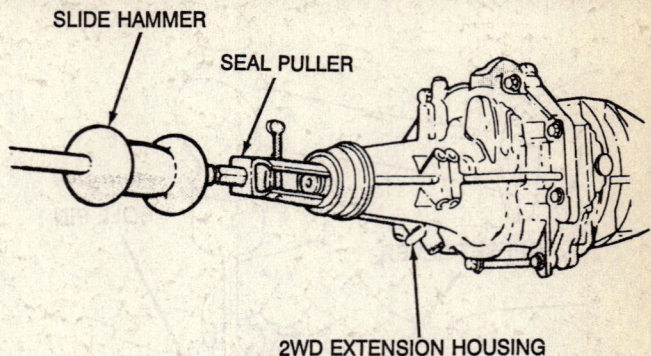

Extension housing seal removal/installation on 2WD

6. Install the driveshaft, making certain to align matchmark. Tighten bolts to 20 ft. lbs.
7. Fill transmission to the level of the fill plug hole. Install plug and lower vehicle.

4-Wheel Drive (4WD)

The extension seal on 4-wheel drive vehicles is located at the rear of the transfer case.
1. Raise and support the vehicle safely.
2. Drain transfer case of lubricant.
3. Matchmark drive shaft to yoke for reassembly and remove drive shaft.
4. Remove old seal using a seal puller or appropriate pry tool.
5. Install new seal, coated with sealing compound, using an appropriate seal installation tool.
6. Install the driveshaft, making certain to align matchmark. Tighten bolts to 20 ft. lbs.
7. Fill transfer case with lubricant. Install plug and lower vehicle.

Warner T4/T5

REMOVAL AND INSTALLATION

1. Remove the gearshift lever boot and remove the upper part of the console.
2. Remove the lower part of the console. Remove the inner gearshift lever boot.
3. Remove the gearshift lever.
4. Raise and support the vehicle safely. Drain the transmission (and transfer case on 4WD) of all lubricant.
5. Matchmark the rear drive shaft and axle yoke for installation alignment. Remove the rear drive shaft.
6. Position a floor jack under the transmission (and transfer case on 4WD) and remove the rear crossmember.

CHILTON TIP: *Tool manufacturers now have available a transmission cradle to fit most floor jacks. This cradle allows the transmission to be tilted horizontally and vertically, thus, easing installation.*

7. Disconnect the speedometer cable, backup light switch, and transfer case vent hose (if equipped).
8. Disconnect all vacuum hoses and linkage from the transmission (and transfer case on 4WD).
9. Remove the clutch slave cylinder attaching nuts and slave cylinder.
10. Matchmark the front drive shaft and axle yoke for installation alignment. Move the front drive shaft aside and secure with wire to the underbody.
11. Remove the transmission (and transfer case on 4WD) using a floor jack. Be sure to tie the assembly to the jack to prevent it from slipping.
12. Separate the transmission from the transfer case (if equipped) and clutch housing.
13. Remove the clutch pivot ball, throwout bearing and lever from the clutch housing.

To Install:
14. Install the clutch pivot ball and throwout lever with the bearing attached.
15. Shift the transmission into gear using the shift lever.
16. With the transmission supported on a floor jack, align the transmission clutch shaft with the splines in the drive plate hub. Mate the transmission to the engine and tighten the mounting bolts to 28 ft. lbs. torque.
17. Install the clutch slave cylinder and attaching nuts.
18. Install the transfer case (if equipped) using a floor jack and tighten attaching bolts to 26 ft. lbs. torque.
19. Connect the transfer case vent hose (if equipped), backup light switch (torque to 27 ft. lbs.), speedometer cable, transfer case vacuum hoses and all linkage.
20. Install the front drive shaft with matchmarks aligned. Torque strap bolts to 14 ft. lbs.; flange-to-transfer case bolts to 35 ft. lbs.
21. Install the crossmember. Tighten crossmember-to-frame bolts to 30 ft. lbs.; crossmember-to-transmission bolts to 33 ft. lbs.
22. Install the rear drive shaft with matchmarks aligned. Torque strap bolts to 14 ft. lbs.
23. Fill the transmission (and transfer case on 4WD) with fluid. Lower vehicle.
24. Install gearshift lever, lower and upper console and shift lever boot.

Warner T4 Overhaul

CASE DISASSEMBLY

1. Drain the transmission lubricant. 2WD models are not equipped with a drain plug; the fluid must be siphoned from the transmission.
2. Use a pin punch and hammer to remove the offset lever-to-shift rail roll pin.
3. Remove the extension housing (2WD) or the adapter (4WD). Remove the housing and the offset lever as an assembly.
4. Remove the detent ball and spring from the offset lever. Remove the roll pin from the extension housing or adapter.

7-7

7 DRIVE TRAIN

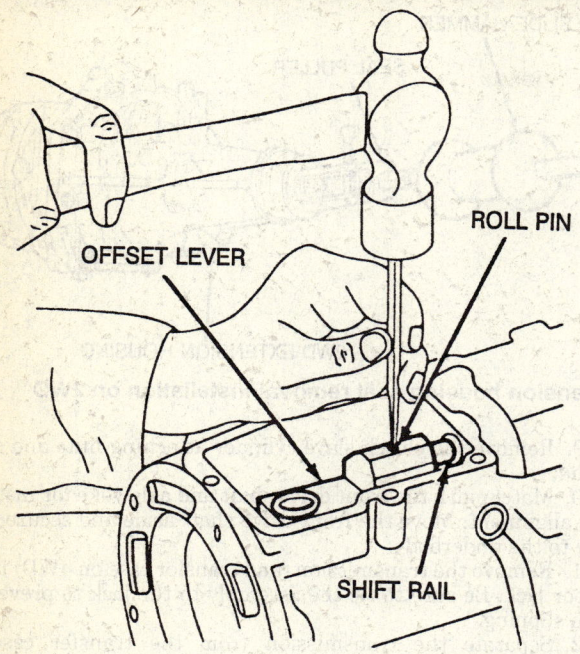

Offset lever and shift rail removal/installation on the T4

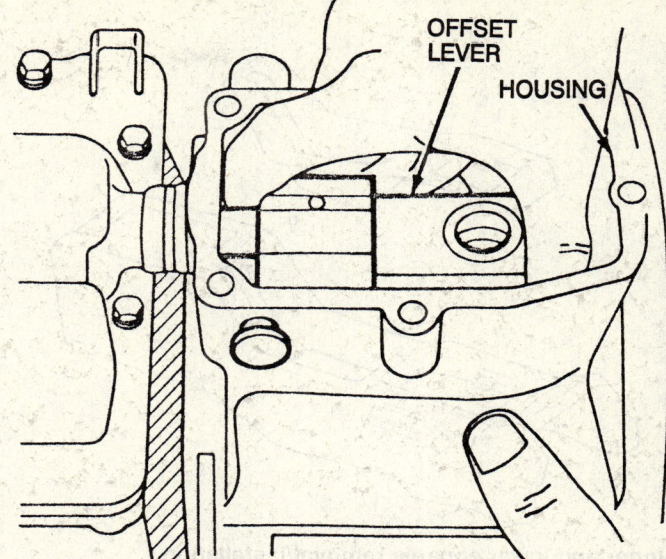

Adapter housing removal/installation on the T4

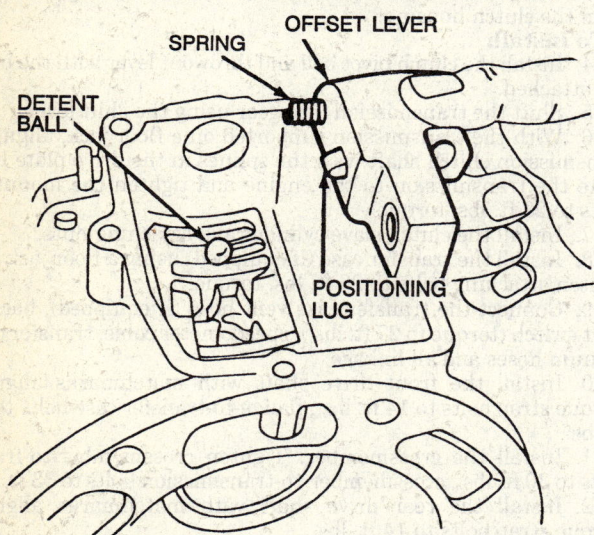

Removing the detent ball and spring from the offset lever on the T4

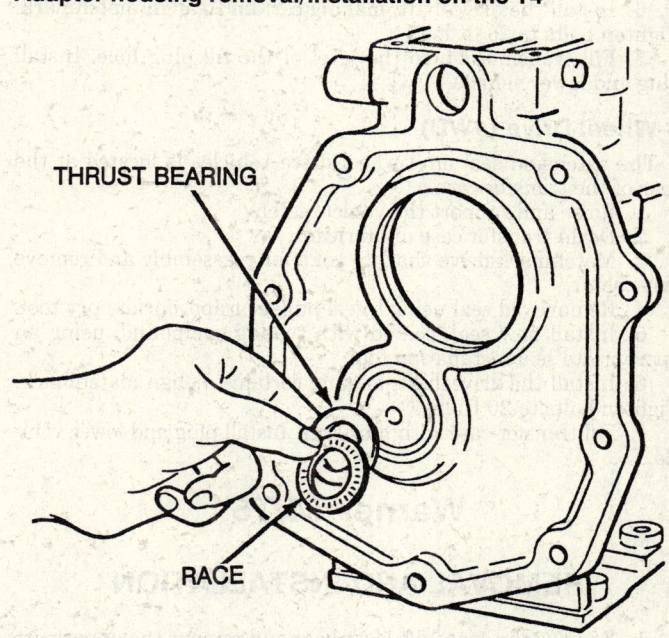

Counter shaft rear thrust bearing and race on the T4

5. Remove the countershaft rear thrust bearing and race.
6. Remove the transmission cover and shift fork assembly. Two of the transmission cover bolts are alignment type dowel pins. Mark their location so that they may be reinstalled in their original locations.
7. Remove the reverse lever to reverse lever pivot bolt C-clip.
8. Remove the reverse lever pivot bolt. Remove the reverse lever and fork as an assembly.
9. Mark the position of the front bearing cap to case, then remove the bearing cap bolts and cap.
10. Remove the front bearing race and the shims from the bearing cap. Use a small pry bar and remove the front seal from the bearing cap.
11. Rotate the main drive gear shaft until the flat portion of the gear faces the countershaft, then remove the main drive gear shaft assembly.

12. Remove the thrust bearing and 15 roller bearings from the clutch shaft. Remove the output shaft bearing race. Tap the output shaft with a plastic hammer to loosen it if necessary.
13. Tilt the output shaft assembly upward and remove the assembly from the case.
14. Carefully pull off the countershaft rear bearing with the proper puller after marking the position for reinstallation.
15. Move the countershaft rearward and tilt it upward to remove it from the transmission case. Remove the countershaft bearing spacer.
16. Remove the reverse idler shaft roll pin, then remove the reverse idler shaft and gear.
17. Press off the countershaft front bearing. Use the appropriate pullers and remove the bearing from the main drive gear shaft.
18. Remove the extension housing or adapter oil seal and remove the back-up light switch from the case.

DRIVE TRAIN 7

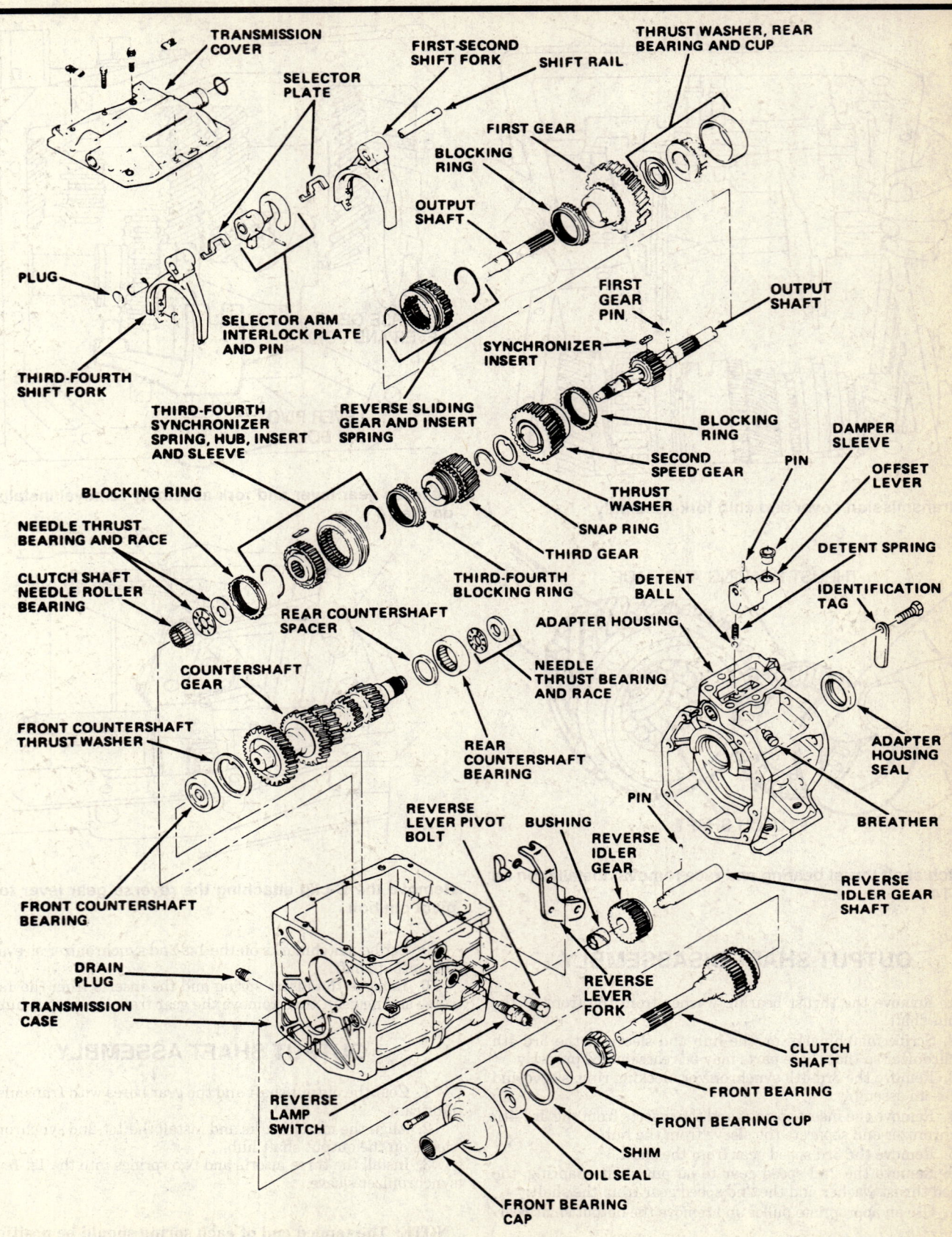

Warner T4 transmission

7-9

7 DRIVE TRAIN

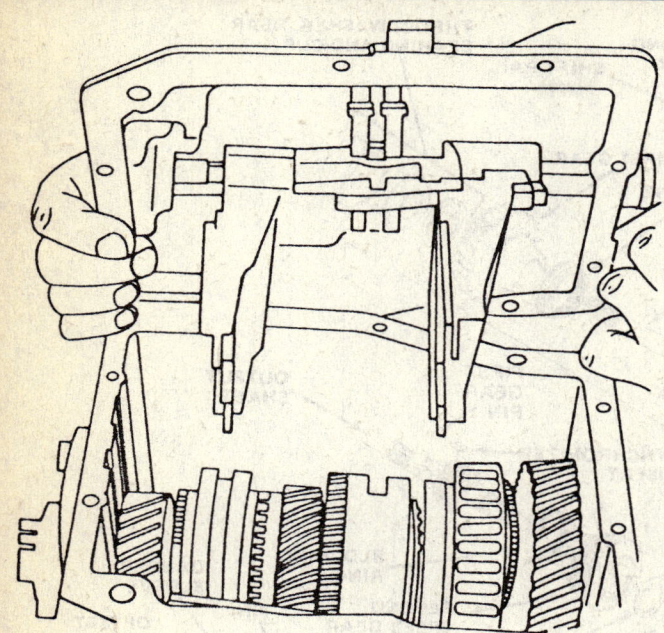

T4 transmission cover and shift fork assembly

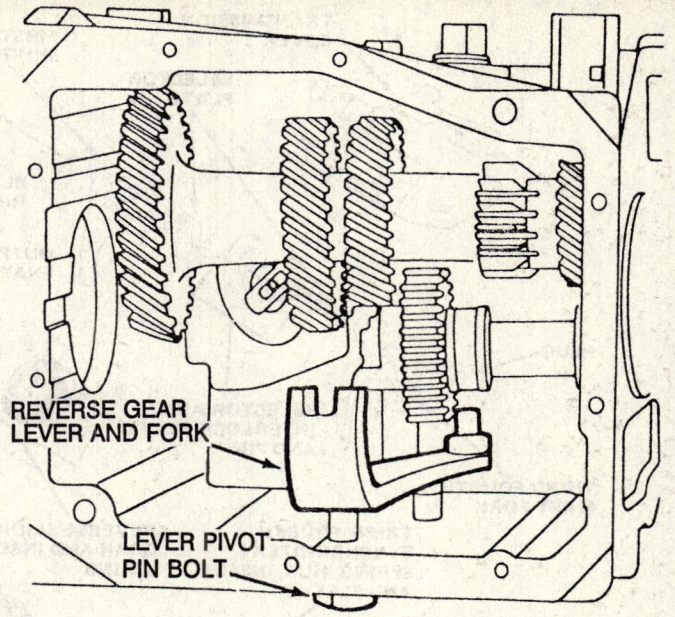

Reverse gear lever and fork assembly removal/installation on the T4

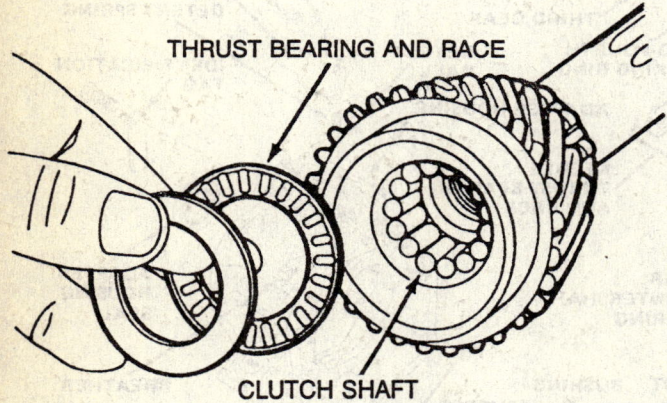

Clutch shaft thrust bearing and race removal/installation on the T4

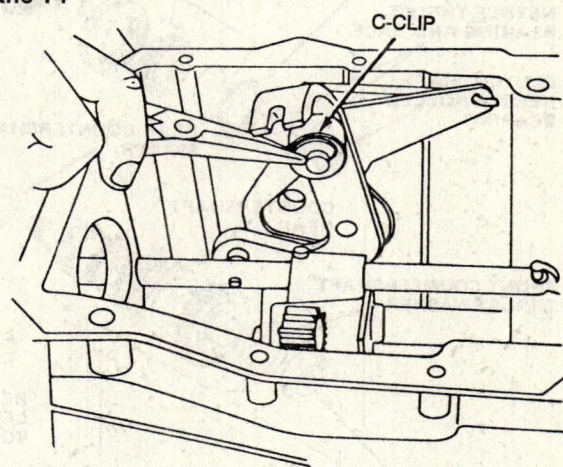

Remove the C-clip attaching the reverse gear lever to the pivot pin bolt

OUTPUT SHAFT DISASSEMBLY

1. Remove the thrust bearing washer from the front of the output shaft.
2. Scribe matchmarks on the hub and sleeve of the 3rd-4th synchronizer so that these parts may be reassembled properly.
3. Remove the 3rd-4th synchronizer blocking ring, sleeve and hub as an assembly.
4. Remove the insert springs and the inserts from the 3rd-4th synchronizer and separate the sleeve from the hub.
5. Remove the 3rd speed gear from the shaft.
6. Remove the 2nd speed gear to output shaft snapring, the tabbed thrust washer and the 2nd speed gear from the shaft.
7. Use an appropriate puller and remove the output shaft bearing.
8. Remove the 1st gear thrust washer, the roll pin, the 1st speed gear and the blocking ring.
9. Scribe matchmarks on the 1st-2nd synchronizer sleeve and the output shaft.
10. Remove the insert spring and the inserts from the 1st-reverse sliding gear, then remove the gear from the output hub.

OUTPUT SHAFT ASSEMBLY

1. Coat the output shaft and the gear bores with transmission lubricant.
2. Align the matchmarks and install the 1st-2nd synchronizer sleeve on the output shaft hub.
3. Install the three inserts and two springs into the 1st-reverse synchronizer sleeve.

NOTE: The tanged end of each spring should be positioned on the same insert but the open face of each spring should be opposite each other.

DRIVE TRAIN 7

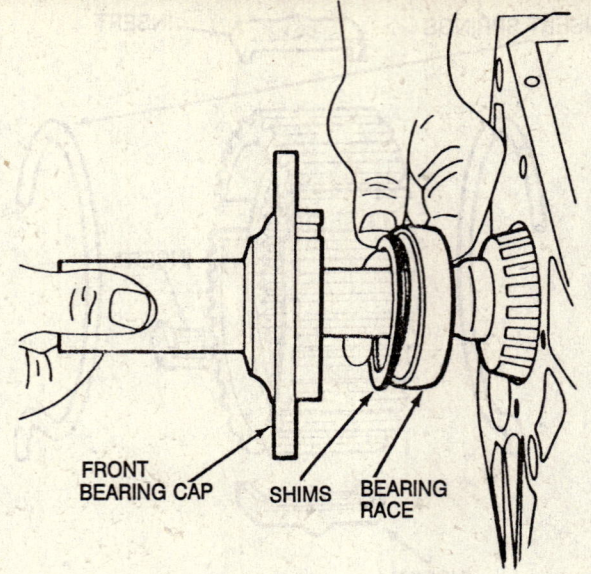

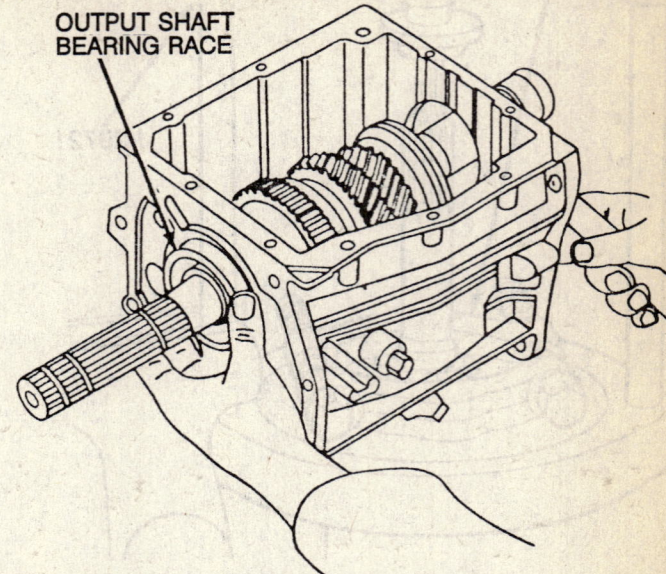

Output shaft removal/installation on the T4

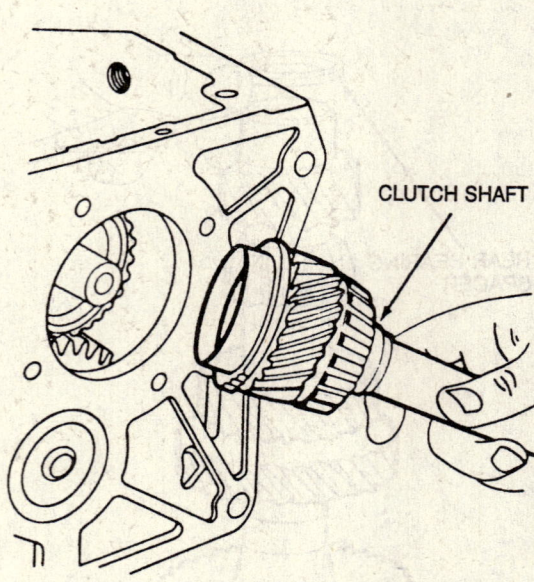

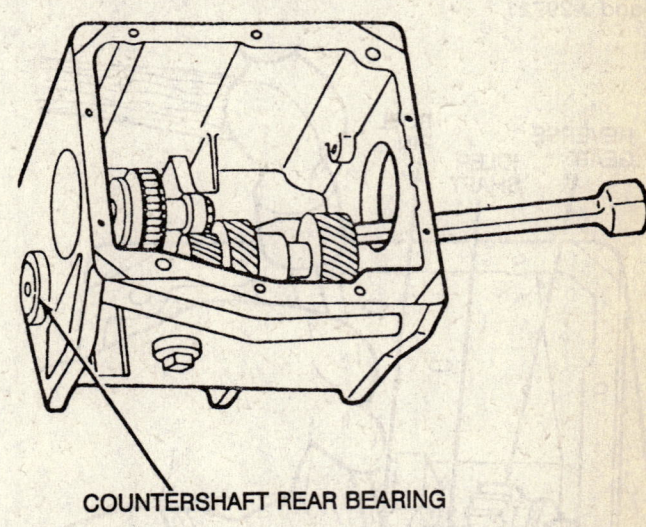

Countershaft rear bearing removal/installation on the T4

Front bearing cap and clutch shaft removal/installation on the T4

4. Install the blocking ring and the 2nd speed gear onto the output shaft.
5. Install the tabbed thrust washer and 2nd gear snapring in the output shaft; be sure that the washer is properly seated in the notch.
6. Install the blocking ring and the 1st speed gear onto the output shaft, then install the 1st gear roll pin.
7. Press the rear bearing onto the shaft.
8. Install the remaining components onto the output shaft: The 1st gear thrust washer. The 3rd speed gear. The 3rd-4th synchronizer hub inserts and the sleeve (the hub offset must face forward). The thrust bearing washer on the rear of the countershaft.

COVER & FORKS DISASSEMBLY

1. Place the selector arm plates and the shift rail centered in the Neutral position.
2. Rotate the shift rail counterclockwise until the selector arm disengages from the selector arm plates; the selector arm roll pin should now be accessible.
3. Pull the shift rail rearward until the selector contacts the 1st-2nd shift fork.
4. Use a ³⁄₁₆ in. (5mm) pin punch and remove the selector arm roll pin and the shift rail.
5. Remove the shift forks, the selector arm, the roll pin and the interlock plate.
6. Remove the shift rail oil seal and O-ring.
7. Remove the nylon inserts and the selector arm plates from the shift forks.

NOTE: Mark the position of the parts so that they may be properly installed.

7-11

7 DRIVE TRAIN

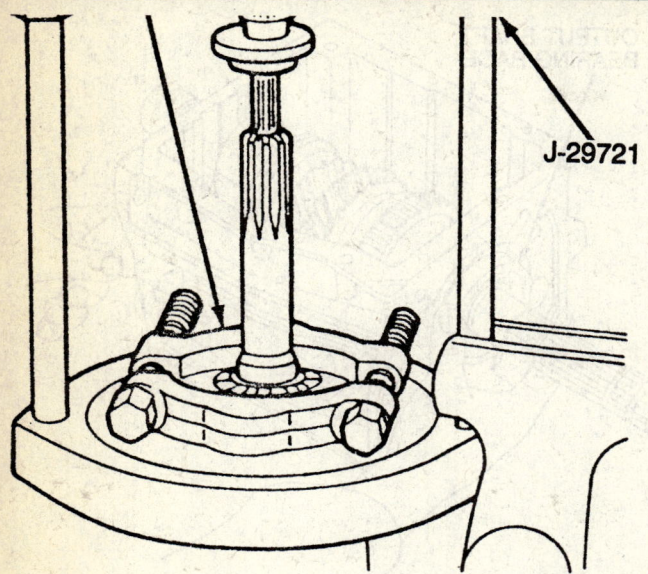

Clutch shaft bearing removal using special tools J-22912-01 and J-29721

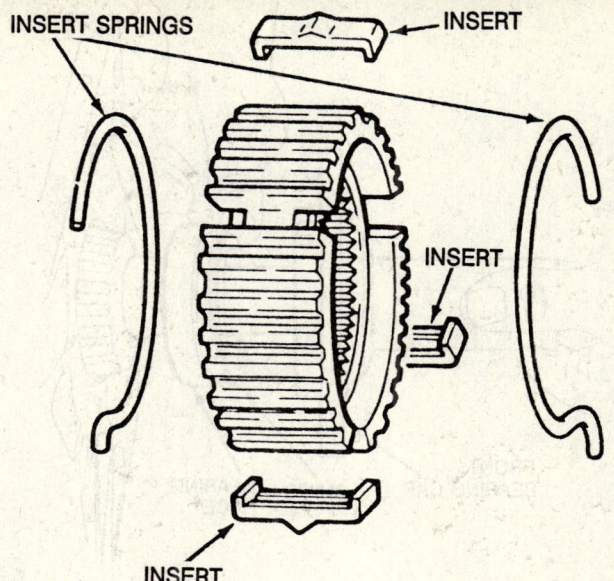

Assembling the 1–2 synchronizer on the T4

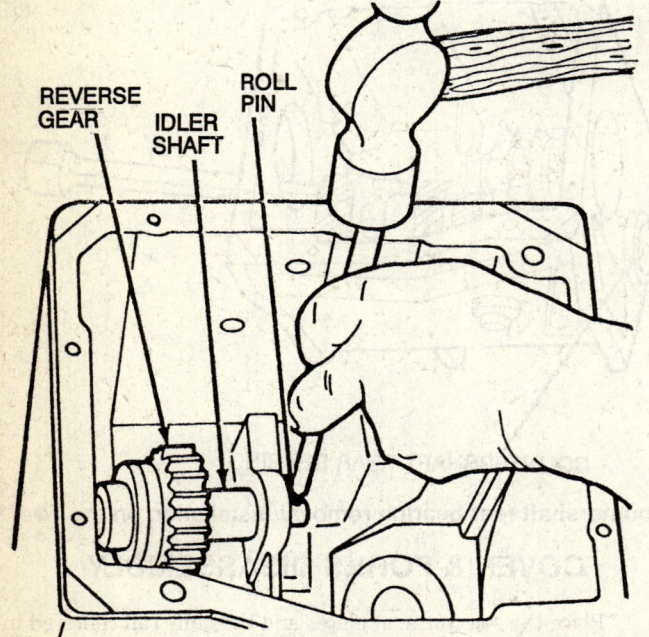

Reverse gear and idler shaft removal on the T4. Note position for installation

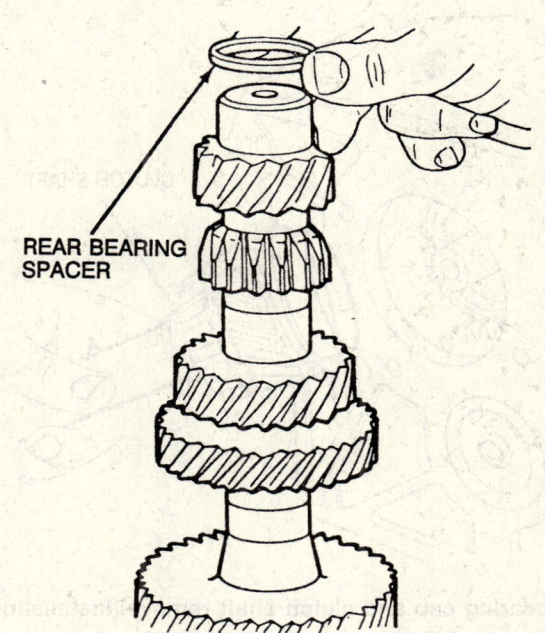

Countershaft rear bearing spacer removal/installation on the T4

COVER & FORK ASSEMBLY

1. Attach the nylon inserts to the selector arm plates and through the shift forks.
2. If removed, coat the edges of the shift rail plug with sealer and install the plug.
3. Coat the shift rail and the rail bores with petroleum jelly, then slide the shift rail into the cover until the end of the rail is flush with the inside edge of the cover.
4. Position the 1st-2nd shift fork into the cover; with the offset of the shift fork facing the rear of the cover. Push the shift rail through the fork. The 1st-2nd fork is the larger of the two forks.
5. Position the selector arm and the C-shaped interlock plate into the cover, then push the shift rail through the arm. The widest part of the interlock plate must face away from the cover and the selector arm roll pin must face downward, toward the rear of the cover.
6. Position the 3rd-4th shift fork into the cover with the fork offset facing the rear of the cover. The 3rd-4th shift selector arm plate must be positioned under the 1st-2nd shift fork selector arm plate.
7. Push the shift rail through the 3rd-4th shift fork and into the front cover rail bore.
8. Rotate the shift rail until the forward selector arm plate faces away from parallel to the cover.
9. Align the roll pin holes of the selector arm and the shift rail

DRIVE TRAIN 7

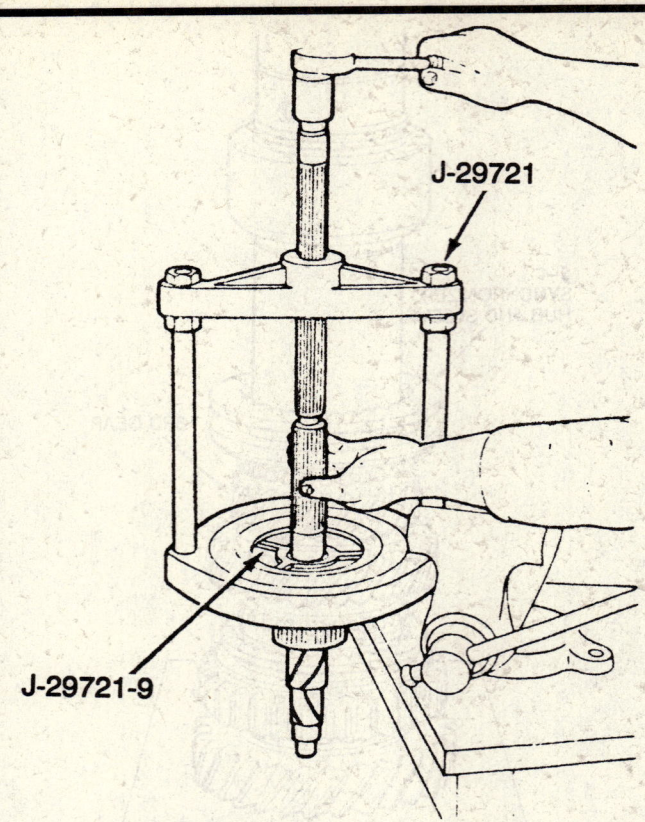

Output shaft removal using special tools J-29721 and J-29721-9

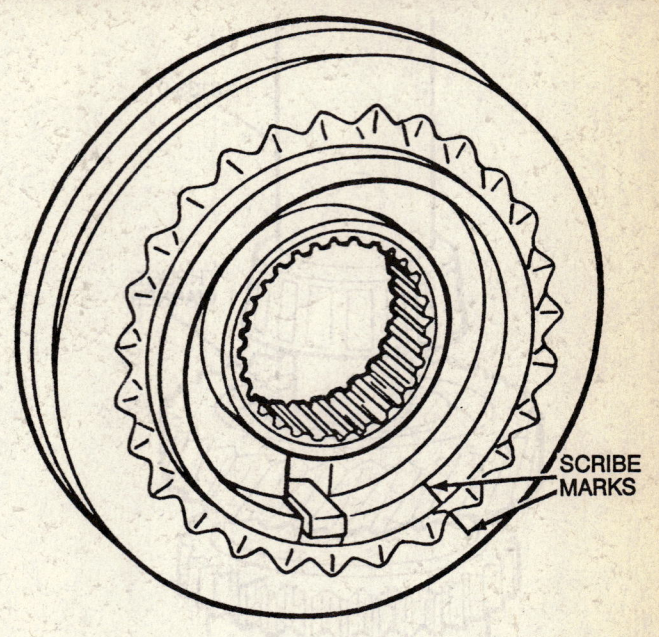

Scribe alignment marks on the 3-4 synchronizer hub and sleeve for reference during assembly

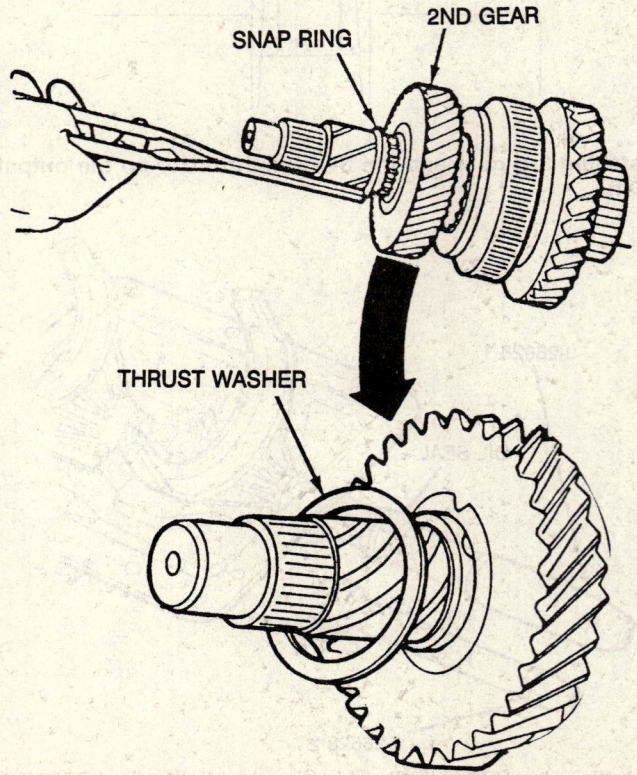

Second gear removal/installation on the T4

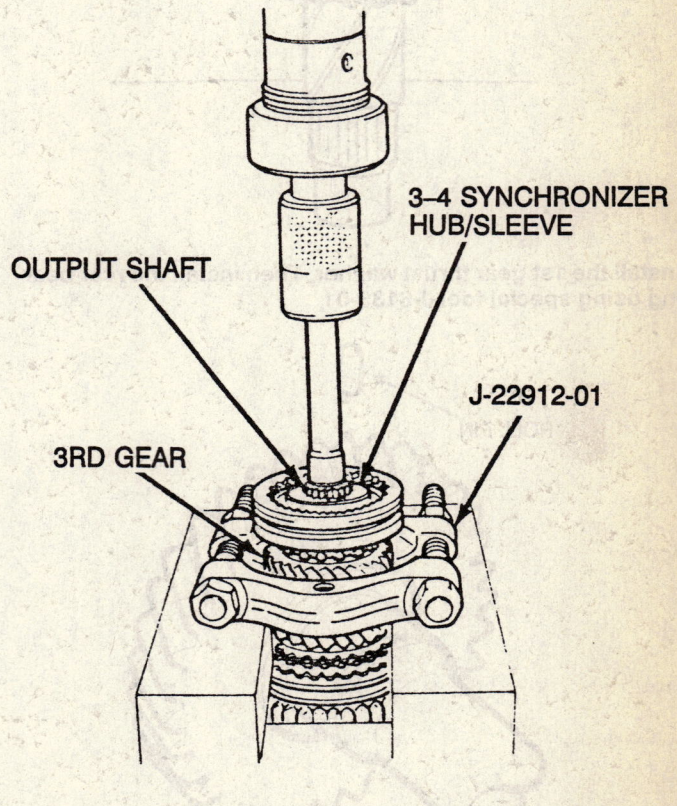

Remove the 3-4 synchronizer and 3rd gear as an assembly using tool J-22912-01

7-13

7 DRIVE TRAIN

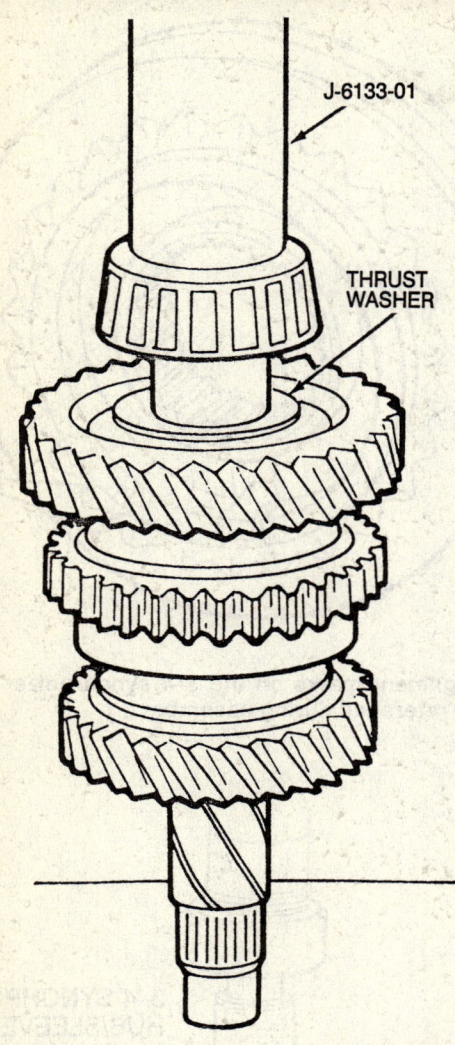

Install the 1st gear thrust washer. Then install the rear bearing using special tool J-6133-01

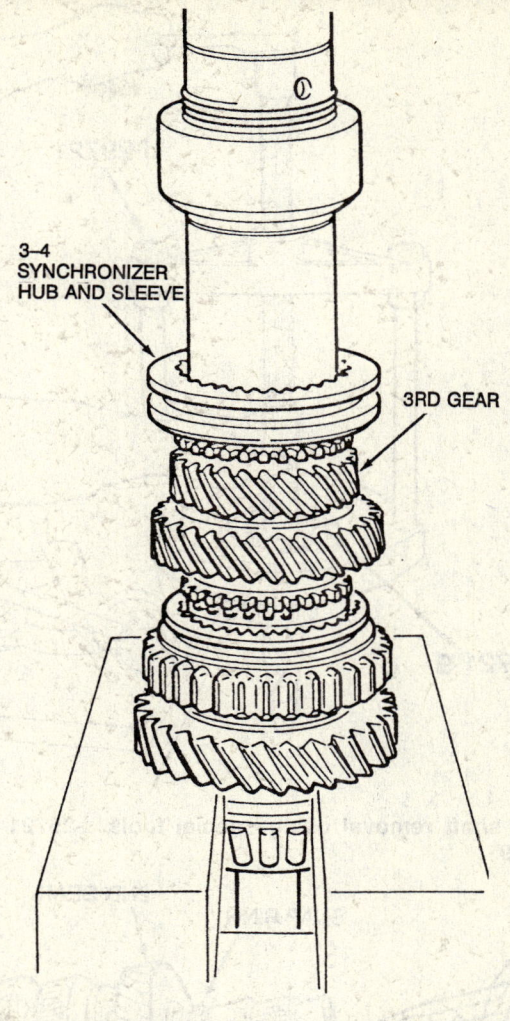

Installing 3rd gear and the 3–4 synchronizer on the output shaft

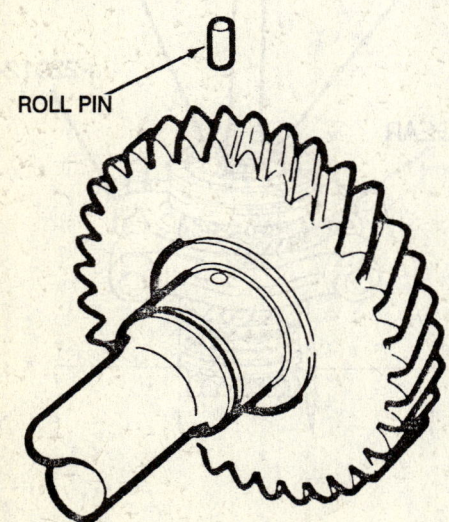

Install the 1st gear roll pin on the output shaft

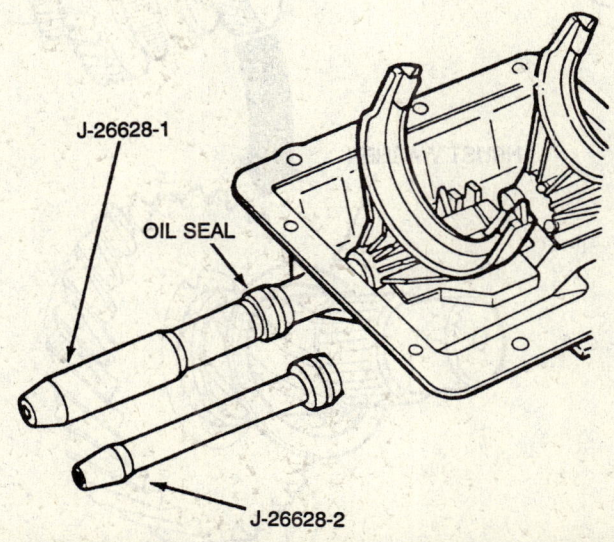

Installing the shift rail oil seal using special tools J-26628-1 and J-26628-2

7-14

DRIVE TRAIN 7

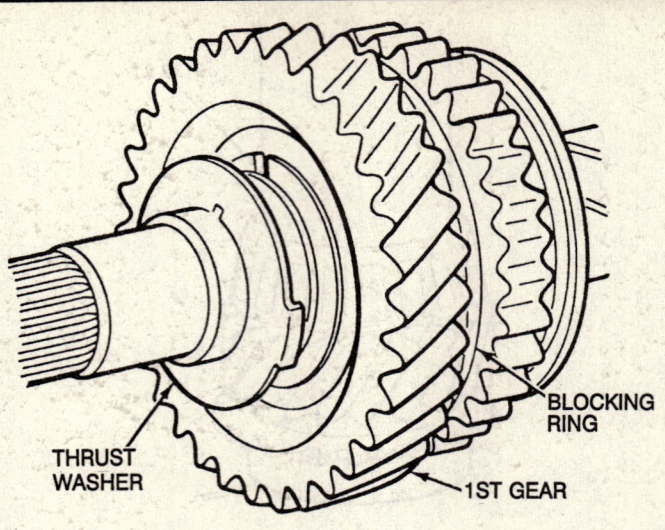

1st gear disassembly on the T4

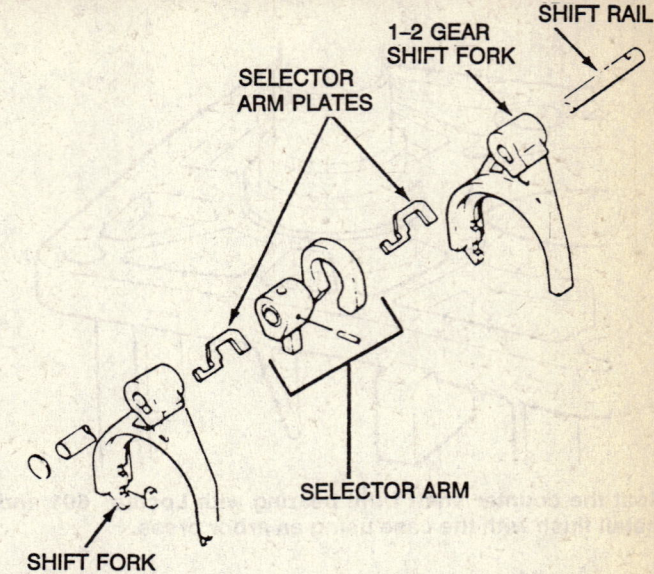

Shift fork and selector arm assembly on the T4

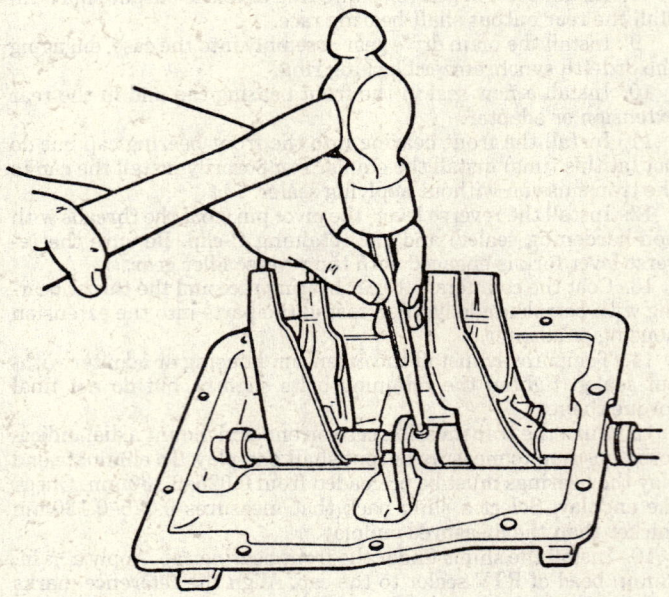

Remove the selector arm roll pin with a 3/16 in. pin punch to remove the shift rail

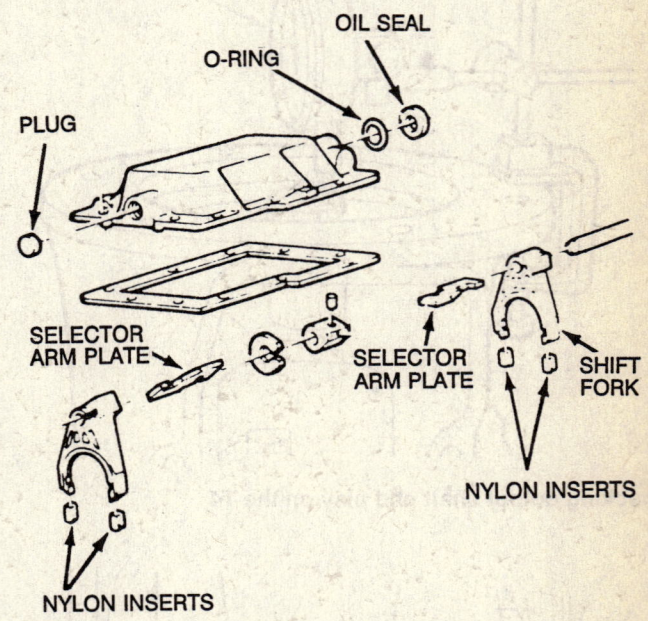

Transmission cover components on the T4

and install the roll pin. The roll pin must be installed flush with the surface of the selector arm to prevent selector arm plate to pin interference.

10. Install the O-ring into the groove of the shift rail oil seal, then install the oil seal carefully after lubricating it.

CASE ASSEMBLY

1. Apply a coat of Loctite® 601, or equivalent, to the outer cage of the front countershaft bearing, then press the bearing into the bore until it is flush with the case.
2. Apply petroleum jelly to the tabbed countershaft thrust washer and install the washer with the tab engaged in the corresponding case depression.

3. Tip the transmission case on end and install the countershaft into the front bearing bore.
4. Install the rear countershaft bearing spacer and coat the rear bearing with petroleum jelly. Install the rear countershaft bearing using the appropriate tools. The rear bearing is properly installed when 3mm is extended beyond the case surface.
5. Position the reverse idler into the case (the shift lever groove must face rearward) and install the reverse idler shaft into the case. Install the shaft retaining pin.
6. Install the output shaft assembly into the transmission case.
7. Install the main drive gear bearing onto the main drive shaft using the appropriate tools. Coat the roller bearings with petroleum jelly and install them in the main drive gear recess. Install the thrust bearing and race.

7-15

7 DRIVE TRAIN

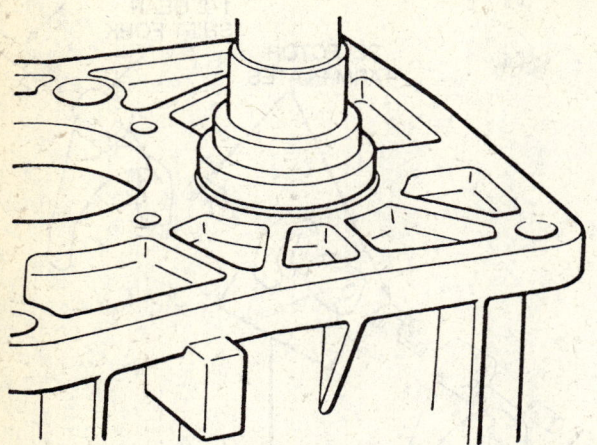

Coat the counter shaft front bearing with Loctite® 601 and install flush with the case using an arbor press.

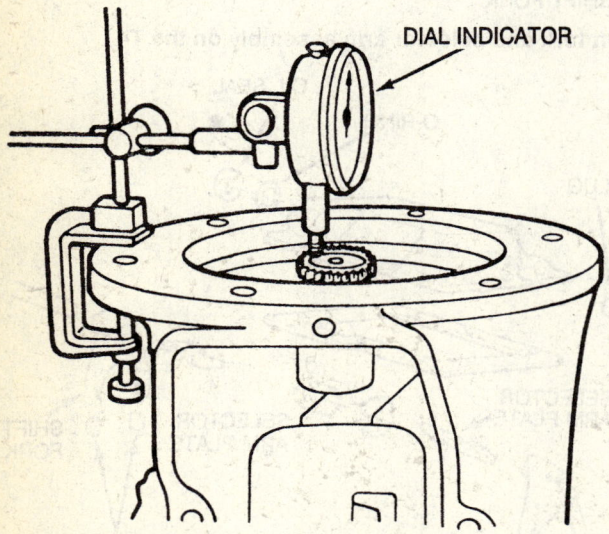

Checking output shaft end play on the T4

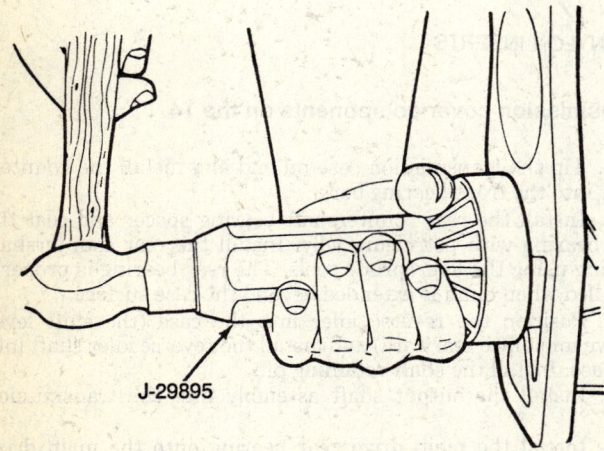

Coat the countershaft rear bearing with petroleum jelly and install with special tool J-29895

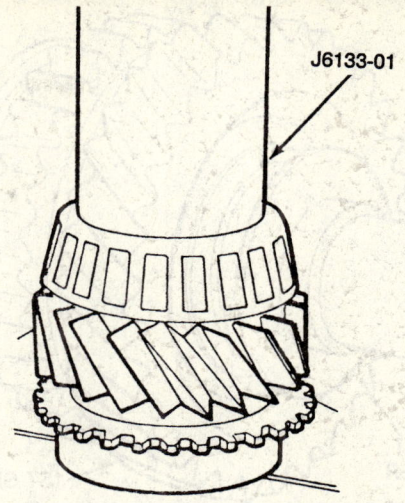

Install the clutch shaft front bearing using special tool J-6133-01

8. Install the 4th gear blocking ring onto the output shaft. Install the rear output shaft bearing race.
9. Install the main drive gear assembly into the case, engaging the 3rd-4th synchronizer blocking ring.
10. Install a new seal in the front bearing cap and in the rear extension or adapter.
11. Install the front bearing into the front bearing cap but do not (at this time) install the shims. Temporarily install the cap to the transmission without applying sealer.
12. Install the reverse lever, the pivot pin (coat the threads with non-hardening sealer) and the retaining C-clip. Be sure the reverse lever fork is engaged with the reverse idler gear.
13. Coat the countershaft rear bearing race and the thrust bearing with petroleum jelly, then install the parts into the extension housing or adapter.
14. Temporarily install the extension housing or adapter without sealer, tighten the retaining bolts slightly, but do not final torque them.
15. Turn the transmission case on end and mount a dial indicator in position to measure output shaft end play. To eliminate end play the bearings must be preloaded from 0.025–0.130mm. Check the endplay. Select a shim pack that measures 0.025–0.130mm thicker than the measured endplay.
16. Install the shims under the front bearing cap. Apply a 1/8 in. (3mm) bead of RTV sealer to the cap. Align the reference marks and install the cap on the front of the transmission. Torque the mounting bolts to 15 ft. lbs. Recheck the output shaft end play, none should exist. Adjust if necessary.
17. Remove the extension housing or adapter. Move the shift forks and synchronizer sleeves to their neutral position. Apply a 1/8 in. (3mm) bead of RTV sealer to the cover to case mounting surface. Align the forks with their sleeves and carefully lower the cover into position. Center the cover and install the alignment dowels. Install the mounting bolts and tighten to 9 ft. lbs.

NOTE: The offset lever to shift rail roll pin must be position vertically; if not, repeat Step 17.

18. Apply a 1/8 in. (3mm) bead of RTV sealer to the extension housing or adapter and install over the output shaft.

NOTE: The shift rail must be positioned so that it just enters the shift cover opening.

19. Install the detent spring into the offset lever and place the steel ball into the Neutral guide plate detent. Apply pressure to the detent spring and offset lever, then slide the offset lever on the shift rail and seat the extension housing or adapter plate against

DRIVE TRAIN 7

the transmission case. Install and tighten the mounting bolts to 25 ft. lbs.

20. Install the roll pin into the offset lever and shift rail. Install the damper sleeve in the offset lever. Coat the back up lamp switch threads with sealer and install the switch, tighten to 15 ft. lbs.

Warner T5 Overhaul

CASE DISASSEMBLY

1. Remove drain bolt on transmission case and drain lubricant.

2. Thoroughly clean the exterior of the transmission assembly.
3. Using pin punch and hammer, remove roll pin attaching offset lever to shift rail.
4. Remove extension housing-to-transmission case bolts and remove housing and offset lever as an assembly.

NOTE: Do not attempt to remove the offset lever while the extension housing is still bolted in place. The lever has a positioning lug engaged in the housing detent plate which prevents moving the lever far enough for removal.

5. Remove detent ball and spring from offset lever and remove roll pin from extension housing or offset lever.
6. Remove plastic funnel, thrust bearing race and thrust bearing from rear of countershaft.

NOTE: The countershaft rear thrust bearing, bearing washer and plastic funnel may be found inside the extension housing.

7. Remove bolts attaching transmission cover and shift fork assembly and remove cover.

NOTE: Two of the transmission cover attaching bolts are alignment-type dowel bolts. Note the location of these bolts for assembly reference.

8. Using a punch and hammer, drive the roll pin from the 5th gearshift fork while supporting the end of the shaft with a block of wood.
9. Remove 5th synchronizer gear snapring, shift fork, 5th gear synchronizer sleeve, blocking ring and 5th speed drive gear from rear of countershaft.
10. Remove snapring from 5th speed driven gear.
11. Using a hammer and punch, mark both bearing cap and case for assembly reference.
12. Remove front bearing cap bolts and remove front bearing cap. Remove front bearing race and end play shims from front bearing cap.
13. Rotate drive gear until flat surface faces countershaft and remove drive gear from transmission case.
14. Remove reverse lever C-clip and pivot bolt.
15. Remove mainshaft rear bearing race and then tilt mainshaft assembly upward and remove assembly from transmission case.
16. Unhook overcenter link spring from front of transmission case.

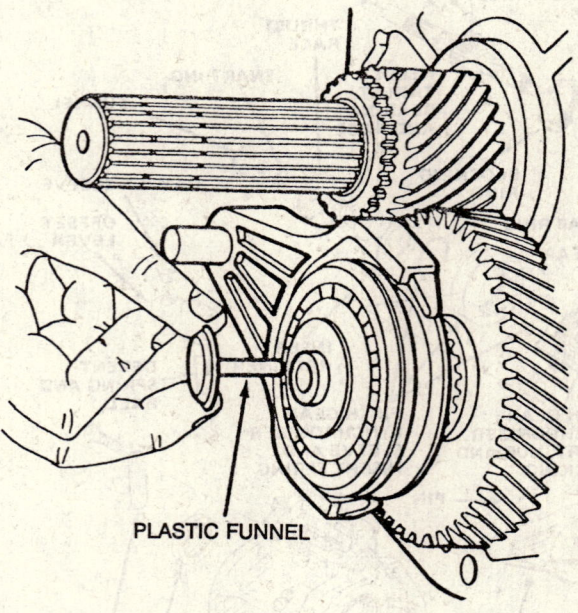

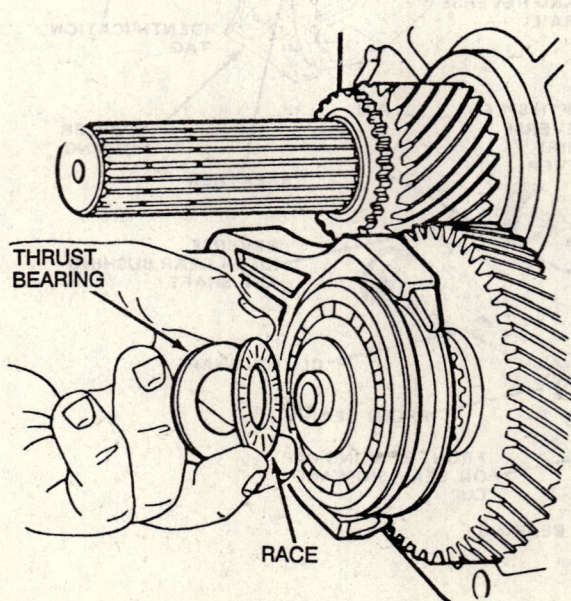

Removing the 5th gear thrust bearing and race on the T5

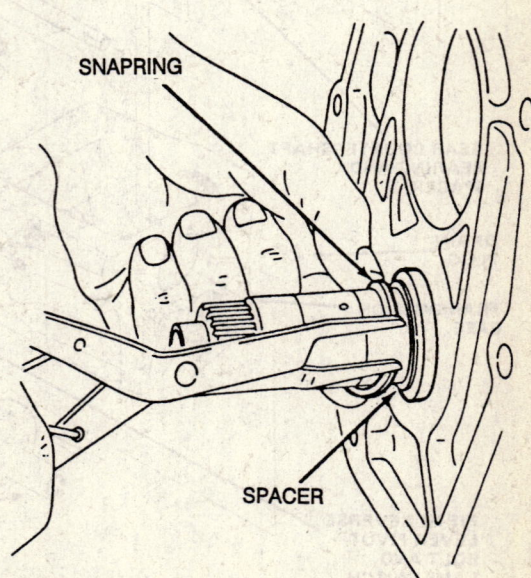

Removing the countershaft rear snapring and spacer

7-17

7 DRIVE TRAIN

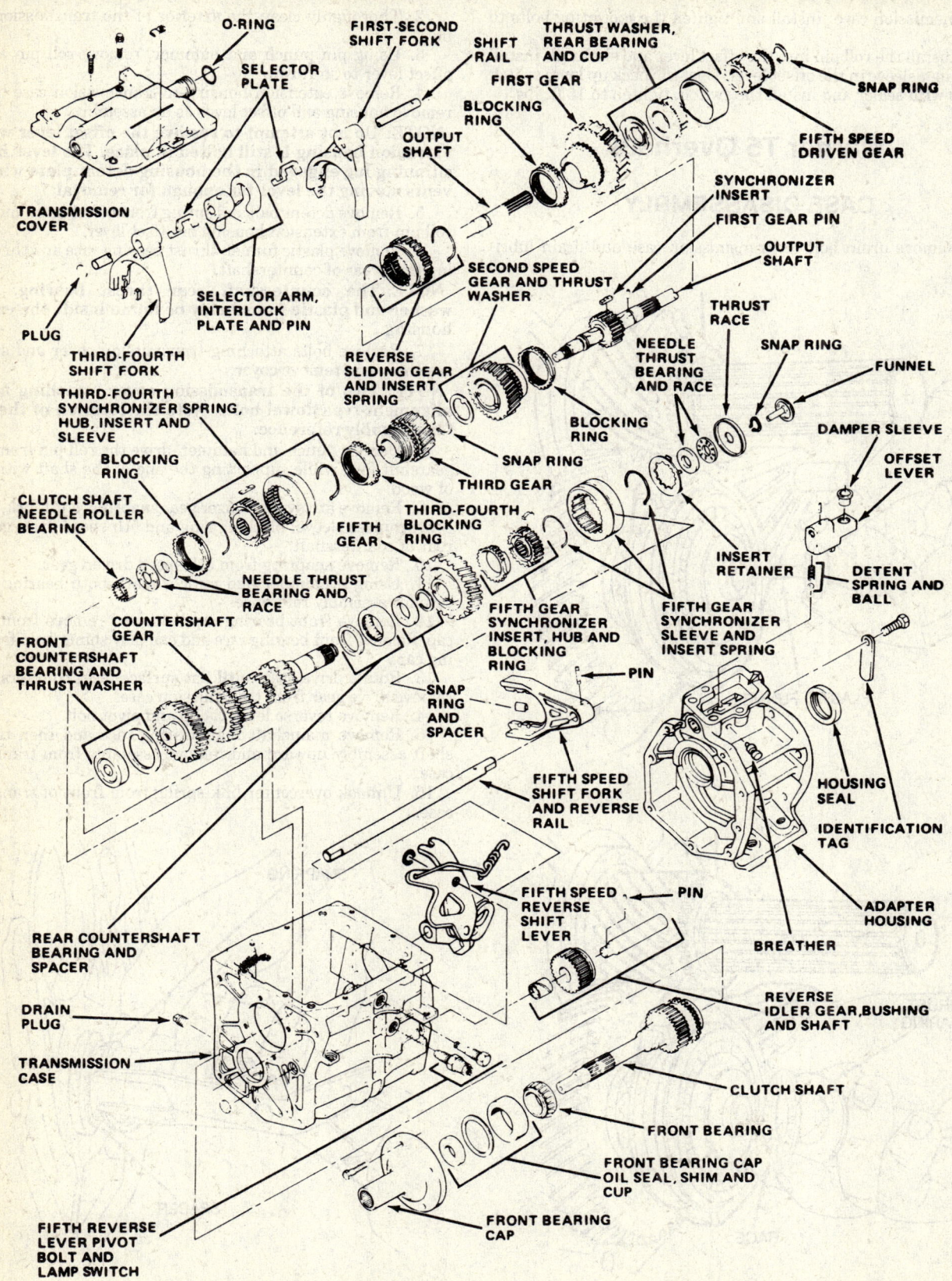

Warner T5 transmission

DRIVE TRAIN 7

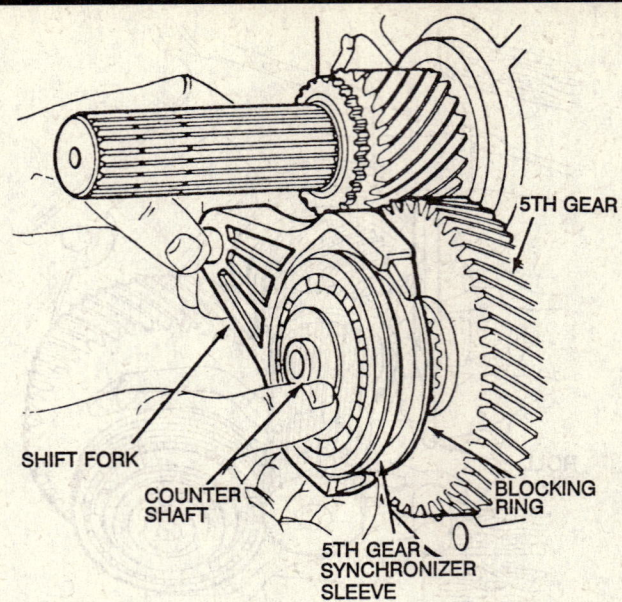

Removing the 5th gear synchronizer assembly on the T5

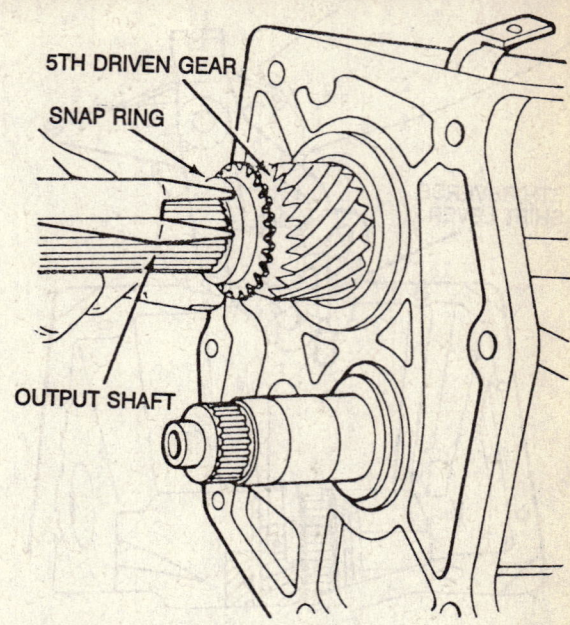

Removing the 5th gear synchronizer assembly on the T5

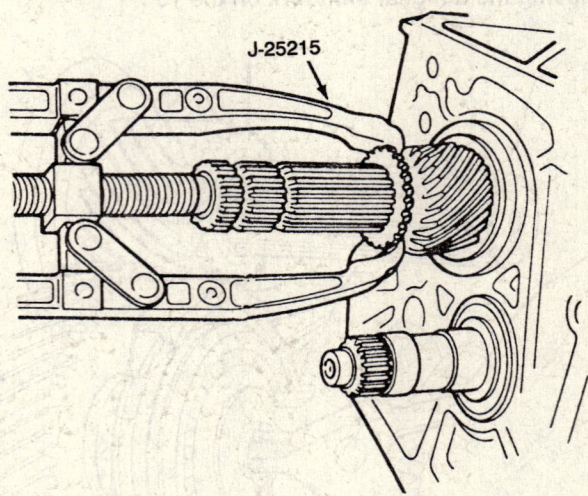

Removing the 5th gear with puller J-25215

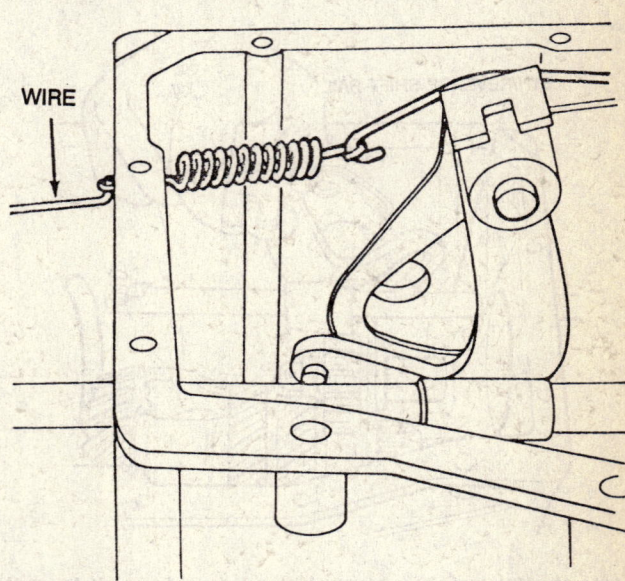

Removing the overcenter link spring with a piece of wire

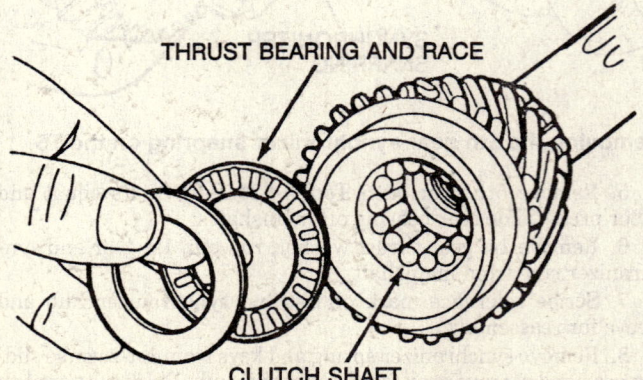

Clutch shaft thrust bearing and race removal/installation on the T5

17. Rotate 5th gear-reverse shift rail to disengage rail from reverse lever assembly. Remove shift rail from rear of transmission case.
18. Remove reverse lever and fork assembly from transmission case.
19. Using hammer and punch, drive roll pin from forward end of reverse idler shaft and remove reverse idler shaft, rubber "O" ring and gear from the transmission case.
20. Remove rear countershaft snapring and spacer.
21. Insert a brass drift through drive gear opening in front of transmission case and, using an arbor press, carefully press countershaft rearward to remove rear countershaft bearing.
22. Move countershaft assembly rearward, tilt countershaft upward and remove from case. Remove countershaft front thrust washer and rear bearing spacer.

7-19

7 DRIVE TRAIN

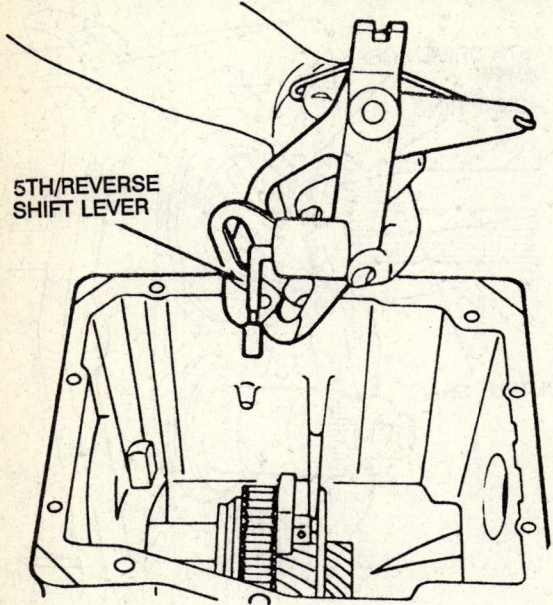

Removing the 5th/reverse gear shift lever on the T5

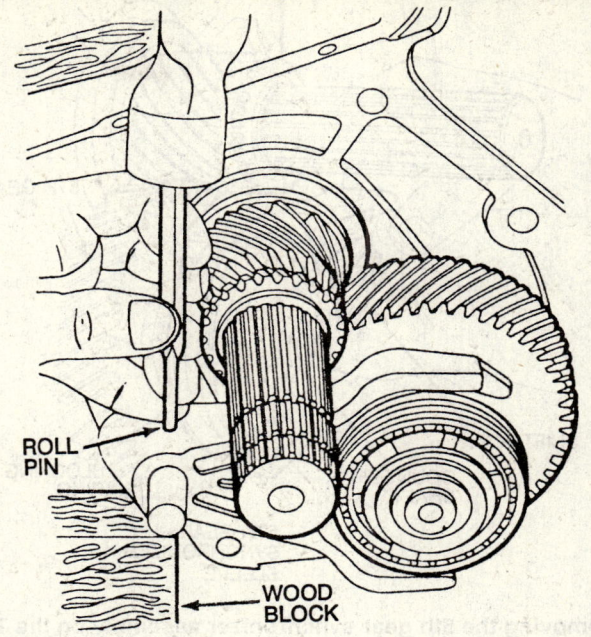

Removing the 5th gear shift fork on the T5

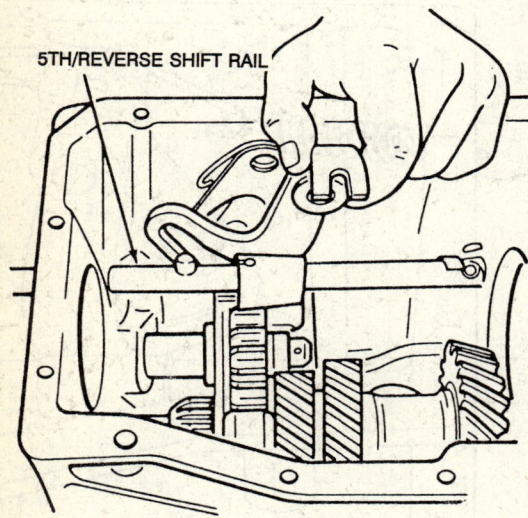

Rotate the 5th/reverse gear shift rail to release it from the gear shift lever assembly. Then remove the shift rail from the rear of the transmission case

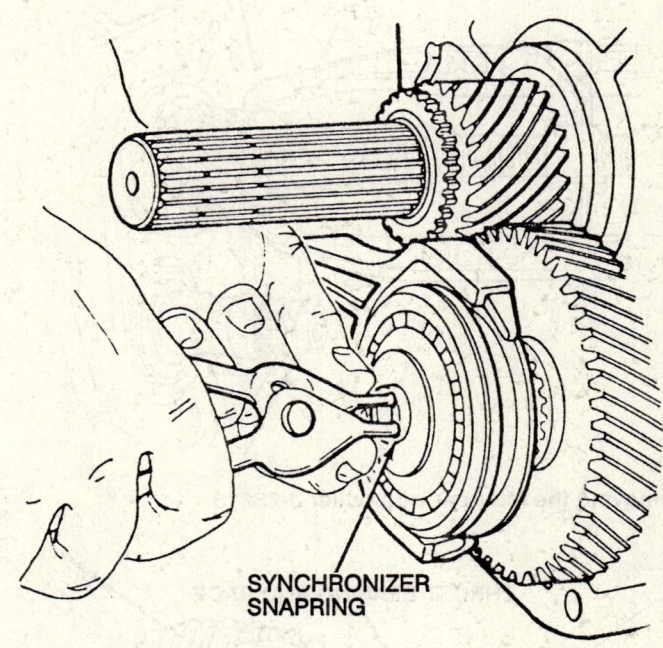

Removing the 5th gear synchronizer snapring on the T5

23. Remove countershaft front bearing from transmission case using an arbor press.

MAINSHAFT DISASSEMBLY

1. Remove thrust bearing washer from front end of mainshaft.
2. Scribe reference mark on 3rd-4th synchronizer hub and sleeve for reassembly.
3. Remove 3rd-4th synchronizer blocking ring, sleeve, hub and 3rd gear as an assembly from mainshaft.
4. Remove snapring, tabbed thrust washer, and 2nd gear from mainshaft.

5. Remove 5th gear with Tool J-22912-01 or its equal and arbor press. Slide rear bearing off mainshaft.
6. Remove 1st gear thrust washer, roll pin, 1st gear and synchronizer ring from mainshaft.
7. Scribe reference mark on 1st-2nd synchronizer hub and sleeve for reassembly.
8. Remove synchronizer spring and keys from 1st-reverse sliding gear and remove gear from mainshaft hub. Do not attempt to remove the 1st-2nd-reverse hub from mainshaft. The hub and shaft are assembled and machined as a matched set.

DRIVE TRAIN 7

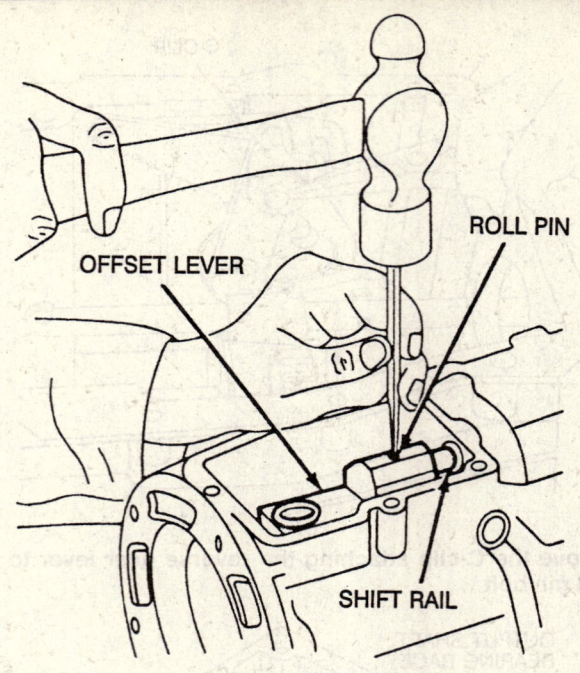

Offset lever and shift rail removal/installation on the T5

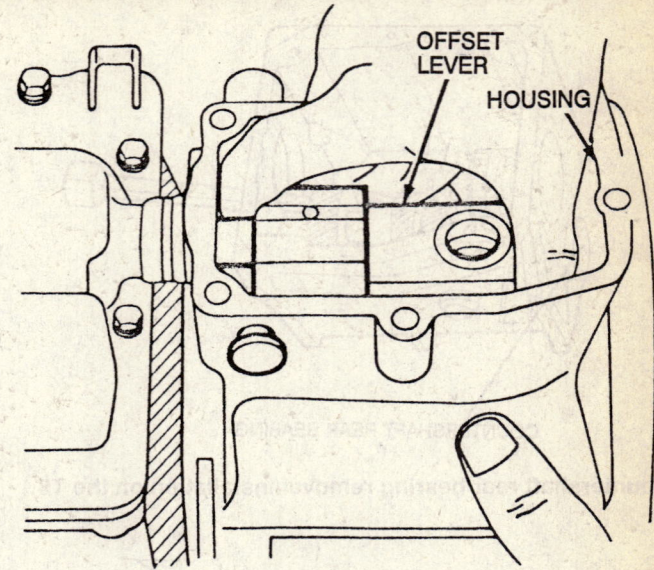

Adapter housing removal/installation on the T5

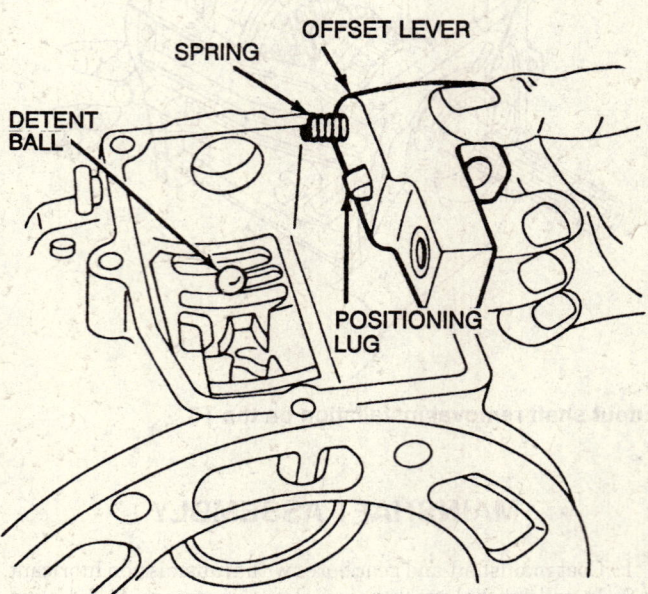

Removing the detent ball and spring from the offset lever on the T5

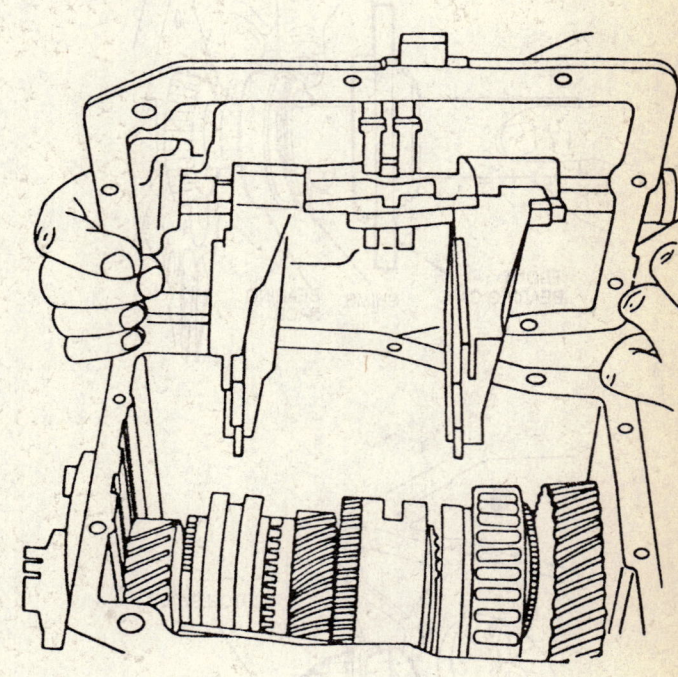

T5 transmission cover and shift fork assembly

DRIVE GEAR DISASSEMBLY

1. Remove bearing race, thrust bearing, and roller bearings from cavity of drive gear.
2. Using Tool J-22912-01 or its equal and arbor press, remove bearing from drive gear.
3. Wash parts in a cleaning solvent.
4. Inspect gear teeth and drive shaft pilot for wear.

DRIVE GEAR ASSEMBLY

1. Using Tool J-22912-01 or its equal with an arbor press, install bearing on drive gear.
2. Coat roller bearings and drive gear bearing bore with grease. Install roller bearings into bore of drive gear.
3. Install thrust bearing and race in drive gear.

7-21

7 DRIVE TRAIN

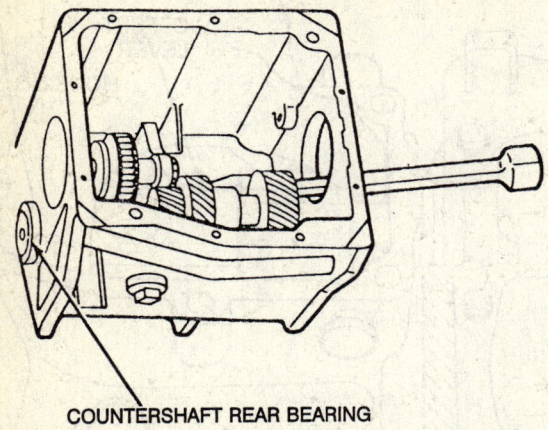

Countershaft rear bearing removal/installation on the T5

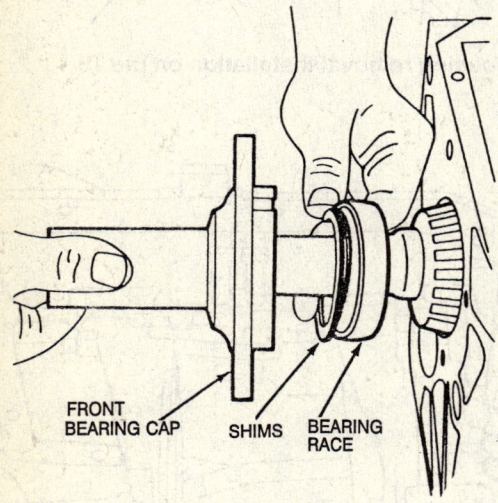

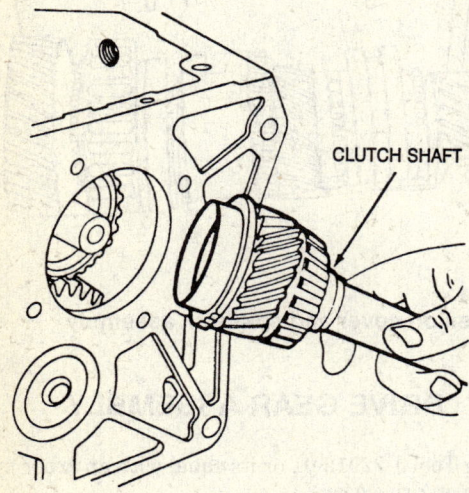

Front bearing cap and clutch shaft removal/installation on the T5

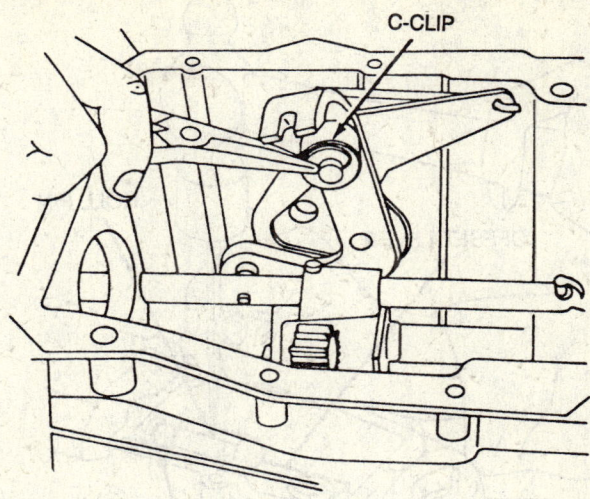

Remove the C-clip attaching the reverse gear lever to the pivot pin bolt

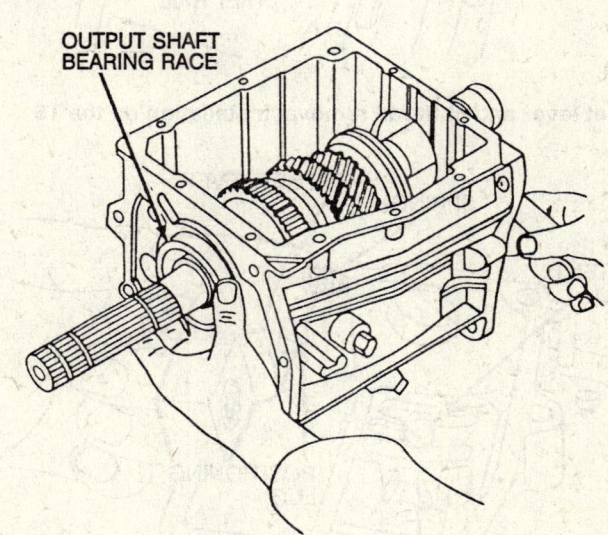

Output shaft removal/installation on the T5

MAINSHAFT ASSEMBLY

1. Coat mainshaft and gear bores with transmission lubricant.
2. Install 1st-2nd synchronizer sleeve on mainshaft hub aligning marks made at disassembly.
3. Install 1st-2nd synchronizer keys and springs. Engage tang end of each spring in same synchronizer key but position open end of springs opposite of each other.
4. Install blocker ring and 2nd gear on mainshaft. Install tabbed thrust washer and 2nd gear retaining snapring on mainshaft. Be sure washer tab is properly seated in mainshaft notch.
5. Install blocker ring and 1st gear on mainshaft. Install 1st gear roll pin and then 1st gear thrust washer.
6. Slide rear bearing on mainshaft.
7. Install 5th speed gear on mainshaft using Tool J-22912-01 and arbor press. Install snapring on mainshaft.
8. Install 3rd gear, 3rd-4th synchronizer assembly and thrust bearing on mainshaft. Synchronizer hub offset must face forward.

DRIVE TRAIN 7

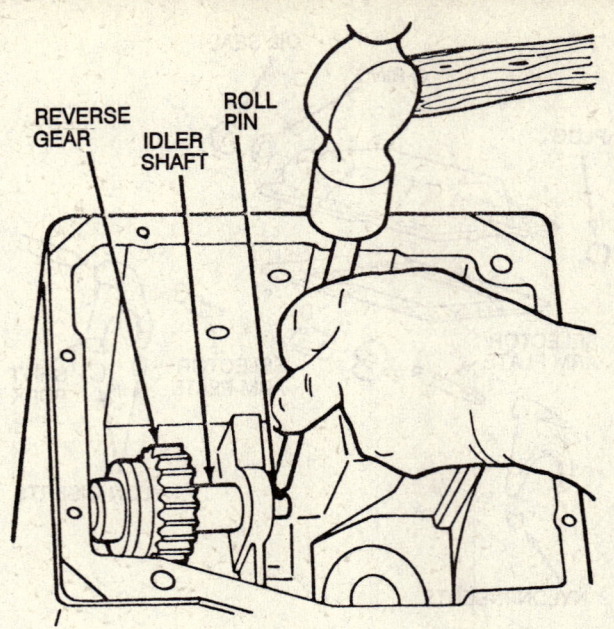

Reverse gear and idler shaft removal on the T5. Note position for installation

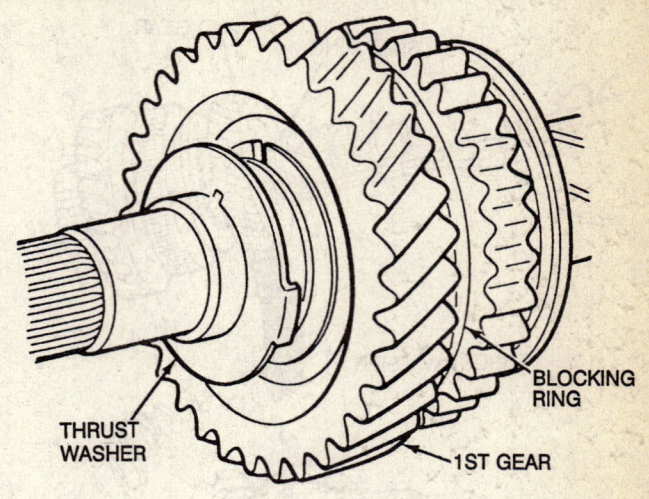

1st gear disassembly on the T5

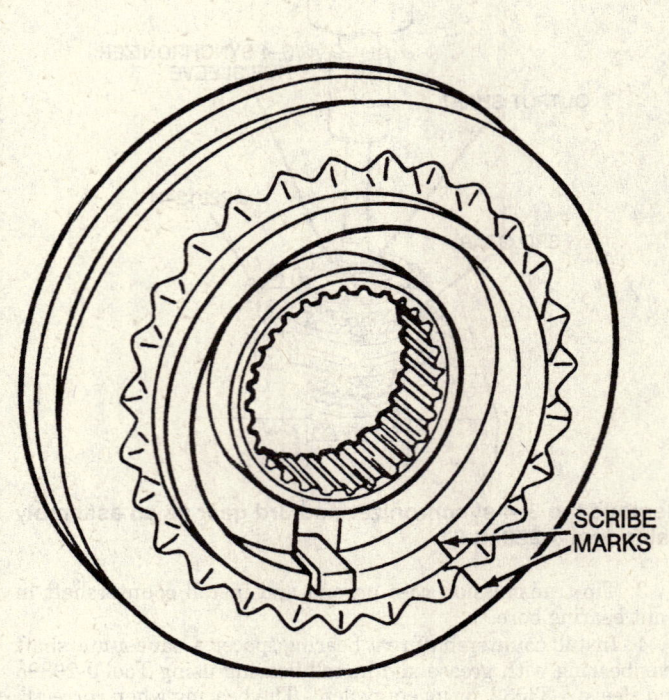

Scribe alignment marks on the 3-4 synchronizer hub and sleeve for reference during assembly

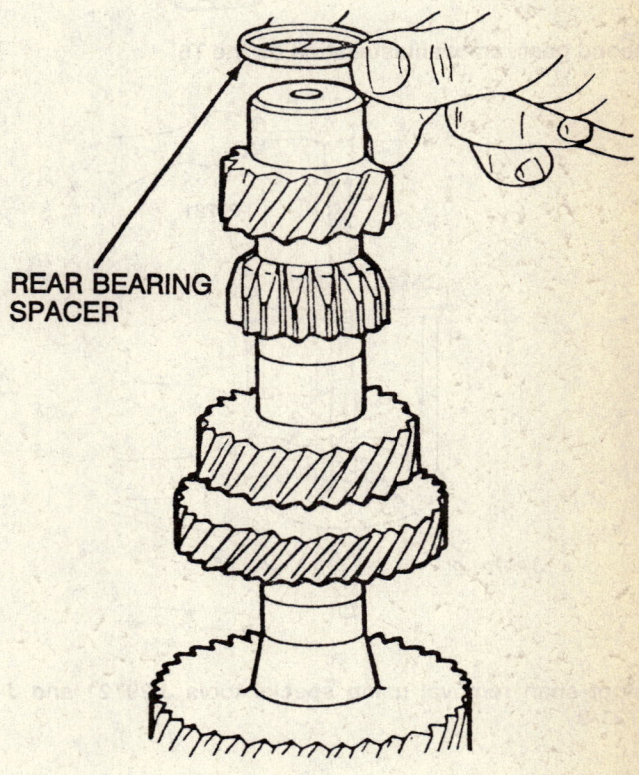

Countershaft rear bearing spacer removal/installation on the T5

7-23

7 DRIVE TRAIN

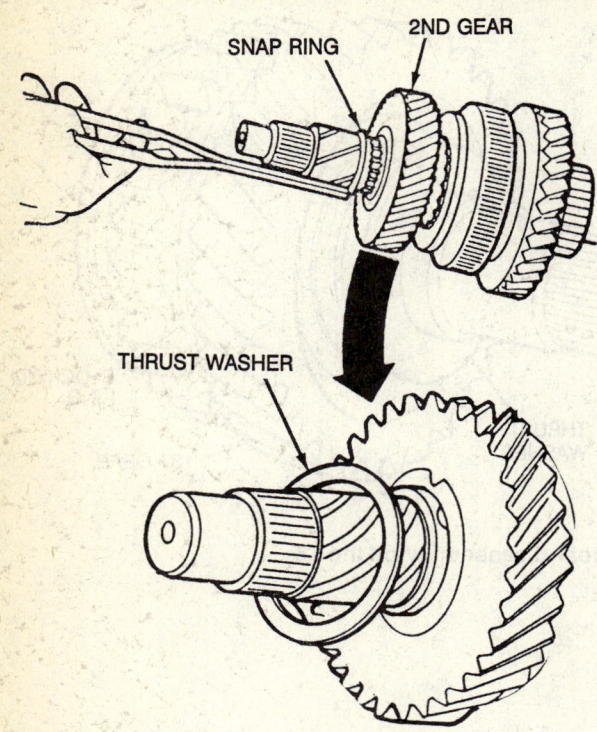

Second gear removal/installation on the T5

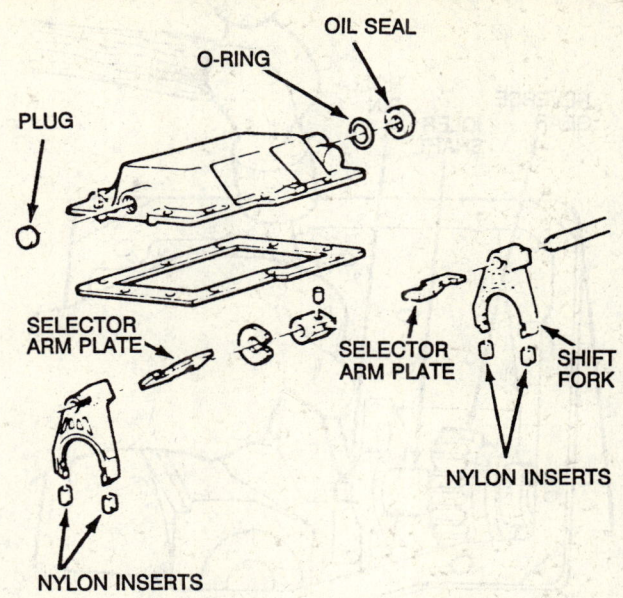

Transmission cover components on the T5

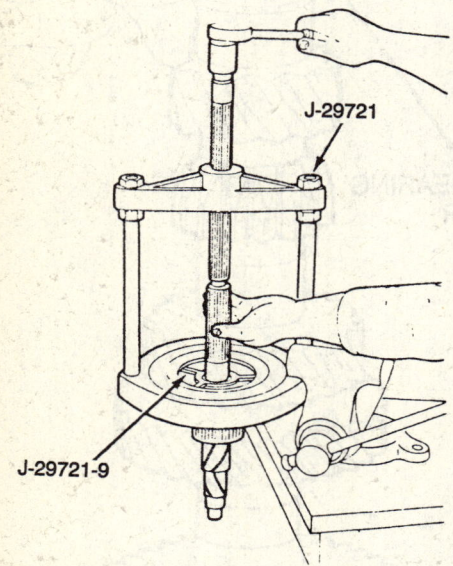

Output shaft removal using special tools J-29721 and J-29721-9

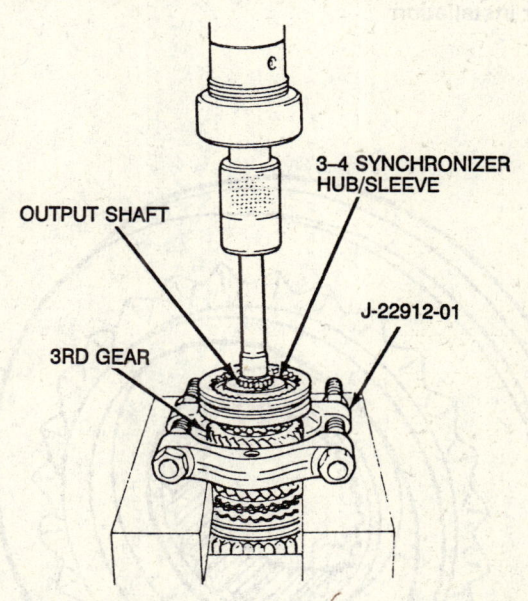

Remove the 3-4 synchronizer and 3rd gear as an assembly using tool J-22912-01

CASE ASSEMBLY

1. Coat countershaft front bearing bore with Loctite 601, or equivalent, and install front countershaft bearing flush with facing of case using an arbor press.
2. Coat countershaft tabbed thrust washer with grease and install washer so tab engages depression in case.
3. Tip transmission case on end and install countershaft in front bearing bore.
4. Install countershaft rear bearing spacer. Coat countershaft rear bearing with grease and install bearing using Tool J-29895 and sleeve J-33032, or its equivalent. The bearing when correctly installed will extend beyond the case surface 3mm.
5. Position reverse idler gear in case with shift lever groove facing rear of case and install reverse idler shaft from rear of case. Install roll pin in idler shaft.
6. Install assembled mainshaft in transmission case. Install rear mainshaft bearing race in case.
7. Install drive gear in case, and engage in 3rd-4th synchronizer sleeve and blocker ring.

DRIVE TRAIN 7

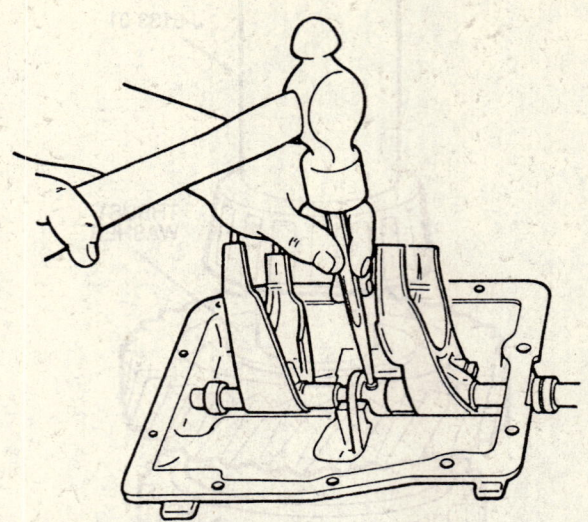

Remove the selector arm roll pin with a ³⁄₁₆ in. pin punch to remove the shift rail

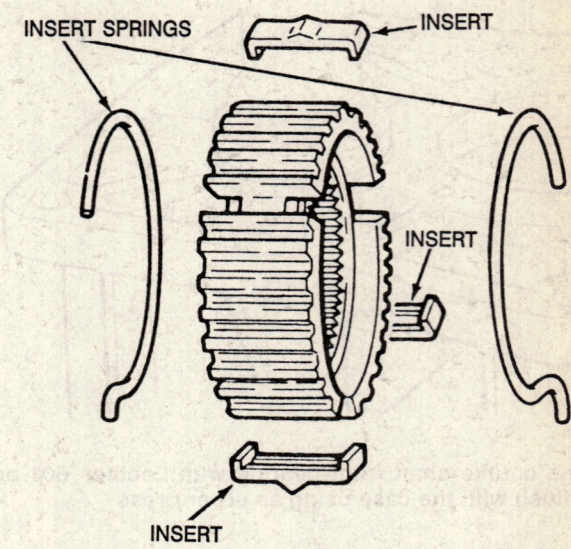

Assembling the 1-2 synchronizer on the T5

8. Install front bearing race in front bearing cap. Do not install shims in front bearing cap at this time.

9. Temporarily install front bearing cap.

10. Install 5th speed-reverse lever, pivot bolt and retaining clip. Coat pivot bolt threads with non-hardening sealer. Be sure to engage reverse lever fork in reverse idler gear.

11. Install countershaft rear bearing spacer and retaining snapring.

12. Install 5th speed gear on countershaft.

13. Insert 5th speed-reverse rail in rear of case and install in to reverse 5th speed lever. Rotate rail during installation to simplify engagement with lever. Connect spring to front of case.

14. Position 5th gear shift fork on 5th gear synchronizer assembly and install synchronizer on countershaft and shift fork on shift rail. Make sure roll pin hole in shift fork and shift rail are aligned.

15. Support 5th gear shift rail and fork on a block of wood and install roll pin.

16. Install thrust race against 5th speed synchronizer hub and install snapring. Install thrust bearing against race on countershaft. Coat both bearing and race with petroleum jelly.

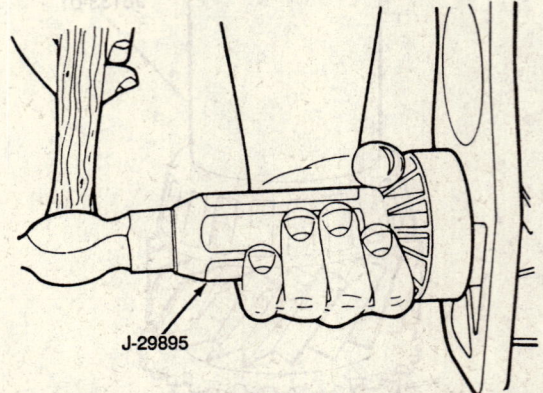

Coat the countershaft rear bearing with petroleum jelly and install with special tool J-29895

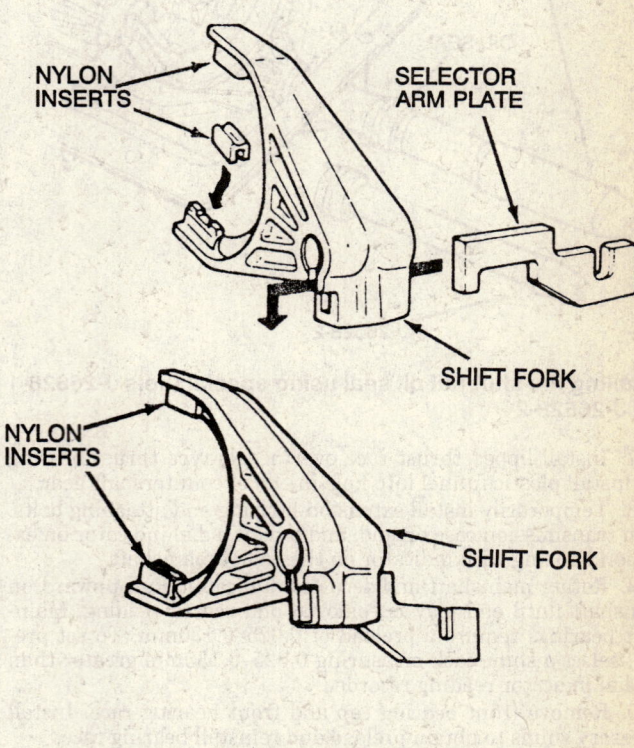

Shift fork assembly on the T5

7-25

7 DRIVE TRAIN

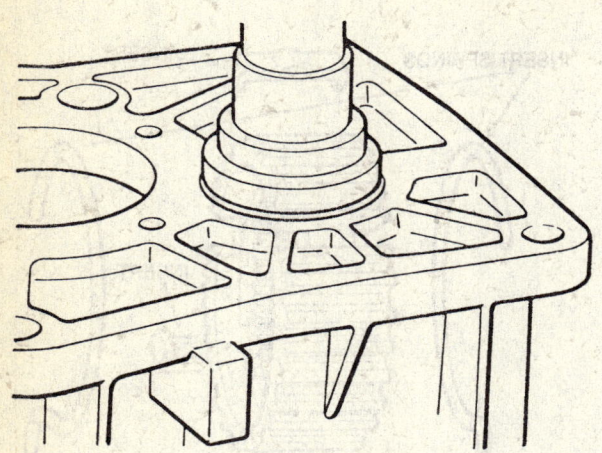

Coat the countershaft front bearing with Loctite® 601 and install flush with the case using an arbor press

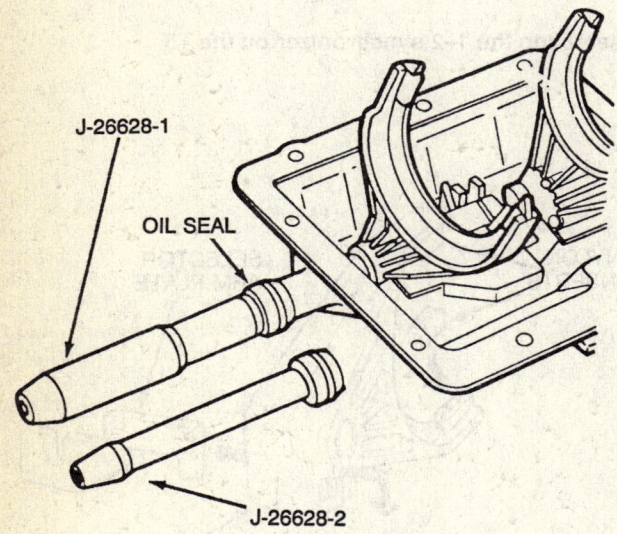

Installing the shift rail oil seal using special tools J-26628-1 and J-26628-2

17. Install lipped thrust race over needle-type thrust bearing and install plastic funnel into hole in end of countershaft gear.
18. Temporarily install extension housing and attaching bolts. Turn transmission case on end, and mount a dial indicator on extension housing with indicator on the end of mainshaft.
19. Rotate mainshaft and zero dial indicator. Pull upward on mainshaft until end play is removed and record reading. Mainshaft bearings require a preload of 0.025–0.130mm. To set preload, select a shim pack measuring 0.025–0.130mm greater than the dial indicator reading recorded.
20. Remove front bearing cap and front bearing race. Install necessary shims to obtain preload and reinstall bearing race.
21. Apply a $1/8$ in. (3mm) bead of RTV sealant, #732 or equivalent, on case mating surface of front bearing cap. Install bearing cap aligning marks made during disassembly and torque bolts to specification.
22. Remove extension housing.
23. Move shift forks on transmission cover and synchronizer sleeves inside transmission to the neutral position.

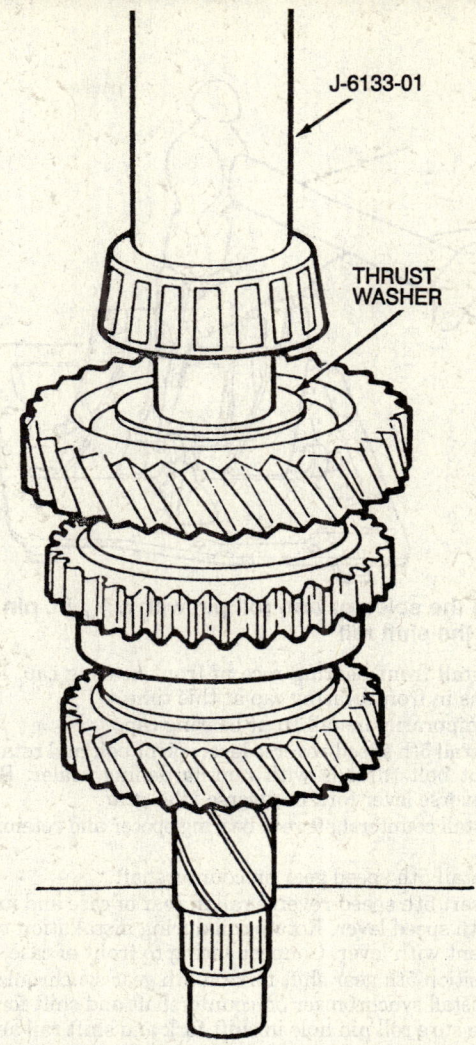

Install the 1st gear thrust washer. Then install the rear bearing using special tool J-6133-01

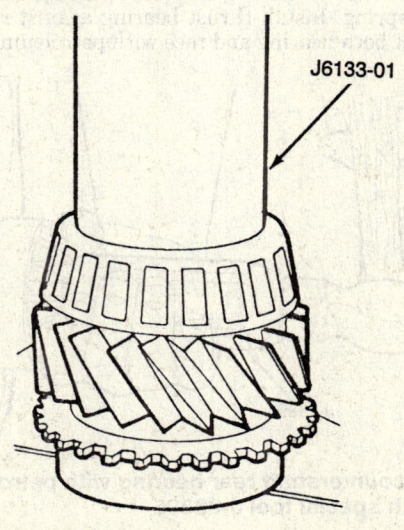

Install the clutch shaft front bearing using special tool J-6133-01

DRIVE TRAIN 7

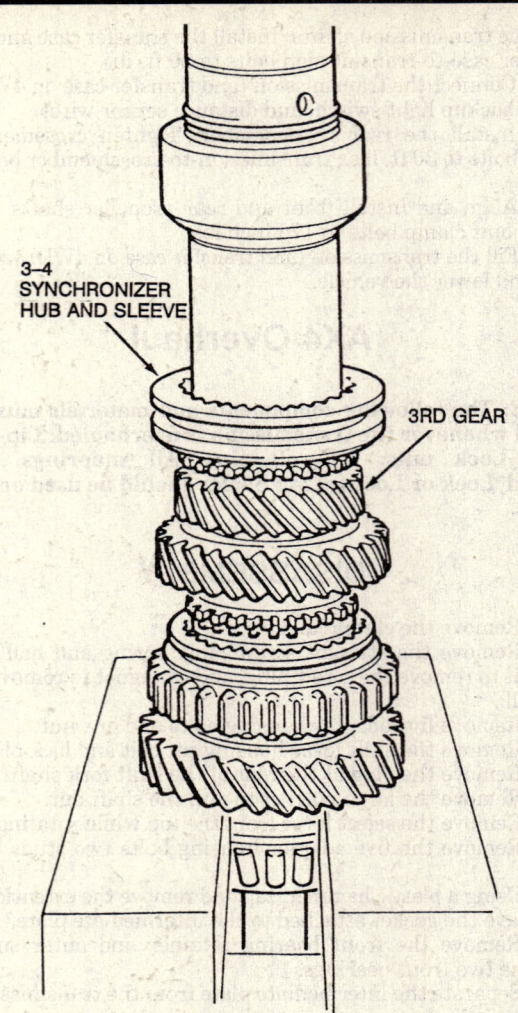

Installing 3rd gear and the 3-4 synchronizer on the output shaft

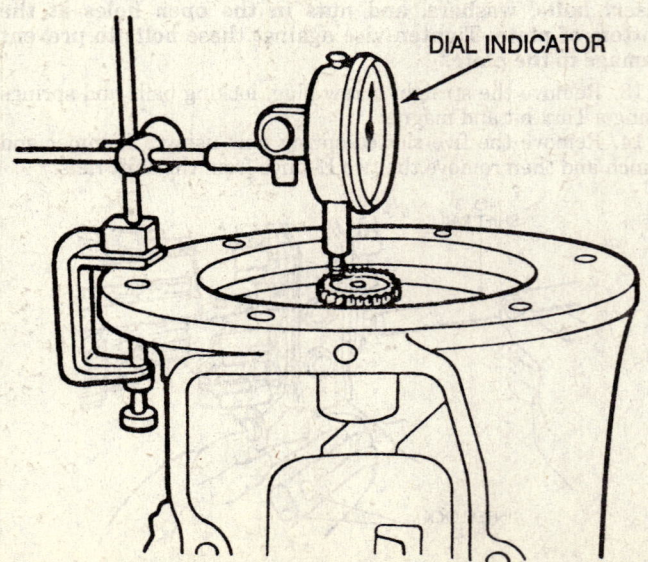

Checking output shaft end play on the T5

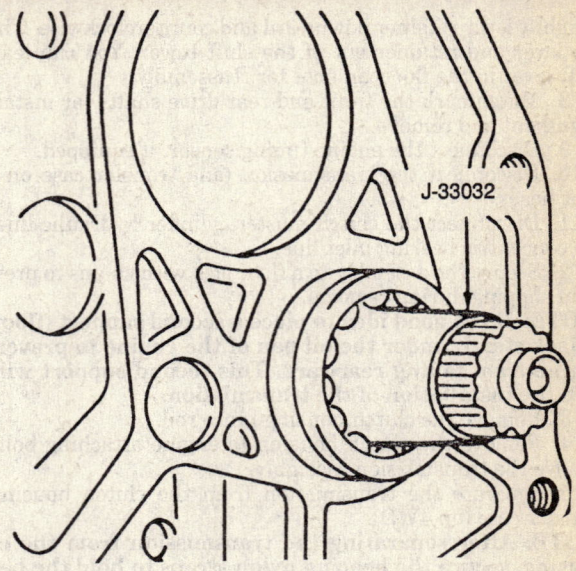

Installing the countershaft rear bearing using protector sleeve tool J-33032

24. Apply a 1/8 in. (3mm) bead of RTV sealant, #732 or equivalent, on cover mating surface of transmission.
25. Lower cover onto case while aligning shift forks and synchronizer sleeves. Center cover and install the 2 dowel bolts. Install remaining bolts and torque to specification. The offset lever to shift rail roll pin hole must be in the vertical position after cover installation.
26. Apply a 1/8 in. (3mm) bead of RTV Sealant, #732 or equivalent, on extension housing to transmission case mating surface.
27. Install extension housing over mainshaft and shift rail to a position where shift rail just enters shift cover opening.
28. Install detent spring into offset lever and place steel ball in neutral guide plate detent. Position offset lever on steel ball and apply pressure on offset lever and at the time seat extension housing against transmission case.
29. Install extension housing bolts and torque to specification.
30. Align and install roll pin in offset lever and shift rail.
31. Fill transmission to its proper level with lubricant.

AX4/5/15

REMOVAL AND INSTALLATION

1. Shift the transmission into first or third gear.
2. Raise and support the vehicle safely.
3. Support the transmission with a floor jack and remove the rear crossmember.

   CHILTON TIP: *Tool manufacturers now have available a transmission cradle to fit most floor jacks. This cradle allows the transmission to be tilted horizontally and vertically, thus, easing installation.*

4. Disconnect the transmission shift linkage, speedometer cable, transfer case vacuum lines (on 4WD) and clutch hydraulic lines.
5. Lower the transmission assembly no more than 3 inches for access to the shift lever.
6. Reach up and around the transmission case to unseat the shifter lever dust boot from the transmission shift tower. Move the boot upward on the shift lever for access to the retainer that secures the lever in the tower.
7. Disengage the shift lever from the transmission by pressing

7 DRIVE TRAIN

the shift lever retainer downward and counterclockwise. Then lift the lever and retainer out of the shift tower. You can leave the shift lever in the floorpan boot for reassembly.

8. Matchmark the front and rear drive shafts for installation alignment and remove.
9. Disconnect the engine timing sensor, if equipped.
10. Disconnect the transmission (and transfer case on 4WD) vent hoses.
11. Disconnect the clutch master cylinder hydraulic line from the concentric bearing inlet line.
12. Secure the assembly to a floor jack with chains to prevent it from slipping during removal.

NOTE: It is a good idea to place a second support (floor jack or jack stand) under the oil pan of the engine to prevent the engine from falling rearward. This second support will also ease the installation of the transmission.

13. Remove the clutch housing brace rod.
14. Remove the clutch housing to engine attaching bolts and remove the transmission assembly.
15. Separate the transmission from the clutch housing and transfer case (on 4WD).

NOTE: After separating the transmission from the clutch housing, secure the bearing nylon straps to hold the bearing piston in place.

To Install:
16. Install the clutch housing on the transmission. Tighten the housing bolts to 27 ft.lbs.
17. Install the concentric bearing. Secure the bearing to the mounting pin with a new retainer clip.
18. Mount the transmission on a floor jack, lightly lubricate the input shaft and install the transmission.
19. Install and tighten the clutch housing-to-engine bolts to 28 ft. lbs.

NOTE: Be sure the housing is properly seated against the engine block before tightening the attaching bolts.

20. Lower the transmission no more than 3 inches to allow installation of the shifter. Insert the shift lever in the shift tower. Press the lever retainer downward and turn clockwise to lock in place. Install the lever dust boot on the shift tower.
21. Connect the concentric bearing hydraulic line and the engine timing sensor wires.
22. Mount the transfer case (if equipped) on a jack and align with the transmission shafts. Install the transfer case and tighten transfer case-to-transmission bolts to 26 ft. lbs.
23. Connect the transmission (and transfer case on 4WD) vent hoses, backup light switch, and distance sensor wires.
24. Install the rear crossmember. Tighten crossmember-to-frame bolts to 30 ft. lbs.; transmission-to-crossmember bolts to 33 ft. lbs.
25. Align and install front and rear propeller shafts. Tighten the U-joint clamp bolts to 170 inch lbs.
26. Fill the transmission (and transfer case on 4WD) with lubricant and lower the vehicle.

AX4 Overhaul

NOTE: The following components and materials must be replaced whenever the transmission is overhauled: Lip-type oil seals. Lock nuts. All roll pins. All snaprings. Loctite Thread®Lock or Loctite®242 Sealer should be used on all fasteners.

DISASSEMBLY

1. Remove the clutch housing.
2. Remove the straight screw plug, spring and ball using a Torx bit to remove the screw plug, and a magnet to remove spring and ball.
3. Remove five adapter housing bolts and one nut.
4. Remove the shift lever housing set bolt and lock plate.
5. Remove the plug at the rear of the shift fork shaft.
6. Remove the large magnet to pull the shaft out.
7. Remove the select lever from the top while rotating.
8. Remove the five adapter housing bolts two studs and one nut.
9. Using a plastic hammer, tap and remove the extension housing. Leave the gasket attached to the intermediate plate.
10. Remove the front bearing retainer and outer snaprings from the two front bearings.
11. Separate the intermediate plate from the transmission case using a small plastic hammer and remove the case.
12. Mount the intermediate plate in a vise. Be careful not to damage the plate.

NOTE: Before placing the intermediate plate in a vise, insert bolts, washers, and nuts in the open holes at the bottom of plate. Tighten vise against these bolts to prevent damage to the plate.

13. Remove the straight screw plug, locking balls and springs using a Torx bit and magnet.
14. Remove the five slotted spring pins using a hammer and punch and then remove the two E-rings from the shift rails.

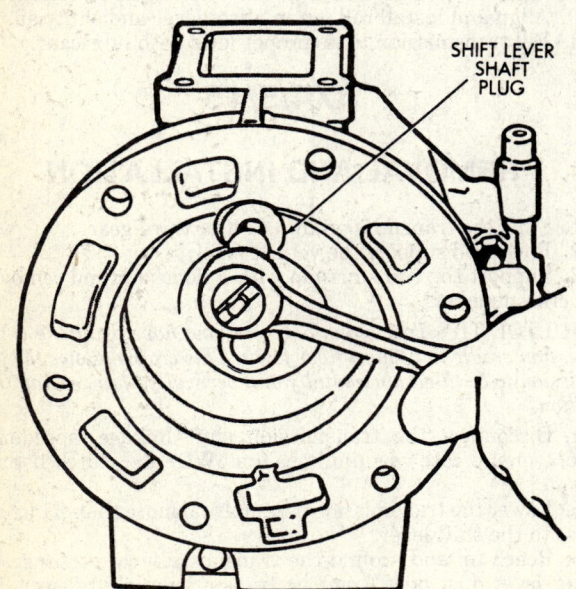

Removing the shift lever shaft plug from the AX4

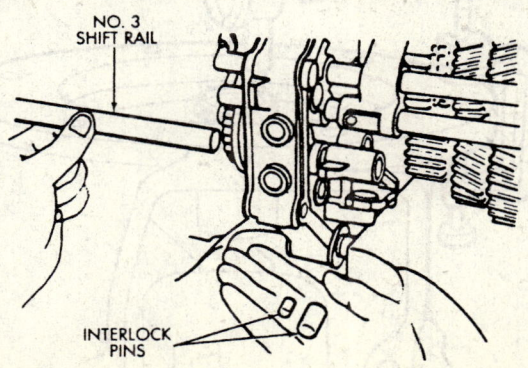

Removing the No. 3 shift rail and interlock pin from the AX4

DRIVE TRAIN 7

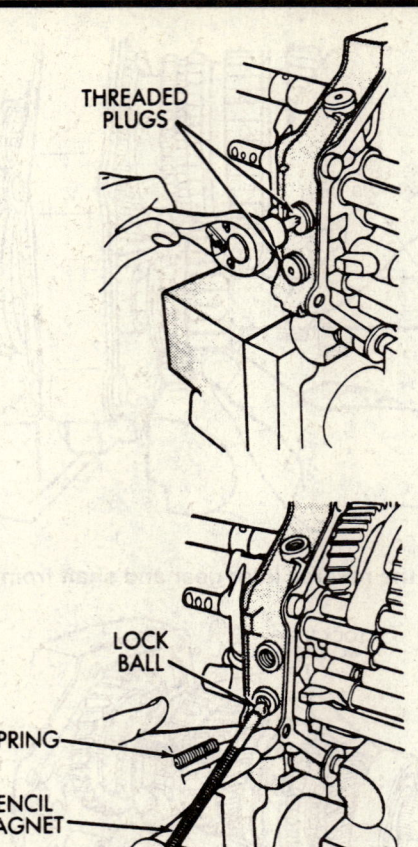

Removing the lock ball and spring from the AX4

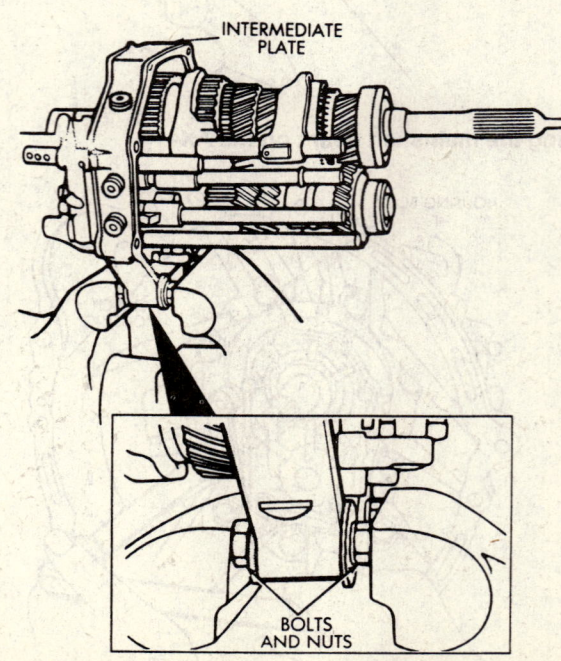

Positioning the AX4 intermediate plate in a vice

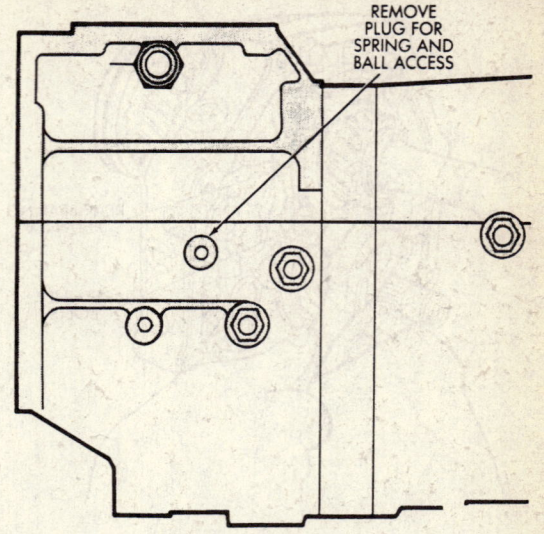

Detent ball plug location on the AX4

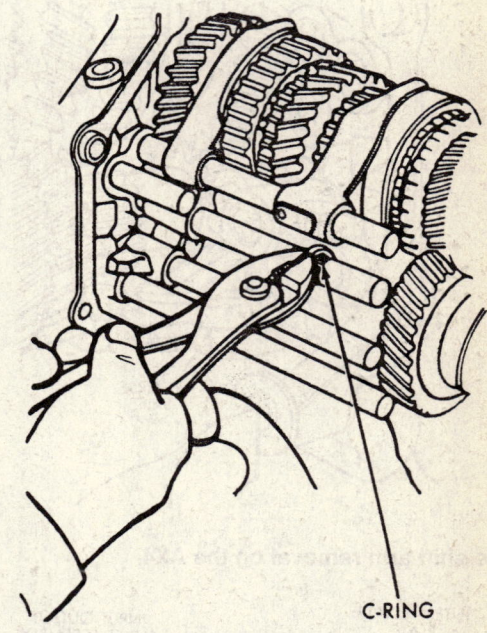

Shift rail C-ring removal on the AX4

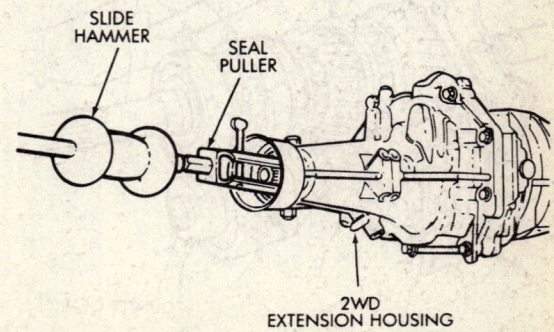

Removing the 2WD extension housing seal from the AX4

7-29

7 DRIVE TRAIN

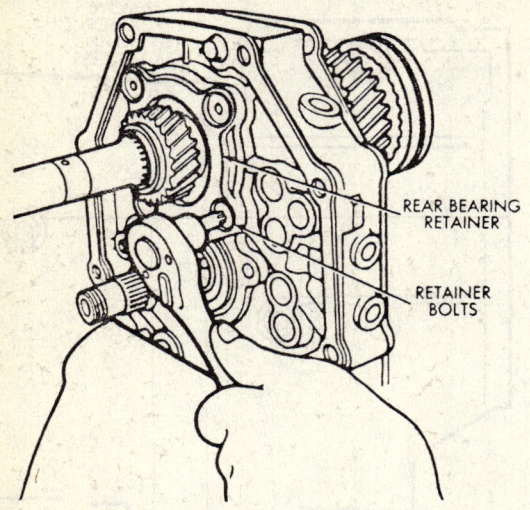

Removing the rear bearing retainer from the AX4

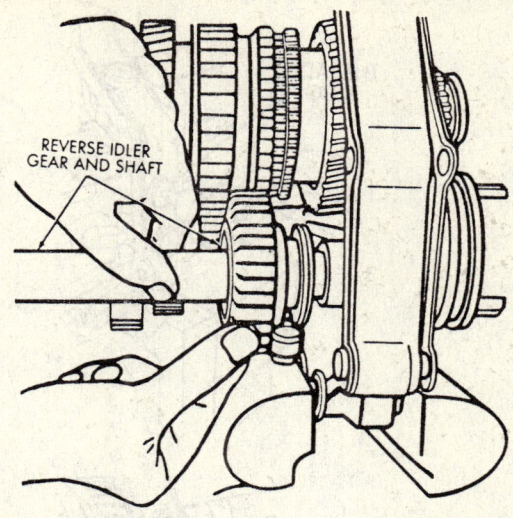

Removing the reverse idler gear and shaft from the AX4

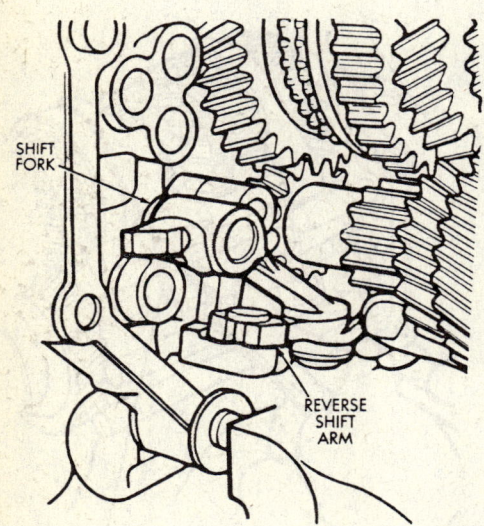

Reverse shift arm removal on the AX4

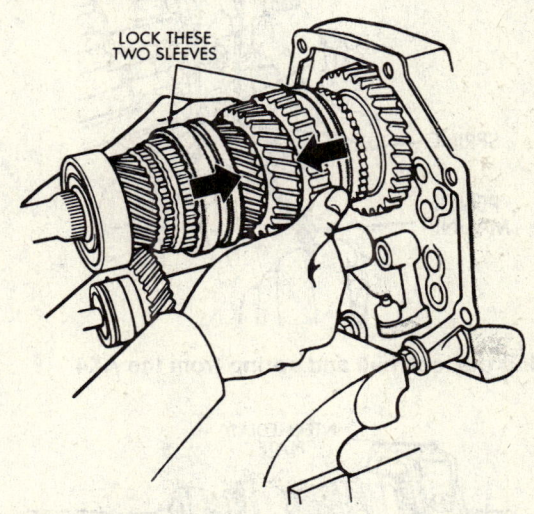

Locking the mainshaft gears on the AX4

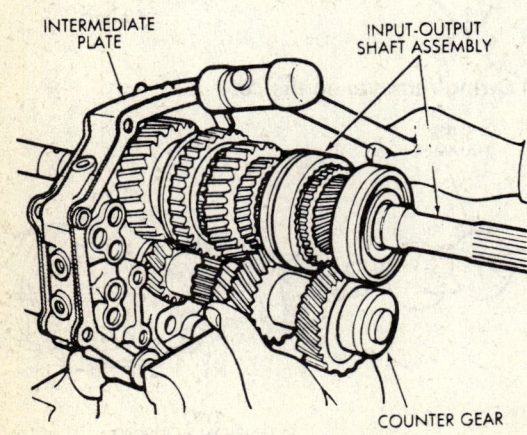

Removing the counter gear and output shaft from the AX4

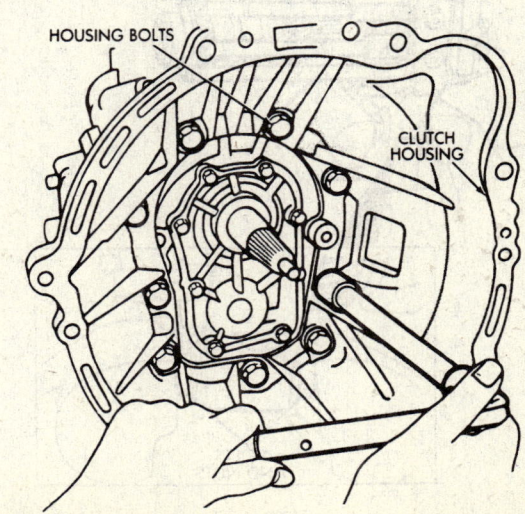

Removing the AX4 clutch housing

DRIVE TRAIN 7

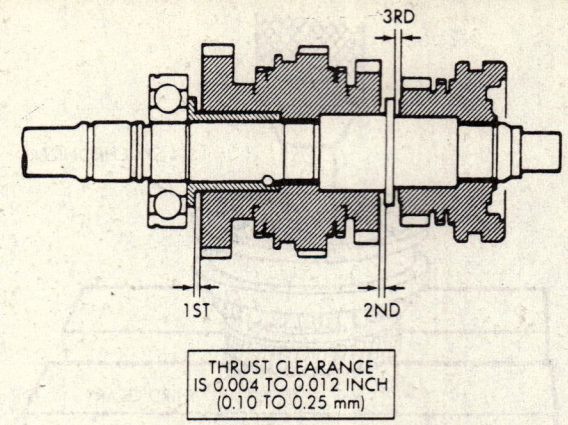

Checking the output shaft gear thrust clearance on the AX4

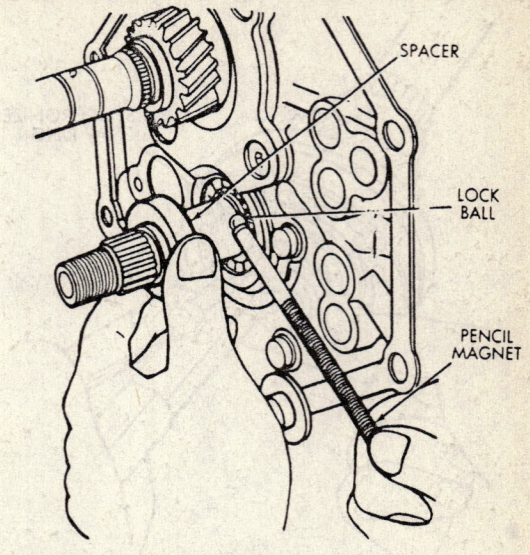

Spacer and lock ball removal on the AX4

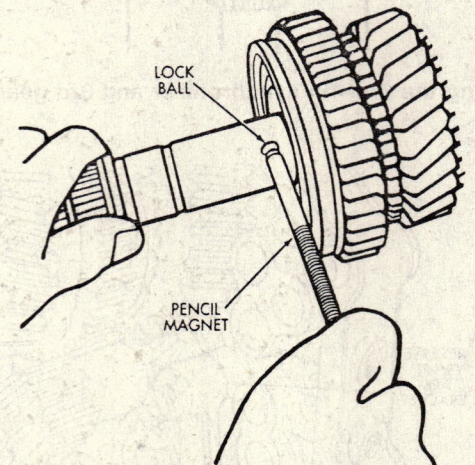

Synchronizer lock ball removal on the AX4

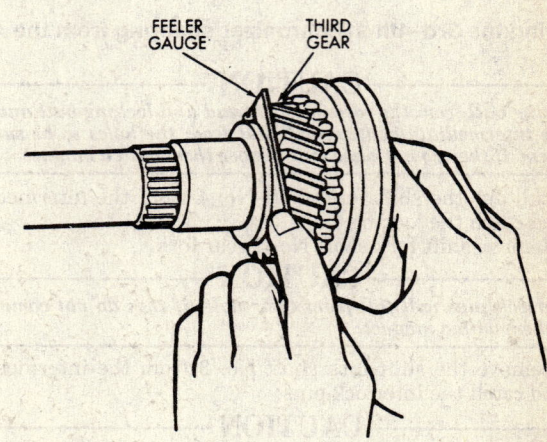

Checking 3rd gear clearance on the AX4

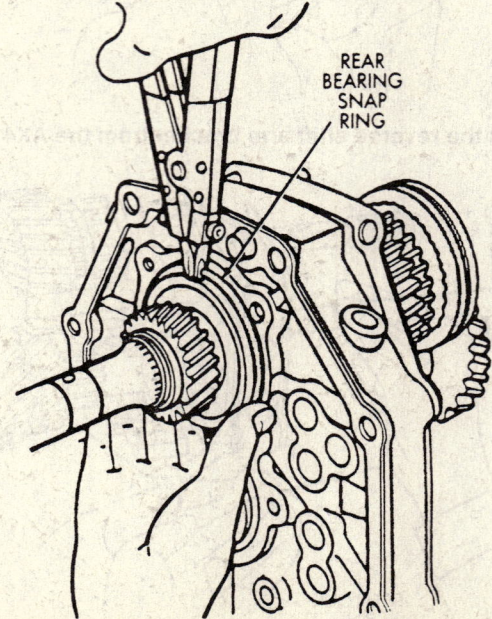

Removing the rear bearing snapring from the AX4

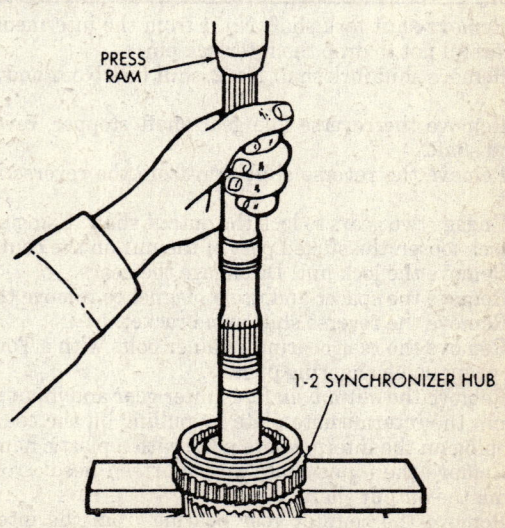

1st–2nd synchronizer and second gear removal from the AX4

7-31

7 DRIVE TRAIN

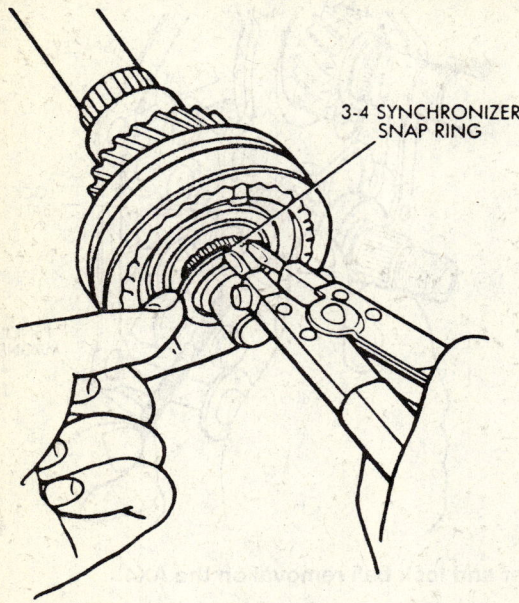

Removing the 3rd–4th synchronizer snapring from the AX4

---- CAUTION ----
The locking ball from the reverse shift head and locking ball and pin from the intermediate housing will fall from the holes so be sure to catch them. If they do not come out, remove them with a magnet.

15. Pull out the shift fork shaft No. 4 from the intermediate plate and catch the locking ball.
16. Remove shift fork shaft No. 4 gear fork.

---- CAUTION ----
The interlock pins will fall from their hole. If they do not come out, remove them with a magnet.

18. Remove the shift fork shaft No. 3 from the intermediate plate and catch the interlock pins.

---- CAUTION ----
The interlock pin will fall from the hole so be sure to catch it. If it does not come out, remove it with a magnet.

19. Remove shift fork shaft No. 1 from the intermediate plate being careful not to drop the interlock pin.
20. Remove shift fork shaft No. 2, shift fork No. 2 and shift fork No. 1.
21. Remove the reverse idle gear shaft stopper, reverse idler gear and shaft.
22. Remove the reverse shift arm from the reverse shift arm bracket.
23. Engage two gears to lock the output shaft. Using a hammer and chisel, loosen the staked part of the nut on the countershaft.
24. Remove the lock nut. Disengage the gears.
25. Remove the spacer and use a magnet to remove the ball.
26. Remove the reverse shift arm bracket.
27. Remove the rear bearing retainer bolts with a Torx bit and the snapring using snapring pliers.
28. Remove the output shaft, counter gear and input shaft as a unit from the intermediate plate by pulling on the counter gear and tapping on the intermediate plate with a plastic hammer.
29. Remove the input shaft with fourteen needle roller bearings from the output shaft.
30. Remove the counter rear bearing from the intermediate plate.
31. Measure the thrust clearance of each gear. Standard Clearance: 0.100–2.540mm.

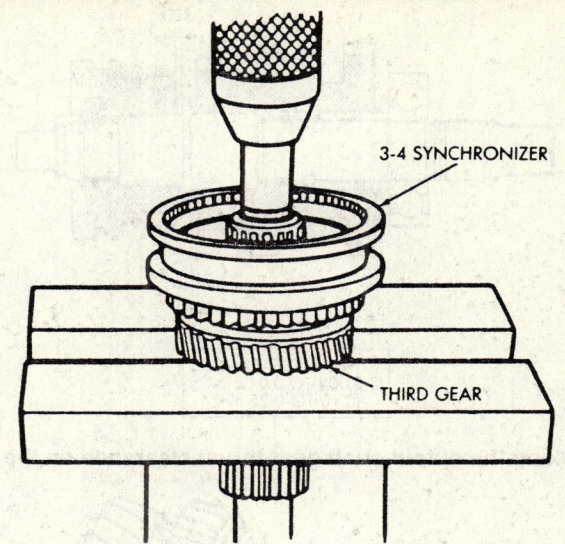

Removing the 3rd–4th synchronizer and 3rd gear from the AX4

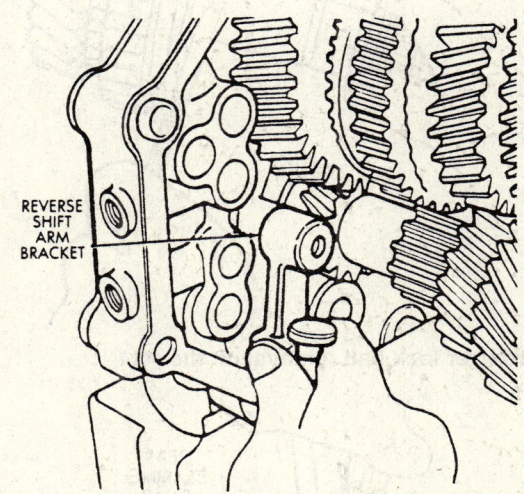

Removing the reverse shift arm bracket from the AX4

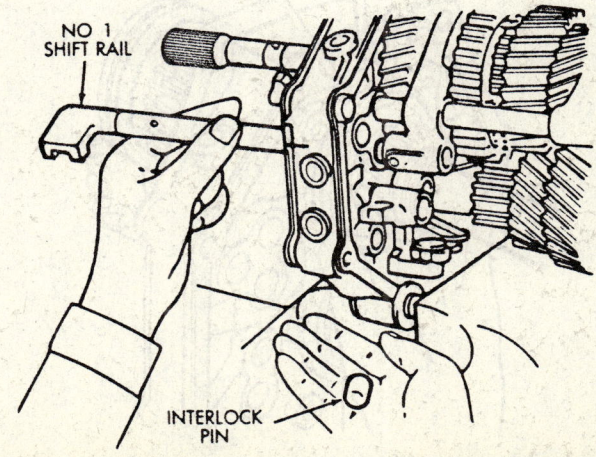

Removing the No. 1 shift rail and interlock pin from the AX4

DRIVE TRAIN 7

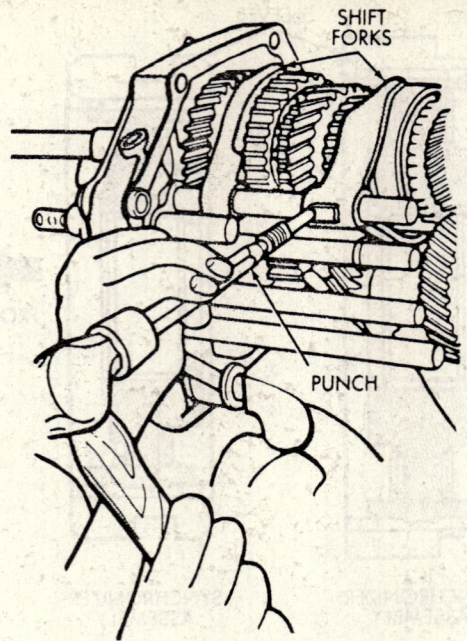

Removing the shift fork pin from the AX4

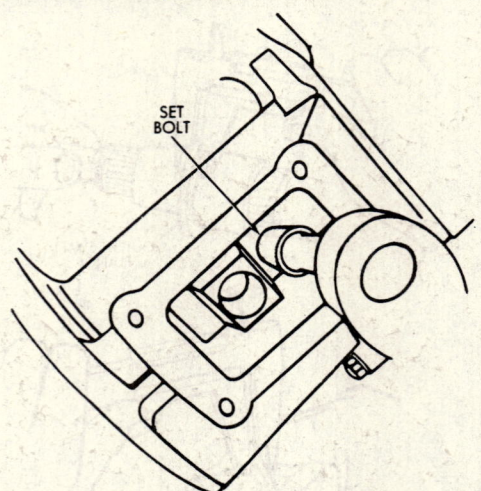

Set bolt removal from the AX4

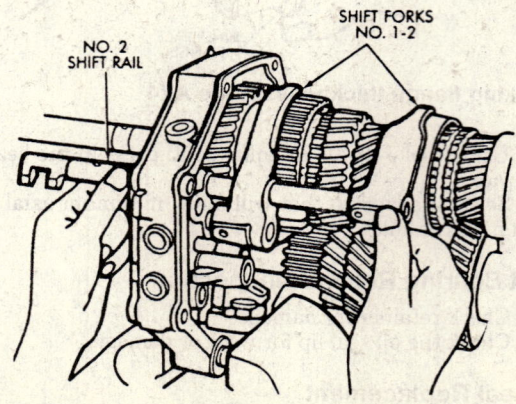

Removing the shift forks and No. 2 shift rail from the AX4

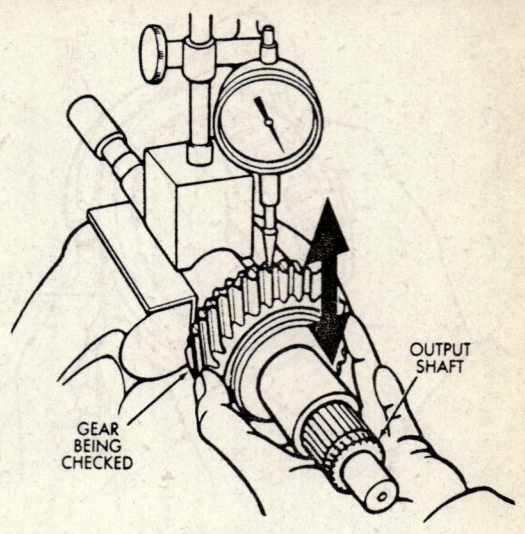

Checking gear-to-shaft clearance on the AX4

32. Using two awls and a hammer, tap out the snapring.
33. Using a press, remove the rear bearing, 1st gear and the inner race.
34. Remove the needle roller bearing.
35. Remove the synchronizer ring and locking ball.
36. Using a press, remove hub sleeve No. 1 assembly, synchronizer ring, 2nd gear.
37. Remove the needle roller bearing.
38. Remove the snapring from hub sleeve No. 2.
39. Using a press, remove the hub sleeve, synchronizer ring, and 3rd gear.
40. Remove the needle roller bearing.

COMPONENT INSPECTION

Output Shaft & Inner Race

1. Check the output shaft and inner race for wear or damage.
2. Using calipers, measure the output shaft flange thickness. Minimum thickness is 4.8mm.
3. Using calipers, measure the inner face flange thickness. Minimum thickness is 4.0mm.
4. Using a micrometer, measure the outer diameter of the output shaft journal surface. 2nd Gear minimum is 38mm; 3rd Gear minimum is 35mm.
5. Using a micrometer, measure the outer diameter of the inner race. Minimum diameter is 39mm.
6. Using a dial indicator, measure the shaft runout. Maximum runout is 0.05mm.

1st Gear Oil Clearance

1. Using a dial indicator, measure the oil clearance between the gear and inner race with the needle roller bearing installed. Standard clearance is 0.010–0.033mm.
2. Using a dial indicator, measure the oil clearance between the gear and shaft with the needle roller bearing installed. Standard clearance for 2nd and 3rd gears is 0.010–0.033mm.

Synchronizer Ring Inspection

1. Check for wear or damage. Turn the ring and push it in to check the braking action.
2. Measure the clearance between the synchronizer ring back and the gear spline end. Standard clearance is 1.00–2.00mm; minimum clearance is 0.8mm.

7-33

7 DRIVE TRAIN

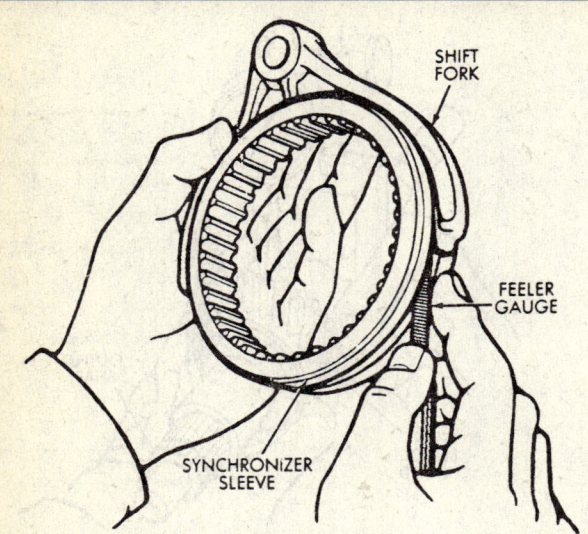

Checking fork-to-hub clearance on the AX4

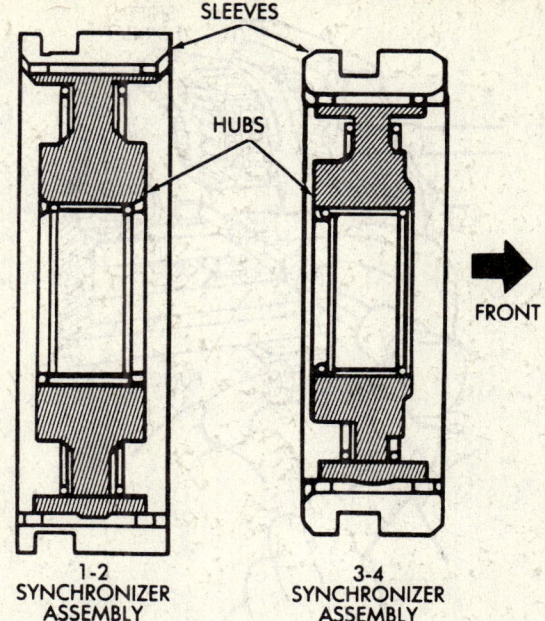

Synchronizer identification on the AX4

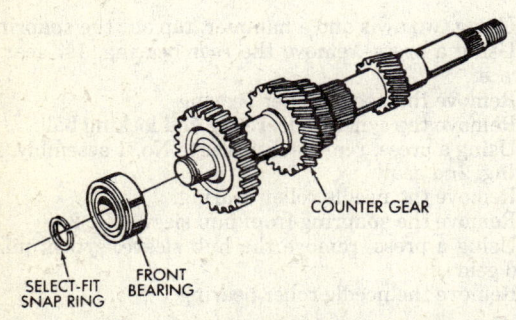

I.D. Mark	Snap Ring Thickness mm (in.)
1	2.05-2.10 (0.0807-0.0827)
2	2.10-2.15 (0.0827-0.0846)
3	2.15-2.20 (0.0846-0.0866)
4	2.20-2.25 (0.0866-0.0886)
5	2.25-2.30 (0.0886-0.0906)
6	2.30-2.35 (0.0906-0.0925)

Installing counter gear front bearing and snapring on the AX4

Shift Fork and Hub Sleeve Clearance

Using a feeler gauge, measure the clearance between the hub sleeve and shift fork. Maximum Clearance: 1.0mm.

Input Shaft and Bearing Inspection and Removal

1. Check for wear or damage. If necessary, remove the bearing snapring using snapring pliers and remove the bearing.
2. Using a press, remove the bearing.
3. Using a press and tool J-34603 or equivalent, install the new bearing.
4. Select a snapring that will allow minimum axial play and install it on the shaft.

Counter Gear and Bearing Inspection

1. Check the gear teeth for wear or damage.
2. Check the bearing for wear or damage.

Counter Gear Front Bearing Replacement

1. Using snapring pliers, remove the snapring.
2. Press out the bearing using tool J-22912-01 or equivalent.
3. Replace the side race.

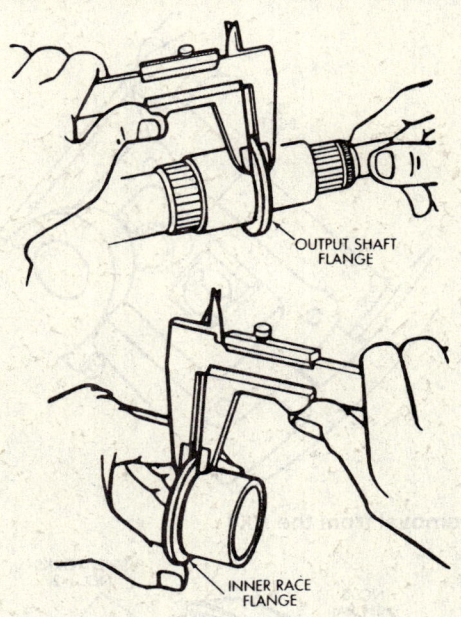

Checking flange thickness on the AX4

4. Using tool J-28406 or equivalent, press in the bearing and inner race.
5. Select a snapring that will allow minimum axial play and install it on the shaft.

Front Bearing Retainer Inspection

1. Check retainer for damage.
2. Check the oil seal lip for wear or damage.

Oil Seal Replacement

1. Using an awl, pry the old seal out of the housing.
2. Press in the new oil seal using tool J-34602 or equivalent.

DRIVE TRAIN 7

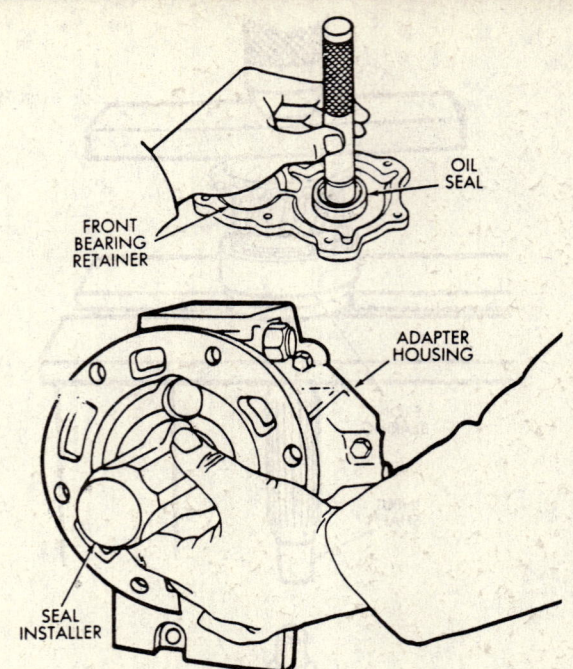

Oil seal installation on the AX4

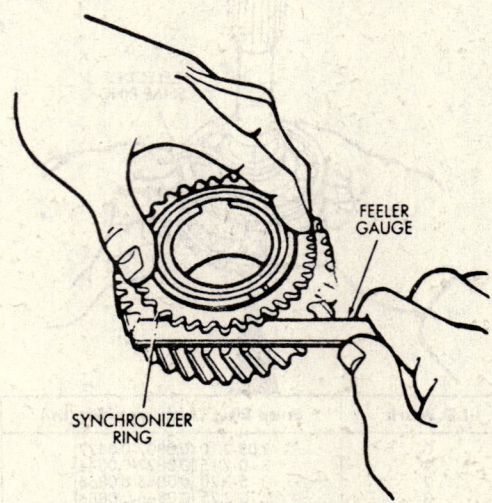

Checking synchronizer ring wear on the AX4

3. The oil seal depth is 11.20–12.20mm from the housing-to-transmission surface to the top edge of the seal.

Reverse Restrict Pin Replacement

1. Check for wear or damage.
2. Using a Torx bit, remove the screw plug.
3. Using a hammer and pin punch, drive out the slotted spring pin.
4. Pull off the lever housing and slide out the shaft.
5. Install the lever housing.
6. Using a hammer and pin punch, drive out the slotted spring pin.
7. Using a Torx bit, install and torque the screw plug to 27 ft. lbs. torque.

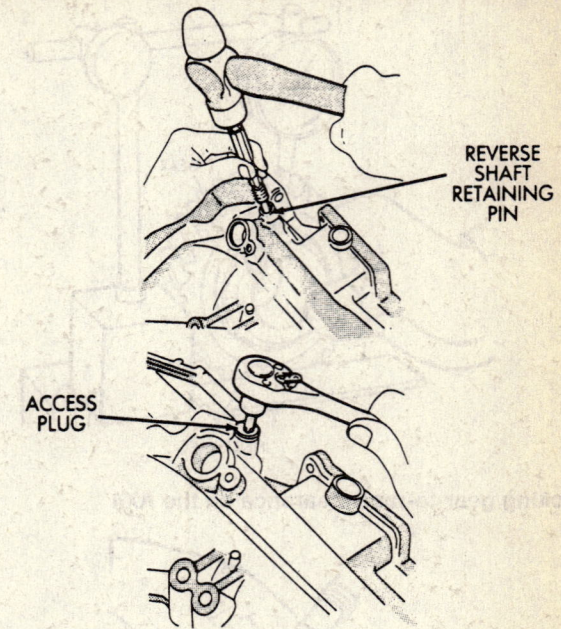

Installing the reverse shaft pin on the AX4

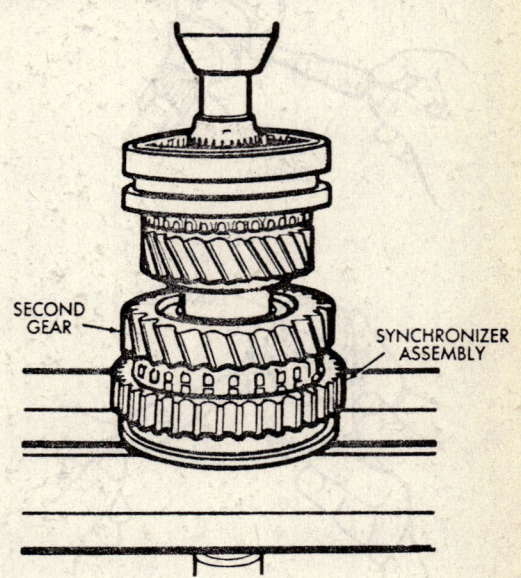

Installing 2nd gear and synchronizer on the AX4

Adapter Housing & Oil Seal Inspection & Replacement

1. Check the adapter housing for wear or damage.
2. Replace the oil seal with tool J-29184 or equivalent.

ASSEMBLY

1. Install the clutch hub No. 1 and No. 2 into hub sleeves along with the shifting keys.
   WARNING: Install the key springs so their gaps are not in line.
2. Install the shifting springs under the shifting keys.
3. Apply gear oil on the output shaft and 3rd gear needle roller bearing.

7 DRIVE TRAIN

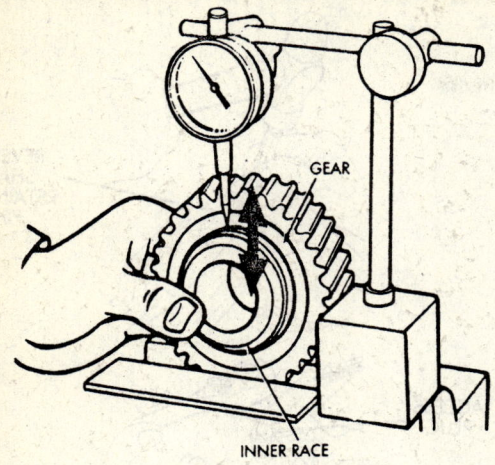

Checking gear-to-race clearance on the AX4

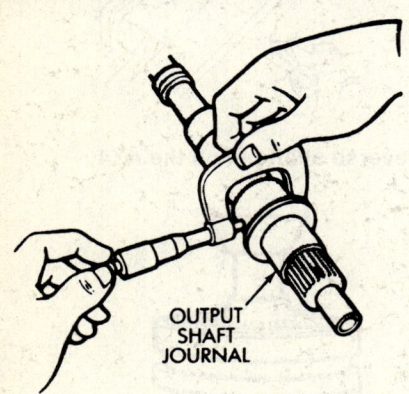

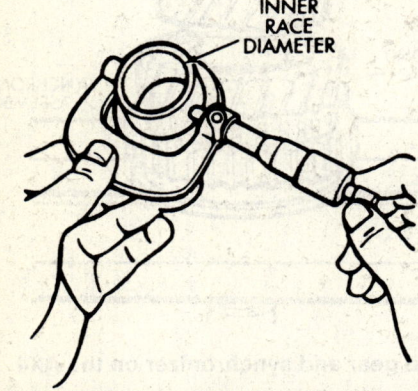

Checking shaft and race diameters on the AX4

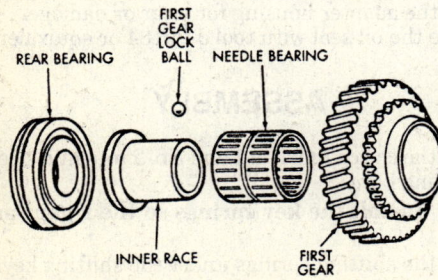

1st gear assembled on the AX4

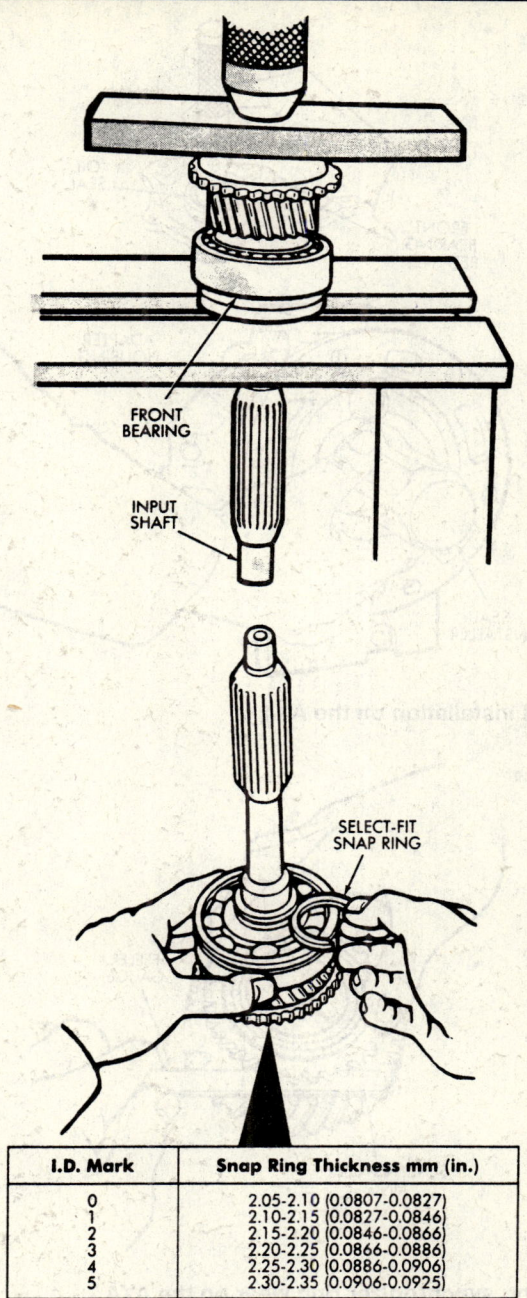

I.D. Mark	Snap Ring Thickness mm (in.)
0	2.05-2.10 (0.0807-0.0827)
1	2.10-2.15 (0.0827-0.0846)
2	2.15-2.20 (0.0846-0.0866)
3	2.20-2.25 (0.0866-0.0886)
4	2.25-2.30 (0.0886-0.0906)
5	2.30-2.35 (0.0906-0.0925)

Installing front bearing and snapring on the AX4

4. Place the 3rd gear synchronizer ring on the gear and align the ring slots with the shifting keys.

5. Install the needle roller bearing in the 3rd gear and hub sleeve No. 2.

6. Select a new snapring (2) that will allow minimum axial play and install it on the shaft.

7. Using a feeler gauge, measure the 3rd gear thrust clearance. Standard clearance is 0.10–0.25mm.

8. Apply gear oil on the output shaft and 2nd gear needle bearing.

9. Place the 2nd gear synchronizer ring on the 2nd gear and align the ring slots with the shifting keys.

10. Install the needle roller bearing in the 2nd gear.

DRIVE TRAIN 7

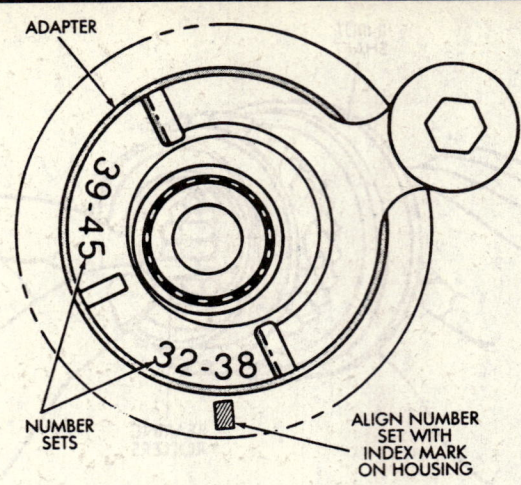

Indexing the speedometer gears on the AX4

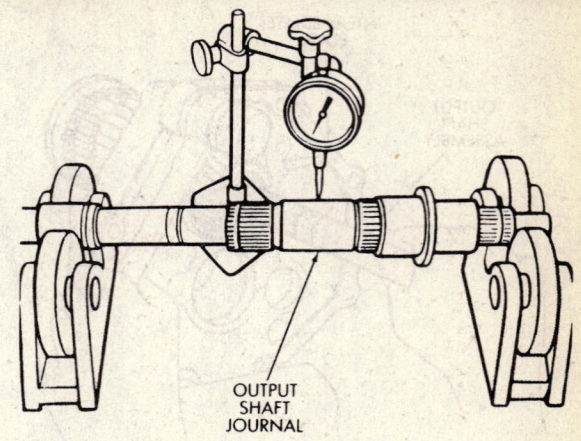

Checking output shaft runout on the AX4

11. Using a press install the 2nd gear and hub sleeve No. 1.
13. Install the 1st gear locking ball in the output shaft.
14. Apply gear oil to the needle roller bearing.
15. Assemble the 1st gear, synchronizer ring, needle roller bearing and bearing inner race.
16. Install the assembly on the output shaft, with the synchronizer ring slots aligned with the shifting keys.
17. Turn the inner race to align it with the locking ball.
18. Install the output shaft rear bearing using tool J-34603 or equivalent and a press.
19. Install the bearing on the output shaft with the outer race snapring groove toward the rear.

NOTE: Hold the 1st gear inner race to prevent it from falling.

20. Measure the 1st and 2nd gear thrust clearance with a feeler gauge. Standard clearance is 0.10–0.25mm.

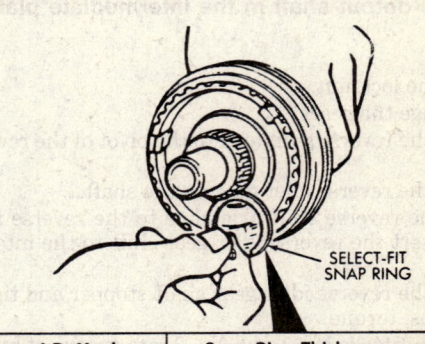

I.D. Mark	Snap Ring Thickness mm (in.)
C-1	1.75-1.80 (0.0689-0.0709)
D	1.80-1.85 (0.0709-0.0728)
D-	1.85-1.90 (0.0728-0.0748)
E	1.90-1.95 (0.0748-0.0768)
E-1	1.95-2.00 (0.0768-0.0787)
F	2.00-2.05 (0.0788-0.0807)
F-1	2.05-2.10 (0.0807-0.0827)

Installing 3rd gear and 3rd–4th synchronizer on the AX4

21. Select a snapring that will allow minimum axial play.
22. Using a screwdriver and a hammer, tap the snap into position.
23. Apply multi-purpose grease to the fourteen needle roller bearings and install them in the input shaft.
24. Install the output shaft into the intermediate plate by pulling on the output shaft and tapping on the intermediate plate.
25. Install the input shaft to the output shaft with the synchronizer ring slots aligned with the shifting keys.
26. Install the counter gear into the intermediate plate while holding the counter gear, and install the counter rear bearing with a suitable driver.
27. Install the bearing snapring using snapring pliers.

NOTE: Be sure the snapring is flush with the intermediate plate surface.

28. Using a Torx bit, install and tighten the screws to 13 ft. lbs. torque.
29. Install the reverse shift arm bracket and tighten the bolts to 13 ft. lbs. torque.
30. Install the ball and spacer.
31. Install shifting key springs under the shifting keys.
32. Install the synchronizer ring on gear spline piece.
33. Engage two gears to lock the output shaft.
34. Install and tighten the lock nut to 90 ft. lbs. torque on the counter shaft.

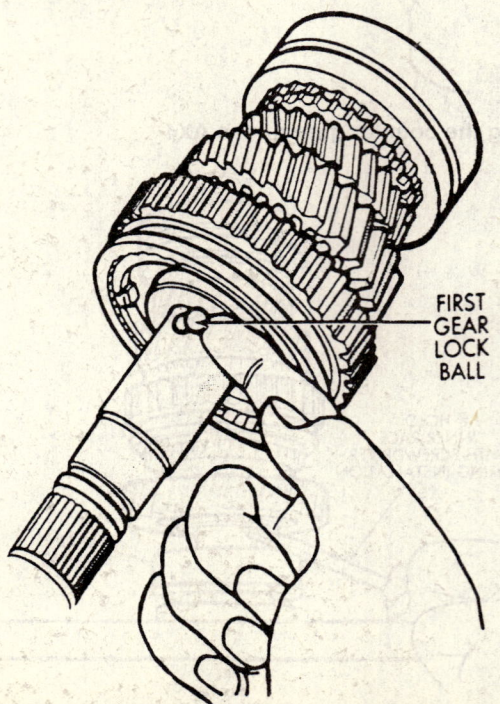

Installing 1st gear and lock ball on the AX4

7 DRIVE TRAIN

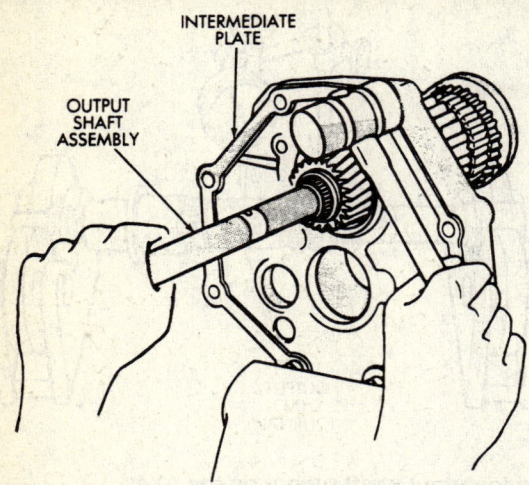

Installing the output shaft in the intermediate plate on the AX4

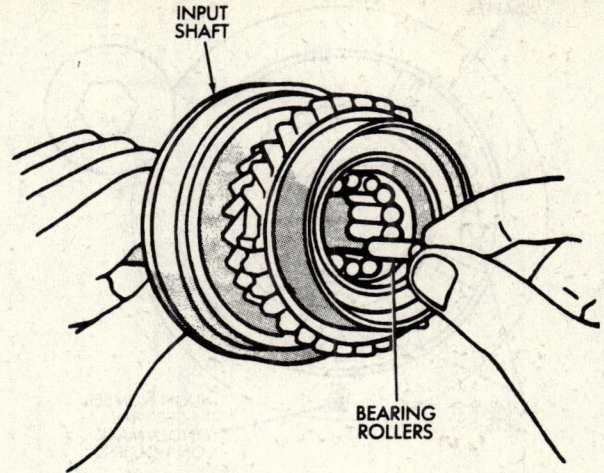

Installing the input shaft bearing rollers on the AX4

35. Stake the lock nut.
36. Disengage the gears.
37. Install the reverse shift arm to the pivot of the reverse shift arm bracket.
38. Install the reverse idler gear on the shaft.
39. Align the reverse shift arm shoe to the reverse idler gear groove and insert the reverse idler gear shift to the intermediate plate.
40. Install the reverse idler gear shaft stopper and tighten the bolt to 13 ft. lbs. torque.
41. Place shift forks No. 1 and No. 2 into groove of hub sleeves No. 1 and No. 2 and install fork shaft No. 2 to the shift forks No. 1 and No. 2 through the intermediate plate.
42. Apply multi-purpose grease to the interlock pins.
43. Using a magnet and screwdriver, install the interlock pin into the intermediate plate.
44. Install the interlock pin into the shaft hole.
45. Install fork shaft No. 1 to shift fork No. 1 through the intermediate plate.
46. Using a magnet and screwdriver, install the interlock pin into the intermediate plate.
47. Install the interlock pin into the shaft hole.
48. Install fork shaft No. 3 to the reverse shift arm through the intermediate plate.
49. Using a magnetic finger and screwdriver, install the locking ball into the reverse shift head hole.
50. Place shift fork No. 3 into the groove of hub sleeve No. 3

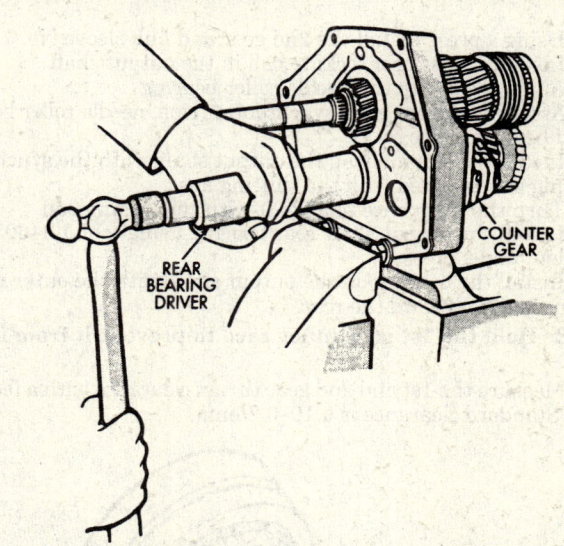

Installing the counter gear on the AX4

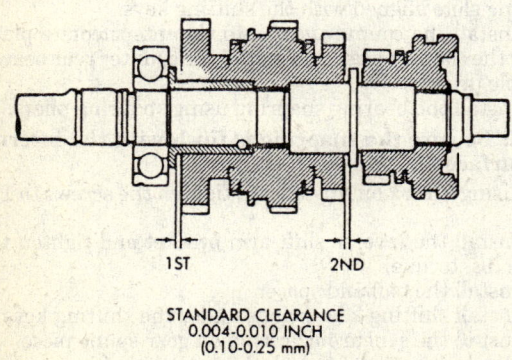

Checking 1st–2nd gear clearance on the AX4

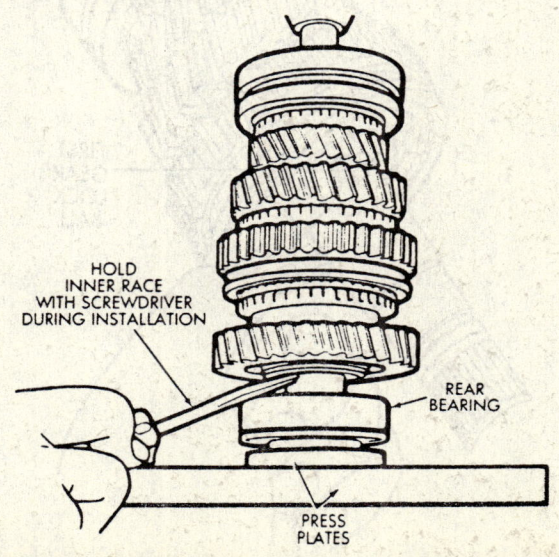

Installing the output shaft rear bearing on the AX4

DRIVE TRAIN 7

and install fork shaft No. 4 to shift fork No. 3 and reverse shift arm.

51. Using a magnet and screwdriver, install the locking ball into the intermediate plate and insert fork shaft No. 4 to the intermediate plate.
52. Check the interlock by positioning the shift fork shaft No. 1 to the 1st speed position.
53. Fork shafts No. 2, No. 3 and No. 4 should not move.
54. Using a pin punch and a hammer, drive in new slotted spring pins in each shift fork, reverse shift arm and reverse shift head.
55. Install two fork shaft E-rings.
56. Apply liquid sealer to the screw plugs.
57. Install the locking balls, springs and screw plugs with a Torx bit and tighten to 14 ft. lbs. torque.

NOTE: Install the short spring into the tower of the intermediate plate.

58. Remove the intermediate plate from the vise.
59. Remove the bolts, nuts, washers and gasket.

CASE INSTALLATION

1. Align each bearing outer race, each fork shaft end and reverse idler gear with the holes in the case and install the case on the intermediate plate. If necessary, tap on the case with a plastic hammer.
2. Install two new bearing snaprings.
3. Install front bearing retainer with a new gasket.
4. Apply liquid sealer to the bolts.
5. Install and tighten the bolts to 12 ft. lbs. torque.
6. Install the new gasket to the intermediate plate.
7. Install the adapter housing.
8. Install and tighten the adapter bolts to 27 ft. lbs. torque.
9. Install the shift lever housing.
10. Insert the shift lever into the adapter and shift lever housing.
11. Install and tighten shift lever housing bolt with a lock plate to 28 ft. lbs. torque. Lock the lock plate.
12. Install and tighten the adapter screw plug to 13 ft. lbs. torque.
13. Apply liquid sealer to the plug.
14. Install the locking ball, spring and screw plug and tighten the plug to 14 ft. lbs. torque.
15. Check to see that the input shaft and output shafts rotate smoothly.

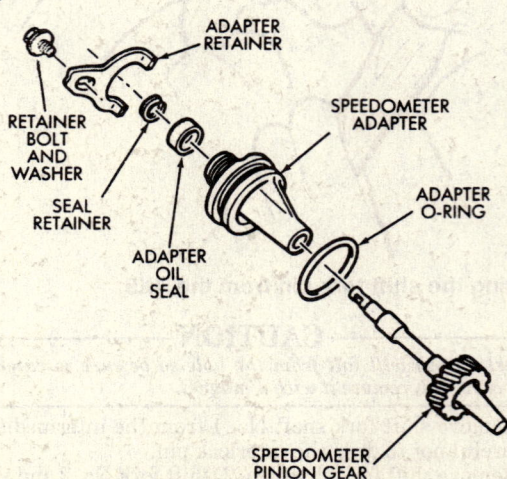

Speedometer gear assembly on the AX5

16. Check to see that shifting can be done smoothly to all positions.
17. Install the black restrict pin on the reverse gear.
18. Install the remaining pin and tighten the pins to 20 ft. lbs. torque.
19. Install the shift lever retainer with a new gasket and tighten the bolts to 13 ft. lbs. torque.
20. Install the back-up light switch and tighten to 27 ft. lbs. torque.
21. Install the clutch housing and tighten the bolts to 27 ft. lbs. torque.

AX 5 Overhaul

NOTE: The following components and materials must be replaced whenever the transmission is overhauled: Lip-type oil seals. Lock nuts. All roll pins. All snaprings. Loctite®Thread Lock or Loctite®242 Sealer should be used on all fasteners.

DISASSEMBLY

1. Remove the clutch housing.
2. Remove the straight screw plug, spring and ball using a Torx bit to remove the screw plug, and a magnet to remove spring and ball.
3. Remove five adapter housing bolts and one nut.
4. Remove the shift lever housing set bolt and lock plate.
5. Remove the plug at the rear of the shift fork shaft.
6. Remove the large magnet to pull the shaft out.
7. Remove the select lever from the top while rotating.
8. Remove the five adapter housing bolts two studs and one nut.
9. Using a plastic hammer, tap and remove the extension housing. Leave the gasket attached to the intermediate plate.
10. Remove the front bearing retainer and outer snaprings from the two front bearings.
11. Separate the intermediate plate from the transmission case using a small plastic hammer and remove the case.
12. Mount the intermediate plate in a vise. Be careful not to damage the plate.

NOTE: Before placing the intermediate plate in a vise, insert bolts, washers, and nuts in the open holes at the bottom of plate. Tighten vise against these bolts to prevent damage to the plate.

13. Remove the straight screw plug, locking balls and springs using a Torx bit and magnet.
14. Remove the five slotted spring pins using a hammer and punch and then remove the two E-rings from the shift rails.

---- **CAUTION** ----
The locking ball from the reverse shift head and locking ball and pin from the intermediate housing will fall from the holes so be sure to catch them. If they do not come out, remove them with a magnet.

15. Pull out the shift fork shaft No. 4 from the intermediate plate and catch the locking ball.
16. Remove shift fork shaft No. 4 and the 5th gear fork.
17. Pull out shift fork shaft No. 5 from the intermediate plate, and remove it with the reverse shift head.

---- **CAUTION** ----
The interlock pins will fall from their hole. If they do not come out, remove them with a magnet.

18. Remove the shift fork shaft No. 3 from the intermediate plate and catch the interlock pins.

7-39

7 DRIVE TRAIN

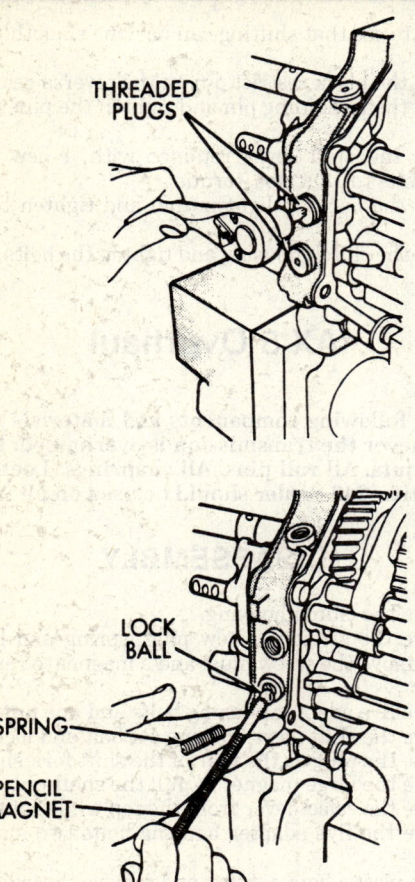

Removing the lock ball and spring from the AX5

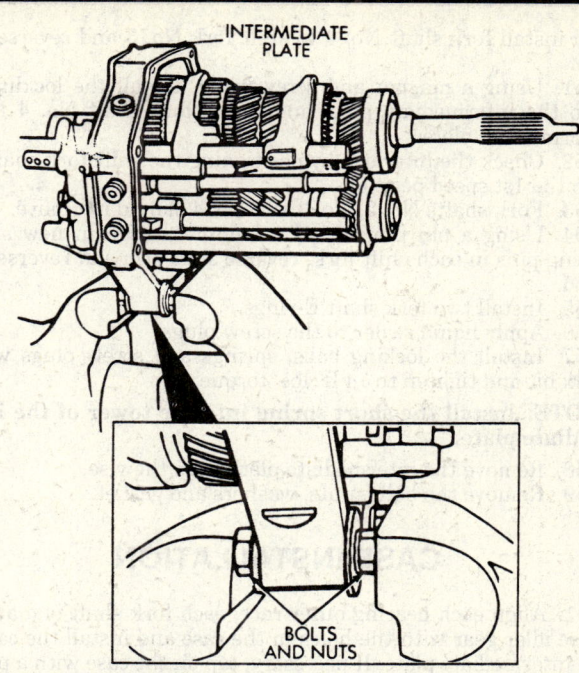

Positioning the AX5 intermediate plate in a vice

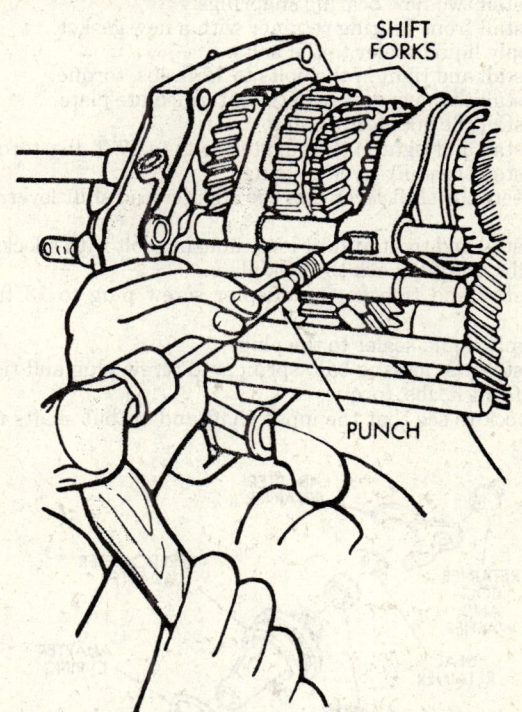

Removing the shift fork pin from the AX5

---- CAUTION ----
The interlock pin will fall from the hole so be sure to catch it. If it does not come out, remove it with a magnet.

19. Remove shift fork shaft No. 1 from the intermediate plate being careful not to drop the interlock pin.
20. Remove shift fork shaft No. 2, shift fork No. 2 and shift fork No. 1.
21. Remove the reverse idle gear shaft stopper, reverse idler gear and shaft.

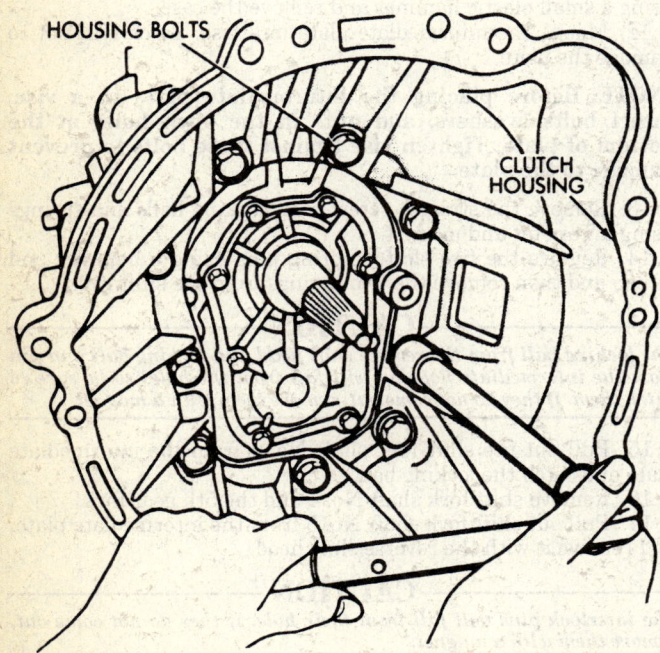

Removing the AX5 clutch housing

7-40

DRIVE TRAIN 7

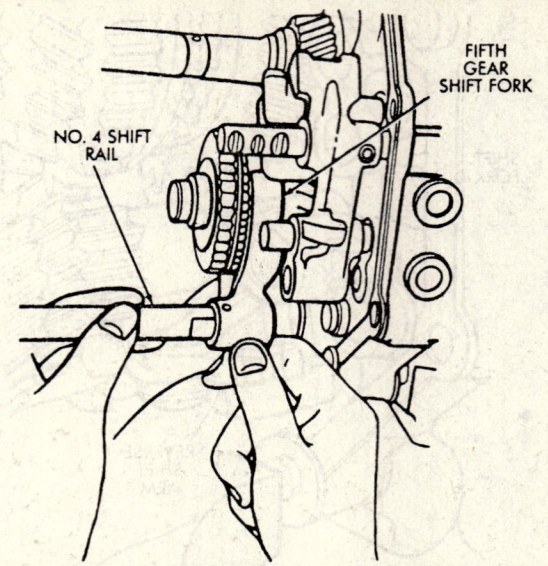

Removing the No. 4 shift rail and the 5th gear shift fork from the AX5

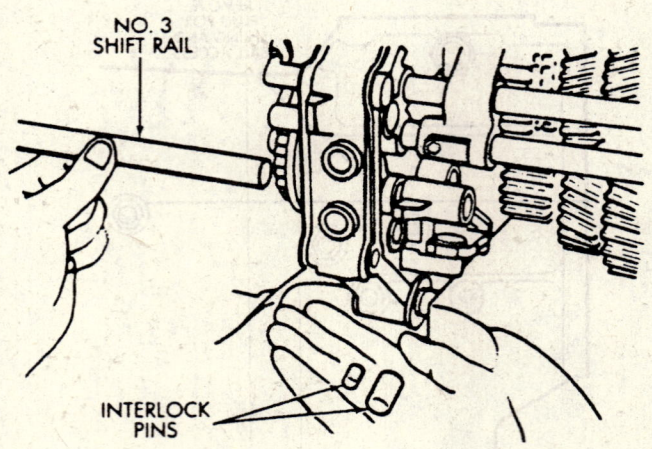

Removing the No. 3 shift rail and interlock pin from the AX5

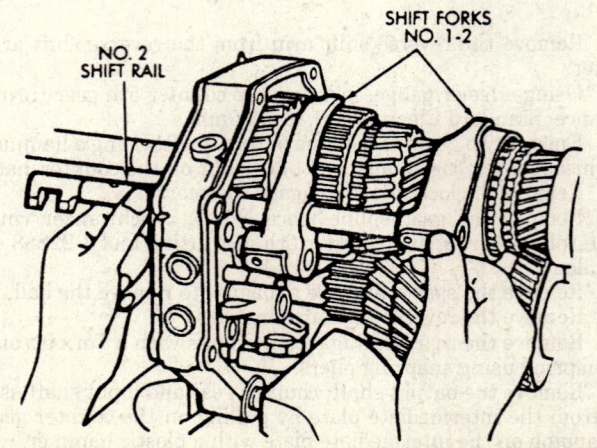

Removing the shift forks and No. 2 shift rail from the AX5

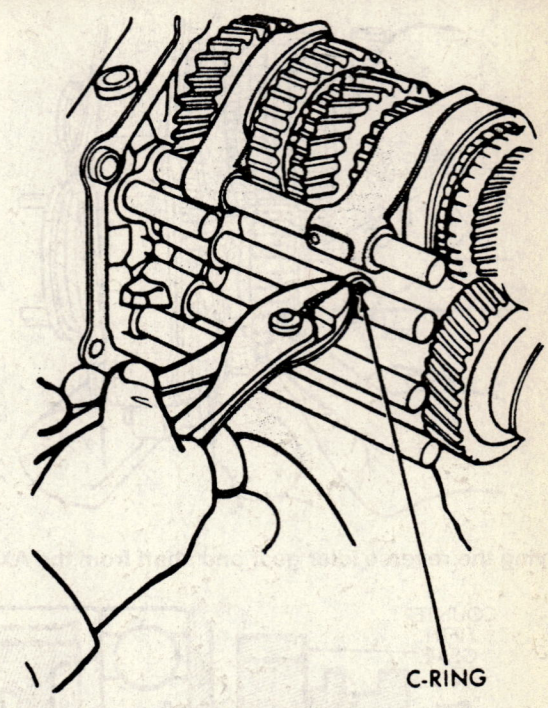

Shift rail C-ring removal on the AX5

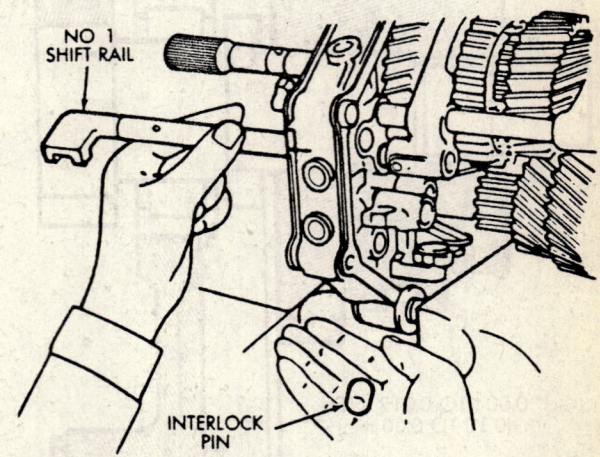

Removing the No. 1 shift rail and interlock pin from the AX5

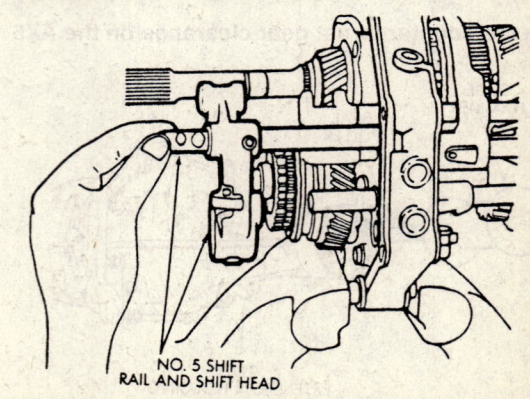

Removing the No. 5 shift rail and shift head from the AX5

7-41

7 DRIVE TRAIN

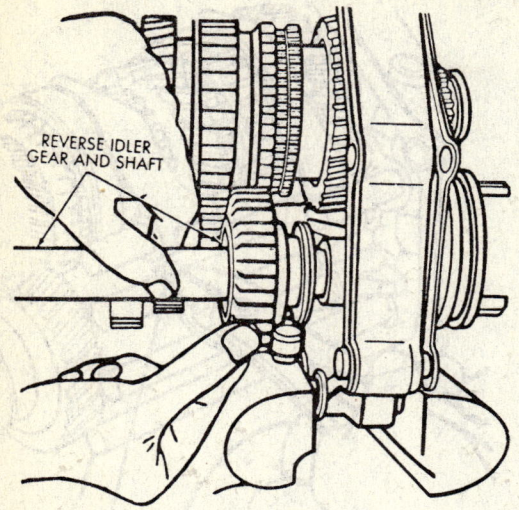

Removing the reverse idler gear and shaft from the AX5

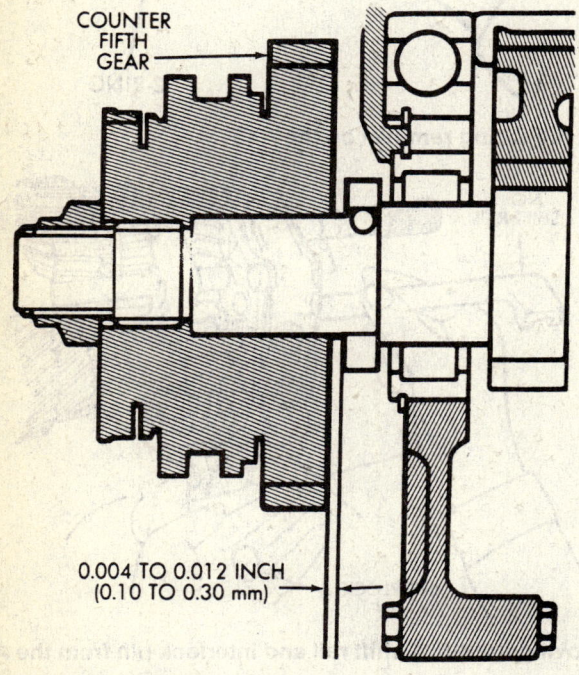

Measuring the counter thrust gear clearance on the AX5

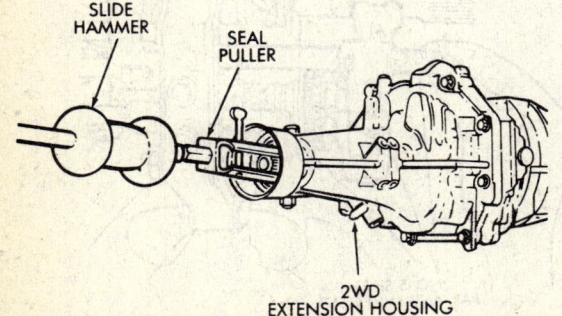

Removing the 2WD extension housing seal from the AX5

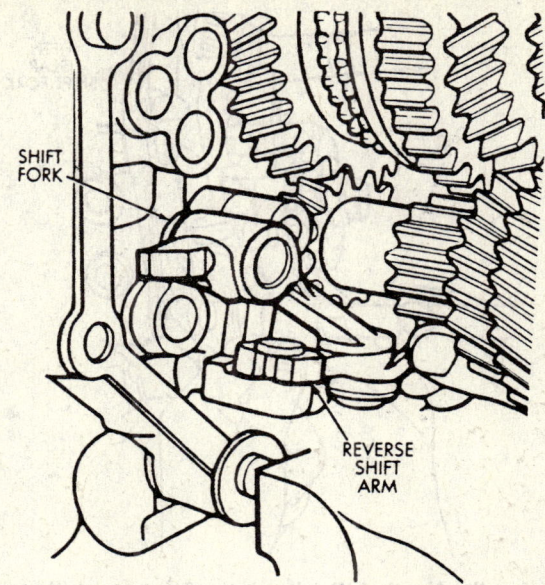

Reverse shift arm removal on the AX5

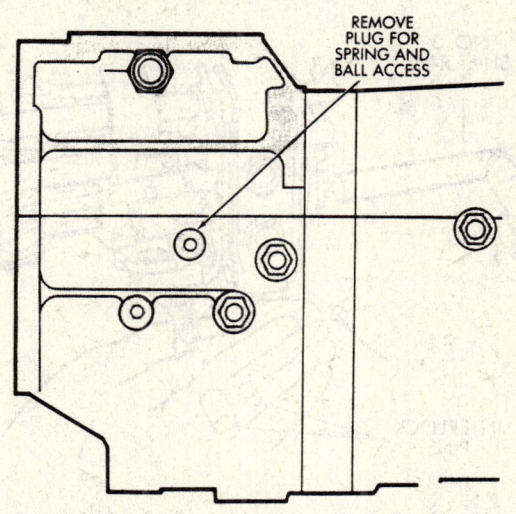

Detent ball plug location on the AX5

22. Remove the reverse shift arm from the reverse shift arm bracket.
23. Using a feeler gauge, measure the counter 5th gear thrust clearance. Standard Clearance: 0.10–0.30mm.
24. Engage two gears to lock the output shaft. Using a hammer and chisel, loosen the staked part of the nut on the countershaft.
25. Remove the lock nut. Disengage the gears.
26. Remove the gear spline piece No. 5, synchronizer ring, needle roller bearing and counter 5th gear using tool J-22888 or equivalent.
27. Remove the spacer and use a magnet to remove the ball.
28. Remove the reverse shift arm bracket.
29. Remove the rear bearing retainer bolts with a Torx bit and the snapring using snapring pliers.
30. Remove the output shaft, counter gear and input shaft as a unit from the intermediate plate by pulling on the counter gear and tapping on the intermediate plate with a plastic hammer.
31. Remove the input shaft with fourteen needle roller bearings from the output shaft.

DRIVE TRAIN 7

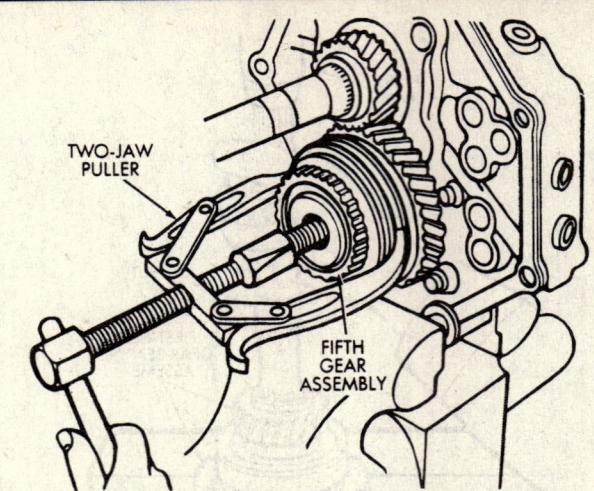

Removing the 5th gear assembly from the AX5

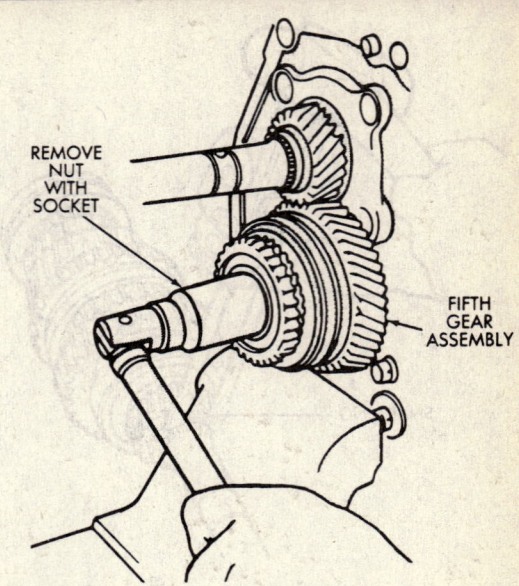

Removing the 5th gear nut from the AX5

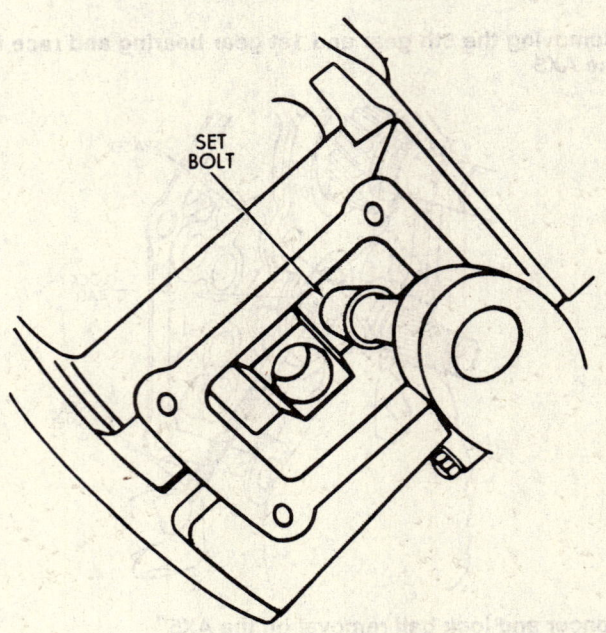

Set bolt removal from the AX5

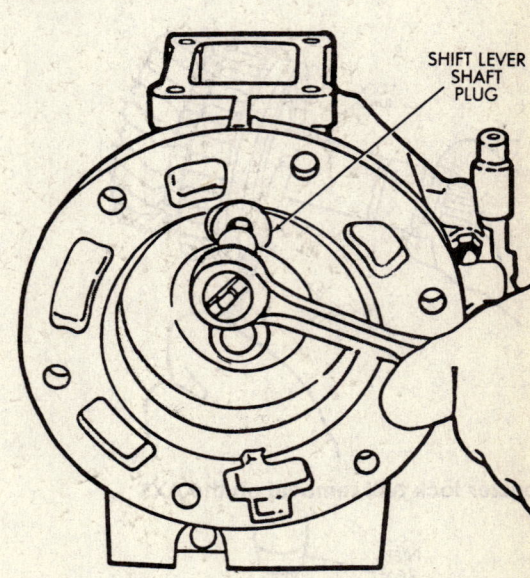

Removing the shift lever shaft plug from the AX5

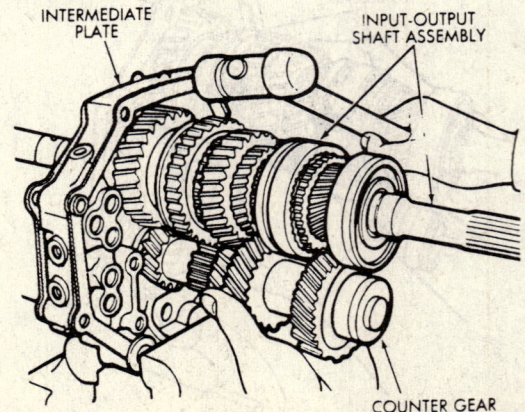

Removing the counter gear and output shaft from the AX5

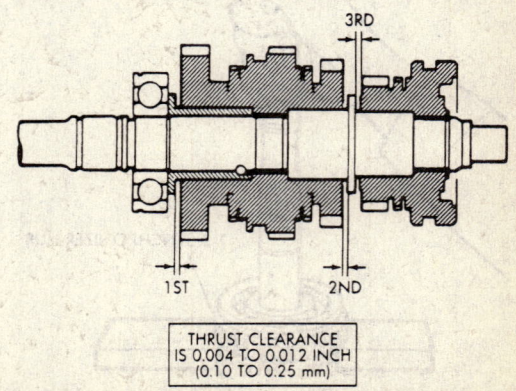

Checking the output shaft gear thrust clearance on the AX5

7 DRIVE TRAIN

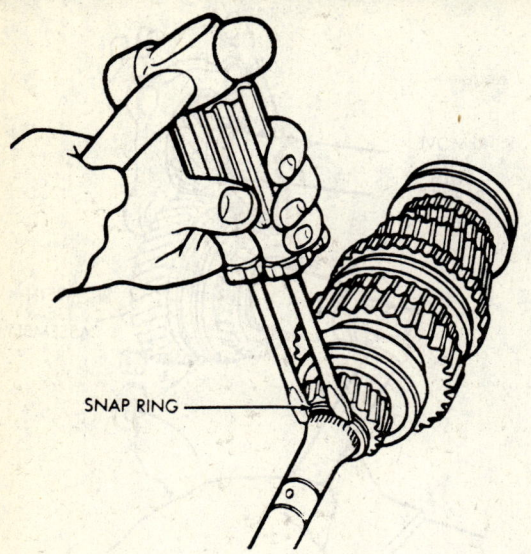

Removing the 5th gear snapring on the AX5

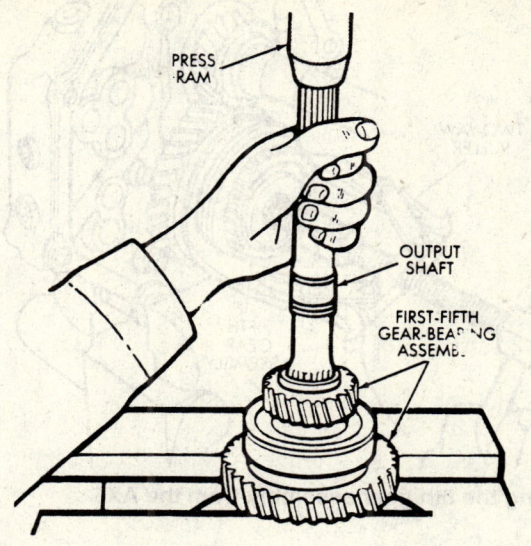

Removing the 5th gear and 1st gear bearing and race from the AX5

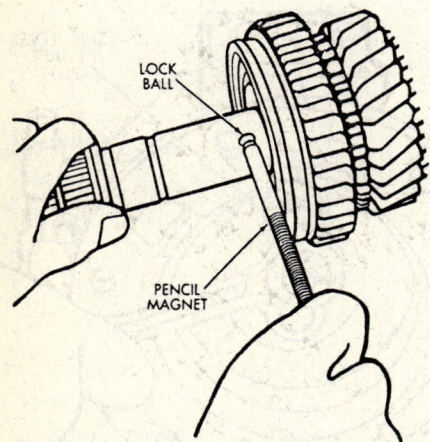

Synchronizer lock ball removal on the AX5

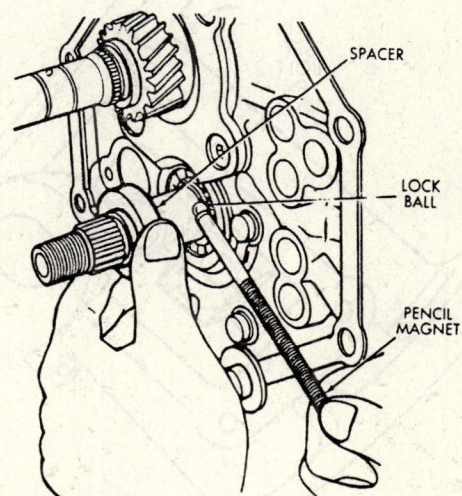

Spacer and lock ball removal on the AX5

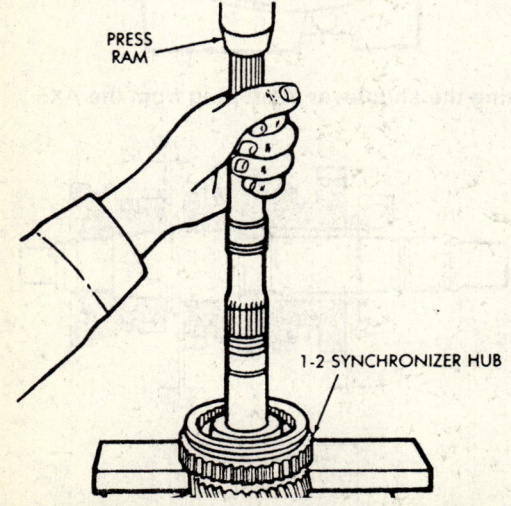

1st–2nd synchronizer and second gear removal from the AX5

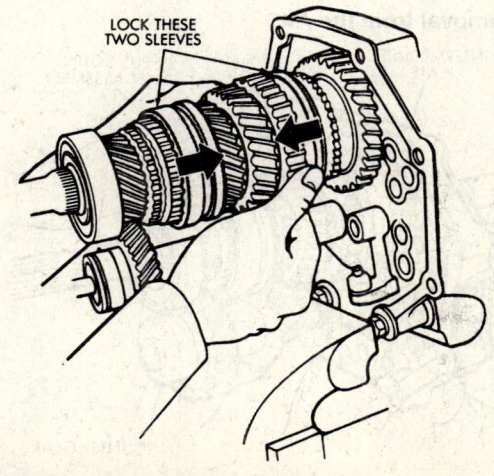

Locking the mainshaft gears on the AX5

DRIVE TRAIN 7

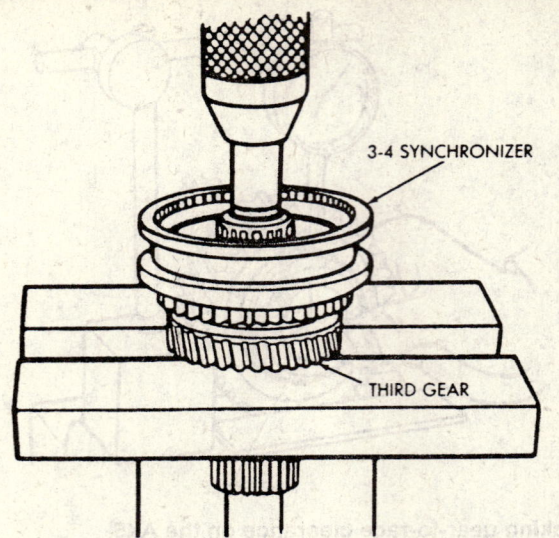

Removing the 3rd–4th synchronizer and 3rd gear from the AX5

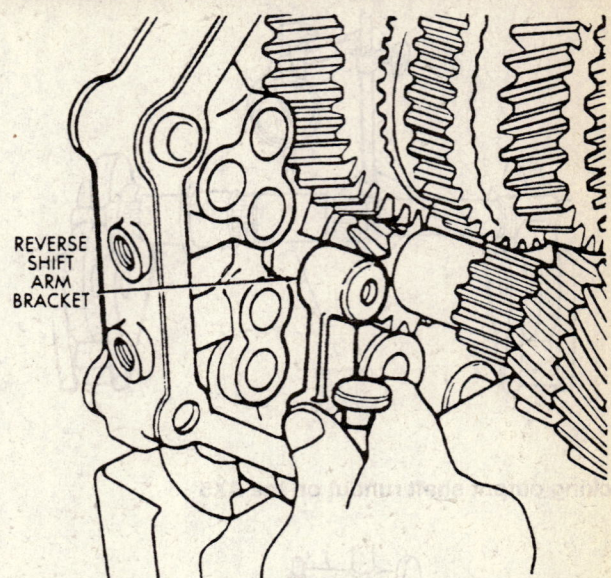

Removing the reverse shift arm bracket from the AX5

COMPONENT INSPECTION

Output Shaft & Inner Race

1. Check the output shaft and inner race for wear or damage.
2. Using calipers, measure the output shaft flange thickness. Minimum thickness is 4.8mm.
3. Using calipers, measure the inner face flange thickness. Minimum thickness is 4.0mm.
4. Using a micrometer, measure the outer diameter of the output shaft journal surface. 2nd gear minimum is 38mm; 3rd gear minimum is 35mm.
5. Using a micrometer, measure the outer diameter of the inner race. Minimum diameter is 39mm.
6. Using a dial indicator, measure the shaft runout. Maximum Runout: 0.05mm.

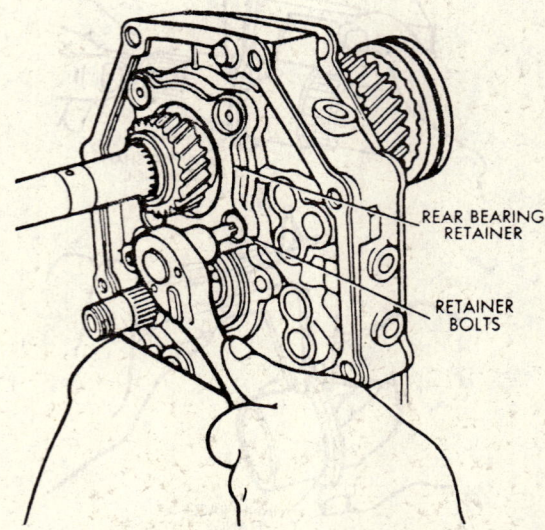

Removing the rear bearing retainer from the AX5

32. Remove the counter rear bearing from the intermediate plate.
33. Measure the thrust clearance of each gear. Standard clearance is 0.10–0.25mm.
34. Using two awls and a hammer, tap out the snapring.
35. Using a press, remove the 5th gear, rear bearing, 1st gear and the inner race.
36. Remove the needle roller bearing.
37. Remove the synchronizer ring and locking ball.
38. Using a press, remove hub sleeve No. 1 assembly, synchronizer ring, 2nd gear.
39. Remove the needle roller bearing.
40. Remove the snapring from hub sleeve No. 2.
41. Using a press, remove the hub sleeve, synchronizer ring, and 3rd gear.
42. Remove the needle roller bearing.

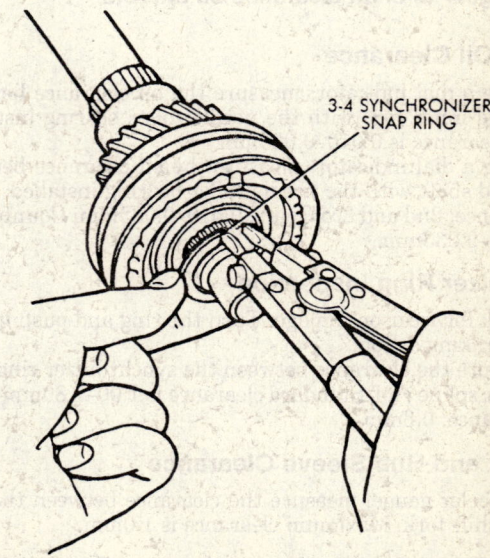

Removing the 3rd–4th synchronizer snapring from the AX5

7-45

7 DRIVE TRAIN

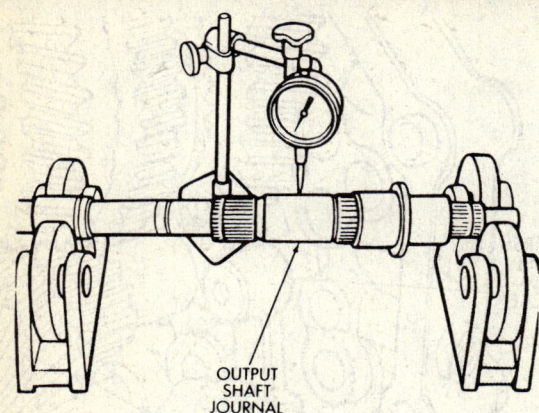

Checking output shaft runout on the AX5

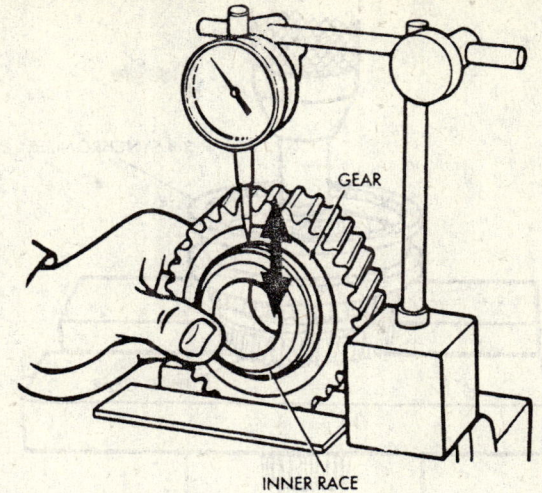

Checking gear-to-race clearance on the AX5

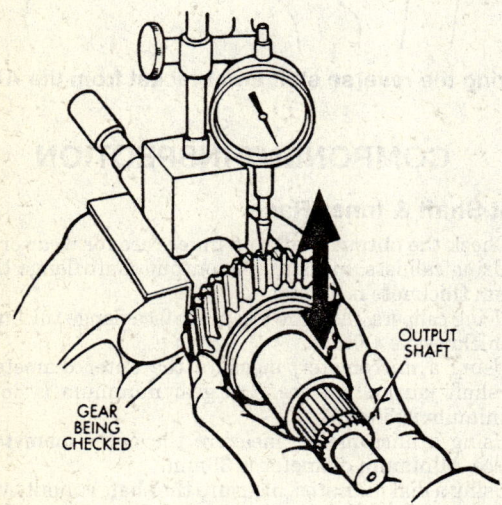

Checking gear-to-shaft clearance on the AX5

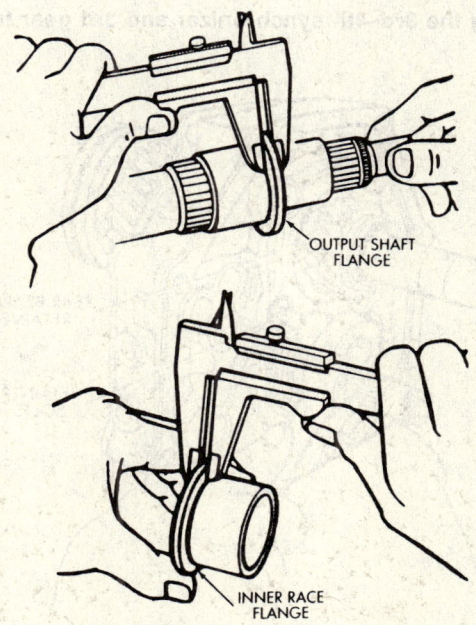

Checking flange thickness on the AX5

1st Gear Oil Clearance

1. Using a dial indicator, measure the oil clearance between the gear and inner race with the needle roller bearing installed. Standard clearance is 0.010–0.033mm.
2. Using a dial indicator, measure the oil clearance between the gear and shaft with the needle roller bearing installed. Standard Clearance: 2nd and 3rd Gears, 0.010–0.033mm; Counter 5th Gear, 0.010–0.033mm.

Synchronizer Ring Inspection

1. Check for wear or damage. Turn the ring and push it in to check the braking action.
2. Measure the clearance between the synchronizer ring back and the gear spline end. Standard clearance is 1.00–1.80mm; minimum clearance: 0.8mm.

Shift Fork and Hub Sleeve Clearance

Using a feeler gauge, measure the clearance between the hub sleeve and shift fork. Maximum clearance is 1.0mm.

Input Shaft and Bearing Inspection and Removal

1. Check for wear or damage. If necessary, remove the bearing snapring using snapring pliers and remove the bearing.

2. Using a press, remove the bearing.
3. Using a press and tool J-34603 or equivalent, install the new bearing.
4. Select a snapring that will allow minimum axial play and install it on the shaft.

Counter Gear and Bearing Inspection

1. Check the gear teeth for wear or damage.
2. Check the bearing for wear or damage.

Counter Gear Front Bearing Replacement

1. Using snapring pliers, remove the snapring.
2. Press out the bearing using tool J-22912-01 or equivalent.
3. Replace the side race.
4. Using tool J-28406 or equivalent, press in the bearing and inner race.
5. Select a snapring that will allow minimum axial play and install it on the shaft.

DRIVE TRAIN 7

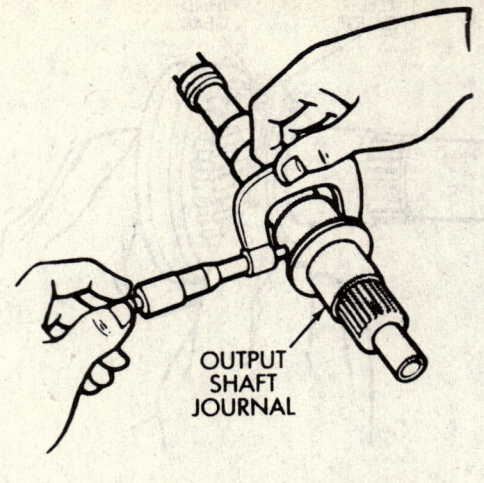

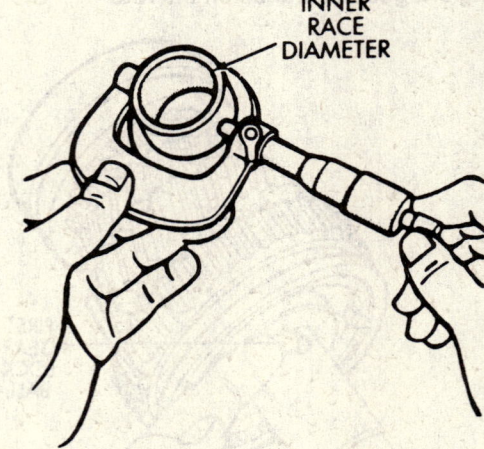

Checking shaft and race diameters on the AX5

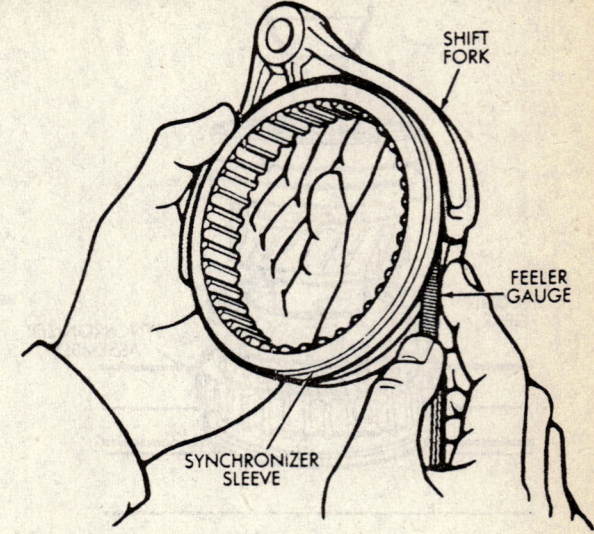

Checking fork-to-hub clearance on the AX5

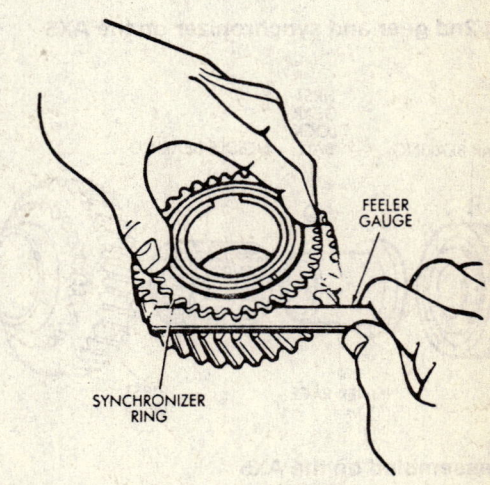

Checking synchronizer ring wear on the AX5

Front Bearing Retainer Inspection

1. Check retainer for damage.
2. Check the oil seal lip for wear or damage.

Oil Seal Replacement

1. Using a awl, pry the old seal out of the housing.
2. Press in the new oil seal using tool J-34602 or equivalent.
3. The oil seal depth is 11.20–12.20mm from the housing-to-transmission surface to the top edge of the seal.

Reverse Restrict Pin Replacement

1. Check for wear or damage.
2. Using a Torx bit, remove the screw plug.
3. Using a hammer and pin punch, drive out the slotted spring pin.
4. Pull off the lever housing and slide out the shaft.
5. Install the lever housing.
6. Using a hammer and pin punch, drive out the slotted spring pin.
7. Using a Torx bit, install and torque the screw plug to 27 ft. lbs. torque.

Adapter Housing & Oil Seal Inspection & Replacement

1. Check the adapter housing for wear or damage.
2. Replace the oil seal with tool J-29184 or equivalent.

ASSEMBLY

1. Install the clutch hub No. 1 and No. 2 into hub sleeves along with the shifting keys.

―――――― **CAUTION** ――――――
Install the key springs so their gaps are not in line.

2. Install the shifting springs under the shifting keys.
3. Apply gear oil on the output shaft and 3rd gear needle roller bearing.
4. Place the 3rd gear synchronizer ring on the gear and align the ring slots with the shifting keys.
5. Install the needle roller bearing in the 3rd gear and hub sleeve No. 2.
6. Select a new snapring (2) that will allow minimum axial play and install it on the shaft.
7. Using a feeler gauge, measure the 3rd gear thrust clearance. Standard clearance is 0.10–0.25mm.
8. Apply gear oil on the output shaft and 2nd gear needle bearing.

7 DRIVE TRAIN

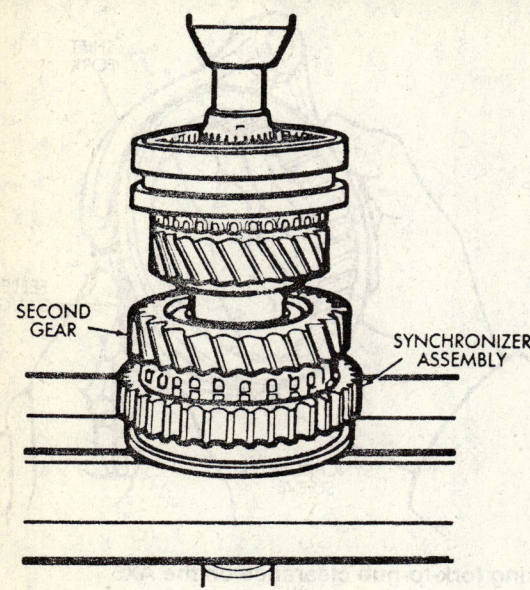

Installing 2nd gear and synchronizer on the AX5

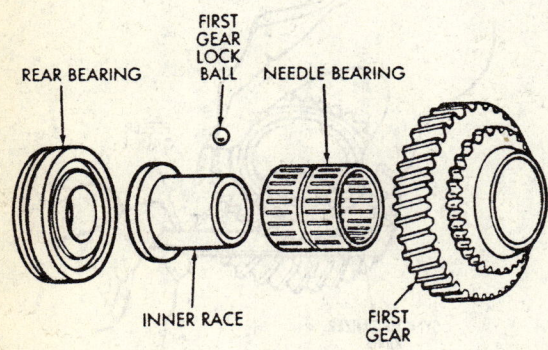

1st gear assembled on the AX5

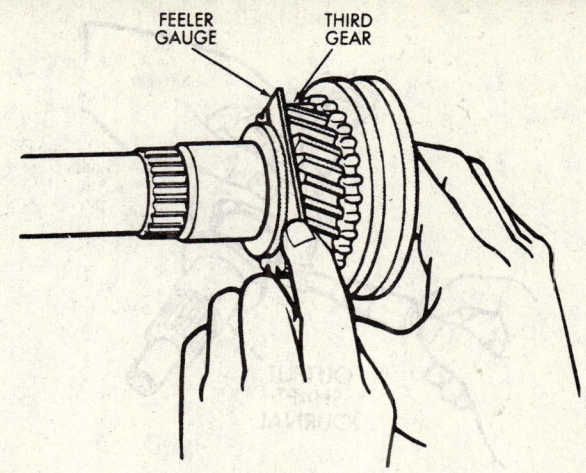

Checking 3rd gear clearance on the AX5

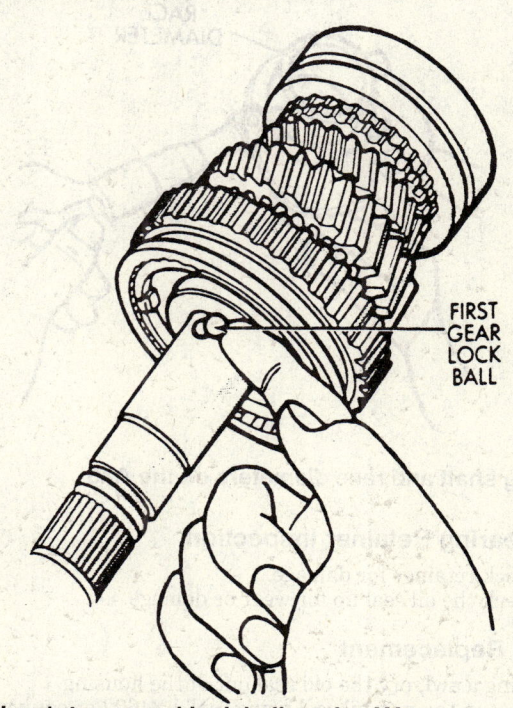

Installing 1st gear and lock ball on the AX5

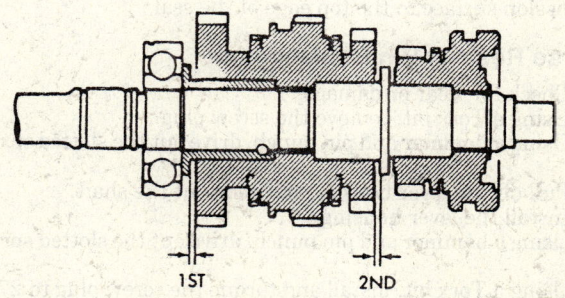

Checking 1st–2nd gear clearance on the AX5

9. Place the 2nd gear synchronizer ring on the 2nd gear and align the ring slots with the shifting keys.
10. Install the needle roller bearing in the 2nd gear.
11. Using a press install the 2nd gear and hub sleeve No. 1.
12. Install the 1st gear locking ball in the output shaft.
13. Apply gear oil to the needle roller bearing.
14. Assemble the 1st gear, synchronizer ring, needle roller bearing and bearing inner race.
15. Install the assembly on the output shaft, with the synchronizer ring slots aligned with the shifting keys.
16. Turn the inner race to align it with the locking ball.
17. Install the output shaft rear bearing using tool J-34603 or equivalent and a press.
18. Install the bearing on the output shaft with the outer race snapring groove toward the rear.

NOTE: Hold the 1st gear inner race to prevent it from falling.

19. Measure the 1st and 2nd gear thrust clearance with a feeler gauge. Standard Clearance: 0.10–0.25mm.
20. Install 5th gear on the output shaft using tool J-34603 or equivalent and a press.
21. Select a snapring that will allow minimum axial play.
22. Using a screwdriver and a hammer, tap the snap into position.

DRIVE TRAIN 7

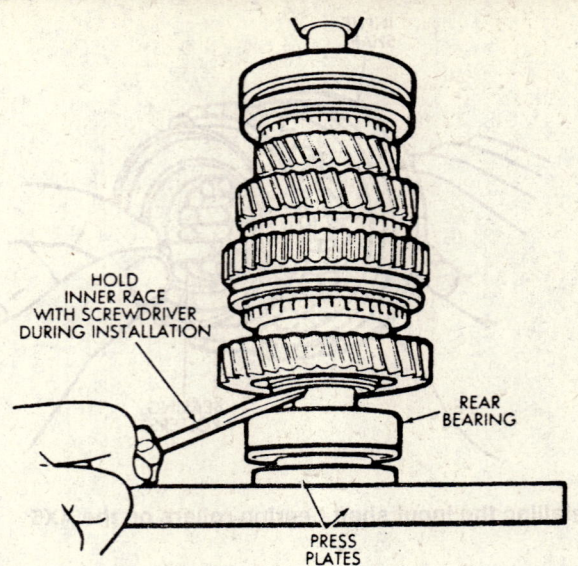

Installing the output shaft rear bearing on the AX5

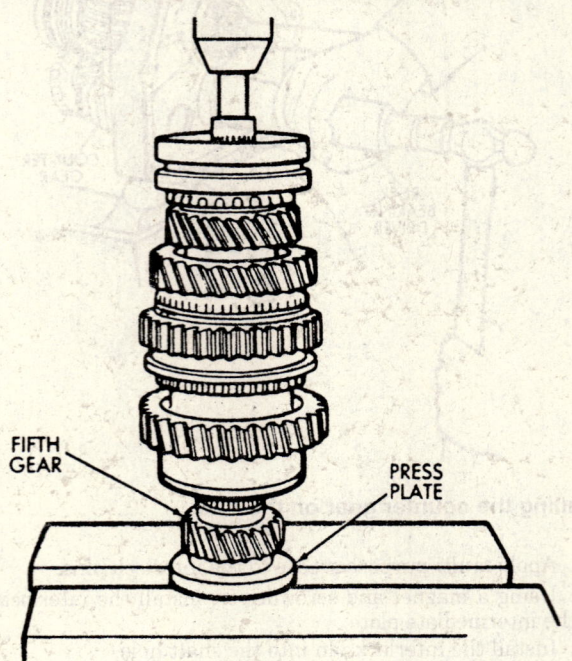

Installing output shaft 5th gear on the AX5

23. Apply multi-purpose grease to the fourteen needle roller bearings and install them in the input shaft.
24. Install the output shaft into the intermediate plate by pulling on the output shaft and tapping on the intermediate plate.
25. Install the input shaft to the output shaft with the synchronizer ring slots aligned with the shifting keys.
26. Install the counter gear into the intermediate plate while holding the counter gear, and install the counter rear bearing with a suitable driver.
27. Install the bearing snapring using snapring pliers.

NOTE: Be sure the snapring is flush with the intermediate plate surface.

28. Using a Torx bit, install and tighten the screws to 13 ft. lbs. torque.

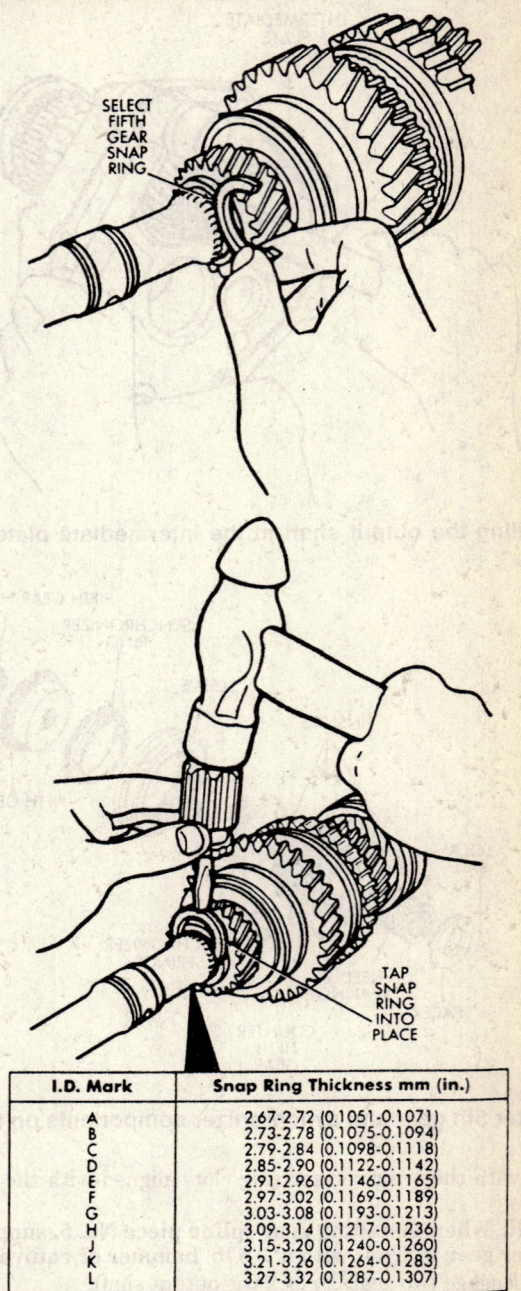

I.D. Mark	Snap Ring Thickness mm (in.)
A	2.67-2.72 (0.1051-0.1071)
B	2.73-2.78 (0.1075-0.1094)
C	2.79-2.84 (0.1098-0.1118)
D	2.85-2.90 (0.1122-0.1142)
E	2.91-2.96 (0.1146-0.1165)
F	2.97-3.02 (0.1169-0.1189)
G	3.03-3.08 (0.1193-0.1213)
H	3.09-3.14 (0.1217-0.1236)
J	3.15-3.20 (0.1240-0.1260)
K	3.21-3.26 (0.1264-0.1283)
L	3.27-3.32 (0.1287-0.1307)

Selecting and installing the 5th gear snapring on the AX5

29. Install the reverse shift arm bracket and tighten the bolts to 13 ft. lbs. torque.
30. Install the ball and spacer.
31. Install the shifting keys and hub sleeve No. 3 onto the counter 5th gear.

── **CAUTION** ──
Install the key springs positioned so the end gaps are not in line.

32. Install shifting key springs under the shifting keys.
33. Apply gear oil to the needle roller bearing and install the counter 5th gear with hub sleeve No. 3 and needle roller bearings.
34. Install the synchronizer ring on gear spline piece.
35. Using tool J-28406 or equivalent drive in gear spline piece

7-49

7 DRIVE TRAIN

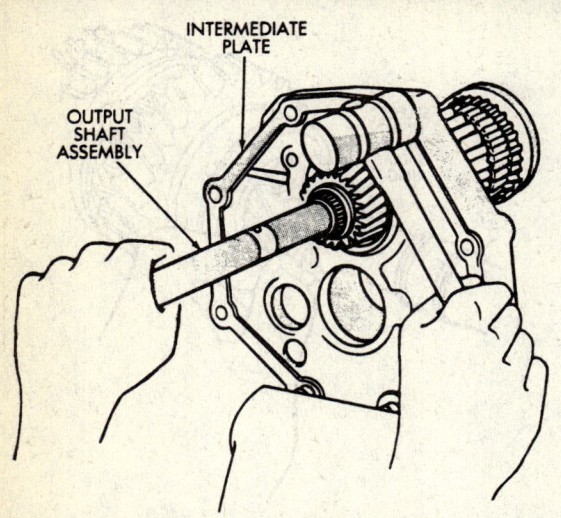

Installing the output shaft in the intermediate plate on the AX5

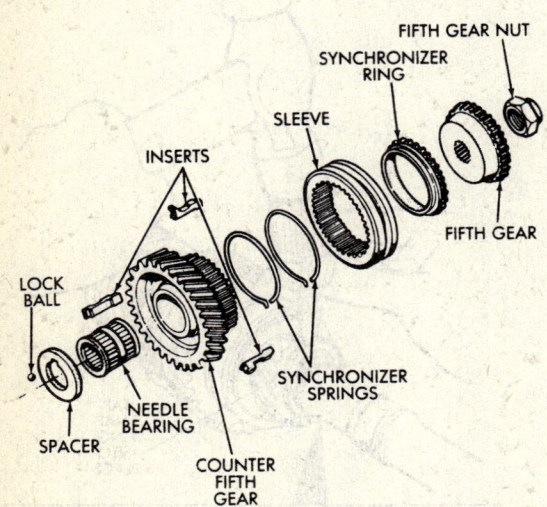

Counter 5th gear and synchronizer components on the AX5

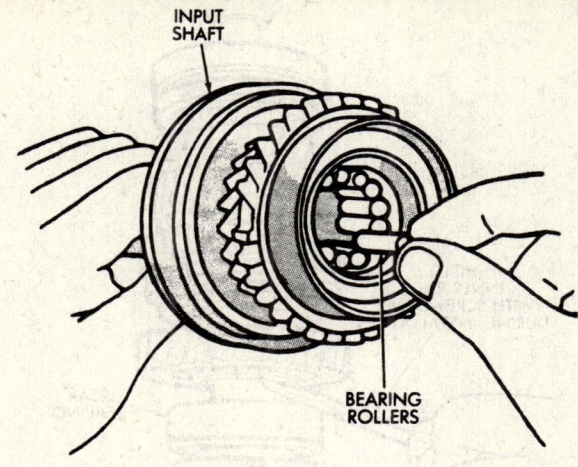

Installing the input shaft bearing rollers on the AX5

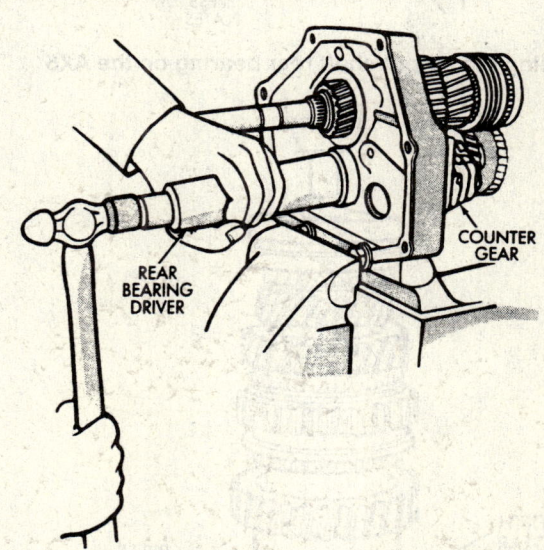

Installing the counter gear on the AX5

No. 5 with the synchronizer ring slots aligned with the shifting keys.

NOTE: When installing gear spline piece No. 5, support the counter gear in front with a 3–5 lb. hammer or equivalent.

36. Engage two gears to lock the output shaft.
37. Install and tighten the lock nut to 90 ft. lbs. torque on the counter shaft.
38. Stake the lock nut.
39. Disengage the gears.
40. Measure the counter 5th gear thrust clearance using a feeler gauge. Standard Clearance: 0.10–0.30mm.
41. Install the reverse shift arm to the pivot of the reverse shift arm bracket.
42. Install the reverse idler gear on the shaft.
43. Align the reverse shift arm shoe to the reverse idler gear groove and insert the reverse idler gear shift to the intermediate plate.
44. Install the reverse idler gear shaft stopper and tighten the bolt to 13 ft. lbs. torque.
45. Place shift forks No. 1 and No. 2 into groove of hub sleeves No. 1 and No. 2 and install fork shaft No. 2 to the shift forks No. 1 and No. 2 through the intermediate plate.

46. Apply multi-purpose grease to the interlock pins.
47. Using a magnet and screwdriver, install the interlock pin into the intermediate plate.
48. Install the interlock pin into the shaft hole.
49. Install fork shaft No. 1 to shift fork No. 1 through the intermediate plate.
50. Using a magnet and screwdriver, install the interlock pin into the intermediate plate.
51. Install the interlock pin into the shaft hole.
52. Install fork shaft No. 3 to the reverse shift arm through the intermediate plate.
53. Install the reverse shift head into fork shaft No. 5.
54. Insert fork shaft No. 5 to the intermediate plate and put in the reverse shift head to the shift fork No. 3.
55. Using a magnetic finger and screwdriver, install the locking ball into the reverse shift head hole.
56. Shift hub sleeve No. 3 to the 5th speed position.
57. Place shift fork No. 3 into the groove of hub sleeve No. 3 and install fork shaft No. 4 to shift fork No. 3 and reverse shift arm.
58. Using a magnet and screwdriver, install the locking ball

DRIVE TRAIN 7

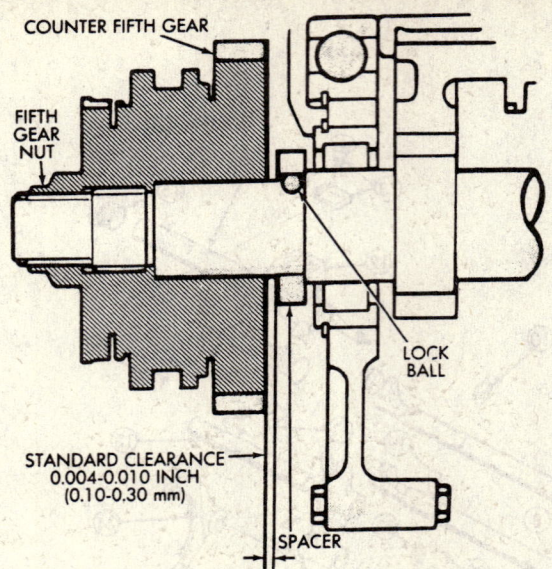

Checking 5th gear thrust clearance on the AX5

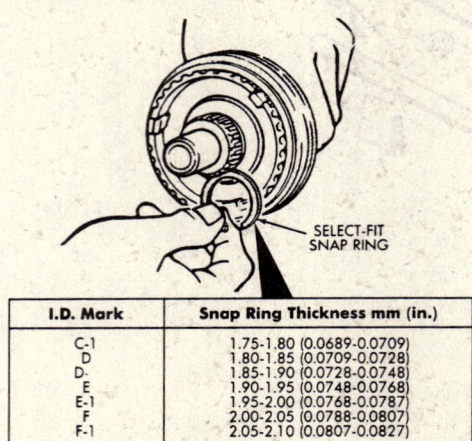

Installing 3rd gear and 3rd–4th synchronizer on the AX5

I.D. Mark	Snap Ring Thickness mm (in.)
C-1	1.75-1.80 (0.0689-0.0709)
D	1.80-1.85 (0.0709-0.0728)
D-	1.85-1.90 (0.0728-0.0748)
E	1.90-1.95 (0.0748-0.0768)
E-1	1.95-2.00 (0.0768-0.0787)
F	2.00-2.05 (0.0788-0.0807)
F-1	2.05-2.10 (0.0807-0.0827)

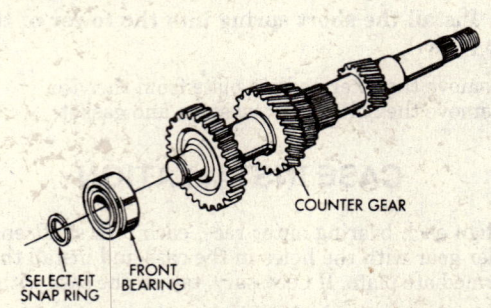

Installing counter gear front bearing and snapring on the AX5

I.D. Mark	Snap Ring Thickness mm (in.)
1	2.05-2.10 (0.0807-0.0827)
2	2.10-2.15 (0.0827-0.0846)
3	2.15-2.20 (0.0846-0.0866)
4	2.20-2.25 (0.0866-0.0886)
5	2.25-2.30 (0.0886-0.0906)
6	2.30-2.35 (0.0906-0.0925)

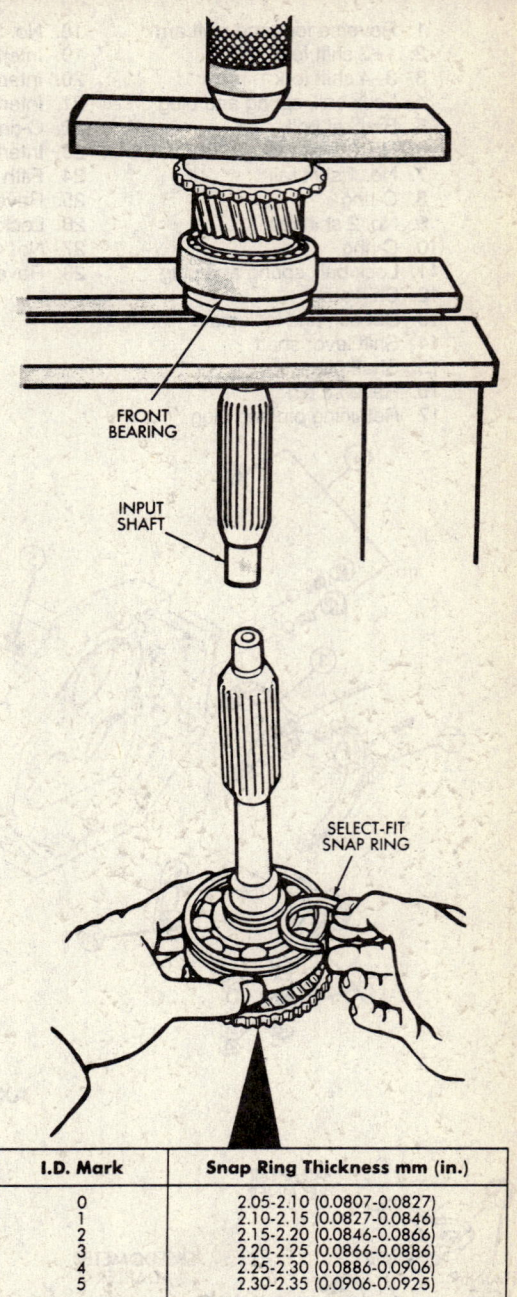

I.D. Mark	Snap Ring Thickness mm (in.)
0	2.05-2.10 (0.0807-0.0827)
1	2.10-2.15 (0.0827-0.0846)
2	2.15-2.20 (0.0846-0.0866)
3	2.20-2.25 (0.0866-0.0886)
4	2.25-2.30 (0.0886-0.0906)
5	2.30-2.35 (0.0906-0.0925)

Installing front bearing and snapring on the AX5

into the intermediate plate and insert fork shaft No. 4 to the intermediate plate.

59. Check the interlock by positioning the shift fork shaft No. 1 to the 1st speed position.

60. Fork shafts No. 2, No. 3, No. 4 and No. 5 should not move.

61. Using a pin punch and a hammer, drive in new slotted spring pins in each shift fork, reverse shift arm and reverse shift head.

62. Install two fork shaft E-rings.

63. Apply liquid sealer to the screw plugs.

64. Install the locking balls, springs and screw plugs with a Torx bit and tighten to 14 ft. lbs. torque.

7 DRIVE TRAIN

1. Reverse fork and shift arm
2. 1–2 shift fork
3. 3–4 shift fork
4. Lock ball, spring and plug
5. Bracket bolt
6. No. 3 shift rail
7. No. 1 shift rail
8. C-ring
9. No. 2 shift rail
10. C-ring
11. Lock ball, spring and plug
12. Shift arm
13. Set bolt and lock plate
14. Shift lever shaft
15. Shaft plug
16. Reverse pin
17. Retaining pin and plug
18. No. 5 shift rail
19. Interlock pin
20. Interlock pin
21. Interlock pin
22. C-ring
23. Interlock pin
24. Fifth-reverse fork
25. Reverse shift head
26. Lock balls
27. No. 4 shift rail
28. Reverse arm bracket

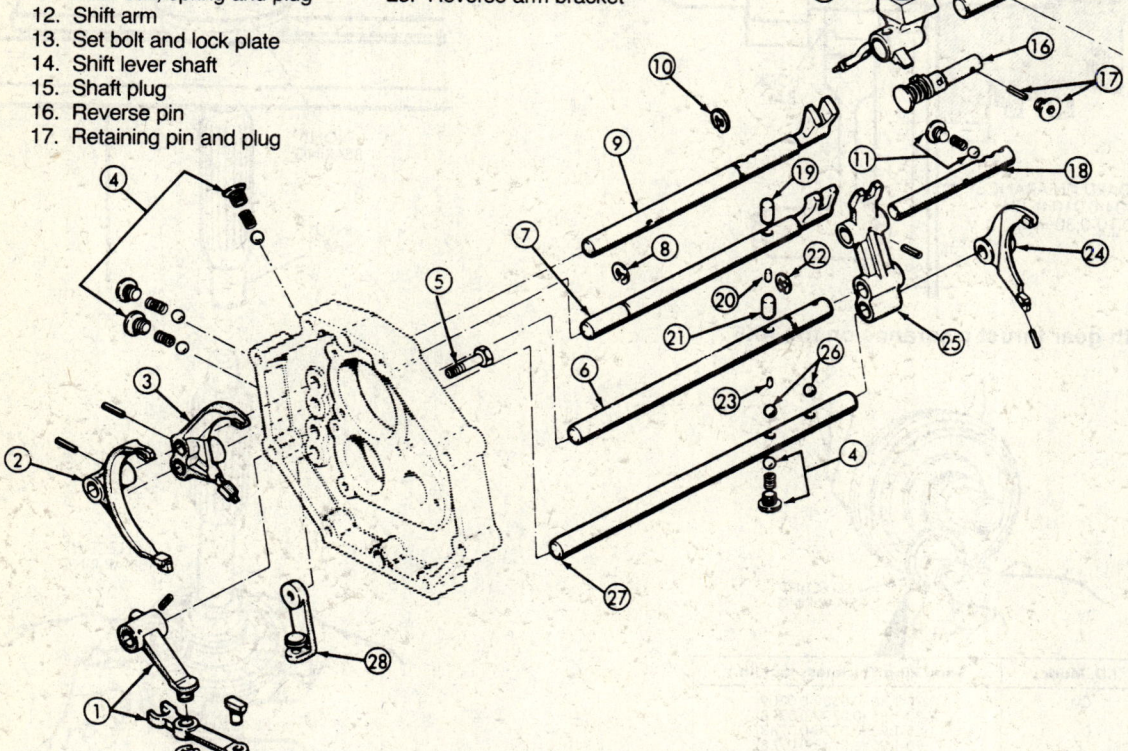

AX5 shift components

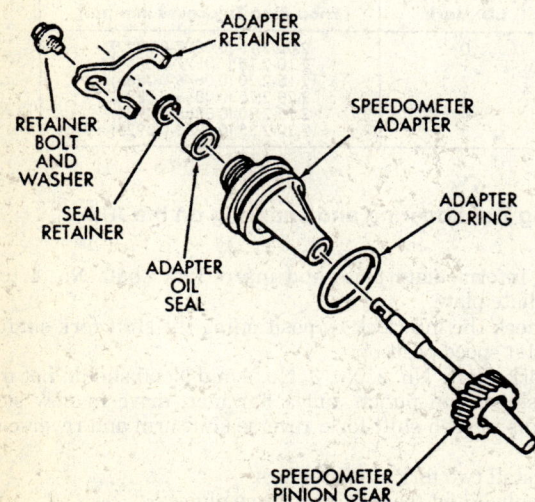

Speedometer gear assembly on the AX5

NOTE: Install the short spring into the tower of the intermediate plate.

65. Remove the intermediate plate from the vise.
66. Remove the bolts, nuts, washers and gasket.

CASE INSTALLATION

1. Align each bearing outer race, each fork shaft end and reverse idler gear with the holes in the case and install the case on the intermediate plate. If necessary, tap on the case with a plastic hammer.
2. Install two new bearing snaprings.
3. Install front bearing retainer with a new gasket.
4. Apply liquid sealer to the bolts.
5. Install and tighten the bolts to 12 ft. lbs. torque.
6. Install the new gasket to the intermediate plate.
7. Install the adapter housing.
8. Install and tighten the adapter bolts to 27 ft. lbs. torque.
9. Install the shift lever housing.
10. Insert the shift lever into the adapter and shift lever housing.

DRIVE TRAIN 7

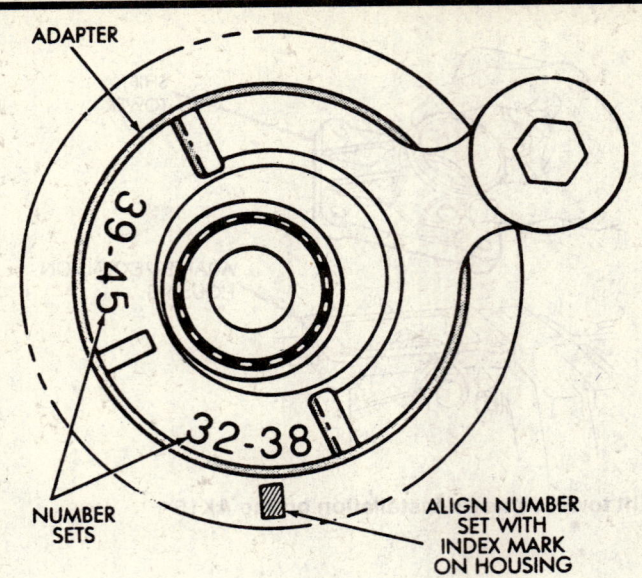

Indexing the speedometer gears on the AX5

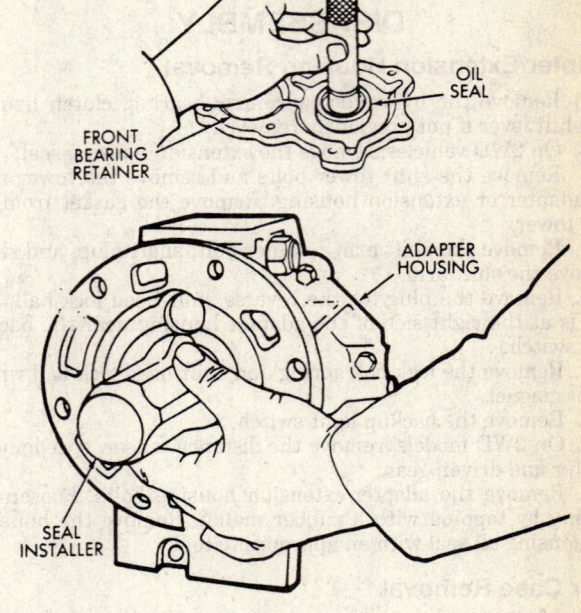

Oil seal installation on the AX5

11. Install and tighten shift lever housing bolt with a lock plate to 28 ft. lbs. torque. Lock the lock plate.
12. Install and tighten the adapter screw plug to 13 ft. lbs. torque.
13. Apply liquid sealer to the plug.
14. Install the locking ball, spring and screw plug and tighten the plug to 14 ft. lbs. torque.
15. Check to see that the input shaft and output shafts rotate smoothly.
16. Check to see that shifting can be done smoothly to all positions.
17. Install the black restrict pin on the reverse gear/5th gear side.

18. Install the remaining pin and tighten the pins to 20 ft. lbs. torque.
19. Install the shift lever retainer with a new gasket and tighten the bolts to 13 ft. lbs. torque.
20. Install the back-up light switch and tighten to 27 ft. lbs. torque.
21. Install the clutch housing and tighten the bolts to 27 ft. lbs. torque.

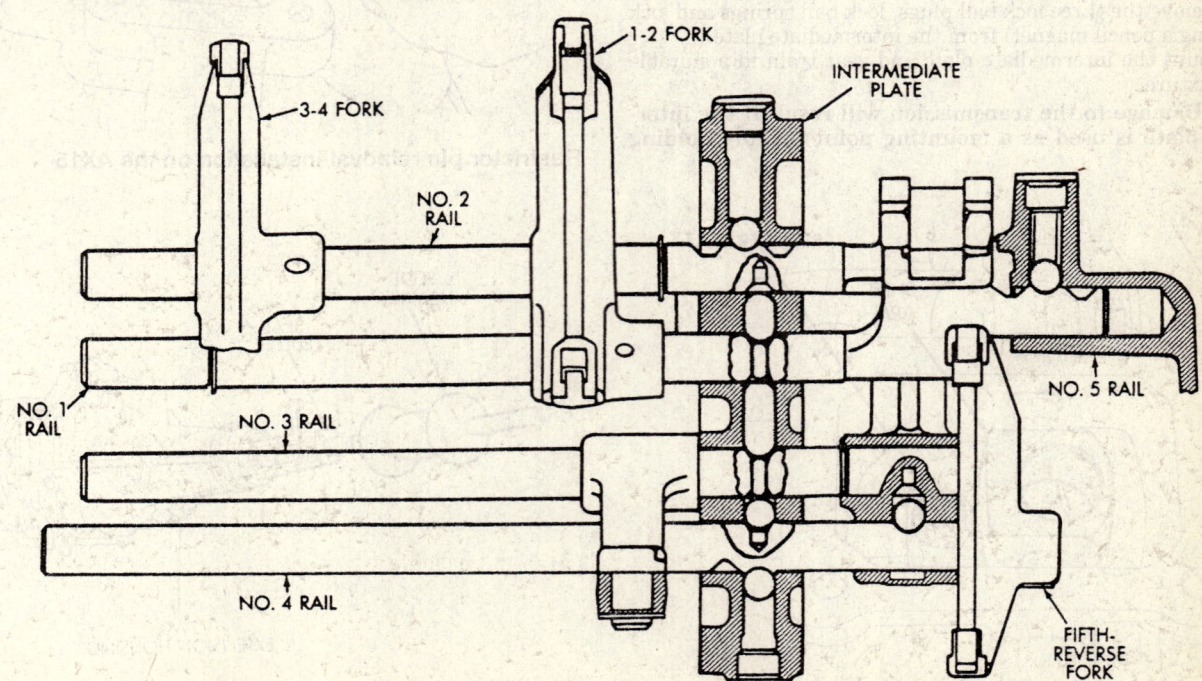

AX5 interlock ball and pin position

7 DRIVE TRAIN

AX 15 Overhaul

DISASSEMBLY

Adapter/Extension Housing Removal

1. Remove the hydraulic concentric bearing, clutch housing and shift lever if not previously removed.
2. On 2WD vehicles, remove the extension housing seal.
3. Remove the shift tower bolts and remove the tower from the adapter or extension housing. Remove the gasket from the shift tower.
4. Remove the shift arm retainer bolt, shaft plug, and shaft. Remove the shift arm.
5. Remove the plug for the reverse shift head lock ball. The plug is at the right side of the adapter housing near the backup light switch.
6. Remove the lock ball spring and shift head lock ball with a pencil magnet.
7. Remove the backup light switch.
8. On 2WD models, remove the distance sensor, speedometer adapter and driven gear.
9. Remove the adapter/extension housing bolts. Loosen the housing by tapping with a rubber mallet. Remove the housing, and housing oil seal with an appropriate tool.

Gear Case Removal

1. Remove the bearing retainer bolts and retainer. Remove the retainer oil seal with an appropriate pry tool.
2. Remove the input bearing snapring. Remove the cluster gear front bearing snapring.
3. Loosen the gear case by tapping it away from the intermediate plate with a rubber mallet. Remove the gear case and intermediate plate.
4. On 2WD models, remove the speedometer gear snapring, speedometer gear and spacer from the output shaft.

Fifth Gear And Synchro Assembly Removal

1. Remove the three lock ball plugs, lock ball springs and lock balls (using a pencil magnet) from the intermediate plate.
2. Mount the intermediate plate and gear train in a suitable holding fixture.

NOTE: Damage to the transmission will result if the intermediate plate is used as a mounting point for any holding fixture.

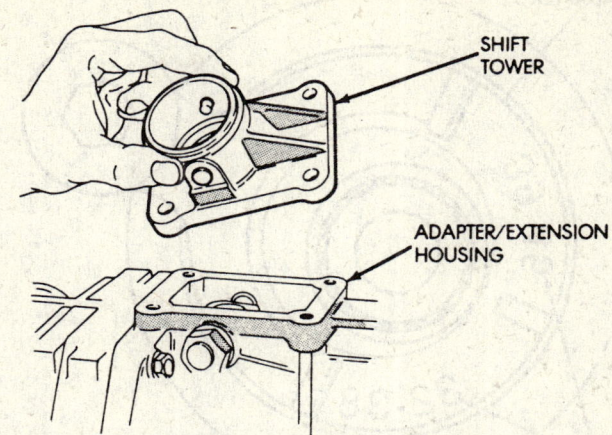

Shift tower removal/installation on the AX15

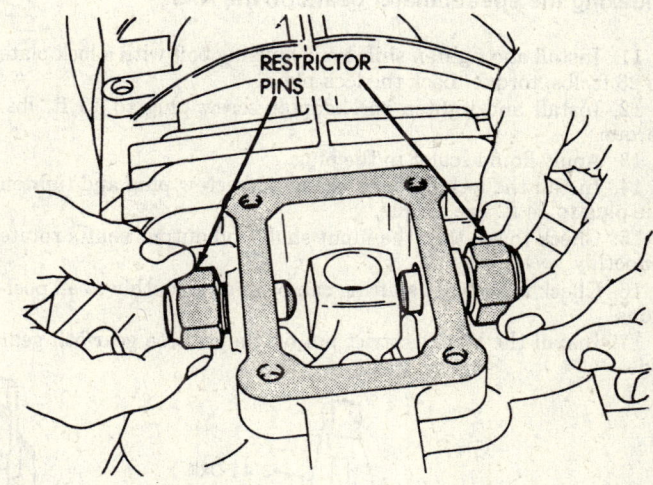

Restrictor pin removal/installation on the AX15

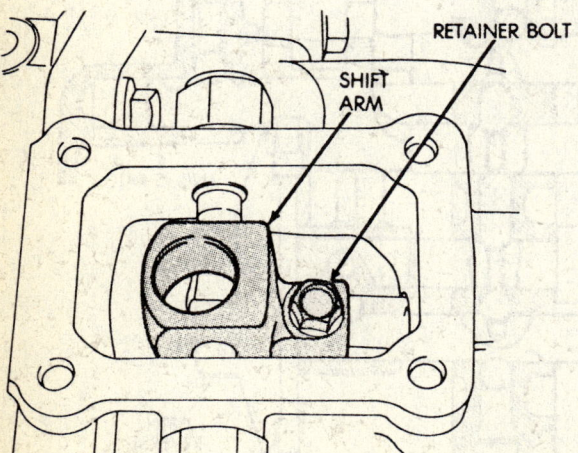

Shift arm retainer bolt removal/installation on the AX15

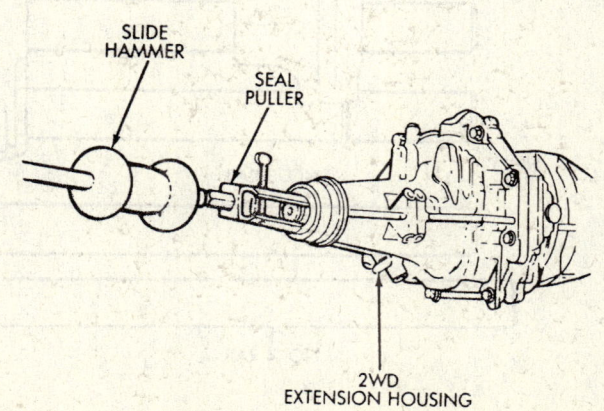

Removing the 2WD extension housing seal

DRIVE TRAIN 7

3. Remove the 5th gear assembly snapring and retain for reference.
4. Remove the E-ring that secures the reverse shift arm to the fork.
5. Remove the bolts attaching the reverse shift arm bracket to the intermediate plate. Then remove the bracket.
6. Remove the reverse shift arm and shoe.
7. Remove the 5th gear shift fork set screw. Move the shift rail forward until it clears the shift fork and remove the shift fork from the synchro sleeve.
8. Remove the reverse shift rail and shift head as an assembly.
9. Measure thrust clearance between the counter 5th gear and the thrust ring with a feeler gauge. Clearance should be 0.003–0.019 in. (0.08–0.48mm). If not within specification, replace the gear and/or ring.
10. Loosen the 5th spline gear with a two-jaw puller. Position the puller jaws behind the 5th counter gear. Remove the 5th spline gear, synchro ring, synchro and sleeve as an assembly.
11. Remove the counter 5th gear thrust ring and lock ball (with a pencil magnet).
12. Remove the bolts attaching the output shaft rear bearing retainer to the intermediate plate. Remove the rear bearing retainer, reverse gear and shaft.

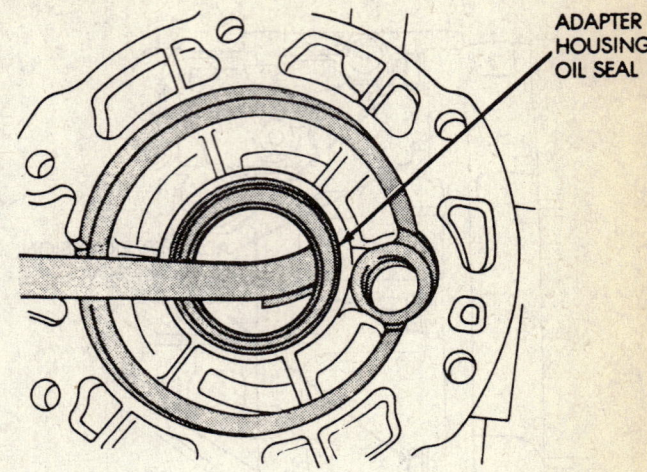

Removing the adapter housing seal

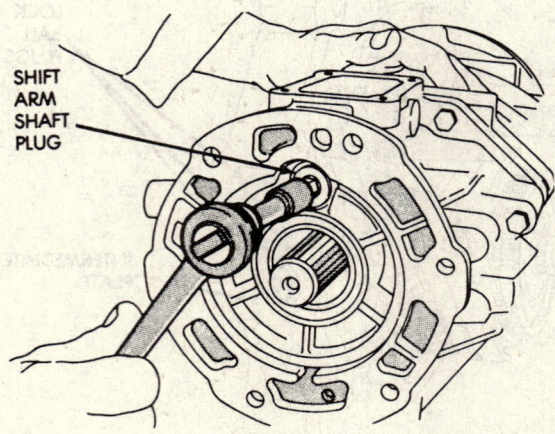

Shift lever shaft plug removal/installation on the AX15

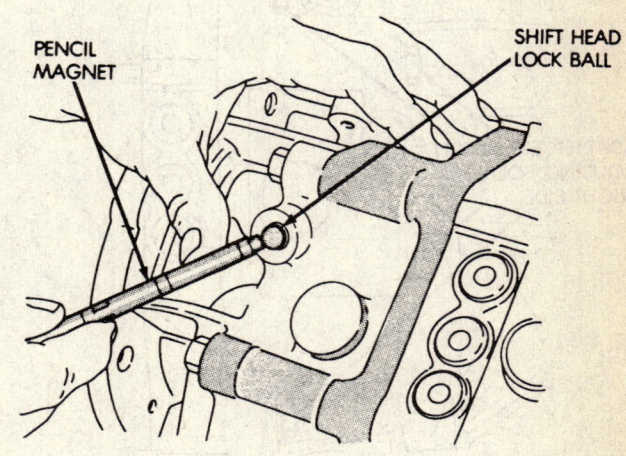

Shift head lock ball removal/installation on the AX15

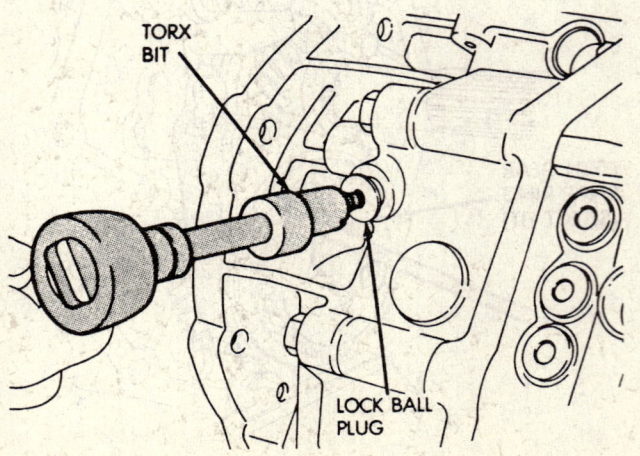

Shift head lock ball plug removal/installation on the AX15

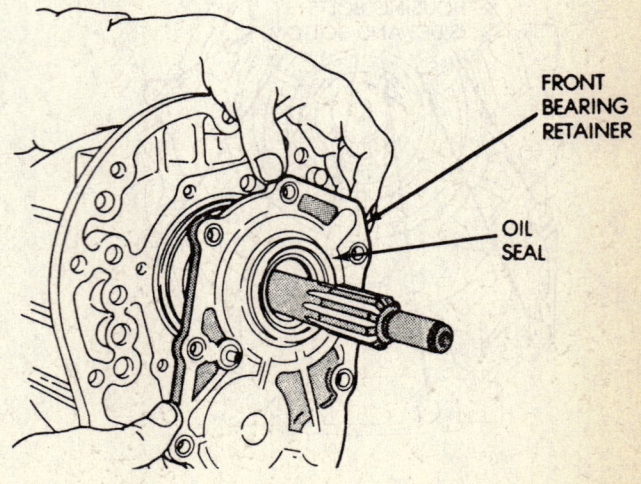

Front bearing retainer removal

7-55

7 DRIVE TRAIN

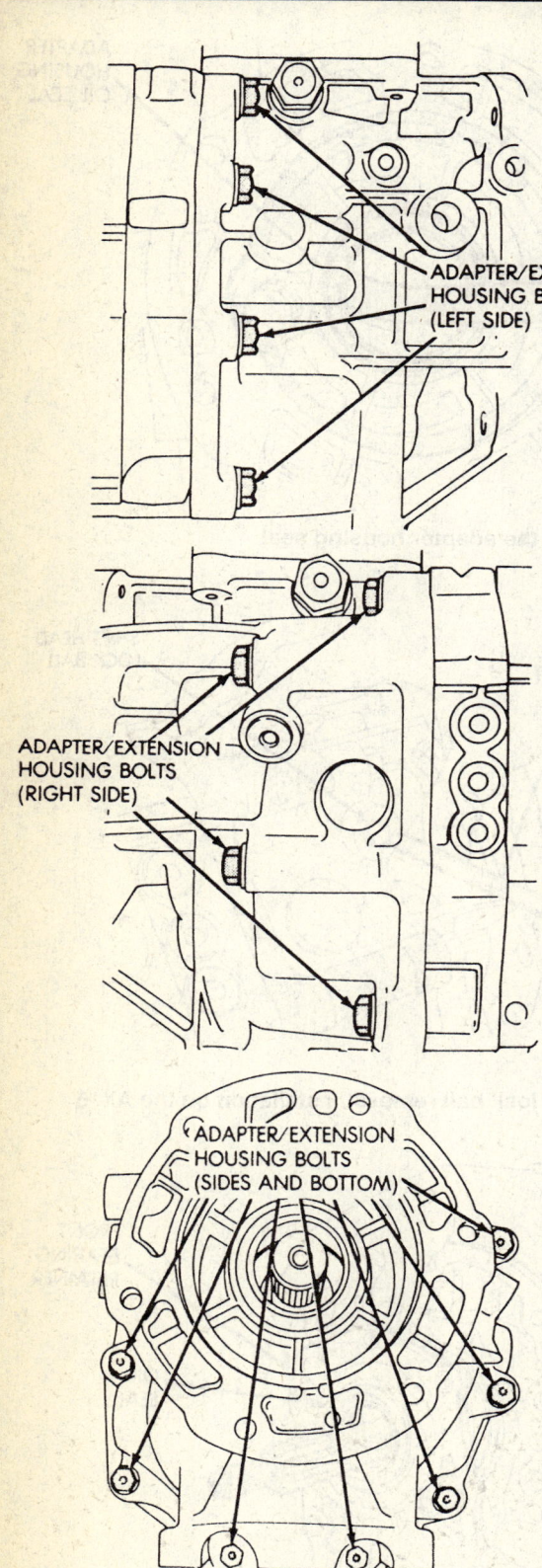

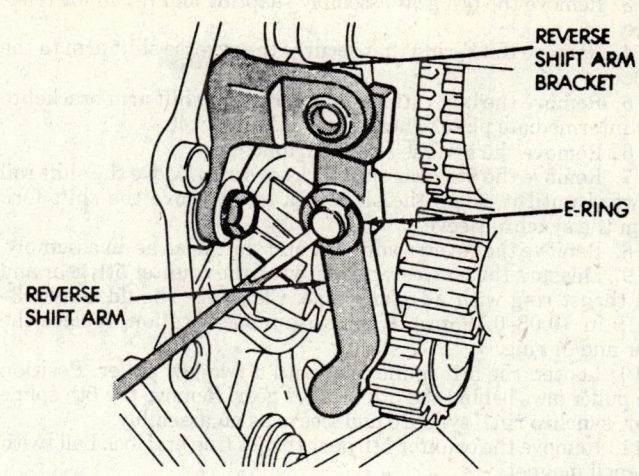

Removing reverse shift arm E-ring

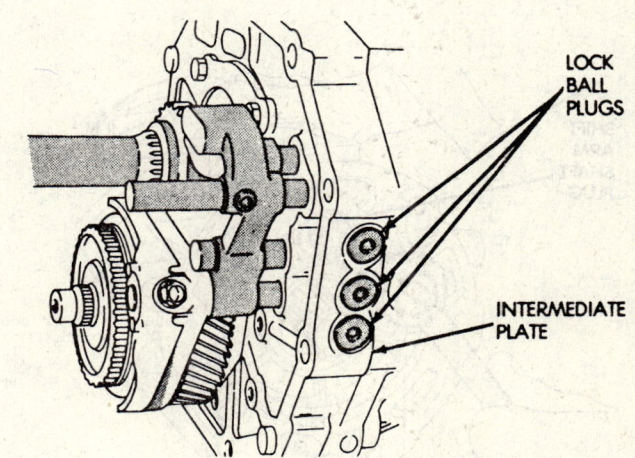

Lock ball plug locations

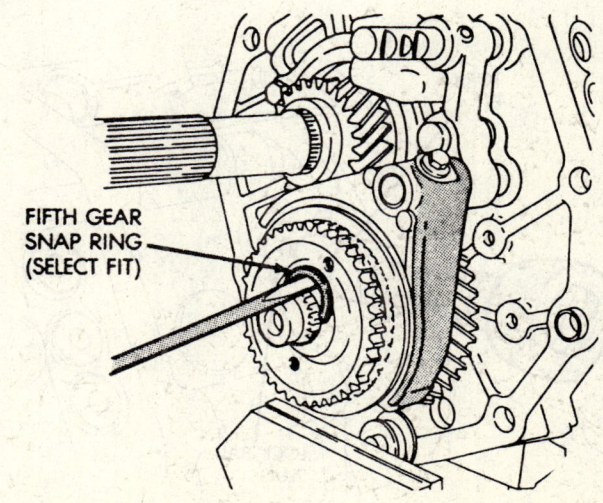

Adapter housing bolt locations on the AX15

5th gear snapring removal

DRIVE TRAIN 7

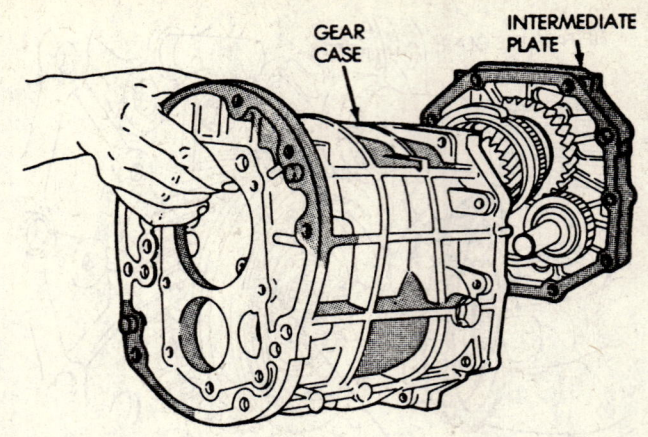

Gear case removal on the AX15

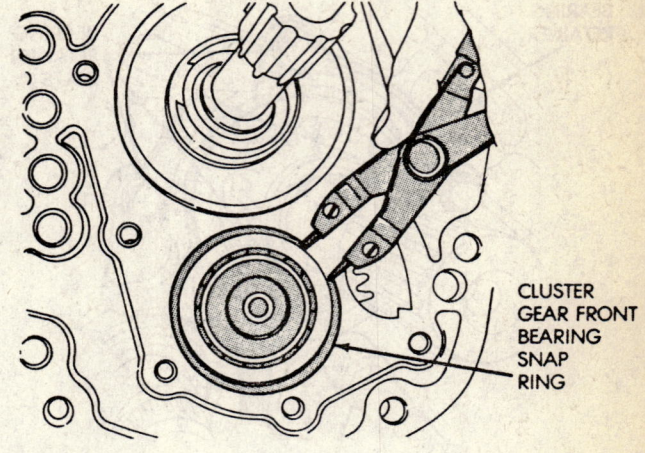

Removing cluster gear front bearing snapring

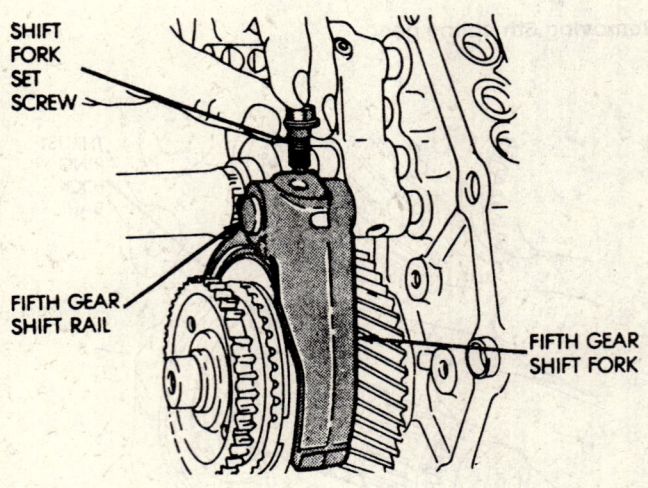

Removing the 5th gear fork set screw

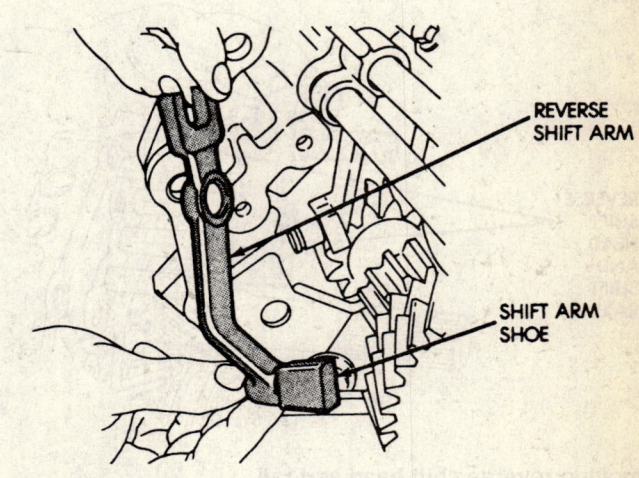

Removing reverse shift arm and shoe

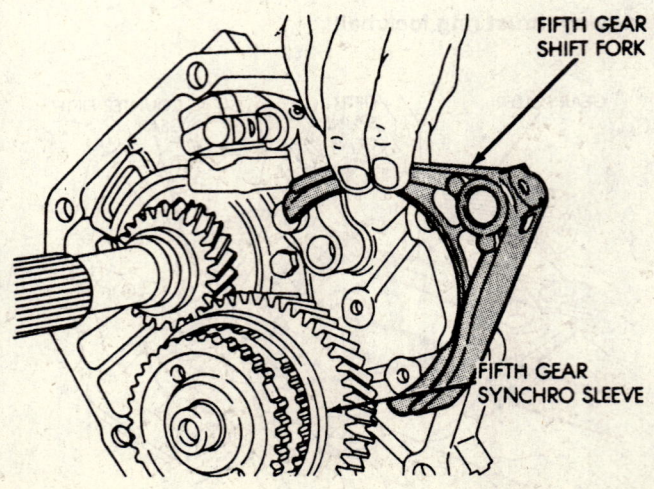

Removing the 5th gear shift fork

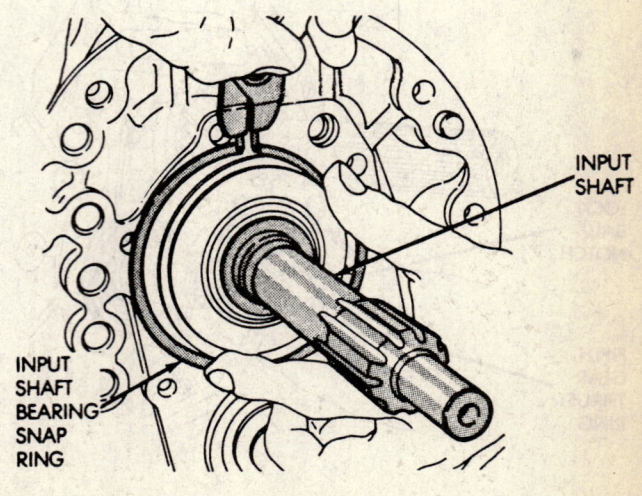

Removing input shaft bearing snapring

7-57

7 DRIVE TRAIN

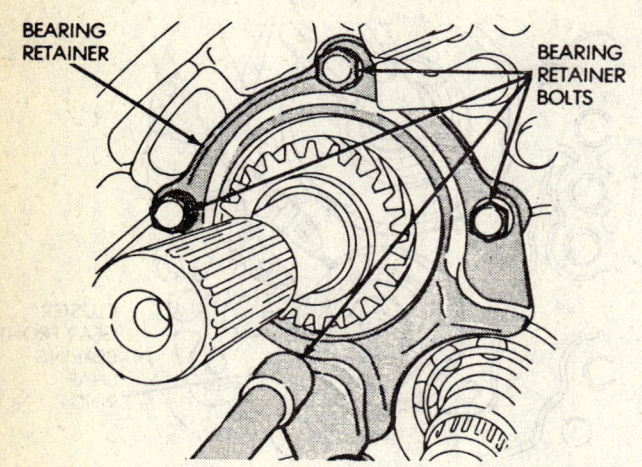

Removing output shaft rear bearing retainer bolts on the AX15

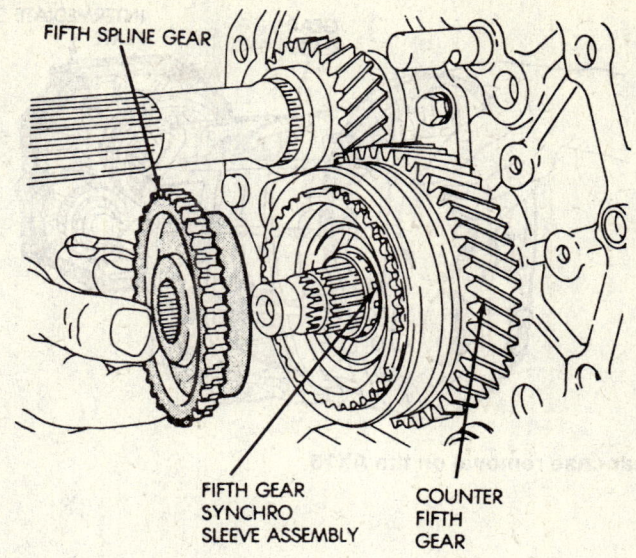

Removing 5th spline gear

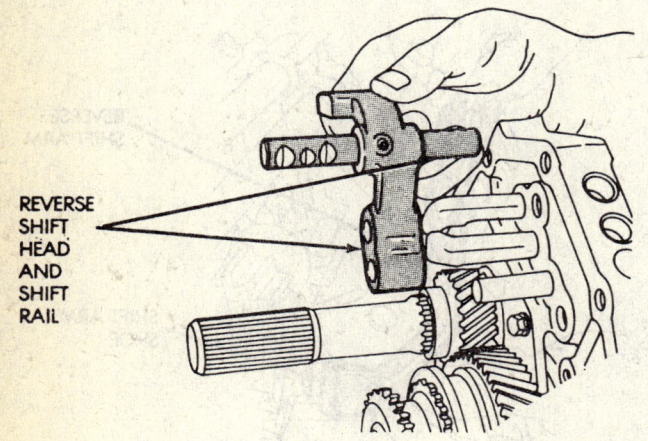

Removing reverse shift head and rail

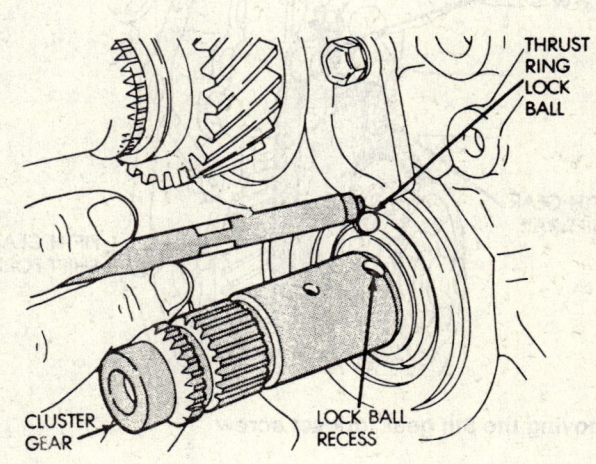

Removing thrust ring lock ball

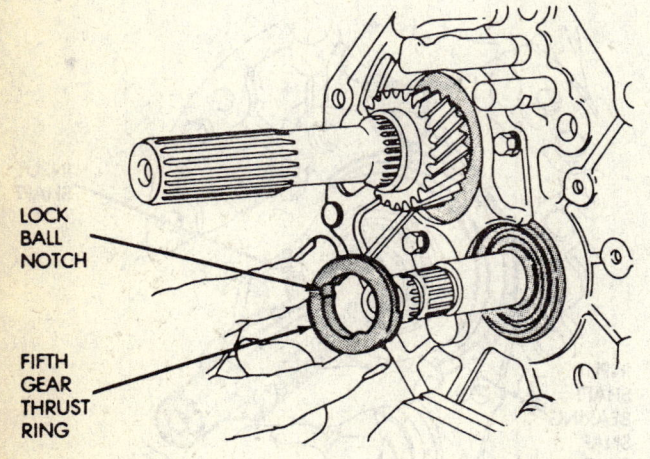

Removing 5th gear thrust ring

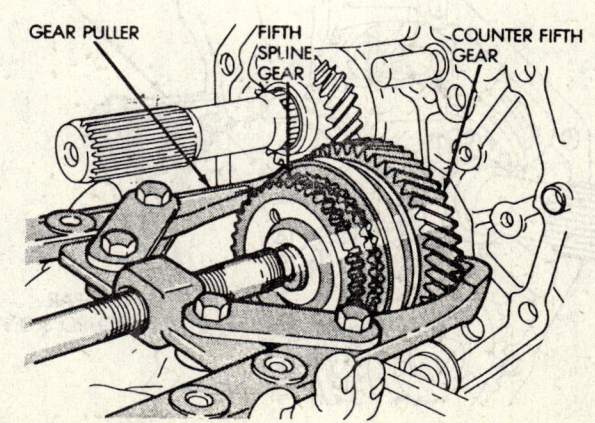

Loosening 5th spline gear

7-58

DRIVE TRAIN 7

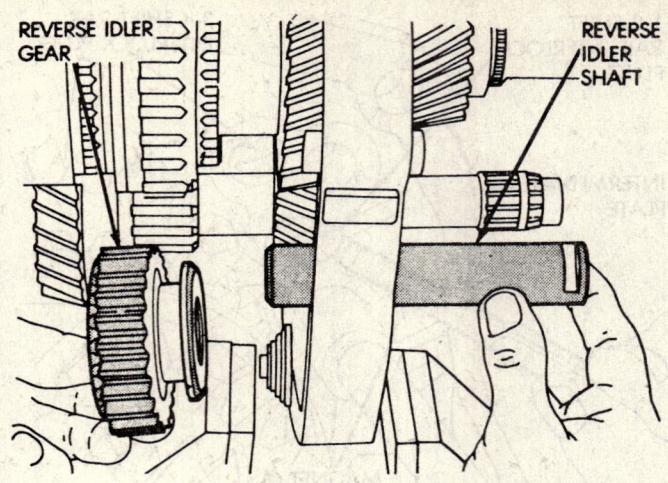

Removing reverse idler gear and shaft on the AX15

Shift Rail And Fork Removal

There are a total of five shift rails in the AX 15 transmission – the 1-2, 3-4, 5th gear and 1st–reverse.

Two shift rails are used for reverse gear range. The front reverse rail is at the forward side of the intermediate plate. The short rear reverse rail and reverse shift head are at the rear side of the intermediate plate.

NOTE: It is NOT necessary to remove the shift rails if they do not require service during overhaul. Only the shift forks need be removed for access to the shafts and gears. Position all removed components in order on a workbench to help in identification during inspection and reassembly.

1. Remove the 5th gear shift rail. Catch the lock ball as it comes out of the intermediate plate.

2. Remove the 1-2 and 3-4 shift rail C-rings. Remove the shift fork set screws.

3. Remove the 3-4 shift rail from the shift fork and intermediate plate. Remove the interlock plug with a magnet.

4. Remove the 1-2 shift rail from the shift fork and intermediate plate. Remove the 1-2 interlock pin and interlock plug.

5. Lift the reverse fork upward and remove the 5th gear shift rail lock ball.

6. Remove the 3-4, then the 1-2 shift fork.

7. Remove the reverse shift rail C-ring, the shift rail and fork.

Shaft and Gear Removal

1. Remove the output shaft and cluster gear rear bearing snapring.

2. Tap the end of the output shaft with a mallet to unseat and start the rear bearing out of the intermediate plate.

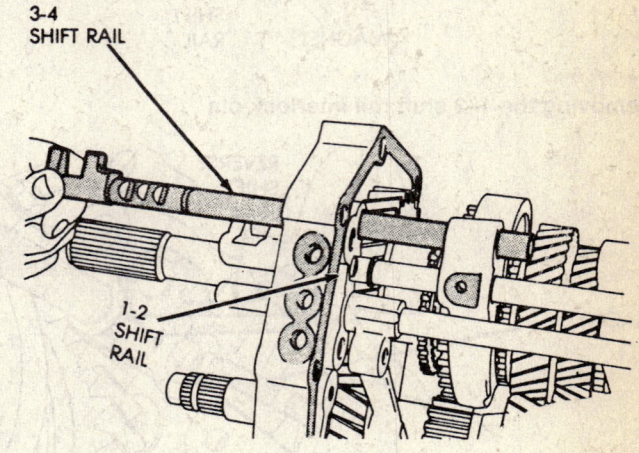

Removing the 3-4 shift rail

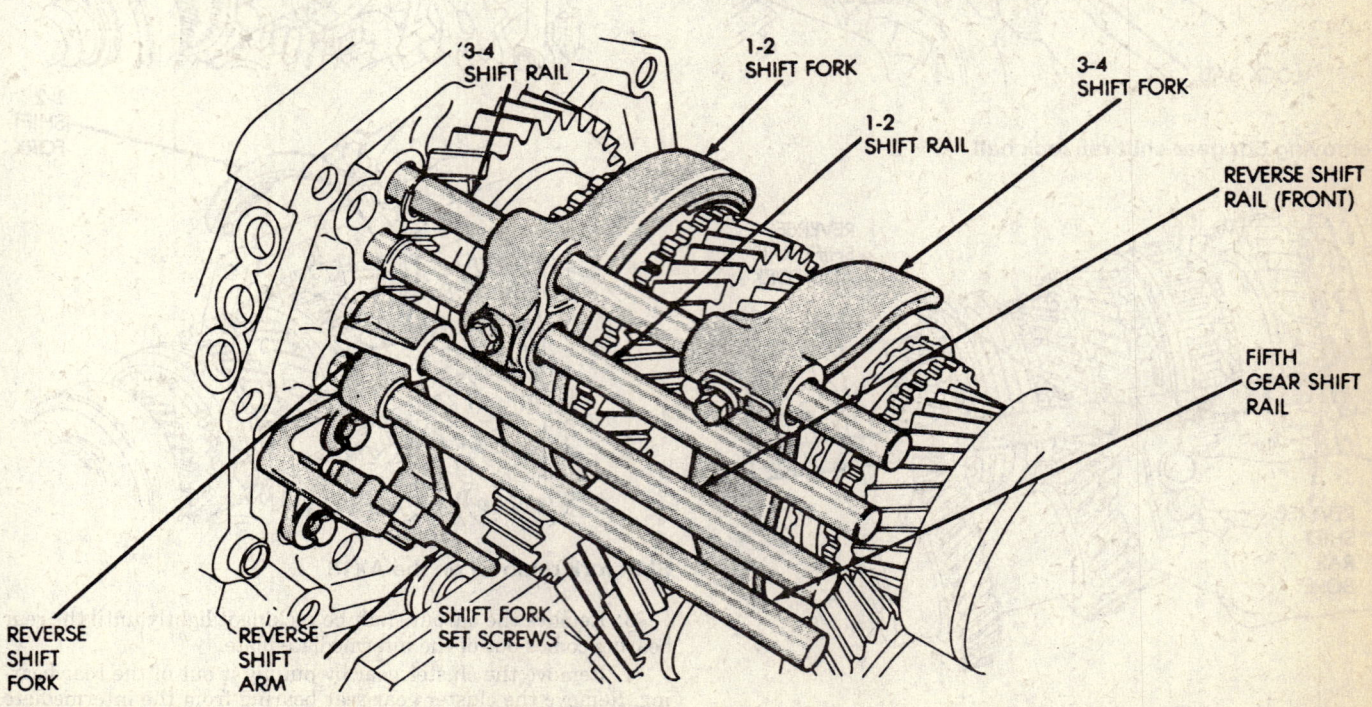

Shift rail identification on the AX15

7-59

7 DRIVE TRAIN

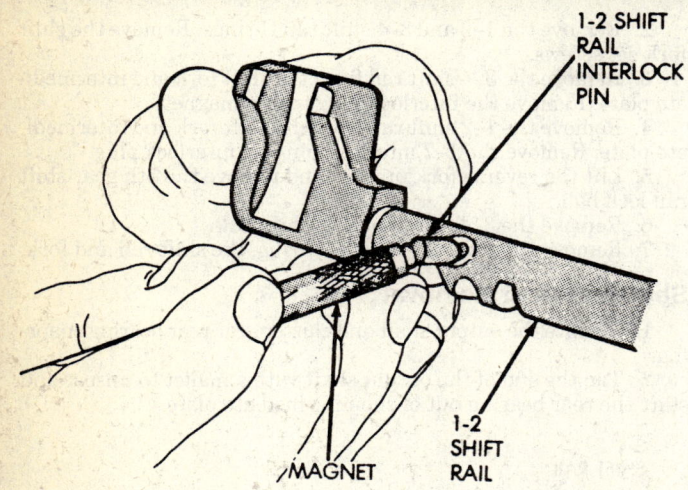

Removing the 1–2 shift rail interlock pin

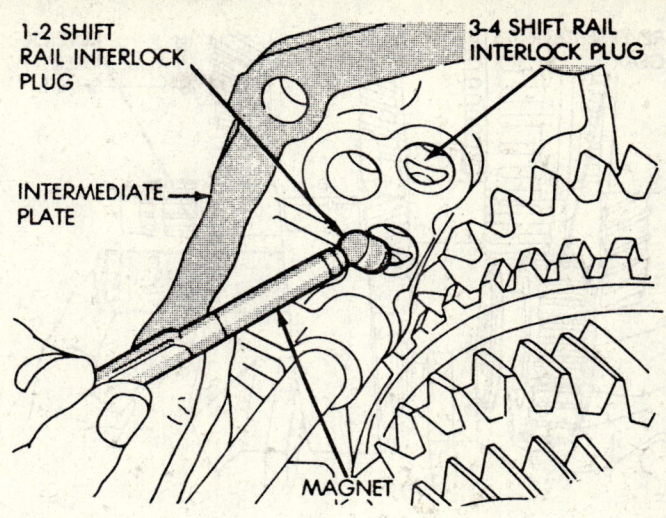

Removing the 1–2 shift rail interlock plug

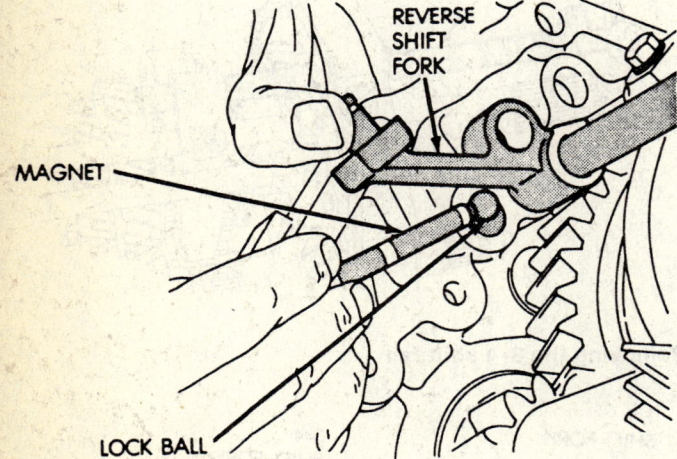

Removing 5th gear shift rail lock ball

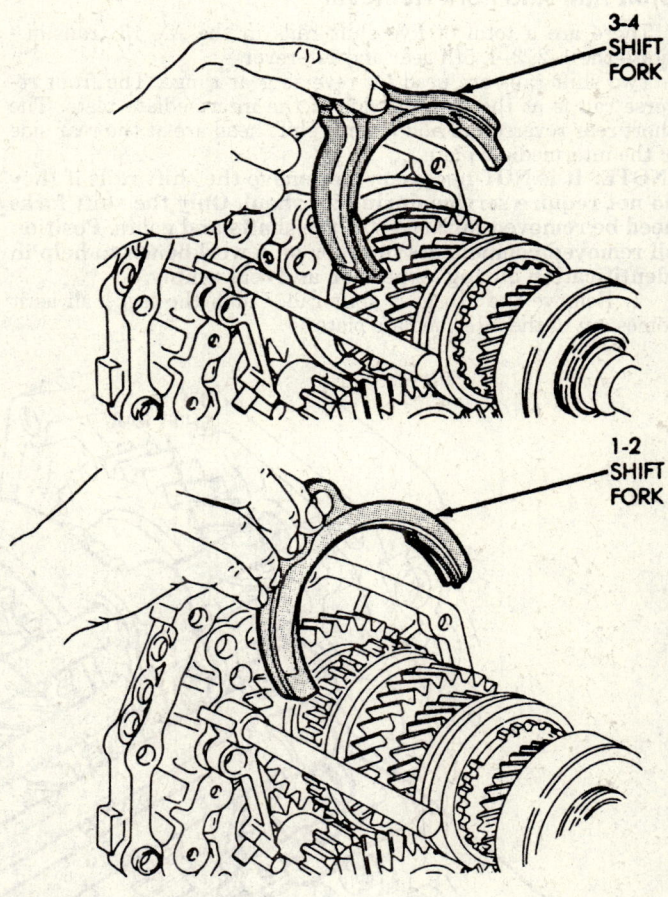

Shift fork removal on the AX15

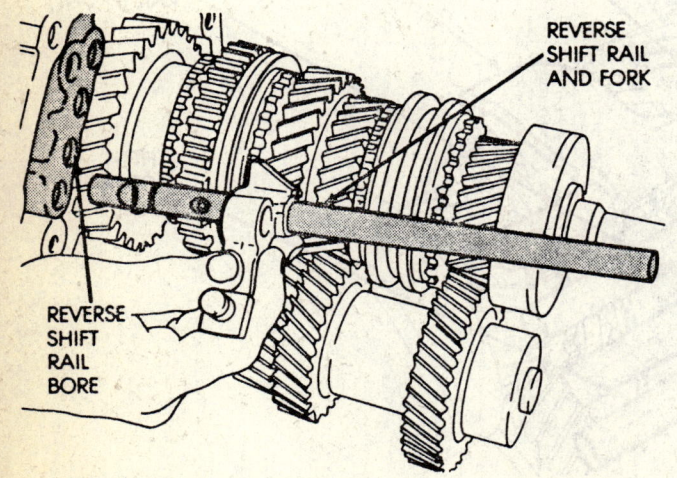

Removing the reverse shift rail and fork on the AX15

3. Remove the output shaft be rocking it lightly until the rear bearing comes out of the intermediate plate.
4. Remove the cluster gear by pulling it out of the rear bearing. Remove the cluster gear rear bearing from the intermediate plate.
5. Remove the input shaft from the output shaft.

DRIVE TRAIN 7

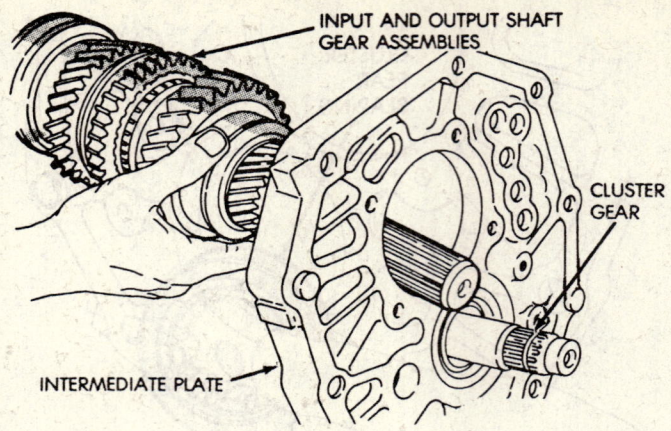

Input output shaft assembly removal

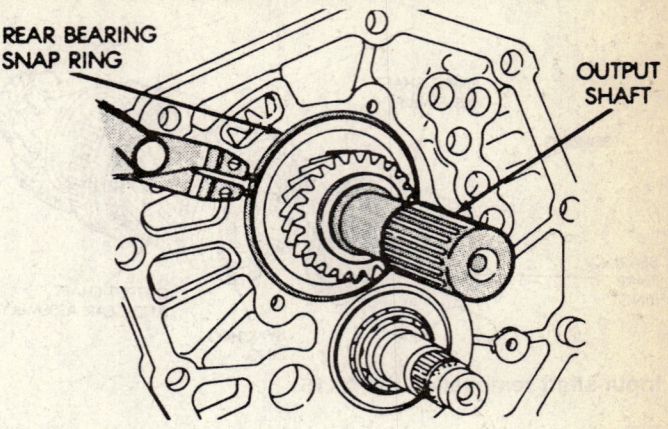

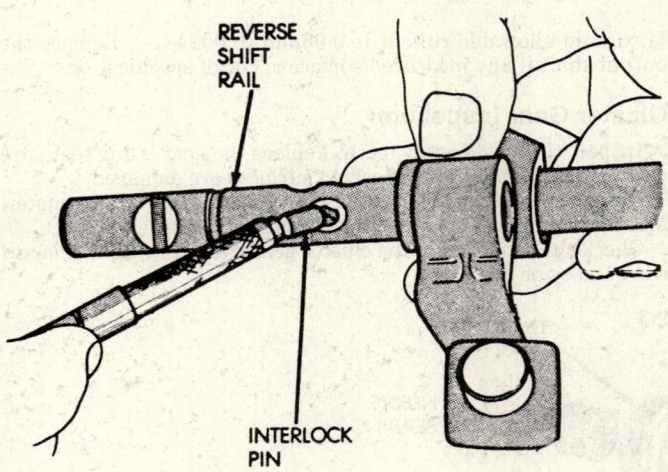

Removing reverse shift rail interlock pin

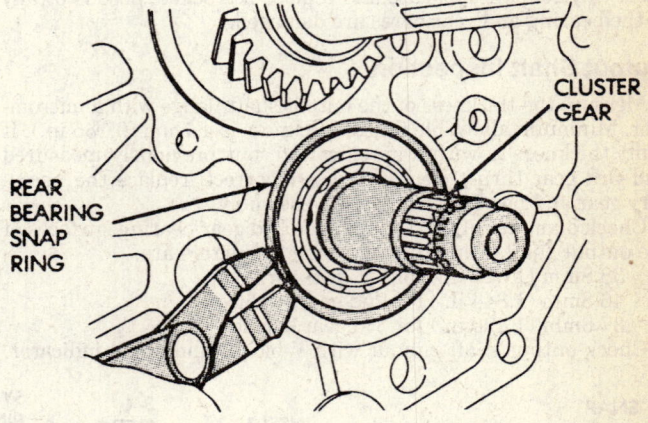

Removing bearing snaprings

6. Remove the output shaft pilot bearing and synchro ring from the input shaft.
7. Remove the bearing snapring and press the bearing off the input shaft.

Output Shaft Disassembly

1. Measure thrust clearance of the output shaft 1st, 2nd and 3rd gears with a feeler gauge. Clearance should be 0.003–0.0197 in. for 1st gear; 0.003–0.0118 in. for 2nd and 3rd gears.
2. If the thrust clearance is incorrect, replace the gear and thrust washer for 1st gear or replace the gear, bearing and/or output shaft for 2nd and 3rd gear.
3. Press the 5th gear and rear bearing off the rear of the output shaft.
4. Remove the thrust washer, pin, 1st gear and bearing.
5. Remove the 1st/reverse hub snapring and synchro ring. Press the reverse gear and 1st/reverse hub off the shaft as an assembly.
6. Remove the remaining synchro ring, 2nd gear and bearing.
7. Remove the snapring at the front of the output shaft. Press the 3–4 hub and sleeve off as an assembly.
8. Remove the synchro ring, 3rd gear and needle bearing.

CLEANING AND INSPECTION

Clean the transmission components in solvent and dry with clean compressed air. Dry bearings with clean, dry shop towels only. Compressed air will damage bearing rollers.

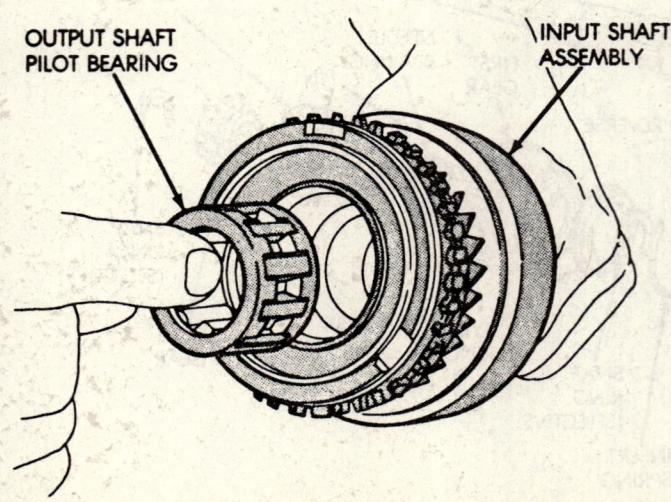

Removing input shaft pilot bearing

7-61

7 DRIVE TRAIN

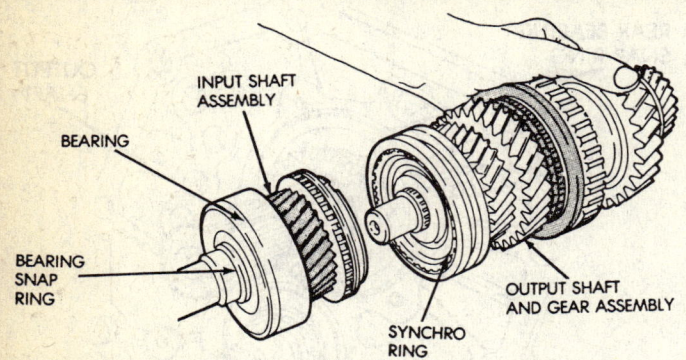

Input shaft removal on the AX15

Replace components that are obviously worn in any way. Inspect the transmission case and replace if cracked, porous or any of the bearing and gear bores are damaged.

Output Shaft Inspection

Measure the thickness of the output shaft flange with a micrometer. Minimum allowable flange thickness is 4.7mm (0.185 in.). If shaft thickness is within specification, but previously measured 2nd–3rd gear thrust clearance was incorrect, replace the necessary gear and needle bearing as an assembly

Check diameter of the 1st, 2nd and 3rd gear bearing surfaces of the output shaft. Minimum allowable diameters are:

38.8mm (1.529 in.) for 1st gear surface
46.8mm (1.844 in.) for 2nd gear surface
37.8mm (1.490 in.) for 3rd gear surface

Check output shaft runout with V-blocks and a dial indicator.

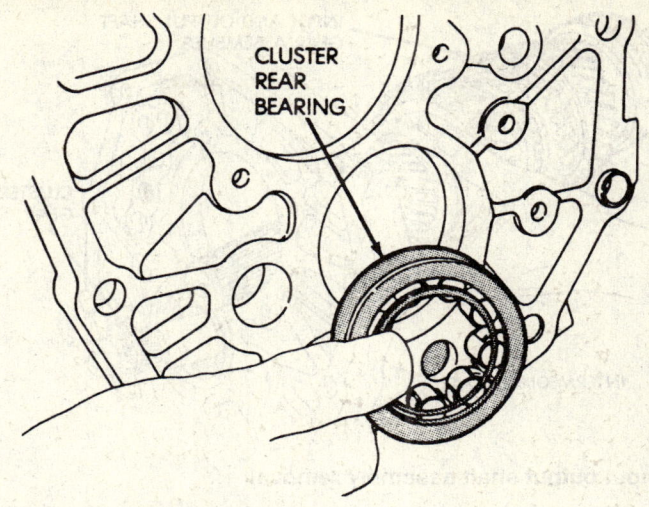

Removing cluster gear rear bearing

Maximum allowable runout is 0.06mm (0.0024 in.). Replace the output shaft if any measured surface is out of specification.

Cluster Gear Inspection

Inspect the cluster gear teeth. Replace the gear if any teeth are worn or damaged or if the bearing surfaces are damaged.

Check diameter of the cluster gear journal with a micrometer. Minimum allowable diameter is 27.8mm (1.096 in.).

Check the condition of the cluster gear front bearing. Replace if worn, noisy or damaged.

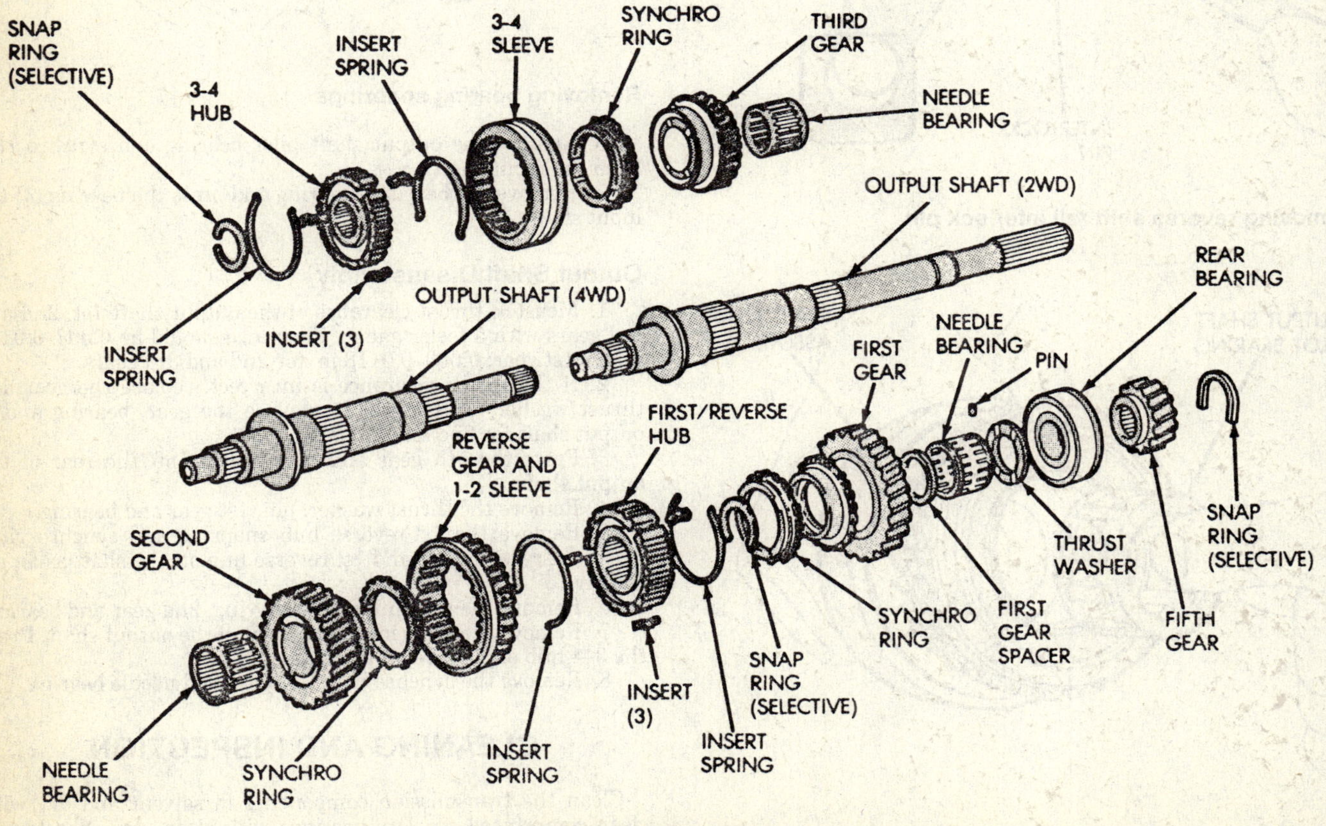

Output shaft and gears

DRIVE TRAIN 7

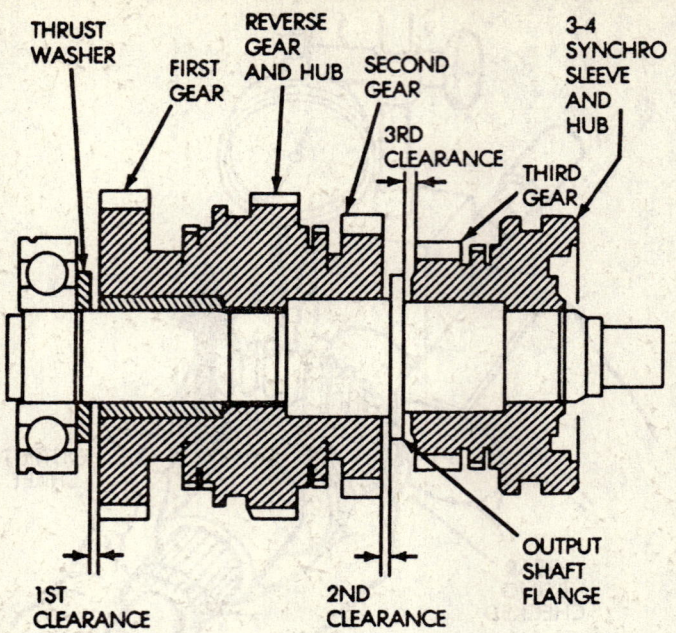

Checking output shaft gear thrust clearance

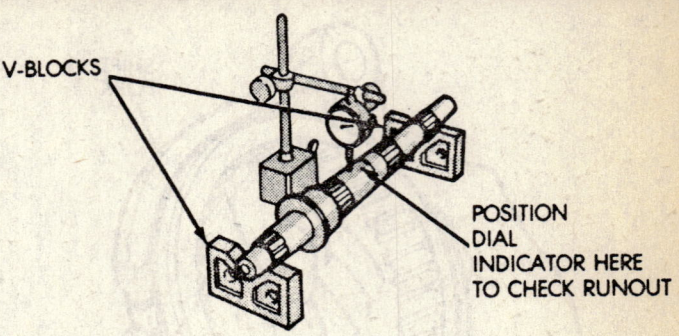

Checking output shaft runout

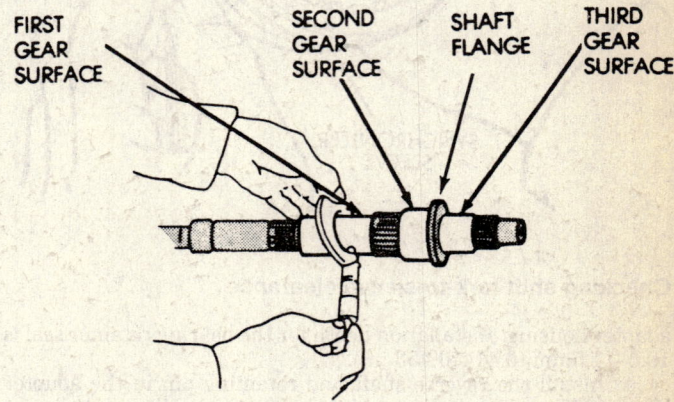

Checking output shaft tolerances

GEAR AND SYNCHRO INSPECTION

Install the synchro rings on their respective gears. Rotate each ring on the gear and note the synchro action. Replace any synchro ring that exhibits a lack of braking action or binds on the gear. Also replace any ring that is worn or has chipped or broken teeth. Measure end clearance between the synchro ring and the gear with a feeler gauge. Clearance should be 0.6–1.6mm (0.024–0.063 in.).

Install the needle bearings in the 1st, 2nd and 3rd gears. Then install the gears on the output shaft and check shaft-to-gear clearance with a dial indicator. Maximum allowable clearance is 1.6mm (0.0063 in.). If any gear exhibits excessive clearance, replace the gear and needle bearing.

Check clearance between the shift forks and synchro sleeves with a feeler gauge. Clearance should not exceed 1mm (0.039 in.). Replace the synchro sleeve and matching hub if clearance is out of specification.

Check condition of the reverse idler gear bushing. Replace the gear if the bushing is damaged or worn.

Gear Case, Housing And Intermediate Plate

Clean the case, housing and plate with solvent and dry wit compressed air. Replace any component that is cracked, warped or damaged in any way.

Inspect the threads in the case, housing and plate. Minor thread damage can be repaired with steel thread inserts if necessary. DO NOT attempt to repair if the cracks are evident around any threaded hole. Inspect the reverse pin in the adapter/extension housing. Replace the pin if worn or damaged.

TRANSMISSION ASSEMBLY

Lubricate all transmission components with 75W-90 gear lubricant during assembly. Use petroleum jelly to lubricate seal lips and/or hold parts in place during installation.

Front Bearing, Seal And Pin Installation

1. Press the front bearing on the input shaft. Then secure the bearing with the thickest snapring that will fit in the groove.
2. Press the front bearing on the cluster gear. Then secure the bearing with the thickest snapring that will fit in the groove.
3. Install new oil seals in the front bearing retainer and

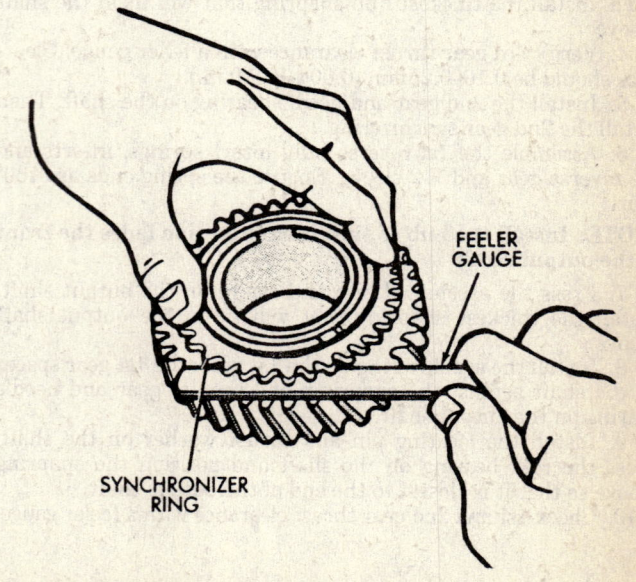

Checking synchronizer ring end clearance

7-63

7 DRIVE TRAIN

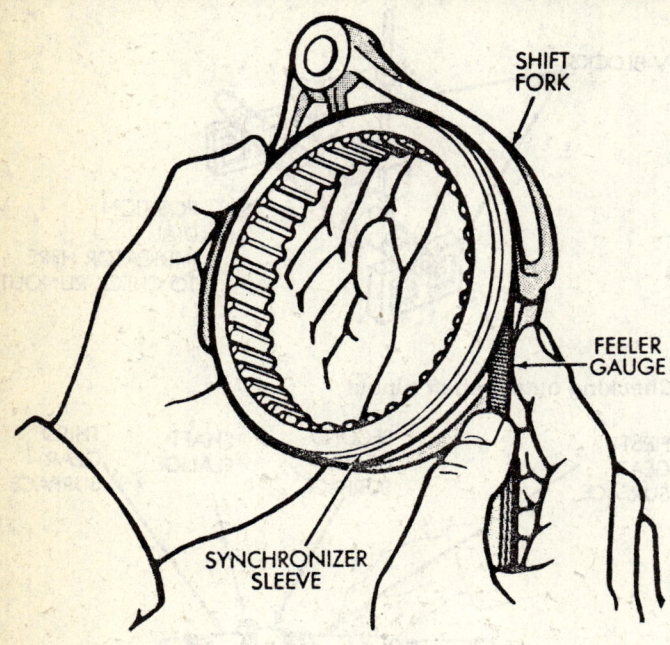

Checking shift fork-to-sleeve clearance

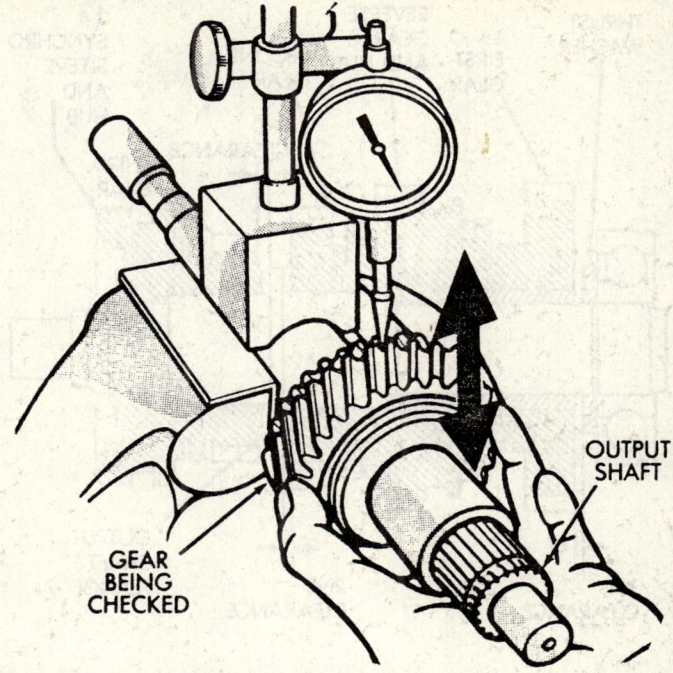

Checking gear-to-shaft clearance

adapter housing. Installation depth for the bearing retainer seal is 10.5–11.5mm (0.414–0.453 in.).

4. Install the reverse shaft and retaining pin in the adapter housing. Then install the access hole plug with a Torx bit.

Output Shaft Assembly

1. Install the third gear and needle bearing on the shaft and synchro ring on the gear.
2. Assemble the 1–2 and 3–4 synchro hubs and sleeves. Install the inserts and springs in the sleeves and position the open ends of the springs 180° apart.
3. Press the 3-4 synchro hub and sleeve onto the output shaft. Then, install the thickest hub snapring that will fit in the shaft groove.
4. Verify 3rd gear thrust clearance with a feller gauge. Clearance should be 0.10–0.25mm (0.004–0.010 in.).
5. Install the 2nd gear and needle bearing on the shaft. Then install the 2nd gear synchro ring.
6. Assemble the 1st/reverse hub, insert springs, inserts and the reverse gear and 1–2 sleeve. Ensure the spring ends are 180° apart.

NOTE: Install the hub so the chamfered side faces the front of the output shaft.

7. Press the assembled hub and sleeve on the output shaft. Install the thickest snapring that will fit in the output shaft groove.
8. Install the synchro ring on the 1st gear; the 1st gear spacer on the shaft against the snapring; and the 1st gear and needle bearing on the output shaft.
9. Install the locating pin and thrust washer on the shaft. Press the rear bearing on the shaft and position the snapring groove so that it is closest to the end of the output shaft.
10. Check 1st and 2nd gear thrust clearance with a feeler gauge.

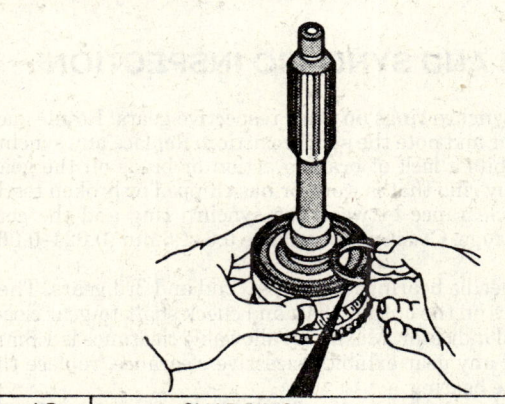

I.D. MARK	SNAP RING THICKNESS	MM (IN.)
A	2.10 - 2.15	(0.0827 - 0.0846)
B	2.15 - 2.20	(0.0846 - 0.0866)
C	2.20 - 2.25	(0.0866 - 0.0886)
D	2.25 - 2.30	(0.0886 - 0.0906)
E	2.30 - 2.35	(0.0906 - 0.0925)
F	2.35 - 2.40	(0.0925 - 0.0945)
G	2.40 - 2.45	(0.0945 - 0.0965)

Selecting input shaft front bearing snapring

1st gear clearance should be 0.08–0.50mm (0.003–0.0197 in.); 2nd gear should be 0.08–0.30mm (0.003–0.0118 in.).

11. Press the 5th gear onto the output shaft. Then install the thickest snapring that will fit in the shaft groove.
12. Lubricate the shaft pilot bearing with petroleum jelly and install the bearing shaft.

DRIVE TRAIN 7

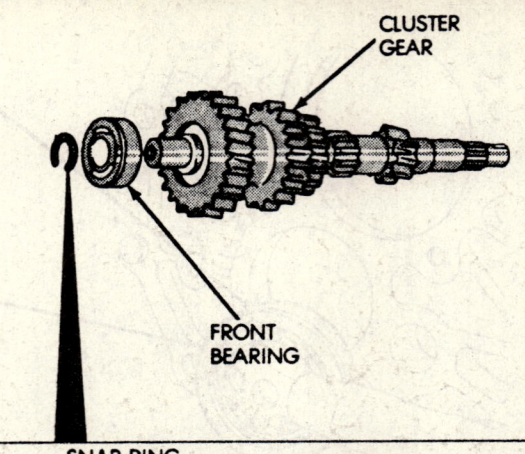

I.D. MARK	SNAP RING THICKNESS	MM (IN.)
A	2.00 - 2.05	(0.0787 - 0.0807)
B	2.05 - 2.10	(0.0807 - 0.0827)
C	2.10 - 2.15	(0.0827 - 0.0846)
D	2.15 - 2.20	(0.0846 - 0.0866)
E	2.20 - 2.25	(0.0866 - 0.0886)

Selecting cluster gear front bearing snapring

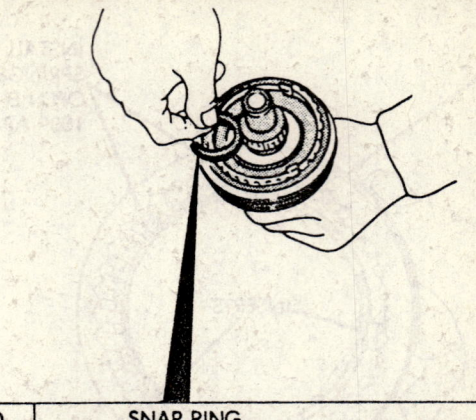

I.D. MARK	SNAP RING THICKNESS	MM (IN.)
A	1.80 - 1.85	(0.0709 - 0.0728)
B	1.85 - 1.90	(0.0728 - 0.0748)
C	1.90 - 1.95	(0.0748 - 0.0768)
D	1.95 - 2.00	(0.0768 - 0.0787)
E	2.00 - 2.05	(0.0787 - 0.0807)
F	2.05 - 2.10	(0.0807 - 0.0827)
G	2.10 - 2.15	(0.0827 - 0.0846)

Installing 3-4 synchronizer hub snapring

13. Install the input shaft on the output shaft. Be sure the output shaft hub is fully seated in the pilot bearing.

Output Shaft And Cluster Gear Installation

1. Mount the intermediate plate in a suitable holding fixture. Lubricate the cluster gear journal and rear bearing with petroleum jelly.
2. Install the cluster gear rear bearing in the intermediate plate. Ensure that the snapring groove in the bearing is rearward.
3. Start the cluster gear into the bearing, then hold the bearing and push the gear into place. Use a rubber mallet if necessary.
4. Install the snaprings on the cluster and output shaft rear bearings only.
5. Install the reverse idler gear and shaft.
6. Position the rear bearing retainer over the output shaft and rear bearing.

NOTE: Ensure the rear bearing is engaged in the reverse idler shaft.

7. Install and tighten the rear bearing retainer to 13 ft. lbs.

Shift Rail And Fork Installation

The shift rail interlock pin, balls and plugs must be installed in the correct sequence for proper shifting. Coat the intermediate plate shift rail bores and interlock ball, pins and plugs with a thick covering of petroleum jelly before assembly. The jelly will hold the

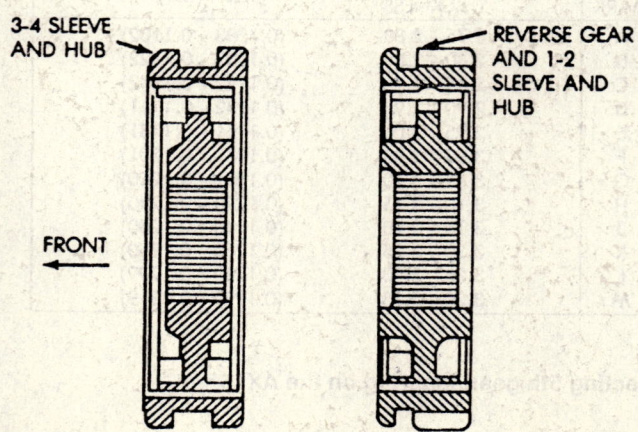

Synchronizer sleeve and hub identification

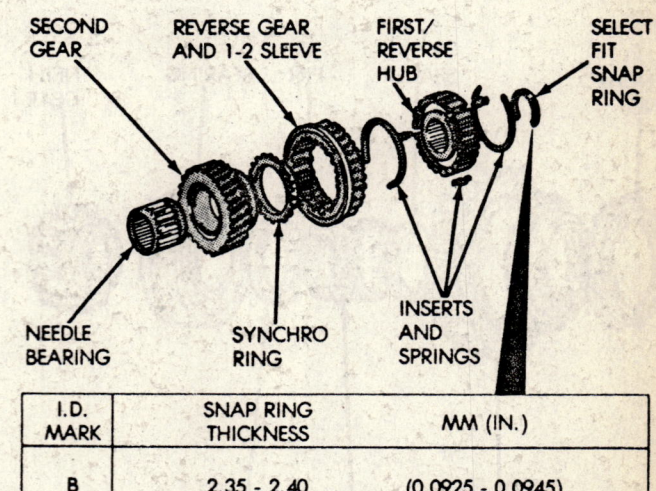

I.D. MARK	SNAP RING THICKNESS	MM (IN.)
B	2.35 - 2.40	(0.0925 - 0.0945)
C	2.40 - 2.45	(0.0945 - 0.0965)
D	2.45 - 2.50	(0.0965 - 0.0984)
E	2.50 - 2.55	(0.0984 - 0.1004)
F	2.55 - 2.60	(0.1004 - 0.1024)
G	2.60 - 2.65	(0.1024 - 0.1043)

2nd gear and synchronizer assembly

7-65

7 DRIVE TRAIN

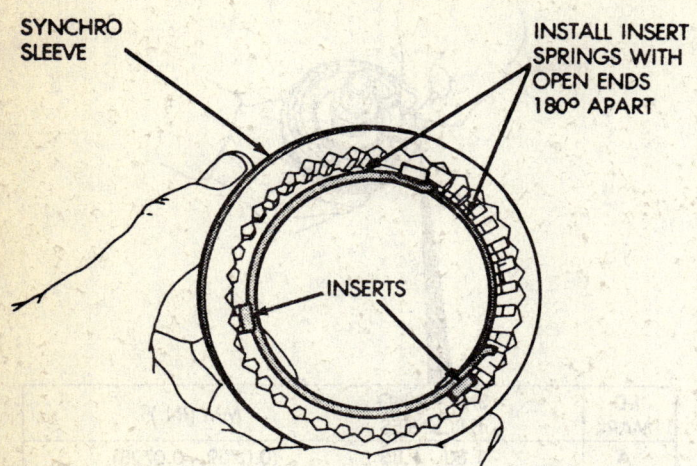

Insert spring position

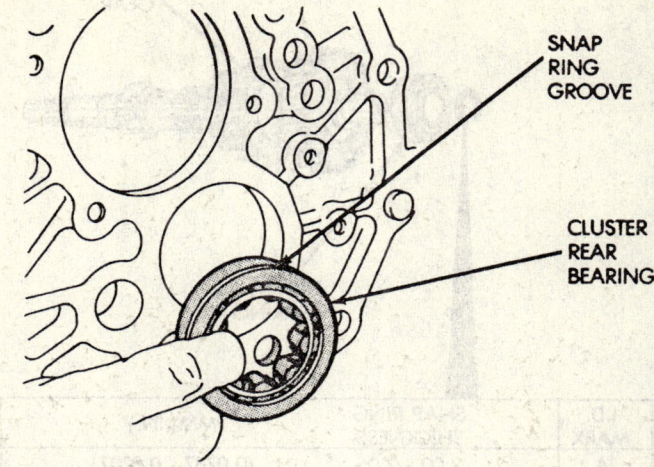

Installing cluster gear rear bearing

interlock components in place during installation. Use a pencil magnet to hold and insert the interlocks. Then use an appropriate tool to push the interlock components into place.

1. Coat the reverse rail interlock pin with petroleum jelly and install in the rail. Install the reverse shift rail in the intermediate plate. Install the reverse rail C-ring.
2. Position the 1–2 and 3–4 shift forks in the synchro sleeves
3. Coat the reverse rail lock ball with petroleum jelly. Then tilt the reverse shift fork upward and insert the ball in the intermediate plate.
4. Coat the 1–2 shift rail interlock plug with petroleum jelly and install it in the intermediate plate bore. Then install the interlock pin in the same manner.

5. Install the 1–2 shift rail and fork in the intermediate plate.
6. Coat the 3–4 shift rail interlock plug with petroleum jelly and install the plug in the intermediate plate. Then install the shift rail, locating it in both forks.
7. Verify all components are in place and have not shifted before continuing.
8. Install and tighten the shift fork setscrews to 14 ft. lbs.
9. Install the 1–2 and 3–4 shift rail C-rings.
10. Insert the 5th gear shift rail through the reverse shift fork. Then slide the rail into the intermediate plate just far enough to hold the interlock ball.

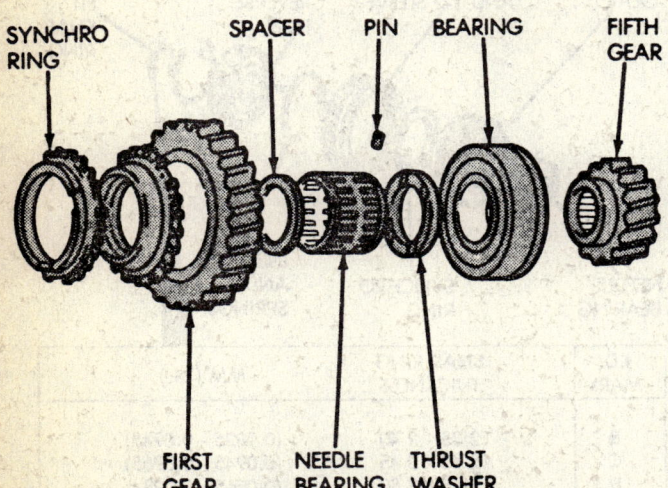

1st and 5th gear components on the AX15

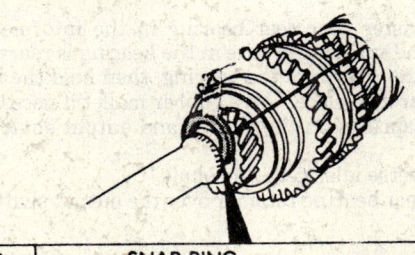

I.D. MARK	SNAP RING THICKNESS	MM (IN.)
A	2.75 – 2.80	(0.1083 – 0.1102)
B	2.80 – 2.85	(0.1002 – 0.1122)
C	2.85 – 2.90	(0.1122 – 0.1142)
D	2.90 – 2.95	(0.1142 – 0.1161)
E	2.95 – 3.00	(0.1161 – 0.1181)
F	3.00 – 3.05	(0.1181 – 0.1201)
G	3.05 – 3.10	(0.1201 – 0.1220)
H	3.10 – 3.15	(0.1220 – 0.1240)
J	3.15 – 3.20	(0.1240 – 0.1260)
K	3.20 – 3.25	(0.1260 – 0.1280)
L	3.25 – 3.30	(0.1280 – 0.1299)
M	3.30 – 3.35	(0.1299 – 0.1319)

Selecting 5th gear snapring on the AX15

DRIVE TRAIN 7

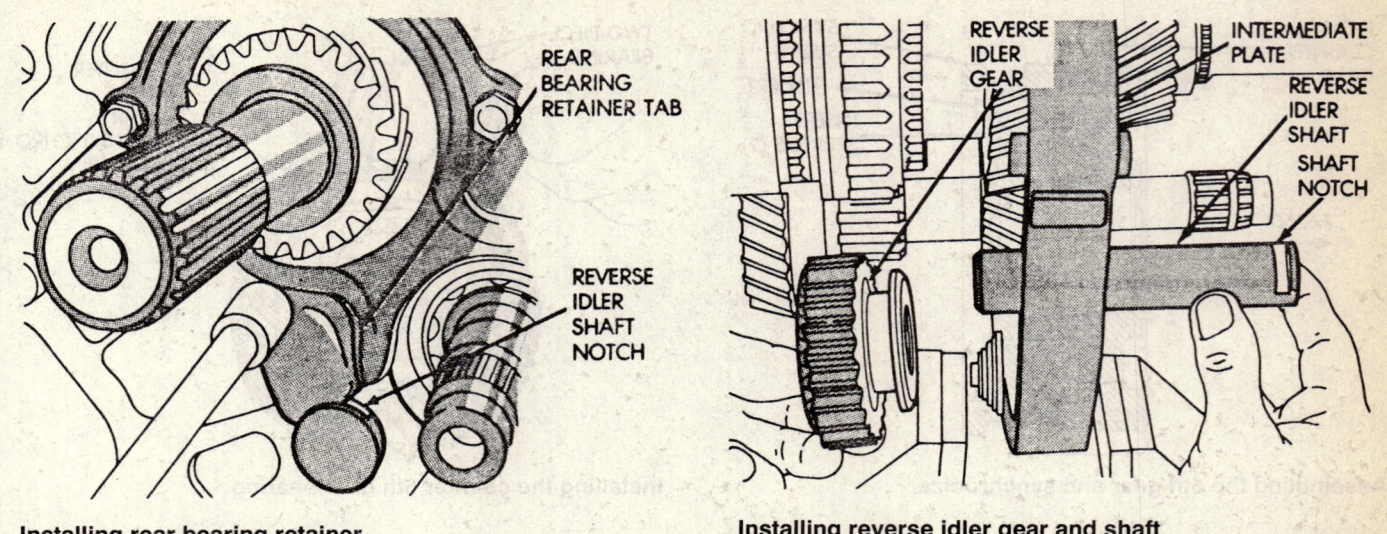

Installing rear bearing retainer

Installing reverse idler gear and shaft

Shift rail ball-plug-pin position

7-67

7 DRIVE TRAIN

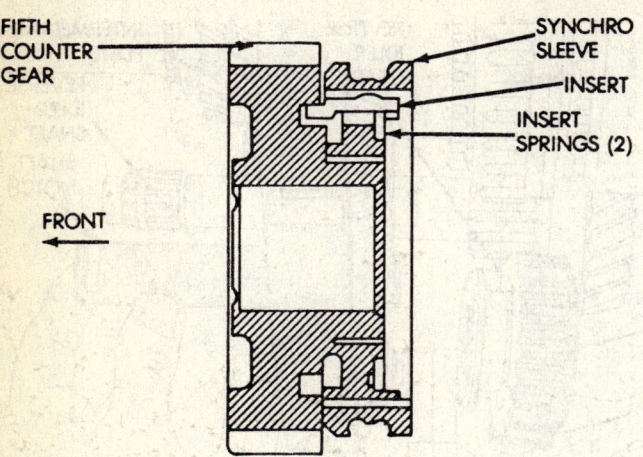

Assembling the 5th gear and synchronizer

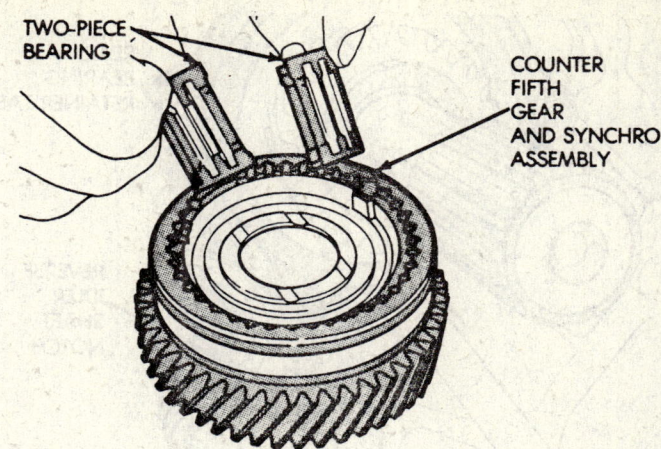

Installing the counter 5th gear bearing

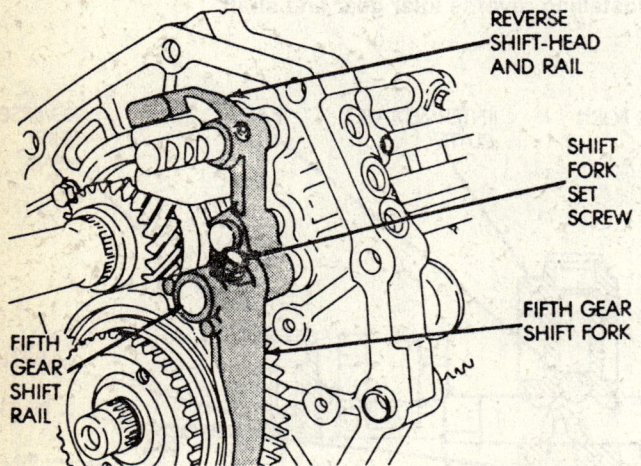

Shift fork set screw installation

NOTE: DO NOT fully install the shift rail at this time.

5th/Reverse Gear And Shift Component Installation

1. Install the thrust ring lock ball in the cluster gear journal. Use petroleum jelly to hold the ball in place.
2. Install the 5th gear thrust ring making sure the thrust ring notch fits over the lock ball.
3. Assemble the counter 5th gear, synchro sleeve, inserts and insert springs.
4. Lubricate the two-piece bearing with petroleum jelly and install it in the counter 5th gear. Install the counter 5th gear and synchro assembly on the cluster gear journal.
5. Install the synchro ring in the sleeve and the 5th spline gear on the cluster journal. Use a rubber mallet to tap it in place if necessary.
6. Install the largest 5th gear snapring that will fit in the groove.

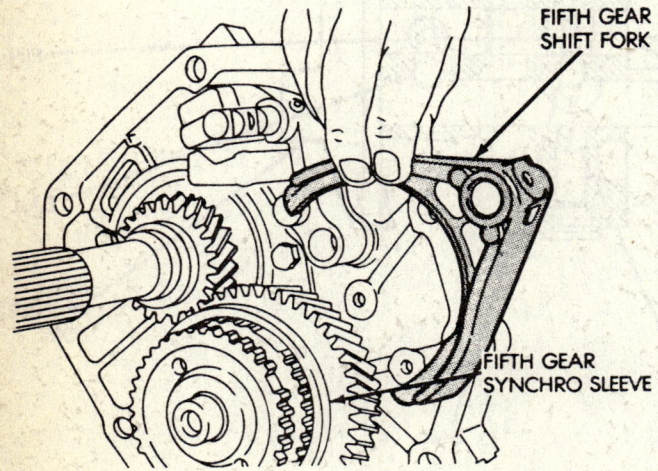

Installing the 5th gear shift fork

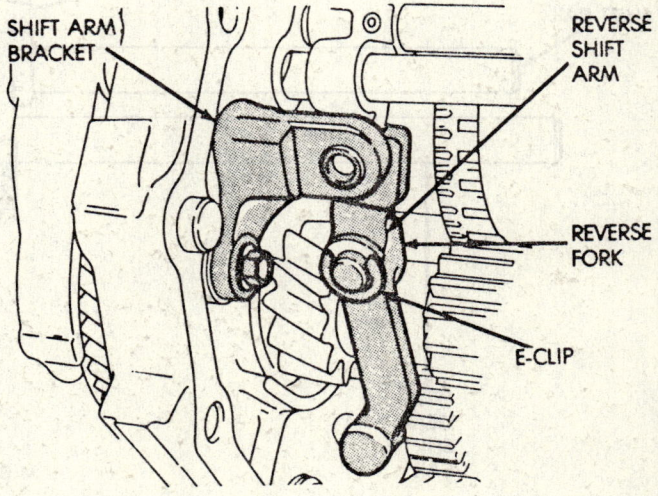

Reverse shift arm and bracket installation

7-68

DRIVE TRAIN 7

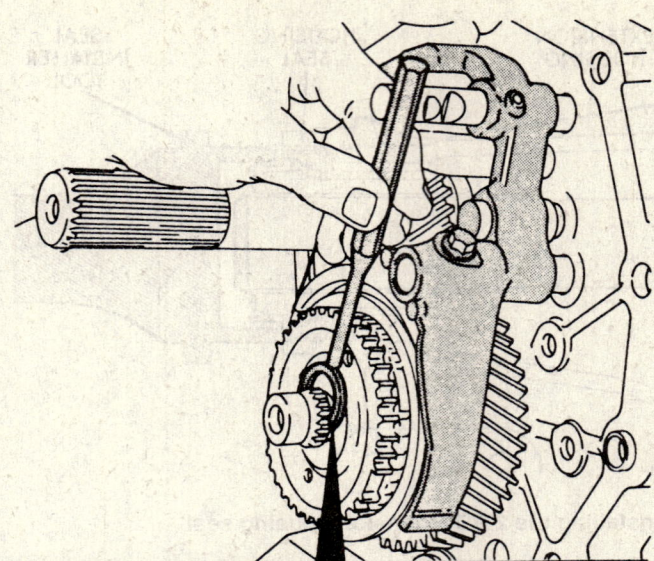

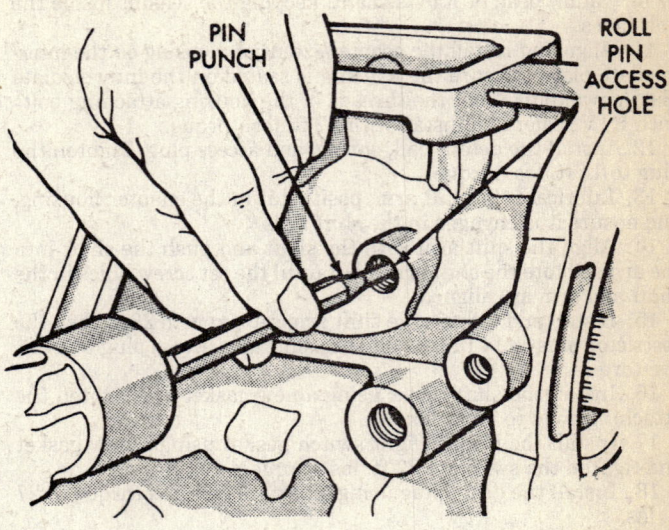

I.D. MARK	SNAP RING THICKNESS	MM (IN.)
A	2.85 – 2.90	(0.1122 – 0.1142)
B	2.90 – 2.95	(0.1142 – 0.1161)
C	2.95 – 3.00	(0.1161 – 0.1181)
D	3.00 – 3.05	(0.1181 – 0.1201)
E	3.05 – 3.10	(0.1201 – 0.1220)
F	3.10 – 3.15	(0.1220 – 0.1240)
G	3.15 – 3.20	(0.1240 – 0.1260)
H	3.20 – 3.25	(0.1260 – 0.1280)

Installing the 5th gear snapring

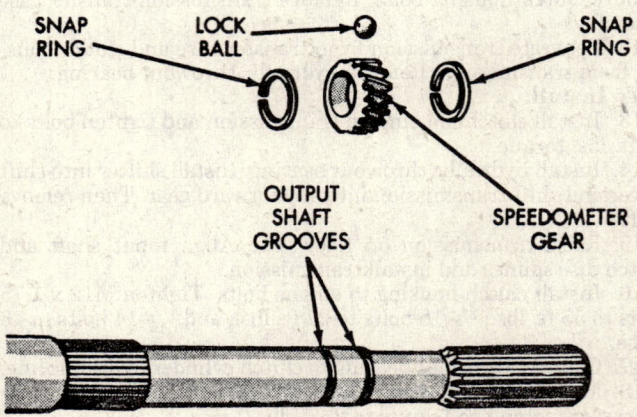

2WD speedometer gear installation

Roll pin removal/installation

Ensure the interlock ball stays in place.

10. Align the screw holes in the shift fork and rail and install the set screw. Tighten to 15 ft. lbs.

11. Install the lock balls and springs in the intermediate plate. Then install and tighten the lock ball plugs to 14 ft. lbs.

12. Install the reverse shift arm bracket and tighten to 13 ft. lbs. Install the reverse shift arm, positioning it on the reverse fork pin. Then engage it with the pin on the shift arm bracket.

13. Verify that the shift arm shoe is engaged in the reverse idler gear. Then secure the shift arm to the pin on the reverse fork with a new E-clip.

Gear Case And Adapter Installation

1. Remove the intermediate and gear assemblies from the holding fixture.

2. Clean the mating surfaces of the intermediate plate and transmission gear case with a wax and grease remover. Apply an 1/8 in. (3mm) bead of RTV sealant to the mating surface of the gear case. Keep the sealer bead inside the bolt holes.

3. Install the gear case, align the shift rails and bearings in the case, and tap the case into position. Verify that the gear case is seated on the intermediate case dowel pins.

4. Install the front bearing snaprings.

5. Clean the gear case and front bearing retainer surfaces with wax and grease remover.

6. Install a new seal in the front bearing retainer to a depth of 10.5–11.5mm (0.413–0.453 in.).

7. Apply an 1/8 in. (3mm) bead of RTV sealant to the front bearing retainer surface. Align and install the front bearing retainer. Ensure the retainer is fully seated on the case and bearings. Install and tighten the retainer bolts to 12 ft. lbs. torque.

8. On 2WD vehicles, install the speedometer gear, lock ball and retaining rings.

9. Inspect the condition of the reverse pin in the adapter/extension housing. If worn, replace the pin by removing the roll pin access plug, removing the old reverse pin, and installing the new reverse pin, roll pin and access plug (torque to 14 ft. lbs.).

10. Clean the mating surfaces of the adapter/extension housing

7. Install the reverse shift head and rail. Then install the lock ball.

8. Position the 5th gear shift fork in the synchro sleeve.

9. Install the 5th gear shift rail. Slide the rail through the fork.

7-69

7 DRIVE TRAIN

and the intermediate plate with wax and grease remover. Apply an 1/8 in. (3mm) bead of RTV sealant, keeping the sealant inside the bolt holes.

11. Align and install the adapter/extension housing on the intermediate plate. Be sure the housing is seated on the intermediate plate dowel pins. Coat the threads of the housing attaching bolts with RTV sealer and install with 27 ft. lbs. torque.
12. Install the detent ball, spring, and access plug. Tighten the plug to 14 ft. lbs. torque.
13. Lubricate the shift arm, position it in the adapter housing, and ensure it is engaged in the shift rails.
14. Align the shift arm with the shaft and push the shaft into the arm. Rotate the shift arm shaft until the set screw holes in the shaft and arm are aligned.
15. Install and tighten the shift arm set screw to 28 ft. lbs.; the restrictor pins to 14 ft. lbs.; and the shift arm access plug to 14 ft. lbs. torque.
16. Install the shift tower using a new gasket and tighten the attaching bolts to 13 ft. lbs.
17. Install the backup light switch gasket using a new gasket and tighten the switch to 27 ft. lbs. torque.
18. Install the drain plug using a new washer and torque to 27 ft. lbs.
19. Place the transmission on a level surface and fill with lubricant to the bottom edge of the fill plug hole. Use 75W-90, grade GL-5 lubricant.

BA10/5

REMOVAL AND INSTALLATION

NOTE: The service tools necessary for removal and installation can be found in service tool kit B.Vi.FM.01. The kit is available through a dealer's parts department.

1. shift transmission into NEUTRAL. Remove shift knob, locknut, boot and bezel. Then remove shifter lever extension.
2. Remove transmission shift lever dust boot.
3. Remove shift lever cover, bushings, washer, pin and lever.

NOTE: On some BA10/5 transmissions, the shift lever may be held in place with a snapring and spring washer.

4. Raise and support the vehicle safely. Drain lubricant from transmission/transfer case.

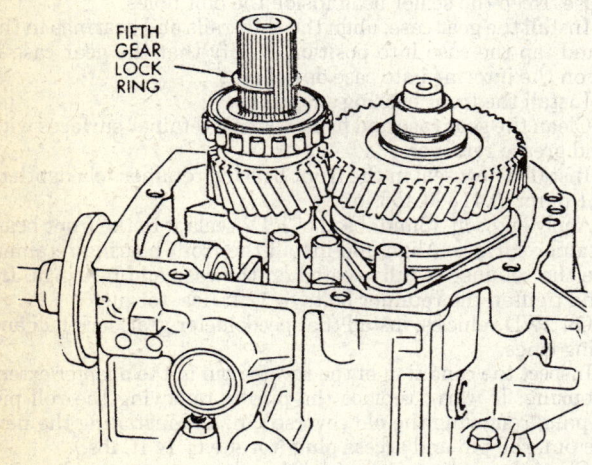

Removing 5th gear lock ring from the BA 10/5

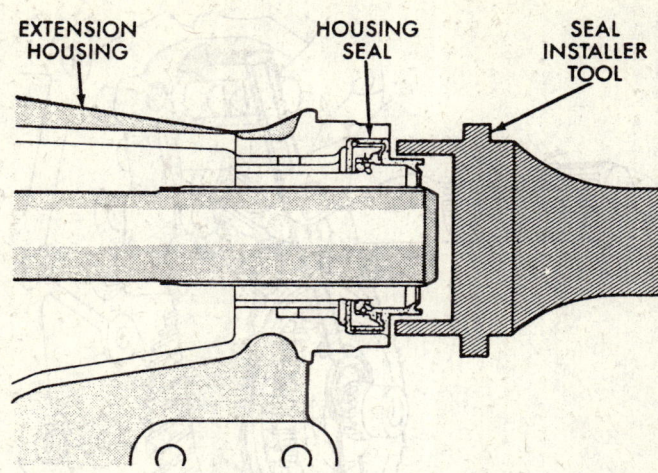

Installing the 2WD extension housing seal

5. Matchmark rear driveshaft for reference during installation and remove.
6. Position a floor jack or support under the transmission/transfer case and remove crossmember.
7. Disconnect speedometer cable, backup light switch, transmission and transfer case vent hoses.
8. Disconnect transfer case vacuum hoses. Then disconnect transfer case range rod from floor shift lever. Mark hoses for assembly reference.
9. Matchmark front driveshaft for reference during installation and remove.
10. Disconnect clutch cylinder hydraulic line from throwout bearing inlet line.
11. Secure transmission/transfer case to a floor jack and remove clutch housing bolts. Remove transmission/transfer case assembly.
12. Separate transmission from transfer case and clutch housing from transmission. Remove hydraulic throwout bearing.

To Install:
13. Install clutch housing on transmission and tighten bolts to 28 ft. lbs. torque.
14. Install hydraulic throwout bearing. Install shifter into shift tower and shift transmission into any forward gear. Then remove shifter.
15. Raise transmission on floor jack. Align input shaft and clutch disc splines and install transmission.
16. Install clutch housing to engine bolts. Tighten M12 x 1.75 bolts to 55 ft. lbs.; 3/8-16 bolts to 27 ft. lbs.; and 7/16-14 bolts to 43 ft lbs.
17. Connect throwout bearing to clutch cylinder hydraulic line.
18. Mount transfer case on floor jack and install. Tighten transfer case attaching bolts/nuts to 26 ft. lbs.
19. Connect transfer case vacuum hoses and linkage. Connect transmission/transfer case vent hoses.
20. Connect backup light switch, speedometer cable and transfer case range rod to floor shift.
21. Install the rear crossmember and torque bolts crossmember-to-frame bolts to 30 ft. lbs.; transmission-to-crossmember bolts to 33 ft. lbs.
22. Align and install front and rear driveshafts. Tighten bolts to 170 inch lbs.
23. Fill transmission/transfer case with lubricant. Lower vehicle.
24. Install transmission shift lever, lever dust boot, shift lever extension, boot, bezel and knob.

DRIVE TRAIN 7

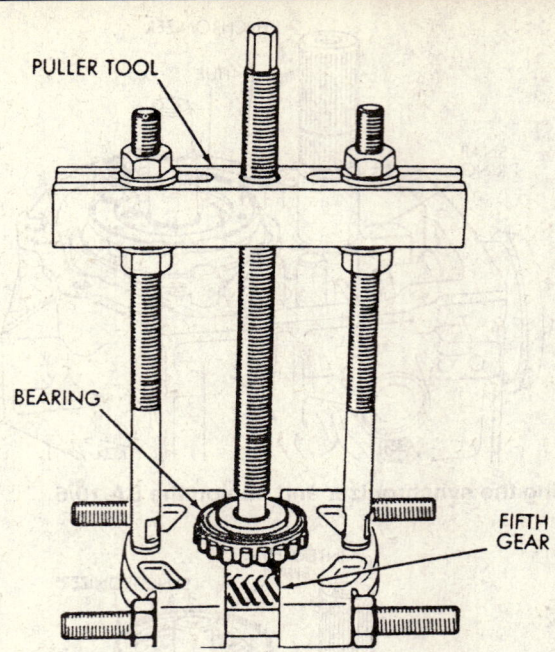

Removing the 5th gear bearing on the BA 10/5

BA 10/5 Overhaul

NOTE: The service tools necessary for overhaul can be found in service tool kit B.Vi.FM.01. The kit is available through a dealer's parts department.

DISASSEMBLY

1. Mount the transmission in a holding fixture or equivalent and drain the lubricant.

2. Remove the speedometer driven gear socket set screw and remove the driven gear socket from the rear extension housing.

3. Position the transmission in the vertical position with the rear upward. Set the gear selectors in the neutral position. Remove the selection lever return spring.

4. Remove the 5th gear cover plate and its gasket. Remove the extension housing bolts.

5. Place an extractor plate tool or equivalent to the rear housing, using the three bolts of the cover plate. Remove the rear housing from the transmission.

6. Remove the 5th speed gear from the mainshaft with an appropriate puller. The rear bearing will be removed as part of the 5th speed gear.

7. Remove the 5th speed drive gear shim washer, the spacer washer, the 5th gear and its needle bearing from the 5th gear stub shaft.

8. Mark the direction of rotation of the 5th/reverse synchronizer and the position of the cage and hub, in relation to each other.

9. Engage the 5th gear and drive the 5th/reverse selector fork roll pin from the fork and rail.

WARNING: Do not damage the mating surface of the housing

10. Reset the rail to the neutral position and remove the 5th/reverse synchronizer cage and selector fork assembly, the synchronizer hub and the 5th gear subshaft.

11. Disengage the selection lever finger from the selector forks spindles. Remove the intermediate housing and retaining bolts.

12. Place the transmission in a horizontal position with the right side up. Remove the clutch fork and release bearing assembly from the front of the transmission. Remove the clutch housing and bolts.

13. Remove the six Allen headed screws from the rear bearing thrust plate. Remove the right hand housing retaining bolts and the housing.

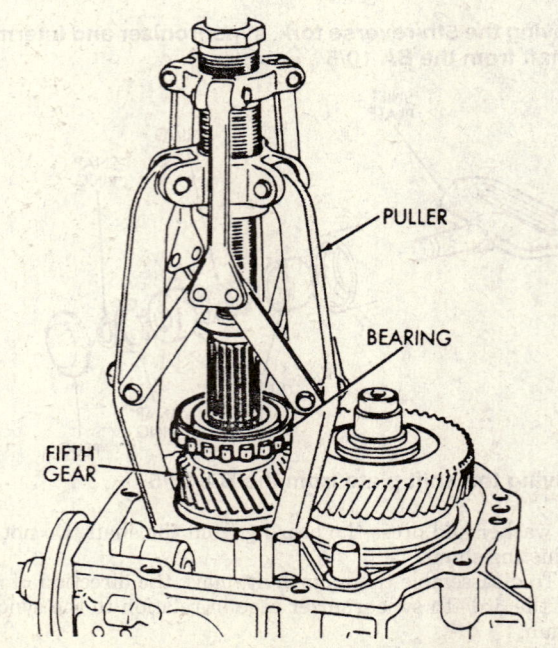

Removing the 5th gear and bearing from the BA 10/5

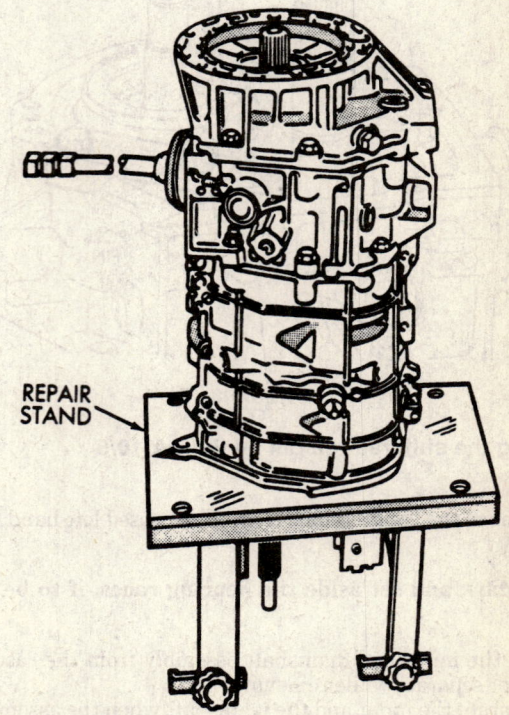

Positioning the BA 10/5 on a stand

7-71

7 DRIVE TRAIN

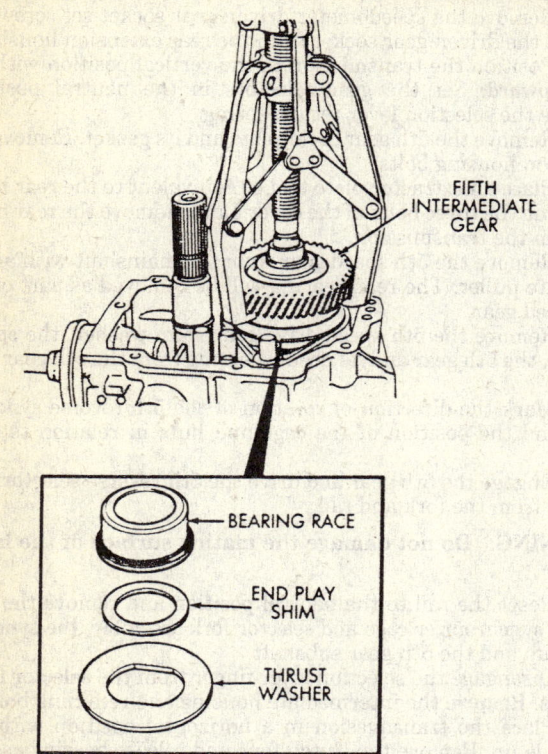

Removing the 5th intermediate gear on the BA 10/5

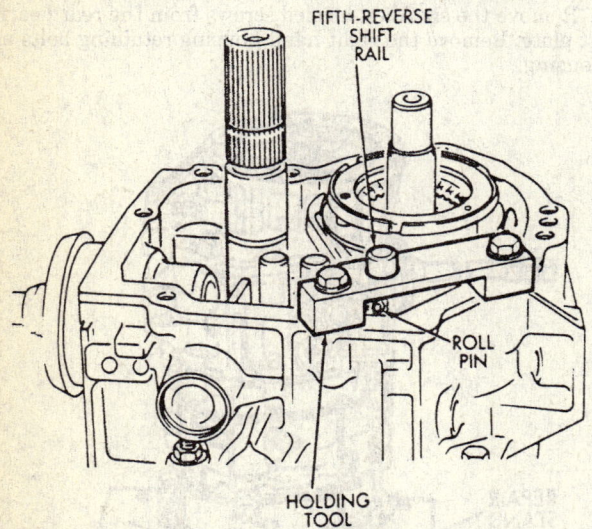

Removing the shift rail roll pin on the BA 10/5

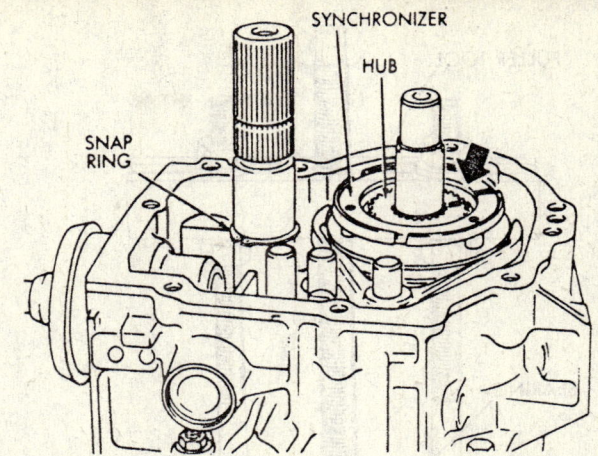

Marking the synchronizer and hub on the BA 10/5

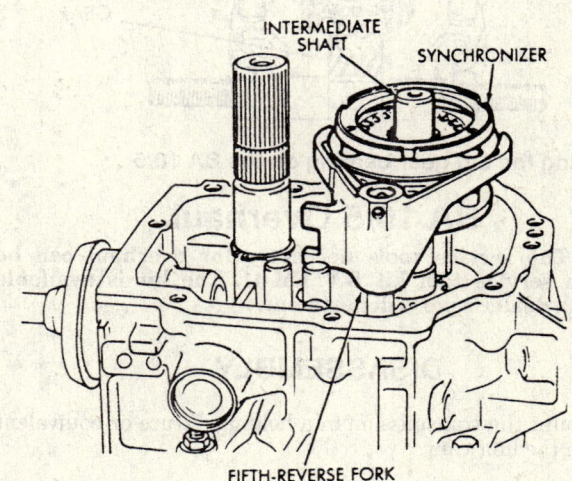

Removing the 5th-reverse fork, synchronizer and intermediate shaft from the BA 10/5

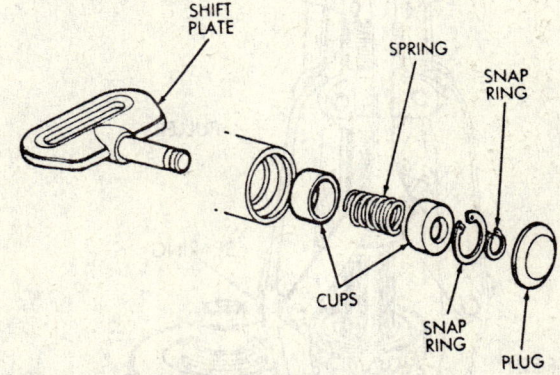

Removing the shift plate from the BA 10/5

14. Remove the countershaft from the exposed left hand housing.

NOTE: Mark and set aside the bearing races, if to be used again.

15. Lift the input and mainshaft assembly from the case as a unit. Do not separate while removing.
16. Separate the input and the mainshaft when the assembly is on a work bench. Remove the needle bearing from the bore of the input shaft. Hold the mainshaft in the 3rd gear position.
17. To disassemble the input shaft, remove the circlips, the spring washer and press the bearing from the shaft. Do not lose the adjusting shims.
18. To disassemble the mainshaft, mark the direction of rotation of the 3rd/4th synchronizer cage in relation to the synchronizer hub.

NOTE: Mark the components with a sharp piece of brass welding rod.

DRIVE TRAIN 7

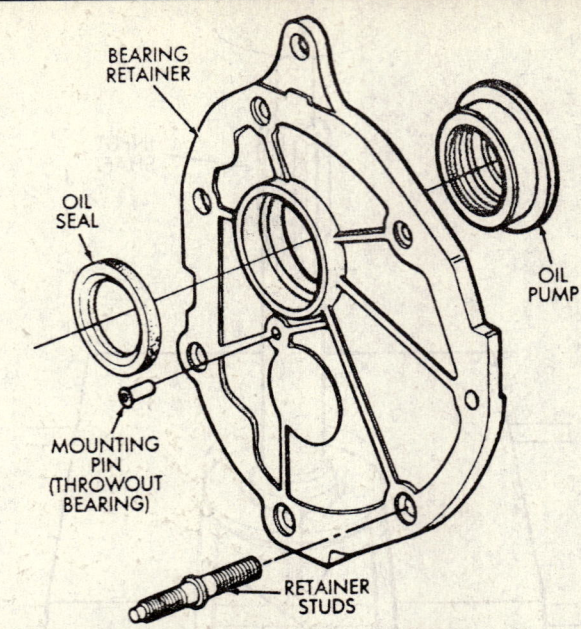

Bearing retainer and components for the BA 10/5

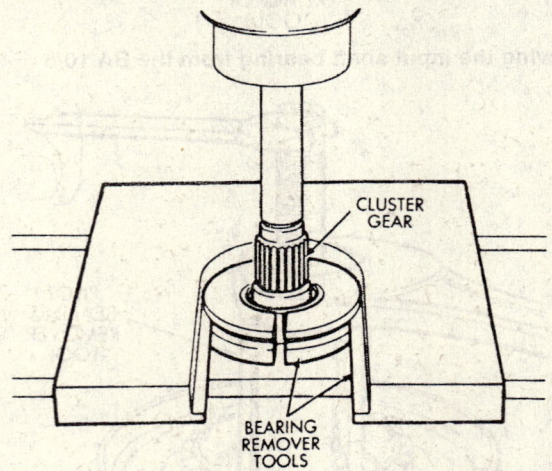

Removing the cluster gear bearings from the BA 10/5

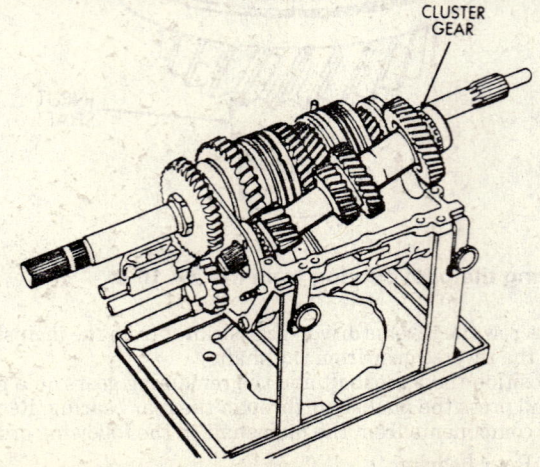

Removing the cluster gear from the BA 10/5

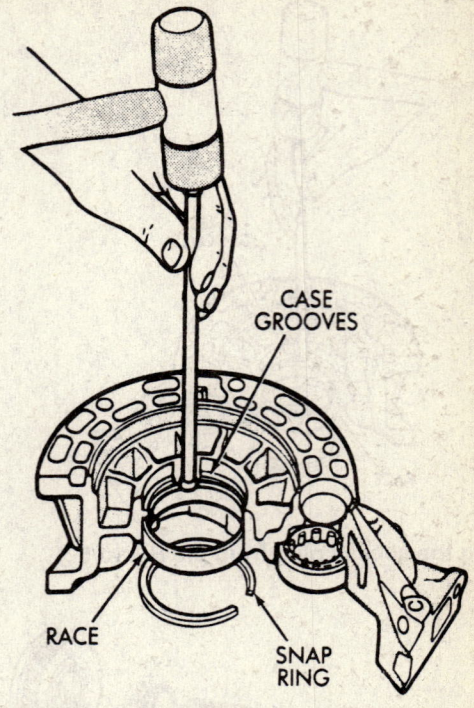

Removing the rear bearing race from the BA 10/5

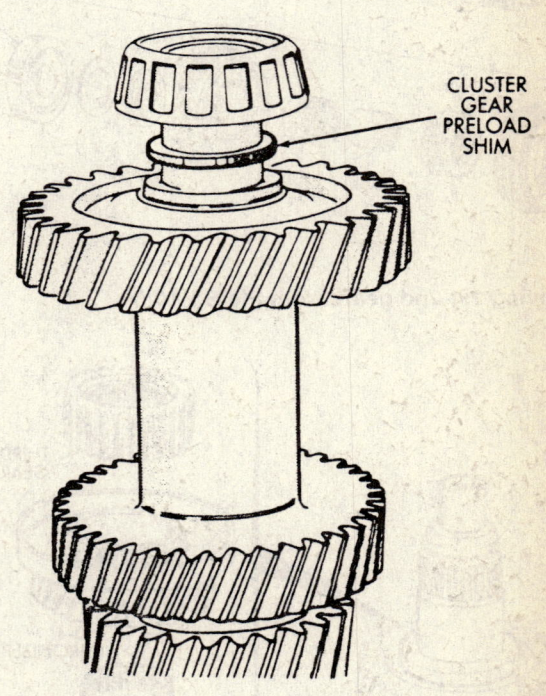

Cluster gear preload shim on the BA 10/5

19. Remove the front synchronizer ring, the circlip and the spring washer from the front of the mainshaft.

20. Remove the 3rd/4th gear synchronizer hub and 3rd gear with an appropriate puller.

21. Invert the mainshaft and lock in a holding device such as a

7-73

7 DRIVE TRAIN

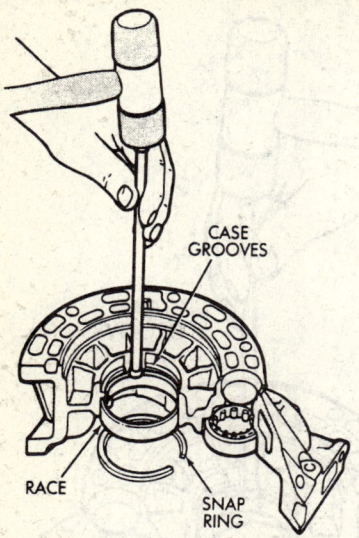

Removing the access plug from the BA 10/5

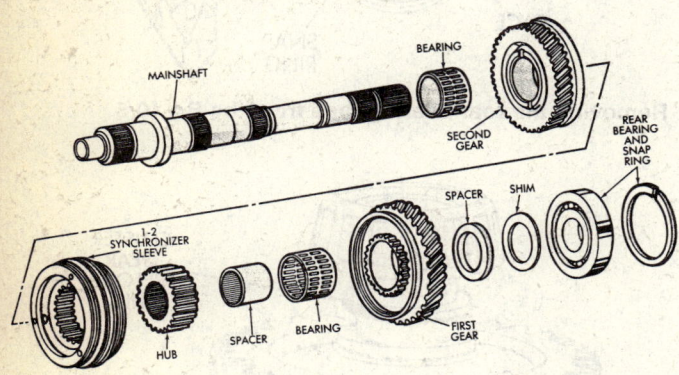

Removing 1st-2nd gears from the BA 10/5

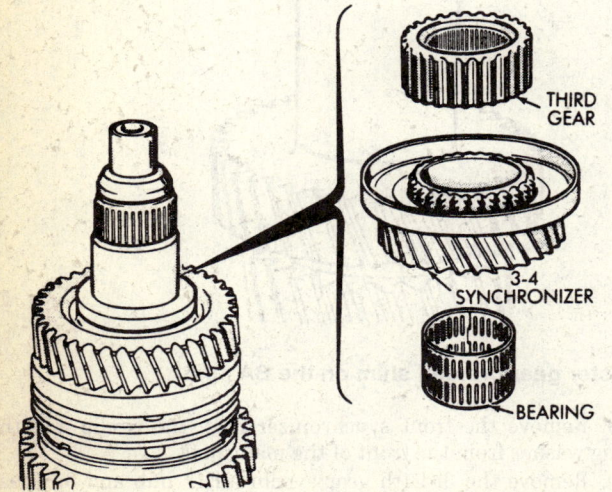

Removing the 3rd gear synchronizer and bearing from the BA 10/5

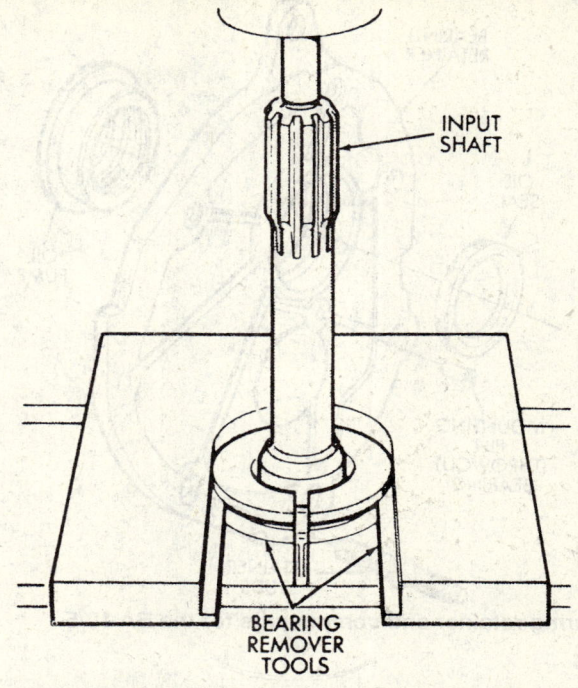

Removing the input shaft bearing from the BA 10/5

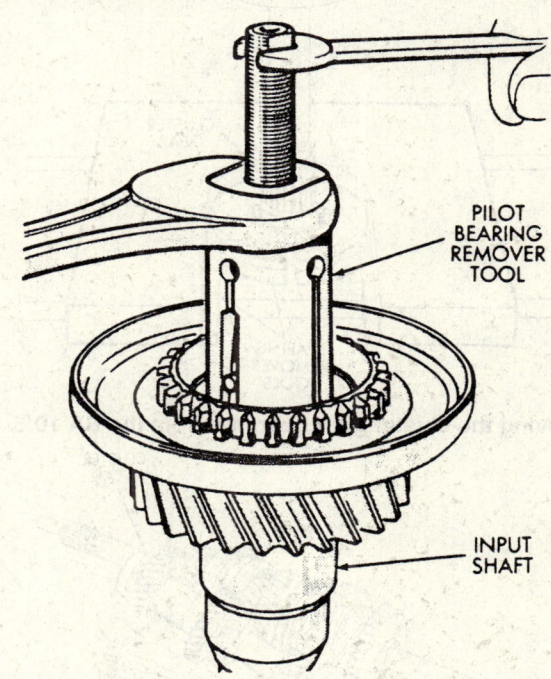

Removing the pilot bearing from the BA 10/5

vise. Unscrew the reverse driven gear locknut from the mainshaft. Remove the reverse gear from the shaft.

22. Position the mainshaft and the remaining gears on a press bench and press the mainshaft through the rear bearing. Remove the gear components from the mainshaft in the following order:

    a. Rear bearing.
    b. Bearing spacer.
    c. Adjustment shim washer.

DRIVE TRAIN 7

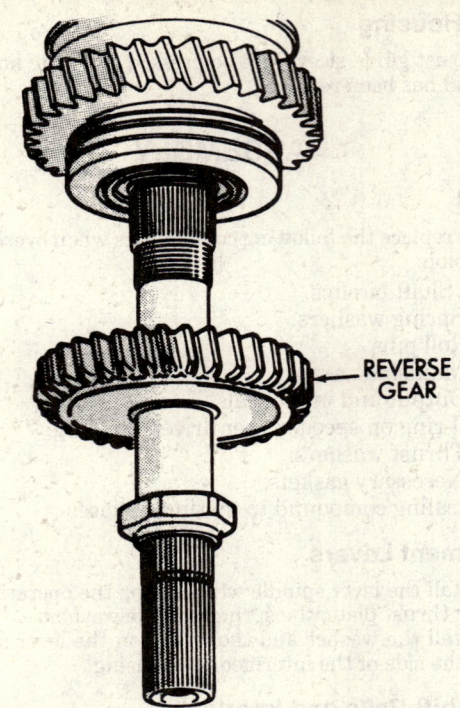

Removing reverse gear from the BA 10/5

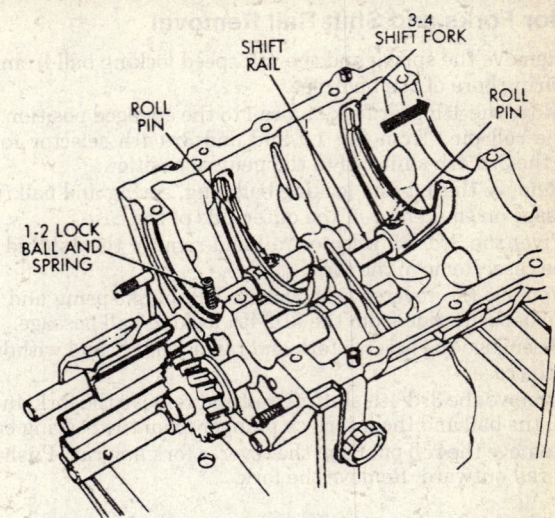

Removing 1st-2nd lock ball and shift for roll pins from the BA 10/5

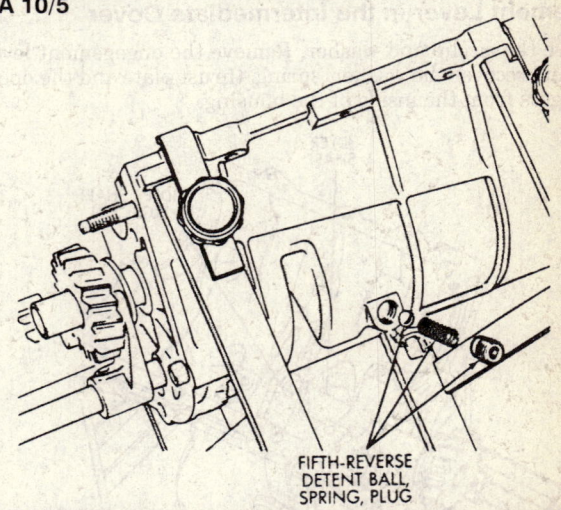

Removing 5th-reverse detent plug, spring and ball from the BA 10/5

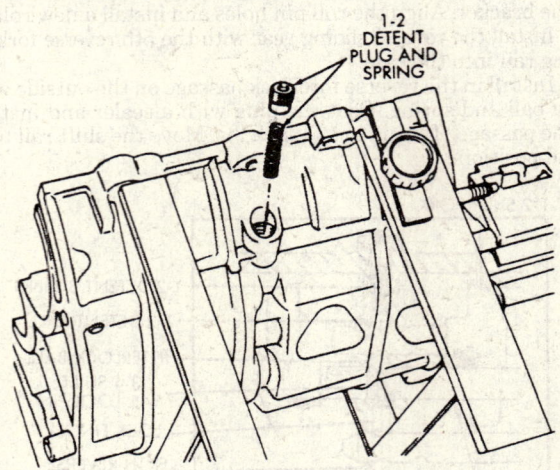

Removing 1st-2nd detent plug and spring from the BA 10/5

d. 1st speed driven gear.
e. Needle bearing.
f. 1st gear bushing.
g. 1st/2nd gear synchronizer and hub.
h. 2nd speed driven gear.
i. Needle bearing.

23. Using a press, remove the front bearing and the shim adjusting washers, Remove the rear bearing.

24. To disassemble the rear housing, the ball bearing, the oil seal and the bearing race is pressed from the housing. Locate the shim washer in the race bore.

WARNING: The press ram should be no bigger than 24mm in diameter.

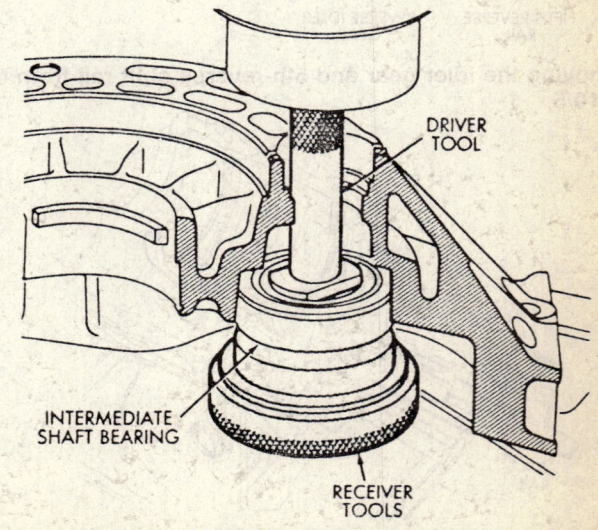

Removing the intermediate shaft bearing from the BA 10/5

7-75

7 DRIVE TRAIN

Selector Forks and Shift Rail Removal

1. Remove the spring and the 4th speed locking ball from the rear bearing bore of the half case.
2. Move the 4th gear fork and rail to the engaged position and drive the roll pins from the 1st/2nd and 3rd/4th selector forks. Return the 3rd/4th shift rail to the neutral position.
3. Remove the 1st/2nd locking ball plug, spring and ball from the passage on the center of the outer side of the case.
4. Pivot the 3rd/4th selector rail and remove the 1st/2nd rail from the case. Remove the fork.
5. Remove the reverse gear locking ball plug, spring and ball from the opposite side from the 3rd/4th locking ball passage.
6. Disengage the reverse fork and rail assembly and withdraw it from the case.
7. Remove the 3rd/4th shifting rail and remove the fork, interlock pin, the ball and the interlock plunger from the bearing bore.
8. Remove the roll pin from the reverse fork and rail. Push the shifting rail outward. Remove the fork.

Engagement Lever in the Intermediate Cover

Remove the circlip and washer. Remove the engagement lever spindle and recover the washer, spring, thrust plate and the operating fingers from the inside of the housing.

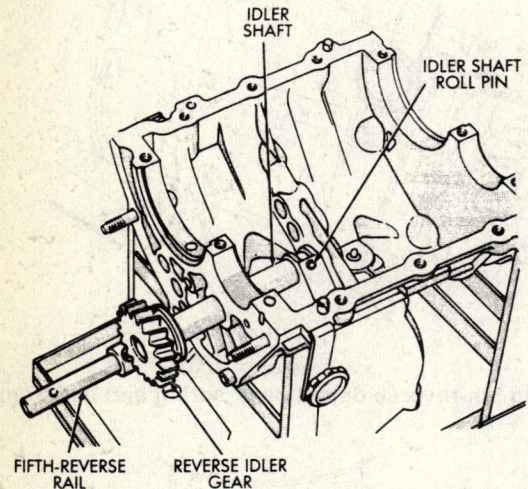

Removing the idler gear and 5th-reverse shift rail from the BA 10/5

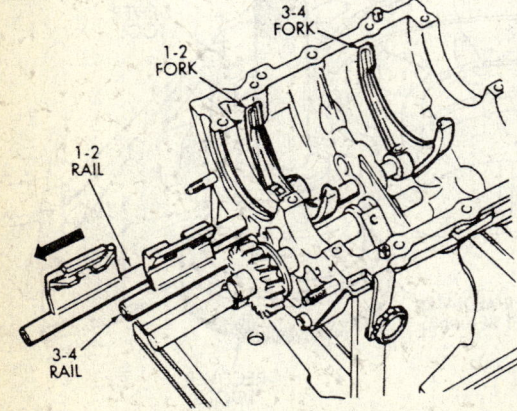

Removing the shift forks and rails from the BA 10/5

Clutch Housing

The thrust guide sleeve can be pressed from the housing after the oil seal has been removed.

ASSEMBLY

General

Always replace the following components when overhauling the transmission:
    a. Shaft circlips.
    b. Spring washers.
    c. Roll pins.
    d. Mainshaft nut.
    e. Output and input seals.
    f. O-ring on speedometer driven bushing.
    g. Thrust washers.
    h. Necessary gaskets.
    i. Sealing compound to mating surfaces

Engagement Levers

1. Install the lever spindle while fitting the operating fingers, the spring thrust plate, the spring and the washer.
2. Install the washer and the circlip on the lever spindle, exposed on the side of the intermediate housing.

Forks, Shift Rails and Interlocks

1. Install the reverse gear sliding shift rail into the case and into the bracket. Align the roll pin holes and install a new roll pin.
2. Install the reverse sliding gear with the 5th/reverse fork and shifting rail into the case.
3. Install in the reverse interlock passage on the outside of the case, a ball and spring. Coat the plug with a sealer and install it into the passage. Torque to 114 inch lbs. Move the shift rail to the neutral position.

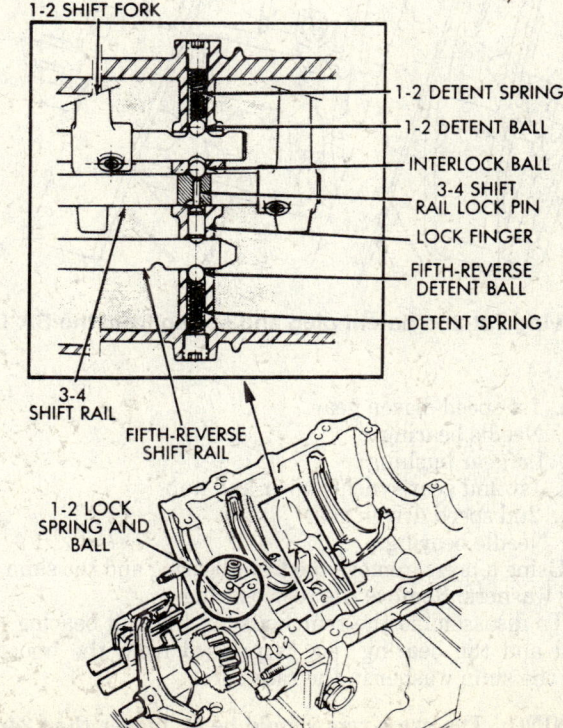

Shift component chart for the BA 10/5

DRIVE TRAIN 7

4. Install the 3rd/4th and 5th/reverse interlock plunger into its passage in the case.

5. Install an interlock pin in the 3rd/4th shift rail and retain with grease. Install the shifting rail into the case. Align the holes in the fork and the rail. Be sure the interlock pin is in the correct position and install a new roll pin.

6. Install an interlock ball in the passage between the 3rd/4th and the 1st/2nd fork rails. Install the 1st/2nd gear fork in the case with the boss towards the front. Install the shifting rail and engage the shifting fork. Align the holes in the fork and the shifting rail and install a new roll pin.

7. Install an interlock ball and spring in the 3rd/4th/2nd/1st interlock passage. Coat the plug with sealer and install it in the passage. Torque to 9.5 ft. lbs.

8. Install the ball and spring in the passage of the rear bearing bore, for the 3rd/4th shifting rail.

Preparing the Input Shaft and Mainshaft for Adjustment

INPUT SHAFT

Press the front bearing on the input shaft with the snapring groove to the front. Do not install any shims.

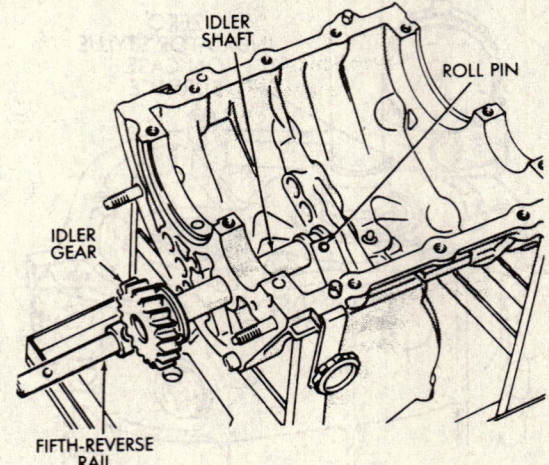

Installing the idler shaft, gear and 5th-reverse rail on the BA 10/5

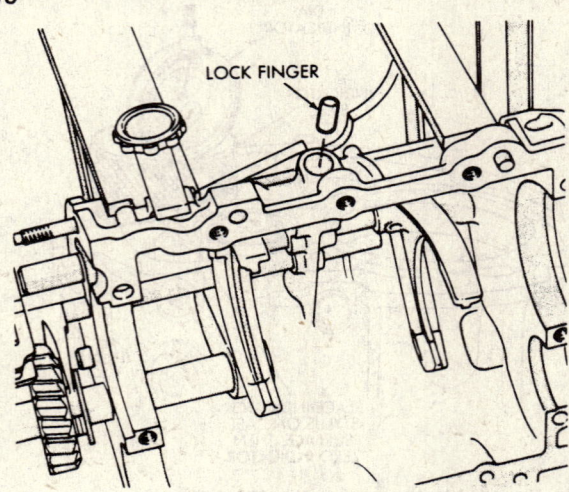

Installing the lock finger on the BA 10/5

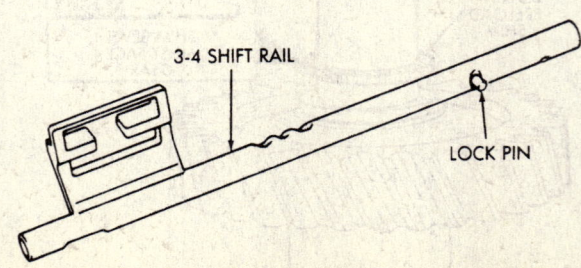

Installing the lock pin in the 3rd-4th shift rail on the BA 10/5

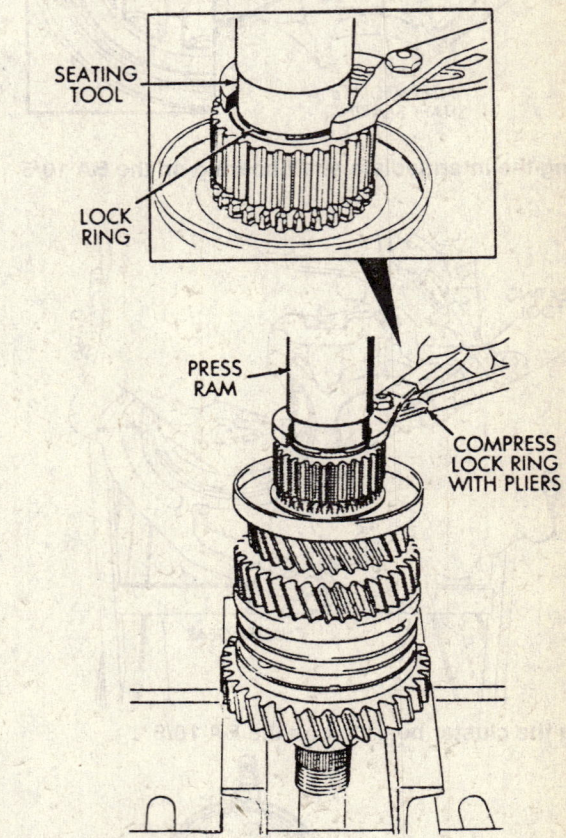

Setting the lock ring on the BA 10/5

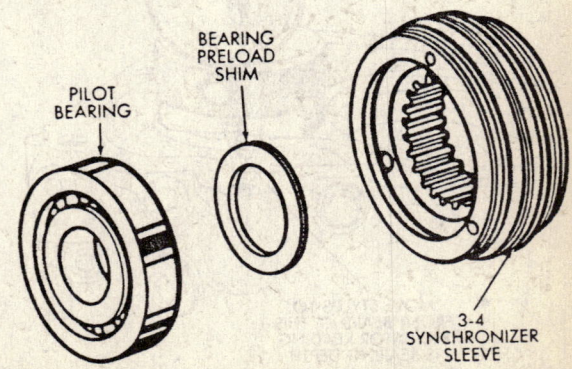

Pilot bearing, shim and 3rd-4th synchronizer sleeve on the BA 10/5

7-77

7 DRIVE TRAIN

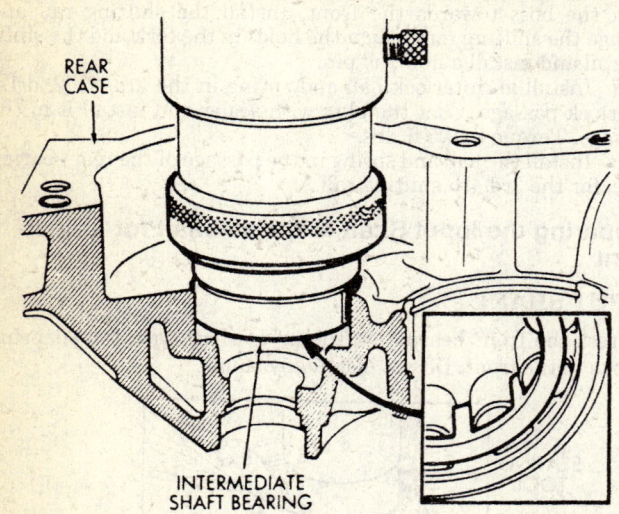

Installing the intermediate shaft bearing on the BA 10/5

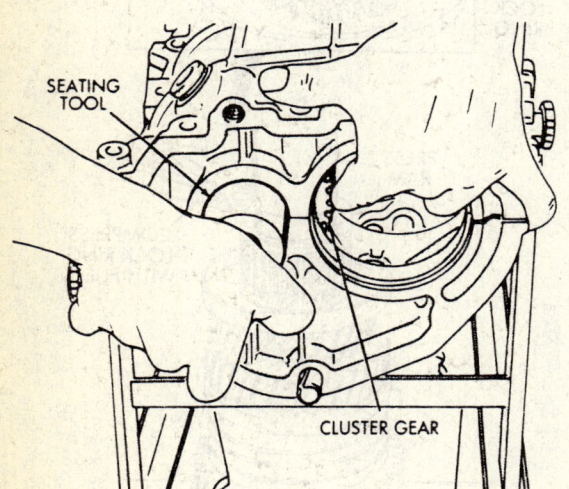

Seating the cluster bearings on the BA 10/5

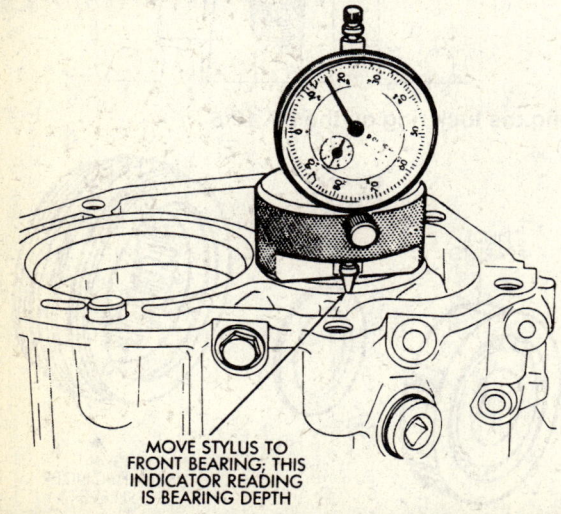

Measuring the cluster gear front bearing depth on the BA 10/5

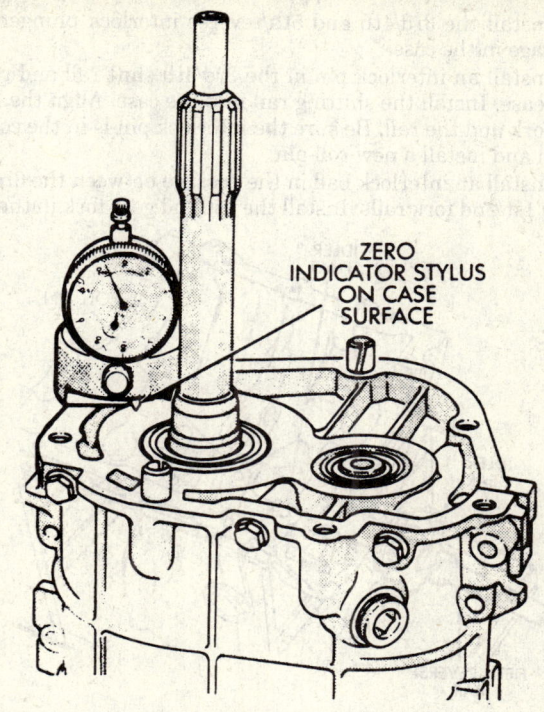

Zeroing the dial indicator on the BA 10/5

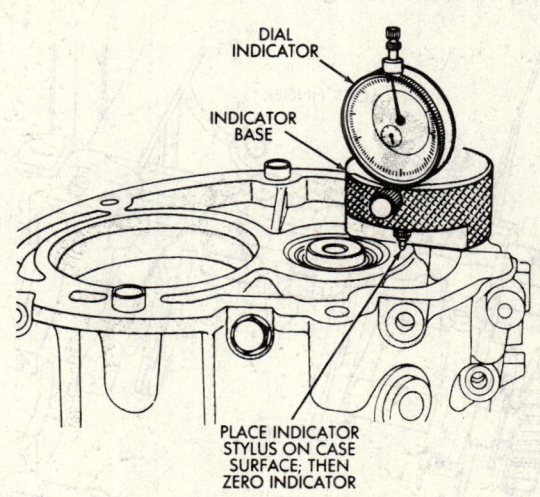

Zeroing the dial indicator on the BA 10/5

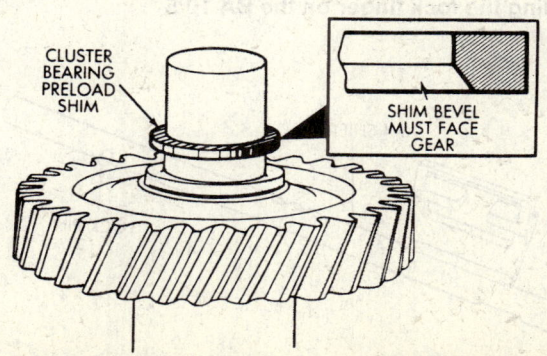

Installing the cluster bearing preload shim on the BA 10/5

7-78

DRIVE TRAIN 7

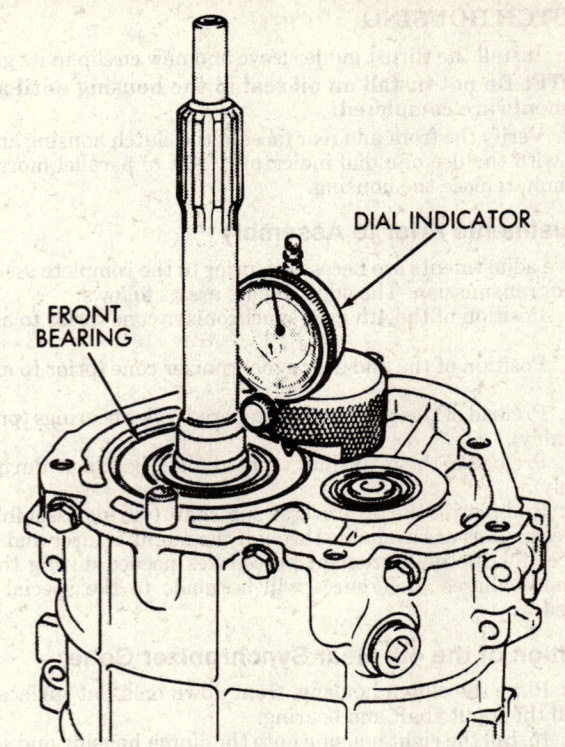

Measuring the input shaft bearing depth on the BA 10/5

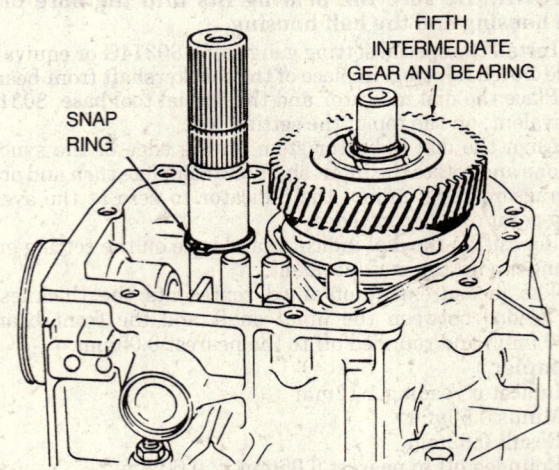

Installing the snapring and 5th intermediate gear on the BA 10/5

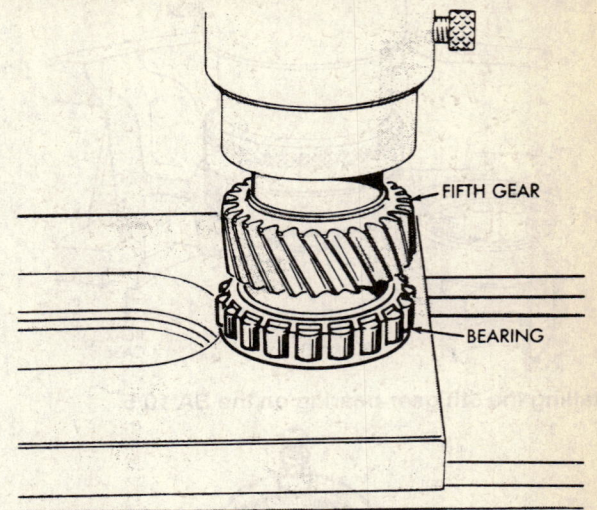

Installing the 5th gear bearing on the BA 10/5

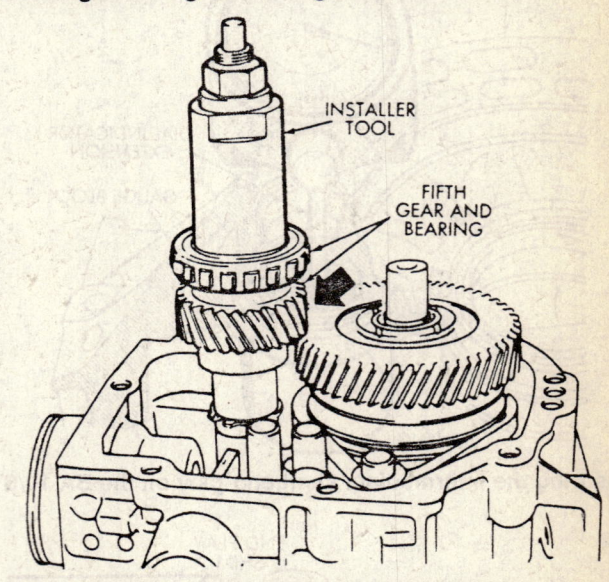

Installing the 5th gear and bearing on the BA 10/5

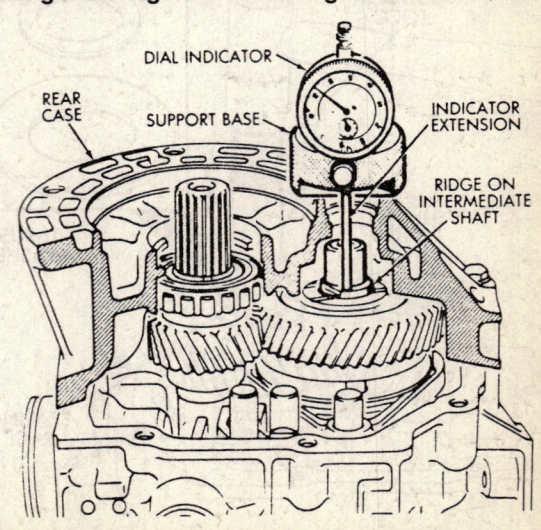

Zero and lock the dial indicator on the BA 10/5

MAINSHAFT

1. Install the 2nd speed gear and its needle bearing, the 1st/2nd synchronizer hub, the 1st speed gear spacer and washer. Install the rear bearing along with a new circlip.

NOTE: The bearing will have to be pressed on the shaft. Do not exceed 3 metric tons pressure after the bearing is seated.

2. Install the adjustment shim removed during the disassembly, the spacer and a new nut on the shaft following the rear bearing. Tighten the nut to 39 ft. lbs.

COUNTERSHAFT

Press the new bearings onto the countershaft, beginning with the rear bearing and then the front

7-79

7 DRIVE TRAIN

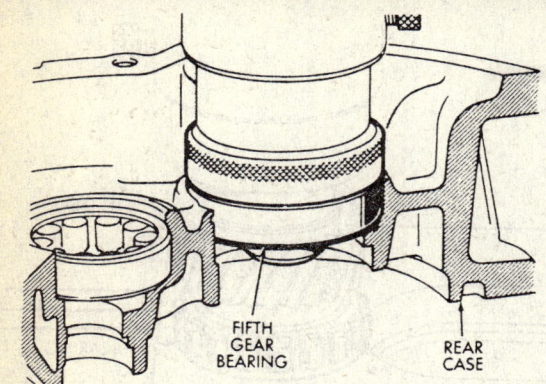

Installing the 5th gear bearing on the BA 10/5

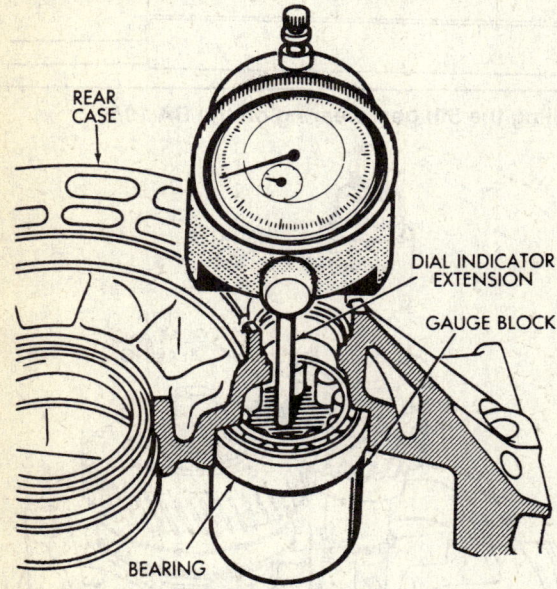

Measuring the intermediate shaft end-play on the BA 10/5

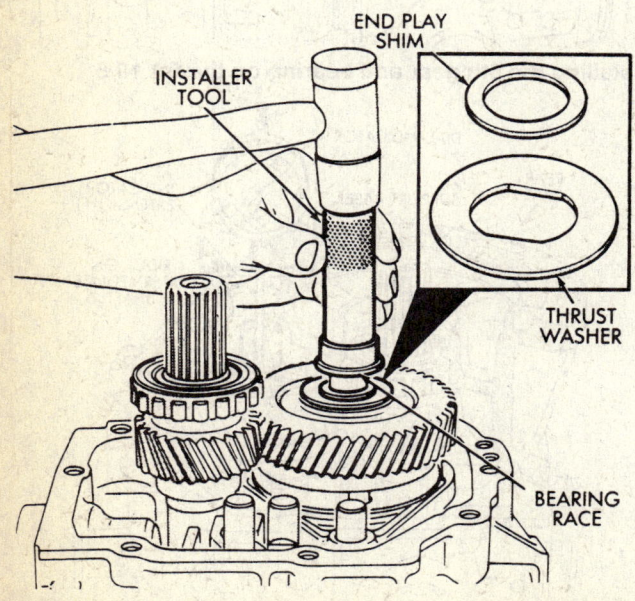

Installing the washer, shim and race on the BA 10/5

CLUTCH HOUSING

1. Install the thrust guide sleeve and new circlip in its groove.

NOTE: Do not install an oil seal in the housing until all adjustments are completed.

2. Verify the front and rear faces of the clutch housing are parallel with the use of a dial indicator. If out of parallel more than 0.10mm, replace the housing.

Adjustments Prior to Assembly

Five adjustments are necessary, prior to the complete assembly of the transmission. The adjustments are as follows:

1. Position of the 4th gear synchronizer cone (prior to assembly).
2. Position of the 2nd gear synchronizer cone (prior to assembly).
3. Preload of the countershaft tapered roller bearings (prior to assembly).
4. Preload of the mainshaft tapered roller bearings (during assembly).
5. End play of the 5th/reverse sub-shaft (during assembly).

Special tools are available through the manufacturer and other sources for the measurement procedures needed during the adjustment phases. References will be made to the special tools needed.

Position of the 4th Gear Synchronizer Cone

1. Place the clutch housing, front down on a flat surface, and install the input shaft and bearing.
2. Install the right housing onto the clutch housing and secure with two bolts. Tighten to 14 ft. lbs.

WARNING: Be sure the bearing fits into the bore of the clutch housing and the half housing.

3. Install the special setting gauge tool, 80314G or equivalent, into the clutch housing, in place of the countershaft front bearing.
4. Place the dial indicator and the special tool base, 80310FZ or equivalent, on the top of the setting tool.
5. Align the dial indicator stem on the edge of the synchronizer cone and rotate the input shaft one complete turn and obtain an average reading. Adjust the indicator to zero at the average reading point on the cone edge.
6. Reposition the dial indicator and base on the setting gauge block and record the measurement.
7. The measurement obtained represents the thickness of shims needed between the input shaft and the front bearing, minus 0.5mm and rounded off to the nearest 0.05mm.

Example:
- Indicator reading 1.12mm
- Minus 0.50mm
- Result 0.62mm
- Rounded off to nearest 0.05mm = 0.60mm

Therefore, a shim pack of 0.60mm is needed between the input shaft and the front bearing to properly position the 4th speed synchronizer cone, in this hypothetical example.

NOTE: Shims are available in steps of 0.05mm, from 0.15mm to 0.50mm.

Position of the 2nd Gear Synchronizer Cone

1. Install the needle bearing into the bore of the input shaft. Install the mainshaft and prepared components into the input shaft, with the rear bearing seated in its bore on the right hand housing.

NOTE: Be sure the bearing circlip is installed in the half housing groove.

2. Install the larger setting tool, 80314K or equivalent, into the countershaft front bearing bore of the clutch housing.
3. Install a longer stem, 80310J or equivalent, onto the indicator. Place the dial indicator and special base on the top of the right

hand half housing, in a position to touch both the setting tool and the 2nd synchronizer cone.

4. With the dial indicator set to zero, position the stem on the top of the setting tool.

5. Reposition the indicator stem to the edge of the 2nd synchronizer cone and record the measurement reading. The amount of movement noted, represents the thickness of shims needed between the 1st gear spacer and the rear bearing, plus 0.50mm, rounded off to the nearest 0.05mm.

Example:
- Indicator reading 2.51mm
- Plus 0.50mm
- Result 3.01mm
- Rounded off to nearest 0.05mm = 3.00mm

6. Remove the input and mainshaft assemblies. Separate the clutch housing and the half housing.

Preload of the Countershaft Tapered Roller Bearings

1. Place the left half housing in the support stand or equivalent. Install the countershaft and its bearings into the housing.

2. Place the right housing in place on the left housing, making sure the dowel pins are in position.

3. Install two bearings center bolts into the housings and hand tighten the bolts. Install bolts into the rear bearing thrust place and hand tighten the bolts.

4. Position the transmission with the front of the housings upward. Apply a downward pressure to the countershaft front bearing while rotating the countershaft, in order to seat the bearings.

5. Tighten the bearing center bolts and the bearing thrust plate bolts to 7 ft. lb.

6. By placing the dial indicator on the end of the countershaft and rotating it one complete turn with the stem contacting the housings, the run-out between the outer race and the face of the half housings must not exceed 0.03mm.

7. Should the run-out exceed the specifications, the race must be realigned by tapping with a mallet. Should the countershaft be difficult to turn, the bearing center bolts and the bearing thrust plate bolts must be loosened and retightened and the run-out rechecked.

8. If the run-out is within specifications, set the dial indicator with a short stem, to number 2 and zero, with the stem resting on the side of the outer race. Move the indicator until the stem is contacting the face of the housing and record the measurement of the movement. Add 0.10mm to the results for the preload of the bearings and round the results to the nearest 0.05mm.

Example:
- Housing reading 4.27mm
- Bearing reading (preset) 2.00mm
- Result 2.27mm
- Plus preload 0.10mm
- Shim pack needed 2.37mm
- Rounded off to nearest 0.05mm = 2.35mm

NOTE: Shims are available from 2.15mm to 3.30mm, in increments of 0.05mm.

9. Remove the countershaft and the front bearing from the countershaft.

10. Install the predetermined shim with the chamfer facing the gear, between the gear and the bearing.

11. Press the bearing in place.

NOTE: The 4th and 5th adjustments are made during the assembly of the transmission as noted in the adjustment list.

FINAL ASSEMBLY

Input Shaft

1. Remove the bearing from the shaft and install the predetermined shim pack between the shaft and the bearing.

2. Reinstall the bearing, with the groove for the large circlip to the front. Press the bearing into position and install the spring washer and circlip on the input shaft. Be sure the circlip engages the groove completely.

Mainshaft

1. Remove the rear bearing and shims from the mainshaft, used in the measurement check.

2. Install in the following order, from the rear to the front of the shaft, the components as listed:
   a. The 2nd gear and its needle bearing (31mm wide).
   b. The synchronizer hub and cage.
   c. The 1st gear and needle bearing (29mm wide).
   d. The spacer and adjusting shim (from measurement check).
   e. The bearing spacer.
   f. Press the bearing onto the shaft with the circlip to the rear.
   g. Install the reverse driven gear with the plain face to the rear.
   h. Install a new nut and tighten to 39 ft. lbs. and lock the collar to the shaft.

3. Invert the mainshaft and install the following in order.
   a. 3rd gear along with its needle bearing (31mm wide).
   b. 3rd-4th synchronizer hub.

4. Install a new spring washer and circlip on the end of the mainshaft. Be sure circlip is in the groove.

5. Insert the needle bearing in the bore of the input shaft, fit the 3rd-4th synchronizer cage and assemble the input and mainshaft together. Set the synchronizers to neutral positions.

Installing Gear Trains Into Transmission Cases

1. Be sure the reverse synchronizer is in the neutral position and the 3rd-4th gear locking ball and spring is in position in the bearing bore.

2. Install the input and mainshaft assembly into the left half housing, engaging the selector forks with the synchronizer cages.

3. Install the outer races to the countershaft and install the countershaft into the housing. Be sure the teeth of both gear trains mate properly.

4. Be sure the alignment dowel pins are in place. Coat the mating surfaces of the half housings with sealer and position the right hand housing onto the left. Position the rear bearing thrust plate.

5. Install the six bearing bolts and tighten to 3 ft. lbs. Install the two thrust plate bolts and tighten to 7 ft. lbs.

6. Be sure the oil seal is installed in the clutch cover and install the clutch cover in place on the transmission housing.

7. Tighten the seven securing bolts to 19 ft. lbs. Rotate the input shaft during the clutch cover retaining bolt tightening.

8. Loosen the six bearing bolts in the housings and tap the half housing with a rubber mallet while rotating the input shaft. Retighten the six bearing bolts to 11 ft. lbs.

9. Install the six assembly bolts in the housing and torque to 7 ft. lbs.

10. Invert the transmission with the rear of the mainshaft upward. Be sure the alignment dowels are in place, coat the mating surfaces of the transmission housing and the intermediate housing with sealing compound and install the intermediate housing in place, while engaging the finger in the selector fork detents.

11. Tighten the five nuts and two bolts to 13 ft. lbs. Place the 5th/reverse spindle to the 5th gear position.

12. Install the 5th/reverse stub shaft and the 5th/reverse synchronizer hub.

NOTE: If a new hub is used, the marking groove should be towards the reverse gear.

7 DRIVE TRAIN

13. As a unit, install the 5th/reverse synchronizer cage and the selector fork, bringing together the marks on the synchronizer hub and the cage.

14. Align the holes and install a new roll pin. Set the unit to the neutral position.

15. Install the 5th gear and needle bearing, along with the spacer.

5th Gear Assembly and Preparation for Measurements 4th and 5th

1. Press the bearing on to the gear pinion.
NOTE: When new parts are used, match the pinion gear to the mainshaft by green or yellow color.

2. Place the 5th gear pinion with the bearing fitted, on a hot plate and place a small piece of solder on the pinion. When the solder melts, place the pinion gear onto the shaft.
NOTE: A drift may have to be used to seat the gear.

3. Remove the alignment dowels from the rear housing and set them aside for later use. Install a shim pack, 4.0mm thick and the bearing race, into the rear housing.

Preload of the Mainshaft Tapered Roller Bearing (Number 4 Measurement)

1. Place the rear housing in position on the transmission case. Fit three bolts to hold housing and hand tighten.

2. Rotate the mainshaft, loosen the three bolts of the rear housing and retighten hand tight only.

3. A gap will exist between the two housings. Measure the gap to check for parallelism and to calculate the shim thickness needed to preload the mainshaft bearing.
Example:
- Thickness of basic shim 4.00mm
- Measurement of gap 1.85mm
- Difference 2.15mm
- Plus preload 0.10mm
- Shim thickness required 2.25mm

NOTE: Shims are available in increments of 0.05mm from 1.5mm to 2.95mm.

4. Remove the rear housing and remove the rear bearing outer race and the basic 4.00 mm shim pack.

CLUTCH

The purpose of the clutch is to disconnect and connect engine power at the transmission. A car at rest requires a lot of engine torque to get all that weight moving. An internal combustion engine does not develop a high starting torque (unlike steam engines), so it must be allowed to operate without any load until it builds up enough torque to move the car. Torque increases with engine rpm. The clutch allows the engine to build up torque by physically disconnecting the engine from the transmission, relieving the engine of any load or resistance. The transfer of engine power to the transmission (the load) must be smooth and gradual; if it weren't, drive line components would wear out or break quickly. This gradual power transfer is made possible by gradually releasing the clutch pedal. The clutch disc and pressure plate are the connecting link between the engine and transmission. When the clutch pedal is released, the disc and plate contact each other (clutch engagement), physically joining the engine and transmission. When the pedal is pushed in, the disc and plate separate (the clutch is disengaged), disconnecting the engine from the transmission.

The clutch assembly consists of the flywheel, the clutch disc, the clutch pressure plate, the throwout bearing and fork, the actuating linkage and the pedal. The flywheel and clutch pressure plate (driving members) are connected to the engine crankshaft and rotate with it. The clutch disc is located between the flywheel and pressure plate, and splined to the transmission shaft. A driving member is one that is attached to the engine and transfers engine power to a driven member (clutch disc) on the transmission shaft. A driving member (pressure plate) rotates (drives) a driven member (clutch disc) on contact and, in so doing, turns the transmission shaft. There is a circular diaphragm spring within the pressure plate cover (transmission side). In a relaxed state (when the clutch pedal is fully released), this spring is convex; that is, it is dished outward toward the transmission. Pushing in the clutch pedal actuates an attached linkage rod. Connected to the other end of this rod is the throwout bearing fork. The throwout bearing is attached to the fork. When the clutch pedal is depressed, the clutch linkage pushes the fork and bearing forward to contact the diaphragm spring of the pressure plate. The outer edges of the spring are secured to the pressure plate and are pivoted on rings so that when the center of the spring is compressed by the throwout bearing, the outer edges bow outward and, by so doing, pull the pressure plate in the same direction – away from the clutch disc. This action separates the disc from the plate, disengaging the clutch and allowing the transmission to be shifted into another gear. A coil type clutch return spring attached to the clutch pedal arm permits full release of the pedal. Releasing the pedal pulls the throwout bearing away from the diaphragm spring resulting in a reversal of spring position. As bearing pressure is gradually released from the spring center, the outer edges of the spring bow outward, pushing the pressure plate into closer contact with the clutch disc. As the disc and plate move closer together, friction between the two increases and slippage is reduced until, when full spring pressure is applied (by fully releasing the pedal), The speed of the disc and plate are the same. This stops all slipping, creating a direct connection between the plate and disc which results in the transfer of power from the engine to the transmission. The clutch disc is now rotating with the pressure plate at engine speed and, because it is splined to the transmission shaft, the shaft now turns at the same engine speed. Understanding clutch operation can be rather difficult at first; if you're still confused after reading this, consider the following analogy. The action of the diaphragm spring can be compared to that of an oil can bottom. The bottom of an oil can is shaped very much like the clutch diaphragm spring and pushing in on the can bottom and then releasing it produces a similar effect. As mentioned earlier, the clutch pedal return spring permits full release of the pedal and reduces linkage slack due to wear. As the linkage wears, clutch free-pedal travel will increase and free-travel will decrease as the clutch wears. Free-travel is actually throwout bearing lash.

The diaphragm spring type clutches used are available in two different designs: flat diaphragm springs or bent spring. The bent fingers are bent back to create a centrifugal boost ensuring quick re-engagement at higher engine speeds. This design enables pressure plate load to increase as the clutch disc wears and makes low pedal effort possible even with a heavy-duty clutch. The throwout bearing used with the bent finger design is 31.75mm (1 1/4 in.) long and is shorter than the bearing used with the flat finger design. These bearings are not interchangeable. If the longer bearing is used with the bent finger clutch, free-pedal travel will not exist. This results in clutch slippage and rapid wear.

The transmission varies the gear ratio between the engine and rear wheels. It can be shifted to change engine speed as driving conditions and loads change. The transmission allows disengaging and reversing power from the engine to the wheels.

DRIVE TRAIN 7

Troubleshooting Basic Clutch Problems

Problem	Cause
Excessive clutch noise	Throwout bearing noises are more audible at the lower end of pedal travel. The usual causes are: • Riding the clutch • Too little pedal free-play • Lack of bearing lubrication A bad clutch shaft pilot bearing will make a high pitched squeal, when the clutch is disengaged and the transmission is in gear or within the first 2″ of pedal travel. The bearing must be replaced. Noise from the clutch linkage is a clicking or snapping that can be heard or felt as the pedal is moved completely up or down. This usually requires lubrication. Transmitted engine noises are amplified by the clutch housing and heard in the passenger compartment. They are usually the result of insufficient pedal free-play and can be changed by manipulating the clutch pedal.
Clutch slips (the car does not move as it should when the clutch is engaged)	This is usually most noticeable when pulling away from a standing start. A severe test is to start the engine, apply the brakes, shift into high gear and SLOWLY release the clutch pedal. A healthy clutch will stall the engine. If it slips it may be due to: • A worn pressure plate or clutch plate • Oil soaked clutch plate • Insufficient pedal free-play
Clutch drags or fails to release	The clutch disc and some transmission gears spin briefly after clutch disengagement. Under normal conditions in average temperatures, 3 seconds is maximum spin-time. Failure to release properly can be caused by: • Too light transmission lubricant or low lubricant level • Improperly adjusted clutch linkage
Low clutch life	Low clutch life is usually a result of poor driving habits or heavy duty use. Riding the clutch, pulling heavy loads, holding the car on a grade with the clutch instead of the brakes and rapid clutch engagement all contribute to low clutch life.

Clutch Pedal

REMOVAL AND INSTALLATION

1. Remove instrument panel lower trim cover for needed clearance.
2. Remove cotter pin securing master cylinder push rod to pedal. Remove flat washer and wave washer, if equipped.
3. Disconnect pedal return spring, if equipped
4. Remove nut securing pedal to pivot shaft, slide pedal off shaft and remove.
5. Lubricate clutch pedal pivot shaft and pedal bushings with chassis grease.
6. Installation is the reverse of removal.

Clutch Disc And Pressure Plate

REMOVAL AND INSTALLATION

NOTE: These vehicles use a hydraulic clutch.

1. Remove the transmission or transmission/transfer case assembly.

―――――― CAUTION ――――――
The clutch driven disc contains asbestos, which has been determined to be a cancer causing agent. Never clean clutch surfaces with compressed air! Avoid inhaling any dust from any clutch surface! When cleaning clutch surfaces, use a commercially available brake cleaning fluid.

2. Matchmark the pressure plate and flywheel. Loosen the pressure plate bolts, a little at a time, in rotation, to avoid warpage.
3. Remove the pressure plate and clutch disc.

7 DRIVE TRAIN

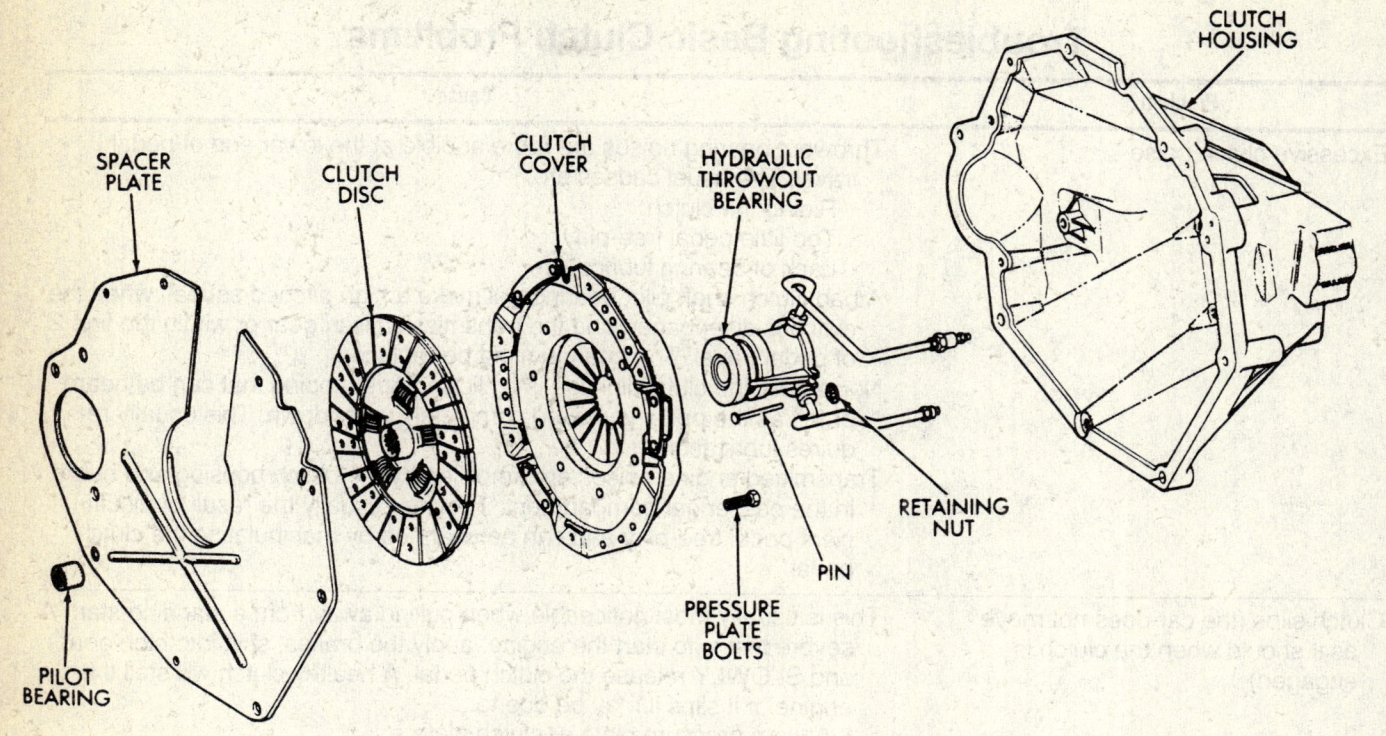

6-cylinder clutch components

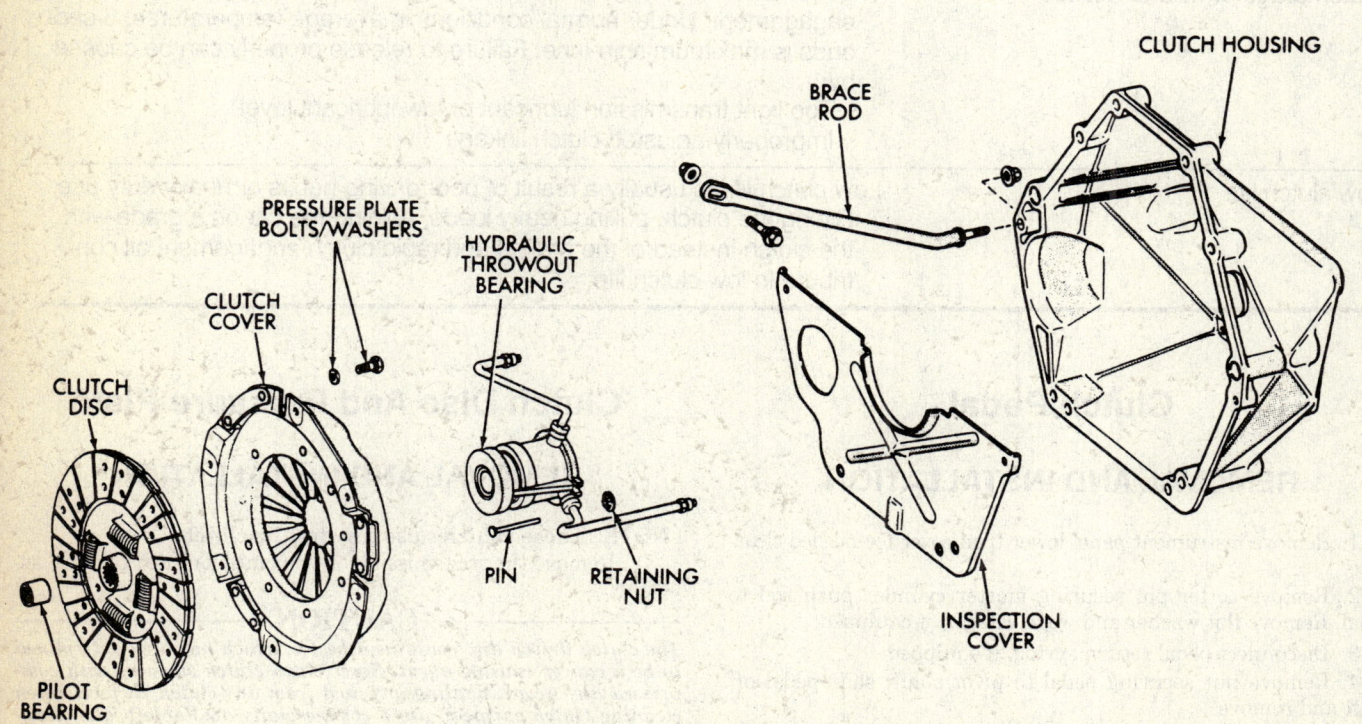

4-cylinder clutch components

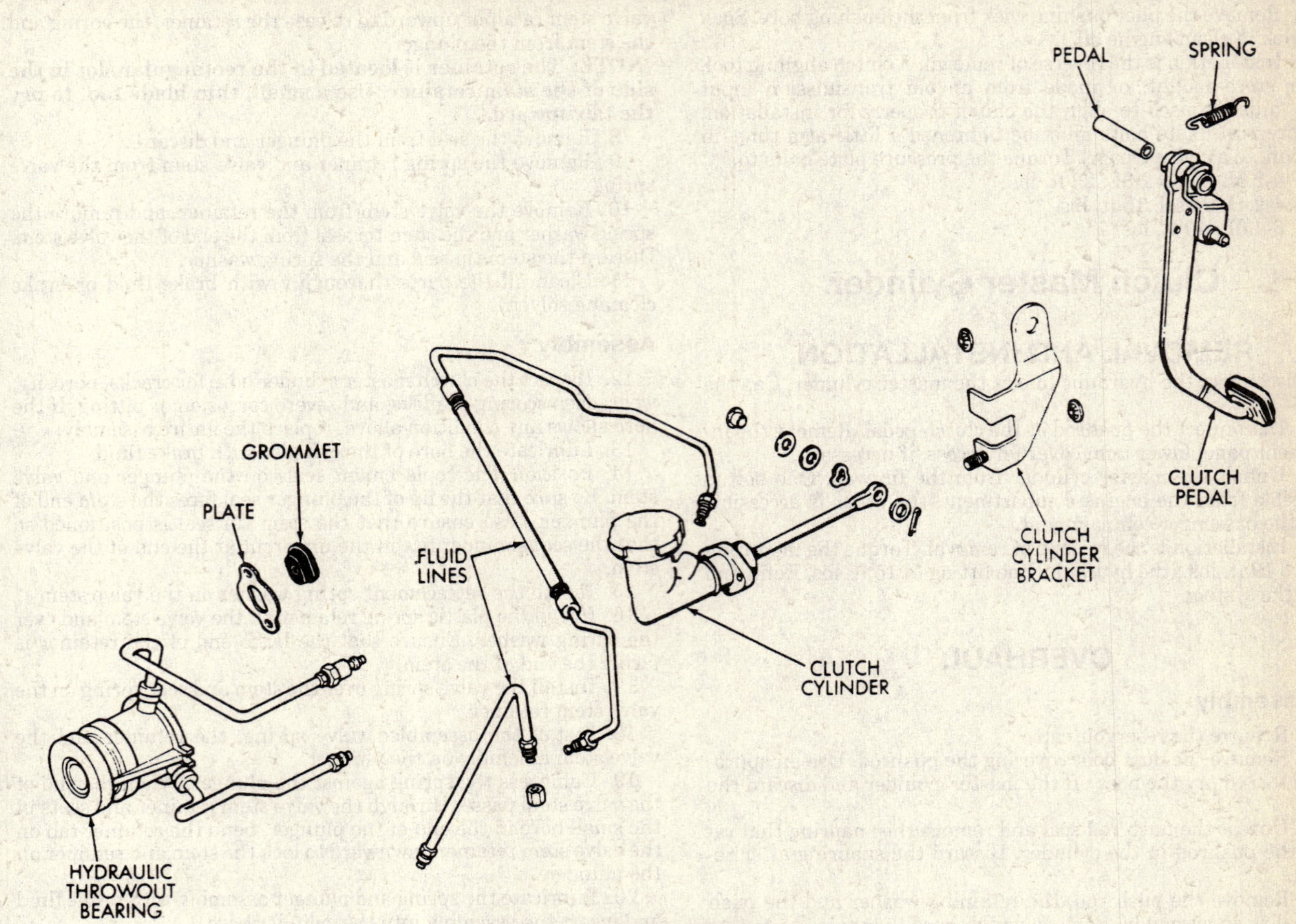

DRIVE TRAIN 7

Clutch hydraulic system

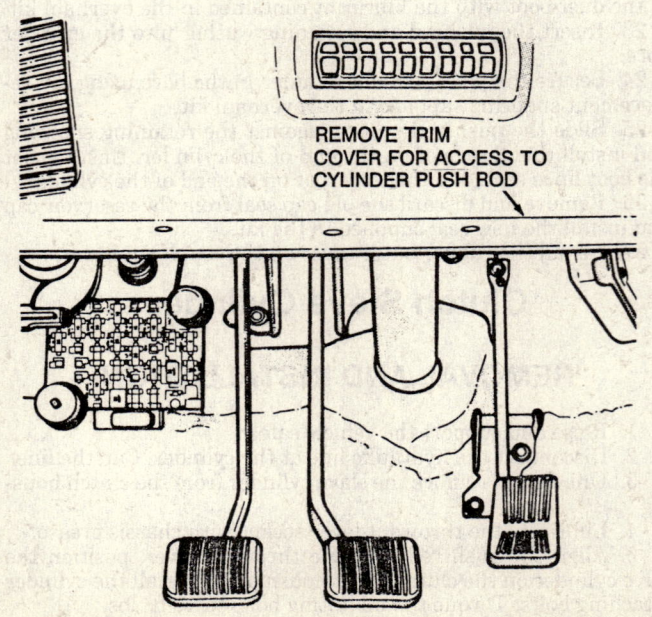

Remove the lower trim cover to gain access to clutch pedal and push rod

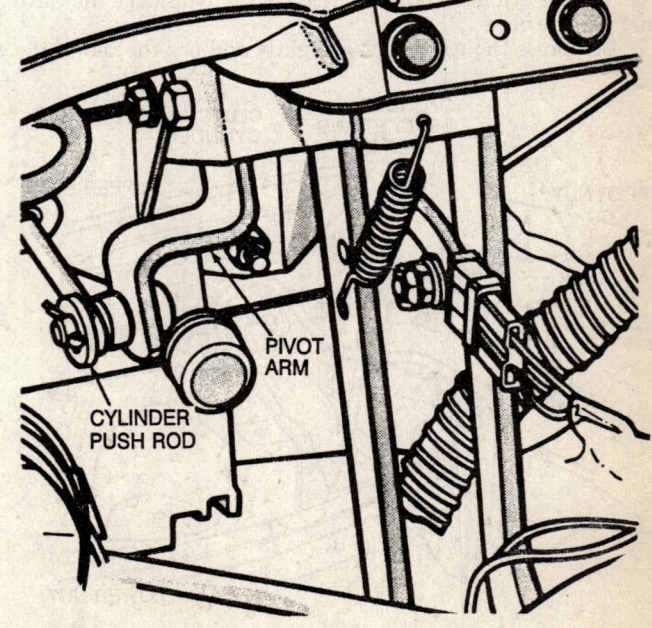

Master cylinder-to-pedal push rod removal/installation

7-85

7 DRIVE TRAIN

4. Remove the pilot bushing wick from the bushing bore. Soak the wick in clean engine oil.
5. Installation is the reverse of removal. A clutch aligning tool, either store-bought, or made from an old transmission input shaft, must be used to align the clutch properly for installation. The pressure plate bolts must be tightened a little at a time, in rotation, to avoid warpage. Torque the pressure plate bolts to:
- 4-2.5L and 6-2.8L: 23 ft. lbs.
- 4-2.1L diesel: 16 ft. lbs.
- 6-4.0L: 40 ft. lbs.

Clutch Master Cylinder

REMOVAL AND INSTALLATION

1. Disconnect the hydraulic line at the master cylinder. Cap the line.
2. Disconnect the pushrod at the clutch pedal. Remove the instrument panel lower trim cover for access, if necessary.
3. Unbolt the master cylinder from the firewall. One bolt is accessible from the engine compartment, the other is accessible from the passenger compartment.
4. Installation is the reverse of removal. Torque the mounting nuts to 19 ft. lbs.; the hydraulic line fitting to 15 ft. lbs. Refill and bleed the system.

OVERHAUL

Disassembly

1. Remove the reservoir cap.
2. Remove the dust boot covering the pushrod. Use an appropriate tool to pry the boot off the master cylinder and discard the boot.
3. Unseat the push rod seal and remove the snapring that retains the pushrod in the cylinder. Discard the snapring after removal.
4. Remove the push rod, the retaining washer and the push rod seal as an assembly. Remove and discard the seal.
5. Remove the plunger, the valve spring and valve stem assembly.
6. Tap the cylinder body on a wood block to dislodge the valve stem from the bore.
7. Compress the valve spring slightly and pry the tab of the valve stem retainer upward to release the retainer, the spring and the stem from the plunger.

NOTE: The retainer is located in the rectangular slot in the side of the stem retainer. Use a small, thin blade tool to pry the tab upward.

8. Remove the seal from the plunger and discard.
9. Remove the spring retainer and valve stem from the valve spring.
10. Remove the valve stem from the retainer, and remove the spring washer and the stem tip seal from the end of the valve stem. Discard the stem tip seal and the spring washer.
11. Clean all the parts thoroughly with brake fluid or brake cleaning solvent.

Assembly

12. Inspect the clutch master cylinder bore for cracks, porosity, wear, deep scoring or nicks, and severe corrosion or pitting. If the bore shows any condition above, replace the entire assembly.
13. Lubricate the bore of the cylinder with brake fluid.
14. Position The replacement seals on the plunger and valve stem. Be sure that the lip of the plunger seal faces the stem end of the plunger. Also ensure that the stem tip seal is positioned so that the seal shoulder fits in the undercut at the end of the valve stem.
15. Install the replacement spring washer on the valve stem.
16. Install the plastic spring retainer on the valve stem and over the spring washer. Ensure that the large end of the retainer is facing the end of the stem.
17. Install the valve spring over the stem and seat spring on the valve stem retainer.
18. Install the assembled valve spring, the retainer and the valve stem assembly on the plunger.
19. Compress the spring against the plunger. When the end of the valve stem passes through the valve stem retainer and seats in the small bore in the end of the plunger, bend the retainer tab on the valve stem retainer downward to lock the stem and retainer on the plunger.
20. Lubricate the spring and plunger assembly with brake fluid and insert the assembly into the cylinder bore.
21. Install the replacement seal and dust boot on the push rod.
22. Lubricate the ball end of the push rod and the seal and lip of the dust boot with the lubricant contained in the overhaul kit.
23. Insert the pushrod and retaining washer into the cylinder bore.
24. Secure the push rod and retainer in the bore using the replacement snapring supplied in the overhaul kit.
25. Slide the push rod seal up against the retaining snapring and install the dust boot on the end of the cylinder. Ensure that the boot lip is seated in the undercut on the end of the cylinder.
26. Remove and discard the old cap seal from the reservoir cap and install the new seal supplied in the kit.
27. Install the rubber outer cover on the cap, if equipped.

Clutch Slave Cylinder

REMOVAL AND INSTALLATION

1. Raise and support the vehicle safely.
2. Disconnect the hydraulic line at the cylinder. Cap the line.
3. Unbolt and remove the slave cylinder from the clutch housing.
4. Lubricate the throwout lever socket with chassis grease.
5. Align the push rod with the throwout lever, position the slave cylinder on the clutch cover housing and install the cylinder attaching bolts. Torque the mounting bolts to 16 ft. lbs.
6. Connect the hydraulic line to the slave cylinder. Lower the vehicle.
7. Fill the reservoir with brake fluid and bleed the system.

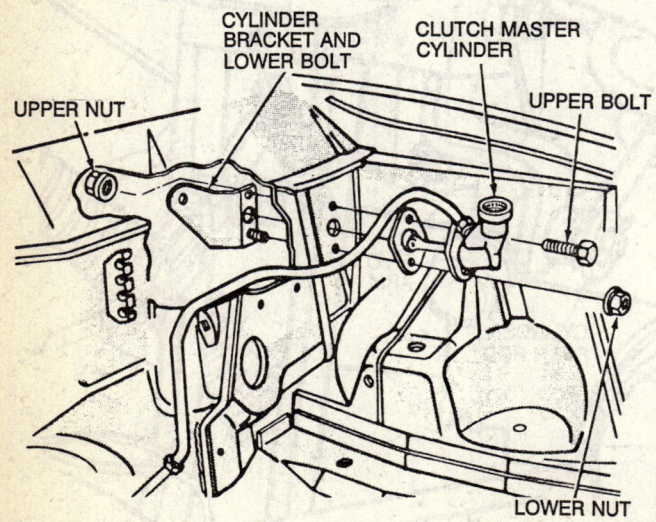

Clutch master cylinder reservoir removal/installation

DRIVE TRAIN 7

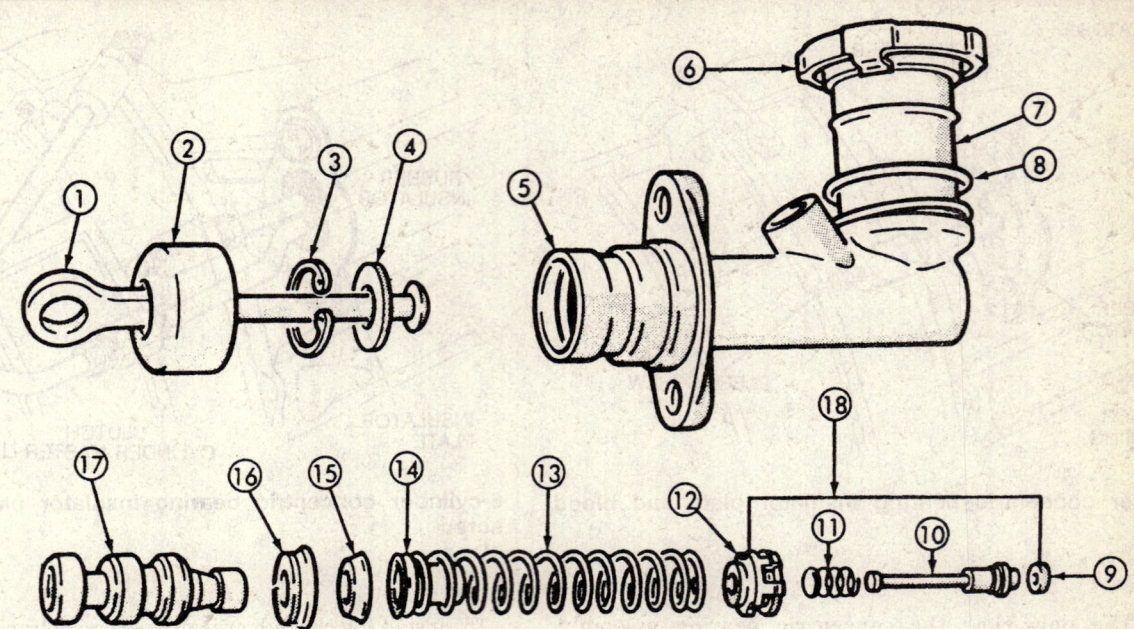

① PUSH ROD
② DUST BOOT
③ SNAP RING
④ WASHER
⑤ CLUTCH MASTER CYLINDER
⑥ RESERVOIR CAP
⑦ RESERVOIR
⑧ RETAINING CLAMP
⑨ STEM TIP SEAL
⑩ VALVE STEM
⑪ RETAINER SPRING
⑫ SPRING RETAINER
⑬ PLUNGER SPRING
⑭ VALVE STEM RETAINER
⑮ PLUNGER REAR SEAL
⑯ PLUNGER FRONT SEAL
⑰ PLUNGER
⑱ VALVE STEM ASSEMBLY

Clutch master cylinder components

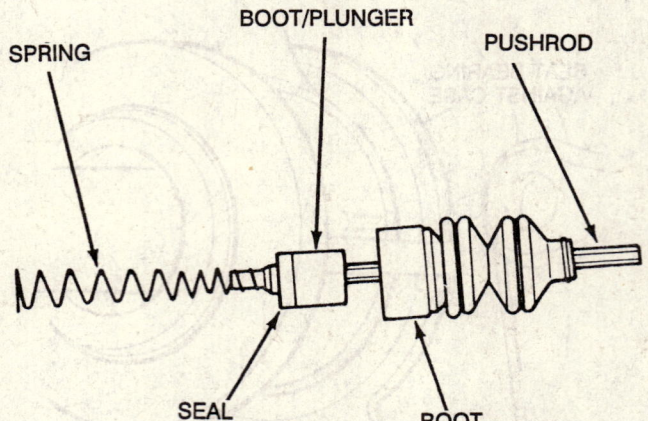

Slave cylinder components

OVERHAUL

Disassembly

1. Clean the outside of the slave cylinder thoroughly.
2. Remove the boot from the cylinder. Remove the cylinder pushrod, boot, plunger and spring as an assembly.
3. Remove the spring and seal from the plunger.
4. Remove the snapring that retains the pushrod in the plunger and remove the push rod and boot. Remove the boot from the push rod.

5. Clean all parts with brake fluid.

Assembly

6. Install the replacement boot on the push rod.
7. Install the pushrod in the plunger and install the replacement push rod retaining snapring.
8. Install the spring on the plunger.
9. Lubricate the cylinder bore and the seal with brake fluid.
10. Install the assembled plunger, spring and push rod in the cylinder. Install and secure the boot on the cylinder.

Concentric Bearing Assembly

REMOVAL AND INSTALLATION

1. Remove the clutch master cylinder reservoir cover and drain all fluid. Replace the reservoir cap.
2. Disconnect the clutch master cylinder line and cap to prevent dirt entry.
3. Remove the clutch housing/transmission/transfer case (if equipped) as an assembly.
4. Disconnect the clutch master cylinder feed line.
5. Remove the insulator plate bolts and slide the plate and rubber insulator off the bleed line.
6. Remove the throwout bearing retaining nut. Pry the nut up and off the mounting pin on the transmission case.
7. Remove the concentric bearing from the transmission input shaft. If the bearing will be reused, secure the bearing and piston with tape or rubber bands.

7 DRIVE TRAIN

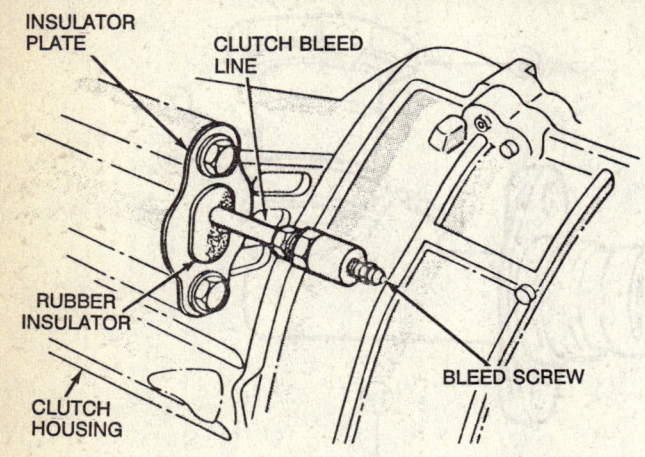

4-cylinder concentric bearing insulator plate and bleed screw

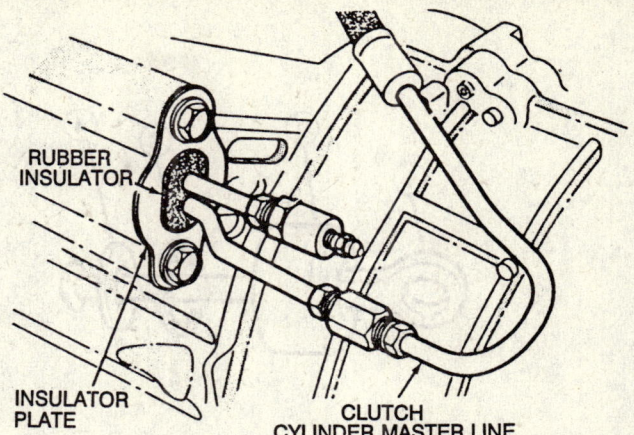

6-cylinder concentric bearing insulator plate and bleed screw

NOTE: The only time the concentric bearing assembly should be replaced is when it is either leaking or obviously damaged. The bearing should never be replaced just because the clutch disc or cover are being serviced. Replace the bearing only when it has actually failed.

To Install:

8. New concentric bearings are equipped with nylon retaining straps to hold the bearing in place during shipment. Unhook the T-shaped ends from the bearing before installation.
9. Inspect the bearing mounting pin and replace if damaged.
10. Install the bearing assembly on the transmission input shaft.
11. Guide the bearing inlet and bleed lines through the openings in the clutch housing.
12. Position the bearing boss on the mounting pin and seat the bearing against the transmission case.
13. Secure the bearing to the mounting pin with a new retaining nut.
14. Unhook the nylon straps that secure the bearing piston. Install the insulator and plate.
15. Install the clutch housing/transmission/transfer case assembly.
16. Connect the clutch master cylinder fluid line. Fill and bleed the system.

Clutch Hydraulic System

BLEEDING THE SYSTEM

With Slave Cylinder

1. Fill the reservoir with clean brake fluid.
2. Raise and support the truck on jackstands.

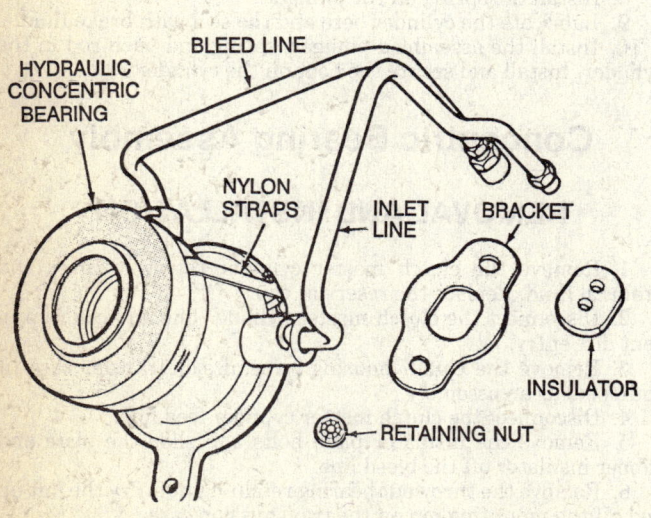

Concentric bearing components

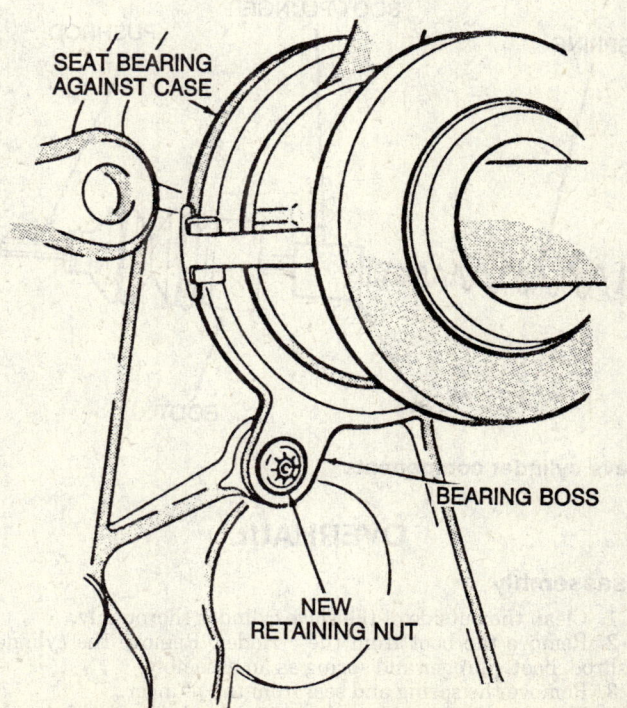

Installing the concentric bearing assembly

DRIVE TRAIN 7

3. Remove the slave cylinder from the clutch housing, but do not disconnect the hydraulic line. There is enough play in the line to do this.
4. Remove the slave cylinder pushrod.
5. Using a wood dowel, compress the slave cylinder plunger.
6. Attach one end of a rubber hose to the slave cylinder bleeder screw and place the other end in a glass jar, filled halfway with clean brake fluid. Make sure that the hose will stay submerged.
7. Loosen the bleeder screw.
8. Have an assistant press and hold the clutch pedal to the floor. Tighten the bleeder screw with the pedal at the floor. Bubbles will have appeared in the jar when the pedal was depressed.
9. Have your assistant release pedal, then perform the sequence again, until bubbles no longer appear in the jar.
10. Install the slave cylinder and lower the truck. Test the clutch.

With Concentric Bearing Assembly

1. Fill the reservoir with clean brake fluid.
2. Raise and support the truck on jackstands.
3. Attach a bleed hose to the bleed screw on the concentric bearing bleed line.
4. Insert the opposite end of the bleed hose in a glass container filled with brake fluid. Ensure the hose end is completely submerged in fluid.
5. Carefully loosen the bleed screw. Hold the bleed screw fitting firmly to prevent it from turning while loosening the screw.
NOTE: DO NOT allow the bleed line to bend or flex when loosening the screw.
6. Have an assistant press and hold the clutch pedal to the floor.
7. Tighten the bolt head screw and have assistant release the clutch pedal.
8. Check clutch master cylinder fluid level. Add fluid if necessary.
9. Repeat the bleeding process until fluid entering the glass container is free of bubbles. Be sure the bleed hose end remains submerged in brake fluid during the bleeding operation.
10. Lower the vehicle and top off the clutch master cylinder with brake fluid.

AUTOMATIC TRANSMISSION

Understanding Automatic Transmissions

The automatic transmission allows engine torque and power to be transmitted to the rear wheels within a narrow range of engine operating speeds. The transmission will allow the engine to turn fast enough to produce plenty of power and torque at very low speeds, while keeping it at a sensible rpm at high vehicle speeds. The transmission performs this job entirely without driver assistance. The transmission uses a light fluid as the medium for the transmission of power. This fluid also works in the operation of various hydraulic control circuits and as a lubricant. Because the transmission fluid performs all of these functions, trouble within the unit can easily travel from one part to another. For this reason, and because of the complexity and unusual operating principles of the transmission, a very sound understanding of the basic principles of operation will simplify troubleshooting.

THE TORQUE CONVERTER

The torque converter replaces the conventional clutch. It has three functions:
1. It allows the engine to idle with the vehicle at a standstill, even with the transmission in gear.
2. It allows the transmission to shift from range to range smoothly, without requiring that the driver close the throttle during the shift.
3. It multiplies engine torque to an increasing extent as vehicle speed drops and throttle opening is increased. This has the effect of making the transmission more responsive and reduces the amount of shifting required.

The torque converter is a metal case which is shaped like a sphere that has been flattened on opposite sides. It is bolted to the rear end of the engine's crankshaft. Generally, the entire metal case rotates at engine speed and serves as the engine's flywheel.

The case contains three sets of blades. One set is attached directly to the case. This set forms the torus or pump. Another set is directly connected to the output shaft, and forms the turbine. The third set is mounted on a hub which, in turn, is mounted on a stationary shaft through a one-way clutch. This third set is known as the stator.

A pump, which is driven by the converter hub at engine speed, keeps the torque converter full of transmission fluid at all times. Fluid flows continuously through the unit to provide cooling.

Under low-speed acceleration, the torque converter functions as follows:

The torus is turning faster than the turbine. It picks up fluid at the center of the converter and, through centrifugal force, slings it outward. Since the outer edge of the converter moves faster than the portions at the center, the fluid picks up speed.

The fluid then enters the outer edge of the turbine blades. It then travels back toward the center of the converter case along the turbine blades. In impinging upon the turbine blades, the fluid loses the energy picked up in the torus.

If the fluid were now to immediately be returned directly into the torus, both halves of the converter would have to turn at approximately the same speed at all times, and torque input and output would both be the same.

In flowing through the torus and turbine, the fluid picks up two types of flow, or flow in two separate directions. It flows through the turbine blades, and it spins with the engine. The stator, whose blades are stationary when the vehicle is being accelerated at low speeds, converts one type of flow into another. Instead of allowing the fluid to flow straight back into the torus, the stator's curved blades turn the fluid almost 90 degrees toward the direction of rotation of the engine. Thus the fluid does not flow as fast toward the torus, but is already spinning when the torus picks it up. This has the effect of allowing the torus to turn much faster than the

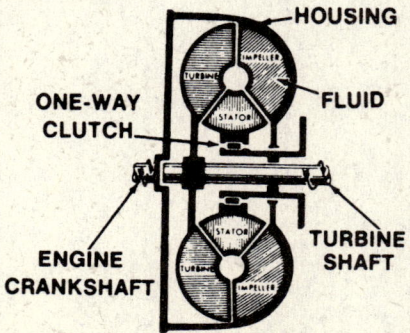

The torque converter housing is rotated by the engine's crankshaft, and turns the impeller. The impeller spins the turbine, which gives motion to the turbine shaft, driving the gears

7 DRIVE TRAIN

Troubleshooting Basic Automatic Transmission Problems

Problem	Cause	Solution
Fluid leakage	• Defective pan gasket	• Replace gasket or tighten pan bolts
	• Loose filler tube	• Tighten tube nut
	• Loose extension housing to transmission case	• Tighten bolts
	• Converter housing area leakage	• Have transmission checked professionally
Fluid flows out the oil filler tube	• High fluid level	• Check and correct fluid level
	• Breather vent clogged	• Open breather vent
	• Clogged oil filter or screen	• Replace filter or clean screen (change fluid also)
	• Internal fluid leakage	• Have transmission checked professionally
Transmission overheats (this is usually accompanied by a strong burned odor to the fluid)	• Low fluid level	• Check and correct fluid level
	• Fluid cooler lines clogged	• Drain and refill transmission. If this doesn't cure the problem, have cooler lines cleared or replaced.
	• Heavy pulling or hauling with insufficient cooling	• Install a transmission oil cooler
	• Faulty oil pump, internal slippage	• Have transmission checked professionally
Buzzing or whining noise	• Low fluid level	• Check and correct fluid level
	• Defective torque converter, scored gears	• Have transmission checked professionally
No forward or reverse gears or slippage in one or more gears	• Low fluid level	• Check and correct fluid level
	• Defective vacuum or linkage controls, internal clutch or band failure	• Have unit checked professionally
Delayed or erratic shift	• Low fluid level	• Check and correct fluid level
	• Broken vacuum lines	• Repair or replace lines
	• Internal malfunction	• Have transmission checked professionally

DRIVE TRAIN 7

Lockup Torque Converter Service Diagnosis

Problem	Cause	Solution

No lockup	• Faulty oil pump
	• Sticking governor valve
	• Valve body malfunction
	   (a) Stuck switch valve
	   (b) Stuck lockup valve
	   (c) Stuck fail-safe valve
	• Failed locking clutch
	• Leaking turbine hub seal
	• Faulty input shaft or seal ring
		• Replace oil pump
		• Repair or replace as necessary
		• Repair or replace valve body or its internal components as necessary
		
		• Replace torque converter
		• Replace torque converter
		• Repair or replace as necessary

Will not unlock	• Sticking governor valve
	• Valve body malfunction
	   (a) Stuck switch valve
	   (b) Stuck lockup valve
	   (c) Stuck fail-safe valve
		• Repair or replace as necessary
		• Repair or replace valve body or its internal components as necessary

Stays locked up at too low a speed in direct	• Sticking governor valve
	• Valve body malfunction
	   (a) Stuck switch valve
	   (b) Stuck lockup valve
	   (c) Stuck fail-safe valve
		• Repair or replace as necessary
		• Repair or replace valve body or its internal components as necessary

Locks up or drags in low or second	• Faulty oil pump
	• Valve body malfunction
	   (a) Stuck switch valve
	   (b) Stuck fail-safe valve
		• Replace oil pump
		• Repair or replace valve body or its internal components as necessary

Sluggish or stalls in reverse	• Faulty oil pump
	• Plugged cooler, cooler lines or fittings
	• Valve body malfunction
	   (a) Stuck switch valve
	   (b) Faulty input shaft or seal ring
		• Replace oil pump as necessary
		• Flush or replace cooler and flush lines and fittings
		• Repair or replace valve body or its internal components as necessary

Loud chatter during lockup engagement (cold)	• Faulty torque converter • Failed locking clutch • Leaking turbine hub seal	• Replace torque converter • Replace torque converter • Replace torque converter
Vibration or shudder during lockup engagement	• Faulty oil pump • Valve body malfunction • Faulty torque converter • Engine needs tune-up	• Repair or replace oil pump as necessary • Repair or replace valve body or its internal components as necessary • Replace torque converter • Tune engine
Vibration after lockup engagement	• Faulty torque converter • Exhaust system strikes underbody • Engine needs tune-up • Throttle linkage misadjusted	• Replace torque converter • Align exhaust system • Tune engine • Adjust throttle linkage

7-91

7 DRIVE TRAIN

Lockup Torque Converter Service Diagnosis

Problem	Cause	Solution
Vibration when revved in neutral Overheating: oil blows out of dip stick tube or pump seal	• Torque converter out of balance • Plugged cooler, cooler lines or fittings • Stuck switch valve	• Replace torque converter • Flush or replace cooler and flush lines and fittings • Repair switch valve in valve body or replace valve body
Shudder after lockup engagement	• Faulty oil pump • Plugged cooler, cooler lines or fittings • Valve body malfunction • Faulty torque converter • Fail locking clutch • Exhaust system strikes underbody • Engine needs tune-up • Throttle linkage misadjusted	• Replace oil pump • Flush or replace cooler and flush lines and fittings • Repair or replace valve body or its internal components as necessary • Replace torque converter • Replace torque converter • Align exhaust system • Tune engine • Adjust throttle linkage

AUTOMATIC TRANSMISSION APPLICATION CHART

Transmission	Years
Chrysler 904 3-speed	1984–86
AISIN/Warner AW4 4-speed	1987–91

turbine. This difference in speed may be compared to the difference in speed between the smaller and larger gears in any gear train. The result is that engine power output is higher, and engine torque is multiplied.

As the speed of the turbine increases, the fluid spins faster and faster in the direction of engine rotation. As a result, the ability of the stator to redirect the fluid flow is reduced. Under cruising conditions, the stator is eventually forced to rotate on its one-way clutch in the direction of engine rotation. Under these conditions, the torque converter begins to behave almost like a solid shaft, with the torus and turbine speeds being almost equal.

THE PLANETARY GEARBOX

The ability of the torque converter to multiply engine torque is limited. Also, the unit tends to be more efficient when the turbine is rotating at relatively high speeds. Therefore, a planetary gearbox is used to carry the power output of the turbine to the driveshaft. Planetary gears function very similarly to conventional transmission gears. However, their construction is different in that three elements make up one gear system, and, in that all three elements are different from one another. The three elements are: an outer gear that is shaped like a hoop, with teeth cut into the inner surface; a sun gear, mounted on a shaft and located at the very center of the outer gear; and a set of three planet gears, held by pins in a ring-like planet carrier, meshing with both the sun

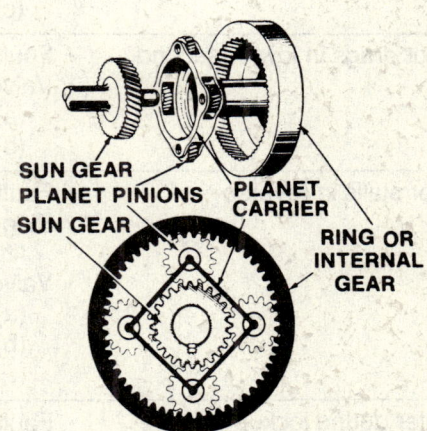

Planetary gears are similar to manual transmission gears but are composed of three parts

gear and the outer gear. Either the outer gear or the sun gear may be held stationary, providing more than one possible torque multiplication factor for each set of gears. Also, if all three gears are forced to rotate at the same speed, the gearset forms, in effect, a solid shaft. Most modern automatics use the planetary gears to provide either a single reduction ratio of about 1.8:1, or two reduction gears: a low of about 2.5:1, and an intermediate of about 1.5:1. Bands and clutches are used to hold various portions of the gearsets to the transmission case or to the shaft on which they are mounted. Shifting is accomplished, then, by changing the portion of each planetary gearset which is held to the transmission case or to the shaft.

THE SERVOS AND ACCUMULATORS

The servos are hydraulic pistons and cylinders. They resemble the hydraulic actuators used on many familiar machines, such as

DRIVE TRAIN 7

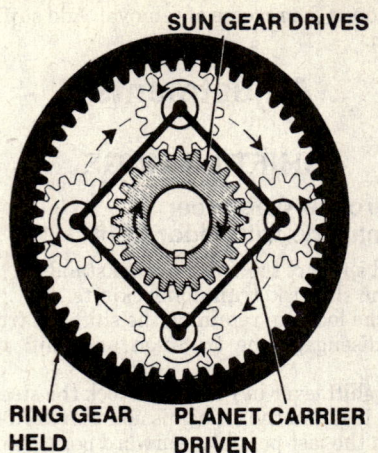

Planetary gears in the maximum reduction (low) range. The ring gear is held and a lower gear ratio is obtained

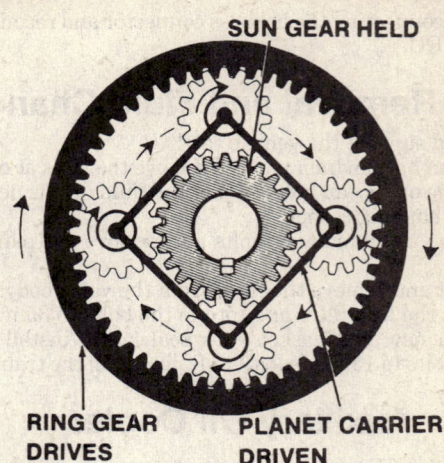

Planetary gears in the minimum reduction (drive) range. The ring gear is allowed to revolve, providing a higher gear ratio

bulldozers. Hydraulic fluid enters the cylinder, under pressure, and forces the piston to move to engage the band or clutches.

The accumulators are used to cushion the engagement of the servos. The transmission fluid must pass through the accumulator on the way to the servo. The accumulator housing contains a thin piston which is sprung away from the discharge passage of the accumulator. When fluid passes through the accumulator on the way to the servo, it must move the piston against spring pressure, and this action smooths out the action of the servo.

THE HYDRAULIC CONTROL SYSTEM

The hydraulic pressure used to operate the servos comes from the main transmission oil pump. This fluid is channeled to the various servos through the shift valves. There is generally a manual shift valve which is operated by the transmission selector lever and an automatic shift valve for each automatic upshift the transmission provides: i.e., two-speed automatics have a low-high shift valve, while three-speeds have a 1-2 valve, and a 2-3 valve.

There are two pressures which effect the operation of these valves. One is the governor pressure which is affected by vehicle speed. The other is the modulator pressure which is affected by intake manifold vacuum or throttle position. Governor pressure rises with an increase in vehicle speed, and modulator pressure rises as the throttle is opened wider. By responding to these two pressures, the shift valves cause the upshift points to be delayed

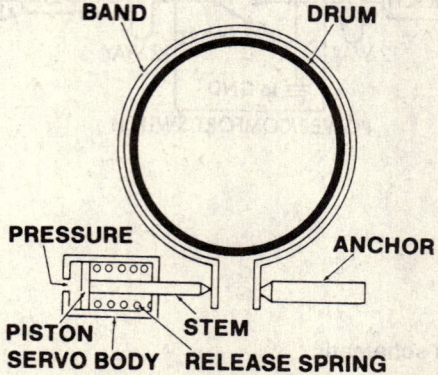

Servos, operated by pressure, are used to apply or release the bands, to either hold the ring gear or allow it to rotate freely

with increased throttle opening to make the best use of the engine's power output.

Most transmissions also make use of an auxiliary circuit for downshifting. This circuit may be actuated by the throttle linkage or the vacuum line which actuates the modulator, or by a cable or solenoid. It applies pressure to a special downshift surface on the shift valve or valves.

The transmission modulator also governs the line pressure, used to actuate the servos. In this way, the clutches and bands will be actuated with a force matching the torque output of the engine.

Identification

Chrysler 904

The Chrysler 904 is a fully automatic, three-speed transmission. The transmission incorporates a wide ratio planetary gear set and uses a lockup type torque converter.

A seven digit transmission part number is stamped on the left side of the case just above the oil pan mating surface. This number is followed by a four digit code number which indicates date of manufacture. The final four digit code stamped on the case represents the transmission serial number.

Lockup torque converters have an identifying decal attached to the front cover. The decal is circular in shape and states the converter type (lockup) and stall ratios (LS-low stall/HS-high stall).

Aisin/Warner AW-4

The AW-4 is a four-speed, electronically controlled transmission. Forward gear ranges are controlled by a Transmission Computer Unit (TCU). The TCU determines shift and converter lockup timing based on signals from the sensors that monitor vehicle speed, throttle opening, shift lever position and brake pedal application. Valve body solenoids are activated/deactivated accordingly.

The transmission I.D. plate is attached to the case. The plate contains the transmission serial and model numbers. Always use the information on the plate when ordering replacement parts.

AW-4 TRANSMISSION CONTROL UNIT (TCU)

The TCU has a self diagnostic program. Component and circuitry malfunctions can be diagnosed with the Diagnostic Readout Box II (DRB II) tester. Once a malfunction is stored in the TCU memory, it is retained even after the problem is corrected. To cancel a stored malfunction, simply disconnect and reconnect the 'Trans.' fuse in the TCU harness.

If the TCU is determined to be at fault, replacement is simply a

7 DRIVE TRAIN

matter of disconnecting the harness connector and reconnecting it to the new TCU.

Pan Removal and Fluid Change

1. Raise and support the vehicle safely.
2. The pan has no drain plug, so remove the bolts at one corner and loosen the other pan bolts so that the fluid drains neatly from the one, low-hanging corner.
3. Remove the remaining bolts and remove the pan. Discard the gasket.
4. Unbolt and remove the filter from the valve body.
5. Install the new filter and torque the bolts to 35 inch lbs.
6. Coat a new pan gasket with sealer and install the pan. Torque the bolts to 150 inch lbs. (12 ft. lbs.). Fill the transmission.

Auxiliary Oil Cooler

REMOVAL AND INSTALLATION

1. Remove the attaching screws and lift off the grille panel.
2. Using masking tape, mark the cooler lines for installation.
3. Place a drain pan on the ground, under the cooler.
4. Loosen the clamps securing the hoses to the cooler and slide them out of the way.
5. Twist the hoses to free them from the cooler pipes and slide the off. Cap the hose ends and cooler outlets to prevent dirt from entering.
6. Unbolt and remove the cooler.

7. Installation is the reverse of removal. Add sufficient fluid to refill the system.

Adjustments

SHIFT LINKAGE

1984–87 Cherokee/Wagoneer
1986–87 Comanche with Floor Shift

1. Raise and support the truck on jackstands.
2. Loosen the shift rod trunnion locknuts.
3. Remove the lock pin retaining the shift rod trunnion to the bellcrank and disengage the trunnion and shift rod from the bellcrank.
4. Place the shift lever in PARK and lock the steering column.
5. Move the lever on the transmission rearward to the PARK detent. PARK is the last possible rearward position.
6. Check to make sure that PARK is engaged, by trying to rotate the driveshaft by hand.
7. Adjust the shift rod trunnion so that the pin fits freely in the bellcrank arm and tighten the trunnion locknuts. Prevent the shift rod from turning while tightening the locknuts.

NOTE: All lash in the linkage must be eliminated to provide for proper adjustment. Lash can be eliminated by pulling downward on the shift rod and pressing upward on the bellcrank.

8. Check that the engine starts in only the PARK and NEUTRAL positions, and that all shift ranges work properly.
9. Lower the truck.

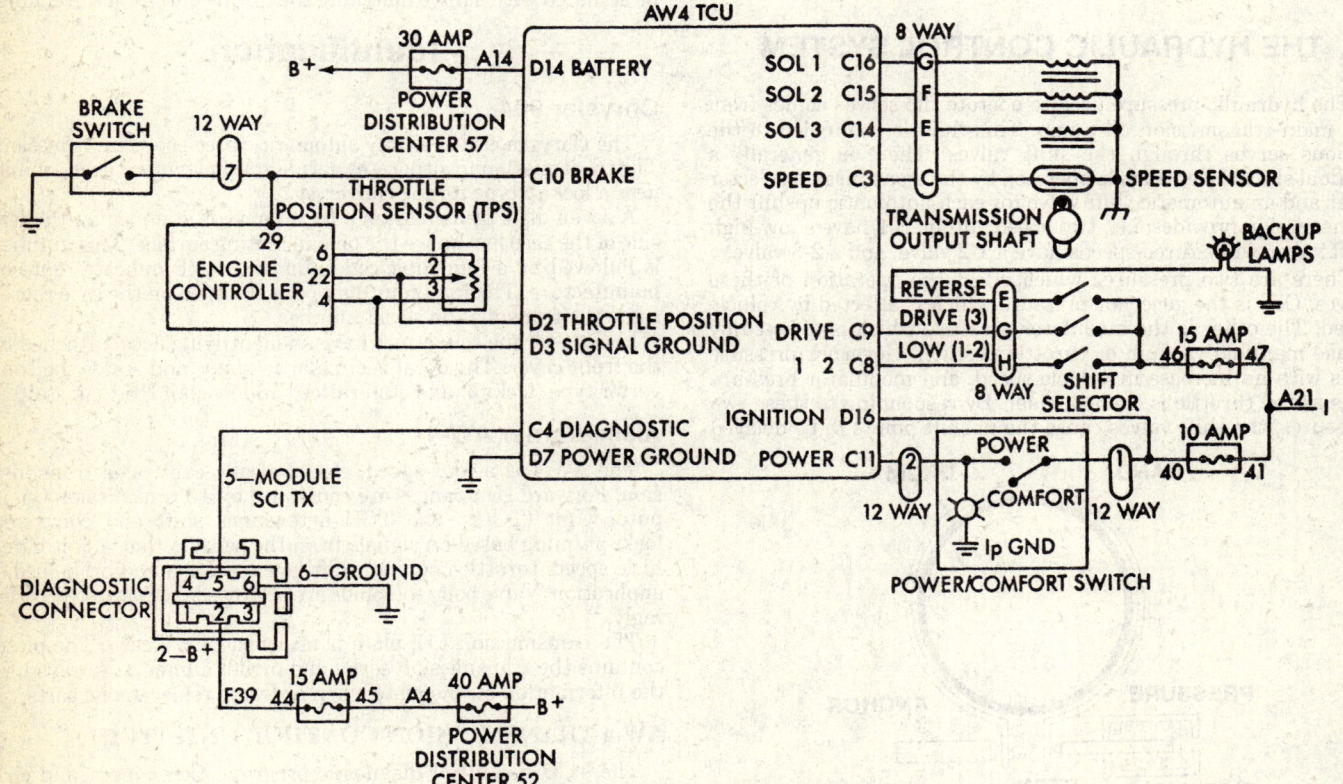

AW-4 transmission control unit (TCU) schematic

DRIVE TRAIN 7

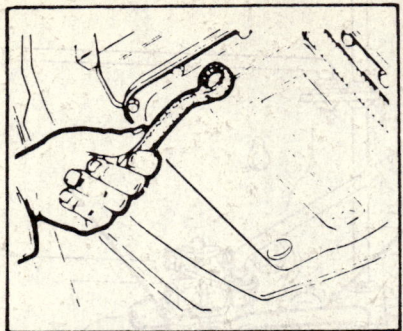

1. Position a catch pan under the transmission. If equipped, remove the drain plug. Be careful; the fluid may be hot.

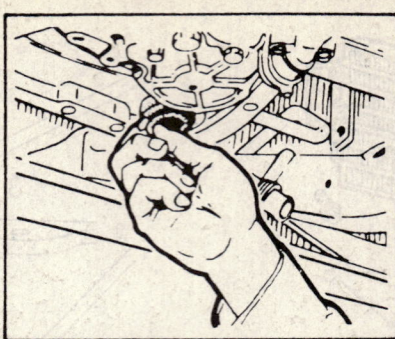

4. Remove the old O-ring from the filter neck and replace with new O-Ring supplied with filter kit.

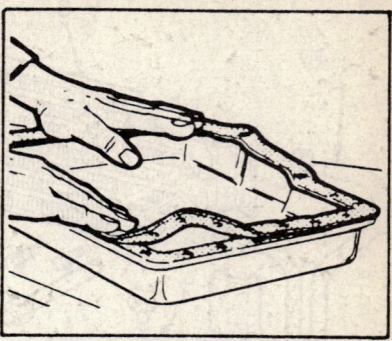

7. Install a new gasket on the pan.

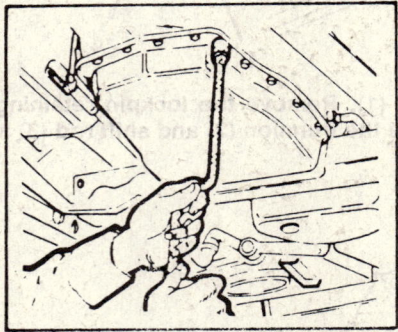

2. Many late-model vehicles have no drain plug. Loosen the pan bolts and allow one corner of the pan to tilt slightly to drain the fluid.

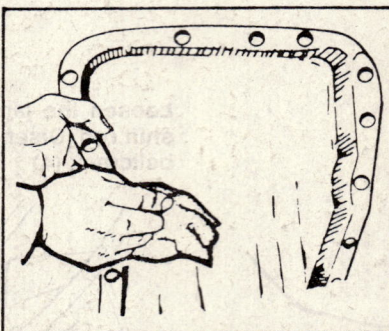

5. Clean the pan thoroughly with gasoline and allow to air dry completely.

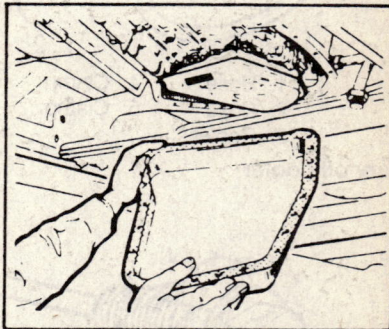

8. Install the new pan and gasket. Do not overtighten the screws.

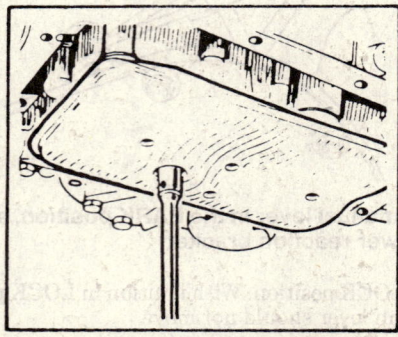

3. The filter or screen is held on by bolts or screws. Remove the filter or screen straight down.

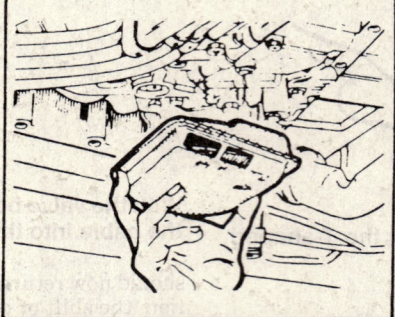

6. Install the new filter. Be sure the intake pipe is seated in the O-ring. Some transmissions use a screen which can be cleaned in gasoline and air dried.

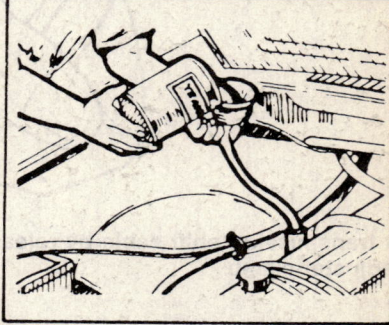

9. Fill the transmission with the required amount of fluid. Do not overfill. Start the engine and shift through all the gears. Check the fluid level and add fluid if necessary.

9 easy steps to transmission fluid and filter service

SHIFT CABLE

1986–88 Comanche with Column Shift

All with AW-4

1. Place gearshift lever in PARK.
2. Raise and support the vehicle safely.
3. Unlock transmission shift control cable by prying upward on the T-shaped adjuster clamp to release.
4. Move valve body manual lever rearward into PARK detent (last rearward detent). Ensure that vehicle is in PARK by attempting to rotate driveshaft. Driveshaft should NOT rotate.
5. With the valve body manual lever in the PARK position, snap the cable into the lower reaction bracket.
6. Lock the cable by pressing the T-shaped adjuster clamp down until it snaps into place.
7. Check engine starting procedure to ensure engine will only start in PARK or NEUTRAL.
8. Lower vehicle.

7 DRIVE TRAIN

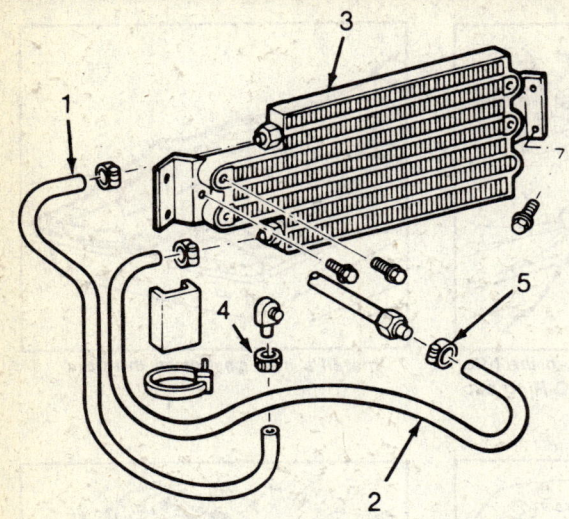

1. Hose
2. Hose
3. Cooler
4. Clamp
5. Clamp

Auxiliary oil cooler

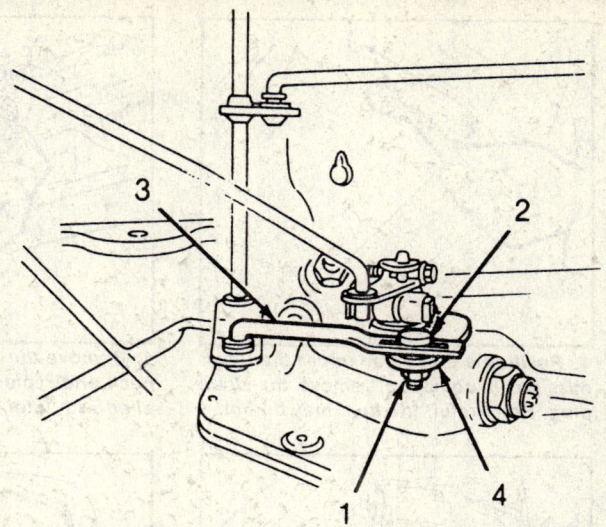

Loosen the jamnut (1). Remove the lockpin retaining the shift rod. Disengage the trunnion (2) and shift rod (3) at the bellcrank (4)

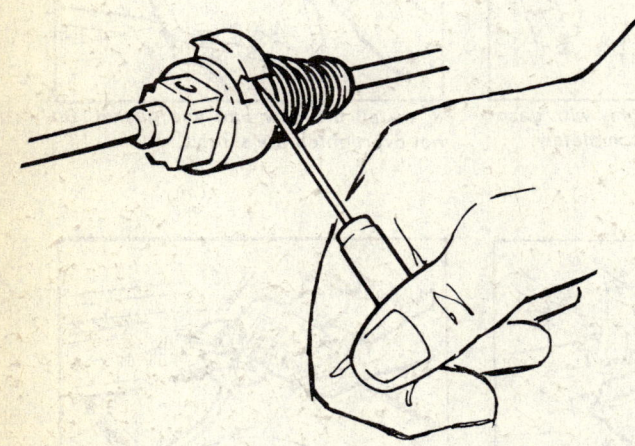

Unlock transmission shift cable by releasing the T-shaped cable adjuster clamp

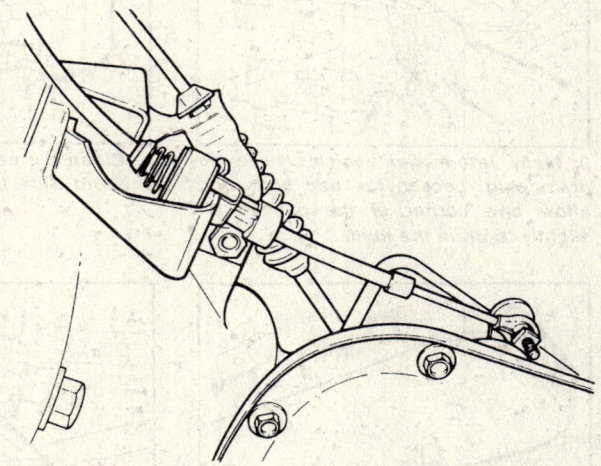

With the valve body manual lever in the PARK position, snap the cable into the lower reaction bracket

should now return to LOCK position. With ignition in LOCK position, the shift or column lever should not move.

PARK LOCK CABLE

1. Shift transmission into PARK.
2. Turn ignition switch to LOCK position.
3. Remove shifter lever bezel and console screws. Raise console for access to cable.
4. Pull cable lock button up to release cable.
5. Pull cable forward. Then release cable and press lock button down until it snaps in place.
6. Check movement of release shift handle button (floor shift) or release lever (column shift). You should not be able to press button inward or move column lever.
7. Turn ignition to ON position. Move shift or column lever into NEUTRAL. If cable adjustment is correct, ignition should not return to LOCK position. Recheck with shift or column lever in DRIVE position.
8. Move shift or column lever to PARK position. Ignition

THROTTLE LINKAGE

4-2.5L with Chrysler 904

1. Disconnect the throttle control rod spring at the carburetor.
2. Raise and support the vehicle safely.
3. Use the spring to hold the transmission control lever forward against the stop.
4. Hook one end of another spring to the throttle control lever and the other end to the throttle linkage bellcrank bracket attached to the converter housing.
5. Lower the vehicle.
6. Block the choke open and set the throttle off of the fast idle cam.
7. Turn the ignition lock to ON to energize the solenoid.
8. Open the throttle halfway to allow the solenoid to lock and return the carburetor to idle.

DRIVE TRAIN 7

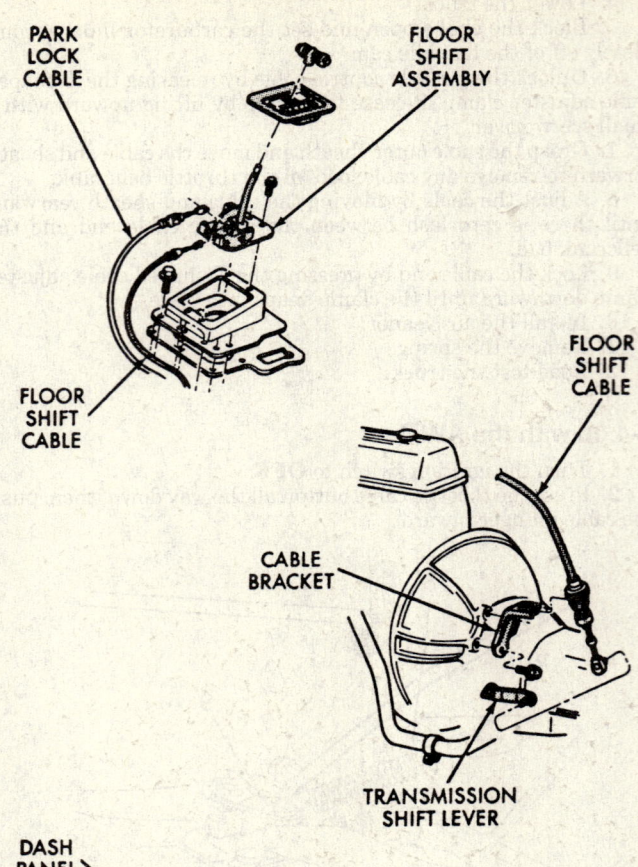

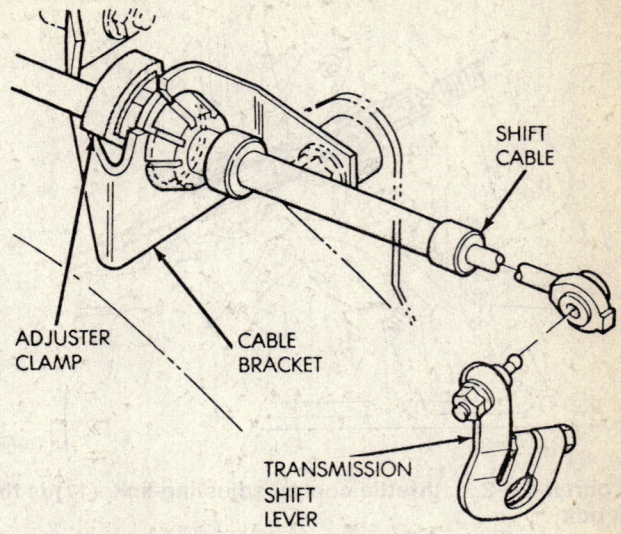

1989–90 lower shift cable and bracket

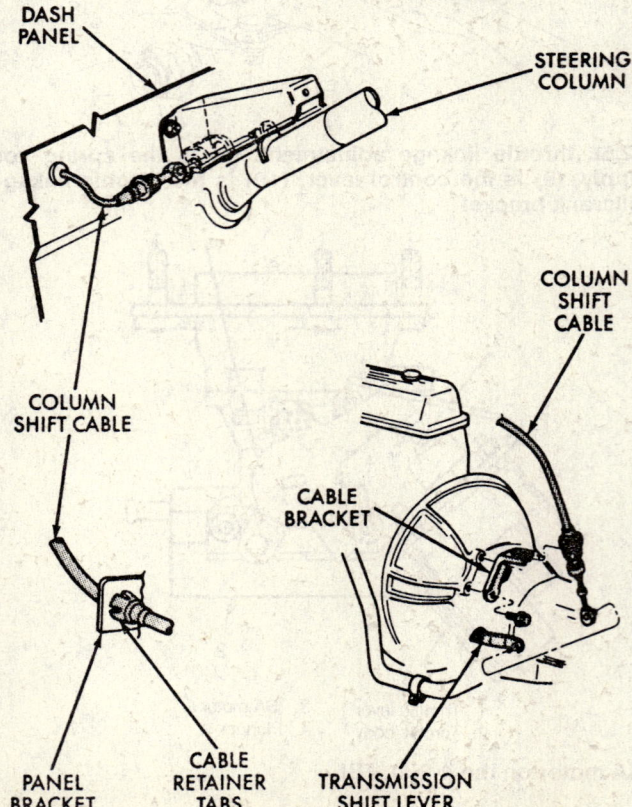

1991 column and floor cable shift assemblies

9. Loosen the retaining bolt on the throttle control adjusting link. DO NOT REMOVE THE SPRING CLIP AND NYLON WASHER!
10. Pull on the end of the link to eliminate play and tighten the link retaining bolt.
11. Turn the ignition off.
12. Raise and support the truck on jackstands and remove the spring. Reconnect the spring in its original position.
13. Lower the truck.

4-2.5L TBI with Chrysler 904

1. Place the ignition switch in the OFF position.
2. Raise and support the front end on jackstands.
3. Obtain a small, about 51mm (2 in.) long, coil spring. Hook one end of the spring on the throttle lever, next to the bell housing, and the other end on the boss which projects from the side of the bell housing, as shown.
4. Lower the truck.
5. Disconnect the idle speed actuator motor (ISA) wiring harness, and connect the idle speed assembly exerciser box. When connected, the ADJUSTMENT light should go out, and the READY light should go on.
6. Press the RETRACK button. The system will, automatically, drive to the proper position with the ADJUST light on and the READY light off.
7. Loosen the retaining bolt (A) on the throttle control adjusting link.
8. Pull on the end of the link to eliminate all play and tighten the bolt.
9. Press the EXTEND button on the exerciser box until the ISA motor ratchets.
10. Disconnect the exerciser box and reconnect the ISA motor harness.
11. Raise the vehicle and remove your spring.
12. Lower the vehicle.

THROTTLE CABLE

6-2.8L with Chrysler 904

1. Remove the air cleaner.
2. Raise and support the truck on jackstands.
3. Hold the throttle control lever rearward against its stop, using a spring selected for that purpose.

7 DRIVE TRAIN

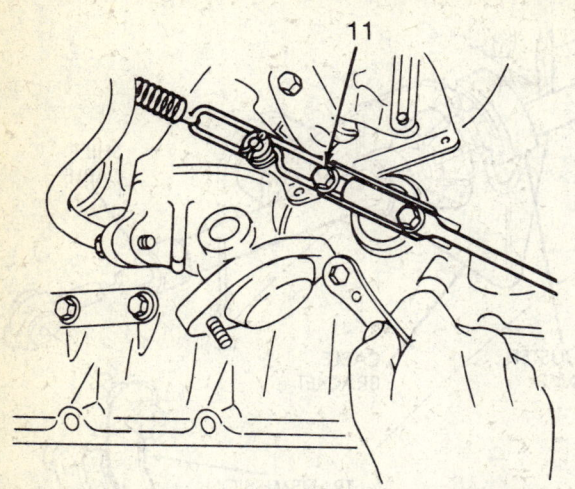

Carbureted 4-2.5L throttle control adjusting link. (11) is the link bolt

4. Lower the truck.
5. Block the choke open and set the carburetor linkage completely off of the fast idle cam.
6. Unlock the throttle control cable by releasing the T-shaped cable adjuster clamp. Release the clamp by lifting upward with a small screwdriver.
7. Grasp the cable outer sheath and move the cable and sheath forward to remove any cable load on the throttle bellcrank.
8. Adjust the cable by moving the cable and sheath rearward until there is zero lash between the plastic cable end and the bellcrank ball.
9. Lock the cable end by pressing the T-shaped cable adjuster clamp downward until the clamp snaps into place.
10. Install the air cleaner.
11. Remove the spring.
12. Road test the truck.

6-4.0L with the AW-4

1. Turn the ignition switch to **OFF**.
2. Press the throttle cable button all the way down, then, push the cable plunger inward.

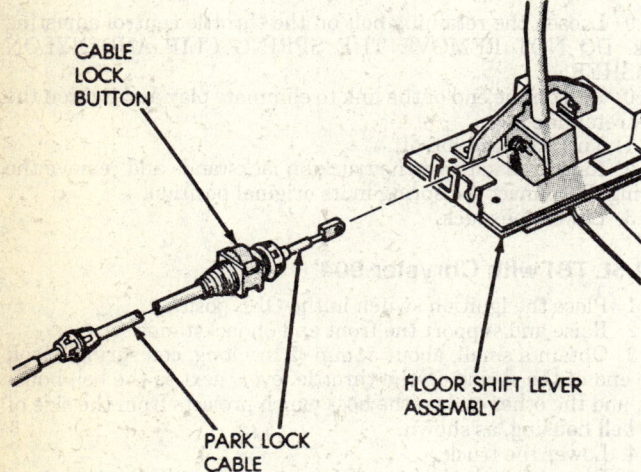

Park lock cable assembly

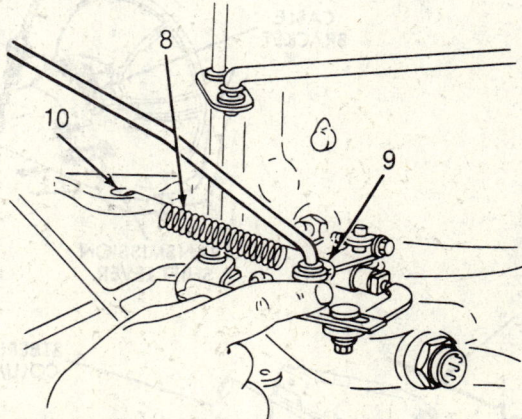

4-2.5L throttle linkage adjustment. (8) is the spring you supply, (9) is the control lever, (10) is the throttle linkage bellcrank bracket

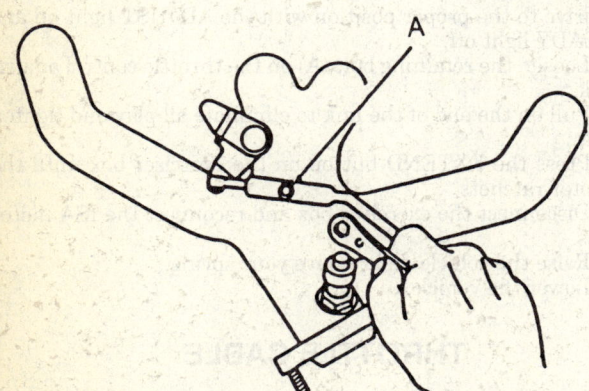

Throttle control adjusting link bolt (A) on the 4-2.5L TBI

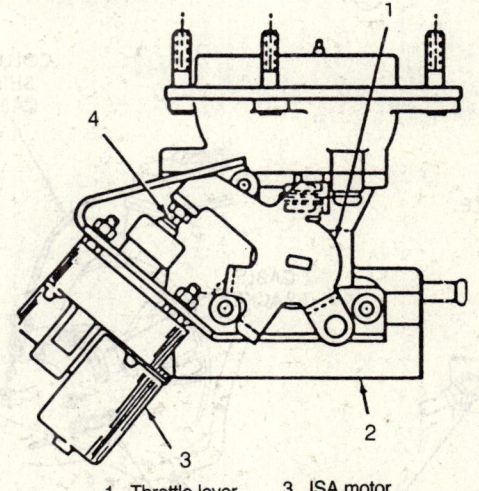

1. Throttle lever
2. Throttle body
3. ISA motor
4. Plunger

ISA motor on the 4-2.5L TBI

DRIVE TRAIN 7

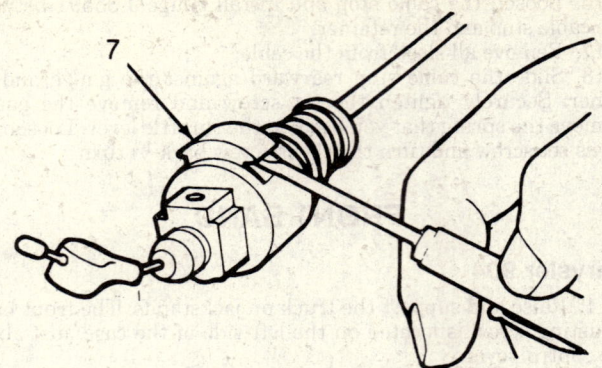

Releasing the T-shaped cable adjuster clamp (7)

3. Rotate the primary throttle lever to the wide open throttle position.
4. Hold the primary throttle lever in this position and let the cable plunger extend.
5. Release the lever when the plunger is fully extended.
6. The cable is now adjusted.

THROTTLE VALVE LEVER AND CABLE

4-2.1L Diesel

NOTE: Special tool J-35514 and gauge J-35591 are necessary for this procedure.

1. Disconnect the throttle valve cable from the pin on the throttle valve lever.
2. Disconnect the cable from the transmission throttle lever. Remove and discard the cable.
3. Set the injection pump automatic advance lever at the curb idle position (seated against the stop).
4. Loosen the set screw and turn the cable clevis 1/4 turn counterclockwise. Tighten the set screw.
5. Install the special tool as shown.
6. Loosen the thumbscrew on the tool and move the sliding legs rearward.
7. Place the notched leg of the tool on the cable bracket. Then, rest the sliding legs on the lever.
8. Move the sliding legs forward until the rear leg lightly touches the cable attaching pin. Tighten the thumbscrew.
9. Move the lever to the wide open throttle position. The cable attaching pin should now lightly touch the forward leg of the sliding legs.
10. If the cable attaching pin does not touch the forward leg, or if the pin tends to move the special tool, hold the lever in the wide open throttle position, loosen the two lever adjusting screws and move the lever to adjust the travel. Tighten the screws to 66 inch lbs. Return the lever to the curb idle position and verify that the pin is, again, lightly touching the rear leg of the sliding legs. If the pin doesn't touch the rear leg at curb idle, loosen the thumbscrew and adjust the tool so that it does, and repeat the adjustment.

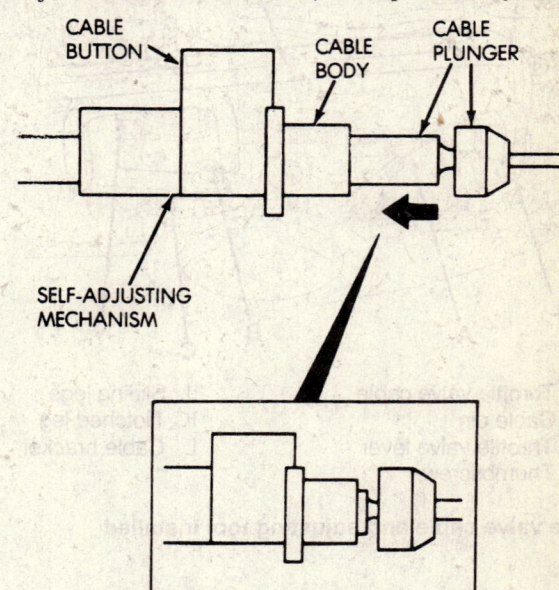

Retract the throttle cable plunger

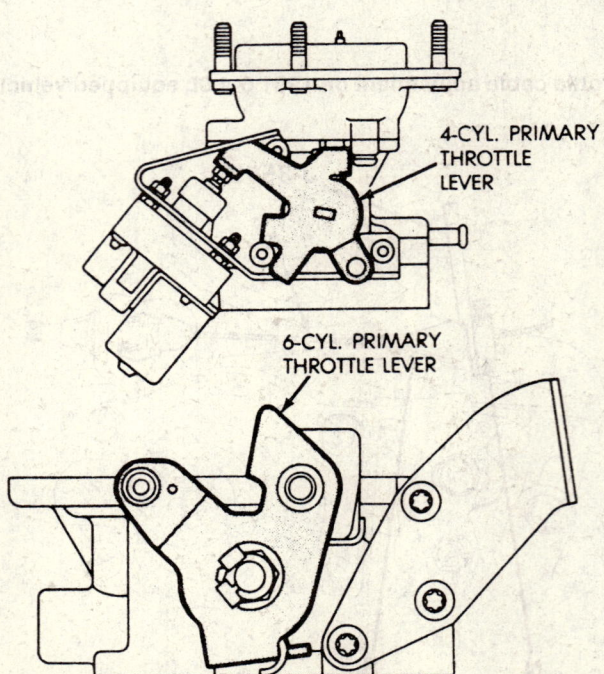

Rotate primary throttle lever to wide open throttle position

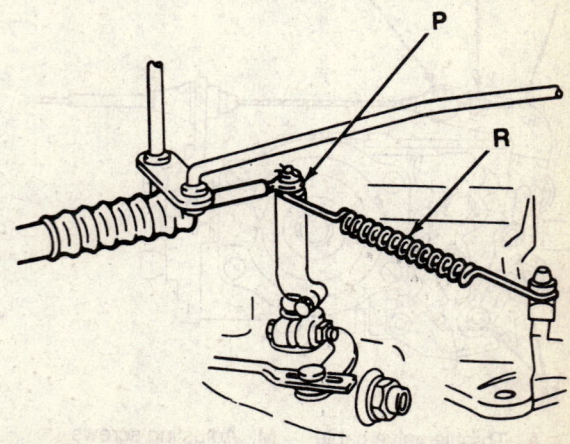

Spring (R), supplied by you, attached to the lever (P)

7-99

7 DRIVE TRAIN

11. Install a new throttle valve cable, part number 8953 001 796.
12. The new cable should be supplied with a cable stop, or one can be obtained from a lawn mower shop, motorcycle repair shop or small engines outlet. The throttle stop should have an inside diameter of 1.07mm.
13. The new cable has a factory installed cable stop crimped onto the end of the cable. Cut this off and slide inner cable stop off the cable. Slide the new cable stop into place and hand tighten the set screw.
14. Connect the new cable to the throttle valve lever pin.
15. Obtain a small coil spring and use it to hold the throttle valve lever against its stop.
16. Loosen the cable stop and install gauge J-35591 between the cable stop and the retainer.
17. Remove all slack from the cable.
18. Slide the cable stop rearward against the gauge and retainer. Securely tighten the set screw and remove the gauge. Remove the spring that you used on the throttle lever. Loosen the clevis set screw and turn the clevis screw back 1/4 turn.

FRONT BAND

Chrysler 904

1. Raise and support the truck on jackstands. The front band adjusting screw is located on the left side of the case, just above the control levers.

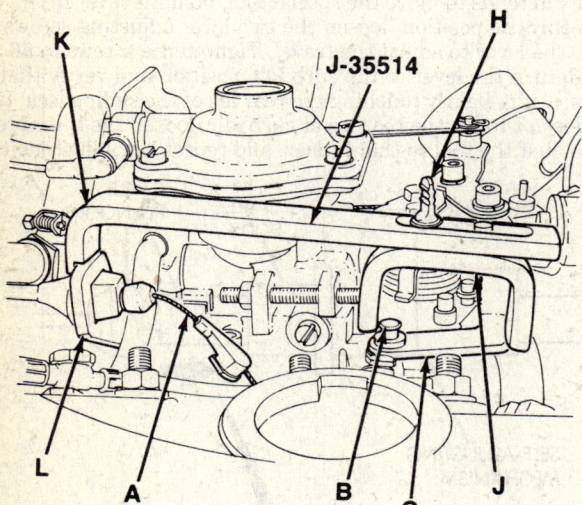

A. Throttle valve cable
B. Cable pin
C. Throttle valve lever
H. Thumbscrew
J. Sliding legs
K. Notched leg
L. Cable bracket

Throttle valve cable and adjusting tool installed

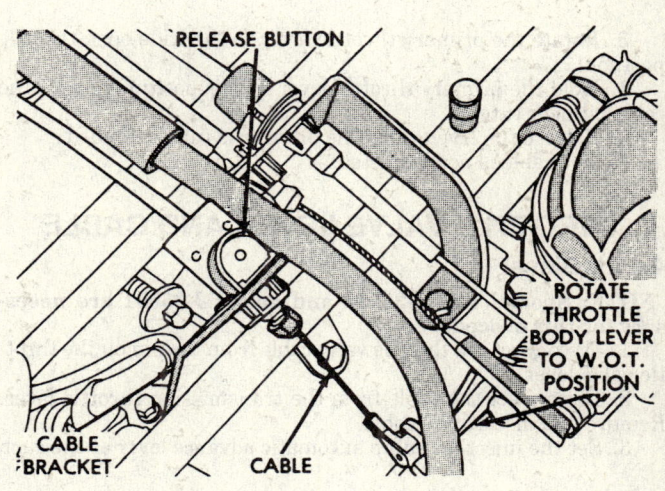

Throttle cable adjustment on 1991 6-4.0L equipped vehicles

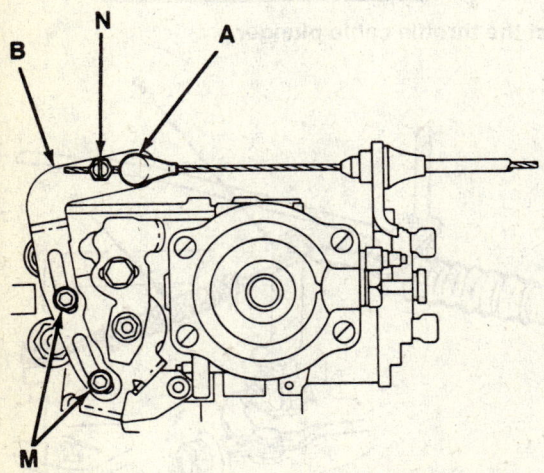

A. Throttle valve cable
B. Lever
M. Adjusting screws
N. Cable stop

Throttle valve cable adjustment points

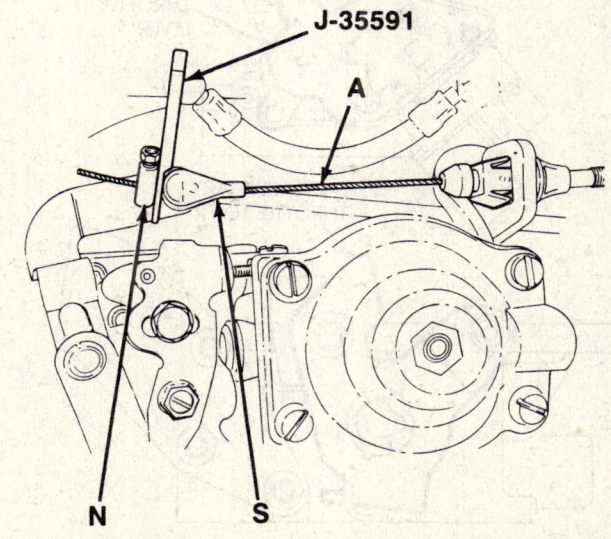

Gauge attached to the cable (A), between the cable stop (N) and the retainer (S)

DRIVE TRAIN 7

2. Loosen the locknut and back it off about five turns.
3. Make sure that the screw turns freely. Use penetrating oil if it binds.
4. Tighten the screw to 72 inch lbs.
5. Back off the screw 2½ turns.
6. Tighten the locknut to 35 ft. lbs. Hold the screw still while tightening the locknut.
7. Lower the truck.

REAR BAND

Chrysler 904

1. Raise and support the truck on jackstands.
2. Drain the fluid and remove the pan.
3. Remove the adjusting screw locknut.
4. Tighten the adjusting screw to 41 inch lbs.
5. Back off the adjusting screw as follows 7 turns.
6. Hold the adjusting screw still and tighten the locknut to 35 ft. lbs.
7. Replace the pan and fill the unit.

Neutral Start/Back-Up Light Switch

ADJUSTMENT AND REPLACEMENT

Chrysler 904

The neutral start switch on the 904 units is non-adjustable. If the truck starts in any position other than PARK or NEUTRAL, and the linkage adjustment is correct, the switch must be replaced. To replace the switch, simply unbolt it from the transmission, disconnect the wires and install a new switch.

AW-4

TESTING

Test continuity with an ohmmeter. Disconnect the switch and check continuity at the connector terminal position and in the gear ranges indicated.
- Continuity should exist between terminals B and C with the transmission in PARK and NEUTRAL only.
- Continuity should exist between terminals A and E with the transmission in REVERSE.
- Continuity should exist between terminals A and G with the transmission in 3rd gear.
- Continuity should exist between terminals A and H with the transmission in 1st and/or 2nd gear.
- Continuity should not exist with the transmission in DRIVE.

REMOVAL

1. Raise and support the front end on jackstands.
2. Disconnect the wiring at the switch.
3. Pry open the lock tabs and remove the switch retaining nut and washer.

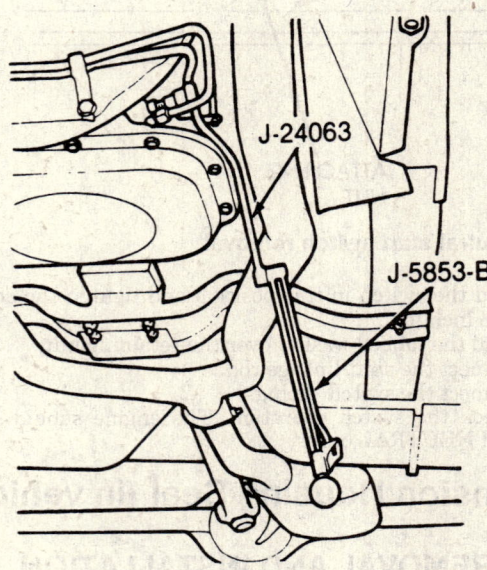

Chrysler 904 front band adjustment

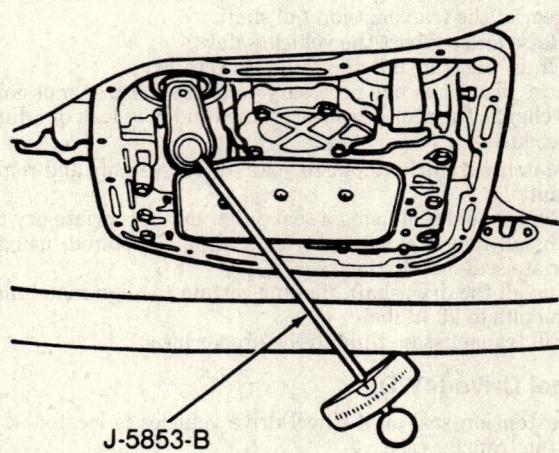

Chrysler 904 intermediate band adjustment

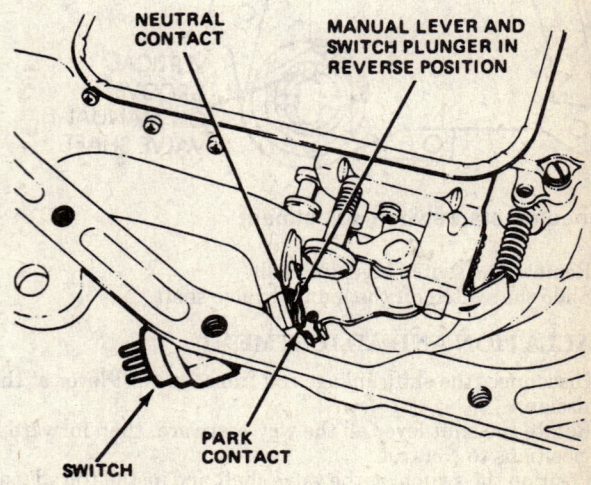

Chrysler 904 neutral start switch location

7-101

7 DRIVE TRAIN

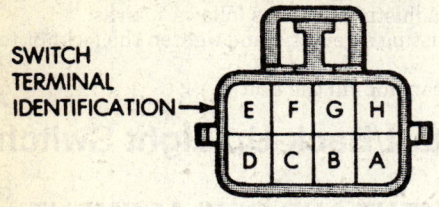

AW-4 neutral start/backup light switch testing

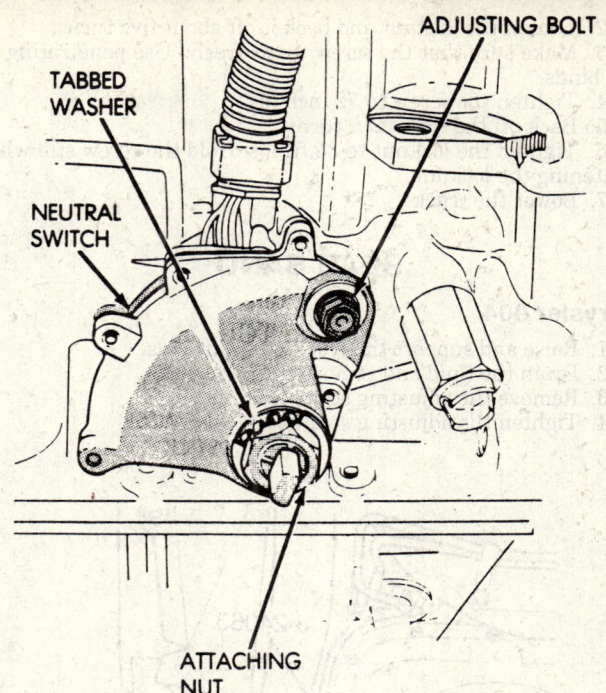

AW-4 neutral start switch removal

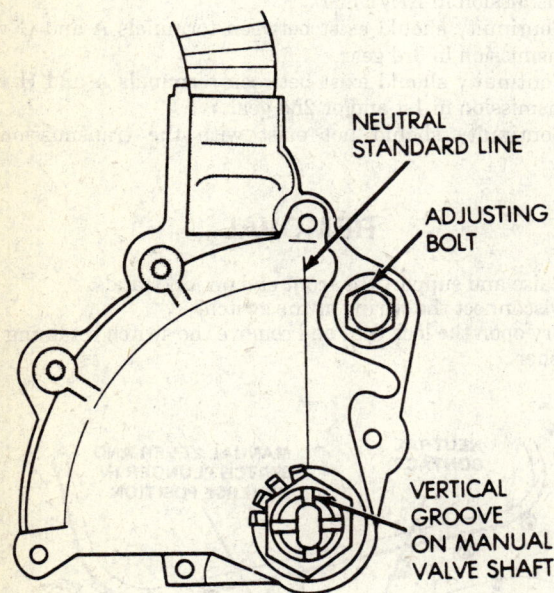

AW-4 neutral start switch adjustment

4. Remove the switch adjusting bolt.
5. Slide the switch off the manual valve shaft.

INSTALLATION AND ADJUSTMENT

1. Disconnect the shift linkage rod from the shift lever at the transmission.
2. Rotate the shift lever all the way rearward, then forward 2 detent positions to Neutral.
3. Position the switch on the valve shaft and install the adjusting bolt finger tightly.
4. Install the washer and attaching nut and torque the nut to 60 inch lbs., but don't bend the tabbed washer yet.
5. With the transmission in neutral, rotate the switch to align the neutral standard line with the groove on the valve shaft.

6. Hold the switch in this position and tighten the adjusting bolt to 108 inch lbs.
7. Bend the tabbed washer over the retaining nut.
8. Connect the shift linkage rod.
9. Connect the switch wiring.
10. Check the switch operation. The engine should start in PARK and NEUTRAL only!

Extension Housing Seal (in vehicle)

REMOVAL AND INSTALLATION

2-Wheel Drive (2WD)

The extension housing seal on 2-wheel drive vehicles is located at the rear of the transmission tail shaft.

1. Raise and support the vehicle safely.
2. Drain the transmission fluid, if necessary.

In most cases it is not necessary to drain the transmission of fluid to change the seal. However, some fluid may leak out during the procedure.

3. Matchmark drive shaft to yoke for reassembly and remove drive shaft.
4. Remove old seal using a seal puller or appropriate pry tool.
5. Install new seal, coated with sealing compound, using an appropriate seal installation tool.
6. Install the driveshaft, making certain to align matchmark. Tighten bolts to 20 ft. lbs.
7. Fill transmission fluid to the proper level.

4-Wheel Drive (4WD)

The extension seal on 4-wheel drive vehicles is located at the rear of the transfer case.

1. Raise and support the vehicle safely.
2. Drain transfer case of lubricant.
3. Matchmark drive shaft to yoke for reassembly and remove drive shaft.
4. Remove old seal using a seal puller or appropriate pry tool.

DRIVE TRAIN 7

5. Install new seal, coated with sealing compound, using an appropriate seal installation tool.
6. Install the driveshaft, making certain to align matchmark. Tighten bolts to 20 ft. lbs.
7. Fill transfer case with lubricant. Install plug and lower vehicle.

Transmission

REMOVAL AND INSTALLATION

2-Wheel Drive (2WD)

1. Disconnect the negative battery cable. Raise and support the vehicle on jackstands.
2. Matchmark the rear driveshaft and yoke for reassembly. Disconnect and remove the rear driveshaft.
3. Remove the torque converter inspection cover. Mark the converter drive plate and converter assembly for reassembly.
4. Remove the bolts attaching the torque converter to the flex plate. Support the transmission assembly on a floor jack.
5. Remove the bolts attaching the rear crossmember to the transmission side rail. Disconnect the exhaust pipe at the catalytic converter.
6. Lower the transmission slightly in order to disconnect the fluid cooler lines.
7. Disconnect the backup light switch wire and the speedometer cable. Disconnect the transmission linkage.
8. Remove the bolts attaching the transmission assembly to the engine. Move the transmission assembly and the torque converter rearward to clear the crankshaft.

CHILTON TIP: *Tool manufacturers now have available a transmission cradle to fit most floor jacks. This cradle allows the transmission to be tilted horizontally and vertically, thus, easing removal and installation.*

9. Carefully lower the transmission assembly from the vehicle.

To install:
10. Carefully raise the transmission into position.
11. Install the bolts attaching the transmission assembly to the engine. Torque the bolts to 25 ft. lbs. for the 904. On the AW-4, torque the 10mm bolts to 25 ft. lbs.; the 12mm bolts to 42 ft. lbs.
12. Connect the backup light switch wire.
13. Connect the speedometer cable.
14. Connect the transmission linkage.
15. Connect the fluid cooler lines.
16. Install the rear crossmember. Torque the crossmember bolts to 30 ft. lbs.; the transmission-to-crossmember bolts to 33 ft. lbs.
17. Connect the exhaust pipe at the catalytic converter.
18. Install the bolts attaching the torque converter to the flex plate. Torque the bolts to 40 ft. lbs.
19. Remove the floor jack.
20. Install the torque converter inspection cover.
21. Install the driveshaft. Torque the nuts to 14 ft. lbs.

NOTE: New strap bolts must be used every time the driveshaft is disconnected.

22. Lower the truck.
23. Connect the negative battery cable.

4-Wheel Drive (4WD)

1. Disconnect the negative battery cable. Raise and support the vehicle safely.
2. Matchmark the rear driveshaft and yoke for reassembly. Disconnect and remove the rear driveshaft.
3. Remove the torque converter inspection cover. Mark the converter drive plate and converter assembly for reassembly.
4. Remove the bolts attaching the torque converter to the flex plate. Support the transmission assembly with a floor jack.

NOTE: If the vehicle is equipped with a diesel engine, support the engine with a jack under the crankshaft damper, and remove the left motor mount and starter in order to gain access to the torque converter drive plate bolts through the starter opening.

5. Remove the rear crossmember-to-side rail attaching bolts. Disconnect the exhaust pipe at the catalytic converter.
6. Lower the transmission slightly in order to disconnect the fluid cooler lines. Matchmark the front driveshaft assembly for installation. Disconnect the driveshaft at the transfer case and secure the assembly out of the way.
7. Disconnect the backup light switch wire and the speedometer cable. Disconnect the transfer case and the transmission linkage. Disconnect the vacuum lines and the vent hose.
8. Remove the bolts attaching the transmission assembly to the engine. Move the transmission assembly and the torque converter rearward to clear the crankshaft.

CHILTON TIP: *Tool manufacturers now have available a transmission cradle to fit most floor jacks. This cradle allows the transmission to be tilted horizontally and vertically, thus, easing removal and installation.*

9. Carefully lower the transmission assembly from the vehicle. Separate the transfer case from the transmission assembly.

To install:
10. If the transmission and transfer case were separated, reassemble the components and torque the bolts to 26 ft. lbs.
11. Carefully raise the transmission into position.
12. Install the bolts attaching the transmission assembly to the engine. Torque the bolts to 25 ft. lbs. for the 904. On the AW-4, torque the 10mm bolts to 25 ft. lbs.; the 12mm bolts to 42 ft. lbs.
13. Connect the backup light switch wire and the speedometer cable.
14. Connect the transfer case and the transmission linkage.
15. Connect the vacuum lines and the vent hose.
16. Connect the fluid cooler lines.
17. Connect the rear driveshaft to the transfer case. Torque the strap bolt nuts to 14 ft. lbs; the flange-to-case bolts to 35 ft. lbs.

NOTE: New strap bolts must be used every time the driveshaft is disconnected.

18. Install the rear crossmember. Torque the crossmember attaching bolts to 30 ft. lbs.; the transmission-to-crossmember bolts to 33 ft. lbs.
19. Connect the exhaust pipe at the catalytic converter.
20. Install the bolts attaching the torque converter to the flex plate. Torque the bolts to 40 ft. lbs.
21. Remove the floor jack.
22. Install the torque converter inspection cover.
23. If the vehicle is equipped with a diesel engine, install the left motor mount and starter.
24. Lower the truck.
25. Connect the negative battery cable.

7 DRIVE TRAIN

TRANSFER CASE

Identification

New Process 207

The Model 207 transfer case is an aluminum case, chain drive, 4 position unit providing 4WD High and Low ranges, a 2WD High range and a Neutral position. The 207 is a part-time 4WD unit used with the Command-Trac® System. Range positions are selected by a floor mounted shift lever. Dexron® II automatic transmission fluid, or equivalent, is the recommended lubricant.

New Process 228

The Model 228 transfer case is very similar to the Model 229 full-time transfer case used on other Jeep vehicles. The main difference in these cases is that the 228 uses a differential unit in place of a viscous coupling. It also uses modified shift collars to prevent engine run away during a delayed shift.

The 228 is used with the Selec-Trac® System. A vacuum shift motor disconnect system is connected to the transfer case to disengage the front differential. The unit operates full-time or part-time and uses Dexron® II automatic transmission fluid, or equivalent, as a lubricant.

New Process 229

The Model 229 full-time transfer case has viscous torque biasing control capability. This is accomplished with a non-serviceable, sealed viscous coupling, which provides a limited-slip feature for the inter-axle differential located between the front and rear output shafts.

The 229 is used with the Selec-Trac® System. It requires 3.5 qts. of Dexron® II automatic transmission fluid for lubrication.

New Process 231

The Model 231 is a part-time transfer case with a built in low range gear reduction system. A front axle disconnect mechanism is used for 2-wheel drive operation. The 231 is used with the Command-Trac® System.

The 231 has three operating ranges — 2-wheel drive High and 4-wheel drive High and Low, plus Neutral. The 4-wheel drive operating ranges are undifferentiated. Dexron® II automatic transmission fluid, or equivalent, is used as a lubricant.

New Process 242

The Model 242 is a full-time transfer case with four operating ranges plus a Neutral position. Used primarily on the Cherokee/Wagoneer, it provides 2-wheel drive and full-time four wheel drive operation. An inter-axle differential is used to control torque transfer to the front and rear axles.

The differential has a locking mechanism for undifferentiated 4-wheel drive in High and Low ranges. These ranges include 2-wheel drive, 4-wheel drive part-time, 4-wheel drive full-time, and 4-wheel drive Low. Dexron® II automatic transmission fluid, or equivalent, is used as a lubricant.

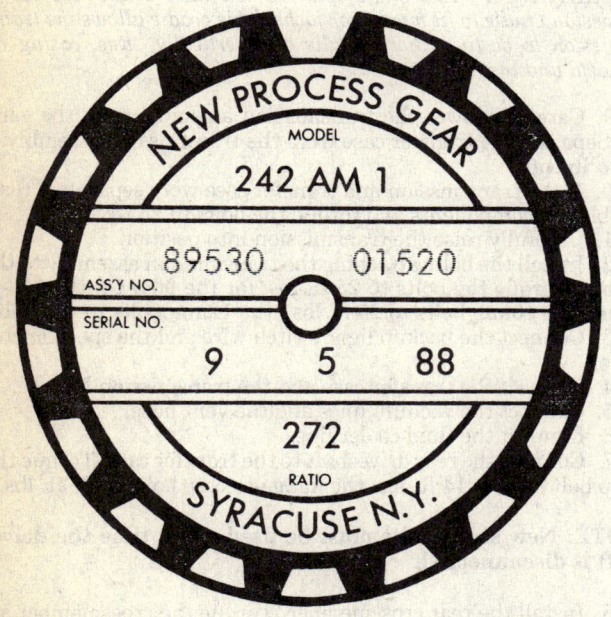

All transfer case identification tags are attached to the rear of the case. The tag provides the transfer case model number, assembly number, serial number (build date) and low range ratio

TRANSFER CASE APPLICATION CHART

Transfer Case Types	Years
New Process 207	1984–87 all
New Process 228	1985–87 w/auto. trans.
New Process 229	1984 w/auto. trans.
New Process 231	1988–91 all
New Process 242	1988–91 Wagoneer and Cherokee

Adjustments

RANGE CONTROL LINKAGE ADJUSTMENT

NP-207

1. Place the range control lever in the 2WD position.
2. Insert a $1/8$ in. (3mm) spacer between the gate and the lever.
3. Hold the lever in this position.
4. Place the transfer case lever in the 2WD position.
5. Adjust the link, at the trunnion, to provide a FREE pin at the case outer lever.

NP-228/229

1. Place the range control lever in the HIGH position.
2. Insert a $1/8$ in. (3mm) spacer between the shift gate and the lever.
3. Hold the lever in this position with tape.
4. Raise and support the vehicle safely.
5. Verify that the range lever is in the HIGH position.
6. Loosen the locknut and adjust the link, at the trunnion, to provide a FREE pin at the case outer lever. Tighten the locknut.
7. Lower the vehicle. Remove the spacer.

NP-231/242

1. Remove the shifter lever bezel.
2. Place the range control lever in the 4 LOW position.
3. Insert a $1/8$ in. (3mm) spacer between the forward edge of the shift gate and the lever.
4. Hold the lever in this position with tape.

DRIVE TRAIN 7

Diagnosis

SERVICE DIAGNOSIS—(COMMAND-TRAC SYSTEM)

Condition	Possible Cause	Correction
TRANSFER CASE DIFFICULT TO SHIFT OR WILL NOT SHIFT INTO DESIRED RANGE	(1) Vehicle speed too great to permit shifting.	(1) Stop vehicle and shift into desired range. Or reduce speed to 3-4 km/h (2-3 mph) before attempting to shift.
	(2) If vehicle was operated for extended period in 4H mode on dry paved surface, driveline torque load may cause difficulty.	(2) Stop vehicle, shift transmission to neutral, shift transfer case to 2H mode and operate vehicle in 2H on dry paved surfaces.
	(3) Transfer case external shift linkage binding.	(3) Lubricate, repair or replace linkage, or tighten loose components as necessary.
	(4) Insufficient or incorrect lubricant.	(4) Drain and refill to edge of fill hole with AMC/Jeep Automatic Transmission Fluid or equivalent labeled DEXRON® II only.
	(5) Internal components binding, worn or damaged.	(5) Disassemble unit and replace worn or damaged components as necessary.
TRANSFER CASE NOISY IN ALL DRIVE MODES	(1) Insufficient or incorrect lubricant.	(1) Drain and refill to edge of fill hole with AMC/Jeep Automatic Transmission Fluid or equivalent labeled DEXRON® II only. Check for leaks and repair if necessary. **Note: If unit is still noisy after drain and refill, disassembly and inspection may be required to locate source of noise.**
NOISY IN — OR JUMPS OUT OF FOUR WHEEL DRIVE LOW RANGE	(1) Transfer case not completely engaged in 4L position.	(1) Stop vehicle, shift transfer case in Neutral, then shift back into 4L position.
	(2) Shift linkage loose or binding.	(2) Tighten, lubricate or repair linkage as necessary.
	(3) Range fork cracked, inserts worn, or fork is binding on shift rail.	(3) Disassemble unit and repair as necessary.
	(4) Annulus gear or lockplate worn or damaged.	(4) Disassemble unit and repair as necessary.
LUBRICANT LEAKING FROM OUTPUT SHAFT SEALS OR FROM VENT	(1) Transfer case overfilled.	(1) Drain to correct level.
	(2) Vent closed or restricted.	(2) Clear or replace vent if necessary.
	(3) Output shaft seals damaged or installed incorrectly.	(3) Replace seals. Be sure seal lip faces interior of case when installed. Also be sure yoke seal surfaces are not scored or nicked. Remove scores and nicks with fine sandpaper or replace yoke(s) if necessary.
ABNORMAL TIRE WEAR	(1) Extended operation on dry hard surface (paved) roads in 4H range.	(1) Operate in 2H on hard surface (paved) roads.

7 DRIVE TRAIN

SERVICE DIAGNOSIS—SELEC-TRAC SYSTEM

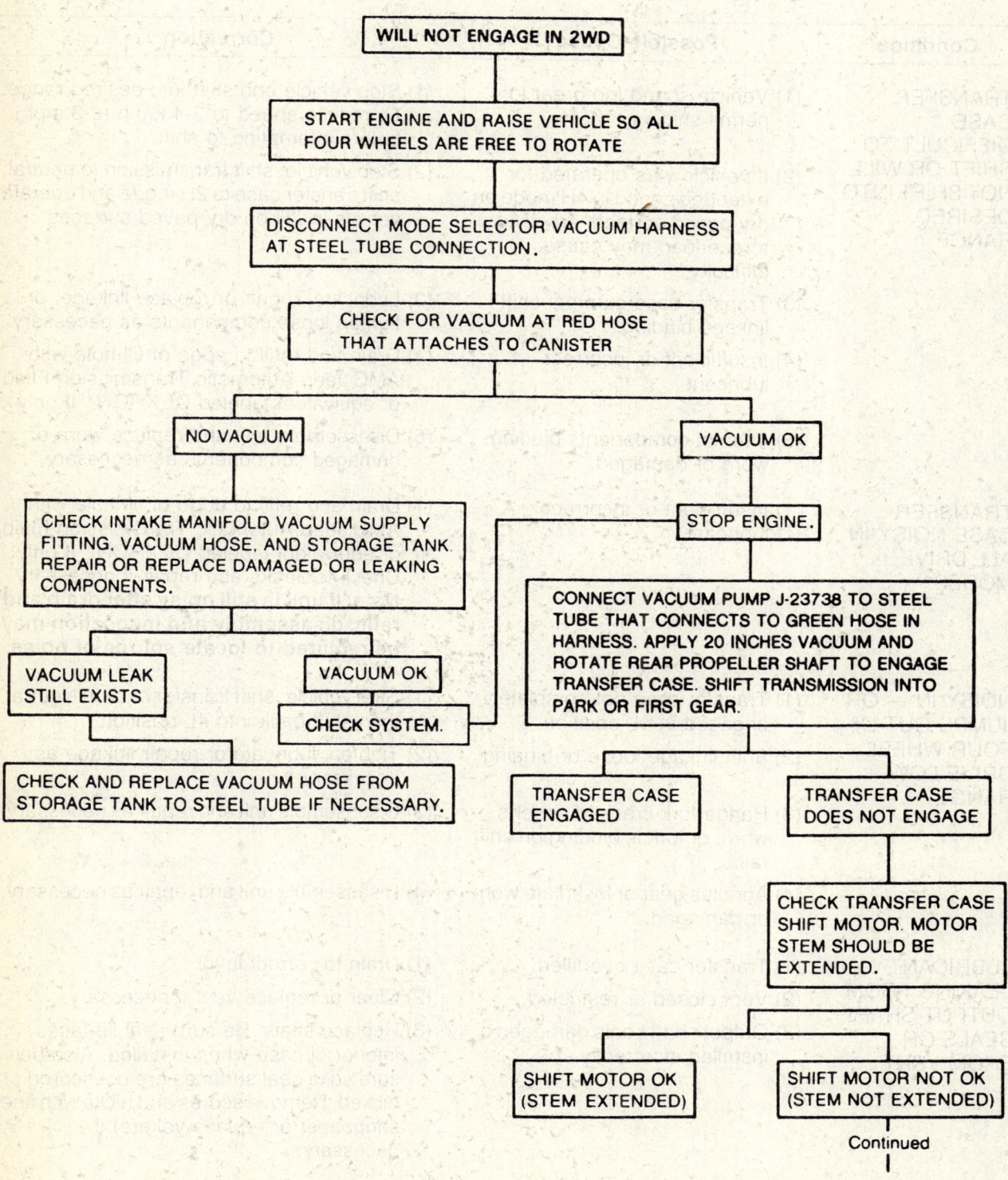

DRIVE TRAIN 7

SERVICE DIAGNOSIS—SELEC-TRAC SYSTEM (Continued)

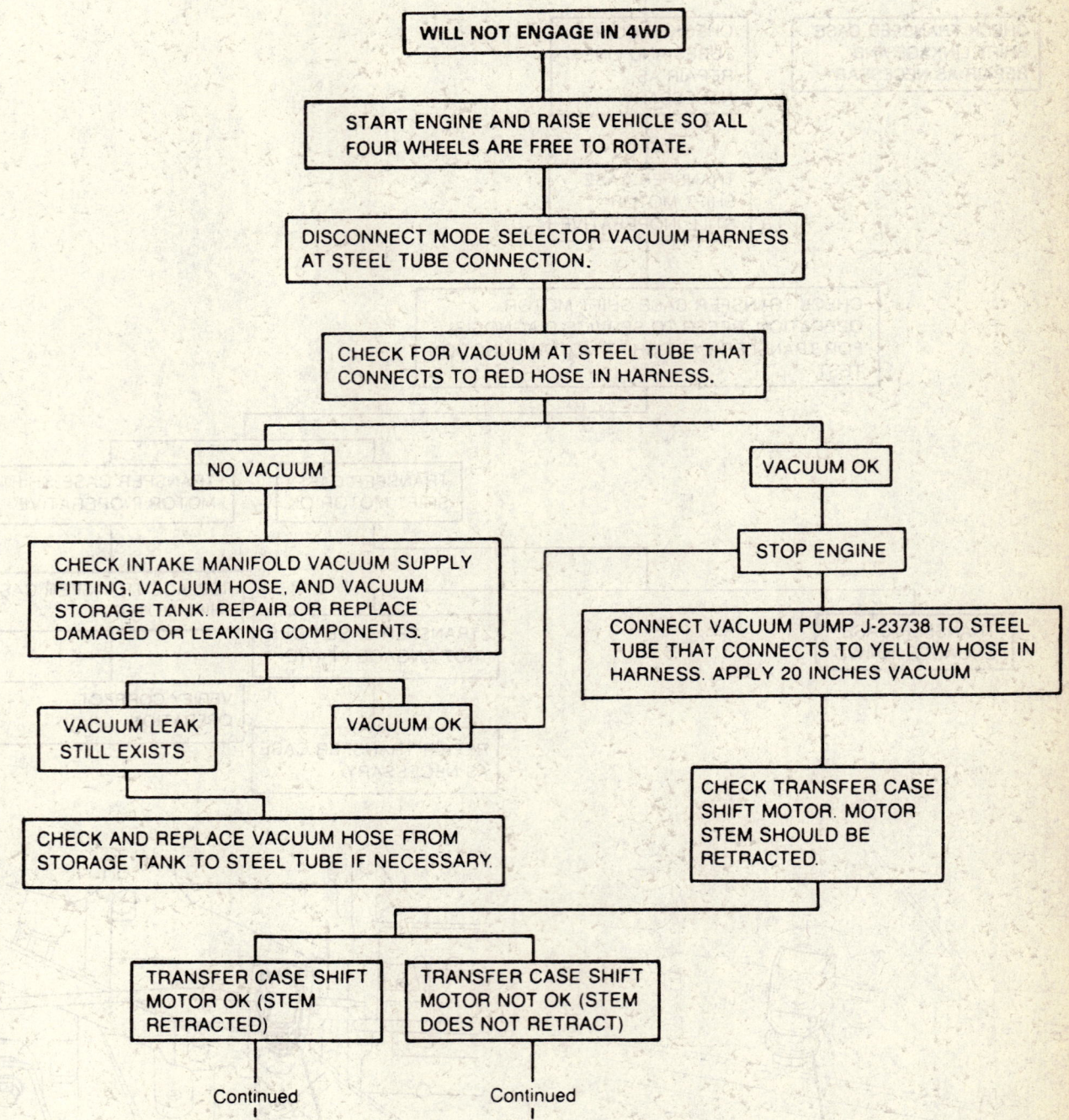

7-107

7 DRIVE TRAIN

SERVICE DIAGNOSIS—SELEC-TRAC SYSTEM (Continued)

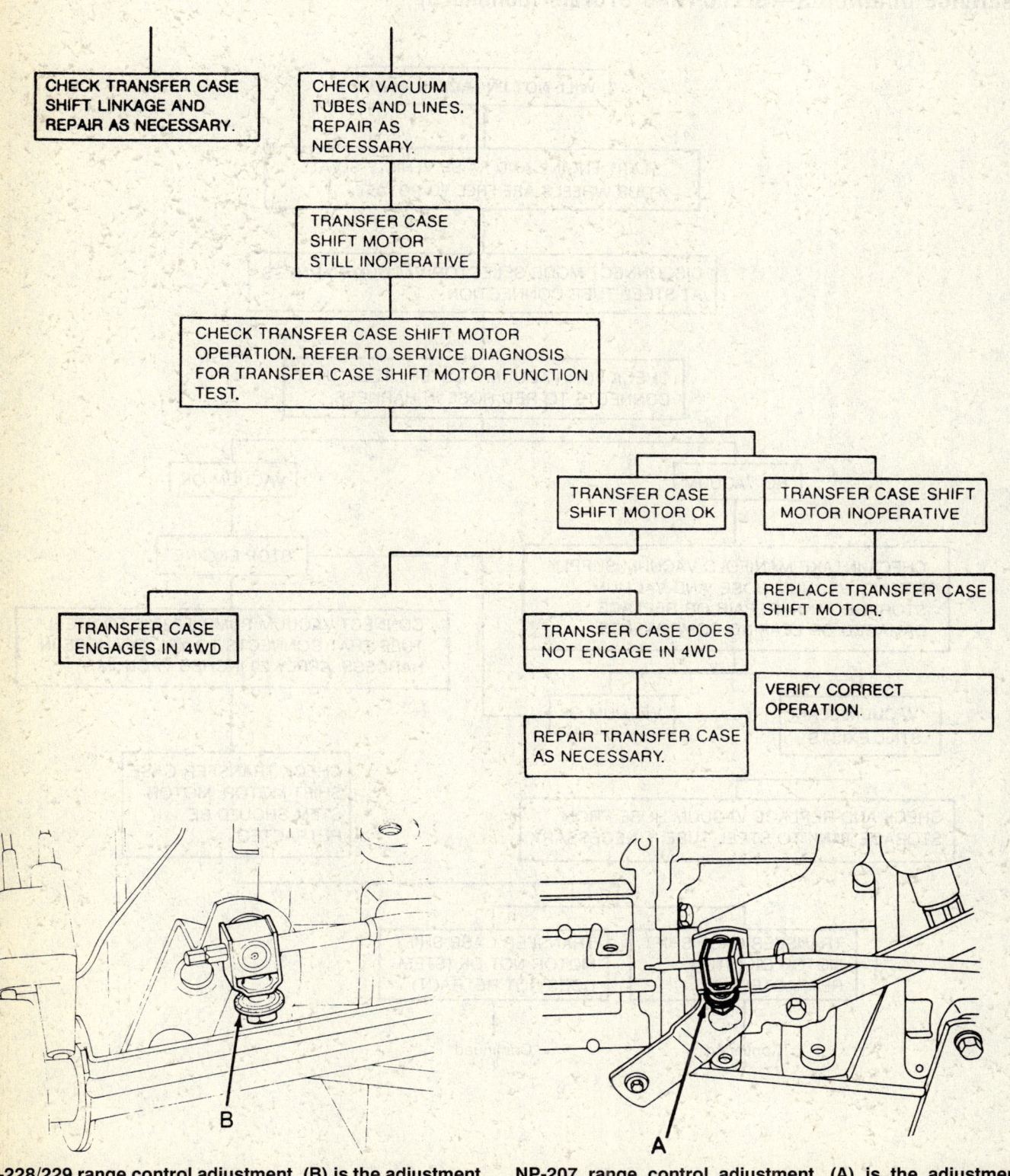

NP-228/229 range control adjustment. (B) is the adjustment point

NP-207 range control adjustment. (A) is the adjustment point

DRIVE TRAIN 7

SERVICE DIAGNOSIS—SELEC-TRAC SYSTEM (Continued)

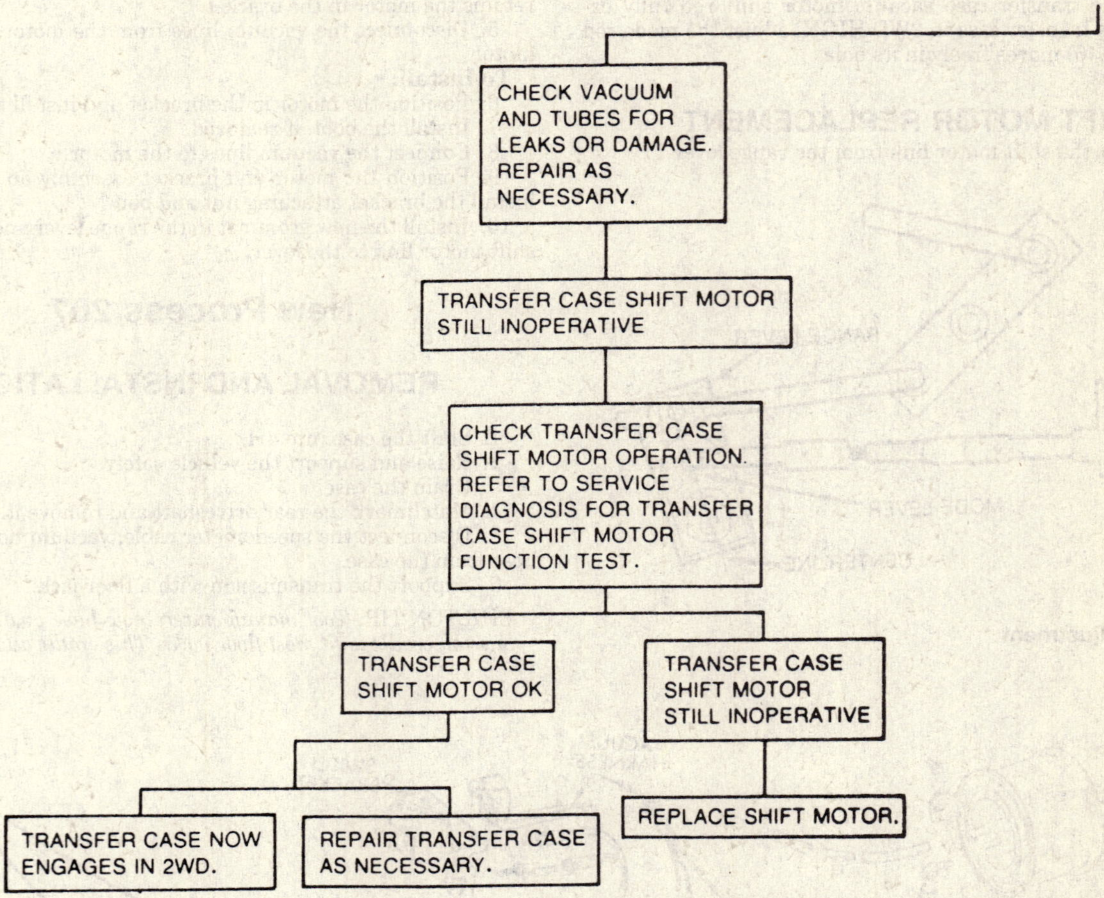

```
CHECK VACUUM
AND TUBES FOR
LEAKS OR DAMAGE.
REPAIR AS
NECESSARY.
        │
        ▼
TRANSFER CASE SHIFT MOTOR
STILL INOPERATIVE
        │
        ▼
CHECK TRANSFER CASE
SHIFT MOTOR OPERATION.
REFER TO SERVICE
DIAGNOSIS FOR TRANSFER
CASE SHIFT MOTOR
FUNCTION TEST.
    │              │
    ▼              ▼
TRANSFER CASE   TRANSFER CASE
SHIFT MOTOR OK  SHIFT MOTOR
                STILL INOPERATIVE
    │              │
    ▼              ▼
TRANSFER CASE NOW    REPAIR TRANSFER CASE    REPLACE SHIFT MOTOR.
ENGAGES IN 2WD.      AS NECESSARY.
```

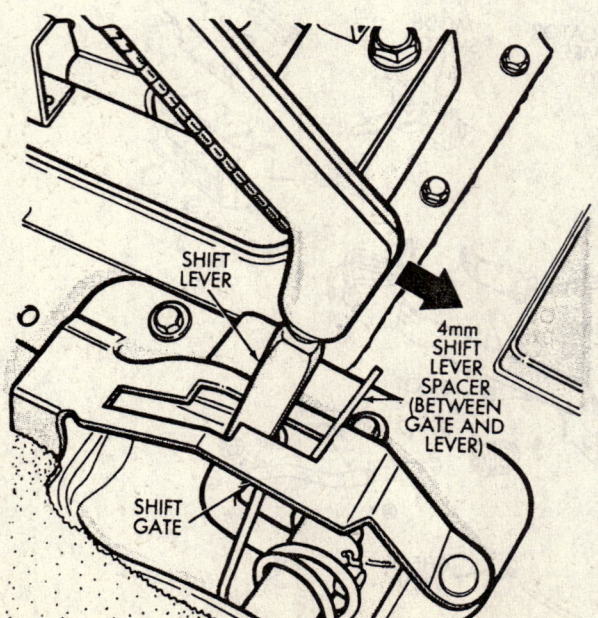

Range control linkage adjustment on the NP-231/242

5. Raise and support the vehicle safely.
6. Loosen the trunnion lock bolt. The linkage rod should now slide freely in the trunnion.
7. Position the linkage rod so it is a free fit in the range lever. Then tighten the locknut.
8. Lower the vehicle. Remove the spacer.

MODE ROD ADJUSTMENT

NP-228, 229

NOTE: If this adjustment is not properly made, the transfer case may not fully engage 2WD/HIGH and internal damage will result.

1. Fully engage the 2WD/HIGH position.
2. Refer to the accompanying illustration. The range lever and the mode lever must be aligned on the same centerline.

NOTE: To correctly position the mode lever, it is sometimes necessary to rotate the transfer case output shaft. To do this, raise and support the rear end on jackstands and rotate the rear driveshaft, while applying a load on the mode lever. Doing this will help align the spline for full engagement of 2WD/HIGH.

3. Adjust the length of the mode rod (4) to approximately 6 in. (152mm), to eliminate all free play.
4. Make sure all vacuum lines are secure.
5. Drive the vehicle a short distance, shifting between 4WD and 2WD/HIGH.

7-109

7 DRIVE TRAIN

6. Check the mode lever position. The lever should be aligned as explained in step 2. If not, repeat steps 3 through 5, increasing the length of the mode rod one turn, until proper alignment is achieved.
7. With the transfer case vacuum motor shift rod fully extended and the transfer case in 2WD/HIGH, adjust the mode rod so that the pin (6) moves freely in its hole.

SHIFT MOTOR REPLACEMENT

1. Disconnect the shift motor link from the range lever.

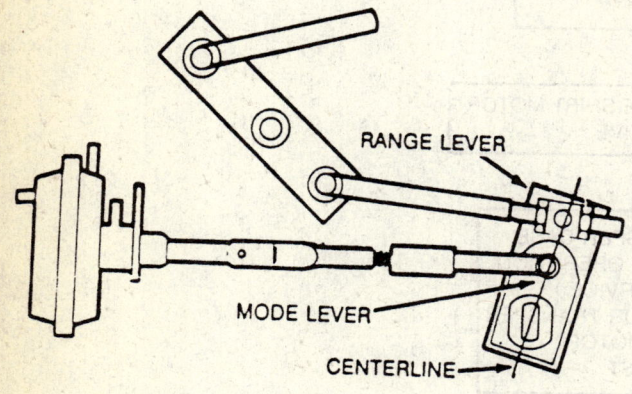

Mode rod adjustment

2. Remove and discard the lever grommet.
3. Remove the nut and bolt attaching the shift motor bracket to the case and remove the bracket and motor as an assembly.
4. Slide the shift motor boot aside and remove the E-ring that retains the motor in the bracket.
5. Disconnect the vacuum lines from the motor. Remove the motor.

To Install:

6. Position the motor in the bracket and install the E-ring.
7. Install the boot, if removed.
8. Connect the vacuum lines to the motor.
9. Position the motor and bracket assembly on the case and install the bracket attaching nut and bolt.
10. Install the new grommet in the range lever and connect the shift motor link to the lever.

New Process 207

REMOVAL AND INSTALLATION

1. Shift the case into 4H.
2. Raise and support the vehicle safely.
3. Drain the case.
4. Matchmark the rear driveshaft and remove it.
5. Disconnect the speedometer cable, vacuum hoses and vent hose from the case.
6. Support the transmission with a floor jack.

CHILTON TIP: *Tool manufacturers now have available a transmission cradle to fit most floor jacks. This cradle allows the trans-*

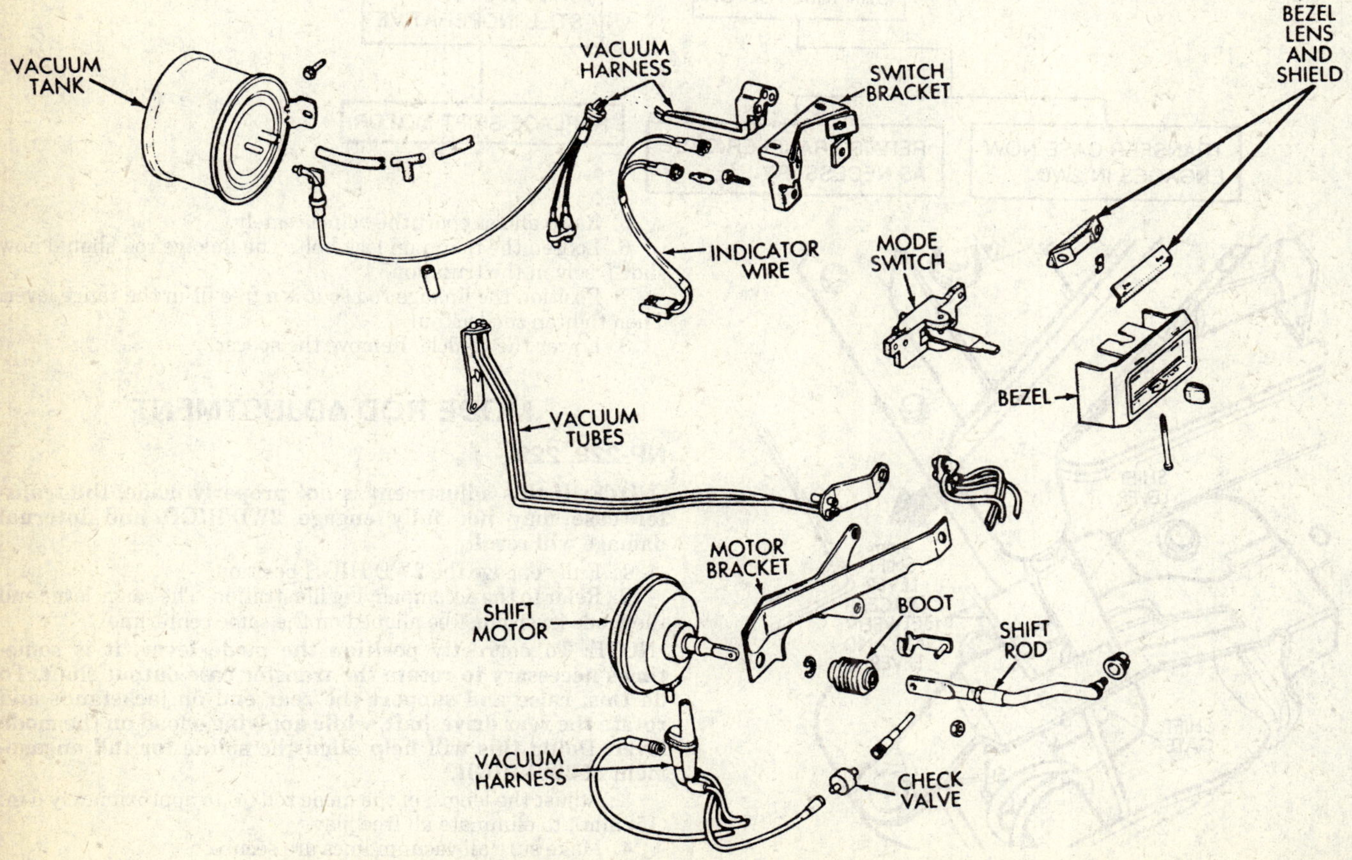

Vacuum shift components on the NP-228/229

DRIVE TRAIN 7

mission to be tilted horizontally and vertically, thus, easing removal/installation.

7. Remove the crossmember.
8. Matchmark the front driveshaft and remove it.
9. Disconnect the shift lever linkage rod at the case.
10. Remove the shift lever bracket bolts.
11. Support the transfer case with a floor jack or transmission jack and remove the attaching bolts.
12. Remove the transfer case from the vehicle.

To install:

13. Raise the transfer case into position. Torque the attaching bolts to 26 ft. lbs.
14. Connect the shift lever linkage rod at the case.
15. Install the shift lever bracket bolts.
16. Install the front driveshaft. Torque the nuts to 14 ft. lbs. Torque the flange bolts to 35 ft. lbs.

NOTE: New strap bolts must be installed each time the driveshaft is removed.

17. Install the crossmember. Torque the crossmember-to-frame bolts to 30 ft. lbs.; the crossmember-to-transmission bolts to 33 ft. lbs.
18. Remove the floor jack.
19. Connect the speedometer cable, vacuum hoses and vent hose at the case.
20. Install the rear driveshaft. Use new strap bolts, torqued to 14 ft. lbs. Torque the flange bolts to 35 ft. lbs.
21. Fill the case.
22. Lower the truck.

New Process 207 — Overhaul

CASE DISASSEMBLY

1. Remove fill and drain plugs.
2. Remove front yoke. Discard yoke seal washer and yoke nut.
3. Turn transfer case on end and position front case on wood blocks.
4. Shift transfer case to 4-Low.
5. Remove extension housing attaching bolts. Using a hammer, tap the shoulder on the extension housing to break sealer loose.
6. Remove the snapring for the rear bearing from the main shaft and discard.
7. Remove the rear retainer attaching bolts. Using a hammer, tap the shoulder on the retainer to break sealer loose.
8. Remove the rear retainer and pump housing from the transfer case.
9. Remove the pump seal from the pump housing and discard.
10. Remove the speedometer drive gear from the main shaft.
11. Remove the pump gear from the main shaft.
12. Remove the bolts attaching the rear case to the front case and remove rear case. To separate the case, insert a pry bar into the slots cast in the case ends and pry upward. DO NOT attempt to wedge the case halves apart at any point on the mating surfaces.
13. Remove the front output shaft and drive chain as an assembly. It may be necessary to raise the main shaft slightly for the output shaft to clear the case.
14. Pull up on the mode fork rail until rail clears range fork and rotate mode fork and rail and remove from transfer case.
15. Pull up on the main shaft until it separates from the planetary assembly. Remove the main shaft from the transfer case.

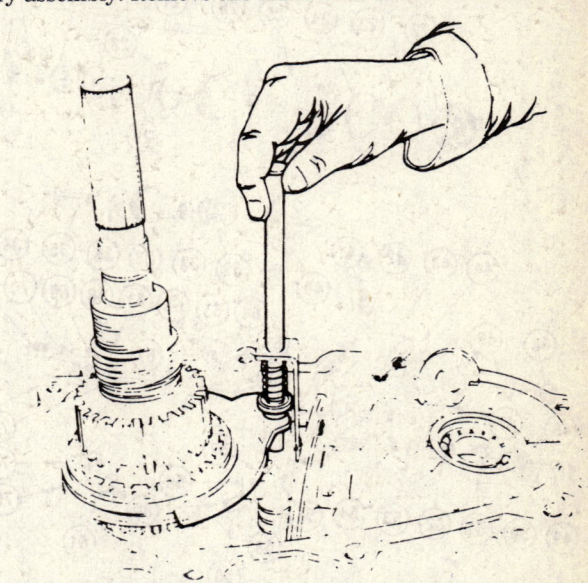

Removing the mode fork and rail from the NP-207

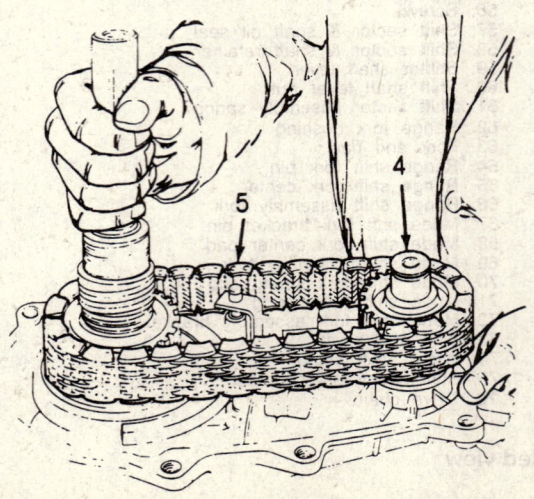

Removing the front output shaft (4) and drive chain (5) from the NP-207

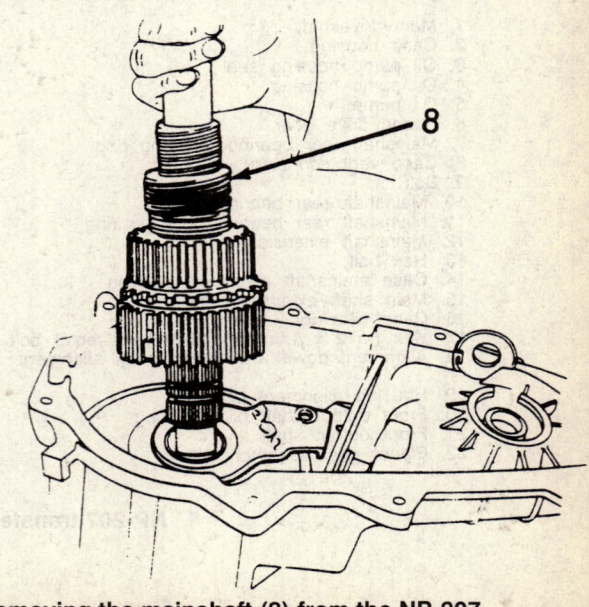

Removing the mainshaft (8) from the NP-207

7-111

7 DRIVE TRAIN

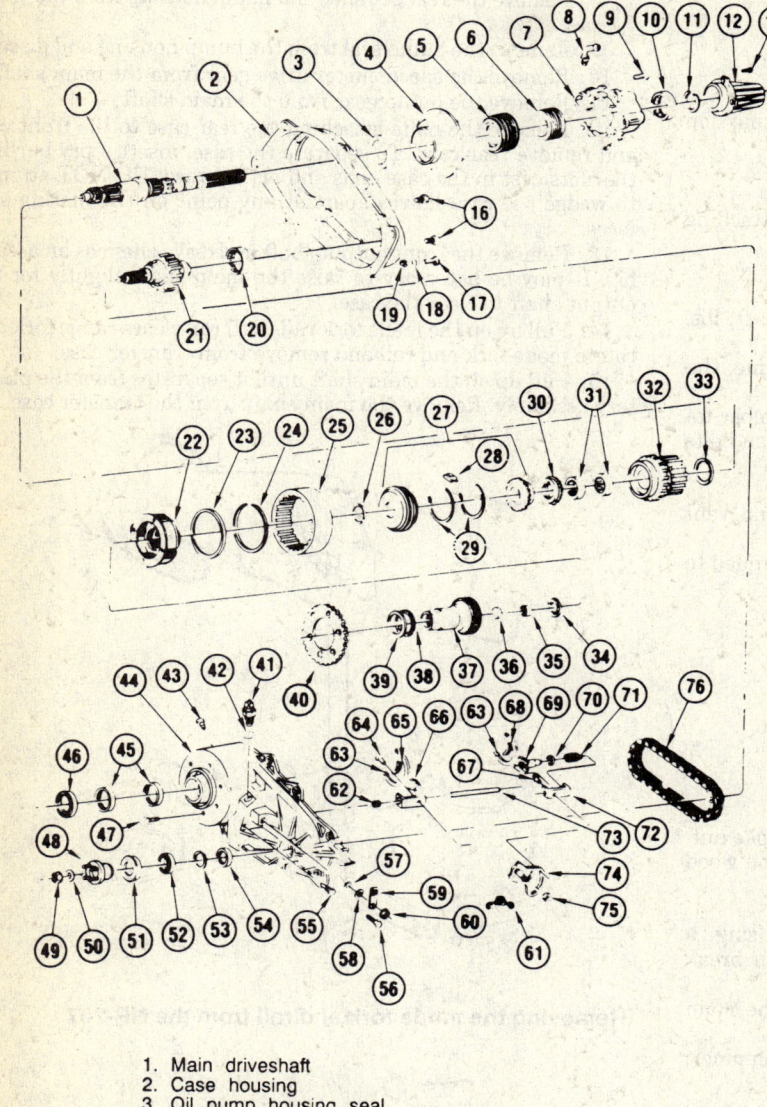

23. Planet gear carrier retaining ring thrust washer
24. Planet gear carrier retaining ring
25. Planet gear carrier annulus gear
26. Main driveshaft synchronizer retaining ring
27. Main driveshaft assembly synchronizer
28. Synchronizer strut
29. Synchronizer strut spring
30. Synchronizer stop ring
31. Drive chain sprocket bearing
32. Drive chain sprocket
33. Drive chain sprocket thrust washer
34. Input main drive gear thrust washer
35. Input drive gear pilot bearing
36. Cup plug
37. Input main drive assembly gear
38. Input drive gear thrust bearing
39. Input drive gear thrust bearing washer
40. Low range lockplate
41. Vacuum four wheel switch
42. Four wheel drive indicator light switch seal
43. Oil access hole plug
44. Case (front half) housing
45. Input drive bearing
46. Input drive gear seal
47. Hex bolt
48. Front output driveshaft flange yoke
49. Front output driveshaft yoke nut
50. Front output driveshaft yoke (rubber)
51. Front output driveshaft yoke deflector
52. Front output driveshaft seal
53. Front output driveshaft retaining ring
54. Front output driveshaft bearing
55. Shift sector spring screw
56. Screw
57. Shift sector & shaft oil seal
58. Shift sector & shaft retainer
59. Shifter shaft lever
60. Shift shaft lever nut
61. Shift sector assembly spring
62. Range fork bushing
63. Fork end pad
64. Range shift fork pin
65. Range shift fork center
66. Range shift assembly fork
67. Mode shft fork bracket pin
68. Mode shift fork center pad
69. Mode shift assembly fork
70. Mode shift fork spring cup
71. Mode shift fork spring
72. Mode shift fork assembly bracket
73. Shift fork shaft
74. W/shf, shift sector
75. Shift sector shaft spacer
76. Drive chain

1. Main driveshaft
2. Case housing
3. Oil pump housing seal
4. Oil pump housing
5. Oil pump
6. Speed drive gear
7. Mainshaft rear bearing retaining ring
8. Case vent connector
9. Bolt
10. Mainshaft rear bearing
11. Mainshaft rear bearing retaining ring
12. Mainshaft extension
13. Hex bolt
14. Case mainshaft extension bushing
15. Main shaft extension seal
16. Case oil plug
17. Hex (m10 x 1.5mm x 35mm) (2 req'd) bolt
18. Alignment dowel washer housing; alignment
19. Housing alignment dowel
20. Front output shaft pilot bearing
21. Front output shaft
22. Planet gear assembly carrier

NP-207 transfer case — exploded view

DRIVE TRAIN 7

16. Remove the planetary assembly with the range fork from the transfer case.
17. Remove the planetary thrust washer, input gear thrust bearing and front thrust washer from the transfer case.
18. Remove the shift sector detent spring and retaining bolt.
19. Remove the shift sector, shaft and spacer from the transfer case.
20. Remove the locking plate retaining bolts and lock plate from the transfer case.
21. Remove the input gear pilot bearing using J-29369-1 or equivalent with a slide hammer.
22. Remove the front output shaft seal, input shaft seal and the rear extension seal using a brass drift.
23. Using J-33841 with J-8092 or equivalent, press the 2 caged roller bearings for the front input shaft gear from the transfer case.
24. Using J-29369-2 with J-33367 or a slide hammer, remove the rear bearing for the front output shaft.
25. Using a hammer and drift, remove the rear main shaft bearing from the rear retainer.
26. Using an awl, remove the snapring retaining the front output shaft bearing. Using a hammer and drift, remove the bearing from the case.
27. Remove the bushing from the extension housing using J-33839 with J-8092 or equivalent. Press bushing from the extension housing.

MAINSHAFT DISASSEMBLY

1. Remove the speedometer gear.
2. Using an awl, pry off the pump gear from the mainshaft.
3. Remove the snapring retaining the synchronizer hub from the mainshaft.
4. Using a brass hammer, tap the synchronizer hub from mainshaft.
5. Remove the drive sprocket.
6. Using J-33826 and J-8092 or equivalent, press 2 caged roller bearings from the drive sprocket.

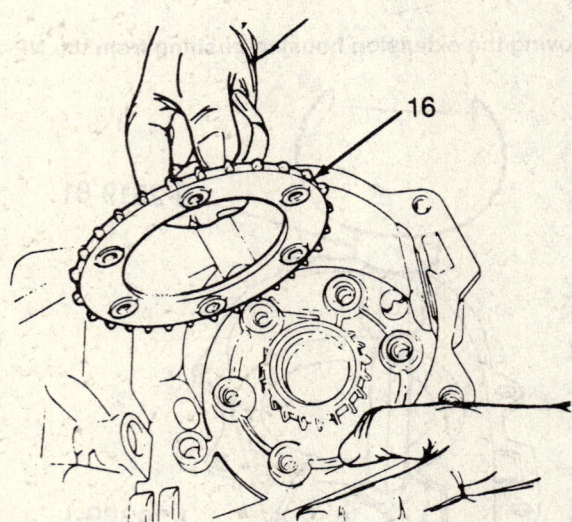

Removing the locking plate (16) from the NP-207

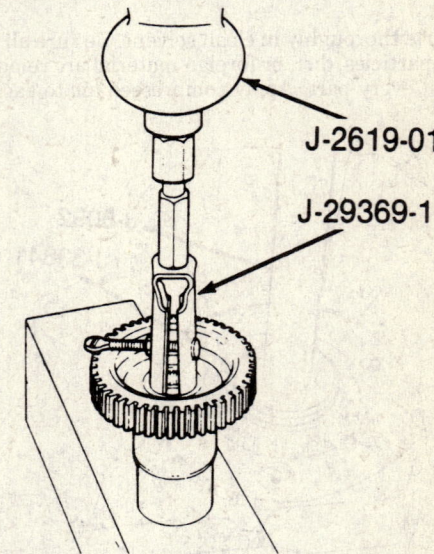

Using a special tool to remove the input gear pilot bearing from the NP-207

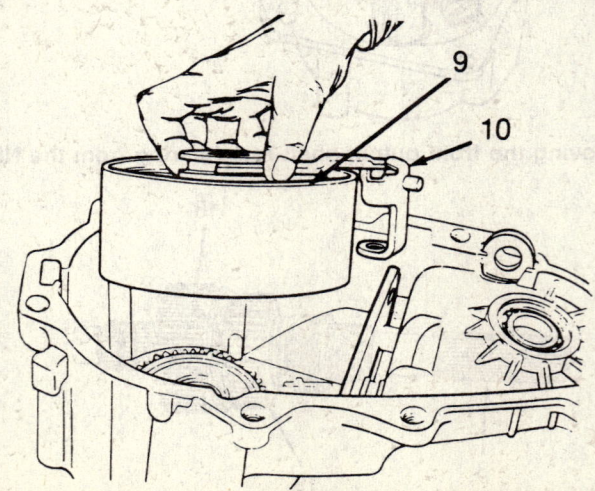

Removing the planetary assembly (9) and range fork (10) from the NP-207

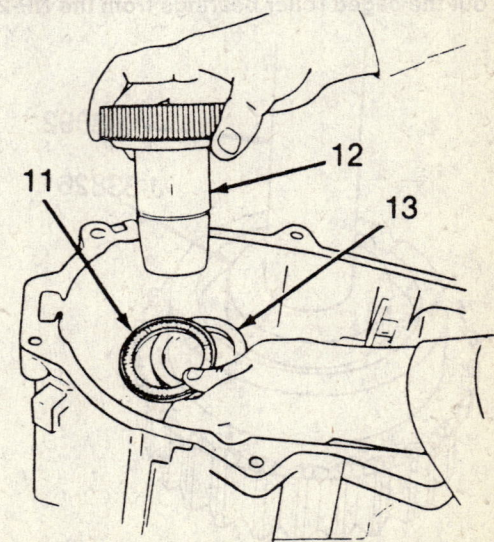

Removing the thrust bearing (11), input gear (12) and thrust washer (13) from the NP-207

7-113

7 DRIVE TRAIN

7. Remove synchronizer keys and retaining rings from the synchronizer hub.

8. Clean and inspect all parts. Replace any parts if they show evidence of excessive wear, distortion or damage.

PLANETARY GEAR DISASSEMBLY

1. Remove the snapring retaining the planetary gear in the annulus gear.
2. Remove outer thrust ring and discard.
3. Remove planetary assembly from the annulus gear.
4. Remove inner thrust ring from the planetary assembly and discard.
5. Clean and inspect parts. Replace any parts if they show evidence of excessive wear, distortion or damage.

CLEANING AND INSPECTION

Wash all parts thoroughly in clean solvent. Be sure all old lubricant, metallic particles, dirt, or foreign material are removed from the surfaces of every part. Apply compressed air to each oil feed

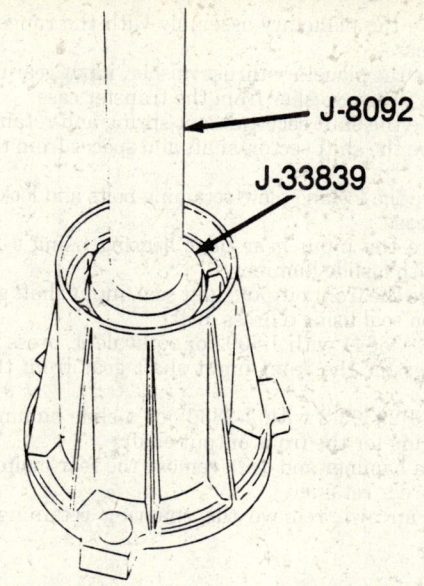

Removing the extension housing bushing from the NP-207

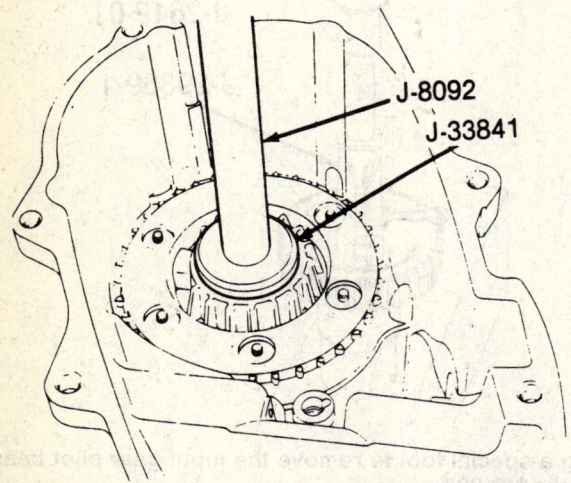

Pressing out the caged roller bearings from the NP-207

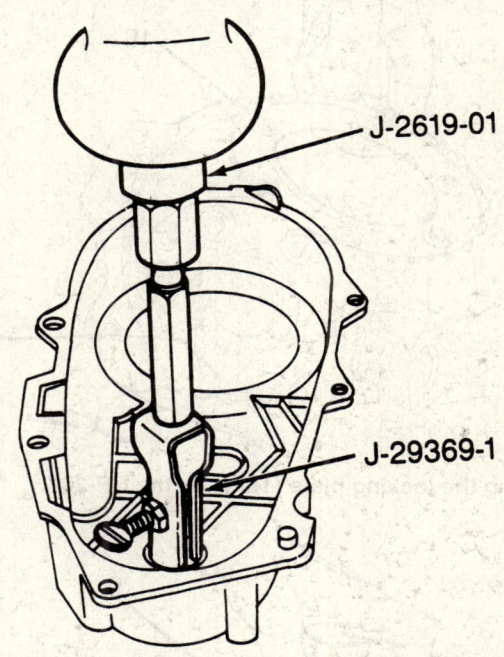

Removing the front output shaft rear bearing from the NP-207

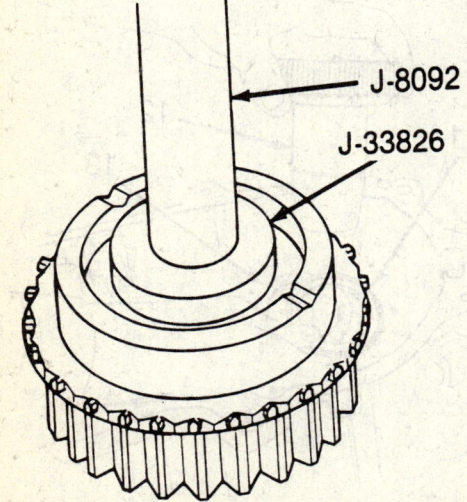

Pressing the caged roller bearings from the drive sprocket on the NP-207

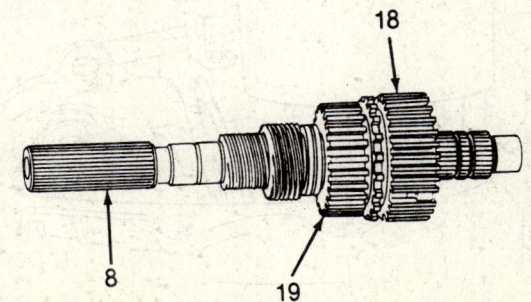

NP-207 mainshaft (8); synchronizer hub (18); and drive sprocket (19)

7-114

DRIVE TRAIN 7

port and channel in each case half to remove any obstructions or cleaning solvent residue.

Inspect all gear teeth for signs of excessive wear or damage and check all gear splines for burrs, nicks, wear or damage. Remove minor nicks or scratches with an oil stone. Replace any part exhibiting excessive wear or damage.

Inspect all snaprings and thrust washers for evidence of excessive wear, distortion or damage. Replace any of these parts if they exhibit these conditions.

Inspect the two case halves for cracks, porosity damaged mating surfaces, stripped bolt threads, or distortion. Replace any part that exhibits these conditions. Inspect the low range lock plate in the front case. If the lock plate teeth or the plate hub is cracked, broken, chipped, or excessively worn, replace the lock plate and the lock plate attaching bolts.

Inspect the condition of all needle, roller and thrust bearings in the front and rear case halves and the input gear. Also, check the condition of the bearing bores in both cases and in the input gear, rear output shaft and rear retainer. Replace any part that exhibits signs of excessive wear or damage.

PLANETARY GEAR ASSEMBLY

1. Install the inner thrust ring on planetary assembly.
2. Install the planetary assembly into the annulus gear.
3. Install the outer thrust ring and then the snapring.

MAINSHAFT ASSEMBLY

1. Using J-33828 and J-8092 or equivalent, install the front drive sprocket bearing. Press bearing until tool bottoms out. Bearing should be flush with front surface. Reverse tool on J-8092 or equivalent and press rear bearing into sprocket until tool bottoms out. The rear bearing should be recessed after installation.
2. Install thrust washer on the mainshaft.
3. Install drive sprocket on the mainshaft.
4. Install blocker ring and synchronizer hub on the mainshaft. Seat hub on main shaft and install a new snapring to retain.
5. Install pump gear on the mainshaft. Tap the gear with a hammer to seat on mainshaft.
6. Install speedometer gear on the mainshaft.

CASE ASSEMBLY

All of the bearings used in the transfer case must be correctly positioned to avoid covering the bearing oil feed holes. After installation of bearings, check the bearing position to be sure the feed hole is not obstructed or blocked by a bearing.

1. Install the lock plate in the transfer case. Coat case and lock plate surfaces around bolt holes with Loctite®515 or equivalent.
2. Position the lock plate to the case and align bolt holes in lock plate with case. Install attaching bolts and torque to specification.
3. Install the roller bearings for the input shaft into the transfer case using J-33830 and J-8092 or equivalent. Press bearings until tool bottoms in bore.
4. Install the front output shaft rear bearing, using J-33832

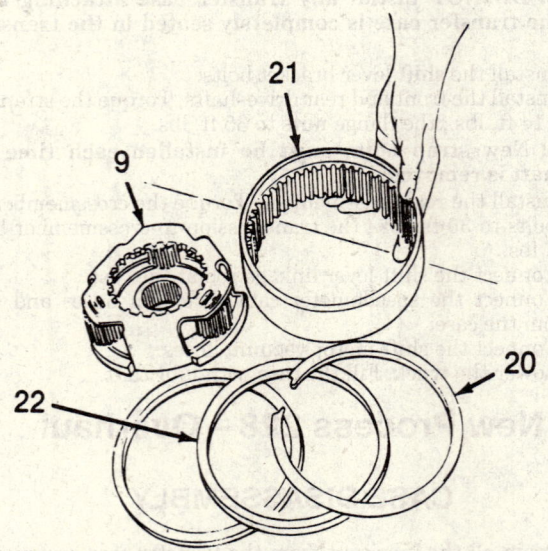

NP-207 planetary gear components. (9) planetary gear; (20) snapring; (21) annulus gear; (22) thrust ring

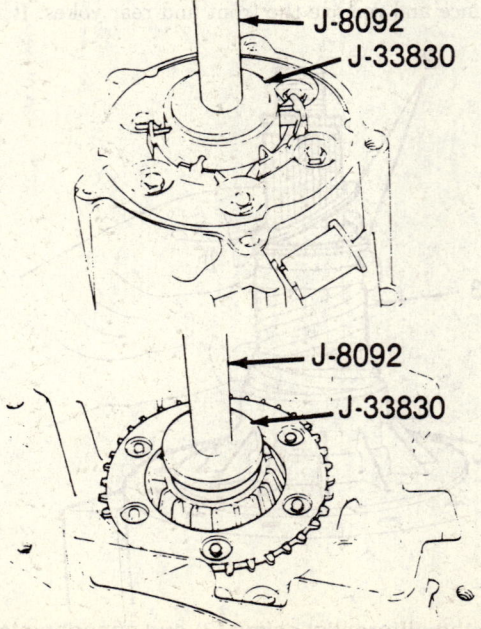

Installing the input shaft roller bearings on the NP-207

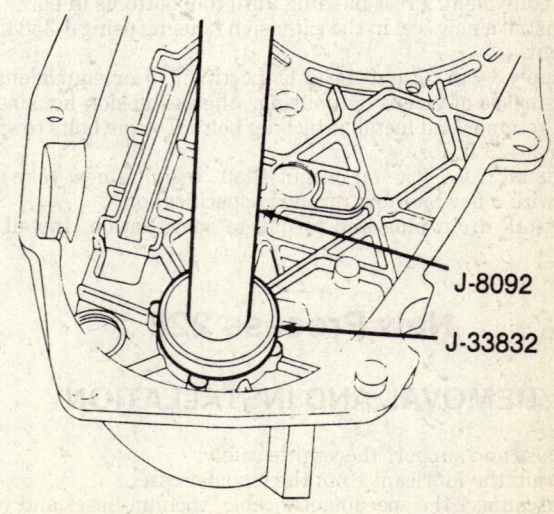

Installing the front output shaft rear bearing on the NP-207

7-115

7 DRIVE TRAIN

and J-8092 or equivalent. Press bearing until tool bottoms in case.

5. Install the front output shaft front bearing using J-33833 and J-8092 or equivalent. Press bearing until tool bottoms in bore.

6. Install the snapring that retains the front output shaft bearing in case.

7. Install the front output shaft seal using J-33834 or equivalent.

8. Install the input shaft seal using J-33831 or equivalent.

9. Install spacer on shift sector shaft and install sector in transfer case. Install shift lever and retaining nut. Torque to specification.

10. Install shift sector detent spring and retaining bolt.

11. Install the pilot bearing into the input gear using J-33829 and J-8092 or equivalent. Press bearing until tool bottoms out.

12. Install the input gear front thrust bearing and input gear in transfer case.

13. Install the planetary gear thrust washer on the input gear. Position range fork on planetary assembly and install planetary assembly into the transfer case.

14. Install the mainshaft into the transfer case. Make sure the thrust washer is aligned with the input gear and planetary assembly before installing mainshaft.

15. Install mode fork on synchronizer sleeve and rotate until mode fork is aligned with range fork. Slide mode fork rail down through range fork until rail is seated in bore of transfer case.

16. Position drive chain on front output shaft and install chain on drive sprocket. Install front output shaft in the transfer case. It may be necessary to slightly raise the main shaft to seat the output shaft in the case.

17. Install the magnet into pocket of transfer case.

18. Apply 1/8 in. (3mm) bead of Loctite®515 or equivalent to the mating surface of the front case. Install rear case on the front case aligning dowel pins. Install bolts and torque to 20–25 ft. lbs. Install the two bolts with washers into the dowel pin holes.

19. Install the output bearing into the rear retainer using J-33833 and J-8092 or equivalent. Press bearing until seated in bore.

20. Install pump seal in pump housing using J-33835 or equivalent. Apply petroleum jelly to pump housing tabs and install housing in rear retainer.

21. Apply 1/8 in. (3mm) bead of Loctite®515 or equivalent to mating surface of rear retainer. Align retainer to case and install retaining bolts. Torque bolts to specification 15–20 ft. lbs.

22. Using a new snapring, install snapring on mainshaft. Pull up on mainshaft and seat snapring in its groove.

23. Install bushing in extension housing using J-33826 and J-8092 or equivalent. Press bushing until tool bottoms in bore.

24. Install a new seal in the extension housing using J-33843 or equivalent.

25. Apply 1/8 in. (3mm) bead of Loctite®515 or equivalent to mating surface of extension housing. Align extension housing to the rear retainer and install attaching bolts. Torque bolts to specification 20–25 ft. lbs.

26. Install front yoke on output shaft. Install a new yoke seal washer with a new nut and torque to specification.

27. Install drain plug and torque to specification. Install fill plug.

New Process 228

REMOVAL AND INSTALLATION

1. Raise and support the vehicle safely.
2. Drain the lubricant from the transfer case.
3. Disconnect the speedometer cable, vacuum hoses and vent hose from the case.
4. Disconnect the shift lever linkage rod at the case.

5. Support the transmission with a floor jack. Remove the rear crossmember.

CHILTON TIP: *Tool manufacturers now have available a transmission cradle to fit most floor jacks. This cradle allows the transmission to be tilted horizontally and vertically, thus, easing installation.*

6. Matchmark the front and rear driveshafts and remove.
7. Disconnect the shift motor vacuum hoses.
8. Remove the shift lever bracket bolts.
9. Support the transfer case with a floor jack or transmission jack and remove the attaching bolts.
10. Pull the case rearward out of the truck.

To install:

11. Position the transfer case in the truck. Torque the attaching bolts to 40 ft. lbs.

NOTE: DO NOT install any transfer case attaching bolts until the transfer case is completely seated in the transmission

12. Install the shift lever bracket bolts.
13. Install the front and rear driveshafts. Torque the strap bolt nuts to 14 ft. lbs.; the flange nuts to 35 ft. lbs.

NOTE: New strap bolts must be installed each time the driveshaft is removed.

14. Install the rear crossmember. Torque the crossmember-to-frame bolts to 30 ft. lbs.; the transmission-to-crossmember bolts to 33 ft. lbs.
15. Connect the shift lever linkage rod at the case.
16. Connect the speedometer cable, vacuum hoses and vent hose from the case.
17. Connect the shift motor vacuum hoses.
18. Lower the truck. Fill the case with lubricant.

New Process 228 – Overhaul

CASE DISASSEMBLY

1. Drain all the lubricant from the transfer case and remove the front and rear yoke nuts along with their seal washers. Discard the seal washers.

2. Mark the front and rear yokes for easy installation alignment reference and remove the front and rear yokes. It may be

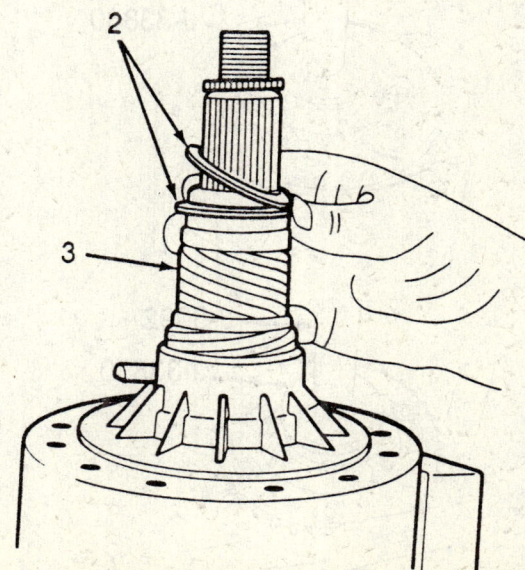

Removing the differential shims (2) and speedometer drive gear (3) from the NP-228

DRIVE TRAIN 7

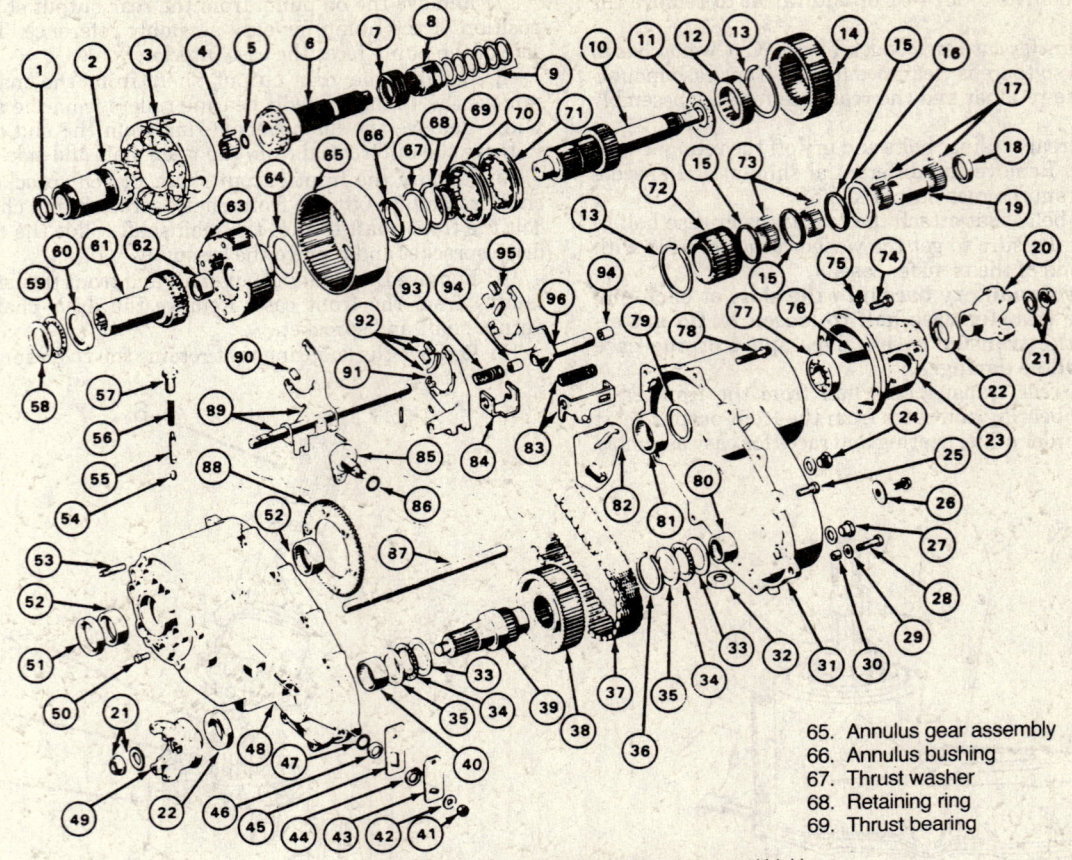

65. Annulus gear assembly
66. Annulus bushing
67. Thrust washer
68. Retaining ring
69. Thrust bearing

1. Spacer
2. Side gear
3. Differential
4. Pilot bearing rollers (15)
5. O-ring seal
6. Rear output shaft
7. Oil pump
8. Speedometer drive gear
9. Shim kit
10. Mainshaft
11. Mainshaft thrust washer
12. Spline gear
13. Retaining ring
14. Sprocket
15. Spacer
16. Sprocket thrust washer
17. Side gear roller (82)
18. Spacer (short)
19. Spacer (long)
20. Rear yoke
21. Nut and seal washer
22. Seal
23. Rear retainer
24. Plug assembly
25. Bolt
26. Identification tag
27. Plug assembly
28. Dowel bolt
29. Dowel bolt washer
30. Case half dowell
31. Rear half case
32. Magnet
33. Front output shaft bearing assembly race (thick)
34. Front output shaft bearing assembly thrust
35. Front output shaft bearing assembly race (thin)
36. Retaining ring
37. Chain
38. Driven sprocket
39. Front output shaft
40. Front output front bearing
41. Nut
42. Washer
43. Mode lever
44. Snap ring
45. Range lever
46. O-ring retainer
47. O-ring seal
48. Front half case
49. Front output yoke
50. Low range plate bolt
51. Input shaft oil seal
52. Input shaft bearing
53. Stud
54. Ball
55. Plunger
56. Plunger spring
57. Screw
58. Input race
59. Input thrust bearing
60. Input race (thick)
61. Input shaft
62. Input bearing
63. Planetary gear assembly
64. Input gear thrust washer
70. High range sliding clutch sleeve
71. Mode sliding clutch sleeve
72. Carrier
73. Carrier rollers (120)
74. Rear retainer bolt
75. Vent
76. Vent seal
77. Output bearing
78. Bolt
79. Seal
80. Front output rear bearing
81. Output shaft inner bearing
82. Range sector
83. Range bracket (outer) and spring
84. Range bracket (inner)
85. Mode sector
86. O-ring seal
87. Range rail
88. Low range lockout plate
89. Mode fork, rail and pin
90. Mode fork pad
91. Range fork
92. Range fork pads
93. Range bracket spring (inner)
94. Locking fork bushing
95. Locking fork pads
96. Locking fork

NP-228 transfer case — exploded view

7 DRIVE TRAIN

necessary to use tool No. J-8614-01 or equivalent to remove the yokes.

3. Place the transfer case on wooden blocks. Cut V-notches in the blocks of wood so there is clearance for the front case mounting studs. Mark the retainer and the rear case for easy assembly reference.

4. Remove the rear retainer bolts and pry off the retainer with a suitable pry bar. Remove the differential shim(s) and speedometer drive gear from the rear output shaft.

5. Remove the bolts that attach the rear transfer case half to the front case half. Be sure to get the washer that are used with the bolts on each end of the transfer case.

NOTE: Insert two small pry bars into the slots at each end of the rear of the transfer case half to loosen it. Do not attempt to wedge the transfer case halves apart or the case mating surface will be damages.

6. Remove the rear transfer case half from the front case. Remove the thrust bearing and races from the front output shaft and be to note the order of the bearing and races for easy assembly reference.

7. Remove the oil pump from the rear output shaft, note the position of the pump for easy assembly reference. The recessed side of the pump faces the case interior.

8. Remove the rear output shaft from the mainshaft and remove the 15 main needle bearing rollers from the shaft or coupling. Remove the mainshaft O-ring from the end of the shaft. Remove the differential from the mainshaft and side gear.

9. Remove the front output shaft, driven sprocket and drive chain assembly. Lift the front shaft, sprocket and chain upward. Tilt the front shaft toward the mainshaft. Slide the chain off the drive sprocket and remove the assembly.

10. Remove the front output shaft and front thrust bearing assembly from the front case. Remove the drive chain from the output shaft and sprocket.

11. Remove the snapring that retains the riven sprocket on the

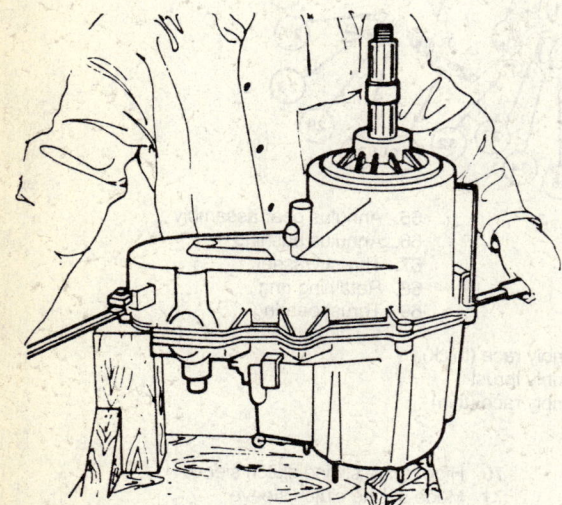

Separating the NP-228 case halves

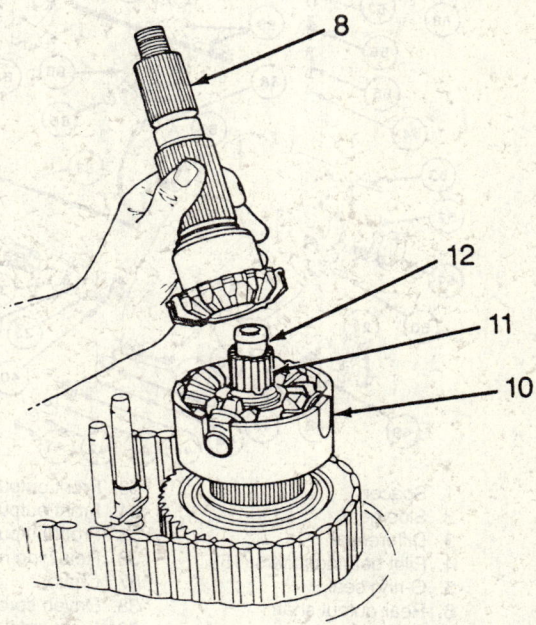

Disassembling the rear output shaft (8), 15 pilot roller (11), and O-ring (12) from the differential (10) on the NP-228

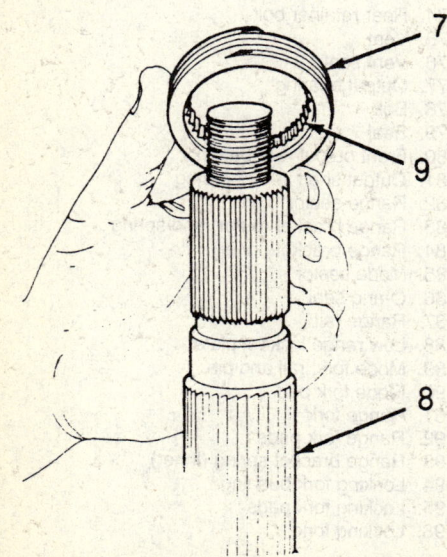

Removing the oil pump (7) from the rear output shaft (8). (9) is the recess in the pump

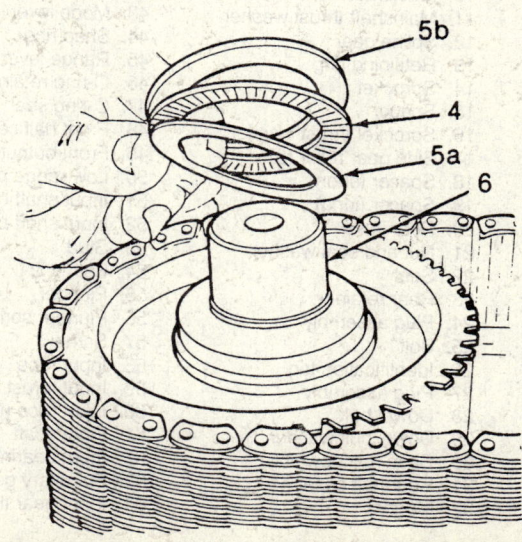

Removing the thrust bearing (4) and races (5a, 5b) from the front output shaft (6) on the NP-228

DRIVE TRAIN 7

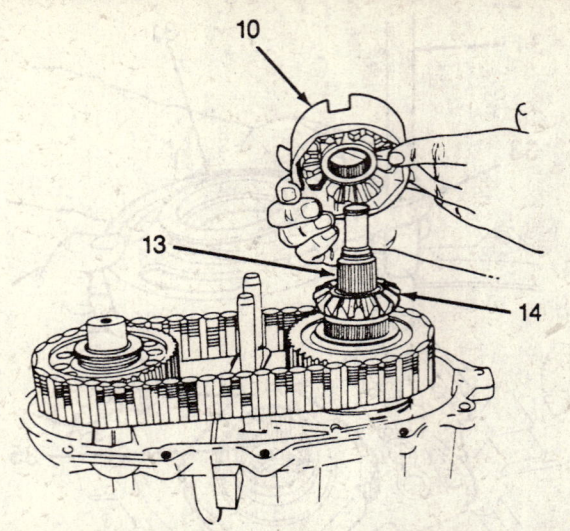

Removing the differential (10) from the mainshaft (13) and side gear (14) on the NP-228

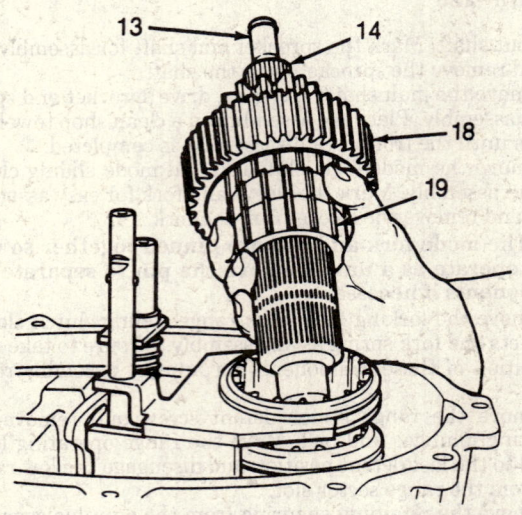

Removing the mainshaft (13), side gear (14), drive sprocket (18) and spline gear (19) from the NP-228

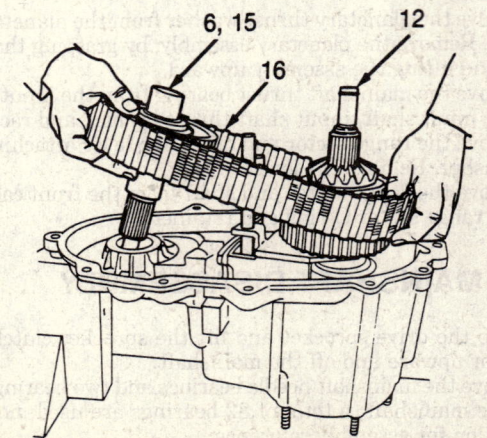

Removing the front output shaft (6), driven sprocket (15) and drive chain (16) from the mainshaft (12) on the NP-228

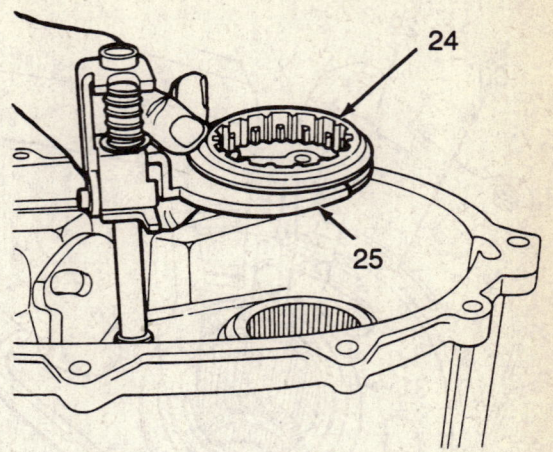

Removing the lock fork (25) and clutch sleeve (24) from the NP-228

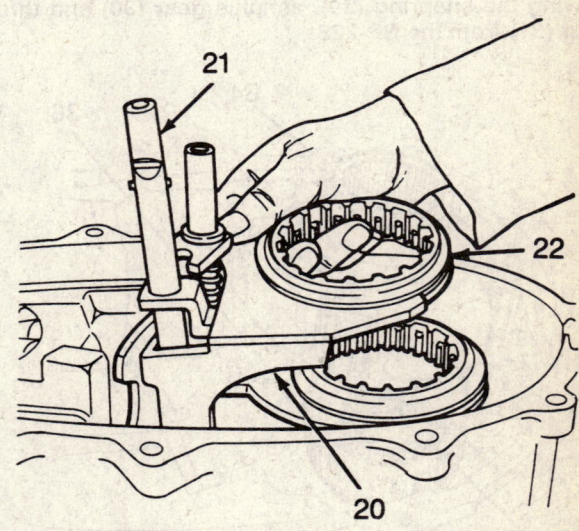

Removing the mode fork (20), shift rail (21) and mode sliding clutch sleeve (22) from the NP-228

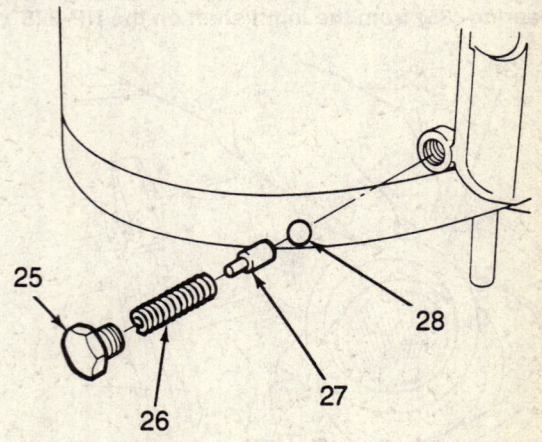

Removing the range selector detent screw, spring, plunger and ball from the NP-228

7-119

7 DRIVE TRAIN

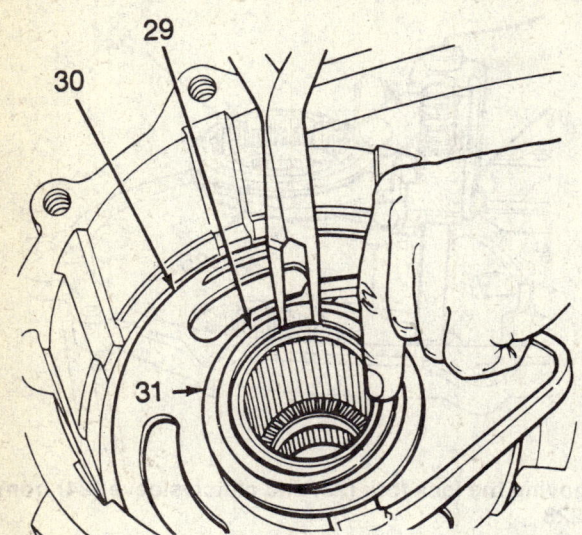

Removing the snapring (29), annulus gear (30) and thrust washer (31) from the NP-228

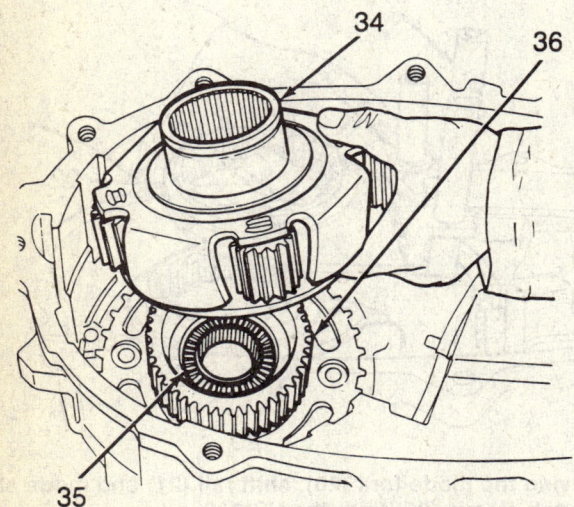

Removing the planetary assembly (34) and the mainshaft thrust bearing (35) from the input shaft on the NP-228

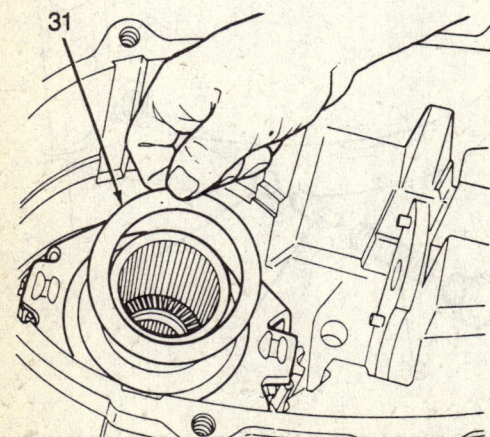

Removing the planetary thrust washer (31) from the NP-228

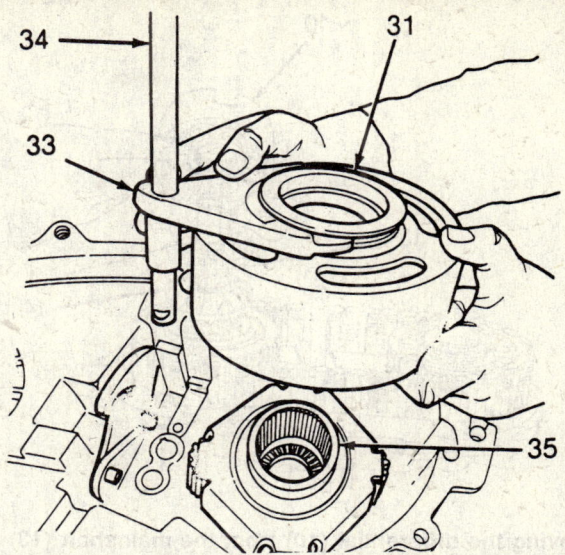

Removing the annulus gear (31), range fork (33) and rail (34) from the NP-228

front output shaft. Mark the sprocket and shaft for assembly reference and remove the sprocket from the shaft.

12. Remove the mainshaft, side gear, drive sprocket and spline gear as an assembly. Place the assembly on a clean shop towel and set it aside until the front case disassembly is completed.

13. Remove the mode fork, shift rail and mode sliding clutch sleeve as an assembly. Mark the sleeve and fork for easy assembly reference and remove the sleeve from the fork.

NOTE: The mode fork and rail are pinned together so that they will operate as a unit. Remove the pin to separate the two components if necessary.

14. Remove the locking fork, high range sliding clutch sleeve, fork brackets and fork spring as an assembly. Be sure to take note of the position of these components for an easy assembly reference.

15. Remove the range sector detent screw and remove the detent spring, plunger and ball. Move the range operating lever downward to the last detent position and disengage the low range fork lug from the range sector slot.

16. Remove the retaining snapring from the annulus gear and remove the thrust washer. Remove the annulus gear, range fork and rail as an assembly and separate the components for cleaning and inspection.

17. Remove the planetary thrust washer from the planetary assembly hub. Remove the planetary assembly, by grasping the planetary hub and lifting the assembly upward.

18. Remove the mainshaft thrust bearing from the input shaft. Remove the input shaft, input shaft thrust bearing and race.

19. Remove the range sector and operating lever attaching nut and lock washer. Remove the lever.

20. Remove the range sector and shaft from the front case and remove the range sector O-ring and retainer.

MAINSHAFT DISASSEMBLY

1. Grasp the drive sprocket and lift the sprocket clutch gear and side gear upward and off the mainshaft.

2. Remove the mainshaft needle bearings and two bearing spacers from the mainshaft; a total of 82 bearings are used; note the spacer position for assembly reference.

3. Remove the spline gear and thrust washer from the mainshaft.

4. Remove the side gear, clutch gear, and clutch gear thrust

DRIVE TRAIN 7

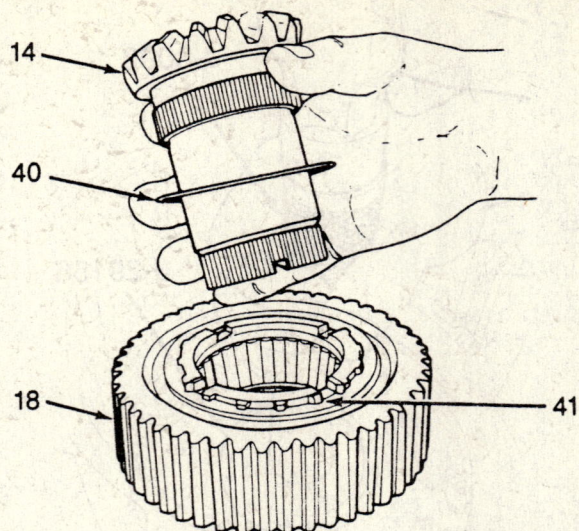

Removing the side gear (14) and thrust washer (40) from the sprocket carrier (41) and drive sprocket (18) on the NP-228

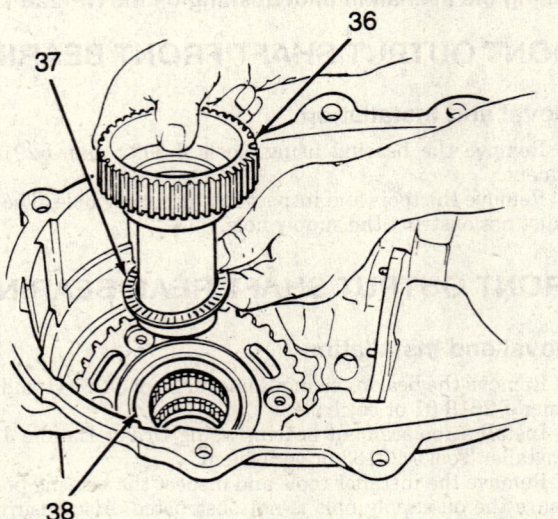

Removing the input shaft (36), input shaft thrust bearing (37) and race (38) from the NP-228

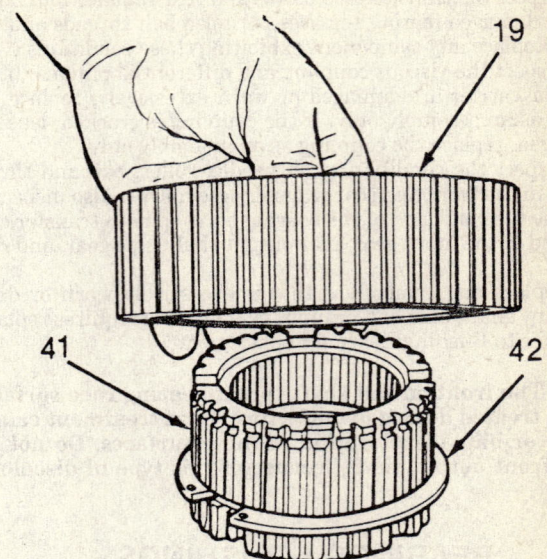

Removing the snapring (42) and drive sprocket (19) from the carrier (41) on the NP-228

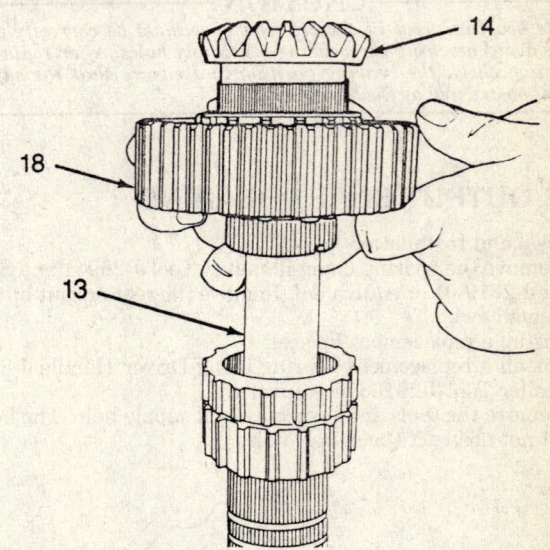

Removing the drive sprocket and side gear from the mainshaft on the NP-228

washer from the sprocket carrier and sprocket.

5. Remove the clutch gear and thrust washer from the side gear.

6. Remove one sprocket carrier snapring and remove the drive sprocket from the carrier; mark for assembly reference.

— **CAUTION** —
The sprocket carrier and mainshaft needle bearings are different in size. Take care to avoid intermixing them.

7. Remove the three bearing spacers and all sprocket carrier needle bearings from the carrier; a total of 120 needle bearings are used.

8. Remove the rear output bearing and rear yoke seal from the rear retainer; the bearing is shielded on one side; note the bearing position for assembly reference.

9. Remove the input gear and front yoke seals from the front case; use a small prybar to pry the seals out of the case.

CLEANING & INSPECTION

1. Wash all components thoroughly in clean solvent. Ensure that all lubricant, metallic particles, dirt, and foreign material are removed from the surfaces of every component.

2. Apply compressed air to each oil supply port and channel in each transfer case half to remove any obstructions or cleaning solvent residue.

3. Inspect all gear teeth for excessive wear or damage. Inspect all gear splines for burrs, nicks, wear or damage.

4. Remove minor nicks or scratches using an oilstone. Replace any component exhibiting excessive wear or damage.

5. Inspect all snaprings and thrust washers for excessive wear, distortion and damage. Replace any component exhibiting these conditions.

7-121

7 DRIVE TRAIN

6. Inspect the transfer case halves and rear retainer for cracks, porosity, damaged mating surfaces, stripped bolt threads and distortion. Replace any component exhibiting these conditions.

7. Inspect the viscous coupling and differential pinions. If the pinions or carrier are damaged or worn excessively, replace the coupling as an assembly only. If the coupling is cracked, leaking, or damaged, replace the coupling as an assembly only.

8. Inspect the condition of all needle, roller, ball and thrust bearings in the front and rear transfer case halves. Also inspect to determine the condition of the bearing bores in both transfer case halves and in the input gear, rear output shaft, side gear, and rear retainer.

9. Replace any component that is excessively worn or damaged. If any shaft, case half or input gear bearing requires replacement, refer to Bushing/Bearing Replacement.

NOTE: The front output shaft thrust bearing race surfaces are heat treated during manufacture. Heat treatment causes a brown or blue discoloration of these surfaces. Do not replace a front output shaft because of this type of discoloration.

BEARINGS & BUSHINGS

---CAUTION---

All of the bearings used in the transfer case must be correctly positioned to avoid blocking the bearing oil supply holes. After replacing any bearing, check the bearing position and ensure that the supply hole is not obstructed by the bearing.

REAR OUTPUT SHAFT BEARING

Removal and Installation

1. Remove the bearing using Remover Tool J-26941 and Slide Hammer J-2619-01 or equivalent. Remove the rear output lip seal using a small awl.
2. Install a replacement lip seal.
3. Install a replacement bearing using Driver Handle J-8092 and Installer Tool J-29166 or equivalent.
4. Remove the tools and inspect the oil supply hole. The bearing must not obstruct the supply hole.

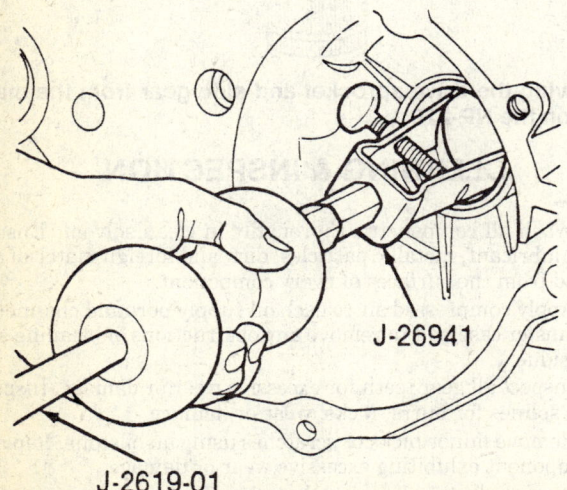
Removing the rear output shaft bearing from the NP-228

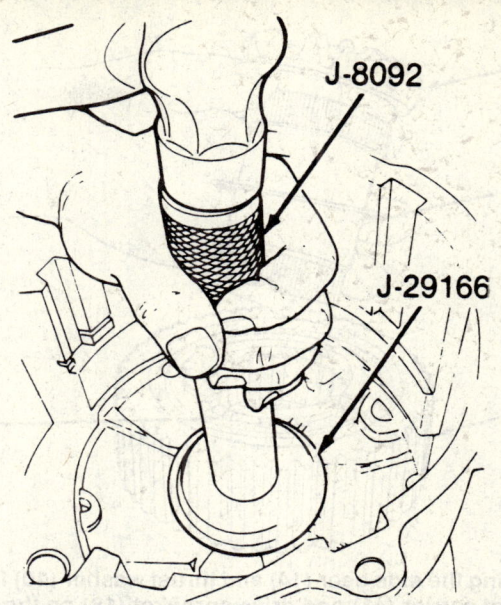
Installing the mainshaft pilot bushing on the NP-228

FRONT OUTPUT SHAFT FRONT BEARING

Removal and Installation

1. Remove the bearing using Tools J-8092 and J-29168 or equivalent.
2. Remove the tools and inspect the oil supply hole. The bearing must not obstruct the supply hole.

FRONT OUTPUT SHAFT REAR BEARING

Removal and Installation

1. Remove the bearing using Remover Tool J-26941 and Slide Hammer J-2619-01 or equivalent.
2. Install a replacement bearing using Driver Handle J-8092 and Installer Tool J-29163 or equivalent.
3. Remove the installer tools and inspect the bearing position to ensure the oil supply hole is not obstructed. Also ensure that

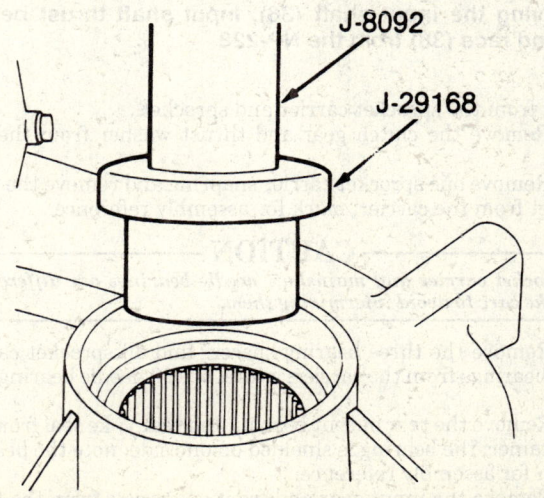
Removing the front output shaft front bearing on the NP-228

DRIVE TRAIN 7

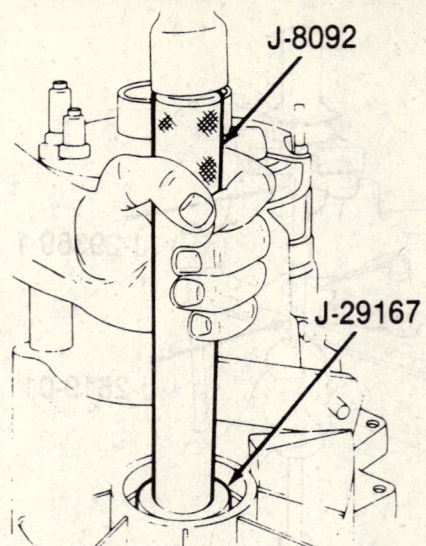
Installing the front output shaft front bearing on the NP-228

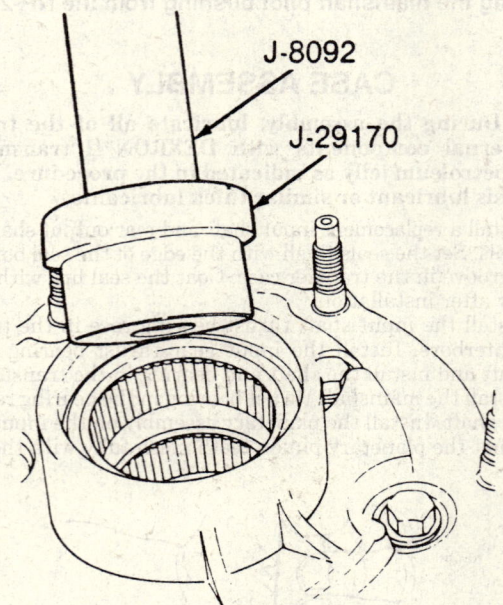
Removing the input gear front and rear bearings on the NP-228

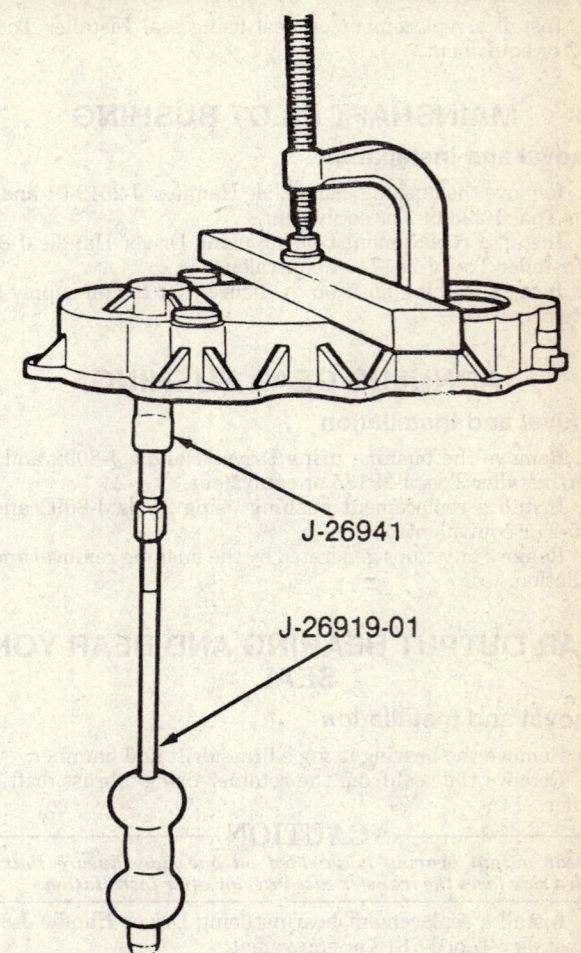
Removing the front output shaft rear bearing on the NP-228

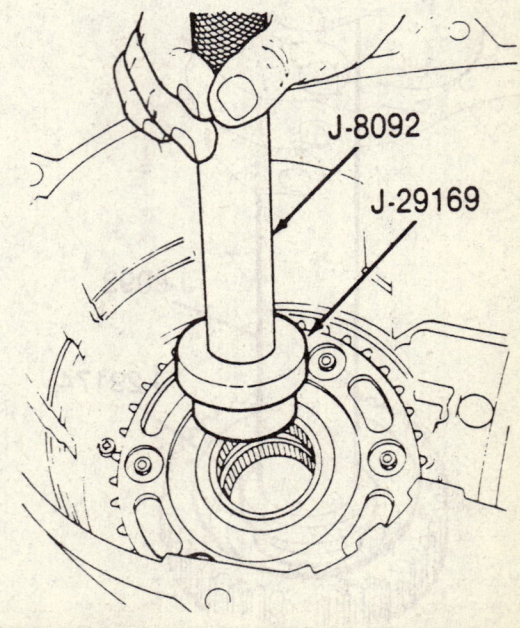
Installing the input gear front and rear bearings on the NP-228

the bearing is seated flush with the edge of the bore in the case to allow clearance for the thrust bearing assembly.

INPUT GEAR FRONT & REAR BEARINGS

Removal and Installation

1. Remove both bearings simultaneously using Driver Handle J-8092 and Remover Tool J-29170 or equivalent.
2. Install the new bearings one at a time. Install the rear bearing first; then install the front bearing. Use Driver Handle J-8092 and Installer Tool J-29169 or equivalent.
3. Remove the installer tools and inspect the bearing position to ensure the oil supply holes are not obstructed. Also ensure that the bearings are flush with the transfer case bore surfaces.

7-123

7 DRIVE TRAIN

4. Install a replacement oil seal using seal Installer Tool J-29162 or equivalent.

MAINSHAFT PILOT BUSHING

Removal and Installation

1. Remove the bushing using Slide Hammer J-2619-01 and Remover Tool J-29369-1 or equivalent.
2. Install a replacement bearing using Driver Handle J-8092 and Installer Tool J-29174 or equivalent.
3. Inspect bushing position to ensure that the oil supply hole is not obstructed.

ANNULUS GEAR BUSHING

Removal and Installation

1. Remove the bushing using Driver Handle J-8092 and Remover/Installer Tool J-29185 or equivalent.
2. Install a replacement bushing using Tools J-8092 and J-29185-2 or equivalent.
3. Remove any chips generated by the bushing removal and/or installation.

REAR OUTPUT BEARING AND REAR YOKE SEAL

Removal and Installation

1. Remove the bearing using a brass drift and hammer.
2. Remove the seal from the retainer using a brass drift and hammer.

---- CAUTION ----
The rear output bearing is shielded on one side. Ensure that the shielded side faces the transfer case interior after installation.

3. Install a replacement bearing using Driver Handle J-8092 and Installer Tool J-7818 or equivalent.
4. Install a replacement seal in the retainer using Tool J-29162 or equivalent.

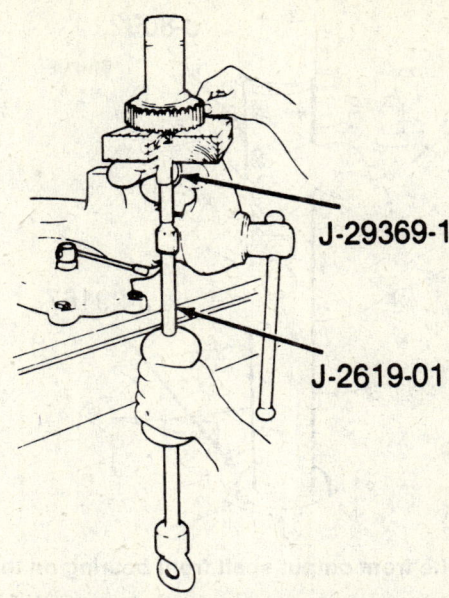
Removing the mainshaft pilot bushing from the NP-228

CASE ASSEMBLY

NOTE: During the assembly, lubricate all of the transfer case internal components with DEXRON®II transmission fluid or petroleum jelly as indicated in the procedure. Do not use chassis lubricant or similar thick lubricants.

1. Install a replacement input shaft and rear output shaft bearing oil seals. Set the seals flush with the edge of the seal bore or in the seal groove in the transfer case. Coat the seal lips with petroleum jelly after installation.
2. Install the input shaft thrust bearing race in the transfer case counterbore. Install the input gear thrust bearing on the input shaft and install the shaft and bearing in the transfer case.
3. Install the mainshaft thrust bearing in the bearing recess in the input shaft. Install the planetary assembly on the input shaft. Ensure that the planetary pinion teeth mesh fully with the input shaft.

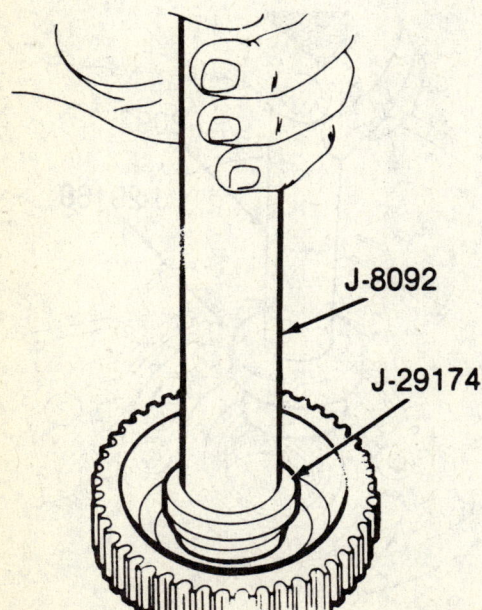
Installing the mainshaft pilot bushing from the NP-228

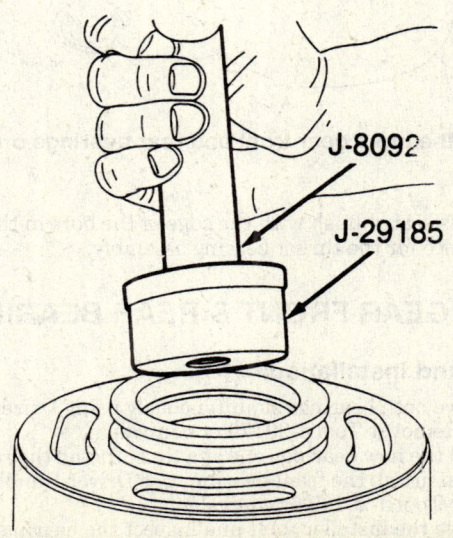
Removing the annulus gear bushing from the NP-228

DRIVE TRAIN 7

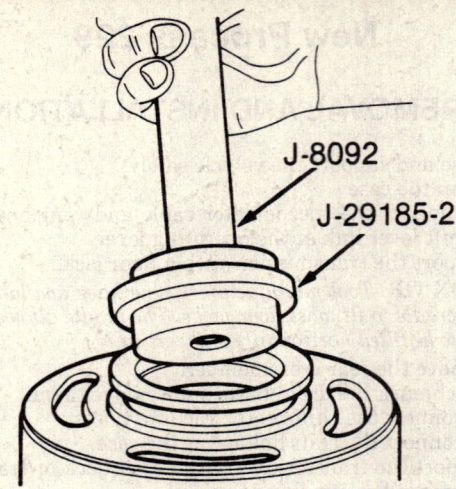

Installing the annulus gear bushing from the NP-228

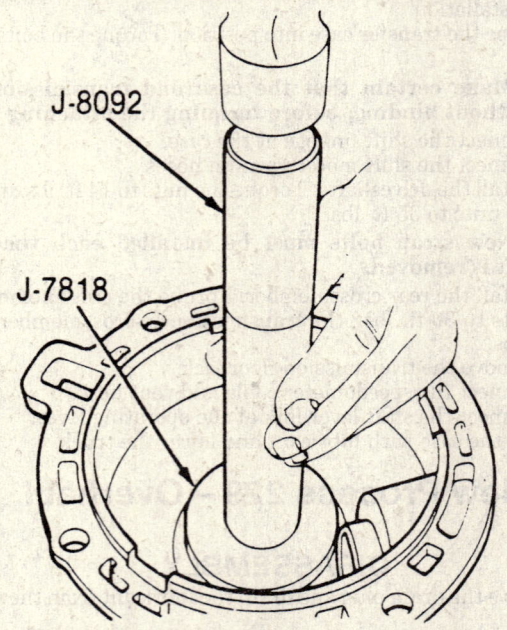

Rear output bearing installation on the NP-228

NOTE: The locking mode clutch sleeve and the high range clutch sleeve are not interchangeable. The sleeve splines are different. So be sure that the correct sleeve is installed in the proper shift fork. Also, the sleeves must be replaced as a set.

9. Assemble and install the locking fork, fork bracket, fork springs and high range clutch sleeves. Be sure that the lug on the fork is seated in the range sector detent slot.

10. Install the range fork lug in the range sector detent notch. Move the range sector to the high range position. Assemble and install the range fork, shift rail and mode clutch sleeve.

NOTE: Steps 11–16 are to be used if the mainshaft was disassembled, when the transfer case was disassembled.

11. Install the thrust washer and a replacement O-ring on the mainshaft. Install the needle bearings and bearing spacers on the mainshaft. Coat the shaft bearing surface and all needle bearings with petroleum jelly.

12. Install the first 41 needle bearings and install the long bearing spacer, the remaining 41 needle bearings and the remaining short spacer. Be careful to avoid displacing the bearing when the spacers are installed. Apply additional petroleum jelly to hold the bearing in place if necessary.

13. Install the spline gear on the mainshaft, be careful not to displace the bearing while installing the gear. Install the sprocket carrier in the drive sprocket and install the sprocket carrier snaprings. Make sure that the carrier and sprockets are aligned according to the reference marks made during disassembly.

NOTE: The sprocket carrier teeth are tapered on one side and the drive sprocket has a deep recess on one side. Be sure that these components are assembles so that the carrier tapered teeth and sprocket recess are on the same side.

14. Install the sprocket carrier bearings and spacers. Coat the carrier bore and all the 120 carrier needle bearings with petroleum jelly. Install the center spacer.

15. Install the 60 needle bearings in each end of the carrier and install the remaining two spacers, one at each side of the carrier. Apply additional petroleum jelly to hold the bearings in place if necessary.

16. Install the assembled sprocket carrier and drive sprocket on the mainshaft. Do not displace the mainshaft bearing during installation. Be sure that the recessed side of the drive sprocket is facing downward.

17. Install the trust washer in the mainshaft, position the washer on the sprocket carrier. Install the side gear on the mainshaft and be sure that the side gear is fully seated in the sprocket carrier. Be careful not to displace any of the carrier or mainshaft needle bearings.

18. Install the mainshaft and gear assembly in the case, making sure that the mainshaft is fully seated in the input gear. Install the driven sprocket on the front output shaft and install the sprocket retaining snapring. Be sure that the sprocket is installed according to the reference marks made during disassembly.

19. Install the front output shaft front thrust bearing assembly in the transfer case front half. Install the thick race in the transfer case and then install the bearing and the thin race.

20. Install the drive chain, front output shaft and driven sprocket. Install the chain on the driven sprocket. Raise and tilt the driven sprocket and chain and install the opposite end of the chain on the drive sprocket.

21. Align the front output shaft with the shaft bore in the transfer case front half and install the shaft in the transfer case. Be sure that the front shaft thrust bearing assembly is seated in the transfer case.

22. Install the front output shaft rear thrust bearing assembly on the front output shaft. Install the tin race first, then install the bearing and the thick race. Install the differential on the side gear, making sure that the differential is fully seated.

23. Coat the mainshaft pilot bearing surface and all 15 needle bearings with petroleum jelly and install the bearing on the shaft.

4. Install the planetary thrust washer on the planetary hub. Install a replacement sector shaft O-ring and install the retainer in the shaft bore in the transfer case.

5. Install the O-ring on the mode sector shaft and insert the mode sector through the range sector. Install the range sector in the front of transfer case half. Install the operating lever and the snapring on the range sector shaft.

6. Install the lever, attaching washer and lock nut on the mode sector shaft. Torque the lock nut to 17 ft. lbs. Assemble the annulus gear, range fork and rail. Install the assembled fork on and over the planetary assembly.

7. Be sure that the annulus gear is fully meshed with the planetary pinions. Engage the range sector lug into the range sector.

8. Install the annulus thrust washer and the annulus retaining ring onto the annulus gear hub. Install the detent ball, plunger, spring and retaining screw in the front transfer case half detent bore. Torque the retaining screw to 22 ft. lbs.

7 DRIVE TRAIN

Apply additional petroleum jelly to hold the bearings in place if necessary.

24. Install the rear output shaft on the mainshaft and into the differential, making sure that the shaft is completely seated. If necessary tap the shaft with a plastic mallet or equivalent to seat the shaft. Do not displace the pilot bearing during shaft installation.

25. Install the oil pump and the rear output shaft. Install the oil pump with the recessed side facing down. Install a replacement rear output shaft bearing seal in the rear transfer case half.

26. Apply a bead of Loctite®515 sealant or equivalent, to the mating surface of the rear transfer case half. Install the magnet in the case and attach the rear transfer case half to the front transfer case half. Be sure that the alignment dowels at the front case half ends are aligned with the bolt holes in the rear case half and mate the rear case half with the front case half.

NOTE: If the rear transfer case half will not mate completely with the front case. Inspect the following; oil in the range fork rail bore, the front output shaft rear thrust bearing assembly is not aligned with the rear case half, the mainshaft is not completely seated or the rear case half is not aligned with the oil pump.

27. Install the rear case half to the front case half bolts. Torque the bolts to 23 ft. lbs. Be sure that the flat washers are used on the bolts at the case end where the alignment dowels are located. Install the speedometer drive gear on the rear output shaft.

28. Measure the thickness of the shim pack and record. Install a 0.76mm (0.030 in.) shim on the rear output shaft. Align the rear retainer on the rear transfer case half and install the retainer. Install the retainer bolts and tighten them securely, do not torque to specifications.

29. Install the front and rear output shaft yokes and the original yoke nuts. Tighten the yoke nuts finger tight and check the differential end play.

30. Set the shift lever in the 4-high range position. Place a dial indicator on the rear retainer and position the indicator stylus so that it contacts the rear yoke nut.

31. Pull upward on the rear output yoke, note the dial indicator pointer position and record it. Remove the retainer and add or subtract differential shims as necessary to correct the end play. The end play should be between 0.05–0.25mm. The recommended end play is 0.15mm.

32. After adjusting the end play, remove the front and rear yokes. Discard the original yoke nuts. Apply a bead of Loctite®515 sealant or equivalent, to the retainer mating surface and install the retainer. Apply the sealer to the retaining bolts and install the bolts. Torque the bolts to 23 ft. lbs.

33. Position the front and rear yokes and install the replacement yoke seal washers and nuts. Using tool # J-8614-01 or equivalent hold the yokes in place and torque the yoke nuts to 120 ft. lbs.

34. Install the detent ball, spring and bolt if these were not installed previously. Apply sealer to the bolt before installing it and torque the bolt to 23 ft. lbs.

35. Install the drain plug and washer. Fill the transfer case with 7 pints of DEXRON®II transmission fluid or equivalent. Install the fill plug and washer and torque the drain and fill plugs to 18 ft. lbs.

36. Install the plug and washer in the front transfer case half (if removed) and torque the plug to 18 ft. lbs. Install the transfer case into the vehicle as described in this section. Road test the vehicle to check for proper operation of the transfer case, stop the engine and check for leaks.

New Process 229

REMOVAL AND INSTALLATION

1. Raise and support the vehicle safely.
2. Drain the case.
3. Disconnect the speedometer cable and vent hose. Disconnect the shift lever link at the operating lever.
4. Support the transmission with a floor jack.

CHILTON TIP: *Tool manufacturers now have available a transmission cradle to fit most floor jacks. The cradle allows the transmission to be tilted horizontally and vertically.*

5. Remove the rear crossmember.
6. Matchmark the driveshafts and remove them.
7. Disconnect the shift motor vacuum hoses.
8. Disconnect the shift linkage at the case.
9. Support the transfer case with a floor jack or transmission jack and remove the attaching bolts.
10. Pull the case rearward and remove it.
11. Clean the gasket mating surfaces and use new gasket material for installation.
12. Raise the transfer case into position. Torque the bolts to 26 ft. lbs.

NOTE: Make certain that the case and transmission are mated without binding, before torquing the attaching bolts.

13. Connect the shift linkage at the case.
14. Connect the shift motor vacuum hoses.
15. Install the driveshafts. Torque the nuts to 14 ft. lbs.; torque the flange nuts to 35 ft. lbs.

NOTE: New strap bolts must be installed each time the driveshaft is removed.

16. Install the rear crossmember. Torque the crossmember-to-frame bolts to 30 ft. lbs.; the transmission-to-crossmember bolts to 33 ft. lbs.
17. Remove the transmission floor jack.
18. Connect the speedometer cable and vent hose.
19. Connect the shift lever link at the operating lever.
20. Fill the case with lubricant and lower the truck.

New Process 229—Overhaul

DISASSEMBLY

1. Remove the drain plug and drain the lubricant from the transfer case.
2. Remove the front and rear yoke nuts and seal washers. Discard the washers.
3. Mark the front and rear yokes for installation alignment reference.
4. Remove the front and rear yokes. Use Tool J-8614-01 or equivalent to remove the yokes if necessary.
5. Place the transfer case on wooden blocks. Cut V-notches in the blocks for clearance for the front case mounting studs.
6. Mark the rear retainer and rear case for assembly reference.
7. Remove the rear retainer bolts and remove the retainer. Use two prybars to pry the retainer off the transfer case. Position the prybars in slots in the retainer and case to pry the retainer loose.
8. Remove the differential shim(s) and speedometer drive gear from the rear output shaft.
9. Remove the bolts attaching the rear transfer case half to

DRIVE TRAIN 7

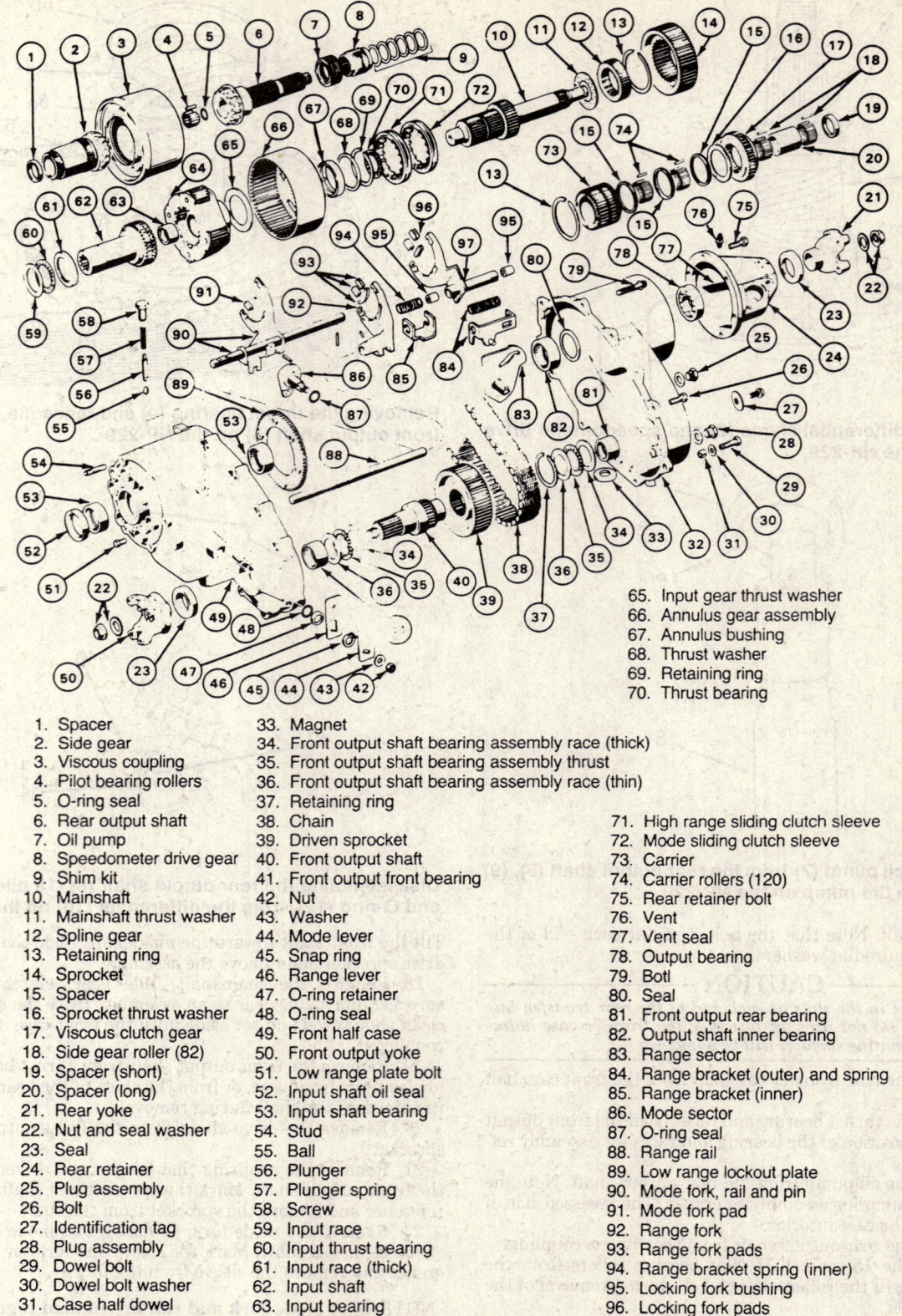

65. Input gear thrust washer
66. Annulus gear assembly
67. Annulus bushing
68. Thrust washer
69. Retaining ring
70. Thrust bearing

1. Spacer
2. Side gear
3. Viscous coupling
4. Pilot bearing rollers
5. O-ring seal
6. Rear output shaft
7. Oil pump
8. Speedometer drive gear
9. Shim kit
10. Mainshaft
11. Mainshaft thrust washer
12. Spline gear
13. Retaining ring
14. Sprocket
15. Spacer
16. Sprocket thrust washer
17. Viscous clutch gear
18. Side gear roller (82)
19. Spacer (short)
20. Spacer (long)
21. Rear yoke
22. Nut and seal washer
23. Seal
24. Rear retainer
25. Plug assembly
26. Bolt
27. Identification tag
28. Plug assembly
29. Dowel bolt
30. Dowel bolt washer
31. Case half dowel
32. Rear half case
33. Magnet
34. Front output shaft bearing assembly race (thick)
35. Front output shaft bearing assembly thrust
36. Front output shaft bearing assembly race (thin)
37. Retaining ring
38. Chain
39. Driven sprocket
40. Front output shaft
41. Front output front bearing
42. Nut
43. Washer
44. Mode lever
45. Snap ring
46. Range lever
47. O-ring retainer
48. O-ring seal
49. Front half case
50. Front output yoke
51. Low range plate bolt
52. Input shaft oil seal
53. Input shaft bearing
54. Stud
55. Ball
56. Plunger
57. Plunger spring
58. Screw
59. Input race
60. Input thrust bearing
61. Input race (thick)
62. Input shaft
63. Input bearing
64. Planetary gear assembly
71. High range sliding clutch sleeve
72. Mode sliding clutch sleeve
73. Carrier
74. Carrier rollers (120)
75. Rear retainer bolt
76. Vent
77. Vent seal
78. Output bearing
79. Botl
80. Seal
81. Front output rear bearing
82. Output shaft inner bearing
83. Range sector
84. Range bracket (outer) and spring
85. Range bracket (inner)
86. Mode sector
87. O-ring seal
88. Range rail
89. Low range lockout plate
90. Mode fork, rail and pin
91. Mode fork pad
92. Range fork
93. Range fork pads
94. Range bracket spring (inner)
95. Locking fork bushing
96. Locking fork pads
97. Locking fork

NP-229 transfer case — exploded view

7 DRIVE TRAIN

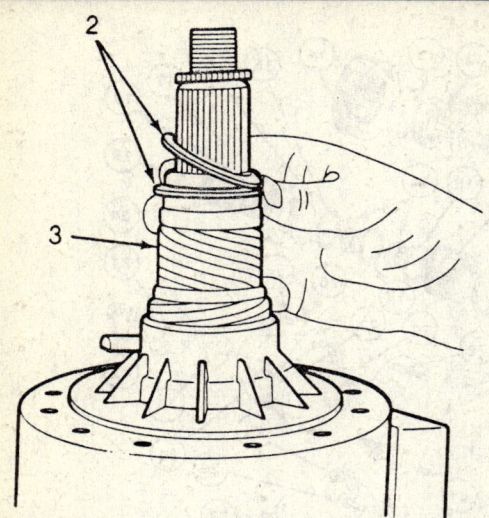

Removing the differential shims (2) and speedometer drive gear (3) from the NP-229

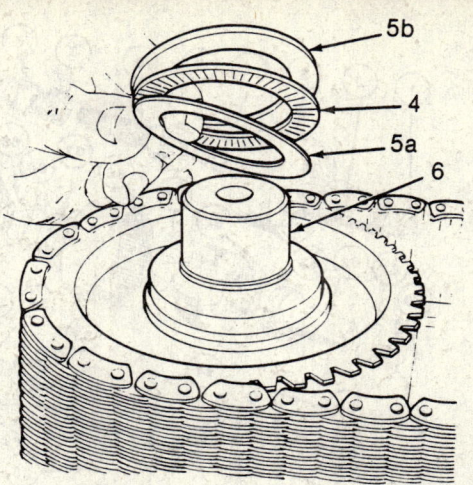

Removing the thrust bearing (4) and races (5a, 5b) from the front output shaft (6) on the NP-229

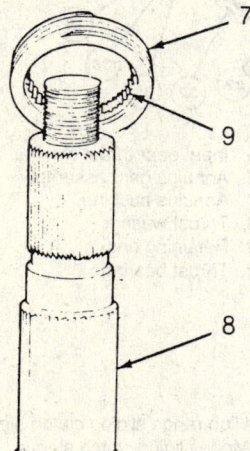

Removing the oil pump (7) from the rear output shaft (8). (9) is the recess in the pump on the NP-229

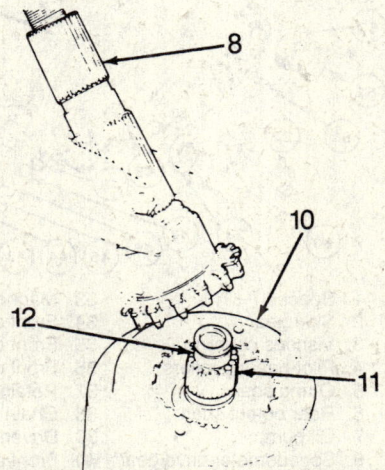

Disassembling the rear output shaft (8), 15 pilot roller (11), and O-ring (12), from the differential (10) on the NP-229

the front case half. Note that the bolts used at each end of the transfer case require flat washers.

── **CAUTION** ──
Insert two prybars in the slots at each end of the rear transfer case half to loosen it. Do not attempt to wedge the transfer case halves apart or the case mating surfaces will be damaged.

10. Remove the rear transfer case half from the front case half using two prybars.
11. Remove the thrust bearing and races from the front output shaft. Note the position of the bearing and races for assembly reference.
12. Remove the oil pump from the rear output shaft. Note the position of the pump for assembly reference. The recessed side of the pump faces the case interior.
13. Remove the rear output shaft from the viscous coupling.
14. Remove the 15 mainshaft pilot bearing rollers from the shaft or coupling (if the rollers dropped off during removal of the rear output shaft).
15. Remove the mainshaft O-ring from the end of the shaft.
16. Remove the viscous coupling from the mainshaft and side gear.
17. Remove the front output shaft, driven sprocket and drive chain assembly. Lift the front shaft, sprocket and chain upward.

Tilt the front shaft toward the mainshaft. Slide the chain off the drive sprocket and remove the assembly.
18. Remove the mainshaft, side gear, clutch gear, drive sprocket and spline gear as an assembly. Place the assembly on a clean shop towel and set aside until the front case disassembly is completed.
19. Remove the front output shaft front thrust bearing assembly from the front case, or from the shaft (if the bearing and races remained on the shaft during removal).
20. Remove the drive chain from the front output shaft and sprocket.
21. Remove the snapring that retains the driven sprocket on the front output shaft. Mark the sprocket and shaft for assembly reference and remove the sprocket from the shaft.
22. Remove the mode fork, shift rail, and mode sliding clutch sleeve as an assembly. Mark the sleeve and fork for assembly reference and remove the sleeve from the fork.

NOTE: The mode fork and rail are pinned together so that they will operate as a unit. Remove the pin to separate the two components if necessary.

23. Remove the locking fork, high range sliding clutch sleeve, fork brackets and fork springs as an assembly. Note the position

DRIVE TRAIN 7

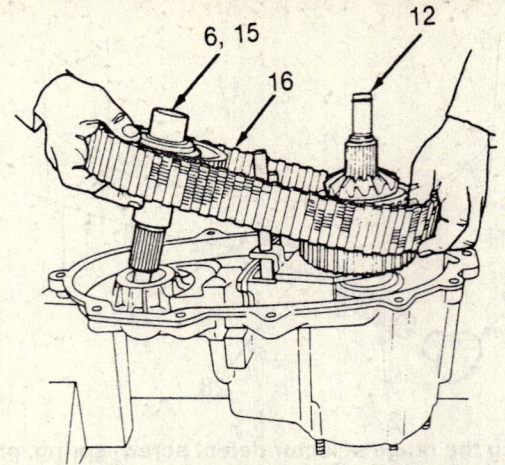

Removing the front output shaft (6), driven sprocket (15) and drive chain (16) from the mainshaft (12) on the NP-229

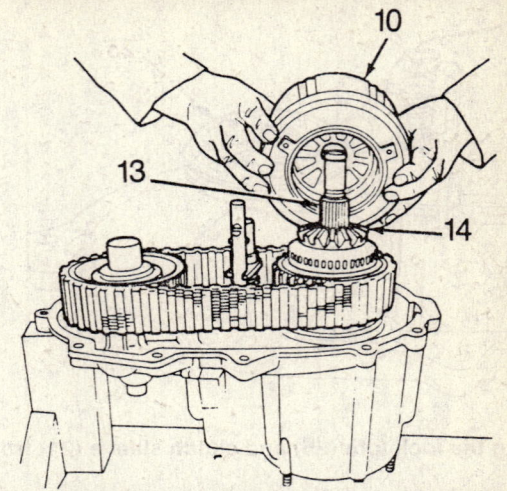

Removing the differential (10) from the mainshaft (13) and side gear (14) on the NP-229

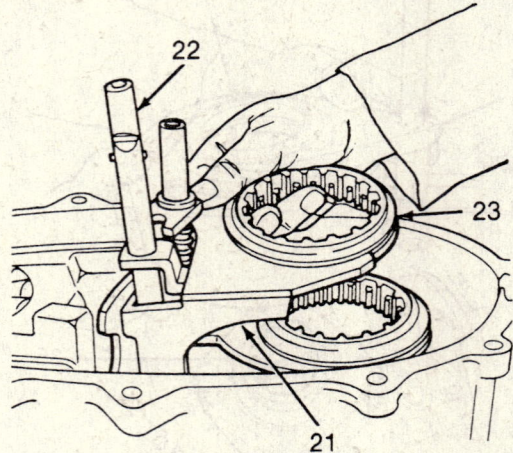

Removing the mode fork (21), shift rail (22) and mode sliding clutch sleeve (23) from the NP-229

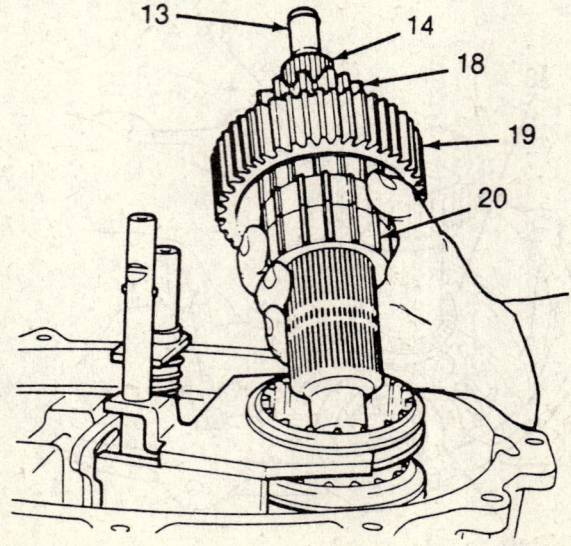

Removing the mainshaft (13), side gear (14), drive sprocket (18) and spline gear (19) from the NP-229

of the components for assembly reference and disassemble the components for cleaning and inspection.

24. Remove the range sector detent screw and remove the detent spring, plunger and ball.
25. Move the range operating lever downward to the last detent position.
26. Disengage the low range fork lug from the range sector slot.
27. Remove the retaining snapring from the annulus gear and remove the thrust washer.
28. Remove the annulus gear, range fork and rail as an assembly. Separate the components for cleaning and inspection.
29. Remove the planetary thrust washer from the planetary assembly hub.
30. Remove the planetary assembly. Grasp the planetary hub and lift the assembly upward to remove it.
31. Remove the mainshaft thrust bearing from the input shaft.
32. Remove the input shaft and remove the input shaft thrust bearing and race.
33. Remove the range sector and operating lever attaching nut and lock washer. Remove the lever.
34. Remove the range sector and shaft from the front case.
35. Remove the range sector O-ring and retainer.

MAINSHAFT DISASSEMBLY

1. Grasp the drive sprocket and lift the sprocket clutch gear and side gear upward and off the mainshaft.
2. Remove the mainshaft needle bearings and two bearing spacers from the mainshaft; a total of 82 bearings are used; note the spacer position for assembly reference.
3. Remove the spline gear and thrust washer from the mainshaft.
4. Remove the side gear, clutch gear, and clutch gear thrust washer from the sprocket carrier and sprocket.
5. Remove the clutch gear and thrust washer from the side gear.
6. Remove one sprocket carrier snapring and remove the drive sprocket from the carrier; mark for assembly reference.

―――― **CAUTION** ――――
The sprocket carrier and mainshaft needle bearings are different in size. Take care to avoid intermixing them.

7. Remove the three bearing spacers and all sprocket carrier needle bearings from the carrier; a total of 120 needle bearings are used.

7-129

7 DRIVE TRAIN

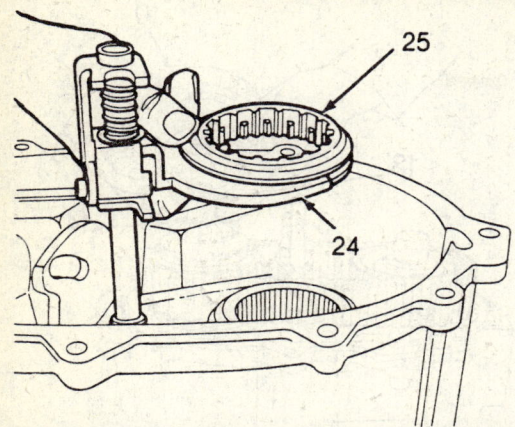

Removing the lock fork (25) and clutch sleeve (24) from the NP-229

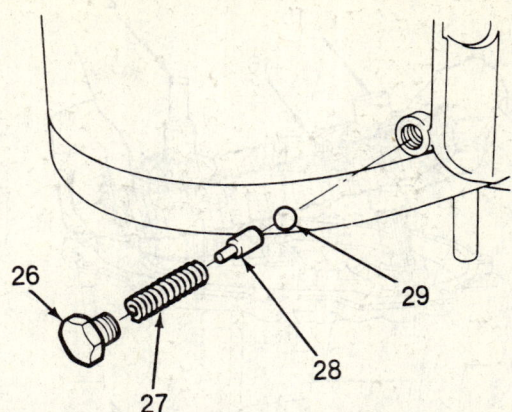

Removing the range selector detent screw, spring, plunger and ball from the NP-229

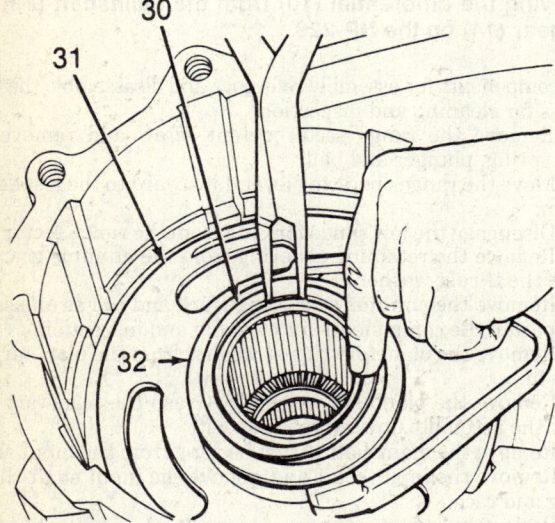

Removing the snapring (30), annulus gear (31) and thrust washer (32) from the NP-229

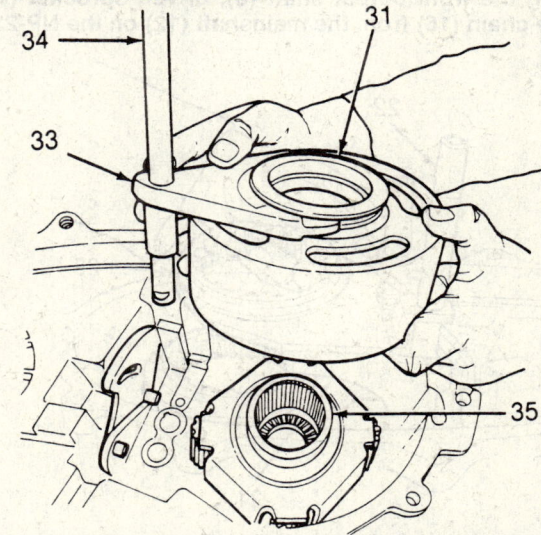

Removing the annulus gear (31), range fork (33) and rail (34) from the NP-229

8. Remove the rear output bearing and rear yoke seal from the rear retainer; the bearing is shielded on one side; note the bearing position for assembly reference.

9. Remove the input gear and front yoke seals from the front case; use a small prybar to pry the seals out of the case.

CLEANING & INSPECTION

1. Wash all components thoroughly in clean solvent. Ensure that all lubricant, metallic particles, dirt, and foreign material are removed from the surfaces of every component.

2. Apply compressed air to each oil supply port and channel in each transfer case half to remove any obstructions or cleaning solvent residue.

3. Inspect all gear teeth for excessive wear or damage. Inspect all gear splines for burrs, nicks, wear or damage.

4. Remove minor nicks or scratches using an oilstone. Replace any component exhibiting excessive wear or damage.

5. Inspect all snaprings and thrust washers for excessive wear, distortion and damage. Replace any component exhibiting these conditions.

6. Inspect the transfer case halves and rear retainer for cracks,

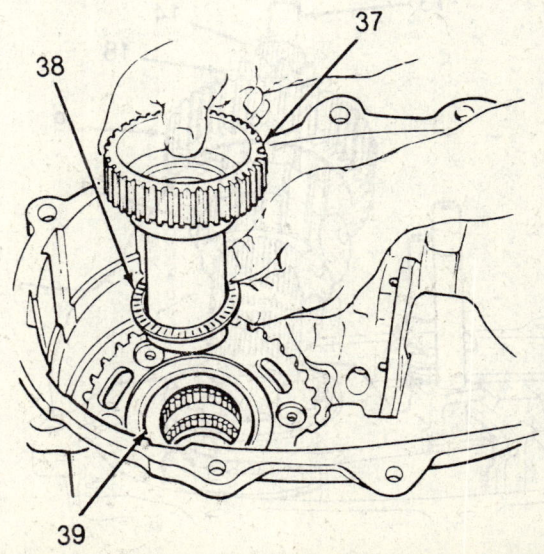

Removing the input shaft (37), input shaft thrust bearing (38) and race (39) from the NP-229

DRIVE TRAIN 7

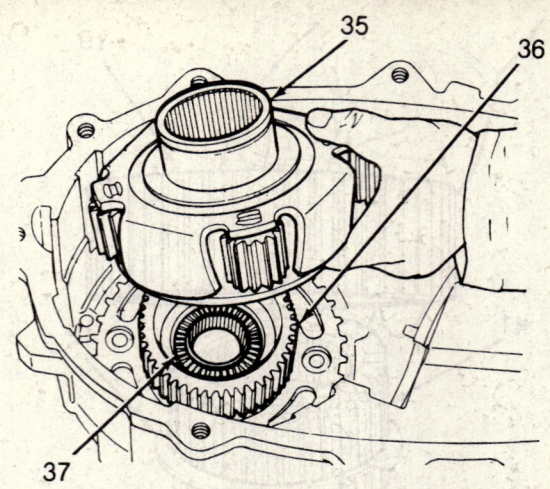

Removing the planetary assembly (35) and the mainshaft thrust bearing (36) from the input shaft on the NP-229

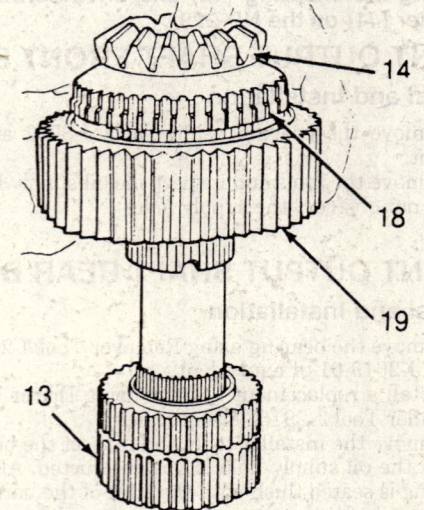

Removing the drive sprocket and side gear from the mainshaft on the NP-229

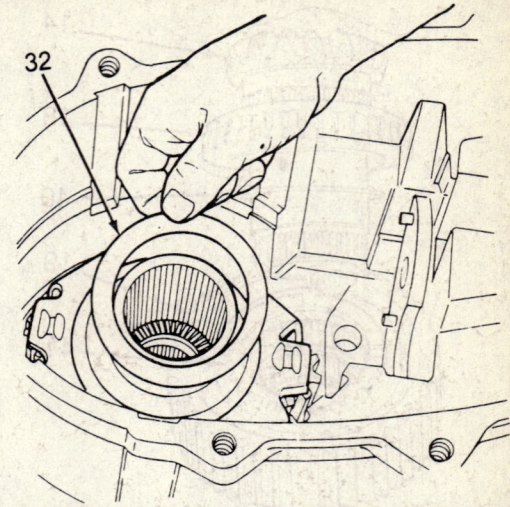

Removing the planetary thrust washer (32) from the NP-229

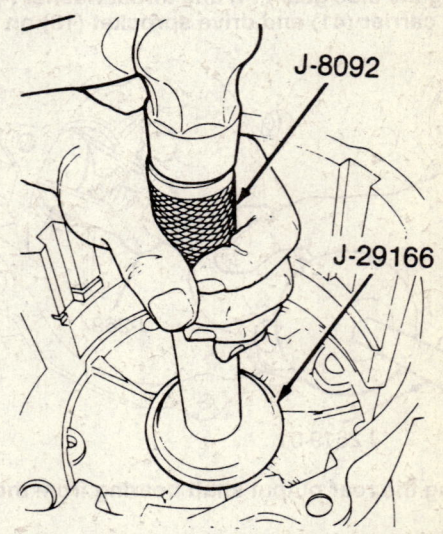

Installing the rear output shaft bearing on the NP-229

porosity, damaged mating surfaces, stripped bolt threads and distortion. Replace any component exhibiting these conditions.

7. Inspect the viscous coupling and differential pinions. If the pinions or carrier are damaged or worn excessively, replace the coupling as an assembly only. If the coupling is cracked, leaking, or damaged, replace the coupling as an assembly only.

8. Inspect the condition of all needle, roller, ball and thrust bearings in the front and rear transfer case halves. Also inspect to determine the condition of the bearing bores in both transfer case halves and in the input gear, rear output shaft, side gear, and rear retainer.

9. Replace any component that is excessively worn or damaged. If any shaft, case half or input gear bearing requires replacement, refer to Bushing/Bearing Replacement.

NOTE: The front output shaft thrust bearing race surfaces are heat treated during manufacture. Heat treatment causes a brown or blue discoloration of these surfaces. Do not replace a front output shaft because of this type of discoloration.

BEARINGS & BUSHINGS

--- CAUTION ---

All of the bearings used in the transfer case must be correctly positioned to avoid blocking the bearing oil supply holes. After replacing any bearing, check the bearing position and ensure that the supply hole is not obstructed by the bearing.

REAR OUTPUT SHAFT BEARING

Removal and Installation

1. Remove the bearing using Remover Tool J-26941 and Slide Hammer J-2619-01 or equivalent. Remove the rear output lip seal using a small awl.
2. Install a replacement lip seal.
3. Install a replacement bearing using Driver Handle J-8092 and Installer Tool J-29166 or equivalent.
4. Remove the tools and inspect the oil supply hole. The bearing must not obstruct the supply hole.

7-131

7 DRIVE TRAIN

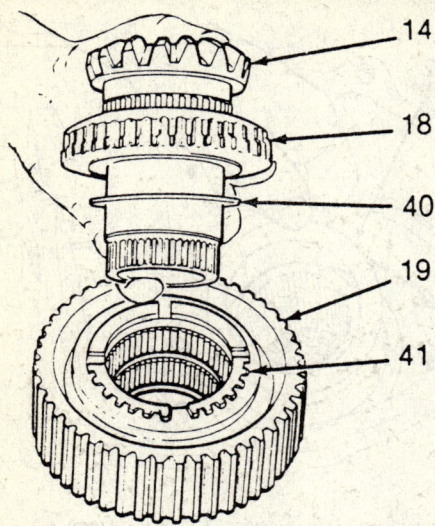

Removing the side gear (14) and thrust washer (40) from the sprocket carrier (41) and drive sprocket (18) on the NP-229

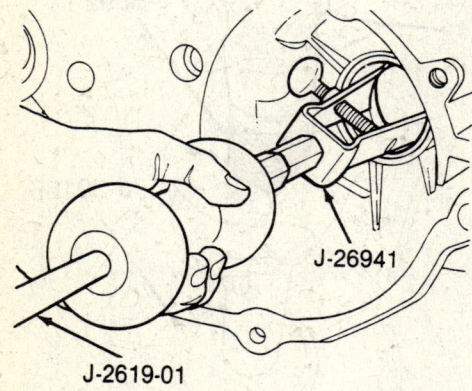

Removing the rear output shaft bearing from the NP-229

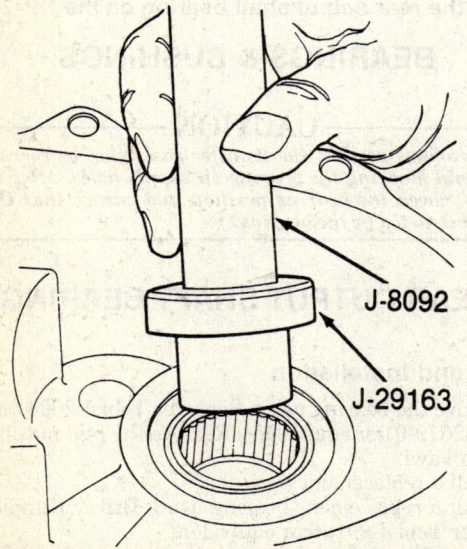

Installing the front output shaft rear bearing on the NP-229

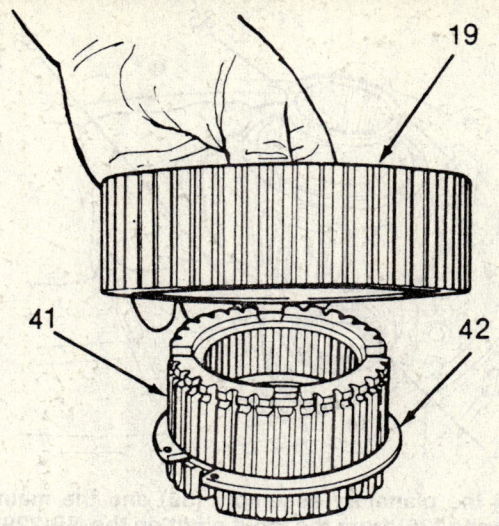

Removing the snapring (42) and drive sprocket (19) from the carrier (41) on the NP-229

FRONT OUTPUT SHAFT FRONT BEARING
Removal and Installation

1. Remove the bearing using Tools J-8092 and J-29168 or equivalent.
2. Remove the tools and inspect the oil supply hole. The bearing must not obstruct the supply hole.

FRONT OUTPUT SHAFT REAR BEARING
Removal and Installation

1. Remove the bearing using Remover Tool J-26941 and Slide Hammer J-2619-01 or equivalent.
2. Install a replacement bearing using Driver Handle J-8092 and Installer Tool J-29163 or equivalent.
3. Remove the installer tools and inspect the bearing position to ensure the oil supply hole is not obstructed. Also ensure that the bearing is seated flush with the edge of the bore in the case to allow clearance for the thrust bearing assembly.

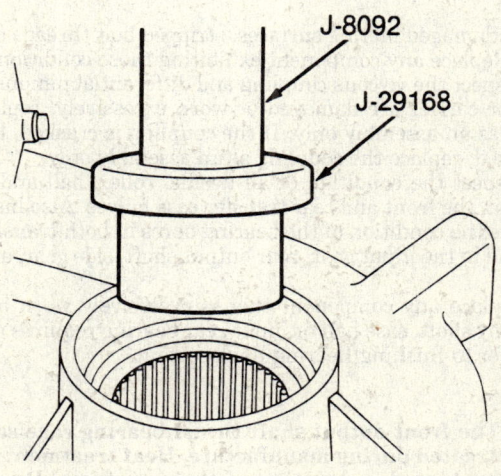

Removing the front output shaft front bearing on the NP-229

DRIVE TRAIN 7

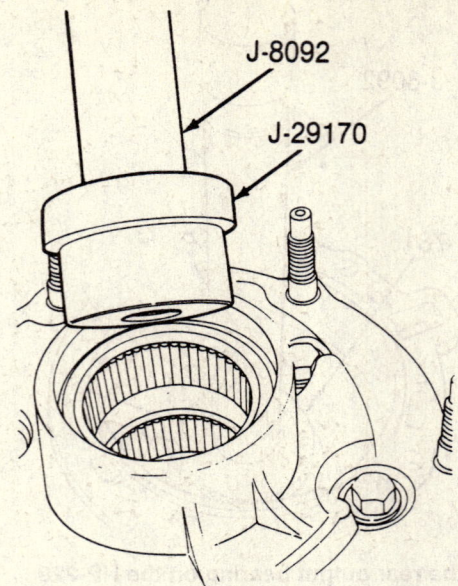

Removing the input gear front and rear bearings from the NP-229

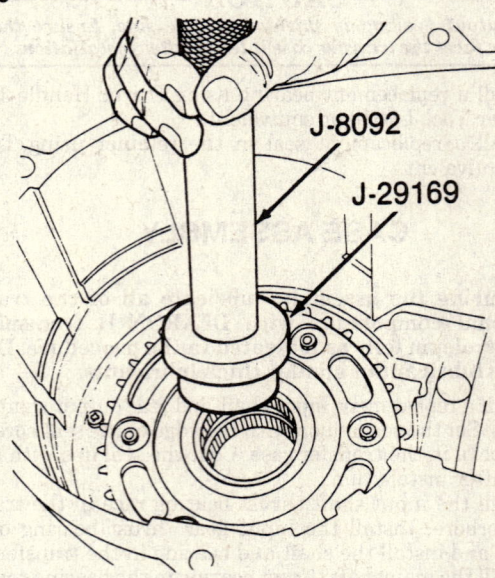

Installing the input gear front and rear bearings from the NP-229

INPUT GEAR FRONT & REAR BEARINGS

Removal and Installation

1. Remove both bearings simultaneously using Driver Handle J-8092 and Remover Tool J-29170 or equivalent.
2. Install the new bearings one at a time. Install the rear bearing first; then install the front bearing. Use Driver Handle J-8092 and Installer Tool J-29169 or equivalent.
3. Remove the installer tools and inspect the bearing position to ensure the oil supply holes are not obstructed. Also ensure that the bearings are flush with the transfer case bore surfaces.

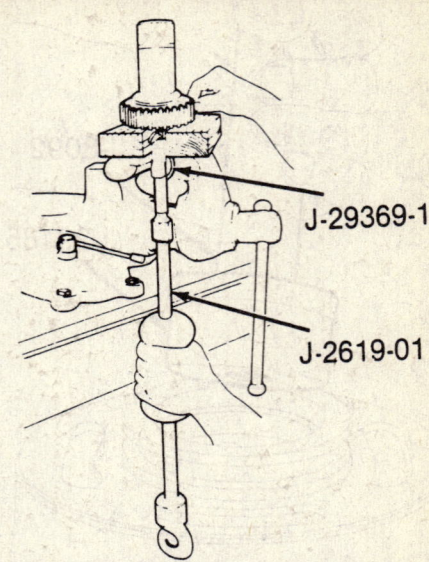

Removing the mainshaft pilot bushing from the NP-229

4. Install a replacement oil seal using seal Installer Tool J-29162 or equivalent.

MAINSHAFT PILOT BUSHING

Removal and Installation

1. Remove the bushing using Slide Hammer J-2619-01 and Remover Tool J-29369-1 or equivalent.
2. Install a replacement bearing using Driver Handle J-8092 and Installer Tool J-29174 or equivalent.
3. Inspect bushing position to ensure that the oil supply hole is not obstructed.

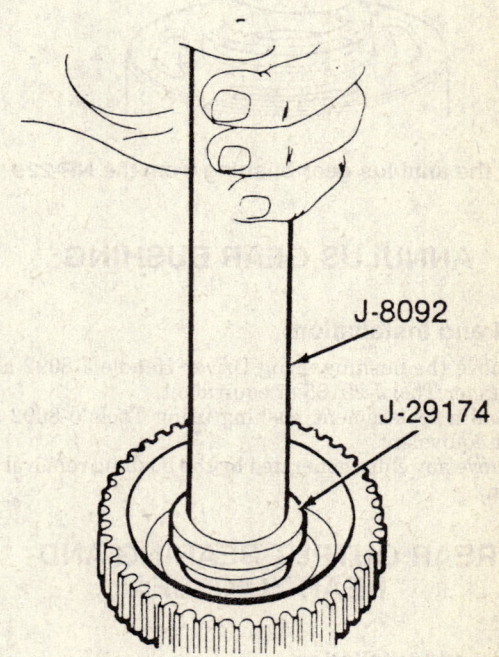

Installing the mainshaft pilot bushing on the NP-229

7-133

7 DRIVE TRAIN

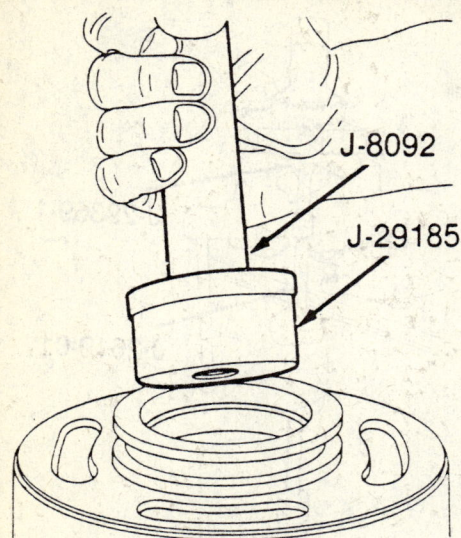

Removing the annulus gear bushing from the NP-229

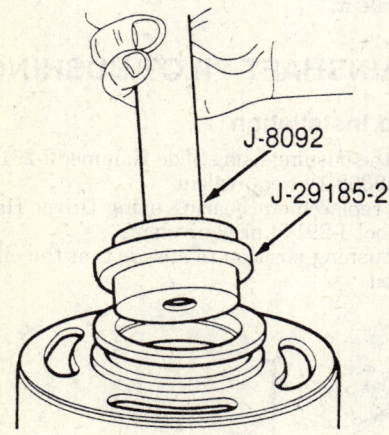

Installing the annulus gear bushing from the NP-229

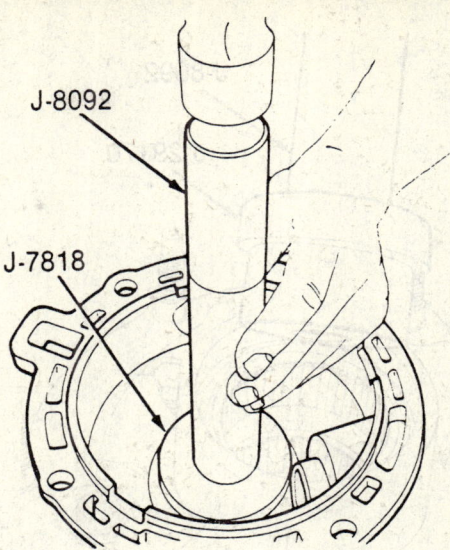

Installing the rear output bearing on the NP-229

ANNULUS GEAR BUSHING

Removal and Installation

1. Remove the bushing using Driver Handle J-8092 and Remover/Installer Tool J-29185 or equivalent.
2. Install a replacement bushing using Tools J-8092 and J-29185-2 or equivalent.
3. Remove any chips generated by the bushing removal and/or installation.

REAR OUTPUT BEARING AND REAR YOKE SEAL

Removal and Installation

1. Remove the bearing using a brass drift and hammer.
2. Remove the seal from the retainer using a brass drift and hammer.

— CAUTION —
The rear output bearing is shielded on one side. Ensure that the shielded side faces the transfer case interior after installation.

3. Install a replacement bearing using Driver Handle J-8092 and Installer Tool J-7818 or equivalent.
4. Install a replacement seal in the retainer using Tool J-29162 or equivalent.

CASE ASSEMBLY

NOTE: During the assembly, lubricate all of the transfer case internal components with DEXRON®II transmission fluid or petroleum jelly as indicated in the procedure. Do not use chassis lubricant or similar thick lubricants.

1. Install a replacement input shaft and rear output shaft bearing oil seals. Set the seals flush with the edge of the seal bore or in the seal groove in the transfer case. Coat the seal lips with petroleum jelly after installation.
2. Install the input shaft thrust bearing race in the transfer case counterbore. Install the input gear thrust bearing on the input shaft and install the shaft and bearing in the transfer case.
3. Install the mainshaft thrust bearing in the bearing recess in the input shaft. Install the planetary assembly on the input shaft. Ensure that the planetary pinion teeth mesh fully with the input shaft.
4. Install the planetary thrust washer on the planetary hub. Install a replacement sector shaft O-ring and install the retainer in the shaft bore in the transfer case.
5. Install the O-ring on the mode sector shaft and insert the mode sector through the range sector. Install the range sector in the front of transfer case half. Install the operating lever and the snapring on the range sector shaft.
6. Install the lever, attaching washer and lock nut on the mode sector shaft. Torque the lock nut to 17 ft. lbs. Assemble the annulus gear, range fork and rail. Install the assembled fork on and over the planetary assembly.
7. Be sure that the annulus gear is fully meshed with the planetary pinions. Engage the range sector lug into the range sector.
8. Install the annulus thrust washer and the annulus retaining ring onto the annulus gear hub. Install the detent ball,

plunger, spring and retaining screw in the front transfer case half detent bore. Torque the retaining screw to 22 ft. lbs.

NOTE: The locking mode clutch sleeve and the high range clutch sleeve are not interchangeable. The sleeve splines are different. So be sure that the correct sleeve is installed in the proper shift fork. Also, the sleeves must be replaced as a set.

9. Assemble and install the locking fork, fork bracket, fork springs and high range clutch sleeves. Be sure that the lug on the fork is seated in the range sector detent slot.

10. Install the range fork lug in the range sector detent notch. Move the range sector to the high range position. Assemble and install the range fork, shift rail and mode clutch sleeve.

NOTE: Steps 11–16 are to be used if the mainshaft was disassembled, when the transfer case was disassembled.

11. Install the thrust washer and a replacement O-ring on the mainshaft. Install the needle bearings and bearing spacers on the mainshaft. Coat the shaft bearing surface and all needle bearings with petroleum jelly.

12. Install the first 41 needle bearings and install the long bearing spacer, the remaining 41 needle bearings and the remaining short spacer. Be careful to avoid displacing the bearing when the spacers are installed. Apply additional petroleum jelly to hold the bearing in place if necessary.

13. Install the spline gear on the mainshaft, be careful not to displace the bearing while installing the gear. Install the sprocket carrier in the drive sprocket and install the sprocket carrier snaprings. Make sure that the carrier and sprockets are aligned according to the reference marks made during disassembly.

NOTE: The sprocket carrier teeth are tapered on one side and the drive sprocket has a deep recess on one side. Be sure that these components are assembles so that the carrier tapered teeth and sprocket recess are on the same side.

14. Install the sprocket carrier bearings and spacers. Coat the carrier bore and all the 120 carrier needle bearings with petroleum jelly. Install the center spacer.

15. Install the 60 needle bearings in each end of the carrier and install the remaining two spacers, one at each side of the carrier. Apply additional petroleum jelly to hold the bearings in place if necessary.

16. Install the assembled sprocket carrier and drive sprocket on the mainshaft. Do not displace the mainshaft bearing during installation. Be sure that the recessed side of the drive sprocket is facing downward.

17. Install the trust washer in the mainshaft, position the washer on the sprocket carrier. Install the side gear on the mainshaft and be sure that the side gear is fully seated in the sprocket carrier. Be careful not to displace any of the carrier or mainshaft needle bearings.

18. Install the mainshaft and gear assembly in the case, making sure that the mainshaft is fully seated in the input gear. Install the driven sprocket on the front output shaft and install the sprocket retaining snapring. Be sure that the sprocket is installed according to the reference marks made during disassembly.

19. Install the front output shaft front thrust bearing assembly in the transfer case front half. Install the thick race in the transfer case and then install the bearing and the thin race.

20. Install the drive chain, front output shaft and driven sprocket. Install the chain on the driven sprocket. Raise and tilt the driven sprocket and chain and install the opposite end of the chain on the drive sprocket.

21. Align the front output shaft with the shaft bore in the transfer case front half and install the shaft in the transfer case. Be sure that the front shaft thrust bearing assembly is seated in the transfer case.

22. Install the front output shaft rear thrust bearing assembly on the front output shaft. Install the tin race first, then install the bearing and the thick race. Install the differential on the side gear, making sure that the differential is fully seated.

23. Coat the mainshaft pilot bearing surface and all 15 needle bearings with petroleum jelly and install the bearing on the shaft. Apply additional petroleum jelly to hold the bearings in place if necessary.

24. Install the rear output shaft on the mainshaft and into the differential, making sure that the shaft is completely seated. If necessary tap the shaft with a plastic mallet or equivalent to seat the shaft. Do not displace the pilot bearing during shaft installation.

25. Install the oil pump and the rear output shaft. Install the oil pump with the recessed side facing down. Install a replacement rear output shaft bearing seal in the rear transfer case half.

26. Apply a bead of Loctite®515 sealant or equivalent, to the mating surface of the rear transfer case half. Install the magnet in the case and attach the rear transfer case half to the front transfer case half. Be sure that the alignment dowels at the front case half ends are aligned with the bolt holes in the rear case half and mate the rear case half with the front case half.

NOTE: If the rear transfer case half will not mate completely with the front case. Inspect the following; oil in the range fork rail bore, the front output shaft rear thrust bearing assembly is not aligned with the rear case half, the mainshaft is not completely seated or the rear case half is not aligned with the oil pump.

27. Install the rear case half to the front case half bolts. Torque the bolts to 23 ft. lbs. Be sure that the flat washers are used on the bolts at the case end where the alignment dowels are located. Install the speedometer drive gear on the rear output shaft.

28. Measure the thickness of the shim pack and record. Install a 0.76mm (0.030 in.) shim on the rear output shaft. Align the rear retainer on the rear transfer case half and install the retainer. Install the retainer bolts and tighten them securely, do not torque to specifications.

29. Install the front and rear output shaft yokes and the original yoke nuts. Tighten the yoke nuts finger tight and check the differential end play.

30. Set the shift lever in the 4-high range position. Place a dial indicator on the rear retainer and position the indicator stylus so that it contacts the rear yoke nut.

31. Pull upward on the rear output yoke, note the dial indicator pointer position and record it. Remove the retainer and add or subtract differential shims as necessary to correct the end play.

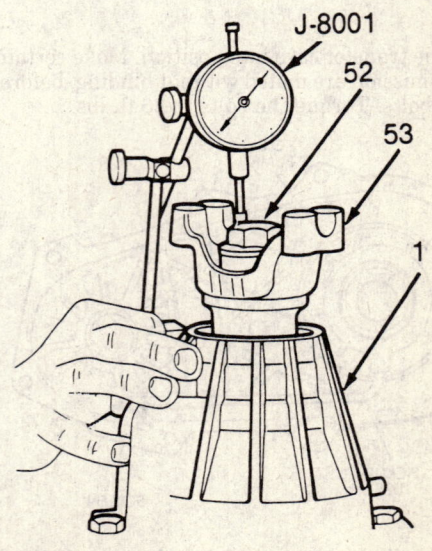

Measuring the NP-229 rear output shaft runout

7 DRIVE TRAIN

The end play should be between 0.05–0.25mm. The recommended end play is 0.15mm.

32. After adjusting the end play, remove the front and rear yokes. Discard the original yoke nuts. Apply a bead of Loctite®515 sealant or equivalent, to the retainer mating surface and install the retainer. Apply the sealer to the retaining bolts and install the bolts. Torque the bolts to 23 ft. lbs.

33. Position the front and rear yokes and install the replacement yoke seal washers and nuts. Using tool # J-8614-01 or equivalent hold the yokes in place and torque the yoke nuts to 120 ft. lbs.

34. Install the detent ball, spring and bolt if these were not installed previously. Apply sealer to the bolt before installing it and torque the bolt to 23 ft. lbs.

35. Install the drain plug and washer. Fill the transfer case with 7 pints of DEXRON®II transmission fluid or equivalent. Install the fill plug and washer and torque the drain and fill plugs to 18 ft. lbs.

36. Install the plug and washer in the front transfer case half (if removed) and torque the plug to 18 ft. lbs. Install the transfer case into the vehicle as described in this section. Road test the vehicle to check for proper operation of the transfer case, stop the engine and check for leaks.

New Process 231

REMOVAL AND INSTALLATION

1. Shift the case into Neutral.
2. Raise and support the truck on jackstands.
3. Drain the lubricant.
4. Matchmark and remove the front and rear driveshafts.
5. Support the transmission with a jackstand.
6. Remove the rear crossmember.
7. Disconnect the speedometer cable.
8. Disconnect the linkage.
9. Disconnect the vent and vacuum hoses and the indicator wire.
10. Support the transfer case with a transmission jack. Make sure that the case is secured to the jack with chains.
11. Remove the transfer case-to-transmission bolts.
12. Pull the case rearward to disengage it and lower it from the truck.

To install:

13. Raise the transfer case into position. Make certain that the case and transmission are mated without binding, before torquing the attaching bolts. Torque the bolts to 26 ft. lbs.
14. Connect the shift linkage at the case.
15. Connect the vacuum hoses.
16. Install the driveshafts. Torque the nuts to 14 ft. lbs.; torque the flange nuts to 35 ft. lbs.

NOTE: New strap bolts must be used each time the driveshaft is removed.

17. Install the rear crossmember. Torque the bolts to 30 ft. lbs.
18. Remove the transmission floor jack.
19. Connect the speedometer cable and vent hose.
20. Connect the shift lever link at the operating lever.
21. Fill the case.
22. Lower the truck.

New Process 231 – Overhaul

DISASSEMBLY

1. Remove the transfer case from the vehicle as described above.
2. Remove the attaching nuts from the front and rear output yokes. Remove the yokes and sealing washers.
3. Move the range lever to 4-LOW. Remove the bolts and tap the extension housing off of the rear retainer.

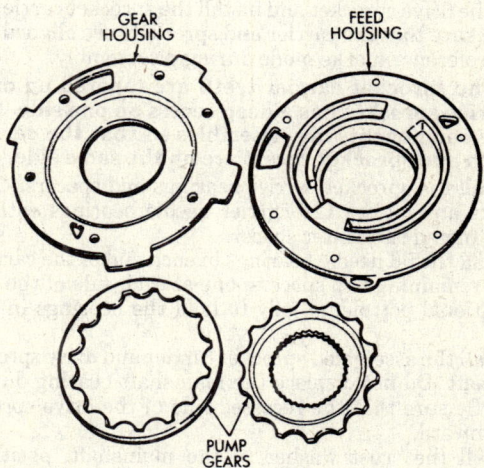

Disassembling the oil pump from the NP-231

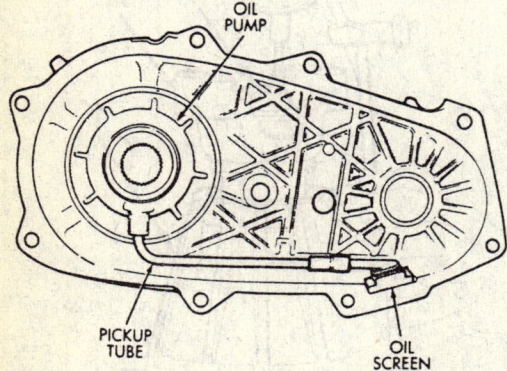

Removing the oil screen and pickup tube from the NP-231

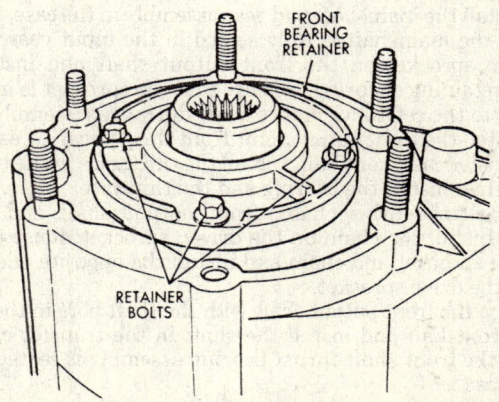

Removing the bearing retainer bolts from the NP-231

DRIVE TRAIN 7

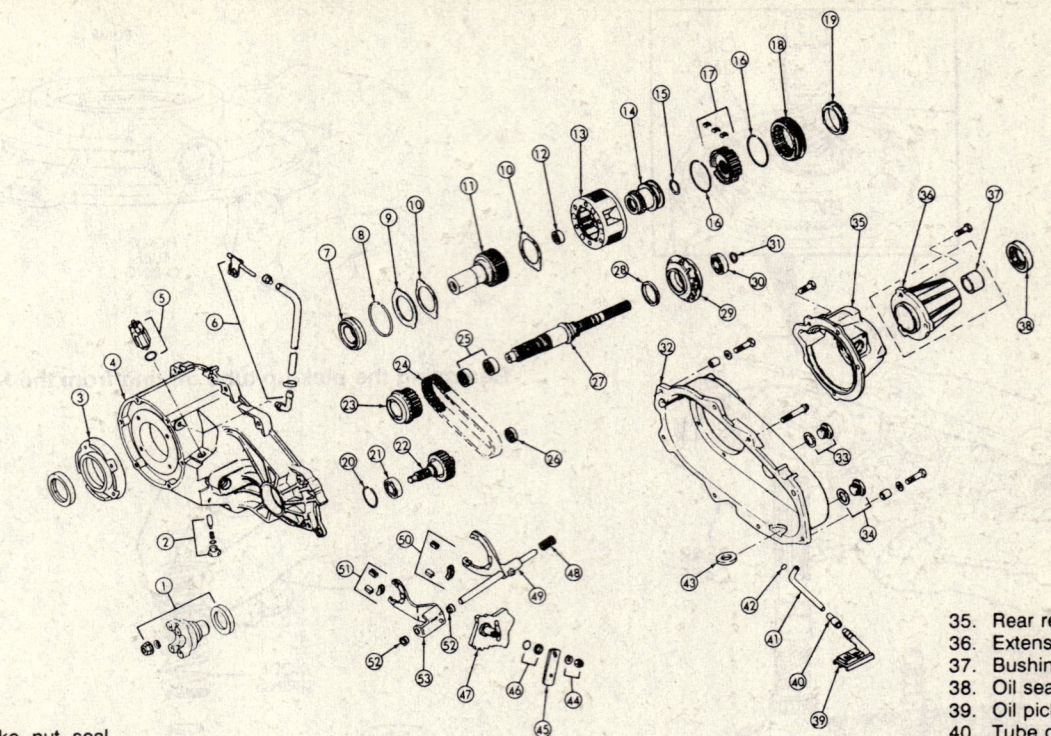

1. Front yoke, nut, seal washer, and oil seal
2. Shift detent plug, spring and pin
3. Front retainer and seal
4. Front case
5. Vacuum switch and seal
6. Vent assembly
7. Input gear bearing and snap ring
8. Low range gear snap ring
9. Input gear retainer
10. Low range gear thrust washers
11. Input gear
12. Input gear pilot bearing
13. Low range gear
14. Range fork shift hub
15. Synchro hub snap ring
16. Synchro hub springs
17. Synchro hub and inserts
18. Synchro sleeve
19. Stop ring
20. Snap ring
21. Output shaft front bearing
22. Output shaft (front)
23. Drive sprocket
24. Drive chain
25. Drive sprocket bearings
26. Output shaft rear bearing
27. Mainshaft
28. Oil seal
29. Oil pump assembly
30. Rear bearing
31. Snap ring
32. Rear case
33. Fill plug and gasket
34. Drain plug and gasket
35. Rear retainer
36. Extension housing
37. Bushing
38. Oil seal
39. Oil pickup screen
40. Tube connector
41. Oil pickup tube
42. Pickup tube O-ring
43. Magnet
44. Range lever nut and washer
45. Range lever
46. O-ring and seal
47. Sector
48. Mode spring
49. Mode fork
50. Mode fork inserts
51. Range fork inserts
52. Range fork bushings
53. Range fork

NP-231 transfer case – exploded view

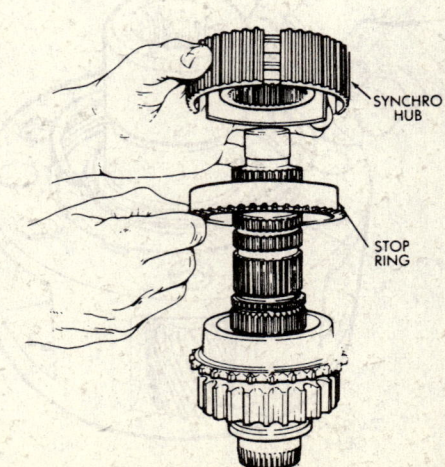

Removing the hub and stop ring from the NP-231

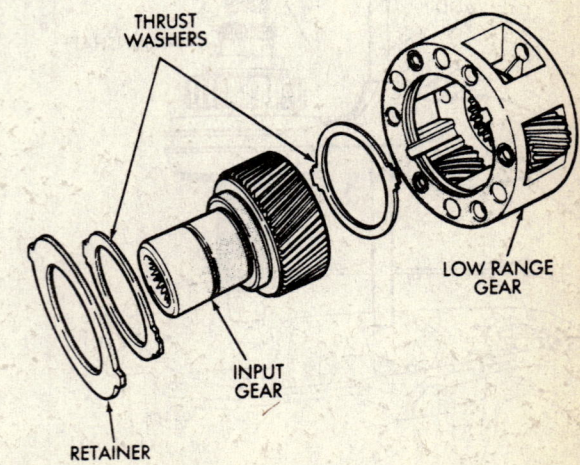

Disassembling the input/low range gear from the NP-231

7-137

7 DRIVE TRAIN

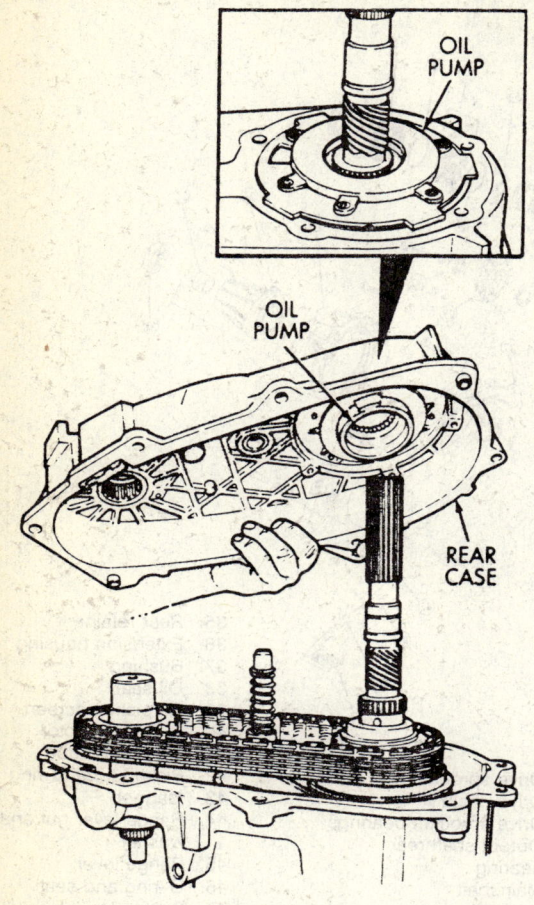

Removing the rear case and oil pump from the NP-231

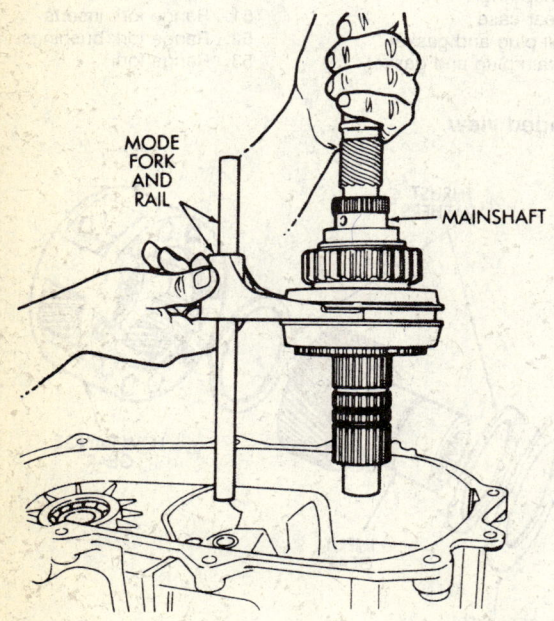

Removing the mainshaft, mode fork and shift rail from the NP-231

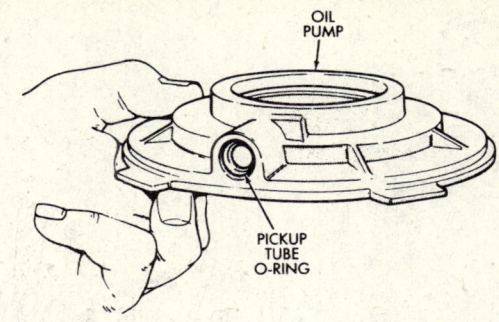

Removing the pick-up tube oil ring from the NP-231

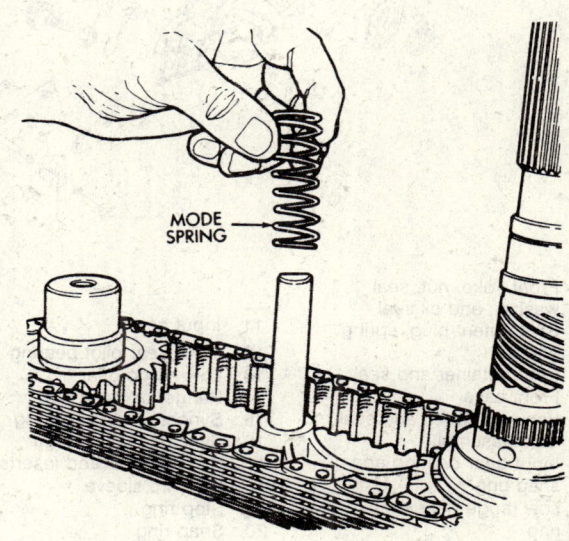

Removing the mode spring from the NP-231

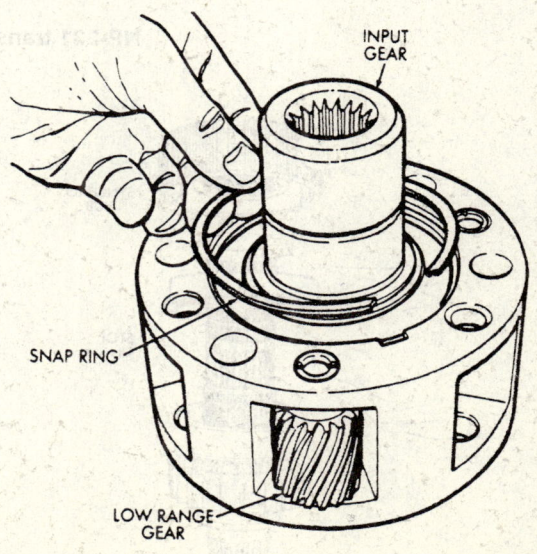

Removing the low range gear snapring from the NP-231

7-138

DRIVE TRAIN 7

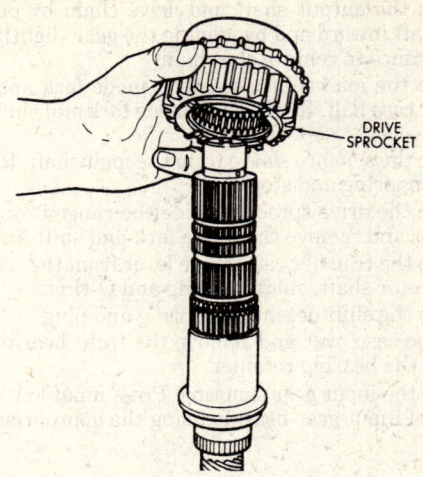

Removing the drive sprocket from the NP-231

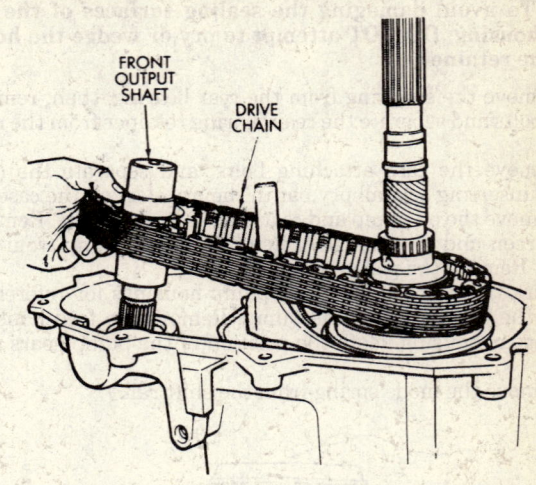

Removing the front output shaft and drive chain from the NP-231

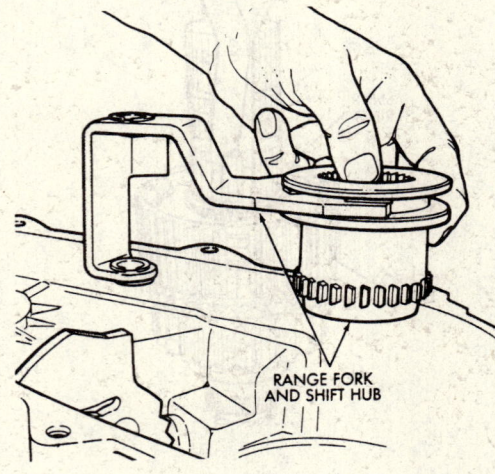

Removing the range fork and hub from the NP-231

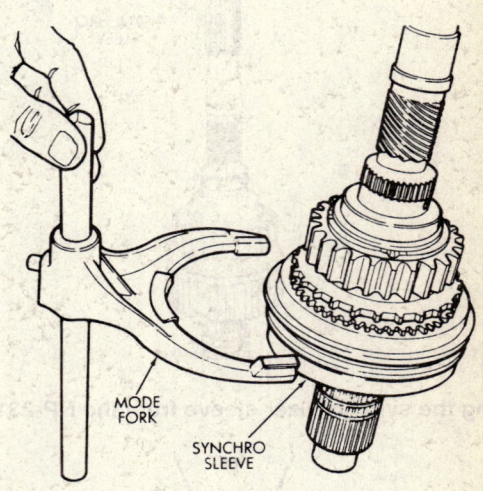

Removing the mode fork from the NP-231

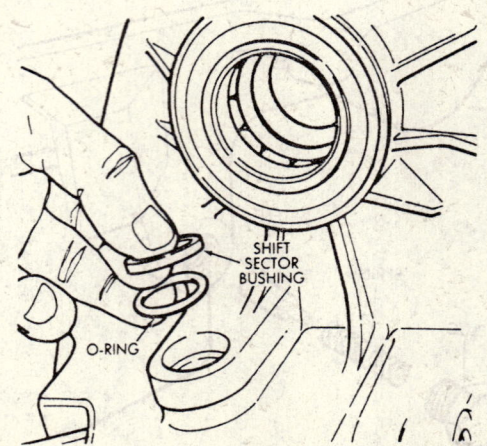

Removing the selector shaft bushing and O-ring from the NP-231

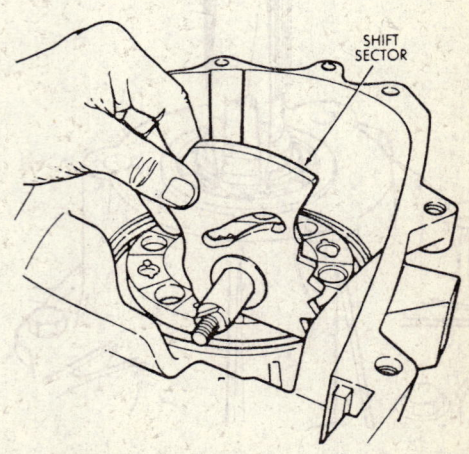

Removing the shift selector from the NP-231

7-139

7 DRIVE TRAIN

NOTE: To avoid damaging the sealing surfaces of the extension housing, DO NOT attempt to pry or wedge the housing off the retainer.

4. Remove the snapring from the rear bearing, then, remove the four bolts and separate the rear bearing retainer from the rear case half.
5. Remove the case attaching bolts, and separate the case halves by inserting a small pry bar in the pry slots on the case.
6. Remove the oil pump and rear case as an assembly. Remove the oil screen and pick-up tube. Remove the oil pump from the rear case. Remove the pickup tube O-ring.
7. Mark the position of the oil pump housings for reference. Separate the two halves of the pump. Remove the feed housing from the gear housing. Note the position of the pump gears and remove.
8. Remove the mode spring from the shift rail.
9. Remove the output shaft and drive chain by pushing the front input shaft inward and by angling the gear slightly to obtain adequate clearance to remove the chain.
10. Remove the mainshaft assembly, mode fork and shift rail from the front case half. Remove the mode fork and shift rail from the synchro sleeve.
11. Remove the synchro sleeve from the mainshaft. Remove the synchro hub snapring and stop ring.
12. Remove the drive sprocket. Slide the range fork pin out of the shift sector and remove the range fork and shift hub.
13. Remove the transfer case range lever from the sector shaft. Remove the sector shaft, shaft bushing and O-ring.
14. Remove the shift detent pin, spring and plug.
15. Turn the case over and remove the front bearing retainer bolts. Remove the bearing retainer.
16. Remove the input gear snapring. Press input/low range gear assembly out of input gear bearing using the appropriate tools.

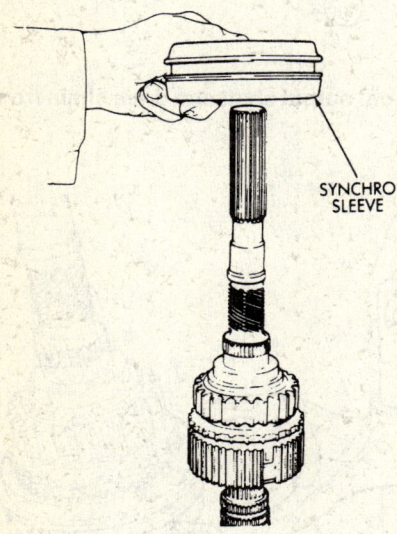

Removing the synchronizer sleeve from the NP-231

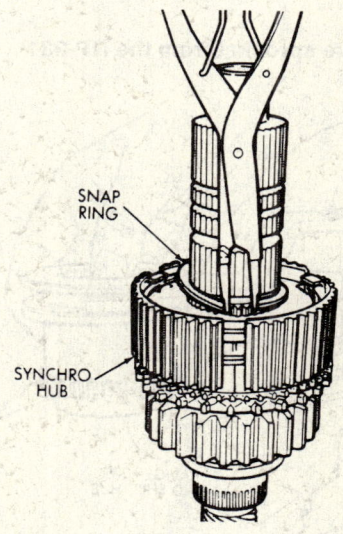

Removing the synchronizer hub snapring from the NP-231

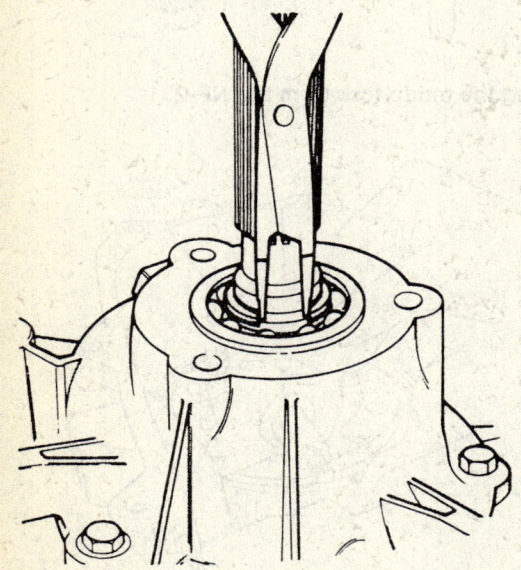

Removing the rear bushing snapring from the NP-231

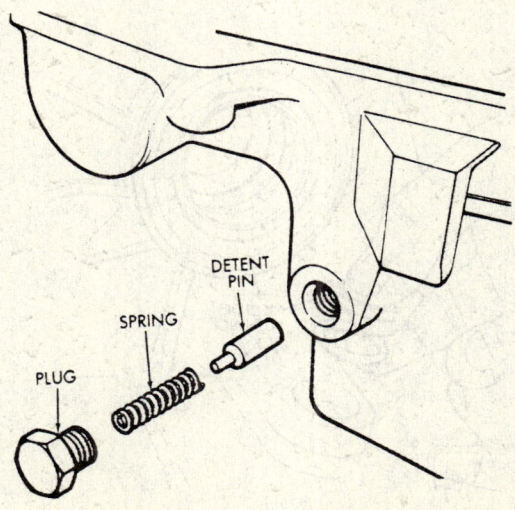

Removing the detent pin, spring and plug from the NP-231

7-140

DRIVE TRAIN 7

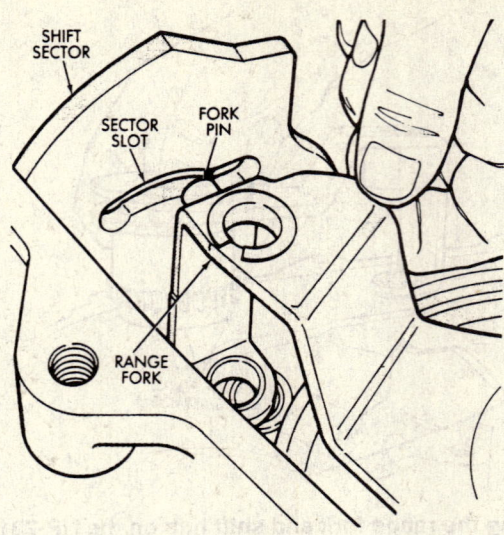

Disengaging the range fork on the NP-231

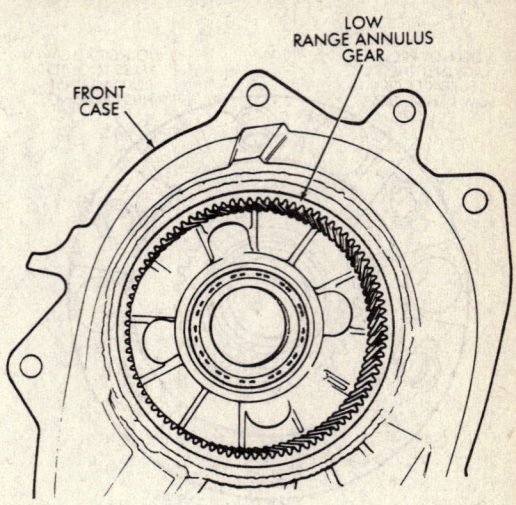

Inspecting the low range annulus gear on the NP-231

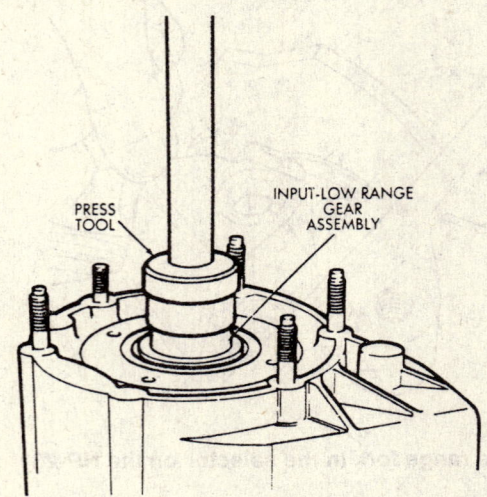

Removing the input/low range gear assembly from the NP-231

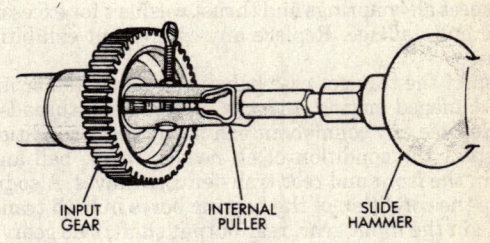

Removing the input gear pilot bearing from the NP-231

17. Remove low range gear snapring. Remove retainer, thrust washers and input gear from low range gear.
18. Remove oil seals from rear retainer, rear extension housing, oil pump feed housing and case halves. Remove magnet from front case.
19. Remove speedometer gear, seals and adaptor.
20. Remove output shaft snapring, oil seal and bearing.

CLEANING & INSPECTION

1. Wash all components thoroughly in clean solvent. Ensure that all lubricant, metallic particles, dirt, and foreign material are removed from the surfaces of every component.
2. Apply compressed air to each oil supply port and channel in each transfer case half to remove any obstructions or cleaning solvent residue.
3. Inspect all gear teeth for excessive wear or damage. Inspect

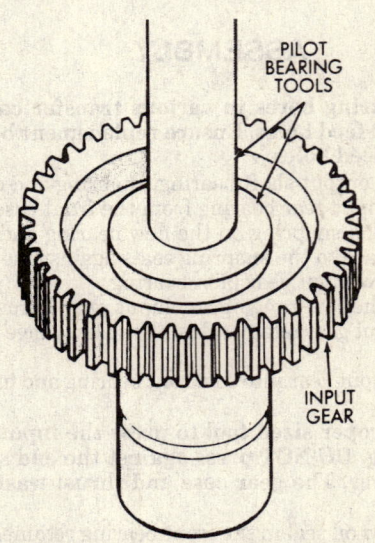

Installing the input gear pilot bearing on the NP-231

all gear splines for burrs, nicks, wear or damage.
4. Inspect the low range annulus gear. If the gear is damaged, replace the gear and front case as an assembly. Do not attempt to remove the gear.
5. Remove minor nicks or scratches using an oilstone. Replace any component exhibiting excessive wear or damage.

7-141

7 DRIVE TRAIN

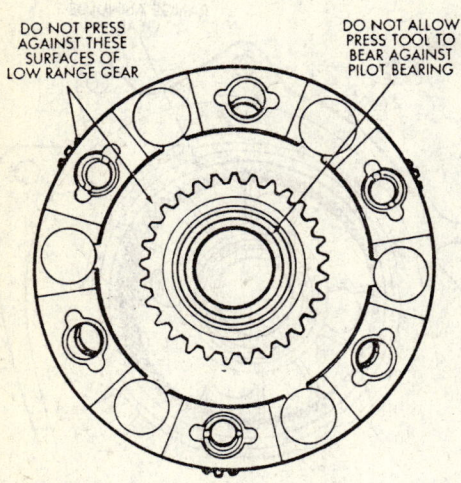

Input gear installation on the NP-231

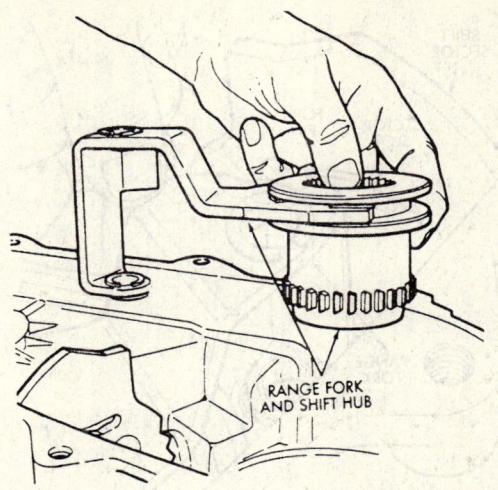

Assembling the range fork and shift hub on the NP-231

6. Inspect all snaprings and thrust washers for excessive wear, distortion and damage. Replace any component exhibiting these conditions.
7. Inspect the transfer case halves and rear retainer for cracks, porosity, damaged mating surfaces, stripped bolt threads and distortion. Replace any component exhibiting these conditions.
8. Inspect the condition of all needle, roller, ball and thrust bearings in the front and rear transfer case halves. Also inspect to determine the condition of the bearing bores in both transfer case halves and in the input gear, rear output shaft, side gear, and rear retainer.
9. Replace any component that is excessively worn or damaged.

ASSEMBLY

NOTE: The bearing bores in various transfer case components contain oil feed holes. Ensure replacement bearings do not block these feed holes.

1. Install new output shaft bearing, snapring and oil seal.
2. Press the input gear bearing from the front case with a remover tool. Install a snapring on the new bearing and install the bearing into the case so the snapring seats against the case.
3. Install a new input gear pilot bearing.
4. Assemble the low range gear, input gear thrust washers, input gear and input gear retainer. Install the low range gear snapring.
5. Press the input gear into the front bearing and install a new snapring.

NOTE: Use a proper sized tool to press the input gear into the front bearing. DO NOT press against the end surfaces of the low range gear. The gear case and thrust washers could be damaged.

6. Install a new oil seal in the front bearing retainer. Apply an 1/8 in. (3mm) bead of RTV sealer to the front bearing retainer sealing surfaces.
7. Install the front bearing retainer on the front case and tighten the bolts to 16 ft. lbs.
8. Install a new sector shaft O-ring and bushing. Install the shift sector. Then install the range lever on the shift sector and tighten the attaching nut to 22 ft. lbs.
9. Install the detent pin, spring and plug. Tighten the plug to 15 ft. lbs.
10. Install new pads and shift rail bushings in the range fork.

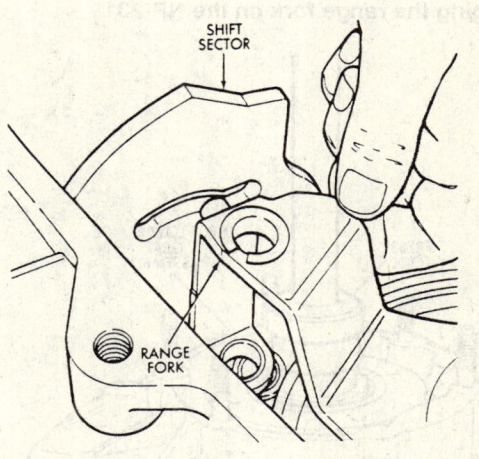

Seating the range fork in the selector on the NP-231

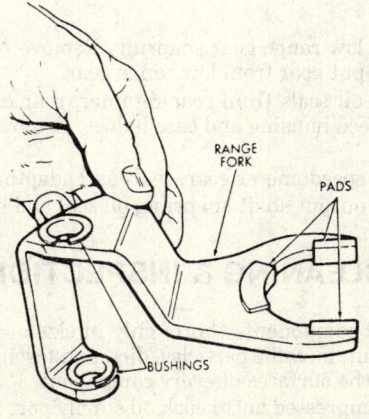

Installing new pads and bushings in the range fork on the NP-231

DRIVE TRAIN 7

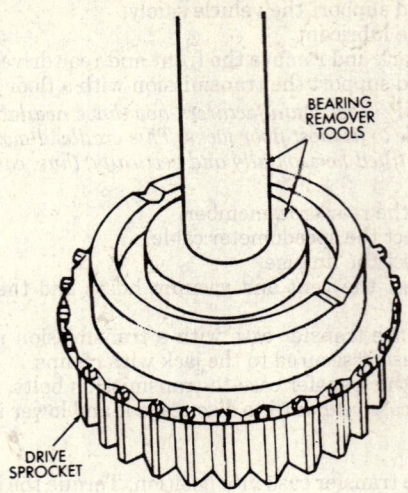

Removing the drive sprocket bearings on the NP-231

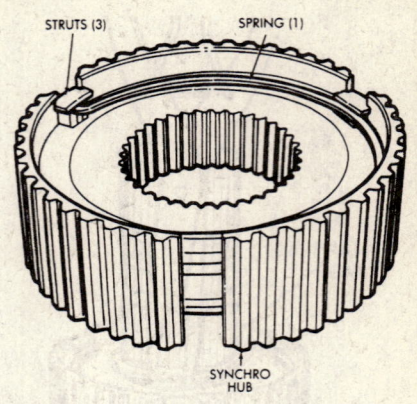

Installing the synchronizer hub, spring and struts on the NP-231

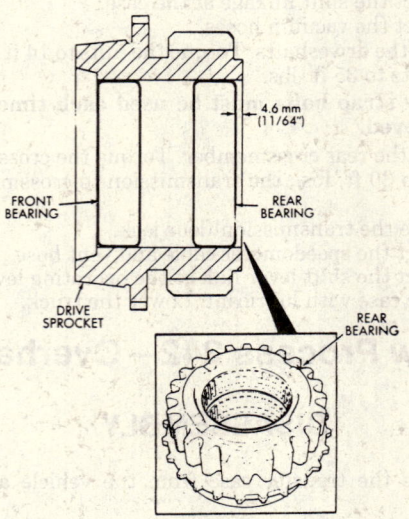

Installing the drive sprocket bearings on the NP-231

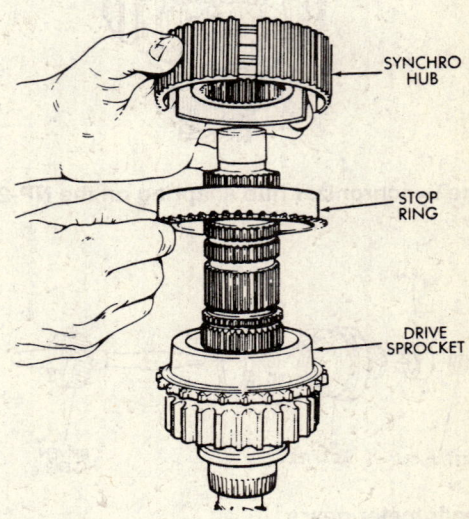

Installing the drive sprocket, stop ring and synchronizer hub on the NP-231

Assemble the range fork and shift hub. Engage the range fork pin in the sector slot.

11. If the drive sprocket bearing are to be replaced, install then as follows:
    a. Press both bearings out of the sprocket at the same time.
    b. Install the front bearing and press flush with the edge of the bore.
    c. Install the rear bearing and press until it is $^3/_{16}$ in. (1.6mm) below the edge of the bore.

NOTE: DO NOT press the bearings any farther into the bore than specified. The mainshaft oil seal may become blocked if the bearings are pressed too deeply.

12. Install the synchro hub spring struts and spring.
13. Lubricate the drive sprocket bearings, the stop ring and synchro hub with automatic transmission fluid and install on the mainshaft. Be sure to seat the hub struts on the stop ring lugs.
14. Install new synchro hub snapring. Install the sleeve on the synchro hub with the beveled spline ends facing the stop ring.
15. Install new pads on the mode fork and install the shift rail in the fork.
16. Engage the mode fork in the synchro sleeve. Install the mode fork mainshaft assembly in the case. Be sure the mode fork rail is seated in both of the range fork bushings.
17. Assemble and install the output shaft and drive chain. Lift the mainshaft slightly to ease chain and shaft installation.
18. Install the mode spring on the shift rail.
19. Install new output shaft rear bearing.
20. Install new seal in oil pump feed housing. Assemble the oil pump and install. Tighten screws to 14 inch lbs. Install new pick-up tube O-ring and install the pick-up tube. Attach the oil screen and connecting hose to the pick-up tube.
21. Install the assembled oil pump in the rear case.
22. Install the magnet in the from case.
23. Apply an $^1/_8$ in. (3mm) bead of RTV sealer to the sealing surface of the front case. Align the case halves and join. Ensure locating dowels are in place and that mainshaft splines are engaged in the oil pump inner gear.
24. Install and tighten attaching bolts/washers to 30 ft. lbs.
25. Install new rear retainer bearing.
26. Apply an $^1/_8$ in. (3mm) bead of RTV sealer to the flange of

7-143

7 DRIVE TRAIN

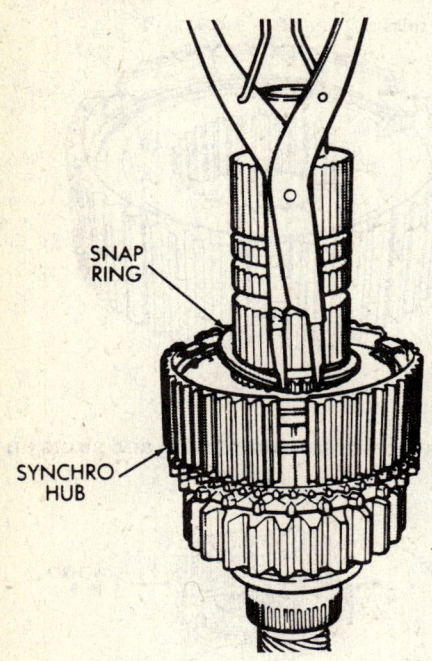

Installing the synchronizer hub snapring on the NP-231

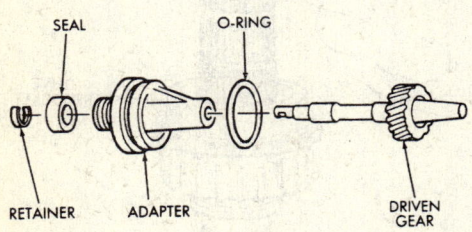

NP-231 speedometer gears

the rear retainer. Install the locating dowels and install retainer on case. Tighten bolts to 18 ft. lbs.
27. Install a new rear bearing snapring. Lift the mainshaft to seat the snapring in the shaft groove.
28. Install new extension housing bushing and seal.
29. Apply an 1/8 in. (3mm) bead of RTV sealer to the flange of the extension housing. Mate the extension housing to the case and tighten bolts to 30 ft. lbs.
30. Install front yoke and seal washer. Tighten nut to 110 ft. lbs.
31. Install a replacement gasket on the vacuum switch and install switch.
32. Install drain plug and tighten to 35 ft. lbs. Install speedometer gear, seals and adaptor.
33. Fill the case with lubricant and install fill plug. Tighten fill plug to 35 ft. lbs.

New Process 242

REMOVAL AND INSTALLATION

1. Shift transfer case into NEUTRAL.
2. Raise and support the vehicle safely.
3. Drain the lubricant.
4. Matchmark and remove the front and rear driveshafts.
5. Raise and support the transmission with a floor jack.

CHILTON TIP: *Tool manufacturers now have available a transmission cradle to fit most floor jacks. This cradle allows the transmission to be tilted horizontally and vertically, thus, easing installation.*

6. Remove the rear crossmember.
7. Disconnect the speedometer cable.
8. Disconnect the linkage.
9. Disconnect the vent and vacuum hoses and the indicator wire.
10. Support the transfer case with a transmission jack. Make sure that the case is secured to the jack with chains.
11. Remove the transfer case-to-transmission bolts.
12. Pull the case rearward to disengage it and lower it from the truck.

To install:
13. Raise the transfer case into position. Torque the bolts to 26 ft. lbs.

NOTE: Make certain that the case and transmission are mated without binding, before torquing the attaching bolts.

14. Connect the shift linkage at the case.
15. Connect the vacuum hoses.
16. Install the driveshafts. Torque the nuts to 14 ft. lbs.; torque the flange nuts to 35 ft. lbs.

NOTE: New strap bolts must be used each time the driveshaft is removed.

17. Install the rear crossmember. Torque the crossmember-to-frame bolts to 30 ft. lbs.; the transmission-to-crossmember bolts to 33 ft. lbs.
18. Remove the transmission floor jack.
19. Connect the speedometer cable and vent hose.
20. Connect the shift lever link at the operating lever.
21. Fill the case with lubricant. Lower the truck.

New Process 242 — Overhaul

DISASSEMBLY

1. Remove the transfer case from the vehicle as described above.

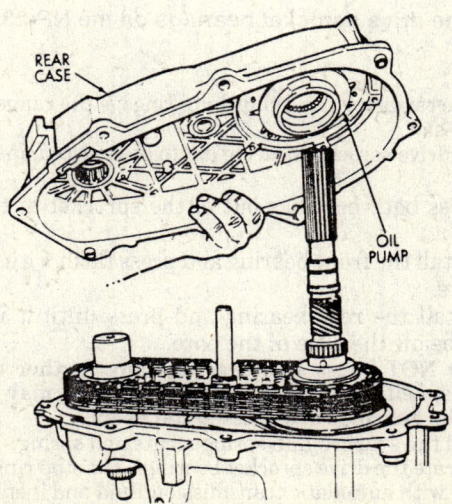

Removing the rear case and oil pump from the NP-242

7-144

DRIVE TRAIN 7

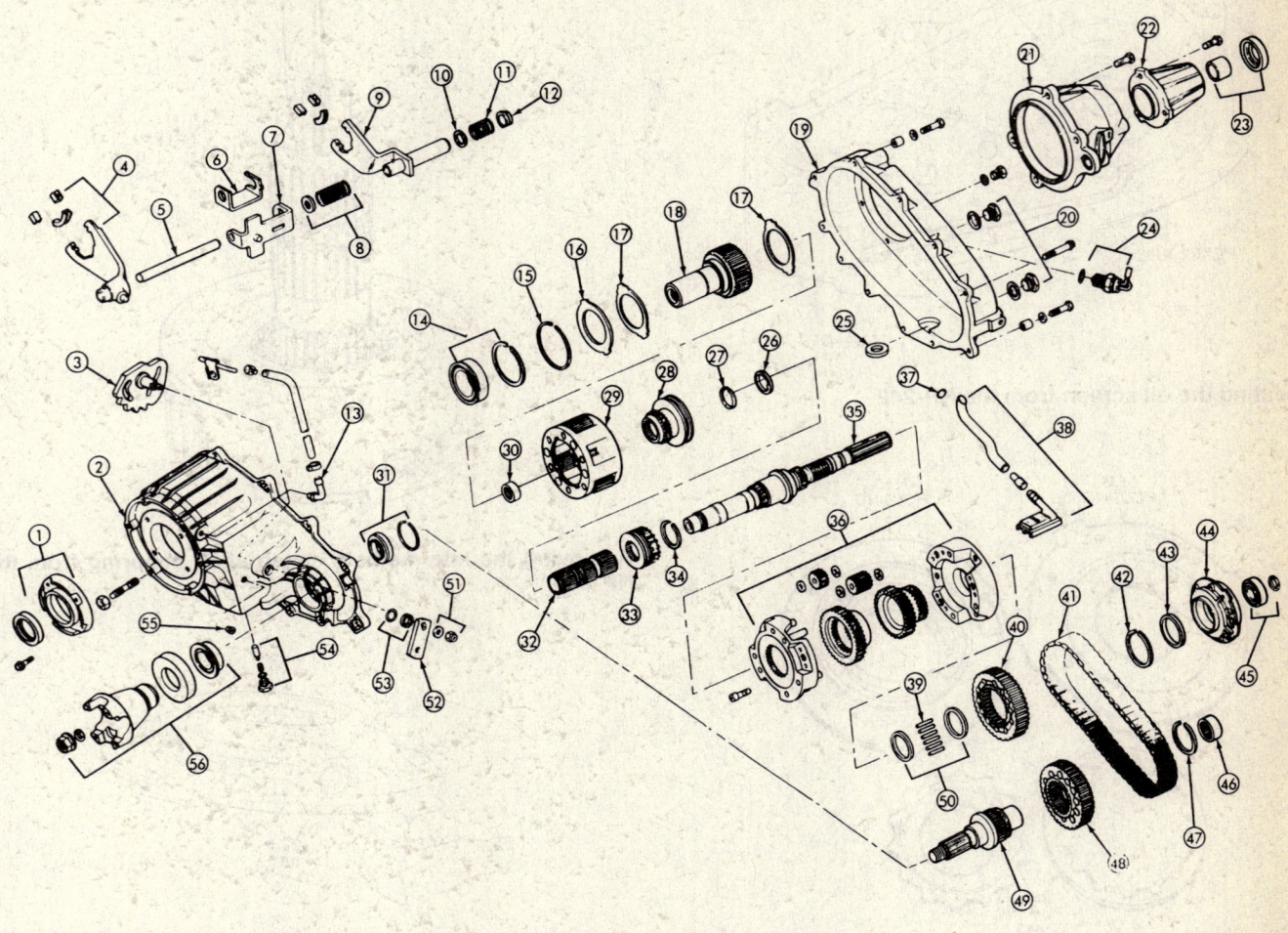

1. Front bearing retainer and seal
2. Front case
3. Shift sector
4. Low range fork and inserts
5. Shift rail
6. Shift bracket
7. Slider bracket
8. Bushing and spring
9. Mode fork and inserts
10. Bushing
11. Fork spring
12. Bushing
13. Vent tube assembly
14. Input gear bearing and snap ring
15. Low range gear snap ring
16. Retainer, low range gear
17. Thrust washer, low range gear
18. Input gear
19. Rear case
20. Drain/fill plugs
21. Rear bearing retainer
22. Extension housing
23. Bushing and oil seal
24. Vacuum switch
25. Magnet
26. Thrust ring
27. Snap ring
28. Shift sleeve
29. Low range gear
30. Pilot bushing (input gear/mainshaft)
31. Front output shaft front bearing and snap ring
32. Intermediate clutch shaft
33. Shift sleeve
34. Snap ring
35. Mainshaft
36. Differential assembly
37. Oil pump tube O-ring
38. Oil pump pickup tube and screen
39. Mainshaft bearing rollers
40. Drive sprocket
41. Drive chain
42. Snap ring
43. Oil pump seal
44. Oil pump
45. Rear bearing and snap ring
46. Front output shaft rear bearing
47. Snap ring
48. Driven sprocket
49. Front output shaft
50. Mainshaft bearing spacers
51. Shift lever washer and nut
52. Shift lever
53. Sector O-ring and seal
54. Detent pin, spring and plug
55. Seal plug
56. Front yoke nut, seal washer, yoke, slinger and oil seal

NP-242 transfer case — exploded view

7 DRIVE TRAIN

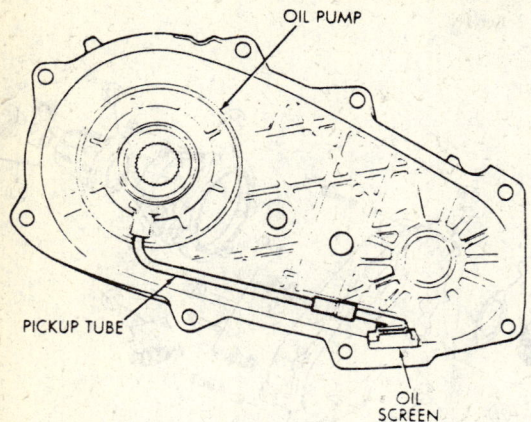

Unseating the oil screen from the NP-242

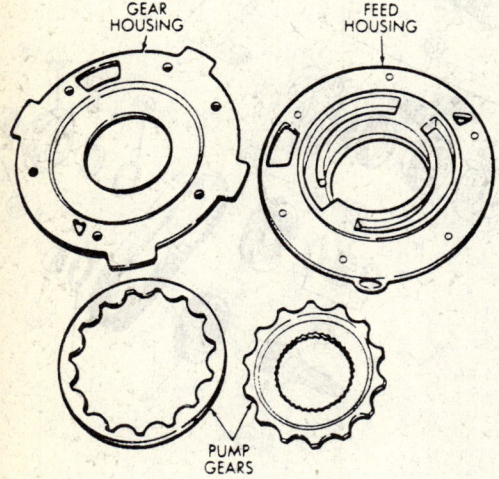

Oil pump components from the NP-242

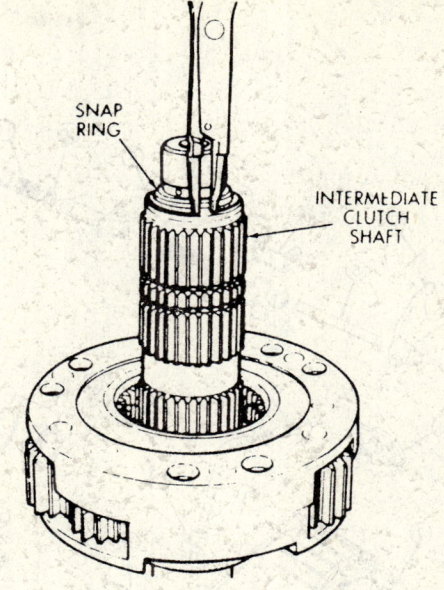

Removing the intermediate clutch shaft snapring from the NP-242

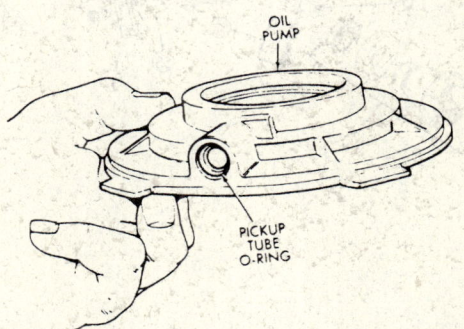

Removing the pick-up tube O-ring from the NP-242

2. Remove the attaching nuts from the front and rear output yokes. Remove the yokes and sealing washers.
3. Move the range lever to 4-LOW. Remove the bolts and tap the extension housing off of the rear retainer.
  NOTE: To avoid damaging the sealing surfaces of the extension housing, DO NOT attempt to pry or wedge the housing off the retainer.
4. Remove the snapring from the rear bearing, then, remove the four bolts and separate the rear bearing retainer from the rear case half.
5. Remove the case attaching bolts, and separate the case halves by inserting a small pry bar in the pry slots on the case.
6. Remove the oil pump and rear case as an assembly. Remove the oil screen and pick-up tube. Remove the oil pump from the rear case. Remove the pickup tube O-ring.
7. Mark the position of the oil pump housings for reference. Separate the two halves of the pump. Remove the feed housing from the gear housing. Note the position of the pump gears and remove.
8. Remove the magnet from the front case.
9. Remove the drive sprocket snapring, drive sprocket and chain.
10. Remove the front output shaft.

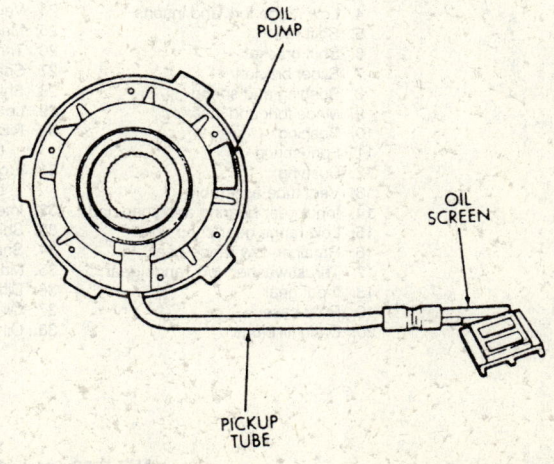

Removing the oil pump, tube and screen from the NP-242

DRIVE TRAIN 7

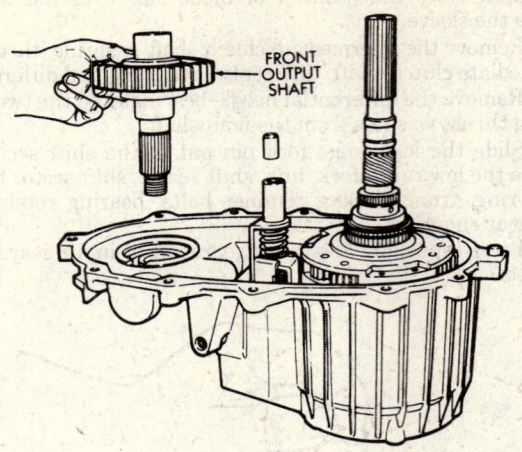

Removing the front output shaft from the NP-242

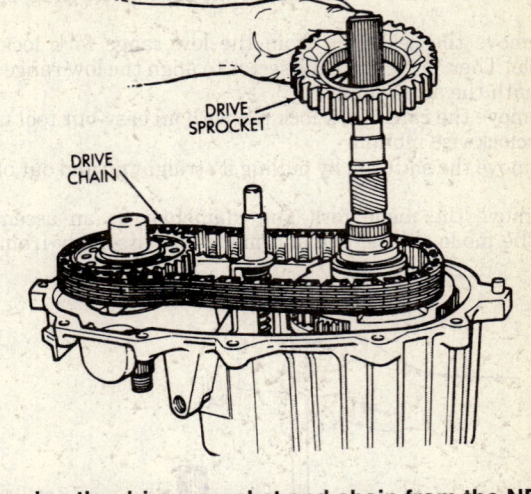

Removing the drive sprocket and chain from the NP-242

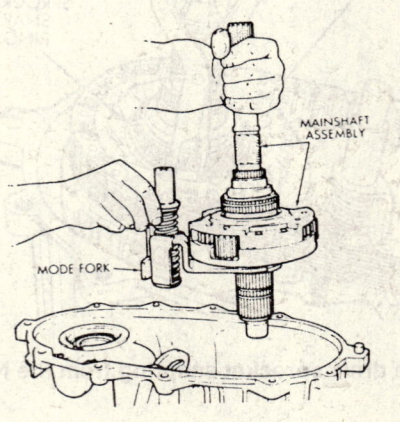

Removing the mode fork and mainshaft from the NP-242

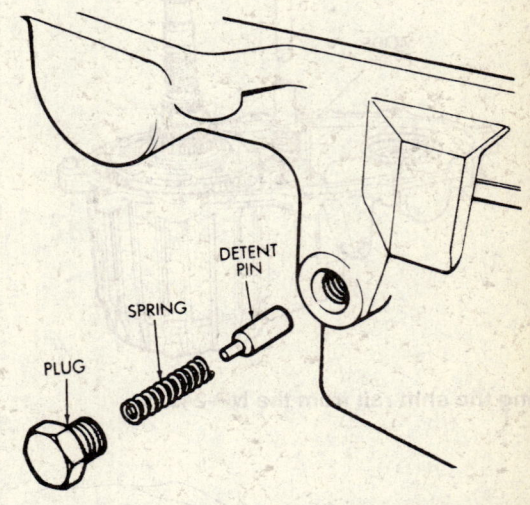

Removing the detent pin, spring and plug from the NP-242

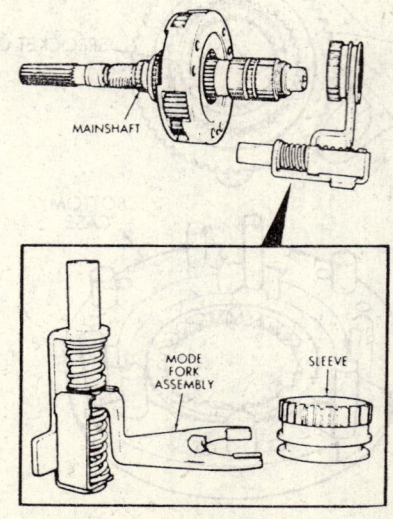

Removing the mode fork and sleeve from the NP-242

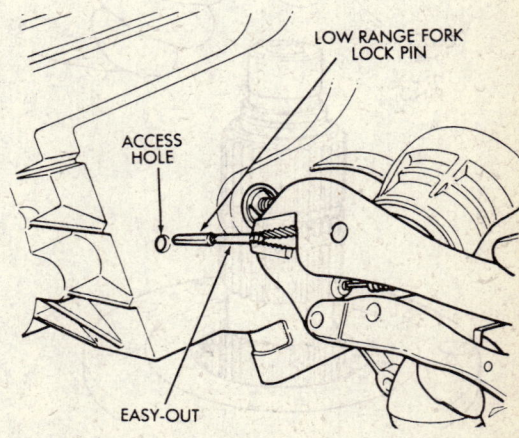

Removing the low range fork lock pin from the NP-242

7-147

7 DRIVE TRAIN

11. Remove the shift lever. Remove the shift detent plug, spring and pin.
12. Remove the seal plug from the low range fork lock pin access hole. Then move the shift sector to align the low range fork lock pin with the access hole.
13. Remove the range fork lock pin with an easy-out tool using a counterclockwise motion.
14. Remove the shift rail by pulling it straight up and out of the fork.
15. Remove the mode fork and mainshaft as an assembly. Remove the mode shift sleeve and mode fork assembly from the mainshaft. Note the position of mode sleeve in the fork and remove the sleeve.
16. Remove the intermediate clutch shaft snapring, thrust ring, intermediate clutch shaft, differential snapring and differential.
17. Remove the differential needle bearings and the two needle bearing thrust washers from the mainshaft.
18. Slide the low range fork pin out of the shift sector slot. Remove the low range fork, hub, shift sector, shift sector bushing and O-ring, front bearing retainer bolts, bearing retainer and input gear snapring.
19. Press input and low range gears out of input gear bearing and case.

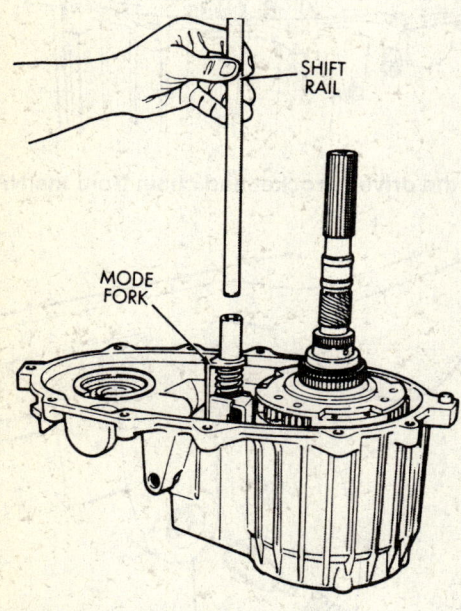

Removing the shift rail from the NP-242

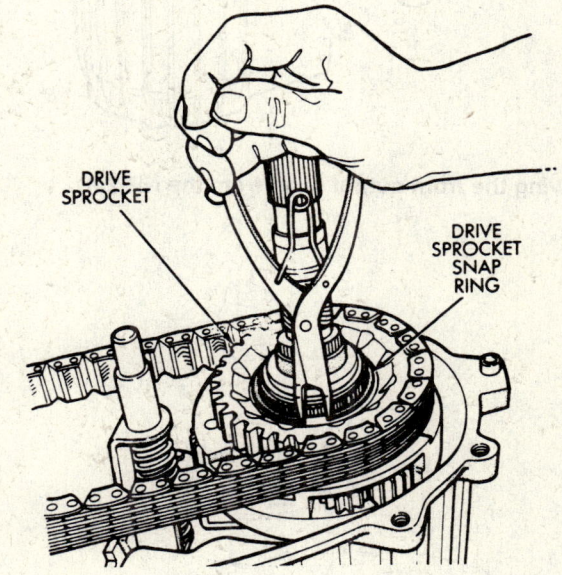

Removing the drive sprocket snapring from the NP-242

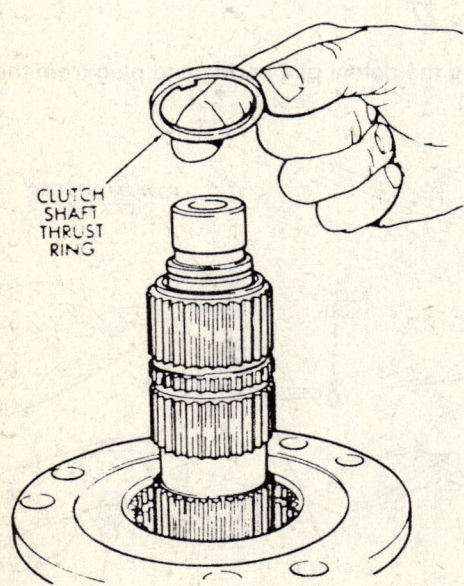

Removing the clutch shaft thrust ring from the NP-242

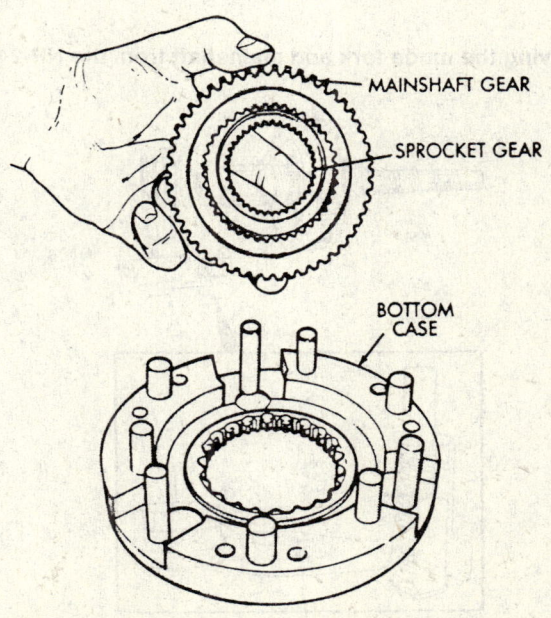

Removing the mainshaft and sprocket gears from the NP-242

DRIVE TRAIN 7

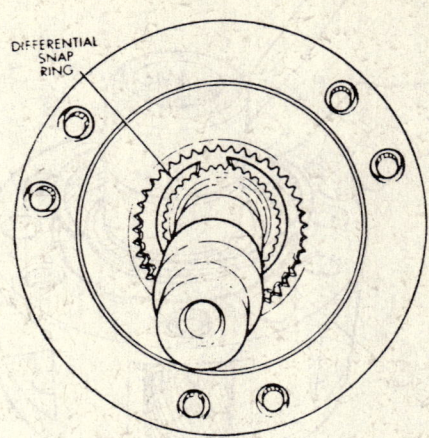

Removing the differential snapring from the NP-242

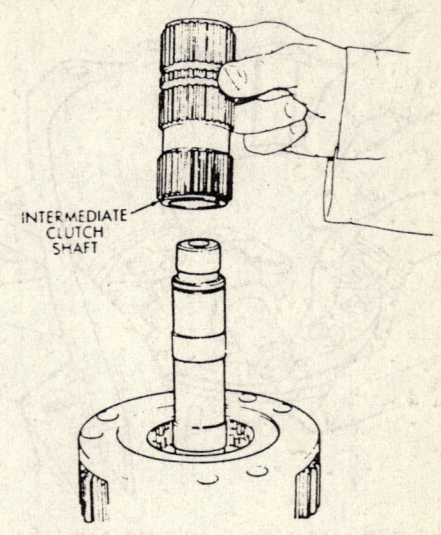

Removing the intermediate clutch shaft from the NP-242

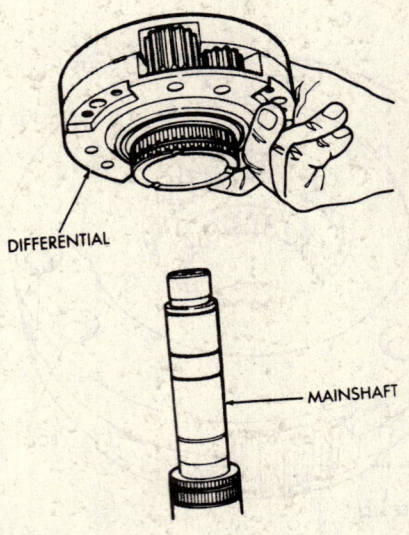

Differential removal from the NP-242

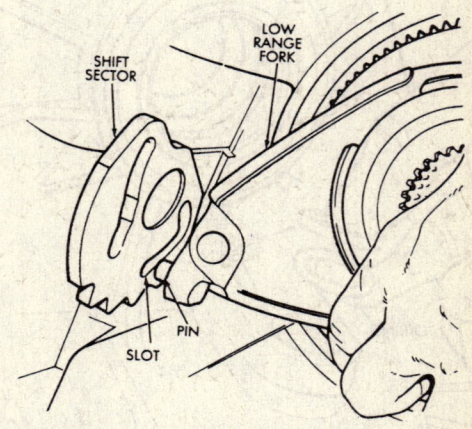

Disengaging the low range fork on the NP-242

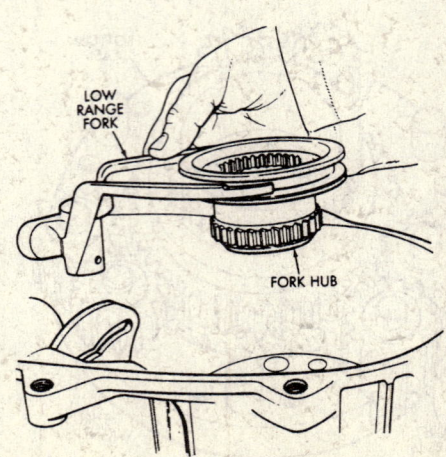

Removing the low range fork and hub from the NP-242

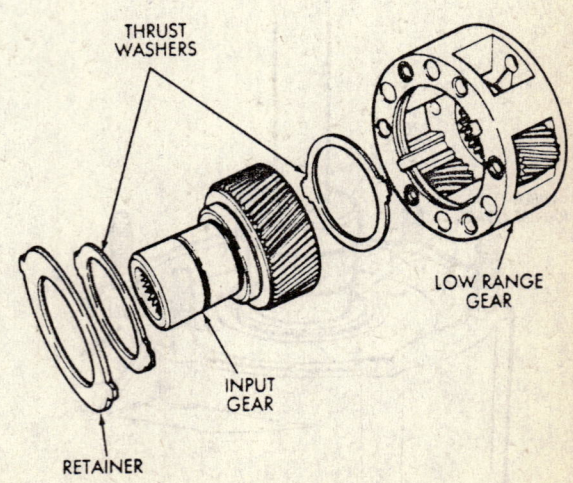

Low range gear components for the NP-242

7-149

7 DRIVE TRAIN

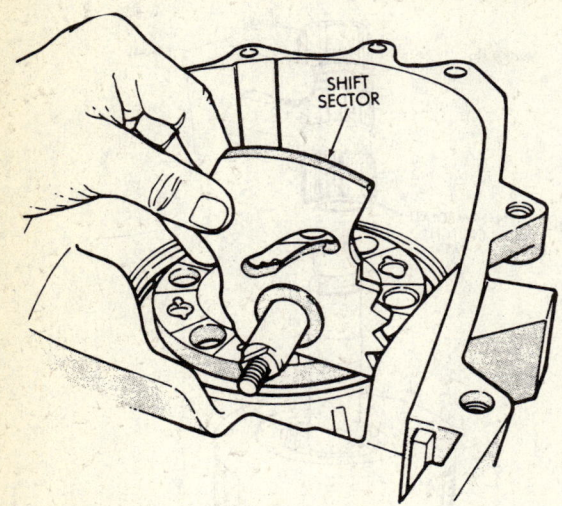

Removing the shift selector from the NP-242

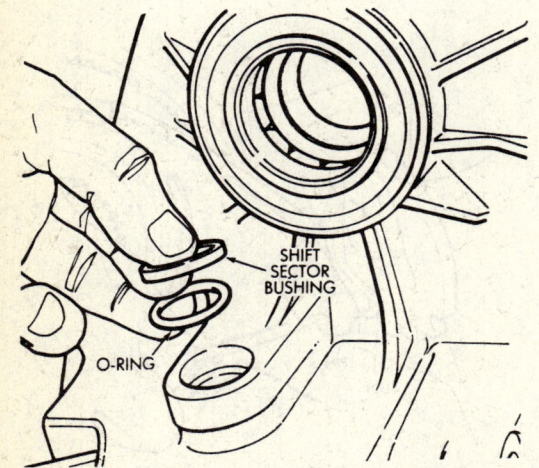

Removing the selector bushing and O-ring from the NP-242

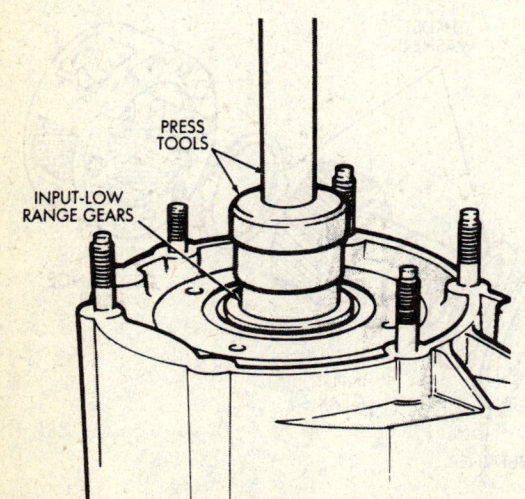

Removing the input and low range gears from the NP-242

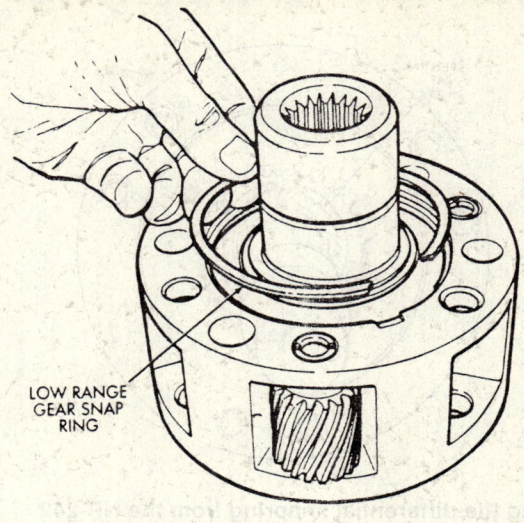

Removing the low range gear snapring from the NP-242

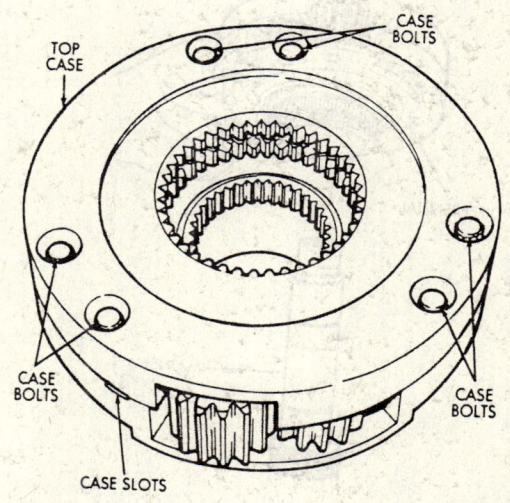

Case bolts securing the NP-242 differential case halves

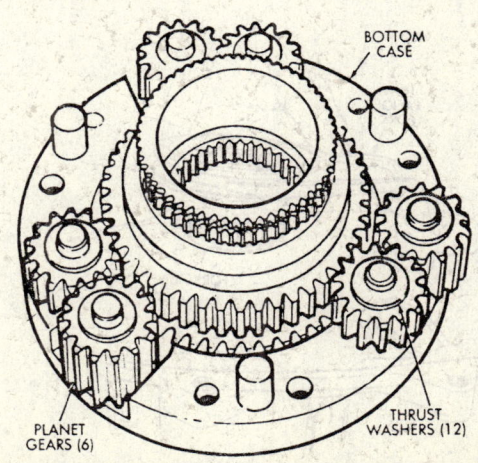

Removing the planet gears and thrust washer from the NP-242

7-150

DRIVE TRAIN 7

20. Remove low range gear snapring, input gear retainer, thrust washers and input gear.
21. Inspect the low range annulus gear. If damaged, replace the gear and front case assembly.
22. Remove the oil seals from the rear retainer, extension housing, oil pump and case halves.
23. Mark case halves for reference. Remove differential case bolts and separate case.
24. Remove thrust washers and planet gears from case pins.
25. Remove mainshaft and sprocket gears from bottom case, noting gear position for assembly.

CLEANING & INSPECTION

1. Wash all components thoroughly in clean solvent. Ensure that all lubricant, metallic particles, dirt, and foreign material are removed from the surfaces of every component.
2. Apply compressed air to each oil supply port and channel in each transfer case half to remove any obstructions or cleaning solvent residue.
3. Inspect all gear teeth for excessive wear or damage. Inspect all gear splines for burrs, nicks, wear or damage.
4. Inspect the low range annulus gear. If the gear is damaged, replace the gear and front case as an assembly. Do not attempt to remove the gear.
5. Remove minor nicks or scratches using an oilstone. Replace any component exhibiting excessive wear or damage.
6. Inspect all snaprings and thrust washers for excessive wear, distortion and damage. Replace any component exhibiting these conditions.
7. Inspect the transfer case halves and rear retainer for cracks, porosity, damaged mating surfaces, stripped bolt threads and distortion. Replace any component exhibiting these conditions.
8. Inspect the condition of all needle, roller, ball and thrust bearings in the front and rear transfer case halves. Also inspect to determine the condition of the bearing bores in both transfer case halves and in the input gear, rear output shaft, side gear, and rear retainer.
9. Replace any component that is excessively worn or damaged.

ASSEMBLY

1. Install new output shaft bearing, snapring and oil seal.
2. Press the input gear bearing from the front case with a re-

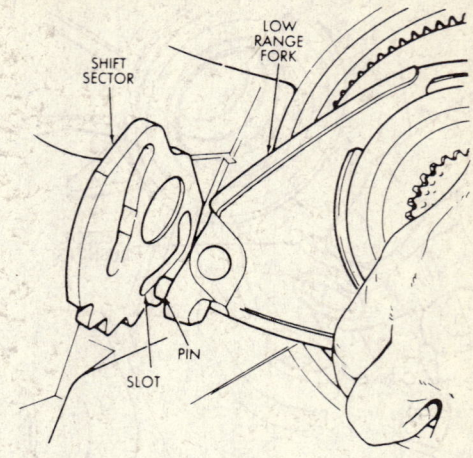
Positioning the low range fork on the NP-242

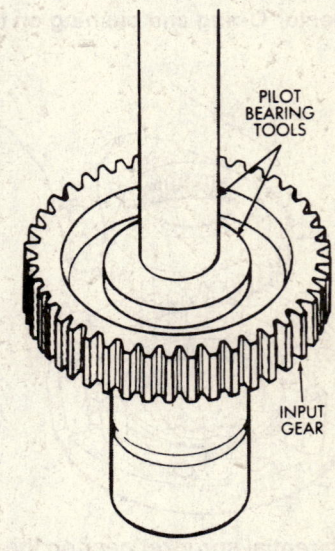
Installing the input gear pilot bearing on the NP-242

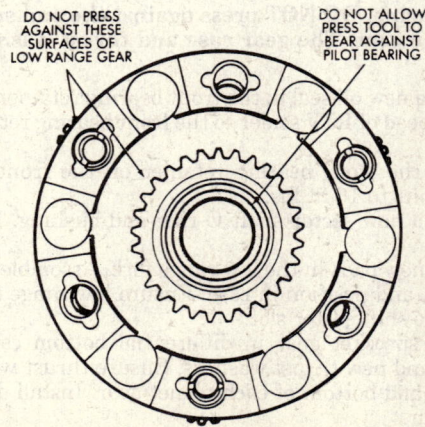
Input gear installation on the NP-242

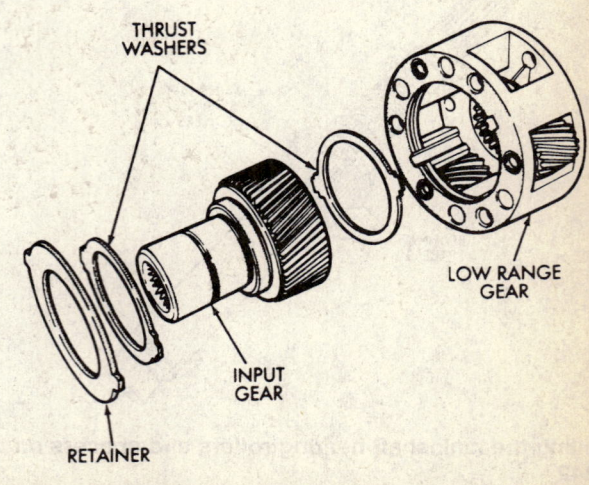
Low range and input gear assembly on the NP-242

7-151

7 DRIVE TRAIN

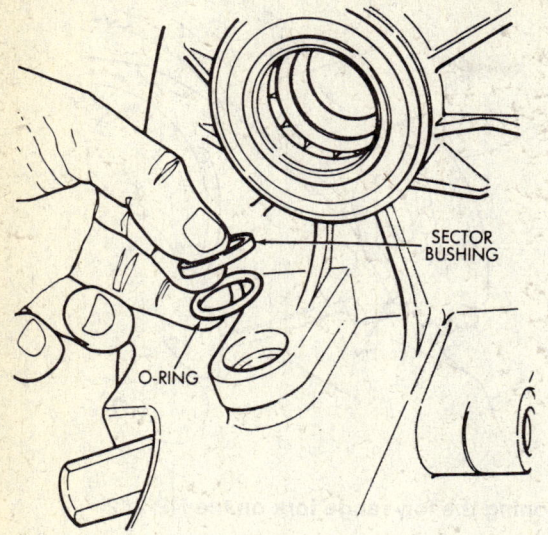

Installing the selector O-ring and bushing on the NP-242

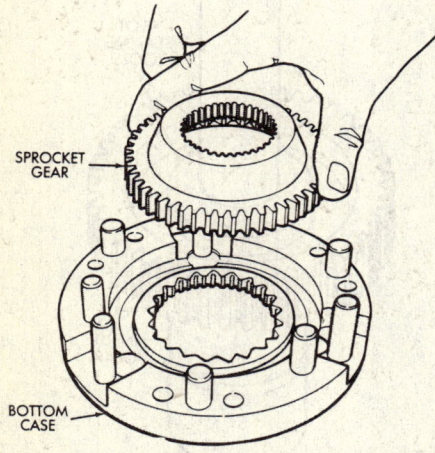

Installing the differential sprocket gear on the NP-242

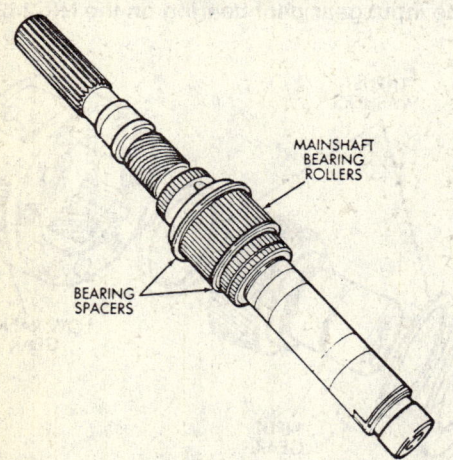

Installing the mainshaft bearing rollers and spacers on the NP-242

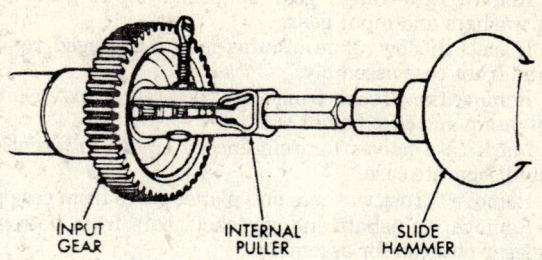

Removing the input gear pilot bearing from the NP-242

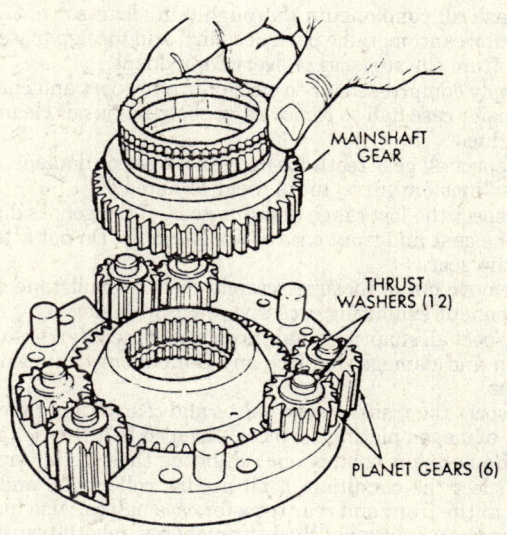

Installing the mainshaft and planet gears on the NP-242

mover tool. Install a snapring on the new bearing and install the bearing into the case so the snapring seats against the case.

3. Install a new input gear pilot bearing.
4. Assemble the low range gear, input gear thrust washers, input gear and input gear retainer. Install the low range gear snapring.
5. Press the input gear into the front bearing and install a new snapring.

NOTE: Use a proper sized tool to press the input gear into the front bearing. DO NOT press against the end surfaces of the low range gear. The gear case and thrust washers could be damaged.

6. Install a new oil seal in the front bearing retainer. Apply an 1/8 in. (3mm) bead of RTV sealer to the front bearing retainer sealing surfaces.
7. Install the front bearing retainer on the front case and tighten the bolts to 16 ft. lbs.
8. Install a new sector shaft O-ring and bushing. Install the shift sector.
9. Install new pads in the low range fork. Assemble low range fork and hub, and position in case. Ensure low range fork pin is engaged in the shift sector slot.
10. Install sprocket gear in differential bottom case. Install planet gears and new thrust washers. Ensure thrust washers are install at top and bottom of each planet gear. Install differential mainshaft gear.
11. Align and position differential top case on bottom case. Align using scribe marks made at disassembly. Install and tighten differential case bolts.

DRIVE TRAIN 7

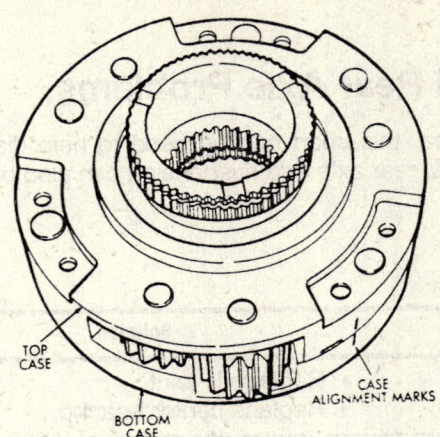

Assembling the differential case halves on the NP-242

12. Install first mainshaft bearing spacer on mainshaft. Install rollers and coat with petroleum jelly to hold in place. Install remaining bearing spacer.
13. Install differential, differential snapring, intermediate clutch shaft, clutch shaft thrust washer and snapring.
14. Inspect mode fork assembly. Replace pads and bushing if necessary. Replace fork tube if bushings are worn. Also check springs and slider bracket for worn components.
15. Install mode sleeve in mode fork and install assembly on mainshaft. Ensure mode sleeve splines are engaged in differential. Install entire assembly in case. Rotate mainshaft slightly to engage shaft with low range gears. Rotate mode fork pin into shift sector slot.
16. Install shift rail and ensure it is seated in both shift forks.
17. Rotate shift sector to align lock pin hole in low range fork with access hole in case. Insert an easy-out in range fork lockpin to hold it securely for installation. Insert tapered end of lock pin into fork and rail. Seat pin with a punch. install plug in lock pin access hole.
18. Install shift lever and tighten to 22 ft. lbs. Install detent plunger, spring and plug.
19. Install front output shaft, drive chain, drive sprocket and drive sprocket snapring.
20. Replace front output shaft rear bearing. Lubricate after installation.
21. Assemble oil pump. Install new oil seal and pick-up tube O-ring. Insert oil pick-up tube in pump and attach oil screen and connector hose. Install pump in rear case.
22. Install magnet in front case.
23. Apply an $1/8$ in. (3mm) bead of RTV sealant to the front case. Align and mate case halves. Ensure case locating dowels are installed and mainshaft splines are engaged in oil pump inner gear. Tighten bolts/washers to 30 ft. lbs.
24. Install new rear retainer bearing. Apply an $1/8$ in. (3mm) bead of RTV sealant to the retainer and install.
25. Install rear bearing snapring, and extension housing seal and bushing.
26. Apply an $1/8$ in. (3mm) bead of RTV sealant to the extension housing and tighten attaching bolts to 30 ft. lbs.
27. Install front yoke with a new seal and torque to 110 ft. lbs.
28. Install new gasket on vacuum switch and install tightening to 20 ft. lbs.
29. Install speedometer components. Install drain plug and tighten to 35 ft. lbs.
30. Fill case with lubricant and tighten fill plug to 35 ft. lbs.
31. Install a replacement gasket on the vacuum switch and install switch.
32. Install drain plug and tighten to 35 ft. lbs. Install speedometer gear, seals and adaptor. retainer bolts to 30 ft. lbs.

DRIVELINE

Front Driveshaft

REMOVAL AND INSTALLATION

Jeep vehicles may come equipped with one of two different type front driveshafts. *Type one* has a conventional universal joint at the axle, but a double offset joint at the transfer case. *Type two* has a conventional universal joint at the axle and a double cardan joint at the transfer case.

Front driveshafts on 1984 vehicles use the type one universal joint only. Front driveshafts on 1985–91 vehicles use either type one or type two.

1. Matchmark the shaft ends, axle and transfer case.
2. Remove the U-joint strap bolts at the front axle yoke.
3. If equipped with a double offset U-joint, remove the double offset joint flange nuts at the transfer case.
4. If equipped with a double cardan U-joint, remove the double cardan joint flange nuts at the transfer case.
5. Installation is the reverse of removal. Install new strap bolts and tighten strap bolts to 170 inch lbs.

FRONT DRIVESHAFT LENGTH ADJUSTMENT

NOTE: The length of the front driveshaft must be checked and adjusted if the shaft has been removed or replaced.

1. Raise the vehicle on ramps.
2. Measure from the rear edge of the groove at the transfer case end of the shaft, to the outer flange of the rubber boot on the double offset joint. The dimension should be 38.0–44.5mm ($1^{1}/_{2}$–$1^{3}/_{4}$ in.).
3. If not, loosen the slip joint locknut and slide the shaft in or out of the double offset joint to correct the length.
4. Tighten the nut to 55 ft. lbs.

FRONT DRIVESHAFT ANGLE MEASUREMENT AND ADJUSTMENT

NOTE: Changes in the front wheel caster adjustment also change the front driveshaft, front U-joint angle. When making caster adjustments, the front driveshaft U-joint angle must be checked. U-joint angle takes precedence over caster angle. A special tool, an inclinometer such as tool J-23498, must be used for this procedure.

1. Before checking the U-joint angle, the ride height must be checked. Record the measurement from the front axle tube to the frame sill, directly above the tubes. Front axle measurement should be 6.2–7.0 inches (157.5–177.8mm).

NOTE: If the vehicle is equipped with P205/75 R15 tires, add 0.345 inch (9mm) to all dimensions. If the vehicle is equipped with P215/75 R15 tires, add 0.787 (20mm) to all dimensions.

7 DRIVE TRAIN

DRIVELINE
Troubleshooting Basic Driveshaft and Rear Axle Problems

When abnormal vibrations or noises are detected in the driveshaft area, this chart can be used to help diagnose possible causes. Remember that other components such as wheels, tires, rear axle and suspension can also produce similar conditions.

BASIC DRIVESHAFT PROBLEMS

Problem	Cause	Solution
Shudder as car accelerates from stop or low speed	• Loose U-joint • Defective center bearing	• Replace U-joint • Replace center bearing
Loud clunk in driveshaft when shifting gears	• Worn U-joints	• Replace U-joints
Roughness or vibration at any speed	• Out-of-balance, bent or dented driveshaft • Worn U-joints • U-joint clamp bolts loose	• Balance or replace driveshaft • Replace U-joints • Tighten U-joint clamp bolts
Squeaking noise at low speeds	• Lack of U-joint lubrication	• Lubricate U-joint; if problem persists, replace U-joint
Knock or clicking noise	• U-joint or driveshaft hitting frame tunnel • Worn CV joint	• Correct overloaded condition • Replace CV joint

2. Place the transmission and transfer case in NEUTRAL.
3. Jack up both the front and rear, and support the truck on jackstands placed under the axle.
4. Attach the inclinometer to the pinion yoke bearing cap and note the angle.
5. Rotate the shaft 90° and take a reading on the driveshaft yoke bearing cap.

NOTE: The inclinometer must face the same direction on both readings.

6. The difference between the readings taken at the driveshaft yoke and the axle yoke is the U-joint angle **B**.
7. The angle can be adjusted by adding or deleting shims.

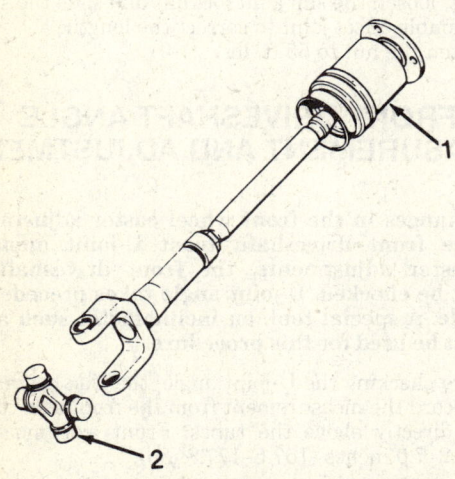

Double offset joint driveshaft used on all 1984 and some 1985–91 Cherokee/Wagoneer models. (1) is the double offset, (2) is the cardan joint

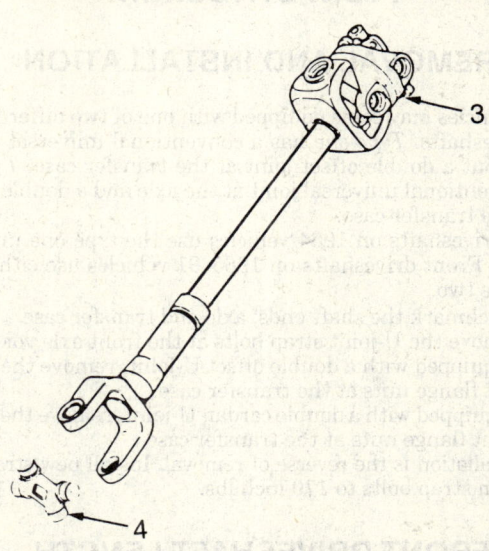

Front driveshaft used on all Comanche models, some 1985–86 Cherokee/Wagoneer models and all 1987–91 Cherokee/Wagoneer models. (3) is the double cardan joint, (4) is the cardan joint

DRIVE TRAIN 7

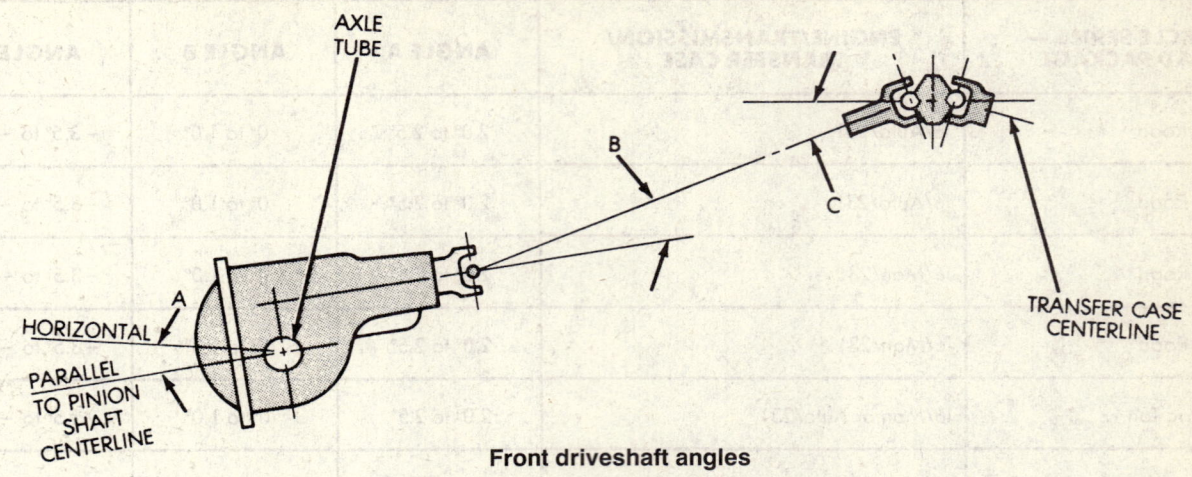

Front driveshaft angles

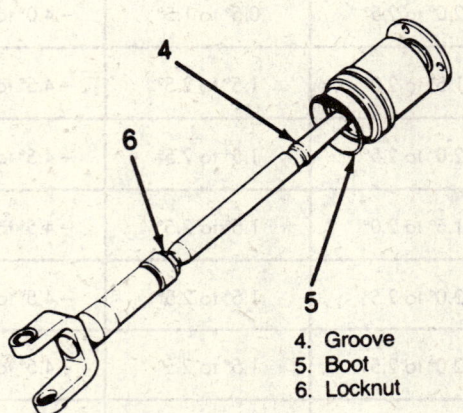

4. Groove
5. Boot
6. Locknut

Double offset joint front driveshaft length adjustment

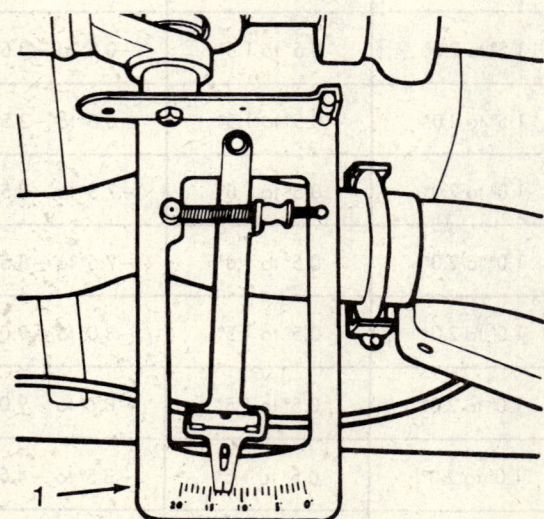

Inclinometer (1) installed for front driveshaft angle adjustment

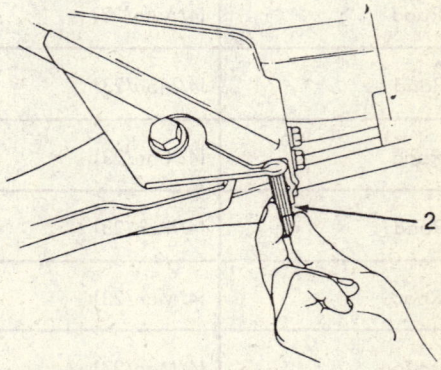

Lower control arm shim (2) location

Adding shims to the lower suspension arms will decrease angle **A**, but will increase the caster angle. Pinion shaft angle **A** has priority over the caster angle if both cannot be adjusted to specifications.

8. If front angle **B** and vehicle height are correct, pinion shaft angle **A** should also be correct.

Rear Driveshaft

NOTE: Two different driveshafts are used on these vehicles. With Command-Trac®, the driveshaft has welded yokes at each end. With Selec-Trac®, a welded yoke is used at the rear and a splined slip yoke is used at the front.

1. Raise and support the vehicle on jackstands.
2. Place the transmission in NEUTRAL.
3. Matchmark the yokes and flanges.
4. On vehicles with Command-Trac®, the driveshaft may be removed by disconnecting it at the axle and sliding it from the front yoke, leaving the front yoke attached to the transfer case. If you do this, however, you MUST matchmark the driveshaft and front yoke BEFORE separation.
5. On vehicles with Selec-Trac®, disconnect the yokes from the axle and transfer case. Remove the driveshaft.
6. Installation is the reverse of removal. Install new strap bolts and tighten strap bolts to 170 inch lbs.

7-155

7 DRIVE TRAIN

VEHICLE SERIES — ROAD PACKAGE	ENGINE/TRANSMISSION/ TRANSFER CASE	ANGLE A	ANGLE B	ANGLE C
63 — Off Road	I6/Auto/231	2.0° to 2.5°	0° to 1.0°	−3.5° to −4.5°
65 — Off Road	I6/Auto/231	2.0° to 2.5°	0° to 1.0°	−3.5° to −4.5°
63 — Off Road	I6/Man/231	2.0° to 2.5°	0° to 1.0°	−3.5° to −4.5°
65 — Off Road	I6/Man/231	2.0° to 2.5°	0° to 1.0°	−3.5° to −4.5°
65 — Metric Ton	I6/Man or Auto/231	2.0° to 2.5°	0° to 1.0°	−3.5° to −4.5°
63 — Off Road	I4/Auto/231	2.0° to 2.5°	0.5° to 1.5°	−4.0° to −5.0°
65 — Off Road	I4/Auto/231	2.0° to 2.5°	0.5° to 1.5°	−4.0° to −5.0°
63 — On Road	I4/Man/231	1.5° to 2.0°	1.5° to 2.5°	−4.5° to −5.5°
63 — Off Road	I4/Man/231	2.0° to 2.5°	1.5° to 2.5°	−4.5° to −5.5°
65 — On Road	I4/Man/231	1.5° to 2.0°	1.5° to 2.5°	−4.5° to −5.5°
65 — Off Road	I4/Man/231	2.0° to 2.5°	1.5° to 2.5°	−4.5° to −5.5°
65 — Metric Ton	I4/Man/231	2.0° to 2.5°	1.5° to 2.5°	−4.5° to −5.5°
63 — On Road	I6/Auto/242	1.5° to 2.0°	0.5° to 1.5°	−0.5° to −3.5°
63 — On Road	I6/Man or Auto/231	1.5° to 2.0°	0.5° to 1.5°	−0.5° to −3.5°
65 — On Road	I6/Auto/242	1.5° to 2.0°	0.5° to 1.5°	−0.5° to −3.5°
65 — On Road	I6/Man or Auto/231	1.5° to 2.0°	0.5° to 1.5°	−0.5° to −3.5°
70 — On Road	I6/Man or Auto/231 or 242	1.0° to 2.0°	0.5° to 1.0°	−7.5° to −8.5°
70 — On Road	I4/Man or Auto/231 or 242	1.0° to 2.0°	0.5° to 1.0°	−7.5° to −8.5°
70 — Off Road	I6/Man/231	1.0° to 2.0°	0.5° to 1.5°	−8.0° to −9.0°
70 — Off Road	I4/Man/231	1.0° to 2.0°	0.5° to 1.5°	−8.0° to −9.0°
70 — Off Road	I6/Auto/231 or 242	1.0° to 2.0°	0.5° to 1.5°	−3.5° to −4.5°
70 — Off Road	I4/Auto/231 or 242	1.0° to 2.0°	0.5° to 1.5°	−3.5° to −4.5°

Front driveshaft angle specifications

DRIVE TRAIN 7

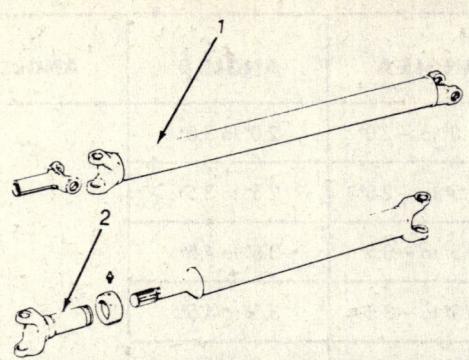

Two types of rear driveshafts used on 1985–91 models. (1) is used with Command-Trac; (2) is used with Selec-Trac

REAR DRIVESHAFT ANGLE MEASUREMENT AND ADJUSTMENT

1. Before checking the U-joint angle, the ride height must be checked. Record the measurement from the front axle tube to the frame sill, directly above the tubes. Front axle measurement should be 5.7–6.5 inches (144.5–165mm).
   NOTE: If the vehicle is equipped with P205/75 R15 tires, add 0.345 inch (9mm) to all dimensions. If the vehicle is equipped with P215/75 R15 tires, add 0.787 (20mm) to all dimensions.
2. Place the transmission and transfer case in NEUTRAL.
3. Jack up both the front and rear, and support the truck on jackstands placed under the axle.
4. Attach the inclinometer to the pinion yoke bearing cap and note the angle.
5. Rotate the shaft 90° and take a reading on the driveshaft yoke bearing cap.
   NOTE: The inclinometer must face the same direction on both readings.
6. The difference between the readings taken at the driveshaft yoke and the axle yoke is the U-joint angle B.
7. To adjust rear U-joint angle:
   a. Raise the rear of the vehicle and place jackstands under the frame.
   b. Position a floor jack under the rear axle and raise just enough to support the weight.
   c. Remove the rear wheels and loosen the spring U-bolts.
   d. Install tapered shims between the springs and brackets to correct the angle.
   e. Tighten the spring U-bolt nuts to 52 ft. lbs.
   f. Remove the jack, install the wheels and lower the vehicle.
8. When angle **A**, **B** and vehicle height are correct, angle **C** should also be correct.

U-Joints

There are five types of universal joints used: the Cardan cross-type with U-bolts and snaprings; a Cardan cross-type with just snaprings; a double Cardan cross-type; ball and trunnion-type universal joints which serve as a combination slip-joint and universal joint. Some models have a front driveshaft which, at the transfer case end, uses a double offset joint. This unit is not repairable and must be serviced by replacement only.

Universal joints fail for numerous reasons, the primary one being lack of lubrication. Others could be structural damage incurred from hitting something, an unbalanced driveshaft, the entrance of dirt or water due to a rotted rubber seal or just plain wear from excessive mileage.

Rebuilding kits are available for both types of universal joints. The kit for a Cardan cross-type universal joint includes the entire cross assembly, the cross bearing journal, roller bearings, bearing cap with new rubber seal and new snaprings.

The rebuilding kit for the ball and trunnion-type universal joint includes a new grease cover and gasket, universal joint body, two centering buttons and spring washers, two ball and roller bearing assemblies, two thrust washers, dust cover and two dust cover clamps.

Although U-joints can be rebuilt, most procedures today call for replacement rather than rebuilding.

OVERHAUL

Cardan Cross-Type with Snaprings

1. Remove the driveshaft from the vehicle.
2. Remove the snaprings by pinching the ends together with a pair of pliers. If the rings do not readily snap out of the groove, tap the end of the bearing lightly to relieve pressure against the rings.
3. After removing the snaprings, press on the end of one bearing until the opposite bearing is pushed from the yoke arm. Turn the joint over and press the first bearing back out of that arm by pressing on the exposed end of the journal shaft. To drive it out, use a soft ground drift with a flat face, about 0.8mm ($\frac{1}{32}$ in.)

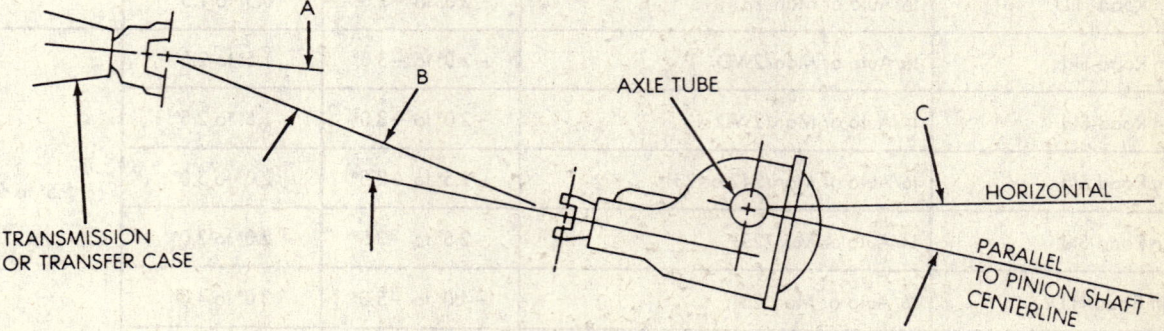

Rear driveshaft angles

7 DRIVE TRAIN

VEHICLE SERIES — ROAD PACKAGE	ENGINE/TRANSMISSION/ TRANSFER CASE OR 2WD	ANGLE A	ANGLE B	ANGLE C
64 — On Road-Std.	I4/Auto or Man/2WD	−1.0° to −2.0°	2.0° to 3.0°	4.5° to 5.5°
64 — On Road-Std.	I6/Auto or Man/2WD	−1.5° to −2.5°	2.5° to 3.5°	
63 — On Road-Std.	I4/Auto or Man/231	−2.5° to −3.5°	3.5° to 4.5°	
63 — Off Road-Std.	I4/Auto or Man/231	−2.5° to −3.5°	3.5° to 4.5°	
63 — On Road-Std.	I6/Auto/242 or Man/231	−3.5° to −4.5°	4.0° to 5.0°	
63 — Off Road-Std.	I6/Auto or Man/231	−3.5° to −4.5°	4.0° to 5.0°	
64 — On Road-H.D.	I6/Auto or Man/2WD	−1.5° to −2.5°	2.5° to 3.5°	
63 — On Road-H.D.	I6/Auto or Man/231	−3.0° to −4.0°	3.5° to 4.5°	
63 — Off Road-H.D.	I6/Auto/231	−3.0° to −4.0°	3.5° to 4.5°	
63 — Off Road-H.D.	I6/Man/231	−3.5° to −4.5°	4.0° to 5.0°	
66 — On Road-Std.	I4/Auto or Man/2WD	0° to −1.0°	0.5° to −0.5°	6.5° to 7.5°
66 — On Road-H.D.	I4/Man/2WD	−1.0° to −2.0°	0.5° to −0.5°	
66 — On Road-Std.	I6/Auto or Man/2WD	−1.0° to −2.0°	0.5° to −0.5°	
66 — On Road-H.D.	I6/Auto or Man/2WD	−1.5° to −2.5°	0.5° to −0.5°	
65 — On Road-Std.	I4/Auto or Man/231	−1.5° to −2.5°	0° to 1.0°	
65 — Off Road-Std.	I4/Auto or Man/231	−1.5° to −2.5°	0° to 1.0°	
65 — On Road-H.D.	I4/Man/231	−1.5° to −2.5°	0° to 1.0°	
65 — On Road-Std.	I6/Auto/242 or Man/231	−2.0° to −3.0°	0.5° to 1.5°	
65 — Off Road-Std.	I6/Auto or Man/231	−2.0° to −3.0°	0.5° to 1.5°	
65 — On Road-H.D.	I6/Auto or Man/231	−2.0° to −3.0°	0.5° to 1.5°	
70 — On Road-Std.	I6/Auto or Man/2WD	−2.0° to −3.0°	1.5° to 2.5°	5.5° to 6.5°
70 — On Road-Std.	I4/Auto or Man/2WD	−2.0° to −3.0°	1.5° to 2.5°	
70 — On Road-Std.	I6/Auto or Man/242 or 231	−2.5° to −3.5°	2.0° to 3.0°	
70 — On Road-Std.	I4/Auto or Man/231	−2.5° to −3.5°	2.0° to 3.0°	
70 — Off Road-H.D.	I6/Auto or Man/231	−4.0° to −5.0°	3.0° to 4.0°	
70 — Off Road-H.D.	I4/Auto or Man/231	−4.0° to −5.0°	3.0° to 4.0°	

Rear driveshaft angle specifications

DRIVE TRAIN 7

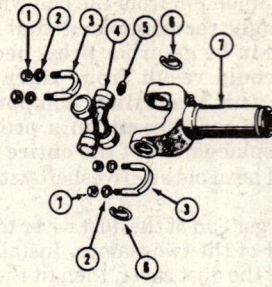

1. U-bolt nut
2. U-bolt washer
3. U-bolt
4. Universal joint journal
5. Lubrication fitting
6. Snap ring
7. Universal joint sleeve yoke

Cardan cross-type with U-bolts and snaprings

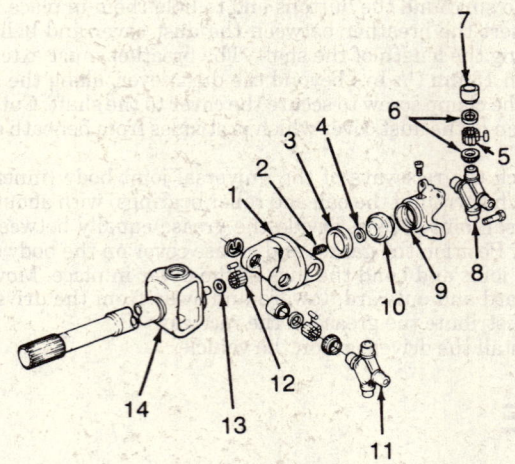

1. Link yoke
2. Socket spring
3. Socket ball retainer
4. Thrust washer
5. Needle bearings
6. Seal
7. Bearing cap
8. Rear spider
9. Socket yoke
10. Socket ball
11. Front spider
12. Socket needle bearings
13. Thrust washer
14. Propeller shaft yoke

Double cardan universal joint

smaller in diameter than the hole in the yoke; otherwise, there is danger of damaging the bearing.

4. Repeat the procedure for the other two bearings, then lift out the journal assembly by sliding it to one side.
5. Wash all parts in cleaning solvent and inspect the parts after cleaning. Replace the journal assembly if it is worn extensively. Make sure that the grease channel in each journal trunnion is open.
6. Pack all of the bearing caps $1/3$ full of grease and install the rollers (bearings).
7. Press one of the cap/bearing assemblies into one of the yoke arms just far enough so that the cap will remain in position.
8. Place the journal in position in the installed cap, with a cap/bearing assembly placed on the opposite end.

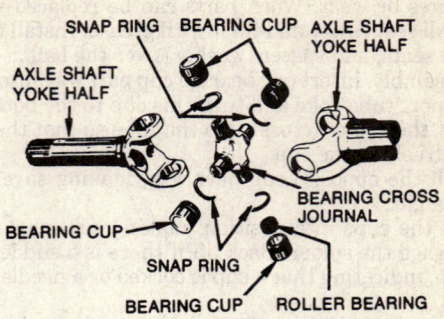

Cardan cross-type universal joint

9. Position the free cap so that when it is driven from the opposite end it will be inserted into the opening of the yoke. Repeat this operation for the other two bearings.
10. Install the retaining clips. If the U-joint binds when it is assembled, tap the arms of the yoke slightly to relieve any pressure on the bearings at the end of the journal.

Cardan Cross-Type with U-Bolts and Snaprings

1. Removal of the attaching U-bolt releases one set of bearing races. Slide the driveshaft into the yoke flange to remove that set of bearing races, being careful not to lose the rollers (bearings).
2. After removal of the first set of bearings, release the other set by pinching the ends of the snaprings with pliers and removing them from the sleeve yoke. Should the rings fail to snap readily from the groove, tap the end of the bearing lightly, to relieve the pressure against them.
3. Press on the end of one bearing, until the opposite bearing is pushed out of the yoke arm.
4. Turn the universal joint over and press the first bearing out by pressing on the exposed end of the journal assembly. Use a soft round drift with a flat face about 0.8mm ($1/32$ in.) smaller in diameter than the hole in the yoke arm. Then drive out the bearing.
5. Lift the journal out by sliding it to one side.
6. Install in the reverse order of removal, using the procedures for the snapring U-joints from Step 4 on as a guide.

Double Cardan Type

1. Use a punch to mark the coupling yoke and the adjoining yokes before disassembly, to ensure proper reassembly and driveline balance.
2. It is easiest to remove the bearings from the coupling yoke first.
3. Support the driveshaft horizontally on a press stand, or on the workbench if a vise is being used.
4. If snaprings are used to retain the bearing cups, remove them. Place the rear car of the coupling yoke over a socket large enough to receive the cup. Place a smaller socket, or a cross press made for the purpose, over the opposite cup. Press the bearing cup out of the coupling yoke ear. If the cup is not completely removed, insert a spacer and complete the operation, or grasp the cup with a pair of slip joint pliers and work it out. If the cups are retained by plastic, this will shear the retainers. Remove any bits of plastic.
5. Rotate the driveshaft and repeat the operation on the opposite cup.
6. Disengage the trunnions of the spider, still attached to the flanged yoke, from the coupling yoke, and pull the flanged yoke and spider from the center ball on the ball support tube yoke.

NOTE: The joint between the shaft and coupling yoke can be serviced without disassembly of the joint between the coupling yoke and flanged yoke.

7. Pry the seal from the ball cavity, remove the washers, spring and three seats. Examine the ball stud seat and the ball

7-159

7 DRIVE TRAIN

stud for scores or wear. Worn parts can be replaced with a kit. Clean the ball seat cavity and fill it with grease. Install the spring, washer, ball seats, and spacer (washer) over the ball.

8. To assembly, insert one bearing cup part way into one ear of the ball support tube yoke and turn this cup to the bottom.
9. Insert the spider (cross) into the tube so that the trunnion (arm) seats freely in the cup.
10. Install the opposite cup part way, making sure that both cups are straight.
11. Press the cups into position, making sure that both cups squarely engage the spider. Back off if there is a sudden increase in resistance, indicating that a cup is cocked or a needle bearing is out of place.
12. As soon as one bearing retainer groove clears the yoke, stop and install the retainer (plastic retainer models). On models with snaprings, press the cups into place, then install the snaprings over the cups.
13. If difficulty is encountered installing the plastic retainers or the snaprings, smack the yoke sharply with a hammer to spring the ears slightly.
14. Install one bearing cup part way into the ear of the coupling yoke, Make sure that the alignment marks are matched, then engaged the coupling yoke over the spider and press in the cups, installing the retainers or snaprings as before.
15. Install the cups and spider into the flanged yoke as with the previous yoke.

NOTE: The flange yoke should snap over center to the right or left and up or down by the pressure of the ball seat spring.

Ball and Trunnion-Type

1. Remove the driveshaft from the vehicle.
2. Position the tube of the driveshaft near the ball-type universal joint, in a bench vise; clamp tightly.
3. Bend the lugs of the grease cover away from the universal joint body and remove the cover and the gasket.
4. Remove the two clamps from the dust cover. Push the joint body toward the driveshaft tube. Remove the two centering buttons and spring washers, the two ball and roller bearings and the two thrust washers from the trunnion pin.
5. Press the trunnion pin from the ball with an arbor press.

NOTE: It is strongly recommended that the trunnion pin be pressed out and in by an arbor press because of the possible damage that could result from other methods such as hammer and drift. This is a critical component in the assembly and any damage could result in a premature failure or even necessitate replacement of the entire driveshaft.

6. Clean the ball head of the driveshaft with a suitable solvent and dry thoroughly.
7. Secure the larger end of the dust cover to the universal joint body with the larger of the two clamps. Install the smaller clamp at the smaller end of the dust cover, then fit the cover over the ball head shaft.
8. Push the universal joint cover toward the driveshaft tube.
9. With an arbor press, press the trunnion pin into a centered position in the ball head.

NOTE: The trunnion pin must project an equal distance from each side of the ball head. If it is not centered within 0.15mm, driveshaft vibration may result.

10. Hold the universal joint body toward the tube of the driveshaft to gain access to the trunnion pin. Install one thrust washer, one ball and roller bearing and one spring washer at one side of the ball head. Compress the centering buttons into the trunnion pin, then move the joint body away from the driveshaft tube, into position to surround the buttons and to hold them in place.
11. Insert the breather between the dust cover and ball head shaft, along the length of the shaft. The breather must extend no more than 13mm ($1/2$ in.) beyond the dust cover, along the shaft. Tighten the clamp screw to secure the cover to the shaft. Cut away any portion of the dust cover which protrudes from beneath either clamp.
12. Pack the raceways of the universal joint body (inner surfaces which surround the ball and roller bearings) with about 2 oz. of universal joint grease. Divide the grease equally between the raceways. Position the gasket and grease cover on the body of the universal joint and bend the lugs of the cover in place. Move the body inward and outward, toward and away from the driveshaft tube, to distribute the grease in the raceways.
13. Install the driveshaft on the vehicle.

REAR AXLE

Understanding Rear Axles

The rear axle is a special type of transmission that reduces the speed of the drive from the engine and transmission and divides the power to the rear wheels. Power enters the rear axle from the driveshaft via the companion flange. The flange is mounted on the drive pinion shaft. The drive pinion shaft and gear which carry the power into the differential turn at engine speed. The gear on the end of the pinion shaft drives a large ring gear the axis of rotation of which is 90 degrees away from the of the pinion. The pinion and gear reduce the gear ratio of the axle, and change the direction of rotation to turn the axle shafts which drive both wheels. The rear axle gear ratio is found by dividing the number of pinion gear teeth into the number of ring gear teeth.

The ring gear drives the differential case. The case provides the two mounting points for the ends of a pinion shaft on which are mounted two pinion gears. The pinion gears drive the two side gears, one of which is located on the inner end of each axle shaft.

By driving the axle shafts through the arrangement, the differential allows the outer drive wheel to turn faster than the inner drive wheel in a turn.

The main drive pinion and the side bearings, which bear the weight of the differential case, are shimmed to provide proper bearing preload, and to position the pinion and ring gears properly.

NOTE: The proper adjustment of the relationship of the ring and pinion gears is critical. It should be attempted only by those with extensive equipment and/or experience.

Limited-slip differentials include clutches which link each axle shaft to the differential case. Clutches may be engaged either by spring action or by pressure produced by the torque on the axles during a turn. During turning on a dry pavement, the effects of the clutches are overcome, and each wheel turns at the required speed. When slippage occurs at either wheel, however, the clutches will transmit some of the power to the wheel which has the greater amount of traction. Because of the presence of clutches, limited-slip units require a special lubricant.

REAR DRIVE AXLE APPLICATION CHART

Axle	Model	Years
AMC 7 9/16 in.	All	1984-86
Dana 35	All	1987-91
Dana 44	Metric Ton Package	1987-91

DRIVE TRAIN 7

Identification

Dana model 35/44 drive axles can be identified by a tag located on the left side of the housing cover. The tag lists part number and gear ratio. Stamped into the right side axle shaft are the production date and manufacturers identification.

The I.D. code for the AMC 7$\frac{9}{16}$ in. (192mm) axle is stamped into the right hand side axle tube boss. Code 'S' indicates a 3.73:1 ratio. Code 'T' indicates a 3.31:1 ratio. Code 'SS' or 'TT' indicate the rear axle is equipped with a Trac-Lok differential.

Determining Axle Ratio

The drive axle is said to have a certain axle ratio. This number (usually a whole number and a decimal fraction) is actually a comparison of the number of gear teeth on the ring gear and the pinion gear. For example, a 4.11 rear means that theoretically, there are 4.11 teeth on the ring gear and one tooth on the pinion gear or, put another way, the driveshaft must turn 4.11 times to turn the wheels once. Actually, on a 4.11 rear, there might be 37 teeth on the ring gear and 9 teeth on the pinion gear. By dividing the number of teeth on the pinion gear into the number of teeth on the ring gear, the numerical axle ratio (4.11) is obtained. This also provides a good method of ascertaining exactly what axle ratio one is dealing with.

Another method of determining gear ratio is to jack up and support the car so that both rear wheels are off the ground. Make a chalk mark on the rear wheel and the driveshaft. Put the transmission in neutral. Turn the rear wheel one complete turn and count the number of turns that the driveshaft makes. The number of turns that the driveshaft makes in one complete revolution of the rear wheel is an approximation of the rear axle ratio.

Axle Shaft, Bearing and Seal

REMOVAL AND INSTALLATION

Dana 44 and AMC 7$\frac{9}{16}$ in. (192mm)

NOTE: An arbor press is necessary for this procedure.

1. Raise and support the vehicle safely.

NOTE: For vehicles equipped with Anti-Lock Brakes (ABS), refer to Section 9 for the proper procedures concerning brake removal.

2. Remove the wheel and tire and brake drum assembly.

CAUTION

Brake linings contain asbestos. Asbestos is a known cancer-causing agent. When working on brakes, remember that the dust which accumulates on the brake parts and/or in the drum contains asbestos. Always wear a protective face covering, such as a painter's mask, when working on the brakes. NEVER blow the dust from the brakes or drum! There are solvents made for the purpose of cleaning brake parts. Use them!

3. Remove the nuts that attach the outer seal retainer (and brake backing plate) to the axle shaft tube. Discard the nuts.
4. Remove the axle shaft from the housing with an axle puller attached to a slide hammer.
5. Discard the inner axle seal. Position the axle shaft in a vise.
6. Remove the retaining ring by drilling a $\frac{1}{4}$ in. (6mm) hole about $\frac{3}{4}$ of the way through the ring, then using a cold chisel over the hole, split the ring.
7. Remove the bearing with an arbor press, discard the seal and remove the retainer plate.

To Install:

8. Clean and then apply a thin coating of wheel bearing lubricant to the bearing and seal contact surfaces. Apply wheel bearing lubricant to the lips of the replacement inner and outer seals.

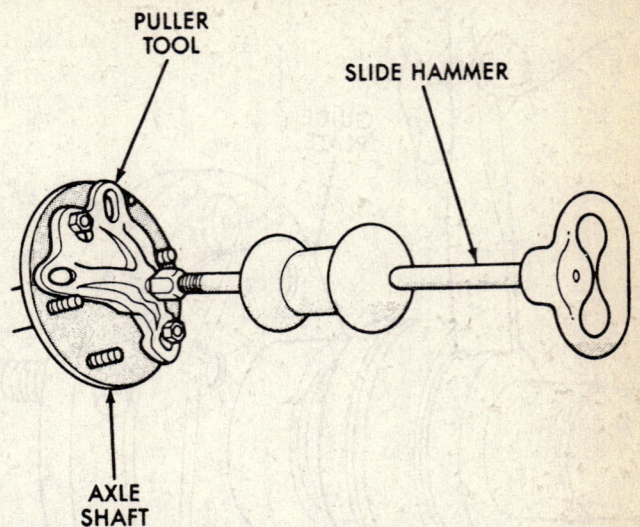

Using a slide hammer-type puller to remove the tapered axle shaft

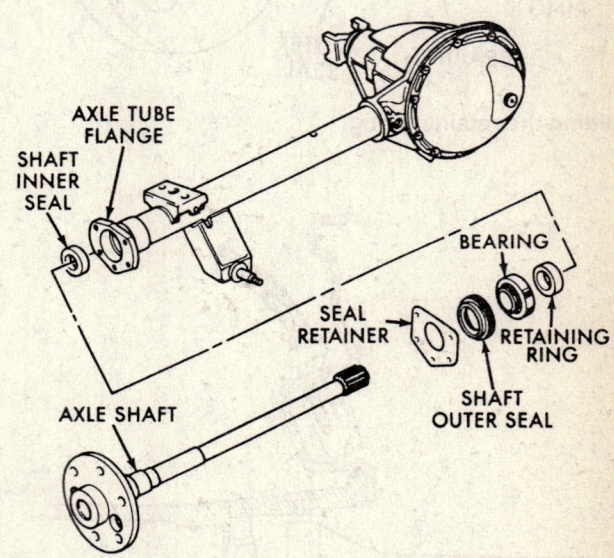

Axle shaft components

9. Install the inner seal with the open end of the seal facing inward. Ensure it is completely seated.

NOTE: It is helpful to cool the axle shaft before pressing on the bearing and retainer. Leave the bearing and retainer at room temperature.

10. Install the retainer plate and the outer seal on the shaft. Ensure the open end of the seal faces toward the axle shaft bearing.
11. Pack the replacement bearing with wheel bearing lubricant and position on axle shaft. Press into place.
12. Press a replacement bearing retainer on the axle shaft against the bearing.
13. Install the axle into the axle tube. Position and align the seal retainer and brake support plate and install replacement attaching nuts. tighten nuts to 32 ft. lbs.
14. Install brake assembly wheels and tires. Lower vehicle.

7 DRIVE TRAIN

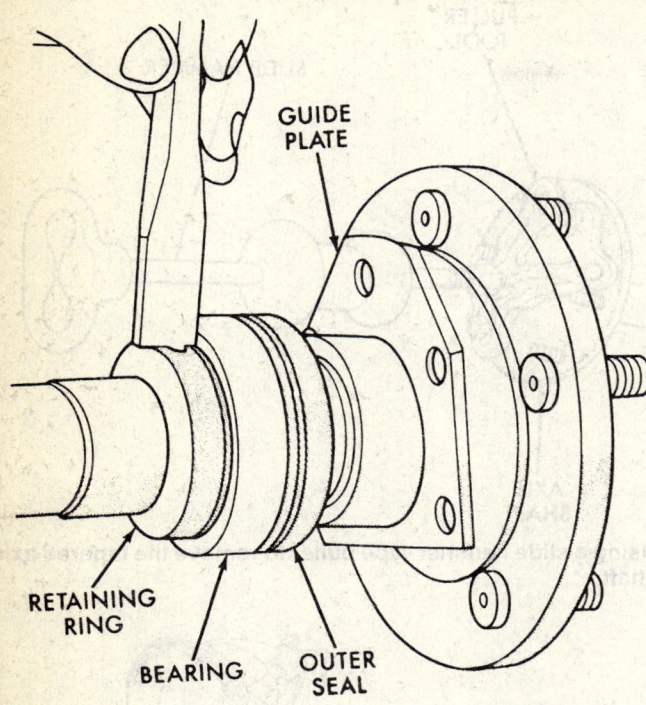

Splitting the retaining ring

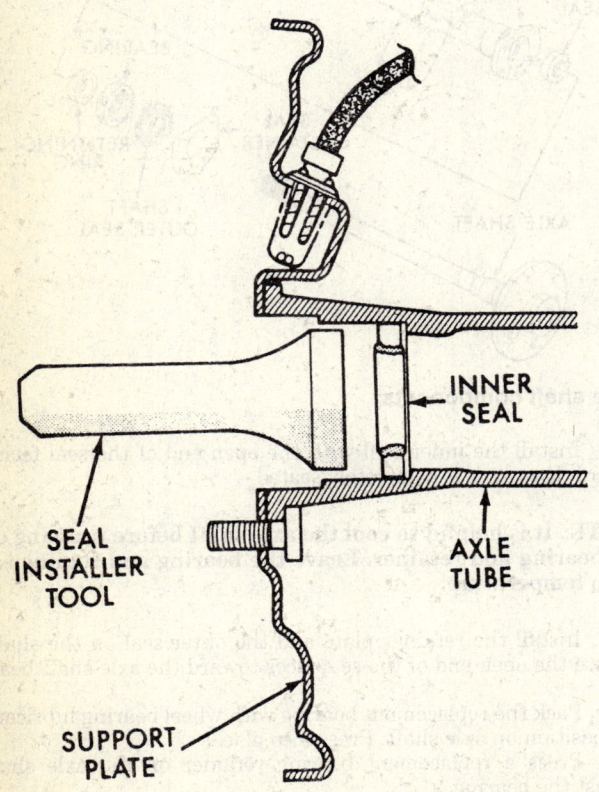

Installing an inner seal in the axle tube with an installer tool

Dana 35

1. Raise and support the vehicle safely.

── **CAUTION** ──
Brake linings contain asbestos. Asbestos is a known cancer-causing agent. When working on brakes, remember that the dust which accumulates on the brake parts and/or in the drum contains asbestos. Always wear a protective face covering, such as a painter's mask, when working on the brakes. NEVER blow the dust from the brakes or drum! There are solvents made for the purpose of cleaning brake parts. Use them!

2. Remove the wheels and brake assemblies.

NOTE: For vehicles equipped with Anti-Lock Brakes (ABS), refer to Section 9 for the proper procedures concerning brake removal.

3. Loosen the differential housing cover and drain the lubricant. Remove the housing cover.
4. Rotate the differential so the pinion gear mate shaft lock screw is accessible. Remove the lock screw and the pinion gear mate shaft.
5. Move the axle shafts inward and remove the C-clip lock from the recessed groove in the axle shaft.
6. Remove the axle shaft from the case.
7. Remove the axle shaft seal and bearing using removal tool set 6310.

To Install:

8. Wipe the bearing bore and axle shaft tube clean.
9. Install the bearing using tools C-4171 and 6436. Seat the bearing against the shoulder in the axle tube.
10. Install the replacement axle shaft seal with tool 6437 and C-4171. When the installation tool face contacts the axle tube, the seal is at the correct depth.
11. Lubricate the bearing bore and the seal lip. Insert the axle shaft into the tube and engage its splines with the differential.
12. Install the C-clip locks and force the axles outward to seat them.
13. Insert the differential pinion gear mate shaft into the case and through the thrust washers and the pinion gears. Align the hole in the shaft with the lock screw hole. Install the lock screw and tighten to 14 ft. lbs.
14. Apply an 1/8 in. (3mm) bead of RTV to the differential cover after cleaning the differential and cover with solvent.

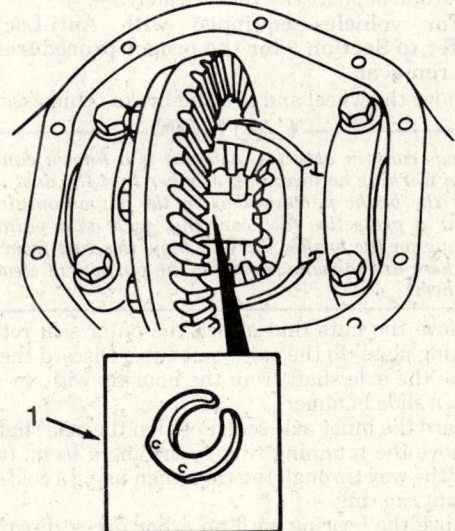

Removing the C-clip axle retainer on Dana 35 model differentials

7-162

DRIVE TRAIN 7

15. Install the cover and tighten bolts to 35 ft. lbs.
16. Install the brake assemblies and wheels.

NOTE: For Trac-Loc differentials, a special limited slip additive is needed.

17. Fill the differential with lubricant. Lower the vehicle and test for proper operation.
18. For vehicles equipped with Trac-Loc differentials, drive the vehicle and make 10 to 12 slow, figure-eight turns to pump lubricant through the clutch discs.

Pinion Seal

REMOVAL AND INSTALLATION

1. Raise and support the vehicle.
2. Mark the driveshaft and yoke for reference during assembly and disconnect the driveshaft at the yoke.
3. Remove the pinion shaft nut and washer. Discard the nut.
4. Remove the yoke from the pinion shaft, using a puller.
5. Remove the pinion shaft oil seal with tool J-25180 on semi-floating axles, or tool J-25144 on full floating axles.
6. Install the new seal with a suitable driver.
7. On pre-1990 models, install the yoke, washer and a new nut. Torque the nut to 210 ft. lbs.
8. On 1990–91 models, set bearing preload as follows:

   a. The required pinion gear bearing preload torque is $1/2$ ft. lbs over the noted release torque as measured above.
   b. Rotate the pinion gear three or four times with a torque wrench attached to the yoke nut. Measure the amount of torque necessary to rotate the pinion.
   c. Using a holding tool and tighten the yoke nut in small increments and remeasure until the specified torque is obtained.

9. Align the index marks on the driveshaft and yoke and install the driveshaft. Tighten the attaching bolts or nuts to 170 inch lbs.
10. Add lubricant to the rear if necessary and lower the vehicle.

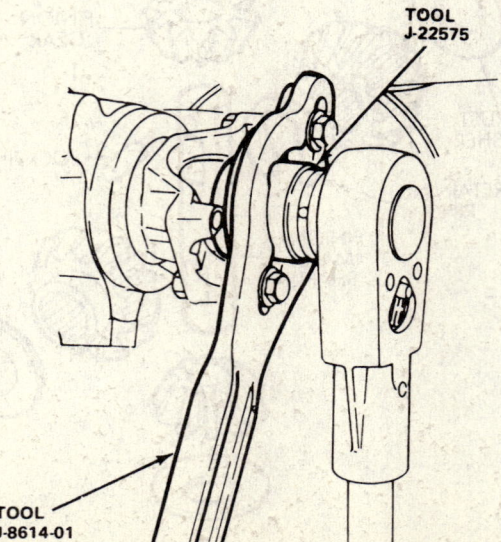

Pinion nut removal on all axles

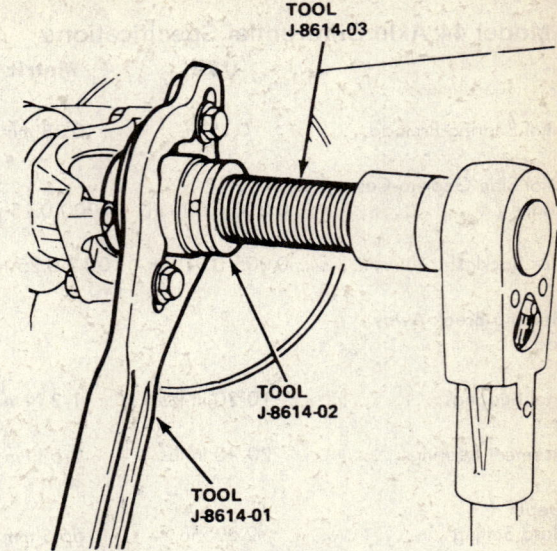

Pinion yoke removal on all axles

Rear Axle Unit

REMOVAL AND INSTALLATION

1. Raise and support the vehicle safely.

CAUTION

Brake linings contain asbestos. Asbestos is a known cancer-causing agent. When working on brakes, remember that the dust which accumulates on the brake parts and/or in the drum contains asbestos. Always wear a protective face covering, such as a painter's mask, when working on the brakes. NEVER blow the dust from the brakes or drum! There are solvents made for the purpose of cleaning brake parts. Use them!

2. Remove the wheels and brake drums.

NOTE: For vehicles equipped with Anti-Lock Brakes (ABS), refer to Section 9 for the proper procedures concerning brake removal.

3. Disconnect the shock absorbers.
4. Disconnect the brake hose at the frame rail and cap to prevent the entry if dirt.

NOTE: On Comanche models a height sensing rear proportioning valve is mounted on the rear axle. This valve must be adjusted after the axle is reinstalled. If not adjusted unsatisfactory brake action could result. See Section 8 for adjustment procedures.

5. Disconnect the parking brake cables at the equalizer.
6. Matchmark the driveshaft and yoke, and disconnect the driveshaft.
7. Place a floor jack under the axle to take up the weight.
8. Remove the axle-to-spring U-bolts and lower the axle.

To Install:

9. Raise the axle into place. Install the axle-to-spring U-bolts and tighten to 52 ft. lbs.
10. Reconnect the driveshaft and tighten U-joint strap bolts 170 inch lb.
11. Connect parking brake cables at the equalizer.
12. Connect brake hoses at the frame rail.
13. Connect shock absorbers and tighten bolts to 44 ft. lbs.
14. Install the wheels and brake drums.
10. Check the differential lubricant, bleed the brakes and road test the vehicle.

7 DRIVE TRAIN

Model 44 Axle Differential Specifications

	USA	Metric
Differential Bearing Preload	0.15 in.	0.38 mm
Differential Side Gear-to-Case Clearance	0.000-0.006 in.	0.000-0.15 mm
Ring Gear Backlash	0.005-0.010 in.	0.12-0.25 mm
Pinion Bearing Break-Away Preload		
Original Bearings	10-20 in-lbs	1-2 N·m
Replacement Bearings	20-40 in-lbs	2-5 N·m
Pinion Depth Standard Setting	2.625 in.	66.6 mm
Lubricant Capacity	3.0 pts.	1.41 liters
Lubricant Type		SAE 75W-90 GL-5

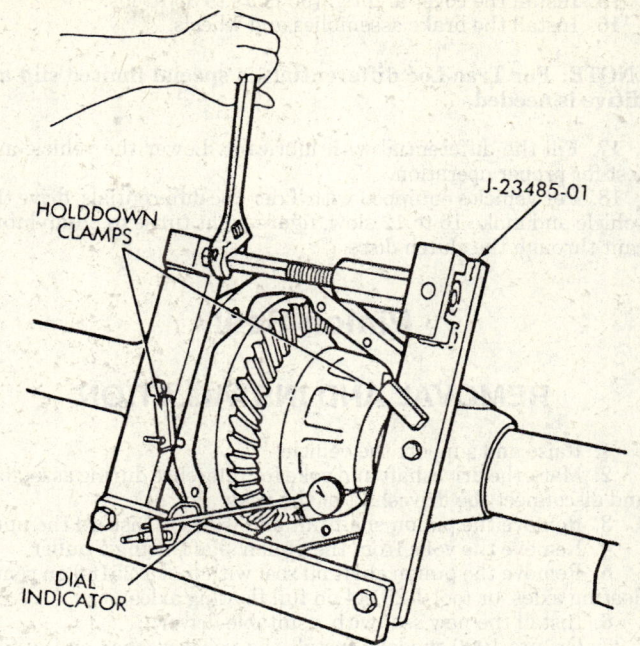

Differential housing separation

9. Remove and discard the ring gear bolts; they are not reusable.
10. Using a brass drift and a hammer, tap the ring gear from the differential.
11. Using a differential bearing puller, remove the differential bearings.
12. Remove the differential bearing shims.
13. Using 2 sets of feeler gauges, insert them between each side of the side gear thrust washer and differential case and measure

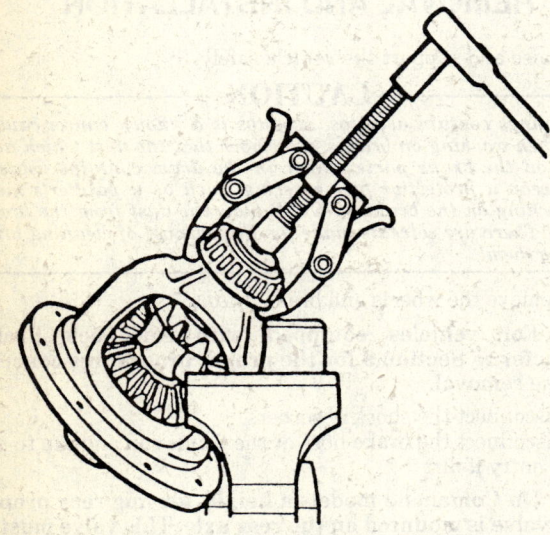

Removing the differential bearing

Dana Model 35—Overhaul

DISASSEMBLY

1. Remove the housing cover and drain the lubricant.
2. Using an axle spreader tool, mount it onto the axle housing and spread the housing enough to remove the differential.
3. Using a dial indicator, measure the amount the opening is being spread; do not spread the housing more than 0.015 in. (0.38mm), for damage to the housing may occur.
4. Mark the differential bearing caps for reassembly purposes.
5. Loosen the bearing caps until 2-3 threads are engaged.
6. Using a prybar, pry the differential loose.
7. Remove the bearing caps and the differential.
8. Mount the differential into a vise.

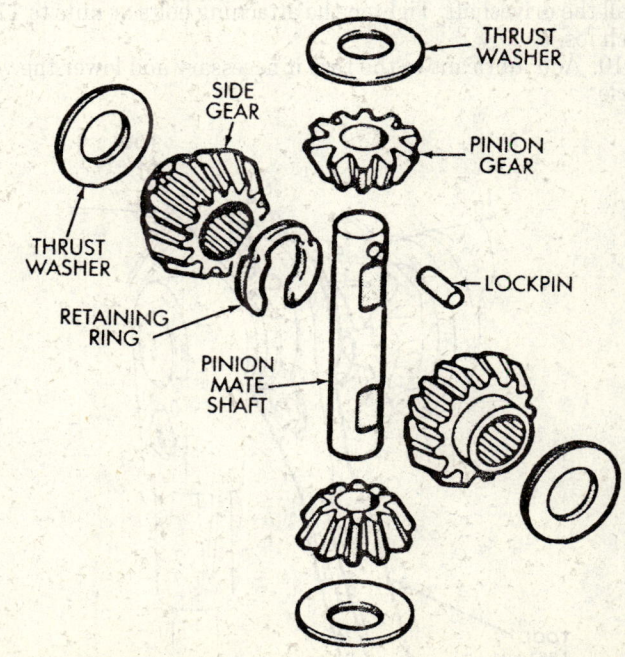

Pinion gear and side gear removal

DRIVE TRAIN 7

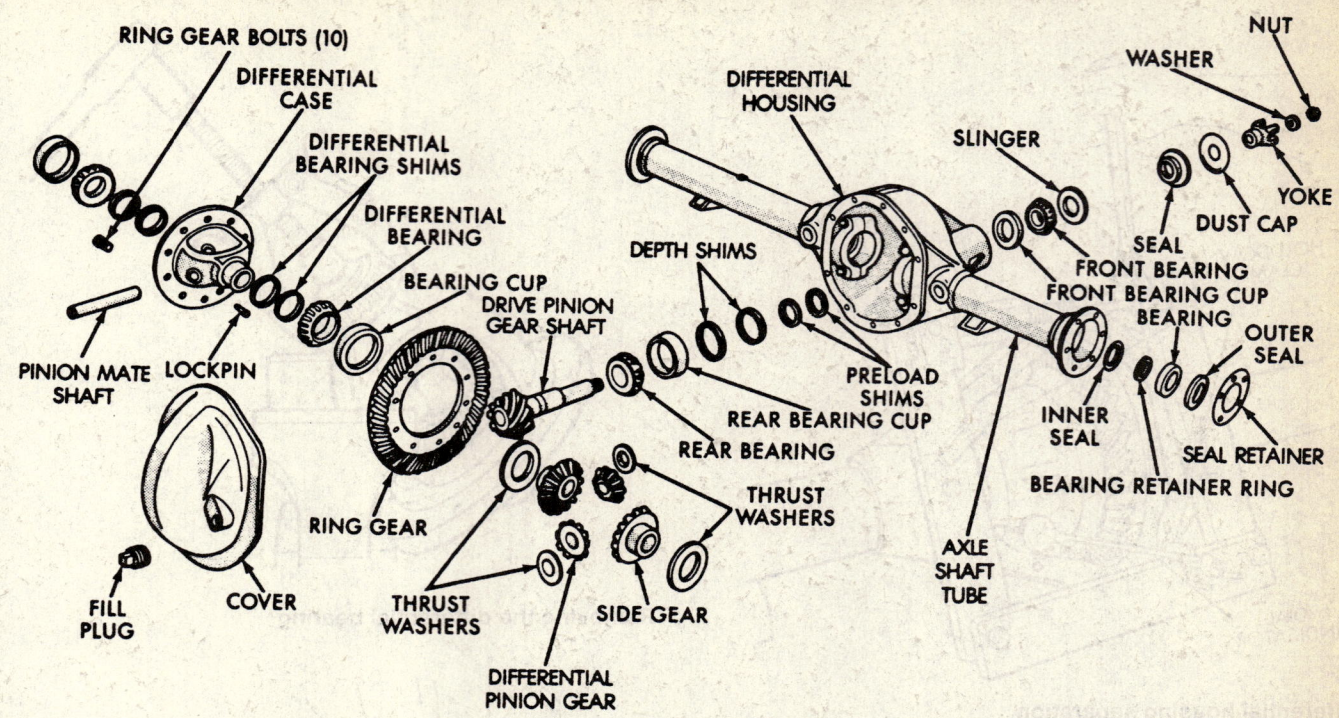

Dana Model 44 differential — exploded view

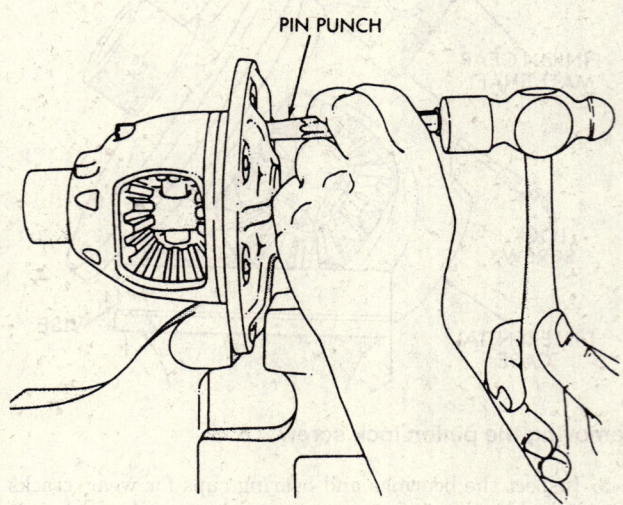

Removing the pinion lock pin

the side gear clearance; the clearance should not exceed 0.007 in. (0.18mm). Replace both thrust washers, if the clearance exceeds the tolerance.

14. Remove the pinion shaft lockpin and pinion shaft.
15. Remove the side gears and thrust washers.

Differential Bearing Removal

1. Mark the bearing cups for reference and remove.
2. Install bearing puller J-22888 on the differential case and bearing.
3. Tighten the puller tool and remove the bearing.

Pinion Gear Removal

1. Using a pinion yoke holding tool, remove the pinion gear nut.
2. Using a pinion yoke holder tool and a pinion puller tool, remove the yoke from the pinion gear. Remove the pinion washer.
3. Using a soft mallet, drive the pinion gear from the axle housing.
4. Remove the pinion gear, the bearings and the preload spacers.
5. Remove and discard the pinion seal.
6. Using a shop press and the bearing removal tool, press the bearing from the pinion gear.

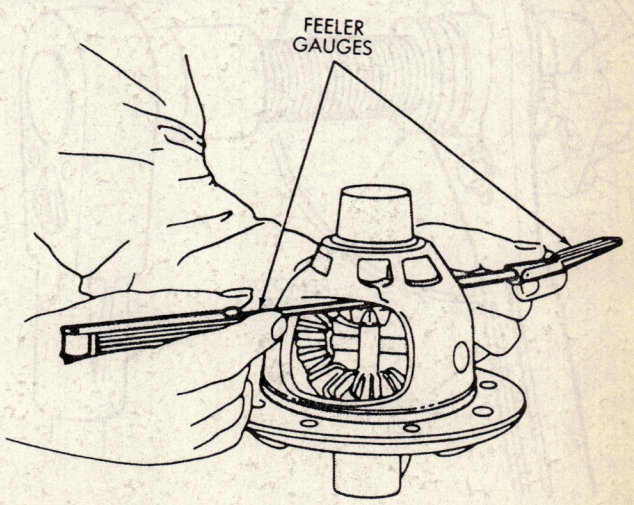

Side gear clearance measurement

7-165

7 DRIVE TRAIN

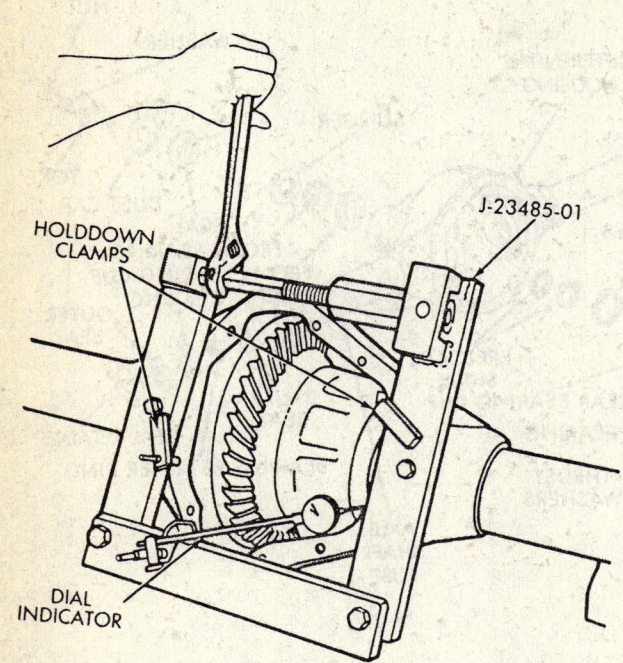

Differential housing separation

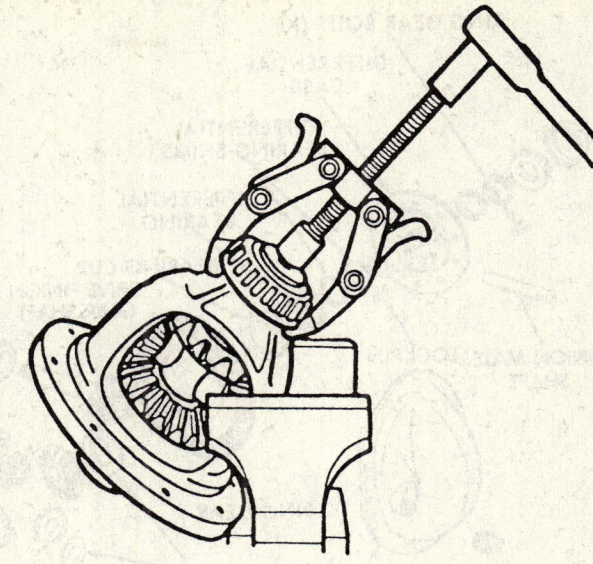

Removing the differential bearing

CLEANING AND INSPECTION

1. Clean the differential components in solvent and use compressed air to dry them; do not use compressed air on the bearings, only shop towels.
2. Check the components for wear or damage; replace them, if necessary.

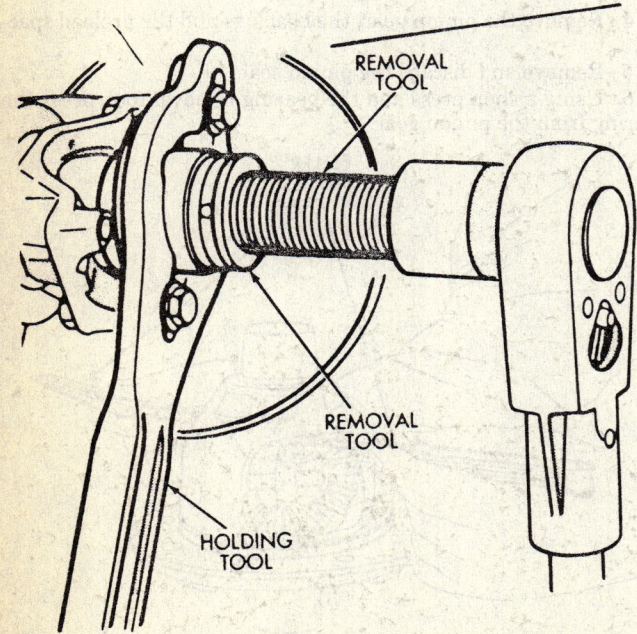

Pinion shaft yoke removal

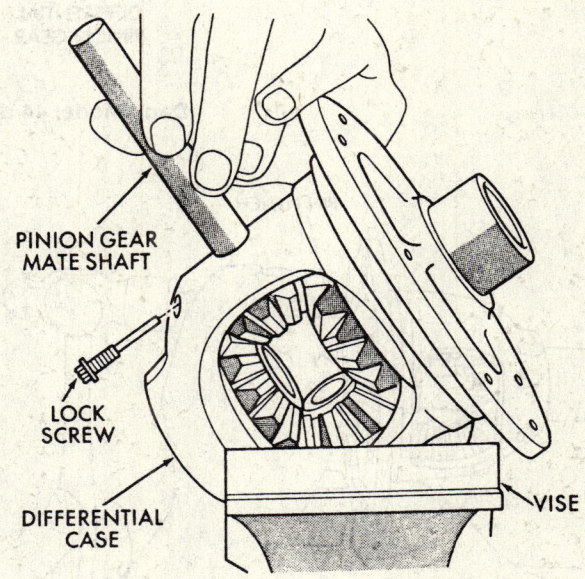

Removing the pinion lock screw

3. Inspect the bearings and bearing cups for wear, cracks or scoring; replace them, if necessary.
4. Inspect the differential side and pinion gears for wear, cracks or chips; replace them, if necessary.
5. Inspect the ring and pinion gears for wear and/or damage; replace them, if necessary.
6. Inspect the differential case for cracks or damage; replace it, if necessary.

ASSEMBLY

The differential ring and pinion gears must be adjusted for the best possible gear teeth contact patterns. The drive pinion gear depth cannot be initially measured and set precisely with shims. If

7-166

DRIVE TRAIN 7

Pinion Gear Depth Variance

Original Pinion Gear Depth Variance	Replacement Pinion Gear Depth Variance								
	−4	−3	−2	−1	0	+1	+2	+3	+4
+4	+0.008	+0.007	+0.006	+0.005	+0.004	+0.003	+0.002	+0.001	0
+3	+0.007	+0.006	+0.005	+0.004	+0.003	+0.002	+0.001	0	−0.001
+2	+0.006	+0.005	+0.004	+0.003	+0.002	+0.001	0	−0.001	−0.002
+1	+0.005	+0.004	+0.003	+0.002	+0.001	0	−0.001	−0.002	−0.003
0	+0.004	+0.003	+0.002	+0.001	0	−0.001	−0.002	−0.003	−0.004
−1	+0.003	+0.002	+0.001	0	−0.001	−0.002	−0.003	−0.004	−0.005
−2	+0.002	+0.001	0	−0.001	−0.002	−0.003	−0.004	−0.005	−0.006
−3	+0.001	0	−0.001	−0.002	−0.003	−0.004	−0.005	−0.006	−0.007
−4	0	−0.001	−0.002	−0.003	−0.004	−0.005	−0.006	−0.007	−0.008

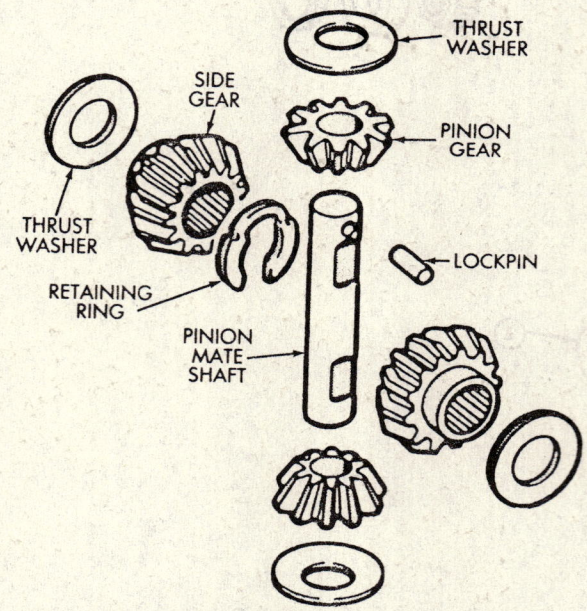

Pinion gear and side gear removal

MODEL 35 AXLE DIFFERENTIAL SPECIFICATIONS

	USA	METRIC
Differential Bearing Preload		
Torque Shims	0.008 in.	0.20 mm
Each Side	0.004 in.	0.10 mm
Differential Side Gear-to-Case		
Clearance (Max. Each Side)	0.000–0.007 in.	0.00–0.18 mm
Ring Gear Backlash	0.005–0.009 in.	0.13–0.23 mm
Pinion Gear Shaft Bearing		
Preload Torque	15-25 in-lbs	2-3 N•m
Pinion Gear Depth		
Standard Setting	2.095 in.	53.21 mm
Lubricant Capacity	2.5 pts.	1.2 liters
Lubricant Type		
Standard	SAE 75W-90, API GL-5	
Trailer Tow	Synthetic Type 80W-140	

the original gear set is installed with the original depth shims, the best possible gear teeth contact patterns are achieved by adjusting the pinion gear depth and the ring gear backlash as necessary.

If a replacement gear set must be installed, the best possible gear teeth contact patterns are achieved by using the Pinion Variance chart. Determine the shims necessary to initially establish the replacement drive pinion gear depth. Adjust the pinion gear depth and the ring gear backlash as necessary.

Installing A Replacement Gear Set

If replacement is necessary, the ring and pinion gear must be replaced as a matched set. They are identified as a matched set by the numbers etched into each gear. The first two identify them as a matched set. The second number etched into the drive pinion is the depth variance. It indicates the amount (in thousandths) that the set varied from the standard setting. The standard for Model 44 differentials is 2.625 in. (66.68 mm).

Refer to the Pinion Gear Depth Variance chart for the required initial depth of a replacement pinion gear. Read the chart as follows:

• Measure the thickness of the original pinion gear depth shims and note the depth variance values etched in the original and replacement drive pinion gears.

7-167

7 DRIVE TRAIN

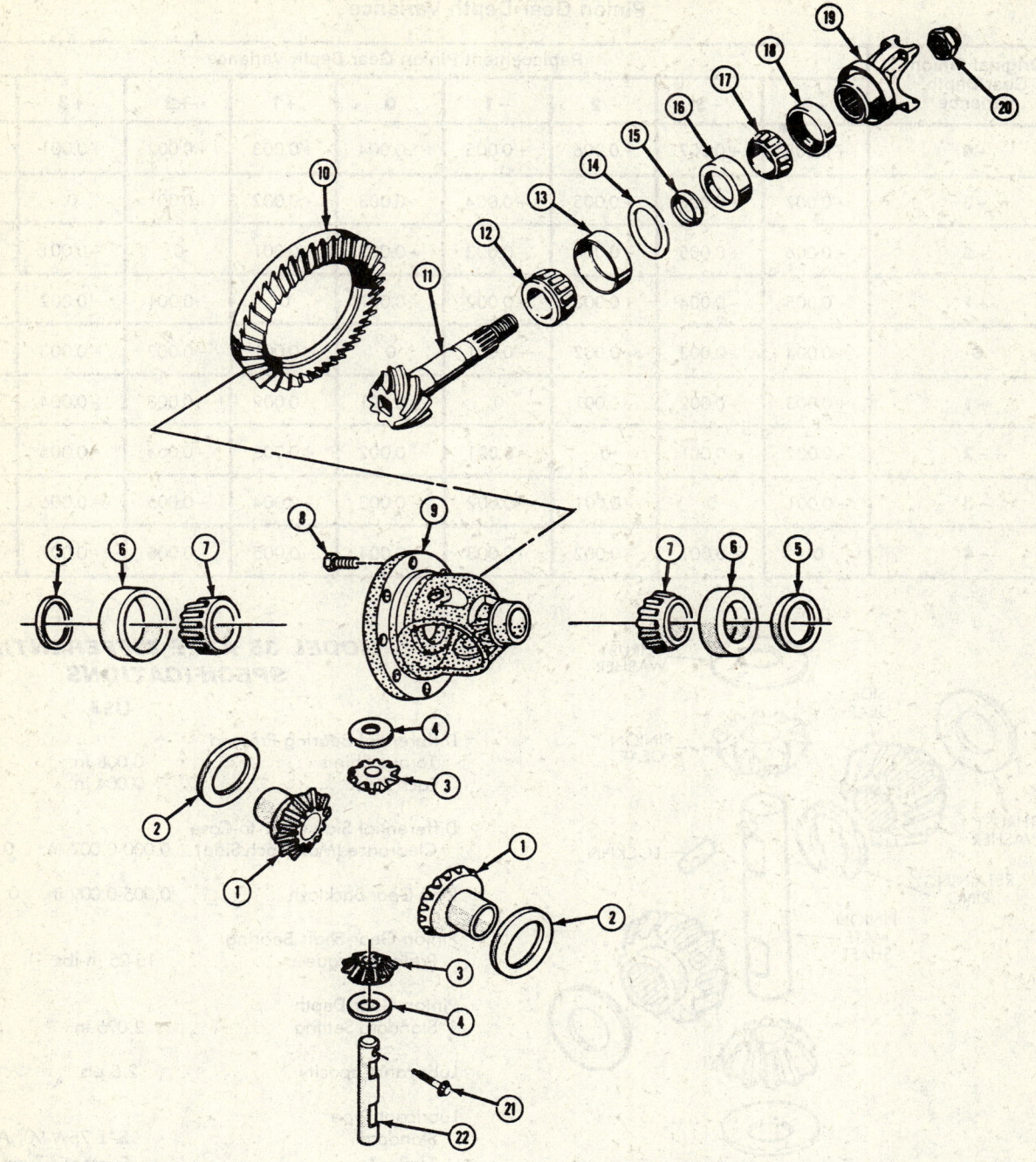

1. DIFFERENTIAL SIDE GEAR
2. SIDE GEAR THRUST WASHER
3. DIFFERENTIAL PINION
4. PINION THRUST WASHER
5. DIFFERENTIAL BEARING SHIM
6. DIFFERENTIAL BEARING CUP
7. DIFFERENTIAL BEARING
8. REAR GEAR BOLT
9. DIFFERENTIAL CASE
10. RING GEAR
11. PINION GEAR
12. PINION GEAR REAR BEARING
13. REAR BEARING CUP
14. PINION DEPTH SHIM
15. PINION BEARING PRELOAD SPACER
16. FRONT BEARING CUP
17. PINION GEAR FRONT BEARING
18. PINION SEAL
19. PINION YOKE
20. PINION NUT
21. PINION SHAFT LOCK SCREW
22. DIFFERENTIAL PINION SHAFT

Dana Model 35 — exploded view

DRIVE TRAIN 7

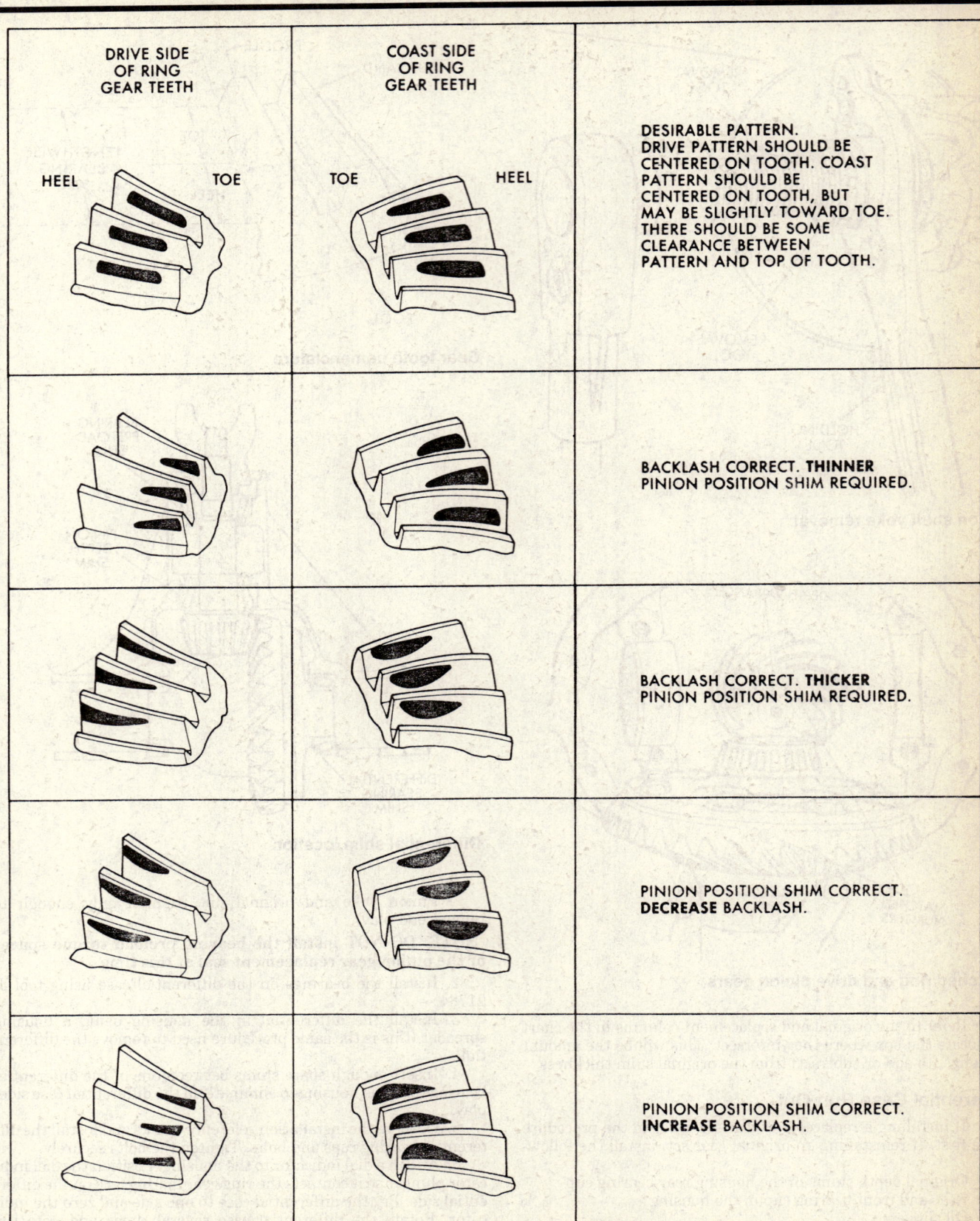

Gear tooth contact pattern chart

7 DRIVE TRAIN

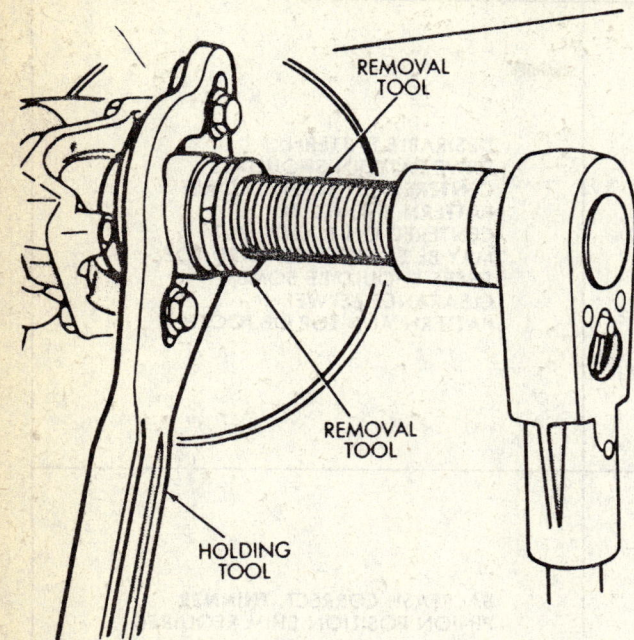

Pinion shaft yoke removal

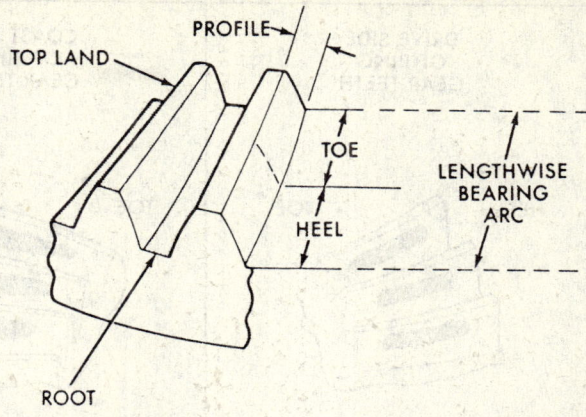

Gear tooth nomenclature

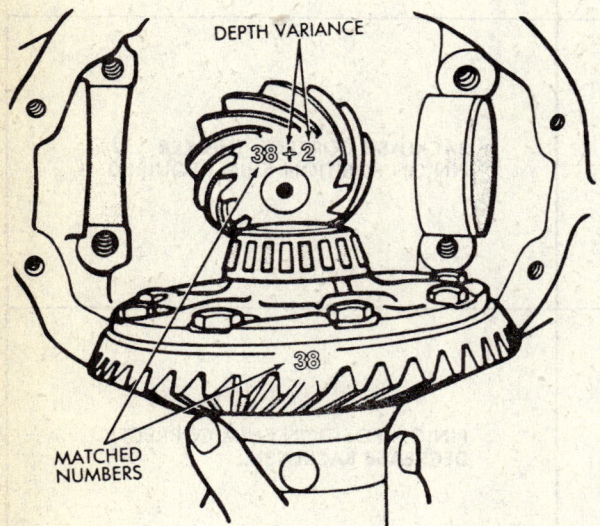

Matched ring and drive pinion gears

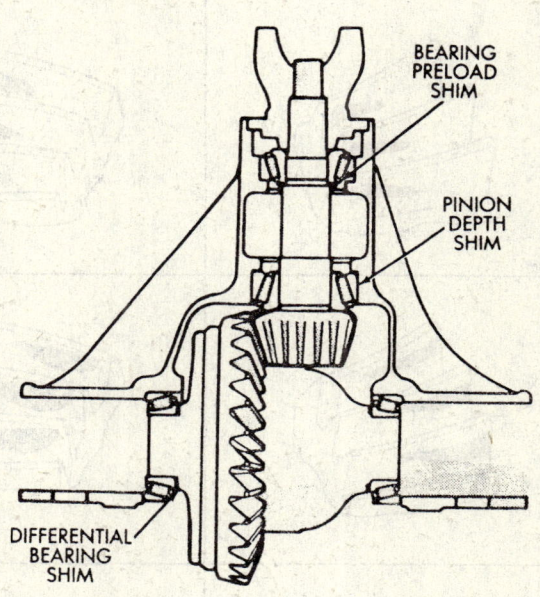

Differential shim location

- Refer to the original and replacement columns in the chart and locate the box where they intersect. This will be the amount of change (to add or subtract) from the original shim thickness.

Differential Case Run-Out

1. If installing a replacement gear set, refer to the procedure above first. If reinstalling an original gear set, install the following:
   - Original depth shims in the housing rear bearing cup
   - Rear and front bearing cup in the housing
   - Oil slinger
   - Rear bearing on the pinion gear with tool J-24433
   - Pinion gear in the housing
   - Front bearing on the pinion gear
   - Pinion yoke and original nut (tighten only enough to remove end-play)

   NOTE: DO NOT install the bearing preload torque spacer or the pinion gear replacement seal at this time

2. Install the bearings on the differential case using tool J-21784.
3. Install the differential in the housing using a housing spreader (this is the same procedure used to remove the differential).
4. Insert enough spare shims between one of the differential bearings and the housing to eliminate all the differential case side-play.
5. Observe the installation reference marks and install the differential bearing caps and bolts. Tighten the bolts securely.
6. Attach a dial indicator to the housing. Position the dial indicator plunger so it contacts the ring gear mating face on the differential side. Pry the differential case to one side and zero the indicator. Rotate the differential case several times and note the pointer position as the case rotates.
7. The differential case run-out should not exceed 0.05mm (0.002 in.). Replace the case if necessary.

DRIVE TRAIN 7

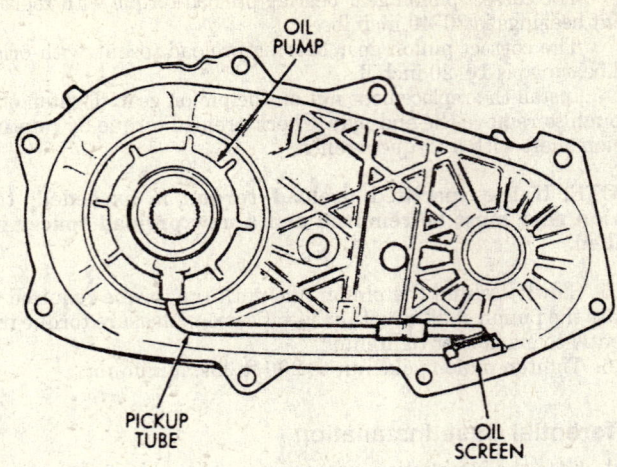

Side gear clearance measurement

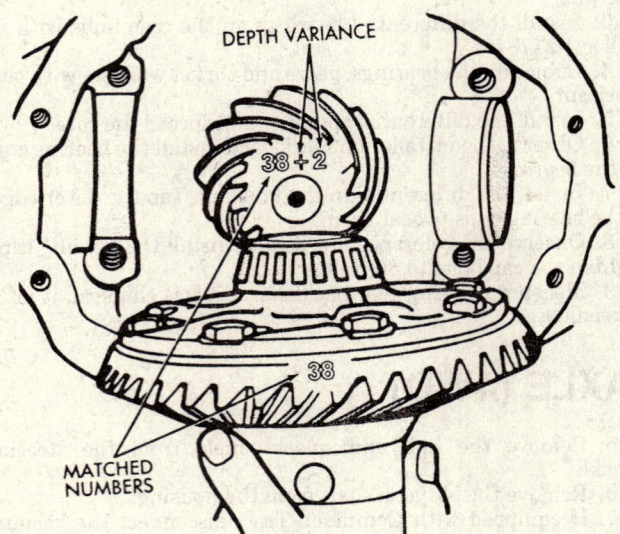

Matched ring and drive pinion gears

Zero End-Play Adjustment

1. Loosen the differential bearing cap bolts.
2. Remove the spare shims that were used to eliminate the differential case side play. Retain the differential case in the same position as it was for the run-out measurement.
3. Install a 0.142 in. (36mm) thick shim between each differential bearing and the housing. These shims will provide an end-play coarse adjustment.
4. Pry the differential case to one side of the housing. Zero the indicator. Pry to the opposite side of the housing and record the indicator end-play. The measurement is the additional thickness required for zero end-play.
5. Obtain the necessary shims and set aside for installation.
6. Install the spreader tool and remove the differential from the housing.

DIFFERENTIAL CASE ASSEMBLY

1. Install the side gears, the thrust washers and the pinion gears into the differential case.

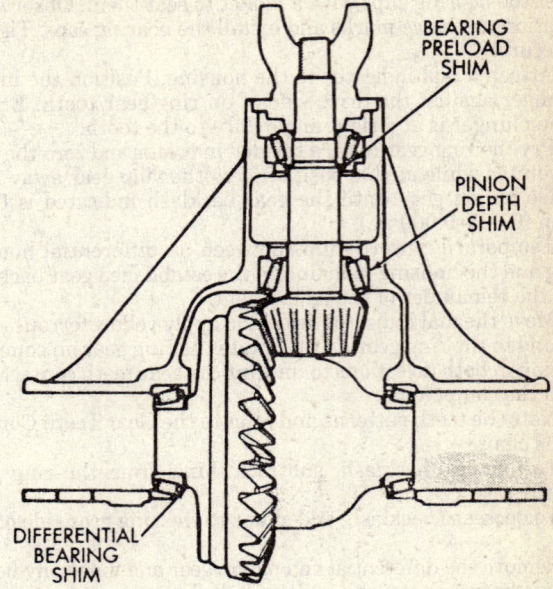

Differential shim location

NOTE: Be sure to install new side gear thrust washers, if the clearance measured at disassembly exceeded 0.007 in. (0.18mm).

2. Using 2 sets of feeler gauges, insert them between each side of the side gear thrust washer and differential case and measure the side gear clearance; the clearance should not exceed 0.007 in. (0.18mm). Replace both thrust washers, if the clearance exceeds the tolerance.
3. Install the pinion shaft and lockpin into the case.
4. Assemble the original differential bearing shim packs, then, remove approximately 0.020 in. (0.50mm) shim thickness from each pack; the remaining shims will serve as a starter shim pack.
5. Install the starter shim packs (zero end-play shims) and bearing onto the case.
6. Align and install the ring gear. Using new bolts, torque the ring gear-to-differential case bolts to 55 ft. lbs. (75 Nm).

Ring Gear Backlash and Pinion Depth Adjustment

1. Apply yellow ferrous oxide compound to both drive and coast sides of the ring gear teeth.
2. Install the differential case in the housing. Tap the outer

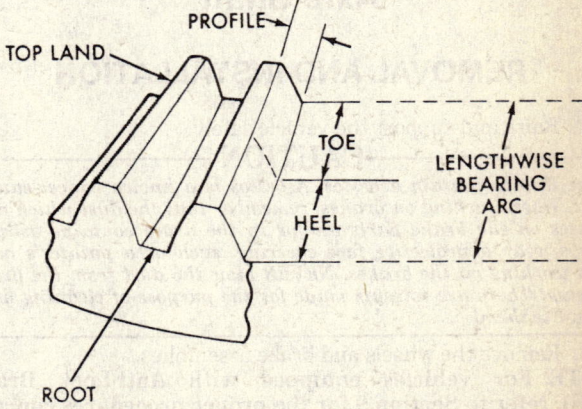

Gear tooth nomenclature

7-171

7 DRIVE TRAIN

edges of the bearing cups with a mallet to seat them. Observe the installation reference marks and install the bearing caps. Tighten bolts securely.

3. Attach a dial indicator to the housing. Position the indicator plunger against the drive side of on ring gear tooth. Ensure that the plunger is at a right angle (90°) to the tooth.

4. Pry the ring gear toward the dial indicator and zero the indicator pointer while at this position. Pry the ring gear away from the drive pinion gear until the gear backlash indicated is 0.13–0.23mm (0.005–0.009 in.).

5. Temporarily insert shims between on differential housing bearing and the housing to maintain the established gear backlash during the remainder of the adjustment.

6. Move the dial indicator aside and apply yellow ferrous oxide compound to the ring gear teeth. Rotate the ring gear on complete revolution in both directions to imprint the gear teeth contact patterns in the compound.

7. Note the teeth patterns and refer to the Gear Teeth Contact Patterns chart.
   - To increase backlash, subtract shims from the ring gear side of the case.
   - To decrease backlash, add shims to the ring gear side of the case.

8. Remove the differential and pinion gear and make any necessary adjustments to the shims. Reinstall the gears and repeat the gear contact pattern test until gear patterns are satisfactory.

Pinion Gear Bearing Preload Adjustment

1. Remove the ferrous oxide compound from the ring gear. Install the differential spreader, remove the differential and pinion gear.

2. Remove the differential bearing cups, the bearings and the shims. Mark the shims for installation reference.

3. Install the replacement bearing preload torque spacer on the pinion gear. Install the pinion gear in the housing. Apply gear lubricant to the pinion seal and install.

   - The correct pinion gear bearing preload torque with replacement bearings is 20–40 inch lbs.
   - The correct pinion gear bearing preload torque with original bearings is 10–20 inch lbs.

4. Install the replacement nut on the pinion gear. Tighten only enough to remove the end-play. Check preload torque by rotating pinion shaft with a torque wrench.

NOTE: If the specified preload torque is exceeded, the pinion gear must be removed and a new preload spacer installed.

5. Slowly tighten the pinion nut until the torque required to rotate the pinion shaft is within specification. Measure torque frequently to avoid over tightening.

6. Tighten pinion yoke nut to 200 ft. lbs. minimum.

Differential Case Installation

1. Note the installation reference marks and install the bearing shims on each case hub.
2. Add an additional 0.38mm (0.015 in.) thick shim to each case hub.
3. Install the differential bearings on the case hubs with installer J-21784.
4. Lubricate the bearings, gears and thrust washers with gear lubricant.
5. Install the differential spreader and spread the case.
6. Observe the installation marks and install the bearing cups on the bearings.
7. Install the differential in the housing. Tap the outer edges of the bearing cups to seat them.
8. Observe the reference marks and install the bearing caps. Tighten the cap bolts to 80 ft. lbs.
9. Measure the ring gear backlash. If it has changed, it must be readjusted.

FRONT DRIVE AXLE (4WD)

Identification

Dana model 30 drive axles can be identified by a tag located on the left side of the housing cover. The tag lists part number and gear ratio. Stamped into the right side axle shaft are the production date and manufacturers identification.

Axle Shaft

REMOVAL AND INSTALLATION

1. Raise and support the vehicle safely.

— CAUTION —

Brake linings contain asbestos. Asbestos is a known cancer-causing agent. When working on brakes, remember that the dust which accumulates on the brake parts and/or in the drum contains asbestos. Always wear a protective face covering, such as a painter's mask, when working on the brakes. NEVER blow the dust from the brakes or drum! There are solvents made for the purpose of cleaning brake parts. Use them!

2. Remove the wheels and brake assemblies.

NOTE: For vehicles equipped with Anti-Lock Brakes (ABS), refer to Section 9 for the proper procedures concerning brake removal.

3. Remove the cotter pin, locknut and axle hub nut.
4. Remove the hub-to-knuckle attaching bolts.
5. Remove the hub and splash shield from the steering knuckle.
6. Remove the left axle shaft from the housing.
7. If equipped with Command-Trac, disconnect the vacuum

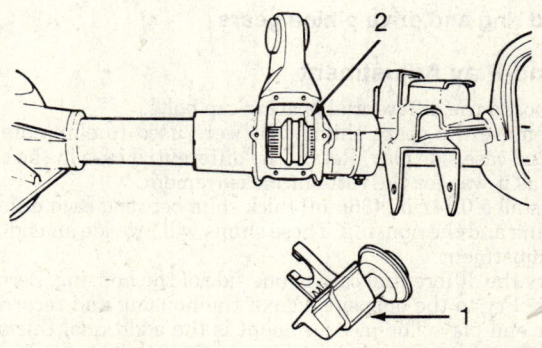

Right side front axle shaft. (1) shift motor (2) shift collar

FRONT DRIVE AXLE APPLICATION CHART

Axle	Model	Years
Dana 30	All	1984–91

DRIVE TRAIN 7

harness from the shift motor and remove the shift motor from the housing.

8. Remove the right axle shaft from the housing.

To Install:

9. Insert the left and right axle shafts into the axle tube.
10. To install the right axle shaft (with Command-Trac) first be sure that the shift collar is in position on the intermediate shaft and that the axle shaft is fully engaged in the intermediate shaft end.
11. If equipped with Command-Trac, install the shift motor, making sure that the fork engages with the collar. Tighten the bolts to 8 ft. lbs.
10. On the left side, install the axle shaft in the housing.
11. Partially fill the hub cavity of the knuckle with chassis lube and install the hub and splash shield.
12. Tighten the hub bolts to 75 ft. lbs.
13. Install the hub washer and nut. Torque the nut to 175 ft. lbs. Install the locknut. Install a new cotter pin.
14. Install the brake assemblies.
15. Lower the vehicle.

Intermediate Shaft

REMOVAL AND INSTALLATION

1. Remove the right side axle shaft.
2. Remove the differential cover and drain the lubricant.
3. Remove the right-side axle shaft.
3. Remove the intermediate shaft C-clip in the differential case.
4. Remove the intermediate shaft.

To Install:

5. Position the intermediate shaft in the housing and engage it with the differential.
6. Install the C-clip. Then install the differential cover.
7. Install the shift collar and outer axle shaft.
8. Fill the differential with lubricant.
9. Install the axle shift motor and complete the installation according to the Axle Shaft Installation procedure.

Axle Tube Bearing

REMOVAL AND INSTALLATION

NOTE: Special tools are needed for this operation.

1. Remove the intermediate shaft.
2. Insert tool J34659-3/J34659-4 into the axle tube.
3. Connect removal tool J34659-1 to the threaded rod via the shift motor housing opening in the axle tube.
4. Position the removal tool behind the axle tube bearing and tighten the nut to remove the bearing. Remove the tool and bearing via the shift motor opening.
5. Position the bearing in the axle tube.
6. Connect removal tool J34659-2 to the threaded rod via the shift motor housing opening in the axle tube and drive the bearing into position.
7. Install the intermediate shaft.

Axle Tube Seal and Guide

REMOVAL AND INSTALLATION

NOTE: Special tools are needed for this operation.

1. Connect removal tool J34659-5 to the threaded rod.
2. Insert the tool into and through the outer end of the axle tube and drive the seal and guide into the shift motor housing. Remove the seal and guide via the opening in the axle tube.
3. Insert the threaded rod into and through the outer end of the axle tube. Position the seal and guide over the threaded rod at the shifter motor housing opening.
4. Attach installation tool J34659-2 to the threaded rod and tighten the nut to pull the seal and guide into position.
5. Remove the installation tool and install the intermediate shaft.

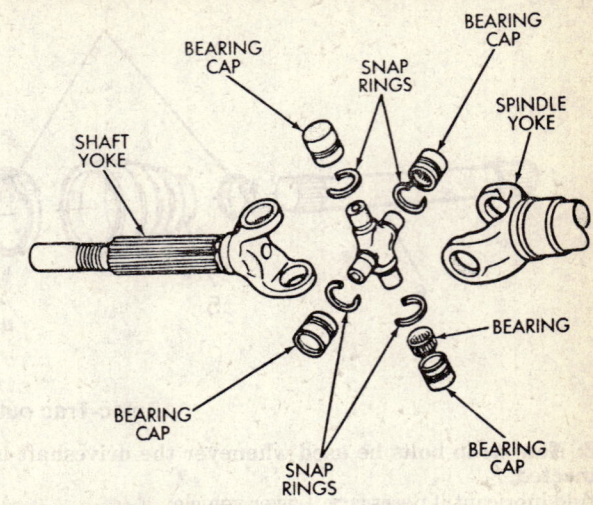

Axle shaft outer U-joint

Pinion Seal

REMOVAL AND INSTALLATION

1. Raise and support the vehicle safely.
2. Matchmark and remove the driveshaft.
3. Rotate the pinion gear three or four times with a torque wrench attached to the yoke nut. Measure the amount of torque necessary to rotate the pinion. Note for installation reference.
4. Matchmark the pinion yoke and gear for installation reference.
5. Using a holding tool, remove the pinion yoke nut and washer. Discard the nut.
6. Punch the seal with a pin punch and pry it from the seal bore.

To Install:

7. Apply gear lubricant to the lip of the replacement seal and install using a seal installation tool.
8. Install the yoke, noting the reference marks. Tighten just enough to remove the end-play.
9. On pre-1990 models, install the yoke, washer and a new nut. Torque the nut to 210 ft. lbs.
10. On 1990–91 models, set bearing preload as follows:

   a. The required pinion gear bearing preload torque is $1/2$ ft. lbs over the noted release torque as measured above.

   b. Rotate the pinion gear three or four times with a torque wrench attached to the yoke nut. Measure the amount of torque necessary to rotate the pinion.

   c. Using a holding tool and tighten the yoke nut in small increments and remeasure until the specified torque is obtained.

11. Install the driveshaft. Torque the strap bolt nuts to 14 ft. lbs.

7-173

7 DRIVE TRAIN

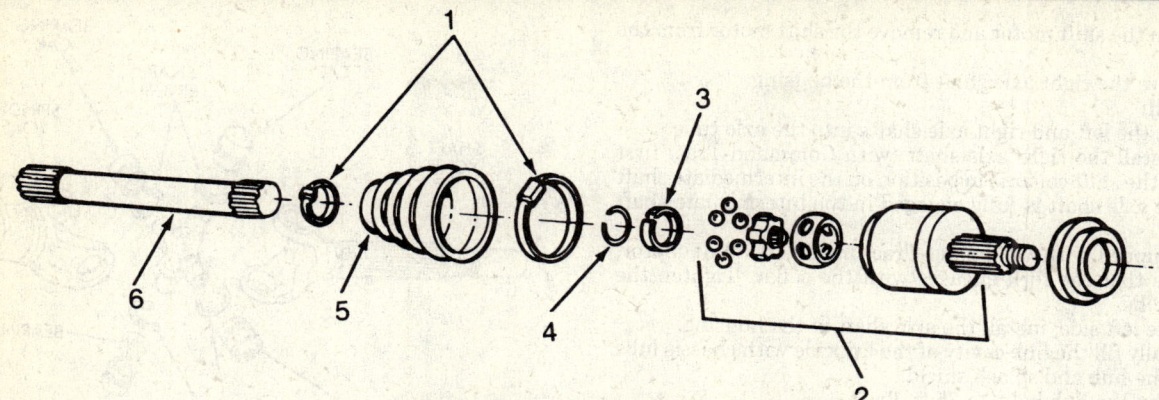

Selec-Trac outer CV joint—exploded view

NOTE: New strap bolts be used whenever the driveshaft is disconnected.

12. Add lubricant if necessary. Lower vehicle.

Front Axle Outer U-Joint Command-Trac System

OVERHAUL

1. Remove the axle shaft.
2. Remove the snaprings by pinching the ends together with a pair of pliers. If the rings do not readily snap out of the groove, tap the end of the bearing lightly to relieve pressure against the rings.
3. After removing the snaprings, press on the end of one bearing until the opposite bearing is pushed from the yoke arm. Turn the joint over and press the first bearing back out of that arm by pressing on the exposed end of the journal shaft. To drive it out, use a soft ground drift with a flat face, about 0.8mm ($\frac{1}{32}$ in.) smaller in diameter than the hole in the yoke; otherwise, there is danger of damaging the bearing.
4. Repeat the procedure for the other two bearings, then lift out the journal assembly by sliding it to one side.
5. Wash all parts in cleaning solvent and inspect the parts after cleaning. Replace the journal assembly if it is worn extensively. Make sure that the grease channel in each journal trunnion is open.
6. Pack all of the bearing caps $\frac{1}{3}$ full of grease and install the rollers (bearings).
7. Press one of the cap/bearing assemblies into one of the yoke arms just far enough so that the cap will remain in position.
8. Place the journal in position in the installed cap, with a cap/bearing assembly placed on the opposite end.
9. Position the free cap so that when it is driven from the opposite end it will be inserted into the opening of the yoke. Repeat this operation for the other two bearings.
10. Install the retaining clips. If the U-joint binds when it is assembled, tap the arms of the yoke slightly to relieve any pressure on the bearings at the end of the journal.

Front Axle Constant Velocity Joint Selec-Trac System

OVERHAUL

1. Secure the shaft in a soft-jawed vise.
2. Cut and remove both outer boot clamps. Slide boot off CV joint.
3. Using a hard wood drift, seated on the inner race, tap the

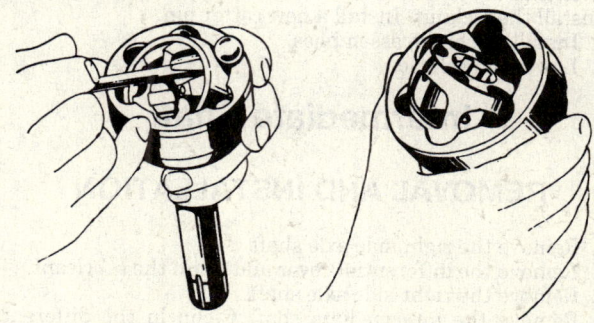

Disassembling the constant velocity joint

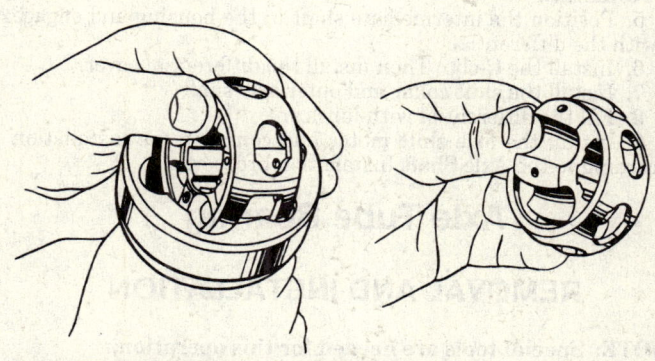

Removing the constant velocity joint

joint off the shaft.
4. Using a brass drift, tap the outer CV-joint cage until it is tilted out far enough to remove the first ball. Remove the remaining ball in this manner.
5. Rotate the cage outward until it is at a 90° angle to the installed position.
6. Align the two oblong holes in the cage with the slots in the interior wall of the spindle housing and remove the cage and inner race.
7. Align the shoulder, between the race groove, with the inside of the oblong holes in the cage. Rotate the inner race out of the cage, using the two larger openings.
8. Clean all parts in a safe solvent and dry with a lint free towel. Inspect all parts for signs of wear, damage, flat spots, cracks, hear checking or any abnormal condition. If any part is defective, all of the parts should be replaced. These joints should be serviced as assemblies only. Kits containing all of the parts, as well and the necessary lubricant, are available. Use only the lubri-

DRIVE TRAIN 7

cant supplied with the kit, Use half the lubricant on the joint and pack the other half in the boot.

9. Coat the spindle hub with lubricant.
10. Install the cage, then install the cage and race assembly in the spindle hub. The smaller diameter of the cage must face outward, and the groove in the race must face inward.
11. Tilt the cage outward, using a brass drift, until the first ball can be installed, then install the remaining ball in the same manner.
12. Pack the joint with half the supplied lubricant.
13. Install the new clamps on the boot and install the boot on the shaft.
14. Install the new retaining ring and spacer ring on the shaft.
15. Install the CV-joint on the shaft until the inner race contacts the inner snapring.
16. Pack the boot with the remaining lubricant, and slide the boot over the joint. Tighten the clamps.

Front Axle Unit

REMOVAL AND INSTALLATION

1. Raise and support the vehicle safely.

CAUTION

Brake linings contain asbestos. Asbestos is a known cancer-causing agent. When working on brakes, remember that the dust which accumulates on the brake parts and/or in the drum contains asbestos. Always wear a protective face covering, such as a painter's mask, when working on the brakes. NEVER blow the dust from the brakes or drum! There are solvents made for the purpose of cleaning brake parts. Use them!

2. Remove the wheels, and brake assemblies.

NOTE: For vehicles equipped with Anti-Lock Brakes (ABS), refer to Section 9 for the proper procedures concerning brake removal.

3. If equipped with Command-Trac, connect the axle shift motor vacuum harness.
4. Matchmark the front driveshaft and yoke.
5. Disconnect the stabilizer bar, rod and center link, front driveshaft, shock absorbers, steering damper, track bar and ABS sensor if equipped.
6. Place a floor jack under the axle to take up the weight.
7. Disconnect the upper and lower control arms at the axle and lower the axle from the truck.

To Install:
8. Install the upper and lower suspension arms to the axle. Tighten upper control arm-to-axle bolts to 55 ft. lbs.; Lower control arm-to-axle bolts to 133 ft. lbs.
9. Connect the following components to the axle observing the torque specifications:
 - Track bar-to-axle: 74 ft. lbs.
 - Steering damper-to-axle: 55 ft. lbs.
 - Shock absorber lower bolt: 14 ft. lbs.
 - Center link-to-knuckle: 35 ft. lbs.
 - Stabilizer bar-to-axle: 70 ft. lbs.
 - U-joint strap nuts: 14 ft. lbs.
 - ABS brake sensor
 - Axle vent hose
 - U-joint straps: 170 inch lbs.

NOTE: New replacement U-joint straps must be used whenever the driveshafts are removed.

10. If equipped with Command-Trac, connect the axle shift motor vacuum harness.
11. Install the brake assemblies and wheels.
12. Lower the vehicle and check the front wheel alignment.

4-Wheel Drive Front Hub Bearings

WARNING: The following procedure requires the use of an arbor press. Chrysler Corp. notes that only the special press tools listed below should be used or damage to the internal machined shoulder of the bearing carrier is probable!

1. Raise and support the front end on jackstands.
2. Remove the wheels.
3. Remove, but do not disconnect, the caliper. Suspend it out of the way.
4. Remove the rotor. See Section 9.
5. Remove the cotter pin, nut retainer, axle nut and washer.
6. Remove the 3 bearing carrier bolts.
7. Remove the hub/bearing carrier and the rotor shield.
8. Using an arbor press, press the hub out of the bearing carrier. Special tools 5073 and 5074 are available for this job. Secure the carrier to the press plate with M12 × 1.75mm × 40mm bolts.
9. Cut and remove the plastic cage from the hub inner bearing. Using diagonal pliers or tin snips, cut the bearing cage. Discard the rollers after removing the cage.
10. Remove what remains of the inner bearing by:
 a. Install a bearing separator tool on the inner bearing.
 b. Position the separator tool and hub in an arbor press.
 c. Force the hub out of the inner bearing with press pin tool 5074.
11. Remove the bearing carrier outer seal and discard it.
12. Drive the inner bearing seal out and discard it. If you're using tool 5078, make sure that the word JEEP faces downward.
13. Attach press plate tool 5073 to the rear of the carrier. Secure it in the press using M12 × 1.75mm × 40mm bolts.
14. Position bearing race remover 5076 in the carrier bore between the inner and outer bearing races.
15. Position the press pin tool 5074 on tool 5076. 16. Place the bearing carrier in the press and force the inner bearing race from the carrier bore. Reverse the position of the carrier and tools and force the outer bearing race from the bore.

To assemble and install
17. Thoroughly clean all reusable parts with a safe solvent. Discard any parts that appear worn or damaged.
18. Attach press plate tool 5073 on the bearing carrier. Secure it in the press using M12 × 1.75mm × 40mm bolts.
19. Position the new outer bearing race in the bore.
20. Position bearing race installation tool 5077 on the race. Make sure that the word JEEP faces the downward. Press the race into the bore. The race should be flush with the machined shoulder of the carrier.
21. Position the new inner bearing race in the carrier bore. Reverse the position of the carrier and tools and force the inner race into the bore.
22. Thoroughly pack the new outer bearing with wheel bearing grease. Make sure that the bearing is fully packed.
23. Coat the race with wheel bearing grease and place the bearing in the bore.
24. Place the new outer seal on the bearing and position bearing installation tool 5079 on the seal. Place the carrier in the press and force the seal into the bore. Apply wheel bearing grease to the seal lip.
25. Insert the hub through the seal and outer bearing and into the bearing carrier bore.
26. Install bearing installation tool 5078 into the rear of the bearing carrier bore and place the race installation tool 5077 on the front of the hub. Make sure that the word JEEP on 5077 is facing the hub.

7 Drive Train

27. Place the assembly in the press and force the hub shaft into the carrier bore.
28. Pack the new inner bearing with wheel bearing grease. Make sure that the bearing is thoroughly packed.
29. Coat the inner seal lip with wheel bearing grease and place it on the inner bearing.
30. Coat the inner bearing race with wheel bearing grease.
31. Place the carrier in a press along with tool 5077. The word JEEP on 5077 must face the hub. Position the bearing and seal in the carrier. Place seal installation tool 5080 on the seal.
32. Force the bearing and seal into the bore and onto the hub shaft.

WARNING: Use extreme care when forcing the assembly into position! The carrier must rotate freely after installation of the bearing! Do not attempt to eliminate bearing lash with the press. Final bearing preload is attained by tightening the drive axle nut.

33. Install the new outer seal on the carrier.
34. Thoroughly clean the axle shaft and apply a thin coating of lithium-based grease to the splines and seal contact surfaces.
35. Install the slinger, rotor shield and hub/bearing assembly on the axle shaft.
36. Coat the carrier bolt threads with Loctite®, install them and torque them to 75 ft. lbs.
37. Install the rotor and caliper. See Section 9.
38. Install the washer and axle shaft nut. Torque the nut to 175 ft. lbs.
39. Install the nut retainer and cotter pin. NEVER back off the nut to install the cotter pin! ALWAYS advance it!
40. Install the wheel.

Axle Shift Motor Command-Trac System

FUNCTIONAL TEST

1. Raise and support the vehicle safely.
2. Disconnect the vacuum harness and connect a hand vacuum pump to the front port. Apply 15 in. Hg of vacuum to the front port and rotate the right front wheel to fully disengage axle shafts.

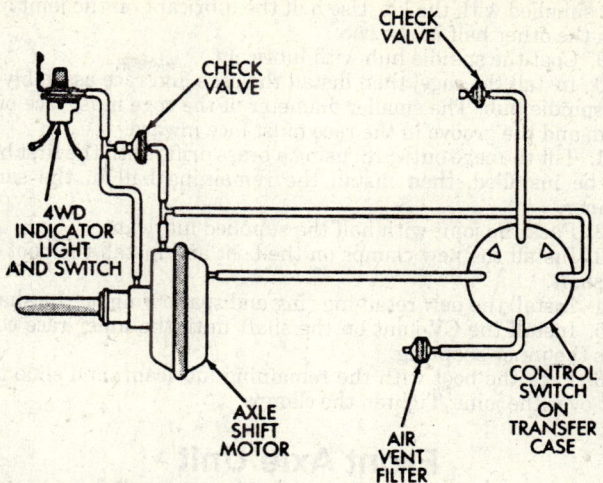

Command-Trac vacuum control system

3. The shift motor should maintain the vacuum applied to the front port for a minimum of 30 seconds. If the motor does not maintain the vacuum, replace it. If the motor does maintain vacuum go to Step 4.
4. Connect the vacuum pump to the rear port. Cap the port for the indicator lamp switch and apply 15 in. Hg.
5. The shift motor should maintain the vacuum applied to the rear port for a minimum of 30 seconds. If the motor does not maintain the vacuum, replace it. If the motor does maintain vacuum go to Step 6.
6. Remove the cap from the port for the indicator lamp switch and determine if vacuum is present. If present, the shift motor is functioning properly. If not, proceed to Step 7.
7. Apply 15 in. Hg of vacuum to the shift motor rear port. Rotate the right front wheel to engage the axle shafts. The axles must be completely engaged!
8. Determine if vacuum is present at the port for the indicator lamp switch. If present, the shift motor is functioning properly. If not, replace the shift motor.

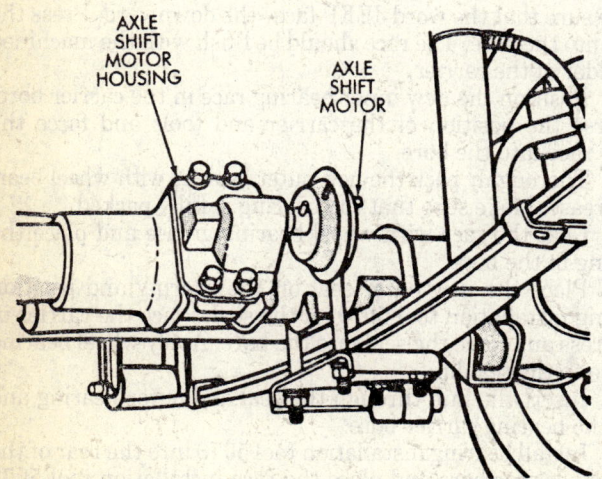

Axle vacuum shift motor housing

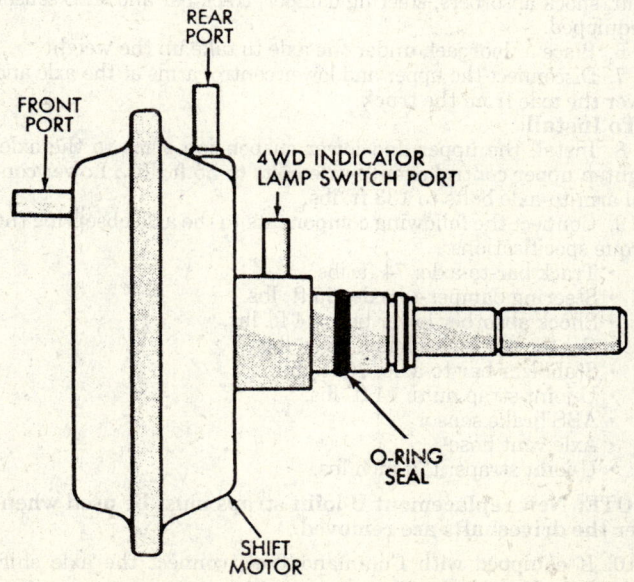

Axle vacuum shift motor

DRIVE TRAIN 7

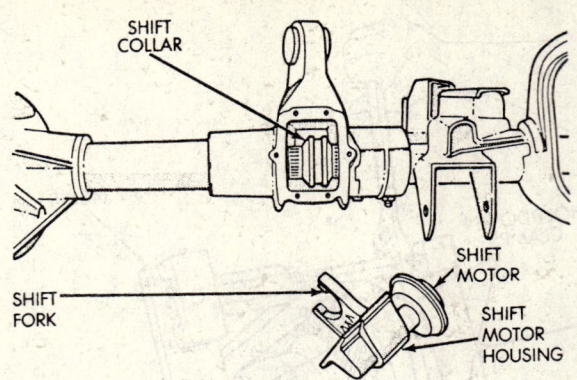

Shift motor and housing removal

Model 30 Axle Differential Specifications

	USA	Metric
Differential Bearing Preload	0.15 in.	0.38 mm
Differential Side Gear-to-Case Clearance	0.000-0.006 in.	0.000-0.15 mm
Ring Gear Backlash	0.005-0.010 in.	0.12-0.25 mm
Pinion Bearing Break-Away Preload		
Original Bearings	15-25 in-lbs	2-3 N·m
Replacement Bearings	20-40 in-lbs	2-5 N·m
Pinion Depth Standard Setting	2.25 in.	57.1 mm
Lubricant Capacity*	2.5 pts.	1.2 liters
Lubricant Type	SAE 75W-90 GL-5	

*Command-Trac – add 5 ounces (148 ml) to front axle shift motor housing.

REMOVAL AND INSTALLATION

1. Raise and support the vehicle safely. Position a drain pan under the shift motor.
2. Disconnect the vacuum harness. Remove the housing attaching bolts. Remove the housing, motor and shift fork as a unit. Mark the shift fork for installation reference.
3. Rotate the shift motor and remove the shift fork and motor retaining snaprings. Remove the shift motor from the housing.
4. Remove the O-ring seal and discard.

To Install:

5. Add 5 ounces of gear lubricant to the axle through the shift motor housing opening.
6. Install a replacement O-ring seal on the shift motor. Install the motor in the housing with the retaining snaprings and slide the shift fork onto the shaft with the reference marks aligned.
7. Engage the shift fork with the shift collar and install the attaching bolts. Tighten to 101 inch lbs.
8. Connect the vacuum harness, lower the vehicle and road test.

Dana Model 30 — Overhaul

DISASSEMBLY

1. Remove the housing cover and drain the lubricant.
2. Using an axle spreader tool, mount it onto the axle housing and spread the housing enough to remove the differential.
3. Using a dial indicator, measure the amount the opening is being spread; do not spread the housing more than 0.015 in. (0.38mm), for damage to the housing may occur.
4. Mark the differential bearing caps for reassembly purposes.
5. Loosen the bearing caps until 2-3 threads are engaged.
6. Using a prybar, pry the differential loose.
7. Remove the bearing caps and the differential.
8. Mount the differential into a vise.
9. Remove and discard the ring gear bolts; they are not reusable.
10. Using a brass drift and a hammer, tap the ring gear from the differential.
11. Using a differential bearing puller, press the differential bearings from the differential.
12. Remove the differential bearing shims.
13. Using 2 sets of feeler gauges, insert them between each side of the side gear thrust washer and differential case and measure the side gear clearance; the clearance should not exceed 0.007 in. (0.18mm). Replace both thrust washers if the clearance exceeds the tolerance.
14. Remove the pinion shaft lockpin and pinion shaft.
15. Rotate the pinions to remove them through the case opening.
16. Remove the side gears and thrust washers.

Pinion Gear

1. Using a pinion yoke holding tool, remove the pinion gear nut.
2. Using a pinion yoke holder tool and a pinion puller tool, press the yoke from the pinion gear. Remove the pinion washer.
3. Using a soft mallet, drive the pinion gear from the axle housing.
4. Remove the pinion gear, the bearings and the preload spacers.
5. Remove and discard the pinion seal.
6. Using a shop press and the bearing removal tool, press the bearing from the pinion gear.

CLEANING AND INSPECTION

1. Clean the differential components in solvent and use compressed air to dry them; do not use compressed air on the bearings, only shop towels.
2. Check the components for wear or damage; replace them, if necessary.
3. Inspect the bearings and bearing cups for wear, cracks or scoring; replace them, if necessary.
4. Inspect the differential side and pinion gears for wear, cracks or chips; replace them, if necessary.
5. Inspect the ring and pinion gears for wear and/or damage; replace them, if necessary.
6. Inspect the differential case for cracks or damage; replace it, if necessary.

ASSEMBLY

The differential ring and pinion gears must be adjusted for the best possible gear teeth contact patterns. The drive pinion gear depth cannot be initially measured and set precisely with shims. If

7-177

7 DRIVE TRAIN

the original gear set is installed with the original depth shims, the best possible gear teeth contact patterns are achieved by adjusting the pinion gear depth and the ring gear backlash as necessary.

If a replacement gear set must be installed, the best possible gear teeth contact patterns are achieved by using the Pinion Variance chart. Determine the shims necessary to initially establish the replacement drive pinion gear depth. Adjust the pinion gear depth and the ring gear backlash as necessary.

Installing A Replacement Gear Set

If replacement is necessary, the ring and pinion gear must be replaced as a matched set. They are identified as a matched set by the numbers etched into each gear. The first two identify them as a matched set. The second number etched into the drive pinion is the depth variance. It indicates the amount (in thousandths) that the set varied from the standard setting. The standard for Model 30 differentials is 2.250 in. (57mm).

Refer to the Pinion Gear Depth Variance chart for the required initial depth of a replacement pinion gear. Read the chart as follows:

- Measure the thickness of the original pinion gear depth shims and note the depth variance values etched in the original and replacement drive pinion gears.
- Refer to the original and replacement columns in the chart and locate the box where they intersect. This will be the amount of change (to add or subtract) from the original shim thickness.

Differential Case Run-Out

1. If installing a replacement gear set, refer to the procedure above first. If reinstalling an original gear set, install the following:
- Original depth shims in the housing rear bearing cup
- Rear and front bearing cup in the housing
- Oil slinger
- Rear bearing on the pinion gear with tool J-24433
- Pinion gear in the housing
- Front bearing on the pinion gear
- Pinion yoke and original nut (tighten only enough to remove end-play)

NOTE: DO NOT install the bearing preload torque spacer or the pinion gear replacement seal at this time

2. Install the bearings on the differential case using tool J-21784.
3. Install the differential in the housing using a housing spreader (this is the same procedure used to remove the differential).
4. Insert enough spare shims between one of the differential bearings and the housing to eliminate all the differential case side-play.
5. Observe the installation reference marks and install the differential bearing caps and bolts. Tighten the bolts securely.
6. Attach a dial indicator to the housing. Position the dial indicator plunger so it contacts the ring gear mating face on the differential side. Pry the differential case to one side and zero the indicator. Rotate the differential case several times and note the pointer position as the case rotates.
7. The differential case run-out should not exceed 0.05mm (0.002 in.). Replace the case if necessary.

Zero End-Play Adjustment

1. Loosen the differential bearing cap bolts.
2. Remove the spar shims that were used to eliminate the differential case side play. Retain the differential case in the same position as it was for the run-out measurement.
3. Install a 0.142 in. (36mm) thick shim between each differential bearing and the housing. These shims will provide an end-play coarse adjustment.
4. Pry the differential case to one side of the housing. Zero the indicator. Pry to the opposite side of the housing and record the

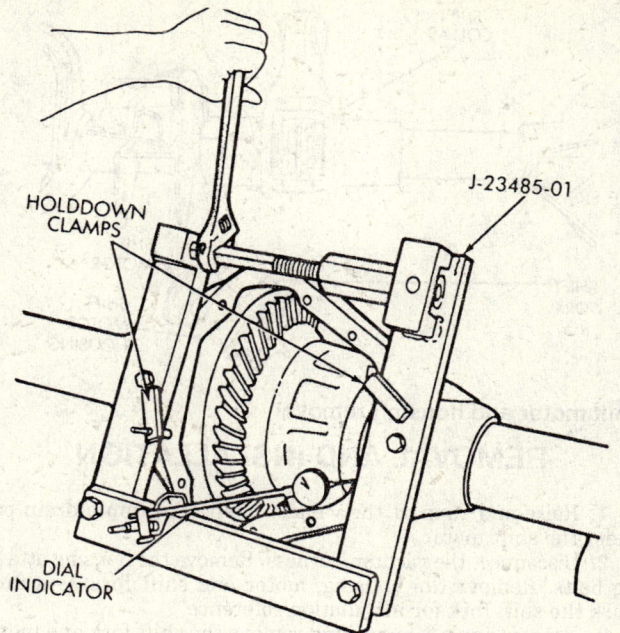

Differential housing separation

indicator end-play. The measurement is the additional thickness required for zero end-play.

5. Obtain the necessary shims and set aside for installation.
6. Install the spreader tool and remove the differential from the housing.

DIFFERENTIAL CASE ASSEMBLY

1. Install the side gears, the thrust washers and the pinion gears into the differential case.

NOTE: Be sure to install new side gear thrust washers, if the clearance measured at disassembly exceeded 0.007 in. (0.18mm).

2. Using 2 sets of feeler gauges, insert them between each side of the side gear thrust washer and differential case and measure the side gear clearance; the clearance should not exceed 0.007 in. (0.18mm). Replace both thrust washers, if the clearance exceeds the tolerance.
3. Install the pinion shaft and lockpin into the case.
4. Assemble the original differential bearing shim packs, then, remove approximately 0.20 in. (0.50mm) shim thickness from each pack; the remaining shims will serve as a starter shim pack.
5. Install the starter shim packs (zero end-play shims) and bearing onto the case.
6. Align and install the ring gear. Using new bolts, torque the ring gear-to-differential case bolts to 55 ft. lbs. (75 Nm).

Ring Gear Backlash and Drive Pinion Depth Adjustment

1. Apply yellow ferrous oxide compound to both drive and coast sides of the ring gear teeth.
2. Install the differential case in the housing. Tap the outer edges of the bearing cups with a mallet to seat them. Observe the installation reference marks and install the bearing caps. Tighten bolts securely.
3. Attach a dial indicator to the housing. Position the indicator plunger against the drive side of on ring gear tooth. Ensure that the plunger is at a right angle (90°) to the tooth.
4. Pry the ring gear toward the dial indicator and zero the indicator pointer while at this position. Pry the ring gear away from

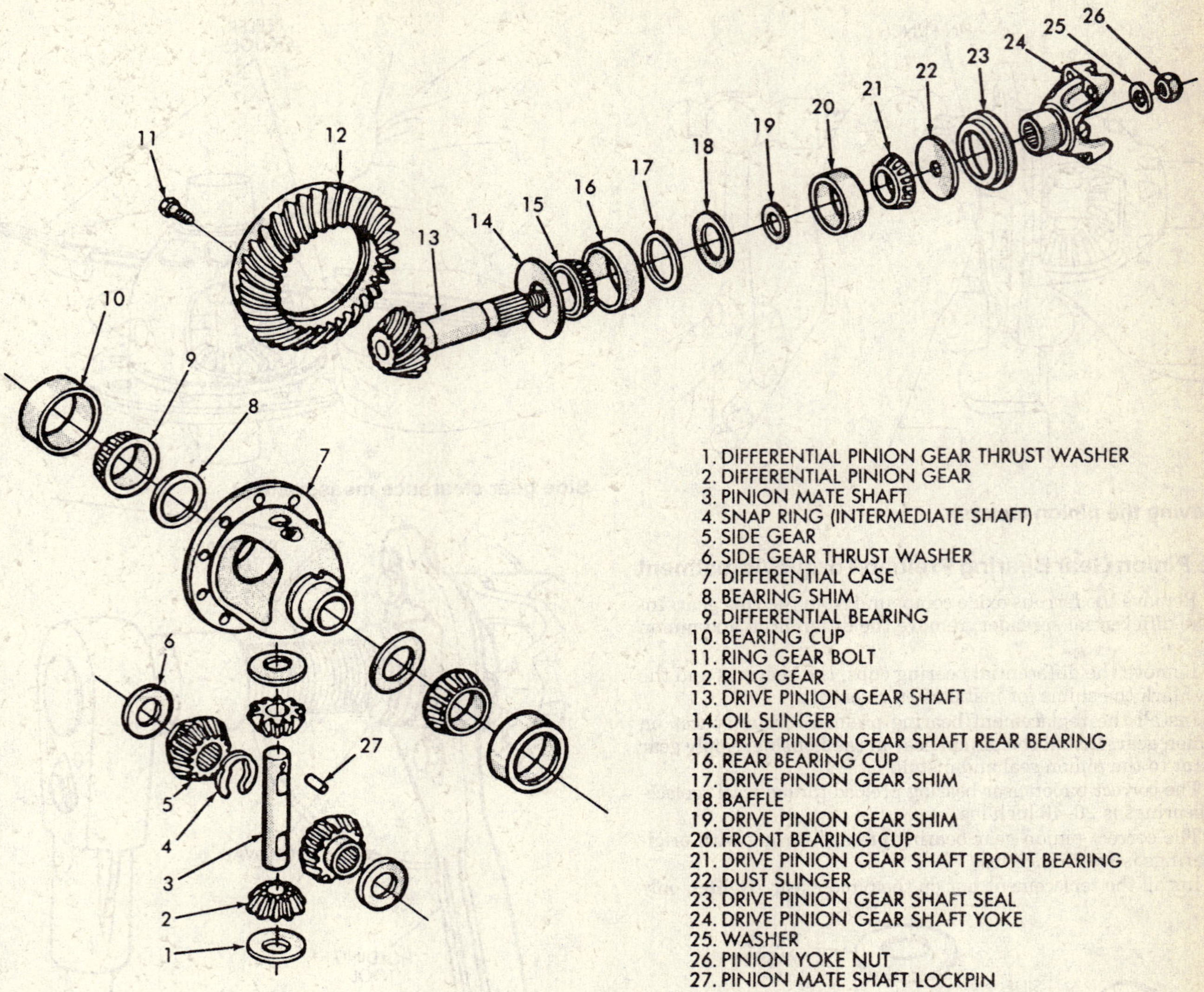

DRIVE TRAIN 7

1. DIFFERENTIAL PINION GEAR THRUST WASHER
2. DIFFERENTIAL PINION GEAR
3. PINION MATE SHAFT
4. SNAP RING (INTERMEDIATE SHAFT)
5. SIDE GEAR
6. SIDE GEAR THRUST WASHER
7. DIFFERENTIAL CASE
8. BEARING SHIM
9. DIFFERENTIAL BEARING
10. BEARING CUP
11. RING GEAR BOLT
12. RING GEAR
13. DRIVE PINION GEAR SHAFT
14. OIL SLINGER
15. DRIVE PINION GEAR SHAFT REAR BEARING
16. REAR BEARING CUP
17. DRIVE PINION GEAR SHIM
18. BAFFLE
19. DRIVE PINION GEAR SHIM
20. FRONT BEARING CUP
21. DRIVE PINION GEAR SHAFT FRONT BEARING
22. DUST SLINGER
23. DRIVE PINION GEAR SHAFT SEAL
24. DRIVE PINION GEAR SHAFT YOKE
25. WASHER
26. PINION YOKE NUT
27. PINION MATE SHAFT LOCKPIN

Dana Model 30 differential — exploded view

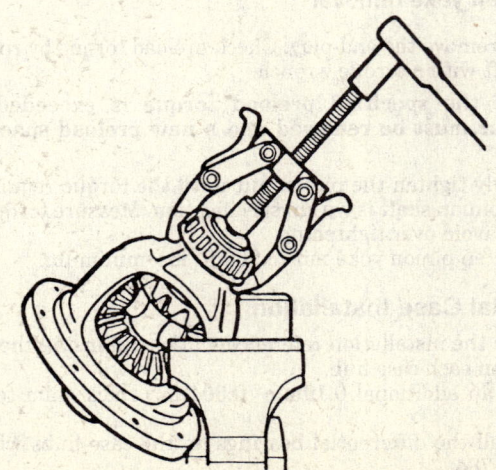

Removing the differential bearing

the drive pinion gear until the gear backlash indicated is 0.13–0.23mm (0.005–0.009in.).

5. Temporarily insert shims between on differential housing bearing and the housing to maintain the established gear backlash during the remainder of the adjustment.

6. Move the dial indicator aside and apply yellow ferrous oxide compound to the ring gear teeth. Rotate the ring gear on complete revolution in both directions to imprint the gear teeth contact patterns in the compound.

7. Note the teeth patterns and refer to the Gear Teeth Contact Patterns chart.

• To increase backlash, use a thinner shim pack on the ring gear side of the case. Subtract the amount needed from the ring gear pack. Add the same amount to the opposite shim pack.

• To decrease backlash, use a thinner shim pack on the ring gear side of the case. Add the amount needed to the ring gear shim pack. Subtract the same amount from the opposite shim pack.

8. Remove the differential and pinion gear and make any necessary adjustments to the shims. Reinstall the gears and repeat the gear contact pattern test until gear patterns are satisfactory.

7-179

7 DRIVE TRAIN

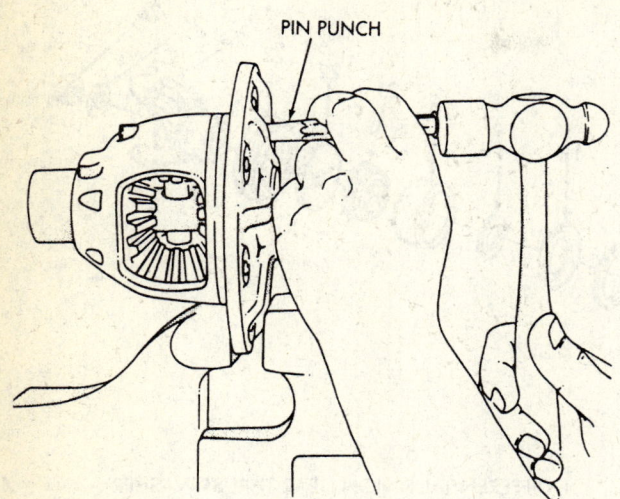

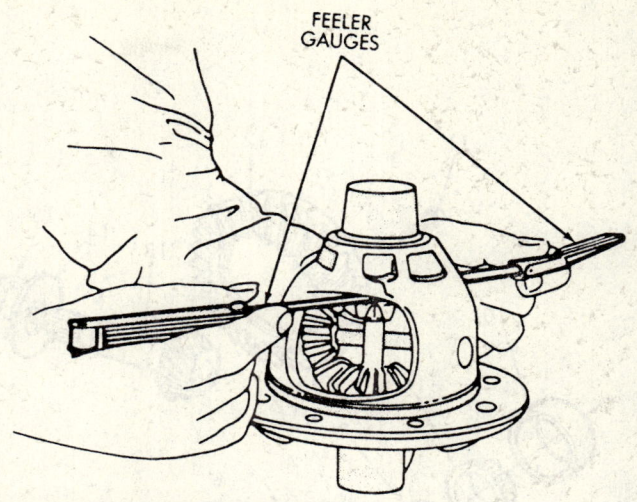

Side gear clearance measurement

Removing the pinion lock pin

Drive Pinion Gear Bearing Preload Torque Adjustment

1. Remove the ferrous oxide compound from the ring gear. Install the differential spreader, remove the differential and pinion gear.
2. Remove the differential bearing cups, the bearings and the shims. Mark the shims for installation reference.
3. Install the replacement bearing preload torque spacer on the pinion gear. Install the pinion gear in the housing. Apply gear lubricant to the pinion seal and install.
 • The correct pinion gear bearing preload torque with replacement bearings is 20–40 inch lbs.
 • The correct pinion gear bearing preload torque with original bearings is 15–25 inch lbs.
4. Install the replacement nut on the pinion gear. Tighten only

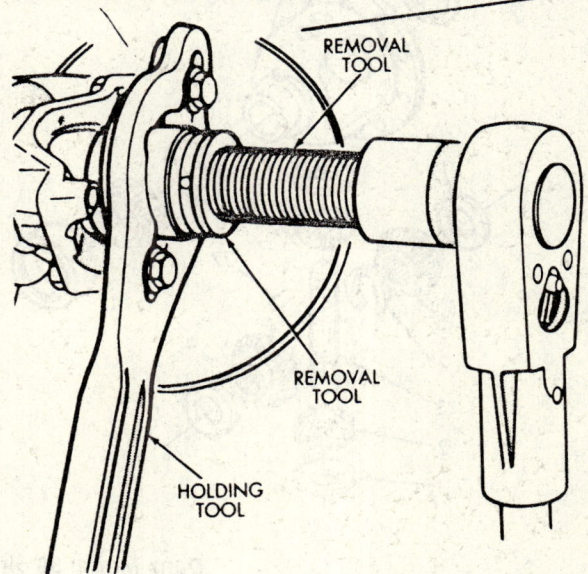

Pinion shaft yoke removal

enough to remove the end-play. Check preload torque by rotating pinion shaft with a torque wrench.

NOTE: If the specified preload torque is exceeded, the pinion gear must be removed and a new preload spacer installed.

5. Slowly tighten the pinion nut until the torque required to rotate the pinion shaft is within specification. Measure torque frequently to avoid over tightening.
6. Tighten pinion yoke nut to 200 ft. lbs. minimum.

Differential Case Installation

1. Note the installation reference marks and install the bearing shims on each case hub.
2. Add an additional 0.10mm (0.004 in.) thick shim to each case hub.
3. Install the differential bearings on the case hubs with installer J-21784.
4. Lubricate the bearings, gears and thrust washers with gear lubricant.

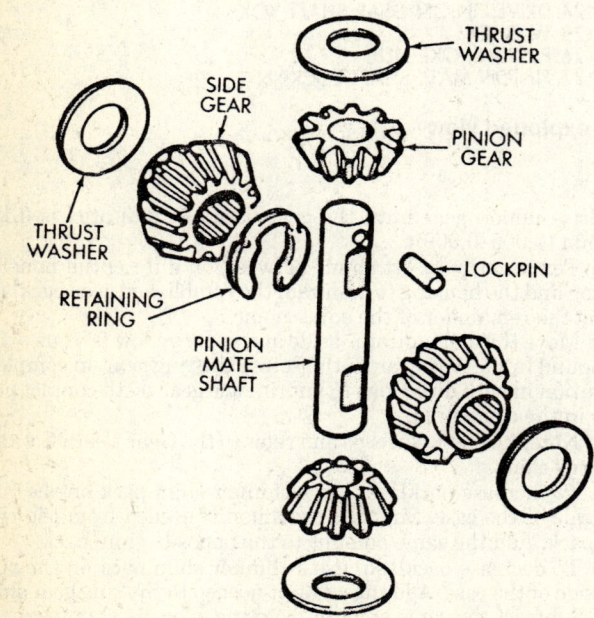

Pinion gear and side gear removal

DRIVE TRAIN 7

Pinion Gear Depth Variance

Original Pinion Gear Depth Variance	Replacement Pinion Gear Depth Variance								
	−4	−3	−2	−1	0	+1	+2	+3	+4
+4	+0.008	+0.007	+0.006	+0.005	+0.004	+0.003	+0.002	+0.001	0
+3	+0.007	+0.006	+0.005	+0.004	+0.003	+0.002	+0.001	0	−0.001
+2	+0.006	+0.005	+0.004	+0.003	+0.002	+0.001	0	−0.001	−0.002
+1	+0.005	+0.004	+0.003	+0.002	+0.001	0	−0.001	−0.002	−0.003
0	+0.004	+0.003	+0.002	+0.001	0	−0.001	−0.002	−0.003	−0.004
−1	+0.003	+0.002	+0.001	0	−0.001	−0.002	−0.003	−0.004	−0.005
−2	+0.002	+0.001	0	−0.001	−0.002	−0.003	−0.004	−0.005	−0.006
−3	+0.001	0	−0.001	−0.002	−0.003	−0.004	−0.005	−0.006	−0.007
−4	0	−0.001	−0.002	−0.003	−0.004	−0.005	−0.006	−0.007	−0.008

5. Install the differential spreader and spread the case.
6. Observe the installation marks and install the bearing cups on the bearings.
7. Install the differential in the housing. Tap the outer edges of the bearing cups to seat them.
8. Observe the reference marks and install the bearing caps. Tighten the cap bolts to 57 ft. lbs.
9. Measure the ring gear backlash. If it has changed, it must be readjusted.

TRAC-LOK DIFFERENTIAL

Operational Test

If a noisy or rough operation such as a chatter occurs when turning corners, the most probable cause of this chatter or noise is incorrect or contaminated lubricant. Before removing the Trac-Lok unit for repair, drain, flush and refill the axle with the specified lubricant. A complete lubricant drain and refill with the specified fluid will usually correct the chatter problem. A quick operational test of the Trac-Lok differential can be done easily by performing the following procedure:
1. Place one wheel on solid dry pavement and the opposite wheel on ice, mud grease or a similar low traction surface.
2. Gradually, increase the engine rpm to obtain the maximum traction prior to a breakaway. The ability to move the vehicle effectively will demonstrate the proper performance.

NOTE: If the test is performed on extremely slick surfaces such as ice or grease coated surfaces, some question may exist as to proper performance. In these extreme cases, a properly performing Trac-Lok will provide greater pulling power by lightly applying the parking brake.

Disassembly

DIFFERENTIAL

1. Remove the differential from the axle housing as previously outlined in this section. Install one axle shaft in the vise with the spline end facing upward and tighten the vise.
2. Do not allow more than 70mm (2³⁄₄ in.) of the shaft to extend above the top of the vise. This prevents the shaft from fully entering the side gear, causing interference with the step plate tool used to remove the differential gears.
3. Mount the differential case on the axle shaft with the ring gear bolt heads facing upward. Place some shop towels under the ring gear to protect the gear when it is removed from the case.
4. Remove and discard the ring gear bolts. Remove the ring gear from the case, using a rawhide hammer. Remove the differential case from the axle shaft and remove the ring gear and remount the differential case on the axle shaft.
5. Use suitable tools to disengage the snaprings from the pinion mate shaft. Place a shop towel on the opposite opening of the case to prevent the snaprings from flying out of the case. Remove the pinion mate shaft using a hammer and brass drift.

NOTE: A special gear rotating tool J–23781–3 or equivalent, is required to perform the following steps. The tool consists of 3 parts; the gear rotating tool, forcing screw and step plate.

6. Install step plate tool into the lower differential side gear. Position the pawl end of the gear rotating tool onto the step plate.
7. Insert the forcing screw tool through the top of the case and thread it into the gear rotating tool. Before using the forcing screw tool, apply a small amount of grease to the centering hole in the step plate and oil the threads of the forcing screw.
8. Center the forcing screw in the step plate and tighten the screw to move the differential side gears away from the differen-

7-181

7 DRIVE TRAIN

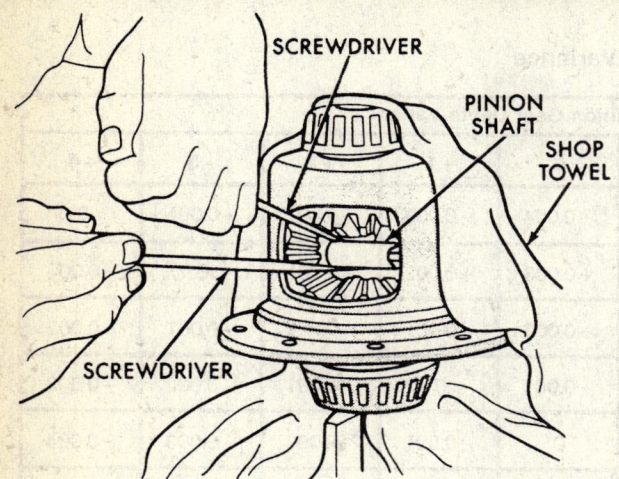

Removing pinion shaft snaprings

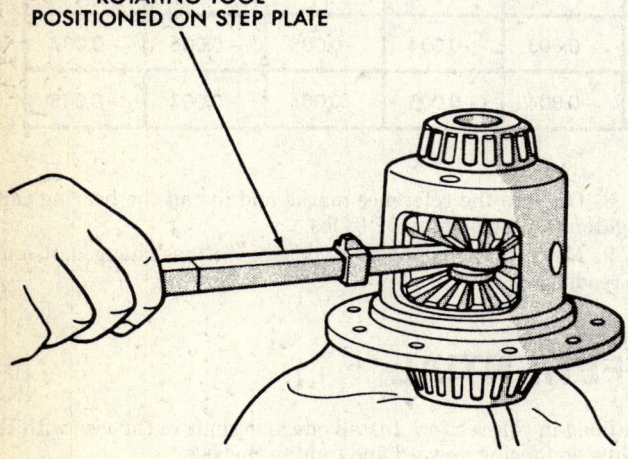

Rotating tool installation

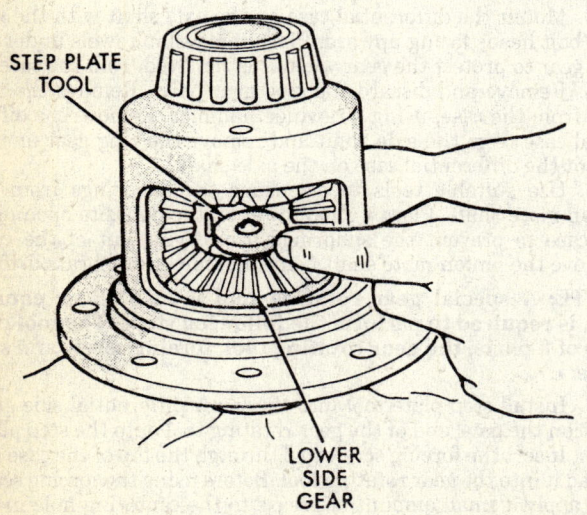

Installing step plate tool

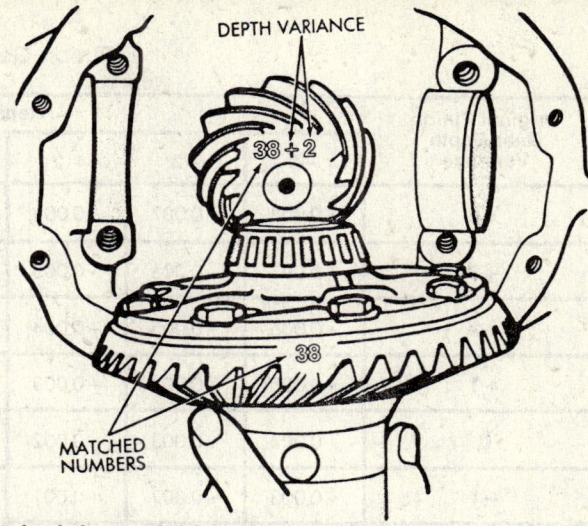

Matched ring and drive pinion gears

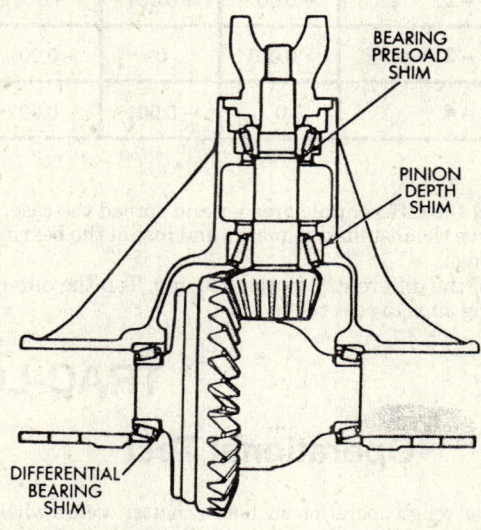

Differential shim location

tial pinion gears. Remove the differential pinion gear thrust washers using a feeler gauge or a shim stock of 0.76mm (0.030 in.) thickness. Insert the feeler gauge or shim stock between the washer and the case and withdraw the shim stock with the thrust washer.

9. Tighten the forcing screw until a slight movement of the differential pinion gear is observed. Insert the pawl end of the gear rotating tool between the teeth of one differential side gear.

10. Pull the handle of the tool to rotate the side gears and pinion gears. Remove the pinion gears as they appear in the case opening. It could be necessary to adjust the tension applied on the belleville springs by the forcing screw before the gears can be rotated in the case.

11. Retain the upper side gear and clutch pack in the case by placing a hand on the bottom of the rotating tool while removing the forcing screw. Remove the rotating tool, upper side gear and clutch pack.

12. Remove the differential case from the axle shaft. Invert the case with the flange or ring gear side up and remove the step plate tool, lower side gear and clutch pack from the case. Remove the retainer clips from both the clutch packs to allow separation of the plates and discs.

DRIVE TRAIN 7

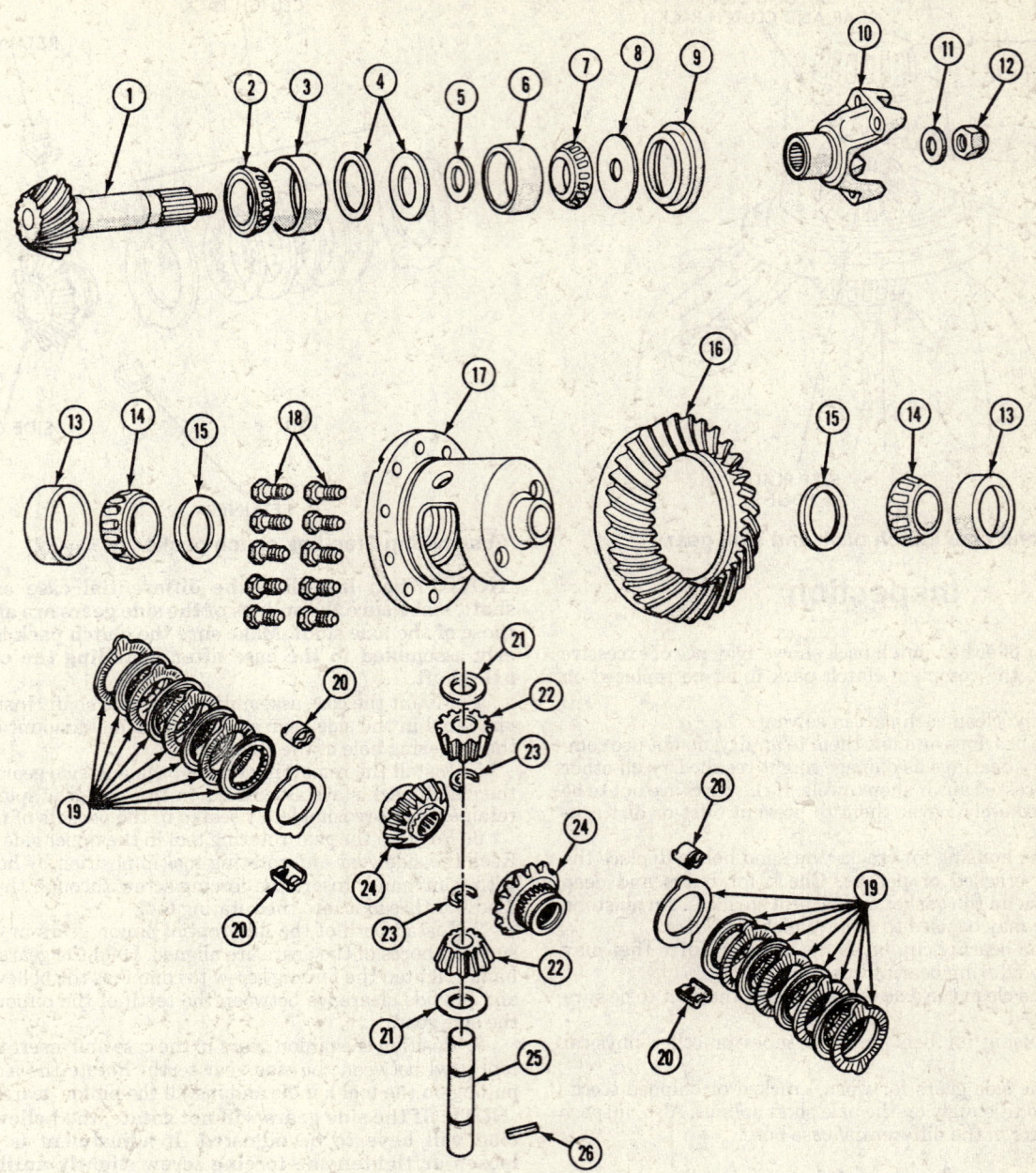

1 PINION GEAR
2 PINION REAR BEARING
3 BEARING CUP
4 PINION DEPTH SHIMS
5 PINION PRELOAD SHIM
6 BEARING CUP
7 PINION FRONT BEARING
8 SLINGER
9 PINION SEAL
10 YOKE
11 WASHER
12 PINION NUT
13 BEARING CUP
14 DIFFERENTIAL BEARING
15 BACKLASH/PRELOAD SHIM
16 RING GEAR
17 DIFFERENTIAL CASE
18 RING GEAR BOLTS
19 CLUTCH PACKS
20 CLUTCH PACK RETAINERS
21 PINION THRUST WASHER
22 DIFFERENTIAL PINIONS
23 PINION SHAFT SNAP RINGS
24 DIFFERENTIAL SIDE GEARS
25 PINION SHAFT
26 PINION SHAFT LOCK PIN

Trac-Lok components

7-183

7 DRIVE TRAIN

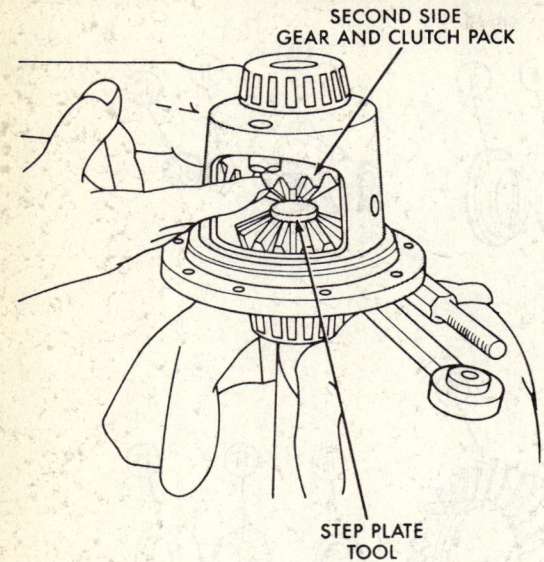

Installing second gear clutch pack and side gear

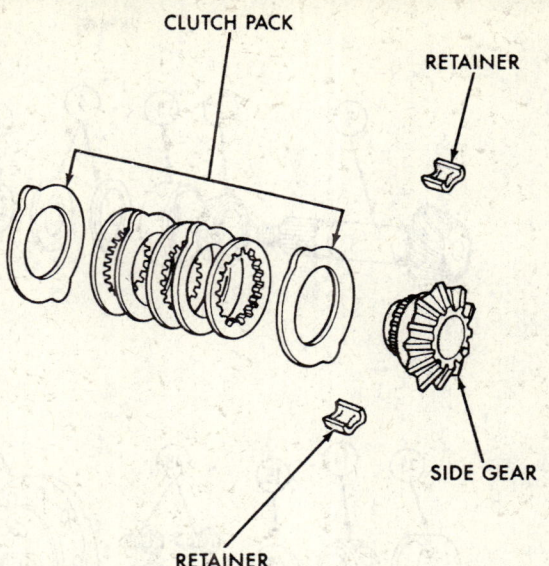

Assembling Trac-Lok clutch packs

Inspection

If any member of either clutch pack shows evidence of excessive wear or scoring, the complete clutch pack must be replaced on both sides.
1. Thoroughly, clean each part in solvent.
2. Towel dry bearings or allow them to air dry, do not use compressed air to dry bearings as damage might result. Dry all other parts with compressed air or shop towels. If the parts are not to be assembled immediately, cover them to prevent dust or dirt contamination.
3. Inspect the housing for cracks and sand holes. Replace the housing if it is cracked or porous. Check for burrs and deep scratches or nicks on the gasket and oil seal surfaces. An oil stone or fine tooth file may be used to remove nicks or burrs.
4. Inspect the bearing cup bores for nicks or burrs that may have been created during bearing cup removal.
5. Inspect and clean the axle tubes. Inspect the vent to be sure it is not obstructed.
6. Check housing for bent or loose tubes or other physical damage.
7. Inspect the side gears for worn, cracked or chipped teeth. The gears should fit snugly on the axle shaft splines. Also, inspect the fit of the gears in the differential case bore.

Assembly

DIFFERENTIAL

1. Lubricate all the differential components with the specified gear lubricant. Assemble the clutch packs. Install the plates and discs in the same position as when removed regardless of whether they are replacement or original parts.
2. Install the clutch retainer clips on the ears of the clutch plates. Be sure the clutch packs are completely assembled and seated on the ears of the plates. Install the clutch packs on the differential side gears and install the assembly in the case.
3. Make sure the clutch pack stays assembled on the side gear splines and the retainer clips are completely seated in the case pockets. To prevent the pack from falling out of the case, it will be necessary to hold it in place by hand while mounting the case on the axle shaft.

NOTE: When installing the differential case on the axle shaft, make sure the splines of the side gears are aligned with those of the axle shaft. Make sure the clutch pack is still properly assembled in the case after installing the case on the axle shaft.

4. Mount the case assembly on the axle shaft. Install the step plate tool in the side gear and apply a small amount of grease in the centering hole of the step plate.
5. Install the remaining clutch pack and side gear. Make sure the clutch pack stays assembled on the side gear splines and the retainer clips are completely seated in the pockets of the case.
6. Position the gear rotating tool in the upper side of the gear. Keep the side gear and rotating tool in position by holding them with your hand. Insert the forcing screw through the top of the case and thread it into the rotating tool.
7. Install both of the differential pinion gears in the case; be sure the bores of the gears are aligned. Hold the gears in place by hand. Tighten the forcing screw to compress the belleville springs and provide clearance between the teeth of the pinion gears and the side gears.
8. Position the pinion gears in the case and insert the rotating tool pawl between the side gear teeth. Rotate the side gears by pulling on the tool handle and install the pinion gears.

NOTE: If the side gears will not rotate, the belleville spring load will have to be adjusted. If adjustment is necessary, loosen or tighten the forcing screw slightly until the gears will rotate.

9. Rotate the side gears, using the rotating tool handle, until the shaft bores in both the pinion gears are aligned with the case bore. Lubricate both sides of the pinion gear thrust washers.
10. Tighten or loosen the forcing screw to permit the thrust washer installation. Install the thrust washers and using a suitable tool, guide the washers into position. Make sure the shaft bores in the washers and gears are aligned with the case bores.
11. Remove the forcing screw, rotating tool and step plate. Lubricate the pinion mate shaft and seat the shaft in the case. Be sure the snapring grooves in the shaft are exposed to allow the snapring installation.
12. Install the pinion mate shaft snaprings, remove the case from the axle shaft and install the ring gear on the case. Be sure to use replacement ring gear bolts only; do not reuse the original bolts.
13. Align the ring gear and case bolt holes and install the ring gear bolts finger tight only. Remove the case on the axle shaft and tighten the bolts evenly to the proper torque specifications.

8 Suspension and Steering

QUICK REFERENCE INDEX

Front Suspension	8-2
Rear Suspension	8-10
Steering	8-13
Wheel Alignment Specifications	8-9

GENERAL INDEX

Alignment, wheel
  Front 8-9
  Rear 8-12
Ball joints 8-5
Front suspension
  Ball joints 8-5
  Knuckle and pivot pins 8-5
  Lower control arm 8-5
  Shock absorbers 8-4
  Springs 8-2
  Stabilizer bar 8-3
  Track bar 8-3
  Upper control arm 8-4
  Wheel alignment 8-9
Front wheel bearings 8-6
Ignition switch
  and lock cylinder 8-15
Knuckles 8-5
Lower ball joint 8-5
Lower control arm
  Front 8-5
  Rear 8-12
Manual steering gear
  Adjustments 8-16
  Overhaul 8-17
  Removal and installation 8-17
  Troubleshooting 8-39
Pitman arm 8-27

Power steering gear
  Adjustments 8-26
  Overhaul 8-22
  Removal and installation 8-22
  Troubleshooting 8-34
Power steering pump
  Bleeding 8-27
  Removal and installation 8-26
  Troubleshooting 8-37
Rear suspension
  Lower control arm 8-12
  Upper control arm 8-12
  Shock absorbers 8-11
  Springs 8-10
  Stabilizer bar 8-11
  Wheel alignment 8-12
Shock absorbers
  Front 8-4
  Rear 8-11
Specifications Charts
  Wheel alignment 8-9
Springs
  Front 8-2
  Rear 8-11
Stabilizer bar
  Front 8-3
  Rear 8-11
Steering column
  Removal and installation 8-16

  Troubleshooting 8-30
Steering gear
  Manual 8-16
  Power 8-22
Steering linkage
  Connecting rod 8-28
  Damper 8-28
  Pitman arm 8-27
  Steering lock 8-15
  Steering wheel 8-13
  Tie rod ends 8-28
  Track bars 8-3
Troubleshooting Charts
  Ignition switch 8-29
  Manual steering gear 8-39
  Power steering gear 8-34
  Power steering pump 8-37
  Steering column 8-30
  Steering ans Suspension .. 8-29
  Turn signal switch 8-32
  Turn signal switch 8-13
Upper control arm
  Front 8-4
  Rear 8-12
Wheel alignment
  Front 8-9
  Rear 8-12
  Specifications 8-9
Wheels 8-2

8 SUSPENSION AND STEERING

WHEELS

Wheels

REMOVAL AND INSTALLATION

1. Remove the wheel cover, if equipped, by prying it off with an appropriate tool.
2. With the vehicle still on the ground loosen the lug nuts just enough to ease removal with the wheel off the ground.
3. Raise and support the vehicle safely.
4. Remove the lug nuts and remove the wheel.
5. Installation is the reverse of removal. Tighten the lug nuts to 75 ft. lbs. observing the tightening sequence in the illustration.

INSPECTION

The wheels should be inspected on a frequent basis. Replace any wheel that is cracked, bent, severely dented, has excessive runout or has a broken weld. The tire inflation valve should also be inspected frequently for wear, leaks, cuts and looseness. It should be replaced if defective or its condition is doubtful.

Clean all the wheels with a mild soap and water solution only and rinse thoroughly with water. Never use abrasive or caustic materials, especially on aluminum or chrome-plated wheels because the surface will be etched or the plating severely damaged. After cleaning aluminum or chrome-plated wheels, apply a coating of protective wax to preserve the finish and luster.

NOTE: DO NOT wax open pore aluminum wheels. The wax will become embedded in the pores and will be very difficult to remove.

Wheel Lug Studs

When replacing wheel lug studs use the following guide:
- Stripped bolts—replace lugs involved.
- One loose bolt—replace all lugs in hub or axle flange.
- One broken bolt—replace all lugs in hub or axle flange.
- Wheel hole elongated—replace wheel

REMOVAL AND INSTALLATION

Rear Drum

1. Raise and support the vehicle safely.
2. Install lug stud nut on lug stud. Using a wheel lug stud removal tool, press the damaged lug stud off the axle flange. Remove lug stud and bolt.
3. Insert the new lug stud into the axle flange. Install four to five thick washers and the lug nut on the stud.
4. Slowly tighten the nut on the lug stud until it seats completely against the axle flange. Then torque to 80 ft. lbs.
5. Remove the nut and washers and install the wheel. Lower the vehicle.

Front Hub/Rotor

1. Raise and support the vehicle safely.
2. Remove the wheel and brake caliper.

NOTE: DO NOT disconnect the caliper hose. Suspend the caliper with a piece of wire.

3. Remove the dust cap, cotter pin, nut retainer, adjusting nut and thrust washer. Remove the outer wheel bearing.
4. Remove the hub/rotor.
5. Place the hub/rotor in a shop press and remove the wheel lug stud.

NOTE: Place the replacement stud in the freezer for a few minutes prior to installation.

6. Press the replacement stud into the hub/rotor until it seats completely.
7. Install hub/rotor, outer wheel bearing, thrust washer and adjusting nut.
8. Tighten the adjusting nut with 21 ft. lbs. torque while spinning the rotor to seat the bearing. Loosen the adjusting nut $1/2$ of-a-turn and retighten to 19 ft. lbs.
9. Install the nut retainer, cotter pin and dust cap. Install the brake caliper.
10. Install the wheel. Lower the vehicle.

FRONT SUSPENSION

Coil Springs

REMOVAL AND INSTALLATION

— CAUTION —
Coil springs are under a great deal of tension when installed in the vehicle. Serious injury or death may result from being hit by an expanding spring. A piece of chain fastened to the frame and wrapped around the coil spring will keep the spring from flying out if it should slip before it is fully expanded.

1. Raise and support the vehicle safely.
2. Support the axle with a floor jack.
3. Remove the wheels.
4. On 4wd trucks, matchmark and disconnect the front driveshaft from the axle.
5. Disconnect the lower control arm at the axle.
6. Disconnect the stabilizer bar links and the shock absorbers at the axle.
7. Disconnect the track bar at the sill bracket.
8. Disconnect the tie rod at the pitman arm.
9. Lower the axle until tension is removed from the spring, then loosen the spring retainer and remove the spring.

To Install:

10. Position the replacement spring on the retainer, tighten the spring retainer bracket screw and lift the rear axle into position.
11. Connect the lower control arm to the axle. Tighten the control arm-to-axle bolt to 133 ft. lbs.
12. Remove the support jack. It is important that the front springs are supporting the weight of the vehicle when the track bar attaching bolts are tightened. Vehicle ride comfort could be adversely affected.
13. Connect the stabilizer bar links and the shock absorbers at the axle. tighten the shock absorber-to-axle bolt to 14 ft. lbs.; the stabilizer bar-to-axle bolt to 70 ft. lbs.
14. Connect the track bar at the sill bracket. Tighten the track bar-to-frame rail bolt to 35 ft. lbs.
15. Connect the tie rod at the pitman arm. Tighten the center link-to-pitman arm bolt to 35 ft. lbs.

NOTE: New strap bolts must be used each time the driveshaft is disconnected.

SUSPENSION AND STEERING 8

16. On 4wd trucks, connect the front driveshaft. Tighten U-joint-to-axle bolt to 14 ft. lbs.
17. Install the wheels and lower the vehicle.

Front Stabilizer Bar

REMOVAL AND INSTALLATION

1. Raise and support the vehicle safely.
2. Disconnect the stabilizer bar at the connecting links. If necessary, disconnect the connecting links from the brackets on the frame rail and steering box.
3. Remove the stabilizer bar-to-frame clamps and cushions, and remove the stabilizer bar.
4. Installation is the reverse of removal. Torque the clamp-to-frame bolts to 55 ft. lbs., the stabilizer bar-to-connecting link nuts to 27 ft. lbs., and, the connecting link-to-axle bolts to 70 ft. lbs.

Track Bar

REMOVAL AND INSTALLATION

1. Raise and support the vehicle safely.
2. Remove the cotter pin and nut securing the track bar to the frame bracket.
3. Remove the bolt and nut securing the track bar to the axle.

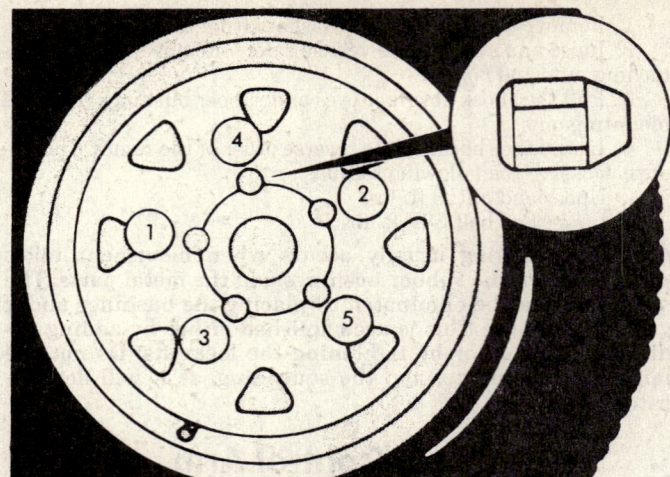
Wheel lug nut tightening sequence

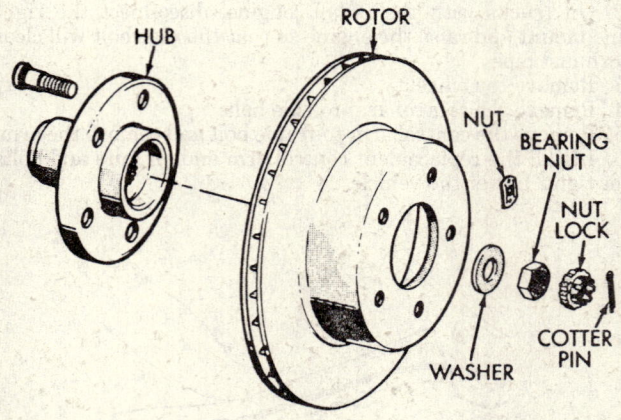
4WD front wheel lug stud removal/installation

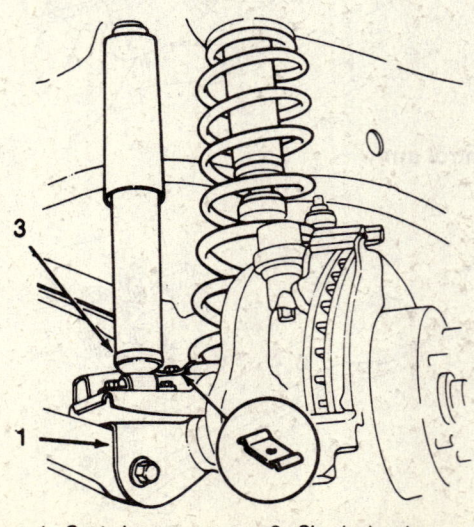
1. Control arm 3. Shock absorber
Removing the coil spring retention clip

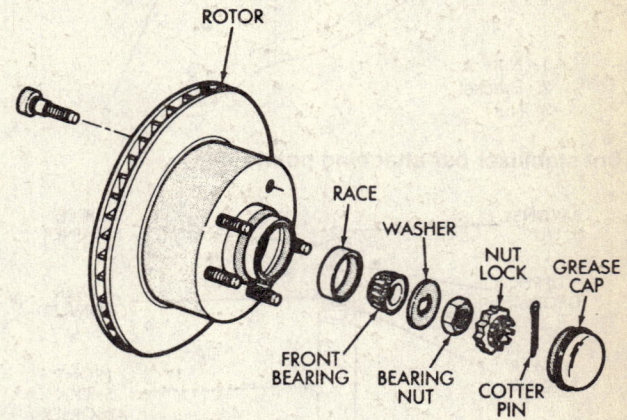
2WD front wheel lug stud removal/installation

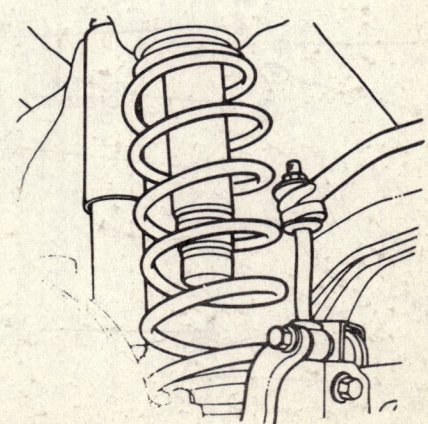
Front coil spring mounting

8-3

8 SUSPENSION AND STEERING

NOTE: A puller tool may be necessary to separate the ball stud from the frame rail bracket.

4. It is important that the front springs are supporting the weight of the vehicle when the track bar attaching bolts are tightened. If the springs are not at their ride height, vehicle ride comfort could be adversely affected.

5. Installation is the reverse of removal. Install both ends loosely, then torque the fasteners. Torque the frame-end nut to 35 ft. lbs.; the axle-end bolt to 55 ft. lbs.

Shock Absorbers

REMOVAL AND INSTALLATION

NOTE: Before installing new shocks, they should be purged of air. To do this, hold the shock upright and fully extend it, then invert and compress it. Do this several times.

1. Remove the locknuts and washers from the upper stud.
2. Raise and support the vehicle safely. Remove the lower attaching nuts and bolts.
3. Pull the shock absorber eyes and rubber bushings from the mounting pins.
4. Install the shocks in the reverse order of the removal procedure. Observe the following torques:
   - Upper end nut: 8 ft. lbs.
   - Lower end bolts: 14 ft. lbs.

NOTE: Squeaking usually occurs when movement takes place between the rubber bushings and the metal parts. The squeaking may be eliminated by placing the bushings under greater pressure. This is accomplished either by adding additional washers or by tightening the locknuts. Do not use mineral lubricant to stop the squeaking, as it will deteriorate the rubber.

Upper Control Arm

REMOVAL AND INSTALLATION

1. Raise and support the vehicle safely.
2. On trucks with the 6-2.8L engine, disconnect the right engine mount and raise the engine so that the rear bolt will clear the exhaust pipe.
3. Remove the wheels.
4. Remove the control arm-to-axle bolt.
5. Remove the control arm-to-frame bolt and remove the arm.
6. Install the replacement control arm and all nuts and bolts finger tight. Lower the vehicle.

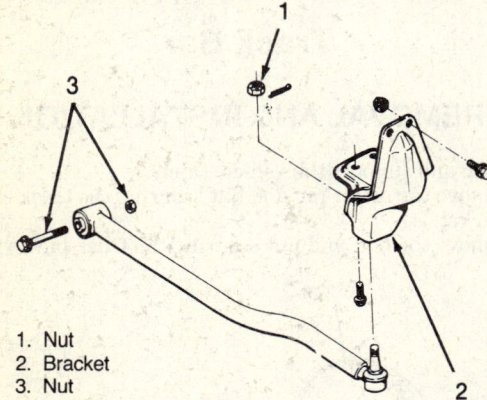

1. Nut
2. Bracket
3. Nut

Front stabilizer bar attaching points

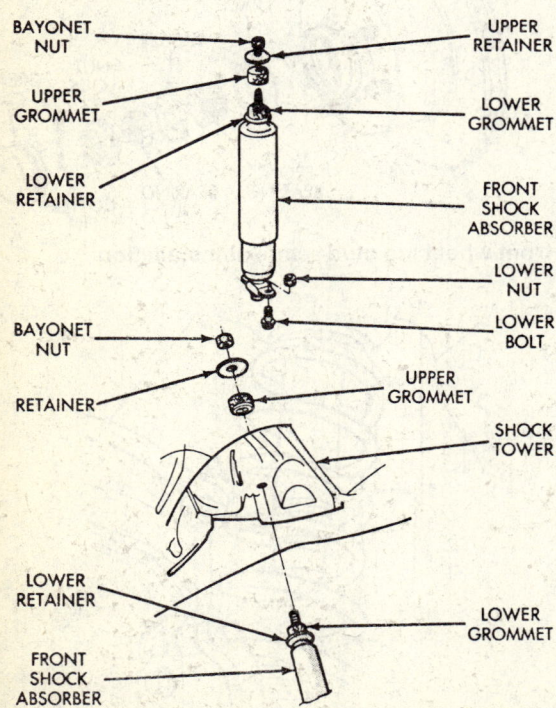

Front shock absorber mounting

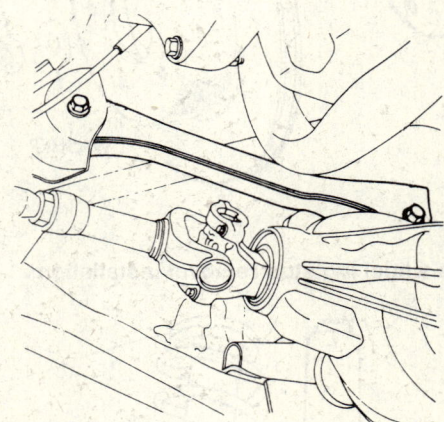

Upper control arm

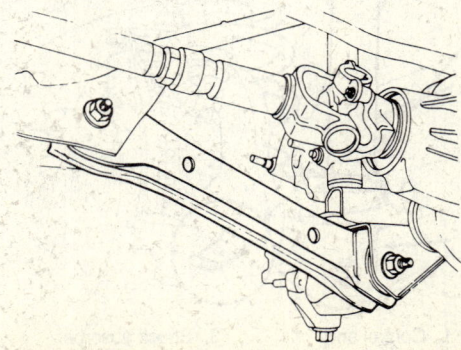

Lower upper control arm

SUSPENSION AND STEERING 8

7. It is important to have the front springs at their normal ride height when the upper control arm attaching nuts are tightened. Vehicle ride comfort could be adversely affected.

8. Torque the control arm bolts to 55 ft. lbs. at the axle; 66 ft. lbs. at the frame.

Lower Control Arm

REMOVAL AND INSTALLATION

1. Raise and support the vehicle safely.
2. Disconnect the lower control arm at the axle and rear bracket. Remove the arm.
3. Install the replacement arm and tighten the attaching bolts finger tight.
4. Lower the vehicle. It is important to have the front springs at their normal ride height when the lower control arm attaching nuts are tightened. Vehicle ride comfort could be adversely affected.
5. Torque lower control arm attaching bolts to 133 ft. lbs.

Upper and Lower Ball Joint

REMOVAL AND INSTALLATION

NOTE: This procedure requires the use of a special tool.

1. Raise and support the vehicle safely.
2. Remove the wheel. Remove the steering knuckle.
3. Position a ball joint removal tool (J-34503-1 and 34503-3), as illustrated, to remove the ball joint.
5. Tighten the clamp screw to remove the joint.
6. Use a ball joint installation tool (J-34503-5 or J-34503-4), as illustrated, to install the ball joint.
7. Install the knuckle. Tighten steering knuckle-to-ball joint nuts to 100 ft. lbs.

Steering Knuckle and Pivot Pins

REMOVAL AND INSTALLATION

1. Remove the axle shaft.

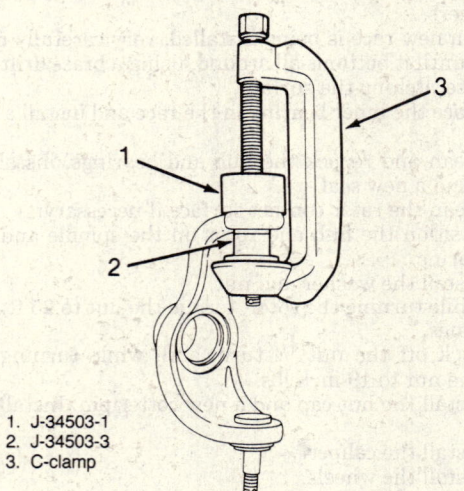

1. J-34503-1
2. J-34503-3
3. C-clamp

Upper ball joint removal

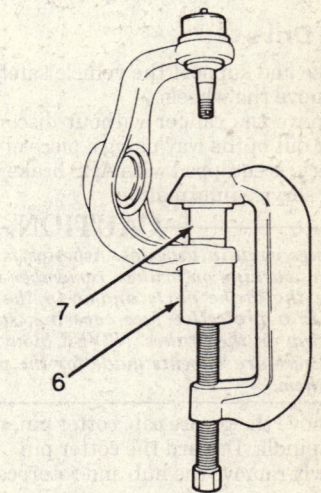

6. J-34503-1
7. J-34503-3

Lower ball joint removal

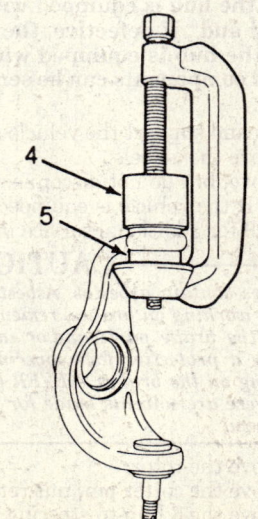

4. J-34503-5
5. J-34503-12

Upper ball joint installation

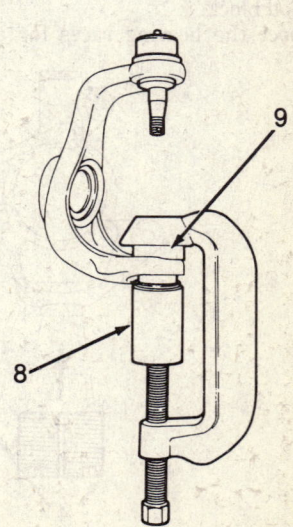

8. J-34503-4
9. J-34503-12

Upper ball joint removal

8-5

8 SUSPENSION AND STEERING

2. Remove the disc brake caliper from the steering knuckle. If equipped with ABS brake system, see Section 9 for additional service information.
3. Remove the knuckle-to-ball joint cotter pins and nuts.
4. Drive the knuckle out with a brass hammer.

NOTE: A split ring seat is located in the bottom of the knuckle. During installation, this ring seat must be set to a depth of 5.23mm. Measure the depth to the top of the ring seat (4).

5. Installation is the reverse of removal. Tighten the knuckle retaining nuts to 75 ft. lbs. and the disc brake caliper bolts to 77 ft. lbs.

Front Wheel Bearings

REPLACEMENT

NOTE: Sodium-based grease is not compatible with lithium-based grease. Read the package labels and be careful not to mix the two types. If there is any doubt as to the type of grease used, completely clean the old grease from the bearing and hub before replacing.

2-Wheel Drive

1. Raise and support the vehicle safely.
2. Remove the wheels.
3. Remove the caliper without disconnecting the brake line. Suspend it out of the way using a piece of wire to prevent damage. If the vehicle is equipped with ABS brake system, see Section 9 for additional service information.

--- **CAUTION** ---

Brake linings contain asbestos. Asbestos is a known cancer-causing agent. When working on brakes, remember that the dust which accumulates on the brake parts and/or in the drum contains asbestos. Always wear a protective face covering, such as a painter's mask, when working on the brakes. NEVER blow the dust from the brakes or drum! There are solvents made for the purpose of cleaning brake parts. Use them!

4. Remove the grease cap, cotter pin, nut cap, nut, and washer from the spindle. Discard the cotter pin.
5. Slowly remove the hub and rotor, catch the outer bearing as it falls.
6. Carefully drive out the inner bearing and seal from the hub, using a wood block.
7. Inspect the bearing races for excessive wear, pitting or grooves. If they are cracked or grooved, or if pitting and excess wear is present, drive them out with a drift or punch.
8. Check the bearing for excess wear, pitting or cracks, or excess looseness.

NOTE: If it is necessary to replace either the bearing or the race, replace both. Never replace just a bearing or a race. These parts wear in a mating pattern. If just one is replaced, premature failure of the new part will result.

To Install:

9. On vehicles with drum brakes, cover the spindle with a cloth and thoroughly brush all dirt from the brakes. Never blow the dirt off the brakes, due to the presence of asbestos in the dirt, which is harmful to your health when inhaled.
10. Remove the cloth and thoroughly clean the spindle and the inside of the hub.
11. Pack the inside of the hub with EP wheel bearing grease. Add grease to the hub until it is flush with the inside diameter of the bearing cup.
12. Pack the bearing with the same grease. A needle-shaped wheel bearing packer is best for this operation. If one is not available, place a large amount of grease in the palm of your hand and slide the edge of the bearing cage through the grease to pick up as much as possible, then work the grease in as best you can with your fingers.
13. If a new race is being installed, very carefully drive it into position until it bottoms all around, using a brass drift. Be careful to avoid scratching the surface.
14. Place the inner bearing in the race and install a new grease seal.
15. Clean and repack the hub and bearings, install the inner bearing and a new seal.
16. Clean the rotor contact surface if necessary.
17. Position the hub and rotor on the spindle and install the outer bearing.
18. Install the washer and nut.
19. While turning the rotor, torque the nut to 25 ft. lbs. to seat the bearings.
20. Back off the nut $1/2$ turn, and, while turning the rotor, torque the nut to 19 inch lbs.
21. Install the nut cap and a new cotter pin. Install the grease cap.
22. Install the caliper.
23. Install the wheels.

4-Wheel Drive

NOTE: If the hub is equipped with ball bearings, it can not be serviced and, if defective, the complete unit must be replaced. If the hub is equipped with tapered roller bearings, its internal components can be serviced or replaced as necessary.

1. Raise and support the vehicle safely.
2. Remove the wheels.
3. Remove, but do not disconnect, the caliper. Suspend it out of the way. If the vehicle is equipped with an ABS brake system, see Section 9 for additional service information.

--- **CAUTION** ---

Brake linings contain asbestos. Asbestos is a known cancer-causing agent. When working on brakes, remember that the dust which accumulates on the brake parts and/or in the drum contains asbestos. Always wear a protective face covering, such as a painter's mask, when working on the brakes. NEVER blow the dust from the brakes or drum! There are solvents made for the purpose of cleaning brake parts. Use them!

4. Remove the rotor.
5. Remove the cotter pin, nut retainer, axle nut and washer.
6. Remove the 3 hub-to-steering knuckle attaching bolts.
7. Remove the hub/bearing carrier and the rotor shield.
8. Using an arbor press, press the hub out of the bearing car-

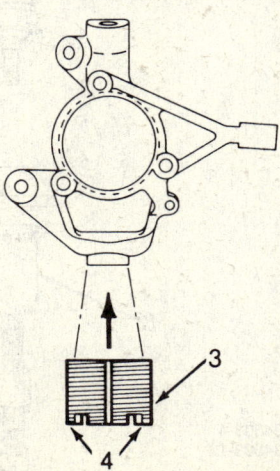

Split ring seat installation details. (3) is the split ring seat, (4) is the top of the seat for measurement purposes

SUSPENSION AND STEERING 8

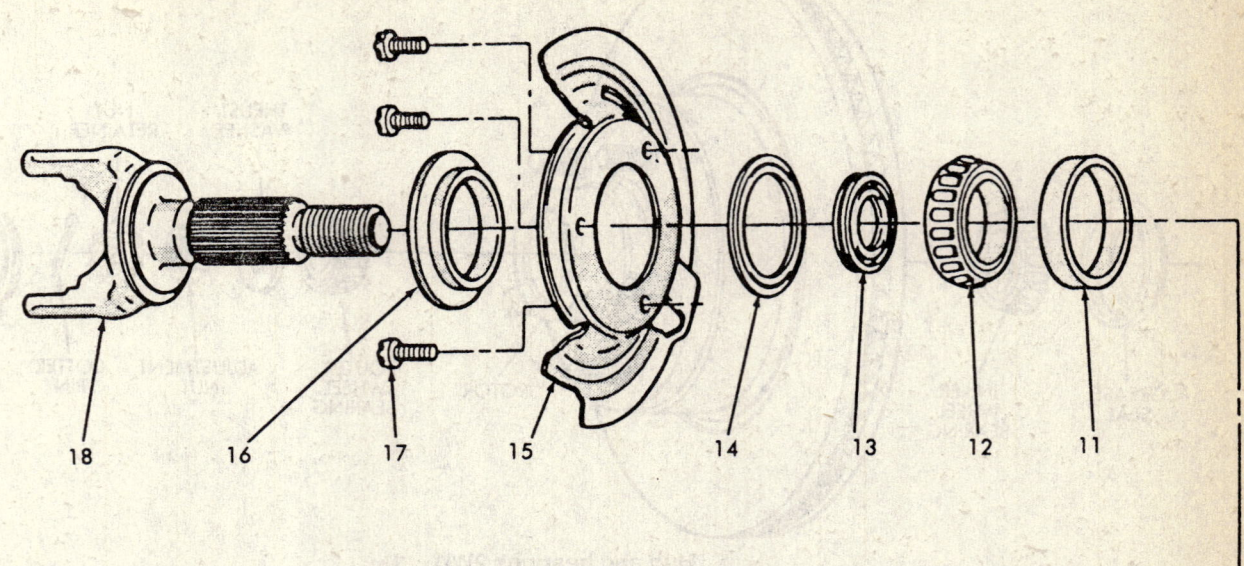

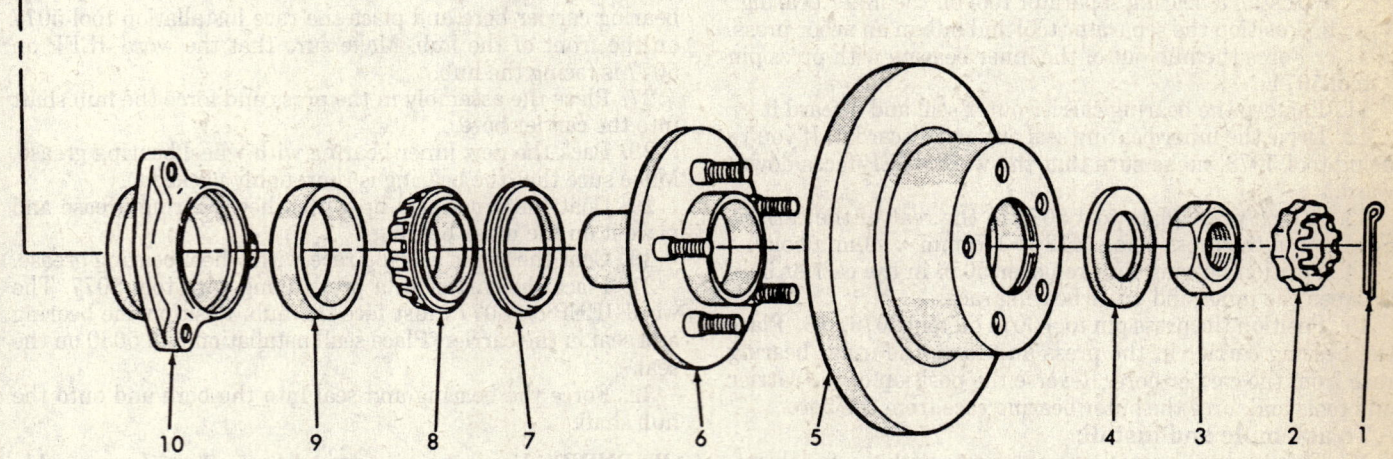

1. COTTER PIN
2. NUT RETAINER
3. NUT
4. WASHER
5. BRAKE ROTOR
6. HUB
7. OUTER BEARING SEAL
8. OUTER BEARING
9. OUTER BEARING RACE
10. BEARING CARRIER
11. INNER BEARING RACE
12. INNER BEARING
13. INNER BEARING SEAL
14. CARRIER SEAL
15. ROTOR SHIELD
16. AXLE SHAFT DUST SLINGER
17. BEARING CARRIER BOLTS
18. AXLE SHAFT

Hub and bearings 4WD

8-7

8 SUSPENSION AND STEERING

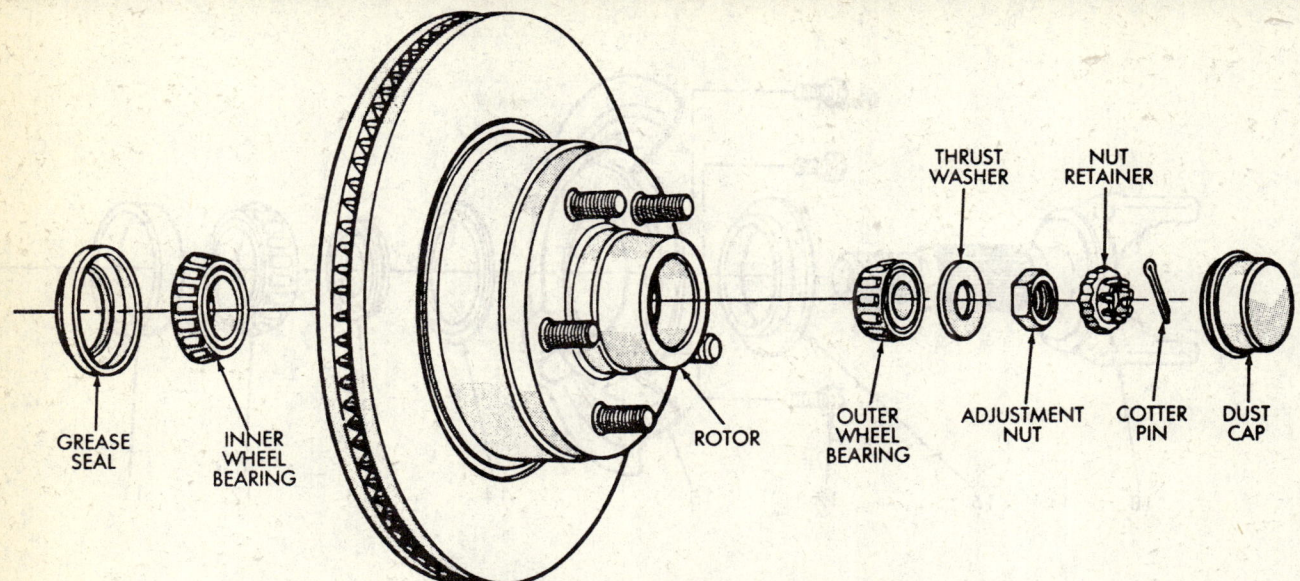

Hub and bearings 2WD

rier. Special tools 5073 and 5074 are available for this job. Secure the carrier to the press plate with M12 × 1.75mm × 40mm bolts.
9. Cut and remove the plastic cage from the hub inner bearing. Using diagonal pliers or tin snips, cut the bearing cage. Discard the rollers after removing the cage.
10. Remove what remains of the inner bearing by:
   a. Install a bearing separator tool on the inner bearing.
   b. Position the separator tool and hub in an arbor press.
   c. Force the hub out of the inner bearing with press pin tool 5074.
11. Remove the bearing carrier outer seal and discard it.
12. Drive the inner bearing seal out and discard it. If you're using tool 5078, make sure that the word JEEP faces downward.
13. Attach press plate tool 5073 to the rear of the carrier. Secure it in the press using M12 × 1.75mm × 40mm bolts.
14. Position bearing race remover 5076 in the carrier bore between the inner and outer bearing races.
15. Position the press pin tool 5074 on tool 5076. 16. Place the bearing carrier in the press and force the inner bearing race from the carrier bore. Reverse the position of the carrier and tools and force the outer bearing race from the bore.

To assemble and install:
17. Thoroughly clean all reusable parts with a safe solvent. Discard any parts that appear worn or damaged.
18. Attach press plate tool 5073 on the bearing carrier. Secure it in the press using M12 × 1.75mm × 40mm bolts.
19. Position the new outer bearing race in the bore.
20. Position bearing race installation tool 5077 on the race. Make sure that the word JEEP faces the downward. Press the race into the bore. The race should be flush with the machined shoulder of the carrier.
21. Position the new inner bearing race in the carrier bore. Reverse the position of the carrier and tools and force the inner race into the bore.
22. Thoroughly pack the new outer bearing with wheel bearing grease. Make sure that the bearing is fully packed.
23. Coat the race with wheel bearing grease and place the bearing in the bore.
24. Place the new outer seal on the bearing and position bearing installation tool 5079 on the seal. Place the carrier in the press and force the seal into the bore. Apply wheel bearing grease to the seal lip.
25. Insert the hub through the seal and outer bearing and into the bearing carrier bore.
26. Install bearing installation tool 5078 into the rear of the bearing carrier bore and place the race installation tool 5077 on the front of the hub. Make sure that the word JEEP on 5077 is facing the hub.
27. Place the assembly in the press and force the hub shaft into the carrier bore.
28. Pack the new inner bearing with wheel bearing grease. Make sure that the bearing is thoroughly packed.
29. Coat the inner seal lip with wheel bearing grease and place it on the inner bearing.
30. Coat the inner bearing race with wheel bearing grease.
31. Place the carrier in a press along with tool 5077. The word JEEP on 5077 must face the hub. Position the bearing and seal in the carrier. Place seal installation tool 5080 on the seal.
32. Force the bearing and seal into the bore and onto the hub shaft.

WARNING: Use extreme care when forcing the assembly into position! The carrier must rotate freely after installation of the bearing! Do not attempt to eliminate bearing lash with the press. Final bearing preload is attained by tightening the drive axle nut.

33. Install the new outer seal on the carrier.
34. Thoroughly clean the axle shaft and apply a thin coating of lithium-based grease to the splines and seal contact surfaces.
35. Install the slinger, rotor shield and hub/bearing assembly on the axle shaft.
36. Coat the carrier bolt threads with Loctite®, install them and torque them to 75 ft. lbs.
37. Install the rotor and caliper.
38. Install the washer and axle shaft nut. Torque the nut to 175 ft. lbs.
39. Install the nut retainer and cotter pin. NEVER back off the nut to install the cotter pin! ALWAYS advance it!
40. Install the wheel.

SUSPENSION AND STEERING 8

WHEEL ALIGNMENT SPECIFICATIONS

Years	Caster (deg.) Range	Pref.	Camber (deg.) Range	Pref.	Toe-in (in.)	Outer Wheel Turning Angle (deg.)
1984–86	7P to 8P	7½P	½N to ½P	0	0①	32–33
1987–89	7P to 8P	7½P	¾N to ½P	0	0①	32–33
1990	5P to 9P	6P	¾N to ½P	0	0①	32–33
1991	②	②	¾N to ½P	0	0①	32–33

① Acceptable range 1/32 in to 1/32 out
② Not adjustable

FRONT END ALIGNMENT

Alignment of the front wheels is essential if your car is to go, stop and turn as designed. Alignment can be altered by collision, overloading, poor repair or bent components.

If you are diagnosing bizarre handling and/or poor road manners, the first place to look is the tires. Although the tires may wear as a result of an alignment problem, worn or poorly inflated tires can make you chase alignment problems which don't exist.

Once you have eliminated all other causes, unload everything from the trunk except the spare tire, set the tire pressures to the correct level and take the car to a reputable alignment facility. Since the alignment settings are measured in very small increments, it is almost impossible for the home mechanic to accurately determine the settings. The explanations that follow will help you understand the three dimensions of alignment: caster, camber and toe.

NOTE: A change in caster angle also changes the front driveshaft angle. See Front Driveshaft Angle Measurement and Adjustment, in Section 7. The driveshaft angle takes precedence.

If the camber and toe-in are correct and it is known that the axle is not twisted, a satisfactory check may be made by testing the vehicle on the road. Before road testing, make sure all tires are properly inflated, being particularly careful that both front tires are inflated to exactly the same pressure.

If the vehicle turns easily to either side but is hard to straighten out, insufficient caster for easy handling of the vehicle is indicated. If correction is necessary, it can usually be accomplished by installing shims between the springs and axle pads to secure the desired result.

CASTER

Caster is the tilting of the steering axis either forward or backward from the vertical, when viewed from the side of the vehicle.
- A backward tilt is said to be positive caster.
- A forward tilt is said to be negative caster.

Changes in caster affect the straight line tendency of the vehicle and the "return to center" of the steering after a turn. If the camber is radically different between the left and right wheels (such as after hitting a major pothole), the car will exhibit a nasty pull to one side.

Caster can be altered by the use of shims at the rear of the lower control arms.

CASTER ADJUSTMENT

Caster angle is established in the axle design by tilting the top of the kingpin toward the rear, and the bottom of the kingpin forward so that an imaginary line through the center of the kingpin would strike the ground at a point ahead of the point of tire contact.

The purpose of caster is to provide steering stability which will keep the front wheels in the straight ahead position and also assist in straightening the wheels when coming out of a turn.

Caster is corrected by adding or installing shims at the rear of the lower control arms.

CAMBER

Camber is the tilting of the wheels from the vertical (leaning in or out) when viewed from the front of the vehicle.

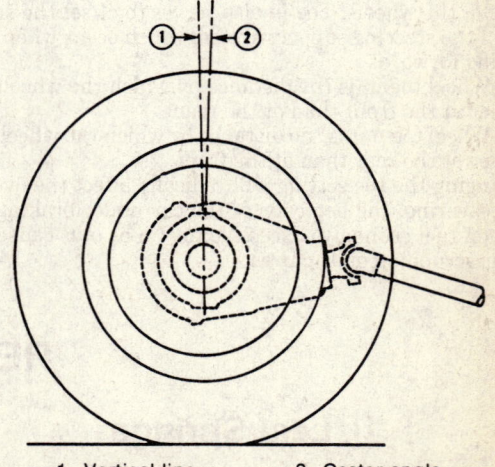

1. Vertical line 2. Caster angle

Axle caster

8-9

8 SUSPENSION AND STEERING

• When the wheels tilt outward at the top, the camber is said to be positive.

• When the wheels tilt inward at the top the camber is said to be negative.

The amount of tilt is measured in degrees from the vertical. This measurement is called camber angle.

This angle affects the position of the tire on the road surface during vertical suspension movement and cornering. Changes in camber affect the handling and ride qualities of the car as well as tire wear. Many tire wear patterns indicate camber related problems from misalignment, overloading or poor driving habits.

When checking wheel alignment, it is important that wheel bearings and knuckle bearings be in proper adjustment. Loose bearings will affect instrument readings when checking the camber, pivot pin inclination, and toe-in. Front wheel camber is preset. Any camber reading outside of specification requires replacement of defective parts.

CAMBER ADJUSTMENT

The purpose of camber is to more nearly place the weight of the vehicle over the tire contact patch on the road to facilitate ease of steering. The result of excessive camber is irregular wear of the tires on the outside shoulders and is usually caused by bent axle parts.

The result of excessive negative or reverse camber will be hard steering and possibly a wandering condition. Tires will also wear on the inside shoulders. Unequal camber may cause any or a combination of the following conditions: unstable steering, wandering, kickback or road shock, shimmy or excessive tire wear. The cause of unequal camber is usually a bent steering knuckle or axle end.

Correct wheel camber is set in the axle at the time of manufacture and cannot be altered by any adjustment. It is important that the camber be the same on both front wheels. Heating of any parts to facilitate straightening usually destroys the heat treatment given them at the factory. Cold bending may cause a fracture of the steel and is also unsafe. Replacement with new parts is recommended, rather than any straightening of damaged parts.

TOE

Toe is the turning in or out (parallelism) of the wheels. The actual amount of toe setting is normally only a fraction of an inch. The purpose of toe-in (or out) specification is to ensure parallel rolling of the wheels. Toe-in also serves to offset the small deflections of the steering support system which occur when the vehicle is rolling forward.

• Wheel toe-in is the distance by which the wheels are closer together at the front than at the rear.

• Wheel toe-out is the distance by which the wheels are closer together at the rear than at the front.

Changing the toe setting will radically affect the overall "feel" of the steering, the behavior of the car under braking, tire wear and even fuel economy. Excessive toe (in or out) causes excessive drag or scrubbing on the tires.

TOE ADJUSTMENT

First raise the front of the vehicle to free the front wheels. Turn the wheels to the straight ahead position. Use a steady rest to scribe a pencil line in the center of each tire tread as the wheel is turned by hand. (A good way to do this is to first run a chalk stripe around the circumference of the tread at the center to form a base for a fine pencil line.) Measure the distance between the scribed lines at the front and rear of the wheels using care that both measurements are made at an equal distance from the floor. The distance between the lines should be within specification.

Specifications for toe are given in two forms. A set-to specification is the ideal amount the toe measurements should differ. The OK-range specification indicates the variance that is allowable without the toe being considered out of specification.

To adjust toe, loosen the clamp bolts and turn the tie rod with a small pipe wrench. The tie rod is threaded with right and left hand threads to provide equal adjustment at both wheels. Do not overlook retightening the clamp bolts to 15–20 ft. lbs.

It is common practice to measure between the wheel rims. This is satisfactory providing the wheels run true. By scribing a line on the tire tread, measurement is taken between the road contact points, reducing error by wheel runout.

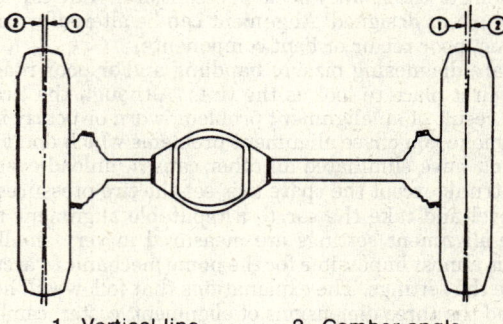

1. Vertical line   2. Camber angle

Wheel camber

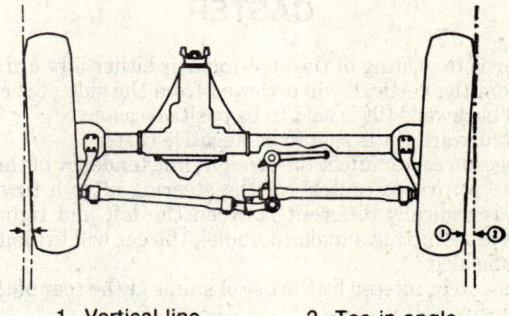

1. Vertical line   2. Toe-in angle

Front wheel toe

REAR SUSPENSION

Leaf Springs

Leaf springs should be examined periodically for broken or shifted leaves, loose or missing clips, angle of the spring shackles, and position of the springs on the saddles. Springs with shifted leaves do not retain their normal strength. Missing clips may permit the spring leaves to fan out or break on rebound. Broken leaves may make the vehicle hard to handle or permit the axle to shift out of line. Weakened springs may break, causing difficulty in steering. Spring attaching clips or bolts must be tight. It is suggested that they be checked at each vehicle inspection.

SUSPENSION AND STEERING 8

REMOVAL AND INSTALLATION

1. Raise and support the vehicle safely.
2. Take up the weight of the axle with a floor jack.
3. Disconnect the shock absorbers at the axle.
4. Remove the wheels.
5. Disconnect the stabilizer bar links at the spring plate.
6. Remove the spring bracket U-bolts and spring plates.
7. Remove the rear spring-to-shackle bolt, then the front spring-to-shackle bolt.
8. Lower the axle and remove the spring.
9. Installation is the reverse of removal. Observe the following torques:
    - Front and rear shackle bolts: 111 ft. lbs. (1984–88); 105 ft. lbs. (1989); 65 ft. lbs. (1990–91)
    - U-bolt nuts: 52 ft. lbs. for Cherokee/Wagoneer, 100 ft. lbs. for Comanche
    - Shock absorber-to-axle nuts: 44 ft. lbs.
    - Stabilizer bar link bolts: 70 ft. lbs.

Shock Absorbers

TESTING

Inspect each shock absorber for signs of fluid leakage (gas-charged shocks will show no signs of leaking). Replace leaking shocks.

Check shock mounting rubber bushings for condition. Shock will rattle, pound and provide poor control if the mounting bushings are worn. Inspect mounting brackets and fasteners. Grab shock and try to shake it sideways, up and down.

Bounce each corner of the car and compare shock action. Bounce vigorously and quickly release at the bottom of the down stroke. Shocks in good condition will allow about one free bounce before stopping any further movement.

REMOVAL AND INSTALLATION

NOTE: Before installing new shocks, they should be purged of air. To do this, hold the shock upright and fully extend it, then invert and compress it. Do this several times.

1. Raise and support the vehicle safely.
2. Remove the locknuts and washers.
3. Pull the shock absorber eyes and rubber bushings from the mounting pins.
4. Install the shocks in the reverse order of the removal procedure. Observe the following torques:
    - Upper end bolts: 44 ft. lbs.
    - Lower end bolts: 15 ft. lbs.

NOTE: Squeaking usually occurs when movement takes place between the rubber bushings and the metal parts. The squeaking may be eliminated by placing the bushings under greater pressure. This is accomplished either by adding additional washers or by tightening the locknuts. Do not use mineral lubricant to stop the squeaking, as it will deteriorate the rubber.

Rear Stabilizer Bar

REMOVAL AND INSTALLATION

1. Raise and support the vehicle safely.
2. Remove the stabilizer bar-to-frame clamps and cushions.
3. Disconnect the stabilizer bar connecting links at the spring tie plates and remove the stabilizer bar.
4. Installation is the reverse of removal. Torque the bracket bolts to 70 ft. lbs.; the stabilizer bar to frame attaching bolts to 55 ft. lbs.

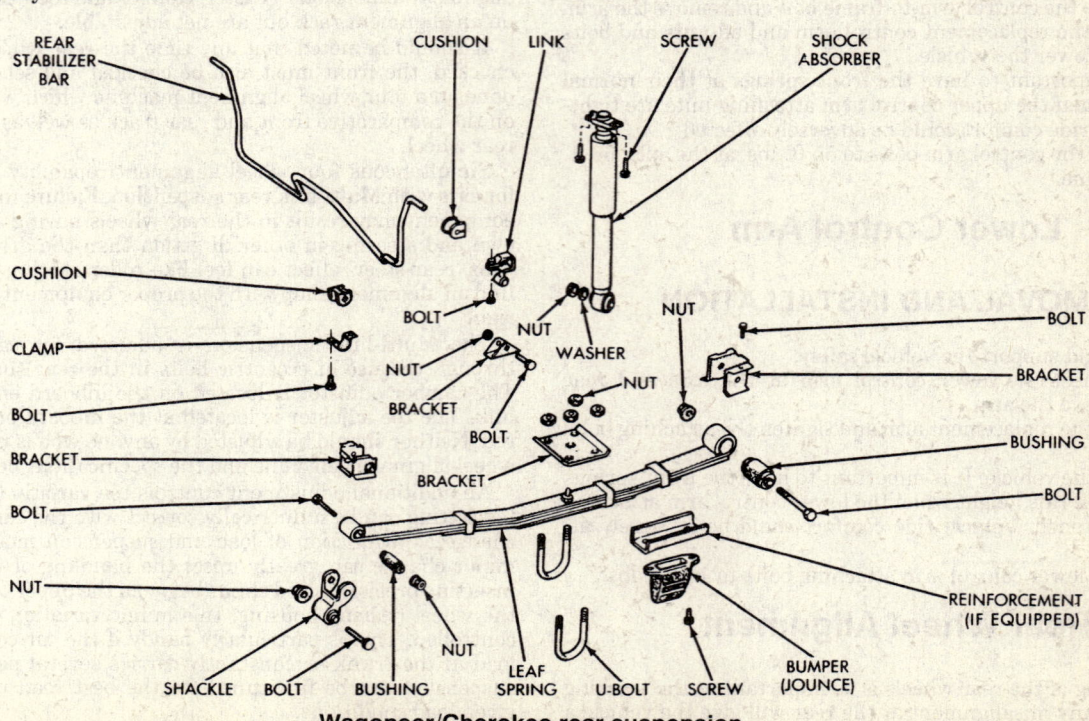

Wagoneer/Cherokee rear suspension

8-11

8 SUSPENSION AND STEERING

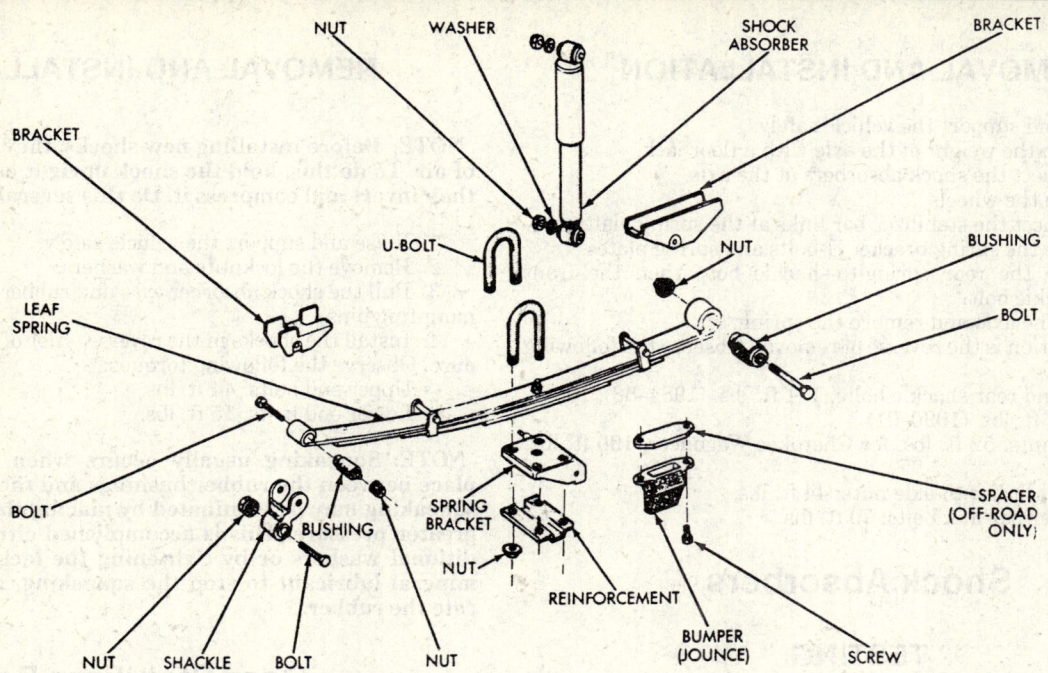

Comanche rear suspension

Upper Control Arm

REMOVAL AND INSTALLATION

1. Raise and support the vehicle safely.
2. Remove the wheels.
3. Remove the control arm-to-axle bolt.
4. Remove the control arm-to-frame bolt and remove the arm.
5. Install the replacement control arm and all nuts and bolts finger tight. Lower the vehicle.
6. It is important to have the front springs at their normal ride height when the upper control arm attaching nuts are tightened. Vehicle ride comfort could be adversely affected.
7. Torque the control arm bolts to 55 ft. lbs. at the axle; 66 ft. lbs. at the frame.

Lower Control Arm

REMOVAL AND INSTALLATION

1. Raise and support the vehicle safely.
2. Disconnect the lower control arm at the axle and rear bracket. Remove the arm.
3. Install the replacement arm and tighten the attaching bolts finger tight.
4. Lower the vehicle. It is important to have the front springs at their normal ride height when the lower control arm attaching nuts are tightened. Vehicle ride comfort could be adversely affected.
5. Torque lower control arm attaching bolts to 133 ft. lbs.

Rear Wheel Alignment

The tracking of the rear wheels is as important as the tracking of the front. Any misalignment at the rear will give the vehicle a loose or slippery feeling under cornering. All the handling and tire wear conditions discussed under front wheel alignment apply equally to the rear; at the rear they are often harder to diagnose and cure.

On all but the Multi-link rear suspensions, the position of the rear wheels is fixed in all three dimensions by the correct location of the components. Any tire or handling problems not traced to other causes will require replacement of suspension parts. The alignment dimensions—caster, camber and toe—can be measured on an alignment rack but are not adjustable.

It should be noted that any time the rear wheel alignment is checked, the front must also be checked and set. Ideally this is done on a four wheel alignment machine which will provide data on the comparative front and rear track as well as each front and rear wheel.

Simultaneous four wheel alignment capability is REQUIRED for cars with Multi-link rear suspension. Failure to use the proper equipment may result in the rear wheels having a mind of their own and steering in other direction than the driver might like. This 'rear steer' effect can feel like roller skating on an ice rink; find an alignment shop with the proper equipment and get it done right.

The Multi-link suspension is adjusted for camber and toe through the use of eccentric bolts in the rear suspension links. The camber adjuster is located on the inboard end of the lower link. The toe adjuster is located at the inboard end of the track rod. Neither should be adjusted by anyone who is not using a four wheel alignment machine and the specifications book.

An additional adjustment controls toe variation. Although the toe setting can be numerically correct with the car at rest, it can change as a function of load and suspension motion. This very minor change can greatly upset the handling of the vehicle. By inserting precisely sized shims between the upper control arm and the wheel bearing housing, this minor variation can be further controlled. This is particularly handy if the car constantly has a load in the trunk or constantly carries several people. The rear suspension can be fine-tuned for the best road manners under given load conditions.

SUSPENSION AND STEERING 8

Steering Wheel

REMOVAL AND INSTALLATION

1. Disconnect the negative battery cable.
2. Set the front tires in a straight ahead position.
3. If equipped with the standard steering wheel:

    a. Remove the trim cover attaching screws from the underside of the wheel and remove the cover.

    b. Disconnect the horn wire connectors from the contact switch.
4. If equipped with the sport steering wheel:

    a. Remove the horn button by prying outward.

    b. Remove the horn contact assembly, bushing, receiver and flex plate from the steering wheel.
5. Remove the steering wheel nut and vibration damper.
6. Scribe a line mark on the steering wheel and steering shaft if there is not one already. Release the turn signal assembly from the steering post and install a puller.
7. Remove the steering wheel and spring.
8. To install, align the scribe marks on the steering shaft with the steering wheel and secure the steering wheel spring, steering wheel, and horn button contact cup with the steering wheel nut.
9. Install the horn button.
10. Connect the battery cable and test the horn.

Turn Signal Switch

REPLACEMENT

NOTE: This procedure requires the use of a special tool.

1. Disconnect the negative battery cable.
2. Remove the steering wheel.
3. Remove the lockplate cover by compressing with tool C-4156 or equivalent and release the steering shaft retaining snapring.

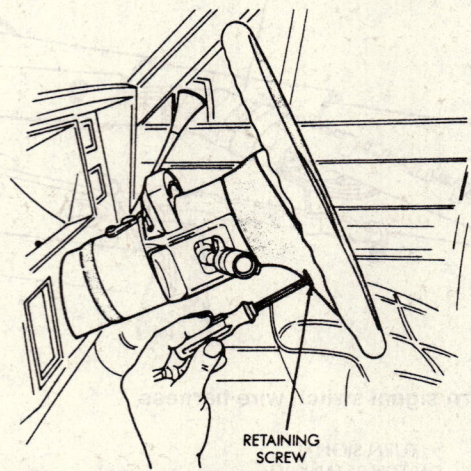
Trim cover removal on the standard wheel

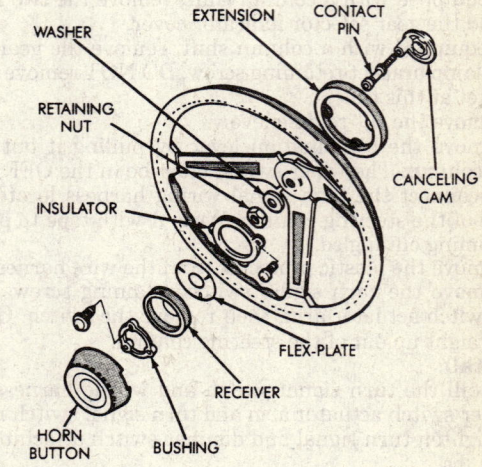
Sport wheel components

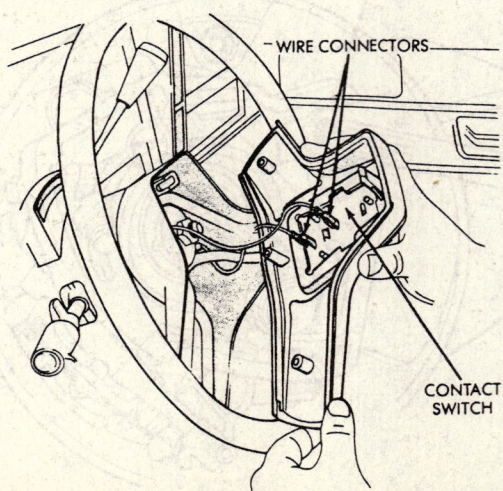
Horn wire connectors on the standard wheel

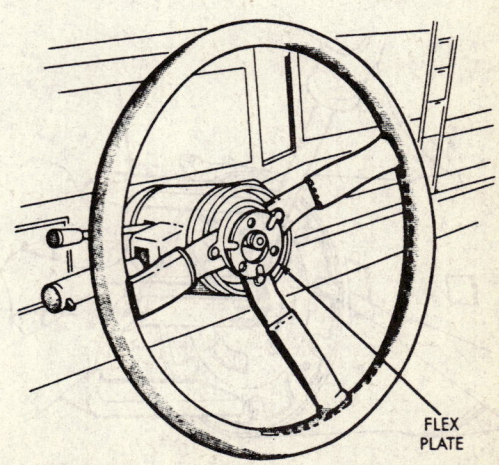
Sport wheel horn flex plate

8-13

8 SUSPENSION AND STEERING

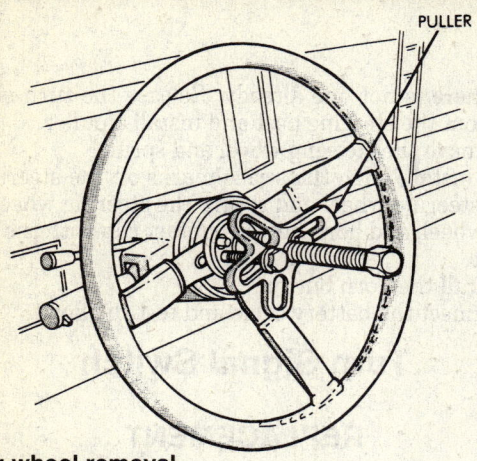

Steering wheel removal

4. Remove the lockplate, canceling cam, upper bearing preload spring, and thrust washer from the steering column.
5. Remove the hazard warning switch knob. Press the knob inward and remove it from the column by turning counterclockwise.
6. If equipped with a column shift, remove the two retaining screws and the gear selector indicator cover.
7. If equipped with a column shift, remove the gear selector indicator lamp bracket retaining screw. DO NOT remove the lamp and bracket at this time.
8. Remove the tilt-release lever.
9. Remove the combination lever by pulling it out straight from the column. The wiper switch must be in the OFF position.
10. Disconnect the turn signal wiring harness located at the lower end of the steering column. Wrap it with tape to prevent it from becoming entangled.
11. Remove the plastic protector from the wire harness.
12. Remove the turn signal switch retaining screws and the dimmer switch actuator arm, then remove the switch. Guide the switch straight up out of the steering column.

To Install:

13. Install the turn signal switch and wiring harness. Install the dimmer switch actuator arm and turn signal switch retaining screws. Tighten turn signal and dimmer switch attaching screws to 35 inch lbs.
14. Install the combination lever and tilt release lever.
15. If equipped with a column shift, install the two retaining screws and the gear selector indicator cover.
16. If equipped with a column shift, install the gear selector indicator lamp bracket retaining screw. DO NOT remove the lamp and bracket at this time.
17. Install the hazard warning switch knob. Press the knob inward and install it from the column by turning clockwise.
18. Install the lockplate, canceling cam, upper bearing preload spring, and thrust washer from the steering column.

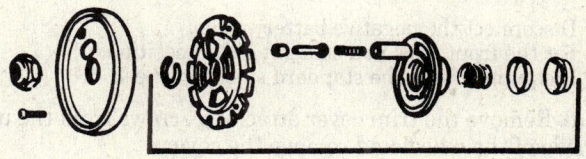

Lockplate components

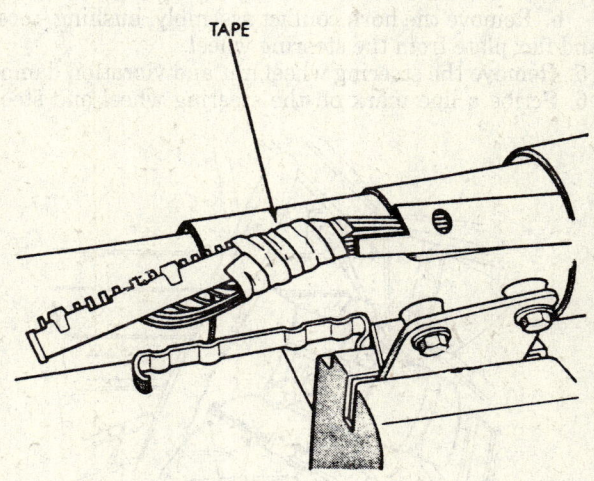

Taped turn signal switch wire harness

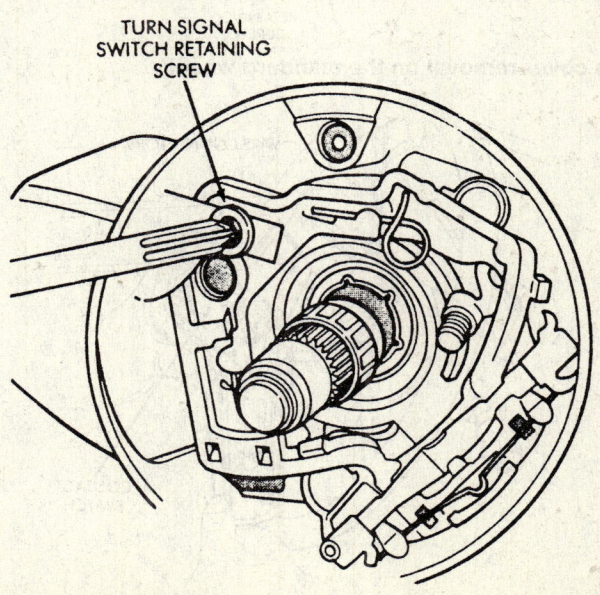

Turn signal switch retaining screw

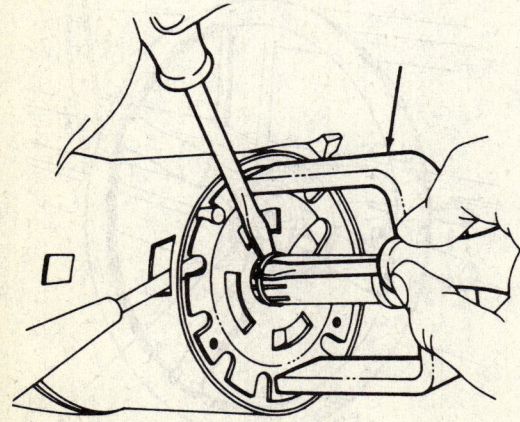

Using the lockplate spring compressor

8-14

SUSPENSION AND STEERING 8

19. Install the lockplate cover and install the steering shaft retaining snapring.
20. Install the steering wheel. Tighten nut to 25 ft. lbs.
21. Connect the negative battery cable.

Ignition Lock Cylinder

REMOVAL AND INSTALLATION

1. Follow the steps under Turn Signal Switch Removal until the switch is removed.
2. Insert the key in the lock cylinder and turn it to the ON position.
3. Remove the key warning buzzer switch and contacts AS AN ASSEMBLY using needle-nosed pliers, or a paper clip with a 90° bend.
4. With the ignition switch still in the ON position, insert a thin screwdriver into the slot adjacent to the switch attaching screw boss (right-hand slot). Depress the spring latch located at the bottom of the clot to release the lock cylinder.
NOTE: Some steering columns may have a retaining screw holding the lock cylinder in the column. When servicing this type, simply remove the retaining screw and remove the lock cylinder.
5. Remove the lock cylinder.
To Install:
6. To install the lock cylinder, turn the key to the LOCK position. Insert the lock cylinder in to the housing far enough to contact the drive shaft. Force it inward and move the ignition switch actuator rod up and down to align the components. When the components align, the cylinder will move inward and the spring-loaded retainer will snap into place locking the lock cylinder in the housing.
NOTE: If the lock cylinder is retained by a screw, tighten the screw to 40 inch lbs.
7. Install the key warning buzzer switch.
8. Ignition switch installation for Non-tilt columns:

a. Move the ignition switch slider to the OFF unlocked position (move the slider all the way down, then back two clicks). The remote rod hole in the ignition switch slider should now be centered.

b. Insert the remote rod in the ignition switch slider hole and install the ignition switch on the steering column. Tighten the attaching screws to 35 inch lbs.
9. Ignition switch installation for Tilt columns: Insert the ignition key in the lock cylinder and turn the cylinder to the OFF UNLOCK position. Move the ignition switch downward to eliminate any slack and tighten the attaching screws to 35 inch lbs.
10. Follow the steps under Turn Signal Switch Installation to complete the installation.

Ignition Switch

The ignition switch is located on the lower part of the steering column. Only vehicles equipped with column shift will have the ignition switch located in the steering column.

REMOVAL AND INSTALLATION

1. Place the ignition lock in the OFF-LOCK position.
2. Remove the two switch mounting screws.
3. Disconnect the switch from the rod.
4. Disconnect the wiring and remove the switch.
To Install:
5. Ignition switch installation for Non-tilt columns:

a. Move the ignition switch slider to the OFF unlocked position (move the slider all the way down, then back two

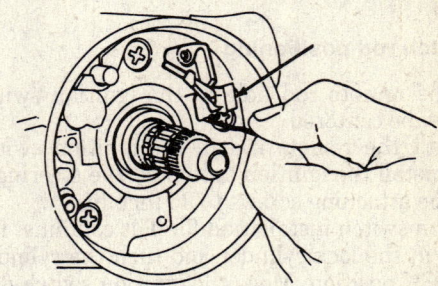

Removing the key warning switch buzzer components

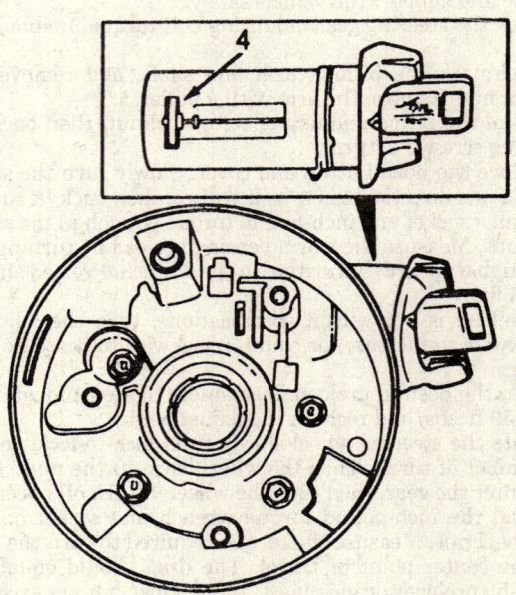

4. Lock cylinder retaining tab

Lock cylinder retaining tab

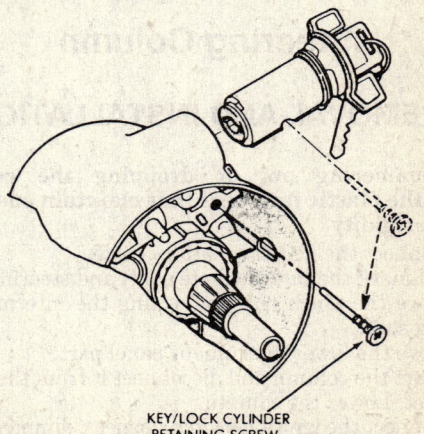

Lock cylinder removal

8-15

8 SUSPENSION AND STEERING

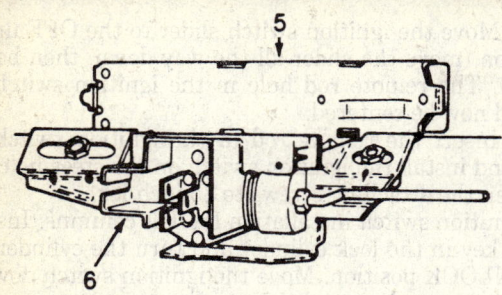

ignition switch/dimmer switch assembly
5. Ignition switch
6. Dimmer switch

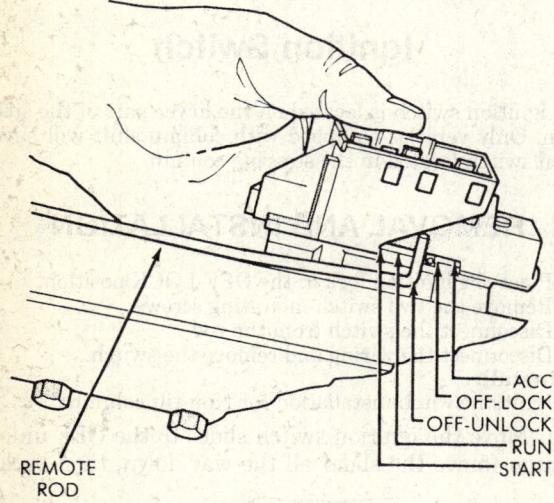

Ignition switch rod positioning

clicks). The remote rod hole in the ignition switch slider should now be centered.

b. Insert the remote rod in the ignition switch slider hole and install the ignition switch on the steering column. Tighten the attaching screws to 35 inch lbs.

6. Ignition switch installation for Tilt columns: Insert the ignition key in the lock cylinder and turn the cylinder to the **OFF UNLOCK** position. Move the ignition switch downward to eliminate any slack and tighten the attaching screws to 35 inch lbs.

Steering Column

REMOVAL AND INSTALLATION

NOTE: Hammering on, or dropping the column will damage to the plastic fasteners that maintain energy absorbing column rigidity.

1. Disconnect the negative battery cable.
2. Matchmark the intermediate shaft and steering shaft.
3. Remove the pinch bolt connecting the intermediate shaft and steering shaft.
4. Remove the lower instrument panel part.
5. Support the column and disconnect it from the instrument panel bracket. Lower the column.
6. Disconnect the ignition switch harness, dimmer switch harness, turn signal switch harness, wiper switch harness, cruise control harness and automatic transmission park/lock cable.

7. Unbolt the column toe plate from the dash panel and pull the column from the truck.

— **CAUTION** —
Use only the specified fasteners when installing the column. If any fastener must be replaced, the replacement part must meet the exact specifications of the original. The use of sub-grade or over-length fasteners will cause a failure in the performance of the impact absorbing column.

NOTE: Install all fasteners finger tight, then, when all the fasteners are installed, tighten to specification. Never allow the column to hang unsupported!

8. Position the steering column in the vehicle, align the matchmarks and connect the steering shaft to the intermediate shaft. Tighten the intermediate shaft-to-steering shaft pinch bolt to 33 ft. lbs.
9. Connect the ignition switch harness, dimmer switch harness, turn signal switch harness, wiper switch harness, cruise control harness and automatic transmission park/lock cable.
10. Support the column and connect it to the instrument panel bracket. tighten the column mounting bracket-to-instrument panel bolts to 22 ft. lbs.
11. Install the column toe plate to the dash panel. Tighten toe plate-to-dash panel bolts to 6 ft. lbs.
12. Install the lower instrument panel part.
13. Connect the negative battery cable.

Manual Steering Gear

ADJUSTMENT — On Vehicle

— **CAUTION** —
Adjust the wormshaft bearing preload and pitman shaft overcenter drag torque in the order listed below. Failure to follow the procedures exactly will result in gear failure.

1. Raise and support the vehicle safely.
2. Check the steering gear mounting bolt torque. It should be 65 ft. lbs.
3. Matchmark the pitman arm and shaft, and remove the pitman arm nut. Remove the arm with a puller.
4. Loosen the pitman adjusting screw locknut, then back off the adjusting screw 2–3 turns.
5. Remove the horn button and cover. Slowly turn the steering wheel in one direction as far as it will go, then back $1/2$ turn.
6. Install a socket and inch-pound torque wrench in the steering wheel nut. Measure the worm bearing preload by turning the wheel through a 90° arc ($1/4$ turn) with the wrench. Preload should be 5–8 inch lbs.
7. If preload is not within specifications, turn the adjuster screw clockwise to increase, or counterclockwise to decrease, the preload.
8. When the desired preload is attained, tighten the adjuster locknut to 50 ft. lbs. and recheck the adjustment.
9. Rotate the steering wheel slowly from lock-to-lock, counting the number of turns. Turn the wheel back, $1/2$ the number of turns to center the gear, then turn the wheel $1/2$ turn off of center.
10. Install the inch-pound torque wrench and socket on the steering wheel nut. Measure the torque required to turn the gear through the center point of travel. The drag should equal the worm bearing preload torque plus 4–10 inch lbs., but not exceed a total of 18 inch lbs.
11. If adjustment is required, loosen the pitman shaft screw locknut and turn the adjusting screw to obtain the desired torque. Tighten the locknut to 25 ft. lbs. and recheck the overcenter drag.
12. Install all parts and check steering wheel alignment.

SUSPENSION AND STEERING 8

REMOVAL AND INSTALLATION

1. Disconnect the steering shaft from the gear.
2. Raise and support the truck on jackstands.
3. Disconnect the center link from the pitman arm.
4. Remove the front stabilizer bar.
5. Remove the pitman arm nut, matchmark the arm and shaft, and remove the arm with a puller.
6. Unbolt and remove the gear.
7. Installation is the reverse of removal. The pitman arm nut MUST be securely staked. Observe the following torques:
   - Steering gear-to-frame: 65 ft. lbs.
   - Pitman arm-to-shaft: 185 ft. lbs.
   - Stabilizer bar-to-frame: 55 ft. lbs.
   - Stabilizer bar-to-link: 27 ft. lbs.
   - Center link-to-pitman arm: 55 ft. lbs.

Manual Steering Gear—Overhaul

DISASSEMBLY

1. Remove the flexible coupling.
2. Position the steering gear in a suitable holding fixture.
3. Rotate the wormshaft from stop-to-stop and count the number of rotations. then rotate it in the reverse direction 1/2 the total rotations to center the gear.
4. Remove the pitman shaft adjustment screw locknut, cover bolts, cover and gasket.
5. Slide the adjustment screw head out of the pitman shaft T-slot and remove it with the shims. Retain the shims for assembly measurement.
6. Remove the pitman shaft, the worm shaft bearing preload cap locknut and cap.
7. Remove the wormshaft and ball nut. Pry the pitman shaft and the wormshaft seals from the housing.

Wormshaft and Ball Nut—Disassembly

1. Remove the upper bearing from the wormshaft.

NOTE: DO NOT allow the ball nut to rotate freely. This could damage the tanks at the ends of the ball guides.

2. Remove the recirculating ball guide clamp screws, clamp and the guides.
3. Hold the ball nut over a cloth and remove the recirculating balls. There are a total of 50 balls.
4. Remove the wormshaft from the ball nut.
5. Clean all components in cleaning solvent and inspect for damage. Replace as necessary.

Wormshaft and Ball Nut—Assembly

1. Position the ball nut with the ball guide holes facing upward and the ball teeth facing down. Install the wormshaft in the ball nut. Rotate the shaft and thread it into the nut until the threads are equal on each side.

NOTE: When assembling the wormshaft and ball nut, position the ball nut so that the wider/deeper side of the tooth is closer to the housing cover opening after installation.

2. Install on ball in each recirculating ball guide in each guide hole. Move the wormshaft around until the ball rolls into the ball nut threads at the bottom of the wormshaft.
3. Assemble and install the ball guides in the ball nut. Divide the remaining balls into two groups and install 24 balls in each ball nut circuit. Insert the balls in the circuits through the holes in the ball guides. Rotate the wormshaft slightly to ease installation.
4. Place the ball guide clamp on the ball nut and install the clamp screws and tighten to 10 ft. lbs.

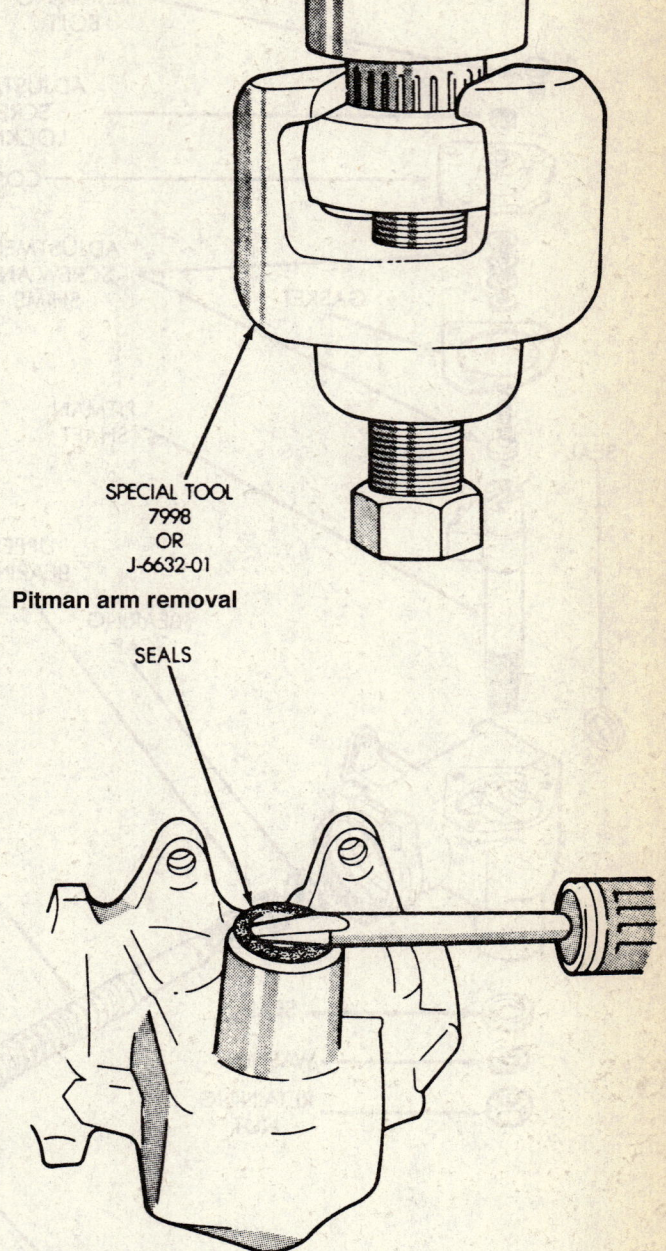

Pitman arm removal

Shaft seal removal

5. Lubricate the wormshaft threads with chassis lube and rotate the shaft to move it in-and-out of the ball nut. Lubricate the upper bearing and install on the wormshaft.

Wormshaft Bearing Adjustment Cap—Disassembly/Assembly

1. Pry out and remove the wormshaft lower bearing retainer. Remove the wormshaft lower bearing.
2. Clean all the components in cleaning solvent and **dry with a clean cloth only**. Inspect for worn components and replace as necessary.
3. If the lower bearing cup must be replaced, remove the original cup and install a replacement cup following this procedure:

8-17

8 SUSPENSION AND STEERING

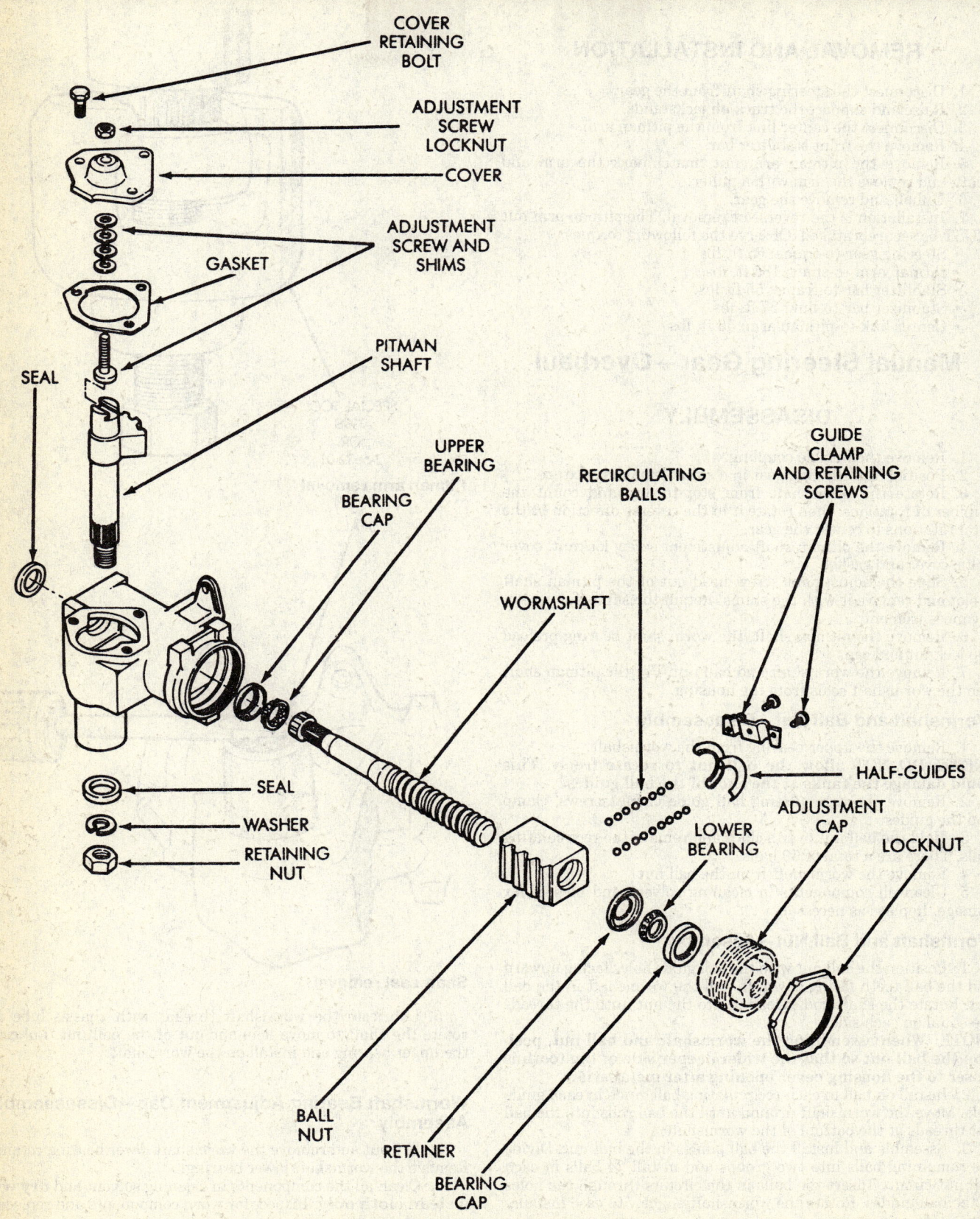

Manual steering gear — exploded view

SUSPENSION AND STEERING 8

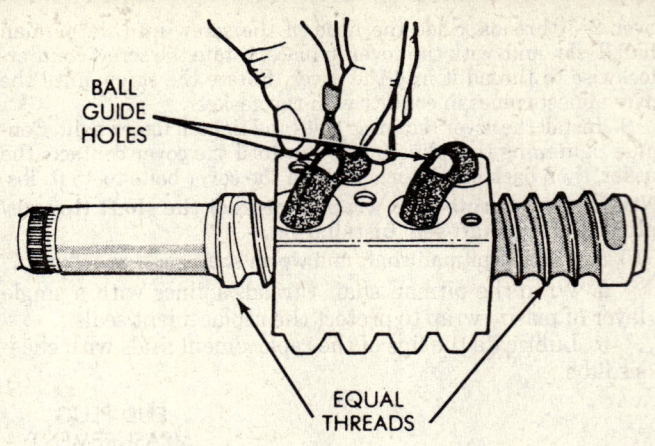

Recirculating ball installation

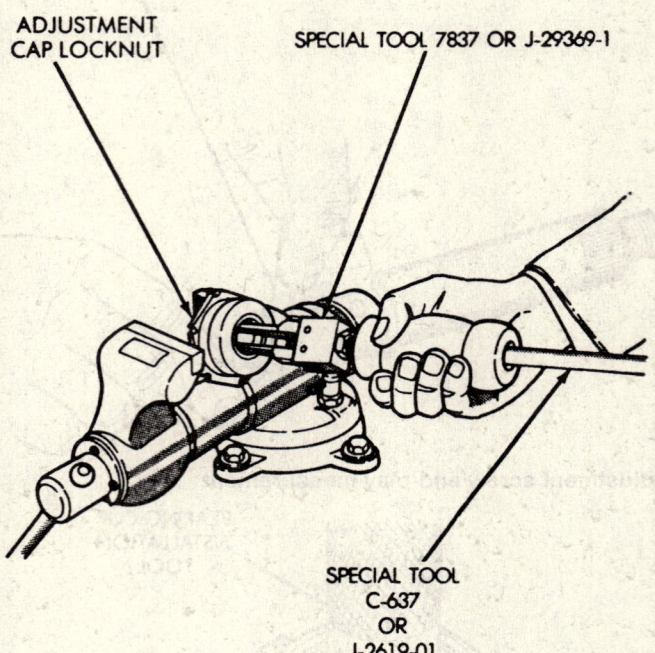

Bearing cup removal

a. Install a spare locknut on the adjustment cap and clamp the cap in a vise. Clamp the vise jaws on the locknut only.

b. Using bearing remover J-29369-1 and a slide hammer, remove the bearing cup from the adjustment cap.

c. Install a replacement cup with an appropriate sized installation tool.

4. Lubricate the wormshaft lower bearing and place it in the bearing cup.

5. Install the bearing retainer on the adjustment cap. If necessary tap the retainer lightly to seat.

CLEANING AND INSPECTION

1. Clean the housing and the pitman shaft with solvent. Dry with a clean cloth.

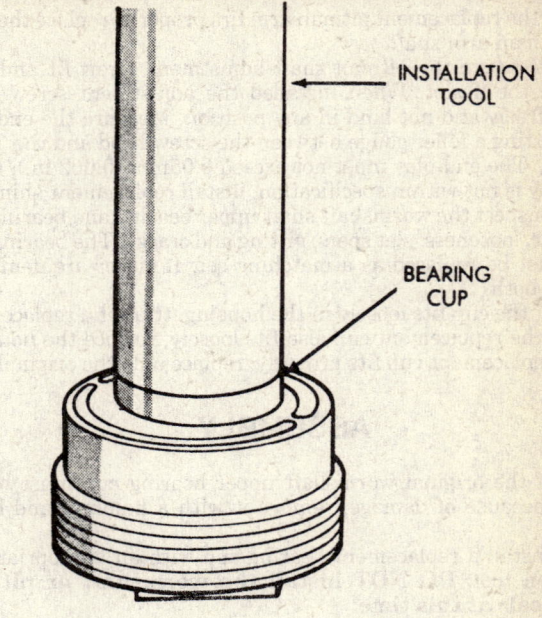

Bearing cup installation

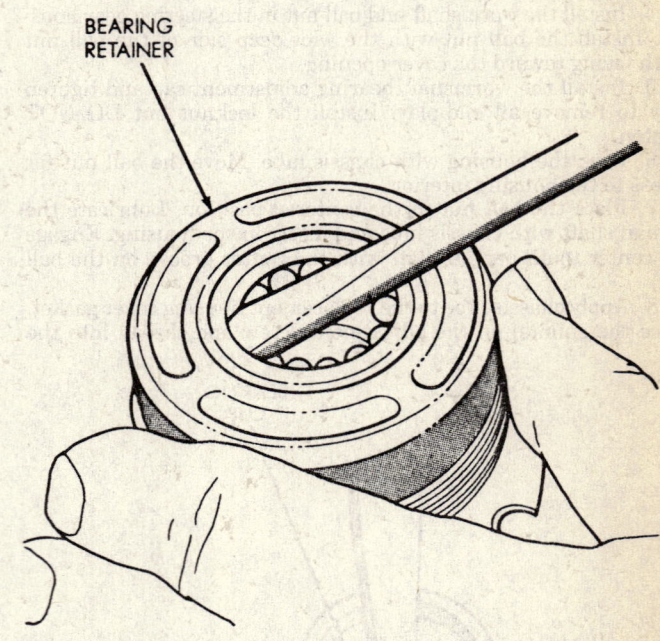

Wormshaft lower bearing retainer removal

2. Inspect the housing for cracks, porosity, damaged threads and scoring of the gasket surface area. Replace as necessary.

3. Inspect the pitman shaft contact surface and the sector teeth for wear, pitting and other damage. Replace as necessary.

4. Insert the pitman arm shaft in the steering gear housing shaft bore and inspect for excessive shaft or housing shaft bore wear. The shaft should have a smooth, bind-free fit with no visible side play when installed in the shaft bore.

5. If the shaft fit is loose but it is not visibly worn, trial fit a replacement pitman arm shaft in the housing shaft bore. If the replacement shaft also has a loose fit, replace the housing. How-

8-19

8 SUSPENSION AND STEERING

ever, if the replacement pitman arm firs properly, replace the original pitman arm shaft.

6. Measure the pitman shaft adjustment screw fit and end-play in the T-slot. When installed the adjustment screw must rotate freely and not bind in any position. Measure the end-play by inserting a feller gauge between the screw head and the T-slot surface. The end-play must not exceed 0.05mm (0.002 in.). If the end-play is not within specification, install replacement shims.

7. Inspect the wormshaft shaft upper bearing and bearing cup for wear, looseness, slat spots, pitting and cracks. The bearing and cup must be replaced as a matching set. If either are damaged, replace both.

8. If the cup fits loosely in the housing, trial fit a replacement cup. If the replacement cup also fits loosely, replace the housing. If the replacement cup fits properly, replace only the original cup.

ASSEMBLY

1. If the original wormshaft upper bearing cup must be replaced because of damage, remove it with a hammer and brass punch.

2. Install a replacement bearing cup with an appropriate installation tool. **DO NOT install the wormshaft or pitman shaft seals at this time.**

Lubricate all components with chassis lube.

3. Place the steering gear housing in a vice. Clamp the housing mounting bosses only.

4. Install the wormshaft and ball nut in the steering gear housing. Install the ball nut with the wide/deep side of the ball nut teeth facing toward the cover opening.

5. Install the wormshaft bearing adjustment cap and tighten only to remove all end-play. Install the locknut but DO NOT tighten.

6. Pack the housing with chassis lube. Move the ball nut for access to the housing interior.

7. Place the ball nut in the centered position. Lubricate the pitman shaft with chassis lube and insert in the housing. Engage the center tooth on the shaft with the center groove on the ball nut.

8. Apply chassis lube to the replacement housing cover gasket. Place the shim(s) on the adjustment screw and thread into the cover 2–3 threads. Slide the head of the screw into the pitman shaft T-slot and, with the cover in place, rotate the screw counterclockwise to thread it into the cover. Rotate the screw until the cover almost comes in contact with the gasket.

9. Install the cover retaining bolts and tighten finger tight. Continue tightening the adjustment nut until the cover contacts the gasket, then back off 1/2 turn. tighten the cover bolts to 45 ft. lbs.

NOTE: Use a protective wrap to protect the shaft threads/splines during shaft seal installation.

10. Install the pitman shaft and worm shaft seals as follows:

   a. Wrap the pitman shaft threads/splines with a single layer of plastic wrap to protect the replacement seals.

   b. Lubricate the lips of the replacement seals with chassis lube.

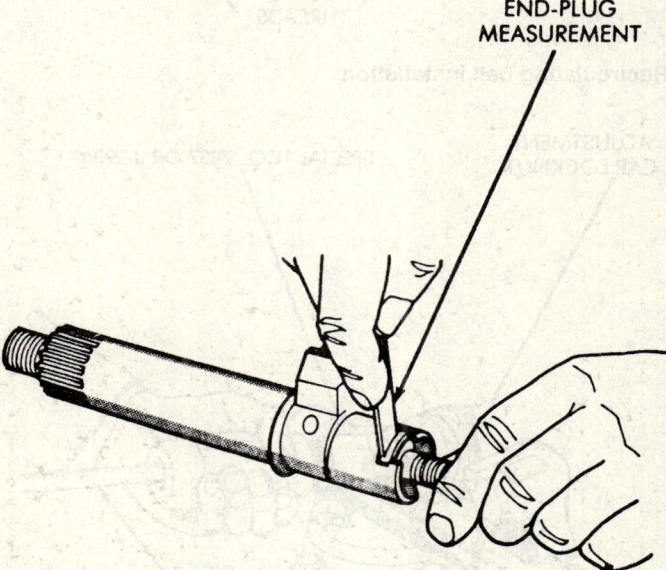

Adjustment screw end-play measurement

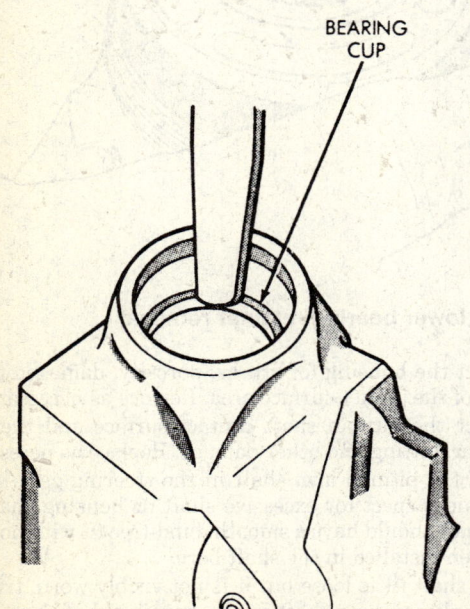

Wormshaft upper bearing cup removal

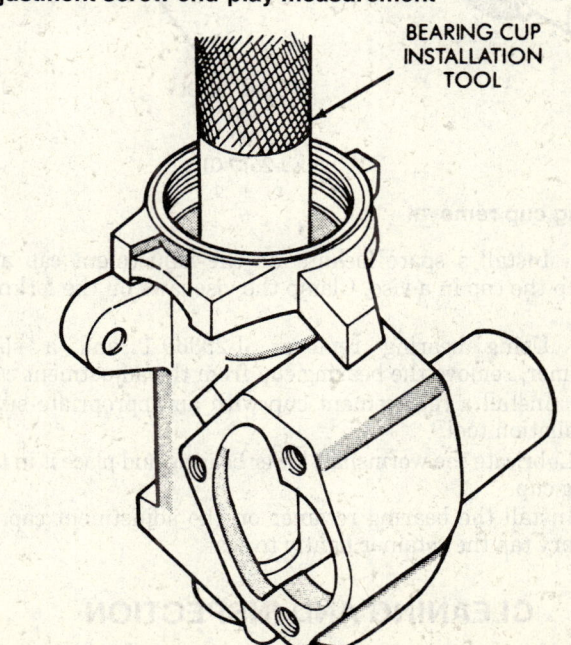

Wormshaft upper bearing cup installation

SUSPENSION AND STEERING

c. Slide the seals over the shaft and into the steering gear housing recess. Then remove the plastic wrap.

d. Complete the installation by tapping the seals into the recess with a small plastic hammer. Ensure each seal is fully seated.

11. Rotate the wormshaft and observe steering gear operation. With the adjustment screw and the cap loose, the shaft should rotate freely and not bind in any position.

12. Inspect for lubricant leakage from the shaft seals. If the is a leak, replace the seal.

STEERING GEAR ADJUSTMENTS

CAUTION
Follow the adjustment procedures in the order listed below. Failure to follow the procedures exactly will result in gear failure.

1. Adjust the wormshaft bearing preload as follows:

a. Tighten the wormshaft bearing adjustment cap until it is snug against the bearing, then loosen 1/4 turn.

b. Install a socket and inch-pound torque wrench on the splined end of the wormshaft. Rotate the wormshaft clockwise or counterclockwise to the stop position and then 1/2 of-a-turn from the stop position.

c. Tighten the wormshaft bearing adjustment cap until the torque required to rotate the wormshaft is 5–8 inch lbs.

d. Tighten the adjustment cap locknut to 50 ft. lbs. Measure the preload torque again.

2. Adjust the pitman shaft overcenter drag torque as follows:

a. Rotate the wormshaft to the center position as explained above.

b. Use a small torque wrench on the wormshaft splines. Rotate the wormshaft back and forth overcenter. Tighten the pitman shaft adjustment screw. The torque required to rotate the wormshaft over center should be 4–10 inch lbs. more than wormshaft bearing preload. torque must not exceed a total of 18 inch lbs.

c. Rotate the wormshaft overcenter. Begin to tighten the pitman shaft adjustment screw. Tighten until the drag torque is increased by an additional 4–10 inch lbs. DO NOT exceed 18 inch lbs.

d. Hold the pitman shaft adjustment screw and tighten the locknut to 25 ft. lbs. Recheck the overcenter drag torque again and readjust if necessary.

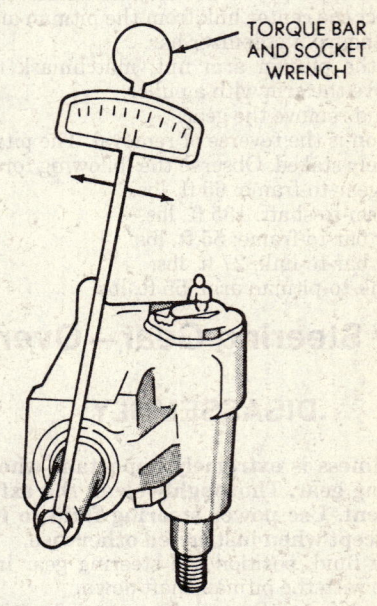

Overcenter drag torque adjustment

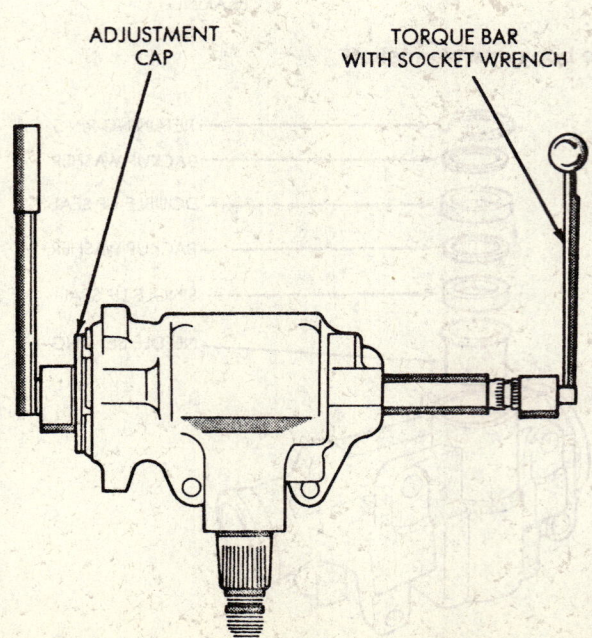

Wormshaft bearing preload torque adjustment

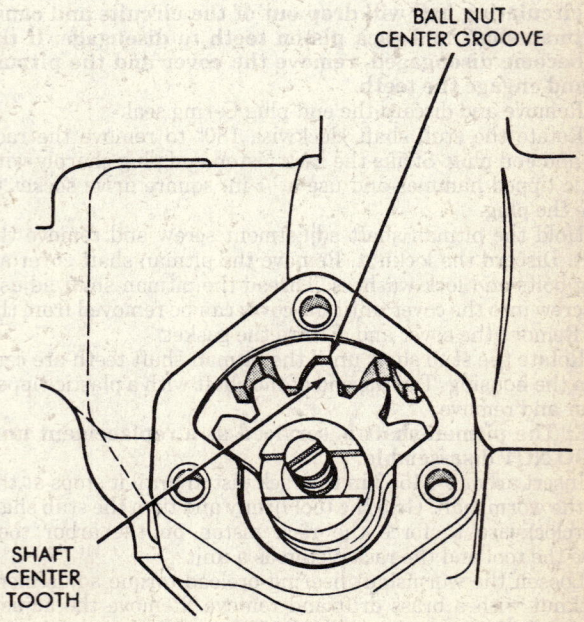

Pitman shaft and ball nut engagement

8 SUSPENSION AND STEERING

Power Steering Gear

REMOVAL AND INSTALLATION

1. Place the front wheels in a straight-ahead position. Place a drain pan under the steering gear.
2. Disconnect the fluid hoses from the steering gear. Raise and secure the hoses above the level of the pump to prevent excess steering loss. Plug the hoses to prevent the entry of dirt.
3. Disconnect the steering shaft from the gear.
4. Raise and support the truck on jackstands.
5. Disconnect the center link from the pitman arm.
6. Remove the front stabilizer bar.
7. Remove the pitman arm nut, matchmark the arm and shaft, and remove the arm with a puller.
8. Unbolt and remove the gear.
9. Installation is the reverse of removal. The pitman arm nut MUST be securely staked. Observe the following torques:
   - Steering gear-to-frame: 65 ft. lbs.
   - Pitman arm-to-shaft: 185 ft. lbs.
   - Stabilizer bar-to-frame: 55 ft. lbs.
   - Stabilizer bar-to-link: 27 ft. lbs.
   - Center link-to-pitman arm: 55 ft. lbs.

Power Steering Gear—Overhaul

DISASSEMBLY

NOTE: Cleanliness is extremely important when repairing a power steering gear. Thoroughly clean the exterior of the gear with solvent. Use power steering fluid to lubricate all components except when instructed otherwise.

1. Drain the fluid, position the steering gear in a vise and clamp it in place with the pitman shaft down.
2. Unseat and force the end plug retaining ring from the groove by inserting a punch through the hole in the housing.
3. Rotate the stub shaft counterclockwise until the rack piston forces the end plug out of the housing.

NOTE: DO NOT rotate the stub and farther than necessary, the recirculating ball will drop out of the circuits and cause the pitman shaft and rack piston teeth to disengage. If the teeth become disengaged, remove the cover and the pitman shaft and engage the teeth.

4. Remove and discard the end-plug O-ring seal.
5. Rotate the stub shaft clockwise 180° to remove the rack piston and end plug. Strike the rack piston end plug sharply with a plastic tipped hammer and use a $1/2$ in. square drive socket to remove the plug.
6. Hold the pitman shaft adjustment screw and remove the locknut. Discard the locknut. Remove the pitman shaft cover attaching bolts and lock washers. Thread the pitman shaft adjustment screw into the cover until the cover can be removed from the screw. Remove the cover and discard the gasket.
7. Rotate the stub shaft until the pitman shaft teeth are centered in the housing. Tap the end of the shaft with a plastic-tipped hammer and remove.

NOTE: The pitman shaft is serviced as a replacement unit only. DO NOT disassemble.

8. Insert arbor J-21552 in the rack piston until it stops at the end of the wormshaft. Grip the tool firmly and turn the stub shaft counterclockwise to force the rack piston on the arbor tool. Remove the tool and the rack piston as a unit.
9. Loosen the wormshaft bearing preload torque adjustment cap locknut with a brass drift and remove. Remove the adjustment cap with a spanner wrench (J-7624).
10. Remove the complete valve body from the housing by pulling outward on the splined end of the stub shaft.
11. Remove the wormshaft lower thrust bearing and the conical bearing races from the wormshaft. Note the position for reassembly.

COMPONENT OVERHAUL

Steering Gear Housing

1. Remove the pitman shaft seal retaining ring from the shaft bore groove with snapring pliers. Remove the outer backup washer from the shaft bore.
2. Remove the pitman shaft needle bearing from the housing inner bore with the appropriate removal tools.
3. Clean the steering gear housing with solvent. Inspect the pitman shaft bore. If badly scored or worn, replace the housing. However, slight scratches in the bore are acceptable.
4. inspect the hose connector seats and the poppet check valve.

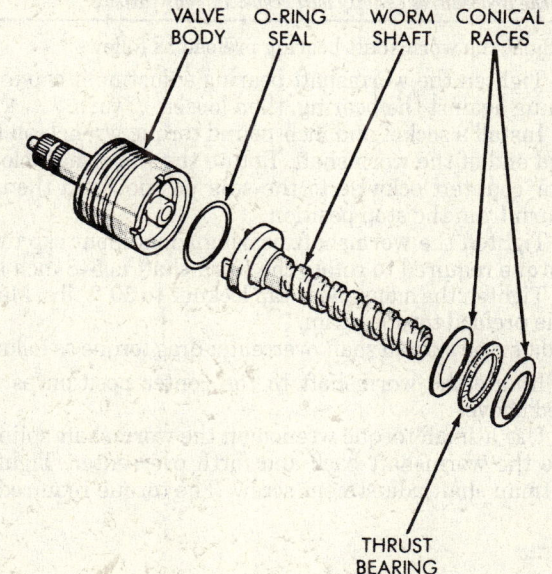

Valve body and wormshaft

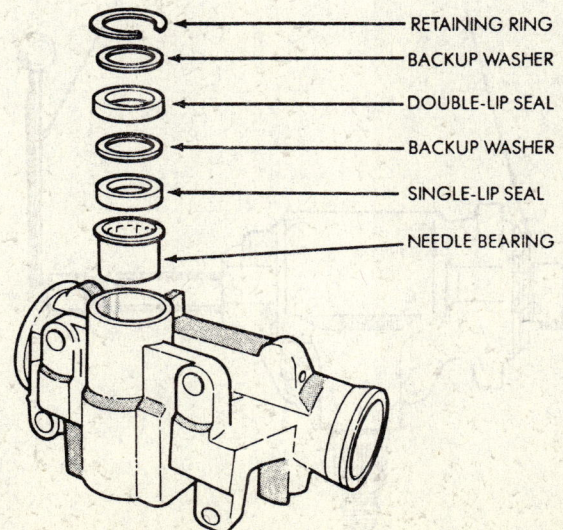

Pitman shaft bearing, seals and washers

SUSPENSION AND STEERING 8

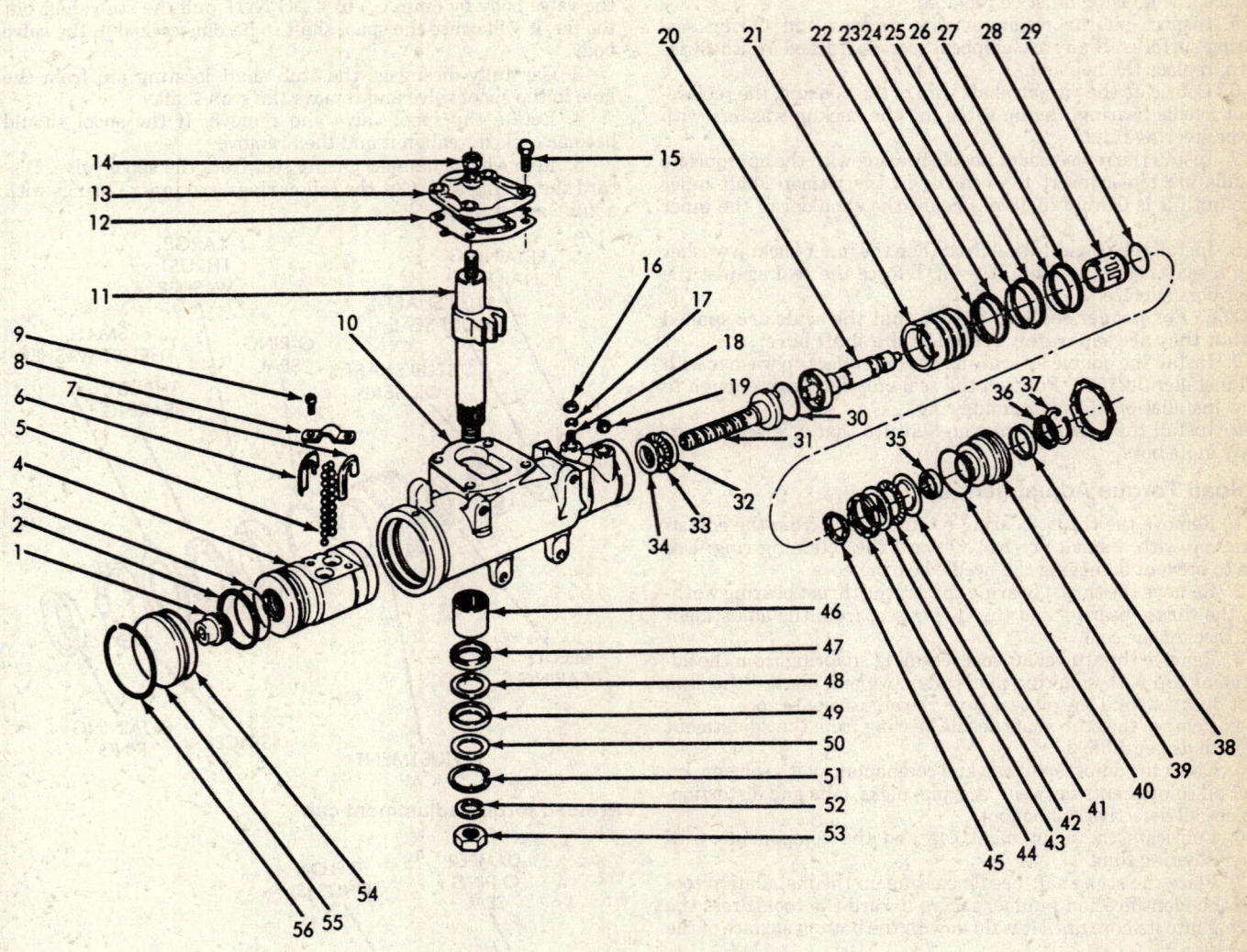

1. PISTON END-PLUG
2. TEFLON RING
3. O-RING SEAL
4. RACK PISTON
5. BLACK & SILVER BALLS
6. BALL HALF-GUIDE
7. BALL HALF-GUIDE
8. CLAMP
9. CLAMP BOLT
10. GEAR HOUSING
11. PITMAN SHAFT
12. COVER GASKET
13. COVER
14. LOCKNUT
15. BOLT
16. HOSE CONNECTOR SEAT
17. CHECK VALVE
18. CHECK VALVE SPRING
19. HOSE CONNECTOR SEAT
20. STUB SHAFT
21. VALVE BODY
22. O-RING SEAL
23. TEFLON RING
24. O-RING SEAL
25. TEFLON RING
26. O-RING SEAL
27. TEFLON RING
28. SPOOL VALVE
29. O-RING SEAL
30. O-RING SEAL
31. WORMSHAFT
32. BEARING RACE
33. THRUST BEARING
34. BEARING RACE
35. NEEDLE BEARING
36. DUST SEAL
37. RETAINING SNAP RING
38. SEAL
39. ADJUSTMENT CAP
40. O-RING SEAL
41. LARGE THRUST WASHER
42. THRUST BEARING
43. SMALL THRUST WASHER
44. SPACER
45. RETAINING RING
46. NEEDLE BEARING
47. SINGLE-LIP SEAL
48. BACK-UP WASHER
49. DOUBLE-LIP SEAL
50. BACK-UP WASHER
51. RETAINING SNAP RING
52. SPRING WASHER
53. RETAINING NUT
54. O-RING SEAL
55. HOUSING END-PLUG
56. RETAINING RING

Power steering gear — exploded view

8 SUSPENSION AND STEERING

if they are deeply scored, cracked or worn, replace them. Inspect the ball plug in the housing. If fluid leakage past the ball plug occurred before disassembly or if it is raised above the housing surface, the housing must be replaced.

5. Inspect all the retaining ring grooves and O-ring seal mating surfaces. If any are chipped, scored, cracked or otherwise worn, replace the housing.

6. Lubricate the pitman shaft bore in the housing, the replacement needle bearing, the lip seals and the backup washers with power steering fluid.

7. Install the replacement needle bearing with the appropriate installation tools. Insert the bearing in the pitman shaft inner bore until it is 0.8mm (0.03 in.) below the shoulder of the inner bore.

8. Install the single lip seal first, then the inner backup washer with a seal installation tool. DO NOT force the seal against the inner bore surface.

NOTE: For proper sealing, ensure that the seals are spaced so that they are separately seated in the shaft bore.

9. Install the double lip seal and the outer backup washer with seal installer J-21553. Position the seal only far down enough to allow installation of the retaining ring.

10. Install the retaining ring and ensure that it is seated correctly in its bore.

Preload Torque Adjustment Cap

1. Remove the thrust bearing retaining ring from the adjustment cap with a small pry bar. Discard the retaining ring. Use care to prevent damaging the needle bearing bore.

2. Remove the thrust bearing spacer, the thrust bearing washers, the thrust bearing and the O-ring seal from the adjustment cap. Discard the seal.

3. Remove the stub shaft seal retaining snapring from the adjustment cap with snapring pliers. Remove and discard the stub shaft dust seal and the oil seal from the adjustment cap.

4. Remove the stub shaft needle bearing from the adjustment cap with driver J-8592.

5. Clean the adjustment cap and components with solvent. Inspect all components for wear, scoring, nicks, cuts and distortion. Replace all defective components.

6. Lubricate the adjustment cap and the components with power steering fluid.

7. Place the stub shaft needle bearing on the installation tool with the identification number facing toward the tool. Press the bearing into its bore until it is flush with the bottom surface of the outer bore.

8. Insert the stub shaft oil seal far enough into the bore to provide sufficient clearance for the dust seal and retaining ring.

9. Lubricate the dust seal with petroleum jelly and install with the rubber side facing out. Install the retaining snapring.

10. Lubricate the O-ring seal with petroleum jelly and install in the cap seal groove.

11. Position the large thrust washer, the thrust bearing, the small thrust washer and the spacer on the adjustment cap. The location of the spacer notches are not important as long as the notches are not damaged during installation.

12. Press the replacement retaining ring into the stub shaft needle bearing bore with a brass drift.

Valve Body and Stub Shaft

— **CAUTION** —

The valve body is precisely manufactured unit. If replacement is necessary, the complete valve body must be replaced. To avoid possible damage, the valve body should not be disassembled unless absolutely necessary. If the valve spool damper O-ring seal requires replacement, remove the valve spool only as instructed in the following procedure.

1. Hold the valve body in both hands with the stub shaft down. Tap the end of the stub shaft lightly against the workbench. The stub shaft cap will disengage from the valve body. Remove and discard the stub shaft cap-to-wormshaft O-ring seal.

2. Pull outward on the cap end of the stub shaft until it clears the valve body by 6mm (1/4 in.). DO NOT pull the stub shaft out too far, it will cause the spool shaft to become cocked in the valve body.

3. Carefully disengage the stub shaft locating pin from the hole in the spool valve and remove the stub shaft.

4. Rotate the spool valve and remove. If the spool should become cocked, realign it and then remove.

5. Remove the damper O-ring seal from the spool valve. Discard the O-ring seal. Cut the teflon rings and inner O-rings with a knife and remove.

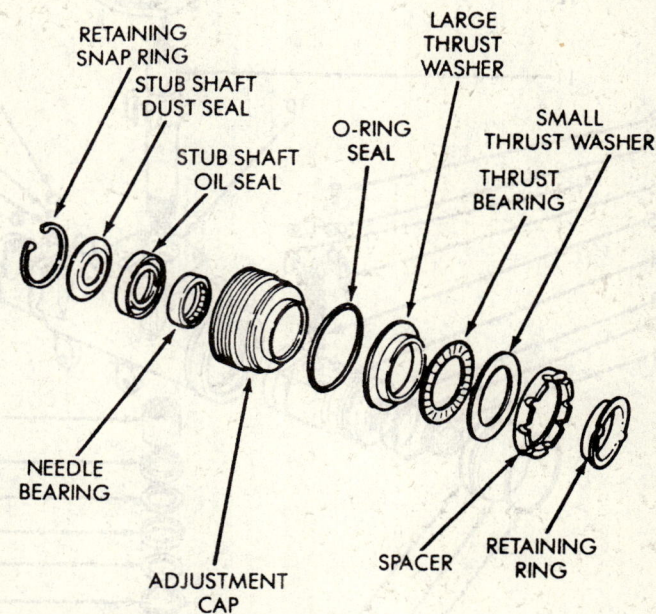

Preload torque adjustment cap

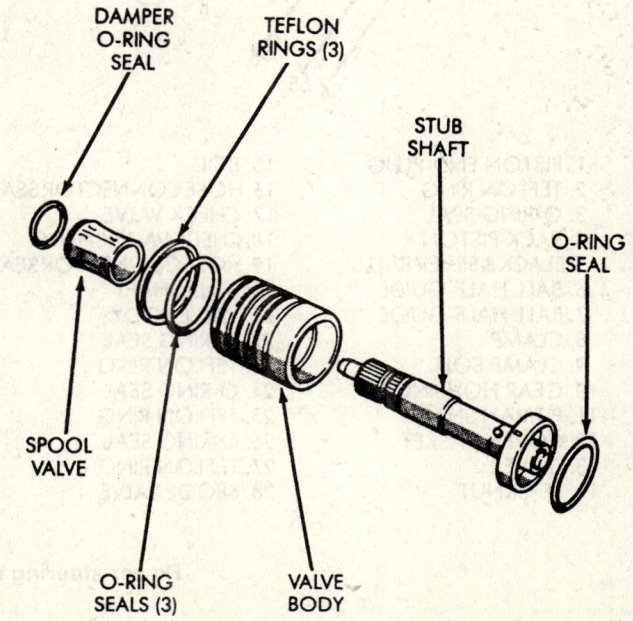

Valve body and stub shaft assembly

SUSPENSION AND STEERING 8

6. Clean all components in solvent and open all fluid passages with compressed air. if the stub shaft locating pin or the spool valve locating hole is cracked, excessively worn or broken, replace the complete valve body. Small flat spots on the side of the stub shaft locating pin head are normal.

7. If the stub shaft ground surfaces has scores, nicked or burrs that cannot be removed by polishing with a crocus cloth, replace the valve body. Inspect the outside surface area of the spool valve and the inside of the valve body for nicks, burrs and wear. Slight wear is normal on the valve mating surfaces.

8. If the small notch in the skirt of the valve body is excessively worn, replace the valve body.

9. Lubricate the spool valve with power steering fluid and check the fit of the spool valve in the valve body without the damper O-ring seal installed. If the spool valve does not rotate freely, replace the valve body.

10. Lubricate the replacement inner O-ring seals and teflon rings with power steering fluid. Install the inner O-ring seals in the valve body ring grooves and install the teflon rings on top of the O-ring seals. Use care to avoid damaging the teflon rings during installation.

11. Lubricate the spool valve damper O-ring seal with petroleum jelly and install it in the groove.

12. Lubricate the spool valve and body with power steering fluid and install the spool valve in the body. Align the stub shaft locating pin hole. Ensure the spool valve is flush with the notched end of the valve body.

13. Carefully insert the stub shaft into the spool valve until the stub shaft locating pin is aligned with the locating pin hole in the spool valve.

14. Align the sub shaft cap notch with the locating pin in the valve body. Press The spool valve and the stub shaft in the valve body. Ensure that the stub shaft cap notch is aligned with the valve body pin before installing the valve body in the steering gear housing.

15. Lubricate the stub shaft cap-to-wormshaft O-ring seal with power steering fluid and position it in the cap groove.

Pitman Shaft and Cover

1. Inspect the cover-to-housing contact surface.
2. Inspect the pitman shaft sector teeth, upper contact surface and bearing/seal contact surface.
3. Replace the cover and the shaft if they are severely worn scored or pitted. if the pitman shaft adjustment screw head fits loose in the T-slot, replace the pitman shaft.

Rack Piston/Wormshaft

1. Remove the ball return guide clamp.
2. Place the complete assembly on clean paper and remove the ball return guides, the wormshaft with an arbor tool, and the recirculating balls. Ensure that all 24 ball are removed.
3. Remove the arbor tool from the wormshaft. Remove the teflon piston ring and the O-ring seal from the rack.
4. Lubricate all of the components with power steering fluid.
5. Install the O-ring seal in the rack piston groove. DO NOT allow the O-ring seal to become twisted during installation.
6. Insert the wormshaft completely into the rack piston.
7. Install the recirculating balls in the rack piston be alternately installing one black ball followed by one silver ball until a total of 18 balls have been installed in the inner return guide hole. After installing each ball, press it downward to provide space for the nest ball.
8. Rotate the wormshaft counterclockwise (viewed from the steering shaft end) to route the balls into the circuit.
9. Fill one ball return half-guide with petroleum jelly and install the six remaining balls. Ensure that the balls are installed alternately by color. and are in alternating color sequence with the balls previously installed in the rack piston.

10. Mate the two half-guides and insert the assembled ball return guide into the guide holes in the rack piston.
11. Install the ball return guide clamp the lock washers and retaining screws. Tighten the retaining screws to 10 ft. lbs.
12. Insert arbor tool J-21552 into the wormshaft and position the end of the assembled rack piston on wooden blocks. Ensure that the rack piston is supported with wooden clocks after it is inverted.
13. DO NOT allow the tool to separate from the wormshaft until the rack piston is completely installed on the wormshaft.

ASSEMBLY

1. Clamp the steering gear housing in a vise with the pitman shaft bore facing downward. Use the unmachined housing bosses for the clamping pads.
2. Install the wormshaft conical bearing races and the lower thrust bearing. Install the first conical bearing race followed by the thrust bearing, and then the second conical bearing race. Install the races so that the top of each cone faces the bottom of the gear housing.
3. Install the stub shaft cap-to-valve body O-ring seal in the valve body so that it is seated against the inner edge of the stub cap.

NOTE: DO NOT press against the stub shaft to seat the valve body. The valve body is correctly seated when all or most of the fluid return hole in the steering gear housing is visible.

4. Align the narrow slot in the valve body with the locating pin in the wormshaft. Insert the valve body into the steering fear housing. Seat the valve body in the housing.
5. Install a seal protector tool over the end of the stub shaft. Install the adjustment cap. Tighten the cap with a spanner wrench until it seats against the valve body (20 ft. lbs.). Remove the seal protector.
6. Insert the rack piston into the steering gear housing until the wormshaft engages with the valve body and the stub shaft.
7. Rotate the stub shaft clockwise to force the rack piston into the steering gear housing. DO NOT remove the arbor tool until the valve body piston ring has entered the housing bore.
8. Rotate the stub shaft until the rack piston center groove is aligned with the center of the pitman shaft bearing bore.
9. Lubricate the pitman shaft bore with petroleum jelly and place it on the cover. Ensure that the rubber seal in the gasket is properly seated in the cover groove.
10. Position the cover over the pitman shaft and thread the cover onto the adjustment screw until it contacts the shaft.
11. Install the pitman shaft with the long, center sector tooth meshing with the rack piston center groove.
12. Ensure that the adjustment screw cover gasket is correctly in place before attaching the cover to the steering fear housing. Install the cover lock washers and bolts to 45 ft. lbs.
13. Thread the adjustment screw locknut halfway on the adjustment screw. If necessary, insert an allen wrench into the adjustment screw head to prevent it from turning while threading the nut on it.
14. Install the end plug in the rack piston. Tighten the plug to 50 ft. lbs. Lubricate the steering gear housing end-plug O-ring seal with power steering fluid and position it on the end plug.
15. Install and seat the end plug in the steering gear housing. If necessary tap the end plug lightly with a plastic mallet. Install the end-plug retaining ring with the ring end gap nor aligned with the hole inside the steering gear housing. Tap lightly on the plug to be sure the ring is seated.
16. Adjust the wormshaft bearing preload and the pitman shaft overcenter drag.

8-25

8 SUSPENSION AND STEERING

ADJUSTMENT

CAUTION

Adjust the wormshaft bearing preload and pitman shaft overcenter drag torque in the order listed below. Failure to follow the procedures exactly will result in gear failure.

1. Ensure the wormshaft bearing adjustment cap is seated. Score an index mark on the steering gear housing adjacent to one of the spanner wrench tightening holes.
2. Measure counterclockwise 5–6mm (3/16–1/4 in.) from the index mark and score an adjustment reference mark on the housing. Rotate the adjustment cap counterclockwise until the spanner wrench tightening hole in the cap is aligned with the adjustment reference mark on the housing.
3. Install the adjustment cap locknut and tighten to 85 ft. lbs. Ensure that the adjustment cap does not rotate. Rotate the stub shaft clockwise to the stop, then rotate it counterclockwise 1/4 of-a-turn.
4. Measure the preload torque by rotating at a constant speed with a torque wrench installed. Specifications call for 4–10 inch lbs.
5. Rotate the pitman shaft adjustment screw counterclockwise until it is fully extended, then rotate it 180° clockwise. Rotate the stub shaft from stop-to-stop, count the number of rotations and toward the shaft in reverse 1/2 the rotations. Make sure the steering gear is centered. The flat area on the stub shaft should face upward and be parallel with the adjustment screw cover.
6. Measure the drag by rotating the stub shaft 45° on each side of vertical and record the highest drag torque measured at or near the steering gear center position.
7. Specifications are as follows:
    a. New Gears: 4–8 inch lbs. greater than wormshaft bearing preload, to a maximum of 18 inch lbs.
    b. Used Gears: 4–5 inch lbs. greater than wormshaft bearing preload, to a maximum of 18 inch lbs.
8. To adjust the overcenter drag torque. Rotate the pitman shaft adjustment screw clockwise torque is obtained. Tighten the locknut to 20 ft. lbs. DO NOT allow the adjustment screw locknut to rotate.
9. Fill the steering pump with fluid and operate the engine until the power steering fluid reaches the normal operating temperature then stop the engine.
10. Turn the wheels to the full left and full right position to circulate the fluid. Add fluid to reservoir to maintain full level. Start the engine and operate at high idle. Check the fluid level and add if necessary.
11. Purge the system of air by turning the wheels from side to side without going to the full left or right position. Fluid with air will have a milky red color.
12. Return the wheels to straight ahead position and operate the engine for 2–3 minutes, then stop the engine. Add fluid if necessary. Road test the vehicle.

Steering Pump

REMOVAL AND INSTALLATION

Engines with a Serpentine Drive Belt

NOTE: A belt tension gauge is needed for this job.

1. Loosen the alternator adjustment and pivot bolts.
2. Insert the drive lug of a 1/2 in. drive ratchet into the adjust-

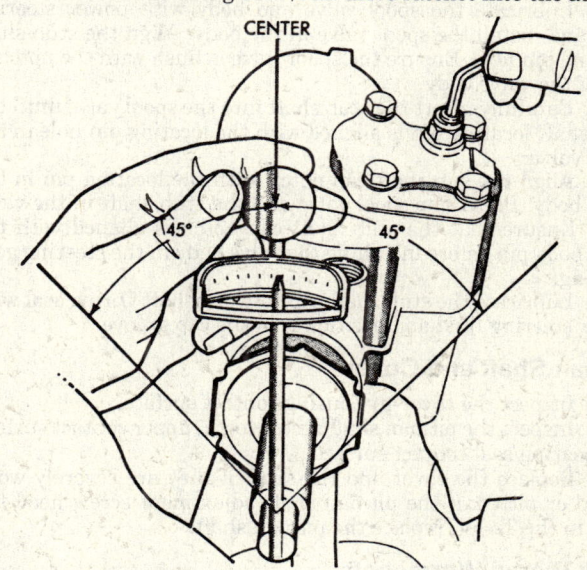

Pitman shaft overcenter drag torque

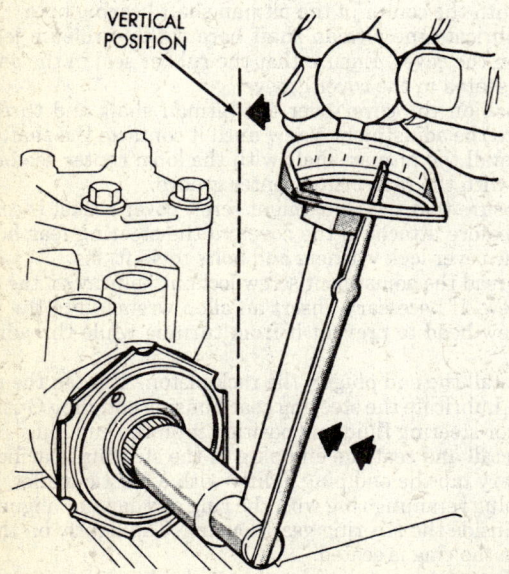

Wormshaft bearing preload torque measurement

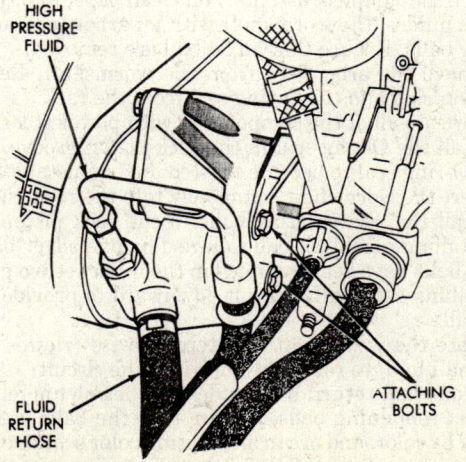

Power steering pump to bracket bolts

SUSPENSION AND STEERING 8

ment hole in the alternator bracket and move the alternator to relieve tension on the belt.

3. Remove the drive belt.
4. Remove the air cleaner.
5. Disconnect the hoses at the pump and cap the hose ends.
6. Remove the front bracket-to-engine bolts.
7. Support the pump with your hand. Remove the pump-to-rear bracket nuts.
8. Lift out the pump.
9. Installation is the reverse of removal. Torque the pump-to-bracket nuts to 28 ft. lbs.; the bracket-to-engine bolts to 33 ft. lbs. Install the drive belt. Using the 1/2 in. drive ratchet, move the alternator to put tension on the belt, tighten the alternator adjustment and pivot bolts and check the belt tension with a tension gauge at the mid-point of its longest straight run. Belt tension should be 180–200 ft. lbs. for a new belt, or 140–160 ft. lbs. for a used belt.
10. When the tension is achieved, tighten the alternator pivot bolt to 28 ft. lbs.; the adjustment bolt to 18 ft. lbs.

Engines with a V-type Drive Belt

1. Loosen the power steering pump adjustment and pivot bolts.
2. Insert the drive lug of a 1/2 in. drive ratchet into the adjustment hole in the pump rear bracket and move the pump to relieve tension on the belt.
3. Remove the drive belt.
4. Remove the air cleaner.
5. Disconnect the hoses at the pump and cap the hose ends.
6. Remove the front bracket-to-engine bolts.
7. Support the pump with your hand. Remove the pump-to-rear bracket nuts.
8. Lift out the pump.
9. Installation is the reverse of removal. Torque the pump-to-bracket nuts to 28 ft. lbs.; the bracket-to-engine bolts to 33 ft. lbs. Install the drive belt. Using the 1/2 in. drive ratchet, move the pump to put tension on the belt, tighten the pump adjustment and pivot bolts and check the belt tension with a tension gauge at the mid-point of its longest straight run. Belt tension should be 120–160 ft. lbs. for a new belt, or 90–115 ft. lbs. for a used belt.
10. When the tension is achieved, tighten the pump pivot nut to 21 ft. lbs.; the adjustment bolt to 21 ft. lbs.

PURGING THE SYSTEM OF AIR

1. Fill the steering pump with fluid and operate the engine until the power steering fluid reaches the normal operating temperature then stop the engine.
2. Turn the wheels to the full left and full right position to circulate the fluid. Add fluid to reservoir to maintain full level. Start the engine and operate at high idle. Check the fluid level and add if necessary.
3. Purge the system of air by turning the wheels from side to side without going to the full left or right position. Fluid with air will have a milky red color.
4. Return the wheels to straight ahead position and operate the engine for 2–3 minutes, then stop the engine. Add fluid if necessary. Road test the vehicle.

Pitman Arm (Steering Arm)

REMOVAL AND INSTALLATION

NOTE: It is recommended that front end alignment be checked after performing this procedure.
1. Raise and support the vehicle safely.
2. Place the wheels in a straight ahead position.

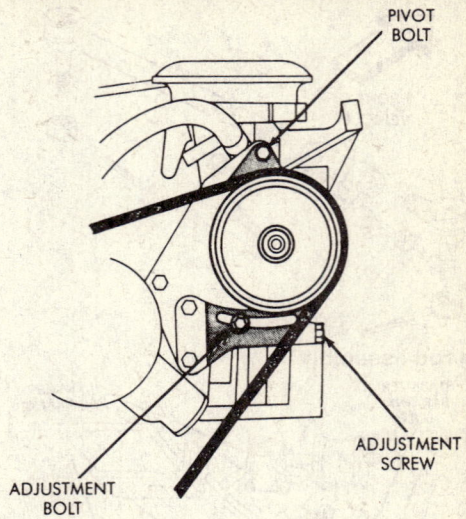

Power steering pump mounting for the 4-2.5L and 6-4.0L with serpentine belt

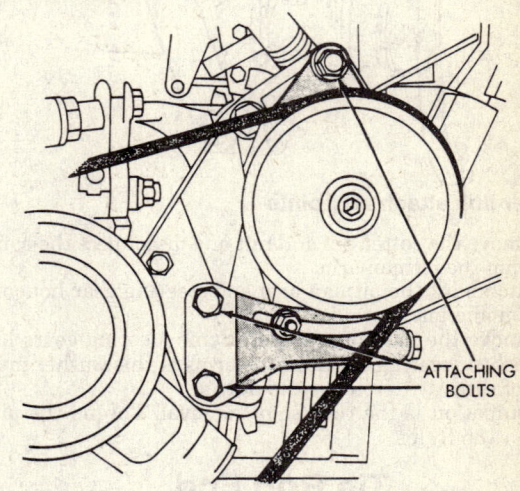

Front bracket bolts

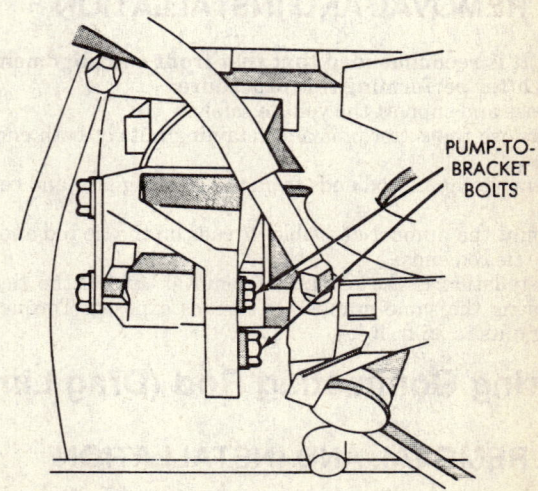

Power steering pump-to-bracket bolts

8-27

8 SUSPENSION AND STEERING

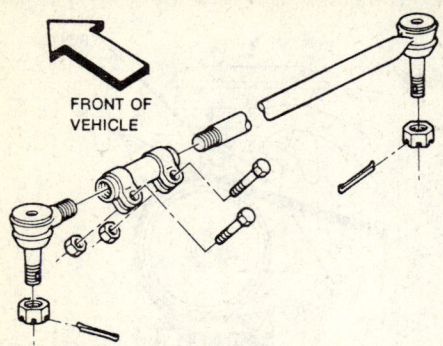

Connecting rod assembly

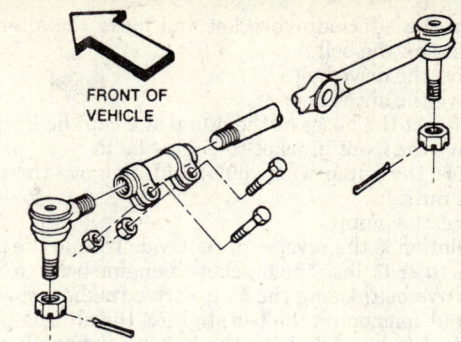

Tie rod assembly

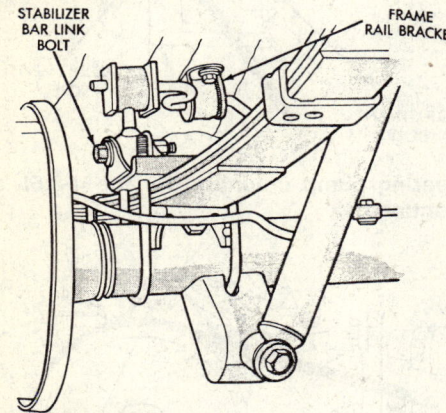

Stabilizer link attaching points

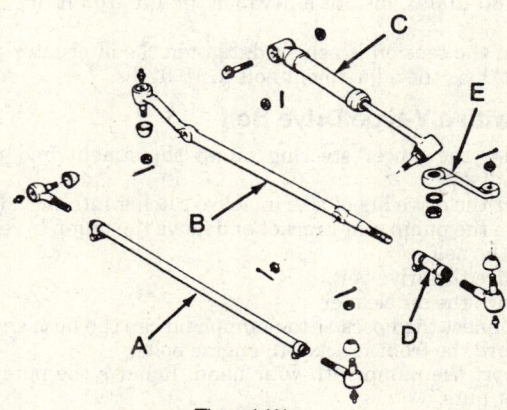

- Tie rod (A)
- Center link (B)
- Damper (C)
- Turn buckle (D)
- Pitman arm (E)

Steering linkage

3. Remove the cotter pin and nut and disconnect the connecting rod from the pitman arm.
4. Matchmark the pitman arm and steering gear housing for installation alignment.
5. Remove the pitman arm nut. Some steering gears have a staked washer securing the nut. The arms of this washer must be bent out of the way to remove the nut.
6. Installation is the reverse of removal. Torque the pitman arm nut to 185 ft. lbs.

Tie Rod End

REMOVAL AND INSTALLATION

NOTE: It is recommended that that front end alignment be checked after performing this procedure.

1. Raise and support the vehicle safely.
2. Remove the cotter pins and retaining nuts at both ends of the tie rod.
3. Remove the tie rod ends from the steering arm and center link.
4. Count the number of visible threads on the tie rod and unscrew the tie rod ends.
5. Installation is the reverse of removal. Install the tie rod ends, leaving the same number of threads exposed. Torque the retaining nuts to 35 ft. lbs.

Steering Connecting Rod (Drag Link)

REMOVAL AND INSTALLATION

NOTE: It is recommended that front end alignment be checked after performing this procedure.

1. Raise and support the vehicle safely.
2. Place the wheels in a straight ahead position.
3. Remove the cotter pin and nut and disconnect the steering damper from the connecting rod.
4. Remove the cotter pins and nuts at each end of the rod, and disconnect the connecting rod from the knuckle and the pitman arm.
5. Install the connecting rod, with the wheels straight ahead and the pitman arm parallel with the vehicle centerline. Install the nuts and torque all three nuts to 35 ft. lbs.

Steering Dampener

REMOVAL AND INSTALLATION

NOTE: It is recommended that front end alignment be checked after performing this procedure.

1. Raise and support the vehicle safely.
2. Place the wheels in a straight ahead position.
3. Remove the steering dampener retaining nut and bolt from the axle bracket.
4. Remove the cotter pin and nut from the piston rod ball stud at the drag link.
5. Remove the steering dampener ball stud with a puller tool.
6. Installation is the reverse of removal. Tighten retaining bolts to 55 ft. lbs.

SUSPENSION AND STEERING 8

Troubleshooting Basic Steering and Suspension Problems

Problem	Cause	Solution
Hard steering (steering wheel is hard to turn)	• Low or uneven tire pressure • Loose power steering pump drive belt • Low or incorrect power steering fluid • Incorrect front end alignment • Defective power steering pump • Bent or poorly lubricated front end parts	• Inflate tires to correct pressure • Adjust belt • Add fluid as necessary • Have front end alignment checked/adjusted • Check pump • Lubricate and/or replace defective parts
Loose steering (too much play in the steering wheel)	• Loose wheel bearings • Loose or worn steering linkage • Faulty shocks • Worn ball joints	• Adjust wheel bearings • Replace worn parts • Replace shocks • Replace ball joints
Car veers or wanders (car pulls to one side with hands off the steering wheel)	• Incorrect tire pressure • Improper front end alignment • Loose wheel bearings • Loose or bent front end components • Faulty shocks	• Inflate tires to correct pressure • Have front end alignment checked/adjusted • Adjust wheel bearings • Replace worn components • Replace shocks
Wheel oscillation or vibration transmitted through steering wheel	• Improper tire pressures • Tires out of balance • Loose wheel bearings • Improper front end alignment • Worn or bent front end components	• Inflate tires to correct pressure • Have tires balanced • Adjust wheel bearings • Have front end alignment checked/adjusted • Replace worn parts
Uneven tire wear	• Incorrect tire pressure • Front end out of alignment • Tires out of balance	• Inflate tires to correct pressure • Have front end alignment checked/adjusted • Have tires balanced

Troubleshooting the Ignition Switch

Problem	Cause	Solution
Ignition switch electrically inoperative	• Loose or defective switch connector • Feed wire open (fusible link) • Defective ignition switch	• Tighten or replace connector • Repair or replace • Replace ignition switch
Engine will not crank	• Ignition switch not adjusted properly	• Adjust switch
Ignition switch wil not actuate mechanically	• Defective ignition switch • Defective lock sector • Defective remote rod	• Replace switch • Replace lock sector • Replace remote rod
Ignition switch cannot be adjusted correctly	• Remote rod deformed	• Repair, straighten or replace

8-29

8 SUSPENSION AND STEERING

Troubleshooting the Steering Column

Problem	Cause	Solution
Will not lock	• Lockbolt spring broken or defective	• Replace lock bolt spring
High effort (required to turn ignition key and lock cylinder)	• Lock cylinder defective • Ignition switch defective • Rack preload spring broken or deformed • Burr on lock sector, lock rack, housing, support or remote rod coupling • Bent sector shaft • Defective lock rack • Remote rod bent, deformed • Ignition switch mounting bracket bent • Distorted coupling slot in lock rack (tilt column)	• Replace lock cylinder • Replace ignition switch • Replace preload spring • Remove burr • Replace shaft • Replace lock rack • Replace rod • Straighten or replace • Replace lock rack
Will stick in "start"	• Remote rod deformed • Ignition switch mounting bracket bent	• Straighten or replace • Straighten or replace
Key cannot be removed in "off-lock"	• Ignition switch is not adjusted correctly • Defective lock cylinder	• Adjust switch • Replace lock cylinder
Lock cylinder can be removed without depressing retainer	• Lock cylinder with defective retainer • Burr over retainer slot in housing cover or on cylinder retainer	• Replace lock cylinder • Remove burr
High effort on lock cylinder between "off" and "off-lock"	• Distorted lock rack • Burr on tang of shift gate (automatic column) • Gearshift linkage not adjusted	• Replace lock rack • Remove burr • Adjust linkage
Noise in column	• One click when in "off-lock" position and the steering wheel is moved (all except automatic column) • Coupling bolts not tightened • Lack of grease on bearings or bearing surfaces • Upper shaft bearing worn or broken • Lower shaft bearing worn or broken • Column not correctly aligned • Coupling pulled apart • Broken coupling lower joint • Steering shaft snap ring not seated	• Normal—lock bolt is seating • Tighten pinch bolts • Lubricate with chassis grease • Replace bearing assembly • Replace bearing. Check shaft and replace if scored. • Align column • Replace coupling • Repair or replace joint and align column • Replace ring. Check for proper seating in groove.

SUSPENSION AND STEERING 8

Troubleshooting the Steering Column (cont.)

Problem	Cause	Solution
Noise in column	• Shroud loose on shift bowl. Housing loose on jacket—will be noticed with ignition in "off-lock" and when torque is applied to steering wheel.	• Position shroud over lugs on shift bowl. Tighten mounting screws.
High steering shaft effort	• Column misaligned • Defective upper or lower bearing • Tight steering shaft universal joint • Flash on I.D. of shift tube at plastic joint (tilt column only) • Upper or lower bearing seized	• Align column • Replace as required • Repair or replace • Replace shift tube • Replace bearings
Lash in mounted column assembly	• Column mounting bracket bolts loose • Broken weld nuts on column jacket • Column capsule bracket sheared	• Tighten bolts • Replace column jacket • Replace bracket assembly
Lash in mounted column assembly (cont.)	• Column bracket to column jacket mounting bolts loose • Loose lock shoes in housing (tilt column only) • Loose pivot pins (tilt column only) • Loose lock shoe pin (tilt column only) • Loose support screws (tilt column only)	• Tighten to specified torque • Replace shoes • Replace pivot pins and support • Replace pin and housing • Tighten screws
Housing loose (tilt column only)	• Excessive clearance between holes in support or housing and pivot pin diameters • Housing support-screws loose	• Replace pivot pins and support • Tighten screws
Steering wheel loose—every other tilt position (tilt column only)	• Loose fit between lock shoe and lock shoe pivot pin	• Replace lock shoes and pivot pin
Steering column not locking in any tilt position (tilt column only)	• Lock shoe seized on pivot pin • Lock shoe grooves have burrs or are filled with foreign material • Lock shoe springs weak or broken	• Replace lock shoes and pin • Clean or replace lock shoes • Replace springs
Noise when tilting column (tilt column only)	• Upper tilt bumpers worn • Tilt spring rubbing in housing	• Replace tilt bumper • Lubricate with chassis grease
One click when in "off-lock" position and the steering wheel is moved	• Seating of lock bolt	• None. Click is normal characteristic sound produced by lock bolt as it seats.
High shift effort (automatic and tilt column only)	• Column not correctly aligned • Lower bearing not aligned correctly • Lack of grease on seal or lower bearing areas	• Align column • Assemble correctly • Lubricate with chassis grease
Improper transmission shifting—automatic and tilt column only	• Sheared shift tube joint • Improper transmission gearshift linkage adjustment • Loose lower shift lever	• Replace shift tube • Adjust linkage • Replace shift tube

8-31

8 SUSPENSION AND STEERING

Troubleshooting the Turn Signal Switch

Problem	Cause	Solution
Turn signal will not cancel	• Loose switch mounting screws • Switch or anchor bosses broken • Broken, missing or out of position detent, or cancelling spring	• Tighten screws • Replace switch • Reposition springs or replace switch as required
Turn signal difficult to operate	• Turn signal lever loose • Switch yoke broken or distorted • Loose or misplaced springs • Foreign parts and/or materials in switch • Switch mounted loosely	• Tighten mounting screws • Replace switch • Reposition springs or replace switch • Remove foreign parts and/or material • Tighten mounting screws
Turn signal will not indicate lane change	• Broken lane change pressure pad or spring hanger • Broken, missing or misplaced lane change spring • Jammed wires	• Replace switch • Replace or reposition as required • Loosen mounting screws, reposition wires and retighten screws
Turn signal will not stay in turn position	• Foreign material or loose parts impeding movement of switch yoke • Defective switch	• Remove material and/or parts • Replace switch
Hazard switch cannot be pulled out	• Foreign material between hazard support cancelling leg and yoke	• Remove foreign material. No foreign material impeding function of hazard switch—replace turn signal switch.
No turn signal lights	• Inoperative turn signal flasher • Defective or blown fuse • Loose chassis to column harness connector • Disconnect column to chassis connector. Connect new switch to chassis and operate switch by hand. If vehicle lights now operate normally, signal switch is inoperative • If vehicle lights do not operate, check chassis wiring for opens, grounds, etc.	• Replace turn signal flasher • Replace fuse • Connect securely • Replace signal switch • Repair chassis wiring as required

SUSPENSION AND STEERING 8

Troubleshooting the Turn Signal Switch (cont.)

Problem	Cause	Solution
Instrument panel turn indicator lights on but not flashing	• Burned out or damaged front or rear turn signal bulb • If vehicle lights do not operate, check light sockets for high resistance connections, the chassis wiring for opens, grounds, etc. • Inoperative flasher • Loose chassis to column harness connection • Inoperative turn signal switch • To determine if turn signal switch is defective, substitute new switch into circuit and operate switch by hand. If the vehicle's lights operate normally, signal switch is inoperative.	• Replace bulb • Repair chassis wiring as required • Replace flasher • Connect securely • Replace turn signal switch • Replace turn signal switch
Stop light not on when turn indicated	• Loose column to chassis connection • Disconnect column to chassis connector. Connect new switch into system without removing old.	• Connect securely • Replace signal switch
Stop light not on when turn indicated (cont.)	Operate switch by hand. If brake lights work with switch in the turn position, signal switch is defective. • If brake lights do not work, check connector to stop light sockets for grounds, opens, etc.	• Repair connector to stop light circuits using service manual as guide
Turn indicator panel lights not flashing	• Burned out bulbs • High resistance to ground at bulb socket • Opens, ground in wiring harness from front turn signal bulb socket to indicator lights	• Replace bulbs • Replace socket • Locate and repair as required
Turn signal lights flash very slowly	• High resistance ground at light sockets • Incorrect capacity turn signal flasher or bulb • If flashing rate is still extremely slow, check chassis wiring harness from the connector to light sockets for high resistance • Loose chassis to column harness connection • Disconnect column to chassis connector. Connect new switch into system without removing old. Operate switch by hand. If flashing occurs at normal rate, the signal switch is defective.	• Repair high resistance grounds at light sockets • Replace turn signal flasher or bulb • Locate and repair as required • Connect securely • Replace turn signal switch

8-33

8 SUSPENSION AND STEERING

Troubleshooting the Turn Signal Switch (cont.)

Problem	Cause	Solution
Hazard signal lights will not flash—turn signal functions normally	• Blow fuse	• Replace fuse
	• Inoperative hazard warning flasher	• Replace hazard warning flasher in fuse panel
	• Loose chassis-to-column harness connection	• Conect securely
	• Disconnect column to chassis connector. Connect new switch into system without removing old. Depress the hazard warning lights. If they now work normally, turn signal switch is defective.	• Replace turn signal switch
	• If lights do not flash, check wiring harness "K" lead for open between hazard flasher and connector. If open, fuse block is defective	• Repair or replace brown wire or connector as required

Troubleshooting the Power Steering Gear

Problem	Cause	Solution
Hissing noise in steering gear	• There is some noise in all power steering systems. One of the most common is a hissing sound most evident at standstill parking. There is no relationship between this noise and performance of the steering. Hiss may be expected when steering wheel is at end of travel or when slowly turning at standstill.	• Slight hiss is normal and in no way affects steering. Do not replace valve unless hiss is extremely objectionable. A replacement valve will also exhibit slight noise and is not always a cure. Investigate clearance around flexible coupling rivets. Be sure steering shaft and gear are aligned so flexible coupling rotates in a flat plane and is not distorted as shaft rotates. Any metal-to-metal contacts through flexible coupling will transmit valve hiss into passenger compartment through the steering column.
Rattle or chuckle noise in steering gear	• Gear loose on frame	• Check gear-to-frame mounting screws.
	• Steering linkage looseness	• Check linkage pivot points for wear. Replace if necessary.
	• Pressure hose touching other parts of car	• Adjust hose position. Do not bend tubing by hand.
	• Loose pitman shaft over center adjustment NOTE: A slight rattle may occur on turns because of increased clearance off the "high point." This is normal and clearance must not be reduced below specified limits to eliminate this slight rattle.	• Adjust to specifications
	• Loose pitman arm	• Tighten pitman arm nut to specifications

SUSPENSION AND STEERING 8

Troubleshooting the Power Steering Gear (cont.)

Problem	Cause	Solution
Squawk noise in steering gear when turning or recovering from a turn	• Damper O-ring on valve spool cut	• Replace damper O-ring
Poor return of steering wheel to center	• Tires not properly inflated • Lack of lubrication in linkage and ball joints • Lower coupling flange rubbing against steering gear adjuster plug • Steering gear to column misalignment • Improper front wheel alignment • Steering linkage binding • Ball joints binding • Steering wheel rubbing against housing • Tight or frozen steering shaft bearings • Sticking or plugged valve spool • Steering gear adjustments over specifications • Kink in return hose	• Inflate to specified pressure • Lube linkage and ball joints • Loosen pinch bolt and assemble properly • Align steering column • Check and adjust as necessary • Replace pivots • Replace ball joints • Align housing • Replace bearings • Remove and clean or replace valve • Check adjustment with gear out of car. Adjust as required. • Replace hose
Car leads to one side or the other (keep in mind road condition and wind. Test car in both directions on flat road)	• Front end misaligned • Unbalanced steering gear valve NOTE: If this is cause, steering effort will be very light in direction of lead and normal or heavier in opposite direction	• Adjust to specifications • Replace valve
Momentary increase in effort when turning wheel fast to right or left	• Low oil level • Pump belt slipping • High internal leakage	• Add power steering fluid as required • Tighten or replace belt • Check pump pressure. (See pressure test)
Steering wheel surges or jerks when turning with engine running especially during parking	• Low oil level • Loose pump belt • Steering linkage hitting engine oil pan at full turn • Insufficient pump pressure • Pump flow control valve sticking	• Fill as required • Adjust tension to specification • Correct clearance • Check pump pressure. (See pressure test). Replace relief valve if defective. • Inspect for varnish or damage, replace if necessary

8 SUSPENSION AND STEERING

Troubleshooting the Power Steering Gear (cont.)

Problem	Cause	Solution
Excessive wheel kickback or loose steering	• Air in system	• Add oil to pump reservoir and bleed by operating steering. Check hose connectors for proper torque and adjust as required.
	• Steering gear loose on frame	• Tighten attaching screws to specified torque
	• Steering linkage joints worn enough to be loose	• Replace loose pivots
	• Worn poppet valve	• Replace poppet valve
	• Loose thrust bearing preload adjustment	• Adjust to specification with gear out of vehicle
	• Excessive overcenter lash	• Adjust to specification with gear out of car
Hard steering or lack of assist	• Loose pump belt • Low oil level **NOTE:** Low oil level will also result in excessive pump noise	• Adjust belt tension to specification • Fill to proper level. If excessively low, check all lines and joints for evidence of external leakage. Tighten loose connectors.
	• Steering gear to column misalignment	• Align steering column
	• Lower coupling flange rubbing against steering gear adjuster plug	• Loosen pinch bolt and assemble properly
	• Tires not properly inflated	• Inflate to recommended pressure
Foamy milky power steering fluid, low fluid level and possible low pressure	• Air in the fluid, and loss of fluid due to internal pump leakage causing overflow	• Check for leak and correct. Bleed system. Extremely cold temperatures will cause system aeration should the oil level be low. If oil level is correct and pump still foams, remove pump from vehicle and separate reservoir from housing. Check welsh plug and housing for cracks. If plug is loose or housing is cracked, replace housing.
Low pressure due to steering pump	• Flow control valve stuck or inoperative	• Remove burrs or dirt or replace. Flush system.
	• Pressure plate not flat against cam ring	• Correct
Low pressure due to steering gear	• Pressure loss in cylinder due to worn piston ring or badly worn housing bore	• Remove gear from car for disassembly and inspection of ring and housing bore
	• Leakage at valve rings, valve body-to-worm seal	• Remove gear from car for disassembly and replace seals

SUSPENSION AND STEERING 8

Troubleshooting the Power Steering Pump

Problem	Cause	Solution
Chirp noise in steering pump	• Loose belt	• Adjust belt tension to specification
Belt squeal (particularly noticeable at full wheel travel and stand still parking)	• Loose belt	• Adjust belt tension to specification
Growl noise in steering pump	• Excessive back pressure in hoses or steering gear caused by restriction	• Locate restriction and correct. Replace part if necessary.
Growl noise in steering pump (particularly noticeable at stand still parking)	• Scored pressure plates, thrust plate or rotor • Extreme wear of cam ring	• Replace parts and flush system • Replace parts
Groan noise in steering pump	• Low oil level • Air in the oil. Poor pressure hose connection.	• Fill reservoir to proper level • Tighten connector to specified torque. Bleed system by operating steering from right to left—full turn.
Rattle noise in steering pump	• Vanes not installed properly • Vanes sticking in rotor slots	• Install properly • Free up by removing burrs, varnish, or dirt
Swish noise in steering pump	• Defective flow control valve	• Replace part
Whine noise in steering pump	• Pump shaft bearing scored	• Replace housing and shaft. Flush system.
Hard steering or lack of assist	• Loose pump belt • Low oil level in reservoir **NOTE:** Low oil level will also result in excessive pump noise • Steering gear to column misalignment • Lower coupling flange rubbing against steering gear adjuster plug • Tires not properly inflated	• Adjust belt tension to specification • Fill to proper level. If excessively low, check all lines and joints for evidence of external leakage. Tighten loose connectors. • Align steering column • Loosen pinch bolt and assemble properly • Inflate to recommended pressure
Foaming milky power steering fluid, low fluid level and possible low pressure	• Air in the fluid, and loss of fluid due to internal pump leakage causing overflow	• Check for leaks and correct. Bleed system. Extremely cold temperatures will cause system aeriation should the oil level be low. If oil level is correct and pump still foams, remove pump from vehicle and separate reservoir from body. Check welsh plug and body for cracks. If plug is loose or body is cracked, replace body.

8 SUSPENSION AND STEERING

Troubleshooting the Power Steering Pump (cont.)

Problem	Cause	Solution
Low pump pressure	• Flow control valve stuck or inoperative • Pressure plate not flat against cam ring	• Remove burrs or dirt or replace. Flush system. • Correct
Momentary increase in effort when turning wheel fast to right or left	• Low oil level in pump • Pump belt slipping • High internal leakage	• Add power steering fluid as required • Tighten or replace belt • Check pump pressure. (See pressure test)
Steering wheel surges or jerks when turning with engine running especially during parking	• Low oil level • Loose pump belt • Steering linkage hitting engine oil pan at full turn • Insufficient pump pressure	• Fill as required • Adjust tension to specification • Correct clearance • Check pump pressure. (See pressure test). Replace flow control valve if defective.
Steering wheel surges or jerks when turning with engine running especially during parking (cont.)	• Sticking flow control valve	• Inspect for varnish or damage, replace if necessary
Excessive wheel kickback or loose steering	• Air in system	• Add oil to pump reservoir and bleed by operating steering. Check hose connectors for proper torque and adjust as required.
Low pump pressure	• Extreme wear of cam ring • Scored pressure plate, thrust plate, or rotor • Vanes not installed properly • Vanes sticking in rotor slots • Cracked or broken thrust or pressure plate	• Replace parts. Flush system. • Replace parts. Flush system. • Install properly • Freeup by removing burrs, varnish, or dirt • Replace part

SUSPENSION AND STEERING 8

Troubleshooting the Manual Steering Gear

Problem	Cause	Solution
Hard or erratic steering	• Incorrect tire pressure	• Inflate tires to recommended pressures
	• Insufficient or incorrect lubrication	• Lubricate as required (refer to Maintenance Section)
	• Suspension, or steering linkage parts damaged or misaligned	• Repair or replace parts as necessary
	• Improper front wheel alignment	• Adjust incorrect wheel alignment angles
	• Incorrect steering gear adjustment	• Adjust steering gear
	• Sagging springs	• Replace springs
Play or looseness in steering	• Steering wheel loose	• Inspect shaft spines and repair as necessary. Tighten attaching nut and stake in place.
	• Steering linkage or attaching parts loose or worn	• Tighten, adjust, or replace faulty components
	• Pitman arm loose	• Inspect shaft splines and repair as necessary. Tighten attaching nut and stake in place
	• Steering gear attaching bolts loose	• Tighten bolts
	• Loose or worn wheel bearings	• Adjust or replace bearings
	• Steering gear adjustment incorrect or parts badly worn	• Adjust gear or replace defective parts
Wheel shimmy or tramp	• Improper tire pressure	• Inflate tires to recommended pressures
	• Wheels, tires, or brake rotors out-of-balance or out-of-round	• Inspect and replace or balance parts
	• Inoperative, worn, or loose shock absorbers or mounting parts	• Repair or replace shocks or mountings
	• Loose or worn steering or suspension parts	• Tighten or replace as necessary
	• Loose or worn wheel bearings	• Adjust or replace bearings
	• Incorrect steering gear adjustments	• Adjust steering gear
	• Incorrect front wheel alignment	• Correct front wheel alignment
Tire wear	• Improper tire pressure	• Inflate tires to recommended pressures
	• Failure to rotate tires	• Rotate tires
	• Brakes grabbing	• Adjust or repair brakes
	• Incorrect front wheel alignment	• Align incorrect angles
	• Broken or damaged steering and suspension parts	• Repair or replace defective parts
	• Wheel runout	• Replace faulty wheel
	• Excessive speed on turns	• Make driver aware of conditions

8 SUSPENSION AND STEERING

Troubleshooting the Manual Steering Gear

Problem	Cause	Solution
Vehicle leads to one side	• Improper tire pressures • Front tires with uneven tread depth, wear pattern, or different cord design (i.e., one bias ply and one belted or radial tire on front wheels) • Incorrect front wheel alignment • Brakes dragging • Pulling due to uneven tire construction	• Inflate tires to recommended pressures • Install tires of same cord construction and reasonably even tread depth, design, and wear pattern • Align incorrect angles • Adjust or repair brakes • Replace faulty tire

8-40

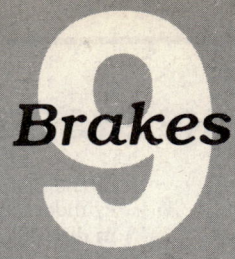

Brakes

QUICK REFERENCE INDEX

Anti-Lock Brake System	9-27
Brake Specifications	9-2
Disc Brakes	9-18
Drum Brakes	9-24
Parking Brake	9-39
Troubleshooting	9-3

GENERAL INDEX

Anti-Lock Brake System
- Diagnosis and testing 9-33
- Electronic control unit 9-39
- Front wheel speed sensor 9-35
- Master cylinder, modulator and accumulator 9-38
- Operation 9-27
- Pump and motor 9-37
- Rear wheel speed sensor 9-36
- Tone wheel 9-37
- Wiring and diagnosis 9-40, 44

Brakes
- Adjustments
  - Brake pedal 9-8
  - Drum brakes 9-7
- Bleeding 9-13
- Brake light switch 9-11
- Caliper 9-19

Disc brakes (Front)
- Operating principals 9-2
- Pads 9-18
- Rotor (Disc) 9-22

Drum brakes
- Adjustment 9-7
- Drum 9-24
- Operating principals 9-2
- Shoes 9-24
- Wheel cylinder 9-26

Hoses and lines 9-13
Master cylinder 9-8
Parking brake
- Adjustment 9-39
- Removal and installation 9-39

Power booster
- Operating principals 9-2
- Removal and installation 9-11

Pressure differential valve 9-10
Proportioning valve 9-10
Specifications 9-2
Troubleshooting 9-3

Calipers
- Overhaul 9-21
- Removal and installation 9-19

Disc brakes 9-18
Drum brakes 9-24
Hoses 9-13
Master cylinder 9-8
Parking brake 9-39
Power brake booster 9-11
Pressure differential valve 9-10
Proportioning valve 9-10
Specifications 9-2
Troubleshooting 9-3
Wheel cylinders 9-26

9-1

9 BRAKES

BRAKE SYSTEMS

Hydraulic System

BASIC OPERATING PRINCIPLES

Except Anti-Lock Braking System

Hydraulic systems are used to actuate the brakes of all modern automobiles. The system transports the power required to force the frictional surfaces of the braking system together from the pedal to the individual brake units at each wheel. A hydraulic system is used for two reasons. First, fluid under pressure can be carried to all parts of an automobile by small hoses-some of which are flexible-without taking up a significant amount of room or posing routing problems. Second, a great mechanical advantage can be given to the brake pedal end of the system, and the foot pressure required to actuate the brakes can be reduced by making the surface area of the master cylinder pistons smaller than that of any of the pistons in the wheel cylinders or calipers.

The master cylinder consists of a fluid reservoir and either a single or double cylinder and piston assembly. Double type master cylinders are designed to separate the front and rear braking systems hydraulically in case of a leak.

Steel lines carry the brake fluid to a point on the vehicle's frame near each of the vehicle's wheels. The fluid is then carried to the wheel cylinders by flexible tubes in order to allow for suspension and steering movements.

Each wheel cylinder contains two pistons, one at either end, which push outward in opposite directions. In disc brake systems, the cylinders are part of the calipers. One or four cylinders are used to force the brake pads against the disc, but all cylinders contain one piston only. All pistons employ some type of seal, usually made of rubber, to minimize fluid leakage. A rubber dust boot seals the outer end of the cylinder against dust and dirt. The boot fits around the outer end of the piston on disc brake calipers, and around the brake actuating rod on wheel cylinders.

The hydraulic system operates as follows: When at rest, the entire system, from the piston(s) in the master cylinder to those in the wheel cylinders or calipers, is full of brake fluid. Upon application of the brake pedal, fluid trapped in front of the master cylinder piston(s) is forced through the lines to the wheel cylinders. Here, it forces the pistons outward, in the case of drum brakes, and inward toward the disc, in the case of disc brakes. The motion of the pistons is opposed by return springs mounted outside the cylinders in drum brakes, and by internal springs or spring seals, in disc brakes.

Upon release of the brake pedal, a spring located inside the master cylinder immediately returns the master cylinder pistons to the normal position. The pistons contain check valves and the master cylinder has compensating ports drilled in it. These are uncovered as the pistons reach their normal position. The piston check valves allow fluid to flow toward the wheel cylinders or calipers as the pistons withdraw. Then, as the return springs force the brake pads or shoes into the released position, the excess returns to the fluid reservoir through the compensating ports. It is during the time the pedal is in the released position that any fluid that has leaked out of the system will be replaced through the compensating ports.

Dual circuit master cylinders employ two pistons, located one behind the other, in the same cylinder. The primary piston is actuated directly by mechanical linkage from the brake pedal. The secondary piston is actuated by fluid trapped between the two pistons. If a leak develops in front of the secondary piston, it moves forward until it bottoms against the front of the master cylinder, and the fluid trapped between the pistons will operate the rear brakes. If the rear brakes develop a leak, the primary piston will move forward until direct contact with the secondary piston takes place, and it will force the secondary piston to actuate the front brakes. In either case, the brake pedal moves farther when the brakes are applied, and less braking power is available.

All dual-circuit systems use a switch to warn the driver when only half of the brake system is operational. This switch is located in a valve body which is mounted on the firewall or the frame below the master cylinder. A hydraulic piston receives pressure from both circuits, each circuit's pressure being applied to one end of the piston. When the pressures are in balance, the piston remains stationary. When one circuit has a leak, however, the greater pressure in that circuit during application of the brakes will push the piston to one side, closing the switch and activating the brake warning light.

In disc brake systems, this valve body also contains a metering valve and, in some cases, a proportioning valve. The metering valve keeps pressure from traveling to the disc brakes on the front wheels until the brake shoes on the rear wheels have contacted the drums, ensuring that the front brakes will never be used

BRAKE SPECIFICATIONS
All specifications in inches

Years	Master Cyl. Bore	Brake Disc Minimum Thickness	Brake Disc Maximum Run-out	Brake Drum Orig. Inside Dia.	Brake Drum Max. Wear Limit	Wheel Cyl. or Caliper Bore Front	Wheel Cyl. or Caliper Bore Rear
1984–86	0.937	0.8150	0.005	10.000	10.060	2.598	0.874
1987–89	0.937	0.8150	0.004	10.000	10.060	2.598	0.874
1990–91	—	0.860 ①	0.005	9.000 ②	9.000 ③	—	—

① 1990 4WD 0.940
   1991 4WD 0.890
② 10.000 w/metric ton package
③ 10.060 w/metric ton package

BRAKES 9

Troubleshooting the Brake System

Problem	Cause	Solution
Low brake pedal (excessive pedal travel required for braking action.)	• Excessive clearance between rear linings and drums caused by inoperative automatic adjusters	• Make 10 to 15 alternate forward and reverse brake stops to adjust brakes. If brake pedal does not come up, repair or replace adjuster parts as necessary.
	• Worn rear brakelining	• Inspect and replace lining if worn beyond minimum thickness specification
	• Bent, distorted brakeshoes, front or rear	• Replace brakeshoes in axle sets
	• Air in hydraulic system	• Remove air from system. Refer to Brake Bleeding.
Low brake pedal (pedal may go to floor with steady pressure applied.)	• Fluid leak in hydraulic system	• Fill master cylinder to fill line; have helper apply brakes and check calipers, wheel cylinders, differential valve tubes, hoses and fittings for leaks. Repair or replace as necessary.
	• Air in hydraulic system	• Remove air from system. Refer to Brake Bleeding.
	• Incorrect or non-recommended brake fluid (fluid evaporates at below normal temp).	• Flush hydraulic system with clean brake fluid. Refill with correct-type fluid.
	• Master cylinder piston seals worn, or master cylinder bore is scored, worn or corroded	• Repair or replace master cylinder
Low brake pedal (pedal goes to floor on first application—o.k. on subsequent applications.)	• Disc brake pads sticking on abutment surfaces of anchor plate. Caused by a build-up of dirt, rust, or corrosion on abutment surfaces	• Clean abutment surfaces
Fading brake pedal (pedal height decreases with steady pressure applied.)	• Fluid leak in hydraulic system	• Fill master cylinder reservoirs to fill mark, have helper apply brakes, check calipers, wheel cylinders, differential valve, tubes, hoses, and fittings for fluid leaks. Repair or replace parts as necessary.
	• Master cylinder piston seals worn, or master cylinder bore is scored, worn or corroded	• Repair or replace master cylinder
Spongy brake pedal (pedal has abnormally soft, springy, spongy feel when depressed.)	• Air in hydraulic system	• Remove air from system. Refer to Brake Bleeding.
	• Brakeshoes bent or distorted	• Replace brakeshoes
	• Brakelining not yet seated with drums and rotors	• Burnish brakes
	• Rear drum brakes not properly adjusted	• Adjust brakes

9 BRAKES

Troubleshooting the Brake System (cont.)

Problem	Cause	Solution
Decreasing brake pedal travel (pedal travel required for braking action decreases and may be accompanied by a hard pedal.)	• Caliper or wheel cylinder pistons sticking or seized • Master cylinder compensator ports blocked (preventing fluid return to reservoirs) or pistons sticking or seized in master cylinder bore • Power brake unit binding internally	• Repair or replace the calipers, or wheel cylinders • Repair or replace the master cylinder • Test unit according to the following procedure: (a) Shift transmission into neutral and start engine (b) Increase engine speed to 1500 rpm, close throttle and fully depress brake pedal (c) Slow release brake pedal and stop engine (d) Have helper remove vacuum check valve and hose from power unit. Observe for backward movement of brake pedal. (e) If the pedal moves backward, the power unit has an internal bind—replace power unit
Grabbing brakes (severe reaction to brake pedal pressure.)	• Brakelining(s) contaminated by grease or brake fluid • Parking brake cables incorrectly adjusted or seized • Incorrect brakelining or lining loose on brakeshoes • Caliper anchor plate bolts loose • Rear brakeshoes binding on support plate ledges • Incorrect or missing power brake reaction disc • Rear brake support plates loose	• Determine and correct cause of contamination and replace brakeshoes in axle sets • Adjust cables. Replace seized cables. • Replace brakeshoes in axle sets • Tighten bolts • Clean and lubricate ledges. Replace support plate(s) if ledges are deeply grooved. Do not attempt to smooth ledges by grinding. • Install correct disc • Tighten mounting bolts
Chatter or shudder when brakes are applied (pedal pulsation and roughness may also occur.)	• Brakeshoes distorted, bent, contaminated, or worn • Caliper anchor plate or support plate loose • Excessive thickness variation of rotor(s)	• Replace brakeshoes in axle sets • Tighten mounting bolts • Refinish or replace rotors in axle sets
Noisy brakes (squealing, clicking, scraping sound when brakes are applied.)	• Bent, broken, distorted brakeshoes • Excessive rust on outer edge of rotor braking surface	• Replace brakeshoes in axle sets • Remove rust

BRAKES 9

Troubleshooting the Brake System (cont.)

Problem	Cause	Solution
Hard brake pedal (excessive pedal pressure required to stop vehicle. May be accompanied by brake fade.)	• Loose or leaking power brake unit vacuum hose • Incorrect or poor quality brakelining • Bent, broken, distorted brakeshoes • Calipers binding or dragging on mounting pins. Rear brakeshoes dragging on support plate. • Caliper, wheel cylinder, or master cylinder pistons sticking or seized • Power brake unit vacuum check valve malfunction • Power brake unit has internal bind	• Tighten connections or replace leaking hose • Replace with lining in axle sets • Replace brakeshoes • Replace mounting pins and bushings. Clean rust or burrs from rear brake support plate ledges and lubricate ledges with molydisulfide grease. **NOTE:** If ledges are deeply grooved or scored, do not attempt to sand or grind them smooth—replace support plate. • Repair or replace parts as necessary • Test valve according to the following procedure: (a) Start engine, increase engine speed to 1500 rpm, close throttle and immediately stop engine (b) Wait at least 90 seconds then depress brake pedal (c) If brakes are not vacuum assisted for 2 or more applications, check valve is faulty • Test unit according to the following procedure: (a) With engine stopped, apply brakes several times to exhaust all vacuum in system (b) Shift transmission into neutral, depress brake pedal and start engine (c) If pedal height decreases with foot pressure and less pressure is required to hold pedal in applied position, power unit vacuum system is operating normally. Test power unit. If power unit exhibits a bind condition, replace the power unit.

9-5

9 BRAKES

Troubleshooting the Brake System (cont.)

Problem	Cause	Solution
Hard brake pedal (excessive pedal pressure required to stop vehicle. May be accompanied by brake fade.)	• Master cylinder compensator ports (at bottom of reservoirs) blocked by dirt, scale, rust, or have small burrs (blocked ports prevent fluid return to reservoirs). • Brake hoses, tubes, fittings clogged or restricted • Brake fluid contaminated with improper fluids (motor oil, transmission fluid, causing rubber components to swell and stick in bores • Low engine vacuum	• Repair or replace master cylinder **CAUTION:** Do not attempt to clean blocked ports with wire, pencils, or similar implements. Use compressed air only. • Use compressed air to check or unclog parts. Replace any damaged parts. • Replace all rubber components, combination valve and hoses. Flush entire brake system with DOT 3 brake fluid or equivalent. • Adjust or repair engine
Dragging brakes (slow or incomplete release of brakes)	• Brake pedal binding at pivot • Power brake unit has internal bind • Parking brake cables incorrrectly adjusted or seized • Rear brakeshoe return springs weak or broken • Automatic adjusters malfunctioning • Caliper, wheel cylinder or master cylinder pistons sticking or seized • Master cylinder compensating ports blocked (fluid does not return to reservoirs).	• Loosen and lubricate • Inspect for internal bind. Replace unit if internal bind exists. • Adjust cables. Replace seized cables. • Replace return springs. Replace brakeshoe if necessary in axle sets. • Repair or replace adjuster parts as required • Repair or replace parts as necessary • Use compressed air to clear ports. Do not use wire, pencils, or similar objects to open blocked ports.
Vehicle moves to one side when brakes are applied	• Incorrect front tire pressure • Worn or damaged wheel bearings • Brakelining on one side contaminated • Brakeshoes on one side bent, distorted, or lining loose on shoe • Support plate bent or loose on one side • Brakelining not yet seated with drums or rotors • Caliper anchor plate loose on one side • Caliper piston sticking or seized • Brakelinings water soaked • Loose suspension component attaching or mounting bolts • Brake combination valve failure	• Inflate to recommended cold (reduced load) inflation pressure • Replace worn or damaged bearings • Determine and correct cause of contamination and replace brakelining in axle sets • Replace brakeshoes in axle sets • Tighten or replace support plate • Burnish brakelining • Tighten anchor plate bolts • Repair or replace caliper • Drive vehicle with brakes lightly applied to dry linings • Tighten suspension bolts. Replace worn suspension components. • Replace combination valve

BRAKES 9

alone. The proportioning valve controls the pressure to the rear brakes to avoid rear wheel lock-up during very hard braking.

Warning lights may be tested by depressing the brake pedal and holding it while opening one of the wheel cylinder bleeder screws. If this does not cause the light to go on, substitute a new lamp, make continuity checks, and, finally, replace the switch as necessary.

The hydraulic system may be checked for leaks by applying pressure to the pedal gradually and steadily. If the pedal sinks very slowly to the floor, the system has a leak. This is not to be confused with a springy or spongy feel due to the compression of air within the lines. If the system leaks, there will be a gradual change in the position of the pedal with a constant pressure.

Check for leaks along all lines and at wheel cylinders. If no external leaks are apparent, the problem is inside the master cylinder.

Disc Brakes

BASIC OPERATING PRINCIPLES

Instead of the traditional expanding brakes that press outward against a circular drum, disc brake systems utilize a disc (rotor) with brake pads positioned on either side of it. Braking effect is achieved in a manner similar to the way you would squeeze a spinning phonograph record between your fingers. The disc (rotor) is a casting with cooling fins between the two braking surfaces. This enables air to circulate between the braking surfaces making them less sensitive to heat buildup and more resistant to fade. Dirt and water do not affect braking action since contaminants are thrown off by the centrifugal action of the rotor or scraped off the by the pads. Also, the equal clamping action of the two brake pads tends to ensure uniform, straight line stops. Disc brakes are inherently self-adjusting.

There are three general types of disc brake:
1. A fixed caliper.
2. A floating caliper.
3. A sliding caliper.

The fixed caliper design uses two pistons mounted on either side of the rotor (in each side of the caliper). The caliper is mounted rigidly and does not move.

The sliding and floating designs are quite similar. In fact, these two types are often lumped together. In both designs, the pad on the inside of the rotor is moved into contact with the rotor by hydraulic force. The caliper, which is not held in a fixed position, moves slightly, bringing the outside pad into contact with the rotor. There are various methods of attaching floating calipers. Some pivot at the bottom or top, and some slide on mounting bolts. In any event, the end result is the same.

Drum Brakes

BASIC OPERATING PRINCIPLES

Drum brakes employ two brake shoes mounted on a stationary backing plate. These shoes are positioned inside a circular drum which rotates with the wheel assembly. The shoes are held in place by springs; this allows them to slide toward the drums (when they are applied) while keeping the linings and drums in alignment. The shoes are actuated by a wheel cylinder which is mounted at the top of the backing plate. When the brakes are applied, hydraulic pressure forces the wheel cylinder's actuating links outward. Since these links bear directly against the top of the brake shoes, the tops of the shoes are then forced against the inner side of the drum. This action forces the bottoms of the two shoes to contact the brake drum by rotating the entire assembly slightly (known as servo action). When pressure within the wheel cylinder is relaxed, return springs pull the shoes back away from the drum.

Most modern drum brakes are designed to self-adjust themselves during application when the vehicle is moving in reverse. This motion causes both shoes to rotate very slightly with the drum, rocking an adjusting lever, thereby causing rotation of the adjusting screw.

Power Boosters

Power brakes operate just as standard brake systems except in the actuation of the master cylinder pistons. A vacuum diaphragm is located on the front of the master cylinder and assists the driver in applying the brakes, reducing both the effort and travel he must put into moving the brake pedal.

The vacuum diaphragm housing is connected to the intake manifold by a vacuum hose. A check valve is placed at the point where the hose enters the diaphragm housing, so that during periods of low manifold vacuum brake assist vacuum will not be lost.

Depressing the brake pedal closes off the vacuum source and allows atmospheric pressure to enter on one side of the diaphragm. This causes the master cylinder pistons to move and apply the brakes. When the brake pedal is released, vacuum is applied to both sides of the diaphragm, and return springs return the diaphragm and master cylinder pistons to the released position. If the vacuum fails, the brake pedal rod will butt against the end of the master cylinder actuating rod, and direct mechanical application will occur as the pedal is depressed.

The hydraulic and mechanical problems that apply to conventional brake systems also apply to power brakes, and should be checked for if the tests below do not reveal the problem.

Test for a system vacuum leak as described below:
1. Operate the engine at idle without touching the brake pedal for at least one minute.
2. Turn off the engine, and wait one minute.
3. Test for the presence of assist vacuum by depressing the brake pedal and releasing it several times. Light application will produce less and less pedal travel, if vacuum was present. If there is no vacuum, air is leaking into the system somewhere.

Test for system operation as follows:
1. Pump the brake pedal (with engine off) until the supply vacuum is entirely gone.
2. Put a light, steady pressure on the pedal.
3. Start the engine, and operate it at idle. If the system is operating, the brake pedal should fall toward the floor if constant pressure is maintained on the pedal.

Power brake systems may be tested for hydraulic leaks just as ordinary systems are tested.

CAUTION
Brake linings contain asbestos. Asbestos is a known cancer-causing agent. When working on brakes, remember that the dust which accumulates on the brake parts and/or in the drum contains asbestos. Always wear a protective face covering, such as a painter's mask, when working on the brakes. NEVER blow the dust from the brakes or drum! There are solvents made for the purpose of cleaning brake parts. Use them!

Adjustments

When the brake linings become worn, effective brake pedal travel is reduced. Adjusting the brake shoes will restore the necessary travel for efficient braking.

Before adjusting the brakes, check the spring nuts, brake dust shield-to-axle flange bolts and wheel adjustments. Any looseness in these parts can cause erratic brake operation.

NOTE: Disc brakes require no manual adjustment, nor are they adjustable. Therefore, the following applies only to drum brakes.

9-7

9 BRAKES

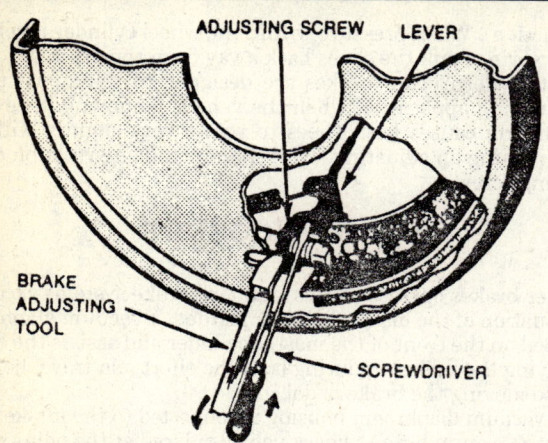

Adjusting drum brakes with starwheel adjusters

1. Jack up the vehicle.
2. Remove the access slot cover and using a brake adjusting tool or screwdriver, rotate the starwheel until the wheel is locked and can't be turned by hand. To tighten, rotate the starwheel in the clockwise direction.
3. Back off the starwheel at least 15 to 20 notches. To back off the starwheel on the brake, insert an ice pick or thin screwdriver in the adjusting screw slot to hold the automatic adjusting lever away from the starwheel. Do not attempt to back off on the adjusting screw without holding the adjusting lever away from the starwheel as the adjuster will be damaged.
4. Test drive vehicle. With hands off the steering wheel, attempt to stop the vehicle. If vehicle pulls to one side, readjust brakes.

BRAKE PEDAL FREE PLAY

NOTE: Pedal free play is measured at the top of the pedal pad.

Proper free play should be 1.5–6.0mm ($1/16$–$1/4$ in.). Free play is not adjustable. If free play is not correct, the problem is the result of worn or damaged parts.

Master Cylinder

REMOVAL AND INSTALLATION

Except Anti-Lock Brakes

1. Disconnect and plug the brake lines.
2. Disconnect the wires from the stoplight switch.
3. Remove all attaching bolts and nuts, and lift the assembly from the vehicle.
4. Prior to installation, fill the master cylinder and operate the pushrod until fluid squirts from the ports.
5. Installation is the reverse of removal. Torque the mounting nuts to 15–18 ft. lbs. Bleed the brake system.

OVERHAUL

NOTE: Do not use any type of mineral oil, gasoline or kerosene to clean any part of any hydraulic brake system. These fluids will cause rubber parts to soften, swell, and distort, resulting in failure. Use only clean brake fluid or alcohol.

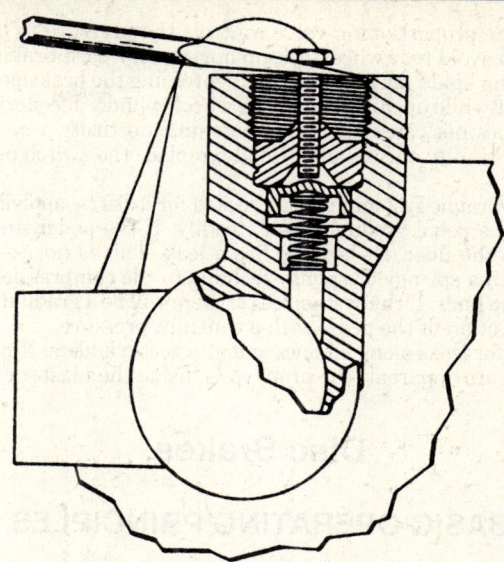

Removing the tube seats from the master cylinder with a screwdriver

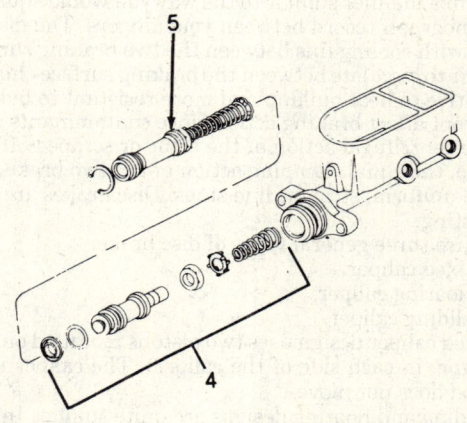

1984–86 master cylinder. (4) secondary piston, (5) primary piston

1984–86

1. Remove the cover, drain the cylinder and mount it in a vise.
2. Using a drift or punch, push the primary piston inward and remove the snapring from its groove.
3. Remove the primary and secondary piston assemblies. It may be necessary to apply air pressure through the piston stop hole to free the secondary piston.
4. Inspect all parts after a thorough cleaning. Inspect the tube seats in the outlet ports. Replace the seats only if they are cracked, cocked or loose. To replace a seat:
   a. Drill out the seats with a $13/64$ in. (5mm) drill bit.
   b. Place a flat washer on each port and thread a $1/4$–20 × $3/4$ in. long self tapping screw into the tube seat. Thread in the screw until the seat is loose.
   c. Pry out the seat.
   d. New seats may be pressed in using spare tube fitting nuts.

Rebuilding kits contain all the necessary parts. Replace all parts with those supplied in the kit. Never reuse a rubber part or any part that appears worn or damaged.

Brakes 9

Imperfections in the bore may be removed by honing. If any imperfection remains after honing, replace the unit.

5. Prior to assembly, coat all parts with clean brake fluid.
6. Install the secondary piston seals. The seal lip of the rear seal must face the inside of the bore. The front seal lip must face outward when installed.
7. Install the seal retainer and return spring on the secondary piston.
8. Install the secondary piston in the bore.
9. Install the primary piston assembly.
10. Push the primary piston inward and install the snapring.
11. Bench-bleed the master cylinder
12. Install the master cylinder, loosely connect the brake lines and bleed the master cylinder. Tighten the brake lines and bleed the system.

1987–91

1. Remove the cover, drain the cylinder and mount it in a vise. Examine the cover seal and replace if worn.
2. Using a drift or punch, push the primary piston inward and remove the snapring from its groove.
3. Remove the primary and secondary piston assemblies. It may be necessary to apply air pressure through the piston stop hole to free the secondary piston.

Rebuilding kits contain all the necessary parts. Replace all parts with those supplied in the kit. Never reuse a rubber part or any part that appears worn or damaged.

4. Clean all parts with brake cleaning solvent only. Prior to assembly, coat all parts with clean brake fluid.

NOTE: DO NOT hone bore to remove imperfections. Replace cylinder bore if doubt exists about its condition.

5. Install the secondary piston seals. The seal lip of the rear seal must face the inside of the bore. The front seal lip must face outward when installed.
6. Install the seal retainer and return spring on the secondary piston.
7. Install the secondary piston in the bore.
8. Install the primary piston assembly.
9. Push the primary piston inward and install the snapring.
10. Bench-bleed the master cylinder
11. Install the master cylinder, loosely connect the brake lines

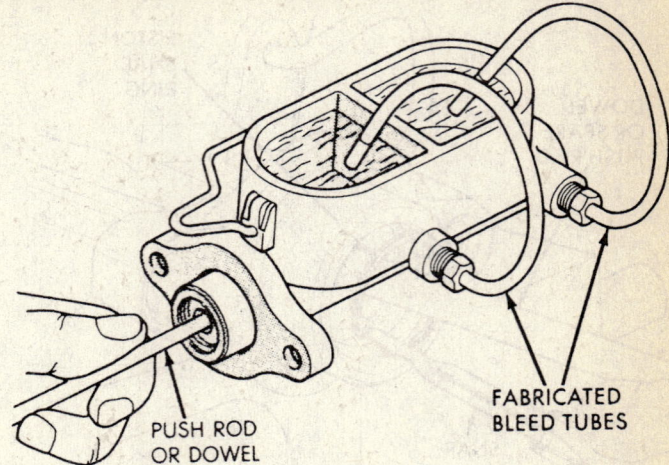

Bleeding the master cylinder

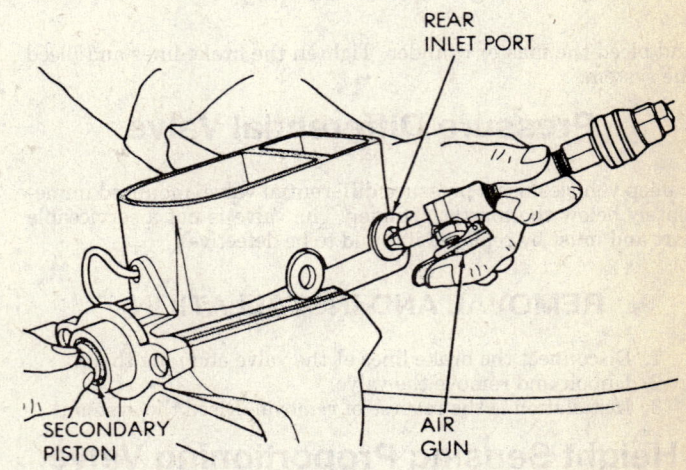

Removing the secondary piston

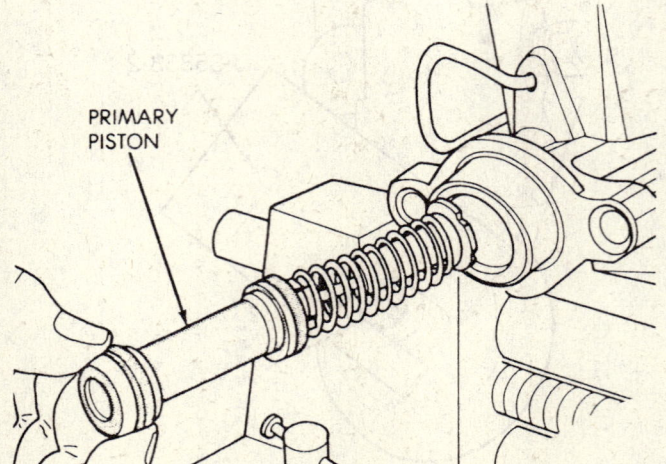

Removing/installing the primary piston

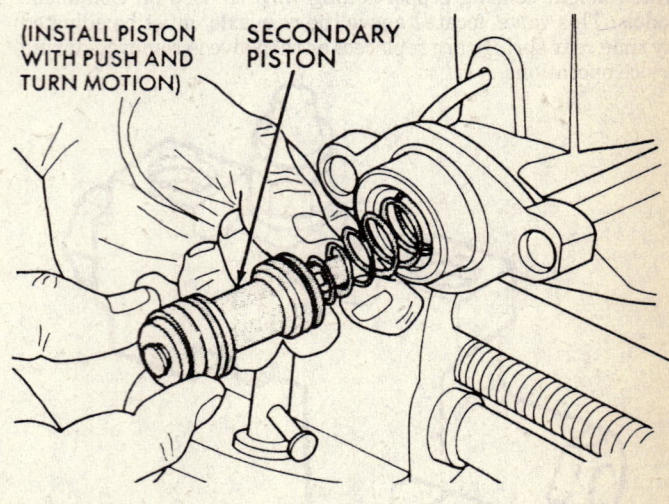

Installing the secondary piston

9-9

9 BRAKES

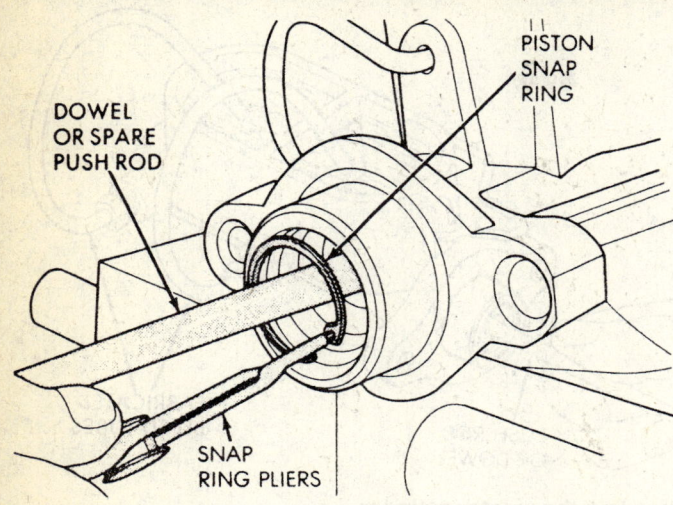

Removing/installing the piston snapring

and bleed the master cylinder. Tighten the brake lines and bleed the system.

Pressure Differential Valve

Jeep vehicles use a pressure differential valve, mounted immediately below the master cylinder. The valve is not a serviceable part and must by replaced if found to be defective.

REMOVAL AND INSTALLATION

1. Disconnect the brake lines at the valve and plug them.
2. Unbolt and remove the valve.
3. Installation is the reverse of removal. Bleed the system.

Height Sensing Proportioning Valve

In addition to the pressure differential valve, a mechanically activated height sensing proportioning valve is used on Comanche models. This valve, located above the rear axle, must be adjusted any time rear springs are replaced, or the valve is removed during service operations.

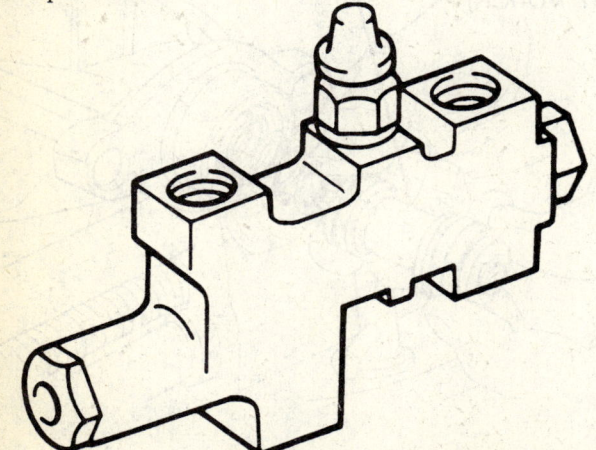

Pressure differential valve

NOTE: Any time the valve is adjusted, the lever bushing must be replaced. The adjustment must be made with the vehicle level and at curb weight. Special tools are needed for this job.

REMOVAL AND INSTALLATION

1. Disconnect the valve lever and spring, if equipped.
2. Disconnect and cap the brake lines.
3. Unbolt and remove the valve.
4. Installation is the reverse of removal. Torque the Valve bracket-to-frame bolts to 155 inch lbs.; the valve-to-bracket bolts to 118 inch lbs.
5. Perform the valve adjusting procedure below.

ADJUSTMENT

Except 1990–91

1. Remove the valve shaft nut and washer.
2. Disconnect the valve lever and remove the spring.
3. Remove and discard the bushing.
4. Rotate the valve shaft and install adjusting gauge tool J–35853–2.

NOTE: The gauge must be properly seated on the D shape of the shaft and the valve lower mounting bolt. All linkage components, except the spring, must be connected before installing the new bushing.

5. Place the bushing in the lever, and, using bushing aligning tool J–35853–1, press the bushing and lever onto the shaft.
6. Remove the lever and adjusting tool J–35853–2 and install the spring.
7. Install the lever, washer and nut. Tighten the nut to 100 inch lbs.
8. Connect the spring.

1990–91

NOTE: Valve adjustment requires Calibration Kit 6229.

1. Unload the vehicle and place on a level surface for accurate valve adjustment.
2. Remove nut attaching lever to valve shaft.

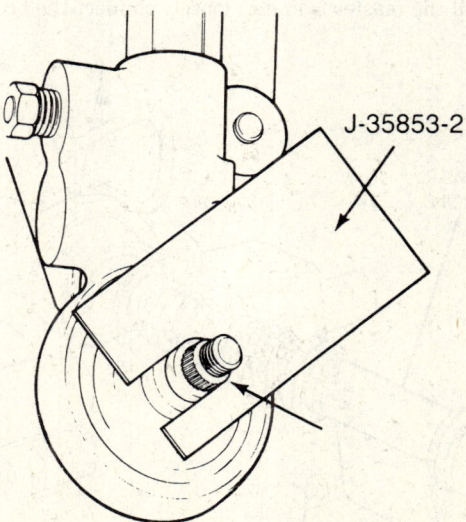

Adjustment tool (from kit 6229) installed on the valve. The arrow points to the valve shaft

BRAKES 9

Tighten valve mounting bolts to 118 inch lbs. Tighten lever nut to 100 inch lbs.

Brake Booster

REMOVAL AND INSTALLATION

Except Anti-Lock Brakes

1. Disconnect the power unit pushrod at the pedal.
2. Disconnect the vacuum line at the power unit check valve.
3. Unbolt the master cylinder from the power unit and move it out of the way without disconnecting the brake lines. Be careful to avoid kinking the lines!
4. Unbolt and remove the power unit from the firewall.
5. Installation is the reverse of removal. Torque the power unit-to-firewall nuts to 30–35 ft. lbs.; the master cylinder-to-booster nuts to 15–18 inch lbs. Torque the pushrod nut to 35 ft. lbs.

Brake Light Switch

REMOVAL AND INSTALLATION

1. Remove the steering column cover and lower trim panel for access, if necessary. Disconnect switch wiring harness.
2. Thread switch out of retainer, or rock switch up/down and pull it rearward.
3. Inspect switch retainer and replace if worn or damaged.
4. Insert replacement switch in retainer. Thread switch into

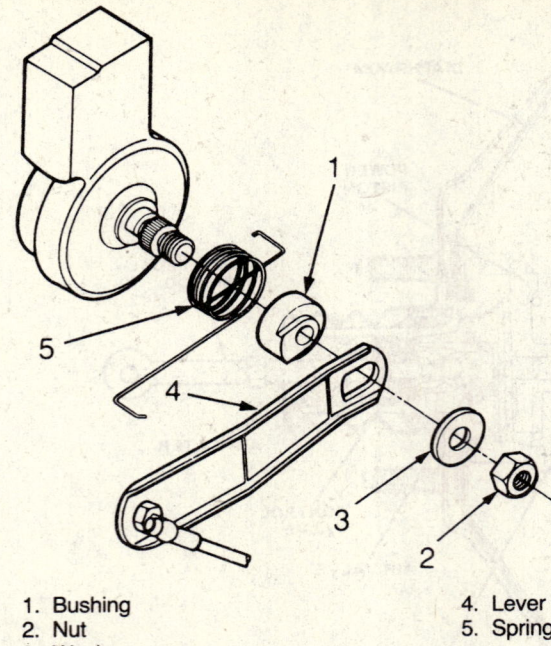

1. Bushing
2. Nut
3. Washer
4. Lever
5. Spring

Height sensing proportioning valve installed on the Comanche. 1990–91 valves DO NOT use a spring (5)

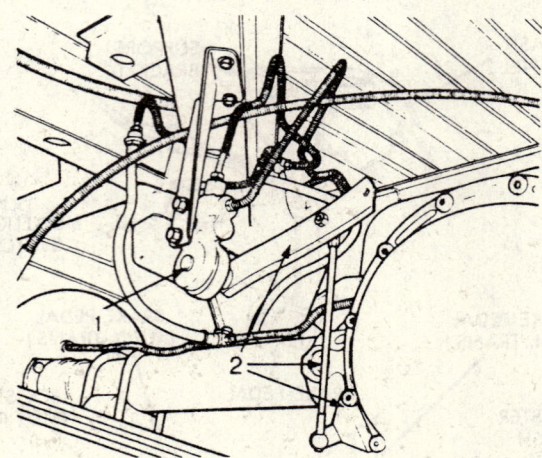

Height sensing proportioning valve (1) and linkage (2)

3. Pull lever and retainer off valve shaft and remove old bushing. Discard bushing.
4. Clean threads and splines on valve shaft. If valve link was disconnected from axle bracket or lever, reconnect link before continuing.
5. Loosen valve mounting bolts two full turns. Then turn valve shaft until shaft flat is approximately between the 5 and 6 O'clock position.
6. Install valve adjusting gauge and position on mounting bolts and shaft. There should be no clearance between gauge, shaft and bolts. Gauge should be seated on the shaft flat.
7. Install retainer on lever and bushing on retainer. Start bushing and lever on valve shaft and press into place with the tools provided in kit 6229.
8. Remove adjustment gauge and bushing installer tool.

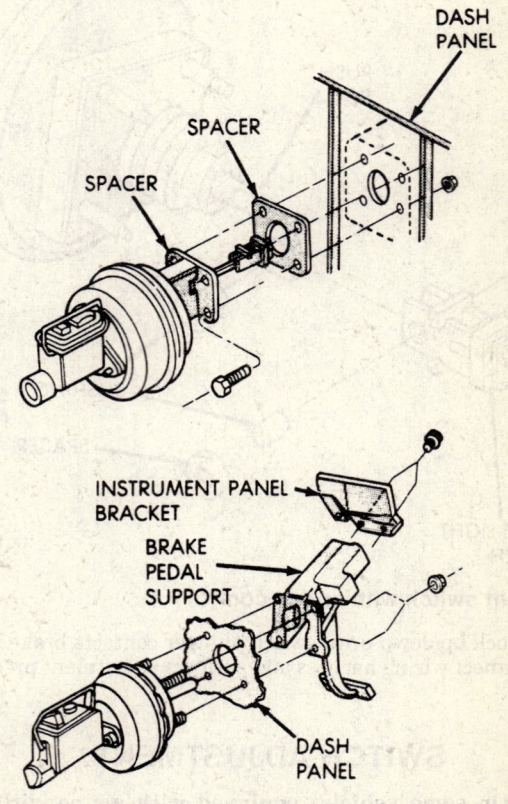

Power brake booster mounting

9 BRAKES

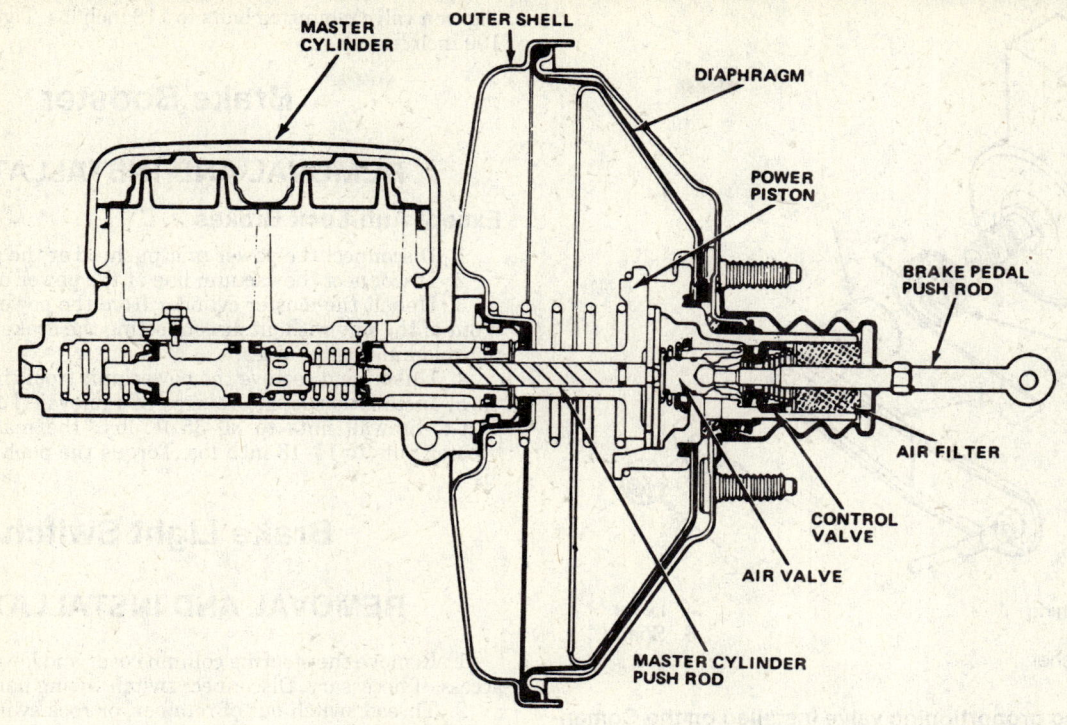

Single diaphragm power booster

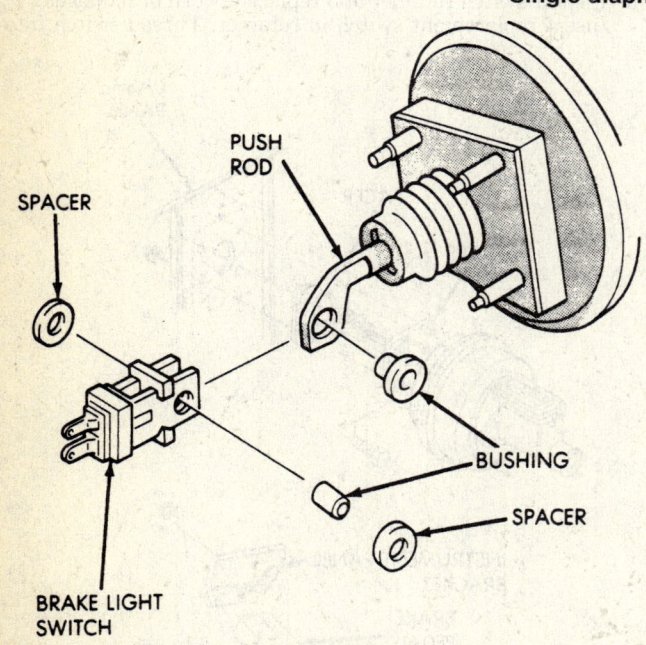

Brakelight switch with cruise control

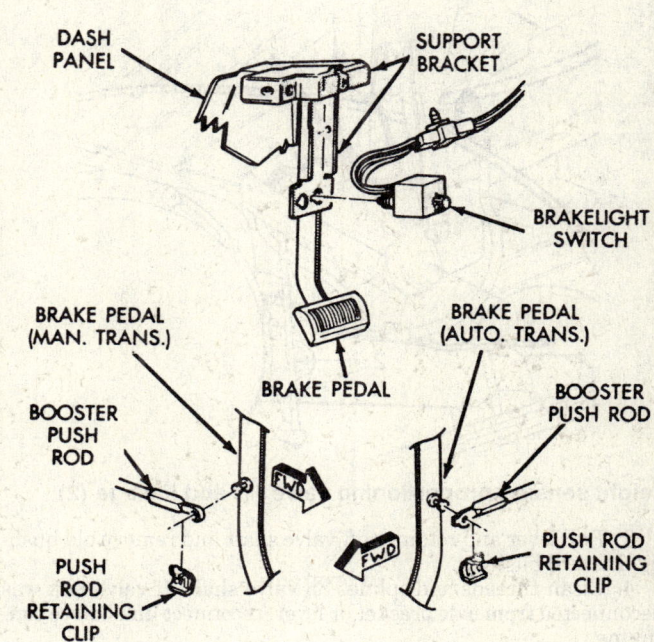

Brake pedal and brake light switch

place or rock up/down until switch plunger contacts brake pedal.

5. Connect wiring harness and perform adjustment procedure below.

SWITCH ADJUSTMENT

NOTE: On some vehicles equipped with air conditioning, remove the screws attaching the evaporator housing to the instrument panel and move the housing away from the panel.

1. Hold the brake pedal in the applied position.
2. Push the stop light switch through the mounting bracket until it stops against the brake pedal bracket. Release the pedal to set the switch in the proper position.
3. Check the position of the switch. The switch plunger should be in the ON position and activate the brake lights after a brake pedal travel of 9.5–15.5mm ($3/8$–$5/8$ in.).

BRAKES 9

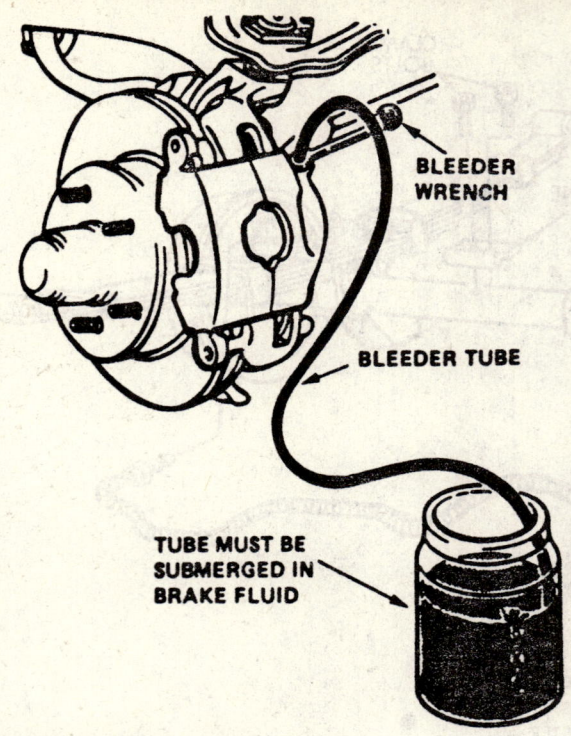

Brake bleeding equipment

Bleeding the Brakes

Except Anti-Lock Brakes

NOTE: This procedure requires the use of a special tool.

The hydraulic brake system must be bled whenever a fluid line has been disconnected or air gets into the system. A leak in the system may sometimes be indicated by the presence of a spongy brake pedal. Air trapped in the system is compressible and does not permit the pressure applied to the brake pedal to be transmitted solidly through to the brakes. The system must be absolutely free from air at all times. When bleeding brakes, begin at the wheel most distant from the master cylinder first, the next most distant second, and so on. During the bleeding operation, the master cylinder must be kept at least $3/4$ full of brake fluid.

NOTE: When bleeding the brakes, the metering section of the pressure differential valve must be held open. Loosen the front mounting bolt of the valve and insert Tool J–23709, or J–26869, or its fabricated equivalent, under the bolt. Push in on the metering valve stem to open it and retighten the bolt to hold the tool in place. When bleeding is finished, loosen the bolt, remove the tool and retighten the bolt.

To bleed the master cylinder, loosen one of the line fittings at the master cylinder. Have an assistant slowly depress the brake pedal and hold it at the floor. When the pedal reaches the floor, tighten the fitting. Repeat this procedure until just fluid emerges at the fitting. Repeat the entire bleeding procedure for the other brake line. Make sure that you have absorbent rags under the fittings to catch the fluid. Wear goggles to avoid any fluid spray from hitting your eyes.

To bleed the brakes, first carefully clean all dirt from around the master cylinder filler plug. If a bleeder tank is used, follow the manufacturer's instructions. Remove the filler plug and fill the master cylinder to the lower edge of the filler neck. Clean off the bleeder connections at all of the wheel cylinders or disc brake calipers. Attach the bleeder hose and fixture to the right rear wheel cylinder bleeder screw and place the end of the tube in a glass jar, submerged in brake fluid. Open the bleeder valve $1/2$–$3/4$ of a turn. Have an assistant depress the brake pedal and allow it to return slowly. Continue this pumping action to force any air out of the system. When bubbles cease to appear at the end of the bleeder hose, close the bleeder valve and remove the hose. Check the level of the brake fluid in the master cylinder and add fluid, if necessary.

After the bleeding operation at each caliper or wheel cylinder has been completed, fill the master cylinder reservoir and replace the filler plug.

NOTE: Never reuse brake fluid which has been removed from the lines through the bleeding process because it contains air bubbles and dirt.

Brake Lines and Hoses

When servicing brake lines several precautions must be taken to prevent damage to the line.
• Clean fittings of rust and road build-up before attempting to remove
• Spray fittings with penetrating oil to loosen rust and allow fitting to be removed easier
• Always use a *flare nut* wrench to prevent rounding the line fittings
• If possible, always use a backup wrench
• To prevent stripping, tighten fittings to the proper torque
• Plug all open lines to prevent contaminates from entering the braking system
• Always refill the system with fresh brake fluid. Never return used brake fluid to the reservoir
• When repairing damaged brake lines (hard line), it is recommended that only hard lines with double flare ends be used. (some states DO NOT allow compression fittings to be used).

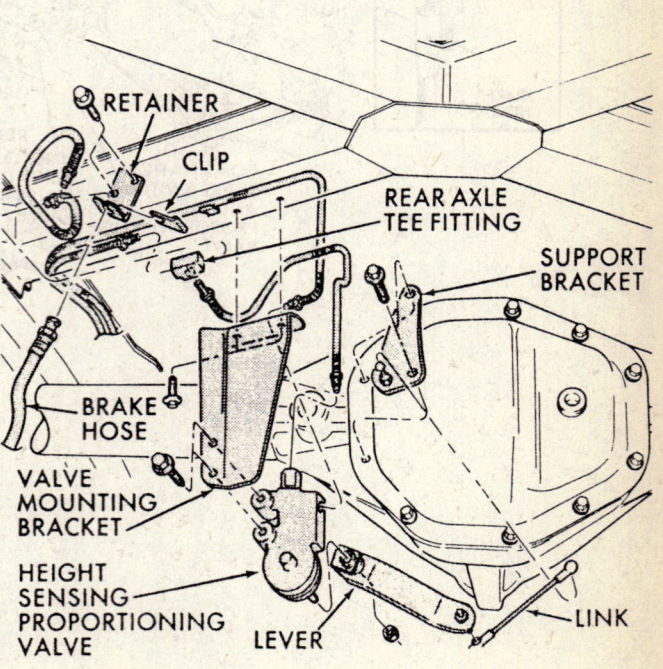

Comanche height sensing valve with Model 35 rear axle

9-13

9 BRAKES

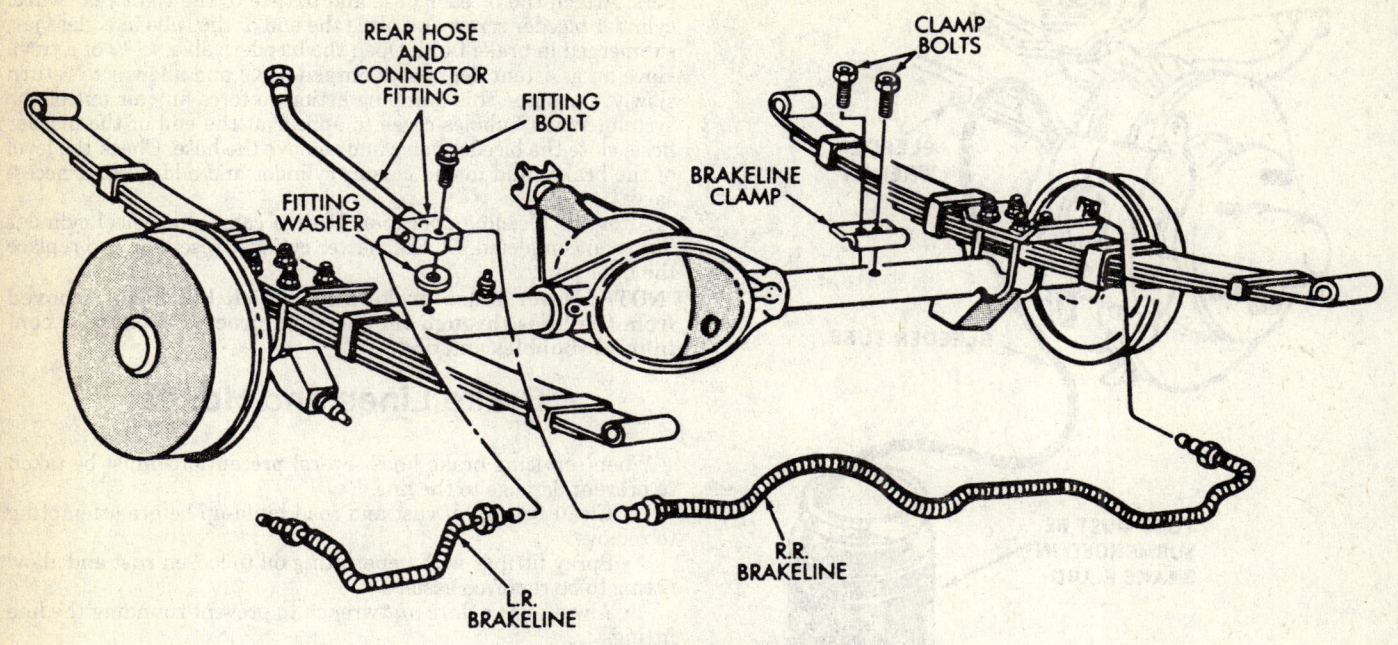

Rear brake line connections

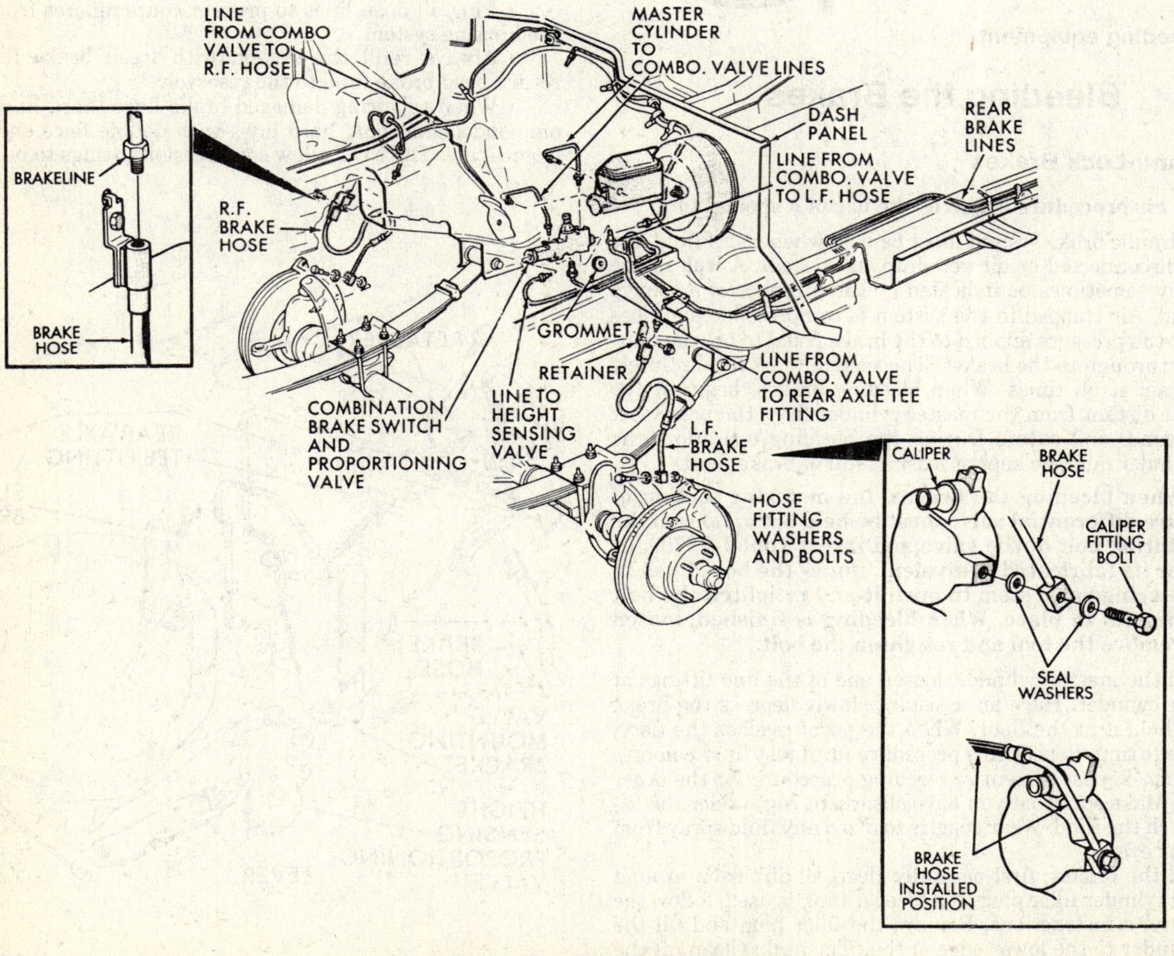

Front end brake line routing

9-14

BRAKES 9

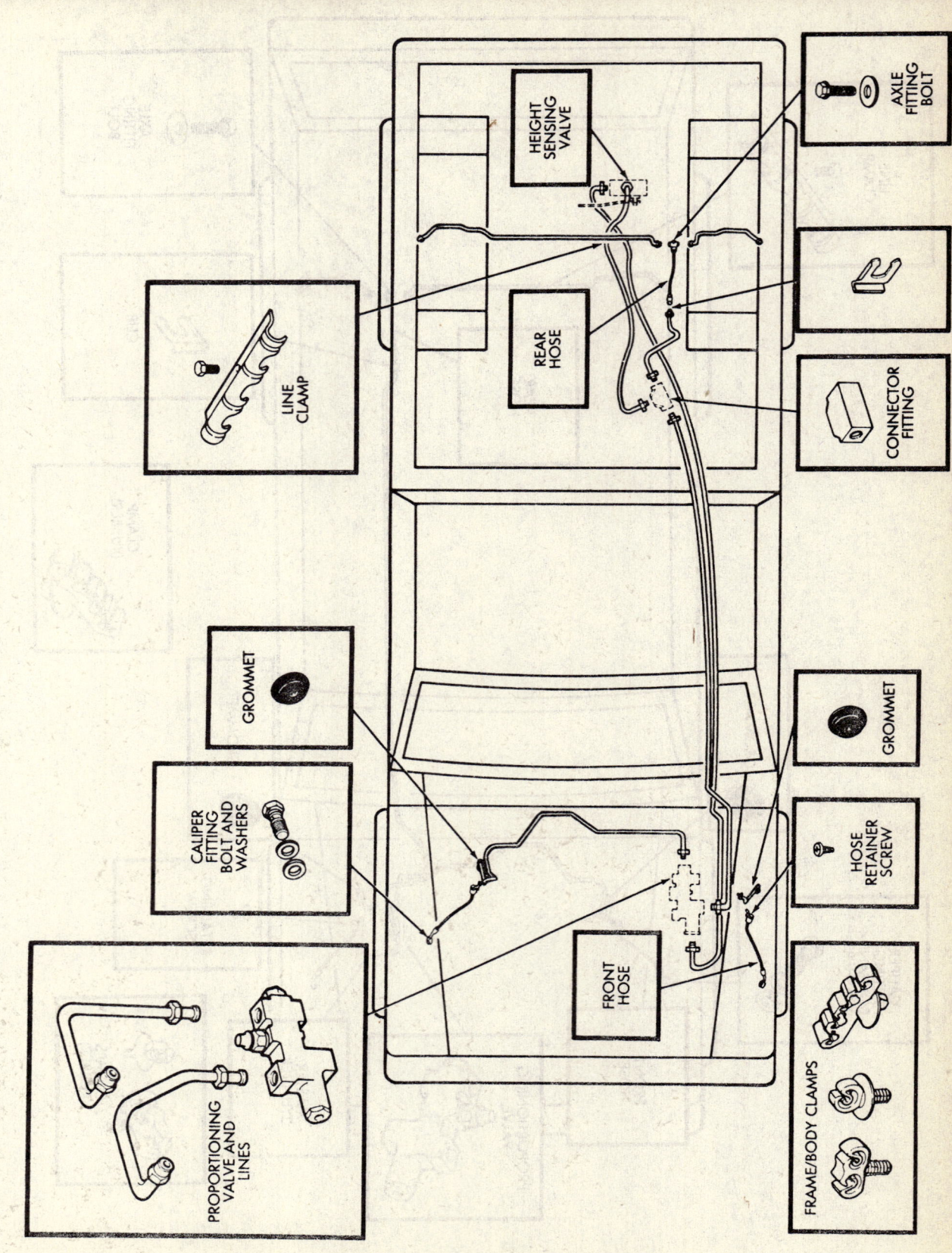

Comanche brake line schematic

9-15

9 BRAKES

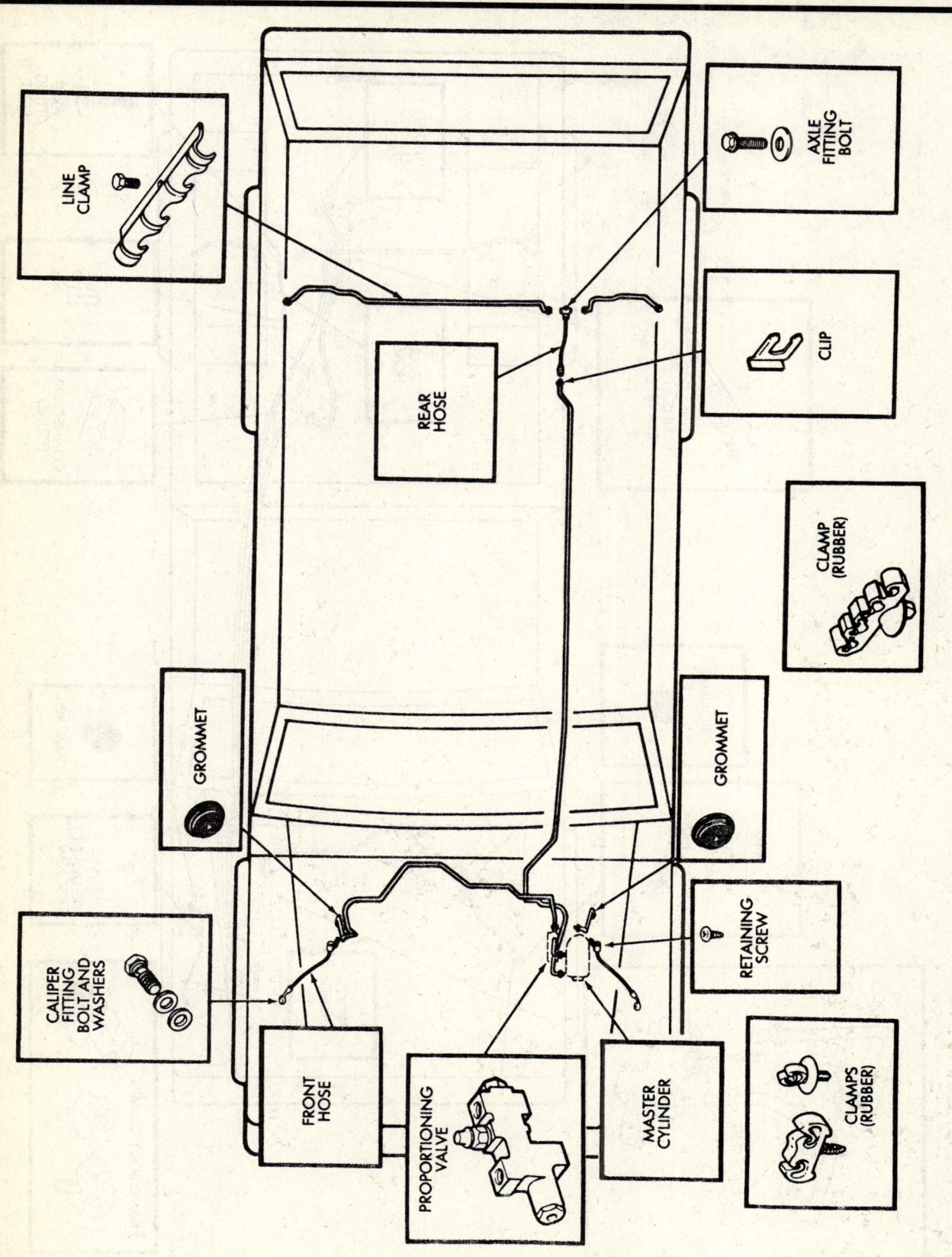

Cherokee/Wagoneer brake line schematic

BRAKES 9

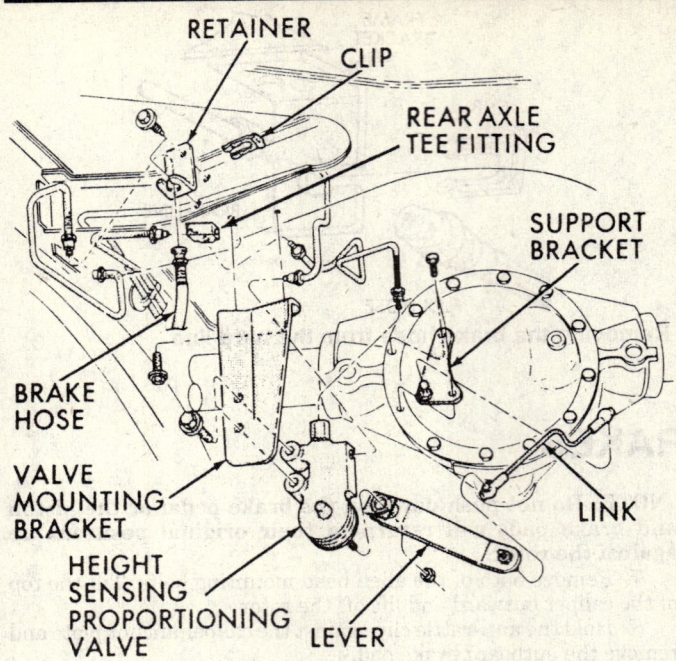

Comanche height sensing valve with Model 44 rear axle

REPLACING RUBBER BRAKE HOSE

Rubber brake hose is located at points on the vehicle where moving suspension parts are encountered—brake caliper-to-frame and rear axle-to-frame. Since these hoses are constantly flexing, they should be checked for wear and damage at regular intervals. When hoses are found to be deteriorating, replace them immediately. A leak in any brake line (hard line or rubber brake hose) will result in decreased braking capacity.

1. Raise and support the vehicle safely and remove the wheel.

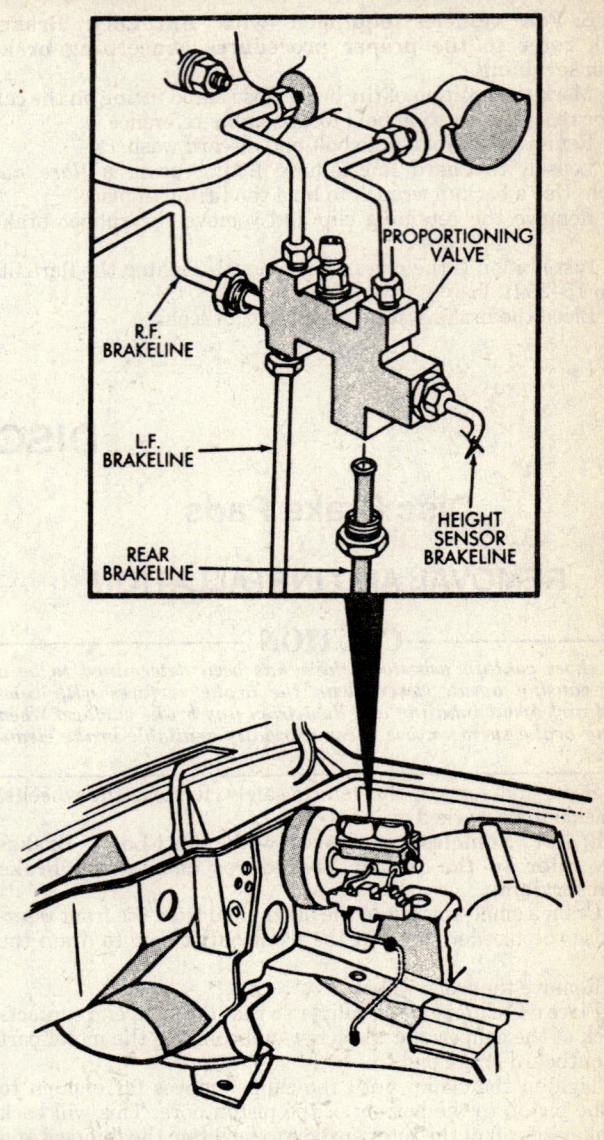

Proportioning valve connections

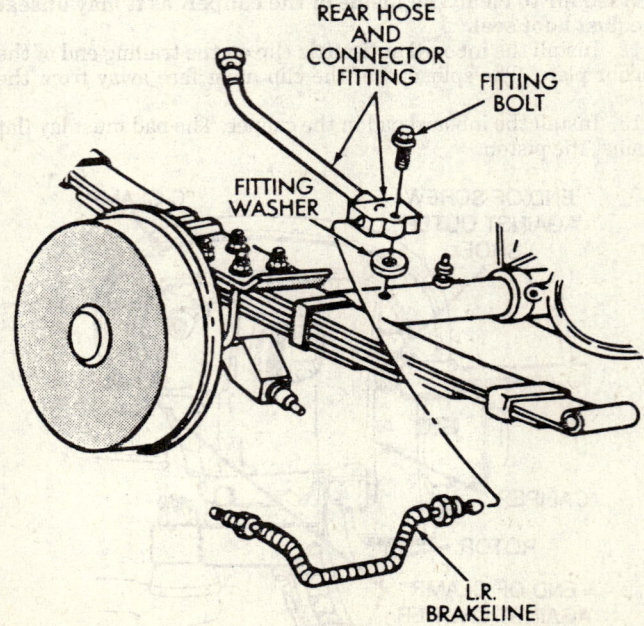

Rear brake hose between rear axle and frame

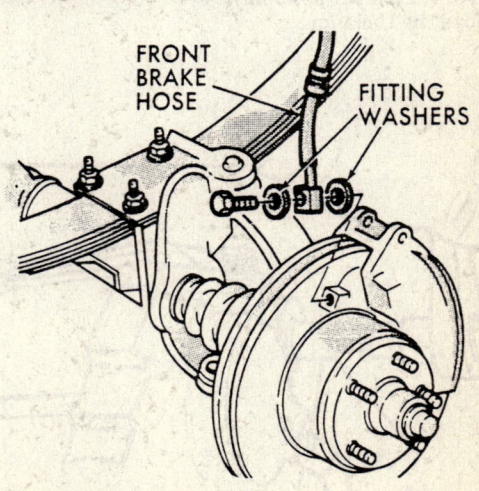

Front brake hose between caliper and frame

9-17

9 BRAKES

NOTE: For vehicles equipped with Anti-Lock Brakes (ABS), refer to the proper procedures concerning brake system servicing.

2. Mark the position of the brake hose banjo fitting on the caliper (or rear axle junction box) for assembly reference.
3. Remove the brake hose bolt and discard washers.
4. Loosen the hard line-to-hose fitting using a *flare nut* wrench. Use a backup wrench to hold the fitting in place.
5. Remove the retaining clip and remove the rubber brake hose.
6. Installation is the reverse of removal. Tighten the flare fitting to 15–25 ft. lbs.
7. Bleed the brake system and check for leaks.

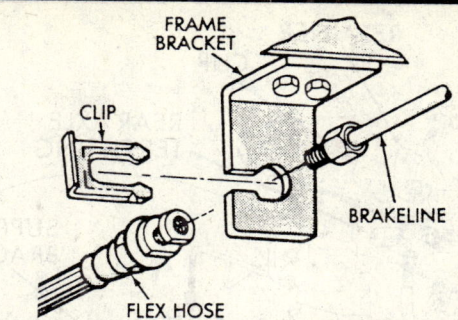
Removing the brake hose from the hard line

DISC BRAKES

Disc Brake Pads

REMOVAL AND INSTALLATION

CAUTION

Brake shoes contain asbestos, which has been determined to be a cancer causing agent. Never clean the brake surfaces with compressed air! Avoid inhaling any dust from any brake surface! When cleaning brake surfaces, use a commercially available brake cleaning fluid.

1. Raise and support the vehicle safely. Remove the wheel(s) on the side to be worked on.

NOTE: For vehicles equipped with Anti-Lock Brakes (ABS), refer to the proper procedures concerning brake system servicing.

2. Drain a small amount of the brake fluid from the front reservoir. Use the bleeder screw at the front outlet port to drain the fluid.
3. Remove the front wheels.
4. Place a C-clamp on the caliper so that the solid end contacts the back of the caliper and the screw end contacts the metal part of the outboard brake pad.
5. Tighten the clamp until the caliper moves far enough to force the piston to the bottom of the piston bore. This will back the brake pads off of the rotor surface to facilitate the removal and installation of the caliper assembly.
6. Remove the C-clamp.

NOTE: Do not push down on the brake pedal or the piston and brake pads will return to their original positions up against the rotor.

7. Remove both of the allen head mounting bolts. Tilt the top of the caliper outward and lift off the rotor.
8. Hold the anti-rattle clip against the caliper anchor plate and remove the outboard brake pad.
9. Remove the inboard pad and its anti-rattle clip.
10. Use a piece of wire to support the caliper so that no tension is placed on the brake hose. DO NOT allow the caliper to hang by the brake hose.

To Install:

11. Clean all the mounting holes and bushing grooves in the caliper ears. Clean the mounting bolts. Replace the bolts if they are corroded or if the threads are damaged. Wipe the inside of the caliper clean, including the exterior of the dust boot. Inspect the dust boot for cuts or cracks and for proper seating in the piston bore. If evidence of fluid leakage is noted, the caliper should be rebuilt.

NOTE: Do not use abrasives on the bolts in order not to destroy their protective plating. You should not use compressed air to clean the inside of the caliper, as it may unseat the dust boot seal.

12. Install the inboard anti-rattle clip on the trailing end of the anchor plate. The split end of the clip must face away from the rotor.
13. Install the inboard pad in the caliper. The pad must lay flat against the piston.

Removing the caliper mounting bolts

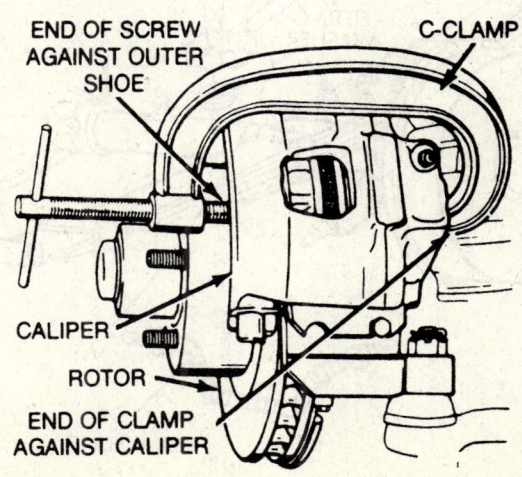
Bottoming the caliper piston

BRAKES 9

14. Install the outboard pad in the caliper while holding the anti-rattle clip.

15. With the pads installed, position the caliper over the rotor.

NOTE: Before securing the caliper, ensure the brake hose is not twisted, kinked or touching any chassis parts.

16. Lubricate the caliper pins and bushings with silicone grease. Line up the mounting holes in the caliper and the support bracket and insert the mounting bolts. Make sure that the bolts pass under the retaining ears on the inboard shoes. Push the bolts through until they engage the holes of the outboard pad and caliper ears. Thread the bolts into the support bracket and tighten them to 7–15 ft. lbs.

— CAUTION —
On models with manual/power brakes, pump the pedal until the caliper pistons and brake shoes are seated. On models with anti-lock brakes, turn the ignition ON and allow the booster pump to build pressure. Pump the brake pedal until the shoes are seated and the indicator lights turn off.

17. Fill the master cylinder with brake fluid and pump the brake pedal to seat the pads.

18. Install the wheel assembly and lower the vehicle. Check the level of the brake fluid in the master cylinder and fill as necessary.

Calipers

REMOVAL AND INSTALLATION

— CAUTION —
Brake shoes contain asbestos, which has been determined to be a cancer causing agent. Never clean the brake surfaces with compressed air! Avoid inhaling any dust from any brake surface! When cleaning brake surfaces, use a commercially available brake cleaning fluid.

1. Raise and support the vehicle safely. Remove the wheel(s) on the side to be worked on.

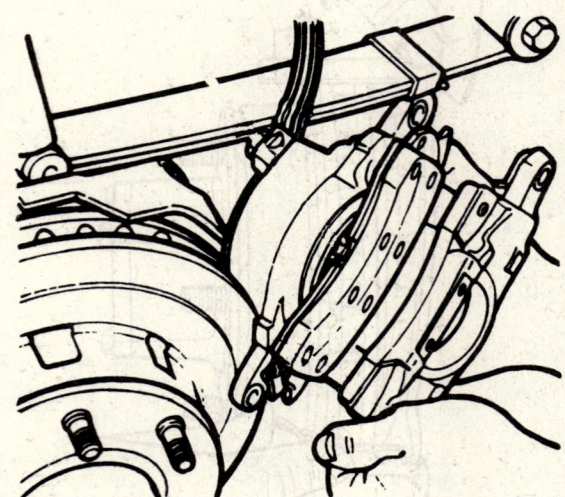

Removing the caliper from the rotor

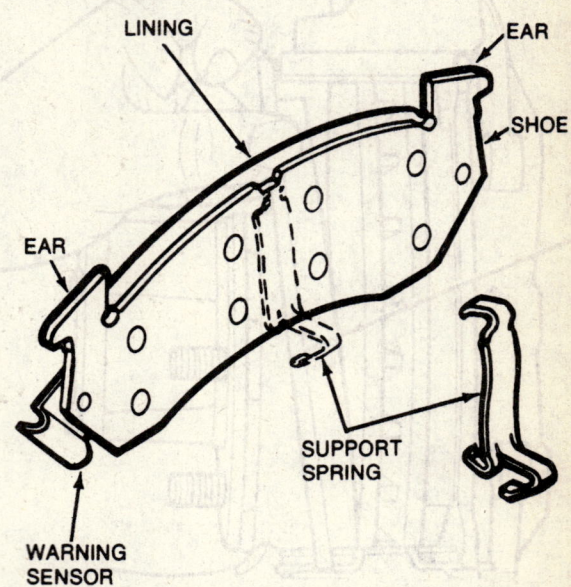

Installing the support spring on the inboard brake pad

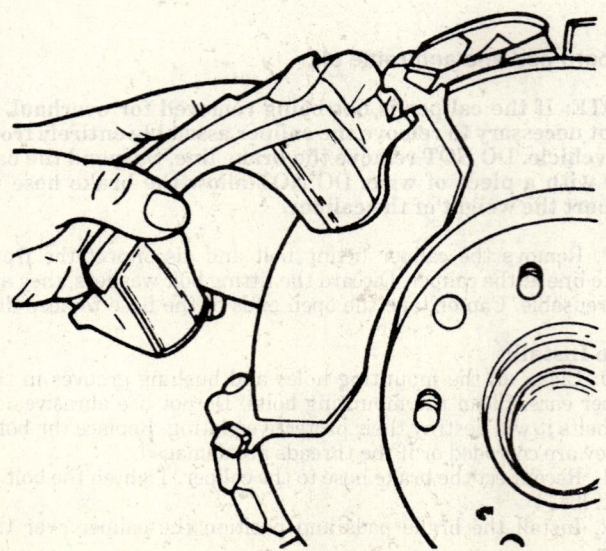

Lifting off the caliper

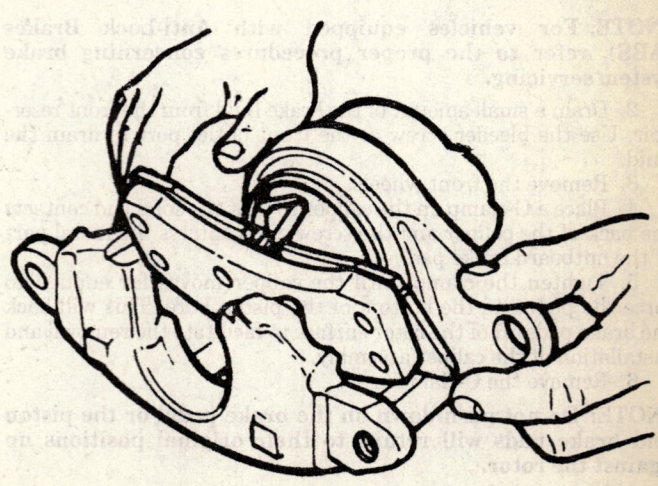

Installing the inboard pad

9-19

9 BRAKES

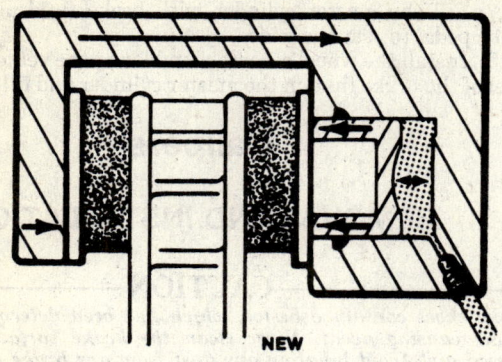 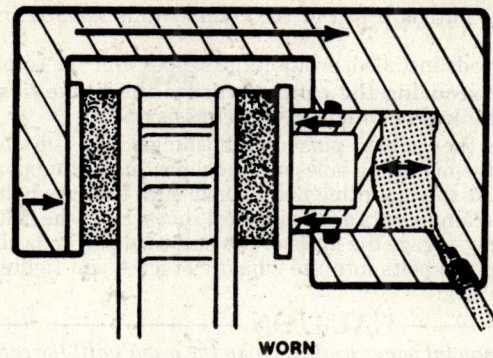

Piston extension on new and worn brake pads

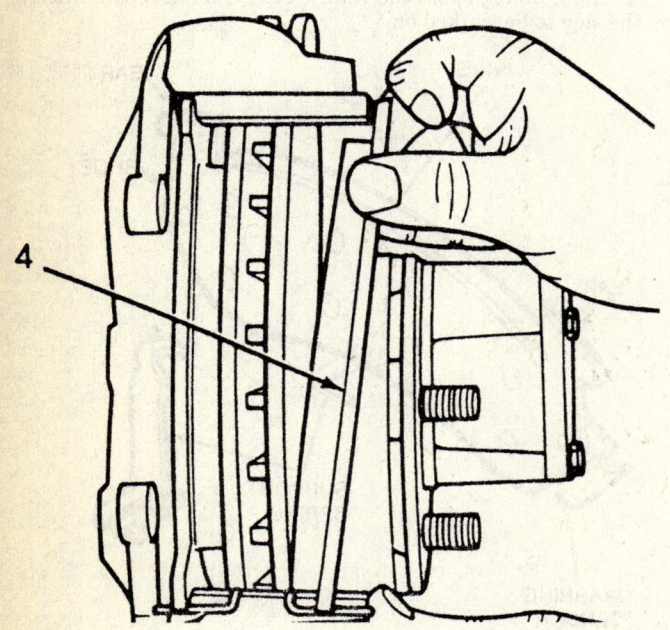

Anti-rattle clip (3) and outboard pad (4)

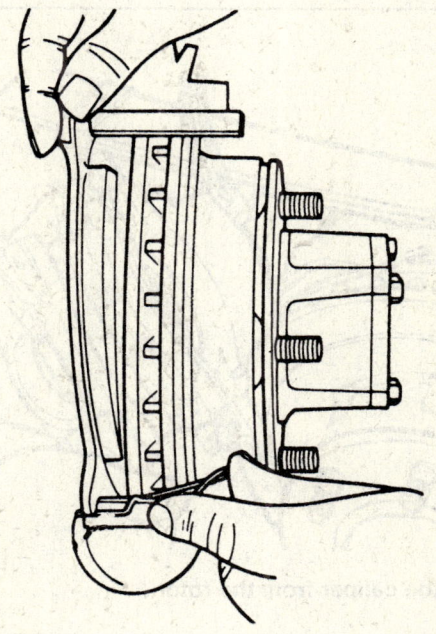

Inboard pad and anti-rattle clip

NOTE: For vehicles equipped with Anti-Lock Brakes (ABS), refer to the proper procedures concerning brake system servicing.

2. Drain a small amount of the brake fluid from the front reservoir. Use the bleeder screw at the front outlet port to drain the fluid.
3. Remove the front wheels.
4. Place a C-clamp on the caliper so that the solid end contacts the back of the caliper and the screw end contacts the metal part of the outboard brake pad.
5. Tighten the clamp until the caliper moves far enough to force the piston to the bottom of the piston bore. This will back the brake pads off of the rotor surface to facilitate the removal and installation of the caliper assembly.
6. Remove the C-clamp.

NOTE: Do not push down on the brake pedal or the piston and brake pads will return to their original positions up against the rotor.

7. Remove both of the allen head mounting bolts. Tilt the top of the caliper outward and lift off the rotor.
8. Remove the brake pads from the caliper.

NOTE: If the caliper is not being removed for overhaul, it is not necessary to remove the caliper assembly entirely from the vehicle. DO NOT remove the brake line. Suspend the caliper with a piece of wire. DO NOT allow the brake hose to support the weight of the caliper.

9. Remove the caliper fitting bolt and disconnect the front brake line at the caliper. Discard the fitting bolt washers, they are not reusable. Cap or tape the open ends of the hose to keep dirt out.

To Install:
10. Clean all the mounting holes and bushing grooves in the caliper ears. Clean the mounting bolts. Do not use abrasives on the bolts it will destroy their protective plating. Replace the bolts if they are corroded or if the threads are damaged.
11. Reconnect the brake hose to the caliper. Tighten the bolt to 23 ft. lbs.
12. Install the brake pads and position the caliper over the rotor.

NOTE: Before securing the caliper, ensure the brake hose is not twisted, kinked or touching any chassis parts.

BRAKES 9

13. Lubricate the caliper pins and bushings with silicone grease. Line up the mounting holes in the caliper and the support bracket and insert the mounting bolts. Make sure that the bolts pass under the retaining ears on the inboard shoes. Push the bolts through until they engage the holes of the outboard pad and caliper ears. Thread the bolts into the support bracket and tighten them to 30 ft. lbs.

CAUTION
On models with manual/power brakes, pump the pedal until the caliper pistons and brake shoes are seated. On models with anti-lock brakes, turn the ignition ON and allow the booster pump to build pressure. Pump the brake pedal until the shoes are seated and the indicator lights turn off.

14. Fill the master cylinder with brake fluid and pump the brake pedal to seat the pads.
15. Install the wheel assembly and lower the vehicle. Check the level of the brake fluid in the master cylinder and fill as necessary.

OVERHAUL

1. Remove the caliper assembly and remove the brake pads. If the pads are to be reused, mark their location in the caliper.

NOTE: For vehicles equipped with Anti-Lock Brakes (ABS), refer to the proper procedures concerning brake system servicing.

2. Clean the caliper exterior with brake cleaning solvent or clean brake fluid. Drain any residual fluid from the caliper and place it on a clean work surface.

NOTE: **Removal of the caliper piston requires the use of compressed air. Do not, under any circumstances, place your fingers in front of the piston in any attempt to catch or protect it when applying compressed air to remove the piston.**

3. Pad the interior of the caliper with clean cloths. Use several cloths and pad the interior well to avoid damaging the piston when it comes out of the bore.
4. Insert an air nozzle into the inlet hole in the caliper and gently apply air pressure on the piston to push it out of the bore. Use only enough air pressure to ease the piston out of the bore.
5. Pry the dust boot out of the bore with a screwdriver. Use caution during this operation to prevent scratching the bore. Discard the dust boot.
6. Remove the piston seal from the piston bore and discard the seal. Use only non-scratching implements such as a pencil, wooden stick or a piece of plastic to remove the seal. Do not use a metal tool, as it could very easily scratch the bore.
7. Remove the bleeder screw. Remove and discard the sleeves and rubber bushings from the mounting ears.
8. Clean all the parts with brake cleaning solvent or clean brake fluid. Blow out all of the passages in the caliper and bleeder valve. Use only dry and filtered compressed air. Replace the mounting bolts if they are corroded or if the threads are damaged.

NOTE: **Do not attempt to clean the attaching bolts with abrasives, as their protective plating may be removed.**

9. Examine the piston for defects. Replace the piston if it is nicked, scratched, corroded or the protective plating is worn off. Examine the caliper piston bore for the same defects as the piston. The bore is not plated and minor stains or corrosion can be polished with crocus cloth.

NOTE: **Do not attempt to refinish the piston in any way. The outside diameter is the sealing surface and is made to very close tolerances. Removal of the nickel-chrome plating will lead to pitting, rusting and eventual cocking of the piston in the piston bore. Do not use emery cloth or similar abrasives on the piston bore. If the bore does not clean up with crocus cloth, replace the caliper. Clean the caliper thoroughly with brake cleaning solvent or brake fluid if the bore was polished with crocus cloth.**

10. Lubricate the bore and new seal with brake fluid and install the seal in the groove in the bore.
11. Lubricate the piston with brake fluid and install the new dust boot on the piston. Assemble the dust boot into the piston groove so that the fold in the boot faces the open end of the piston. Slide the metal portion of the dust boot over the open end of the piston and push the retainer toward the back of the piston until the lip on the fold seats in the piston groove. Then push the retainer portion of the boot forward until the boot is flush with the rim at the open end of the piston and snaps into place.
12. Insert the piston in the bore, being careful not to unseat the piston seal. Push the piston to the bottom of the bore. It requires 50–100 lb. of force to bottom the piston.
13. Position the dust boot retainer in the counter bore at the top of the piston bore. Seat the dust boot retainer with a flat-ended punch by tapping the metal ring of the dust boot into place.

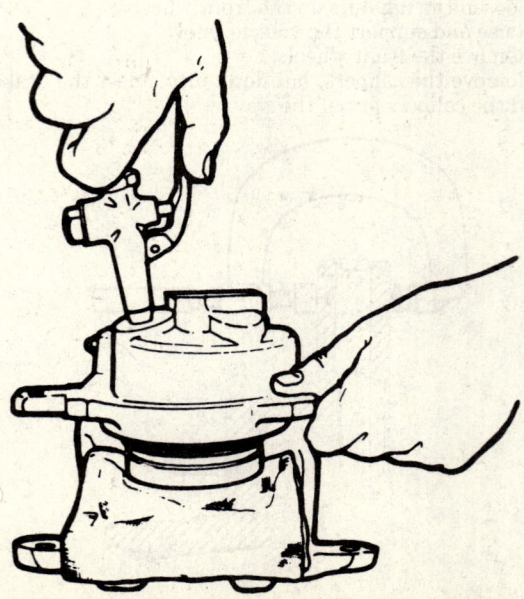

Removing the piston with compressed air

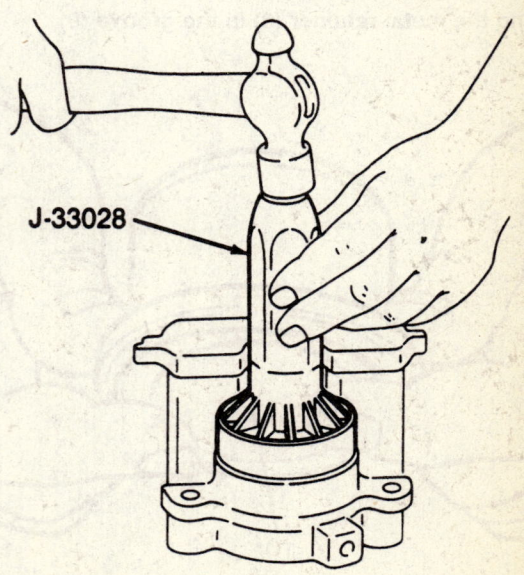

Seating the metal retainer

9 BRAKES

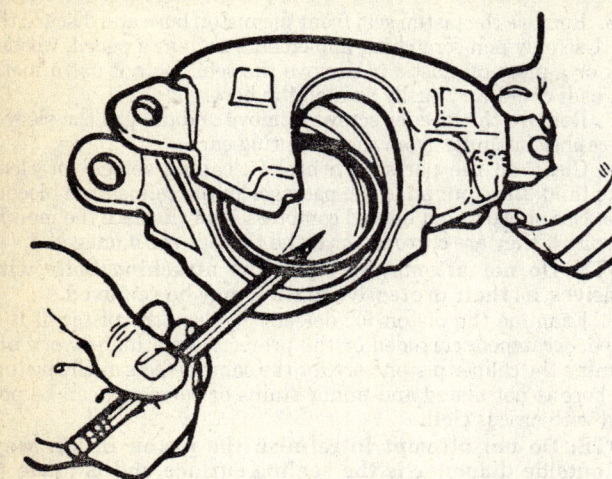

Removing the O-ring

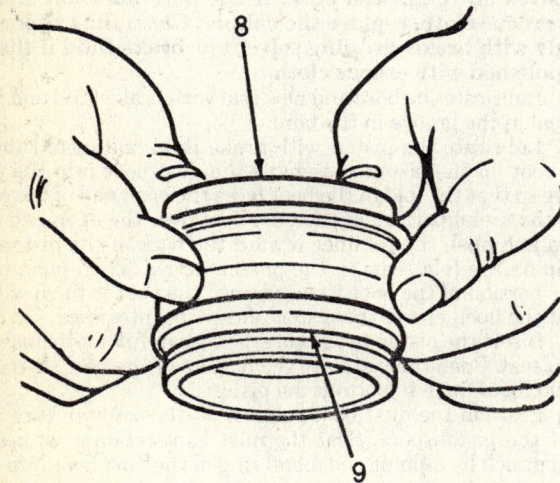

Installing the metal retainer (8) in the groove (9)

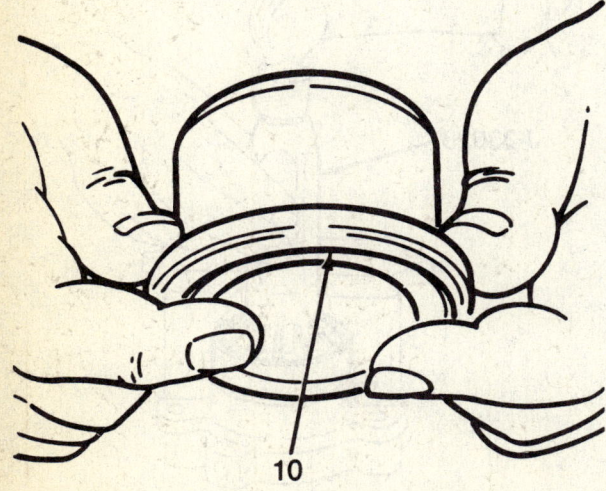

Dust seal (10) installation

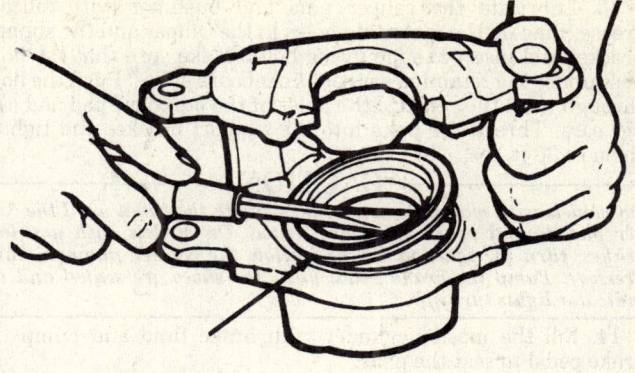

Removing the dust seal

Be careful not do damage the rubber portion of the dust boot. The metal retainer portion of the boot must be evenly seated in the counterbore, using tool J–33028 or J–22904, and fit below the face of the caliper.

14. Install the bleeder screw. Tighten it to 50–140 inch lbs.
15. Connect the brake line to the caliper using new copper gaskets. tighten to 23 ft. lbs.
16. Install the brake pads, sleeves and rubber bushings.
17. Install the caliper and tighten the mounting bolts to 30 ft. lbs. Bleed the hydraulic system.

Brake Rotor

REMOVAL AND INSTALLATION

CAUTION

Brake shoes contain asbestos, which has been determined to be a cancer causing agent. Never clean the brake surfaces with compressed air! Avoid inhaling any dust from any brake surface! When cleaning brake surfaces, use a commercially available brake cleaning fluid.

4-Wheel Drive

1. Loosen the lug nuts on the front wheels.
2. Raise and support the vehicle safely.
3. Remove the front wheels.
4. Remove the calipers, but don't disconnect the brake lines. Suspend the calipers out of the way.

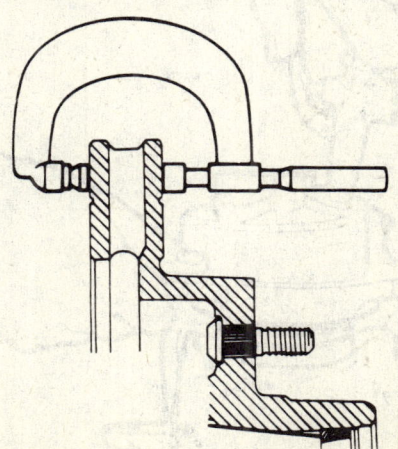

Measuring the rotor thickness with a micrometer

BRAKES 9

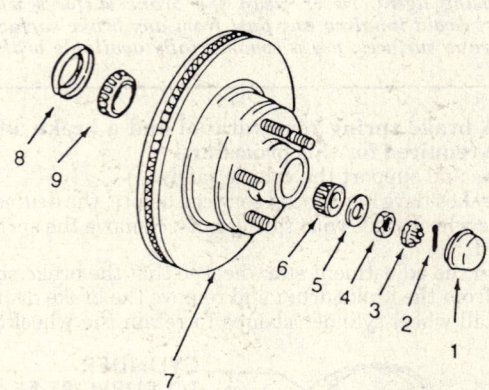

Rotor and hub assembly used on 4WD vehicles

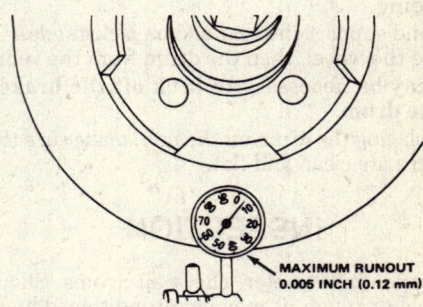

Checking the rotor lateral runout

1. Grease cap
2. Cotter pin
3. Nut cap
4. Nut
5. Washer
6. Outer bearing
7. Hub and rotor
8. Inner seal
9. Inner bearing

Rotor used on 2WD vehicles

5. Remove the rotor.
6. Installation is the reverse of removal. Tighten wheel lug nuts to 75 ft. lbs.

2-Wheel Drive

1. Raise and support the front end on jackstands.
2. Remove the wheels.
3. Remove the caliper without disconnecting the brake line. Suspend it out of the way.
4. Remove the grease cap, cotter pin, nut cap, nut, and washer from the spindle.
5. Pull slowly on the hub and catch the outer bearing as it falls.
6. Remove the hub and rotor. The inner bearing and seal can be removed by prying out and discarding the inner seal.
7. Clean and repack the hub and bearings, install the inner bearing and a new seal.
8. Position the hub and rotor on the spindle and install the outer bearing.
9. Install the washer and nut.
10. While turning the rotor, torque the nut to 25 ft. lbs. to seat the bearings.
11. Back off the nut 1/2 turn, and, while turning the rotor, torque the nut to 19 inch lbs.
12. Install the nut cap and a new cotter pin. Install the grease cap.
13. Install the caliper.
14. Install the wheels.

Wheel Bearings

For detailed front wheel bearing service, see Section 1.

INSPECTION AND MEASUREMENT

Check the rotor for surface cracks, nicks, broken cooling fins and scoring of both contact surfaces. Some scoring of the surfaces may occur during normal use. Scoring that is 0.38mm (0.015 in.) deep or less is not detrimental to the operation of the brakes.

NOTE: Remember to adjust the preload on the wheel bearings after the runout measurement has been taken.

If the rotor surface is heavily rusted or scaled, clean both surfaces on a disc brake lathe using flat sanding discs before attempting any measurements.

With the hub and rotor assembly mounted on the spindle of the

9-23

9 BRAKES

vehicle or a disc brake lathe and all play removed from the wheel bearings, assemble a dial indicator so that the stem contacts the center of the rotor braking surface. Zero the dial indicator before taking any measurements. Lateral runout must not exceed 0.127mm (0.005 in.) with a maximum rate of change not to exceed 0.025mm (0.001 in.) in 30° of rotation.

Excessive runout will cause the rotor to wobble and knock the piston back into the caliper, causing increased pedal travel, noise and vibration.

Check the Brake Specifications Chart for rotor thickness. Discard the rotor if it is not within the specification.

DRUM BRAKES

Brake Drums

REMOVAL AND INSTALLATION

—— CAUTION ——
Brake shoes contain asbestos, which has been determined to be a cancer causing agent. Never clean the brake surfaces with compressed air! Avoid inhaling any dust from any brake surface! When cleaning brake surfaces, use a commercially available brake cleaning fluid.

NOTE: For vehicles equipped with Anti-Lock Brakes (ABS), refer to the proper procedures concerning brake system servicing.

1. Raise and support the rear end on jackstands.
2. Remove the wheel, then the drum from the vehicle.

NOTE: It may be necessary to back off the brake adjusters to remove the drum.

3. When placing the drum on the hub, make sure that the contacting surfaces are clean and flat.

INSPECTION

Using an inside micrometer, check all drums. Should a brake drum be scored or rough, it may be reconditioned by grinding or turning on a lathe. Do not remove more than 0.76mm (0.030 in.) thickness of metal. If a drum is reconditioned in this manner, it is recommended that either the correct factory supplied 0.76mm (0.030 in.) oversize lining must be installed, or a shim equal in thickness to the metal removed must be placed between the lining and the brake shoe so that the arc of the lining will be the same as that of the drum.

Brake Shoes

REMOVAL AND INSTALLATION

—— CAUTION ——
Brake shoes contain asbestos, which has been determined to be a cancer causing agent. Never clean the brake surfaces with compressed air! Avoid inhaling any dust from any brake surface! When cleaning brake surfaces, use a commercially available brake cleaning fluid.

NOTE: A brake spring removal tool and a brake adjusting gauge are required for this procedure.

1. Raise and support the vehicle safely.
2. If brakes have never been serviced before, the drums will be held on the wheel studs with spring nuts. Remove the spring nuts and discard.
3. Turn the adjustment starwheel so that the brake shoes are retracted from the brake drum and remove the brake drum.
4. Install wheel cylinder clamps to retain the wheel cylinder

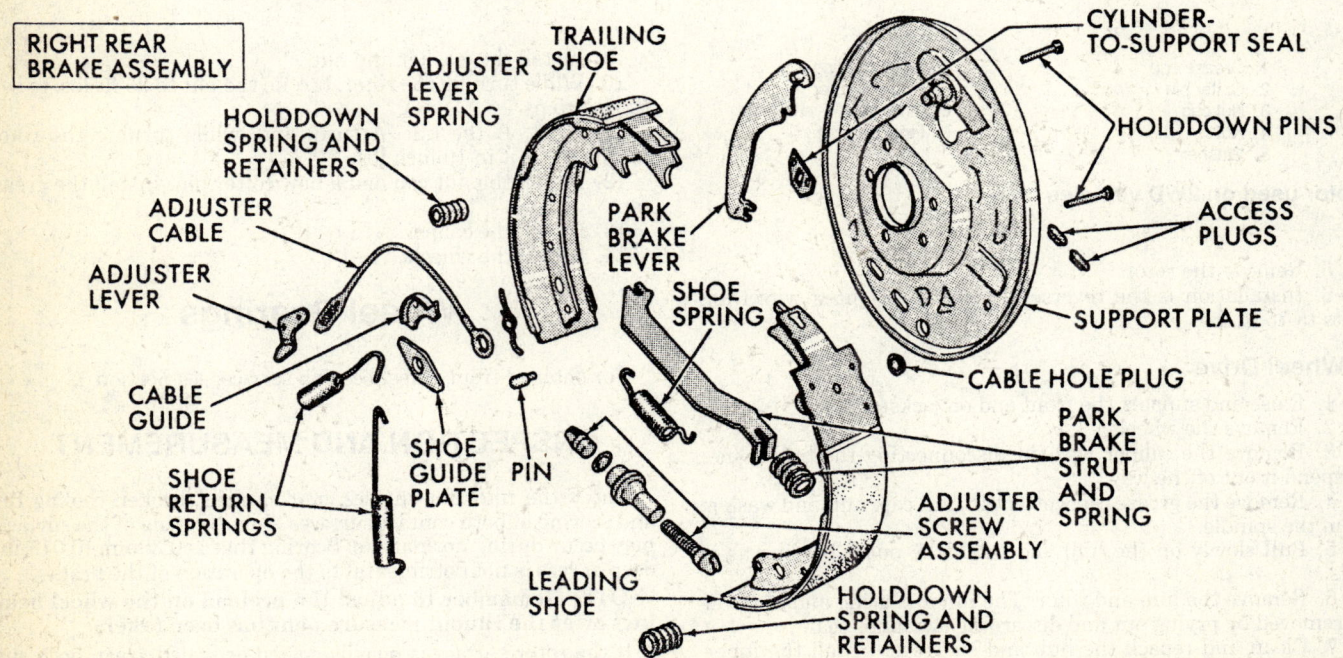

9-inch drum brake components

Brakes 9

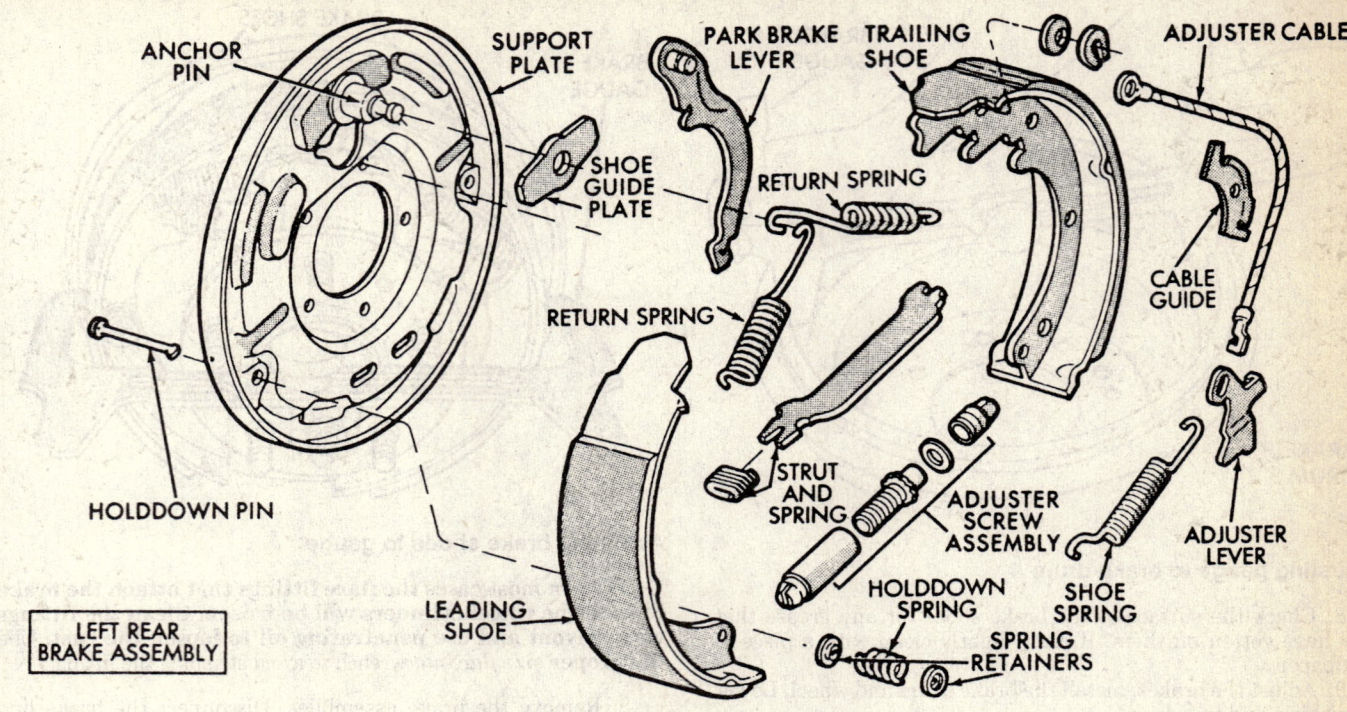

10-inch drum brake components

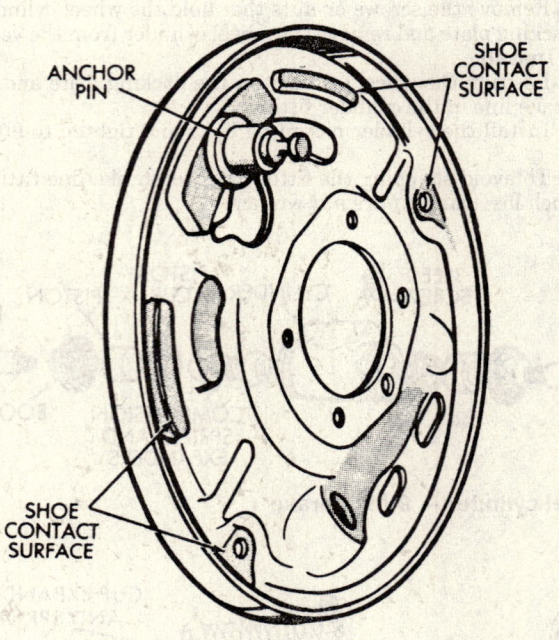

Lubricate shoe contact surfaces — 10-inch drum brake backing plate shown

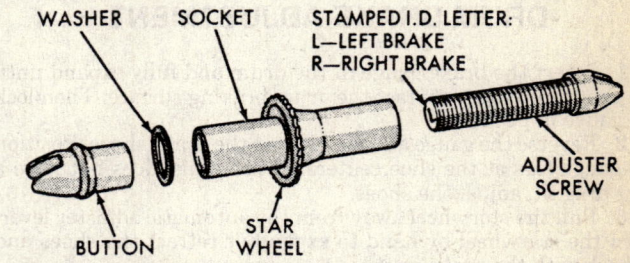

Starwheel adjuster screw components

pistons in place and prevent leakage of brake fluid while replacing the shoes.

5. Remove the U-clip and washer securing the adjuster cable to the parking brake lever.
6. Remove the adjuster cable, cable guide, adjuster lever and adjuster springs. Remove the return springs with a brake spring remover tool.
7. Remove the holddown washers and springs and remove the brake shoes.

To Install:

8. Clean the backing plate with a brush or cloth. Place a dab of Lubriplate® on each spot where the brake shoes rub on the backing plate.

NOTE: Always replace brake linings in axle sets. Never replace linings on one side or just on one wheel.

9. Thoroughly clean and lubricate adjuster cable guides, adjuster screw and pivot, parking brake lever and lever pivot pin with multi purpose grease.
10. Apply a thin coat of multi-purpose chassis lube to the mounting pads on the backing plate.
11. Transfer the parking brake actuating lever to the new secondary shoe.
12. Position the brake shoes on the backing plate and install the holddown springs. Don't forget to engage the parking brake lever with the cable.
13. Install the parking brake actuating bar and spring between the parking brake lever and primary shoe.
14. Install the self-adjusting cable, cable guide and upper return springs.
15. Thoroughly clean the starwheel and lightly lubricate the threads with lithium based grease.
16. Install the starwheel.
17. Install the self-adjusting cam and lower spring. A big pair of locking pliers is good for this job.

9 BRAKES

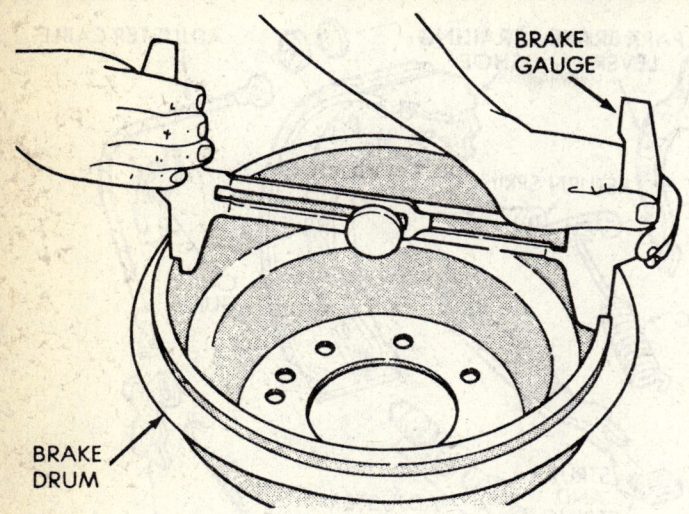

Adjusting gauge to brake drum

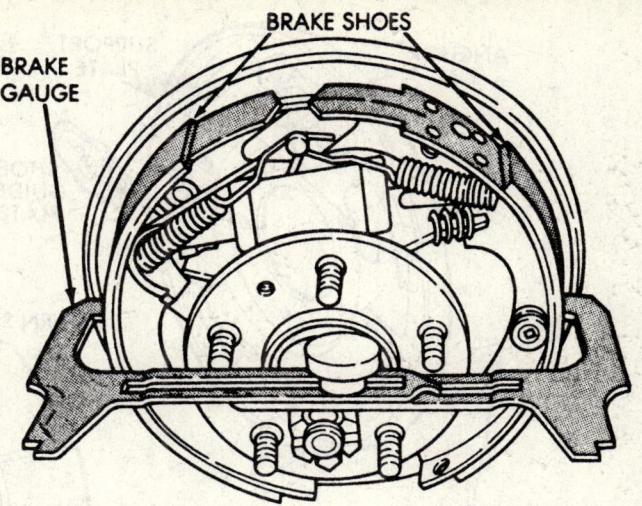

Adjusting brake shoes to gauge

18. Check the surface of the brake shoes for any grease that may have gotten on them. If dirty, lightly clean with a piece of sandpaper.
19. Adjust the brakes, install the brake drum and wheel. Lower the vehicle and test drive.

DRUM BRAKE ADJUSTMENT

1. Insert the brake gauge in the drum and fully expand until the gauge inner legs contact the drum braking surface. Then lock the gauge in position.
2. Reverse the gauge and install it on the brake shoes. Position the gauge legs at the shoe centers. If the gauge does not have a light drag fit, adjust the shoes.
3. Pull the starwheel away from the automatic adjuster lever. Turn the starwheel by hand to expand or retract the shoes and recheck with the brake gauge.
4. Install the brake drums, lower vehicle and make final adjustment.
5. Final adjustments on drum brakes take advantage of the systems self-adjustment mechanism. Drive the vehicle and make one forward stop followed by on reverse stop. Repeat the procedure 8–10 times to equalize adjustment between the two sides. Bring the vehicle to a complete stop each time. Rolling stops will not activate the self-adjuster mechanism

Wheel Cylinders

REMOVAL AND INSTALLATION

— CAUTION —
Brake shoes contain asbestos, which has been determined to be a cancer causing agent. Never clean the brake surfaces with compressed air! Avoid inhaling any dust from any brake surface! When cleaning brake surfaces, use a commercially available brake cleaning fluid.

NOTE: For vehicles equipped with Anti-Lock Brakes (ABS), refer to the proper procedures concerning brake system servicing.

1. Raise and support the vehicle safely. Remove the wheel.
2. Disconnect the brake line at the fitting on the brake backing plate.

NOTE: In most cases the flare fittings that attach the brake lines to the wheel cylinders will be frozen. Clean the fittings with solvent and use penetrating oil to loosen the rust. Use the proper size *flare nut* wrench to avoid stripping the fitting.

3. Remove the brake assemblies. Disconnect the brake line from the rear of the wheel cylinder.
4. Remove the screws or nuts that hold the wheel cylinder to the backing plate and remove the wheel cylinder from the vehicle.

To Install:
5. Position the wheel cylinder on the backing plate and start the brake line in the cylinder fitting.
6. Install the cylinder mounting bolts and tighten to 90 inch lbs.
7. To avoid stripping the fitting, tighten brake line fitting to 160 inch lbs. using a *flare nut* wrench.

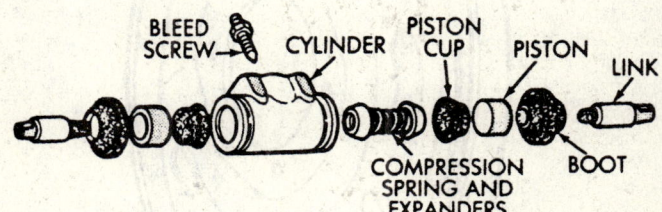

Wheel cylinder — 9-inch brake

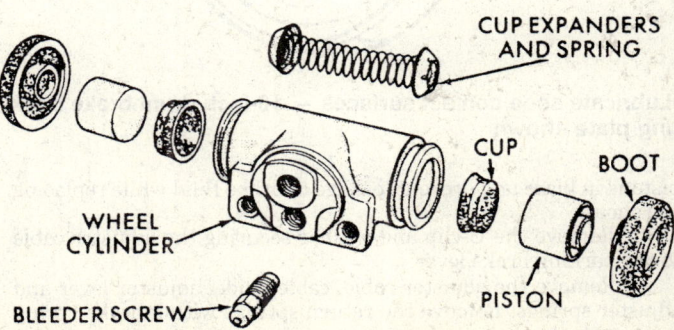

Wheel cylinder — 10-inch brake

BRAKES 9

OVERHAUL

1. Remove the wheel cylinder from the vehicle.
2. Remove the rubber dust covers on the ends of the cylinder.
3. Remove the pistons and piston cups and the spring.
4. Remove the bleeder screw and make sure it is not plugged.

NOTE: Wheel cylinder rebuilding kits are available for reconditioning wheel cylinders. The kits contain new cup springs, cylinder cups and new boots. The most important factor when rebuilding wheel cylinders is cleanliness. Keep all dirt away from the wheel cylinders when you are reassembling them.

6. Discard all of the parts that the rebuilding kit will replace.
7. Examine the inside of the cylinder. If it is severely rusted, pitted or scratched, then the cylinder must be replaced, as the piston cups won't be able to seal against the walls of the cylinder. DO NOT hone cylinder bores or polish pistons. Replace cylinder as an assembly if bore is damaged.
8. When reassembling the cylinder, dip all of the parts in clean brake fluid.
9. Ensure the piston cup lips face the expander and reassemble in the reverse order of removal.

BENDIX ANTI-LOCK BRAKE SYSTEM

General Information

The Bendix anti-lock braking system is available on 1989–91 Jeep Cherokee and Wagoneer vehicles (model designation XJ) with Selec–Trac 4-wheel drive. Anti-lock Brake Systems (ABS) are designed to prevent wheel lockup under heavy braking conditions on virtually any type of road surface. The Jeep ABS limits wheel lockup by modulating the brake fluid pressure to the brakes at each wheel. A vehicle which is stopped without locking the wheels will normally stop in a shorter distance than a vehicle with locked wheels. Additionally, vehicle control can be maintained during hard braking because the front wheels do not lock. The Jeep system is an electronically operated, power assisted brake system controlled by an isolated ECU.

Under normal braking conditions, the ABS system functions in the same manner as a standard brake system. The primary difference is that power assist is gained from hydraulic pressure rather than a conventional vacuum booster. The system also prevents excessive pedal travel in the event of a hydraulic leak. Anti–lock braking is available above approximately 12 mph; the system disengages at approximately 4 mph.

There are conditions for which the ABS system provides no benefit. Hydroplaning is possible when the tires ride on a film of water, losing contact with the paved surface. This renders the vehicle totally uncontrollable until road contact is regained. Extreme steering maneuvers at high speed or cornering beyond the limits of tire adhesion can result in skidding which is independent of vehicle braking. For this reason, the system is named anti-lock rather than anti–skid.

SYSTEM OPERATION

The booster pump and accumulator provide the fluid pressure needed for power assist. The accumulator is connected to the pump by a high-pressure feed line; a second high-pressure line connects the accumulator to the booster section of the master cylinder. The fluid reservoir is connected to the booster pump by a low-pressure line. Brake fluid from the master cylinder is sent to the calipers and brake cylinders through the pressure modulator. Each modulator channel contains 3 control solenoid valves; the valves are used to increase, decrease or maintain line pressure.

The electronic control module (ECU) receives data from the wheel speed sensors located at each wheel. Based on the sensor inputs, the ECU activates the proper solenoid valve to control braking effort at the wheels.

The ABS system is activated when the ignition switch is in the **ON** or **RUN** position. The system indicator light(s) are energized in the **START** position to serve as a bulb check. When the vehicle is motionless (no speed signal received by the ECU) and the ignition switch is in the **ON** or **RUN** position, the ECU will momentarily activate the control solenoids and operate them through full range. This allows the ECU to perform a system check. A slight whirring noise may be noticed by the operator if starting the car in a quiet environment.

The main fluid supply is contained within the master cylinder reservoir and the accumulator as well as in the booster pump accumulator. The pump and the main accumulator provide the reserve fluid pressure needed for power brake assist. The accumulator holds enough pressurized fluid for 25–30 power assisted brake applications should the pump fail.

CAUTION

The accumulator holds fluid at a normal pressure of 1650–2050 psi. Never attempt to work on or around the ABS hydraulic system without fully depressurizing the system. Severe injury may result.

Operation of the pump motor is controlled the pump relay and by an internal line pressure switch within the pump. The pump will only operate when the ignition switch is in the **ON** or **RUN** position. The pump does not run continuously, but on demand of the line pressure switch. The pump is capable of running without connection to the ECU; thus, anti–lock function may be lost but pressure within the system will still provide power assist for normal braking. If for any reason the pump motor overheats, a thermal fuse inside the pump will blow shutting off the motor. The fuse is not serviceable and cannot be reset.

At each wheel, a fixed sensor generates an electrical signal based on the revolutions of a toothed tone wheel. This low–voltage signal is sent to the ECU as wheel speed. The ECU compares the wheel speed signals to each other and to pre-programmed values; when excessive deceleration is indicated during a brake application, the system will enter ANTI-LOCK mode. During anti-lock braking, hydraulic pressure in the wheel circuits is modulated to prevent any wheel from locking. The ABS system controls pressure to the front wheels individually and to the rear wheels together. The control of the rear channel is usually based on the wheel with the greatest rate of deceleration. The system can build (increase), hold (maintain) or decay (reduce) pressure in each circuit as dictated by the ECU. Rapid changes in input data result in equally rapid changes in pressure modulation. Solenoid operation occurs in brief rapid cycles, both front-to-rear and side-to-side. Function change and cycle times are measured in milliseconds.

As the solenoids in each channel operate to control line pressures, the operator may experience a slight pulsing sensation within the vehicle. A firmer brake pedal and/or some pedal pulsation may be noticed during anti-lock operation. The pulsing results from the rapid changes within the system and is completely normal during ABS stops.

The operator may hear a clicking or whirring sound as the booster pump and/or relay cycle on and off during normal operation. The sounds are due to normal pump motor operation and are not indicative of a system problem. Under most conditions, the sounds are only faintly audible.

Although the ABS system prevents wheel lock-up under hard

9-27

9 Brakes

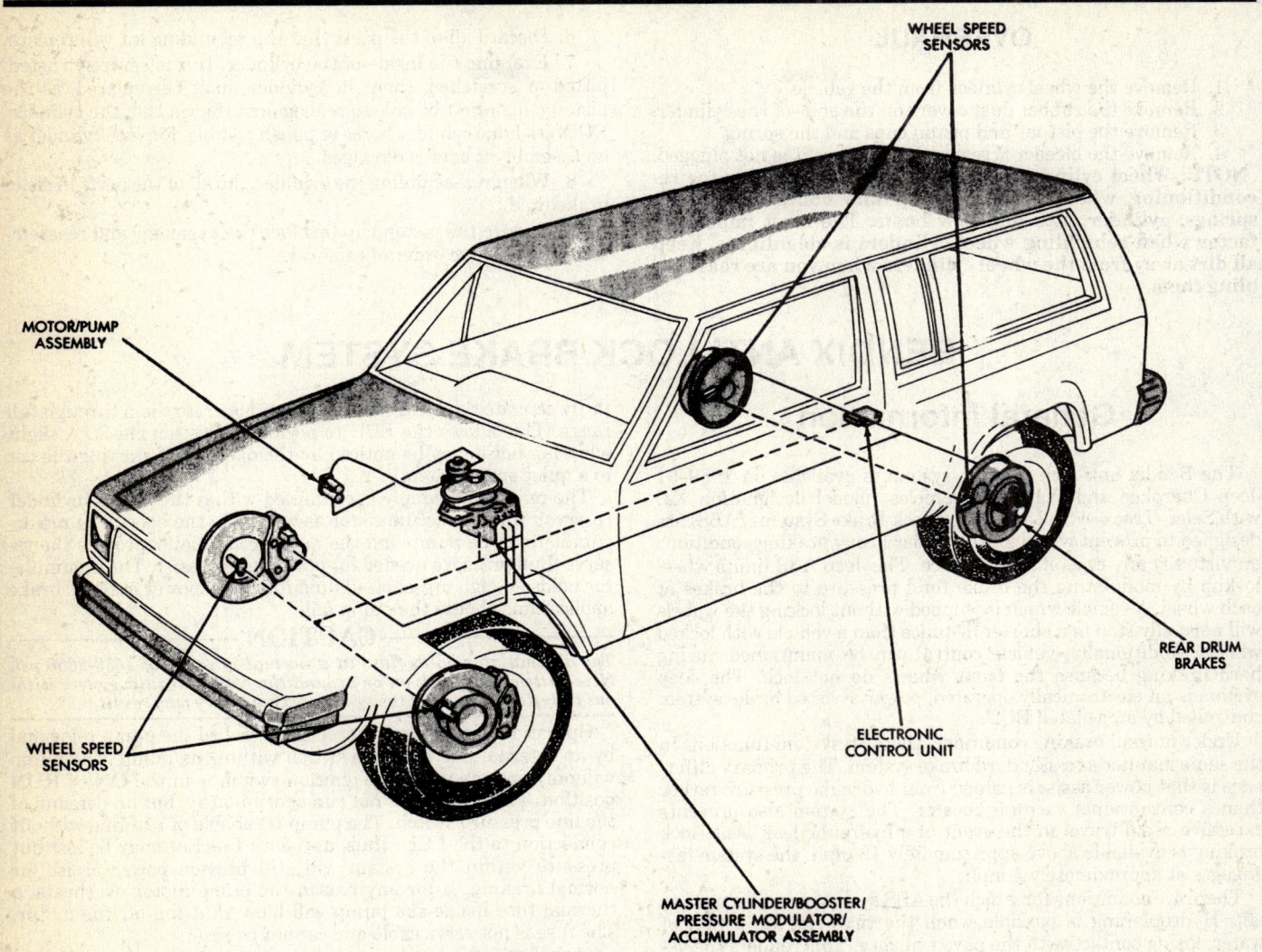

Anti-lock brake system component location

braking, as brake pressure increases, wheel slip is allowed to reach as high as 30%. This means that the rolling velocity of a given wheel is 30% less than that of a free-rolling wheel at a given speed. This slip will result in some tire chirp during ABS operation. The sound should not be interpreted as lock-up but rather than as indication of the system holding the wheel(s) just outside the point of lock-up. Additionally, since the ABS system turns off below 4 mph, the final few feet of an ABS-engaged stop may be completed with the wheels locked.

SYSTEM COMPONENTS

Master Cylinder/Power Booster

The integrated master cylinder and power booster is made from cast aluminum and mounted on the left side firewall within the engine compartment. A fluid reservoir is attached to the unit with rubber seals. The master cylinder portion is of the conventional split-system design. The brake pedal rod activates a ball valve at the end of the primary piston, providing boost pressure to the master cylinder and pressurized fluid to the modulator during an anti-lock stop.

The power booster only provides boost when the brake pedal is depressed. Assist is through high pressure brake fluid supplied by an electric pump. The pump is connected to the booster unit by high-pressure brake lines.

Booster Pump and Motor

Located on the right side of the engine compartment, the booster pump is powered by an electric motor. The pump piston operates from an eccentric drive. The motor is controlled through a relay by the pressure switch located next to the pump and motor assembly. The pump and motor are equipped with an accumulator to provide additional fluid supply for working pressure.

Normal pump operating pressures are approximately 1700–2000 psi. The pressure switch engages the pump when the line pressure drops below 1700 psi. once the pressure returns to 2000 psi, the relay is de-energized and the pump shuts off. If the pump remains on for more than 4 minutes without the brakes being applied, the ECU will illuminate the red brake warning lamp on the instrument panel. If the internal pressure reaches 3000 psi, an internal relief valve will open, allowing the pressure to drop.

The pump motor is also equipped with an internal thermal fuse. If operating temperature exceeds 385°F (196°C), the fuse will fail and stop operation of the motor.

Brakes 9

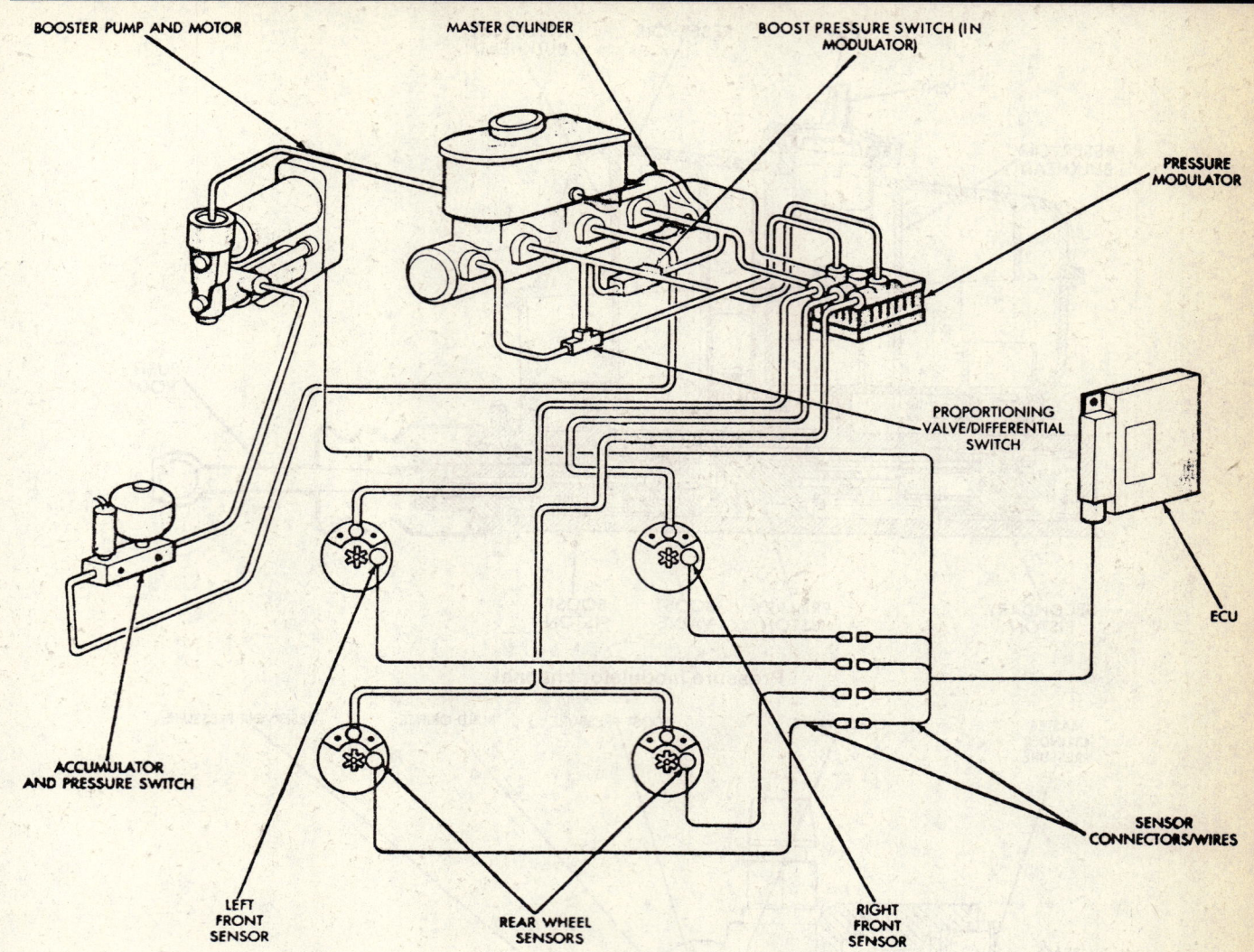

System component connections

Pressure Modulator

The pressure modulator is a hydro-electric unit attached to the master cylinder/power booster assembly. It provides 3-function control to each of 3 brake circuits — left front, right front and both rear wheels. The modulator contains 9 solenoids. Each brake channel has a separate isolate, build and decay solenoid assigned to it. Each solenoid performs its single task at the direction of the ECU whenever anti–lock is engaged.

Under normal brake operation, master cylinder pressure passes through the isolation solenoids to the individual wheel brake units. When ABS is engaged, the isolation solenoids block the master cylinder ports, allowing pressure to the wheels to be controlled through the build and decay solenoids by the ECU.

The ECU activates the decay solenoid to reduce brake line pressure so the wheel can increase speed and avoid lock-up. When the ECU determines that wheel speed has increased above lock-up, the build solenoid is engaged to add braking force at the wheel. By quickly building and releasing line pressures, an individual wheel may be kept just outside the point of locking or skidding.

NOTE: All 3 channels operate independently. It is quite possible at any given moment during an ABS stop that one circuit has the build solenoid energized while another has the decay solenoid energized.

Electronic Control Module (ECU)

Located under the rear seat, the ECU monitors and controls the ABS system. It is connected to the wiring harness through 2 multi–pin connectors. The micro–processor within the unit receives input from the a variety of sources, compares the data against pre-programmed values and controls the output drivers. Sources of ECU input are:
- Speed sensors at 4 wheels
- Boost pressure differential switch
- Low fluid level switch
- Proportioning valve/pressure differential switch
- Brake pedal switch
- Parking brake switch
- Ignition switch
- Booster Pump and motor
- Modulator

The ECU contains self-check and system diagnostic capabilities. If a system fault or an internal ECU fault is detected, the ECU will assign a fault code, store it for later retrieval and turn either

9-29

9 BRAKES

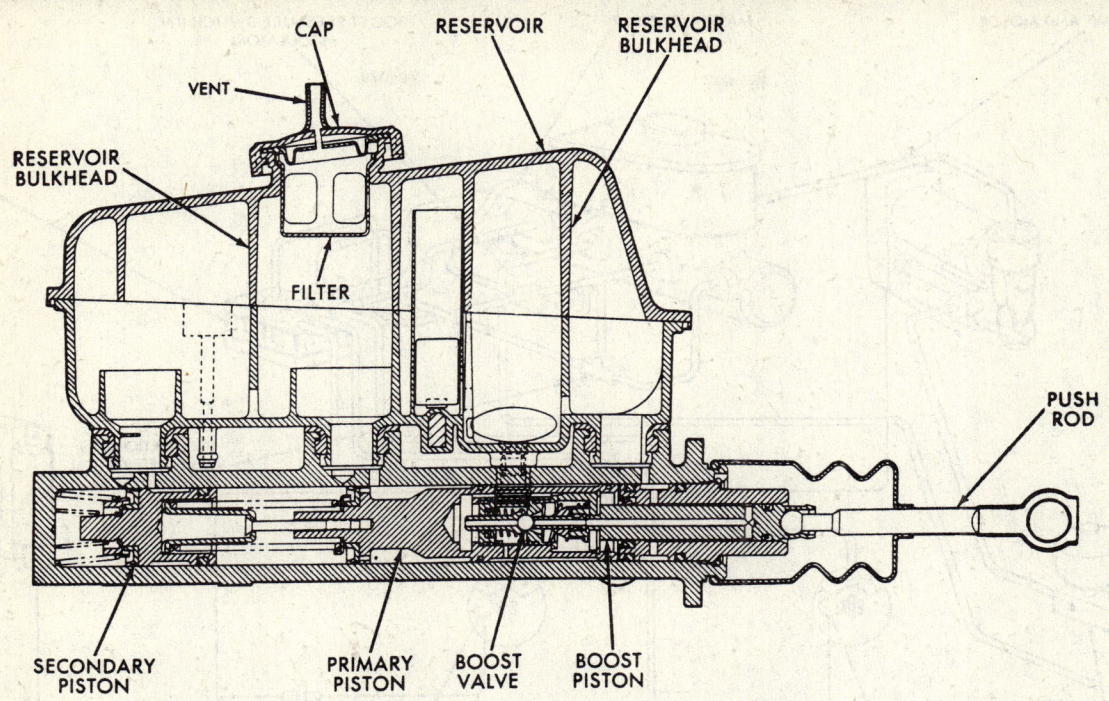

Pressure modulator channel

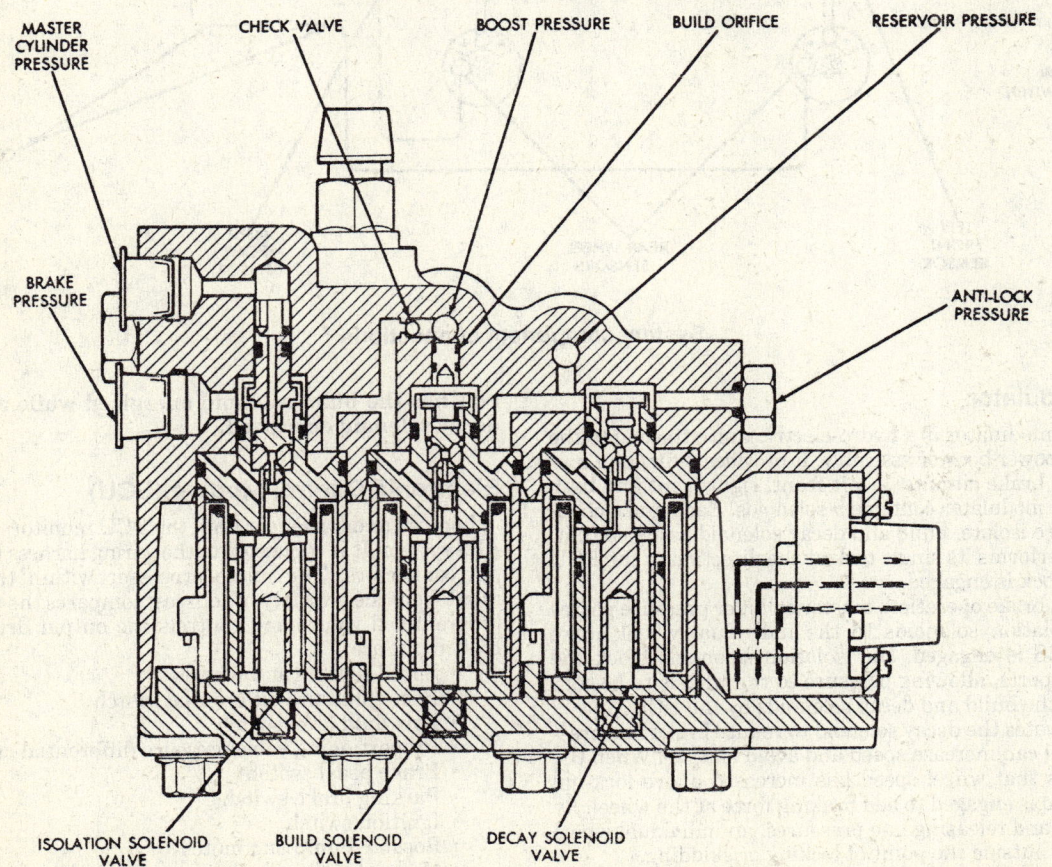

Typical channel within pressure regulator

BRAKES 9

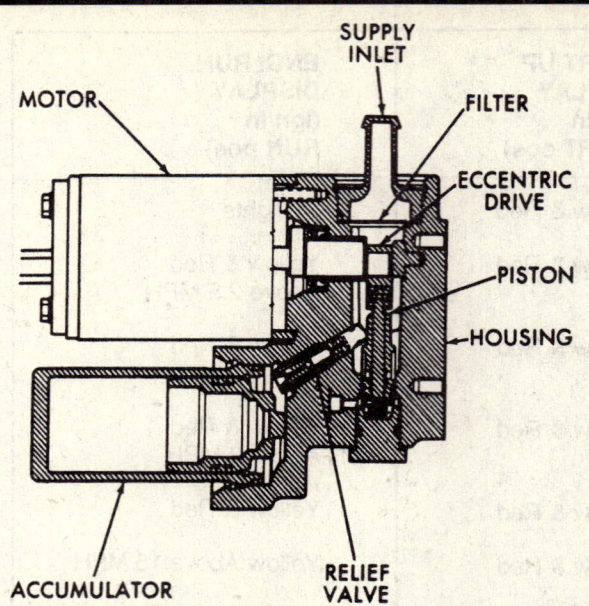

Pump and motor assembly

or both of the dash warning lamps. There are 14 different faults that may be detected by the ECU, but only 1 fault code will be stored each time. The fault code will remain in memory until the battery is disconnected from the ECU. The stored fault code may be read with the DRB-II tester or equivalent hand-scanner.

When the ECU is brought out of stand-by by turning the ignition switch to **ON** or **RUN**, the unit checks itself internally as well as checking the solenoid driver circuits and certain external components. This self-check is continuously performed throughout the driving cycle. If any fault is found, the ECU will engage the yellow dash warning light and disable itself. Under these conditions, anti-lock function is disabled but normal, power-assisted braking is still available. This provides a system fail-safe (sometimes termed default) whereby the vehicle may still be driven without the benefits of ABS.

NOTE: The ECU contains a mercury switch which monitors the degree of vehicle deceleration to determine what type of surface the vehicle is on. The switch provides input to the ECU for improved operation when in 4wd on slippery surfaces. Proper mounting angle of the ECU is critical to the correct operation of the mercury switch.

Warning Lights

The ABS system uses 2 warning lamps on the instrument panel. Both the red and yellow lights are in circuit with the self-diagnostic program in the ECU.

The red BRAKE light serves as the normal brake system warning lamp. It warns of conditions which can affect the normal or service brakes on the vehicle. The red lamp will illuminate for low fluid level, parking brake **ON**, system pressure differential too great, and other similar conditions.

The yellow CK ANTI LOCK light indicates conditions affecting the anti-lock brake system. The lamp is on during start up and will go out if the ECU finds no errors during the first system check. If a fault is found, the ECU will engage the yellow light until the fault is corrected, the battery is disconnected or the ignition switch is cycled **OFF** and **ON**. If the fault is still present after cycling the ignition, the ECU will re-light the lamp.

The yellow light is in circuit with the pressure modulator solenoids. When the light is on, the solenoids are disabled and ABS function is not available. If only the yellow warning lamp is lit, the car will have normal braking without benefit of ABS.

There are certain time delays built into the ECU warning lamp outputs. If certain faults occur, the yellow lamp will illuminate first. If, after a period of seconds, the fault has not been corrected, the red warning lamp will be brought on. An example would be that under certain circumstances, accumulator pressure might be reduced below minimum during a high-speed panic stop. The low pressure switch engages the yellow lamp. If, within 20 seconds, the pump can restore the pressure, the lamp will go off. If the pressure is still low after 20 seconds, the ECU will trip the red warning lamp to warn of a possible fluid leak or similar system failure. Various combinations of inputs will cause the ECU to illuminate either or both warning lamps.

Wheel Speed Sensors and Tone Wheels

A toothed tone wheel is attached to each axle and rotates with the wheel. Sensors or pick-ups are mounted at each tone wheel; as the teeth turn past the sensor, an alternating current is generated proportional to wheel speed. This signal is transmitted to the ECU which translates the signal into a digital reference for each wheel. The air gap between the sensor and the tone wheel is critical; replacement sensors usually contain a self-locating tab to insure correct placement. Diagnostic work may require checking the air gap if the sensor is not being replaced.

Tone wheels on the front and rear wheels may be different by both number of teeth and air gap. Do not assume that tone wheels or sensors are interchangeable front to rear.

Boost Pressure Differential Switch

Located in the pressure modulator, this switch compares the modulated boost pressure to the master cylinder primary system pressure. If an abnormal pressure differential exists, the switch will ground through the vehicle body, signaling the ECU. The control unit reads this signal as a significant fault and will illuminate both warning lights on the instrument panel.

Proportioning Valve/Pressure Differential Switch

The combination front/rear brake pressure switch and proportioning valve is connected between the master cylinder and modulator. Hydraulic pressure from the master cylinder is applied through opposite ends of the valve, providing balancing forces to hold the piston centered in the bore. As long as the piston remains centered, the switch is in the **OFF** position.

If pressure loss occurs in either the front or rear circuit, a pressure differential of 70-300 psi will cause the piston to move to the low pressure side, engaging the switch and grounding the red warning lamp on the dashboard.

During normal operation, the valve is positioned to allow proportional braking to the rear wheels. When ABS is engaged, the proportioning valve and the master cylinder are isolated to allow pressure modulation of the system. Continuity through the switch is checked each time the ignition switch is turned to **START** by illuminating the red warning lamp.

Fluid Level Switch

A reed switch located in the master cylinder reservoir is connected to the ECU. When a low fluid condition exists, the switch closes grounding the circuit. When the ECU senses the grounded circuit, the red dash warning lamp is lit.

Accumulators and Low Pressure Switch

One accumulator is located within the pump/motor assembly; the other is located with the low pressure switch next to the master cylinder and power booster assembly. Each stores brake fluid at extremely high pressures (approximately 1700-2000 psi) for system operation.

The pump accumulator is the smaller of the 2. It contains a piston and is pre-charged with 450 psi of nitrogen. The external accumulator is a diaphragm type and contains nitrogen charged to 1000 psi.

9-31

9 BRAKES

CONDITION	INITIAL. DISPLAY (ign in ON pos)	START UP DISPLAY (ign in START pos)	ENG. RUN. DISPLAY (ign in RUN pos)
Normal	Yellow On For 2 Sec	Yellow & Red	No lights
Low Fluid or Parking Brake	Red	Yellow & Red	Yellow & Red Above 2.5 MPH
Low Accumulator	Yellow & Red After 20 sec	Yellow & Red	Yellow & Red
Front to Rear Pressure Differential	Red	Yellow & Red	Yellow & Red Above 3 MPH
Low Boost Pressure	Yellow & Red	Yellow & Red	Yellow & Red
Sensor Faults	Yellow On For 2 Sec	Yellow & Red	Yellow Above 15 MPH
Excess Decay	Yellow On For 2 Sec	Yellow & Red	Yellow
Solenoid Faults	Yellow	Yellow & Red	Yellow
Pump Fault	Yellow On For 2 Sec	Yellow & Red	Red
Low Voltage	Yellow	Yellow & Red	Yellow
Brake Switch	Yellow On For 2 Sec	Yellow & Red	Red During Stop Only
Relay	Yellow	Yellow & Red	Yellow
ECU Self-test	Yellow	Yellow & Red	Yellow

System warning lights display

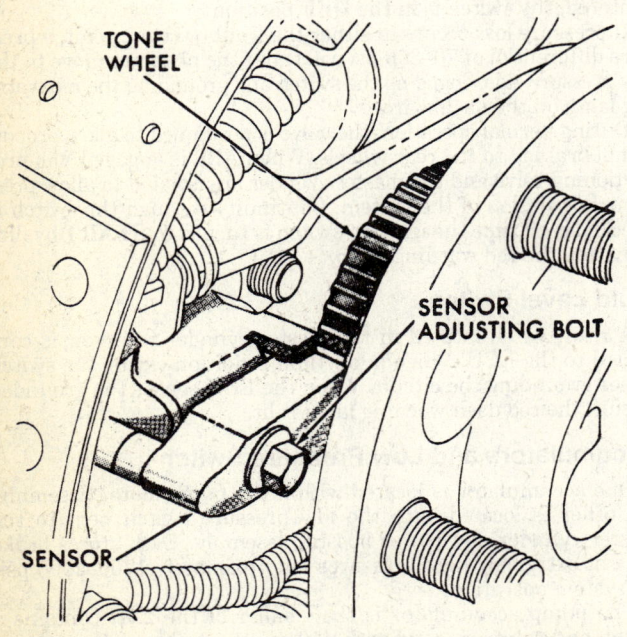

Rear wheel speed sensor and tone wheel. Not all sensors are adjustable

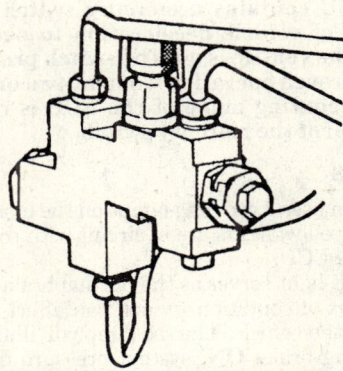

Proportioning valve and pressure differential switch

The low pressure switch is grounded to the body during normal operation. If the line pressure drops below approximately 1050 psi, the switch signals the ECU by opening. The ECU will illuminate the yellow dash warning lamp for 20 seconds. If pressure is not regained within 20 seconds, the ECU engages the red warning lamp on the dash.

Switch Inputs

The ABS ECU receives input from the brake pedal switch, the ignition switch and the parking brake switch. The brake pedal

BRAKES 9

switch communicates with the ECU independently of the brake lamps; once notified that the brakes are applied, the ECU is prepared to enter ABS if wheel speed signals indicate the need.

The parking brake switch grounds the low fluid switch when the brake is applied. This will cause the red dash warning lamp to be illuminated. if the car is drive with the parking brake applied (or not fully released), the yellow warning lamp will come on and a LOW FLUID trouble code will be stored in the ECU.

The anti–lock ECU and the indicator lamps are in standby whenever the ignition switch is in either **OFF** or **ACCESSORY** position. In the **ON** or **RUN** positions, power is supplied to the ECU, the pump motor and the indicator lights. In **START**, only the indicator lamps are powered to serve as a bulb check.

Diagnosis and Testing

SERVICE PRECAUTIONS

— CAUTION —
This brake system uses a hydraulic accumulator which, when fully charged, contains brake fluid at very high pressure. Before disconnecting any hydraulic lines, hoses or fittings be certain that the accumulator pressure is completely relieved. Failure to depressurize the accumulator may result in personal injury and/or vehicle damage.

- Certain components within the ABS system are not intended to be serviced or repaired individually. Only those components with removal and installation procedures should be serviced.
- Both the external accumulator and the smaller accumulator within the pump contain high pressure nitrogen charges to assist in pressurizing the system. The gas pressure is maintained even after fluid pressure in the system is reduced. Never puncture or attempt to disassemble either of these components.
- Do not use rubber hoses or other parts not specifically specified for the ABS system. When using repair kits, replace all parts included in the kit. Partial or incorrect repair may lead to functional problems and require the replacement of components.
- Lubricate rubber parts with clean, fresh brake fluid to ease assembly. Do not use lubricated shop air to clean parts; damage to rubber components may result.
- Use only DOT 3 brake fluid from an unopened container.
- If any hydraulic component or line is removed or replaced, it may be necessary to bleed the entire system.
- A clean repair area is essential. Always clean the reservoir and cap thoroughly before removing the cap. The slightest amount of dirt in the fluid may plug an orifice and impair the system function. Perform repairs after components have been thoroughly cleaned; use only denatured alcohol to clean components. Do not allow ABS components to come into contact with any substance containing mineral oil; this includes used shop rags.
- The anti-lock ECU is a microprocessor similar to other computer units in the vehicle. Insure that the ignition switch is **OFF** before removing or installing controller harnesses. Avoid static electricity discharge at or near the controller.

DEPRESSURIZING THE SYSTEM

— CAUTION —
Depressurize the ABS accumulator and master cylinder assembly before performing any service operations. Failure to completely relieve the system could result in brake fluid under high pressure being sprayed on the technician and the vehicle. This can result in serious personal injury and vehicle damage.

1. Turn the ignition switch **OFF** and leave it **OFF** during repairs unless specifically directed otherwise.

2. Firmly apply and release the brake pedal a minimum of 45–50 times.

3. The pedal feel will become noticeably harder when the accumulator is completely discharged.

4. Do not turn the ignition switch **ON** after depressurizing the system unless service procedures specifically require it or all service operations have been performed.

NOTE: After the reserve pressure is depleted, the fluid level in the reservoir will rise above the MAX fill mark. This is normal; the reservoir will not overflow unless the system was overfilled to begin with.

5. Always wear safety goggles when disconnecting lines and fittings.

PRE–DIAGNOSIS INSPECTION

Before diagnosing an apparent ABS problem, make absolutely certain that the normal braking system is in correct working order. Many common brake problems (dragging shoe, seepage, etc) will affect the ABS system. A visual check of specific system components may reveal problems creating an apparent ABS malfunction. Performing this inspection may reveal a simple failure, thus eliminating extended diagnostic time. The steps should be performed in order.

1. Depressurize the system.
2. Inspect the brake fluid level in the reservoir.
3. Inspect brake lines, hoses, master cylinder assembly, brake calipers and cylinders for leakage.
4. Visually check brake lines and hoses for excessive wear, heat damage, punctures, contact with other parts, missing clips or holders, blockage or crimping.
5. Check the calipers and wheel cylinders for rust or corrosion. Check for proper sliding action if applicable.

FAULT CODE	FAULT DESCRIPTION
800	No voltage at ABS module
801	No serial data from ABS module
802	Parking brake not seen
803	ABS lights inoperative
804	Yellow light off
805	Differential pressure fault
806	Boost pressure fault
807	Low accumulator
808	Modulator fault
809	Self-Test failure
810	Solenoid undervoltage
811	Relay fault
812	Motor pump fault
813	Brake fault
814	Low fluid
815	Wheel speed sensor fault — right rear —
816	Wheel speed sensor fault — left rear —
817	Wheel speed sensor fault — right front —
818	Wheel speed sensor fault — left front —
819	Open circuit at D2-14

ABS fault codes shown by DRB-II

9 BRAKES

SYSTEM FAULT	POSSIBLE CAUSE	INDICATOR LIGHT DISPLAY
LOW FLUID	SYSTEM LEAK. ACCUMULATOR CHARGE LOW OR LOST.	RED LIGHT ON. YELLOW LIGHT ON WITHIN 1/2 SECOND WHEN VEHICLE SPEED EXCEEDS 2.5 MPH.
PARKING BRAKES APPLIED	PARKING BRAKES NOT RELEASED BEFORE DRIVING VEHICLE.	RED LIGHT ON. YELLOW LIGHT ON IF VEHICLE SPEED EXCEEDS 2.5 MPH.
PRESSURE DROP AT ACCUMULATOR	ACCUMLATOR GAS CHARGE LOST. SYSTEM LEAK. PUMP/MOTOR MALFUNCTION. PROLONGED STOP ON ICY SURFACE WITH TRANSMISSION IN GEAR.	YELLOW LIGHT ON. RED LIGHT WILL ALSO COME ON WITHIN 20 SECONDS.
DIFFERENTIAL PRESSURE SWITCH (IN PROPORTIONING VALVE) ACTUATED	SYSTEM LEAK. MASTER CYLINDER MALFUNCTION (SECONDARY PISTON). AIR IN SYSTEM.	RED LIGHT ON. YELLOW LIGHT COMES ON AT VEHICLE SPEED OF 3 MPH.
PRESSURE DROP AT BOOST PRESSURE SWITCH AND PRESSURE DIFFERENTIAL SWITCH	MASTER CYLINDER MALFUNCTION (PRIMARY PISTON). SYSTEM LEAK. AIR IN SYSTEM.	RED LIGHT ON. YELLOW LIGHT COMES ON AT VEHICLE SPEED OF 3 MPH.
WHEEL SENSOR FAULT (FRONT ONLY)	SENSOR-TO-TONE WHEEL SPACING INCORRECT (SPACE TOO LARGE). DAMAGED SENSOR WIRE, SENSOR, OR TONE WHEEL. SENSOR AND TONE WHEEL MISALIGNED. SENSOR DISCONNECTED.	YELLOW LIGHT ON. (AFTER 15 MPH)
WHEEL SENSOR FAULT (FRONT OR REAR ONE OR TWO MISSING SIGNALS)	DAMAGED SENSOR, WIRE, OR CONNECTOR. SENSOR DISCONNECTED. EXCESSIVE WHEEL SPIN. MISALIGNED OR DAMAGED TONE WHEEL. OPEN SENSOR OR WIRE.	YELLOW LIGHT ON AT 15 MPH IF FAULT OCCURRED BEFORE VEHICLE DRIVE-OFF. OR, YELLOW LIGHT ON AT 8 MPH IF FAULT OCCURRED AFTER VEHICLE DRIVE-OFF.
EXCESSIVE DECAY SOLENOID OPERATION	MODULATOR/SOLENOID FAULT. WHEEL SENSOR FAULT. EXTREMELY LOW AMBIENT TEMPERATURES. VEHICLE ON ICE COVERED SURFACE. TIRES HYDROPLANING ON WATER COVERED ROAD SURFACE.	YELLOW LIGHT ON WITHIN 1-2 SECONDS.
PRESSURE MODULATOR SOLENOID FAULT	SOLENOID SHORTED OR OPEN. DECAY AND BUILD SOLENOID ON AT SAME TIME. OPEN/SHORT IN MODULATOR HARNESS.	YELLOW LIGHT ON.
PUMP/MOTOR RUN-ON	EXCESSIVE RUN TIME. RELAY SHORTED, MOTOR SWITCH SHORTED.	RED LIGHT ON IF PUMP RUNS MORE THAN 4 MINUTES WITH NO BRAKE.
PUMP/MOTOR INOPERATIVE	PUMP RELAY FAULT. NO VOLTAGE TO MOTOR. DAMAGED PUMP OR MOTOR. PUMP GAS CHARGE LOST.	YELLOW LIGHT ON. RED LIGHT ON AFTER 20 SECONDS.
LOW VOLTAGE	SYSTEM VOLTAGE BELOW 9V. SHORT, OPEN IN FEED WIRES OR RELAY. FUSE BAD. POOR GROUND. LOOSE, DISCONNECTED WIRE IN SYSTEM. BATTERY LOW OR DISCHARGED	YELLOW LIGHT ON.
NO BRAKE SIGNAL	SYSTEM LEAK. MASTER CYLINDER MALFUNCTION. PUMP/MOTOR MALFUNCTION. ACCUMULATOR OR MODULATOR FAULT.	RED LIGHT ON DURING BRAKING.
RELAY FAULT	RELAY SHORTED OR OPEN.	YELLOW LIGHT ON.
ECU SELF DIAGNOSTIC FEATURE INOPERATIVE (SOLENOIDS NOT TEST-EXERCISED AT START-UP)	IGNITION SWITCH IN OFF POSITION. PARKING BRAKES ON (NOT RELEASED AT DRIVE-OFF). SYSTEM COMPONENT HAS MALFUNCTIONED. LOW FLUID LEVEL/LEAK IN SYSTEM.	YELLOW LIGHT ON.

Warning lamp display and possible system causes

BRAKES 9

6. Check the caliper and wheel cylinder pistons for freedom of motion during application and release.

7. Inspect the wheel speed sensors for proper mounting and connections.

8. Inspect the tone wheels for broken teeth or poor mounting.

9. Inspect the wheels and tires on the vehicle. They must be of the same size and type to generate accurate speed signals.

10. Confirm the fault occurrence with the operator. Certain driver induced faults, such as not releasing the parking brake fully, will set a fault code and trigger the dash warning light(s). Excessive wheel spin on low-traction surfaces, high speed acceleration or riding the brake pedal may also set fault codes and trigger a warning lamp. These induced faults are not system failures but examples of vehicle performance outside the parameters of the ECU.

11. Many system shut–downs are due to loss of sensor signals to or from the ECU. The most common cause is not a failed sensor but a loose, corroded or dirty connector. Incorrect adjustment of the wheel speed sensor will cause a loss of wheel speed signal. Check harness and component connectors carefully.

DIAGNOSIS

After performing the preliminary visual checks, observe the behavior and timing of the dashboard warning lamps. Their function, when used in diagnostics, can point to possible causes and eliminate others.

Use the DRB-II with the correct cartridge to determine the specific circuit at fault. The tester with the correct adapter should be connected to the diagnostic connector on the right side of the engine compartment. Any fault read by the tester on initial hookup should be considered as a guide only. After initial repairs, clear the fault code, drive the vehicle and recheck for any stored code. Once the fault is identified, the DRB-II may be used to test or energize system components.

ABS FAULT CODE DIAGNOSTIC CHARTS

Component Replacement

---CAUTION---
Certain components within the ABS system are not repairable. If any fault is found with any of these components, they must be removed and replaced as a unit. Any attempt to disassemble or repair these components may result in impaired system function and/or personal injury.

The master cylinder/power booster assembly, the pressure modulator, the external accumulator, the pump and motor (with internal accumulator) and the proportioning valve are not repairable components; they must be replaced as complete assemblies. Additionally, the fluid level switch in the master cylinder and the boost pressure switch within the modulator cannot be serviced because they cannot be removed from their components.

FILLING THE SYSTEM

The only recommended brake fluid for the ABS system is fluid meeting SAE standard J-1703 and DOT 3. Use of any other fluid may result in improper function and/or component damage. Never use reclaimed fluid or fluid from a previously opened container.

The fluid level indicator mark is on the side of the plastic reservoir. Check the fluid with the engine off, after driving or running the engine. This allows the pump to charge the system and gives a true indication of fluid level. Checking the fluid when the system has not been pressurized may result in a false level within the reservoir.

Completely clean the reservoir and cap area before removing the cap. Add fluid only to the MAX mark. Overfilling may result in fluid overflow and possible reservoir damage during pump operation. Also check the reservoir filter when the cap is off; remove and clean the filter with clean brake fluid if necessary.

BLEEDING THE SYSTEM

1. Fill the reservoir to the MAX mark with clean, fresh brake fluid.

2. The brake system must be bled in the correct order. For all vehicles, the wheel order is right rear, left rear, right front, left front. For 1991 vehicles, the master cylinder/power booster must be bled before the wheels are bled.

3. For 1991 vehicles, bleed the master cylinder/booster assembly. Loosen and bleed the brake lines at the side of the modulator one at a time. Have a helper turn the ignition **ON** and operate the brake pedal in the usual manner while each line is loosened, bled and re-tightened. Bleed each circuit until the fluid is clear and free of air bubbles.

4. Attach a clear plastic bleed hose to the caliper or wheel cylinder fitting. Place the other end of the hose in a clear container of fresh brake fluid. Make certain the hose end is submerged in the fluid.

5. Turn the ignition switch **ON** to cycle the pump.

6. Have an assistant apply and hold brake pedal pressure to pressurize the system.

7. Open the bleed screw $1/2$–turn. Close the bleed screw when the fluid entering the container is free of bubbles.

8. Check the reservoir level and refill to the MAX mark. Do not allow the master cylinder reservoir to run dry while bleeding. If the reservoir runs dry, air re-enters the system; the pump may be severely damaged if a constant supply of fluid is not available.

9. Repeat the bleeding procedure at the remaining wheels.

SPEED SENSORS

Removal and Installation

FRONT WHEEL

1. Elevate and safely support the vehicle. Turn the front wheel outward for easier access to the sensor.

2. Before disassembly, note sensor wire routing including location of all clips and retainers. The sensor wire must be routed correctly during reassembly to avoid damage from moving parts.

3. Carefully remove the wire ties holding the sensor wire to the brake lines and the steering knuckle.

4. If the sensor is coated with mud, slush, etc., clean the sensor and surrounding area. This will prevent damage to the sensor and tone wheel during removal.

5. Remove the sensor attaching screw and remove the sensor from the steering knuckle.

6. Loosen the grommet holding the sensor wire from the wheel arch panel.

7. In the engine compartment, disconnect the sensor wire connector from the ABS harness. Carefully remove the sensor and harness from the car.

To install:

8. The wheel sensors have a plastic spacing strip attached to

9 BRAKES

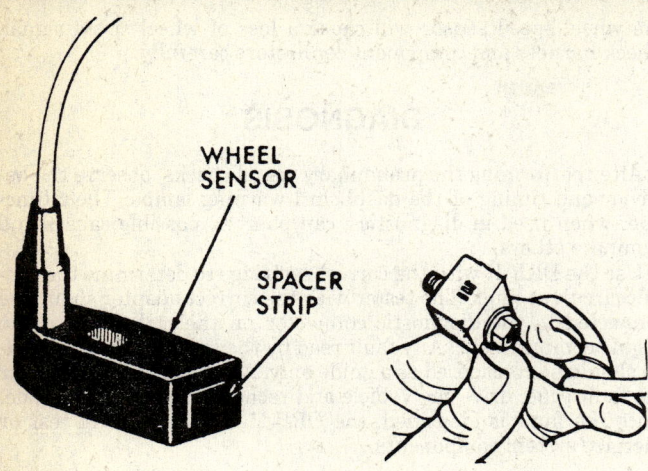

Typical wheel sensor with and without spacer

the contact face. Inspect this spacer and note the condition. If the strip is securely attached and in good condition, no adjustment will be needed after installation. If the strip is damaged or not present, an air gap adjustment will be required.

9. Feed the sensor wire through the grommet hole in the wheel well panel. Connect the sensor connector to the ABS harness and seat the rubber grommet in the panel.

10. Position the sensor on the steering knuckle and install the attaching bolt finger tight.

11. If the spacer strip was intact and in good condition, lightly press the sensor against the tone wheel. Hold the sensor in this position and tighten the retaining bolt to 11 ft. lbs (14 Nm).

12. If the spacer was missing or damaged, clean the contacts on the sensor with a clean shop towel. Remove the spacer strip completely if loose or torn. After the sensor is loosely held in position by the retaining bolt, use a brass feeler gauge to set the air gap from the sensor to the tone wheel. Correct air gap is 0.33–0.48mm (0.013–0.019 in.). Tighten the retaining bolt to 11 ft. lbs. (14 Nm) and recheck the air gap with the feeler gauge.

NOTE: Use of a brass or non-magnetic gauge is required. Do not use common steel feelers; the small magnets within the sensor may be damaged. Correct air gap is critical to the proper operation of the sensor.

13. Use new wire ties to secure the sensor wire to the brake lines and steering knuckle.

REAR WHEEL

1. Raise and fold forward the rear seat to gain access to the rear sensor connectors.
2. Disconnect the sensor connector from the ABS harness; push the sensor grommet and wiring through the floor pan.
3. Elevate and safely support the vehicle.
4. Remove the wheel and brake drum.
5. Carefully remove the wire ties holding the sensor wires to the brake lines and rear axle.
6. Loosen or unseat the backing plate grommet holding the sensor wire.
7. Remove the bolt holding the sensor to the bracket. Remove the sensor by pulling the wire through the grommet hole in the backing plate.

To install:

8. The wheel sensors have a plastic spacing strip attached to the contact face. Inspect this spacer and note the condition. If the strip is securely attached and in good condition, no adjustment

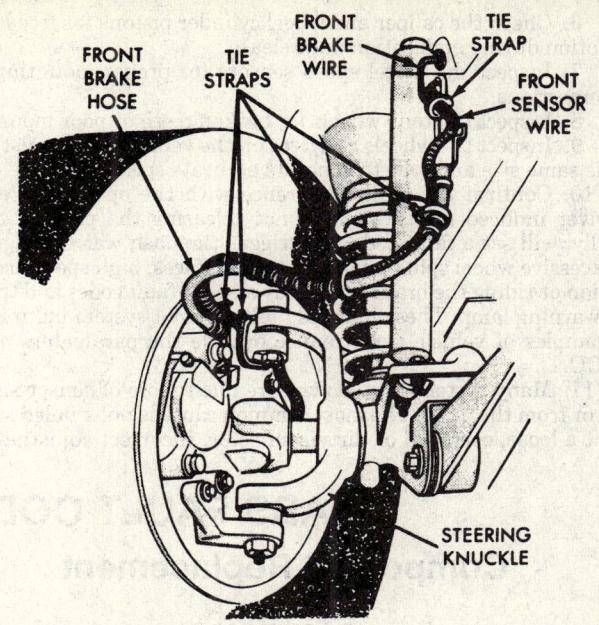

Front sensor wire routing

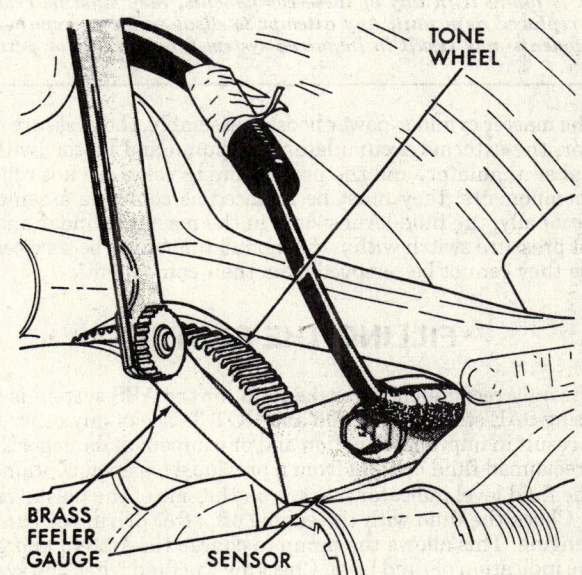

Adjusting the sensor-to-tone wheel air gap

will be needed after installation. If the strip is damaged or not present, an air gap adjustment will be required.

9. Feed the sensor wire through the grommet hole in the backing plate and seat the grommet in the plate.

10. If the spacer strip was intact and in good condition, lightly press the sensor against the tone wheel. Hold the sensor in this position and tighten the retaining bolt to 11 ft. lbs (14 Nm).

11. If the spacer was missing or damaged, clean the contacts on the sensor with a clean shop towel. Remove the spacer strip completely if loose or torn. After the sensor is loosely held in position by the retaining bolt, use a brass feeler gauge to set the air gap from the sensor to the tone wheel. Correct air gap is 0.76–0.91mm (0.030–0.036 in.). Tighten the retaining bolt to 11 ft. lbs. (14 Nm) and recheck the air gap with the feeler gauge.

BRAKES 9

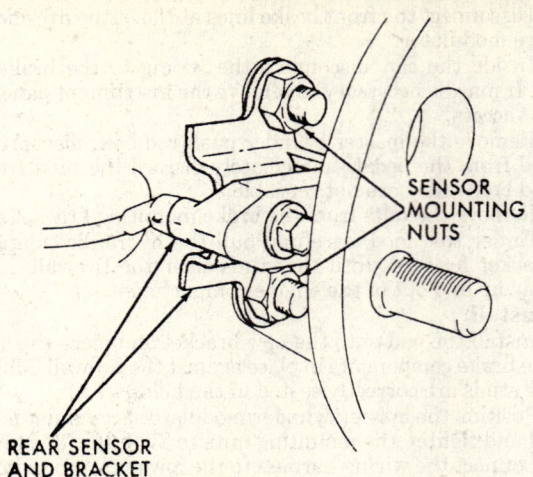

Rear wheel sensor installation

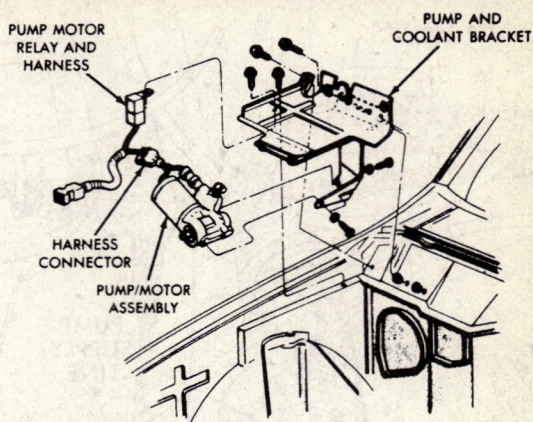

Pump/motor and coolant tank bracket

NOTE: Use of a brass or non-magnetic gauge is required. Do not use common steel feelers; the small magnets within the sensor may be damaged. Correct air gap is critical to the proper operation of the sensor.

12. Route the sensor wire to the rear seat area and feed through the access hole. Seat the sensor wire grommets in the floorpan.
13. Use new wire ties to secure the sensor wiring to the brake lines and rear axle. Make certain that the wiring is clear of all moving and/or hot components.
14. Install the brake drum and wheel. Lower the vehicle to the ground.
15. Within the car, connect the sensor to the ABS harness. Reposition the seat and carpet.

TONE WHEELS
Removal and Installation

The toothed tone wheels are permanently mounted to the axles and are not replaceable In the event of damage to a tone wheel, the axle shaft assembly must be replaced with the new tone wheel attached.

PUMP AND MOTOR
Removal and Installation

— CAUTION —
This brake system uses hydraulic accumulators, which, when fully charged, contain brake fluid at very high pressure. Before disconnecting any components, hydraulic lines, hoses or fittings be certain that the accumulator pressure is completely relieved. Failure to depressurize the system may result in personal injury and/or vehicle damage.

1. Depressurize the brake system
2. Disconnect the negative battery cable.
3. Remove the strap holding the coolant reserve bottle and move the bottle aside. The hoses may be left attached; moving the bottle allows better access.
4. Remove the bolts holding the 2-piece mounting bracket to the firewall and inner fender panels.
5. Move or rotate the bracket with the pump assembly to one side for access to the wiring and hoses. Disconnect the pump motor wiring harness from the engine harness.
6. Slowly loosen the high pressure line at the pump and allow any residual high pressure to bleed off. Wear eye protection and wrap the joint in a clean shop towel to suppress any spray. Disconnect the line from the pump.
7. Place a container or catch pan under the return line to the pump. Loosen the hose clamp and remove the line. Do not reuse the brake fluid which drains from the line.
8. Remove the pump/motor and bracket as a complete assembly.
9. Remove the screw holding the relay to the bracket. Remove the screws holding the pump and motor to the bracket and remove the bracket.

To install:

10. Position the pump assembly onto the bracket and install the assembly attaching screws. Attach the pump/motor to the mounting bracket and attach the pump relay to the mounting bracket.
11. Connect the high-pressure and return lines to the pump.
12. Connect the electrical harness from the pump to the engine harness.
13. Place the bracket with the pump/motor and relay in place and install the retaining bolts.
14. Inspect the high-pressure and return lines; make certain they are not kinked or touching the engine.
15. Fill the master cylinder to the MAX level.

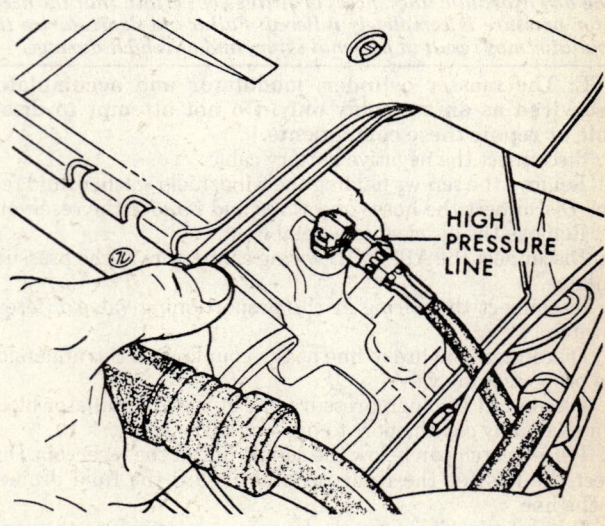

Always wear eye protection when disconnecting the high pressure hose

9-37

9 BRAKES

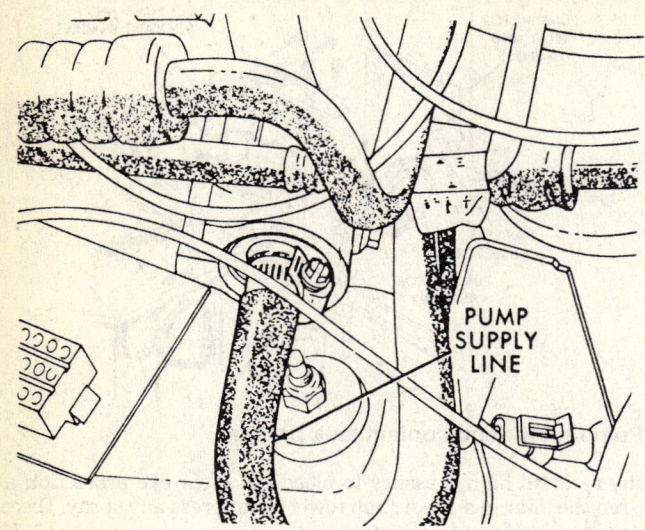

Use a catch pan when disconnecting the supply/return line

16. Connect the negative battery cable.
17. Turn the ignition switch **ON**; the pump should start running. Listen for a drop in pump rpm; this shows the pump is pressurizing the system. If there is no drop in pump rpm within 20 seconds, immediately shut the ignition **OFF** and check for hydraulic leaks.

NOTE: Severe pump damage will result if the pump runs without pressurizing the system for any length of time.

18. Add fluid to the reservoir as necessary. Do not overfill.
19. Reposition and secure the coolant reservoir.

MASTER CYLINDER, MODULATOR AND ACCUMULATOR

Removal and Installation

— CAUTION —
This brake system uses a hydraulic accumulator which, when fully charged, contains brake fluid at very high pressure. Before disconnecting any hydraulic lines, hoses or fittings be certain that the accumulator pressure is completely relieved. Failure to depressurize the accumulator may result in personal injury and/or vehicle damage.

NOTE: The master cylinder, modulator and accumulator are serviced as an assembly only. Do not attempt to disassemble or repair these components.

1. disconnect the negative battery cable.
2. Remove the screws holding the windshield washer fluid reservoir. Disconnect the hoses and wires and remove the reservoir.
3. Remove the air cleaner assembly.
4. Disconnect the ABS ECU wiring connectors at the pressure modulator.
5. disconnect the wiring at the proportioning valve/differential switch.
6. Disconnect the brake line at the coupling on the underside of the proportioning valve.
7. Disconnect the high pressure line at the accumulator block and immediately cap the port to prevent entry of dirt.
8. Place a catch pan below the supply line at the reservoir. Disconnect the hose at the reservoir and discard the fluid drained from the line.
9. Remove the wires from the low pressure switch on the accumulator block, the modulator boost pressure switch and the fluid level switch.

10. Disconnect the front brake lines at the outboard side of the pressure modulator.
11. Inside the car, disconnect the wiring to the brake pedal switch. It may be necessary to remove the instrument panel lower trim for access.
12. Remove the master cylinder push rod bolt; disconnect the pushrod from the pedal. Immediately discard the nuts from the pushrod bolt—they are not reusable.
13. Remove the nuts from the brake mounting bracket studs.
14. Under the hood, carefully pull the hydraulic components and bracket forward until the studs clear the firewall. Lift the assembly up and out of the engine compartment.

To install:

15. Install the pad onto the new bracket and place the bracket with the brake components in place against the firewall. Make certain the studs are correctly seated in the holes.
16. Position the master cylinder/modulator/accumulator on the firewall and tighten the mounting nuts to 27 ft. lbs (31 Nm).
17. Connect the wiring harness to the low pressure switch, the differential switch, the pressure modulator, the low fluid and boost pressure switches.
18. Inside the vehicle, install the nuts on the mounting studs and tighten them to 31 ft. lbs (42 Nm).
19. Align the brake pedal, the brake lamp switch and the master cylinder pushrod. Install the pushrod bolt. The pushrod bolt must be correctly installed to avoid interference with the bracket. The bolt head must be on the left side of the brake pedal.
20. Use new nuts on the pushrod bolt. The inner lock nut should be tightened to 25 ft. lbs. (34 Nm); the outer jam nut should be tightened to 75 inch lbs. (8.5 Nm).
21. Connect the wiring to the brake switch and replace the lower dashboard trim if it was removed.
22. In the engine compartment, connect the brake lines to the proportioning valve.
23. Connect the pressure and return lines to the accumulator.
24. Install the air cleaner assembly.
25. Connect hoses and wires to the windshield washer fluid reservoir and install it in position.

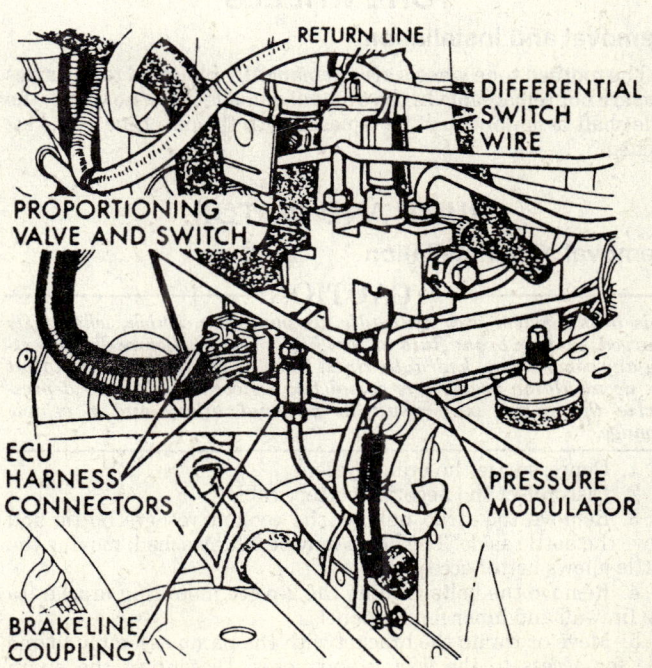

Master cylinder connectors

BRAKES 9

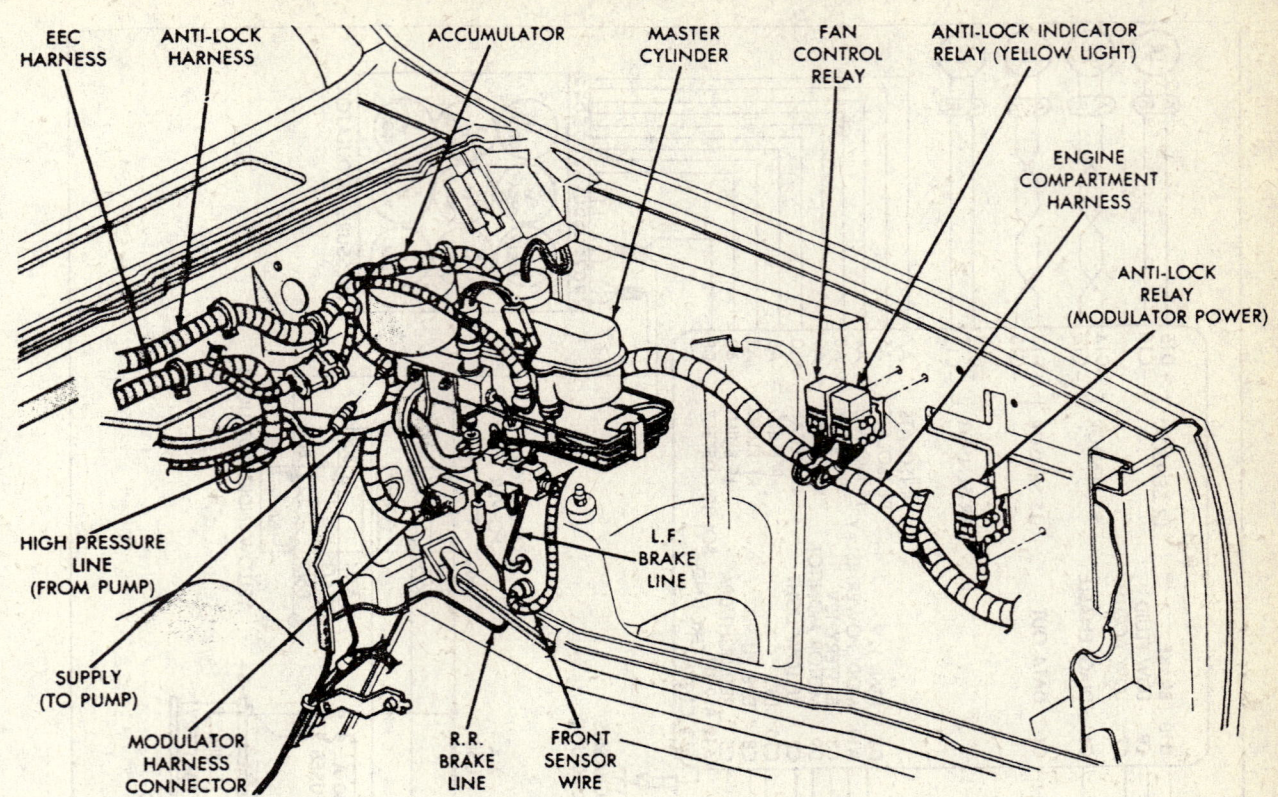

ABS left-side underhood component location

26. Inspect the high-pressure and return lines; make certain they are not kinked or touching the engine.
27. Fill the master cylinder to the MAX level.
28. Connect the negative battery cable.
29. Turn the ignition switch **ON**; the pump should start running. Listen for a drop in pump rpm; this shows the pump is pressurizing the system. If there is no drop in pump rpm within 20 seconds, immediately shut the ignition **OFF** and check for hydraulic leaks.

NOTE: Severe pump damage will result if the pump runs without pressurizing the system for any length of time.

30. Add fluid to the reservoir as necessary. Do not overfill.
31. Bleed the brake system.

ELECTRONIC CONTROL UNIT (ECU)

Removal and Installation

1. Confirm that the ignition switch is **OFF**.
2. Fold the rear seat cushion forward for access to the ECU.
3. Remove the bracket holding the ECU from the floor pan, then remove the control unit from the bracket.
4. Carefully disconnect the wiring connectors from the ECU.

To install:

5. Connect the wiring harnesses to the replacement unit.
6. Mount the control unit on the bracket, then install the bracket to the floor pan. Make certain the bracket is in the correct position.
7. Reposition the rear seat cushion.

PARKING BRAKE

ADJUSTMENT

NOTE: This procedure requires the use of a special tool.

1. Ensure the rear brakes are properly adjusted. Place the parking brake lever in the fifth notch.
2. Raise and support the vehicle safely.
3. Place the adjustment tool J-34651 on the rear cable (Cherokee/Wagoneer) or the front cable (Comanche). Using a torque wrench, apply a torque of 45–50 inch lbs.
4. Adjust the equalizer adjusting nut so that the gauge pointer is in the green band on the tool.
5. Apply and release the brake lever fully, five times, and re-check the adjustment.
6. When adjustment is correct, stake the adjusting nut.

REPLACEMENT

Rear Cable

1. Raise and support the vehicle safely. Fully release the parking brake.

9-39

9 BRAKES

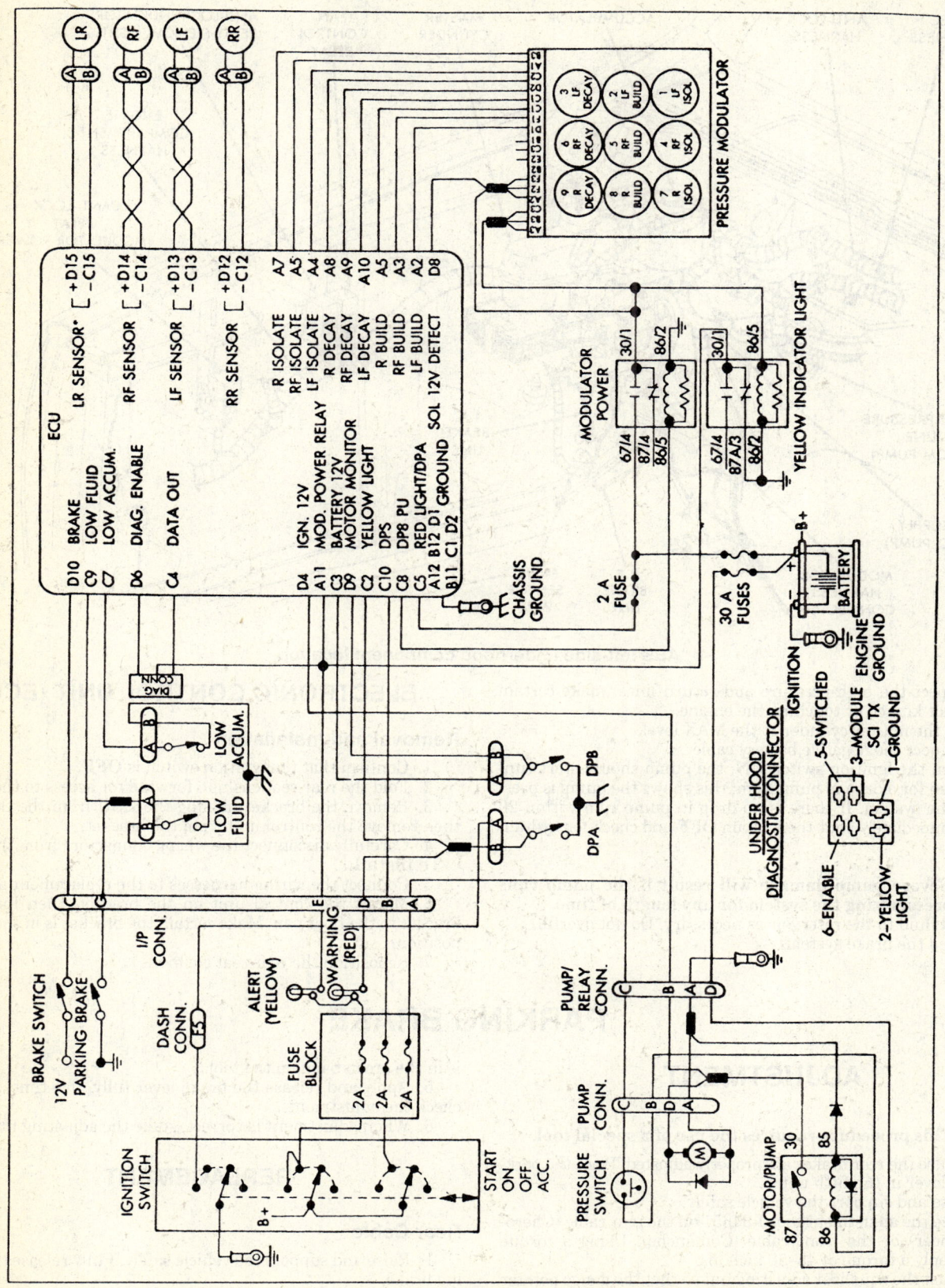

9-40

BRAKES 9

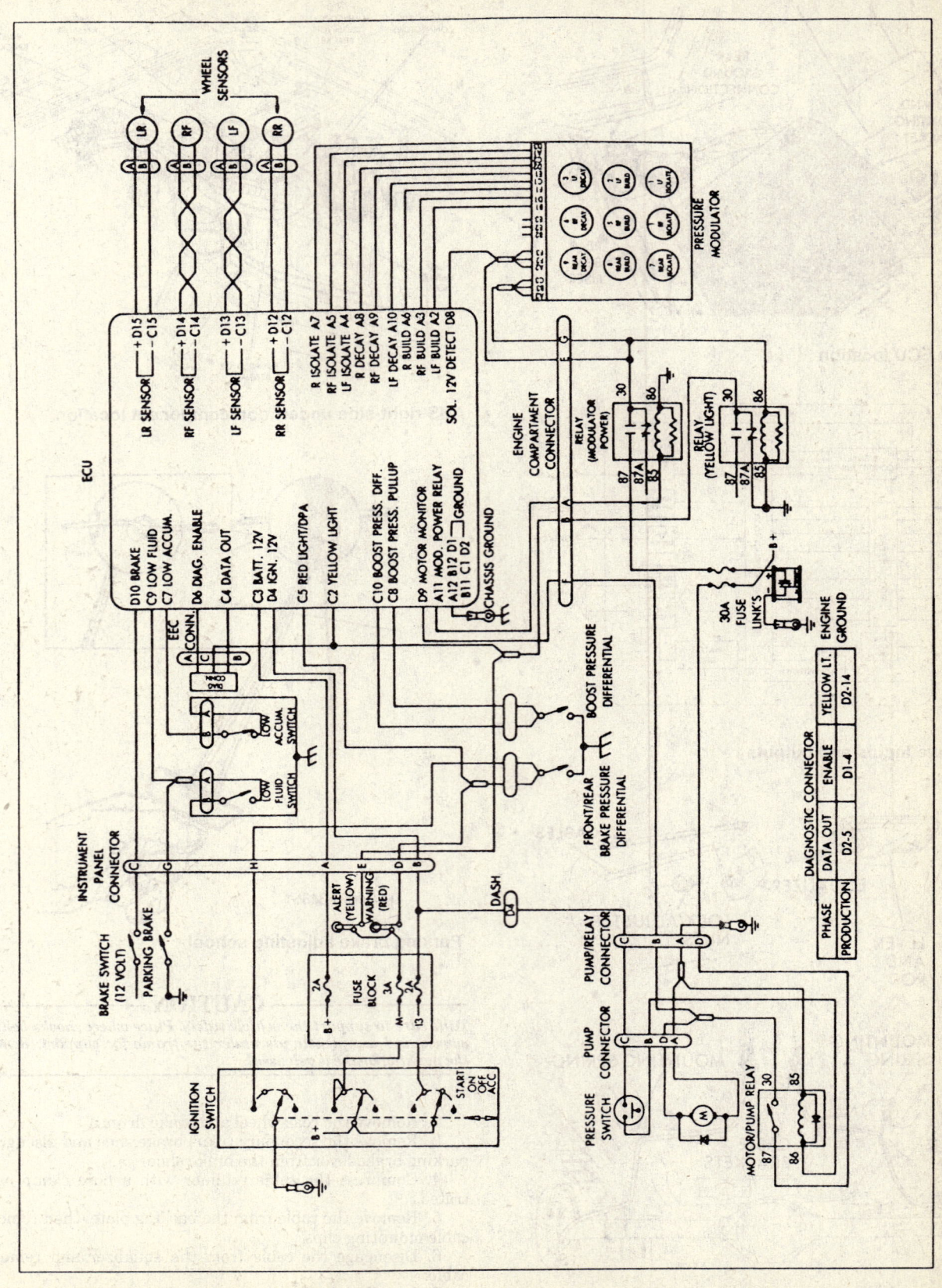

9-41

9 Brakes

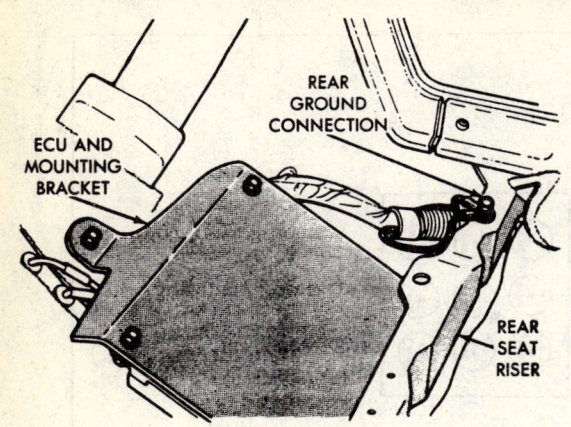

Anti-lock ECU location

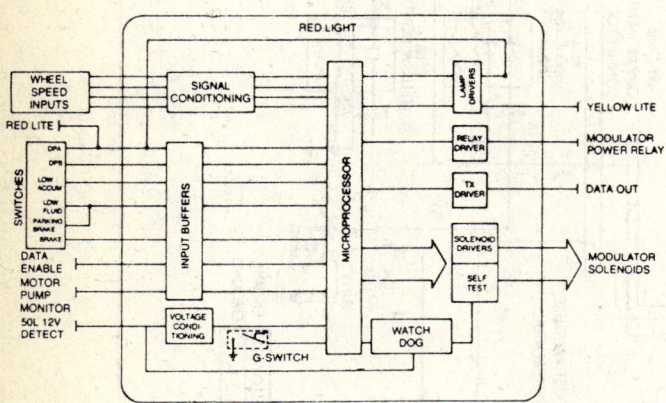

ABS module inputs and outputs

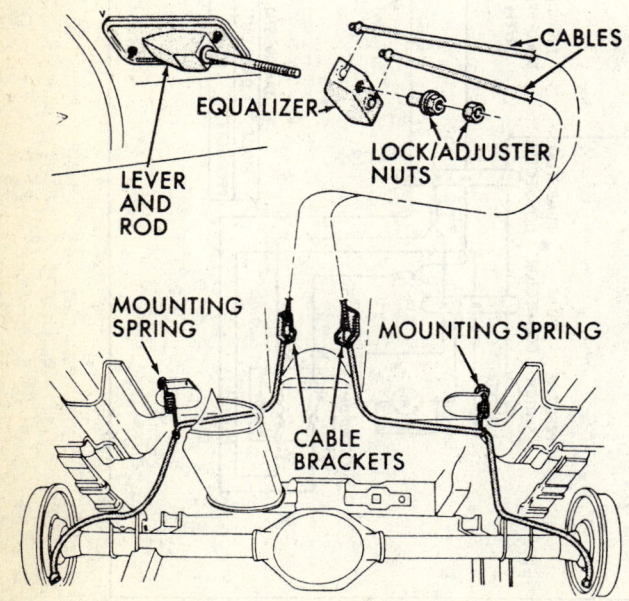

Parking brake cables — Cherokee/Wagoneer

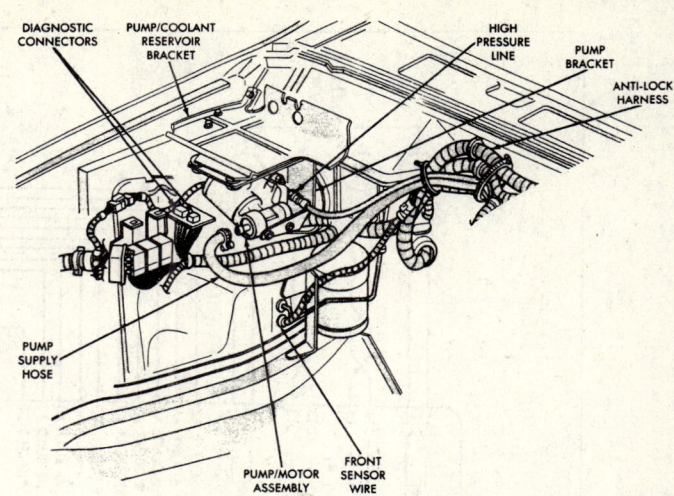

ABS right-side underhood component location

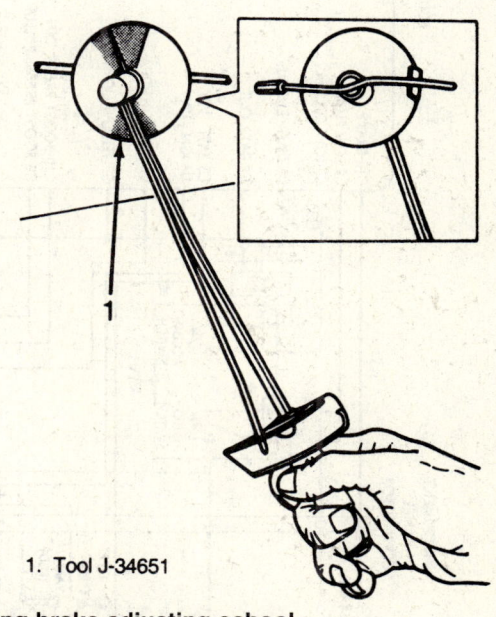

1. Tool J-34651

Parking brake adjusting school

CAUTION

Take care to support the vehicle safely. Place wheel chocks behind the wheels and use jackstands under the frame for support. Remember, the parking brake is released!.

---

2. Remove the rear wheel and brake drum.
3. Remove the secondary (rear) brake shoe and disengage the parking brake lever from the brake shoe.
4. Compress the cable retainer with a hose clamp as illustrated.
5. Remove the cable from the backing plate, then remove the cable mounting clips.
6. Disengage the cable from the equalizer and remove the cable.
7. Installation is the reverse of removal. Adjust the rear brakes. Adjust the parking brake cable.

BRAKES 9

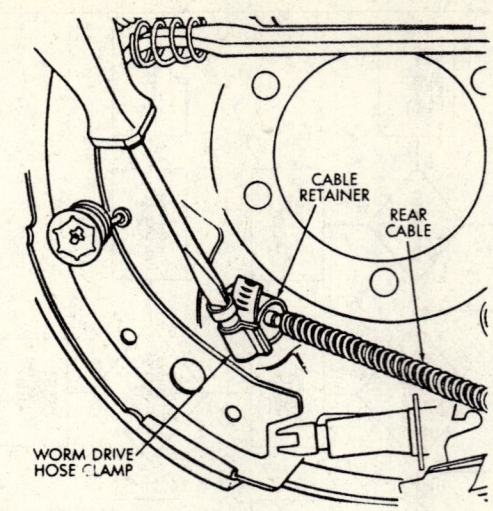

Compressing the cable retainer

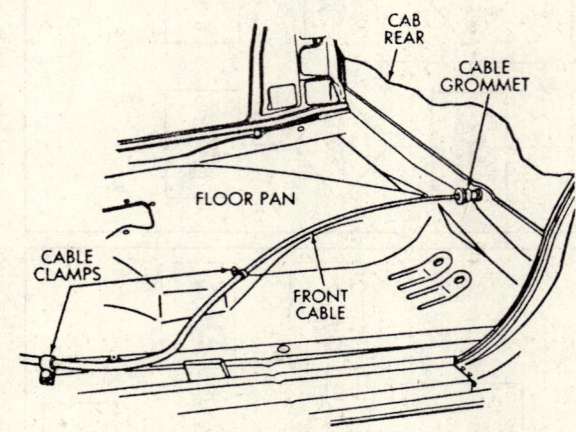

Front cable floor pan attachment — Comanche Only

Front Cable (Comanche Only)

1. Raise and support the vehicle safely. Fully release the parking brake.

CAUTION

Take care to support the vehicle safely. Place wheel chocks behind the wheels and use jackstands under the frame for support. Remember, the parking brake is released!.

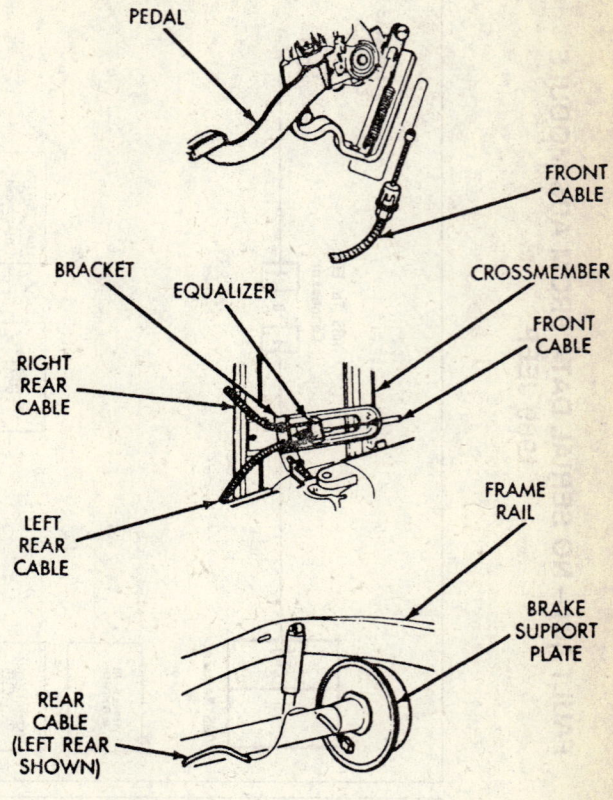

Parking brake cable — Comanche

2. Remove the equalizer nuts and remove the front cable from the equalizer and cable bracket.

3. Lower the vehicle.

4. Move the carpet away from the pedal assembly. Then remove the pedal mounting bolts and move the pedal assembly away from the kick panel. Disconnect the front cable from the pedal.

5. Move the carper at the drivers side and rear of the cab to gain access to the cable floor pan clamps. Remove the clamps, unseat the cable grommet and remove the cable through the floor pan.

6. Installation is the reverse of removal. Adjust the parking brake cable.

9-43

FAULT 800—NO VOLTAGE AT ABS MODULE 1989 JEEP

FAULT 801—NO SERIAL DATA FROM ABS MODULE 1989 JEEP

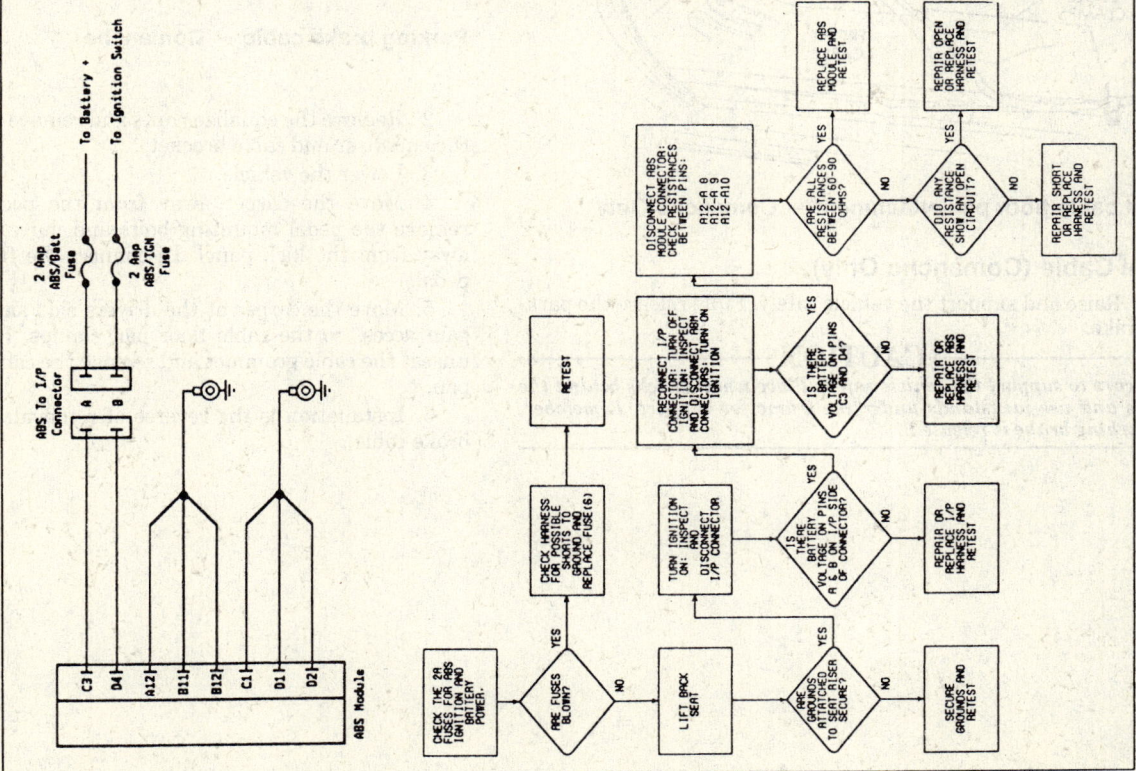

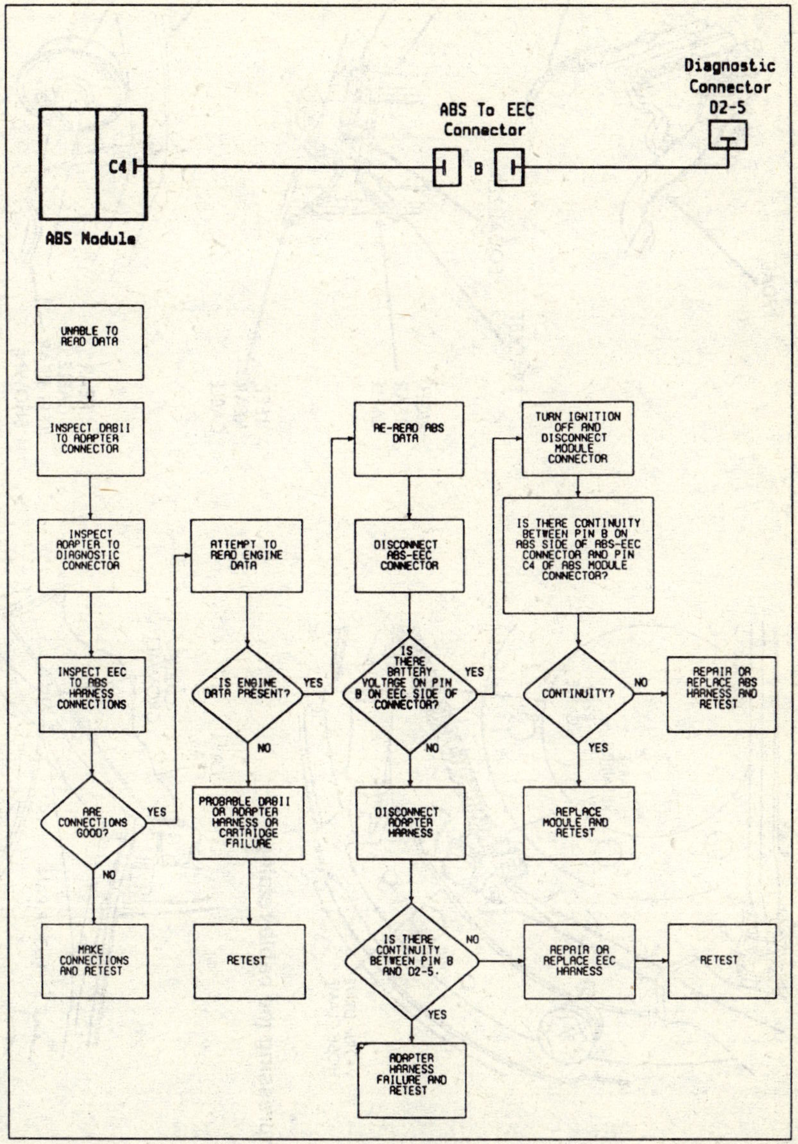

BRAKES 9

FAULT 803 – ABS LIGHTS INOPERATIVE – 1989 JEEP

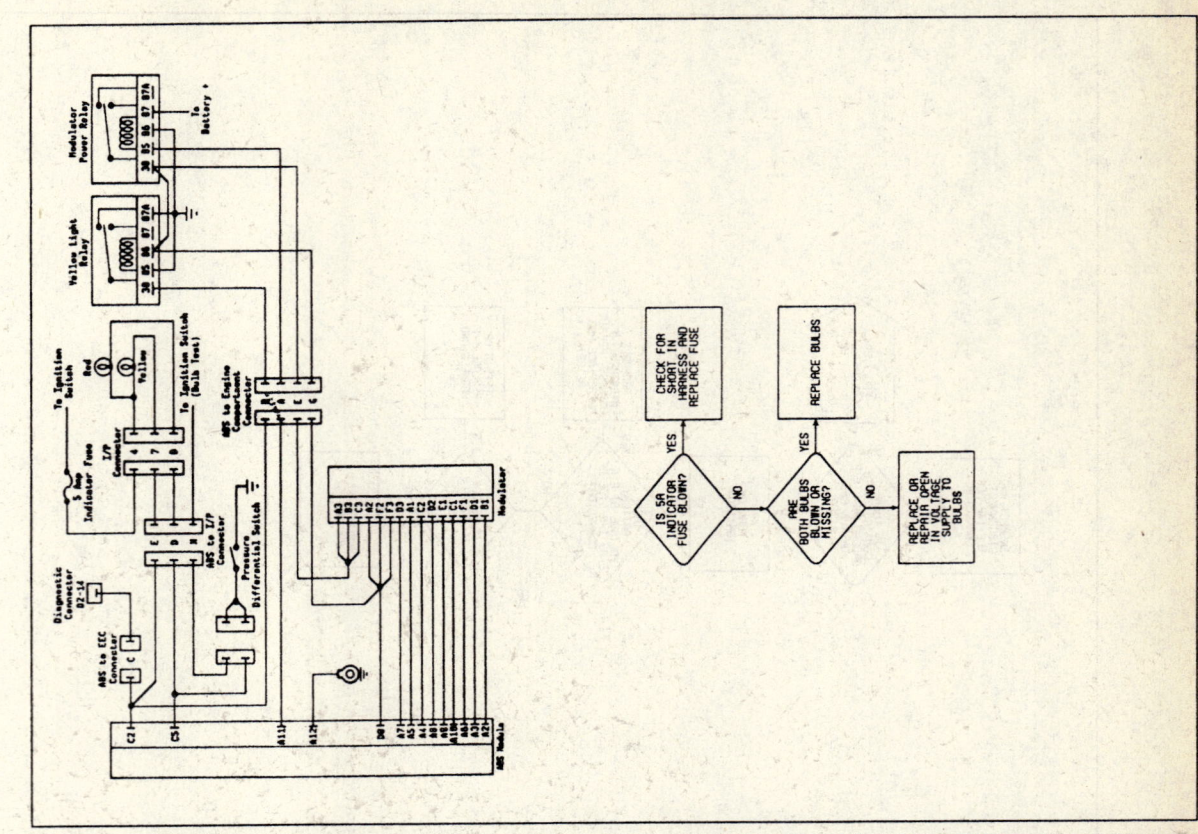

FAULT 802 – PARKING BRAKE NOT SEEN – 1989 JEEP

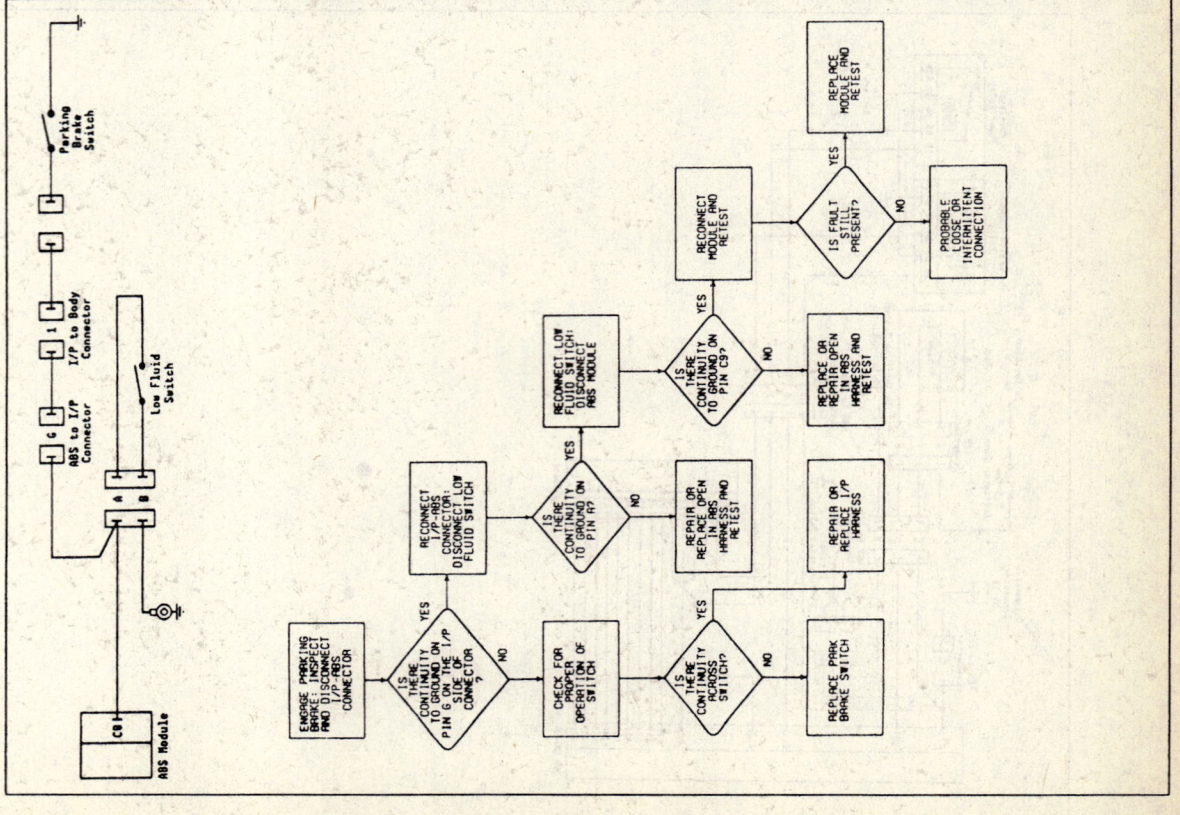

9-45

9 BRAKES

FAULT 804 — YELLOW LIGHT OFF — 1989 JEEP

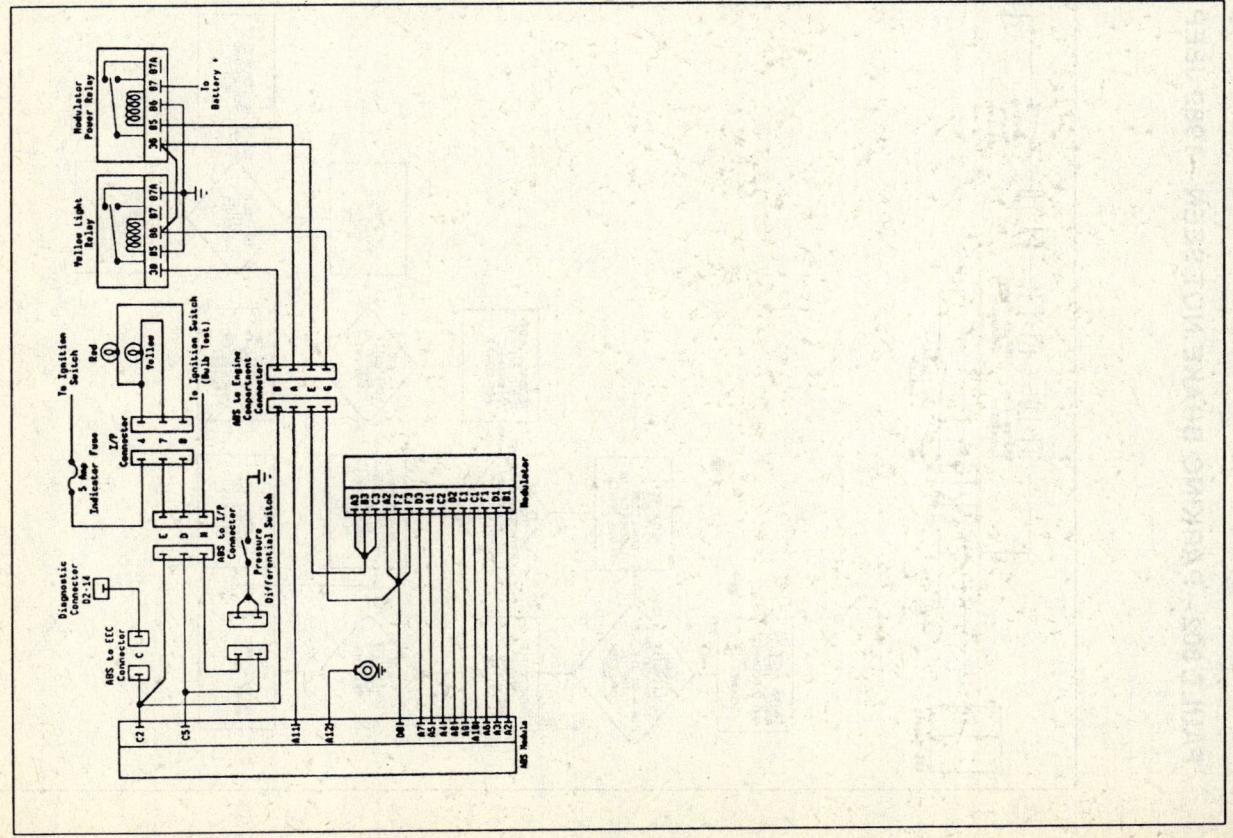

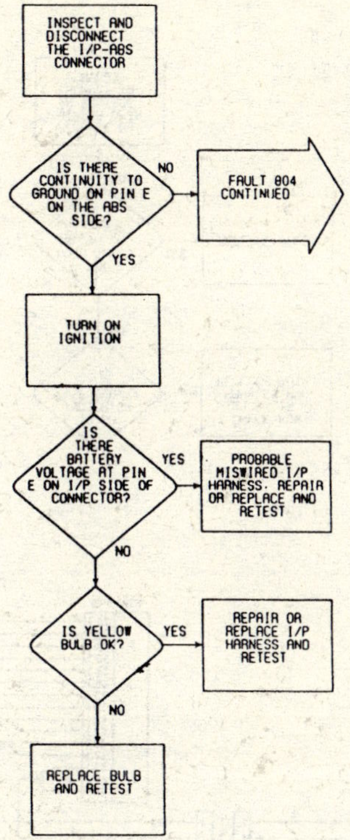

9-46

BRAKES 9

FAULT 804 — YELLOW LIGHT OFF (CONTINUED) — 1989 JEEP

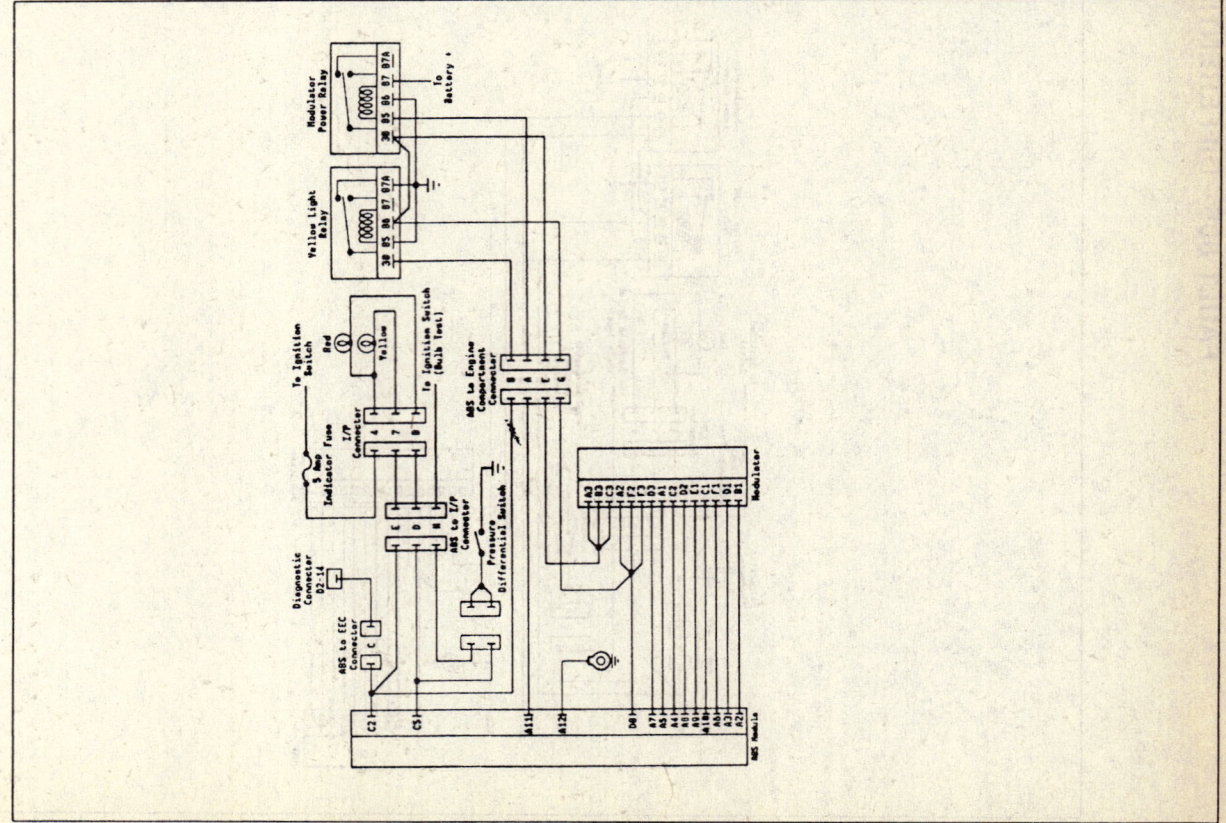

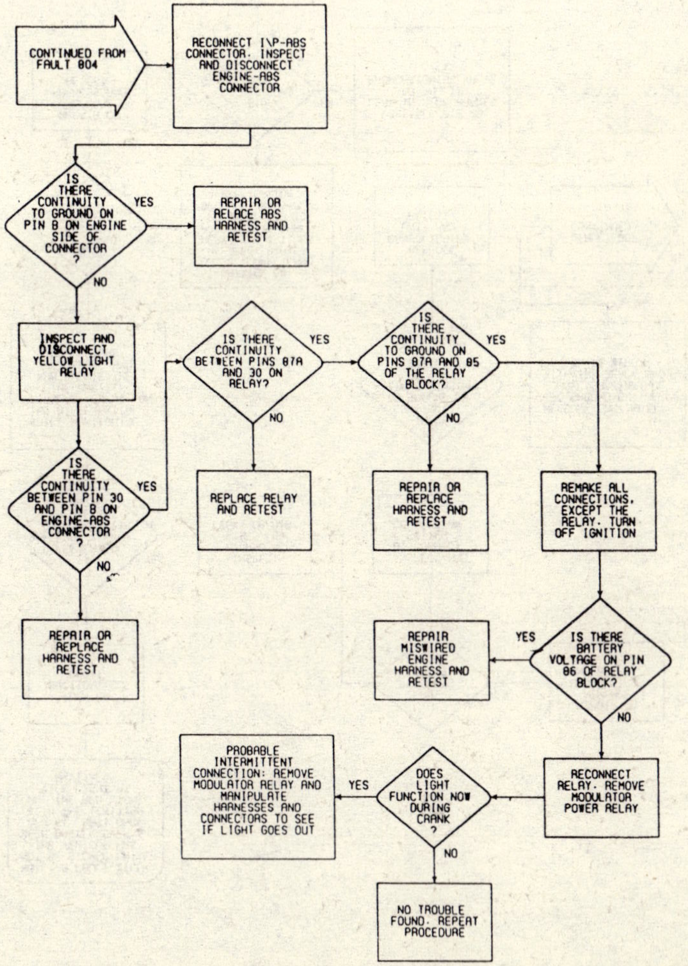

9-47

9 BRAKES

FAULT 805 – DIFFERENTIAL PRESSURE – 1989 JEEP

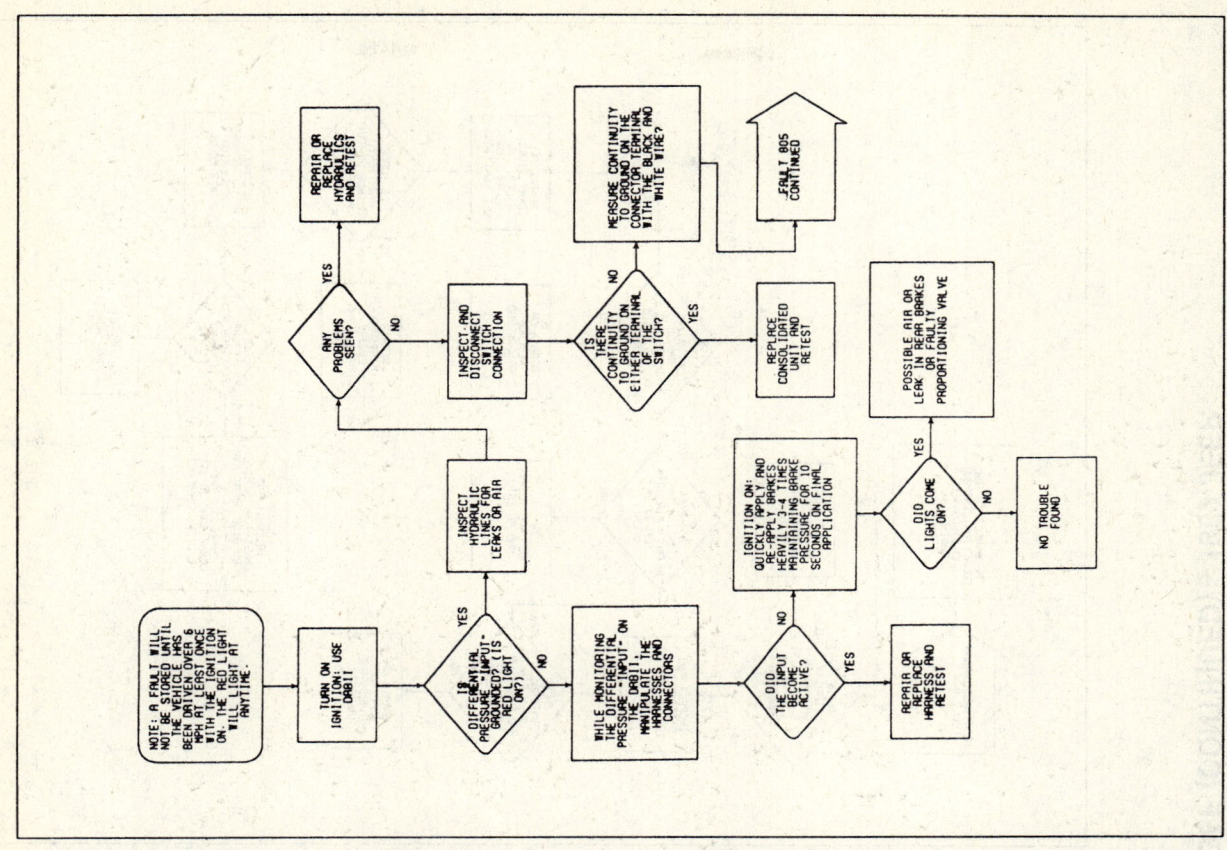

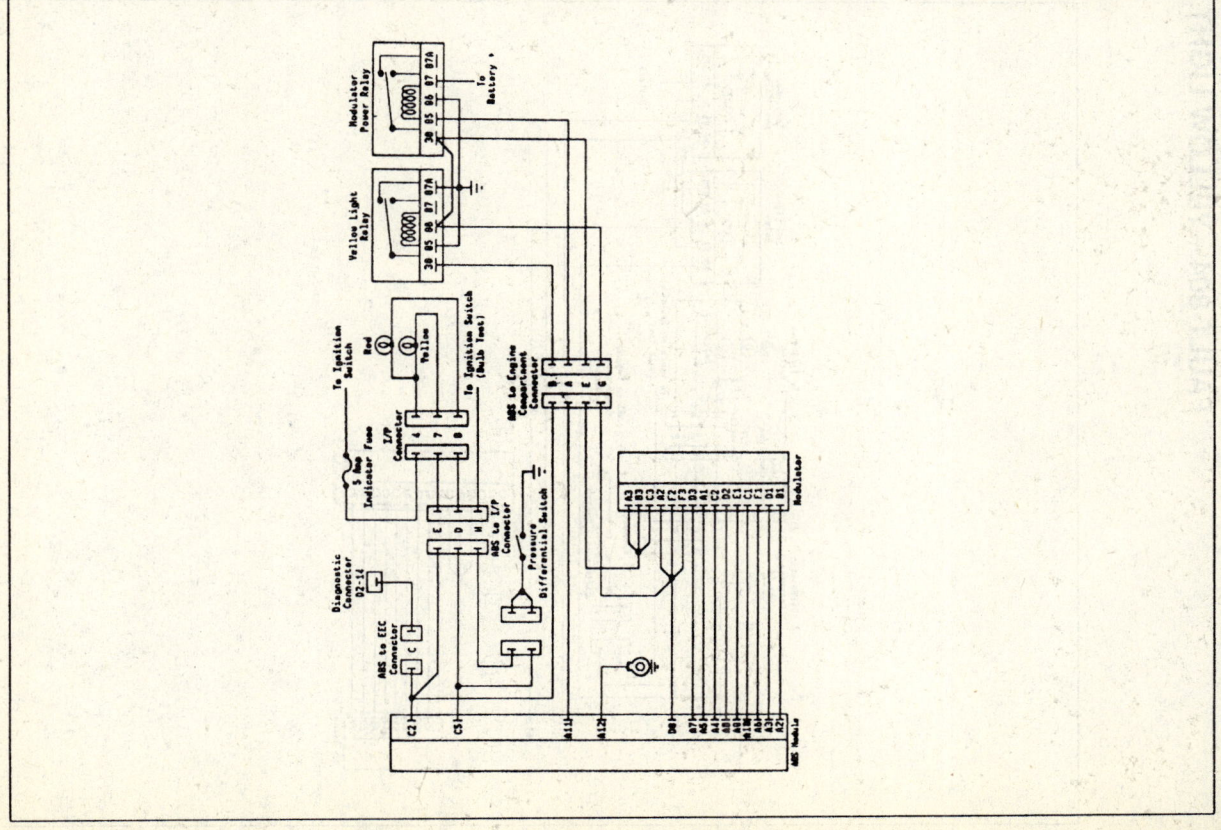

9-48

BRAKES 9

FAULT 805 – DIFFERENTIAL PRESSURE (CONTINUED) – 1989 JEEP

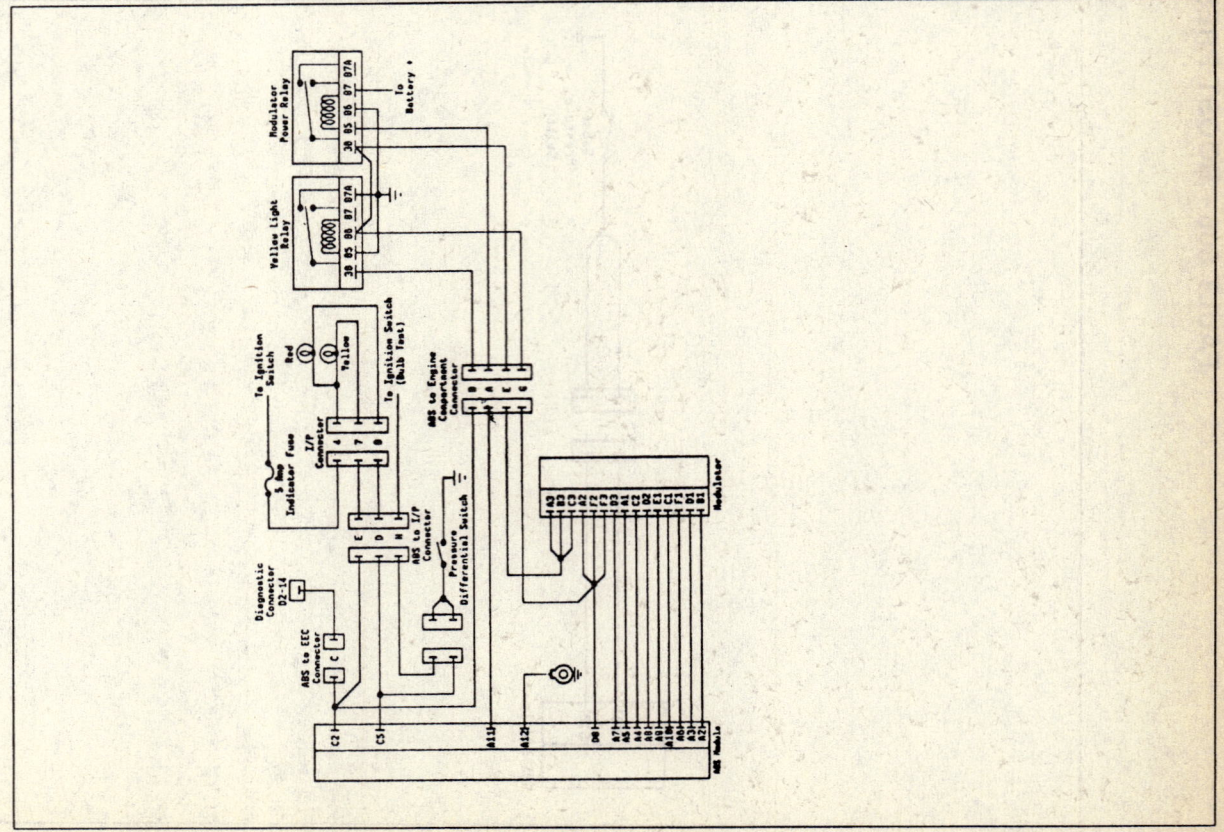

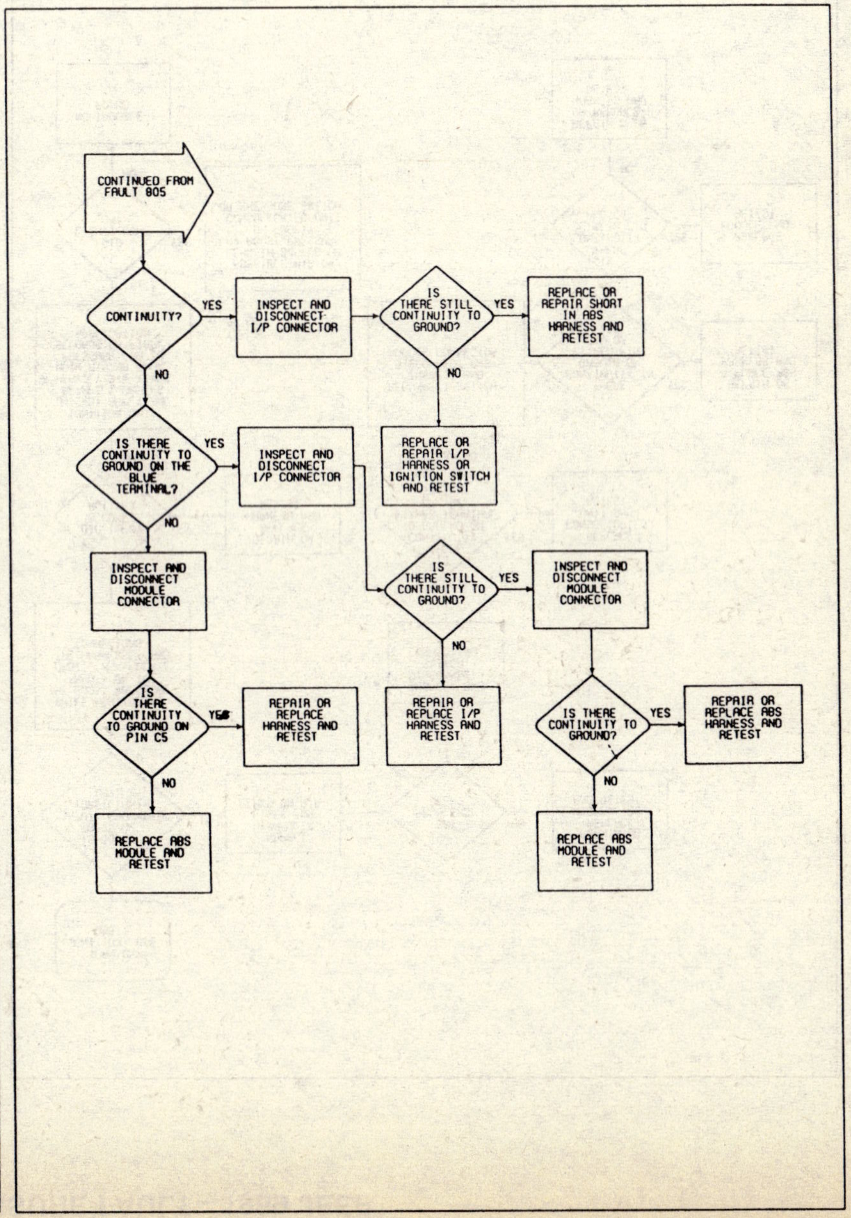

9-49

9 BRAKES

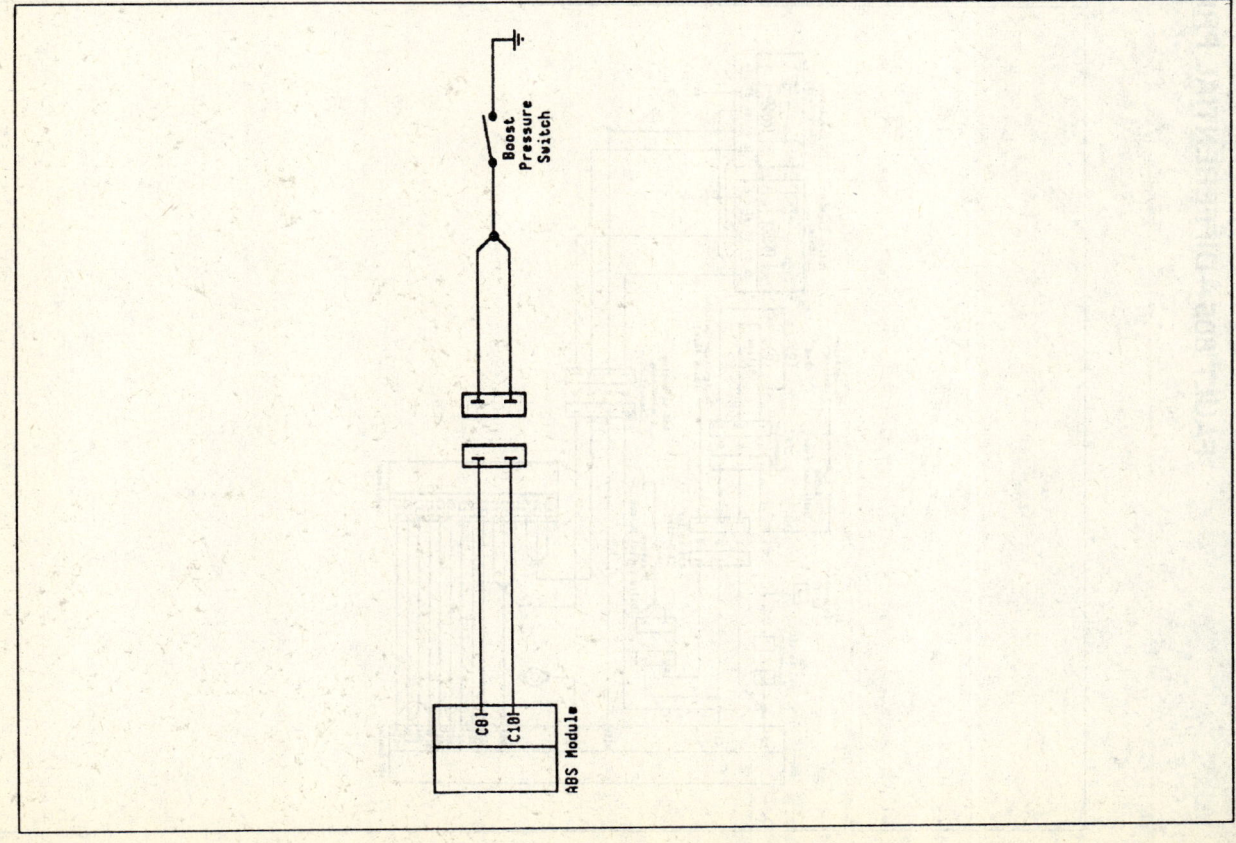

FAULT 806 — BOOST PRESSURE FAULT — 1989 JEEP

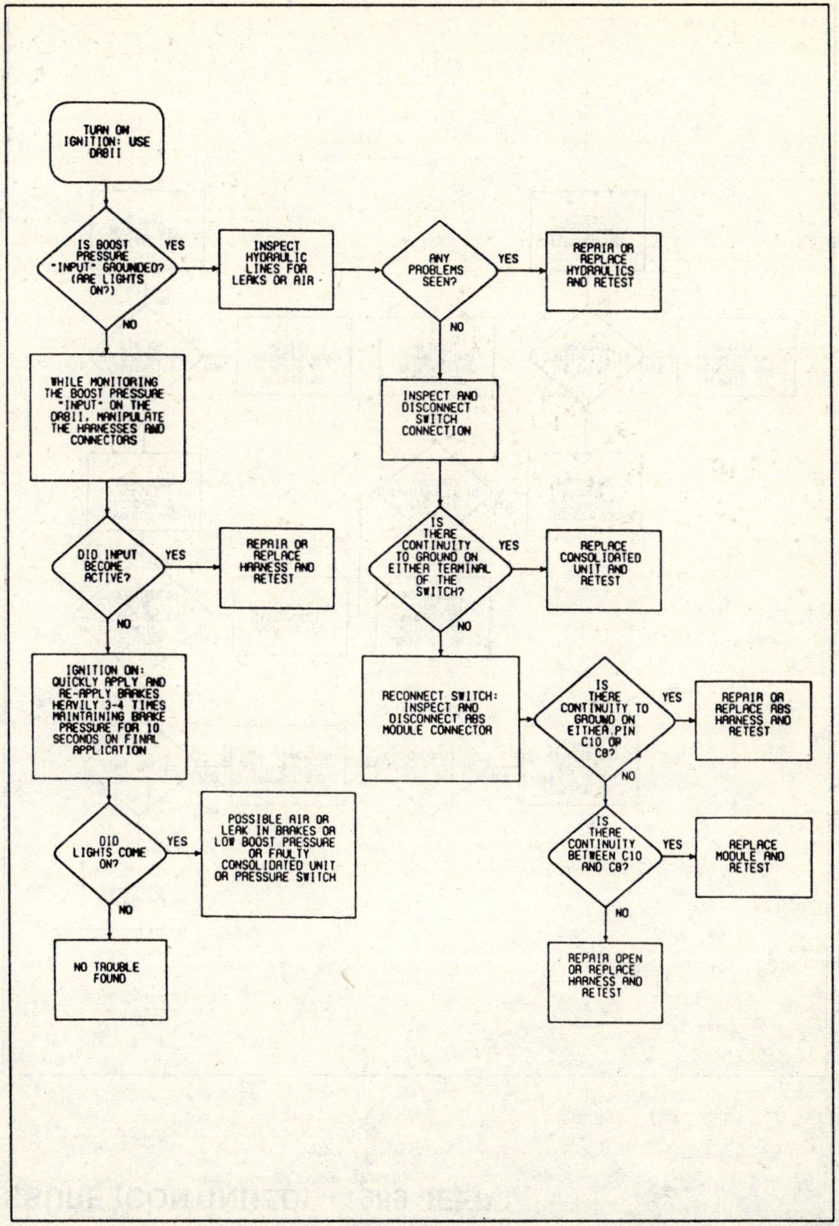

9-50

BRAKES 9

FAULT 807 – LOW ACCUMULATOR – 1989 JEEP

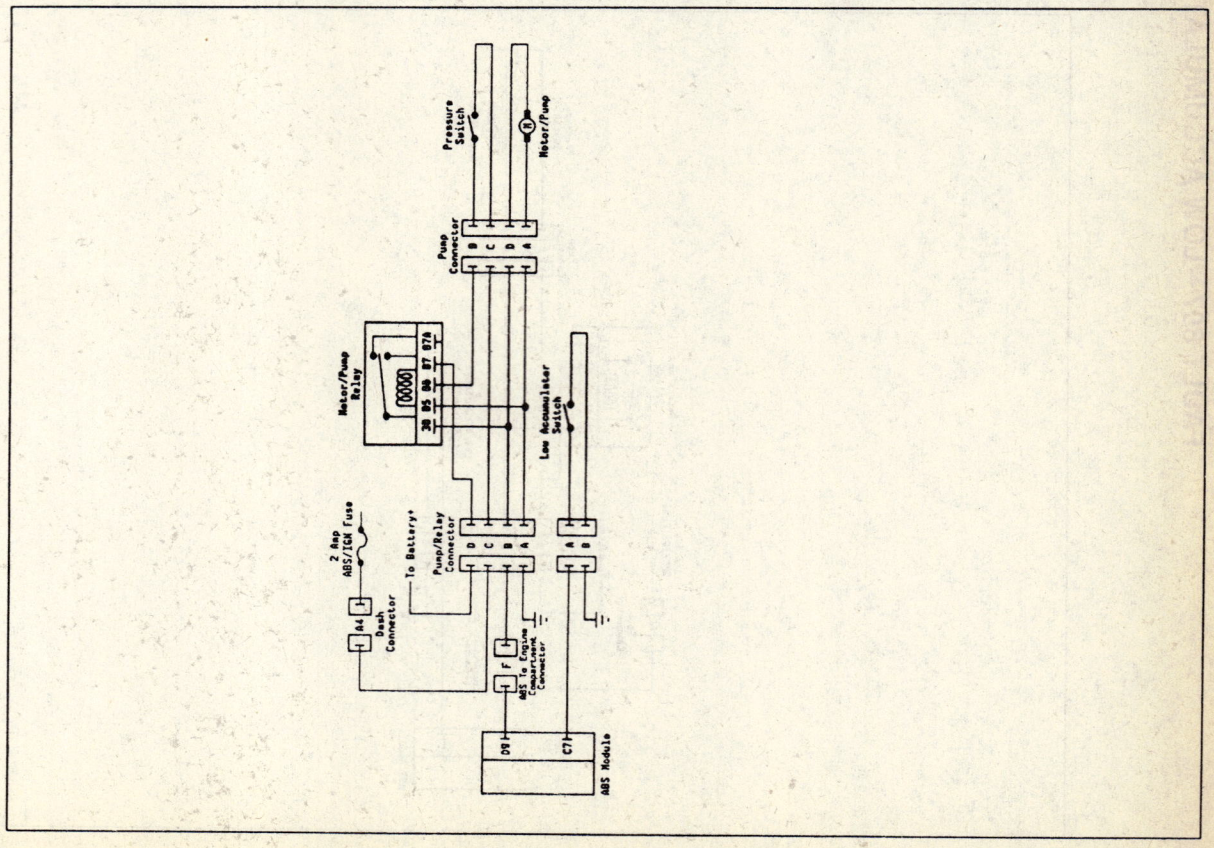

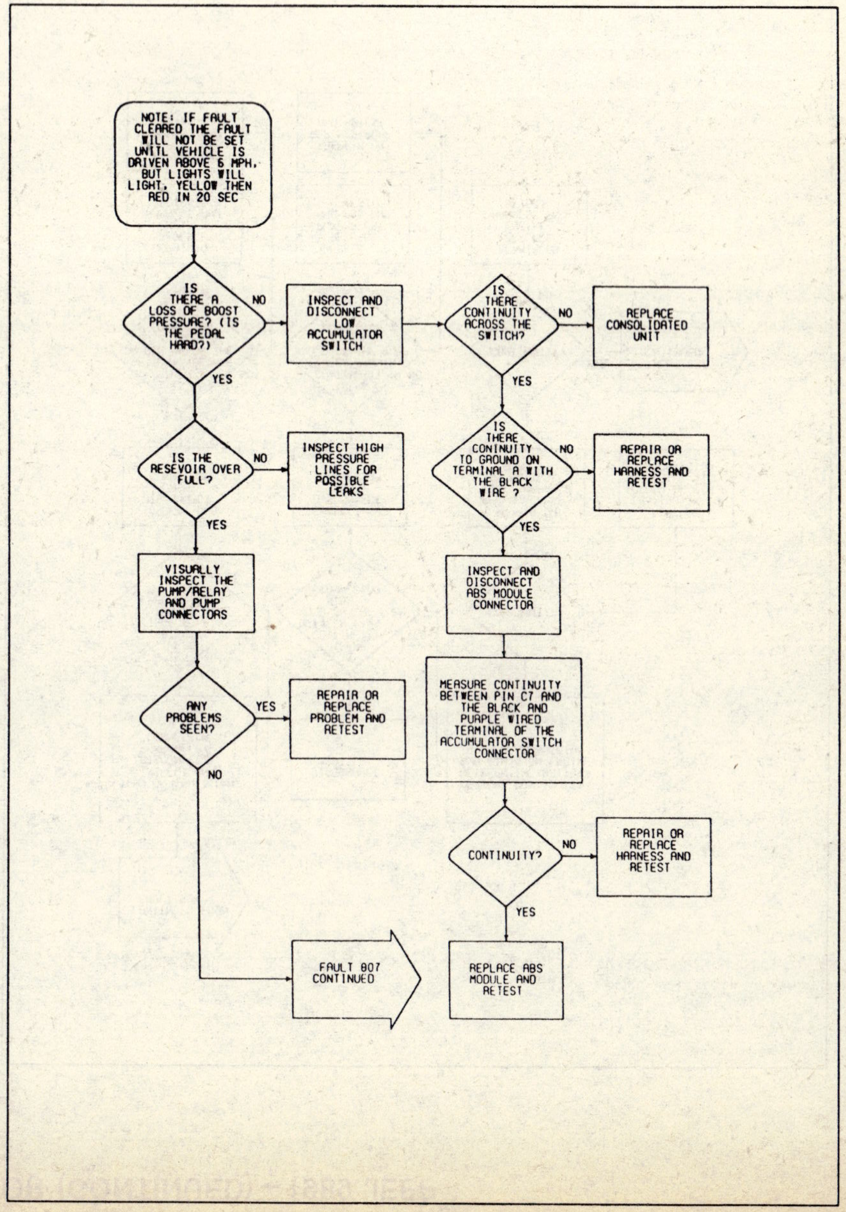

9-51

9 BRAKES

FAULT 807 – LOW ACCUMULATOR (CONTINUED) – 1989 JEEP

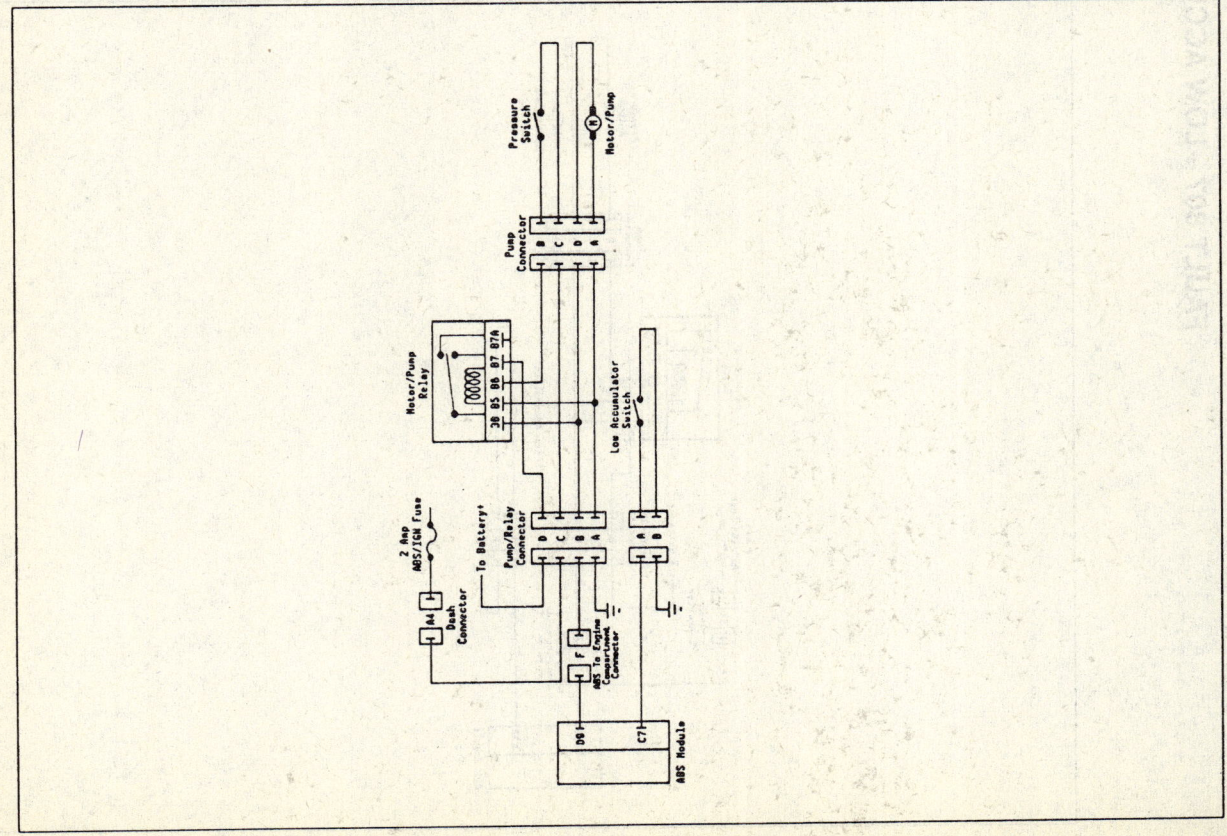

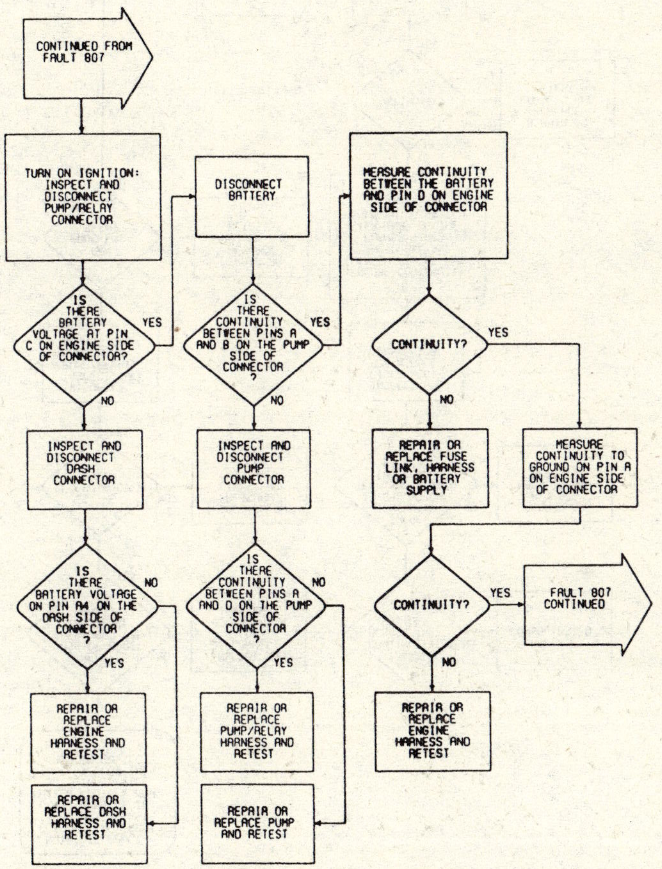

BRAKES 9

FAULT 807 — LOW ACCUMULATOR (CONTINUED) — 1989 JEEP

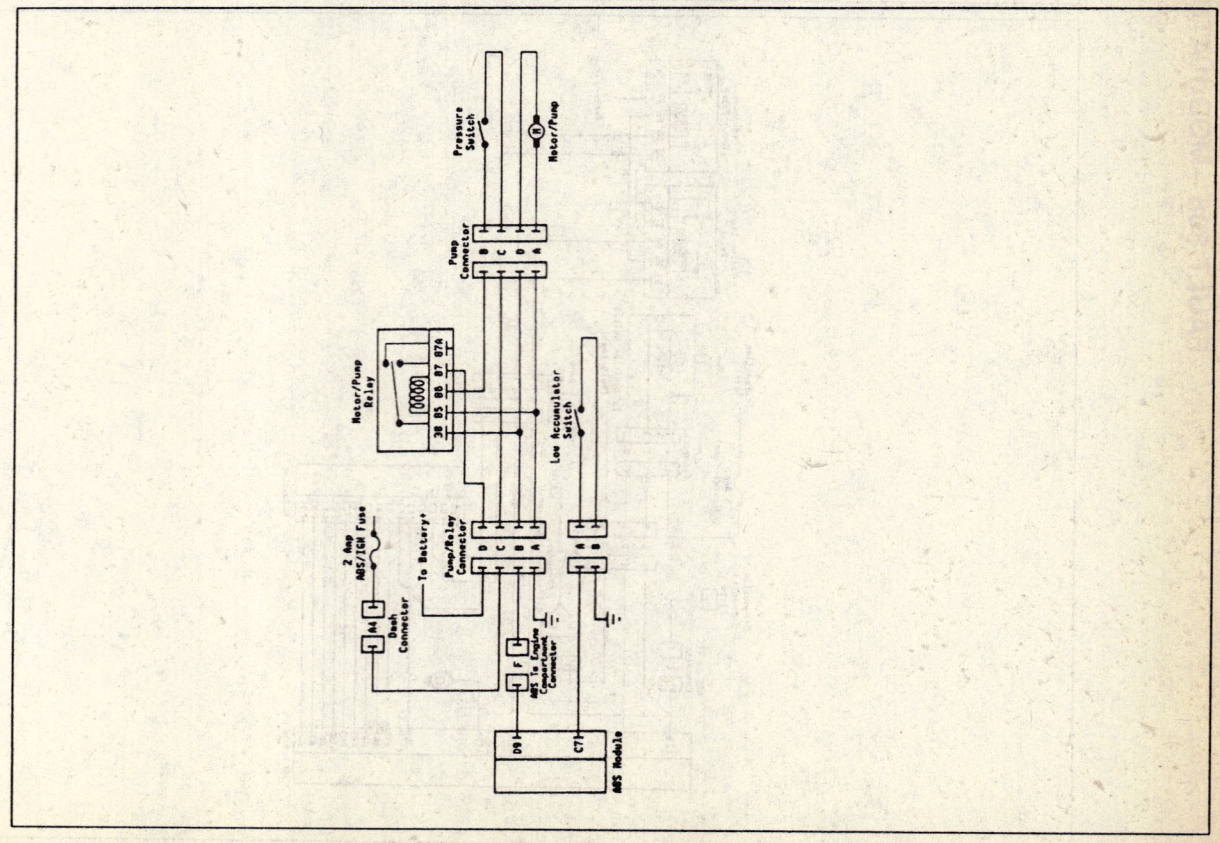

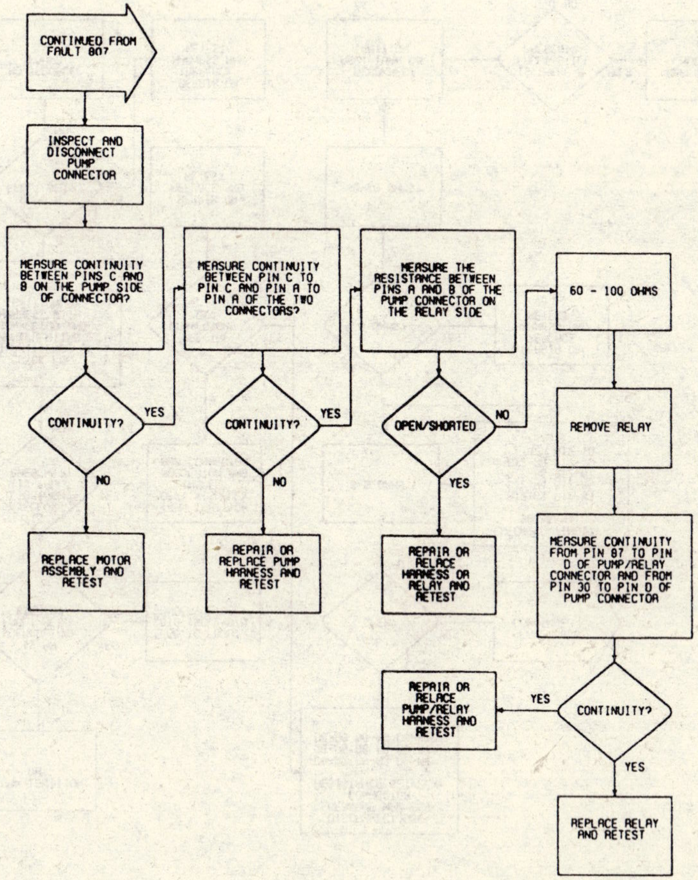

9-53

9 BRAKES

FAULT 808 – MODULATOR FAULT – 1989 JEEP

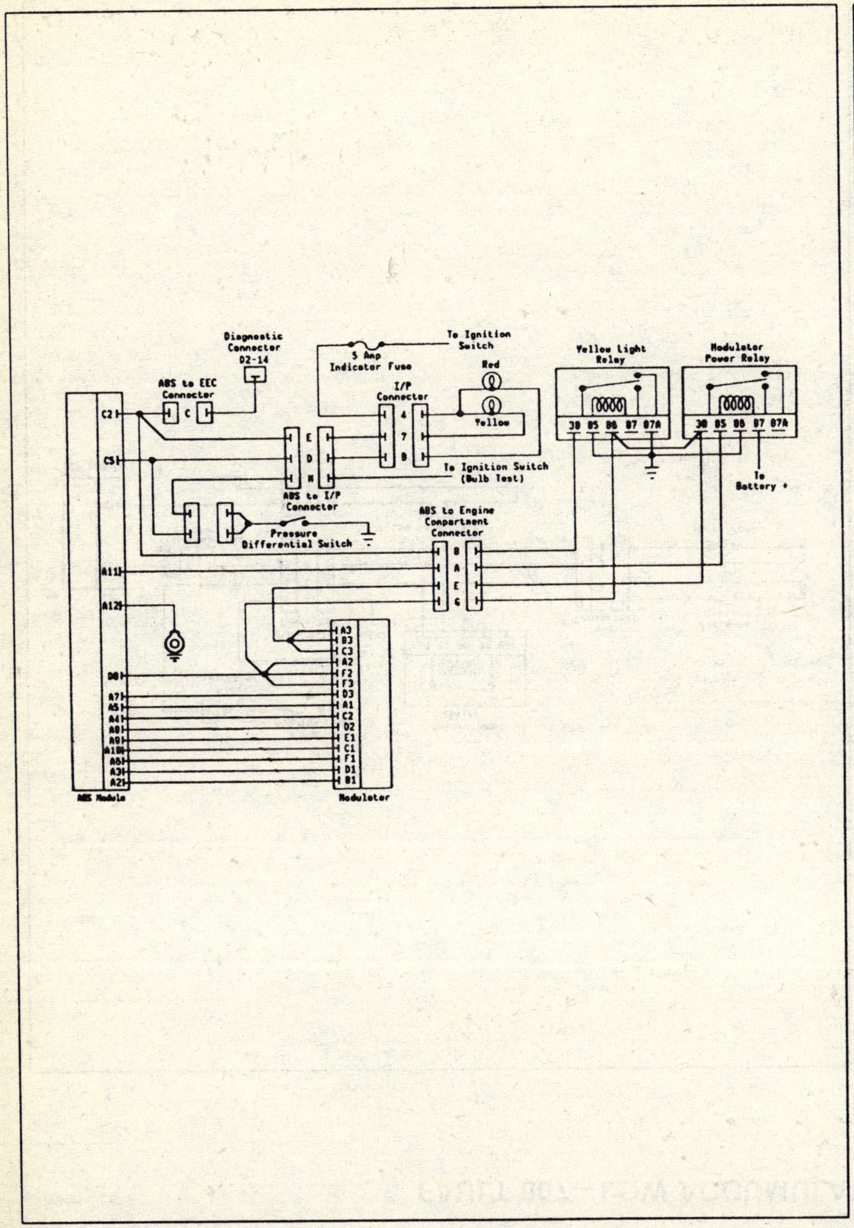

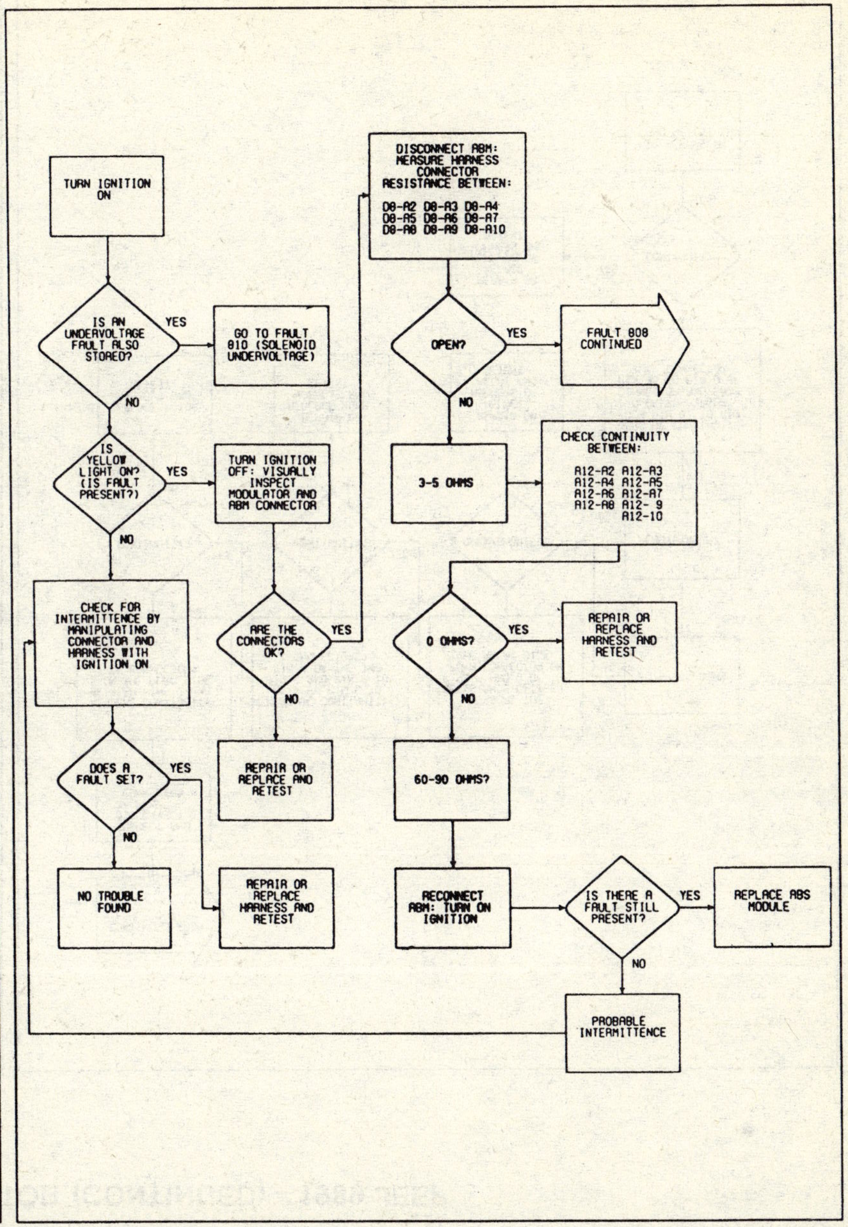

9-54

BRAKES 9

FAULT 808—MODULATOR FAULT (CONTINUED)—1989 JEEP

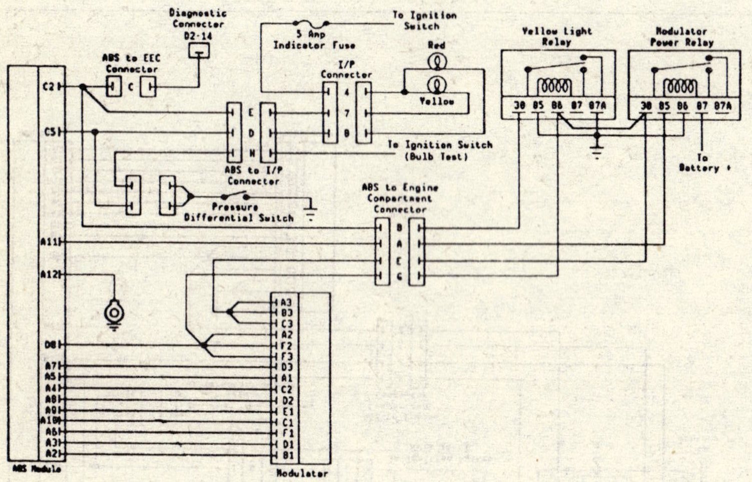

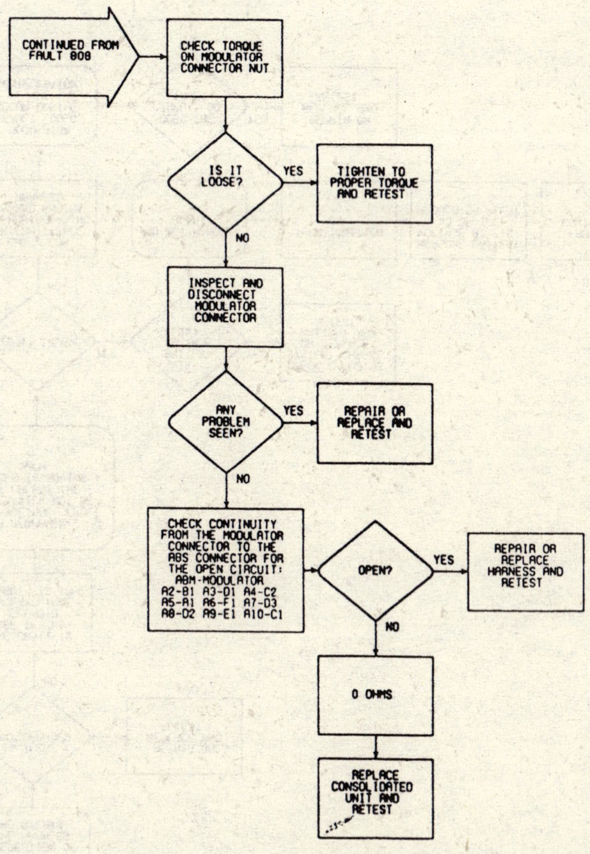

9-55

FAULT 810—SOLENOID UNDER VOLTAGE—1989 JEEP

FAULT 809—SELF TEST FAILURE—1989 JEEP

REPLACE ABS MODULE

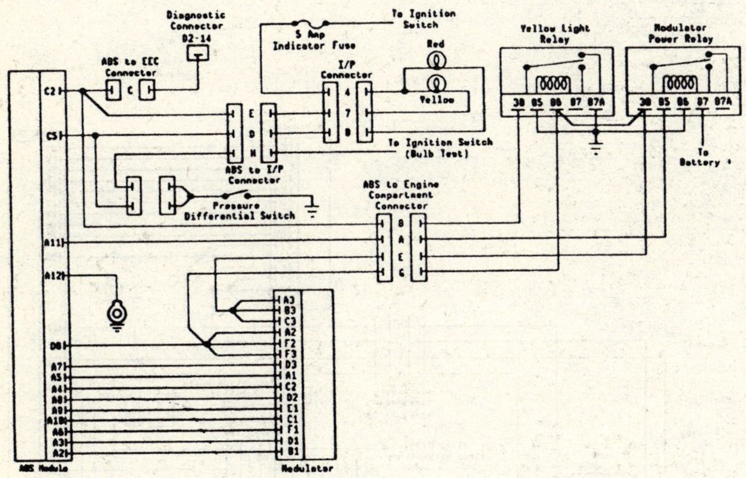

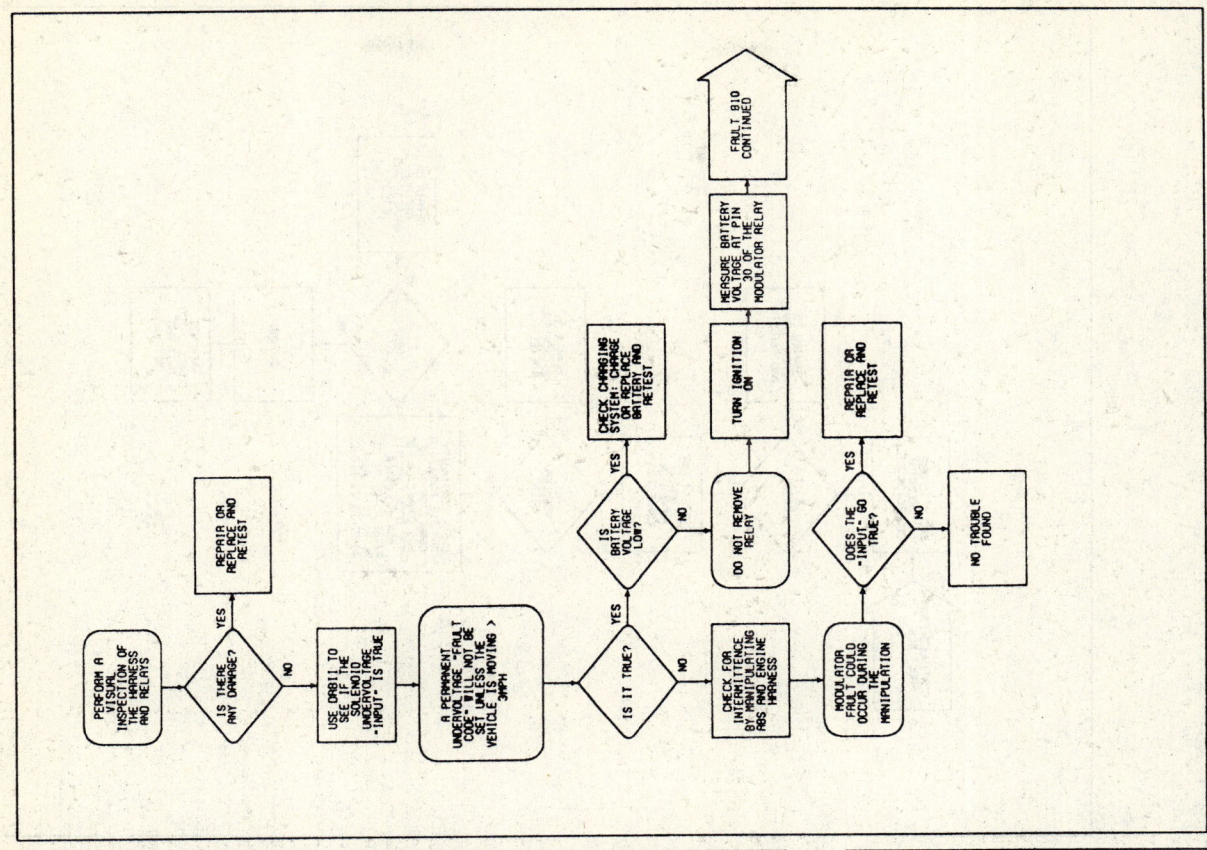

BRAKES 9

FAULT 810—SOLENOID UNDER VOLTAGE (CONTINUED)—1989 JEEP

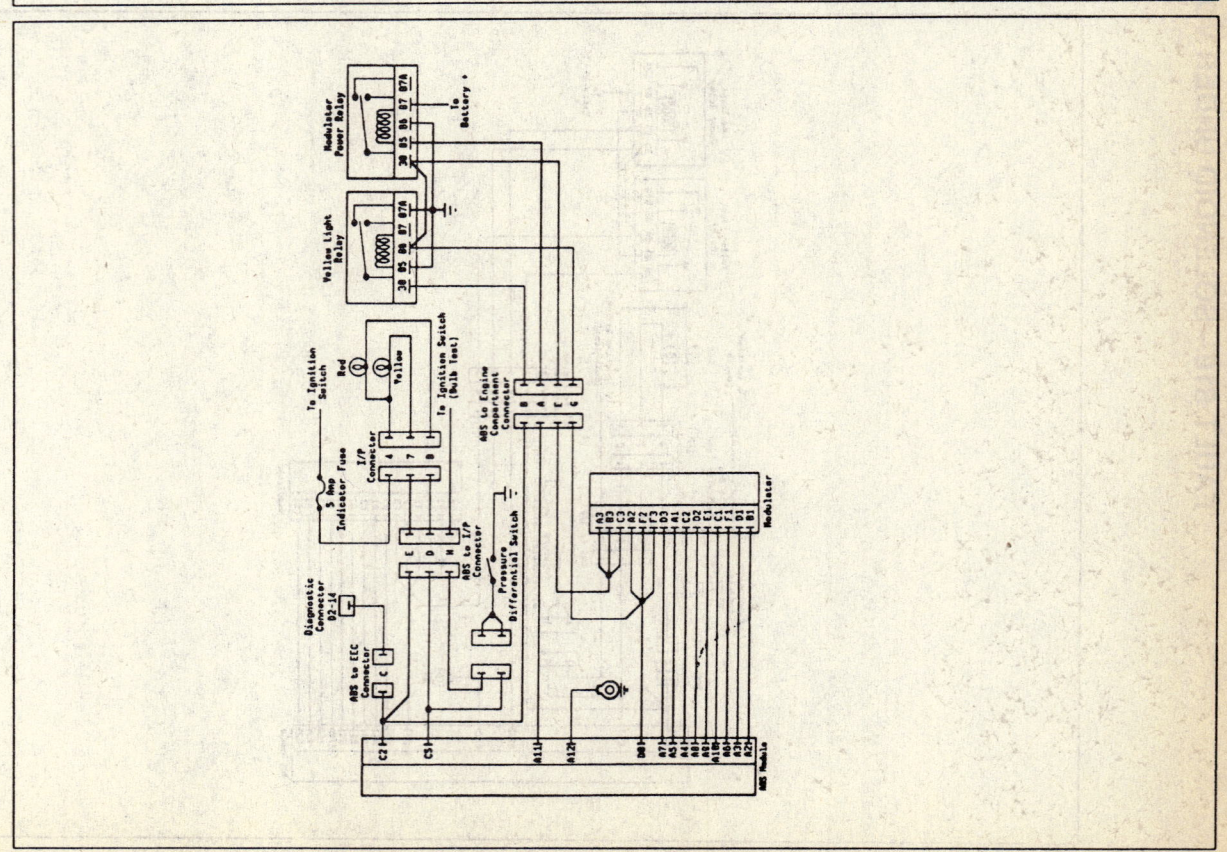

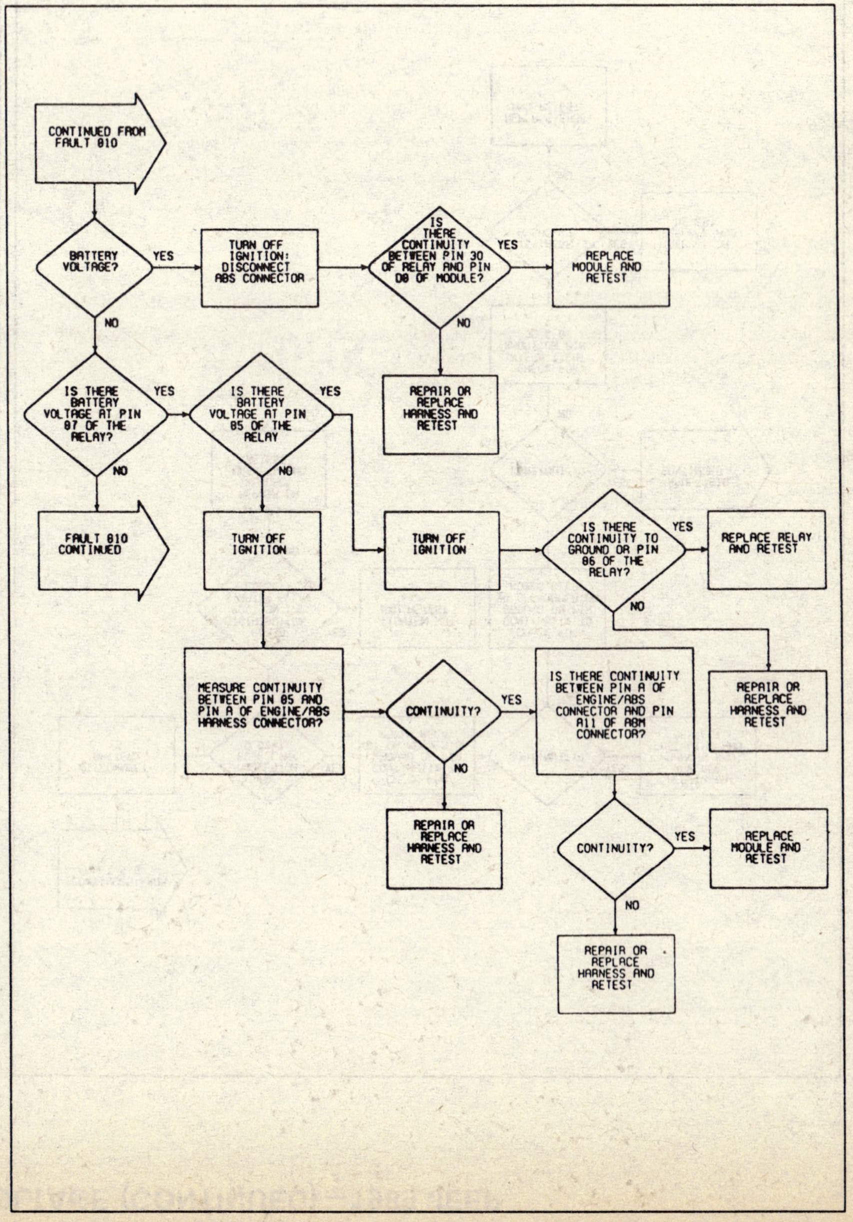

9-57

9 BRAKES

FAULT 810—SOLENOID UNDER VOLTAGE (CONTINUED)—1989 JEEP

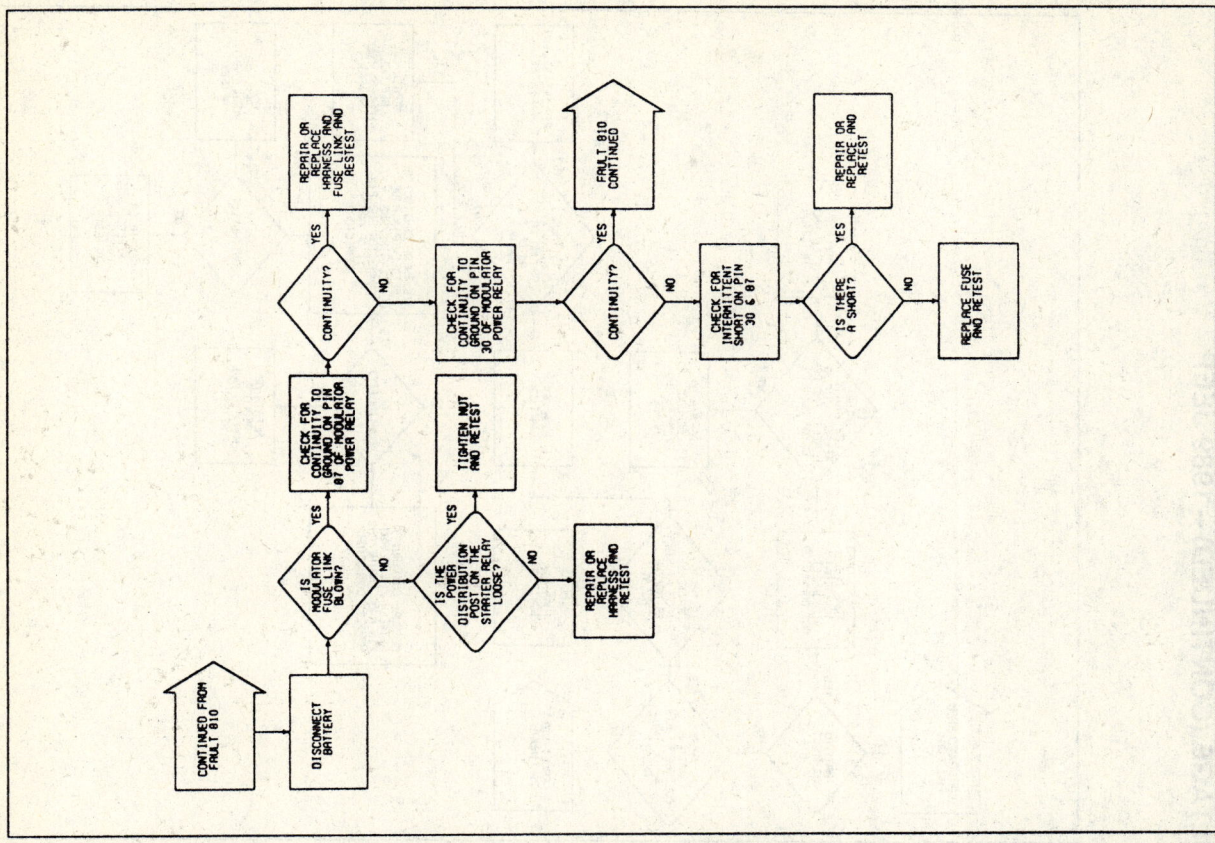

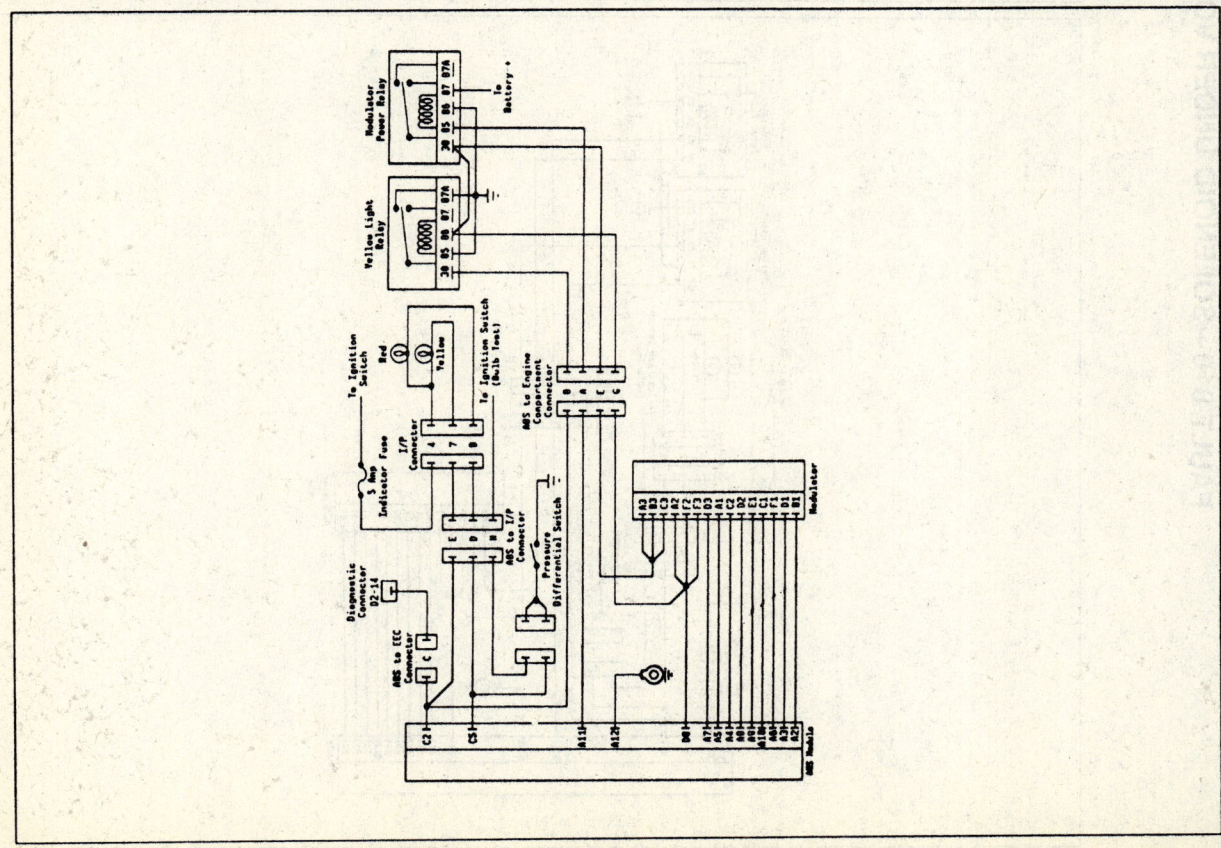

9-58

BRAKES 9

FAULT 810 – SOLENOID UNDER VOLTAGE (CONTINUED) – 1989 JEEP

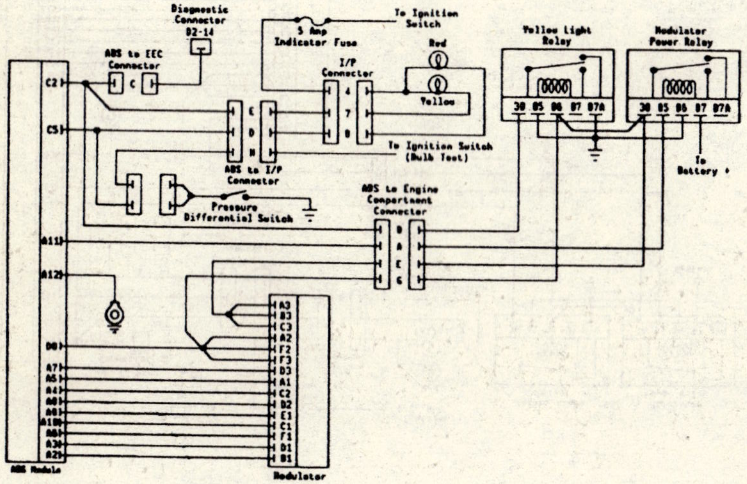

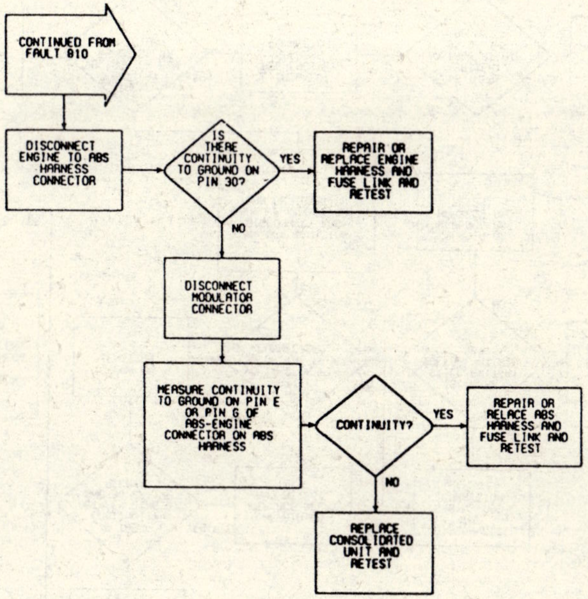

9-59

9 BRAKES

FAULT 811 — RELAY FAULT — 1989 JEEP

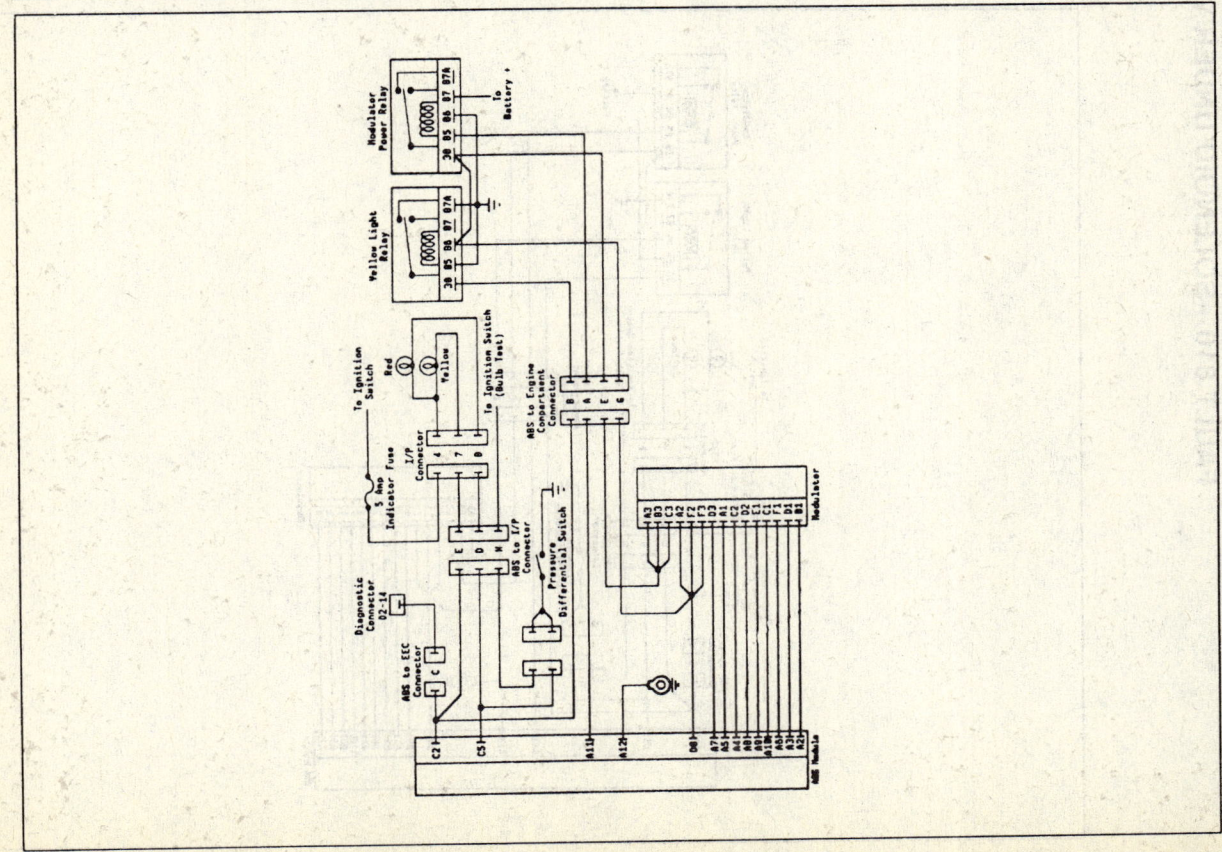

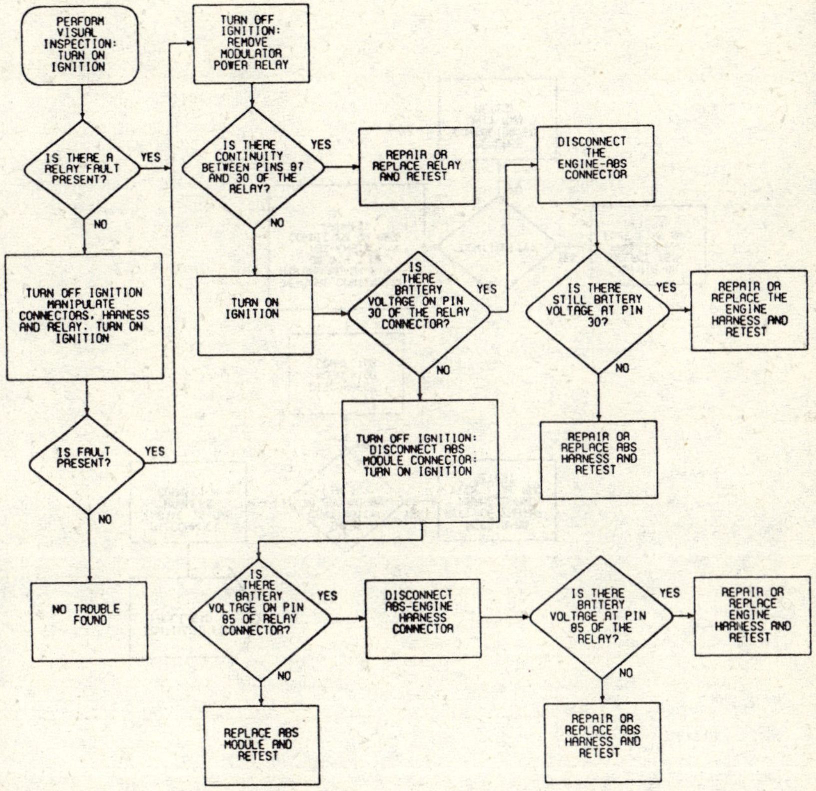

9-60

BRAKES 9

FAULT 812—MOTOR/PUMP FAULT—1989 JEEP

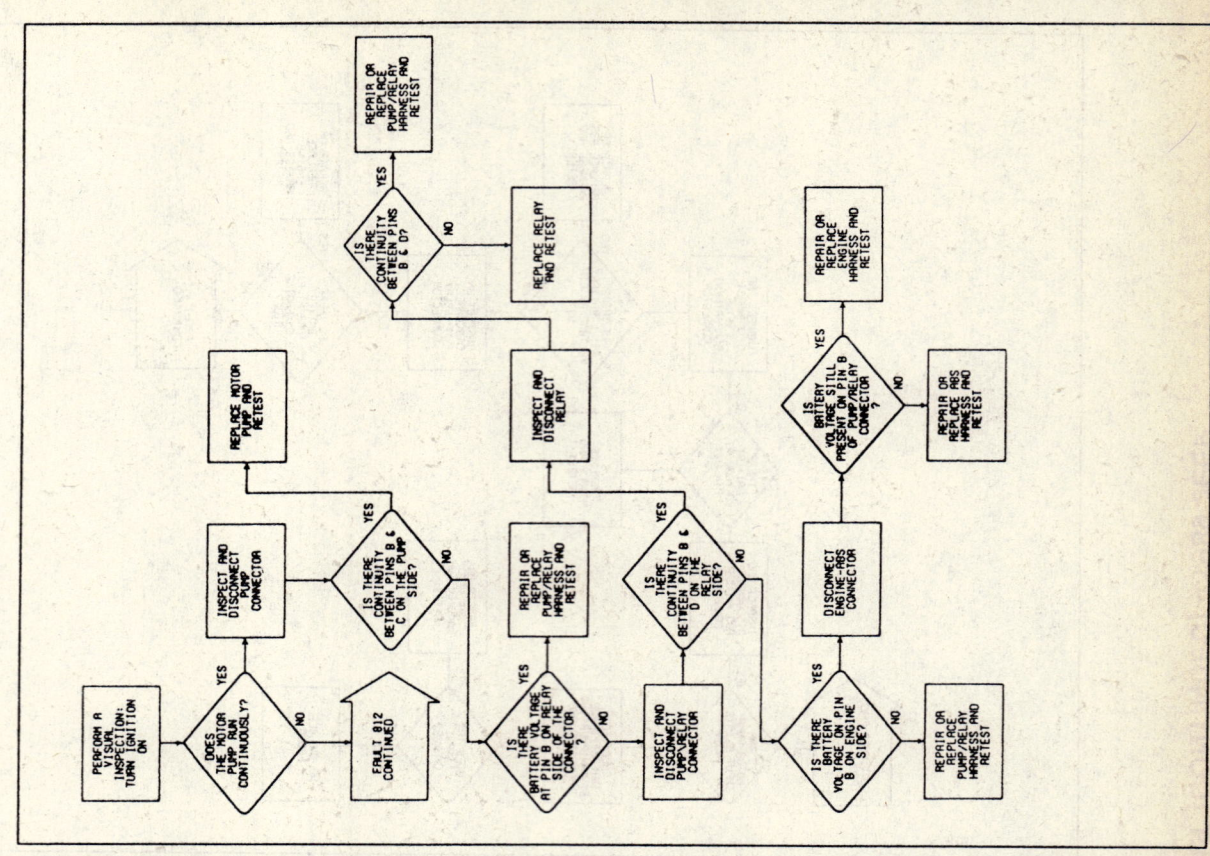

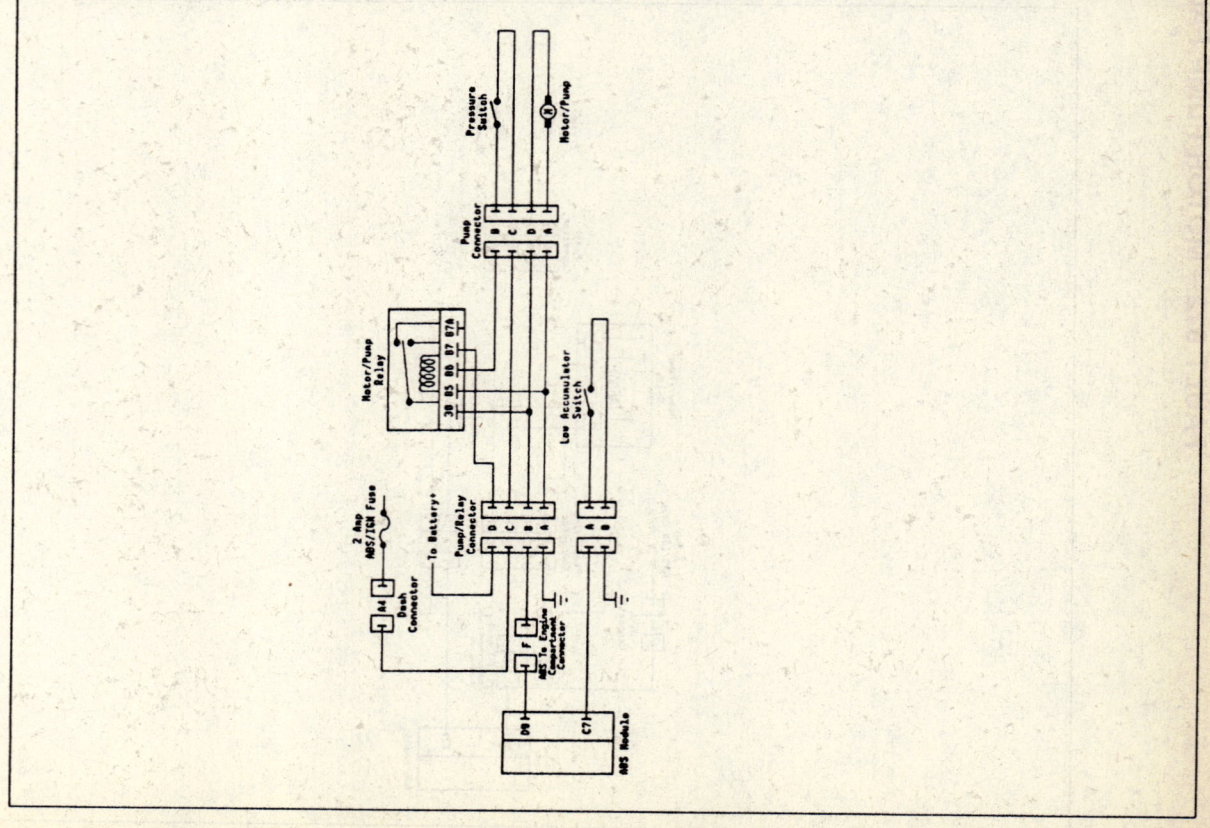

9 BRAKES

FAULT 812—MOTOR/PUMP FAULT (CONTINUED)—1989 JEEP

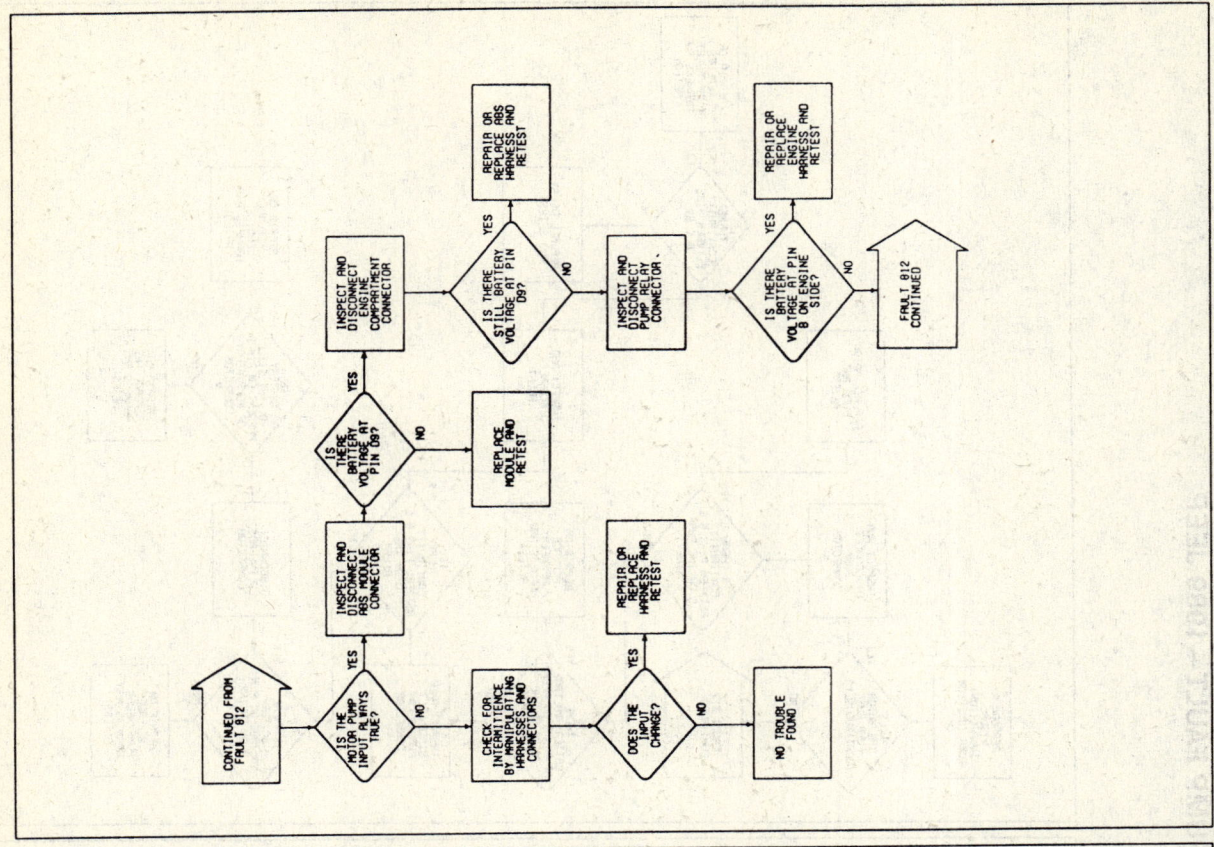

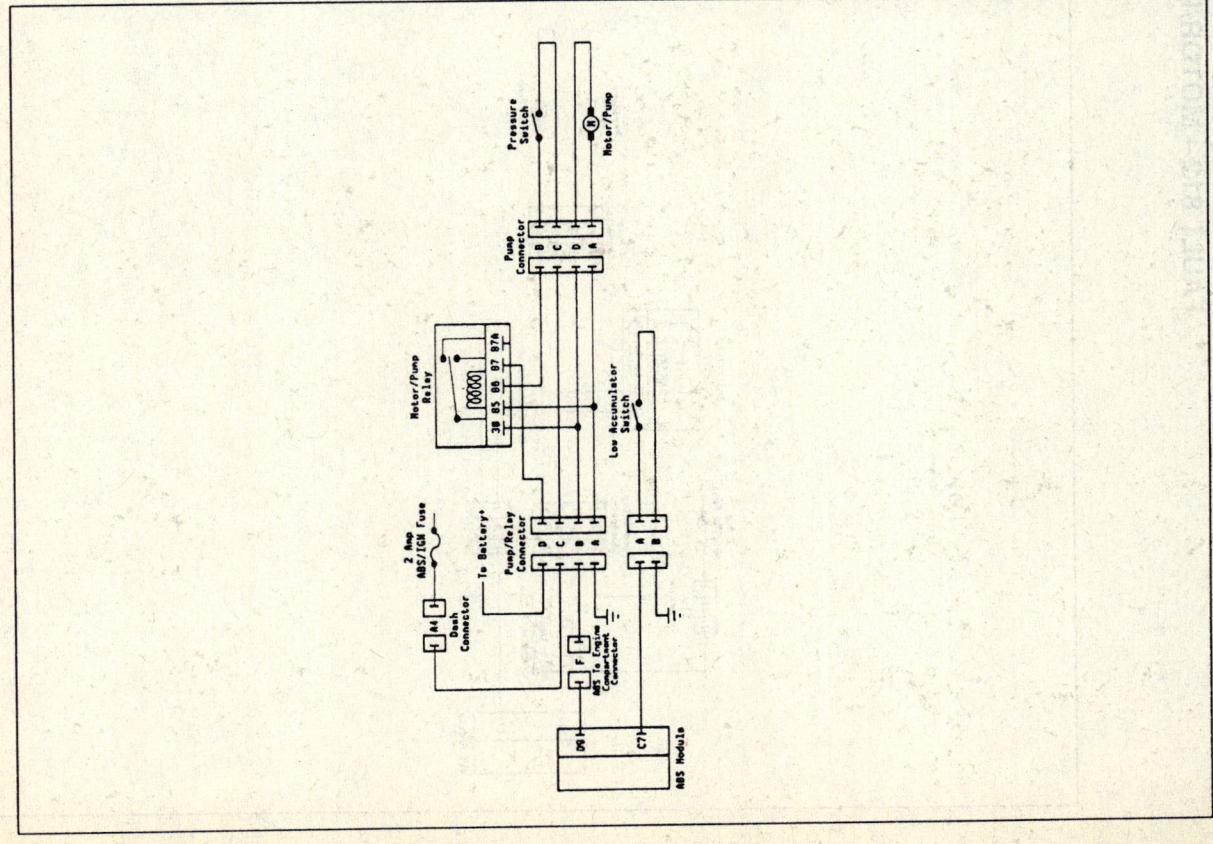

9-62

BRAKES 9

FAULT 812—MOTOR/PUMP FAULT (CONTINUED) – 1989 JEEP

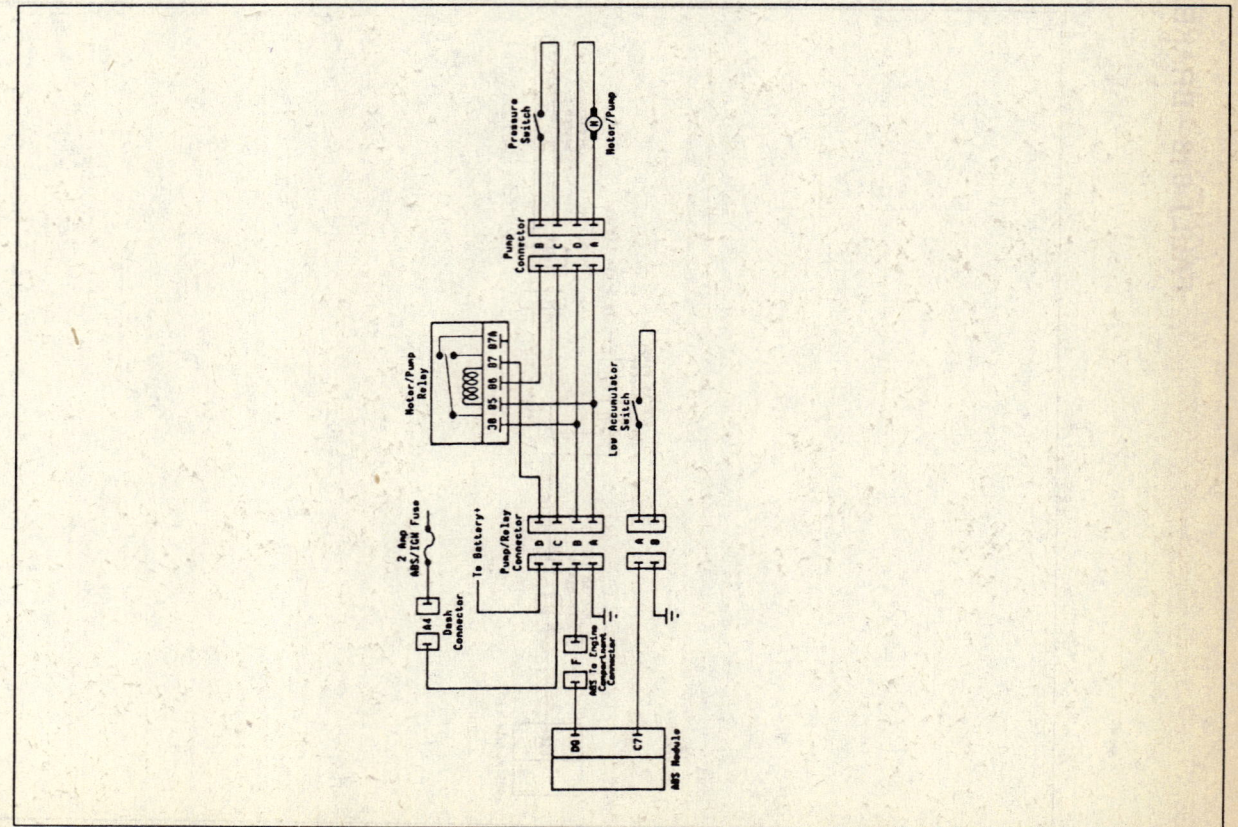

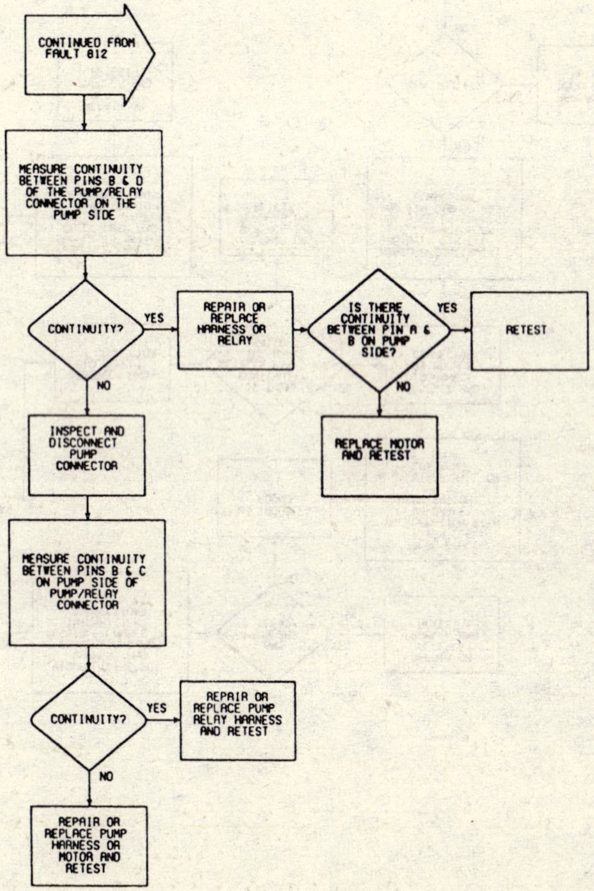

9-63

9 BRAKES

FAULT 813 – BRAKE FAULT – 1989 JEEP

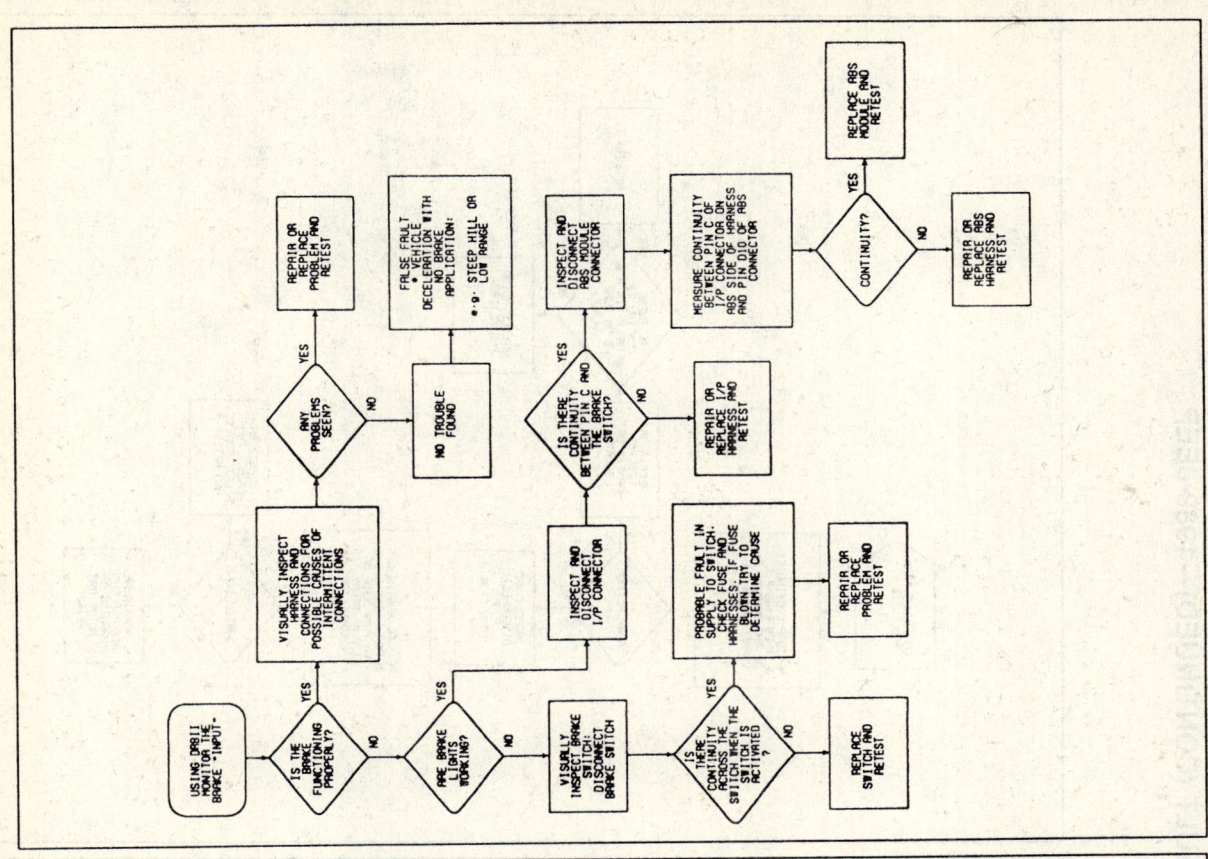

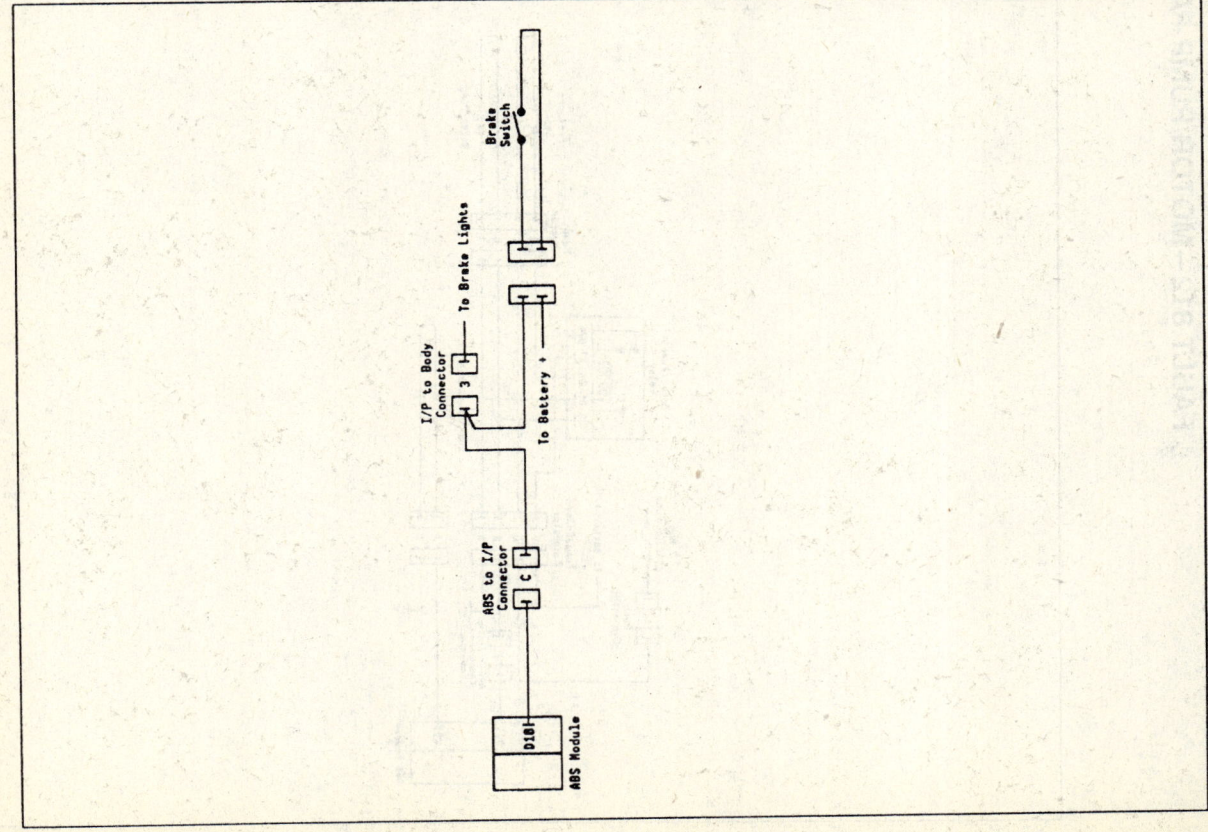

BRAKES 9

FAULT 814 – LOW FLUID – 1989 JEEP

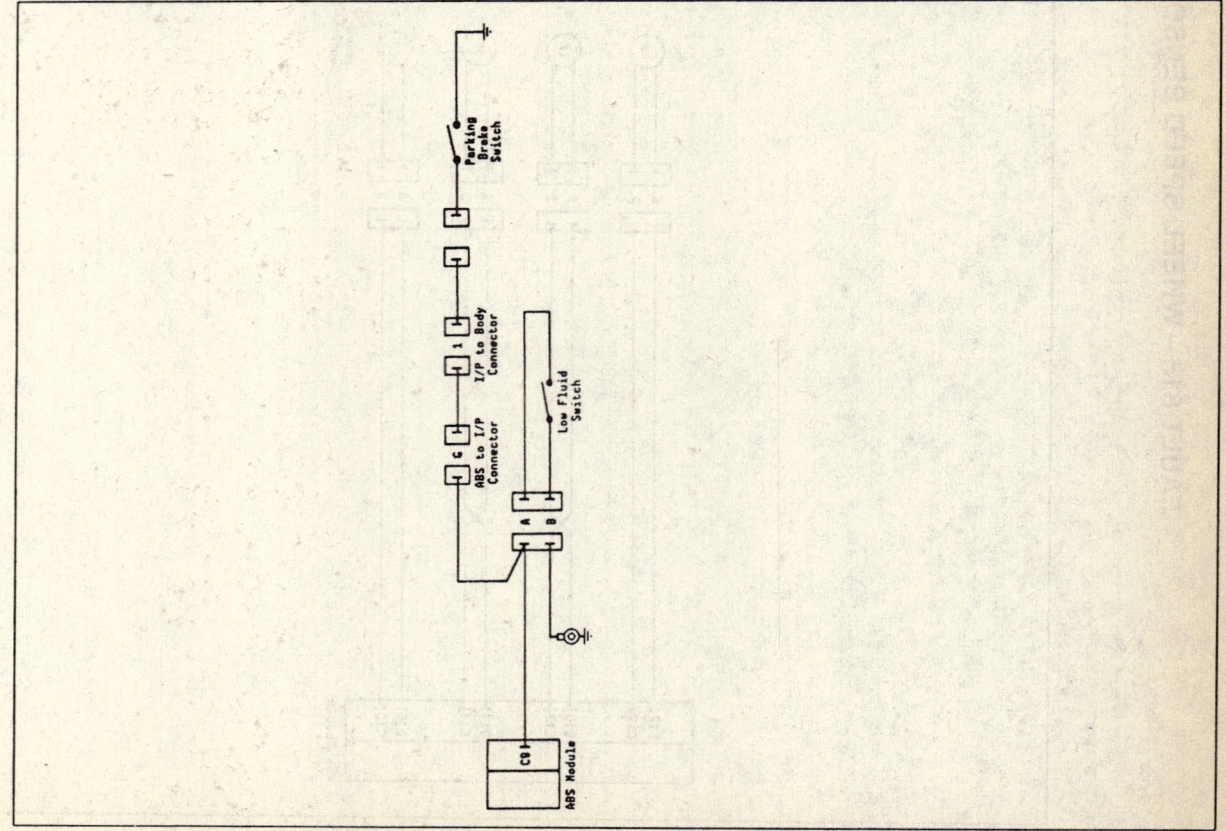

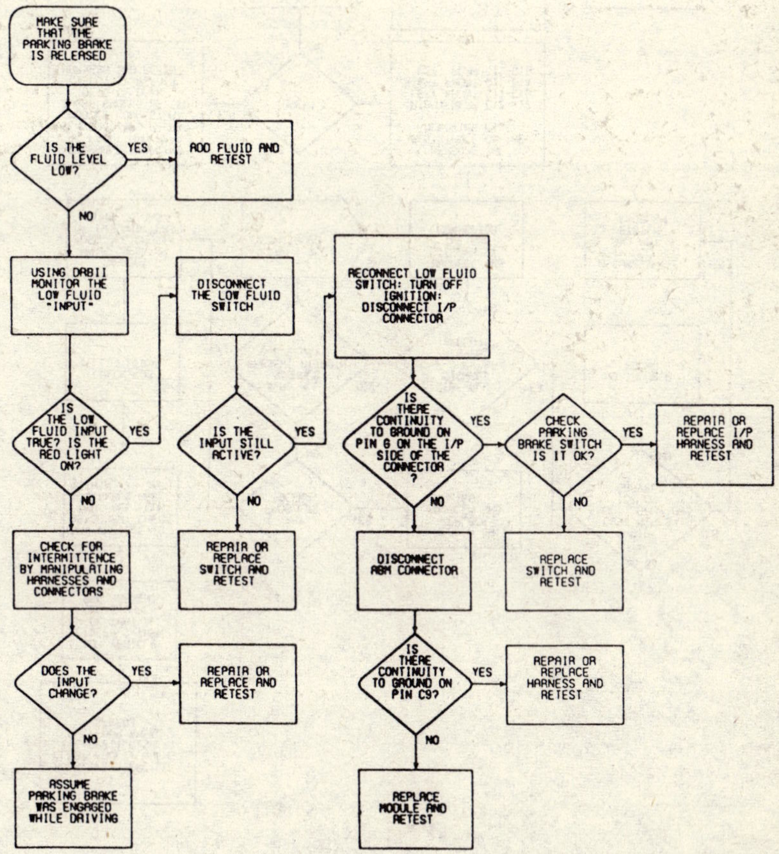

9-65

9 BRAKES

FAULT 815—WHEEL SPEED SENSOR FAULT: RIGHT REAR—1989 JEEP

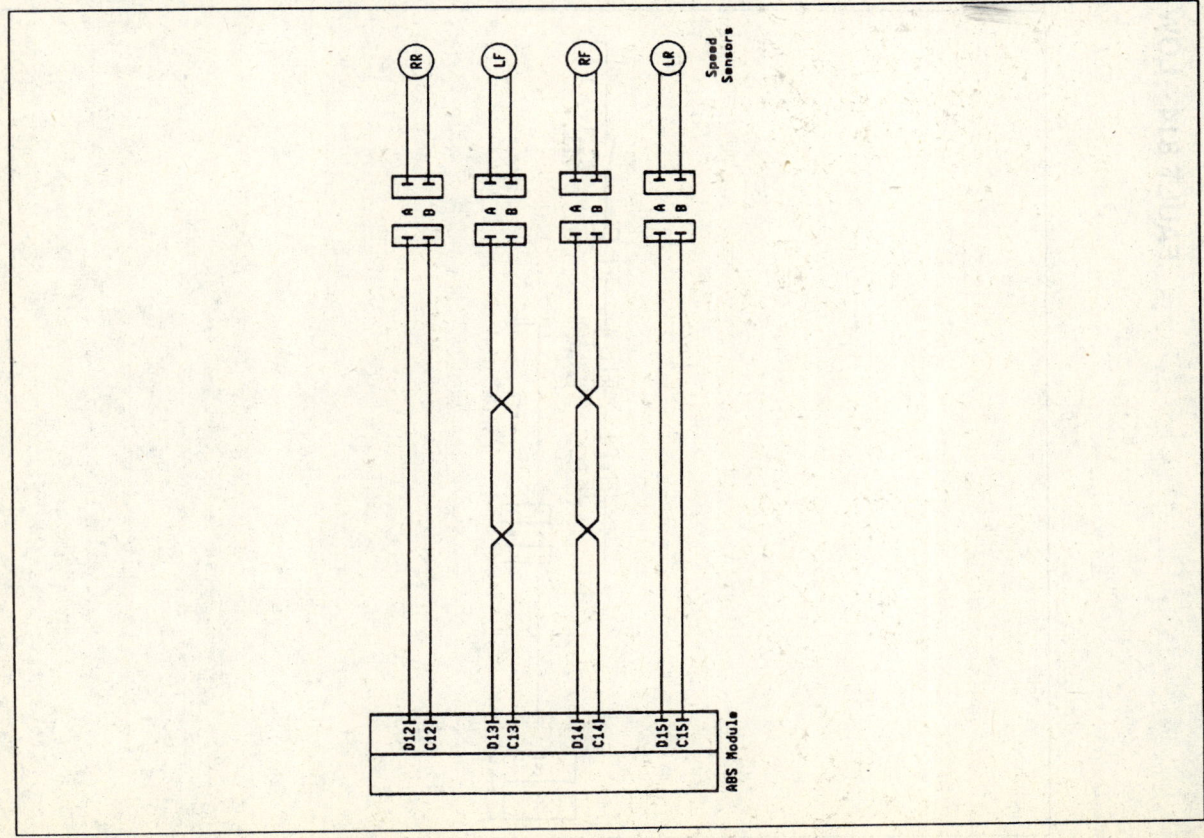

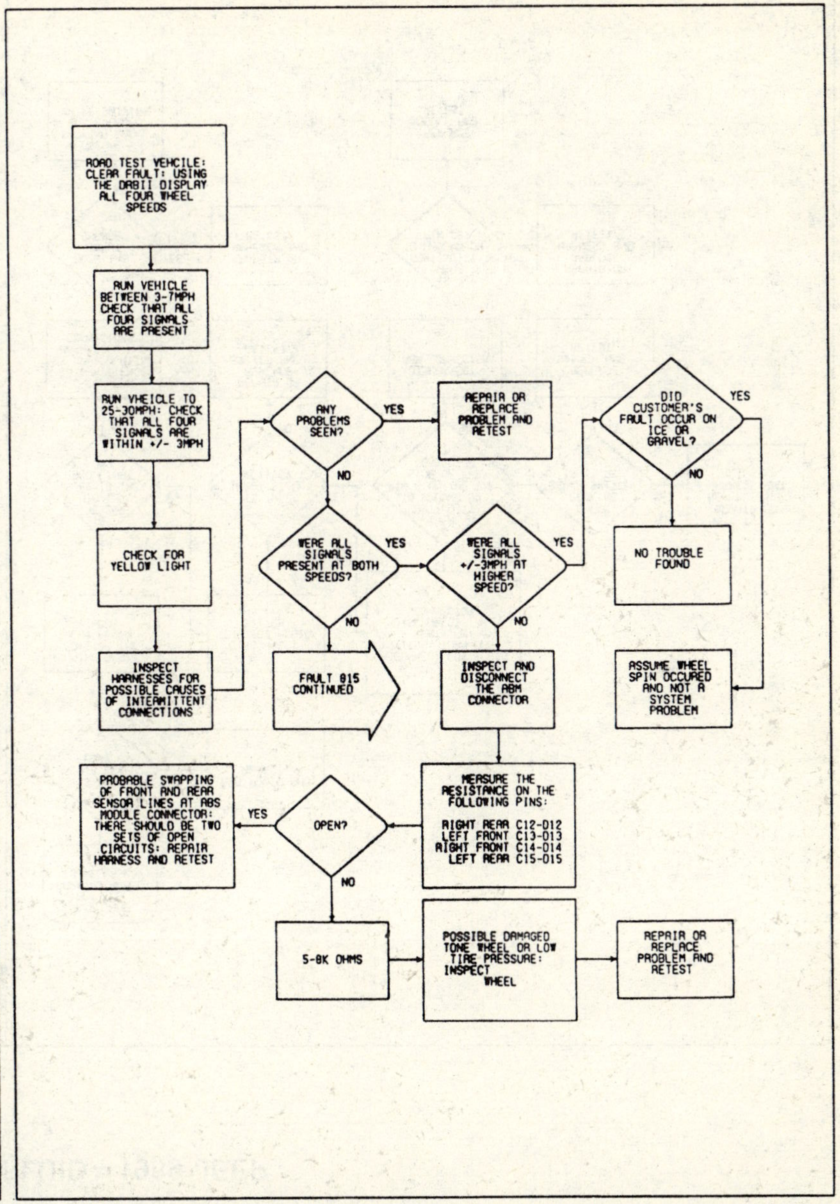

9-66

BRAKES 9

FAULT 815—WHEEL SPEED SENSOR FAULT: RIGHT REAR (CONTINUED)—1989 JEEP

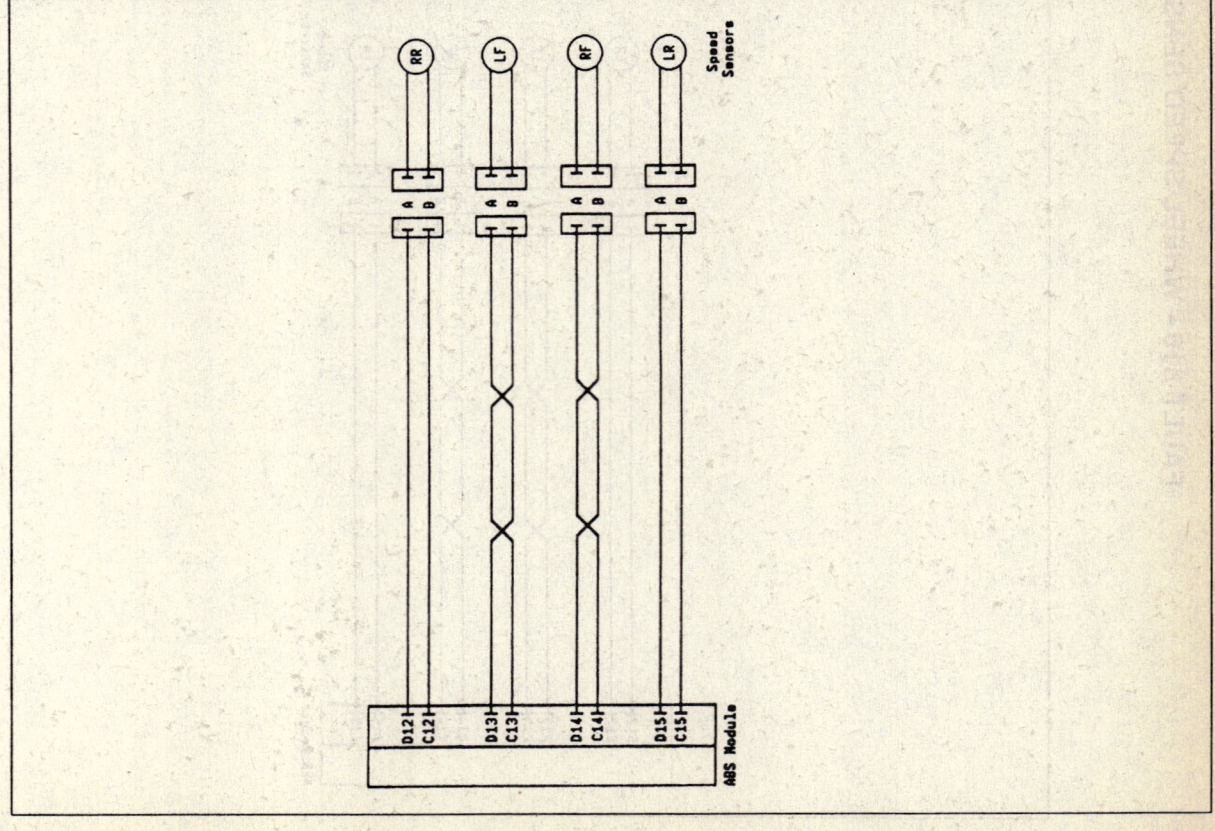

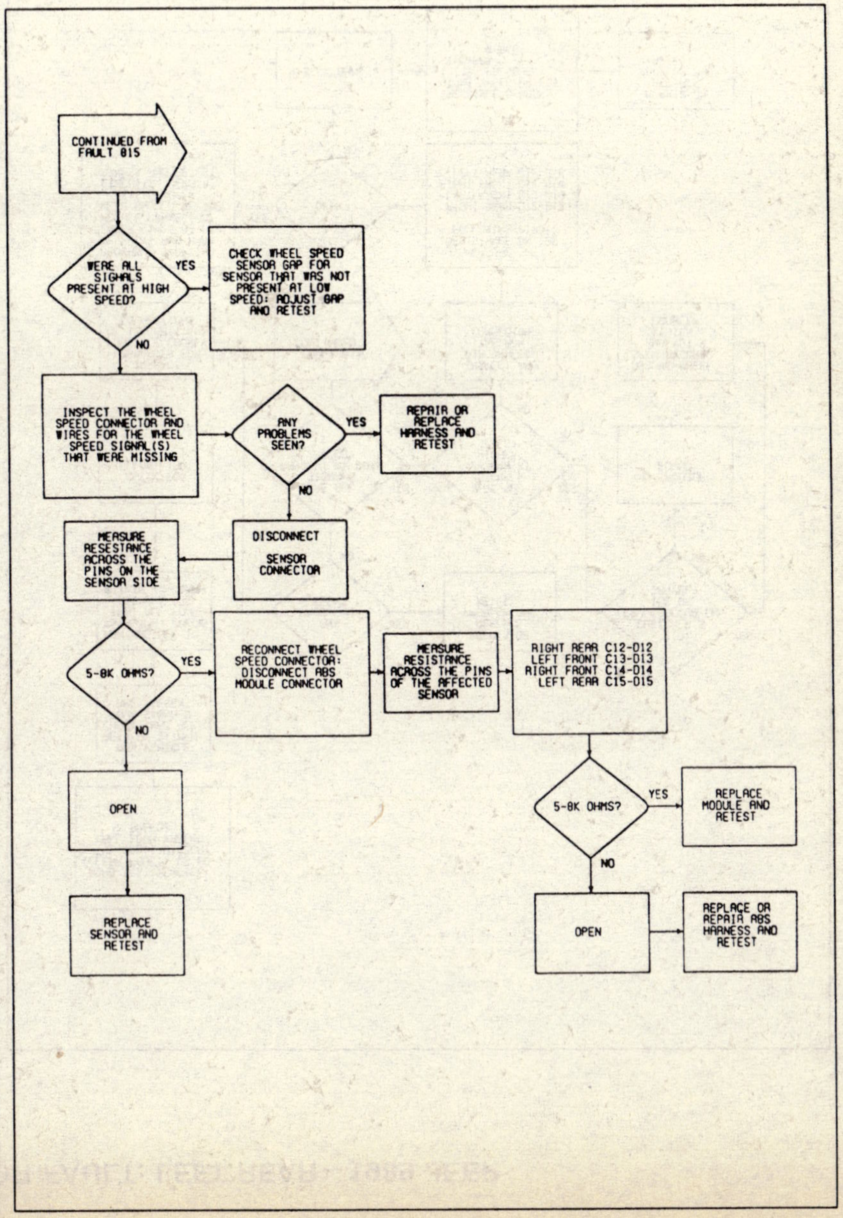

9-67

9 BRAKES

FAULT 816 – WHEEL SPEED SENSOR FAULT: LEFT REAR – 1989 JEEP

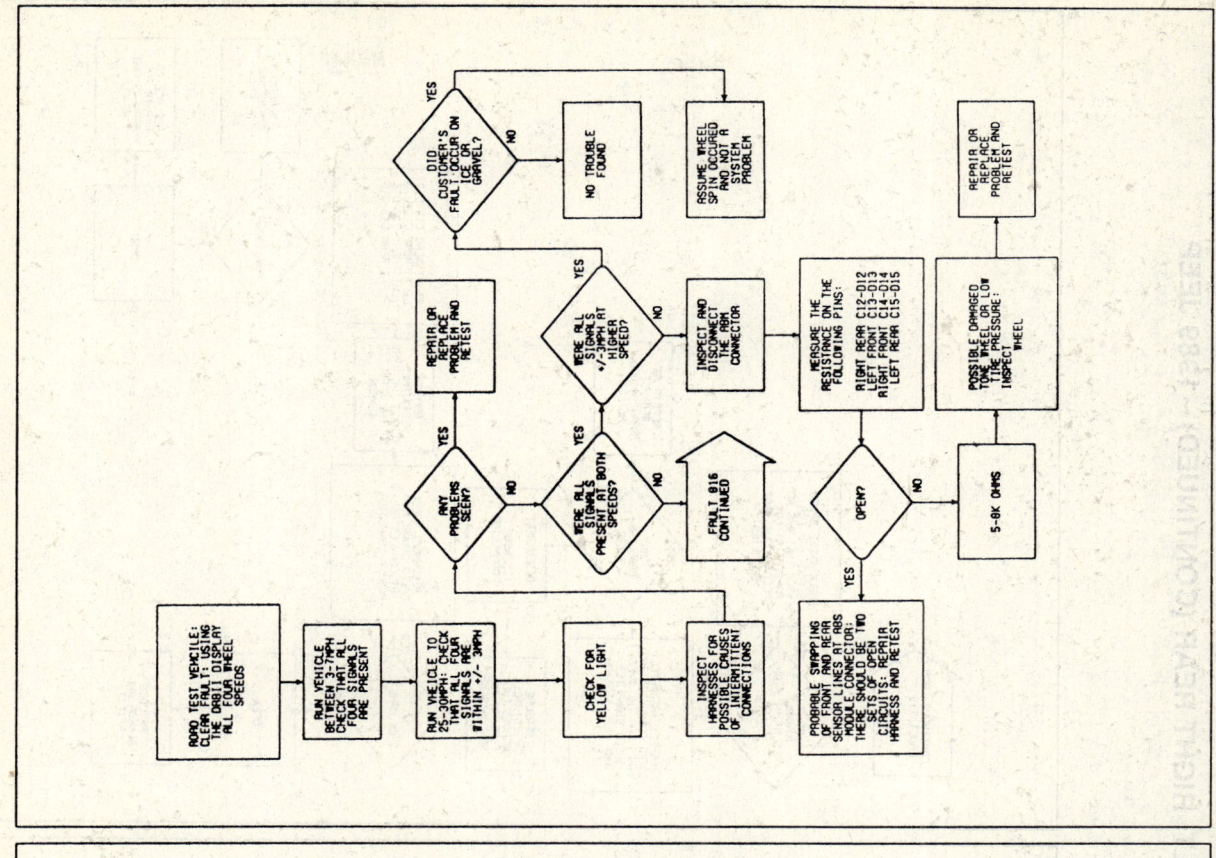

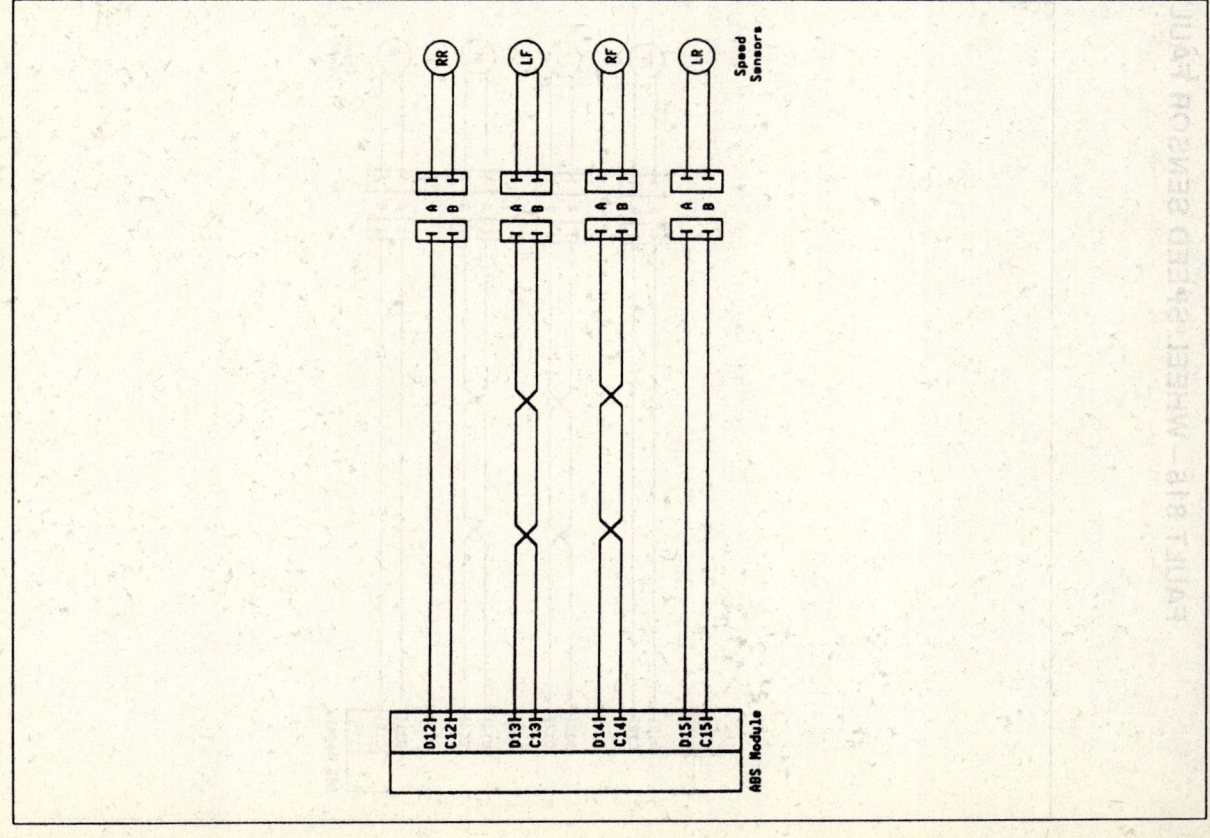

9-68

BRAKES 9

FAULT 816 – WHEEL SPEED SENSOR FAULT: LEFT REAR (CONTINUED) – 1989 JEEP

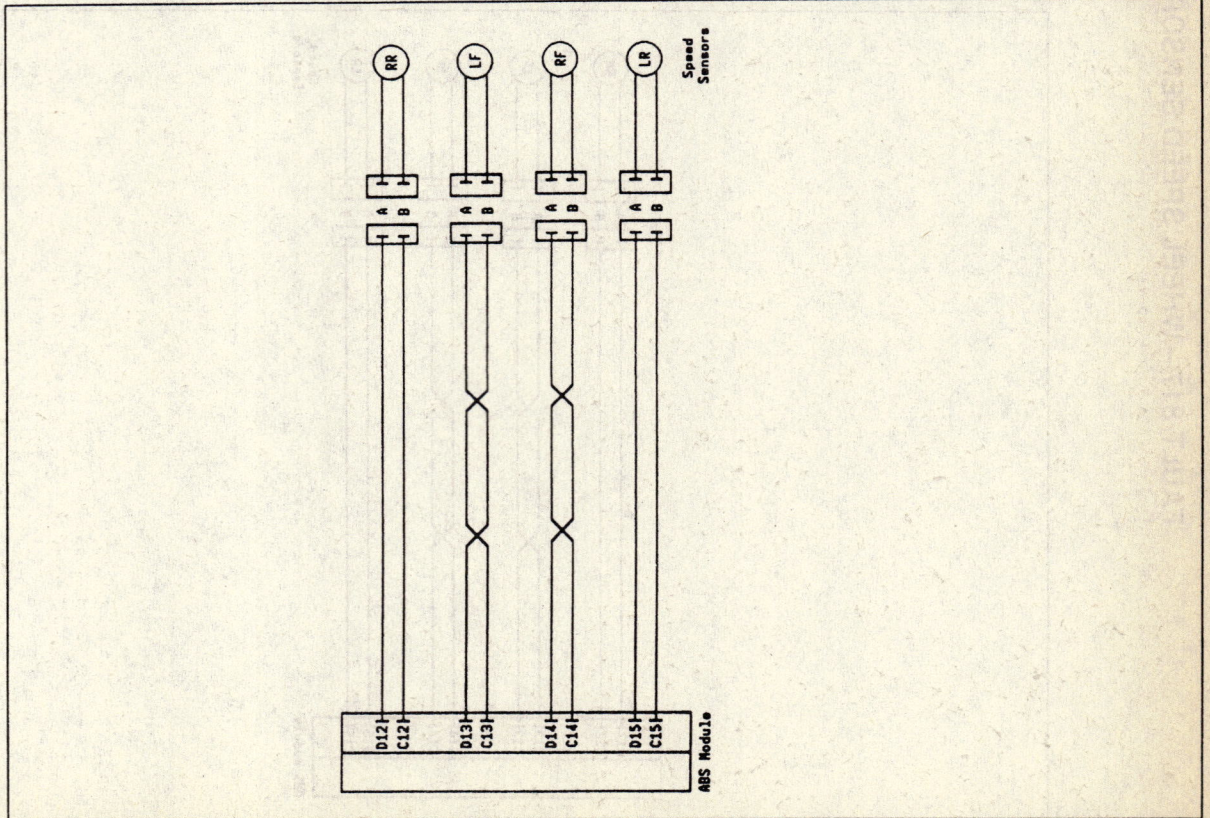

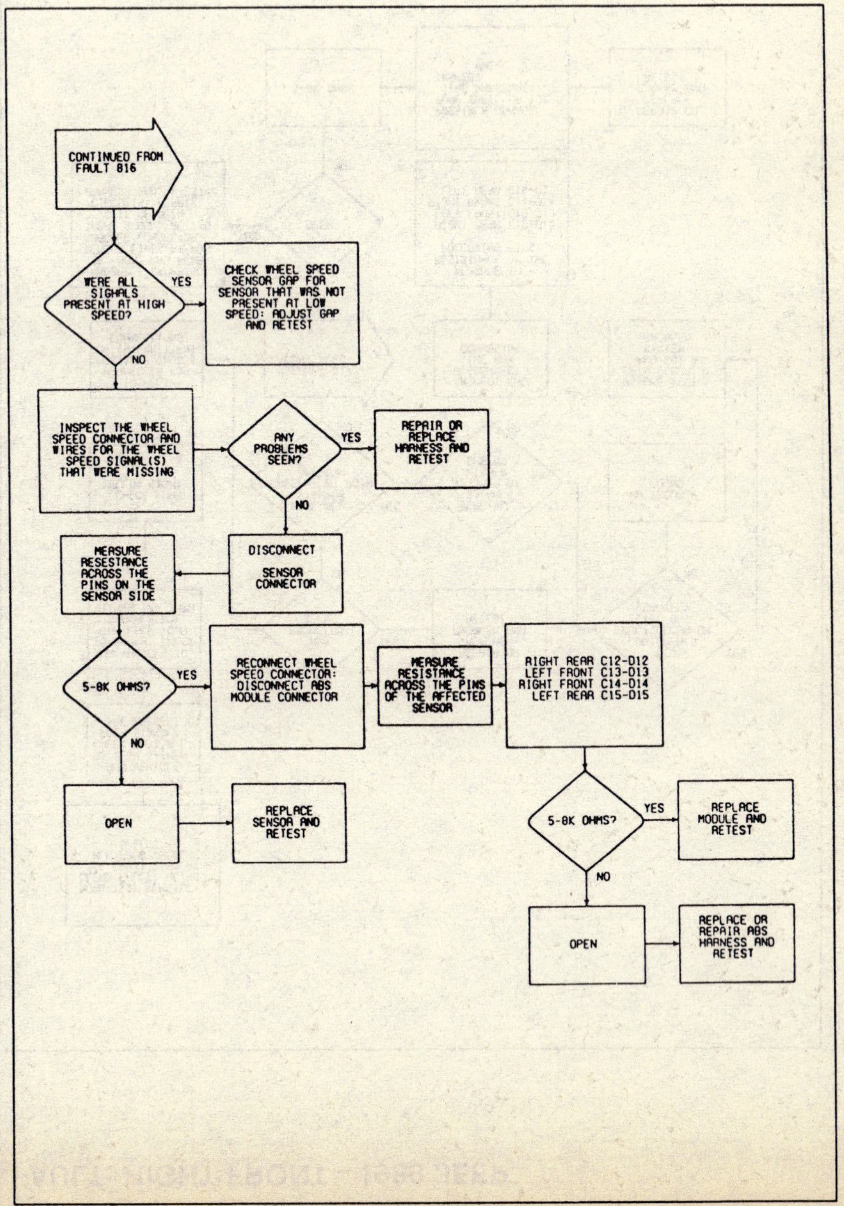

9-69

9 BRAKES

FAULT 817 – WHEEL SPEED SENSOR FAULT: RIGHT FRONT – 1989 JEEP

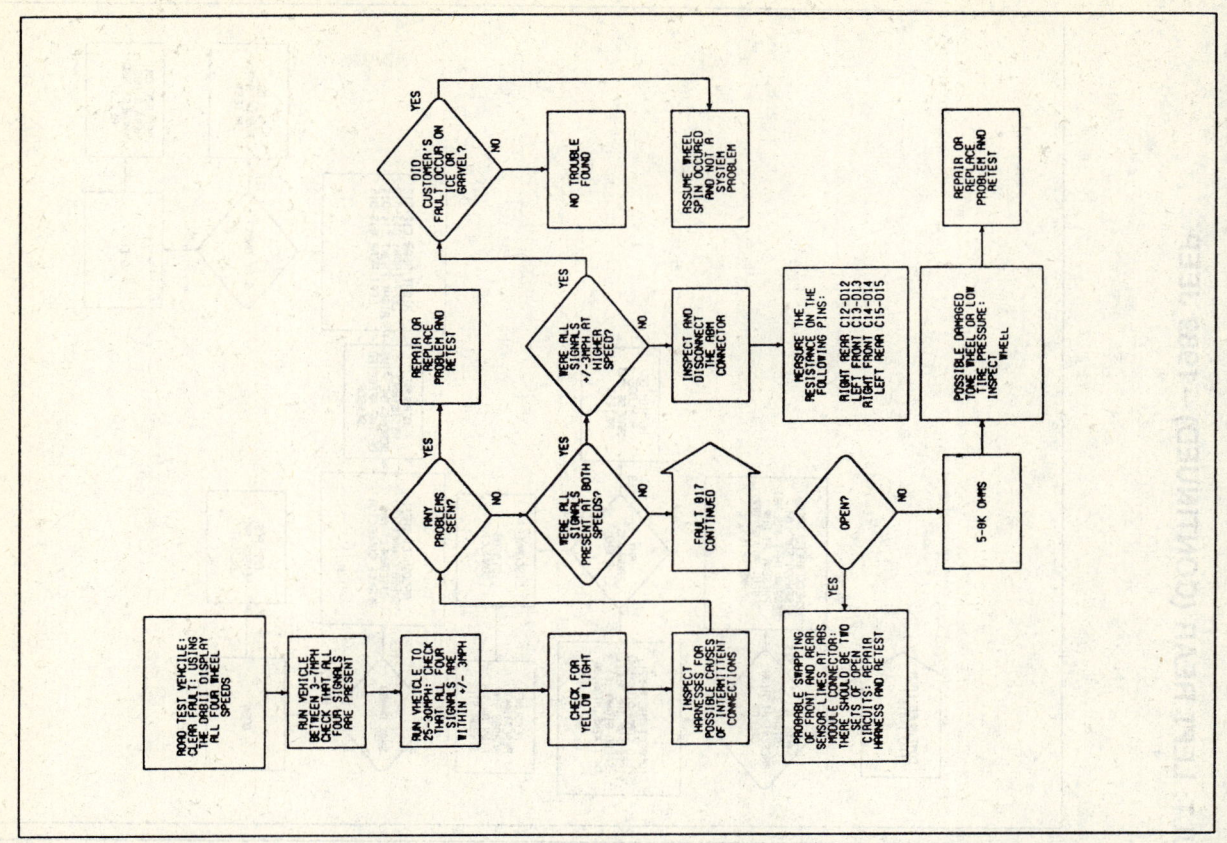

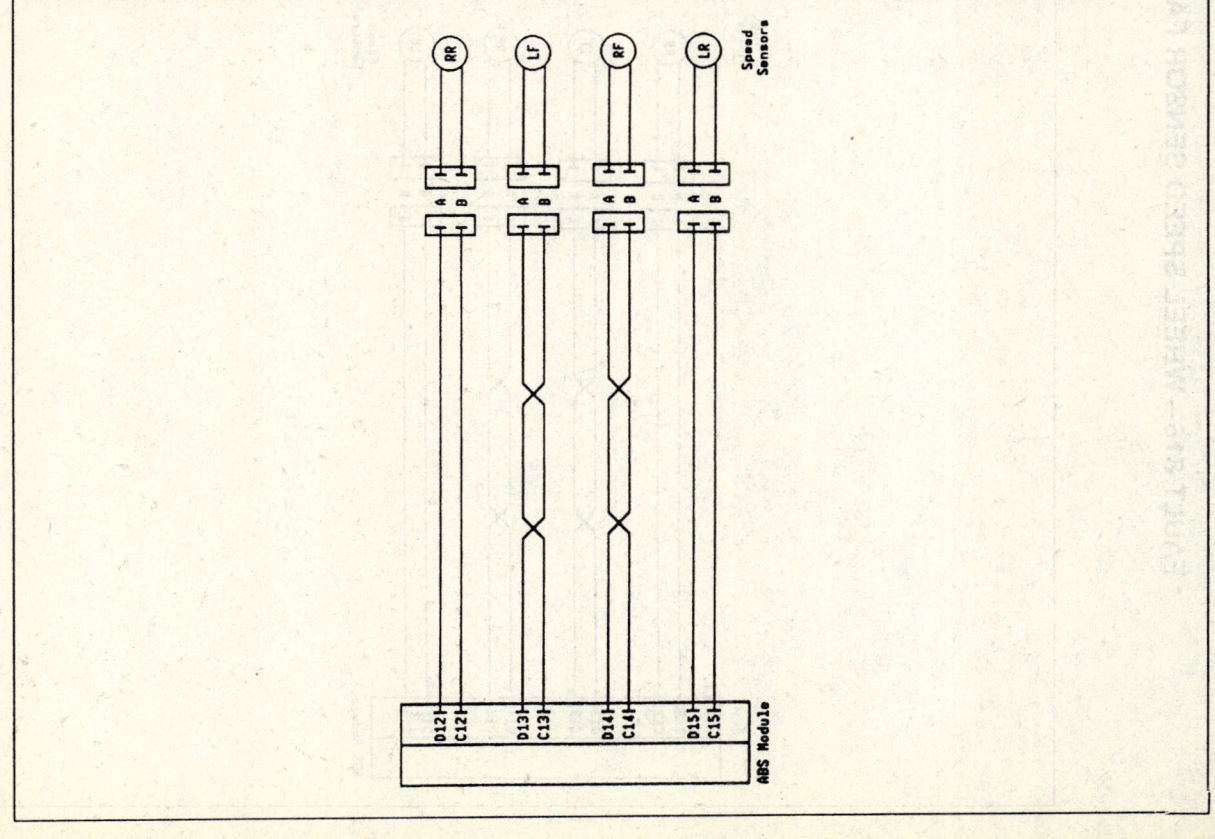

BRAKES 9

FAULT 817 – WHEEL SPEED SENSOR FAULT: RIGHT FRONT (CONTINUED) – 1989 JEEP

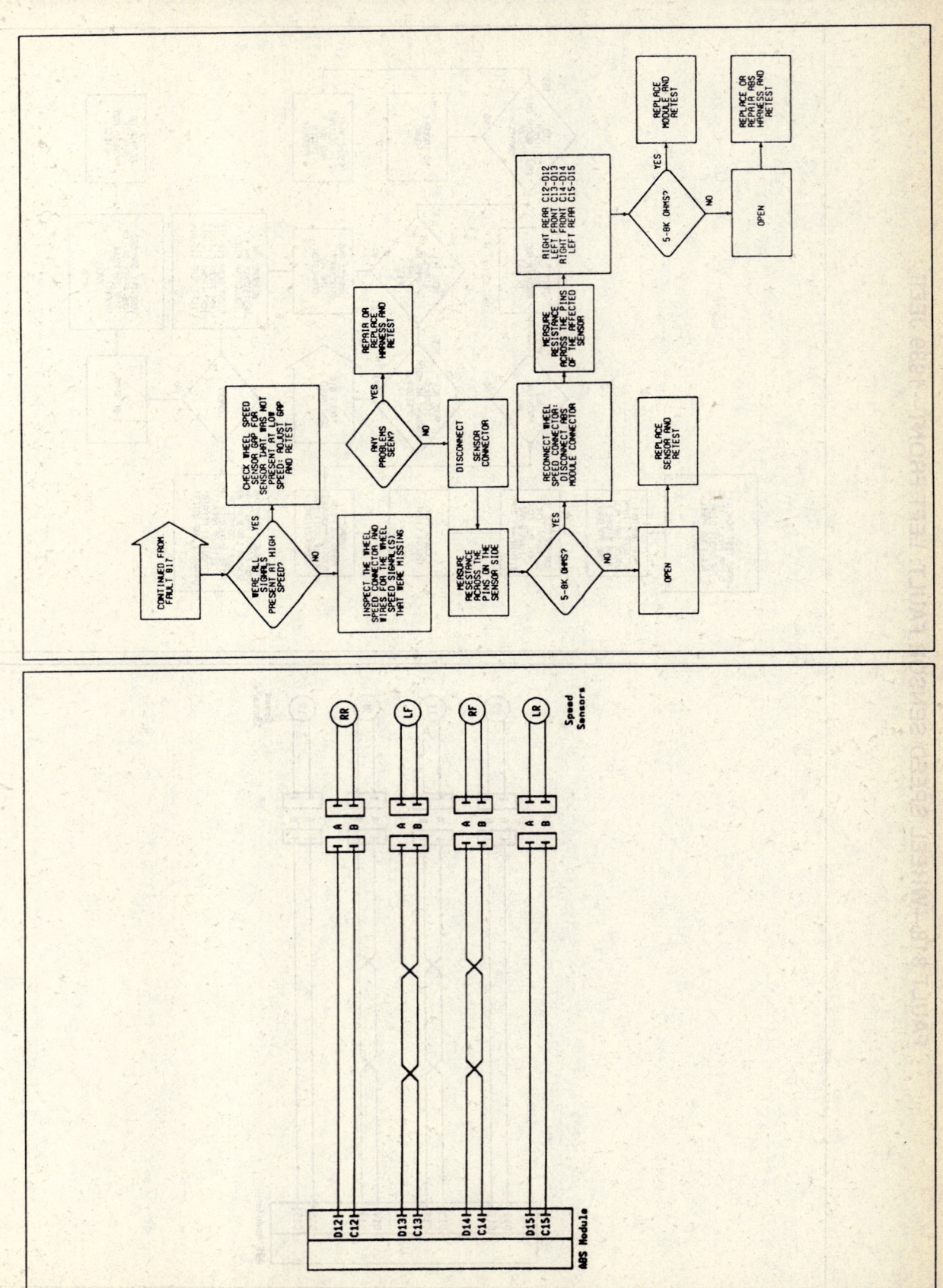

9-71

9 BRAKES

FAULT 818—WHEEL SPEED SENSOR FAULT: LEFT FRONT—1989 JEEP

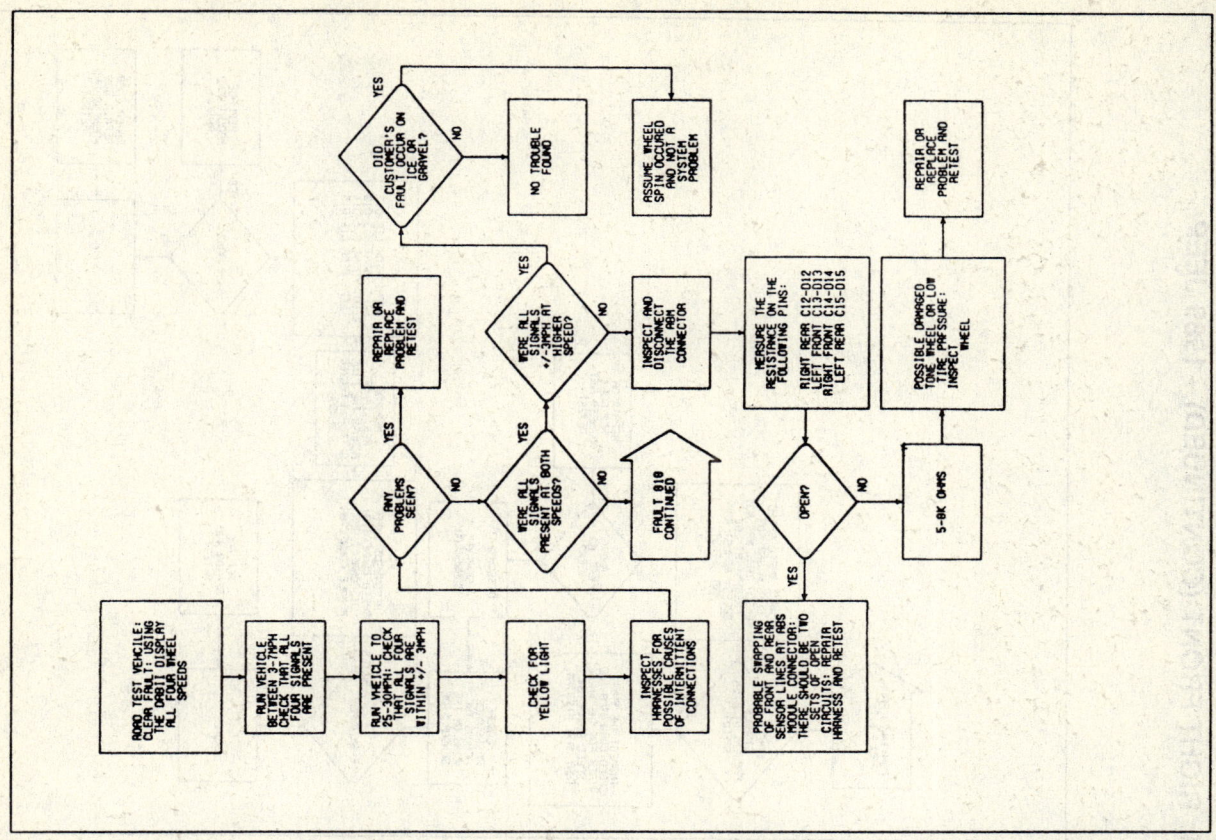

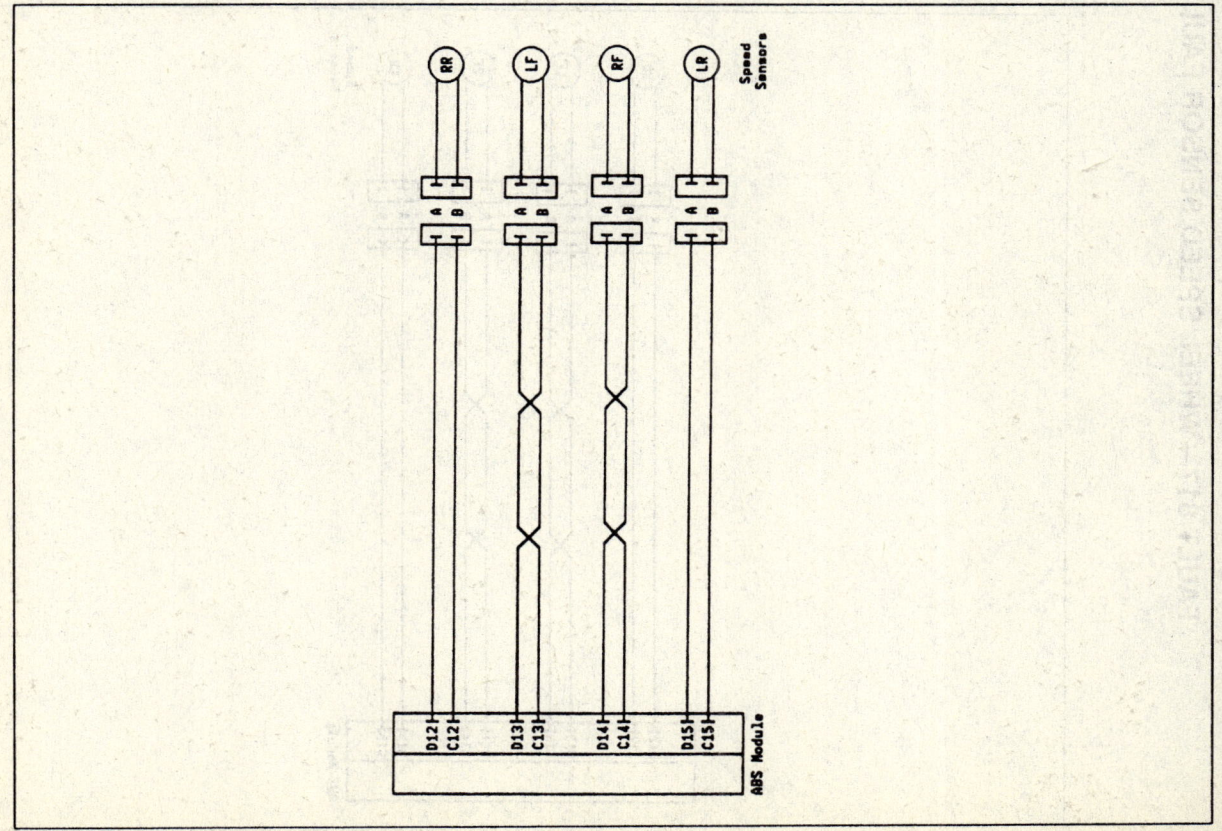

9-72

BRAKES 9

FAULT 818—WHEEL SPEED SENSOR FAULT: LEFT FRONT (CONTINUED)—1989 JEEP

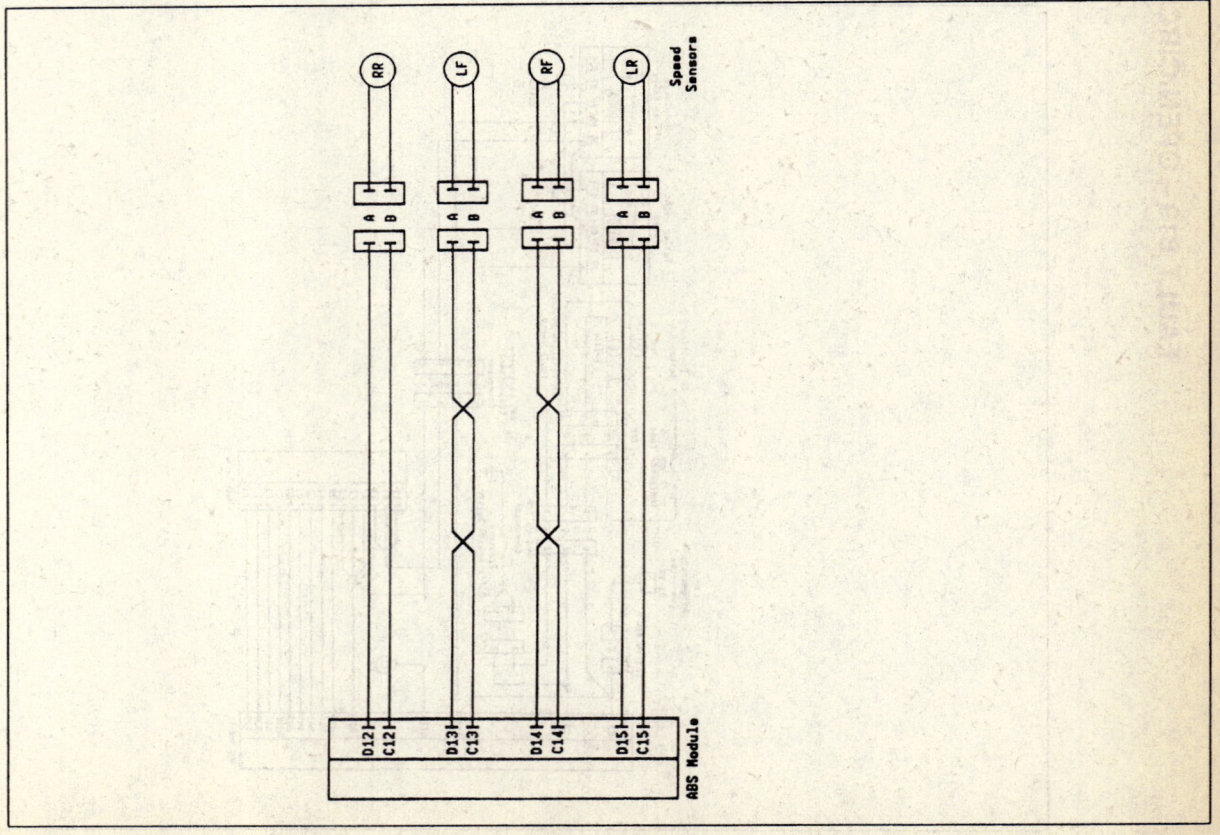

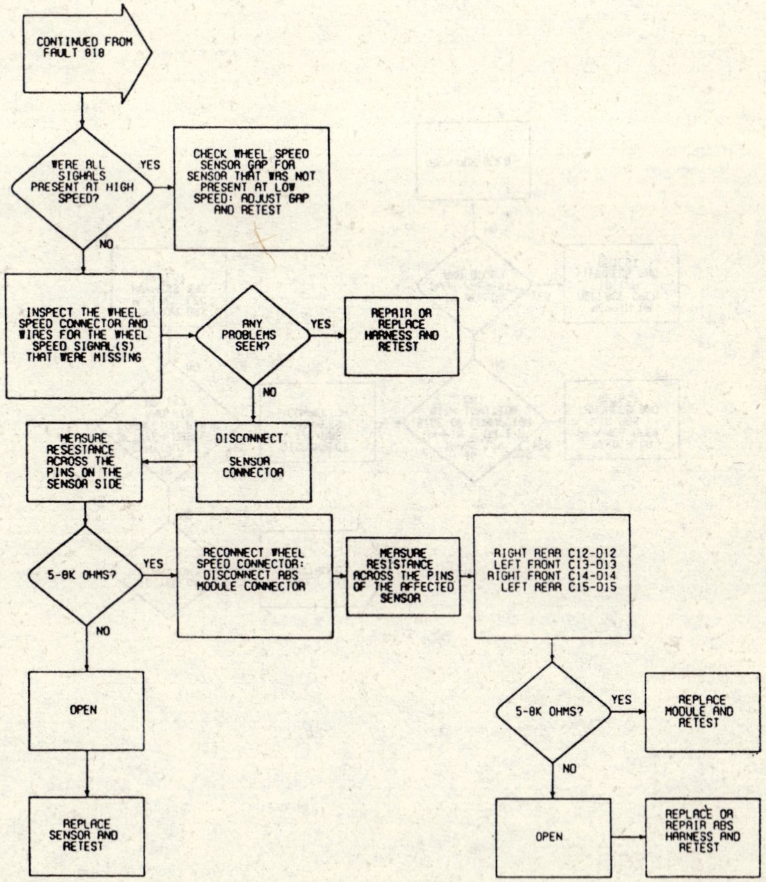

9 BRAKES

FAULT 819 – OPEN CIRCUIT AT D2-14 – 1989 JEEP

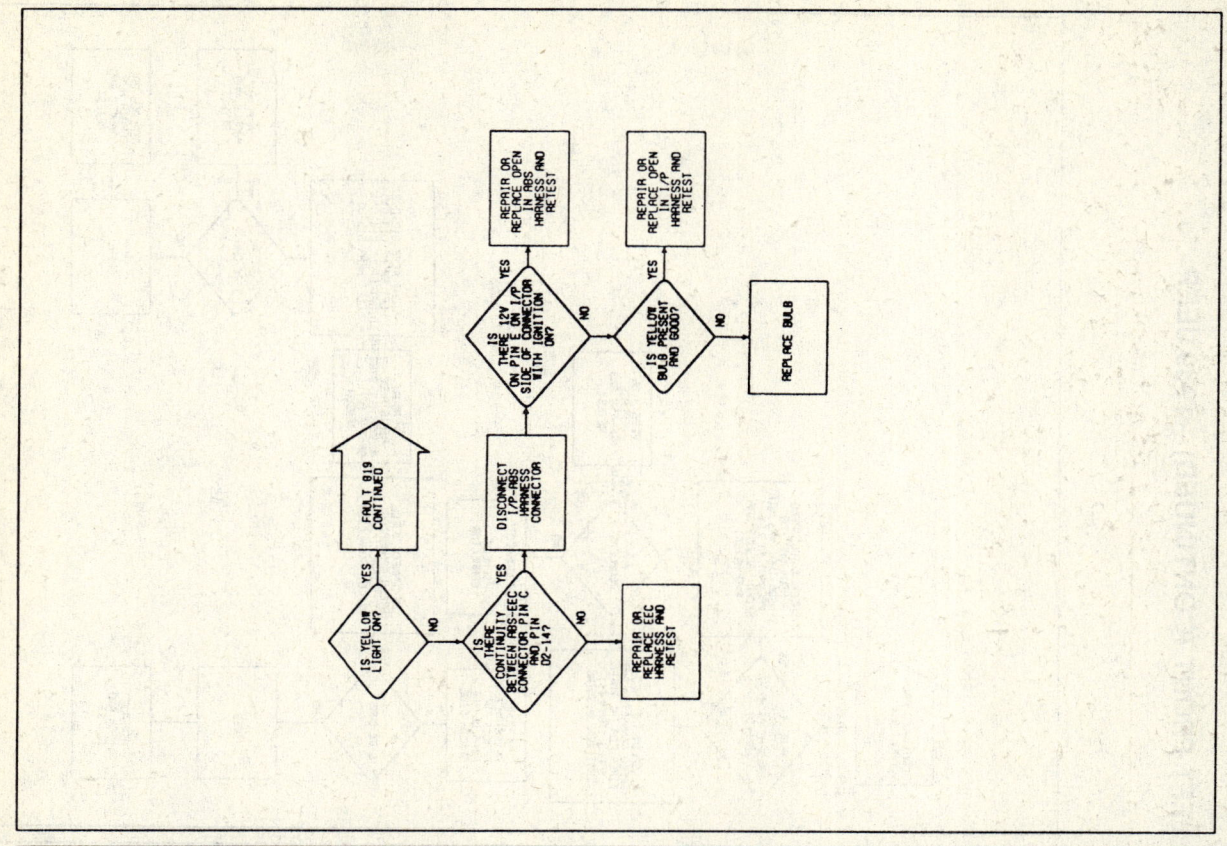

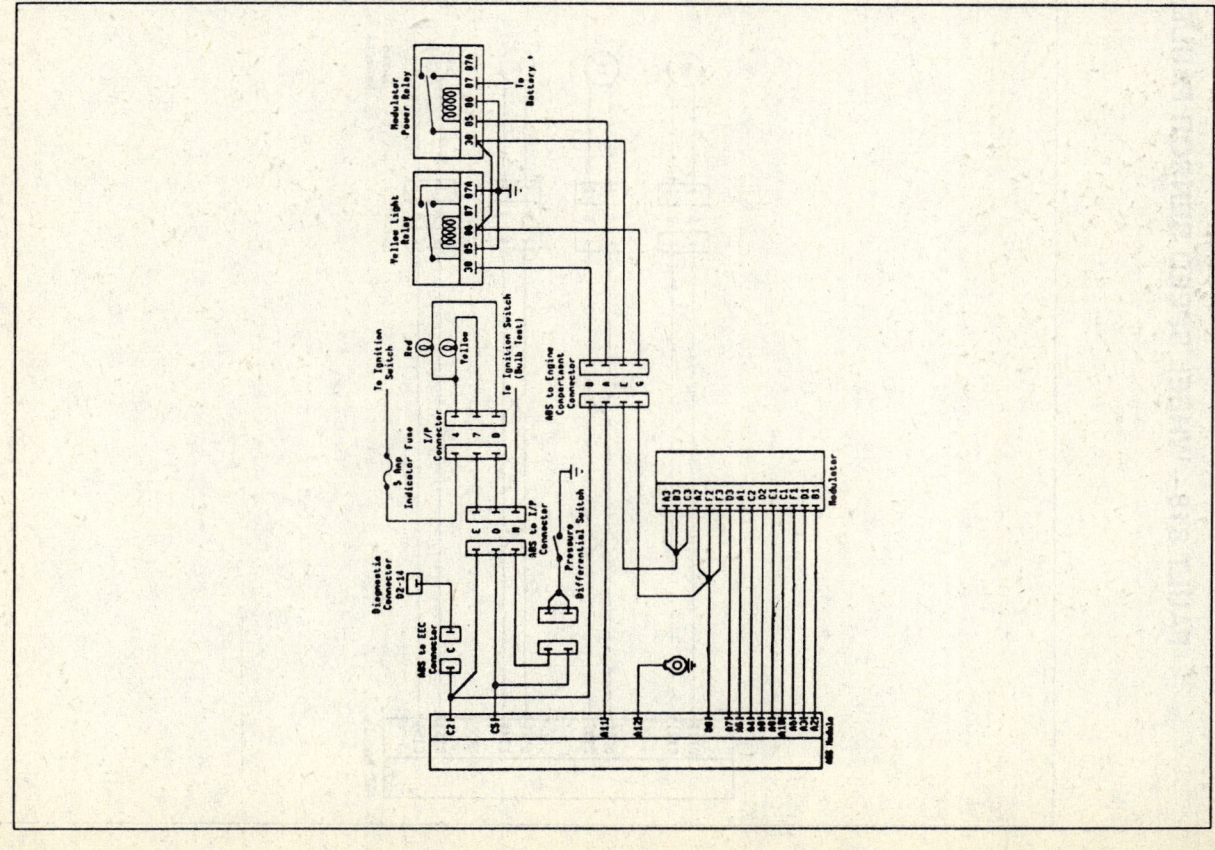

BRAKES 9

FAULT 819 – OPEN CIRCUIT AT D2-14 (CONTINUED) – 1989 JEEP

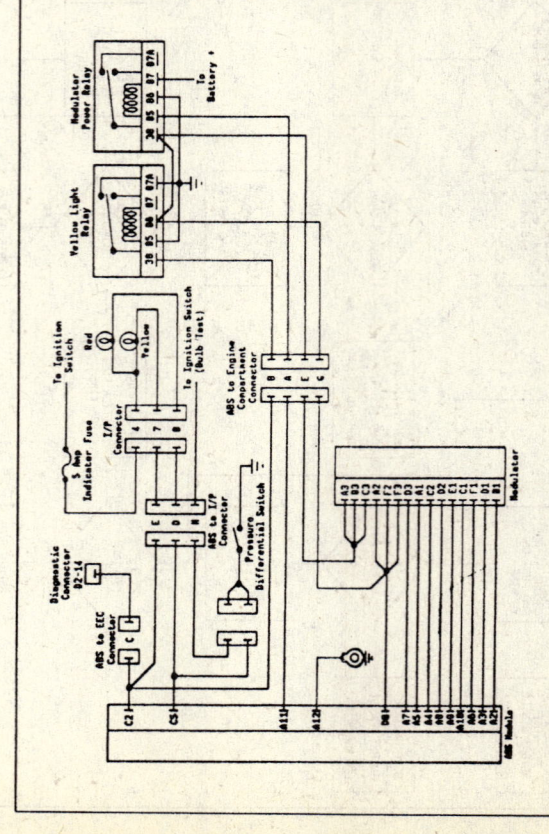

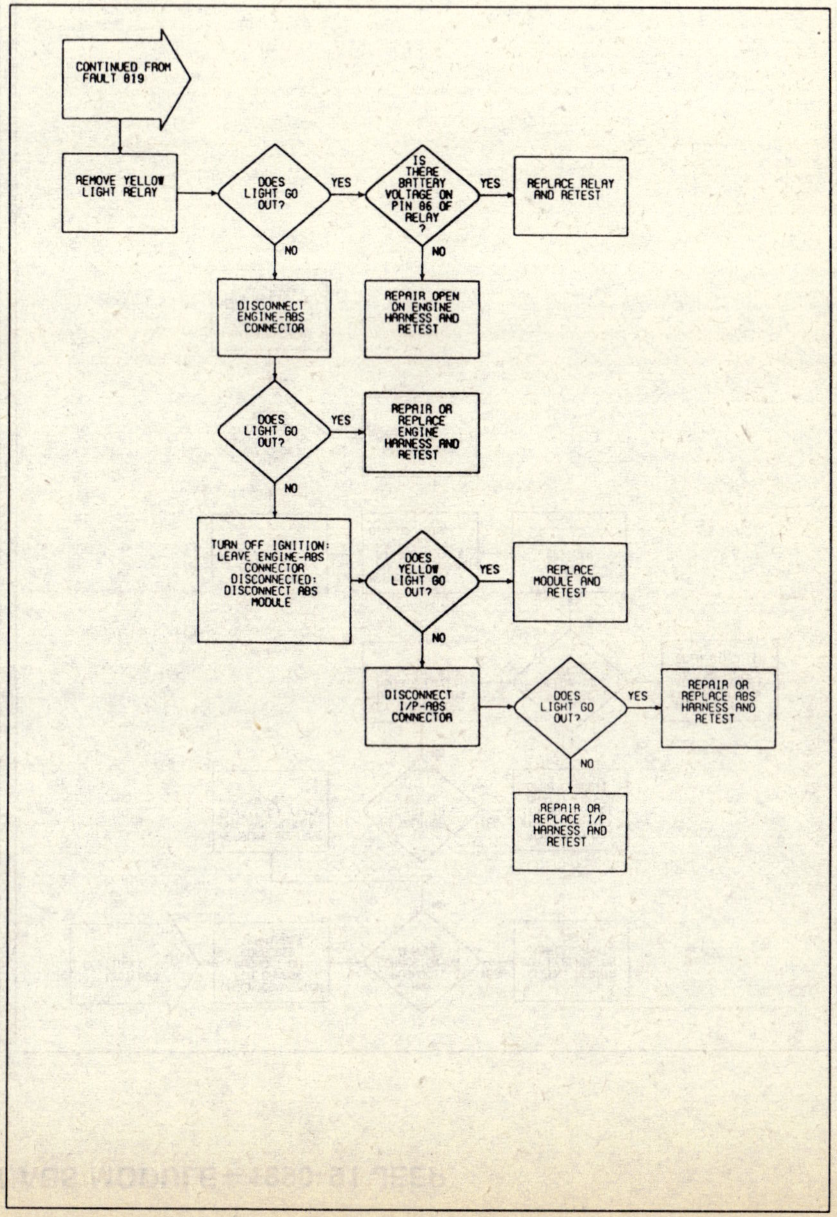

CONNECTOR PROFILES AND PIN DESIGNATION

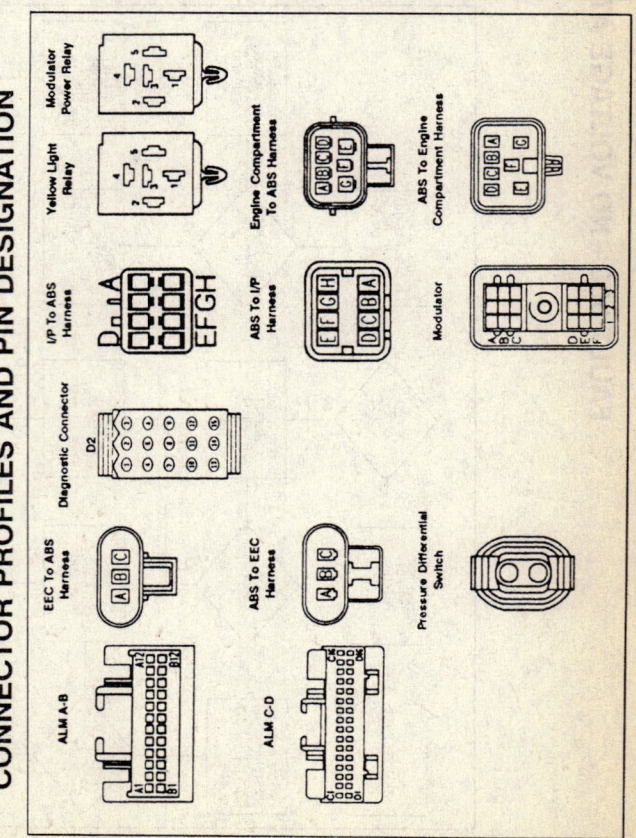

9-75

9 Brakes

FAULT 800 — NO VOLTAGE AT ABS MODULE — 1990-91 JEEP

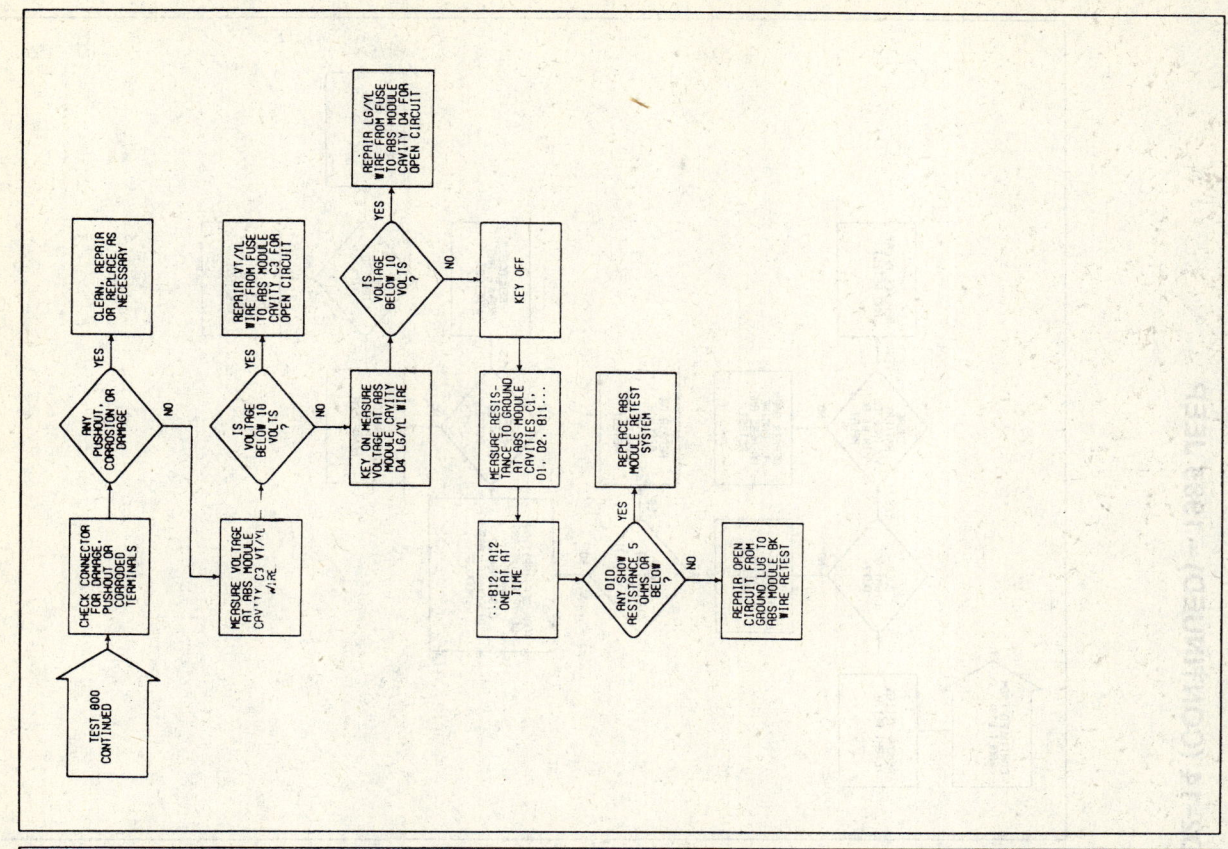

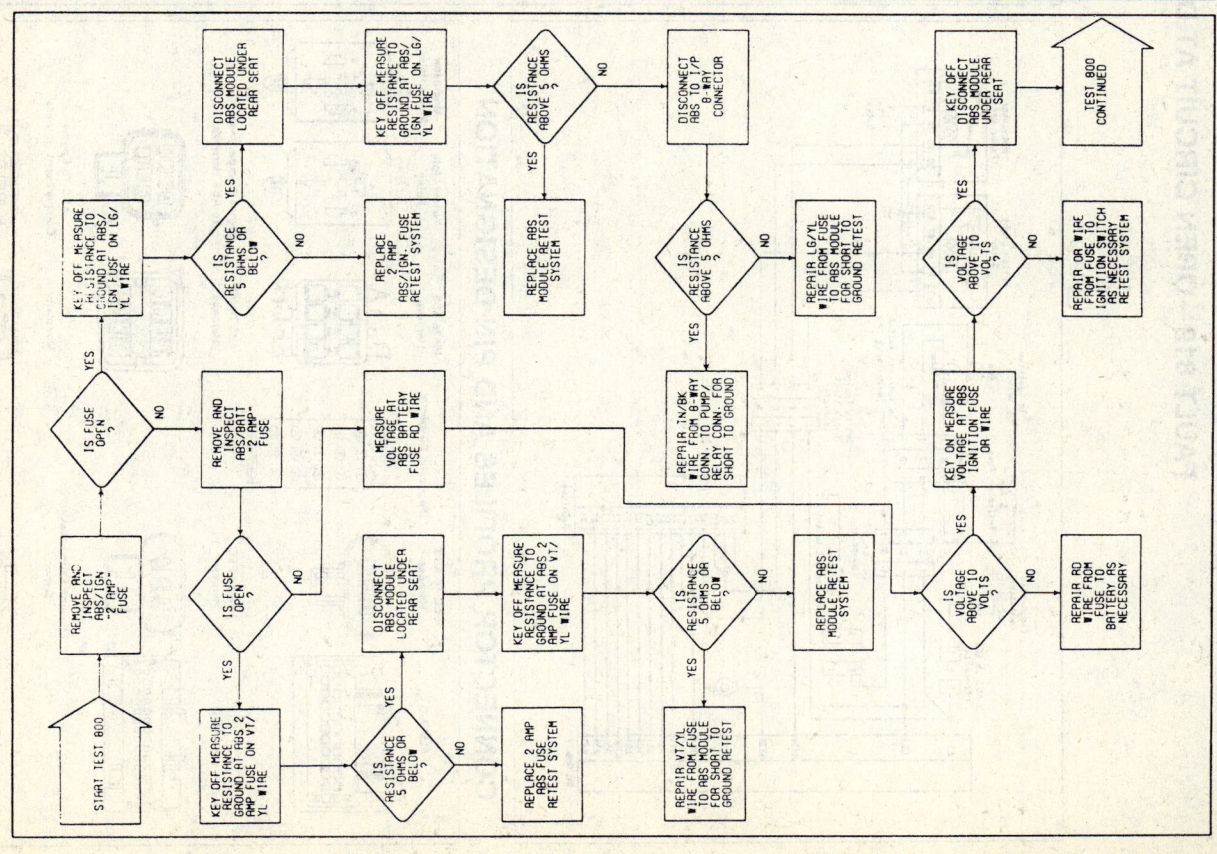

BRAKES 9

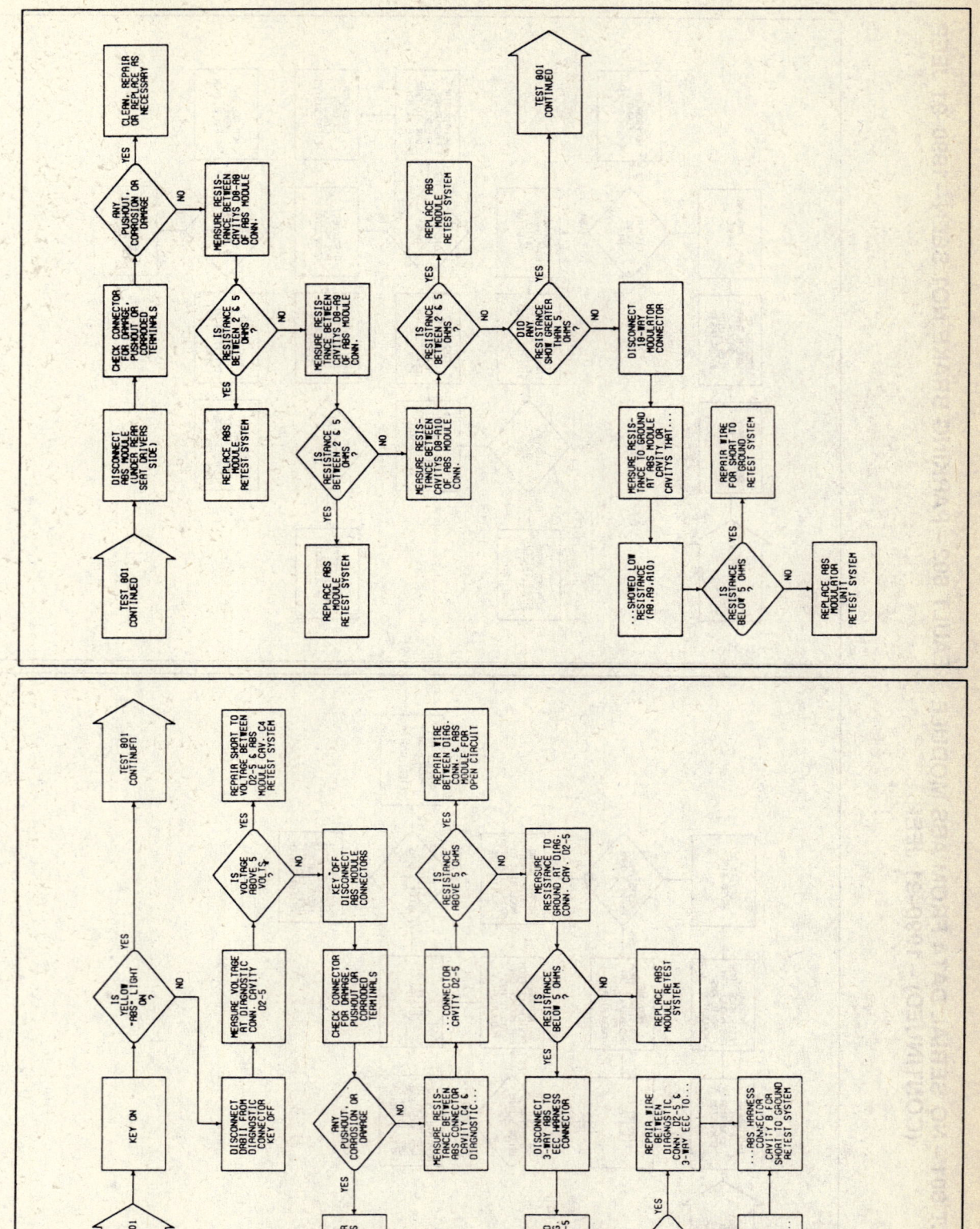

FAULT 801 – NO SERIAL DATA FROM ABS MODULE – 1990-91 JEEP

9-77

9 BRAKES

FAULT 802 – PARKING BRAKE NOT SEEN – 1990-91 JEEP

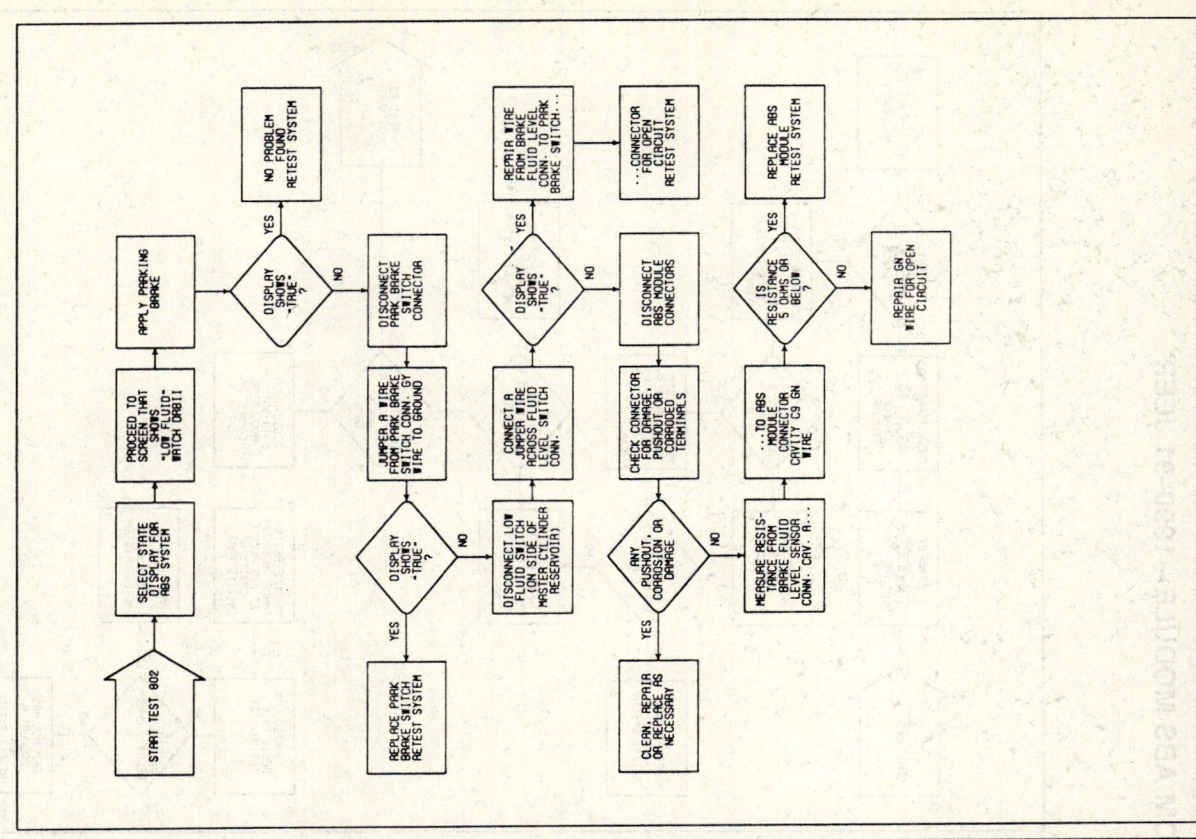

FAULT 801 – NO SERIAL DATA FROM ABS MODULE (CONTINUED) – 1990-91 JEEP

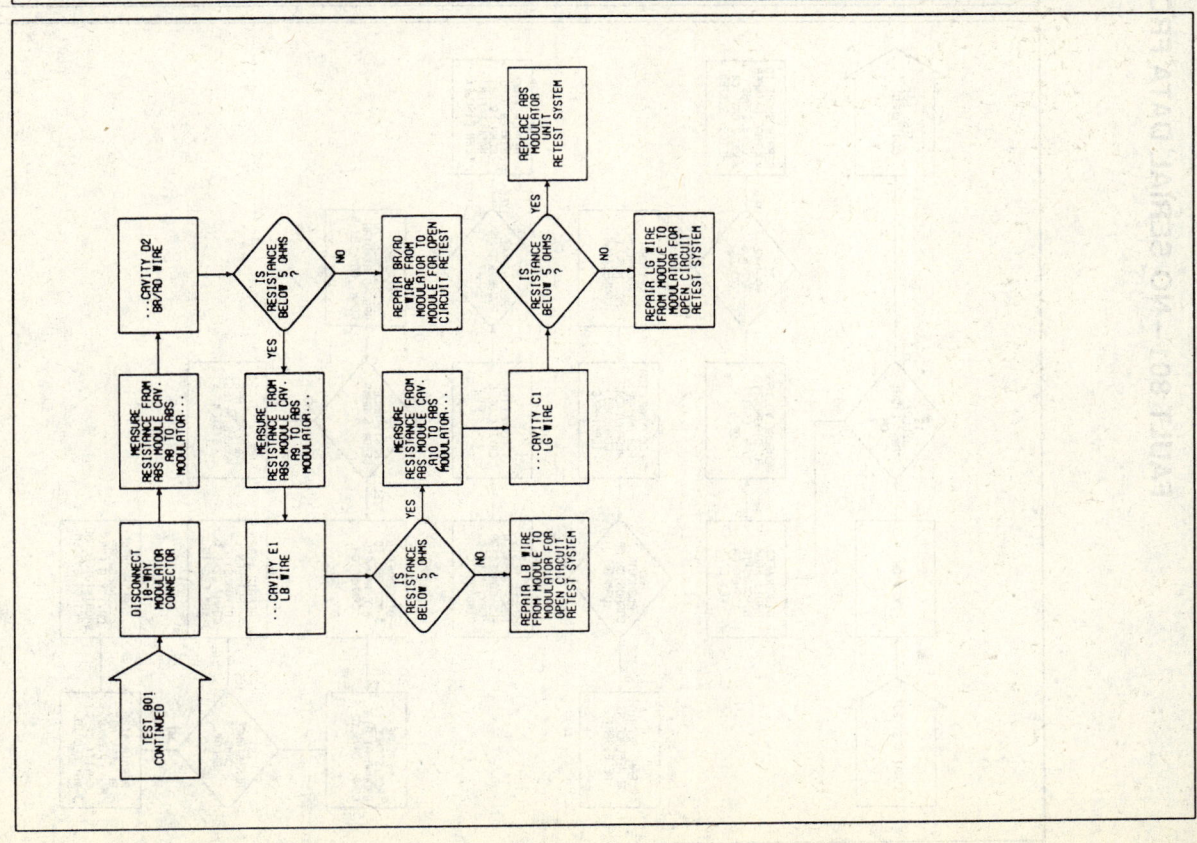

BRAKES 9

FAULT 804 — YELLOW LIGHT OFF — 1990-91 JEEP

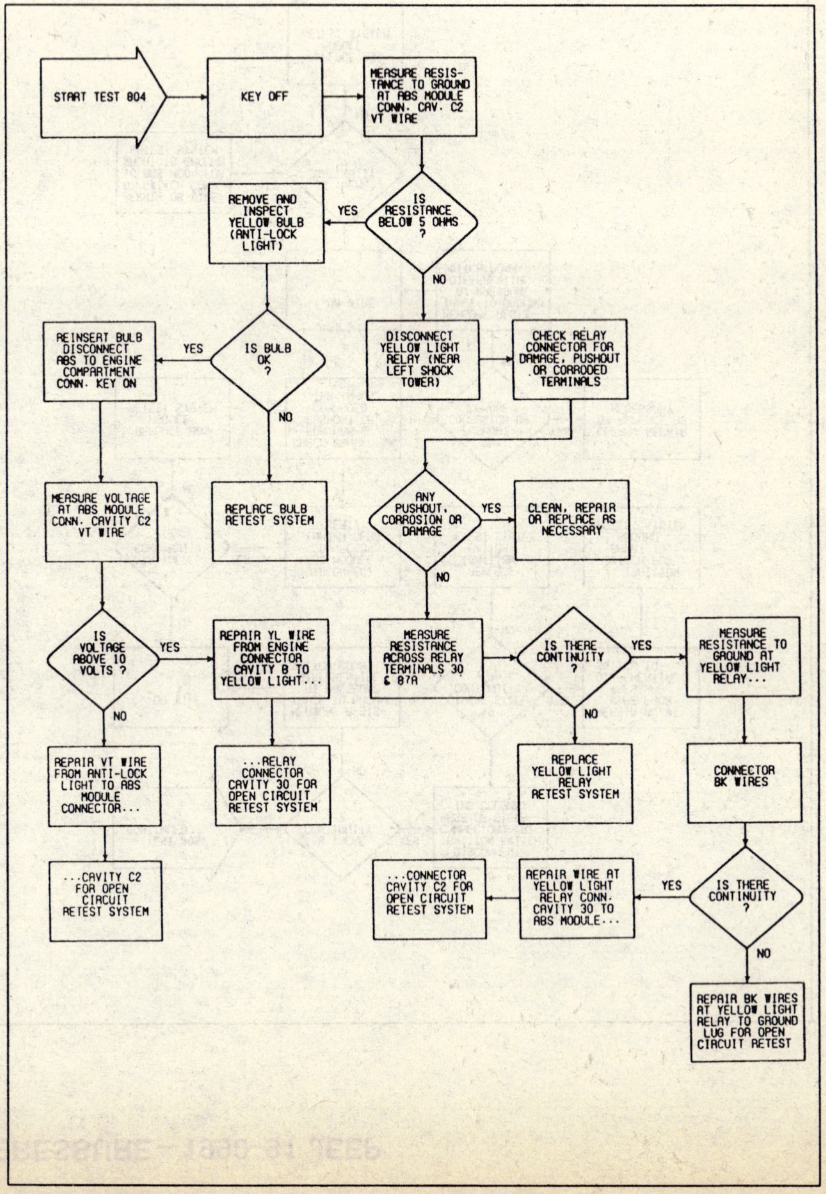

FAULT 803 — ABS LIGHTS INOPERATIVE — 1990-91 JEEP

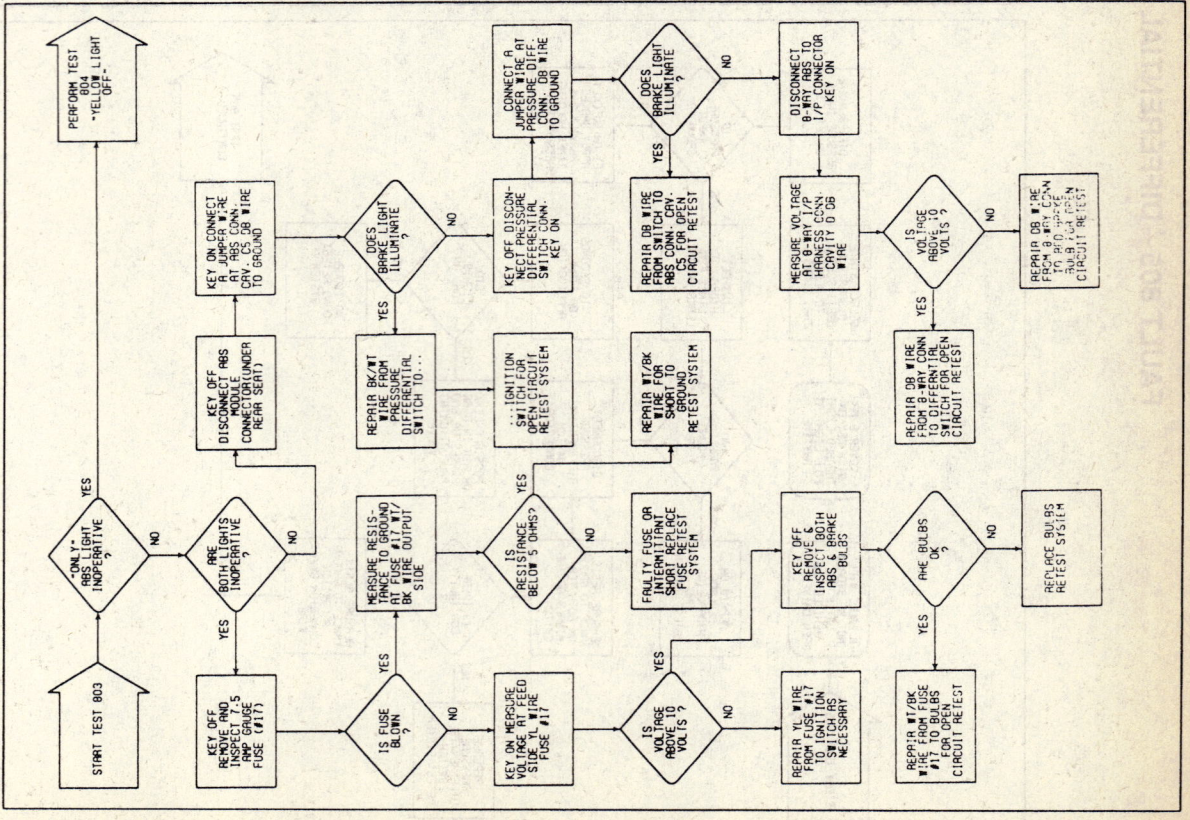

9-79

9 BRAKES

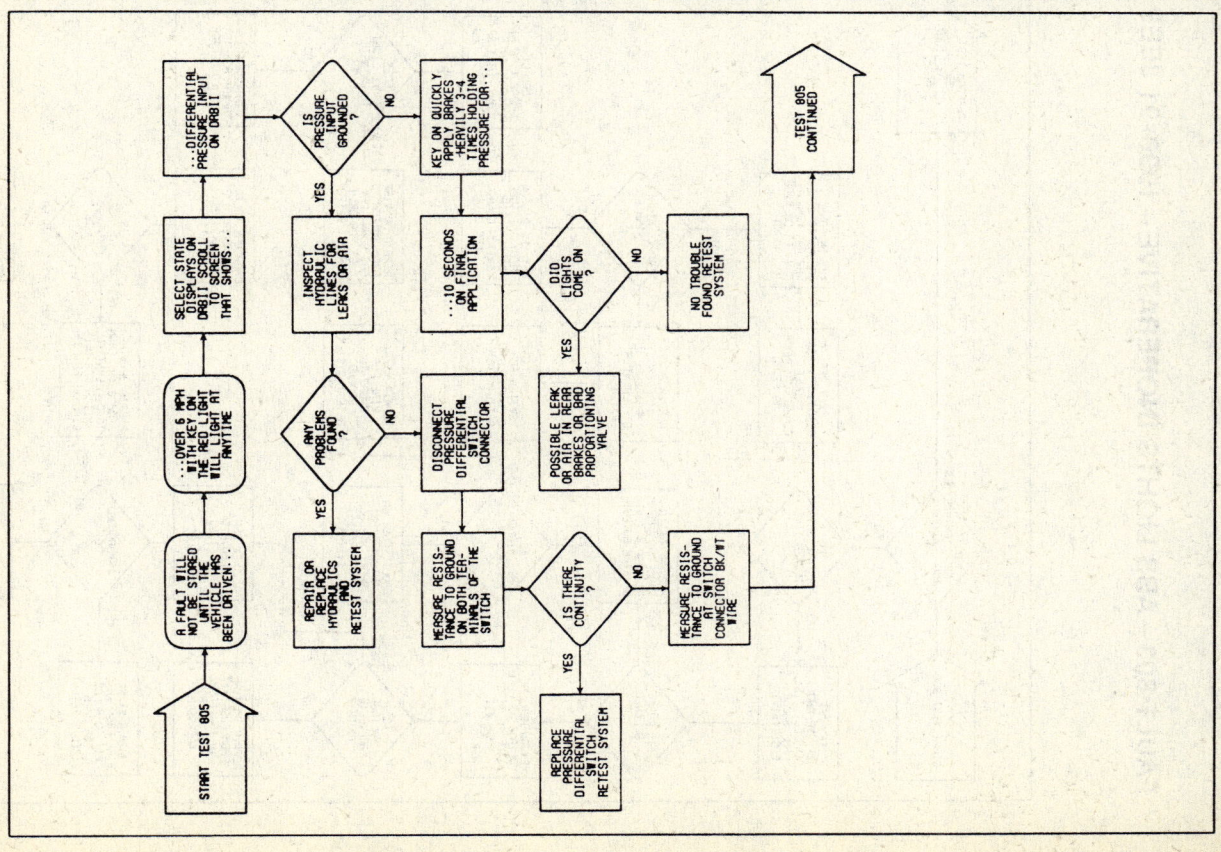

FAULT 805 – DIFFERENTIAL PRESSURE – 1990-91 JEEP

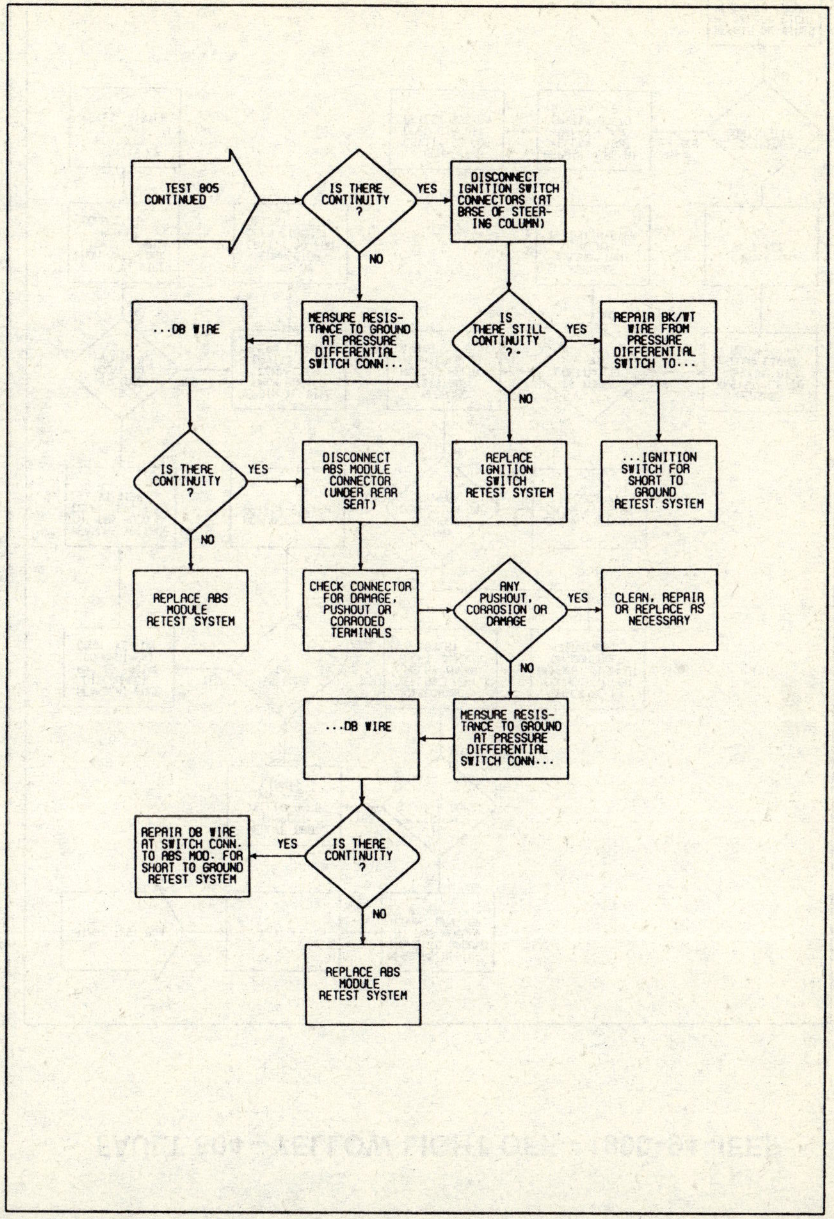

9-80

BRAKES 9

FAULT 807 — LOW ACCUMULATOR — 1990-91 JEEP

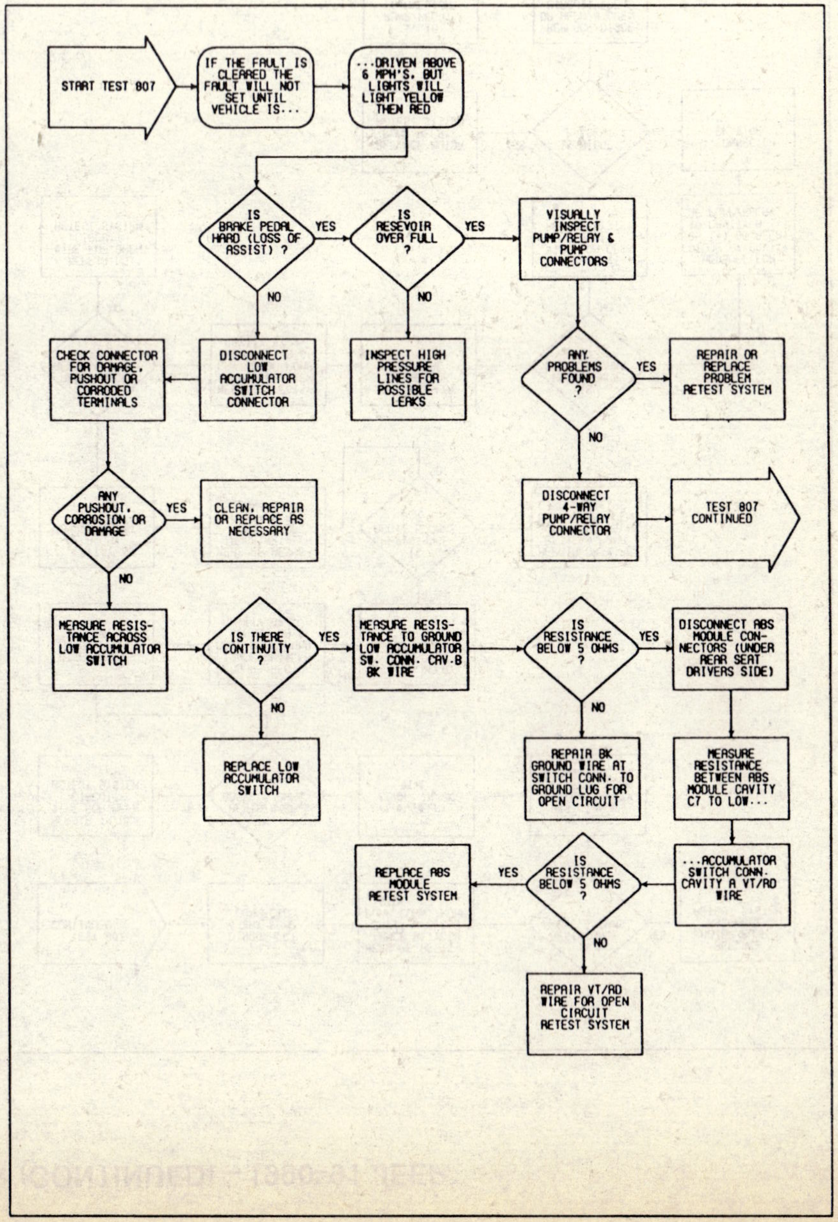

FAULT 806 — BOOST PRESSURE FAULT — 1990-91 JEEP

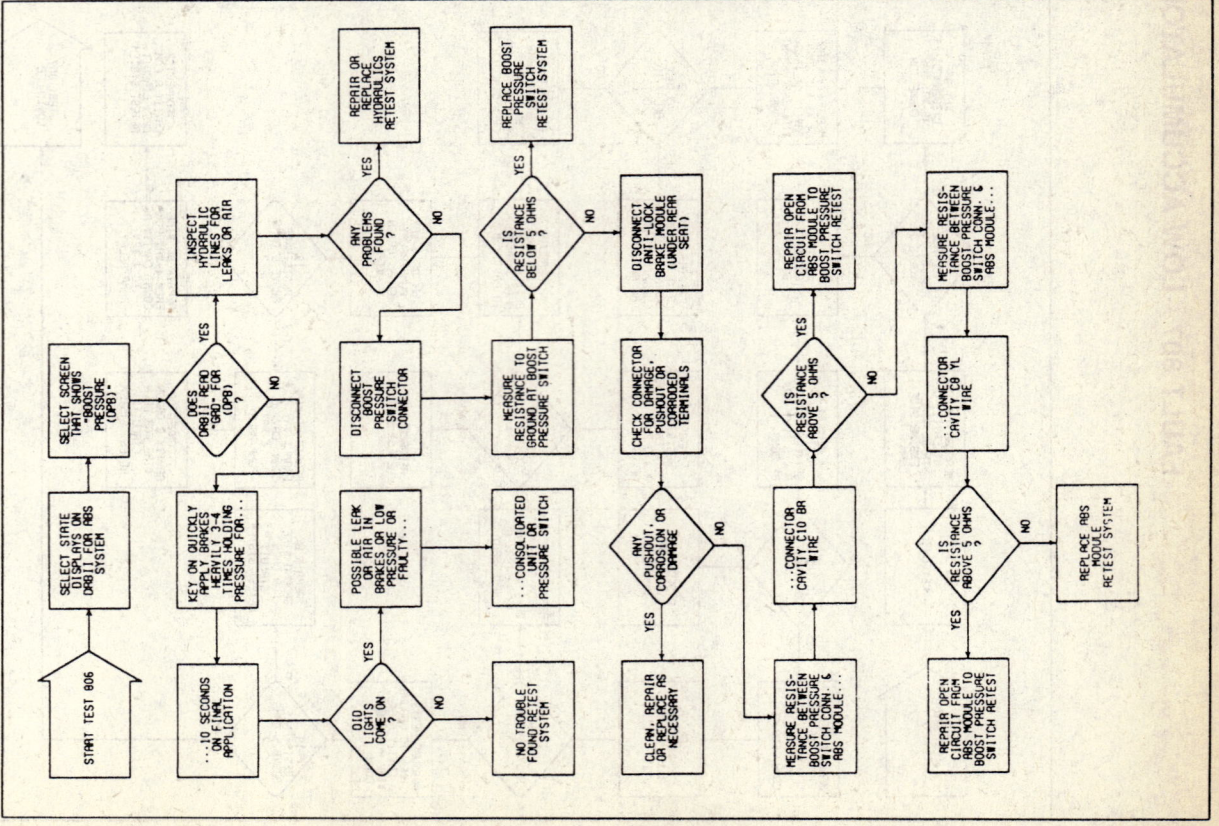

9-81

9 BRAKES

FAULT 807 — LOW ACCUMULATOR (CONTINUED) — 1990-91 JEEP

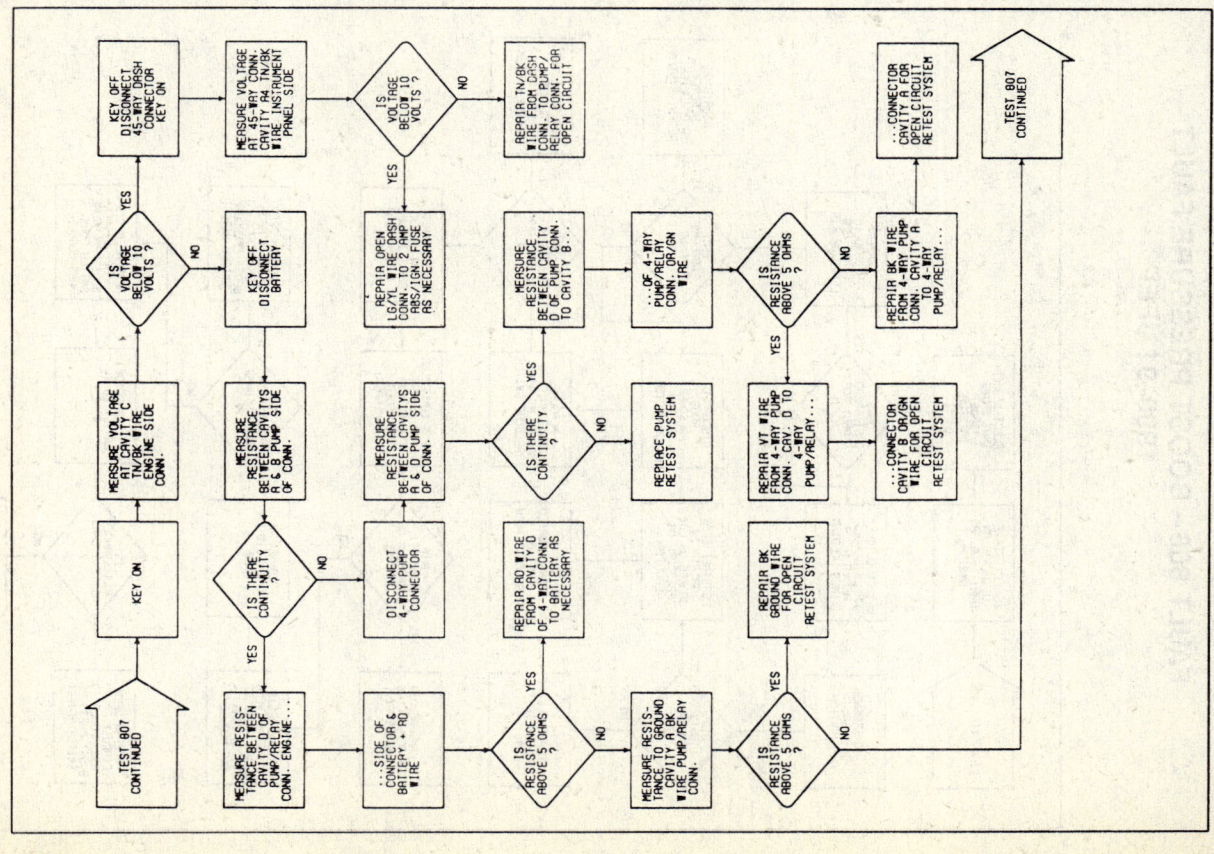

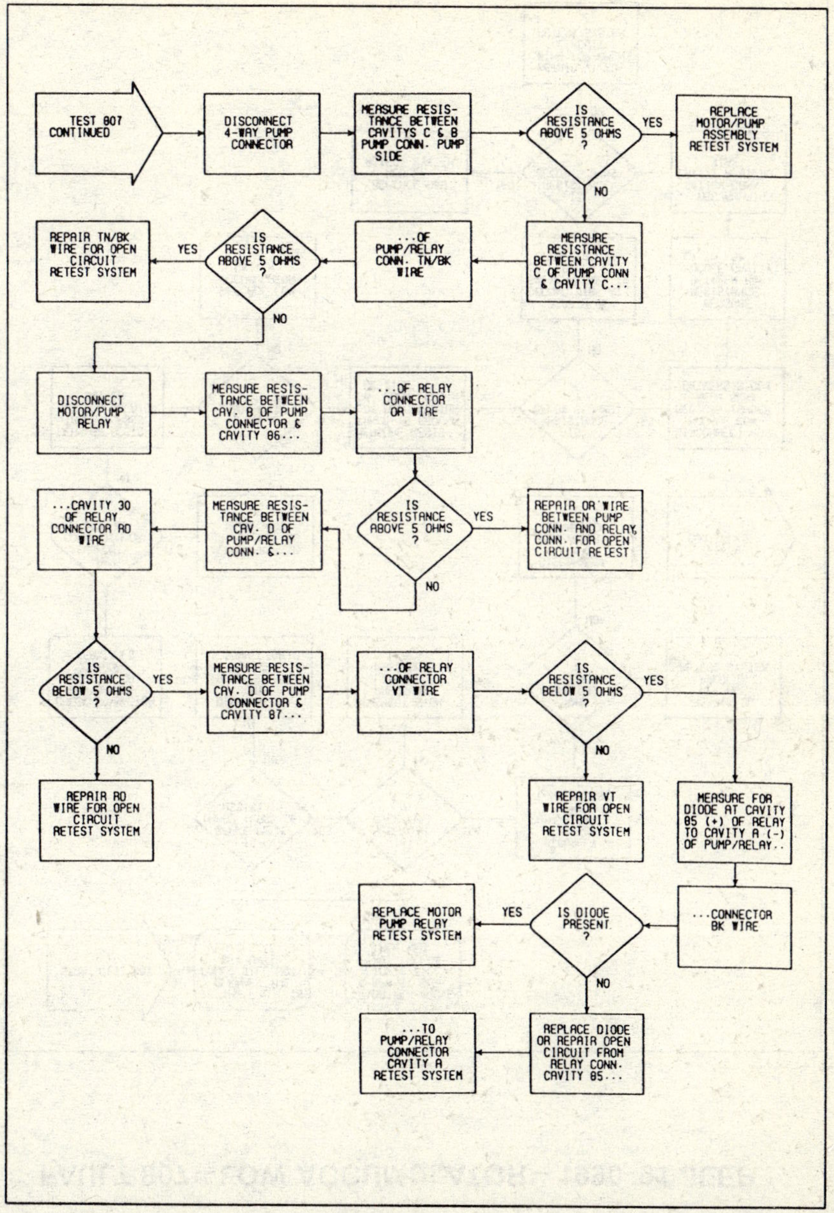

9-82

BRAKES 9

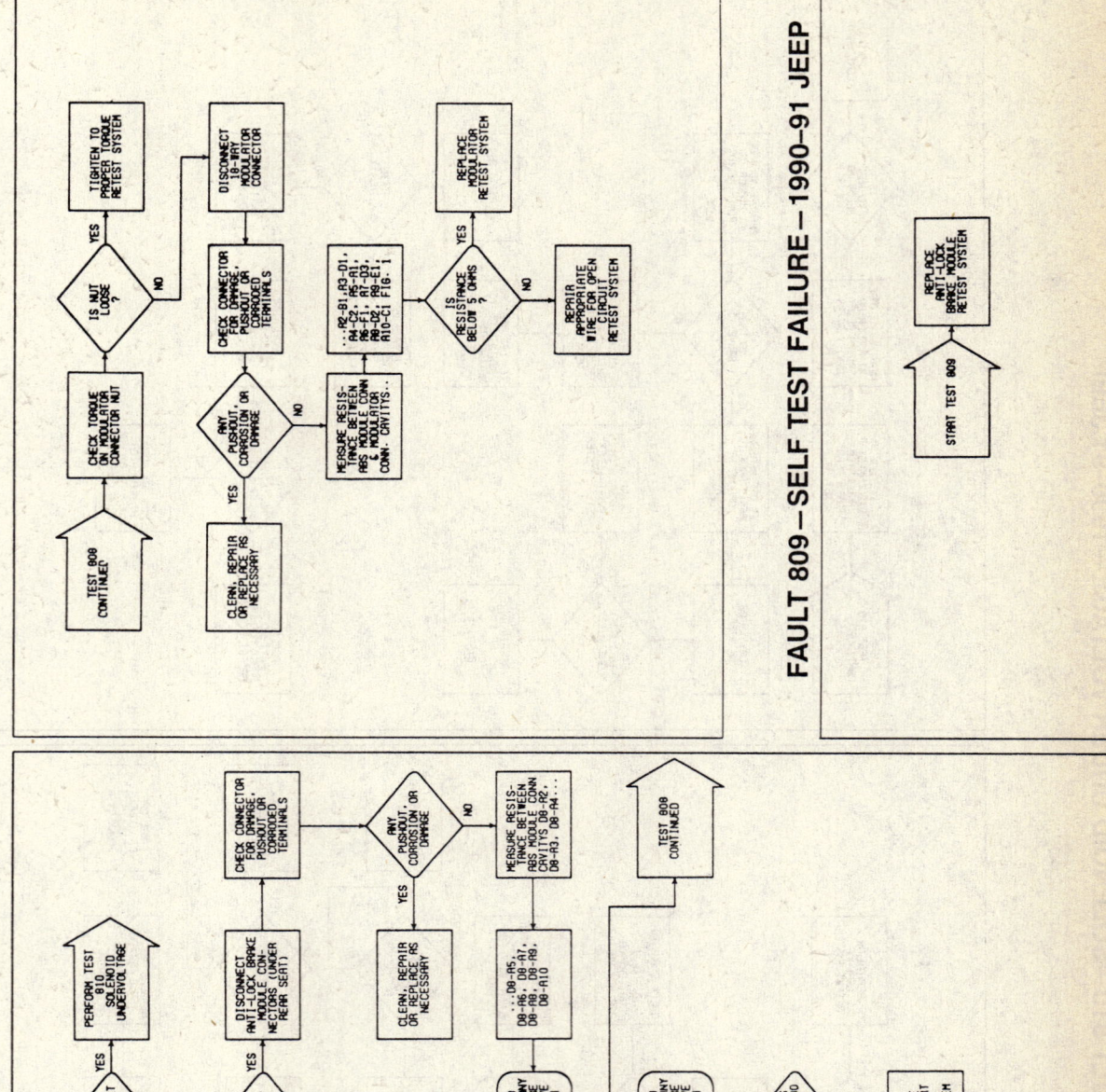

9-83

9 BRAKES

FAULT 810 – SOLENOID UNDER VOLTAGE – 1990-91 JEEP

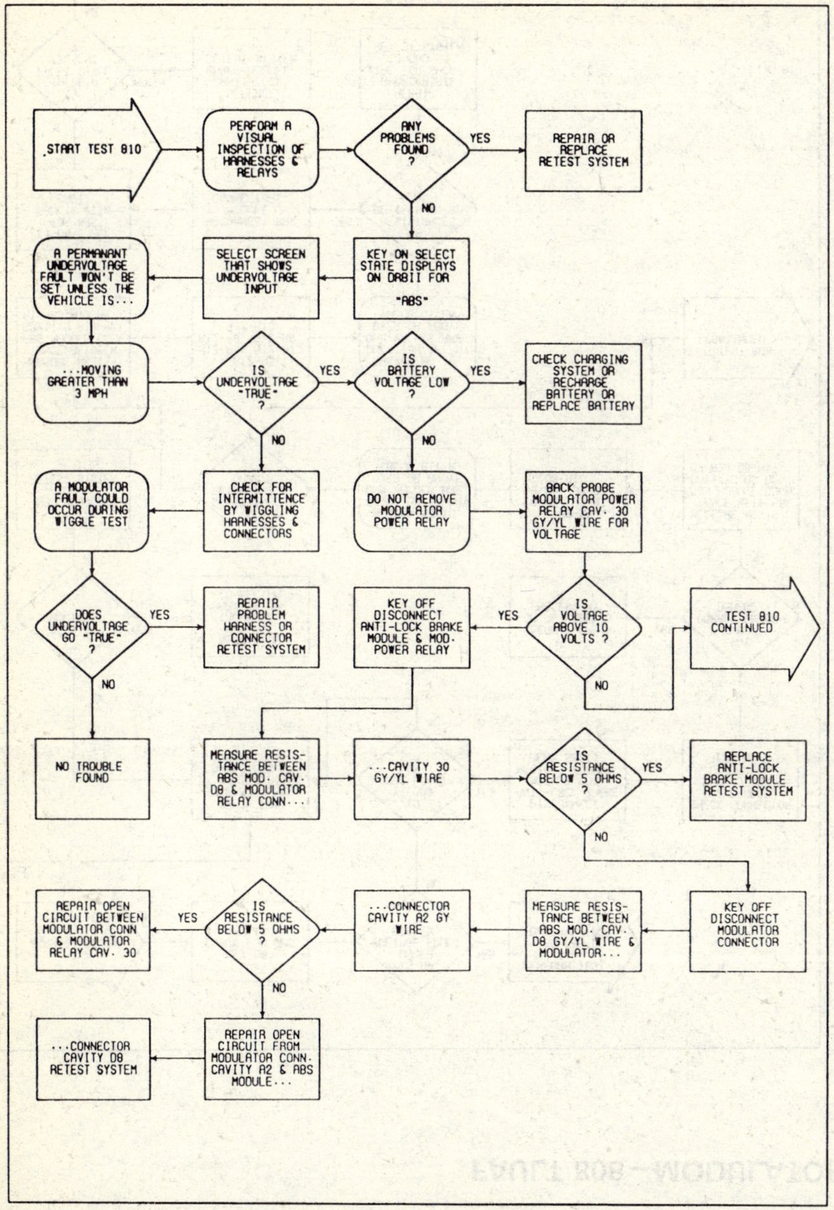

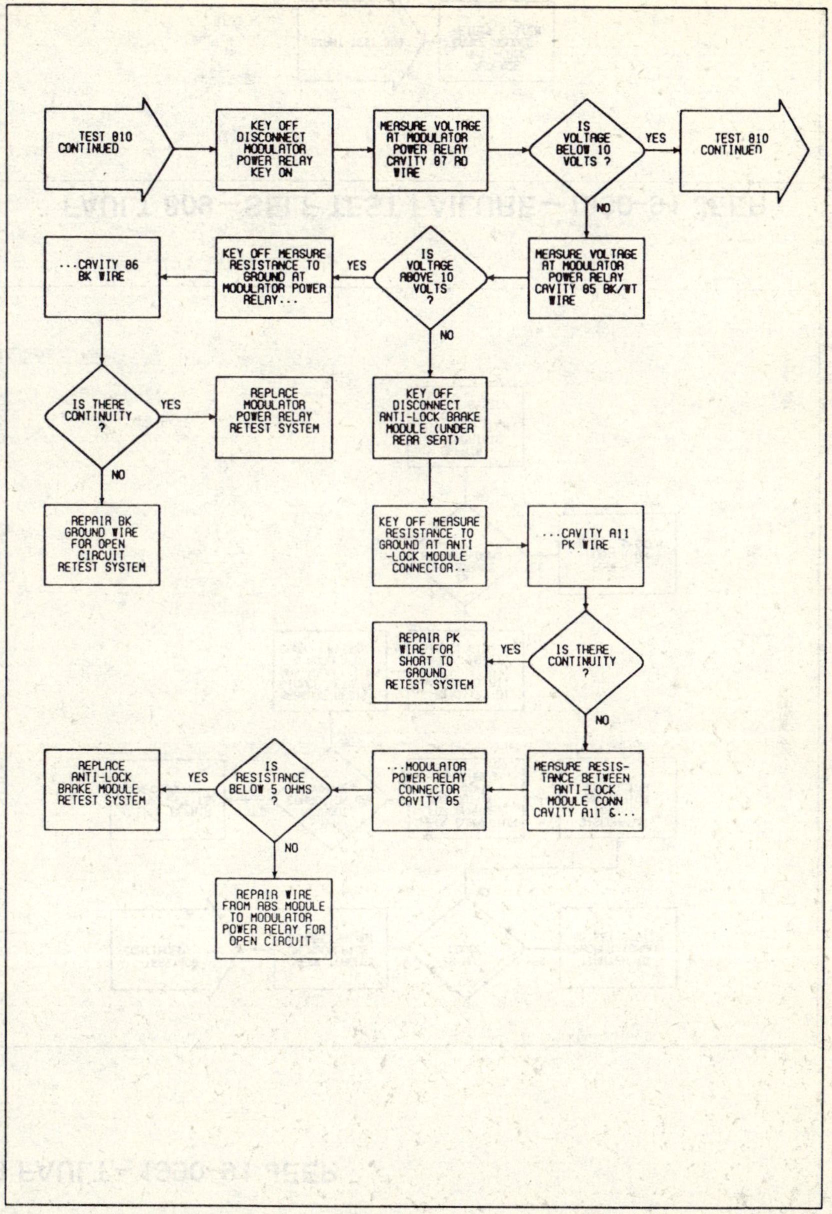

9-84

BRAKES 9

FAULT 811 – RELAY FAULT – 1990-91 JEEP

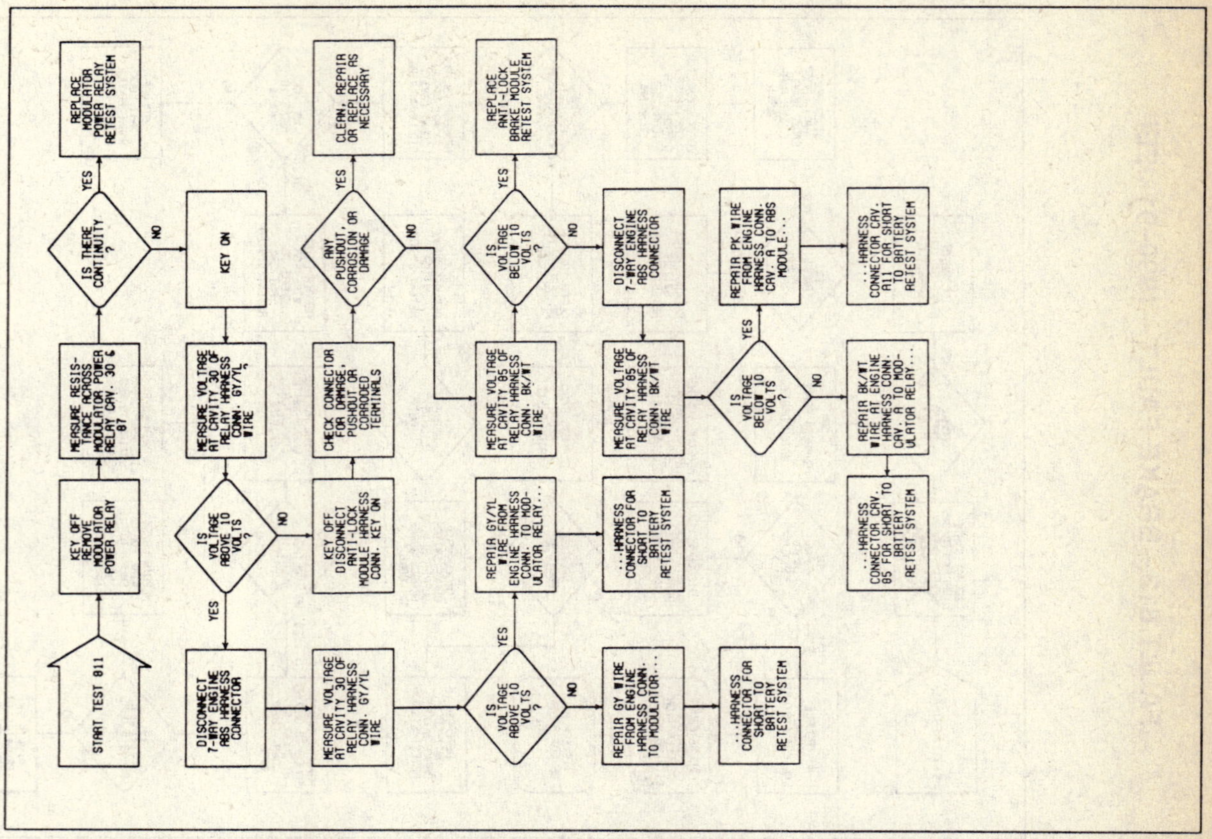

FAULT 810 – SOLENOID UNDER VOLTAGE (CONTINUED) – 1990-91 JEEP

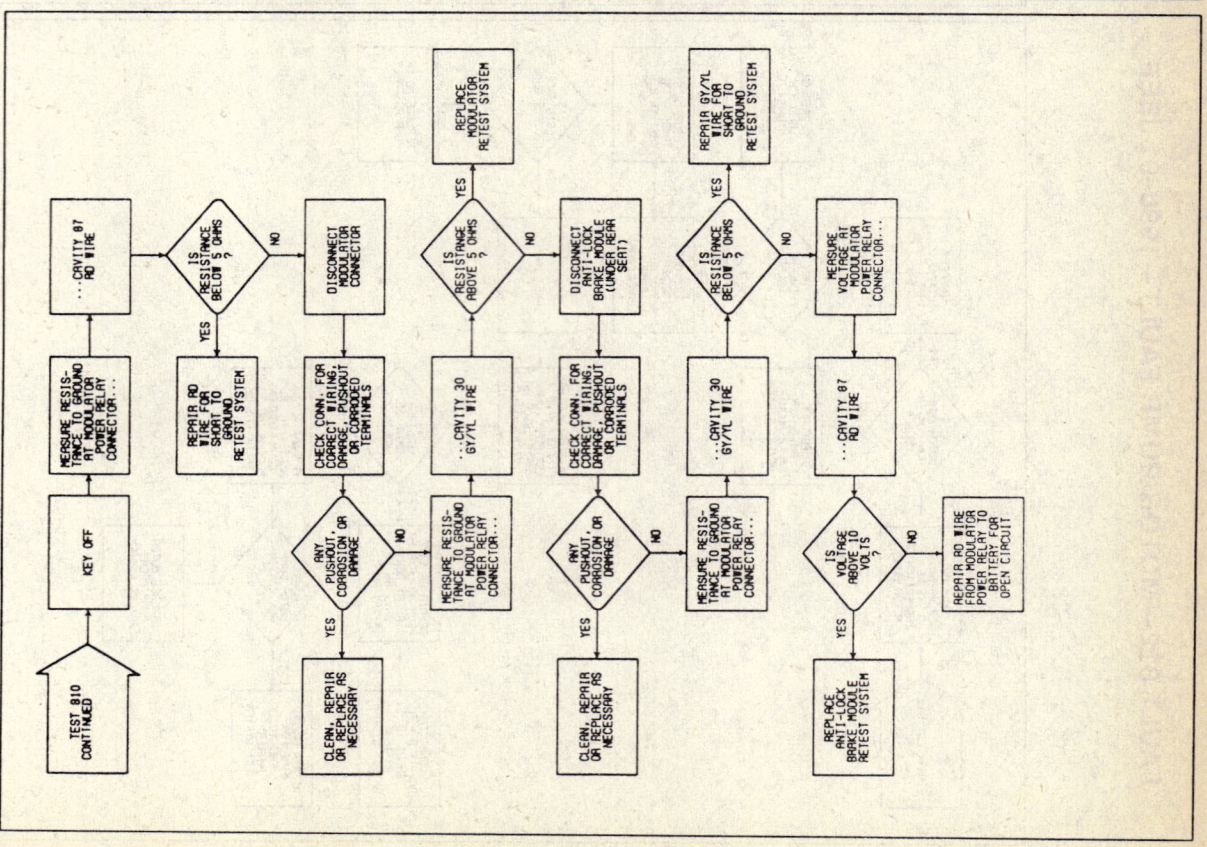

9-85

9 BRAKES

FAULT 813 — BRAKE FAULT — 1990-91 JEEP

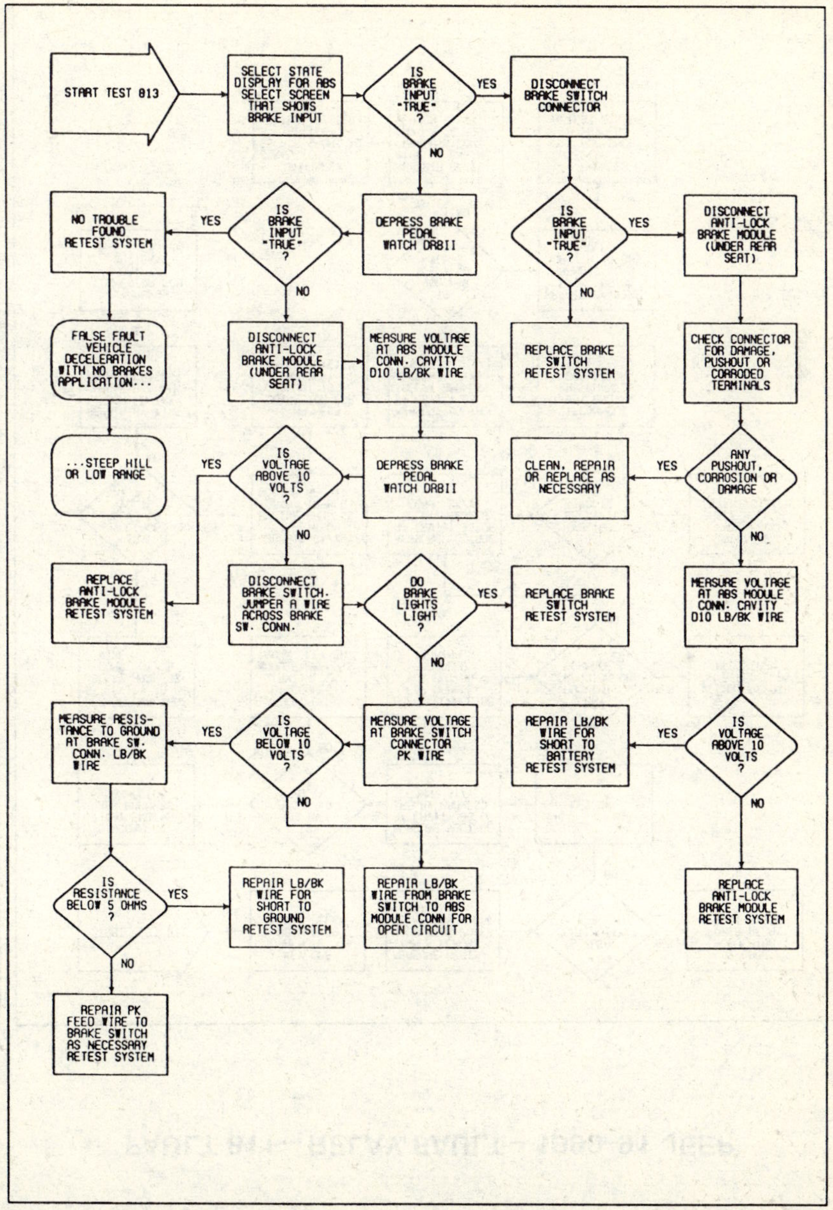

FAULT 812 — MOTOR/PUMP FAULT — 1990-91 JEEP

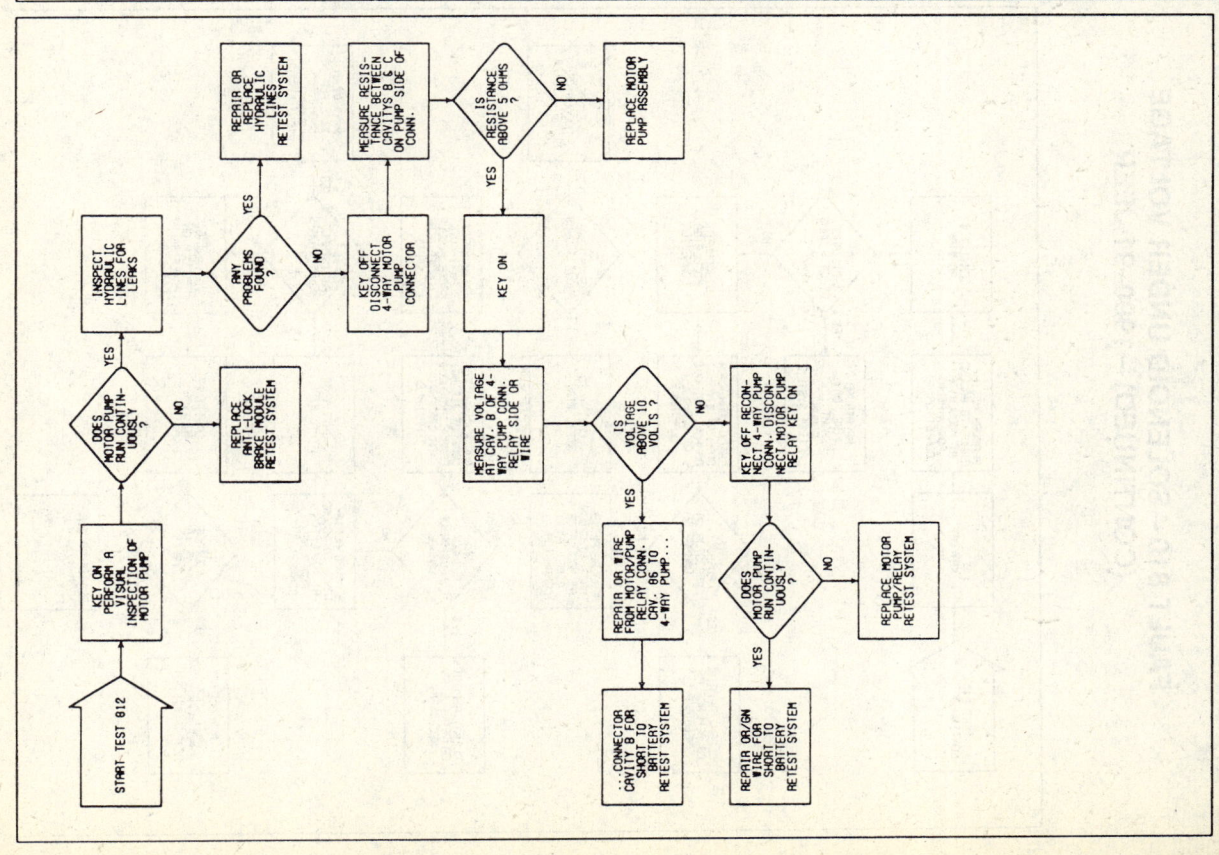

BRAKES 9

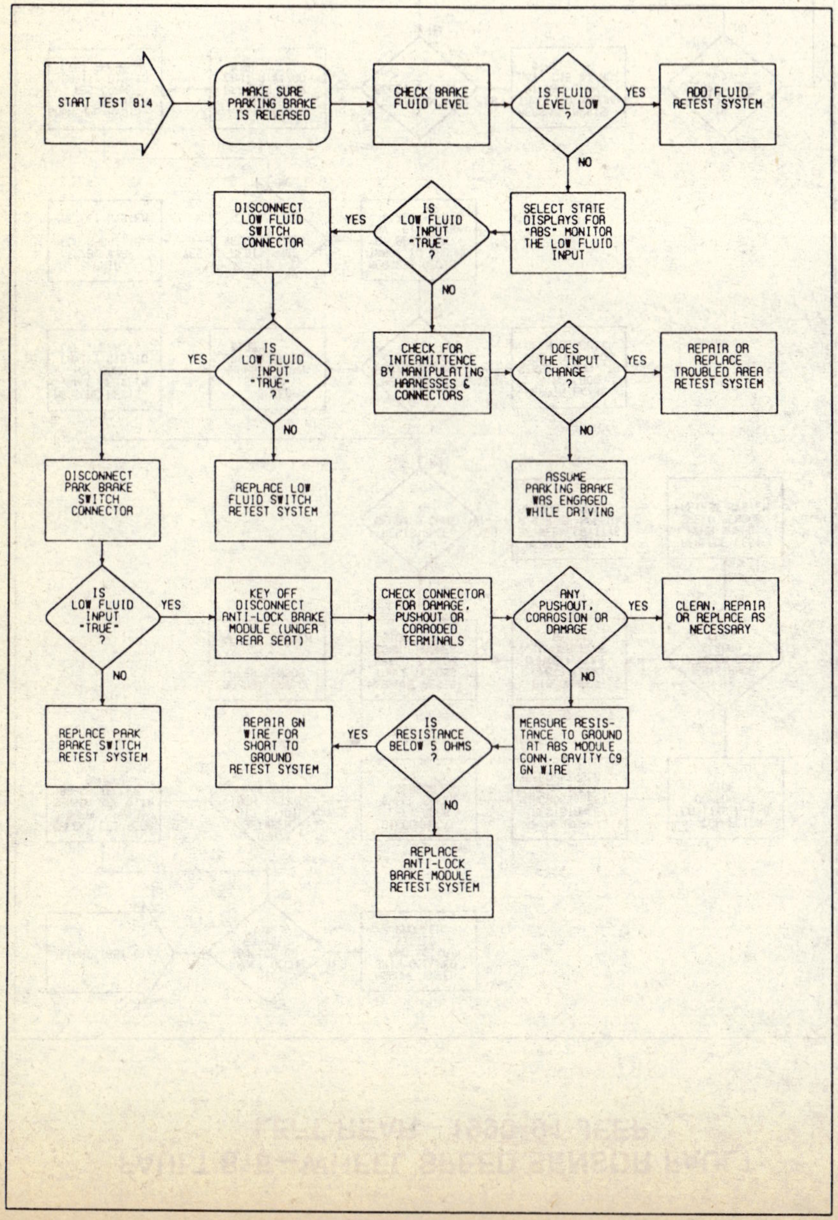

FAULT 815 – WHEEL SPEED SENSOR FAULT: RIGHT REAR – 1990-91 JEEP

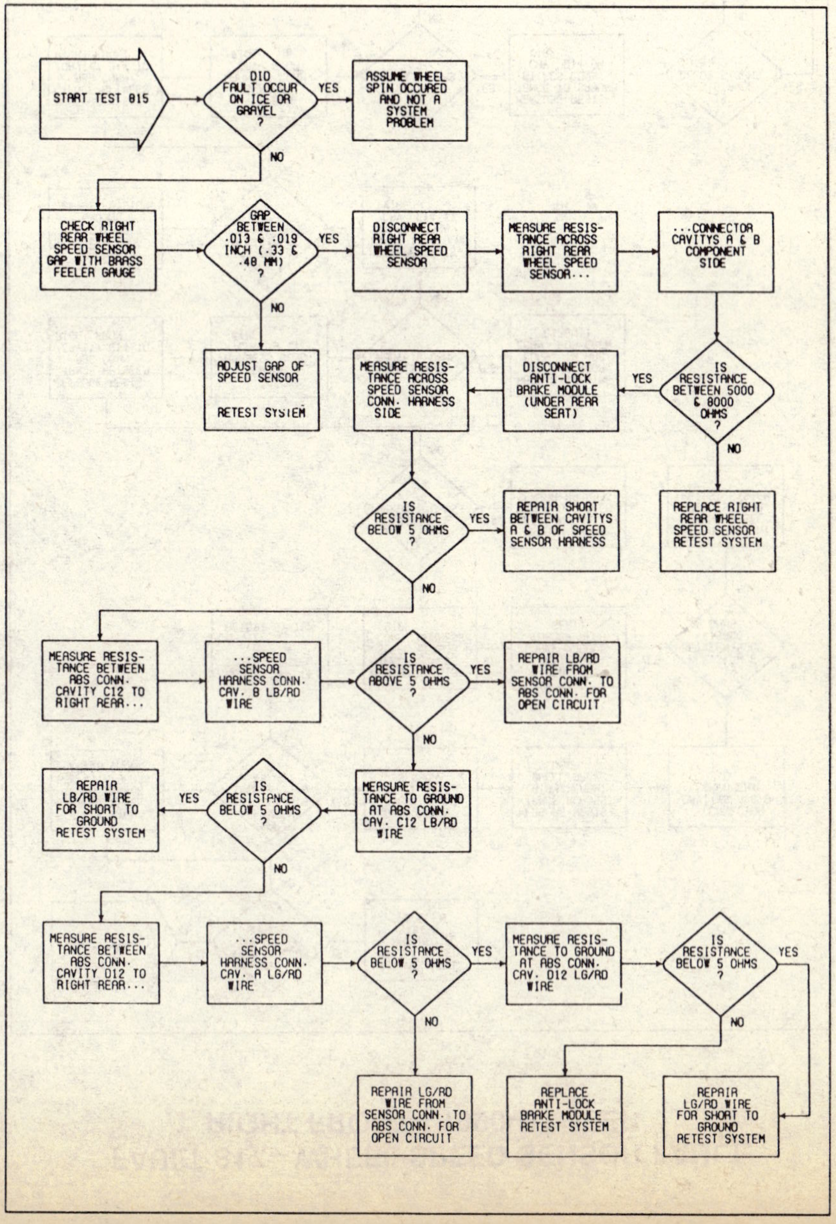

FAULT 814 – LOW FLUID – 1990-91 JEEP

9-87

9 BRAKES

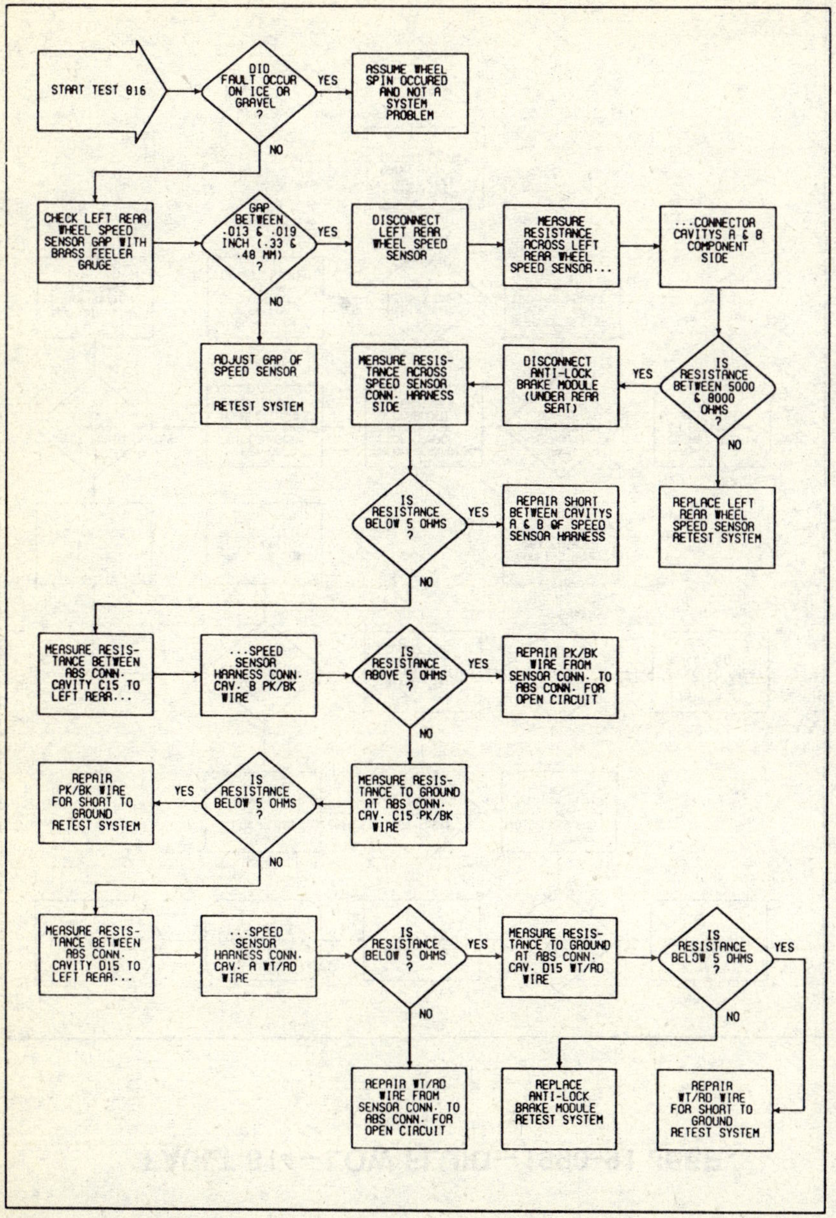

FAULT 817 – WHEEL SPEED SENSOR FAULT: RIGHT FRONT – 1990-91 JEEP

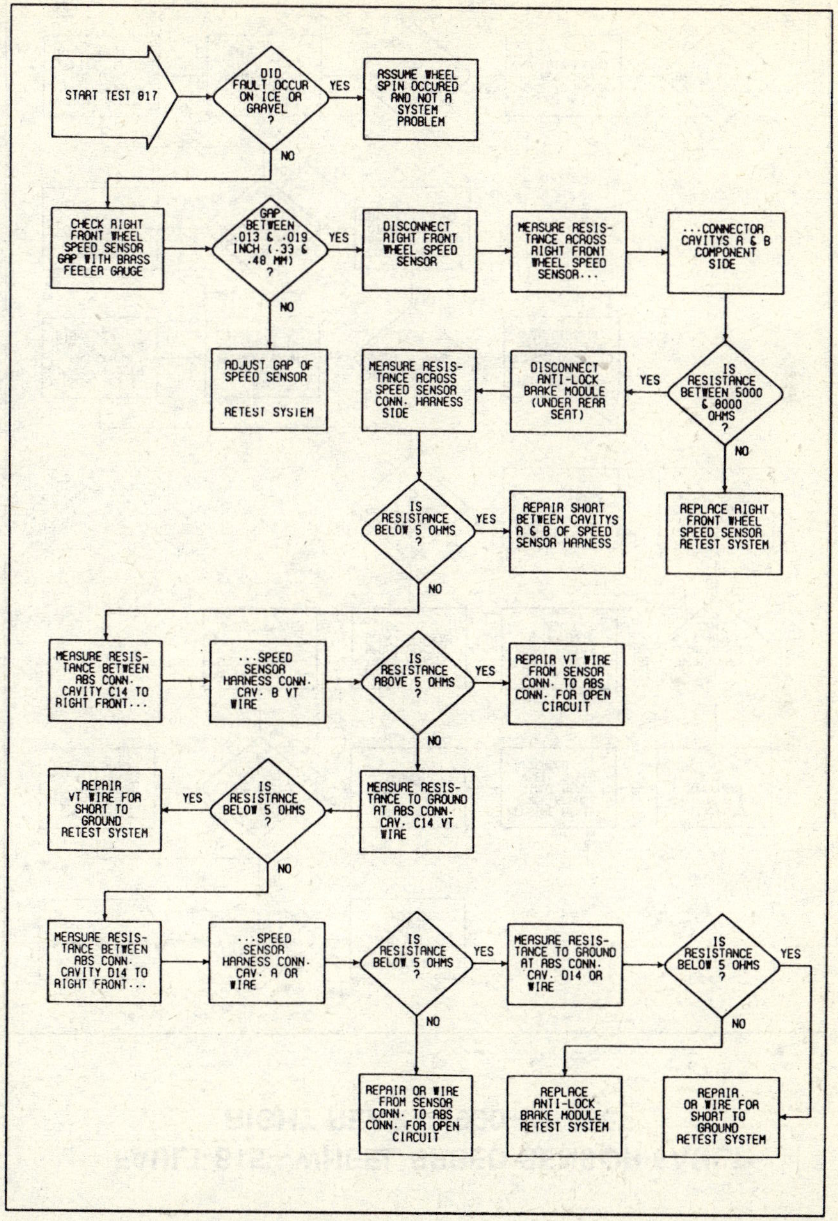

FAULT 816 – WHEEL SPEED SENSOR FAULT: LEFT REAR – 1990-91 JEEP

BRAKES 9

FAULT 819—OPEN CIRCUIT AT D2-14—1990-91 JEEP

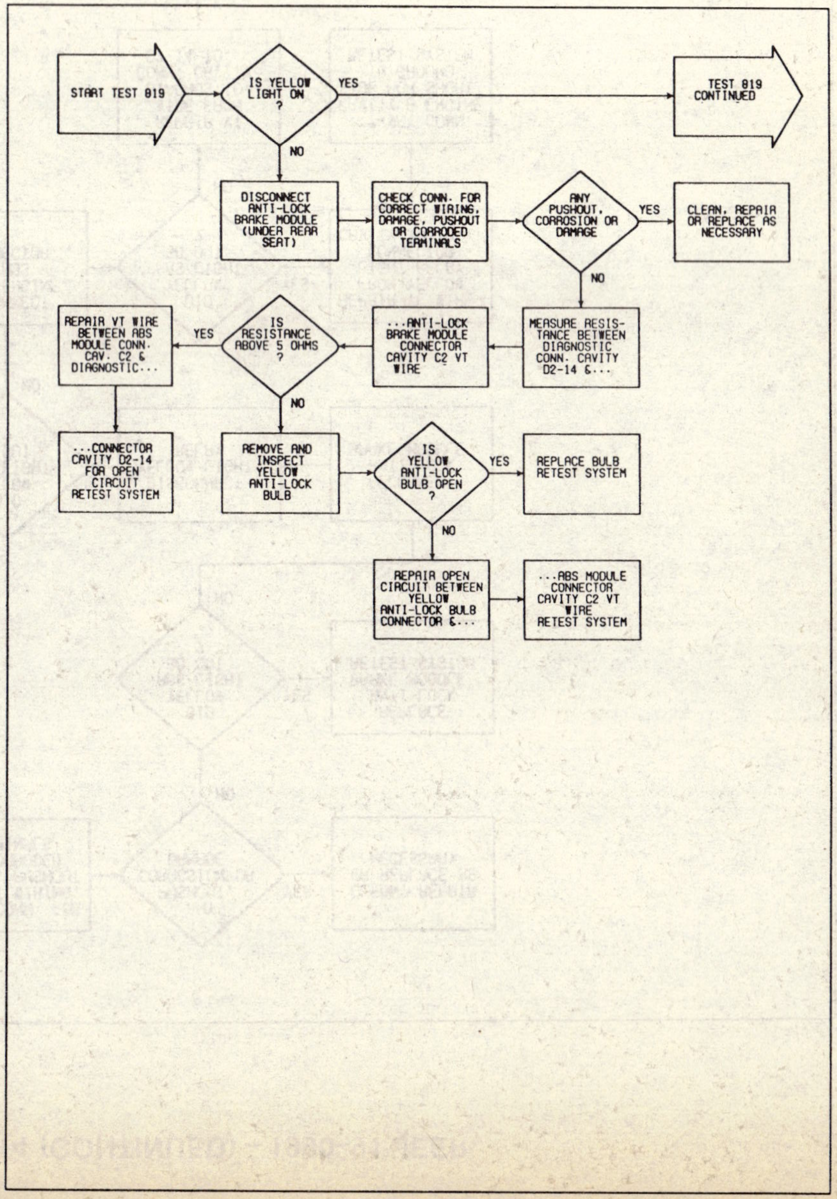

FAULT 818—WHEEL SPEED SENSOR FAULT: LEFT FRONT—1990-91 JEEP

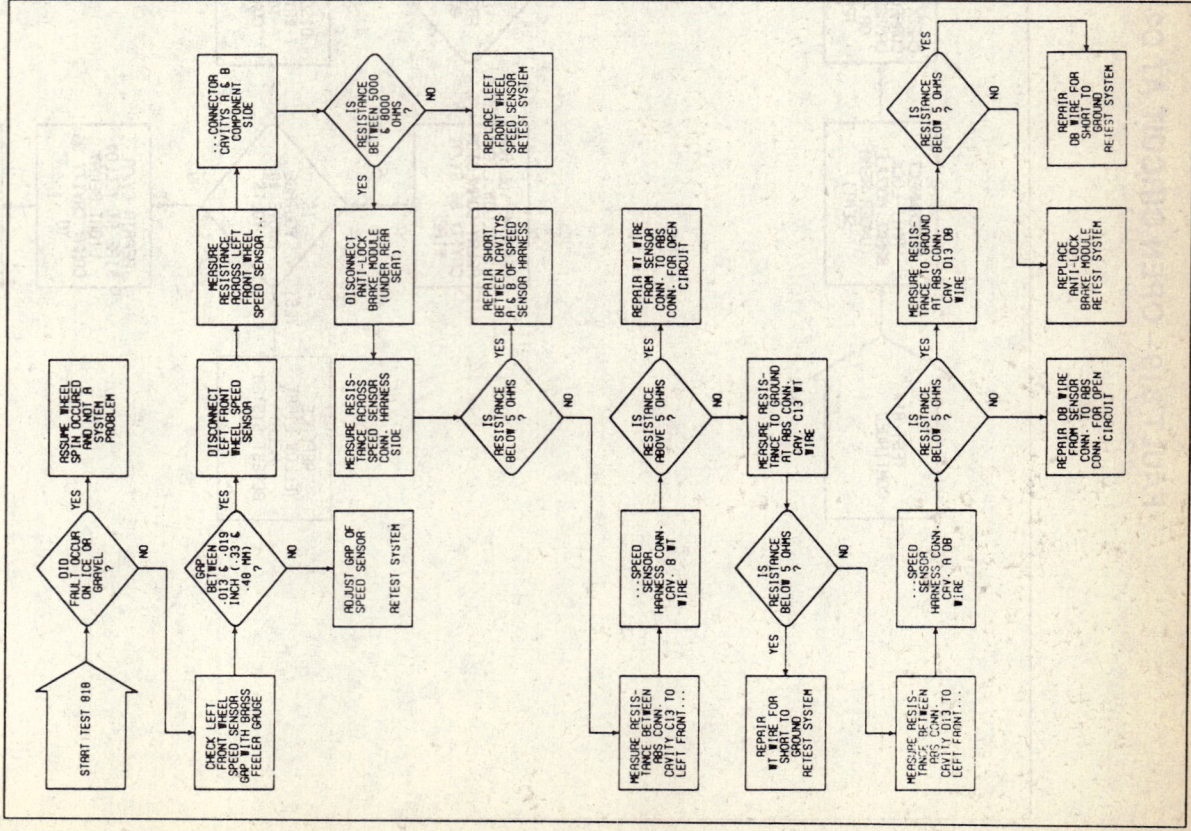

9-89

9 BRAKES

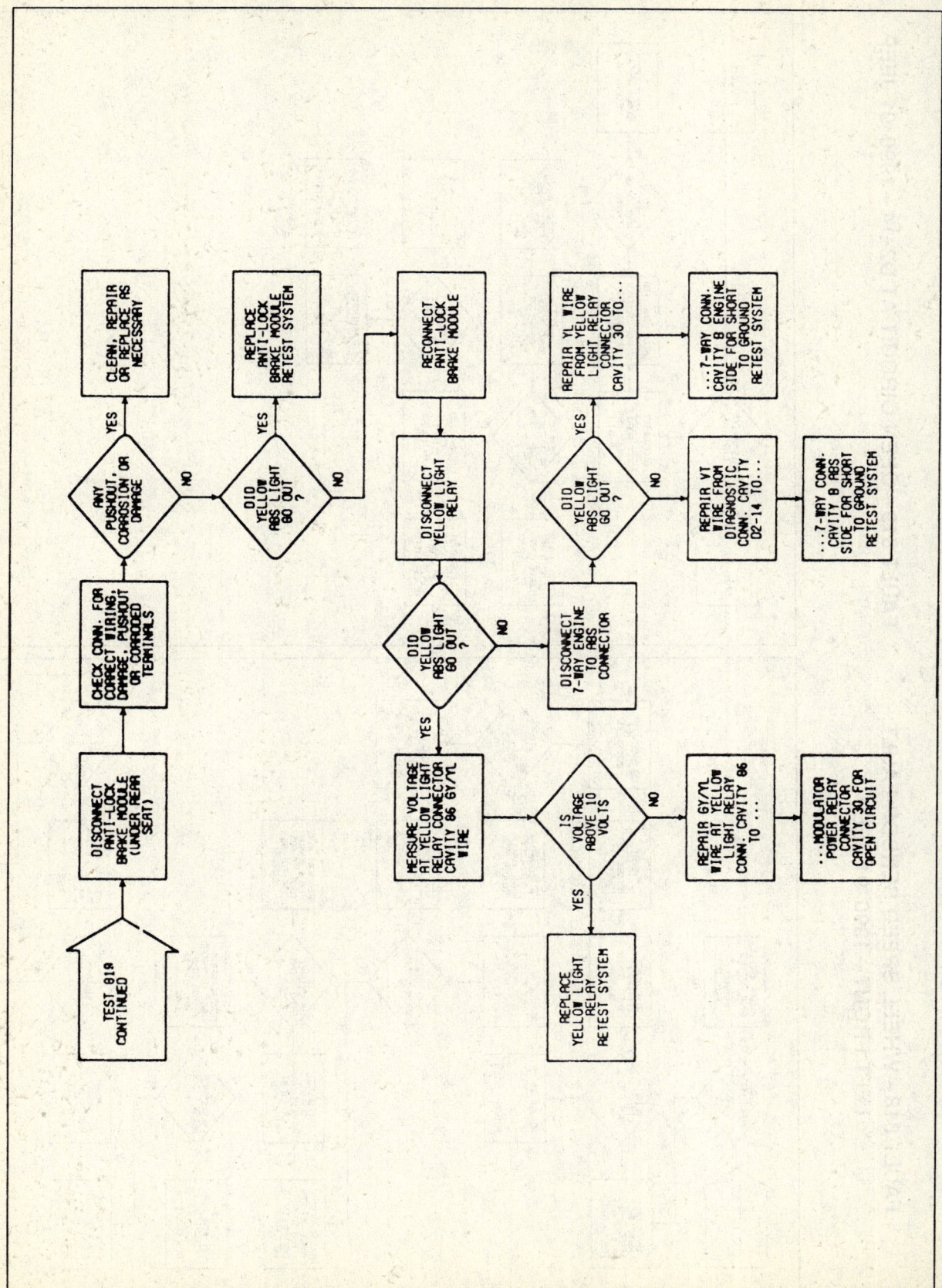

FAULT 819—OPEN CIRCUIT AT D2-14 (CONTINUED)—1990-91 JEEP

10 Body

QUICK REFERENCE INDEX

Exterior	10-3
Interior	10-18
Stain Removal	10-2

GENERAL INDEX

Antenna	10-13	Glass		Power window motor	10-24
Bumpers	10-10	Door	10-22	Rear bumper	10-10
Cargo box	10-15	Rear window	10-24, 30	Rear window	10-24, 30
Door glass	10-22	Windshield	10-24	Seat belts	10-34
Doors		Fenders	10-15	Seats	10-30
Adjustment	10-3	Grille	10-11	Spare tire carrier	10-16
Glass	10-22	Headliner	10-35	Stain removal	10-2
Locks	10-21, 22	Hood	10-3	Tailgate	10-9
Removal and installation	10-3	Interior trim panels	10-18	Window glass	10-22, 24, 30
Trim panels	10-18	Liftgate	10-10	Window regulator	10-22
Front bumper	10-10	Mirrors	10-12, 30	Windshield	10-24

10 BODY

How to Remove Stains from Fabric Interior

For best results, spots and stains should be removed as soon as possible. Never use gasoline, lacquer thinner, acetone, nail polish remover or bleach. Use a 3' x 3" piece of cheesecloth. Squeeze most of the liquid from the fabric and wipe the stained fabric from the outside of the stain toward the center with a lifting motion. Turn the cheesecloth as soon as one side becomes soiled. When using water to remove a stain, be sure to wash the entire section after the spot has been removed to avoid water stains. Encrusted spots can be broken up with a dull knife and vacuumed before removing the stain.

Type of Stain	How to Remove It
Surface spots	Brush the spots out with a small hand brush or use a commercial preparation such as K2R to lift the stain.
Mildew	Clean around the mildew with warm suds. Rinse in cold water and soak the mildew area in a solution of 1 part table salt and 2 parts water. Wash with upholstery cleaner.
Water stains	Water stains in fabric materials can be removed with a solution made from 1 cup of table salt dissolved in 1 quart of water. Vigorously scrub the solution into the stain and rinse with clear water. Water stains in nylon or other synthetic fabrics should be removed with a commercial type spot remover.
Chewing gum, tar, crayons, shoe polish (greasy stains)	Do not use a cleaner that will soften gum or tar. Harden the deposit with an ice cube and scrape away as much as possible with a dull knife. Moisten the remainder with cleaning fluid and scrub clean.
Ice cream, candy	Most candy has a sugar base and can be removed with a cloth wrung out in warm water. Oily candy, after cleaning with warm water, should be cleaned with upholstery cleaner. Rinse with warm water and clean the remainder with cleaning fluid.
Wine, alcohol, egg, milk, soft drink (non-greasy stains)	Do not use soap. Scrub the stain with a cloth wrung out in warm water. Remove the remainder with cleaning fluid.
Grease, oil, lipstick, butter and related stains	Use a spot remover to avoid leaving a ring. Work from the outisde of the stain to the center and dry with a clean cloth when the spot is gone.
Headliners (cloth)	Mix a solution of warm water and foam upholstery cleaner to give thick suds. Use only foam—liquid may streak or spot. Clean the entire headliner in one operation using a circular motion with a natural sponge.
Headliner (vinyl)	Use a vinyl cleaner with a sponge and wipe clean with a dry cloth.
Seats and door panels	Mix 1 pint upholstery cleaner in 1 gallon of water. Do not soak the fabric around the buttons.
Leather or vinyl fabric	Use a multi-purpose cleaner full strength and a stiff brush. Let stand 2 minutes and scrub thoroughly. Wipe with a clean, soft rag.
Nylon or synthetic fabrics	For normal stains, use the same procedures you would for washing cloth upholstery. If the fabric is extremely dirty, use a multi-purpose cleaner full strength with a stiff scrub brush. Scrub thoroughly in all directions and wipe with a cotton towel or soft rag.

BODY 10

EXTERIOR

Replacement of exterior body panels is a fairly straight forward procedure. Most panels are fastened to the chassis with an assortment of bolts, nuts, screws and clips. Professional body shops use many specialty tools designed to quicken the time required to replace and align body panels but the average do-it-yourselfer can perform the same procedures with basic hand tools—it just takes a little longer. However, there are some areas which require special a attention to detail in order to achieve a professional appearance.

The first area that requires special attention is the alignment of body panels. When aligning body panels, most of the time is spent trying to achieve straight body lines. If the body lines down the side of a vehicle are not straight, the vehicle will have a distorted appearance and anyone, even another do-it-yourselfer, will be able to tell the panel was replaced.

Before you begin replacing the panel, measure all the air gaps between the panel that is being replaced and the adjacent panels. Use this information to properly align the replacement panel. If you are repairing a vehicle that has damage on one side, measure the other side to ensure your measurements are accurate.

When installing the new replacement panel, wrap the edges with masking tape to ensure you do not nick the paint. Install all bolts in the panel loosely and then align the panel. After aligning, tighten all bolts to specification.

Doors

REMOVAL AND INSTALLATION

1. On vehicles with power windows or locks, remove the trim panel and water shield. Disconnect the speaker wiring.
2. Matchmark the hinge-to-door position.
3. Have an assistant support the door.
4. Remove the door stop-to-pillar pin.
5. Remove the hinge-to-door bolts, catch the shims, and lift off the door.
6. Position the door and shims and install, but do not tighten the bolts.
7. Adjust the door, as described below, then, torque the bolts to 26 ft. lbs.
8. Connect the wiring and install the trim panel.

ADJUSTMENT

Door adjustment is made by means of shims located between the door and the hinge. The shims are placed in shim plates. Add or remove shims as necessary to obtain proper door fit. When adjustment is complete, torque the mounting bolts to 26 ft. lbs.

Hood

REMOVAL AND INSTALLATION

1. If the hood is properly aligned, prior to removal, matchmark the position of the hinges and hood reinforcement.
2. Raise the hood fully.
3. Disconnect the underhood lamp wiring.
4. While your assistant supports the hood, remove the hood-to-hinge bolts and lift off the hood.
5. Installation is the reverse of removal. Torque the bolts to 15 ft. lbs.

ALIGNMENT

NOTE: Hood hinge mounting holes are oversized to permit movement for hood alignment. If the hood is to be moved to either side, the hood lock striker, hood lever lock and safety hook assembly must first be loosened.

1. Loosen the hinge mounting bolts slightly on one side and tap the hinge in the direction opposite to that in which the hood is to be moved.
2. Tighten the bolts.
3. Repeat this procedure for the opposite hinge.
4. Check that the lock striker, lever lock and safety hook are

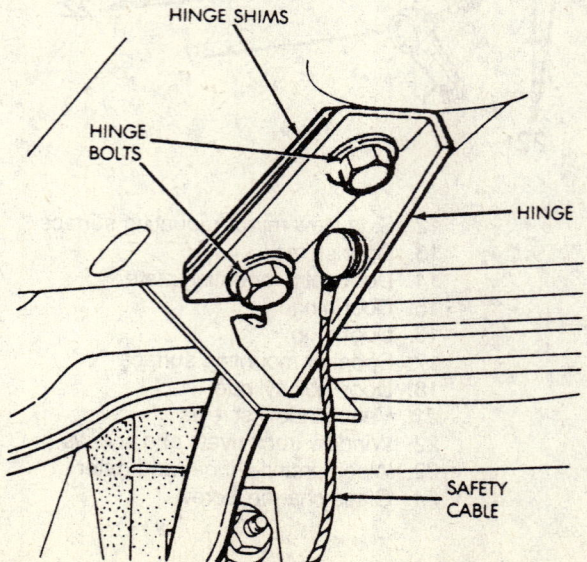
Hood hinge and shim position

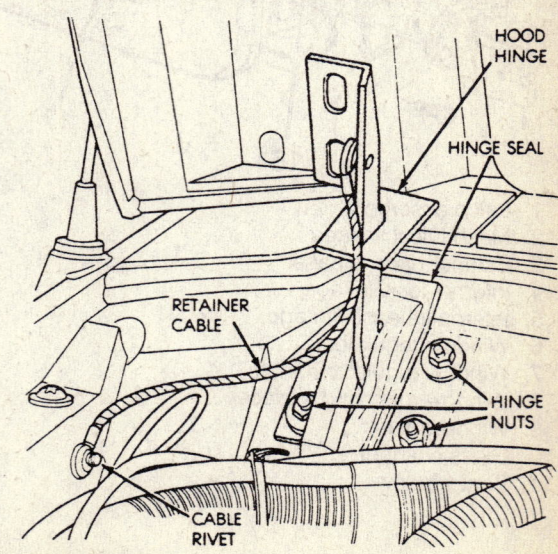
Hood hinge removal

10-3

10 BODY

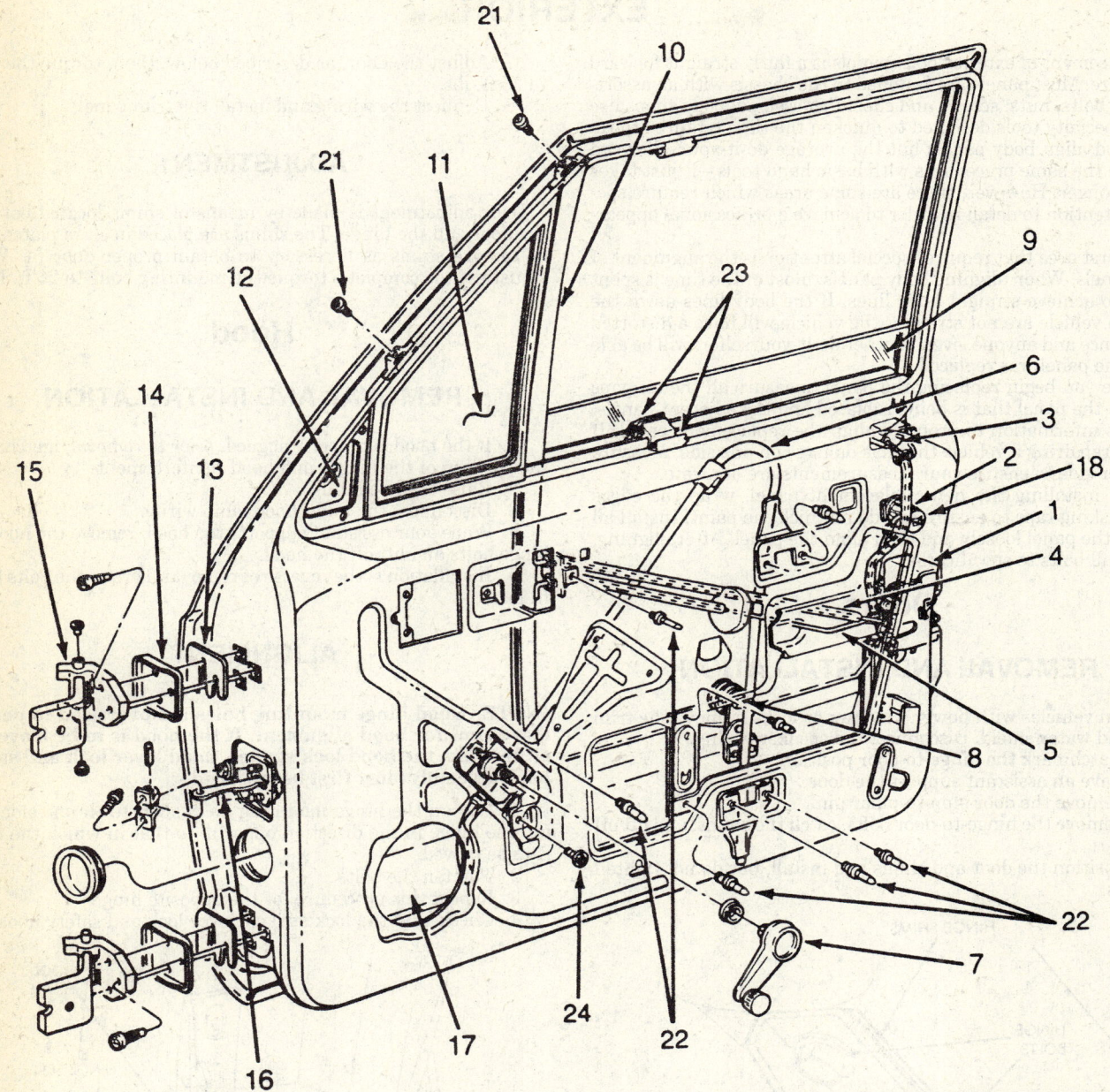

1. Latch assembly
2. Mechanical linkage
3. Exterior door release
4. Internal lock linkage
5. Internal release linkage
6. Window regulator
7. Window regulator handle
8. Window mounting surface
9. Window glass
10. Glass channel
11. Vent window
12. Side view mirror mounting surface
13. Door shims
14. Door shim mounting plate
15. Door hinge
16. Door stop
17. Speaker mounting surface
18. Door lock cylinder
21. Vent window screws
22. Window track rivets and screws
23. Weatherstrip—inner and outer
24. Glass channel screw

Front door with manual windows and locks

BODY 10

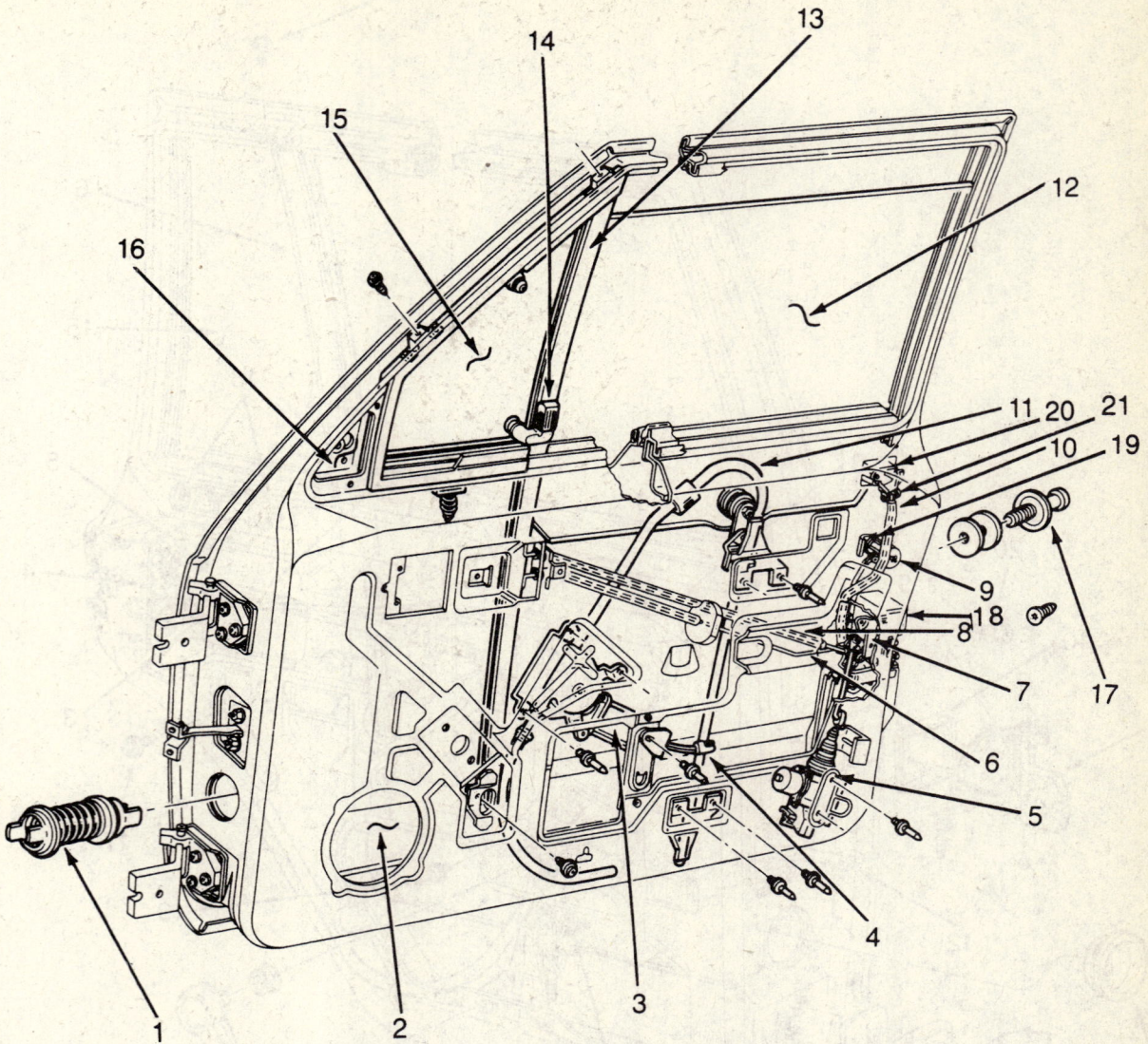

1. Wire harness boot
2. Speaker mounting surface
3. Power window motor
4. Motor wire harness connector
5. Power lock actuator
6. Internal latch release linkage
7. Door latch
8. Internal lock linkage
9. External lock
10. External latch release linkage
11. Window regulator
12. Window glass
13. Window channel
14. Vent window latch
15. Vent window
16. Side view mirror mounting surface
17. Striker
18. Latch assembly
19. External lock cylinder retainer clip
20. External door handle
21. Access plug (external door handle)

Front door with power windows and locks

10 BODY

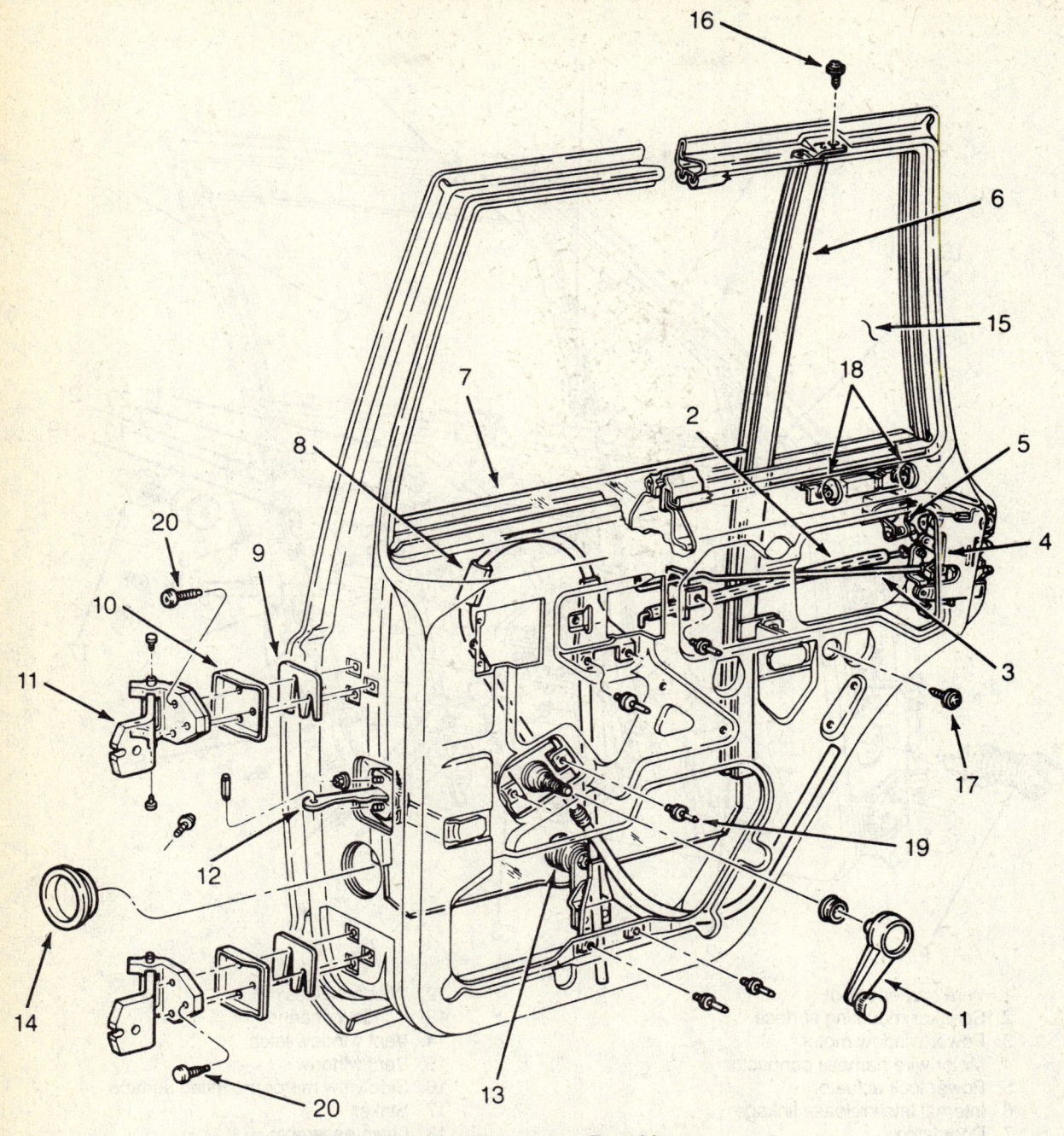

1. Window regulator crank handle
2. Internal latch release linkage
3. Internal lock linkage
4. Latch assembly
5. Exterior door handle
6. Window channel
7. Door glass
8. Window regulator
9. Shims
10. Shim retainer plate
11. Door hinge
12. Door stop
13. Glass attaching surface
14. Access plug
15. Stationary glass
16. Glass channel upper screw
17. Glass channel lower screw
18. Stationary glass frame screws
19. Regulator rivet (typical)
20. Door hinge screw

Rear door with manual windows and locks

BODY 10

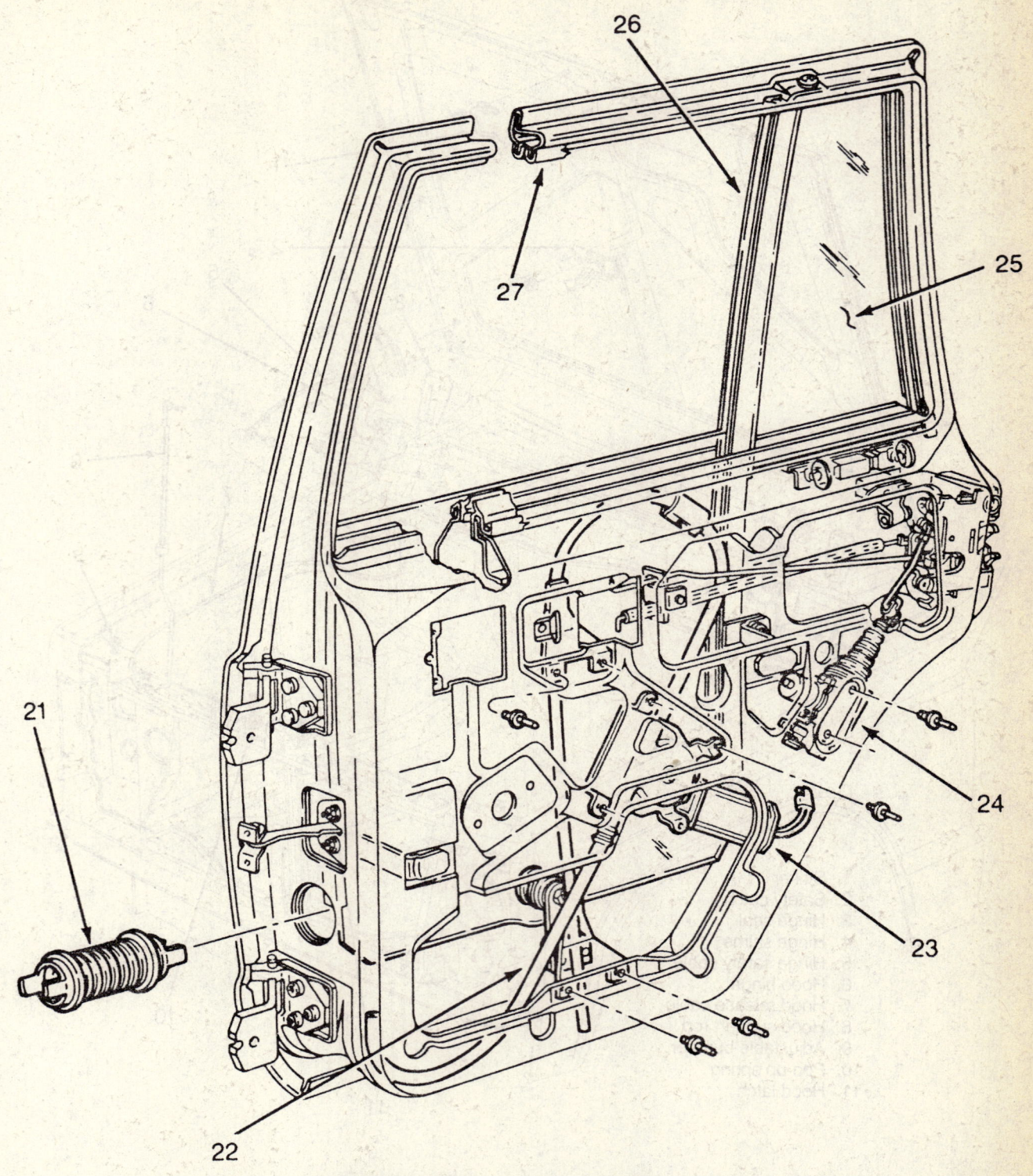

21. Wire harness boot
22. Window regulator
23. Power window motor
24. Power door lock actuator
25. Stationary glass
26. Glass channel
27. Glass slide channel

Rear door with power windows and locks

10-7

10 BODY

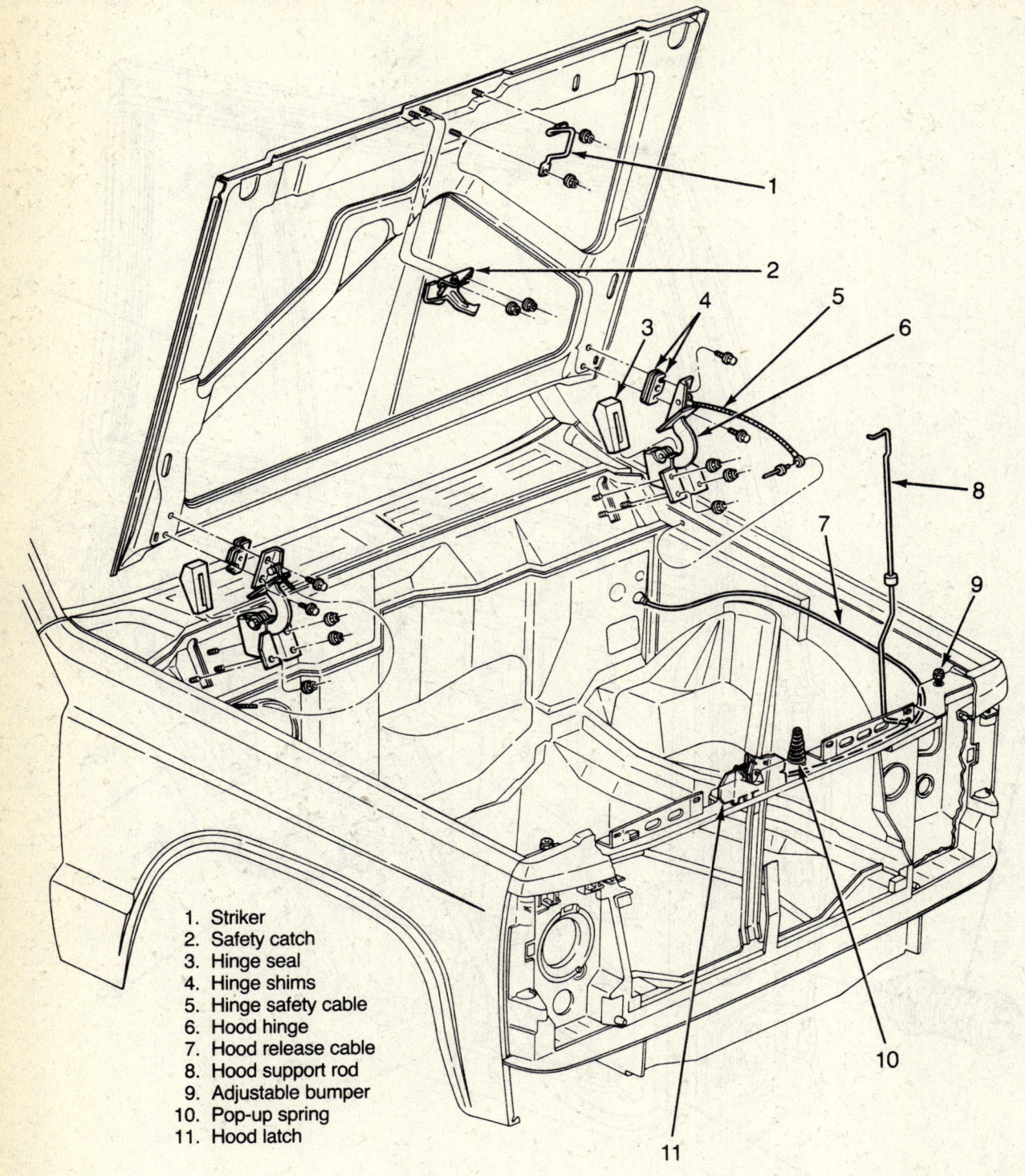

1. Striker
2. Safety catch
3. Hinge seal
4. Hinge shims
5. Hinge safety cable
6. Hood hinge
7. Hood release cable
8. Hood support rod
9. Adjustable bumper
10. Pop-up spring
11. Hood latch

Hood components

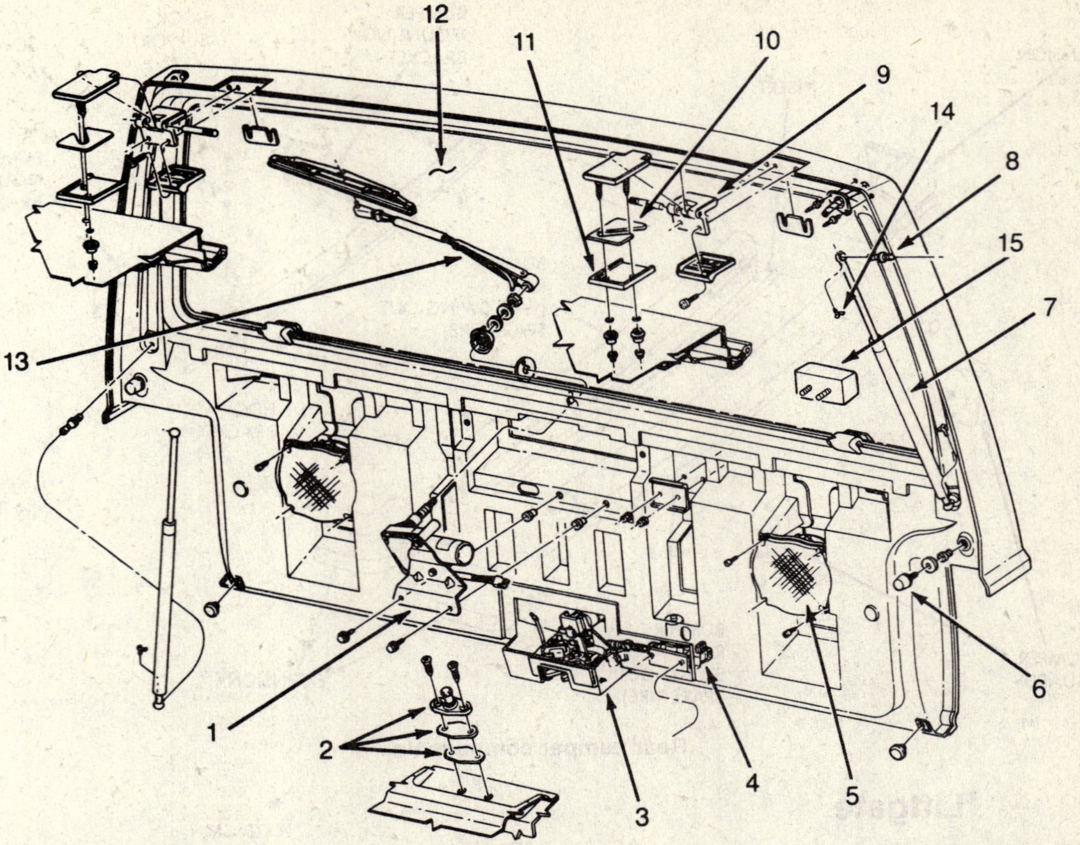

BODY 10

1. Wiper motor assembly
2. Striker and shims
3. Latch assembly
4. Power lock actuator
5. Speaker location
6. Liftgate stop
7. Support cylinder
8. Support cylinder attaching location
9. Liftgate hinge
10. Hinge shim

Liftgate components

properly adjusted to ensure positive locking. Torque the lock bolts to 10-12 ft. lbs.

5. If the rear edge of the hood is not flush with the cowl, add or subtract shims (caster and camber adjusting shims will work)

or flat washers between the hinge and the hood at the rear bolt (hood too low) or front bolt (hood too high).

6. Adjust the hood-to-fender height using the front bumpers, located at the left and right front corners of the vehicle.

Tailgate

REMOVAL AND INSTALLATION

Comanche

1. Lower the tailgate.
2. Pull each support up at the center and force the upper end forward, then inward, to disengage it from the retaining dowel.
3. Pull the right side of the tailgate rearward to disengage the hinge.
4. Move the tailgate to the right to disengage the left hinge.
5. Installation is the reverse of removal.

ADJUSTMENT

The only adjustment possible to the Comanche's tailgate is the striker adjustment. This is performed by loosening the striker plate screws and moving the striker to properly position it.

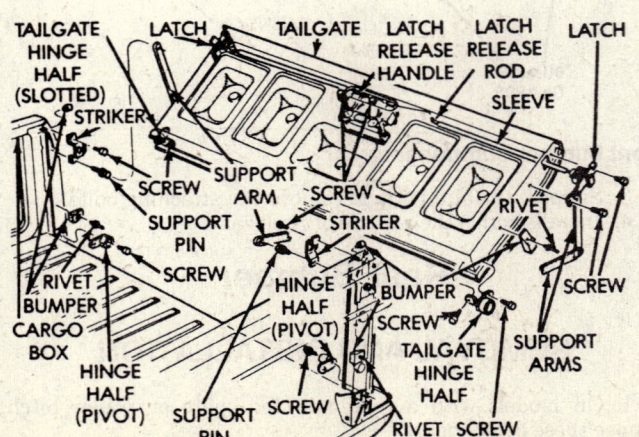

Tailgate components

10 BODY

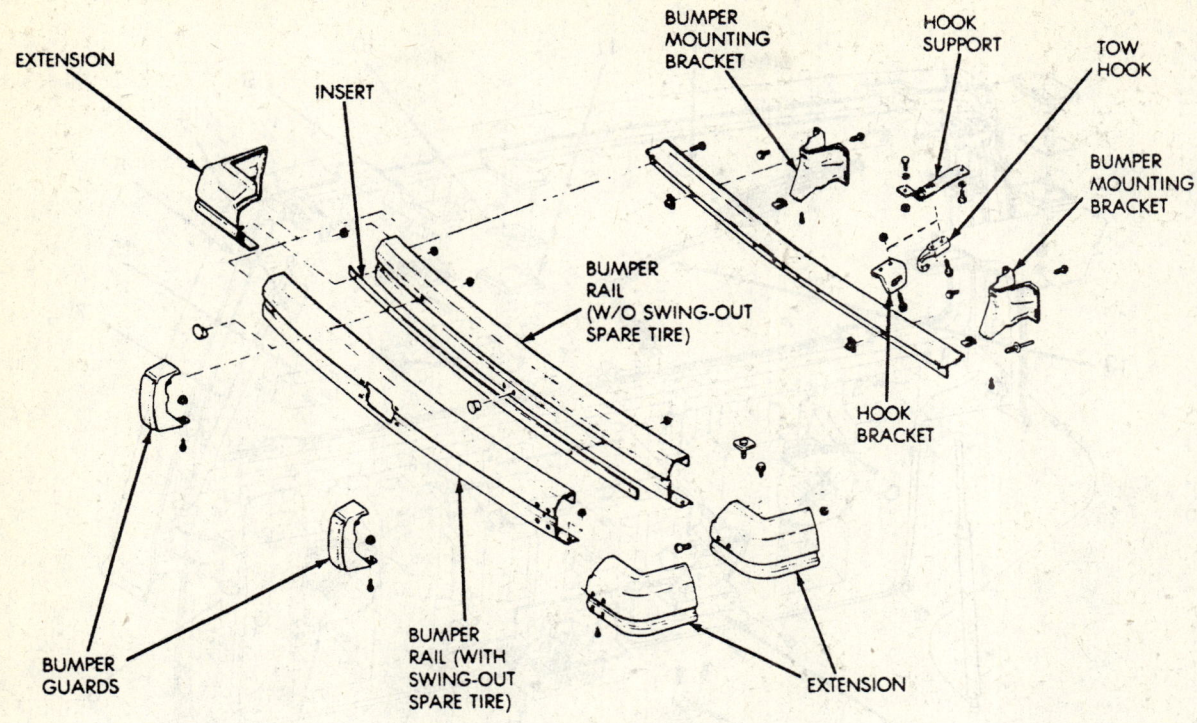

Rear bumper components

Liftgate

REMOVAL AND INSTALLATION

Wagoneer and Cherokee

1. Open the liftgate.
2. Remove the trim panel.

—— CAUTION ——
Never attempt to remove a support cylinder with the liftgate closed. The cylinders contain gas under high pressure. Severe personal injury may occur if the cylinders are disconnect with the liftgate closed!

3. Remove the retainer clips from the ball studs at the ends of the liftgate support cylinders.
4. Pull the support cylinders off of the ball studs.
5. Disconnect and remove the wiring harness.
6. Have a helper support the liftgate and remove the liftgate hinge bolts.
7. Installation is the reverse of removal. Tighten fasteners to 7 ft. lbs. Check alignment.

ADJUSTMENT

The hinge-to-body bolt holes are slotted to permit satisfactory alignment.

Front Bumper

REMOVAL AND INSTALLATION

1. Remove the fog lamps.
2. Disconnect the vacuum reservoir harness.

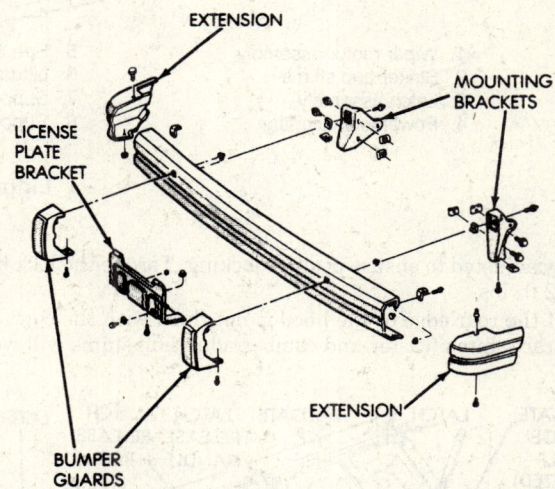

Front bumper components

3. Support the bumper and remove the attaching bolts.
4. Installation is the reverse of removal.

Rear Bumper

REMOVAL AND INSTALLATION

1. On models with a rear mounted spare or trailer hitch, remove these components.
2. Support the bumper and remove the attaching bolts.
3. Installation is the reverse of removal.

BODY 10

Grille and Grille Panel

REMOVAL AND INSTALLATION

1. Remove the grille attaching screws and lift the grille from the grille panel.
2. Remove the upper and lower moldings.
3. Remove the air deflector.
4. Remove the radiator supports.
5. Raise and support the front end on jackstands.
6. Remove the front wheels.
7. Remove the fender flare nuts.
8. Carefully pry out the push rivets and remove the fender liners.
9. Carefully remove the fender flare and valance panel push rivets.
10. Remove the fender flare and flare retainers.
11. Remove the nuts at each side of the grille panel through the

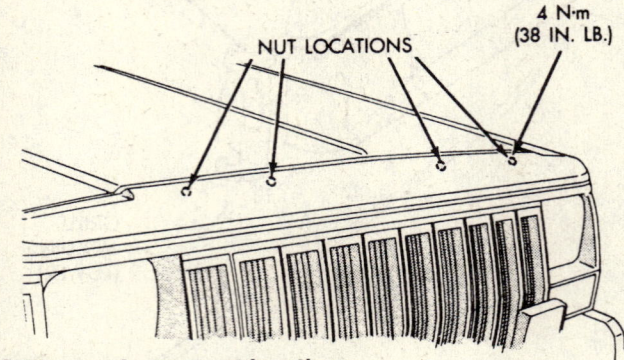

Grille panel upper nut locations

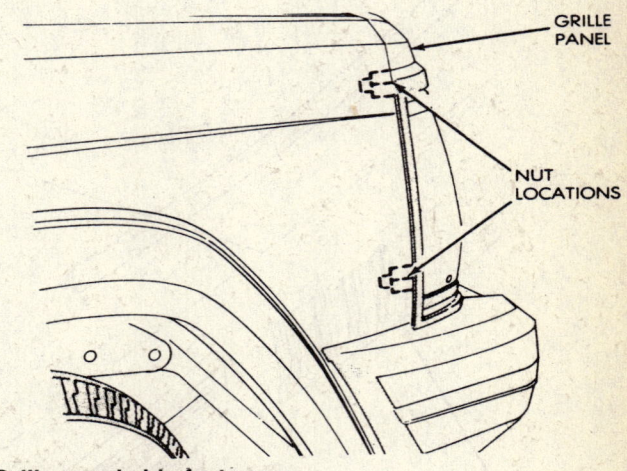

Grille panel side fasteners

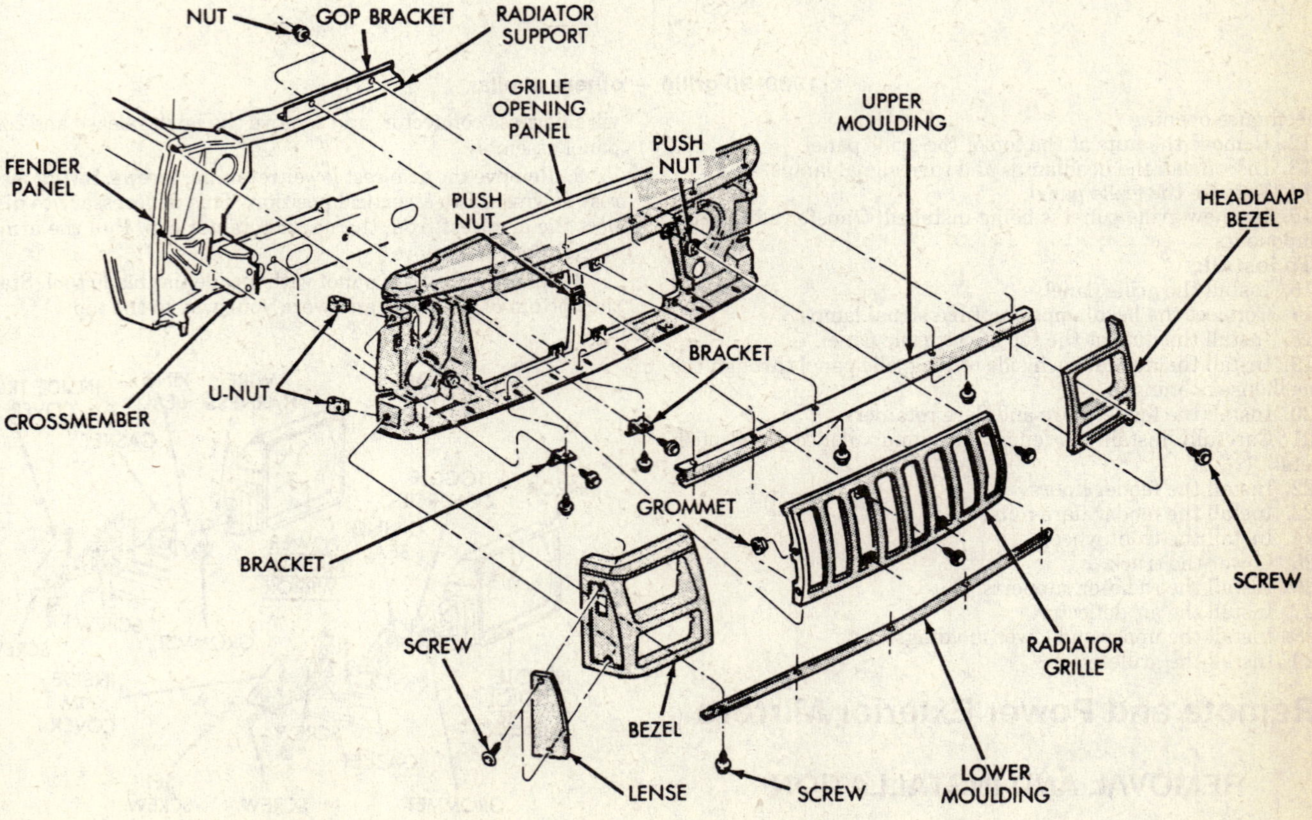

1991 grille — exploded view

10-11

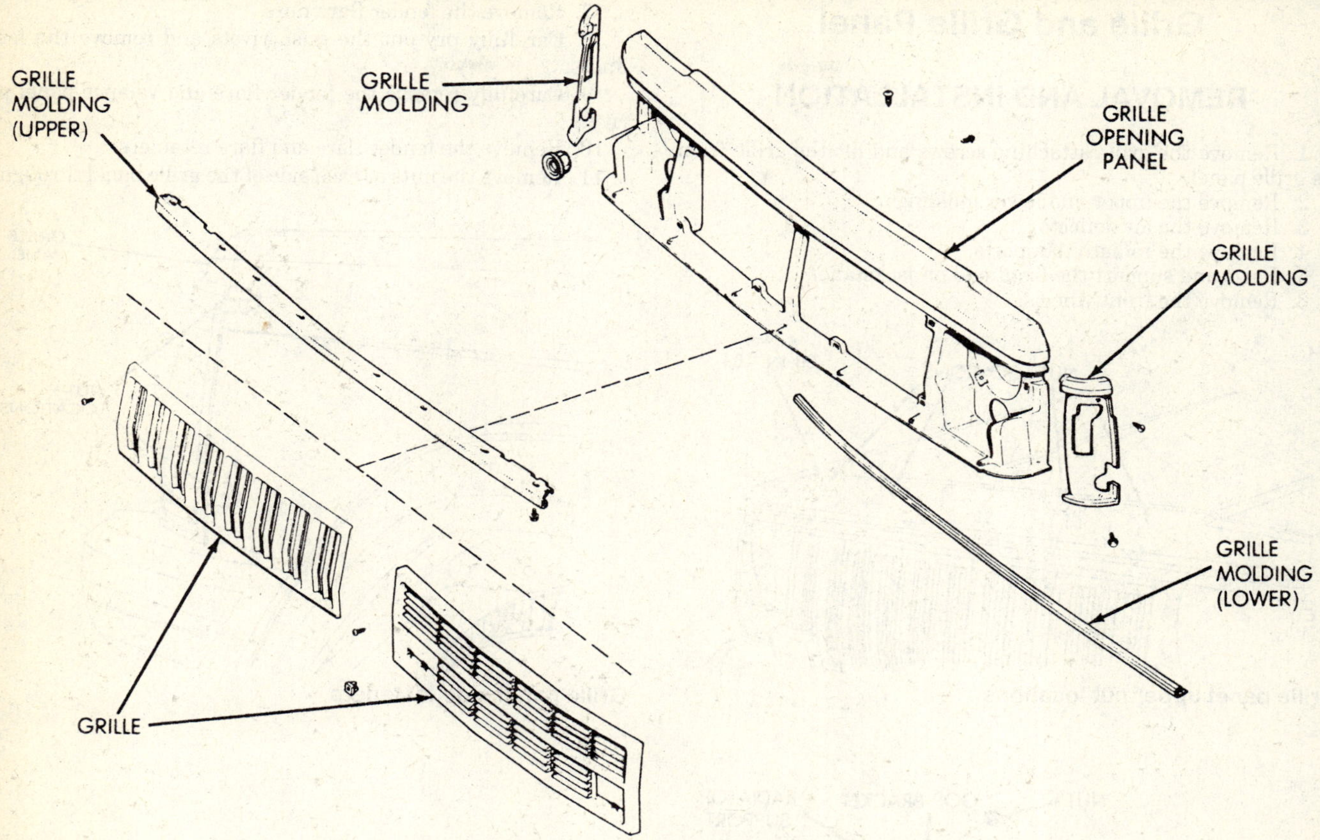

10 BODY

1989–90 grille — others similar

wheelhouse opening.
12. Remove the nuts at the top of the grille panel.
13. Disconnect the headlamps and turn signal lamps.
14. Remove the grille panel.
15. If a new grille panel is being installed, transfer all lighting components.

To install:
16. Install the grille panel.
17. Connect the headlamps and turn signal lamps.
18. Install the nuts at the top of the grille panel.
19. Install the nuts at each side of the grille panel through the wheelhouse opening.
20. Install the fender flare and flare retainers.
21. Carefully install the fender flare and valance panel push rivets.
22. Install the fender liners.
23. Install the fender flare nuts.
24. Install the front wheels.
25. Lower the truck.
26. Install the radiator supports.
27. Install the air deflector.
28. Install the upper and lower moldings.
29. Install the grille.

Remote and Power Exterior Mirrors

REMOVAL AND INSTALLATION

1. Remove the interior door latch release assembly and control panel retaining screws. Disconnect the control linkage and the wire harness connector, and remove the latch release and control panel assembly.
2. Remove the arm rest lower retaining screws. Swing the arm rest downward to a vertical position. This is necessary to disconnect the arm rest from the upper retainer clip. Pull the arm rest straight out to remove.
3. Remove the trim panel with a wide flat blade tool. Start at the bottom of the panel and work your way to the top.

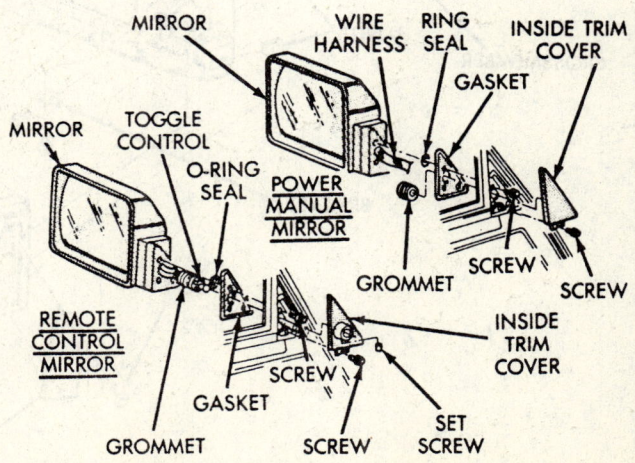

Remote and power/manual mirrors

BODY 10

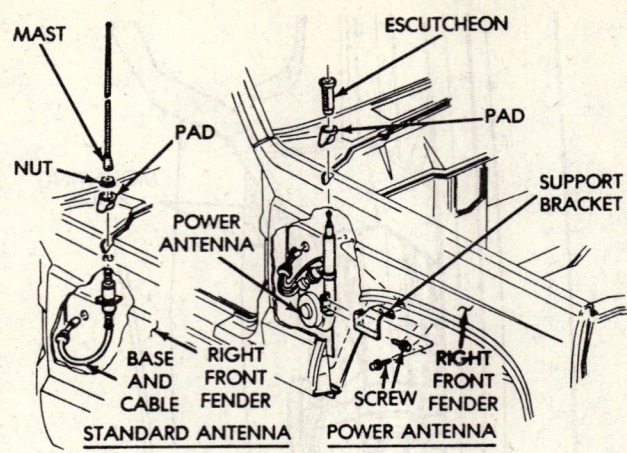

Manual and power antenna

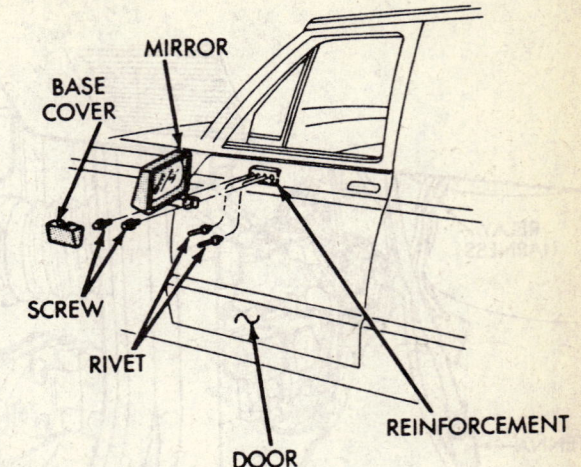

Wide-view exterior mirror

4. If equipped with remote mirror, loosen the set screw which holds the toggle control.
5. Remove the screws holding the window trim cover and remove.
6. If equipped with power windows, disconnect the wire harness at the connector in the door. Pull the harness up through the door.
7. Remove the mirror retaining screws. Remove the mirror from the door.
8. Installation is the reverse of removal.

Wide-View Exterior Mirror

REMOVAL AND INSTALLATION

1. Remove the mirror base cover.
2. Remove the mirror base attaching screws. The mirror base reinforcement is attached to the inside of the door with rivets.

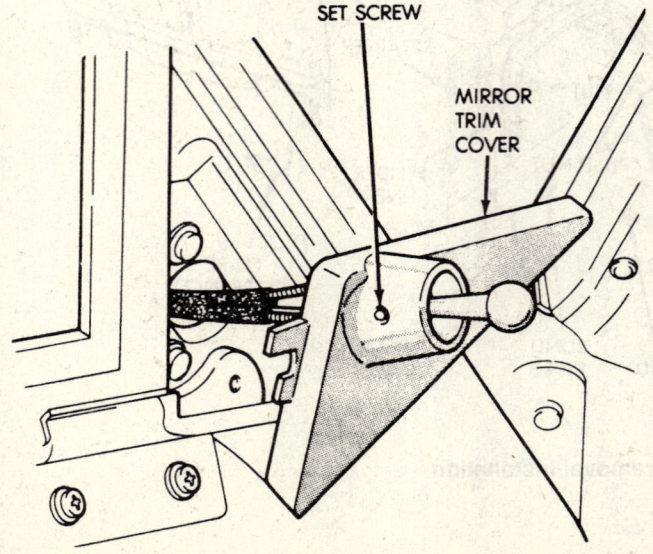

Remote mirror toggle control

3. Remove the mirror from the door panel.
4. Installation is the reverse of removal.

Antenna

POWER ANTENNA RELAY DIAGNOSIS

1. With the radio ON and both relay connectors disconnected, measure the voltage at connector with red wire pin 'A'. There should be 12 volts. If not, repair open to ANT fuse.
2. Measure the voltage at connector with red wire pin 'B'. There should be 12 volts. If not, repair open to radio.
3. Turn radio OFF. Measure the resistance at connector with red wire pin 'C'. Meter should read zero ohms. If not, repair open to ground.

POWER ANTENNA DIAGNOSIS

1. With both relay connectors disconnected, connect a jumper wire between red wire connector pin 'C' and the other connector 'B'.
2. Connect a jumper wire between the connector with the red wire pin 'A' and the other connector 'A'. The antenna should extend. If not, replace the antenna.
3. Move the jumper wire between the connector with the red wire pin 'A' to the other connector pin 'C'. The antenna should retract. If not, replace the power antenna.
4. If the antenna extends and retracts, replace the relay.

REMOVAL AND INSTALLATION

1. Remove the fender inner splash shield nuts and move the panel aside far enough to get at the antenna cable and base.
2. Unscrew the antenna mast and nut and remove the antenna pad from the top of the fender.
3. Remove the passenger side kick panel.
4. If equipped with a power antenna:
   a. Disconnect the harness from the relay. The relay is located behind the right hand side of the dash just above the lower edge.
   b. Remove the antenna mounting bolts and washers.
   c. Pull the antenna motor harness through the hole in the kick panel.

10-13

10 BODY

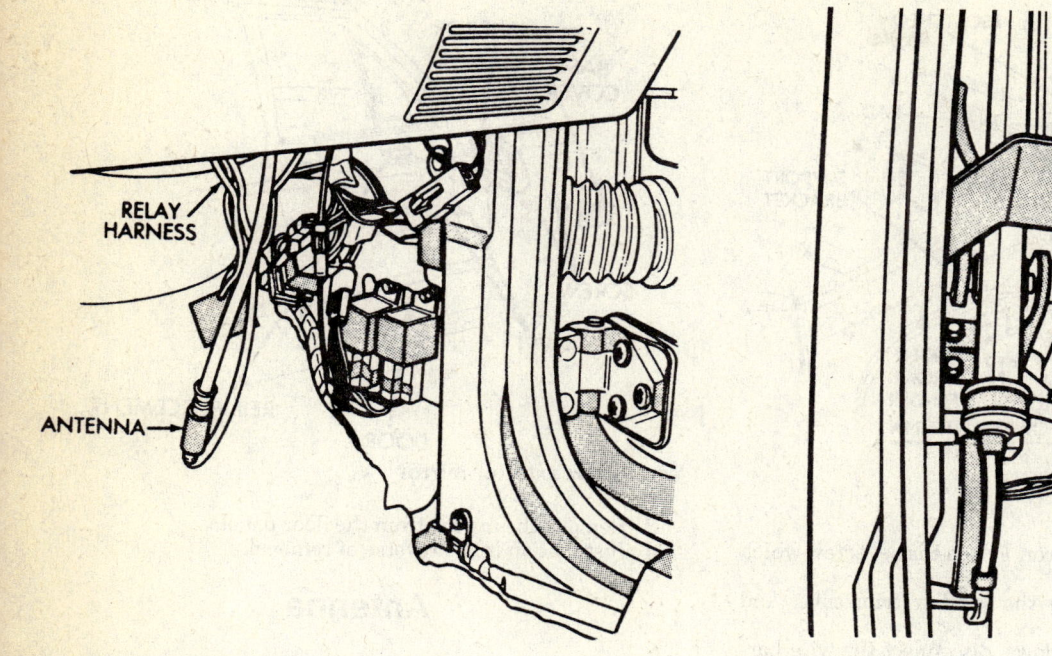

Power antenna relay harness

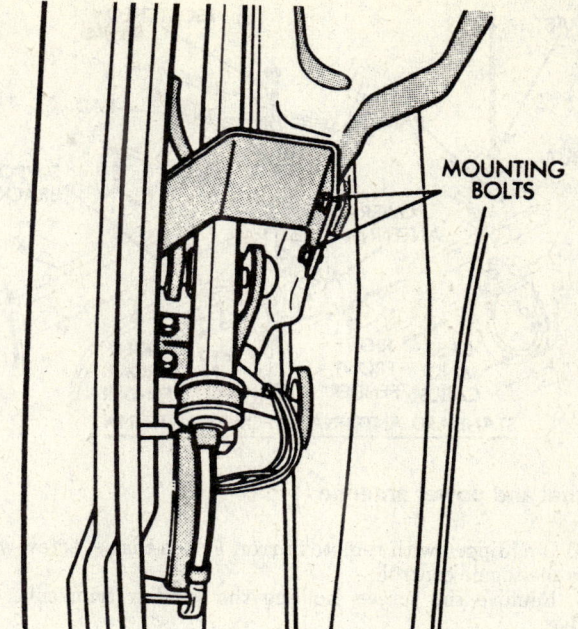

Power antenna mounting bolts

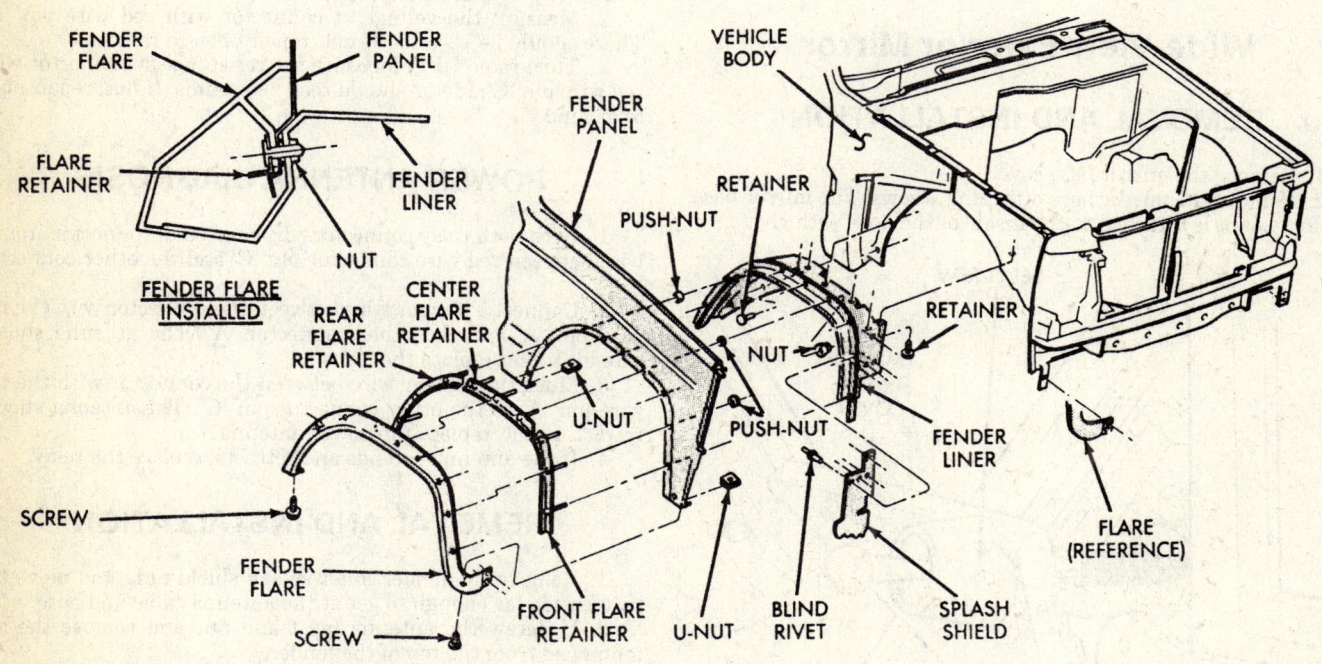

Front fender flare and liner removal/installation

BODY 10

Fenders

REMOVAL AND INSTALLATION

1. Remove the front bumper. See the Bumper Removal and Installation in this Section.
2. If removing the Right fender, remove the radio antenna.
3. Raise and support the vehicle safely.
4. Remove the following:
   - the front wheel
   - the fender liner, the fender flare and retainers
   - the grille
   - the air deflector
   - the rocker panel molding
   - all fender braces
5. Remove the fender braces. Then remove the fender lower attaching screws.
6. Remove all other fender attaching screws.
7. Remove the front fender from the inner fender panel.
8. Installation is the reverse of removal.

Cargo Box (Comanche)

REMOVAL AND INSTALLATION

1. Remove the left tail lamp and disconnect the wire harness connector.
2. Disconnect the license plate lamp wire harness.
3. Support the fuel tank and remove the fuel tank support strap retaining nuts.
4. Remove the parking brake cable housing bolts.
5. Support the exhaust system and disconnect the support hanger.
6. Remove the cotter pin from the spare tire winch rod.

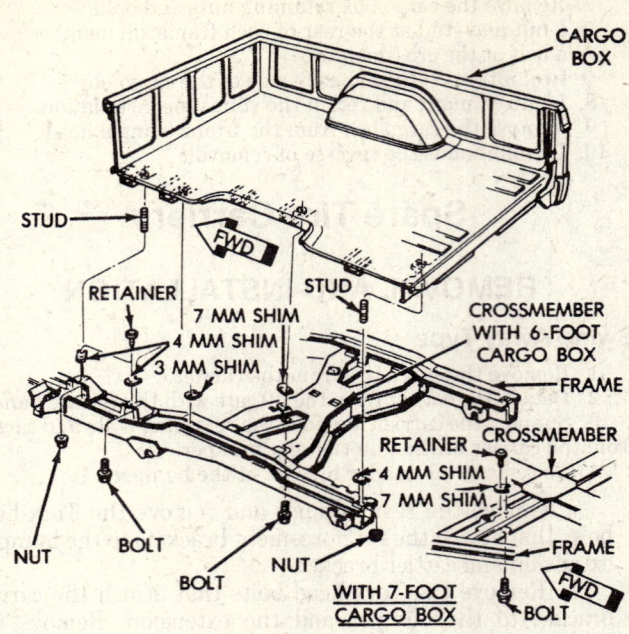

Cargo box removal/installation

5. Disconnect the antenna lead by pull and twisting the metal connectors. NEVER pull on the cable!
6. Pull the rubber grommet out of the kick panel.
7. Remove the antenna assembly from the inside of the wheelhouse.
8. Installation is the reverse of removal.

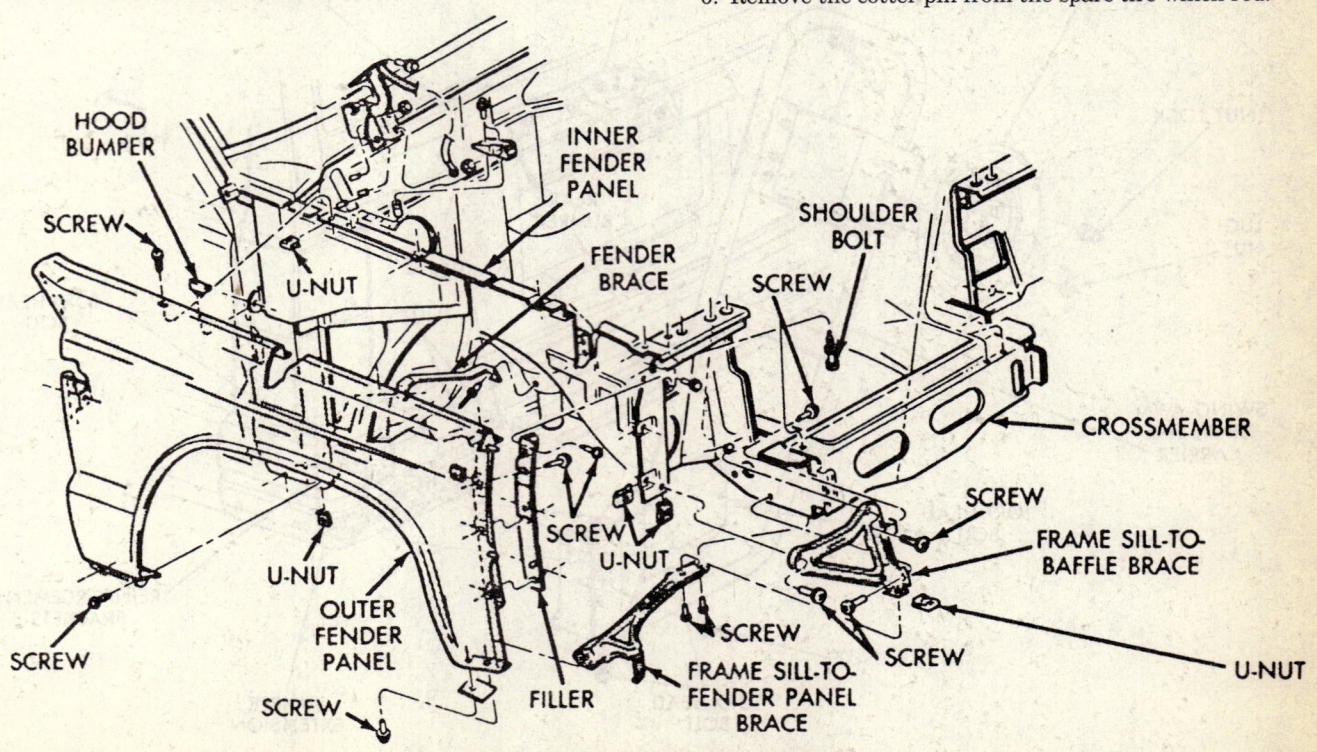

Front fender removal/installation

10-15

10 BODY

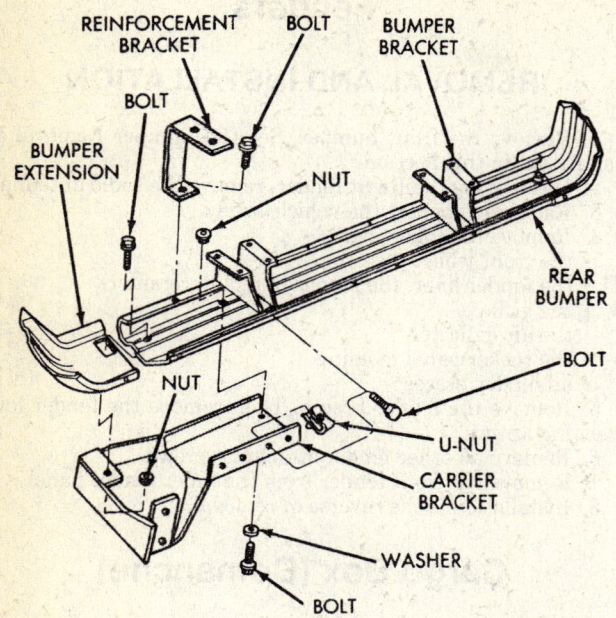

Swing-away type spare tire carrier bracket

7. Remove the cargo box retaining nuts and bolts:
   - a nut and stud at the rear of each frame sill member
   - a bolt at the crossmember
   - two nuts and studs at each side of the cargo box
8. Identify, mark and retain the shims for installation.
9. Remove the cargo box from the frame using a hoist.
10. Installation is the reverse of removal.

Spare Tire Carriers

REMOVAL AND INSTALLATION

Swing Away Type

1. Remove the spare tire from the carrier.
2. Detach the cattier from the liftgate with the release handle.
3. Support the carrier. Remove the retaining bolts and carrier from the carrier bracket on the rear bumper.
4. To remove the carrier bracket at the bumper:

   a. Remove the rear bumper and remove the Torx-head bolts that attach the reinforcement brackets to the bumper, extension and cattier bracket.

   b. Remove the Torx-head bolts that attach the carrier bracket to the bumper and the extension. Remove the bracket from the bumper.

   c. Remove the bolts that attach the reinforcement brackets to the cross sill.

5. To remove the carrier bracket at the liftgate:

   a. Remove the liftgate trim panel.

   b. Remove the Torx-head bolts that attach the outer re-

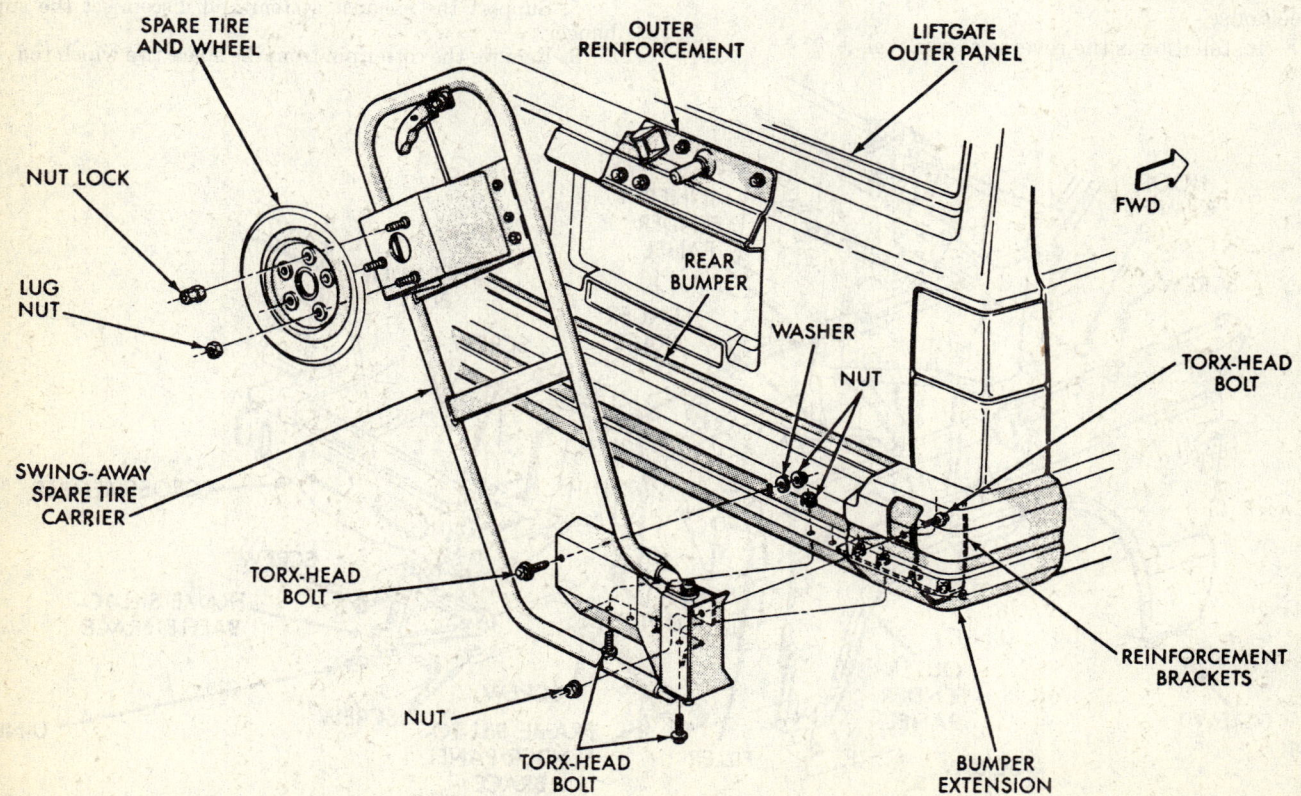

Swing-away type spare tire carrier

10-16

BODY 10

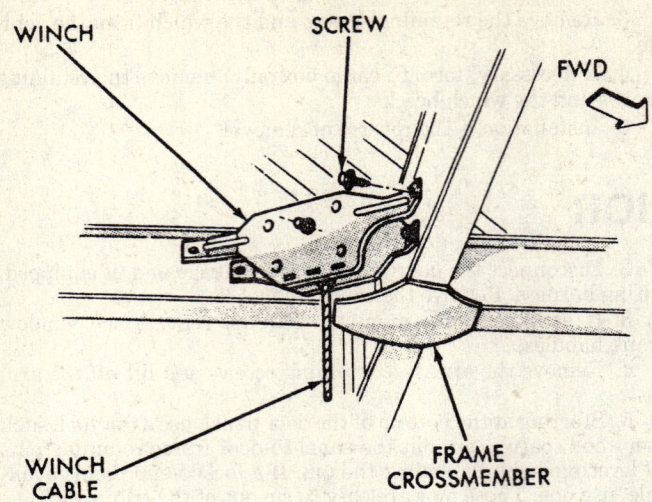

Spare tire winch — 7-foot cargo box

inforcement bracket to the liftgate and the inner reinforcement bracket.
   c. Remove the shoulder bolts that attach the outer reinforcement bracket.
   d. Remove the reinforcement brackets from the liftgate.
6. Installation is the reverse of removal.

Interior Type (Cherokee/Wagoneer)

1. Remove the spare tire and wheel.
2. Remove the floor bracket retaining screws.

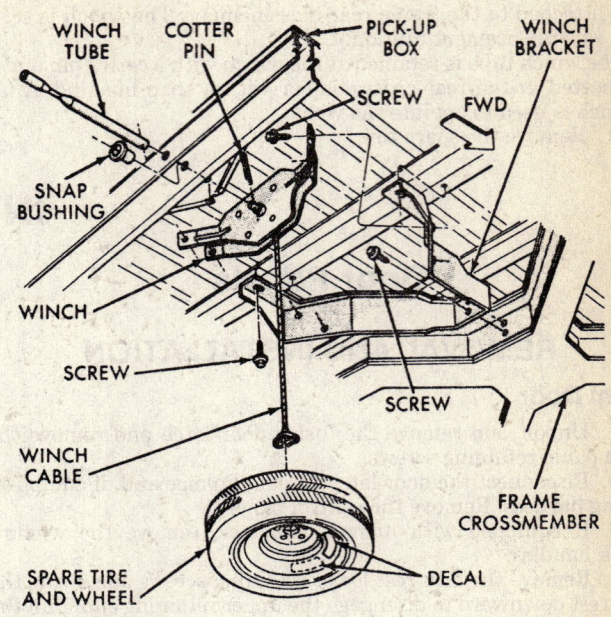

Spare tire winch — 6-foot cargo box

3. Remove the quarter trim panel.
4. Remove the retaining screws and the wheel holddown bracket.
5. Installation is the reverse of removal.

Spare Tire Winch (Comanche)

The spare tire winch is located under the cargo box. On the 6 ft. cargo box it is located on a bracket attached to the cargo box cross-

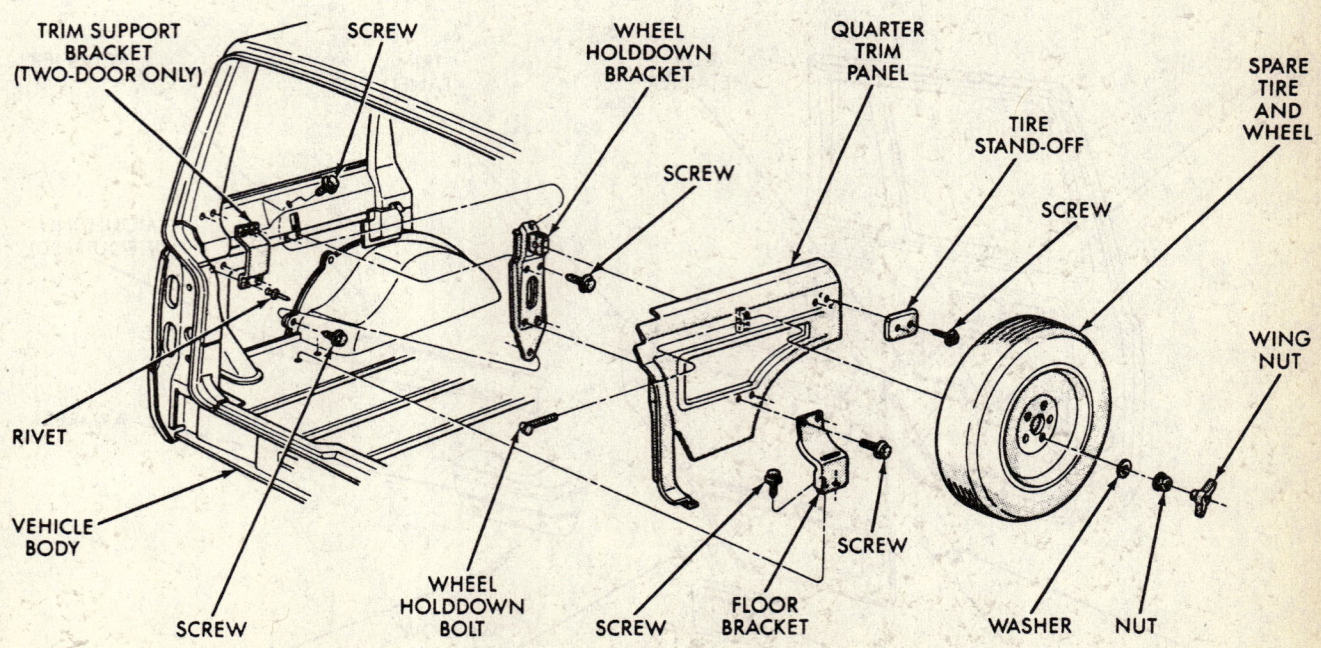

Interior spare tire carrier — Cherokee/Wagoneer

10-17

10 BODY

member and the frame rear crossmember. On the 7 ft. cargo box it is attached to the frame rear crossmember. The winch is serviced as a replacement unit only.

The winch tube is retained at the winch with a cotter pin and is supported in the rear crossmember with a snap bushing. A lug wrench is used to operate the winch.

1. Remove the spare tire.
2. Remove the cotter pin and the winch tube.
3. Remove the retaining screws and the winch from the vehicle.
4. If necessary (for 6 ft. cargo box only), remove the retaining screws and the winch bracket.
5. Installation is the reverse of removal.

INTERIOR

Door Panels

REMOVAL AND INSTALLATION

Front Door

1. Unbolt and remove the inside door latch and remove the latch panel retaining screws.
2. Disconnect the door latch control linkage and, if equipped, wiring harness. Remove the control panel.
3. If equipped with manual windows, remove the window crank handles.
4. Remove the arm rest lower retaining screws and swing the arm rest downward to disengage the upper retaining clip. Pull the arm rest straight out from the door panel.
5. Starting at the bottom of the door panel, use a flat tool, such as a wood spatula, pry out the panel-to-door frame retaining pins by levering right up against the pin. If a forked-end tool is available, use one. These pins are easy to rip out of the trim panel.
6. Installation is the reverse of removal. A firm hit with the heel of your palm is usually enough to drive the retainers into the holes in the door panel. Make sure that the retainer is directly over the hole before knocking it in, or it may be damaged.

Rear Door

1. Unbolt and remove the inside door latch and remove the latch panel retaining screws.
2. Disconnect the door latch control linkage and, if equipped, wiring harness. Remove the control panel.
3. If equipped with manual windows, remove the window crank handles.
4. Remove the arm rest retaining screws and lift off the arm rest.
5. Starting at the bottom of the door panel, use a flat tool, such as a wood spatula, pry out the panel-to-door frame retaining pins by levering right up against the pin. If a forked-end tool is available, use one. These pins are easy to rip out of the trim panel.
6. Installation is the reverse of removal. A firm hit with the heel of your palm is usually enough to drive the retainers into the holes in the door panel. Make sure that the retainer is directly over the hole before knocking it in, or it may be damaged.

Interior Trim Panels

Interior trim panels are attached to the chassis using a variety of clips and fasteners. When removing the panels, work slowly and carefully. Most panels are made of plastic and can be easily damaged. DO NOT bend or attempt to remove a trim panel until the interfering adjacent panels and attached components have first been removed. The panels are have limited flexibility. Refer to the following illustrations when removing/installing interior trim panels.

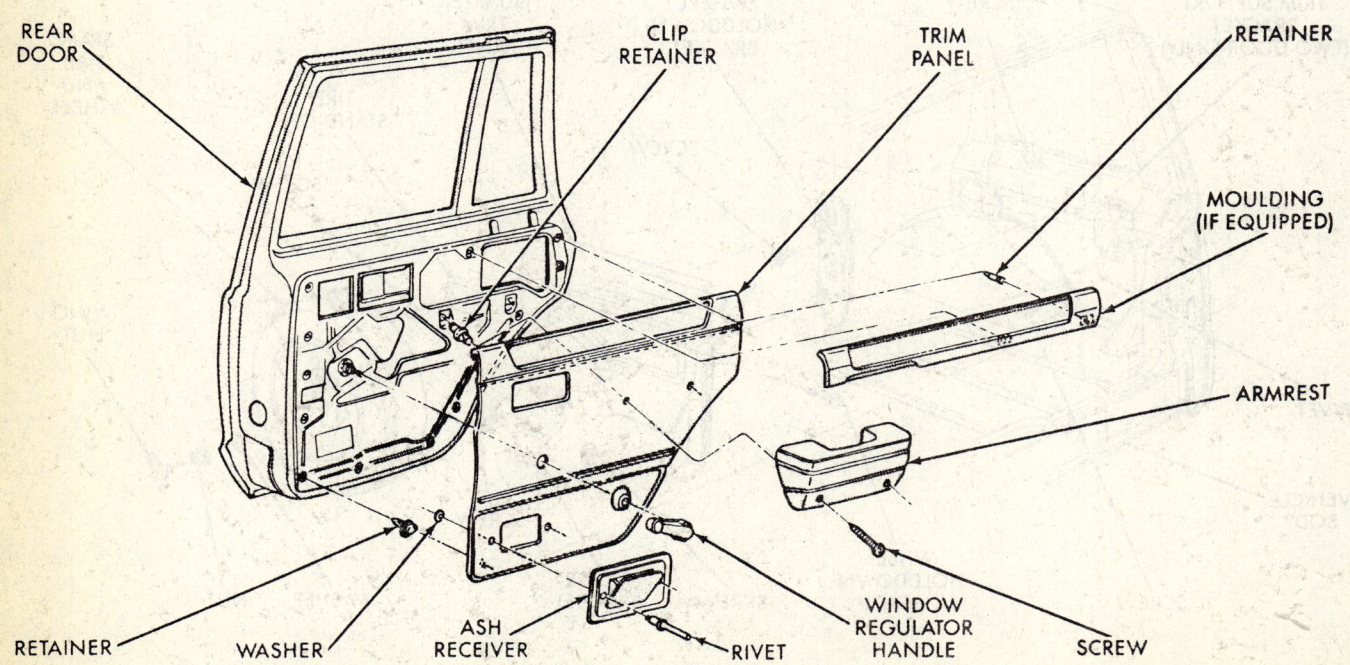

Rear door interior panel

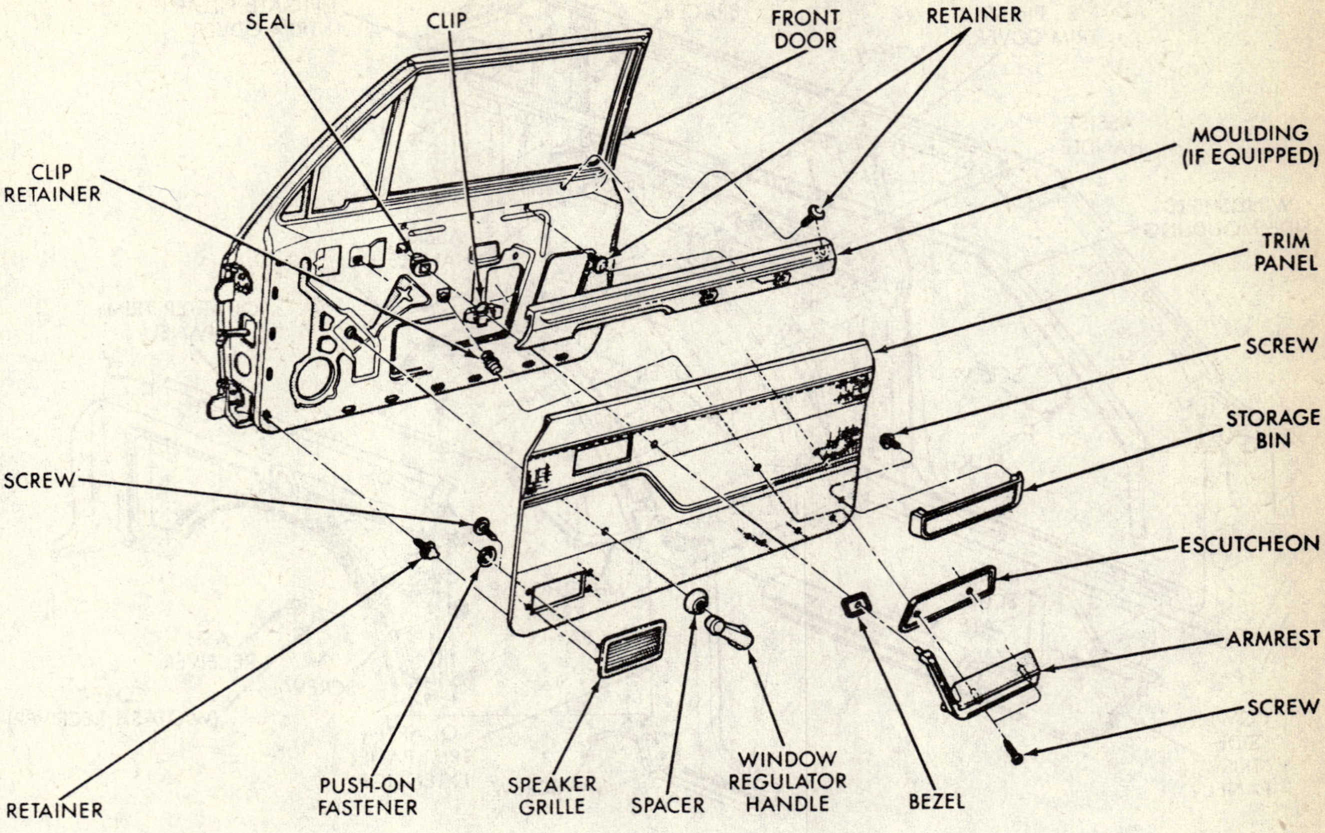

BODY 10

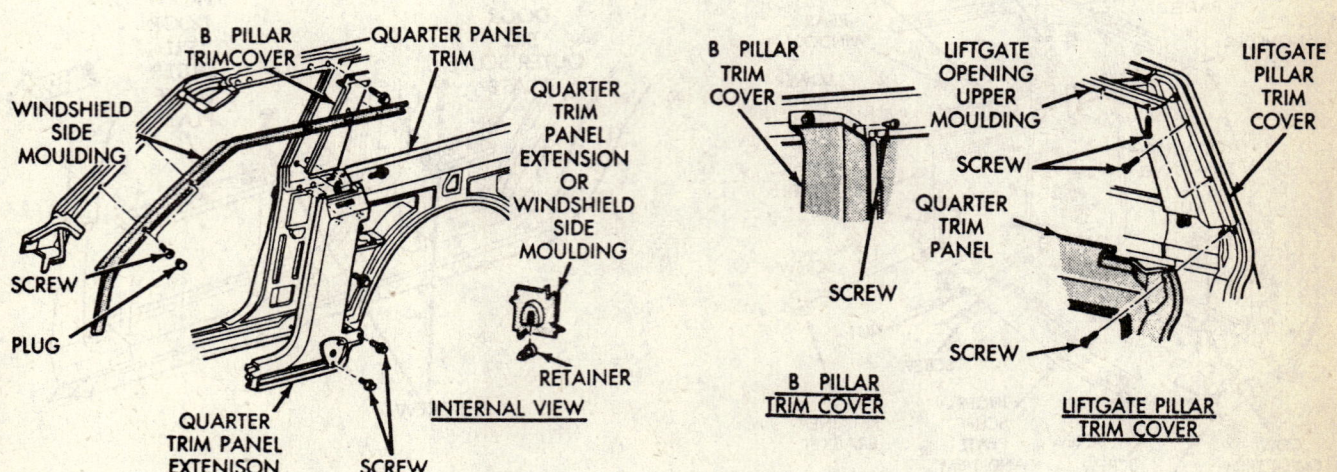

Front door interior panel

Windshield molding, quarter trim and extension panels — Cherokee/Wagoneer

B-pillar and liftgate pillar trim covers — Cherokee/Wagoneer

10-19

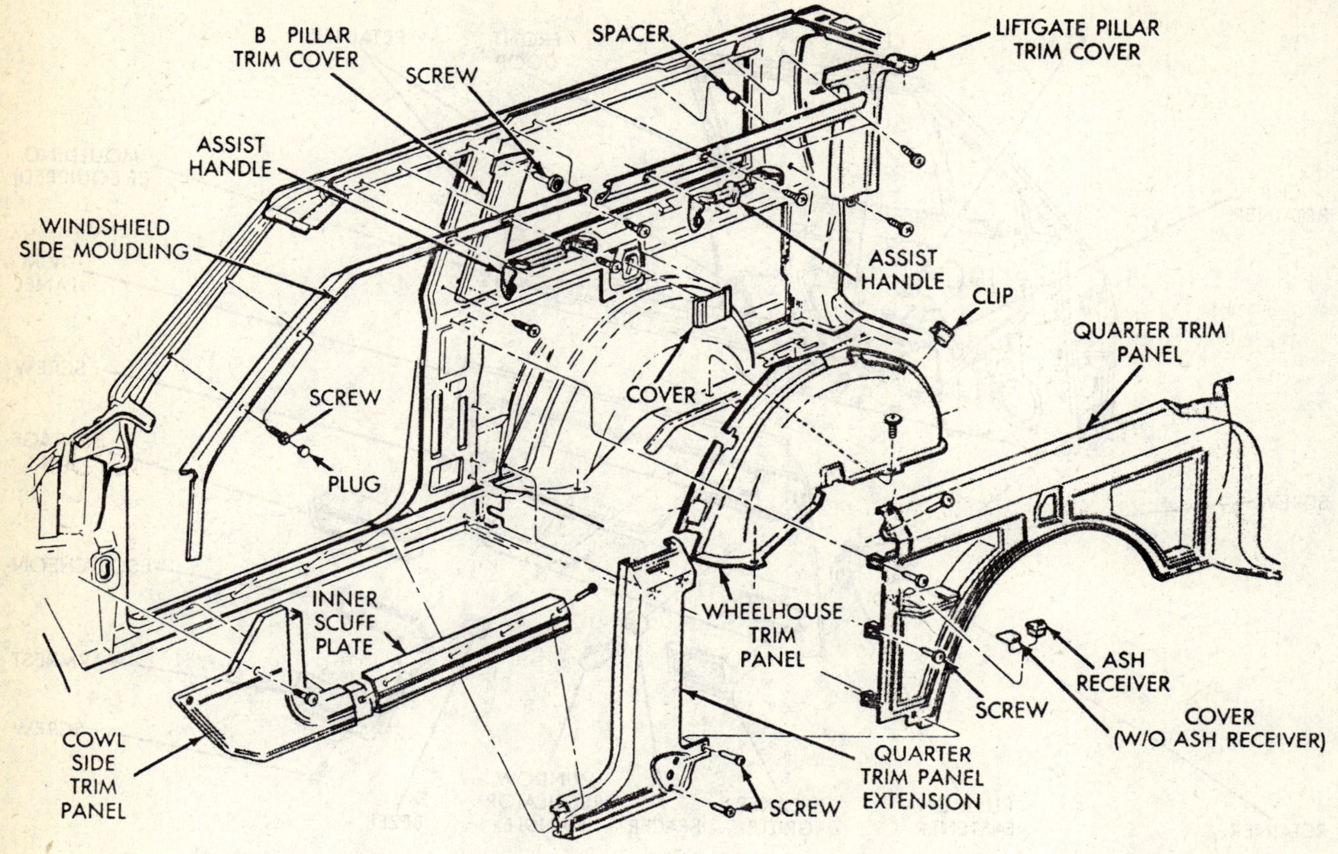

10 BODY

Interior trim panels, moldings and scuff plates — Cherokee/Wagoneer

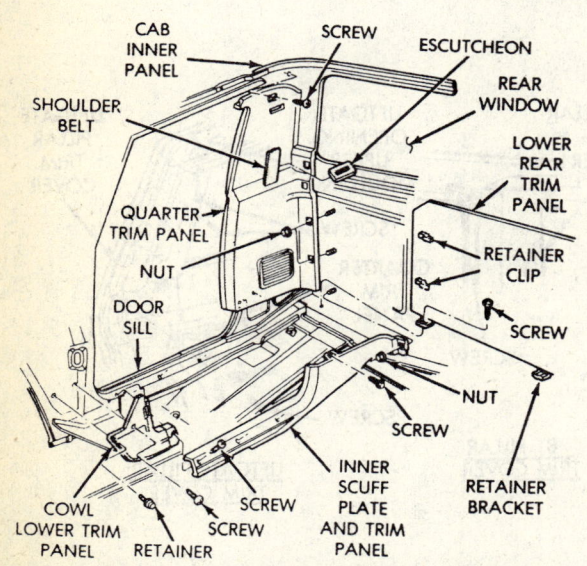

Inner scuff plate, quarter and rear lower trim panels Comanche

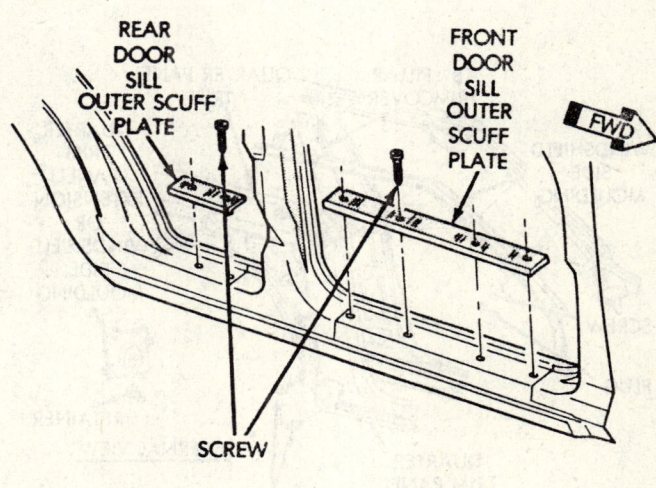

Outer scuff plates on the 4-door Cherokee/Wagoneer

10-20

BODY 10

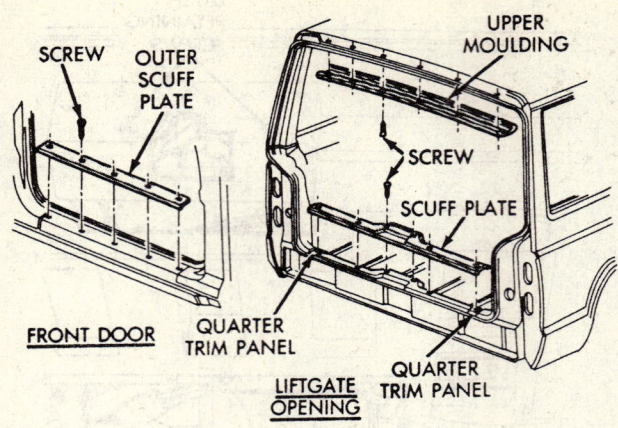

Liftgate and door sill outer scuff plate — Cherokee/Wagoneer

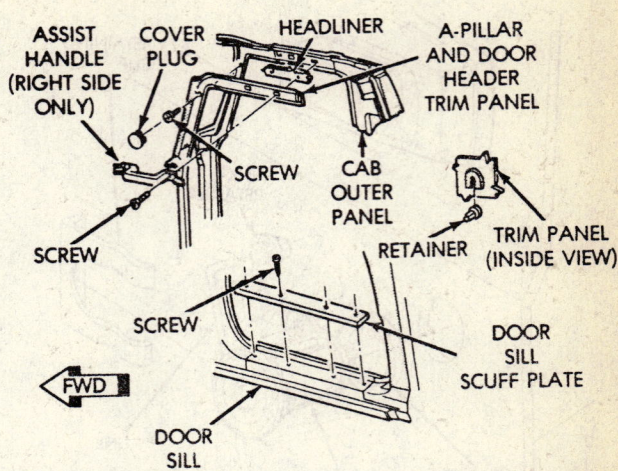

A-pillar trim panel and door sill outer scuff plate — Comanche

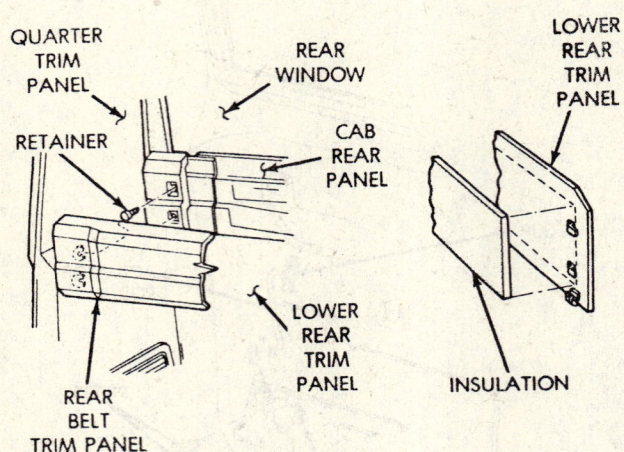

Rear trim panels — Comanche

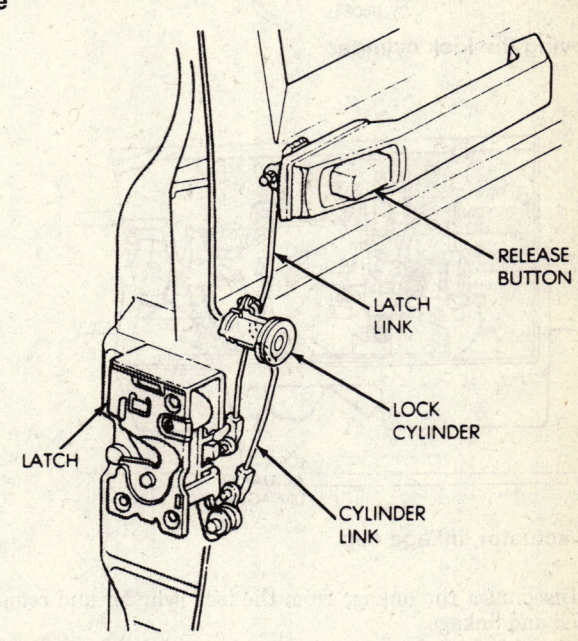

Manual door lock components

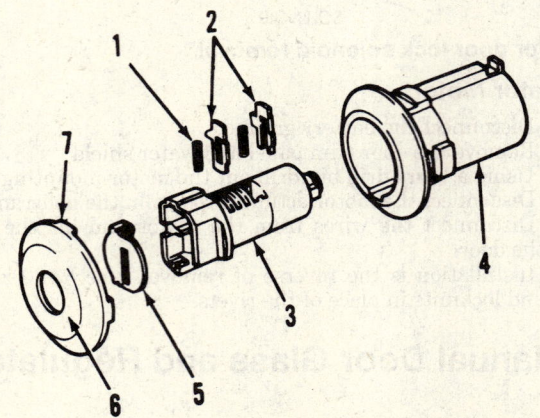

1. Spring
2. Tumblers
3. Cylinder
4. Casing
5. Key door
6. Lock cover
7. Retaining tab

Door lock cylinder components

Manual Door Locks

REMOVAL AND INSTALLATION

Lock Cylinder

1. Remove the door trim panel and plastic waterproof sheet.
2. Working through an access hole, remove the lock cylinder retaining clip.
3. Disconnect the lock control linkage.
4. Push the lock cylinder from the door.
5. Installation is the reverse of removal.

Latch and Linkage

1. Remove the door trim panel and plastic waterproof sheet.
2. Remove the latch retaining bolts from the rear edge of the door.

10-21

10 BODY

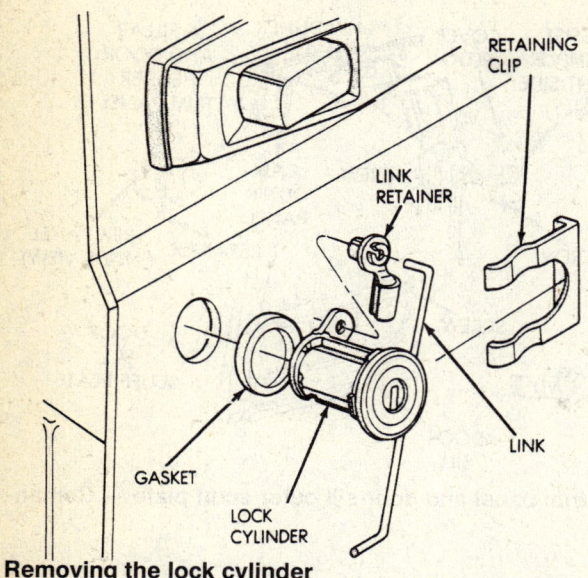
Removing the lock cylinder

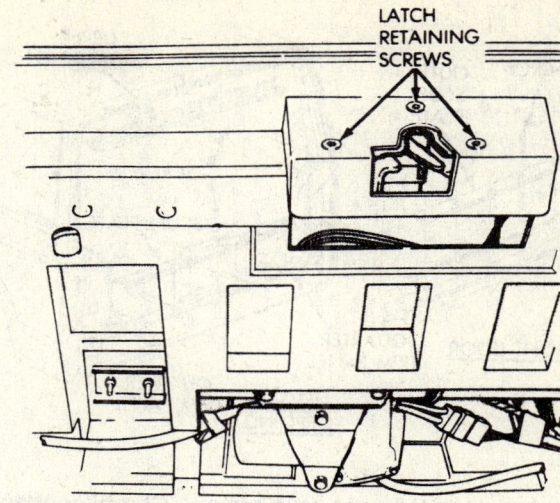
Latch assembly removal

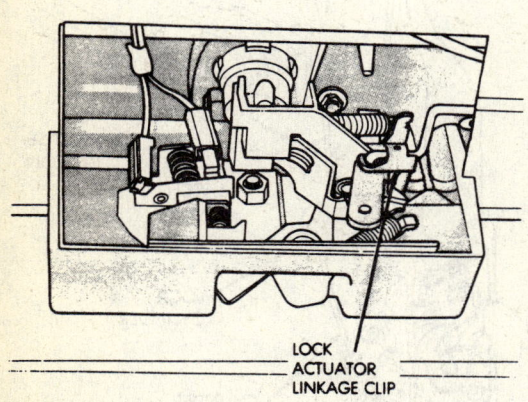
Lock actuator linkage clip

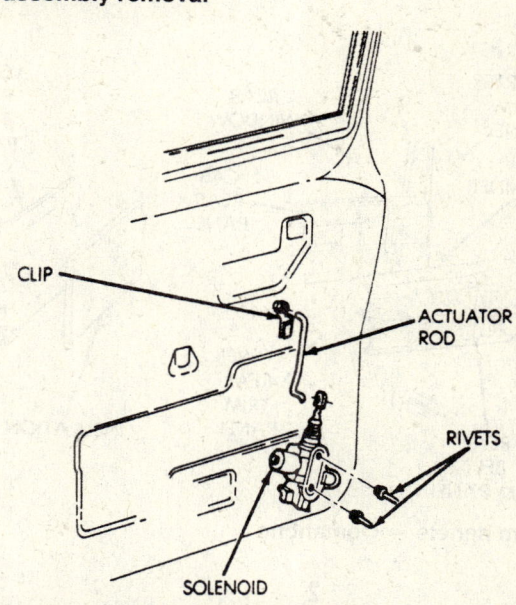
Power door lock solenoid removal

3. Disconnect the linkage from the lock cylinder and remove the latch and linkage.

NOTE: With power locks, it will be necessary to drill out the lock solenoid rivets and remove the solenoid and latch assembly. During installation, the solenoid will have to be attached with pop rivets or bolt/nut assemblies.

4. Installation is the reverse of removal. Torque the latch retaining bolts to 7 ft. lbs.

Power Door Locks

REMOVAL AND INSTALLATION

Switch

1. Disconnect the battery ground.
2. Remove the door trim panel and water shield.
3. Remove the switch housing from the inner door panel.
4. Disconnect the wiring and pry up the switch retaining clips. Remove the switch.
5. Installation is the reverse of removal.

Actuator Motor

1. Disconnect the battery ground.
2. Remove the door trim panel and water shield.
3. Using a $1/4$ in. drill bit, drill out the motor mounting rivets.
4. Disconnect the motor actuator rod from the bellcrank.
5. Disconnect the wires from the motor and lift the motor from the door.
6. Installation is the reverse of removal. Use $1/4$-20 x $1/2$ in. bolts and locknuts in place of the rivets.

Manual Door Glass and Regulator

REMOVAL AND INSTALLATION

Front Door

1. Remove the trim panel and waterproof plastic sheet.
2. Remove the window frame trim molding.
3. Remove the glass channel bottom screw.

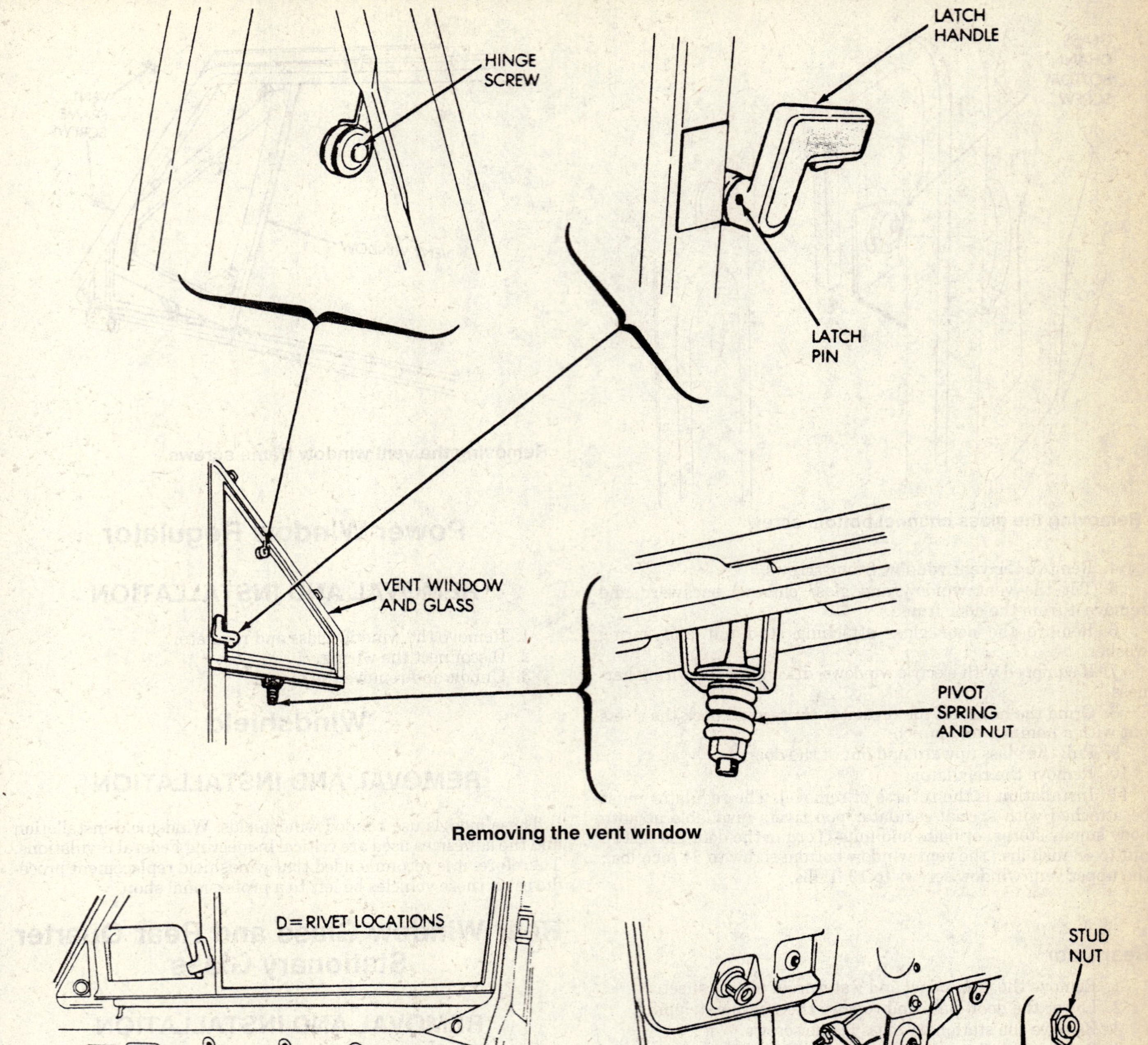

BODY 10

Removing the vent window

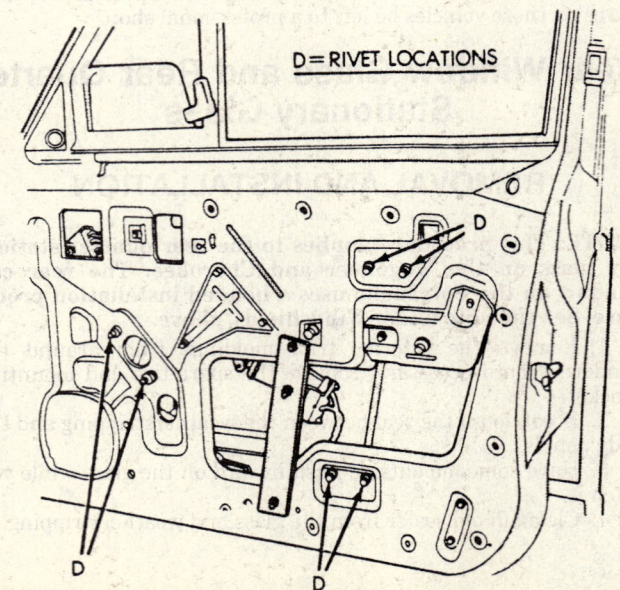

Manual window glass regulator rivet locations

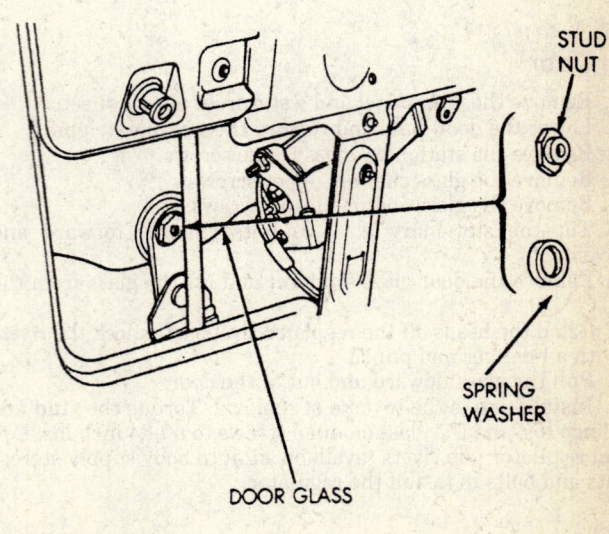

Removing the door glass stud

10-23

10 BODY

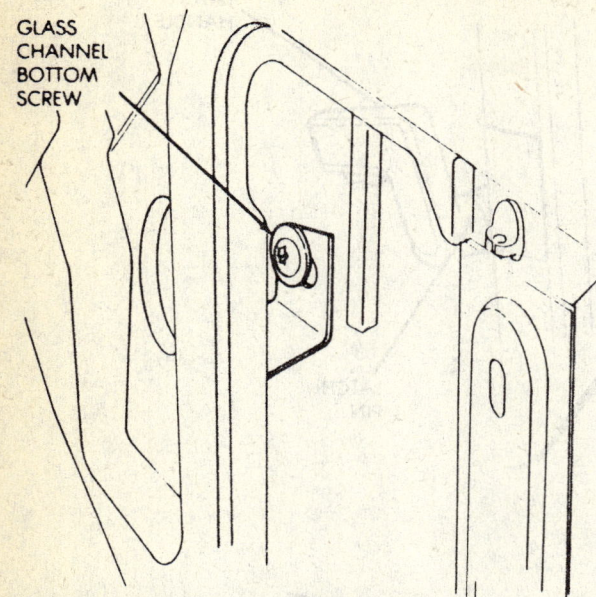

Removing the glass channel bottom screw

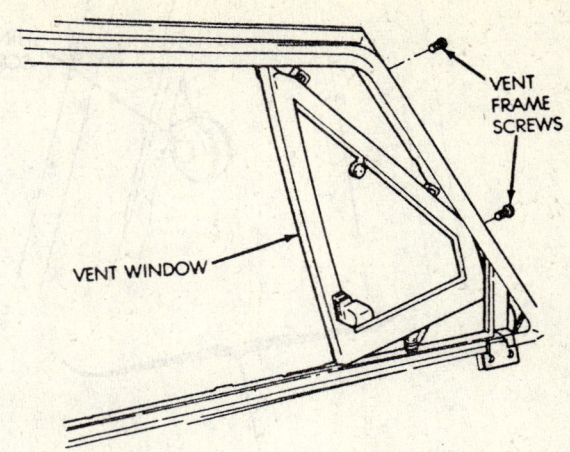

Removing the vent window frame screws

4. Remove the vent window frame screws.
5. Tilt the vent window and glass channel backward and remove it from the door frame.
6. Remove the door glass attaching stud nut and spring washer.
7. If equipped with electric windows, disconnect the wiring harness.
8. Grind the heads off the regulator rivets and knock the rivets out with a hammer and punch.
9. Pull the glass upward and out of the door.
10. Remove the regulator.
11. Installation is the reverse of removal. The regulator must be attached with special regulator pop rivets (available at auto body supply stores) or bolts and nuts. Torque the door glass stud nut to 48 inch lbs.; the vent window bottom screw to 84 inch lbs.; the upper vent window screws to 10 ft. lbs.

Rear Door

1. Remove the trim panel and waterproof plastic sheet.
2. Lower the door glass and remove the weatherstripping.
3. Remove the stationary glass frame screws.
4. Remove the glass channel upper screws.
5. Remove the glass channel lower screws.
6. Tilt the stationary glass and its channel forward and remove it.
7. Remove the door glass stud nut and lift the glass from the door.
8. Grind the heads off the regulator rivets and knock the rivets out with a hammer and punch.
9. Pull the glass upward and out of the door.
10. Installation is the reverse of removal. Torque the stud nut to 48 inch lbs. and the glass channel screws to 60-84 inch lbs. Use special regulator pop rivets (available at auto body supply stores) or nuts and bolts to install the regulator.

Power Window Regulator

REMOVAL AND INSTALLATION

1. Remove the window glass and regulator.
2. Disconnect the wiring.
3. Unbolt and remove the motor.

Windshield

REMOVAL AND INSTALLATION

These models use bonded windshields. Windshield installation and the adhesives used are critical in meeting Federal regulations. Therefore, it is recommended that windshield replacement procedures on these vehicles be left to a professional shop.

Rear Window Glass and Rear Quarter Stationary Glass

REMOVAL AND INSTALLATION

NOTE: This procedure applies to the rear quarter stationary glass on the Wagoneer and Cherokee. The rear cab window on the Comanche uses a bonded installation procedure. See the note under Windshields, above.

1. Remove the interior trim moldings from around the window. Where necessary, remove the spare tire and mounting bracket.
2. Break loose the seal between the weatherstripping and the body panels.
3. Have someone outside push inward on the glass while you catch it.
4. Clean all old sealer from the glass and weatherstripping.

BODY 10

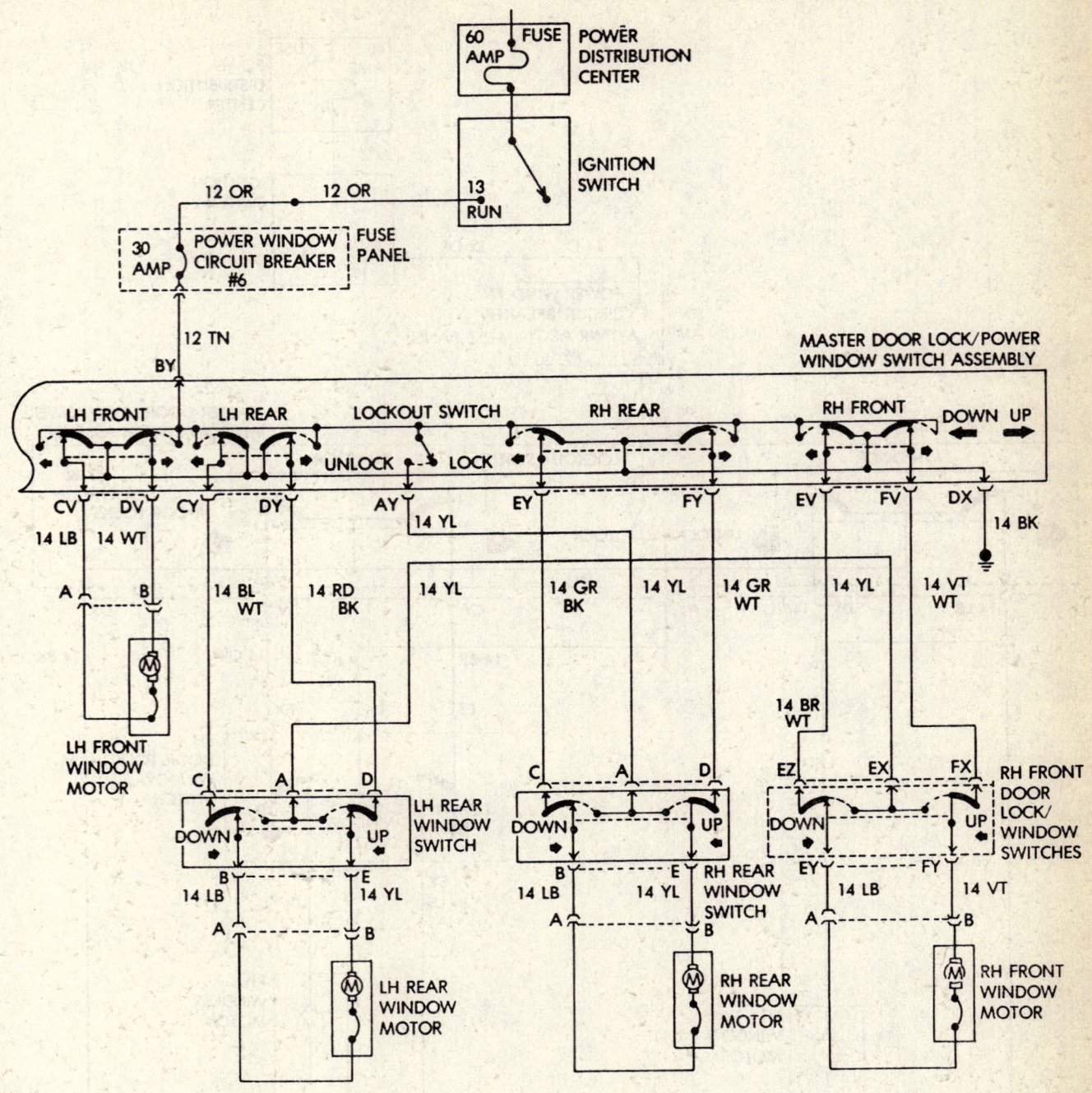

Power window wiring diagram — 4-door Cherokee/Wagoneer

10-25

10 BODY

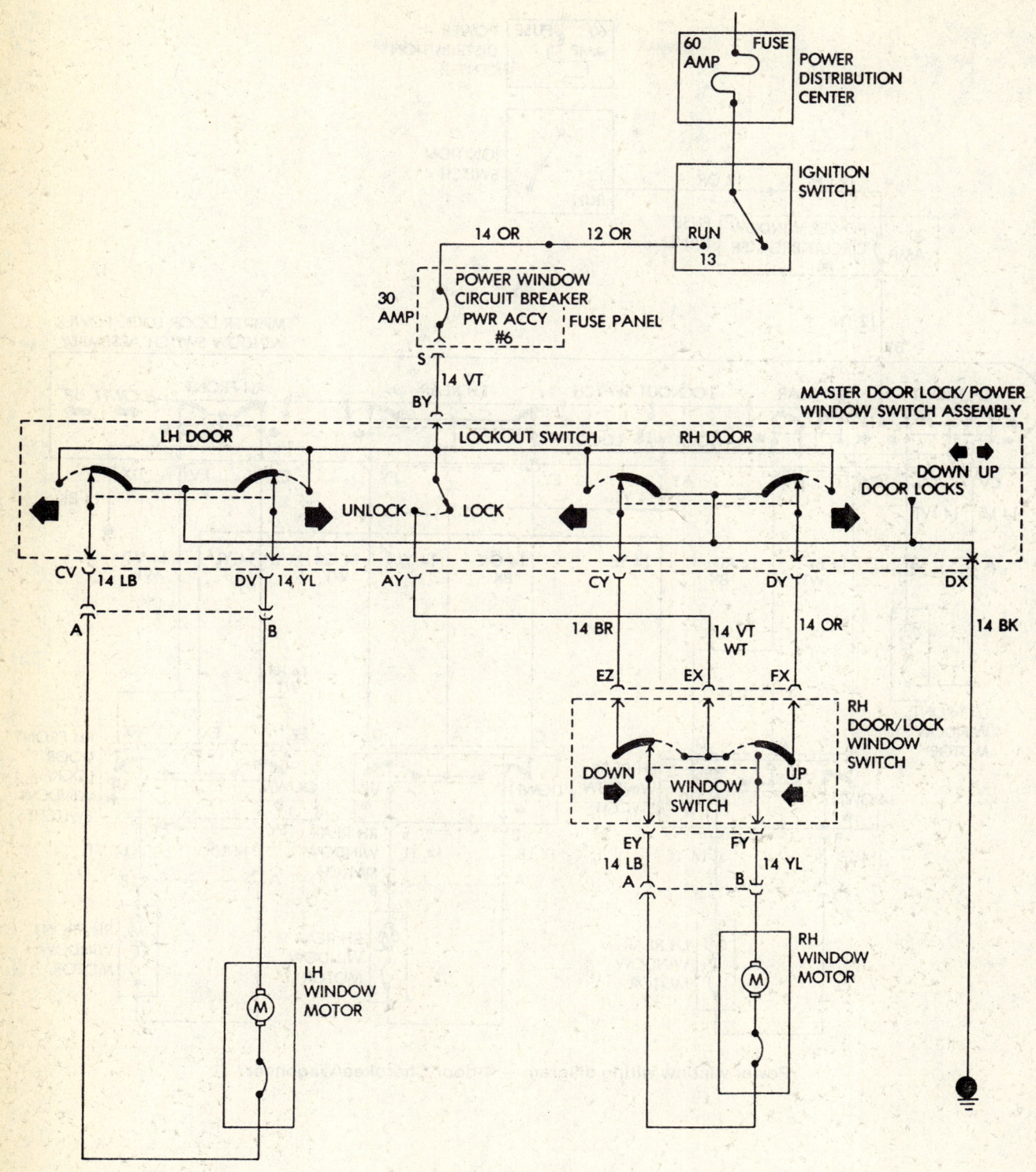

Power window wiring diagram — 2-door Cherokee/Wagoneer

BODY 10

DRIVERS DOOR POWER WINDOW SWITCH—2-DOOR

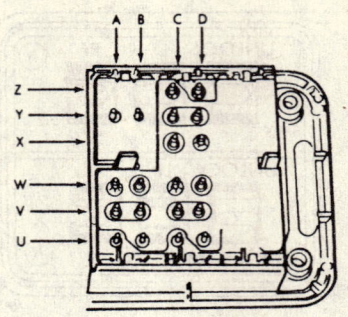
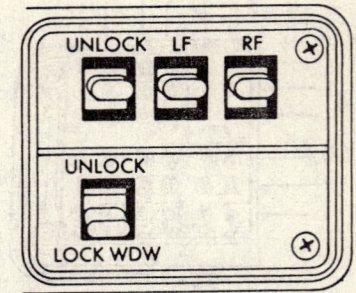

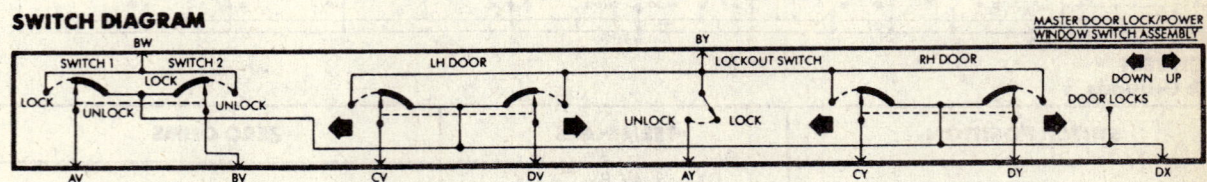

SWITCH DIAGRAM

SWITCH TEST
Switch Grounds

SWITCH POSITION	TERMINALS	ZERO OHMS
Off (Normal)	DX and: AV, BV, CV DV, CY, DY	Yes
	BW and DX	No
	BY and DX	No

SWITCH TEST
LH Door

SWITCH POSITION	TERMINALS	ZERO OHMS
Up	BY and DV	Yes
Down	BY and CV	Yes

SWITCH TEST
RH Door

SWITCH POSITION	TERMINALS	ZERO OHMS
Up	BY and DY	Yes
Down	BY and CY	Yes

SWITCH TEST
Lockout Switch

SWITCH POSITION	TERMINALS	ZERO OHMS
Up (Unlock)	AY and BY	Yes
Down (Lock)	AY and BY	No

10 BODY

DRIVERS DOOR POWER WINDOW SWITCH—4-DOOR

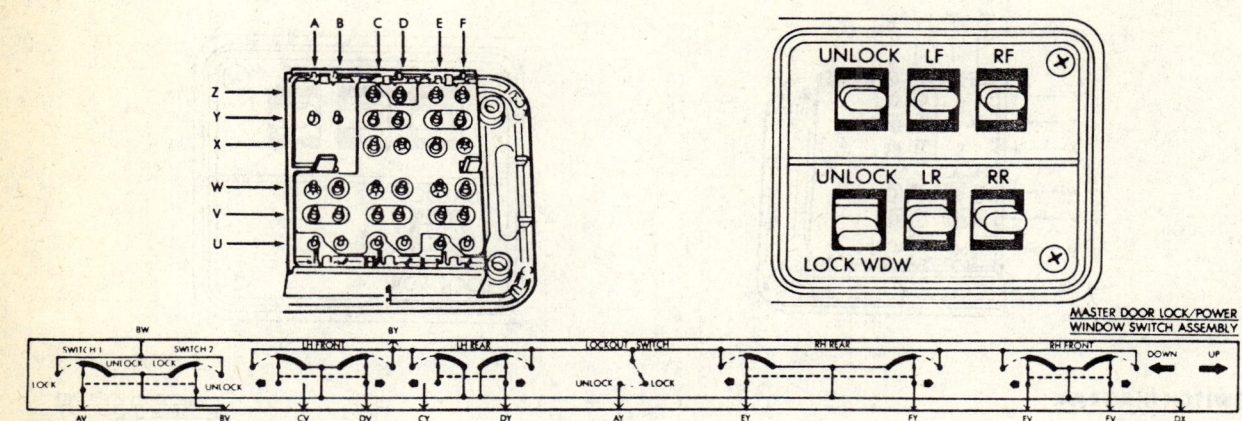

SWITCH TEST
Switch Grounds

SWITCH POSITION	TERMINALS	ZERO OHMS
Off (Normal)	DX and: AV, BV, CV, DV, CY, DY, EY, FY, EV, FV	Yes
	BW and DX	No
	BY and DX	No

SWITCH TEST
LH Front

SWITCH POSITION	TERMINALS	ZERO OHMS
Up	BY and DV	Yes
Down	BY and CV	Yes

SWITCH TEST
LH Rear

SWITCH POSITION	TERMINALS	ZERO OHMS
Up	BY and DY	Yes
Down	BY and CY	Yes

SWITCH TEST
Lockout Switch

SWITCH POSITION	TERMINALS	ZERO OHMS
Up (Unlock)	AY and BY	Yes
Down (Lock)	AY and BY	No

SWITCH TEST
RH Rear

SWITCH POSITION	TERMINALS	ZERO OHMS
Up	BY and FY	Yes
Down	BY and EY	Yes

SWITCH TEST
RH Front

SWITCH POSITION	TERMINALS	ZERO OHMS
Up	BY and FV	Yes
Down	BY and EV	Yes

BODY 10

PASSENGER DOOR WINDOW SWITCH

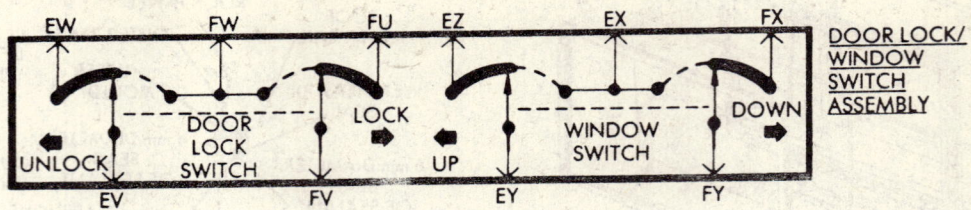

SWITCH TEST
Window Switch

SWITCH POSITION	TERMINALS	ZERO OHMS
Off (Normal)	EY and EZ	Yes
	FY and FX	Yes
	All Others	No
Up	EY and EZ	Yes
	EX and FY	Yes
	All Others	No
Down	EX and EY	Yes
	FX and FY	Yes
	All Others	No

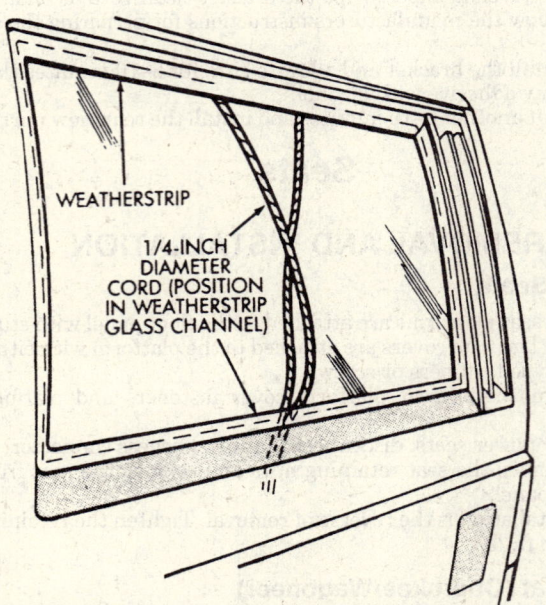

Quarter window glass installation with cord

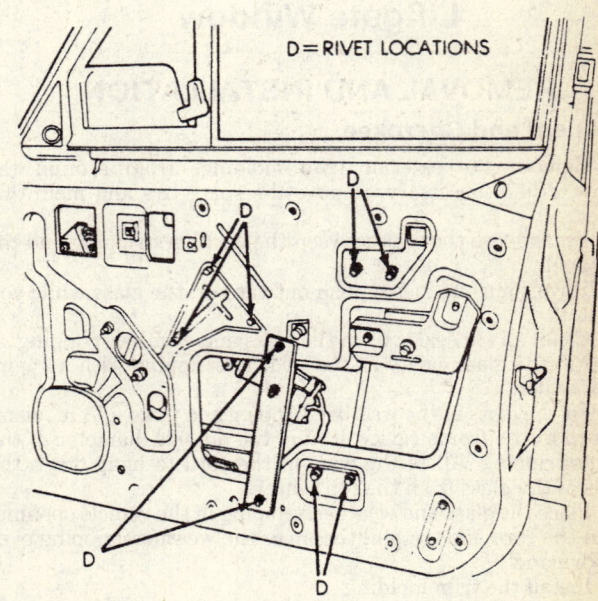

Power window glass regulator rivet locations

10-29

10 BODY

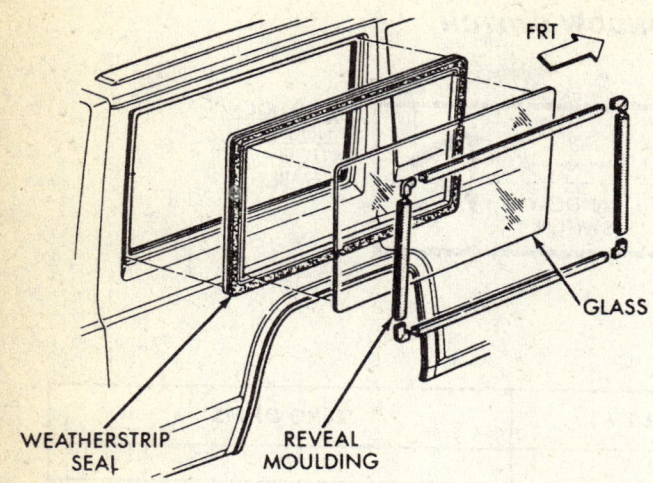

Quarter window molding, glass and seal

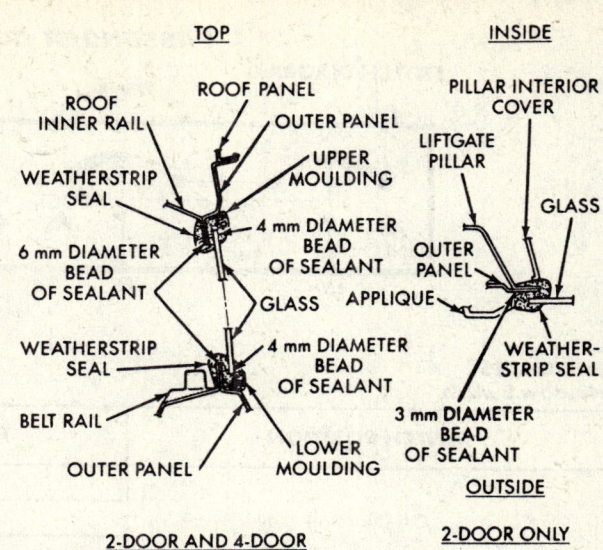

Quarter window glass installation

5. Fill the glass cavity in the weatherstripping with a 3/16 in. bead of sealer.
6. Fit the glass in the weatherstripping and place a 1/4 in. diameter cord in the frame cavity around the outside diameter of the weatherstripping. Allow the ends of the cord to hang down the outside of the glass from the top center.
7. Place the glass and weatherstripping in the vehicle opening. Pull on the cord ends to pull the lip of the weatherstripping over the body panel.
8. Install the trim molding.

Liftgate Window

REMOVAL AND INSTALLATION

Wagoneer and Cherokee

1. Remove the exterior trim moldings from around the window. Where necessary, remove the spare tire and mounting bracket.
2. Break loose the seal between the weatherstripping and the body panel.
3. Have someone inside push outward on the glass while you catch it.
4. Clean all old sealer from the glass and weatherstripping.
5. Fill the glass cavity in the weatherstripping with a 3/16 in. bead of sealer.
6. Fit the glass in the weatherstripping and place a 1/4 in. diameter cord in the frame cavity around the outside diameter of the weatherstripping. Allow the ends of the cord to hang down the outside of the glass from the top center.
7. Place the glass and weatherstripping in the vehicle opening. Pull on the cord ends to pull the lip of the weatherstripping over the body panel.
8. Install the trim molding.

Inside Rear View Mirror

To replace the rear view mirror, loosen the mirror set screw and slide the mirror base up and off the retaining bracket. Install the replacement mirror on to the retaining bracket and tighten the set screw. DO NOT over tighten the set screw as this will chip or break the windshield.

To replace the retaining bracket use the following procedure:
1. Mark installation reference position lines on the outside of the windshield glass with a grease pencil. Mark both horizontal and vertical reference marks.
2. If the vinyl pad remained on the windshield glass, soften and remove it with a hear gun.
3. Thoroughly clean the bracket contact surface area on the glass. Use a mild abrasive cleaning solution and final clean with isopropyl alcohol.
4. Lightly sand the contact area on the replacement bracket with fine grit sand paper. Wipe the bracket clean with alcohol.
5. Follow the manufacturers instructions for preparing the adhesive.
6. Install the bracket and allow to cure for 8-10 minutes then remove any adhesive with alcohol.
7. Wait another 8-10 minutes and install the rear view mirror.

Seats

REMOVAL AND INSTALLATION

Bucket Seats

Bucket seat platforms are attached to the floor panel with studs and nuts. The trim covers are attached to the platform with either push-on type fasteners or screws.
1. Remove the seat platform cover fasteners and platform cover.
2. For power seats, disconnect the wire harness connector.
3. Remove the seat retaining nuts and remove the seat from the floor panel.
4. Installation is the reverse of removal. Tighten the retaining nuts to 18 ft. lbs.

Rear Seat (Cherokee/Wagoneer)

1. Disengage the seat cushion at the rear by pulling upward on the release strap.
2. Tilt the sear cushion forward and disengage the seat cushion latch with the release lever knob. Separate the right side latch and the left side seat bracket from the floor anchor bolts, then remove the cushion from the vehicle.
3. Remove the shoulder/lap belt buckles from the elastic straps. Release the seat back lock.

BODY 10

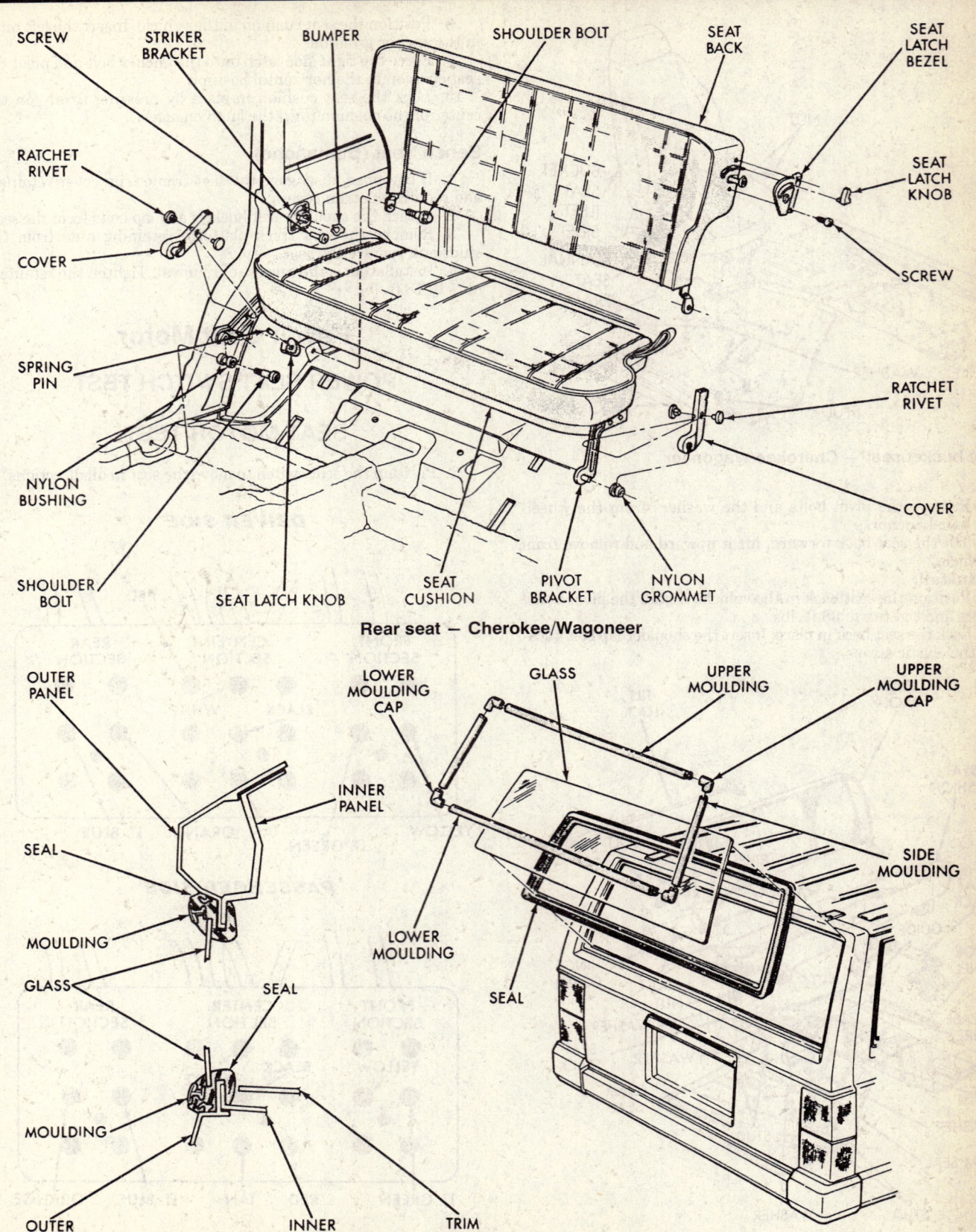

Rear seat — Cherokee/Wagoneer

Liftgate window glass revel molding, glass and seal

10-31

10　BODY

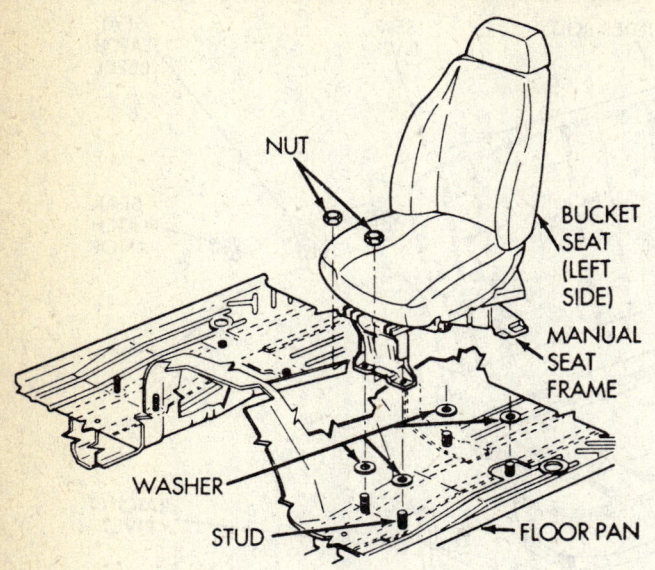

Front bucket seat — Cherokee/Wagoneer

8. Position the seat cushion in the vehicle. Insert the left pivot in the anchor grommet.
9. Force the tight side latch onto the anchor bolt and pivot the seat cushion to the horizontal position.
10. Lock the seat cushion in-place by pressing firmly on the center of the cushion until the latch engages.

Bench Seat (Comanche)

1. If equipped, disengage the seat frame trim cover retainers and remove the trim covers.
2. Detach the shoulder belt buckles and lap belts from the seat.
3. Remove the seat track platform retaining nuts from the studs and remove the seat.
4. Installation is the reverse of removal. Tighten the retaining nuts to 18 ft. lbs.

Power Seat Motor

POWER SEAT SWITCH TEST

SEAT MOTOR TEST

1. Position the seat switch to move the seat in all directions. If

4. Remove the pivot bolts and the washers from the wheelhouse panel anchors.
5. Tilt the seat back forward, lift it upward and remove from the vehicle.

To Install:

6. Position the seat back in the vehicle. Install the pivot bolts/washers and tighten to 38 ft. lbs.
7. Lock the seat back in place. Insert the shoulder/lap belt buckles in the elastic straps.

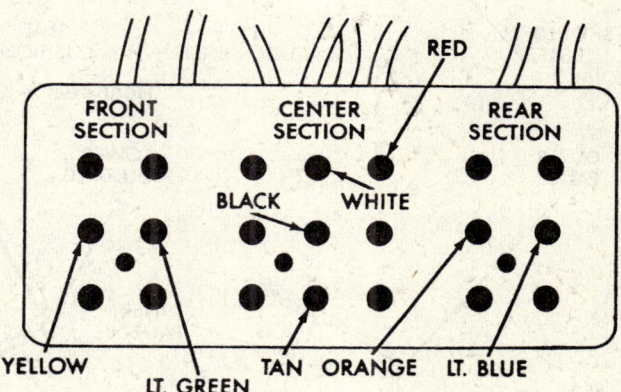

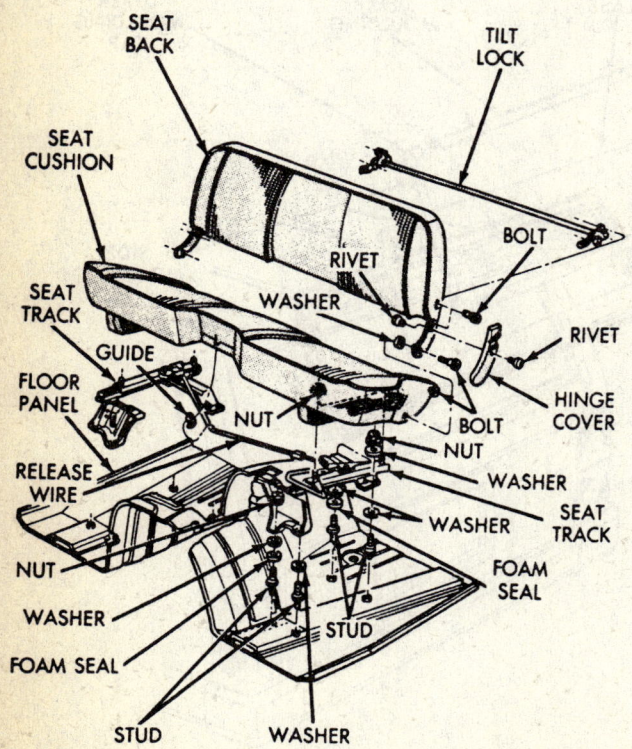

Front bench seat — Comanche

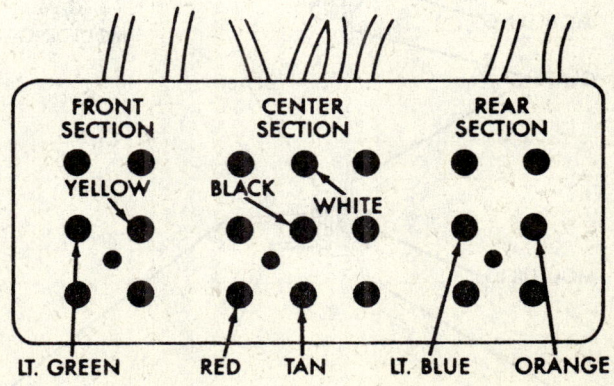

Power seat switch terminal diagram

BODY 10

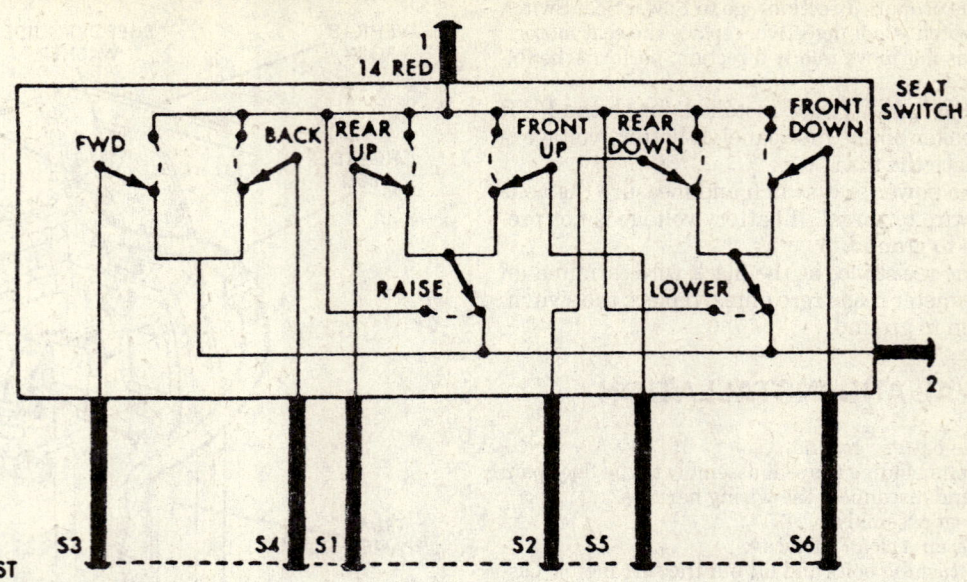

SWITCH TEST
SWITCHES 1, 2 AND 3 (GROUNDS)

SWITCH POSITION	TERMINALS	ZERO OHMS
OFF (NORMAL)	2 AND: S1, S2, S3, S4, S5 AND S6	YES
	1 AND 2	NO

SWITCH TEST
SWITCH 1

SWITCH POSITION	TERMINALS	ZERO OHMS
UP (FRONT)	1 AND S5	YES
DOWN (FRONT)	1 AND S6	YES

SWITCH TEST
SWITCH 2

SWITCH POSITION	TERMINALS	ZERO OHMS
UP (RAISE)	1 AND S1	YES
	1 AND S5	YES
DOWN (LOWER)	1 AND S2	YES
	1 AND S6	YES
FORWARD (FWD)	1 AND S3	YES
BACKWARD (BACK)	1 AND S4	YES

SWITCH TEST
SWITCH 3

SWITCH POSITION	TERMINALS	ZERO OHMS
UP (REAR)	1 AND S1	YES
DOWN (REAR)	1 AND S2	YES

10 BODY

the seat moves in one or more directions, go to Power Seat Switch Test above. If the switch is not defective, replace the seat motor.

2. If the seat does not move in any direction, perform the following test sequence:

    a. With the PWR ACCY fuse installed, probe the PWR ACCY circuit breaker on the fuse panel. If battery voltage is not present, replace the fuse.

    b. Remove the power seat switch and measure the voltage at the RED wire terminal. If battery voltage is not present, repair open to ground.

    c. Measure the resistance at the black wire terminal on the switch. If the meter reads zero ohms, replace the switch. If not, repair open to ground.

REMOVAL AND INSTALLATION

1. Disconnect the battery ground.
2. Remove the bolts holding the seat assembly to the floor pan.
3. Tilt the seat and disconnect the wiring harness.
4. Remove the seat assembly.
5. Invert the seat on a clean surface.
6. Remove the attaching bolts and lift out the seat motor. Disconnect the wiring and cables.
7. Installation is the reverse of removal.

NOTE: If the seat transmission fails, it is not replaceable. The entire seat adjuster assembly will have to be replaced.

Seat Belt Systems

REMOVAL AND INSTALLATION

Front Shoulder Belt

1. Move the front seat to the forward position. Disconnect the wiring harness (if equipped with power seats) and remove the anchor bolt covers.
2. Remove the shoulder belt buckle anchor bolt with a Torx bit. Remove the shoulder belt buckle.
3. Remove the cap concealing the shoulder belt upper anchor bolt and use a Torx bit to remove the bolt. Remove the support/guide washer.
4. Remove the inner scuff plate/trim panel from the door sill and remove the shoulder belt lower anchor bolts.

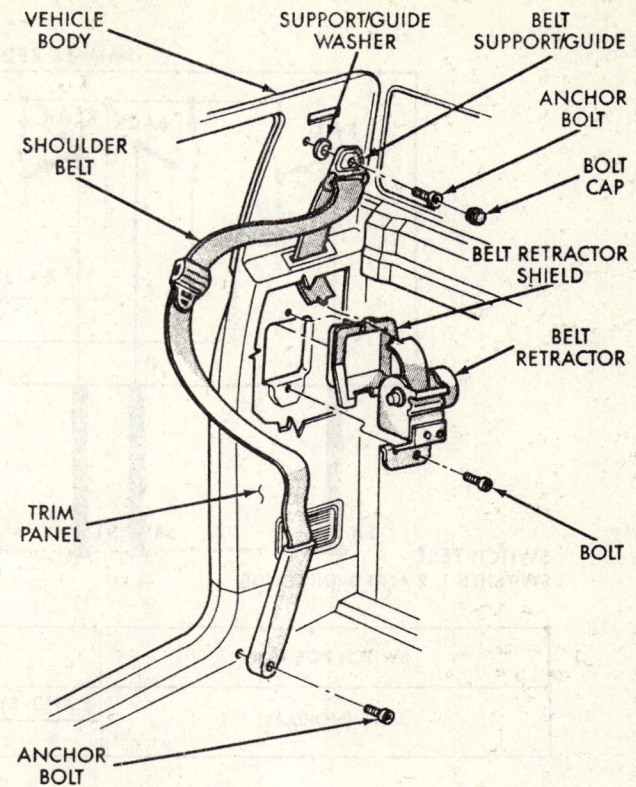

Shoulder belt — Comanche

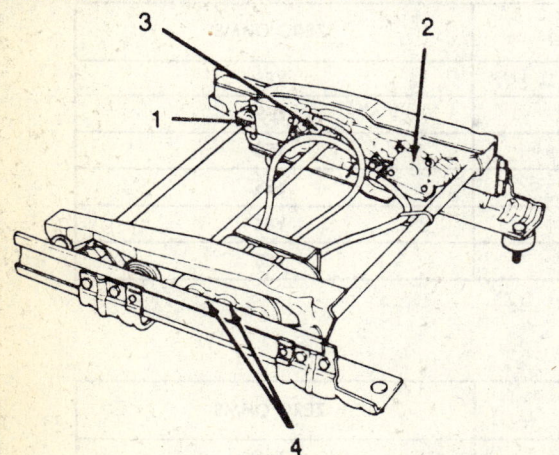

1. Front transmission
2. Rear transmission
3. Horizontal transmission
4. Motor attaching bolts

Power seat track assembly

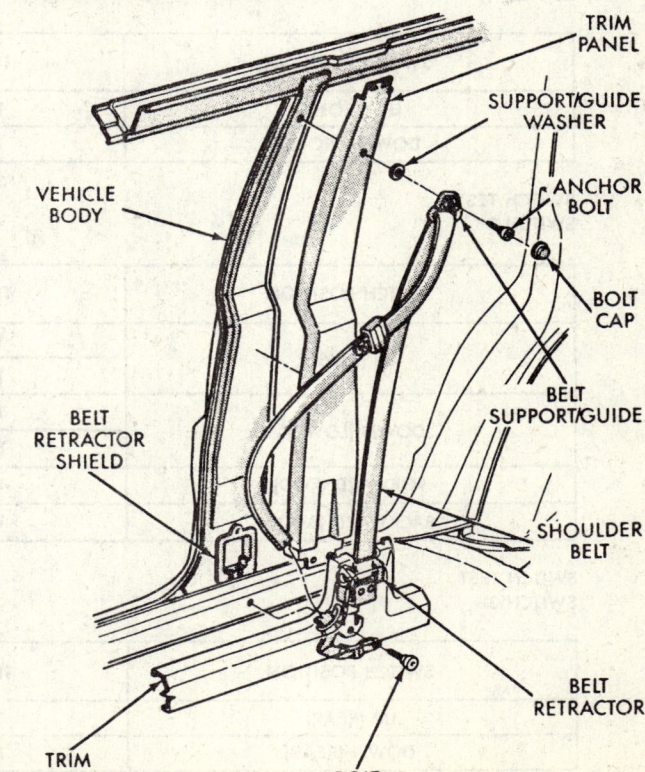

Front shoulder belt — 4-door Cherokee/Wagoneer

10-34

BODY 10

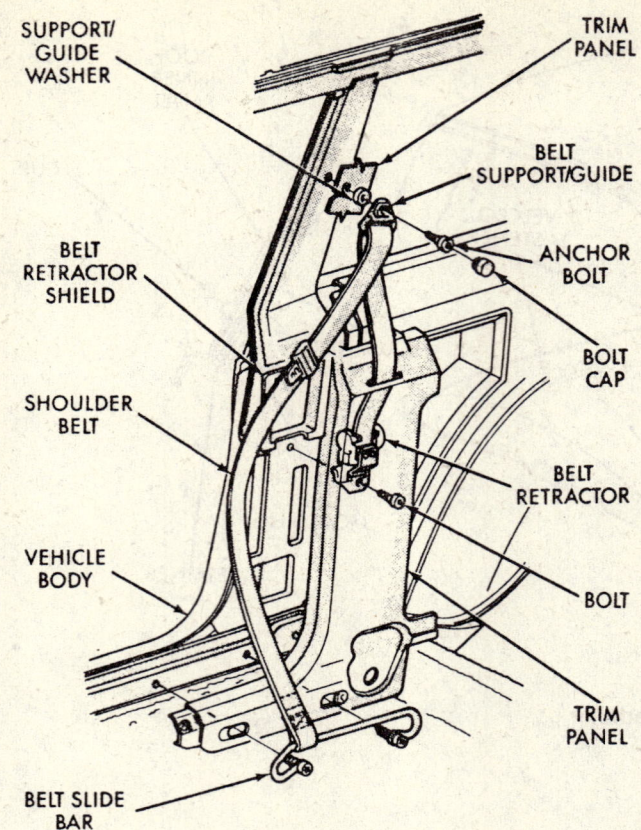

Front shoulder belt — 2-door Cherokee/Wagoneer

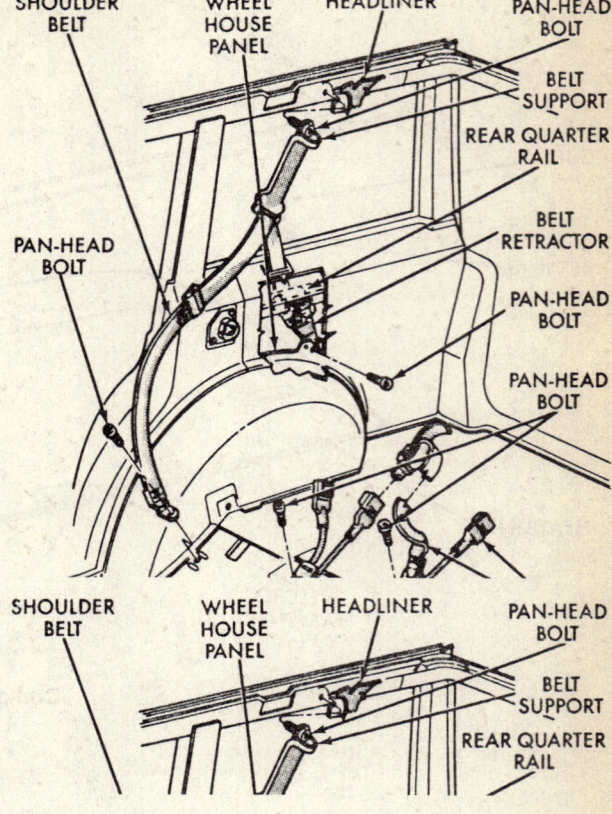

Rear shoulder belt — Cherokee/Wagoneer

5. Remove the shoulder belt and retractor.
NOTE: Inspect the belts and buckles thoroughly. Replace any belt that is either cut, frayed, torn or damaged in any way. Remember! the seat belts are the only thing between you and the windshield in an accident. You are wearing you seat belts aren't you?
6. Installation is the reverse of removal. Tighten all anchor bolts to 27 ft. lbs.

Rear Shoulder Belt—Cherokee/Wagoneer Only

1. Tilt the rear seat forward.
2. Remove the shoulder belt buckle and lap belt buckle anchor plate bolts from the floor panel.
3. Remove the shoulder belt lower anchor bolt.
4. Remove the quarter trim panel and remove the shoulder belt retractor support retaining screw from the rear quarter rail.
5. Remove the retractor and shoulder belt from the trim panel.
NOTE: Inspect the belts and buckles thoroughly. Replace any belt that is either cut, frayed, torn or damaged in any way. Remember! in the event of an accident, the seat belts are the only thing between your rear seat passengers and you. Friends don't let friends ride without seat belts.
6. Installation is the reverse of removal. Tighten all anchor bolts to 27 ft. lbs.

Headliner

REMOVAL AND INSTALLATION

1. Remove the following:
- the sun visors
- the dome/cargo light
- the overhead console (if equipped)
- the keyless entry receiver module (if equipped)
- the sunroof retainer (if equipped)
- the assist handle
- the coat hooks
- all other attached components
2. Remove the side and rear trim panels.

NOTE: The headliner is a one-piece, molded unit, and MUST NOT be bent during removal or installation.

3. Make sure that all trim clips are removed. Remove the headliner through the tailgate opening (Cherokee/Wagoneer) or through the door (Comanche).
4. Installation is the reverse of removal.

10 BODY

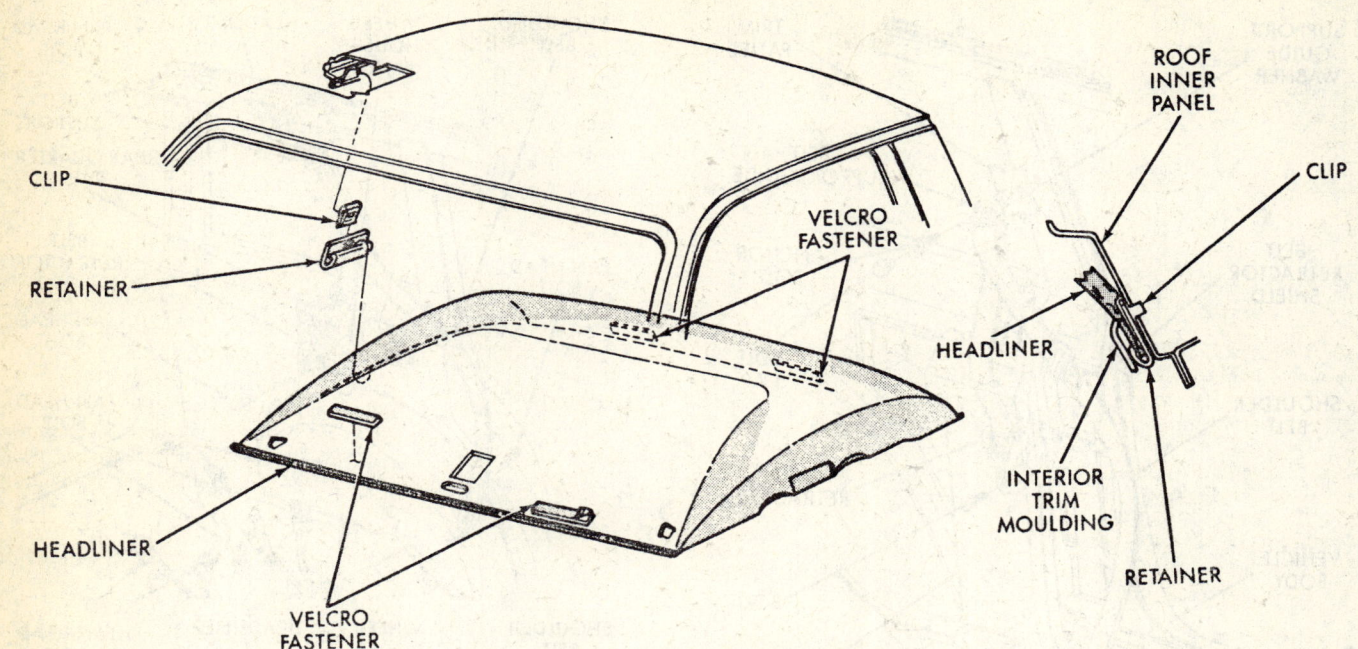

Comanche headliner

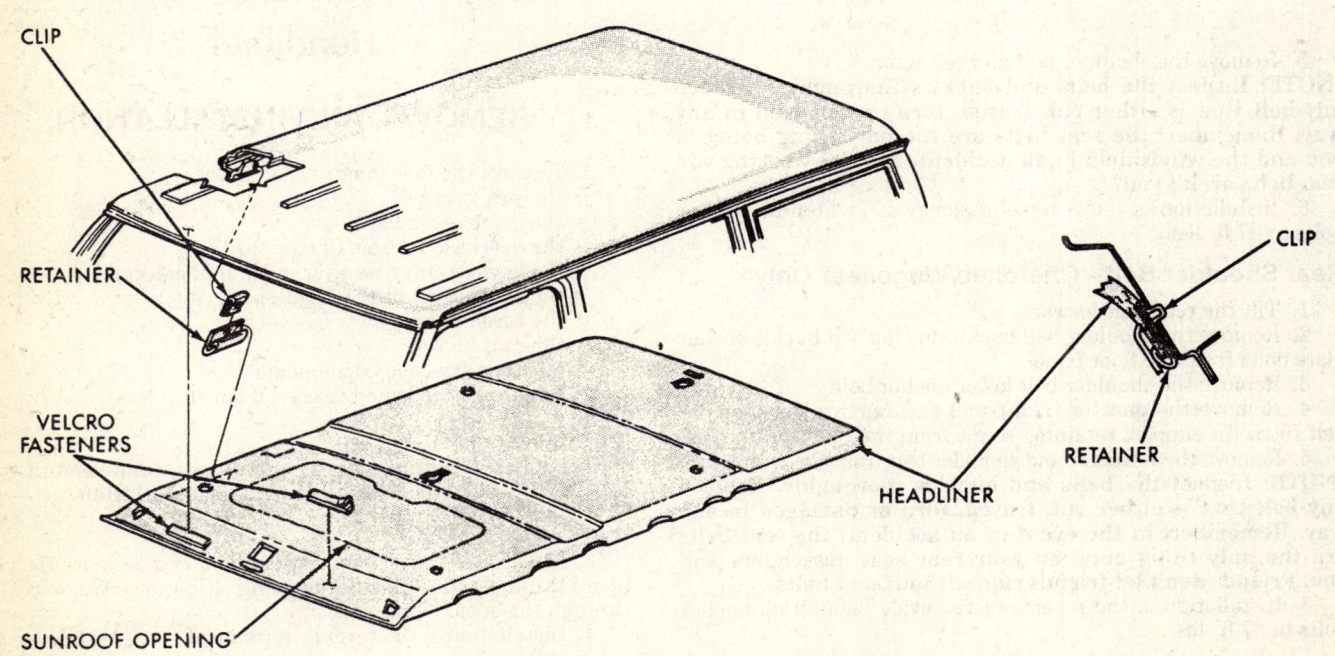

Cherokee/Wagoneer headliner

Glossary

AIR/FUEL RATIO: The ratio of air to gasoline by weight in the fuel mixture drawn into the engine.

AIR INJECTION: One method of reducing harmful exhaust emissions by injecting air into each of the exhaust ports of an engine. The fresh air entering the hot exhaust manifold causes any remaining fuel to be burned before it can exit the tailpipe.

ALTERNATOR: A device used for converting mechanical energy into electrical energy.

AMMETER: An instrument, calibrated in amperes, used to measure the flow of an electrical current in a circuit. Ammeters are always connected in series with the circuit being tested.

AMPERE: The rate of flow of electrical current present when one volt of electrical pressure is applied against one ohm of electrical resistance.

ANALOG COMPUTER: Any microprocessor that uses similar (analogous) electrical signals to make its calculations.

ARMATURE: A laminated, soft iron core wrapped by a wire that converts electrical energy to mechanical energy as in a motor or relay. When rotated in a magnetic field, it changes mechanical energy into electrical energy as in a generator.

ATMOSPHERIC PRESSURE: The pressure on the Earth's surface caused by the weight of the air in the atmosphere. At sea level, this pressure is 14.7 psi at 32°F (101 kPa at 0°C).

ATOMIZATION: The breaking down of a liquid into a fine mist that can be suspended in air.

AXIAL PLAY: Movement parallel to a shaft or bearing bore.

BACKFIRE: The sudden combustion of gases in the intake or exhaust system that results in a loud explosion.

BACKLASH: The clearance or play between two parts, such as meshed gears.

BACKPRESSURE: Restrictions in the exhaust system that slow the exit of exhaust gases from the combustion chamber.

BAKELITE: A heat resistant, plastic insulator material commonly used in printed circuit boards and transistorized components.

BALL BEARING: A bearing made up of hardened inner and outer races between which hardened steel balls roll.

BALLAST RESISTOR: A resistor in the primary ignition circuit that lowers voltage after the engine is started to reduce wear on ignition components.

BEARING: A friction reducing, supportive device usually located between a stationary part and a moving part.

BIMETAL TEMPERATURE SENSOR: Any sensor or switch made of two dissimilar types of metal that bend when heated or cooled due to the different expansion rates of the alloys. These types of sensors usually function as an on/off switch.

BLOWBY: Combustion gases, composed of water vapor and unburned fuel, that leak past the piston rings into the crankcase during normal engine operation. These gases are removed by the PCV system to prevent the buildup of harmful acids in the crankcase.

BRAKE PAD: A brake shoe and lining assembly used with disc brakes.

BRAKE SHOE: The backing for the brake lining. The term is, however, usually applied to the assembly of the brake backing and lining.

BUSHING: A liner, usually removable, for a bearing; an anti-friction liner used in place of a bearing.

BYPASS: System used to bypass ballast resistor during engine cranking to increase voltage supplied to the coil.

CALIPER: A hydraulically activated device in a disc brake system, which is mounted straddling the brake rotor (disc). The caliper contains at least one piston and two brake pads. Hydraulic pressure on the piston(s) forces the pads against the rotor.

CAMSHAFT: A shaft in the engine on which are the lobes (cams) which operate the valves. The camshaft is driven by the crankshaft, via a belt, chain or gears, at one half the crankshaft speed.

CAPACITOR: A device which stores an electrical charge.

CARBON MONOXIDE (CO): A colorless, odorless gas given off as a normal byproduct of combustion. It is poisonous and extremely dangerous in confined areas, building up slowly to toxic levels without warning if adequate ventilation is not available.

CARBURETOR: A device, usually mounted on the intake manifold of an engine, which mixes the air and fuel in the proper proportion to allow even combustion.

CATALYTIC CONVERTER: A device installed in the exhaust system, like a muffler, that converts harmful byproducts of combustion into carbon dioxide and water vapor by means of a heat-producing chemical reaction.

CENTRIFUGAL ADVANCE: A mechanical method of advancing the spark timing by using fly weights in the distributor that react to centrifugal force generated by the distributor shaft rotation.

CHECK VALVE: Any one-way valve installed to permit the flow of air, fuel or vacuum in one direction only.

GLOSSARY

CHOKE: A device, usually a movable valve, placed in the intake path of a carburetor to restrict the flow of air.

CIRCUIT: Any unbroken path through which an electrical current can flow. Also used to describe fuel flow in some instances.

CIRCUIT BREAKER: A switch which protects an electrical circuit from overload by opening the circuit when the current flow exceeds a predetermined level. Some circuit breakers must be reset manually, while most reset automatically

COIL (IGNITION): A transformer in the ignition circuit which steps up the voltage provided to the spark plugs.

COMBINATION MANIFOLD: An assembly which includes both the intake and exhaust manifolds in one casting.

COMBINATION VALVE: A device used in some fuel systems that routes fuel vapors to a charcoal storage canister instead of venting them into the atmosphere. The valve relieves fuel tank pressure and allows fresh air into the tank as the fuel level drops to prevent a vapor lock situation.

COMPRESSION RATIO: The comparison of the total volume of the cylinder and combustion chamber with the piston at BDC and the piston at TDC.

CONDENSER: 1. An electrical device which acts to store an electrical charge, preventing voltage surges.
2. A radiator-like device in the air conditioning system in which refrigerant gas condenses into a liquid, giving off heat.

CONDUCTOR: Any material through which an electrical current can be transmitted easily.

CONTINUITY: Continuous or complete circuit. Can be checked with an ohmmeter.

COUNTERSHAFT: An intermediate shaft which is rotated by a mainshaft and transmits, in turn, that rotation to a working part.

CRANKCASE: The lower part of an engine in which the crankshaft and related parts operate.

CRANKSHAFT: The main driving shaft of an engine which receives reciprocating motion from the pistons and converts it to rotary motion.

CYLINDER: In an engine, the round hole in the engine block in which the piston(s) ride.

CYLINDER BLOCK: The main structural member of an engine in which is found the cylinders, crankshaft and other principal parts.

CYLINDER HEAD: The detachable portion of the engine, fastened, usually, to the top of the cylinder block, containing all or most of the combustion chambers. On overhead valve engines, it contains the valves and their operating parts. On overhead cam engines, it contains the camshaft as well.

DEAD CENTER: The extreme top or bottom of the piston stroke.

DETONATION: An unwanted explosion of the air/fuel mixture in the combustion chamber caused by excess heat and compression, advanced timing, or an overly lean mixture. Also referred to as "ping".

DIAPHRAGM: A thin, flexible wall separating two cavities, such as in a vacuum advance unit.

DIESELING: A condition in which hot spots in the combustion chamber cause the engine to run on after the key is turned off.

DIFFERENTIAL: A geared assembly which allows the transmission of motion between drive axles, giving one axle the ability to turn faster than the other.

DIODE: An electrical device that will allow current to flow in one direction only.

DISC BRAKE: A hydraulic braking assembly consisting of a brake disc, or rotor, mounted on an axle, and a caliper assembly containing, usually two brake pads which are activated by hydraulic pressure. The pads are forced against the sides of the disc, creating friction which slows the vehicle.

DISTRIBUTOR: A mechanically driven device on an engine which is responsible for electrically firing the spark plug at a predetermined point of the piston stroke.

DOWEL PIN: A pin, inserted in mating holes in two different parts allowing those parts to maintain a fixed relationship.

DRUM BRAKE: A braking system which consists of two brake shoes and one or two wheel cylinders, mounted on a fixed backing plate, and a brake drum, mounted on an axle, which revolves around the assembly. Hydraulic action applied to the wheel cylinders forces the shoes outward against the drum, creating friction, slowing the vehicle.

DWELL: The rate, measured in degrees of shaft rotation, at which an electrical circuit cycles on and off.

ELECTRONIC CONTROL UNIT (ECU): Ignition module, amplifier or igniter. See Module for definition.

ELECTRONIC IGNITION: A system in which the timing and firing of the spark plugs is controlled by an electronic control unit, usually called a module. These systems have no points or condenser.

ENDPLAY: The measured amount of axial movement in a shaft.

ENGINE: A device that converts heat into mechanical energy.

EXHAUST MANIFOLD: A set of cast passages or pipes which conduct exhaust gases from the engine.

FEELER GAUGE: A blade, usually metal, of precisely predetermined thickness, used to measure the clearance between two parts. These blades usually are available in sets of assorted thicknesses.

F-HEAD: An engine configuration in which the intake valves are in the cylinder head, while the camshaft and exhaust valves are located in the cylinder block. The camshaft operates the intake valves via lifters and pushrods, while it operates the exhaust valves directly.

FIRING ORDER: The order in which combustion occurs in the cylinders of an engine. Also the order in which spark is distributed to the plugs by the distributor.

FLATHEAD: An engine configuration in which the camshaft and all the valves are located in the cylinder block.

GLOSSARY

RACE: The surface on the inner or outer ring of a bearing on which the balls, needles or rollers move.

REGULATOR: A device which maintains the amperage and/or voltage levels of a circuit at predetermined values.

RELAY: A switch which automatically opens and/or closes a circuit.

RESISTANCE: The opposition to the flow of current through a circuit or electrical device, and is measured in ohms. Resistance is equal to the voltage divided by the amperage.

RESISTOR: A device, usually made of wire, which offers a preset amount of resistance in an electrical circuit.

RING GEAR: The name given to a ring-shaped gear attached to a differential case, or affixed to a flywheel or as part a planetary gear set.

ROLLER BEARING: A bearing made up of hardened inner and outer races between which hardened steel rollers move.

ROTOR: 1. The disc-shaped part of a disc brake assembly, upon which the brake pads bear; also called, brake disc.
2. The device mounted atop the distributor shaft, which passes current to the distributor cap tower contacts.

SECONDARY CIRCUIT: The high voltage side of the ignition system, usually above 20,000 volts. The secondary includes the ignition coil, coil wire, distributor cap and rotor, spark plug wires and spark plugs.

SENDING UNIT: A mechanical, electrical, hydraulic or electromagnetic device which transmits information to a gauge.

SENSOR: Any device designed to measure engine operating conditions or ambient pressures and temperatures. Usually electronic in nature and designed to send a voltage signal to an on-board computer, some sensors may operate as a simple on/off switch or they may provide a variable voltage signal (like a potentiometer) as conditions or measured parameters change.

SHIM: Spacers of precise, predetermined thickness used between parts to establish a proper working relationship.

SLAVE CYLINDER: In automotive use, a device in the hydraulic clutch system which is activated by hydraulic force, disengaging the clutch.

SOLENOID: A coil used to produce a magnetic field, the effect of which is to produce work.

SPARK PLUG: A device screwed into the combustion chamber of a spark ignition engine. The basic construction is a conductive core inside of a ceramic insulator, mounted in an outer conductive base. An electrical charge from the spark plug wire travels along the conductive core and jumps a preset air gap to a grounding point or points at the end of the conductive base. The resultant spark ignites the fuel/air mixture in the combustion chamber.

SPLINES: Ridges machined or cast onto the outer diameter of a shaft or inner diameter of a bore to enable parts to mate without rotation.

TACHOMETER: A device used to measure the rotary speed of an engine, shaft, gear, etc., usually in rotations per minute.

THERMOSTAT: A valve, located in the cooling system of an engine, which is closed when cold and opens gradually in response to engine heating, controlling the temperature of the coolant and rate of coolant flow.

TOP DEAD CENTER (TDC): The point at which the piston reaches the top of its travel on the compression stroke.

TORQUE: The twisting force applied to an object.

TORQUE CONVERTER: A turbine used to transmit power from a driving member to a driven member via hydraulic action, providing changes in drive ratio and torque. In automotive use, it links the driveplate at the rear of the engine to the automatic transmission.

TRANSDUCER: A device used to change a force into an electrical signal.

TRANSISTOR: A semi-conductor component which can be actuated by a small voltage to perform an electrical switching function.

TUNE-UP: A regular maintenance function, usually associated with the replacement and adjustment of parts and components in the electrical and fuel systems of a vehicle for the purpose of attaining optimum performance.

TURBOCHARGER: An exhaust driven pump which compresses intake air and forces it into the combustion chambers at higher than atmospheric pressures. The increased air pressure allows more fuel to be burned and results in increased horsepower being produced.

VACUUM ADVANCE: A device which advances the ignition timing in response to increased engine vacuum.

VACUUM GAUGE: An instrument used to measure the presence of vacuum in a chamber.

VALVE: A device which control the pressure, direction of flow or rate of flow of a liquid or gas.

VALVE CLEARANCE: The measured gap between the end of the valve stem and the rocker arm, cam lobe or follower that activates the valve.

VISCOSITY: The rating of a liquid's internal resistance to flow.

VOLTMETER: An instrument used for measuring electrical force in units called volts. Voltmeters are always connected parallel with the circuit being tested.

WHEEL CYLINDER: Found in the automotive drum brake assembly, it is a device, actuated by hydraulic pressure, which, through internal pistons, pushes the brake shoes outward against the drums.

GLOSSARY

FLOODING: The presence of too much fuel in the intake manifold and combustion chamber which prevents the air/fuel mixture from firing, thereby causing a no-start situation.

FLYWHEEL: A disc shaped part bolted to the rear end of the crankshaft. Around the outer perimeter is affixed the ring gear. The starter drive engages the ring gear, turning the flywheel, which rotates the crankshaft, imparting the initial starting motion to the engine.

FOOT POUND (ft.lb. or sometimes, ft. lbs.): The amount of energy or work needed to raise an item weighing one pound, a distance of one foot.

FUSE: A protective device in a circuit which prevents circuit overload by breaking the circuit when a specific amperage is present. The device is constructed around a strip or wire of a lower amperage rating than the circuit it is designed to protect. When an amperage higher than that stamped on the fuse is present in the circuit, the strip or wire melts, opening the circuit.

GEAR RATIO: The ratio between the number of teeth on meshing gears.

GENERATOR: A device which converts mechanical energy into electrical energy.

HEAT RANGE: The measure of a spark plug's ability to dissipate heat from its firing end. The higher the heat range, the hotter the plug fires. **HUB:** The center part of a wheel or gear.

HYDROCARBON (HC): Any chemical compound made up of hydrogen and carbon. A major pollutant formed by the engine as a byproduct of combustion.

HYDROMETER: An instrument used to measure the specific gravity of a solution.

INCH POUND (in.lb. or sometimes, in. lbs.): One twelfth of a foot pound.

INDUCTION: A means of transferring electrical energy in the form of a magnetic field. Principle used in the ignition coil to increase voltage.

INJECTION PUMP: A device, usually mechanically operated, which meters and delivers fuel under pressure to the fuel injector.

INJECTOR: A device which receives metered fuel under relatively low pressure and is activated to inject the fuel into the engine under relatively high pressure at a predetermined time.

INPUT SHAFT: The shaft to which torque is applied, usually carrying the driving gear or gears.

INTAKE MANIFOLD: A casting of passages or pipes used to conduct air or a fuel/air mixture to the cylinders.

JOURNAL: The bearing surface within which a shaft operates.

KEY: A small block usually fitted in a notch between a shaft and a hub to prevent slippage of the two parts.

MANIFOLD: A casting of passages or set of pipes which connect the cylinders to an inlet or outlet source.

MANIFOLD VACUUM: Low pressure in an engine intake manifold formed just below the throttle plates. Manifold vacuum is highest at idle and drops under acceleration.

MASTER CYLINDER: The primary fluid pressurizing device in a hydraulic system. In automotive use, it is found in brake and hydraulic clutch systems and is pedal activated, either directly or, in a power brake system, through the power booster.

MODULE: Electronic control unit, amplifier or igniter of solid state or integrated design which controls the current flow in the ignition primary circuit based on input from the pick-up coil. When the module opens the primary circuit, the high secondary voltage is induced in the coil.

NEEDLE BEARING: A bearing which consists of a number (usually a large number) of long, thin rollers.

OHM:(Ω) The unit used to measure the resistance of conductor to electrical flow. One ohm is the amount of resistance that limits current flow to one ampere in a circuit with one volt of pressure.

OHMMETER: An instrument used for measuring the resistance, in ohms, in an electrical circuit.

OUTPUT SHAFT: The shaft which transmits torque from a device, such as a transmission.

OVERDRIVE: A gear assembly which produces more shaft revolutions than that transmitted to it.

OVERHEAD CAMSHAFT (OHC): An engine configuration in which the camshaft is mounted on top of the cylinder head and operates the valves either directly or by means of rocker arms.

OVERHEAD VALVE (OHV): An engine configuration in which all of the valves are located in the cylinder head and the camshaft is located in the cylinder block. The camshaft operates the valves via lifters and pushrods.

OXIDES OF NITROGEN (NOx): Chemical compounds of nitrogen produced as a byproduct of combustion. They combine with hydrocarbons to produce smog.

OXYGEN SENSOR: Used with the feedback system to sense the presence of oxygen in the exhaust gas and signal the computer which can reference the voltage signal to an air/fuel ratio.

PINION: The smaller of two meshing gears.

PISTON RING: An open ended ring which fits into a groove on the outer diameter of the piston. Its chief function is to form a seal between the piston and cylinder wall. Most automotive pistons have three rings: two for compression sealing; one for oil sealing.

PRELOAD: A predetermined load placed on a bearing during assembly or by adjustment.

PRIMARY CIRCUIT: Is the low voltage side of the ignition system which consists of the ignition switch, ballast resistor or resistance wire, bypass, coil, electronic control unit and pick-up coil as well as the connecting wires and harnesses.

PRESS FIT: The mating of two parts under pressure, due to the inner diameter of one being smaller than the outer diameter of the other, or vice versa; an interference fit.

1 GENERAL INFORMATION AND MAINTENANCE

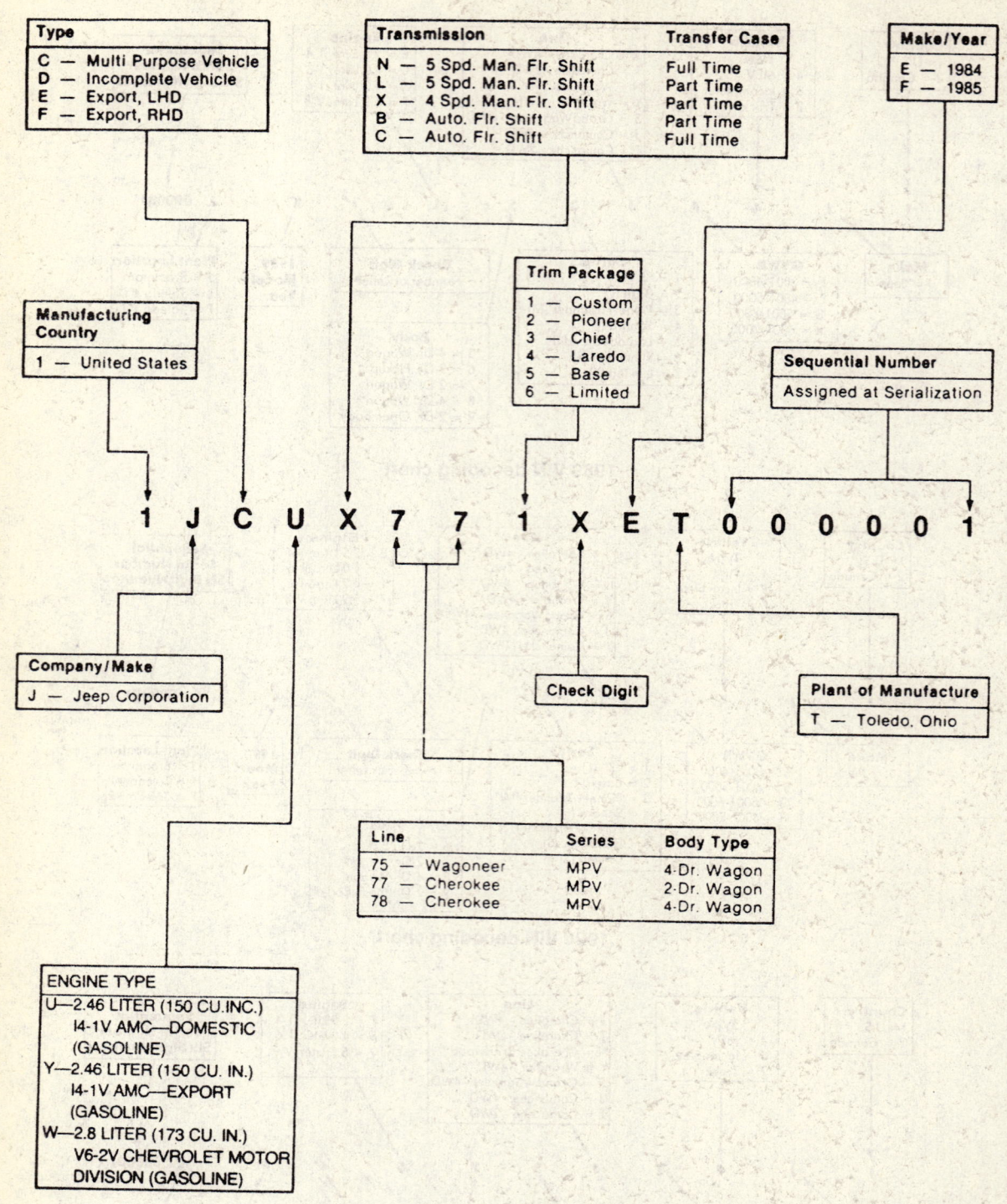

1984-88 Cherokee and Wagoneer VIN decoding chart

GENERAL INFORMATION AND MAINTENANCE

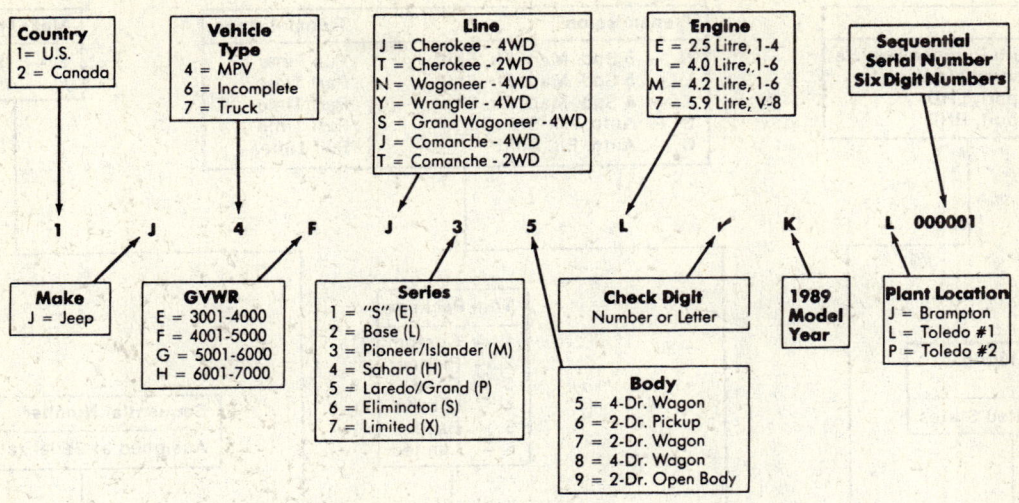

1989 VIN decoding chart

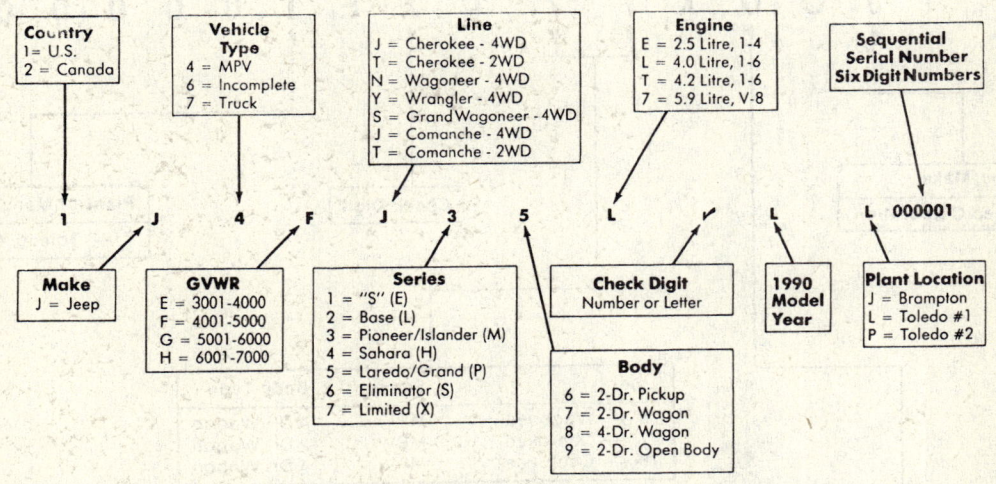

1990 VIN decoding chart

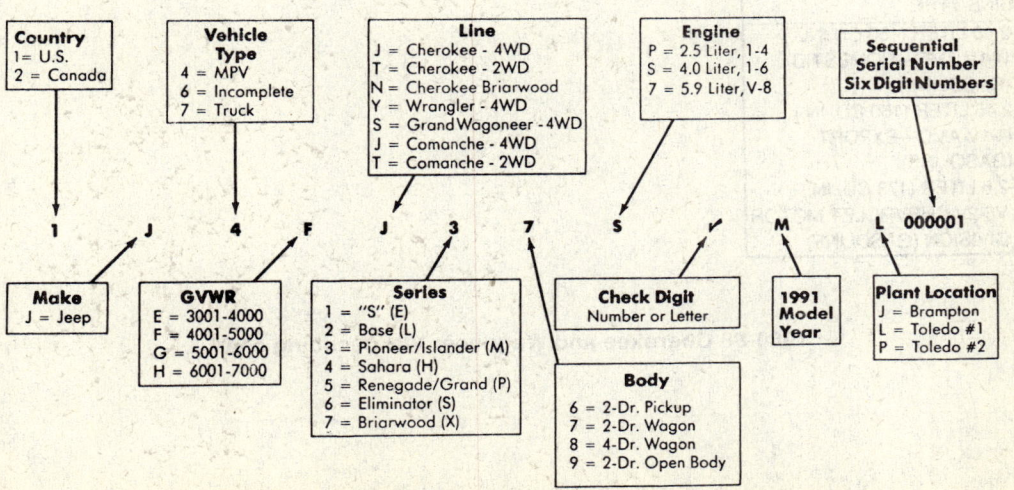

1991 VIN decoding chart

1 GENERAL INFORMATION AND MAINTENANCE

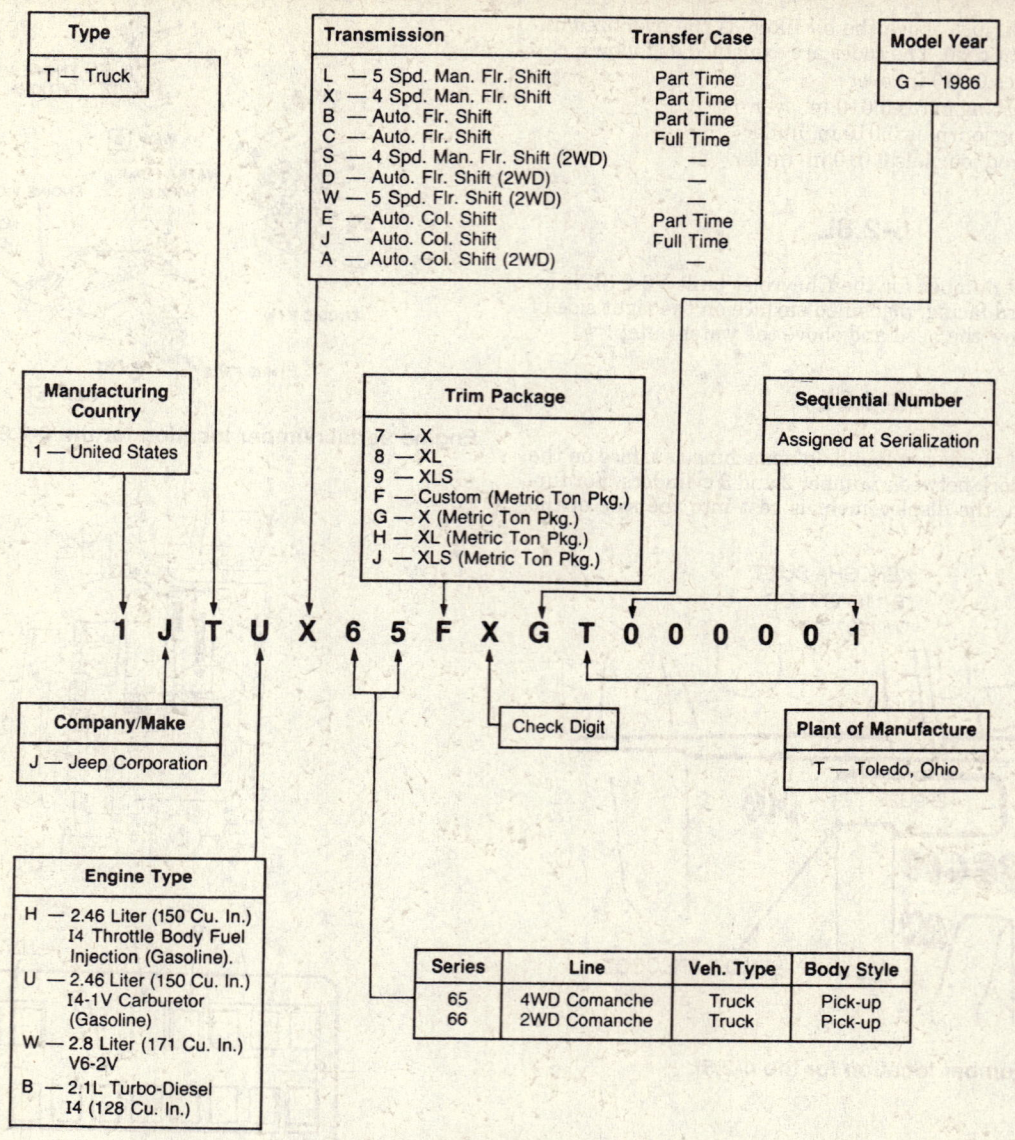

1986-88 Comanche VIN decoding chart

ENGINE IDENTIFICATION CHART

No. of Cylinders and Cu. In. Displacement	Actual Displacement			Fuel System	Engine Type	Built by	Years
	Cu. In.	CC	Liters				
4-126	126.09	2066.36	2.1	Diesel	OHC	Renault	1986–87
4-150	150.46	2465.67	2.5	1-bbl	OHC	AMC	1984–85
				TBI	OHV	AMC/Chrysler	1986–90
				MFI	OHV	Chrysler	1991
6-173	172.60	2828.45	2.8	2-bbl	OHV	Chevrolet	1984–86
6-243	243.35	3987.89	4.0	MFI	OHV	Chrysler	1987–91

TBI: Throttle Body Fuel Injection
MFI: Multi-point Fuel Injection
OHV: Overhead Valve
OHC: Overhead Camshaft

GENERAL INFORMATION AND MAINTENANCE 1

Also on the block, just above the oil filter, is the oversized/undersized component code. The codes are explained as follows:
- B: cylinder bores 0.010 in. over
- C: camshaft bearing bores 0.010 in. over
- M: main bearing journals 0.010 in. under
- P: connecting rod journals 0.010 in. under

6-2.8L

The engine serial number for the Chevrolet built V6-2.8L is located on an upward facing, machined surface on the right side of the block, just below the head and above the water pump.

6-4.0L

The engine serial number is found on a machined surface on the right side of the block between number 2 and 3 cylinders. For further identification, the displacement is cast into the side of the

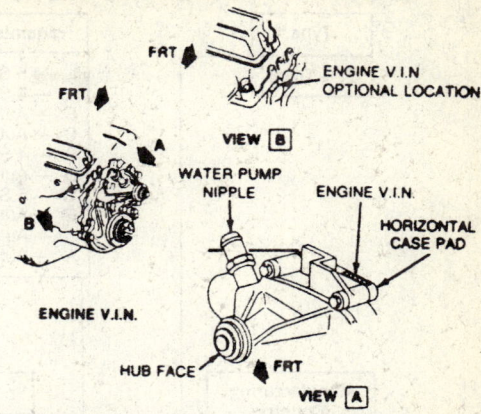

Engine serial number location for the 6-2.8L

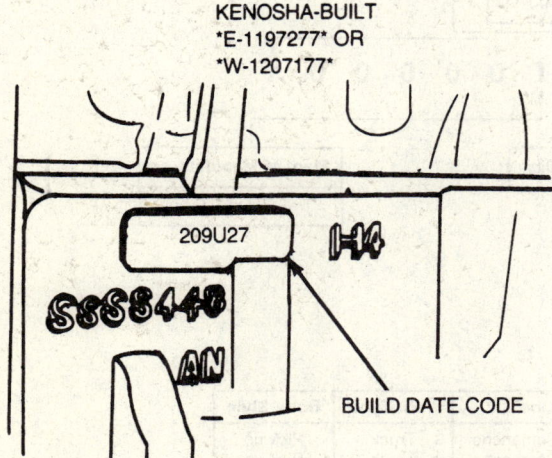

Engine serial number location for the 4-2.5L

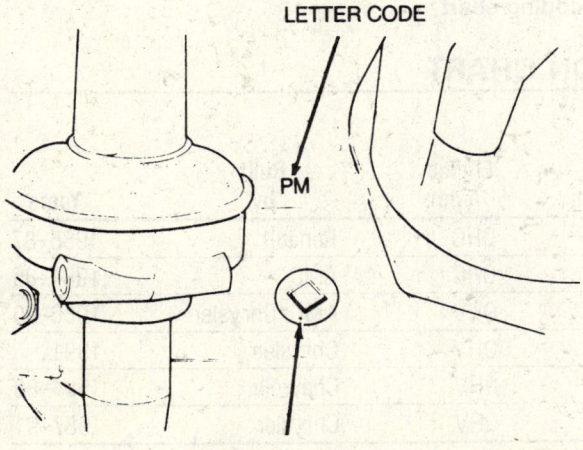

4-2.5L oversized/undersized component code location

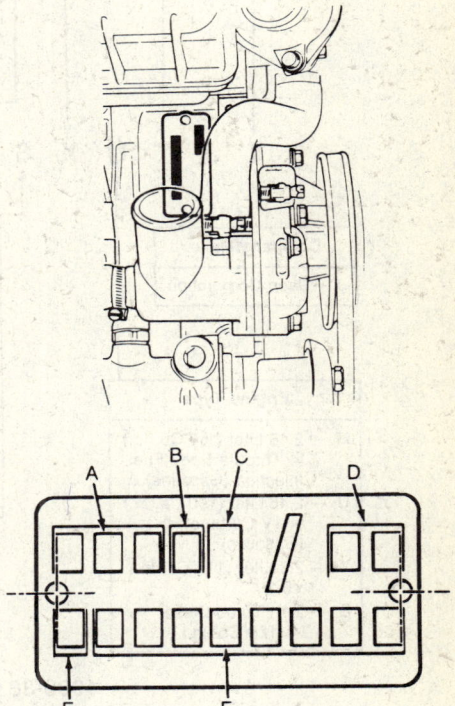

The plate contains the following engine coded information.

The engine type code (A):
- J—the engine family
- 8—the engine has indirect fuel injection (precombustion chambers)
- S—the engine has a cubic displacement of 2068 cc/2.1 liters/126 in^3

The engine certification code letter (B):
- A—50-state
- B—49-state, Canada and altitude
- C—California
- D—Europe (if unique)

The application index code (C):
- 8—Jeep vehicles

The engine index code (D):
- 14—manual transmission
- 15—automatic transmission

The manufacturer's location code (E):
- F—France

The engine serial number (F).

Engine serial number location for the 4-2.1L diesel

1 GENERAL INFORMATION AND MAINTENANCE

TOOLS AND EQUIPMENT

Naturally, without the proper tools and equipment it is impossible to properly service your vehicle. It would be impossible to catalog each tool that you would need to perform each or every operation in this book. It would also be unwise for the amateur to rush out and buy an expensive set of tools an the theory that he may need one or more of them at sometime.

The best approach is to proceed slowly, gathering together a good quality set of those tools that are used most frequently. Don't be misled by the low cost of bargain tools. It is far better to spend a little more for better quality. Forged wrenches, 6- or 12-point sockets and fine tooth ratchets are by far preferable to their less expensive counterparts. As any good mechanics can tell you, there are few worse experiences than trying to work on a truck with bad tools. Your monetary savings will be far outweighed by frustration and mangled knuckles.

Certain tools, plus a basic ability to handle tools, are required to get started. A basic mechanics tool set, a torque wrench, and, for 1976 and later models, a Torx bits set. Torx bits are hexlobular drivers which fit both inside and outside on special Torx head fasteners used in various places on Jeep vehicles.

A special wheel bearing nut socket would be helpful when removing the front wheel bearings on 4×4 models.

Begin accumulating those tools that are used most frequently; those associated with routine maintenance and tune-up.

In addition to the normal assortment of screwdrivers and pliers you should have the following tools for routine maintenance jobs (your Jeep, depending on the model year, uses both SAE and metric fasteners):

1. SAE/Metric wrenches, sockets and combination open end/box end wrenches in sizes from $4^1/_8$ in. (3mm) to $3/_4$ in. (19mm); and a spark plug socket ($^{13}/_{16}$ in.) If possible, buy various length socket drive extensions. One break in this department is that the metric sockets available in the U.S. will all fit the ratchet handles and extensions you may already have ($4^1/_4$ in., $3/_8$ in., and $4^1/_2$ in. drive).
2. Jackstands for support
3. Oil filter wrench
4. Oil filter spout for pouring oil
5. Grease gun for chassis lubrication
6. Hydrometer for checking the battery
7. A container for draining oil
8. Many rags for wiping up the inevitable mess.

In addition to the above items there are several others that are not absolutely necessary, but handy to have around. These include oil-dry (cat box litter works just as well and may be cheaper), a transmission funnel and the usual supply of lubricants, antifreeze and fluids, although these can be purchased as needed. This is a basic list for routine maintenance, but only your personal needs and desires can accurately determine your list of necessary tools.

The second list of tools is for tune-ups. While the tools involved here are slightly more sophisticated, they need not be outrageously expensive. There are several inexpensive tach/dwell meters on the market that are every bit as good for the average mechanic as a $100.00 professional model. Just be sure that it goes to at least 1,200-1,500 rpm on the tach scale and that it works on 4, 6 and 8 cylinder engines. A basic list of tune-up equipment could include:

1. Tach-dwell meter
2. Spark plug wrench
3. Timing light (a DC light that works from the truck's battery is best, although an AC light that plugs into 110V house current will suffice at some sacrifice in brightness)
4. Wire spark plug gauge/adjusting tools
5. Set of feeler blades.

Here again, be guided by your own needs. A feeler blade will set the point gap as easily as dwell meter will read dwell, but slightly less accurately. And since you will need a tachometer anyway ... well, make your own decision.

In addition to these basic tools, there are several other tools and gauges you may find useful. These include:

1. A compression gauge. The screw-in type is slower to use, but eliminates the possibility of a faulty reading due to escaping pressure
2. A manifold vacuum gauge
3. A test light
4. An induction meter. This is used for determining whether or not there is current in a wire. These are handy for use if a wire is broken somewhere in a wiring harness.

As a final note, you will probably find a torque wrench necessary for all but the most basic work. The beam type models are perfectly adequate, although the newer click (breakaway) type are more precise, and you don't have to crane your neck to see a torque reading in awkward situations. The breakaway torque wrenches are more expensive and should be recalibrated periodically.

Torque specification for each fastener will be given in the procedure in any case that a specific torque value is required. If no torque specifications are given, use the following values as a guide, based upon fastener size:

Bolts marked 6T
  6mm bolt/nut — 5-7 ft. lbs.
  8mm bolt/nut — 12-17 ft. lbs.
  10mm bolt/nut — 23-34 ft. lbs.
  12mm bolt/nut — 41-59 ft. lbs.
  14mm bolt/nut — 56-76 ft. lbs.

Bolts marked 8T
  6mm bolt/nut — 6-9 ft. lbs.
  8mm bolt/nut — 13-20 ft. lbs.
  10mm bolt/nut — 27-40 ft. lbs.
  12mm bolt/nut — 46-69 ft. lbs.
  14mm bolt/nut — 75-101 ft. lbs.

Special Tools

Normally, the use of special factory tools is avoided for repair procedures, since these are not readily available for the do-it-yourself mechanic. When it is possible to perform the job with more commonly available tools, it will be pointed out, but occasionally, a special tool was designed to perform a specific function and should be used. Before substituting another tool, you should be convinced that neither your safety nor the performance of the vehicle will be compromised.

Some special tools are available commercially from major tool manufacturers. These manufacturers include:

Service Tool Divison
Kent-Moore
29784 Little Mack
Roseville, MI 48066-2298
Miller Special Tools
Utica Tool Co.
32615 Park La.
Garden City, MI 48135

Others can be purchased through your Chrysler/Jeep dealer.

GENERAL INFORMATION AND MAINTENANCE

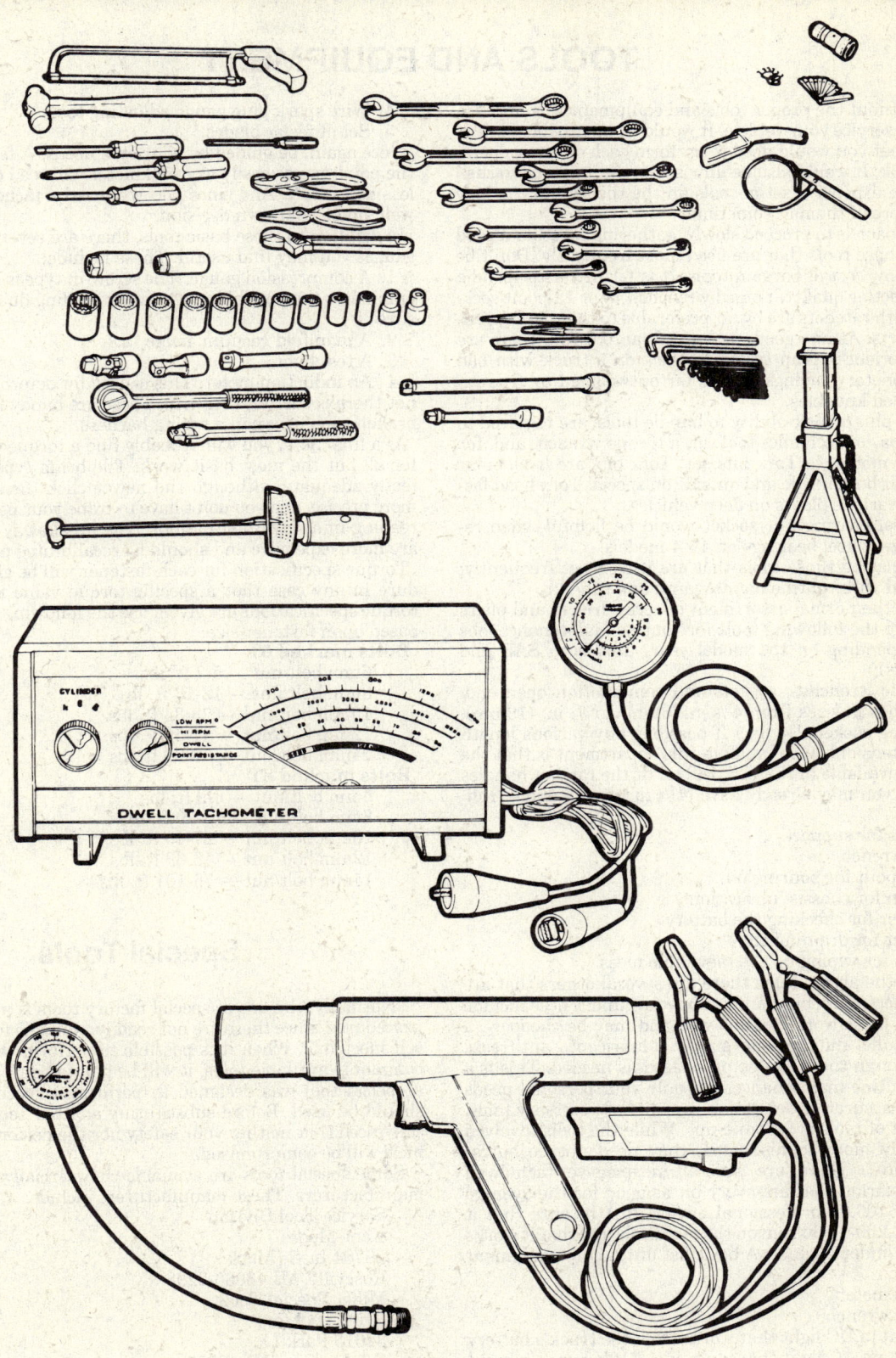

You need only a basic assortment of hand tools for most maintenance and repair jobs

1 GENERAL INFORMATION AND MAINTENANCE

HOW TO USE THIS BOOK

This book covers all Wagoneer, Cherokee, and Comanche models from 1984 through 1991.

The first two Sections will be the most used, since they contain maintenance and tune-up information and procedures. Studies have shown that a properly tuned and maintained truck can get at least 10% better gas mileage (which translates into lower operating costs) and periodic maintenance will catch minor problems before they turn into major repair bills. The other Sections deal with the more complex systems of your truck. Operating systems from engine through brakes are covered to the extent that the average do-it-yourselfer becomes mechanically involved. This book will not explain such things as rebuilding the differential for the simple reason that the expertise required and the investment in special tools make this task impractical and uneconomical. It will give you the detailed instructions to help you change your own brake pads and shoes, tune-up the engine, replace spark plugs and filters, and do many more jobs that will save you money, give you personal satisfaction and help you avoid expensive problems.

A secondary purpose of this book is a reference guide for owners who want to understand their truck and/or their mechanics better. In this case, no tools at all are required. Knowing just what a particular repair job requires in parts and labor time will allow you to evaluate whether or not you're getting a fair price quote and help decipher itemized bills from a repair shop.

Before attempting any repairs or service on your truck, read through the entire procedure outlined in the appropriate Section. This will give you the overall view of what tools and supplies will be required. There is nothing more frustrating than having to walk to the bus stop on Monday morning because you were short one gasket on Sunday afternoon. So read ahead and plan ahead. Each operation should be approached logically and all procedures thoroughly understood before attempting any work. Some special tools that may be required can often be rented from local automotive jobbers or places specializing in renting tools and equipment. Check the yellow pages of your phone book.

All Sections contain adjustments, maintenance, removal and installation procedures, and overhaul procedures. When overhaul is not considered practical, we tell you how to remove the failed part and then how to install the new or rebuilt replacement. In this way, you at least save the labor costs. Backyard overhaul of some components (such as the alternator or water pump) is just not practical, but the removal and installation procedure is often simple and well within the capabilities of the average truck owner.

Two basic mechanic's rules should be mentioned here. First, whenever the LEFT side of the truck or engine is referred to, it is meant to specify the DRIVER'S side of the truck. Conversely, the RIGHT side of the truck means the PASSENGER'S side. Second, all screws and bolts are removed by turning counterclockwise, and tightened by turning clockwise, unless otherwise noted.

Safety is always the most important rule. Constantly be aware of the dangers involved in working on or around an automobile and take proper precautions to avoid the risk of personal injury or damage to the vehicle. See the section in this Section, Servicing Your Vehicle Safely, and the SAFETY NOTICE on the acknowledgment page before attempting any service procedures and pay attention to the instructions provided. There are 3 common mistakes in mechanical work:

1. Incorrect order of assembly, disassembly or adjustment. When taking something apart or putting it together, doing things in the wrong order usually just costs you extra time; however it CAN break something. Read the entire procedure before beginning disassembly. Do everything in the order in which the instructions say you should do it, even if you can't immediately see a reason for it. When you're taking apart something that is very intricate (for example, a carburetor), you might want to draw a picture of how it looks when assembled at one point in order to make sure you get everything back in its proper position. We will supply exploded views whenever possible, but sometimes the job requires more attention to detail than an illustration provides. When making adjustments (especially tune-up adjustments), do them in order. One adjustment often affects another and you cannot expect satisfactory results unless each adjustment is made only when it cannot be changed by any other.

2. Overtorquing (or undertorquing) nuts and bolts. While it is more common for overtorquing to cause damage, undertorquing can cause a fastener to vibrate loose and cause serious damage, especially when dealing with aluminum parts. Pay attention to torque specifications and utilize a torque wrench in assembly. If a torque figure is not available remember that, if you are using the right tool to do the job, you will probably not have to strain yourself to get a fastener tight enough. The pitch of most threads is so slight that the tension you put on the wrench will be multiplied many times in actual force on what you are tightening. A good example of how critical torque is can be seen in the case of spark plug installation, especially where you are putting the plug into an aluminum cylinder head. Too little torque can fail to crush the gasket, causing leakage of combustion gases and consequent overheating of the plug and engine parts. Too much torque can damage the threads or distort the plug, which changes the spark gap at the electrode. Since more and more manufacturers are using aluminum in their engine and chassis parts to save weight, a torque wrench should be in any serious do-it-yourselfer's tool box.

There are many commercial chemical products available for ensuring that fasteners won't come loose, even if they are not torqued just right (a very common brand is Loctite®). If you're worried about getting something together tight enough to hold, but loose enough to avoid mechanical damage during assembly, one of these products might offer substantial insurance. Read the label on the package and make sure the product is compatible with the materials, fluids, etc. involved before choosing one.

3. Crossthreading. This occurs when a part such as a bolt is screwed into a nut or casting at the wrong angle and forced, causing the threads to become damaged. Crossthreading is more likely to occur if access is difficult. It helps to clean and lubricate fasteners, and to start threading with the part to be installed going straight in, using your fingers. If you encounter resistance, unscrew the part and start over again at a different angle until it can be inserted and turned several times without much effort. Keep in mind that many parts, especially spark plugs, use tapered threads so that gentle turning will automatically bring the part you're threading to the proper angle if you don't force it or resist a change in angle. Don't put a wrench on the part until it's been turned in a couple of times by hand. If you suddenly encounter resistance and the part has not seated fully, don't force it. Pull it back out and make sure it's clean and threading properly.

Always take your time and be patient; once you have some experience, working on your truck will become an enjoyable hobby.

General Information and Maintenance

QUICK REFERENCE INDEX

Air Cleaner	1-13	Jump starting	1-49
Air Conditioning	1-24	Manual Transmission Application Chart	1-11
Automatic Transmission Application Chart	1-12	Oil and filter change (engine)	1-36
Capacities Chart	1-54	Preventive Maintenance Schedules	1-54
Cooling system	1-41	Windshield wipers	1-30
Fuel filter	1-13		

GENERAL INDEX

Air cleaner	1-13	Oil	1-36	Transmission	1-39
Air conditioning		Fluids and lubricants		Outside vehicle maintenance	1-44
Charging	1-27	Automatic transmission	1-39	PCV valve	1-14
Discharging	1-27	Battery	1-17	Power steering pump	1-44
Evacuating	1-27	Chassis greasing	1-44	Preventive Maintenance Charts	1-54
Gauge sets	1-25	Coolant	1-41	Pushing	1-51
General service	1-24	Drive axle	1-41	Radiator	1-42
Isolating the compressor	1-26	Engine oil	1-36	Rear axle	
Inspection	1-26	Fuel recommendations	1-35	Identification	1-12
Leak testing	1-27	Manual transmission	1-39	Lubricant level	1-41
Oil level check	1-30	Master cylinder	1-43	Routine maintenance	1-13
Preventive maintenance	1-24	Power steering pump	1-44	Safety measures	1-5
Safety precautions	1-24	Transfer case	1-39	Serial number location	1-6
Service valves	1-25	Front drive axle		Special tools	1-4
System tests	1-26	Identification	1-12	Specifications Charts	
Troubleshooting	1-28	Lubricant level	1-41	Capacities	1-54
Antifreeze	1-41	Fuel filter	1-13	Preventive Maintenance	1-54
Automatic transmission		History	1-6	Tires	
Application chart	1-12	Hoses	1-22	Design	1-32
Fluid change	1-39	How to Use This Book	1-2	Rotation	1-30
Battery		Identification		Size chart	1-33
Cables	1-17	Drive axle	1-12	Tread depth	1-32
Charging	1-16	Engine	1-6	Troubleshooting	1-34
General maintenance	1-16	Model	1-6	Usage	1-32
Fluid level and maintenance	1-17	Serial number	1-6	Wear problems	1-35
Jump starting	1-49	Transfer case	1-11	Tools and equipment	1-4
Replacement	1-16	Transmission		Towing	1-51
Testing	1-18	Automatic	1-12	Trailer towing	1-51
Belts		Manual	1-11	Transfer Case	
Capacities Chart	1-54	Vehicle	1-6	Fluid level	1-39
Chassis lubrication	1-44	Jacking points	1-51	Identification	1-11
Cooling system	1-41	Jump starting	1-49	Transmission	
Crankcase ventilation valve	1-14	Maintenance Intervals Chart	1-54	Application charts	1-11, 12
Drive axle		Master cylinder	1-43	Routine maintenance	1-39
Identification	1-12	Model identification	1-6	Troubleshooting Charts	
Lubricant level	1-41	Oil and fuel recommendations	1-35	Air conditioning	1-28
Evaporative canister	1-15	Oil and filter change (engine)	1-36	Tires	1-34
Filters		Oil level check		Wheels	1-34
Air	1-13	Differential	1-41	Vehicle identification	1-6
Crankcase	1-14	Engine	1-36	Wheel bearings	1-45, 48
Fuel	1-13	Transfer case	1-39	Wheels	1-30

1 GENERAL INFORMATION AND MAINTENANCE

is not safe working around a truck. Long hair should be hidden under a hat or cap.
• Don't use pockets for toolboxes. A fall or bump can drive a screwdriver deep into you body. Even a wiping cloth hanging from the back pocket can wrap around a spinning shaft or fan.
• Don't smoke when working around gasoline, cleaning solvent or other flammable material.
• Don't smoke when working around the battery. When the battery is being charged, it gives off explosive hydrogen gas.
• Don't use gasoline to wash your hands; there are excellent soaps available. Gasoline may contain lead, and lead can enter the body through a cut, accumulating in the body until you are very ill. Gasoline also removes all the natural oils from the skin so that bone dry hands will suck up oil and grease.
• Don't service the air conditioning system unless you are equipped with the necessary tools and training. The refrigerant, R-12, is extremely cold and when exposed to the air, will instantly freeze any surface it comes in contact with, including your eyes. Although the refrigerant is normally non-toxic, R-12 becomes a deadly poisonous gas in the presence of an open flame. One good whiff of the vapors from burning refrigerant can be fatal.

HISTORY AND MODEL IDENTIFICATION

In 1984 a new, redesigned, downsized version of the Wagoneer/Cherokee line was introduced. These smaller, fuel efficient models incorporated features such as a standard 4-cylinder, 2.5L engine, with a V6-2.8L engine as an option, new transfer case/transmission combinations, and for the first time, integrated frames.

For 1985, the Jeep line-up remained unchanged.

For 1986, Jeep introduced the Comanche. The Comanche is a pick-up version of the downsized Wagoneer and is available in both 2- and 4-wheel drive. The engine selection for the Wagoneer/Cherokee/Comanche remains the same as previous years, with the exception of an optional 4-cylinder, 126 cu.in. turbocharged, Renault-made Diesel. Throttle body fuel injection replaced the carburetor on the 4-2.5L.

The line-up continued unchanged in 1987, with one, notable exception. The V6-2.8L engine made by General Motors was no longer offered. In its place was a 6-4.0L, inline engine made by AMC. The engine is mechanically similar to the older 6-258 AMC engines with a redesigned cylinder head and Multi-point Fuel Injection.

In 1988 Chrysler Corporation bought the Jeep division from AMC. The model line-up remained unchanged but the diesel engine was discontinued.

For 1989, Jeep introduced a four-wheel anti-lock brake system on Cherokee and Wagoneer models equipped with the 4.0L 6-cylinder engine and Selec-Trac full-time four-wheel-drive system. This was a first for the light truck industry.

In 1990, the Jeep line continued unchanged.

New for 1991 is a vehicle theft security system, available as an option on all models. The familiar Wagoneer name has been dropped and replaced with the Cherokee Briarwood. The Grand Wagoneer is still offered.

SERIAL NUMBER IDENTIFICATION

Vehicle

The VIN plate is located on the left side of the instrument panel pad, visible through the windshield.

In addition to the VIN plate, the truck is equipped with a Vehicle Identification Plate affixed to the left side of the firewall in the engine compartments. Pre-1990 model vehicles may have the plate attached to the left side of the radiator support. The VIN plate and the Vehicle Identification plate can be interpreted by the accompanying illustrations.

A metal identification plate is riveted to the driver side of the dash panel in the engine compartment.
1. Order number
2. Paint gun number
3. Vehicle identification number (VIN)
4. Vehicle deviation or special sales request and order (SSR & O)
5. Trim option number
6. Paint option number

Pre-1990 Vehicle identification plate

Engine

4-126 TURBO DIESEL

The serial number for the Renault built Diesel is found on a machined pad located at the front of the block.

4-2.5L

The engine serial number for the American Motors built 4-2.5L is located on a machined pad on the rear right side of the block, between cylinders number 3 and 4.

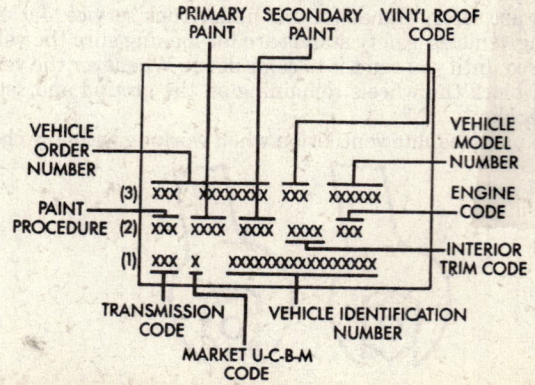

1990-91 Vehicle identification plate

1-6

GENERAL INFORMATION AND MAINTENANCE 1

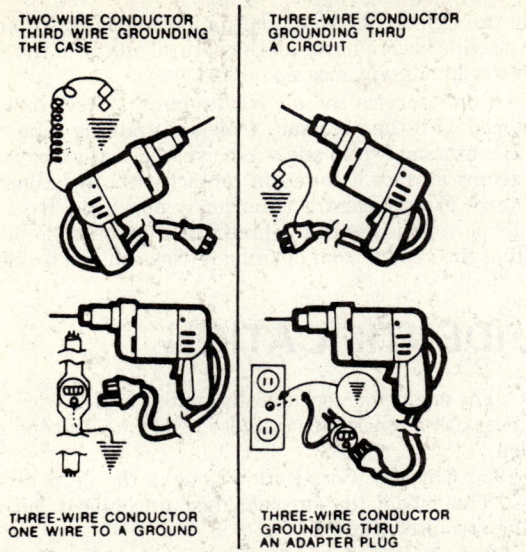

When using electric tools make sure they are properly grounded

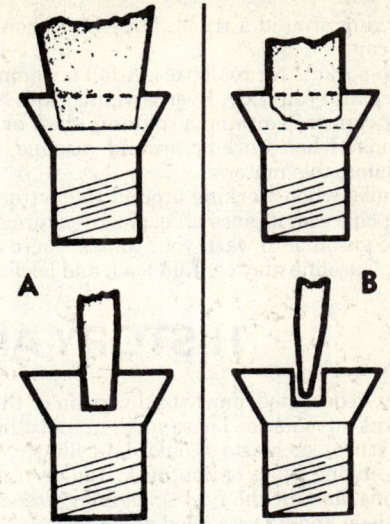

Keep screwdriver tips in good shape. They should fit the slot as shown in 'A'. If they look like those in 'B', they need grinding or replacing

SERVICING YOUR VEHICLE SAFELY

It is virtually impossible to anticipate all of the hazards involved with automotive maintenance and service, but care and common sense will prevent most accidents.

The rules of safety for mechanics range from "don't smoke around gasoline," to "use the proper tool for the job." The trick to avoiding injuries is to develop safe work habits and take every possible precaution.

Dos

• Do keep a fire extinguisher and first aid kit within easy reach.

• Do wear safety glasses or goggles when cutting, drilling or prying, even if you have 20-20 vision. If you wear glasses for the sake of vision, they should be made of hardened glass that can also serve as safety glasses, or wear safety goggles over your regular glasses.

• Do shield your eyes whenever you work around the battery. Batteries contain sulphuric acid; in case of contact with the eyes or skin, flush the area with water or a mixture of water and baking soda and get medical attention immediately.

• Do use safety stands for any undertruck service. Jacks are for raising vehicles; safety stands are for making sure the vehicle stays raised until you want it to come down. Whenever the vehicle is raised, block the wheels remaining on the ground and set the parking brake.

• Do use adequate ventilation when working with any chemi-

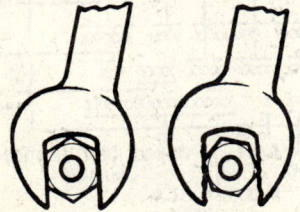

If you're using an open end wrench, use the correct size, and position it properly on the nut or bolt

cals. Like carbon monoxide, the asbestos dust resulting from brake lining wear can be poisonous in sufficient quantities.

• Do disconnect the negative battery cable when working on the electrical system. The primary ignition system can contain up to 40,000 volts.

• Do follow manufacturer's directions whenever working with potentially hazardous materials. Both brake fluid and antifreeze are poisonous if taken internally.

• Do properly maintain your tools. Loose hammerheads, mushroomed punches and chisels, frayed or poorly grounded electrical cords, excessively worn screwdrivers, spread wrenches (open end), cracked sockets, slipping ratchets, or faulty droplight sockets can cause accidents.

• Do use the proper size and type of tool for the job being done.

• Do when possible, pull on a wrench handle rather than push on it, and adjust your stance to prevent a fall.

• Do be sure that adjustable wrenches are tightly adjusted on the nut or bolt and pulled so that the face is on the side of the fixed jaw.

• Do select a wrench or socket that fits the nut or bolt. The wrench or socket should sit straight, not cocked.

• Do strike squarely with a hammer—avoid glancing blows.

• Do set the parking brake and block the drive wheels if the work requires that the engine be running.

Don'ts

• Don't run an engine in a garage or anywhere else without proper ventilation—EVER! Carbon monoxide is poisonous; it takes a long time to leave the human body and you can build up a deadly supply of it in your system by simply breathing in a little every day. You may not realize you are slowly poisoning yourself. Always use power vents, windows, fans or open the garage doors.

• Don't work around moving parts while wearing a necktie or other loose clothing. Short sleeves are much safer than long, loose sleeves and hard-toed shoes with neoprene soles protect your toes and give a better grip on slippery surfaces. Jewelry such as watches, fancy belt buckles, beads or body adornment of any kind

1-5

SAFETY NOTICE

Proper service and repair procedures are vital to the safe, reliable operation of all motor vehicles, as well as the personal safety of those performing repairs. This manual outlines procedures for servicing and repairing vehicles using safe, effective methods. The procedures contain many NOTES, CAUTIONS and WARNINGS which should be followed along with standard safety procedures to eliminate the possibility of personal injury or improper service which could damage the vehicle or compromise its safety.

It is important to note that the repair procedures and techniques, tools and parts for servicing motor vehicles, as well as the skill and experience of the individual performing the work vary widely. It is not possible to anticipate all of the conceivable ways or conditions under which vehicles may be serviced, or to provide cautions as to all of the possible hazards that may result. Standard and accepted safety precautions and equipment should be used when handling toxic or flammable fluids, and safety goggles or other protection should be used during cutting, grinding, chiseling, prying, or any other process that can cause material removal or projectiles.

Some procedures require the use of tools specially designed for a specific purpose. Before substituting another tool or procedure, you must be completely satisfied that neither your personal safety, nor the performance of the vehicle will be endangered

Although information in this manual is based on industry sources and is complete as possible at the time of publication, the possibility exists that some car manufacturers made later changes which could not be included here. While striving for total accuracy, Chilton Book Company cannot assume responsibility for any errors, changes or omissions that may occur in the compilation of this data.

PART NUMBERS

Part numbers listed in this reference are not recommendations by Chilton for any product by brand name. They are references that can be used with interchange manuals and aftermarket supplier catalogs to locate each brand supplier's discrete part number.

SPECIAL TOOLS

Special tools are recommended by the vehicle manufacturer to perform their specific job. Use has been kept to a minimum, but where absolutely necessary, they are referred to in the text by the part number of the tool manufacturer. These tools can be purchased, under the appropiate part number, from your Jeep dealer or regional distributor, or an equivalent tool can be purchased locally from a tool supplier or parts outlet. Before substituting any tool for the one recommended, read the SAFETY NOTICE at the top of this page.

ACKNOWLEDGMENTS

The Chilton Book Company expresses appreciation to Jeep Division, Chrysler Corp., Detroit, Michigan for their generous assistance.

No part of this publication may be reproduced, transmitted or stored in any form or by any means, electronic or mechanical, including photocopy, recording, or by information storage or retrieval system without prior written permission from the publisher.

Contents

6 — Chassis Electrical
- 6-8 Heating and Air Cond.
- 6-13 Radio
- 6-14 Windshield Wipers
- 6-15 Cruise Control
- 6-28 Instruments and Switches
- 6-31 Lighting
- 6-39 Circuit Protection
- 6-49 Wiring Diagrams

7 — Drive Train
- 7-2 Manual Transmission
- 7-82 Clutch
- 7-89 Automatic Tramsmission
- 7-104 Transfer Case
- 7-153 Driveshaft and U-Joints
- 7-160 Rear Axle
- 7-172 Front Drive Axle

8 — Suspension and Steering
- 8-2 Front Suspension
- 8-9 Wheel Alignment Specs.
- 8-10 Rear Suspension
- 8-13 Steering

9 — Brakes
- 9-2 Brake Specifications
- 9-18 Disc Brakes
- 9-24 Drum Brakes
- 9-27 Anti-Lock Brake System
- 9-39 Parking Brake

10 — Body
- 10-2 Stain Removal
- 10-3 Exterior
- 10-18 Interior

Contents

1. General Information and Maintenance
- 1-2 How to Use this Book
- 1-3 Tools and Equipment
- 1-13 Routine Maintenance and Lubrication
- 1-49 Jump Starting
- 1-54 Capacities Chart

2. Engine Performance and Tune-Up
- 2-2 Tune-Up Procedures
- 2-3 Tune-Up Specifications
- 2-4 Firing Orders
- 2-5 Electronic Ignition

3. Engine and Engine Overhaul
- 3-2 Engine Electrical Systems
- 3-25 Engine Mechanical Service
- 3-28 Engine Specifications
- 3-30 Engine Troubleshooting
- 3-92 Exhaust Systems

4. Emission Controls
- 4-2 Engine Emission Control System And Service
- 4-12 Electronic Engine Control System
- 4-147 Vacuum Diagrams

5. Fuel System
- 5-2 Carbureted Fuel System
- 5-20 Gasoline Fuel Injection System
- 5-27 Diesel Fuel System
- 5-31 Fuel Tank

JEEP WAGONEER/COM[MANCHE] 1984-91 REPAIR MANUAL

CHILTON'S

President, Chilton Enterprises	David S. Loewith
Senior Vice President	Ronald A. Hoxter
Publisher and Editor-In-Chief	Kerry A. Freeman, S.A.E.
Managing Editors	Peter M. Conti, Jr. □ W. Calvin Settle, Jr., S.A.E.
Assistant Managing Editor	Nick D'Andrea
Senior Editors	Debra Gaffney □ Ken Grabowski, A.S.E., S.A.E. Michael L. Grady □ Richard J. Rivele, S.A.E. Richard T. Smith □ Jim Taylor Ron Webb
Director of Manufacturing	Mike D'Imperio

CHILTON BOOK COMPANY
ONE OF THE **ABC PUBLISHING COMPANIES**,
A PART OF **CAPITAL CITIES/ABC, INC.**

Manufactured in USA
© 1991 Chilton Book Company
Chilton Way, Radnor, PA 19089
ISBN 0–8019–8143–3
Library of Congress Catalog Card No. 90–056133
34567890 0987654